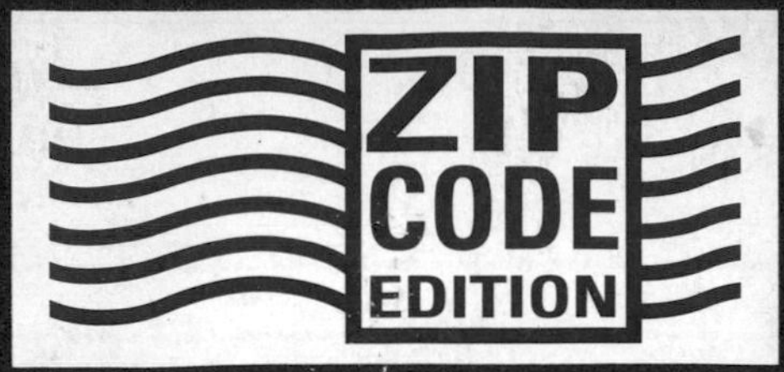

The Thomas Guide®

1998 GOLDEN GATE COUNTIES

This version of the Thomas Guide is overprinted with postal ZIP code boundary lines and numbers as determined by the U.S. Postal Service. The information within this atlas is useful to anyone in need of a detailed ZIP code directory.

94133 ZIP CODE NUMBER

ZIP CODE BOUNDARY

ZIP CODE EDITION

1998 ZIP CODE POSTAL ZONES

NUMERICAL LISTING
(FOR ALPHABETICAL LISTING SEE CITIES AND COMMUNITIES INDEX)

MARIN COUNTY

ZIP CODE	NAME	PAGE
94901	GLENWOOD	567
94901	SAN RAFAEL	566
94903	SAN RAFAEL	566
94903	SANTA VENETIA	566
94904	KENTFIELD	586
94904	SAN RAFAEL	586
94920	BELVEDERE	627
94920	TIBURON	607
94924	BOLINAS	604
94925	CORTE MADERA	606
94930	FAIRFAX	565
94933	FOREST KNOLLS	564
94937	INVERNESS	522
94938	LAGUNITAS	564
94939	LARKSPUR	586
94940	MARSHALL	482
94941	MILL VALLEY	606
94945	NOVATO (SAN MARIN)	545
94946	NICASIO	525
94947	NAVOTO	525
94949	NOVATO	546
94949	NOVATO (IGNACIO)	546
94950	OLEMA	543
94952	BLOOMFIELD	442
94956	POINT REYES STATION	523
94957	ROSS	586
94960	SAN ANSELMO	566
94963	SAN GERONIMO	565
94964	SAN QUENTIN	587
94965	MARIN CITY	626
94965	SAUSALITO	627
94970	STINSON BEACH	605
94971	TOMALES	462
94972	FALLON	441
94973	WOODACRE	565

POST OFFICE BOXES

ZIP CODE	NAME
94912	SAN RAFAEL
94913	SAN RAFAEL
94914	SAN RAFAEL
94915	SAN RAFAEL
94942	MILL VALLEY
94948	NOVATO
94966	SAUSALITO
94974	SAN QUENTIN PENITENTIARY
94976	CORTE MADERA
94977	LARKSPUR
94978	FAIRFAX
94979	SAN ANSELMO

SAN FRANCISCO COUNTY

ZIP CODE	NAME	PAGE
94102	CIVIC CENTER (MAIN OFFICE N)	6
94103	SOUTH OF MARKET (MAIN OFC S)	10
94104	FINANCIAL DISTRICT	7
94105	SOUTH OF MARKET	7
94107	POTRERO HILL	11
94108	CHINATOWN	7
94108	NOB HILL	7
94109	POLK GULCH	6
94110	BERNAL HEIGHTS	14
94110	MISSION DISTRICT	10
94111	RINCON EAST	7
94112	EXCELSIOR	19
94112	INGLESIDE	19
94114	EUREKA VALLEY	10
94114	NOE VALLEY	10
94115	PACIFIC HEIGHTS	6
94115	WESTERN ADDITION	6
94116	FOREST HILL	12
94116	PARKSIDE	13
94117	HAIGHT-ASHBURY	10
94118	LAUREL HEIGHTS	5
94118	PRESIDIO HEIGHTS	5
94121	RICHMOND	5
94121	SEACLIFF	4
94122	SUNSET	8
94122	WEST OF TWIN PEAKS	9
94123	COW HOLLOW	2
94123	MARINA	2
94124	BAYVIEW	15
94124	HUNTER'S POINT	15
94127	MIRALOMA PARK	13
94127	SAINT FRANCIS WOOD	13
94127	WEST PORTAL	13
94127	WESTWOOD PARK	13
94129	PRESIDIO OF SAN FRANCISCO	5
94130	TREASURE ISLAND	3
94131	DIAMOND HEIGHTS	14
94131	GLEN PARK	14
94132	LAKESIDE	12
94132	PARK MERCED	18
94132	STONESTOWN	18
94133	NORTH BEACH	3
94133	RUSSIAN HILL	3
94133	TELEGRAPH HILL	7
94134	PORTOLA	14
94134	VISITACION VALLEY	20
94143	U. C. MEDICAL CENTER	9

POST OFFICE BOXES

ZIP CODE	NAME
94119	RINCON CENTER
94126	STATION B
94140	STATION C
94141	MISSION ANNEX
94142	CIVIC CENTER
94146	NOE VALLEY
94147	MARINA
94159	GOLDEN GATE
94164	POLK GULCH
94188	GENERAL MAIL FACILITY

SAN MATEO COUNTY

ZIP CODE	NAME	PAGE
94002	BELMONT	769
94005	BRISBANE	688
94010	BURLINGAME	728
94010	HILLSBOROUGH	728
94014	DALY CITY	708
94014	COLMA	687
94015	DALY CITY	687
94018	EL GRANADA	767
94019	HALF MOON BAY	767
94020	LA HONDA	829
94020	PORTOLA VALLEY	809
94021	LOMA MAR	848
94025	MENLO PARK	790
94027	ATHERTON	790
94028	PORTOLA VALLEY	830
94030	MILLBRAE	728
94037	MONTARA	746
94038	MOSS BEACH	746
94038	PRINCETON BY THE SEA	766
94044	PACIFICA	706
94060	PESCADERO	848
94061	REDWOOD CITY	790
94062	KINGS MOUNTAIN	788
94062	WOODSIDE	789
94063	REDWOOD CITY	770
94065	REDWOOD CITY (REDWOOD SHORES)	769
94066	SAN BRUNO	707
94070	SAN CARLOS	769
94074	SAN GREGORIO	828
94080	SOUTH SAN FRANCISCO	708
94128	S.F. INTERNATIONAL AIRPORT	728
94303	EAST PALO ALTO	771
94401	SAN MATEO	728
94402	SAN MATEO	748
94403	SAN MATEO (HILLSDALE)	749
94404	FOSTER CITY	749

POST OFFICE BOXES

ZIP CODE	NAME
94011	BURLINGAME

1998 SANTA CLARA COUNTY
ZIP CODE POSTAL ZONES

NUMERICAL LISTING
(FOR ALPHABETICAL LISTING SEE CITIES AND COMMUNITIES INDEX)

ZIP CODE	COMMUNITY NAME	PAGE
94022	LOS ALTOS	811
94024	LOS ALTOS HILLS	831
94025	MENLO PARK	790
94027	ATHERTON	790
94028	PORTOLA VALLEY	830
94035	MILPITAS	812
94040	MTN VIEW (BLOSSOM VALLEY STATION)	811
94041	MOUNTAIN VIEW	811
94043	MOUNTAIN VIEW	811
94061	REDWOOD CITY	790
94062	REDWOOD CITY (WOODSIDE BRANCH)	790
94063	REDWOOD CITY (MAIN OFFICE)	790
94086	SUNNYVALE	812
94087	SUNNYVALE (ENCINAL STATION)	832
94089	SUNNYVALE	812
94301	PALO ALTO	791
94303	PALO ALTO (EAST PALO ALTO STATION)	791
94304	PALO ALTO (VETERANS HOSP BRANCH)	810
94305	PALO ALTO (STANFORD UNIV)	790
94306	PALO ALTO (A STATION)	811
95002	ALVISO	792
95008	CAMPBELL	853
95014	CUPERTINO	832
95020	GILROY	957
95030	LOS GATOS	873
95032	LOS GATOS	873
95035	MILPITAS	794
95037	MORGAN HILL	937
95046	SAN MARTIN	937
95050	SANTA CLARA	833
95051	SANTA CLARA	833
95053	SANTA CLARA	833
95054	SANTA CLARA	813
95070	SARATOGA	872
95110	SAN JOSE (CITY HALL)	833
95111	SAN JOSE	854
95112	SAN JOSE	834
95113	SAN JOSE	834
95116	SAN JOSE	834
95117	SAN JOSE	853
95118	SAN JOSE	874
95119	SAN JOSE	875
95120	SAN JOSE	895
95121	SAN JOSE	855
95122	SAN JOSE	834
95123	SAN JOSE	874
95124	SAN JOSE	873
95125	SAN JOSE	854
95126	SAN JOSE	833
95127	SAN JOSE	815
95128	SAN JOSE	853
95129	SAN JOSE	852
95130	SAN JOSE	853
95131	SAN JOSE	814
95132	SAN JOSE	814
95133	SAN JOSE	834
95134	SAN JOSE	813
95135	SAN JOSE	856
95136	SAN JOSE	874
95137	SAN JOSE	896
95138	SAN JOSE	855
95139	SAN JOSE	895
95140	SAN JOSE (MT HAMILTON)	858
95141	SAN JOSE	915
95148	SAN JOSE	835
95192	SAN JOSE (SAN JOSE STATE UNIV)	834

	POST OFFICE BOXES
95009	CAMPBELL
95011	CAMPBELL
95013	COYOTE
95015	CUPERTINO
95021	GILROY
95026	HOLY CITY
95031	LOS GATOS
95036	MILPITAS
95038	MORGAN HILL
95042	NEW ALMADEN
95044	REDWOOD ESTATES
95052	SANTA CLARA
95055	SANTA CLARA (MISSION STATION)
95056	SANTA CLARA
95071	SARATOGA
95103	SAN JOSE
95106	SAN JOSE
95108	SAN JOSE
95109	SAN JOSE
95150	SAN JOSE
95151	SAN JOSE
95152	SAN JOSE
95153	SAN JOSE
95154	SAN JOSE
95155	SAN JOSE
95156	SAN JOSE
95157	SAN JOSE
95158	SAN JOSE
95159	SAN JOSE
95160	SAN JOSE
95161	SAN JOSE
95164	SAN JOSE
95172	SAN JOSE

The Thomas Guide®

1998 EDITION

MARIN COUNTY

ZIP

How To Use This Thomas Guide
Modo De Empleo Del Thomas Guide

To Find a City or Community:
Manera de Localizar una Ciudad o Comunidad:

Start with the Key Map to Detail Pages, then turn to the Detail Page indicated.

Empiece con el mapa clave de páginas detalladas, luego pase a la página detallada que se indica.

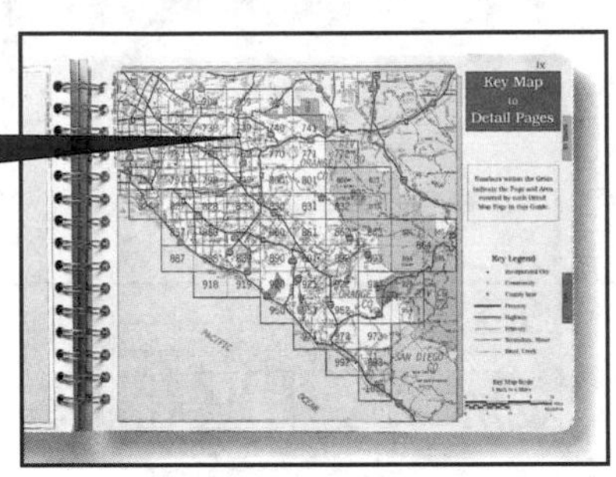

or

o

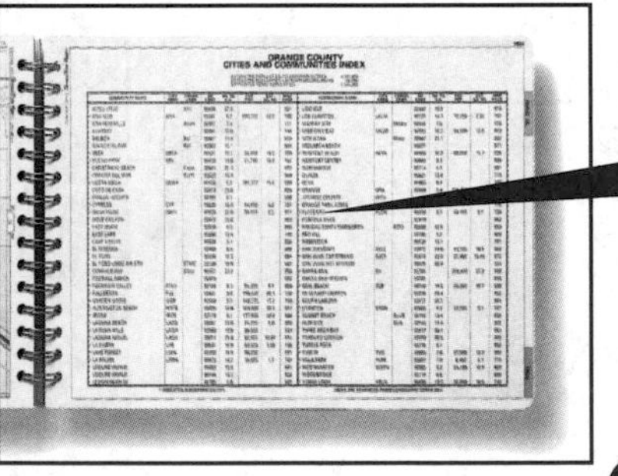

Look up the name in the Cities and Communities Index, then turn to the Detail Page indicated.

Busque el nombre en el Indice de Ciudades y Comunidades, luego pase a la página detallada que se indica.

or

o

Refer to the enclosed Foldout Map and its Index, then turn to the Detail Page indicated.

Consulte el mapa desplegable y el Indice del mismo adjunto, luego pase a la página detallada que se indica.

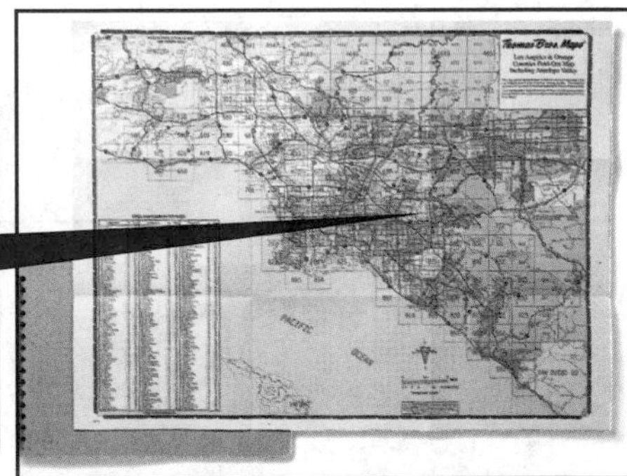

To Find an Address:
Manera de Localizar una Dirección:

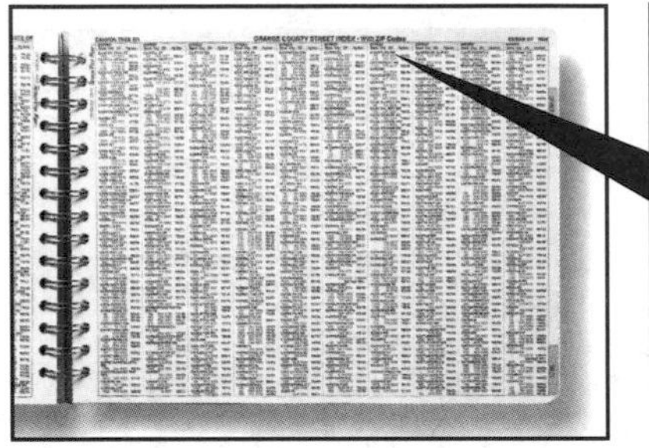

1 Look up the street name in the Street Index. If there are multiple listings, choose the proper city and/or address range. (All city abbreviations are listed in the Cities and Communities Index.)

Localice el nombre de la calle en el Indice de Calles. Si aparecen varias listas, seleccione el área apropiada de la ciudad y/o el domicilio. (Todas las abreviaturas de las ciudades figuran en la lista del Indice de Ciudades y Comunidades).

2 The street name will include a Thomas Bros. Maps Page and Grid™ where the address is located.

El nombre de la calle incluye un cuadro de Thomas Bros. Maps Page and Grid™ con el número de página y de coordenadas que indican la ubicación del domicilio.

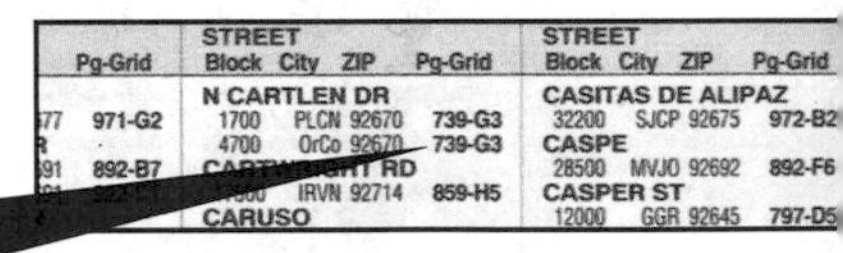

Pg-Grid	STREET Block City ZIP	Pg-Grid	STREET Block City ZIP	Pg-Grid
	N CARTLEN DR		CASITAS DE ALIPAZ	
971-G2	1700 PLCN 92670	739-G3	32200 SJCP 92675	972-B2
	4700 OrCo 92670	739-G3	CASPE	
892-B7	CARTWRIGHT RD		28500 MVJO 92692	892-F6
	IRVN 92714	859-H5	CASPER ST	
	CARUSO		12000 GGR 92645	797-D5

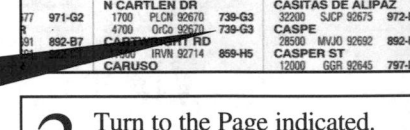

3 Turn to the Page indicated.

Pase a la página que se indica.

4 Locate the address by following the indicated Letter column and Number row until the two intersect. The street name is within this Grid area.

Localice el domicilio siguiendo la columna con letras y la hilera con números indicadas hasta que intersecten. El nombre de la calle se encuentra dentro de dicho cuadro.

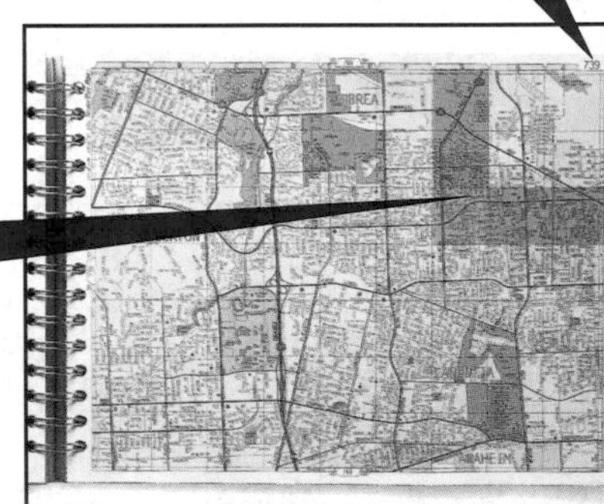

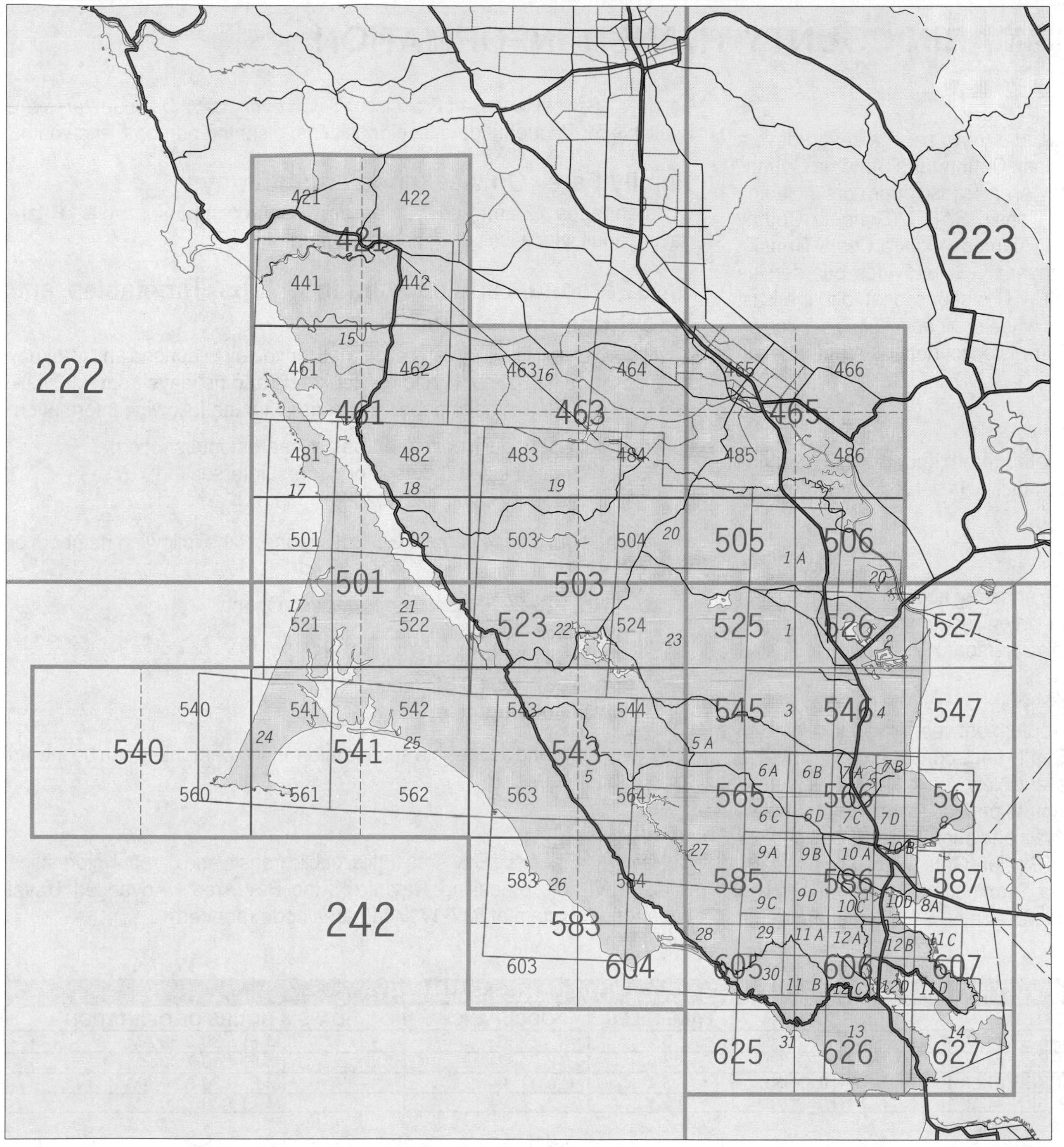

How The New Pages Work With The Old Pages

Finding New Page Numbers

This key map shows our old page layout in green and the new page layout in red. You can locate an old page number on this key map to determine the new page number.

Use of Quad-Pages

To provide important new area coverage, we have created the Quad-Page, a single map page that contains four regular pages of coverage. On the Key Map, Quad-Pages are designated by enlarged numbers in the "Quad" center, and surrounded by the page numbers of the pages included in that "Quad." Normal-size page numbers within a Quad-Page indicate that, in addition to appearing on the Quad-Page, the page is also shown in normal detail and size in the Guide. Small page numbers within the Quad-Pages indicate pages found only on Quad-Pages.

Conversion Help

As you convert to the new Thomas Bros. Maps page and grid® reference system, you may have questions or need conversion assistance. If we can be of help, please call the toll-free customer service number below for additional conversion information.

Call toll-free 1 800-899-MAPS and ask for Extension 99.

1998 MARIN COUNTY TRANSIT INFORMATION

Introduction

Golden Gate Transit (GGT) provides Bus and Ferry service seven days a week linking downtown San Francisco, Marin County, and Sonoma County. GGT provides connections with other Bay Area Transit operators including San Francisco MUNI, Bay Area Rapid Transit (BART), Sonoma County Transit, Santa Rosa City Bus, AC Transit (Alameda/Contra Costa Transit), and SamTrans (San Mateo County Transit). GGT provides bus service connecting Marin County with Del Norte BART stations located in the East Bay, Contra Costa County. GGT provides wheelchair accessible service on all ferries and most bus routes. Call numbers listed for details. All information is subject to change.

Park and Ride Facilities

There are 25 Park and Ride facilities located throughout the GGT service area. Parking is complimentary and each facility is served by GGT buses during commute hours.

Bus Fares

Bus fares are determined by travel zones and vary according to the length of trip, and range from $1.25 to $4.50 one-way. Discount fares are available for frequent riders, senior citizens, disabled persons, and youth.

Ferry Service

Golden Gate Transit operates two ferry routes; between Larkspur and San Francisco and between Sausalito and San Francisco. Service is provided daily (except on Thanksgiving, Christmas, and New Year's Day). Free shuttle bus service is available during peak commute periods to the ferry terminals providing direct connections with ferry arrivals and departures. Free transfers to San Francisco MUNI are available to Golden Gate Transit ferry riders. Free parking is available at the Larkspur Terminal. One-way adult cash fares: Larkspur to San Francisco: $2.50 weekdays, $4.25 weekends and holidays. Sausalito to San Francisco: $4.25 every day. Discount fares are available for frequent riders, senior citizens, disabled persons, and youth.

Family Fare - On weekends and holidays

Children, ages 12 and under, ride free when accompanied by a full-fare paying adult with a limit of two children per adult.

Free Personalized Trip Planning, Maps, Timetables, and Telephone Information

Your public transit itinerary can be planned for you by telephone any weekday from 6:00 a.m. to 8:00 p.m. and on weekends and holidays from 6:30 a.m. to 8:00 p.m. Please have paper and pencil with the following information:

- Your departure point (address or nearest intersection)
- Your destination (address or nearest intersection)
- Day and time you wish to travel

For information, please contact GGT using one of the following numbers or web site:

(415) 923-2000 from San Francisco County
(415) 455-2000 from Marin County
(707) 541-2000 from Sonoma County
(415) 257-4554 TDD number
www.goldengate.org

Map, timetable, and accessible service information pamphlets can be mailed to you upon request.

TravInfo™

Current San Francisco Bay Area traffic, public transit, and carpool information is also available by calling TravInfo™, the Bay Area's Advanced Travel Information System at **817-1717** (no area code required).

EXISTING HIGH OCCUPANCY VEHICLE (HOV) LANES SUMMARY

COUNTY	ROUTE DESCRIPTION	DIRECTION	LANE MILES	OCCUPANCY	DAYS & HOURS OF OPERATION
MARIN	**HWY 101** - MILEAGE MARKER #4.7/8.4	SOUTHBOUND	3.7	2+	(M-F) 6:30-8:30 AM
MARIN	**HWY 101** - MILEAGE MARKER #4.0/7.5	NORTHBOUND	3.5	2+	(M-F) 4:30-7:00 PM
MARIN	**HWY 101** - MILEAGE MARKER #12.8/18.9	SOUTHBOUND	6.1	2+	(M-F) 6:30-8:30 AM
MARIN	**HWY 101** - MILEAGE MARKER #12.8/18.9	NORTHBOUND	6.1	2+	(M-F) 4:30-7:00 PM

1998 MARIN COUNTY CITIES AND COMMUNITIES

ESTIMATED POPULATION INCORPORATED CITIES	177,305
ESTIMATED POPULATION UNINCORPORATED AREAS	68,195
ESTIMATED TOTAL POPULATION	245,500

COMMUNITY NAME	ABBR.	ZIP CODE	AREA SQ. MI.	EST. POP.	PAGE
ALMONTE		94941			606
ALTO		94941			606
BEL AIRE		94920			607
BEL MARIN KEYS		94949			526
* BELVEDERE	BLV	94920	2.20	2,300	627
BLACK POINT		94945			526
BOLINAS		94924			604
BURDELL		94945			506
* CORTE MADERA	CMAD	94925	4.00	8,750	606
DILLON BEACH		94929			461
DRAKES BEACH		94956			542
* FAIRFAX	FRFX	94930	2.20	7,175	565
FALLON		94972			442
FOREST KNOLLS		94933			564
GALLINAS		94903			566
GLENWOOD		94901			567
GREENBRAE		94904			586
GREEN POINT		94945			526
HARBOR POINT		94941			606
HILL HAVEN		94920			607
HOMESTEAD VALLEY		94941			606
IGNACIO		94949			546
INVERNESS		94937			522
INVERNESS PARK		94937			543
KENTFIELD		94904			586
LAGUNITAS		94938			564
* LARKSPUR	LKSP	94939	3.22	11,850	586
LITTLE REEDS HGTS		94920			607
LOS RANCHITOS		94903			566
MANZANITA		94941			606
MARIN BAY		94901			567
MARIN CITY		94965			626
-- MARIN COUNTY	MarC			245,500	
MARIN VILLAGE		94947			526
MARINWOOD		94903			546
MARSHALL		94940			502
* MILL VALLEY	MLV	94941	4.70	14,000	606
MUIR BEACH		94965			625
NICASIO		94946			544
NICASIO REDWOODS		94946			544
* NOVATO	NVTO	94949	23.00	49,050	526
OLEMA		94950			543
PARADISE CAY		94920			607
PEACOCK GAP		94901			567
PT REYES STATION		94956			543
REED		94920			607
* ROSS	ROSS	94957	2.50	2,280	586
* SAN ANSELMO	SANS	94960	2.67	12,400	566
SAN GERONIMO		94963			564
SAN MARIN		94945			525
SAN QUENTIN		94964			587
* SAN RAFAEL	SRFL	94901	22.00	53,200	566
SANTA VENETIA		94903			566
* SAUSALITO	SAUS	94965	2.14	7,800	627
SLEEPY HOLLOW		94960			566
STINSON BEACH		94970			605
STRAWBERRY MANOR		94941			606
TAMALPAIS VALLEY		94941			626
TERRA LINDA		94903			566
* TIBURON	TBRN	94920	5.90	8,500	607
TOCALOMA		94950			544
TOMALES		94971			462
WOODACRE		94973			565

* INDICATES INCORPORATED CITY

ZIP CODE POSTAL ZONES

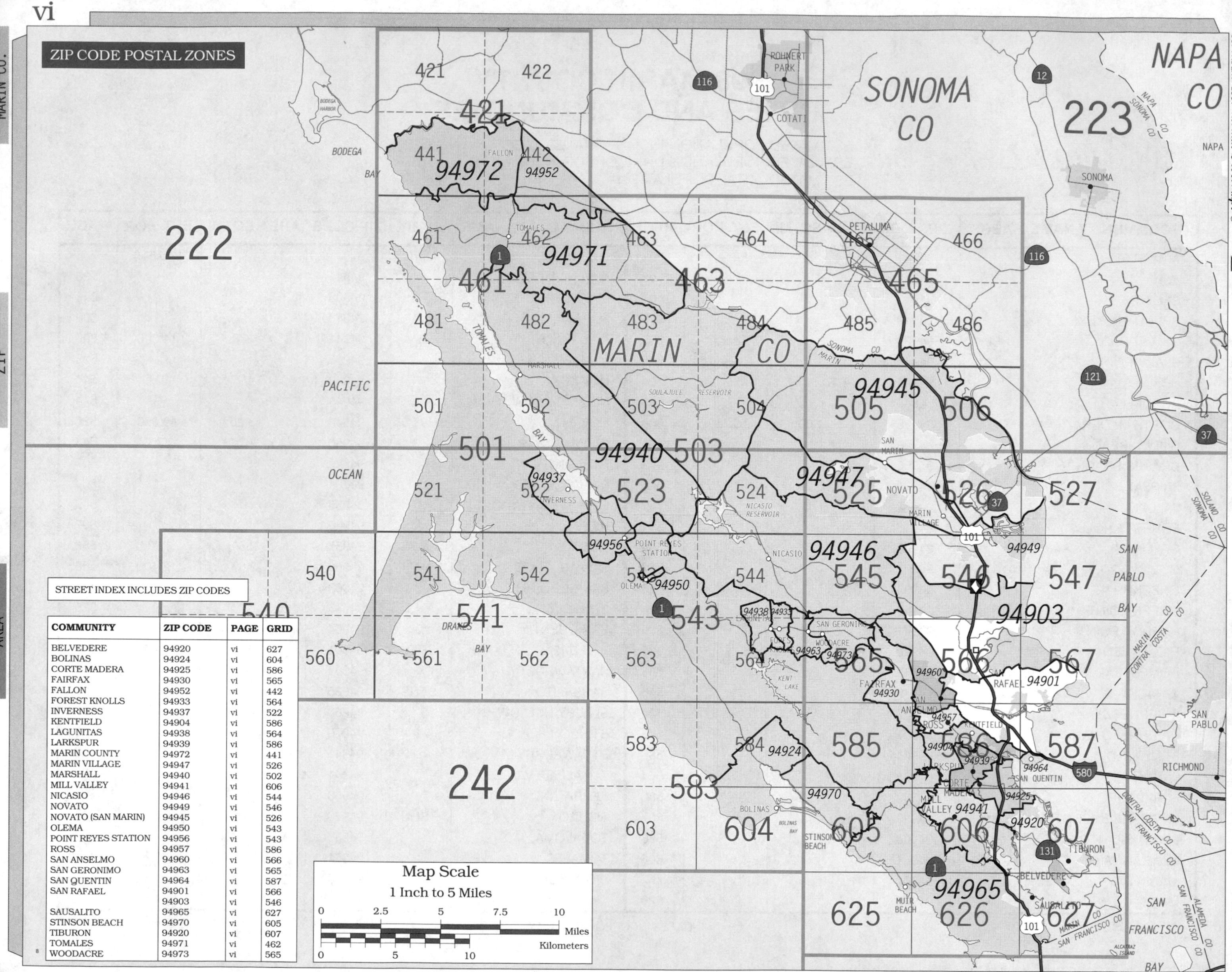

STREET INDEX INCLUDES ZIP CODES

COMMUNITY	ZIP CODE	PAGE	GRID
BELVEDERE	94920	vi	627
BOLINAS	94924	vi	604
CORTE MADERA	94925	vi	586
FAIRFAX	94930	vi	565
FALLON	94952	vi	442
FOREST KNOLLS	94933	vi	564
INVERNESS	94937	vi	522
KENTFIELD	94904	vi	586
LAGUNITAS	94938	vi	564
LARKSPUR	94939	vi	586
MARIN COUNTY	94972	vi	441
MARIN VILLAGE	94947	vi	526
MARSHALL	94940	vi	502
MILL VALLEY	94941	vi	606
NICASIO	94946	vi	544
NOVATO	94949	vi	546
NOVATO (SAN MARIN)	94945	vi	526
OLEMA	94950	vi	543
POINT REYES STATION	94956	vi	543
ROSS	94957	vi	586
SAN ANSELMO	94960	vi	566
SAN GERONIMO	94963	vi	565
SAN QUENTIN	94964	vi	587
SAN RAFAEL	94901	vi	566
	94903	vi	546
SAUSALITO	94965	vi	627
STINSON BEACH	94970	vi	605
TIBURON	94920	vi	607
TOMALES	94971	vi	462
WOODACRE	94973	vi	565

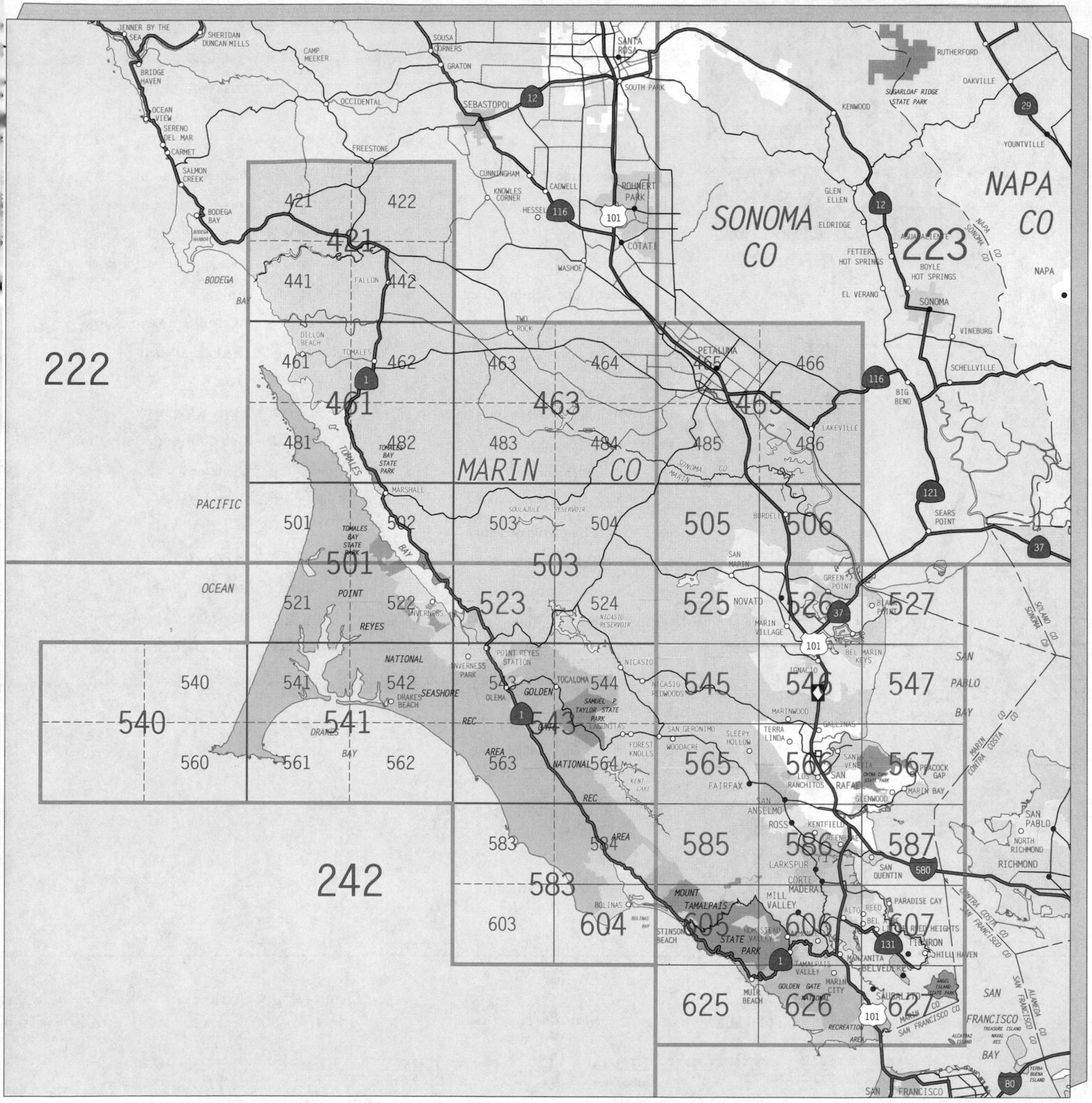

Key Map to Detail Pages

The Thomas Guide® contains several types of map pages:
Arterial, Detail, and Quad

243 Arterial Page– Small scale area map, shown with a wide border

525 Detail Page– Full scale map page, shown with a solid thin border

465 Quad Page– A single map page containing four interior pages at half the detail scale, shown with a bold border subdivided by thin dashed lines

466 Interior pages are shown only inside Quad pages

Key Legend

- Incorporated City
- Community
- County Seat
- Freeway
- Highway
- Primary
- Secondary, Minor
- River, Creek

Key Map Scale

1 Inch to 6 Miles

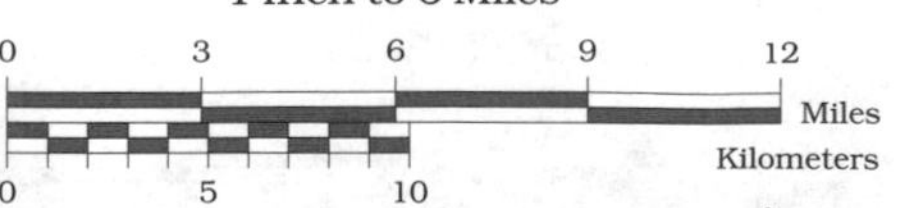

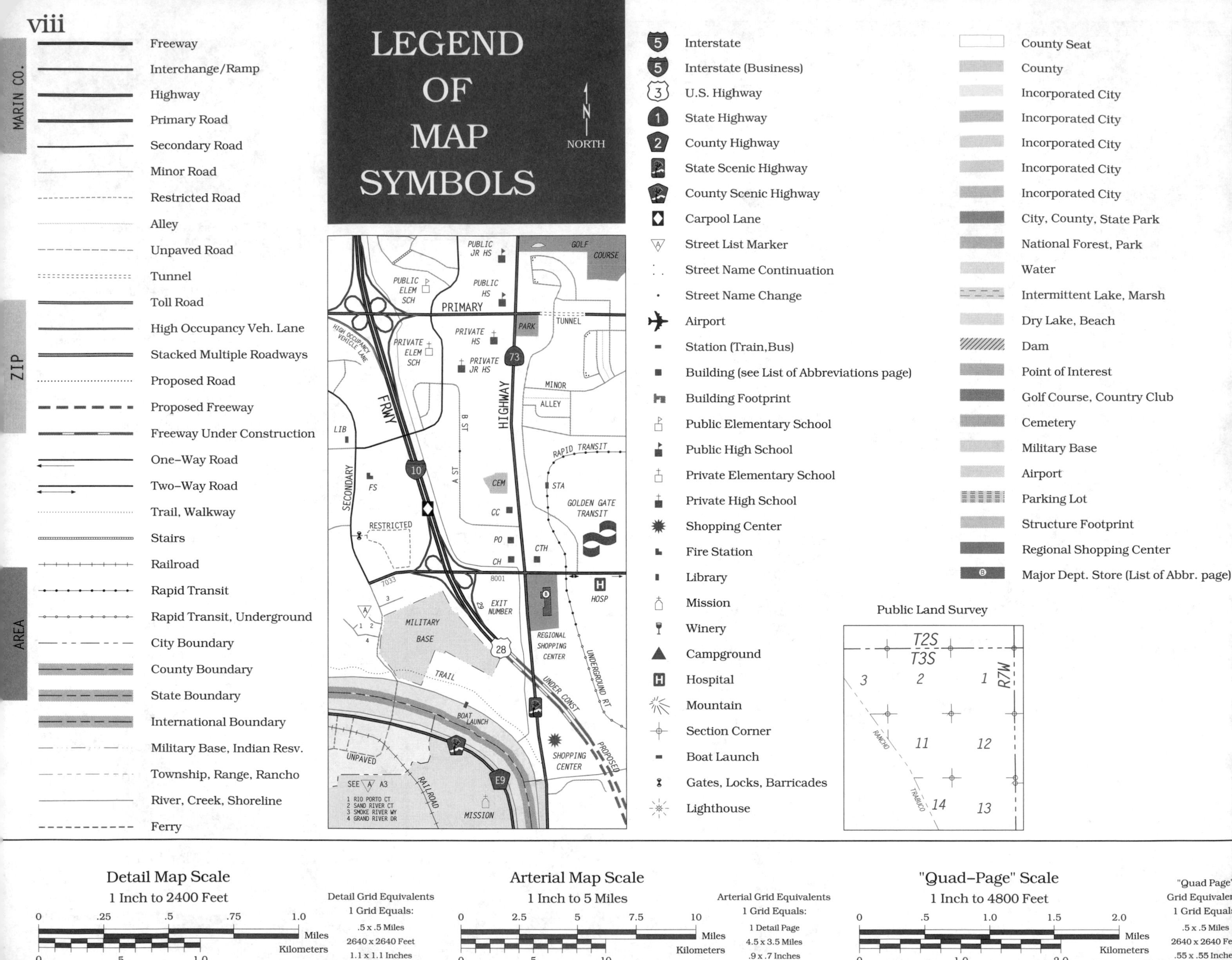
MARIN CO.
ZIP
AREA
Freeway
Interchange/Ramp
Highway
Primary Road
Secondary Road
Minor Road
Restricted Road
Alley
Unpaved Road
Tunnel
Toll Road
High Occupancy Veh. Lane
Stacked Multiple Roadways
Proposed Road
Proposed Freeway
Freeway Under Construction
One-Way Road
Two-Way Road
Trail, Walkway
Stairs
Railroad
Rapid Transit
Rapid Transit, Underground
City Boundary
County Boundary
State Boundary
International Boundary
Military Base, Indian Resv.
Township, Range, Rancho
River, Creek, Shoreline
Ferry
LEGEND OF MAP SYMBOLS
NORTH
PUBLIC JR HS
GOLF COURSE
PUBLIC ELEM SCH
PUBLIC HS
PRIMARY
TUNNEL
PARK
HIGH OCCUPANCY VEHICLE LANE
PRIVATE ELEM SCH
PRIVATE HS
PRIVATE JR HS
73
MINOR
ALLEY
FRWY
B ST
HIGHWAY
LIB
RAPID TRANSIT
10
A ST
SECONDARY
FS
CEM
STA
GOLDEN GATE TRANSIT
RESTRICTED
CC
PO
CTH
CH
7033
8001
HOSP
3
29
EXIT NUMBER
MILITARY BASE
1 2
4
28
REGIONAL SHOPPING CENTER
UNDERGROUND RT
TRAIL
UNDER CONST
BOAT LAUNCH
SHOPPING CENTER
PROPOSED
UNPAVED
E9
SEE A A3
1 RIO PORTO CT
2 SAND RIVER CT
3 SMOKE RIVER WY
4 GRAND RIVER DR
RAILROAD
MISSION
Interstate
Interstate (Business)
U.S. Highway
State Highway
County Highway
State Scenic Highway
County Scenic Highway
Carpool Lane
Street List Marker
Street Name Continuation
Street Name Change
Airport
Station (Train,Bus)
Building (see List of Abbreviations page)
Building Footprint
Public Elementary School
Public High School
Private Elementary School
Private High School
Shopping Center
Fire Station
Library
Mission
Winery
Campground
Hospital
Mountain
Section Corner
Boat Launch
Gates, Locks, Barricades
Lighthouse
County Seat
County
Incorporated City
Incorporated City
Incorporated City
Incorporated City
Incorporated City
City, County, State Park
National Forest, Park
Water
Intermittent Lake, Marsh
Dry Lake, Beach
Dam
Point of Interest
Golf Course, Country Club
Cemetery
Military Base
Airport
Parking Lot
Structure Footprint
Regional Shopping Center
Major Dept. Store (List of Abbr. page)
Public Land Survey
T2S
T3S
3 2 1
R7W
RANCHO
11 12
TRABUCO
14 13
Detail Map Scale
1 Inch to 2400 Feet
0 .25 .5 .75 1.0
Miles
Kilometers
0 .5 1.0
Detail Grid Equivalents
1 Grid Equals:
.5 x .5 Miles
2640 x 2640 Feet
1.1 x 1.1 Inches
Arterial Map Scale
1 Inch to 5 Miles
0 2.5 5 7.5 10
Miles
Kilometers
0 5 10
Arterial Grid Equivalents
1 Grid Equals:
1 Detail Page
4.5 x 3.5 Miles
.9 x .7 Inches
"Quad-Page" Scale
1 Inch to 4800 Feet
0 .5 1.0 1.5 2.0
Miles
Kilometers
0 1.0 2.0
"Quad Page"
Grid Equivalent
1 Grid Equals:
.5 x .5 Miles
2640 x 2640 Feet
.55 x .55 Inches

SEE 566 MAP

Downtown San Rafael

Points of Interest

1 Administration Building D2
2 Albert Park D7
3 Beach Park F7
4 Boyd Memorial Park D5
5 Childrens Island D1
6 Court House Square D6
7 Diversified Financial Centre D6
8 Dominican College F5
9 Embassy Suites Hotel D1
10 Exhibit Hall/Convention Center D1
11 Forest Meadows Performing Arts Center F5
12 Grestle Memorial Park C7
13 Hall of Justice D1
14 Harry A Barrier Memorial Park F3
15 Kaiser Permanente Hospital A1
16 Lagoon Park D1
17 Marin County Civic Center & Library D2
18 Marin Co Historical Society Museum D6
19 Mission San Rafael D6
20 Montecito Plaza F7
21 Mount Olivet Cemetery B1
22 Mount Tamalpais Cemetery A3
23 Panama Hotel D7
24 San Pedro Mountain Preserve E2
25 San Rafael Chamber of Commerce E6
26 San Rafael City Hall D6
27 San Rafael Library D6
28 San Rafael Yacht Harbor F7
29 Sun Valley Park B4
30 Terra Linda–Sleepy Hollow Divide Pres. Southern Area A3
31 The Mall At Northgate B1
32 Veterans Memorial Auditorium D1

Map Scale

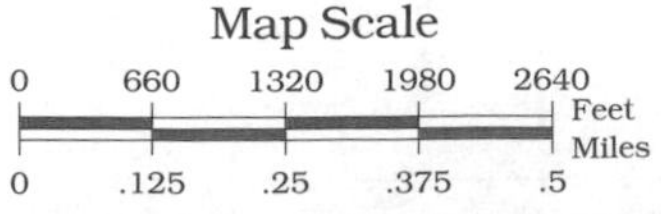

SEE 566 MAP
SEE 566 MAP
SEE 586 MAP

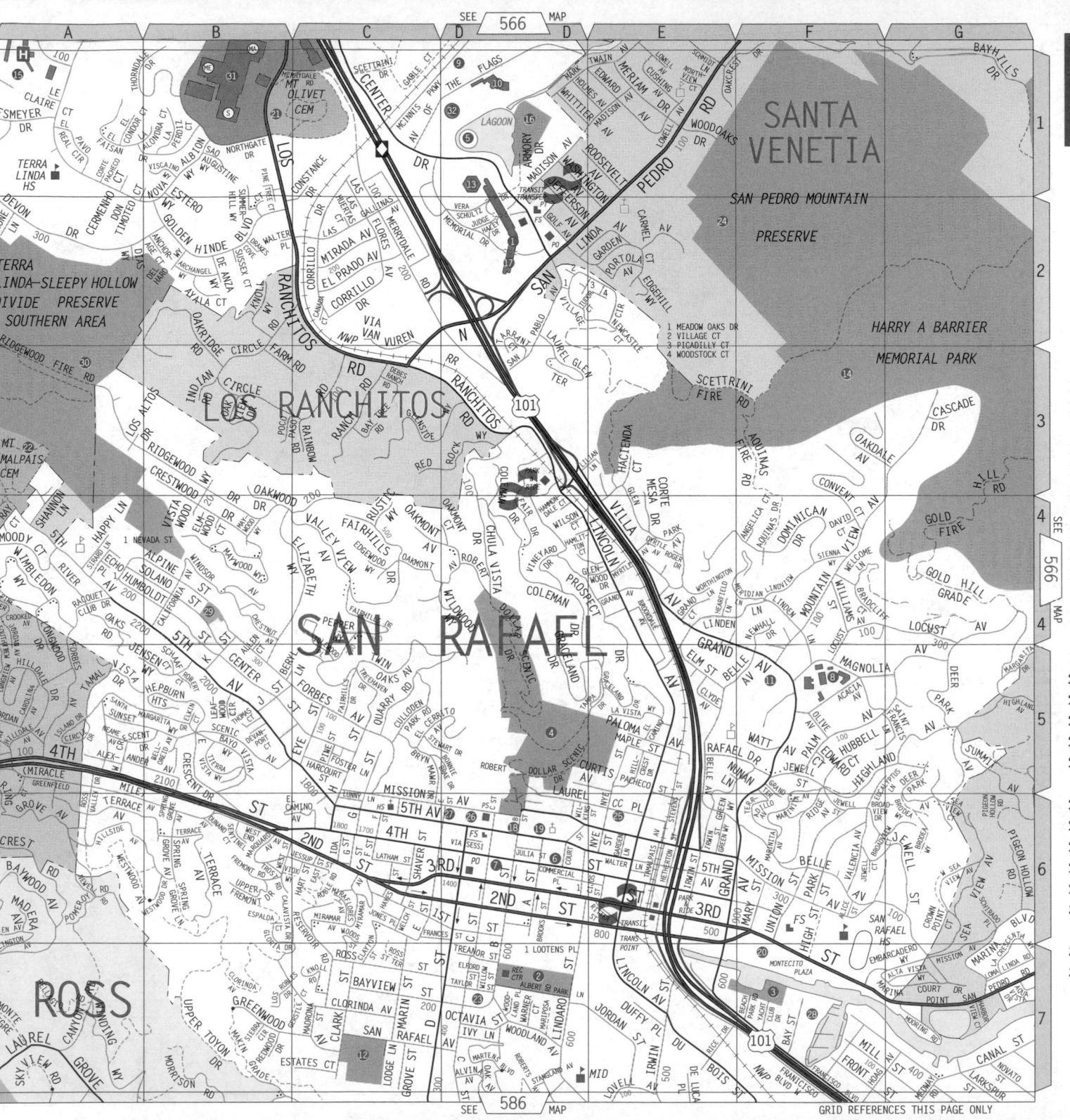

GRID REFERENCES THIS PAGE ONLY

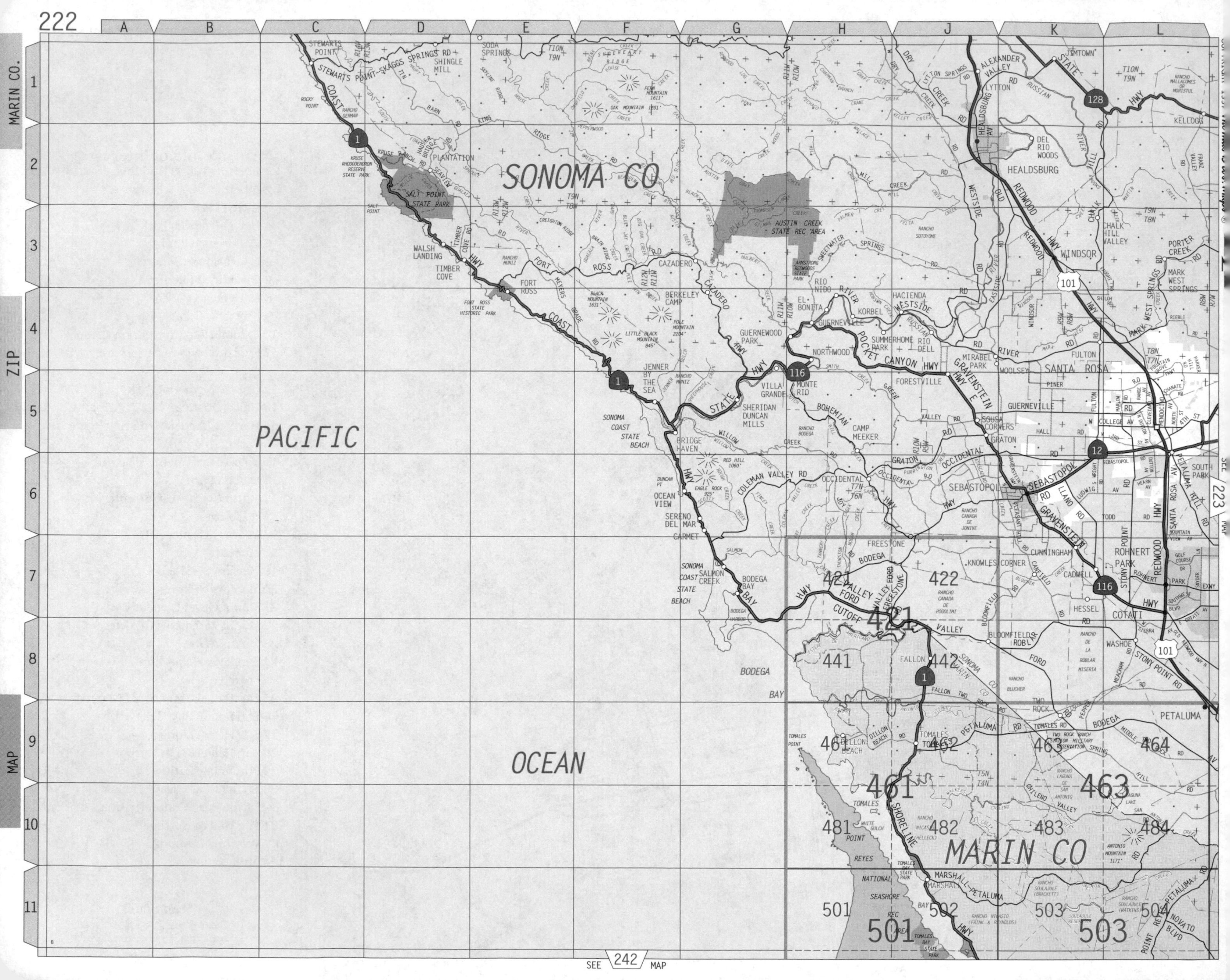
222
A
B
C
D
E
F
G
H
J
K
L
MARIN CO.
ZIP
MAP
1
2
3
4
5
6
7
8
9
10
11
SONOMA CO
MARIN CO
PACIFIC
OCEAN
STEWARTS POINT
STEWARTS POINT-SKAGGS SPRINGS RD
SODA SPRINGS
SHINGLE MILL
ROCKY POINT
RANCHO GERMAN
KRUSE RHODODENDRON RESERVE STATE PARK
PLANTATION
SALT POINT STATE PARK
SALT POINT
WALSH LANDING
TIMBER COVE
FORT ROSS
FORT ROSS STATE HISTORIC PARK
CREIGHTON RIDGE
CAZADERO
BERKELEY CAMP
AUSTIN CREEK STATE REC AREA
ARMSTRONG REDWOODS STATE PARK
RIO NIDO
EL BONITA
GUERNEVILLE
GUERNEWOOD PARK
NORTHWOOD
KORBEL
HACIENDA
SUMMERHOME PARK
RIO DELL
MIRABEL PARK
FORESTVILLE
JENNER BY THE SEA
VILLA GRANDE
MONTE RIO
SHERIDAN DUNCAN MILLS
SONOMA COAST STATE BEACH
BRIDGE HAVEN
CAMP MEEKER
OCCIDENTAL
DUNCAN PT
OCEAN VIEW
SERENO DEL MAR
CARMET
SALMON CREEK
BODEGA BAY
BODEGA HARBOR
BODEGA
FREESTONE
VALLEY FORD
CUTOFF
KNOWLES CORNER
CUNNINGHAM
CADWELL
HESSEL
COTATI
ROHNERT PARK
BLOOMFIELD
FALLON
TWO ROCK
DILLON BEACH
TOMALES
TOMALES POINT
WHITE GULCH
POINT REYES NATIONAL SEASHORE
MARSHALL
TOMALES BAY STATE PARK
PETALUMA
ALEXANDER VALLEY
LYTTON
HEALDSBURG
DEL RIO WOODS
JIMTOWN
KELLOGG
CHALK HILL VALLEY
WINDSOR
PORTER CREEK
MARK WEST SPRINGS
FULTON
SANTA ROSA
WOOLSEY
PINER
SOUSA CORNERS
GRATON
SEBASTOPOL
SOUTH PARK
WASHOE
REDWOOD HWY
GRAVENSTEIN HWY
SHORELINE HWY
COAST HWY
BOHEMIAN HWY
RIVER RD
WESTSIDE RD
COLEMAN VALLEY RD
BODEGA HWY
STONY POINT RD
PETALUMA HILL RD
CHILENO VALLEY
ANTONIO MOUNTAIN 1171'
FERN MOUNTAIN 1611'
OAK MOUNTAIN 1891'
BLACK MOUNTAIN 1631'
POLE MOUNTAIN 2204'
LITTLE BLACK MOUNTAIN 845'
RED HILL 1060'
EAGLE ROCK 925'
1
101
116
12
128
421
422
441
442
461
462
463
464
481
482
483
484
501
502
503
504
T10N
T9N
T8N
T7N
T6N
T5N
T4N
SEE 223 MAP
SEE 242 MAP

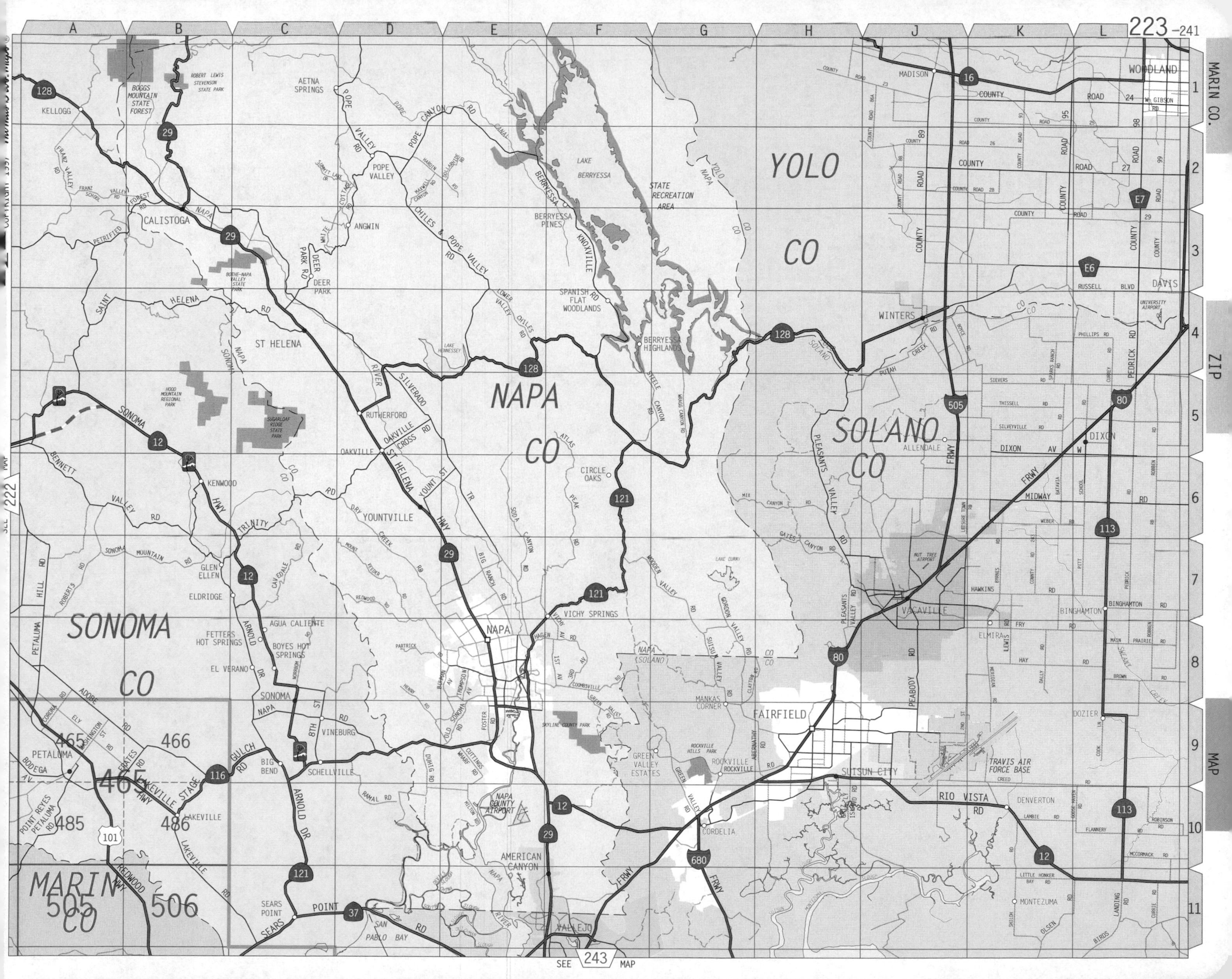

223-241
A
B
C
D
E
F
G
H
J
K
L
1
2
3
4
5
6
7
8
9
10
11
MARIN CO.
ZIP
MAP
SEE 222 MAP
SEE 243 MAP
YOLO
CO
NAPA
CO
SOLANO
CO
SONOMA
CO
MARIN
CO
KELLOGG
BOGGS MOUNTAIN STATE FOREST
ROBERT LEWIS STEVENSON STATE PARK
AETNA SPRINGS
POPE VALLEY
ANGWIN
CALISTOGA
DEER PARK
ST HELENA
RUTHERFORD
OAKVILLE
YOUNTVILLE
KENWOOD
GLEN ELLEN
ELDRIDGE
AGUA CALIENTE
FETTERS HOT SPRINGS
BOYES HOT SPRINGS
EL VERANO
SONOMA
VINEBURG
BIG BEND
SCHELLVILLE
PETALUMA
LAKEVILLE
SEARS POINT
NAPA
VICHY SPRINGS
AMERICAN CANYON
NAPA COUNTY AIRPORT
VALLEJO
SAN PABLO BAY
LAKE BERRYESSA
BERRYESSA PINES
SPANISH FLAT WOODLANDS
BERRYESSA HIGHLANDS
STATE RECREATION AREA
CIRCLE OAKS
MADISON
WOODLAND
WINTERS
DAVIS
UNIVERSITY AIRPORT
ALLENDALE
DIXON
VACAVILLE
NUT TREE AIRPORT
ELMIRA
BINGHAMTON
DOZIER
FAIRFIELD
MANKAS CORNER
ROCKVILLE
GREEN VALLEY ESTATES
CORDELIA
SUISUN CITY
TRAVIS AIR FORCE BASE
DENVERTON
MONTEZUMA
SKYLINE COUNTY PARK
ROCKVILLE HILLS PARK
HOOD MOUNTAIN REGIONAL PARK
SUGARLOAF RIDGE STATE PARK
BOTHE-NAPA VALLEY STATE PARK
465
466
485
486
505
506

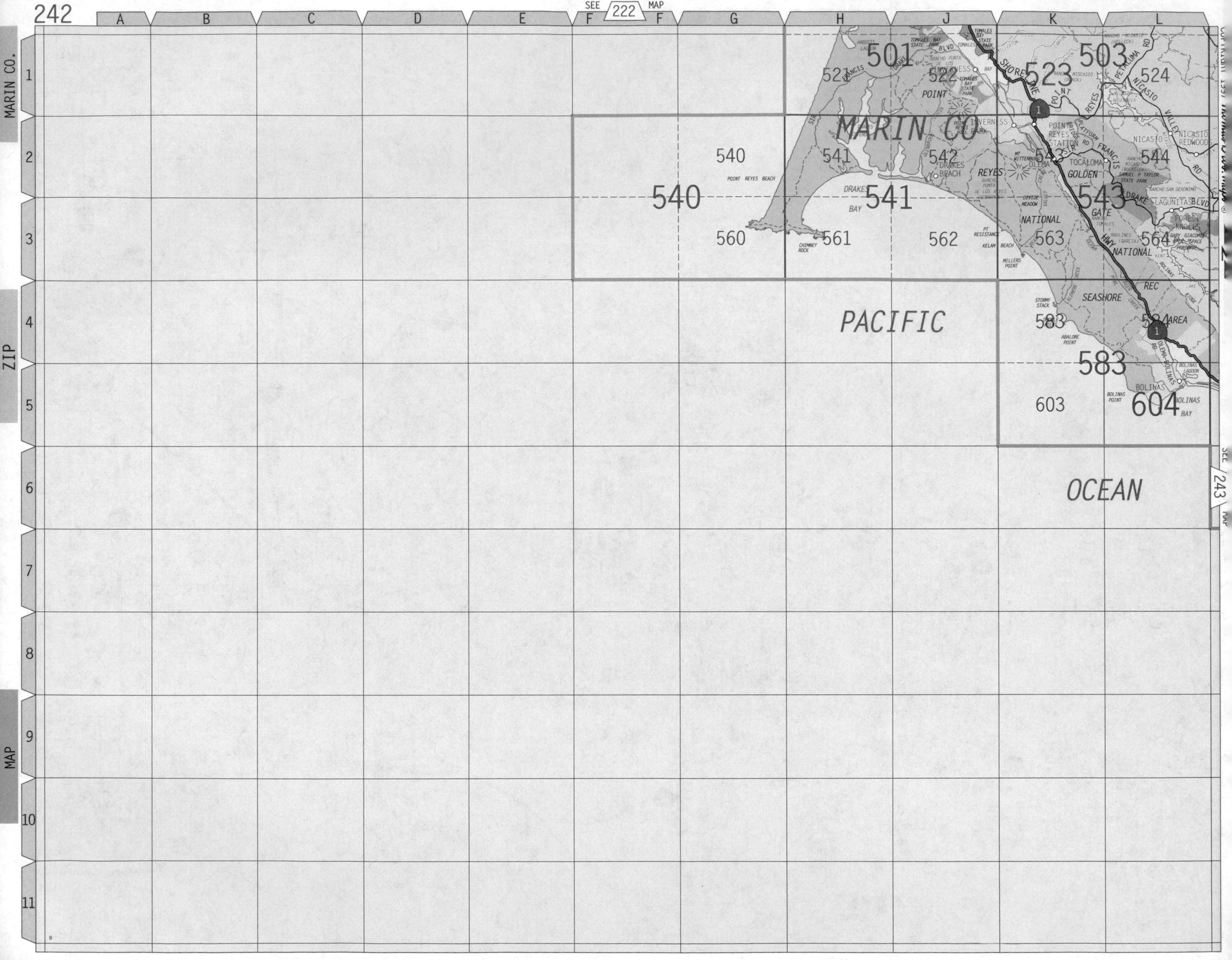

SEE 222 MAP
MARIN CO.
ZIP
MAP
MARIN CO
PACIFIC
OCEAN
540
541
560
561
562
563
583
603
604
501
503
521
522
523
524
542
543
544
564
DRAKES BAY
POINT REYES BEACH
CHIMNEY ROCK
DRAKES BEACH
INVERNESS
POINT REYES STATION
OLEMA
TOCALOMA
NICASIO
LAGUNITAS
FOREST KNOLLS
BOLINAS
BOLINAS POINT
BOLINAS BAY
BOLINAS LAGOON
SEASHORE
NATIONAL
GOLDEN GATE
REC AREA
SHORELINE HWY
SIR FRANCIS DRAKE BLVD
PLATFORM BRIDGE RD
PETALUMA RD
NICASIO VALLEY RD
OLEMA-BOLINAS RD
KELAM BEACH
MILLERS POINT
STORMY STACK
ABALONE POINT
PT RESISTANCE
DIVIDE MEADOW
SAMUEL P TAYLOR STATE PARK
TOMALES BAY STATE PARK
SEE 243 MAP

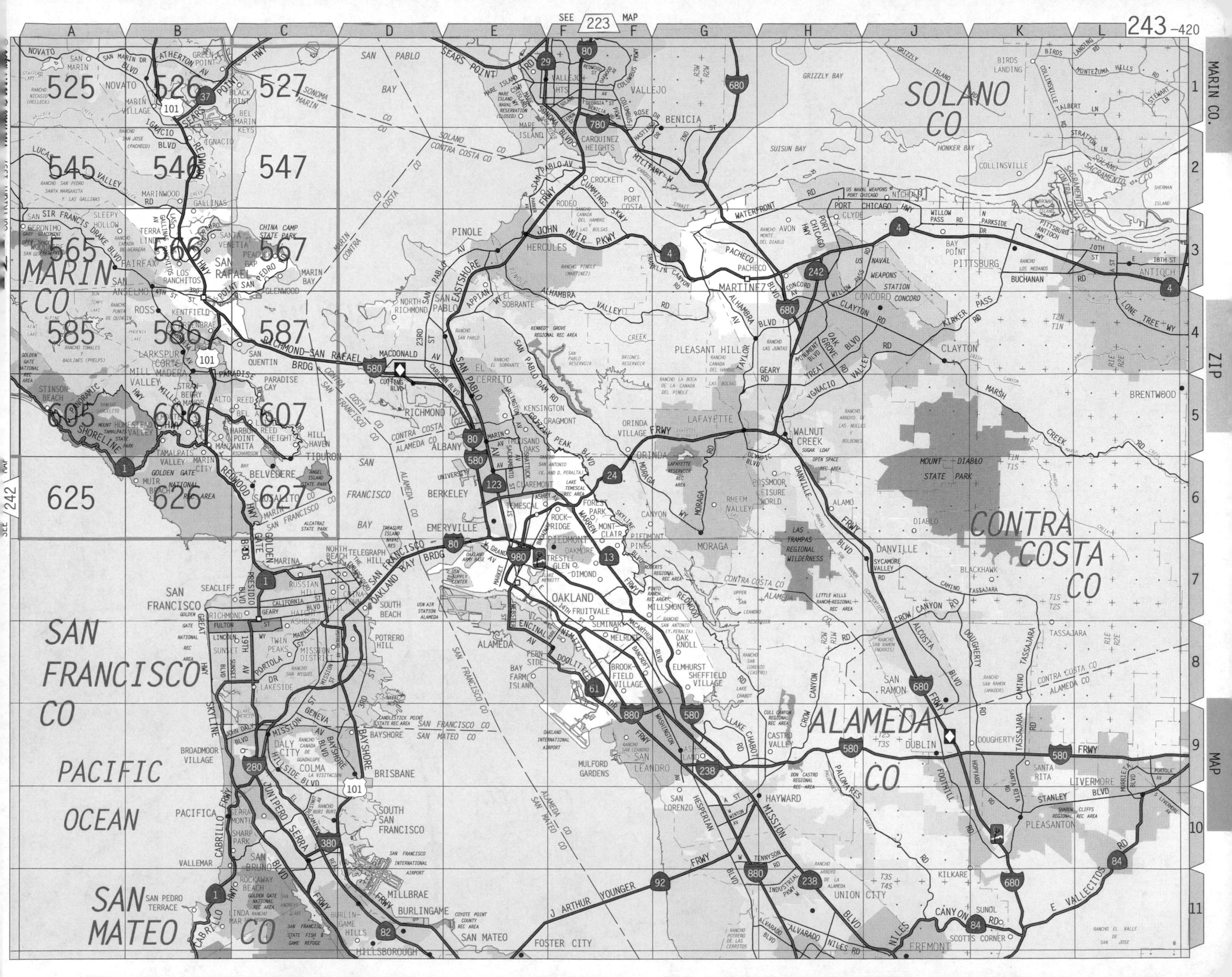
SEE 223 MAP
A
B
C
D
E
F
G
H
J
K
L
1
2
3
4
5
6
7
8
9
10
11
MARIN CO.
ZIP
MAP
SEE 242
SOLANO CO
MARIN CO
CONTRA COSTA CO
ALAMEDA CO
SAN FRANCISCO CO
SAN MATEO CO
PACIFIC OCEAN
SAN PABLO BAY
SAN FRANCISCO BAY
GRIZZLY BAY
SUISUN BAY
HONKER BAY
525
526
527
545
546
547
565
566
567
585
586
587
605
606
607
625
626
627
NOVATO
VALLEJO
BENICIA
SAN RAFAEL
RICHMOND
BERKELEY
OAKLAND
ALAMEDA
SAN FRANCISCO
DALY CITY
SOUTH SAN FRANCISCO
HAYWARD
SAN LEANDRO
MARTINEZ
CONCORD
PITTSBURG
ANTIOCH
WALNUT CREEK
LAFAYETTE
ORINDA
MORAGA
DANVILLE
SAN RAMON
DUBLIN
PLEASANTON
LIVERMORE
UNION CITY
FREMONT
FOSTER CITY
SAN MATEO
BURLINGAME
MILLBRAE
PACIFICA
BRENTWOOD
CLAYTON
EMERYVILLE
ALBANY
EL CERRITO
PINOLE
HERCULES
CROCKETT
MOUNT DIABLO STATE PARK
SAN FRANCISCO INTERNATIONAL AIRPORT
OAKLAND INTERNATIONAL AIRPORT

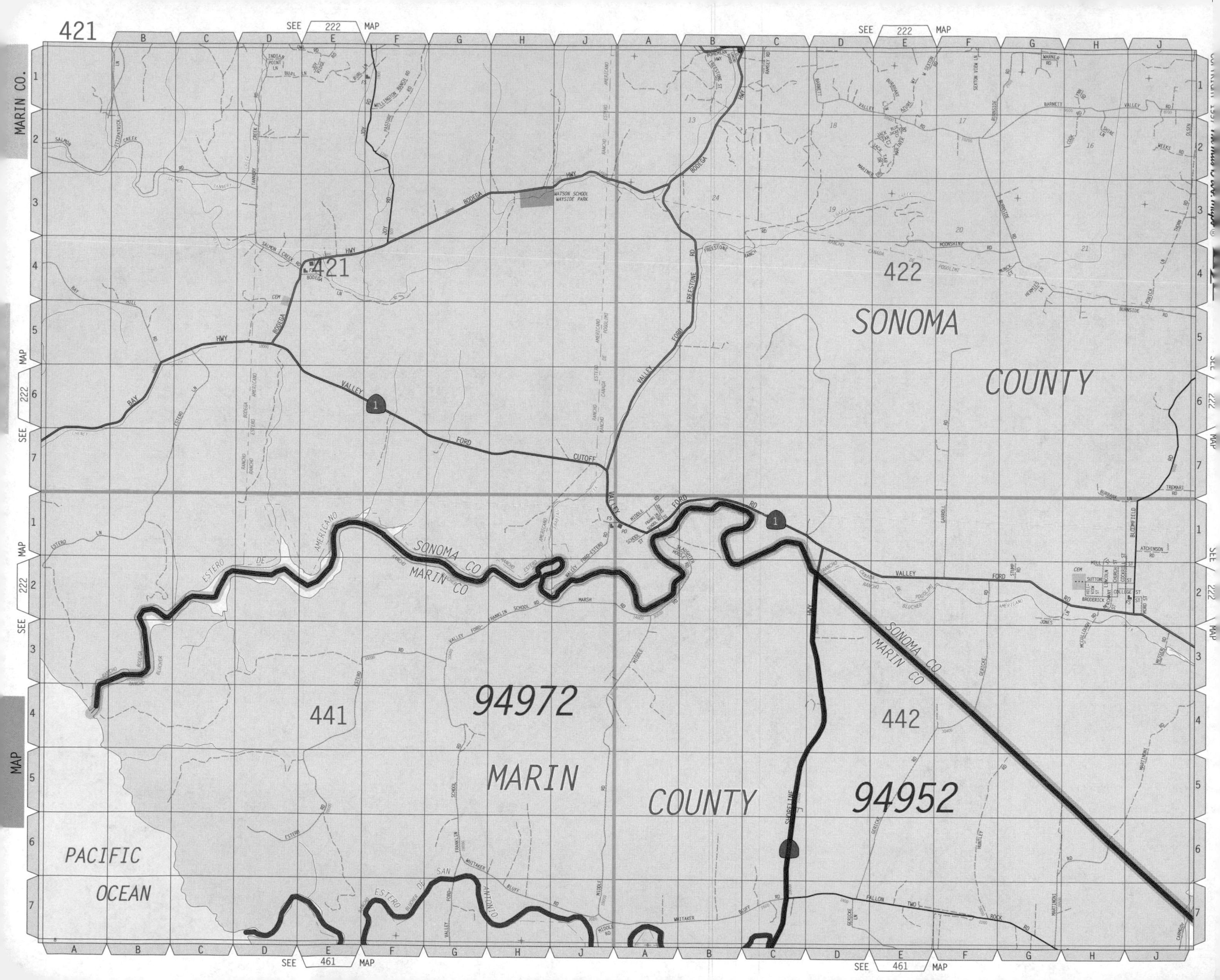
SEE 222 MAP
SEE 222 MAP
MARIN CO.
SONOMA
COUNTY
MARIN
COUNTY
94972
94952
421
422
441
442
PACIFIC
OCEAN
SONOMA CO
MARIN CO
BODEGA HWY
VALLEY FORD CUTOFF
VALLEY FORD RD
FREESTONE
VALLEY FORD RD
WATSON SCHOOL WAYSIDE PARK
BODEGA
SALMON CREEK RD
BAY HILL RD
ESTERO AMERICANO
ESTERO DE SAN ANTONIO
SHORELINE HWY
FRANKLIN SCHOOL RD
MARSH RD
WHITAKER BLUFF RD
FALLON TWO ROCK RD
BLOOMFIELD
BURNSIDE
MOONSHINE RD
BARNETT VALLEY RD
SEE 222 MAP
SEE 222 MAP
SEE 461 MAP
SEE 461 MAP
MAP

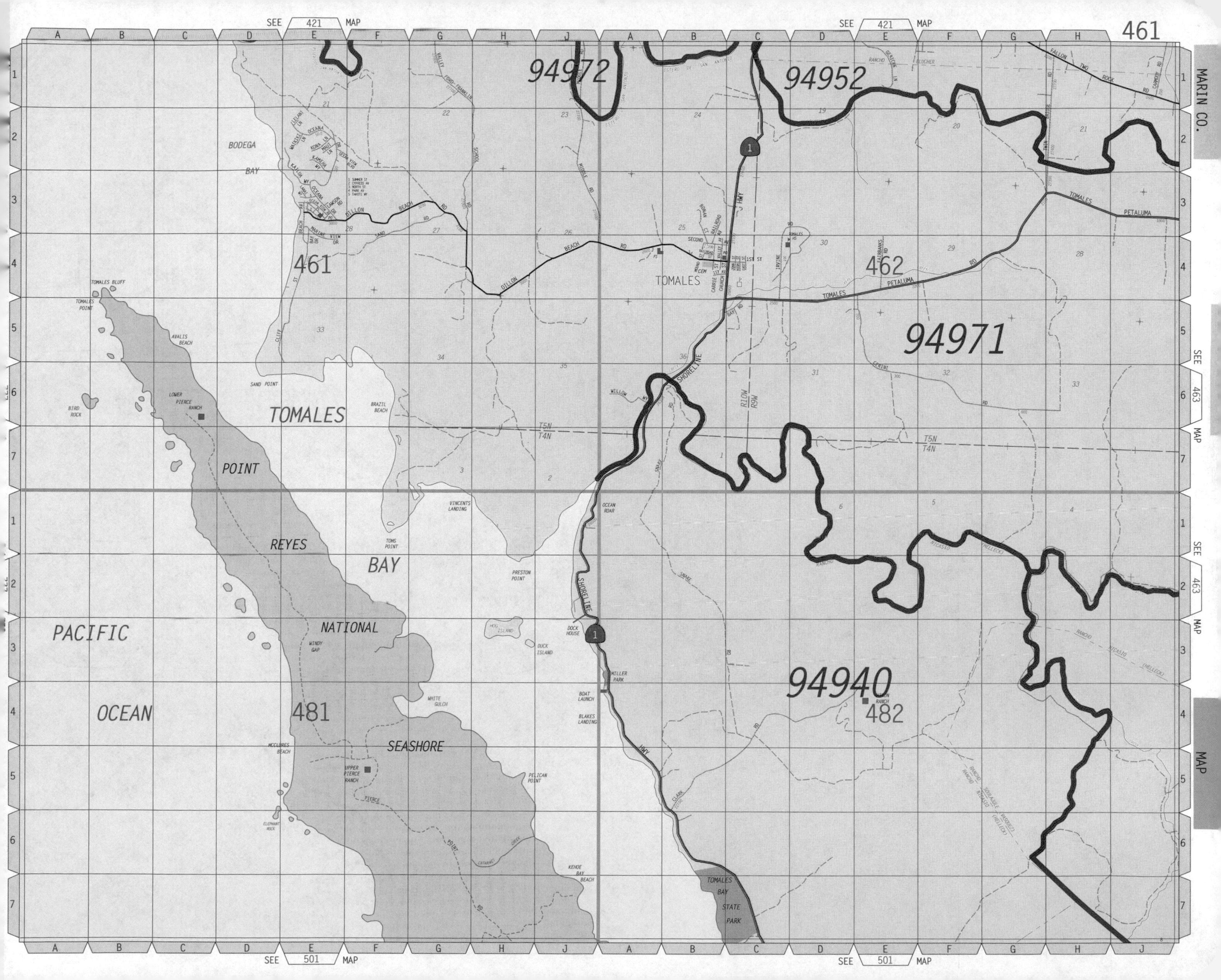

SEE 421 MAP
SEE 421 MAP
94972
94952
94971
94940
MARIN CO.
BODEGA BAY
461
462
481
482
TOMALES
TOMALES BLUFF
TOMALES POINT
AVALIS BEACH
SAND POINT
LOWER PIERCE RANCH
BIRD ROCK
TOMALES
POINT
REYES
NATIONAL
SEASHORE
BAY
PACIFIC
OCEAN
BRAZIL BEACH
VINCENTS LANDING
TOMS POINT
PRESTON POINT
HOG ISLAND
DUCK ISLAND
DOCK HOUSE
MILLER PARK
BOAT LAUNCH
BLAKES LANDING
OCEAN ROAR
WINDY GAP
WHITE GULCH
MCCLURES BEACH
UPPER PIERCE RANCH
PELICAN POINT
ELEPHANT ROCK
KEHOE BAY BEACH
TOMALES BAY STATE PARK
DILLON BEACH RD
SHORELINE HWY
TOMALES PETALUMA RD
FALLON TWO ROCK RD
T5N
T4N
R10W
R9W
SEE 463 MAP
SEE 463 MAP
SEE 501 MAP
SEE 501 MAP

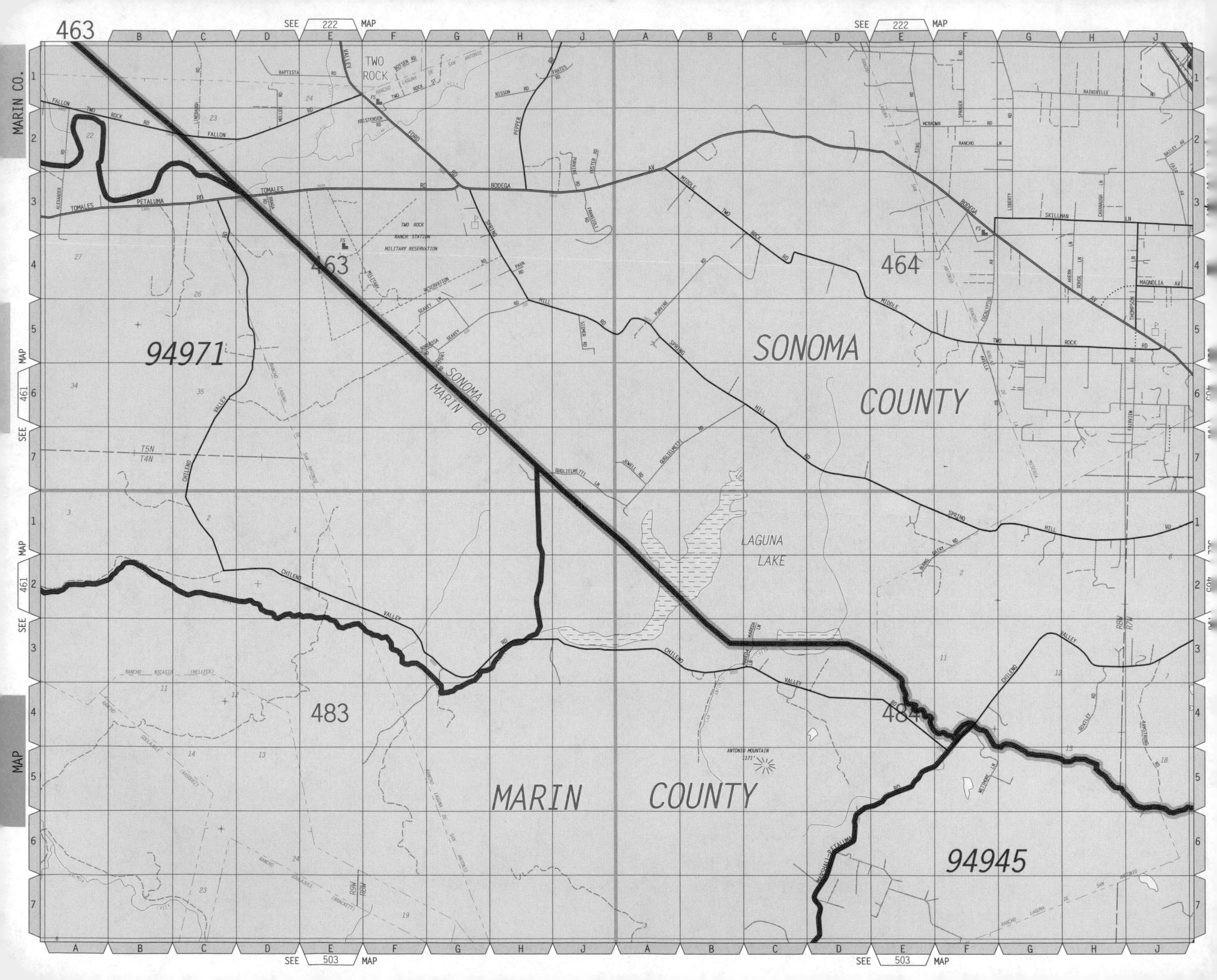

463
SEE 222 MAP
MARIN CO.
TWO ROCK
SONOMA COUNTY
MARIN COUNTY
94971
94945
463
464
483
484
TWO ROCK RANCH STATION MILITARY RESERVATION
LAGUNA LAKE
ANTONIO MOUNTAIN 1171'
SONOMA CO
MARIN CO
SEE 461 MAP
SEE 503 MAP
T5N
T4N
FALLON TWO ROCK RD
TOMALES PETALUMA RD
BODEGA AV
MIDDLE TWO ROCK RD
SPRING HILL RD
CHILENO VALLEY RD
SKILLMAN LN
MAGNOLIA AV

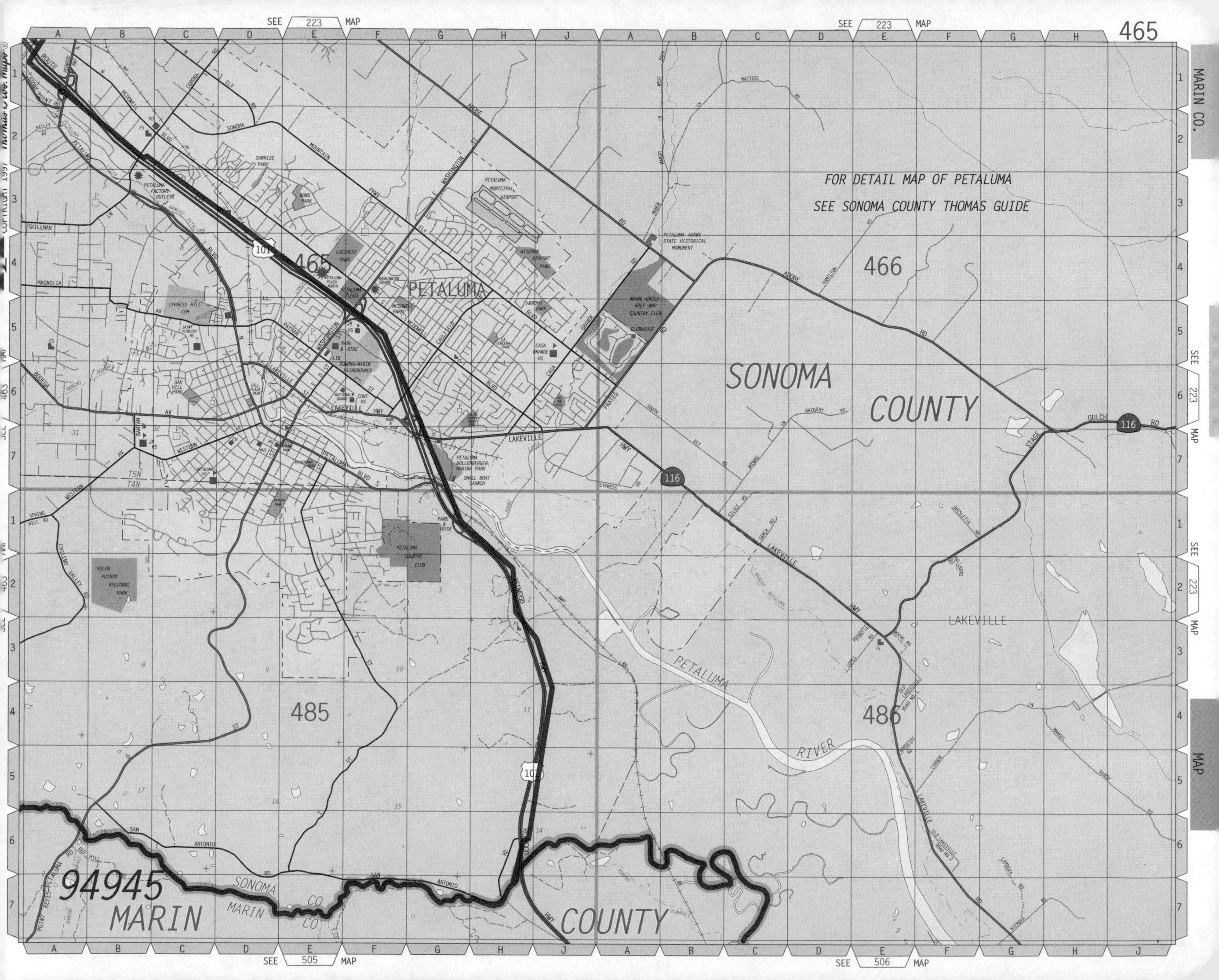

SEE 223 MAP
FOR DETAIL MAP OF PETALUMA
SEE SONOMA COUNTY THOMAS GUIDE
PETALUMA
SONOMA COUNTY
LAKEVILLE
PETALUMA RIVER
94945
MARIN
COUNTY
465
466
485
486
MARIN CO.
SEE 505 MAP
SEE 506 MAP

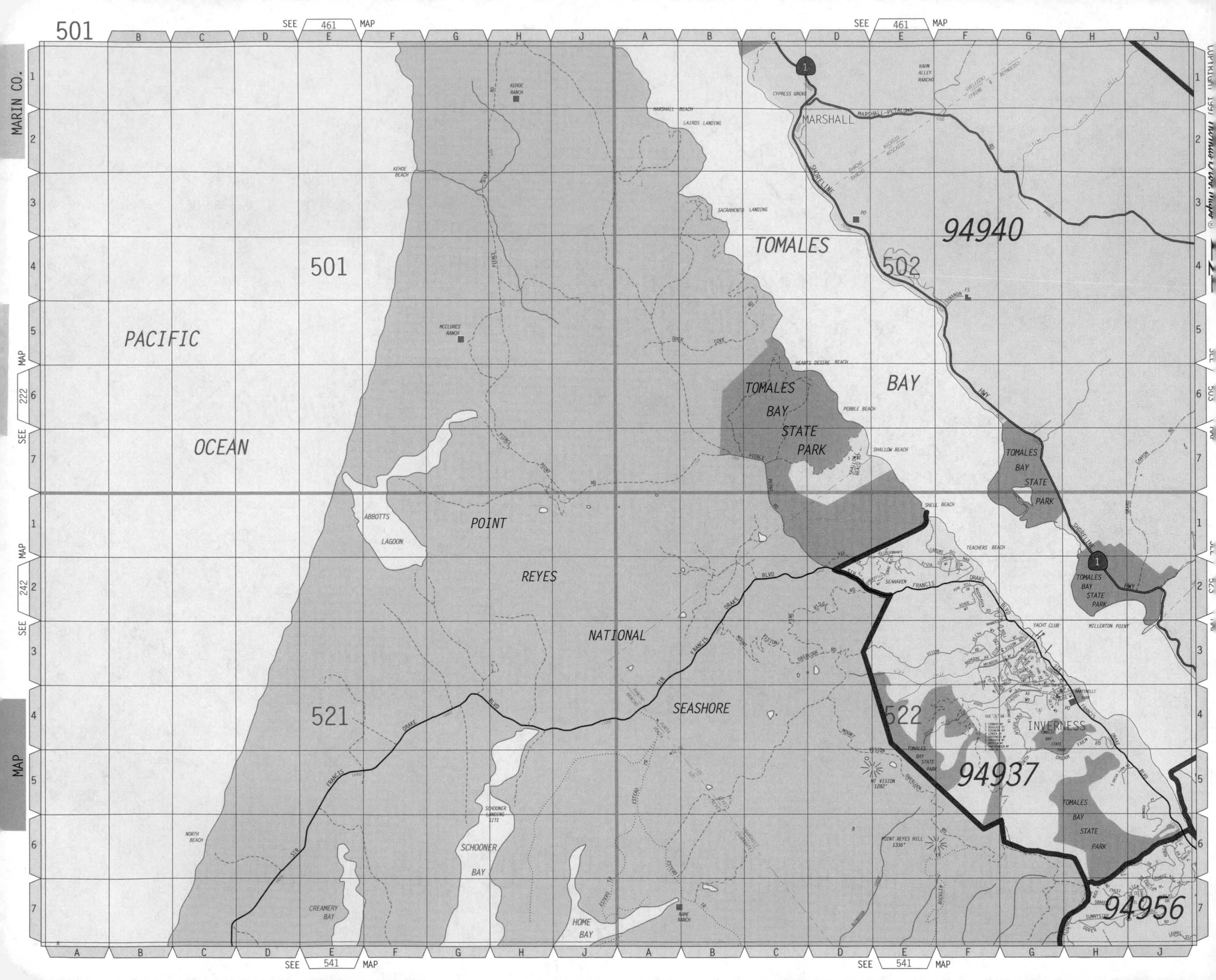
SEE 461 MAP
MARIN CO.
PACIFIC
OCEAN
501
521
522
502
TOMALES
BAY
94940
94937
94956
MARSHALL
TOMALES BAY STATE PARK
POINT
REYES
NATIONAL
SEASHORE
ABBOTTS LAGOON
SCHOONER BAY
HOME BAY
CREAMERY BAY
INVERNESS
SEE 222 MAP
SEE 242 MAP
SEE 541 MAP
Copyright 1997 Thomas Bros. Maps

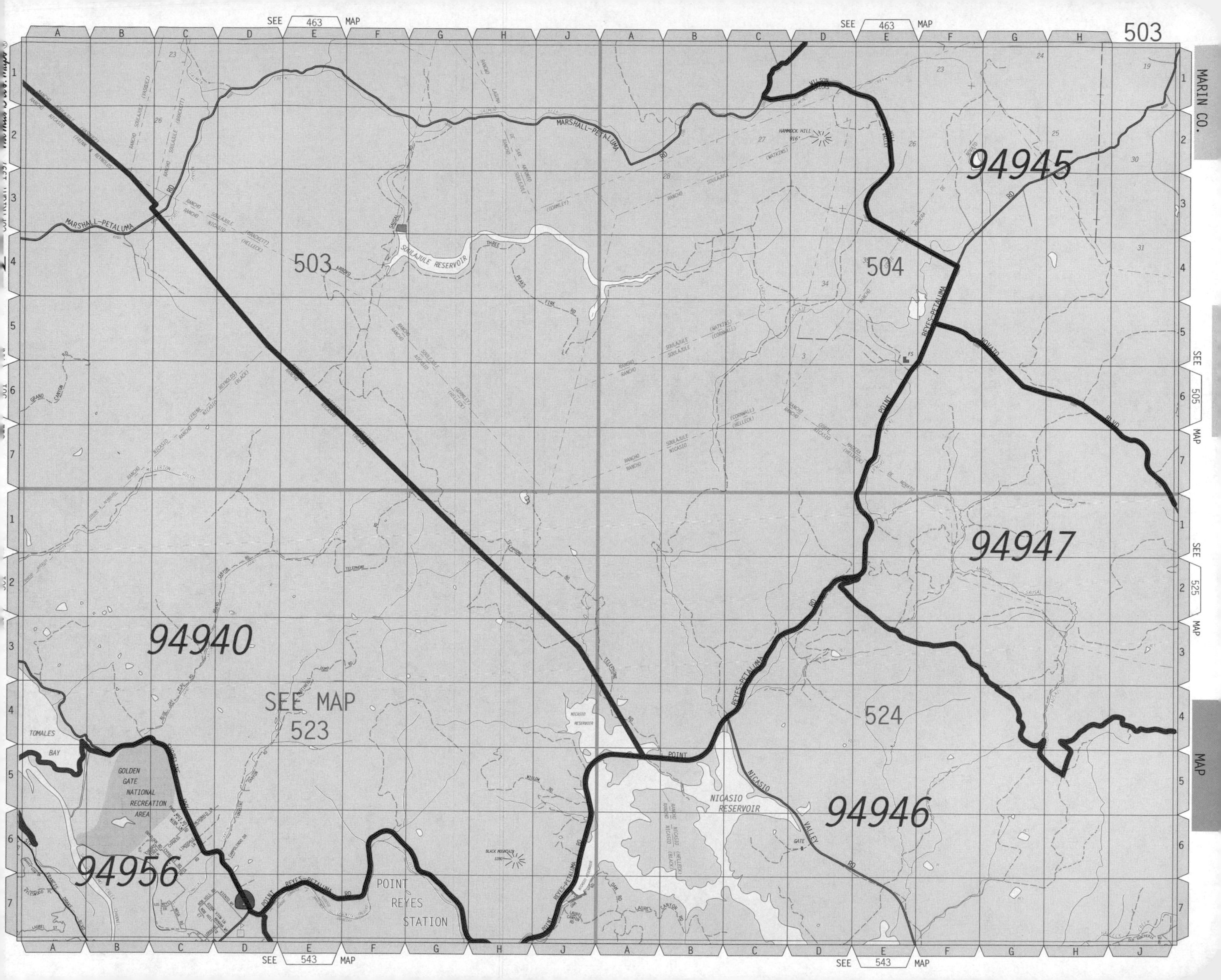
503
SEE 463 MAP
SEE 463 MAP
MARIN CO.
MARSHALL-PETALUMA RD
SOULAJULE RESERVOIR
HAMMOCK HILL 916'
THREE PEAKS FIRE RD
503
504
94945
94947
94940
94946
94956
NOVATO BLVD
POINT REYES-PETALUMA RD
SEE 505 MAP
SEE 525 MAP
SEE MAP 523
524
NICASIO RESERVOIR
NICASIO VALLEY RD
TOMALES BAY
GOLDEN GATE NATIONAL RECREATION AREA
POINT REYES STATION
BLACK MOUNTAIN
LAURELS CANYON RD
GRAND CANYON RD
TELEPHONE RD
SEE 543 MAP
SEE 543 MAP
MAP

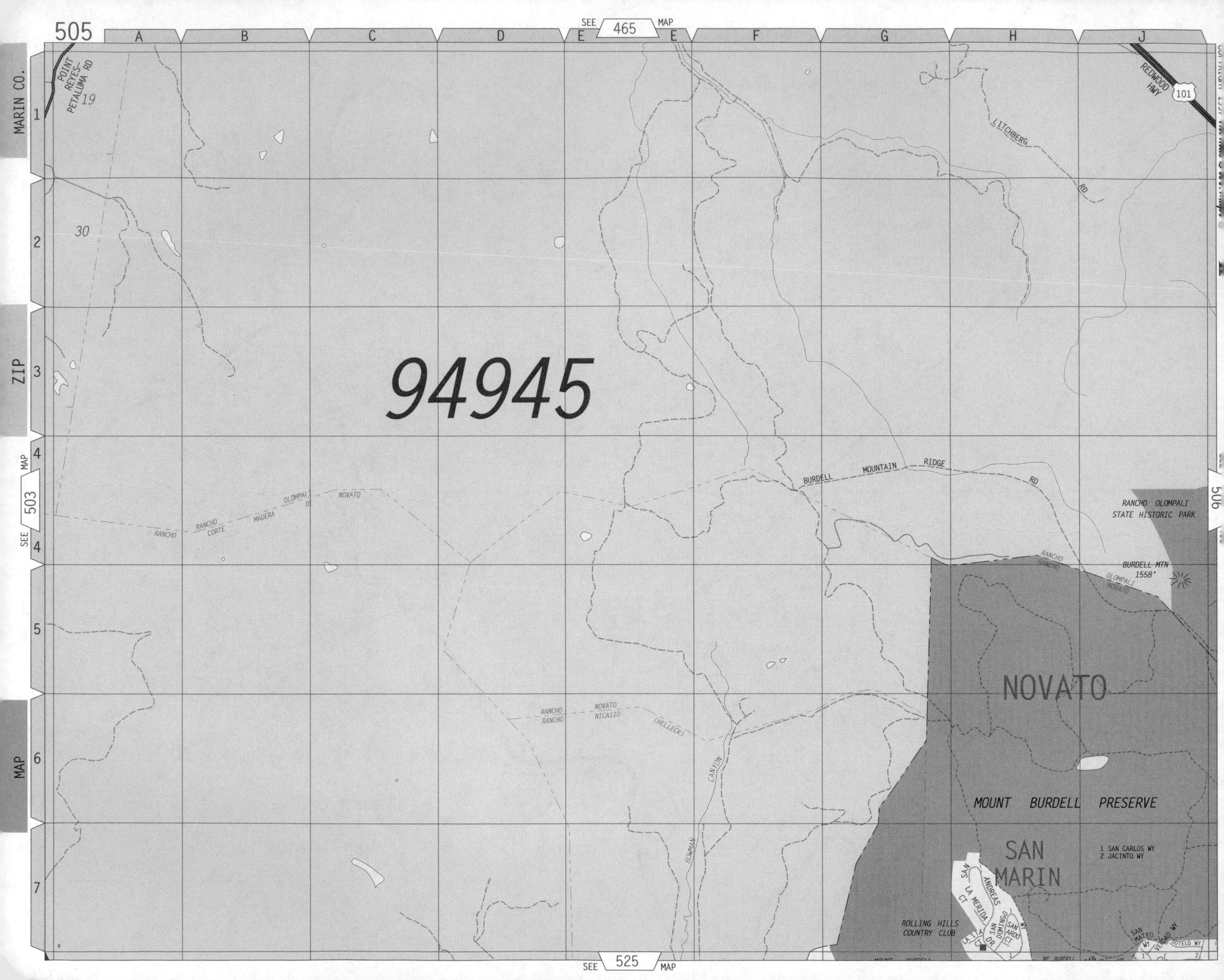
SEE 465 MAP
A
B
C
D
E
F
G
H
J
MARIN CO.
ZIP
MAP
1
2
3
4
5
6
7
POINT REYES-PETALUMA RD
19
30
REDWOOD HWY
101
LITCHBERG RD
94945
BURDELL MOUNTAIN RIDGE RD
RANCHO OLOMPALI STATE HISTORIC PARK
SEE MAP 503
506
RANCHO CORTE MADERA DE NOVATO
RANCHO OLOMPALI
RANCHO NOVATO
BURDELL MTN 1558'
NOVATO
RANCHO NOVATO
RANCHO NICASIO
(HELLECK)
CANYON
BOWMAN
MOUNT BURDELL PRESERVE
SAN MARIN
1 SAN CARLOS WY
2 JACINTO WY
ROLLING HILLS COUNTRY CLUB
SAN ANDREAS
LA MERIDA CT
SAN DOMINGO
SAN ARDO CT
SAN MATEO WY
VERDAD WY
SOTELO WY
SEE 525 MAP

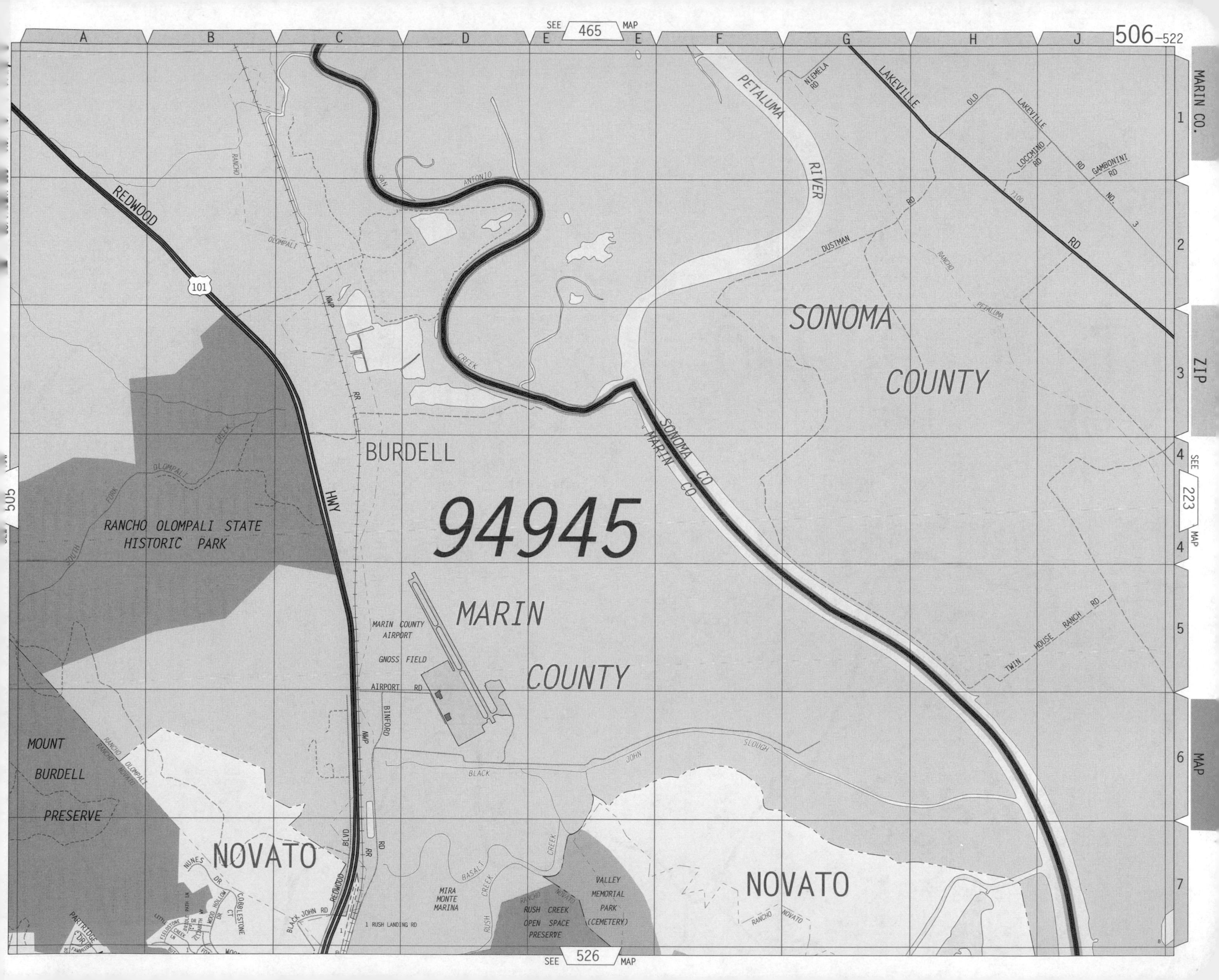
SEE 465 MAP
A
B
C
D
E
F
G
H
J
1
2
3
4
5
6
7
MARIN CO.
ZIP
MAP
SEE 223 MAP
505
REDWOOD
101
HWY
PETALUMA RIVER
LAKEVILLE
OLD LAKEVILLE
LOCCMIND RD
GAMBONINI RD
RD NO. 3
RD
NIEMELA RD
DUSTMAN RD
RANCHO PETALUMA
SAN ANTONIO CREEK
OLOMPALI
RANCHO
NWP RR
SONOMA COUNTY
SONOMA CO
MARIN CO
BURDELL
94945
RANCHO OLOMPALI STATE HISTORIC PARK
SOUTH FORK CREEK
MARIN COUNTY
MARIN COUNTY AIRPORT
GNOSS FIELD
AIRPORT RD
BINFORD RD
TWIN HOUSE RANCH RD
JOHN SLOUGH
BLACK
MOUNT BURDELL PRESERVE
RANCHO OLOMPALI
RANCHO NOVATO
NOVATO
NUNES DR
COBBLESTONE CT
WOOD HOLLOW DR
FIELDSTONE
LITTLE CREEK LN
PARTRIDGE DR
BLACK JOHN RD
REDWOOD BLVD
1 RUSH LANDING RD
MIRA MONTE MARINA
BASALT CREEK
RUSH CREEK
RUSH CREEK OPEN SPACE PRESERVE
VALLEY MEMORIAL PARK (CEMETERY)
NOVATO
RANCHO NOVATO
SEE 526 MAP

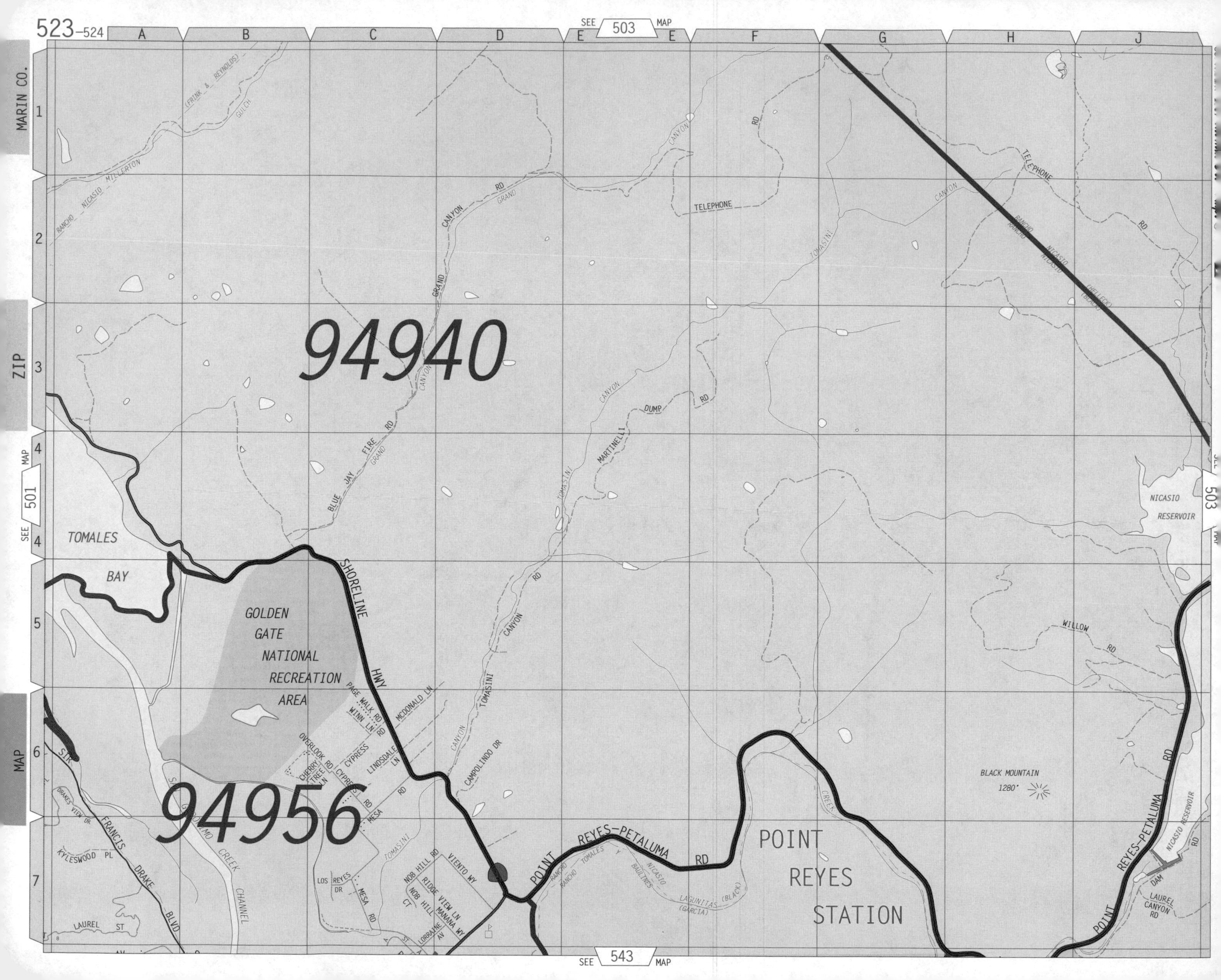

SEE 503 MAP
MARIN CO.
ZIP
MAP
94940
94956
TOMALES BAY
GOLDEN GATE NATIONAL RECREATION AREA
SHORELINE HWY
POINT REYES-PETALUMA RD
POINT REYES STATION
NICASIO RESERVOIR
BLACK MOUNTAIN 1280'
RANCHO NICASIO MILLERTON
(FRINK & REYNOLDS) GULCH
CANYON RD
GRAND CANYON RD
BLUE JAY FIRE RD
TELEPHONE
TOMASINI CANYON RD
MARTINELLI DUMP RD
RANCHO NICASIO RD
WILLOW RD
MCDONALD LN
PAGE WALK
WINN LN
OVERLOOK RD
CHERRY TREE LN
CYPRESS RD
LINDSDALE LN
MESA RD
CAMPOLINDO DR
SIR FRANCIS DRAKE BLVD
DRAKES VIEW DR
KYLESWOOD PL
LAUREL ST
LOS REYES DR
NOB HILL RD
VIENTO WY
RIDGE VIEW LN
MANANA WY
NOB HILL CT
LORRAINE AV
LAGUNITAS (BLACK) (GARCIA) CREEK
CHANNEL
DAM
LAUREL CANYON RD
SEE 501 MAP
SEE 503 MAP

SEE 543 MAP

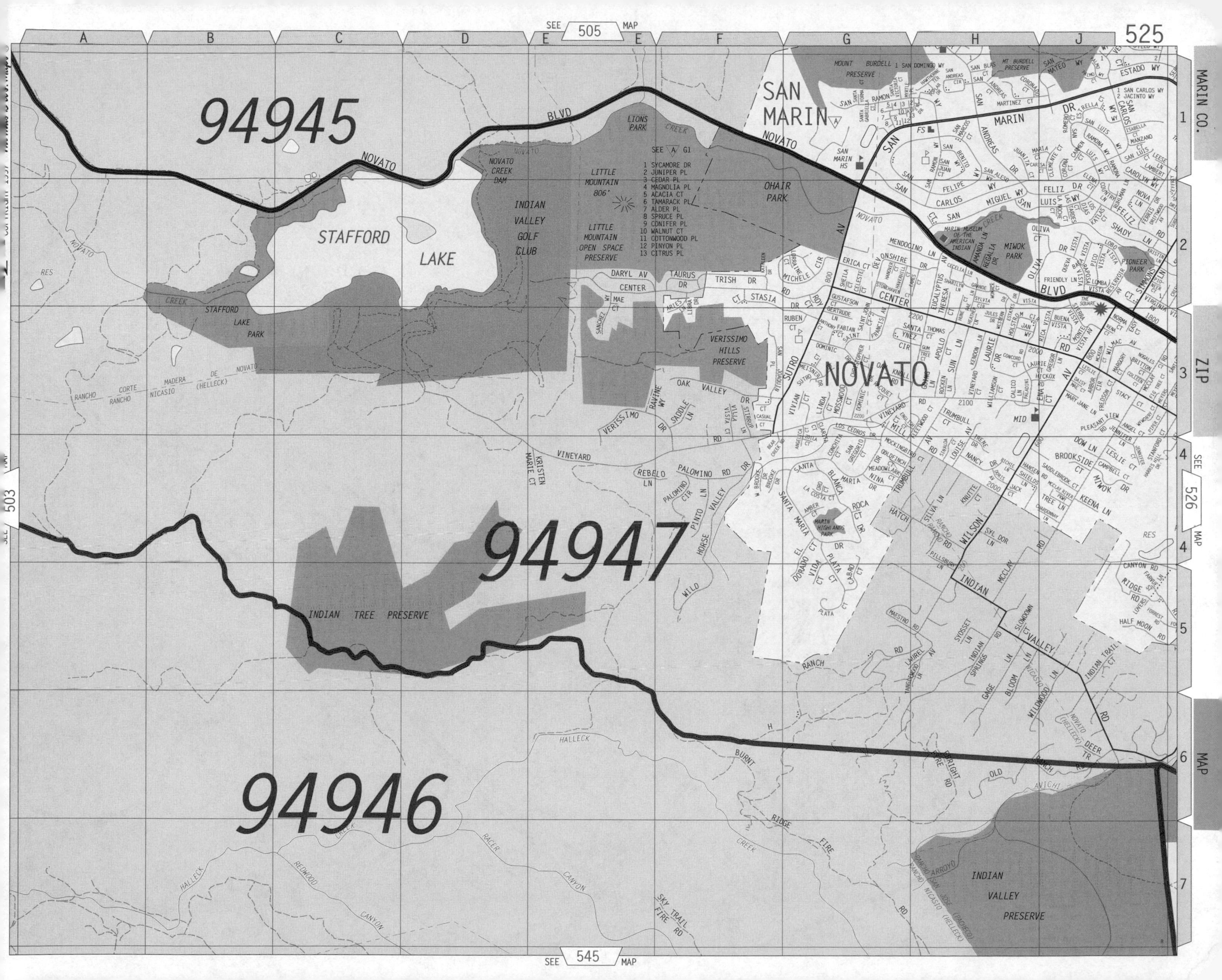
SEE 505 MAP
SEE 545 MAP
SEE 503 MAP
SEE 526 MAP
MARIN CO.
ZIP
MAP
94945
94947
94946
STAFFORD LAKE
STAFFORD LAKE PARK
NOVATO CREEK DAM
INDIAN VALLEY GOLF CLUB
LITTLE MOUNTAIN 806'
LITTLE MOUNTAIN OPEN SPACE PRESERVE
LIONS PARK
OHAIR PARK
VERISSIMO HILLS PRESERVE
INDIAN TREE PRESERVE
INDIAN VALLEY PRESERVE
MOUNT BURDELL PRESERVE
SAN MARIN
NOVATO
MIWOK PARK
PIONEER PARK
MARIN MUSEUM OF THE AMERICAN INDIAN
MARIN HIGHLANDS PARK
SAN MARIN HS
NOVATO BLVD
SEE A G1
1 SYCAMORE DR
2 JUNIPER PL
3 CEDAR PL
4 MAGNOLIA PL
5 ACACIA CT
6 TAMARACK PL
7 ALDER PL
8 SPRUCE PL
9 CONIFER PL
10 WALNUT CT
11 COTTONWOOD PL
12 PINYON PL
13 CITRUS PL
RANCHO CORTE MADERA DE NOVATO
RANCHO NICASIO (HELLECK)
HALLECK CREEK
REDWOOD CANYON
RACER CANYON
BURNT RIDGE FIRE RD
SKY TRAIL FIRE RD

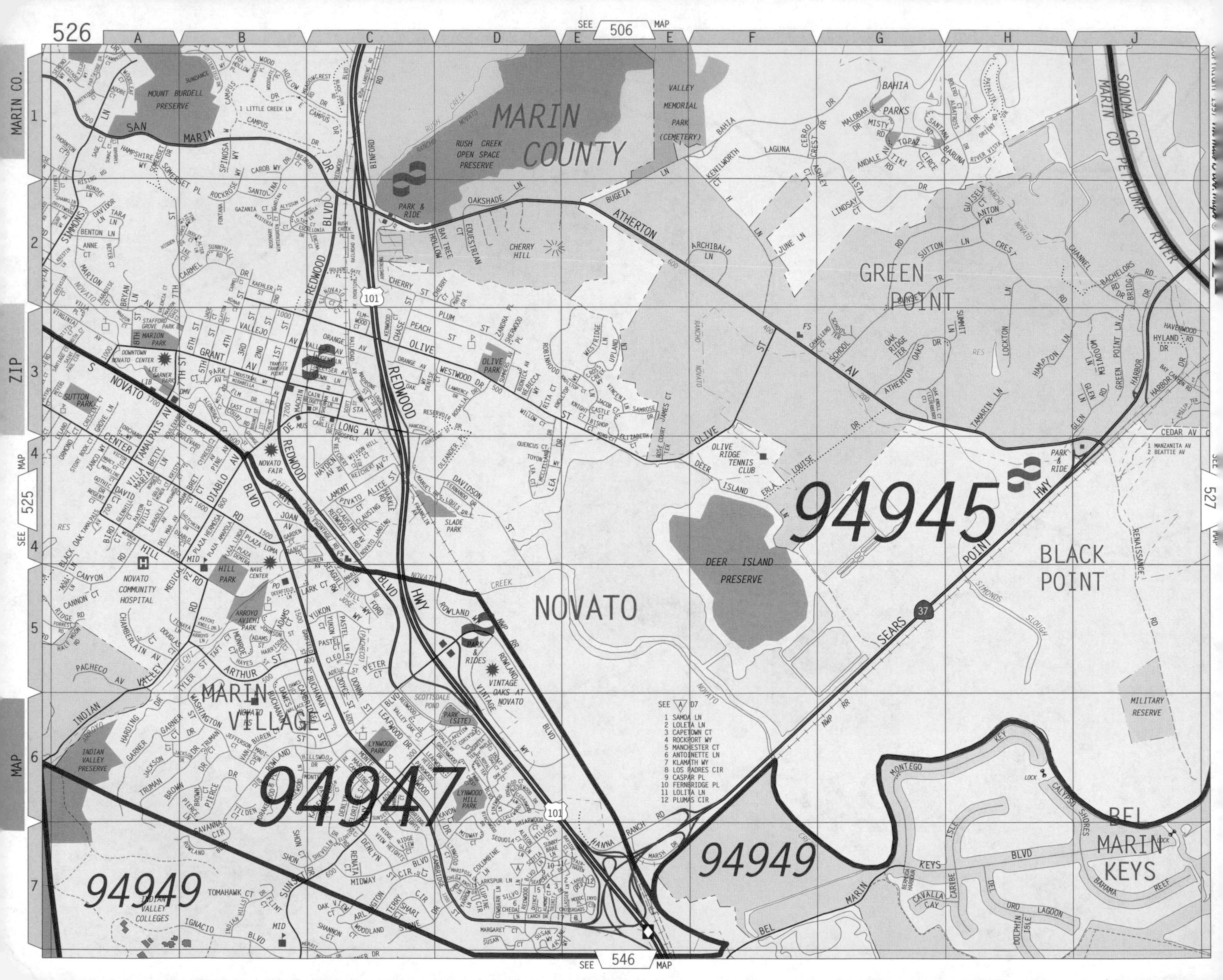
SEE 506 MAP
A
B
C
D
E
F
G
H
J
MARIN CO.
ZIP
MAP
SEE MAP 525
527
MARIN COUNTY
MOUNT BURDELL PRESERVE
RUSH CREEK OPEN SPACE PRESERVE
VALLEY MEMORIAL PARK (CEMETERY)
BAHIA
PARKS
MARIN CO
SONOMA CO
PETALUMA RIVER
PARK & RIDE
CHERRY HILL
GREEN POINT
ATHERTON AV
SAN MARIN DR
REDWOOD BLVD
REDWOOD HWY
101
DOWNTOWN NOVATO CENTER
STAFFORD GROVE PARK
MARION PARK
OLIVE PARK
SUTTON PARK
NOVATO FAIR
SLADE PARK
OLIVE RIDGE TENNIS CLUB
94945
BLACK POINT
DEER ISLAND PRESERVE
NOVATO
NOVATO COMMUNITY HOSPITAL
HILL PARK
NAVE CENTER
ARROYO AVICHI PARK
PARK & RIDES
VINTAGE OAKS AT NOVATO
SEARS POINT HWY
37
MILITARY RESERVE
MARIN VILLAGE
INDIAN VALLEY PRESERVE
LYNWOOD PARK
LYNWOOD HILL PARK
94947
SCOTTSDALE POND
PARK (SITE)
SEE A D7
1 SAMOA LN
2 LOLETA LN
3 CAPETOWN CT
4 ROCKPORT WY
5 MANCHESTER CT
6 ANTOINETTE LN
7 KLAMATH WY
8 LOS PADRES CIR
9 CASPAR PL
10 FERNBRIDGE PL
11 LOLITA LN
12 PLUMAS CIR
1 MANZANITA AV
2 BEATTIE AV
94949
BEL MARIN KEYS
BEL MARIN KEYS BLVD
HANNA RANCH RD
INDIAN VALLEY COLLEGES
IGNACIO BLVD
SEE 546 MAP

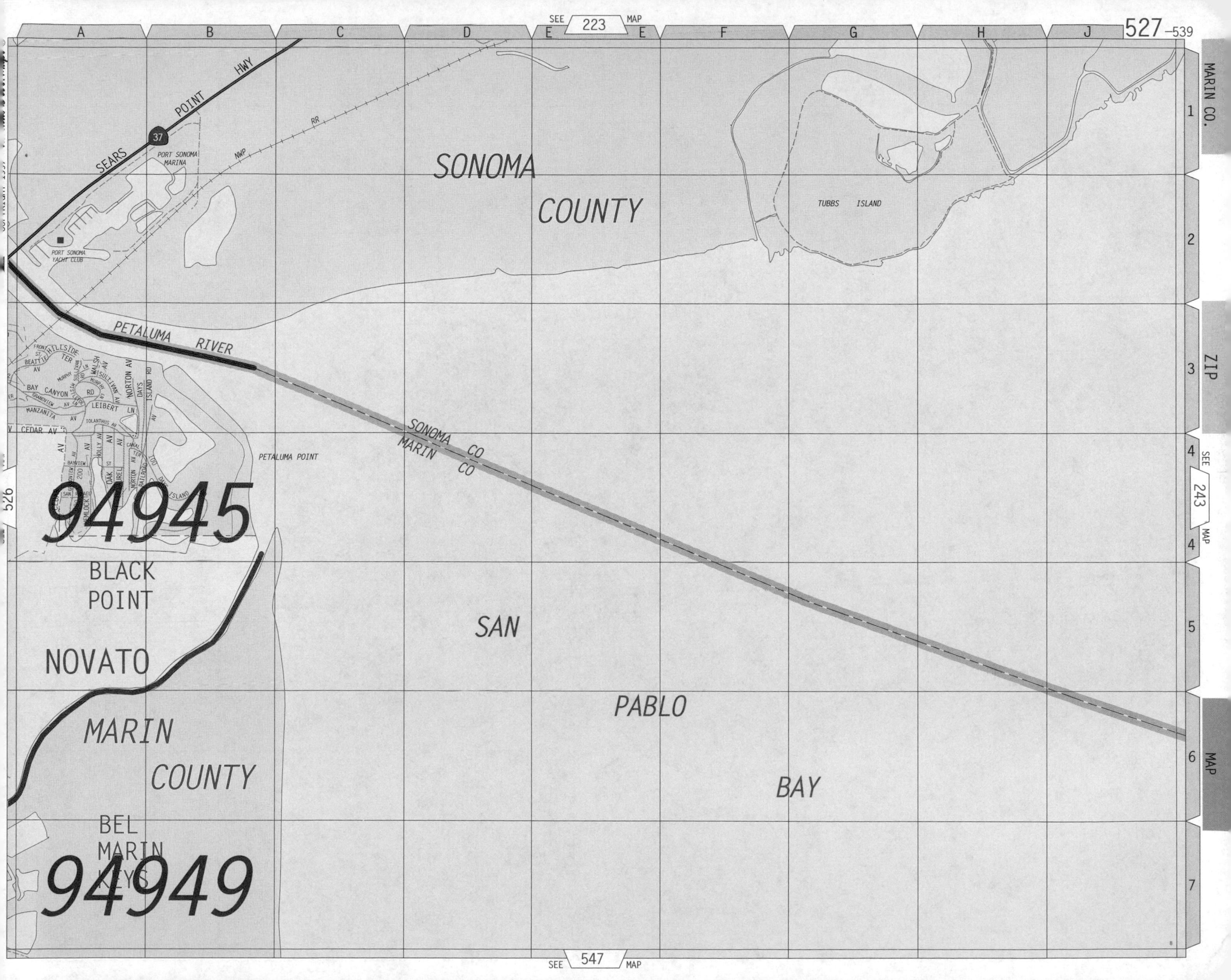

SEE 223 MAP
A
B
C
D
E
F
G
H
J
1
2
3
4
5
6
7
MARIN CO.
ZIP
MAP
SEARS POINT HWY
37
NWP RR
PORT SONOMA MARINA
PORT SONOMA YACHT CLUB
SONOMA COUNTY
TUBBS ISLAND
PETALUMA RIVER
SONOMA CO
MARIN CO
PETALUMA POINT
HILLSIDE TER
BEATTIE AV
BAY CANYON RD
MANZANITA AV
LEIBERT LN
NORTON AV
DAYS ISLAND RD
CEDAR AV
IOLANTHUS AV
HOLLY AV
OAK
LAUREL
BAYVIEW
HEMLOCK
SAN RAFAEL
DAYS ISLAND
CANAL
RAILROAD
94945
BLACK POINT
NOVATO
MARIN COUNTY
BEL MARIN KEYS
94949
SAN PABLO BAY
SEE 243 MAP
526
SEE 547 MAP

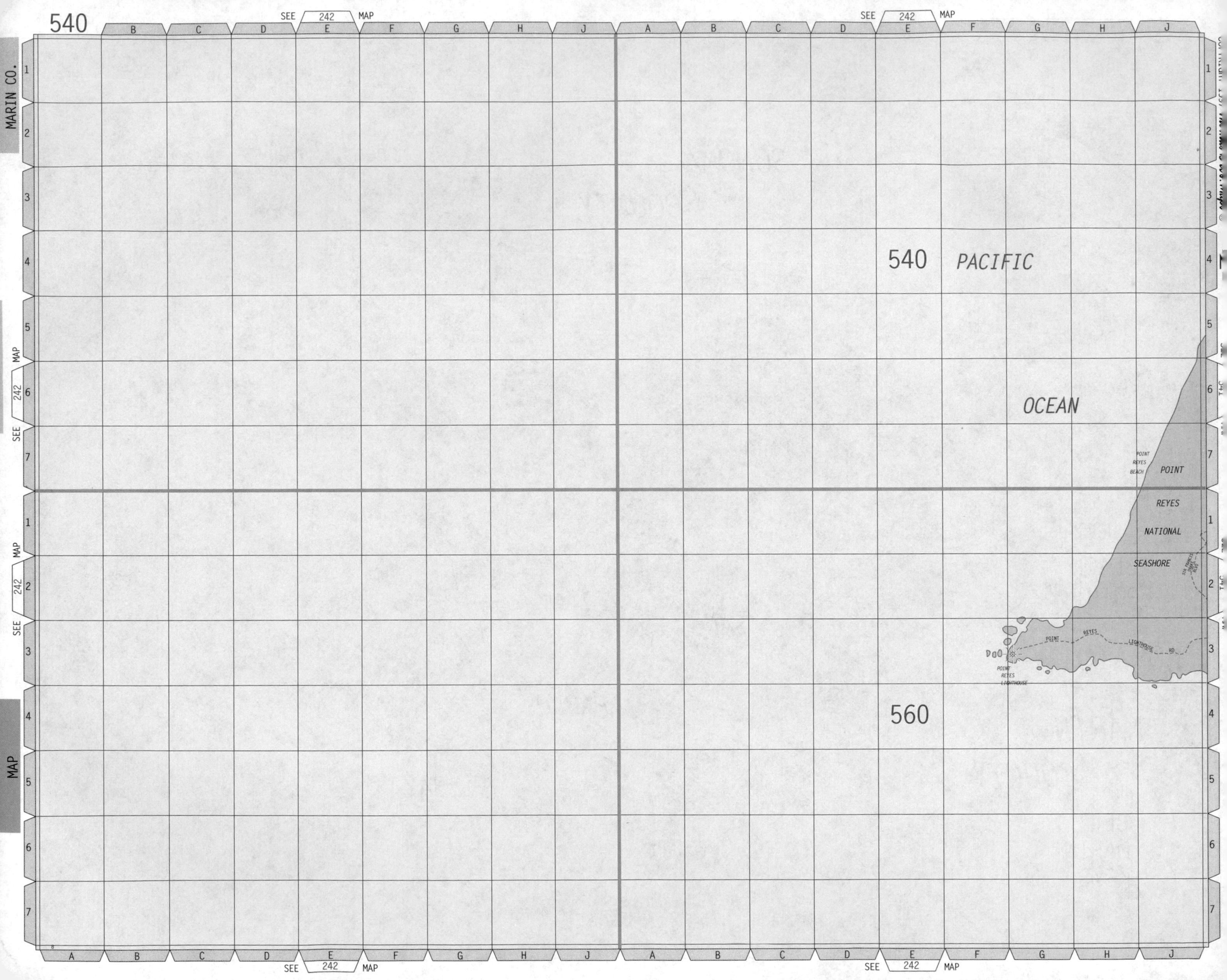
540
MARIN CO.
SEE 242 MAP
540
PACIFIC
OCEAN
POINT REYES BEACH
POINT
REYES
NATIONAL
SEASHORE
POINT REYES LIGHTHOUSE RD
POINT REYES LIGHTHOUSE
560
MAP

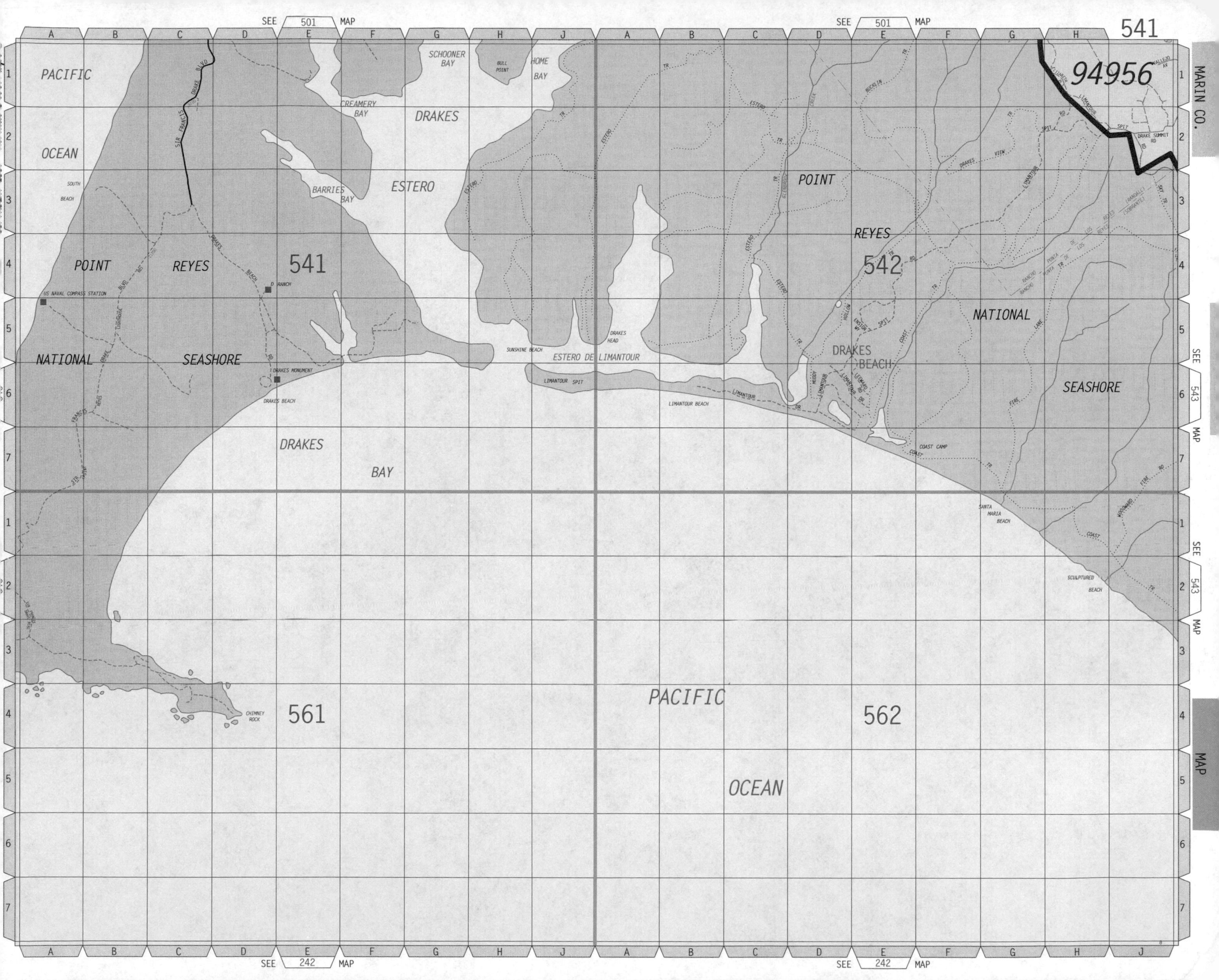

SEE 501 MAP
SEE 501 MAP
MARIN CO.
94956
PACIFIC
OCEAN
POINT
REYES
NATIONAL
SEASHORE
541
542
561
562
DRAKES
ESTERO
SCHOONER BAY
HOME BAY
BULL POINT
CREAMERY BAY
BARRIES BAY
ESTERO DE LIMANTOUR
DRAKES HEAD
SUNSHINE BEACH
LIMANTOUR SPIT
LIMANTOUR BEACH
DRAKES BEACH
D RANCH
DRAKES MONUMENT
US NAVAL COMPASS STATION
SOUTH BEACH
SIR FRANCIS DRAKE BLVD
DRAKES BEACH RD
DRAKES BAY
COAST CAMP
SANTA MARIA BEACH
SCULPTURED BEACH
CHIMNEY ROCK
DRAKE SUMMIT RD
SEE 543 MAP
SEE 543 MAP
SEE 242 MAP
SEE 242 MAP
MAP

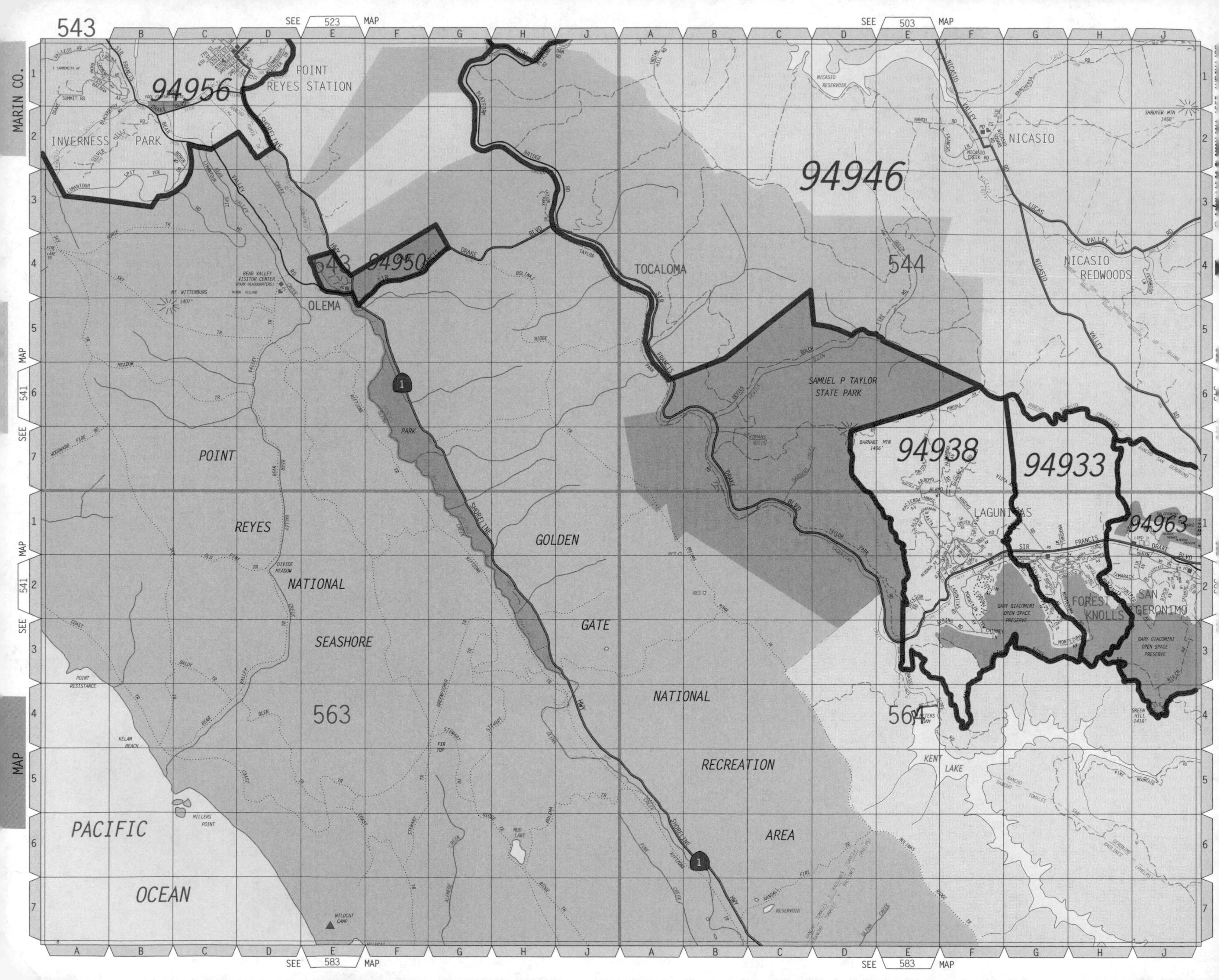

SEE 523 MAP
SEE 503 MAP
MARIN CO.
94956
POINT REYES STATION
INVERNESS PARK
94946
NICASIO
NICASIO RESERVOIR
SHROYER MTN 1458'
NICASIO REDWOODS
TOCALOMA
544
543
94950
OLEMA
BEAR VALLEY VISITOR CENTER (PARK HEADQUARTERS)
MT WITTENBURG 1407'
SAMUEL P TAYLOR STATE PARK
BARNABE MTN 1466'
94938
94933
LAGUNITAS
94963
FOREST KNOLLS
SAN GERONIMO
GARY GIACOMINI OPEN SPACE PRESERVE
GREEN HILL 1418'
SEE 541 MAP
POINT REYES NATIONAL SEASHORE
GOLDEN GATE NATIONAL RECREATION AREA
DIVIDE MEADOW
POINT RESISTANCE
KELAM BEACH
563
564
KENT LAKE
PACIFIC OCEAN
MILLERS POINT
FIR TOP
MUD LAKE
WILDCAT CAMP
SHORELINE HWY
SIR FRANCIS DRAKE BLVD
LUCAS VALLEY RD
NICASIO VALLEY RD
PLATFORM BRIDGE RD
SEE 583 MAP
SEE 583 MAP

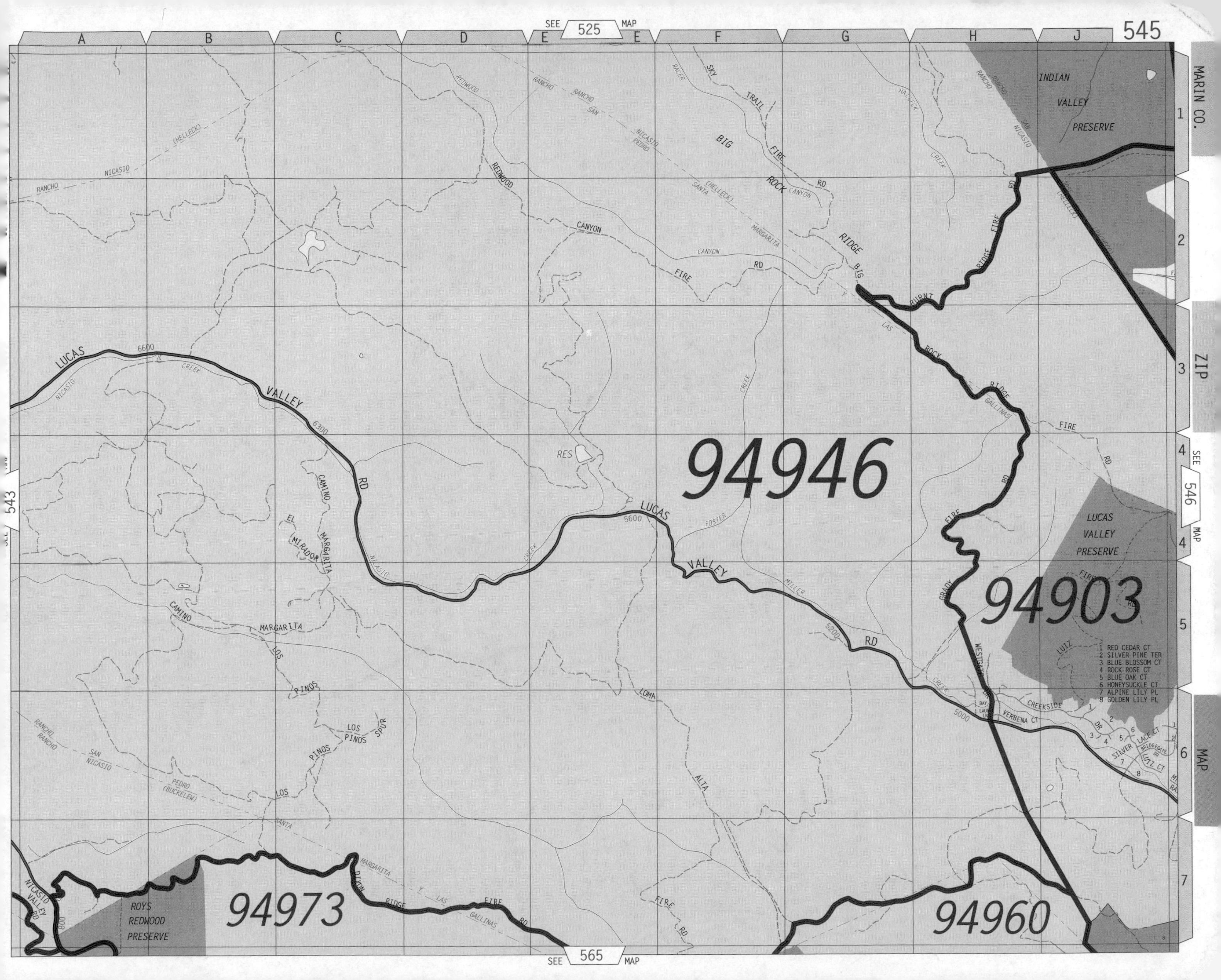

SEE 525 MAP
A
B
C
D
E
F
G
H
J
1
2
3
4
5
6
7
MARIN CO.
ZIP
MAP
SEE 543 MAP
SEE 546 MAP
SEE 565 MAP
94946
94903
94973
94960
INDIAN VALLEY PRESERVE
LUCAS VALLEY PRESERVE
ROYS REDWOOD PRESERVE
LUCAS VALLEY RD
6600
6300
5600
5200
5000
NICASIO CREEK
CAMINO EL MIRADOR
CAMINO MARGARITA
LOS PINOS
LOS PINOS SPUR
LOMA ALTA
FIRE RD
RES
BIG ROCK RIDGE
BIG ROCK FIRE RD
SKY TRAIL FIRE RD
REDWOOD CANYON FIRE RD
CANYON
BURNT RIDGE FIRE RD
LAS GALLINAS RIDGE FIRE RD
GRADY
WESTVIEW DR
CREEKSIDE DR
VERBENA CT
SILVER LACE CT
LUIZ CT
LUIZ
BAY LAUREL
FOSTER
MILLER CREEK
RANCHO SAN PEDRO SANTA MARGARITA Y LAS GALLINAS
RANCHO NICASIO
(HELLECK)
(BUCKELEW)
NICASIO VALLEY RD
DIXON RIDGE FIRE RD
1 RED CEDAR CT
2 SILVER PINE TER
3 BLUE BLOSSOM CT
4 ROCK ROSE CT
5 BLUE OAK CT
6 HONEYSUCKLE CT
7 ALPINE LILY PL
8 GOLDEN LILY PL

SEE 526 MAP

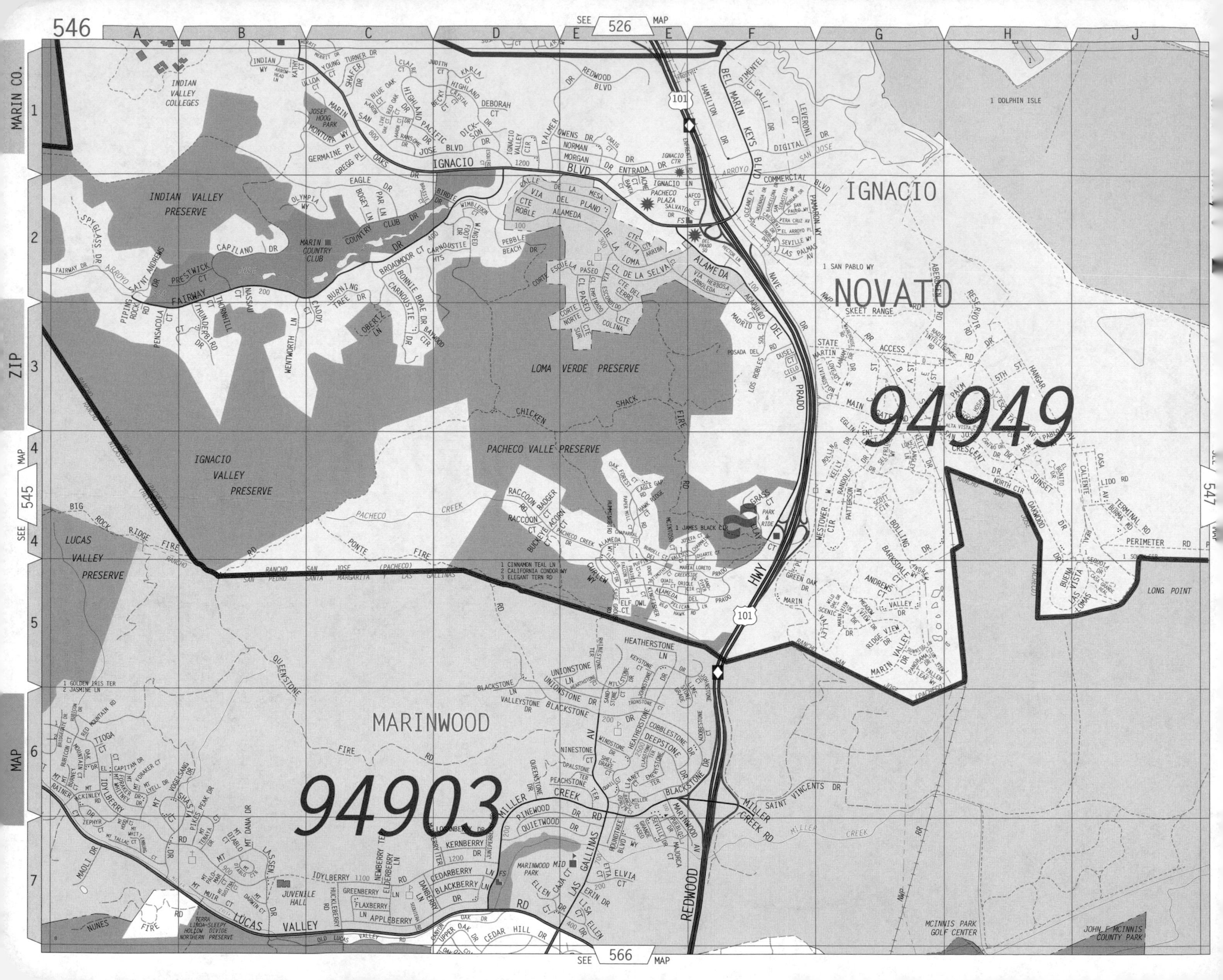

SEE 566 MAP

SEE 527 MAP

A B C D E E F G H J

94949

NOVATO

PERIMETER RD

94903

SAN PABLO BAY

SEE 546 MAP
SEE 243 MAP

1 2 3 4 4 5 6 7

SEE 567 MAP

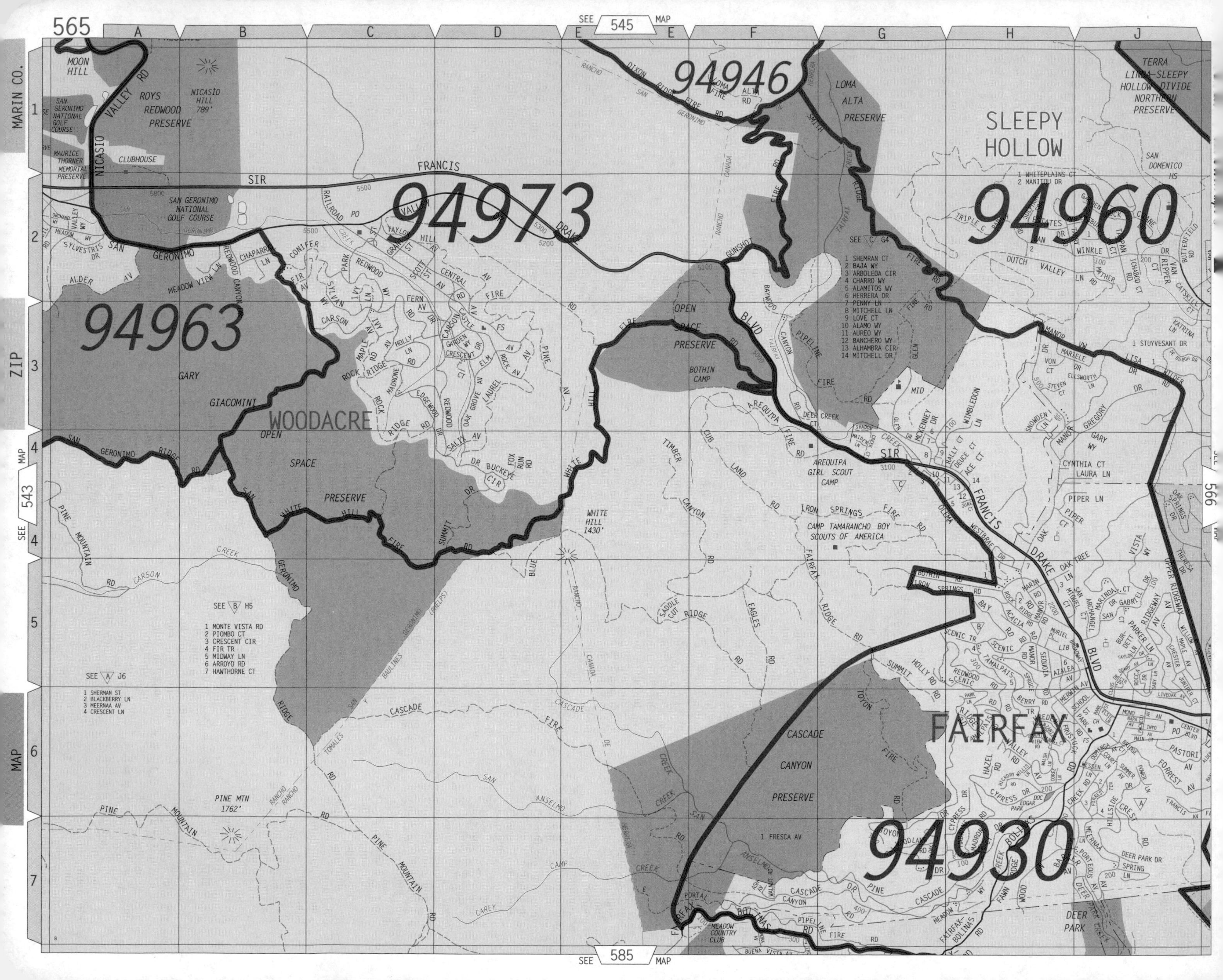
SEE 545 MAP
A
B
C
D
E
F
G
H
J
MARIN CO.
ZIP
MAP
SEE 543 MAP
566
SEE 585 MAP
94946
94973
94960
94963
94930
MOON HILL
ROYS REDWOOD PRESERVE
NICASIO HILL 789'
SAN GERONIMO NATIONAL GOLF COURSE
MAURICE THORNER MEMORIAL PRESERVE
CLUBHOUSE
LOMA ALTA PRESERVE
TERRA LINDA-SLEEPY HOLLOW DIVIDE NORTHERN PRESERVE
SLEEPY HOLLOW
SIR FRANCIS DRAKE BLVD
WOODACRE
WOODACRE OPEN SPACE PRESERVE
OPEN SPACE PRESERVE
BOTHIN CAMP
AREQUIPA GIRL SCOUT CAMP
CAMP TAMARANCHO BOY SCOUTS OF AMERICA
WHITE HILL 1430'
PINE MTN 1762'
CASCADE CANYON PRESERVE
FAIRFAX
MEADOW COUNTRY CLUB
DEER PARK
1 SHERMAN CT
2 BAJA WY
3 ARBOLEDA CIR
4 CHARRO WY
5 ALAMITOS WY
6 HERRERA DR
7 PENNY LN
8 MITCHELL LN
9 LOVE CT
10 ALAMO WY
11 AUREO WY
12 BANCHERO WY
13 ALHAMBRA CIR
14 MITCHELL DR
1 MONTE VISTA RD
2 PIOMBO CT
3 CRESCENT CIR
4 FIR TR
5 MIDWAY LN
6 ARROYO RD
7 HAWTHORNE CT
1 SHERMAN ST
2 BLACKBERRY LN
3 MEERNAA AV
4 CRESCENT LN
1 WHITEPLAINS CT
2 MANITOU DR
1 STUYVESANT DR
1 FRESCA AV

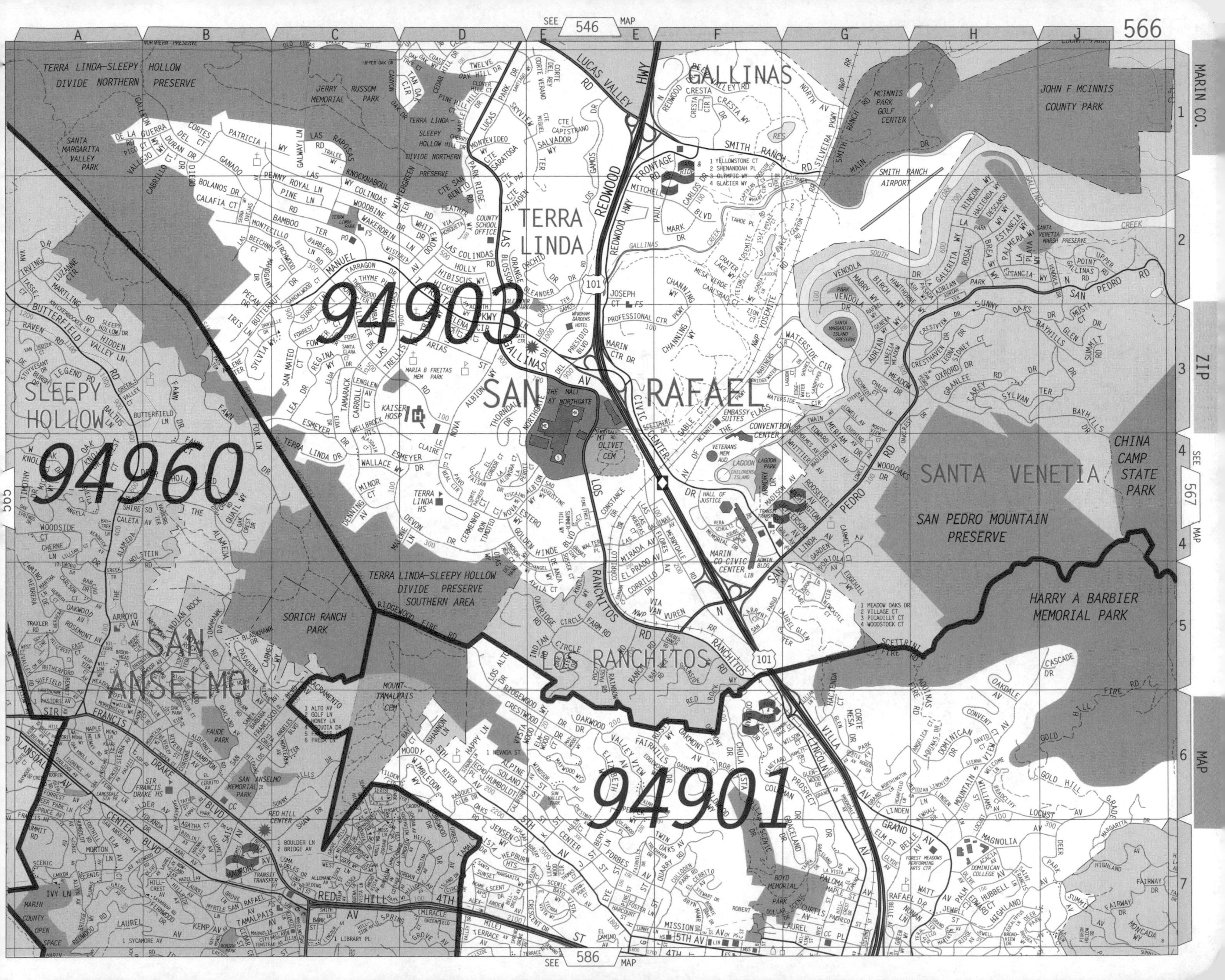
SEE 546 MAP
SEE 586 MAP
SEE 567 MAP
MARIN CO.
ZIP
MAP
TERRA LINDA–SLEEPY HOLLOW DIVIDE NORTHERN PRESERVE
JERRY RUSSOM MEMORIAL PARK
SANTA MARGARITA VALLEY PARK
GALLINAS
JOHN F MCINNIS COUNTY PARK
MCINNIS PARK GOLF CENTER
SMITH RANCH AIRPORT
TERRA LINDA
94903
SAN RAFAEL
THE MALL AT NORTHGATE
MT OLIVET CEM
KAISER HOSP
MARIA B FREITAS MEM PARK
TERRA LINDA HS
EMBASSY SUITES
CONVENTION CENTER
VETERANS MEM AUD
LAGOON PARK
HALL OF JUSTICE
MARIN CO CIVIC CENTER
SANTA VENETIA
CHINA CAMP STATE PARK
SAN PEDRO MOUNTAIN PRESERVE
HARRY A BARBIER MEMORIAL PARK
SLEEPY HOLLOW
94960
TERRA LINDA–SLEEPY HOLLOW DIVIDE PRESERVE SOUTHERN AREA
SORICH RANCH PARK
LOS RANCHITOS
SAN ANSELMO
MOUNT TAMALPAIS CEM
FAUDE PARK
SAN ANSELMO MEMORIAL PARK
SIR FRANCIS DRAKE HS
RED HILL CENTER
TRANSIT TRANSFER
94901
BOYD MEMORIAL PARK
FOREST MEADOWS PERFORMING ARTS CTR
DOMINICAN COLLEGE
MARIN COUNTY OPEN SPACE
LUCAS VALLEY RD
REDWOOD HWY
SMITH RANCH RD
N SAN PEDRO RD
LAS GALLINAS AV
MANUEL T FREITAS PKWY
LOS RANCHITOS RD
CIVIC CENTER DR
SIR FRANCIS DRAKE BLVD
RED HILL AV
LINCOLN AV
GRAND AV
4TH ST
5TH AV
1 YELLOWSTONE CT
2 SHENANDOAH PL
3 OLYMPIC WY
4 GLACIER WY
1 MEADOW OAKS DR
2 VILLAGE CT
3 PICADILLY CT
4 WOODSTOCK CT
1 ALTO AV
2 GOLF LN
3 HONEY LN
4 SEQUOIA DR
5 FRANCIS CT
6 FREDA LN
1 BOULDER LN
2 BRIDGE AV
1 NEVADA ST
1 SYCAMORE AV
1 LIBRARY PL

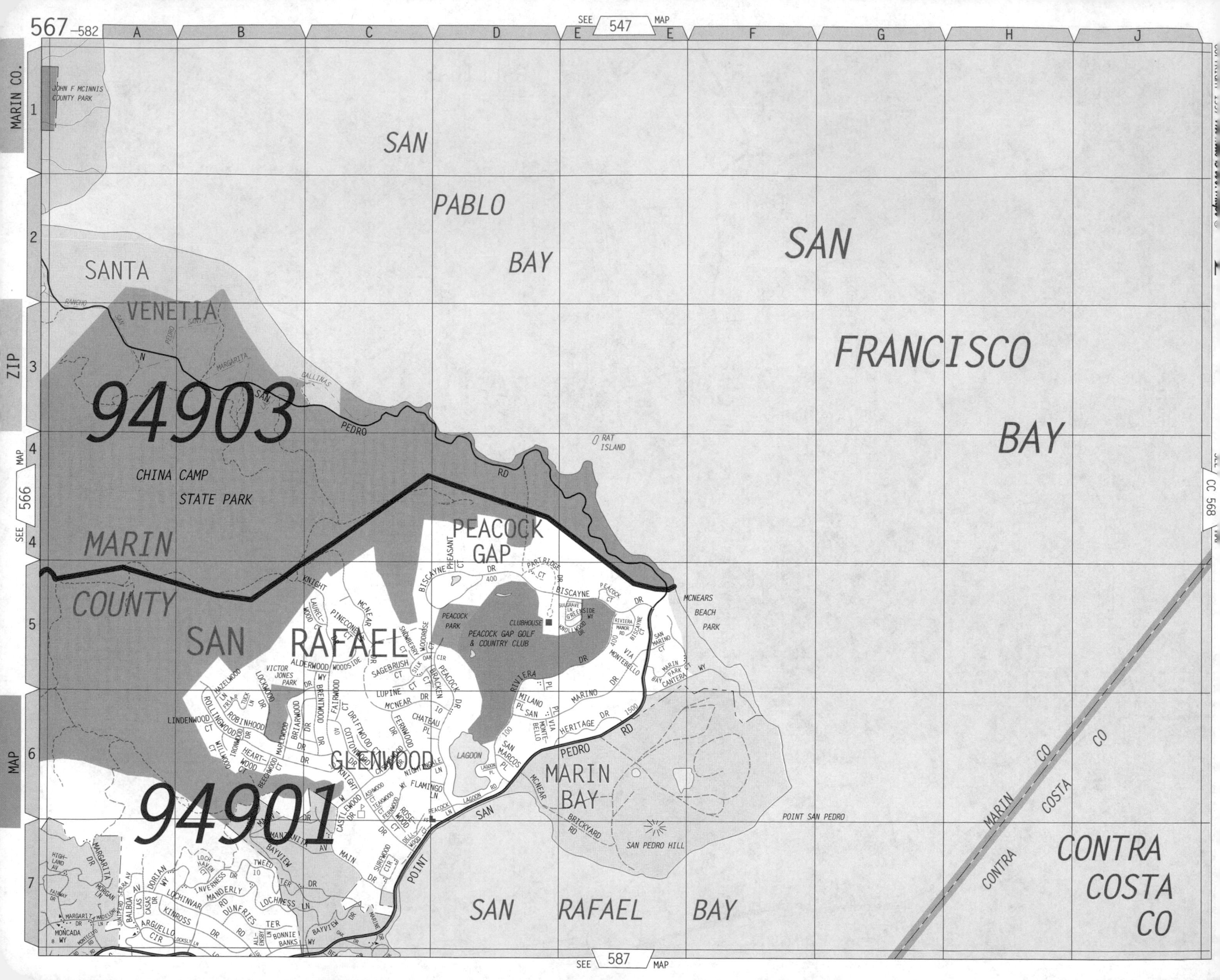
A
B
C
D
E
F
G
H
J
SEE 547 MAP
SEE 566 MAP
CC 568
SEE 587 MAP
MARIN CO.
ZIP
MAP
JOHN F MCINNIS COUNTY PARK
SAN PABLO BAY
SAN FRANCISCO BAY
SANTA VENETIA
94903
94901
RAT ISLAND
CHINA CAMP STATE PARK
MARIN COUNTY
SAN RAFAEL
PEACOCK GAP
PEACOCK PARK
PEACOCK GAP GOLF & COUNTRY CLUB
CLUBHOUSE
MCNEARS BEACH PARK
VICTOR JONES PARK
GLENWOOD
LAGOON
MARIN BAY
SAN PEDRO HILL
POINT SAN PEDRO
SAN RAFAEL BAY
CONTRA COSTA CO
MARIN CO
CONTRA COSTA CO
N SAN PEDRO RD
POINT SAN PEDRO RD
BISCAYNE DR
RIVIERA DR
HERITAGE DR
MCNEAR BRICKYARD RD

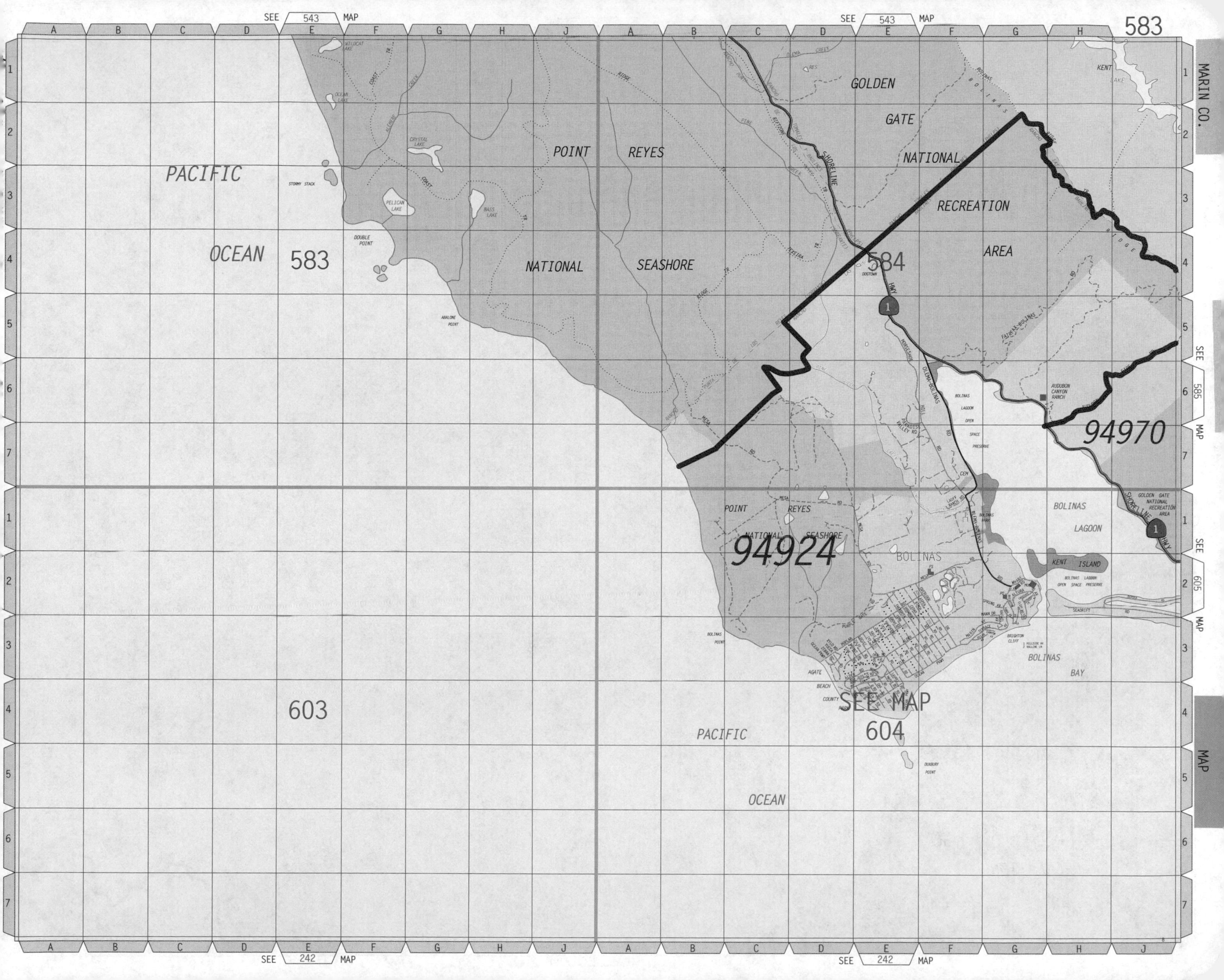

MARIN CO.
SEE 543 MAP
SEE 585 MAP
SEE 605 MAP
SEE 242 MAP
PACIFIC
OCEAN
583
POINT REYES
NATIONAL SEASHORE
GOLDEN
GATE
NATIONAL
RECREATION
AREA
584
WILDCAT LAKE
OCEAN LAKE
CRYSTAL LAKE
PELICAN LAKE
BASS LAKE
STORMY STACK
DOUBLE POINT
ABALONE POINT
KENT LAKE
DOGTOWN
SHORELINE HWY
BOLINAS LAGOON OPEN SPACE PRESERVE
AUDUBON CANYON RANCH
94970
94924
POINT REYES
NATIONAL SEASHORE
BOLINAS
BOLINAS LAGOON
KENT ISLAND
BOLINAS LAGOON OPEN SPACE PRESERVE
GOLDEN GATE NATIONAL RECREATION AREA
BOLINAS POINT
AGATE BEACH COUNTY PARK
BRIGHTON CLIFF
BOLINAS BAY
SEE MAP
604
603
PACIFIC
OCEAN
DUXBURY POINT
MAP

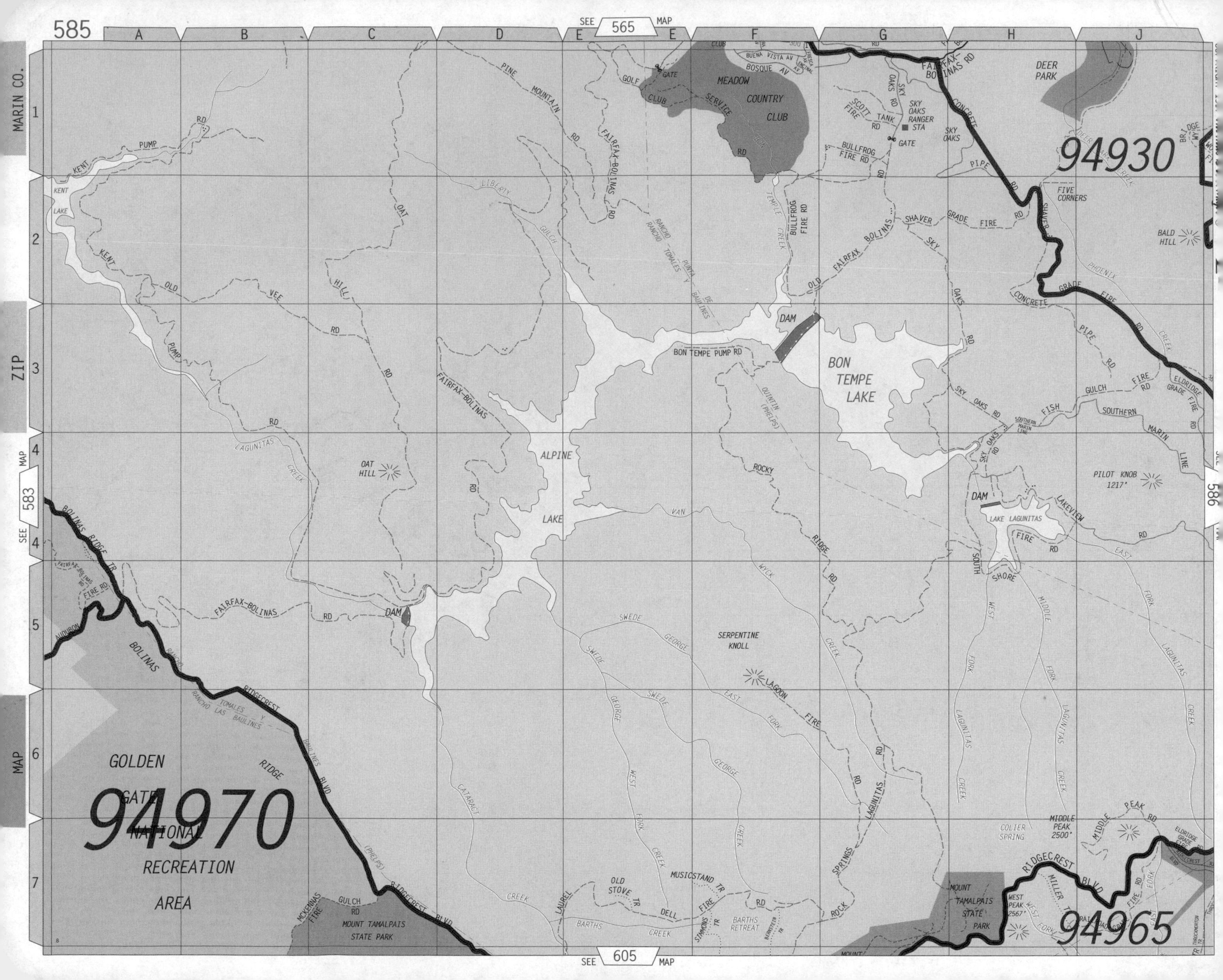
SEE 565 MAP
MARIN CO.
ZIP
MAP
SEE 583 MAP
586
SEE 605 MAP
MEADOW
COUNTRY
CLUB
DEER
PARK
94930
SKY
OAKS
RANGER
STA
FIVE
CORNERS
BALD
HILL
BON
TEMPE
LAKE
ALPINE
LAKE
OAT
HILL
PILOT KNOB
1217'
LAKE LAGUNITAS
SERPENTINE
KNOLL
GOLDEN
GATE
NATIONAL
RECREATION
AREA
94970
MIDDLE
PEAK
2500'
COLIER
SPRING
MOUNT
TAMALPAIS
STATE
PARK
MOUNT TAMALPAIS
STATE PARK
WEST
PEAK
2567'
94965
BARTHS
RETREAT

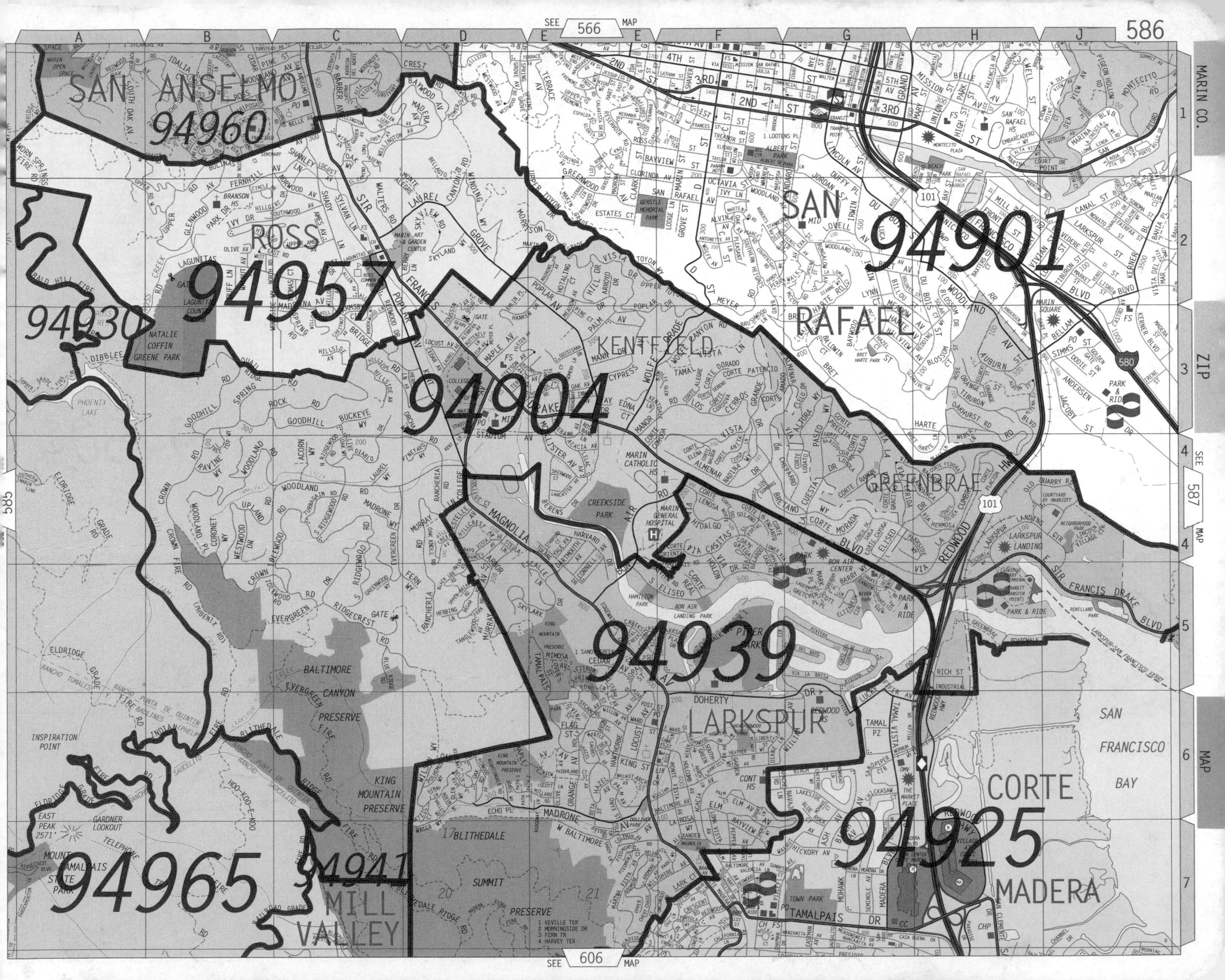
SEE 566 MAP
A
B
C
D
E
F
G
H
J
MARIN CO.
ZIP
MAP
SAN ANSELMO
94960
ROSS
94957
94930
94904
KENTFIELD
SAN RAFAEL
94901
GREENBRAE
94939
LARKSPUR
94925
CORTE MADERA
94965
94941
MILL VALLEY
SAN FRANCISCO BAY
PHOENIX LAKE
NATALIE COFFIN GREENE PARK
MARIN CATHOLIC HS
MARIN GENERAL HOSPITAL
CREEKSIDE PARK
PIPER PARK
BALTIMORE CANYON PRESERVE
KING MOUNTAIN PRESERVE
BLITHEDALE SUMMIT PRESERVE
MOUNT TAMALPAIS STATE PARK
EAST PEAK 2571'
GARDNER LOOKOUT
INSPIRATION POINT
LARKSPUR LANDING
LARKSPUR-SAN FRANCISCO FERRY
SEE 585 MAP
SEE 587 MAP
SEE 606 MAP
1
2
3
4
5
6
7

SEE 567 MAP

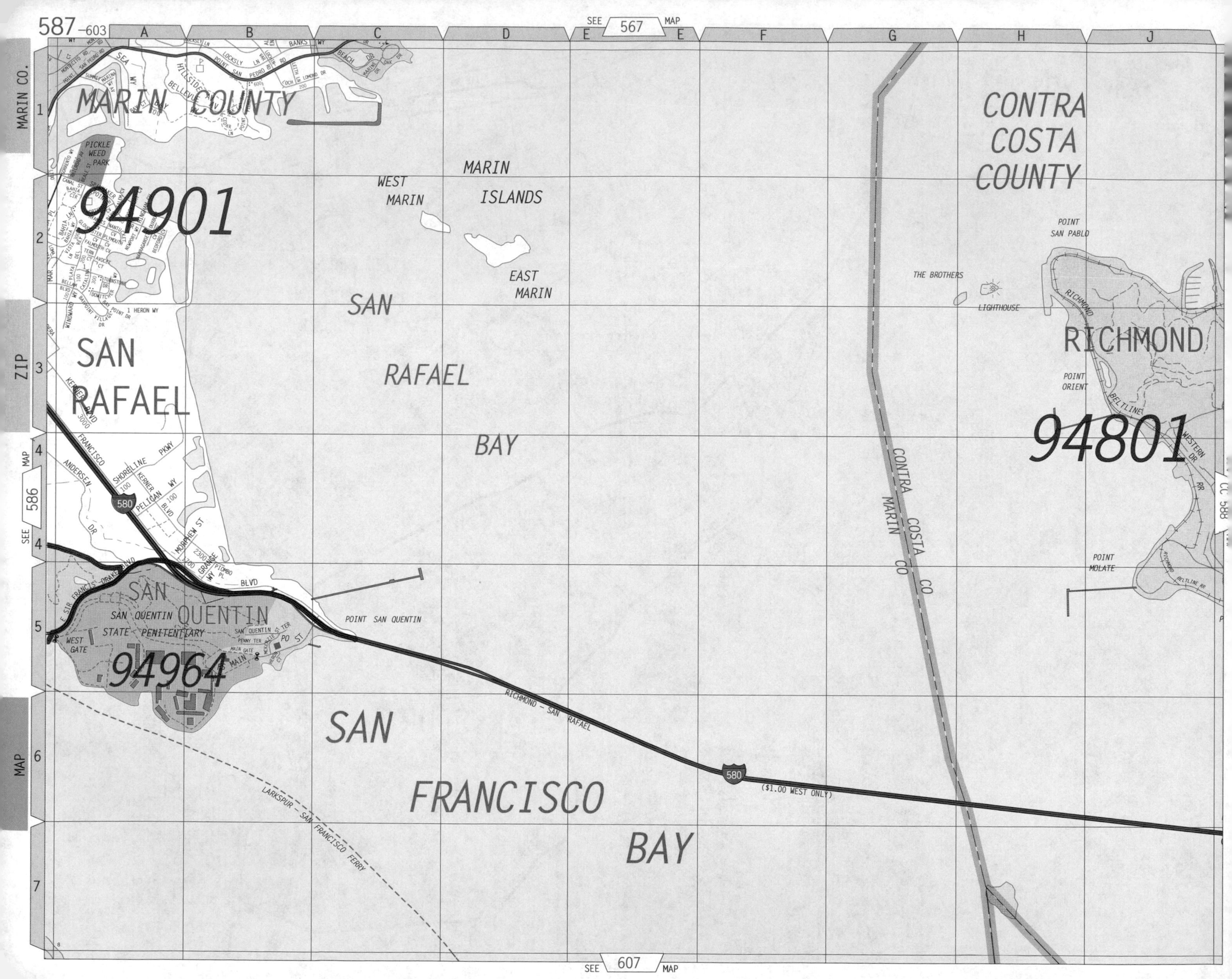

SEE 586 MAP

CC 588

SEE 607 MAP

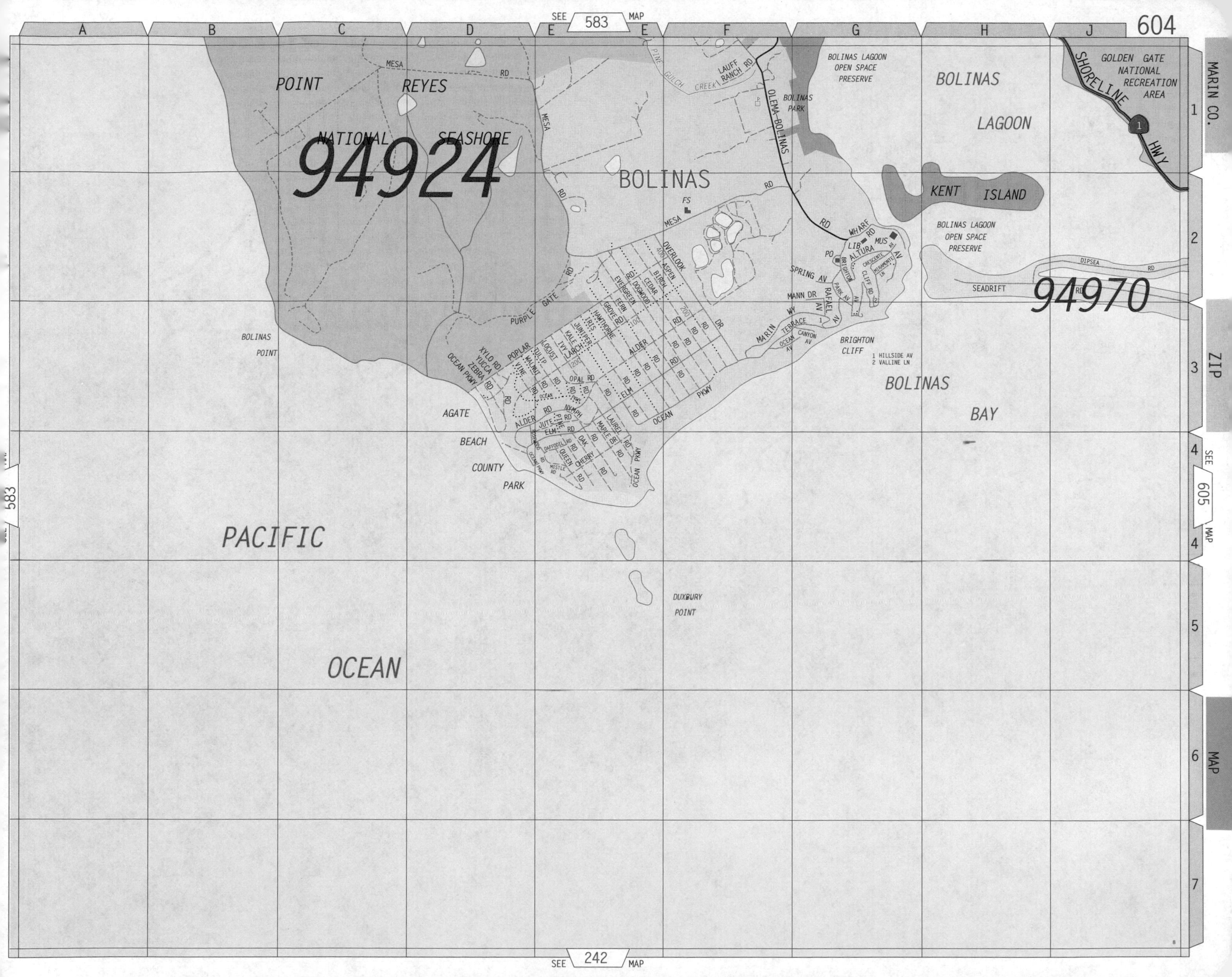

SEE 583 MAP
POINT REYES NATIONAL SEASHORE
94924
BOLINAS
BOLINAS LAGOON OPEN SPACE PRESERVE
BOLINAS PARK
BOLINAS LAGOON
GOLDEN GATE NATIONAL RECREATION AREA
SHORELINE HWY
KENT ISLAND
94970
BOLINAS POINT
AGATE BEACH COUNTY PARK
BRIGHTON CLIFF
1 HILLSIDE AV
2 VALLINE LN
BOLINAS BAY
PACIFIC OCEAN
DUXBURY POINT
MARIN CO.
ZIP
MAP
SEE 605 MAP
SEE 242 MAP

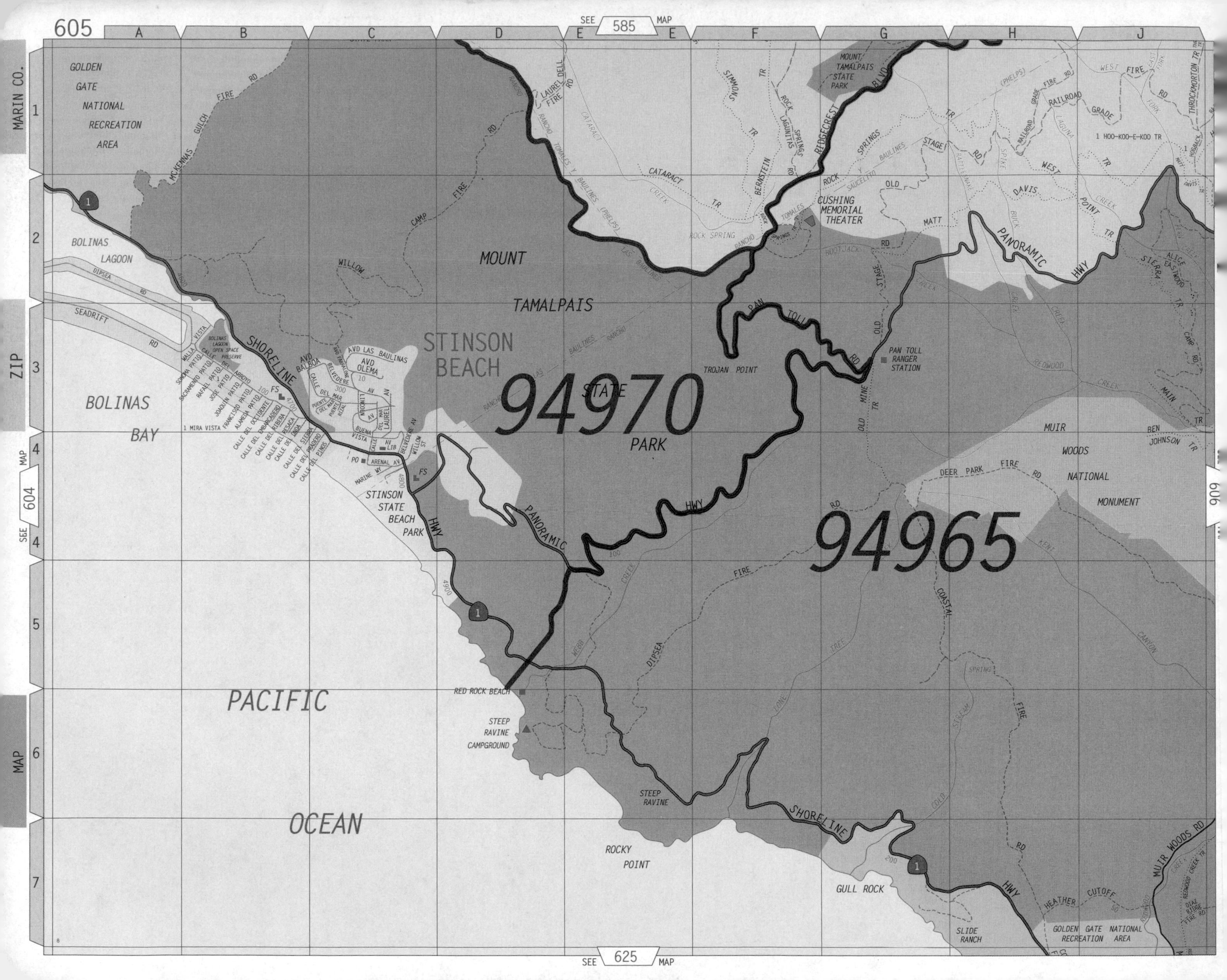
SEE 585 MAP
MARIN CO.
ZIP
MAP
SEE 604 MAP
606
SEE 625 MAP
GOLDEN GATE NATIONAL RECREATION AREA
BOLINAS LAGOON
BOLINAS BAY
PACIFIC
OCEAN
MOUNT TAMALPAIS
STINSON BEACH
94970
STATE PARK
94965
MUIR WOODS NATIONAL MONUMENT
MOUNT TAMALPAIS STATE PARK
CUSHING MEMORIAL THEATER
TROJAN POINT
PAN TOLL RANGER STATION
STINSON STATE BEACH PARK
RED ROCK BEACH
STEEP RAVINE CAMPGROUND
STEEP RAVINE
ROCKY POINT
GULL ROCK
SLIDE RANCH
GOLDEN GATE NATIONAL RECREATION AREA
SHORELINE HWY
PANORAMIC HWY
RIDGECREST BLVD
PAN TOLL RD
SEADRIFT RD
DIPSEA RD
MUIR WOODS RD
DEER PARK FIRE RD
HEATHER CUTOFF
BOLINAS LAGOON OPEN SPACE PRESERVE
1 HOO-KOO-E-KOO TR
1 MIRA VISTA
BEN JOHNSON TR
THROCKMORTON TR

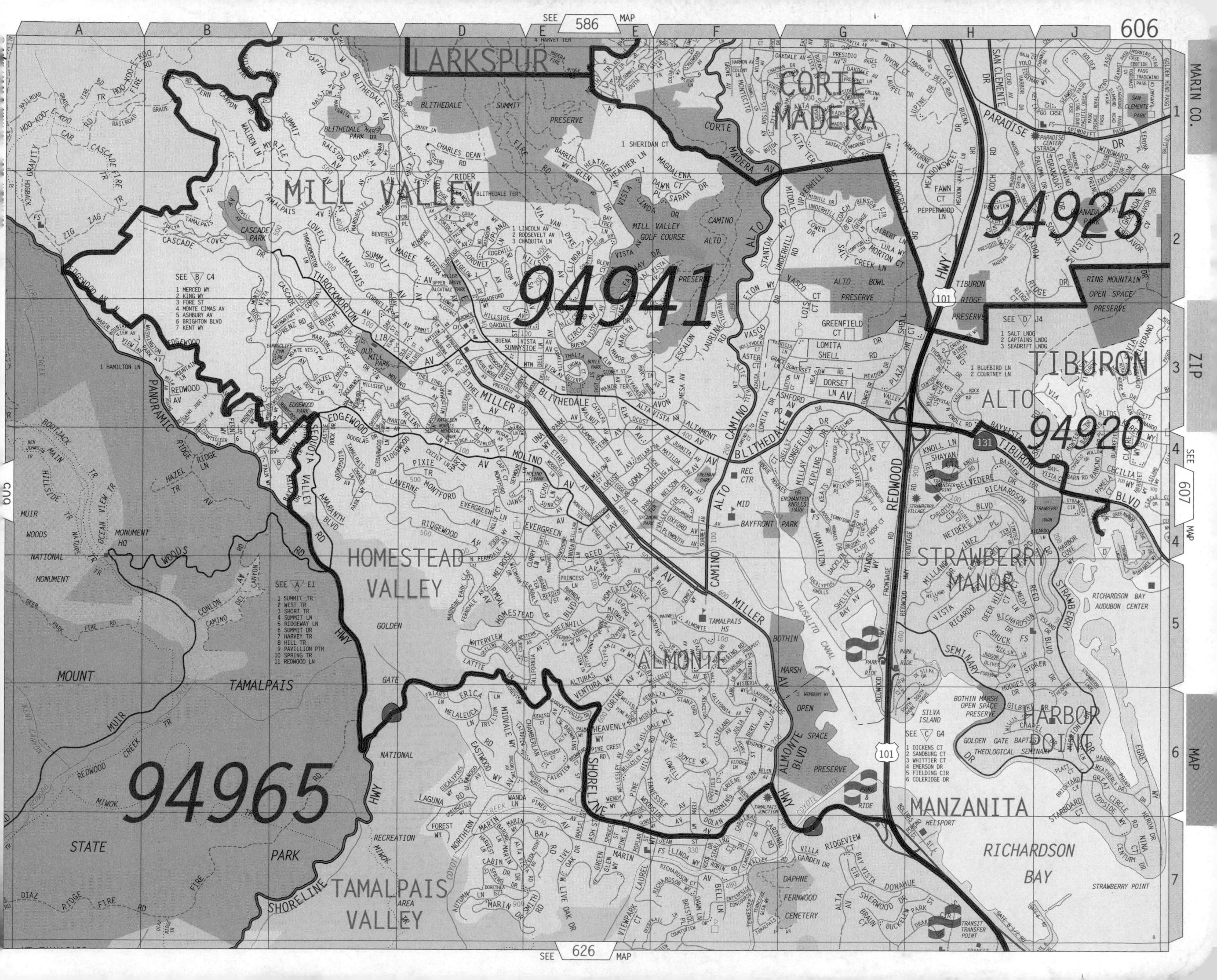

SEE 586 MAP
SEE 626 MAP
SEE 607 MAP
MARIN CO.
ZIP MAP
A B C D E F G H J
1 2 3 4 5 6 7
LARKSPUR
CORTE MADERA
MILL VALLEY
94941
94925
94920
94965
TIBURON
ALTO
STRAWBERRY MANOR
HOMESTEAD VALLEY
ALMONTE
MANZANITA
HARBOR POINT
TAMALPAIS VALLEY
MOUNT TAMALPAIS STATE PARK
MUIR WOODS NATIONAL MONUMENT
MONUMENT HQ
BLITHEDALE SUMMIT PRESERVE
MILL VALLEY GOLF COURSE
ALTO BOWL PRESERVE
TIBURON RIDGE PRESERVE
RING MOUNTAIN OPEN SPACE PRESERVE
BOTHIN MARSH OPEN SPACE PRESERVE
RICHARDSON BAY
RICHARDSON BAY AUDUBON CENTER
STRAWBERRY POINT
GOLDEN GATE BAPTIST THEOLOGICAL SEMINARY
SILVA ISLAND
FERNWOOD CEMETERY
TAMALPAIS HS
CASCADE PARK
EDGEWOOD PARK
OLD MILL PARK
ENCHANTED KNOLLS PARK
BAYFRONT PARK
HWY 101
SHORELINE HWY
PANORAMIC HWY
MILLER AV
BLITHEDALE AV
CAMINO ALTO
REDWOOD HWY
TIBURON BLVD
SEE B C4
1 MERCED WY
2 KING WY
3 FORE ST
4 MONTE CIMAS AV
5 ASHBURY AV
6 BRIGHTON BLVD
7 KENT WY
SEE A E1
1 SUMMIT TR
2 WEST TR
3 SHORT TR
4 SUMMIT LN
5 RIDGEWAY LN
6 SUMMIT DR
7 HARVEY TR
8 HILL TR
9 PAVILLION PTH
10 SPRING TR
11 REDWOOD LN
SEE C G4
1 DICKENS CT
2 SANDBURG CT
3 WHITTIER CT
4 EMERSON DR
5 FIELDING CIR
6 COLERIDGE DR
SEE D J4
1 SALT LNDG
2 CAPTAINS LNDG
3 SEADRIFT LNDG
1 LINCOLN AV
2 ROOSEVELT AV
3 CHAQUITA LN
1 BLUEBIRD LN
2 COURTNEY LN

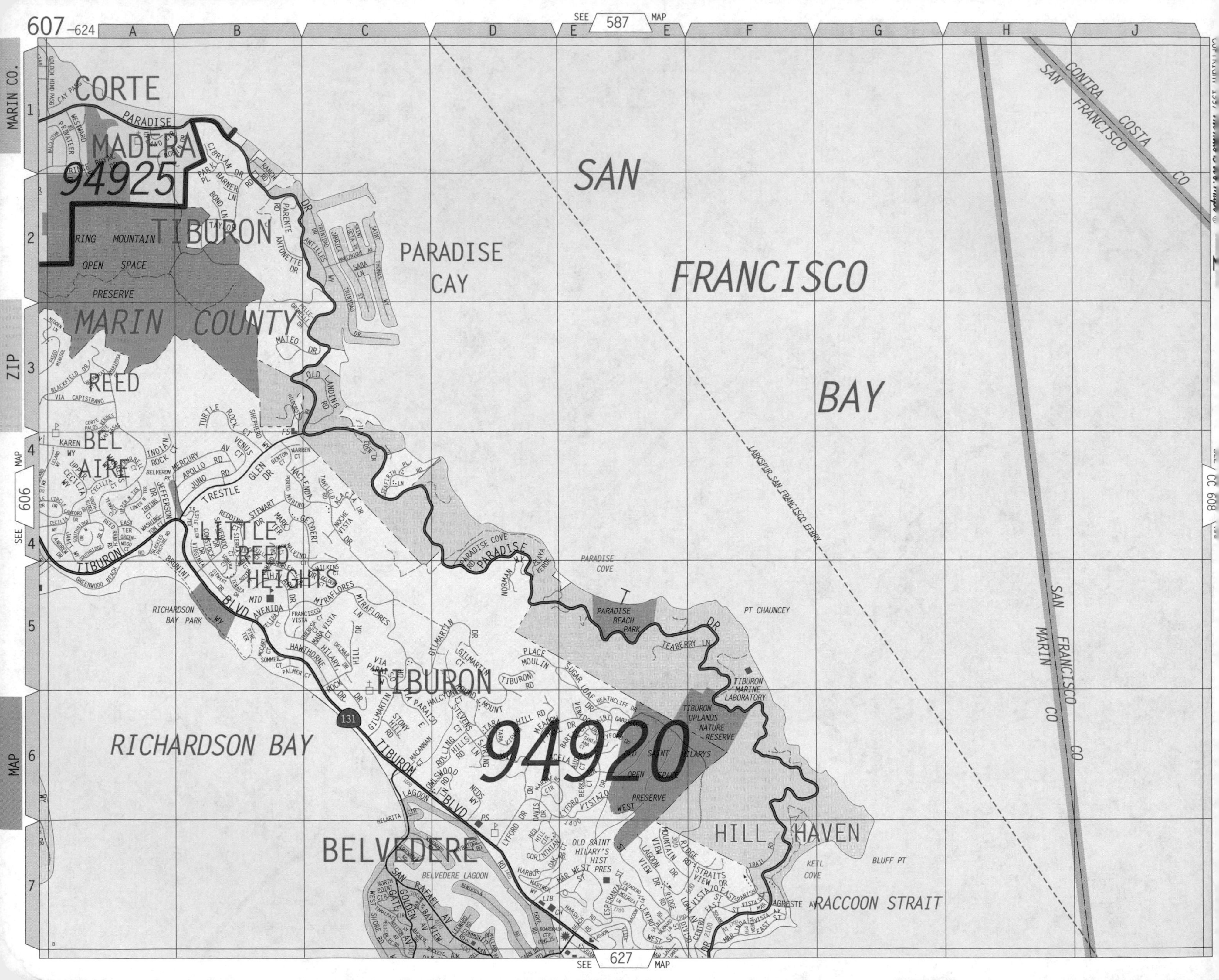
SEE 587 MAP
MARIN CO.
ZIP
MAP
SEE 606 MAP
CC 608
SEE 627 MAP
CORTE
MADERA
94925
TIBURON
RING MOUNTAIN
OPEN SPACE
PRESERVE
MARIN COUNTY
REED
BEL
AIRE
LITTLE
REED
HEIGHTS
RICHARDSON BAY PARK
RICHARDSON BAY
TIBURON
94920
BELVEDERE
BELVEDERE LAGOON
PARADISE
CAY
SAN
FRANCISCO
BAY
LARKSPUR-SAN FRANCISCO FERRY
PARADISE COVE
PARADISE BEACH PARK
PT CHAUNCEY
TIBURON MARINE LABORATORY
TIBURON UPLANDS NATURE RESERVE
OLD SAINT HILARY'S HIST
HILL HAVEN
KETL COVE
BLUFF PT
RACCOON STRAIT
CONTRA COSTA CO
SAN FRANCISCO CO
MARIN CO
SAN FRANCISCO CO
TIBURON BLVD
PARADISE DR
131

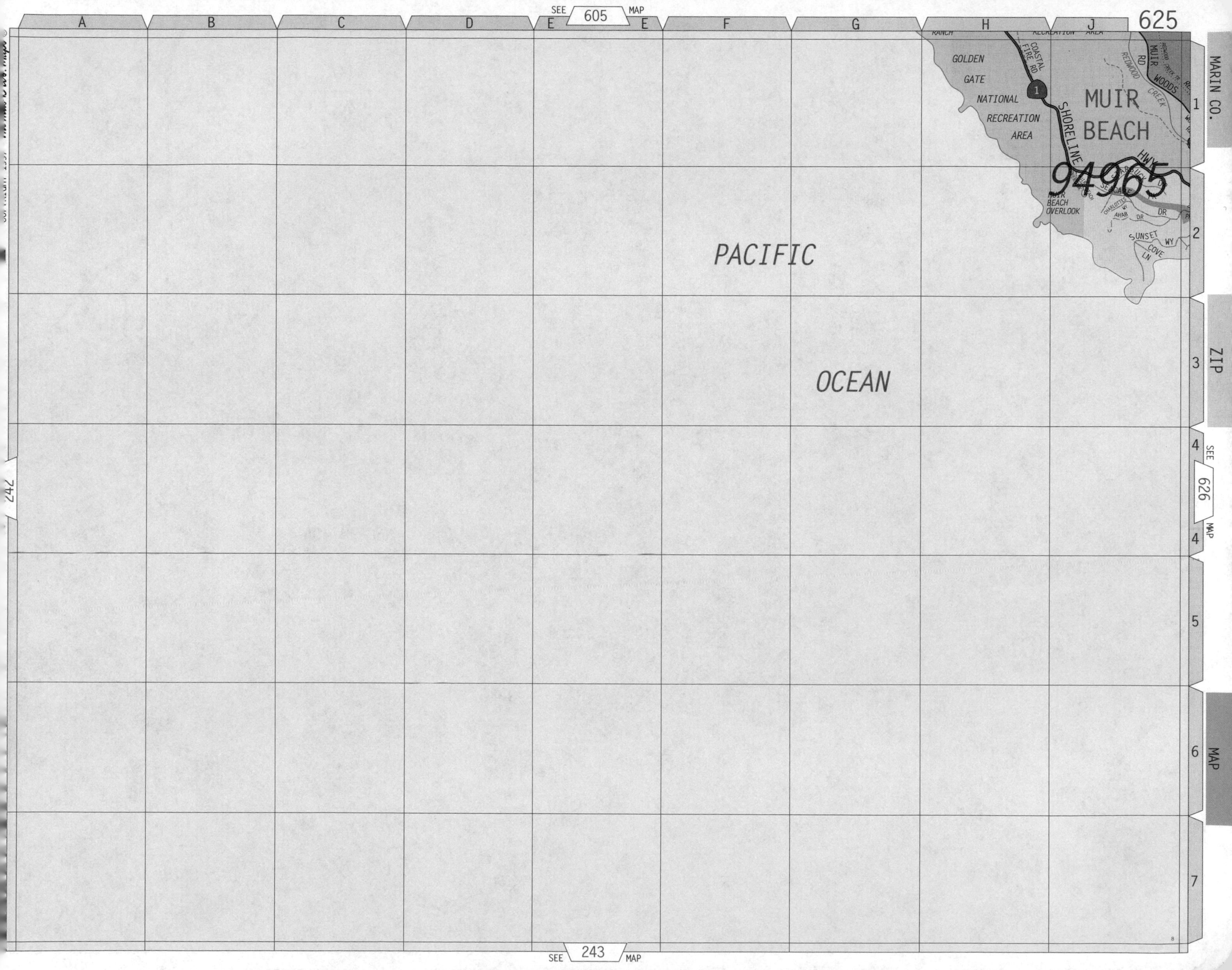

SEE 605 MAP
A
B
C
D
E
F
G
H
J
GOLDEN
GATE
NATIONAL
RECREATION
AREA
COASTAL FIRE RD
SHORELINE
HWY
MUIR
BEACH
94965
MUIR BEACH OVERLOOK
REDWOOD CREEK
MUIR WOODS
RD
AHAB
DR
SUNSET
WY
COVE
LN
PACIFIC
OCEAN
MARIN CO.
ZIP
MAP
SEE 626 MAP
SEE 243 MAP
247
1
2
3
4
5
6
7

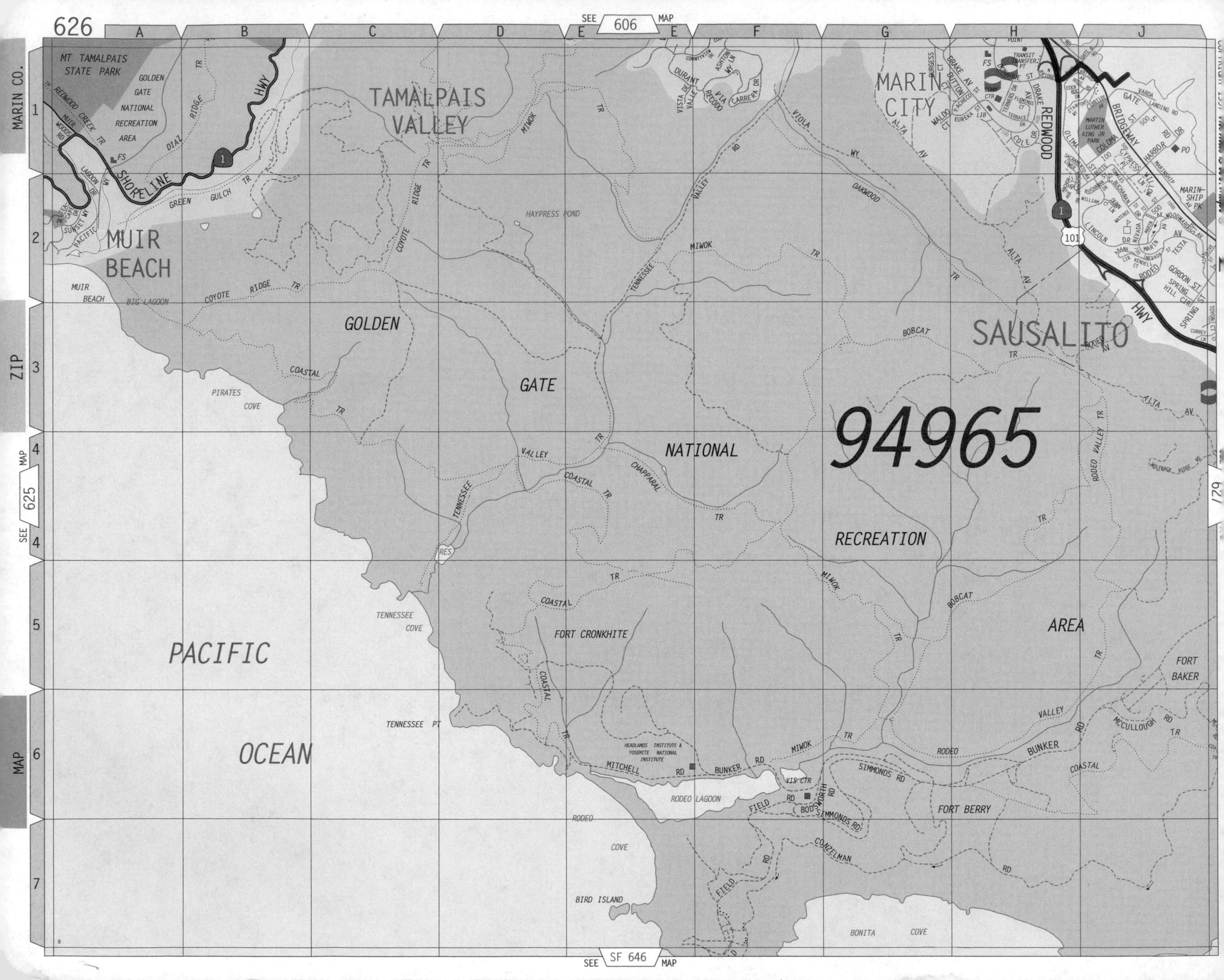

SEE 606 MAP
A B C D E E F G H J
MARIN CO.
ZIP
MAP
SEE 625 MAP
627
SEE SF 646 MAP
MT TAMALPAIS STATE PARK
GOLDEN GATE NATIONAL RECREATION AREA
TAMALPAIS VALLEY
MARIN CITY
MUIR BEACH
SAUSALITO
94965
GOLDEN
GATE
NATIONAL
RECREATION
AREA
PACIFIC
OCEAN
PIRATES COVE
TENNESSEE COVE
TENNESSEE PT
HAYPRESS POND
FORT CRONKHITE
RODEO LAGOON
RODEO COVE
BIRD ISLAND
BONITA COVE
FORT BERRY
FORT BAKER
HEADLANDS INSTITUTE & YOSEMITE NATIONAL INSTITUTE
VIS CTR
SHORELINE HWY
REDWOOD HWY
COYOTE RIDGE TR
COASTAL TR
MIWOK TR
TENNESSEE VALLEY RD
BOBCAT TR
RODEO VALLEY TR
ALTA AV
BRIDGEWAY
MITCHELL RD
BUNKER RD
CONZELMAN RD
FIELD RD
SIMMONDS RD

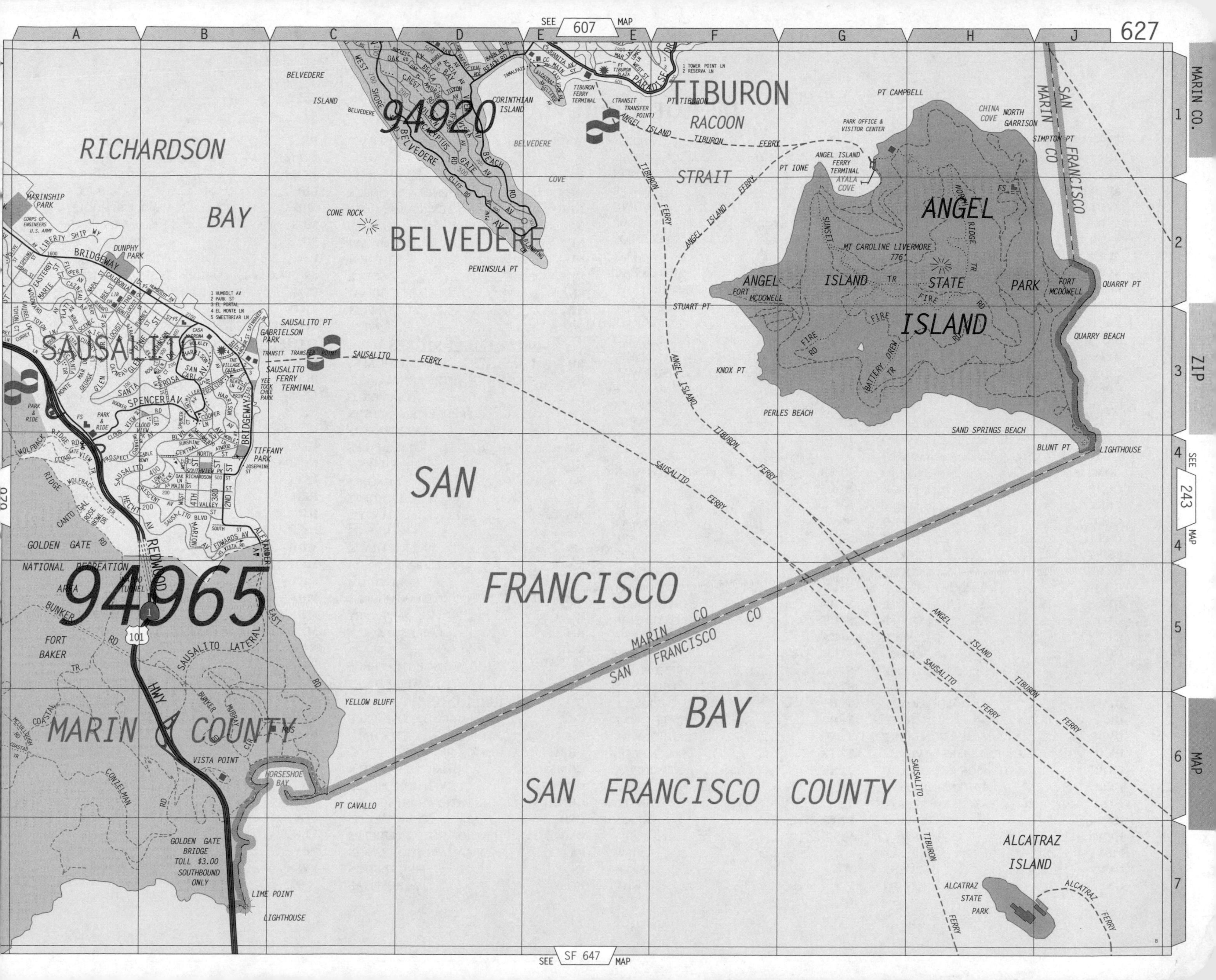
SEE 607 MAP
A
B
C
D
E
F
G
H
J
MARIN CO.
ZIP
MAP
SEE 243 MAP
RICHARDSON
BAY
BELVEDERE
ISLAND
94920
CORINTHIAN ISLAND
TIBURON
RACOON
STRAIT
TIBURON FERRY TERMINAL
PT TIBURON
PT CAMPBELL
CHINA COVE
NORTH GARRISON
SIMPTON PT
PARK OFFICE & VISITOR CENTER
ANGEL ISLAND FERRY TERMINAL
AYALA COVE
PT IONE
ANGEL ISLAND STATE PARK
MT CAROLINE LIVERMORE 776'
FORT MCDOWELL
QUARRY PT
QUARRY BEACH
STUART PT
KNOX PT
PERLES BEACH
SAND SPRINGS BEACH
BLUNT PT
LIGHTHOUSE
MARINSHIP PARK
CORPS OF ENGINEERS U.S. ARMY
DUNPHY PARK
CONE ROCK
BELVEDERE
PENINSULA PT
COVE
SAUSALITO
SAUSALITO PT
GABRIELSON PARK
SAUSALITO FERRY TERMINAL
YEE TOCK CHEE PARK
TIFFANY PARK
SAUSALITO FERRY
ANGEL ISLAND FERRY
TIBURON FERRY
SAN FRANCISCO BAY
GOLDEN GATE NATIONAL RECREATION AREA
94965
FORT BAKER
MARIN CO
SAN FRANCISCO CO
YELLOW BLUFF
MARIN COUNTY
VISTA POINT
HORSESHOE BAY
PT CAVALLO
SAN FRANCISCO COUNTY
GOLDEN GATE BRIDGE TOLL $3.00 SOUTHBOUND ONLY
LIME POINT
LIGHTHOUSE
ALCATRAZ ISLAND
ALCATRAZ STATE PARK
ALCATRAZ FERRY
SEE SF 647 MAP

LIST OF ABBREVIATIONS

PREFIXES AND SUFFIXES

AL . . . ALLEY
ARC . . . ARCADE
AV, AVE . . . AVENUE
AVCT . . . AVENUE COURT
AVD . . . AVENIDA
AVDR . . . AVENUE DRIVE
AVEX . . . AVENUE EXTENSION
BLEX . . . BOULEVARD EXTENSION
BL, BLVD . . . BOULEVARD
BLCT . . . BOULEVARD COURT
BRCH . . . BRANCH
BRDG . . . BRIDGE
BYPS . . . BYPASS
CIDR . . . CIRCLE DRIVE
CIR . . . CIRCLE
CL . . . CALLE
CLJ . . . CALLEJON
CM . . . CAMINO
CMTO . . . CAMINITO
COM . . . COMMON
CORR . . . CORRIDOR
CRES . . . CRESCENT
CRLO . . . CIRCULO
CRSG . . . CROSSING
CSWY . . . CAUSEWAY
CT . . . COURT
CTAV . . . COURT AVENUE
CTE . . . CORTE
CTO . . . CUT OFF
CTR . . . CENTER
CUR . . . CURVE
CV . . . COVE
D . . . DE
DIAG . . . DIAGONAL
DR . . . DRIVE
DVDR . . . DIVISION DRIVE
EXAV . . . EXTENSION AVENUE
EXBL . . . EXTENSION BOULEVARD
EXRD . . . EXTENSION ROAD
EXST . . . EXTENSION STREET
EXT . . . EXTENSION
EXWY . . . EXPRESSWAY
FRWY . . . FREEWAY
GDNS . . . GARDENS
GN . . . GLEN
GRN . . . GREEN
HWY . . . HIGHWAY
JCT . . . JUNCTION
LN . . . LANE
LNDG . . . LANDING
LP . . . LOOP
LS . . . LAS, LOS
MNR . . . MANOR
MTWY . . . MOTORWAY
OH . . . OUTER HIGHWAY
OVL . . . OVAL
OVPS . . . OVERPASS
PAS . . . PASEO
PK . . . PARK
PKWY . . . PARKWAY
PL . . . PLACE
PLZ, PZ . . . PLAZA
PT . . . POINT
PTH . . . PATH
RD . . . ROAD
RDEX . . . ROAD EXTENSION
RDGE . . . RIDGE
RW . . . ROW
SKWY . . . SKYWAY
SQ . . . SQUARE
ST . . . STREET
STAV . . . STREET AVENUE
STCT . . . STREET COURT
STDR . . . STREET DRIVE
STEX . . . STREET EXTENSION
STLN . . . STREET LANE
STLP . . . STREET LOOP
STPL . . . STREET PLACE
STXP . . . STREET EXPRESSWAY
TER . . . TERRACE
TFWY . . . TRAFFICWAY
THWY . . . THROUGHWAY
TKTR . . . TRUCKTRAIL
TPKE . . . TURNPIKE
TR . . . TRAIL
TUN . . . TUNNEL
UNPS . . . UNDERPASS
VIS . . . VISTA
VW . . . VIEW
WK . . . WALK
WY . . . WAY
WYPL . . . WAY PLACE

DIRECTIONS

E . . . EAST
KPN . . . KEY PENINSULA NORTH
KPS . . . KEY PENINSULA SOUTH
N . . . NORTH
NE . . . NORTHEAST
NW . . . NORTHWEST
S . . . SOUTH
SE . . . SOUTHEAST
SW . . . SOUTHWEST
W . . . WEST

DEPARTMENT STORES

BD . . . BLOOMINGDALES
BN . . . THE BON MARCHE
D . . . DIAMONDS
FN . . . FREDERICK & NELSON
G . . . GOLDWATERS
GT . . . GOTTSCHALKS
H . . . HARRIS
IM . . . I MAGNIN
L . . . LAMONTS
MA . . . MACY'S
ME . . . MERVYN'S
MF . . . MEIER & FRANK
MW . . . MONTGOMERY WARD
N . . . NORDSTROM
NM . . . NEIMAN-MARCUS
P . . . J C PENNEY
RM . . . ROBINSONS MAY
S . . . SEARS
SF . . . SAKS FIFTH AVENUE
W . . . WEINSTOCKS

BUILDINGS

CC . . . CHAMBER OF COMMERCE
CH . . . CITY HALL
CHP . . . CALIFORNIA HIGHWAY PATROL
COMM CTR . . . COMMUNITY CENTER
CON CTR . . . CONVENTION CENTER
CONT HS . . CONTINUATION HIGH SCHOOL
CTH . . . COURT HOUSE
DMV . . . DEPT OF MOTOR VEHICLES
FAA . . . FEDERAL AVIATION ADMIN
FS . . . FIRE STATION
HOSP . . . HOSPITAL
HS . . . HIGH SCHOOL
INT . . . INTERMEDIATE SCHOOL
JR HS . . . JUNIOR HIGH SCHOOL
LIB . . . LIBRARY
MID . . . MIDDLE SCHOOL
MUS . . . MUSEUM
PO . . . POST OFFICE
PS . . . POLICE STATION
SR CIT CTR . . . SENIOR CITIZENS CENTER
STA . . . STATION
THTR . . . THEATER
VIS BUR . . . VISITORS BUREAU

OTHER COMMON ABBREVIATIONS

BCH . . . BEACH
BLDG . . . BUILDING
CEM . . . CEMETERY
CK . . . CREEK
CO . . . COUNTY
CTR . . . CENTER
COMM . . . COMMUNITY
EST . . . ESTATE
HIST . . . HISTORIC
HTS . . . HEIGHTS
LK . . . LAKE
MDW . . . MEADOW
MED . . . MEDICAL
MEM . . . MEMORIAL
MHP . . . MOBILE HOME PARK
MT . . . MOUNT
MTN . . . MOUNTAIN
NATL . . . NATIONAL
PKG . . . PARKING
PLGD . . . PLAYGROUND
RCH . . . RANCH
RCHO . . . RANCHO
REC . . . RECREATION
RES . . . RESERVOIR
RIV . . . RIVER
RR . . . RAILROAD
SPG . . . SPRING
STA . . . SANTA
VLG . . . VILLAGE
VLY . . . VALLEY
VW . . . VIEW

STREET
Block City ZIP Pg-Grid

A

A ST
- NVTO 94949 546-G3
100 MrnC 94956 543-C1
400 PET 94952 465-D7
700 MrnC 94956 523-C7
700 SRFL 94901 586-F1
AARON CT
- NVTO 94949 546-C1
2200 PET 94954 465-G3
AARON DR
- NVTO 94949 546-C1
ABERCROMBIE WY
1500 PET 94954 465-D2
ABERDEEN RD
- NVTO 94949 546-G2
ABERDEEN WY
- MrnC 94937 (522-F3
See Page 501)
ACACIA AV
- BLV 94920 627-D1
- LKSP 94939 586-F6
- MrnC 94904 586-E4
- SRFL 94901 566-H7
ACACIA CT
500 NVTO 94945 525-E2
ACACIA DR
- TBRN 94920 607-C4
ACACIA RD
- FRFX 94930 565-H5
ACADIA LN
300 SRFL 94903 566-F2
ACAPULCO CT
- NVTO 94949 546-F2
1600 PET 94954 465-H5
ACE CT
- FRFX 94930 565-H4
ACELA DR
- TBRN 94920 607-D6
ACME CT
1000 NVTO 94949 546-E2
ACORN CIR
- PET 94952 465-C4
ACORN CT
- NVTO 94949 546-D4
ACORN DR
100 PET 94952 465-D4
ACORN WY
- MrnC 94904 586-C4
ADAMS AV
- MrnC 94965 606-B3
ADAMS CT
- NVTO 94947 526-B5
ADAMS LN
- PET 94952 (485-E1
See Page 465)
ADAMS ST
100 NVTO 94947 526-B5
ADELE ST
200 NVTO 94947 526-C5
ADOBE CT
- NVTO 94945 526-A1
ADOBE RD
- SonC 95476 (466-C4
See Page 465)
1900 SonC 94954 465-G1
8200 SonC 94954 (466-C4
See Page 465)
ADOBE CREEK DR
- PET 94954 (466-A5
See Page 465)
ADOBESTONE CT
200 MrnC 94903 546-F6
ADRIAN TER
- MrnC 94903 566-H2
ADRIAN WY
- MrnC 94903 566-H2
ADRIENNE DR
500 PET 94954 465-F5
ADRIENNE ST
600 NVTO 94945 526-C4
AGATHA CT
- SANS 94960 566-B7
AGRESTE AV
2500 TBRN 94920 607-F7
2500 MrnC 94920 607-F7
AHAB DR
- MrnC 94965 625-J2
AHERN LN
100 SonC 94952 (464-H4
See Page 463)
AIRPORT RD
300 MrnC 94945 506-C5
AJAX ST
- LKSP 94939 586-E5
ALAM RD
- SonC 94952 (464-F4
See Page 463)
ALAMEDA DE LA LOMA
- NVTO 94949 546-D2
- MrnC 94949 546-D2
ALAMEDA DEL PRADO
- NVTO 94949 546-F2
- MrnC 94949 546-F2
ALAMEDA PATIO
- MrnC 94970 605-B3
ALAMITOS WY
- FRFX 94930 565-G2

ALAMO WY
- FRFX 94930 565-G3
- MrnC 94938 (564-E1
See Page 543)
ALASDAIR CT
- SRFL 94903 566-C4
ALBATROSS DR
600 NVTO 94945 526-H1
ALBERT LN
- MLV 94941 606-G2
ALBERT WY
300 PET 94954 465-G4
ALBERT PARK LN
1000 SRFL 94901 586-F1
ALBIN WY
1600 PET 94954 465-H5
ALBION CT
300 NVTO 94947 526-D7
ALBION ST
- MrnC 94901 586-H3
ALCATRAZ AV
- BLV 94920 627-E1
- TBRN 94920 627-E1
ALCATRAZ FERRY
- SF - 627-J7
ALDER AV
- MrnC 94963 565-A2
- SANS 94960 566-A6
ALDER CT
- FRFX 94930 566-A6
ALDER PL
200 NVTO 94945 525-E2
ALDER RD
- MrnC 94924 604-D3
ALDERNEY RD
- SANS 94960 566-B6
ALDERWOOD CT
900 PET 94954 465-G6
ALDERWOOD WY
- SRFL 94901 567-B5
ALEXANDER AV
- LKSP 94939 586-F7
- SRFL 94901 566-D7
- SAUS 94965 627-B4
- MrnC 94965 627-B4
ALEXANDER RD
- MrnC 94952 463-A3
200 MrnC 94971 463-A3
ALHAMBRA AV
- MrnC 94938 (544-F7
See Page 543)
ALHAMBRA CIR
- FRFX 94930 565-G3
ALHAMBRA CT
1700 PET 94954 465-G4
ALICE ST
- SRFL 94901 586-H1
700 NVTO 94945 526-C4
ALICE WY
- SANS 94960 566-B6
ALICE EASTWOOD
CAMP RD
- MrnC 94965 606-A2
- MrnC 94965 605-J2
ALLEGANY CT
- PET 94954 465-D2
ALLEMAND AV
- SANS 94960 566-C7
ALLEN AV
- ROSS 94957 586-C2
ALLEN CT
- SRFL 94901 566-E7
ALLEN LN
- ROSS 94957 586-C2
ALLENSBY LN
- SRFL 94901 567-B7
- SRFL 94901 587-B1
ALLYN AV
- SANS 94960 566-A7
ALMA CT
- PET 94952 465-E5
ALMENAR DR
- MrnC 94904 586-F4
N ALMENAR DR
200 MrnC 94904 586-F3
200 LKSP 94904 586-F3
ALMOND CT
- NVTO 94947 526-D7
ALMONTE BLVD
100 MrnC 94941 606-F6
100 MLV 94941 606-F5
ALOHA CT
- SonC 94952 465-B4
ALPINE ST
100 SRFL 94901 566-D6
ALPINE TER
- SANS 94960 566-C6
ALPINE LILY PL
- MrnC 94903 545-J6
ALTA AV
- MrnC 94938 (564-E1
See Page 543)
- MrnC 94965 606-G7
- MrnC 94965 626-G1
300 SAUS 94965 626-H2
500 MrnC 94965 627-A4
500 SAUS 94965 627-A4
ALTA DR
- PET 94954 465-G4

ALTA ST
- LKSP 94939 586-E5
ALTA TER
- CMAD 94925 606-G1
ALTA WY
- CMAD 94925 606-G1
500 MrnC 94965 606-E6
ALTAMIRA AV
- MrnC 94904 586-D3
ALTAMONT AV
- MLV 94941 606-F3
ALTA VISTA AV
- MLV 94941 606-E3
- SANS 94960 586-C1
ALTA VISTA CT
- NVTO 94949 546-H3
ALTA VISTA RD
700 MrnC 94965 606-D7
ALTA VISTA WY
- SRFL 94901 586-H1
- MrnC 94901 586-H1
ALTENA ST
- MrnC 94901 586-H3
ALTER LN
- NVTO 94945 526-B2
ALTO AV
- SANS 94960 566-C6
ALTO ST
- SRFL 94901 586-J2
ALTURA AV
- MrnC 94924 604-G2
ALTURA WY
- SRFL 94901 586-G3
- MrnC 94904 586-G3
- LKSP 94904 586-G3
ALTURAS WY
400 MrnC 94941 606-E6
ALVARADO AV
- MLV 94941 606-E3
ALVINA AV
- SRFL 94901 586-F2
ALYSSUM CT
- NVTO 94945 526-B2
AMALFI PL
- SRFL 94901 586-J1
AMANDA LN
- NVTO 94945 525-H2
AMARANTH BLVD
600 MrnC 94941 606-C4
AMBER CT
- NVTO 94947 525-G4
AMBER WY
400 PET 94952 465-C6
AMBERWOOD LN
- SANS 94960 566-C7
AMES AV
- ROSS 94957 586-C2
AMICITA AV
- MLV 94941 606-E4
ANA CT
- SRFL 94903 566-D3
ANCHOR ST
- SAUS 94965 627-B3
ANCHORAGE CT
- SRFL 94903 566-D4
ANCHORAGE RD
- SAUS 94965 626-H1
ANCHO VISTA AV
- SANS 94960 566-C7
ANDALE AV
600 NVTO 94945 526-G1
ANDERSEN DR
700 SRFL 94901 586-H3
800 SRFL 94901 587-A4
ANDRADE RD
- SonC 94952 (464-E4
See Page 463)
ANDREW DR
- TBRN 94920 607-A4
ANDREWS CT
- NVTO 94949 546-G5
ANDREWS WY
- NVTO 94949 546-G5
ANGEL CT
- NVTO 94947 525-J3
ANGELA AV
- MrnC 94960 566-A4
- SANS 94960 566-A4
ANGELICA CT
- NVTO 94947 525-G4
- SRFL 94901 566-H6
ANGEL ISLAND FERRY
- TBRN - 627-F2
ANGEL ISLAND
TIBURON FERRY
- MrnC - 627-F3
- SF - 627-H5
- TBRN - 627-E1
ANNA WY
1500 PET 94954 465-H6
ANNE CT
- NVTO 94945 526-A2
ANNE LN
- MrnC 94963 (564-J2
See Page 543)
ANNETTA DR
1500 PET 94954 465-G4
ANTHONY CT
- NVTO 94947 525-G3

ANTILLES WY
- MrnC 94920 607-B2
ANTOINETTE LN
200 NVTO 94947 526-E6
ANTON WY
- MrnC 94945 526-H2
ANTONE WY
1000 PET 94952 465-C5
ANTONETTE AV
- SRFL 94901 586-F2
ANTONETTE DR
- TBRN 94920 607-B2
APACHE RD
- CMAD 94925 586-F6
APOLLO CT
100 NVTO 94947 525-H3
APOLLO RD
- TBRN 94920 607-B4
APPALOOSA CIR
2100 PET 94954 465-H3
APPALOOSA CT
- PET 94954 465-H3
APPALOOSA DR
600 PET 94954 465-H4
APPLEBERRY DR
500 MrnC 94903 546-C7
AQUA VISTA DR
- SRFL 94901 586-J1
AQUINAS DR
- SRFL 94901 566-H6
AQUINAS FIRE RD
- SRFL 94901 566-H5
ARAM CT
- NVTO 94947 526-B4
ARANA CIR
- SAUS 94965 626-J2
ARBOLEDA CIR
- FRFX 94930 565-G2
ARBOR CIR
- NVTO 94947 525-J3
ARBOR ST
- LKSP 94939 586-D4
ARCH ST
- LKSP 94939 586-E6
ARCHANGEL CT
- FRFX 94930 565-J5
ARCHANGEL WY
- SRFL 94903 566-D5
ARCHIBALD LN
- MrnC 94945 526-F2
ARDEN WY
800 PET 94952 465-E5
ARDMORE AV
- LKSP 94939 586-E7
ARENAL AV
- MrnC 94970 605-C4
AREQUIPA FIRE RD
6600 MrnC - 565-F3
ARGUELLO CIR
- SRFL 94901 567-A7
ARGYLE ST
- MrnC 94937 (522-G3
See Page 501)
ARIAS ST
200 SRFL 94903 566-D3
ARIES LN
- NVTO 94947 525-F3
ARLENE CT
- PET 94952 (485-F1
See Page 465)
ARLENE TER
100 SRFL 94903 566-B3
ARLENE WY
800 NVTO 94947 526-D7
800 NVTO 94947 546-D1
ARLINGTON CIR
- NVTO 94949 526-C7
500 NVTO 94947 526-C7
ARLINGTON CT
- NVTO 94947 526-C7
ARLINGTON DR
- PET 94952 465-E4
ARMADA DR
600 PET 94954 465-G4
ARMORY DR
- SRFL 94903 566-F4
ARMSBY CIR
- ROSS 94957 586-C3
ARMSTRONG AV
1500 NVTO 94945 526-C2
1500 MrnC 94945 526-C2
ARMSTRONG RD
- SonC 94952 (484-J4
See Page 463)
ARONIA LN
- NVTO 94945 526-B2
ARROWHEAD CT
- PET 94954 465-J5
ARROWHEAD LN
- CMAD 94925 586-G6
- NVTO 94949 546-B1
ARROYO AV
- SANS 94960 566-A5
ARROYO DR
- MrnC 94904 586-E2
ARROYO LN
- NVTO 94947 526-B5
ARROYO RD
- FRFX 94930 565-B5

ARROYO RD
- MrnC 94938 (564-E1
See Page 543)
- MrnC 94933 (564-F1
See Page 543)
100 MrnC 94938 (544-E7
See Page 543)
ARROYO SAUSAL RD
- MrnC - 503-E4
ARTHUR CT
1000 PET 94954 465-H6
ARTHUR ST
400 NVTO 94947 526-B5
ASCALON RD
- MrnC 94933 (564-G2
See Page 543)
ASH AV
- CMAD 94925 586-G7
- FRFX 94930 565-F7
- MrnC 94904 586-D3
- SANS 94960 566-A6
ASH ST
400 MrnC 94965 606-E7
ASH WY
100 MrnC 94903 566-H2
ASHBURY AV
- MrnC 94965 606-B3
ASHFORD AV
- MLV 94941 606-F3
ASHLEY CT
- NVTO 94945 526-F1
ASHTON LN
300 MrnC 94965 626-F1
ASHWOOD CT
- SRFL 94901 567-C6
900 PET 94954 465-G6
ASPEN CT
- SANS 94960 566-B6
ASPEN DR
100 NVTO 94945 525-G1
ASPEN RD
- MrnC 94924 604-E2
ASPEN WY
900 PET 94954 465-G6
ASTER CT
- MLV 94941 606-F3
ATCHINSON RD
11300 SonC 95472 (442-J1
See Page 421)
ATHERTON AV
- MrnC 94945 526-E2
- NVTO 94945 526-E2
ATHERTON OAKS DR
- MrnC 94945 526-G3
ATLANTIC CT
- PET 94954 465-G6
ATWOOD AV
- SAUS 94965 627-B4
AUBURN CT
- TBRN 94920 607-B5
AUBURN ST
100 MrnC 94901 586-H3
AUDREY CT
- TBRN 94920 607-E6
AUDUBON FIRE RD
- MrnC 94924 585-A5
- MrnC 94924 (584-H6
See Page 583)
- MrnC 94970 585-A5
- MrnC 94970 (584-H6
See Page 583)
AUREO WY
- FRFX 94930 565-G3
AUSTIN AV
- SANS 94960 586-B1
AUTO CENTER DR
1100 PET 94952 465-A2
AUTUMN LN
800 MrnC 94965 606-D7
AVELLA RD
- SonC 94952 (464-F5
See Page 463)
AVENIDA BALBOA
400 MrnC 94970 605-B3
AVENIDA FARRALONE
- MrnC 94970 605-C3
AVENIDA LAS
BAULINAS
- MrnC 94970 605-C3
AVENIDA MIRAFLORES
100 TBRN 94920 607-C5
AVENIDA OLEMA
- MrnC 94970 605-C3
AVENUE DEL NORTE
- SANS 94960 566-C7
- SANS 94960 586-C1
AVENUE OF THE FLAGS
100 SRFL 94903 566-F4
AVERYE WY
- PET 94952 465-E5
AVICHI KNOLL DR
- NVTO 94947 526-B5
AVOCET CT
- SRFL 94901 587-A2
AVON AV
- MLV 94941 606-F3
AVON ST
- LKSP 94939 586-E6
AYALA CT
- SRFL 94903 566-E5

AZALEA AV
- FRFX 94930 565-H5
AZALEA CT
- PET 94954 465-H4
AZALEA DR
- MLV 94941 606-F3
AZEVEDO RD
500 SonC 94952 (464-H3
See Page 463)
AZTEC AV
- MrnC 94933 (564-G2
See Page 543)
AZURE WY
2800 SonC 95472 (422-E1
See Page 421)

B

B ST
- NVTO 94949 546-G3
100 MrnC 94956 543-C1
100 PET 94952 465-D6
400 SRFL 94901 586-F1
900 PET 94952 (485-D1
See Page 465)
1100 SRFL 94901 566-F7
BACA VISTA
- NVTO 94945 525-J2
BACCHARIS PL
- MrnC 94920 606-J4
BACHELORS RD
- MrnC 94945 526-J2
BADGER CT
- NVTO 94949 546-D4
BAHAMA REEF
- MrnC 94949 526-J7
BAHIA CIR
100 SRFL 94901 587-A2
BAHIA DR
400 NVTO 94945 526-F1
500 MrnC 94945 526-F1
BAHIA LN
200 SRFL 94901 587-A2
200 SRFL 94901 586-J2
BAHIA PL
200 SRFL 94901 587-A2
200 SRFL 94901 586-J2
BAHIA WY
- SRFL 94901 587-A2
300 SRFL 94901 586-J2
BAHR LN
- CMAD 94925 586-F7
BAILEY AV
- SonC 94952 (464-J2
See Page 463)
100 SonC 94952 465-A2
BAJA CT
- CMAD 94925 606-H1
BAJA WY
- FRFX 94930 565-G2
BAKER CT
- PET 94952 (485-F1
See Page 465)
BAKER RD
100 SonC 94952 (464-J6
See Page 463)
BAKER ST
200 PET 94952 465-C6
BALBOA AV
- MrnC 94956 543-A1
- SRFL 94901 567-A7
- SRFL 94901 587-A1
BALCLUTHA DR
- CMAD 94925 607-A1
BALD HILL FIRE RD
- MrnC 94904 586-A2
- MrnC 94930 586-A2
BALDWIN CT
- SRFL 94901 586-G3
BALDY TR
- MrnC - (563-C3
See Page 543)
BALMORAL WY
- MrnC 94937 (522-G3
See Page 501)
BALRA DR
- NVTO 94947 526-C6
BALTIMORE AV
- CMAD 94925 586-F7
- LKSP 94939 586-E6
W BALTIMORE AV
200 LKSP 94939 586-E7
BALTUS LN
- MrnC 94960 566-A3
BAMBOO TER
600 SRFL 94903 566-C2
BANCHERO WY
- FRFX 94930 565-G4
BANFF WY
100 PET 94954 465-E3
BANK ST
- FRFX 94930 565-J6
- SANS 94960 566-C7
BANTA CT
1000 NVTO 94949 546-E2
BANTAM WY
700 SonC 94952 465-B7
700 PET 94952 465-B7
BAPTISTA RD
- SonC 94952 463-D1

BARBAREE WY
- MrnC 94920 606-J5
BARBER AV
- SANS 94960 586-C1
100 ROSS 94957 586-C1
BARBERRY LN
600 SRFL 94903 566-C2
BARCELONA DR
200 NVTO 94949 546-F2
BARKER AV
- FRFX 94930 565-H7
BARKSDALE CT
- NVTO 94949 546-G4
BARN RD
- BLV 94920 607-D7
- BLV 94920 627-D1
- MrnC 94920 606-J4
BARNER LN
- TBRN 94920 607-B2
BARNETT VALLEY RD
8700 SonC 95472 (422-D1
See Page 421)
BARONE LN
- MrnC 94965 606-D7
BARRANCA RD
- MrnC 94938 (544-F7
See Page 543)
BARRE RD
- SonC 94952 465-A7
BARRIE WY
- MLV 94941 606-E1
BARRY WY
- LKSP 94939 586-G5
BARTEL CT
- TBRN 94920 607-E6
BARUNA CT
100 NVTO 94945 526-G1
BASSETT ST
- PET 94952 465-D7
BATCHELOR TER
- PET 94952 465-D7
- PET 94952 (485-D1
See Page 465)
BATTERY DREW TR
- TBRN - 627-G3
BAXTERS CT
- SRFL 94901 586-H2
BAY CT
- SRFL 94901 587-A1
BAY DR
- MrnC 94971 461-E4
BAY HWY Rt#-1
18000 SonC 94923 421-B6
BAY RD
- FRFX 94930 565-H5
200 MrnC 94971 (462-B6
See Page 461)
700 MrnC 94965 606-E7
BAY ST
- SAUS 94965 627-B3
- SRFL 94901 586-H2
BAY WY
- SRFL 94901 587-A1
BAY CANYON RD
- MrnC 94945 526-J3
- MrnC 94945 527-A3
BAY HILL RD
600 SonC 94923 421-A4
BAYHILLS DR
- MrnC 94903 566-H3
BAY LAUREL LN
- MrnC 94903 545-H6
BAYLIS ST
100 PET 94952 465-D6
BAYO VISTA AV
- LKSP 94939 586-D4
- MrnC 94904 586-D4
BAYO VISTA WY
- SRFL 94901 566-E7
BAY POINT DR
- SRFL 94901 587-A2
BAYPOINT VILLAGE DR
- SRFL 94901 587-A2
BAYSIDE CT
800 NVTO 94947 526-D7
BAY TREE LN
- MLV 94941 606-E2
BAYTREE LN
- SANS 94960 566-A4
BAY TREE RD
- MrnC 94903 566-E5
BAY TREE HOLLOW
- MrnC 94945 526-D2
BAY VIEW AV
- BLV 94920 607-C7
- BLV 94920 627-D1
BAYVIEW AV
- LKSP 94939 586-F7
100 MLV 94941 606-D3
BAYVIEW DR
- MrnC 94901 587-C1
- MrnC 94901 567-B7
100 SRFL 94901 567-C7
100 MrnC 94941 606-C4
100 MrnC 94965 606-C4
BAYVIEW RD
- LKSP 94939 586-E4
- MrnC 94904 586-E4
BAYVIEW ST
- SRFL 94901 586-E1

BAYVIEW ST
100 MrnC 94945 527-A4
BAYVIEW TER
- MrnC 94941 606-H4
BAYVIEW WY
- MrnC 94937 (522-F4
See Page 501)
BAYVISTA CIR
200 MrnC 94965 606-G7
BAYVISTA CT
- MrnC 94941 606-J4
BAYVISTA DR
- MrnC 94941 606-H3
- MrnC 94920 606-H3
BAYWOOD AV
- ROSS 94957 586-D1
BAYWOOD CIR
- NVTO 94949 546-C3
BAYWOOD CT
1700 PET 94954 465-H5
BAYWOOD DR
1100 PET 94954 465-H5
BAYWOOD PL
- MrnC 94956 (522-J6
See Page 501)
BAYWOOD RD
- FRFX 94930 566-A6
BAYWOOD TER
200 SRFL 94901 586-G3
BAYWOOD CANYON RD
- MrnC 94930 565-F2
BEACH AV
- MrnC 94971 461-E3
BEACH DR
- MrnC 94901 587-C1
BEACH RD
- TBRN 94920 607-E7
- TBRN 94920 627-D1
100 BLV 94920 627-D1
BEACH PARK RD
- SRFL 94901 586-H2
BEALE ST
- SRFL 94901 587-A2
BEAR CREEK CT
- PET 94952 (485-F1
See Page 465)
BEAR CREEK RD
- NVTO 94947 525-F4
BEAR VALLEY RD
- MrnC - 543-B2
- MrnC 94950 543-B2
1900 MrnC 94956 543-B2
BEAR VALLEY TR
- MrnC - 543-D7
- MrnC - (563-C4
See Page 543)
BEATTIE AV
- MrnC 94945 527-A3
- MrnC 94945 526-J4
BECKY CT
300 NVTO 94949 546-D1
BEDFORD CV
- SRFL 94901 587-A2
BEE ST
300 SAUS 94965 627-A2
BEECHNUT CT
700 SRFL 94903 566-B2
BEECHWOOD CT
- SRFL 94901 567-B6
BEECHWOOD DR
1200 PET 94954 465-H6
BELL LN
300 MrnC 94965 606-F7
BELLAGIO RD
- ROSS 94957 586-D1
BELLAM BLVD
- SRFL 94901 586-J3
300 SRFL 94901 587-A2
BELLA VISTA AV
- BLV 94920 627-D1
- SANS 94960 566-B7
BELLE AV
- FRFX 94930 566-A6
- SANS 94960 586-C1
- SRFL 94901 586-H1
600 SRFL 94901 566-G7
BELLE DR
- PET 94952 465-C2
- PET 94954 465-C2
BELLE RIVE PL
- LKSP 94939 586-D6
BELLE VIEW AV
100 PET 94952 (485-C1
See Page 465)
BELLEVUE AV
- BLV 94920 627-E1
- SRFL 94901 587-A1
BELLOREID AV
- SRFL 94901 566-D7
BEL MARIN KEYS BLVD
100 NVTO 94949 546-F1
400 NVTO 94949 526-F7
500 MrnC 94949 526-F7
BELMONT AV
- FRFX 94930 566-A6
BELVEDERE AV
- MrnC 94970 605-C3
- BLV 94920 627-D1
BELVEDERE DR
- MrnC 94941 606-H4

BELVEDERE ST
- SRFL 94901 586-J2
BELVEDERE WY
- BLV 94920 627-C1
BENJAMIN LN
- PET 94952 465-C7
BEN JOHNSON TR
- MrnC 94965 606-A4
- MrnC 94965 605-J4
BENNETT RD
- SonC 94952 (464-J5
See Page 463)
BENNIT AV
- SANS 94960 566-A5
BENSON CIR
200 MLV 94941 606-G2
BENSON WY
- PET 94952 465-A2
BENTON LN
1900 NVTO 94945 526-A2
BERENS DR
- MrnC 94904 586-E4
BERGER LN
- PET 94952 465-B5
- SonC 94952 465-B5
BERKE CT
- TBRN 94920 607-E6
BERKELEY AV
- SANS 94960 566-B5
BERLIN AV
- SANS 94960 566-B7
BERMUDA HARBOUR
- MrnC 94949 526-G7
BERNARD LN
- MLV 94941 606-D3
BERNARD ST
- MLV 94941 606-D3
BERNICE CT
- PET 94952 465-D5
BERNSTEIN TR
- MrnC - 585-F7
- MrnC - 605-F2
BERRY LN
- ROSS 94957 586-D2
BERRY TR
- FRFX 94930 565-H6
BERRYDALE DR
1200 PET 94954 465-G5
BERYL AV
200 MrnC 94941 606-F6
BERYL LN
- SRFL 94901 566-E7
BETA ST
- LKSP 94939 586-E6
BETTINELLI RD
- SonC 94952 (484-H3
See Page 463)
BETTY CT
- PET 94952 465-D5
BETTY LN
- NVTO 94947 526-A4
BEVERLEY WY
- SANS 94960 566-B6
BEVERLY TER
- MLV 94941 606-C2
BEYER CT
- NVTO 94945 526-A2
BIGELOW AV
- MLV 94941 606-D2
BIG ROCK RIDGE
FIRE RD
- MrnC 94946 545-G2
100 MrnC 94903 545-G2
200 MrnC 94903 546-A4
600 NVTO 94949 546-A4
BILLOU ST
- SRFL 94901 586-G2
BILLYS LN
- CMAD 94925 606-E1
BINFORD RD
8000 MrnC 94945 526-C1
8000 NVTO 94945 526-C1
8000 MrnC 94945 506-C6
8000 NVTO 94945 506-C6
BIONDA LN
- PET 94954 465-E2
BIONDA RD
- SonC 94954 465-F1
BIRCH AV
- CMAD 94925 586-G6
- MrnC 94963 (564-J2
See Page 543)
BIRCH CT
- PET 94952 465-B5
BIRCH RD
- MrnC 94924 604-E2
BIRCH ST
- MLV 94941 606-D4
BIRCH WY
- MrnC 94903 566-G2
BIRCHWOOD CT
700 SRFL 94903 566-C2
BIRCHWOOD DR
- NVTO 94947 526-D6
500 PET 94954 465-D3
BIRD CT
600 NVTO 94947 526-A4
BIRDIE DR
- NVTO 94949 546-D2

BIRDS NEST CT
- MrnC 94920 606-H3
BIRNAM WOOD CT
- PET 94954 465-J5
BISCAYNE CT
100 SRFL 94901 567-E5
BISCAYNE DR
- SRFL 94901 567-C5
BISHOP CT
100 NVTO 94945 526-E3
BLACKBERRY LN
- FRFX 94930 565-A6
500 MrnC 94903 546-D7
BLACKBERRY WY
- MrnC 94956 543-A2
BLACKFIELD DR
- MrnC 94941 606-J4
- MrnC 94920 606-J4
- TBRN 94920 606-J4
200 TBRN 94920 607-A3
BLACKHAWK DR
- MrnC 94960 566-B5
- SANS 94960 566-B5
BLACKIES PASTURE RD
400 TBRN 94920 607-A4
BLACK JOHN RD
100 NVTO 94945 526-C1
100 NVTO 94945 506-C7
100 MrnC 94945 506-C7
BLACK LOG RD
- MrnC 94904 586-D5
BLACK OAK DR
200 PET 94952 (485-E3
See Page 465)
BLACK OAK LN
- NVTO 94947 526-A5
BLACKSTONE DR
- MrnC 94903 546-D6
BLACKSTONE LN
- MrnC 94903 546-D6
BLANCA DR
- NVTO 94947 525-G4
BLANDING LN
- BLV 94920 627-D2
BLITHEDALE AV
800 MLV 94941 606-F4
E BLITHEDALE AV
- MLV 94941 606-E3
W BLITHEDALE AV
- MLV 94941 606-C1
400 MLV 94941 586-C7
BLITHEDALE TER
- MLV 94941 606-D2
BLITHEDALE RIDGE RD
- LKSP 94939 586-C7
- MLV 94941 586-C7
- MrnC 94904 586-C7
BLITHEDALE RIDGE
FIRE RD
- MrnC 94904 586-B6
- MrnC 94965 586-B6
BLOGETT LN
800 NVTO 94945 526-B3
BLOOM LN
- MrnC 94947 525-H6
BLOOMFIELD RD
4600 SonC 95472 (422-J6
See Page 421)
5600 SonC 95472 (442-J1
See Page 421)
6700 SonC 94952 (442-J1
See Page 421)
BLOSSOM CT
100 SRFL 94901 586-H3
800 PET 94952 465-B5
BLOSSOM DR
- MrnC 94901 586-H2
- SRFL 94901 586-H2
BLUEBIRD LN
- MrnC 94920 606-H3
BLUE BLOSSOM CT
- MrnC 94903 545-J5
BLUEGRASS DR
700 PET 94954 465-H4
BLUE HERON PL
- PET 94954 465-J5
BLUE JACKET CT
10800 SonC 95472 (422-E2
See Page 421)
BLUE JAY FIRE RD
- MrnC 94940 523-C4
BLUE OAK CT
- MrnC 94903 545-J5
- NVTO 94949 546-C1
BLUE RIDGE RD
- MrnC 94904 586-C5
6500 MrnC - 565-D5
BLUE ROCK CT
- CMAD 94925 586-G6
BOARDWALK NUMBER 1
- LKSP 94939 586-F5
BODEGA AV
- PET 94952 465-A6
900 SonC 94952 465-A6
3000 SonC 94952 (464-F3
See Page 463)
6300 SonC 94952 463-H3
BODEGA HWY
13000 SonC 95465 (422-B2
See Page 421)

STREET	Block	City	ZIP	Pg-Grid
BODEGA HWY	13000	SonC	95472	(422-B2 See Page 421)
	14400	SonC	94922	(422-B2 See Page 421)
	14500	SonC	94922	421-G3
	14500	SonC	95465	421-G3
	17000	SonC	94923	421-D5
BODEGA LN	15900	SonC	94922	421-E4
	17100	SonC	94923	421-E4
BODSWORTH RD	-	MrnC	94965	626-F6
BOGEY LN	-	NVTO	94949	546-C2
BOHEMIAN HWY	200	SonC	95465	(422-B1 See Page 421)
BOLANOS DR	-	SRFL	94903	566-B2
BOLEMA TR	-	MrnC	-	(563-H6 See Page 543)
BOLERO CT	700	NVTO	94945	526-H1
BOLINAS AV	-	SANS	94960	586-B1
	-	ROSS	94957	586-B1
BOLINAS RD	-	FRFX	94930	565-H7
BOLINAS ST	-	MrnC	94941	606-G6
BOLINAS RIDGE TR	-	MrnC	-	543-H4
	-	MrnC	-	(564-B1 See Page 543)
	-	MrnC	-	585-A4
	-	MrnC	94924	585-A4
	-	MrnC	94924	(584-F1 See Page 583)
BOLLING DR	100	NVTO	94949	546-G4
BOLSA AV	-	MLV	94941	606-D2
BON AIR RD	-	LKSP	94939	586-E5
	100	MrnC	94904	586-E5
BONAN CT	-	MrnC	94971	(462-B3 See Page 461)
BOND AV	100	PET	94954	465-J6
BOND LN	-	TBRN	94920	607-B2
BOND ST	-	LKSP	94939	586-E5
BONITA ST	-	SAUS	94965	627-A3
BONNIE BANKS WY	-	SRFL	94901	587-B1
	-	SRFL	94901	567-B7
	-	MrnC	94901	567-B7
BONNIE BRAE DR	-	NVTO	94949	546-C2
	-	SRFL	94901	566-F7
BON TEMPE PUMP RD	-	MrnC	-	585-E3
BOOKER AV	-	SAUS	94965	627-A3
BOOM LN	-	SonC	94952	465-A4
BOOTJACK TR	-	MrnC	94965	606-A3
BORDEAUX CT	-	PET	94954	465-H4
BORDEAUX DR	600	PET	94954	465-H4
BORDESSA RD	-	SonC	94952	463-F5
BORDESSI RD	-	SonC	94954	(486-E5 See Page 465)
BOREAL PL	-	PET	94954	465-H4
BORGES CT	-	NVTO	94947	526-A4
BOSQUE AV	-	MrnC	-	585-F1
	-	MrnC	-	565-F7
BOTHIN RD	-	FRFX	94930	565-G5
BOULDER LN	-	SANS	94960	566-C7
BOULEVARD CT	-	NVTO	94947	526-A3
BOULEVARD TER	-	NVTO	94947	526-A4
BOURKE RD	-	SonC	94954	(466-G7 See Page 465)
BOVIN WY	-	LKSP	94939	586-D6
BOXWOOD DR	500	PET	94954	465-D3
BOYSEN RD	-	SonC	94952	463-F1
BRABO TER	200	MrnC	94941	606-E5
BRACKEN CT	-	SRFL	94901	567-C5
BRADCLIFF CT	-	SRFL	94901	566-H6
BRADFORD WY	-	MLV	94941	606-D2
BRADLEY AV	700	NVTO	94947	526-A4
BRADY RD	-	SonC	94952	(464-J7 See Page 463)
BRAGA RD	-	SonC	94952	463-D3
BRAINERD AV	-	PET	94952	465-C7
BRANCH AV	-	LKSP	94939	586-F7
BRANCHING WY	-	PET	94952	465-E7
	-	PET	94952	(485-E1 See Page 465)
BRANDY CT	-	PET	94954	465-H4
BRASSIE CT	-	NVTO	94949	546-C2
BRAUN CT	-	MrnC	94965	606-G7
BRENGLE CT	-	PET	94954	465-J4
BRENNFLECK AV	-	SANS	94960	566-B7
BRENTWOOD DR	-	SRFL	94901	567-C6
BRET AV	-	SRFL	94901	586-G2
BRET CT	-	NVTO	94947	526-B4
BRETANO WY	-	MrnC	94904	586-F4
	300	LKSP	94904	586-F4
BRET HARTE LN	-	SRFL	94901	586-G3
BRET HARTE RD	-	MrnC	94901	586-G3
	100	SRFL	94901	586-G3
BRIAR RD	-	MrnC	94904	586-D5
	-	LKSP	94939	586-D5
BRIARWOOD CT	-	NVTO	94947	526-D7
BRIARWOOD DR	-	SRFL	94901	567-B6
BRICKYARD CV	-	MrnC	94941	606-J6
BRIDGE AV	-	SANS	94960	566-C7
BRIDGE CT	-	FRFX	94930	565-J6
BRIDGE RD	-	LKSP	94939	586-E7
	-	MrnC	94945	526-J2
	-	ROSS	94957	586-C3
	-	MrnC	94904	586-C3
N BRIDGE RD	-	MrnC	94965	606-H7
	-	MrnC	94965	626-H1
BRIDGE WY	-	MrnC	94930	586-A1
	-	MrnC	94930	585-J1
	-	SANS	94960	566-A7
BRIDGEGATE DR	-	MrnC	94903	545-J6
	-	MrnC	94903	546-A6
BRIDGEWATER DR	-	SRFL	94903	566-F3
BRIDGEWAY	-	MrnC	94941	626-J1
	-	MrnC	94965	626-J1
	-	SAUS	94965	626-J1
	1200	SAUS	94965	627-A2
BRIDLE PATH LN	-	NVTO	94945	506-B7
BRIGHTON AV	-	MrnC	94924	604-G2
BRIGHTON BLVD	-	MrnC	94965	606-B3
BRISTOL PL	300	MrnC	94965	606-F7
BRITTON AV	-	BLV	94920	607-C7
	-	BLV	94920	627-C1
BRITTON CT	-	NVTO	94947	525-J3
BROADMOOR AV	-	SANS	94960	566-A5
BROADMOOR CT	-	NVTO	94949	546-C2
	100	SANS	94960	566-B5
BROADVIEW CT	-	SRFL	94901	586-H1
BROADVIEW DR	-	SRFL	94901	566-H7
	-	SRFL	94901	586-H1
BROADWAY	-	MrnC	94904	586-E3
	100	FRFX	94930	565-H5
BROADWAY ST	300	PET	94952	465-C7
BRODEA WY	-	SRFL	94901	566-H7
	-	SRFL	94901	586-H1
BRODERICK ST	11700	SonC	95472	(442-H2 See Page 421)
BROOK LN	-	SANS	94960	566-A6
BROOKDALE AV	-	SRFL	94901	566-G6
BROOKE CIR	-	MLV	94941	606-G4
BROOKE DR	-	NVTO	94947	525-F4
W BROOKE DR	-	NVTO	94947	525-F4
	-	MrnC	94947	525-F4
BROOKLINE AV	500	MrnC	94965	606-D6
BROOKMEAD CT	-	SANS	94960	566-A5
BROOKMEAD PL	-	SANS	94960	566-A5
BROOKMONT CIR	-	SANS	94960	566-B5
BROOKS ST	800	SRFL	94901	586-F1
BROOKSIDE CT	-	NVTO	94947	525-J4
	-	SANS	94960	566-B6
BROOKSIDE DR	-	SANS	94960	566-A5
BROOKSIDE WY	-	PET	94952	(485-E1 See Page 465)
BROOKWOOD LN	-	ROSS	94957	586-C3
BROWN CT	-	NVTO	94947	526-B6
	-	PET	94952	(485-D1 See Page 465)
BROWN DR	-	NVTO	94947	526-A6
BROWNING CT	500	MrnC	94965	606-E6
BROWNING ST	500	MrnC	94965	606-E6
BROWNS LN	300	SonC	94954	(466-C7 See Page 465)
	300	SonC	94954	(486-C1 See Page 465)
BRUCE ST	-	MrnC	94937	(522-G3 See Page 501)
BRUNINI WY	-	TBRN	94920	607-A4
BRUNO ST	900	NVTO	94945	526-B3
BRUSHWOOD LN	-	SRFL	94901	586-F3
BRYAN LN	-	NVTO	94945	526-A2
BRYCE CANYON RD	100	SRFL	94903	566-F2
BRYN MAWR DR	-	SRFL	94901	566-F7
BUCCANEER CT	-	CMAD	94925	606-J1
BUCHANAN CT	100	SAUS	94965	626-J2
BUCHANAN DR	-	SAUS	94965	626-J2
BUCHANAN ST	1400	NVTO	94947	526-B5
BUCK PT	-	MrnC	94956	(522-H7 See Page 501)
BUCKELEW ST	-	MrnC	94965	606-G7
	-	MrnC	94965	626-G1
BUCKEYE CIR	-	MrnC	94973	565-D4
BUCKEYE CT	-	NVTO	94949	546-D4
	-	PET	94952	(485-E2 See Page 465)
BUCKEYE RD	-	BLV	94920	607-C7
	-	BLV	94920	627-C1
BUCKEYE WY	-	MrnC	94904	586-C3
BUCKLIN TR	-	MrnC	-	(522-F7 See Page 501)
	-	MrnC	-	(542-E1 See Page 541)
BUCKWHEAT CT	-	TBRN	94920	607-A3
BUENA VISTA	-	NVTO	94947	525-J3
	200	NVTO	94949	546-H5
BUENA VISTA AV	-	MLV	94941	606-E2
	-	MrnC	-	585-F1
	-	MrnC	94956	543-A1
	-	MrnC	94970	605-C3
	100	CMAD	94925	606-G1
BUENA VISTA LN	-	SANS	94960	566-C7
BUGEIA LN	600	MrnC	94945	526-E2
	600	NVTO	94945	526-E2
BUIDA CT	-	CMAD	94925	606-F1
BULKLEY AV	-	SAUS	94965	627-B3
BULLFROG FIRE RD	-	MrnC	-	585-G1
BUNDESEN RD	-	SonC	94952	465-A5
BUNGALOW AV	-	SANS	94960	566-C7
	-	SRFL	94901	586-G2
BUNGALOW LN	1500	PET	94954	465-H5
BUNKER RD	-	MrnC	94965	627-A5
	-	MrnC	94965	626-F6
BURBANK LN	11500	SonC	95472	(422-H7 See Page 421)
	11500	SonC	95472	(442-H1 See Page 421)
BURDELL CT	-	NVTO	94949	546-E4
BURDELL MOUNTAIN RIDGE RD	-	MrnC	94945	505-F4
	-	NVTO	94945	505-F4
BURDETT LN	-	FRFX	94930	565-J5
BURGESS CT	-	MrnC	94965	606-G7
	-	MrnC	94965	626-G1
BURKHART LN	2800	SonC	95472	(422-E1 See Page 421)
BURKSHIRE SQ	-	SANS	94960	566-A4
BURL LN	16400	SonC	95465	421-D1
BURLINGTON DR	-	PET	94952	465-E4
BURMA RD	-	NVTO	94949	546-J4
BURNING TREE DR	-	NVTO	94949	546-C2
BURNS DAIRY RD	-	SonC	94952	(484-E2 See Page 463)
BURNSIDE RD	2400	SonC	95472	(422-F2 See Page 421)
BURNT RIDGE FIRE RD	-	MrnC	94903	545-H2
	-	MrnC	94946	525-F6
	-	MrnC	94946	545-H2
BURRELL CT	-	TBRN	94920	607-A4
BUTTE ST	600	SAUS	94965	626-J2
BUTTERFIELD DR	100	NVTO	94945	526-B1
BUTTERFIELD LN	-	MrnC	94960	566-A3
BUTTERFIELD RD	-	MrnC	94960	565-J2
	400	MrnC	94960	566-A3
	1000	SANS	94960	566-A3
BUTTERFLY LN	-	MrnC	94904	586-D3
BUTTERNUT DR	700	SRFL	94903	566-B3
BYRON CIR	-	MLV	94941	606-G4

C

STREET	Block	City	ZIP	Pg-Grid
C ST	-	PET	94952	465-E6
	-	SRFL	94901	586-F1
	300	MrnC	94956	543-C1
	800	PET	94952	(485-D1 See Page 465)
	900	NVTO	94949	546-G3
	1100	SRFL	94901	566-F7
CABIN DR	700	MrnC	94965	606-D7
CABLE RDWY	-	SAUS	94965	627-A4
CABRILLO CT	-	SRFL	94903	566-B2
CABRO CT	1000	NVTO	94947	525-G5
CADDY CT	-	NVTO	94949	546-C3
CADER CT	-	PET	94952	465-C6
CADER LN	-	PET	94954	465-J7
CAIN LN	800	NVTO	94945	526-C3
CAJA CT	-	MrnC	94903	546-D7
CALAFIA CT	-	SRFL	94903	566-B2
CALAVISTA DR	-	SRFL	94901	586-E1
CALEDONIA ST	-	SAUS	94965	627-A2
CALETA AV	-	SANS	94960	566-A4
CALICO LN	-	NVTO	94947	525-H3
CALIENTA REAL	-	NVTO	94949	546-H4
CALIENTE REAL	-	NVTO	94949	546-J4
CALIFORNIA AV	-	MrnC	94941	606-E5
	-	SRFL	94901	566-D6
W CALIFORNIA AV	900	MrnC	94941	606-E5
CALIFORNIA LN	-	CMAD	94925	586-F7
CALIFORNIA CONDOR WY	-	NVTO	94949	546-D5
CALLE ARBOLEDA	300	MrnC	94949	546-F2
	600	NVTO	94949	546-F2
CALLE DE LA MESA	200	MrnC	94949	546-E2
CALLE DEL ARROYO	-	MrnC	94970	605-B3
CALLE DE LA SELVA	200	MrnC	94949	546-E2
CALLE DEL EMBARCADERO	-	MrnC	94970	605-B4
CALLE DEL MAR	-	MrnC	94970	605-B3
CALLE DEL OCCIDENTE	-	MrnC	94970	605-B4
CALLE DEL ONDA	-	MrnC	94970	605-B4
CALLE DEL PINOS	-	MrnC	94970	605-B4
CALLE DEL PRADERO	-	MrnC	94970	605-B4
CALLE DEL RESACA	-	MrnC	94970	605-B4
CALLE DEL RIBERA	-	MrnC	94970	605-B4
CALLE DEL SIERRA	-	MrnC	94970	605-B4
CALLE EMPINADO	1000	MrnC	94949	546-E2
CALLENDER WY	-	MrnC	94937	(522-G3 See Page 501)
CALLE PASEO	900	MrnC	94949	546-E2
CALLE RANCHERO	1600	PET	94954	465-J6
	1600	PET	94954	(466-A6 See Page 465)
CALUMET AV	-	SANS	94960	566-B7
CALYPSO SHORES	-	MrnC	94949	526-H6
CAMA LN	-	NVTO	94947	526-D7
CAMBRIDGE CT	100	NVTO	94947	526-C6
CAMBRIDGE HTS	-	NVTO	94947	526-C6
CAMBRIDGE LN	200	PET	94952	(485-B1 See Page 465)
CAMBRIDGE ST	1000	NVTO	94947	526-B5
CAMERON ST	-	MrnC	94937	(522-G3 See Page 501)
CAMINO CT	-	PET	94952	(485-F2 See Page 465)
CAMINO DR	200	NVTO	94949	546-H4
CAMINO ALTO	-	MLV	94941	606-F2
	300	CMAD	94925	606-F2
CAMINO ALTO CT	200	MLV	94941	606-F4
CAMINO DE HERRERA	-	SANS	94960	566-A5
CAMINO DEL CANYON RD	100	MrnC	94965	606-B5
CAMINO DEL MAR	-	MrnC	94937	(522-F2 See Page 501)
CAMINO MARGARITA	-	MrnC	94946	545-C4
CAMM RD	-	SonC	94952	(464-B6 See Page 463)
CAMPBELL CT	-	NVTO	94947	525-J4
CAMPOLINDO DR	-	MrnC	94940	523-D6
CAMPUS DR	-	NVTO	94945	526-B1
E CAMPUS DR	-	NVTO	94945	526-C1
W CAMPUS DR	200	NVTO	94945	526-B1
CANADA CT	-	SRFL	94903	566-E5
CANAL ST	-	SRFL	94901	587-A2
	-	SRFL	94901	586-J2
CANAL TER	-	MrnC	94945	527-A4
CANDELERO RD	-	MrnC	94933	(564-G2 See Page 543)
CANDLEWOOD DR	-	PET	94954	465-E3
CANE ST	400	LKSP	94939	586-F6
CANNON CT	-	NVTO	94947	526-A5
CANNON LN	-	SonC	94954	(486-F5 See Page 465)
	-	SonC	95476	(486-F5 See Page 465)
CANTERA WY	200	SRFL	94901	567-E5
CANTERBURY CT	-	PET	94954	465-H4
CANTO GAL	-	SAUS	94965	627-A4
CANYON AV	-	MrnC	94924	604-G3
CANYON DR	1300	PET	94952	(485-F2 See Page 465)
CANYON RD	-	FRFX	94930	565-F7
	-	SANS	94960	566-A7
	-	ROSS	94957	586-D2
	500	NVTO	94947	526-A5
	600	NVTO	94947	525-J4
	600	MrnC	94947	525-J4
CANYON OAK DR	-	SRFL	94903	566-C1
	-	SRFL	94903	546-D7
CAPE CT	300	MrnC	94941	606-D4
CAPETOWN CT	300	NVTO	94947	526-E6
CAPILANO DR	-	NVTO	94949	546-B2
CAPISTRANO WY	1700	PET	94954	465-H5
CAPRI AV	1400	PET	94954	465-D2
CAPRI CT	-	SRFL	94901	586-J2
CAPTAINS LNDG	-	MrnC	94920	606-H3
CAPTAINS COVE DR	100	SRFL	94903	566-F2
CARACAS CT	1700	PET	94954	465-H5
CARDINAL CT	300	MrnC	94965	606-F7
CARDINAL RD	200	MrnC	94965	606-F7
CARDOZA RD	-	SonC	94954	(486-G6 See Page 465)
CAREY DR	-	MrnC	94903	566-H3
CARIBE ISL	-	MrnC	94949	526-H7
CARISA CT	-	NVTO	94945	525-H1
CARLETON DR	-	PET	94952	465-E4
CARLILE DR	800	NVTO	94945	526-C3
CARLIN CT	700	PET	94954	465-G5
CARLOS DR	100	SRFL	94903	566-F2
CARLOTTA CIR	100	MrnC	94941	606-H4
CARLSBAD CT	200	SRFL	94903	566-F2
CARLSON AV	-	SANS	94960	566-A5
CARLSON CT	-	SANS	94960	566-A5
CARLTON PL	-	MrnC	94956	(522-J7 See Page 501)
CARMEL CT	-	MrnC	94903	566-G4
	-	NVTO	94945	526-B2
CARMEL DR	-	NVTO	94945	526-B2
CARMEL WY	-	MrnC	94960	566-B5
CARMELITA AV	-	MLV	94941	606-E3
CARMEN CT	-	NVTO	94945	525-J1
CARMENCITA AV	-	MrnC	94956	543-A1
CARMODY RD	100	MrnC	94952	(442-J7 See Page 421)
	100	MrnC	94952	(462-J1 See Page 461)
CARNOUSITE DR	-	NVTO	94949	546-C3
CARNOUSTIE DR	-	NVTO	94949	546-C2
CARNOUSTIE HTS	-	NVTO	94949	546-C2
CAROB CT	1000	PET	94954	465-G6
CAROB WY	-	NVTO	94945	526-B1
CAROLINA AV	-	SANS	94960	566-D7
CAROLYN LN	-	MrnC	94941	606-F5
CAROLYN WY	2000	NVTO	94945	525-J1
CARRERA DR	300	MrnC	94965	606-F7
	300	MrnC	94965	626-F1
CARRIE ST	-	MrnC	94971	(462-B4 See Page 461)
CARROLL CT	-	SRFL	94903	566-C3
CARROLL RD	5000	SonC	95472	(422-F5 See Page 421)
	7200	SonC	95472	(442-F1 See Page 421)
CARSON RD	-	MrnC	94973	565-C3
CASA AV	-	NVTO	94949	546-J4
CASA BUENA DR	-	CMAD	94925	586-G7
	500	CMAD	94925	606-H1
CASA DE ARROYO DR	200	PET	94954	465-H6
CASA GRANDE RD	-	PET	94954	465-J6
	700	SonC	94954	465-J6
CASA GRANDE REAL	200	NVTO	94949	546-J5
CASA VERDE CIR	400	PET	94954	465-H6
CASA VERDE CT	600	PET	94954	465-J6
CASCADE CT	600	PET	94954	465-D3
CASCADE DR	-	FRFX	94930	565-F7
	-	MLV	94941	606-B2
	-	SRFL	94901	566-J5
CASCADE WY	-	MLV	94941	606-C3
CASCADE FIRE RD	-	FRFX	94930	565-C6
	6200	MrnC	-	565-C6
CASPAR PL	100	NVTO	94947	526-E6
CASTLE CT	200	NVTO	94945	526-E3
CASTLE ROCK AV	-	MrnC	94973	565-D3
CASTLE ROCK DR	-	MrnC	94941	606-C4
CASTLEWOOD DR	-	SRFL	94901	567-C6
W CASTLEWOOD DR	-	SRFL	94901	567-C7
	-	MrnC	94901	567-C7
CASTRO AV	-	SRFL	94901	586-J3
CASTRO ST	-	MrnC	94933	(564-F2 See Page 543)
	200	MrnC	94938	(564-F2 See Page 543)
CASUAL CT	-	NVTO	94947	525-F3
CATALINA BLVD	-	SRFL	94901	587-A2
CATALPA AV	-	MLV	94941	606-E3
CATALPA WY	900	PET	94954	465-G6
CATARACT TR	-	MrnC	-	605-E2
CATSKILL CT	-	MrnC	94960	565-J2
CAULFIELD CT	-	PET	94954	465-H4
CAULFIELD LN	-	PET	94952	465-G5
	1600	PET	94954	465-G5
CAVALLA CAY	-	MrnC	94949	526-G7
CAVALLERO CT	-	MrnC	94945	526-F3
CAVANAUGH LN	-	SonC	94952	(464-H3 See Page 463)
CAY PASG	-	CMAD	94925	607-A1
CAYFORD DR	-	TBRN	94920	607-A4
CAZADERO LN	-	TBRN	94920	607-E7
CAZNEAU AV	-	SAUS	94965	627-A2
CECELIA LN	-	NVTO	94947	525-H2
CECIL RD	-	MrnC	94963	565-A2
	-	MrnC	94963	(564-J2 See Page 543)
CECILIA CT	-	TBRN	94920	607-A4
CECILIA WY	-	TBRN	94920	607-A4
	200	MrnC	94920	606-J4
	200	TBRN	94920	606-J4
CECILY LN	-	MrnC	94941	606-D4
CEDAR AV	-	LKSP	94939	586-E5
	-	NVTO	94945	526-J3
	-	MrnC	94904	586-D3
	100	MrnC	94945	526-J3
	100	NVTO	94945	527-A3
	100	MrnC	94945	527-A3
CEDAR LN	-	SRFL	94901	587-B1
CEDAR PL	600	NVTO	94945	525-E2
CEDAR RD	-	MrnC	94924	604-E2
CEDAR ST	-	SANS	94960	566-B7
	-	SANS	94960	586-B1
CEDARBERRY LN	500	MrnC	94903	546-C7
CEDAR GROVE PK	-	PET	94952	465-D5
CEDAR HILL DR	400	SRFL	94903	566-D1
	400	SRFL	94903	546-D7
CEDARWOOD LN	-	MrnC	94941	606-C4
	-	NVTO	94947	526-D6
	800	PET	94954	465-G6
CELESTE CT	-	NVTO	94947	525-G2
CEMETERY LN	-	SonC	94952	465-C5
CENTER BLVD	-	FRFX	94930	566-A6
	-	FRFX	94930	565-J6
	100	SANS	94960	566-A6
CENTER RD	1500	NVTO	94947	526-A4
	1800	NVTO	94947	525-E2
	2500	MrnC	94947	525-E2
CENTER ST	-	SRFL	94901	566-E7
CENTRAL AV	-	MrnC	94973	565-D2
	-	SAUS	94965	627-B4
	500	PET	94952	465-C6
CENTRAL CT	-	MrnC	94920	606-H3
CENTRAL DR	-	MrnC	94920	606-H3
CENTRO WY	900	MrnC	94941	606-E5
CENTRO EAST ST	2000	TBRN	94920	627-F1
	2000	TBRN	94920	607-F7
CENTRO WEST ST	1700	TBRN	94920	607-E7
	1800	TBRN	94920	627-E1
CENTURY DR	-	MrnC	94941	606-J7
CENTURY LN	-	SonC	94952	465-B3
CERINI RD	200	MrnC	94971	(462-E5 See Page 461)
CERMENHO CT	-	SRFL	94903	566-D4
CERRA SONOMA WY	-	PET	94954	465-J6
CERRO CREST DR	100	NVTO	94945	526-F1
CERRO SONOMA CIR	1500	PET	94954	465-J6
CHABOT CT	100	PET	94954	465-D3
CHALDA CT	-	MrnC	94903	566-G3
CHAMBERLAIN AV	-	NVTO	94947	526-A5
CHAMBERLAIN CT	-	NVTO	94947	526-A5
CHAMBERLAN CT	800	MrnC	94965	606-E6
CHANNEL DR	-	CMAD	94925	606-J1
	-	CMAD	94925	586-J7
	200	MrnC	94945	526-H2
CHANNEL LNDG	200	MrnC	94920	606-J4
CHANNING WY	-	SAUS	94965	627-A4
	200	SRFL	94903	566-F2
CHANTICLEER AV	-	LKSP	94939	586-F6
	-	MrnC	94965	606-B4
CHAPARRAL CT	-	NVTO	94949	546-E4
CHAPARRAL LN	-	MrnC	94963	565-B2
CHAPARRAL LN	-	MrnC	94973	565-B2
CHAPARRO AV	-	MrnC	94938	(564-E1 See Page 543)
CHAPEL DR	-	MrnC	94941	606-H6
CHAPMAN DR	200	CMAD	94925	586-F7
	200	CMAD	94925	606-F1
CHAPMAN LN	-	SonC	94952	465-A7
	200	MrnC	94941	606-E4
	200	SonC	94952	(464-J6 See Page 463)
CHAQUITA LN	-	MLV	94941	606-D2
CHARDONNAY LN	-	NVTO	94947	525-H4
CHARLES LN	-	MrnC	94938	(564-E2 See Page 543)
	500	MrnC	94941	606-C4
CHARLES DEAN RD	-	MLV	94941	606-D1
CHARLOTTE DR	-	SRFL	94901	586-J2
CHARLOTTES WY	-	MrnC	94965	625-J2
CHARMAINE CT	-	NVTO	94949	546-F4
CHARRO WY	-	FRFX	94930	565-G2
CHASE ST	1200	NVTO	94945	526-C3
CHATEAU PL	-	SRFL	94901	567-C6
CHAUCER CT	-	MLV	94941	606-G4
CHEDA LN	100	NVTO	94947	526-D7
CHEDA KNOLLS DR	-	NVTO	94947	526-D7
CHEHALIS DR	1600	PET	94954	465-F3
CHERNE LN	-	SANS	94960	566-A4
CHERRY CT	-	NVTO	94945	526-D2
CHERRY DR	200	MrnC	94924	604-E4
CHERRY ST	-	PET	94952	465-C5
	600	NVTO	94945	526-C2
CHERRY HILL DR	-	SRFL	94903	566-D1
CHERRY TREE LN	-	MrnC	94956	523-B6
CHESTER AV	-	FRFX	94930	565-J5
CHESTNUT AV	-	ROSS	94957	586-C3
	-	SRFL	94901	566-E6
CHEVY CHASE CT	-	LKSP	94939	586-E7
CHEYENNE WY	-	CMAD	94925	586-G6
CHIAPAS AV	-	MrnC	94938	(564-F2 See Page 543)
CHICKASAW CT	-	CMAD	94925	586-G6
CHICKEN SHACK FIRE RD	-	NVTO	94949	546-D3
CHILENO VALLEY RD	200	MrnC	-	(484-A3 See Page 463)
	200	SonC	94952	(485-A1 See Page 465)
	900	SonC	94952	(484-G3 See Page 463)
	1700	MrnC	-	(483-D2 See Page 463)
	2100	MrnC	94945	(484-G3 See Page 463)
	2700	MrnC	94971	(483-D2 See Page 463)
	5100	MrnC	94971	463-C7
CHIMNEY LN	-	MrnC	94938	(564-F3 See Page 543)
CHIPMAN PL	-	SANS	94960	586-B1
CHRISDUMAR LN	-	SonC	94952	465-A4
CHRISTOPHER CT	-	NVTO	94947	525-G3
CHULA VISTA DR	-	SRFL	94901	566-F6
CHURCH CT	-	CMAD	94925	586-F7
CHURCH ST	-	MrnC	94971	(462-B4 See Page 461)
	6500	SonC	95472	(442-H2 See Page 421)
CIBRIAN DR	-	TBRN	94920	607-B1
CIELO DR	-	LKSP	94904	586-G3
CIELO LN	-	NVTO	94949	546-F3
CIJOS ST	900	SRFL	94901	586-G1
CINDY LN	700	PET	94952	465-C5
CINNABAR AV	100	PET	94952	465-D4
CINNAMON TEAL LN	-	NVTO	94949	546-D5
E CINTURA AV	-	MrnC	94938	(564-F1 See Page 543)
W CINTURA AV	-	MrnC	94938	(564-F2 See Page 543)
CIRCE CT	-	NVTO	94945	526-G1
CIRCLE AV	-	MLV	94941	606-E3
CIRCLE DR	-	SANS	94960	566-D7
	-	SRFL	94901	566-D7
	-	ROSS	94957	586-B2
	-	TBRN	94920	607-A4
	-	TBRN	94920	606-J4
CIRCLE RD	-	MrnC	94903	566-E5
CIRCLE WY	-	MrnC	94941	606-E5
CITRON AV	-	LKSP	94939	586-E5
CITRUS PL	700	NVTO	94945	525-E2
CITY HALL AV	-	SANS	94960	566-B7
CIVIC CENTER DR	-	SRFL	94903	566-E3
CLAIRE CT	-	NVTO	94949	546-C1
CLAIRE WY	-	TBRN	94920	606-J4
CLAIRMONT CT	1700	PET	94954	465-G4
CLARITA CT	-	NVTO	94947	525-G3
CLARK RD	22700	MrnC	94940	(482-B5 See Page 461)
CLARK ST	-	PET	94952	465-D6
	-	SRFL	94901	586-E2
CLAUS CIR	-	FRFX	94930	565-J5
CLAUS DR	-	FRFX	94930	565-J6
CLAUSING AV	700	NVTO	94945	526-C4
CLAUSING CT	-	NVTO	94945	526-C4
CLAY CT	-	NVTO	94949	546-F4
CLAYTON CT	1100	NVTO	94945	526-B3
CLAYTON ST	-	SRFL	94901	586-E1
CLEARVIEW CT	400	PET	94952	(485-E2 See Page 465)
CLEARVIEW PL	400	PET	94952	(485-E2 See Page 465)
CLEGG CT	1000	PET	94954	465-B2
CLEGG ST	1300	PET	94954	465-B2
CLELIA CT	1100	PET	94954	465-H6
CLELIA LN	2000	PET	94954	465-H6
CLEMENTE CT	-	NVTO	94945	525-J1
CLEO ST	-	NVTO	94947	526-C5
CLEVELAND AV	-	SonC	94952	465-A7
	200	MrnC	94941	606-F6
CLEVELAND CT	200	MrnC	94941	606-F6
CLEVELAND LN	-	SonC	94952	465-B6
CLIFF RD	-	BLV	94920	627-D2
	-	MrnC	94924	604-G2
CLIFF ST	-	MrnC	94971	461-D5
CLORINDA AV	-	SRFL	94901	586-E1
CLOTILDA CT	-	MrnC	94941	606-H4
CLOUD VIEW CIR	-	SAUS	94965	627-B3
CLOUD VIEW RD	-	SAUS	94965	627-A4
CLOUD VIEW TR	-	SAUS	94965	627-A4
	-	MrnC	94965	627-A4

STREET
Block City ZIP Pg-Grid

CLOVER HILL CT
- SRFL 94903 566-D1
CLUB VW
- NVTO 94949 546-G5
CLYDE AV
- SRFL 94901 566-G7
CLYDESDALE WY
1900 PET 94954 465-H4
COACH RD
- MLV 94941 606-G2
COADY CT
- PET 94952 465-D7
COAST TR
- MrnC - (542-E5
See Page 541)
- MrnC - (563-D5
See Page 543)
- MrnC - (562-H1
See Page 541)
- MrnC - 583-G3
COASTAL TR
- MrnC 94965 627-A6
COASTAL FIRE RD
400 MrnC 94965 605-G5
400 MrnC 94965 625-H1
COAST OAK WY
- SRFL 94903 546-D7
- SRFL 94903 566-D1
COBBLESTONE CT
- NVTO 94945 506-B7
COBBLESTONE DR
100 MrnC 94903 546-E6
COCHRANE AV
- PET 94952 465-F7
- PET 94952 (485-F1
See Page 465)
COCKRILL ST
6400 SonC 95472 (442-H2
See Page 421)
CODEROLLI RD
- SonC 94952 (464-H7
See Page 463)
COHEN CT
1000 PET 94952 (485-F1
See Page 465)
COLBY AV
- MrnC 94941 606-E5
COLE DR
- MrnC 94965 626-H1
COLEMAN AV
- LKSP 94939 586-E7
COLEMAN DR
100 SRFL 94901 566-F6
COLERIDGE DR
- MLV 94941 606-H6
COLIMA AV
- MrnC 94938 (564-G2
See Page 543)
COLINDA WY
- PET 94952 (485-F1
See Page 465)
COLLEEN CT
- NVTO 94947 525-J3
COLLEGE AV
700 LKSP 94939 586-D4
700 MrnC 94904 586-D4
COLLEGE CT
- LKSP 94939 586-D4
COLLEGE ST
11500 SonC 95472 (442-H2
See Page 421)
COLOMA ST
- SAUS 94965 626-J1
COLONY LN
- CMAD 94925 606-F1
COLONY WY
- CMAD 94925 606-F1
COLUMBIA AV
100 MrnC 94941 606-F5
COLUMBINE LN
- NVTO 94947 526-D7
COLWOOD DR
1400 PET 94954 465-G5
COMMERCE ST
- PET 94954 465-D3
COMMERCIAL BLVD
- NVTO 94949 546-F2
COMMERCIAL PL
800 SRFL 94901 586-F1
COMMODORE WEBSTER DR
- MrnC 94956 543-D1
COMMUNITY RD
- BLV 94920 607-D7
- BLV 94920 627-D1
COMPTON CIR
- MLV 94941 606-G2
COMSTOCK DR
500 TBRN 94920 607-B4
CONCHITA CT
- NVTO 94947 525-G4
CONCORD CT
- NVTO 94947 525-H3
CONCRETE PIPE RD
- MrnC - 585-H2
- MrnC 94930 585-H1
CONIFER LN
1000 PET 94954 465-H6
CONIFER PL
300 NVTO 94945 525-E2
CONIFER WY
- MrnC 94963 565-B2
- MrnC 94973 565-B2
CONLON AV
200 MrnC 94965 606-B5
CONOW ST
100 CMAD 94925 586-H7
100 CMAD 94925 606-H1
CONSTANCE DR
- SRFL 94903 566-E4
CONSTITUTION DR
- CMAD 94925 606-J2
CONVENT CT
- SRFL 94901 566-H6
CONZELMAN RD
- MrnC 94965 627-A6
- MrnC 94965 626-F7
COOGAN AV
- SANS 94960 566-C7
COOK RD
3000 SonC 95472 (422-H2
See Page 421)
COOLIDGE AV
- FRFX 94930 566-A6
COOPER LN
- SAUS 94965 627-B3
COPELAND ST
- PET 94952 465-D6
CORDELIA DR
- PET 94952 465-D5
CORDONE DR
- SANS 94960 566-B6
COREE LN
- FRFX 94930 565-H6
CORINTHIA CT
- NVTO 94947 526-D6
CORINTHIAN CT
- TBRN 94920 607-D7
CORNELIA AV
- MLV 94941 606-C2
CORNELL AV
- LKSP 94939 586-E5
CORNILSEN LN
- SonC 94952 465-A6
CORNWALL ST
- MLV 94941 606-C3
COROGUA DR
- PET 94952 465-D5
CORONA AV
- MrnC 94938 (564-F2
See Page 543)
CORONA CT
- NVTO 94945 525-J1
CORONA RD
- SonC 94952 465-C1
- PET 94952 465-C1
200 PET 94954 465-C1
300 SonC 94954 465-C1
CORONADO CT
- NVTO 94945 525-H1
CORONADO DR
300 PET 94954 465-F5
CORONET AV
- MLV 94941 606-D2
CORONET WY
- MrnC 94904 586-B4
CORRILLO DR
- SRFL 94903 566-E5
CORTE ALEGRE
- MrnC 94904 586-F3
CORTE ALEJO
- LKSP 94904 586-G4
CORTE ALMADEN
- SRFL 94903 566-D2
CORTE ALTA
- MrnC 94949 546-E2
CORTE AMADO
- MrnC 94904 586-F3
- LKSP 94904 586-F3
CORTE ANITA
100 MrnC 94904 586-F4
CORTE ARRIBA
- MrnC 94949 546-E2
CORTE BALBOA
100 MrnC 94904 586-F4
CORTE BARISTO
- LKSP 94904 586-G4
CORTE CAPISTRANO
- SRFL 94903 566-E1
CORTE CAYUGA
- MrnC 94904 586-G4
CORTE COLINA
200 MrnC 94949 546-E3
CORTE COMODA
- MrnC 94904 586-E4
CORTE CORDOVA
- MrnC 94904 586-F3
CORTE DEL BAYO
- LKSP 94939 586-G5
CORTE DEL CERRO
200 MrnC 94949 546-E2
CORTE DEL CORONADO
- LKSP 94939 586-G5
CORTE DEL NORTE
- LKSP 94939 586-F4
CORTE DEL REY
- SRFL 94903 566-E1
CORTE DE SABLA
- MrnC 94904 586-G4
CORTE DORADO
- MrnC 94904 586-F3
CORTE ELENA
100 MrnC 94904 586-F4
CORTE ENCANTO
- LKSP 94939 586-F4
CORTE ESCUELA
400 MrnC 94949 546-D2
CORTE FEDORA
- LKSP 94904 586-H4
CORTE GRACITAS
- LKSP 94904 586-G4
CORTE LA PAZ
- SRFL 94903 566-D2
CORTE LAS CASAS
- TBRN 94920 607-A4
CORTE LENOSA
- LKSP 94939 586-F4
CORTE LODATO
- MrnC 94904 586-G4
CORTE LOS SOMBRAS
- MrnC 94904 586-F4
CORTE LOYOLA
- LKSP 94904 586-G4
CORTE MADERA AV
- CMAD 94925 586-F7
- MLV 94941 606-D2
200 CMAD 94925 606-F1
CORTE MESA DR
- SRFL 94901 566-G6
CORTE MIGUEL
- SRFL 94903 566-E1
CORTE MORADA
- MrnC 94904 586-G4
CORTE NORTE
400 MrnC 94949 546-E3
CORTE ORIENTAL
- LKSP 94939 586-F4
CORTE ORTEGA
- LKSP 94939 586-F4
CORTE PACHECO
- SRFL 94903 566-D4
CORTE PALOS VERDES
- TBRN 94920 607-A3
CORTE PATENCIO
- MrnC 94904 586-F3
CORTE PLACIDA
- LKSP 94904 586-H4
CORTE PRECITA
- LKSP 94904 586-G3
CORTE RAMON
- LKSP 94904 586-G4
CORTE REAL
- LKSP 94939 586-F5
CORTE ROBLE
- MrnC 94949 546-D2
CORTES CT
- SRFL 94903 566-B1
CORTE SAN BENITO
- SRFL 94903 566-D2
CORTE SAN FERNANDO
- TBRN 94920 606-J3
CORTE SARATOGA
- SRFL 94903 566-D1
CORTE SERENO
- MrnC 94904 586-F3
CORTE SOLANO
- LKSP 94939 586-F4
CORTE SUR
400 MrnC 94949 546-E3
CORTE TOLUCA
- LKSP 94904 586-H4
CORTE VERANO
- SRFL 94903 546-E7
- SRFL 94903 566-E1
CORTEZ AV
- MrnC 94933 (564-H2
See Page 543)
CORTEZ CIR
100 NVTO 94949 546-H3
CORTEZ DR
300 PET 94954 465-F5
COTTAGE AV
- MLV 94941 606-D2
- SANS 94960 566-C7
1600 SRFL 94901 566-C7
COTTAGE CT
800 PET 94954 465-G5
COTTONWOOD CT
900 PET 94954 465-G6
COTTONWOOD DR
- SRFL 94901 567-C6
COTTONWOOD PL
- NVTO 94945 525-E2
COUNCIL CREST DR
- CMAD 94925 586-G7
COUNTRY LN
- NVTO 94945 525-J2
COUNTRY CLUB DR
- MLV 94941 606-E2
- NVTO 94949 546-C2
1000 PET 94952 (485-F1
See Page 465)
COUNTRYWOOD CT
100 PET 94954 465-J6
COUNTYVIEW DR
300 MrnC 94965 626-E1
300 MrnC 94965 606-F7
COURT LN
- FRFX 94930 565-J6
COURT RD
- MLV 94941 606-D2
1000 NVTO 94945 526-B3
COURT ST
100 PET 94952 465-D6
1000 SRFL 94901 586-G1
COURTNEY LN
- MrnC 94920 606-H3
COURTRIGHT RD
100 SRFL 94901 586-F2
COVE LN
- MrnC 94965 625-J2
COVE PL
- BLV 94920 607-D7
COVE RD
- BLV 94920 607-D7
- BLV 94920 627-D1
COVEY WY
- PET 94954 465-G5
COWBARN LN
- NVTO 94947 526-D7
CRAIG CT
500 NVTO 94949 546-E1
CRANE DR
- MrnC 94960 565-J2
CRATER LAKE WY
200 SRFL 94903 566-F2
CREAMERY RD
- MrnC 94963 (564-J2
See Page 543)
300 MrnC 94963 565-A2
CRECIENTA DR
- SAUS 94965 627-A3
CRECIENTA LN
- SAUS 94965 627-A3
CREEK LN
- MLV 94941 606-D3
CREEK RD
- FRFX 94930 565-H6
100 FRFX 94930 566-A6
100 SANS 94960 566-A6
CREEK TR
- SANS 94960 566-A5
CREEKSIDE CT
- CMAD 94925 606-H2
- NVTO 94945 526-A2
CREEKSIDE DR
- LKSP 94939 586-E5
- MrnC 94903 545-H6
1500 PET 94954 465-F4
CREEK SIDE WY
- MrnC 94920 606-H3
CREEK VIEW CIR
- LKSP 94939 586-E5
CREEKVIEW CIR
1600 PET 94954 465-F3
CREEKVIEW CT
1600 PET 94954 465-F3
CRESCENT AV
- SAUS 94965 627-A4
CRESCENT CIR
- FRFX 94930 565-B5
CRESCENT CT
- MrnC 94973 565-D3
- NVTO 94947 526-A3
CRESCENT DR
- MrnC 94973 565-D3
100 NVTO 94949 546-H4
E CRESCENT DR
- SRFL 94901 566-E7
W CRESCENT DR
- SRFL 94901 566-D7
CRESCENT LN
- FRFX 94930 565-A6
- SANS 94960 586-B1
CRESCENT RD
- CMAD 94925 586-F7
100 SANS 94960 586-B1
CRESCENTE AV
- MrnC 94924 604-G2
CREST RD
- SANS 94960 566-C7
- SANS 94960 586-D1
- BLV 94920 627-D1
- FRFX 94930 565-J6
- MrnC 94945 526-H2
- ROSS 94957 586-D1
CRESTA CIR
- SRFL 94903 566-F1
CRESTA DR
100 SRFL 94903 566-F1
CRESTA WY
- SRFL 94903 566-F1
CRESTHAVEN DR
- MrnC 94903 566-H3
CRESTVIEW CT
- PET 94952 (485-D1
See Page 465)
CRESTVIEW DR
- MrnC 94903 566-H3
CRESTWOOD DR
- SRFL 94901 566-D6
CRICKLEWOOD DR
- NVTO 94947 526-D7
CRINELLA DR
500 PET 94954 465-G4
CROMARY WY
- MrnC 94937 (522-F4
See Page 501)
CROOKED AV
- SANS 94960 566-D6
CROSS CREEK PL
- LKSP 94939 586-E5
CROSS CREEK WY
- NVTO 94945 526-E3
CROSSROADS
700 NVTO 94947 526-D7
CROWN CT
- MLV 94941 606-E3
CROWN RD
100 MrnC 94904 586-B4
1500 PET 94954 465-D2
CROWN FIRE RD
100 MrnC 94904 586-B4
CROWN POINT CT
- MrnC 94901 586-J1
- SRFL 94901 586-J1
CRYSTAL CT
- MrnC 94920 606-H3
100 NVTO 94949 546-D1
CRYSTAL CREEK
- LKSP 94939 586-E5
CUB LAND RD
6600 MrnC - 565-F3
CULLODEN PARK RD
- SRFL 94901 566-F7
CULVER ST
- SRFL 94901 586-H2
CURLEW WY
- NVTO 94949 546-E5
CURREY AV
- SAUS 94965 627-A3
CURREY LN
200 SAUS 94965 626-J3
200 SAUS 94965 627-A3
CURRY LN
200 MrnC 94941 606-E5
CURTIS AV
- SRFL 94901 566-G7
CUSHING AV
- MrnC 94903 566-G3
CUSHING DR
- MLV 94941 606-D1
CYNTHIA CT
- MrnC 94930 565-H4
CYPRESS AV
- MLV 94941 606-B3
- MrnC 94904 586-E3
- MrnC 94971 461-F3
800 NVTO 94947 526-B4
CYPRESS CT
- NVTO 94947 526-B3
CYPRESS DR
- PET 94954 (466-A7
See Page 465)
- PET 94954 465-J7
- FRFX 94930 565-H6
CYPRESS PL
- SAUS 94965 626-J1
CYPRESS RD
- MrnC 94956 523-C6
- SANS 94960 566-C7
CYPRESS HOLLOW DR
- MrnC 94920 606-J4

D

D ST
- NVTO 94949 546-G3
- SRFL 94901 586-F2
100 PET 94952 465-D7
800 PET 94952 (485-B5
See Page 465)
1400 SonC 94952 (485-B5
See Page 465)
E D ST
400 PET 94952 465-E6
DAFFODIL LN
- MLV 94941 606-C3
DAFFODIL RD
300 MrnC 94924 604-E4
DAISY MAE CT
- NVTO 94947 525-J3
DAM RD
- MrnC 94946 (524-A7
See Page 503)
- MrnC 94946 523-J7
- MrnC 94946 543-J1
DANA ST
- PET 94952 465-C7
DANBERRY LN
2100 MrnC 94903 546-C7
DANDELION WY
1400 PET 94954 465-D2
DANIEL DR
700 PET 94954 465-G5
DANIELLE DR
100 SRFL 94903 566-B3
DARLENE DR
100 SonC 94952 (464-F2
See Page 463)
DARTMOUTH AV
- LKSP 94939 586-E5
DARYL AV
- MrnC 94947 525-E2
DAVENPORT CT
- SRFL 94901 566-E7
DAVID CT
- NVTO 94947 526-A4
DAVID CT
- SRFL 94901 566-H6
DAVIDOR LN
- NVTO 94945 526-A2
DAVIDSON ST
500 NVTO 94945 526-D4
DAVIS DR
- TBRN 94920 607-D7
DAWES CT
- NVTO 94947 526-B5
DAWES ST
1400 NVTO 94947 526-B5
DAWN LN
300 MrnC 94965 606-F7
DAWN PL
- MLV 94941 606-E2
100 PET 94952 (485-E2
See Page 465)
DAYS ISLAND RD
- MrnC 94945 527-A3
DEAN CT
- PET 94952 465-F5
- PET 94954 465-F5
DE ANZA WY
- SRFL 94903 566-E4
DEBES RANCH RD
- MrnC 94903 566-F5
DEBORAH CT
100 NVTO 94949 546-D1
DEBRA DR
1400 PET 94954 465-H5
DE BURGH DR
- MrnC 94960 566-A3
- MrnC 94960 565-J3
DEEPSTONE DR
100 MrnC 94903 546-E6
DEER RUN
- CMAD 94925 606-H1
DEER TR
- MrnC 94947 525-J6
DEER CREEK CT
- MrnC 94930 565-F3
DEERFIELD LN
- NVTO 94947 526-B5
DEER HILL CT
300 MrnC 94941 606-H5
DEER HOLLOW RD
- MrnC 94960 566-A4
DEER ISLAND LN
300 MrnC 94945 526-F4
300 NVTO 94945 526-F4
DEER PARK AV
- SRFL 94901 566-H7
DEER PARK DR
- FRFX 94930 565-J7
DEER PARK LN
- SANS 94960 566-A6
DEER PARK FIRE RD
- MrnC 94965 606-A5
- MrnC 94965 605-G4
DEERTRAIL LN
300 MrnC 94965 606-E7
300 MrnC 94965 626-E1
DEER VALLEY RD
100 SRFL 94903 566-F1
DE FORD DR
- SRFL 94903 566-C3
DE LA GUERRA RD
- SRFL 94903 566-A1
DEL CASA DR
- MLV 94941 606-E3
DEL GANADO RD
600 SRFL 94903 566-B1
DEL HARO WY
- SRFL 94903 566-D5
DELL LN
- MLV 94941 606-E3
DELL ST
- MLV 94941 606-E3
DELLWOOD CT
- SRFL 94901 567-C7
DEL MAR AV
700 NVTO 94947 526-A4
DELMAR DR
- TBRN 94920 607-C5
DEL MONTE
- LKSP 94939 586-G5
DE LONG AV
600 NVTO 94945 526-B3
DEL ORO CIR
1600 PET 94954 465-J6
DEL ORO LAGOON
- MrnC 94949 526-H7
DEL PRESIDIO BLVD
900 SRFL 94903 566-E3
DEL RANCHO WY
- PET 94954 465-J6
DEL SOL CT
- PET 94954 465-J6
DEL SOL WY
1200 PET 94954 465-J6
DE LUCA PL
- SRFL 94901 586-G2
DENISE CT
- NVTO 94945 526-C3
800 MrnC 94965 606-E6
DENLYN ST
1100 NVTO 94947 526-C6
DENMAN RD
- PET 94952 465-A1
DENMAN RD
- PET 94952 (464-J1
See Page 463)
DENNING AV
- SRFL 94903 566-C4
DESCANSO WY
800 MrnC 94903 566-H2
DE SILVA CT
- MrnC 94941 606-G5
DE SILVA DR
- MrnC 94941 606-H5
DEUCE CT
- FRFX 94930 565-H4
DEVILS GULCH FIRE RD
- MrnC - (544-B6
See Page 543)
- MrnC 94946 (544-B6
See Page 543)
DEVON DR
100 SRFL 94903 566-D4
DEVONSHIRE DR
- NVTO 94947 525-G2
DE WITT DR
- ROSS 94957 586-C2
DIABLO AV
- NVTO 94945 526-B4
700 NVTO 94947 526-B4
DIABLO CT
- NVTO 94947 526-A4
DIABLO DR
- MrnC 94904 586-C4
DIAMOND HEAD PASG
- CMAD 94925 606-J1
DIANE LN
- LKSP 94939 586-F6
DIANNE WY
- SRFL 94901 586-G2
DIAS WY
- SRFL 94903 566-D4
DIAZ RIDGE TR
- MrnC 94965 606-B7
- MrnC 94965 626-A1
DIAZ RIDGE FIRE RD
- MrnC 94965 606-A7
- MrnC 94965 605-J7
DIBBLEE RD
- MrnC 94904 586-A3
- ROSS 94957 586-A3
DICKENS CT
- MLV 94941 606-H6
DICKSON DR
1100 NVTO 94949 546-D1
DICKSON RD
- MrnC 94938 (564-E2
See Page 543)
DICKSON HILL
800 PET 94952 465-C6
DIEGO DR
- SRFL 94903 566-B1
DIGITAL DR
- NVTO 94949 546-F1
DILLON BEACH RD
2500 MrnC 94971 (462-A4
See Page 461)
2800 MrnC 94971 461-F3
DIPSEA RD
- MrnC 94970 605-A2
- MrnC 94970 604-J2
DIPSEA TR
100 MrnC 94941 606-C4
100 MrnC 94965 606-C4
DIPSEA FIRE RD
- MrnC 94965 605-E5
DIVISO ST
200 TBRN 94920 607-E7
200 TBRN 94920 627-E1
DIXON RIDGE FIRE RD
- MrnC 94946 545-C7
- MrnC 94946 565-E1
- MrnC 94973 545-C7
- MrnC 94973 565-E1
DOCKSIDE CIR
- SRFL 94903 566-F2
DODIE ST
- SRFL 94901 586-J3
DOGWOOD CT
- NVTO 94947 526-D6
- PET 94952 (485-E3
See Page 465)
DOGWOOD RD
- MrnC 94924 604-E2
DOHERTY DR
200 LKSP 94939 586-F6
DOLAN AV
300 MrnC 94941 606-F7
DOLORES ST
- SRFL 94901 586-G2
DOLPHIN ISL
- MrnC 94949 526-H7
- MrnC 94949 546-H1
DOMINGA AV
- FRFX 94930 565-J6
DOMINIC DR
2300 NVTO 94947 525-G3
DOMINICAN DR
- SRFL 94901 566-H6
DONAHUE ST
- MrnC 94965 606-G7
300 MrnC 94965 626-H1
DONNA ST
1300 NVTO 94947 526-C5
DONNER AV
400 PET 94954 465-G4
DONNER CT
400 PET 94954 465-G4
DON TIMOTEO CT
- SRFL 94903 566-D4
DOOLEY CT
- NVTO 94945 526-B2
DORETHEA ST
800 MrnC 94965 606-D7
DORIAN WY
- SRFL 94901 567-A7
DORIS AV
- NVTO 94947 525-H4
DORIS WY
- PET 94952 465-E5
DORSET LN
- MrnC 94941 606-G3
- MLV 94941 606-G3
DOTS LN
- MLV 94941 606-C3
DOUGLAS CT
- NVTO 94947 526-A5
DOUGLAS DR
600 MrnC 94941 606-C4
DOUGLAS RD
100 MrnC 94956 (522-J7
See Page 501)
DOUGLAS ST
- PET 94952 465-D7
DOUGLASS ST
- MrnC 94937 (522-F4
See Page 501)
DOVE PL
- NVTO 94949 546-E5
DOVER RD
- MrnC 94956 (522-H7
See Page 501)
DOW LN
- NVTO 94947 525-J4
DOWITCHER WY
- SRFL 94901 587-A2
DRACO DR
600 PET 94954 465-E2
DRAKE AV
- MrnC 94965 606-H7
200 MrnC 94965 626-G1
DRAKE WY
- MrnC 94937 (522-F2
See Page 501)
DRAKES CV
- SRFL 94903 566-E4
DRAKES BEACH RD
- MrnC - 541-C4
DRAKES LANDING RD
- LKSP 94939 586-G5
DRAKE SUMMIT RD
- MrnC 94956 543-A1
- MrnC 94956 (542-J2
See Page 541)
DRAKES VIEW CIR
- LKSP 94939 586-G5
DRAKES VIEW DR
- MrnC 94956 523-A6
400 MrnC - (522-H7
See Page 501)
DRAKES VIEW TR
- MrnC - (542-F2
See Page 541)
DRAKEWOOD LN
- NVTO 94947 526-B6
DRAKEWOOD PL
100 NVTO 94947 526-B6
N DREAM FARM RD
- MrnC 94937 (522-G5
See Page 501)
S DREAM FARM RD
- MrnC 94937 (522-H5
See Page 501)
DRIFTWOOD AV
- NVTO 94945 526-A2
- NVTO 94945 525-J2
DRIFTWOOD CT
- SRFL 94901 567-C6
DUARTE CT
- NVTO 94949 546-F4
DUBLIN CT
100 PET 94952 (485-C1
See Page 465)
DU BOIS ST
100 SRFL 94901 586-G2
DUCK COVE RD
- MrnC - (502-A5
See Page 501)
DUFF LN
- ROSS 94957 586-B2
DUFFY PL
- SRFL 94901 586-G1
DUNAND AV
- SRFL 94901 566-E7
- SRFL 94901 586-E1
DUNDEE WY
- MrnC 94937 (522-G3
See Page 501)
DUNFRIES TER
- SRFL 94901 567-B7
DUNLIN CT
- MrnC 94903 546-E6
DUNN LN
- SAUS 94965 626-J2
DUPREE LN
- PET 94954 465-D2
DURAN DR
- SRFL 94903 566-B1
DURANT WY
300 MrnC 94965 626-E1
DURHAM RD
- SANS 94960 566-B6
DUSEL CT
- NVTO 94949 546-F3
DUSTMAN RD
- SonC 94954 506-G2
DUTCH HILL DR
- SonC 94954 (466-A1
See Page 465)
- SonC 94954 465-J1
DUTCH VALLEY LN
- MrnC 94960 565-H2
DUTTON CT
- MrnC 94965 626-G1
DUXBURY CV
- SRFL 94901 587-A2
DYNAMIC ST
1300 PET 94954 465-D3
DYRTLE AV
- SRFL 94901 566-G6

E

E ST
- NVTO 94949 546-G3
100 PET 94952 465-E7
600 SRFL 94901 586-F1
1000 SRFL 94901 566-F7
E TER
- TBRN 94920 607-A4
EAGLE DR
- NVTO 94949 546-C2
EAGLE GAP CT
- NVTO 94949 546-E4
EAGLE GAP RD
- NVTO 94949 546-E4
EAGLE ROCK RD
- MrnC 94920 606-H3
EAGLES RD
6500 MrnC - 565-F5
EAMES CT
- NVTO 94947 525-H2
EARLS CT
500 PET 94952 465-B6
EAST CT
- SANS 94960 566-A5
100 PET 94952 465-F6
1100 NVTO 94945 526-B3
EAST DR
- MLV 94941 606-E3
EAST RD
- MrnC 94965 627-C5
- ROSS 94957 586-B2
EAST ST
- MrnC 94971 (462-C4
See Page 461)
- SRFL 94901 586-E1
EAST TER
- TBRN 94920 607-A4
EASTERBY ST
500 SAUS 94965 627-A2
EASTMAN AV
100 CMAD 94925 586-G7
100 CMAD 94925 606-G1
EASTMAN CT
100 SonC 94952 (464-J6
See Page 463)
EASTMAN LN
- SonC 94952 465-A6
400 SonC 94952 (464-G5
See Page 463)
EASTSIDE CIR
- PET 94954 465-F4
EAST VIEW AV
- BLV 94920 627-E1
- TBRN 94920 627-E1
EASTWOOD DR
300 PET 94954 465-G3
EASTWOOD WY
600 MrnC 94965 606-D6
EASY CT
- NVTO 94947 525-J3
EBBTIDE AV
- SAUS 94965 626-H1
EBBTIDE PASG
- CMAD 94925 606-J1
- CMAD 94925 607-A1
EBRIGHT FIRE RD
400 MrnC 94947 525-H6
600 MrnC 94946 525-H6
ECHO AV
- CMAD 94925 606-H1
- CMAD 94925 586-H7
ECHO CT
- SANS 94960 586-B1
800 PET 94954 465-G5
ECHO LN
- MLV 94941 606-E4
ECHO PL
- LKSP 94939 586-D6
- SRFL 94901 566-D6
ECKMANN PL
100 PET 94952 (485-E2
See Page 465)
EDDIE CT
- PET 94952 465-B5
EDDIE WY
- PET 94952 465-B5
EDEN LN
4000 MrnC 94920 607-C4
EDEN ST
- LKSP 94939 586-E6
EDEN ROC DR
100 SAUS 94965 626-H1
EDGEHILL RD
- MLV 94941 606-D2
EDGEHILL WY
- MrnC 94903 566-G5
EDGEMAR WY
- CMAD 94925 606-H1
EDGEMONT WY
- MrnC 94937 (522-G3
See Page 501)
EDGEWATER CT
- SRFL 94903 566-G3
EDGEWATER PL
- LKSP 94939 586-E5
EDGEWATER RD
- BLV 94920 607-C7
EDGEWOOD AV
- MrnC 94937 (522-F4
See Page 501)
- MrnC 94941 606-C3
- MLV 94941 606-B3
600 MrnC 94965 606-B3
EDGEWOOD AV N
900 MrnC 94965 606-A2
900 MLV 94941 606-A2
EDGEWOOD DR
- MrnC 94973 565-C3
EDGEWOOD WY
- SRFL 94901 566-E6
EDINBORO LN
- MrnC 94937 (522-G4
See Page 501)
EDINBURGH LN
200 PET 94952 (485-B1
See Page 465)
EDISON AV
- CMAD 94925 586-F7
EDITH ST
- PET 94952 465-D5
EDNA CT
- MrnC 94904 586-E3
EDWARD AV
- MrnC 94903 566-G3
EDWARD CT
- SRFL 94901 566-H7
EDWARDS AV
- SAUS 94965 627-B4
EGGERS PZ
- MLV 94941 606-E4
EGLIN LN
- NVTO 94949 546-G3
EGRET WY
- MrnC 94941 606-J6
ELAINE AV
- MLV 94941 606-C1
ELAINE WY
- SRFL 94901 586-J2
ELANOR CT
- PET 94952 465-D5
EL ARROYO PL
600 NVTO 94949 546-F2
EL BONITO DR
200 NVTO 94949 546-H4
EL CAMINO
- SRFL 94901 566-G7
EL CAMINO AV
- SRFL 94901 586-E1
- SRFL 94901 566-E7
EL CAMINO DR
- CMAD 94925 606-J1
EL CAMINO BODEGA
- SonC 95465 (422-B1
See Page 421)
EL CAMINO BUENO
- ROSS 94957 586-C2
EL CAPITAN AV
- MLV 94941 606-C1
EL CAPITAN DR
- MrnC 94903 546-A6
EL CERRITO
- MrnC 94933 (564-G1
See Page 543)
- MrnC 94938 (564-G1
See Page 543)
EL CERRITO AV
- SANS 94960 566-B6
- SRFL 94901 566-F7
EL CIDE CT
1200 MrnC 94941 606-D5
EL CONDOR CT
- SRFL 94903 566-D4
ELDA CT
- SRFL 94903 566-C3
ELDA DR
- SRFL 94903 566-C3
ELDERBERRY DR
300 PET 94952 (485-E3
See Page 465)

MARIN CO.

STREET Block City ZIP Pg-Grid

ELDERBERRY LN
2100 MrnC 94903 546-C7
EL DORADO CT
2000 NVTO 94947 525-G4
ELDRIDGE AV
- MLV 94941 606-C1
ELDRIDGE CT
600 NVTO 94947 526-C7
ELDRIDGE ST
500 NVTO 94947 526-C7
ELDRIDGE GRADE RD
- MrnC - 586-A4
ELDRIDGE GRADE FIRE RD
- MrnC - 585-J3
- MrnC 94930 585-J3
- MrnC 94965 586-A6
- MrnC 94965 585-J7
- MrnC - 586-A5
ELEGANT TERN RD
- NVTO 94949 546-D5
ELENA CIR
- SRFL 94903 566-D3
ELENA CT
- NVTO 94945 525-J1
- PET 94954 465-F6
EL FAISAN DR
200 SRFL 94903 566-D4
ELFORD ST
- SRFL 94901 586-F1
ELF OWL CT
- NVTO 94949 546-E5
ELGIN WY
- MrnC 94937 (522-G3
See Page 501)
ELINOR AV
- MLV 94941 606-E2
ELIOT CT
- MLV 94941 606-G4
ELISEO DR
- MrnC 94904 586-G4
- LKSP 94904 586-G4
S ELISEO DR
400 LKSP 94939 586-E5
ELIZABETH CIR
- LKSP 94939 586-G5
ELIZABETH CT
- NVTO 94945 526-E4
ELIZABETH DR
1400 PET 94954 465-H5
ELIZABETH PL
100 MrnC 94956 (522-H7
See Page 501)
100 MrnC 94956 (542-H1
See Page 541)
200 MrnC - (522-H7
See Page 501)
ELIZABETH WY
- NVTO 94945 506-B7
- SRFL 94901 566-E6
ELK HORN WY
- SANS 94960 566-B5
ELKIN CT
- SRFL 94901 566-E7
ELLEN CT
300 MrnC 94903 546-D7
ELLEN DR
200 MrnC 94903 546-E7
ELLIS CT
- PET 94952 465-C6
ELLIS ST
100 PET 94952 465-E5
ELLSWORTH LN
- MrnC 94930 565-H3
ELM AV
- LKSP 94939 586-F6
- MLV 94941 606-E3
- MrnC 94904 586-D3
- MrnC 94973 565-D3
- SANS 94960 566-A7
ELM CIR
500 PET 94952 465-B6
ELM CT
100 SANS 94960 566-A7
ELM DR
- PET 94952 465-C5
1000 NVTO 94945 526-B3
ELM RD
- MrnC 94924 604-E3
ELM ST
- SRFL 94901 566-G7
ELMA ST
- MLV 94941 606-C3
EL MIRADOR
- MrnC 94946 545-C4
EL MONTE LN
- SAUS 94965 627-B3
ELMWOOD CT
- NVTO 94945 526-C3
- SRFL 94901 566-E6
ELMWOOD DR
500 PET 94954 465-D3
EL NAVATO CIR
- NVTO 94945 526-C2
EL NOVATO CIR
- NVTO 94945 526-C2
EL NOVATO CT
- NVTO 94945 526-C2
EL PAVO REAL CIR
- SRFL 94903 566-D4

EL PORTAL
- SAUS 94965 627-B3
EL PORTAL DR
- LKSP 94939 586-F4
EL PRADO AV
100 SRFL 94903 566-E5
EL ROSE DR
- PET 94952 (485-C1
See Page 465)
ELSIE LN
- FRFX 94930 565-J6
ELVIA CT
200 MrnC 94903 546-E7
ELY BLVD
- PET 94954 (466-A6
See Page 465)
- SonC 94954 465-G3
200 PET 94954 465-G3
N ELY RD
400 SonC 94954 465-D1
700 PET 94954 465-D1
EMBARCADERO WY
- MrnC 94901 586-H1
- SRFL 94901 586-H1
EMERSON DR
- MLV 94941 606-H6
EMERYSTONE TER
200 MrnC 94903 546-E6
EMLIN PL
- MrnC 94904 586-D3
ENA CT
- NVTO 94947 525-J3
ENCINA AV
- CMAD 94925 606-G1
ENCINA CT
- NVTO 94945 526-C2
ENCINA PL
- SANS 94960 586-B1
ENCINAL AV
- MrnC - 585-F1
ENDEAVOR CV
- CMAD 94925 606-J2
ENDEAVOR DR
- CMAD 94925 606-J2
100 MrnC 94920 606-J2
ENFRENTE RD
300 NVTO 94949 546-E1
ENGLISH CT
- NVTO 94947 525-G3
ENGLISH ST
- PET 94952 465-D7
ENSENADA DR
100 NVTO 94949 546-F2
ENSIGN WY
- MrnC - (542-E5
See Page 541)
ENT CT
- NVTO 94949 546-G4
ENTERPRISE DR
- CMAD 94925 606-J2
ENTERPRISE CONCOURSE
300 MrnC 94965 606-F7
ENTRADA DR
200 NVTO 94949 546-E1
ENTRATA AV
- SANS 94960 586-C1
- SANS 94960 566-C7
EQUESTRIAN CT
- MrnC 94945 526-D2
ERIC CT
1500 PET 94954 465-H5
ERICA CT
- NVTO 94947 525-G2
ERICA RD
1000 MrnC 94965 606-D6
ERIN DR
- MrnC 94903 546-E7
ERLA LOUISE DR
- MrnC 94945 526-F4
200 NVTO 94945 526-F4
ERWIN ST
300 PET 94952 465-E6
ESCALLE LN
- LKSP 94939 586-D5
ESCALLONIA DR
100 NVTO 94945 526-B2
ESCALON DR
- MLV 94941 606-F3
ESCOLTA AV
- NVTO 94949 546-H3
ESCONDIDA LN
- MrnC 94938 (564-F2
See Page 543)
ESCONDIDO WY
- MrnC 94937 (522-F2
See Page 501)
ESMEYER DR
- SRFL 94903 566-C3
ESPALDA CT
- SRFL 94901 586-E1
ESPERANZA ST
100 TBRN 94920 607-E7
ESQUIRE CT
- NVTO 94949 546-D1
ESSEX LN
- SANS 94960 566-C7
ESSEX ST
- SANS 94960 566-C7

ESTADO CT
- NVTO 94945 525-J1
ESTADO WY
400 NVTO 94945 526-A1
400 NVTO 94945 525-J1
ESTANCIA WY
700 MrnC 94903 566-H2
ESTATES CT
- SRFL 94901 586-E2
ESTATES DR
- MrnC 94960 565-H2
- NVTO 94947 525-H3
ESTELLE AV
- LKSP 94939 586-D4
- MrnC 94904 586-D4
ESTERO LN
1300 SonC 94923 421-C6
1300 SonC 94923 (441-A1
See Page 421)
ESTERO RD
27000 MrnC 94972 (441-E4
See Page 421)
ESTERO TR
- MrnC - (521-J7
See Page 501)
- MrnC - (542-C1
See Page 541)
- MrnC - 541-G3
ESTERO WY
- SRFL 94903 566-D4
ESTRADA LN
- CMAD 94925 606-H1
ESTRELLA CT
- NVTO 94945 525-J1
ESTRELLA WY
- NVTO 94945 525-J1
ESTUARY WY
1900 PET 94954 465-H4
ETHEL AV
- MLV 94941 606-E3
500 MrnC 94941 606-E4
ETHEL CT
- MLV 94941 606-D3
ETHEL LN
- MrnC 94941 606-E4
ETON WY
- MLV 94941 606-F3
ETTA CT
200 MrnC 94903 546-E7
EUCALYPTUS AV
200 SonC 94952 (464-F5
See Page 463)
700 NVTO 94947 525-H3
EUCALYPTUS LN
- SRFL 94901 566-H7
EUCALYPTUS RD
- BLV 94920 627-D1
EUCALYPTUS WY
600 MrnC 94965 606-D6
EUCALYPTUS KNOLLS
- MLV 94941 606-G5
EUGENE ST
- MLV 94941 606-C3
EUGENIA DR
100 SonC 94952 465-A6
EUREKA ST
- MrnC 94965 626-H1
EUTERPE ST
- MLV 94941 606-E3
EVA ST
- SRFL 94901 586-G2
EVELYN AV
- MLV 94941 606-B2
EVEREST CT
800 MrnC 94965 606-E6
EVERGREEN AV
- MLV 94941 606-D4
- MrnC 94941 606-D4
EVERGREEN DR
- MrnC 94904 586-B5
EVERGREEN LN
300 MrnC 94941 606-D4
1300 PET 94954 465-H6
EVERGREEN RD
- MrnC 94924 604-E2
EVERGREEN FIRE RD
- MrnC 94904 586-C5
EXCELSIOR
- SAUS 94965 627-B3
EXECUTIVE DR
- PET 94954 465-G3
EYE ST
- SRFL 94901 566-E7

F

F ST
- NVTO 94949 546-G3
- SRFL 94901 586-F1
100 PET 94952 465-E7
100 SRFL 94901 566-F7
800 PET 94952 (485-D1
See Page 465)
FABIAN CT
- NVTO 94947 525-G3
FAIR AV
- SonC 94952 (464-J2
See Page 463)
FAIR DR
- SRFL 94901 566-F6

FAIR ST
- PET 94952 465-C7
N FAIR ST
600 PET 94952 465-C7
FAIRBANKS RD
200 MrnC 94971 (462-E4
See Page 461)
FAIRFAX ST
- SRFL 94901 586-J2
FAIRFAX-BOLINAS RD
- MrnC - 565-E7
- MrnC - 585-E1
- MrnC 94924 585-B5
- MrnC 94924 (584-G5
See Page 583)
- MrnC 94970 585-B5
- MrnC 94930 565-G7
300 MrnC - 585-G1
300 MrnC 94930 585-G1
FAIRFAX RIDGE RD
- FRFX 94930 565-F4
6500 MrnC - 565-F4
FAIRGROUNDS DR
- PET 94952 465-E5
FAIRHAVEN
600 NVTO 94947 526-E7
FAIRHILLS DR
- SRFL 94901 566-E6
FAIRVIEW AV
- CMAD 94925 606-G1
100 SonC 94952 (464-J7
See Page 463)
500 MrnC 94965 606-D6
FAIRVIEW CT
- SANS 94960 566-A5
FAIRVIEW TER
- PET 94952 (485-F1
See Page 465)
FAIRWAY DR
- MLV 94941 606-E2
- MrnC 94901 566-J7
- NVTO 94949 546-A3
- NVTO 94949 545-J2
100 MrnC 94901 567-A7
FAIRWOOD CT
- SRFL 94901 567-C6
FALCON RIDGE DR
- PET 94954 (466-A5
See Page 465)
- PET 94954 465-J5
FALLEN LEAF AV
- ROSS 94957 586-C1
FALLEN LEAF WY
- NVTO 94949 546-G6
FALLON RD
- SonC 94952 463-C2
FALLON TWO ROCK RD
1000 MrnC 94952 463-A1
1400 MrnC 94952 (462-H1
See Page 461)
2100 MrnC 94952 (442-D7
See Page 421)
FALMOUTH CV
- SRFL 94901 587-A2
FARM RD
- MrnC 94903 566-E5
FARVUE ST
- NVTO 94947 525-J5
FAWN CT
- MrnC 94960 566-B4
FAWN DR
- MrnC 94960 566-B3
FAWN LN
- CMAD 94925 606-H2
FAWN RDGE
- FRFX 94930 565-H7
FAWNRIDGE CT
- NVTO 94945 526-A1
FAY DR
- MrnC 94904 586-E3
FAYE CT
- PET 94952 465-E4
FELIPA CT
- TBRN 94920 607-B5
FELIZ DR
2100 NVTO 94945 525-J2
FELIZ RD
2000 NVTO 94945 526-A2
2000 NVTO 94945 525-J2
FERN AV
- BLV 94920 627-D1
- MLV 94941 606-E4
- MrnC 94973 565-C3
FERN LN
- CMAD 94925 606-G1
- SANS 94960 566-A6
FERN RD
- MrnC 94904 586-D5
- MrnC 94924 604-E2
FERN TR
- CMAD 94925 586-E7
FERN WY
- MrnC 94904 586-D5
- MrnC 94941 606-F6
- MrnC 94965 606-B3
FERNANDO DR
500 NVTO 94945 526-D4
FERNBRIDGE PL
400 NVTO 94947 526-E6

FERN CANYON RD
- MLV 94941 606-B1
- MrnC 94965 606-B1
FERNDALE AV
200 MrnC 94941 606-D5
N FERNDALE AV
300 MrnC 94941 606-D5
FERNHILL AV
- ROSS 94957 586-B2
FERNWOOD DR
- SANS 94960 566-A6
- SRFL 94901 567-C6
FERNWOOD LN
- MrnC 94946 (544-J4
See Page 543)
FERNWOOD WY
- SRFL 94901 567-C7
FERRIS DR
1100 NVTO 94945 525-J2
1100 NVTO 94945 526-A1
FIELD RD
- MrnC 94965 626-F6
FIELDING CIR
- MLV 94941 606-H6
FIELDSTONE DR
400 NVTO 94945 506-B7
FIFER AV
- CMAD 94925 586-G5
FIG TREE CT
- NVTO 94947 525-J3
FILBERT AV
- SAUS 94965 627-A2
FILIPPINI WY
1500 PET 94954 465-H6
FIR AV
- MrnC 94963 (564-J2
See Page 543)
- MrnC 94973 565-B2
FIR TR
- FRFX 94930 565-B5
FIRE RD
- MLV 94941 606-D1
- MrnC 94965 606-B7
- MrnC 94973 565-D2
- TBRN - 627-H2
FIRE LANE TR
- MrnC - 543-A4
- MrnC - (542-G6
See Page 541)
FISHER DR
- PET 94954 465-J7
FISH GULCH FIRE RD
- MrnC - 585-H3
FITZPATRICK LN
16000 SonC 95465 421-B2
FLAG ST
- LKSP 94939 586-E6
FLAGSTONE TER
200 MrnC 94903 546-E6
FLAMINGO LN
- SRFL 94901 567-C6
FLAMINGO RD
200 MrnC 94965 606-F7
FLAXBERRY LN
800 MrnC 94903 546-C7
FLEETWOOD CT
- NVTO 94947 525-H3
FLEMINGS CT
800 MrnC 94965 626-H1
FLICKER DR
- NVTO 94949 546-E4
FLINT CT
- NVTO 94949 526-B7
FLORENCE AV
- MLV 94941 606-C3
- SANS 94960 566-A6
FLORENCE WY
1500 PET 94954 465-D3
FLORIBEL AV
- SANS 94960 566-A7
FLYING CLOUD CRSE
- CMAD 94925 606-J1
FOCHA DR
- SonC 94952 465-A6
FOLEY LN
- LKSP 94939 586-E7
FOLIUM AV
- MrnC 94938 (564-F2
See Page 543)
FONTANA
- NVTO 94945 526-B2
FOOTHILL RD
- SANS 94960 566-A7
FORBES AV
- SANS 94960 566-D7
- SRFL 94901 566-E7
FORD WY
- NVTO 94947 526-C5
FORE ST
- MLV 94941 606-B3
FOREMAN LN
- MrnC 94941 606-H5
FOREMAST CV
- CMAD 94925 606-J1
FOREST DR
- MrnC 94933 (564-G2
See Page 543)
FOREST WY
600 MrnC 94965 606-D7

FOREST TRAIL DR
- PET 94952 (485-E1
See Page 465)
FORRES WY
- MrnC 94937 (522-G3
See Page 501)
FORREST AV
- FRFX 94930 565-J6
- FRFX 94930 566-A6
- SANS 94960 566-A6
FORREST CT
- MrnC 94960 566-A4
FORREST LN
- SRFL 94903 566-C3
FORREST RD
- MrnC 94947 526-A5
- NVTO 94947 526-A5
- NVTO 94947 525-J5
FORREST ST
- MLV 94941 606-D3
FORREST TER
- FRFX 94930 565-J6
FOSS AV
- SANS 94960 586-B1
FOSTER AV
100 MrnC 94904 586-D3
FOSTER LN
- SRFL 94901 566-E7
FOSTER RD
- SonC 94952 463-J3
FOWLER CT
- SRFL 94903 566-C3
FOX CT
- NVTO 94945 526-C4
FOX DR
- MrnC 94956 543-B3
FOX LN
- MrnC 94960 566-B3
FOX HOLLOW PL
- NVTO 94945 526-B1
FOX RUN RD
- MrnC 94973 565-D4
FRANCES AV
- LKSP 94939 586-D4
- MrnC 94904 586-D4
FRANCES ST
- SRFL 94901 586-F1
FRANCIS AV
- SANS 94960 566-A6
- FRFX 94930 566-A6
- FRFX 94930 565-J6
FRANCIS LN
- SANS 94960 566-C6
FRANCISCO BLVD
300 SRFL 94901 586-H2
1100 SRFL 94901 587-A4
FRANCISCO PATIO
- MrnC 94970 605-B3
FRANCISCO VISTA CT
- TBRN 94920 607-B5
FRANICISCO BLVD W
200 SRFL 94901 586-H2
FRANKLIN AV
600 NVTO 94945 526-C4
FRANKLIN WY
800 PET 94952 465-E5
FRANKLIN SCHOOL RD
13900 SonC 95472 (442-A1
See Page 421)
FRANSIOLI RD
- SonC 94952 463-J3
FRATES RD
- SonC 94952 463-J1
100 PET 94954 465-J6
1800 SonC 94954 (466-A6
See Page 465)
1800 PET 94954 (466-A6
See Page 465)
FREDA LN
- SANS 94960 566-C6
FREDSON CT
- NVTO 94947 525-J3
FREESTONE ST
12000 SonC 95465 (422-B1
See Page 421)
FREESTONE RANCH RD
- SonC 94952 (422-B4
See Page 421)
- SonC 95472 (422-B4
See Page 421)
FREMONT RD
- SRFL 94901 586-E1
FRESCA AV
- MrnC - 565-F7
- MrnC - 585-F1
FRIARS LN
- MrnC 94965 606-D6
FRIAR TUCK LN
- SRFL 94901 567-B6
FRIENDLY LN
- NVTO 94945 526-A2
- NVTO 94945 525-J2
FRONT ST
- MrnC 94945 527-A3
- SRFL 94901 586-H2
900 NVTO 94945 526-B3
FRONT TER
- CMAD 94925 586-F7
FRONTAGE RD
7000 NVTO 94945 526-C4

FROST CT
- MLV 94941 606-G4
FROSTY LN
- NVTO 94949 546-E1
FRUSTUCK AV
- FRFX 94930 565-H6
FUJITA RD
- SonC 94954 465-C1
FULLERTON RD
- SonC 94952 (464-C3
See Page 463)

G

G ST
- PET 94952 465-E7
- SRFL 94901 586-E1
100 SRFL 94901 566-E7
700 PET 94952 (485-E1
See Page 465)
GABLE CT
- SRFL 94903 566-F4
GAGE LN
- MrnC 94947 525-H6
GALE RD
- PET 94952 (464-J1
See Page 463)
- SonC 94952 (464-J1
See Page 463)
GALERITA WY
600 MrnC 94903 566-H2
GALLAND ST
100 PET 94952 465-D6
GALLEON WY
- SRFL 94903 566-A1
GALLI DR
- NVTO 94949 546-F1
GALWAY LN
- SRFL 94903 566-C1
GAMBINI RD
- SonC 94952 (485-J4
See Page 465)
- SonC 94954 (485-J3
See Page 465)
GAMBONINI RD
- SonC 94954 506-J1
GARDEN AV
- MrnC 94903 566-G4
- ROSS 94957 586-C1
GARDEN CT
- NVTO 94947 526-B4
800 PET 94954 465-G5
GARDEN LN
1100 SRFL 94901 586-G1
GARDEN WY
- LKSP 94939 586-F6
- MrnC 94973 565-D3
GARDEN ROCK RD
- MrnC 94960 565-J2
GARDEN VALLEY DR
500 MrnC 94965 606-E6
GARDNER ST
- MLV 94941 606-D3
GARFIELD DR
200 PET 94954 465-G3
GARFIELD ST
1400 NVTO 94947 526-B5
GARNER CT
100 NVTO 94947 526-A6
GARNER DR
- NVTO 94947 526-A6
- NVTO 94949 526-A6
GARRETT WY
- PET 94954 465-D2
GARY PL
- SRFL 94901 586-H3
GARY WY
- MrnC 94930 565-J4
GARZOLI RD
- SonC 94952 (464-H7
See Page 463)
W GATE WY
- SANS 94960 566-C7
GATE 5 RD
- SAUS 94965 626-J1
GATE 6 RD
- MrnC 94941 606-J7
- MrnC 94941 626-J1
GATE 6 1/2 RD
- MrnC 94941 606-H7
- MrnC 94941 626-H1
GAZANIA CT
- NVTO 94945 526-B2
GEARY AV
- FRFX 94930 565-J5
- MrnC 94904 586-D3
GEARY DR
1200 PET 94954 465-G6
GEARY LN
- FRFX 94930 565-J5
GELDERT CT
- TBRN 94920 607-C5
GELDERT DR
- TBRN 94920 607-B4
GENEVA WY
- MrnC 94903 566-G3
GEORGE LN
- MLV 94941 606-G2
- SAUS 94965 627-A3

GEORGE ST
900 NVTO 94945 526-B3
GEORGE TER
- PET 94952 (485-F1
See Page 465)
GERICKE LN
25000 MrnC 94952 (442-D7
See Page 421)
25000 MrnC 94952 (462-E1
See Page 461)
GERICKE RD
28000 MrnC 94952 (442-E6
See Page 421)
30400 SonC 94952 (442-F3
See Page 421)
30400 SonC 95472 (442-F3
See Page 421)
GERLACK RD
- SANS 94960 586-A1
GERMAINE PL
- NVTO 94949 546-C1
GERSTLE CT
- SRFL 94901 586-E2
GERTRUDE LN
- NVTO 94947 525-G3
GHISLETTA RD
- SonC 94954 (486-F1
See Page 465)
GIBSON AV
200 MrnC 94941 606-F6
GILARDI DR
800 PET 94952 465-C6
GILBERT DR
- MrnC 94941 606-H6
GILBERT ST
- MrnC 94901 586-H3
GILMARTIN CT
- TBRN 94920 607-D5
GILMARTIN DR
- TBRN 94920 607-D5
GILRIX CT
- PET 94954 465-G3
GILRIX ST
1700 PET 94954 465-G3
GIRARD AV
- SAUS 94965 627-A2
GLACIER CT
100 PET 94954 465-E3
GLACIER WY
300 SRFL 94903 566-F2
GLEN AV
- SRFL 94901 586-F2
GLEN CT
- MLV 94941 606-E2
- SAUS 94965 627-B3
GLEN DR
- FRFX 94930 565-G3
- MrnC 94903 566-J3
- SAUS 94965 627-A3
- MLV 94941 606-E1
GLEN LN
- MrnC 94945 526-J3
GLEN RD
- NVTO 94945 526-J3
- SANS 94960 566-A6
- MrnC 94945 526-J3
GLEN TR
- MrnC - (563-D4
See Page 543)
GLEN WY
- LKSP 94939 586-D6
- MrnC 94937 (522-G4
See Page 501)
GLENAIRE DR
- SRFL 94901 586-G3
GLENDON WY
100 PET 94952 (485-F1
See Page 465)
GLEN EAGLE DR
1000 PET 94952 (485-F1
See Page 465)
GLEN FIRE RD
- MrnC 94930 565-G3
GLENHILL CT
700 NVTO 94947 526-A4
GLENICE ST
700 PET 94954 465-G5
GLEN PARK AV
- SRFL 94901 566-G6
GLENSIDE WY
- MrnC 94903 566-F5
GLENWOOD AV
- ROSS 94957 586-B2
600 MrnC 94965 606-D6
GLENWOOD DR
- SRFL 94901 566-G6
1200 PET 94954 465-G6
GLORIA DR
- SRFL 94901 586-E1
GLOUCESTER CV
- SRFL 94901 587-A2
GOATLEY RD
- SonC 94952 (484-H4
See Page 463)
GOING LN
700 NVTO 94947 525-H3
GOLDEN GATE AV
- BLV 94920 607-C7
- BLV 94920 627-D1

GOLDEN GATE BRDG U.S.-101
- SF - 627-B7
GOLDEN GATE DR
- SRFL 94901 586-J3
GOLDEN GATE PL
900 NVTO 94945 526-C2
GOLDEN HIND PASG
- CMAD 94925 606-J1
100 CMAD 94925 586-J7
200 CMAD 94925 607-A1
GOLDEN HINDE BLVD
- SRFL 94903 566-D4
GOLDEN IRIS TER
- MrnC 94903 546-A6
- MrnC 94903 545-J6
GOLDEN LILY PL
- MrnC 94903 545-J6
GOLDFINCH CT
- NVTO 94947 525-G4
GOLD HILL FIRE RD
- SRFL 94901 566-J6
100 SRFL 94901 567-A5
GOLD HILL GRADE
- MrnC 94901 566-J6
- SRFL 94901 566-J6
GOLDMAN RD
- SonC 94952 (464-G5
See Page 463)
GOLD MINER CT
- NVTO 94947 526-A4
GOLF AV
- SRFL 94903 566-F4
- MrnC 94903 566-F4
GOLF LN
- SANS 94960 566-C6
GOLF CLUB SERVICE RD
- MrnC - 585-E1
GOMEZ WY
- MLV 94941 606-F5
GOODHILL RD
100 MrnC 94904 586-B3
GORDON ST
- SAUS 94965 626-J2
GOSSAGE AV
- PET 94952 465-C3
- SonC 94952 465-C3
GOSSAGE WY
- SonC 94952 465-B4
GOTHIC DR
- NVTO 94947 526-A4
GRACE CT
200 CMAD 94925 606-G1
GRACE LN
- MrnC 94941 606-F3
GRACELAND DR
- SRFL 94901 566-G7
GRADY FIRE RD
- MrnC 94903 545-H5
- MrnC 94946 545-H5
GRANADA CT
1700 PET 94954 465-H5
GRANADA DR
- CMAD 94925 606-J1
GRAND AV
600 SRFL 94901 586-G1
1300 SRFL 94901 566-G6
GRAND CT
- SRFL 94901 566-G6
GRAND TER
- SRFL 94901 566-H7
GRAND CANYON RD
- MrnC 94940 503-A5
- MrnC 94940 (502-J6
See Page 501)
- MrnC 94940 523-D2
- MrnC 94940 (522-J1
See Page 501)
GRANDE RD
- PET 94954 (466-A5
See Page 465)
- PET 94954 465-J5
- SonC 94954 (466-A4
See Page 465)
- SonC 94954 465-J5
GRANDE PASEO
- MrnC 94903 546-E7
GRANDE VISTA
- NVTO 94947 525-H2
GRAND VIEW AV
- PET 94952 465-F7
GRANDVIEW AV
- PET 94952 465-F7
- MrnC 94945 527-A3
GRANGE WY
100 SRFL 94901 587-B5
GRANLEE RD
- MrnC 94903 566-H3
GRANT AV
- PET 94952 (485-F1
See Page 465)
700 NVTO 94945 526-B3
GRANT CT
- PET 94952 (485-E1
See Page 465)
GRANT ST
- MrnC 94973 565-C2
GRASS CT
- NVTO 94949 546-F4

GRASSY SLOPE RD
- MrnC - (564-E3
See Page 543)
GRAVEL PLANT RD
- SonC 94952 465-G7
- SonC 94952 (485-G1
See Page 465)
GRAVES RD
6000 SonC 94954 465-C1
GRAVITY CAR RD
- MrnC 94965 606-A2
GRAYLAWN AV
- PET 94952 465-D4
GREAT CIRCLE DR
- MrnC 94941 606-J6
GREEN WY
- SRFL 94901 566-G7
- SRFL 94901 566-G1
GREENBERRY LN
800 MrnC 94903 546-C7
GREENBRAE BOARDWLK
- CMAD 94904 586-H5
- CMAD 94925 586-H5
- MrnC 94925 586-H5
2100 LKSP 94904 586-H5
2100 MrnC 94904 586-H5
GREEN BRIAR CIR
300 PET 94954 465-F4
GREENE ST
200 MrnC 94941 606-F6
GREENFIELD AV
- SANS 94960 566-D7
- SRFL 94901 566-D7
GREENFIELD CT
- MLV 94941 606-G3
- SANS 94960 566-D7
GREEN GLEN WY
400 MrnC 94965 606-E7
GREENHILL RD
900 MrnC 94941 606-E5
GREEN OAK DR
1000 NVTO 94949 546-F5
GREEN OAK PL
1000 NVTO 94949 546-F4
GREENOCH WY
- MrnC 94937 (522-F4
See Page 501)
GREENPICHER TR
- MrnC - (563-G4
See Page 543)
GREEN POINT LN
- MrnC 94945 526-J3
GREENRIDGE CT
100 PET 94952 (485-E2
See Page 465)
GREENSBURGH LN
- MrnC 94960 565-H2
GREENSIDE WY
- SRFL 94901 567-E5
GREEN VALLEY CT
- MrnC 94960 566-A3
GREENWOOD AV
- SRFL 94901 586-E1
GREENWOOD CT
- TBRN 94920 607-A4
GREENWOOD DR
1000 NVTO 94947 526-D6
GREENWOOD WY
- MLV 94941 606-D2
- MrnC 94904 586-C5
GREENWOOD BAY DR
- TBRN 94920 606-J4
- MrnC 94941 606-J4
GREENWOOD BEACH RD
400 TBRN 94920 607-A5
GREENWOOD COVE DR
- MrnC 94920 606-J4
100 TBRN 94920 607-A5
100 TBRN 94920 606-J4
GREGG PL
- NVTO 94949 546-C1
GREGOR LN
- NVTO 94947 525-J3
GREGORY CT
- PET 94954 465-H4
GREGORY DR
- MrnC 94930 565-J3
GREGORY PL
- LKSP 94939 586-G5
GREGORY RD
900 SonC 94954 (466-D6
See Page 465)
GRETCHEN PL
- LKSP 94939 586-G5
GREVILLIA DR
100 PET 94952 (485-F3
See Page 465)
GREY ST
- PET 94952 465-D6
GROSSLAND WY
- PET 94952 (485-D1
See Page 465)
GROUSE LN
800 PET 94954 465-G5
GROVE AV
- CMAD 94925 586-F7
- CMAD 94925 606-F1
GROVE LN
- NVTO 94947 526-A3
- SANS 94960 566-B7

INDEX

STREET / Block City ZIP Pg-Grid

GROVE RD
- MrnC 94924 604-E3
GROVE ST
- MLV 94941 606-D3
- SRFL 94901 586-F2
GROVE HILL AV
- SANS 94960 566-C7
GUADALUPE PL
- MrnC 94933 (564-G2 See Page 543)
GUGLIELMETTI LN
- SonC 94952 463-J7
- SonC 94952 (484-A1 See Page 463)
- SonC 94952 (483-J1 See Page 463)
GUGLIELMETTI RD
- SonC 94952 (464-A7 See Page 463)
- SonC 94952 (484-A1 See Page 463)
GUISELA CT
- MrnC 94945 526-H2
GUM TREE CT
- NVTO 94947 525-H3
GUMWOOD LN
1100 PET 94954 465-G6
GUNSHOT FIRE RD
- MrnC 94930 565-F2
- MrnC 94973 565-F2
GUSTAFSON CT
- NVTO 94947 525-G2

H

H LN
- MrnC 94945 526-F2
- NVTO 94945 526-F2
H ST
- PET 94952 465-E7
- SRFL 94901 566-E7
- SRFL 94901 586-E1
700 PET 94952 (485-E1 See Page 465)
HACIENDA AV
- MrnC 94938 (564-E1 See Page 543)
HACIENDA CT
- SRFL 94901 566-G6
HACIENDA DR
- TBRN 94920 607-B4
HACIENDA WY
700 MrnC 94903 566-H2
HALCYON CT
- TBRN 94920 607-C6
HALE LN
- MLV 94941 606-C3
HALF MOON RD
- MrnC 94947 526-A5
- NVTO 94947 526-A5
- NVTO 94947 525-J5
HALSEY AV
- PET 94952 (485-E1 See Page 465)
HAMILTON CT
- SRFL 94901 566-G6
HAMILTON DR
- MLV 94941 606-G4
- NVTO 94949 546-F1
- SonC 94952 465-A5
HAMILTON LN
- MrnC 94965 606-A3
HAMILTON RD
800 SonC 94954 (466-D4 See Page 465)
HAMMONDALE CT
- SRFL 94901 566-G6
HAMPSHIRE WY
- NVTO 94945 526-A1
HAMPTON AV
- SANS 94960 566-B6
HAMPTON LN
- MrnC 94945 526-H3
HANCOCK ST
600 NVTO 94945 526-C3
HANDY WK
- SRFL 94901 586-F2
HANGAR AV
- NVTO 94949 546-H3
HANKEN DR
100 MrnC 94904 586-D3
HANNA RANCH RD
- NVTO 94945 526-E7
200 NVTO 94947 526-E7
HANOVER CT
- NVTO 94947 525-G2
HANSEN RD
- NVTO 94947 525-H4
HAPPY LN
- SRFL 94901 566-D6
HARBOR DR
- CMAD 94925 606-H1
- MrnC 94945 526-J3
- SAUS 94965 626-J1
100 CMAD 94925 586-H7
HARBOR ST
- SRFL 94901 586-H2
HARBOR COVE WY
- MrnC 94941 606-J4
HARBOR OAK DR
- TBRN 94920 607-D7
HARBOR POINT DR
- MrnC 94941 606-J6
HARBOR VIEW CT
- MrnC 94901 586-J1
HARCOURT ST
- SRFL 94901 566-E7
HARDING DR
- NVTO 94947 526-A6
HARKLE RD
100 NVTO 94945 526-C4
HARMON AV
- CMAD 94925 606-F1
HARN CT
100 TBRN 94920 607-B4
HARRIET WY
- TBRN 94920 606-J4
HARRIS ST
- PET 94952 465-D7
HARRIS HILL DR
- NVTO 94947 526-A4
- NVTO 94947 525-J4
HARRISON AV
- SAUS 94965 627-B3
HARRISON CT
- NVTO 94947 526-B5
HARRISON ST
2000 PET 94954 465-G3
HART AV
100 CMAD 94925 586-F7
HART LN
- MrnC 94941 606-D4
HART ST
- SRFL 94901 586-E1
100 CMAD 94925 586-F7
HARTE AV
- SRFL 94901 586-G3
HARVARD AV
100 MrnC 94941 606-F5
HARVARD DR
- LKSP 94939 586-E4
HARVEST LN
- MrnC 94965 606-D7
HARVEY TER
- CMAD 94925 586-E7
HARVEY TR
- CMAD 94925 606-C5
200 CMAD 94925 586-F7
HASH CT
300 PET 94952 (485-E3 See Page 465)
HASSOLD RD
- SonC 94952 (484-J3 See Page 463)
HATCH RD
2000 MrnC 94947 525-G4
HATZIC CT
- LKSP 94939 586-D7
HAVEN DR
- PET 94952 (485-C1 See Page 465)
HAVENWOOD RD
- MrnC 94945 527-A3
- MrnC 94945 526-J3
HAVERHILL CT
- NVTO 94947 525-G2
HAWKINS WY
- LKSP 94939 586-F6
HAWK RIDGE CT
- NVTO 94949 546-E4
HAWTHORNDEN WY
- MrnC 94937 (522-F4 See Page 501)
HAWTHORNE AV
- LKSP 94939 586-E6
- SANS 94960 566-A6
HAWTHORNE CT
- FRFX 94930 565-B5
- PET 94952 465-D5
HAWTHORNE DR
600 TBRN 94920 607-B5
HAWTHORNE LN
- CMAD 94925 606-G1
HAWTHORNE RD
- MrnC 94924 604-E3
HAWTHORNE ST
200 MrnC 94941 606-E5
HAWTHORNE TER
2000 NVTO 94945 525-H1
HAWTHORNE WY
100 MrnC 94903 566-G2
HAYDEN AV
800 NVTO 94945 526-C4
HAYES AV
1000 PET 94952 (485-D1 See Page 465)
HAYES LN
- PET 94952 (485-C1 See Page 465)
HAYES ST
- NVTO 94947 526-B5
- SRFL 94901 586-F1
HAZEL AV
- LKSP 94939 586-E6
- MLV 94941 606-C3
- MrnC 94938 (564-F1 See Page 543)
- SANS 94960 566-B7
HAZEL CT
- SRFL 94901 586-G3
HAZEL LN
100 MLV 94941 606-C3
HAZEL RD
- FRFX 94930 565-H6
HAZEL TR
- MrnC 94965 606-B4
HAZELWOOD LN
- SRFL 94901 567-B6
HEARFIELD LN
- SRFL 94901 566-G6
HEARTHSTONE CT
- MrnC 94903 546-E5
HEARTHWOOD CT
- SRFL 94901 567-B6
HEATHCLIFF DR
- TBRN 94920 607-E6
HEATHER CTO
- MrnC 94965 605-H7
HEATHER LN
- MLV 94941 606-E1
- MrnC 94937 (522-F3 See Page 501)
- NVTO 94947 525-H3
HEATHER WY
- LKSP 94939 586-F6
- MLV 94941 606-E1
500 SRFL 94903 566-D2
HEATHERSTONE DR
2500 MrnC 94903 546-E6
HEATHERSTONE LN
- MrnC 94903 546-E5
HEAVENLY WY
- MrnC 94941 606-E6
HECHT AV
- SAUS 94965 627-A4
HECTOR LN
- NVTO 94949 546-F2
HELEN AV
200 MrnC 94941 606-F6
HELEN CT
1000 PET 94954 465-H6
HELEN LN
- LKSP 94939 586-E7
HELENS LN
- MLV 94941 606-D3
HEMLOCK
- MrnC 94933 (564-H2 See Page 543)
- MrnC 94963 (564-H2 See Page 543)
HEMLOCK AV
200 MrnC 94945 527-A4
HENRY WY
1500 PET 94954 465-J6
HEPBURN HTS
- SRFL 94901 566-D7
HERBING LN
- MrnC 94904 586-D5
HERITAGE DR
- SRFL 94901 567-E6
HERMIES LN
10000 SonC 95472 (422-G4 See Page 421)
HERMIT LN
- MrnC 94904 586-D3
HERON CT
- MrnC 94964 587-B5
HERON DR
- MrnC 94941 607-A7
- MrnC 94941 606-J6
HERON WY
- SRFL 94901 587-A3
HERRERA CT
- SANS 94960 566-A5
HERRERA DR
- FRFX 94930 565-G2
HERRING DR
- MrnC 94941 606-J6
HETHERTON ST
800 SRFL 94901 586-G1
HEUTERS LN
- MLV 94941 606-D3
HIBISCUS WY
300 SRFL 94903 566-D2
HICKORY AV
- CMAD 94925 586-G7
HICKORY LN
300 SRFL 94903 566-D2
HICKORY RD
- FRFX 94930 565-H6
HICKOX RD
- NVTO 94947 525-H3
HIDALGO AV
- MrnC 94938 (564-G3 See Page 543)
HIDDEN LN
- MrnC 94941 606-F6
HIDDEN OAKS DR
- NVTO 94945 526-A2
HIDDEN VALLEY LN
- MrnC 94960 566-A3
HIGH ST
- SRFL 94901 586-H1
- MrnC 94971 (462-C4 See Page 461)
- PET 94952 465-D6
HIGHLAND AV
- MrnC 94901 567-A7
- MrnC 94901 566-J7
100 SRFL 94901 566-H7
HIGHLAND CT
- LKSP 94939 586-E6
HIGHLAND DR
1000 NVTO 94949 546-C1
HIGHLAND LN
100 MrnC 94941 606-F5
HIGHLAND RD
- PET 94952 (485-E1 See Page 465)
HIGHLAND WY
- MrnC 94937 (522-G4 See Page 501)
HILARITA AV
- MLV 94941 606-E4
HILARITA CIR
- BLV 94920 607-C7
HILARY DR
300 TBRN 94920 607-B5
HILL AV
- FRFX 94930 566-A6
- MrnC 94973 565-C2
- SANS 94960 566-A6
HILL BLVD
100 PET 94952 (485-C1 See Page 465)
300 PET 94952 465-C7
HILL DR
- PET 94952 465-C7
- MrnC 94904 586-E2
HILL PTH
- CMAD 94925 586-F7
100 CMAD 94925 606-F1
HILL RD
- NVTO 94947 526-A4
- ROSS 94957 586-B2
HILL ST
- MLV 94941 606-D3
HILL TR
- CMAD 94925 586-E7
- CMAD 94925 606-C5
HILLCREST AV
- LKSP 94939 586-D4
- SANS 94960 566-B7
100 MrnC 94904 586-D4
HILLCREST CT
- SANS 94960 566-A5
HILLCREST DR
- SRFL 94901 566-G7
HILLCREST RD
- MLV 94941 606-E3
- MrnC 94920 607-B3
- TBRN 94920 607-B3
HILLDALE AV
- SANS 94960 566-D7
HILLDALE DR
- SANS 94960 566-D7
HILLDALE WY
400 MrnC 94941 606-E6
HILLGIRT DR
- ROSS 94957 586-B2
HILLSIDE AV
- SRFL 94901 586-B7
- MLV 94941 606-E2
- MrnC 94904 586-E3
- MrnC 94924 604-G3
- SANS 94960 566-B7
- SRFL 94901 587-A1
- ROSS 94957 586-C3
200 SRFL 94901 586-D1
HILLSIDE DR
- FRFX 94930 565-J7
HILLSIDE RD
- MrnC 94904 586-E3
HILLSIDE TER
- MrnC 94945 527-A3
HILLSWOOD DR
- NVTO 94947 526-B6
HILLTOP AV
- MrnC 94963 (564-J2 See Page 543)
HILLVIEW AV
- SRFL 94901 586-G3
HILLVIEW ST
6600 SonC 95472 (442-H2 See Page 421)
HINGHAM CV
- SRFL 94901 587-A2
HINMAN ST
- PET 94952 465-D7
- PET 94952 (485-D1 See Page 465)
HI VISTA RD
100 SAUS 94965 627-B4
HOAG AV
- SRFL 94901 586-H2
HODGES DR
- MrnC 94941 606-H5
HOGBACK
- MrnC 94965 606-A2
- MrnC 94965 605-J1
HOLCOMB AV
100 LKSP 94939 586-F6
HOLLY AV
- LKSP 94939 586-E6
200 MrnC 94945 527-A4
HOLLY CT
300 MrnC 94941 606-D4
HOLLY DR
300 SRFL 94903 566-D2
HOLLY HTS
- PET 94952 465-B6
HOLLY LN
- MrnC 94973 565-C3
800 PET 94952 465-E5
HOLLY RD
- FRFX 94930 565-G5
HOLLYHOCK CT
- MLV 94941 606-F3
HOLM RD
1000 PET 94952 465-B2
1000 PET 94954 465-A1
HOLMES AV
100 MrnC 94903 566-G4
HOLSTEIN RD
- SANS 94960 566-A4
HOLSTROM CIR
- NVTO 94947 525-H3
HOMESTEAD BLVD
- MrnC 94941 606-D5
- MLV 94941 606-E5
HONEY LN
- SANS 94960 566-C6
HONEYSUCKLE CT
- MrnC 94903 545-J5
HONTAR LN
- PET 94952 465-B5
HOO-KOO-E-KOO TR
- MrnC 94965 606-A1
- MrnC 94965 605-J1
HOO-KOO-E-KOO FIRE RD
- MrnC 94965 586-B6
- MrnC 94965 606-A1
HOOPER
- SANS 94960 566-A6
HOPKINS RD
- SonC 94952 (484-H1 See Page 463)
HOPPER ST
- PET 94952 465-E6
HORN AV
- SonC 94952 465-A4
HORSE TR
- MrnC - 543-A4
HORSESHOE BAY CT
- PET 94954 (466-A6 See Page 465)
HORSESHOE HILL RD
- MrnC 94924 604-F1
- MrnC 94924 (584-E5 See Page 583)
HOSPITAL RD
- NVTO 94949 546-H3
HOTALING CT
- MrnC 94904 586-E2
HOTCHKIN DR
1600 NVTO 94947 526-B4
HOWARD DR
100 TBRN 94920 607-B5
HOWARD ST
- PET 94952 465-C6
H RANCH RD
- MrnC 94946 525-F6
HUBBELL CT
- SRFL 94901 566-H7
HUCKLEBERRY RD
2000 MrnC 94903 546-C7
2000 SRFL 94903 546-C7
HUMBOLDT AV
- SANS 94960 566-A7
500 SAUS 94965 627-B2
HUMBOLDT ST
100 SRFL 94901 586-D6
HUMBOLT AV
- SAUS - 627-B3
- SAUS 94965 627-B3
HUMMINGBIRD WY
- NVTO 94949 546-E4
HUNE CT
- NVTO 94947 525-H3
HUNINGTON WY
- PET 94952 465-E5
HUNTLEY RD
28000 MrnC 94952 (442-F6 See Page 421)
HYACINTH WY
300 SRFL 94903 566-D2
HYANNIS CV
- SRFL 94901 587-A2
HYATT RD
- SonC 94952 (464-F5 See Page 463)
HYLAND DR
- MrnC 94945 526-J3

I

I ST
300 PET 94952 465-E7
600 PET 94952 (485-E2 See Page 465)
2000 SonC 94952 (485-E6 See Page 465)
ICHABOD CT
- MrnC 94960 565-J2
IDA ST
- SRFL 94901 586-E1
IDALIA CT
- SANS 94960 586-B1
IDALIA RD
- SANS 94960 586-B1
IDLEWOOD DR
- SANS 94960 566-A5
IDLEWOOD PL
- SRFL 94901 566-E7
IDLEWOOD RD
- MrnC 94904 586-C5
IDYLBERRY RD
500 MrnC 94903 546-A6
IGNACIO BLVD
300 NVTO 94949 526-B7
400 NVTO 94949 546-C1
1300 MrnC 94949 546-D1
IGNACIO LN
- NVTO 94949 546-E2
IGNACIO VALLEY CIR
100 NVTO 94949 546-D1
IKE CT
- NVTO 94945 526-B2
INDEPENDENCE WY
1700 PET 94952 (485-E1 See Page 465)
INDIAN RD
- MrnC 94903 566-E5
INDIAN WY
100 NVTO 94949 526-B7
100 NVTO 94949 546-B1
INDIAN FIRE RD
- MrnC - 586-B6
- MrnC 94904 586-B6
- MrnC 94965 586-B6
INDIAN HILL RD
- MrnC 94946 (524-A7 See Page 503)
- MrnC 94946 (544-A1 See Page 543)
INDIAN HILLS DR
- NVTO 94949 526-B7
INDIAN POINT LN
17100 SonC 95465 421-D1
INDIAN ROCK CT
- SANS 94960 566-B5
- TBRN 94920 607-A4
INDIAN ROCK RD
- SANS 94960 566-B5
INDIAN SPRINGS RD
400 MrnC 94947 525-H5
INDIAN TRAIL CT
- MrnC 94947 525-J5
INDIAN VALLEY RD
1400 NVTO 94947 526-A6
1500 MrnC 94947 526-A6
1500 MrnC 94947 525-H5
INDUSTRIAL AV
1100 PET 94952 465-A2
INDUSTRIAL DR
- PET 94952 465-B3
INDUSTRIAL WY
- LKSP 94904 586-H5
1000 NVTO 94945 526-B3
INEZ PL
100 MrnC 94941 606-H4
INGERSON RD
- SonC 94952 (464-F5 See Page 463)
INMAN AV
- MrnC 94904 586-E3
INVERNESS DR
- SRFL 94901 567-B7
INVERNESS WY
- MrnC 94937 (522-G4 See Page 501)
INYO AV
- FRFX 94930 565-J6
INYO CIR
- NVTO 94947 526-E7
IOLANTHUS AV
- MrnC 94945 527-A3
IRENE DR
- NVTO 94947 525-H4
IRENE ST
100 SRFL 94901 586-J3
200 SRFL 94901 587-A3
IRIS LN
100 SRFL 94903 566-B3
IRIS RD
- MrnC 94924 604-E3
IRON SPRINGS RD
- FRFX 94930 565-G5
6500 MrnC - 565-G5
IRON SPRINGS FIRE RD
6600 MrnC - 565-F4
IRONSTONE CT
200 MrnC 94903 546-E6
IRONWOOD DR
- SRFL 94901 567-B6
IRVINE RD
- MrnC 94971 (462-C4 See Page 461)
IRVING CT
400 TBRN 94920 607-A4
IRVING DR
- MrnC 94960 566-A2
IRWIN ST
- SRFL 94901 586-G1
1200 SRFL 94901 566-G7
ISABELLA CT
- NVTO 94945 525-J1
ISLAND DR
- SANS 94960 566-D7
- SRFL 94901 566-D7
300 MrnC 94941 606-J5
ISLA VISTA LN
- SRFL 94901 587-A2
100 SRFL 94901 586-J2
ISLE ROYALE CT
100 SRFL 94903 566-F2
IVY AV
- MrnC 94973 565-C3
IVY DR
- ROSS 94957 586-B2
IVY LN
- FRFX 94930 565-H7
- MrnC 94973 565-C2
- SRFL 94901 586-F2
- SANS 94960 566-A7
1400 PET 94954 465-H5
IVY RD
300 MrnC 94924 604-E3

J

J ST
- SRFL 94901 566-E7
500 PET 94952 465-E7
JACINTO WY
- NVTO 94945 505-J7
- NVTO 94945 525-J1
JACK CT
- NVTO 94947 525-H4
JACKLYN TER
- MLV 94941 606-G5
JACKSON CT
- NVTO 94947 526-A6
JACKSON DR
- NVTO 94947 526-A6
JACK TAR CT
10900 SonC 95472 (422-E2 See Page 421)
JACK TAR DR
10000 SonC 95472 (422-D2 See Page 421)
JACOB CT
- NVTO 94945 526-E3
JACOBSEN RD
- SonC 94952 (464-J7 See Page 463)
JACOBY ST
500 SRFL 94901 586-J3
JADE CT
- NVTO 94945 526-B3
JAFCO CT
- NVTO 94949 546-E2
JAMAICA ST
100 MrnC 94920 607-C2
JAMES CT
- MrnC 94945 526-E3
JAMES WY
1200 PET 94952 465-B5
JAMES BLACK CIR
- NVTO 94949 546-E4
JAN WY
- NVTO 94947 525-H3
JANES ST
- MrnC 94941 606-D4
- MLV 94941 606-D4
JANET ST
- PET 94954 465-F3
JANET WY
- TBRN 94920 607-A4
JASMINE LN
- MrnC 94903 546-A6
- MrnC 94903 545-J6
400 PET 94952 465-B6
JASON CT
- PET 94954 465-D2
JEAN ST
- PET 94952 (485-E1 See Page 465)
300 MrnC 94965 606-F7
JEFFERSON AV
- MrnC 94903 566-F4
JEFFERSON CT
- NVTO 94947 526-B6
JEFFERSON DR
100 TBRN 94920 607-A4
JEFFERSON ST
400 PET 94952 465-F6
JEFFREY CT
- NVTO 94945 526-A2
JEFFREY DR
100 PET 94954 465-F4
JENNIFER CT
- NVTO 94947 525-J4
JENNIFER LN
- NVTO 94947 525-J3
JENSEN DR
- PET 94952 (485-F1 See Page 465)
JENSEN WY
- SRFL 94901 566-D7
JERSEY DR
500 SANS 94960 566-C6
JESS AV
- PET 94952 465-D5
JESSIE LN
- SonC 94952 465-C4
JESSUP ST
- SRFL 94901 586-E1
JEWELL CT
- SRFL 94901 586-H1
JEWELL RD
- SonC 94952 (464-A7 See Page 463)
JEWELL ST
- SRFL 94901 586-H1
200 SRFL 94901 566-H7
JOAN AV
- NVTO 94947 526-B4
JOAN DR
1400 PET 94954 465-F4
JOAQUIN PATIO
- MrnC 94970 605-B3
JOELLE HTS
- PET 94952 465-B6
JOERGER
- SonC 94952 465-A2
JOHN ST
- MrnC 94971 (462-C4 See Page 461)
JOHNS ST
- SonC 95472 (442-A1 See Page 421)
JOHNSON ST
300 SAUS 94965 627-B3
1400 NVTO 94947 526-B5
JOHNSTONE CT
- MrnC 94903 546-F5
JOHNSTONE DR
200 MrnC 94903 546-E6
JONAS LN
600 PET 94952 (485-E2 See Page 465)
JONES LN
- SonC 94952 (442-G2 See Page 421)
JONES PL
- SRFL 94901 586-F1
JONES ST
- SANS 94960 586-B1
JONES WY
- LKSP 94939 586-D6
JORDAN AV
- SANS 94960 566-D6
JORDAN ST
- SRFL 94901 586-G1
JOSEFA CT
- NVTO 94949 546-E4
JOSE PATIO
- MrnC 94970 605-B3
JOSEPH CT
- SRFL 94903 566-E2
JOSEPH LN
- SonC 94952 (464-J5 See Page 463)
JOSEPHINE ST
- MLV 94941 606-C3
- SAUS 94965 627-B4
JOSETTE CT
- PET 94952 (485-E2 See Page 465)
JOY RD
500 SonC 94922 421-F3
500 SonC 95465 421-F2
JOYCE ST
1300 NVTO 94947 526-C5
JOYCE WY
300 MrnC 94941 606-F6
JOY RIDGE RD
1900 SonC 95465 421-E1
JUANITA AV
- MLV 94941 606-F4
1600 TBRN 94920 607-E7
1600 TBRN 94920 627-E1
JUANITA CT
- NVTO 94945 525-H1
JUAREZ AV
- MrnC 94933 (564-G2 See Page 543)
JUDGE HALEY DR
- SRFL 94903 566-F4
JUDITH CT
200 NVTO 94949 546-C1
JUDSON LN
- MrnC 94941 606-H5
JULES DR
- NVTO 94947 525-H3
JULIA AV
200 MrnC 94941 606-F6
JULIA ST
- SRFL 94901 586-F1
JULIET DR
1600 PET 94954 465-J5
JUNE CT
- FRFX 94930 565-H4
JUNE LN
- MrnC 94945 526-F2
- NVTO 94945 526-F2
JUNIPER AV
- MrnC 94963 565-A3
- MrnC 94963 (564-H2 See Page 543)
JUNIPER CT
- FRFX 94930 565-J5
- PET 94952 465-B6
JUNIPER PL
800 NVTO 94945 525-E1
JUNIPER RD
- MrnC 94924 604-E3
JUNIPERBERRY DR
2200 MrnC 94903 546-D7
JUNIPERO SERRA AV
- SRFL 94901 567-A7
JUNO RD
- TBRN 94920 607-B4
JUTE RD
200 MrnC 94924 604-E3

K

K ST
- SRFL 94901 566-E7
300 PET 94952 465-F7
KADEN CT
- NVTO 94947 526-C6
KADEN DR
- NVTO 94947 526-C6
KAEHLER ST
1200 NVTO 94945 526-B2
KAILUA WY
- MrnC 94971 461-E2
KALE RD
100 MrnC 94924 604-E3
KAMEHA WY
- MrnC 94971 461-E2
KANDACE CT
- PET 94952 465-E7
KAREN WY
200 TBRN 94920 606-J3
300 TBRN 94920 607-A4
KARL AV
- SANS 94960 566-B7
KARLA CT
400 NVTO 94949 546-D1
KASTANIA RD
2700 SonC 94952 (485-H2 See Page 465)
KATHLEEN DR
- NVTO 94947 525-F2
KATHLEEN WY
1200 PET 94952 465-B4
KATHY CT
- NVTO 94949 546-B1
KATLAS CT
- NVTO 94945 525-J2
KATRINA LN
- MrnC 94960 565-J3
KAUFMAN RD
- SonC 94952 (464-G6 See Page 463)
KAVON CT
- NVTO 94947 526-D6
KAZEN WY
- PET 94952 465-C6
KEARNY CT
1600 PET 94954 465-G4
KEARNY ST
1700 PET 94954 465-G4
KEATS DR
- MLV 94941 606-G4
KEEL CT
- SRFL 94903 566-F2
KEENA LN
- NVTO 94947 525-J4
KEHOE WY
- MrnC 94937 (522-F2 See Page 501)
KEITH WY
- MrnC 94937 (522-F3 See Page 501)
KELLER ST
- PET 94952 465-D5
E KELLY DR
100 NVTO 94949 546-G4
W KELLY DR
100 NVTO 94949 546-G4
KELLY LN
- PET 94952 (485-E1 See Page 465)
KEMP AV
- SANS 94960 566-B7
KENDELL CT
- SAUS 94965 626-J2
KENDON LN
700 NVTO 94947 525-H3
KENDRICK AV
- SANS 94960 566-A4
KENILWORTH CT
- PET 94952 465-F5
- NVTO 94945 526-F2
KENNETH WY
- MrnC 94937 (522-G4 See Page 501)
KENSINGTON CT
- SANS 94960 586-B1
KENSINGTON RD
- SANS 94960 586-B1
KENT AV
- FRFX 94930 566-A6
- MrnC 94904 586-D3
KENT LN
- MrnC 94904 586-D4
KENT ST
- PET 94952 465-D6
KENT WY
- MrnC 94965 606-B3
KENTDALE LN
- MrnC 94904 586-E3
KENT PUMP RD
- MrnC - 585-A2
KENTUCKY ST
- PET 94952 465-D5
KENWOOD CT
100 NVTO 94945 526-C3
KEOKUK ST
200 PET 94952 465-C5
KERNBERRY DR
500 MrnC 94903 546-D7
KERNER BLVD
2300 SRFL 94901 587-A3
3000 SRFL 94901 586-J2
KEVILLE TER
- CMAD 94925 586-E7
100 LKSP 94939 586-E7
KEVILLE TR
- CMAD 94925 606-E1
100 LKSP 94939 606-E1
KEY LARGO CV
- CMAD 94925 606-J1
KEY LARGO CRSE
- CMAD 94925 606-J1
KEYSTONE CT
300 MrnC 94903 546-E5
KIENTZ LN
- SANS 94960 566-C7
KILGORE CT
- SANS 94960 566-A5
KILLOP CT
- SonC 94952 465-A6
KILMER CT
- MLV 94941 606-G4
KILPATRICK RD
- SonC 94952 (484-E1 See Page 463)
KING LN
- MLV 94941 606-D1
KING RD
100 SonC 94952 (464-E2 See Page 463)
KING ST
- LKSP 94939 586-E6
- MLV 94941 606-D1
KING WY
- MLV 94941 606-B2
KINGFISHER CT
- NVTO 94949 546-E5
KINROSS DR
- SRFL 94901 567-A7
100 SRFL 94901 587-B1
KIPLING DR
- MLV 94941 606-G4
KITE HILL LN
- MLV 94941 606-F3
KIWI CT
- PET 94954 465-H4
KLAMATH WY
- NVTO 94947 526-E6
KLARE AV
- SANS 94960 566-A6
KNICKERBOCKER LN
- MrnC 94960 566-A2
KNIGHT AV
2000 PET 94954 465-G3
KNIGHT CT
100 NVTO 94945 526-E3
KNIGHT DR
- SRFL 94901 567-C5
KNOCKNABOUL WY
600 SRFL 94903 566-C1
KNOLL LN
- MrnC 94941 606-H4
KNOLL RD
- SANS 94960 566-C7
- SRFL 94901 586-E1
N KNOLL RD
- MrnC 94920 606-H3
- MrnC 94941 606-H3
S KNOLL RD
- MrnC 94941 606-H4
KNOLL WY
- MrnC 94903 566-E5
KNOLLTOP CT
- NVTO 94945 526-C3
KNOLLTOP WY
- NVTO 94945 526-D3
KNOLLWOOD DR
- SRFL 94901 567-E5
KNUDTSEN RD
- SonC 94952 465-A6
KNUTTE CT
- MrnC 94947 525-H4
KOCH RD
- CMAD 94925 606-H2
KONA LN
- MrnC 94971 461-E2
KRESKY CIR
- PET 94954 465-F5
KRESKY CT
- PET 94954 465-F5
KRESKY WY
1200 PET 94954 465-G5
KRISTEN MARIE CT
- MrnC 94947 525-E4

STREET Block City ZIP Pg-Grid

KRISTENSEN RD
- SonC 94952 463-E2
KRISTIN LN
- NVTO 94945 526-A2
- NVTO 94945 525-J2
KRISTY CT
- NVTO 94947 526-A4
KUCK LN
100 SonC 94952 (464-F3 See Page 463)
KULLBERG RD
- SonC 94954 (486-F2 See Page 465)
KYLESWOOD PL
- MrnC 94956 523-A7

L

LA ALONDRA CT
100 SRFL 94903 566-D4
LA BREA WY
- MrnC 94903 566-H2
LA COSTA CT
- NVTO 94947 525-G4
LA CRESCENTA DR
- NVTO 94949 546-F2
LA CRESCENTA WY
- SRFL 94901 586-J1
LA CRESTA DR
- PET 94952 (485-C1 See Page 465)
LA CUESTA DR
- MrnC 94904 586-G4
- LKSP 94904 586-G4
LA CUESTA LN
- MrnC 94938 (564-F1 See Page 543)
LADERMAN LN
- LKSP 94939 586-G5
LA FRANCHI LN
- MrnC 94946 (544-E2 See Page 543)
LA GOMA ST
- MLV 94941 606-E4
LAGOON CT
- SRFL 94903 566-G3
LAGOON DR
- MrnC 94965 626-A1
LAGOON PL
- SRFL 94901 567-D6
LAGOON RD
- SRFL 94901 567-D6
- TBRN 94920 607-C6
- BLV 94920 607-C6
LAGOON FIRE RD
- MrnC - 585-F5
LAGOON VIEW DR
1700 TBRN 94920 607-E7
LAGOON VISTA
- TBRN 94920 607-E7
LAGUNA RD
600 MrnC 94965 606-D6
LAGUNA VISTA DR
2000 NVTO 94945 526-F1
2300 MrnC 94945 526-F1
LAGUNITAS RD
- MrnC 94938 (564-F2 See Page 543)
- ROSS 94957 586-B2
LAGUNITAS SCHOOL RD
- MrnC 94963 (564-H1 See Page 543)
LA ITA CT
100 NVTO 94945 505-H7
LAKESIDE DR
- CMAD 94925 586-G6
LAKEVIEW CT
- NVTO 94947 526-D6
LAKEVIEW RD
100 MrnC - 586-A4
100 MrnC - 585-H4
LAKEVILLE CIR
- PET 94954 (466-A6 See Page 465)
- PET 94954 465-J6
LAKEVILLE HWY
800 PET 94952 465-E6
LAKEVILLE HWY Rt#-116
- PET 94952 465-H7
- PET 94954 (466-A6 See Page 465)
- SonC 94954 (466-B7 See Page 465)
- SonC 94954 (486-C1 See Page 465)
1800 PET 94954 465-H7
LAKEVILLE RD
- SonC 94954 506-G1
5800 SonC 94954 (486-F5 See Page 465)
LAKEVILLE ST
- PET 94952 465-D6
LA LOMA CT
- SRFL 94901 586-G2
LAMBERT WY
- NVTO 94945 525-J1
LA MERIDA CT
100 NVTO 94945 505-H7

LAMONT AV
700 NVTO 94945 526-C4
LANAI WY
- MrnC 94971 461-E3
LANCASTER AV
- MrnC 94904 586-E4
LANGLEY LN
- NVTO 94949 546-G4
LANHAM DR
- NVTO 94949 546-G3
LA NOCHE CT
- NVTO 94945 525-J2
LANSDALE AV
- FRFX 94930 566-A6
- SANS 94960 566-A6
LANYARD CV
- CMAD 94925 606-J1
LA PALOMA WK
- MLV 94941 606-D2
LA PASADA
100 MrnC 94903 566-H2
LA PERDIZ CT
100 SRFL 94903 566-D4
LA PLAYA WY
800 MrnC 94903 566-H2
LARCH DR
- NVTO 94947 526-D7
- PET 94952 465-B6
LARCH RD
- MrnC 94924 604-E3
LARK CT
- LKSP 94939 586-F7
1000 NVTO 94947 526-B5
LARK LN
100 MrnC 94941 606-F6
LARKSPUR LN
- NVTO 94947 526-D7
LARKSPUR ST
- SRFL 94901 586-J2
LARKSPUR-SAN FRANCISCO FERRY
- CMAD - 587-B6
- LKSP - 586-J5
- MrnC - 587-B6
- MrnC - 586-J5
- SF - 607-F4
- SF - 627-J1
- TBRN - 587-C7
- TBRN - 607-F4
LARKSPUR LANDING CIR
- LKSP 94904 586-H4
LARKSPUR PLAZA DR
- LKSP 94939 586-F5
LA ROSA WY
- LKSP 94939 586-F7
LAS CASAS DR
- SRFL 94901 567-A7
LAS COLINDAS RD
300 SRFL 94903 566-C1
LAS FLORES AV
100 SRFL 94903 566-E4
LAS GALLINAS AV
100 MrnC 94903 546-E7
100 SRFL 94903 566-D2
1000 SRFL 94903 546-E7
LAS HUERTAS CT
- SRFL 94903 566-E4
LAS LOMAS
200 NVTO 94949 546-J5
LAS LOMAS LN
100 TBRN 94920 607-E7
100 TBRN 94920 627-E1
LAS OVEJAS AV
700 SRFL 94903 566-B2
LAS PALMAS AV
800 NVTO 94949 546-F2
LAS PAVADAS AV
800 SRFL 94903 566-C3
LAS RAPOSAS RD
1000 SRFL 94903 566-C1
LASSEN DR
- PET 94954 465-E3
LASSEN LN
- NVTO 94947 526-E7
LAS TARDES CT
- NVTO 94945 525-J2
LATHAM ST
- SRFL 94901 586-F1
LATTIE LN
1200 MrnC 94941 606-D5
LAUFF RANCH RD
- MrnC 94924 604-F1
LAURA LN
- FRFX 94930 565-J4
- MrnC 94930 565-J4
LAUREL AV
- BLV 94920 627-D1
- LKSP 94939 586-E6
- MrnC 94904 586-D3
- MrnC 94937 (522-G4 See Page 501)
- MrnC 94970 605-C3
- MrnC 94973 565-D3
- PET 94952 (485-D1 See Page 465)
- SANS 94960 566-A7
200 MrnC 94945 527-A4
300 MrnC 94947 525-G5
400 SANS 94960 586-A1

LAUREL DR
- CMAD 94925 606-G1
- FRFX 94930 565-H7
LAUREL LN
- SAUS 94965 627-A2
LAUREL PL
- SRFL 94901 566-G7
LAUREL RD
- MrnC 94924 604-E3
LAUREL ST
- MLV 94941 606-C3
- MrnC 94956 523-A7
- MrnC 94956 (522-J7 See Page 501)
500 PET 94952 465-C5
LAUREL WY
- MrnC 94904 586-C4
300 MrnC 94965 606-E7
LAUREL CANYON RD
- MrnC 94946 (524-A7 See Page 503)
- MrnC 94946 523-J7
LAUREL DELL FIRE RD
- MrnC - 585-D7
- MrnC - 605-D1
LAUREL GLEN TER
- SRFL 94903 566-F5
LAUREL GROVE AV
- MrnC 94904 586-D2
- ROSS 94957 586-D2
LAUREL VIEW WY
- MrnC 94937 (522-G3 See Page 501)
LAURELWOOD AV
- MLV 94941 606-D3
LAURELWOOD CT
- SRFL 94901 567-C5
LAUREN AV
- NVTO 94947 526-B4
LAUREN DR
1400 PET 94954 465-F4
LAURIE CT
- NVTO 94947 525-H3
LAURIE DR
- NVTO 94947 525-H3
LAURINA RD
- MLV 94941 606-F3
LAVENDER LN
100 MrnC 94941 606-F6
LAVERNE AV
- MrnC 94941 606-C4
LAVERNE LN
- MrnC 94941 606-E5
LAVIO DR
100 PET 94952 (485-E2 See Page 465)
LAVIO RD
100 SonC 94952 (485-A5 See Page 465)
LA VISTA WY
- SRFL 94901 566-G7
LA VUELTA AV
- MrnC 94938 (564-F2 See Page 543)
LAWRENCE DR
- NVTO 94945 526-D3
LAWRENCE RD
- SonC 94952 (464-J5 See Page 463)
LAWSON RD
- MrnC 94971 461-E3
LEA CT
400 NVTO 94945 526-D4
LEA DR
900 SRFL 94903 566-C3
1100 NVTO 94945 526-D4
LEAFWOOD CIR
- SRFL 94901 566-E7
LEAFWOOD DR
1300 NVTO 94947 526-C6
LEAFWOOD HTS
1100 NVTO 94947 526-C6
LE CLAIRE CT
- SRFL 94903 566-D4
LEE ST
- MLV 94941 606-C1
LEESE LN
2000 NVTO 94945 526-A1
2000 NVTO 94945 525-J1
LEEWARD RD
- MrnC - (542-E6 See Page 541)
- BLV 94920 607-D7
LEGEND RD
- MrnC 94960 566-A3
LEHMAN LN
100 MrnC 94941 606-E4
LEIBERT LN
- MrnC 94945 527-A3
LEIGH LN
4200 SonC 94952 465-A2
LEITH LN
- SRFL 94901 587-B1
LELAND CT
- NVTO 94947 526-A4
LELAND WY
100 TBRN 94920 607-A4
100 TBRN 94920 606-J4
LELANI LN
- MrnC 94971 461-E2

LENGLEN AV
- SRFL 94903 566-C3
LEO LN
- MrnC 94941 606-E6
LEONA DR
- MrnC 94903 566-H3
LESLIE CT
- NVTO 94947 525-J3
LESLIE WY
- PET 94954 465-H5
LEVERONI CT
- NVTO 94949 546-F1
LEYTON CT
- MLV 94941 606-G3
LIBERTY RD
200 SonC 94952 (464-G3 See Page 463)
LIBERTY ST
- LKSP 94939 586-F6
- PET 94952 465-C5
LIBERTY SHIP WY
- SAUS 94965 627-A2
LIBERTY VALLEY GOLF COURSE
- PET 94954 465-E3
LIBRA DR
- NVTO 94947 525-F3
- MrnC 94947 525-F3
LIBRARY PL
- SANS 94960 566-C7
LIDO LN
- SRFL 94901 586-J1
LIDO RD
- NVTO 94949 546-J4
LILAC AV
- MrnC 94904 586-E4
LILAC LN
- MrnC 94941 606-F6
LILIAN LN
- SRFL 94901 566-G6
LILLIAN CT
- SANS 94960 566-A4
LILLIAN LN
- MrnC 94941 606-E4
LILY AV
- SANS 94960 586-B1
LIMANTOUR DR
900 MrnC - (542-C6 See Page 541)
LIMANTOUR SPIT RD
- MrnC - 543-C2
100 MrnC 94956 543-A3
200 MrnC - (542-D6 See Page 541)
300 MrnC 94956 (542-D6 See Page 541)
LIMESTONE GRADE
- MrnC 94903 546-E5
LINARES AV
- MrnC 94933 (564-H2 See Page 543)
LINCOLN AV
- MLV 94941 606-D2
- MrnC 94970 605-C3
- SANS 94960 566-C7
600 SRFL 94901 586-G1
1200 SRFL 94901 566-G6
2100 SRFL 94903 566-G6
LINCOLN CT
- SANS 94960 566-C7
LINCOLN DR
- SAUS 94965 626-J2
LINCOLN LN
500 PET 94954 465-G3
LINCOLN ST
6400 SonC 95472 (442-H2 See Page 421)
LINCOLN VILLAGE CIR
100 LKSP 94904 586-J4
LINDA AV
- MrnC 94903 566-G4
LINDA CT
- NVTO 94947 525-G3
LINDA WY
300 MrnC 94965 606-F7
LINDARO ST
600 SRFL 94901 586-G2
LINDA VISTA AV
- TBRN 94920 607-F7
LINDA VISTA TER
- PET 94952 (485-C1 See Page 465)
LINDBERG CT
- PET 94952 465-F6
- PET 94954 465-F6
LINDBERG LN
800 PET 94952 465-F6
1200 PET 94954 465-G5
LINDEN AV
- MrnC 94937 (522-F4 See Page 501)
LINDEN LN
- MrnC 94941 606-E5
100 SRFL 94901 566-G6
LINDENWOOD CT
- SRFL 94901 567-B6
LINDSAY CT
- NVTO 94945 526-G2
LINDSDALE LN
- MrnC 94956 523-C6

LINDVIEW
- SRFL 94901 566-H6
LINEBAUGH RD
7600 SonC 94952 463-C2
LINNET CT
- MrnC 94903 546-E6
LISA CT
- MrnC 94903 546-E7
LISA DR
- MrnC 94960 565-J3
- MrnC 94930 565-J3
LISBON ST
- SRFL 94901 586-J2
LITCHBERG RD
- MrnC 94945 505-H1
LITHO ST
400 SAUS 94965 627-A3
LITTLE CREEK LN
- NVTO 94945 526-B1
- NVTO 94945 506-B7
LIVEOAK AV
- FRFX 94930 565-J6
LIVE OAK CT
- NVTO 94949 546-C1
LIVE OAK DR
400 MrnC 94965 606-E7
W LIVE OAK DR
400 MrnC 94965 606-E7
LIVE OAK TR
1100 PET 94952 465-B5
LIVE OAK WY
- MrnC 94904 586-C4
LIVINGSTON CT
- NVTO 94949 546-G3
LOBO VISTA
100 NVTO 94945 525-J2
LOCCMIND RD
- SonC 94954 506-H1
LOCH HAVEN CT
- SRFL 94901 567-B7
LOCHINVAR RD
- SRFL 94901 587-B1
- SRFL 94901 567-A7
LOCH LOMOND DR
- SRFL 94901 587-B1
LOCHNESS LN
- SRFL 94901 567-B7
- MrnC 94901 567-B7
LOCKE LN
- MLV 94941 606-E4
LOCKSLY LN
- SRFL 94901 567-A7
- SRFL 94901 587-B1
LOCKTON LN
- MrnC 94945 526-H3
LOCKWOOD DR
- SRFL 94901 567-B5
LOCKWOOD LN
- MLV 94941 606-D4
LOCUST AV
- LKSP 94939 586-E6
- MLV 94941 606-E3
- ROSS 94957 586-C1
- SRFL 94901 566-H6
- MrnC 94904 586-D3
LOCUST RD
400 MrnC 94924 604-E3
600 SAUS 94965 627-A3
LOCUST ST
300 SAUS 94965 627-A3
LODGE LN
- SRFL 94901 586-F2
LOGAN ST
600 NVTO 94945 526-C3
LOGANBERRY DR
500 MrnC 94903 546-D7
LOHRMAN LN
- SonC 94952 465-A4
LOIS CT
- MLV 94941 606-G3
LOLETA LN
500 NVTO 94947 526-E6
LOLITA LN
500 NVTO 94947 526-E6
LOMA AV
- TBRN 94920 607-E7
LOMA ALTA FIRE RD
- MrnC 94946 545-E6
- MrnC 94946 565-F1
LOMA LINDA AV
- ROSS 94957 586-C1
LOMA LINDA RD
- SRFL 94901 586-J1
LOMA ROBLES DR
- SANS 94960 566-C7
LOMA VISTA AV
- LKSP 94939 586-F6
LOMA VISTA PL
- SRFL 94901 586-J2
LOMBARDI AV
1100 PET 94954 465-G5
LOMBARDI CT
- PET 94954 465-G6
LOMBA VISTA
- NVTO 94945 525-J2
LOMITA DR
- MrnC 94941 606-G3
- MLV 94941 606-G3
- MrnC 94941 606-G3

LONE OAK CT
- PET 94952 (485-E2 See Page 465)
LONE TREE AV
- MLV 94941 606-B4
100 MrnC 94965 606-B4
LONE TREE TR
- MrnC 94965 606-C4
- MLV 94941 606-C4
LONG RD
- SonC 94952 465-A5
LONGFELLOW DR
- MLV 94941 606-G4
LONGHORN LN
1000 SonC 94952 (485-C5 See Page 465)
LONGVIEW AV
- SANS 94960 566-D7
LONGWOOD DR
- SRFL 94901 566-D6
- SANS 94960 566-D6
LOOTENS PL
900 SRFL 94901 586-F1
LOPES RD
- SonC 94954 (486-D3 See Page 465)
LORETTA LN
- MrnC 94963 (564-J2 See Page 543)
LORING AV
- MrnC 94941 606-E5
LORRAINE AV
- MrnC 94956 523-C7
- MrnC 94956 543-C1
LORRAINE CT
- NVTO 94947 525-G2
LOS ALONDRAS CT
- NVTO 94945 526-B3
LOS ALTOS DR
- SRFL 94901 566-D5
LOS ANGELES BLVD
100 SANS 94960 566-B6
200 MrnC 94901 566-B6
LOS CEDROS DR
- NVTO 94947 525-G3
LOS CERROS DR
- MrnC 94904 586-F3
LOS DIAS CT
- NVTO 94945 525-J2
LOS GAMOS DR
1000 SRFL 94903 566-E2
LOS GAMOS RD
1000 SRFL 94903 566-E3
LOS PADRES CIR
- NVTO 94947 526-E6
LOS PINOS
- MrnC 94946 545-B5
LOS PINOS SPUR
- MrnC 94946 545-C6
LOS RANCHITOS RD
- SRFL 94903 566-E4
100 MrnC 94903 566-E4
LOS REYES DR
- MrnC 94956 523-C7
LOS ROBLES DR
- SRFL 94901 586-E1
LOS ROBLES RD
- NVTO 94949 546-F3
LOTUS CT
- NVTO 94945 526-B2
LOUIS DR
500 NVTO 94945 526-D4
LOUISE AV
600 NVTO 94947 525-H4
LOUISE DR
700 PET 94954 465-H5
LOUISE ST
- SRFL 94901 586-J2
LOVE CT
- FRFX 94930 565-G3
LOVEJOY WY
- NVTO 94949 546-G3
LOVELL AV
- MLV 94941 606-B2
- SRFL 94901 586-G2
LOVERS LN
- NVTO 94947 525-J5
- NVTO 94947 526-A5
LOWELL AV
- MrnC 94903 566-G3
200 MrnC 94941 606-F6
LOWER DR
- MLV 94941 606-G2
LOWER LN
- CMAD 94925 586-F7
- CMAD 94925 606-F1
LOWER ALCATRAZ PL
- MLV 94941 606-D3
LOWER ANCHORAGE RD
100 SAUS 94965 626-H1
LOWER CRESCENT AV
- SAUS 94965 627-B4
LOWER N TER
- TBRN 94920 607-A4
LOWER NORTH TER
- TBRN 94920 607-A4
LOWER VIA CASITAS
- LKSP 94939 586-F4
LUCAS PARK DR
- SRFL 94903 566-D1

LUCAS VALLEY RD
100 MrnC 94903 545-E4
400 MrnC 94903 546-B7
800 SRFL 94903 546-B7
1900 SRFL 94903 566-E1
1900 MrnC 94903 566-E1
5000 MrnC 94946 545-A3
6600 MrnC 94946 (544-G3 See Page 543)
LUCIA LN
- MrnC 94938 (564-F1 See Page 543)
LUCKY DR
- CMAD 94925 586-G6
- MrnC 94939 586-G6
100 LKSP 94925 586-G6
100 LKSP 94939 586-G6
LUISA CT
- SRFL 94903 566-D3
LUIZ CT
- MrnC 94903 545-J6
LUIZ FIRE RD
- MrnC 94903 546-A4
- MrnC 94903 545-J5
LUKE LN
- NVTO 94949 546-G4
LULA WY
- MLV 94941 606-G2
LUNA LN
- SANS 94960 566-C7
LUNADA CT
- MrnC 94901 587-A1
LUNDBERG LN
- SonC 94952 (464-F5 See Page 463)
LUNNY LN
1700 SRFL 94901 566-E7
LUPINE CIR
- NVTO 94947 526-D7
LUPINE CT
- SRFL 94901 567-C5
LUPINE DR
- CMAD 94925 606-H1
LUZANNE CIR
- MrnC 94960 566-A2
LYDIA CT
300 PET 94952 (485-E3 See Page 465)
LYFORD DR
- TBRN 94920 607-E6
LYNCH CREEK PKWY
- PET 94954 465-E4
LYNCH CREEK WY
- PET 94954 465-E4
LYNN CT
- SRFL 94901 586-G2
LYNN RD
2800 SonC 95472 (422-H1 See Page 421)
LYNWOOD CT
- NVTO 94947 526-D7
LYNWOOD DR
1100 NVTO 94947 526-C6
LYON PL
- MLV 94941 606-C2

M

MABRY WY
- MrnC 94903 566-G2
MACANNAN CT
- TBRN 94920 607-C6
MACHIN AV
900 NVTO 94945 526-B3
MAC MAHAN WY
800 PET 94954 465-D2
MADELENE LN
- MrnC 94901 567-A7
MADELINE CT
- NVTO 94947 526-A4
MADERA AV
- ROSS 94957 586-D1
- SANS 94960 566-C7
MADERA BLVD
- CMAD 94925 586-G7
MADERA ST
- SRFL 94901 587-A3
- SRFL 94901 586-J3
MADERA WY
200 MLV 94941 606-B3
200 MrnC 94965 606-B3
MADERA DEL PRESIDIO DR
- CMAD 94925 606-H1
MADERA RIDGE FIRE RD
- CMAD 94925 606-E1
- LKSP 94939 586-D7
- LKSP 94939 606-E1
- MLV 94941 606-E1
MADISON AV
100 MrnC 94903 566-G4
100 SRFL 94903 566-F4
MADISON CT
- NVTO 94947 526-B6
MADISON ST
400 PET 94952 465-E5
E MADISON ST
1400 PET 94954 465-F3

MADRID CT
- NVTO 94949 546-F3
MADRONA AV
- BLV 94920 627-D1
- ROSS 94957 586-C3
MADRONA ST
- MLV 94941 606-D3
- SRFL 94901 586-E2
MADRONE AV
- LKSP 94939 586-E6
- MrnC 94904 586-E2
- MrnC 94937 (522-F3 See Page 501)
- MrnC 94973 565-C3
- SANS 94960 566-B7
MADRONE CT
- FRFX 94930 565-H7
MADRONE LN
900 PET 94952 465-D5
MADRONE RD
- FRFX 94930 565-H7
MADRONE ST
1000 NVTO 94945 526-C3
MADRONE WY
- MrnC 94904 586-C4
MADRONE PARK CIR
- MrnC 94941 606-D5
MADRONO AV
- CMAD 94925 606-G1
MADRONO CT
- CMAD 94925 606-G1
MAE CT
- MrnC 94947 525-E2
MAESTRO RD
- MrnC 94947 525-G5
MAGDALENA CT
- MLV 94941 606-F1
MAGEE AV
- MLV 94941 606-C2
MAGNOLIA AV
- PET 94952 465-A4
- SANS 94960 566-B7
- SRFL 94901 566-H7
- CMAD 94925 586-D4
- LKSP 94939 586-D4
- SonC 94952 465-A4
3000 SonC 94952 (464-J4 See Page 463)
MAGNOLIA PL
500 NVTO 94945 525-E2
MAHOGANY DR
- SRFL 94903 566-B2
MAIDEN LN
- FRFX 94930 565-G4
MAIER LN
- PET 94952 (485-E1 See Page 465)
MAIN CT
- FRFX 94930 565-J6
MAIN DR
- MrnC 94901 567-B7
- SRFL 94901 567-C7
200 SRFL 94903 566-G1
MAIN ST
- SRFL 94901 587-B5
- SRFL 94964 587-B5
- BLV 94920 627-E1
- TBRN 94920 627-E1
- MrnC 94964 587-B5
100 SAUS 94965 627-B4
MAIN TR
- MrnC 94965 606-A3
- MrnC 94965 605-J3
MAIN GATE RD
- NVTO 94949 546-G3
MAJORCA CT
- MrnC 94903 546-E7
MAKENA CT
- PET 94954 (466-A5 See Page 465)
MAKIN GRADE
- ROSS 94957 586-D2
- SRFL 94901 586-E2
- MrnC 94904 586-D2
MALLARD RD
- BLV 94920 607-D7
- BLV 94920 627-D1
MALLORY RD
- SonC 94952 (464-G5 See Page 463)
MALOBAR DR
500 NVTO 94945 526-G1
MALONE LN
- SRFL 94903 566-C4
MALVINO CT
- TBRN 94920 607-B4
MANANA WY
- MrnC 94956 523-D7
MANCHESTER CT
- NVTO 94947 526-E6
MANDERLY RD
- SRFL 94901 587-B1
- SRFL 94901 567-B7
MANGEL RANCH RD
- SonC 94954 (486-H4 See Page 465)
MANITOU DR
- MrnC 94960 565-H2
MANN DR
- MrnC 94904 586-E3

MANN DR
- MrnC 94924 604-F2
MANOR DR
100 MLV 94941 606-E3
E MANOR DR
- MLV 94941 606-E3
MANOR LN
800 SonC 94954 (466-A3 See Page 465)
MANOR RD
- FRFX 94930 565-H5
- MrnC 94904 586-E3
MANOR TER
- MLV 94941 606-E3
MANOR VW
- MrnC 94930 565-H3
- MrnC 94960 565-H3
MANOR WY
- PET 94952 (485-C1 See Page 465)
MANOR LN WEST BRCH
800 SonC 94954 (466-B2 See Page 465)
MANUEL DR
600 NVTO 94945 526-C4
MANUEL T FREITAS PKWY
600 SRFL 94903 566-C2
MANZANITA AV
- MrnC 94901 567-B7
- MrnC 94933 (564-H2 See Page 543)
- MrnC 94945 526-J4
- MrnC 94963 (564-H2 See Page 543)
- MrnC 94945 527-A3
400 CMAD 94925 586-F7
700 CMAD 94925 606-G1
MANZANITA CT
- FRFX 94930 565-H6
200 CMAD 94925 586-G7
200 CMAD 94925 606-G1
MANZANITA PL
- MLV 94941 606-C1
MANZANITA RD
- FRFX 94930 565-H6
MANZANO CT
- NVTO 94945 525-J1
MAOLI DR
1600 MrnC 94903 546-A7
MAPLE AV
- FRFX 94930 565-J5
- LKSP 94939 586-D6
- MrnC 94904 586-D3
MAPLE CT
- NVTO 94947 526-D6
MAPLE DR
- NVTO 94945 526-D2
800 PET 94954 465-G6
MAPLE LN
- SANS 94960 566-A6
MAPLE RD
- MrnC 94924 604-E3
- MrnC 94973 565-C3
MAPLE ST
- SRFL 94901 566-G7
400 MrnC 94965 606-E7
MAPLE HILL DR
- SRFL 94903 566-D1
MAPLEWOOD DR
- SRFL 94901 567-B6
500 PET 94954 465-D3
MARA VISTA CT
- TBRN 94920 607-C5
MARCY CT
- NVTO 94947 526-A4
MAR EAST ST
2100 TBRN 94920 607-F7
2300 MrnC 94920 607-F7
MAREDA LN
- MrnC - (484-C3 See Page 463)
- SonC 94952 (484-C3 See Page 463)
MARGARET CT
1000 NVTO 94947 526-D7
MARGARITA DR
- MrnC 94901 567-A7
- MrnC 94901 587-A1
300 SRFL 94901 567-A7
300 MrnC 94901 566-J7
300 SRFL 94901 566-J7
MARGARITA TER
- NVTO 94947 526-D6
MARGO LN
100 PET 94952 465-E5
MARGORY CT
- NVTO 94947 525-J3
MARGUERITE AV
- MLV 94941 606-C2
MARGUERITE WY
800 PET 94954 465-G5
MARI LN
2200 PET 94954 465-G3
MARIA CT
- NVTO 94945 525-H1
MARIA DR
- PET 94954 465-D2
MARIA LORETO CT
- NVTO 94949 546-E5

MARIAN CT
- SRFL 94901 586-J2
MARIAN WY
1200 PET 94954 465-G5
MARIE ST
- SAUS 94965 627-A2
MARIELE DR
- MrnC 94930 565-H3
MARILYN CIR
- PET 94954 465-H4
MARIN AV
- BLV 94920 607-C7
- SAUS 94965 626-J2
200 MrnC 94965 606-D7
MARIN DR
700 MrnC 94965 606-D7
MARIN RD
- FRFX 94930 565-H5
MARIN ST
- SRFL 94901 586-F2
MARIN WY
- MrnC 94924 604-F3
- MrnC 94965 606-D7
700 PET 94952 465-E5
MARINA AV
- PET 94954 465-G7
MARINA BLVD
- MrnC 94901 586-J1
- SRFL 94901 586-J1
MARINA WY
- SRFL 94901 587-A1
100 NVTO 94947 526-C5
MARINA COURT DR
- MrnC 94901 586-H1
100 SRFL 94901 586-H1
MARINA VISTA AV
- LKSP 94939 586-E7
200 CMAD 94925 586-E7
MARIN BAY PARK CT
- SRFL 94901 567-E5
MARIN CENTER DR
100 SRFL 94903 566-E3
MARINDA CT
- FRFX 94930 565-J5
MARINDA DR
- FRFX 94930 565-J5
MARINE DR
- MrnC 94901 567-C7
- MrnC 94901 587-C1
MARINE WY
- MrnC 94970 605-C4
MARINER DR
1600 SonC 95472 (422-D2 See Page 421)
MARINER WY
- TBRN 94920 607-D7
MARINER GREEN CT
100 CMAD 94925 606-J1
MARINER GREEN DR
- CMAD 94925 606-J1
MARINERO CIR
- TBRN 94920 607-D6
MARINERS CIR
- SRFL 94903 566-F3
MARINE VIEW DR
- MrnC 94971 461-E3
MARINITA AV
- SRFL 94901 586-H1
- SRFL 94901 566-H7
MARIN OAKS DR
200 NVTO 94949 546-C1
MARINSHIP AV
900 SAUS 94965 626-J1
2000 SAUS 94965 627-A2
MARIN VALLEY DR
- NVTO 94949 546-F5
MARIN VIEW AV
- MrnC 94965 606-A3
MARIN VIEW DR
- NVTO 94949 546-G5
MARINWOOD AV
100 MrnC 94903 546-E6
MARION AV
- MLV 94941 606-C3
- SAUS 94965 627-B4
1700 NVTO 94945 526-A2
MARION CT
- NVTO 94945 526-A3
MARION OAKS CT
- NVTO 94945 526-A3
MARIPOSA AV
- SANS 94960 586-B1
MARIPOSA CT
- TBRN 94920 607-A3
MARIPOSA LN
- NVTO 94947 526-D7
MARIPOSA RD
- SRFL 94901 586-F2
MARK DR
- SRFL 94903 566-F2
1000 PET 94954 465-H5
MARK PL
- LKSP 94939 586-G5
MARK TER
- TBRN 94920 607-B4
MARKET ST
- SRFL 94901 586-J2
MARK TWAIN AV
100 MrnC 94903 566-G4

STREET
Block City ZIP Pg-Grid

MARLIN AV
- MLV 94941 606-E3
MARQUARD AV
- SRFL 94901 586-E1
MARSH DR
- NVTO 94945 526-E7
- MLV 94941 606-C1
MARSH RD
- TBRN 94920 607-E7
14000 MrnC 94972 (442-A2 See Page 421)
14000 MrnC 94972 (441-J2 See Page 421)
MARSHALL AV
- SonC 94952 465-A3
MARSHALL WY
- MrnC 94933 (564-G1 See Page 543)
MARSHALL-PETALUMA RD
- MrnC 94945 (484-D7 See Page 463)
- MrnC - (484-D7 See Page 463)
600 MrnC - (504-B1 See Page 503)
600 MrnC 94945 (504-D1 See Page 503)
1700 MrnC - 503-J2
6000 MrnC 94940 503-J2
6200 MrnC 94940 (502-D2 See Page 501)
MARTENS BLVD
- SRFL 94901 586-F2
MARTHA LN
- SANS 94960 566-A5
MARTHA ST
- PET 94952 465-D6
MARTIN CIR
900 PET 94952 465-E5
MARTIN DR
- NVTO 94949 546-F3
MARTINELLI DUMP RD
- MrnC 94940 523-E4
MARTINEZ CT
- NVTO 94945 525-H1
MARTINIQUE AV
200 MrnC 94920 607-C2
MARTINONI RD
28000 MrnC 94952 (442-G7 See Page 421)
28000 MrnC 94952 (462-G1 See Page 461)
28900 SonC 94952 (442-J5 See Page 421)
MARTLING RD
- MrnC 94960 566-A2
MARTY RD
500 SonC 94952 (464-J6 See Page 463)
MARVIN CT
100 PET 94954 465-D3
MAR WEST ST
1100 TBRN 94920 607-D7
1100 BLV 94920 607-D7
1700 TBRN 94920 627-E1
MARY ST
- PET 94952 465-D6
- SRFL 94901 586-H1
MARY JANE LN
- NVTO 94947 525-J3
MARYLYN CIR
100 PET 94954 465-H4
MARYLYNN CIR
- PET 94954 465-H4
MATEO DR
- TBRN 94920 607-B3
MATHER RD
- MrnC 94960 565-J2
MATILDA AV
- MLV 94941 606-F4
MATT DAVIS TR
- MrnC 94965 606-A2
- MrnC 94965 605-G2
MATTERI RD
- SonC 94954 (466-C1 See Page 465)
MATZEN RD
1900 SonC 94952 (484-J3 See Page 463)
MAUI LN
- MrnC 94971 461-E2
MAXWELL LN
- MrnC 94941 606-F5
MAYBRIDGE RD
- BLV 94920 607-D7
MAYWOOD WY
- SRFL 94901 566-E6
MCALLISTER AV
- MrnC 94904 586-E3
MCBROWN RD
- SonC 94952 (464-E2 See Page 463)
MCCART CT
- TBRN 94920 607-B5
MCCLAY RD
500 MrnC 94947 525-H5
500 NVTO 94947 525-J3
800 NVTO 94947 526-A3

MCCLAY RIVER PKWY
- NVTO 94947 525-J4
MCCLELLAND DR
1100 NVTO 94945 526-D4
MCCOY RD
- SRFL 94901 586-G2
MCCULLOUGH RD
- MrnC 94965 627-A6
- MrnC 94965 626-J6
- SonC 94952 (442-H3 See Page 421)
MCDONALD DR
100 PET 94952 (485-E2 See Page 465)
MCDONALD LN
- MrnC 94940 523-C6
MC DOWELL BLVD
1300 PET 94954 465-A1
MCDOWELL BLVD
- PET 94954 465-J7
N MCDOWELL BLVD
- PET 94954 465-B1
S MCDOWELL BLVD
200 PET 94954 465-F5
MCDOWELL EXT
- PET 94954 (466-A7 See Page 465)
- PET 94954 465-J7
MCGREGOR AV
1200 PET 94954 465-G4
MCINNIS PKWY
- SRFL 94903 566-F4
MCINTOSH CT
- NVTO 94949 546-E4
MCKENNAS GULCH FIRE RD
- MrnC 94970 585-B7
- MrnC 94970 605-A2
MCKENNEY DR
- FRFX 94930 565-G4
MCKENZIE AV
1200 PET 94954 465-F5
MCKENZIE ST
- MrnC 94964 587-B5
MCKEON CT
- NVTO 94947 525-J3
MCKILLOP CT
800 PET 94954 465-H5
MC NEAR AV
- SonC 94952 465-F7
- PET 94952 465-F7
MCNEAR AV
- PET 94952 (485-F1 See Page 465)
- SonC 94952 (485-F1 See Page 465)
MCNEAR DR
- SRFL 94901 567-C5
MCNEAR BRICKYARD RD
200 MrnC 94901 567-D6
MCNEIL AV
1300 PET 94954 465-F5
MCRAE RD
100 MrnC 94941 606-F5
MEADOW AV
- MrnC 94904 586-E3
- SRFL 94901 586-G3
MEADOW CT
- SANS 94960 566-A6
MEADOW DR
- MrnC 94903 566-G3
- MrnC 94941 606-G3
MEADOW RD
- MLV 94941 606-G3
MEADOW TR
- MrnC - 543-B6
MEADOW WY
- FRFX 94930 565-G7
- MrnC 94963 565-A2
100 MrnC 94963 (564-J1 See Page 543)
MEADOW CREEK DR
100 CMAD 94925 606-H2
MEADOWCREST DR
- MLV 94941 606-G1
1100 CMAD 94925 606-G1
MEADOWCREST RD
- NVTO 94945 526-B1
MEADOWCROFT DR
- SANS 94960 566-A5
MEADOWGLEN DR
- PET 94952 (485-F1 See Page 465)
MEADOW HILL DR
- TBRN 94920 607-D6
MEADOWLARK CT
- NVTO 94947 525-G4
MEADOWLARK LN
1400 PET 94954 465-G5
MEADOW OAKS DR
- SRFL 94903 566-G5
MEADOWOOD DR
- LKSP 94939 586-F6
MEADOW RIDGE DR
- CMAD 94925 606-H2
MEADOWSWEET DR
600 CMAD 94925 586-G7
800 CMAD 94925 606-H2
MEADOW VALLEY LN
1400 CMAD 94925 606-H2

MEADOW VIEW DR
- NVTO 94949 546-G5
MEADOWVIEW DR
1800 PET 94954 465-J4
MEADOW VIEW LN
- MrnC 94963 565-A2
MEDA CT
200 MrnC 94941 606-H5
MEDA LN
200 MrnC 94941 606-H5
MEDIAN WY
400 MrnC 94941 606-E6
MEDICAL PZ
100 NVTO 94947 526-A5
MEDWAY RD
- SANS 94960 566-A6
- SRFL 94901 586-H2
MEERNAA AV
- FRFX 94930 565-J7
MEGAN CT
- PET 94954 465-D2
MEISNER CT
- NVTO 94947 525-G3
MEISNER DR
- NVTO 94947 525-G3
MELALEUCA LN
1000 MrnC 94965 606-D6
MELANIE CT
900 PET 94952 (485-E1 See Page 465)
MELINDA LN
- SonC 94952 465-A6
MELODY LN
- MLV 94941 606-D2
MELROSE AV
200 MrnC 94941 606-D5
MELVILLE AV
- SANS 94960 586-B1
MELVIN ST
400 PET 94952 465-C7
MEMORIAL DR
- SRFL 94903 566-F4
MENDOCINO DR
500 PET 94954 465-C3
MENDOCINO LN
- NVTO 94947 525-G2
MERCED AV
- SANS 94960 566-A6
MERCED WY
- MLV 94941 606-B2
MERCHANT ST
6600 SonC 95472 (442-H2 See Page 421)
6700 SonC 94952 (442-H2 See Page 421)
MERCURY AV
- TBRN 94920 607-B4
MERIAM DR
- MrnC 94903 566-G3
MERIDIAN LN
- SRFL 94901 566-G6
MERRIT DR
1500 NVTO 94949 526-B7
1500 NVTO 94949 546-C1
MERRY LN
- CMAD 94925 606-F1
MERRYDALE RD
- SRFL 94903 566-F4
MERTENS RD
- SonC 94952 (484-G1 See Page 463)
MERWIN AV
- FRFX 94930 565-H6
MESA AV
- MLV 94941 606-F3
MESA RD
- MrnC 94924 604-C1
- MrnC 94956 523-C6
300 MrnC 94924 (584-B6 See Page 583)
700 MrnC 94956 543-D1
MESA WY
- MrnC 94937 (522-G3 See Page 501)
MESA VERDE WY
300 SRFL 94903 566-F2
MESSER RD
- SonC 94952 (442-J3 See Page 421)
METZ LN
100 SonC 94952 465-A2
MEYER PL
- MrnC 94904 586-D3
MEYER RD
- SRFL 94901 586-F2
MEYERS CT
- NVTO 94947 526-A3
- NVTO 94947 525-J3
MEYLING RD
6400 SonC 94954 465-C1
MICHAEL DR
- PET 94954 465-C2
MICHAEL WY
- SANS 94960 566-A4
- MrnC 94960 566-A4
MICHELE CIR
- NVTO 94947 525-F2
MIDDEN LN
- TBRN 94920 607-A3
- TBRN 94920 606-J3

MIDDLE CT
- MLV 94941 606-G2
MIDDLE RD
- SonC 95472 (442-A1 See Page 421)
27000 MrnC 94971 (462-A3 See Page 461)
27000 MrnC 94971 461-J2
27700 MrnC 94972 461-J2
27700 MrnC 94972 (442-A3 See Page 421)
27700 MrnC 94972 (441-J7 See Page 421)
MIDDLEFIELD DR
800 PET 94952 (485-F1 See Page 465)
MIDDLE PEAK RD
- MrnC - 585-J7
MIDDLE TWO ROCK RD
- SonC 94952 (464-B3 See Page 463)
MIDHILL DR
- MLV 94941 606-G2
MIDVALE WY
500 MrnC 94965 606-D6
MIDWAY AV
- MrnC 94941 606-E5
MIDWAY BLVD
300 NVTO 94947 526-C7
MIDWAY CT
1100 NVTO 94947 526-D7
MIDWAY LN
- FRFX 94930 565-B5
MIDWAY RD
- LKSP 94939 586-F6
MILANO PL
- SRFL 94901 567-D6
MILITARY RESERVATION RD
- SonC 94952 463-F4
MILL RD
2000 NVTO 94947 525-G3
2000 MrnC 94947 525-G3
MILL ST
- SRFL 94901 586-H2
11500 SonC 95472 (442-H2 See Page 421)
MILLAND CT
- MrnC 94941 606-H5
MILLAND DR
- MrnC 94941 606-H5
MILLARD RD
- LKSP 94939 586-E6
MILLAY PL
- MLV 94941 606-G4
MILLBRAE AV
- SANS 94960 566-C7
MILLER AV
- MLV 94941 606-D3
- SAUS 94965 627-B3
- MrnC 94941 606-D3
MILLER LN
- MLV 94941 606-D3
- SAUS 94965 627-B3
MILLER RD
- SonC 94952 465-G7
- SonC 94952 (485-G1 See Page 465)
MILLER TR
- MrnC 94965 585-H7
MILLER CREEK RD
200 MrnC 94903 546-F6
200 SRFL 94903 546-D7
MILLER RANCH CT
- MrnC 94903 546-E6
MILLSIDE LN
- MLV 94941 606-C3
MILLSTONE DR
- MrnC 94903 546-E5
MILLWOOD ST
- MLV 94941 606-E3
MIMOSA AV
- LKSP 94939 586-E5
MING CT
100 NVTO 94945 526-E4
MINOR CT
- SRFL 94903 566-C4
MIRABEL AV
- MLV 94941 606-D3
MIRABELLA AV
1000 NVTO 94945 526-B3
MIRADA AV
200 SRFL 94903 566-E5
MIRAFLORES AV
- SRFL 94901 586-E1
MIRAFLORES LN
- TBRN 94920 607-C5
MIRAMAR AV
- SRFL 94901 586-E1
MIRAMONTE LN
- MrnC 94924 604-G2
MIRANDA CT
- NVTO 94947 526-A4
MIRA VISTA
- MrnC 94970 605-B3
MISSION AV
- MrnC 94901 586-J1
- SRFL 94901 586-H1
900 SRFL 94901 566-F7

MISSION DR
- PET 94952 (485-E1 See Page 465)
100 MrnC 94941 606-J6
MISSION PASS TER
- MrnC 94960 566-B3
- SRFL 94903 566-B3
MISTLE RD
300 MrnC 94924 604-E4
MISTLETOE LN
- MrnC 94945 527-A3
MISTY RD
- NVTO 94945 526-G1
MITCHELL BLVD
- SRFL 94903 566-E2
MITCHELL DR
- FRFX 94930 565-G3
MITCHELL LN
- FRFX 94930 565-G3
MITCHELL RD
- MrnC 94965 626-E6
MIWOK DR
- NVTO 94947 525-J4
- SANS 94960 566-B5
MIWOK WY
- MLV 94941 606-G5
MLISS LN
- SRFL 94901 586-H4
MOCKINGBIRD CT
- NVTO 94947 525-G4
MOCLIPS DR
1600 PET 94954 465-F3
MODOC PL
- NVTO 94947 526-E7
MOHAVE CT
- CMAD 94925 586-G6
MOHAWK AV
- CMAD 94925 586-G7
MOITOZA LN
100 TBRN 94920 607-E7
MOLINO AV
- MLV 94941 606-C3
300 MrnC 94941 606-D4
MOLL WY
- MrnC 94937 (522-G3 See Page 501)
MOLLER RD
7600 SonC 94952 463-D2
MONCADA WY
- MrnC 94901 567-A7
- MrnC 94901 566-J7
MONO AV
- FRFX 94930 565-J6
MONO LN
- SANS 94960 566-A6
W MONO WY
- MLV 94941 606-B3
MONONA DR
- CMAD 94925 586-G7
MONONA LN
- CMAD 94925 586-G7
MONROE CT
- NVTO 94947 526-B5
1600 PET 94954 465-F3
MONROE ST
- PET 94954 465-F3
MONTCLAIR CT
- PET 94952 465-F5
- PET 94954 465-F5
MONTE ALEGRE
- ROSS 94957 586-C1
MONTECILLO RD
- SRFL 94903 566-B2
MONTE CIMAS AV
- MrnC 94965 606-B3
MONTECITO DR
- CMAD 94925 586-F7
300 CMAD 94925 606-F1
MONTECITO RD
- MrnC 94901 586-J1
100 MrnC 94901 587-A1
100 MrnC 94901 567-A7
MONTEGO KEY
- MrnC 94949 526-G6
MONTE MAR DR
- SAUS 94965 627-A3
MONTE MARIA AV
1300 NVTO 94947 526-B6
MONTEREY AV
- SANS 94960 566-C6
MONTEREY DR
- MrnC 94920 606-J4
MONTEREY TER
- SANS 94960 566-C6
MONTEVIDEO WY
- SRFL 94903 566-D1
MONTE VISTA
- MrnC 94904 586-E3
MONTE VISTA AV
- LKSP 94939 586-F6
- MLV 94941 606-B3
- NVTO 94947 525-J3
MONTE VISTA LN
100 SonC 94952 (464-F3 See Page 463)
MONTE VISTA RD
- FRFX 94930 565-B5
100 MrnC - 565-B5

MONTEZUMA AV
- MrnC 94938 (564-G3 See Page 543)
MONTEZUMA RD
- MrnC 94933 (564-G2 See Page 543)
300 MrnC 94938 (564-G2 See Page 543)
MONTFORD AV
- MrnC 94941 606-D4
- MLV 94941 606-D4
MONTFORD PL
300 MrnC 94941 606-D4
MONTFORD ST
- MLV 94941 606-E4
- MrnC 94941 606-E4
MONTGOMERY LN
- MrnC 94904 586-E3
MONTURA WY
100 NVTO 94949 546-C1
MOODY CT
- SRFL 94901 566-D6
MOONSHINE RD
10200 SonC 95472 (422-F4 See Page 421)
MOORING RD
- SRFL 94901 586-H2
- MrnC 94901 586-H2
MORA AV
- MrnC - 565-F7
- MrnC - 585-F1
MORA LN
- NVTO 94947 526-A5
MOREDA RD
- SonC 94952 465-B7
MORELOS AV
- MrnC 94933 (564-G2 See Page 543)
MORGAN DR
600 NVTO 94949 546-E1
MORGAN LN
- MrnC 94901 567-A7
MORNING DOVE CT
- PET 94952 465-B5
- SonC 94952 465-B5
MORNING GLORY DR
1400 PET 94954 465-D2
MORNINGSIDE DR
- CMAD 94925 586-E7
- SANS 94960 566-A6
100 CMAD 94925 606-F1
MORNING STAR CRSE
- CMAD 94925 606-J1
MORNING SUN AV
- MrnC 94941 606-E5
MORNING SUN DR
- PET 94952 (485-D1 See Page 465)
MORO ST
6700 SonC 94952 (442-J2 See Page 421)
6700 SonC 95472 (442-J2 See Page 421)
MORPHEW ST
100 SRFL 94901 587-A4
MORRISON RD
- ROSS 94957 586-D2
MORTON CT
- MLV 94941 606-G2
MORTON LN
- SANS 94960 566-A7
MOSS LN
- SANS 94960 566-C7
MOSSWOOD CT
- NVTO 94947 525-G3
MOUND ST
100 MrnC 94971 (462-B4 See Page 461)
MOUNTAIN LN
- MrnC 94965 606-B3
MOUNTAIN KING RD
- MrnC 94938 (544-D7 See Page 543)
MOUNTAIN VIEW AV
- MLV 94941 606-A3
- MrnC 94938 (564-F2 See Page 543)
- MrnC 94965 606-A3
- SANS 94960 566-B6
- SRFL 94901 566-H6
300 PET 94952 465-F7
500 PET 94952 (485-F1 See Page 465)
MOUNTAIN VIEW DR
1800 TBRN 94920 607-E7
MOUNTAIN VIEW RD
- PET 94952 (485-F1 See Page 465)
- SonC 94952 (485-F1 See Page 465)
- FRFX 94930 565-H6
MOUNT TIBURON RD
- TBRN 94920 607-D6
MOUNT VISION OVERLOOK RD
14200 MrnC - (522-C3 See Page 501)
MOUNT WHITNEY CT
- MrnC 94903 546-A6
- SRFL 94903 546-A6

MUDDY HOLLOW TR
- MrnC - (542-D6 See Page 541)
MUIR AV
- MrnC 94965 606-B3
MUIR CT
100 PET 94954 465-E4
MUIR BEACH OVLK
- MrnC 94965 625-J2
MUIR WOODS RD
- MrnC 94965 606-A6
200 MrnC 94965 605-J7
300 MrnC 94965 626-A1
300 MrnC 94965 625-J1
MULBERRY TER
2200 MrnC 94903 546-D7
MUNCK CT
10200 SonC 95472 (422-G4 See Page 421)
MUNROE
- PET 94952 465-E5
MURIEL PL
- FRFX 94930 565-H5
MURPHY LN
- MrnC 94945 527-A3
MURRAY AV
- MrnC 94904 586-D5
200 LKSP 94939 586-D5
MURRAY CIR
- MrnC 94965 627-B6
MURRAY DR
500 PET 94954 465-F5
MURRAY LN
- LKSP 94939 586-D4
- MrnC 94904 586-D4
MUSICSTAND TR
- MrnC - 585-E7
MUSTA CT
- MrnC 94903 566-J3
MYRTLE AV
- LKSP 94939 586-E6
- MLV 94941 606-B1
- SRFL 94901 566-G6
MYRTLE CT
- PET 94952 465-E5
MYRTLE LN
- SANS 94960 566-B7
MYRTLE PL
1000 NVTO 94945 525-G1

N

NADINA WY
100 MrnC 94904 586-F4
NANCY DR
- NVTO 94947 525-H4
NANDINA CT
- NVTO 94945 526-B2
NANTUCKET CV
100 SRFL 94901 587-A2
NAPA AV
- FRFX 94930 565-J6
NAPA CT
1000 PET 94954 465-C3
E NAPA DR
- PET 94954 465-C2
W NAPA DR
- PET 94952 465-C3
- PET 94954 465-C2
NAPA ST
300 SAUS 94965 627-A2
NARRAGANSETT CV
- SRFL 94901 587-A2
NASSAU CT
- NVTO 94949 546-B2
NATALLE CIR
- PET 94952 465-D5
NAVAJO LN
- CMAD 94925 586-G6
NAVE CT
- NVTO 94947 526-B4
NAVE DR
5300 NVTO 94949 546-F2
NEAME AV
- SRFL 94901 566-D7
NEDS WY
- TBRN 94920 607-D6
NEIDER LN
100 MrnC 94941 606-H4
NEILA WY
- MrnC 94920 606-H3
NELLEN DR
100 CMAD 94925 586-G6
100 LKSP 94925 586-G6
300 LKSP 94904 586-G6
NELSON AV
- MLV 94941 606-F4
NEVADA ST
- SRFL 94901 566-D6
500 SAUS 94965 626-J2
NEWBERRY TER
- MrnC 94903 546-C7
NEWCASTLE CT
- SRFL 94903 566-G5
NEWELL RD
- ROSS 94957 586-D1
NEWHALL DR
- SRFL 94901 566-H7
NEWPORT WY
- SRFL 94901 587-A2

NICASIO CREEK RD
- MrnC 94946 (544-F2 See Page 543)
NICASIO SQUARE RD
- MrnC 94946 (544-F2 See Page 543)
NICASIO VALLEY RD
- MrnC 94963 565-A2
- MrnC 94973 565-A2
600 MrnC 94946 (524-C5 See Page 503)
600 MrnC 94973 545-A7
600 MrnC 94963 545-A7
700 MrnC 94946 565-A2
700 MrnC 94946 545-A7
1100 MrnC 94946 (544-F1 See Page 543)
NIEMELA RD
- SonC 94954 (486-G7 See Page 465)
- SonC 94954 506-G1
NIGHTINGALE LN
- SRFL 94901 567-C6
NIGHTINGALE RD
- LKSP 94939 586-D6
NIKKI DR
600 PET 94954 465-D3
NINA CT
- MrnC 94941 606-J7
NINA DR
- NVTO 94947 525-G4
NINESTONE CT
- MrnC 94903 546-E6
NISSON RD
- SonC 94952 463-H1
NIVEN WY
- LKSP 94939 586-F6
NOB HILL CT
- MrnC 94956 523-C7
NOB HILL RD
- MrnC 94956 523-C7
NOB HILL TER
- PET 94952 (485-C1 See Page 465)
NOBLE LN
- SAUS 94965 627-B4
NOCHE VISTA
- TBRN 94920 607-C4
NOGALES CT
- NVTO 94947 526-A3
- NVTO 94947 525-J3
NOKOMIS AV
- SANS 94960 566-B7
NOREN WY
- MrnC 94956 543-C2
NORMA CT
- NVTO 94947 525-J3
NORMAN DR
300 NVTO 94949 546-E1
NORMAN WY
- TBRN 94920 607-D5
NORTH AV
- SRFL 94903 566-G1
NORTH CIR
- NVTO 94949 546-H4
NORTH RD
- ROSS 94957 586-B2
NORTH ST
- MrnC 94971 461-F3
200 SAUS 94965 627-B4
NORTH TR
- MLV 94941 606-E1
- CMAD 94925 606-E1
NORTH BRIDGE BLVD
- MrnC 94941 626-J1
- SAUS 94965 626-H1
- MrnC 94965 626-H1
NORTHERN AV
500 MrnC 94965 606-E6
NORTHGATE DR
500 SRFL 94903 566-E3
NORTH POINT CIR
- BLV 94920 607-C7
NORTH RIDGE TR
- TBRN - 627-H2
NORTHSTAR DR
1600 PET 94954 465-E3
NORTHVIEW CT
- MrnC 94903 566-G3
NORTON AV
200 MrnC 94945 527-A3
NORWOOD AV
- ROSS 94957 586-C1
NOSECCHI RD
- SonC 94952 (464-D2 See Page 463)
NOVA LN
- NVTO 94945 525-J2
NOVA ALBION WY
- SRFL 94903 566-D4
NOVAK DR
100 PET 94954 465-F4
NOVATO BLVD
1500 NVTO 94947 526-A3
1600 NVTO 94947 525-F1
1600 NVTO 94945 525-F1
2400 MrnC 94945 525-C1
2400 MrnC 94947 525-C1
3700 MrnC 94945 (524-J1 See Page 503)

NOVATO BLVD
3700 MrnC 94947 (524-J1 See Page 503)
4000 MrnC 94945 (504-F5 See Page 503)
4000 MrnC 94947 (504-F5 See Page 503)
S NOVATO BLVD
1300 NVTO 94947 526-A3
1400 NVTO 94945 526-A3
NOVATO ST
- SRFL 94901 586-J2
NOVATO LANDING CT
700 NVTO 94945 526-C4
NUGENT LN
800 NVTO 94945 526-C3
NUMES RD
- SonC 94952 465-A4
NUNAN LN
- SRFL 94901 566-G7
NUNES DR
- NVTO 94945 506-B7
NUNES FIRE RD
- SRFL 94903 546-A7
- MrnC 94903 546-A7
NYE ST
1100 SRFL 94901 586-G1
1200 SRFL 94901 566-G7
NYMPH RD
- MrnC 94924 604-E3

O

OAK AV
- BLV 94920 627-C1
- MrnC 94904 586-E3
- SANS 94960 586-A1
- SRFL 94901 586-F2
200 MrnC 94945 527-A4
600 ROSS 94957 586-B1
S OAK AV
- SANS 94960 586-A1
OAK DR
- MrnC 94901 567-C7
- MrnC 94901 587-C1
OAK LN
- SRFL 94901 587-B1
- SonC 94952 465-C4
- MLV 94941 606-C2
- PET 94952 (485-C1 See Page 465)
- CMAD 94925 586-F7
200 SAUS 94965 627-B4
OAK PL
- BLV 94920 627-D1
OAK RD
- FRFX 94930 565-G7
- LKSP 94939 586-D6
- MrnC 94924 604-E4
OAK ST
- MLV 94941 606-C3
- PET 94952 465-D6
OAK WY
- NVTO 94945 526-C3
- ROSS 94957 586-C1
OAK CREST CT
- NVTO 94947 526-D6
OAK CREST DR
100 MrnC 94960 566-B4
OAKCREST DR
- MrnC 94903 566-G4
OAK CREST RD
- MrnC 94960 566-B4
OAKDALE AV
- MLV 94941 606-E2
- SRFL 94901 566-H5
300 CMAD 94925 606-F1
OAK FOREST RD
- NVTO 94949 546-E4
OAK GROVE AV
- MrnC 94973 565-D3
OAK HILL DR
- SANS 94960 566-C7
OAKHURST RD
- MrnC 94901 586-H3
OAK KNOLL AV
- SANS 94960 566-A6
OAK KNOLL CT
- MrnC 94945 526-G3
OAK KNOLL DR
- MrnC 94960 566-A4
W OAK KNOLL DR
- MrnC 94960 566-A4
OAK KNOLL RD
- MrnC 94904 586-D4
- NVTO 94947 525-G3
OAKLAND AV
- SANS 94960 566-B6
OAK MANOR DR
- FRFX 94930 565-H4
- MrnC 94930 565-H4
OAKMONT AV
- SRFL 94901 566-F6
OAKMONT CT
- SRFL 94901 566-F6
OAK MOUNTAIN CT
- MrnC 94903 546-A6
OAK MOUNTAIN DR
- MrnC 94903 546-A6

OAKRIDGE RD
- MrnC 94903 566-E5
OAK RIDGE TER
- MrnC 94945 526-G3
OAKSHADE LN
- MrnC 94945 526-D2
OAK SPRINGS DR
- SANS 94960 565-J4
100 SANS 94960 566-A4
OAK TERRACE WY
- PET 94952 465-C7
OAK TREE CT
- SRFL 94903 566-D1
OAK TREE LN
- FRFX 94930 565-H5
OAK VALLEY DR
- NVTO 94947 525-F3
- MrnC 94947 525-F3
OAK VIEW CT
- NVTO 94949 526-C7
OAK VIEW DR
100 MrnC 94903 566-E5
OAKWOOD AV
- SANS 94960 566-A5
OAKWOOD DR
- PET 94954 465-E3
- SRFL 94901 566-E6
200 NVTO 94949 546-H4
N OAKWOOD DR
500 NVTO 94949 546-H3
OAT HILL RD
- MrnC - 585-C2
OBERTZ LN
- NVTO 94949 546-C3
OCEAN AV
- MrnC 94924 604-F3
OCEAN PKWY
- MrnC 94924 604-D3
OCEAN WY
- MLV 94941 606-C3
OCEANA DR
- MrnC 94971 461-E2
OCEANO PL
- NVTO 94949 546-F2
OCEAN VIEW AV
- MrnC 94971 461-E3
OCEAN VIEW BLVD
400 MrnC 94971 461-E2
OCTAVIA ST
- SRFL 94901 586-F2
OELTJEN RD
200 SonC 94952 465-A7
OLD CORONA RD
- PET 94952 465-B2
- SonC 94952 465-B3
OLD CREEK RD
- SonC 94952 465-A7
OLD FAIRFAX BOLINAS RD
- MrnC - 585-F2
OLD KING RD
- PET 94954 465-E3
OLD LAKEVILLE ROAD NUMBER 1
5200 SonC 94954 (486-E4 See Page 465)
OLD LAKEVILLE ROAD NUMBER 2
7000 SonC 94954 (486-F6 See Page 465)
OLD LAKEVILLE ROAD NUMBER 3
- SonC 94954 506-H1
OLD LANDING RD
- MrnC 94920 607-C3
OLD LUCAS VALLEY RD
- SRFL 94903 546-C7
OLD MILL ST
- MLV 94941 606-D3
OLD MINE TR
- MrnC 94965 605-G3
OLD PINE TR
- MrnC - (563-C2 See Page 543)
OLD QUARRY RD
100 LKSP 94904 586-H4
OLD RANCH RD
- MrnC 94947 525-H6
- MrnC 94946 525-H6
OLD RANCHERIA RD
- MrnC 94946 (524-J7 See Page 503)
- MrnC 94946 (544-F2 See Page 543)
OLD REDWOOD HWY N
- PET 94952 465-A2
- PET 94954 465-A2
- SonC 94952 465-A2
OLD STAGE RD
- MrnC 94965 605-G2
OLD STOVE TR
- MrnC - 585-E7
OLD VEE RD
- MrnC - 585-A2
OLEANDER DR
100 SRFL 94903 566-D2
OLEANDER PL
800 NVTO 94945 526-D4
OLEMA RD
- FRFX 94930 565-G4

STREET
Block City ZIP Pg-Grid

OLEMA RD
6500 MrnC - 565-G4
OLEMA-BOLINAS RD
- MrnC 94924 604-F1
200 MrnC 94924 (584-F6
See Page 583)
OLIMA ST
500 SAUS 94965 626-H1
OLIVA CT
100 NVTO 94945 525-H2
OLIVA DR
- NVTO 94945 525-H2
OLIVE AV
- LKSP 94939 586-E6
- ROSS 94957 586-B2
- SANS 94960 566-B7
- SRFL 94901 566-H7
OLIVE ST
- MLV 94941 606-D3
100 MrnC 94945 526-F4
100 PET 94952 (485-F1
See Page 465)
200 NVTO 94945 526-C3
500 SAUS 94965 627-A2
OLIVER LN
- MrnC 94941 606-H5
OLSEN RD
2600 SonC 95472 (422-J2
See Page 421)
OLYMPIA WY
- NVTO 94949 546-B2
OLYMPIC CT
300 PET 94954 465-E3
OLYMPIC WY
200 SRFL 94903 566-F2
ONEEL DR
1600 PET 94954 465-H5
ONYX ST
- LKSP 94939 586-E6
OPAL RD
- MrnC 94924 604-E3
OPAL ST
- LKSP 94939 586-E5
OPALSTONE TER
2500 MrnC 94903 546-E6
ORANGE AV
- LKSP 94939 586-E6
600 NVTO 94945 526-C3
ORANGE CT
- MrnC 94901 586-H3
ORANGE ST
- MrnC 94901 586-H3
ORANGE BLOSSOM LN
100 SRFL 94903 566-D2
ORCHARD LN
- PET 94952 (485-C1
See Page 465)
ORCHARD WY
- MrnC 94904 586-D3
- MrnC 94963 565-A2
- MrnC 94963 (564-J2
See Page 543)
- NVTO 94947 526-A3
ORCHID DR
300 SRFL 94903 566-D2
ORIENT DR
700 NVTO 94945 526-H1
ORINDA AV
400 PET 94954 465-G4
ORINDA CT
1700 PET 94954 465-G4
ORIOLE CIR
100 NVTO 94949 546-E5
ORMOND CT
- NVTO 94947 526-A4
ORO CT
- NVTO 94947 525-G4
ORRIS TER
200 SRFL 94903 566-E3
OSPREY PL
- PET 94954 465-J5
OVER ST
- LKSP 94939 586-E5
OVERHILL RD
- MLV 94941 606-F2
OVERLAND DR
- PET 94954 465-G6
OVERLOOK DR
- MrnC 94924 604-E2
OVERLOOK RD
- MrnC 94956 523-B6
OWENS DR
600 NVTO 94949 546-D1
OWL RD
17000 SonC 95465 421-D1
OWLSWOOD LN
- TBRN 94920 607-C6
OWLSWOOD RD
- LKSP 94939 586-E7
- TBRN 94920 607-C6
OXFORD AV
- MLV 94941 606-F4
OXFORD CT
- PET 94952 (485-C1
See Page 465)
OXFORD DR
- MrnC 94903 566-H3

P

PACHECHO RD
- SonC 94952 (464-C6
See Page 463)
PACHECO AV
- FRFX 94930 565-J6
100 MrnC 94947 526-A5
PACHECO LN
4400 SonC 94952 465-A2
PACHECO ST
- MrnC 94965 626-H1
- SRFL 94901 566-G7
PACHECO CREEK DR
- NVTO 94949 546-D4
PACIFIC AV
1200 PET 94954 465-G5
PACIFIC DR
- NVTO 94949 546-C1
PACIFIC WY
- MrnC 94965 626-A2
PACIFIC QUEEN PASG
- CMAD 94925 606-J1
PACKARD LN
100 SonC 94952 (464-G2
See Page 463)
PAGE WALK RD
- MrnC 94956 523-C5
PALADINI RD
- NVTO 94947 525-H3
PALAZZI CT
- SANS 94960 566-A6
PALM AV
- CMAD 94925 586-F7
- LKSP 94939 586-E6
- SANS 94960 566-C7
- SRFL 94901 566-H7
300 MrnC 94904 586-E3
PALM CT
- LKSP 94939 586-F6
PALM DR
- NVTO 94949 546-H3
PALM WY
- MrnC 94965 606-B4
PALMA WY
500 MrnC 94965 606-E6
PALMER CT
- TBRN 94920 607-B5
PALMER DR
1000 NVTO 94949 546-D1
PALMER ST
600 PET 94952 465-E6
PALMERA WY
800 MrnC 94903 566-H2
PALMETTO WY
900 PET 94954 465-G6
PALMO CT
- NVTO 94945 525-J1
PALMO WY
- NVTO 94945 525-J1
PALOMA AV
200 SRFL 94901 566-G7
PALOMA DR
- CMAD 94925 606-H1
PALOMINO CIR
- MrnC 94947 525-F4
PALOMINO CT
- PET 94954 465-H4
PALOMINO RD
- MrnC 94947 525-F4
PALO VERDE WY
- PET 94954 465-D3
PAMARON WY
- NVTO 94949 546-F2
PAMELA CT
- MrnC 94920 606-J4
PAMELA DR
- PET 94954 465-B2
PANORAMA DR
- NVTO 94949 546-G5
PANORAMIC HWY
800 MrnC 94965 605-H2
800 MrnC 94970 605-D4
1200 MrnC 94965 606-B3
1700 MrnC 94941 606-B3
PAN TOLL RD
- MrnC 94965 605-F3
- MrnC 94970 605-F3
PAPER MILL CT
- NVTO 94949 546-E4
PAR LN
- NVTO 94949 546-C2
PARADISE CT
- NVTO 94945 526-A2
PARADISE DR
200 TBRN 94920 627-E1
1000 TBRN 94920 607-D5
1800 MrnC 94920 607-A1
4500 MrnC 94920 607-A1
5000 CMAD - 607-A1
5100 CMAD 94925 607-A1
5400 CMAD 94925 606-H1
5800 CMAD 94925 586-H7
PARADISE COVE RD
- MrnC 94920 607-D5
PARADISE VALLEY RD
- MrnC 94924 (584-E6
See Page 583)
PARENT WY
800 PET 94954 465-H5
PARENTE RD
- TBRN 94920 607-B2
PARK AV
- MLV 94941 606-E4
- MrnC 94924 604-G2
- MrnC 94937 (522-G3
See Page 501)
- MrnC 94965 606-E4
- MrnC 94971 461-F3
- PET 94952 465-C6
1400 NVTO 94945 526-B3
PARK CIR
- MrnC 94965 606-H7
PARK CT
1500 NVTO 94945 526-B3
PARK DR
- ROSS 94957 586-B2
- SANS 94960 566-B6
PARK LN
- CMAD 94925 606-G1
- FRFX 94930 565-H6
200 SANS 94960 566-C6
500 PET 94954 465-F4
PARK PL
- TBRN 94920 607-B2
PARK RD
- FRFX 94930 565-H6
PARK ST
- LKSP 94939 586-E6
- MrnC 94973 565-C2
- SRFL 94901 566-H7
- SRFL 94901 586-H1
- SAUS 94965 627-B2
PARK TER
- MLV 94941 606-E4
PARK WY
- LKSP 94939 586-F7
- SANS 94960 566-C7
500 MrnC 94941 606-C4
PARK CREST CT
1100 NVTO 94947 526-D6
PARKER LN
- FRFX 94930 565-J5
PARKER RD
- SonC 94952 (464-J6
See Page 463)
PARKLAND WY
2200 PET 94954 465-G3
PARK RIDGE RD
- SRFL 94903 566-D1
PARKSIDE CT
- SANS 94960 566-B6
PARKSIDE WY
- MrnC 94904 586-G4
- LKSP 94904 586-G4
100 PET 94952 465-C6
PARKVIEW CIR
- CMAD 94925 606-H2
PARKVIEW CT
300 PET 94952 (485-E2
See Page 465)
PARKWOOD AV
- MLV 94941 606-D3
PARKWOOD DR
1200 NVTO 94947 526-C6
PARRAL WY
- MrnC 94938 (564-G2
See Page 543)
PARTRIDGE CT
- NVTO 94945 526-A1
- SRFL 94901 567-D5
PARTRIDGE DR
- NVTO 94945 526-A1
- SRFL 94901 567-D5
100 NVTO 94945 506-A7
PASADENA AV
- MrnC 94960 566-B5
- SANS 94960 566-B5
PASEO WY
- LKSP 94904 586-G4
PASEO MIRASOL
- TBRN 94920 606-J3
- TBRN 94920 607-A3
PASTEL CT
- NVTO 94947 526-C5
PASTEL LN
1400 NVTO 94947 526-C5
PASTORI AV
- FRFX 94930 566-A6
- SANS 94960 566-A6
- FRFX 94930 565-J6
PASTURE RD
15500 SonC 95465 421-F2
PATALITA DR
700 NVTO 94945 526-H1
PATH 1
- LKSP 94939 586-D6
PATH 2
- LKSP 94939 586-E6
PATH 3
- LKSP 94939 586-D6
PATOCCHI RD
- SonC 94954 (466-C6
See Page 465)
PATRICIA LN
- MrnC 94941 606-F3
PATRICIA WY
800 SRFL 94903 566-B1
PATTERSON LN
- NVTO 94949 546-G4
PAUL DR
- SRFL 94903 566-F2
PAULA LN
- SonC 94952 465-B5
500 PET 94952 465-B5
PAULINE WY
1700 PET 94954 465-H4
PAULSEN LN
100 SonC 94952 (464-E1
See Page 463)
PAVILLION PTH
- CMAD 94925 606-C5
PAVN RD
- SonC 94952 463-H4
PAXTON VILLA CT
800 NVTO 94947 526-A4
PAYRAN
100 PET 94952 465-E5
PAYRAN ST
400 PET 94952 465-E5
W PAYRAN ST
100 PET 94952 465-D5
PEACH ST
600 NVTO 94945 526-C3
PEACHSTONE TER
300 MrnC 94903 546-D6
PEACOCK CT
- SRFL 94901 567-E5
PEACOCK DR
- SRFL 94901 567-D5
PEACOCK LN
- SRFL 94901 567-D6
PEARCE RD
- SRFL 94901 586-F2
PEARCE ST
- PET 94952 (485-C1
See Page 465)
PEARL ST
- SAUS 94965 627-A2
PEBBLE BEACH DR
- NVTO 94949 546-D2
PECAN DR
- SRFL 94903 566-B2
PECAN WY
900 PET 94954 465-G6
PEDOTTI RD
- SonC 94952 (485-C4
See Page 465)
PEDRINI LN
- MrnC 94938 (564-F2
See Page 543)
PEDRINI WY
- MrnC 94938 (564-F2
See Page 543)
PEGGY CT
1700 PET 94954 465-H5
PEGGY LN
1600 PET 94954 465-H5
PELICAN CT
- PET 94954 465-J5
PELICAN LN
100 NVTO 94949 546-E5
PELICAN WY
- SRFL 94901 587-A4
PELICAN PT RD
- BLV 94920 607-C7
- BLV 94920 627-C1
PELLEGRINELLI DR
- TBRN 94920 607-B3
PENINSULA RD
- BLV 94920 627-D1
- BLV 94920 607-D7
PENNY LN
- FRFX 94930 565-G3
- LKSP 94939 586-D6
PENNY TER
- MrnC 94964 587-B5
PENNY ROYAL LN
700 SRFL 94903 566-B2
PENROD DR
100 PET 94954 465-F4
PENSACOLA CT
- NVTO 94949 546-A3
PEPPER AV
- CMAD 94925 586-F7
- LKSP 94939 586-F7
PEPPER RD
2700 SonC 94952 463-H2
PEPPER WY
- SRFL 94901 566-E6
PEPPERWOOD LN
- CMAD 94925 606-H2
900 PET 94952 465-C5
PERALTA AV
100 MrnC 94941 606-E6
PEREIERA RD
- SonC 94952 (464-J7
See Page 463)
PEREIRA RD
- SonC 94952 (464-J7
See Page 463)
PERIERA RD
- SonC 94954 (466-D6
See Page 465)
PERIMETER RD
- NVTO 94949 547-A4
- NVTO 94949 546-J4
PERRY RD
- PET 94954 465-G7
PERRY ST
200 MrnC 94941 606-F6
PERRY WALK AV
- SRFL 94901 586-F2
PERSIMMON CT
- PET 94954 465-H4
PERTH WY
- MrnC 94937 (522-F4
See Page 501)
PETALUMA BLVD N
200 PET 94952 465-A2
1700 SonC 94952 465-A2
PETALUMA BLVD S
- PET 94952 465-E7
900 SonC 94952 465-E7
PETALUMA WY
- PET 94954 465-C2
PETER CT
- NVTO 94947 526-C5
PETERSEN LN
300 SonC 94952 465-B6
PETERSEN RD
6400 SonC 94954 465-C1
PETRA AV
- MrnC 94938 (564-F2
See Page 543)
PHEASANT CT
- SRFL 94901 567-D5
PHEASANT DR
1400 PET 94954 465-H5
PHILIP TER
- MrnC 94945 527-A3
- MrnC 94945 526-J3
PHILLIPS AV
900 PET 94952 (485-F1
See Page 465)
PHOTINIA PL
200 PET 94952 (485-E3
See Page 465)
PICADILLY CT
- SRFL 94903 566-G5
PICNIC AV
100 SRFL 94901 586-G2
PICO CT
- SRFL 94903 566-A1
PICO VISTA
- NVTO 94945 525-J2
PIDGEON CT
- PET 94952 465-D5
PIEDMONT CT
- LKSP 94939 586-E7
PIEDMONT RD
- LKSP 94939 586-E7
PIERCE DR
- NVTO 94947 526-B6
PIERCE LN
- NVTO 94947 526-B6
PIERCE POINT RD
- MrnC - (522-C1
See Page 501)
1300 MrnC - 501-H4
1300 MrnC - (521-J1
See Page 501)
4300 MrnC - (481-F5
See Page 461)
PIGEON HOLLOW RD
- MrnC 94901 566-J7
- MrnC 94901 586-J1
PIKES PEAK DR
- MrnC 94903 546-B7
PILLSBURY LN
- MrnC 94947 525-H4
PIMENTEL CT
- NVTO 94949 546-F1
PIMLOTT LN
- MLV 94941 606-D4
PINE AV
- BLV 94920 627-D2
- MrnC 94973 565-D3
800 NVTO 94947 526-B4
1700 PET 94954 465-G4
PINE CT
- MrnC 94904 586-E3
PINE DR
- FRFX 94930 565-G7
200 MrnC 94930 565-G7
PINE LN
700 SRFL 94903 566-C2
PINE RD
- MrnC 94924 604-E3
PINE ST
- SRFL 94901 566-E7
100 SANS 94960 586-B1
300 SAUS 94965 627-A3
400 MrnC 94965 606-E7
PINE TER
- TBRN 94920 607-B5
PINECONE CT
- SRFL 94901 567-C5
PINE CREST
- MrnC 94956 (522-H7
See Page 501)
PINE CREST RD
500 MrnC 94941 606-E6
PINE HILL CT
- SRFL 94903 566-D1
PINE HILL DR
- MrnC 94937 (522-F2
See Page 501)
PINE HILL RD
300 MrnC 94941 606-E6
PINE MOUNTAIN RD
- MrnC - 585-D1
6400 MrnC - 565-A4
6900 MrnC - (564-H5
See Page 543)
PINEO AV
500 MrnC 94965 606-E6
PINE RIDGE RD
15300 MrnC - (522-C3
See Page 501)
PINE RIDGE WY
400 MrnC 94941 606-E6
PINE TREE CT
- SRFL 94903 566-E4
PINE TREE LN
4100 SonC 94952 465-B2
PINE VIEW LN
- NVTO 94945 526-B2
PINE VIEW WY
- PET 94954 (466-A7
See Page 465)
PINEWOOD CT
800 PET 94954 465-G6
PINEWOOD DR
300 MrnC 94903 546-D7
PINEWOOD LN
- NVTO 94947 526-D6
PINTO LN
- MrnC 94947 525-F4
PINYON PL
- NVTO 94945 525-E2
PIOMBO CT
- FRFX 94930 565-B5
PIOMBO PL
- SRFL 94901 587-B4
PIONEER CT
- NVTO 94945 525-J2
PIPELINE FIRE RD
- FRFX 94930 565-F3
- MrnC 94930 565-F3
PIPER CT
- FRFX 94930 565-H4
- NVTO 94947 525-J3
PIPER LN
- FRFX 94930 565-H4
PIPING ROCK RD
- NVTO 94949 546-A3
PIVATO CT
- NVTO 94945 526-C4
PIXIE TR
400 MrnC 94941 606-D4
PIXLEY AV
- CMAD 94925 586-F7
PIZARO
- MrnC 94933 (564-H1
See Page 543)
PLACE MOULIN
- TBRN 94920 607-D5
PLATA CT
- NVTO 94947 525-G4
PLATFORM BRIDGE RD
- MrnC 94946 543-G1
PLATT AV
- SAUS 94965 627-A3
PLATT CT
- MrnC 94941 606-J6
PLAYA DEL REY
100 SRFL 94901 587-A2
PLAYA VERDE
- MrnC 94920 607-D5
PLAZA DR
- MrnC 94941 606-G3
PLAZA AMAPOLA
700 NVTO 94947 526-B4
PLAZA DEMIRA
- NVTO 94947 526-B4
PLAZA HERMOSA
700 NVTO 94947 526-B4
PLAZA LINDA
700 NVTO 94947 526-B4
PLAZA LOMA
- NVTO 94947 526-B4
PLEASANT AV
- CMAD 94925 606-G1
PLEASANT LN
- SRFL 94901 586-F2
PLEASANT ST
- PET 94952 465-C6
PLEASANT VIEW RD
- NVTO 94947 525-J3
PLUM ST
600 NVTO 94945 526-D3
PLUMAS AV
- SANS 94960 566-A7
PLUMAS CIR
- NVTO 94947 526-E6
PLUMMER RD
- SonC 94952 (464-E4
See Page 463)
PLYMOUTH AV
- MLV 94941 606-F4
PLYMOUTH CV
100 SRFL 94901 587-A2
POCO PASO
- MrnC 94903 566-E5
POHONO ST
- MrnC 94941 606-H7
POINT GALLINAS RD
- MrnC 94903 566-J2
POINT REYES-PETALUMA RD
- MrnC - 523-G7
- MrnC - 543-H1
- MrnC 94940 (524-B5
See Page 503)
- MrnC 94946 (524-B5
See Page 503)
- MrnC 94946 523-J7
- MrnC 94947 (524-B5
See Page 503)
- MrnC 94940 523-D7
- MrnC 94956 523-D7
- MrnC - 523-D7
600 MrnC 94946 543-H1
600 MrnC 94940 543-H1
700 MrnC 94946 523-J7
700 MrnC 94946 543-H1
700 MrnC 94940 523-G7
700 MrnC 94940 543-H1
5200 MrnC 94945 (485-A7
See Page 465)
5700 MrnC 94945 505-A1
5700 MrnC 94945 (504-E6
See Page 503)
7300 MrnC 94947 (504-E6
See Page 503)
POINT REYES LIGHTHOUSE RD
2000 MrnC - (561-A3
See Page 541)
2000 MrnC - (560-G3
See Page 540)
2000 MrnC - (561-A3
See Page 541)
2000 MrnC - (560-G3
See Page 540)
POINT SAN PEDRO RD
- MrnC 94901 586-H1
- SRFL 94901 586-H1
100 SRFL 94901 587-B1
100 MrnC 94901 587-A1
600 MrnC 94901 587-B1
700 MrnC 94901 567-C7
800 SRFL 94901 567-C7
POLHEMUS WY
- LKSP 94939 586-D6
POLONSKY RD
- SonC 94952 (464-H5
See Page 463)
POMEROY RD
- ROSS 94957 586-D1
PONDEROSA DR
1100 PET 94954 465-G6
PONICA LN
2500 SonC 95472 (422-J3
See Page 421)
PONTE FIRE RD
- NVTO 94949 546-C4
100 MrnC 94903 546-C4
POPLAR AV
- ROSS 94957 586-C2
100 MrnC 94904 586-C2
POPLAR DR
- MrnC 94904 586-E2
1000 NVTO 94945 525-H1
POPLAR LN
200 SonC 94952 465-A7
POPLAR RD
- MrnC 94924 604-D3
POPLAR ST
300 MrnC 94965 606-E7
POPPY CT
1600 PET 94954 465-F3
E PORTAL PIPELINE FIRE RD
- FRFX 94930 565-E7
- MrnC 94930 565-E7
- MrnC 94930 585-G1
6200 MrnC - 565-E7
PORTEOUS AV
- FRFX 94930 565-J7
PORTER RD
- SonC 94952 (464-B3
See Page 463)
PORTERO LN
- MrnC 94938 (564-F1
See Page 543)
PORTO BELLO DR
- SRFL 94901 586-J1
PORTOFINO RD
- SRFL 94901 586-J2
PORTOLA AV
- MrnC 94903 566-G5
- MrnC 94938 (544-F6
See Page 543)
- MrnC 94956 543-A1
PORTOLA LN
- MLV 94941 606-D2
PORTOLA WY
- CMAD 94925 586-F7
PORTO MARINO DR
- TBRN 94920 607-B4
PORTSMOUTH CV
- SRFL 94901 587-A2
POSADA DEL SOL
100 NVTO 94949 546-F3
POST ST
- LKSP 94939 586-E6
- PET 94952 465-D7
POWELL RD
- SonC 94952 (464-D2
See Page 463)
POWER LN
- FRFX 94930 565-J6
PRAIRIE FALCON DR
- NVTO 94949 546-E5
PRESCOTT WY
- PET 94954 465-G4
PRESIDIO AV
- MLV 94941 606-D3
500 CMAD 94925 606-G1
PRESIDIO CT
- CMAD 94925 606-H2
PRESTWICK CT
- NVTO 94949 546-A2
PRICE DR
- SonC 94952 465-B6
PRIMROSE PTH
100 MrnC 94941 606-F5
PRINCE ALBERT ST
100 PET 94954 465-E3
PRINCE ROYAL DR
- CMAD 94925 606-J2
400 CMAD 94925 607-A1
PRINCE ROYAL PASG
- CMAD 94925 606-J1
PRINCESS LN
- SAUS 94965 627-B3
200 MrnC 94941 606-E5
PRINCESS ST
- SAUS 94965 627-B3
PRINCETON AV
200 MrnC 94941 606-F6
PRINCE VILLE CT
- PET 94954 (466-A6
See Page 465)
PRIVATEER DR
- CMAD 94925 607-A1
PROFESSIONAL DR
- PET 94954 465-E3
PROFESSIONAL CTR PKWY
- SRFL 94903 566-E3
PROGOTTI
- SonC 94954 (486-E3
See Page 465)
PROSPECT AV
- SANS 94960 586-C1
- SAUS 94965 627-B3
100 ROSS 94957 586-C1
PROSPECT DR
- SRFL 94901 566-G6
PROSPECT LN
- CMAD 94925 606-G1
PROSPECT PL
700 NVTO 94945 526-C3
PROSPECT PTH
- MrnC 94941 606-F5
PROSPECT ST
- PET 94952 465-D6
PUEBLO DR
- MrnC 94903 546-E7
PUENTE DEL MAR
- MrnC 94970 605-C3
PUENTE RIZAL
- MrnC 94970 605-C3
PUFFIN CT
- NVTO 94949 546-E5
PURPLE GATE RD
- MrnC 94924 604-D3
PURRINGTON RD
- SonC 94952 (485-F2
See Page 465)
PURVINE RD
- SonC 94952 463-J2
100 SonC 94952 (464-A5
See Page 463)
PUTNAM WY
1600 PET 94954 465-H4

Q

QUAIL CT
- MrnC 94903 546-E6
- NVTO 94949 546-E5
QUAIL DR
1400 PET 94954 465-H5
QUAIL RDGE
- ROSS 94957 586-B3
- MrnC 94904 586-B3
QUAIL WY
- MrnC 94960 566-B4
QUARRY RD
- MLV 94941 606-C1
- SRFL 94901 566-F7
QUEEN RD
- MrnC 94924 604-E4
QUEENS LN
- SonC 94952 (464-D1
See Page 463)
QUEENSTONE DR
2400 MrnC 94903 546-D6
QUEENSTONE FIRE RD
- MrnC 94903 546-B5
QUERCUS CT
400 NVTO 94945 526-D4
QUEVA VISTA
- NVTO 94945 525-J2
QUIETWOOD DR
300 MrnC 94903 546-D7
QUINCE CT
- NVTO 94947 526-D7
QUISISANA DR
- MrnC 94904 586-E3

R

RACCOON CT
- NVTO 94949 546-D4
RACCOON RD
- NVTO 94949 546-D4
RACOON LN
- TBRN 94920 607-E7
RACQUET CT
- NVTO 94947 525-G3
RACQUET CLUB DR
- SRFL 94901 566-D6
RADIO INTELLIGENCE RD
- NVTO 94949 546-G3
RAE LN
800 NVTO 94947 525-H3
RAFAEL AV
- MrnC 94924 604-G2
RAFAEL DR
- SRFL 94901 566-G7
RAFAEL WY
- MrnC 94903 566-G3
RAFAEL PATIO
- MrnC 94970 605-B3
RAFFLES CT
- PET 94954 (466-A5
See Page 465)
- PET 94954 465-J5
RAILROAD AV
- MrnC 94945 527-A4
- MrnC 94971 (462-B3
See Page 461)
- MrnC 94973 565-C2
- SRFL 94901 587-A2
800 NVTO 94945 526-C2
RAILROAD ST
- MrnC 94971 (462-B4
See Page 461)
RAILROAD GRADE FIRE RD
- MLV 94941 586-B7
- MLV 94941 606-B1
- MrnC 94965 586-B7
- MrnC 94965 585-J7
- MrnC 94965 606-A1
- MrnC 94965 605-H1
RAINBOW LN
- MLV 94941 606-D4
RAINBOW RD
- MrnC 94903 566-E5
RAINER AV
1500 PET 94954 465-E3
RAINSVILLE RD
- SonC 94952 (464-H1
See Page 463)
700 PET 94952 (464-H1
See Page 463)
RALLY CT
- FRFX 94930 565-G4
RALSTON AV
- MLV 94941 606-C1
400 MLV 94941 586-C7
RAMEN RD
- SonC 94952 (464-B2
See Page 463)
RAMONA AV
- MrnC 94933 (564-H2
See Page 543)
RAMONA CT
- NVTO 94945 525-J1
- PET 94952 465-F6
- PET 94954 465-F6
RAMONA LN
1100 PET 94954 465-G5
RAMONA WY
- NVTO 94945 525-J1
- SANS 94960 566-A6
RAMSEY RD
12500 SonC 95472 (422-C1
See Page 421)
RANCH LN
- LKSP 94939 586-F6
RANCH RD
- MrnC 94946 (544-E2
See Page 543)
- MrnC 94903 566-E5
4900 MrnC 94920 607-B1
4900 TBRN 94920 607-B1
RANCHERIA RD
- MrnC 94904 586-D4
600 LKSP 94939 586-D4
RANCHITOS RD
- MrnC 94903 566-F5
- SRFL 94903 566-F5
RANCHO DR
- MrnC 94920 606-J4
- SANS 94960 566-A5
RANCHO LN
100 SonC 94952 (464-F2
See Page 463)
RANCHO WY
700 PET 94954 465-H5
RANCHO BONITO CIR
100 PET 94954 465-J6
RANCHO LINDO RD
1000 PET 94952 (485-F2
See Page 465)
RAND ST
1300 PET 94952 465-B2
1300 PET 94954 465-B2
RANDALL FIRE TR
- MrnC - (564-C7
See Page 543)
RANDOLF DR
100 NVTO 94949 546-G4
RANNOCH WY
- MrnC 94937 (522-F3
See Page 501)
RANSOME DR
1100 NVTO 94949 546-C1
RAPOSA VISTA
- NVTO 94945 525-J2
RASMUSSEN LN
200 SonC 94952 465-A4
RAVEN RD
- MrnC 94960 566-A3
RAVINE WY
- MrnC 94904 586-B4
- MrnC 94947 525-E3
RAY CT
- SRFL 94901 566-D6
- MrnC 94901 566-D6
RAYMOND AV
- SANS 94960 586-B1
- SANS 94960 566-B7
RAYMOND HTS
- PET 94952 465-E7
- PET 94952 (485-E1
See Page 465)
READE LN
- SAUS 94965 627-B3
REBECCA WY
- NVTO 94945 526-D3
REBELO LN
- MrnC 94947 525-E4
REDBUD CT
- NVTO 94945 526-B1
RED CEDAR CT
- MrnC 94903 545-J5
REDDING CT
- TBRN 94920 607-B4
REDDING WY
- SRFL 94901 586-H3
RED HAWK RD
100 NVTO 94949 546-E5
RED HILL AV
- SANS 94960 566-C7
RED HILL CIR
- TBRN 94920 607-D7
RED HILL RD
5200 SonC 94952 (485-A6
See Page 465)
5400 MrnC 94945 (485-A6
See Page 465)
RED MOUNTAIN RD
- MrnC 94903 546-A6
RED OAK CT
- NVTO 94949 546-C1
REDONDA AV
- MrnC 94938 (564-E2
See Page 543)
RED ROCK WY
- SRFL 94901 566-F6
- MrnC 94903 566-F6
REDWOOD AV
- CMAD 94925 586-F7
- LKSP 94939 586-D6
- MrnC 94937 (522-J6
See Page 501)
- MrnC 94965 606-B3
200 CMAD 94925 606-F1
REDWOOD BLVD
- NVTO 94947 546-E1
- NVTO 94949 546-E1
500 NVTO 94947 526-C6
6900 NVTO 94945 526-C2
7800 NVTO 94945 506-C7
7800 MrnC 94945 506-C7
REDWOOD CIR
200 PET 94954 465-G3
REDWOOD DR
- MrnC 94973 565-C2
- ROSS 94957 586-C2
- SRFL 94901 586-E2
200 MrnC 94904 586-C2
N REDWOOD DR
100 SRFL 94903 566-F1
REDWOOD HWY
- LKSP 94904 586-H6
- SRFL 94903 566-E1
1700 CMAD 94925 586-H6
1900 LKSP 94925 586-H6
3700 SonC 94952 (485-H2
See Page 465)
3700 SonC 94954 (485-H2
See Page 465)

STREET
Block City ZIP Pg-Grid

REDWOOD HWY
5300 MrnC 94945 (485-H2
See Page 465)
REDWOOD HWY U.S.-101
- CMAD - 586-H5
- CMAD - 606-G4
- LKSP - 586-H5
- LKSP - 586-H5
- MLV - 606-G4
- MrnC - 506-A2
- MrnC - 546-F6
- MrnC - 546-F7
- MrnC - 566-F1
- MrnC - 566-E2
- MrnC - 586-H5
- MrnC - 606-G4
- MrnC - 626-H1
- MrnC - 627-B4
- NVTO - 506-A2
- NVTO - 526-C3
- NVTO - 546-F7
- PET - 465-A1
- SF - 627-B4
- SRFL - 566-F5
- SRFL - 566-E1
- SAUS - 627-B4
- SAUS - 626-H1
- SRFL - 586-H5
- SRFL - 566-E2
- SonC - (485-H6
See Page 465)
5500 MrnC - (485-H6
See Page 465)
5500 MrnC - 505-J1
REDWOOD LN
- CMAD 94925 606-C3
- MLV 94941 606-C3
REDWOOD RD
- FRFX 94930 565-H5
- SANS 94960 566-A7
400 SANS 94960 586-A1
7000 NVTO 94945 526-C4
REDWOOD WY
1300 PET 94954 465-A1
REDWOOD CANYON DR
- MrnC 94963 565-B2
REDWOOD CANYON FIRE RD
- MrnC 94946 545-D1
REDWOOD CREEK TR
- MrnC 94965 606-A6
- MrnC 94965 605-J7
REDWOOD HIGHWAY FRONTAGE RD
- MrnC 94920 606-G5
200 MLV 94941 606-G6
500 MrnC 94941 606-G5
3500 SRFL 94903 566-E2
REED BLVD
- MrnC 94941 606-H4
REED CIR
200 MrnC 94941 606-H5
REED ST
- MrnC 94941 606-E5
- MLV 94941 606-E5
REEDLAND WOODS WY
- TBRN 94920 606-J3
REED RANCH RD
- TBRN 94920 607-A4
REGALIA DR
- NVTO 94945 525-H2
REGENT CT
- NVTO 94947 526-A4
REGINA CT
700 PET 94954 465-G5
REGINA WY
- SRFL 94903 566-C3
REICHERT AV
800 NVTO 94945 526-C4
REICHERT CT
- NVTO 94945 526-C4
RENA CT
- NVTO 94947 525-J3
RENAISSANCE RD
- MrnC 94945 526-J4
- NVTO 94945 526-J4
RENATA CT
- NVTO 94947 526-C7
RENE DR
100 PET 94954 465-F4
RENZ RD
- MLV 94941 606-C3
RESACA AV
- MrnC 94933 (564-G2
See Page 543)
- MrnC 94938 (564-G2
See Page 543)
RESERVA LN
- TBRN 94920 627-F1
RESERVOIR AV
- NVTO 94945 525-J2
RESERVOIR DR
600 NVTO 94945 526-C3
RESERVOIR RD
- NVTO 94949 546-H2
- SRFL 94901 586-E1
REYNOLDS DR
500 PET 94954 465-F5

RHINESTONE TER
- MrnC 94903 546-E5
RHONDA WY
200 MrnC 94941 606-E5
RICARDO LN
- MrnC 94941 606-H4
RICARDO RD
100 MrnC 94941 606-H5
RICA VISTA
- NVTO 94947 525-J3
RICCI CT
- PET 94952 465-C6
RICE DR
- SRFL 94901 586-G2
RICE LN
- LKSP 94939 586-F6
- MrnC 94941 606-H5
RICH ST
- LKSP 94904 586-H6
RICHARDSON CT
300 MrnC 94965 606-F7
RICHARDSON DR
100 MrnC 94941 606-H4
RICHARDSON ST
200 SAUS 94965 627-B4
RICHARDSON WY
300 MrnC 94965 606-F7
RICHIE LN
- NVTO 94947 525-H4
RICHMOND RD
- SANS 94960 586-C1
RICHMOND-SAN RAFAEL BRDG I-580
- MrnC - 587-C5
- RCH - 587-H6
- SRFL - 587-C5
RIDER LN
- MLV 94941 606-D2
RIDGE AV
- MrnC 94965 606-B4
- SRFL 94901 566-H7
RIDGE CT
- CMAD 94925 606-H2
RIDGE LN
- MrnC 94965 606-B4
RIDGE RD
- FRFX 94930 565-H6
- SANS 94960 566-B5
- SAUS 94965 627-A4
- MrnC 94965 627-A4
300 NVTO 94947 526-A5
300 NVTO 94947 525-J5
400 TBRN 94920 607-E7
500 MrnC 94920 607-E7
RIDGE TR
- MrnC - (563-G6
See Page 543)
- MrnC - (584-A1
See Page 583)
RIDGE WY
- CMAD 94925 586-F7
RIDGECREST BLVD
- MrnC - 585-B5
- MrnC - 605-G1
- MrnC 94965 605-G1
- MrnC 94970 585-C7
- MrnC 94970 605-G1
100 MrnC 94965 586-A7
100 MrnC 94965 585-J7
RIDGECREST RD
- MrnC 94904 586-C5
RIDGE VIEW CT
1200 NVTO 94947 526-C7
RIDGEVIEW CT
- MrnC 94965 606-G7
RIDGE VIEW DR
- NVTO 94949 546-G5
RIDGEVIEW DR
100 PET 94952 (485-E2
See Page 465)
800 MrnC 94965 606-D5
RIDGE VIEW HTS
1200 NVTO 94947 526-C7
RIDGE VIEW LN
- MrnC 94956 523-C7
RIDGEWAY
- LKSP 94939 586-D6
RIDGEWAY AV
- FRFX 94930 565-J5
RIDGEWAY LN
- CMAD 94925 606-C5
- LKSP 94939 586-E7
- LKSP 94939 606-C5
RIDGEWOOD AV
300 MrnC 94941 606-C4
RIDGEWOOD DR
- SRFL 94901 566-D5
N RIDGEWOOD RD
- MrnC 94904 586-C4
S RIDGEWOOD RD
- MrnC 94904 586-C4
RIDGEWOOD FIRE RD
- MrnC 94960 566-C5
- SANS 94960 566-C5
200 SRFL 94903 566-C5
200 MrnC 94901 566-C5
RIFTZONE TR
- MrnC - 543-E6
- MrnC - (564-A6
See Page 543)

RIFTZONE TR
- MrnC - (563-G1
See Page 543)
- MrnC - (584-B1
See Page 583)
RINCON WY
800 MrnC 94903 566-H2
RIO NIDO CT
1500 PET 94954 465-J6
RIO NIDO WY
1500 PET 94954 465-J6
RIO VISTA WY
- PET 94952 465-D5
RISCIONI RD
- SonC 94954 (466-H7
See Page 465)
- SonC 95476 (466-H7
See Page 465)
RISING RD
- NVTO 94945 526-A1
100 MrnC 94941 606-F5
RITA CT
- NVTO 94945 526-D3
RITTER ST
- SRFL 94901 586-G1
RIVERA ST
- SANS 94960 566-B6
RIVER OAKS RD
- SRFL 94901 566-D6
RIVER VISTA LN
- NVTO 94945 526-H1
RIVIERA CIR
- LKSP 94939 586-F5
RIVIERA DR
- SRFL 94901 567-D6
RIVIERA PL
- SRFL 94901 567-D5
RIVIERA MANOR RD
- SRFL 94901 567-E5
ROBERT CT
- SRFL 94901 566-E7
E ROBERT DR
- MrnC 94956 (522-J6
See Page 501)
W ROBERT DR
- MrnC 94956 (522-J6
See Page 501)
ROBERT DOLLAR SCENIC DR
- SRFL 94901 566-F6
ROBERTS AV
- SRFL 94901 586-F2
ROBERTSON TER
- MLV 94941 606-E4
ROBIN DR
300 CMAD 94925 607-A1
ROBIN RD
300 MrnC 94965 606-F7
ROBIN WY
800 PET 94954 465-G5
ROBINHOOD DR
- SRFL 94901 567-B6
ROBINHOOD LN
- NVTO 94945 526-D3
ROBLAR DR
100 NVTO 94949 546-F2
ROBLE CT
- SANS 94960 566-A5
ROBLE RD
- SRFL 94901 586-E1
ROCA CT
- NVTO 94947 525-G4
ROCCA DR
- FRFX 94930 565-J5
- PET 94952 465-D6
ROCHE RD
- SonC 94954 (486-E3
See Page 465)
ROCK RD
- ROSS 94957 586-B3
- MrnC 94904 586-B3
ROCKEN LN
700 NVTO 94947 525-H3
ROCK HILL DR
- TBRN 94920 607-C5
ROCKLYN CT
- CMAD 94925 586-F7
ROCKPORT CV
- SRFL 94901 587-A2
ROCKPORT WY
200 NVTO 94947 526-E6
ROCK RIDGE RD
- FRFX 94930 565-H5
- MrnC 94973 565-C3
ROCK ROSE CT
- MrnC 94903 545-J5
ROCKROSE WY
- NVTO 94945 526-B2
ROCK SPRINGS TR
- MrnC - 605-F2
- MrnC 94965 605-G2
ROCK SPRINGS LAGUNITAS RD
- MrnC - 585-G7
- MrnC - 605-F1
ROCKY RIDGE RD
- MrnC - 585-F4
RODEO AV
- MrnC 94938 (564-F1
See Page 543)

RODEO AV
- SAUS 94965 626-J2
ROGER AV
- SANS 94960 566-C7
ROGER DR
- SRFL 94901 566-G6
ROGERS LN
1900 PET 94954 465-J4
ROHDE LN
100 SonC 94952 (464-H4
See Page 463)
ROLLING HILLS RD
- TBRN 94920 607-D6
ROLLINGWOOD DR
- SRFL 94901 567-B6
ROMAR CT
- NVTO 94945 526-B2
ROMERO CT
- NVTO 94945 525-J1
RONDEE LN
- NVTO 94945 526-A2
ROOSEVELT AV
- MLV 94941 606-D2
- MrnC 94903 566-G4
ROQUE MORAES CT
- MLV 94941 606-F4
ROQUE MORAES DR
- MLV 94941 606-G4
ROSAL WY
600 MrnC 94903 566-H2
ROSALIA DR
1000 NVTO 94945 526-D3
ROSARIO RD
- MrnC 94933 (564-G2
See Page 543)
ROSE AV
- MLV 94941 606-B3
- SANS 94960 586-B1
ROSE CT
- SAUS 94965 627-B3
ROSE ST
- NVTO 94945 526-C3
- SRFL 94901 586-H3
- MrnC 94901 586-H3
ROSEBANK AV
- MrnC 94904 586-E3
ROSEBANK LN
- MrnC 94904 586-E3
ROSE BOWL DR
- SAUS 94965 627-A4
ROSE COURT TER
- MrnC 94945 526-E4
ROSEMARY CT
- NVTO 94945 526-B2
2100 PET 94954 465-J4
ROSEMONT AV
- SANS 94960 566-A5
200 MrnC 94941 606-F6
ROSE PETAL CT
100 PET 94954 465-F3
ROSEVILLE CT
- TBRN 94920 607-B4
ROSEWOOD CIR
500 PET 94954 465-D3
ROSEWOOD CT
- SRFL 94901 567-C6
ROSEWOOD DR
- NVTO 94947 526-D6
ROSEWOOD RD
100 MrnC 94924 604-D3
ROSINA CT
600 PET 94954 465-F6
ROSS AV
- SANS 94960 586-B1
ROSS COM
- ROSS 94957 586-C2
ROSS DR
300 MrnC 94965 606-F7
ROSS RD
- SAUS 94965 626-H1
ROSS ST
- SRFL 94901 586-E1
1300 PET 94954 465-B1
ROSS STREET TER
- SRFL 94901 586-F1
ROSS VALLEY DR
- SRFL 94901 566-D7
- SRFL 94901 586-D1
ROUND CT
100 PET 94952 (485-E2
See Page 465)
ROUND HILL RD
- TBRN 94920 607-D5
ROUNDTREE BLVD
- MrnC 94903 546-E7
ROUNDTREE WY
100 MrnC 94903 546-E7
ROVINA LN
- SonC 94952 465-F7
- SonC 94952 (485-F1
See Page 465)
ROWAN WY
- MLV 94941 606-C1
ROWLAND AV
- SANS 94960 566-B7
ROWLAND BLVD
- NVTO 94949 526-B7
300 NVTO 94947 526-D5
ROWLAND CT
- NVTO 94947 526-B6

ROWLAND WY
- NVTO 94945 526-D5
- NVTO 94947 526-D5
ROWLEY CIR
- TBRN 94920 607-B5
ROY CT
- NVTO 94947 525-G2
ROYAL CT
- SRFL 94901 586-J1
ROYAL OAK DR
1500 PET 94954 465-D2
ROYAL OAK TER
1200 NVTO 94947 526-D6
RUBEN CT
- NVTO 94947 525-G3
RUBICON CT
- MrnC 94903 546-A6
RUBICON DR
- MrnC 94903 546-A6
RUDNICK AV
- NVTO 94945 526-D3
RUHLMAN LN
1100 NVTO 94945 525-J2
RUSH CREEK PL
900 NVTO 94945 526-C2
RUSH LANDING RD
100 NVTO 94945 526-C1
200 NVTO 94945 506-C7
RUSHMORE AV
100 PET 94954 465-E3
RUSSEL AV
- MrnC 94904 586-D3
RUSTIC WY
- SRFL 94901 566-F6
RUTH CT
- NVTO 94945 526-A3
800 PET 94952 465-B6
RUTHERFORD AV
- SANS 94960 566-A5
RUTTENBERRY RD
- SonC 94952 465-B5
RYAN AV
- MLV 94941 606-F4
RYAN LN
4300 SonC 94952 465-A2
RYDAL AV
300 MrnC 94941 606-D5

S

SABA LN
- MrnC 94920 607-C2
SACRAMENTO AV
- MrnC 94901 566-C5
- MrnC 94960 566-C5
- SAUS 94965 626-H1
100 SANS 94960 566-C5
SACRAMENTO WY
- SAUS 94965 627-B3
SACRAMENTO PATIO
- MrnC 94970 605-B3
SADDLE LN
- MrnC 94947 525-F3
SADDLEBROOK CT
- NVTO 94947 525-J4
SADDLE CUT
600 MrnC - 565-E5
SADY LN
- FRFX 94930 565-J6
SAGE CT
- NVTO 94945 526-A1
SAGEBRUSH CT
- SRFL 94901 567-C5
SAGE GROUSE RD
- NVTO 94949 546-E5
SAGHALIE LN
- SAUS 94965 627-B3
SAILMAKER CT
- SRFL 94901 566-G2
SAINT ANDREW CT
1200 PET 94954 465-H6
SAINT ANDREWS DR
- NVTO 94949 546-A2
SAINT ANNE WY
1600 PET 94954 465-G4
SAINT ANTHONY LN
1100 PET 94954 465-H6
SAINT AUGUSTINE CIR
2100 PET 94954 465-H4
SAINT AUGUSTINE CT
- PET 94954 465-H4
SAINT AUGUSTINE WY
1900 PET 94954 465-H4
SAINT BERNARD LN
- TBRN 94920 607-E7
SAINT BERNARD RD
- TBRN 94920 607-E7
SAINT FRANCIS AV
700 NVTO 94947 525-G3
SAINT FRANCIS DR
600 PET 94954 465-F6
SAINT FRANCIS LN
100 SRFL 94901 566-H7
SAINT GABRIELLE CT
- TBRN 94920 607-E6
SAINT JOHN CT
- NVTO 94947 525-G3
SAINT JOSEPH WY
1200 PET 94954 465-H6

SAINT JUDE LN
- MrnC 94965 606-B3
SAINT LOUIS CT
800 PET 94954 465-G5
SAINT LUCIA PL
- MrnC 94920 607-C2
SAINT PAUL CIR
- NVTO 94947 526-A3
SAINT THOMAS WY
- MrnC 94920 607-C2
SAINT VINCENT CT
1100 PET 94954 465-H6
SAINT VINCENTS DR
- MrnC 94903 546-F6
SAIS AV
- SANS 94960 566-B7
SALEM CV
- SRFL 94901 587-A2
SALINAS AV
- SANS 94960 566-B5
SALIX AV
- MrnC 94973 565-D4
SALMON CREEK RD
200 SonC 94923 421-A2
300 SonC 95465 421-A2
SALT LNDG
- MrnC 94920 606-H3
SALT CREEK LN
- MLV 94941 606-G2
SALVADOR WY
- SRFL 94903 566-E1
SALVATORE DR
- NVTO 94949 546-E2
SAMOA LN
700 NVTO 94947 526-E6
SAMROSE DR
- NVTO 94945 526-E3
100 MrnC 94945 526-E3
SAMUEL DR
900 PET 94952 465-C4
SAN ALESO WY
- NVTO 94945 525-H1
SAN ANDREAS CIR
- NVTO 94945 525-H1
SAN ANDREAS CT
- NVTO 94945 525-H1
SAN ANDREAS DR
- NVTO 94945 525-H1
300 NVTO 94945 505-H7
SAN ANSELMO AV
- SANS 94960 566-A7
1400 SANS 94960 586-C1
1700 ROSS 94957 586-C1
SAN ANTONIO RD
100 SonC 94952 (485-B6
See Page 465)
SAN ARDO CT
- NVTO 94945 505-H7
SAN BENITO WY
- NVTO 94945 525-H1
SAN BLAS CT
- NVTO 94945 525-H1
SAN CARLOS AV
- SAUS 94965 627-B3
SAN CARLOS DR
- PET 94952 465-E5
SAN CARLOS WY
- NVTO 94945 525-J1
400 NVTO 94945 505-J7
SANCHEZ RD
- MrnC 94933 (564-G2
See Page 543)
SANCHEZ WY
- MrnC 94947 525-E3
SAN CLEMENTE DR
- CMAD 94925 586-H7
- CMAD 94925 606-H1
SAND RD
3200 MrnC 94971 461-F4
SANDALWOOD CT
- SRFL 94903 566-C2
SANDBURG CT
- MLV 94941 606-H6
SAN DOMINGO WY
- NVTO 94945 505-H7
- NVTO 94945 525-G1
SANDPIPER CIR
- CMAD 94925 586-G6
SANDPIPER CT
- SRFL 94903 566-G3
100 NVTO 94949 546-F5
SANDSTONE CT
- MrnC 94903 546-E5
SANDY CREEK WY
- LKSP 94939 586-E5
SAN FELIPE WY
- NVTO 94945 525-G1
SANFORD ST
- CMAD 94925 586-G7
SAN FRANCISCO BLVD
- SANS 94960 566-B6
400 MrnC 94901 566-B6
500 MrnC 94960 566-B6
SAN GABRIEL CT
- FRFX 94930 565-J5
SAN GABRIEL DR
- FRFX 94930 565-J5

SAN GERONIMO RIDGE RD
- MrnC 94963 (564-F4
See Page 543)
6600 MrnC - 565-A4
6800 MrnC 94973 565-B4
6900 MrnC 94963 565-A4
6900 MrnC - (564-F4
See Page 543)
7200 MrnC 94933 (564-F4
See Page 543)
7200 MrnC 94938 (564-F4
See Page 543)
SAN GERONIMO VALLEY DR
5200 MrnC 94973 565-A2
5600 MrnC 94963 565-A2
5900 MrnC 94963 (564-J2
See Page 543)
SAN GREGORIO CT
- NVTO 94947 525-G4
SAN JOAQUIN CT
- NVTO 94947 525-F3
SAN JOAQUIN PL
- NVTO 94947 525-F3
SAN JOSE BLVD
800 NVTO 94949 546-C1
SAN JOSE DR
100 NVTO 94949 546-H4
SAN JOSE WY
1200 PET 94954 465-H6
SAN JUAN CT
- NVTO 94945 525-H1
SAN JUAN WY
1200 PET 94954 465-H6
SAN LUIS CT
- NVTO 94945 525-J1
SAN LUIS WY
100 NVTO 94945 525-J1
SAN MARCOS CT
- NVTO 94945 525-H1
SAN MARCOS PL
- SRFL 94901 567-D6
SAN MARIN DR
- NVTO 94945 526-A1
300 NVTO 94945 525-G1
SAN MARINO CT
- SRFL 94901 567-E5
SAN MARINO DR
- SRFL 94901 567-D6
1600 PET 94954 465-H5
SAN MARINO PL
- SRFL 94901 567-D6
SAN MATEO CT
- SRFL 94903 566-C3
SAN MATEO WY
- NVTO 94945 525-J1
100 NVTO 94945 505-J7
SAN MIGUEL CT
- FRFX 94930 565-H5
- NVTO 94945 525-H2
SAN MIGUEL WY
- NVTO 94945 525-H2
SAN PABLO AV
- NVTO 94949 546-H4
- MrnC 94903 566-F5
- SRFL 94903 566-F5
SAN PABLO WY
900 NVTO 94949 546-G2
SAN PAULO WY
400 NVTO 94949 546-F2
N SAN PEDRO CT
- MrnC 94903 566-H3
N SAN PEDRO RD
- SRFL 94901 567-B3
- SRFL 94903 566-F5
100 MrnC 94903 566-J2
400 MrnC 94903 567-B3
SAN QUENTIN TER
- MrnC 94964 587-B5
SAN RAFAEL AV
- SANS 94960 566-B7
- SRFL 94901 586-E2
- TBRN 94920 607-C7
- BLV 94920 607-C7
400 BLV 94920 627-D1
SAN RAFAEL ST
100 MrnC 94945 527-A4
SAN RAFAEL WY
1100 PET 94954 465-H6
SAN RAMON WY
- NVTO 94945 525-G1
SAN SEBASTIAN DR
300 NVTO 94949 546-F2
SANTA ANA CT
- TBRN 94920 607-E6
SANTA BARBARA AV
- SANS 94960 566-B6
SANTA BARBARA WY
1100 PET 94954 465-H6
SANTA CLARA CT
- SRFL 94903 566-C3
SANTA CLARA LN
1000 PET 94954 465-H6
SANTA CRUZ AV
- SANS 94960 566-B6
SANTA GABRIELLA CT
- NVTO 94945 525-G1
SANTA INES CT
1200 PET 94954 465-H6

SANTA INES WY
1200 PET 94954 465-H6
SANTA MARGARITA DR
- SRFL 94901 566-D7
SANTA MARIA CT
100 NVTO 94947 525-G3
SANTA MARIA DR
- NVTO 94947 525-G4
SANTANA RD
500 NVTO 94945 526-G1
SANTA ROSA AV
- SAUS 94965 627-A3
SANTA VICTORIA CT
- NVTO 94945 525-G1
SANTA YNEZ CIR
- NVTO 94947 525-G3
SANTA YORMA CT
- NVTO 94945 525-G1
SANTIAGO CT
- NVTO 94947 526-A3
SANTIAGO WY
- SRFL 94903 546-D7
- SRFL 94903 566-D1
SANTOLINA DR
1100 NVTO 94945 526-B2
SAO AUGUSTINE WY
- SRFL 94903 566-E4
SAPPORO CT
- PET 94954 (466-A5
See Page 465)
SARAH DR
- MLV 94941 606-F2
SARAH WY
300 PET 94954 465-G3
SARATOGA CT
100 PET 94954 465-D3
SARKESIAN DR
1400 PET 94954 465-G4
SARTORI DR
600 PET 94954 465-J6
SARTORI RD
- SonC 94952 463-G6
SAUNDERS AV
- SANS 94960 566-B6
SAUSALITO BLVD
- SAUS 94965 627-A4
SAUSALITO ST
200 CMAD 94925 586-G7
200 CMAD 94925 606-G1
SAUSALITO FERRY
- BLV - 627-C3
- MrnC - 627-C3
- SAUS - 627-C3
- SF - 627-H5
- TBRN - 627-C3
SAUSALITO FISHERMANS WARF FER
- MrnC - 627-F4
- SF - 627-F4
- TBRN - 627-F4
SAUSALITO-LATERAL
- SAUS 94965 627-B5
SAUSALITO TIBURON FERRY
- SF - 627-H6
SAUTTER RD
- SonC 94952 (464-J6
See Page 463)
SAVANNA CIR
- NVTO 94947 526-B7
SAVANNAH RD
- SANS 94960 566-B7
SCENIC AV
- SANS 94960 566-A7
- SRFL 94901 566-E7
SCENIC DR
- NVTO 94949 546-G5
SCENIC LN
- SAUS 94965 627-A3
SCENIC RD
- FRFX 94930 565-H5
SCENIC TR
- FRFX 94930 565-G5
SCENIC WY
- PET 94952 (485-C1
See Page 465)
SCETTRINI DR
- SRFL 94903 566-E3
SCETTRINI FIRE RD
100 SRFL 94903 566-G5
200 SRFL 94901 566-G5
200 MrnC 94903 566-G5
SCHAAF CT
- SRFL 94901 566-D7
SCHIRADO PL
- MrnC 94901 586-J1
SCHMIDT LN
- MrnC 94903 566-G3
SCHOOL RD
300 MrnC 94945 526-G3
SCHOOL ST
- FRFX 94930 565-J6
14400 SonC 94972 (442-A1
See Page 421)
SCHOOL TER
- MrnC 94945 526-G3
SCHUMAN LN
800 PET 94952 465-B5
SCHWMAN LN
1200 PET 94952 465-B5

SCOTIA LN
100 NVTO 94947 526-D7
SCOTT CIR
- NVTO 94949 546-G4
SCOTT LN
- LKSP 94939 586-E6
SCOTT PL
- LKSP 94939 586-G5
SCOTT RD
800 SonC 94954 (466-F3
See Page 465)
SCOTT ST
- MrnC 94973 565-C2
200 MrnC 94941 606-E4
700 NVTO 94945 526-C3
1300 PET 94954 465-B1
SCOTTSDALE WY
- NVTO 94947 526-C6
SCOTT TANK FIRE RD
- MrnC - 585-G1
SCOWN LN
800 NVTO 94945 526-C3
SEA WY
- SRFL 94901 587-A1
SEACAPE DR
- MrnC 94965 626-A2
- MrnC 94965 625-J2
SEADRIFT LNDG
- MrnC 94920 606-H3
SEADRIFT RD
- MrnC 94970 605-A3
- MrnC 94970 604-H2
SEAFIRTH LN
- TBRN 94920 607-C4
SEAFIRTH PL
- TBRN 94920 607-C4
SEAFIRTH RD
- TBRN 94920 607-C4
- MrnC 94920 607-C4
SEAGULL RW
100 NVTO 94947 526-C4
SEAMAST PASG
- CMAD 94925 606-J1
- CMAD 94925 586-J7
SEARLES LN
- SANS 94960 566-C6
SEARS POINT HWY Rt#-37
- MrnC 94945 526-G5
- NVTO 94945 526-G5
- SonC - 527-A2
- SonC - 526-G5
- SonC 94954 527-A2
SEASCAPE DR
500 NVTO 94947 526-D7
SEAVER DR
500 MLV 94941 606-G4
SEAVEY LN
- SonC 94952 463-F5
SEAVEY RD
- SonC 94952 463-G5
SEA VIEW AV
- MrnC 94901 586-J1
W SEA VIEW AV
- MrnC 94901 586-J1
- SRFL 94901 586-J1
SEA VIEW CT
- MrnC 94901 566-J7
- MrnC 94901 586-J1
- SRFL 94901 566-J7
SEAWOLF PASG
- CMAD 94925 606-J1
SECOND AV
- MrnC 94971 (462-B4
See Page 461)
SEIBEL ST
- SRFL 94901 586-F2
SELFRIDGE WY
- NVTO 94949 546-G4
SEMINARY DR
100 MrnC 94941 606-H5
SEMINARY RD
- SANS 94960 586-B1
SEMINOLE AV
- CMAD 94925 586-G7
SENTINEL CT
- SRFL 94901 566-E7
- SRFL 94901 586-E1
SEQUIERA RD
- MrnC 94903 546-C7
- SRFL 94903 546-C7
SEQUOIA DR
- NVTO 94949 546-J5
- SANS 94960 566-C6
SEQUOIA RD
- FRFX 94930 565-H5
SEQUOIA GLEN LN
- NVTO 94947 526-D7
SEQUOIA VALLEY RD
600 MLV 94941 606-C3
600 MrnC 94941 606-C3
SERENO WY
- NVTO 94945 526-A1
SERPILIO WY
1400 PET 94954 465-D3
SERRA ST
- CMAD 94925 586-F7
SERRA WY
- SRFL 94903 566-B2

SEVILLE DR
- MrnC 94903 546-E7
SEVILLE WY
700 NVTO 94949 546-F2
W SEXTON RD
- SonC 95472 (422-E1
See Page 421)
SEXTON VIEW LN
1500 SonC 95472 (422-F1
See Page 421)
SEYMOUR LN
300 MrnC 94941 606-D4
SHADOW CREEK CT
- FRFX 94930 565-G3
SHADY LN
- LKSP 94939 586-E7
- ROSS 94957 586-C2
- SonC 94952 465-A4
300 MLV 94941 606-D1
2000 NVTO 94945 525-J2
SHAFER DR
1000 NVTO 94949 546-C1
SHAKIN CT
- MrnC 94956 (522-J7
See Page 501)
SHALLOW BEACH RD
- MrnC - (502-D7
See Page 501)
SHAMROCK RD
- SonC 94952 (484-H1
See Page 463)
SHANKLIN CT
- NVTO 94945 526-A2
SHANLEY LN
- ROSS 94957 586-C1
SHANNON CT
- NVTO 94949 546-C1
- NVTO 94949 526-C7
SHANNON LN
- SRFL 94901 566-D6
- MrnC 94901 566-D6
SHARI CT
- NVTO 94947 526-C7
SHARILYN LN
- NVTO 94947 525-H2
SHASTA AV
- PET 94952 465-D5
SHASTA WY
500 MrnC 94965 606-E6
SHAVER ST
- SRFL 94901 586-F1
SHAVER GRADE FIRE
- MrnC - 585-G2
SHAVER GRADE FIRE RD
- MrnC - 585-H2
- MrnC 94904 586-A3
- MrnC 94930 586-A3
- MrnC 94930 585-H2
SHAW DR
- MrnC 94901 566-C7
- SANS 94960 566-C7
SHAYAN CT
- MrnC 94941 606-H4
SHEFFIELD AV
300 MrnC 94941 606-F6
SHEILA CT
- NVTO 94947 525-G2
- SANS 94960 566-A4
SHELASKY RD
- SonC 94952 465-A4
SHELDON ST
400 PET 94952 465-C7
SHELDRAKE CT
- MrnC 94903 546-E6
SHELL CT
- MrnC 94941 606-G3
SHELL RD
- MLV 94941 606-G3
- MrnC 94941 606-G3
SHELLEY DR
- MLV 94941 606-G4
SHELTER BAY AV
1000 MLV 94941 606-G5
SHEMRAN CT
- FRFX 94930 565-G2
SHENANDOAH PL
- SRFL 94903 566-F1
SHEPHERD WY
- TBRN 94920 607-B3
SHERIDAN CT
- MLV 94941 606-E1
SHERMAN AV
900 NVTO 94945 526-C3
SHERMAN ST
- FRFX 94930 565-A6
SHERRI CT
300 PET 94952 (485-E1
See Page 465)
SHERWOOD CT
- MrnC 94904 586-E4
SHERWOOD DR
400 MrnC 94945 606-G7
SHERWOOD PL
- NVTO 94945 526-D3
SHEVELIN RD
100 NVTO 94947 526-C7
SHIELDS LN
- NVTO 94947 525-H4

STREET	Block	City	ZIP	Pg-Grid
SHIRE LN				
	-	SonC	95472	(422-H2 See Page 421)
SHON CT				
	-	NVTO	94947	526-B7
SHON DR				
	-	NVTO	94947	526-B7
SHORELINE HWY RT#-1				
	8200	MrnC	-	(564-A5 See Page 543)
	8500	MrnC	-	(563-H2 See Page 543)
	10000	MrnC	-	543-D2
	10100	MrnC	94950	543-D2
	10800	MrnC	94956	543-D2
	11800	MrnC	94940	523-C5
	11800	MrnC	94956	523-C5
SHORELINE PKWY				
	100	SRFL	94901	587-A4
SHORES CT				
	-	SRFL	94903	566-G3
SHORT LN				
	-	LKSP	94939	586-F6
SHORT TR				
	-	CMAD	94925	606-C5
SHORT WY				
	-	LKSP	94939	586-F7
SHUCK DR				
	-	MrnC	94941	606-H5
SIDNEY CT				
	-	MrnC	94903	566-H3
SIDNEY ST				
	-	MLV	94941	606-E3
SIEMER RD				
	-	SonC	94952	463-J5
SIENNA WY				
	-	SRFL	94901	566-H6
SIERRA AV				
	-	SANS	94960	566-A6
SIERRA CIR				
	-	SRFL	94901	586-E2
SIERRA CT				
	-	TBRN	94920	607-B4
SIERRA DR				
	1400	PET	94954	465-G5
SIERRA TR				
	-	MrnC	94965	605-J2
SIERRA VISTA				
	-	NVTO	94947	525-J2
SILACE RD				
	-	SonC	94954	(486-C1 See Page 465)
SILK OAK CIR				
	-	SRFL	94901	567-C5
SILVA LN				
	-	MrnC	94947	525-H4
SILVA RD				
	-	PET	94954	465-G7
	-	SonC	94952	(464-J4 See Page 463)
SILVEIRA PKWY				
	1500	SRFL	94903	566-G1
SILVERADO CIR				
	-	PET	94954	465-J5
SILVERADO DR				
	500	TBRN	94920	607-B4
SILVER HILLS RD				
	-	MrnC	94956	543-A2
SILVER LACE CT				
	-	MrnC	94903	545-J6
SILVER PINE TER				
	-	MrnC	94903	545-J5
SILVO LN				
	300	NVTO	94947	526-D7
SIMMONDS RD				
	-	MrnC	94965	626-F6
SIMMONS CT				
	-	NVTO	94945	525-J2
SIMMONS LN				
	900	NVTO	94945	525-J2
	1000	NVTO	94945	526-A2
SIMMONS TR				
	-	MrnC	-	585-F7
	-	MrnC	-	605-F1
SIMMS ST				
	-	SRFL	94901	586-J3
SIMON DR				
	200	PET	94952	(485-E3 See Page 465)
SINALOA CT				
	-	NVTO	94947	525-H4
SINOLA AV				
	-	MrnC	94938	(564-G2 See Page 543)
SIRARD LN				
	-	SRFL	94901	566-D6
SIR FRANCIS DRAKE BLVD				
	-	FRFX	94930	565-G4
	-	LKSP	94904	586-C2
	-	MrnC	94904	586-C2
	-	LKSP	94939	586-C2
	200	MrnC	94930	565-G4
	400	SANS	94960	566-A6
	600	FRFX	94930	566-A6
	1200	SANS	94960	586-C2
	1300	ROSS	94957	586-C2
	5000	MrnC	94973	565-B2
	6000	MrnC	94963	(564-G1 See Page 543)
	6400	MrnC	94933	(564-G1 See Page 543)
	6700	MrnC	-	565-G4
	7000	MrnC	94938	(564-G1 See Page 543)
	7300	MrnC	-	(564-G1 See Page 543)
	8300	MrnC	-	(544-A4 See Page 543)
	9000	MrnC	94946	(544-A4 See Page 543)
	9800	MrnC	94946	543-F4
	10000	MrnC	-	543-F4
	10200	MrnC	94950	543-F4
	11100	MrnC	94956	543-B1
	12400	MrnC	94956	523-A6
	12900	MrnC	94956	(522-G3 See Page 501)
	13300	MrnC	94937	(522-D2 See Page 501)
	18700	MrnC	-	(521-D6 See Page 501)
	22600	MrnC	-	541-C2
	25800	MrnC	-	(561-A1 See Page 541)
	25800	MrnC	-	(560-J2 See Page 540)
E SIR FRANCIS DRAKE BLVD				
	-	SRFL	94901	587-A5
	-	SRFL	94964	587-A5
	-	LKSP	94904	586-J5
	300	MrnC	94904	586-J5
	400	MrnC	94964	587-A5
	400	MrnC	94964	586-J5
	400	MrnC	94904	587-A5
SKEET RANGE RD				
	-	NVTO	94949	546-G3
SKILLMAN LN				
	100	SonC	94952	465-A3
	1400	SonC	94952	(464-G3 See Page 463)
SKINNER RD				
	-	SonC	94952	(485-H5 See Page 465)
	-	SonC	94954	(485-J5 See Page 465)
SKY RD				
	-	MrnC	94920	606-J4
SKY TR				
	-	MrnC	-	543-A4
	-	MrnC	-	(542-J3 See Page 541)
	-	MrnC	-	(563-B1 See Page 543)
SKYLAND WY				
	-	ROSS	94957	586-D2
SKYLARK DR				
	-	LKSP	94939	586-D5
SKYLINE				
	-	SANS	94960	566-A5
SKYLINE TER				
	-	MrnC	94941	606-D5
SKY OAKS RD				
	200	MrnC	-	585-G1
SKY RANCH DR				
	-	PET	94954	465-G3
SKY TRAIL FIRE RD				
	-	MrnC	94946	525-F7
	-	MrnC	94946	545-F1
SKYVIEW RD				
	-	ROSS	94957	586-D2
SKYVIEW TER				
	-	SRFL	94903	566-D1
SLAUGHTER HOUSE RD				
	500	SonC	94972	(442-A1 See Page 421)
	500	SonC	95472	(442-A1 See Page 421)
	600	MrnC	94972	(442-A1 See Page 421)
SLEEPY HOLLOW DR				
	-	MrnC	94960	566-A3
SLOWDOWN CT				
	500	MrnC	94947	525-H5
SMITH CT				
	400	PET	94952	(485-E2 See Page 465)
SMITH DR				
	300	PET	94952	(485-E2 See Page 465)
SMITH LN				
	-	SANS	94960	566-C7
SMITH RD				
	800	MrnC	94965	606-E7
SMITH RANCH RD				
	-	SRFL	94903	566-F1
	400	SRFL	94903	546-H7
	400	MrnC	94903	546-H7
	400	MrnC	94903	566-F1
SMITH RIDGE FIRE RD				
	-	MrnC	94930	565-F1
	-	MrnC	94960	565-F1
SNAKE RD				
	22700	MrnC	94940	(482-B2 See Page 461)
	23100	MrnC	94940	(462-A7 See Page 461)
SNOWBERRY CT				
	-	SRFL	94901	567-C5
SNOWDEN LN				
	-	MrnC	94930	565-H4
	-	FRFX	94930	565-H4
SOBRE VISTA				
	-	MrnC	94937	(522-E2 See Page 501)
SOLANO ST				
	100	SRFL	94901	566-D6
	100	TBRN	94920	607-F7
SOLAR CT				
	-	SRFL	94901	586-H2
SOLDATE RD				
	-	SonC	94952	(464-D7 See Page 463)
	800	SonC	94954	(466-H6 See Page 465)
SOMERSET DR				
	-	NVTO	94945	526-A1
SOMERSET LN				
	-	MLV	94941	606-G3
SOMERSET PL				
	-	NVTO	94945	526-A1
SOMMER CT				
	-	TBRN	94920	607-B5
SONOMA AV				
	800	PET	94952	465-C7
SONOMA CT				
	1000	PET	94952	465-C3
	1000	PET	94954	465-C2
SONOMA DR				
	500	PET	94954	465-C2
SONOMA ST				
	-	SRFL	94901	586-J2
SONOMA MOUNTAIN PKWY				
	1000	PET	94954	465-D2
SONOMA PATIO				
	-	MrnC	94970	605-A3
SONORA CT				
	-	TBRN	94920	607-B4
SONORA WY				
	-	CMAD	94925	606-J2
SORRENTO WY				
	-	SRFL	94901	587-A1
SOTELO WY				
	-	NVTO	94945	505-J7
SOUSA CT				
	700	PET	94952	465-B5
SOUSA RD				
	-	SonC	94952	(464-H2 See Page 463)
SOUTH CIR				
	200	NVTO	94949	546-J4
SOUTH ST				
	-	SAUS	94965	627-B4
SOUTH TR				
	-	CMAD	94925	606-E1
SOUTH WY				
	-	CMAD	94925	606-G1
SOUTH ELY RD				
	3700	PET	94954	(466-A6 See Page 465)
	3700	SonC	94954	(466-A6 See Page 465)
SOUTHERN HEIGHTS BLVD				
	-	MrnC	94904	586-F2
	-	SRFL	94901	586-F2
SOUTHERN MARIN LINE				
	100	MrnC	-	586-A4
	100	MrnC	-	585-H3
SOUTHGREEN				
	-	LKSP	94939	586-F6
SOUTHPOINT BLVD				
	700	PET	94954	465-D3
SOUTHRIDGE DR				
	-	TBRN	94920	607-A4
SOUTHRIDGE DR E				
	-	TBRN	94920	607-A5
SOUTHRIDGE DR W				
	-	TBRN	94920	607-A4
SOUTH SHORE E				
	-	MrnC	94941	606-H6
SOUTH SHORE W				
	-	MrnC	94941	606-G6
SOUTH SHORE FIRE RD				
	-	MrnC	-	585-H4
SOUTHVIEW TER				
	-	SANS	94960	566-D6
SOUTHWOOD AV				
	-	ROSS	94957	586-B2
SOUZA CT				
	700	PET	94952	465-B5
SPANISH BAY CT				
	-	PET	94954	465-J5
SPANISH TRAIL DR				
	2400	TBRN	94920	607-F7
	2400	MrnC	94920	607-F7
SPANISH TRAIL RD				
	2300	TBRN	94920	607-F7
	2300	MrnC	94920	607-F7
SPAULDING ST				
	100	SANS	94960	566-C7
SPELDRAKE LN				
	1900	PET	94954	465-J4
SPENCER AV				
	-	SAUS	94965	627-A3
SPENCER CT				
	-	SAUS	94965	627-B3
SPINDRIFT PASG				
	-	CMAD	94925	606-J1
SPINNAKER DR				
	-	SAUS	94965	627-B3
SPINNAKER POINT DR				
	-	SRFL	94901	587-A2
SPINOSA WY				
	-	NVTO	94945	526-B1
SPOONBILL AV				
	1800	PET	94954	465-J5
SPRAUER RD				
	-	SonC	94952	(464-F2 See Page 463)
SPRING AV				
	-	MrnC	94924	604-F2
SPRING DR				
	800	MrnC	94965	606-D7
SPRING LN				
	-	FRFX	94930	565-J7
	-	LKSP	94939	586-E5
	-	TBRN	94920	607-D6
SPRING RD				
	-	MrnC	94904	586-B3
	-	MrnC	94938	(564-E3 See Page 543)
	-	ROSS	94957	586-C3
SPRING ST				
	-	PET	94952	465-D7
	100	SRFL	94901	586-G2
	500	SAUS	94965	626-J3
	500	SAUS	94965	627-A2
SPRING TR				
	-	CMAD	94925	606-C5
SPRINGFIELD WY				
	600	MrnC	94965	606-D7
SPRING GROVE AV				
	-	SANS	94960	586-D1
	-	SRFL	94901	566-D7
	-	SRFL	94901	586-D1
	-	SANS	94960	566-C7
SPRING GROVE LN				
	200	SRFL	94901	586-D1
SPRING HILL CIR				
	-	SAUS	94965	626-J2
SPRING HILL RD				
	100	SonC	94952	(485-A1 See Page 465)
	900	SonC	94952	(484-F1 See Page 463)
	2100	SonC	94952	(464-A5 See Page 463)
	3900	SonC	94952	463-G3
SPRINGSIDE WY				
	300	MrnC	94941	606-E7
SPRUCE AV				
	-	SANS	94960	566-A6
SPRUCE PL				
	100	NVTO	94945	525-E2
SPRUCE RD				
	-	FRFX	94930	565-H5
SPRUCE ST				
	400	MrnC	94965	606-E7
SPRUCEWOOD CT				
	800	PET	94954	465-G6
SPYGLASS DR				
	-	NVTO	94949	546-A2
SPYGLASS RD				
	-	PET	94954	465-J5
STACY CT				
	-	NVTO	94947	525-J3
STADIUM AV				
	-	MrnC	94904	586-D3
	100	MrnC	94941	606-F5
STADIUM WY				
	-	MrnC	94904	586-D3
STADLER LN				
	100	SonC	94952	(464-H6 See Page 463)
STAGE GULCH RD Rt#-116				
	1000	SonC	94954	(466-G7 See Page 465)
	1000	SonC	94954	(486-G1 See Page 465)
	1400	SonC	95476	(466-G7 See Page 465)
STAGHOUND PASG				
	-	CMAD	94925	606-J1
STANFORD AV				
	100	MrnC	94941	606-F6
STANFORD CT				
	-	LKSP	94939	586-E4
	-	NVTO	94947	526-A3
	-	NVTO	94947	525-J4
STANFORD WY				
	-	SAUS	94965	626-H1
STANGLAND AV				
	-	SRFL	94901	586-F2
STANLEY ST				
	-	PET	94952	465-D6
STANTON WY				
	-	MLV	94941	606-F2
STARBOARD CT				
	-	MrnC	94941	606-J7
STARBUCK DR				
	-	MrnC	94965	625-J2
STARLING CT				
	300	MrnC	94965	606-F7
STARLING DR				
	-	PET	94954	465-J4
STARLING RD				
	300	MrnC	94965	606-F7
STASIA CT				
	100	NVTO	94947	525-F2
STASIA DR				
	-	NVTO	94947	525-F2
STATE ACCESS RD				
	800	NVTO	94949	546-G3
STELLA LN				
	-	LKSP	94939	586-D4
STETSON AV				
	-	CMAD	94925	606-F1
	-	MLV	94941	606-D2
	-	MrnC	94904	586-D3
STEVEN CT				
	-	MrnC	94930	565-H3
STEVEN DR				
	-	PET	94952	(485-F1 See Page 465)
STEVEN WY				
	-	MrnC	94903	566-G3
STEVENS CT				
	-	TBRN	94920	607-D6
STEVENS ST				
	-	SRFL	94901	566-G7
	-	SRFL	94901	586-G1
STEWART DR				
	-	SRFL	94901	566-F7
	-	TBRN	94920	607-B4
STEWART TR				
	-	MrnC	-	(563-G4 See Page 543)
STILLSON DR				
	800	PET	94954	465-D2
STIRLING WY				
	-	MrnC	94937	(522-F3 See Page 501)
STIRRUP LN				
	-	MrnC	94947	525-F3
STITTS CT				
	-	NVTO	94945	526-A3
STOCKSTILL WY				
	-	MrnC	94937	(522-D2 See Page 501)
STOKES CT				
	200	PET	94954	465-H6
STONE CT				
	-	SANS	94960	566-B5
STONE DR				
	400	NVTO	94947	526-C7
	500	NVTO	94949	526-C7
STONEHAVEN CT				
	-	NVTO	94947	525-G2
STONY HILL RD				
	800	TBRN	94920	607-C6
STONY POINT RD				
	-	PET	94952	(464-J1 See Page 463)
	-	SonC	94952	465-A1
	-	SonC	94952	(464-J1 See Page 463)
	100	PET	94952	465-A1
STORER DR				
	300	MrnC	94941	606-H5
STORY BOOK CT				
	700	NVTO	94947	526-A4
STRAITS VIEW DR				
	1900	TBRN	94920	607-F7
STRAUB LN				
	-	SonC	94952	465-A6
STRAWBERRY CIR				
	-	MrnC	94941	606-J4
STRAWBERRY DR				
	100	MrnC	94941	606-J5
STRAWBERRY LN				
	-	MrnC	94941	606-J6
STRAWBERRY LNDG				
	-	MrnC	94941	606-J5
STUART DR				
	300	PET	94954	465-F5
	300	PET	94952	465-F5
STUB RD				
	-	PET	94954	465-B1
STUMP RD				
	7500	SonC	95472	(442-G2 See Page 421)
STURDIVANT AV				
	-	SANS	94960	586-C1
STUYVESANT DR				
	-	MrnC	94960	565-J3
	200	MrnC	94960	566-A3
SUCCETTI RD				
	-	SonC	94952	(464-D4 See Page 463)
SUFFIELD AV				
	-	SANS	94960	566-A5
SUGARLOAF CT				
	-	PET	94954	(466-A6 See Page 465)
SUGAR LOAF DR				
	-	TBRN	94920	607-E5
SULGRAVE LN				
	-	SRFL	94901	567-E5
SULLIVAN AV				
	-	MrnC	94945	527-A3
SULLIVAN RD				
	-	MrnC	94945	527-A3
SULPHUR SPA				
	-	MrnC	94960	565-H2
SULTANA DR				
	2000	PET	94954	465-G3
SUMAC CT				
	-	NVTO	94945	526-A1
SUMMER AV				
	-	FRFX	94930	565-J6
SUMMER ST				
	-	MrnC	94971	461-F3
SUMMERHILL CT				
	-	SRFL	94903	566-E4
SUMMERHILL WY				
	-	SRFL	94903	566-E4
SUMMERS AV				
	-	NVTO	94945	526-D3
SUMMIT AV				
	-	MrnC	94965	606-C1
	-	MLV	94941	606-C1
	-	SRFL	94901	587-A1
	100	MrnC	94901	587-A1
	100	MrnC	94901	586-J1
	200	MrnC	94901	566-J7
	300	SRFL	94901	566-J7
SUMMIT DR				
	-	CMAD	94925	606-E1
	-	MrnC	94973	565-D4
	100	CMAD	94925	586-F7
	100	LKSP	94939	586-F7
SUMMIT LN				
	-	CMAD	94925	606-C5
	-	MrnC	94945	526-H3
SUMMIT RD				
	-	FRFX	94930	565-G5
	-	MrnC	94903	566-J3
	-	SANS	94960	566-A7
	-	FRFX	94930	566-A7
SUMMIT TR				
	-	CMAD	94925	606-C5
	-	MLV	94941	606-C5
SUMMIT WY				
	-	PET	94952	(485-C1 See Page 465)
SUN LN				
	700	NVTO	94947	525-H3
SUNCREST HILL DR				
	100	PET	94952	(485-D1 See Page 465)
SUNDANCE WY				
	300	NVTO	94945	526-B1
	300	NVTO	94945	506-B7
SUNNY DR				
	-	SANS	94960	566-C7
SUNNYBRAE LN				
	900	NVTO	94947	526-D7
SUNNYCREST AV				
	-	MLV	94941	606-C3
SUNNY HILL DR				
	-	PET	94952	(485-E1 See Page 465)
SUNNYHILL RD				
	-	NVTO	94945	526-B2
SUNNY HILLS DR				
	-	SANS	94960	566-C6
	300	MrnC	94901	566-C6
SUNNY OAKS DR				
	-	MrnC	94903	566-H3
SUNNYSIDE AV				
	-	CMAD	94925	606-G1
	-	MLV	94941	606-D3
	-	SANS	94960	586-B1
SUNNYSIDE CT				
	-	CMAD	94925	586-F7
SUNNYSIDE DR				
	-	MrnC	94956	(522-H7 See Page 501)
SUNNY SLOPE AV				
	200	PET	94952	(485-E1 See Page 465)
SUNNY SLOPE CT				
	-	PET	94952	(485-E2 See Page 465)
SUNNY SLOPE RD				
	-	PET	94952	(485-D1 See Page 465)
E SUNNY SLOPE RD				
	1000	PET	94952	(485-E2 See Page 465)
SUNRISE AV				
	-	MLV	94941	606-E4
SUNRISE LN				
	-	LKSP	94939	586-E7
	-	MrnC	94965	606-B4
	-	CMAD	94925	586-E7
	100	NVTO	94949	546-G5
SUNRISE PKWY				
	1400	PET	94954	465-D2
SUNSET CT				
	-	NVTO	94947	526-C6
SUNSET DR				
	200	NVTO	94949	546-H4
	1300	PET	94952	465-B6
	1400	SonC	94952	465-B6
SUNSET LN				
	-	MLV	94941	606-C4
SUNSET PKWY				
	200	NVTO	94947	526-B7
	800	NVTO	94949	526-B7
	1000	NVTO	94949	546-B1
SUNSET TER				
	2400	PET	94952	(485-E3 See Page 465)
SUNSET TR				
	-	TBRN	-	627-G2
	300	MrnC	94945	526-G2
SUNSET WY				
	-	MrnC	94965	626-A2
	-	SRFL	94901	566-D7
	-	MrnC	94965	625-J2
	300	MrnC	94941	606-E7
SUNSHINE AV				
	-	SAUS	94965	627-B4
SUNSHINE CT				
	-	MrnC	94956	(522-J7 See Page 501)
	100	PET	94952	(485-E2 See Page 465)
SUNSHINE LN				
	-	MrnC	94963	(564-J2 See Page 543)
SUNVIEW AV				
	-	SANS	94960	566-B5
SURF WY				
	-	NVTO	94945	526-A2
SURFWOOD CIR				
	-	SRFL	94901	567-C7
SURREY AV				
	-	MLV	94941	606-F4
SURREY LN				
	-	SRFL	94903	566-C3
SUSAN CT				
	900	NVTO	94947	526-D7
SUSAN WY				
	900	NVTO	94947	526-D7
SUSSEX CT				
	-	SRFL	94903	566-E4
SUTRO AV				
	700	NVTO	94947	525-G3
SUTRO CT				
	-	NVTO	94947	525-G3
SUTTER CT				
	-	TBRN	94920	607-B5
	1600	PET	94954	465-G4
SUTTER ST				
	200	PET	94954	465-F4
SUTTON LN				
	-	MrnC	94945	526-G2
SUTTON ST				
	11500	SonC	95472	(442-H2 See Page 421)
SWANSON RD				
	-	SonC	94952	(464-G5 See Page 463)
SWEETBRIAR LN				
	-	SAUS	94965	627-B3
SWEETSER AV				
	700	NVTO	94945	526-C3
SWIFT CT				
	-	MLV	94941	606-G4
SYCAMORE AV				
	-	LKSP	94939	586-E6
	-	MLV	94941	606-E3
	100	SANS	94960	566-A7
SYCAMORE DR				
	900	NVTO	94945	525-E1
SYCAMORE LN				
	700	PET	94952	465-C5
	1100	SonC	94952	465-C5
SYL DOR LN				
	-	MrnC	94947	525-H4
SYLVAN LN				
	-	ROSS	94957	586-C2
SYLVAN TER				
	-	MrnC	94903	566-H3
SYLVAN WY				
	-	MrnC	94973	565-C2
SYLVESTRIS DR				
	-	MrnC	94963	565-A2
	-	MrnC	94963	(564-J2 See Page 543)
SYLVIA CIR				
	-	NVTO	94947	525-H2
SYLVIA WY				
	100	SRFL	94903	566-B3
SYNANON				
	-	MrnC	94940	(502-F5 See Page 501)
SYOSSET LN				
	-	MrnC	94947	525-H5

T

STREET	Block	City	ZIP	Pg-Grid
TAFT CT				
	-	NVTO	94947	526-B5
TAHITI WY				
	-	MrnC	94971	461-F3
TAHOE CIR				
	-	NVTO	94947	526-E7
TAHOE PL				
	100	SRFL	94903	566-F2
TAHOLA LN				
	200	PET	94954	465-F3
TAINTER PTH				
	300	CMAD	94925	606-F1
TAMAL AV				
	-	SANS	94960	566-B6
TAMAL PZ				
	100	CMAD	94925	586-G6
TAMAL RD				
	-	MrnC	94933	(564-G1 See Page 543)
	100	MrnC	94938	(564-G1 See Page 543)
TAMALPAIS AV				
	-	BLV	94920	607-C7
	-	LKSP	94939	586-E5
	-	MLV	94941	606-B2
	-	MrnC	94965	606-F7
	-	SANS	94960	566-B7
	-	TBRN	94920	627-D1
	600	NVTO	94947	526-A4
	800	SRFL	94901	586-G1
TAMALPAIS CIR				
	-	BLV	94920	607-C7
TAMALPAIS DR				
	200	CMAD	94925	586-G7
	500	MrnC	94941	606-C4
TAMALPAIS RD				
	-	FRFX	94930	565-H5
	-	LKSP	94939	586-F5
	-	MrnC	94904	586-F5
TAMAL VISTA BLVD				
	-	CMAD	94925	586-G6
TAMAL VISTA DR				
	-	SANS	94960	566-D7
	-	SRFL	94901	566-D7
TAMAL VISTA LN				
	-	MrnC	94904	586-F3
TAMARACK DR				
	500	SRFL	94903	566-C3
TAMARACK PL				
	400	NVTO	94945	525-E2
TAMARACK RD				
	-	MrnC	94963	(564-H2 See Page 543)
TAMARIN LN				
	-	MrnC	94945	526-H3
TAMPA DR				
	-	SRFL	94901	566-G7
TAMPICO CT				
	1700	PET	94954	465-H4
TANAGER LN				
	1400	PET	94954	465-G5
TANAR DR				
	1500	PET	94954	465-G5
TANBARK CT				
	-	NVTO	94945	526-A1
TANBARK TER				
	500	SRFL	94903	566-C2
TANFIELD RD				
	-	TBRN	94920	607-C4
TANGLEWOOD AV				
	-	MrnC	94904	586-D5
TANGLEWOOD LN				
	-	MrnC	94947	525-G6
TANNERY CREEK RD				
	500	SonC	95465	421-D3
TAN OAK CIR				
	-	SRFL	94903	566-D1
TANOAK CT				
	-	CMAD	94925	606-G1
TANZI WY				
	-	PET	94952	465-C6
TAPPAN CT				
	-	MrnC	94960	565-J2
TAPPAN RD				
	-	MrnC	94960	565-J2
TARA LN				
	-	NVTO	94945	526-A2
TARA HILL RD				
	-	TBRN	94920	607-D6
TARA VIEW RD				
	-	TBRN	94920	607-D6
TARCA RD				
	-	SonC	94954	(486-C1 See Page 465)
TARRAGON CT				
	-	PET	94954	465-H4
TARRAGON DR				
	500	SRFL	94903	566-C2
TARRANT CT				
	-	SRFL	94903	566-F5
TARRY RD				
	-	MrnC	94960	565-J2
TARTAN RD				
	-	MLV	94941	606-E1
TAURUS DR				
	-	MrnC	94947	525-F2
TAYLOR AV				
	-	MrnC	94973	565-C2
TAYLOR DR				
	-	FRFX	94930	565-J5
TAYLOR LN				
	-	CMAD	94925	586-F7
	-	LKSP	94939	586-F7
TAYLOR RD				
	-	TBRN	94920	607-B2
	-	MrnC	94920	607-B2
TAYLOR ST				
	-	SANS	94960	566-B6
	-	SRFL	94901	586-F1
TAYLOR PARK RD				
	7300	MrnC	94938	(564-D1 See Page 543)
	7400	MrnC	-	(564-D1 See Page 543)
	9100	MrnC	-	543-H3
TEABERRY LN				
	-	MrnC	94920	607-E5
TEAKWOOD CT				
	-	SRFL	94901	567-C6
TEAL RD				
	-	BLV	94920	627-D1
TELEPHONE RD				
	-	MrnC	-	523-H1
	-	MrnC	94940	(524-A3 See Page 503)
	-	MrnC	94940	523-F2
TELEPHONE TR				
	-	MrnC	94965	586-A7
TEMPLEMAN CT				
	400	CMAD	94925	606-F1
TENAYA DR				
	500	TBRN	94920	607-B5
TENAYA LN				
	-	NVTO	94947	526-A5
TENNESSEE AV				
	-	MrnC	94965	606-E6
	300	MrnC	94941	606-E6
TENNESSEE GLEN WY				
	200	MrnC	94965	606-F7
TENNESSEE VALLEY RD				
	-	MrnC	94965	606-F7
	200	MrnC	94965	626-E2
TENNYSON DR				
	-	MLV	94941	606-G4
TERESA CT				
	700	PET	94954	465-G5
TERMINAL RD				
	-	NVTO	94949	546-J4
TERN CT				
	-	SRFL	94901	587-A2
TERNERS DR				
	800	MrnC	94965	626-H1
TERRACE AV				
	-	MrnC	94904	586-D3
	-	MrnC	94924	604-F3
	-	SRFL	94901	566-D7
	-	SANS	94960	566-D7
	100	PET	94952	(485-E2 See Page 465)
	100	SRFL	94901	586-D1
TERRACE CT				
	-	TBRN	94920	607-A4
TERRACE DR				
	600	MrnC	94965	626-H1
TERRADILLO AV				
	-	SRFL	94901	586-H1
	-	SRFL	94901	566-H7
TERRA LINDA DR				
	-	SRFL	94903	566-C4
TERRY CIR				
	-	NVTO	94947	526-C7
	-	NVTO	94949	526-C7
TESTA ST				
	-	SAUS	94965	626-J2
TETON CT				
	200	SRFL	94903	566-F2
TEXEIRA TR				
	-	MrnC	-	(584-C4 See Page 583)
THALIA ST				
	-	MLV	94941	606-E3
THE ALAMEDA				
	-	SANS	94960	566-A5
	300	MrnC	94960	566-B4
THERESA CT				
	-	NVTO	94947	525-H3
	-	TBRN	94920	607-C5
THERESA DR				
	-	SANS	94960	565-J4
THOMAS CT				
	-	NVTO	94947	525-H3
	-	ROSS	94957	586-C2
	-	SRFL	94901	566-E7
THOMAS DR				
	-	MrnC	94920	606-H3
THOMAS LN				
	-	SonC	94952	(464-J5 See Page 463)
THOMAS RD				
	-	PET	94952	(464-J1 See Page 463)
THOMPSON LN				
	-	SonC	94952	(464-J5 See Page 463)
THOREAU DR				
	-	MLV	94941	606-G4
THORN RD				
	2500	SonC	95472	(422-J3 See Page 421)
THORNDALE DR				
	-	SRFL	94903	566-D3
THORNHILL CT				
	-	NVTO	94949	546-B2
THORNTON CT				
	-	NVTO	94945	526-A1
THORNWOOD TER				
	500	SRFL	94903	566-C2
THREE PEAKS FIRE RD				
	-	MrnC	-	(504-B4 See Page 503)
	-	MrnC	-	503-H4
THROCKMORTON AV				
	-	MLV	94941	606-C2
THROCKMORTON LN				
	-	MLV	94941	606-C2
THROCKMORTON TR				
	-	MrnC	94965	586-A7
	-	MrnC	94965	585-J7
	-	MrnC	94965	605-J1
THUNDERBIRD CT				
	-	NVTO	94949	546-B3
THUNDERBIRD DR				
	-	NVTO	94949	546-B3
THYME PL				
	500	SRFL	94903	566-C2
TIBURON BLVD				
	100	MrnC	94901	586-H3
TIBURON BLVD Rt#-131				
	-	MrnC	94920	606-H4
	-	TBRN	94920	606-H4
	-	MrnC	94941	606-H4
	100	MrnC	94920	607-A5
	100	TBRN	94920	607-A5
	1500	BLV	94920	607-C6
	1700	TBRN	94920	627-E1
TIBURON ST				
	-	SRFL	94901	586-J2
TIBURON FERRY				
	-	TBRN	-	627-E1
	-	TBRN	-	627-E1
TIERRA VISTA WY				
	-	SRFL	94901	566-E7
TIKI RD				
	2700	NVTO	94945	526-G1
TILDEN CIR				
	-	SRFL	94901	566-C6
TILDEN CT				
	-	NVTO	94947	526-B6
TIMBER CANYON RD				
	6600	MrnC	-	565-E4
TIMOTEO DR				
	-	MrnC	94941	606-H4
TIMOTEO TER				
	-	MrnC	94941	606-H4
TIMOTHY CT				
	-	NVTO	94949	546-E5
TIMOTHY DR				
	-	SANS	94960	566-A4
TIOGA CT				
	-	MrnC	94903	546-A6
TIOGA LN				
	100	MrnC	94904	586-F4
TODD WY				
	300	MrnC	94941	606-D4
TOMAHAWK CT				
	-	NVTO	94949	526-B7
TOMAHAWK DR				
	-	SANS	94960	566-B5
TOMALES PL				
	-	MrnC	94956	(522-J6 See Page 501)
TOMALES RD				
	-	SonC	94952	463-D3
TOMALES ST				
	-	SAUS	94965	626-J1
TOMALES PETALUMA RD				
	1000	MrnC	94971	463-A3
	1700	MrnC	94971	(462-H3 See Page 461)
TOMASETTI RD				
	-	SonC	94952	(484-F4 See Page 463)
TOMASINI CANYON RD				
	-	MrnC	94940	523-D6
TOPAZ DR				
	2400	NVTO	94945	526-G1
TOPSIDE WY				
	-	MrnC	94941	606-J6
TOUSSIN AV				
	-	MrnC	94904	586-D3
TOWER DR				
	-	MrnC	94941	606-G3
TOWER POINT LN				
	-	TBRN	94920	607-F7
	-	TBRN	94920	627-F1
TOWNVIEW LN				
	-	PET	94952	465-C7
TOYON AV				
	-	BLV	94920	627-D1
TOYON CT				
	-	CMAD	94925	606-G1
	-	SAUS	94965	627-A3
TOYON DR				
	-	FRFX	94930	565-G7
TOYON LN				
	-	SAUS	94965	627-A3
	-	SAUS	94965	626-J3
TOYON TER				
	-	SANS	94960	566-B5
TOYON WY				
	-	NVTO	94945	526-D4
	-	SRFL	94901	586-E2
TOYON FIRE RD				
	-	FRFX	94930	565-G6
	-	MrnC	94930	565-G6
TRADEWIND PASG				
	-	CMAD	94925	606-J1
	-	CMAD	94925	607-A1
TRALEE WY				
	-	SRFL	94903	566-C1
TRANSPORT WY				
	-	PET	94954	465-D3
TRAXLER RD				
	-	SANS	94960	566-A5

STREET Block City ZIP Pg-Grid

TREANOR ST
- SRFL 94901 586-F1
TREE LN
- NVTO 94947 525-J4
TREEHAVEN DR
- SRFL 94901 566-E7
TREE TOP WY
- MrnC 94904 586-B4
TRELLIS DR
- SRFL 94903 566-C3
TRELLIS LN
1500 PET 94954 465-H6
TREMARI RD
11300 SonC 95472 (422-J7 See Page 421)
TRESTLE GLEN DR
300 TBRN 94920 607-B4
300 MrnC 94920 607-B4
TRESTLE GLEN TER
100 TBRN 94920 607-B4
TRILLIUM LN
1000 MrnC 94965 606-D6
TRINIDAD DR
- MrnC 94920 607-C2
TRINITY DR
- NVTO 94947 526-D7
TRINITY WY
- SRFL 94903 566-D3
TRIPLE C RANCH RD
- MrnC 94960 565-H2
TRISH DR
- NVTO 94947 525-F2
- NVTO 94947 525-F2
TROSSACH WY
- MrnC 94937 (522-F3 See Page 501)
TROST RD
- SRFL 94901 586-E1
TROUDY LN
4100 SonC 94952 465-A2
TROY CT
- PET 94952 (485-F1 See Page 465)
TRUMAN CT
- NVTO 94947 526-B6
TRUMAN DR
- NVTO 94947 526-A6
- NVTO 94949 526-A6
TRUMBULL AV
500 MrnC 94947 525-G4
500 NVTO 94947 525-G4
TRUMBULL CT
- NVTO 94947 525-H3
TUDOR CT
- SRFL 94903 566-G5
TULANE DR
- LKSP 94939 586-E4
TULIP RD
200 MrnC 94924 604-D3
TUNNEL LN
400 CMAD 94925 606-F1
TUNSTEAD AV
- SANS 94960 566-B7
- SANS 94960 586-C1
TUNZI LN
800 SonC 94954 (466-F4 See Page 465)
TUNZI RD
- SonC 94952 (485-J4 See Page 465)
- SonC 94954 (485-J4 See Page 465)
TURNAGAIN RD
- MrnC 94904 586-C4
TURNBERRY CT
- PET 94952 (485-F1 See Page 465)
TURNER DR
1000 NVTO 94949 546-C1
TURNEY ST
300 SAUS 94965 627-A3
TURNSTONE DR
- SRFL 94901 587-A2
TURTLE ROCK CT
- TBRN 94920 607-B3
TWAIN HARTE LN
- SRFL 94901 586-G3
TWEED TER
- SRFL 94901 567-B7
- MrnC 94901 567-B7
TWELVE OAK HILL DR
- SRFL 94903 546-D7
- SRFL 94903 566-D1
TWIN BRIDGE RD
27300 MrnC 94971 (462-H2 See Page 461)
27300 MrnC 94952 (462-H2 See Page 461)
TWIN HOUSE RANCH RD
- SonC 94954 506-H5
TWIN OAKS AV
- SRFL 94901 566-F7
TWO ROCK ST
- SonC 94952 463-F1
TYLER ST
- NVTO 94947 526-A5

U

ULLOA CT
900 NVTO 94949 546-B1
UNA WY
- MLV 94941 606-E4
UNDERHILL RD
- MLV 94941 606-G2
UNION ST
- SRFL 94901 586-H1
100 SRFL 94901 566-H7
400 PET 94952 465-D6
UNIONSTONE DR
- MrnC 94903 546-D5
UNIONSTONE LN
- MrnC 94903 546-D5
UPHAM ST
100 PET 94952 465-C6
UPLAND CIR
100 CMAD 94925 607-A1
UPLAND LN
- MLV 94941 606-D2
- NVTO 94945 526-E3
UPLAND RD
- MrnC 94904 586-B4
UPPER RD
- ROSS 94957 586-B2
100 MrnC 94903 566-J2
UPPER RD W
- ROSS 94957 586-A2
UPPER ALCATRAZ PL
- MLV 94941 606-D2
UPPER AMES AV
- ROSS 94957 586-C2
UPPER ARDMORE
- LKSP 94939 586-E7
UPPER BRIAR RD
- MrnC 94904 586-D5
UPPER CECILIA WY
- TBRN 94920 607-A4
UPPER FREMONT DR
- SRFL 94901 586-E1
UPPERHILL RD
- MLV 94941 606-G2
UPPER N TER
- TBRN 94920 607-A4
UPPER OAK DR
- SRFL 94903 566-C1
- SRFL 94903 546-D7
UPPER RIDGEWAY AV
- FRFX 94930 565-J4
UPPER TOYON DR
- SRFL 94901 586-E1
- MrnC 94904 586-E2
- ROSS 94957 586-E1
UPPER VIA CASITAS
- LKSP 94939 586-F4
URSA MAJOR CT
600 PET 94954 465-E2

V

VALENCIA AV
- SRFL 94901 586-H1
VALENCIA CT
- NVTO 94945 526-A3
VALENCIA LN
300 CMAD 94925 586-F7
VALESCO CT
- NVTO 94949 546-E4
VALLEJO AV
- MrnC 94956 543-B1
100 MrnC 94956 (542-J1 See Page 541)
800 NVTO 94945 526-B3
VALLEJO ST
- PET 94952 465-D5
VALLEJO WY
- SRFL 94903 566-A2
VALLEJO SAN FRANCISCO FERRY
- SF - 607-J1
VALLEY AV
100 MrnC 94971 (462-B4 See Page 461)
VALLEY CIR
- MLV 94941 606-F4
VALLEY DR
100 NVTO 94949 546-G5
VALLEY RD
- FRFX 94930 565-H6
- MrnC 94941 606-G3
- SANS 94960 566-A5
VALLEY ST
200 SAUS 94965 627-B4
VALLEY WY
- MrnC 94963 565-A2
100 LKSP 94939 586-D6
VALLEY FORD CUTOFF Rt#-1
15000 SonC 94922 421-E6
17000 SonC 94923 421-E6
VALLEY FORD RD
7000 SonC 94952 463-E1
11200 SonC 94952 (442-E2 See Page 421)
12000 SonC 95472 (442-E2 See Page 421)
VALLEY FORD RD Rt#-1
13000 SonC 95472 (442-B1 See Page 421)
13900 SonC 94972 (442-A1 See Page 421)
14400 SonC 94922 421-J7
14400 SonC 94972 421-J7
14400 SonC 94972 (441-J1 See Page 421)
VALLEY FORD-ESTERO RD
30500 MrnC 94972 (441-J2 See Page 421)
30500 SonC 94972 (441-J2 See Page 421)
30900 SonC 94972 (442-A1 See Page 421)
VALLEY FORD-FRANKLIN SCHL RD
27000 MrnC 94971 461-G1
27800 MrnC 94971 (441-G7 See Page 421)
27900 MrnC 94972 (441-G3 See Page 421)
VALLEY FORD FREESTONE RD
3000 SonC 94922 (422-A6 See Page 421)
3000 SonC 95465 (422-A6 See Page 421)
5000 SonC 94922 421-J7
VALLEY OAK CT
1200 NVTO 94947 526-C6
VALLEYSTONE DR
- MrnC 94903 546-D6
VALLEY VIEW AV
- SRFL 94901 566-E6
VALLEY VIEW LN
900 MrnC 94941 606-E5
VALLINE LN
- MrnC 94924 604-G3
VAL VISTA AV
- MLV 94941 606-E2
VAN BUREN CT
- NVTO 94947 526-B6
VANESSA WY
700 PET 94952 465-C5
VAN HOOTEN CT
300 MrnC 94960 566-A3
VAN RIPPER CT
- MrnC 94960 565-J2
VAN TASSEL CT
- MrnC 94960 566-A2
VAN WINKLE DR
- MrnC 94960 565-H2
VARBORG TER
- SANS 94960 566-B4
VARDA LANDING RD
- SAUS 94965 626-J1
VASCO CT
- MLV 94941 606-G2
VASCO DR
- MLV 94941 606-F3
VENADO DR
- TBRN 94920 607-E6
VENDOLA DR
- MrnC 94903 566-G2
VENETIA MEADOW
- MrnC 94903 566-G3
VENTURA WY
900 MrnC 94941 606-E6
VENUS CT
- TBRN 94920 607-B4
VERA CRUZ AV
500 NVTO 94949 546-F2
VERA SCHULTZ DR
- SRFL 94903 566-F4
VERBENA CT
- MrnC 94903 545-H6
VERDAD WY
- NVTO 94945 505-J7
- NVTO 94945 525-J1
VERDE CT
100 PET 94954 465-D3
VERDI ST
- SRFL 94901 586-J2
VEREDA PTH
- TBRN 94920 607-F7
VERISSIMO DR
- MrnC 94947 525-E3
VERNAL AV
900 MrnC 94941 606-E5
VERNAL AV N
900 MrnC 94941 606-E5
VERNAL AV S
900 MrnC 94941 606-E5
VERNAL AV W
900 MrnC 94941 606-E5
VERONA PL
- CMAD 94925 606-J1
VETERANS PL
- SANS 94960 566-B6
VIA BARRANCA
- LKSP 94904 586-G4
VIA BELARDO
- LKSP 94939 586-F5
VIA CAPISTRANO
- TBRN 94920 607-A3
- TBRN 94920 606-J3
VIA CASITAS
200 LKSP 94939 586-F4
VIA CHEPARRO
- MrnC 94904 586-G4
100 LKSP 94904 586-G4
VIA DE LA VISTA
- MrnC 94937 (522-E2 See Page 501)
500 MrnC - (522-E2 See Page 501)
VIA DEL PLANO
400 MrnC 94949 546-E2
VIA ELVERANO
- TBRN 94920 606-J3
VIA ESCONDIDO
800 MrnC 94949 546-E2
1100 NVTO 94949 546-E2
VIA HERBOSA
400 MrnC 94949 546-F2
VIA HERMOSA
- LKSP 94904 586-H4
VIA HIDALGO
300 LKSP 94939 586-F4
VIA HOLON
- LKSP 94939 586-F4
VIA HORQUETA
1100 SRFL 94903 566-D2
VIA LA BRISA
- LKSP 94939 586-G5
VIA LA CUMBRE
- LKSP 94904 586-H4
300 MrnC 94901 586-H4
VIA LA PAZ
- LKSP 94904 586-G4
VIA LERIDA
- LKSP 94904 586-G4
VIA LOS ALTOS
- TBRN 94920 606-J3
- MrnC 94920 606-J3
VIA MONTEBELLO
- SRFL 94901 567-E5
VIA NAVARRO
- LKSP 94904 586-H4
VIA PARAISO E
- TBRN 94920 607-C6
VIA PARAISO W
- TBRN 94920 607-C5
VIA RECODO
300 MrnC 94965 626-F1
VIA SAN FERNANDO
- TBRN 94920 606-J3
VIA SESSI
1300 SRFL 94901 586-F1
VIA SOBRANTE
- MrnC 94937 (522-E1 See Page 501)
VIA VAN DYKE
- MLV 94941 606-E2
VIA VAN VUREN
- SRFL 94903 566-E5
VICTOR CT
- NVTO 94947 526-A4
VICTORIA DR
800 PET 94954 465-H5
VICTORIA WY
- LKSP 94904 586-H5
VIDA CT
100 NVTO 94947 525-G5
VIEJO WY
- NVTO 94945 526-A1
VIENTO WY
- MrnC 94956 523-D7
VIEW ST
- LKSP 94939 586-E6
VIEWPARK CT
400 MrnC 94965 606-E7
400 MrnC 94965 626-E1
VIEW POINT RD
700 MrnC 94965 606-E7
VILLA AV
- SRFL 94901 566-G6
VILLA CT
- MrnC 94904 586-E3
VILLA PL
- NVTO 94945 526-A2
VILLA GARDEN DR
- MrnC 94965 606-G7
VILLAGE CIR
- SRFL 94903 566-G5
100 NVTO 94947 526-D7
VILLAGE CT
- SRFL 94903 566-G5
VILLAGE EAST CT
- PET 94954 465-J5
VILLAGE EAST DR
1800 PET 94954 465-J5
VILLA MARIA
- NVTO 94947 526-A4
VILLA VISTA CT
- MrnC 94947 525-F3
VINA ROSE DR
500 PET 94952 465-C3
500 PET 94954 465-C2
VINCENT LN
- NVTO 94945 526-E3
VINE AV
- SANS 94960 586-B1
VINE RD
300 MrnC 94924 604-D3
VINE ST
- LKSP 94939 586-E6
VINEYARD AV
- SANS 94960 586-B1
VINEYARD CT
- NVTO 94947 525-H3
VINEYARD DR
- SRFL 94901 566-F6
VINEYARD RD
2000 NVTO 94947 525-G3
2400 MrnC 94947 525-E4
VINEYARD WY
- MrnC 94960 586-D4
VINTAGE CT
- PET 94954 (466-A5 See Page 465)
VINTAGE WY
100 NVTO 94947 526-D5
VIOLA WY
- MrnC 94965 626-F1
VIOX WY
- SRFL 94901 586-E1
VIRGINIA AV
1700 NVTO 94945 526-A2
1800 NVTO 94945 525-J2
VIRGINIA DR
500 PET 94954 465-G4
500 TBRN 94920 607-B4
VISCAINO WY
- SRFL 94903 566-D4
VISION RD
- MrnC 94937 (522-E3 See Page 501)
VISTA AV
200 MrnC 94938 (544-F7 See Page 543)
VISTA CT
- CMAD 94925 606-J2
VISTA DR
- MrnC 94904 586-E2
VISTA LN
- SANS 94960 566-A6
2000 PET 94954 465-H3
VISTA WY
- FRFX 94930 565-J4
VISTA CLARA
- SAUS 94965 627-A3
VISTA DEL MAR
- TBRN 94920 607-F7
100 SRFL 94901 586-J2
200 SRFL 94901 587-A2
1500 MrnC 94920 607-F7
VISTA DEL SOL
- MrnC 94941 606-H4
VISTA DE VALLE
300 MrnC 94965 626-E1
VISTA GRANDE
- LKSP 94904 586-F3
100 MrnC 94904 586-F3
VISTA LINDA DR
300 MLV 94941 606-E2
VISTA REAL
- MrnC 94941 606-H5
VISTA TIBURON DR
- TBRN 94920 606-J3
VISTA VIEW PL
100 PET 94952 (485-E2 See Page 465)
VISTA WOOD WY
- SRFL 94901 566-E6
VISTAZO EAST ST
1500 TBRN 94920 607-F7
VISTAZO WEST ST
1400 TBRN 94920 607-E6
VIVIAN CT
- NVTO 94947 525-G3
VIVIAN ST
- SRFL 94901 586-H2
VOGELSANG DR
- MrnC 94903 546-A6
VOLKERS DR
- SonC 94952 465-A5
VON CT
- MrnC 94930 565-H3

W

WAGNER LN
1800 SonC 94954 465-E1
WAIKIKI LN
- MrnC 94971 461-E2
WAINWRIGHT PL
- MrnC 94941 606-C3
WAKEROBIN LN
500 SRFL 94903 566-C2
WALDEN LN
- MLV 94941 606-B1
WALDO CT
- MrnC 94965 626-G1
WALKER ST
- MrnC 94920 606-H3
WALLACE CT
- NVTO 94947 526-B6
- PET 94952 465-C8
WALLACE WY
- SRFL 94903 566-C4
WALLA VISTA
- MrnC 94970 605-B3
WALNUT AV
- CMAD 94925 586-F7
- LKSP 94939 586-E6
- MLV 94941 606-E3
- ROSS 94957 586-B2
200 PET 94952 465-C6
WALNUT CT
700 NVTO 94945 525-E2
WALNUT RD
- FRFX 94930 565-F7
300 MrnC 94924 604-D3
WALSH AV
- MrnC 94945 527-A3
WALSH DR
100 MrnC 94941 606-C4
100 MrnC 94965 606-C4
WALSH LN
- FRFX 94930 565-H6
WALTER LN
700 SRFL 94901 586-G1
WALTER PL
- LKSP 94904 566-E4
WALTERS RD
- ROSS 94957 586-C2
WANDA LN
600 MrnC 94965 606-D6
WARD ST
- LKSP 94939 586-E6
E WARD ST
100 LKSP 94939 586-F6
WAREHOUSE RD
- NVTO 94949 546-G3
WARNER CT
- SRFL 94901 586-F2
WARNER RD
- SonC 95472 (422-G1 See Page 421)
WARRENS WY
- TBRN 94920 607-A4
WARRICK CT
- PET 94954 465-J4
WASHINGTON AV
- MrnC 94903 566-G4
WASHINGTON CT
400 TBRN 94920 607-A4
WASHINGTON ST
- SonC 94954 465-H1
- NVTO 94947 526-B6
- PET 94952 465-E6
E WASHINGTON ST
- SonC 94954 465-G3
400 PET 94952 465-E5
2100 PET 94954 465-G3
WASHINGTON PARK AV
- MrnC 94965 606-B3
WATER WY
- LKSP 94939 586-D7
WATEREE ST
600 SAUS 94965 626-J2
WATERSIDE CIR
- SRFL 94903 566-F3
WATERVIEW DR
1200 MrnC 94941 606-D5
WATT AV
- SRFL 94901 566-H7
WAVERLY RD
- SANS 94960 586-B1
WEATHERBY CT
- PET 94954 465-H4
WEATHERBY WY
2000 PET 94954 465-H4
WEATHERLY DR
- MrnC 94941 606-J6
WEAVERLY DR
1400 PET 94954 465-G4
WEBER LN
- MrnC 94901 586-H4
WEBSTER ST
- PET 94952 (485-C1 See Page 465)
100 PET 94952 465-C7
N WEBSTER ST
600 PET 94952 465-C6
WEDGEWOOD CT
- PET 94954 (466-A5 See Page 465)
WEEKS RD
- SonC 95472 (422-J2 See Page 421)
WELCH ST
- SRFL 94901 586-F1
WELCOME LN
- SRFL 94901 566-H6
WELLBROCK HTS
- SRFL 94903 566-C4
WELLER
200 PET 94952 465-E6
WELLESLEY AV
400 MrnC 94941 606-E6
WELLESLY CT
400 MrnC 94941 606-E6
WELLINGTON AV
- ROSS 94957 586-C1
WELLINGTON RANCH RD
16000 SonC 95465 421-F1
WELSH CT
- PET 94954 465-G4
WEMBURY WY
- MrnC 94941 606-G6
WENDY LN
800 PET 94952 465-C5
WENDY WY
400 MrnC 94941 606-E6
WENTWORTH LN
- NVTO 94949 546-B3
WERNER CT
- NVTO 94947 526-A4
WESSEN LN
- FRFX 94930 565-J6
WEST CT
- SANS 94960 566-A5
- SAUS 94965 627-B4
1400 NVTO 94945 526-B3
WEST LN
- SANS 94960 566-C7
WEST RD
- ROSS 94957 586-B2
WEST ST
- SRFL 94901 586-E1
- PET 94952 465-D5
100 SAUS 94965 627-B4
WEST TR
- CMAD 94925 606-C5
WESTBRAE DR
- FRFX 94930 565-H4
WEST END AV
200 SRFL 94901 586-E1
WESTERN AV
- PET 94952 465-C7
1100 SonC 94952 465-C7
1100 MrnC 94941 606-D5
2300 SonC 94952 (485-A1 See Page 465)
WESTERN DR
- NVTO 94947 525-H3
- RCH 94801 587-J4
WESTGATE DR
- MrnC 94903 545-H5
WESTOVER CIR
100 NVTO 94949 546-G4
WEST POINT TR
- MrnC 94965 605-H1
WESTRIDGE DR
100 PET 94952 (485-E2 See Page 465)
WESTRIDGE LN
- NVTO 94945 526-E3
WESTRIDGE PL
300 PET 94952 (485-E2 See Page 465)
WEST SHORE RD
- BLV 94920 607-C7
- BLV 94920 627-C1
WESTWARD DR
- CMAD 94925 607-A1
WESTWOOD AV
- SRFL 94901 586-D1
WESTWOOD DR
- NVTO 94945 526-D3
- SRFL 94901 586-D1
- MrnC 94904 586-B4
WETTMORE LN
- MrnC 94945 (484-F5 See Page 463)
WHARF CIR
- SRFL 94903 566-F2
WHARF RD
- MrnC 94924 604-G2
WHITAKER BLUFF RD
2600 MrnC 94972 (442-A7 See Page 421)
2900 MrnC 94972 (441-G6 See Page 421)
WHITE WY
- SANS 94960 566-A7
- SANS 94960 586-A1
WHITE HILL FIRE RD
6500 MrnC 94973 565-B4
6500 MrnC - 565-B4
WHITEPLAINS CT
- MrnC 94960 565-H2
WHITEWOOD DR
500 SRFL 94903 566-D2
WHITNEY WY
800 PET 94954 465-H5
WHITTIER AV
100 MrnC 94903 566-G4
WHITTIER CT
- MLV 94941 606-H6
WICKHAM DR
200 MrnC 94941 606-D5
WILIAM AV
400 LKSP 94939 586-F6
WILDER RD
- MrnC 94930 565-J3
200 MrnC 94960 565-J3
WILDFLOWER CT
- CMAD 94925 606-H2
WILDFLOWER DR
- CMAD 94925 606-H2
WILD HORSE VALLEY DR
- MrnC 94947 525-F5
WILD OAK DR
- NVTO 94949 546-G5
WILDOMAR AV
- MLV 94941 606-D3
WILDWOOD AV
- CMAD 94925 606-G1
WILDWOOD LN
- MrnC 94947 525-H6
WILDWOOD WY
- SRFL 94901 566-F6
WILKINS CT
- TBRN 94920 607-C5
WILKINS PL
- MLV 94941 606-G4
WILKINS ST
- SRFL 94901 566-G7
WILLIAM AV
- LKSP 94939 586-E6
WILLIAM CT
- SAUS 94965 626-J2
WILLIAMS DR
500 PET 94954 465-F5
WILLIAMS ST
- SRFL 94901 566-H6
WILLIAMSON CT
- NVTO 94947 525-H3
WILLIS DR
- MrnC 94941 606-H6
WILLIS LN
- FRFX 94930 565-H6
WILLOW AV
- CMAD 94925 586-F7
- FRFX 94930 565-J5
- LKSP 94939 586-E6
- ROSS 94957 586-C3
- SRFL 94903 566-F4
- FRFX 94930 566-A5
200 CMAD 94925 606-F1
WILLOW CT
400 NVTO 94945 526-D3
WILLOW DR
1900 PET 94954 465-G3
WILLOW LN
- SAUS 94965 626-J2
WILLOW RD
400 MrnC 94940 523-H5
WILLOW ST
- MLV 94941 606-E4
- MrnC 94970 605-C4
- SRFL 94901 586-F1
WILLOW WK
- SANS 94960 566-A6
WILLOW WY
- SANS 94960 566-A5
2600 MrnC 94940 (462-A6 See Page 461)
2600 MrnC 94971 (462-A6 See Page 461)
WILLOW CAMP FIRE RD
- MrnC 94970 605-C2
WILLOW HILL RD
- ROSS 94957 586-C3
WILLWOOD CT
- SRFL 94901 567-B6
WILMAC AV
800 NVTO 94947 525-J3
WILMINGTON DR
- PET 94952 465-E5
WILSON AV
- MrnC 94947 525-H4
500 NVTO 94947 525-H4
WILSON CT
- SRFL 94901 566-G6
WILSON LN
- SonC 94952 (464-H5 See Page 463)
WILSON RD
- SonC 94952 (464-F4 See Page 463)
WILSON ST
100 PET 94952 465-D6
WILSON WY
- MrnC 94904 586-D6
200 LKSP 94939 586-D6
WILSON HILL CT
- NVTO 94945 526-C4
WILSON HILL RD
- MrnC 94945 (504-D1 See Page 503)
WILTSHIRE AV
- LKSP 94939 586-E7
WIMBLEDON CT
- NVTO 94949 546-D2
WIMBLEDON LN
- FRFX 94930 565-H3
WIMBLEDON WY
- SRFL 94901 566-D6
WINDING WY
- ROSS 94957 586-D1
WINDMILL PL
- NVTO 94945 526-B1
WINDSOR AV
- SRFL 94901 566-E6
WINDSOR DR
100 PET 94952 (485-B1 See Page 465)
200 SonC 94952 465-A7
200 SonC 94952 (485-B1 See Page 465)
WINDSOR LN
- PET 94952 (485-C1 See Page 465)
WINDSTONE DR
- MrnC 94903 546-E6
WINDWARD DR
- CMAD 94925 606-J1
WINDWARD RD
- BLV 94920 607-C7
WINDWARD WY
100 SRFL 94901 587-A3
WINGED FOOT DR
- NVTO 94949 546-D2
WINN LN
- MrnC 94956 523-C6
WINSHIP AV
- ROSS 94957 586-C1
WINTERGREEN CT
- NVTO 94945 526-B2
WINTERGREEN TER
- SRFL 94903 566-C2
WINTON DR
800 PET 94954 465-D2
WINWOOD PL
- MLV 94941 606-D2
WISHKAH LN
200 PET 94954 465-F3
WISTERIA CT
- NVTO 94945 526-B2
WISTERIA WY
100 MrnC 94941 606-F5
500 SRFL 94903 566-C2
WITT RD
- SonC 94952 (464-C1 See Page 463)
WOLFBACK RIDGE RD
- MrnC 94965 627-A4
- MrnC 94965 626-J4
- SAUS 94965 627-A4
WOLFBACK RIDGE TER
- SAUS 94965 627-A4
WOLFE AV
- SRFL 94901 586-F2
WOLFE CANYON RD
- MrnC 94904 586-F3
WOLFE GLEN WY
- MrnC 94904 586-E3
WOLFE GRADE
- MrnC 94904 586-E3
100 SRFL 94901 586-E3
WOMACK CT
- NVTO 94947 525-H2
WOOD CT
- SANS 94960 566-B6
WOOD LN
- FRFX 94930 565-H7
100 MrnC 94930 565-H7
800 PET 94954 465-G6
WOODALE DR
- PET 94952 465-C7
WOODBINE DR
- MLV 94941 606-D2
500 SRFL 94903 566-C2
WOODGATE PL
- NVTO 94945 526-B1
WOODHAVEN RD
- MrnC 94937 (522-F2 See Page 501)
- ROSS 94957 586-A1
- SANS 94960 586-A1
WOOD HOLLOW DR
- NVTO 94945 526-B1
300 NVTO 94945 506-B7
WOODHUE LN
- CMAD 94925 606-G1
WOODLAND AV
- MrnC 94901 586-H2
- SANS 94960 586-B1
- SRFL 94901 586-F2
WOODLAND CT
- FRFX 94930 565-G7
- NVTO 94949 526-C7
WOODLAND PL
- MrnC 94904 586-B4
- SRFL 94901 586-B4
WOODLAND RD
- FRFX 94930 565-G7
- MrnC 94904 586-B4
WOODLEAF CT
- NVTO 94945 526-A1
WOODOAKS DR
- MrnC 94903 566-G4
WOODROSE CT
- SRFL 94901 567-C5
WOODRUFF RD
- SANS 94960 566-C1
WOODS ST
- SRFL 94901 586-E1
WOODSIDE AV
300 MrnC 94941 606-E6
WOODSIDE CT
- SANS 94960 566-A4
WOODSIDE DR
- SANS 94960 566-A4
WOODSIDE LN
- MLV 94941 606-E4
WOODSIDE WY
- ROSS 94957 586-C3
- SRFL 94901 567-C5
WOODSON WY
700 PET 94952 465-E5
WOOD SORREL DR
700 PET 94954 465-C2
WOODSTOCK CT
- SRFL 94903 566-G5
WOODVIEW LN
- MrnC 94945 526-J3
WOODWARD AV
- SAUS 94965 626-J2
100 SAUS 94965 627-A2
WOODWARD FIRE RD
- MrnC - 543-A6
- MrnC - (542-J7 See Page 541)
- MrnC - (562-J1 See Page 541)
WOODWORTH WY
- PET 94952 465-D5
WORDSWORTH CT
- MLV 94941 606-G4
WORN SPRINGS FIRE RD
- MrnC 94904 586-A2
- MrnC 94930 586-A2
- ROSS 94957 586-A1
- ROSS 94957 585-J1
WORNUM WY
- CMAD 94925 586-G6
- LKSP 94925 586-G6
WOROPIEFF RD
- SonC 94952 (464-H7 See Page 463)
WORTHINGTON LN
- SRFL 94901 566-G6
WRAY AV
- SAUS 94965 627-A3
WREDEN AV
- FRFX 94930 565-H6
WREN CT
- PET 94954 465-J5
WREN DR
1000 PET 94954 465-J5
WYNOOCHEE WY
1600 PET 94954 465-F3
WYWORRY CT
- NVTO 94947 525-J3

X

XYLO RD
- MrnC 94924 604-D3

Y

YACHT CLUB DR
- SRFL 94901 586-H2
YALE AV
- LKSP 94939 586-E4
100 MrnC 94941 606-F5
YARBERY DR
1500 PET 94954 465-D2
YARROW LN
- NVTO 94947 526-D7
YELLOWSTONE CT
- SRFL 94903 566-F1
500 PET 94954 465-D3
YOLANDA DR
- SANS 94960 566-B6
YOLO ST
- CMAD 94925 606-H1
YOSEMITE CT
400 PET 94954 465-E3
YOSEMITE RD
- SRFL 94903 566-F2
YOUNG CT
1000 NVTO 94949 546-C1
YUCCA RD
400 MrnC 94924 604-D3
YUKON CT
- NVTO 94947 526-C5
YUKON WY
1200 NVTO 94947 526-C5

Z

ZANCO WY
- NVTO 94947 526-A4
ZANDRA PL
- NVTO 94945 526-D3
ZEBRA RD
400 MrnC 94924 604-D3
ZEPHYR CT
- MrnC 94903 546-A7
ZIG ZAG TR
- MrnC 94965 606-A2
ZION CT
300 SRFL 94903 566-F3
ZOILA CT
- NVTO 94947 525-G4

#

1ST AV
- MrnC 94971 (462-B4 See Page 461)
1ST ST
- CMAD 94925 586-F7
- MrnC 94956 543-D1
- MrnC 94971 (462-C4 See Page 461)
- PET 94952 465-D6
- SRFL 94901 586-F1
900 NVTO 94945 526-B3
2ND ST
- MrnC 94956 543-C1
- PET 94952 465-D6
- SAUS 94965 627-B4
400 SRFL 94901 586-E1

STREET Block	City	ZIP	Pg-Grid
2ND ST			
900	NVTO	94945	526-B2
3RD ST			
-	MrnC	94956	543-C1
-	SAUS	94965	627-B4
-	SRFL	94901	586-F1
-	MrnC	94901	586-G1
1000	NVTO	94945	526-B3
4TH ST			
-	MrnC	94956	543-C1
-	PET	94952	465-D7
100	SANS	94960	566-D7
100	SAUS	94965	627-B4
300	SRFL	94901	586-F1
900	NVTO	94945	526-B3
1900	SRFL	94901	566-D7
5TH AV			
-	MrnC	94901	566-D6
500	SRFL	94901	586-G1
1400	SRFL	94901	566-D7
5TH ST			
-	NVTO	94949	546-H3
-	MrnC	94956	543-C1
-	PET	94952	465-D7
900	NVTO	94945	526-B3
6TH ST			
-	MrnC	94956	543-C1
-	PET	94952	465-D7
700	PET	94952	(485-E1 See Page 465)
1000	NVTO	94945	526-B3
7TH ST			
-	PET	94952	(485-E1 See Page 465)
-	PET	94952	465-D7
100	MrnC	94956	543-C1
900	NVTO	94945	526-A2
8TH ST			
-	PET	94952	465-D7
400	PET	94952	(485-D1 See Page 465)
1000	NVTO	94945	526-A3
9TH ST			
300	PET	94952	(485-D1 See Page 465)
10TH ST			
-	PET	94952	465-D7
-	PET	94952	(485-D1 See Page 465)
11TH ST			
300	PET	94952	(485-D1 See Page 465)
12TH ST			
200	PET	94952	(485-D1 See Page 465)
I-580 FWY			
-	MrnC	-	587-C5
-	SRFL	-	586-H2
-	SRFL	-	587-A3
-	SRFL	-	587-A4
I-580 RICHMOND-SAN RAFAEL BRD			
-	MrnC	-	587-C5
-	RCH	-	587-H6
-	SRFL	-	587-C5
-	SRFL	94901	587-C5
Rt#-1 BAY HWY			
18000	SonC	94923	421-B6
Rt#-1 SHORELINE HWY			
-	MrnC	94965	605-F6
200	MrnC	94941	606-E6
200	MrnC	94965	606-E6
400	MrnC	94965	625-J1
500	MrnC	94965	626-A2
4600	MrnC	94970	605-B3
4600	MrnC	94970	(584-D2 See Page 583)
4600	MrnC	94970	604-J1
5300	MrnC	94924	(584-D2 See Page 583)
7500	MrnC	-	(564-A5 See Page 543)
8800	MrnC	-	543-F5
8800	MrnC	-	(563-G1 See Page 543)
11400	MrnC	94956	523-D7
11600	MrnC	94940	523-A3
16100	MrnC	94940	(502-D2 See Page 501)
19900	MrnC	94940	(482-A3 See Page 461)
22800	MrnC	94940	(481-J2 See Page 461)
23900	MrnC	94940	461-J7
23900	MrnC	94940	(462-B6 See Page 461)
25200	MrnC	94971	(462-B6 See Page 461)
27800	MrnC	94952	(442-C6 See Page 421)
27800	MrnC	94952	(462-B6 See Page 461)
27800	MrnC	94972	(442-C6 See Page 421)
27800	MrnC	94972	(462-B6 See Page 461)
30500	SonC	94952	(442-C6 See Page 421)
30500	SonC	95472	(442-C6 See Page 421)
Rt#-1 VALLEY FORD CUTOFF			
15000	SonC	-	421-E6
17000	SonC	-	421-E6
Rt#-1 VALLEY FORD RD			
13000	SonC	-	(442-B1 See Page 421)
13900	SonC	-	(442-A1 See Page 421)
14400	SonC	-	421-J7
14400	SonC	-	421-J7
14400	SonC	-	(441-J1 See Page 421)
Rt#-37 SEARS POINT HWY			
-	MrnC	94945	526-G5
-	NVTO	94945	526-G5
-	SonC	-	526-G5
-	SonC	-	527-A2
-	SonC	94954	527-A2
Rt#-116 LAKEVILLE HWY			
-	PET	94952	465-H7
-	PET	94954	(466-A6 See Page 465)
-	SonC	94954	(466-B7 See Page 465)
-	SonC	94954	(486-C1 See Page 465)
1800	PET	94954	465-H7
Rt#-116 STAGE GULCH RD			
1000	SonC	94954	(466-G7 See Page 465)
1000	SonC	94954	(486-G1 See Page 465)
1400	SonC	95476	(466-G7 See Page 465)
Rt#-131 TIBURON BLVD			
-	MrnC	94920	606-H4
-	TBRN	94920	606-H4
-	MrnC	94941	606-H4
100	MrnC	94920	607-A5
100	TBRN	94920	607-A5
1500	BLV	94920	607-C6
1700	TBRN	94920	627-E1
U.S.-101 ROUTE 101 FRWY			
-	PET	94952	(464-J1 See Page 463)
-	PET	94952	465-A1
-	PET	94954	465-A1
-	SonC	94952	465-A1
-	SonC	94952	(485-G1 See Page 465)
U.S.-101 GOLDEN GATE BRDG			
-	SF	-	627-B7
U.S.-101 REDWOOD HWY			
-	CMAD	-	586-H5
-	CMAD	-	606-G4
-	LKSP	-	586-H5
-	MLV	-	606-G4
-	MrnC	-	506-A2
-	MrnC	-	546-F6
-	MrnC	-	546-F7
-	MrnC	-	566-F1
-	MrnC	-	566-E2
-	MrnC	-	586-H5
-	MrnC	-	606-G4
-	MrnC	-	626-H1
-	MrnC	-	627-B4
-	NVTO	-	506-A2
-	NVTO	-	526-C3
-	NVTO	-	546-F7
-	PET	-	465-A1
-	SF	-	627-B4
-	SRFL	-	566-E1
-	SRFL	-	566-E2
-	SRFL	-	566-F5
-	SRFL	-	586-H5
-	SAUS	-	626-H1
-	SAUS	-	627-B4
-	SonC	-	(485-H6 See Page 465)
5500	MrnC	-	(485-H6 See Page 465)
5500	MrnC	-	505-J1

AIRPORTS

FEATURE NAME / Address City, ZIP Code	PAGE-GRID
MARIN COUNTY AIRPORT GNOSS FIELD 451 AIRPORT RD, MrnC, 94945, (415)897-5185	506 - D5
SMITH RANCH AIRPORT 2173 SAN FRANCISCO BLVD, SRFL, 94903, (415)453-0212	566 - G1

BEACHES & HARBORS

FEATURE NAME / Address City, ZIP Code	PAGE-GRID
AGATE BEACH COUNTY PARK OCEAN PKWY, MrnC, 94924	604 - D4
AVALIS BEACH POINT REYES NATIONAL SEASHORE, MrnC	461 - C5
BRAZIL BEACH TOMALES BAY, MrnC, 94971	461 - F6
DRAKES BEACH DRAKES BEACH RD, MrnC	541 - D6
HEARTS DESIRE BEACH (SEE PAGE 501) MrnC	502 - C6
KEHOE BAY BEACH (SEE PAGE 461) POINT REYES NATIONAL SEASHORE, MrnC	481 - J7
KEHOE BEACH MrnC	501 - F3
KELAM BEACH (SEE PAGE 543) MrnC	563 - B4
LIMANTOUR BEACH (SEE PAGE 541) MrnC	542 - B6
MARSHALL BEACH (SEE PAGE 501) MrnC	502 - A2
MCCLURES BEACH (SEE PAGE 461) POINT REYES NATIONAL SEASHORE, MrnC	481 - D5
MCNEARS BEACH PARK PT SAN PEDRO RD, SRFL, 94901	567 - F5
MUIR BEACH SUNSET WY, MrnC, 94965, (415)388-2595	626 - A2
NORTH BEACH (SEE PAGE 501) MrnC	521 - C6
PEBBLE BEACH (SEE PAGE 501) MrnC	502 - D6
PERLES BEACH TBRN	627 - G3
POINT REYES BEACH MrnC	540 - H7
QUARRY BEACH TBRN	627 - J3
RED ROCK BEACH MrnC, 94965	605 - D6
SAND SPRINGS BEACH TBRN	627 - H3
SANTA MARIA BEACH (SEE PAGE 541) MrnC	562 - G1
SCULPTURED BEACH (SEE PAGE 541) MrnC	562 - H2
SHALLOW BEACH (SEE PAGE 501) MrnC	502 - E7
SHELL BEACH (SEE PAGE 501) MrnC	522 - E1
SOUTH BEACH MrnC	541 - A3
STINSON STATE BEACH PARK SHORELINE HWY, MrnC, 94970	605 - C4
SUNSHINE BEACH MrnC	541 - H5
TEACHERS BEACH (SEE PAGE 501) MrnC, 94937	522 - F1

BED & BREAKFAST

FEATURE NAME / Address City, ZIP Code	PAGE-GRID
BEAR VALLEY 88 BEAR VALLEY RD, MrnC, 94950, (415)663-1777	543 - E4
HOLLY TREE INN 3 SILVER HILLS RD, MrnC, 94956, (415)663-1554	543 - B2
PANAMA HOTEL 4 BAYVIEW ST, SRFL, 94901, (415)457-3993	586 - F1
PELICAN INN BED AND BREAKFAST 10 PACIFIC WY, MrnC, 94965, (415)383-6000	626 - A1

BUILDINGS

FEATURE NAME / Address City, ZIP Code	PAGE-GRID
FOR DOWNTOWN BUILDINGS SEE PAGE IX	-
COURT HOUSE SQUARE 1000 4TH ST, SRFL, 94901	586 - G1
DIVERSIFIED FINANCIAL CENTRE 1299 4TH ST, SRFL, 94901	586 - F1
THIRTY-THIRTY BRIDGEWAY BUILDING 3030 BRIDGEWAY BLVD, SAUS, 94965, (415)332-3800	627 - B3
VETERANS MEMORIAL AUDITORIUM AV OF THE FLAGS, SRFL, 94903	566 - F4

BUILDINGS - GOVERNMENTAL

FEATURE NAME / Address City, ZIP Code	PAGE-GRID
HALL OF JUSTICE 3501 CIVIC CENTER DR, SRFL, 94903, (415)499-6211	566 - F4
JUVENILE HALL IDYLBERRY RD, MrnC, 94903, (415)499-6705	546 - B7
MARIN COUNTY ADMIN BUILDING 3501 CIVIC CENTER DR, SRFL, 94903, (415)499-6151	566 - F4
SAN QUENTIN STATE PENITENTIARY MAIN ST, MrnC, 94964	587 - A5

CEMETERIES

FEATURE NAME / Address City, ZIP Code	PAGE-GRID
CEMETERY BODEGA HWY, SonC, 94923	421 - D4
CEMETERY (SEE PAGE 421) SUTTON ST & HILLVIEW ST, SonC, 95472	442 - H2
CYPRESS HILL CEMETERY MAGNOLIA AV & SYCAMORE LN, SonC, 94952	465 - C5
DAPHNE FERNWOOD CEMETERY 301 TENNESSEE VALLEY BLVD, MrnC, 94965, (415)383-7100	606 - G7
MOUNT OLIVET CEMETRY LOS RANCHITOS RD, SRFL, 94903	566 - E4
MOUNT TAMALPAIS CEMETERY 2500 W 5TH AV, MrnC, 94901, (415)479-9020	566 - C5
VALLEY MEMORIAL PARK 650 BUGEIA LN, NVTO, 94945, (415)897-9609	526 - E1

CHAMBERS OF COMMERCE

FEATURE NAME / Address City, ZIP Code	PAGE-GRID
BELVEDERE-TIBURON PENNINSULA C OF C 96 MAIN ST, TBRN, 94920, (415)435-5633	627 - E1
CORTE MADERA CHAMBER OF COMMERCE 121 CTE TOWN CENTER CTE MADERA, CMAD, 94925, (415)924-0441	586 - G7
MILL VALLEY / LARKSPUR C OF C 85 THROCKMORTON AV, MLV, 94941, (415)388-9700	606 - D3
NOVATO CHAMBER OF COMMERCE 807 DE LONG AV, NVTO, 94945, (415)897-1164	526 - C3
SAN ANSELMO CHAMBER OF COMMERCE 1000 SIR FRANCIS DRAKE BLVD, SANS, 94960, (415)454-2510	566 - B6
SAN RAFAEL CHAMBER OF COMMERCE 817 MISSION AV, SRFL, 94901, (415)454-4163	566 - G7
SAUSALITO CHAMBER OF COMMERCE 333 CALEDONIA AV, SAUS, 94966, (415)331-7262	627 - A2
WEST MARIN CHAMBER OF COMMERCE P.O. BOX 1045, MrnC, 94956, (415)663-9232	543 - D1

CITY HALLS

FEATURE NAME / Address City, ZIP Code	PAGE-GRID
BELVEDERE CITY HALL 450 SAN RAFAEL AV, BLV, 94920, (415)435-3838	607 - D7
CORTE MADERA CITY HALL 300 TAMALPAIS DR, CMAD, 94925, (415)924-1700	586 - F7
FAIRFAX CITY HALL 142 BOLINAS RD, FRFX, 94930, (415)453-1584	565 - J6
LARKSPUR CITY HALL 400 MAGNOLIA AV, LKSP, 94939, (415)927-5110	586 - F6
MILL VALLEY CITY HALL 26 CTE MADERA AV, MLV, 94941, (415)388-4033	606 - D3
NOVATO CITY HALL 901 SHERMAN AV, NVTO, 94945, (415)897-4311	526 - C3
ROSS CITY HALL 31 SIR FRANCIS DRAKE BLVD, ROSS, 94957, (415)453-1453	586 - C2
SAN ANSELMO CITY HALL 525 SAN ANSELMO AV, SANS, 94960, (415)258-4600	566 - C7
SAN RAFAEL CITY HALL 1400 5TH AV, SRFL, 94901, (415)485-3066	566 - F7
SAUSALITO CITY HALL 420 LITHO ST, SAUS, 94965, (415)332-0310	627 - A3
TIBURON CITY HALL 1505 TIBURON BLVD, TBRN, 94920, (415)435-0956	607 - D7

COLLEGES & UNIVERSITIES

FEATURE NAME / Address City, ZIP Code	PAGE-GRID
COLLEGE OF MARIN 885 COLLEGE AV, MrnC, 94904, (415)457-8811	586 - D3
DOMINICAN COLLEGE 1520 GRAND AV, SRFL, 94901, (415)457-4440	566 - H7
GLDN GATE BAPTIST THEOLOGICAL-SEMINARY SEMINARY DR, MrnC, 94941, (415)388-8080	606 - H6
INDIAN VALLEY COLLEGES 1800 IGNACIO BLVD, NVTO, 94949, (415)883-2211	526 - A7
SAN FRANCISCO THEOLOGICAL SEMINARY 2 KENSINGTON RD, SANS, 94960, (415)258-6500	586 - B1

DEPARTMENT OF MOTOR VEHICLES

FEATURE NAME / Address City, ZIP Code	PAGE-GRID
DEPARTMENT OF MOTOR VEHICLES 75 TAMAL VISTA BLVD, CMAD, 94925, (415)924-5560	586 - G6
NOVATO FIELD OFFICE DMV 936 7TH ST, NVTO, 94945, (415)897-0490	526 - A3

ENTERTAINMENT & SPORTS

FEATURE NAME / Address City, ZIP Code	PAGE-GRID
CONVENTION CENTER AV OF THE FLAGS, SRFL, 94903	566 - F3
SONOMA-MARIN FAIRGROUNDS PAYRAN & WASHINGTON ST, PET, 94952	465 - F6

GOLF COURSES

FEATURE NAME / Address City, ZIP Code	PAGE-GRID
INDIAN VALLEY GOLF CLUB 3035 NOVATO BLVD, MrnC, 94947, (415)897-1118	525 - D2
LAGUNITAS COUNTRY CLUB LAGUNITAS RD & GLENWOOD AV, ROSS, 94957, (415)453-8706	586 - B3
MARIN COUNTRY CLUB 500 COUNTRY CLUB DR, NVTO, 94949, (415)382-6700	546 - B2
MCINNIS PARK GOLF CENTER 350 SMITH RANCH RD, SRFL, 94903, (415)492-1800	566 - G1
MEADOW COUNTRY CLUB 1001 BOLINAS RD, MrnC, (415)453-3274	585 - F1
MILL VALLEY GOLF COURSE 280 BUENA VISTA AV, MLV, 94941, (415)388-9982	606 - F2
PEACOCK GAP GOLF & COUNTRY CLUB 333 BISCAYNE DR, SRFL, 94901, (415)453-3111	567 - D5
SAN GERONIMO NATIONAL GOLF COURSE 5800 SIR FRANCIS DRAKE BLVD, MrnC, 94973, (415)488-9849	565 - A2

HOSPITALS

FEATURE NAME / Address City, ZIP Code	PAGE-GRID
KAISER PERMANENTE MEDICAL HOSPITAL 99 MONTECILLO RD, SRFL, 94903, (415)444-2000	566 - D3
MARIN GENERAL HOSPITAL 250 BON AIR RD, MrnC, 94904, (415)925-7000	586 - E4
NOVATO COMMUNITY HOSPITAL 1625 HILL RD, NVTO, 94947, (415)897-3111	526 - A5

HOTELS & MOTELS

FEATURE NAME / Address City, ZIP Code	PAGE-GRID
BEST WESTERN CORTE MADERA INN 1815 REDWOOD HWY, CMAD, 94925, (415)924-1502	586 - H7
BEST WESTERN NOVATO OAKS INN 215 ALAMEDA DEL PRADO, NVTO, 94949, (415)833-4400	546 - F4
CASA MADRONA 801 BRIDGEWAY BLVD, SAUS, 94965, (415)332-0502	627 - B3
COURTYARD BY MARRIOTT 2500 LARKSPUR LANDING CIR, LKSP, 94904, (415)925-1800	586 - J4
EMBASSY SUITES HOTEL 101 MCINNIS PKWY, SRFL, 94903, (415)499-9223	566 - F3
HOLIDAY INN EXPRESS 160 SHORELINE HWY, MrnC, 94965, (415)332-5700	606 - G7
WYNDHAM GARDENS HOTEL 1010 NORTHGATE DR, SRFL, 94903, (415)479-8800	566 - E3

LIBRARIES

FEATURE NAME / Address City, ZIP Code	PAGE-GRID
BELVEDERE TIBURON LIBRARY 1501 TIBURON BLVD, TBRN, 94920	607 - D7
BOLINAS LIBRARY WHARF RD, MrnC, 94924, (415)868-1171	604 - G2
CORTE MADERA LIBRARY 707 MEADOWSWEET DR, CMAD, 94925, (415)924-4844	586 - G7
FAIRFAX LIBRARY 2097 SIR FRANCIS DRAKE BLVD, FRFX, 94930, (415)453-8092	565 - H5
INVERNESS LIBRARY (SEE PAGE 501) 15 PARK AV, MrnC, 94937, (415)669-1288	522 - G4
LARKSPUR LIBRARY 400 MAGNOLIA AV, LKSP, 94939, (415)927-5005	586 - F6
MARIN CITY LIBRARY 630 DRAKE AV ANNEX B, MrnC, 94965, (415)332-1128	626 - H1
MARIN COUNTY CIVIC CENTER LIBRARY 3501 CIVIC CENTER DR, SRFL, 94903, (415)499-6211	566 - F5
MILL VALLEY LIBRARY 375 THROCKMORTON AV, MLV, 94941, (415)388-2190	606 - C3
NOVATO LIBRARY 1720 S NOVATO BLVD, NVTO, 94945, (415)898-4623	526 - A3
POINT REYES LIBRARY 4TH & A ST, MrnC, 94956, (415)663-8375	543 - D1
SAN ANSELMO LIBRARY 110 TUNSTEAD AV, SANS, 94960, (415)258-4656	566 - C7
SAN GERONIMO LIBRARY-(SEE PAGE 543) 7282 SIR FRANCIS DRAKE BLVD, MrnC, 94963, (707)488-0430	564 - J1
SAN RAFAEL LIBRARY 1100 E ST, SRFL, 94901, (415)485-3320	566 - F7
SAUSALITO LIBRARY 420 LITHO ST, SAUS, 94965, (415)289-4120	627 - A2
STINSON BEACH LIBRARY 3470 SHORELINE HWY, MrnC, 94970, (415)868-0252	605 - C4

MILITARY INSTALLATIONS

FEATURE NAME / Address City, ZIP Code	PAGE-GRID
ARMORY PET, 94952	465 - E6
FORT BAKER MrnC, 94965	627 - A6
FORT BERRY MrnC, 94965	626 - H7
FORT CRONKHITE MrnC, 94965	626 - D5
MILITARY RESERVE RENAISSANCE RD, NVTO, 94945	526 - J6
TWO ROCK RANCH STA MILITARY RESERVE TOMALES RD & VALLEY FORD RD, SonC, 94952	463 - F4
US NAVAL COMPASS STATION MrnC	541 - A4

MUSEUMS

FEATURE NAME / Address City, ZIP Code	PAGE-GRID
BAY AREA DISCOVERY MUSEUM 557 EAST RD, MrnC, 94965, (415)487-4398	627 - C6
BOLINAS MUSEUM 48 WHARF RD, MrnC, 94924, (415)868-0330	604 - G2
MARIN COUNTY HISTORICAL SOCIETY-MUSEUM 1125 B ST, SRFL, 94901, (415)454-8538	586 - F1
MARIN MUSEUM OF THE AMERICAN INDIAN 2200 NOVATO BLVD, NVTO, 94945, (415)897-4064	525 - H2
NOVATO HISTORY MUSEUM & ARCHIVES 815 DE LONG AV, NVTO, 94945, (415)897-4320	526 - B3

OPEN SPACE PRESERVES

FEATURE NAME / Address City, ZIP Code	PAGE-GRID
ALTO BOWL PRESERVE LOMITA DR, MLV, 94941	606 - G2
BALTIMORE CANYON PRESERVE BLUE RIDGE RD, MrnC, 94904	586 - C5
BLITHEDALE SUMMIT PRESERVE SUMMIT DR, LKSP, 94939	586 - D7
BOLINAS LAGOON OPEN SPACE PRESERVE OLEMA-BOLINAS RD, MrnC, 94924	604 - G1
BOTHIN MARSH OPEN SPACE PRESERVE ALMONTE BL & ROSEMONT AV, MrnC, 94941	606 - G6
CAMINO ALTO PRESERVE CAMINO ALTO & CORTE MADERA AV, MLV, 94941	606 - F2
CASCADE CANYON PRESERVE FAIRFAX-BOLINAS RD, MrnC, 94930	565 - F6
DEER ISLAND PRESERVE DEER ISLAND LN, NVTO, 94945	526 - F5
GIACOMINI, GARY OPEN SPACE PRESERVE MrnC, 94963	565 - A3
IGNACIO VALLEY PRESERVE CHICKEN SHACK FIRE RD, NVTO, 94949	546 - B4
INDIAN TREE PRESERVE MrnC, 94947	525 - C5
INDIAN VALLEY PRESERVE NVTO, 94949	546 - B2
KING MOUNTAIN PRESERVE EVERGREEN FIRE RD, MrnC, 94904	586 - C6
KING MOUNTAIN PRESERVE TAMALPAIS AV & MIMOSA AV, LKSP, 94939	586 - E5
LITTLE MOUNTAIN OPEN SPACE PRESERVE MrnC, 94947	525 - E2
LOMA ALTA PRESERVE BAYWOOD CANNON RD, MrnC, 94930	565 - G1
LOMA VERDE PRESERVE NVTO, 94949	546 - D3
LUCAS VALLEY PRESERVE LUIZ FIRE RD, MrnC, 94903	545 - J4
MARIN COUNTY OPEN SPACE REDWOOD RD, SANS, 94960	565 - J7
MARIN OPEN SPACE REDWOOD RD, SANS, 94960	586 - A1
MAURICE THORNER MEMORIAL PRESERVE NICASIO VALLEY RD, MrnC, 94963	565 - A1
MOUNT BURDELL PRESERVE SAN MARIN DR & SAGE CT, NVTO, 94945	505 - H6
OLD SAINT HILARYS OPEN SPACE-PRESERVE TBRN, 94920	607 - E6
OPEN SPACE PRESERVE SIR FRANCIS DRAKE BLVD, MrnC	565 - E3
PACHECO VALLE PRESERVE NVTO, 94949	546 - D4
RING MOUNTAIN OPEN SPACE PRESERVE MrnC, 94920	606 - J2
ROYS REDWOOD PRESERVE NICASIO VLY RD & SIR FRANCIS, MrnC, 94973	565 - A1
RUSH CREEK OPEN SPACE PRESERVE ATHERTON AV, MrnC, 94945	506 - E7
SAN PEDRO MOUNTAIN PRESERVE WOODOAKS DR, MrnC, 94903	566 - H4
SANTA MARGARITA ISLAND PRESERVE VENDOLA DR, MrnC, 94903	566 - G3
SANTA VENETIA MARSH PRESERVE VENDOLA DR & SAND PEDRO RD, MrnC, 94903	566 - J2
TERRA LINDA-SLEEPY HOLLOW DIVIDE-NORTH LUCAS VALLEY RD, SRFL, 94903	566 - A1
TIBURON RIDGE PRESERVE HWY 101 REDWOOD HWY FRONTAGE, CMAD, 94925	606 - H3
TIBURON UPLANDS NATURE RESERVE PARADISE DR, MrnC, 94920	607 - F6
VERISSIMO HILLS PRESERVE OAK VALLEY DR, NVTO, 94947	525 - F3

PARK & RIDE

FEATURE NAME / Address City, ZIP Code	PAGE-GRID
PARK & RIDE (SEE PAGE 465) SonC, 94952	485 - G1
PARK & RIDE 1100 ANDERSEN DR, SRFL, 94901	586 - J3
PARK & RIDE 3RD ST & HETHERTON ST, SRFL, 94901	586 - G1
PARK & RIDE ALAMEDA DEL PRADO & HWY 101, NVTO, 94949	546 - F4
PARK & RIDE E SIR FRANCIS DRAKE BLVD, LKSP, 94904	586 - H5
PARK & RIDE HART ST & REDWOOD AV, CMAD, 94925	586 - F7
PARK & RIDE HWY 1 & HWY 101, MrnC, 94965	606 - G6
PARK & RIDE HWY 101 & ATHERTON AVE, NVTO, 94945	526 - C2
PARK & RIDE HWY 101 & REDWOOD FRONTAGE RD, MLV, 94941	606 - G5
PARK & RIDE HWY 101 & SMITH RANCH RD, SRFL, 94903	566 - F1
PARK & RIDE HWY 101 & SPENCER AVE, SAUS, 94965	627 - A3
PARK & RIDE LINCOLN AV & HWY 101, SRFL, 94901	566 - F6
PARK & RIDE REDWOOD HWY & ROWLAND BL, NVTO, 94947	526 - D5
PARK & RIDE SEARS POINT HWY & ATHERTON AV, MrnC, 94945	526 - H4
PARK & RIDE SIR FRANCIS DRAKE & DEL MONTE, LKSP, 94939	586 - G5
PARK & RIDE SIR FRANCIS DRAKE & LA CUESTA, LKSP, 94939	586 - G4

PARKS & RECREATION

FEATURE NAME	Address City, ZIP Code	PAGE-GRID
ALBERT PARK	B ST & TREANOR ST, SRFL, 94901	586 - F1
ALCATRAZ STATE PARK	SF, (415)546-2700	627 - H7
ANGEL ISLAND STATE PARK	TBRN, (415)435-1915	627 - H2
ARROYO AVICHI PARK	HILL RD, NVTO, 94947	526 - B5
BAHIA PARKS	SANTANA RD, NVTO, 94945	526 - G1
BARRIER, HARRY A MEMORIAL PARK	MOUNTAIN VIEW AV, SRFL, 94901	566 - J5
BAYFRONT PARK	ROQUE MORAES DR & HAMILTON DR, MLV, 94941	606 - F4
BEACH PARK	FRANCISCO BLVD, SRFL, 94901	586 - H1
BELVERON PARK	TRESTLE GLEN DR & MERCURY AV, TBRN, 94920	607 - A4
BLITHEDALE PK	W BLITHEDALE AV &MARGUERITE AV, MLV, 94941	606 - C1
BOLINAS PARK	OLEMA-BOLINAS RD, MrnC, 94924	604 - F1
BON AIR LANDING PARK	S ELISEO DR & CORTE REAL, LKSP, 94939	586 - F5
BOYD MEMORIAL PARK	B ST & MISSION AV, SRFL, 94901	566 - F7
BOYLE PARK	E BLITHEDALE AV & E DR, MLV, 94941	606 - E3
BRET HARTE PARK	IRWIN ST & BAYWOOD TER, SRFL, 94901	586 - G3
CASCADE PARK	LOVELL AV, MLV, 94941	606 - B2
CHINA CAMP STATE PARK	N SAN PEDRO RD, MrnC, 94903, (415)456-0766	567 - B4
CLOUD VIEW PARK	CLOUD VIEW RD & BOOKER AV, SAUS, 94965	627 - A3
CREEK PARK	CENTER BLVD & SIR FRANCIS DRAK, SANS, 94960	566 - C7
CREEKSIDE PARK	BON AIR RD, MrnC, 94904	586 - E4
CREEKSIDE PARK	JAMES BLACK CIR & ALAMEDA DEL, NVTO, 94949	546 - E5
DEER PARK	PORTEOUS AV, FRFX, 94930	565 - H7
DOC EDGAR PARK	CASCADE DR, FRFX, 94930	565 - H6
DOLLIVER PARK	MADRONE AV & MAGNOLIA AV, LKSP, 94939	586 - E6
DUNPHY PARK	BRIDGEWAY BLVD & NAPA ST, SAUS, 94965	627 - A2
EARNSCLIFF CANYON PARK	HAZEL AV & MONTE VISTA AV, MLV, 94941	606 - C3
EDGEWOOD PARK	SUNNY CREST AV & EDGEWOOD AV, MLV, 94941	606 - C3
ENCHANTED KNOLLS PARK	ROQUE MORAES & HAMILTON DR, MLV, 94941	606 - G4
FAUDE PARK	OAKLAND AV, SANS, 94960	566 - B6
FREEMAN PARK	BLITHEDALE AV & RYAN AV, MLV, 94941	606 - F4
GABRIELSON PARK	BRIDGEWAY BLVD & ANCHOR ST, SAUS, 94965	627 - B3
GERSTLE MEMORIAL PARK	SAN RAFAEL AV & CLARK ST, SRFL, 94901	586 - E2
GOLDEN GATE NATIONAL RECREATION-AREA	MrnC, 94965	626 - C3
GOLDEN GATE NATIONAL RECREATION-AREA	MrnC, 94965	563 - H1
GRANADA PARK	GRANADA DR & VISTA CT, CMAD, 94925	606 - J2
HAMILTON PARK	S ELISEO DR, LKSP, 94939	586 - E5
HEATHERWOOD PARK	HEATHER WY & MIDWAY RD, LKSP, 94939	586 - F6
HELEN PUTNAM REGIONAL PARK-(SEE PAGE 465)	SonC, 94952	485 - B2
HILL PARK	HILL RD & INDIAN VALLEY RD, NVTO, 94947	526 - B5
JERRY RUSSOM MEMORIAL PARK	OLD LUCAS VALLEY RD, SRFL, 94903	566 - C1
JONES, VICTOR PARK	ROBINHOOD DR & MAPLEWOOD DR, SRFL, 94901	567 - B5
JOSEF HOOG PARK	MARIN OAKS DR & MONTURA WY, NVTO, 94949	546 - C1
LAGOON PARK	ARMORY DR, SRFL, 94903	566 - F4
LANDSDALE STATION PARK	FORREST AV & GLEN RD, SANS, 94960	566 - A6
LEE GARNER PARK	NOVATO BLVD & TAMALPAIS AV, NVTO, 94945	526 - A3
LIONS PARK	NOVATO BLVD, MrnC, 94947	525 - E1
LYNWOOD HILL PARK	LEAFWOOD HGHTS & GREENWOOD DR, NVTO, 94947	526 - D6
LYNWOOD PARK	S NOVATO BLVD & ROWLAND BLVD, NVTO, 94947	526 - C6
MAGNOLIA PARK	MAGNOLIA AV & ALEXANDER AV, LKSP, 94939	586 - F7
MARIA B FREITAS MEMORIAL PARK	MONTECILLO RD, SRFL, 94903	566 - D3
MARIN HIGHLANDS PARK	BLANCA DR & SANTA MARIA DR, NVTO, 94947	525 - G4
MARINSHIP PARK	MARINSHIP AV & LIBERTY SHIP WY, SAUS, 94965	627 - A2
MARINWOOD PARK	LUCAS VALLEY RD & MILLER CREEK, MrnC, 94903	546 - D7
MARION PARK	GRANT AV & 8TH ST, NVTO, 94945	526 - A3
MARTIN LUTHER KING JR PARK	OLIMA ST & COLOMA ST, SAUS, 94965	626 - J1
MARTINELLI PARK (SEE PAGE 501)	MrnC, 94937	522 - H4
MCINNIS, JOHN F COUNTY PARK	SMITH RANCH RD, SRFL, 94903	566 - C1
MILLER GROVE PARK	ELDRIGE AV & BLITHEDALE AV, MLV, 94941	606 - D2
MILLER PARK (SEE PAGE 461)	NICKS COVE AT TOM BAY, MrnC, 94940	482 - A3
MIWOK PARK	NOVATO BLVD & REGALIA DR, NVTO, 94945	525 - H2
MOLINO PARK	MOLINO AV, MLV, 94941	606 - E4
MOUNT TAMALPAIS STATE PARK	801 PANORAMIC HWY, MrnC, 94965, (415)388-2070	605 - D2
NATALIE COFFIN GREENE PARK	LAGUNITAS RD & GLENWOOD AV, ROSS, 94957	586 - B3
NEIGHBORHOOD PARK	LARKSPUR LANDING CIR, LKSP, 94904	586 - J4
NIVEN PARK	DRAKES LANDING RD, LKSP, 94939	586 - G5
NORRIS, KATHLEEN MEMORIAL PARK	WILDOMAR ST & FLORENCE AV, MLV, 94941	606 - D3
OAK PARK	RIDGE PARKSIDE CT, SANS, 94960	566 - B6
OHAIR PARK	NOVATO BLVD & SUTRO AV, NVTO, 94947	525 - F2
OLD MILL PARK	THROCKMORTON AV & LAUREL ST, MLV, 94941	606 - C3
OLEANDER PARK	OLEANDER DR, SRFL, 94903	566 - D2
OLIVE PARK	OLIVE ST & SUMMERS AV, NVTO, 94945	526 - D3
PARADISE BEACH PARK	PARADISE DR, MrnC, 94920	607 - E5
PARK (SEE PAGE 501)	MrnC	502 - B7
PARK	MrnC, 94950	543 - F4
PARK	ADRIAN WY & ROSAL WY, MrnC, 94903	566 - H2
PARK	HACIENDA WY, MrnC, 94903	566 - H2
PARK	REDWOOD AV & CORTE MADERA AV, CMAD, 94925	586 - F7
PARK	SEASCAPE DR, MrnC, 94965	625 - J2
PARK	VENDOLA DR & MABRY WY, MrnC, 94903	566 - G2
PEACOCK PARK	BISCAYNE DR, SRFL, 94901	567 - D5
PICKLE WEED PARK	SPINNAKER POINT & RAILROAD AV, SRFL, 94901	587 - A1
PIONEER PARK	SIMMONS LN & SHADY LN, NVTO, 94945	525 - J2
PIPER PARK	DOHERTY DR, LKSP, 94939	586 - F5
POINT REYES NATIONAL SEASHORE	MESA RD, MrnC, (415)663-1092	604 - C1
REMILLARD PARK	E SIR FRANCIS DRAKE BLVD, LKSP, 94904	586 - J5
RICHARDSON BAY PARK	TIBURON BLVD & SILVERADO DR, TBRN, 94920	607 - B5
ROBSON PARK	RAYMOND AV & CRESCENT RD, SANS, 94960	566 - B7
ROSS COMMON PARK	LAGUNITAS RD & ROSS COM, ROSS, 94957	586 - C2
SAMUEL P TAYLOR STATE PARK-(SEE PAGE 543)	SIR FRANCIS DRAKE BLVD, MrnC, (415)488-9897	544 - D6
SAN ANSELMO MEMORIAL PARK	VETERANS PL, SANS, 94960	566 - B6
SAN CLEMENTE PARK	PARADISE DR & HIND PASSAGE, CMAD, 94925	606 - J1
SANTA MARGARITA VALLEY PARK	DE LA GUERRA RD, SRFL, 94903	566 - A1
SLADE PARK	MANUEL DR & LOUIS DR, NVTO, 94945	526 - D4
SORICH RANCH PARK	SAN FRANCISCO BLVD, SANS, 94960	566 - C5
SOUTHVIEW PARK	RICHARDSON ST & 4TH ST, SAUS, 94965	627 - B4
STAFFORD GROVE PARK	MARION AV, NVTO, 94945	526 - A3
STAFFORD LAKE PARK	NOVATO BLVD, MrnC, 94947	525 - B3
STRAWBERRY PARK	BELVEDERE DR & RICARDO LN, MrnC, 94941	606 - J4
SUN VALLEY PARK	SOLANO ST, SRFL, 94901	566 - E6
SUTTON PARK	CENTER RD & MEYERS CT, NVTO, 94947	526 - A3
SYCAMORE PARK	PARK TER & SYCAMORE AV, MLV, 94941	606 - E4
TERRA LINDA PARK	670 DEL GANADO RD, SRFL, 94903	566 - C2
TIFFANY PARK	BRIDGEWAY BLVD & NOBLE LN, SAUS, 94965	627 - B4
TOMALES BAY STATE PARK-(SEE PAGE 501)	PIERCE POINT RD, MrnC, (415)669-1140	502 - C7
TOWN PARK	TAMALPAIS DR, CMAD, 94925	586 - G7
WATSON SCHOOL WAYSIDE PARK	BODEGA HWY, SonC, 94922	421 - J3
WHITE HOUSE POOL FISHING ACCESS	SIR FRANCIS DRAKE BLVD, MrnC, 94956	543 - B1
YEE TOCK CHEE PARK	BRIDGEWAY BLVD & PRINCESS ST, SAUS, 94965	627 - B3

PERFORMING ARTS

FEATURE NAME	Address City, ZIP Code	PAGE-GRID
CUSHING MEMORIAL THEATER	E RIDGECREST BLVD, MrnC, 94965, (415)383-1100	605 - F2
FOREST MEDWS PERFRMNG ARTS CTR	1500 GRAND AV, SRFL, 94901, (415)457-4440	566 - H7

POINTS OF INTEREST

FEATURE NAME	Address City, ZIP Code	PAGE-GRID
AREQUIPA GIRL SCOUT CAMP	AREQUIPA FIRE RD, MrnC	565 - F4
AUDUBON CANYON RANCH-(SEE PAGE 583)	4900 SHORELINE HWY, MrnC, 94924, (415)663-8203	584 - H6
BLUNT POINT LIGHTHOUSE	TBRN	627 - J4
BROTHERS LIGHTHOUSE, THE	POINT SAN PABLO, RCH, 94801, (510)233-2385	587 - H2
CAMP TAMARANCHO BOY SCOUTS OF-AMERICA	1000 IRON SPRINGS RD, MrnC, (415)459-9530	565 - G4
COAST CAMP (SEE PAGE 541)	COAST TR, MrnC	542 - F7
CYPRESS GROVE (SEE PAGE 501)	MrnC, 94940	502 - C1
KAHN ALLEY RANCHO (SEE PAGE 501)	MrnC, 94940	502 - E1
LIME POINT LIGHTHOUSE	SF	627 - B7
MARIN ART & GARDEN CENTER	SIR FRANCIS DRAKE BLVD, ROSS, 94957, (415)454-5597	586 - D2
POINT REYES LIGHTHOUSE-(SEE PAGE 540)	SIR FRANCIS DRAKE BLVD, MrnC	560 - F3
RICHARDSON BAY AUDUBON CENTER	376 GREENWOOD BEACH RD, TBRN, 94920, (415)388-2524	606 - J5
TIBURON MARINE LABORATORY	PARADISE RD, MrnC, 94920	607 - F5
VISTA POINT	N END GOLDEN GATE BRIDGE, MrnC, 94965	627 - B6

POINTS OF INTEREST - HISTORIC

FEATURE NAME	Address City, ZIP Code	PAGE-GRID
ALCATRAZ ISLAND	ALCATRAZ ISLAND, SF, (415)546-2700	627 - H7
DRAKES MONUMENT	DRAKES BEACH RD, MrnC	541 - D6
MISSION SAN RAFAEL	1104 5TH AV, SRFL, 94901, (415)454-8141	586 - F1
MUIR WOODS NATIONAL MONUMENT	MUIR WOODS RD, MrnC, 94965, (415)388-2595	606 - A4
OLD SAINT HILARY'S HISTORIC-PRESERVE	ESPERANZA ST & MAR WEST ST, TBRN, 94920	607 - E7

POST OFFICES

FEATURE NAME	Address City, ZIP Code	PAGE-GRID
BELVEDERE - TIBURON POST OFFICE	6 BEACH RD, TBRN, 94920, (415)435-1361	627 - D1
BODEGA POST OFFICE	17160 BODEGA HWY, SonC, 95465, (707)876-3186	421 - E4
BOLINAS POST OFFICE	20 BRIGHTON AV, MrnC, 94924, (415)868-1314	604 - G2
CORTE MADERA POST OFFICE	7 PIXLEY AV, CMAD, 94925, (415)924-4463	586 - F7
DILLON BEACH POST OFFICE	52 CYPRESS AV, MrnC, 94971, (707)878-2343	461 - E3
FAIRFAX POST OFFICE	733 CENTER BLVD, FRFX, 94930, (415)453-3146	565 - J6
FOREST KNOLLS POST OFFICE-(SEE PAGE 543)	6 CASTRO ST, MrnC, 94933, (707)488-0533	564 - G1
INVERNESS POST OFFICE-(SEE PAGE 501)	12781 SIR FRANCIS DRAKE BLVD, MrnC, 94937, (415)669-1675	522 - H4
KENTFIELD POST OFFICE	822 COLLEGE AV, MrnC, 94904, (415)454-9627	586 - D3
LAGUNITAS POST OFFICE-(SEE PAGE 543)	7120 SIR FRANCIS DRAKE BLVD, MrnC, 94938, (707)488-9708	564 - F2
LARKSPUR POST OFFICE	120 WARD ST, LKSP, 94939, (415)924-4792	586 - E6
MILL VALLEY POST OFFICE	751 E BLITHEDALE AV, MLV, 94941, (415)388-9656	606 - F3
MISSION RAFAEL STATION POST OFFICE	910 D ST, SRFL, 94901, (415)453-1153	586 - F1
NICASIO POST OFFICE (SEE PAGE 543)	1 OLD RANCHERIA RD, MrnC, 94946, (415)662-2000	544 - F2
NOVATO POST OFFICE	1537 S NOVATO BLVD, NVTO, 94947, (415)897-3171	526 - B5
OLEMA POST OFFICE	10155 SHORELINE HWY, MrnC, 94950, (415)663-1761	543 - E4
POINT REYES STATION	11260 HIGHWAY 1, MrnC, 94956, (415)663-1305	543 - C1
POST OFFICE (SEE PAGE 501)	19200 HIGHWAY 1, MrnC, 94940	502 - D3
ROSS POST OFFICE	1 ROSS COM, ROSS, 94957, (415)454-4123	586 - C2
SAN ANSELMO POST OFFICE	121 SAN ANSELMO AV, SANS, 94960, (415)453-0830	586 - C1
SAN GERONIMO POST OFFICE-(SEE PAGE 543)	630 SAN GERONIMO VALLEY DR, MrnC, 94963, (415)488-4644	564 - J2
SAN QUENTIN POST OFFICE	1 MAIN ST, MrnC, 94964, (415)456-4741	587 - B5
SAN RAFAEL CIVIC CENTER BRANCH PO	2 CIVIC CENTER DR, SRFL, 94903, (415)479-6338	566 - G4
SAN RAFAEL POST OFFICE	40 BELLAM BLVD, SRFL, 94901, (415)459-0944	586 - J3
SAUSALITO POST OFFICE	150 HARBOR DR, SAUS, 94965, (415)332-4656	626 - J1
STINSON BEACH POST OFFICE	15 CL DL MAR, MrnC, 94970, (415)868-1504	605 - C4
TERRA LINDA BRANCH POST OFFICE	603 DEL GANADO RD, SRFL, 94903, (415)479-1850	566 - C2
TOMALES POST OFFICE (SEE PAGE 461)	27005 SHORELINE HWY, MrnC, 94971, (707)878-2364	462 - B4
WOODACRE POST OFFICE	183 SAN GERONIMO VALLEY DR, MrnC, 94973, (415)488-9337	565 - C2

SCHOOLS - PRIVATE ELEMENTARY

FEATURE NAME	Address City, ZIP Code	PAGE-GRID
BRANDEIS-HILLEL PRIVATE SCHOOL	170 N SAN PEDRO RD, MrnC, 94903, (415)472-1833	566 - G4
CHRISTIAN LIFE SCHOOL	1370 S NOVATO BLVD, NVTO, 94947, (415)892-5713	526 - C6
LYCEE FRANCAIS INTL ELEM SCHOOL	330 GOLDEN HIND PASSAGE, CMAD, 94925, (415)924-4202	606 - J1
MARIN COUNTRY DAY ELEM SCHOOL	5221 PARADISE DR, CMAD, 94925, (415)927-5900	607 - A1
MARIN HORIZON SCHOOL	305 MONTFORD AV, MrnC, 94941, (415)388-8408	606 - D4
MARIN PRIMARY ELEM SCHOOL	20 MAGNOLIA AV, LKSP, 94939, (415)924-2608	586 - F7
MARIN WALDORF ELEM SCHOOL	755 IDYLBERRY RD, MrnC, 94903, (415)479-8190	546 - B7
MOUNT TAMALPAIS	100 HARVARD AV, MrnC, 94941, (415)383-9434	606 - F5
NORTH BAY CHRISTIAN ACADEMY	1055 LAS OVEJAS, SRFL, 94903, (415)492-0550	566 - B1
OUR LADY OF LORETTO ELEM SCHOOL	1811 VIRGINIA AV, NVTO, 94945, (415)892-8621	526 - A3
SAINT ANSELM ELEM SCHOOL	40 BELLE AV, SANS, 94960, (415)454-8667	586 - C1
SAINT ISABELLAS PAROCHIAL	S 1 TRINITY WY, SRFL, 94903, (415)479-3727	566 - D3
SAINT MARKS ELEM SCHOOL	39 TRELLIS DR, SRFL, 94903, (415)472-8000	566 - D3
SAINT PATRICK ELEM SCHOOL	120 KING ST, LKSP, 94939, (415)924-0501	586 - E6
SAINT RAPHAELS ELEM SCHOOL	1100 5TH AV, SRFL, 94901, (415)454-4455	586 - F1
SAN DOMENICO LOWER/MIDDLE	S 1500 BUTTERFIELD RD, MrnC, 94960, (415)454-0200	565 - J2
ST HILARY ELEM SCHOOL	765 HILARY DR, TBRN, 94920, (415)435-2224	607 - C5
ST RITA ELEM SCHOOL	102 MARINDA DR, FRFX, 94930, (415)456-1003	565 - J5

SCHOOLS - PRIVATE HIGH

FEATURE NAME	Address City, ZIP Code	PAGE-GRID
BRANSON HIGH SCHOOL	39 FERNHILL AV, ROSS, 94957, (415)454-3612	586 - B2
MARIN ACADEMY HIGH SCHOOL	1600 MISSION AV, SRFL, 94901, (415)453-4550	566 - F7
MARIN CATHOLIC HIGH SCHOOL	675 SIR FRANCIS DRAKE BLVD, MrnC, 94904, (415)461-8844	586 - E4
SAN DOMENICO HIGH SCHOOL	1500 BUTTERFIELD RD, MrnC, 94960, (415)454-0200	565 - J2

SCHOOLS - PUBLIC ELEMENTARY

FEATURE NAME	Address City, ZIP Code	PAGE-GRID
BACICH, ANTHONY G ELEM SCHOOL	25 MCALLISTER AV, MrnC, 94904, (415)925-2220	586 - E4
BAHIA VISTA ELEM SCHOOL	125 BAHIA WY, SRFL, 94901, (415)485-2415	587 - A2
BAYSIDE ELEM SCHOOL	630 NEVADA ST, SAUS, 94965, (415)332-1024	626 - J2
BEL AIRE ELEM SCHOOL	277 KAREN WY, TBRN, 94920, (415)388-7100	607 - A3
BOLINAS-STINSON ELEM SCHOOL	STAR ROUTE, MrnC, 94924, (415)868-1603	604 - F1
BROOKSIDE ELEM SCHOOL	116 BUTTERFIELD RD, SANS, 94960, (415)453-2948	566 - A5
BROOKSIDE UPPER CAMPUS SCHOOL	46 GREEN VALLEY CT, MrnC, 94960, (415)454-7409	566 - B3
COLEMAN ELEM SCHOOL	140 RAFAEL DR, SRFL, 94901, (415)485-2420	566 - G7
CUMMINS, NEIL ELEM SCHOOL	58 MOHAWK AV, CMAD, 94925, (415)927-6965	586 - G7
DIXIE ELEM SCHOOL	1175 IDYLBERRY RD, MrnC, 94903, (415)479-6200	546 - C7

FEATURE NAME Address City, ZIP Code	PAGE-GRID
GALLINAS ELEM SCHOOL 177 N SAN PEDRO RD, MrnC, 94903, (415)492-3150	566 - G4
GLENWOOD ELEM SCHOOL 25 CASTLEWOOD DR, SRFL, 94901, (415)485-2430	567 - C6
HAMILTON ELEM SCHOOL 601 BOLLING DR, NVTO, 94949, (415)883-4691	546 - G4
LAGUNITAS ELEM SCHOOL- (SEE PAGE 543) SIR FRANCIS DRAKE BLVD & MEADO, MrnC, 94963, (415)488-9437	564 - J1
LOMA VERDE ELEM SCHOOL 399 ALAMEDA DE LA LOMA, MrnC, 94949, (415)883-4681	546 - E2
LU SUTTON ELEM SCHOOL 1800 CENTER RD, NVTO, 94947, (415)897-3196	526 - A3
LYNWOOD ELEM SCHOOL 1320 LYNWOOD DR, NVTO, 94947, (415)897-4161	526 - C6
MAGUIRE, EDNA ELEM SCHOOL 80 LOMITA DR, MLV, 94941, (415)389-7733	606 - G3
MANOR ELEM SCHOOL 150 OAK MANOR DR, FRFX, 94930, (415)453-1544	565 - H4
OLD MILL ELEM SCHOOL 352 THROCKMORTON AV, MLV, 94941, (415)389-7727	606 - C3
OLIVE ELEM SCHOOL 629 PLUM ST, NVTO, 94945, (415)897-2131	526 - D3
PARK ELEM SCHOOL 360 E BLITHEDALE AV, MLV, 94941, (415)389-7735	606 - E3
PLEASANT VALLEY ELEM SCHOOL 755 SUTRO AV, NVTO, 94947, (415)897-5104	525 - G3
RANCHO ELEM SCHOOL 1430 JOHNSON ST, NVTO, 94947, (415)897-3101	526 - B5
REED ELEM SCHOOL 1199 TIBURON BLVD, TBRN, 94920, (415)435-3302	607 - D7
ROSS ELEM SCHOOL LAGUNITAS RD & ALLEN AV, ROSS, 94957, (415)457-2705	586 - C2
SAN GERONIMO VALLEY ELEM SCHOOL- (SEE PAGE 543) SIR FRANCIS DRAKE BLVD & MEADO, MrnC, 94963, (707)488-9421	564 - J1
SAN PEDRO ELEM SCHOOL 498 POINT SAN PEDRO RD, SRFL, 94901, (415)485-2450	587 - B1
SAN RAMON ELEM SCHOOL 45 SAN RAMON WY, NVTO, 94945, (415)897-1196	525 - H1
SILVEIRA, MARY E ELEM SCHOOL 375 BLACKSTONE DR, MrnC, 94903, (415)479-8373	546 - E6
STINSON BEACH ELEM SCHOOL SHORELINE HWY, MrnC, 94970, (415)868-0844	605 - A2
SUN VALLEY ELEM SCHOOL 75 HAPPY LN, SRFL, 94901, (415)485-2440	566 - D6
TAMALPAIS VALLEY ELEM SCHOOL 350 BELL LN, MrnC, 94965, (415)389-7731	606 - F7
THOMAS, WADE ELEM SCHOOL ROSS AV, SANS, 94960, (415)454-4603	586 - B1
TOMALES ELEM SCHOOL (SEE PAGE 461) 40 JOHN ST, MrnC, 94971, (707)878-2214	462 - C4
VALLECITO ELEM SCHOOL 50 NOVA ALBION WY, SRFL, 94903, (415)479-2032	566 - D3
WEST MARIN ELEM SCHOOL 11550 SHORELINE HWY, MrnC, 94956, (415)663-1014	523 - D7

SCHOOLS - PUBLIC HIGH

FEATURE NAME Address City, ZIP Code	PAGE-GRID
NOVATO HIGH SCHOOL 625 ARTHUR ST, NVTO, 94947, (415)898-2125	526 - B6
REDWOOD HIGH SCHOOL 395 DOHERTY DR, LKSP, 94939, (415)924-6200	586 - G6
SAN ANDREAS CONT HIGH SCHOOL 599 WILLIAM AV, LKSP, 94939, (415)945-3770	586 - F6
SAN MARIN HIGH SCHOOL 15 SAN MARIN DR, NVTO, 94945, (415)898-2121	525 - G1
SAN RAFAEL HIGH SCHOOL 185 MISSION AV, SRFL, 94901, (415)485-2330	586 - H1
SIR FRANCIS DRAKE HIGH SCHOOL 1327 SIR FRANCIS DRAKE BLVD, SANS, 94960, (415)453-8770	566 - B6
TAMALPAIS HIGH SCHOOL 700 MILLER AV, MLV, 94941, (415)388-3292	606 - F5
TERRA LINDA HIGH SCHOOL 320 NOVA ALBION WY, SRFL, 94903, (415)492-3100	566 - D4
TOMALES HIGH SCHOOL (SEE PAGE 461) IRVINE RD, MrnC, 94971, (707)878-2286	462 - D4

SCHOOLS - PUBLIC MIDDLE

FEATURE NAME Address City, ZIP Code	PAGE-GRID
DAVIDSON, JAMES B MIDDLE SCHOOL 280 WOODLAND AV, SRFL, 94901, (415)485-2400	586 - G2
DEL MAR INTERMEDIATE SCHOOL 105 AVD MIRAFLORES, TBRN, 94920, (415)435-1468	607 - B5
HALL MIDDLE SCHOOL 200 DOHERTY DR, LKSP, 94939, (415)927-6978	586 - F5
HILL MIDDLE SCHOOL 720 DIABLO AV, NVTO, 94947, (415)899-9300	526 - B4
KENT, ADALINE E MIDDLE SCHOOL 250 STADIUM WY, MrnC, 94904, (415)925-2200	586 - D3
MILL VALLEY MIDDLE SCHOOL 425 SYCAMORE AV, MLV, 94941, (415)389-7711	606 - F4
MILLER CREEK MIDDLE SCHOOL 2255 LAS GALLINAS AV, MrnC, 94903, (415)479-1660	546 - D7
SAN JOSE MIDDLE SCHOOL 1000 SUNSET PKWY, NVTO, 94949, (415)883-7831	526 - B7
SINALOA MIDDLE SCHOOL 2045 VINEYARD RD, NVTO, 94947, (415)897-2111	525 - H3
WHITE HILL MIDDLE SCHOOL 101 GLEN DR, FRFX, 94930, (415)454-8390	565 - G3

SHOPPING CENTERS - COMMUNITY

FEATURE NAME Address City, ZIP Code	PAGE-GRID
BOARDWALK SHOPPING CENTER TIBURON BLVD & BEACH RD, TBRN, 94920, (415)435-2822	607 - D7
BON AIR CENTER SIR FRANCIS DRAKE & LA CUESTA, LKSP, 94939, (415)461-0200	586 - G4
DEL PRADO SQUARE SHOPPING CENTER HWY 101 & IGNACIO BL, NVTO, 94949	546 - F2
DOWNTOWN NOVATO CENTER TAMALPAIS AVE & GRANT AVE, NVTO, 94945, (415)897-9601	526 - A3
IGNACIO CENTER 455 ENTRADA DR, NVTO, 94949, (415)883-4012	546 - E1
LARKSPUR LANDING 101 FRWY & E SIR FRANCIS DRAKE, LKSP, 94904, (415)461-3424	586 - H4
MARIN SQUARE 75 BELLAM BLVD, SRFL, 94901, (415)563-6200	586 - J3
MONTECITO PLAZA 3RD ST & GRAND AV, SRFL, 94901, (415)453-2843	586 - H1
NAVE SHOPPING CENTER 1535 S NOVATO BLVD, NVTO, 94947, (415)479-8788	526 - B5
NORTHGATE CENTER FREITAS PKWY & NORTHGATE DR, SRFL, 94903, (415)546-0696	566 - D3
NOVATO FAIR SHOPPING CENTER REDWOOD BLVD & DIABLO AV, NVTO, 94945	526 - B4
PACHECO PLAZA IGNACIO BLVD, NVTO, 94949, (415)883-4646	546 - E2
PARADISE CENTER PARADISE DR & EL CAMINO DR, CMAD, 94925	606 - J1
PT TIBURON PLAZA SHOPPING CENTER PARADISE DR & MAIN ST, TBRN, 94920	627 - E1
RED HILL CENTER 900 SIR FRANCIS DRAKE BLVD, SANS, 94960	566 - B6
STRAWBERRY VILLAGE SHOPPING CENTER BELVEDERE DR & REED BL, MrnC, 94941	606 - H4
TAMALPAIS JUNCTION SHOPPING CENTER HWY 1 & FLAMINGO RD, MrnC, 94965	606 - F6
THE MARKET PLACE TAMAL VISTA BL & SANDPIPER CIR, CMAD, 94925, (415)924-0441	586 - G6
THE SQUARE SHOPPING CENTER WILSON AV & NOVATO BLVD, NVTO, 94947	525 - J2
THE VILLAGE FAIR 777 BRIDGEWAY BLVD, SAUS, 94965	627 - B3
VINTAGE OAKS AT NOVATO 208 VINTAGE WY, NVTO, 94947, (415)897-9999	526 - D5

SHOPPING MALLS

FEATURE NAME Address City, ZIP Code	PAGE-GRID
THE MALL AT NORTHGATE 580 NORTHGATE DR, SRFL, 94903, (415)479-5955	566 - E3
TOWN CENTER CORTE MADERA 706 TAMALPAIS DR, CMAD, 94925, (415)924-2961	586 - G7
VILLAGE AT CORTE MADERA 1852 REDWOOD HWY, CMAD, 94925, (415)924-8557	586 - H7

TRANSPORTATION

FEATURE NAME Address City, ZIP Code	PAGE-GRID
ANGEL ISLAND FERRY TERMINAL TBRN	627 - G1
GOLDEN GATE LARKSPUR FERRY TERMINAL E SIR FRANCIS DRAKE BLVD, LKSP, 94904	586 - H5
GOLDEN GATE SAUSALITO FERRY-TERMINAL ANCHOR SPINNAKER DR & PARK ST, SAUS, 94965	627 - B3
LARKSPUR FERRY TERMINAL E SIR FRANCIS DRAKE BLVD, LKSP, 94904	586 - H5
RAILROAD STATION GRANT AVE & SCOTT CT, NVTO, 94945	526 - C3
TIBURON FERRY TERMINAL PARADISE DR, TBRN, 94920	627 - E1

1998 MARIN NEW TO OLD Page Conversion List

MARIN CO.

NEW-OLD	
New 441	
A2	15 - A1
A3	15 - A2
A4	15 - A2
A6	15 - A3
A7	15 - A3
B1	15 - A1
B2	15 - A1
B3	15 - A2
B4	15 - A2
B5	15 - A2
B6	15 - A3
B7	15 - A3
C1	15 - A1
C2	15 - A1
C3	15 - A2
C4	15 - A2
C5	15 - A2
C6	15 - A3
C7	15 - A3
D1	15 - B1
D2	15 - B1
D3	15 - B2
D4	15 - B2
D5	15 - B2
D6	15 - B3
D7	15 - B3
E1	15 - B1
E2	15 - B1
E3	15 - B2
E4	15 - B2
E5	15 - B2
E6	15 - B3
E7	15 - B3
F1	15 - B1
F2	15 - B1
F3	15 - B2
F4	15 - B2
F5	15 - B2
F6	15 - B3
F7	15 - B3
G1	15 - C1
G2	15 - C1
G3	15 - C2
G4	15 - C2
G5	15 - C2
G6	15 - C3
G7	15 - C3
H1	15 - C1
H2	15 - C1
H3	15 - C2
H4	15 - C2
H5	15 - C2
H6	15 - C3
H7	15 - C3
J1	15 - C1
J2	15 - C1
J3	15 - C2
J4	15 - D2
J5	15 - D2
J6	15 - D3
J7	15 - D3
New 442	
A1	15 - D1
A2	15 - D1
A3	15 - D2
A4	15 - D2
A5	15 - D2
A6	15 - D3
A7	15 - D3
B1	15 - D1
B2	15 - D1
B3	15 - D2
B4	15 - D2
B5	15 - D2
B6	15 - D3
B7	15 - D3
C1	15 - E1
C2	15 - E1
C3	15 - E2
C4	15 - E2
C5	15 - E2
C6	15 - E3
C7	15 - E3
D1	15 - E1
D2	15 - E1
D3	15 - E2
D4	15 - E2
D5	15 - E2
D6	15 - E3
D7	15 - E3
E1	15 - E1
E2	15 - E1
E3	15 - E2
E4	15 - E2
E5	15 - E2
E6	15 - E3
E7	15 - E3
F1	15 - F1
F2	15 - F1
F3	15 - F2
F4	15 - F2
F5	15 - F2
F6	15 - F3
F7	15 - F3
G1	15 - F1
G2	15 - F1
G3	15 - F2

NEW-OLD	
New 442	
G4	15 - F2
G5	15 - F2
G6	15 - F3
G7	15 - F3
H1	15 - F1
H2	15 - F1
H4	15 - F2
H5	15 - F2
H6	15 - F3
H7	16 - A2
J5	16 - A1
J6	16 - A1
J7	16 - A2
New 461	
A1	15 - A4
A2	15 - A4
A3	15 - A5
A4	15 - A5
A5	15 - A5
A6	15 - A6
A7	15 - A6
B1	15 - A4
B2	15 - A4
B3	15 - A5
B4	15 - A5
B5	15 - A5
B6	15 - A6
B7	15 - A6
C1	15 - A4
C2	15 - A4
C3	15 - A5
C4	15 - A5
C5	15 - A5
C6	15 - A6
C7	15 - A6
D1	15 - B4
D2	15 - B4
D3	15 - B5
D4	15 - B5
D5	15 - B5
D6	15 - B6
D7	15 - B6
E1	15 - B4
E2	15 - B4
E3	15 - B5
E4	15 - B5
E5	15 - B5
E6	15 - B6
E7	15 - B6
F1	15 - B4
F2	15 - B4
F3	15 - B5
F4	15 - B5
F5	15 - B5
F6	15 - C6
F7	15 - C6
G1	15 - C4
G2	15 - C4
G3	15 - C5
G4	15 - C5
G5	15 - C5
G6	15 - C6
G7	15 - C6
H1	15 - C4
H2	15 - C4
H3	15 - C5
H4	15 - C5
H5	15 - C5
H6	15 - C6
H7	15 - C6
J1	15 - D4
J2	15 - D4
J3	15 - D5
J4	15 - D5
J5	15 - D5
J6	15 - D6
J7	15 - D6
New 462	
A1	15 - D4
A2	15 - D4
A3	15 - D5
A4	15 - D5
A5	15 - D5
A6	15 - D6
A7	15 - D6
B1	15 - D4
B2	15 - D4
B3	15 - D5
B4	15 - D5
B5	15 - D5
B6	15 - D6
B7	15 - D6
C1	15 - E4
C2	15 - E4
C3	15 - E5
C4	15 - E5
C5	15 - E5
C6	15 - E6
C7	15 - E6
D1	15 - E4
D2	15 - E4
D3	15 - E5
D4	15 - E5
D5	15 - E5
D6	15 - E6
D7	15 - E6
E1	15 - E4

NEW-OLD	
New 462	
E2	15 - E4
E3	15 - E5
E4	15 - E5
E5	15 - E5
E6	15 - E6
E7	15 - E6
F1	15 - F4
F2	15 - F4
F3	15 - F4
F4	15 - F5
F5	15 - F5
F6	15 - F6
F7	15 - F6
G1	15 - F4
G2	15 - F4
G3	15 - F4
G4	15 - F5
G5	15 - F5
G6	15 - F6
G7	15 - F6
H1	16 - A2
H2	16 - A3
H3	16 - A3
H4	16 - A4
H5	16 - A5
H6	16 - A5
H7	16 - A6
J1	16 - A2
J2	16 - A3
J3	16 - A3
J4	16 - A4
J5	16 - A5
J6	16 - A5
J7	16 - A6
New 463	
A1	16 - B2
A2	16 - B3
A3	16 - B3
A4	16 - B4
A5	16 - B5
A6	16 - B5
A7	16 - B6
B1	16 - B2
B2	16 - B3
B3	16 - B3
B4	16 - B4
B5	16 - B4
B6	16 - B5
B7	16 - B6
C1	16 - C2
C2	16 - C3
C3	16 - C3
C4	16 - C4
C5	16 - C4
C6	16 - C5
C7	16 - C6
D1	16 - C2
D2	16 - C3
D3	16 - C3
D4	16 - C4
D5	16 - C4
D6	16 - C5
D7	16 - C6
E1	16 - D2
E2	16 - D3
E3	16 - D3
E4	16 - D4
E5	16 - D4
E6	16 - D5
E7	16 - D6
F1	16 - D2
F2	16 - D3
F3	16 - D3
F4	16 - D4
F5	16 - D4
F6	16 - D5
F7	16 - D6
G1	16 - E2
G2	16 - E3
G3	16 - E3
G4	16 - E4
G5	16 - E4
G6	16 - E5
G7	16 - E5
H1	16 - E2
H2	16 - E3
H3	16 - E3
H4	16 - E4
H5	16 - E4
H6	16 - E5
H7	16 - E5
J1	16 - F2
J2	16 - F3
J3	16 - F3
J4	16 - F4
J5	16 - F4
J6	16 - F5
J7	16 - F5
New 464	
A1	16 - F2
A2	16 - F3
A3	16 - F3
A4	16 - F4
A5	16 - F4
A6	16 - F5
A7	16 - F5
New 481	

NEW-OLD	
New 481	
A1	15 - A6
B1	15 - A6
B4	17 - A2
B5	17 - A3
B6	17 - A3
B7	17 - A4
C1	15 - A6
C2	17 - A1
C3	17 - A2
C4	17 - A2
C5	17 - A3
C6	17 - A3
C7	17 - A4
D1	15 - B6
D2	17 - B1
D3	17 - B2
D4	17 - B2
D5	17 - B3
D6	17 - B3
D7	17 - B4
E1	15 - B6
E2	17 - B1
E3	17 - B2
E4	17 - B2
E5	17 - B3
E6	17 - B3
E7	17 - B4
F1	15 - C6
F2	17 - C1
F3	17 - C2
F4	17 - C2
F5	17 - C3
F6	17 - C3
F7	17 - C4
G1	15 - C6
G2	17 - C1
G3	17 - C1
G4	17 - C2
G5	17 - C3
G6	17 - C3
G7	17 - C4
H1	15 - C6
H2	18 - A1
H3	18 - A1
H4	18 - A2
H5	18 - A3
H6	18 - A3
H7	18 - A4
J1	15 - D6
J2	18 - A1
J3	18 - A1
J4	18 - A2
J5	18 - A3
J6	18 - A3
J7	18 - A4
New 482	
A1	15 - D6
A2	18 - B1
A3	18 - B1
A4	18 - B2
A5	18 - B3
A6	18 - B3
A7	18 - B4
B1	15 - D6
B2	18 - B1
B3	18 - B1
B4	18 - B2
B5	18 - B3
B6	18 - B3
B7	18 - B4
C1	15 - E6
C2	18 - C1
C3	18 - C1
C4	18 - C2
C5	18 - C3
C6	18 - C3
C7	18 - C4
D1	15 - E6
D2	18 - C1
D3	18 - C1
D4	18 - C2
D5	18 - C2
D6	18 - C3
D7	18 - C4
E1	15 - E6
E2	18 - D1
E3	18 - D1
E4	18 - D2
E5	18 - D2
E6	18 - D3
E7	18 - D4
F1	15 - F6
F2	18 - D1
F3	18 - D1
F4	18 - D2
F5	18 - D2
F6	18 - D3
F7	18 - D4
G1	15 - F6
G2	18 - E1
G3	18 - E1
G4	18 - E2
G5	18 - E2
G6	18 - E3
G7	18 - E4
H1	16 - A6
H2	18 - E1

NEW-OLD	
New 482	
H3	18 - E1
H4	18 - E2
H5	18 - E2
H6	18 - E3
H7	18 - E3
J1	16 - A6
J2	18 - F1
J3	18 - F1
J4	18 - F2
J5	18 - F2
J6	18 - F3
J7	18 - F3
New 483	
A1	16 - B6
A2	18 - F1
A3	18 - F1
A4	18 - F2
A5	18 - F2
A6	18 - F3
A7	18 - F3
B1	16 - B6
B2	19 - A1
B3	19 - A1
B4	19 - A2
B5	19 - A2
B6	19 - A3
B7	19 - A3
C1	16 - C6
C2	19 - A1
C3	19 - A1
C4	19 - A2
C5	19 - A2
C6	19 - A3
C7	19 - A3
D1	16 - C6
D2	19 - B1
D3	19 - B1
D4	19 - B2
D5	19 - B2
D6	19 - B3
D7	19 - B3
E1	16 - D6
E2	19 - B1
E3	19 - B1
E4	19 - B2
E5	19 - B2
E6	19 - B3
E7	19 - B3
F1	16 - D6
F2	19 - C1
F3	19 - C1
F4	19 - C2
F5	19 - C2
F6	19 - C3
F7	19 - C3
G1	16 - E6
G2	19 - C1
G3	19 - C1
G4	19 - C2
G5	19 - C2
G6	19 - C3
G7	19 - C3
H1	16 - E6
H2	19 - D1
H3	19 - D1
H4	19 - D2
H5	19 - D2
H6	19 - D3
H7	19 - D3
J1	16 - F6
J2	19 - D1
J3	19 - D1
J4	19 - D2
J5	19 - D2
J6	19 - D3
J7	19 - D3
New 484	
A1	16 - F6
A2	19 - E1
A3	19 - E1
A4	19 - E2
A5	19 - E2
A6	19 - E3
A7	19 - E3
B3	19 - E1
B4	19 - E2
B5	19 - E2
B6	19 - E3
B7	19 - E3
C3	19 - F1
C4	19 - F2
C5	19 - F2
C6	19 - F3
C7	19 - F3
D3	19 - F1
D4	19 - F2
D5	19 - F2
D6	20 - A3
D7	20 - A3
E3	20 - A1
E4	20 - A2
E5	20 - A2
E6	20 - A3
E7	20 - A3
F3	20 - B1
F4	20 - B2
F5	20 - B2

NEW-OLD	
New 484	
F6	20 - B3
F7	20 - B3
G3	20 - B1
G4	20 - B2
G5	20 - B2
G6	20 - B3
G7	20 - B3
H7	20 - C3
J7	20 - C3
New 485	
A7	20 - D3
B7	20 - D3
C7	20 - E3
D7	20 - E3
E7	20 - F3
New 501	
B1	17 - A4
B2	17 - A5
B3	17 - A5
B4	17 - A6
B5	17 - D1
B6	17 - D1
B7	17 - D2
C1	17 - A4
C2	17 - A5
C3	17 - A5
C4	17 - A6
C5	17 - D1
C6	17 - D1
C7	17 - D2
D1	17 - B4
D2	17 - B5
D3	17 - B5
D4	17 - B6
D5	17 - E1
D6	17 - E1
D7	17 - E2
E1	17 - B4
E2	17 - B5
E3	17 - B5
E4	17 - B6
E5	17 - E1
E6	17 - E1
E7	17 - E2
F1	17 - C4
F2	17 - C5
F3	17 - C5
F4	17 - C6
F5	17 - F1
F6	17 - F1
F7	17 - F2
G1	17 - C4
G2	17 - C5
G3	17 - C5
G4	17 - C6
G5	17 - F1
G6	17 - F1
G7	17 - F2
H1	18 - A4
H2	18 - A5
H3	18 - A5
H4	18 - A6
H5	21 - A1
H6	21 - A1
H7	21 - A2
J1	18 - A4
J2	18 - A5
J3	18 - A5
J4	18 - A6
J5	21 - A1
J6	21 - A1
J7	21 - A2
New 502	
A1	18 - B4
A2	18 - B5
A3	18 - B5
A4	18 - B6
A5	18 - B6
A6	21 - B1
A7	21 - B2
B1	18 - B4
B2	18 - B5
B3	18 - B5
B4	18 - B6
B5	18 - B6
B6	21 - B1
B7	21 - B2
C1	18 - C4
C2	18 - C5
C3	18 - C5
C4	18 - C6
C5	18 - C6
C6	21 - C1
C7	21 - C2
D1	18 - C4
D2	18 - C5
D3	18 - C5
D4	18 - C6
D5	18 - C6
D6	21 - C1
D7	21 - C1
E1	18 - D4
E2	18 - D5
E3	18 - D5
E4	18 - D6
E5	18 - D6
E6	21 - D1

NEW-OLD	
New 502	
E7	21 - D1
F1	18 - D4
F2	18 - D5
F3	18 - D5
F4	18 - D6
F5	18 - D6
F6	21 - D1
F7	21 - D1
G1	18 - E4
G2	18 - E5
G3	18 - E5
G4	18 - E6
G5	18 - E6
G6	21 - E1
G7	21 - E1
H1	18 - E4
H2	18 - E5
H3	18 - E5
H4	18 - E6
H5	18 - E6
H6	21 - E1
H7	21 - E1
J1	18 - F4
J2	18 - F5
J3	18 - F5
J4	18 - F6
J5	18 - F6
J6	21 - F1
J7	21 - F1
New 503	
A1	18 - F4
A2	18 - F5
A3	18 - F5
A4	18 - F6
A5	18 - F6
A6	21 - F1
A7	21 - F1
B1	19 - A4
B2	19 - A5
B3	19 - A5
B4	19 - A6
B5	19 - A6
B6	22 - A1
B7	22 - A1
C1	19 - A4
C2	19 - A4
C3	19 - A5
C4	19 - A6
C5	19 - A6
C6	22 - A1
C7	22 - A1
D1	19 - B4
D2	19 - B4
D3	19 - B5
D4	19 - B6
D5	19 - B6
D6	22 - B1
D7	22 - B1
E1	19 - B4
E2	19 - B4
E3	19 - B5
E4	19 - B6
E5	19 - B6
E6	22 - B1
E7	22 - C1
F1	19 - C4
F2	19 - C4
F3	19 - C5
F4	19 - C6
F5	19 - C6
F6	22 - C1
F7	22 - C1
G1	19 - C4
G2	19 - C4
G3	19 - C5
G4	19 - C5
G5	19 - D6
G6	22 - D1
G7	22 - D1
H1	19 - D4
H2	19 - D4
H3	19 - D5
H4	19 - D5
H5	19 - D6
H6	22 - D1
H7	22 - D1
J1	19 - D4
J2	19 - D4
J3	19 - D5
J4	19 - E5
J5	19 - E6
J6	22 - E1
J7	22 - E1
New 504	
A1	19 - E4
A2	19 - E4
A3	19 - E5
A4	19 - E5
A5	19 - E6
A6	19 - E6
A7	22 - E1
B1	19 - E4
B2	19 - F4
B3	19 - F5
B4	19 - F5
B5	19 - F6
B6	19 - F6

NEW-OLD	
New 504	
B7	22 - F1
C1	19 - F4
C2	19 - F4
C3	19 - F5
C4	19 - F5
C5	19 - F6
C6	19 - F6
C7	22 - F1
D1	20 - A4
D2	20 - A4
D3	20 - A5
D4	20 - A5
D5	20 - A6
D6	20 - A6
D7	23 - A1
E1	20 - A4
E2	20 - A4
E3	20 - A5
E4	20 - A5
E5	20 - A6
E6	20 - B6
E7	23 - B1
F1	20 - B4
F2	20 - B4
F3	20 - B5
F4	20 - B5
F5	20 - B6
F6	20 - B6
F7	23 - B1
G1	20 - B4
G2	20 - B4
G3	20 - B5
G4	20 - C5
G5	20 - C6
G6	20 - C6
G7	23 - C1
H1	20 - C4
H2	20 - C4
H3	20 - C5
H4	20 - C5
H5	20 - C6
H6	20 - C6
H7	23 - C1
J1	20 - C4
J2	20 - C4
J3	20 - D5
J4	20 - D5
J5	20 - D6
J6	20 - D6
J7	23 - D1
New 505	
A1	20 - D4
A2	20 - D4
A3	20 - D5
A4	20 - D5
A5	20 - D6
A6	20 - D6
A7	23 - D1
B1	20 - D4
B2	20 - D4
B3	20 - E5
B4	20 - E5
B5	20 - E6
B6	20 - E6
B7	23 - E1
C1	20 - E4
C2	20 - E4
C3	20 - E5
C4	20 - E5
C5	20 - E6
C6	20 - E6
C7	23 - E1
D1	20 - E4
D2	20 - F4
D3	20 - F5
D4	20 - F5
D5	20 - F6
D6	20 - F6
D7	23 - F1
E1	20 - F4
E2	20 - F4
E3	20 - F5
E4	20 - F5
E5	20 - F6
E6	20 - F6
E7	23 - F1
F2	20 - F4
F3	1A - A2
F4	1A - A3
F5	1A - A4
F6	1A - A5
F7	1A - A6
G2	1A - A1
G3	1A - A2
G4	1A - A3
G5	1A - A4
G6	1A - A5
G7	1A - A6
H2	1A - B1
H3	1A - B2
H4	1A - B3
H5	1A - B4
H6	1A - B5
H7	1A - B6
J2	1A - C1
J3	1A - C2
J4	1A - C3

NEW-OLD	
New 505	
J5	1A - C4
J6	1A - C5
J7	1A - C6
New 506	
A2	1A - D1
A3	1A - D2
A4	1A - D3
A5	1A - D4
A6	1A - D5
A7	1A - D6
B2	1A - E1
B3	1A - E2
B4	1A - E3
B5	1A - E4
B6	1A - E5
B7	1A - E6
C2	1A - E1
C3	1A - E2
C4	1A - E3
C5	1A - F4
C6	1A - F5
C7	1A - F6
D2	1A - F1
D3	1A - F2
D4	1A - F3
D5	1A - F4
D6	1A - F5
F6	20 - D1
F7	20 - D2
G6	20 - E1
G7	20 - E2
H6	20 - F1
H7	20 - F2
J6	20 - F1
J7	20 - F2
New 521	
B1	17 - D2
B2	17 - D3
B3	17 - D3
B4	17 - D4
B5	17 - D5
B6	17 - D5
B7	17 - D6
C1	17 - D2
C2	17 - D3
C3	17 - D3
C4	17 - D4
C5	17 - D5
C6	17 - D5
C7	17 - D6
D1	17 - E2
D2	17 - E3
D3	17 - E3
D4	17 - E4
D5	17 - E5
D6	17 - E5
D7	17 - E6
E1	17 - E2
E2	17 - E3
E3	17 - E3
E4	17 - E4
E5	17 - E5
E6	17 - E5
E7	17 - E6
F1	17 - F2
F2	17 - F3
F3	17 - F3
F4	17 - F4
F5	17 - F5
F6	17 - F5
F7	17 - F6
G1	17 - F2
G2	17 - F3
G3	17 - F3
G4	17 - F4
G5	17 - F5
G6	17 - F5
G7	17 - F6
H1	21 - A2
H2	21 - A3
H3	21 - A3
H4	21 - A4
H5	21 - A4
H6	21 - A5
H7	21 - A6
J1	21 - A2
J2	21 - A3
J3	21 - A3
J4	21 - A4
J5	21 - A4
J6	21 - A5
J7	21 - A6
New 522	
A1	21 - B2
A2	21 - B3
A3	21 - B3
A4	21 - B4
A5	21 - B4
A6	21 - B5
A7	21 - B5
B1	21 - B2
B2	21 - B3
B3	21 - B3
B4	21 - B4
B5	21 - B4
B6	21 - B5
B7	21 - B5

NEW-OLD	
New 522	
C1	21 - C2
C2	21 - C3
C3	21 - C3
C4	21 - C4
C5	21 - C4
C6	21 - C5
C7	21 - C5
D1	21 - C2
D2	21 - C3
D3	21 - C3
D4	21 - C4
D5	21 - C4
D6	21 - C5
D7	21 - D5
E1	21 - D2
E2	21 - D3
E3	21 - D3
E4	21 - D4
E5	21 - D4
E6	21 - D5
E7	21 - D5
F1	21 - D2
F2	21 - D3
F3	21 - D3
F4	21 - D4
F5	21 - E4
F6	21 - E5
F7	21 - E5
G1	21 - E2
G2	21 - E2
G3	21 - E3
G4	21 - E4
G5	21 - E4
G6	21 - E5
G7	21 - E5
H1	21 - E2
H2	21 - E2
H3	21 - F3
H4	21 - F4
H5	21 - F4
H6	21 - F5
H7	21 - F5
J1	21 - F2
J2	21 - F2
J3	21 - F3
J4	21 - F3
J5	21 - F4
J6	21 - F5
J7	21 - F5
New 523	
A1	21 - F2
A2	21 - F2
A3	22 - A3
A4	22 - A3
A5	22 - A4
A6	22 - A5
A7	22 - A5
B1	22 - A2
B2	22 - A2
B3	22 - A3
B4	22 - A3
B5	22 - A4
B6	22 - A4
B7	22 - A5
C1	22 - B2
C2	22 - B2
C3	22 - B3
C4	22 - B3
C5	22 - B4
C6	22 - B4
C7	22 - B5
D1	22 - B2
D2	22 - B2
D3	22 - B3
D4	22 - B3
D5	22 - B4
D6	22 - B4
D7	22 - B5
E1	22 - C2
E2	22 - C2
E3	22 - C3
E4	22 - C3
E5	22 - C4
E6	22 - C4
E7	22 - C5
F1	22 - C2
F2	22 - C2
F3	22 - C3
F4	22 - C3
F5	22 - C4
F6	22 - C4
F7	22 - C5
G1	22 - D2
G2	22 - D2
G3	22 - D3
G4	22 - D3
G5	22 - D4
G6	22 - D4
G7	22 - D5
H1	22 - D2
H2	22 - D2
H3	22 - D3
H4	22 - D3
H5	22 - D4
H6	22 - D4
H7	22 - D5
J1	22 - E2

NEW-OLD	
New 523	
J2	22 - E2
J3	22 - E3
J4	22 - E3
J5	22 - E4
J6	22 - E4
J7	22 - E5
New 524	
A1	22 - E2
A2	22 - E2
A3	22 - E3
A4	22 - E3
A5	22 - E4
A6	22 - E4
A7	22 - E5
B1	22 - F2
B2	22 - F2
B3	22 - F3
B4	22 - F3
B5	22 - F4
B6	22 - F4
B7	22 - F5
C1	22 - F2
C2	22 - F2
C3	22 - F3
C4	22 - F3
C5	22 - F4
C6	22 - F4
C7	22 - F5
D1	23 - A2
D2	23 - A2
D3	23 - A3
D4	23 - A3
D5	23 - A4
D6	23 - A4
D7	23 - A5
E1	23 - B2
E2	23 - B2
E3	23 - B3
E4	23 - B3
E5	23 - B4
E6	23 - B4
E7	23 - B5
F1	23 - B2
F2	23 - B2
F3	23 - B3
F4	23 - B3
F5	23 - B4
F6	23 - B4
F7	23 - B5
G1	23 - C2
G2	23 - C2
G3	23 - C3
G4	23 - C3
G5	23 - C4
G6	23 - C4
G7	23 - C5
H1	23 - C2
H2	23 - C2
H3	23 - C3
H4	23 - C3
H5	23 - D4
H6	23 - D4
H7	23 - D5
J1	23 - D2
J2	23 - D2
J3	23 - D3
J4	23 - D3
J5	23 - D4
J6	23 - D4
J7	23 - D5
New 525	
A1	23 - D2
A2	23 - D2
A3	23 - D3
A4	23 - D3
A5	23 - D4
A6	23 - D4
A7	23 - D5
B1	23 - E2
B2	23 - E2
B3	23 - E3
B4	23 - E3
B5	23 - E4
B6	23 - E4
B7	23 - E5
C1	23 - E1
C2	23 - E2
C3	23 - E3
C4	23 - E3
C5	23 - E4
C6	23 - E4
C7	23 - E5
D1	23 - F2
D2	23 - F2
D3	23 - F3
D4	23 - F3
D5	23 - F4
D6	23 - F4
D7	23 - F5
E1	23 - F1
E2	23 - F2
E3	23 - F3
E4	23 - F3
E5	23 - F4
E6	23 - F4
E7	23 - F5
F1	1A - A6

NEW-OLD	
New 525	
F2	1 - A1
F3	1 - A2
F4	1 - A3
F5	1 - A4
F6	1 - A5
F7	1 - A6
G1	1A - B6
G2	1 - B1
G3	1 - B2
G4	1 - B3
G5	1 - B4
G6	1 - B5
G7	1 - B6
H1	1A - B6
H2	1 - B1
H3	1 - B2
H4	1 - B3
H5	1 - C4
H6	1 - C5
H7	1 - C6
J1	1A - C6
J2	1 - C1
J3	1 - C2
J4	1 - C3
J5	1 - C4
J6	1 - C5
J7	1 - C6
New 526	
A1	1A - D6
A2	1 - D1
A3	1 - D2
A4	1 - D3
A5	1 - D4
A6	1 - D5
A7	1 - D6
B1	1A - E6
B2	1 - E1
B3	1 - E2
B4	1 - E3
B5	1 - E4
B6	1 - E5
B7	1 - E6
C1	1A - F6
C2	1 - F1
C3	1 - F2
C4	1 - F3
C5	1 - F4
C6	1 - F5
C7	1 - F6
D1	1A - F6
D2	2 - A1
D3	2 - A2
D4	2 - A3
D5	2 - A4
D6	2 - A5
D7	2 - A6
E2	2 - A1
E3	2 - A2
E4	2 - A3
E5	2 - A4
E6	2 - A5
E7	2 - B6
F1	20 - D2
F2	2 - B1
F3	2 - B2
F4	2 - B3
F5	2 - B4
F6	2 - B5
F7	2 - B6
G1	20 - E2
G2	2 - C1
G3	2 - C2
G4	2 - C3
G5	2 - C4
G6	2 - C5
G7	2 - C6
H1	20 - F2
H2	2 - D1
H3	2 - D2
H4	2 - D3
H5	2 - D4
H6	2 - D5
H7	2 - D6
J1	20 - F2
J2	2 - E1
J3	2 - E2
J4	2 - E3
J5	2 - E4
J6	2 - E5
J7	2 - E6
New 527	
A2	2 - F1
A3	2 - F2
A4	2 - F3
A5	2 - F4
A6	2 - F5
A7	2 - F6
B2	2 - F1
B3	2 - F2
B4	2 - F3
New 540	
F2	24 - A1
F3	24 - A2
F4	24 - A2
F5	24 - A3
F6	24 - A3
F7	24 - A4

NEW-OLD	
New 540	
G2	24 - A1
G3	24 - A2
G4	24 - A2
G5	24 - A3
G6	24 - B3
G7	24 - B4
H2	24 - B1
H3	24 - B2
H4	24 - B2
H5	24 - B3
H6	24 - B3
H7	24 - B4
J2	24 - C1
J3	24 - C2
J4	24 - C2
J5	24 - C3
J6	24 - C3
J7	24 - C4
New 541	
A2	24 - C1
A3	24 - C2
A4	24 - C2
A5	24 - C3
A6	24 - C3
A7	24 - C4
B1	17 - D6
B2	24 - D1
B3	24 - D1
B4	24 - D2
B5	24 - D3
B6	24 - D3
B7	24 - D4
C1	17 - D6
C2	24 - D1
C3	24 - D1
C4	24 - D2
C5	24 - D3
C6	24 - D3
C7	24 - D4
D1	17 - E6
D2	24 - E1
D3	24 - E1
D4	24 - E2
D5	24 - E3
D6	24 - E3
D7	24 - E4
E1	17 - E6
E2	24 - E1
E3	24 - E1
E4	24 - E2
E5	24 - E3
E6	24 - E3
E7	24 - E4
F1	17 - F6
F2	24 - F1
F3	24 - F1
F4	24 - F2
F5	24 - F2
F6	24 - F3
F7	24 - F4
G1	17 - F6
G2	24 - F1
G3	24 - F1
G4	24 - F2
G5	24 - F2
G6	24 - F3
G7	24 - F4
H1	21 - A6
H2	25 - A1
H3	25 - A1
H4	25 - A2
H5	25 - A2
H6	25 - A3
H7	25 - A4
J1	21 - A6
J2	25 - A1
J3	25 - A1
J4	25 - A2
J5	25 - A2
J6	25 - A3
J7	25 - A4
New 542	
A1	21 - B6
A2	25 - B1
A3	25 - B1
A4	25 - B2
A5	25 - B2
A6	25 - B3
A7	25 - B3
B1	21 - B6
B2	25 - B1
B3	25 - B1
B4	25 - B2
B5	25 - B2
B6	25 - B3
B7	25 - B3
C1	21 - C6
C2	21 - C6
C3	25 - C1
C4	25 - C2
C5	25 - C2
C6	25 - C3
C7	25 - C3
D1	21 - D6
D2	25 - C1
D3	25 - C1
D4	25 - C2

NEW-OLD	
New 542	
D5	25 - C2
D6	25 - C3
D7	25 - C3
E1	21 - D6
E2	21 - D6
E3	25 - C1
E4	25 - C2
E5	25 - D2
E6	25 - D3
E7	25 - D3
F1	21 - E6
F2	21 - E6
F3	25 - D1
F4	25 - D2
F5	25 - D2
F6	25 - D3
F7	25 - D3
G1	21 - E6
G2	21 - E6
G3	25 - D1
G4	25 - D1
G5	25 - D2
G6	25 - D3
G7	25 - D3
H1	21 - F6
H2	21 - F6
H3	25 - E1
H4	25 - E1
H5	25 - E2
H6	25 - E3
H7	25 - E3
J1	21 - F6
J2	21 - F6
J3	25 - E1
J4	25 - E1
J5	25 - E2
J6	25 - E3
J7	25 - E3
New 543	
A1	22 - A6
A2	22 - A6
A3	25 - F1
A4	25 - F1
A5	25 - F2
A6	25 - F3
A7	25 - F3
B1	22 - A6
B2	22 - A6
B3	25 - F1
B4	25 - F1
B5	25 - F2
B6	25 - F2
B7	25 - F3
C1	22 - B6
C2	22 - B6
C3	5 - A1
C4	5 - A1
C5	5 - A2
C6	5 - A2
C7	5 - A3
D1	22 - B6
D2	22 - B6
D3	5 - A1
D4	5 - A1
D5	5 - A2
D6	5 - A2
D7	5 - A3
E1	22 - C6
E2	22 - C6
E3	5 - B1
E4	5 - B1
E5	5 - B2
E6	5 - B2
E7	5 - B3
F1	22 - C6
F2	22 - C6
F3	5 - B1
F4	5 - B1
F5	5 - B2
F6	5 - B2
F7	5 - B3
G1	22 - D6
G2	22 - D6
G3	5 - C1
G4	5 - C1
G5	5 - C2
G6	5 - C2
G7	5 - C3
H1	22 - D5
H2	22 - D6
H3	5 - C1
H4	5 - C1
H5	5 - C2
H6	5 - C2
H7	5 - C3
J1	22 - E5
J2	22 - E6
J3	5 - D1
J4	5 - D1
J5	5 - D2
J6	5 - D2
J7	5 - D3
New 544	
A1	22 - E5
A2	22 - E6
A3	5 - D1
A4	5 - D1

NEW-OLD	
New 544	
A5	5 - D2
A6	5 - D2
A7	5 - D3
B1	22 - F5
B2	22 - F6
B3	5 - E1
B4	5 - E1
B5	5 - E2
B6	5 - E2
B7	5 - E3
C1	22 - F5
C2	23 - A6
C3	5 - E1
C4	5 - E1
C5	5 - E2
C6	5 - E2
C7	5 - E3
D1	23 - A5
D2	23 - A6
D3	5 - F1
D4	5 - F1
D5	5 - F2
D6	5 - F3
D7	5 - F3
E1	23 - B5
E2	23 - B6
E3	23 - B6
E4	5 - F1
E5	5 - F2
E6	5 - F3
E7	5 - F3
F1	23 - B5
F2	23 - B6
F3	5A - A1
F4	5A - A1
F5	5A - A2
F6	5A - A3
F7	5A - A4
G1	23 - C5
G2	23 - C6
G3	23 - C6
G4	5A - B1
G5	5A - B2
G6	5A - B3
G7	5A - B4
H1	23 - D5
H2	23 - D6
H3	23 - D6
H4	5A - B1
H5	5A - B2
H6	5A - B3
H7	5A - B4
J1	23 - D5
J2	23 - D6
J3	23 - D6
J4	5A - C1
J5	5A - C2
J6	5A - C3
J7	5A - C4
New 545	
A1	23 - D5
A2	23 - E6
A3	23 - E6
A4	5A - D1
A5	5A - D2
A6	5A - D3
A7	5A - D4
B1	23 - E5
B2	23 - E6
B3	23 - E6
B4	5A - D1
B5	5A - D2
B6	5A - D3
B7	5A - D4
C1	23 - E5
C2	23 - E6
C3	23 - E6
C4	5A - E1
C5	5A - E2
C6	5A - E3
C7	5A - E4
D1	23 - F5
D2	23 - F6
D3	23 - F6
D4	5A - F1
D5	5A - F2
D6	5A - F3
D7	5A - F4
E1	23 - F5
E2	23 - F6
E3	23 - F6
E4	5A - F1
E5	5A - F2
E6	5A - F3
E7	5A - F4
F1	3 - A1
F2	3 - A2
F3	3 - A2
F4	3 - A3
F5	3 - A4
F6	3 - A5
F7	3 - A6
G1	3 - B1
G2	3 - B2
G3	3 - B2
G4	3 - B3
G5	3 - B4

NEW-OLD	
New 545	
G6	3 - B5
G7	3 - B6
H1	3 - C1
H2	3 - C2
H3	3 - C2
H4	3 - C3
H5	3 - C4
H6	3 - C5
H7	3 - C6
J1	3 - C1
J2	3 - C2
J3	3 - C2
J4	3 - C3
J5	3 - C4
J6	3 - C5
J7	3 - C6
New 546	
A1	3 - D1
A2	3 - D2
A3	3 - D2
A4	3 - D3
A5	3 - D4
A6	3 - D5
A7	3 - D6
B1	3 - E1
B2	3 - E2
B3	3 - E2
B4	3 - E3
B5	3 - E4
B6	3 - E5
B7	3 - E6
C1	3 - F1
C2	3 - F2
C3	3 - F2
C4	3 - F3
C5	3 - F4
C6	3 - F5
C7	3 - F6
D1	4 - A1
D2	4 - A1
D3	4 - A2
D4	4 - A3
D5	4 - A4
D6	4 - A5
D7	4 - A6
E1	4 - B1
E2	4 - B1
E3	4 - B2
E4	4 - B3
E5	4 - B4
E6	4 - B5
E7	4 - B6
F1	4 - B1
F2	4 - B1
F3	4 - B2
F4	4 - B3
F5	4 - B4
F6	4 - B5
F7	4 - B6
G1	2 - C6
G2	4 - C1
G3	4 - C2
G4	4 - C3
G5	4 - C4
G6	4 - C5
G7	4 - C6
H1	2 - D6
H2	4 - D1
H3	4 - D2
H4	4 - D3
H5	4 - D4
H6	4 - D5
H7	4 - D6
J1	2 - E6
J2	4 - E1
J3	4 - E2
J4	4 - E3
J5	4 - E4
J6	4 - E5
J7	4 - E6
New 547	
A1	2 - F6
A2	4 - F1
A3	4 - F2
A4	4 - F3
A5	4 - F4
A6	4 - F5
A7	4 - F6
New 560	
F1	24 - A5
F2	24 - A5
F3	24 - A6
F4	24 - A6
G1	24 - B4
G2	24 - B5
G3	24 - B6
G4	24 - B6
H1	24 - B4
H2	24 - B5
H3	24 - B6
H4	24 - B6
J1	24 - C4
J2	24 - C5
J3	24 - C6
J4	24 - C6
New 561	
A1	24 - C4

NEW-OLD	
New 561	
A2	24 - C5
A3	24 - C5
A4	24 - C6
B1	24 - D4
B2	24 - D5
B3	24 - D5
B4	24 - D6
C1	24 - D4
C2	24 - D5
C3	24 - D5
C4	24 - D6
D1	24 - E4
D2	24 - E5
D3	24 - E5
D4	24 - E6
E1	24 - E4
E2	24 - E5
E3	24 - E5
E4	24 - E6
F1	24 - F4
F2	24 - F5
F3	24 - F5
F4	24 - F6
F5	24 - F6
G1	24 - F4
G2	24 - F5
G3	24 - F5
G4	24 - F6
G5	24 - F6
H1	25 - A4
H2	25 - A5
H3	25 - A5
H4	25 - A6
H5	25 - A6
J1	25 - A4
J2	25 - A5
J3	25 - A5
J4	25 - A6
J5	25 - A6
New 562	
A1	25 - B4
A2	25 - B5
A3	25 - B5
A4	25 - B6
A5	25 - B6
B1	25 - B4
B2	25 - B5
B3	25 - B5
B4	25 - B6
B5	25 - B6
C1	25 - C4
C2	25 - C5
C3	25 - C5
C4	25 - C6
C5	25 - C6
D1	25 - C4
D2	25 - C5
D3	25 - C5
D4	25 - C6
D5	25 - C6
E1	25 - D4
E2	25 - D4
E3	25 - D5
E4	25 - D6
E5	25 - D6
F1	25 - D4
F2	25 - D4
F3	25 - D5
F4	25 - D6
F5	25 - D6
G1	25 - D4
G2	25 - D4
G3	25 - D5
G4	25 - D6
G5	25 - E6
H1	25 - E4
H2	25 - E4
H3	25 - E5
H4	25 - E6
H5	25 - E6
J1	25 - E4
J2	25 - E4
J3	25 - E5
J4	25 - E6
J5	25 - E6
New 563	
A1	25 - F4
A2	25 - F4
A3	25 - F5
A4	25 - F5
A5	25 - F6
B1	25 - F4
B2	25 - F4
B3	25 - F5
B4	25 - F5
B5	25 - F6
C1	5 - A4
C2	5 - A4
C3	5 - A5
C4	5 - A5
C5	5 - A6
C6	26 - A1
C7	26 - A1
D1	5 - A4
D2	5 - A4
D3	5 - A5
D4	5 - A5

NEW-OLD	
New 563	
D5	5 - A6
D6	26 - A1
D7	26 - A1
E1	5 - B4
E2	5 - B4
E3	5 - B5
E4	5 - B5
E5	5 - B6
E6	26 - B1
E7	26 - B1
F1	5 - B4
F2	5 - B4
F3	5 - B5
F4	5 - B5
F5	5 - B6
F6	26 - B1
F7	26 - B1
G1	5 - C4
G2	5 - C4
G3	5 - C5
G4	5 - C5
G5	5 - C6
G6	26 - C1
G7	26 - C1
H1	5 - C4
H2	5 - C4
H3	5 - C5
H4	5 - C5
H5	5 - C6
H6	26 - C1
H7	26 - C1
J1	5 - D4
J2	5 - D4
J3	5 - D5
J4	5 - D5
J5	5 - D6
J6	26 - D1
J7	26 - D1
New 564	
A1	5 - D4
A2	5 - D4
A3	5 - D5
A4	5 - D5
A5	5 - D6
A6	26 - D1
A7	26 - D1
B1	5 - E4
B2	5 - E4
B3	5 - E5
B4	5 - E5
B5	5 - E6
B6	5 - E6
B7	26 - E1
C1	5 - E4
C2	5 - E4
C3	5 - E5
C4	5 - E5
C5	5 - E6
C6	5 - E6
C7	26 - F1
D1	5 - F4
D2	5 - F4
D3	5 - F5
D4	5 - F5
D5	5 - F6
D6	5 - F6
D7	26 - F1
E1	5 - F4
E2	5 - F4
E3	5 - F5
E4	27 - A1
E5	5 - F6
E6	27 - A3
E7	26 - F1
F1	5A - A5
F2	5A - A5
F3	5A - A6
F4	27 - A1
F5	27 - A2
F6	27 - A3
F7	27 - A3
G1	5A - B5
G2	5A - B5
G3	5A - B6
G4	27 - B1
G5	27 - B2
G6	27 - B3
G7	27 - B3
H1	5A - B5
H2	5A - B5
H3	5A - B6
H4	27 - B1
H5	27 - B2
H6	27 - B3
H7	27 - B3
J1	5A - C5
J2	5A - C5
J3	5A - C6
J4	27 - C1
J5	27 - C2
J6	27 - C2
J7	27 - C3
New 565	
A1	5A - D4
A2	5A - D5
A3	5A - D6
A4	27 - D1

NEW-OLD	
New 565	
A5	27 - D2
A6	27 - D2
A7	27 - D3
B1	5A - D4
B2	5A - D5
B3	5A - D6
B4	27 - D1
B5	27 - D2
B6	27 - D2
B7	27 - D3
C1	5A - E4
C2	5A - E5
C3	5A - E6
C4	27 - E1
C5	27 - E2
C6	27 - E2
C7	27 - E3
D1	5A - F4
D2	5A - F5
D3	5A - F6
D4	27 - F1
D5	27 - F2
D6	27 - F2
D7	27 - F3
E1	5A - F4
E2	5A - F5
E3	5A - F6
E4	27 - F1
E5	27 - F2
E6	27 - F2
E7	27 - F3
F1	6A - A1
F2	6A - A2
F3	6A - A3
F4	6C - A4
F5	6C - A5
F6	6C - A6
F7	9A - A1
G1	6A - B1
G2	6A - B2
G3	6A - B3
G4	6C - B4
G5	6C - B5
G6	6C - B6
G7	9A - B1
H1	6A - C1
H2	6A - C2
H3	6A - C3
H4	6C - C4
H5	6C - C5
H6	6C - C6
H7	6C - C6
J1	6A - C1
J2	6A - C2
J3	6B - D3
J4	6D - D4
J5	6D - D5
J6	6D - D6
J7	6D - D6
New 566	
A1	6B - D1
A2	6B - D2
A3	6B - D3
A4	6D - D4
A5	6D - D5
A6	6D - D6
A7	6D - D6
B1	6B - E1
B2	6B - E2
B3	6B - E3
B4	6D - E4
B5	6D - E5
B6	6D - E6
B7	6D - E6
C1	6B - F1
C2	6B - F2
C3	6B - F3
C4	6D - F4
C5	6D - F5
C6	6D - F5
C7	6D - F6
D1	7A - A1
D2	7A - A2
D3	7A - A3
D4	7C - A4
D5	7C - A5
D6	7C - A5
D7	7C - A6
E1	7A - B1
E2	7A - B2
E3	7A - B3
E4	7C - B4
E5	7C - B5
E6	7C - B5
E7	7C - B6
F1	7A - B1
F2	7A - C2
F3	7A - C3
F4	7C - C4
F5	7C - C5
F6	7C - C5
F7	7C - C6
G1	7A - C1
G2	7A - C2
G3	7A - C3
G4	7C - C4
G5	7C - C5

NEW-OLD	
New 566	
G6	7C - C5
G7	7C - C6
H1	7B - D1
H2	7B - D2
H3	7B - D3
H4	7D - D4
H5	7D - D4
H6	7D - D5
H7	7D - D6
J1	7B - E1
J2	7B - E2
J3	7B - E3
J4	7D - E4
J5	7D - E4
J6	7D - E5
J7	7D - E6
New 567	
A1	7B - F1
A2	7B - F2
A3	7B - F3
A4	7B - F3
A5	7D - F4
A6	7D - F5
A7	7D - F6
B2	8 - A1
B3	8 - A2
B4	8 - A2
B5	8 - A3
B6	8 - A4
B7	8 - A5
C2	8 - B1
C3	8 - B2
C4	8 - B2
C5	8 - B3
C6	8 - B4
C7	8 - B5
D2	8 - B1
D3	8 - B2
D4	8 - B2
D5	8 - B3
D6	8 - B4
D7	8 - B5
E2	8 - C1
E3	8 - C2
E4	8 - C2
E5	8 - C3
E6	8 - C4
E7	8 - C5
F3	8 - D2
F4	8 - D2
F5	8 - D3
F6	8 - D4
F7	8 - D5
New 583	
B7	26 - A5
C1	26 - A2
C2	26 - A2
C3	26 - A3
C4	26 - A3
C5	26 - A4
C6	26 - A5
C7	26 - A5
D1	26 - A2
D2	26 - A2
D3	26 - A3
D4	26 - A3
D5	26 - B4
D6	26 - B5
D7	26 - B5
E1	26 - B2
E2	26 - B2
E3	26 - B3
E4	26 - B3
E5	26 - B4
E6	26 - B5
E7	26 - B5
F1	26 - B2
F2	26 - B2
F3	26 - B3
F4	26 - C3
F5	26 - C4
F6	26 - C5
F7	26 - C5
G1	26 - C2
G2	26 - C2
G3	26 - C3
G4	26 - C3
G5	26 - C4
G6	26 - C4
G7	26 - C5
H1	26 - C2
H2	26 - C2
H3	26 - D3
H4	26 - D3
H5	26 - D4
H6	26 - D4
H7	26 - D5
J1	26 - D2
J2	26 - D2
J3	26 - D3
J4	26 - D3
J5	26 - D4
J6	26 - D4
J7	26 - D5
New 584	
A1	26 - D2
A2	26 - E2

NEW-OLD	
New 584	
A3	26 - E3
A4	26 - E3
A5	26 - E4
A6	26 - E4
A7	26 - E5
B1	26 - E2
B2	26 - E2
B3	26 - E3
B4	26 - E3
B5	26 - E4
B6	26 - E4
B7	26 - E5
C1	26 - F2
C2	26 - F2
C3	26 - F3
C4	26 - F3
C5	26 - F4
C6	26 - F4
C7	26 - F5
D1	26 - F2
D2	26 - F2
D3	26 - F3
D4	26 - F3
D5	26 - F4
D6	26 - F4
D7	26 - F5
E1	27 - A4
E2	27 - A5
E3	27 - A6
E4	28 - A1
E5	28 - A1
E6	28 - A2
E7	28 - A3
F1	27 - A4
F2	27 - A5
F3	27 - A6
F4	27 - A6
F5	28 - A1
F6	28 - A2
F7	28 - A3
G1	27 - B4
G2	27 - B5
G3	27 - B6
G4	27 - B6
G5	28 - B1
G6	28 - B2
G7	28 - B3
H1	27 - B4
H2	27 - C5
H3	27 - C6
H4	27 - C6
H5	28 - C1
H6	28 - C2
H7	28 - C3
J1	27 - C4
J2	27 - C5
J3	27 - C6
J4	27 - C6
J5	28 - C1
J6	28 - C2
J7	28 - C2
New 585	
A1	27 - D4
A2	27 - D5
A3	27 - D5
A4	27 - D6
A5	28 - D1
A6	28 - D2
A7	28 - D2
B1	27 - D4
B2	27 - D5
B3	27 - D5
B4	27 - D6
B5	28 - D1
B6	28 - D2
B7	28 - E2
C1	27 - E4
C2	27 - E5
C3	27 - E5
C4	27 - E6
C5	28 - E1
C6	28 - E2
C7	28 - E2
D1	27 - F4
D2	27 - F5
D3	27 - F5
D4	27 - F6
D5	28 - F1
D6	28 - F2
D7	28 - F2
E1	27 - F4
E2	27 - F5
E3	27 - F5
E4	27 - F6
E5	28 - F1
E6	9C - A6
E7	28 - F2
F1	9A - A1
F2	9A - A2
F3	9A - A3
F4	9C - A4
F5	9C - A5
F6	9C - A6
F7	29 - A1
G1	9A - B1
G2	9A - B2
G3	9A - B3

INDEX

1998 MARIN NEW TO OLD Page Conversion List

NEW	OLD
New 585	
G4	9C - B4
G5	9C - B5
G6	9C - B6
G7	29 - B1
H1	9A - C1
H2	9A - C2
H3	9A - C3
H4	9C - C4
H5	9C - C5
H6	9C - C6
H7	29 - C1
J1	9B - D1
J2	9B - D2
J3	9B - D3
J4	9D - D4
J5	9D - D5
J6	9D - D6
J7	11A - A1
New 586	
A1	9B - D1
A2	9B - D2
A3	9B - E3
A4	9D - E4
A5	9D - E5
A6	9D - E6
A7	11A - B1
B1	9B - E1
B2	9B - E2
B3	9B - E3
B4	9D - E4
B5	9D - E5
B6	9D - E6
B7	11A - B1
C1	9B - F1
C2	9B - F2
C3	9B - F3
C4	9D - F4
C5	9D - F5
C6	9D - F6
C7	11A - C1
D1	10A - A1
D2	10A - A2
D3	10A - A3
D4	10C - A4
D5	10C - A5
D6	10C - A6
D7	12A - A1
E1	10A - B1
E2	10A - B2
E3	10A - B3
E4	10C - B4
E5	10C - B5
E6	10C - B6
E7	12A - B1
F1	10A - C1
F2	10A - C2
F3	10A - C3
F4	10C - C4
F5	10C - C5
F6	10C - C6
F7	12A - C1
G1	10A - C1
G2	10B - D2
G3	10B - D3
G4	10D - D4
G5	10D - D5
G6	10D - D6
G7	12B - D1
H1	10B - D1
H2	10B - D2
H3	10B - D3
H4	10D - D4
H5	10D - D5
H6	10D - D6
H7	12B - D1
J1	10B - E1
J2	10B - E2
J3	10B - E3
J4	10D - E4
J5	10D - E5
J6	10D - E6
J7	12B - E1
New 587	
A1	10B - F1
A2	10B - F2
A3	10B - F3
A4	10D - F4
A5	10D - F5
A6	10D - F6
A7	12B - F1
B1	8 - A6
B2	8A - E1
B3	8A - E2
B4	8A - E3
B5	8A - E4
B6	8A - E5
B7	11C - D1
C1	8 - B6
C2	8A - F1
C3	8A - F2
C4	8A - F3
C5	8A - F4
C6	8A - F5
C7	8A - F5
D1	8 - B6
E1	8 - C6
F1	8 - D6
New 603	
B1	26 - A5
B2	26 - A6
B3	26 - A6
C1	26 - A5
C2	26 - A6
C3	26 - A6
D1	26 - B5
D2	26 - B6
D3	26 - B6
E1	26 - B5
E2	26 - B6
E3	26 - B6
F1	26 - C5
F2	26 - C6
F3	26 - C6
G1	26 - C5
G2	26 - C6
G3	26 - C6
H1	26 - D5
H2	26 - D6
H3	26 - D6
J1	26 - D5
J2	26 - D6
J3	26 - D6
New 604	
A1	26 - E5
A2	26 - E6
A3	26 - E6
B1	26 - E5
B2	26 - E6
B3	26 - E6
C1	26 - F5
C2	26 - F6
C3	26 - F6
D1	26 - F5
D2	26 - F6
D3	26 - F6
E1	28 - A3
E2	28 - A4
E3	28 - A5
E4	28 - A5
E5	28 - A6
F1	28 - A3
F2	28 - A4
F3	28 - A5
F4	28 - A5
F5	28 - B6
G1	28 - B3
G2	28 - B4
G3	28 - B5
G4	28 - B5
G5	28 - B6
H1	28 - C3
H2	28 - C4
H3	28 - C5
H4	28 - C5
H5	28 - C6
J1	28 - C3
J2	28 - C4
J3	28 - C5
J4	28 - C5
J5	28 - C6
New 605	
A1	28 - D3
A2	28 - D4
A3	28 - D5
A4	28 - D5
A5	28 - D6
A6	28 - D6
B1	28 - E3
B2	28 - E4
B3	28 - E5
B4	28 - E5
B5	28 - E6
B6	28 - E6
C1	28 - E3
C2	28 - E4
C3	28 - E4
C4	28 - E5
C5	28 - E6
C6	28 - E6
D1	28 - F3
D2	28 - F4
D3	28 - F4
D4	28 - F5
D5	28 - F6
D6	28 - F6
E1	28 - F3
E2	28 - F4
E3	30 - A4
E4	28 - F5
E5	30 - A5
E6	30 - A6
E7	31 - A1
F1	29 - A2
F2	29 - A3
F3	30 - A4
F4	30 - A4
F5	30 - A5
F6	30 - A6
F7	31 - B1
G1	29 - B2
G2	29 - B3
G3	30 - B4
G4	30 - B4
G5	30 - B5
G6	30 - B6
New 605	
G7	31 - B1
H1	29 - C2
H2	29 - C3
H3	29 - C3
H4	30 - C4
H5	30 - C5
H6	30 - C6
H7	31 - C1
J1	11A - A2
J2	11A - A3
J3	11A - A3
J4	11B - A4
J5	11B - A5
J6	11B - A6
J7	31 - D1
New 606	
A1	11A - B2
A2	11A - B3
A3	11A - B3
A4	11B - B4
A5	11B - B5
A6	11B - B6
A7	31 - E1
B1	11A - B2
B2	11A - B3
B3	11A - B3
B4	11B - C4
B5	11B - C5
B6	11B - C6
B7	31 - F1
C1	11A - C2
C2	11A - C3
C3	11A - C3
C4	11B - C4
C5	11B - C5
C6	11B - C6
C7	31 - F1
D1	12A - A2
D2	12A - A2
D3	12A - A3
D4	12C - A4
D5	12C - A5
D6	12C - A6
D7	13 - A1
E1	12A - B2
E2	12A - B2
E3	12A - B3
E4	12C - B4
E5	12C - B5
E6	12C - B6
E7	13 - B1
F1	12A - C2
F2	12A - C2
F3	12A - C3
F4	12C - C4
F5	12C - C5
F6	12C - C6
F7	13 - C1
G1	12B - D2
G2	12B - D2
G3	12B - D3
G4	12D - D4
G5	12D - D5
G6	12D - D6
G7	13 - D1
H1	12B - D1
H2	12B - E2
H3	12B - E3
H4	12D - E4
H5	12D - E5
H6	12D - E6
H7	13 - E1
J1	12B - E1
J2	12B - E2
J3	12B - E3
J4	12D - E4
J5	12D - E5
J6	12D - E6
J7	13 - F1
New 607	
A1	12B - F1
A2	12B - F2
A3	12B - F3
A4	12D - F4
A5	12D - F5
A6	12D - F6
A7	13 - F1
B1	11C - D1
B2	11C - D2
B3	11C - D3
B4	11D - D4
B5	11D - D5
B6	11D - D6
B7	14 - A1
C1	11C - E1
C2	11C - E2
C3	11C - E3
C4	11D - E4
C5	11D - E5
C6	11D - E6
C7	14 - B1
D1	11C - F1
D2	11C - F2
D3	11C - F3
D4	11D - F4
D5	11D - F5
D6	11D - F6
New 607	
D7	14 - C1
E1	11C - F1
E2	11C - F2
E3	11C - F3
E4	11D - F4
E5	11D - F5
E6	11D - F6
E7	14 - C1
F5	14 - E4
F6	14 - E5
F7	14 - D1
G7	14 - E1
H7	14 - F1
New 625	
E1	31 - A2
E2	31 - A3
E3	31 - A4
E4	31 - A5
E5	31 - A5
E6	31 - A6
F1	31 - B2
F2	31 - B3
F3	31 - B4
F4	31 - B5
F5	31 - B5
F6	31 - B6
G1	31 - B2
G2	31 - B3
G3	31 - B4
G4	31 - B5
G5	31 - B5
G6	31 - B6
H1	31 - C2
H2	31 - C3
H3	31 - C4
H4	31 - C5
H5	31 - C5
H6	31 - C6
J1	31 - D2
J2	31 - D3
J3	31 - D4
J4	31 - D5
J5	31 - D5
J6	31 - D6
New 626	
A1	31 - E2
A2	31 - E3
A3	31 - E4
A4	31 - E5
A5	31 - E5
A6	31 - E6
B1	31 - F2
B2	31 - F3
B3	31 - F4
B4	31 - F5
B5	31 - F5
B6	31 - F6
C1	31 - F2
C2	31 - F3
C3	31 - F4
C4	13 - A5
C5	13 - A5
C6	13 - A6
D1	13 - A2
D2	13 - A3
D3	13 - A4
D4	13 - A4
D5	13 - A5
D6	13 - A6
E1	13 - B2
E2	13 - B3
E3	13 - B4
E4	13 - B4
E5	13 - B5
E6	13 - B6
F1	13 - C2
F2	13 - C3
F3	13 - C4
F4	13 - C4
F5	13 - C5
F6	13 - C6
G1	13 - D2
G2	13 - D3
G3	13 - D4
G4	13 - D4
G5	13 - D5
G6	13 - D6
H1	13 - E2
H2	13 - E3
H3	13 - E4
H4	13 - E4
H5	13 - E5
H6	13 - E6
J1	13 - F2
J2	13 - F3
J3	13 - F4
J4	13 - F4
J5	13 - F5
J6	13 - F6
New 627	
A1	13 - F2
A2	13 - F3
A3	13 - F4
A4	13 - F4
A5	13 - F5
A6	13 - F6
B1	14 - A2
New 627	
B2	14 - A3
B3	14 - A3
B4	14 - A4
B5	14 - A5
B6	14 - A6
C1	14 - B2
C2	14 - B3
C3	14 - B3
C4	14 - B4
C5	14 - B5
C6	14 - B6
D1	14 - C2
D2	14 - C3
D3	14 - C3
D4	14 - C4
D5	14 - C5
D6	14 - C6
E1	14 - C2
E2	14 - D3
E3	14 - D3
E4	14 - D4
E5	14 - D5
E6	14 - D6
F1	14 - D2
F2	14 - D3
F3	14 - D3
F4	14 - D4
F5	14 - E5
F6	14 - E6
G1	14 - E2
G2	14 - E2
G3	14 - E3
G4	14 - E4
G5	14 - E5
G6	14 - E6
H1	14 - F2
H2	14 - F2
H3	14 - F3
H4	14 - F4
H5	14 - F5
H6	14 - F6

1998 MARIN OLD TO NEW Page Conversion List

OLD-NEW	
Old 1	
A1	525 - F2
A2	525 - F3
A3	525 - F4
A4	525 - F5
A5	525 - F6
A6	525 - F7
B1	525 - H2
B2	525 - H3
B3	525 - G4
B4	525 - G5
B5	525 - G6
B6	525 - G7
C1	525 - J2
C2	525 - J3
C3	525 - J4
C4	525 - J5
C5	525 - J6
C6	525 - H7
D1	526 - A2
D2	526 - A3
D3	526 - A4
D4	526 - A5
D5	526 - A6
D6	526 - A7
E1	526 - B2
E2	526 - B3
E3	526 - B4
E4	526 - B5
E5	526 - B6
E6	526 - B7
F1	526 - C2
F2	526 - C3
F3	526 - C4
F4	526 - C5
F5	526 - C6
F6	526 - C7
Old 1A	
A1	505 - G2
A2	505 - G3
A3	505 - G4
A4	505 - F5
A5	505 - F6
A6	505 - F7
B1	505 - H2
B2	505 - H3
B3	505 - H4
B4	505 - H5
B5	505 - H6
B6	505 - H7
C1	505 - J2
C2	505 - J3
C3	505 - J4
C4	505 - J5
C5	505 - J6
C6	505 - J7
D1	506 - A2
D2	506 - A3
D3	506 - A4
D4	506 - A5
D5	506 - A6
D6	526 - A1
E1	506 - C2
E2	506 - B3
E3	506 - B4
E4	506 - B5
E5	506 - B6
E6	526 - B1
F1	506 - D2
F2	506 - D3
F3	506 - D4
F4	506 - D5
F5	506 - D6
F6	526 - C1
Old 2	
A1	526 - E2
A2	526 - E3
A3	526 - E4
A4	526 - D5
A5	526 - D6
A6	526 - D7
B1	526 - F2
B2	526 - F3
B3	526 - F4
B4	526 - F5
B5	526 - F6
B6	526 - F7
C1	526 - G2
C2	526 - G3
C3	526 - G4
C4	526 - G5
C5	526 - G6
C6	526 - G7
D1	526 - H2
D2	526 - H3
D3	526 - H4
D4	526 - H5
D5	526 - H6
D6	526 - H7
E1	526 - J2
E2	526 - J3
E3	526 - J4
E4	526 - J5
E5	526 - J6
E6	546 - J1
F1	527 - B2
F2	527 - A3
F3	527 - A4

OLD-NEW	
Old 2	
F4	527 - A5
F5	527 - A6
F6	547 - A1
Old 3	
A1	545 - F1
A2	545 - F3
A3	545 - F4
A4	545 - F5
A5	545 - F6
A6	545 - F7
B1	545 - G1
B2	545 - G3
B3	545 - G4
B4	545 - G5
B5	545 - G6
B6	545 - G7
C1	545 - H1
C2	545 - H3
C3	545 - H4
C4	545 - H5
C5	545 - H6
C6	545 - H7
D1	546 - A1
D2	546 - A3
D3	546 - A4
D4	546 - A5
D5	546 - A6
D6	546 - A7
E1	546 - B1
E2	546 - B3
E3	546 - B4
E4	546 - B5
E5	546 - B6
E6	546 - B7
F1	546 - C1
F2	546 - C3
F3	546 - C4
F4	546 - C5
F5	546 - C6
F6	546 - C7
Old 4	
A1	546 - D1
A2	546 - D3
A3	546 - D4
A4	546 - D5
A5	546 - D6
A6	546 - D7
B1	546 - F2
B2	546 - F3
B3	548 - E4
B4	546 - E5
B5	546 - E6
B6	546 - E7
C1	546 - G2
C2	546 - G3
C3	546 - G4
C4	546 - G5
C5	546 - G6
C6	546 - G7
D1	546 - H2
D2	546 - H3
D3	546 - H4
D4	546 - H5
D5	546 - H6
D6	546 - H7
E1	546 - J2
E2	546 - J3
E3	546 - J4
E4	546 - J5
E5	546 - J6
E6	546 - J7
F1	547 - A2
F2	547 - A3
F3	547 - A4
F4	547 - A5
F5	547 - A6
F6	547 - A7
Old 5	
A1	543 - D4
A2	543 - D5
A3	543 - D7
A4	563 - D2
A5	563 - D3
A6	563 - C5
B1	543 - F4
B2	543 - F5
B3	543 - F7
B4	563 - F2
B5	563 - E3
B6	563 - E5
C1	543 - H4
C2	543 - H5
C3	543 - H7
C4	563 - G2
C5	563 - G3
C6	563 - G5
D1	544 - A4
D2	544 - A5
D3	543 - J7
D4	563 - J2
D5	563 - J3
D6	563 - J5
E1	544 - C4
E2	544 - B5
E3	544 - B7
E4	564 - B2
E5	564 - B3

OLD-NEW	
Old 5	
E6	564 - B5
F1	544 - D4
F2	544 - D5
F3	544 - D7
F4	564 - D2
F5	564 - D3
F6	564 - D5
Old 5A	
A1	544 - F4
A2	544 - F5
A3	544 - F6
A4	544 - F7
A5	564 - F1
A6	564 - F3
B1	544 - H4
B2	544 - H5
B3	544 - H6
B4	544 - H7
B5	564 - G2
B6	564 - G3
C1	544 - J4
C2	544 - J5
C3	544 - J6
C4	544 - J7
C5	564 - J2
C6	564 - J3
D1	545 - B4
D2	545 - B5
D3	545 - B6
D4	545 - B7
D5	565 - B2
D6	565 - B3
E1	545 - C4
E2	545 - C5
E3	545 - C6
E4	545 - C7
E5	565 - C2
E6	565 - C3
F1	545 - E4
F2	545 - E5
F3	545 - E6
F4	565 - E1
F5	565 - E2
F6	565 - E3
Old 6A	
A1	565 - F1
A2	565 - F2
A3	565 - F3
B1	565 - G1
D2	566 - G2
B3	565 - G3
C1	565 - H1
C2	565 - H2
C3	565 - H3
Old 6B	
D1	566 - A1
D2	566 - A2
D3	566 - A3
E1	566 - B1
E2	566 - B2
E3	566 - B3
F1	566 - C1
F2	566 - C2
F3	566 - C3
Old 6C	
A4	565 - F4
A5	565 - F5
A6	565 - F6
B4	565 - G4
B5	565 - G5
B6	565 - G6
C4	565 - H4
C5	565 - H5
C6	565 - H6
Old 6D	
D4	565 - J4
D5	565 - J5
D6	565 - J6
E4	566 - B4
E5	566 - B5
E6	566 - B7
F4	566 - C4
F5	566 - C5
F6	566 - C7
Old 7A	
A1	566 - D1
A2	566 - D2
A3	566 - D3
B1	566 - E1
B2	566 - E2
B3	566 - E3
C1	566 - G1
C2	566 - G2
C3	566 - G3
Old 7B	
D1	566 - H1
D2	566 - H2
D3	566 - H3
E1	566 - J1
E2	566 - J2
E3	566 - J3
F1	567 - A1
F2	567 - A2
F3	567 - A3
Old 7C	
A4	566 - D4
A5	566 - D5

OLD-NEW	
Old 7C	
A6	566 - D7
B4	566 - E4
B5	566 - E6
B6	566 - E7
C4	566 - G4
C5	566 - F6
C6	566 - F7
Old 7D	
D4	566 - H4
D5	566 - H6
D6	566 - H7
E4	566 - J5
E5	566 - J6
E6	566 - J7
F4	567 - A5
F5	567 - A6
F6	567 - A7
Old 8	
A1	567 - B2
A2	567 - B3
A3	567 - B5
A4	567 - B6
A5	567 - B7
A6	587 - B1
B1	567 - D2
B2	567 - C3
B3	567 - C5
B4	567 - C6
B5	567 - C7
B6	587 - C1
C1	567 - E2
C2	567 - E4
C3	567 - E5
C4	567 - E6
C5	567 - E7
C6	587 - E1
D1	567 - F2
D2	567 - F4
D3	567 - F5
D4	567 - F6
D5	567 - F7
D6	587 - F1
Old 8A	
E1	587 - B2
E2	587 - B3
E3	587 - B4
E4	587 - B5
E5	587 - B6
F1	587 - C2
F2	587 - C3
F3	587 - C4
F4	587 - C5
F5	587 - C6
Old 9A	
A1	585 - F1
A2	585 - F2
A3	585 - F3
B1	585 - G1
B2	585 - G2
B3	585 - G3
C1	585 - H1
C2	585 - H2
C3	585 - H3
Old 9B	
D1	585 - J1
D2	585 - J2
D3	585 - J3
E1	586 - B1
E2	586 - B2
E3	586 - B3
F1	586 - C1
F2	586 - C2
F3	586 - C3
Old 9C	
A4	585 - F4
A5	585 - F5
A6	585 - F6
B4	585 - G4
B5	585 - G5
B6	585 - G6
C4	585 - H4
C5	585 - H5
C6	585 - H6
Old 9D	
D4	585 - J4
D5	585 - J5
D6	585 - J6
E4	586 - B4
E5	586 - B5
E6	586 - A6
F4	586 - C4
F5	586 - C5
F6	586 - C6
Old 10A	
A1	586 - D1
A2	586 - D2
A3	586 - D3
B1	586 - E1
B2	586 - E2
B3	586 - E3
C1	586 - F1
C2	586 - F2
C3	586 - F3
Old 10B	
D1	586 - H1
D2	586 - H2
D3	586 - H3

OLD-NEW	
Old 10B	
E1	586 - J1
E2	586 - J2
E3	586 - J3
F1	587 - A1
F2	587 - A2
F3	587 - A3
Old 10C	
A4	586 - D4
A5	586 - D5
A6	586 - D6
B4	586 - E4
B5	586 - E5
B6	586 - E6
C4	586 - F4
C5	586 - F5
C6	586 - F6
Old 10D	
D4	586 - H4
D5	586 - H5
D6	586 - G6
E4	586 - J4
E5	586 - J5
E6	586 - J6
F4	587 - A4
F5	587 - A5
F6	587 - A6
Old 11A	
A1	585 - J7
A2	605 - J1
A3	605 - J2
B1	586 - A7
B2	606 - A1
B3	606 - A3
C1	586 - C7
C2	606 - C1
C3	606 - C3
Old 11B	
A4	605 - J4
A5	605 - J5
A6	605 - J6
B4	606 - A4
B5	606 - A5
B6	606 - A6
C4	606 - C4
C5	606 - C5
C6	606 - B6
Old 11C	
D1	607 - B1
D2	607 - B2
D3	607 - B3
E1	607 - C1
E2	607 - C2
E3	607 - C3
F1	607 - D1
F2	607 - D2
F3	607 - E3
Old 11D	
D4	607 - B4
D5	607 - B5
D6	607 - B6
E4	607 - C4
E5	607 - C5
E6	607 - C6
F4	607 - E4
F5	607 - D5
F6	607 - D6
Old 12A	
A1	586 - D7
A2	606 - D1
A3	606 - D3
B1	586 - E7
B2	606 - E1
B3	606 - E3
C1	586 - F7
C2	606 - F2
C3	606 - F3
Old 12B	
D1	586 - G7
D2	606 - G2
D3	606 - G3
E1	586 - J7
E2	606 - J2
E3	606 - J3
F1	587 - A7
F2	607 - A2
F3	607 - A3
Old 12C	
A4	606 - D4
A5	606 - D5
A6	606 - D6
B4	606 - E4
B5	606 - E5
B6	606 - E6
C4	606 - F4
C5	606 - F5
C6	606 - F6
Old 12D	
D4	606 - G4
D5	606 - G5
D6	606 - G6
E4	606 - J4
E5	606 - H5
E6	606 - H6
F4	607 - A4
F5	607 - A5
F6	607 - A6
Old 13	

OLD-NEW	
Old 13	
A1	606 - D7
A2	626 - D1
A3	626 - D2
A4	626 - D3
A5	626 - D5
A6	626 - D6
B1	606 - E7
B2	626 - E1
B3	626 - E2
B4	626 - E3
B5	626 - E5
B6	626 - E6
C1	606 - F7
C2	626 - F1
C3	626 - F2
C4	626 - F3
C5	626 - F5
C6	626 - F6
D1	606 - G7
D2	626 - G1
D3	626 - G2
D4	626 - G3
D5	626 - G5
D6	626 - G6
E1	606 - H7
E2	626 - H1
E3	626 - H2
E4	626 - H4
E5	626 - H5
E6	626 - H6
F1	607 - A7
F2	627 - A1
F3	627 - A2
F4	627 - A4
F5	627 - A5
F6	626 - J6
Old 14	
A1	607 - B7
A2	627 - B1
A3	627 - B2
A4	627 - B4
A5	627 - B5
A6	627 - B6
B1	607 - C7
B2	627 - C1
B3	627 - C2
B4	627 - C4
B5	627 - C5
B6	627 - C6
C1	607 - D7
C2	627 - D1
C3	627 - D3
C4	627 - D4
C5	627 - D5
C6	627 - D6
D1	607 - F7
D2	627 - F1
D3	627 - F3
D4	627 - E4
D5	627 - E5
D6	627 - E6
E1	607 - G7
E2	627 - G1
E3	627 - G3
E4	627 - G4
E5	627 - G5
E6	627 - G6
F1	607 - H7
F2	627 - H1
F3	627 - H3
F4	627 - H4
F5	627 - H5
F6	627 - H6
Old 15	
A1	441 - B1
A2	441 - B4
A3	441 - B6
A4	461 - B1
A5	461 - B4
A6	461 - B6
B1	441 - E1
B2	441 - E4
B3	441 - E6
B4	461 - D2
B5	461 - D4
B6	461 - D6
C1	441 - G1
C2	441 - G4
C3	441 - G6
C4	461 - G2
C5	461 - G4
C6	461 - G6
D1	442 - A1
D2	442 - A4
D3	442 - A6
D4	462 - A2
D5	462 - A4
D6	462 - A6
E1	442 - D2
E2	442 - D4
E3	442 - D6
E4	462 - D2
E5	462 - C4
E6	462 - C6
F1	442 - F2
F2	442 - F4
F3	442 - F6

OLD-NEW	
Old 15	
F4	462 - F2
F5	462 - F4
F6	462 - F6
Old 16	
A2	442 - J7
A3	462 - J2
A4	462 - J4
A5	462 - J6
A6	482 - J1
B3	463 - B2
B4	463 - B4
B5	463 - B6
B6	483 - B1
C3	463 - D2
C4	463 - D4
C5	463 - D6
C6	483 - D1
D3	463 - F2
D4	463 - F4
D5	463 - F6
D6	483 - F1
E3	463 - H3
E4	463 - H4
E5	463 - H6
E6	483 - G1
F3	464 - A3
F4	464 - A4
F5	464 - A6
F6	483 - J1
Old 17	
A1	481 - C2
A2	481 - C4
A3	481 - C6
A4	481 - C7
A5	501 - C2
A6	501 - C4
B1	481 - E2
B2	481 - E4
B3	481 - E6
B4	481 - E7
B5	501 - E2
B6	501 - D4
C1	481 - G2
C2	481 - G4
C3	481 - F6
C4	481 - F7
C5	501 - F2
C6	501 - F4
D1	501 - C6
D2	501 - C7
D0	521 - C2
D4	521 - C4
D5	521 - C6
D6	541 - C1
E1	501 - D6
E2	521 - D1
E3	521 - D2
E4	521 - D4
E5	521 - D6
E6	541 - D1
F1	501 - F6
F2	521 - F1
F3	521 - F2
F4	521 - F4
F5	521 - F6
F6	541 - F1
Old 18	
A1	481 - J2
A2	481 - J4
A3	481 - H6
A4	481 - H7
A5	501 - H2
A6	501 - H4
B1	482 - B2
B2	482 - B4
B3	482 - A6
B4	502 - A1
B5	502 - A2
B6	502 - A4
C1	482 - D2
C2	482 - D4
C3	482 - C6
C4	502 - C1
C5	502 - C2
C6	502 - C4
D1	482 - F2
D2	482 - F4
D3	482 - E6
D4	502 - E1
D5	502 - E3
D6	502 - E4
E1	482 - H2
E2	482 - H4
E3	482 - H6
E4	502 - G1
E5	502 - G3
E6	502 - G4
F1	483 - A3
F2	483 - A4
F3	483 - A6
F4	502 - J1
F5	502 - J3
F6	502 - J5
Old 19	
A1	483 - C3
A2	483 - C4
A3	483 - B6

OLD-NEW	
Old 19	
A4	503 - B1
A5	503 - B3
A6	503 - B5
B1	483 - E3
B2	483 - D4
B3	483 - D6
B4	503 - D1
B5	503 - D3
B6	503 - D5
C1	483 - F3
C2	483 - F5
C3	483 - F6
C4	503 - F1
C5	503 - F3
C6	503 - F5
D1	483 - H3
D2	483 - H5
D3	483 - H6
D4	503 - H1
D5	503 - H3
D6	503 - H5
E1	484 - A3
E2	484 - A5
E3	484 - A7
E4	504 - A1
E5	504 - A3
E6	504 - A5
F1	484 - C3
F2	484 - C5
F3	484 - C7
F4	504 - C2
F5	504 - C3
F6	504 - C5
Old 20	
A1	484 - E3
A2	484 - E5
A3	484 - E7
A4	504 - E2
A5	504 - E3
A6	504 - D5
B1	484 - G3
B2	484 - G5
B3	484 - F7
B4	504 - F2
B5	504 - F3
B6	504 - F5
C3	484 - H7
C4	504 - H2
C5	504 - H4
C6	504 - H5
D1	506 - F6
D2	526 - F1
D3	485 - A7
D4	505 - A2
D5	505 - A4
D6	505 - A5
E1	506 - G6
E2	526 - G1
E3	485 - C7
E4	505 - C2
E5	505 - C4
E6	505 - C5
F1	506 - J6
F2	526 - H1
F3	485 - E7
F4	505 - E2
F5	505 - E4
F6	505 - E6
Old 21	
A1	501 - H6
A2	521 - H1
A3	521 - H2
A4	521 - H4
A5	521 - H6
A6	541 - H1
B1	502 - A6
B2	522 - A1
B3	522 - A3
B4	522 - A4
B5	522 - A6
B6	542 - A1
C1	502 - C6
C2	522 - C1
C3	522 - C3
C4	522 - C4
C5	522 - C6
C6	542 - C1
D1	502 - E6
D2	522 - E1
D3	522 - E3
D4	522 - E5
D5	522 - E6
D6	542 - E1
E1	502 - G6
E2	522 - G1
E3	522 - G3
E4	522 - G5
E5	522 - G7
E6	542 - G2
F1	502 - J6
F2	522 - J1
F3	522 - J3
F4	522 - J5
F5	522 - J7
F6	542 - J2
Old 22	
A1	503 - B7

OLD-NEW	
Old 22	
A2	523 - B1
A3	523 - B3
A4	523 - B5
A5	523 - B7
A6	543 - B2
B1	503 - D7
B2	523 - D1
B3	523 - D3
B4	523 - D5
B5	523 - D7
B6	543 - C2
C1	503 - F7
C2	523 - F2
C3	523 - F3
C4	523 - F5
C5	523 - E7
C6	543 - E2
D1	503 - H7
D2	523 - H2
D3	523 - H3
D4	523 - H5
D5	523 - G7
D6	543 - G2
E1	504 - A7
E2	524 - A2
E3	524 - A4
E4	523 - J5
E5	523 - J7
E6	543 - J2
F1	504 - C7
F2	524 - C2
F3	524 - B4
F4	524 - B5
F5	524 - B7
F6	544 - B2
Old 23	
A1	504 - D7
A2	524 - D2
A3	524 - D4
A4	524 - D5
A5	524 - D7
A6	544 - D2
B1	504 - F7
B2	524 - F2
B3	524 - E4
B4	524 - E5
B5	524 - E7
B6	544 - E2
C1	504 - G7
C2	524 - G2
C3	524 - G4
C4	524 - G6
C5	524 - G7
C6	544 - G2
D1	504 - J7
D2	524 - J2
D3	524 - J4
D4	524 - J6
D5	524 - J7
D6	544 - J2
E1	505 - B7
E2	525 - B2
E3	525 - B4
E4	525 - B6
E5	525 - B7
E6	545 - B2
F1	505 - E7
F2	525 - E2
F3	525 - D4
F4	525 - D6
F5	525 - D7
F6	545 - D2
Old 24	
A1	540 - F2
A2	540 - F4
A3	540 - F5
A4	540 - F7
A5	560 - F2
A6	560 - F4
B1	540 - H2
B2	540 - H4
B3	540 - H5
B4	540 - H7
B5	560 - H2
B6	560 - H4
C1	541 - A2
C2	541 - A4
C3	541 - A6
C4	541 - A7
C5	561 - A2
C6	561 - A4
D1	541 - B2
D2	541 - B4
D3	541 - B6
D4	541 - B7
D5	561 - B2
D6	561 - B4
E1	541 - D2
E2	541 - D4
E3	541 - D6
E4	561 - D1
E5	561 - D2
E6	561 - D4
F1	541 - F2
F2	541 - F4
F3	541 - F6
F4	561 - F1

OLD-NEW	
Old 24	
F5	561 - F2
F6	561 - F4
Old 25	
A1	541 - J3
A2	541 - H4
A3	541 - H6
A4	561 - H1
A5	561 - H3
A6	561 - H4
B1	542 - A3
B2	542 - A4
B3	542 - A6
B4	562 - A1
B5	562 - A3
B6	562 - A4
C1	542 - D3
C2	542 - D5
C3	542 - D6
C4	562 - D1
C5	562 - D3
C6	562 - D5
D1	542 - F3
D2	542 - F5
D3	542 - F7
D4	562 - F1
D5	562 - F3
D6	562 - F5
E1	542 - H3
E2	542 - H5
E3	542 - H7
E4	562 - H1
E5	562 - H3
E6	562 - H5
F1	543 - B4
F2	543 - B5
F3	543 - A7
F4	563 - B2
F5	563 - A3
F6	563 - A5
Old 26	
A1	563 - C7
A2	583 - C1
A3	583 - C3
A4	583 - C5
A5	583 - C7
A6	603 - C2
B1	563 - E7
B2	583 - E1
B3	583 - E3
B4	583 - E5
B5	583 - E7
B6	603 - E2
C1	563 - G7
C2	583 - G1
C3	583 - G3
C4	583 - G5
C5	583 - G7
C6	603 - G2
D1	563 - J7
D2	583 - J1
D3	583 - J3
D4	583 - J5
D5	583 - J7
D6	603 - J2
E1	564 - B7
E2	584 - B1
E3	584 - B3
E4	584 - B5
E5	584 - B7
E6	604 - B2
F1	564 - D7
F2	584 - D2
F3	584 - D3
F4	584 - D5
F5	584 - D7
F6	604 - D2
Old 27	
A1	564 - F4
A2	564 - F5
A3	564 - F6
A4	584 - F1
A5	584 - F2
A6	584 - F3
B1	564 - G4
B2	564 - G5
B3	564 - G7
B4	584 - G1
B5	584 - G2
B6	584 - G3
C1	564 - J4
C2	564 - J5
C3	564 - J7
C4	584 - J1
C5	584 - J2
C6	584 - J4
D1	565 - B4
D2	565 - A5
D3	565 - A7
D4	585 - A1
D5	585 - A2
D6	585 - A4
E1	565 - C4
E2	565 - C6
E3	565 - C7
E4	585 - C1
E5	585 - C3
E6	585 - C4

OLD-NEW	
Old 27	
F1	565 - E4
F2	565 - E6
F3	565 - E7
F4	585 - E1
F5	585 - E3
F6	585 - D4
Old 28	
A1	584 - F5
A2	584 - E6
A3	584 - E7
A4	604 - E2
A5	604 - E4
A6	604 - E5
B1	584 - G5
B2	584 - G6
B3	604 - G1
B4	604 - G2
B5	604 - G4
B6	604 - G5
C1	584 - J5
C2	584 - J6
C3	604 - J1
C4	604 - H2
C5	604 - H4
C6	604 - H5
D1	585 - A5
D2	585 - A6
D3	605 - A1
D4	605 - A2
D5	605 - A4
D6	605 - A5
E1	585 - C5
E2	585 - C6
E3	605 - C1
E4	605 - C2
E5	605 - C4
E6	605 - B5
F1	585 - D5
F2	585 - D7
F3	605 - D1
F4	605 - D2
F5	605 - D4
F6	605 - D5
Old 29	
A1	585 - F7
A2	605 - F1
A3	605 - F2
B1	585 - G7
B2	605 - G1
B3	605 - G2
C1	585 - H7
C2	605 - H1
C3	605 - H2
Old 30	
A4	605 - F3
A5	605 - E5
A6	605 - E6
B4	605 - G4
B5	605 - G5
B6	605 - G6
C4	605 - H4
C5	605 - H5
C6	605 - H6
Old 31	
A1	605 - E7
A2	625 - E1
A3	625 - E2
A4	625 - E3
A5	625 - E5
A6	625 - E6
B1	605 - G7
B2	625 - G1
B3	625 - G2
B4	625 - G3
B5	625 - F5
B6	625 - F6
C1	605 - H7
C2	625 - H1
C3	625 - H2
C4	625 - H3
C5	625 - H5
C6	625 - H6
D1	605 - J7
D2	625 - J1
D3	625 - J2
D4	625 - J3
D5	625 - J5
D6	625 - J6
E1	606 - A7
E2	626 - A1
E3	626 - A2
E4	626 - A3
E5	626 - A5
E6	626 - A6
F1	606 - B7
F2	626 - B1
F3	626 - B2
F4	626 - B3
F5	626 - B5
F6	626 - B6

The Thomas Guide®

1998 EDITION

SAN FRANCISCO COUNTY

ZIP

How To Use This Thomas Guide
Modo De Empleo Del Thomas Guide

To Find a City or Community: Manera de Localizar una Ciudad o Comunidad:

Start with the Key Map to Detail Pages, then turn to the Detail Page indicated.

Empiece con el mapa clave de páginas detalladas, luego pase a la página detallada que se indica.

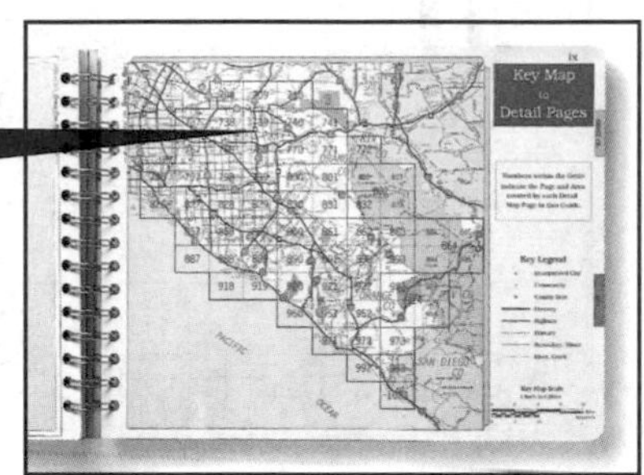

or
o

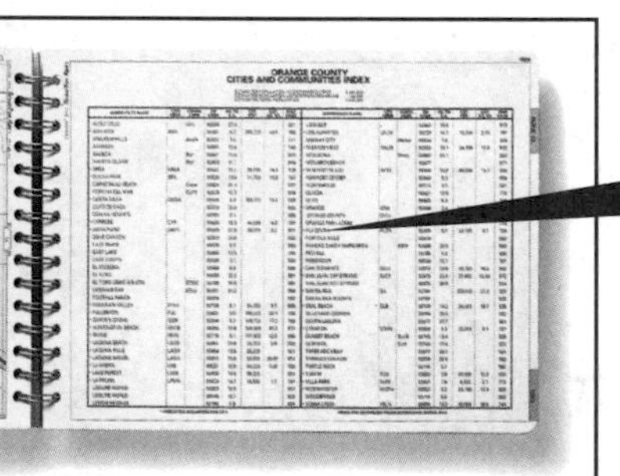

Look up the name in the Cities and Communities Index, then turn to the Detail Page indicated.

Busque el nombre en el Indice de Ciudades y Comunidades, luego pase a la página detallada que se indica.

or
o

Refer to the enclosed Foldout Map and its Index, then turn to the Detail Page indicated.

Consulte el mapa desplegable y el Indice del mismo adjunto, luego pase a la página detallada que se indica.

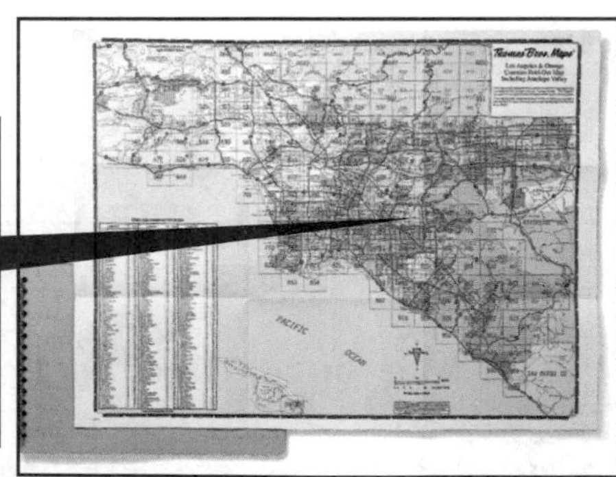

To Find an Address: Manera de Localizar una Dirección:

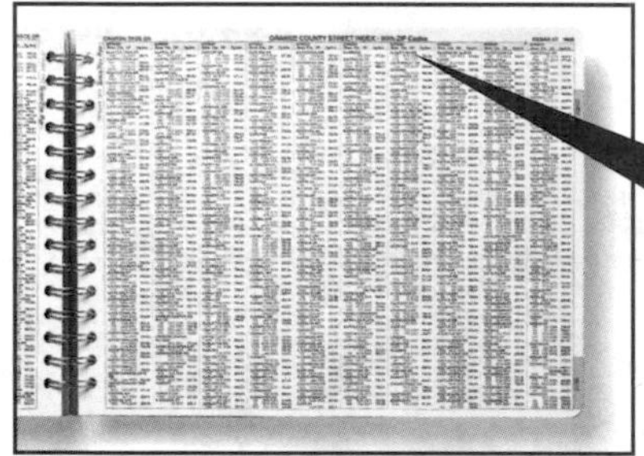

1 Look up the street name in the Street Index. If there are multiple listings, choose the proper city and/or address range. (All city abbreviations are listed in the Cities and Communities Index.)

Localice el nombre de la calle en el Indice de Calles. Si aparecen varias listas, seleccione el área apropiada de la ciudad y/o el domicilio. (Todas las abreviaturas de las ciudades figuran en la lista del Indice de Ciudades y Comunidades).

2 The street name will include a Thomas Bros. Maps Page and Grid™ where the address is located.

El nombre de la calle incluye un cuadro de Thomas Bros. Maps Page and Grid™ con el número de página y de coordenadas que indican la ubicación del domicilio.

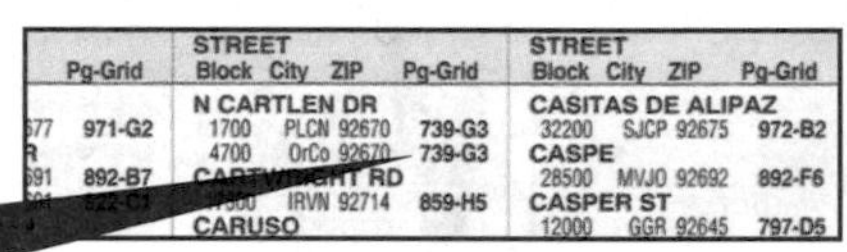

	Pg-Grid	STREET Block City ZIP	Pg-Grid	STREET Block City ZIP	Pg-Grid
		N CARTLEN DR		CASITAS DE ALIPAZ	
77	971-G2	1700 PLCN 92670	739-G3	32200 SJCP 92675	972-B2
R		4700 OrCo 92670	739-G3	CASPE	
91	892-B7	CART[illegible]HT RD		28500 MVJO 92692	892-F6
[illegible]	[illegible]	[illegible] IRVN 92714	859-H5	CASPER ST	
		CARUSO		12000 GGR 92645	797-D5

3 Turn to the Page indicated.

Pase a la página que se indica.

4 Locate the address by following the indicated Letter column and Number row until the two intersect. The street name is within this Grid area.

Localice el domicilio siguiendo la columna con letras y la hilera con números indicadas hasta que intersecten. El nombre de la calle se encuentra dentro de dicho cuadro.

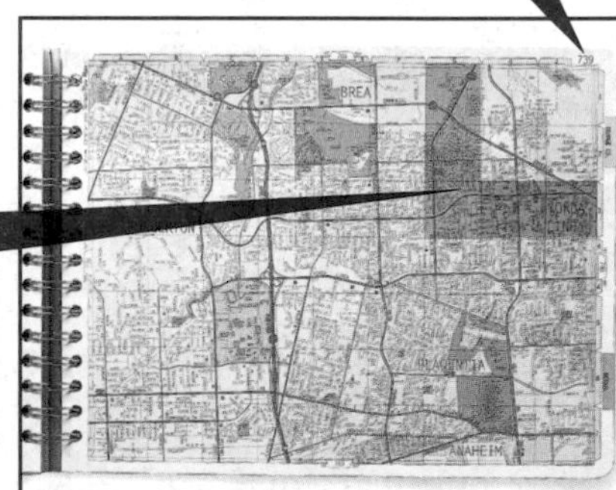

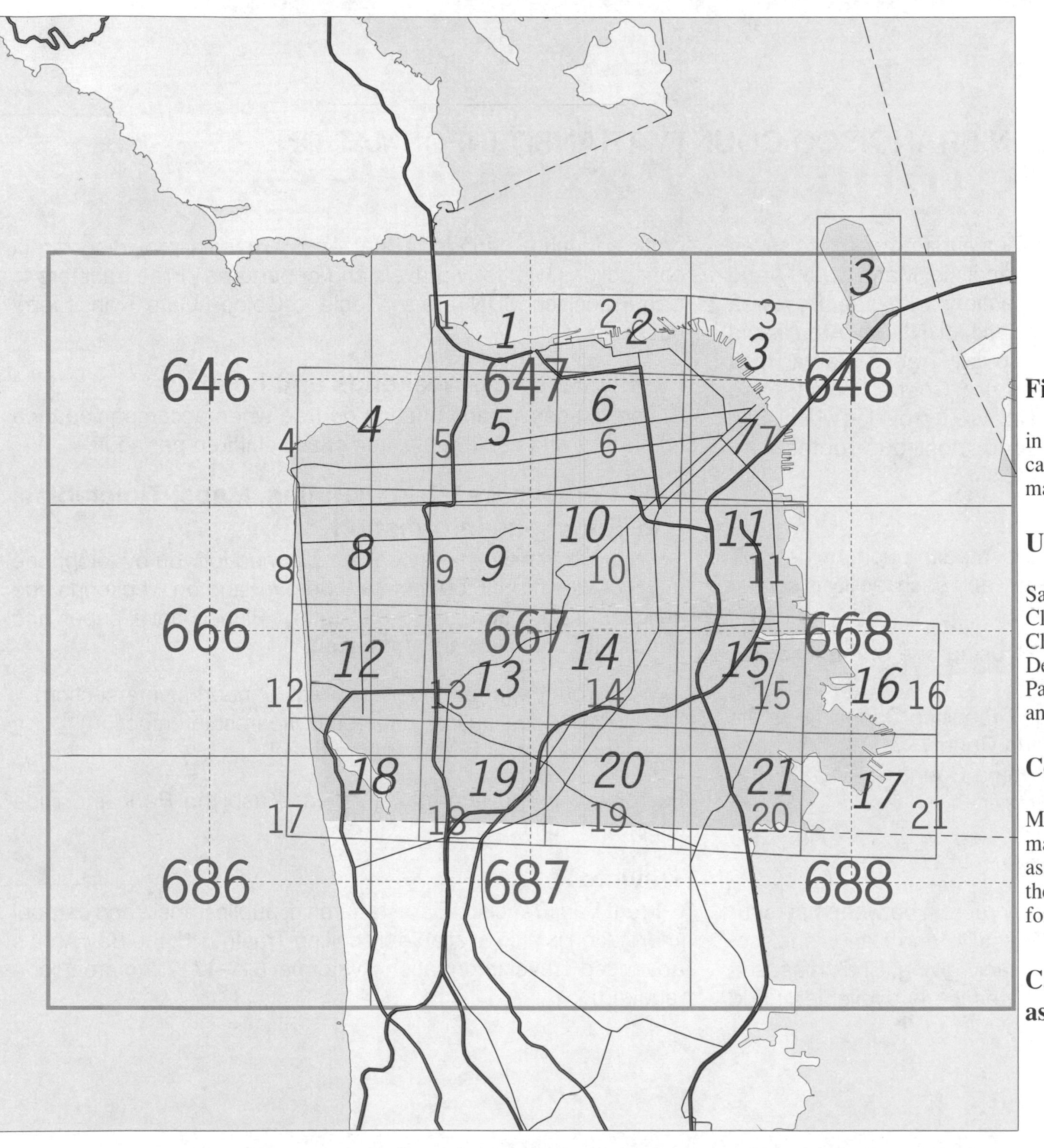

How The New Pages Work With The Old Pages

Finding New Page Numbers

This key map shows our old page layout in green and the new page layout in red. You can locate an old page number on this key map to determine the new page number.

Use of Close-Up Pages

To provide greater coverage detail for the San Francisco area, we have created the Close-Up Page. From a scale perspective, Close-Up Pages correspond to a quarter of a Detail Page. On the Key Map, Close-Up Pages are designated by the smaller numbers and Detail Pages by the larger numbers.

Conversion Help

As you convert to the new Thomas Bros. Maps page and grid® reference system, you may have questions or need conversion assistance. If we can be of help, please call the toll-free customer service number below for additional conversion information.

Call toll-free 1 800-899-MAPS and ask for Extension 99.

SAN FRANCISCO
ZIP
INTRO

1998 SAN FRANCISCO COUNTY TRANSIT INFORMATION

Golden Gate Transit (GGT) provides Bus and Ferry service seven days a week linking downtown San Francisco, Marin County, and Sonoma County. GGT provides connections with other Bay Area Transit operators including San Francisco MUNI, Bay Area Rapid Transit (BART), CalTrain, Sonoma County Transit, Santa Rosa City Bus, AC Transit (Alameda/Contra Costa Transit), and SamTrans (San Mateo County Transit). GGT provides wheelchair accessible service on all ferries and most bus routes. All information is subject to change.

Park and Ride Facilities

There are 25 Park and Ride facilities located throughout the GGT service area. Parking is complimentary and each facility is served by GGT buses during commute hours.

For information, please contact GGT using one of the following numbers or web site:

(415) 923-2000 from San Francisco County
(415) 455-2000 from Marin County
(707) 541-2000 from Sonoma County
(415) 257-4554 TDD number
www.goldengate.org

Ferry Service

Golden Gate Transit operates two ferry routes; between Larkspur and San Francisco and between Sausalito and San Francisco. Service is provided daily (except on Thanksgiving, Christmas, and New Year's Day). Free shuttle bus service is available during peak commute periods to the ferry terminals providing direct connections with ferry arrivals and departures. Free transfers to San Francisco MUNI are available to Golden Gate Transit ferry riders.

Family Fare - On weekends and holidays

Children, ages 12 and under, ride free when accompanied by a full-fare paying adult with a limit of two children per adult.

Free Personalized Trip Planning, Maps, Timetables, and Telephone Information

Your public transit itinerary can be planned for you by telephone any weekday from 6:00 a.m. to 8:00 p.m. and on weekends and holidays from 6:30 a.m. to 8:00 p.m. Please have paper and pencil with the following information:

- Your departure point (address or nearest intersection)
- Your destination (address or nearest intersection)
- Day and time you wish to travel

For planning and information, please use the Park and Ride telephone numbers.

TravInfo™

Current San Francisco Bay Area traffic, public transit, and carpool information is also available by calling TravInfo™, the Bay Area's Advanced Travel Information System at **817-1717** (no area code required).

1998 SAN FRANCISCO COUNTY COMMUNITIES

ESTIMATED POPULATION 759,300 AREA IN SQUARE MILES 44.75

COMMUNITY NAME	POST OFFICE NAME	ZIP CODE	PAGE
ALAMO SQUARE	STATION A	94115	647
ANZA VISTA	STATION A	94115	647
BALBOA TERRACE	WEST PORTAL	94127	667
BAYVIEW	BAYVIEW	94124	668
BAYVIEW HEIGHTS	BAYVIEW	94124	688
BERNAL HEIGHTS	STATION C	94110	667
CHINATOWN	RINCON WEST	94108	648
CLARENDON HEIGHTS	STATION G	94114	667
CORONA HEIGHTS	STATION G	94114	667
COW HOLLOW	MARINA	94123	647
CROCKER AMAZON	STATION F	94112	687
DIAMOND HEIGHTS	DIAMOND HTS	94131	667
DUBOCE TRIANGLE	STATION G	94114	667
EUREKA VLY/DOLORES HTS	STATION G	94114	667
EXCELSIOR	STATION F	94112	687
FINANCIAL DISTRICT	RINCON WEST	94104	648
FOREST HILL	PARKSIDE	94116	667
FOREST KNOLLS	STATION G	94131	667
GLEN PARK	DIAMOND HTS	94131	667
GOLDEN GATE HEIGHTS	SUNSET	94122	667
HAIGHT-ASHBURY	STATION J	94117	667
HAYES VALLEY	40 BELL BAZAAR	94103	667
HUNTERS POINT	BAYVIEW	94124	668
INGLESIDE	STATION F	94112	667
INGLESIDE HEIGHTS	STATION F	94112	667
INGLESIDE TERRACE	STATION F	94112	667
JORDAN HTS/LAUREL HTS	GOLDEN GATE	94118	647
LAKE	GOLDEN GATE	94118	647
LAKESIDE	STONESTOWN	94132	667
LAKE SHORE	STONESTOWN	94132	686
LONE MOUNTAIN	GOLDEN GATE	94118	647
MARINA	MARINA	94123	647
MERCED HEIGHTS	STATION F	94112	687
MERCED MANOR	STONESTOWN	94132	667
MIDTOWN TERRACE	STATION G	94131	667
MIRALOMA PARK	WEST PORTAL	94127	667
MISSION BAY	STATION E	94107	668
MISSION DISTRICT	STATION C	94110	667
MISSION DOLORES	STATION G	94110	667
MISSION TERRACE	STATION F	94112	667
MONTEREY HEIGHTS	WEST PORTAL	94127	667
MT DAVIDSON MANOR	WEST PORTAL	94127	667
NOB HILL	RINCON WEST	94108	648
NOE VALLEY	STATION G	94114	667
NORTH BEACH	NORTH BEACH	94133	648
NORTH PANHANDLE	STATION J	94117	647
NORTH WATERFRONT	NORTH BEACH	94133	648
OCEANVIEW	STATION F	94112	687
OUTER MISSION	STATION F	94112	687
PACIFIC HEIGHTS	STATION A	94115	647
PARK MERCED	STONESTOWN	94132	687
PARKSIDE	PARKSIDE	94116	667
PARNASSUS/ASHBURY HTS	STATION J	94117	667
PINE LAKE PARK	STONESTOWN	94132	667
PORTOLA	VISITACION	94134	667
POTRERO HILL	STATION E	94107	668
PRESIDIO HEIGHTS	GOLDEN GATE	94118	647
PRESIDIO OF SAN FRANCISCO	PRESIDIO	94129	647
RICHMOND	STATION P	94121	647
RUSSIAN HILL	NORTH BEACH	94133	648
ST FRANCIS WOOD	WEST PORTAL	94127	667
* SAN FRANCISCO			
-- SAN FRANCISCO COUNTY			
SEACLIFF	STATION P	94121	647
SHERWOOD FOREST	WEST PORTAL	94127	667
SILVER TERRACE	BAYVIEW	94124	668
SOUTH BEACH	STATION E	94107	648
SOUTH OF MARKET	MAIN OFC. SOUTH	94103	648
STONESTOWN	STONESTOWN	94132	667
SUNNYSIDE	STATION F	94112	667
SUNSET	SUNSET	94122	666
TELEGRAPH HILL	NORTH BEACH	94133	648
TWIN PEAKS	STATION G	94131	667
VISITACION VALLEY	VISITACION	94134	688
WEST PORTAL	WEST PORTAL	94127	667
WESTWOOD HIGHLANDS	WEST PORTAL	94127	667
WESTWOOD PARK	WEST PORTAL	94127	667

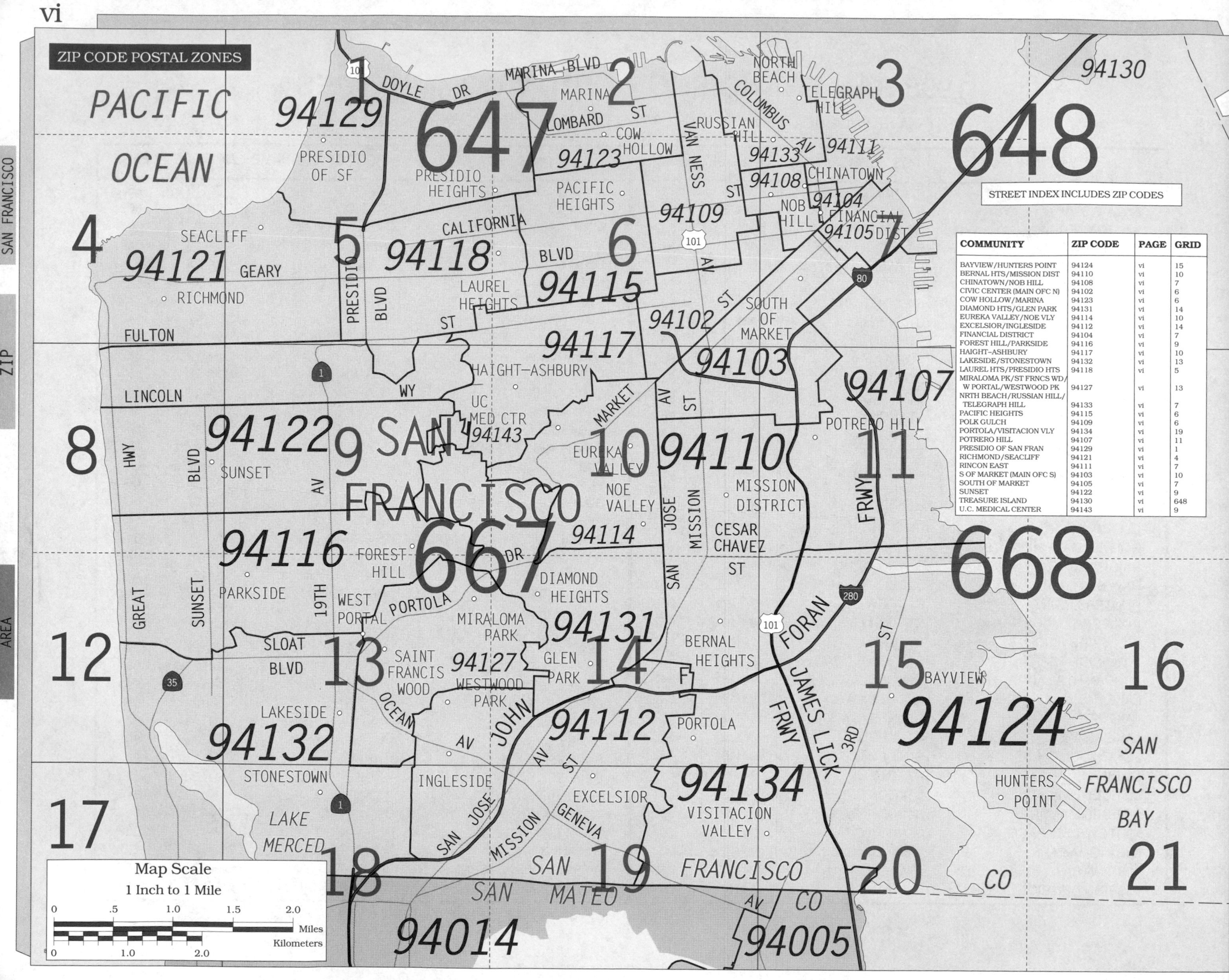

COMMUNITY	ZIP CODE	PAGE	GRID
BAYVIEW/HUNTERS POINT	94124	vi	15
BERNAL HTS/MISSION DIST	94110	vi	10
CHINATOWN/NOB HILL	94108	vi	7
CIVIC CENTER (MAIN OFC N)	94102	vi	6
COW HOLLOW/MARINA	94123	vi	6
DIAMOND HTS/GLEN PARK	94131	vi	14
EUREKA VALLEY/NOE VLY	94114	vi	10
EXCELSIOR/INGLESIDE	94112	vi	14
FINANCIAL DISTRICT	94104	vi	7
FOREST HILL/PARKSIDE	94116	vi	9
HAIGHT-ASHBURY	94117	vi	10
LAKESIDE/STONESTOWN	94132	vi	13
LAUREL HTS/PRESIDIO HTS	94118	vi	5
MIRALOMA PK/ST FRNCS WD/ W PORTAL/WESTWOOD PK	94127	vi	13
NRTH BEACH/RUSSIAN HILL/ TELEGRAPH HILL	94133	vi	7
PACIFIC HEIGHTS	94115	vi	6
POLK GULCH	94109	vi	6
PORTOLA/VISITACION VLY	94134	vi	19
POTRERO HILL	94107	vi	11
PRESIDIO OF SAN FRAN	94129	vi	1
RICHMOND/SEACLIFF	94121	vi	4
RINCON EAST	94111	vi	7
S OF MARKET (MAIN OFC S)	94103	vi	10
SOUTH OF MARKET	94105	vi	7
SUNSET	94122	vi	9
TREASURE ISLAND	94130	vi	648
U.C. MEDICAL CENTER	94143	vi	9

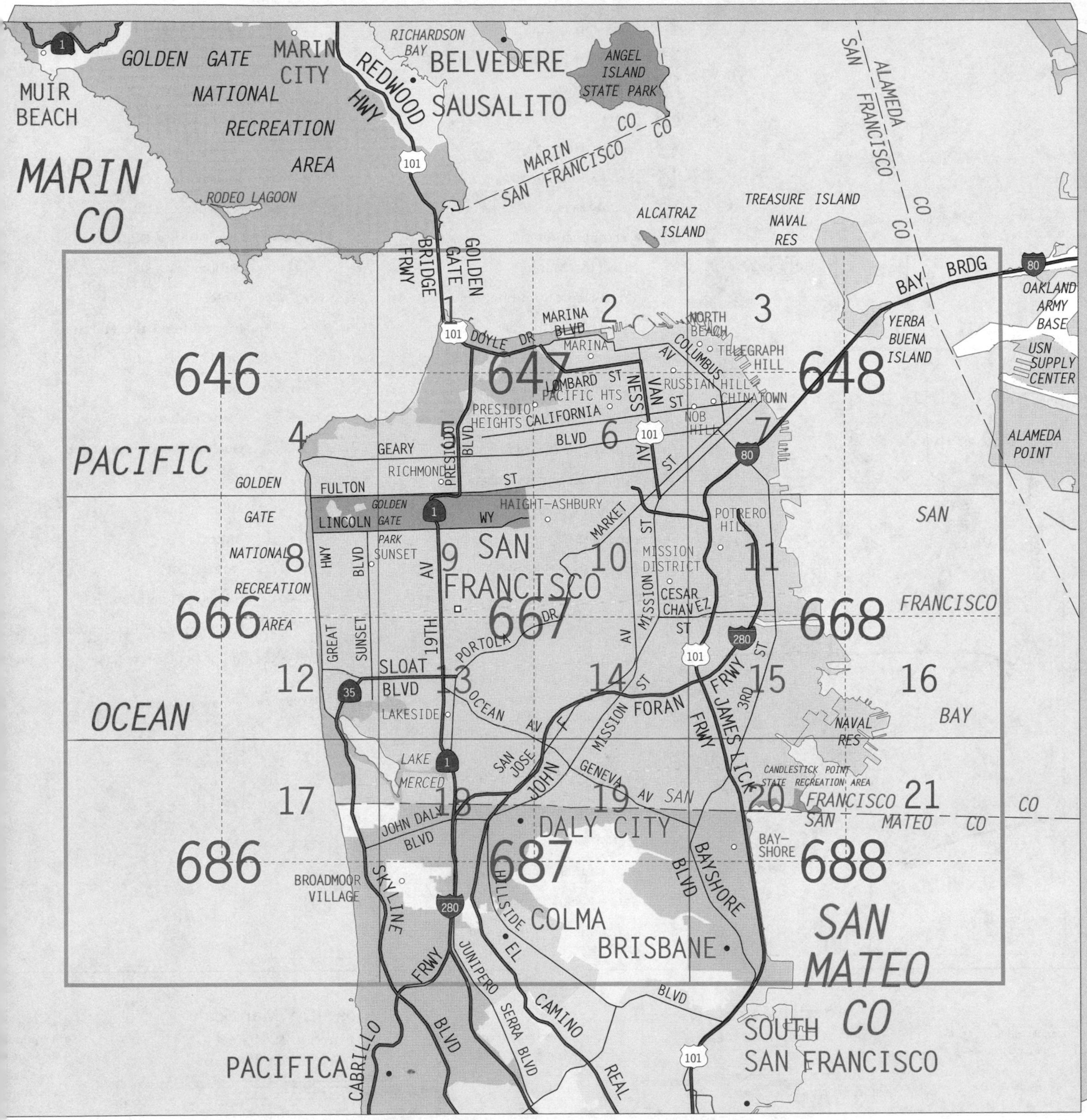

Key Map to Detail Pages

This Thomas Guide® contains three types of map pages:
Arterial, Detail, and Close–up

243	**Arterial Page–** Small scale area map, shown with a wide border
648	**Detail Page–** Full scale map page, shown with a solid thin border
10	**Close–Up Page–** One quarter of a Detail page at twice the scale, shown with dashed lines

Key Legend

- Incorporated City
- Community
- County Seat
- Freeway
- Highway
- Primary
- Secondary, Minor
- River, Creek

Key Map Scale

1 Inch to 2 Miles

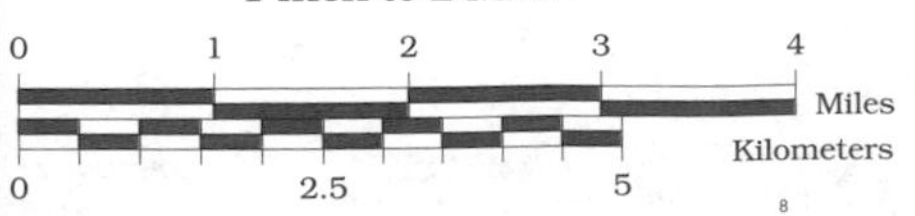

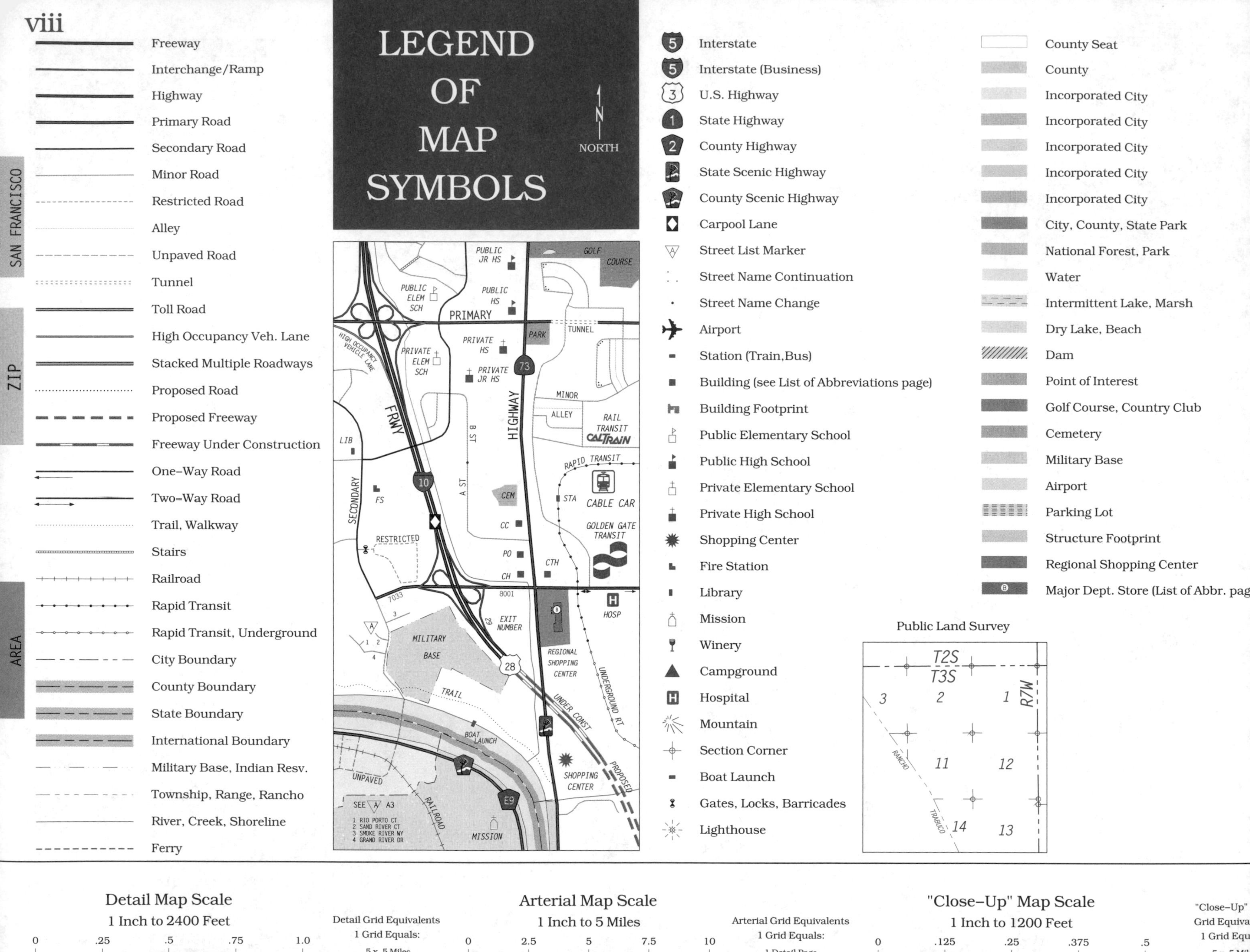

Detail Map Scale
1 Inch to 2400 Feet
0 .25 .5 .75 1.0 Miles
0 .5 1.0 Kilometers

Detail Grid Equivalents
1 Grid Equals:
.5 x .5 Miles
2640 x 2640 Feet
1.1 x 1.1 Inches

Arterial Map Scale
1 Inch to 5 Miles
0 2.5 5 7.5 10 Miles
0 5 10 Kilometers

Arterial Grid Equivalents
1 Grid Equals:
1 Detail Page
4.5 x 3.5 Miles
.9 x .7 Inches

"Close-Up" Map Scale
1 Inch to 1200 Feet
0 .125 .25 .375 .5 Miles
0 .25 .5 Kilometers

"Close-Up" F
Grid Equival
1 Grid Equa
.5 x .5 Mile
2640 x 2640 F
2.2 x 2.2 Inch

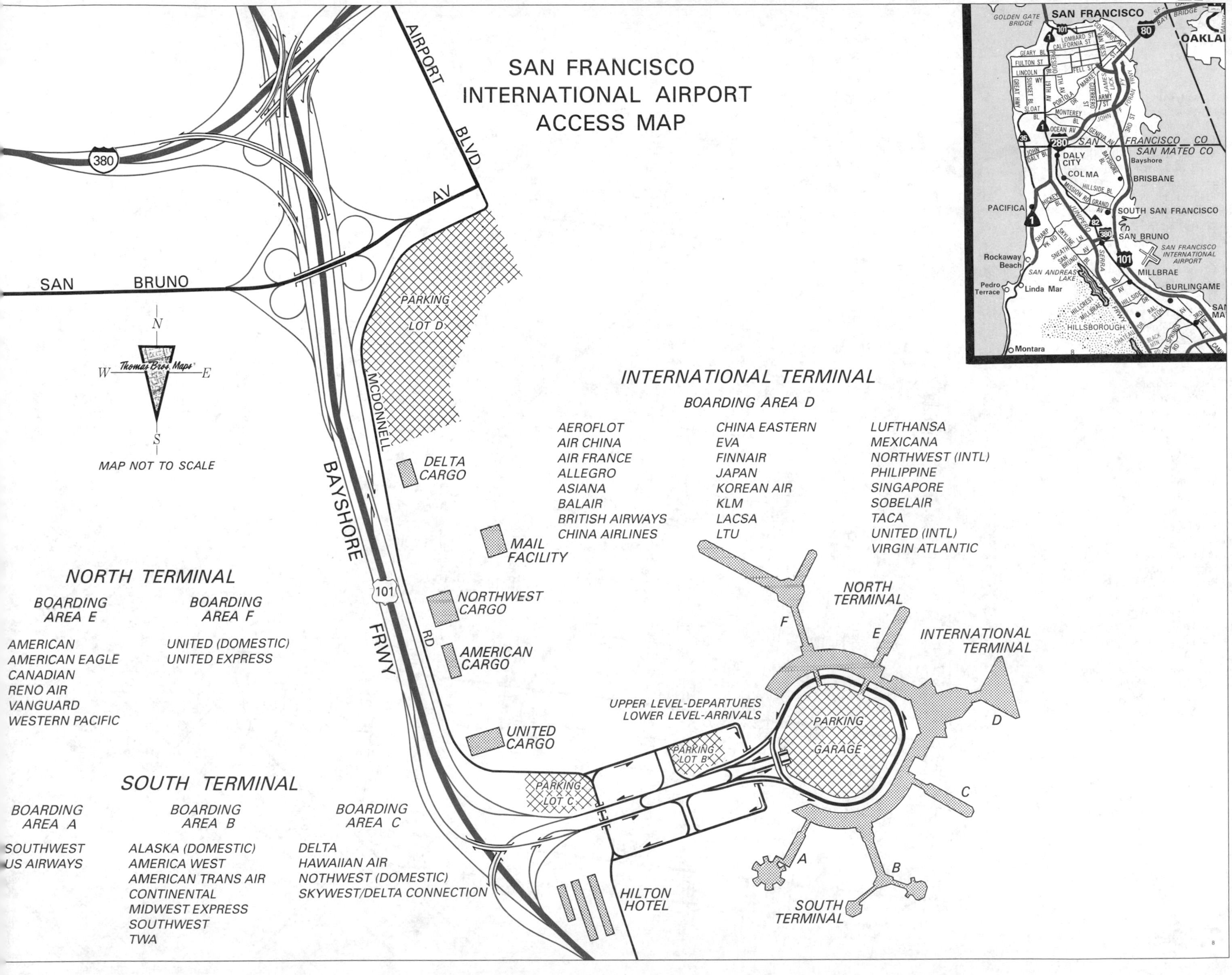

SAN FRANCISCO INTERNATIONAL AIRPORT ACCESS MAP

AIRPORT BLVD
AV
380
SAN BRUNO
BAYSHORE 101 FRWY
MCDONNELL RD
PARKING LOT D
DELTA CARGO
MAIL FACILITY
NORTHWEST CARGO
AMERICAN CARGO
UNITED CARGO
PARKING LOT C
PARKING LOT B
PARKING GARAGE
UPPER LEVEL-DEPARTURES
LOWER LEVEL-ARRIVALS
HILTON HOTEL
NORTH TERMINAL
INTERNATIONAL TERMINAL
SOUTH TERMINAL
A B C D E F

N S W E
Thomas Bros. Maps
MAP NOT TO SCALE

INTERNATIONAL TERMINAL

BOARDING AREA D

AEROFLOT
AIR CHINA
AIR FRANCE
ALLEGRO
ASIANA
BALAIR
BRITISH AIRWAYS
CHINA AIRLINES
CHINA EASTERN
EVA
FINNAIR
JAPAN
KOREAN AIR
KLM
LACSA
LTU
LUFTHANSA
MEXICANA
NORTHWEST (INTL)
PHILIPPINE
SINGAPORE
SOBELAIR
TACA
UNITED (INTL)
VIRGIN ATLANTIC

NORTH TERMINAL

BOARDING AREA E

AMERICAN
AMERICAN EAGLE
CANADIAN
RENO AIR
VANGUARD
WESTERN PACIFIC

BOARDING AREA F

UNITED (DOMESTIC)
UNITED EXPRESS

SOUTH TERMINAL

BOARDING AREA A

SOUTHWEST
US AIRWAYS

BOARDING AREA B

ALASKA (DOMESTIC)
AMERICA WEST
AMERICAN TRANS AIR
CONTINENTAL
MIDWEST EXPRESS
SOUTHWEST
TWA

BOARDING AREA C

DELTA
HAWAIIAN AIR
NOTHWEST (DOMESTIC)
SKYWEST/DELTA CONNECTION

SAN FRANCISCO
GOLDEN GATE BRIDGE
OAKLAND
80 101 280 380 1 35 82
DALY CITY
COLMA
BRISBANE
Bayshore
PACIFICA
SOUTH SAN FRANCISCO
SAN BRUNO
SAN FRANCISCO INTERNATIONAL AIRPORT
MILLBRAE
Rockaway Beach
SAN ANDREAS LAKE
Pedro Terrace
Linda Mar
BURLINGAME
HILLSBOROUGH
Montara
SAN FRANCISCO CO
SAN MATEO CO

ZIP

AREA

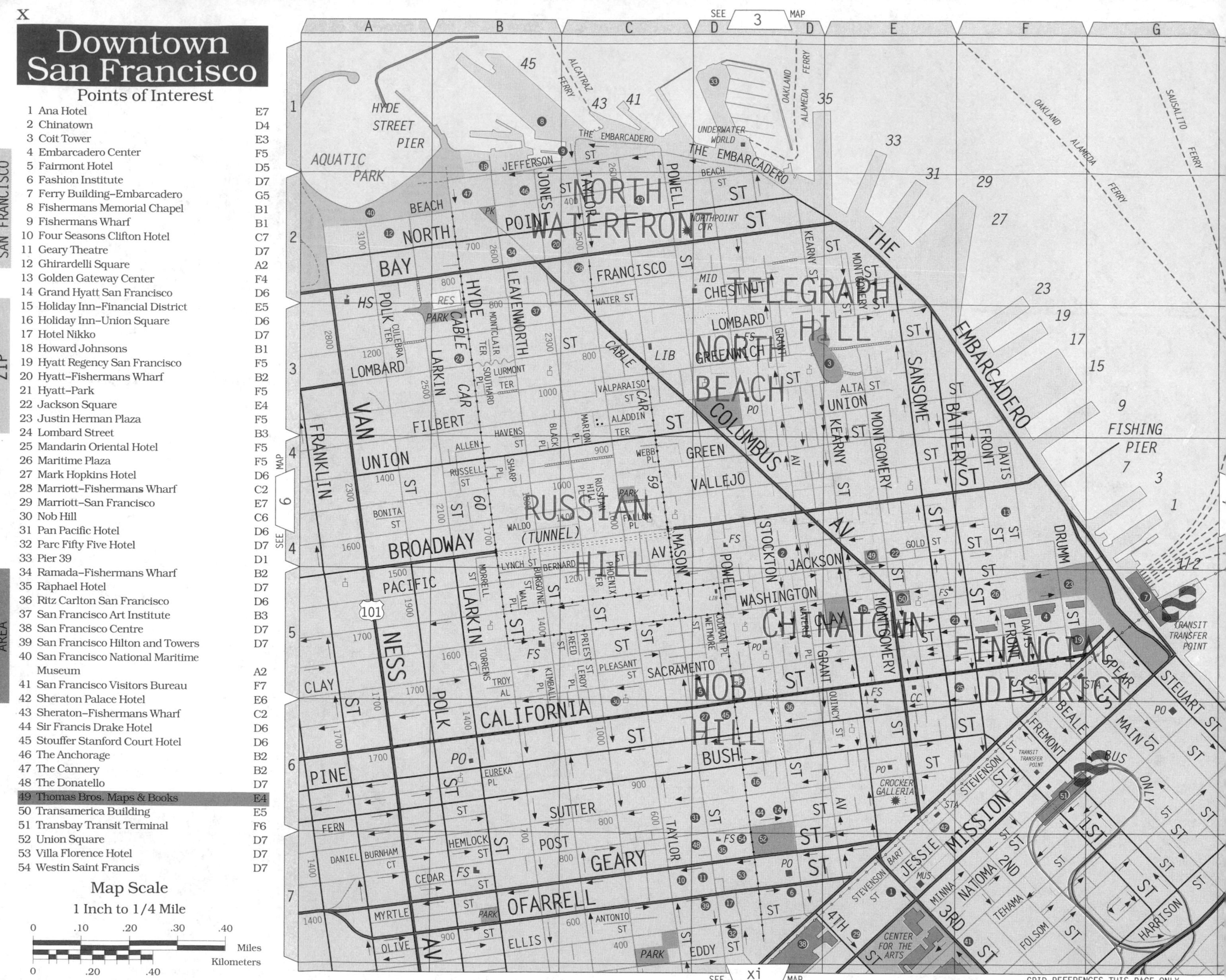
Downtown San Francisco
Points of Interest
1 Ana Hotel E7
2 Chinatown D4
3 Coit Tower E3
4 Embarcadero Center F5
5 Fairmont Hotel D5
6 Fashion Institute D7
7 Ferry Building–Embarcadero G5
8 Fishermans Memorial Chapel B1
9 Fishermans Wharf B1
10 Four Seasons Clifton Hotel C7
11 Geary Theatre D7
12 Ghirardelli Square A2
13 Golden Gateway Center F4
14 Grand Hyatt San Francisco D6
15 Holiday Inn–Financial District E5
16 Holiday Inn–Union Square D6
17 Hotel Nikko D7
18 Howard Johnsons B1
19 Hyatt Regency San Francisco F5
20 Hyatt–Fishermans Wharf B2
21 Hyatt–Park F5
22 Jackson Square E4
23 Justin Herman Plaza F5
24 Lombard Street B3
25 Mandarin Oriental Hotel F5
26 Maritime Plaza F5
27 Mark Hopkins Hotel D6
28 Marriott–Fishermans Wharf C2
29 Marriott–San Francisco E7
30 Nob Hill C6
31 Pan Pacific Hotel D6
32 Parc Fifty Five Hotel D7
33 Pier 39 D1
34 Ramada–Fishermans Wharf B2
35 Raphael Hotel D7
36 Ritz Carlton San Francisco D6
37 San Francisco Art Institute B3
38 San Francisco Centre D7
39 San Francisco Hilton and Towers D7
40 San Francisco National Maritime Museum A2
41 San Francisco Visitors Bureau F7
42 Sheraton Palace Hotel E6
43 Sheraton–Fishermans Wharf C2
44 Sir Francis Drake Hotel D6
45 Stouffer Stanford Court Hotel D6
46 The Anchorage B2
47 The Cannery B2
48 The Donatello D7
49 Thomas Bros. Maps & Books E4
50 Transamerica Building E5
51 Transbay Transit Terminal F6
52 Union Square D7
53 Villa Florence Hotel D7
54 Westin Saint Francis D7
Map Scale
1 Inch to 1/4 Mile
Miles
Kilometers
SAN FRANCISCO
ZIP
AREA
SEE 3 MAP
SEE 6 MAP
SEE xi MAP
GRID REFERENCES THIS PAGE ONLY

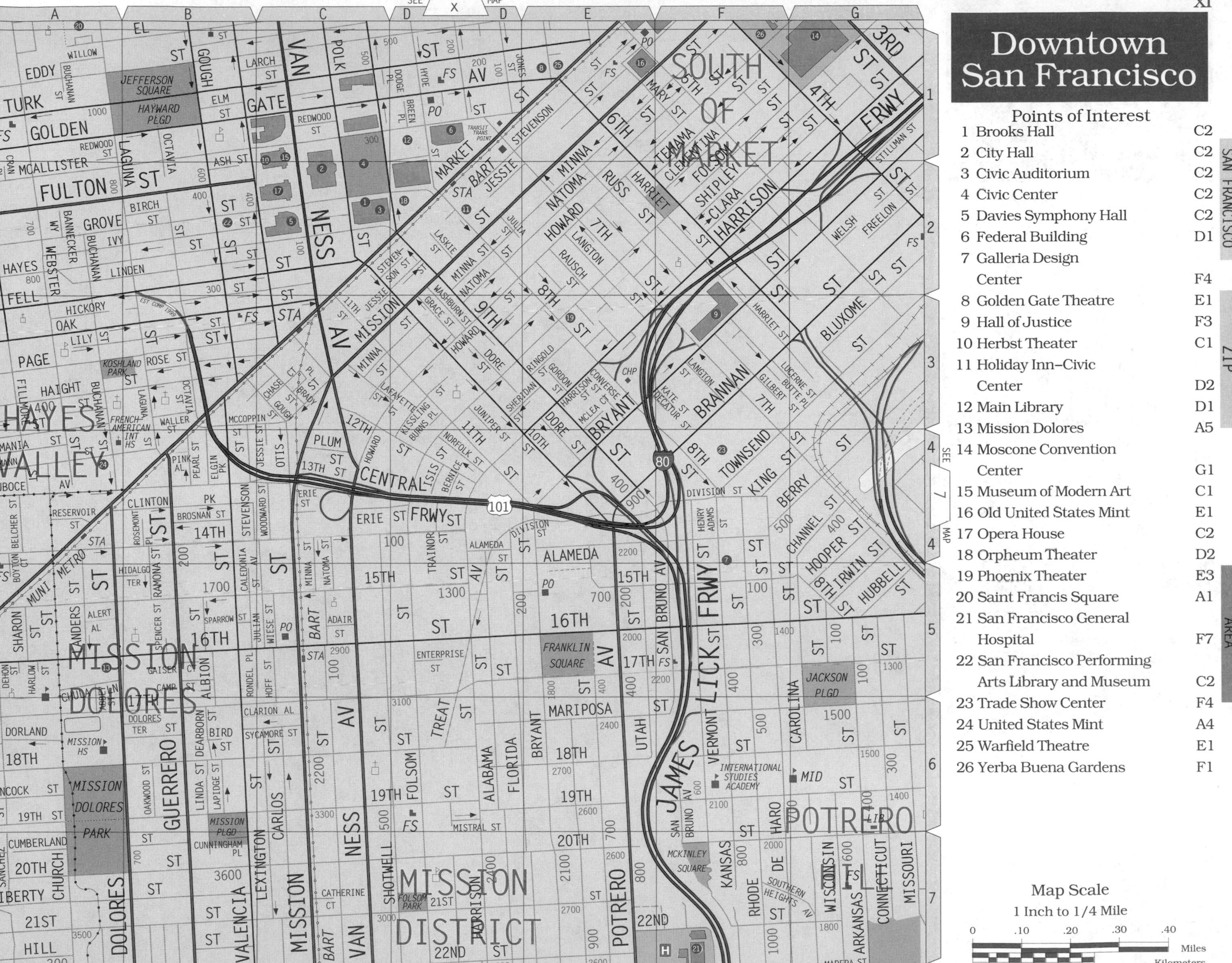
Downtown San Francisco
Points of Interest
1 Brooks Hall C2
2 City Hall C2
3 Civic Auditorium C2
4 Civic Center C2
5 Davies Symphony Hall C2
6 Federal Building D1
7 Galleria Design Center F4
8 Golden Gate Theatre E1
9 Hall of Justice F3
10 Herbst Theater C1
11 Holiday Inn–Civic Center D2
12 Main Library D1
13 Mission Dolores A5
14 Moscone Convention Center G1
15 Museum of Modern Art C1
16 Old United States Mint E1
17 Opera House C2
18 Orpheum Theater D2
19 Phoenix Theater E3
20 Saint Francis Square A1
21 San Francisco General Hospital F7
22 San Francisco Performing Arts Library and Museum C2
23 Trade Show Center F4
24 United States Mint A4
25 Warfield Theatre E1
26 Yerba Buena Gardens F1
Map Scale
1 Inch to 1/4 Mile
0 .10 .20 .30 .40 Miles
0 .20 .40 Kilometers
SAN FRANCISCO
ZIP
AREA
SEE X MAP
SEE 11 MAP
SEE 7 MAP
GRID REFERENCES THIS PAGE ONLY
SOUTH OF MARKET
HAYES VALLEY
MISSION DOLORES
MISSION DISTRICT
POTRERO HILL
JEFFERSON SQUARE
HAYWARD PLGD
KOSHLAND PARK
FRANKLIN SQUARE
JACKSON PLGD
MISSION DOLORES PARK
MISSION PLGD
MCKINLEY SQUARE
FOLSOM PARK
CENTRAL FRWY
JAMES LICK FRWY
MARKET ST
MISSION ST
VAN NESS AV
FOLSOM
HOWARD
HARRISON
BRYANT
BRANNAN
TOWNSEND
KING ST
16TH
POTRERO
VALENCIA
GUERRERO
DOLORES

Key Map To The Detail And Close–up Pages

Detail Page - Full scale map pages, shown with a solid thin border. A Detail Page provides street detail and is labeled with a 3 digit number. The scale is 1" equals 2400'

Close-Up Page - One quarter of a Detail Page at twice the scale, shown with dashed lines.
The Close-Up Pages display enlarged views of each Detail Page, providing full street name detail at an easy-to-read map scale (1" equals 1200').
Four Close-Up Pages equal one Detail Page.

DETAIL PAGE	CLOSE-UP PAGES
646	4
647	1,2,5,6
648	3,7
666	8,12
667	9,10,13,14
668	11,15,16
686	17
687	18,19
688	20,21

Key Map Scale
1 Inch to 2 Miles

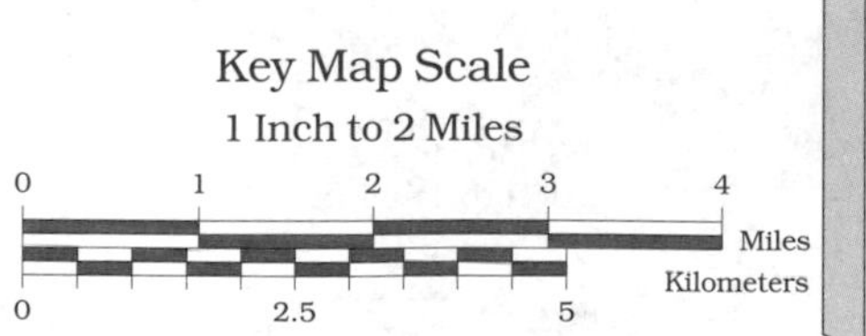

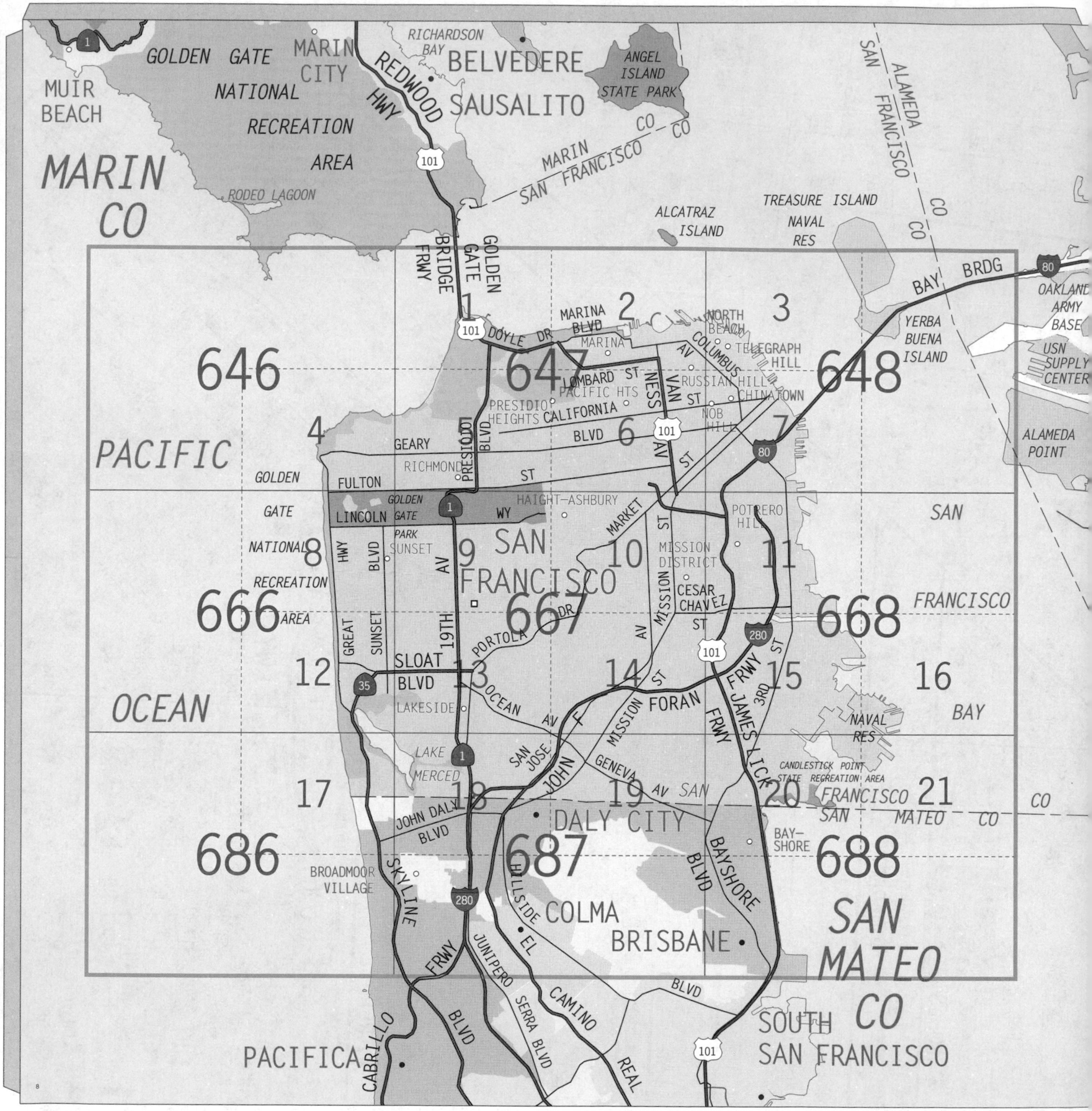

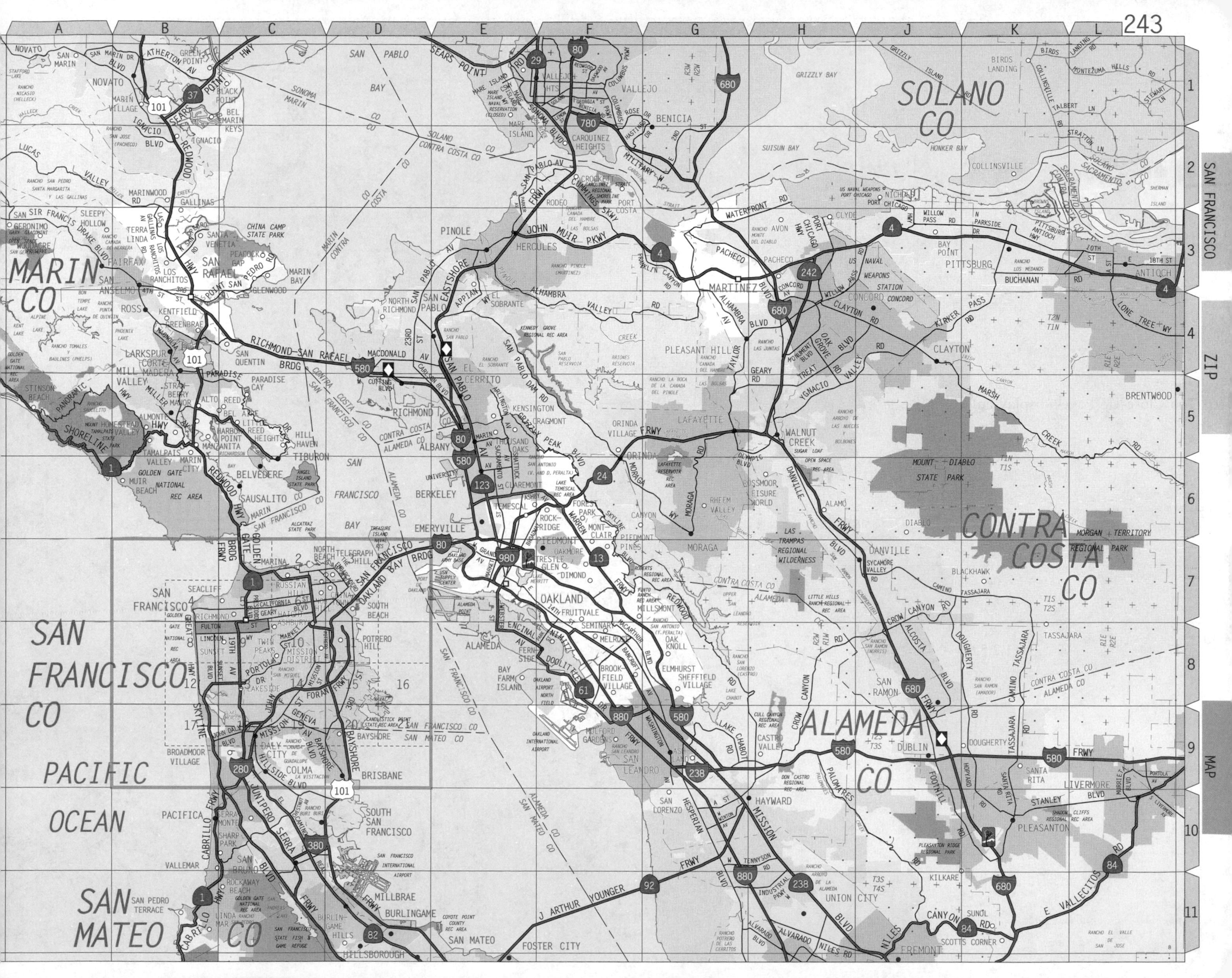
A
B
C
D
E
F
G
H
J
K
L
1
2
3
4
5
6
7
8
9
10
11
SAN FRANCISCO
ZIP
MAP
NOVATO
SAN MARIN
SAN MARIN DR
BLVD
ATHERTON AV
GREEN POINT
HWY
SEARS POINT
SAN PABLO BAY
SONOMA
MARIN
CO
SOLANO
CONTRA COSTA CO
VALLEJO
BENICIA
GRIZZLY BAY
SOLANO CO
HONKER BAY
SUISUN BAY
COLLINSVILLE
BIRDS LANDING
MONTEZUMA HILLS
TALBERT LN
STRATTON LN
SACRAMENTO CO
MARIN VILLAGE
BEL MARIN KEYS
BLACK POINT
IGNACIO
REDWOOD
LUCAS
VALLEY
MARINWOOD
GALLINAS
SLEEPY HOLLOW
SIR FRANCIS DRAKE BLVD
TERRA LINDA
SANTA VENETIA
CHINA CAMP STATE PARK
SAN RAFAEL
MARIN CO
FAIRFAX
SAN ANSELMO
ROSS
KENTFIELD
GREENBRAE
LARKSPUR
CORTE MADERA
MILL VALLEY
STINSON BEACH
PANORAMIC
SHORELINE
HWY
TAMALPAIS VALLEY
MUIR BEACH
GOLDEN GATE NATIONAL REC AREA
MARIN CITY
SAUSALITO
BELVEDERE
TIBURON
SAN QUENTIN
PARADISE CAY
RICHMOND-SAN RAFAEL BRDG
MACDONALD AV
CUTTING BLVD
RICHMOND
NORTH RICHMOND
SAN PABLO
EL SOBRANTE
PINOLE
HERCULES
RODEO
CROCKETT
PORT COSTA
CARQUINEZ HEIGHTS
JOHN MUIR PKWY
MARTINEZ
PACHECO
CONCORD
CLAYTON
PITTSBURG
ANTIOCH
BAY POINT
WATERFRONT RD
WILLOW PASS RD
BUCHANAN
LONE TREE WY
KIRKER PASS RD
CLAYTON RD
PLEASANT HILL
TAYLOR
ALHAMBRA VALLEY RD
EL CERRITO
KENSINGTON
ALBANY
BERKELEY
EMERYVILLE
OAKLAND
PIEDMONT
ORINDA
LAFAYETTE
MORAGA
WALNUT CREEK
MOUNT DIABLO STATE PARK
CONTRA COSTA CO
DANVILLE
ALAMO
DIABLO
BLACKHAWK
BRENTWOOD
MARSH CREEK
MORGAN TERRITORY REGIONAL PARK
SAN RAMON
DUBLIN
PLEASANTON
LIVERMORE
STANLEY BLVD
ALAMEDA CO
HAYWARD
SAN LORENZO
SAN LEANDRO
CASTRO VALLEY
UNION CITY
FREMONT
SUNOL
NILES
KILKARE
ALAMEDA
BAY FARM ISLAND
OAKLAND INTERNATIONAL AIRPORT
SAN FRANCISCO BAY
SAN FRANCISCO CO
TREASURE ISLAND
SAN FRANCISCO OAKLAND BAY BRDG
GOLDEN GATE BRDG
SAN FRANCISCO
SEACLIFF
RICHMOND
FULTON ST
SUNSET
MISSION DISTRICT
POTRERO HILL
BAYSHORE
BRISBANE
DALY CITY
COLMA
SOUTH SAN FRANCISCO
SAN BRUNO
PACIFICA
BROADMOOR VILLAGE
PACIFIC OCEAN
SAN FRANCISCO INTERNATIONAL AIRPORT
MILLBRAE
BURLINGAME
HILLSBOROUGH
SAN MATEO
FOSTER CITY
SAN MATEO CO
J ARTHUR YOUNGER FRWY
E VALLECITOS RD
CANYON RD
FOOTHILL
MISSION BLVD
HESPERIAN BLVD
580
680
880
80
101
1
4
24
13
61
92
84
238
242
280
380
780
980
123
29
37
82

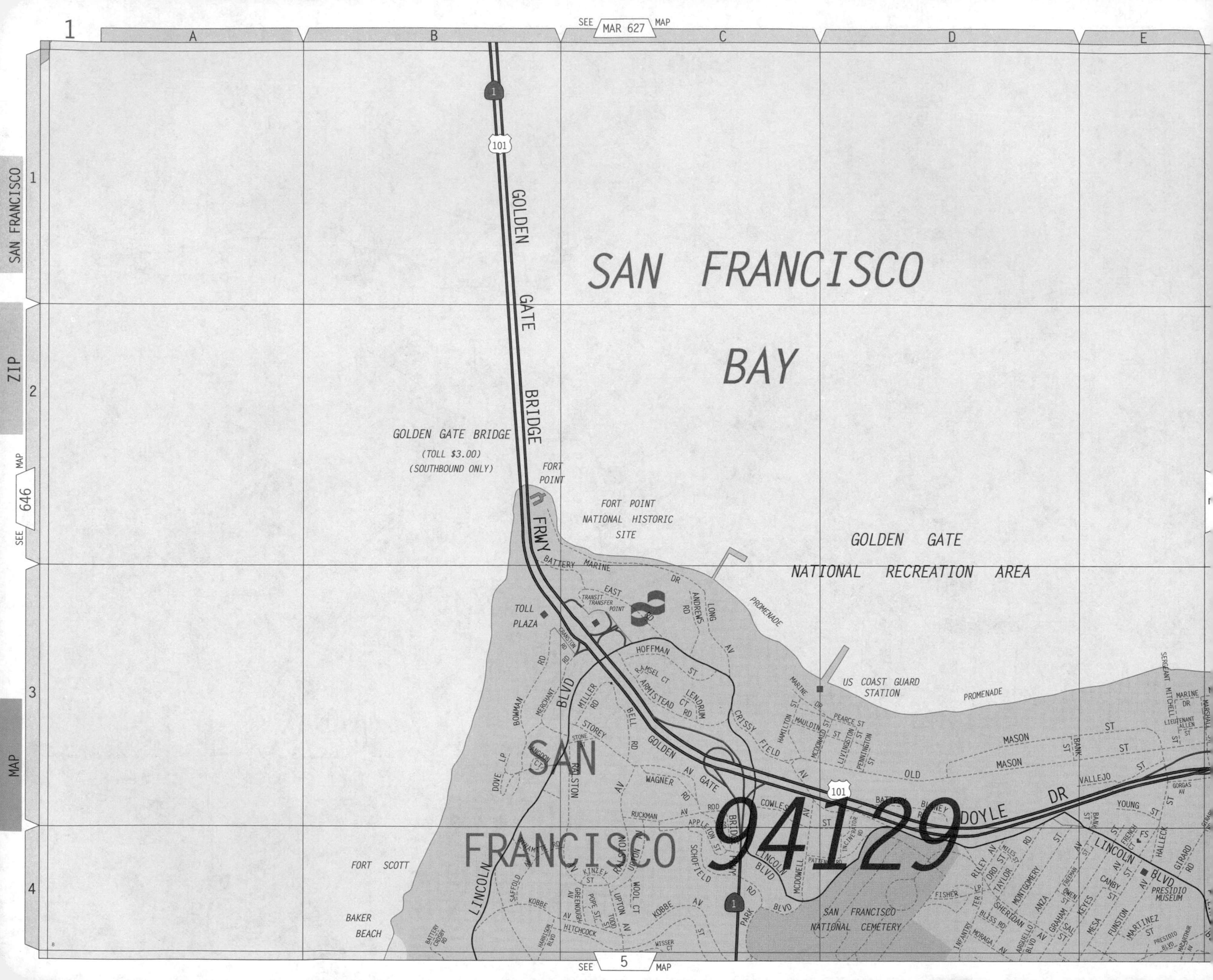
SEE MAR 627 MAP
A
B
C
D
E
1
2
3
4
SAN FRANCISCO
ZIP
MAP
SEE 646 MAP
SAN FRANCISCO
BAY
GOLDEN GATE BRIDGE
GOLDEN GATE BRIDGE
(TOLL $3.00)
(SOUTHBOUND ONLY)
FORT POINT
FORT POINT
NATIONAL HISTORIC
SITE
GOLDEN GATE
NATIONAL RECREATION AREA
FRWY
TOLL PLAZA
US COAST GUARD STATION
PROMENADE
SAN FRANCISCO
94129
FORT SCOTT
BAKER BEACH
SAN FRANCISCO
NATIONAL CEMETERY
PRESIDIO MUSEUM
LINCOLN BLVD
DOYLE DR
MASON ST
OLD MASON ST
VALLEJO ST
CRISSY FIELD AV
HOFFMAN ST
MARINE DR
LONG AV
ANDREWS RD
GOLDEN GATE AV
WAGNER RD
RUCKMAN AV
KOBBE AV
RALSTON
BOWMAN
MERCHANT RD
MILLER RD
BELL RD
STOREY
ARMISTEAD RD
LENDRUM CT
HAMILTON ST
MCDOWELL AV
LIVINGSTON ST
PENNINGTON ST
PEARCE ST
SCHOFIELD
PARK BLVD
BRIDGE
HALLECK ST
GIRARD RD
MONTGOMERY ST
SHERIDAN AV
TAYLOR RD
ANZA
GRAHAM ST
FUNSTON AV
MARTINEZ ST
MESA ST
KEYES AV
CANBY ST
YOUNG ST
FISHER
INFANTRY TER
MORAGA AV
ARGUELLO BLVD
HITCHCOCK
WISSER CT
SAFFOLD
UPTON AV
WOOL CT
KINZEY ST
POPE ST
TODD
GREENOUGH AV
HARRISON BLVD
BATTERY CROSBY RD
DOVE LP
SEE 5 MAP

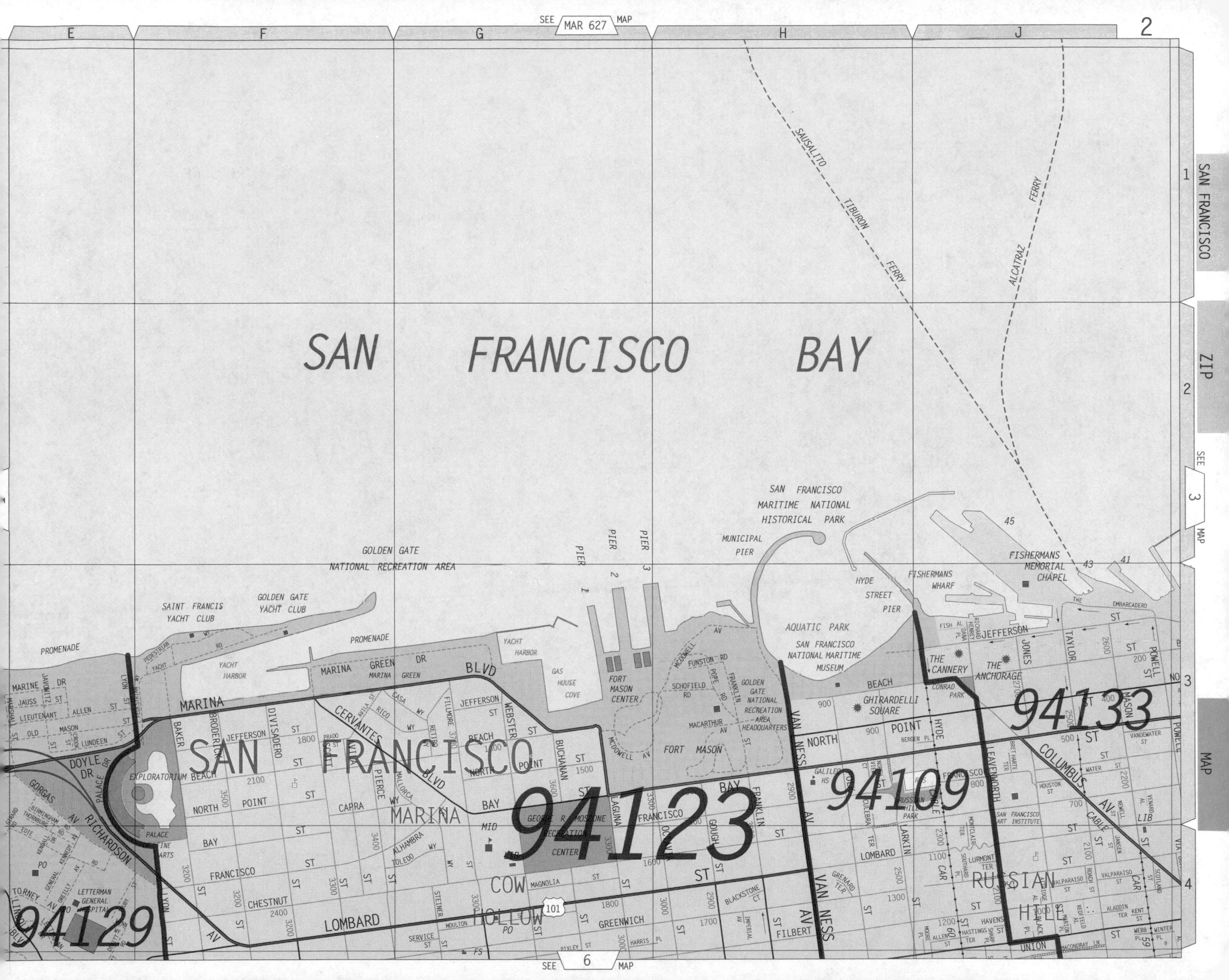
SAN FRANCISCO BAY
SAUSALITO TIBURON FERRY
ALCATRAZ FERRY
SAN FRANCISCO MARITIME NATIONAL HISTORICAL PARK
MUNICIPAL PIER
GOLDEN GATE NATIONAL RECREATION AREA
SAINT FRANCIS YACHT CLUB
GOLDEN GATE YACHT CLUB
PROMENADE
YACHT HARBOR
GAS HOUSE COVE
FORT MASON CENTER
FORT MASON
GOLDEN GATE NATIONAL RECREATION AREA HEADQUARTERS
AQUATIC PARK
SAN FRANCISCO NATIONAL MARITIME MUSEUM
HYDE STREET PIER
FISHERMANS WHARF
FISHERMANS MEMORIAL CHAPEL
THE CANNERY
THE ANCHORAGE
GHIRARDELLI SQUARE
SAN FRANCISCO
MARINA
COW HOLLOW
RUSSIAN HILL
EXPLORATORIUM
PALACE OF FINE ARTS
GEORGE R MOSCONE RECREATION CENTER
LETTERMAN GENERAL HOSPITAL
SAN FRANCISCO ART INSTITUTE
RUSSIAN HILL PARK
94123
94109
94133
94129
MARINA BLVD
LOMBARD ST
VAN NESS AV
COLUMBUS AV
CHESTNUT ST
FRANCISCO ST
NORTH POINT ST
BEACH ST
JEFFERSON ST
BAY ST
GREENWICH ST
FILBERT ST
UNION
RICHARDSON AV
DOYLE DR
101
SAN FRANCISCO
ZIP
MAP

SEE 3 MAP

SEE 243 MAP
A
B
C
D
E
1
2
3
4
SAN FRANCISCO
ZIP
MAP
SEE 2 MAP
SEE 7 MAP
94130
TREASURE
ISLAND
NAVAL
RESERVATION
SAN FRANCISCO
BAY
ANGEL ISLAND
TIBURON FERRY
SAUSALITO FERRY
LARKSPUR
SAN FRANCISCO FERRY
VALLEJO FERRY
OAKLAND ALAMEDA FERRY
TREASURE ISLAND MUSEUM
CALIFORNIA AV
YERBA
BUENA
ISLAND
BAY BRIDGE
80
BART TRANSBAY TUBE
PIER 39
MARINA
UNDERWATER WORLD
THE EMBARCADERO
NORTH WATERPOINT
NORTHPOINT CENTRE
94133
94111
TELEGRAPH HILL
NORTH BEACH
PIONEER PARK
COIT TOWER
WASHINGTON SQUARE
SAN FRANCISCO
FISHING PIER
COLUMBUS AV
EMBARCADERO
BATTERY
SANSOME
MONTGOMERY
KEARNY
GRANT
POWELL
LOMBARD
CHESTNUT
FILBERT
GREENWICH
UNION
GREEN
VALLEJO
FRONT
DAVIS
35
33
31
29
27
23
19
17
15
9
7

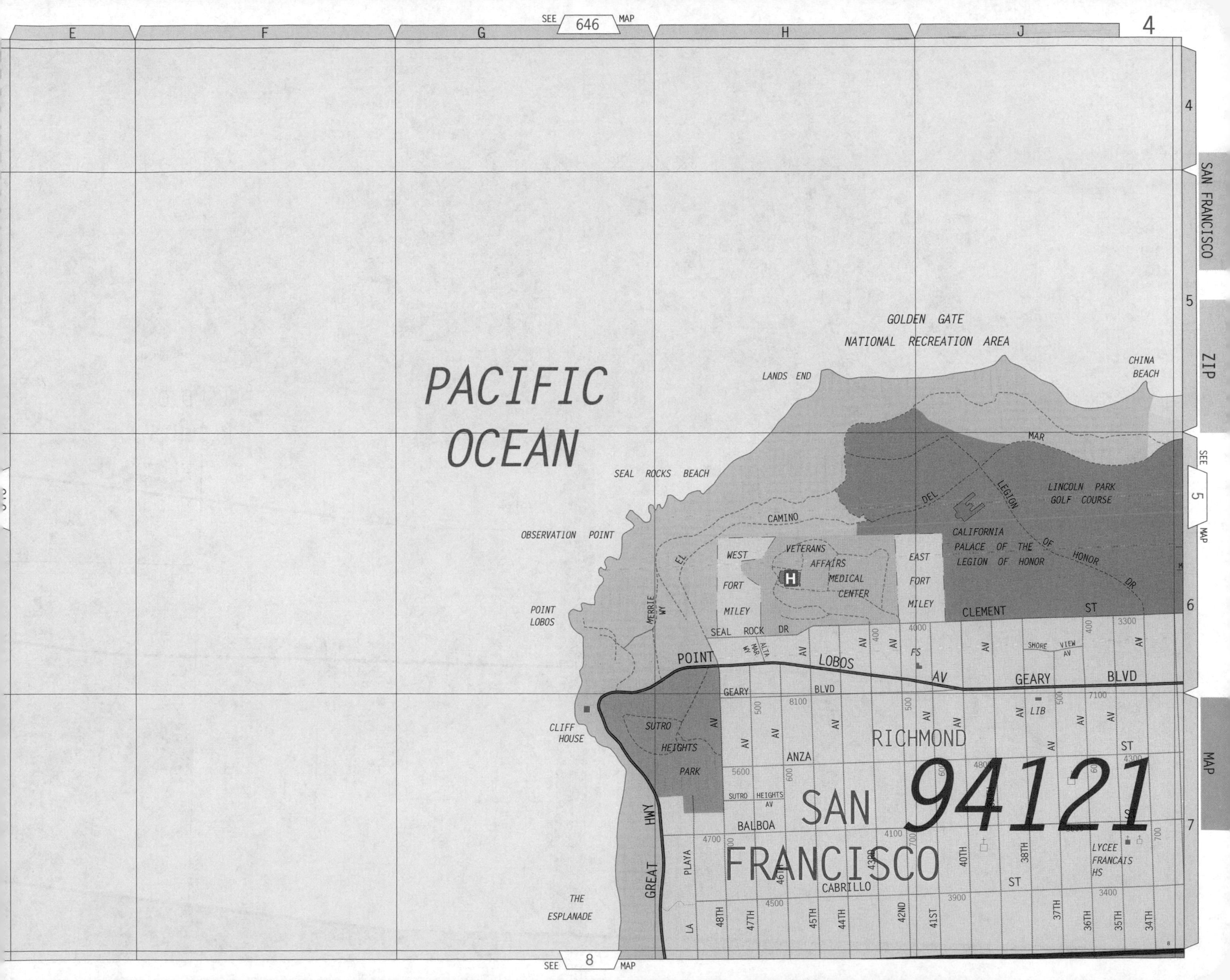
SEE 646 MAP
E
F
G
H
J
PACIFIC OCEAN
GOLDEN GATE NATIONAL RECREATION AREA
LANDS END
CHINA BEACH
SEAL ROCKS BEACH
OBSERVATION POINT
POINT LOBOS
CLIFF HOUSE
THE ESPLANADE
LINCOLN PARK GOLF COURSE
CALIFORNIA PALACE OF THE LEGION OF HONOR
LEGION OF HONOR DR
EL CAMINO DEL MAR
WEST FORT MILEY
VETERANS AFFAIRS MEDICAL CENTER
EAST FORT MILEY
MERRIE WY
SEAL ROCK DR
CLEMENT ST
POINT LOBOS AV
GEARY BLVD
SHORE VIEW AV
SUTRO HEIGHTS PARK
SUTRO HEIGHTS AV
ANZA
BALBOA
CABRILLO ST
GREAT HWY
PLAYA
LA PLAYA
48TH
47TH
46TH
45TH
44TH
43RD
42ND
41ST
40TH
38TH
37TH
36TH
35TH
34TH
RICHMOND
SAN FRANCISCO
94121
FS
LIB
LYCEE FRANCAIS HS
SEE 5 MAP
SAN FRANCISCO
ZIP
MAP
4
5
6
7
SEE 8 MAP

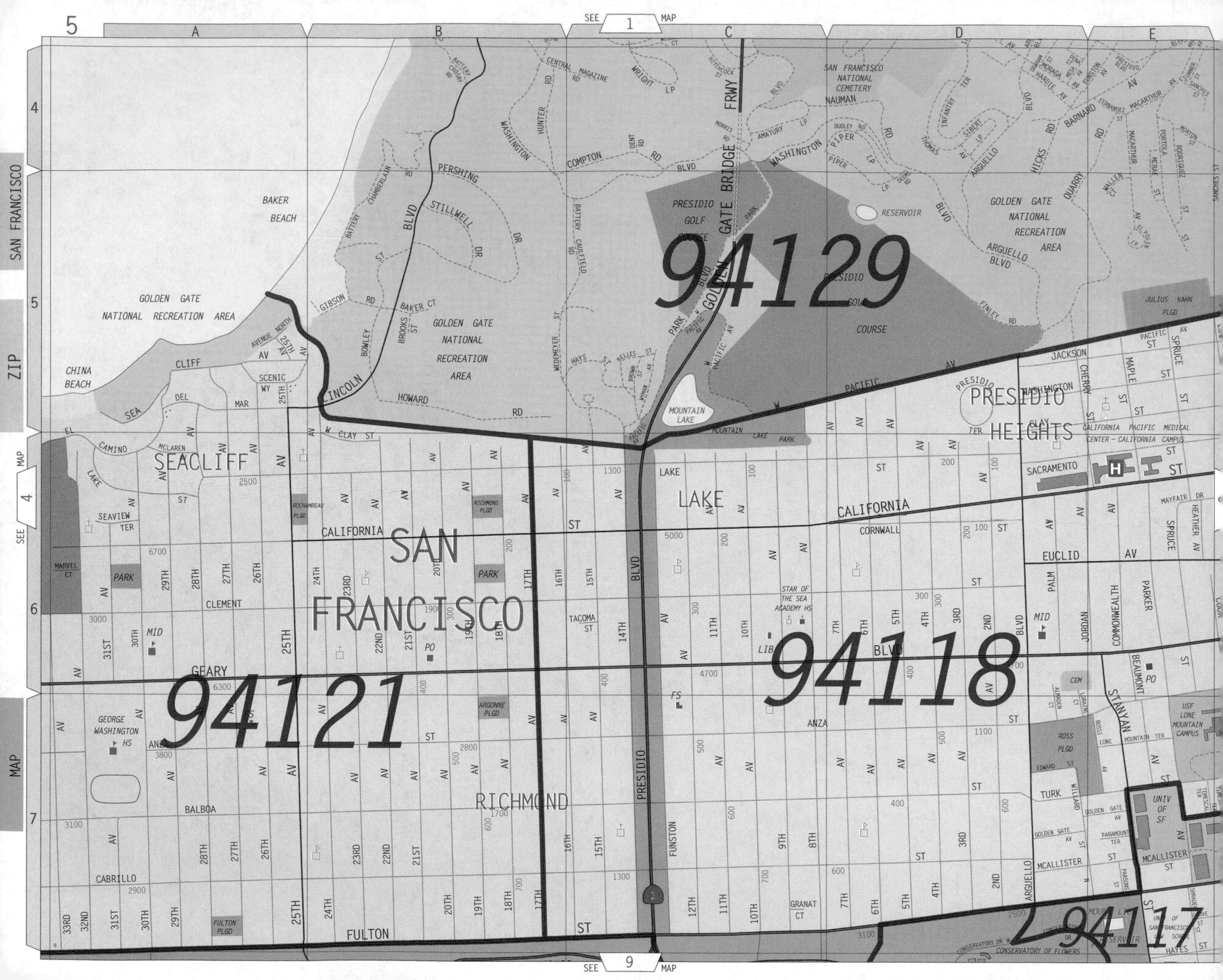
SEE 1 MAP
SEE 9 MAP
SEE 4 MAP
SAN FRANCISCO
ZIP
MAP
A
B
C
D
E
4
5
6
7
94129
94121
94118
94117
SAN FRANCISCO
SEACLIFF
LAKE
PRESIDIO HEIGHTS
RICHMOND
BAKER BEACH
CHINA BEACH
GOLDEN GATE NATIONAL RECREATION AREA
SAN FRANCISCO NATIONAL CEMETERY
PRESIDIO GOLF COURSE
MOUNTAIN LAKE
RESERVOIR
JULIUS KAHN PLGD
ROCHAMBEAU PLGD
RICHMOND PLGD
ARGONNE PLGD
FULTON PLGD
ROSS PLGD
PARK
MARVEL CT
GEORGE WASHINGTON HS
STAR OF THE SEA ACADEMY HS
CALIFORNIA PACIFIC MEDICAL CENTER - CALIFORNIA CAMPUS
USF LONE MOUNTAIN CAMPUS
UNIV OF SF
UNIV OF SAN FRANCISCO LAW SCHOOL
CONSERVATORY OF FLOWERS
CEM
PO
LIB
FS
MID
GOLDEN GATE BRIDGE FRWY
PARK PRESIDIO BLVD
LINCOLN BLVD
GEARY BLVD
CALIFORNIA ST
CLEMENT ST
FULTON ST
BALBOA ST
CABRILLO ST
ANZA ST
LAKE ST
EL CAMINO DEL MAR
SEA CLIFF AV
PACIFIC AV
W PACIFIC AV
JACKSON ST
WASHINGTON ST
CLAY ST
SACRAMENTO ST
EUCLID AV
TURK ST
MCALLISTER ST
GOLDEN GATE AV
STANYAN ST
ARGUELLO BLVD
FUNSTON AV
HAYES ST
CONSERVATORY DR W

SEE 2 MAP
E
F
G
H
J
6
94123
94133
94129
94108
94109
94118
94115
94117
94102
94103
PACIFIC HEIGHTS
SAN FRANCISCO
JORDAN HEIGHTS/LAUREL HEIGHTS
ANZA VISTA
ALAMO SQUARE
LONE MOUNTAIN
PRESIDIO
GOLDEN GATE NATIONAL RECREATION AREA
ALTA PLAZA
LAFAYETTE PARK
JEFFERSON SQUARE
JAPAN CENTER
CIVIC CENTER
SAN FRANCISCO UNIVERSITY HS
UNIVERSITY OF THE PACIFIC
LIBRARY FOR THE BLIND
DREW COLLEGE PREPARATORY HS
SAINT ROSE ACADEMY HS
PIONEER MEMORIAL MUSEUM
UCSF MOUNT ZION HOSPITAL
HAMILTON SQUARE
RAYMOND KIMBELL PLGD
KAISER PERMANENTE MEDICAL CENTER
SACRED HEART CATHEDRAL PREPARATORY
CALIFORNIA PACIFIC MEDICAL CEN HOSP
NEWCOMER HS
CONVENT OF THE SACRED HEART HS
SHERMAN HOUSE
USF LONE MOUNTAIN CAMPUS
UNIV OF SAN FRANCISCO
RAOUL WALLENBERG TRADITIONAL HS
IDA B WELLS HS
FEDERAL BUILDING
STATE BUILDING
CITY HALL
MAIN LIBRARY
OPERA HOUSE
DAVIES SYMPHONY HALL
CIVIC AUDITORIUM
SAN FRANCISCO PERFORMING ARTS LIBRARY & MUSEUM
TRANSIT TRANS POINT
BOEDDEKER PARK
UNION
GREENWICH
FILBERT
LOMBARD
BROADWAY
VALLEJO
GREEN
PACIFIC
JACKSON
WASHINGTON
CLAY
SACRAMENTO
CALIFORNIA
PINE
BUSH
SUTTER
POST
GEARY
OFARRELL
ELLIS
EDDY
TURK
GOLDEN GATE
MCALLISTER
FULTON
GROVE
HAYES
FELL
OAK
MARKET
MISSION
VAN NESS
FRANKLIN
GOUGH
OCTAVIA
LAGUNA
BUCHANAN
WEBSTER
FILLMORE
STEINER
PIERCE
SCOTT
DIVISADERO
BRODERICK
BAKER
LYON
PRESIDIO
MASONIC
POLK
LARKIN
HYDE
LEAVENWORTH
JONES
TAYLOR
MASON
SEE 10 MAP
SAN FRANCISCO
ZIP
SEE 7 MAP
MAP

SEE 3 MAP
94133
94111
94108
94104
94105
94102
94103
94107
SAN FRANCISCO
FINANCIAL DISTRICT
CHINATOWN
SOUTH OF MARKET
SOUTH BEACH
SAN FRANCISCO—OAKLAND BAY BRIDGE
(TOLL $1.00 WESTBOUND ONLY)
(TWO LEVEL FRWY)
SAN FRANCISCO BAY
RINCON POINT
CHINA BASIN
SOUTH BEACH MARINA
OAKLAND ALAMEDA FERRY
HARBOR BAY ISLE FERRY
FISHING PIER
GOLDEN GATEWAY CENTER
JUSTIN HERMAN PLAZA
UNION SQUARE
YERBA BUENA GARDENS
MOSCONE CONVENTION CENTER
SEE A B5
1 ONE EMBARCADERO CENTER
2 TWO EMBARCADERO CENTER
3 THREE EMBARCADERO CENTER
4 FOUR EMBARCADERO CENTER
5 HYATT REGENCY
SEE 6 MAP
SEE 11 MAP
SAN FRANCISCO
ZIP
MAP

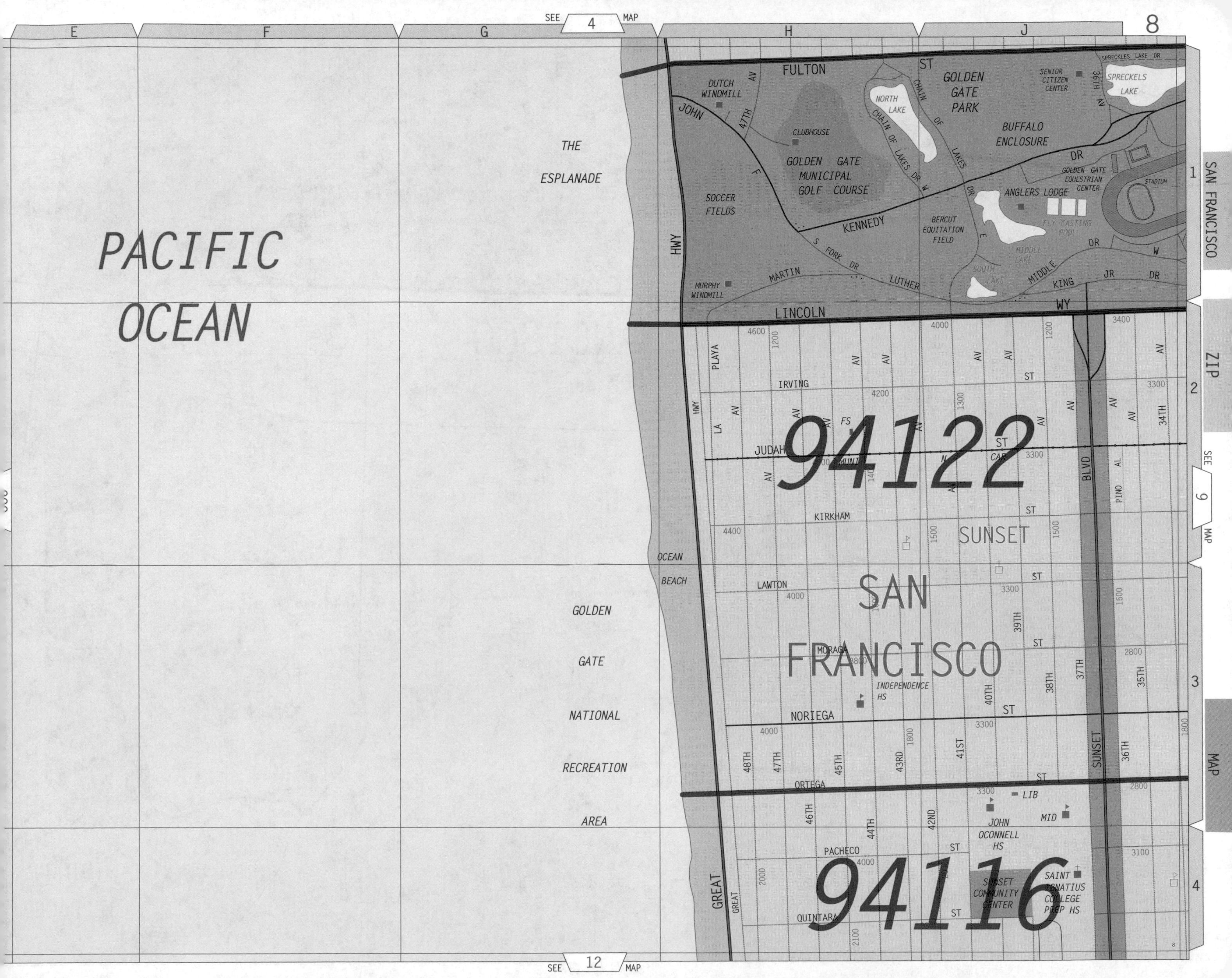

SEE 4 MAP
E
F
G
H
J
PACIFIC OCEAN
THE ESPLANADE
GOLDEN GATE NATIONAL RECREATION AREA
OCEAN BEACH
FULTON ST
GOLDEN GATE PARK
DUTCH WINDMILL
MURPHY WINDMILL
CLUBHOUSE
GOLDEN GATE MUNICIPAL GOLF COURSE
NORTH LAKE
CHAIN OF LAKES DR W
CHAIN OF LAKES DR E
BUFFALO ENCLOSURE
SENIOR CITIZEN CENTER
SPRECKLES LAKE DR
SPRECKELS LAKE
GOLDEN GATE EQUESTRIAN CENTER
STADIUM
ANGLERS LODGE
FLY CASTING POOL
BERCUT EQUITATION FIELD
SOCCER FIELDS
JOHN F KENNEDY DR
S FORK DR
MARTIN LUTHER KING JR DR
MIDDLE DR W
MIDDLE LAKE
SOUTH LAKE
LINCOLN WY
HWY
GREAT HWY
LA PLAYA
IRVING ST
JUDAH ST
KIRKHAM ST
LAWTON ST
MORAGA ST
NORIEGA ST
ORTEGA ST
PACHECO ST
QUINTARA ST
SUNSET BLVD
PINO AL
48TH AV
47TH AV
46TH AV
45TH AV
44TH AV
43RD AV
42ND AV
41ST AV
40TH AV
39TH AV
38TH AV
37TH AV
36TH AV
35TH AV
34TH AV
94122
94116
SUNSET
SAN FRANCISCO
FS
INDEPENDENCE HS
LIB
MID
JOHN OCONNELL HS
SUNSET COMMUNITY CENTER
SAINT IGNATIUS COLLEGE PREP HS
1
2
3
4
SAN FRANCISCO
ZIP
MAP
SEE 9 MAP
SEE 12 MAP

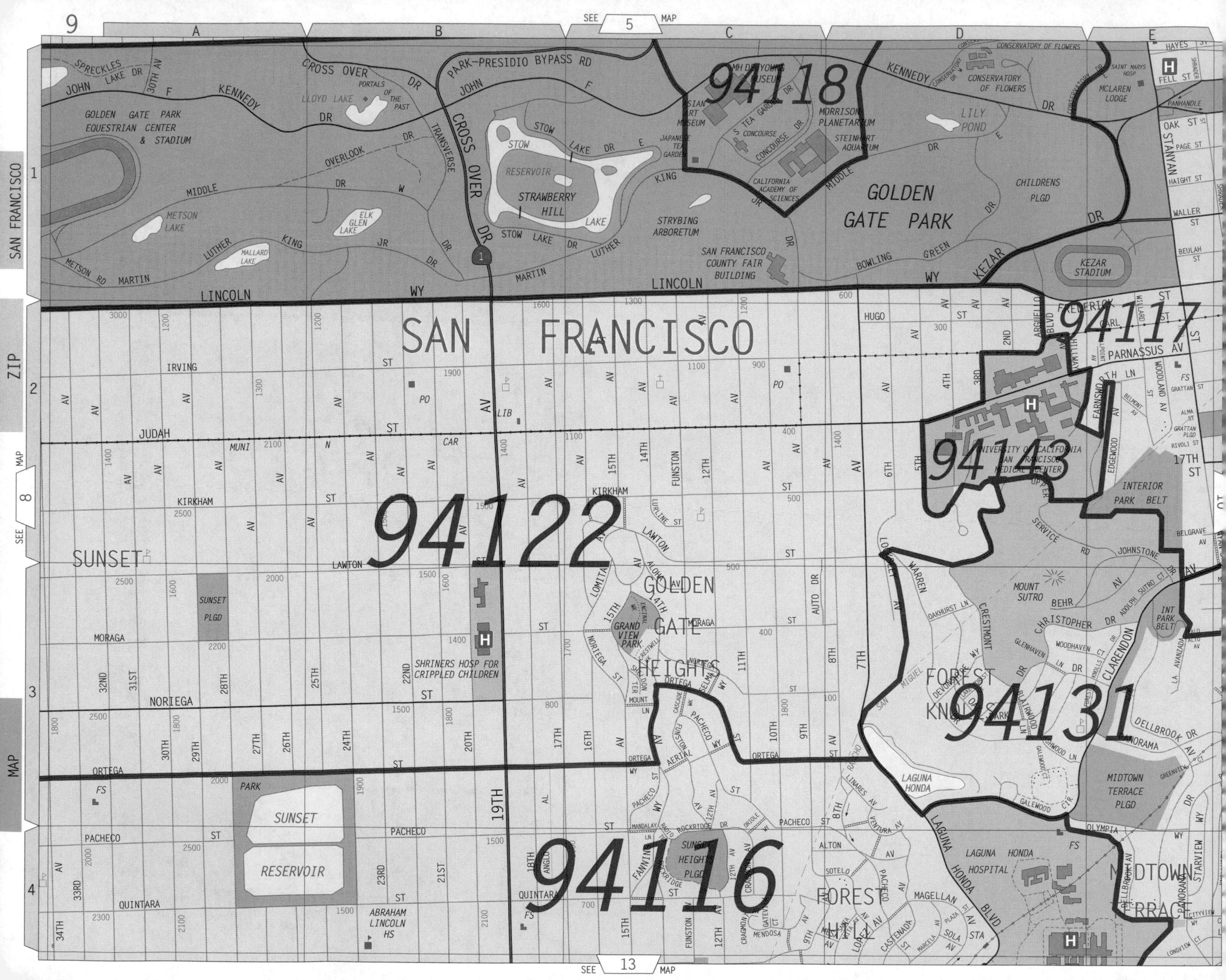
9
SEE 5 MAP
SAN FRANCISCO
ZIP
MAP
SEE 8 MAP
SEE 13 MAP
94118
94117
94143
94122
94131
94116
GOLDEN GATE PARK
SAN FRANCISCO
GOLDEN GATE PARK EQUESTRIAN CENTER & STADIUM
STRAWBERRY HILL
STRYBING ARBORETUM
SAN FRANCISCO COUNTY FAIR BUILDING
MORRISON PLANETARIUM
STEINHART AQUARIUM
CALIFORNIA ACADEMY OF SCIENCES
CONSERVATORY OF FLOWERS
MCLAREN LODGE
CHILDRENS PLGD
KEZAR STADIUM
UNIVERSITY OF CALIFORNIA SAN FRANCISCO MEDICAL CENTER
INTERIOR PARK BELT
MOUNT SUTRO
SUNSET
SUNSET PLGD
SHRINERS HOSP FOR CRIPPLED CHILDREN
GOLDEN GATE HEIGHTS
GRAND VIEW PARK
FOREST KNOLLS
LAGUNA HONDA
MIDTOWN TERRACE PLGD
LAGUNA HONDA HOSPITAL
MIDTOWN TERRACE
SUNSET RESERVOIR
ABRAHAM LINCOLN HS
SUNSET HEIGHTS PLGD
FOREST HILL
LINCOLN WY
IRVING ST
JUDAH ST
KIRKHAM ST
LAWTON ST
MORAGA ST
NORIEGA ST
ORTEGA ST
PACHECO ST
QUINTARA ST
19TH AV
7TH AV
PARNASSUS AV
FREDERICK ST
CLARENDON AV
LAGUNA HONDA BLVD

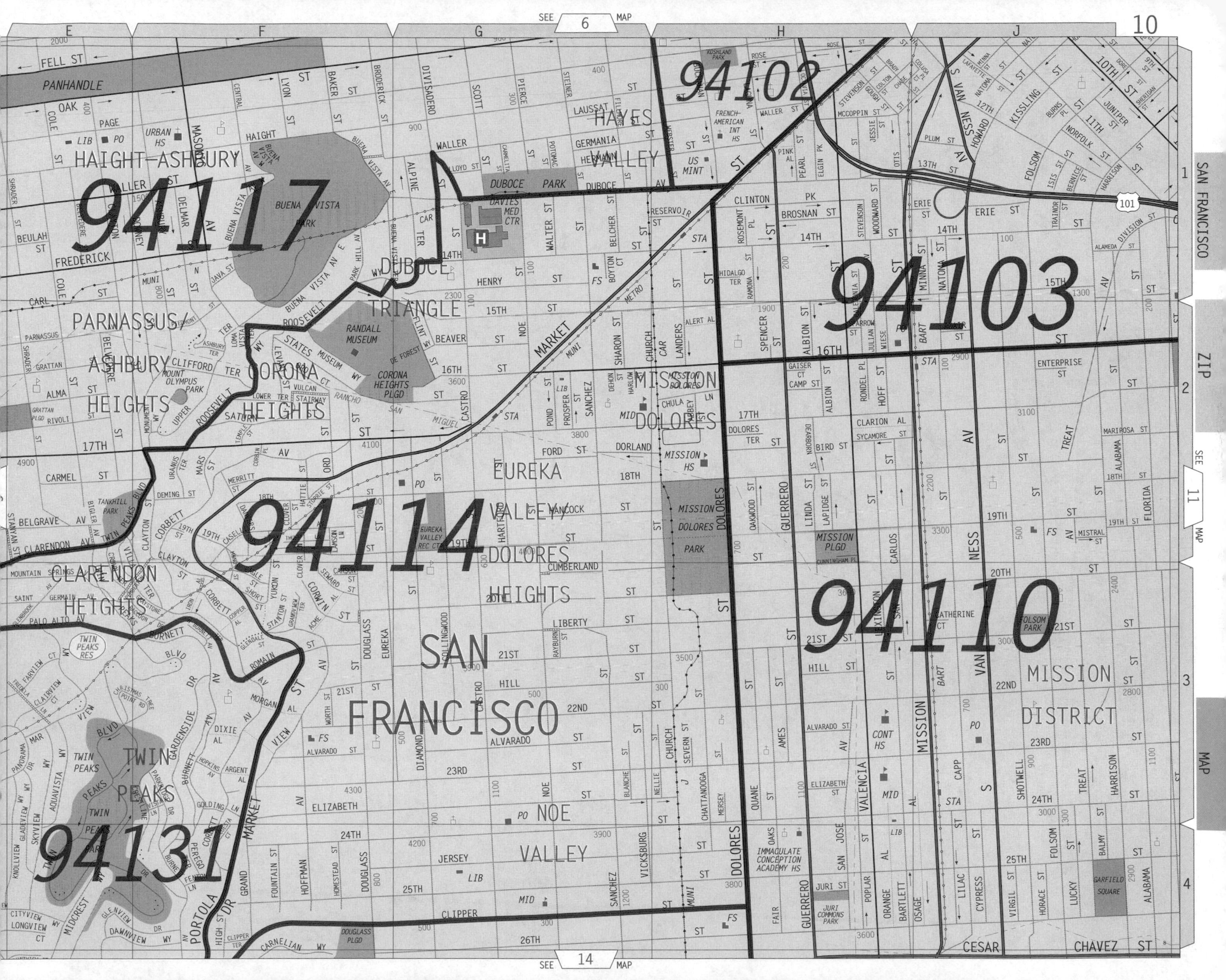

10
SEE 6 MAP
SEE 14 MAP
SEE 11 MAP
SAN FRANCISCO
ZIP
MAP
E
F
G
H
J
1
2
3
4
94117
94102
94103
94114
94110
94131
SAN FRANCISCO
HAIGHT-ASHBURY
HAYES VALLEY
DUBOCE TRIANGLE
PARNASSUS/ ASHBURY HEIGHTS
CORONA HEIGHTS
MISSION DOLORES
EUREKA VALLEY/ DOLORES HEIGHTS
CLARENDON HEIGHTS
TWIN PEAKS
NOE VALLEY
MISSION DISTRICT
PANHANDLE
BUENA VISTA PARK
DUBOCE PARK
DAVIES MED CTR
RANDALL MUSEUM
CORONA HEIGHTS PLGD
MOUNT OLYMPUS PARK
TANKHILL PARK
MISSION DOLORES PARK
MISSION PLGD
FOLSOM PARK
GARFIELD SQUARE
JURI COMMONS PARK
DOUGLASS PLGD
TWIN PEAKS RES
EUREKA VALLEY REC CTR
IMMACULATE CONCEPTION ACADEMY HS
MISSION HS
CONT HS
URBAN HS
FRENCH-AMERICAN INT HS
US MINT
KOSHLAND PARK
FELL ST
OAK ST
PAGE ST
HAIGHT
WALLER ST
FREDERICK
CARL
17TH
CARMEL ST
BELGRAVE AV
CLARENDON AV
MARKET
DUBOCE AV
14TH
15TH
16TH
17TH
18TH
19TH
20TH
21ST
22ND
23RD
24TH
25TH
26TH
CLIPPER
CESAR CHAVEZ ST
DOLORES
GUERRERO
VALENCIA
MISSION
VAN NESS AV
S VAN NESS AV
CASTRO
NOE
SANCHEZ
CHURCH
DIVISADERO
DOUGLASS
DIAMOND
PORTOLA DR
TWIN PEAKS BLVD
101

SEE 7 MAP
SEE 15 MAP
SEE 10 MAP
ZIP
MAP
SAN FRANCISCO
94103
94107
94110
94124
MISSION BAY
SAN FRANCISCO BAY
SAN FRANCISCO
POTRERO HILL
CENTRAL BASIN
MISSION ROCK TERMINAL
BOAT LAUNCH
OLD SP RAIL FERRY PIER
AGUA VISTA PARK
FISHING PIER
SF DRYDOCK
POTRERO POINT
NORTH CONTAINER TERMINAL
FRANKLIN SQUARE
JACKSON PLGD
MCKINLEY SQUARE
INTERNATIONAL STUDIES ACADEMY
POTRERO HILL RECREATION CENTER
SAN FRANCISCO GENERAL HOSPITAL
POTRERO DEL SOL PARK
RALPH PLGD
JOHN F FORAN (SOUTHERN FRWY)
JAMES LICK FRWY
CENTRAL FRWY
CESAR CHAVEZ ST
CALTRAIN
3RD ST
TERRY A FRANCOIS BLVD
HUMBOLDT ST
TUBBS ST
MARIPOSA
16TH
17TH ST
18TH
19TH
20TH
21ST
22ND
23RD
24TH
25TH
26TH
BRANNAN
TOWNSEND
KING ST
BERRY ST
CHANNEL ST
OWENS ST
HOOPER
IRWIN
HUBBELL
DAGGETT
DIVISION
HENRY ADAMS ST
RHODE ISLAND
DE HARO
BRUNO
UTAH
VERMONT
KANSAS
CAROLINA
WISCONSIN
ARKANSAS
CONNECTICUT
MISSOURI
TEXAS
MISSISSIPPI
PENNSYLVANIA
INDIANA
IOWA
MINNESOTA
TENNESSEE
ILLINOIS
MICHIGAN
MARIN
EVANS AV
BRYANT
YORK
HAMPSHIRE
POTRERO
FLORIDA
ALAMEDA
MERRIMAC ST
EL DORADO ST
MISSION ROCK ST
SOUTHERN HEIGHTS AV
TURNER TER
WATCHMAN WY
CORAL RD
CAIRE TER
LITTLEFIELD TER
BLAIR TER
FONTINELLA TER
SERPENTINE AV
MADERA ST
SIERRA
DAKOTA
HARRISON
GORDON ST
CONVERSE
LANGTON
GILBERT
LUCERNE ST
HARRIET
9TH
10TH
8TH
7TH
6TH
5TH
4TH ST

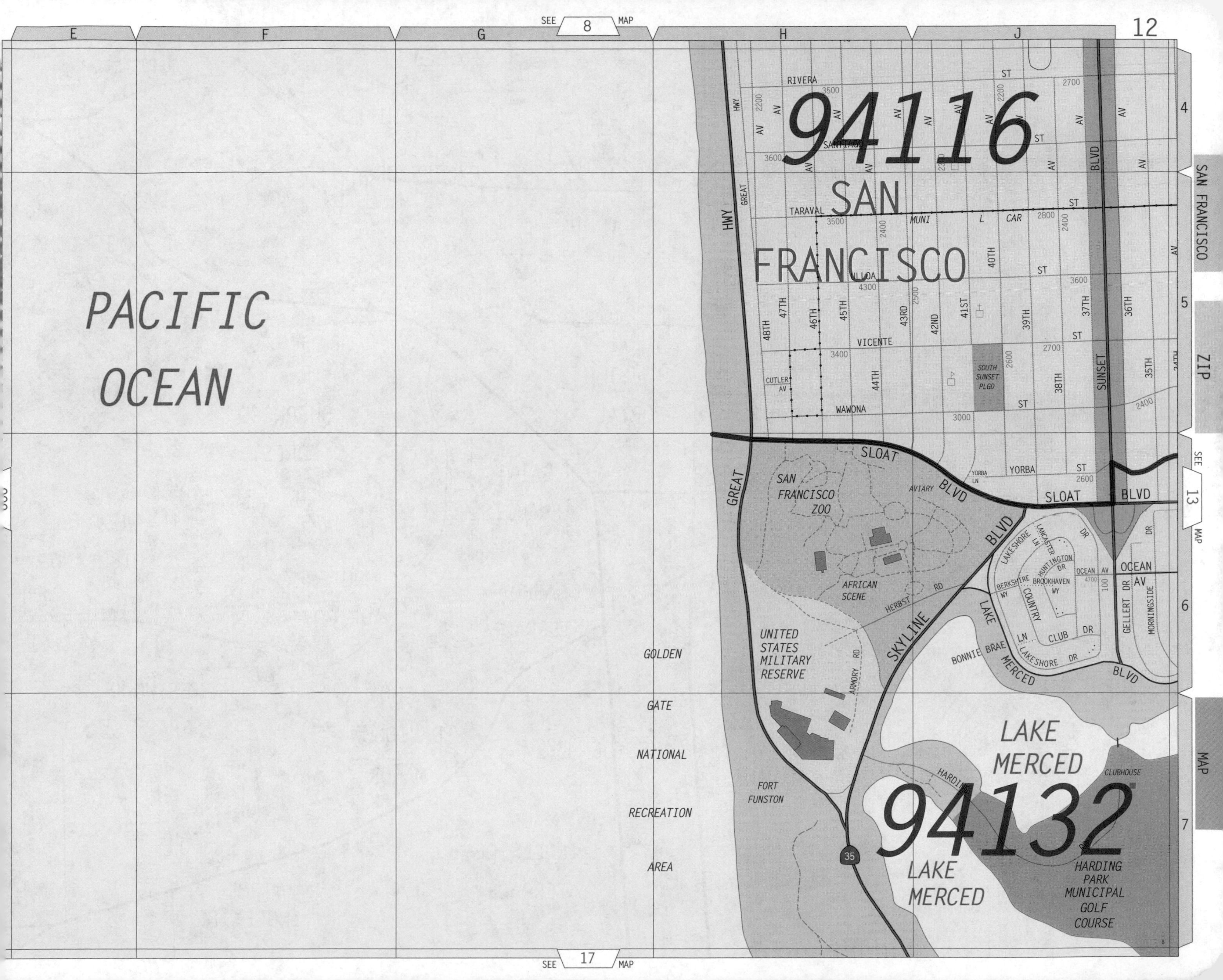

SEE 8 MAP
E
F
G
H
J
4
5
6
7
SAN FRANCISCO
ZIP
MAP
SEE 13 MAP
PACIFIC OCEAN
94116
SAN FRANCISCO
RIVERA
SANTIAGO
TARAVAL
MUNI L CAR
ULLOA
VICENTE
WAWONA
CUTLER AV
GREAT HWY
SUNSET BLVD
48TH
47TH
46TH
45TH
44TH
43RD
42ND
41ST
40TH
39TH
38TH
37TH
36TH
35TH
SOUTH SUNSET PLGD
SLOAT BLVD
YORBA ST
YORBA LN
SAN FRANCISCO ZOO
AVIARY
AFRICAN SCENE
HERBST RD
SKYLINE BLVD
LAKESHORE DR
LANCASTER LN
HUNTINGTON DR
BERKSHIRE WY
BROOKHAVEN WY
COUNTRY CLUB DR
OCEAN AV
GELLERT DR
MORNINGSIDE
LAKE MERCED BLVD
BONNIE BRAE LN
UNITED STATES MILITARY RESERVE
ARMORY RD
GOLDEN GATE NATIONAL RECREATION AREA
FORT FUNSTON
35
LAKE MERCED
HARDING
CLUBHOUSE
94132
HARDING PARK MUNICIPAL GOLF COURSE
SEE 17 MAP

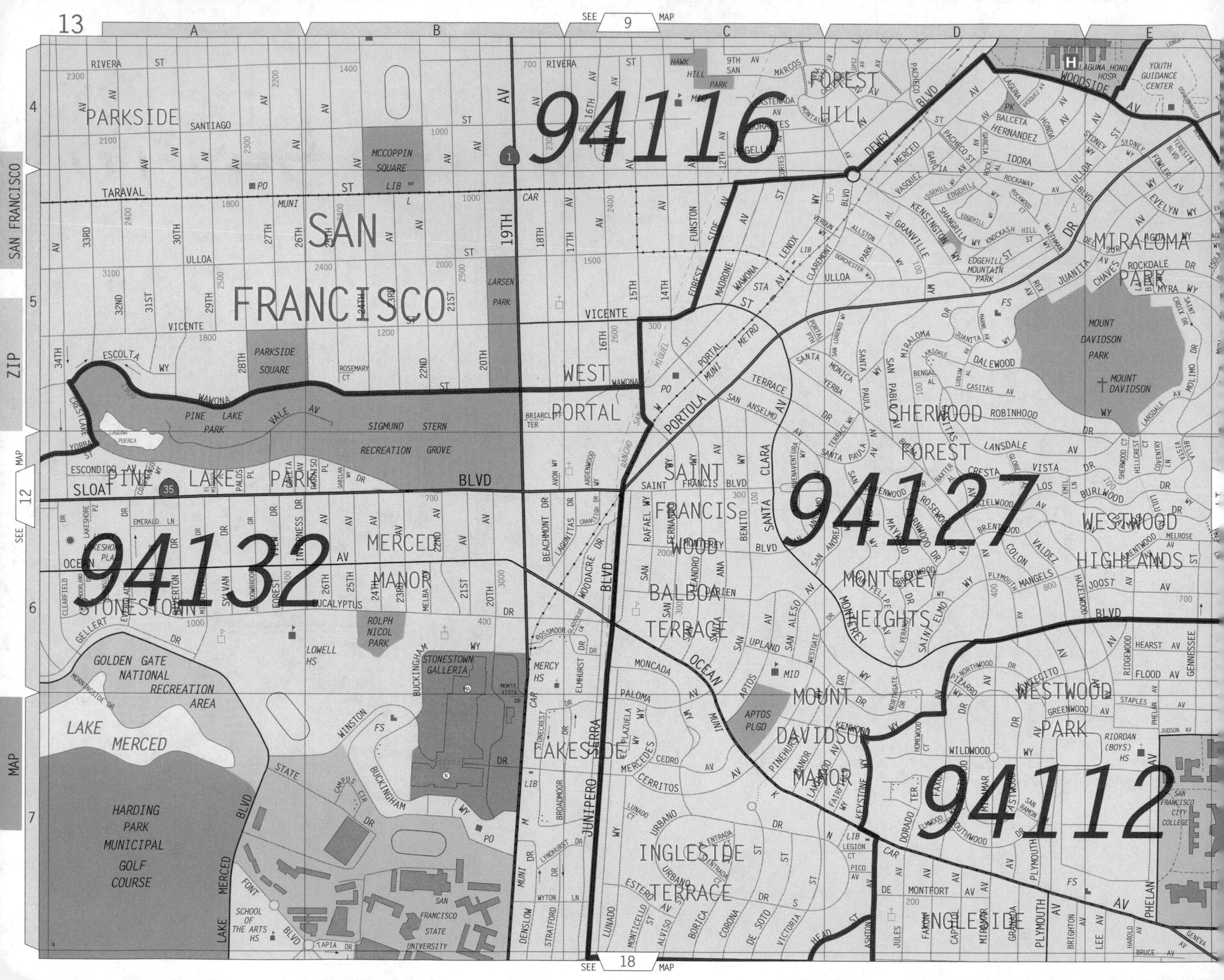
SEE 9 MAP
A
B
C
D
E
4
5
6
7
SAN FRANCISCO
ZIP
MAP
SEE 12 MAP
94116
94127
94132
94112
SAN
FRANCISCO
PARKSIDE
RIVERA ST
SANTIAGO
TARAVAL
MUNI
ULLOA
VICENTE
ESCOLTA
WAWONA
SLOAT
BLVD
OCEAN
EUCALYPTUS
GELLERT
MCCOPPIN SQUARE
LIB
PO
LARSEN PARK
PARKSIDE SQUARE
ROSEMARY CT
PINE LAKE PARK
LAGUNA PUERCA
SIGMUND STERN RECREATION GROVE
PINE LAKE PARK
MERCED MANOR
STONESTOWN
ROLPH NICOL PARK
LOWELL HS
STONESTOWN GALLERIA
GOLDEN GATE NATIONAL RECREATION AREA
LAKE MERCED
HARDING PARK MUNICIPAL GOLF COURSE
SCHOOL OF THE ARTS HS
SAN FRANCISCO STATE UNIVERSITY
WINSTON
BUCKINGHAM
FS
LAKE MERCED BLVD
19TH AV
WEST PORTAL
BRIARCLIFF TER
MERCY HS
LAKESIDE
JUNIPERO SERRA BLVD
HAWK HILL PARK
FOREST HILL
DEWEY BLVD
LAGUNA HONDA HOSP
YOUTH GUIDANCE CENTER
WOODSIDE AV
PORTOLA
SAINT FRANCIS WOOD
BALBOA TERRACE
MONTEREY HEIGHTS
SHERWOOD FOREST
MIRALOMA PARK
MOUNT DAVIDSON PARK
MOUNT DAVIDSON
WESTWOOD HIGHLANDS
WESTWOOD PARK
MOUNT DAVIDSON MANOR
APTOS PLGD
INGLESIDE TERRACE
INGLESIDE
RIORDAN (BOYS) HS
SAN FRANCISCO CITY COLLEGE
OCEAN AV
MONTEREY BLVD
PHELAN AV
SEE 18 MAP

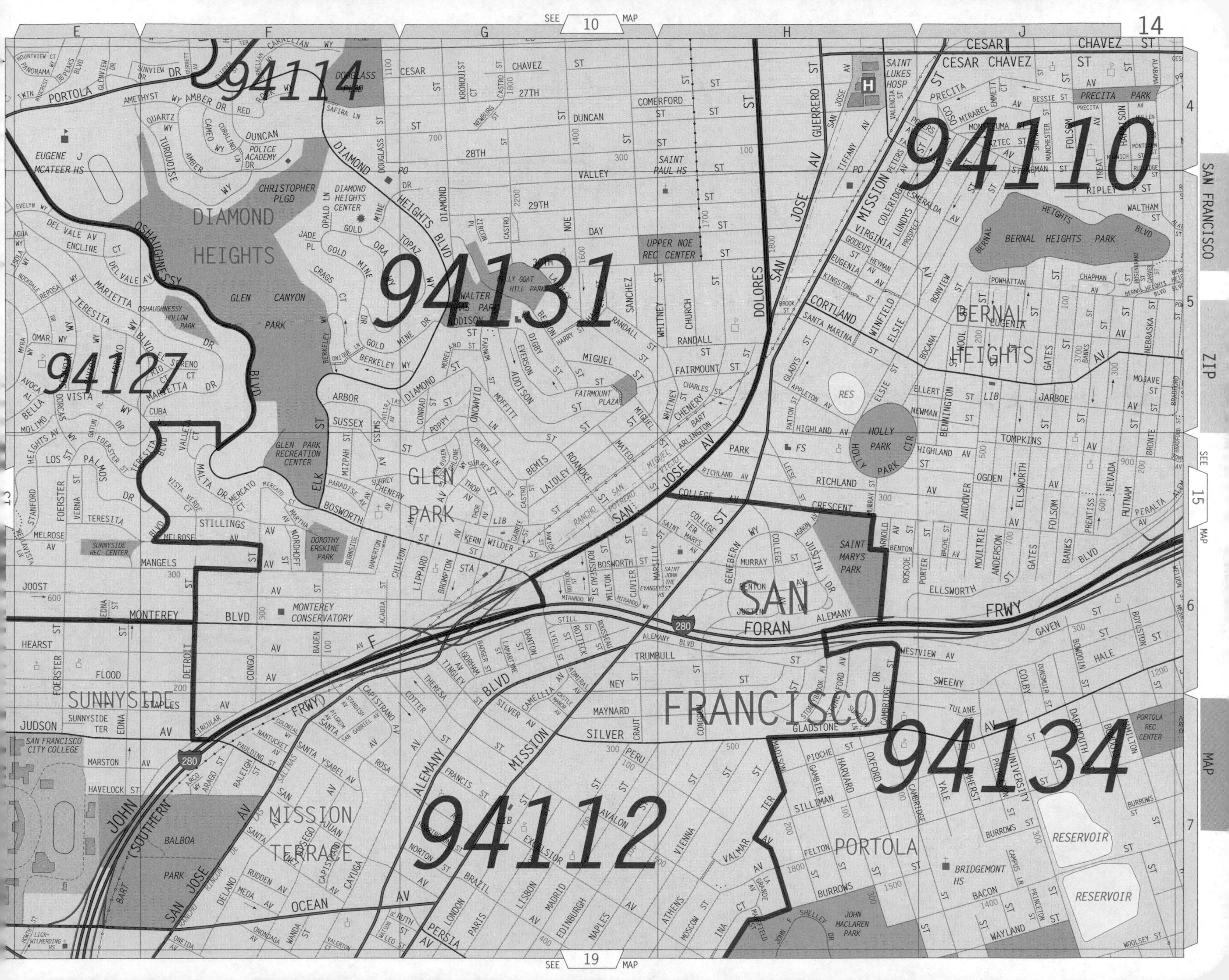

SEE 10 MAP
SEE 19 MAP
SEE 15 MAP
SAN FRANCISCO ZIP MAP
94114
94110
94131
94127
94112
94134
DIAMOND HEIGHTS
GLEN PARK
BERNAL HEIGHTS
SUNNYSIDE
MISSION TERRACE
PORTOLA
SAN FRANCISCO
GLEN CANYON PARK
BERNAL HEIGHTS PARK
SAINT MARYS PARK
HOLLY PARK
BALBOA PARK
JOHN MACLAREN PARK
RESERVOIR

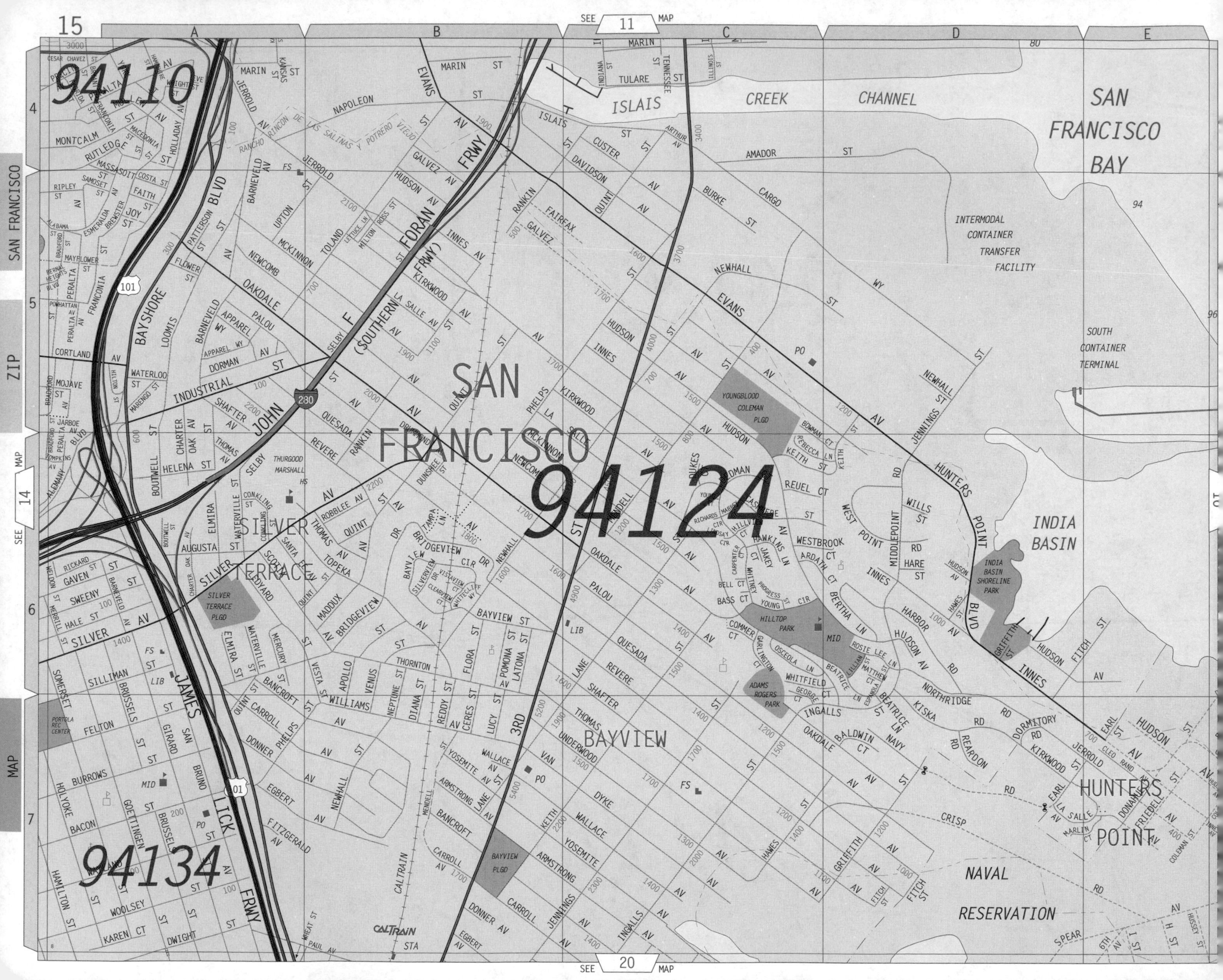
SEE 11 MAP
SEE 20 MAP
SEE 14 MAP
SAN FRANCISCO
ZIP
MAP
A
B
C
D
E
4
5
6
7
94110
94124
94134
SAN FRANCISCO
ISLAIS CREEK CHANNEL
SAN FRANCISCO BAY
INTERMODAL CONTAINER TRANSFER FACILITY
SOUTH CONTAINER TERMINAL
INDIA BASIN
INDIA BASIN SHORELINE PARK
YOUNGBLOOD COLEMAN PLGD
HILLTOP PARK
ADAMS ROGERS PARK
SILVER TERRACE
SILVER TERRACE PLGD
BAYVIEW
BAYVIEW PLGD
HUNTERS POINT
NAVAL RESERVATION
PORTOLA REC CENTER
THURGOOD MARSHALL HS
JOHN F FORAN FRWY
(SOUTHERN FRWY)
JAMES LICK FRWY
BAYSHORE BLVD
HUNTERS POINT BLVD
EVANS AV
3RD ST
CALTRAIN
CALTRAIN STA
101
280
MARIN ST
ISLAIS ST
AMADOR ST
CARGO WY
OAKDALE AV
PALOU AV
QUESADA AV
REVERE AV
SHAFTER AV
THOMAS AV
INNES AV
HUDSON AV
NEWHALL ST
INDUSTRIAL ST
SILVER AV
INGALLS ST
CRISP RD

SEE 668 MAP
E
F
G
H
J
4
5
6
7
SAN FRANCISCO
ZIP
MAP
SEE ALA 669 MAP
96
98
INDIA
BASIN
SAN FRANCISCO
BAY
POINT
AVISADERO
HUNTERS
POINT
94124
DONAHUE ST
ENGLISH ST
MCCANN ST
LOCKWOOD
AV
GALVEZ
AV
HUDSON AV
COLEMAN ST
INNES AV
ROBINSON ST
HILL
AV
VAN KEUREN AV
ST
C
AV
ST
A
AV
FISHER
HORNE
DR
DR
SPEAR
BLANDY
ST
NIMITZ
COCHRANE ST
MORRELL ST
E ST
NAVAL
RESERVATION
SEE 21 MAP

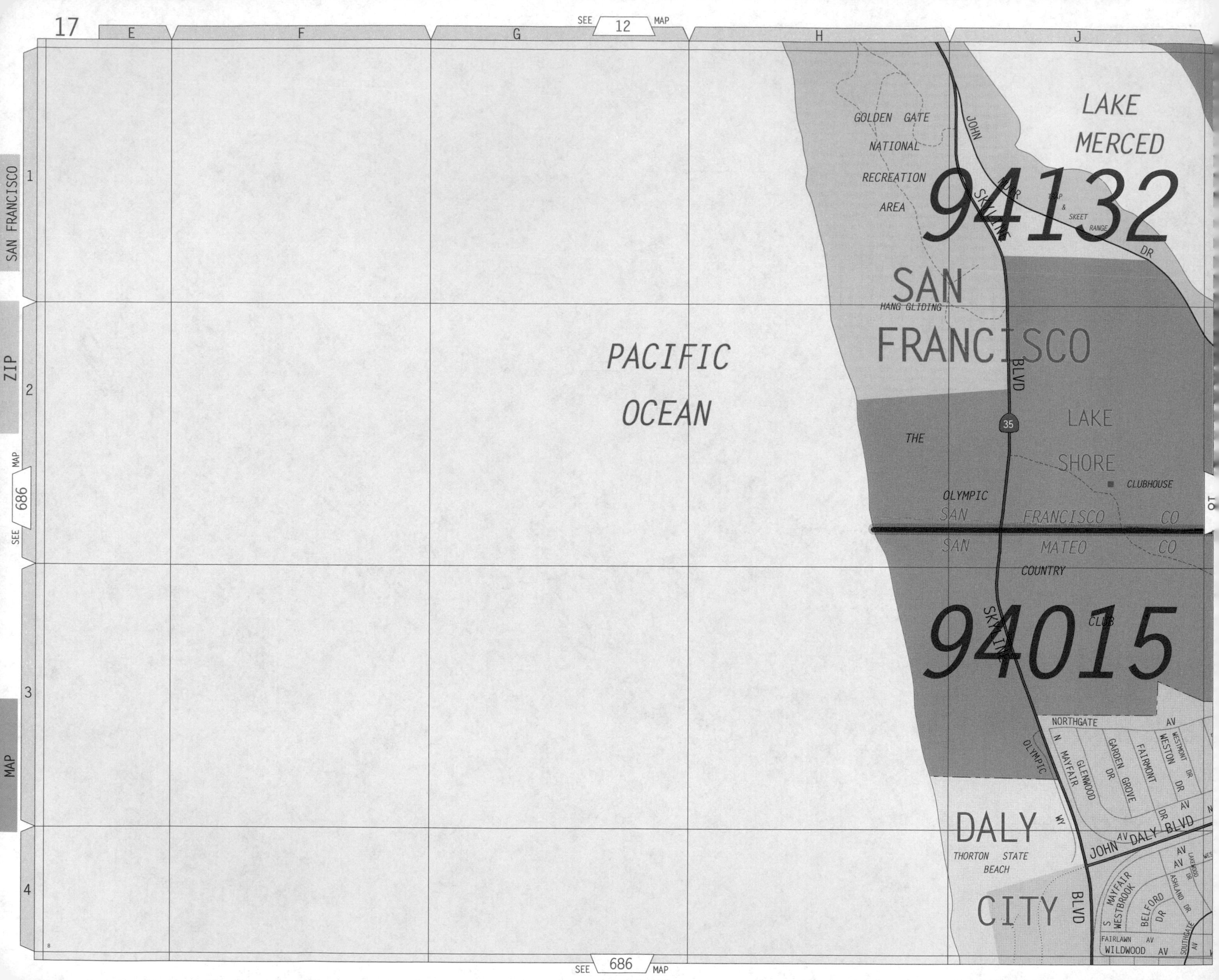
SEE 12 MAP
E
F
G
H
J
1
2
3
4
SAN FRANCISCO
ZIP
MAP
SEE 686 MAP
PACIFIC
OCEAN
GOLDEN GATE
NATIONAL
RECREATION
AREA
LAKE
MERCED
94132
JOHN
MUIR
SKYLINE
DR
TRAP
&
SKEET
RANGE
SAN
FRANCISCO
HANG GLIDING
BLVD
35
LAKE
SHORE
CLUBHOUSE
THE
OLYMPIC
SAN FRANCISCO CO
SAN MATEO CO
COUNTRY
CLUB
94015
SKYLINE
NORTHGATE AV
OLYMPIC
WY
N MAYFAIR
GLENWOOD
DR
GARDEN GROVE
DR
FAIRMONT
WESTON
DR
WESTMONT DR
AV
DR
JOHN DALY BLVD
AV
DALY
CITY
THORTON STATE
BEACH
BLVD
S MAYFAIR
WESTBROOK
BELFORD
DR
ASHLAND DR
LAKEWOOD DR
FAIRLAWN AV
WILDWOOD AV
SOUTHGATE
SEE 686 MAP

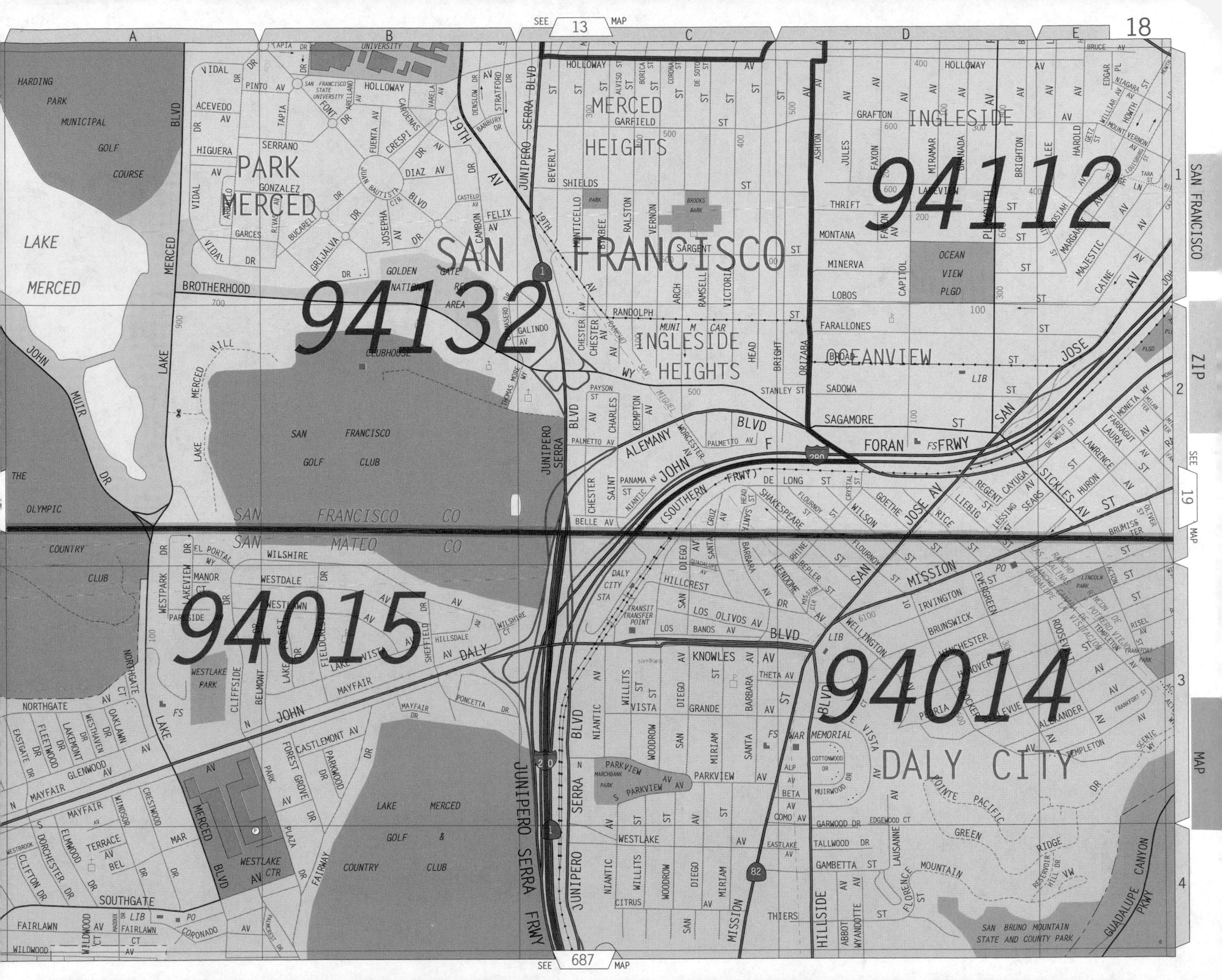
SEE 13 MAP
SAN FRANCISCO
ZIP
MAP
SEE 19 MAP
SEE 687 MAP
94132
94112
94015
94014
SAN FRANCISCO
PARK MERCED
MERCED HEIGHTS
INGLESIDE
INGLESIDE HEIGHTS
OCEANVIEW
DALY CITY
LAKE MERCED
HARDING PARK MUNICIPAL GOLF COURSE
SAN FRANCISCO GOLF CLUB
THE OLYMPIC COUNTRY CLUB
LAKE MERCED GOLF & COUNTRY CLUB
SAN FRANCISCO CO
SAN MATEO CO
SAN BRUNO MOUNTAIN STATE AND COUNTY PARK
JUNIPERO SERRA FRWY
JOHN DALY BLVD
ALEMANY BLVD
FORAN FRWY
MISSION ST
SAN JOSE AV
GUADALUPE CANYON PKWY

SEE 14 MAP

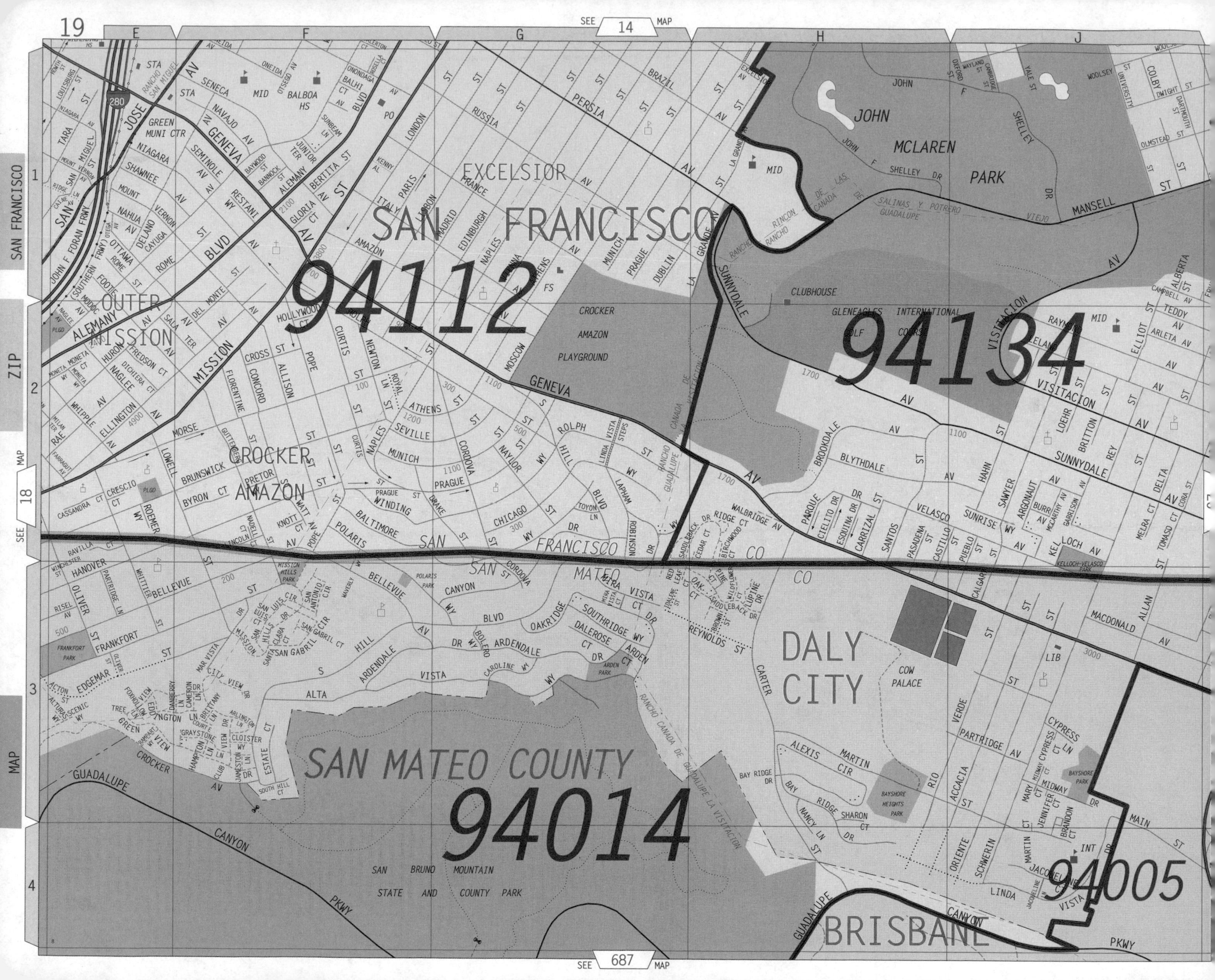

SEE 18 MAP

SEE 687 MAP

SEE 15 MAP

SEE 21 MAP

SEE 688 MAP

SEE 16 MAP
E
F
G
H
J
1
2
3
4
SAN FRANCISCO
ZIP
MAP
SEE 20 MAP
HUSSEY
COCHRANE ST
MORRELL ST
E ST
MANSEAU ST
SAN
94124
FRANCISCO
NAVAL
RESERVATION
H ST
J ST
MAHAN
ST
SAN FRANCISCO
NAVAL
SHIPYARD
SAN FRANCISCO
BAY
SAN FRANCISCO CO
SAN MATEO CO
SEE 688 MAP

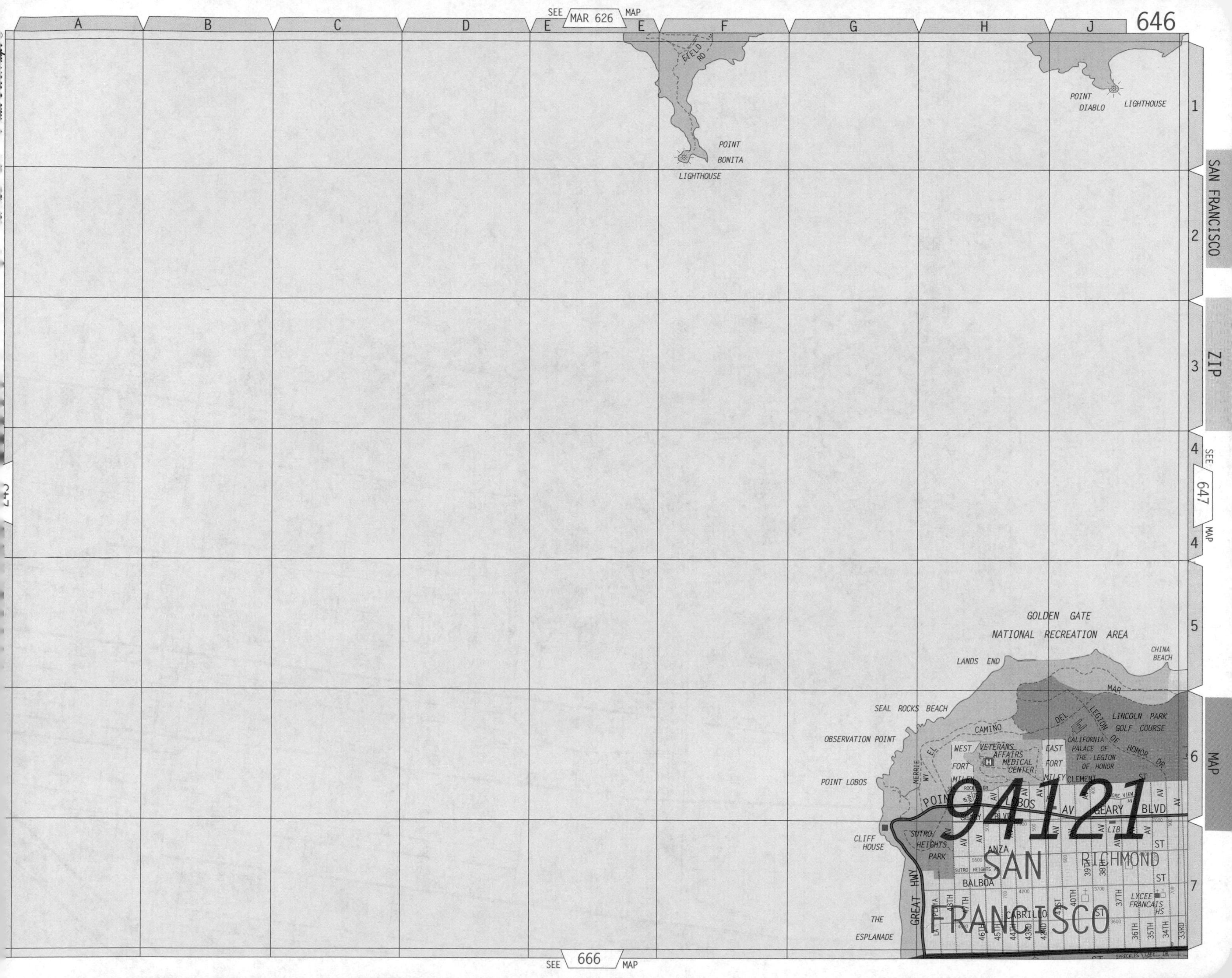
SEE MAR 626 MAP
A
B
C
D
E
F
G
H
J
1
2
3
4
5
6
7
FIELD RD
POINT BONITA
LIGHTHOUSE
POINT DIABLO
LIGHTHOUSE
SAN FRANCISCO
ZIP
MAP
SEE 647 MAP
GOLDEN GATE
NATIONAL RECREATION AREA
LANDS END
CHINA BEACH
SEAL ROCKS BEACH
OBSERVATION POINT
POINT LOBOS
CLIFF HOUSE
THE ESPLANADE
LINCOLN PARK GOLF COURSE
CALIFORNIA PALACE OF THE LEGION OF HONOR
LEGION OF HONOR DR
EL CAMINO DEL MAR
WEST FORT MILEY
VETERANS AFFAIRS MEDICAL CENTER
EAST FORT MILEY
CLEMENT ST
POINT LOBOS AV
GEARY BLVD
SUTRO HEIGHTS PARK
ANZA
BALBOA
CABRILLO
GREAT HWY
94121
SAN FRANCISCO
RICHMOND
LYCEE FRANCAIS HS
LIB
48TH
47TH
46TH
45TH
44TH
43RD
42ND
41ST
40TH
39TH
38TH
37TH
36TH
35TH
34TH
33RD
SEE 666 MAP

SAN FRANCISCO BAY
GOLDEN GATE BRIDGE
(TOLL $3.00)
(SOUTHBOUND ONLY)
GOLDEN GATE BRIDGE FRWY
FORT POINT
FORT POINT NATIONAL HISTORIC SITE
GOLDEN GATE NATIONAL RECREATION AREA
US COAST GUARD STATION
SAUSALITO
TIBURON
FERRY
ALCATRAZ
SAN FRANCISCO MARITIME NATIONAL HISTORICAL PARK
MUNICIPAL PIER
FISHERMANS WHARF
HYDE STREET PIER
AQUATIC PARK
SAINT FRANCIS YACHT CLUB
GOLDEN GATE YACHT CLUB
PROMENADE
MARINA
COW HOLLOW
RUSSIAN
PACIFIC HEIGHTS
PRESIDIO HEIGHTS
JORDAN HEIGHTS/LAUREL HEIGHTS
ANZA VISTA
LAKE
SEACLIFF
RICHMOND
LONE MOUNTAIN
ALAMO SQUARE
SAN FRANCISCO NATIONAL CEMETERY
PRESIDIO GOLF COURSE
FORT SCOTT
BAKER BEACH
CHINA BEACH
LINCOLN BLVD
PRESIDIO BLVD
94129
94123
94133
94115
94118
94121
94108
94109
94102
94103
94117
SEE MAR 627 MAP
SEE 646 MAP
SEE 667 MAP
SAN FRANCISCO
ZIP
MAP

SEE 243 MAP
A
B
C
D
E
F
G
H
J
94130
TREASURE ISLAND
NAVAL RESERVATION
TREASURE ISLAND MUSEUM
ALAMEDA
COUNTY
94649
OUTER HARBOR
YERBA BUENA
ISLAND
MATSON TERMINAL
OAKLAND
7TH STREET
MARINE CONTAINER
TERMINAL
PORTVIEW PARK
94625
BART TRANSBAY TUBE
SAN FRANCISCO COUNTY
ANGEL ISLAND TIBURON FERRY
SAUSALITO FERRY
LARKSPUR SAN FRANCISCO FERRY
VALLEJO FERRY
OAKLAND ALAMEDA FERRY
HARBOR BAY ISLE FERRY
SAN FRANCISCO CO
ALAMEDA CO
SAN FRANCISCO
BAY
ALAMEDA
94501
ALAMEDA POINT
(FORMERLY US NAVAL AIR STATION AT ALAMEDA)
SAN FRANCISCO - OAKLAND BAY BRIDGE
(TWO LEVEL FRWY)
(TOLL $1.00 WESTBOUND ONLY)
80
NORTH WATERFRONT
TELEGRAPH HILL
NORTH BEACH
94133
94111
FISHING PIER
CHINATOWN
94108
94104
94105
94102
SAN FRANCISCO
SOUTH OF MARKET
SOUTH BEACH
94107
94103
EMBARCADERO
RINCON POINT
SOUTH BEACH MARINA
CHINA BASIN
MISSION ROCK
MOSCONE CONV CTR
CALTRAIN
1 ONE EMBARCADERO CENTER
2 TWO EMBARCADERO CENTER
3 THREE EMBARCADERO CENTER
4 FOUR EMBARCADERO CENTER
5 HYATT REGENCY
SEE B4
SAN FRANCISCO ZIP MAP
SEE ALA 649 MAP
SEE 668 MAP

SEE 646 MAP
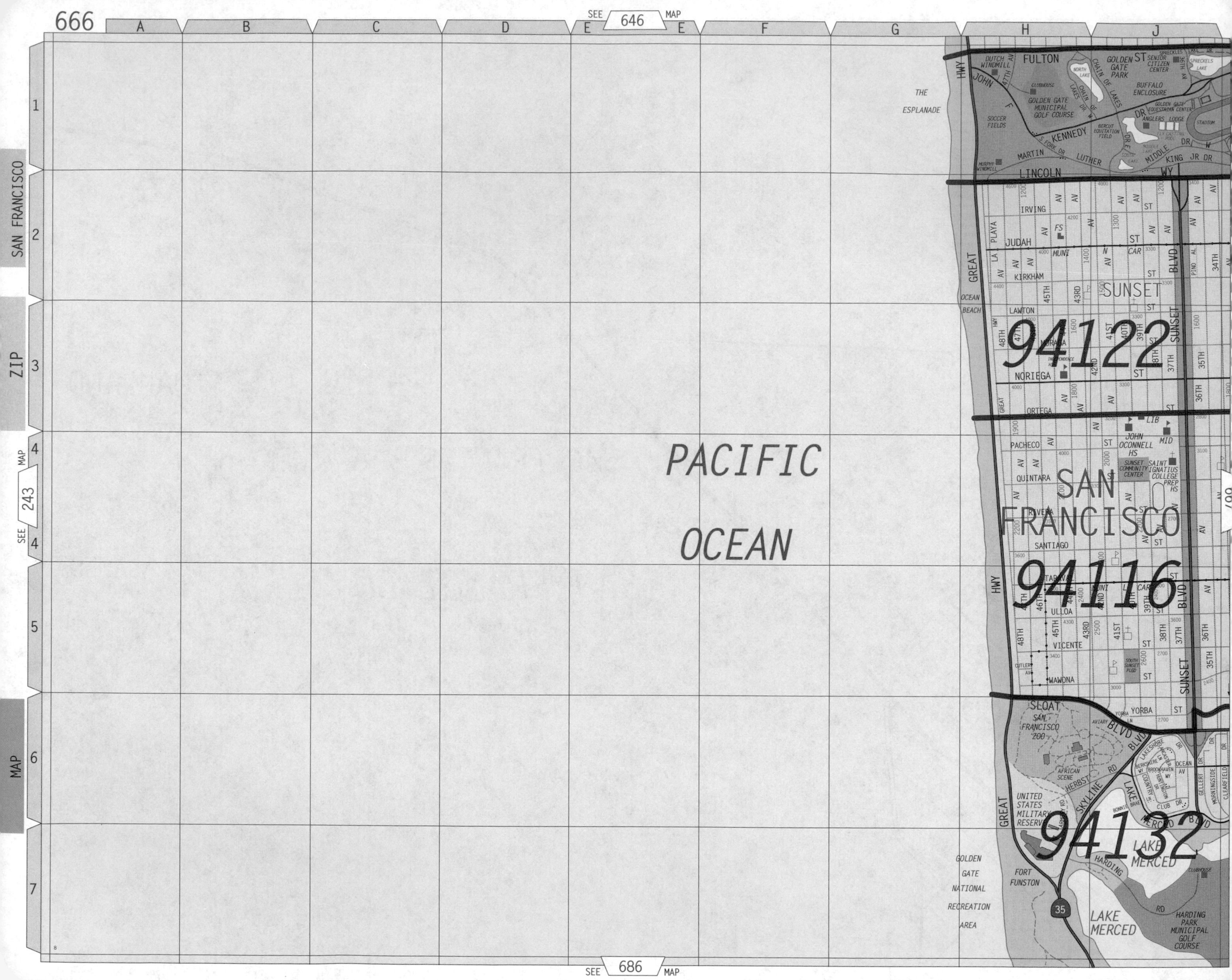

SEE 686 MAP

SEE 647 MAP
SEE 687 MAP
SEE 668 MAP
SAN FRANCISCO
ZIP
MAP
94118
94117
94103
94143
94122
94114
94116
94110
94131
94127
94132
94112
94134
GOLDEN GATE PARK
HAIGHT ASHBURY
HAYES VALLEY
BUENA VISTA PARK
DUBOCE TRIANGLE
PARNASSUS/ASHBURY HEIGHTS
CORONA HEIGHTS
MISSION DOLORES
EUREKA VALLEY/DOLORES HEIGHTS
SUNSET
GOLDEN GATE HEIGHTS
CLARENDON HEIGHTS
FOREST KNOLLS
TWIN PEAKS
MIDTOWN TERRACE
NOE VALLEY
MISSION DISTRICT
PARKSIDE
FOREST HILL
SAN FRANCISCO
DIAMOND HEIGHTS
MIRALOMA PARK
BERNAL HEIGHTS
WEST PORTAL
SHERWOOD
SAINT FRANCIS WOOD
MONTEREY HEIGHTS
WESTWOOD HIGHLANDS
GLEN PARK
PINE LAKE PARK
MERCED MANOR
STONETOWN
BALBOA TERRACE
MOUNT DAVIDSON MANOR
WESTWOOD PARK
SUNNYSIDE
LAKESIDE
INGLESIDE TERRACE
INGLESIDE
MISSION TERRACE
PORTOLA
LAKE MERCED
HARDING PARK MUNICIPAL GOLF COURSE
SUNSET RESERVOIR
MOUNT DAVIDSON PARK
GLEN CANYON PARK
SIGMUND STERN RECREATION GROVE
SAN FRANCISCO CITY COLLEGE

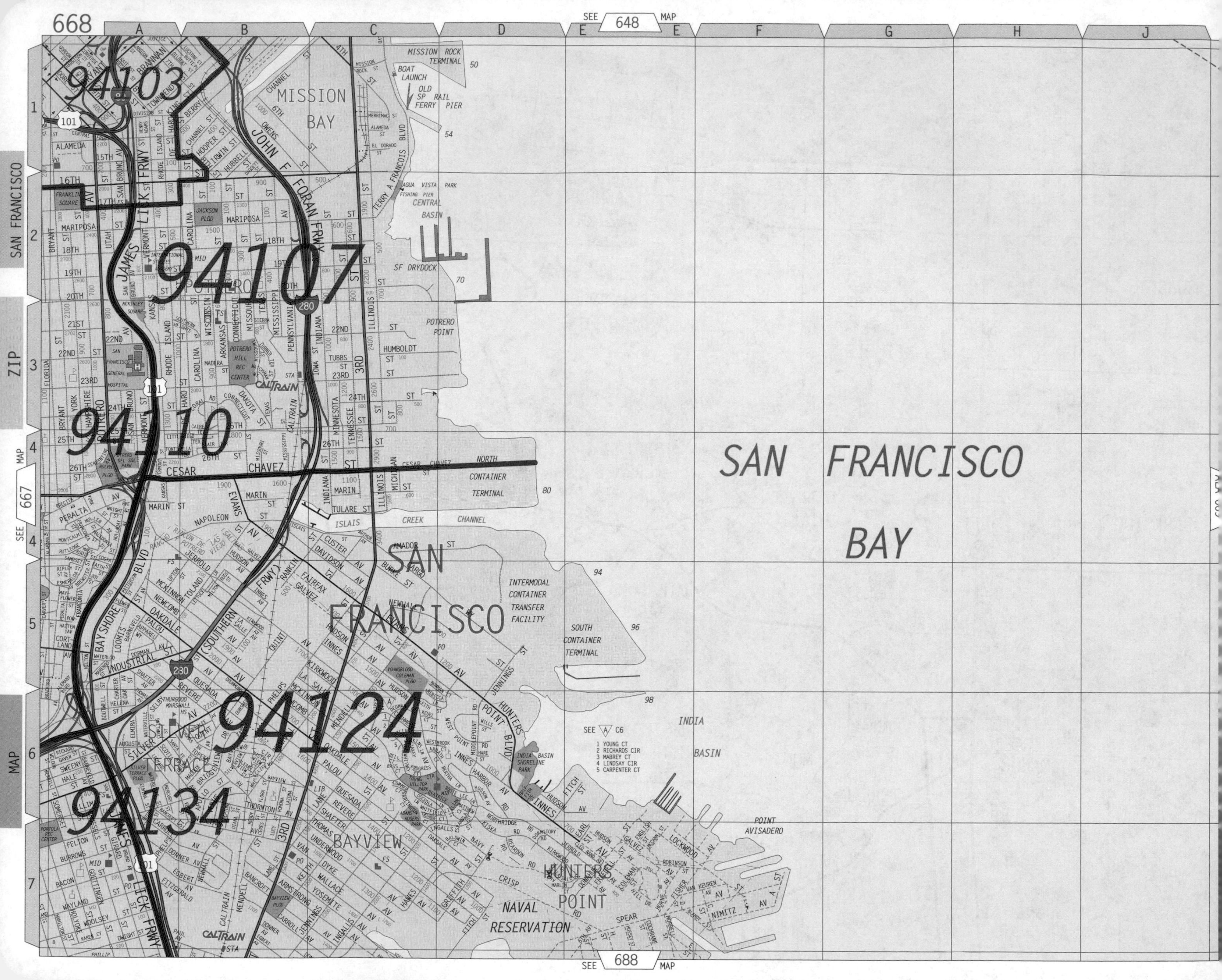
SEE 648 MAP
SEE 688 MAP
SEE 667 MAP
SAN FRANCISCO
ZIP
MAP
94103
94107
94110
94124
94134
MISSION BAY
MISSION ROCK TERMINAL
BOAT LAUNCH
OLD SP RAIL FERRY PIER
AGUA VISTA PARK
CENTRAL BASIN
SF DRYDOCK
POTRERO POINT
JOHN F FORAN FRWY
JAMES LICK FRWY
NORTH CONTAINER TERMINAL
ISLAIS CREEK CHANNEL
SAN FRANCISCO BAY
SAN FRANCISCO
INTERMODAL CONTAINER TRANSFER FACILITY
SOUTH CONTAINER TERMINAL
INDIA BASIN
INDIA BASIN SHORELINE PARK
POINT AVISADERO
SEE A C6
1 YOUNG CT
2 RICHARDS CIR
3 MABREY CT
4 LINDSAY CIR
5 CARPENTER CT
SILVER TERRACE
BAYVIEW
HUNTERS POINT
NAVAL RESERVATION
SAN FRANCISCO GENERAL HOSPITAL
POTRERO HILL REC CENTER
CALTRAIN
YOUNGBLOOD COLEMAN PLGD
FRANKLIN SQUARE
JACKSON PLGD
MCKINLEY SQUARE
PORTOLA REC CENTER
BAYSHORE BLVD
HUNTERS POINT BLVD
CESAR CHAVEZ ST
3RD ST
EVANS AV
INNES AV
PALOU AV
OAKDALE AV
QUESADA AV
REVERE AV
MARIPOSA ST
16TH ST
INDUSTRIAL ST
CRISP RD
SPEAR AV

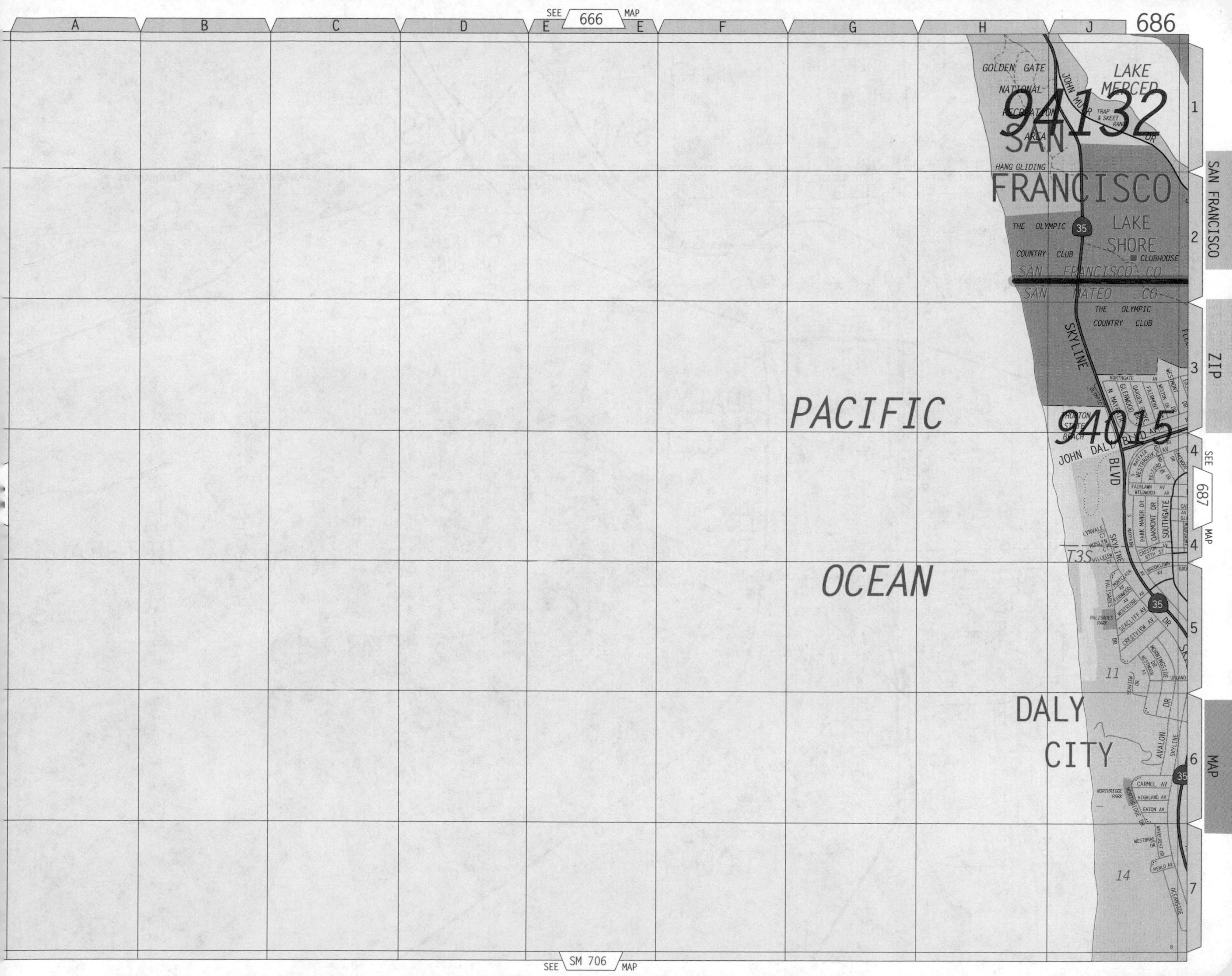

SEE 666 MAP
A
B
C
D
E
F
G
H
J
1
2
3
4
5
6
7
GOLDEN GATE NATIONAL RECREATION AREA
HANG GLIDING
JOHN MUIR DR
TRAP & SKEET RANGE
LAKE MERCED
94132
SAN FRANCISCO
THE OLYMPIC COUNTRY CLUB
35
LAKE SHORE
CLUBHOUSE
SAN FRANCISCO CO
SAN MATEO CO
THE OLYMPIC COUNTRY CLUB
SKYLINE
NORTHGATE AV
GLENWOOD
N MAYFAIR DR
GARDEN GROVE
FAIRMONT
WESTMONT
WESTON DR
94015
THORNTON STATE BEACH
JOHN DALY BLVD
BLVD
WESTBROOK
BELFORD DR
FAIRLAWN AV
WILDWOOD AV
PARK MANOR DR
OAKMONT DR
SOUTHGATE
LYNVALE CT
ROSLYN CT
HILLVIEW CT
SKYLINE
CRESTON
87TH ST
BROOKLAWN AV
T3S
PACIFIC
OCEAN
PALISADES
FERNWOOD
WESTRIDGE AV
MONTCLAIR AV
PALISADES PARK
SEACLIFF AV
CRESTVIEW AV
DR
MORNINGSIDE DR
WESTMOOR AV
SEAVIEW
URLAND
11
DALY
CITY
AVALON
SKYLINE
DR
CARMEL AV
HIGHLAND AV
EATON AV
NORTHRIDGE PARK
NORTHRIDGE DR
WESTBRAE DR
WAVECREST DR
MENLO AV
14
OCEANSIDE
SAN FRANCISCO
ZIP
MAP
SEE 687 MAP
SEE SM 706 MAP

SEE 667 MAP

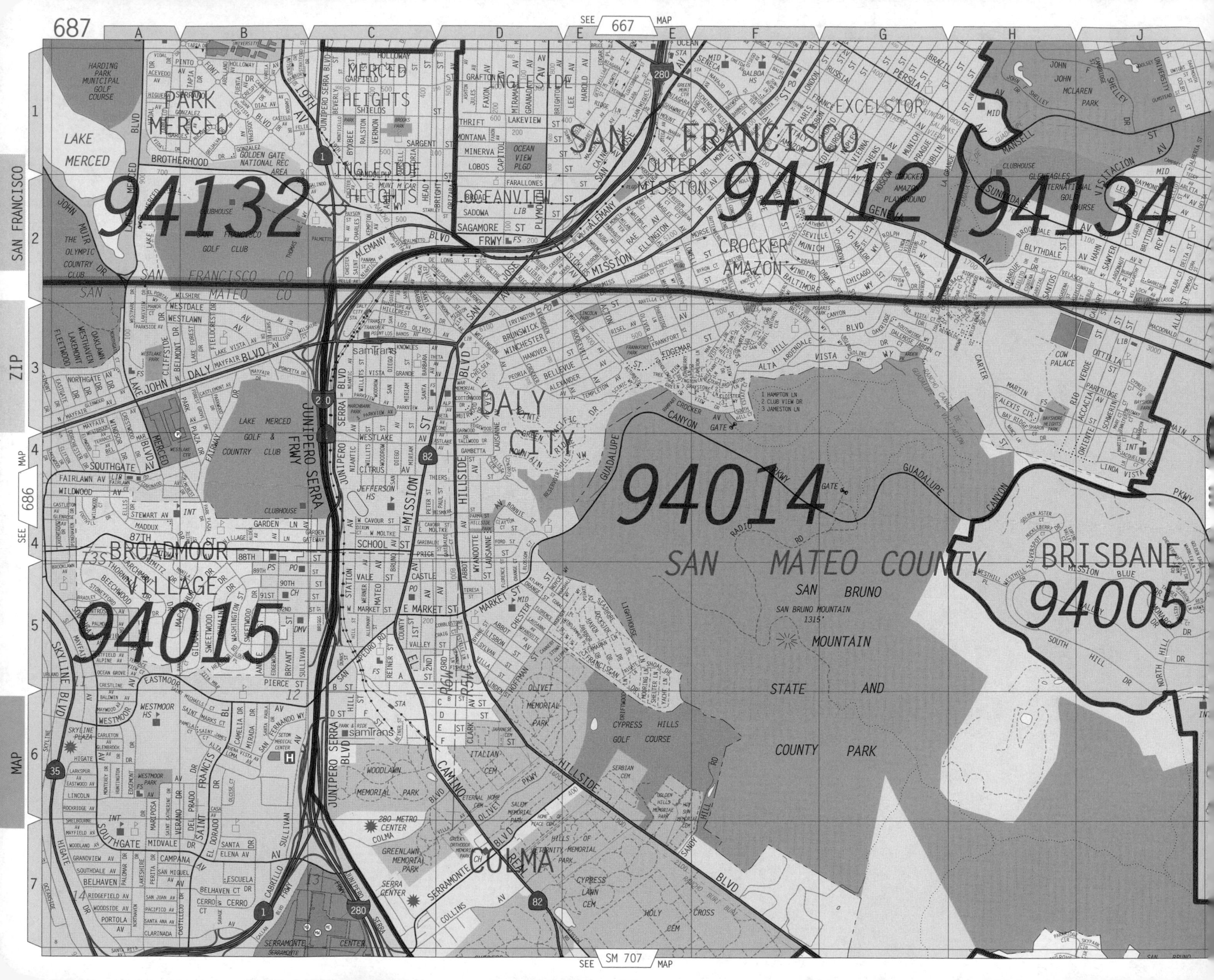

SEE 686 MAP

SEE SM 707 MAP

SEE 668 MAP
A
B
C
D
E
F
G
H
J
SAN 94124
FRANCISCO
HUNTERS
NAVAL
RESERVATION
POINT
SAN FRANCISCO
NAVAL
SHIPYARD
SOUTH BASIN
CANDLESTICK POINT
3COM PARK
(CANDLESTICK PARK)
HOME OF SF GIANTS & 49ERS
CANDLESTICK POINT STATE RECREATION AREA
BAYVIEW HEIGHTS
VISITACION VALLEY
94134
94014
BAYSHORE
SAN FRANCISCO CO
SAN MATEO CO
SAN MATEO
COUNTY
SAN FRANCISCO
BAY
BRISBANE
94005
GUADALUPE CANAL
LAGOON
SIERRA POINT
MARINA
1 SAN MATEO LN
2 PLACER WY
94014
1
2
3
4
5
6
7
SAN FRANCISCO
ZIP
SEE 243 MAP
MAP
SEE SM 708 MAP

LIST OF ABBREVIATIONS

PREFIXES AND SUFFIXES

AL .... ALLEY
ARC .... ARCADE
AV, AVE .... AVENUE
AVCT .... AVENUE COURT
AVD .... AVENIDA
AVDR .... AVENUE DRIVE
AVEX .... AVENUE EXTENSION
BLEX .... BOULEVARD EXTENSION
BL, BLVD .... BOULEVARD
BLCT .... BOULEVARD COURT
BRCH .... BRANCH
BRDG .... BRIDGE
BYPS .... BYPASS
CIDR .... CIRCLE DRIVE
CIR .... CIRCLE
CL .... CALLE
CLJ .... CALLEJON
CM .... CAMINO
CMTO .... CAMINITO
COM .... COMMON
CORR .... CORRIDOR
CRES .... CRESCENT
CRLO .... CIRCULO
CRSG .... CROSSING
CSWY .... CAUSEWAY
CT .... COURT
CTAV .... COURT AVENUE
CTE .... CORTE
CTO .... CUT OFF
CTR .... CENTER
CUR .... CURVE
CV .... COVE
D .... DE
DIAG .... DIAGONAL
DR .... DRIVE
DVDR .... DIVISION DRIVE
EXAV .... EXTENSION AVENUE
EXBL .... EXTENSION BOULEVARD
EXRD .... EXTENSION ROAD
EXST .... EXTENSION STREET
EXT .... EXTENSION
EXWY .... EXPRESSWAY
FRWY .... FREEWAY
GDNS .... GARDENS
GN .... GLEN
GRN .... GREEN
HWY .... HIGHWAY
JCT .... JUNCTION
LN .... LANE
LNDG .... LANDING
LP .... LOOP
LS .... LAS, LOS
MNR .... MANOR
MTWY .... MOTORWAY
OH .... OUTER HIGHWAY
OVL .... OVAL
OVPS .... OVERPASS
PAS .... PASEO
PK .... PARK
PKWY .... PARKWAY
PL .... PLACE
PLZ, PZ .... PLAZA
PT .... POINT
PTH .... PATH
RD .... ROAD
RDEX .... ROAD EXTENSION
RDGE .... RIDGE
RW .... ROW
SKWY .... SKYWAY
SQ .... SQUARE
ST .... STREET
STAV .... STREET AVENUE
STCT .... STREET COURT
STDR .... STREET DRIVE
STEX .... STREET EXTENSION
STLN .... STREET LANE
STLP .... STREET LOOP
STPL .... STREET PLACE
STXP .... STREET EXPRESSWAY
TER .... TERRACE
TFWY .... TRAFFICWAY
THWY .... THROUGHWAY
TKTR .... TRUCKTRAIL
TPKE .... TURNPIKE
TR .... TRAIL
TUN .... TUNNEL
UNPS .... UNDERPASS
VIS .... VISTA
VW .... VIEW
WK .... WALK
WY .... WAY
WYPL .... WAY PLACE

DIRECTIONS

E .... EAST
KPN .... KEY PENINSULA NORTH
KPS .... KEY PENINSULA SOUTH
N .... NORTH
NE .... NORTHEAST
NW .... NORTHWEST
S .... SOUTH
SE .... SOUTHEAST
SW .... SOUTHWEST
W .... WEST

DEPARTMENT STORES

BD .... BLOOMINGDALES
BN .... THE BON MARCHE
D .... DIAMONDS
FN .... FREDERICK & NELSON
G .... GOLDWATERS
GT .... GOTTSCHALKS
H .... HARRIS
IM .... I MAGNIN
L .... LAMONTS
MA .... MACY'S
ME .... MERVYN'S
MF .... MEIER & FRANK
MW .... MONTGOMERY WARD
N .... NORDSTROM
NM .... NEIMAN-MARCUS
P .... J C PENNEY
RM .... ROBINSONS MAY
S .... SEARS
SF .... SAKS FIFTH AVENUE
W .... WEINSTOCKS

BUILDINGS

CC .... CHAMBER OF COMMERCE
CH .... CITY HALL
CHP .... CALIFORNIA HIGHWAY PATROL
COMM CTR .... COMMUNITY CENTER
CON CTR .... CONVENTION CENTER
CONT HS .... CONTINUATION HIGH SCHOOL
CTH .... COURT HOUSE
DMV .... DEPT OF MOTOR VEHICLES
FAA .... FEDERAL AVIATION ADMIN
FS .... FIRE STATION
HOSP .... HOSPITAL
HS .... HIGH SCHOOL
INT .... INTERMEDIATE SCHOOL
JR HS .... JUNIOR HIGH SCHOOL
LIB .... LIBRARY
MID .... MIDDLE SCHOOL
MUS .... MUSEUM
PO .... POST OFFICE
PS .... POLICE STATION
SR CIT CTR .... SENIOR CITIZENS CENTER
STA .... STATION
THTR .... THEATER
VIS BUR .... VISITORS BUREAU

OTHER COMMON ABBREVIATIONS

BCH .... BEACH
BLDG .... BUILDING
CEM .... CEMETERY
CK .... CREEK
CO .... COUNTY
CTR .... CENTER
COMM .... COMMUNITY
EST .... ESTATE
HIST .... HISTORIC
HTS .... HEIGHTS
LK .... LAKE
MDW .... MEADOW
MED .... MEDICAL
MEM .... MEMORIAL
MHP .... MOBILE HOME PARK
MT .... MOUNT
MTN .... MOUNTAIN
NATL .... NATIONAL
PKG .... PARKING
PLGD .... PLAYGROUND
RCH .... RANCH
RCHO .... RANCHO
REC .... RECREATION
RES .... RESERVOIR
RIV .... RIVER
RR .... RAILROAD
SPG .... SPRING
STA .... SANTA
VLG .... VILLAGE
VLY .... VALLEY
VW .... VIEW

STREET	Block	City	ZIP	Pg-Grid
A				
A ST				
	600	SF	94124	16-F7
ABBEY ST				
	-	SF	94114	10-H2
ABBOT AV				
	-	DALY	94014	18-D4
ACADIA ST				
	100	SF	94131	14-F6
ACCACIA ST				
	-	DALY	94014	19-J3
ACEVEDO AV				
	-	SF	94132	18-A1
ACME AL				
	-	SF	94114	10-F3
ACORN AL				
	1400	SF	94109	6-J5
ACTON ST				
	-	SF	94112	18-E2
	-	DALY	94014	18-E3
	400	DALY	94014	19-E3
ADA CT				
	-	SF	94109	6-J6
ADAIR ST				
	-	SF	94103	10-J2
ADDISON ST				
	-	SF	94131	14-G5
ADELE CT				
	-	SF	94133	7-A4
ADMIRAL AV				
	-	SF	94112	14-G6
ADOLPH SUTRO CT				
	-	SF	94131	9-E3
AERIAL WY				
	-	SF	94116	9-C3
AGATE AL				
	600	SF	94109	6-J5
AGNON AV				
	-	SF	94112	14-H6
AGUA WY				
	-	SF	94127	13-E5
	-	SF	94127	14-E5
AHERN WY				
	-	SF	94103	7-A7
AHLERS CT				
	-	SF	94123	6-G4
ALABAMA ST				
	100	SF	94103	10-J2
	300	SF	94110	10-J2
	800	SF	94110	15-A5
	1400	SF	94110	14-J4
ALADDIN TER				
	-	SF	94133	2-J4
ALAMEDA ST				
	300	SF	94107	11-C1
	1700	SF	94103	11-A1
	2200	SF	94103	10-J1
ALANA WY				
	-	BSBN	94005	20-B2
	-	SF	94134	20-B2
ALBERTA ST				
	-	SF	94134	19-J1
ALBION ST				
	-	SF	94103	10-H2
	100	SF	94110	10-H2
ALCATRAZ FERRY				
	-	SF	94133	2-J1
ALDER ST				
	-	SF	94134	20-A1
ALDRICH AL				
	-	SF	94105	7-B6
ALEMANY BLVD				
	-	SF	94110	15-A6
	-	SF	94110	14-H6
	-	SF	94124	15-A6
	800	SF	94112	14-G6
	1900	SF	94112	19-F1
	2500	SF	94112	18-C2
	3200	SF	94132	18-C2
ALERT AL				
	-	SF	94114	10-H2
ALEXANDER AV				
	-	DALY	94014	18-E3
ALEXIS CIR				
	500	DALY	94014	19-H3
ALHAMBRA ST				
	-	SF	94123	2-F4
ALLAN ST				
	400	DALY	94014	19-J3
	400	SF	94134	19-J3
ALLEN ST				
	-	SF	94109	2-J4
ALLISON ST				
	-	SF	94112	19-F2
ALLSTON WY				
	-	SF	94127	13-D5
ALMA ST				
	-	SF	94117	10-E2
	200	SF	94117	9-E2
ALMADEN CT				
	500	SF	94118	5-D6
ALOHA AV				
	-	SF	94122	9-C3
ALP AV				
	-	DALY	94014	18-D3
ALPHA ST				
	-	SF	94134	20-A2
ALPINE TER				
	-	SF	94117	10-G1
ALTA ST				
	-	SF	94133	3-A4
ALTA MAR WY				
	-	SF	94121	4-H6
ALTA VISTA TER				
	1600	SF	94133	6-J4
ALTA VISTA WY				
	-	SMCo	94014	19-F3
	-	DALY	94014	19-F3
ALTON AV				
	-	SF	94116	9-D4
ALTURAS WY				
	-	DALY	94014	19-E3
ALVARADO ST				
	-	SF	94110	10-H3
	400	SF	94114	10-F3
ALVISO ST				
	-	SF	94132	18-C1
	-	SF	94127	13-C7
AMADOR ST				
	-	SF	94124	15-C4
AMATURY LP				
	400	SF	94129	5-C4
AMAZON AV				
	-	SF	94112	19-F1
AMBER DR				
	-	SF	94131	14-F4
AMES ST				
	-	SF	94110	10-H3
AMETHYST WY				
	-	SF	94131	14-E4
AMHERST ST				
	-	SF	94134	14-J7
AMITY AL				
	600	SF	94109	6-J6
ANDERSON ST				
	-	SF	94110	14-J6
ANDOVER ST				
	-	SF	94110	14-J6
ANDREWS RD				
	-	SF	94129	1-C3
ANGEL ISLAND TIBURON FERRY				
	-	SF	-	3-B1
	-	SF	-	7-C4
ANGLO AL				
	-	SF	94116	9-B4
ANKENY ST				
	-	SF	94134	20-A1
ANNAPOLIS TER				
	-	SF	94118	6-E7
ANNIE ST				
	-	SF	94105	7-A6
	-	SF	94103	7-A6
ANSON PL				
	-	SF	94108	7-A5
ANTHONY ST				
	-	SF	94105	7-B5
ANTONIO ST				
	-	SF	94102	6-J6
ANZA ST				
	-	SF	94129	1-D4
	100	SF	94118	6-E6
	500	SF	94118	5-C7
	2600	SF	94121	5-A7
	4200	SF	94121	4-H7
ANZAVISTA AV				
	-	SF	94115	6-F7
APOLLO ST				
	-	SF	94124	15-B6
APPAREL WY				
	-	SF	94124	15-A5
APPLETON AV				
	-	SF	94110	14-H5
APPLETON ST				
	-	SF	94129	1-C3
APTOS AV				
	-	SF	94127	13-C6
AQUAVISTA WY				
	-	SF	94131	10-E3
ARAGO ST				
	-	SF	94112	14-F7
ARBALLO DR				
	200	SF	94132	18-A1
ARBOL LN				
	-	SF	94115	6-F7
ARBOR ST				
	-	SF	94131	14-F5
ARCH ST				
	-	SF	94132	18-C1
ARCO WY				
	-	SF	94112	14-F7
ARDATH CT				
	-	SF	94124	15-C6
ARDEN CT				
	-	DALY	94014	19-G3
ARDENDALE DR				
	-	DALY	94014	19-F3
ARDENWOOD WY				
	-	SF	94132	13-C6
ARELIOUS WALKER DR				
	2800	SF	94124	20-C1
ARELLANO AV				
	-	SF	94132	18-B1
ARGENT AL				
	-	SF	94131	10-F3
ARGONAUT AV				
	-	SF	94134	19-J2
ARGUELLO BLVD				
	-	SF	94118	5-D7
	300	SF	94129	1-D4
	300	SF	94129	5-D4
	800	SF	94117	5-D7
	1200	SF	94117	9-D2
	1200	SF	94122	9-D2
	1200	SF	94143	9-D2
ARKANSAS ST				
	-	SF	94107	11-B3
ARLETA AV				
	-	SF	94134	19-J2
	-	SF	94134	20-A2
ARLINGTON LN				
	-	DALY	94014	19-F3
ARLINGTON ST				
	-	SF	94131	14-H6
ARMISTEAD RD				
	1200	SF	94129	1-C3
ARMORY RD				
	-	SF	94132	12-H6
ARMSTRONG AV				
	1200	SF	94124	20-C1
	1300	SF	94124	15-B7
ARNOLD AV				
	-	SF	94110	14-H6
ARROYO WY				
	-	SF	94127	14-E5
ARTHUR AV				
	600	SF	94124	15-C4
ASH ST				
	300	SF	94102	6-H7
ASHBURY ST				
	-	SF	94117	6-E7
	200	SF	94117	10-F1
ASHBURY TER				
	-	SF	94117	10-F2
ASHLAND DR				
	-	DALY	94015	17-J4
ASHTON AV				
	-	SF	94112	18-D1
	200	SF	94112	13-D7
	200	SF	94132	13-D7
	200	SF	94127	13-D7
ASHWOOD LN				
	-	SF	94131	9-D3
ATALAYA TER				
	-	SF	94117	6-F7
ATHENS ST				
	-	SF	94112	14-H7
	300	SF	94112	19-G1
ATTRIDGE AL				
	-	SF	94133	2-J4
AUBURN ST				
	-	SF	94133	6-J4
AUGUSTA AL				
	-	SF	94133	3-A4
AUGUSTA ST				
	-	SF	94124	15-A6
AUSTIN ST				
	-	SF	94109	6-H5
AUTO DR				
	1600	SF	94122	9-D3
AVALON AV				
	-	SF	94112	14-G7
AVENUE B				
	-	SF	94130	3-E1
AVENUE C				
	-	SF	94130	3-E1
AVENUE D				
	-	SF	94130	3-E1
AVENUE E				
	-	SF	94130	3-E1
AVENUE NORTH				
	-	SF	94121	5-A5
AVENUE OF THE PALMS				
	-	SF	94130	3-E1
AVERY ST				
	-	SF	94115	6-G6
AVILA ST				
	-	SF	94123	2-F3
AVOCA AL				
	-	SF	94127	14-E5
AVON WY				
	2800	SF	94132	13-B6
AZTEC ST				
	-	SF	94110	14-J4
B				
BACHE ST				
	-	SF	94110	14-J6
BACON ST				
	-	SF	94124	15-A7
	-	SF	94134	15-A7
	600	SF	94134	14-J7
BADEN ST				
	-	SF	94131	14-F6
BADGER ST				
	-	SF	94112	14-G6
BAKER CT				
	1700	SF	94129	5-B5
BAKER ST				
	-	SF	94117	10-F1
	200	SF	94117	6-F7
	700	SF	94115	6-F5
	2500	SF	94123	6-F5
	2900	SF	94123	2-F3
BALANCE ST				
	-	SF	94133	7-B4
BALBOA ST				
	-	SF	94118	5-A7
	1600	SF	94121	5-A7
	3200	SF	94121	4-H7
BALCETA AV				
	-	SF	94127	13-D4
BALDWIN CT				
	-	SF	94124	15-D7
BALHI CT				
	-	SF	94112	19-F1
BALMY ST				
	-	SF	94110	10-J4
BALTIMORE WY				
	-	SF	94112	19-F2
	100	DALY	94014	19-F2
BANBURY DR				
	-	SF	94132	18-B1
BANCROFT AV				
	1400	SF	94124	15-A6
BANK ST				
	-	SF	94129	1-E3
BANKS ST				
	-	SF	94110	14-J5
BANNAM PL				
	-	SF	94133	3-A4
BANNECKER WY				
	800	SF	94102	6-H7
BANNOCK ST				
	-	SF	94112	19-F1
BARCELONA AV				
	-	SF	94115	6-F6
BARNARD AV				
	-	SF	94129	5-D4
	-	SF	94129	1-E4
BARNEVELD AV				
	-	SF	94124	15-A5
	700	SF	94134	15-A6
BARTLETT ST				
	-	SF	94110	10-J4
BARTOL ST				
	-	SF	94133	7-A4
BASS CT				
	-	SF	94124	15-C6
BATTERY ST				
	-	SF	94104	7-B4
	-	SF	94111	7-B4
	800	SF	94111	3-B3
BATTERY BLANEY RD				
	-	SF	94129	1-D3
BATTERY CAULFIELD RD				
	-	SF	94129	5-C5
BATTERY CHAMBERLAIN RD				
	-	SF	94129	5-B5
BATTERY CROSBY RD				
	-	SF	94129	1-B4
	-	SF	94129	5-B4
BATTERY EAST RD				
	-	SF	94129	1-B2
BAXTER AL				
	-	SF	94127	13-D6
BAY ST				
	-	SF	94111	3-A3
	-	SF	94133	3-A3
	300	SF	94133	2-H3
	700	SF	94109	2-H3
	1100	SF	94123	2-G3
BAY RIDGE DR				
	500	DALY	94014	19-H3
BAYSHORE BLVD				
	-	SF	94134	20-A3
	-	SF	94124	15-A5
	1700	SF	94124	20-A3
	3000	BSBN	94005	20-A3
	3000	DALY	94014	20-A3
BAYSHORE FRWY U.S.-101				
	-	BSBN	-	20-B3
	-	SF	-	20-B3
BAYSIDE VILLAGE PL				
	-	SF	94107	7-C6
BAYVIEW CIR				
	100	SF	94124	15-B6
BAYVIEW ST				
	-	SF	94124	15-B6
BAYVIEW PARK RD				
	-	SF	94124	20-B1
BAYWOOD ST				
	-	SF	94112	19-F1
BEACH ST				
	-	SF	94133	3-A3
	100	SF	94133	2-H3
	600	SF	94109	2-H3
	1500	SF	94123	2-F3
BEACHMONT DR				
	-	SF	94132	13-B6
BEACON ST				
	100	SF	94131	14-G5
BEALE ST				
	-	SF	94105	7-B5
	400	SF	94107	7-B5
BEATRICE LN				
	-	SF	94124	15-D6
BEATTY AV				
	-	BSBN	94005	20-A3
BEAUMONT AV				
	-	SF	94118	5-E6
BEAVER ST				
	-	SF	94114	10-G2
BECKETT ST				
	-	SF	94133	7-A4
BEDFORD PL				
	-	SF	94133	7-A4
BEHR AV				
	-	SF	94131	9-D3
BEIDEMAN ST				
	-	SF	94115	6-G6
BELCHER ST				
	-	SF	94114	10-G1
BELDEN ST				
	-	SF	94104	7-A5
BELFORD DR				
	-	DALY	94015	17-J4
BELGRAVE AV				
	-	SF	94117	10-E2
	200	SF	94117	9-E2
BELL CT				
	-	SF	94124	15-C6
BELL RD				
	-	SF	94129	1-C3
BELLAIR PL				
	-	SF	94133	3-A3
BELLAVISTA LN				
	-	SF	94127	13-E6
	-	SF	94127	14-E6
BELLA VISTA WY				
	-	SF	94127	14-E5
	200	SF	94127	13-E6
BELLE AV				
	-	SF	94132	18-C2
BELLES ST				
	-	SF	94129	5-C5
BELLEVUE AV				
	-	DALY	94014	19-E3
	-	SF	94112	19-F3
	500	DALY	94014	18-D3
BEL MAR AV				
	-	DALY	94015	18-A4
BELMONT AV				
	-	SF	94117	9-E2
BELMONT DR				
	-	DALY	94015	18-B3
BELVEDERE ST				
	-	SF	94117	10-E1
BEMIS ST				
	-	SF	94131	14-G6
BENGAL AL				
	-	SF	94127	13-D5
BENNINGTON ST				
	-	SF	94110	14-J5
BENTON AV				
	-	SF	94110	14-H6
	-	SF	94112	14-H6
BEPLER ST				
	-	DALY	94014	18-D2
BERGEN PL				
	800	SF	94109	2-H3
BERKELEY WY				
	-	SF	94131	14-F5
BERKSHIRE WY				
	-	SF	94132	12-J6
BERNAL HEIGHTS BLVD				
	-	SF	94110	15-A5
	-	SF	94110	14-J5
BERNARD ST				
	-	SF	94133	6-J4
	100	SF	94109	6-J4
BERNICE ST				
	-	SF	94103	10-J1
BERRY ST				
	-	SF	94107	7-B7
	200	SF	94107	11-B1
BERTHA LN				
	-	SF	94124	15-D6
BERTIE MINOR LN				
	-	SF	94115	6-E2
BERTITA ST				
	100	SF	94112	19-F1
BERWICK PL				
	-	SF	94103	7-A7
BESSIE ST				
	-	SF	94110	14-J4
BETA AV				
	-	DALY	94014	18-D3
BEULAH ST				
	-	SF	94117	10-E1
	100	SF	94117	9-E1
BEVERLY ST				
	-	SF	94132	18-C1
BIGLER AV				
	-	SF	94117	10-E2
BIRCH ST				
	500	SF	94102	6-H7
BIRCHWOOD CT				
	-	SF	94134	19-H2
BIRD ST				
	-	SF	94110	10-H2
BIRMINGHAM RD				
	-	SF	94129	2-E3
BISHOP ST				
	-	SF	94134	20-A1
BLACK PL				
	2000	SF	94133	2-J4
BLACKSTONE CT				
	-	SF	94123	2-H4
BLAIR TER				
	-	SF	94107	11-B4
BLAIRWOOD LN				
	-	SF	94131	9-D3
BLAKE ST				
	-	SF	94118	6-E6
BLANCHE ST				
	-	SF	94114	10-G3
BLANDY ST				
	-	SF	94124	16-E7
BLANKEN AV				
	-	SF	94134	20-A2
BLISS RD				
	-	SF	94129	1-D4
BLUXOME ST				
	-	SF	94107	7-B7
BLYTHDALE AV				
	-	SF	94134	19-H2
BOARDMAN PL				
	-	SF	94103	7-A7
BOCANA ST				
	-	SF	94110	14-J5
BOLERO WY				
	-	DALY	94014	19-G3
BONIFACIO ST				
	-	SF	94107	7-B6
BONITA ST				
	-	SF	94109	6-H4
BONNIE BRAE LN				
	-	SF	94132	12-J6
BONVIEW ST				
	-	SF	94110	14-J5
BORICA ST				
	-	SF	94127	13-C7
	-	SF	94132	18-C1
BOSWORTH ST				
	-	SF	94112	14-G6
	500	SF	94131	14-G6
BOUTWELL ST				
	-	SF	94124	15-A6
BOWDOIN ST				
	-	SF	94134	14-J6
	600	SF	94134	20-A1
BOWLEY ST				
	-	SF	94129	5-B5
BOWLING GREEN DR				
	-	SF	-	9-D1
BOWMAN CT				
	-	SF	94124	15-C5
BOWMAN RD				
	-	SF	94129	1-B3
BOYLSTON ST				
	-	SF	94134	14-J6
BOYTON CT				
	-	SF	94114	10-G1
BRADFORD ST				
	-	SF	94110	15-A5
BRADY ST				
	-	SF	94103	10-H1
BRANDON CT				
	-	DALY	94014	19-J4
BRANNAN ST				
	-	SF	94103	11-A1
	-	SF	94107	7-B7
	700	SF	94103	7-B7
BRAZIL AV				
	-	SF	94112	14-G7
	600	SF	94112	19-G1
	1100	SF	94134	19-G1
BREEN PL				
	-	SF	94102	6-J6
BRENTWOOD AV				
	-	SF	94127	13-D6
BRET HARTE TER				
	-	SF	94133	2-J3
BREWSTER ST				
	-	SF	94110	15-A5
BRIARCLIFF TER				
	-	SF	94132	13-B5
BRIDGEVIEW DR				
	-	SF	94124	15-B6
BRIGHT ST				
	-	SF	94132	18-D2
BRIGHTON AV				
	-	SF	94112	18-D1
	200	SF	94112	13-D7
BRITTANY LN				
	-	DALY	94014	19-F3
BRITTON ST				
	-	SF	94134	19-J2
BROAD ST				
	-	SF	94112	18-D2
	200	SF	94132	18-D2
BROADMOOR DR				
	-	SF	94132	13-C7
BROADWAY				
	300	SF	94133	7-A4
	900	SF	94133	6-H4
	1100	SF	94109	6-H4
BROADWAY ST				
	-	SF	94111	7-A4
	2000	SF	94115	6-H4
W BROADWAY ST				
	-	SF	94129	6-F5
BRODERICK ST				
	100	SF	94117	10-F1
	300	SF	94117	6-F6
	900	SF	94115	6-F6
	2600	SF	94123	6-F4
	3000	SF	94123	2-F3
BROMLEY PL				
	-	SF	94115	6-G5
BROMPTON AV				
	-	SF	94131	14-G6
BRONTE ST				
	-	SF	94110	14-J6
BROOK ST				
	-	SF	94110	14-H5
BROOKDALE AV				
	-	SF	94134	19-H2
BROOKHAVEN WY				
	-	SF	94132	12-J6
BROOKLYN PL				
	-	SF	94108	7-A5
BROOKS ST				
	-	SF	94129	5-B5
BROSNAN ST				
	-	SF	94103	10-H1
BROTHERHOOD WY				
	500	SF	94132	18-A1
BROWN ST				
	-	DALY	94014	19-H3
	-	SF	94129	5-C5
BRUCE AV				
	-	SF	94112	13-E7
BRUMISS TER				
	-	DALY	94014	18-E2
BRUNSWICK ST				
	-	SF	94112	19-F2
	700	DALY	94014	19-F2
	800	DALY	94014	18-D3
BRUSH PL				
	-	SF	94103	7-A7
BRUSSELS ST				
	-	SF	94134	15-A6
	1100	SF	94134	20-A1
BRYANT AL				
	-	SF	94133	3-A4
BRYANT ST				
	-	SF	94105	7-C6
	100	SF	94107	7-B6
	800	SF	94103	7-B7
	900	SF	94103	11-A1
	1700	SF	94110	11-A2
BUCARELI DR				
	-	SF	94132	18-B1
BUCHANAN ST				
	-	SF	94102	10-H1
	400	SF	94102	6-H7
	600	SF	94115	6-G6
	2800	SF	94123	6-G4
	3100	SF	94123	2-G3
BUCKINGHAM WY				
	100	SF	94132	13-B7
BUENA VISTA AV E				
	-	SF	94117	10-F1
BUENA VISTA AV W				
	-	SF	94117	10-F1
BUENA VISTA TER				
	-	SF	94117	10-G2
BURGOYNE ST				
	-	SF	94109	6-J5
BURKE ST				
	-	SF	94124	15-C5
BURLWOOD DR				
	-	SF	94127	13-E6
BURNETT AV				
	-	SF	94131	10-F3
	900	SF	94131	14-F4
N BURNETT AV				
	-	SF	94131	10-F3
BURNS PL				
	-	SF	94103	10-J1
BURNSIDE AV				
	-	SF	94131	14-F6
BURR AV				
	-	SF	94134	19-J2
BURRITT ST				
	-	SF	94108	7-A5
BURROWS ST				
	-	SF	94134	15-A7
	600	SF	94134	14-H7
	2000	SF	94112	14-H7
BUSH ST				
	-	SF	94111	7-A5
	100	SF	94104	7-A5
	300	SF	94108	7-A5
	700	SF	94102	7-A5
	800	SF	94108	6-F6
	800	SF	94102	6-F6
	900	SF	94109	6-F6
	1900	SF	94115	6-F6
BUTTE PL				
	-	SF	94103	11-A1
BYINGTON ST				
	-	SF	94115	6-G6
BYRON CT				
	-	SF	94112	19-F2
BYXBEE ST				
	-	SF	94132	18-C1
C				
C ST				
	-	SF	-	16-F7
	-	SF	94124	16-F7
CABRILLO ST				
	-	SF	94118	5-A7
	1600	SF	94121	5-A7
	3200	SF	94121	4-H7
CADELL PL				
	-	SF	94133	3-A4
CAINE AV				
	-	SF	94112	18-E1
	-	SF	94112	19-E1
CAIRE TER				
	-	SF	94107	11-B3
CALEDONIA ST				
	-	SF	94103	10-H2
CALGARY ST				
	-	SF	94134	19-J3
	-	DALY	94014	19-J3
CALHOUN TER				
	-	SF	94133	3-A4
CALIFORNIA AV				
	-	SF	94130	3-E2
CALIFORNIA ST				
	-	SF	94111	7-A5
	300	SF	94104	7-A5
	600	SF	94108	7-A5
	1000	SF	94108	6-E6
	1200	SF	94109	6-E6
	2100	SF	94115	6-E6
	3300	SF	94118	6-E6
	3500	SF	94118	5-D6
	5500	SF	94121	5-B6
CAMBON DR				
	-	SF	94132	18-B1
CAMBRIDGE ST				
	-	SF	94134	14-H7
	-	SF	94112	14-H7
	600	SF	94134	19-J1
CAMELLIA AV				
	-	SF	94112	14-G7
CAMEO WY				
	-	SF	94131	14-F4
CAMERON LN				
	-	DALY	94014	19-F3
CAMERON WY				
	-	SF	94124	20-C1
CAMP ST				
	-	SF	94110	10-H2
CAMPBELL AV				
	-	SF	94134	19-J1
	-	SF	94134	20-A1
CAMPTON PL				
	-	SF	94108	7-A5
CAMPUS CIR				
	-	SF	94132	13-B7
CAMPUS LN				
	-	SF	94134	14-J7
CANBY ST				
	-	SF	94129	1-E4
CANYON DR				
	-	SF	94112	19-G3
	-	DALY	94014	19-G3
CAPISTRANO AV				
	-	SF	94112	14-F7
CAPITOL AV				
	-	SF	94112	18-D1
	1100	SF	94112	13-D7
CAPP ST				
	-	SF	94103	10-J3
	100	SF	94110	10-J3
CAPRA WY				
	-	SF	94123	2-F3
CARD AL				
	-	SF	94133	7-A4
CARDENAS AV				
	-	SF	94132	18-B1
CARGO WY				
	-	SF	94124	15-C5
CARL ST				
	-	SF	94117	10-E1
	100	SF	94117	9-E2
	400	SF	94143	9-E2
CARMEL ST				
	-	SF	94117	10-E2

STREET Block	City	ZIP	Pg-Grid
CARMELITA ST			
-	SF	94117	10-G1
CARNELIAN WY			
-	SF	94131	10-F4
-	SF	94131	14-F4
CAROLINA ST			
-	SF	94107	11-B2
100	SF	94103	11-B2
CAROLINE WY			
-	DALY	94014	19-G3
CARPENTER CT			
-	SF	94124	15-C6
CARR ST			
-	SF	94124	20-B1
CARRIE ST			
-	SF	94131	14-G6
CARRIZAL ST			
-	SF	94134	19-H2
CARROLL AV			
700	SF	94124	20-C1
1200	SF	94124	15-A7
CARSON ST			
-	SF	94114	10-F3
CARTER ST			
500	DALY	94014	19-H3
500	SF	94134	19-H3
600	SMCo	94014	19-H3
CARVER ST			
-	SF	94110	14-J5
CASA WY			
-	SF	94123	2-G3
CASCADE WK			
-	SF	94116	9-C3
CASELLI AV			
-	SF	94114	10-F2
CASHMERE ST			
-	SF	94124	15-C6
CASITAS AV			
100	SF	94127	13-D5
CASSANDRA CT			
-	SF	94112	19-E2
CASTELO AV			
-	SF	94132	18-B1
CASTENADA AV			
-	SF	94116	9-D4
200	SF	94116	13-D4
CASTILLO ST			
-	DALY	94014	19-H2
-	SF	94134	19-H2
CASTLE ST			
-	SF	94133	3-A4
CASTLE MANOR AV			
-	SF	94112	14-G7
CASTLEMONT AV			
-	DALY	94015	18-B3
CASTRO ST			
-	SF	94114	10-G2
-	SF	94117	10-G2
1600	SF	94131	10-G3
1700	SF	94131	14-G4
CATHERINE CT			
-	SF	94110	10-J3
CAYUGA AV			
-	SF	94112	19-E1
1300	SF	94112	14-F7
2100	SF	94112	18-D2
CECILIA AV			
2200	SF	94116	13-C4
CEDAR CT			
-	DALY	94014	19-H2
-	SF	94134	19-H2
CEDAR ST			
-	SF	94109	6-H6
CEDRO AV			
-	SF	94127	13-C7
CENTRAL AV			
-	SF	94117	10-F1
400	SF	94117	6-F7
900	SF	94115	6-F7
CENTRAL FRWY U.S.-101			
-	SF	-	6-H7
-	SF	-	10-J1
-	SF	-	11-A1
CENTRAL MAGAZINE RD			
-	SF	94129	5-C4
CENTURY PL			
-	SF	94104	7-B5
CERES ST			
-	SF	94124	15-B7
CERRITOS AV			
-	SF	94127	13-C7
CERVANTES BLVD			
-	SF	94123	2-F3
CESAR CHAVEZ ST			
500	SF	94107	11-A4
500	SF	94124	11-A4
2700	SF	94110	11-A4
2900	SF	94110	15-A4
2900	SF	94110	14-J4
3800	SF	94131	14-G4
CHABOT TER			
-	SF	94118	6-E7
CHAIN OF LAKES DR E			
-	SF	-	8-J1
CHAIN OF LAKES DR W			
-	SF	-	8-H1
CHANNEL ST			
-	SF	94107	7-C7
-	SF	94107	11-B1
CHAPMAN ST			
-	SF	94110	14-J5
CHARLES ST			
100	SF	94131	14-H5
CHARLESTOWN PL			
-	SF	94105	7-B6
CHARLTON CT			
-	SF	94123	6-G4
CHARTER OAK AV			
-	SF	94124	15-A6
CHASE CT			
-	SF	94103	10-H1
CHATHAM PL			
-	SF	94108	7-A5
CHATTANOOGA ST			
-	SF	94114	10-H3
CHAVES AV			
-	SF	94127	13-E5
CHELSEA CT			
-	DALY	94014	18-D3
CHELSEA PL			
-	SF	94108	7-A5
CHENERY ST			
-	SF	94131	14-H5
CHERRY ST			
-	SF	94118	5-D5
CHESLEY ST			
-	SF	94103	7-A7
CHESTER AV			
-	SF	94132	18-C2
CHESTNUT ST			
-	SF	94111	3-A3
100	SF	94133	3-A3
500	SF	94133	2-F4
900	SF	94109	2-F4
1300	SF	94123	2-F4
CHICAGO WY			
-	SF	94112	19-G2
CHILD ST			
-	SF	94133	3-A3
CHILTON AV			
-	SF	94131	14-F6
CHRISTMAS TREE POINT RD			
100	SF	94131	10-E3
CHRISTOPHER DR			
-	SF	94131	9-D3
CHULA LN			
-	SF	94114	10-H2
CHUMASERO DR			
-	SF	94132	18-B2
CHURCH ST			
-	SF	94117	10-H3
-	SF	94114	10-H3
1300	SF	94131	10-H3
1400	SF	94131	14-H5
CIELITO DR			
-	SF	94134	19-H2
CIRCULAR AV			
200	SF	94131	14-F7
600	SF	94112	14-F7
CITRUS AV			
-	DALY	94014	18-C4
CITY VIEW DR			
-	DALY	94014	19-F3
CITYVIEW WY			
-	SF	94131	10-E4
-	SF	94131	9-E4
CLAIRVIEW CT			
-	SF	94131	10-E3
CLARA ST			
100	SF	94107	7-A7
CLAREMONT BLVD			
-	SF	94127	13-C5
CLARENCE PL			
-	SF	94107	7-B7
CLARENDON AV			
-	SF	94117	10-E2
-	SF	94114	10-E2
100	SF	94114	9-E3
100	SF	94117	9-E3
100	SF	94131	9-E3
400	SF	94116	9-E3
CLARION AL			
-	SF	94110	10-H2
CLARKE ST			
-	SF	94129	6-E4
CLAUDE LN			
-	SF	94108	7-A5
CLAY ST			
100	SF	94111	7-A5
700	SF	94108	7-A5
1100	SF	94108	6-H5
1300	SF	94109	6-H5
2200	SF	94115	6-E5
3400	SF	94118	6-E5
3600	SF	94118	5-D5
W CLAY ST			
-	SF	94121	5-B6
CLAYTON ST			
-	SF	94117	6-E7
200	SF	94117	10-E1
1200	SF	94114	10-F2
CLEARFIELD DR			
-	SF	94132	13-A6
CLEARVIEW CT			
-	SF	94124	15-B6
CLEARY CT			
-	SF	94109	6-H6
CLEMENT ST			
-	SF	94118	5-A6
1600	SF	94121	5-A6
3200	SF	94121	4-J6
CLEMENTINA ST			
-	SF	94105	7-A7
300	SF	94103	7-A7
700	SF	94103	6-J7
CLEO RAND AV			
100	SF	94124	15-E7
CLEVELAND ST			
-	SF	94103	7-A7
CLIFFORD TER			
-	SF	94117	10-F2
CLIFFSIDE DR			
-	DALY	94015	18-A3
CLIFTON DR			
-	DALY	94015	18-A4
CLINTON PK			
-	SF	94103	10-H1
CLIPPER ST			
-	SF	94131	10-G4
-	SF	94114	10-G4
700	SF	94114	14-F4
700	SF	94131	14-F4
CLIPPER TER			
800	SF	94114	10-F4
CLOISTER WY			
-	DALY	94014	19-F3
CLOVER LN			
-	SF	94114	10-F3
CLOVER ST			
-	SF	94114	10-F2
CLUB VIEW DR			
-	DALY	94014	19-F3
CLYDE ST			
-	SF	94107	7-B7
COCHRANE ST			
-	SF	94124	16-E7
-	SF	94124	21-E1
CODMAN PL			
100	SF	94108	7-A5
COHEN PL			
-	SF	94109	6-J6
COLBY ST			
-	SF	94134	14-J6
600	SF	94134	19-J1
COLE ST			
-	SF	94117	6-E7
200	SF	94117	10-E1
COLEMAN ST			
2700	SF	94124	16-E7
3000	SF	94124	15-E7
COLERIDGE ST			
-	SF	94110	14-H5
COLIN PL			
-	SF	94102	6-J6
COLIN P KELLY JR ST			
-	SF	94107	7-C6
COLLEGE AV			
-	SF	94112	14-H6
COLLEGE TER			
-	SF	94112	14-H6
COLLINGWOOD ST			
-	SF	94114	10-G3
COLLINS ST			
-	SF	94118	6-E6
COLON AV			
-	SF	94112	13-D6
300	SF	94127	13-D6
COLONIAL WY			
-	SF	94112	14-F7
COLTON ST			
-	SF	94103	10-H1
COLUMBIA SQUARE ST			
-	SF	94103	7-A7
COLUMBUS AV			
-	SF	94111	7-A4
-	SF	94133	7-A4
300	SF	94133	3-A4
700	SF	94133	2-J3
1300	SF	94109	2-J3
COLUSA PL			
-	SF	94103	10-J1
COMERFORD ST			
-	SF	94131	14-G4
COMMER CT			
-	SF	94124	15-C6
COMMERCIAL ST			
400	SF	94111	7-A5
700	SF	94108	7-A5
COMMONWEALTH AV			
-	SF	94118	5-E6
COMO AV			
-	DALY	94014	18-D3
COMPTON RD			
-	SF	94129	5-C4
CONCORD ST			
-	SF	94112	19-F2
CONCOURSE DR			
-	SF	94118	9-C1
CONGDON ST			
-	SF	94112	14-H7
CONGO ST			
-	SF	94131	14-F6
500	SF	94127	14-F6
CONKLING ST			
-	SF	94124	15-A6
CONNECTICUT ST			
-	SF	94107	11-B3
CONRAD ST			
-	SF	94131	14-G5
CONSERVATORY DR E			
-	SF	94117	9-D1
-	SF	94117	5-D7
CONSERVATORY DR W			
-	SF	-	9-D1
-	SF	-	5-D7
CONSTANSO WY			
-	SF	94132	13-A6
CONVERSE ST			
-	SF	94103	11-A1
COOK ST			
-	SF	94118	6-E6
COOPER AL			
-	SF	94108	7-A4
COPPER AL			
-	SF	94114	10-F3
CORA ST			
-	SF	94134	19-J2
-	SF	94134	20-A2
CORAL RD			
-	SF	94107	11-B3
CORALINO LN			
-	SF	94131	14-F4
CORBETT AV			
-	SF	94114	10-F2
700	SF	94131	10-F4
CORBIN PL			
-	SF	94114	10-F2
CORDELIA ST			
-	SF	94133	7-A4
CORDOVA ST			
-	SF	94112	19-G2
500	DALY	94014	19-G2
CORNWALL ST			
-	SF	94118	5-D6
CORONA ST			
-	SF	94127	13-C7
-	SF	94132	18-C1
CORONADO AV			
-	DALY	94015	18-A4
CORONADO ST			
-	SF	94124	20-B1
CORTES AV			
-	SF	94116	13-C4
CORTLAND AV			
-	SF	94110	14-H5
1400	SF	94110	15-A5
1600	SF	94124	15-A5
CORWIN ST			
-	SF	94114	10-F3
COSMO PL			
-	SF	94109	6-J6
COSO AV			
-	SF	94110	14-J4
COSTA ST			
-	SF	94110	15-A5
COTTAGE RW			
-	SF	94115	6-G6
COTTER ST			
-	SF	94112	14-G7
COTTONWOOD DR			
-	DALY	94014	18-D3
COUNTRY CLUB DR			
-	SF	94132	12-J6
COURT E			
-	DALY	94014	19-F3
COVENTRY LN			
-	SF	94127	13-E6
COWELL PL			
-	SF	94111	3-B4
-	SF	94111	7-B4
COWLES ST			
-	SF	94129	1-C3
CRAGMONT AV			
-	SF	94116	9-C4
CRAGS CT			
-	SF	94131	14-F5
CRAN PL			
-	SF	94117	6-G7
CRANE ST			
-	SF	94124	20-B1
CRANLEIGH DR			
-	SF	94132	13-C6
CRANSTON RD			
-	SF	94129	1-C3
CRAUT ST			
100	SF	94112	14-G7
CRESCENT AV			
-	SF	94112	14-H6
-	SF	94110	14-H6
CRESCIO CT			
-	SF	94112	19-E2
CRESPI DR			
-	SF	94132	18-B1
CRESTA VISTA DR			
-	SF	94127	13-D6
CRESTLAKE DR			
-	SF	94132	13-A5
500	SF	94116	13-A5
CRESTLINE DR			
-	SF	94131	10-F3
CRESTMONT DR			
-	SF	94131	9-D3
-	SF	94122	9-D3
CRESTWELL WK			
-	SF	94122	9-C3
CRESTWOOD DR			
-	DALY	94015	18-A3
CRISP RD			
-	SF	94124	15-D7
CRISSY FIELD AV			
-	SF	94129	1-C3
CROCKER AV			
-	DALY	94014	18-D3
800	DALY	94014	19-E3
900	SMCo	94014	19-E3
CROOK ST			
-	SF	94129	2-E3
CROSS ST			
-	SF	94112	19-F2
CROSS OVER DR			
300	SF	-	5-A7
300	SF	-	9-B1
CROSS OVER DR Rt#-1			
1000	SF	-	9-B1
CROWN TER			
-	SF	94114	10-E2
CRYSTAL ST			
-	SF	94112	18-D2
CUBA AL			
-	SF	94127	14-F5
CUESTA CT			
-	SF	94131	10-F4
CULEBRA TER			
-	SF	94109	2-H3
CUMBERLAND ST			
-	SF	94110	10-G2
200	SF	94114	10-G2
CUNNINGHAM PL			
-	SF	94110	10-H2
CURTIS ST			
-	SF	94112	19-F2
CUSTER AV			
1400	SF	94124	15-C4
CUSTOM HOUSE PL			
-	SF	94111	7-B4
CUTLER AV			
3600	SF	94116	12-H5
CUVIER ST			
-	SF	94112	14-G6
CYPRESS CT			
-	DALY	94014	19-J3
CYPRESS LN			
-	DALY	94014	19-J3
CYPRESS ST			
-	SF	94110	10-J4
CYRIL MAGIN ST			
-	SF	94102	7-A6
CYRUS PL			
-	SF	94109	6-J4
D			
D ST			
-	SF	94124	16-E7
DAGGETT ST			
-	SF	94107	11-B2
DAKOTA ST			
-	SF	94107	11-B3
DALE PL			
-	SF	94102	6-J6
DALEROSE CT			
-	DALY	94014	19-G3
DALEWOOD WY			
-	SF	94127	13-D5
DANBERRY LN			
-	DALY	94014	19-F3
DANIEL BURNHAM CT			
-	SF	94109	6-H6
DANTON ST			
-	SF	94112	14-G6
DANVERS ST			
-	SF	94114	10-F2
DARIEN WY			
-	SF	94127	13-C6
DARRELL PL			
-	SF	94133	3-A4
DARTMOUTH ST			
-	SF	94134	14-J7
600	SF	94134	19-J1
900	SF	94134	20-A1
DASHELLE HAMMETT ST			
-	SF	94108	7-A5
DAVIDSON AV			
1400	SF	94124	15-C4
DAVIS ST			
-	SF	94111	7-B4
700	SF	94111	3-B4
DAWNVIEW WY			
-	SF	94131	10-E4
DAWSON PL			
-	SF	94108	7-A5
DAY ST			
-	SF	94110	14-G5
100	SF	94131	14-G5
DEARBORN ST			
-	SF	94110	10-H2
DE BOOM ST			
-	SF	94107	7-C6
DECATUR ST			
-	SF	94103	11-A1
DECKER AL			
100	SF	94103	7-A7
DEDMAN CT			
-	SF	94124	15-C6
DEEMS RD			
-	SF	94129	5-D4
DE FOREST WY			
-	SF	94114	10-G2
DE HARO ST			
-	SF	94107	11-B3
-	SF	94103	11-A3
DEHON ST			
-	SF	94114	10-G2
DELANCEY ST			
500	SF	94107	7-C6
DELANO AV			
-	SF	94112	14-F7
500	SF	94112	19-E1
DELGADO PL			
-	SF	94109	6-J4
DELLBROOK AV			
-	SF	94131	9-E3
DELMAR ST			
-	SF	94117	10-F1
DEL MONTE ST			
-	SF	94112	19-F2
DE LONG ST			
-	SF	94112	18-C2
500	DALY	94014	18-C2
DEL SUR AV			
-	SF	94127	13-E5
DELTA PL			
-	SF	94102	7-A5
DELTA ST			
-	SF	94134	19-J2
100	SF	94134	20-A1
DEL VALE AV			
-	SF	94127	14-E5
DEMING ST			
-	SF	94114	10-F2
DE MONTFORT AV			
-	SF	94112	13-D7
DENSLOW DR			
-	SF	94132	13-B7
100	SF	94132	18-B1
DENT RD			
-	SF	94129	5-C4
DERBY ST			
-	SF	94102	7-A6
DESMOND ST			
-	SF	94134	20-A2
DE SOTO ST			
-	SF	94127	13-C7
-	SF	94132	18-C1
DETROIT ST			
100	SF	94131	14-F6
100	SF	94112	14-F6
500	SF	94127	14-F6
DEVONSHIRE WY			
-	SF	94131	9-D3
DEWEY BLVD			
400	SF	94116	13-D4
400	SF	94127	13-D4
DEWITT RD			
-	SF	94129	2-E4
-	SF	94129	6-E4
DE WOLF ST			
-	SF	94112	18-E2
DIAMOND ST			
-	SF	94114	10-G3
1100	SF	94131	10-G3
1200	SF	94131	14-G5
DIAMOND HEIGHTS BLVD			
5000	SF	94114	14-F4
5000	SF	94131	14-F4
DIANA ST			
-	SF	94124	15-B7
DIAZ AV			
-	SF	94132	18-B1
DICHA AL			
-	SF	94118	6-E6
DICHIERA CT			
-	SF	94112	19-E2
DIGBY ST			
-	SF	94131	14-G5
DIVISADERO ST			
-	SF	94117	10-G1
-	SF	94114	10-G1
400	SF	94117	6-F4
1000	SF	94115	6-F4
2700	SF	94123	6-F4
3100	SF	94123	2-F3
DIVISION ST			
-	SF	94103	11-A1
-	SF	94107	11-A1
300	SF	94103	10-J1
DIXIE AL			
-	SF	94114	10-F3
-	SF	94131	10-F3
DODGE PL			
-	SF	94102	6-J6
DOLORES ST			
-	SF	94114	10-H3
-	SF	94103	10-H3
300	SF	94110	10-H3
1300	SF	94131	10-H3
1400	SF	94110	14-H5
1400	SF	94131	14-H5
DOLORES TER			
-	SF	94110	10-H2
DONAHUE ST			
700	SF	94124	16-E6
DONAHUE ST			
700	SF	94124	15-E7
700	SF	94124	20-C2
DONNER AV			
700	SF	94124	20-B1
1400	SF	94124	15-A7
DORADO TER			
-	SF	94112	13-D7
DORANTES AV			
-	SF	94116	13-C4
DORCAS WY			
-	SF	94127	14-E5
DORCHESTER DR			
-	DALY	94015	18-A4
DORCHESTER WY			
-	SF	94127	13-D5
DORE ST			
-	SF	94103	6-J7
-	SF	94103	10-J1
300	SF	94103	11-A1
DORIC AL			
-	SF	94108	7-A5
DORLAND ST			
-	SF	94110	10-G2
200	SF	94114	10-G2
DORMAN AV			
-	SF	94124	15-A5
DORMITORY RD			
-	SF	94124	15-D7
DOUBLE ROCK ST			
-	SF	94124	20-C1
DOUGLASS ST			
-	SF	94114	10-F3
1000	SF	94131	10-F4
1100	SF	94131	14-F4
DOVE LP			
-	SF	94129	1-B3
DOVER ST			
-	SF	94107	7-C6
DOW PL			
-	SF	94107	7-B6
DOWNEY ST			
-	SF	94117	10-F1
DOYLE DR			
-	SF	94123	2-E3
-	SF	94129	2-E3
DOYLE DR U.S.-101			
-	SF	94129	1-D3
-	SF	94129	2-E3
DRAKE ST			
-	DALY	94014	19-G2
-	SF	94112	19-G2
DRUMM ST			
-	SF	94111	7-B4
DRUMMOND AL			
-	SF	94124	15-B5
DUBLIN ST			
-	SF	94112	19-G1
DUBOCE AV			
-	SF	94103	10-G1
300	SF	94102	10-G1
300	SF	94114	10-G1
300	SF	94117	10-G1
DUDLEY RD			
-	SF	94129	5-D4
DUKES CT			
-	SF	94124	15-C6
DUNBAR ST			
-	SF	94111	7-A5
DUNCAN ST			
-	SF	94110	14-G4
200	SF	94131	14-F4
DUNCOMBE AL			
-	SF	94133	7-A4
DUNNES AL			
-	SF	94133	7-A4
DUNSHEE ST			
-	SF	94124	15-B6
DUNSMUIR ST			
-	SF	94134	14-J6
DWIGHT ST			
-	SF	94134	15-A7
300	SF	94134	20-A1
700	SF	94134	19-J1
DYNAMITE RD			
-	SF	94129	1-B4
E			
E ST			
300	SF	94124	16-E7
300	SF	94124	21-F1
EAGLE ST			
-	SF	94114	10-F3
EARL ST			
700	SF	94124	20-C1
800	SF	94124	15-D7
EASTGATE DR			
-	DALY	94015	18-A3
EASTLAKE AV			
-	DALY	94014	18-C4
EASTMAN ST			
-	SF	94109	6-J4
-	SF	94109	2-J4
EASTWOOD DR			
-	SF	94112	13-D7
EATON PL			
-	SF	94133	7-A4
ECKER ST			
-	SF	94105	7-B5
EDDINGTON LN			
-	DALY	94014	19-E3
EDDY ST			
-	SF	94102	7-A6
200	SF	94102	6-F6
400	SF	94109	6-F6
1200	SF	94115	6-F6
EDGAR PL			
-	SF	94112	18-E1
EDGARDO PL			
-	SF	94133	3-A3
EDGEHILL WY			
-	SF	94127	13-D5
EDGEMAR ST			
-	DALY	94014	19-E3
EDGEWOOD AV			
100	SF	94117	9-E2
EDGEWOOD CT			
-	DALY	94014	18-D3
EDIE RD			
-	SF	94129	2-E4
EDINBURGH ST			
-	SF	94112	14-G7
300	SF	94112	19-G1
EDITH ST			
-	SF	94133	3-A4
EDNA ST			
-	SF	94112	14-E7
600	SF	94127	14-E7
EDWARD ST			
-	SF	94118	5-D7
EGBERT AV			
600	SF	94124	20-B1
1300	SF	94124	15-A7
EL CAMINO DEL MAR			
200	SF	94121	5-A5
2500	SF	94121	4-H6
EL DORADO ST			
-	SF	94107	11-C1
ELGIN PK			
-	SF	94103	10-H1
ELIM AL			
-	SF	94105	7-B5
ELIZABETH ST			
-	SF	94110	10-H3
300	SF	94114	10-F3
ELK ST			
-	SF	94131	14-F6
ELKHART ST			
-	SF	94105	7-C6
ELLERT ST			
-	SF	94110	14-J5
ELLINGTON AV			
-	SF	94112	19-E2
ELLIOT ST			
100	SF	94134	19-J2
ELLIS ST			
-	SF	94102	7-A6
-	SF	94108	7-A6
300	SF	94102	6-H6
500	SF	94109	6-H6
1300	SF	94115	6-F6
ELLSWORTH ST			
-	SF	94110	14-J6
ELM ST			
-	SF	94102	6-H6
1100	SF	94115	6-G7
ELMHURST DR			
-	SF	94132	13-C6
ELMIRA ST			
-	SF	94124	15-A6
EL MIRASOL PL			
-	SF	94132	13-A6
ELMWOOD DR			
-	DALY	94015	18-A4
ELMWOOD WY			
100	SF	94112	13-D7

STREET	Block	City	ZIP	Pg-Grid
EL PLAZUELA WY				
	-	SF	94127	13-C7
EL POLIN LP				
	-	SF	94129	5-E5
EL PORTAL WY				
	-	DALY	94015	18-A2
EL SERENO CT				
	-	SF	94127	14-F5
ELSIE ST				
	-	SF	94110	14-H5
EL VERANO WY				
	-	SF	94127	13-D6
ELWOOD ST				
	-	SF	94102	7-A6
EMERALD LN				
	-	SF	94132	13-A6
EMERSON ST				
	-	SF	94118	6-E6
EMERY LN				
	-	SF	94133	7-A4
EMIL LN				
	-	SF	94127	13-D6
EMMA ST				
	-	SF	94108	7-A5
EMMETT CT				
	-	SF	94110	14-J4
EMPRESS LN				
	-	SF	94134	20-A2
ENCANTO AV				
	-	SF	94115	6-F6
ENCINAL WK				
	-	SF	94122	9-C3
ENCLINE CT				
	-	SF	94127	14-E5
ENGLISH ST				
	-	SF	94124	16-E7
ENTERPRISE ST				
	-	SF	94110	10-J2
N ENTRADA CT				
	-	SF	94127	13-C7
S ENTRADA CT				
	100	SF	94127	13-C7
ERIE ST				
	-	SF	94103	10-J1
ERKSON CT				
	-	SF	94115	6-F6
ERVINE ST				
	-	SF	94134	20-A1
ESCOLTA WY				
	-	SF	94116	13-A5
ESCONDIDO AV				
	-	SF	94132	13-A6
ESMERALDA AV				
	900	SF	94110	15-A5
	900	SF	94110	14-H5
ESPANOLA ST				
	-	SF	94124	15-D7
ESQUINA DR				
	-	SF	94134	19-H2
ESSEX ST				
	-	SF	94105	7-B6
ESTATE CT				
	600	DALY	94014	19-F3
ESTERO AV				
	-	SF	94127	13-C7
EUCALYPTUS DR				
	-	SF	94132	13-B6
EUCLID AV				
	-	SF	94115	6-E6
	-	SF	94118	6-E6
	300	SF	94118	5-D6
EUGENIA AV				
	-	SF	94110	14-H5
EUREKA PL				
	-	SF	94109	6-J5
EUREKA ST				
	-	SF	94114	10-F3
EVA TER				
	-	SF	94117	6-G7
EVANS AV				
	900	SF	94124	15-B4
	2100	SF	94124	11-B4
EVE ST				
	-	SF	94110	15-A4
EVELYN WY				
	-	SF	94127	13-E5
	100	SF	94127	14-E5
EVERGLADE DR				
	-	SF	94132	13-A6
EVERGREEN AV				
	-	DALY	94014	18-D3
EVERSON ST				
	-	SF	94131	14-G5
EWER PL				
	-	SF	94108	7-A5
EWING TER				
	-	SF	94118	6-E7
EXCELSIOR AV				
	-	SF	94112	14-G7
	900	SF	94112	19-H1
EXECUTIVE PARK BLVD				
	100	SF	94134	20-B2
EXETER ST				
	-	SF	94124	20-B1
F				
FAIR AV				
	-	SF	94110	14-H4
FAIRFAX AV				
	500	SF	94124	15-B5
FAIRFIELD WY				
	-	SF	94127	13-D7
FAIRLAWN AV				
	-	DALY	94015	17-J4
	-	DALY	94015	18-A4
FAIRLAWN CT				
	-	DALY	94015	18-A4
FAIRMONT DR				
	-	DALY	94015	17-J3
FAIRMOUNT ST				
	-	SF	94131	14-H5
FAIR OAKS ST				
	-	SF	94110	10-H4
FAIRWAY DR				
	-	DALY	94015	18-B4
FAITH ST				
	-	SF	94110	15-A5
FALLON PL				
	-	SF	94133	6-J4
FALMOUTH ST				
	-	SF	94107	7-A7
FANNING WY				
	-	SF	94116	9-C4
FARALLONES ST				
	-	SF	94112	18-D2
	200	SF	94132	18-D2
FARGO PL				
	-	SF	94103	7-A7
FARNSWORTH LN				
	-	SF	94117	9-E2
FARNUM ST				
	-	SF	94131	14-G5
FARRAGUT AV				
	-	SF	94112	18-E2
	100	SF	94112	19-E2
FARVIEW CT				
	-	SF	94131	10-E3
FAXON AV				
	-	SF	94112	18-D1
	400	SF	94112	13-D7
	900	SF	94127	13-D7
FEDERAL ST				
	-	SF	94107	7-B6
FELIX AV				
	-	SF	94132	18-B1
FELL ST				
	-	SF	94102	6-F7
	700	SF	94117	6-F7
	1600	SF	94117	10-E1
	2000	SF	94117	9-E1
FELLA PL				
	-	SF	94108	7-A5
FELTON ST				
	-	SF	94134	15-A7
	500	SF	94134	14-H7
FENTON LN				
	-	SF	94131	10-F4
FERN ST				
	-	SF	94109	6-H6
FERNANDEZ ST				
	800	SF	94129	5-E4
FERNWOOD DR				
	-	SF	94127	13-D6
FIELDCREST DR				
	-	DALY	94015	18-B3
FIELDING ST				
	-	SF	94133	3-A3
FILBERT ST				
	200	SF	94133	3-A4
	700	SF	94133	2-H4
	1100	SF	94109	2-H4
	1500	SF	94123	2-H4
	1800	SF	94123	6-F4
FILLMORE ST				
	-	SF	94117	10-G1
	400	SF	94117	6-G4
FILLMORE ST				
	1100	SF	94115	6-G4
	2800	SF	94123	6-G4
	3100	SF	94123	2-G3
FINLEY RD				
	-	SF	94129	5-D5
FISH AL				
	400	SF	94133	2-J3
FISHER AL				
	-	SF	94133	7-A4
FISHER AV				
	-	SF	94124	16-E7
FISHER LP				
	-	SF	94129	1-D4
FITCH ST				
	-	SF	94124	15-E6
	2600	SF	94124	20-C1
FITZGERALD AV				
	500	SF	94124	20-B1
	1700	SF	94124	15-A7
FLEETWOOD DR				
	-	DALY	94015	18-A3
FLINT ST				
	-	SF	94114	10-G2
FLOOD AV				
	-	SF	94131	14-E6
	200	SF	94112	14-E6
	400	SF	94112	13-E6
FLORA ST				
	-	SF	94124	15-B6
FLORENCE ST				
	-	DALY	94014	18-D4
	-	SF	94133	6-J4
FLORENTINE ST				
	-	SF	94112	19-F2
FLORIDA ST				
	-	SF	94103	10-J2
	300	SF	94110	10-J2
	800	SF	94110	11-A4
	1400	SF	94110	15-A4
FLOURNOY ST				
	-	DALY	94014	18-D2
	100	SF	94112	18-D2
FLOWER ST				
	-	SF	94124	15-A5
FOERSTER ST				
	-	SF	94112	14-E6
	400	SF	94127	14-E6
FOLSOM ST				
	-	SF	94105	7-B6
	400	SF	94110	14-J4
	600	SF	94107	7-B6
	600	SF	94103	7-A7
	1300	SF	94103	6-J7
	1300	SF	94103	10-J1
	2000	SF	94110	10-J4
FONT BLVD				
	-	SF	94132	13-A7
	200	SF	94132	18-B1
FONTINELLA TER				
	-	SF	94107	11-A4
FOOTE AV				
	-	SF	94112	19-E1
FORD ST				
	-	SF	94114	10-G2
FOREST GROVE DR				
	-	DALY	94015	18-B3
FOREST KNOLLS DR				
	-	SF	94131	9-E3
FOREST SIDE AV				
	-	SF	94116	13-C5
	-	SF	94127	13-C5
FOREST VIEW DR				
	-	SF	94132	13-A6
S FORK DR				
	1700	SF	-	8-H1
FORTUNA AV				
	-	SF	94115	6-F6
FOUNTAIN ST				
	-	SF	94114	10-F4
FOWLER AV				
	-	SF	94127	13-E4
FOXHOLLOW LN				
	-	DALY	94014	19-E3
FRANCE AV				
	-	SF	94112	19-G1
FRANCIS ST				
	-	SF	94112	14-G7
FRANCISCO ST				
	-	SF	94133	3-A3
	400	SF	94133	2-J3
	800	SF	94109	2-J3
	1200	SF	94123	2-G3
FRANCONIA ST				
	-	SF	94110	15-A4
FRANKFORT ST				
	-	DALY	94014	19-E3
	200	DALY	94014	18-E3
FRANKLIN ST				
	-	SF	94102	6-H4
	900	SF	94109	6-H4
	2400	SF	94123	6-H4
	2600	SF	94123	2-H3
FRATESSA CT				
	-	SF	94134	20-A2
FREDELA LN				
	-	SF	94131	10-E3
FREDERICK ST				
	-	SF	94117	10-E1
	400	SF	94117	9-D1
FREDSON CT				
	-	SF	94112	19-E2
FREELON ST				
	-	SF	94107	7-B7
FREEMAN CT				
	-	SF	94108	7-A5
FREEMAN ST				
	-	SF	94129	1-E4
FRWY I-80				
	-	SF	-	3-E4
	-	SF	-	7-B7
	-	SF	-	11-A1
FREMONT ST				
	-	SF	94105	7-B5
FRENCH CT				
	-	SF	94129	1-E4
FRESNO ST				
	-	SF	94133	7-A4
FRIEDELL ST				
	900	SF	94124	15-E7
FRONT ST				
	-	SF	94111	7-B4
	800	SF	94111	3-B4
FUENTA AV				
	-	SF	94132	18-B1
FULTON ST				
	300	SF	94102	6-F7
	800	SF	94117	6-F7
	2100	SF	94117	5-B7
	2300	SF	94118	5-B7
	2500	SF	-	5-B7
	4100	SF	94121	5-B7
	5700	SF	94121	4-J7
	6700	SF	-	4-J7
	5900	SF	94121	8-H1
	5900	SF	-	8-H1
FUNSTON AV				
	-	SF	94118	5-C7
	-	SF	94129	1-E4
	-	SF	94129	5-E4
	1200	SF	94122	9-C2
	1800	SF	94116	9-C3
	2100	SF	94116	13-C5
FUNSTON RD				
	-	SF	94123	2-H3
G				
GABILAN WY				
	-	SF	94132	13-B6
GAISER CT				
	-	SF	94110	10-H2
GALEWOOD CIR				
	-	SF	94131	9-D3
GALEWOOD CT				
	-	SF	94131	9-D3
GALILEE LN				
	-	SF	94115	6-H6
GALINDO AV				
	-	SF	94132	18-C2
GALLAGHER LN				
	-	SF	94103	7-A6
GALVEZ AV				
	500	SF	94124	16-E7
	600	SF	94124	15-B4
GAMBETTA ST				
	-	DALY	94014	18-D4
GAMBIER ST				
	-	SF	94134	14-H7
GARCES DR				
	-	SF	94132	18-A1
GARCIA AV				
	-	SF	94127	13-D4
GARDEN ST				
	-	SF	94115	6-F6
GARDEN GROVE DR				
	-	DALY	94015	17-J3
GARDENSIDE DR				
	-	SF	94131	10-F3
GARFIELD ST				
	-	SF	94112	18-C1
	-	SF	94132	18-C1
GARLINGTON CT				
	-	SF	94124	15-C6
GARRISON AV				
	-	SF	94134	19-J2
GARWOOD DR				
	-	DALY	94014	18-D3
GATES ST				
	-	SF	94110	14-J6
GATEVIEW CT				
	-	SF	94116	9-C4
GATEWAY AV				
	-	SF	94130	3-D1
GATUN AL				
	-	SF	94127	14-E5
GAVEN ST				
	-	SF	94134	15-A6
	200	SF	94134	14-J6
GAVIOTA WY				
	-	SF	94127	14-E5
GEARY BLVD				
	1100	SF	94109	6-E6
	1500	SF	94115	6-E6
	2700	SF	94118	6-E6
	3100	SF	94118	5-A6
	5300	SF	94121	5-A6
	6900	SF	94121	4-H6
GEARY ST				
	-	SF	94108	7-A6
	300	SF	94102	7-A6
	400	SF	94102	6-J6
	700	SF	94109	6-J6
GELLERT DR				
	-	SF	94132	12-J6
	100	SF	94132	13-A6
GENEBERN WY				
	-	SF	94112	14-H6
GENERAL KENNEDY AV				
	-	SF	94129	2-E4
GENEVA AV				
	-	SF	94112	13-E7
	-	SF	94112	19-F1
	1600	SF	94134	19-G2
	2100	DALY	94014	19-G2
	3100	BSBN	94005	19-G2
	3200	BSBN	94005	20-A3
	3200	DALY	94014	20-A3
GENNESSEE ST				
	-	SF	94112	13-E6
	400	SF	94127	13-E6
GENOA PL				
	100	SF	94133	3-A4
GEORGE CT				
	-	SF	94124	15-C6
GERKE AL				
	-	SF	94133	3-A4
GERMANIA ST				
	-	SF	94117	10-G1
GETZ ST				
	-	SF	94112	18-E1
GIANTS DR				
	3000	SF	94124	20-C1
GIBB ST				
	-	SF	94111	7-A4
GIBBON CT				
	-	SF	94129	6-F4
GIBSON RD				
	1700	SF	94129	5-B5
GILBERT ST				
	-	SF	94103	7-A7
	-	SF	94103	11-A1
GILLETTE AV				
	-	SF	94134	20-B2
GILMAN AV				
	500	SF	94124	20-B1
GILROY ST				
	-	SF	94124	20-C2
GIRARD RD				
	-	SF	94129	2-E4
	-	SF	94129	1-E4
GIRARD ST				
	-	SF	94134	15-A7
	700	SF	94134	20-A1
GLADEVIEW WY				
	-	SF	94131	10-E4
GLADIOLUS LN				
	-	SF	94132	13-C6
GLADSTONE DR				
	-	SF	94112	14-H7
GLADYS ST				
	-	SF	94110	14-H5
GLENBROOK AV				
	-	SF	94114	10-E3
GLENDALE ST				
	-	SF	94114	10-F3
GLENHAVEN LN				
	100	SF	94131	9-D3
GLENVIEW DR				
	-	SF	94131	10-E4
	200	SF	94131	14-E4
GLENWOOD AV				
	100	DALY	94015	18-A3
	200	DALY	94015	17-J3
GLOBE AL				
	-	SF	94127	13-D6
GLORIA CT				
	-	SF	94112	19-F1
GLOVER ST				
	-	SF	94109	6-J4
GODEUS ST				
	-	SF	94110	14-H5
GOETHE ST				
	-	DALY	94014	18-D2
	-	SF	94112	18-D2
GOETTINGEN ST				
	-	SF	94134	15-A7
	800	SF	94134	20-A1
GOLD ST				
	-	SF	94133	7-A4
GOLDEN CT				
	-	SF	94109	6-J5
GOLDEN GATE AV				
	-	SF	94102	7-A6
	-	SF	94102	6-F7
	1000	SF	94115	6-F7
	1200	SF	94117	6-F7
	2200	SF	94118	6-F7
	2500	SF	94118	5-D7
	2500	SF	94117	5-E7
GOLDEN GATE BRIDGE FRWY Rt#-1				
	-	SF	-	5-C5
	-	SF	-	1-C3
GOLDEN GATE BRG FRWY U.S.-101				
	-	SF	-	1-B1
GOLDING LN				
	-	SF	94131	10-F3
GOLD MINE DR				
	-	SF	94131	14-F5
GOLETA AV				
	-	SF	94132	13-A6
GONZALEZ DR				
	-	SF	94132	18-B1
GORDON ST				
	-	SF	94103	11-A1
GORGAS AV				
	-	SF	94129	1-E3
	-	SF	94129	2-E3
GORHAM AV				
	-	SF	94112	14-G6
GOUGH ST				
	-	SF	94103	10-H1
	100	SF	94102	6-H4
	100	SF	94102	10-H1
	300	SF	94109	6-H4
	2500	SF	94123	6-H4
	2700	SF	94123	2-H3
GOULD ST				
	-	SF	94124	20-B1
GRACE ST				
	-	SF	94103	6-J7
GRAFTON AV				
	-	SF	94112	18-D1
GRAHAM ST				
	-	SF	94129	1-D4
	-	SF	94129	5-D4
GRANADA AV				
	-	SF	94112	18-D1
	200	SF	94112	13-D7
GRANAT CT				
	-	SF	94118	5-C7
GRAND VIEW AV				
	-	SF	94114	10-F4
GRANDVIEW TER				
	-	SF	94114	10-F3
GRANT AV				
	-	SF	94108	7-A5
	1000	SF	94133	7-A4
	1300	SF	94133	3-A3
GRANVILLE WY				
	-	SF	94127	13-D5
GRATTAN ST				
	-	SF	94117	10-E2
	200	SF	94117	9-E2
GRAYSTONE LN				
	-	DALY	94014	19-F3
GRAYSTONE TER				
	-	SF	94114	10-F3
GREAT HWY				
	-	SF	-	8-H4
	500	SF	94121	4-G7
	700	SF	94116	8-H4
	700	SF	94122	8-H4
	800	SF	94121	8-H4
	1700	SF	94116	12-H5
	2700	SF	94132	12-H6
GREEN ST				
	-	SF	94111	3-A4
	200	SF	94133	3-A4
	700	SF	94133	6-F4
	1000	SF	94109	6-F4
	1500	SF	94123	6-F4
GREEN RDGE				
	-	DALY	94014	18-D4
GREENOUGH AV				
	-	SF	94129	1-C4
GREENVIEW CT				
	-	SF	94131	9-E3
GREEN VIEW DR				
	-	DALY	94014	19-E3
GREENWICH ST				
	100	SF	94111	3-A4
	200	SF	94133	3-A4
	700	SF	94133	2-G4
	1100	SF	94109	2-G4
	1500	SF	94123	2-G4
	2300	SF	94123	6-F4
GREENWOOD AV				
	-	SF	94112	13-D7
GRENARD TER				
	-	SF	94109	2-H4
GRIFFITH ST				
	900	SF	94124	15-D7
	1000	SF	94124	20-C1
GRIJALVA DR				
	-	SF	94132	18-B1
GROTE PL				
	-	SF	94105	7-B6
GROVE ST				
	-	SF	94102	6-G7
	800	SF	94117	6-E7
	2100	SF	94117	5-E7
GUADALUPE AV				
	-	DALY	94014	18-C2
GUADALUPE CANYON PKWY				
	-	SMCo	94014	18-E4
	300	SMCo	94014	19-E3
	300	BSBN	94005	19-H4
GUERRERO ST				
	-	SF	94103	10-H4
	400	SF	94110	10-H4
	1400	SF	94110	14-H4
GUTTENBERG ST				
	-	SF	94112	19-F2
	300	DALY	94014	19-F2
GUY PL				
	-	SF	94105	7-B6
H				
H ST				
	-	SF	94124	21-E1
	100	SF	94124	20-E1
	300	SF	94124	15-E7
HAHN ST				
	-	SF	94134	19-J2
HAIGHT ST				
	-	SF	94102	10-F1
	400	SF	94117	10-F1
	1800	SF	94117	9-E1
HALE ST				
	-	SF	94134	15-A6
	200	SF	94134	14-J6
HALLAM ST				
	-	SF	94103	7-A7
HALLECK ST				
	-	SF	94129	1-E4
	-	SF	94111	7-B5
	100	SF	94104	7-B5
HAMERTON AV				
	-	SF	94131	14-F6
HAMILTON ST				
	-	SF	94129	1-C3
	-	SF	94134	14-J7
HAMILTON ST				
	300	SF	94134	15-A7
	600	SF	94134	20-A1
HAMLIN ST				
	-	SF	94109	6-J4
HAMPSHIRE ST				
	100	SF	94103	11-A1
	300	SF	94110	11-A3
	1500	SF	94110	15-A4
HAMPTON LN				
	1700	DALY	94014	19-F3
HANCOCK ST				
	-	SF	94114	10-G2
HANOVER ST				
	-	SF	94112	19-E3
	400	DALY	94014	19-E3
	600	DALY	94014	18-D3
HARBOR RD				
	-	SF	94124	15-D6
HARBOR BAY ISLE FERRY				
	-	SF	-	7-D5
HARDIE AV				
	-	SF	94129	5-D4
HARDIE PL				
	-	SF	94108	7-A5
HARDING RD				
	-	SF	94132	12-J7
HARE ST				
	-	SF	94124	15-D6
HARKNESS AV				
	-	SF	94134	20-A1
HARLAN PL				
	-	SF	94108	7-A5
HARLEM AL				
	-	SF	94109	6-J6
HARLOW ST				
	-	SF	94114	10-G2
HARNEY RD				
	-	BSBN	94005	20-B3
	-	SF	94134	20-B3
HARNEY WY				
	-	SF	94134	20-C2
	-	SF	94124	20-C2
HAROLD AV				
	-	SF	94112	18-E1
	200	SF	94112	13-E7
HARPER ST				
	-	SF	94131	14-G5
HARRIET ST				
	-	SF	94103	7-A7
	400	SF	94103	11-B1
HARRINGTON ST				
	-	SF	94112	14-G7
HARRIS PL				
	-	SF	94123	2-G4
HARRISON BLVD				
	-	SF	94129	1-B4
	-	SF	94129	5-B4
HARRISON ST				
	-	SF	94105	7-A7
	600	SF	94107	7-A7
	1000	SF	94103	7-A7
	1100	SF	94103	11-A1
	1300	SF	94103	10-J1
	2000	SF	94110	10-J1
	3000	SF	94110	14-J4
HARRY ST				
	-	SF	94131	14-G5
HARTFORD ST				
	-	SF	94114	10-G2
HARVARD ST				
	-	SF	94134	14-H7
HARWOOD AL				
	-	SF	94133	3-A4
HASTINGS TER				
	-	SF	94109	2-J4
HATTIE ST				
	-	SF	94114	10-F2
HAVELOCK ST				
	-	SF	94112	14-E7
HAVENS ST				
	-	SF	94109	2-J4
HAVENSIDE DR				
	100	SF	94132	13-A6
HAWES ST				
	1200	SF	94124	15-C7
	2300	SF	94124	20-B1
HAWKINS LN				
	-	SF	94124	15-C6
HAWTHORNE ST				
	-	SF	94105	7-B6
	-	SF	94103	7-B6
	100	SF	94107	7-B6
HAYES ST				
	-	SF	94102	6-E7
	800	SF	94117	6-E7
	2100	SF	94117	5-E7
HAYS ST				
	-	SF	94129	5-C5
HAZELWOOD AV				
	-	SF	94112	13-D6
	200	SF	94127	13-D6
HEAD ST				
	-	SF	94112	18-C2
	200	SF	94132	18-C2
	900	SF	94132	13-C7
	900	SF	94127	13-C7
HEARST AV				
	-	SF	94131	14-E6
	300	SF	94112	14-E6
	500	SF	94112	13-E6
HEATHER AV				
	-	SF	94118	5-E6
HELEN ST				
	-	SF	94109	6-J5
HELENA ST				
	-	SF	94124	15-A6
HEMLOCK ST				
	-	SF	94109	6-H6
	600	SF	94115	6-H6
HEMWAY TER				
	-	SF	94117	6-E7
HENRY ST				
	-	SF	94114	10-G1
HENRY ADAMS ST				
	-	SF	94103	11-A1
HERBST RD				
	3100	SF	94132	12-H6
HERMANN ST				
	-	SF	94102	10-G1
	200	SF	94117	10-G1
HERNANDEZ AV				
	-	SF	94127	13-D4
HERON ST				
	-	SF	94103	7-A7
HESTER AV				
	-	SF	94134	20-B2
HEYMAN AV				
	-	SF	94110	14-H5
HICKORY ST				
	-	SF	94102	6-H7
HICKS RD				
	-	SF	94129	5-D4
HIDALGO TER				
	-	SF	94103	10-H1
HIGH ST				
	-	SF	94114	10-F4
HIGHLAND AV				
	-	SF	94131	14-H5
	-	SF	94110	14-H5
HIGUERA AV				
	-	SF	94132	18-A1
HILIRITAS AV				
	-	SF	94131	14-F5
S HILL BLVD				
	-	SF	94112	19-G2
	300	DALY	94014	19-F3
HILL DR				
	-	SF	94124	16-E7
HILL ST				
	-	SF	94110	10-H3
	300	SF	94114	10-G3
HILLCREST CT				
	-	SF	94127	13-E6
HILLCREST DR				
	-	DALY	94014	18-C3
HILLPOINT AV				
	-	SF	94117	9-E2
HILLSDALE AV				
	-	DALY	94015	18-B3
HILLSIDE BLVD				
	-	DALY	94014	18-D4
HILLVIEW CT				
	-	SF	94124	15-C6
HILLWAY AV				
	-	SF	94143	9-D2
	-	SF	94117	9-D2
HILTON ST				
	-	SF	94124	15-A5
HIMMELMANN PL				
	-	SF	94133	6-J4
HITCHCOCK ST				
	-	SF	94129	1-C4
	-	SF	94129	5-C4
HOBART AL				
	-	SF	94102	7-A5
	-	SF	94102	6-J5

STREET Block	City	ZIP	Pg-Grid
HODGES AL			
-	SF	94133	3-A4
HOFF ST			
-	SF	94110	10-H2
HOFFMAN AV			
-	SF	94114	10-F4
HOFFMAN ST			
-	SF	94129	1-C3
HOLLADAY AV			
100	SF	94110	15-A4
HOLLAND CT			
-	SF	94103	7-A6
HOLLIS ST			
-	SF	94115	6-G6
HOLLISTER AV			
900	SF	94124	20-B1
HOLLOWAY AV			
-	SF	94112	18-D1
900	SF	94112	18-B1
HOLLY PARK CIR			
-	SF	94110	14-H6
HOLLYWOOD CT			
-	SF	94112	19-F2
HOLYOKE ST			
-	SF	94134	15-A7
-	SF	94134	20-A1
HOMER ST			
-	SF	94103	7-A7
HOMESTEAD ST			
-	SF	94114	10-F4
HOMEWOOD CT			
-	SF	94112	13-D7
HOOKER AL			
-	SF	94108	7-A5
HOOPER ST			
100	SF	94107	11-B1
HOPKINS AV			
-	SF	94131	10-F3
HORACE ST			
-	SF	94110	10-J4
HORNE AV			
-	SF	94124	16-E7
HOTALING ST			
-	SF	94111	7-A4
HOUSTON ST			
-	SF	94133	2-J3
HOWARD RD			
-	SF	94129	5-B5
HOWARD ST			
-	SF	94105	7-B6
600	SF	94103	7-B6
1200	SF	94103	6-J7
1400	SF	94103	10-J1
HOWTH ST			
-	SF	94112	18-E1
100	SF	94112	19-E1
400	SF	94112	14-E7
HUBBELL ST			
100	SF	94107	11-B1
HUDSON AV			
600	SF	94124	15-B4
600	SF	94124	16-E7
HUGO ST			
-	SF	94122	9-D2
HULBERT AL			
-	SF	94107	7-A7
HUMBOLDT ST			
100	SF	94107	11-C3
HUNTER RD			
-	SF	94129	5-B4
HUNTERS POINT BLVD			
-	SF	94124	15-D6
HUNTERS POINT EXWY			
-	SF	94124	20-C2
HUNTINGTON DR			
-	SF	94132	12-J6
HURON AV			
-	DALY	94014	18-E2
400	SF	94112	19-E2
700	SF	94112	18-E2
HUSSEY ST			
-	SF	94124	21-E1
300	SF	94124	15-E7
HYDE ST			
-	SF	94102	6-J6
300	SF	94109	6-J4
1900	SF	94109	2-J3
2800	SF	94133	2-J3
I			
I ST			
200	SF	94124	20-E1
500	SF	94124	15-E7
ICEHOUSE AL			
-	SF	94111	3-B4
IDALENE ST			
-	DALY	94014	19-G3
IDORA AV			
-	SF	94127	13-D4
IGNACIO ST			
-	SF	94124	20-C2
ILLINOIS ST			
-	SF	94107	11-C3
1600	SF	94124	11-C4
1600	SF	94124	15-C4
ILS LN			
-	SF	94111	7-A5
IMPERIAL AV			
-	SF	94123	2-H4
INA CT			
-	SF	94112	14-H7
INCA LN			
-	SF	94115	6-H6
INCINERATOR RD			
-	SF	94129	1-D4
INDIANA ST			
500	SF	94107	11-C3
1600	SF	94124	11-C4
1700	SF	94124	15-C4
INDUSTRIAL ST			
-	SF	94124	15-A5
INDUSTRIAL WY			
-	BSBN	94005	20-A4
INFANTRY TER			
-	SF	94129	1-D4
-	SF	94129	5-D4
INGALLS ST			
1200	SF	94124	15-C7
2500	SF	94124	20-B1
INGERSON AV			
700	SF	94124	20-B1
INNES AV			
400	SF	94124	15-B5
400	SF	94124	16-E7
INVERNESS DR			
-	SF	94132	13-A6
IOWA ST			
700	SF	94107	11-C3
IRIS AV			
-	SF	94118	6-E6
IRON AL			
-	SF	94114	10-F3
IRVING ST			
-	SF	94143	9-A2
-	SF	94122	9-A2
3200	SF	94122	8-H2
IRVINGTON ST			
100	DALY	94014	18-D3
IRWIN ST			
400	SF	94107	11-B1
ISADORA DUNCAN LN			
-	SF	94102	7-A6
-	SF	94102	6-J6
ISIS ST			
-	SF	94103	10-J1
ISLAIS ST			
-	SF	94124	15-B4
ISOLA WY			
-	SF	94127	14-E5
ITALY AV			
-	SF	94112	19-F1
IVY ST			
200	SF	94102	6-H7
J			
J ST			
-	SF	94124	21-E1
-	SF	94124	20-D1
JACK KEROUAC AL			
-	SF	94133	7-A4
JACK LONDON AL			
-	SF	94107	7-B6
JACKSON ST			
-	SF	94111	7-A4
400	SF	94133	7-A4
600	SF	94108	7-A4
1000	SF	94133	6-F5
1000	SF	94108	6-F5
1200	SF	94109	6-F5
2100	SF	94115	6-F5
3300	SF	94118	6-F5
3500	SF	94118	5-D5
JACQUELINE CT			
-	DALY	94014	19-J4
JACQUELINE LN			
-	DALY	94014	19-J4
JADE PL			
-	SF	94131	14-F5
JAKEY CT			
-	SF	94124	15-C6
JAMES LICK FRWY U.S.-101			
-	SF	-	11-A2
-	SF	-	15-A6
-	SF	-	20-A1
JAMESTON LN			
-	DALY	94014	19-F3
JAMESTOWN AV			
800	SF	94124	20-B1
JAMESTOWN AVEX			
700	SF	94124	20-C2
JANSEN ST			
-	SF	94133	2-J4
JARBOE AV			
600	SF	94110	14-J5
1200	SF	94110	15-A5
JASON CT			
-	SF	94133	7-A4
JASPER PL			
-	SF	94133	3-A4
JAUSS ST			
-	SF	94129	2-E3
JAVA ST			
-	SF	94117	10-F1
JAVOWITZ ST			
-	SF	94129	2-E3
JEAN WY			
-	SF	94118	6-E6
JEFFERSON ST			
-	SF	94133	2-J3
500	SF	94109	2-J3
1400	SF	94123	2-F3
JENNIFER CT			
-	DALY	94014	19-J3
JENNINGS ST			
100	SF	94124	15-D6
2700	SF	94124	20-B1
JEROME AL			
-	SF	94133	7-A4
JERROLD AV			
400	SF	94124	15-A4
JERSEY ST			
-	SF	94114	10-G4
JESSIE ST			
-	SF	94105	7-A6
100	SF	94103	7-A6
600	SF	94103	6-J7
1300	SF	94103	10-H1
JOHN ST			
-	SF	94133	7-A4
JOHN DALY BLVD			
400	DALY	94014	18-B3
500	DALY	94015	18-B3
800	DALY	94015	17-J4
JOHN F FORAN FRWY I-280			
-	DALY	-	18-C2
-	SF	-	15-A6
-	SF	-	11-B1
-	SF	-	14-E7
-	SF	-	18-C2
-	SF	-	19-E1
JOHN F KENNEDY DR			
-	SF	94117	9-B1
-	SF	94118	9-B1
200	SF	-	9-A1
1200	SF	-	8-H1
JOHN F SHELLEY DR			
-	SF	94134	19-H1
-	SF	94134	14-H7
JOHN MAHER ST			
-	SF	94111	3-B4
JOHN MUIR DR			
100	SF	94132	18-A2
100	SMCo	94015	18-A2
600	SF	94132	17-J1
JOHNSTONE DR			
-	SF	94131	9-E2
JOICE ST			
-	SF	94108	7-A5
JONES ST			
-	SF	94102	6-J4
800	SF	94109	6-J4
900	SF	94108	6-J4
1500	SF	94133	6-J4
1900	SF	94133	2-J3
1900	SF	94109	2-J3
JOOST AV			
-	SF	94131	14-E6
400	SF	94127	14-E6
JOOST AV			
600	SF	94127	13-E6
JORDAN AV			
-	SF	94118	5-E6
JOSEPHA AV			
-	SF	94132	18-B1
JOSIAH AV			
-	SF	94112	18-E1
JOY ST			
-	SF	94110	15-A5
JUAN BAUTISTA CIR			
-	SF	94132	18-B1
JUANITA WY			
-	SF	94127	13-D5
JUDAH ST			
-	SF	94122	9-A2
2800	SF	94122	8-H2
JUDSON AV			
100	SF	94131	14-E7
100	SF	94112	14-E7
300	SF	94112	13-E7
JULES AV			
-	SF	94112	18-D1
200	SF	94112	13-D7
JULIA ST			
-	SF	94103	6-J7
JULIAN AV			
-	SF	94103	10-H2
JULIUS ST			
-	SF	94133	3-A3
JUNIOR TER			
-	SF	94112	19-F1
JUNIPER ST			
-	SF	94103	10-J1
JUNIPERO SERRA BLVD			
-	SF	94127	13-C7
-	SF	94132	13-C7
900	SF	94132	18-C1
1800	DALY	94014	18-C4
JUNIPERO SERRA BLVD Rt#-1			
1100	SF	94132	18-C2
JUNIPERO SERRA FRWY I-280			
-	DALY	-	18-C3
-	SF	-	18-C3
JUNIPERO SERRA FRWY Rt#-1			
-	DALY	-	18-C3
-	SF	-	18-C3
JURI ST			
-	SF	94110	10-H4
JUSTIN DR			
-	SF	94112	14-H6
K			
KANSAS ST			
100	SF	94103	11-A1
400	SF	94107	11-A3
1600	SF	94124	11-A4
1600	SF	94124	15-A4
KAPLAN LN			
-	SF	94103	7-B6
KAREN CT			
-	SF	94134	15-A7
KATE ST			
-	SF	94103	11-A1
KEARNY ST			
-	SF	94108	7-A5
300	SF	94104	7-A5
600	SF	94111	7-A5
900	SF	94133	7-A5
1200	SF	94133	3-A3
KEITH ST			
-	SF	94124	15-C6
-	SF	94124	20-B1
KELLOCH AV			
-	SF	94134	19-J2
KEMPTON AV			
-	SF	94132	18-C2
KENDALL DR			
-	SF	94129	2-E4
KENNY AL			
-	SF	94112	19-F1
KENSINGTON WY			
-	SF	94127	13-D5
KENT ST			
-	SF	94133	2-J4
KENWOOD WY			
-	SF	94112	13-D7
-	SF	94127	13-D7
KERN ST			
100	SF	94131	14-G6
KEY AV			
900	SF	94124	20-B1
KEYES AL			
-	SF	94133	7-A4
KEYES AV			
-	SF	94129	1-E4
KEYSTONE WY			
-	SF	94127	13-D7
-	SF	94112	13-D7
KEZAR DR			
500	SF	94117	9-D1
500	SF	-	9-D1
KIMBALL PL			
-	SF	94109	6-J5
KING ST			
-	SF	94107	7-B7
400	SF	94107	11-A1
400	SF	94103	11-A1
KINGSTON ST			
-	SF	94110	14-H5
KINZEY ST			
-	SF	94129	1-C4
KIRKHAM ST			
-	SF	94143	9-C2
100	SF	94122	9-A2
2900	SF	94122	8-H2
KIRKWOOD AV			
500	SF	94124	15-B5
KISKA RD			
-	SF	94124	15-D7
KISSLING ST			
-	SF	94103	10-J1
KITTREDGE TER			
-	SF	94118	6-E7
KNOCKASH HILL ST			
-	SF	94127	13-D5
KNOLLVIEW WY			
-	SF	94131	10-E4
KNOTT CT			
-	SF	94112	19-F2
KNOWLES AV			
-	DALY	94014	18-C3
KOBBE AV			
-	SF	94129	5-C4
1300	SF	94129	1-B4
KRAMER PL			
-	SF	94133	3-A4
KRAUSGRILL PL			
-	SF	94133	3-A4
KRONQUIST CT			
-	SF	94131	14-G4
L			
LA AVANZADA			
-	SF	94131	9-E3
LA BICA WY			
-	SF	94127	13-E5
LAFAYETTE ST			
-	SF	94103	10-J1
LA FERRERA TER			
-	SF	94133	3-A3
LA GRANDE AV			
-	SF	94112	14-H7
100	SF	94112	19-H1
LAGUNA ST			
-	SF	94102	10-H1
200	SF	94102	6-H6
1000	SF	94115	6-G4
1200	SF	94109	6-H6
2700	SF	94123	6-G4
3000	SF	94123	2-G3
LAGUNA HONDA BLVD			
200	SF	94131	9-D4
200	SF	94116	9-D4
300	SF	94116	13-D4
400	SF	94127	13-D4
LAGUNITAS DR			
-	SF	94132	13-C6
LAIDLEY ST			
-	SF	94131	14-G5
LAKE ST			
-	SF	94118	5-C6
1600	SF	94121	5-A6
LAKE FOREST CT			
-	SF	94131	9-D3
LAKE FOREST DR			
-	DALY	94015	18-B3
LAKE MERCED BLVD			
-	SF	94132	12-J6
-	SF	94132	18-A2
-	SF	94132	13-A7
100	DALY	94015	18-A3
100	SMCo	94015	18-A2
LAKE MERCED HILL			
-	SF	94132	18-A2
LAKEMONT DR			
-	DALY	94015	18-A3
LAKESHORE DR			
-	SF	94132	12-J6
LAKESHORE PZ			
-	SF	94132	13-A6
LAKEVIEW AV			
-	SF	94112	18-D1
LAKEVIEW DR			
-	DALY	94015	18-A3
LAKE VISTA AV			
-	DALY	94015	18-B3
LAKEWOOD AV			
-	SF	94127	13-C7
LAKEWOOD DR			
-	DALY	94015	18-A4
-	DALY	94015	17-J4
LAMARTINE ST			
-	SF	94112	14-G6
LAMSON LN			
-	SF	94114	10-F2
LANCASTER LN			
-	SF	94132	12-J6
LANDERS ST			
-	SF	94114	10-H2
LANE ST			
1100	SF	94124	15-C6
LANGDON CT			
-	SF	94129	1-B3
LANGTON ST			
-	SF	94103	11-A1
-	SF	94103	7-A7
LANSDALE AV			
-	SF	94127	13-D5
LANSING ST			
-	SF	94105	7-B6
LAPHAM WY			
-	SF	94112	19-G2
LAPIDGE ST			
-	SF	94110	10-H2
LA PLAYA			
200	SF	94121	4-H7
800	SF	94121	8-H2
1200	SF	94122	8-H2
LAPU LAPU ST			
-	SF	94107	7-B6
LARCH ST			
200	SF	94102	6-H6
LARKIN ST			
-	SF	94102	6-J5
600	SF	94109	6-J5
2300	SF	94109	2-H4
LARKSPUR SAN FRANCISCO FERRY			
-	SF	-	3-C1
-	SF	-	7-C4
LA SALLE AV			
-	SF	94124	15-B5
LASKIE ST			
-	SF	94103	6-J7
LATHROP AV			
100	SF	94134	20-A2
LATONA ST			
-	SF	94124	15-B6
LAURA ST			
-	SF	94112	18-E2
LAUREL ST			
-	SF	94118	6-E5
LAUSANNE AV			
-	DALY	94014	18-D4
LAUSSAT ST			
-	SF	94102	10-G1
200	SF	94117	10-G1
LAWRENCE AV			
-	SF	94112	18-E2
LAWTON ST			
-	SF	94122	9-C2
2700	SF	94122	8-H3
LEAVENWORTH ST			
-	SF	94102	6-J5
300	SF	94109	6-J5
1900	SF	94109	2-J3
2000	SF	94133	2-J3
LECH WALESA			
-	SF	94102	6-J7
LE CONTE AV			
700	SF	94124	20-B1
LEDYARD ST			
-	SF	94124	15-A6
LEE AV			
-	SF	94112	18-E1
200	SF	94112	13-E7
LEESE ST			
-	SF	94110	14-H6
LEGION CT			
-	SF	94127	13-D7
LEGION OF HONOR DR			
-	SF	94121	4-J6
LEIDESDORFF ST			
-	SF	94104	7-B5
200	SF	94111	7-B5
LELAND AV			
-	SF	94134	19-J2
300	SF	94134	20-A2
LENDRUM CT			
-	SF	94129	1-C3
LENOX WY			
-	SF	94127	13-C5
LEO ST			
-	SF	94112	14-F7
LEONA TER			
-	SF	94115	6-F6
LEROY PL			
-	SF	94109	6-J5
LESSING ST			
-	SF	94112	18-D2
LETTERMAN DR			
-	SF	94129	2-E4
-	SF	94129	6-E4
LETTUCE LN			
-	SF	94124	15-B5
LEVANT ST			
-	SF	94114	10-F2
LEXINGTON ST			
-	SF	94110	10-H3
LIBERTY ST			
-	SF	94110	10-G3
200	SF	94114	10-G3
LICK PL			
-	SF	94108	7-A5
-	SF	94104	7-A5
LIEBIG ST			
-	DALY	94014	18-D2
-	SF	94112	18-D2
LIEUTENANT ALLEN ST			
-	SF	94129	1-E3
-	SF	94129	2-E3
LIGGETT AV			
700	SF	94129	6-E4
LILAC ST			
-	SF	94110	10-J4
LILLIAN ST			
-	SF	94124	15-D6
LILY ST			
-	SF	94102	6-H7
LINARES AV			
-	SF	94116	9-D3
LINCOLN BLVD			
-	SF	94129	2-E4
-	SF	94129	1-B4
-	SF	94129	5-B5
100	SF	94121	5-B5
LINCOLN CT			
-	SF	94112	19-F2
LINCOLN WY			
-	SF	94122	9-A1
-	SF	94117	9-C1
200	SF	-	9-A1
3200	SF	-	8-H2
3200	SF	94122	8-H2
LINDA ST			
-	SF	94110	10-H2
LINDA VISTA DR			
100	DALY	94014	19-J4
LINDA VISTA STEPS			
-	SF	94112	19-G2
LINDEN ST			
200	SF	94102	6-H7
LINDSAY CIR			
-	SF	94124	15-C6
LIPPARD AV			
-	SF	94131	14-G6
LISBON ST			
-	SF	94112	14-G7
400	SF	94112	19-F1
LITTLEFIELD TER			
-	SF	94107	11-A4
LIVINGSTON ST			
-	SF	94129	1-D3
LLOYD ST			
-	SF	94117	10-G1
LOBOS ST			
-	SF	94112	18-D1
200	SF	94132	18-D1
LOCKSLEY AV			
-	SF	94122	9-D3
LOCKWOOD ST			
-	SF	94124	16-E7
LOCUST ST			
-	SF	94118	6-E5
LOEHR ST			
-	SF	94134	19-J2
LOMA VISTA TER			
-	SF	94117	10-F2
-	SF	94114	10-F2
LOMBARD ST			
-	SF	94129	6-E4
-	SF	94129	2-H4
-	SF	94111	3-A3
100	SF	94133	3-A3
1300	SF	94109	2-H4
2600	SF	94123	2-H4
LOMBARD ST Rt#-1			
500	SF	94133	2-J3
1000	SF	94109	2-J4
LOMBARD ST U.S.-101			
1400	SF	94123	2-F4
LOMITA AV			
-	SF	94122	9-C3
LONDON ST			
200	SF	94112	14-G7
500	SF	94112	19-F1
LONE MOUNTAIN TER			
-	SF	94118	5-E7
LONG AV			
-	SF	94129	1-C3
LONGVIEW CT			
-	SF	94131	9-E4
-	SF	94131	10-E4
LOOMIS ST			
-	SF	94124	15-A5
LOPEZ AV			
-	SF	94116	9-D4
-	SF	94116	13-D4
LORAINE CT			
100	SF	94118	5-E6
LORI LN			
-	SF	94131	9-E3
LOS BANOS AV			
100	DALY	94014	18-C3
LOS OLIVOS AV			
-	DALY	94014	18-C3
LOS PALMOS DR			
-	SF	94127	14-E6
400	SF	94127	13-D6
LOTTIE BENNETT LN			
-	SF	94115	6-E5
LOUISBURG ST			
100	SF	94112	18-E1
100	SF	94112	19-E1
LOWELL ST			
-	SF	94112	19-E2
300	DALY	94014	19-E2
LOWER TER			
-	SF	94114	10-F2
LOYOLA TER			
-	SF	94117	6-E7
LUCERNE ST			
100	SF	94103	11-B1
LUCKY ST			
-	SF	94110	10-J4
LUCY ST			
-	SF	94124	15-B7
LUDLOW AL			
-	SF	94127	13-D5
LULU AL			
-	SF	94127	13-E6
LUNADO CT			
100	SF	94127	13-C7
LUNADO WY			
-	SF	94127	13-C7
LUNDEEN ST			
-	SF	94123	2-E3
-	SF	94129	2-E3
LUNDYS LN			
-	SF	94110	14-H5
LUPINE AV			
-	SF	94118	6-E6
LUPINE DR			
-	DALY	94014	19-H3
LURLINE ST			
-	SF	94122	9-C2
LURMONT TER			
-	SF	94109	2-J4
LUSK ST			
-	SF	94107	7-B7
LYELL ST			
-	SF	94112	14-G6
-	SF	94131	14-G6
LYNCH ST			
-	SF	94109	6-J4
LYNDHURST DR			
-	SF	94132	13-B7
LYON ST			
-	SF	94117	10-F1
300	SF	94117	6-F7
800	SF	94115	6-F5
2300	SF	94129	6-F4
2500	SF	94123	6-F4
2900	SF	94123	2-E3
2900	SF	94129	2-F4
LYSETTE ST			
-	SF	94109	6-J5
M			
MABINI ST			
-	SF	94107	7-B6
MABREY CT			
-	SF	94124	15-C6
MACARTHUR AV			
-	SF	94123	2-H3
-	SF	94129	1-E4
800	SF	94129	5-E4
MACDONALD AV			
-	DALY	94014	19-J3
-	DALY	94014	20-A3
MACEDONIA ST			
-	SF	94110	15-A4
MACONDRAY LN			
-	SF	94133	2-J4
-	SF	94109	2-J4
-	SF	94109	6-J4
MADDUX AV			
-	SF	94124	15-B6
MADDUX DR			
900	SMCo	94015	18-A4
900	DALY	94015	18-A4
MADERA ST			
-	SF	94107	11-B3
MADISON ST			
-	SF	94112	14-H7
-	SF	94134	14-H7
MADRID ST			
-	SF	94112	14-G7
400	SF	94112	19-G1
MADRONE AV			
-	SF	94127	13-C5
MAGELLAN AV			
-	SF	94116	9-D4
200	SF	94116	13-C4
MAGNOLIA ST			
-	SF	94123	2-G4
MAHAN ST			
600	SF	94124	21-E1
MAIDEN LN			
-	SF	94108	7-A6
MAIN ST			
-	SF	94105	7-B5
100	BSBN	94005	19-J3
100	BSBN	94005	20-A4
MAJESTIC AV			
-	SF	94112	18-E1
MALDEN AL			
-	SF	94105	7-B6
MALLORCA WY			
-	SF	94123	2-G3
MALTA DR			
-	SF	94131	14-F6
MALVINA PL			
-	SF	94108	7-A5
-	SF	94108	6-J5
MANCHESTER ST			
-	SF	94110	14-J4
MANDALAY LN			
1000	SF	94116	9-C3
MANGELS AV			
-	SF	94131	14-F6
200	SF	94127	14-F6
500	SF	94127	13-D6
MANOR CT			
-	DALY	94015	18-A3
MANOR DR			
-	SF	94127	13-C7
MANSEAU ST			
600	SF	94124	21-E1
600	SF	94124	20-E1
MANSELL ST			
-	SF	94134	20-A1
400	SF	94134	19-J1
MANSFIELD ST			
-	SF	94112	14-H7

1998 SAN FRANCISCO COUNTY STREET INDEX - With ZIP Codes

STREET
Block City ZIP Pg-Grid

MANZANITA AV
- SF 94118 6-E6
MAPLE ST
- SF 94118 5-E5
MARCELA AV
- SF 94116 9-D4
MARCY PL
- SF 94108 6-J5
MARENGO ST
- SF 94124 15-A5
MARGARET AV
- SF 94112 18-E1
MARGRAVE PL
- SF 94133 3-A4
- SF 94133 7-A4
MARIETTA DR
- SF 94127 14-E5
MARIN ST
600 SF 94124 11-C4
1400 SF 94124 15-A4
MARINA BLVD
- SF 94123 2-F3
MARINA GREEN DR
- SF 94123 2-F3
MARINE DR
- SF 94129 1-C2
- SF 94129 2-E3
MARION PL
- SF 94133 2-J4
MARIPOSA ST
400 SF 94107 11-B2
2200 SF 94110 11-A2
2700 SF 94110 10-J2
MARK LN
- SF 94108 7-A5
MARKET ST
- SF 94105 7-A6
- SF 94111 7-A6
500 SF 94104 7-A6
600 SF 94108 7-A6
600 SF 94103 7-A6
800 SF 94102 7-A6
1000 SF 94102 6-J7
1000 SF 94103 6-J7
1600 SF 94102 10-G2
1600 SF 94103 10-G2
1900 SF 94114 10-G2
3400 SF 94131 10-F4
MARLIN CT
100 SF 94124 15-D7
MARNE AV
- SF 94127 13-D5
MARS ST
- SF 94114 10-F2
MARSHALL ST
- SF 94129 2-E3
MARSILLY ST
- SF 94112 14-H6
MARSTON AV
- SF 94112 14-E7
MARTHA AV
- SF 94131 14-F6
MARTIN CT
- DALY 94014 19-J4
MARTIN ST
- DALY 94014 19-H3
MARTINEZ ST
- SF 94129 1-E4
MARTIN LUTHER KING JR DR
- SF - 9-A1
300 SF 94118 9-B1
1200 SF - 8-H1
MARVEL CT
- SF 94121 5-A6
MAR VIEW WY
- SF 94131 10-E3
MAR VISTA DR
- DALY 94014 19-F3
MARY CT
- DALY 94014 19-J3
MARY ST
- SF 94103 7-A6
MASON ST
- SF 94129 1-D3
- SF 94102 7-A4
700 SF 94108 7-A4
1300 SF 94133 7-A4
1400 SF 94133 6-J4
1700 SF 94133 2-J3
MASONIC AV
- SF 94118 6-F6
- SF 94115 6-F6
300 SF 94117 6-F6
600 SF 94117 10-F1
MASSASOIT ST
- SF 94110 15-A4
MASSET PL
- SF 94103 7-B6
MATEO ST
- SF 94131 14-G6
MATTHEW CT
- SF 94124 15-D6
MAULDIN ST
- SF 94129 1-C3
N MAYFAIR AV
- DALY 94015 18-A3
500 DALY 94015 17-J3
S MAYFAIR AV
100 DALY 94015 18-A3
700 DALY 94015 17-J4
MAYFAIR DR
- DALY 94015 18-B3
- SF 94118 6-E6
100 SF 94118 5-E6
MAYFLOWER ST
300 SF 94110 15-A5
MAYNARD ST
- SF 94112 14-G7
MAYWOOD DR
- SF 94127 13-D6
MCALLISTER ST
- SF 94102 6-F7
1000 SF 94117 6-F7
2500 SF 94117 5-E7
2600 SF 94118 5-D7
MCCANN ST
- SF 94124 16-E7
MCCARTHY AV
- SF 94134 19-J2
MCCOPPIN ST
- SF 94103 10-H1
MCCORMICK ST
- SF 94109 6-J5
MCDONALD ST
- SF 94129 1-D3
MCDOWELL AV
- SF 94123 2-G3
- SF 94129 1-C4
MCKINNON AV
1400 SF 94124 15-A5
MCLAREN AV
- SF 94121 5-A6
MCLEA CT
- SF 94103 11-A1
MCRAE ST
- SF 94129 5-E4
MEACHAM PL
- SF 94109 6-J6
MEADE AV
700 SF 94124 20-B1
MEADOWBROOK DR
- SF 94132 13-A6
MEDA AV
- SF 94112 14-F7
MELBA AV
- SF 94132 13-B6
MELRA CT
- SF 94134 19-J2
MELROSE AV
- SF 94127 14-E6
- SF 94131 14-F6
400 SF 94127 13-E6
MENDELL ST
- SF 94124 15-C6
MENDOSA AV
- SF 94116 9-C4
MERCATO CT
- SF 94131 14-F6
MERCED AV
- SF 94127 13-D4
MERCEDES WY
- SF 94127 13-C7
MERCHANT RD
- SF 94129 1-B3
MERCHANT ST
400 SF 94111 7-B5
MERCURY ST
- SF 94124 15-A6
MERLIN ST
- SF 94107 7-A7
MERRIE WY
- SF 94121 4-H6
MERRILL ST
- SF 94134 15-A6
MERRIMAC ST
- SF 94107 11-C1
MERRITT ST
- SF 94114 10-F2
MERSEY ST
- SF 94114 10-H3
MESA AV
- SF 94129 1-E4
- SF 94129 5-D4
- SF 94116 9-D4
METSON RD
- SF - 9-A1
MICHIGAN ST
800 SF 94107 11-C4
1600 SF 94124 11-C4
MIDCREST WY
- SF 94131 10-E4
100 SF 94131 14-E4
MIDDLE DR E
- SF 94118 9-D1
MIDDLE DR W
- SF - 9-A1
- SF - 8-J1
MIDDLEFIELD DR
- SF 94132 13-A6
MIDDLEPOINT RD
- SF 94124 15-D6
MIDWAY CT
- DALY 94014 19-J3
MIDWAY DR
- DALY 94014 19-J3
MIDWAY ST
- SF 94133 3-A3
MIGUEL ST
- SF 94131 14-G5
MILAN TER
- SF 94112 18-E2
- SF 94112 19-E2
MILES PL
- SF 94108 7-A5
MILES ST
- SF 94129 1-D4
MILEY ST
- SF 94123 6-F4
MILL ST
- SF 94134 20-A1
MILLER PL
- SF 94108 7-A5
MILLER RD
- SF 94129 1-C3
MILTON ST
- SF 94112 14-G6
MILTON ROSS ST
- SF 94124 15-B5
MINERVA ST
- SF 94112 18-D1
200 SF 94132 18-D1
MINNA ST
- SF 94106 7-B6
100 SF 94103 7-B6
600 SF 94103 6-J7
1000 SF 94103 10-J1
MINNESOTA ST
500 SF 94107 11-C3
MINT ST
- SF 94103 7-A6
MIRABEL AV
- SF 94110 14-J4
MIRALOMA DR
- SF 94127 13-D5
MIRAMAR AV
- SF 94112 18-D1
200 SF 94112 13-D7
MIRANDO WY
- SF 94112 14-G6
MIRA VISTA CT
- DALY 94014 19-G3
MIRIAM ST
- DALY 94014 18-C3
MISSION CIR
- DALY 94014 18-D3
MISSION ST
- SF 94105 7-A6
600 SF 94103 7-A6
1100 SF 94103 6-J7
1500 SF 94103 10-J3
2000 SF 94110 10-J3
3000 SF 94110 14-H5
3800 SF 94112 14-G7
4100 SF 94112 19-F2
5300 SF 94112 18-D3
5900 DALY 94014 18-D3
MISSION ST Rt#-82
6300 DALY 94014 18-C4
MISSION HILLS DR
- DALY 94014 19-F3
MISSION ROCK ST
- SF 94107 11-C1
MISSISSIPPI ST
- SF 94107 11-B3
MISSOURI ST
- SF 94107 11-B3
MISTRAL ST
- SF 94110 10-J2
MIZPAH ST
- SF 94131 14-F6
MODOC AV
- SF 94112 19-E1
MOFFITT ST
- SF 94131 14-G5
MOJAVE ST
- SF 94110 15-A5
- SF 94110 14-J5
MOLIMO DR
- SF 94127 14-E5
200 SF 94127 13-E5
MONCADA WY
- SF 94127 13-C6
MONETA CT
- SF 94112 19-E2
MONETA WY
- SF 94112 19-E2
- SF 94112 18-E2
MONO ST
- SF 94114 10-F3
MONTAGUE PL
- SF 94133 3-A4
MONTALVO AV
- SF 94116 13-C4
MONTANA ST
- SF 94112 18-D1
200 SF 94132 18-D1
MONTCALM ST
- SF 94110 15-A4
300 SF 94110 14-J4
MONTCLAIR TER
- SF 94109 2-J3
MONTECITO AV
- SF 94112 13-D6
MONTEREY BLVD
- SF 94131 14-E6
400 SF 94127 14-E6
400 SF 94112 14-E6
600 SF 94127 13-C6
600 SF 94112 13-D6
MONTE VISTA DR
- SF 94132 13-B6
MONTEZUMA ST
- SF 94110 14-J4
MONTGOMERY ST
- SF 94108 7-A5
- SF 94104 7-A5
- SF 94129 1-D4
500 SF 94111 7-A5
800 SF 94133 7-A4
1100 SF 94133 3-A3
1600 SF 94111 3-A3
MONTICELLO ST
- SF 94127 13-C7
- SF 94132 18-C1
MONUMENT WY
- SF 94117 10-F2
MOORE PL
- SF 94109 2-J4
MORAGA AV
- SF 94129 1-D4
- SF 94129 5-D4
MORAGA ST
200 SF 94122 9-A3
2800 SF 94122 8-H3
MORELAND ST
100 SF 94131 14-G5
MORGAN AL
- SF 94114 10-F3
- SF 94131 10-F3
MORNINGSIDE DR
- SF 94132 13-A6
- SF 94132 12-J6
MORRELL ST
- SF 94109 6-J4
300 SF 94124 16-E7
300 SF 94124 21-E1
MORRIS RD
- SF 94129 5-C4
MORRIS ST
- SF 94107 7-A7
MORSE ST
- SF 94112 19-F2
MORTON ST
700 SF 94129 5-E4
MOSCOW ST
200 SF 94112 14-H7
300 SF 94112 19-G2
MOSS ST
- SF 94103 7-A7
MOULTON ST
- SF 94123 2-G4
MOULTRIE ST
100 SF 94110 14-J6
MOUNT LN
- SF 94122 9-C3
MOUNTAIN VW
300 DALY 94014 18-D4
MOUNTAIN SPRINGS AV
- SF 94114 10-E3
- SF 94114 9-E3
MOUNT VERNON AV
- SF 94112 18-E1
100 SF 94112 19-E1
MOUNTVIEW CT
- SF 94131 14-E4
MUIR LP
- SF 94129 6-F4
MUIRWOOD DR
- DALY 94014 18-D3
MULFORD AL
- SF 94108 6-J5
MULLEN AV
- SF 94110 15-A4
200 SF 94110 14-J4
MUNICH ST
100 SF 94112 19-G1
MURRAY ST
- SF 94112 14-H6
400 SF 94110 14-H6
MUSEUM WY
- SF 94114 10-F2
MYRA WY
300 SF 94127 13-E5
400 SF 94127 14-E5
MYRTLE ST
- SF 94109 6-H6

N

NADELL CT
- SF 94112 19-F2
NAGLEE AV
- SF 94112 19-E2
NAHUA AV
- SF 94112 19-E1
NANCY LN
- DALY 94014 19-H3
NANTUCKET AV
- SF 94112 14-F7
NAPIER LN
- SF 94133 3-A3
NAPLES ST
- SF 94112 14-G7
300 SF 94112 19-G1
NAPOLEON ST
- SF 94124 15-B4
NATICK ST
- SF 94131 14-G6
NATOMA ST
- SF 94105 7-B6
400 SF 94103 7-A7
600 SF 94103 6-J7
900 SF 94103 10-J1
NAUMAN RD
- SF 94129 5-D4
NAVAJO AV
- SF 94112 19-F1
NAVY RD
- SF 94124 15-D7
NAYLOR ST
- SF 94112 19-G2
NEBRASKA ST
- SF 94110 14-J5
NELLIE ST
- SF 94114 10-H3
NELSON AV
3600 SF 94124 20-B1
NEPTUNE ST
- SF 94124 15-B6
NEVADA ST
- SF 94110 14-J6
NEWBURG ST
- SF 94131 14-G4
NEWCOMB AV
1300 SF 94124 15-A5
NEWELL ST
2100 SF 94133 2-J3
NEWHALL ST
- SF 94124 15-C5
NEWMAN ST
- SF 94110 14-H5
NEW MONTGOMERY ST
- SF 94105 7-B6
NEWTON ST
- SF 94112 19-F2
NEY ST
- SF 94112 14-G6
NIAGARA AV
- SF 94112 18-E1
- SF 94112 19-E1
NIANTIC AV
- SF 94132 18-C2
400 DALY 94014 18-C3
NIBBI CT
- SF 94134 20-B2
NICHOLS WY
- SF 94124 20-C1
NIDO AV
- SF 94115 6-F7
NIMITZ AV
600 SF 94124 16-F7
NOB HILL CIR
- SF 94108 7-A5
NOB HILL PL
- SF 94108 7-A5
NOBLES AL
- SF 94133 3-A4
NOE ST
- SF 94114 10-G2
1200 SF 94131 10-G3
1300 SF 94131 14-G5
NORDHOFF ST
- SF 94131 14-F6
NORFOLK ST
- SF 94103 10-J1
NORIEGA ST
100 SF 94122 9-A3
2700 SF 94122 8-H3
NORMANDIE TER
- SF 94115 6-F5
NORTHGATE AV
- DALY 94015 18-A3
200 DALY 94015 17-J3
NORTHGATE CT
- DALY 94015 18-A3
NORTHGATE DR
- SF 94127 13-D7
NORTH POINT ST
- SF 94133 3-A3
200 SF 94133 2-H3
700 SF 94109 2-H3
1500 SF 94123 2-F3
NORTHRIDGE RD
- SF 94124 15-D6
NORTH VIEW CT
2800 SF 94109 2-H3
NORTHWOOD DR
- SF 94112 13-D6
NORTON ST
- SF 94112 14-G7
NORWICH ST
- SF 94110 14-J4
NOTTINGHAM PL
- SF 94133 7-A4
NUEVA AV
- SF 94134 20-B2

O

OAK CT
- DALY 94014 19-H3
OAK ST
- SF 94102 6-G7
600 SF 94117 6-G7
1000 SF 94117 10-E1
2000 SF 94117 9-E1
OAKDALE AV
1000 SF 94124 15-A5
OAK GROVE ST
- SF 94107 7-A7
OAKHURST LN
- SF 94131 9-D3
OAKLAND ALAMEDA FERRY
- SF - 3-B2
- SF - 7-D4
OAKLAWN DR
- DALY 94015 18-A3
OAK PARK DR
- SF 94131 9-D3
OAKRIDGE DR
- DALY 94014 19-G3
200 SMCo 94014 19-G3
OAKWOOD ST
- SF 94110 10-H2
OCEAN AV
- SF 94112 14-F7
900 SF 94112 13-C6
1800 SF 94127 13-C6
2500 SF 94132 13-A6
4500 SF 94132 12-J6
OCTAVIA ST
- SF 94102 10-H1
100 SF 94102 6-H7
1600 SF 94109 6-H5
2600 SF 94123 6-H4
2800 SF 94123 2-H3
OFARRELL ST
- SF 94108 7-A6
200 SF 94102 7-A6
400 SF 94102 6-J6
600 SF 94109 6-J6
1500 SF 94115 6-F6
OGDEN AV
- SF 94110 14-J6
OHLONE WY
- SF 94131 14-G6
OLD CHINATOWN LN
- SF 94108 7-A5
OLD MASON ST
- SF 94129 1-D3
800 SF 94123 2-E3
800 SF 94129 2-E3
OLIVE ST
- SF 94109 6-H6
OLIVER ST
- DALY 94014 19-E3
- SF 94112 18-E2
- SF 94112 19-E3
OLMSTEAD ST
600 SF 94134 20-A1
700 SF 94134 19-J1
OLYMPIA WY
- SF 94131 9-E3
OLYMPIC WY
2100 SMCo 94015 17-J3
2200 DALY 94015 17-J3
OMAR WY
- SF 94127 14-E5
ONEIDA AV
- SF 94112 19-F1
- SF 94112 14-F7
ONIQUE LN
- SF 94131 14-F6
ONONDAGA AV
- SF 94112 14-F7
100 SF 94112 19-F1
OPAL PL
- SF 94102 7-A6
OPALO LN
- SF 94131 14-F5
OPHIR AL
- SF 94109 6-J6
ORA WY
- SF 94131 14-F5
ORANGE AL
- SF 94110 10-H4
ORBEN PL
- SF 94115 6-G5
ORD CT
- SF 94114 10-F2
ORD ST
- SF 94129 1-D4
- SF 94114 10-F2
ORDWAY ST
- SF 94134 20-A1
OREILLY AV
- SF 94129 2-E4
ORIENTE ST
- DALY 94014 19-J4
ORIOLE WY
- SF 94116 9-C3
ORIZABA AV
- SF 94132 18-D2
ORTEGA ST
- SF 94116 9-A3
- SF 94122 9-A3
2700 SF 94122 8-H3
2700 SF 94116 8-H3
ORTEGA WY
700 SF 94122 9-C3
700 SF 94116 9-C3
OSAGE AL
- SF 94110 10-J4
OSCAR AL
- SF 94105 7-B6
OSCEOLA LN
- SF 94124 15-C6
OSGOOD PL
- SF 94133 7-A4
OSHAUGHNESSY BLVD
- SF 94127 13-E4
- SF 94127 14-E5
- SF 94131 13-E4
- SF 94131 14-E5
OTEGA AV
- SF 94112 19-E1
OTIS ST
- SF 94103 10-H1
OTSEGO AV
- SF 94112 19-F1
- SF 94112 14-F7
OTTAWA AV
- SF 94112 19-E1
OTTILIA ST
300 DALY 94014 19-H3
OVERLOOK DR
- SF - 9-B1
OWEN ST
- SF 94129 1-D4
OWENS ST
- SF 94107 11-B1
OXFORD ST
- SF 94134 14-H7
500 SF 94134 19-J1

P

PACHECO ST
- SF 94127 13-D4
- SF 94116 13-D4
200 SF 94116 9-C3
3000 SF 94116 8-H4
PACIFIC AV
- SF 94129 5-C5
- SF 94111 7-A4
400 SF 94133 7-A4
1000 SF 94133 6-F5
1200 SF 94109 6-F5
2100 SF 94115 6-F5
2300 SF 94118 6-F5
2500 SF 94118 5-E6
3100 SF 94129 6-F5
W PACIFIC AV
- SF 94118 5-C5
- SF 94129 5-C5
3300 SF 94129 6-E5
3300 SF 94118 6-E5
PAGE ST
- SF 94102 6-H7
400 SF 94102 10-E1
500 SF 94117 10-E1
1900 SF 94117 9-E1
PAGODA PL
- SF 94108 7-A5
PALACE DR
- SF 94123 2-E3
- SF 94129 2-E3
PALM AV
- SF 94118 5-D6
PALMCREST DR
100 DALY 94015 18-B4
PALMETTO AV
200 SF 94132 18-C2
PALO ALTO AV
- SF 94131 10-E3
200 SF 94114 10-E3
200 SF 94114 9-E3
200 SF 94131 9-E3
PALOMA AV
- SF 94127 13-C6
PALOS PL
- SF 94132 13-A6
PALOU AV
900 SF 94124 15-A5
PANAMA ST
100 SF 94132 18-C2
PANORAMA DR
- SF 94131 9-E3
100 SF 94131 10-E3
500 SF 94131 14-E4
PANTON AL
- SF 94109 6-J5
PARADISE AV
- SF 94131 14-F6
PARAISO PL
- SF 94132 13-B6
PARAMOUNT TER
- SF 94118 5-E7
PARDEE AL
- SF 94133 3-A4
PARIS ST
200 SF 94112 14-G7
400 SF 94112 19-F1
PARK AL
300 SF 94127 13-D5
S PARK AV
- SF 94107 7-B7
PARK BLVD
- SF 94129 1-C4
- SF 94129 5-C5
PARK ST
- SF 94110 14-H6
PARKER AV
- SF 94118 5-E6
500 SF 94117 5-E6
PARK HILL AV
- SF 94117 10-F1
PARKHURST AL
- SF 94108 7-A5
PARK PLAZA DR
- DALY 94015 18-B3
PARKRIDGE DR
- SF 94131 10-F3
PARKSIDE AV
- DALY 94015 18-A3
PARKVIEW AV
- DALY 94014 18-C3
N PARKVIEW AV
200 DALY 94014 18-C3
S PARKVIEW AV
- DALY 94014 18-C3
PARKWOOD DR
- DALY 94015 18-B3
PARNASSUS AV
- SF 94117 10-E2
100 SF 94117 9-E2
300 SF 94143 9-E2
500 SF 94122 9-E2
PARQUE DR
100 SF 94134 19-H2
PARSONS ST
- SF 94118 5-E7
PARTRIDGE AV
100 DALY 94014 19-J3
PARTRIDGE LN
- DALY 94014 19-E3
PASADENA ST
- DALY 94014 19-H2
- SF 94134 19-H2
PATTEN RD
- SF 94129 1-C4
PATTERSON ST
- SF 94124 15-A5
PATTON ST
- SF 94110 14-H5
PAUL AV
- SF 94124 20-B1
200 SF 94124 15-B7
500 SF 94134 15-B7
PAULDING ST
- SF 94131 14-F7
- SF 94112 14-F7
PAYSON ST
- SF 94132 18-C2
PEABODY ST
- SF 94134 20-A2
PEARCE ST
- SF 94129 1-D3
PEARL ST
- SF 94103 10-H1
PEDESTRIAN WY
- SF 94123 2-F3
PELTON PL
- SF 94133 7-A4
PEMBERTON PL
- SF 94114 10-E3
PENA ST
- SF 94129 1-D4
- SF 94129 5-D4
PENINSULA AV
200 SF 94134 20-A2
PENNINGTON ST
- SF 94129 1-D3
PENNSYLVANIA AV
100 SF 94107 11-B3
PENNY LN
- SF 94131 14-G6
PEORIA ST
- DALY 94014 18-D3

1998 SAN FRANCISCO COUNTY STREET INDEX - With ZIP Codes

STREET Block	City	ZIP	Pg-Grid
PERALTA AV			
-	SF	94110	15-A4
900	SF	94110	14-J6
PEREGO TER			
-	SF	94131	10-F4
PERINE PL			
-	SF	94115	6-G5
PERRY ST			
-	SF	94107	7-B6
PERSHING DR			
1500	SF	94129	5-B5
PERSIA AV			
-	SF	94112	14-G7
200	SF	94112	19-G1
900	SF	94134	19-G1
PERU AV			
100	SF	94112	14-G7
700	SF	94134	14-G7
PETERS AV			
-	SF	94110	14-H4
PETER YORKE WY			
-	SF	94109	6-H6
PETRARCH PL			
-	SF	94104	7-B5
PFEIFFER ST			
-	SF	94133	3-A3
PHELAN AV			
-	SF	94112	13-E7
PHELPS ST			
200	SF	94124	15-B6
PHOENIX TER			
-	SF	94133	6-J4
PICO AV			
-	SF	94127	13-D7
PIEDMONT ST			
-	SF	94117	10-F2
PIERCE ST			
-	SF	94117	10-G1
300	SF	94117	6-G7
1000	SF	94115	6-G5
2700	SF	94123	6-G4
3100	SF	94123	2-F3
PILGRIM AV			
-	SF	94112	14-F7
PINAR LN			
-	SF	94115	6-F7
PINE CT			
-	DALY	94014	19-H3
PINE ST			
-	SF	94111	7-A5
200	SF	94104	7-A5
500	SF	94108	7-A5
900	SF	94108	6-F6
1100	SF	94109	6-F6
2000	SF	94115	6-F6
PINEHURST WY			
-	SF	94127	13-C7
PINK AL			
-	SF	94103	10-H1
PINO AL			
-	SF	94122	8-J2
PINTO AV			
-	SF	94132	18-A1
PIOCHE ST			
100	SF	94134	14-H7
PIPER LP			
-	SF	94129	5-D4
PIXLEY ST			
-	SF	94123	2-G4
-	SF	94123	6-G4
PIZARRO WY			
-	SF	94112	13-D6
PLAZA ST			
-	SF	94116	9-D4
PLEASANT ST			
-	SF	94108	6-J5
PLUM ST			
-	SF	94103	10-J1
PLYMOUTH AV			
-	SF	94112	18-D1
1100	SF	94112	13-D7
1600	SF	94127	13-D6
POINTE PACIFIC DR			
700	DALY	94014	18-D3
POINT LOBOS AV			
-	SF	94121	4-H6
POLARIS WY			
200	DALY	94014	19-F2
200	SF	94112	19-F2
POLK ST			
-	SF	94102	6-H4
700	SF	94109	6-H4
2400	SF	94109	2-H3

STREET Block	City	ZIP	Pg-Grid
POLLARD PL			
-	SF	94133	3-A4
-	SF	94133	7-A4
POMONA ST			
-	SF	94124	15-B6
PONCETTA DR			
-	DALY	94015	18-B3
POND ST			
-	SF	94114	10-G2
POPE RD			
-	SF	94123	2-H3
POPE ST			
-	DALY	94014	19-F2
-	SF	94129	1-C4
-	SF	94112	19-F2
POPLAR ST			
-	SF	94110	10-H4
POPPY LN			
-	SF	94131	14-G5
W PORTAL AV			
-	SF	94127	13-C5
300	SF	94132	13-C5
PORTAL PTH			
-	SF	94127	13-C5
PORTER ST			
-	SF	94110	14-J6
PORTOLA DR			
-	SF	94114	14-E4
-	SF	94114	10-F4
-	SF	94131	14-E4
-	SF	94131	10-F4
400	SF	94131	13-C5
500	SF	94127	13-C5
PORTOLA ST			
700	SF	94129	5-E4
POST ST			
-	SF	94108	7-A6
-	SF	94104	7-A6
400	SF	94102	7-A6
500	SF	94102	6-F6
600	SF	94109	6-F6
1600	SF	94115	6-F6
POTOMAC ST			
-	SF	94117	10-G1
POTRERO AV			
-	SF	94103	11-A4
400	SF	94110	11-A4
POWELL ST			
-	SF	94102	7-A4
100	SF	94108	7-A4
1200	SF	94133	7-A4
1500	SF	94133	3-A3
2300	SF	94133	2-J3
POWERS AV			
-	SF	94110	14-H4
POWHATTAN AV			
300	SF	94110	14-J5
1000	SF	94110	15-A5
PRADO ST			
-	SF	94123	2-F3
PRAGUE ST			
-	SF	94112	19-G1
PRATT PL			
-	SF	94108	7-A5
PRECITA AV			
-	SF	94110	14-J4
500	SF	94110	15-A4
PRENTISS ST			
-	SF	94110	14-J6
PRESCOTT CT			
-	SF	94133	7-A4
PRESIDIO AV			
-	SF	94115	6-F5
PRESIDIO BLVD			
-	SF	94129	5-E4
-	SF	94129	6-E4
-	SF	94129	1-E4
100	SF	94129	2-E4
PRESIDIO BLVD Rt#-1			
-	SF	-	5-C7
-	SF	94118	5-C7
PRESIDIO TER			
-	SF	94118	5-D5
PRETOR WY			
-	SF	94112	19-F2
PRICE RW			
-	SF	94133	3-A4
PRIEST ST			
-	SF	94109	6-J5
PRINCETON ST			
-	SF	94134	14-J7
PROGRESS ST			
-	SF	94124	15-C6

STREET Block	City	ZIP	Pg-Grid
PROSPECT AV			
-	SF	94110	14-H5
PROSPER ST			
-	SF	94114	10-G2
PUEBLO ST			
-	DALY	94014	19-J2
100	SF	94134	19-J2
PUTNAM ST			
-	SF	94110	14-J6
Q			
QUANE ST			
-	SF	94110	10-H3
QUARRY RD			
-	SF	94129	5-D5
QUARTZ WY			
-	SF	94131	14-F4
QUESADA AV			
1000	SF	94124	15-B5
QUICKSTEP LN			
-	SF	94115	6-E5
QUINCY ST			
-	SF	94108	7-A5
QUINT ST			
-	SF	94124	15-B5
QUINTARA ST			
-	SF	94116	9-A4
2500	SF	94116	8-H4
R			
RACCOON DR			
-	SF	94114	10-F3
RACINE LN			
-	SF	94134	20-A2
RADIO TER			
-	SF	94116	9-C3
RAE AV			
-	SF	94112	19-E2
RALEIGH ST			
-	SF	94112	14-F7
RALSTON AV			
-	SF	94129	1-C3
RALSTON ST			
-	SF	94132	18-C1
RAMONA ST			
-	SF	94103	10-H1
RAMPART WY			
-	DALY	94014	19-E3
RAMSEL CT			
-	SF	94129	1-C3
RAMSELL ST			
-	SF	94132	18-C1
RANDALL ST			
-	SF	94110	14-H5
-	SF	94131	14-G5
RANDOLPH ST			
-	SF	94132	18-C2
RANKIN ST			
-	SF	94124	15-B5
RAUSCH ST			
-	SF	94103	7-A7
RAVENWOOD DR			
-	SF	94127	13-D6
RAVILLA CT			
-	DALY	94014	19-E2
RAWLES ST			
-	SF	94129	6-E4
RAYBURN ST			
-	SF	94114	10-G3
RAYCLIFF TER			
-	SF	94115	6-F5
RAYMOND AV			
-	SF	94134	19-J2
200	SF	94134	20-A2
REARDON RD			
-	SF	94124	15-D7
REBECCA LN			
-	SF	94124	15-C6
REDDY ST			
-	SF	94124	15-B7
REDFIELD AL			
-	SF	94133	2-J4
RED LEAF CT			
-	DALY	94014	19-G3
REDONDO ST			
-	SF	94124	20-B1
RED ROCK WY			
-	SF	94131	14-F4
REDWOOD ST			
100	SF	94102	6-H7
REED ST			
-	SF	94109	6-J5

STREET Block	City	ZIP	Pg-Grid
REGENT ST			
-	SF	94112	18-D2
REPOSA WY			
-	SF	94127	14-E5
RESERVOIR ST			
-	SF	94114	10-H1
RESERVOIR HILL DR			
-	DALY	94014	18-E4
RESTANI WY			
-	SF	94112	19-F1
RETIRO WY			
-	SF	94123	2-G3
REUEL CT			
-	SF	94124	15-C6
REVERE AV			
1000	SF	94124	15-B6
REX AV			
-	SF	94127	13-D5
REY ST			
-	SF	94134	19-J2
REYNOLDS ST			
-	DALY	94014	19-H3
RHINE ST			
-	SF	94112	18-D2
200	DALY	94014	18-D2
RHODE ISLAND ST			
-	SF	94103	11-A2
400	SF	94107	11-A3
RICE ST			
-	DALY	94014	18-D2
-	SF	94112	18-D2
RICHARD HENREY DANA PL			
-	SF	94133	2-J3
RICHARDS CIR			
-	SF	94124	15-C6
RICHARDSON AV U.S.-101			
-	SF	94123	2-E3
100	SF	94129	2-E3
RICHLAND AV			
-	SF	94110	14-H6
RICKARD ST			
-	SF	94134	15-A6
RICO WY			
-	SF	94123	2-F3
RIDGE CT			
1200	SF	94134	19-H2
RIDGE LN			
-	SF	94112	18-E1
100	SF	94112	19-E1
RIDGEWOOD AV			
-	SF	94112	13-E6
200	SF	94127	13-E6
RILEY AV			
100	SF	94129	1-D4
RINCON ST			
100	SF	94107	7-C6
RINGOLD ST			
-	SF	94103	7-A7
RIO CT			
-	SF	94127	14-F5
RIO VERDE ST			
-	SF	94134	19-H3
-	DALY	94014	19-H3
RIPLEY ST			
-	SF	94110	15-A5
-	SF	94110	14-J5
RISEL AV			
-	DALY	94014	18-E3
-	DALY	94014	19-E3
RITCH ST			
200	SF	94107	7-B7
RIVAS AV			
-	SF	94132	18-B1
RIVERA ST			
300	SF	94116	13-B4
2400	SF	94116	12-H4
RIVERTON DR			
-	SF	94132	13-A6
RIVOLI ST			
-	SF	94117	10-E2
200	SF	94117	9-E2
RIZAL ST			
-	SF	94107	7-B6
ROACH ST			
-	SF	94133	2-J4
ROANOKE ST			
-	SF	94131	14-G6
ROBBLEE AV			
-	SF	94124	15-B6
ROBERT KIRK LN			
-	SF	94108	7-A5

STREET Block	City	ZIP	Pg-Grid
ROBINHOOD DR			
-	SF	94127	13-D5
ROBINSON DR			
-	SF	94112	19-G2
-	DALY	94014	19-G2
ROBINSON ST			
-	SF	94124	16-E7
ROCK AL			
-	SF	94127	13-D5
ROCKAWAY AV			
-	SF	94127	13-D5
ROCKDALE DR			
500	SF	94127	13-E5
500	SF	94127	14-E5
ROCKLAND ST			
-	SF	94109	6-H4
ROCKRIDGE DR			
-	SF	94116	9-C4
ROCKWOOD CT			
-	SF	94127	13-D5
ROD RD			
-	SF	94129	1-C3
RODGERS ST			
-	SF	94103	7-A7
RODRIGUEZ ST			
700	SF	94129	5-E4
ROEMER WY			
-	SF	94112	19-E2
ROLPH ST			
-	SF	94112	19-F2
ROMAIN ST			
-	SF	94114	10-F3
200	SF	94131	10-F3
ROME ST			
-	SF	94112	19-E1
ROMOLO ST			
-	SF	94133	7-A4
RONDEL PL			
-	SF	94110	10-H2
ROOSEVELT AV			
-	DALY	94014	18-E3
ROOSEVELT WY			
-	SF	94117	10-F2
-	SF	94114	10-F2
ROSCOE ST			
-	SF	94110	14-H6
ROSE ST			
-	SF	94102	6-H7
-	SF	94102	10-H1
ROSELLA CT			
-	SF	94112	19-F1
ROSELYN TER			
-	SF	94118	6-E7
ROSEMARY CT			
-	SF	94116	13-B5
ROSEMONT PL			
-	SF	94103	10-H1
ROSENKRANZ ST			
-	SF	94110	14-J5
ROSEWOOD DR			
-	SF	94127	13-D6
ROSIE LEE LN			
-	SF	94124	15-D6
ROSS AL			
-	SF	94108	7-A4
ROSSI AV			
-	SF	94118	5-E7
ROSSMOOR DR			
-	SF	94132	13-B6
ROTTECK ST			
-	SF	94112	14-G6
ROUSSEAU ST			
-	SF	94112	14-G6
ROWLAND ST			
-	SF	94133	7-A4
ROYAL LN			
-	SF	94112	19-F2
RUCKMAN AV			
1200	SF	94129	1-C3
RUDDEN AV			
-	SF	94112	14-F7
RUGER ST			
-	SF	94129	6-F4
RUSS ST			
-	SF	94103	7-A7
RUSSELL ST			
-	SF	94109	6-J4
RUSSIA AV			
-	SF	94112	19-G1
RUSSIAN HILL PL			
-	SF	94133	6-J4
RUTH ST			
-	SF	94112	14-F7

STREET Block	City	ZIP	Pg-Grid
RUTLAND ST			
-	SF	94134	20-A2
500	DALY	94014	20-A3
500	DALY	94014	19-J3
RUTLEDGE ST			
-	SF	94110	15-A4
300	SF	94110	14-J4
S			
SABIN PL			
-	SF	94108	7-A5
SACRAMENTO ST			
100	SF	94111	7-A5
400	SF	94104	7-A5
700	SF	94108	7-A5
1100	SF	94108	6-E5
1300	SF	94109	6-E5
2200	SF	94115	6-E5
3400	SF	94118	6-E5
3600	SF	94118	5-D6
SADDLEBACK DR			
-	DALY	94014	19-G2
-	SF	94134	19-H2
SADOWA ST			
-	SF	94112	18-D2
200	SF	94132	18-D2
SAFFOLD AV			
-	SF	94129	1-B4
SAFIRA LN			
-	SF	94131	14-F4
SAGAMORE ST			
200	SF	94112	18-D2
200	SF	94132	18-D2
SAINT CHARLES AV			
-	SF	94132	18-C2
SAINT CROIX DR			
-	SF	94127	13-E5
SAINT ELMO WY			
-	SF	94127	13-D6
SAINT FRANCIS BLVD			
-	SF	94127	13-C6
SAINT FRANCIS PL			
-	SF	94107	7-B6
SAINT GEORGE AL			
-	SF	94108	7-A5
SAINT GERMAIN AV			
-	SF	94114	10-E3
100	SF	94114	9-E3
SAINT JAMES AL			
-	SF	94108	7-A4
100	SF	94133	7-A4
SAINT JOSEPHS AV			
-	SF	94115	6-F6
SAINT LOUIS AL			
-	SF	94108	7-A4
SAINT MARYS AV			
-	SF	94112	14-H6
100	SF	94131	14-H6
SAINT TENNY PL			
-	SF	94105	7-B6
SAL ST			
-	SF	94129	1-D4
SALA TER			
-	SF	94112	19-E2
SALINAS AV			
100	SF	94124	20-B1
SALMON ST			
-	SF	94133	6-J4
SAMOSET ST			
-	SF	94110	15-A5
SAN ALESO AV			
-	SF	94127	13-C6
SAN ANDREAS WY			
-	SF	94127	13-D6
SAN ANSELMO AV			
-	SF	94127	13-C5
SAN ANTONIO CIR			
-	DALY	94014	19-F3
SAN ANTONIO PL			
-	SF	94133	3-A4
-	SF	94133	7-A4
SAN BENITO WY			
-	SF	94127	13-C6
SAN BRUNO AV			
-	SF	94103	11-A2
400	SF	94110	11-A3
500	SF	94107	11-A2
2100	SF	94110	15-A7
2100	SF	94134	15-A7
3100	SF	94134	20-A1
SAN BUENAVENTURA WY			
-	SF	94127	13-C6

STREET Block	City	ZIP	Pg-Grid
SAN CARLOS ST			
-	SF	94110	10-H3
SANCHES ST			
-	SF	94129	5-E4
-	SF	94129	6-E5
SANCHEZ ST			
-	SF	94114	10-G1
1200	SF	94131	10-G4
1300	SF	94131	14-G5
SAN DIEGO AV			
-	SF	94112	18-C3
100	DALY	94014	18-C3
SAN FELIPE AV			
-	SF	94127	13-D6
SAN FERNANDO WY			
-	SF	94127	13-C6
SAN GABRIEL AV			
-	SF	94112	14-F7
SAN GABRIL CIR			
-	DALY	94014	19-F3
SAN GABRIL CT			
-	DALY	94014	19-F3
SAN JACINTO WY			
-	SF	94127	13-D6
SAN JOSE AV			
-	SF	94110	10-H4
-	SF	94110	14-H4
200	SF	94131	14-G6
600	SF	94112	14-F7
2200	SF	94112	19-E1
2400	SF	94112	18-D2
3200	DALY	94014	18-D3
SAN JUAN AV			
-	SF	94112	14-F7
SAN LEANDRO WY			
-	SF	94127	13-C6
SAN LORENZO WY			
-	SF	94127	13-D5
SAN LUIS CIR			
-	DALY	94014	19-F3
SAN LUIS CT			
-	DALY	94014	19-F3
SAN MARCOS AV			
-	SF	94116	13-C4
SAN MIGUEL ST			
300	SF	94112	19-E1
SAN PABLO AV			
-	SF	94127	13-D5
SAN RAFAEL WY			
-	SF	94127	13-C6
SAN RAMON WY			
100	SF	94112	13-D7
SANSOME ST			
-	SF	94104	7-B4
400	SF	94111	7-B4
700	SF	94133	7-B4
900	SF	94111	3-A4
900	SF	94133	3-A4
SANTA ANA AV			
-	SF	94127	13-C6
SANTA BARBARA AV			
-	SF	94112	18-C2
-	DALY	94014	18-C3
SANTA CLARA AV			
-	SF	94127	13-C6
SANTA CLARA CT			
-	DALY	94014	19-F3
SANTA CRUZ AV			
-	DALY	94014	18-C2
-	SF	94112	18-C2
SANTA FE AV			
-	SF	94124	15-A6
SANTA MARINA ST			
-	SF	94110	14-H5
SANTA MONICA WY			
-	SF	94127	13-C5
SANTA PAULA AV			
-	SF	94127	13-D5
SANTA RITA AV			
-	SF	94116	9-D4
-	SF	94116	13-C4
SANTA ROSA AV			
-	SF	94112	14-F7
SANTA YNEZ AV			
-	SF	94112	14-F7
SANTA YSABEL AV			
-	SF	94112	14-F7
SANTIAGO ST			
200	SF	94116	13-A4
2300	SF	94116	12-H4
SANTOS ST			
-	SF	94134	19-H3
200	DALY	94014	19-H3

STREET Block	City	ZIP	Pg-Grid
SARGENT ST			
-	SF	94132	18-C1
SATURN ST			
-	SF	94114	10-F2
SAUSALITO FERRY			
-	SF	-	3-B1
-	SF	-	7-C4
SAUSALITO TIBURON FERRY			
-	SF	-	2-H1
SAWYER ST			
200	SF	94134	19-J2
SCENIC WY			
-	DALY	94014	18-E3
-	DALY	94014	19-E3
-	SF	94121	5-A5
SCHOFIELD RD			
-	SF	94123	2-H3
-	SF	94129	1-C4
SCHOOL AL			
100	SF	94133	3-A4
SCHWERIN ST			
-	SF	94134	19-J4
300	DALY	94014	19-J4
SCOTIA AV			
-	SF	94124	15-A6
SCOTLAND ST			
-	SF	94133	2-J4
SCOTT ST			
-	SF	94117	10-G1
300	SF	94117	6-G6
1000	SF	94115	6-G6
2700	SF	94123	6-F4
3100	SF	94123	2-F3
SEA CLIFF AV			
-	SF	94121	5-A5
SEAL ROCK DR			
-	SF	94121	4-H6
SEARS ST			
-	SF	94112	18-D2
SEAVIEW TER			
-	SF	94121	5-A6
SECURITY PAC PL			
-	SF	94108	7-A6
SELBY ST			
300	SF	94124	15-B5
SELMA WY			
-	SF	94122	9-C3
SEMINOLE AV			
-	SF	94112	19-F1
SENECA AV			
-	SF	94112	19-F1
SEQUOIA WY			
-	SF	94127	14-E5
SERGEANT MITCHELL ST			
-	SF	94129	1-E3
SERPENTINE AV			
-	SF	94110	11-A4
SERRANO DR			
-	SF	94132	18-B1
SERVICE ST			
2200	SF	94123	2-G4
SEVERN ST			
-	SF	94114	10-H3
SEVILLE ST			
-	SF	94112	19-F2
SEWARD ST			
-	SF	94114	10-F3
SEYMOUR ST			
-	SF	94115	6-G7
SHAFTER AV			
1000	SF	94124	15-A5
SHAFTER RD			
-	SF	94129	6-E4
SHAKESPEARE ST			
-	DALY	94014	18-C2
100	SF	94112	18-C2
SHANGRILA WY			
-	SF	94127	13-D5
SHANNON ST			
-	SF	94102	6-J6
SHARON CT			
-	DALY	94014	19-H3
SHARON ST			
-	SF	94114	10-G2
SHARP PL			
-	SF	94109	2-J4
-	SF	94109	6-J4
SHAW ST			
-	SF	94105	7-B5
SHAWNEE AV			
-	SF	94112	19-E1
SHEFFIELD DR			
-	DALY	94015	18-B3

STREET Block	City	ZIP	Pg-Grid
SHELDON TER			
-	SF	94122	9-C3
SHEPHARD PL			
-	SF	94108	7-A5
SHERIDAN AV			
-	SF	94129	1-D4
SHERIDAN ST			
-	SF	94103	10-J1
SHERMAN RD			
-	SF	94129	6-E4
SHERMAN ST			
-	SF	94103	7-A7
SHERWOOD CT			
-	SF	94127	13-E6
SHIELDS ST			
-	SF	94132	18-C1
SHIPLEY ST			
100	SF	94107	7-A7
SHORE VIEW AV			
-	SF	94121	4-J6
SHORT ST			
-	SF	94114	10-F3
SHOTWELL ST			
-	SF	94103	10-J3
200	SF	94110	10-J3
1200	SF	94110	14-J4
SHRADER ST			
-	SF	94117	5-E7
200	SF	94117	9-E1
400	SF	94117	10-E1
SIBERT LP			
-	SF	94129	5-D4
SIBLEY RD			
700	SF	94129	6-E4
SICKLES AV			
100	SF	94112	18-E2
SIERRA ST			
-	SF	94107	11-B3
SILLIMAN ST			
-	SF	94134	15-A6
400	SF	94134	14-H7
SILVER AV			
200	SF	94112	14-G7
600	SF	94134	14-G7
1200	SF	94134	15-A6
1600	SF	94124	15-A6
SILVERVIEW DR			
-	SF	94124	15-B6
SIMONDS LP			
-	SF	94129	6-E4
SKYLINE BLVD Rt#-35			
-	DALY	94015	17-J3
-	SF	94132	12-H6
-	SF	94132	17-J1
2100	SMCo	94015	17-J3
SKYVIEW WY			
-	SF	94131	10-E4
SLOAN AL			
-	SF	94105	7-B5
SLOAT BLVD			
-	SF	94132	13-A6
1600	SF	94132	12-J6
2300	SF	94116	12-H6
SOLA AV			
-	SF	94116	9-D4
SOMERSET ST			
-	SF	94134	15-A6
-	SF	94134	20-A1
SONOMA ST			
-	SF	94133	3-A4
SOTELO AV			
-	SF	94116	9-D4
SOUTHARD PL			
-	SF	94109	2-J4
SOUTHERN FRWY I-280			
-	DALY	-	18-C4
-	SF	-	15-B4
-	SF	-	7-C7
-	SF	-	11-B1
-	SF	-	14-E7
-	SF	-	19-E1
-	SF	-	18-D2
SOUTHERN HEIGHTS AV			
-	SF	94107	11-A3
SOUTHGATE AV			
-	DALY	94015	18-A4
400	DALY	94015	17-J4
SOUTH HILL CT			
200	DALY	94014	19-F3
SOUTHRIDGE WY			
-	DALY	94014	19-G3
SOUTHWOOD DR			
-	SF	94112	13-D7

SAN FRANCISCO

INDEX

STREET Block	City	ZIP	Pg-Grid
SPARROW ST			
-	SF	94103	10-H2
SPARTA ST			
-	SF	94134	20-A1
SPEAR AV			
600	SF	94124	16-E7
900	SF	94124	15-D7
1000	SF	94124	20-D1
SPEAR ST			
-	SF	94105	7-B5
SPENCER ST			
-	SF	94103	10-H2
SPOFFORD LN			
-	SF	94108	7-A5
SPRECKLES LAKE DR			
-	SF	-	9-A1
-	SF	-	8-J1
SPRING ST			
100	SF	94104	7-A5
SPRINGFIELD DR			
-	SF	94132	13-A6
SPROULE LN			
-	SF	94108	6-J5
SPRUCE ST			
-	SF	94118	5-E5
STANDISH AV			
-	SF	94131	14-F7
-	SF	94112	14-F7
STANFORD ST			
-	SF	94107	7-C7
STANFORD HEIGHTS AV			
-	SF	94127	14-E6
STANLEY ST			
-	SF	94132	18-C2
STANTON ST			
-	SF	94114	10-F3
STANYAN ST			
-	SF	94117	5-E6
-	SF	94118	5-E6
100	SF	94117	9-E1
1200	SF	94117	10-E2
STAPLES AV			
-	SF	94131	14-F7
100	SF	94112	14-F7
300	SF	94112	13-E7
STARK ST			
-	SF	94133	7-A4
STARR KING WY			
-	SF	94109	6-H6
STARVIEW WY			
-	SF	94131	9-E4
STATE DR			
-	SF	94132	13-A7
STATES ST			
-	SF	94114	10-F2
STEINER ST			
-	SF	94117	10-G1
400	SF	94117	6-G6
1100	SF	94115	6-G6
2800	SF	94123	6-G4
3100	SF	94123	2-G4
STERLING ST			
-	SF	94107	7-B6
STEUART ST			
-	SF	94111	7-C5
-	SF	94105	7-C5
STEVELOE PL			
-	SF	94102	6-J6
STEVENS AL			
-	SF	94111	7-B4
STEVENSON ST			
-	SF	94105	7-B5
100	SF	94103	7-A6
500	SF	94103	6-J7
1300	SF	94103	10-H1
STILL ST			
-	SF	94112	14-G6
STILLINGS AV			
-	SF	94131	14-F6
STILLMAN ST			
-	SF	94107	7-B7
STILLWELL DR			
1500	SF	94129	5-B5
STOCKTON ST			
-	SF	94102	7-A4
-	SF	94108	7-A4
1100	SF	94133	7-A4
1400	SF	94133	3-A3
STONE ST			
-	SF	94129	1-C3
-	SF	94108	7-A5
STONECREST DR			
-	SF	94132	13-B7
STONEMAN ST			
-	SF	94110	14-J4
STONEYBROOK AV			
-	SF	94112	14-H7
STONEYFORD AV			
-	SF	94112	14-H7
STOREY AV			
1200	SF	94129	1-C3
STORRIE ST			
-	SF	94114	10-F2
STOW LAKE DR			
-	SF	-	9-B1
STOW LAKE DR E			
-	SF	-	9-B1
STRATFORD DR			
-	SF	94132	13-B7
100	SF	94132	18-B1
SUMMIT ST			
-	SF	94112	18-E1
SUMNER ST			
-	SF	94129	1-E4
-	SF	94129	2-E4
-	SF	94129	5-E4
-	SF	94129	6-E4
-	SF	94103	7-A7
SUNBEAM LN			
-	SF	94112	19-F1
SUNGLOW LN			
-	SF	94112	14-H7
SUNNYDALE AV			
-	SF	94134	20-A2
400	SF	94134	19-H2
2200	SF	94112	19-H2
SUNNYSIDE TER			
-	SF	94112	14-E7
SUNRISE WY			
300	SF	94134	19-J2
SUNSET BLVD			
-	SF	94116	8-J3
-	SF	94116	12-J5
-	SF	94122	8-J3
1800	SF	94132	12-J5
SUNVIEW DR			
-	SF	94131	14-F4
SURREY ST			
-	SF	94131	14-F6
SUSSEX ST			
-	SF	94131	14-F5
SUTRO HEIGHTS AV			
-	SF	94121	4-H7
SUTTER ST			
-	SF	94104	7-A5
100	SF	94108	7-A5
500	SF	94102	7-A5
600	SF	94102	6-F6
700	SF	94109	6-F6
1700	SF	94115	6-F6
SWEENY ST			
-	SF	94134	15-A6
200	SF	94134	14-J6
SWISS AV			
-	SF	94131	14-F5
SYCAMORE ST			
-	SF	94110	10-H2
SYDNEY WY			
-	SF	94127	13-E4
SYLVAN DR			
-	SF	94132	13-A6

T

STREET Block	City	ZIP	Pg-Grid
TABER PL			
-	SF	94107	7-B7
TACOMA ST			
-	SF	94118	5-C6
TALBERT CT			
-	SF	94134	20-A2
TALBERT ST			
-	SF	94134	20-A3
200	DALY	94014	20-A3
400	DALY	94014	19-J3
TALLWOOD DR			
100	DALY	94014	18-D4
TAMALPAIS TER			
-	SF	94118	6-E7
TAMPA LN			
-	SF	94124	15-B6
TANDANG SORA			
-	SF	94107	7-B6
TAPIA DR			
-	SF	94132	13-B7
-	SF	94132	18-B1
TARA ST			
100	SF	94112	18-E1
TARA ST			
100	SF	94112	19-E1
TARAVAL ST			
-	SF	94127	13-A5
-	SF	94116	13-A5
2400	SF	94116	12-H5
TAYLOR RD			
-	SF	94129	1-D4
TAYLOR ST			
-	SF	94102	7-A6
400	SF	94102	6-J5
600	SF	94109	6-J5
800	SF	94108	6-J5
1400	SF	94133	6-J4
1800	SF	94133	2-J3
S TEA GARDEN DR			
-	SF	94118	9-C1
TEDDY AV			
-	SF	94134	19-J2
-	SF	94134	20-A2
TEHAMA ST			
-	SF	94105	7-B6
300	SF	94103	7-A7
700	SF	94103	6-J7
TELEGRAPH PL			
-	SF	94133	3-A3
TELEGRAPH HILL BLVD			
-	SF	94133	3-A3
TEMESCAL TER			
-	SF	94118	5-E7
TEMPLE ST			
-	SF	94114	10-F2
TEMPLETON AV			
-	DALY	94014	18-E3
TENNESSEE ST			
600	SF	94107	11-C4
1700	SF	94124	11-C4
1800	SF	94124	15-C4
TERESITA BLVD			
-	SF	94127	13-E4
200	SF	94127	14-E5
600	SF	94131	14-E5
TERRACE AV			
-	DALY	94015	18-A4
TERRACE DR			
-	SF	94127	13-C5
TERRACE WK			
200	SF	94127	13-D6
TERRA VISTA AV			
-	SF	94115	6-F6
TERRY A FRANCOIS BLVD			
-	SF	94107	7-C7
100	SF	94107	11-C2
TEXAS ST			
100	SF	94107	11-B3
THE EMBARCADERO			
-	SF	94105	7-C6
-	SF	94107	7-C6
100	SF	94111	7-C6
500	SF	94111	3-A3
1300	SF	94133	3-A3
1600	SF	94133	2-J3
THERESA ST			
-	SF	94112	14-G6
THETA AV			
-	DALY	94014	18-C3
THIERS ST			
-	DALY	94014	18-C4
THOMAS AV			
-	SF	94129	5-D4
1200	SF	94124	15-A6
THOMAS MELLON DR			
-	SF	94134	20-B2
THOMAS MORE WY			
-	SF	94132	18-B2
THOR AV			
-	SF	94131	14-G6
THORNBURG RD			
-	SF	94129	2-E3
THORNTON AV			
-	SF	94124	15-B6
THORP LN			
-	SF	94114	10-F2
THRIFT ST			
-	SF	94112	18-D1
200	SF	94132	18-D1
TIFFANY AV			
-	SF	94110	14-H4
TILLMAN PL			
-	SF	94108	7-A5
TINGLEY ST			
-	SF	94112	14-G6
TIOGA AV			
-	SF	94134	20-A1
TOCOLOMA AV			
100	SF	94134	20-B2
TODD ST			
-	SF	94129	1-C4
TOLAND ST			
-	SF	94124	15-B5
TOLEDO WY			
-	SF	94123	2-G4
TOMASO CT			
-	SF	94134	19-J2
TOMPKINS AV			
-	SF	94110	14-J6
1000	SF	94110	15-A6
TOPAZ WY			
-	SF	94131	14-G5
TOPEKA AV			
-	SF	94124	15-B6
TORNEY AV			
-	SF	94129	2-E4
TORRENS CT			
-	SF	94109	6-J5
TOUCHARD ST			
-	SF	94109	6-J5
TOWNSEND ST			
-	SF	94107	7-B7
400	SF	94107	11-A1
600	SF	94103	11-A1
TOYON LN			
-	SF	94112	19-G2
TRACY PL			
-	SF	94133	7-A4
TRAINOR ST			
-	SF	94103	10-J1
TRANSVERSE DR			
-	SF	-	9-B1
TREASURY PL			
-	SF	94104	7-B5
TREAT AV			
200	SF	94103	10-J2
400	SF	94110	10-J2
1500	SF	94110	14-J4
TREE VIEW DR			
200	DALY	94014	19-E3
TRENTON ST			
-	SF	94108	7-A5
TRINITY ST			
-	SF	94104	7-A5
-	SF	94108	7-A5
TROY AL			
-	SF	94109	6-J5
TRUBY ST			
-	SF	94129	2-E4
TRUETT ST			
-	SF	94108	7-A5
-	SF	94108	6-J5
TRUMBULL ST			
-	SF	94134	14-H6
-	SF	94112	14-H6
TUBBS ST			
-	SF	94107	11-C3
TUCKER AV			
-	SF	94134	20-A1
TULANE ST			
-	SF	94134	14-J7
TULARE ST			
900	SF	94124	15-C4
TULIP AL			
-	SF	94103	7-A7
TUNNEL AV			
100	SF	94134	20-A2
500	BSBN	94005	20-A4
TURK ST			
-	SF	94102	7-A6
100	SF	94102	6-G6
1000	SF	94115	6-G6
2200	SF	94118	6-G6
2700	SF	94118	5-D7
2900	SF	94117	5-D7
TURK MURPHY LN			
-	SF	94133	7-A4
TURNER TER			
-	SF	94107	11-B3
TURQUOISE WY			
-	SF	94131	14-F4
TUSCANY AL			
-	SF	94133	3-A3
TWAIN ST			
600	SF	94111	7-A5
TWIN PEAKS BLVD			
-	SF	94117	10-E3
-	SF	94114	10-E3
200	SF	94131	10-E4
TWIN PEAKS BLVD			
300	SF	94131	14-E4

U

STREET Block	City	ZIP	Pg-Grid
ULLOA ST			
-	SF	94127	13-E4
1200	SF	94116	13-A5
3300	SF	94116	12-H5
UNDERWOOD AV			
1200	SF	94124	15-C7
UNION ST			
-	SF	94111	3-A4
200	SF	94133	3-A4
700	SF	94133	2-J4
1000	SF	94109	2-J4
1200	SF	94109	6-H4
1500	SF	94123	6-F4
UNIVERSITY ST			
-	SF	94134	14-J7
500	SF	94134	19-J1
UPLAND DR			
-	SF	94112	13-C6
-	SF	94127	13-C6
UPPER TER			
-	SF	94117	10-F2
UPPER SERVICE RD			
-	SF	94131	9-D2
-	SF	94143	9-D2
UPTON AV			
-	SF	94129	1-C4
UPTON ST			
400	SF	94124	15-A5
URANUS TER			
-	SF	94114	10-F2
URBANO DR N			
-	SF	94127	13-C7
URBANO DR S			
400	SF	94127	13-C7
UTAH ST			
100	SF	94103	11-A2
400	SF	94110	11-A2

V

STREET Block	City	ZIP	Pg-Grid
VALDEZ AV			
-	SF	94112	13-D6
200	SF	94127	13-D6
VALE AV			
-	SF	94132	13-A5
VALENCIA ST			
-	SF	94103	10-H3
500	SF	94110	10-H3
1500	SF	94110	14-H4
VALERTON CT			
-	SF	94112	14-F7
VALLEJO ST			
-	SF	94129	1-D3
-	SF	94111	3-B4
300	SF	94133	7-A4
300	SF	94133	3-B4
800	SF	94133	6-F5
1100	SF	94109	6-F5
1600	SF	94123	6-F5
2000	SF	94115	6-F5
VALLEJO TER			
-	SF	94133	6-J4
VALLEJO FERRY			
-	SF	-	7-C4
-	SF	-	3-D1
VALLETA CT			
-	SF	94131	14-F6
VALLEY ST			
-	SF	94110	14-G5
100	SF	94131	14-G5
VALMAR TER			
-	SF	94112	14-H7
-	SF	94134	14-H7
VALPARAISO ST			
-	SF	94133	2-J4
VAN BUREN ST			
-	SF	94131	14-G6
VANDEWATER ST			
300	SF	94133	3-A3
300	SF	94133	2-J3
VAN DYKE AV			
1200	SF	94124	15-B7
VAN KEUREN AV			
-	SF	94124	16-F7
VAN NESS AV			
-	SF	94103	10-J1
2700	SF	94109	2-H3
2700	SF	94123	2-H3
VAN NESS AV U.S.-101			
-	SF	94102	6-H5
-	SF	94103	6-H5
800	SF	94109	6-H5
2200	SF	94123	6-H5
2400	SF	94109	2-H4
2400	SF	94123	2-H4
S VAN NESS AV			
200	SF	94103	10-J1
500	SF	94110	10-J1
1500	SF	94110	14-J4
S VAN NESS AV U.S.-101			
-	SF	94103	10-J3
VARELA AV			
-	SF	94132	18-B1
VARENNES ST			
-	SF	94133	3-A4
VARNEY PL			
-	SF	94107	7-B7
VASQUEZ AV			
-	SF	94127	13-D4
VASSAR PL			
-	SF	94107	7-B6
VEGA ST			
-	SF	94115	6-F7
VELASCO AV			
-	DALY	94014	19-H2
-	SF	94134	19-H2
VENARD AL			
2100	SF	94133	2-J3
VENDOME AV			
-	DALY	94014	18-D2
VENTURA AV			
-	SF	94116	9-D3
VENUS ST			
-	SF	94124	15-B6
VERDUN WY			
-	SF	94127	13-D5
VERMEHR PL			
-	SF	94108	7-A5
VERMONT ST			
-	SF	94103	11-A2
400	SF	94107	11-A2
1000	SF	94110	11-A4
VERNA ST			
-	SF	94127	14-E6
VERNON ST			
-	SF	94132	18-C1
VESTA ST			
-	SF	94124	15-B6
VIA BUFANO			
-	SF	94133	3-A4
VICENTE ST			
-	SF	94127	13-B5
200	SF	94116	13-A5
2300	SF	94116	12-H5
VICKSBURG ST			
-	SF	94114	10-G4
VICTORIA ST			
-	SF	94132	18-C2
600	SF	94127	13-C7
VIDAL DR			
-	SF	94132	18-A1
VIENNA ST			
-	SF	94112	14-H7
300	SF	94112	19-G1
VILLA TER			
-	SF	94114	10-F2
VINE TER			
-	SF	94108	7-A5
VINTON CT			
-	SF	94108	7-A5
VIRGIL ST			
-	SF	94110	10-J4
VIRGINIA AV			
-	SF	94110	14-H5
VISITACION AV			
200	SF	94134	19-J2
1200	SF	94134	20-A2
E VISTA AV			
-	DALY	94014	18-D3
VISTA CT			
-	SF	94129	6-E5
VISTA LN			
-	SF	94131	10-F3
VISTA GRANDE AV			
-	DALY	94014	18-C3
VISTA VERDE CT			
-	SF	94131	14-F6
VISTAVIEW CT			
-	SF	94124	15-B6
VULCAN STAIRWAY			
-	SF	94114	10-F2

W

STREET Block	City	ZIP	Pg-Grid
WABASH TER			
-	SF	94134	20-A2
WAGNER AL			
-	SF	94102	6-J6
WAGNER RD			
-	SF	94129	1-C3
WAITHMAN WY			
900	SF	94127	13-D5
WALBRIDGE AV			
-	SF	94134	19-H2
WALDO AL			
-	SF	94109	6-J4
WALL PL			
-	SF	94109	6-J5
WALLACE AV			
1300	SF	94124	15-C7
WALLEN CT			
-	SF	94129	5-E5
WALLER ST			
-	SF	94102	10-H1
300	SF	94117	10-E1
1700	SF	94117	9-E1
WALNUT ST			
-	SF	94118	6-E5
-	SF	94115	6-E5
WALTER ST			
-	SF	94114	10-G1
WALTER LUM PL			
-	SF	94108	7-A5
WALTHAM ST			
-	SF	94110	14-J5
WANDA ST			
-	SF	94112	14-F7
WARD ST			
100	SF	94134	20-A1
WARNER PL			
-	SF	94109	6-J4
WARREN DR			
-	SF	94131	9-D3
WASHBURN ST			
-	SF	94103	6-J7
WASHINGTON BLVD			
-	SF	94129	5-B4
WASHINGTON ST			
-	SF	94111	7-A5
700	SF	94108	7-A5
1100	SF	94108	6-G5
1300	SF	94109	6-G5
2200	SF	94115	6-G5
3400	SF	94118	6-E5
3600	SF	94118	5-D6
WASHOE PL			
-	SF	94133	7-A4
WATCHMAN WY			
-	SF	94107	11-B3
WATER ST			
-	SF	94133	2-J3
WATERLOO ST			
-	SF	94124	15-A5
WATERVILLE ST			
-	SF	94124	15-A6
WATSON PL			
-	SF	94112	14-F7
WATT AV			
-	SF	94112	19-F2
WAVERLY PL			
-	SF	94108	7-A5
WAVERLY WY			
-	DALY	94014	19-F3
-	SF	94112	19-F3
WAWONA ST			
-	SF	94127	13-C5
400	SF	94116	13-A5
400	SF	94132	13-A5
2300	SF	94116	12-H5
WAYLAND ST			
-	SF	94134	15-A7
700	SF	94134	14-J7
1500	SF	94134	19-J1
WAYNE PL			
-	SF	94133	7-A4
WEBB PL			
-	SF	94133	2-J4
WEBSTER ST			
-	SF	94117	10-H1
-	SF	94102	10-H1
300	SF	94102	6-G6
300	SF	94117	6-G6
1000	SF	94115	6-G6
2700	SF	94123	6-G4
3000	SF	94123	2-G3
WEDEMEYER ST			
-	SF	94129	5-B5
WELDON ST			
-	SF	94134	15-A6
WELLINGTON AV			
-	DALY	94014	18-D3
WELSH ST			
-	SF	94107	7-B7
WENTWORTH PL			
-	SF	94108	7-A4
WESTBROOK AV			
-	DALY	94015	18-A4
100	DALY	94015	17-J4
WESTBROOK CT			
-	SF	94124	15-C6
WESTDALE AV			
-	DALY	94015	18-B3
WESTERN SHORE LN			
-	SF	94115	6-E5
WESTGATE DR			
-	SF	94127	13-C6
WESTHAVEN DR			
-	DALY	94015	18-A3
WESTLAKE AV			
-	DALY	94014	18-C4
WESTLAWN AV			
-	DALY	94015	18-B3
WESTMONT DR			
-	DALY	94015	17-J3
WESTMOORLAND DR			
100	SF	94132	13-A6
WESTON DR			
-	DALY	94015	17-J3
WESTPARK DR			
-	DALY	94015	18-A3
WEST POINT RD			
-	SF	94124	15-D6
WESTSIDE DR			
-	SF	94130	3-D1
WESTVIEW AV			
-	SF	94134	14-H6
WESTWOOD DR			
-	SF	94112	13-D7
WETMORE ST			
-	SF	94108	7-A5
WHEAT ST			
-	SF	94124	15-B7
WHEELER AV			
200	SF	94134	20-A2
WHIPPLE AV			
-	SF	94112	19-E2
WHITE ST			
-	SF	94109	6-J4
WHITECLIFF WY			
-	SF	94124	15-B6
WHITFIELD CT			
-	SF	94124	15-C6
WHITING ST			
-	SF	94133	3-A3
WHITNEY ST			
-	SF	94131	14-H5
WHITNEY YOUNG CIR			
-	SF	94124	15-C6
WHITTIER ST			
-	SF	94112	19-E3
100	DALY	94014	19-E3
WIESE ST			
-	SF	94103	10-H2
WILDE AV			
-	SF	94134	20-A1
WILDER ST			
-	SF	94131	14-G6
WILDFLOWER CT			
-	DALY	94014	19-H3
WILDWOOD AV			
800	SMCo	94015	18-A4
900	DALY	94015	18-A4
900	DALY	94015	17-J4
WILDWOOD WY			
500	SF	94112	13-D7
WILLARD ST			
1200	SF	94117	9-E1
WILLARD ST N			
-	SF	94118	5-D7
WILLIAMS AV			
-	SF	94124	15-B7
WILLIAR AV			
200	SF	94112	18-E1
WILLITS ST			
-	DALY	94014	18-C3
WILLOW ST			
-	SF	94109	6-H6
600	SF	94115	6-H6
WILLS ST			
-	SF	94124	15-D6
WILMOT ST			
-	SF	94115	6-G6
WILSHIRE AV			
-	DALY	94015	18-B2
WILSHIRE CT			
-	DALY	94015	18-B3
WILSON ST			
-	DALY	94014	18-D2
100	SF	94112	18-D2
WINCHESTER ST			
100	DALY	94014	18-D3
100	DALY	94014	19-E3
WINDING WY			
-	SF	94112	19-F2
WINDSOR DR			
-	DALY	94015	18-A3
WINDSOR PL			
-	SF	94133	3-A4
WINFIELD ST			
-	SF	94110	14-H5
WINN WY			
-	SF	94129	2-E4
WINSTON DR			
-	SF	94132	13-B7
WINTER PL			
-	SF	94133	3-A4
-	SF	94133	2-J4
WINTHROP ST			
-	SF	94133	3-A3
WISCONSIN ST			
-	SF	94107	11-B3
-	SF	94103	11-B3
WISSER CT			
-	SF	94129	1-C4
WOOD ST			
-	SF	94118	6-E6
WOODACRE DR			
-	SF	94132	13-C6
WOODHAVEN CT			
-	SF	94131	9-D3
WOODLAND AV			
-	SF	94117	9-E2
WOODROW ST			
-	DALY	94014	18-C3
WOODSIDE AV			
-	SF	94127	13-D4
-	SF	94116	13-D4
200	SF	94131	13-D4
WOODWARD ST			
-	SF	94103	10-H1
WOOL CT			
-	SF	94129	1-C4
WOOL ST			
-	SF	94110	14-J5
WOOLSEY ST			
-	SF	94134	15-A7
700	SF	94134	14-J7
800	SF	94134	19-J1
WORCESTER AV			
-	SF	94132	18-C2
WORDEN ST			
-	SF	94133	3-A3
WORTH ST			
-	SF	94114	10-F3
WRIGHT LP			
-	SF	94129	5-C4
1300	SF	94129	1-C4
WRIGHT ST			
-	SF	94110	15-A4
WYANDOTTE AV			
900	DALY	94014	18-D4
WYMAN AV			
-	SF	94129	5-C5
WYTON LN			
-	SF	94132	13-B7

Y

STREET Block	City	ZIP	Pg-Grid
YACHT RD			
-	SF	94123	2-F3
YALE ST			
-	SF	94134	14-J7
500	SF	94134	19-J1
YERBA BUENA AV			
-	SF	94127	13-D5
YORBA LN			
2900	SF	94116	12-J6
2900	SF	94132	12-J6
YORBA ST			
2200	SF	94116	13-A6
2200	SF	94132	13-A6
2300	SF	94116	12-J6

STREET Block	City	ZIP	Pg-Grid
YORBA ST			
2300	SF	94132	12-J6
YORK ST			
500	SF	94110	11-A3
1500	SF	94110	15-A4
YOSEMITE AV			
1200	SF	94124	15-C7
1200	SF	94124	20-C1
YOUNG CT			
-	SF	94124	15-C6
YOUNG ST			
-	SF	94129	1-E3
YUKON ST			
-	SF	94114	10-F3
Z			
ZAMPA LN			
-	SF	94115	6-G6
ZENO PL			
-	SF	94105	7-C6
ZIRCON PL			
-	SF	94131	14-G5
ZOE ST			
-	SF	94107	7-B7
#			
1ST ST			
-	SF	94105	7-B5
-	SF	94130	3-E2
2ND AV			
-	SF	94118	5-D6
1200	SF	94122	9-D2
2ND ST			
-	SF	94105	7-B6
300	SF	94107	7-B6
3RD AV			
-	SF	94118	5-D6
700	SF	94124	20-E1
1200	SF	94122	9-D2
1300	SF	94143	9-D2
3RD ST			
-	SF	94134	20-B1
-	SF	94103	7-B6
-	SF	94130	3-E1
300	SF	94107	7-B6
900	SF	94107	11-C3
3100	SF	94124	11-C3
3200	SF	94124	15-B7
5800	SF	94124	20-B1
4TH AV			
-	SF	94118	5-D6
1200	SF	94122	9-D2
1400	SF	94143	9-D2
4TH ST			
-	SF	94103	7-A6
-	SF	94130	3-E1
300	SF	94107	7-A6
800	SF	94107	11-C1
5TH AV			
-	SF	94118	5-D6
1200	SF	94122	9-D2
1400	SF	94143	9-D2
5TH ST			
-	SF	94103	7-A6
300	SF	94107	7-A6
800	SF	94107	11-B1
6TH AV			
-	SF	94118	5-D6
1200	SF	94122	9-D2
1300	SF	94124	15-E7
1300	SF	94124	20-D1
6TH ST			
-	SF	94103	7-A7
300	SF	94107	7-B7
600	SF	94103	11-B1
600	SF	94107	11-B1
7TH AV			
-	SF	-	9-D3
-	SF	94118	5-D6
1200	SF	94122	9-D3
1600	SF	94131	9-D3
1600	SF	94116	9-D3
7TH ST			
-	SF	94102	6-J7
-	SF	94103	6-J7
-	SF	94103	7-A7
500	SF	94103	11-A1
800	SF	94107	11-A1
8TH AV			
-	SF	94118	9-D3
-	SF	94118	5-C7
1200	SF	94122	9-D3
8TH AV			
1900	SF	94116	9-D3
8TH ST			
-	SF	94103	6-J7
200	SF	94103	7-A7
300	SF	94103	11-A1
1200	SF	94107	11-B1
9TH AV			
-	SF	94118	5-C7
1200	SF	94122	9-C3
1900	SF	94116	9-C4
2200	SF	94116	13-C4
9TH ST			
-	SF	94103	6-J7
-	SF	94130	3-E1
200	SF	94103	10-J1
300	SF	94103	11-A1
10TH AV			
-	SF	94118	9-C3
-	SF	94118	5-C6
1200	SF	94122	9-C3
1900	SF	94116	9-C3
10TH ST			
-	SF	94103	6-J7
200	SF	94103	10-J1
400	SF	94103	11-A1
11TH AV			
-	SF	94118	5-C6
1200	SF	94122	9-C3
1900	SF	94116	9-C3
11TH ST			
-	SF	94103	6-J7
100	SF	94103	10-J1
12TH AV			
-	SF	94118	5-C7
1200	SF	94122	9-C2
1900	SF	94116	9-C3
2100	SF	94116	13-C4
12TH ST			
-	SF	94103	6-H7
-	SF	94103	10-J1
13TH ST			
100	SF	94103	10-J1
14TH AV			
-	SF	94118	5-C6
-	SF	94129	5-C6
1200	SF	94122	9-C2
1700	SF	94116	9-C3
2100	SF	94116	13-C5
2700	SF	94127	13-C5
14TH ST			
-	SF	94103	10-H1
600	SF	94114	10-H1
1000	SF	94117	10-H1
15TH AV			
-	SF	94129	5-C6
-	SF	94118	5-C6
1200	SF	94122	9-C2
1900	SF	94116	9-C4
2100	SF	94116	13-C5
2600	SF	94127	13-C5
2700	SF	94132	13-C5
15TH ST			
-	SF	94103	11-A1
-	SF	94107	11-A1
1000	SF	94103	10-J1
1900	SF	94114	10-G2
2500	SF	94117	10-G2
16TH AV			
-	SF	94118	5-C6
1200	SF	94122	9-C3
1900	SF	94116	9-C3
2100	SF	94116	13-C4
16TH ST			
200	SF	94107	11-A2
1300	SF	94103	11-A2
2100	SF	94110	11-A2
2400	SF	94103	10-H2
2400	SF	94110	10-H2
3300	SF	94114	10-G2
17TH AV			
-	SF	94121	5-B6
-	SF	94118	5-B6
1200	SF	94122	9-B3
1900	SF	94116	9-B3
2100	SF	94116	13-C5
17TH ST			
400	SF	94107	11-C2
1800	SF	94103	11-A2
2100	SF	94110	11-A2
2700	SF	94110	10-H2
3600	SF	94114	10-E2
4500	SF	94117	10-E2
4900	SF	94117	9-E2
18TH AV			
-	SF	94121	5-B6
1200	SF	94122	9-B4
1900	SF	94116	9-B4
2100	SF	94116	13-B5
18TH ST			
500	SF	94107	11-B2
2400	SF	94110	11-A2
2800	SF	94110	10-J2
3700	SF	94114	10-F2
19TH AV			
-	SF	94121	5-B6
4000	SF	94132	18-C1
19TH AV Rt#-1			
1200	SF	94122	9-B3
1900	SF	94116	9-B3
2100	SF	94116	13-B5
2700	SF	94132	13-B5
3500	SF	94132	18-B1
19TH ST			
500	SF	94107	11-B2
2500	SF	94110	11-A2
2800	SF	94110	10-J2
3700	SF	94114	10-F2
20TH AV			
-	SF	94121	5-B6
1200	SF	94122	9-B3
1900	SF	94116	9-B3
2100	SF	94116	13-B5
2900	SF	94132	13-B6
20TH ST			
400	SF	94107	11-B2
2400	SF	94110	11-A2
2900	SF	94110	10-J3
3800	SF	94114	10-J3
3900	SF	94114	10-H3
21ST AV			
-	SF	94121	5-B6
1200	SF	94122	9-B4
1900	SF	94116	9-B4
2100	SF	94116	13-B5
2900	SF	94132	13-B6
21ST ST			
2600	SF	94110	11-A3
2800	SF	94110	10-H3
3500	SF	94114	10-F3
22ND AV			
-	SF	94121	5-B6
1200	SF	94122	9-B3
1900	SF	94116	9-B3
2100	SF	94116	13-B5
2900	SF	94132	13-B5
22ND ST			
500	SF	94107	11-C3
2300	SF	94110	11-A3
2800	SF	94110	10-G3
3500	SF	94114	10-G3
23RD AV			
100	SF	94121	5-B6
1200	SF	94122	9-B4
1900	SF	94116	9-B4
2400	SF	94116	13-B5
2900	SF	94132	13-B6
23RD ST			
400	SF	94107	11-C3
2300	SF	94110	11-A3
2900	SF	94110	10-J3
3700	SF	94114	10-G3
24TH AV			
-	SF	94121	5-B6
1200	SF	94122	9-B3
1900	SF	94116	9-B3
2100	SF	94116	13-B5
2900	SF	94132	13-B6
24TH ST			
500	SF	94107	11-C3
2400	SF	94110	11-A3
2900	SF	94110	10-J3
3700	SF	94114	10-F4
25TH AV			
-	SF	94121	5-A5
1100	SF	-	9-B3
1200	SF	94122	9-B3
2100	SF	94116	9-B3
2100	SF	94116	13-B5
2900	SF	94132	13-B6
25TH ST			
700	SF	94107	11-B3
2500	SF	94110	11-A4
2900	SF	94110	10-J4
3800	SF	94114	10-G4
26TH AV			
-	SF	94121	5-A6
1200	SF	94122	9-A3
26TH AV			
2100	SF	94116	9-A3
2100	SF	94116	13-B6
2900	SF	94132	13-B6
26TH ST			
700	SF	94107	11-B4
2800	SF	94110	11-A4
3000	SF	94110	10-G4
3800	SF	94131	10-G4
27TH AV			
-	SF	94121	5-A6
1200	SF	94122	9-A3
2100	SF	94116	9-A3
2100	SF	94116	13-A5
27TH ST			
-	SF	94110	14-G4
200	SF	94131	14-G4
28TH AV			
100	SF	94121	5-A6
1200	SF	94122	9-A3
1900	SF	94116	9-A3
2100	SF	94116	13-A5
28TH ST			
-	SF	94110	14-G4
100	SF	94131	14-G4
29TH AV			
100	SF	94121	5-A6
1200	SF	94122	9-A3
1900	SF	94116	9-A3
2100	SF	94116	13-A5
29TH ST			
-	SF	94110	14-G5
200	SF	94131	14-G5
30TH AV			
100	SF	94121	5-A6
900	SF	-	5-A7
900	SF	-	9-A3
1200	SF	94122	9-A3
1900	SF	94116	9-A3
2100	SF	94116	13-A5
30TH ST			
-	SF	94110	14-G5
200	SF	94131	14-G5
31ST AV			
200	SF	94121	5-A6
1200	SF	94122	9-A3
1900	SF	94116	9-A3
2100	SF	94116	13-A5
32ND AV			
-	SF	94121	5-A7
1200	SF	94122	9-A3
1900	SF	94116	9-A3
2100	SF	94116	13-A5
33RD AV			
400	SF	94121	5-A7
1200	SF	94122	9-A4
1900	SF	94116	9-A4
2100	SF	94116	13-A5
34TH AV			
400	SF	94121	4-J7
1200	SF	94122	8-J2
1600	SF	94122	9-A4
1900	SF	94116	9-A4
2100	SF	94116	13-A5
2800	SF	94132	13-A5
35TH AV			
400	SF	94121	4-J7
1200	SF	94122	8-J3
1900	SF	94116	8-J3
2100	SF	94116	12-J5
2800	SF	94132	12-J5
36TH AV			
400	SF	94121	4-J7
800	SF	-	8-J1
1200	SF	94122	8-J3
1900	SF	94116	8-J3
2500	SF	94116	12-J5
2800	SF	94132	12-J5
37TH AV			
400	SF	94121	4-J7
800	SF	94121	8-J3
1200	SF	94122	8-J3
1900	SF	94116	8-J3
2100	SF	94116	12-J5
2800	SF	94132	12-J5
38TH AV			
400	SF	94121	4-J7
800	SF	94121	8-J3
1200	SF	94122	8-J3
2200	SF	94116	12-J5
39TH AV			
400	SF	94121	4-J7
800	SF	94121	8-J2
1200	SF	94122	8-J2
39TH AV			
2100	SF	94116	8-J2
2100	SF	94116	12-J5
2800	SF	94132	12-J5
40TH AV			
400	SF	94121	4-J7
800	SF	94121	8-J3
1200	SF	94122	8-J3
2100	SF	94116	8-J3
2100	SF	94116	12-J5
41ST AV			
400	SF	94121	4-J7
800	SF	94121	8-J3
1200	SF	94122	8-J3
1900	SF	94116	8-J3
2100	SF	94116	12-J5
2700	SF	94132	12-J5
42ND AV			
400	SF	94121	4-H7
800	SF	94121	8-J3
1200	SF	94122	8-J3
1900	SF	94116	8-J3
2100	SF	94116	12-J5
43RD AV			
400	SF	94121	4-H7
800	SF	94121	8-H3
1200	SF	94122	8-H3
1900	SF	94116	8-H3
2100	SF	94116	12-H5
44TH AV			
400	SF	94121	4-H7
800	SF	94121	8-H2
1200	SF	94122	8-H2
1900	SF	94116	8-H2
2100	SF	94116	12-H5
45TH AV			
400	SF	94121	4-H7
800	SF	94121	8-H3
1200	SF	94122	8-H3
1900	SF	94116	8-H3
2100	SF	94116	12-H5
46TH AV			
400	SF	94121	4-H7
800	SF	94121	8-H3
1200	SF	94122	8-H3
1900	SF	94116	8-H3
2100	SF	94116	12-H5
47TH AV			
400	SF	94121	4-H7
800	SF	94121	8-H1
900	SF	-	8-H1
1200	SF	94122	8-H3
1900	SF	94116	8-H3
2100	SF	94116	12-H5
48TH AV			
400	SF	94121	4-H7
800	SF	94121	8-H3
1200	SF	94122	8-H3
1900	SF	94116	8-H3
2100	SF	94116	12-H5
I-80 FRWY			
-	SF	-	3-E4
-	SF	-	7-B7
-	SF	-	11-A1
I-280 JOHN F FORAN FRWY			
-	DALY	-	18-C2
-	SF	-	15-A6
-	SF	-	11-B1
-	SF	-	14-E7
-	SF	-	18-C2
-	SF	-	19-E1
I-280 JUNIPERO SERRA FRWY			
-	DALY	-	18-C3
-	SF	-	18-C3
I-280 SOUTHERN FRWY			
-	DALY	-	18-C4
-	SF	-	15-B4
-	SF	-	7-C7
-	SF	-	11-B1
-	SF	-	14-E7
-	SF	-	19-E1
-	SF	-	18-D2
Rt#-1 CROSS OVER DR			
1000	SF	-	9-B1
Rt#-1 GOLDEN GATE BRIDGE FRWY			
-	SF	-	5-C5
-	SF	-	1-C3
Rt#-1 JUNIPERO SERRA BLVD			
1100	SF	94132	18-C2
JUNIPERO SERRA FRWY Rt#-1			
-	DALY	-	18-C3
-	SF	-	18-C3
Rt#-1 LOMBARD ST			
500	SF	94133	2-J3
1000	SF	94109	2-J4
Rt#-1 PRESIDIO BLVD			
-	SF	-	5-C7
-	SF	94118	5-C7
Rt#-1 19TH AV			
1200	SF	94122	9-B3
1900	SF	94116	9-B3
2100	SF	94116	13-B5
2700	SF	94132	13-B5
3500	SF	94132	18-B1
Rt#-35 SKYLINE BLVD			
-	DALY	94015	17-J3
-	SF	94132	12-H6
-	SF	94132	17-J1
2100	SMCo	94015	17-J3
Rt#-82 MISSION ST			
6300	DALY	94014	18-C4
U.S.-101 BAYSHORE FRWY			
-	BSBN	-	20-B3
-	SF	-	20-B3
U.S.-101 CENTRAL FRWY			
-	SF	-	6-H7
-	SF	-	10-J1
-	SF	-	11-A1
U.S.-101 DOYLE DR			
-	SF	94129	1-D3
-	SF	94129	2-E3
U.S.-101 GOLDEN GATE BRG FRWY			
-	SF	-	1-B1
U.S.-101 JAMES LICK FRWY			
-	SF	-	20-A1
-	SF	-	15-A6
-	SF	-	11-A2
U.S.-101 LOMBARD ST			
1400	SF	94123	2-F4
U.S.-101 RICHARDSON AV			
-	SF	94123	2-E3
100	SF	94129	2-E3
U.S.-101 VAN NESS AV			
-	SF	94102	6-H5
-	SF	94103	6-H5
800	SF	94109	6-H5
2200	SF	94123	6-H5
2400	SF	94109	2-H4
2400	SF	94123	2-H4
U.S.-101 S VAN NESS AV			
-	SF	94103	10-J3

1998 SAN FRANCISCO COUNTY POINTS OF INTEREST

BEACHES & HARBORS

FEATURE NAME	Address City, ZIP Code	PAGE-GRID
BAKER BEACH	GIBSON RD & BTTRY CHAMBERLAIN, SF, 94129, (415)556-0560	5 - A5
CHINA BEACH	EL CAMINO DEL MAR & 32ND AV, SF, 94121	5 - A5
OCEAN BEACH	GREAT HWY & JUDAH ST, SF, 94122	8 - H3
SEAL ROCKS BEACH	EL CAMINO DEL MAR, SF, 94121	4 - G6
THORTON STATE BEACH	SKYLINE BLVD & THORNTON STATE, DALY, 94015	17 - J4

BUILDINGS

FEATURE NAME	Address City, ZIP Code	PAGE-GRID
FOR DOWNTOWN BUILDINGS SEE PAGES x- & xi		-
1 HARRISON STREET	1 HARRISON ST, SF, 94105	7 - C5
100 CALIFORNIA ST	100 CALIFORNIA ST, SF, 94111	7 - B5
100 FIRST PLAZA	100 1ST ST, SF, 94105	7 - B5
100 PINE ST	100 PINE ST, SF, 94111, (415)986-6469	7 - B5
101 CALIFORNIA ST	101 CALIFORNIA ST, SF, 94111, (415)398-8655	7 - B5
120 MONTGOMERY STREET	120 MONTGOMERY ST, SF, 94104	7 - B5
123 MISSION ST	123 MISSION ST, SF, 94105, (415)974-1722	7 - B5
160 SPEAR ST	160 SPEAR ST, SF, 94105	7 - B5
201 CALIFORNIA ST	201 CALIFORNIA ST, SF, 94111	7 - B5
221 MAIN ST	221 MAIN ST, SF, 94105	7 - C5
301 HOWARD ST	301 HOWARD ST, SF, 94105	7 - C5
333 BUSH ST	333 BUSH ST, SF, 94108, (415)982-2278	7 - A5
333 MARKET ST	333 MARKET ST, SF, 94105, (415)546-0333	7 - B5
343 SANSOME	343 SANSOME ST, SF, 94104	7 - B5
353 SACRAMENTO ST	353 SACRAMENTO ST, SF, 94104	7 - B5
388 MARKET ST	388 MARKET ST, SF, 94111	7 - B5
425 MARKET ST	425 MARKET ST, SF, 94105	7 - B5
455 MARKET ST	455 MARKET ST, SF, 94105	7 - B5
475 SANSOME ST	475 SANSOME ST, SF, 94111	7 - B5
49 STEVENSON ST	49 STEVENSON ST, SF, 94103	7 - A6
50 FREMONT STREET	50 FREMONT ST, SF, 94105, (415)543-5600	7 - B5
505 MONTGOMERY ST	505 MONTGOMERY ST, SF, 94111	7 - A5
55 HAWTHORNE ST	55 HAWTHORNE ST, SF, 94105	7 - B6
580 CALIFORNIA ST	580 CALIFORNIA ST, SF, 94104	7 - A5
595 MARKET ST	595 MARKET ST, SF, 94108	7 - A6
60 SPEAR ST	60 SPEAR ST, SF, 94105	7 - B5
601 MONTGOMERY ST	601 MONTGOMERY ST, SF, 94111	7 - A5
605 MARKET STREET	605 MARKET ST, SF, 94103, (415)495-0239	7 - A6
650 CALIFORNIA ST	650 CALIFORNIA ST, SF, 94108	7 - A5
660 MARKET ST	660 MARKET ST, SF, 94108, (415)788-4820	7 - A6
71 STEVENSON ST	71 STEVENSON ST, SF, 94103	7 - A6
75 HAWTHORNE ST PLAZA	75 HAWTHORNE ST PZ, SF, 94105	7 - B6
90 NEW MONTGOMERY	90 NEW MONTGOMERY ST, SF, 94105, (415)777-0952	7 - B6
ABC	900 FRONT ST, SF, 94111, (415)954-7777	3 - B4
ADAM GRANT	114 SANSOME ST, SF, 94104, (415)981-0375	7 - B5
AEROFLOT AIRLINES	291 GEARY ST, SF, 94108, (415)434-2300	7 - A6
AIR FRANCE AIRLINES	360 POST ST, SF, 94102	7 - A5
AMERICAN AIRLINES	51 O'FARREL ST, SF, 94108, (415)433-7300	7 - A6
AMERICAN SAVINGS	MARKET & KEARNY STS, SF, 94108, (415)362-8220	7 - A6
AT&T	795 FOLSOM ST, SF, 94107	7 - B6
BANK OF CALIFORNIA COMPUTER CENTER	640 BATTERY ST, SF, 94111	7 - B4
BANK OF CANTON	555 MONTGOMERY ST, SF, 94104	7 - A5
BANK OF SAN FRANCISCO	550 MONTGOMERY ST, SF, 94104	7 - A5
BANKERS INVESTMENT	742 MARKET ST, SF, 94108, (415)781-2836	7 - A6
BAYSIDE PLAZA	188 THE EMBARCADERO ST, SF, 94105, (415)979-2300	7 - C6
BRITISH AIRWAYS	51 OFARRELL ST, SF, 94108, (415)247-9297	7 - A6
BROOKS BROTHERS	209 POST ST, SF, 94108	7 - A5
BUILDERS EXCHANGE	850 S VAN NESS AV, SF, 94109, (415)282-8220	6 - H6
CENTRAL TOWER	703 MARKET ST, SF, 94105, (415)982-1935	7 - B5
CHEVRON	225 BUSH ST, SF, 94108, (415)894-7700	7 - A5
CHINA AIRLINES	391 STOCKTON ST, SF, 94108, (415)391-3954	7 - A5
CHRONICLE	5TH ST & MISSION ST, SF, 94103, (415)777-1111	7 - A6
CITICORP CENTER	1 SANSOME ST, SF, 94104	7 - B5
COMMERCIAL	833 MARKET ST, SF, 94103, (415)362-4915	7 - A6
CONTINENTAL AIRLINES	433 CALIFORNIA ST, SF, 94104, (415)397-8818	7 - B5
CONVENTION PLAZA	201 3RD ST, SF, 94103	7 - B6
DELTA AIRLINES	250 STOCKTON ST, SF, 94108, (415)552-5700	7 - A6
ECKER SQUARE	25 ECKER ST, SF, 94105	7 - B5
EIGHT THIRTY MARKET	830 MARKET ST, SF, 94102	7 - A6
EMBARCADERO CENTER W	275 BATTERY ST, SF, 94104, (415)772-0500	7 - B5
EXCHANGE BLOCK	369 PINE ST, SF, 94104, (415)421-0422	7 - B5
FASHION INSTITUTE	55 STOCKTON ST, SF, 94108, (415)433-6691	7 - A6
FEDERAL HOME LOAN BANK	600 CALIFORNIA ST, SF, 94108	7 - A5
FERRY BUILDING	EMBARCADERO & WASHINGTON ST, SF, 94111	7 - C4
FIFTEEN CALIFORNIA ST	15 CALIFORNIA ST, SF, 94111	7 - B5
FIFTY HAWTHORNE	50 HAWTHORNE ST, SF, 94103	7 - B6
FILBERT LANDING	201 FILBERT ST, SF, 94133	3 - A4
FIRST INTERSTATE CENTER	BATTERY ST & PINE ST, SF, 94104	7 - B5
FIRST MARKET TOWER	525 MARKET ST, SF, 94108	7 - A5
FIVE FREMONT CENTER	5 MISSION ST & FREMONT ST, SF, 94105	7 - B5
FLATIRON	1 SUTTER ST, SF, 94105	7 - B5
FLOOD	870 MARKET ST, SF, 94102, (415)982-3298	7 - A6
FOLGER	101 HOWARD ST, SF, 94105	7 - C5
FORTY FOUR MONTGOMERY	44 MONTGOMERY ST, SF, 94104, (415)392-2433	7 - B5
FOUR EMBARCADERO CENTER	EMBARCADERO CTR, SF, 94111, (415)772-0500	7 - B5
FOUR SEVENTEEN MONTGOMERY	417 MONTGOMERY ST, SF, 94104, (415)392-2470	7 - A5
FOX PLAZA	1390 MARKET ST, SF, 94102, (415)626-6900	6 - J7
FREMONT CENTER	215 FREMONT ST, SF, 94105	7 - B5
GALLERIA DESIGN CENTER	101 HENRY ADAMS ST, SF, 94103, (415)863-3388	11 - A1
GOLDEN GATE	25 TAYLOR ST, SF, 94102, (415)775-3890	7 - A6
GOLDEN GATEWAY CENTER	460 DAVIS ST, SF, 94111, (415)434-2000	7 - B4
GRANT	1095 MARKET ST, SF, 94103, (415)621-8139	6 - J7
GREAT WESTERN BANK	425 CALIFORNIA ST, SF, 94104	7 - B5
GUNST, ELKAN	323 GEARY ST, SF, 94102, (415)421-4762	7 - A6
GUZZARDO	836 MONTGOMERY ST, SF, 94133, (415)433-4672	7 - A4
HASS	1255 SANSOME ST, SF, 94133	3 - A3
HEARST	669 MARKET ST, SF, 94105, (415)777-0600	7 - B5
HILLS PLAZA 1	345 SPEAR ST, SF, 94105	7 - C5
HILLS PLAZA 2	1 HARRISON ST, SF, 94105	7 - C5
HOBART	582 MARKET ST, SF, 94104, (415)362-8783	7 - B5
HONG KONG BANK	160 SANSOME ST, SF, 94104	7 - B5
HUMBOLDT BANK	785 MARKET ST, SF, 94103	7 - A6
INDUSTRIAL INDEMNITY	255 CALIFORNIA ST, SF, 94111	7 - B5
INSURANCE EXCHANGE	433 CALIFORNIA ST, SF, 94104, (415)362-0529	7 - A5
INTERNATIONAL	601 CALIFORNIA ST, SF, 94108, (415)981-7878	7 - A5
JAPAN AIRLINES	POWELL ST & OFARRELL ST, SF, 94102, (415)765-8555	7 - A6
KOHL	400 MONTGOMERY ST, SF, 94104, (415)392-2470	7 - A5
KOREAN AIR	251 POST ST, SF, 94108, (415)956-6373	7 - A5
KOSHLAND	1160 BATTERY ST, SF, 94111	3 - B3
KPIX	855 BATTERY ST, SF, 94111, (415)362-5550	3 - B4
KRESS	939 MARKET ST, SF, 94103, (415)495-8748	7 - A6
LEVI STRAUSS	1155 BATTERY ST, SF, 94111, (415)544-6000	3 - B3
LUFTHANSA	240 STOCKTON ST, SF, 94108, (415)398-7400	7 - A6
MARATHON PLAZA	303 2ND ST, SF, 94105	7 - B6
MARINE FIREMANS UNION	240 2ND ST, SF, 94105	7 - B6
MARITIME ADMINISTRATION	211 MAIN ST, SF, 94105, (415)744-3125	7 - B5
MEDICO/DENTAL	490 POST ST, SF, 94102, (415)781-1427	7 - A6
MERCANTILE CENTER	706 MISSION ST, SF, 94103	7 - A6
MERCHANTS EXCHANGE	465 CALIFORNIA ST, SF, 94104, (415)421-7730	7 - B5
MEXICANA AIRLINES	421 POWELL ST, SF, 94102, (415)982-1424	7 - A6
MILLS BUILDING & TOWER	220 MONTGOMERY ST, SF, 94104, (415)421-1444	7 - B5
MONADNOCK	685 MARKET ST, SF, 94103, (415)781-1361	7 - A6
MONTEREY CONSERVATORY	MONTEREY BLVD & CONGO ST, SF, 94131	14 - F6
MONTGOMERY WASHINGTON TOWER	655 MONTGOMERY ST, SF, 94111, (415)981-2655	7 - A4
NATIVE SONS	414 MASON ST, SF, 94102, (415)392-0943	7 - A6
NEW MONTGOMERY TOWER	33 NEW MONTGOMERY ST, SF, 94105	7 - B6
NORTHWEST	433 CALIFORNIA ST, SF, 94104, (415)225-2525	7 - B5
ONE BUSH ST	1 BUSH ST, SF, 94111	7 - B5
ONE CALIFORNIA ST	1 CALIFORNIA ST, SF, 94111, (415)421-4144	7 - B5
ONE ELEVEN SUTTER	111 SUTTER ST, SF, 94108, (415)477-3274	7 - A5
ONE EMBARCADERO CENTER	EMBARCADERO CTR, SF, 94111, (415)772-0500	7 - B5
ONE JACKSON PLACE	633 BATTERY ST, SF, 94111, (415)362-1800	7 - B4
ONE MARITIME PLAZA	1 MARITIME PZ, SF, 94111, (415)397-2339	7 - B5
ONE MARKET PLAZA	1 MARKET PZ, SF, 94105	7 - B5
ONE POST BLDG	1 POST ST, SF, 94104, (415)546-1300	7 - B5
ORPHEUM THEATRE	1192 MARKET ST, SF, 94102, (415)474-3800	6 - J7
PACIFIC BANK	351 CALIFORNIA ST, SF, 94104	7 - B5
PACIFIC BELL	140 NEW MONTGOMERY ST, SF, 94105, (415)811-9000	7 - B6
PACIFIC CENTRE	22 4TH ST, SF, 94103, (415)398-7333	7 - A6
PACIFIC COAST STOCK EXCHANGE	301 PINE ST, SF, 94104, (415)393-4000	7 - B5
PACIFIC GATEWAY	201 MISSION ST, SF, 94105	7 - B5
PACIFIC TELESIS TOWER	1 MONTGOMERY ST, SF, 94108	7 - B5
PHELAN	760 MARKET ST, SF, 94108, (415)392-7552	7 - A6
PHILIPPINE AIRLINES	447 SUTTER ST, SF, 94108, (415)391-0270	7 - A5
QANTAS AIRWAYS	360 POST ST, SF, 94102, (415)445-1461	7 - A5
RAY	181 FREMONT ST, SF, 94105, (415)392-3870	7 - B5
REDWOOD BANK	735 MONTGOMERY ST, SF, 94133, (415)788-3700	7 - A4
RIALTO	116 NEW MONTGOMERY ST, SF, 94105, (415)421-0704	7 - B6
RINCON CENTER	101 SPEAR ST, SF, 94105	7 - B5
ROBERT DOLLAR	311 CALIFORNIA ST, SF, 94104, (415)392-8454	7 - B5
ROTHSCHILD	165 POST ST, SF, 94108	7 - A5
RUCKER FULLER	731 SANSOME ST, SF, 94133, (415)627-4600	7 - B4
RUSS	235 MONTGOMERY ST, SF, 94104, (415)421-7424	7 - A5
SAILORS UNION OF PACIFIC	450 HARRISON ST, SF, 94105	7 - C6
SAINT FRANCIS MEDICAL	909 HYDE ST, SF, 94109, (415)673-1317	6 - J5
SAN FRANCISCO FEDERAL SAVINGS	POST ST & KEARNY ST, SF, 94108	7 - A5
SEVENTY NINE NEW MONTGOMERY	79 NEW MONTGOMERY ST, SF, 94105	7 - B6
SHAKLEE TERRACES	444 MARKET ST, SF, 94104	7 - B5
SHARON	55 NEW MONTGOMERY ST, SF, 94105, (415)982-9281	7 - B6
SHELL	100 BUSH ST, SF, 94104, (415)986-0647	7 - B5
SINGAPORE AIRLINES	476 POST ST, SF, 94102, (415)781-7304	7 - A6
SIXTY FOUR PINE ST	64 PINE ST, SF, 94111	7 - B5
SOUTHERN PACIFIC	1 MARKET PZ, SF, 94105, (415)541-1000	7 - B5
SPEAR STREET TERRACE	201 SPEAR ST, SF, 94105	7 - C5
SPEAR STREET TOWER	1 MARKET PZ, SF, 94105	7 - B5
STEUART ST TOWER	1 MARKET PZ, SF, 94105	7 - B5
STOCK EXCHANGE TOWER	155 SANSOME ST, SF, 94104	7 - B5
SUMITOMO BANK	320 CALIFORNIA ST, SF, 94104	7 - B5
SUTTER MEDICAL DENTAL	450 SUTTER ST, SF, 94108, (415)421-7221	7 - A5
TACA	870 MARKET ST, SF, 94108	7 - A6
THREE EMBARCADERO CENTER	EMBARCADERO CTR, SF, 94111, (415)772-0500	7 - B5
TRADE SHOW CENTER	2 HENRY ADAMS ST, SF, 94103, (415)864-1500	11 - A1
TRANS WORLD AIRLINES	595 MARKET ST, SF, 94104, (415)864-5731	7 - B5
TRANSAMERICA	701 MONTGOMERY ST, SF, 94133	7 - A4
TRANSAMERICA (PYRAMID)	600 MONTGOMERY ST, SF, 94111, (415)983-4000	7 - A5
TWO EMBARCADERO CENTER	EMBARCADERO CTR, SF, 94111, (415)772-0500	7 - B5
TWO RINCON CENTER	121 SPEAR ST, SF, 94105	7 - B5
TWO TRANSAMERICA CENTER	505 SANSOME ST, SF, 94111	7 - B5
UNION BANK	350 CALIFORNIA ST, SF, 94104, (415)445-0224	7 - B5
UNITED AIRLINES	124 GEARY ST, SF, 94108, (415)397-2100	7 - A6
US AIRWAYS	433 CALIFORINIA ST, SF, 94104, (415)956-8636	7 - A5
WELLS FARGO	464 CALIFORNIA ST, SF, 94104, (415)396-0123	7 - B5
YERBA BUENA WEST	150 4TH ST, SF, 94103, (415)495-3433	7 - A6
YOUTH GUIDANCE CENTER	WOODSIDE AV & TWIN PEAKS RD, SF, 94131	13 - E4

BUILDINGS - GOVERNMENTAL

FEATURE NAME	Address City, ZIP Code	PAGE-GRID
BILL GRAHAM CIVIC AUDITORIUM	99 GROVE ST AT POLK ST, SF, 94102, (415)974-4060	6 - J7
CALIFORNIA STATE BUILDING	350 MCALLISTER ST, SF, 94102	6 - H6
CIVIC CENTER	VAN NESS AV & POLK ST, SF, 94102	6 - J7
FEDERAL BUILDING	450 GOLDEN GATE AV, SF, 94102, (415)556-6600	6 - J6
FEDERAL BUILDING	MCALLISTER ST & HYDE ST, SF, 94102	6 - J7
FEDERAL RESERVE BANK	101 MARKET ST, SF, 94105, (415)974-2000	7 - B5
HALL OF JUSTICE	850 BRYANT ST, SF, 94103, (415)553-9395	7 - A7
MARITIME COMMISSION	525 MARKET ST, SF, 94105, (415)974-9756	7 - B5
MECHANICS INSTITUTE	57 POST ST, SF, 94108, (415)956-2260	7 - A5
UNITED STATES MINT	155 HERMANN ST, SF, 94102, (415)556-6704	10 - H1
US APPRAISERS BUILDING	630 SANSOME ST, SF, 94111	7 - B4
US CUSTOMS HOUSE	555 BATTERY ST, SF, 94111, (415)705-4440	7 - B5
VETERANS ADMINISTRATION	211 MAIN ST, SF, 94105	7 - C5

CEMETERIES

FEATURE NAME	Address City, ZIP Code	PAGE-GRID
SAN FRANCISCO COLUMBARIUM	1 LORAINE CT, SF, 94118, (415)752-7891	5 - D6
SAN FRANCISCO NATIONAL CEMETERY	LINCOLN BLVD & SHERIDAN AV, SF, 94129	1 - D4

CHAMBERS OF COMMERCE

FEATURE NAME	Address City, ZIP Code	PAGE-GRID
SAN FRANCISCO CHAMBER OF COMMERCE	465 CALIFORNIA ST, SF, 94104, (415)392-4511	7 - B5
SAN FRANCISCO VISITORS BUREAU	201 3RD ST, SF, 94103, (415)974-6900	7 - B6

COLLEGES & UNIVERSITIES

FEATURE NAME	Address City, ZIP Code	PAGE-GRID
CITY COLLEGE OF SAN FRANCISCO	50 PHELAN AV, SF, 94112, (415)239-3000	14 - E7
GOLDEN GATE UNIVERSITY	550 MISSION ST, SF, 94105, (415)442-7225	7 - B5

FEATURE NAME	Address City, ZIP Code	PAGE-GRID
POLICE ACADEMY	350 AMBER DR, SF, 94131	14 - F4
SAN FRANCISCO ART INSTITUTE	800 CHESTNUT ST, SF, 94133, (415)771-7020	2 - J3
SAN FRANCISCO STATE UNIVERSITY	1600 HOLLOWAY AV, SF, 94132, (415)469-1111	13 - B7
UNIV OF CALIF SAN FRANCISCO	501 PARNASSUS AV, SF, 94143, (415)476-9000	9 - D2
UNIVERSITY OF SAN FRANCISCO	2130 FULTON ST, SF, 94117, (415)422-5555	6 - E7
UNIV OF SAN FRANCISCO LAW SCHOOL	STANYAN ST & HAYES ST, SF, 94117	5 - E7
UNIVERSITY OF THE PACIFIC	2155 WEBSTER ST, SF, 94115, (415)929-6450	6 - G5
USF LONE MOUNTAIN CAMPUS	2130 FULTON ST, SF, 94118, (415)422-5555	6 - E7

DEPARTMENT OF MOTOR VEHICLES

FEATURE NAME	Address City, ZIP Code	PAGE-GRID
SAN FRANCISCO DMV	1377 FELL ST, SF, 94117, (415)557-1179	6 - F7

ENTERTAINMENT & SPORTS

FEATURE NAME	Address City, ZIP Code	PAGE-GRID
3COM PARK (CANDLESTICK PARK)	GIANTS DR, SF, 94124	20 - C2
COW PALACE	GENEVA & RIO VERDE, DALY, 94014, (415)469-6000	19 - H3
GOLDEN GATE PARK STADIUM	36TH ST & JOHN F KENNEDY DR, SF	9 - A1
KEZAR STADIUM	FREDERICK ST, SF, 94117, (415)753-7032	9 - D1
MOSCONE CONVENTION CENTER	747 HOWARD ST, SF, 94103, (415)974-4000	7 - B6

GOLF COURSES

FEATURE NAME	Address City, ZIP Code	PAGE-GRID
GLENEAGLES INTL GOLF COURSE	2100 SUNNYDALE AV, SF, 94134, (415)587-2425	19 - H2
GOLDEN GATE MUNICIPAL GOLF COURSE	47TH AV & FULTON ST, SF, (415)751-8987	8 - H1
HARDING PARK MUNICIPAL GOLF COURSE	HARDING RD & SKYLINE BLVD, SF, 94132, (415)878-4427	12 - J7
LAKE MERCED GOLF & COUNTRY CLUB	2300 JUNIPERO SERRA BLVD, DALY, 94015, (650)755-2233	18 - B4
LINCOLN PARK GOLF COURSE	34TH AV & CLEMENT ST, SF, 94121, (415)221-9911	4 - J6
PRESIDIO GOLF COURSE	300 FINLEY RD, SF, 94129, (415)561-4653	5 - C5
SAN FRANCISCO GOLF CLUB	JUNIPERO SERRA & BROTHERHOOD, SF, 94132, (415)469-4100	18 - B2
THE OLYMPIC COUNTRY CLUB	599 SKYLINE BLVD, SMCo, 94015, (415)587-4800	17 - J3

HOSPITALS

FEATURE NAME	Address City, ZIP Code	PAGE-GRID
CALIFORNIA PACIFIC MEDICAL CENTER	2333 BUCHANAN ST, SF, 94115, (415)563-4321	6 - G5
CALIFORNIA PACIFIC MEDICAL CENTER	3700 CALIFORNIA ST, SF, 94118, (415)387-8700	5 - D6
CHINESE HOSPITAL	845 JACKSON ST, SF, 94108, (415)982-2400	7 - A4
DAVIES MEDICAL CENTER	CASTRO ST & DUBOCE AV, SF, 94114, (415)565-6000	10 - G1
KAISER PERMANENTE MEDICAL CENTER	2425 GEARY BLVD, SF, 94115, (405)929-4000	6 - F6
LAGUNA HONDA HOSPITAL	375 LAGUNA HONDA BLVD, SF, 94116, (415)664-1580	9 - D4
LETTERMAN GENERAL HOSPITAL	LETTERMAN DR & DEWITT RD, SF, 94129	2 - E4
SAINT FRANCIS MEMORIAL HOSPITAL	900 HYDE ST, SF, 94109, (415)353-6000	6 - J5
SAINT LUKES HOSPITAL	3555 CESAR CHAVEZ ST, SF, 94110, (415)647-8600	14 - H4
SAINT MARYS HOSPITAL	450 STANYAN ST, SF, 94117, (415)668-1000	9 - E1
SAN FRANCISCO GENERAL HOSPITAL	1001 POTRERO AV, SF, 94110, (415)206-8000	11 - A3
SHRINERS HOSP FOR CRIPPLED CHILDREN	1701 19TH AV, SF, 94122, (415)665-1100	9 - B3
UCSF MEDICAL CENTER	500 PARNASSUS AV, SF, 94131, (415)476-1000	9 - D2
UCSF MOUNT ZION HOSPITAL	1600 DIVISADERO ST, SF, 94115, (415)567-6600	6 - G6
VETERANS AFFAIRS MEDICAL CENTER	4150 CLEMENT ST, SF, 94121, (415)750-2041	4 - H6

HOTELS & MOTELS

FEATURE NAME	Address City, ZIP Code	PAGE-GRID
AMERICANA	121 7TH ST, SF, 94103, (415)626-0200	7 - A7
ANA HOTEL	50 3RD ST, SF, 94103, (415)974-6400	7 - A6
BERESFORD ARMS	701 POST ST, SF, 94102, (415)673-2600	6 - J6
BEST WESTERN CANTERBURY HOTEL	750 SUTTER ST, SF, 94109, (415)474-6464	6 - J5
CAMPTON PLACE	340 STOCKTON ST, SF, 94108, (415)781-5555	7 - A5
CATHEDRAL HILL	VAN NESS AV & GEARY ST, SF, 94109, (415)776-8200	6 - H6
CHANCELLOR HOTEL	433 POWELL ST, SF, 94102, (415)362-1403	7 - A5
CLIFT HOTEL	495 GEARY ST, SF, 94102, (415)775-4700	7 - A6
DOWNTOWN TRAVELODGE	790 ELLIS ST, SF, 94109, (415)775-7612	6 - J6
FAIRMONT	950 MASON ST, SF, 94108, (415)772-5000	7 - A5
FOUR SEASONS CLIFTON	495 GEARY ST, SF, 94102, (415)775-4700	6 - J6
GALLERIA PARK HOTEL	191 SUTTER ST, SF, 94108, (415)781-3060	7 - A5
GRAND HYATT SAN FRANCISCO	345 STOCKTON ST, SF, 94108, (415)398-1234	7 - A5
GROSVENOR INN	1050 VAN NESS AV, SF, 94109, (415)673-4711	6 - H6
HOLIDAY INN-CIVIC CENTER	50 8TH ST, SF, 94103, (415)626-6103	6 - J7
HOLIDAY INN-FINANCIAL DISTRICT	750 KEARNY ST, SF, 94111, (415)433-6600	7 - A5
HOLIDAY INN-FISHERMANS WHARF	1300 COLUMBUS AV, SF, 94133, (415)771-9000	2 - J3
HOLIDAY INN-GOLDEN GATE	1500 VAN NESS AV, SF, 94109, (415)441-4000	6 - H5
HOLIDAY INN-UNION SQUARE	480 SUTTER ST, SF, 94108, (415)398-8900	7 - A5
HOTEL NIKKO	222 MASON ST, SF, 94102, (415)394-1111	7 - A6
HOWARD JOHNSONS	580 BEACH ST, SF, 94133, (415)775-3800	2 - J3
HUNTINGTON HOTEL - NOB HILL	1075 CALIFORNIA ST, SF, 94108, (415)474-5400	6 - J5
HYATT REGENCY SAN FRANCISCO	5 EMBARCADERO CTR, SF, 94111, (415)788-1234	7 - B5
HYATT-FISHERMANS WHARF	555 N POINT ST, SF, 94133, (415)563-1234	2 - J3
MANDARIN ORIENTAL	222 SANSOME ST, SF, 94104, (415)885-0999	7 - B5
MARINES MEMORIAL CLUB/HOTEL	609 SUTTER ST, SF, 94102, (415)673-6672	7 - A5
MARK HOPKINS	1 NOB HILL CIR, SF, 94108, (415)392-3434	7 - A5
MARRIOTT-FISHERMANS WHARF	1250 COLUMBUS AV, SF, 94133, (415)775-7555	2 - J3
MARRIOTT-MOSCONE CENTER	55 4TH ST, SF, 94103, (415)896-1600	7 - A6
MCLAREN LODGE	FELL ST & STANYON ST, SF, 94117, (415)666-7200	9 - E1
MIYAKO	1625 POST ST, SF, 94115, (415)922-3200	6 - H6
MIYAKO INN	1800 SUTTER ST, SF, 94115, (415)921-4000	6 - G6
PALACE HOTEL	2 NEW MONTGOMERY ST, SF, 94105, (415)392-8600	7 - B6
PAN PACIFIC	500 POST ST, SF, 94102, (415)771-8600	7 - A6
PARC FIFTY FIVE	55 CYRL MAGNIN ST, SF, 94102, (415)392-8000	7 - A6
PARK HYATT	333 BATTERY ST, SF, 94104, (415)392-1234	7 - B5
RAMADA-FISHERMANS WHARF	590 BAY ST, SF, 94133, (415)885-4700	2 - J3
RAPHAEL	386 GEARY ST, SF, 94102, (415)986-2000	7 - A6
RENAISSANCE STANFORD COURT	905 CALIFORNIA ST, SF, 94108, (415)989-3500	7 - A5
RENAISSANCE STANFORD COURT HOTEL	905 CALIFORNIA ST, SF, 94108, (415)989-3500	7 - A5
RITZ CARLTON SAN FRANCISCO	600 STOCKTON ST, SF, 94108, (415)296-7465	7 - A5
SAN FRANCISCO HILTON AND TOWERS	333 OFARRELL ST, SF, 94102, (415)771-1400	7 - A6
SHANNON COURT HOTEL	550 GEARY ST, SF, 94102, (415)775-5000	6 - J6
SHERATON PALACE	2 NEW MONTGOMERY ST, SF, 94105, (415)392-8600	7 - B5
SHERATON-FISHERMANS WHARF	2500 MASON ST, SF, 94133, (415)362-5500	2 - J3
SIR FRANCIS DRAKE	450 POWELL ST, SF, 94108, (415)392-7755	7 - A5
THE DONATELLO	150 POST ST, SF, 94102, (415)441-7100	7 - A6
THE HANDLERY UNION SQUARE	351 GEARY ST, SF, 94102, (415)781-7800	7 - A6
THE PRESCOTT HOTEL	545 POST ST, SF, 94102, (415)563-0303	7 - A6
TRAVELODGE AT FISHERMANS WHARF	250 BEACH ST, SF, 94133, (415)392-6700	2 - J3
TRAVELODGE SAN FRANCISCO CENTRAL	1707 MARKET ST, SF, 94103, (415)621-6775	10 - H1
TRAVELODGE, GOLDEN GATE	2230 LOMBARD ST, SF, 94123, (415)922-3900	2 - G4
TRAVELODGE-FISHERMANS WHARF	1201 COLUMBUS AV, SF, 94133, (415)776-7070	2 - J3
VAGABOND INN, MIDTOWN	2550 VAN NESS AV, SF, 94123, (415)776-7500	2 - H4
VILLA FLORENCE	225 POWELL ST, SF, 94102, (415)397-7700	7 - A6
WESTIN SAINT FRANCIS	335 POWELL ST, SF, 94102, (415)397-7000	7 - A6

LIBRARIES

FEATURE NAME	Address City, ZIP Code	PAGE-GRID
ANZA LIBRARY	550 37TH AV, SF, 94121, (415)666-7160	4 - J7
BAYSHORE LIBRARY	2960 GENEVA AV, DALY, 94014, (650)991-8074	19 - J3
BAYVIEW-ANNA WARDEN LIBRARY	5075 3RD ST, SF, 94124, (415)715-4100	15 - C6
BERNAL HEIGHTS LIBRARY	500 CORTLAND AV, SF, 94110, (415)695-5160	14 - J5
CHINATOWN LIBRARY	1135 POWELL ST, SF, 94108, (415)274-0275	7 - A5
DALY, JOHN D LIBRARY	6351 MISSION ST, DALY, 94014, (650)991-8073	18 - D3
EUREKA VALLEY-HARVEY MILK LIBRARY	3555 16TH ST, SF, 94114, (415)554-9445	10 - G2
EXCELSIOR LIBRARY	4400 MISSION ST, SF, 94112, (415)337-4735	14 - G7
GLEN PARK LIBRARY	653 CHENERY ST, SF, 94131, (415)337-4740	14 - G6
GOLDEN GATE VALLEY LIBRARY	1801 GREEN ST, SF, 94123, (415)292-2195	6 - H4
INGLESIDE LIBRARY	387 ASHTON AV, SF, 94127, (415)337-4745	13 - D7
LIBRARY FOR THE BLIND	3150 SACRAMENTO ST, SF, 94115, (415)292-2022	6 - F5
MARINA LIBRARY	1890 CHESTNUT ST, SF, 94123, (415)292-2150	2 - G4
MERCED LIBRARY	155 WINSTON DR, SF, 94132, (415)337-4780	13 - B7
MISSION LIBRARY	3359 24TH ST, SF, 94110, (415)695-5090	10 - H4
NOE VALLEY-SALLY BURN LIBRARY	451 JERSEY ST, SF, 94114, (415)695-5095	10 - G4
NORTH BEACH LIBRARY	2000 MASON ST, SF, 94133, (415)274-0270	2 - J3
OCEAN VIEW	111 BROAD ST, SF, 94112, (415)337-4785	18 - D2
ORTEGA LIBRARY	3223 ORTEGA ST, SF, 94116, (415)753-7120	8 - J3
PARK LIBRARY	1833 PAGE ST, SF, 94117, (415)666-7155	10 - E1
PARKSIDE LIBRARY	1200 TARAVAL ST, SF, 94116, (415)753-7125	13 - B5
PORTOLA LIBRARY	2450 SAN BRUNO AV, SF, 94134, (415)715-4090	15 - A6
POTRERO LIBRARY	1616 20TH ST, SF, 94107, (415)695-6640	11 - B2
PRESIDIO LIBRARY	3150 SACRAMENTO ST, SF, 94115, (415)292-2155	6 - F5
RICHMOND LIBRARY	351 9TH AV, SF, 94118, (415)666-7165	5 - C6
SAN FRANCISCO MAIN LIBRARY	100 LARKIN ST, SF, 94102, (415)557-4400	6 - J7
SUNSET LIBRARY	1305 18TH AV, SF, 94122, (415)753-7130	9 - B2
VISITACION VALLEY LIBRARY	45 LELAND AV, SF, 94134, (415)337-4790	20 - A2
WEST PORTAL LIBRARY	190 LENOX WY, SF, 94127, (415)753-7135	13 - C5
WESTERN ADDITION LIBRARY	1550 SCOTT ST, SF, 94115, (415)292-2160	6 - G6
WESTLAKE BRANCH LIBRARY	275 SOUTHGATE AV, DALY, 94015, (650)991-8071	18 - A4

MILITARY INSTALLATIONS

FEATURE NAME	Address City, ZIP Code	PAGE-GRID
EAST FORT MILEY	CLEMENT ST, SF, 94121	4 - J6
FORT FUNSTON	HERBST RD, SF, 94132	12 - H6
NAVAL RESERVATION	INNES AV & DONAHUE ST, SF, 94124	15 - D7
TREASURE ISLAND NAVAL RESERVATION	SF-OAKLAND BAY BRIDGE, SF, 94130, (415)395-1000	3 - D1
UNITED STATES MILITARY RESERVE	HERBST RD & SKYLINE BLVD, SF, 94132	12 - H6
US COAST GUARD STATION	MARINE DR, SF, 94129	1 - D3
WEST FORT MILEY	CLEMENT ST, SF, 94121	4 - H6

MUSEUMS

FEATURE NAME	Address City, ZIP Code	PAGE-GRID
ASIAN ART MUSEUM	S TEA GARDEN DR, SF, 94118, (415)668-8921	9 - C1
CALIFORNIA HIST SOCIETY MUSEUM	687 MISSION ST, SF, 94103, (415)357-1848	7 - B6
CALIF PALACE OF THE LEGION OF HONOR	LEGION OF HONOR DR, SF, 94121, (415)750-3614	4 - J6
CENTER FOR THE ARTS	701 MISSION ST, SF, 94103, (415)978-2700	7 - A6
MH DE YOUNG MUSEUM	S TEA GARDEN DR, SF, 94118, (415)863-3330	9 - C1
PALACE OF FINE ARTS EXPLORATORIUM	3601 LYON ST, SF, 94123, (415)563-7337	2 - E3
PIONEER MEMORIAL MUSEUM	PRESIDIO AV & MASONIC AV, SF, 94115	6 - F6
PRESIDIO MUSEUM	LINCOLN BLVD & FUNSTON AV, SF, 94129, (415)561-4323	1 - E4
RANDALL MUSEUM	199 MUSEUM WY, SF, 94114, (415)554-9600	10 - F2
SAN FRANCISCO NATL MARITIME MUS	HYDE ST & JEFFERSON ST, SF, 94109, (415)556-3002	2 - H3
SAN FRANCISCO PERF ARTS LIBRARY	399 GROVE ST, SF, 94102, (415)255-4800	6 - H7
TREASURE ISLAND MUSEUM	AV OF THE PALMS, SF, 94130, (415)395-5067	3 - E2

PARKS & RECREATION

FEATURE NAME	Address City, ZIP Code	PAGE-GRID
ADAMS ROGERS PARK	OAKDALE AV & INGALLS ST, SF, 94124	15 - C6
AGUA VISTA PARK	100 TERRY A FRANCIOS BLVD, SF, 94107	11 - C2
ALAMO SQUARE	FULTON ST & SCOTT ST, SF, 94117	6 - G7
ALTA PLAZA	JACKSON ST & SCOTT ST, SF, 94115	6 - G5
APTOS PLAYGROUND	APTOS AV & OCEAN AV, SF, 94127	13 - C7
ARDEN PARK	ALTA VISTA WY & ARDENDALE DR, DALY, 94014	19 - G3
ARGONNE PLAYGROUND	19TH AV, SF, 94121	5 - B7
BALBOA PARK	OCEAN AV & SAN JOSE AV, SF, 94112, (415)337-4715	14 - F7
BAYSHORE HEIGHTS PARK	400 MARTIN ST, DALY, 94014	19 - H3
BAYSHORE PARK	45 MIDWAY DR, DALY, 94014	19 - J3
BAYVIEW PARK	JAMESTOWN AV, SF, 94124	20 - B2
BAYVIEW PLAYGROUND	3RD ST & CARROLL AV, SF, 94124	15 - B7
BERCUT EQUITATION FIELD	CHAIN OF LAKES & JF KENNEDY DR, SF, (415)668-7360	8 - J1
BERNAL HEIGHTS PARK	BERNAL HEIGHTS BLVD, SF, 94110	14 - J5
BILLY GOAT HILL PARK	BEACON ST & LAIDLEY ST, SF, 94131	14 - G5
BOEDDEKER PARK	JONES ST & EDDY ST, SF, 94102	6 - J6
BROOKS PARK	SHIELDS ST & ARCH ST, SF, 94132	18 - C1
BUENA VISTA PARK	BUENA VISTA AV & HAIGHT ST, SF, 94117	10 - F1
CANDLESTICK POINT STATE REC AREA	JAMESTOWN AV & HARNEY WY, SF, 94124	20 - D2
CHRISTOPHER PLAYGROUND	DIAMOND HEIGHTS BLVD, SF, 94131	14 - F5
CIVIC CENTER	POLK ST & GROVE ST, SF, 94102	6 - J7
CONRAD PARK	BEACH ST & COLUMBUS AV, SF, 94133	2 - J3
CORONA HEIGHTS PLAYGROUND	MUSEUM WY, SF, 94114	10 - F2
CROCKER AMAZON PLAYGROUND	GENEVA AV & MOSCOW ST, SF, 94112	19 - G2
DOUGLASS PLAYGROUND	26TH ST & DOUGLASS ST, SF, 94131, (415)695-5017	14 - F4
DUBOCE PARK	DUBOCE AV & STEINER ST, SF, 94117	10 - G1
EDGEHILL MOUNTAIN PARK	SHANGRILA WY, SF, 94127	13 - D5
ERSKINE, DOROTHY PARK	MARTHA AV & BURNSIDE AV, SF, 94131	14 - F6
EUREKA VALLEY RECREATION CENTER	DIAMOND ST & 19TH ST, SF, 94114	10 - G2
FAIRMOUNT PLAZA	FAIRMOUNT ST & MIGUEL ST, SF, 94131	14 - G5
FOLSOM PARK	FOLSOM ST & 21ST ST, SF, 94110	10 - J3
FRANKFORT PARK	FRANKFORT ST & OLIVER ST, DALY, 94014	18 - E3
FRANKFORT PARK	FRANKFORT ST & OLIVER ST, DALY, 94014	19 - E3
FRANKLIN SQUARE	17TH ST & HAMPSHIRE ST, SF, 94110	11 - A2
FULTON PLAYGROUND	28TH AV, SF, 94121	5 - A7
GARFIELD SQUARE	26TH ST & HARRISON ST, SF, 94110, (415)695-5010	10 - J4
GEORGE R MOSCONE REC CENTER	CHESTNUT ST & BUCHANAN ST, SF, 94123, (415)292-2006	2 - G3
GILMAN PARK	GILMAN AV & GIANTS DR, SF, 94124	20 - C1
GLEN CANYON PARK	OSHAUGHNESSY BLVD, SF, 94131	14 - F5
GLEN PARK RECREATION CENTER	BOSWORTH ST & ELK ST, SF, 94131, (415)337-4705	14 - F6
GOLDEN GATE NATIONAL REC AREA	SF, 94129, (415)556-0560	1 - D2
GOLDEN GATE PARK	FELL ST & STANYAN ST, SF, (415)666-7200	9 - D1
GRAND VIEW PARK	14TH AV & 15TH AV, SF, 94122	9 - C3
GRATTAN PLAYGROUND	STANYON ST & ALMA ST, SF, 94117	10 - E2
HAAS, WALTER PARK	ADDISON ST & BEACON ST, SF, 94131	14 - G5
HAMILTON SQUARE	GEARY BLVD & STEINER ST, SF, 94115	6 - G6
HAWK HILL PARK	RIVERA ST & FUNSTON AV, SF, 94116	13 - C4
HAYWARD PLAYGROUND	TURK ST & GOUGH ST, SF, 94102	6 - H6
HERMAN, JUSTIN PLAZA	MARKET ST & THE EMBARCADERO, SF, 94111	7 - B4
HILLTOP PARK	LA SALLE AV & NEWCOMB AV, SF, 94124	15 - C6
HOLLY PARK	HOLLY PARK CIR, SF, 94110	14 - H5
INDIA BASIN SHORELINE PARK	HUNTERS POINT BLVD, SF, 94124	15 - D6
INTERIOR PARK BELT	STANYON ST, SF, 94117	9 - E2

FEATURE NAME	Address City, ZIP Code	PAGE-GRID
JACKSON PLAYGROUND	ARKANSAS ST & MARIPOSA ST, SF, 94107	11 - B2
JEFFERSON SQUARE	TURK ST & GOUGH ST, SF, 94102	6 - H6
JULIUS KAHN PLAYGROUND	W PACIFIC AV & SPRUCE ST, SF, 94129, (415)292-2004	5 - E5
JURI COMMONS PARK	SAN JOSE AV & JURI ST, SF, 94110	10 - H4
KELLOCH-VELASCO PARK	KELLOCH AV & VELASCO AV, SF, 94134	19 - J3
KOSHLAND PARK	BUCHANAN ST & PAGE ST, SF, 94102	10 - H1
LAFAYETTE PARK	GOUGH ST & WASHINGTON ST, SF, 94109	6 - H5
LARSEN PARK	ULLOA ST & 19TH AV, SF, 94116	13 - B5
LINCOLN PARK	901 BRUNSWICK ST, DALY, 94014	18 - E3
MARCHBANK PARK	PARKVIEW AV & WOODROW ST, DALY, 94014	18 - C3
MCCOPPIN SQUARE	SANTIAGO ST & 24TH AV, SF, 94116	13 - B4
MCKINLEY SQUARE	VERMONT ST & 20TH ST, SF, 94107	11 - A3
MCLAREN, JOHN PARK	MANSELL ST & JOHN F SHELLEY DR, SF, 94134	19 - J1
MIDTOWN TERRACE PLAYGROUND	CLARENDON AV & OLYMPIA WY, SF, 94131, (415)753-7036	9 - E3
MISSION DOLORES PARK	DOLORES ST & 18TH ST, SF, 94114, (415)554-9529	10 - H2
MISSION HILLS PARK	FRANKFORT ST & GUTTENBERG ST, DALY, 94014	19 - F3
MISSION PLAYGROUND	19TH ST & VALENCIA ST, SF, 94110	10 - H2
MOUNT DAVIDSON PARK	MYRA WY & DALEWOOD WY, SF, 94127	13 - E5
MOUNT OLYMPUS PARK	UPPER TER, SF, 94117	10 - F2
MOUNTAIN LAKE PARK	W PACIFIC BLVD, SF, 94129	5 - C5
NICOL, ROLPH PARK	EUCALYPTUS DR & 25TH AV, SF, 94132	13 - B6
OCEAN VIEW PLAYGROUND	PLYMOUTH AV & MONTANA ST, SF, 94112	18 - D1
OSHAUGHNESSY HOLLOW PARK	OSHAUGHNESSY BLVD, SF, 94127	14 - F5
PALACE OF FINE ARTS	PALACE DR & MARINA BLVD, SF, 94123	2 - F4
PANHANDLE	OAK ST & STANYAN ST, SF, 94117	10 - E1
PARK	18TH AV, SF, 94121	5 - B6
PARK	30TH AV, SF, 94121	5 - A6
PARK	LARKIN ST & MYRTLE ST, SF, 94109	6 - J6
PARK	LATHROP AV & TOCOLOMA AV, SF, 94134	20 - B2
PARK	ORTEGA ST & 28TH AV, SF, 94116	9 - A3
PARK	SHIELDS ST & MONTICELLO ST, SF, 94132	18 - C1
PARK	SUNSET BLVD & SLOAT BLVD, SF, 94116	8 - J3
PARK	TAYLOR ST & VALLEJO ST, SF, 94133	6 - J4
PARK	VASQUEZ AV & LAGUNA HONDA BLVD, SF, 94127	13 - D4
PARKSIDE SQUARE	VICENTE ST & 28TH AV, SF, 94116	13 - A5
PINE LAKE PARK	WAWONA ST & 28TH AV, SF, 94132	13 - A5
PIONEER PARK	TELEGRAPH HILL BLVD, SF, 94133	3 - A3
PLAYGROUND	BRUNSWICK ST & LOWELL ST, SF, 94112	19 - E2
PLAYGROUND	CAYUGA AV & NAGLEE AV, SF, 94112	18 - E2
POLARIS PARK	POLARIS WY & CANYON DR, DALY, 94014	19 - F3
PORTOLA RECREATION CENTER	SILLIMAN ST & SOMERSET ST, SF, 94134	14 - J7
PORTSMOUTH SQUARE	WASHINGTON ST & KEARNY ST, SF, 94108	7 - A5
POTRERO DEL SOL PARK	1500 SAN BRUNO AV, SF, 94110	11 - A4
POTRERO HILL RECREATION CENTER	ARKANSAS ST & MADERA ST, SF, 94107	11 - B3
PRECITA PARK	PRECITA AV & FOLSOM ST, SF, 94110	14 - J4
RAYMOND KIMBELL PLAYGROUND	GEARY BLVD & STEINER ST, SF, 94115	6 - G6
RICHMOND PLAYGROUND	19TH AV, SF, 94121	5 - B6
ROCHAMBEAU PLAYGROUND	25TH AV, SF, 94121	5 - A6
ROLPH PLAYGROUND	HAMPSHIRE ST & 26TH ST, SF, 94110	11 - A4
ROSS PLAYGROUND	ARGUELLO BLVD & EDWARD ST, SF, 94118	5 - D7
RUSSIAN HILL PARK	LARKIN ST & CHESTNUT ST, SF, 94109	2 - H3
SAINT MARYS PARK	CRESENT AV & AGNON AV, SF, 94112, (415)695-5006	14 - H6
SAN BRUNO MTN STATE AND COUNTY PARK	GUADALUPE CANYON PKWY, SMCo, 94014	19 - F4
SILVER TERRACE PLAYGROUND	SILVER AV & ELMIRA ST, SF, 94124	15 - A6
SOUTH OF MARKET PARK	FOLSOM ST & 6TH ST, SF, 94103	7 - A7
SOUTH PARK	SOUTH PARK AV & LONDON AL, SF, 94107	7 - B6
SOUTH SUNSET PLAYGROUND	VICENTE ST & 40TH AV, SF, 94116	12 - J5
STERN, SIGMUND RECREATION GROVE	WAWONA ST & 19TH AV, SF, 94132	13 - B5
SUNNYSIDE RECREATION CENTER	EDNA ST, SF, 94127	14 - E6
SUNSET COMMUNITY CENTER	QUINTARA ST & 29TH AV, SF, 94116, (415)753-7047	8 - J4
SUNSET HEIGHTS PLAYGROUND	ROCKRIDGE DR, SF, 94116	9 - C4
SUNSET PLAYGROUND	LAWTON ST & 29TH AV, SF, 94122	9 - A3
SUTRO HEIGHTS PARK	POINT LOBOS AV & 48TH AV, SF, 94121	4 - H7
TANKHILL PARK	TWINPEAKS BLVD, SF, 94117	10 - E2
TRAP & SKEET RANGE	JOHN MUIR DR & SKYLINE BLVD, SF, 94132	17 - J1
TWIN PEAKS PARK	TWIN PEAKS BLVD, SF, 94131	10 - E3
UNION SQUARE	GEARY ST & POWELL ST, SF, 94108	7 - A6
UPPER NOE RECREATION CENTER	SANCHEZ ST & DAY ST, SF, 94131	14 - G5
WASHINGTON SQUARE	COLUMBUS AV & FILBERT ST, SF, 94133	3 - A4
WESTLAKE PARK	149 LAKE MERCED BLVD, DALY, 94015	18 - A3
YOUNGBLOOD COLEMAN PLAYGROUND	1801 MENDELL ST, SF, 94124	15 - C5

PERFORMING ARTS

FEATURE NAME	Address City, ZIP Code	PAGE-GRID
BROOKS HALL	99 GROVE ST, SF, 94102, (415)974-4060	6 - J7
CURRAN THEATER	445 GEARY ST, SF, 94102, (415)474-3800	7 - A6
GEARY THEATRE	415 GEARY ST, SF, 94102, (415)749-2228	7 - A6
GOLDEN GATE THEATRE	6TH ST & MARKET ST, SF, 94103, (415)474-3800	7 - A6
HERBST THEATRE	401 VAN NESS AV & MCALLISTER S, SF, 94102, (415)392-4400	6 - H7
LOUISE M. DAVIES SYMPHONY HALL	201 VAN NESS AV & GROVE ST, SF, 94102, (415)431-5400	6 - H7
MUSIC CONCOURSE	CONCOURSE DR, SF, 94118	9 - C1
PHOENIX THEATRE	301 8TH ST, SF, 94103, (415)621-4423	7 - A7
WAR MEMORIAL OPERA HOUSE	301 VAN NESS AV & GROVE ST, SF, 94102, (415)621-6600	6 - H7
WARFIELD THEATRE	982 MARKET ST, SF, 94102, (415)775-7722	7 - A6

POINTS OF INTEREST

FEATURE NAME	Address City, ZIP Code	PAGE-GRID
ANGLERS LODGE	JOHN F KENNEDY & 36TH AV, SF, (415)386-2630	8 - J1
CALIFORNIA ACADEMY OF SCIENCES	CONCOURSE DR, SF, 94118, (415)750-7145	9 - C1
CLIFF HOUSE	1066 POINT LOBOS AV, SF, 94121, (415)386-3330	4 - G7
CONSERVATORY OF FLOWERS	CONSERVATORY DR W, SF, (415)666-7017	9 - D1
DUTCH WINDMILL	GREAT HWY & JOHN F KENNEDY DR, SF	8 - H1
FISHERMANS MEMORIAL CHAPEL	THE EMBARCADERO & TAYLOR ST, SF, 94133	2 - J2
FISHERMANS WHARF	JEFFERSON ST & TAYLOR ST, SF, 94133	2 - H3
GOLDEN GATE EQUESTRIAN CENTER	36TH AV & JOHN F KENNEDY DR, SF	8 - J1
GOLDEN GATE YACHT CLUB	YACHT RD, SF, 94123, (415)346-2628	2 - F3
JAPANESE TEA GARDEN	MARTIN LUTHER KING JR DR, SF, 94118, (415)752-1171	9 - C1
MORRISON PLANETARIUM	CONCOURSE DR, SF, 94118, (415)750-7000	9 - C1
MURPHY WINDMILL	M L KING JR DR & GRE, SF	8 - H1
SAINT FRANCIS YACHT CLUB	YACHT RD, SF, 94123, (415)563-6363	2 - F3
SAN FRANCISCO COUNTY FAIR BUILDING	MARTIN LUTHER KING JR DR, SF	9 - C1
SAN FRANCISCO ZOO	SLOAT BLVD & 45TH AV, SF, 94132, (415)753-7061	12 - H6
SHERMAN HOUSE	2160 GREEN ST, SF, 94123, (415)563-3600	6 - G4
STEINHART AQUARIUM	CONCOURSE DR, SF, 94118, (415)221-5100	9 - C1
THOMAS BROTHERS MAPS STORE	550 JACKSON ST, SF, 94133, (415)981-7520	7 - A4
UNDERWATER WORLD	THE EMBARCADERO AT BEACH ST, SF, 94133, (415)623-5300	3 - A3
UNION STREET PLAZA	UNION ST, SF, 94123, (415)931-2445	6 - G4
YERBA BUENA GARDENS	MISSION ST & 3RD ST, SF, 94103, (415)978-2787	7 - A6
YMCA	WESTERN SHORE LN, SF, 94115	6 - H6

POINTS OF INTEREST - HISTORIC

FEATURE NAME	Address City, ZIP Code	PAGE-GRID
COIT TOWER	TELEGRAPH HILL BLVD, SF, 94133, (415)362-0808	3 - A4
FORT MASON	MARINA BLVD & BUCHANAN ST, SF, 94123, (415)979-3010	2 - H3
FORT MASON CENTER	MARINA BLVD & BUCHANAN ST, SF, 94123, (415)979-3010	2 - G3
FORT POINT NATIONAL HISTORIC SITE	MARINE DR, SF, 94129, (415)556-1693	1 - C2
FORT SCOTT	LINCOLN BLVD & DYNAMITE RD, SF, 94129	1 - B4
GOLDEN GATE BRIDGE	HWY 101 & BATTERY EAST RD, SF, 94129, (415)921-5858	1 - B2
MISSION DOLORES	3321 16TH ST, SF, 94114, (415)621-8203	10 - H2
MOUNT DAVIDSON CROSS	SF, 94127	13 - E5
OLD FEDERAL RESERVE	400 SANSOME ST, SF, 94111	7 - B5
OLD UNITED STATES MINT	88 5TH ST, SF, 94103, (415)744-6830	7 - A6
PIER 39	THE EMBARCADERO & PIER 39, SF, 94133	3 - A2
PORTALS OF THE PAST	CROSS OVER DR & TRANSVERSE DR, SF	9 - B1
SF NATIONAL MARITIME HIST PARK	HYDE ST & JEFFERSON ST, SF, 94109, (415)556-3002	2 - H2
WAR MEMORIAL	6655 MISSION ST, DALY, 94014, (650)991-8020	18 - D3

POST OFFICES

FEATURE NAME	Address City, ZIP Code	PAGE-GRID
A POST OFFICE	1550 STEINER ST, SF, 94115, (415)563-5954	6 - G6
BAYVIEW POST OFFICE	2111 LANE ST, SF, 94124, (415)822-7619	15 - B7
BERNAL	30 29TH ST, SF, 94110, (415)695-1703	14 - H4
C POST OFFICE	1198 S VAN NESS AV, SF, 94110, (415)285-7382	10 - J3
CHINATOWN POST OFFICE	867 STOCKTON ST, SF, 94108, (415)956-3566	7 - A5
CITY HALL POST OFFICE	VAN NESS AV, SF, 94102, (415)621-6325	6 - H7
CIVIC CENTER POST OFFICE	101 HYDE ST, SF, 94102, (415)441-8399	6 - J6
DIAMOND HEIGHTS POST OFFICE	5262 DIAMOND HEIGHTS BLVD, SF, 94131, (415)550-6412	14 - G4
E POST OFFICE	460 BRANNAN ST, SF, 94107, (415)543-7729	7 - B7
EMPORIUM POST OFFICE	835 MARKET ST, SF, 94103, (415)543-2606	7 - A6
FEDERAL BUILDING POST OFFICE	450 GOLDEN GATE AV, SF, 94102, (415)621-7505	6 - J6
FISK POST OFFICE	1317 9TH AV, SF, 94122, (415)759-1901	9 - C2
G POST OFFICE	4304 18TH ST, SF, 94114, (415)621-5317	10 - G2
GEARY POST OFFICE	5654 GEARY BLVD, SF, 94121, (415)752-0231	5 - B6
GOLDEN GATE POST OFFICE	3245 GEARY BLVD, SF, 94118, (415)751-1645	5 - E6
J POST OFFICE	554 CLAYTON ST, SF, 94117, (415)621-7445	10 - E1
LETTERMAN POST OFFICE	1100 LETTERMAN DR, SF, 94129, (415)563-7196	2 - E4
MACYS UNION SQUARE POST OFFICE	180 OFARREL ST, SF, 94108, (415)956-3570	7 - A6
MARINA POST OFFICE	2055 LOMBARD ST, SF, 94123, (415)563-4674	2 - G4
MCLAREN POST OFFICE	2755 SAN BRUNO AV, SF, 94134, (415)467-3560	15 - A7
MISSION ANNEX POST OFFICE	1600 BRYANT ST, SF, 94103, (415)621-8646	11 - A1
NOE VALLEY POST OFFICE	4083 24TH ST, SF, 94114, (415)821-0776	10 - G3
NORTH BEACH POST OFFICE	1640 STOCKTON ST, SF, 94133, (415)956-3581	3 - A4
NUMBER 40 BELL BAZAAR POST OFFICE	3030 16TH ST, SF, 94103, (415)621-6053	10 - H2
P & DC POST OFFICE	1300 EVANS AV, SF, 94124, (415)550-5247	15 - C5
PARKSIDE POST OFFICE	1800 TARAVAL ST, SF, 94116, (415)759-1601	13 - A5
PINE STREET POST OFFICE	1400 PINE ST, SF, 94109, (415)289-0755	6 - J5
POST OFFICE F	15 ONONDAGA AV, SF, 94112, (415)334-0739	19 - F1
PRESIDIO POST OFFICE	950 LINCOLN BLVD, SF, 94129, (415)563-4975	2 - E4
RINCON CENTER POST OFFICE	180 STEAURT ST, SF, 94105, (415)543-3340	7 - C5
STONESTOWN POST OFFICE	565 BUCKINGHAM WY, SF, 94132, (415)759-1660	13 - B7
SUNSET POST OFFICE	1314 22ND AV, SF, 94122, (415)759-1707	9 - B2
SUTTER POST OFFICE	150 SUTTER ST, SF, 94108, (415)956-3169	7 - A5
VISITATION POST OFFICE	68 LELAND AV, SF, 94134, (415)333-1150	20 - A2
VISTA GRANDE STATION	6025 MISSION ST, DALY, 94014, (415)334-7884	18 - D3
WEST PORTAL POST OFFICE	317 W PORTAL AV, SF, 94127, (415)759-1811	13 - C5
WESTLAKE STATION POST OFFICE	199 SOUTHGATE AV, DALY, 94015, (650)756-1842	18 - A4

SCHOOLS - PRIVATE ELEMENTARY

FEATURE NAME	Address City, ZIP Code	PAGE-GRID
BRANDEIS HILLEL DAY ELEM SCHOOL	655 BROTHERHOOD WY, SF, 94132, (415)406-1035	18 - B2
CATHEDRAL SCHOOL FOR BOYS	1275 SACRAMENTO ST, SF, 94108, (415)771-6600	6 - J5
CONVENT OF THE SACRED HEART	2200 BROADWAY ST, SF, 94115, (415)563-2900	6 - G5
CORNERSTONE ACADEMY BAPTIST	801 SILVER AV, SF, 94134, (415)587-7256	14 - H7
CORPUS CHRISTI ELEM SCHOOL	75 FRANCIS ST, SF, 94112, (415)587-7014	14 - G7
DELMAR BURKE, KATHERINE ELEM	7070 CALIFORNIA ST, SF, 94121, (415)751-0177	5 - A6
DISCOVERY CENTER ELEM SCHOOL	65 OCEAN AV, SF, 94112, (415)333-6609	14 - F7
EPIPHANY ELEM SCHOOL	600 ITALY AV, SF, 94112, (415)337-4030	19 - G1
FIRST BAPTIST CHURCH SCHOOL	42 WALLER ST, SF, 94102, (415)863-1691	10 - H1
FRENCH-AMERICAN INTL ELEM	220 BUCHANAN ST, SF, 94102, (415)626-8564	10 - H1
HAMLIN	2129 VALLEJO ST, SF, 94115, (415)922-0600	6 - G5
HEBREW ACADEMY OF SAN FRANCISCO	645 14TH AV, SF, 94118, (415)752-7490	5 - C7
HOLY NAME ELEM SCHOOL	1560 40TH AV, SF, 94122, (415)731-4077	8 - J2
IMMACULATE CONCEPTION ELEM	1550 TREAT AV, SF, 94110, (415)824-6860	14 - J4
KITTREDGE SCHOOL	2355 LAKE ST, SF, 94121, (415)750-8390	5 - A6
KROUZIAN-ZEKARIAN OF ST. GREGORY-ARMEN	825 BROTHERHOOD WY, SF, 94132, (415)586-8686	18 - B2
LYCEE FRANCAIS INTL-LAPEROUSE	3301 BALBOA ST, SF, 94121, (415)668-1833	4 - J7
MISSION DOLORES ELEM SCHOOL	3371 16TH ST, SF, 94103, (415)861-7673	10 - H2
NOTRE DAME VICTORIES ELEM SCHOOL	659 PINE ST, SF, 94108, (415)421-0069	7 - A5
OUR LADY OF MERCY ELEM SCHOOL	7 ELMWOOD DR, DALY, 94015, (650)756-3395	18 - A4
OUR LADY OF PERPETUAL HELP	80 WELLINGTON AV, DALY, 94014, (650)755-4438	18 - D3
OUR LADY OF THE VISITACION	785 SUNNYDALE AV, SF, 94134, (415)239-7840	19 - J2
PRESIDIO HILL	3839 WASHINGTON ST, SF, 94118, (415)751-9318	5 - E5
SACRED HEART GRAMMAR ELEM SCHOOL	735 FELL ST, SF, 94117, (415)621-8035	6 - G7
SAINT ANNE ELEM SCHOOL	1320 14TH AV, SF, 94122, (415)664-7977	9 - C2
SAINT ANTHONY ELEM SCHOOL	299 PRECITA AV, SF, 94110, (415)648-2008	14 - J4
SAINT BRENDAN ELEM SCHOOL	234 ULLOA ST, SF, 94127, (415)731-2665	13 - D5
SAINT BRIGID ELEM SCHOOL	2250 FRANKLIN ST, SF, 94109, (415)673-4523	6 - H5
SAINT CECILIA ELEM SCHOOL	660 VICENTE ST, SF, 94116, (415)731-8400	13 - B5
SAINT CHARLES BORROMEO SCHOOL	3250 18TH ST, SF, 94110, (415)861-7652	10 - J2
SAINT DOMINIC ELEM SCHOOL	2445 PINE ST, SF, 94115, (415)346-9500	6 - G5
SAINT ELIZABETHS ELEM SCHOOL	450 SOMERSET ST, SF, 94134, (415)468-3247	15 - A7
SAINT EMYDIUS ELEM SCHOOL	301 DE MONTFORT AV, SF, 94112, (415)333-4877	13 - D7
SAINT FINN BARR ELEM SCHOOL	419 HEARST AV, SF, 94112, (415)333-1800	14 - E6
SAINT GABRIEL ELEM SCHOOL	2550 41ST AV, SF, 94116, (415)566-0314	12 - J5
SAINT JAMES ELEM SCHOOL	321 FAIR OAKS ST, SF, 94110, (415)647-8972	10 - H4
SAINT JOHN ELEM SCHOOL	925 CHENERY ST, SF, 94131, (415)584-8383	14 - F6
SAINT JOHN THE EVANGELIST	4056 MISSION ST, SF, 94112, (415)334-4646	14 - G6
SAINT JOSEPH ELEM SCHOOL	220 10TH ST, SF, 94103, (415)431-1206	10 - J1
SAINT MARY CHINESE DAY ELEM SCHOOL	910 BROADWAY ST, SF, 94133, (415)929-4690	6 - J4
SAINT MONICA ELEM SCHOOL	5920 GEARY BLVD, SF, 94121, (415)751-9564	5 - B6
SAINT PAUL ELEM SCHOOL	180 FAIR OAKS ST, SF, 94110, (415)648-2055	10 - H3
SAINT PETER ELEM SCHOOL	1266 FLORIDA ST, SF, 94110, (415)647-8662	10 - J4
SAINT PHILIP ELEM SCHOOL	665 ELIZABETH ST, SF, 94114, (415)824-8467	10 - G3
SAINT STEPHEN ELEM SCHOOL	401 EUCALYPTUS DR, SF, 94132, (415)664-8331	13 - B6
SAINT THOMAS MORE ELEM SCHOOL	50 THOMAS MORE WY, SF, 94132, (650)377-0100	18 - C2

FEATURE NAME	Address City, ZIP Code	PAGE-GRID
SAINT THOMAS THE APOSTLE	3801 BALBOA ST, SF, 94121, (415)221-2711	4 - J7
SAINT VINCENT DE PAUL ELEM SCHOOL	2350 GREEN ST, SF, 94123, (415)346-5505	6 - G4
SAINTS PETER & PAUL	600 FIBERT ST, SF, 94133, (415)421-5219	3 - A4
SAN FRANCISCO CHRISTIAN ELEM SCHOOL	25 WHITTIER ST, SF, 94112, (415)586-1117	19 - E2
SAN FRANCISCO DAY	350 MASONIC AV, SF, 94115, (415)931-2422	6 - F7
SAN FRANCISCO JUNIOR ACADEMY ELEM	66 GENEVA AV, SF, 94112, (415)585-5550	19 - F1
SAN FRANCISCO MONTESSORI	300 GAVEN ST, SF, 94134, (415)239-5065	14 - J6
SAN FRANCISCO WALDORF ELEM SCHOOL	2938 WASHINGTON ST, SF, 94115, (415)931-2750	6 - F5
SF CHINESE PARENT COMMUNITY ELEM	843 STOCKTON ST, SF, 94108, (415)391-5564	7 - A5
ST PAUL OF THE SHIPWRECK ACADEMY	1060 KEY AV, SF, 94124, (415)467-1798	20 - B1
STAR OF THE SEA ELEM SCHOOL	360 9TH AV, SF, 94118, (415)221-8558	5 - C6
STUART HALL FOR BOYS ELEM SCHOOL	2252 BROADWAY ST, SF, 94115, (415)563-2900	6 - G4
TOWN SCHOOL FOR BOYS ELEM SCHOOL	2750 JACKSON ST, SF, 94115, (415)921-3747	6 - F5
WEST PORTAL LUTHERAN ELEM SCHOOL	200 SLOAT BLVD, SF, 94132, (415)665-6330	13 - C6
ZION LUTHERAN ELEM SCHOOL	495 9TH AV, SF, 94118, (415)221-7500	5 - C7

SCHOOLS - PRIVATE HIGH

FEATURE NAME	Address City, ZIP Code	PAGE-GRID
BRIDGEMONT HIGH SCHOOL	501 CAMBRIDGE ST, SF, 94134, (415)333-7600	14 - J7
CONVENT OF THE SACRED HEART HS	2222 BROADWAY ST, SF, 94115, (415)292-3122	6 - G5
DREW COLLEGE PREPARATORY HS	2901 CALIFORNIA ST, SF, 94115, (415)346-4831	6 - F5
FRENCH-AMERICAN INTERNATIONAL HS	220 BUCHANAN ST, SF, 94102, (415)626-8564	10 - H1
IMMACULATE CONCEPTION ACADEMY	3625 24TH ST, SF, 94110, (415)824-2052	10 - H4
LICK-WILMERDING HIGH SCHOOL	755 OCEAN AV, SF, 94112, (415)333-4021	14 - E7
LYCEE FRANCAIS INTL-LAPEROUSE	3301 BALBOA ST, SF, 94121, (415)668-1833	4 - J7
MERCY HIGH SCHOOL (GIRLS)	3250 19TH AV, SF, 94132, (415)334-0525	13 - B6
RIORDAN HIGH SCHOOL (BOYS)	175 PHELAN AV, SF, 94112, (415)586-8200	13 - E7
SACRED HEART CATHEDRAL PREP HS	1055 ELLIS ST, SF, 94109, (415)775-6626	6 - H6
SAINT IGNATIUS COLLEGE PREP HS	2001 37TH AV, SF, 94116, (415)731-7500	8 - J4
SAINT JOHN THE EVANGELIST HS	4056 MISSION ST, SF, 94112, (415)334-4646	14 - H6
SAINT PAUL HIGH SCHOOL	317 29TH ST, SF, 94131, (415)648-0505	14 - H4
SAINT ROSE ACADEMY	2475 PINE ST, SF, 94115, (415)921-3584	6 - G5
SAN FRANCISCO UNIVERSITY HS	3065 JACKSON ST, SF, 94115, (415)346-8400	6 - F5
STAR OF THE SEA ACADEMY	350 9TH AV, SF, 94118, (415)221-8558	5 - C6
URBAN HIGH SCHOOL	1563 PAGE ST, SF, 94117, (415)626-2919	10 - F1

SCHOOLS - PUBLIC ELEMENTARY

FEATURE NAME	Address City, ZIP Code	PAGE-GRID
ALAMO ELEM SCHOOL	250 23RD AV, SF, 94121, (415)750-8456	5 - B6
ALVARADO ELEM SCHOOL	625 DOUGLASS ST, SF, 94114, (415)695-5695	10 - F3
ARGONNE ELEM SCHOOL	3950 SACRAMENTO ST, SF, 94118, (415)750-8460	5 - D6
BAYSHORE ELEM SCHOOL	155 ORIENTE ST, DALY, 94014, (415)467-0442	19 - J3
BRYANT ELEM SCHOOL	1050 YORK ST, SF, 94110, (415)695-5780	11 - A3
BUENA VISTA ANNEX SCHOOL	2641 25TH ST, SF, 94110, (415)695-5875	11 - A4
CABRILLO ELEM SCHOOL	735 24TH AV, SF, 94121, (415)750-8464	5 - B7
CARMICHAEL, BESSIE ELEM SCHOOL	55 SHERMAN ST, SF, 94103, (415)241-6294	7 - A7
CARVER, GEORGE WASHINGTON ELEM	1360 OAKDALE AV, SF, 94124, (415)330-1540	15 - C6
CHAVEZ, CESAR ELEM SCHOOL	825 SHOTWELL ST, SF, 94110, (415)695-5765	10 - J3
CHIN, JOHN YEHALL	350 BROADWAY ST, SF, 94133, (415)291-7946	7 - A4
CHINESE EDUCATION CENTER ELEM	657 MERCHANT ST, SF, 94111, (415)291-7918	7 - B5
CLARENDON ELEM SCHOOL	500 CLARENDON AV, SF, 94131, (415)759-2796	9 - D3
CLEVELAND ELEM SCHOOL	455 ATHENS ST, SF, 94112, (415)469-4709	19 - G1
COBB, WILLIAM L ELEM SCHOOL	2725 CALIFORNIA ST, SF, 94115, (415)749-3505	6 - F6
COMMODORE SLOAT ELEM SCHOOL	50 DARIEN WY, SF, 94127, (415)759-2807	13 - C6
COMMODORE STOCKTON ELEM SCHOOL	950 CLAY ST, SF, 94108, (415)291-7921	7 - A5
DE AVILA, WILLIAM ELEM SCHOOL	1351 HAIGHT ST, SF, 94117, (415)241-6325	10 - F1
DREW, CHARLES R ELEM SCHOOL	50 POMONA ST, SF, 94124, (415)330-1526	15 - B6
EDISON ELEM SCHOOL	3531 22ND ST, SF, 94114, (415)695-5848	10 - H3
EL DORADO ELEM SCHOOL	70 DELTA ST, SF, 94134, (415)330-1537	20 - A1
FAIRMOUNT ELEM SCHOOL	65 CHENERY ST, SF, 94131, (415)695-5669	14 - H5
FLYNN, LEONARD ELEM SCHOOL	3125 CESAR CHAVEZ ST, SF, 94110, (415)695-5770	14 - J4
GARFIELD ELEM SCHOOL	420 FILBERT ST, SF, 94133, (415)291-7924	3 - A4
GLEN PARK ELEM SCHOOL	151 LIPPARD AV, SF, 94131, (415)469-4713	14 - G6
GOLDEN GATE ELEM SCHOOL	1601 TURK ST, SF, 94115, (415)749-3509	6 - G7
GRATTAN ELEM SCHOOL	165 GRATTAN ST, SF, 94117, (415)759-2815	10 - E2
GUADALUPE ELEM SCHOOL	859 PRAGUE ST, SF, 94112, (415)469-4718	19 - G2
HARTE, BRET ELEM SCHOOL	1035 GILMAN AV, SF, 94124, (415)330-1520	20 - C1
HILLCREST ELEM SCHOOL	810 SILVER AV, SF, 94134, (415)469-4722	14 - H7
JEFFERSON ELEM SCHOOL	1725 IRVING ST, SF, 94122, (415)759-2821	9 - B2
KEY, FRANCIS SCOTT ELEM SCHOOL	1530 43RD AV, SF, 94122, (415)759-2811	8 - H2
KING, STARR ELEM SCHOOL	1215 CAROLINA ST, SF, 94107, (415)695-5797	11 - B3
LAFAYETTE ELEM SCHOOL	4545 ANZA ST, SF, 94121, (415)750-8543	4 - J7
LAKESHORE ELEM SCHOOL	220 MIDDLEFIELD DR, SF, 94132, (415)759-2825	13 - A6
LAWTON ELEM SCHOOL	1570 31ST AV, SF, 94122, (415)759-2832	9 - A2
LILIENTHAL, CLAIRE ELEM SCHOOL	3630 DIVISADERO ST, SF, 94123, (415)749-3516	2 - F3
LONGFELLOW ELEM SCHOOL	755 MORSE ST, SF, 94112, (415)469-4730	19 - E2
MALCOLM X ELEM SCHOOL	350 HARBOR RD, SF, 94124, (415)695-5950	15 - D6
MARSHALL ELEM SCHOOL	1575 15TH ST, SF, 94103, (415)241-6280	10 - J2
MCCOPPIN, FRANK ELEM SCHOOL	651 6TH AV, SF, 94118, (415)750-8475	5 - D7
MCKINLEY ELEM SCHOOL	1025 14TH ST, SF, 94114, (415)241-6300	10 - G1
MILK, HARVEY ELEM SCHOOL	4235 19TH ST, SF, 94114, (415)241-6276	10 - G3
MIRALOMA ELEM SCHOOL	175 OMAR WY, SF, 94127, (415)469-4734	14 - E5
MISSION EDUCATION CENTER	1670 NOE ST, SF, 94131, (415)695-5313	14 - G5
MONROE ELEM SCHOOL	260 MADRID ST, SF, 94112, (415)469-4736	14 - G7
MOSCONE, GEORGE R ELEM SCHOOL	2355 FOLSOM ST, SF, 94110, (415)695-5736	10 - J3
MUIR, JOHN ELEM SCHOOL	380 WEBSTER ST, SF, 94102, (415)241-6335	6 - H7
ORTEGA, JOSE ELEM SCHOOL	400 SARGENT ST, SF, 94132, (415)469-4726	18 - C1
PANORAMA ELEM SCHOOL	25 BELLEVUE AV, DALY, 94014, (415)586-6595	19 - F3
PARKER, JEAN ELEM SCHOOL	840 BROADWAY ST, SF, 94133, (415)291-7990	7 - A4
PARKS, ROSA ELEM SCHOOL	1501 OFARRELL ST, SF, 94115, (415)749-3519	6 - G6
PEABODY, GEORGE ELEM SCHOOL	251 6TH AV, SF, 94118, (415)750-8480	5 - D6
REDDING ELEM SCHOOL	1421 PINE ST, SF, 94109, (415)749-3525	6 - J5
REVERE, PAUL ANNEX	610 TOMPKINS AV, SF, 94110, (415)695-5974	14 - J5
REVERE, PAUL ELEM SCHOOL	555 TOMPKINS AV, SF, 94110, (415)695-5656	14 - J6
ROOFTOP ALTERNATIVE ELEM SCHOOL	443 BURNETT AV, SF, 94131, (415)695-5691	10 - F3
SAN FRANCISCO COMMUNITY ELEM SCHOOL	125 EXCELSIOR AV, SF, 94112, (415)469-4739	14 - G7
SANCHEZ ELEM SCHOOL	325 SANCHEZ ST, SF, 94114, (415)241-6380	10 - G2
SERRA, JUNIPERO ELEM SCHOOL	625 HOLLY PARK CIR, SF, 94110, (415)695-5685	14 - H6
SHERIDAN ELEM SCHOOL	431 CAPITOL AV, SF, 94112, (415)469-4743	18 - D2
SHERMAN ELEM SCHOOL	1651 UNION ST, SF, 94123, (415)749-3530	6 - H4
SPRING VALLEY ELEM SCHOOL	1451 JACKSON ST, SF, 94109, (415)749-3535	6 - J5
STEVENSON, ROBERT LOUIS ELEM	2051 34TH AV, SF, 94116, (415)759-2837	8 - J4
SUNNYSIDE ELEM SCHOOL	250 FOERSTER ST, SF, 94112, (415)469-4746	14 - E6
SUNSET ELEM SCHOOL	3045 SANTIAGO, SF, 94116, (415)759-2760	12 - J4
SUTRO ELEM SCHOOL	235 12TH AV, SF, 94118, (415)750-8525	5 - C6
SWETT, JOHN ELEM SCHOOL	727 GOLDEN GATE AV, SF, 94102, (415)241-6320	6 - H7
TAYLOR, EDWARD R ELEM SCHOOL	423 BURROWS ST, SF, 94134, (415)330-1530	15 - A7
ULLOA ELEM SCHOOL	2650 42ND AV, SF, 94116, (415)759-2841	12 - J5
VISITACION VALLEY ELEM SCHOOL	55 SCHWERIN ST, SF, 94134, (415)469-4796	19 - J2
WASHINGTON, GEORGE ELEM SCHOOL	251 WHITTIER ST, DALY, 94014, (650)991-1236	19 - E2
WEBSTER, DANIEL ELEM SCHOOL	465 MISSOURI ST, SF, 94107, (415)695-5787	11 - B2
WEST PORTAL ELEM SCHOOL	5 LENOX WY, SF, 94127, (415)759-2846	13 - D5
WESTLAKE ELEM SCHOOL	80 FIELDCREST DR, DALY, 94015, (650)991-1252	18 - B3
WILSON, WOODROW ELEM SCHOOL	43 MIRIAM ST, DALY, 94014, (650)991-1255	18 - C3
WO, YICK ELEM SCHOOL	2245 JONES ST, SF, 94133, (415)749-3540	2 - J4
YU, ALICE FONG ELEM SCHOOL	1541 12TH AV, SF, 94122, (415)759-2764	9 - C2

SCHOOLS - PUBLIC HIGH

FEATURE NAME	Address City, ZIP Code	PAGE-GRID
BALBOA HIGH SCHOOL	1000 CAYUGA AV, SF, 94112, (415)469-4090	19 - F1
BURTON, PHILLIP & SALA HIGH SCHOOL	400 MANSELL ST, SF, 94134, (415)469-4550	20 - A1
DOWNTOWN CONTINUATION HIGH SCHOOL	110 BARTLETT ST, SF, 94110, (415)695-5860	10 - H3
GALILEO HIGH SCHOOL	1150 FRANCISCO ST, SF, 94109, (415)749-3430	2 - H3
INDEPENDENCE HIGH SCHOOL	1717 44TH AV, SF, 94122, (415)242-2528	8 - H3
INTERNATIONAL STUDIES ACADEMY	693 VERMONT ST, SF, 94107, (415)595-5866	11 - A2
LINCOLN, ABRAHAM HIGH SCHOOL	2162 24TH AV, SF, 94116, (415)759-2700	9 - B4
LOWELL HIGH SCHOOL	1101 EUCALYPTUS DR, SF, 94132, (415)759-2730	13 - B6
MARSHALL, THURGOOD ACADEMIC HS	45 CONKLING ST, SF, 94124, (415)695-5612	15 - A6
MCATEER, EUGENE J HIGH SCHOOL	555 PORTOLA DR, SF, 94131, (415)695-5700	14 - E4
MISSION HIGH SCHOOL	3750 18TH ST, SF, 94114, (415)241-6240	10 - H2
NEWCOMER HIGH (LEP) SCHOOL	2340 JACKSON ST, SF, 94115, (415)241-6584	6 - G5
OCONNELL, JOHN HIGH SCHOOL	1920 41ST AV, SF, 94116, (415)759-2724	8 - J3
SCHOOL OF THE ARTS HIGH SCHOOL	700 FONT BLVD, SF, 94132, (415)469-4027	13 - A7
WALLENBERG, RAOUL TRADITIONAL HS	40 VEGA ST, SF, 94115, (415)749-3469	6 - F7
WASHINGTON, GEORGE HIGH SCHOOL	600 32ND AV, SF, 94121, (415)750-8400	5 - A7
WELLS, IDA B / TWAIN, MARK HS	1099 HAYES ST, SF, 94117, (415)241-6315	6 - G7

SCHOOLS - PUBLIC INTERMEDIATE

FEATURE NAME	Address City, ZIP Code	PAGE-GRID
ROBERTSON, GARNET J INT	1 MARTIN ST, DALY, 94014, (415)467-5443	19 - J4

SCHOOLS - PUBLIC MIDDLE

FEATURE NAME	Address City, ZIP Code	PAGE-GRID
APTOS MIDDLE SCHOOL	105 APTOS AV, SF, 94127, (415)469-4520	13 - C6
BURBANK, LUTHER MIDDLE SCHOOL	325 LA GRANDE AV, SF, 94112, (415)469-4547	19 - H1
DAVIS, GLORIA B. MIDDLE SCHOOL	1195 HUDSON ST, SF, 94124, (415)469-4547	15 - D6
DENMAN, JAMES MIDDLE SCHOOL	241 ONEIDA AV, SF, 94112, (415)469-4535	19 - F1
EVERETT MIDDLE SCHOOL	450 CHURCH ST, SF, 94114, (415)241-6344	10 - G2
FRANCISCO MIDDLE SCHOOL	2190 POWELL ST, SF, 94133, (415)291-7900	3 - A3
FRANKLIN, BENJAMIN MIDDLE SCHOOL	1430 SCOTT ST, SF, 94115, (415)749-3476	6 - G6
GIANNINI, A P MIDDLE SCHOOL	3151 ORTEGA ST, SF, 94116, (415)759-2770	8 - J3
HOOVER, HERBERT MIDDLE SCHOOL	2290 14TH AV, SF, 94116, (415)759-2783	13 - C4
KING, MARTIN LUTHER ACADEMIC MID	350 GIRARD ST, SF, 94134, (415)330-1500	15 - A7
LICK, JAMES MIDDLE SCHOOL	1220 NOE ST, SF, 94114, (415)695-5675	10 - G4
MANN, HORACE MIDDLE SCHOOL	3351 23RD ST, SF, 94110, (415)695-5881	10 - H3
MARINA MIDDLE SCHOOL	3500 FILLMORE ST, SF, 94123, (415)749-3495	2 - G4
POTRERO HILL MIDDLE SCHOOL	655 DE HARO ST, SF, 94107, (415)695-5905	11 - B2
PRESIDIO MIDDLE SCHOOL	450 30TH AV, SF, 94121, (415)750-8435	5 - A6
ROOSEVELT MIDDLE SCHOOL	460 ARGUELLO BLVD, SF, 94118, (415)750-8446	5 - D6
VISITACION VALLEY MIDDLE SCHOOL	450 RAYMOND AV, SF, 94134, (415)469-4590	19 - J2

SHOPPING CENTERS - COMMUNITY

FEATURE NAME	Address City, ZIP Code	PAGE-GRID
CROCKER GALLERIA	50 POST ST, SF, 94108, (415)393-1500	7 - A5
DIAMOND HEIGHTS CENTER	DIAMOND HTS BL & GOLD MINE DR, SF, 94131	14 - F5
EMBARCADERO CENTER	4 EMBARCADERO CTR, SF, 94111, (415)772-0500	7 - B5
GHIRARDELLI SQUARE	900 NORTH POINT ST, SF, 94109, (415)775-5500	2 - H3
JAPAN CENTER	1737 POST ST, SF, 94115, (415)922-6776	6 - H6
LUCKY LAKESHORE PLAZA	1501 SLOAT BLVD, SF, 94132	13 - A6
NORTHPOINT CENTRE	2351 POWELL ST, SF, 94133, (415)391-1313	3 - A3
THE ANCHORAGE	2800 LEAVENWORTH ST, SF, 94133, (415)775-6000	2 - J3
THE CANNERY	2801 LEAVENWORTH ST, SF, 94133, (415)771-3112	2 - J3

SHOPPING MALLS

FEATURE NAME	Address City, ZIP Code	PAGE-GRID
SAN FRANCISCO CENTRE	5TH ST & MARKET ST, SF, 94103, (415)495-5656	7 - A6
STONESTOWN GALLERIA	19TH AV & WINSTON DR, SF, 94132, (415)759-2623	13 - B6
WESTLAKE CENTER	285 LAKE MERCED BLVD, DALY, 94015, (650)756-2161	18 - A5

TRANSPORTATION

FEATURE NAME	Address City, ZIP Code	PAGE-GRID
16TH ST & MISSION ST STATION	16TH ST & MISSION ST, SF, 94110	10 - J2
24TH ST & MISSION ST STATION	24TH ST & MISSION ST, SF, 94110	10 - J3
BALBOA PARK STATION	OCEAN AV & SAN JOSE AV, SF, 94112	19 - E1
BAYSHORE CALTRAIN STATION	TUNNEL AV & VISITACION AV, SF, 94134	20 - A2
CALTRAIN 22ND STREET STATION	22ND ST & PENNSYLVANIA AV, SF, 94107	11 - B3
CALTRAIN PAUL AVENUE STATION	PAUL AV & GOULD ST, SF, 94124	15 - B7
CALTRAIN TERMINAL	FOURTH ST & TOWNSEND ST, SF, 94107	7 - B7
CASTRO STREET STATION	CASTRO ST & MARKET ST, SF, 94114	10 - G2
CHURCH STREET STATION	CHURCH ST & MARKET ST, SF, 94114	10 - H1
CIVIC CENTER STATION	7TH ST & MARKET ST, SF, 94103	6 - J7
DALY CITY STATION	JOHN DALY BLVD & DE LONG ST, DALY, 94014	18 - C3
EMBARCADERO STATION	MAIN ST & MARKET ST, SF, 94105	7 - B5
FOREST HILLS STATION	LAGUNA HONDA BLVD & DEWEY BLVD, SF, 94116	9 - D4
GLEN PARK STATION	BOSWORTH ST & DIAMOND ST, SF, 94131	14 - G6
GREEN MUNI CENTER	SAN JOSE AV & GENEVA AV, SF, 94112	19 - F1
MONTGOMERY ST STATION	MONTGOMERY ST & MARKET ST, SF, 94105	7 - B5
POWELL STATION	POWELL ST & MARKET ST, SF, 94103	7 - A6
TRANSBAY TRANSIT TERMINAL	1ST ST & NATOMA ST, SF, 94105	7 - B5
VAN NESS STATION	12TH ST & MARKET ST, SF, 94103	6 - H7
WEST PORTAL STATION	W PORTAL AV & VICENTE ST, SF, 94127	13 - C5

A

PRIMARY STREET / Address	Cross Street	ZIP	CITY Pg-Grid
A ST			SF
680	NIMITZ AV	94124	16-F7
	SPEAR AV	94124	16-F7
ABBEY ST			SF
1	CHULA LN	94114	10-H2
100	17TH ST	94114	10-H2
ACADIA ST			SF
100	MONTEREY BLVD	94131	14-F6
200	JOOST AV	94131	14-F6
ACEVEDO AV			SF
1	VIDAL DR	94132	18-A1
100	ARBALLO DR	94132	18-A1
ACORN AL			SF
1400	LEAVENWORTH ST	94109	6-J5
ACTON ST			SF
1	MISSION ST	94112	18-E2
1	SICKLES AV	94112	18-E2
ADA CT			SF
1	OFARRELL ST	94109	6-J6
50	AMITY AL	94109	6-J6
ADAIR ST			SF
1	S VAN NESS AV	94103	10-J2
100	CAPP ST	94103	10-J2
ADDISON ST			SF
250	DIGBY ST	94131	14-G5
300	FARNUM ST	94131	14-G5
400	DIAMOND HEIGHTS BLVD	94131	14-G5
400	GOLD MINE DR	94131	14-G5
1	BEMIS ST	94131	14-G5
ADELE CT			SF
1	JACKSON ST	94133	7-A4
ADMIRAL AV			SF
1	MISSION ST	94112	14-G6
50	CAMELLIA AV	94112	14-G6
100	ALEMANY BLVD	94112	14-G6
ADOLPH SUTRO CT			SF
1	JOHNSTONE DR	94131	9-E3
AERIAL WY			SF
40	PACHECO ST	94116	9-C3
70	FUNSTON AV	94116	9-C3
AGATE AL			SF
600	POST ST	94109	6-J6
650	COSMO PL	94109	6-J6
AGNON AV			SF
1	CRESCENT AV	94112	14-H6
100	JUSTIN DR	94112	14-H6
AGUA WY			SF
1	TERESITA BLVD	94127	13-E5
100	CHAVES AV	94127	13-E5
AHERN WY			SF
	6TH ST	94103	7-A7
	HARRIET ST	94103	7-A7
AHLERS CT			SF
	FILBERT ST	94123	6-G4
ALABAMA ST			SF
100	ALAMEDA ST	94103	10-J1
150	TREAT AV	94103	10-J1
200	15TH ST	94103	10-J2
300	16TH ST	94110	10-J2
400	17TH ST	94110	10-J2
500	MARIPOSA ST	94110	10-J2
600	18TH ST	94110	10-J2
700	19TH ST	94110	10-J2
800	20TH ST	94110	10-J3
900	21ST ST	94110	10-J3
1000	22ND ST	94110	10-J3
1100	23RD ST	94110	10-J3
1200	24TH ST	94110	10-J4
1300	25TH ST	94110	10-J4
1400	26TH ST	94110	10-J4
1500	CESAR CHAVEZ ST	94110	14-J4
1560	PRECITA AV	94110	14-J4
1640	PRECITA AV	94110	14-J4
1600	PRECITA AV	94110	14-J4
1650	MULLEN AV	94110	14-J4
1700	MONTCALM ST	94110	14-J4
1720	NORWICH ST	94110	14-J4
1750	RUTLEDGE ST	94110	14-J5
1800	RIPLEY ST	94110	14-J5
800	WALTHAM ST	94110	14-J5
900	BRADFORD ST	94110	15-A5
900	ESMERALDA AV	94110	15-A5
900	PERALTA AV	94110	15-A5
ALADDIN TER			SF
1	REDFIELD AL	94133	2-J4
1	TAYLOR ST	94133	2-J4
ALAMEDA ST			SF
	ILLINOIS ST	94107	11-C1
1700	DE HARO ST	94103	11-A1
1800	RHODE ISLAND ST	94103	11-A1
1900	KANSAS ST	94103	11-A1
1900	HENRY ADAMS ST	94103	11-A1
2000	VERMONT ST	94103	11-A1
2100	SAN BRUNO AV	94103	11-A1
2200	UTAH ST	94103	11-A1
2300	POTRERO AV	94103	11-A1
2400	HAMPSHIRE ST	94103	11-A1
2500	BRYANT ST	94103	11-A1
2200	FLORIDA ST	94103	10-J1
2230	TREAT AV	94103	10-J1
2230	DIVISION ST	94103	10-J1
2270	ALABAMA ST	94103	10-J1
2300	HARRISON ST	94103	10-J1
ALANA WY			SF
1	HARNEY RD	94134	20-B2
1	HARNEY WY	94134	20-B2
20	THOMAS MELLON DR	94134	20-B2
70	HARNEY RD	94134	20-B2
150	EXECUTIVE PARK BLVD	94134	20-B2
ALBERTA ST			SF
1	CAMPBELL AV	94134	19-J1
ALBION ST			SF
1	15TH ST	94103	10-H2
100	16TH ST	94103	10-H2
100	16TH ST	94110	10-H2
150	CAMP ST	94110	10-H2
200	17TH ST	94110	10-H2
ALDER ST			SF
1	HARKNESS AV	94134	20-A1
100	ANKENY ST	94134	20-A1
100	ORDWAY ST	94134	20-A1
ALEMANY BLVD			SF
	BAYSHORE BLVD	94124	15-A5
	WATERLOO ST	94124	15-A5
	HILTON ST	94124	15-A5
	BAYSHORE BLVD	94124	15-A6
	INDUSTRIAL ST	94124	15-A6
	SAN BRUNO AV	94110	15-A6
100	PUTNAM ST	94110	14-J6
400	FOLSOM ST	94110	14-J6
800	ELLSWORTH ST	94110	14-J6
	SAN BRUNO AV	94110	15-A6
1000	CONGDON ST	94112	14-G6
1070	MISSION ST	94112	14-G6
1100	ROUSSEAU ST	94112	14-G6
1180	ADMIRAL AV	94112	14-G6
1200	LYELL ST	94112	14-G6
1330	SILVER AV	94112	14-G7
1380	TINGLEY ST	94112	14-G7
1430	THERESA ST	94112	14-G7
1480	COTTER ST	94112	14-G7
1530	FRANCIS ST	94112	14-G7
1600	SANTA ROSA AV	94112	14-G7
1650	HARRINGTON ST	94112	14-G7
1700	NORTON ST	94112	14-G7
1750	SAN JUAN AV	94112	14-F7
1840	OCEAN AV	94112	14-F7
1900	LEO ST	94112	14-F7
1970	ONONDAGA AV	94112	19-F1
2140	SENECA AV	94112	19-F1
2200	GENEVA AV	94112	19-F1
2230	RESTANI WY	94112	19-F1
2260	NIAGARA AV	94112	19-F1
2330	MOUNT VERNON AV	94112	19-F1
2400	HURON AV	94112	19-E1
2400	OTTAWA AV	94112	19-E1
2460	FOOTE AV	94112	19-E2
2550	NAGLEE AV	94112	19-E2
2700	FARRAGUT AV	94112	18-E2
2740	LAURA ST	94112	18-E2
2770	LAWRENCE AV	94112	18-E2
2790	CAYUGA AV	94112	18-E2
2850	SICKLES AV	94112	18-D2
2940	REGENT ST	94112	18-D2
2940	SAN JOSE AV	94112	18-D2
	CRYSTAL ST	94112	18-D2
3200	BROTHERHOOD WY	94132	18-D2
3200	ORIZABA AV	94132	18-D2
3200	SAGAMORE ST	94132	18-D2
3600	BRIGHT ST	94132	18-C2
3700	VICTORIA ST	94132	18-C2
3750	RAMSELL ST	94132	18-C2
3800	ARCH ST	94132	18-C2
3800	WORCESTER AV	94132	18-C2
3850	KEMPTON AV	94132	18-C2
3900	SAINT CHARLES AV	94132	18-C2
3900	PALMETTO AV	94132	18-C2
ALHAMBRA ST			SF
1	CERVANTES BLVD	94123	2-G3
100	MALLORCA WY	94123	2-G4
200	PIERCE ST	94123	2-F4
250	AVILA ST	94123	2-F4
300	FRANCISCO ST	94123	2-F4
300	SCOTT ST	94123	2-F4
ALLEN ST			SF
1	HASTINGS TER	94109	2-J4
1	HYDE ST	94109	2-J4
100	EASTMAN ST	94109	2-J4
ALLISON ST			SF
1	MISSION ST	94112	19-F2
1	MOUNT VERNON AV	94112	19-F2
90	CROSS ST	94112	19-F2
220	MORSE ST	94112	19-F2
330	BRUNSWICK ST	94112	19-F2
450	HANOVER ST	94112	19-F2
ALLSTON WY			SF
1	ULLOA ST	94127	13-D5
60	PARK AL	94127	13-D5
100	CLAREMONT BLVD	94127	13-D5
ALMA ST			SF
1	BELVEDERE ST	94117	10-E2
100	COLE ST	94117	10-E2
200	SHRADER ST	94117	10-E2
300	STANYAN ST	94117	10-E2
ALMADEN CT			SF
600	ANZA ST	94118	5-D6
ALOHA AV			SF
100	15TH AV	94122	9-C3
200	LOMITA AV	94122	9-C3
1	FUNSTON AV	94122	9-C3
ALPHA ST			SF
1	GOETTINGEN ST	94134	20-A1
1	WILDE AV	94134	20-A1
	TIOGA AV	94134	20-A2
140	TUCKER AV	94134	20-A2
260	TEDDY AV	94134	20-A2
340	ARLETA AV	94134	20-A2
420	RAYMOND AV	94134	20-A2
500	LELAND AV	94134	20-A2
ALPINE TER			SF
1	WALLER ST	94117	10-G1
100	DUBOCE AV	94117	10-G1
200	14TH ST	94117	10-G1
200	ROOSEVELT WY	94117	10-G1
ALTA ST			SF
100	MONTGOMERY ST	94133	3-A4
ALTA MAR WY			SF
1	SEAL ROCK DR	94121	4-H6
100	POINT LOBOS AV	94121	4-H6
ALTA VISTA TER			SF
1600	VALLEJO ST	94133	6-J4
ALTON AV			SF
1	CASTENADA AV	94116	9-D4
100	PACHECO ST	94116	9-D4
200	9TH AV	94116	9-D4
ALVARADO ST			SF
1	SAN JOSE AV	94110	10-H3
100	GUERRERO ST	94110	10-H3
400	SANCHEZ ST	94114	10-G3
500	NOE ST	94114	10-G3
600	CASTRO ST	94114	10-G3
700	DIAMOND ST	94114	10-G3
800	DOUGLASS ST	94114	10-F3
900	HOFFMAN AV	94114	10-F3
1000	GRAND VIEW AV	94114	10-F3
ALVISO ST			SF
	HOLLOWAY AV	94127	13-C7
50	ESTERO AV	94127	13-C7
100	URBANO DR S	94127	13-C7
AMADOR ST			SF
1	CARGO WY	94124	15-C4
AMATURY LP			SF
450	PARK BLVD	94129	5-C4
400	NAUMAN RD	94129	5-C4
AMAZON AV			SF
1	MISSION ST	94112	19-F1
100	LONDON ST	94112	19-F1
200	PARIS ST	94112	19-F1
290	LISBON ST	94112	19-F1
390	MADRID ST	94112	19-F1
490	EDINBURGH ST	94112	19-G1
590	NAPLES ST	94112	19-G1
690	VIENNA ST	94112	19-G2
790	ATHENS ST	94112	19-G2
900	MOSCOW ST	94112	19-G2
AMBER DR			SF
1	DUNCAN ST	94131	14-F4
1	RED ROCK WY	94131	14-F4
40	CAMEO WY	94131	14-F4
80	AMETHYST WY	94131	14-F4
100	QUARTZ WY	94131	14-F4
280	CORALINO LN	94131	14-F4
300	TURQUOISE WY	94131	14-F4
400	DUNCAN ST	94131	14-F4
AMES ST			SF
1	21ST ST	94110	10-H3
100	22ND ST	94110	10-H3
200	23RD ST	94110	10-H3
AMETHYST WY			SF
1	TURQUOISE WY	94131	14-F4
80	AMBER DR	94131	14-F4
AMHERST ST			SF
1	SILVER AV	94134	14-J7
70	SILLIMAN ST	94134	14-J7
200	FELTON ST	94134	14-J7
300	BURROWS ST	94134	14-J7
400	BACON ST	94134	14-J7
500	WAYLAND ST	94134	14-J7
AMITY AL			SF
700	ADA CT	94109	6-J6
ANDERSON ST			SF
1	BERNAL HEIGHTS BLVD	94110	14-J5
100	POWHATTAN AV	94110	14-J5
200	EUGENIA AV	94110	14-J5
300	CORTLAND AV	94110	14-J5
400	JARBOE AV	94110	14-J5
500	TOMPKINS AV	94110	14-J6
600	OGDEN AV	94110	14-J6
700	CRESCENT AV	94110	14-J6
ANDOVER ST			SF
100	POWHATTAN AV	94110	14-J5
200	EUGENIA AV	94110	14-J5
300	CORTLAND AV	94110	14-J5
400	ELLERT ST	94110	14-J5
450	NEWMAN ST	94110	14-J5
500	TOMPKINS AV	94110	14-J6
530	HIGHLAND AV	94110	14-J6
580	PARK ST	94110	14-J6
600	OGDEN AV	94110	14-J6
630	RICHLAND AV	94110	14-J6
680	CRESCENT AV	94110	14-J6
760	BENTON AV	94110	14-J6
ANDREWS RD			SF
	LINCOLN BLVD	94129	1-C3
ANKENY ST			SF
1	DELTA ST	94134	20-A1
1	HAMILTON ST	94134	20-A1
90	HOLYOKE ST	94134	20-A1
110	MILL ST	94134	20-A1
170	ORDWAY ST	94134	20-A1
170	ALDER ST	94134	20-A1
230	BISHOP ST	94134	20-A1
300	SPARTA ST	94134	20-A1
300	WARD ST	94134	20-A1
ANNAPOLIS TER			SF
1	TURK ST	94118	6-E7
100	GOLDEN GATE AV	94118	6-E7
ANNIE ST			SF
1	MARKET ST	94105	7-A6
1	MARKET ST	94103	7-A6
30	STEVENSON ST	94105	7-B6
30	STEVENSON ST	94103	7-B6
60	JESSIE ST	94105	7-B6
60	JESSIE ST	94103	7-B6
80	ALDRICH AL	94105	7-B6
80	ALDRICH AL	94103	7-B6
100	MISSION ST	94105	7-B6
100	MISSION ST	94103	7-B6
ANSON PL			SF
100	POWELL ST	94108	7-A5
ANTHONY ST			SF
1	STEVENSON ST	94105	7-B5
50	JESSIE ST	94105	7-B5
100	MISSION ST	94105	7-B5
ANTONIO ST			SF
1	JONES ST	94102	6-J6
ANZA ST			SF
	LINCOLN BLVD	94129	1-E4
	FREEMAN ST	94129	1-D4
	OWEN ST	94129	1-D4
	ARGUELLO BLVD	94129	1-D4
	SHERIDAN AV	94129	1-D4
100	MASONIC AV	94118	6-F6
100	OFARRELL ST	94118	6-F6
180	WOOD ST	94118	6-E6
250	JEAN WY	94118	6-E6
300	COLLINS ST	94118	6-E6
400	BLAKE ST	94118	6-E6
500	COOK ST	94118	6-E6
600	SPRUCE ST	94118	5-E6
700	PARKER AV	94118	5-E6
800	BEAUMONT AV	94118	5-E7
820	BEAUMONT AV	94118	5-E7
900	STANYAN ST	94118	5-E7
920	ROSSI AV	94118	5-E7
940	LORAINE CT	94118	5-D7
970	ALMADEN CT	94118	5-D7
1000	ARGUELLO BLVD	94118	5-D7
1100	2ND AV	94118	5-D7
1200	3RD AV	94118	5-D7
1300	4TH AV	94118	5-D7
1400	5TH AV	94118	5-D7
1500	6TH AV	94118	5-D7
1600	7TH AV	94118	5-D7
1700	8TH AV	94118	5-C7
1800	9TH AV	94118	5-C7
1900	10TH AV	94118	5-C7
2000	11TH AV	94118	5-C7
2100	12TH AV	94118	5-C7
2200	FUNSTON AV	94118	5-C7
2250	PRESIDIO BLVD	94118	5-C7
2300	14TH AV	94118	5-C7
2400	15TH AV	94118	5-C7
2500	16TH AV	94118	6-B7
2600	17TH AV	94121	5-B7
2700	18TH AV	94121	5-B7
2800	19TH AV	94121	5-B7
2900	20TH AV	94121	5-B7
3000	21ST AV	94121	5-B7
3100	22ND AV	94121	5-B7
3200	23RD AV	94121	5-B7
3300	24TH AV	94121	5-B7
3400	25TH AV	94121	5-A7
3500	26TH AV	94121	5-A7
3600	27TH AV	94121	5-A7
3700	28TH AV	94121	5-A7
3800	29TH AV	94121	5-A7
3900	30TH AV	94121	5-A7
4100	32ND AV	94121	5-A7
4200	33RD AV	94121	5-A7
4300	34TH AV	94121	4-J7
4400	35TH AV	94121	4-J7
4500	36TH AV	94121	4-J7
4600	37TH AV	94121	4-J7
4700	38TH AV	94121	4-J7
4800	39TH AV	94121	4-J7
4900	40TH AV	94121	4-J7
5000	41ST AV	94121	4-J7
5100	42ND AV	94121	4-H7
5200	43RD AV	94121	4-H7
5300	44TH AV	94121	4-H7
5400	45TH AV	94121	4-H7
5500	46TH AV	94121	4-H7
5600	47TH AV	94121	4-H7
5700	48TH AV	94121	4-H7
ANZAVISTA AV			SF
1	BAKER ST	94115	6-F7
60	FORTUNA AV	94115	6-F7
110	ENCANTO AV	94115	6-F7
180	BARCELONA AV	94115	6-F7
290	VEGA ST	94115	6-F6
360	TERRA VISTA AV	94115	6-F6
400	OFARRELL ST	94115	6-F6
APOLLO ST			SF
1	TOPEKA AV	94124	15-B6
100	THORNTON AV	94124	15-B6
100	WILLIAMS AV	94124	15-B6
200	THORNTON AV	94124	15-B6
APPAREL WY			SF
1	BARNEVELD AV	94124	15-A5
100	BARNEVELD AV	94124	15-A5
APPLETON AV			SF
1	MISSION ST	94110	14-H5
50	GLADYS ST	94110	14-H5
100	PATTON ST	94110	14-H5
200	HOLLY PARK CIR	94110	14-H5
APPLETON ST			SF
1	STOREY AV	94129	1-C4
140	SCHOFIELD RD	94129	1-C4
160	RUCKMAN AV	94129	1-C3
APTOS AV			SF
1	DARIEN WY	94127	13-C6
100	UPLAND DR	94127	13-C6
200	OCEAN AV	94127	13-C7
AQUAVISTA WY			SF
1	MAR VIEW WY	94131	10-E3
100	SKYVIEW WY	94131	10-E3
ARAGO ST			SF
1	PAULDING ST	94112	14-F7
100	HAVELOCK ST	94112	14-F7
ARBALLO DR			SF
200	VIDAL DR	94132	18-A1
250	PINTO AV	94132	18-A1
300	ACEVEDO AV	94132	18-A1
360	SERRANO DR	94132	18-A1
400	HIGUERA AV	94132	18-A1
500	GONZALEZ DR	94132	18-A1
620	GARCES DR	94132	18-A1
700	VIDAL DR	94132	18-A1
ARBOR ST			SF
1	DIAMOND ST	94131	14-G5
100	CONRAD ST	94131	14-G5
170	HILIRITAS AV	94131	14-F5
200	SWISS AV	94131	14-F5
300	ELK ST	94131	14-F5
300	DIAMOND HEIGHTS BLVD	94131	14-F5
ARCH ST			SF
400	SHIELDS ST	94132	18-C1
500	GARFIELD ST	94132	18-C1
600	HOLLOWAY AV	94132	18-C1
1	ALEMANY BLVD	94132	18-C2
1	WORCESTER AV	94132	18-C2
100	BROTHERHOOD WY	94132	18-C2
200	RANDOLPH ST	94132	18-C1
300	SARGENT ST	94132	18-C1
ARCO WY			SF
100	HAVELOCK ST	94112	14-F7
ARDATH CT			SF
1	HUDSON AV	94124	15-C6
ARDENWOOD WY			SF
10	SLOAT BLVD	94132	13-C6
ARELIOUS WALKER DR			SF
2800	EGBERT AV	94124	20-C1
2800	FITCH ST	94124	20-C1
2900	FITZGERALD AV	94124	20-C1
3000	GILMAN AV	94124	20-C1
ARELLANO AV			SF
1	SERRANO DR	94132	18-B1
100	HOLLOWAY AV	94132	18-B1
ARGONAUT AV			SF
1	GARRISON AV	94134	19-J2
90	MCCARTHY AV	94134	19-J2
310	BURR AV	94134	19-J2
600	VELASCO AV	94134	19-J2
ARGUELLO BLVD			SF
340	SHERIDAN AV	94129	1-D4
340	ANZA ST	94129	1-D4
	MORAGA AV	94129	5-D4
	HARDIE AV	94129	5-D4
340	INFANTRY TER	94129	5-D4
340	THOMAS AV	94129	5-D5
	WASHINGTON BLVD	94129	5-D5
	FINLEY RD	94129	5-D5
1	W PACIFIC AV	94118	5-D5
20	JACKSON ST	94118	5-D5
80	WASHINGTON ST	94118	5-D5
90	PRESIDIO TER	94118	5-D5
140	CLAY ST	94118	5-D6
180	LAKE ST	94118	5-D6
200	SACRAMENTO ST	94118	5-D6
260	CALIFORNIA ST	94118	5-D6
300	CORNWALL ST	94118	5-D6
370	EUCLID AV	94118	5-D6
400	CLEMENT ST	94118	5-D6
500	GEARY BLVD	94118	5-D6
600	ANZA ST	94118	5-D7
650	EDWARD ST	94118	5-D7
700	BALBOA ST	94118	5-D7
700	TURK ST	94118	5-D7
750	GOLDEN GATE AV	94118	5-D7
780	CABRILLO ST	94118	5-D7
800	MCALLISTER ST	94118	5-D7
840	FULTON ST	94117	5-D7
900	CONSERVATORY DR E	94117	5-D7
900	CONSERVATORY DR W	94117	5-D7
1200	KEZAR DR	94117	9-D1
1230	LINCOLN WY	94117	9-D1
1230	LINCOLN WY	94122	9-D1
1230	FREDERICK ST	94122	9-D1
1250	HUGO ST	94117	9-D2
1250	HUGO ST	94122	9-D2
1280	CARL ST	94143	9-D2
1280	CARL ST	94122	9-D2
1300	IRVING ST	94143	9-D2
1300	IRVING ST	94122	9-D2
ARKANSAS ST			SF
1	16TH ST	94107	11-B2
100	17TH ST	94107	11-B2
200	MARIPOSA ST	94107	11-B2
300	18TH ST	94107	11-B2
400	19TH ST	94107	11-B2
500	20TH ST	94107	11-B3
800	MADERA ST	94107	11-B3
900	23RD ST	94107	11-B3
ARLETA AV			SF
1	ELLIOT ST	94134	19-J2

PRIMARY STREET / Address Cross Street / ZIP / CITY Pg-Grid

ARLETA AV SF
100 DELTA ST 94134 20-A2
200 RUTLAND ST 94134 20-A2
290 ALPHA ST 94134 20-A2
400 BAYSHORE BLVD 94134 20-A2
400 BLANKEN AV 94134 20-A2
400 SAN BRUNO AV 94134 20-A2

ARLINGTON ST SF
1 RANDALL ST 94131 14-H5
100 FAIRMOUNT ST 94131 14-H5
160 CHARLES ST 94131 14-H5
300 MIGUEL ST 94131 14-H6
400 MATEO ST 94131 14-G6
450 SAINT MARYS AV 94131 14-G6
500 ROANOKE ST 94131 14-G6
700 WILDER ST 94131 14-G6
700 NATICK ST 94131 14-G6

ARMISTEAD RD SF
1200 LINCOLN BLVD 94129 1-C3
1210 LENDRUM CT 94129 1-C3
1280 RAMSEL CT 94129 1-C3
1290 HOFFMAN ST 94129 1-C3
1300 LINCOLN BLVD 94129 1-C3

ARMSTRONG AV SF
1300 HAWES ST 94124 20-C1
1400 INGALLS ST 94124 15-C7
1500 JENNINGS ST 94124 15-B7
1600 KEITH ST 94124 15-B7
1700 3RD ST 94124 15-B7
1740 LANE ST 94124 15-B7
1800 MENDELL ST 94124 15-B7

ARNOLD AV SF
1 CRESCENT AV 94110 14-H6
100 BENTON AV 94110 14-H6

ARROYO WY SF
1 MARIETTA DR 94127 14-E5
10 TERESITA BLVD 94127 14-E5
100 BELLA VISTA WY 94127 14-E5

ARTHUR AV SF
600 3RD ST 94124 15-C4
600 CARGO WY 94124 15-C4
700 QUINT ST 94124 15-C4

ASH ST SF
400 GOUGH ST 94102 6-H7

ASHBURY ST SF
1 FULTON ST 94117 6-E7
100 GROVE ST 94117 6-E7
200 HAYES ST 94117 6-E7
300 FELL ST 94117 10-F1
400 OAK ST 94117 10-F1
500 PAGE ST 94117 10-F1
600 HAIGHT ST 94117 10-F1
700 WALLER ST 94117 10-F1
800 FREDERICK ST 94117 10-F1
900 PIEDMONT ST 94117 10-F2
970 CLIFFORD TER 94117 10-F2
1000 DOWNEY ST 94117 10-F2
1050 CLAYTON ST 94117 10-F2
1100 17TH ST 94117 10-F2
1100 CLAYTON ST 94117 10-F2

ASHBURY TER SF
1 UPPER TER 94117 10-F2
100 PIEDMONT ST 94117 10-F2
100 DELMAR ST 94117 10-F2

ASHTON AV SF
100 GARFIELD ST 94112 18-D1
100 GRAFTON AV 94112 18-D1
200 HOLLOWAY AV 94132 18-D1
200 HOLLOWAY AV 94112 18-D1
210 HOLLOWAY AV 94132 18-D1
210 HOLLOWAY AV 94112 18-D1
290 HEAD ST 94127 13-D7
290 HEAD ST 94112 13-D7
320 DE MONTFORT AV 94127 13-D7
320 DE MONTFORT AV 94112 13-D7
340 PICO AV 94127 13-D7
340 PICO AV 94112 13-D7
360 LEGION CT 94127 13-D7
360 LEGION CT 94112 13-D7
400 OCEAN AV 94127 13-D7
400 OCEAN AV 94112 13-D7

ASHWOOD LN SF
1 WARREN DR 94131 9-D3
100 CLARENDON AV 94131 9-D3

ATALAYA TER SF
100 FULTON ST 94117 6-F7

ATHENS ST SF
1 MADISON ST 94112 14-H7
120 PERU AV 94112 14-H7
200 VALMAR TER 94112 14-H7
200 AVALON AV 94112 14-H7
300 EXCELSIOR AV 94112 19-G1
400 BRAZIL AV 94112 19-G1
510 PERSIA AV 94112 19-G1
650 RUSSIA AV 94112 19-G1
780 FRANCE AV 94112 19-G1
910 ITALY AV 94112 19-G2
970 AMAZON AV 94112 19-G2
1070 GENEVA AV 94112 19-G2
1130 ROLPH ST 94112 19-G2
1190 CORDOVA ST 94112 19-F2
1300 NAPLES ST 94112 19-F2

ATTRIDGE AL SF
1 FILBERT ST 94133 2-J4

AUBURN ST SF
1 JACKSON ST 94133 6-J4
100 PACIFIC AV 94133 6-J4
100 SALMON ST 94133 6-J4

AUGUSTA ST SF
1 BAYSHORE BLVD 94124 15-A6
90 CHARTER OAK AV 94124 15-A6
170 ELMIRA ST 94124 15-A6
250 WATERVILLE ST 94124 15-A6
300 SILVER AV 94124 15-A6

AUSTIN ST SF
1 LARKIN ST 94109 6-J5
100 POLK ST 94109 6-H5
200 VAN NESS AV 94109 6-H5
300 FRANKLIN ST 94109 6-H5
400 GOUGH ST 94109 6-H5
500 OCTAVIA ST 94109 6-H5

AUTO DR SF
1600 LAWTON ST 94122 9-D3
1700 MORAGA ST 94122 9-D3

AVALON AV SF
1 MISSION ST 94112 14-G7
1 THERESA ST 94112 14-G7
90 LONDON ST 94112 14-G7
200 PARIS ST 94112 14-G7
300 LISBON ST 94112 14-G7
380 MADRID ST 94112 14-G7
470 EDINBURGH ST 94112 14-G7
550 NAPLES ST 94112 14-H7
630 VIENNA ST 94112 14-H7
720 ATHENS ST 94112 14-H7
800 MOSCOW ST 94112 14-H7
910 LA GRANDE AV 94112 14-H7
1000 PERU AV 94112 14-H7
1000 FELTON ST 94112 14-H7

AVENUE B SF
1 9TH ST 94130 3-E1
1 GATEWAY AV 94130 3-E1
1 3RD ST 94130 3-E1
100 CALIFORNIA AV 94130 3-E1

AVENUE C SF
100 4TH ST 94130 3-E1

AVENUE D SF
1 9TH ST 94130 3-E1

AVENUE E SF
1 9TH ST 94130 3-E1

AVENUE NORTH SF
50 25TH AV 94121 5-A5

AVENUE OF THE PALMS SF
1 9TH ST 94130 3-D1
1 3RD ST 94130 3-E2

AVERY ST SF
1 GEARY BLVD 94115 6-G6
100 POST ST 94115 6-G6

AVILA ST SF
1 CHESTNUT ST 94123 2-F4
100 ALHAMBRA ST 94123 2-F4
200 CAPRA WY 94123 2-F3
300 BEACH ST 94123 2-F3
350 PRADO ST 94123 2-F3
400 CERVANTES BLVD 94123 2-F3
450 RICO WY 94123 2-F3
500 MARINA BLVD 94123 2-F3
500 CASA WY 94123 2-F3

AVON WY SF
2900 SLOAT BLVD 94132 13-B6

AZTEC ST SF
100 COSO AV 94110 14-J4

B

BACHE ST SF
1 CRESCENT AV 94110 14-J6
100 BENTON AV 94110 14-J6

BACON ST SF
1 BAYSHORE BLVD 94124 15-A7
100 SAN BRUNO AV 94134 15-A7
200 GIRARD ST 94134 15-A7
300 BRUSSELS ST 94134 15-A7
400 GOETTINGEN ST 94134 15-A7
500 SOMERSET ST 94134 15-A7
600 HOLYOKE ST 94134 15-A7
700 HAMILTON ST 94134 14-J7
800 BOWDOIN ST 94134 14-J7
1100 UNIVERSITY ST 94134 14-J7
1200 PRINCETON ST 94134 14-J7
1230 CAMPUS LN 94134 14-J7
1300 AMHERST ST 94134 14-J7
1500 CAMBRIDGE ST 94134 14-J7
1590 OXFORD ST 94134 14-H7
1700 HARVARD ST 94134 14-H7

BADEN ST SF
500 MARTHA AV 94131 14-F6
1 CIRCULAR AV 94131 14-F6
1 STANDISH AV 94131 14-F6
100 HEARST AV 94131 14-F6
200 MONTEREY BLVD 94131 14-F6
300 JOOST AV 94131 14-F6
400 MANGELS AV 94131 14-F6

BADGER ST SF
1 GORHAM AV 94112 14-G6
100 CAYUGA AV 94112 14-G6

BAKER CT SF
1750 LINCOLN BLVD 94129 5-B5
1750 GIBSON RD 94129 5-B5
1700 BROOKS ST 94129 5-B5

BAKER ST SF
2500 VALLEJO ST 94123 6-F5
2600 GREEN ST 94123 6-F4
2700 UNION ST 94123 6-F4
2800 FILBERT ST 94123 6-F4
2850 MILEY ST 94123 6-F4
2900 GREENWICH ST 94123 6-F4
3000 LOMBARD ST 94123 2-F4
3100 CHESTNUT ST 94123 2-F4
3120 RICHARDSON AV 94123 2-F4
3200 FRANCISCO ST 94123 2-F4
3300 BAY ST 94123 2-F4
3340 BAY ST 94123 2-F4
3400 NORTH POINT ST 94123 2-F3
3500 BEACH ST 94123 2-F3
3600 JEFFERSON ST 94123 2-F3
3700 MARINA BLVD 94123 2-F3
1310 GEARY BLVD 94115 6-F6
1310 SAINT JOSEPHS AV 94115 6-F6
1400 POST ST 94115 6-F6
1500 SUTTER ST 94115 6-F6
1600 BUSH ST 94115 6-F6
1700 PINE ST 94115 6-F6
1800 CALIFORNIA ST 94115 6-F5
1900 SACRAMENTO ST 94115 6-F5
2000 CLAY ST 94115 6-F5
2100 WASHINGTON ST 94115 6-F5
2200 JACKSON ST 94115 6-F5
2300 PACIFIC AV 94115 6-F5
2400 BROADWAY ST 94115 6-F5
1 BUENA VISTA AV E 94117 10-F1
1 HAIGHT ST 94117 10-F1
100 PAGE ST 94117 10-F1
200 OAK ST 94117 10-F1
300 FELL ST 94117 6-F7
400 HAYES ST 94117 6-F7
500 GROVE ST 94117 6-F7
600 FULTON ST 94117 6-F7
690 MCALLISTER ST 94117 6-F7
780 GOLDEN GATE AV 94115 6-F7
870 TURK ST 94115 6-F7
930 ANZAVISTA AV 94115 6-F7
960 PINAR LN 94115 6-F6
1100 TERRA VISTA AV 94115 6-F6

BALANCE ST SF
1 GOLD ST 94133 7-B4
100 JACKSON ST 94133 7-B4

BALBOA ST SF
20 ARGUELLO BLVD 94118 5-D7
20 TURK ST 94118 5-D7
100 2ND AV 94118 5-D7
200 3RD AV 94118 5-D7
300 4TH AV 94118 5-D7
400 5TH AV 94118 5-D7
500 6TH AV 94118 5-D7
600 7TH AV 94118 5-D7
700 8TH AV 94118 5-C7
800 9TH AV 94118 5-C7
900 10TH AV 94118 5-C7
1000 11TH AV 94118 5-C7
1100 12TH AV 94118 5-C7
1200 FUNSTON AV 94118 5-C7
1250 PRESIDIO BLVD 94118 5-C7
1300 14TH AV 94118 5-C7
1400 15TH AV 94118 6-C7
1500 16TH AV 94118 5-B7
1600 17TH AV 94121 5-B7
1700 18TH AV 94121 5-B7
1800 19TH AV 94121 5-B7
1900 20TH AV 94121 5-B7
2000 21ST AV 94121 5-B7
2100 22ND AV 94121 5-B7
2200 23RD AV 94121 5-B7
2300 24TH AV 94121 5-B7
2400 25TH AV 94121 5-A7
2500 26TH AV 94121 5-A7
2600 27TH AV 94121 5-A7
2700 28TH AV 94121 5-A7
2800 29TH AV 94121 5-A7
2900 30TH AV 94121 5-A7
3000 31ST AV 94121 5-A7
3100 32ND AV 94121 5-A7
3200 33RD AV 94121 5-A7
3300 34TH AV 94121 4-J7
3400 35TH AV 94121 4-J7
3500 36TH AV 94121 4-J7
3600 37TH AV 94121 4-J7
3700 38TH AV 94121 4-J7
3800 39TH AV 94121 4-J7
3900 40TH AV 94121 4-J7
4000 41ST AV 94121 4-J7
4100 42ND AV 94121 4-H7
4200 43RD AV 94121 4-H7
4300 44TH AV 94121 4-H7
4400 45TH AV 94121 4-H7
4500 46TH AV 94121 4-H7
4600 47TH AV 94121 4-H7
4700 48TH AV 94121 4-H7
4750 LA PLAYA 94121 4-H7

BALCETA AV SF
100 LAGUNA HONDA BLVD 94127 13-D4
200 VASQUEZ AV 94127 13-D4
1 WOODSIDE AV 94127 13-D4

BALDWIN CT SF
1 OAKDALE AV 94124 15-D7

BALHI CT SF
1 CAYUGA AV 94112 19-F1

BALMY ST SF
1 24TH ST 94110 10-J4
100 25TH ST 94110 10-J4

BALTIMORE WY SF
1 S HILL BLVD 94112 19-G2
60 TOYON LN 94112 19-G2
130 NAYLOR ST 94112 19-G2
400 POPE ST 94112 19-F2

BANBURY DR SF
1 19TH AV 94132 18-B1
10 DENSLOW DR 94132 18-B1
50 STRATFORD DR 94132 18-B1

BANCROFT AV SF
2000 QUINT ST 94124 15-A7
1900 PHELPS ST 94124 15-B7
2000 NEWHALL ST 94124 15-B7
1700 3RD ST 94124 15-B7
1800 MENDELL ST 94124 15-B7
1400 INGALLS ST 94124 15-C7
1500 JENNINGS ST 94124 15-B7
1600 KEITH ST 94124 15-B7

BANK ST SF
MASON ST 94129 1-E3
OLD MASON ST 94129 1-E3
LINCOLN BLVD 94129 1-E3

BANKS ST SF
1 POWHATTAN AV 94110 14-J5
200 EUGENIA AV 94110 14-J5
300 CORTLAND AV 94110 14-J5
400 JARBOE AV 94110 14-J5
500 TOMPKINS AV 94110 14-J6
600 OGDEN AV 94110 14-J6
700 CRESCENT AV 94110 14-J6

BANNAM PL SF
1 GREEN ST 94133 3-A4
100 UNION ST 94133 3-A4

BANNECKER WY SF
800 GROVE ST 94102 6-H7

BANNOCK ST SF
1 GENEVA AV 94112 19-F1
100 SENECA AV 94112 19-F1

BARCELONA AV SF
1 ANZAVISTA AV 94115 6-F7
100 TERRA VISTA AV 94115 6-F7

BARNARD AV SF
HARDIE AV 94129 5-D4
FUNSTON AV 94129 5-D4
FERNANDEZ ST 94129 5-E4
PRESIDIO BLVD 94129 5-E4

BARNEVELD AV SF
1 JERROLD AV 94124 15-A4
110 LOOMIS ST 94124 15-A5
240 MCKINNON AV 94124 15-A5
300 NEWCOMB AV 94124 15-A5
400 OAKDALE AV 94124 15-A5
450 PALOU AV 94124 15-A5
490 APPAREL WY 94124 15-A5
580 APPAREL WY 94124 15-A5
640 DORMAN AV 94124 15-A5
700 INDUSTRIAL ST 94124 15-A5
700 SHAFTER AV 94124 15-A5
700 RICKARD ST 94134 15-A6
740 GAVEN ST 94134 15-A6
790 SWEENY ST 94134 15-A6
840 HALE ST 94134 15-A6
900 SILVER AV 94134 15-A6

BARTLETT ST SF
1 21ST ST 94110 10-H3
100 22ND ST 94110 10-H3
200 23RD ST 94110 10-H3
300 24TH ST 94110 10-H4
400 25TH ST 94110 10-J4
500 26TH ST 94110 10-J4
600 CESAR CHAVEZ ST 94110 10-J4

BARTOL ST SF
100 BROADWAY 94133 7-A4

BASS CT SF
1 WHITNEY YOUNG CIR 94124 15-C6

BATTERY ST SF
1 MARKET ST 94104 7-B5
1 MARKET ST 94111 7-B5
40 BUSH ST 94104 7-B5
40 BUSH ST 94111 7-B5
100 PINE ST 94104 7-B5
100 PINE ST 94111 7-B5
200 CALIFORNIA ST 94104 7-B5
200 CALIFORNIA ST 94111 7-B5
230 HALLECK ST 94104 7-B5
230 HALLECK ST 94111 7-B5
300 SACRAMENTO ST 94111 7-B5
350 COMMERCIAL ST 94111 7-B5
400 CLAY ST 94111 7-B5
430 MERCHANT ST 94111 7-B5
500 WASHINGTON ST 94111 7-B4
600 JACKSON ST 94111 7-B4
700 PACIFIC AV 94111 7-B4
800 BROADWAY ST 94111 7-B4
900 VALLEJO ST 94111 3-B4
1000 GREEN ST 94111 3-B4
1050 JOHN MAHER ST 94111 3-B4
1100 UNION ST 94111 3-B4
1300 GREENWICH ST 94111 3-B3
1400 THE EMBARCADERO 94111 3-B3

BATTERY BLANEY RD SF
INCINERATOR RD 94129 1-D3

BATTERY CAULFIELD RD SF
WASHINGTON BLVD 94129 5-C5
WEDEMEYER ST 94129 5-C5

BATTERY CHAMBERLAIN RD SF
GIBSON RD 94129 5-B5
LINCOLN BLVD 94129 5-B4

BATTERY CROSBY RD SF
LINCOLN BLVD 94129 5-B4

BATTERY EAST RD SF
LINCOLN BLVD 94129 1-C3

BAY ST SF
1 THE EMBARCADERO 94133 3-A3
50 KEARNY ST 94133 3-A3
120 MIDWAY ST 94133 3-A3
200 STOCKTON ST 94133 3-A3
300 POWELL ST 94133 3-A3
400 MASON ST 94133 2-J3
500 TAYLOR ST 94133 2-J3
600 JONES ST 94133 2-J3
620 COLUMBUS AV 94133 2-J3
700 LEAVENWORTH ST 94109 2-J3
800 HYDE ST 94109 2-J3
900 LARKIN ST 94109 2-H3
950 NORTH VIEW CT 94109 2-H3
1000 POLK ST 94109 2-H3
1100 VAN NESS AV 94123 2-H3
1190 FRANKLIN ST 94123 2-H3
1300 GOUGH ST 94123 2-H3
1400 OCTAVIA ST 94123 2-G3
1500 LAGUNA ST 94123 2-G3
1600 BUCHANAN ST 94123 2-G3
1700 WEBSTER ST 94123 2-G3
1800 CERVANTES BLVD 94123 2-G3
1800 FILLMORE ST 94123 2-G3
2100 SCOTT ST 94123 2-F4
2200 DIVISADERO ST 94123 2-F4
2300 BRODERICK ST 94123 2-F4
2400 BAKER ST 94123 2-F4
2500 LYON ST 94123 2-F4

BAYSHORE BLVD SF
CESAR CHAVEZ ST 94110 11-A4
180 CESAR CHAVEZ ST 94110 11-A4
60 JERROLD AV 94124 15-A4
330 OAKDALE AV 94124 15-A5
370 FLOWER ST 94124 15-A5
520 CORTLAND AV 94124 15-A5
540 ALEMANY BLVD 94124 15-A5
540 WATERLOO ST 94124 15-A5
570 MARENGO ST 94124 15-A5
600 ALEMANY BLVD 94124 15-A6
600 INDUSTRIAL ST 94124 15-A6
680 HELENA ST 94124 15-A6
870 BOUTWELL ST 94124 15-A6
800 AUGUSTA ST 94124 15-A6
980 SILVER AV 94124 15-A6
1160 CARROLL AV 94124 15-A6
1160 THORNTON AV 94124 15-A6
1220 QUINT ST 94124 15-A7
1190 DONNER AV 94124 15-A7
1190 BACON ST 94124 15-A7
1300 EGBERT AV 94124 15-A7
1440 FITZGERALD AV 94124 15-A7
1700 PAUL AV 94124 15-A7
1710 WHEAT ST 94124 20-A1
1740 CRANE ST 94124 20-B1
1750 SALINAS AV 94124 20-B1
1760 KEY AV 94124 20-B1
1 3RD ST 94124 20-B1
KEY AV 94124 20-B1
180 3RD ST 94134 20-B1
100 HESTER AV 94134 20-B2
2300 HESTER AV 94134 20-A2
2310 TUNNEL AV 94134 20-A2
2380 BLANKEN AV 94134 20-A2
2360 RAYMOND AV 94134 20-A2
2400 BLANKEN AV 94134 20-A2
2400 ARLETA AV 94134 20-A2
2400 SAN BRUNO AV 94134 20-A2
2400 RAYMOND AV 94134 20-A2
2460 LELAND AV 94134 20-A2
2520 VISITACION AV 94134 20-A2
2650 SUNNYDALE AV 94134 20-A2

BAYSIDE VILLAGE PL SF
BRYANT ST 94107 7-C6
DELANCEY ST 94107 7-C6

BAYVIEW CIR SF
100 NEWHALL ST 94124 15-B6
100 BAYVIEW ST 94124 15-B6
180 WHITECLIFF WY 94124 15-B6
300 SILVERVIEW DR 94124 15-B6
400 SILVERVIEW DR 94124 15-B6
470 WHITECLIFF WY 94124 15-B6
500 NEWHALL ST 94124 15-B6

BAYVIEW ST SF
1 3RD ST 94124 15-B6
1 REVERE AV 94124 15-B6
20 LATONA ST 94124 15-B6
50 POMONA ST 94124 15-B6
80 FLORA ST 94124 15-B6
100 BAYVIEW CIR 94124 15-B6
100 NEWHALL ST 94124 15-B6

BAYVIEW PARK RD SF
LE CONTE AV 94124 20-B1

BAYWOOD ST SF
1 GENEVA AV 94112 19-F1

BEACH ST SF
1 THE EMBARCADERO 94133 3-A3
1 GRANT AV 94133 3-A3
100 STOCKTON ST 94133 3-A3
200 POWELL ST 94133 2-J3
300 MASON ST 94133 2-J3
400 TAYLOR ST 94133 2-J3
500 JONES ST 94133 2-J3
600 LEAVENWORTH ST 94133 2-J3
640 COLUMBUS AV 94109 2-J3
640 COLUMBUS AV 94133 2-J3
700 HYDE ST 94109 2-J3
800 LARKIN ST 94109 2-H3
900 POLK ST 94109 2-H3
1500 BUCHANAN ST 94123 2-G3
1600 WEBSTER ST 94123 2-G3
1700 FILLMORE ST 94123 2-G3
1760 RETIRO WY 94123 2-G3
1840 CERVANTES BLVD 94123 2-G3
1850 MALLORCA WY 94123 2-F3
1900 PIERCE ST 94123 2-F3
1950 AVILA ST 94123 2-F3

PRIMARY STREET Address	Cross Street	ZIP	CITY Pg-Grid
BEACH ST			**SF**
2000	SCOTT ST	94123	2-F3
2100	DIVISADERO ST	94123	2-F3
2200	BRODERICK ST	94123	2-F3
2300	BAKER ST	94123	2-F3
BEACHMONT DR			**SF**
1	SLOAT BLVD	94132	13-B6
100	LAGUNITAS DR	94132	13-B6
BEACON ST			**SF**
100	DIAMOND ST	94131	14-G5
410	HARRY ST	94131	14-G5
450	MIGUEL ST	94131	14-G5
500	EVERSON ST	94131	14-G5
BEALE ST			**SF**
1	DAVIS ST	94105	7-B5
1	MARKET ST	94105	7-B5
100	MISSION ST	94105	7-B5
200	HOWARD ST	94105	7-B5
300	FOLSOM ST	94105	7-C6
	BRYANT ST	94105	7-C6
	BRYANT ST	94107	7-C6
BEATRICE LN			**SF**
1	INGALLS ST	94124	15-D6
20	ESPANOLA ST	94124	15-D6
50	LILLIAN ST	94124	15-D6
100	LA SALLE AV	94124	15-C6
BEAUMONT AV			**SF**
1	GEARY BLVD	94118	5-E6
100	ANZA ST	94118	5-E6
150	LONE MOUNTAIN TER	94118	5-E7
200	TURK ST	94118	5-E7
BEAVER ST			**SF**
100	CASTRO ST	94114	10-G2
150	DE FOREST WY	94114	10-G2
200	15TH ST	94114	10-G2
1	NOE ST	94114	10-G2
BECKETT ST			**SF**
1	JACKSON ST	94133	7-A4
100	PACIFIC AV	94133	7-A4
BEDFORD PL			**SF**
1	JACKSON ST	94133	7-A4
BEHR AV			**SF**
1	JOHNSTONE DR	94131	9-E3
130	JOHNSTONE DR	94131	9-D3
BEIDEMAN ST			**SF**
1	ELLIS ST	94115	6-G6
100	OFARRELL ST	94115	6-G6
BELCHER ST			**SF**
1	DUBOCE AV	94114	10-G1
100	14TH ST	94114	10-G1
BELDEN ST			**SF**
1	BUSH ST	94104	7-A5
100	PINE ST	94104	7-A5
BELGRAVE AV			**SF**
100	SHRADER ST	94117	10-E2
200	STANYAN ST	94117	9-E2
BELL CT			**SF**
1	WHITNEY YOUNG CIR	94124	15-C6
BELL RD			**SF**
	STOREY AV	94129	1-C3
	MILLER RD	94129	1-C3
BELLAIR PL			**SF**
1	CHESTNUT ST	94133	3-A3
60	PFEIFFER ST	94133	3-A3
100	FRANCISCO ST	94133	3-A3
BELLAVISTA LN			**SF**
1	LOS PALMOS DR	94127	14-E6
100	MELROSE AV	94127	14-E6
100	BELLA VISTA WY	94127	14-E6
100	STANFORD HEIGHTS AV	94127	14-E6
BELLA VISTA WY			**SF**
1	CUBA AL	94127	14-F5
1	TERESITA BLVD	94127	14-F5
1	MARIETTA DR	94127	14-F5
30	TERESITA BLVD	94127	14-E5
90	ARROYO WY	94127	14-E5
100	GATUN AL	94127	14-E5
130	GAVIOTA WY	94127	14-E5
170	SEQUOIA WY	94127	14-E5
200	DORCAS WY	94127	14-E5
210	AVOCA AL	94127	14-E5
300	MOLIMO DR	94127	13-E6
400	CRESTA VISTA DR	94127	13-E6
500	BURLWOOD DR	94127	13-E6
550	LOS PALMOS DR	94127	14-E6
600	MELROSE AV	94127	14-E6
600	BELLAVISTA LN	94127	14-E6
600	STANFORD HEIGHTS AV	94127	14-E6
BELLE AV			**SF**
20	CHESTER AV	94132	18-C2
100	NIANTIC AV	94132	18-C2
100	SAINT CHARLES AV	94132	18-C2
BELLES ST			**SF**
	WYMAN AV	94129	5-C5
	BROWN ST	94129	5-C5
	HAYS ST	94129	5-C5
	BROWN ST	94129	5-C5
BELLEVUE AV			**SF**
80	POPE ST	94112	19-F2
BELMONT AV			**SF**
1	WILLARD ST	94117	9-E2
100	EDGEWOOD AV	94117	9-E2
BELVEDERE ST			**SF**
1	HAIGHT ST	94117	10-E1
100	WALLER ST	94117	10-E1
200	FREDERICK ST	94117	10-E1
400	PARNASSUS AV	94117	10-E2
450	GRATTAN ST	94117	10-E2
500	ALMA ST	94117	10-E2
550	RIVOLI ST	94117	10-E2
600	17TH ST	94117	10-E2
700	CARMEL ST	94117	10-E2
BEMIS ST			**SF**
10	MIGUEL ST	94131	14-G5
70	ADDISON ST	94131	14-G5
100	MATEO ST	94131	14-G5
200	ROANOKE ST	94131	14-G6
200	MOFFITT ST	94131	14-G6
300	CASTRO ST	94131	14-G6
300	SUSSEX ST	94131	14-G6
BENNINGTON ST			**SF**
1	EUGENIA AV	94110	14-J5
100	CORTLAND AV	94110	14-J5
200	ELLERT ST	94110	14-J5
300	NEWMAN ST	94110	14-J5
400	HIGHLAND AV	94110	14-J5
BENTON AV			**SF**
1	ARNOLD AV	94110	14-H6
220	ROSCOE ST	94110	14-J6
380	PORTER ST	94110	14-J6
530	BACHE ST	94110	14-J6
700	ANDOVER ST	94110	14-J6
110	GENEBERN WY	94112	14-H6
190	COLLEGE AV	94112	14-H6
270	JUSTIN DR	94112	14-H6
BERGEN PL			**SF**
800	HYDE ST	94109	2-J3
BERKELEY WY			**SF**
1	DIAMOND HEIGHTS BLVD	94131	14-G5
200	CRAGS CT	94131	14-F5
300	DIAMOND HEIGHTS BLVD	94131	14-F5
BERKSHIRE WY			**SF**
30	COUNTRY CLUB DR	94132	12-J6
1	LAKESHORE DR	94132	12-J6
20	LAKE MERCED BLVD	94132	12-J6
BERNAL HEIGHTS BLVD			**SF**
	FOLSOM ST	94110	14-J5
	CARVER ST	94110	14-J5
	ELLSWORTH ST	94110	14-J5
920	ANDERSON ST	94110	14-J5
900	MOULTRIE ST	94110	14-J5
1	BRADFORD ST	94110	15-A5
50	CARVER ST	94110	14-J5
50	ROSENKRANZ ST	94110	14-J5
100	NEVADA ST	94110	14-J5
100	POWHATTAN AV	94110	14-J5
BERNARD ST			**SF**
1	TAYLOR ST	94133	6-J4
100	JONES ST	94109	6-J4
200	LEAVENWORTH ST	94109	6-J4
BERNICE ST			**SF**
1	12TH ST	94103	10-J1
BERRY ST			**SF**
	KING ST	94107	7-C7
	THE EMBARCADERO	94107	7-C7
20	2ND ST	94107	7-C7
100	3RD ST	94107	7-C7
100	3RD ST	94107	7-B7
200	4TH ST	94107	7-B7
	5TH ST	94107	11-B1
500	7TH ST	94107	11-B1
600	DE HARO ST	94107	11-B1
BERTHA LN			**SF**
1	HARBOR RD	94124	15-D6
200	HUDSON AV	94124	15-D6
BERTITA ST			**SF**
100	SENECA AV	94112	19-F1
BERWICK PL			**SF**
30	HARRISON ST	94103	7-A7
1	HERON ST	94103	7-A7
BESSIE ST			**SF**
1	MIRABEL AV	94110	14-J4
1	SHOTWELL ST	94110	14-J4
50	MANCHESTER ST	94110	14-J4
100	FOLSOM ST	94110	14-J4
100	PRECITA AV	94110	14-J4
BEULAH ST			**SF**
1	COLE ST	94117	10-E1
100	SHRADER ST	94117	10-E1
200	STANYAN ST	94117	10-E1
BEVERLY ST			**SF**
1	19TH AV	94132	18-C1
100	SHIELDS ST	94132	18-C1
200	GARFIELD ST	94132	18-C1
300	HOLLOWAY AV	94132	18-C1
BIRCH ST			**SF**
500	OCTAVIA ST	94102	6-H7
600	LAGUNA ST	94102	6-H7
BIRCHWOOD CT			**SF**
	SADDLEBACK DR	94134	19-H2
BIRD ST			**SF**
100	DEARBORN ST	94110	10-H2
BIRMINGHAM RD			**SF**
	GENERAL KENNEDY AV	94129	2-E4
	KENDALL DR	94129	2-E3
	GORGAS AV	94129	2-E3
BISHOP ST			**SF**
100	ANKENY ST	94134	20-A1
BLACK PL			**SF**
2000	UNION ST	94133	2-J4
BLACKSTONE CT			**SF**
1	FRANKLIN ST	94123	2-H4
BLAIR TER			**SF**
1	WISCONSIN ST	94107	11-B4
100	26TH ST	94107	11-B4
BLAIRWOOD LN			**SF**
150	OAK PARK DR	94131	9-D3
BLAKE ST			**SF**
100	GEARY BLVD	94118	6-E6
200	ANZA ST	94118	6-E6
BLANCHE ST			**SF**
100	23RD ST	94114	10-G3
200	ELIZABETH ST	94114	10-G3
BLANDY ST			**SF**
	NIMITZ AV	94124	16-E7
	SPEAR AV	94124	16-E7
	C ST	94124	16-F7
BLANKEN AV			**SF**
1	BAYSHORE BLVD	94134	20-A2
1	ARLETA AV	94134	20-A2
1	SAN BRUNO AV	94134	20-A2
50	BAYSHORE BLVD	94134	20-A2
160	TUNNEL AV	94134	20-A2
240	WHEELER AV	94134	20-B2
320	PENINSULA AV	94134	20-B2
390	TOCOLOMA AV	94134	20-B2
470	NUEVA AV	94134	20-B2
550	GILLETTE AV	94134	20-B2
700	EXECUTIVE PARK BLVD	94124	20-B2
700	EXECUTIVE PARK BLVD	94134	20-B2
BLISS RD			**SF**
	MONTGOMERY ST	94129	1-D4
	INFANTRY TER	94129	1-D4
BLUXOME ST			**SF**
1	4TH ST	94107	7-B7
100	5TH ST	94107	7-B7
200	6TH ST	94107	7-B7
BLYTHDALE AV			**SF**
1	HAHN ST	94134	19-J2
100	SANTOS ST	94134	19-H2
300	BROOKDALE AV	94134	19-H2
BOARDMAN PL			**SF**
1	BRYANT ST	94103	7-A7
10	FARGO PL	94103	7-A7
30	BRANNAN ST	94103	11-A1
BOCANA ST			**SF**
100	POWHATTAN AV	94110	14-J5
200	EUGENIA AV	94110	14-J5
300	CORTLAND AV	94110	14-J5
380	ELLERT ST	94110	14-H5
400	HOLLY PARK CIR	94110	14-H5
BONIFACIO ST			**SF**
1	TANDANG SORA	94107	7-B6
50	MABINI ST	94107	7-B6
100	LAPU LAPU ST	94107	7-B6
BONITA ST			**SF**
1	POLK ST	94109	6-H4
BONVIEW ST			**SF**
1	COSO AV	94110	14-J4
1	STONEMAN ST	94110	14-J4
200	EUGENIA AV	94110	14-J5
300	CORTLAND AV	94110	14-J5
BORICA ST			**SF**
1	HOLLOWAY AV	94127	13-C7
100	URBANO DR S	94127	13-C7
120	S ENTRADA CT	94127	13-C7
100	N ENTRADA CT	94127	13-C7
120	URBANO DR N	94127	13-C7
BOSWORTH ST			**SF**
1	MISSION ST	94112	14-H6
1	MURRAY ST	94112	14-H6
100	MARSILLY ST	94112	14-G6
200	CUVIER ST	94112	14-G6
300	MILTON ST	94112	14-G6
400	ROUSSEAU ST	94112	14-G6
420	ROTTECK ST	94112	14-G6
420	LYELL ST	94112	14-G6
500	LYELL ST	94131	14-G6
600	DIAMOND ST	94131	14-G6
700	BROMPTON AV	94131	14-G6
800	LIPPARD AV	94131	14-G6
900	CHILTON AV	94131	14-G6
1100	BURNSIDE AV	94131	14-F6
1220	MERCATO CT	94131	14-F6
1220	ELK ST	94131	14-F6
1300	OSHAUGHNESSY BLVD	94131	14-F6
BOUTWELL ST			**SF**
1	INDUSTRIAL ST	94124	15-A5
1	LOOMIS ST	94124	15-A5
160	HELENA ST	94124	15-A6
200	BAYSHORE BLVD	94124	15-A6
BOWDOIN ST			**SF**
50	GAVEN ST	94134	14-J6
160	SWEENY ST	94134	14-J6
280	HALE ST	94134	14-J6
400	SILVER AV	94134	14-J6
400	SILVER AV	94134	14-J7
480	SILLIMAN ST	94134	14-J7
590	FELTON ST	94134	14-J7
700	BURROWS ST	94134	14-J7
1	BACON ST	94134	14-J7
300	WAYLAND ST	94134	14-J7
500	WOOLSEY ST	94134	14-J7
800	DWIGHT ST	94134	20-A1
1100	OLMSTEAD ST	94134	20-A1
1400	MANSELL ST	94134	20-A1
BOWLEY ST			**SF**
	HOWARD RD	94129	5-B5
	LINCOLN BLVD	94129	5-B5
	GIBSON RD	94129	5-B5
BOWLING GREEN DR			**SF**
	MIDDLE DR E	-	9-D1
	7TH AV	-	9-D1
	MARTIN LUTHER KING JR DR	-	9-D1
BOWMAN CT			**SF**
1	KEITH ST	94124	15-D6
BOWMAN RD			**SF**
	CRANSTON RD	94129	1-B3
	DOVE LP	94129	1-B3
BOYLSTON ST			**SF**
50	GAVEN ST	94134	14-J6
100	SWEENY ST	94134	14-J6
150	HALE ST	94134	14-J6
200	SILVER AV	94134	14-J6
300	SILLIMAN ST	94134	14-J6
BOYTON CT			**SF**
1	14TH ST	94114	10-G1
BRADFORD ST			**SF**
1	ESMERALDA AV	94110	15-A5
1	PERALTA AV	94110	15-A5
1	ALABAMA ST	94110	15-A5
50	MAYFLOWER ST	94110	15-A5
70	BERNAL HEIGHTS BLVD	94110	15-A5
100	POWHATTAN AV	94110	15-A5
200	CORTLAND AV	94110	15-A5
240	MOJAVE ST	94110	15-A5
300	JARBOE AV	94110	15-A5
400	TOMPKINS AV	94110	15-A6
BRADY ST			**SF**
1	MARKET ST	94103	10-H1
30	STEVENSON ST	94103	10-H1
50	COLTON ST	94103	10-H1
	CHASE CT	94103	10-J1
100	OTIS ST	94103	10-J1
BRANNAN ST			**SF**
1	THE EMBARCADERO	94107	7-C6
100	DELANCEY ST	94107	7-C6
200	DOVER ST	94107	7-C6
270	COLIN P KELLY JR ST	94107	7-C6
300	2ND ST	94107	7-C6
320	STANFORD ST	94107	7-C7
350	JACK LONDON AL	94107	7-B7
400	3RD ST	94107	7-B7
420	RITCH ST	94107	7-B7
440	ZOE ST	94107	7-B7
500	4TH ST	94107	7-B7
600	5TH ST	94107	7-B7
	6TH ST	94103	7-B7
730	HARRIET ST	94103	7-B7
750	LUCERNE ST	94103	7-A7
750	BOARDMAN PL	94103	11-A1
760	BUTTE PL	94103	11-A1
780	GILBERT ST	94103	11-A1
	7TH ST	94103	11-A1
	LANGTON ST	94103	11-A1
900	8TH ST	94103	11-A1
1000	9TH ST	94103	11-A1
1	DIVISION ST	94103	11-A1
50	POTRERO AV	94103	11-A1
	BRYANT ST	94103	11-A1
	DECATUR ST	94103	11-A1
	8TH ST	94103	11-A1
BRAZIL AV			**SF**
1	MISSION ST	94112	14-G7
1	NORTON ST	94112	14-G7
100	LONDON ST	94112	14-G7
200	PARIS ST	94112	14-G7
300	LISBON ST	94112	14-G7
400	MADRID ST	94112	14-G7
	EDINBURGH ST	94112	19-G1
600	NAPLES ST	94112	19-G1
700	VIENNA ST	94112	19-G1
800	ATHENS ST	94112	19-G1
900	MOSCOW ST	94112	19-H1
1000	MUNICH ST	94112	19-H1
1100	PRAGUE ST	94112	19-H1
1200	LA GRANDE AV	94134	19-H1
1200	LA GRANDE AV	94112	19-H1
1500	MANSELL ST	94134	19-H1
1500	MANSELL ST	94112	19-H1
1500	PERSIA AV	94112	19-H1
BREEN PL			**SF**
1	MCALLISTER ST	94102	6-J6
BRENTWOOD AV			**SF**
1	LULU AL	94127	13-E6
1	MELROSE AV	94127	13-E6
80	MANGELS AV	94127	13-E6
100	MANGELS AV	94127	13-E6
200	HAZELWOOD AV	94127	13-D6
230	VALDEZ AV	94127	13-D6
260	COLON AV	94127	13-D6
300	YERBA BUENA AV	94127	13-D6
350	FERNWOOD DR	94127	13-D6
400	MAYWOOD DR	94127	13-D6
BRET HARTE TER			**SF**
1	FRANCISCO ST	94133	2-J3
BREWSTER ST			**SF**
1	MONTCALM ST	94110	15-A4
1	MULLEN AV	94110	15-A4
50	MACEDONIA ST	94110	15-A4
100	MULLEN AV	94110	15-A4
100	RUTLEDGE ST	94110	15-A4
120	COSTA ST	94110	15-A5
140	FAITH ST	94110	15-A5
160	JOY ST	94110	15-A5
200	FRANCONIA ST	94110	15-A5
BRIARCLIFF TER			**SF**
100	19TH AV	94132	13-B5
BRIDGEVIEW DR			**SF**
1	NEWHALL ST	94124	15-B6
1	REVERE AV	94124	15-B6
200	TAMPA LN	94124	15-B6
300	TOPEKA AV	94124	15-B6
400	THORNTON AV	94124	15-B6
400	SCOTIA AV	94124	15-B6
BRIGHT ST			**SF**
30	STANLEY ST	94132	18-D2
200	RANDOLPH ST	94132	18-D1
300	SARGENT ST	94132	18-D1
400	SHIELDS ST	94132	18-D1
500	GARFIELD ST	94132	18-D1
600	HOLLOWAY AV	94132	18-D1
30	ALEMANY BLVD	94132	18-D2
BRIGHTON AV			**SF**
1	LAKEVIEW AV	94112	18-D1
100	GRAFTON AV	94112	18-D1
200	HOLLOWAY AV	94112	13-D7
400	OCEAN AV	94112	13-D7
BRITTON ST			**SF**
1	LELAND AV	94134	19-J2
100	VISITACION AV	94134	19-J2
BROAD ST			**SF**
210	ORIZABA AV	94112	18-D2
100	CAPITOL AV	94112	18-D2
1	PLYMOUTH AV	94112	18-D2
100	SAN JOSE AV	94112	18-D2
BROADMOOR DR			**SF**
1	STONECREST DR	94132	13-C7
100	WINSTON DR	94132	13-C7
200	STONECREST DR	94132	13-C7
BROADWAY			**SF**
300	SANSOME ST	94133	7-B4
300	BROADWAY ST	94133	7-B4
340	OSGOOD PL	94133	7-A4
370	BARTOL ST	94133	7-A4
400	MONTGOMERY ST	94133	7-A4
450	ROWLAND ST	94133	7-A4
500	KEARNY ST	94133	7-A4
530	ROMOLO ST	94133	7-A4
560	COLUMBUS AV	94133	7-A4
600	GRANT AV	94133	7-A4
700	STOCKTON ST	94133	7-A4
740	CORDELIA ST	94133	7-A4
730	TURK MURPHY LN	94133	7-A4
770	TURK MURPHY LN	94133	7-A4
	POWELL ST	94133	7-A4
	WAYNE PL	94133	7-A4
	MASON ST	94133	6-J4
	HIMMELMANN PL	94133	6-J4
1000	TAYLOR ST	94133	6-J4
1100	JONES ST	94109	6-J4
	LEAVENWORTH ST	94109	6-J4
	CYRUS PL	94109	6-J4
	HYDE ST	94109	6-J4
	JONES ST	94133	6-J4
	TAYLOR ST	94133	6-J4
1400	LARKIN ST	94109	6-H4
1500	POLK ST	94109	6-H4
1600	VAN NESS AV	94109	6-H4
1700	FRANKLIN ST	94109	6-H4
1800	GOUGH ST	94109	6-H5
1900	OCTAVIA ST	94109	6-H5
2000	BROADWAY ST	94109	6-H5
2000	LAGUNA ST	94109	6-H5
BROADWAY ST			**SF**
1	THE EMBARCADERO	94111	7-B4
50	DAVIS ST	94111	7-B4
100	FRONT ST	94111	7-B4
200	BATTERY ST	94111	7-B4
300	BROADWAY	94111	7-B4
300	SANSOME ST	94111	7-B4
2000	LAGUNA ST	94115	6-G5
2000	BROADWAY	94115	6-G5
2100	BUCHANAN ST	94115	6-G5
2200	WEBSTER ST	94115	6-G5
2300	FILLMORE ST	94115	6-G5
2400	STEINER ST	94115	6-G5
2500	PIERCE ST	94115	6-G5
2600	SCOTT ST	94115	6-F5
2650	NORMANDIE TER	94115	6-F5
2700	DIVISADERO ST	94115	6-F5
2800	BRODERICK ST	94115	6-F5
2900	BAKER ST	94115	6-F5
3000	W BROADWAY ST	94115	6-F5
3000	LYON ST	94115	6-F5
W BROADWAY ST			**SF**
	BROADWAY ST	94129	6-F5
	LYON ST	94129	6-F5
	PRESIDIO BLVD	94129	6-F5
BRODERICK ST			**SF**
2600	VALLEJO ST	94123	6-F5
2700	GREEN ST	94123	6-F4
2800	UNION ST	94123	6-F4
2900	FILBERT ST	94123	6-F4
3000	GREENWICH ST	94123	6-F4
3100	LOMBARD ST	94123	2-F4
3200	CHESTNUT ST	94123	2-F4
3300	FRANCISCO ST	94123	2-F4
3400	BAY ST	94123	2-F4
3500	NORTH POINT ST	94123	2-F3
3600	BEACH ST	94123	2-F3
3700	JEFFERSON ST	94123	2-F3
3800	MARINA BLVD	94123	2-F3
1400	GEARY BLVD	94115	6-F6
1450	GARDEN ST	94115	6-F6
1500	POST ST	94115	6-F6
1600	SUTTER ST	94115	6-F6
1700	BUSH ST	94115	6-F6
1800	PINE ST	94115	6-F6
1900	CALIFORNIA ST	94115	6-F5
2000	SACRAMENTO ST	94115	6-F5
2100	CLAY ST	94115	6-F5
2200	WASHINGTON ST	94115	6-F5
2300	JACKSON ST	94115	6-F5
2400	PACIFIC AV	94115	6-F5
2500	BROADWAY ST	94115	6-F5
100	HAIGHT ST	94117	10-F1
200	PAGE ST	94117	10-F1
300	OAK ST	94117	10-F1

PRIMARY STREET Address	Cross Street	ZIP	CITY Pg-Grid
BRODERICK ST			SF
400	FELL ST	94117	6-F7
500	HAYES ST	94117	6-F7
600	GROVE ST	94117	6-F7
700	FULTON ST	94117	6-F7
800	MCALLISTER ST	94117	6-F7
900	GOLDEN GATE AV	94115	6-F7
1000	TURK ST	94115	6-F7
1100	EDDY ST	94115	6-F6
1200	ELLIS ST	94115	6-F6
1300	OFARRELL ST	94115	6-F6
BROMLEY PL			SF
	WEBSTER ST	94115	6-G5
BROMPTON AV			SF
1	CHENERY ST	94131	14-G6
50	KERN ST	94131	14-G6
100	BOSWORTH ST	94131	14-G6
200	JOOST AV	94131	14-G6
BRONTE ST			SF
1	CORTLAND AV	94110	14-J5
40	MOJAVE ST	94110	14-J5
100	JARBOE AV	94110	14-J5
200	TOMPKINS AV	94110	14-J5
BROOK ST			SF
1	SAN JOSE AV	94110	14-H5
100	MISSION ST	94110	14-H5
100	SANTA MARINA ST	94110	14-H5
BROOKDALE AV			SF
1	SANTOS ST	94134	19-H2
170	BLYTHDALE AV	94134	19-H2
200	GENEVA AV	94134	19-H2
BROOKLYN PL			SF
1	SACRAMENTO ST	94108	7-A5
BROOKS ST			SF
	BAKER CT	94129	5-B5
BROSNAN ST			SF
1	VALENCIA ST	94103	10-H1
100	GUERRERO ST	94103	10-H1
BROTHERHOOD WY			SF
500	ALEMANY BLVD	94132	18-D2
500	ORIZABA AV	94132	18-D2
500	SAGAMORE ST	94132	18-D2
600	ARCH ST	94132	18-C2
690	JUNIPERO SERRA BLVD	94132	18-C2
720	THOMAS MORE WY	94132	18-B1
720	CHUMASERO DR	94132	18-B1
1000	LAKE MERCED BLVD	94132	18-B1
BROWN ST			SF
	BELLES ST	94129	5-C5
	HAYS ST	94129	5-C5
	WYMAN AV	94129	5-C5
	PACIFIC AV	94129	5-C5
BRUCE AV			SF
70	EDGAR PL	94112	13-E7
100	HAROLD AV	94112	13-E7
BRUNSWICK ST			SF
1	NEWTON ST	94112	19-F2
70	CURTIS ST	94112	19-F2
150	POPE ST	94112	19-F2
220	ALLISON ST	94112	19-F2
290	CONCORD ST	94112	19-F2
330	FLORENTINE ST	94112	19-F2
380	GUTTENBERG ST	94112	19-F2
540	LOWELL ST	94112	19-E2
630	ROEMER WY	94112	19-E2
700	WHITTIER ST	94112	19-E2
BRUSH PL			SF
1	HALLAM ST	94103	7-A7
BRUSSELS ST			SF
1	SILVER AV	94134	15-A6
100	SILLIMAN ST	94134	15-A7
200	FELTON ST	94134	15-A7
300	BURROWS ST	94134	15-A7
1000	BACON ST	94134	15-A7
1040	WAYLAND ST	94134	15-A7
1100	WOOLSEY ST	94134	15-A7
1200	DWIGHT ST	94134	15-A7
1300	OLMSTEAD ST	94134	20-A1
1200	MANSELL ST	94134	20-A1
1230	ORDWAY ST	94134	20-A1
1270	WARD ST	94134	20-A1
1310	HARKNESS AV	94134	20-A1
1350	WILDE AV	94134	20-A2
1400	CAMPBELL AV	94134	20-A2
BRYANT ST			SF
1	THE EMBARCADERO	94105	7-C6
40	MAIN ST	94105	7-C6
120	BEALE ST	94107	7-C6
100	BAYSIDE VILLAGE PL	94107	7-C6
250	DELANCEY ST	94107	7-C6
300	RINCON ST	94107	7-C6
360	STERLING ST	94107	7-B6
400	2ND ST	94107	7-B6
450	JACK LONDON AL	94107	7-B6
500	3RD ST	94107	7-B7
520	RITCH ST	94107	7-B7
540	ZOE ST	94107	7-B7
600	4TH ST	94107	7-B7
700	5TH ST	94107	7-B7
750	OAK GROVE ST	94107	7-B7
770	MORRIS ST	94107	7-A7
800	6TH ST	94103	7-A7
830	HARRIET ST	94103	7-A7
850	BOARDMAN PL	94103	7-A7
880	GILBERT ST	94103	7-A7
900	7TH ST	94103	7-A7
980	LANGTON ST	94103	11-A1
990	KATE ST	94103	11-A1
1000	BRANNAN ST	94103	11-A1
1000	8TH ST	94103	11-A1
1030	CONVERSE ST	94103	11-A1
1100	9TH ST	94103	11-A1
1140	DORE ST	94103	11-A1
1200	10TH ST	94103	11-A1
	11TH ST	94103	11-A1
	DIVISION ST	94103	11-A1
	ALAMEDA ST	94103	11-A1
	15TH ST	94103	11-A2
1700	16TH ST	94110	11-A2
1800	17TH ST	94110	11-A2
1900	MARIPOSA ST	94110	11-A2
2000	18TH ST	94110	11-A2
2100	19TH ST	94110	11-A2
2190	20TH ST	94110	11-A3
2240	21ST ST	94110	11-A3
2400	22ND ST	94110	11-A3
2500	23RD ST	94110	11-A3
2600	24TH ST	94110	11-A4
2700	25TH ST	94110	11-A4
2800	26TH ST	94110	11-A4
2900	CESAR CHAVEZ ST	94110	15-A4
3000	PRECITA AV	94110	15-A4
2290	19TH ST	94110	11-A2
2400	20TH ST	94110	11-A2
BUCARELI DR			SF
1	JUAN BAUTISTA CIR	94132	18-B1
100	GONZALEZ DR	94132	18-B1
190	GARCES DR	94132	18-B1
200	RIVAS AV	94132	18-B1
BUCHANAN ST			SF
3600	BAY ST	94123	2-G3
3700	NORTH POINT ST	94123	2-G3
	BEACH ST	94123	2-G3
	MARINA BLVD	94123	2-G3
1800	SUTTER ST	94115	6-G6
1900	BUSH ST	94115	6-G5
2000	PINE ST	94115	6-G5
2100	CALIFORNIA ST	94115	6-G5
2200	SACRAMENTO ST	94115	6-G5
2300	CLAY ST	94115	6-G5
2400	WASHINGTON ST	94115	6-G5
2500	JACKSON ST	94115	6-G5
2600	PACIFIC AV	94115	6-G5
2700	BROADWAY ST	94115	6-G4
2800	VALLEJO ST	94123	6-G4
2900	GREEN ST	94123	6-G4
3000	UNION ST	94123	6-G4
3100	FILBERT ST	94123	6-G4
3150	PIXLEY ST	94123	2-G4
3200	GREENWICH ST	94123	2-G4
3250	MOULTON ST	94123	2-G4
3300	LOMBARD ST	94123	2-G4
3360	MAGNOLIA ST	94123	2-G4
3400	CHESTNUT ST	94123	2-G4
	ZAMPA LN	94115	6-G6
	GEARY BLVD	94115	6-G6
680	EDDY ST	94115	6-H6
700	WILLOW ST	94115	6-H6
1	DUBOCE AV	94102	10-H1
100	HERMANN ST	94102	10-H1
200	WALLER ST	94102	10-H1
250	LAUSSAT ST	94102	10-H1
300	HAIGHT ST	94102	10-H1
400	PAGE ST	94102	6-H7
420	LILY ST	94102	6-H7
500	OAK ST	94102	6-H7
520	HICKORY ST	94102	6-H7
600	FELL ST	94102	6-H7
630	LINDEN ST	94102	6-H7
700	HAYES ST	94102	6-H7
730	IVY ST	94102	6-H7
800	GROVE ST	94102	6-H7
BUCKINGHAM WY			SF
100	20TH AV	94132	13-B6
300	WINSTON DR	94132	13-B7
580	20TH AV	94132	13-B7
600	19TH AV	94132	13-B7
500	20TH AV	94132	13-B6
600	19TH AV	94132	13-B6
600	MONTE VISTA DR	94132	13-B6
BUENA VISTA AV E			SF
1	BAKER ST	94117	10-F1
1	HAIGHT ST	94117	10-F1
190	DUBOCE AV	94117	10-F1
200	BUENA VISTA TER	94117	10-F1
300	PARK HILL AV	94117	10-F1
500	UPPER TER	94117	10-F1
500	BUENA VISTA AV W	94117	10-F1
BUENA VISTA AV W			SF
1	HAIGHT ST	94117	10-F1
100	WALLER ST	94117	10-F1
200	CENTRAL AV	94117	10-F1
300	FREDERICK ST	94117	10-F1
400	JAVA ST	94117	10-F1
500	UPPER TER	94117	10-F1
500	BUENA VISTA AV E	94117	10-F1
BUENA VISTA TER			SF
1	BUENA VISTA AV E	94117	10-F1
100	14TH ST	94117	10-G1
150	ROOSEVELT WY	94117	10-G1
150	ROOSEVELT WY	94117	10-F1
200	15TH ST	94117	10-F1
BURGOYNE ST			SF
1	PACIFIC AV	94109	6-J5
BURKE ST			SF
400	3RD ST	94124	15-C5
BURLWOOD DR			SF
1	BELLA VISTA WY	94127	13-E6
100	LULU AL	94127	13-E6
200	LOS PALMOS DR	94127	13-E6
BURNETT AV			SF
1	TWIN PEAKS BLVD	94131	10-F3
180	N BURNETT AV	94131	10-F3
230	GARDENSIDE DR	94131	10-F3
390	DIXIE AL	94131	10-F3
430	HOPKINS AV	94131	10-F3
550	GOLDING LN	94131	10-F3
610	PEREGO TER	94131	10-F4
650	GARDENSIDE DR	94131	10-F4
690	PARKRIDGE DR	94131	10-F4
770	FENTON LN	94131	10-F4
760	CRESTLINE DR	94131	10-F4
870	GLENVIEW DR	94131	10-F4
900	DAWNVIEW WY	94131	14-F4
1000	DIAMOND HEIGHTS BLVD	94131	14-F4
1000	PORTOLA DR	94131	14-F4
N BURNETT AV			SF
200	BURNETT AV	94131	10-F3
BURNS PL			SF
1	11TH ST	94103	10-J1
BURNSIDE AV			SF
1	CHENERY ST	94131	14-F6
50	PARADISE AV	94131	14-F6
100	BOSWORTH ST	94131	14-F6
200	MANGELS AV	94131	14-F6
BURR AV			SF
1	MCCARTHY AV	94134	19-J2
100	ARGONAUT AV	94134	19-J2
BURRITT ST			SF
1	BUSH ST	94108	7-A5
BURROWS ST			SF
100	SAN BRUNO AV	94134	15-A7
200	GIRARD ST	94134	15-A7
300	BRUSSELS ST	94134	15-A7
400	GOETTINGEN ST	94134	15-A7
500	SOMERSET ST	94134	15-A7
600	HOLYOKE ST	94134	15-A7
700	HAMILTON ST	94134	14-J7
800	BOWDOIN ST	94134	14-J7
1100	UNIVERSITY ST	94134	14-J7
1300	AMHERST ST	94134	14-J7
1500	CAMBRIDGE ST	94134	14-J7
1600	OXFORD ST	94134	14-H7
1700	HARVARD ST	94134	14-H7
1800	GAMBIER ST	94134	14-H7
1900	MADISON ST	94134	14-H7
2000	PERU AV	94134	14-H7
2000	PERU AV	94112	14-H7
2100	MANSFIELD ST	94134	14-H7
2100	MANSFIELD ST	94112	14-H7
BUSH ST			SF
1	1ST ST	94111	7-B5
1	MARKET ST	94111	7-B5
100	BATTERY ST	94104	7-B5
200	SANSOME ST	94104	7-B5
210	TREASURY PL	94104	7-B5
300	MONTGOMERY ST	94104	7-A5
310	TRINITY ST	94108	7-A5
310	TRINITY ST	94104	7-A5
360	BELDEN ST	94108	7-A5
360	BELDEN ST	94104	7-A5
410	KEARNY ST	94108	7-A5
400	SAINT GEORGE AL	94108	7-A5
410	CLAUDE LN	94108	7-A5
460	MARK LN	94108	7-A5
500	GRANT AV	94108	7-A5
550	CHATHAM PL	94108	7-A5
600	STOCKTON ST	94108	7-A5
620	BURRITT ST	94108	7-A5
640	DASHELLE HAMMETT ST	94108	7-A5
650	CHELSEA PL	94108	7-A5
700	POWELL ST	94102	7-A5
700	POWELL ST	94108	7-A5
800	MASON ST	94102	7-A5
800	MASON ST	94108	7-A5
900	TAYLOR ST	94109	6-J5
900	TAYLOR ST	94108	6-J5
1000	JONES ST	94109	6-J5
1100	LEAVENWORTH ST	94109	6-J5
1200	HYDE ST	94109	6-J5
1300	LARKIN ST	94109	6-J5
1400	POLK ST	94109	6-H5
1500	VAN NESS AV	94109	6-H5
1600	FRANKLIN ST	94109	6-H5
1700	GOUGH ST	94109	6-H5
1800	OCTAVIA ST	94109	6-H6
1900	LAGUNA ST	94115	6-H6
2000	BUCHANAN ST	94115	6-G6
2100	WEBSTER ST	94115	6-G6
2120	COTTAGE RW	94115	6-G6
2200	FILLMORE ST	94115	6-G6
2300	STEINER ST	94115	6-G6
2400	PIERCE ST	94115	6-G6
2500	SCOTT ST	94115	6-F6
2600	DIVISADERO ST	94115	6-F6
2700	BRODERICK ST	94115	6-F6
2800	BAKER ST	94115	6-F6
2900	LYON ST	94115	6-F6
3000	EUCLID AV	94115	6-F6
3000	PRESIDIO AV	94115	6-F6
BUTTE PL			SF
	BRANNAN ST	94103	11-A1
BYINGTON ST			SF
100	FILLMORE ST	94115	6-G6
BYRON CT			SF
1	LOWELL ST	94112	19-F2
BYXBEE ST			SF
1	19TH AV	94132	18-C1
100	SARGENT ST	94132	18-C1
200	SHIELDS ST	94132	18-C1
300	GARFIELD ST	94132	18-C1
400	HOLLOWAY AV	94132	18-C1
C			
C ST			SF
	BLANDY ST	94124	16-F7
	NIMITZ AV	94124	16-F7
	SPEAR AV	94124	16-F7
	VAN KEUREN AV	94124	16-F7
CABRILLO ST			SF
1	ARGUELLO BLVD	94118	5-D7
100	2ND AV	94118	5-D7
200	3RD AV	94118	5-D7
300	4TH AV	94118	5-D7
400	5TH AV	94118	5-D7
500	6TH AV	94118	5-D7
600	7TH AV	94118	5-D7
700	8TH AV	94118	5-C7
800	9TH AV	94118	5-C7
900	10TH AV	94118	5-C7
1000	11TH AV	94118	5-C7
1100	12TH AV	94118	5-C7
1200	FUNSTON AV	94118	5-C7
1250	PRESIDIO BLVD	94118	5-C7
1300	14TH AV	94118	5-C7
1400	15TH AV	94118	5-C7
1500	16TH AV	94118	5-B7
1600	17TH AV	94121	5-B7
1700	18TH AV	94121	5-B7
1800	19TH AV	94121	5-B7
1900	20TH AV	94121	5-B7
2000	21ST AV	94121	5-B7
2100	22ND AV	94121	5-B7
2200	23RD AV	94121	5-B7
2300	24TH AV	94121	5-B7
2400	25TH AV	94121	5-A7
2500	26TH AV	94121	5-A7
2600	27TH AV	94121	5-A7
2700	28TH AV	94121	5-A7
2800	29TH AV	94121	5-A7
2900	30TH AV	94121	5-A7
3000	31ST AV	94121	5-A7
3100	32ND AV	94121	5-A7
3200	33RD AV	94121	5-A7
3300	34TH AV	94121	4-J7
3400	35TH AV	94121	4-J7
3500	36TH AV	94121	4-J7
3600	37TH AV	94121	4-J7
3700	38TH AV	94121	4-J7
3800	39TH AV	94121	4-J7
3900	40TH AV	94121	4-J7
4000	41ST AV	94121	4-J7
4100	42ND AV	94121	4-H7
4200	43RD AV	94121	4-H7
4300	44TH AV	94121	4-H7
4400	45TH AV	94121	4-H7
4500	46TH AV	94121	4-H7
4600	47TH AV	94121	4-H7
4700	48TH AV	94121	4-H7
4800	LA PLAYA	94121	4-H7
CADELL PL			SF
1	UNION ST	94133	3-A4
CAINE AV			SF
1	LOBOS ST	94112	18-E1
100	LAKEVIEW AV	94112	18-E1
200	MOUNT VERNON AV	94112	19-E1
200	SAN MIGUEL ST	94112	19-E1
CAIRE TER			SF
1	CAROLINA ST	94107	11-B3
CALEDONIA ST			SF
100	15TH ST	94103	10-H2
150	SPARROW ST	94103	10-H2
200	16TH ST	94103	10-H2
CALGARY ST			SF
1	SAWYER ST	94134	19-J2
1	VELASCO AV	94134	19-J2
CALHOUN TER			SF
100	UNION ST	94133	3-A4
CALIFORNIA AV			SF
1	AVENUE B	94130	3-E2
CALIFORNIA ST			SF
	MARKET ST	94111	7-B5
	SPEAR ST	94111	7-B5
40	DRUMM ST	94111	7-B5
100	DAVIS ST	94111	7-B5
200	FRONT ST	94111	7-B5
300	BATTERY ST	94104	7-B5
400	SANSOME ST	94104	7-B5
450	LEIDESDORFF ST	94104	7-B5
500	MONTGOMERY ST	94104	7-A5
550	SPRING ST	94104	7-A5
600	KEARNY ST	94108	7-A5
650	QUINCY ST	94108	7-A5
700	GRANT AV	94108	7-A5
740	SABIN PL	94108	7-A5
800	STOCKTON ST	94108	7-A5
840	PRATT PL	94108	7-A5
850	JOICE ST	94108	7-A5
890	MILES PL	94108	7-A5
900	POWELL ST	94108	7-A5
1000	MASON ST	94108	7-A5
1060	SPROULE LN	94108	6-J5
1100	TAYLOR ST	94108	6-J5
1200	JONES ST	94109	6-J5
1230	LYSETTE ST	94109	6-J5
1300	LEAVENWORTH ST	94109	6-J5
1330	HELEN ST	94109	6-J5
1400	HYDE ST	94109	6-J5
1500	LARKIN ST	94109	6-J5
1600	POLK ST	94109	6-H5
1700	VAN NESS AV	94109	6-H5
1800	FRANKLIN ST	94109	6-H5
1900	GOUGH ST	94109	6-H5
2000	OCTAVIA ST	94109	6-H5
2100	LAGUNA ST	94115	6-H5
2200	BUCHANAN ST	94115	6-G5
2300	WEBSTER ST	94115	6-G5
2350	ORBEN PL	94115	6-G5
2400	FILLMORE ST	94115	6-G5
2500	STEINER ST	94115	6-G5
2600	PIERCE ST	94115	6-G5
2700	SCOTT ST	94115	6-F5
2800	DIVISADERO ST	94115	6-F5
2900	BRODERICK ST	94115	6-F5
3000	BAKER ST	94115	6-F6
3100	LYON ST	94115	6-F6
3200	PRESIDIO AV	94115	6-F6
3300	WALNUT ST	94118	6-E6
3400	LAUREL ST	94118	6-E6
3500	LOCUST ST	94118	6-E6
3600	SPRUCE ST	94118	5-E6
3650	PARKER AV	94118	5-E6
3700	MAPLE ST	94118	5-E6
3750	COMMONWEALTH AV	94118	5-E6
3780	CHERRY ST	94118	5-E6
3800	JORDAN AV	94118	5-E6
3850	PALM AV	94118	5-E6
3900	ARGUELLO BLVD	94118	5-D6
4000	2ND AV	94118	5-D6
4100	3RD AV	94118	5-D6
4200	4TH AV	94118	5-D6
4300	5TH AV	94118	5-D6
4400	6TH AV	94118	5-D6
4500	7TH AV	94118	5-D6
4560	CORNWALL ST	94118	5-C6
4600	8TH AV	94118	5-C6
4700	9TH AV	94118	5-C6
4800	10TH AV	94118	5-C6
4900	11TH AV	94118	5-C6
5000	12TH AV	94118	5-C6
5100	FUNSTON AV	94118	5-C6
5150	PRESIDIO BLVD	94118	5-C6
5200	14TH AV	94118	5-C6
5300	15TH AV	94118	5-C6
5400	16TH AV	94118	5-B6
5500	17TH AV	94121	5-B6
5600	18TH AV	94121	5-B6
5700	19TH AV	94121	5-B6
5800	20TH AV	94121	5-B6
5900	21ST AV	94121	5-B6
6000	22ND AV	94121	5-B6
6100	23RD AV	94121	5-B6
6200	24TH AV	94121	5-B6
6300	25TH AV	94121	5-A6
6400	26TH AV	94121	5-A6
6500	27TH AV	94121	5-A6
6600	28TH AV	94121	5-A6
6700	29TH AV	94121	5-A6
6800	30TH AV	94121	5-A6
6900	31ST AV	94121	5-A6
7000	32ND AV	94121	5-A6
CAMBON DR			SF
1	CARDENAS AV	94132	18-B1
100	CASTELO AV	94132	18-B1
150	FELIX AV	94132	18-B1
200	FONT BLVD	94132	18-B1
CAMBRIDGE ST			SF
1	STONEYBROOK AV	94134	14-H6
1	STONEYBROOK AV	94112	14-H6
1	TRUMBULL ST	94112	14-H6
50	STONEYFORD AV	94134	14-H6
50	STONEYFORD AV	94112	14-H6
90	GLADSTONE DR	94134	14-H6
90	GLADSTONE DR	94112	14-H6
160	WESTVIEW AV	94134	14-H6
160	WESTVIEW AV	94112	14-H6
250	SWEENY ST	94134	14-H6
250	SWEENY ST	94112	14-H6
310	SILVER AV	94134	14-H7
330	PIOCHE ST	94134	14-H7
420	SILLIMAN ST	94134	14-H7
510	FELTON ST	94134	14-J7
610	BURROWS ST	94134	14-J7
700	BACON ST	94134	14-J7
800	WAYLAND ST	94134	19-J1
900	JOHN F SHELLEY DR	94134	19-J1
CAMELLIA AV			SF
40	SILVER AV	94112	14-G7
1	CASTLE MANOR AV	94112	14-G6
50	ADMIRAL AV	94112	14-G6
CAMEO WY			SF
1	AMBER DR	94131	14-F4
100	DUNCAN ST	94131	14-F4
CAMERON WY			SF
1	GRIFFITH ST	94124	20-C1
1	NICHOLS WY	94124	20-C1
180	DOUBLE ROCK ST	94124	20-C1
240	NICHOLS WY	94124	20-C1
300	FITZGERALD AV	94124	20-C1
CAMP ST			SF
1	ALBION ST	94110	10-H2
100	GUERRERO ST	94110	10-H2
CAMPBELL AV			SF
	ELLIOT ST	94134	19-J1
40	ALBERTA ST	94134	19-J1
90	ERVINE ST	94134	20-A1
130	DELTA ST	94134	20-A2
270	RUTLAND ST	94134	20-A2
440	HOLYOKE ST	94134	20-A2

PRIMARY STREET Address	Cross Street	ZIP	CITY Pg-Grid
CAMPBELL AV			SF
500	SOMERSET ST	94134	20-A2
520	SOMERSET ST	94134	20-A2
570	GOETTINGEN ST	94134	20-A2
630	BRUSSELS ST	94134	20-A2
700	SAN BRUNO AV	94134	20-A2
CAMPTON PL			SF
1	GRANT AV	94108	7-A5
	STOCKTON ST	94108	7-A5
CAMPUS CIR			SF
	STATE DR	94132	13-B7
CAMPUS LN			SF
100	BACON ST	94134	14-J7
CANBY ST			SF
	KEYES AV	94129	1-E4
	MESA AV	94129	1-E4
CANYON DR			SF
1	ROBINSON DR	94112	19-G2
10	S HILL BLVD	94112	19-G2
CAPISTRANO AV			SF
1	SAN JOSE AV	94112	14-F6
70	SAN GABRIEL AV	94112	14-F7
200	SANTA ROSA AV	94112	14-F7
270	SANTA YSABEL AV	94112	14-F7
400	SAN JUAN AV	94112	14-F7
500	SANTA YNEZ AV	94112	14-F7
CAPITOL AV			SF
60	SAGAMORE ST	94112	18-D2
160	SADOWA ST	94112	18-D2
250	BROAD ST	94112	18-D2
340	FARALLONES ST	94112	18-D2
440	LOBOS ST	94112	18-D1
530	MINERVA ST	94112	18-D1
620	MONTANA ST	94112	18-D1
710	THRIFT ST	94112	18-D1
800	LAKEVIEW AV	94112	18-D1
990	GRAFTON AV	94112	18-D1
1100	HOLLOWAY AV	94112	18-D1
1200	DE MONTFORT AV	94112	13-D7
1300	OCEAN AV	94112	13-D7
CAPP ST			SF
1	15TH ST	94103	10-J2
50	ADAIR ST	94103	10-J2
100	16TH ST	94103	10-J2
100	16TH ST	94110	10-J2
200	17TH ST	94110	10-J2
300	18TH ST	94110	10-J2
400	19TH ST	94110	10-J2
500	20TH ST	94110	10-J3
600	21ST ST	94110	10-J3
700	22ND ST	94110	10-J3
800	23RD ST	94110	10-J3
900	24TH ST	94110	10-J4
1000	25TH ST	94110	10-J4
1100	26TH ST	94110	10-J4
1200	CESAR CHAVEZ ST	94110	10-J4
1200	MISSION ST	94110	10-J4
CAPRA WY			SF
1	MALLORCA WY	94123	2-G3
100	PIERCE ST	94123	2-F3
150	AVILA ST	94123	2-F3
330	SCOTT ST	94123	2-F3
CARDENAS AV			SF
1	HOLLOWAY AV	94132	18-B1
100	SERRANO DR	94132	18-B1
	CRESPI DR	94132	18-B1
200	CRESPI DR	94132	18-B1
300	GONZALEZ DR	94132	18-B1
400	CAMBON DR	94132	18-B1
CARGO WY			SF
1	JENNINGS ST	94124	15-D5
440	MENDELL ST	94124	15-C5
560	AMADOR ST	94124	15-C4
600	3RD ST	94124	15-C4
600	ARTHUR AV	94124	15-C4
CARL ST			SF
1	CLAYTON ST	94117	10-E1
100	COLE ST	94117	10-E1
150	SHRADER ST	94117	10-E2
200	STANYAN ST	94117	9-E2
300	WILLARD ST	94117	9-E2
400	HILLWAY AV	94143	9-D2
400	HILLWAY AV	94117	9-D2
500	ARGUELLO BLVD	94143	9-D2
500	ARGUELLO BLVD	94117	9-D2
CARMEL ST			SF
1	CLAYTON ST	94117	10-F2
1	TWIN PEAKS BLVD	94117	10-F2
50	BELVEDERE ST	94117	10-E2
100	COLE ST	94117	10-E2
200	SHRADER ST	94117	10-E2
CARMELITA ST			SF
100	WALLER ST	94117	10-G1
CARNELIAN WY			SF
100	DIAMOND HEIGHTS BLVD	94131	10-F4
CAROLINA ST			SF
1	CHANNEL ST	94107	11-B1
100	15TH ST	94103	11-B1
100	8TH ST	94103	11-B1
200	16TH ST	94107	11-B2
300	17TH ST	94107	11-B2
400	MARIPOSA ST	94107	11-B2
500	18TH ST	94107	11-B2
600	19TH ST	94107	11-B2
700	20TH ST	94107	11-B3
890	SOUTHERN HEIGHTS AV	94107	11-B3
900	22ND ST	94107	11-B3
1100	23RD ST	94107	11-B3
1150	CORAL RD	94107	11-B3
1160	CORAL RD	94107	11-B3
1220	CORAL RD	94107	11-B3
1280	CAIRE TER	94107	11-B3
1300	WISCONSIN ST	94107	11-B3
CARPENTER CT			SF
1	WHITNEY YOUNG CIR	94124	15-C6
CARR ST			SF
1	PAUL AV	94124	20-B1
100	SALINAS AV	94124	20-B1
CARRIE ST			SF
1	CHENERY ST	94131	14-G6
100	WILDER ST	94131	14-G6
CARRIZAL ST			SF
1	GENEVA AV	94134	19-H2
100	PARQUE DR	94134	19-H2
100	VELASCO AV	94134	19-H2
CARROLL AV			SF
1900	NEWHALL ST	94124	15-B7
2000	PHELPS ST	94124	15-A7
2100	QUINT ST	94124	15-A6
2200	BAYSHORE BLVD	94124	15-A6
2200	THORNTON AV	94124	15-A6
700	FITCH ST	94124	20-C1
990	HAWES ST	94124	20-C1
1200	INGALLS ST	94124	15-C7
1400	JENNINGS ST	94124	15-B7
1600	KEITH ST	94124	15-B7
1700	3RD ST	94124	15-B7
1800	MENDELL ST	94124	15-B7
CARSON ST			SF
1	DOUGLASS ST	94114	10-F3
CARTER ST			SF
500	GENEVA AV	94134	19-H2
CARVER ST			SF
1	BERNAL HEIGHTS BLVD	94110	14-J5
20	CHAPMAN ST	94110	14-J5
100	BERNAL HEIGHTS BLVD	94110	14-J5
CASA WY			SF
1	RETIRO WY	94123	2-G3
100	MARINA BLVD	94123	2-G3
100	AVILA ST	94123	2-G3
CASELLI AV			SF
1	DOUGLASS ST	94114	10-F2
50	LAMSON LN	94114	10-F2
100	CLOVER LN	94114	10-F2
140	CLOVER ST	94114	10-F2
200	YUKON ST	94114	10-F2
250	DANVERS ST	94114	10-F2
300	19TH ST	94114	10-F2
300	MONO ST	94114	10-F2
400	EAGLE ST	94114	10-F2
CASHMERE ST			SF
100	HUDSON AV	94124	15-C6
200	WHITNEY YOUNG CIR	94124	15-C6
200	DEDMAN CT	94124	15-C6
240	DUKES CT	94124	15-C6
300	LA SALLE AV	94124	15-C6
CASITAS AV			SF
180	LUDLOW AL	94127	13-D5
200	LANSDALE AV	94127	13-D5
200	LANSDALE AV	94127	13-D5
300	BAXTER AL	94127	13-D5
300	CRESTA VISTA DR	94127	13-D6
400	YERBA BUENA AV	94127	13-D6
400	HAZELWOOD AV	94127	13-D6
CASSANDRA CT			SF
100	WHITTIER ST	94112	19-E2
CASTELO AV			SF
1	CAMBON DR	94132	18-B1
100	GONZALEZ DR	94132	18-B1
CASTENADA AV			SF
1	VENTURA AV	94116	9-D4
50	ALTON AV	94116	9-D4
100	MAGELLAN AV	94116	9-D4
200	PACHECO ST	94116	9-D4
350	LOPEZ AV	94116	13-D4
390	SANTA RITA AV	94116	13-D4
400	SAN MARCOS AV	94116	13-D4
500	MONTALVO AV	94116	13-C4
CASTILLO ST			SF
100	VELASCO AV	94134	19-J2
CASTLE ST			SF
1	GREEN ST	94133	3-A4
100	UNION ST	94133	3-A4
CASTLE MANOR AV			SF
1	CAMELLIA AV	94112	14-G7
50	MAYNARD ST	94112	14-G7
50	MISSION ST	94112	14-G7
CASTRO ST			SF
1	DIVISADERO ST	94117	10-G1
1	DIVISADERO ST	94114	10-G1
1	WALLER ST	94114	10-G1
30	LLOYD ST	94117	10-G1
30	LLOYD ST	94114	10-G1
50	DUBOCE AV	94114	10-G1
100	14TH ST	94114	10-G1
150	HENRY ST	94114	10-G1
200	15TH ST	94114	10-G2
	BEAVER ST	94114	10-G2
250	BEAVER ST	94114	10-G2
300	16TH ST	94114	10-G2
350	STATES ST	94114	10-G2
	17TH ST	94114	10-G2
	MARKET ST	94114	10-G2
400	17TH ST	94114	10-G2
500	18TH ST	94114	10-G2
600	19TH ST	94114	10-G3
700	20TH ST	94114	10-G3
750	LIBERTY ST	94114	10-G3
800	21ST ST	94114	10-G3
850	HILL ST	94114	10-G3
900	22ND ST	94114	10-G3
1000	ALVARADO ST	94114	10-G3
1100	23RD ST	94114	10-G3
1200	ELIZABETH ST	94114	10-G3
1300	24TH ST	94114	10-G4
1400	JERSEY ST	94114	10-G4
1500	25TH ST	94114	10-G4
1600	CLIPPER ST	94131	10-G4
1700	26TH ST	94131	14-G4
1800	CESAR CHAVEZ ST	94131	14-G4
1900	27TH ST	94131	14-G4
1900	NEWBURG ST	94131	14-G4
2000	DUNCAN ST	94131	14-G4
2100	28TH ST	94131	14-G4
2200	VALLEY ST	94131	14-G5
2310	29TH ST	94131	14-G5
2320	29TH ST	94131	14-G5
2410	DAY ST	94131	14-G5
2500	30TH ST	94131	14-G5
3000	SUSSEX ST	94131	14-G6
3000	BEMIS ST	94131	14-G6
3130	LAIDLEY ST	94131	14-G6
3160	SURREY ST	94131	14-G6
3200	CHENERY ST	94131	14-G6
CATHERINE CT			SF
100	MISSION ST	94110	10-J3
CAYUGA AV			SF
60	ALEMANY BLVD	94112	19-E2
140	SICKLES AV	94112	19-E1
220	REGENT ST	94112	19-E1
290	STILL ST	94112	19-E1
360	ROTTECK ST	94112	19-E1
500	LYELL ST	94112	19-F1
570	DANTON ST	94112	19-F1
640	LAMARTINE ST	94112	19-F1
710	BADGER ST	94112	19-F1
770	GORHAM AV	94112	19-F1
840	TINGLEY ST	94112	19-F1
910	THERESA ST	94112	19-F1
1000	COTTER ST	94112	19-F1
1150	SANTA ROSA AV	94112	19-F1
1220	SAN JUAN AV	94112	19-F1
1300	SANTA YNEZ AV	94112	19-F1
1350	OCEAN AV	94112	14-F7
1380	VALERTON CT	94112	14-F7
1400	ONONDAGA AV	94112	14-F7
1510	BALHI CT	94112	14-F7
1700	ONEIDA AV	94112	14-G7
1840	JUNIOR TER	94112	14-G7
1900	SENECA AV	94112	14-G7
1950	NAVAJO AV	94112	14-G6
1990	GENEVA AV	94112	14-G6
2010	SEMINOLE AV	94112	14-G6
2060	NIAGARA AV	94112	14-G6
2110	SHAWNEE AV	94112	14-G6
2160	MOUNT VERNON AV	94112	14-G6
2200	OTTAWA AV	94112	14-G6
2250	ROME ST	94112	14-G6
2200	FOOTE AV	94112	18-D2
2100	MODOC AV	94112	18-E2
2200	NAGLEE AV	94112	18-E2
CECILIA AV			SF
2200	RIVERA ST	94116	13-C4
2300	SANTIAGO ST	94116	13-C4
2400	16TH AV	94116	13-C4
CEDAR ST			SF
1	LARKIN ST	94109	6-J6
130	POLK ST	94109	6-H6
200	VAN NESS AV	94109	6-H6
CEDRO AV			SF
1	OCEAN AV	94127	13-C7
100	MONCADA WY	94127	13-C7
200	MERCEDES WY	94127	13-C7
CENTRAL AV			SF
400	FELL ST	94117	6-F7
500	HAYES ST	94117	6-F7
600	GROVE ST	94117	6-F7
700	FULTON ST	94117	6-F7
800	MCALLISTER ST	94117	6-F7
900	GOLDEN GATE AV	94115	6-F7
1000	TURK ST	94115	6-F7
1	BUENA VISTA AV W	94117	10-F1
50	WALLER ST	94117	10-F1
100	HAIGHT ST	94117	10-F1
200	PAGE ST	94117	10-F1
300	OAK ST	94117	10-F1
CENTRAL MAGAZINE RD			SF
	HARRISON BLVD	94129	5-B4
	WASHINGTON BLVD	94129	5-B4
	HUNTER RD	94129	5-C4
CENTURY PL			SF
1	PINE ST	94104	7-B5
CERES ST			SF
1	THORNTON AV	94124	15-B7
100	WILLIAMS AV	94124	15-B7
CERRITOS AV			SF
1	OCEAN AV	94127	13-C7
100	MONCADA WY	94127	13-C7
200	MERCEDES WY	94127	13-C7
CERVANTES BLVD			SF
1	FILLMORE ST	94123	2-G3
1	BAY ST	94123	2-G3
30	ALHAMBRA ST	94123	2-G3
100	BEACH ST	94123	2-F3
200	AVILA ST	94123	2-F3
300	MARINA BLVD	94123	2-F3
300	MARINA GREEN DR	94123	2-F3
300	SCOTT ST	94123	2-F3
CESAR CHAVEZ ST			SF
800	MICHIGAN ST	94124	11-C4
800	MICHIGAN ST	94107	11-C4
900	ILLINOIS ST	94124	11-C4
900	ILLINOIS ST	94107	11-C4
1000	3RD ST	94124	11-C4
1000	3RD ST	94107	11-C4
1100	TENNESSEE ST	94124	11-C4
1100	TENNESSEE ST	94107	11-C4
1200	MINNESOTA ST	94124	11-C4
1200	MINNESOTA ST	94107	11-C4
1300	INDIANA ST	94124	11-C4
1300	INDIANA ST	94107	11-C4
1420	PENNSYLVANIA AV	94124	11-B4
1420	PENNSYLVANIA AV	94107	11-B4
1590	PENNSYLVANIA AV	94124	11-B4
1590	PENNSYLVANIA AV	94107	11-B4
1600	MISSISSIPPI ST	94124	11-B4
1600	MISSISSIPPI ST	94107	11-B4
1770	MISSOURI ST	94124	11-B4
1770	MISSOURI ST	94107	11-B4
1890	CONNECTICUT ST	94124	11-B4
1890	CONNECTICUT ST	94107	11-B4
1980	EVANS AV	94124	11-B4
1980	EVANS AV	94107	11-B4
2600	KANSAS ST	94124	11-A4
2600	KANSAS ST	94107	11-A4
2650	VERMONT ST	94124	11-A4
2650	VERMONT ST	94107	11-A4
2820	BAYSHORE BLVD	94110	11-A4
2850	HAMPSHIRE ST	94110	11-A4
2860	HAMPSHIRE ST	94110	11-A4
	PRECITA AV	94110	15-A4
	YORK ST	94110	15-A4
	BRYANT ST	94110	15-A4
	FLORIDA ST	94110	15-A4
3000	ALABAMA ST	94110	14-J4
3100	HARRISON ST	94110	14-J4
3200	FOLSOM ST	94110	14-J4
3250	SHOTWELL ST	94110	14-J4
3300	S VAN NESS AV	94110	14-J4
3400	MISSION ST	94110	14-J4
3400	CAPP ST	94110	14-J4
3450	BARTLETT ST	94110	14-H4
3500	VALENCIA ST	94110	14-H4
3600	SAN JOSE AV	94110	14-H4
3700	GUERRERO ST	94110	14-H4
3800	DOLORES ST	94131	14-H4
3900	CHURCH ST	94131	14-H4
4000	SANCHEZ ST	94131	14-G4
4100	NOE ST	94131	14-G4
4200	CASTRO ST	94131	14-G4
4300	DIAMOND ST	94131	14-G4
4400	DOUGLASS ST	94131	14-G4
CHABOT TER			SF
1	TURK ST	94118	6-E7
100	GOLDEN GATE AV	94118	6-E7
CHAIN OF LAKES DR E			SF
	CHAIN OF LAKES DR W	-	8-H1
	JOHN F KENNEDY DR	-	8-J1
	MIDDLE DR W	-	8-J1
	MARTIN LUTHER KING JR DR	-	8-J1
	41ST AV	-	8-J1
	LINCOLN WY	-	8-J1
CHAIN OF LAKES DR W			SF
	FULTON ST	-	8-H1
	43RD AV	-	8-H1
	CHAIN OF LAKES DR E	-	8-H1
	JOHN F KENNEDY DR	-	8-H1
CHANNEL ST			SF
1	4TH ST	94107	7-C7
330	6TH ST	94107	11-B1
400	OWENS ST	94107	11-B1
400	7TH ST	94107	11-B1
500	CAROLINA ST	94107	11-B1
CHAPMAN ST			SF
1	MAYFLOWER ST	94110	15-A5
1	CARVER ST	94110	14-J5
300	PRENTISS ST	94110	14-J5
460	FOLSOM ST	94110	14-J5
CHARLES ST			SF
100	CHENERY ST	94131	14-H5
200	ARLINGTON ST	94131	14-H5
CHARLESTOWN PL			SF
100	HARRISON ST	94105	7-B6
CHARLTON CT			SF
100	UNION ST	94123	6-G4
CHARTER OAK AV			SF
1	INDUSTRIAL ST	94124	15-A6
100	HELENA ST	94124	15-A6
200	AUGUSTA ST	94124	15-A6
300	SILVER AV	94124	15-A6
CHASE CT			SF
1	COLUSA PL	94103	10-J1
100	BRADY ST	94103	10-J1
CHATHAM PL			SF
1	BUSH ST	94108	7-A5
CHATTANOOGA ST			SF
1	21ST ST	94114	10-H3
100	22ND ST	94114	10-H3
200	23RD ST	94114	10-H3
300	24TH ST	94114	10-H4
400	JERSEY ST	94114	10-H4
CHAVES AV			SF
110	MYRA WY	94127	13-E5
110	ROCKDALE DR	94127	13-E5
70	DEL SUR AV	94127	13-E5
1	AGUA WY	94127	13-E5
70	EVELYN WY	94127	13-E5
CHELSEA PL			SF
1	BUSH ST	94108	7-A5
CHENERY ST			SF
1	30TH ST	94131	14-H5
100	RANDALL ST	94131	14-H5
200	FAIRMOUNT ST	94131	14-H5
230	CHARLES ST	94131	14-H5
290	WHITNEY ST	94131	14-H5
300	MIGUEL ST	94131	14-H6
400	MATEO ST	94131	14-G6
500	ROANOKE ST	94131	14-G6
580	NATICK ST	94131	14-G6
600	CASTRO ST	94131	14-G6
610	CARRIE ST	94131	14-G6
700	DIAMOND ST	94131	14-G6
710	THOR AV	94131	14-G6
750	BROMPTON AV	94131	14-G6
800	LIPPARD AV	94131	14-G6
910	CHILTON AV	94131	14-G6
910	HAMERTON AV	94131	14-F6
970	BURNSIDE AV	94131	14-F6
1030	SURREY ST	94131	14-F6
1030	MIZPAH ST	94131	14-F6
1100	ELK ST	94131	14-F6
CHERRY ST			SF
100	JACKSON ST	94118	5-D5
200	WASHINGTON ST	94118	5-E5
300	CLAY ST	94118	5-E5
400	SACRAMENTO ST	94118	5-E6
500	CALIFORNIA ST	94118	5-E6
CHESLEY ST			SF
	HARRISON ST	94103	7-A7
	HOMER ST	94103	7-A7
CHESTER AV			SF
1	19TH AV	94132	18-C1
40	RANDOLPH ST	94132	18-C2
100	PAYSON ST	94132	18-C2
300	PALMETTO AV	94132	18-C2
400	BELLE AV	94132	18-C2
CHESTNUT ST			SF
1	SANSOME ST	94111	3-A3
100	MONTGOMERY ST	94133	3-A3
150	WINTHROP ST	94133	3-A3
300	GRANT AV	94133	3-A3
360	BELLAIR PL	94133	3-A3
400	STOCKTON ST	94133	3-A3
500	POWELL ST	94133	3-A3
570	VENARD AL	94133	2-J3
600	MASON ST	94133	2-J3
700	COLUMBUS AV	94133	2-J3
700	TAYLOR ST	94133	2-J3
800	JONES ST	94133	2-J3
900	LEAVENWORTH ST	94109	2-J3
1000	HYDE ST	94109	2-J3
1100	LARKIN ST	94109	2-J3
1150	CULEBRA TER	94109	2-H4
1200	POLK ST	94109	2-H4
1300	VAN NESS AV	94123	2-H4
1400	FRANKLIN ST	94123	2-H4
1500	GOUGH ST	94123	2-H4
1600	OCTAVIA ST	94123	2-G4
1700	LAGUNA ST	94123	2-G4
1800	BUCHANAN ST	94123	2-G4
1900	WEBSTER ST	94123	2-G4
2000	FILLMORE ST	94123	2-G4
2050	MALLORCA WY	94123	2-G4
2100	STEINER ST	94123	2-G4
2200	PIERCE ST	94123	2-F4
2250	AVILA ST	94123	2-F4
2300	SCOTT ST	94123	2-F4
2400	DIVISADERO ST	94123	2-F4
2500	BRODERICK ST	94123	2-F4
2590	RICHARDSON AV	94123	2-F4
2600	BAKER ST	94123	2-F4
2700	LYON ST	94123	2-F4
CHICAGO WY			SF
120	LAPHAM WY	94112	19-G2
190	S HILL BLVD	94112	19-G2
280	NAYLOR ST	94112	19-G2
400	CORDOVA ST	94112	19-G2
CHILD ST			SF
1	GREENWICH ST	94133	3-A4
60	TELEGRAPH PL	94133	3-A3
100	LOMBARD ST	94133	3-A3
CHILTON AV			SF
1	CHENERY ST	94131	14-G6
100	BOSWORTH ST	94131	14-G6
CHRISTMAS TREE POINT RD			SF
100	TWIN PEAKS BLVD	94131	10-E3
CHRISTOPHER DR			SF
1	CLARENDON AV	94131	9-E3
50	FOREST KNOLLS DR	94131	9-D3
310	CRESTMONT DR	94131	9-D3
480	OAK PARK DR	94131	9-D3
CHULA LN			SF
1	DOLORES ST	94114	10-H2
50	ABBEY ST	94114	10-H2
100	CHURCH ST	94114	10-H2
CHUMASERO DR			SF
1	FONT BLVD	94132	18-B1
70	GALINDO AV	94132	18-C2
100	BROTHERHOOD WY	94132	18-C2
100	THOMAS MORE WY	94132	18-C2
CHURCH ST			SF
1	HERMANN ST	94117	10-G1
50	DUBOCE AV	94114	10-H1
110	RESERVOIR ST	94114	10-H1
180	14TH ST	94114	10-H1
200	MARKET ST	94114	10-H1
300	15TH ST	94114	10-H2
400	16TH ST	94114	10-H2
450	CHULA LN	94114	10-H2

Address	Cross Street	ZIP	City / Pg-Grid
CHURCH ST			SF
500	17TH ST	94114	10-H2
550	DORLAND ST	94114	10-H2
600	18TH ST	94114	10-H2
650	HANCOCK ST	94114	10-H2
700	19TH ST	94114	10-H2
750	CUMBERLAND ST	94114	10-H3
800	20TH ST	94114	10-H3
850	LIBERTY ST	94114	10-H3
900	21ST ST	94114	10-H3
950	HILL ST	94114	10-H3
1000	22ND ST	94114	10-H3
1100	23RD ST	94114	10-H3
1150	ELIZABETH ST	94114	10-H3
1200	24TH ST	94114	10-H4
1250	JERSEY ST	94114	10-H4
1300	25TH ST	94114	10-H4
1350	CLIPPER ST	94131	10-H4
1400	26TH ST	94131	10-H4
1450	CESAR CHAVEZ ST	94131	14-H4
1500	27TH ST	94131	14-H4
1530	COMERFORD ST	94131	14-H4
1550	DUNCAN ST	94131	14-H4
1600	28TH ST	94131	14-H4
1650	VALLEY ST	94131	14-H5
1700	29TH ST	94131	14-H5
1750	DAY ST	94131	14-H5
1800	30TH ST	94131	14-H5
1900	RANDALL ST	94131	14-H5
CIELITO DR			SF
1	PARQUE DR	94134	19-H2
100	GENEVA AV	94134	19-H2
CIRCULAR AV			SF
200	MONTEREY BLVD	94131	14-G6
300	HEARST AV	94131	14-F6
330	BADEN ST	94131	14-F6
330	STANDISH AV	94131	14-F6
400	FLOOD AV	94131	14-F6
470	CONGO ST	94131	14-F7
500	STAPLES AV	94131	14-F7
600	JUDSON AV	94112	14-F7
600	PAULDING ST	94112	14-F7
650	MARSTON AV	94112	14-F7
700	HAVELOCK ST	94112	14-F7
CITYVIEW WY			SF
10	MIDCREST WY	94131	10-E4
30	SKYVIEW WY	94131	10-E4
70	KNOLLVIEW WY	94131	9-E4
100	PANORAMA DR	94131	9-E4
CLAIRVIEW CT			SF
200	PANORAMA DR	94131	10-E3
CLARA ST			SF
100	4TH ST	94107	7-B7
170	HULBERT AL	94107	7-A7
200	5TH ST	94107	7-A7
300	6TH ST	94107	7-A7
CLAREMONT BLVD			SF
1	TARAVAL ST	94127	13-D5
50	GRANVILLE WY	94127	13-D5
100	ALLSTON WY	94127	13-D5
130	VERDUN WY	94127	13-D5
200	DORCHESTER WY	94127	13-D5
300	ULLOA ST	94127	13-C5
400	PORTAL PTH	94127	13-C5
400	PORTOLA DR	94127	13-C5
CLARENCE PL			SF
100	TOWNSEND ST	94107	7-C7
CLARENDON AV			SF
1	TWIN PEAKS BLVD	94114	10-E2
1	TWIN PEAKS BLVD	94117	10-E2
170	JOHNSTONE DR	94131	9-E3
200	DELLBROOK AV	94131	9-E3
230	CHRISTOPHER DR	94131	9-E3
230	OAK PARK DR	94131	9-E3
380	PANORAMA DR	94131	9-E3
430	GALEWOOD CIR	94131	9-E3
490	OLYMPIA WY	94116	9-D3
490	OLYMPIA WY	94131	9-D3
700	LAGUNA HONDA BLVD	94116	9-D3
700	LAGUNA HONDA BLVD	94131	9-D3
CLARKE ST			SF
	LIGGETT AV	94129	6-E5
CLAUDE LN			SF
1	SUTTER ST	94108	7-A5
100	BUSH ST	94108	7-A5
CLAY ST			SF
100	DRUMM ST	94111	7-B5
200	DAVIS ST	94111	7-B5
300	FRONT ST	94111	7-B5
400	BATTERY ST	94111	7-B5
500	SANSOME ST	94111	7-B5
550	LEIDESDORFF ST	94111	7-A5
600	MONTGOMERY ST	94111	7-A5
700	KEARNY ST	94108	7-A5
750	WALTER LUM PL	94108	7-A5
800	GRANT AV	94108	7-A5
830	WAVERLY PL	94108	7-A5
860	SPOFFORD LN	94108	7-A5
900	STOCKTON ST	94108	7-A5
950	JOICE ST	94108	7-A5
970	PARKHURST AL	94108	7-A5
1000	POWELL ST	94108	7-A5
1020	FREEMAN CT	94108	7-A5
1050	WETMORE ST	94108	7-A5
1100	MASON ST	94108	7-A5
1160	SPROULE LN	94108	6-J5
1200	TAYLOR ST	94108	6-J5
1300	JONES ST	94109	6-J5
1400	LEAVENWORTH ST	94109	6-J5
1500	HYDE ST	94109	6-J5
1550	TORRENS CT	94109	6-J5
1600	LARKIN ST	94109	6-J5
1700	POLK ST	94109	6-H5
1800	VAN NESS AV	94109	6-H5
1900	FRANKLIN ST	94109	6-H5
2000	GOUGH ST	94109	6-H5
2200	LAGUNA ST	94115	6-G5
2300	BUCHANAN ST	94115	6-G5
2400	WEBSTER ST	94115	6-G5
2500	FILLMORE ST	94115	6-G5
2600	STEINER ST	94115	6-G5
2700	PIERCE ST	94115	6-G5
2800	SCOTT ST	94115	6-F5
2900	DIVISADERO ST	94115	6-F5
3000	BRODERICK ST	94115	6-F5
3100	BAKER ST	94115	6-F5
3200	LYON ST	94115	6-F5
3300	PRESIDIO AV	94115	6-F5
3400	WALNUT ST	94118	6-E5
3500	LAUREL ST	94118	6-E5
3600	LOCUST ST	94118	5-E5
3700	SPRUCE ST	94118	5-E5
3800	MAPLE ST	94118	5-E5
3900	CHERRY ST	94118	5-D5
4000	ARGUELLO BLVD	94118	5-D5
W CLAY ST			SF
1	22ND AV	94121	5-B6
1	24TH AV	94121	5-B6
100	24TH AV	94121	5-B6
100	LAKE ST	94121	5-B6
CLAYTON ST			SF
1	FULTON ST	94117	6-E7
100	GROVE ST	94117	6-E7
200	HAYES ST	94117	6-E7
300	FELL ST	94117	10-E1
400	OAK ST	94117	10-E1
500	PAGE ST	94117	10-E1
600	HAIGHT ST	94117	10-E1
700	WALLER ST	94117	10-E1
800	FREDERICK ST	94117	10-E1
950	CARL ST	94117	10-E1
1000	PARNASSUS AV	94117	10-E2
1200	ASHBURY ST	94117	10-E2
1200	17TH ST	94117	10-F2
1200	17TH ST	94114	10-F2
1200	ASHBURY ST	94114	10-F2
1230	CARMEL ST	94114	10-F2
1230	TWIN PEAKS BLVD	94114	10-F2
1280	DEMING ST	94114	10-F2
1400	CORBETT AV	94114	10-F2
1460	IRON AL	94114	10-F3
1500	MARKET ST	94114	10-F3
CLEARFIELD DR			SF
	SLOAT BLVD	94132	13-A6
1	MORNINGSIDE DR	94132	13-A6
100	OCEAN AV	94132	13-A6
150	EUCALYPTUS DR	94132	13-A6
	GELLERT DR	94132	13-A6
	LAKE MERCED BLVD	94132	13-A6
CLEARVIEW CT			SF
1	WHITECLIFF WY	94124	15-B6
CLEARY CT			SF
1	GEARY BLVD	94109	6-H6
100	GALILEE LN	94109	6-H6
200	LAGUNA ST	94109	6-H6
CLEMENT ST			SF
1	ARGUELLO BLVD	94118	5-D6
100	2ND AV	94118	5-D6
200	3RD AV	94118	5-D6
300	4TH AV	94118	5-D6
400	5TH AV	94118	5-D6
500	6TH AV	94118	5-D6
600	7TH AV	94118	5-D6
700	8TH AV	94118	5-C6
800	9TH AV	94118	5-C6
900	10TH AV	94118	5-C6
1000	11TH AV	94118	5-C6
1100	12TH AV	94118	5-C6
1200	FUNSTON AV	94118	5-C6
1250	PRESIDIO BLVD	94118	5-C6
1300	14TH AV	94118	5-C6
1400	15TH AV	94118	5-C6
1500	16TH AV	94118	5-B6
1600	17TH AV	94121	5-B6
1700	18TH AV	94121	5-B6
1800	19TH AV	94121	5-B6
1900	20TH AV	94121	5-B6
2000	21ST AV	94121	5-B6
2100	22ND AV	94121	5-B6
2200	23RD AV	94121	5-B6
2300	24TH AV	94121	5-B6
2400	25TH AV	94121	5-A6
2500	26TH AV	94121	5-A6
2600	27TH AV	94121	5-A6
2700	28TH AV	94121	5-A6
2800	29TH AV	94121	5-A6
2900	30TH AV	94121	5-A6
3000	31ST AV	94121	5-A6
3100	32ND AV	94121	5-A6
3200	33RD AV	94121	5-A6
3300	34TH AV	94121	4-J6
3300	LEGION OF HONOR DR	94121	4-J6
3400	35TH AV	94121	4-J6
3500	36TH AV	94121	4-J6
3700	38TH AV	94121	4-J6
3800	39TH AV	94121	4-J6
3900	40TH AV	94121	4-J6
4000	41ST AV	94121	4-J6
4100	42ND AV	94121	4-J6
4200	43RD AV	94121	4-H6
4300	44TH AV	94121	4-H6
4400	45TH AV	94121	4-H6
4400	SEAL ROCK DR	94121	4-H6
CLEMENTINA ST			SF
1	1ST ST	94105	7-B6
30	ECKER ST	94105	7-B6
80	OSCAR AL	94105	7-B6
100	2ND ST	94105	7-B6
300	KAPLAN LN	94103	7-B6
400	3RD ST	94103	7-B6
300	4TH ST	94103	7-A6
350	GALLAGHER LN	94103	7-A6
400	5TH ST	94103	7-A7
500	6TH ST	94103	7-A7
650	SUMNER ST	94103	7-A7
700	8TH ST	94103	7-A7
800	9TH ST	94103	6-J7
CLEO RAND AV			SF
200	DONAHUE ST	94124	15-E7
CLEVELAND ST			SF
1	SHERMAN ST	94103	7-A7
100	7TH ST	94103	7-A7
CLIFFORD TER			SF
1	ROOSEVELT WY	94117	10-F2
100	UPPER TER	94117	10-F2
200	ASHBURY ST	94117	10-F2
CLINTON PK			SF
100	STEVENSON ST	94103	10-H1
100	VALENCIA ST	94103	10-H1
200	GUERRERO ST	94103	10-H1
400	DOLORES ST	94103	10-H1
CLIPPER ST			SF
1	DOLORES ST	94131	10-H4
1	DOLORES ST	94114	10-H4
100	CHURCH ST	94131	10-G4
100	CHURCH ST	94114	10-G4
200	SANCHEZ ST	94131	10-G4
200	SANCHEZ ST	94114	10-G4
300	NOE ST	94131	10-G4
300	NOE ST	94114	10-G4
400	CASTRO ST	94131	10-G4
400	CASTRO ST	94114	10-G4
500	DIAMOND ST	94131	10-G4
500	DIAMOND ST	94114	10-G4
600	DOUGLASS ST	94131	10-F4
600	DOUGLASS ST	94114	10-F4
790	CLIPPER TER	94131	10-F4
790	CLIPPER TER	94114	10-F4
800	GRAND VIEW AV	94114	10-F4
900	DIAMOND HEIGHTS BLVD	94131	14-F4
900	DIAMOND HEIGHTS BLVD	94114	14-F4
CLIPPER TER			SF
800	CLIPPER ST	94114	10-F4
800	GRAND VIEW AV	94114	10-F4
900	HIGH ST	94114	10-F4
CLOVER LN			SF
30	CASELLI AV	94114	10-F2
40	THORP LN	94114	10-F2
70	19TH ST	94114	10-F2
CLOVER ST			SF
1	18TH ST	94114	10-F2
	CASELLI AV	94114	10-F2
CLYDE ST			SF
	TOWNSEND ST	94107	7-B7
COCHRANE ST			SF
1	MANSEAU ST	94124	21-E1
100	SPEAR AV	94124	21-E1
CODMAN PL			SF
200	WASHINGTON ST	94108	7-A5
COHEN PL			SF
1	ELLIS ST	94109	6-J6
COLBY ST			SF
1	SWEENY ST	94134	14-J6
120	SILVER AV	94134	14-J6
120	SILVER AV	94134	14-J7
180	SILLIMAN ST	94134	14-J7
300	FELTON ST	94134	14-J7
600	WOOLSEY ST	94134	19-J1
800	DWIGHT ST	94134	19-J1
1100	OLMSTEAD ST	94134	19-J1
1400	MANSELL ST	94134	19-J1
COLE ST			SF
1	FULTON ST	94117	6-E7
100	GROVE ST	94117	6-E7
200	HAYES ST	94117	6-E7
300	FELL ST	94117	10-E1
400	OAK ST	94117	10-E1
500	PAGE ST	94117	10-E1
600	HAIGHT ST	94117	10-E1
700	WALLER ST	94117	10-E1
750	BEULAH ST	94117	10-E1
800	FREDERICK ST	94117	10-E1
900	CARL ST	94117	10-E2
1000	PARNASSUS AV	94117	10-E2
1100	GRATTAN ST	94117	10-E2
1200	ALMA ST	94117	10-E2
1300	RIVOLI ST	94117	10-E2
1400	17TH ST	94117	10-E2
1500	CARMEL ST	94117	10-E2
COLEMAN ST			SF
2700	HILL DR	94124	16-E7
2700	HUDSON AV	94124	16-E7
3000	INNES AV	94124	15-E7
3400	JERROLD AV	94124	15-E7
COLERIDGE ST			SF
1	COSO AV	94110	14-J4
40	POWERS AV	94110	14-J4
100	FAIR AV	94110	14-H5
150	ESMERALDA AV	94110	14-H5
200	VIRGINIA AV	94110	14-H5
230	GODEUS ST	94110	14-H5
270	HEYMAN AV	94110	14-H5
300	EUGENIA AV	94110	14-H5
340	KINGSTON ST	94110	14-H5
400	CORTLAND AV	94110	14-H5
COLIN PL			SF
1	TAYLOR ST	94102	6-J6
50	SHANNON ST	94102	6-J6
100	JONES ST	94102	6-J6
COLIN P KELLY JR ST			SF
1	BRANNAN ST	94107	7-C6
100	TOWNSEND ST	94107	7-C6
COLLEGE AV			SF
1	SAINT MARYS AV	94112	14-H6
200	MISSION ST	94112	14-H6
200	CRESCENT ST	94112	14-H6
300	GENEBERN WY	94112	14-H6
300	JUSTIN DR	94112	14-H6
400	MURRAY ST	94112	14-H6
500	BENTON AV	94112	14-H6
600	JUSTIN DR	94112	14-H6
COLLEGE TER			SF
1	MISSION ST	94112	14-H6
COLLINGWOOD ST			SF
1	17TH ST	94114	10-G2
20	MARKET ST	94114	10-G2
100	18TH ST	94114	10-G2
200	19TH ST	94114	10-G3
300	20TH ST	94114	10-G3
400	21ST ST	94114	10-G3
460	22ND ST	94114	10-G3
COLLINS ST			SF
1	MAYFAIR DR	94118	6-E6
100	EUCLID AV	94118	6-E6
200	GEARY BLVD	94118	6-E6
300	ANZA ST	94118	6-E6
COLON AV			SF
100	GREENWOOD AV	94112	13-D6
200	MONTECITO AV	94112	13-D6
300	MONTEREY BLVD	94127	13-D6
400	MANGELS AV	94127	13-D6
500	BRENTWOOD AV	94127	13-D6
COLONIAL WY			SF
1	SAN JOSE AV	94112	14-F7
COLTON ST			SF
1	COLUSA PL	94103	10-J1
100	BRADY ST	94103	10-H1
200	GOUGH ST	94103	10-H1
COLUMBIA SQUARE ST			SF
1	HARRISON ST	94103	7-A7
100	FOLSOM ST	94103	7-A7
COLUMBUS AV			SF
1	MONTGOMERY ST	94111	7-A4
1	WASHINGTON ST	94111	7-A4
60	ILS LN	94111	7-A4
90	JACKSON ST	94133	7-A4
150	KEARNY ST	94133	7-A4
170	PACIFIC AV	94133	7-A4
240	JACK KEROUAC AL	94133	7-A4
270	BROADWAY	94133	7-A4
300	GRANT AV	94133	7-A4
380	VALLEJO ST	94133	7-A4
380	STOCKTON ST	94133	3-A4
500	GREEN ST	94133	3-A4
600	UNION ST	94133	3-A4
660	POWELL ST	94133	3-A4
700	FILBERT ST	94133	3-A4
720	VIA BUFANO	94133	3-A4
750	SCOTLAND ST	94133	2-J4
800	GREENWICH ST	94133	2-J4
820	MASON ST	94133	2-J4
900	LOMBARD ST	94133	2-J3
1000	CHESTNUT ST	94133	2-J3
1000	TAYLOR ST	94133	2-J3
1060	HOUSTON ST	94133	2-J3
1100	FRANCISCO ST	94133	2-J3
1170	JONES ST	94133	2-J3
1200	BAY ST	94133	2-J3
1300	NORTH POINT ST	94133	2-J3
1330	LEAVENWORTH ST	94109	2-J3
1330	LEAVENWORTH ST	94133	2-J3
1400	BEACH ST	94109	2-J3
1400	BEACH ST	94133	2-J3
COLUSA PL			SF
1	COLTON ST	94103	10-J1
50	CHASE CT	94103	10-J1
COMERFORD ST			SF
1	CHURCH ST	94131	14-H4
100	SANCHEZ ST	94131	14-H4
COMMER CT			SF
10	GARLINGTON CT	94124	15-C6
COMMERCIAL ST			SF
400	BATTERY ST	94111	7-B5
500	SANSOME ST	94111	7-B5
550	LEIDESDORFF ST	94111	7-A5
600	MONTGOMERY ST	94111	7-A5
700	KEARNY ST	94108	7-A5
800	GRANT AV	94108	7-A5
COMMONWEALTH AV			SF
1	CALIFORNIA ST	94118	5-E6
100	EUCLID AV	94118	5-E6
200	GEARY BLVD	94118	5-E6
COMPTON RD			SF
	HUNTER RD	94129	5-B4
	WASHINGTON BLVD	94129	5-B4
	DENT RD	94129	5-C4
	WASHINGTON BLVD	94129	5-C4
CONCORD ST			SF
1	MISSION ST	94112	19-F2
40	CROSS ST	94112	19-F2
130	MORSE ST	94112	19-F2
210	BRUNSWICK ST	94112	19-F2
250	PRETOR WY	94112	19-F2
300	HANOVER ST	94112	19-F2
300	WATT AV	94112	19-F2
CONCOURSE DR			SF
	JOHN F KENNEDY DR	94118	9-C1
	S TEA GARDEN DR	94118	9-C1
	MARTIN LUTHER KING JR DR	94118	9-C1
CONGDON ST			SF
50	ALEMANY BLVD	94112	14-H6
100	TRUMBULL ST	94112	14-H6
200	NEY ST	94112	14-H7
300	MAYNARD ST	94112	14-H7
400	SILVER AV	94112	14-H7
CONGO ST			SF
1	CIRCULAR AV	94131	14-F7
100	FLOOD AV	94131	14-F6
200	HEARST AV	94131	14-F6
300	MONTEREY BLVD	94131	14-F6
400	JOOST AV	94131	14-F6
500	MANGELS AV	94127	14-F6
500	MANGELS AV	94131	14-F6
600	MELROSE AV	94131	14-F6
700	STILLINGS AV	94131	14-F6
900	MERCATO CT	94131	14-F6
CONKLING ST			SF
1	SILVER AV	94124	15-A6
100	WATERVILLE ST	94124	15-A6
CONNECTICUT ST			SF
1	16TH ST	94107	11-B2
100	17TH ST	94107	11-B2
200	MARIPOSA ST	94107	11-B2
300	18TH ST	94107	11-B2
400	19TH ST	94107	11-B2
500	20TH ST	94107	11-B3
900	WISCONSIN ST	94107	11-B3
1100	25TH ST	94107	11-B4
1200	26TH ST	94107	11-B4
1300	CESAR CHAVEZ ST	94107	11-B4
CONRAD ST			SF
1	DIAMOND ST	94131	14-G5
100	ARBOR ST	94131	14-G5
150	POPPY LN	94131	14-G6
200	SUSSEX ST	94131	14-G6
CONSERVATORY DR E			SF
	JOHN F KENNEDY DR	94117	9-E1
	ARGUELLO BLVD	94117	5-E7
	CONSERVATORY DR W	94117	5-E7
CONSERVATORY DR W			SF
	JOHN F KENNEDY DR	-	9-D1
	ARGUELLO BLVD	-	5-D7
	CONSERVATORY DR E	-	5-D7
CONSTANSO WY			SF
1	CRESTLAKE DR	94132	13-A6
50	ESCONDIDO AV	94132	13-A6
100	SLOAT BLVD	94132	13-A6
CONVERSE ST			SF
	BRYANT ST	94103	11-A1
COOK ST			SF
100	GEARY BLVD	94118	6-E6
200	ANZA ST	94118	6-E6
CORA ST			SF
1	SUNNYDALE AV	94134	19-J2
1	TOMASO CT	94134	19-J2
100	VISITACION AV	94134	20-A2
200	LELAND AV	94134	20-A2
CORAL RD			SF
1	WISCONSIN ST	94107	11-B3
100	CAROLINA ST	94107	11-B3
100	CAROLINA ST	94107	11-B3
200	CAROLINA ST	94107	11-B3
CORALINO LN			SF
1	AMBER DR	94131	14-F4
CORBETT AV			SF
1	17TH ST	94114	10-F2
1	DOUGLASS ST	94114	10-F2
100	ORD ST	94114	10-F2
130	HATTIE ST	94114	10-F2
200	CORBIN PL	94114	10-F2
250	DANVERS ST	94114	10-F2
300	MARS ST	94114	10-F2
350	19TH ST	94114	10-F2
400	CLAYTON ST	94114	10-F3
500	IRON AL	94114	10-F3
600	COPPER AL	94114	10-F3
670	GLENDALE ST	94114	10-F3
670	GRAYSTONE TER	94114	10-F3
700	ROMAIN ST	94131	10-F3
750	MORGAN AL	94131	10-F3
790	DIXIE AL	94131	10-F3
800	DIXIE AL	94131	10-F3
850	ARGENT AL	94131	10-F3
850	HOPKINS AV	94131	10-F3
900	GOLDING LN	94131	10-F3
900	GOLDING LN	94131	10-F4
1000	CUESTA CT	94131	10-F4
1050	FENTON LN	94131	10-F4
1100	PORTOLA DR	94131	10-F4
1100	MARKET ST	94131	10-F4
CORBIN PL			SF
1	17TH ST	94114	10-F2
100	CORBETT AV	94114	10-F2
CORDELIA ST			SF
1	PACIFIC AV	94133	7-A4
100	BROADWAY	94133	7-A4
CORDOVA ST			SF
1	ROLPH ST	94112	19-G2
100	ATHENS ST	94112	19-G2
200	SEVILLE ST	94112	19-G2

SAN FRANCISCO INDEX

PRIMARY STREET Address	Cross Street	ZIP	CITY Pg-Grid
CORDOVA ST			SF
300	MUNICH ST	94112	19-G2
400	PRAGUE ST	94112	19-G2
500	WINDING WY	94112	19-G2
550	CHICAGO WY	94112	19-G2
CORNWALL ST			SF
1	ARGUELLO BLVD	94118	5-D6
100	2ND AV	94118	5-D6
200	3RD AV	94118	5-D6
300	4TH AV	94118	5-D6
400	5TH AV	94118	5-D6
500	6TH AV	94118	5-D6
600	7TH AV	94118	5-D6
700	CALIFORNIA ST	94118	5-D6
CORONA ST			SF
1	HOLLOWAY AV	94127	13-C7
100	URBANO DR S	94127	13-C7
200	URBANO DR N	94127	13-C7
CORONADO ST			SF
	INGERSON AV	94124	20-C1
	JAMESTOWN AV	94124	20-C1
CORTES AV			SF
1	DORANTES AV	94116	13-C4
100	MAGELLAN AV	94116	13-C4
200	TARAVAL ST	94116	13-C4
CORTLAND AV			SF
1	MISSION ST	94110	14-H5
50	COLERIDGE ST	94110	14-H5
100	PROSPECT AV	94110	14-H5
130	WINFIELD ST	94110	14-H5
160	ELSIE ST	94110	14-H5
200	ELSIE ST	94110	14-H5
230	BONVIEW ST	94110	14-J5
300	BOCANA ST	94110	14-J5
400	BENNINGTON ST	94110	14-J5
440	WOOL ST	94110	14-J5
500	ANDOVER ST	94110	14-J5
600	MOULTRIE ST	94110	14-J5
610	MOULTRIE ST	94110	14-J5
700	ANDERSON ST	94110	14-J5
720	ANDERSON ST	94110	14-J5
800	ELLSWORTH ST	94110	14-J5
900	GATES ST	94110	14-J5
910	GATES ST	94110	14-J5
1000	FOLSOM ST	94110	14-J5
1110	BANKS ST	94110	14-J5
1200	PRENTISS ST	94110	14-J5
1300	NEVADA ST	94110	14-J5
1400	PUTNAM ST	94110	14-J5
1420	NEBRASKA ST	94110	14-J5
1450	BRONTE ST	94110	14-J5
1500	BRADFORD ST	94110	15-A5
1520	BRADFORD ST	94110	15-A5
1600	PERALTA AV	94110	15-A5
1750	HILTON ST	94124	15-A5
1800	BAYSHORE BLVD	94124	15-A5
CORWIN ST			SF
100	ACME AL	94114	10-F3
200	DOUGLASS ST	94114	10-F3
COSMO PL			SF
1	TAYLOR ST	94109	6-J6
50	AGATE AL	94109	6-J6
	OPHIR AL	94109	6-J6
	JONES ST	94109	6-J6
COSO AV			SF
1	PRECITA AV	94110	14-J4
50	COLERIDGE ST	94110	14-J4
1	MIRABEL AV	94110	14-J4
80	PRECITA AV	94110	14-J4
80	MIRABEL AV	94110	14-J4
100	LUNDYS LN	94110	14-J4
100	MONTEZUMA ST	94110	14-J4
130	PROSPECT AV	94110	14-J4
200	WINFIELD ST	94110	14-J4
210	AZTEC ST	94110	14-J4
250	ELSIE ST	94110	14-J4
300	BONVIEW ST	94110	14-J4
300	STONEMAN ST	94110	14-J4
COSTA ST			SF
1	HOLLADAY AV	94110	15-A5
100	BREWSTER ST	94110	15-A5
COTTAGE RW			SF
100	BUSH ST	94115	6-G6
COTTER ST			SF
1	MISSION ST	94112	14-G7
100	ALEMANY BLVD	94112	14-G7
200	CAYUGA AV	94112	14-G7
300	SAN JOSE AV	94112	14-G7
COUNTRY CLUB DR			SF
1	LAKESHORE DR	94132	12-J6
200	BERKSHIRE WY	94132	12-J6
400	HUNTINGTON DR	94132	12-J6
430	OCEAN AV	94132	12-J6
480	HUNTINGTON DR	94132	12-J6
COVENTRY LN			SF
1	CRESTA VISTA DR	94127	13-E6
COWELL PL			SF
1	VALLEJO ST	94111	7-B4
COWLES ST			SF
	LINCOLN BLVD	94129	1-C3
	MCDOWELL AV	94129	1-C3
	INCINERATOR RD	94129	1-D4
	MCDOWELL AV	94129	1-D4
CRAGMONT AV			SF
1	ROCKRIDGE DR	94116	9-C4
80	QUINTARA ST	94116	9-C4
100	MENDOSA AV	94116	9-C4
CRAGS CT			SF
1	BERKELEY WY	94131	14-F5
CRAN PL			SF
1	MCALLISTER ST	94117	6-G7
CRANE ST			SF
1	PAUL AV	94124	15-B7
100	BAYSHORE BLVD	94124	15-B7
CRANLEIGH DR			SF
1	SLOAT BLVD	94132	13-C6
100	LAGUNITAS DR	94132	13-C6
CRANSTON RD			SF
	MERCHANT RD	94129	1-C3
	BOWMAN RD	94129	1-C3
CRAUT ST			SF
100	TRUMBULL ST	94112	14-G6
200	NEY ST	94112	14-G6
300	MAYNARD ST	94112	14-G7
400	SILVER AV	94112	14-G7
CRESCENT AV			SF
1	COLLEGE AV	94110	14-H6
1	COLLEGE AV	94112	14-H6
1	MISSION ST	94112	14-H6
100	LEESE ST	94110	14-H6
100	LEESE ST	94112	14-H6
120	AGNON AV	94110	14-H6
120	AGNON AV	94112	14-H6
200	MURRAY ST	94110	14-H6
270	ARNOLD AV	94110	14-H6
380	ROSCOE ST	94110	14-J6
450	PORTER ST	94110	14-J6
520	BACHE ST	94110	14-J6
600	ANDOVER ST	94110	14-J6
680	MOULTRIE ST	94110	14-J6
750	ANDERSON ST	94110	14-J6
830	ELLSWORTH ST	94110	14-J6
900	GATES ST	94110	14-J6
980	FOLSOM ST	94110	14-J6
1050	BANKS ST	94110	14-J6
1120	PRENTISS ST	94110	14-J6
1150	NEVADA ST	94110	14-J6
1200	PUTNAM ST	94110	14-J6
1200	PERALTA AV	94110	14-J6
CRESCIO CT			SF
1	WHITTIER ST	94112	19-E2
CRESPI DR			SF
1	19TH AV	94132	18-B1
20	CARDENAS AV	94132	18-B1
100	JUAN BAUTISTA CIR	94132	18-B1
100	CARDENAS AV	94132	18-B1
200	JUAN BAUTISTA CIR	94132	18-B1
CRESTA VISTA DR			SF
1	BELLA VISTA WY	94127	13-E6
50	COVENTRY LN	94127	13-E6
100	LULU AL	94127	13-E6
200	EMIL LN	94127	13-D6
	GLOBE AL	94127	13-D6
300	GLOBE AL	94127	13-D6
400	BAXTER AL	94127	13-D6
400	CASITAS AV	94127	13-D6
CRESTLAKE DR			SF
10	23RD AV	94132	13-B6
10	SLOAT BLVD	94132	13-B6
50	GABILAN WY	94132	13-B6
100	PARAISO PL	94132	13-B6
150	GOLETA AV	94132	13-A6
200	VALE AV	94132	13-A6
250	PALOS PL	94132	13-A6
300	EL MIRASOL PL	94132	13-A6
400	CONSTANSO WY	94132	13-A6
500	YORBA ST	94116	13-A5
500	YORBA ST	94132	13-A5
600	WAWONA ST	94116	13-A5
600	WAWONA ST	94132	13-A5
CRESTLINE DR			SF
10	PARKRIDGE DR	94131	10-F3
40	VISTA LN	94131	10-F4
100	BURNETT AV	94131	10-F4
CRESTMONT DR			SF
260	OAKHURST LN	94131	9-D3
380	DEVONSHIRE WY	94131	9-D3
600	CHRISTOPHER DR	94131	9-D3
CRISP RD			SF
1	SPEAR AV	94124	15-D7
70	GRIFFITH ST	94124	15-D7
80	PALOU AV	94124	15-D7
90	QUESADA AV	94124	15-D7
100	REVERE AV	94124	15-D7
CRISSY FIELD AV			SF
50	LINCOLN BLVD	94129	1-D3
	INCINERATOR RD	94129	1-D3
	MCDOWELL AV	94129	1-C3
50	MASON ST	94129	1-C3
60	LINCOLN BLVD	94129	1-C3
CROOK ST			SF
	OLD MASON ST	94129	2-E3
	LUNDEEN ST	94129	2-E3
CROSS ST			SF
100	CONCORD ST	94112	19-F2
1	ALLISON ST	94112	19-F2
100	POPE ST	94112	19-F2
CROSS OVER DR			SF
300	FULTON ST	-	5-A7
300	25TH AV	-	5-A7
350	TRANSVERSE DR	-	9-B1
1000	PRESIDIO BLVD	-	9-B1
1050	JOHN F KENNEDY DR	-	9-B1
1150	MARTIN LUTHER KING JR DR	-	9-B1
1200	19TH AV	-	9-B1
1200	LINCOLN WY	-	9-B1
CROWN TER			SF
1	TWIN PEAKS BLVD	94114	10-E3
100	RACCOON DR	94114	10-E3
CRYSTAL ST			SF
	ALEMANY BLVD	94112	18-D2
100	DE LONG ST	94112	18-D2
CUESTA CT			SF
	CORBETT AV	94131	10-F4
CULEBRA TER			SF
100	CHESTNUT ST	94109	2-H3
CUMBERLAND ST			SF
1	GUERRERO ST	94110	10-H2
100	DOLORES ST	94110	10-H2
200	CHURCH ST	94114	10-G3
300	SANCHEZ ST	94114	10-G3
CUNNINGHAM PL			SF
1	VALENCIA ST	94110	10-H2
CURTIS ST			SF
1	ROLPH ST	94112	19-F2
100	MORSE ST	94112	19-F2
150	BRUNSWICK ST	94112	19-F2
230	MUNICH ST	94112	19-F2
230	NAPLES ST	94112	19-F2
1	NAPLES ST	94112	19-F2
1	NEWTON ST	94112	19-F2
100	NAPLES ST	94112	19-F2
100	SEVILLE ST	94112	19-F2
300	PRAGUE ST	94112	19-F2
CUSTER AV			SF
1500	QUINT ST	94124	15-C4
1600	RANKIN ST	94124	15-C4
1400	3RD ST	94124	15-C5
1500	QUINT ST	94124	15-C5
CUSTOM HOUSE PL			SF
1	WASHINGTON ST	94111	7-B4
100	JACKSON ST	94111	7-B4
CUTLER AV			SF
3600	47TH AV	94116	12-H5
3700	48TH AV	94116	12-H5
CUVIER ST			SF
100	BOSWORTH ST	94112	14-G6
200	MIRANDO WY	94112	14-G6
CYPRESS ST			SF
1	24TH ST	94110	10-J4
100	25TH ST	94110	10-J4
200	26TH ST	94110	10-J4
CYRIL MAGIN ST			SF
1	5TH ST	94102	7-A6
1	MARKET ST	94102	7-A6
40	EDDY ST	94102	7-A6
100	ELLIS ST	94102	7-A6
200	OFARRELL ST	94102	7-A6
CYRUS PL			SF
	BROADWAY	94109	6-J4

D

PRIMARY STREET Address	Cross Street	ZIP	CITY Pg-Grid
D ST			SF
	SPEAR AV	94124	16-E7
	VAN KEUREN AV	94124	16-E7
DAGGETT ST			SF
1	7TH ST	94107	11-B2
200	16TH ST	94107	11-B2
DAKOTA ST			SF
1	23RD ST	94107	11-B3
200	25TH ST	94107	11-B3
DALE PL			SF
100	GOLDEN GATE AV	94102	6-J6
DALEWOOD WY			SF
1	LANSDALE AV	94127	13-D5
300	LANSDALE AV	94127	13-D5
DANIEL BURNHAM CT			SF
1	VAN NESS AV	94109	6-H6
1	HEMLOCK ST	94109	6-H6
100	FRANKLIN ST	94109	6-H6
DANTON ST			SF
1	LAMARTINE ST	94112	14-G6
100	CAYUGA AV	94112	14-G6
DANVERS ST			SF
1	CORBETT AV	94114	10-F2
50	MERRITT ST	94114	10-F2
100	MARKET ST	94114	10-F2
100	18TH ST	94114	10-F2
200	CASELLI AV	94114	10-F2
300	19TH ST	94114	10-F2
DARIEN WY			SF
1	JUNIPERO SERRA BLVD	94127	13-C6
100	SAN RAFAEL WY	94127	13-C6
200	SAN FERNANDO WY	94127	13-C6
300	SAN LEANDRO WY	94127	13-C6
400	SANTA ANA AV	94127	13-C6
500	SAN BENITO WY	94127	13-C6
550	APTOS AV	94127	13-C6
600	SAN ALESO AV	94127	13-C6
700	WESTGATE DR	94127	13-C6
700	WESTGATE DR	94127	13-D6
800	MANOR DR	94127	13-D6
900	NORTHGATE DR	94127	13-D6
1000	UPLAND DR	94127	13-D6
DARRELL PL			SF
1	FILBERT ST	94133	3-A4
DARTMOUTH ST			SF
1	SWEENY ST	94134	14-J6
70	SILVER AV	94134	14-J7
100	SILLIMAN ST	94134	14-J7
200	FELTON ST	94134	14-J7
600	WOOLSEY ST	94134	14-J7
800	DWIGHT ST	94134	19-J1
1100	OLMSTEAD ST	94134	19-J1
970	MANSELL ST	94134	20-A1
DASHELLE HAMMETT ST			SF
1	BUSH ST	94108	7-A5
100	PINE ST	94108	7-A5
DAVIDSON AV			SF
1400	3RD ST	94124	15-C5
1410	PHELPS ST	94124	15-C5
1500	QUINT ST	94124	15-C4
1600	RANKIN ST	94124	15-B4
1600	ISLAIS ST	94124	15-B4
1700	ISLAIS ST	94124	15-B4
DAVIS ST			SF
500	JACKSON ST	94111	7-B4
700	BROADWAY ST	94111	7-B4
800	VALLEJO ST	94111	3-B4
1	BEALE ST	94111	7-B5
1	MARKET ST	94111	7-B5
10	PINE ST	94111	7-B5
100	CALIFORNIA ST	94111	7-B5
200	SACRAMENTO ST	94111	7-B5
300	CLAY ST	94111	7-B5
DAWNVIEW WY			SF
1	BURNETT AV	94131	10-F4
100	GLENVIEW DR	94131	10-F4
DAWSON PL			SF
1	MALVINA PL	94108	7-A5
1	MASON ST	94108	7-A5
100	WETMORE ST	94108	7-A5
DAY ST			SF
1	SAN JOSE AV	94110	14-H5
100	DOLORES ST	94131	14-H5
200	CHURCH ST	94131	14-H5
300	SANCHEZ ST	94131	14-G5
400	NOE ST	94131	14-G5
500	CASTRO ST	94131	14-G5
DEARBORN ST			SF
1	17TH ST	94110	10-H2
60	BIRD ST	94110	10-H2
100	18TH ST	94110	10-H2
DE BOOM ST			SF
100	2ND ST	94107	7-C6
DECATUR ST			SF
	BRANNAN ST	94103	11-A1
DEDMAN CT			SF
100	CASHMERE ST	94124	15-C6
100	WHITNEY YOUNG CIR	94124	15-C6
DEEMS RD			SF
	PIPER LP	94129	5-D4
	WASHINGTON BLVD	94129	5-D4
DE FOREST WY			SF
1	BEAVER ST	94114	10-G2
100	FLINT ST	94114	10-G2
DE HARO ST			SF
1	DIVISION ST	94107	11-A1
1	DIVISION ST	94103	11-A1
80	BERRY ST	94107	11-A1
80	BERRY ST	94103	11-A1
100	ALAMEDA ST	94107	11-A1
100	ALAMEDA ST	94103	11-A1
200	15TH ST	94103	11-A1
300	16TH ST	94107	11-A2
300	16TH ST	94103	11-A2
400	17TH ST	94107	11-B2
500	MARIPOSA ST	94107	11-B2
600	18TH ST	94107	11-B2
700	19TH ST	94107	11-B2
800	20TH ST	94107	11-B3
920	SOUTHERN HEIGHTS AV	94107	11-B3
1000	22ND ST	94107	11-B3
1200	23RD ST	94107	11-B3
1300	24TH ST	94107	11-B3
1400	25TH ST	94107	11-B3
1400	25TH ST	94107	11-B4
1430	LITTLEFIELD TER	94107	11-B4
1480	FONTINELLA TER	94107	11-B4
1500	26TH ST	94107	11-B4
DEHON ST			SF
1	16TH ST	94114	10-G2
DELANCEY ST			SF
500	BRYANT ST	94107	7-C6
520	FEDERAL ST	94107	7-C6
560	BAYSIDE VILLAGE PL	94107	7-C6
610	BRANNAN ST	94107	7-C6
DELANO AV			SF
1	SANTA YSABEL AV	94112	14-F7
130	SAN JUAN AV	94112	14-F7
250	SANTA YNEZ AV	94112	14-F7
340	RUDDEN AV	94112	14-F7
400	MEDA AV	94112	14-F7
500	OCEAN AV	94112	14-F7
600	ONEIDA AV	94112	14-F7
500	SENECA AV	94112	19-F1
550	NAVAJO AV	94112	19-F1
610	GENEVA AV	94112	19-F1
670	SEMINOLE AV	94112	19-F1
740	NIAGARA AV	94112	19-E1
800	SHAWNEE AV	94112	19-E1
870	MOUNT VERNON AV	94112	19-E1
920	NAHUA AV	94112	19-E1
1000	OTTAWA AV	94112	19-E1
DELGADO PL			SF
	HYDE ST	94109	6-J4
DELLBROOK AV			SF
1	CLARENDON AV	94131	9-E3
40	LA AVANZADA	94131	9-E3
140	LORI LN	94131	9-E3
240	PANORAMA DR	94131	9-E3
270	GREENVIEW CT	94131	9-E3
360	OLYMPIA WY	94131	9-E4
600	OLYMPIA WY	94131	9-E4
DELMAR ST			SF
1	WALLER ST	94117	10-F1
100	FREDERICK ST	94117	10-F1
200	PIEDMONT ST	94117	10-F1
200	ASHBURY TER	94117	10-F1
DEL MONTE ST			SF
100	MOUNT VERNON AV	94112	19-F1
1	OTTAWA AV	94112	19-F1
DE LONG ST			SF
20	SAN DIEGO AV	94112	18-C2
80	SANTA CRUZ AV	94112	18-C2
110	SHAKESPEARE ST	94112	18-C2
170	FLOURNOY ST	94112	18-D2
230	WILSON ST	94112	18-D2
280	CRYSTAL ST	94112	18-D2
280	RHINE ST	94112	18-D2
330	RICE ST	94112	18-D2
400	LIEBIG ST	94112	18-D2
400	SAN JOSE AV	94112	18-D2
DEL SUR AV			SF
100	CHAVES AV	94127	13-E5
1	JUANITA WY	94127	13-E5
100	PORTOLA DR	94127	13-E5
DELTA PL			SF
100	MASON ST	94102	7-A5
DELTA ST			SF
700	WILDE AV	94134	20-A1
750	HARKNESS AV	94134	20-A1
800	ANKENY ST	94134	20-A1
800	HAMILTON ST	94134	20-A1
100	TIOGA AV	94134	20-A1
130	WILDE AV	94134	20-A1
200	LELAND AV	94134	19-J2
320	RAYMOND AV	94134	19-J2
450	ARLETA AV	94134	20-A2
570	TEDDY AV	94134	20-A2
700	CAMPBELL AV	94134	20-A2
1	SUNNYDALE AV	94134	19-J2
1	MELRA CT	94134	19-J2
200	VISITACION AV	94134	19-J2
DEL VALE AV			SF
100	OSHAUGHNESSY BLVD	94127	14-E5
1	ENCLINE CT	94127	14-E5
100	EVELYN WY	94127	14-E5
DEMING ST			SF
40	URANUS TER	94114	10-F2
100	CLAYTON ST	94114	10-F2
DE MONTFORT AV			SF
1	MIRAMAR AV	94112	13-D7
100	CAPITOL AV	94112	13-D7
200	FAXON AV	94112	13-D7
300	JULES AV	94112	13-D7
400	ASHTON AV	94112	13-D7
DENSLOW DR			SF
250	19TH AV	94132	13-B7
1	LYNDHURST DR	94132	13-B7
100	WYTON LN	94132	13-B7
200	HOLLOWAY AV	94132	18-B1
300	BANBURY DR	94132	18-B1
DENT RD			SF
	COMPTON RD	94129	5-C4
DERBY ST			SF
1	MASON ST	94102	7-A6
DESMOND ST			SF
1	LELAND AV	94134	20-A2
100	VISITACION AV	94134	20-A2
200	SUNNYDALE AV	94134	20-A2
300	SUNNYDALE AV	94134	20-A2
DE SOTO ST			SF
1	HOLLOWAY AV	94127	13-C7
100	URBANO DR S	94127	13-C7
200	URBANO DR N	94127	13-C7
DETROIT ST			SF
800	MELROSE AV	94131	14-F6
900	STILLINGS AV	94131	14-F6
900	VISTA VERDE CT	94131	14-F6
600	JOOST AV	94127	14-F6
600	JOOST AV	94131	14-F6
700	MANGELS AV	94127	14-F6
100	JUDSON AV	94112	14-F7
100	JUDSON AV	94131	14-F7
200	STAPLES AV	94112	14-F7
200	STAPLES AV	94131	14-F7
300	FLOOD AV	94112	14-F6
300	FLOOD AV	94131	14-F6
400	HEARST AV	94112	14-F6
400	HEARST AV	94131	14-F6
DEVONSHIRE WY			SF
1	CRESTMONT DR	94131	9-D3
100	OAK PARK DR	94131	9-D3
200	WARREN DR	94131	9-D3
DEWEY BLVD			SF
400	WOODSIDE AV	94127	13-D4
400	WOODSIDE AV	94116	13-D4
400	LAGUNA HONDA BLVD	94116	13-D4
500	PACHECO ST	94127	13-D4
500	PACHECO ST	94116	13-D4
	TARAVAL ST	94116	13-D4
	TARAVAL ST	94127	13-D4
	MONTALVO AV	94116	13-D4
	MONTALVO AV	94127	13-D4
DEWITT RD			SF
	WINN WY	94129	2-E4
	LETTERMAN DR	94129	6-E4
DE WOLF ST			SF
1	LAWRENCE AV	94112	18-E2
100	SICKLES AV	94112	18-E2
DIAMOND ST			SF
1	17TH ST	94114	10-G2
30	MARKET ST	94114	10-G2
100	18TH ST	94114	10-G2
200	19TH ST	94114	10-G3
300	20TH ST	94114	10-G3
400	21ST ST	94114	10-G3

PRIMARY STREET Address	Cross Street	ZIP	CITY Pg-Grid
DIAMOND ST			SF
500	22ND ST	94114	10-G3
550	ALVARADO ST	94114	10-G3
600	23RD ST	94114	10-G3
700	ELIZABETH ST	94114	10-G3
800	24TH ST	94114	10-G4
900	JERSEY ST	94114	10-G4
1000	25TH ST	94114	10-G4
1100	CLIPPER ST	94131	10-G4
1200	26TH ST	94131	14-G4
1300	CESAR CHAVEZ ST	94131	14-G4
1400	27TH ST	94131	14-G4
1500	DUNCAN ST	94131	14-G4
1600	28TH ST	94131	14-G4
1600	VALLEY ST	94131	14-G5
1800	29TH ST	94131	14-G5
1850	BEACON ST	94131	14-G5
1900	DIAMOND HEIGHTS BLVD	94131	14-G5
2300	DIAMOND HEIGHTS BLVD	94131	14-G5
2350	HILIRITAS AV	94131	14-G5
2400	CONRAD ST	94131	14-G5
2450	MORELAND ST	94131	14-G5
2500	MOFFITT ST	94131	14-G5
2530	ARBOR ST	94131	14-G5
2570	POPPY LN	94131	14-G5
2600	SUSSEX ST	94131	14-G5
2700	PENNY LN	94131	14-G6
2730	SURREY ST	94131	14-G6
2860	CHENERY ST	94131	14-G6
2880	WILDER ST	94131	14-G6
2900	KERN ST	94131	14-G6
2930	BOSWORTH ST	94131	14-G6
DIAMOND HEIGHTS BLVD			SF
5000	PORTOLA DR	94114	14-F4
5000	PORTOLA DR	94131	14-F4
5000	BURNETT AV	94131	14-F4
5050	CLIPPER ST	94131	14-F4
5080	DUNCAN ST	94131	14-F4
5120	CARNELIAN WY	94131	14-F4
5300	DUNCAN ST	94131	14-F4
5450	GOLD MINE DR	94131	14-G5
5630	DIAMOND ST	94131	14-G5
5710	ADDISON ST	94131	14-G5
5710	GOLD MINE DR	94131	14-G5
5800	BERKELEY WY	94131	14-G5
5820	DIAMOND ST	94131	14-F5
5870	BERKELEY WY	94131	14-F5
5900	ELK ST	94131	14-F5
5900	ARBOR ST	94131	14-F5
DIANA ST			SF
100	WILLIAMS AV	94124	15-B7
DIAZ AV			SF
1	JUAN BAUTISTA CIR	94132	18-B1
100	GONZALEZ DR	94132	18-B1
DICHA AL			SF
	LUPINE AV	94118	6-E6
	WOOD ST	94118	6-E6
DICHIERA CT			SF
100	ELLINGTON AV	94112	19-E2
DIGBY ST			SF
1	EVERSON ST	94131	14-G5
90	EVERSON ST	94131	14-G5
	ADDISON ST	94131	14-G5
DIVISADERO ST			SF
1	14TH ST	94117	10-G1
1	14TH ST	94114	10-G1
100	DUBOCE AV	94117	10-G1
100	DUBOCE AV	94114	10-G1
140	CASTRO ST	94117	10-G1
140	WALLER ST	94117	10-G1
200	HAIGHT ST	94117	10-G1
300	PAGE ST	94117	10-G1
400	OAK ST	94117	10-G1
500	FELL ST	94117	6-G7
600	HAYES ST	94117	6-G7
700	GROVE ST	94117	6-G7
800	FULTON ST	94117	6-G7
900	MCALLISTER ST	94117	6-G7
1000	GOLDEN GATE AV	94115	6-G7
1100	TURK ST	94115	6-F7
1200	EDDY ST	94115	6-F6
1300	ELLIS ST	94115	6-F6
1400	OFARRELL ST	94115	6-F6
1500	GEARY BLVD	94115	6-F6
1550	GARDEN ST	94115	6-F6
1600	POST ST	94115	6-F6
1700	SUTTER ST	94115	6-F6
1800	BUSH ST	94115	6-F6
1900	PINE ST	94115	6-F6
2000	CALIFORNIA ST	94115	6-F5
2100	SACRAMENTO ST	94115	6-F5
2200	CLAY ST	94115	6-F5
2300	WASHINGTON ST	94115	6-F5
2400	JACKSON ST	94115	6-F5
2500	PACIFIC AV	94115	6-F5
2600	BROADWAY ST	94115	6-F5
2700	VALLEJO ST	94123	6-F5
2800	GREEN ST	94123	6-F4
2900	UNION ST	94123	6-F4
3000	FILBERT ST	94123	6-F4
3100	GREENWICH ST	94123	6-F4
3200	LOMBARD ST	94123	2-F4
3300	CHESTNUT ST	94123	2-F4
3400	FRANCISCO ST	94123	2-F4
3500	BAY ST	94123	2-F3
3600	NORTH POINT ST	94123	2-F3
3700	BEACH ST	94123	2-F3
3800	JEFFERSON ST	94123	2-F3
3900	MARINA BLVD	94123	2-F3
DIVISION ST			SF
1	DE HARO ST	94103	11-A1
1	DE HARO ST	94107	11-A1
20	KING ST	94103	11-A1
50	RHODE ISLAND ST	94103	11-A1
110	8TH ST	94103	11-A1
70	HENRY ADAMS ST	94103	11-A1
100	TOWNSEND ST	94103	11-A1
140	VERMONT ST	94103	11-A1
190	SAN BRUNO AV	94103	11-A1
190	9TH ST	94103	11-A1
200	SAN BRUNO AV	94103	11-A1
270	BRANNAN ST	94103	11-A1
300	POTRERO AV	94103	11-A1
300	10TH ST	94103	11-A1
370	BRYANT ST	94103	11-A1
560	FLORIDA ST	94103	10-J1
600	ALAMEDA ST	94103	10-J1
600	TREAT AV	94103	10-J1
DODGE PL			SF
100	TURK ST	94102	6-J6
DOLORES ST			SF
1	MARKET ST	94103	10-H1
1	MARKET ST	94114	10-H1
10	CLINTON PK	94103	10-H1
10	CLINTON PK	94114	10-H1
100	14TH ST	94103	10-H1
100	14TH ST	94114	10-H1
150	HIDALGO TER	94103	10-H1
150	HIDALGO TER	94114	10-H1
200	15TH ST	94103	10-H2
200	15TH ST	94114	10-H2
250	ALERT AL	94103	10-H2
250	ALERT AL	94114	10-H2
300	16TH ST	94110	10-H2
300	16TH ST	94114	10-H2
350	CHULA LN	94110	10-H2
350	CHULA LN	94114	10-H2
400	17TH ST	94110	10-H2
400	17TH ST	94114	10-H2
450	DOLORES TER	94110	10-H2
450	DOLORES TER	94114	10-H2
500	DORLAND ST	94110	10-H2
500	DORLAND ST	94114	10-H2
600	18TH ST	94110	10-H2
600	18TH ST	94114	10-H2
700	19TH ST	94110	10-H2
700	19TH ST	94114	10-H2
750	CUMBERLAND ST	94110	10-H3
750	CUMBERLAND ST	94114	10-H3
800	20TH ST	94110	10-H3
800	20TH ST	94114	10-H3
850	LIBERTY ST	94110	10-H3
850	LIBERTY ST	94114	10-H3
900	21ST ST	94110	10-H3
900	21ST ST	94114	10-H3
1000	22ND ST	94110	10-H3
1000	22ND ST	94114	10-H3
1100	23RD ST	94110	10-H3
1100	23RD ST	94114	10-H3
1200	24TH ST	94110	10-H4
1200	24TH ST	94114	10-H4
1250	JERSEY ST	94110	10-H4
1250	JERSEY ST	94114	10-H4
1300	25TH ST	94110	10-H4
1300	25TH ST	94114	10-H4
1350	CLIPPER ST	94110	10-H4
1350	CLIPPER ST	94131	10-H4
1400	26TH ST	94110	10-H4
1400	26TH ST	94131	10-H4
1450	CESAR CHAVEZ ST	94110	14-H4
1450	CESAR CHAVEZ ST	94131	14-H4
1500	27TH ST	94110	14-H4
1500	27TH ST	94131	14-H4
1550	DUNCAN ST	94110	14-H4
1550	DUNCAN ST	94131	14-H4
1600	28TH ST	94110	14-H4
1600	28TH ST	94131	14-H4
1650	VALLEY ST	94110	14-H5
1650	VALLEY ST	94131	14-H5
1700	29TH ST	94110	14-H5
1700	29TH ST	94131	14-H5
1750	DAY ST	94110	14-H5
1750	DAY ST	94131	14-H5
1780	30TH ST	94110	14-H5
1780	30TH ST	94131	14-H5
1800	SAN JOSE AV	94110	14-H5
1800	SAN JOSE AV	94131	14-H5
DOLORES TER			SF
100	DOLORES ST	94110	10-H2
DONAHUE ST			SF
700	LOCKWOOD ST	94124	16-E6
800	GALVEZ AV	94124	15-E7
900	HUDSON AV	94124	15-E7
1000	INNES AV	94124	15-E7
1020	INNES AV	94124	15-E7
1040	CLEO RAND AV	94124	15-E7
1100	JERROLD AV	94124	15-E7
1200	KIRKWOOD AV	94124	15-E7
700	EGBERT AV	94124	20-D2
890	FITZGERALD AV	94124	20-C2
1100	GILMAN AV	94124	20-C2
DONNER AV			SF
	NEWHALL ST	94124	15-B7
1900	PHELPS ST	94124	15-A7
2000	BAYSHORE BLVD	94124	15-A7
1500	3RD ST	94124	15-B7
700	HAWES ST	94124	20-C1
1340	INGALLS ST	94124	20-B1
2000	JENNINGS ST	94124	20-B1
2000	HUNTERS POINT EXWY	94124	20-D2
DORADO TER			SF
1	OCEAN AV	94112	13-D7
1	JULES AV	94112	13-D7
DORANTES AV			SF
1	MAGELLAN AV	94116	13-D4
1	PACHECO ST	94116	13-D4
100	SAN MARCOS AV	94116	13-D4
200	MONTALVO AV	94116	13-C4
300	CORTES AV	94116	13-C4
DORCAS WY			SF
1	BELLA VISTA WY	94127	14-E5
100	MOLIMO DR	94127	14-E5
200	FOERSTER ST	94127	14-E5
DORCHESTER WY			SF
1	PORTOLA DR	94127	13-D5
100	ULLOA ST	94127	13-D5
150	PARK AL	94127	13-D5
200	CLAREMONT BLVD	94127	13-D5
DORE ST			SF
1	HOWARD ST	94103	6-J7
100	FOLSOM ST	94103	10-J1
300	HARRISON ST	94103	11-A1
400	BRYANT ST	94103	11-A1
DORLAND ST			SF
1	GUERRERO ST	94110	10-H2
100	DOLORES ST	94110	10-H2
200	CHURCH ST	94114	10-G2
300	SANCHEZ ST	94114	10-G2
DORMAN AV			SF
1	BARNEVELD AV	94124	15-A5
100	PALOU AV	94124	15-A5
DORMITORY RD			SF
1	KIRKWOOD AV	94124	15-D7
1	KISKA RD	94124	15-D7
100	JERROLD AV	94124	15-D7
100	NORTHRIDGE RD	94124	15-D7
DOUBLE ROCK ST			SF
1	CAMERON WY	94124	20-C1
DOUGLASS ST			SF
100	17TH ST	94114	10-F2
100	CORBETT AV	94114	10-F2
150	MARKET ST	94114	10-F2
200	18TH ST	94114	10-F2
250	CASELLI AV	94114	10-F2
300	19TH ST	94114	10-F3
320	CARSON ST	94114	10-F3
360	SEWARD ST	94114	10-F3
400	20TH ST	94114	10-F3
430	CORWIN ST	94114	10-F3
450	ROMAIN ST	94114	10-F3
500	21ST ST	94114	10-F3
600	22ND ST	94114	10-F3
650	ALVARADO ST	94114	10-F3
700	23RD ST	94114	10-F3
720	ELIZABETH ST	94114	10-F3
800	24TH ST	94114	10-F4
850	JERSEY ST	94114	10-F4
900	25TH ST	94114	10-F4
1000	CLIPPER ST	94131	10-F4
1100	26TH ST	94131	14-F4
1200	CESAR CHAVEZ ST	94131	14-F4
1300	27TH ST	94131	14-F4
1400	28TH ST	94131	14-F4
1400	DUNCAN ST	94131	14-F4
DOVE LP			SF
	BOWMAN RD	94129	1-B3
DOVER ST			SF
1	BRANNAN ST	94107	7-C6
DOW PL			SF
100	2ND ST	94107	7-B6
DOWNEY ST			SF
1	WALLER ST	94117	10-F1
100	FREDERICK ST	94117	10-F1
300	ASHBURY ST	94117	10-F2
DOYLE DR			SF
	MARINA BLVD	94123	2-F3
	PALACE DR	94129	2-E3
	PEDESTRIAN WY	94129	2-E3
	MARSHALL ST	94129	2-E3
DRAKE ST			SF
130	WINDING WY	94112	19-G2
220	PRAGUE ST	94112	19-F2
300	MUNICH ST	94112	19-F2
DRUMM ST			SF
1	MARKET ST	94111	7-B5
30	CALIFORNIA ST	94111	7-B5
100	SACRAMENTO ST	94111	7-B5
200	CLAY ST	94111	7-B4
300	WASHINGTON ST	94111	7-B4
400	JACKSON ST	94111	7-B4
DUBLIN ST			SF
1	LA GRANDE AV	94112	19-H1
70	PERSIA AV	94112	19-H1
200	RUSSIA AV	94112	19-G1
DUBOCE AV			SF
140	MISSION ST	94103	10-J1
70	OTIS ST	94103	10-H1
30	STEVENSON ST	94103	10-H1
20	WOODWARD ST	94103	10-H1
30	OTIS ST	94103	10-H1
100	VALENCIA ST	94103	10-H1
130	ELGIN PK	94103	10-H1
160	PEARL ST	94103	10-H1
200	GUERRERO ST	94103	10-H1
200	MARKET ST	94114	10-H1
300	MARKET ST	94102	10-H1
330	BUCHANAN ST	94114	10-H1
330	BUCHANAN ST	94102	10-H1
400	CHURCH ST	94114	10-G1
400	CHURCH ST	94117	10-G1
450	FILLMORE ST	94114	10-G1
450	FILLMORE ST	94117	10-G1
470	BELCHER ST	94114	10-G1
470	BELCHER ST	94117	10-G1
500	SANCHEZ ST	94114	10-G1
500	SANCHEZ ST	94117	10-G1
510	STEINER ST	94114	10-G1
510	STEINER ST	94117	10-G1
550	WALTER ST	94114	10-G1
550	WALTER ST	94117	10-G1
600	NOE ST	94114	10-G1
600	NOE ST	94117	10-G1
700	SCOTT ST	94114	10-G1
700	SCOTT ST	94117	10-G1
740	CASTRO ST	94114	10-G1
800	DIVISADERO ST	94117	10-G1
900	ALPINE TER	94117	10-G1
1000	BUENA VISTA AV E	94117	10-G1
DUDLEY RD			SF
	PIPER LP	94129	5-D4
DUKES CT			SF
1	CASHMERE ST	94124	15-C6
DUNBAR ST			SF
1	TWAIN ST	94111	7-A5
100	WASHINGTON ST	94111	7-A5
DUNCAN ST			SF
1	VALENCIA ST	94110	14-H4
10	TIFFANY AV	94110	14-H4
80	SAN JOSE AV	94110	14-H4
100	GUERRERO ST	94110	14-H4
200	DOLORES ST	94131	14-H4
300	CHURCH ST	94131	14-H4
400	SANCHEZ ST	94131	14-G4
500	NOE ST	94131	14-G4
600	CASTRO ST	94131	14-G4
650	NEWBURG ST	94131	14-G4
700	DIAMOND ST	94131	14-G4
800	28TH ST	94131	14-F4
800	DOUGLASS ST	94131	14-F4
930	DIAMOND HEIGHTS BLVD	94131	14-F4
940	AMBER DR	94131	14-F4
1000	CAMEO WY	94131	14-F4
1050	AMBER DR	94131	14-F4
1050	RED ROCK WY	94131	14-F4
1100	DIAMOND HEIGHTS BLVD	94131	14-F4
DUNSHEE ST			SF
1	PALOU AV	94124	15-B6
100	DRUMMOND AL	94124	15-B6
DUNSMUIR ST			SF
1	SWEENY ST	94134	14-J6
100	SILVER AV	94134	14-J6
DWIGHT ST			SF
1	SAN BRUNO AV	94134	15-A7
100	GIRARD ST	94134	15-A7
200	BRUSSELS ST	94134	15-A7
300	GOETTINGEN ST	94134	20-A1
600	HAMILTON ST	94134	20-A1
700	BOWDOIN ST	94134	20-A1
800	DARTMOUTH ST	94134	19-J1
900	COLBY ST	94134	19-J1
1000	UNIVERSITY ST	94134	19-J1
DYNAMITE RD			SF
	LINCOLN BLVD	94129	1-B4
	SAFFOLD AV	94129	1-B4
	RALSTON AV	94129	1-B4

E

PRIMARY STREET Address	Cross Street	ZIP	CITY Pg-Grid
E ST			SF
300	MANSEAU ST	94124	21-F1
500	MORRELL ST	94124	21-F1
EAGLE ST			SF
1	YUKON ST	94114	10-F3
160	MONO ST	94114	10-F3
200	CASELLI AV	94114	10-F3
EARL ST			SF
900	INNES AV	94124	15-E7
900	JERROLD AV	94124	15-E7
1000	KIRKWOOD AV	94124	15-D7
1100	LA SALLE AV	94124	15-D7
1100	NAVY RD	94124	15-D7
700	EGBERT AV	94124	20-C1
890	FITZGERALD AV	94124	20-C1
1100	GILMAN AV	94124	20-C1
EASTMAN ST			SF
1	GREEN ST	94109	6-J4
30	RUSSELL ST	94109	6-J4
50	ROCKLAND ST	94109	6-J4
70	UNION ST	94109	2-J4
100	ALLEN ST	94109	2-J4
EASTWOOD DR			SF
1	MIRAMAR AV	94112	13-D7
1	WESTWOOD DR	94112	13-D7
30	SAN RAMON WY	94112	13-D7
100	WILDWOOD WY	94112	13-D7
180	MONTECITO AV	94112	13-D6
200	MIRAMAR AV	94112	13-D6
200	WESTWOOD DR	94112	13-D6
EATON PL			SF
	GREEN ST	94133	7-A4
ECKER ST			SF
1	STEVENSON ST	94105	7-B5
50	JESSIE ST	94105	7-B5
60	ELIM AL	94105	7-B5
100	MISSION ST	94105	7-B5
100	CLEMENTINA ST	94105	7-B6
200	FOLSOM ST	94105	7-B6
EDDY ST			SF
50	CYRIL MAGIN ST	94102	7-A6
100	MASON ST	94102	7-A6
200	TAYLOR ST	94102	7-A6
300	JONES ST	94102	6-J6
340	WAGNER AL	94102	6-J6
400	LEAVENWORTH ST	94102	6-J6
400	LEAVENWORTH ST	94109	6-J6
500	HYDE ST	94102	6-J6
500	HYDE ST	94109	6-J6
600	LARKIN ST	94102	6-J6
600	LARKIN ST	94109	6-J6
700	POLK ST	94102	6-J6
700	POLK ST	94109	6-J6
800	VAN NESS AV	94102	6-H6
800	VAN NESS AV	94109	6-H6
900	FRANKLIN ST	94102	6-H6
900	FRANKLIN ST	94109	6-H6
1000	GOUGH ST	94102	6-H6
1000	GOUGH ST	94109	6-H6
1200	LAGUNA ST	94115	6-H6
1300	BUCHANAN ST	94115	6-H6
1410	WEBSTER ST	94115	6-G6
1520	FILLMORE ST	94115	6-G6
1620	STEINER ST	94115	6-G6
1730	PIERCE ST	94115	6-G6
1840	SCOTT ST	94115	6-G6
1950	DIVISADERO ST	94115	6-F6
2060	BRODERICK ST	94115	6-F7
2100	SAINT JOSEPHS AV	94115	6-F7
EDGAR PL			SF
1	NIAGARA AV	94112	18-E1
100	BRUCE AV	94112	18-E1
EDGARDO PL			SF
1	GRANT AV	94133	3-A3
EDGEHILL WY			SF
1	GARCIA AV	94127	13-D5
100	SHANGRILA WY	94127	13-D5
200	PACHECO ST	94127	13-D5
500	PACHECO ST	94127	13-D5
EDGEWOOD AV			SF
100	FARNSWORTH LN	94117	9-E2
150	BELMONT AV	94117	9-E2
EDIE RD			SF
	GORGAS AV	94129	2-E4
	OREILLY AV	94129	2-E4
	GENERAL KENNEDY AV	94129	2-E4
	KENDALL DR	94129	2-E4
	GIRARD RD	94129	2-E4
EDINBURGH ST			SF
1	SILVER AV	94112	14-H7
60	PERU AV	94112	14-H7
140	AVALON AV	94112	14-G7
220	EXCELSIOR AV	94112	14-G7
300	BRAZIL AV	94112	19-G1
450	PERSIA AV	94112	19-G1
550	RUSSIA AV	94112	19-G1
690	FRANCE AV	94112	19-G1
820	ITALY AV	94112	19-G1
900	AMAZON AV	94112	19-G1
1000	GENEVA AV	94112	19-G1
EDITH ST			SF
1	GRANT AV	94133	3-A4
EDNA ST			SF
600	MONTEREY BLVD	94127	14-E6
1	HAVELOCK ST	94112	14-E7
100	MARSTON AV	94112	14-E7
200	JUDSON AV	94112	14-E7
300	STAPLES AV	94112	14-E6
400	FLOOD AV	94112	14-E6
500	HEARST AV	94112	14-E6
EDWARD ST			SF
1	WILLARD ST N	94118	5-D7
100	ARGUELLO BLVD	94118	5-D7
EGBERT AV			SF
1880	NEWHALL ST	94124	15-A7
1990	PHELPS ST	94124	15-A7
2000	BAYSHORE BLVD	94124	15-A7
800	HAWES ST	94124	20-C1
1180	INGALLS ST	94124	20-B1
1300	JENNINGS ST	94124	15-B7
1500	3RD ST	94124	15-B7
600	DONAHUE ST	94124	20-D1
700	EARL ST	94124	20-C1
800	ARELIOUS WALKER DR	94124	20-C1
890	FITCH ST	94124	20-C1
EL CAMINO DEL MAR			SF
200	25TH AV	94121	5-A5
200	LINCOLN BLVD	94121	5-A5
300	26TH AV	94121	5-A5
400	27TH AV	94121	5-A5
500	28TH AV	94121	5-A5
680	MCLAREN AV	94121	5-A6
700	30TH AV	94121	5-A6
800	LAKE ST	94121	5-A6
	32ND AV	94121	5-A6
	LEGION OF HONOR DR	94121	4-J6
2600	SEAL ROCK DR	94121	4-H6
2700	48TH AV	94121	4-H6
2700	POINT LOBOS AV	94121	4-H6
EL DORADO ST			SF
	ILLINOIS ST	94107	11-C1
ELGIN PK			SF
1	MCCOPPIN ST	94103	10-H1
100	DUBOCE AV	94103	10-H1
ELIZABETH ST			SF
1	SAN JOSE AV	94110	10-H3
100	GUERRERO ST	94110	10-H3
300	CHURCH ST	94114	10-H3
310	NELLIE ST	94114	10-H3
350	VICKSBURG ST	94114	10-G3
360	BLANCHE ST	94114	10-G3

PRIMARY STREET / Address Cross Street / ZIP / CITY Pg-Grid

ELIZABETH ST SF
400 SANCHEZ ST 94114 10-G3
500 NOE ST 94114 10-G3
600 CASTRO ST 94114 10-G3
700 DIAMOND ST 94114 10-G3
800 DOUGLASS ST 94114 10-F3
900 HOFFMAN AV 94114 10-F3
1000 GRAND VIEW AV 94114 10-F3

ELK ST SF
1 ARBOR ST 94131 14-F5
1 DIAMOND HEIGHTS BLVD 94131 14-F5
30 SUSSEX ST 94131 14-F5
70 CHENERY ST 94131 14-F6
80 PARADISE AV 94131 14-F6
100 BOSWORTH ST 94131 14-F6
100 MERCATO CT 94131 14-F6

ELKHART ST SF
1 MAIN ST 94105 7-C6

ELLERT ST SF
1 BOCANA ST 94110 14-J5
100 BENNINGTON ST 94110 14-J5
200 ANDOVER ST 94110 14-J5

ELLINGTON AV SF
100 MOUNT VERNON AV 94112 19-F1
100 MOUNT VERNON AV 94112 19-F2
190 OTTAWA AV 94112 19-F2
240 SALA TER 94112 19-F2
280 FOOTE AV 94112 19-E2
340 DICHIERA CT 94112 19-E2
380 NAGLEE AV 94112 19-E2
490 WHIPPLE AV 94112 19-E2
600 FARRAGUT AV 94112 19-E2

ELLIOT ST SF
100 LELAND AV 94134 19-J2
170 RAYMOND AV 94134 19-J2
250 ARLETA AV 94134 19-J2
320 TEDDY AV 94134 19-J1
400 CAMPBELL AV 94134 19-J1

ELLIS ST SF
1 4TH ST 94102 7-A6
1 4TH ST 94108 7-A6
1 MARKET ST 94108 7-A6
20 STOCKTON ST 94102 7-A6
20 STOCKTON ST 94108 7-A6
100 POWELL ST 94102 7-A6
140 CYRIL MAGIN ST 94102 7-A6
200 MASON ST 94102 7-A6
300 TAYLOR ST 94102 7-A6
400 JONES ST 94102 6-J6
500 LEAVENWORTH ST 94109 6-J6
540 COHEN PL 94109 6-J6
600 HYDE ST 94109 6-J6
700 LARKIN ST 94109 6-J6
800 POLK ST 94109 6-J6
900 VAN NESS AV 94109 6-H6
1000 FRANKLIN ST 94109 6-H6
1100 GOUGH ST 94109 6-H6
1300 LAGUNA ST 94115 6-H6
1330 QUICKSTEP LN 94115 6-H6
1380 QUICKSTEP LN 94115 6-H6
1400 HOLLIS ST 94115 6-G6
1500 WEBSTER ST 94115 6-G6
1700 STEINER ST 94115 6-G6
1800 PIERCE ST 94115 6-G6
1900 SCOTT ST 94115 6-G6
1950 BEIDEMAN ST 94115 6-G6
2000 DIVISADERO ST 94115 6-F6
2100 BRODERICK ST 94115 6-F6
2200 SAINT JOSEPHS AV 94115 6-F6
2200 TERRA VISTA AV 94115 6-F6

ELLSWORTH ST SF
1 BERNAL HEIGHTS BLVD 94110 14-J5
100 POWHATTAN AV 94110 14-J5
200 EUGENIA AV 94110 14-J5
300 CORTLAND AV 94110 14-J5
400 JARBOE AV 94110 14-J5
500 TOMPKINS AV 94110 14-J6
600 OGDEN AV 94110 14-J6
700 CRESCENT AV 94110 14-J6
1000 ALEMANY BLVD 94110 14-J6

ELM ST SF
1 POLK ST 94102 6-J6
200 VAN NESS AV 94102 6-J6
FRANKLIN ST 94102 6-H6
GOUGH ST 94102 6-H6
1120 PIERCE ST 94115 6-G7

ELMHURST DR SF
1 ROSSMOOR DR 94132 13-C6
90 GLADIOLUS LN 94132 13-C6
100 ROSSMOOR DR 94132 13-C6

ELMIRA ST SF
1 SHAFTER AV 94124 15-A5
120 THOMAS AV 94124 15-A6
200 HELENA ST 94124 15-A6
400 AUGUSTA ST 94124 15-A6
500 SILVER AV 94124 15-A6
500 THORNTON AV 94124 15-A6

EL MIRASOL PL SF
1 CRESTLAKE DR 94132 13-A6
90 SLOAT BLVD 94132 13-A6

ELMWOOD WY SF
100 WESTWOOD DR 94112 13-D7
180 FAXON AV 94112 13-D7
180 SOUTHWOOD DR 94112 13-D7

EL PLAZUELA WY SF
1 JUNIPERO SERRA BLVD 94127 13-C7

EL POLIN LP SF
MACARTHUR AV 94129 5-E5

EL SERENO CT SF
1 TERESITA BLVD 94127 14-F5
50 RIO CT 94127 14-F5

ELSIE ST SF
1 COSO AV 94110 14-J5
100 ESMERALDA AV 94110 14-J5
180 VIRGINIA AV 94110 14-J5
200 EUGENIA AV 94110 14-J5
200 EUGENIA AV 94110 14-H5
300 CORTLAND AV 94110 14-H5
320 SANTA MARINA ST 94110 14-H5
400 HOLLY PARK CIR 94110 14-H5

EL VERANO WY SF
1 SAINT ELMO WY 94127 13-D6
30 FERNWOOD DR 94127 13-D6
70 MAYWOOD DR 94127 13-D6
100 SAN FELIPE AV 94127 13-D6

ELWOOD ST SF
1 MASON ST 94102 7-A6
100 OFARRELL ST 94102 7-A6

EMERALD LN SF
1 RIVERTON DR 94132 13-A6
50 SPRINGFIELD DR 94132 13-A6
100 EVERGLADE DR 94132 13-A6

EMERSON ST SF
100 GEARY BLVD 94118 6-E6

EMERY LN SF
1 VALLEJO ST 94133 7-A4

EMIL LN SF
1 LOS PALMOS DR 94127 13-D6
100 CRESTA VISTA DR 94127 13-D6

EMMA ST SF
1 STOCKTON ST 94108 7-A5

EMMETT CT SF
1 PRECITA AV 94110 14-J4

EMPRESS LN SF
1 SAN BRUNO AV 94134 20-A2
1 SOMERSET ST 94134 20-A2

ENCANTO AV SF
1 ANZAVISTA AV 94115 6-F7
100 TERRA VISTA AV 94115 6-F7

ENCLINE CT SF
100 MARIETTA DR 94127 14-E5
1 DEL VALE AV 94127 14-E5

ENGLISH ST SF
ROBINSON ST 94124 16-E7
MCCANN ST 94124 16-E7
LOCKWOOD ST 94124 16-E7

ENTERPRISE ST SF
100 FOLSOM ST 94110 10-J2

N ENTRADA CT SF
1 BORICA ST 94127 13-C7
50 S ENTRADA CT 94127 13-C7
100 S ENTRADA CT 94127 13-C7

S ENTRADA CT SF
N ENTRADA CT 94127 13-C7
100 N ENTRADA CT 94127 13-C7
200 BORICA ST 94127 13-C7

ERIE ST SF
1 FOLSOM ST 94103 10-J1
100 S VAN NESS AV 94103 10-J1
200 MISSION ST 94103 10-J1

ERKSON CT SF
1 POST ST 94115 6-F6

ERVINE ST SF
80 WILDE AV 94134 20-A1
100 CAMPBELL AV 94134 20-A1

ESCOLTA WY SF
1 30TH AV 94116 13-A5
100 31ST AV 94116 13-A5
200 WAWONA ST 94116 13-A5
200 33RD AV 94116 13-A5

ESCONDIDO AV SF
1 CONSTANSO WY 94132 13-A6
100 34TH AV 94132 13-A6

ESMERALDA AV SF
900 BRADFORD ST 94110 15-A5
900 PERALTA AV 94110 15-A5
900 ALABAMA ST 94110 15-A5
940 PERALTA AV 94110 15-A5
1020 SAMOSET ST 94110 15-A5
1060 MASSASOIT ST 94110 15-A4
1100 FRANCONIA ST 94110 15-A4
1100 RUTLEDGE ST 94110 15-A4
1140 COLERIDGE ST 94110 14-J5
1100 LUNDYS LN 94110 14-J5
1140 PROSPECT AV 94110 14-J5
900 WINFIELD ST 94110 14-J5
1000 ELSIE ST 94110 14-J5

ESPANOLA ST SF
1 ROSIE LEE LN 94124 15-D6
50 MATTHEW CT 94124 15-D6
100 BEATRICE LN 94124 15-D6

ESQUINA DR SF
1 PARQUE DR 94134 19-H2
100 GENEVA AV 94134 19-H2

ESSEX ST SF
1 HARRISON ST 94105 7-B6
100 FOLSOM ST 94105 7-B6

ESTERO AV SF
1 ALVISO ST 94127 13-C7
60 MONTICELLO ST 94127 13-C7
140 LUNADO WY 94127 13-C7
200 JUNIPERO SERRA BLVD 94127 13-C7

EUCALYPTUS DR SF
JUNIPERO SERRA BLVD 94132 13-C6
OCEAN AV 94132 13-C6
20 GLADIOLUS LN 94132 13-C6
200 19TH AV 94132 13-B6
300 20TH AV 94132 13-B6
400 21ST AV 94132 13-B6
430 22ND AV 94132 13-B6
500 MELBA AV 94132 13-B6
600 23RD AV 94132 13-B6
700 24TH AV 94132 13-B6
800 25TH AV 94132 13-B6
900 26TH AV 94132 13-B6
1000 INVERNESS DR 94132 13-B6
1100 FOREST VIEW DR 94132 13-A6
1200 MEADOWBROOK DR 94132 13-A6
1300 SYLVAN DR 94132 13-A6
1400 MIDDLEFIELD DR 94132 13-A6
1500 RIVERTON DR 94132 13-A6
1600 SPRINGFIELD DR 94132 13-A6
1700 EVERGLADE DR 94132 13-A6
1730 HAVENSIDE DR 94132 13-A6
1770 WESTMOORLAND DR 94132 13-A6
1800 CLEARFIELD DR 94132 13-A6

EUCLID AV SF
1 PRESIDIO AV 94115 6-F6
1 BUSH ST 94115 6-F6
80 MASONIC AV 94118 6-F6
200 LAUREL ST 94118 6-E6
250 COLLINS ST 94118 6-E6
300 MANZANITA AV 94118 6-E6
340 IRIS AV 94118 6-E6
400 HEATHER AV 94118 5-E6
450 SPRUCE ST 94118 5-E6
500 PARKER AV 94118 5-E6
600 COMMONWEALTH AV 94118 5-E6
700 JORDAN AV 94118 5-E6
800 PALM AV 94118 5-D6
900 ARGUELLO BLVD 94118 5-D6

EUGENIA AV SF
1 MISSION ST 94110 14-H5
100 COLERIDGE ST 94110 14-H5
200 PROSPECT AV 94110 14-H5
300 WINFIELD ST 94110 14-H5
380 ELSIE ST 94110 14-J5
400 ELSIE ST 94110 14-J5
470 BONVIEW ST 94110 14-J5
560 BOCANA ST 94110 14-J5
580 BENNINGTON ST 94110 14-J5
670 WOOL ST 94110 14-J5
760 ANDOVER ST 94110 14-J5
840 MOULTRIE ST 94110 14-J5
930 ANDERSON ST 94110 14-J5
1020 ELLSWORTH ST 94110 14-J5
1100 GATES ST 94110 14-J5
1190 FOLSOM ST 94110 14-J5
1270 BANKS ST 94110 14-J5
1460 PRENTISS ST 94110 14-J5
1500 NEVADA ST 94110 14-J5

EUREKA PL SF
1 LARKIN ST 94109 6-J5

EUREKA ST SF
1 17TH ST 94114 10-F2
40 MARKET ST 94114 10-F2
100 18TH ST 94114 10-F2
200 19TH ST 94114 10-F3
300 20TH ST 94114 10-G3
360 21ST ST 94114 10-G3
430 21ST ST 94114 10-G3
500 22ND ST 94114 10-G3
600 23RD ST 94114 10-G3

EVA TER SF
1 OAK ST 94117 6-G7

EVANS AV SF
900 HUNTERS POINT BLVD 94124 15-D6
900 JENNINGS ST 94124 15-D6
900 MIDDLEPOINT RD 94124 15-D6
1200 KEITH ST 94124 15-D5
1500 MENDELL ST 94124 15-C5
1600 NEWHALL ST 94124 15-C5
1660 3RD ST 94124 15-C5
1700 PHELPS ST 94124 15-C5
1800 QUINT ST 94124 15-B5
1900 RANKIN ST 94124 15-B4
SELBY ST 94124 15-B4
2100 NAPOLEON ST 94124 15-B4
2100 TOLAND ST 94124 15-B4
2150 MARIN ST 94124 11-B4
2200 CESAR CHAVEZ ST 94124 11-B4

EVE ST SF
1 HOLLADAY AV 94110 15-A4

EVELYN WY SF
130 TERESITA BLVD 94127 13-E5
100 CHAVES AV 94127 13-E5
1 JUANITA WY 94127 13-E5
100 PORTOLA DR 94127 13-E5
200 DEL VALE AV 94127 14-E5
300 TERESITA BLVD 94127 14-E5

EVERGLADE DR SF
1 SLOAT BLVD 94132 13-A6
20 EMERALD LN 94132 13-A6
100 OCEAN AV 94132 13-A6
200 EUCALYPTUS DR 94132 13-A6
300 GELLERT DR 94132 13-A6

EVERSON ST SF
90 BEACON ST 94131 14-G5
100 DIGBY ST 94131 14-G5
200 DIGBY ST 94131 14-G5

EWER PL SF
1 MASON ST 94108 7-A5

EWING TER SF
1 JEAN WY 94118 6-E6
100 MASONIC AV 94118 6-F7

EXCELSIOR AV SF
1 MISSION ST 94112 14-G7
100 LONDON ST 94112 14-G7
210 PARIS ST 94112 14-G7
330 LISBON ST 94112 14-G7
440 MADRID ST 94112 14-G7
550 EDINBURGH ST 94112 14-G7
660 NAPLES ST 94112 14-G7
770 VIENNA ST 94112 14-G7
900 ATHENS ST 94112 14-H7
970 MOSCOW ST 94112 14-H7
1050 MUNICH ST 94112 19-H1

EXECUTIVE PARK BLVD SF
100 ALANA WY 94134 20-B2
170 BLANKEN AV 94124 20-B2
170 BLANKEN AV 94134 20-B2
230 THOMAS MELLON DR 94124 20-B2
230 THOMAS MELLON DR 94134 20-B2
300 HARNEY WY 94124 20-B2
300 HARNEY WY 94134 20-B2

EXETER ST SF
1 PAUL AV 94124 20-B1
100 SALINAS AV 94124 20-B1

F

FAIR AV SF
1 MISSION ST 94110 14-H4
1 VALENCIA ST 94110 14-H4
50 PETERS AV 94110 14-J4
100 COLERIDGE ST 94110 14-J4
150 LUNDYS LN 94110 14-J4
200 PROSPECT AV 94110 14-J4

FAIRFAX AV SF
1600 RANKIN ST 94124 15-B5
1600 3RD ST 94124 15-C5
1700 PHELPS ST 94124 15-C5
600 KEITH ST 94124 15-C5
800 MENDELL ST 94124 15-C5
900 NEWHALL ST 94124 15-C5

FAIRFIELD WY SF
1 OCEAN AV 94127 13-D7
70 LAKEWOOD AV 94127 13-D7
100 KENWOOD WY 94127 13-D7

FAIRMOUNT ST SF
1 ARLINGTON ST 94131 14-H5
100 CHENERY ST 94131 14-H5
200 WHITNEY ST 94131 14-H5
300 LAIDLEY ST 94131 14-G5
400 MIGUEL ST 94131 14-G5

FAIR OAKS ST SF
1 21ST ST 94110 10-H3
100 22ND ST 94110 10-H3
200 23RD ST 94110 10-H3
300 24TH ST 94110 10-H4
400 25TH ST 94110 10-H4
500 26TH ST 94110 10-H4

FAITH ST SF
1 HOLLADAY AV 94110 15-A5
100 BREWSTER ST 94110 15-A5

FALLON PL SF
1 TAYLOR ST 94133 6-J4

FALMOUTH ST SF
1 SHIPLEY ST 94107 7-A7
100 FOLSOM ST 94107 7-A7

FANNING WY SF
1 14TH AV 94116 9-C4
100 15TH AV 94116 9-C4
100 QUINTARA ST 94116 9-C4

FARALLONES ST SF
210 ORIZABA AV 94112 18-D2
100 CAPITOL AV 94112 18-D2
1 PLYMOUTH AV 94112 18-E2
100 SAN JOSE AV 94112 18-E2

FARGO PL SF
1 BOARDMAN PL 94103 7-A7

FARNSWORTH LN SF
1 WILLARD ST 94117 9-E2
100 EDGEWOOD AV 94117 9-E2

FARNUM ST SF
1 ADDISON ST 94131 14-G5
100 MORELAND ST 94131 14-G5
200 MOFFITT ST 94131 14-G5

FARRAGUT AV SF
1 ALEMANY BLVD 94112 18-E2
30 MONETA WY 94112 18-E2
90 HURON AV 94112 18-E2
130 RAE AV 94112 19-E2
180 ELLINGTON AV 94112 19-E2
200 MISSION ST 94112 19-E2

FARVIEW CT SF
1 MAR VIEW WY 94131 10-E3

FAXON AV SF
1100 OCEAN AV 94112 13-D7
1190 ELMWOOD WY 94112 13-D7
1190 SOUTHWOOD DR 94112 13-D7
1350 WILDWOOD WY 94112 13-D7
1450 UPLAND DR 94127 13-D7
1450 UPLAND DR 94112 13-D7
1460 NORTHWOOD DR 94127 13-D6
1460 NORTHWOOD DR 94112 13-D6
980 PIZARRO WY 94127 13-D6
980 PIZARRO WY 94112 13-D6
1000 MONTEREY BLVD 94112 13-D6
1000 MONTEREY BLVD 94127 13-D6
200 LAKEVIEW AV 94112 18-D1
300 GRAFTON AV 94112 18-D1
400 HOLLOWAY AV 94112 13-D7
500 DE MONTFORT AV 94112 13-D7
600 OCEAN AV 94112 13-D7
1 MONTANA ST 94112 18-D1
100 THRIFT ST 94112 18-D1

FEDERAL ST SF
1 DELANCEY ST 94107 7-C6
40 RINCON ST 94107 7-C6
100 2ND ST 94107 7-C6

FELIX AV SF
1 CAMBON DR 94132 18-B1

FELL ST SF
1 POLK ST 94102 6-J7
100 VAN NESS AV 94102 6-J7
200 FRANKLIN ST 94102 6-H7
300 GOUGH ST 94102 6-H7
400 OCTAVIA ST 94102 6-H7
500 LAGUNA ST 94102 6-H7
600 BUCHANAN ST 94102 6-H7
700 WEBSTER ST 94117 6-G7
800 FILLMORE ST 94117 6-G7
900 STEINER ST 94117 6-G7
1000 PIERCE ST 94117 6-G7
1100 SCOTT ST 94117 6-G7
1200 DIVISADERO ST 94117 6-G7
1300 BRODERICK ST 94117 6-F7
1400 BAKER ST 94117 6-F7
1500 LYON ST 94117 6-F7
1600 CENTRAL AV 94117 6-F7
1700 MASONIC AV 94117 10-F1
1800 ASHBURY ST 94117 10-E1
1900 CLAYTON ST 94117 10-E1
2000 COLE ST 94117 10-E1
SHRADER ST 94117 9-E1
STANYAN ST 94117 9-E1
KEZAR DR 94117 9-E1
OAK ST 94117 9-E1

FELLA PL SF
1 POWELL ST 94108 7-A5

FELTON ST SF
1 SAN BRUNO AV 94134 15-A7
100 GIRARD ST 94134 15-A7
200 BRUSSELS ST 94134 15-A7
300 GOETTINGEN ST 94134 15-A7
400 SOMERSET ST 94134 15-A7
500 HOLYOKE ST 94134 15-A7
600 HAMILTON ST 94134 14-J7
700 BOWDOIN ST 94134 14-J7
800 DARTMOUTH ST 94134 14-J7
900 COLBY ST 94134 14-J7
1000 UNIVERSITY ST 94134 14-J7
1100 PRINCETON ST 94134 14-J7
1200 AMHERST ST 94134 14-J7
1300 YALE ST 94134 14-J7
1400 CAMBRIDGE ST 94134 14-J7
1500 OXFORD ST 94134 14-H7
1600 HARVARD ST 94134 14-H7
1700 GAMBIER ST 94134 14-H7
1800 MADISON ST 94134 14-H7
1900 PERU AV 94134 14-H7
1900 AVALON AV 94134 14-H7

FENTON LN SF
1 CORBETT AV 94131 10-F4
100 BURNETT AV 94131 10-F4

FERN ST SF
1 LARKIN ST 94109 6-J5
100 POLK ST 94109 6-H5
200 VAN NESS AV 94109 6-H6
300 FRANKLIN ST 94109 6-H6
400 GOUGH ST 94109 6-H6

FERNANDEZ ST SF
830 BARNARD AV 94129 5-E4
800 QUARRY RD 94129 5-E4
830 MACARTHUR AV 94129 5-E4

FERNWOOD DR SF
1 RAVENWOOD DR 94127 13-D6
1 ROSEWOOD DR 94127 13-D6
90 ROSEWOOD DR 94127 13-D6
100 BRENTWOOD AV 94127 13-D6
200 EL VERANO WY 94127 13-D6

FILBERT ST SF
200 SANSOME ST 94133 3-A4
220 NAPIER LN 94133 3-A4
260 DARRELL PL 94133 3-A4
270 MONTGOMERY ST 94133 3-A4
400 KEARNY ST 94133 3-A4
420 GENOA PL 94133 3-A4
450 VARENNES ST 94133 3-A4
470 HARWOOD AL 94133 3-A4
500 GRANT AV 94133 3-A4
520 KRAMER PL 94133 3-A4
550 JASPER PL 94133 3-A4
570 KRAUSGRILL PL 94133 3-A4
600 STOCKTON ST 94133 3-A4
700 POWELL ST 94133 3-A4
720 COLUMBUS AV 94133 3-A4
780 SCOTLAND ST 94133 2-J4
800 MASON ST 94133 2-J4
900 TAYLOR ST 94133 2-J4
940 REDFIELD AL 94133 2-J4
1000 JONES ST 94133 2-J4
1030 ATTRIDGE AL 94133 2-J4
1100 LEAVENWORTH ST 94109 2-J4
1200 HYDE ST 94109 2-J4
1300 LARKIN ST 94109 2-H4
1400 POLK ST 94109 2-H4
1500 VAN NESS AV 94123 2-H4
1600 FRANKLIN ST 94123 2-H4
1700 GOUGH ST 94123 2-H4
1800 OCTAVIA ST 94123 6-G4
1900 LAGUNA ST 94123 6-G4
2000 BUCHANAN ST 94123 6-G4
2060 AHLERS CT 94123 6-G4
2100 WEBSTER ST 94123 6-G4
2200 FILLMORE ST 94123 6-G4
2300 STEINER ST 94123 6-G4
2400 PIERCE ST 94123 6-F4
2500 SCOTT ST 94123 6-F4

Address	Cross Street	ZIP	City / Pg-Grid
FILBERT ST			SF
2600	DIVISADERO ST	94123	6-F4
2700	BRODERICK ST	94123	6-F4
2800	BAKER ST	94123	6-F4
2900	LYON ST	94123	6-F4
FILLMORE ST			SF
1	DUBOCE AV	94117	10-G1
100	HERMANN ST	94117	10-G1
150	GERMANIA ST	94117	10-G1
200	WALLER ST	94117	10-G1
250	LAUSSAT ST	94117	10-G1
300	HAIGHT ST	94117	10-G1
400	PAGE ST	94117	10-G1
500	OAK ST	94117	6-G7
600	FELL ST	94117	6-G7
700	HAYES ST	94117	6-G7
800	GROVE ST	94117	6-G7
900	FULTON ST	94117	6-G7
1000	MCALLISTER ST	94117	6-G7
1100	GOLDEN GATE AV	94115	6-G7
1200	TURK ST	94115	6-G7
1300	EDDY ST	94115	6-G6
1450	BYINGTON ST	94115	6-G6
1500	OFARRELL ST	94115	6-G6
1600	GEARY BLVD	94115	6-G6
1700	POST ST	94115	6-G6
1800	SUTTER ST	94115	6-G6
1900	BUSH ST	94115	6-G6
1920	WILMOT ST	94115	6-G6
2000	PINE ST	94115	6-G5
2100	CALIFORNIA ST	94115	6-G5
2200	SACRAMENTO ST	94115	6-G5
2300	CLAY ST	94115	6-G5
2400	WASHINGTON ST	94115	6-G5
2500	JACKSON ST	94115	6-G5
2600	PACIFIC AV	94115	6-G5
2700	BROADWAY ST	94115	6-G5
2800	VALLEJO ST	94123	6-G4
2900	GREEN ST	94123	6-G4
3000	UNION ST	94123	6-G4
3100	FILBERT ST	94123	6-G4
3140	PIXLEY ST	94123	2-G4
3200	GREENWICH ST	94123	2-G4
3200	MOULTON ST	94123	2-G4
3300	LOMBARD ST	94123	2-G4
3400	CHESTNUT ST	94123	2-G4
3600	CERVANTES BLVD	94123	2-G3
3600	BAY ST	94123	2-G3
3650	NORTH POINT ST	94123	2-G3
3650	BEACH ST	94123	2-G3
3710	BEACH ST	94123	2-G3
3750	JEFFERSON ST	94123	2-G3
3790	RETIRO WY	94123	2-G3
3800	MARINA BLVD	94123	2-G3
FINLEY RD			SF
	ARGUELLO BLVD	94129	5-D5
FISHER AV			SF
	LOCKWOOD ST	94124	16-F7
	ROBINSON ST	94124	16-F7
	VAN KEUREN AV	94124	16-E7
	SPEAR AV	94124	16-E7
	MORRELL ST	94124	16-E7
FISHER LP			SF
	SHERIDAN AV	94129	1-D4
	INFANTRY TER	94129	1-D4
FITCH ST			SF
1	INNES AV	94124	15-D6
80	HUDSON AV	94124	15-E6
1400	QUESADA AV	94124	15-D7
1500	REVERE AV	94124	15-D7
1600	SHAFTER AV	94124	15-D7
2600	CARROLL AV	94124	20-C1
2800	ARELIOUS WALKER DR	94124	20-C1
2800	EGBERT AV	94124	20-C1
FITZGERALD AV			SF
1700	BAYSHORE BLVD	94124	15-A7
1000	GRIFFITH ST	94124	20-C1
1160	CAMERON WY	94124	20-C1
1200	HAWES ST	94124	20-C1
1390	INGALLS ST	94124	20-B1
1580	JENNINGS ST	94124	20-B1
1800	3RD ST	94124	20-B1
500	DONAHUE ST	94124	20-C2
750	EARL ST	94124	20-C1
1000	ARELIOUS WALKER DR	94124	20-C1
FLINT ST			SF
50	DE FOREST WY	94114	10-G2
100	16TH ST	94114	10-G2
FLOOD AV			SF
1	CIRCULAR AV	94131	14-F6
100	CONGO ST	94131	14-F6
220	DETROIT ST	94112	14-F6
300	EDNA ST	94112	14-F6
400	FOERSTER ST	94112	14-E6
500	GENNESSEE ST	94112	13-E6
570	PHELAN AV	94112	13-E6
590	RIDGEWOOD AV	94112	13-E6
600	HAZELWOOD AV	94112	13-E6
FLORA ST			SF
1	BAYVIEW ST	94124	15-B6
100	THORNTON AV	94124	15-B6
FLORENCE ST			SF
1	VALLEJO ST	94133	6-J4
FLORENTINE ST			SF
1	MISSION ST	94112	19-F2
100	MORSE ST	94112	19-F2
200	BRUNSWICK ST	94112	19-F2
FLORIDA ST			SF
1	DIVISION ST	94103	10-J1
100	ALAMEDA ST	94103	10-J1
220	15TH ST	94103	10-J2
300	16TH ST	94110	10-J2
400	17TH ST	94110	10-J2
500	MARIPOSA ST	94110	10-J2
600	18TH ST	94110	10-J2
700	19TH ST	94110	10-J2
800	20TH ST	94110	10-J2
800	20TH ST	94110	10-J3
900	21ST ST	94110	10-J3
	22ND ST	94110	11-A3
1100	23RD ST	94110	11-A3
1200	24TH ST	94110	11-A4
1300	25TH ST	94110	11-A4
1400	26TH ST	94110	11-A4
1500	CESAR CHAVEZ ST	94110	15-A4
1600	PRECITA AV	94110	15-A4
1700	PERALTA AV	94110	15-A4
FLOURNOY ST			SF
200	RHINE ST	94112	18-D2
300	DE LONG ST	94112	18-D2
FLOWER ST			SF
50	LOOMIS ST	94124	15-A5
1	PATTERSON ST	94124	15-A5
50	BAYSHORE BLVD	94124	15-A5
FOERSTER ST			SF
1	JUDSON AV	94112	14-E7
30	SUNNYSIDE TER	94112	14-E7
100	STAPLES AV	94112	14-E6
200	FLOOD AV	94112	14-E6
300	HEARST AV	94112	14-E6
400	MONTEREY BLVD	94127	14-E6
500	JOOST AV	94127	14-E6
600	MANGELS AV	94127	14-E6
650	MELROSE AV	94127	14-E6
700	TERESITA BLVD	94127	14-E6
800	LOS PALMOS DR	94127	14-E6
810	DORCAS WY	94127	14-E6
850	GATUN AL	94127	14-E6
900	TERESITA BLVD	94127	14-E6
FOLSOM ST			SF
1	THE EMBARCADERO	94105	7-C5
40	STEUART ST	94105	7-C5
100	SPEAR ST	94105	7-C5
200	MAIN ST	94105	7-C5
300	BEALE ST	94105	7-C6
350	ZENO PL	94105	7-B6
400	FREMONT ST	94105	7-B6
420	GROTE PL	94105	7-B6
500	1ST ST	94105	7-B6
520	ECKER ST	94105	7-B6
	ESSEX ST	94105	7-B6
600	2ND ST	94107	7-B6
600	2ND ST	94105	7-B6
650	HAWTHORNE ST	94107	7-B6
650	HAWTHORNE ST	94103	7-B6
720	3RD ST	94107	7-B6
720	3RD ST	94103	7-B6
700	MABINI ST	94107	7-B6
700	MABINI ST	94103	7-B6
800	4TH ST	94107	7-A7
800	4TH ST	94103	7-A7
900	5TH ST	94107	7-A7
900	5TH ST	94103	7-A7
940	FALMOUTH ST	94107	7-A7
940	FALMOUTH ST	94103	7-A7
1000	6TH ST	94103	7-A7
1020	HARRIET ST	94103	7-A7
1020	HARRIET ST	94103	7-A7
1030	COLUMBIA SQUARE ST	94103	7-A7
1050	RUSS ST	94103	7-A7
1060	SHERMAN ST	94103	7-A7
1070	MOSS ST	94103	7-A7
1100	7TH ST	94103	7-A7
1130	LANGTON ST	94103	7-A7
1120	HALLAM ST	94103	7-A7
1150	RAUSCH ST	94103	7-A7
1150	RODGERS ST	94103	7-A7
1200	8TH ST	94103	7-A7
1330	9TH ST	94103	10-J1
1350	DORE ST	94103	10-J1
1400	10TH ST	94103	10-J1
1450	JUNIPER ST	94103	10-J1
1500	11TH ST	94103	10-J1
1540	NORFOLK ST	94103	10-J1
1600	12TH ST	94103	10-J1
1750	ERIE ST	94103	10-J1
1800	14TH ST	94103	10-J1
1900	15TH ST	94103	10-J2
2000	16TH ST	94110	10-J2
2040	ENTERPRISE ST	94110	10-J2
2100	17TH ST	94110	10-J2
2200	18TH ST	94110	10-J2
2300	19TH ST	94110	10-J2
2400	20TH ST	94110	10-J3
2500	21ST ST	94110	10-J3
2600	22ND ST	94110	10-J3
2700	23RD ST	94110	10-J3
2800	24TH ST	94110	10-J4
2900	25TH ST	94110	10-J4
3000	26TH ST	94110	10-J4
3100	CESAR CHAVEZ ST	94110	14-J4
3200	PRECITA AV	94110	14-J4
3220	PRECITA AV	94110	14-J4
3220	BESSIE ST	94110	14-J4
3300	STONEMAN ST	94110	14-J5
3400	RIPLEY ST	94110	14-J5
3600	BERNAL HEIGHTS BLVD	94110	14-J5
460	CHAPMAN ST	94110	14-J5
3600	POWHATTAN AV	94110	14-J5
3700	EUGENIA AV	94110	14-J5
3800	CORTLAND AV	94110	14-J5
3900	JARBOE AV	94110	14-J5
4000	TOMPKINS AV	94110	14-J6
4100	OGDEN AV	94110	14-J6
4190	CRESCENT AV	94110	14-J6
4300	ALEMANY BLVD	94110	14-J6
FONT BLVD			SF
1	LAKE MERCED BLVD	94132	13-A7
	TAPIA DR	94132	13-B7
	VIDAL DR	94132	13-B7
270	HOLLOWAY AV	94132	18-B1
	TAPIA DR	94132	18-B1
	SERRANO DR	94132	18-B1
500	JUAN BAUTISTA CIR	94132	18-B1
	GONZALEZ DR	94132	18-B1
	CAMBON DR	94132	18-B1
	CHUMASERO DR	94132	18-C1
900	JUNIPERO SERRA BLVD	94132	18-C2
FONTINELLA TER			SF
1	DE HARO ST	94107	11-B4
FOOTE AV			SF
240	CAYUGA AV	94112	19-E1
200	ALEMANY BLVD	94112	19-E2
100	HURON AV	94112	19-E2
1	ELLINGTON AV	94112	19-F2
100	MISSION ST	94112	19-F2
FORD ST			SF
1	SANCHEZ ST	94114	10-G2
100	NOE ST	94114	10-G2
FOREST KNOLLS DR			SF
1	CHRISTOPHER DR	94131	9-E3
250	WOODHAVEN CT	94131	9-E3
400	OAK PARK DR	94131	9-E3
FOREST SIDE AV			SF
1	TARAVAL ST	94127	13-C5
1	TARAVAL ST	94116	13-C5
100	ULLOA ST	94127	13-C5
100	ULLOA ST	94116	13-C5
200	VICENTE ST	94127	13-C5
200	VICENTE ST	94116	13-C5
FOREST VIEW DR			SF
1	SLOAT BLVD	94132	13-A6
100	OCEAN AV	94132	13-A6
200	EUCALYPTUS DR	94132	13-A6
S FORK DR			SF
1700	MARTIN LUTHER KING JR DR	-	8-H1
1800	JOHN F KENNEDY DR	-	8-H1
FORTUNA AV			SF
1	ANZAVISTA AV	94115	6-F6
100	TERRA VISTA AV	94115	6-F6
FOUNTAIN ST			SF
1	24TH ST	94114	10-F4
100	25TH ST	94114	10-F4
FOWLER AV			SF
1	PORTOLA DR	94127	13-E4
100	JUANITA WY	94127	13-E5
200	TERESITA BLVD	94127	13-E5
FRANCE AV			SF
1	MISSION ST	94112	19-F1
100	LONDON ST	94112	19-F1
200	PARIS ST	94112	19-G1
300	LISBON ST	94112	19-G1
400	MADRID ST	94112	19-G1
500	EDINBURGH ST	94112	19-G1
600	NAPLES ST	94112	19-G1
700	VIENNA ST	94112	19-G1
800	ATHENS ST	94112	19-G1
900	MOSCOW ST	94112	19-G1
FRANCIS ST			SF
1	MISSION ST	94112	14-G7
100	ALEMANY BLVD	94112	14-G7
FRANCISCO ST			SF
1	MONTGOMERY ST	94133	3-A3
100	KEARNY ST	94133	3-A3
200	GRANT AV	94133	3-A3
250	MIDWAY ST	94133	3-A3
260	BELLAIR PL	94133	3-A3
300	STOCKTON ST	94133	3-A3
320	WORDEN ST	94133	3-A3
400	POWELL ST	94133	3-A3
500	MASON ST	94133	2-J3
600	TAYLOR ST	94133	2-J3
650	COLUMBUS AV	94133	2-J3
700	JONES ST	94133	2-J3
750	BRET HARTE TER	94133	2-J3
800	LEAVENWORTH ST	94109	2-J3
900	HYDE ST	94109	2-J3
1000	LARKIN ST	94109	2-H3
1100	POLK ST	94109	2-H3
1200	VAN NESS AV	94123	2-H3
1300	FRANKLIN ST	94123	2-H3
1400	GOUGH ST	94123	2-H3
1500	OCTAVIA ST	94123	2-G3
1600	LAGUNA ST	94123	2-G3
2200	SCOTT ST	94123	2-F4
2200	ALHAMBRA ST	94123	2-F4
2300	DIVISADERO ST	94123	2-F4
2400	BRODERICK ST	94123	2-F4
2500	BAKER ST	94123	2-F4
2570	RICHARDSON AV	94123	2-F4
2590	GORGAS AV	94123	2-F4
2590	LYON ST	94123	2-F4
FRANCONIA ST			SF
1	PERALTA AV	94110	15-A4
100	MULLEN AV	94110	15-A4
170	RUTLEDGE ST	94110	15-A4
200	ESMERALDA AV	94110	15-A4
200	RUTLEDGE ST	94110	15-A4
400	BREWSTER ST	94110	15-A5
500	MAYFLOWER ST	94110	15-A5
600	POWHATTAN AV	94110	15-A5
FRANKLIN ST			SF
1	MARKET ST	94102	6-H7
20	PAGE ST	94102	6-H7
60	LILY ST	94102	6-H7
100	OAK ST	94102	6-H7
140	HICKORY ST	94102	6-H7
200	FELL ST	94102	6-H7
250	LINDEN ST	94102	6-H7
300	HAYES ST	94102	6-H7
350	IVY ST	94102	6-H7
400	GROVE ST	94102	6-H7
500	FULTON ST	94102	6-H7
600	MCALLISTER ST	94102	6-H7
700	GOLDEN GATE AV	94102	6-H6
750	ELM ST	94102	6-H6
800	TURK ST	94102	6-H6
850	LARCH ST	94102	6-H6
900	EDDY ST	94109	6-H6
950	WILLOW ST	94109	6-H6
960	WILLOW ST	94109	6-H6
1000	ELLIS ST	94109	6-H6
1030	OLIVE ST	94109	6-H6
1100	OFARRELL ST	94109	6-H6
1100	STARR KING WY	94109	6-H6
1150	MYRTLE ST	94109	6-H6
1200	GEARY BLVD	94109	6-H6
1300	POST ST	94109	6-H6
1340	DANIEL BURNHAM CT	94109	6-H6
1400	SUTTER ST	94109	6-H6
1440	FERN ST	94109	6-H6
1500	BUSH ST	94109	6-H5
1530	AUSTIN ST	94109	6-H5
1600	PINE ST	94109	6-H5
1700	CALIFORNIA ST	94109	6-H5
1800	SACRAMENTO ST	94109	6-H5
1900	CLAY ST	94109	6-H5
2000	WASHINGTON ST	94109	6-H5
2100	JACKSON ST	94109	6-H5
2200	PACIFIC AV	94109	6-H5
2300	BROADWAY	94109	6-H4
2400	VALLEJO ST	94123	6-H4
2500	GREEN ST	94123	6-H4
2600	UNION ST	94123	6-H4
2700	FILBERT ST	94123	2-H4
2800	GREENWICH ST	94123	2-H4
2850	BLACKSTONE CT	94123	2-H4
2900	LOMBARD ST	94123	2-H4
3000	CHESTNUT ST	94123	2-H3
3100	FRANCISCO ST	94123	2-H3
	BAY ST	94123	2-H3
	MACARTHUR AV	94123	2-H3
	POPE RD	94123	2-H3
	FUNSTON RD	94123	2-H3
FRATESSA CT			SF
60	GIRARD ST	94134	20-B1
100	SAN BRUNO AV	94134	20-B1
FREDERICK ST			SF
1	BUENA VISTA AV W	94117	10-F1
100	MASONIC AV	94117	10-F1
120	DELMAR ST	94117	10-F1
200	ASHBURY ST	94117	10-F1
230	DOWNEY ST	94117	10-E1
300	CLAYTON ST	94117	10-E1
350	BELVEDERE ST	94117	10-E1
400	COLE ST	94117	10-E1
450	SHRADER ST	94117	10-E1
500	STANYAN ST	94117	9-E1
600	WILLARD ST	94117	9-D1
800	ARGUELLO BLVD	94117	9-D1
800	LINCOLN WY	94117	9-D1
FREDSON CT			SF
100	HURON AV	94112	19-E2
FREELON ST			SF
1	ZOE ST	94107	7-B7
100	4TH ST	94107	7-B7
FREEMAN CT			SF
100	CLAY ST	94108	7-A5
FREEMAN ST			SF
	ANZA ST	94129	1-E4
	OWEN ST	94129	1-E4
FREMONT ST			SF
1	FRONT ST	94105	7-B5
1	MARKET ST	94105	7-B5
100	MISSION ST	94105	7-B5
150	NATOMA ST	94106	7-B5
200	HOWARD ST	94105	7-B5
300	FOLSOM ST	94105	7-C6
400	HARRISON ST	94105	7-C6
FRENCH CT			SF
	LINCOLN BLVD	94129	1-E4
FRIEDELL ST			SF
900	HUDSON AV	94124	15-E7
1000	INNES AV	94124	15-E7
1100	JERROLD AV	94124	15-E7
1200	KIRKWOOD AV	94124	15-E7
FRONT ST			SF
600	JACKSON ST	94111	7-B4
700	PACIFIC AV	94111	7-B4
800	BROADWAY ST	94111	7-B4
900	VALLEJO ST	94111	3-B4
1000	GREEN ST	94111	3-B4
1050	JOHN MAHER ST	94111	3-B4
1100	UNION ST	94111	3-B4
1	FREMONT ST	94111	7-B5
1	MARKET ST	94111	7-B5
100	PINE ST	94111	7-B5
200	CALIFORNIA ST	94111	7-B5
250	HALLECK ST	94111	7-B5
300	SACRAMENTO ST	94111	7-B5
400	CLAY ST	94111	7-B5
FUENTA AV			SF
1	JUAN BAUTISTA CIR	94132	18-B1
100	SERRANO DR	94132	18-B1
FULTON ST			SF
300	FRANKLIN ST	94102	6-H7
400	GOUGH ST	94102	6-H7
500	OCTAVIA ST	94102	6-H7
600	LAGUNA ST	94102	6-H7
800	WEBSTER ST	94117	6-G7
900	FILLMORE ST	94117	6-G7
1000	STEINER ST	94117	6-G7
1100	PIERCE ST	94117	6-G7
1200	SCOTT ST	94117	6-G7
1300	DIVISADERO ST	94117	6-F7
1400	BRODERICK ST	94117	6-F7
1500	BAKER ST	94117	6-F7
1600	LYON ST	94117	6-F7
1700	CENTRAL AV	94117	6-F7
1800	MASONIC AV	94117	6-F7
1860	ATALAYA TER	94117	6-E7
1900	ASHBURY ST	94117	6-E7
1910	HEMWAY TER	94117	6-E7
1950	LOYOLA TER	94117	6-E7
2000	CLAYTON ST	94117	6-E7
2100	COLE ST	94117	6-E7
2200	PARKER AV	94117	5-E7
2210	SHRADER ST	94117	5-E7
2300	STANYAN ST	94117	5-E7
2300	STANYAN ST	94118	5-E7
2340	PARSONS ST	94117	5-E7
2340	PARSONS ST	94118	5-E7
2400	WILLARD ST N	94117	5-D7
2400	WILLARD ST N	94118	5-D7
2500	ARGUELLO BLVD	94118	5-D7
2600	2ND AV	94118	5-D7
2700	3RD AV	94118	5-D7
2800	4TH AV	94118	5-D7
2900	5TH AV	94118	5-D7
3000	6TH AV	94118	5-D7
3100	7TH AV	94118	5-D7
3200	8TH AV	94118	5-C7
3300	9TH AV	94118	5-C7
3400	10TH AV	94118	5-C7
3500	11TH AV	94118	5-C7
3600	12TH AV	94118	5-C7
3700	FUNSTON AV	94118	5-C7
3740	PRESIDIO BLVD	94118	5-C7
3800	14TH AV	94118	5-C7
3900	15TH AV	94118	5-C7
4000	16TH AV	94118	5-B7
4100	17TH AV	94121	5-B7
4200	18TH AV	94121	5-B7
4300	19TH AV	94121	5-B7
4400	20TH AV	94121	5-B7
4500	21ST AV	94121	5-B7
4600	22ND AV	94121	5-B7
4700	23RD AV	94121	5-B7
4800	24TH AV	94121	5-B7
4900	CROSS OVER DR	94121	5-A7
4900	25TH AV	94121	5-A7
5000	26TH AV	94121	5-A7
5100	27TH AV	94121	5-A7
5200	28TH AV	94121	5-A7
5300	29TH AV	94121	5-A7
5300	30TH AV	94121	5-A7
5400	30TH AV	94121	5-A7
5500	31ST AV	94121	5-A7
5600	32ND AV	94121	5-A7
5700	33RD AV	94121	5-A7
5800	34TH AV	94121	4-J7
5900	35TH AV	94121	4-J7
6000	36TH AV	94121	8-J1
6100	37TH AV	94121	8-J1
6200	38TH AV	94121	8-J1
6300	39TH AV	94121	8-J1
6400	40TH AV	94121	8-J1
6500	41ST AV	94121	8-J1
6600	42ND AV	94121	8-H1
6700	CHAIN OF LAKES DR W	94121	8-H1
6700	43RD AV	94121	8-H1
6800	44TH AV	94121	8-H1
6900	45TH AV	94121	8-H1
7000	46TH AV	94121	8-H1
7100	47TH AV	94121	8-H1
7200	48TH AV	94121	8-H1
7300	LA PLAYA	94121	8-H1
7400	GREAT HWY	94121	8-H1
FUNSTON AV			SF
30	HICKS RD	94129	5-D4
	BARNARD AV	94129	5-D4
	HARDIE AV	94129	5-D4
	MORAGA AV	94129	5-E4
30	PRESIDIO BLVD	94129	1-E4
30	MARTINEZ ST	94129	1-E4
1	LINCOLN BLVD	94129	1-E4
100	LAKE ST	94118	5-C6
200	CALIFORNIA ST	94118	5-C6
300	CLEMENT ST	94118	5-C6
400	GEARY BLVD	94118	5-C6
500	ANZA ST	94118	5-C7
600	BALBOA ST	94118	5-C7
700	CABRILLO ST	94118	5-C7
800	FULTON ST	94118	5-C7
1200	LINCOLN WY	94122	9-C1
1300	IRVING ST	94122	9-C2
1400	JUDAH ST	94122	9-C2
1500	KIRKHAM ST	94122	9-C2
1550	LURLINE ST	94122	9-C2
1600	LAWTON ST	94122	9-C3

PRIMARY STREET / Address Cross Street / ZIP / CITY Pg-Grid

FUNSTON AV SF
1640 ALOHA AV 94122 9-C3
1700 MORAGA ST 94122 9-C3
1800 NORIEGA ST 94122 9-C3
1800 PACHECO ST 94116 9-C3
1900 AERIAL WY 94116 9-C3
1990 ROCKRIDGE DR 94116 9-C3
1990 12TH AV 94116 9-C3
2100 QUINTARA ST 94116 9-C4
2200 RIVERA ST 94116 9-C4
2400 TARAVAL ST 94116 13-C5
2500 ULLOA ST 94116 13-C5

FUNSTON RD SF
FRANKLIN ST 94123 2-H3
POPE RD 94123 2-H3

G

GABILAN WY SF
1 CRESTLAKE DR 94132 13-B6
90 SLOAT BLVD 94132 13-B6

GAISER CT SF
100 GUERRERO ST 94110 10-H2

GALEWOOD CIR SF
1 CLARENDON AV 94131 9-D3
100 GALEWOOD CT 94131 9-D3

GALEWOOD CT SF
1 GALEWOOD CIR 94131 9-D3

GALILEE LN SF
1 LAGUNA ST 94115 6-H6
1 CLEARY CT 94115 6-H6

GALINDO AV SF
1 CHUMASERO DR 94132 18-C2

GALLAGHER LN SF
TEHAMA ST 94103 7-A6
CLEMENTINA ST 94103 7-A6

GALVEZ AV SF
2100 TOLAND ST 94124 15-B4
1500 MENDELL ST 94124 15-C5
1600 NEWHALL ST 94124 15-C5
1640 3RD ST 94124 15-C5
1700 PHELPS ST 94124 15-C5
1900 RANKIN ST 94124 15-C5
500 HORNE AV 94124 16-E7
580 HILL DR 94124 16-E7
600 ROBINSON ST 94124 16-E7
800 DONAHUE ST 94124 15-E7

GAMBIER ST SF
1 SILVER AV 94134 14-H7
70 PIOCHE ST 94134 14-H7
180 SILLIMAN ST 94134 14-H7
280 FELTON ST 94134 14-H7
400 BURROWS ST 94134 14-H7

GARCES DR SF
50 VIDAL DR 94132 18-A1
100 ARBALLO DR 94132 18-A1
200 RIVAS AV 94132 18-B1
210 BUCARELI DR 94132 18-B1
300 GRIJALVA DR 94132 18-B1
500 GONZALEZ DR 94132 18-B1

GARCIA AV SF
1 HERNANDEZ AV 94127 13-D4
1 VASQUEZ AV 94127 13-D4
50 IDORA AV 94127 13-D4
100 PACHECO ST 94127 13-D4
130 EDGEHILL WY 94127 13-D4
180 VASQUEZ AV 94127 13-D4
200 MERCED AV 94127 13-D4

GARDEN ST SF
1 DIVISADERO ST 94115 6-F6
100 BRODERICK ST 94115 6-F6

GARDENSIDE DR SF
1 BURNETT AV 94131 10-F3
400 BURNETT AV 94131 10-F3

GARFIELD ST SF
ASHTON AV 94112 18-D1
GRAFTON AV 94112 18-D1
10 ORIZABA AV 94132 18-D1
100 BRIGHT ST 94132 18-D1
200 HEAD ST 94132 18-C1
300 VICTORIA ST 94132 18-C1
400 RAMSELL ST 94132 18-C1
500 ARCH ST 94132 18-C1
600 VERNON ST 94132 18-C1
700 RALSTON ST 94132 18-C1
800 BYXBEE ST 94132 18-C1
900 MONTICELLO ST 94132 18-C1
1000 BEVERLY ST 94132 18-C1
1100 JUNIPERO SERRA BLVD 94132 18-C1

GARLINGTON CT SF
1 LA SALLE AV 94124 15-C6
30 COMMER CT 94124 15-C6

GARRISON AV SF
1 SCHWERIN ST 94134 19-J2
150 ARGONAUT AV 94134 19-J2
200 SUNNYDALE AV 94134 19-J2

GATES ST SF
100 POWHATTAN AV 94110 14-J5
200 EUGENIA AV 94110 14-J5
300 CORTLAND AV 94110 14-J5
400 JARBOE AV 94110 14-J5
500 TOMPKINS AV 94110 14-J6
600 OGDEN AV 94110 14-J6
700 CRESCENT AV 94110 14-J6

GATEVIEW CT SF
100 MENDOSA AV 94116 9-C4

GATEWAY AV SF
1 AVENUE B 94130 3-D1
1 WESTSIDE DR 94130 3-D1

GAVEN ST SF
1 SAN BRUNO AV 94134 15-A6
100 BARNEVELD AV 94134 15-A6
200 MERRILL ST 94134 15-A6
300 BOYLSTON ST 94134 14-J6
400 BOWDOIN ST 94134 14-J6

GAVIOTA WY SF
1 TERESITA BLVD 94127 14-E5
100 BELLA VISTA WY 94127 14-E5

GEARY BLVD SF
1100 VAN NESS AV 94109 6-H6
1100 GEARY ST 94109 6-H6
1200 FRANKLIN ST 94109 6-H6
1300 GOUGH ST 94109 6-H6
1300 PETER YORKE WY 94109 6-H6
1300 STARR KING WY 94109 6-H6
1400 CLEARY CT 94109 6-H6
1500 LAGUNA ST 94115 6-H6
1620 BUCHANAN ST 94115 6-G6
1700 WEBSTER ST 94115 6-G6
1850 AVERY ST 94115 6-G6
1900 STEINER ST 94115 6-G6
2100 SCOTT ST 94115 6-G6
2200 DIVISADERO ST 94115 6-F6
2300 BRODERICK ST 94115 6-F6
2400 BAKER ST 94115 6-F6
2400 SAINT JOSEPHS AV 94115 6-F6
2500 LYON ST 94115 6-F6
2600 PRESIDIO AV 94115 6-F6
2700 MASONIC AV 94118 6-F6
2740 EMERSON ST 94118 6-E6
2800 WOOD ST 94118 6-E6
2900 COLLINS ST 94118 6-E6
3000 BLAKE ST 94118 6-E6
3100 COOK ST 94118 5-E6
3200 SPRUCE ST 94118 5-E6
3300 PARKER AV 94118 5-E6
3350 BEAUMONT AV 94118 5-E6
3400 COMMONWEALTH AV 94118 5-E6
3450 STANYAN ST 94118 5-E6
3500 JORDAN AV 94118 5-D6
3600 PALM AV 94118 5-D6
3700 ARGUELLO BLVD 94118 5-D6
3800 2ND AV 94118 5-D6
3900 3RD AV 94118 5-D6
4000 4TH AV 94118 5-D6
4100 5TH AV 94118 5-D6
4200 6TH AV 94118 5-D6
4300 7TH AV 94118 5-D6
4400 8TH AV 94118 5-C6
4500 9TH AV 94118 5-C6
4600 10TH AV 94118 5-C6
4700 11TH AV 94118 5-C6
4800 12TH AV 94118 5-C6
4900 FUNSTON AV 94118 5-C6
4950 PRESIDIO BLVD 94118 5-C6
5000 14TH AV 94118 5-C6
5100 15TH AV 94118 5-C6
5200 16TH AV 94118 5-B6
5300 17TH AV 94121 5-B6
5400 18TH AV 94121 5-B6
5500 19TH AV 94121 5-B6
5600 20TH AV 94121 5-B6
5700 21ST AV 94121 5-B6
5800 22ND AV 94121 5-B6
5900 23RD AV 94121 5-B6
6000 24TH AV 94121 5-B6
6100 25TH AV 94121 5-A6
6200 26TH AV 94121 5-A6
6300 27TH AV 94121 5-A6
6400 28TH AV 94121 5-A6
6500 29TH AV 94121 5-A6
6600 30TH AV 94121 5-A6
6700 31ST AV 94121 5-A6
6800 32ND AV 94121 5-A6
6900 33RD AV 94121 5-A6
7000 34TH AV 94121 4-J6
7100 35TH AV 94121 4-J6
7200 36TH AV 94121 4-J6
7300 37TH AV 94121 4-J6
7400 38TH AV 94121 4-J6
7500 39TH AV 94121 4-J6
7600 40TH AV 94121 4-J6
7600 POINT LOBOS AV 94121 4-J6
7700 41ST AV 94121 4-J6
7800 42ND AV 94121 4-H6
7900 43RD AV 94121 4-H6
8000 44TH AV 94121 4-H6
8100 45TH AV 94121 4-H6
8200 46TH AV 94121 4-H7
8300 47TH AV 94121 4-H7
8400 48TH AV 94121 4-H7

GEARY ST SF
1 MARKET ST 94108 7-A6
20 KEARNY ST 94108 7-A6
100 GRANT AV 94108 7-A6
200 STOCKTON ST 94108 7-A6
300 POWELL ST 94102 7-A6
400 MASON ST 94102 7-A6
500 TAYLOR ST 94102 6-J6
550 SHANNON ST 94102 6-J6
600 JONES ST 94102 6-J6
700 LEAVENWORTH ST 94109 6-J6
800 HYDE ST 94109 6-J6
900 LARKIN ST 94109 6-J6
1000 POLK ST 94109 6-J6
1100 GEARY BLVD 94109 6-J6
1100 VAN NESS AV 94109 6-J6

GELLERT DR SF
100 OCEAN AV 94132 12-J6
300 MORNINGSIDE DR 94132 13-A6
400 CLEARFIELD DR 94132 13-A6
500 EVERGLADE DR 94132 13-A6
600 MIDDLEFIELD DR 94132 13-A6

GENEBERN WY SF
1 COLLEGE AV 94112 14-H6
1 JUSTIN DR 94112 14-H6
150 MURRAY ST 94112 14-H6
220 BENTON AV 94112 14-H6
300 JUSTIN DR 94112 14-H6

GENERAL KENNEDY AV SF
GORGAS AV 94129 2-E4
BIRMINGHAM RD 94129 2-E4
THORNBURG RD 94129 2-E4
EDIE RD 94129 2-E4

GENEVA AV SF
1 OCEAN AV 94112 14-E7
60 HOWTH ST 94112 19-E1
80 LOUISBURG ST 94112 19-E1
240 SAN JOSE AV 94112 19-F1
340 DELANO AV 94112 19-F1
470 CAYUGA AV 94112 19-F1
500 BAYWOOD ST 94112 19-F1
540 BANNOCK ST 94112 19-F1
580 ALEMANY BLVD 94112 19-F1
640 GLORIA CT 94112 19-F1
720 MISSION ST 94112 19-F1
770 LONDON ST 94112 19-F1
830 PARIS ST 94112 19-F1
890 LISBON ST 94112 19-F1
940 MADRID ST 94112 19-F2
1000 EDINBURGH ST 94112 19-F2
1060 NAPLES ST 94112 19-G2
1110 VIENNA ST 94112 19-G2
1170 ATHENS ST 94112 19-G2
1230 MOSCOW ST 94112 19-G2
1230 S HILL BLVD 94112 19-G2
1270 MUNICH ST 94112 19-G2
1280 PRAGUE ST 94112 19-G2
1900 BROOKDALE AV 94134 19-H2
1990 WALBRIDGE AV 94134 19-H2
2010 CARTER ST 94134 19-H2
2040 PARQUE DR 94134 19-H2
2090 CIELITO DR 94134 19-H2
2140 ESQUINA DR 94134 19-H2
2190 CARRIZAL ST 94134 19-H2

GENNESSEE ST SF
1 JUDSON AV 94112 13-E7
100 STAPLES AV 94112 13-E6
200 FLOOD AV 94112 13-E6
300 HEARST AV 94112 13-E6
400 MONTEREY BLVD 94127 13-E6
500 JOOST AV 94127 13-E6
600 MANGELS AV 94127 13-E6
700 MELROSE AV 94127 13-E6

GENOA PL SF
100 UNION ST 94133 3-A4
200 FILBERT ST 94133 3-A4

GEORGE CT SF
1 INGALLS ST 94124 15-C6

GERMANIA ST SF
1 WEBSTER ST 94117 10-G1
80 FILLMORE ST 94117 10-G1
200 STEINER ST 94117 10-G1

GETZ ST SF
100 GRAFTON AV 94112 18-E1
200 MOUNT VERNON AV 94112 18-E1

GIANTS DR SF
3000 GILMAN AV 94124 20-C1
3200 INGERSON AV 94124 20-C1

GIBB ST SF
1 ILS LN 94111 7-A4

GIBBON CT SF
SIMONDS LP 94129 6-F4

GIBSON RD SF
1780 BATTERY CHAMBERLAIN RD 94129 5-B5
BOWLEY ST 94129 5-B5
BAKER ST 94129 5-B5
LINCOLN BLVD 94129 5-B5

GILBERT ST SF
1 BRANNAN ST 94103 11-A1
100 BRYANT ST 94103 7-A7

GILLETTE AV SF
140 LATHROP AV 94134 20-B2
100 NIBBI CT 94134 20-B2
1 BLANKEN AV 94134 20-B2

GILMAN AV SF
500 HUNTERS POINT EXWY 94124 20-C2
540 DONAHUE ST 94124 20-C2
660 EARL ST 94124 20-C1
780 ARELIOUS WALKER DR 94124 20-C1
820 GIANTS DR 94124 20-C1
910 GRIFFITH ST 94124 20-C1
1030 HAWES ST 94124 20-C1
1150 INGALLS ST 94124 20-B1
1300 JENNINGS ST 94124 20-B1
1400 3RD ST 94124 20-B1
1400 PAUL AV 94124 20-B1

GILROY ST SF
1 INGERSON AV 94124 20-C1
70 IGNACIO ST 94124 20-C2

GIRARD RD SF
50 EDIE RD 94129 1-E4
40 LINCOLN BLVD 94129 1-E4

GIRARD ST SF
1 SILVER AV 94134 15-A6
100 SILLIMAN ST 94134 15-A6
200 FELTON ST 94134 15-A7
300 BURROWS ST 94134 15-A7
400 BACON ST 94134 15-A7
500 WAYLAND ST 94134 15-A7
600 WOOLSEY ST 94134 15-A7
700 DWIGHT ST 94134 15-A7
800 OLMSTEAD ST 94134 20-A1
900 MANSELL ST 94134 20-A1
1010 ORDWAY ST 94134 20-A1
1120 WARD ST 94134 20-A1
1240 HARKNESS AV 94134 20-A1
1360 WILDE AV 94134 20-A1
1400 FRATESSA CT 94134 20-A1

GLADEVIEW WY SF
1 PANORAMA DR 94131 10-E3
200 SKYVIEW WY 94131 10-E3

GLADIOLUS LN SF
1 EUCALYPTUS DR 94132 13-C6
100 ELMHURST DR 94132 13-C6

GLADSTONE DR SF
1 CAMBRIDGE ST 94112 14-H6
200 STONEYFORD AV 94112 14-H7
300 STONEYBROOK AV 94112 14-H7
400 MAYNARD ST 94112 14-H7

GLADYS ST SF
1 SANTA MARINA ST 94110 14-H5
100 APPLETON AV 94110 14-H5

GLENBROOK AV SF
1 MOUNTAIN SPRINGS AV 94114 10-E3
100 SAINT GERMAIN AV 94114 10-E3
200 PALO ALTO AV 94114 10-E3

GLENDALE ST SF
1 GRAND VIEW AV 94114 10-F3
1 MARKET ST 94114 10-F3
1 STANTON ST 94114 10-F3
100 CORBETT AV 94114 10-F3
100 GRAYSTONE TER 94114 10-F3

GLENVIEW DR SF
1 BURNETT AV 94131 10-F4
250 DAWNVIEW WY 94131 10-E4
400 PORTOLA DR 94131 14-E4

GLORIA CT SF
1 GENEVA AV 94112 19-F1

GODEUS ST SF
1 MISSION ST 94110 14-H5
100 COLERIDGE ST 94110 14-H5

GOETHE ST SF
20 RHINE ST 94112 18-D2
1 SAN JOSE AV 94112 18-D2

GOETTINGEN ST SF
1 SILVER AV 94134 15-A6
90 SILLIMAN ST 94134 15-A7
190 FELTON ST 94134 15-A7
280 BURROWS ST 94134 15-A7
380 BACON ST 94134 15-A7
480 WAYLAND ST 94134 15-A7
580 WOOLSEY ST 94134 15-A7
800 DWIGHT ST 94134 15-A7
1100 OLMSTEAD ST 94134 20-A1
910 MANSELL ST 94134 20-A1
1000 ORDWAY ST 94134 20-A1
1100 WARD ST 94134 20-A1
1200 HARKNESS AV 94134 20-A1
1300 ALPHA ST 94134 20-A2
1300 WILDE AV 94134 20-A2
1400 CAMPBELL AV 94134 20-A2

GOLD ST SF
1 SANSOME ST 94133 7-B4
20 BALANCE ST 94133 7-B4
100 MONTGOMERY ST 94133 7-A4

GOLDEN CT SF
1 SACRAMENTO ST 94109 6-J5

GOLDEN GATE AV SF
1 6TH ST 94102 7-A6
1 MARKET ST 94102 7-A6
30 TAYLOR ST 94102 7-A6
100 JONES ST 94102 6-J6
200 LEAVENWORTH ST 94102 6-J6
250 DALE PL 94102 6-J6
300 HYDE ST 94102 6-J6
400 LARKIN ST 94102 6-J6
500 POLK ST 94102 6-J6
600 VAN NESS AV 94102 6-H6
700 FRANKLIN ST 94102 6-H7
800 GOUGH ST 94102 6-H7
900 OCTAVIA ST 94102 6-H7
1000 LAGUNA ST 94102 6-H7
1000 LAGUNA ST 94115 6-H7
1200 WEBSTER ST 94117 6-G7
1200 WEBSTER ST 94115 6-G7
1300 FILLMORE ST 94117 6-G7
1300 FILLMORE ST 94115 6-G7
1400 STEINER ST 94117 6-G7
1400 STEINER ST 94115 6-G7
1500 PIERCE ST 94117 6-G7
1500 PIERCE ST 94115 6-G7
1600 SCOTT ST 94117 6-G7
1600 SCOTT ST 94115 6-G7
1650 SEYMOUR ST 94117 6-G7
1650 SEYMOUR ST 94115 6-G7
1700 DIVISADERO ST 94117 6-F7
1700 DIVISADERO ST 94115 6-F7
1800 BRODERICK ST 94117 6-F7
1800 BRODERICK ST 94115 6-F7
1900 BAKER ST 94117 6-F7
1900 BAKER ST 94115 6-F7
2000 LYON ST 94117 6-F7
2000 LYON ST 94115 6-F7
2100 CENTRAL AV 94117 6-F7
2100 CENTRAL AV 94115 6-F7
2200 MASONIC AV 94117 6-F7
2200 MASONIC AV 94118 6-F7
2250 ANNAPOLIS TER 94117 6-E7
2250 ANNAPOLIS TER 94118 6-E7
2300 TAMALPAIS TER 94117 6-E7
2300 TAMALPAIS TER 94118 6-E7
2370 ROSELYN TER 94117 6-E7
2370 ROSELYN TER 94118 6-E7
2430 KITTREDGE TER 94117 6-E7
2430 KITTREDGE TER 94118 6-E7
2500 CHABOT TER 94117 6-E7
2500 CHABOT TER 94118 6-E7
2550 TEMESCAL TER 94117 5-E7
2550 TEMESCAL TER 94118 5-E7
2600 PARKER AV 94117 5-E7
2600 PARKER AV 94118 5-E7
2700 STANYAN ST 94118 5-E7
2800 WILLARD ST N 94118 5-E7
2800 WILLARD ST N 94118 5-D7
2900 ARGUELLO BLVD 94118 5-D7

GOLDING LN SF
10 CORBETT AV 94131 10-F3
50 CORBETT AV 94131 10-F3
90 BURNETT AV 94131 10-F3

GOLD MINE DR SF
80 DIAMOND HEIGHTS BLVD 94131 14-F5
100 TOPAZ WY 94131 14-F5
130 ORA WY 94131 14-F5
180 OPALO LN 94131 14-F5
200 JADE PL 94131 14-F5
300 TOPAZ WY 94131 14-F5
500 DIAMOND HEIGHTS BLVD 94131 14-F5
500 ADDISON ST 94131 14-F5

GOLETA AV SF
1 CRESTLAKE DR 94132 13-A6
90 SLOAT BLVD 94132 13-A6

GONZALEZ DR SF
100 CARDENAS AV 94132 18-B1
130 DIAZ AV 94132 18-B1
200 CASTELO AV 94132 18-B1
300 FONT BLVD 94132 18-B1
BUCARELI DR 94132 18-B1
800 RIVAS AV 94132 18-B1
900 ARBALLO DR 94132 18-B1
GRIJALVA DR 94132 18-B1
430 JOSEPHA AV 94132 18-B1
500 GARCES DR 94132 18-B1

GORDON ST SF
HARRISON ST 94103 11-A1

GORGAS AV SF
HALLECK ST 94129 1-E3
MARSHALL ST 94129 2-E3
BIRMINGHAM RD 94129 2-E3
KENDALL DR 94129 2-E3
GENERAL KENNEDY AV 94129 2-E4
EDIE RD 94129 2-E4
TRUBY ST 94129 2-F4
LYON ST 94129 2-F4
FRANCISCO ST 94129 2-F4

GORHAM AV SF
20 BADGER ST 94112 14-G6
100 CAYUGA AV 94112 14-G6

GOUGH ST SF
100 MARKET ST 94102 10-H1
130 HAIGHT ST 94102 10-H1
140 ROSE ST 94102 6-H7
100 PAGE ST 94102 6-H7
150 LILY ST 94102 6-H7
200 OAK ST 94102 6-H7
230 HICKORY ST 94102 6-H7
300 FELL ST 94102 6-H7
350 LINDEN ST 94102 6-H7
400 HAYES ST 94102 6-H7
450 IVY ST 94102 6-H7
500 GROVE ST 94102 6-H7
600 FULTON ST 94102 6-H7
650 ASH ST 94102 6-H7
700 MCALLISTER ST 94102 6-H7
800 GOLDEN GATE AV 94102 6-H6
840 ELM ST 94102 6-H6
900 TURK ST 94102 6-H6
1000 EDDY ST 94109 6-H6
1050 WILLOW ST 94109 6-H6
1100 ELLIS ST 94109 6-H6
300 GEARY BLVD 94109 6-H6
300 PETER YORKE WY 94109 6-H6
300 STARR KING WY 94109 6-H6
1400 POST ST 94109 6-H6
1500 SUTTER ST 94109 6-H6
1520 FERN ST 94109 6-H6
1600 BUSH ST 94109 6-H5
1630 AUSTIN ST 94109 6-H5
1700 PINE ST 94109 6-H5
1800 CALIFORNIA ST 94109 6-H5
1900 SACRAMENTO ST 94109 6-H5
2000 CLAY ST 94109 6-H5
2100 WASHINGTON ST 94109 6-H5
2200 JACKSON ST 94109 6-H5
2300 PACIFIC AV 94109 6-H5
2400 BROADWAY 94109 6-H4
2500 VALLEJO ST 94123 6-H4
2600 GREEN ST 94123 6-H4
2700 UNION ST 94123 6-H4
2800 FILBERT ST 94123 2-H4
2900 GREENWICH ST 94123 2-H4
3000 LOMBARD ST 94123 2-H4
3100 CHESTNUT ST 94123 2-H4
3200 FRANCISCO ST 94123 2-H3
3300 BAY ST 94123 2-H3
1 MCCOPPIN ST 94103 10-H1
1 OTIS ST 94103 10-H1
50 COLTON ST 94103 10-H1
80 STEVENSON ST 94103 10-H1

Address	Cross Street	ZIP	Pg-Grid
GOUGH ST			SF
100	HAIGHT ST	94103	10-H1
100	MARKET ST	94103	10-H1
GOULD ST			SF
1	PAUL AV	94124	20-B1
100	SALINAS AV	94124	20-B1
GRACE ST			SF
1	MISSION ST	94103	6-J7
60	HOWARD ST	94103	6-J7
GRAFTON AV			SF
1	GETZ ST	94112	18-E1
1	MOUNT VERNON AV	94112	18-E1
60	HAROLD AV	94112	18-E1
160	LEE AV	94112	18-E1
260	BRIGHTON AV	94112	18-D1
370	PLYMOUTH AV	94112	18-D1
470	GRANADA AV	94112	18-D1
580	MIRAMAR AV	94112	18-D1
680	CAPITOL AV	94112	18-D1
780	FAXON AV	94112	18-D1
890	JULES AV	94112	18-D1
1000	ASHTON AV	94112	18-D1
1000	GARFIELD ST	94112	18-D1
GRAHAM ST			SF
	MORAGA AV	94129	5-D4
	SHERIDAN AV	94129	1-D4
	SAL ST	94129	1-D4
	OWEN ST	94129	1-E4
	LINCOLN BLVD	94129	1-E4
GRANADA AV			SF
300	OCEAN AV	94112	13-D7
400	SOUTHWOOD DR	94112	13-D7
1	LAKEVIEW AV	94112	18-D1
100	GRAFTON AV	94112	18-D1
200	HOLLOWAY AV	94112	18-D1
300	OCEAN AV	94112	18-D1
GRANAT CT			SF
100	9TH AV	94118	5-C7
GRAND VIEW AV			SF
30	GLENDALE ST	94114	10-F3
30	MARKET ST	94114	10-F3
30	STANTON ST	94114	10-F3
50	GRANDVIEW TER	94114	10-F3
80	ACME AL	94114	10-F3
100	ROMAIN ST	94114	10-F3
150	21ST ST	94114	10-F3
200	MORGAN AL	94114	10-F3
210	HOFFMAN AV	94114	10-F3
300	DIXIE AL	94114	10-F3
310	ALVARADO ST	94114	10-F3
400	23RD ST	94114	10-F3
500	ELIZABETH ST	94114	10-F3
600	24TH ST	94114	10-F4
700	25TH ST	94114	10-F4
800	CLIPPER ST	94114	10-F4
800	CLIPPER TER	94114	10-F4
GRANDVIEW TER			SF
100	GRAND VIEW AV	94114	10-F3
GRANT AV			SF
2200	NORTH POINT ST	94133	3-A3
2300	BEACH ST	94133	3-A3
1	MARKET ST	94108	7-A6
20	OFARRELL ST	94108	7-A6
100	GEARY ST	94108	7-A6
130	MAIDEN LN	94108	7-A5
200	POST ST	94108	7-A5
270	CAMPTON PL	94108	7-A5
280	TILLMAN PL	94108	7-A5
300	SUTTER ST	94108	7-A5
360	HARLAN PL	94108	7-A5
400	BUSH ST	94108	7-A5
500	PINE ST	94108	7-A5
520	VINTON CT	94108	7-A5
600	CALIFORNIA ST	94108	7-A5
700	SACRAMENTO ST	94108	7-A5
740	COMMERCIAL ST	94108	7-A5
800	CLAY ST	94108	7-A5
900	WASHINGTON ST	94108	7-A5
1000	JACKSON ST	94133	7-A4
1100	PACIFIC AV	94133	7-A4
1180	JACK KEROUAC AL	94133	7-A4
1200	BROADWAY	94133	7-A4
1230	COLUMBUS AV	94133	7-A4
1270	FRESNO ST	94133	7-A4
1300	VALLEJO ST	94133	7-A4
1400	GREEN ST	94133	3-A4
1500	UNION ST	94133	3-A4
1550	NOBLES AL	94133	3-A4
1600	FILBERT ST	94133	3-A4
1670	GERKE AL	94133	3-A4
1680	PARDEE AL	94133	3-A4
1700	GREENWICH ST	94133	3-A4
1730	EDITH ST	94133	3-A3
1740	EDGARDO PL	94133	3-A3
1850	LOMBARD ST	94133	3-A3
1830	WHITING ST	94133	3-A3
1900	CHESTNUT ST	94133	3-A3
1980	PFEIFFER ST	94133	3-A3
1930	PFEIFFER ST	94133	3-A3
2000	FRANCISCO ST	94133	3-A3
GRANVILLE WY			SF
1	PORTOLA DR	94127	13-D5
100	ULLOA ST	94127	13-D5
200	PARK AL	94127	13-D5
280	CLAREMONT BLVD	94127	13-D5
GRATTAN ST			SF
1	BELVEDERE ST	94117	10-E2
100	COLE ST	94117	10-E2
200	SHRADER ST	94117	10-E2
300	STANYAN ST	94117	10-E2
GRAYSTONE TER			SF
1	TWIN PEAKS BLVD	94114	10-E2
1	VILLA TER	94114	10-E2
150	VILLA TER	94114	10-F3
200	IRON AL	94114	10-F3
300	COPPER AL	94114	10-F3
400	CORBETT AV	94114	10-F3
400	GLENDALE ST	94114	10-F3
GREAT HWY			SF
500	POINT LOBOS AV	94121	4-G7
800	CABRILLO ST	94121	4-H7
	FULTON ST	-	8-H1
	JOHN F KENNEDY DR	-	8-H1
700	LINCOLN WY	94122	8-H2
2710	SLOAT BLVD	94132	12-H6
	SKYLINE BLVD	94132	12-H7
	LINCOLN WY	94122	8-H2
	IRVING ST	94122	8-H2
	JUDAH ST	94122	8-H2
	KIRKHAM ST	94122	8-H2
	LA PLAYA	94122	8-H3
	LAWTON ST	94122	8-H3
	MORAGA ST	94122	8-H3
	NORIEGA ST	94122	8-H3
	ORTEGA ST	94116	8-H3
	PACHECO ST	94116	8-H4
	QUINTARA ST	94116	8-H4
	RIVERA ST	94116	12-H4
2300	SANTIAGO ST	94116	12-H4
2400	TARAVAL ST	94116	12-H5
2480	48TH AV	94116	12-H5
2480	ULLOA ST	94116	12-H5
3600	SKYLINE BLVD	94132	12-H7
GREEN ST			SF
1	THE EMBARCADERO	94111	3-B4
50	FRONT ST	94111	3-B4
100	BATTERY ST	94111	3-B4
160	ICEHOUSE AL	94111	3-B4
200	SANSOME ST	94133	3-A4
300	MONTGOMERY ST	94133	3-A4
350	CASTLE ST	94133	3-A4
370	WINDSOR PL	94133	3-A4
400	KEARNY ST	94133	3-A4
430	SONOMA ST	94133	3-A4
450	VARENNES ST	94133	3-A4
500	GRANT AV	94133	3-A4
520	BANNAM PL	94133	3-A4
550	JASPER PL	94133	3-A4
600	STOCKTON ST	94133	3-A4
600	COLUMBUS AV	94133	3-A4
700	POWELL ST	94133	3-A4
780	AUGUSTA AL	94133	7-A4
770	EATON PL	94133	7-A4
800	MASON ST	94133	6-J4
900	TAYLOR ST	94133	6-J4
1000	JONES ST	94109	6-J4
1100	LEAVENWORTH ST	94109	6-J4
1130	HAMLIN ST	94109	6-J4
1200	HYDE ST	94109	6-J4
1270	EASTMAN ST	94109	6-J4
1300	LARKIN ST	94109	6-H4
1400	POLK ST	94109	6-H4
1500	VAN NESS AV	94109	6-H4
1600	FRANKLIN ST	94123	6-H4
1700	GOUGH ST	94123	6-H4
1800	OCTAVIA ST	94123	6-H4
1900	LAGUNA ST	94123	6-G4
2000	BUCHANAN ST	94123	6-G4
2100	WEBSTER ST	94123	6-G4
2200	FILLMORE ST	94123	6-G4
2300	STEINER ST	94123	6-G4
2400	PIERCE ST	94123	6-F4
2500	SCOTT ST	94123	6-F4
2600	DIVISADERO ST	94123	6-F4
2700	BRODERICK ST	94123	6-F4
2800	BAKER ST	94123	6-F5
2900	LYON ST	94123	6-F5
GREENOUGH AV			SF
	RALSTON AV	94129	1-C4
	POPE ST	94129	1-C4
	KOBBE AV	94129	1-C4
GREENVIEW CT			SF
100	DELLBROOK AV	94131	9-E3
GREENWICH ST			SF
100	BATTERY ST	94111	3-B3
200	SANSOME ST	94133	3-A3
420	CHILD ST	94133	3-A4
500	GRANT AV	94133	3-A4
520	KRAMER PL	94133	3-A4
540	JASPER PL	94133	3-A4
600	STOCKTON ST	94133	3-A4
650	BRYANT AL	94133	3-A4
700	POWELL ST	94133	3-A4
730	VIA BUFANO	94133	2-J4
780	COLUMBUS AV	94133	2-J4
800	MASON ST	94133	2-J4
850	JANSEN ST	94133	2-J4
900	TAYLOR ST	94133	2-J4
920	ROACH ST	94133	2-J4
1000	JONES ST	94133	2-J4
1100	LEAVENWORTH ST	94133	2-J4
1160	SOUTHARD PL	94109	2-J4
1200	HYDE ST	94109	2-J4
1300	LARKIN ST	94109	2-H4
1400	POLK ST	94109	2-H4
1420	GRENARD TER	94109	2-H4
1500	VAN NESS AV	94123	2-H4
1600	FRANKLIN ST	94123	2-H4
1660	IMPERIAL AV	94123	2-H4
1700	GOUGH ST	94123	2-H4
1800	OCTAVIA ST	94123	2-H4
1900	LAGUNA ST	94123	2-G4
2000	BUCHANAN ST	94123	2-G4
2100	WEBSTER ST	94123	2-G4
2200	FILLMORE ST	94123	2-G4
2300	STEINER ST	94123	2-G4
2400	PIERCE ST	94123	6-F4
2500	SCOTT ST	94123	6-F4
2600	DIVISADERO ST	94123	6-F4
2700	BRODERICK ST	94123	6-F4
2800	BAKER ST	94123	6-F4
2900	LYON ST	94123	6-F4
GREENWOOD AV			SF
1	HAZELWOOD AV	94112	13-E7
50	VALDEZ AV	94112	13-E7
100	COLON AV	94112	13-D7
200	PLYMOUTH AV	94112	13-D7
GRENARD TER			SF
1	GREENWICH ST	94109	2-H4
GRIFFITH ST			SF
1000	INNES AV	94124	15-D6
1000	NAVY RD	94124	15-D7
1100	OAKDALE AV	94124	15-D7
1170	CRISP RD	94124	15-D7
1200	PALOU AV	94124	15-D7
1300	QUESADA AV	94124	15-D7
1400	REVERE AV	94124	15-D7
1500	SHAFTER AV	94124	15-D7
1600	THOMAS AV	94124	15-D7
1000	CAMERON WY	94124	20-C1
1000	NICHOLS WY	94124	20-C1
1750	FITZGERALD AV	94124	20-C1
1790	GILMAN AV	94124	20-C1
2900	INGERSON AV	94124	20-C1
3000	JAMESTOWN AV	94124	20-C1
GRIJALVA DR			SF
1	JUAN BAUTISTA CIR	94132	18-B1
100	GONZALEZ DR	94132	18-B1
200	GARCES DR	94132	18-B1
GROTE PL			SF
1	FOLSOM ST	94105	7-B6
GROVE ST			SF
1	MARKET ST	94102	6-J7
50	LARKIN ST	94102	6-J7
100	POLK ST	94102	6-J7
200	VAN NESS AV	94102	6-H7
300	FRANKLIN ST	94102	6-H7
400	GOUGH ST	94102	6-H7
500	OCTAVIA ST	94102	6-H7
600	LAGUNA ST	94102	6-H7
700	BUCHANAN ST	94102	6-H7
750	BANNECKER WY	94102	6-H7
800	WEBSTER ST	94102	6-H7
900	FILLMORE ST	94117	6-G7
1000	STEINER ST	94117	6-G7
1200	SCOTT ST	94117	6-G7
1300	DIVISADERO ST	94117	6-G7
1400	BRODERICK ST	94117	6-F7
1500	BAKER ST	94117	6-F7
1600	LYON ST	94117	6-F7
1700	CENTRAL AV	94117	6-F7
1800	MASONIC AV	94117	6-F7
1900	ASHBURY ST	94117	6-E7
2000	CLAYTON ST	94117	6-E7
2100	COLE ST	94117	6-E7
2200	SHRADER ST	94117	6-E7
GUERRERO ST			SF
1	MARKET ST	94103	10-H1
100	DUBOCE AV	94103	10-H1
130	CLINTON PK	94103	10-H1
160	BROSNAN ST	94103	10-H1
200	14TH ST	94103	10-H1
300	15TH ST	94103	10-H2
400	16TH ST	94110	10-H2
430	GAISER CT	94110	10-H2
450	CAMP ST	94110	10-H2
500	17TH ST	94110	10-H2
550	DORLAND ST	94110	10-H2
600	18TH ST	94110	10-H2
700	19TH ST	94110	10-H2
750	CUMBERLAND ST	94110	10-H3
800	20TH ST	94110	10-H3
850	LIBERTY ST	94110	10-H3
900	21ST ST	94110	10-H3
950	HILL ST	94110	10-H3
1000	22ND ST	94110	10-H3
1020	ALVARADO ST	94110	10-H3
1070	23RD ST	94110	10-H3
1130	ELIZABETH ST	94110	10-H3
1190	24TH ST	94110	10-H4
1300	25TH ST	94110	10-H4
1400	26TH ST	94110	10-H4
1450	CESAR CHAVEZ ST	94110	14-H4
1500	27TH ST	94110	14-H4
1600	DUNCAN ST	94110	14-H4
1650	28TH ST	94110	14-H4
1700	SAN JOSE AV	94110	14-H4
GUTTENBERG ST			SF
1	LINCOLN CT	94112	19-F2
100	HANOVER ST	94112	19-F2
150	PRETOR WY	94112	19-F2
200	BRUNSWICK ST	94112	19-F2
310	MORSE ST	94112	19-F2
400	MISSION ST	94112	19-F2
GUY PL			SF
1	1ST ST	94105	7-B6
100	LANSING ST	94105	7-B6
H			
H ST			SF
100	MAHAN ST	94124	21-E1
350	MANSEAU ST	94124	20-E1
600	SPEAR AV	94124	20-E1
HAHN ST			SF
1	SUNRISE WY	94134	19-J2
30	BLYTHDALE AV	94134	19-J2
130	SUNNYDALE AV	94134	19-J2
230	VISITACION AV	94134	19-J2
300	LELAND AV	94134	19-J2
HAIGHT ST			SF
1	MARKET ST	94102	10-H1
1	GOUGH ST	94102	10-H1
10	GOUGH ST	94102	10-H1
100	OCTAVIA ST	94102	10-H1
200	LAGUNA ST	94102	10-H1
300	BUCHANAN ST	94102	10-H1
400	WEBSTER ST	94117	10-G1
500	FILLMORE ST	94117	10-G1
600	STEINER ST	94117	10-G1
700	PIERCE ST	94117	10-G1
800	SCOTT ST	94117	10-G1
900	DIVISADERO ST	94117	10-G1
1000	BRODERICK ST	94117	10-F1
1100	BAKER ST	94117	10-F1
1100	BUENA VISTA AV E	94117	10-F1
1220	LYON ST	94117	10-F1
1200	BUENA VISTA AV W	94117	10-F1
1300	CENTRAL AV	94117	10-F1
1400	MASONIC AV	94117	10-F1
1500	ASHBURY ST	94117	10-F1
1610	CLAYTON ST	94117	10-E1
1600	BELVEDERE ST	94117	10-E1
1690	COLE ST	94117	10-E1
1680	COLE ST	94117	10-E1
1800	SHRADER ST	94117	9-E1
1900	STANYAN ST	94117	9-E1
HALE ST			SF
1	SAN BRUNO AV	94134	15-A6
100	BARNEVELD AV	94134	15-A6
200	MERRILL ST	94134	15-A6
300	BOYLSTON ST	94134	14-J6
400	BOWDOIN ST	94134	14-J6
HALLAM ST			SF
1	FOLSOM ST	94103	7-A7
30	DECKER AL	94103	7-A7
70	BRUSH PL	94103	7-A7
HALLECK ST			SF
	LINCOLN BLVD	94129	1-E4
	MESA AV	94129	1-E3
	YOUNG ST	94129	1-E3
	GORGAS AV	94129	1-E3
	VALLEJO ST	94129	1-E3
	MASON ST	94129	1-E3
	OLD MASON ST	94129	1-E3
1	FRONT ST	94111	7-B5
100	BATTERY ST	94104	7-B5
200	SANSOME ST	94104	7-B5
300	LEIDESDORFF ST	94104	7-B5
HAMERTON AV			SF
1	CHENERY ST	94131	14-F6
200	MANGELS AV	94131	14-F6
HAMILTON ST			SF
	MAULDIN ST	94129	1-C3
	PEARCE ST	94129	1-C3
	MARINE DR	94129	1-C3
1	SILVER AV	94134	14-J6
80	SILLIMAN ST	94134	14-J7
180	FELTON ST	94134	14-J7
280	BURROWS ST	94134	14-J7
380	BACON ST	94134	14-J7
400	WAYLAND ST	94134	15-A7
600	WOOLSEY ST	94134	15-A7
800	DWIGHT ST	94134	15-A7
900	MANSELL ST	94134	20-A1
1000	ANKENY ST	94134	20-A1
1000	DELTA ST	94134	20-A1
HAMLIN ST			SF
1	GREEN ST	94109	6-J4
HAMPSHIRE ST			SF
100	ALAMEDA ST	94103	11-A1
200	15TH ST	94103	11-A1
400	17TH ST	94110	11-A2
500	MARIPOSA ST	94110	11-A2
600	18TH ST	94110	11-A2
700	19TH ST	94110	11-A2
800	20TH ST	94110	11-A2
900	21ST ST	94110	11-A3
1000	22ND ST	94110	11-A3
1100	23RD ST	94110	11-A3
1200	24TH ST	94110	11-A3
1300	25TH ST	94110	11-A4
1400	26TH ST	94110	11-A4
1500	CESAR CHAVEZ ST	94110	11-A4
1500	CESAR CHAVEZ ST	94110	15-A4
1600	PERALTA AV	94110	15-A4
HANCOCK ST			SF
1	CHURCH ST	94114	10-H2
100	SANCHEZ ST	94114	10-G2
200	NOE ST	94114	10-G2
HANOVER ST			SF
1	POPE ST	94112	19-F2
80	ALLISON ST	94112	19-F2
150	CONCORD ST	94112	19-F2
150	WATT AV	94112	19-F2
240	GUTTENBERG ST	94112	19-F2
420	LOWELL ST	94112	19-F2
HARBOR RD			SF
1	BERTHA LN	94124	15-D6
120	INGALLS ST	94124	15-D6
300	NORTHRIDGE RD	94124	15-D6
HARDIE AV			SF
	BARNARD AV	94129	5-D4
	FUNSTON AV	94129	5-D4
	ARGUELLO BLVD	94129	5-D4
HARDIE PL			SF
100	KEARNY ST	94108	7-A5
HARDING RD			SF
100	SKYLINE BLVD	94132	12-H7
HARE ST			SF
1	MIDDLEPOINT RD	94124	15-D6
HARKNESS AV			SF
470	DELTA ST	94134	20-A1
400	MILL ST	94134	20-A1
380	ALDER ST	94134	20-A1
330	RUTLAND ST	94134	20-A1
300	SPARTA ST	94134	20-A1
200	GOETTINGEN ST	94134	20-A1
100	BRUSSELS ST	94134	20-A1
1	GIRARD ST	94134	20-A1
100	SAN BRUNO AV	94134	20-A1
HARLAN PL			SF
1	MARK LN	94108	7-A5
30	GRANT AV	94108	7-A5
HARLEM AL			SF
1	OFARRELL ST	94109	6-J6
HARLOW ST			SF
1	16TH ST	94114	10-G2
HARNEY RD			SF
1	ALANA WY	94134	20-B2
1	HARNEY WY	94134	20-B2
100	ALANA WY	94134	20-B2
HARNEY WY			SF
1	ALANA WY	94134	20-B2
1	ALANA WY	94124	20-B2
1	HARNEY RD	94124	20-B2
90	EXECUTIVE PARK BLVD	94124	20-C2
200	JAMESTOWN AV	94124	20-C2
200	JAMESTOWN AVEX	94124	20-C2
HAROLD AV			SF
80	GRAFTON AV	94112	18-E1
200	HOLLOWAY AV	94112	18-E1
220	BRUCE AV	94112	13-E7
300	OCEAN AV	94112	13-E7
HARPER ST			SF
1	30TH ST	94131	14-G5
60	RANDALL ST	94131	14-G5
100	LAIDLEY ST	94131	14-G5
HARRIET ST			SF
1	HOWARD ST	94103	7-A7
100	FOLSOM ST	94103	7-A7
200	HARRISON ST	94103	7-A7
240	AHERN WY	94103	7-A7
300	BRYANT ST	94103	7-A7
400	BRANNAN ST	94103	7-B7
HARRINGTON ST			SF
1	MISSION ST	94112	14-G7
100	ALEMANY BLVD	94112	14-G7
HARRIS PL			SF
100	LAGUNA ST	94123	2-G4
HARRISON BLVD			SF
	CENTRAL MAGAZINE RD	94129	1-B4
	WASHINGTON BLVD	94129	1-B4
	HITCHCOCK ST	94129	1-B4
	KOBBE AV	94129	1-B4
HARRISON ST			SF
1	THE EMBARCADERO	94105	7-C5
1	STEUART ST	94105	7-C5
100	SPEAR ST	94105	7-C6
200	MAIN ST	94105	7-C6
300	BEALE ST	94105	7-C6
400	FREMONT ST	94105	7-C6
500	1ST ST	94105	7-B6
550	ESSEX ST	94105	7-B6
590	CHARLESTOWN PL	94105	7-B6
600	2ND ST	94107	7-B6
620	VASSAR PL	94107	7-B6
650	HAWTHORNE ST	94107	7-B6
700	3RD ST	94107	7-B6
720	LAPU LAPU ST	94107	7-B6
800	4TH ST	94107	7-B7
900	5TH ST	94107	7-A7
920	MERLIN ST	94107	7-A7
950	OAK GROVE ST	94107	7-A7
970	MORRIS ST	94107	7-A7
1000	6TH ST	94103	7-A7
1020	HARRIET ST	94103	7-A7
1040	COLUMBIA SQUARE ST	94103	7-A7
1060	SHERMAN ST	94103	7-A7
1100	7TH ST	94103	7-A7
1120	LANGTON ST	94103	7-A7
1150	CHESLEY ST	94103	7-A7
1160	BERWICK PL	94103	7-A7
	8TH ST	94103	11-A1
	GORDON ST	94103	11-A1
1300	9TH ST	94103	11-A1
	DORE ST	94103	11-A1
1400	10TH ST	94103	10-J1
1500	11TH ST	94103	10-J1
1550	NORFOLK ST	94103	10-J1
1600	12TH ST	94103	10-J1
1800	14TH ST	94103	10-J1
1840	ALAMEDA ST	94103	10-J1
1900	15TH ST	94103	10-J1
1930	15TH ST	94103	10-J2
1970	TREAT AV	94103	10-J2
2000	TREAT AV	94103	10-J2

Address	Cross Street	ZIP	City Pg-Grid
HARRISON ST			SF
2010	16TH ST	94110	10-J2
2090	17TH ST	94110	10-J2
2160	MARIPOSA ST	94110	10-J2
2200	18TH ST	94110	10-J2
2250	18TH ST	94110	10-J2
2300	19TH ST	94110	10-J2
2320	19TH ST	94110	10-J2
2350	MISTRAL ST	94110	10-J2
2400	20TH ST	94110	10-J3
2500	21ST ST	94110	10-J3
2600	22ND ST	94110	10-J3
2700	23RD ST	94110	10-J3
2800	24TH ST	94110	10-J3
2900	25TH ST	94110	10-J4
3000	26TH ST	94110	10-J4
3100	CESAR CHAVEZ ST	94110	14-J4
3200	PRECITA AV	94110	14-J4
3300	NORWICH ST	94110	14-J4
3400	RIPLEY ST	94110	14-J5
HARRY ST			SF
100	BEACON ST	94131	14-G5
HARTFORD ST			SF
1	17TH ST	94114	10-G2
100	18TH ST	94114	10-G2
200	19TH ST	94114	10-G2
300	20TH ST	94114	10-G2
HARVARD ST			SF
1	SILVER AV	94134	14-H7
50	PIOCHE ST	94134	14-H7
160	SILLIMAN ST	94134	14-H7
270	FELTON ST	94134	14-H7
380	BURROWS ST	94134	14-H7
500	BACON ST	94134	14-H7
HASTINGS TER			SF
1	ALLEN ST	94109	2-J4
1	HYDE ST	94109	2-J4
HATTIE ST			SF
1	CORBETT AV	94114	10-F2
50	MARKET ST	94114	10-F2
100	18TH ST	94114	10-F2
100	STORRIE ST	94114	10-F2
HAVELOCK ST			SF
200	CIRCULAR AV	94112	14-F7
370	EDNA ST	94112	14-E7
1	SAN JOSE AV	94112	14-F7
150	ARAGO ST	94112	14-F7
100	ARCO WY	94112	14-F7
HAVENS ST			SF
1	LEAVENWORTH ST	94109	2-J4
HAVENSIDE DR			SF
100	OCEAN AV	94132	13-A6
200	EUCALYPTUS DR	94132	13-A6
HAWES ST			SF
3000	INNES AV	94124	15-D6
3100	HUNTERS POINT BLVD	94124	15-D6
1200	PALOU AV	94124	15-D7
1300	QUESADA AV	94124	15-C7
1400	REVERE AV	94124	15-C7
1500	SHAFTER AV	94124	15-C7
1600	THOMAS AV	94124	15-C7
1700	UNDERWOOD AV	94124	15-C7
2300	YOSEMITE AV	94124	15-C7
2400	ARMSTRONG AV	94124	20-C1
2600	CARROLL AV	94124	20-C1
2700	DONNER AV	94124	20-C1
2800	EGBERT AV	94124	20-C1
2900	FITZGERALD AV	94124	20-C1
3000	GILMAN AV	94124	20-C1
3100	HOLLISTER AV	94124	20-C1
3200	INGERSON AV	94124	20-B1
3300	JAMESTOWN AV	94124	20-B1
HAWKINS LN			SF
1	WHITNEY YOUNG CIR	94124	15-C6
20	JAKEY CT	94124	15-C6
HAWTHORNE ST			SF
1	HOWARD ST	94105	7-B6
1	HOWARD ST	94103	7-B6
100	FOLSOM ST	94107	7-B6
200	HARRISON ST	94107	7-B6
HAYES ST			SF
1	9TH ST	94102	6-J7
1	LARKIN ST	94102	6-J7
1	MARKET ST	94102	6-J7
100	POLK ST	94102	6-J7
200	VAN NESS AV	94102	6-J7
300	FRANKLIN ST	94102	6-H7
400	GOUGH ST	94102	6-H7
500	OCTAVIA ST	94102	6-H7
600	LAGUNA ST	94102	6-H7
700	BUCHANAN ST	94102	6-H7
770	LINDEN ST	94102	6-H7
800	WEBSTER ST	94117	6-G7
900	FILLMORE ST	94117	6-G7
1000	STEINER ST	94117	6-G7
1100	PIERCE ST	94117	6-G7
1200	SCOTT ST	94117	6-G7
1300	DIVISADERO ST	94117	6-F7
1400	BRODERICK ST	94117	6-F7
1500	BAKER ST	94117	6-F7
1600	LYON ST	94117	6-F7
1700	CENTRAL AV	94117	6-F7
1800	MASONIC AV	94117	6-F7
1900	ASHBURY ST	94117	6-E7
2000	CLAYTON ST	94117	6-E7
2100	COLE ST	94117	6-E7
2200	SHRADER ST	94117	5-E7
2300	STANYAN ST	94117	5-E7
HAYS ST			SF
	WEDEMEYER ST	94129	5-C5
	BELLES ST	94129	5-C5
	BROWN ST	94129	5-C5
HAZELWOOD AV			SF
	GLOBE AL	94127	13-D6
	LOS PALMOS DR	94127	13-D6
500	YERBA BUENA AV	94127	13-D6
500	CASITAS AV	94127	13-D6
1	JUDSON AV	94112	13-E7
20	GREENWOOD AV	94112	13-E7
40	STAPLES AV	94112	13-E6
70	FLOOD AV	94112	13-E6
100	MONTECITO AV	94112	13-E6
200	MONTEREY BLVD	94127	13-E6
250	JOOST AV	94127	13-E6
300	MANGELS AV	94127	13-D6
370	BRENTWOOD AV	94127	13-D6
HEAD ST			SF
300	RANDOLPH ST	94132	18-C1
500	SARGENT ST	94132	18-C1
630	SHIELDS ST	94132	18-C1
770	GARFIELD ST	94132	18-C1
900	HOLLOWAY AV	94127	13-D7
900	HOLLOWAY AV	94132	13-D7
	ASHTON AV	94127	13-D7
	ASHTON AV	94132	13-D7
200	PALMETTO AV	94132	18-C2
1	SHAKESPEARE ST	94112	18-C2
200	SANTA BARBARA AV	94112	18-C2
HEARST AV			SF
1	CIRCULAR AV	94131	14-F6
100	BADEN ST	94131	14-F6
200	CONGO ST	94131	14-F6
300	DETROIT ST	94112	14-F6
400	EDNA ST	94112	14-E6
500	FOERSTER ST	94112	14-E6
600	GENNESSEE ST	94112	13-E6
700	RIDGEWOOD AV	94112	13-E6
HEATHER AV			SF
1	MAYFAIR DR	94118	5-E6
100	EUCLID AV	94118	5-E6
HELEN ST			SF
	CALIFORNIA ST	94109	6-J5
HELENA ST			SF
1	ELMIRA ST	94124	15-A6
120	CHARTER OAK AV	94124	15-A6
270	BOUTWELL ST	94124	15-A6
400	BAYSHORE BLVD	94124	15-A6
HEMLOCK ST			SF
1	LARKIN ST	94109	6-J6
100	POLK ST	94109	6-H6
200	DANIEL BURNHAM CT	94109	6-H6
200	VAN NESS AV	94109	6-H6
600	LAGUNA ST	94115	6-H6
HEMWAY TER			SF
	FULTON ST	94117	6-E7
HENRY ST			SF
1	SANCHEZ ST	94114	10-G1
100	NOE ST	94114	10-G1
200	CASTRO ST	94114	10-G1
HENRY ADAMS ST			SF
1	DIVISION ST	94103	11-A1
100	ALAMEDA ST	94103	11-A1
100	KANSAS ST	94103	11-A1
HERBST RD			SF
3100	SKYLINE BLVD	94132	12-J6
HERMANN ST			SF
1	LAGUNA ST	94102	10-H1
100	BUCHANAN ST	94102	10-H1
200	WEBSTER ST	94117	10-H1
250	CHURCH ST	94117	10-G1
300	FILLMORE ST	94117	10-G1
400	STEINER ST	94117	10-G1
HERNANDEZ AV			SF
1	WOODSIDE AV	94127	13-D4
100	LAGUNA HONDA BLVD	94127	13-D4
200	GARCIA AV	94127	13-D4
200	VASQUEZ AV	94127	13-D4
300	MERCED AV	94127	13-D4
HERON ST			SF
1	BERWICK PL	94103	7-A7
100	8TH ST	94103	7-A7
HESTER AV			SF
1	BAYSHORE BLVD	94134	20-B2
300	BAYSHORE BLVD	94134	20-B2
HEYMAN AV			SF
1	COLERIDGE ST	94110	14-H5
100	PROSPECT AV	94110	14-H5
HICKORY ST			SF
1	VAN NESS AV	94102	6-H7
100	FRANKLIN ST	94102	6-H7
200	GOUGH ST	94102	6-H7
	OCTAVIA ST	94102	6-H7
400	LAGUNA ST	94102	6-H7
500	BUCHANAN ST	94102	6-H7
600	WEBSTER ST	94102	6-H7
HICKS RD			SF
	FUNSTON AV	94129	5-D4
HIDALGO TER			SF
100	DOLORES ST	94103	10-H1
HIGH ST			SF
90	CLIPPER TER	94114	10-F4
HIGHLAND AV			SF
	ARLINGTON ST	94131	14-H5
20	SAN JOSE AV	94110	14-H5
100	MISSION ST	94110	14-H5
200	PATTON ST	94110	14-H5
300	HOLLY PARK CIR	94110	14-H5
300	HOLLY PARK CIR	94110	14-J6
350	BENNINGTON ST	94110	14-J6
400	ANDOVER ST	94110	14-J6
HIGUERA AV			SF
1	VIDAL DR	94132	18-A1
100	ARBALLO DR	94132	18-A1
HILIRITAS AV			SF
1	DIAMOND ST	94131	14-G5
100	ARBOR ST	94131	14-G5
S HILL BLVD			SF
80	CANYON DR	94112	19-G2
110	TOYON LN	94112	19-G2
160	BALTIMORE WY	94112	19-G2
200	CHICAGO WY	94112	19-G2
240	ROLPH ST	94112	19-G2
240	WINDING WY	94112	19-G2
290	PRAGUE ST	94112	19-G2
290	MUNICH ST	94112	19-G2
340	GENEVA AV	94112	19-G2
340	MOSCOW ST	94112	19-G2
HILL DR			SF
	GALVEZ AV	94124	16-E7
	COLEMAN ST	94124	16-E7
	HUDSON AV	94124	16-E7
HILL ST			SF
1	VALENCIA ST	94110	10-H3
100	GUERRERO ST	94110	10-H3
300	CHURCH ST	94114	10-H3
400	SANCHEZ ST	94114	10-G3
500	NOE ST	94114	10-G3
600	CASTRO ST	94114	10-G3
HILLCREST CT			SF
1	LANSDALE AV	94127	13-E6
HILLPOINT AV			SF
100	PARNASSUS AV	94117	9-E2
HILLVIEW CT			SF
1	LINDSAY CIR	94124	15-C6
1	WHITNEY YOUNG CIR	94124	15-C6
HILLWAY AV			SF
1	CARL ST	94117	9-D2
1	CARL ST	94143	9-D2
100	PARNASSUS AV	94117	9-D2
100	PARNASSUS AV	94143	9-D2
HILTON ST			SF
1	CORTLAND AV	94124	15-A5
100	ALEMANY BLVD	94124	15-A5
HIMMELMANN PL			SF
1	PACIFIC AV	94133	6-J4
100	BROADWAY	94133	6-J4
HITCHCOCK ST			SF
	PARK BLVD	94129	5-C4
	UPTON AV	94129	1-C4
	WRIGHT LP	94129	1-C4
	HARRISON BLVD	94129	1-C4
HOFF ST			SF
1	16TH ST	94110	10-H2
100	17TH ST	94110	10-H2
HOFFMAN AV			SF
1	GRAND VIEW AV	94114	10-F3
10	22ND ST	94114	10-F3
100	ALVARADO ST	94114	10-F3
200	23RD ST	94114	10-F3
300	ELIZABETH ST	94114	10-F4
400	24TH ST	94114	10-F4
500	25TH ST	94114	10-F4
HOFFMAN ST			SF
	LINCOLN BLVD	94129	1-C3
	ARMISTEAD RD	94129	1-C3
HOLLADAY AV			SF
100	PERALTA AV	94110	15-A4
130	EVE ST	94110	15-A4
150	WRIGHT ST	94110	15-A4
210	YORK ST	94110	15-A4
300	RUTLEDGE ST	94110	15-A4
340	COSTA ST	94110	15-A5
370	FAITH ST	94110	15-A5
400	JOY ST	94110	15-A5
500	MAYFLOWER ST	94110	15-A5
HOLLAND CT			SF
1	HOWARD ST	94103	7-A6
HOLLIS ST			SF
1	ELLIS ST	94115	6-G6
60	OFARRELL ST	94115	6-G6
HOLLISTER AV			SF
1000	HAWES ST	94124	20-B1
1100	INGALLS ST	94124	20-B1
1200	JENNINGS ST	94124	20-B1
1300	3RD ST	94124	20-B1
HOLLOWAY AV			SF
	ASHTON AV	94112	18-D1
	ASHTON AV	94132	18-D1
900	ORIZABA AV	94132	18-D1
950	BRIGHT ST	94132	18-D1
1000	HEAD ST	94132	18-C1
1000	HEAD ST	94127	18-C1
	VICTORIA ST	94132	18-C1
	VICTORIA ST	94127	18-C1
1050	VICTORIA ST	94132	18-C1
1050	VICTORIA ST	94127	18-C1
1100	RAMSELL ST	94132	18-C1
1100	RAMSELL ST	94127	18-C1
1120	DE SOTO ST	94132	18-C1
1120	DE SOTO ST	94127	18-C1
1170	ARCH ST	94132	18-C1
1170	ARCH ST	94127	18-C1
1730	CORONA ST	94132	18-C1
1730	CORONA ST	94127	18-C1
1730	VERNON ST	94132	18-C1
1730	VERNON ST	94127	18-C1
1730	BORICA ST	94132	18-C1
1730	BORICA ST	94127	18-C1
1730	RALSTON ST	94132	18-C1
1730	RALSTON ST	94127	18-C1
1730	ALVISO ST	94132	18-C1
1730	ALVISO ST	94127	18-C1
1730	BYXBEE ST	94132	18-C1
1730	BYXBEE ST	94127	18-C1
1730	MONTICELLO ST	94132	18-C1
1730	MONTICELLO ST	94127	18-C1
1730	BEVERLY ST	94132	18-C1
1730	BEVERLY ST	94127	18-C1
	LUNADO WY	94132	18-C1
	LUNADO WY	94127	18-C1
	JUNIPERO SERRA BLVD	94132	18-C1
	JUNIPERO SERRA BLVD	94127	18-C1
1730	STRATFORD DR	94132	18-B1
1470	DENSLOW DR	94132	18-B1
1500	19TH AV	94132	18-B1
1730	VARELA AV	94132	18-B1
1730	CARDENAS AV	94132	18-B1
1730	ARELLANO AV	94132	18-B1
1730	TAPIA DR	94132	18-B1
1800	FONT BLVD	94132	18-B1
1	HAROLD AV	94112	18-E1
90	LEE AV	94112	18-E1
190	BRIGHTON AV	94112	18-D1
280	PLYMOUTH AV	94112	18-D1
370	GRANADA AV	94112	18-D1
470	MIRAMAR AV	94112	18-D1
570	CAPITOL AV	94112	18-D1
660	FAXON AV	94112	18-D1
760	JULES AV	94112	18-D1
900	ASHTON AV	94112	18-D1
HOLLY PARK CIR			SF
90	BOCANA ST	94110	14-H5
180	NEWMAN ST	94110	14-J5
270	HIGHLAND AV	94110	14-H6
400	PARK ST	94110	14-H6
500	MURRAY ST	94110	14-H6
600	PARK ST	94110	14-H6
700	HIGHLAND AV	94110	14-H5
750	APPLETON AV	94110	14-H5
1	ELSIE ST	94110	14-H5
100	BOCANA ST	94110	14-H5
HOLLYWOOD CT			SF
1	POPE ST	94112	19-F2
HOLYOKE ST			SF
1	FELTON ST	94134	15-A7
300	BURROWS ST	94134	15-A7
600	BACON ST	94134	15-A7
800	WAYLAND ST	94134	15-A7
1100	WOOLSEY ST	94134	15-A7
1200	KAREN CT	94134	15-A7
1	ANKENY ST	94134	20-A1
1500	MANSELL ST	94134	20-A1
1500	CAMPBELL AV	94134	20-A2
HOMER ST			SF
	CHESLEY ST	94103	7-A7
HOMESTEAD ST			SF
1	24TH ST	94114	10-F4
100	25TH ST	94114	10-F4
HOMEWOOD CT			SF
100	WILDWOOD WY	94112	13-D7
HOOPER ST			SF
100	7TH ST	94107	11-B1
200	8TH ST	94107	11-B1
HOPKINS AV			SF
1	CORBETT AV	94131	10-F3
100	BURNETT AV	94131	10-F3
HORACE ST			SF
1	25TH ST	94110	10-J4
100	26TH ST	94110	10-J4
HORNE AV			SF
	SPEAR AV	94124	16-E7
	GALVEZ AV	94124	16-E7
	ROBINSON ST	94124	16-E7
HOTALING ST			SF
1	WASHINGTON ST	94111	7-A4
100	JACKSON ST	94111	7-A4
HOUSTON ST			SF
1	COLUMBUS AV	94133	2-J3
100	JONES ST	94133	2-J3
HOWARD RD			SF
	BOWLEY ST	94129	5-B5
	LINCOLN BLVD	94129	5-B5
HOWARD ST			SF
1	STEUART ST	94105	7-C5
100	SPEAR ST	94105	7-C5
200	MAIN ST	94105	7-B5
300	BEALE ST	94105	7-B5
400	FREMONT ST	94105	7-B5
500	1ST ST	94105	7-B6
580	MALDEN AL	94105	7-B6
600	2ND ST	94105	7-B6
640	NEW MONTGOMERY ST	94105	7-B6
650	HAWTHORNE ST	94103	7-B6
700	3RD ST	94103	7-B6
800	4TH ST	94103	7-A6
820	HOLLAND CT	94103	7-A6
900	5TH ST	94103	7-A6
930	MARY ST	94103	7-A7
1000	6TH ST	94103	7-A7
1020	HARRIET ST	94103	7-A7
	RUSS ST	94103	7-A7
1070	MOSS ST	94103	7-A7
1100	7TH ST	94103	7-A7
1130	LANGTON ST	94103	7-A7
1160	RAUSCH ST	94103	7-A7
1190	SUMNER ST	94103	7-A7
1220	8TH ST	94103	6-J7
1300	9TH ST	94103	6-J7
1400	WASHBURN ST	94103	6-J7
1390	DORE ST	94103	6-J7
1410	GRACE ST	94103	6-J7
1440	10TH ST	94103	6-J7
1500	11TH ST	94103	10-J1
1550	LAFAYETTE ST	94103	10-J1
1600	12TH ST	94103	10-J1
1700	S VAN NESS AV	94103	10-J1
HOWTH ST			SF
1	MOUNT VERNON AV	94112	18-E1
1	JOSIAH AV	94112	18-E1
190	NIAGARA AV	94112	18-E1
400	GENEVA AV	94112	14-E7
500	OCEAN AV	94112	14-E7
HUBBELL ST			SF
100	7TH ST	94107	11-B1
200	16TH ST	94107	11-B1
HUDSON AV			SF
2100	TOLAND ST	94124	15-B5
1310	INGALLS ST	94124	15-D6
1310	BERTHA LN	94124	15-D6
1350	WHITNEY YOUNG CIR	94124	15-C6
1380	ARDATH CT	94124	15-C6
1390	WESTBROOK CT	94124	15-C6
1410	CASHMERE ST	94124	15-C6
1420	REUEL CT	94124	15-C6
1440	KEITH ST	94124	15-C6
1500	MENDELL ST	94124	15-C5
1600	NEWHALL ST	94124	15-C5
1620	3RD ST	94124	15-C5
1700	PHELPS ST	94124	15-C5
1300	HUNTERS POINT BLVD	94124	15-D6
1000	FITCH ST	94124	15-D6
600	COLEMAN ST	94124	16-E7
600	HILL DR	94124	16-E7
700	FRIEDELL ST	94124	15-E7
800	DONAHUE ST	94124	15-E7
HUGO ST			SF
1	ARGUELLO BLVD	94122	9-D2
100	2ND AV	94122	9-D2
200	3RD AV	94122	9-D2
300	4TH AV	94122	9-D2
400	5TH AV	94122	9-D2
500	6TH AV	94122	9-D2
600	7TH AV	94122	9-D2
HULBERT AL			SF
	CLARA ST	94107	7-B7
HUMBOLDT ST			SF
100	ILLINOIS ST	94107	11-C3
HUNTER RD			SF
	COMPTON RD	94129	5-B4
	WASHINGTON BLVD	94129	5-B4
	CENTRAL MAGAZINE RD	94129	5-B4
HUNTERS POINT BLVD			SF
1	INNES AV	94124	15-D6
110	HAWES ST	94124	15-D6
140	HUDSON AV	94124	15-D6
500	EVANS AV	94124	15-D6
500	JENNINGS ST	94124	15-D6
500	MIDDLEPOINT RD	94124	15-D6
HUNTERS POINT EXWY			SF
1	GILMAN AV	94124	20-D2
190	DONNER AV	94124	20-C2
500	JAMESTOWN AVEX	94124	20-C2
HUNTINGTON DR			SF
1	COUNTRY CLUB DR	94132	12-J6
200	COUNTRY CLUB DR	94132	12-J6
HURON AV			SF
400	ALEMANY BLVD	94112	19-E2
400	OTTAWA AV	94112	19-E2
440	SALA TER	94112	19-E2
490	FOOTE AV	94112	19-E2
540	FREDSON CT	94112	19-E2
600	NAGLEE AV	94112	19-E2
650	MONETA WY	94112	19-E2
700	WHIPPLE AV	94112	19-E2
750	MILAN TER	94112	18-E2
810	FARRAGUT AV	94112	18-E2
860	LAURA ST	94112	18-E2
900	LAWRENCE AV	94112	18-E2
1010	SICKLES AV	94112	18-E2
HUSSEY ST			SF
300	MANSEAU ST	94124	21-E1
600	SPEAR AV	94124	21-E1
1	MAHAN ST	94124	21-E1
300	MANSEAU ST	94124	21-E1
HYDE ST			SF
1	8TH ST	94102	6-J7
1	MARKET ST	94102	6-J7
60	MCALLISTER ST	94102	6-J6
100	GOLDEN GATE AV	94102	6-J6
200	TURK ST	94102	6-J6
300	EDDY ST	94109	6-J6
400	ELLIS ST	94109	6-J6
500	OFARRELL ST	94109	6-J6
600	GEARY ST	94109	6-J6
700	POST ST	94109	6-J6
800	SUTTER ST	94109	6-J5
900	BUSH ST	94109	6-J5
1000	PINE ST	94109	6-J5
1100	CALIFORNIA ST	94109	6-J5
1200	SACRAMENTO ST	94109	6-J5
1230	TROY AL	94109	6-J5
1300	CLAY ST	94109	6-J5
1400	WASHINGTON ST	94109	6-J5
1500	JACKSON ST	94109	6-J5
1600	PACIFIC AV	94109	6-J4
1630	LYNCH ST	94109	6-J4
1660	MORRELL ST	94109	6-J4
1630	BROADWAY	94109	6-J4
1800	VALLEJO ST	94109	6-J4
1900	GREEN ST	94109	6-J4

Address	Cross Street	ZIP	City Pg-Grid
HYDE ST			SF
1920	DELGADO PL	94109	6-J4
1940	RUSSELL ST	94109	6-J4
1960	WARNER PL	94109	6-J4
2000	UNION ST	94109	2-J4
2030	ALLEN ST	94109	2-J4
2030	HASTINGS TER	94109	2-J4
2100	FILBERT ST	94109	2-J4
2200	GREENWICH ST	94109	2-J4
2300	LOMBARD ST	94109	2-J4
2400	CHESTNUT ST	94109	2-J3
2500	FRANCISCO ST	94109	2-J3
2600	BAY ST	94109	2-J3
2630	BERGEN PL	94109	2-J3
2700	NORTH POINT ST	94109	2-J3
2800	BEACH ST	94109	2-J3
2800	BEACH ST	94133	2-J3
2900	JEFFERSON ST	94109	2-J3
2900	JEFFERSON ST	94133	2-J3

I

Address	Cross Street	ZIP	City Pg-Grid
I ST			SF
200	J ST	94124	20-E1
350	3RD AV	94124	20-E1
350	MANSEAU ST	94124	20-E1
700	SPEAR AV	94124	20-E1
IDORA AV			SF
1	WOODSIDE AV	94127	13-E4
50	SYDNEY WY	94127	13-D4
100	LAGUNA HONDA BLVD	94127	13-D4
180	ROCK AL	94127	13-D4
200	GARCIA AV	94127	13-D4
IGNACIO ST			SF
1	GILROY ST	94124	20-C2
ILLINOIS ST			SF
1	4TH ST	94107	11-C1
40	MERRIMAC ST	94107	11-C1
70	ALAMEDA ST	94107	11-C1
100	EL DORADO ST	94107	11-C1
200	16TH ST	94107	11-C2
300	17TH ST	94107	11-C2
400	MARIPOSA ST	94107	11-C2
400	TERRY A FRANCOIS BLVD	94107	11-C2
500	18TH ST	94107	11-C2
600	19TH ST	94107	11-C2
700	20TH ST	94107	11-C3
900	22ND ST	94107	11-C3
990	HUMBOLDT ST	94107	11-C3
1100	23RD ST	94107	11-C3
1200	24TH ST	94107	11-C3
1300	25TH ST	94107	11-C3
1700	CESAR CHAVEZ ST	94124	11-C4
1600	MARIN ST	94124	11-C4
1700	TULARE ST	94124	11-C4
ILS LN			SF
1	COLUMBUS AV	94111	7-A4
10	GIBB ST	94111	7-A4
IMPERIAL AV			SF
100	GREENWICH ST	94123	2-H4
INA CT			SF
1	MANSFIELD ST	94112	14-H7
1	LA GRANDE AV	94112	14-H7
INCINERATOR RD			SF
	BATTERY BLANEY RD	94129	1-D3
	CRISSY FIELD AV	94129	1-D4
	COWLES ST	94129	1-D4
	PATTEN RD	94129	1-D4
INDIANA ST			SF
500	MARIPOSA ST	94107	11-C2
700	19TH ST	94107	11-C2
1000	22ND ST	94107	11-C3
1100	TUBBS ST	94107	11-C3
1200	23RD ST	94107	11-C3
1400	25TH ST	94107	11-C4
1500	26TH ST	94107	11-C4
1600	CESAR CHAVEZ ST	94124	11-C4
1710	MARIN ST	94124	15-C4
1800	TULARE ST	94124	15-C4
INDUSTRIAL ST			SF
1	OAKDALE AV	94124	15-B5
50	PALOU AV	94124	15-A5
90	QUESADA AV	94124	15-A5
140	REVERE AV	94124	15-A5
190	BARNEVELD AV	94124	15-A5
190	SHAFTER AV	94124	15-A5
220	CHARTER OAK AV	94124	15-A5
250	BOUTWELL ST	94124	15-A5
250	LOOMIS ST	94124	15-A5
300	ALEMANY BLVD	94124	15-A5
300	BAYSHORE BLVD	94124	15-A5
INFANTRY TER			SF
	ARGUELLO BLVD	94129	5-D4
	THOMAS AV	94129	5-D4
	MORAGA AV	94129	1-D4
	BLISS RD	94129	1-D4
	FISHER LP	94129	1-D4
	SHERIDAN AV	94129	1-D4
INGALLS ST			SF
1200	INNES AV	94124	15-D6
1200	MIDDLEPOINT RD	94124	15-D6
1230	HARBOR RD	94124	15-D6
1260	HUDSON AV	94124	15-D6
1280	NORTHRIDGE RD	94124	15-D6
1280	ROSIE LEE LN	94124	15-D6
1300	KISKA RD	94124	15-D6
1320	BEATRICE LN	94124	15-D7
1360	LA SALLE AV	94124	15-D7
1380	GEORGE CT	94124	15-C7
1400	OAKDALE AV	94124	15-C7
1500	PALOU AV	94124	15-C7
1600	QUESADA AV	94124	15-C7
1700	REVERE AV	94124	15-C7
1800	SHAFTER AV	94124	15-C7
1900	THOMAS AV	94124	15-C7
2000	UNDERWOOD AV	94124	15-C7
2100	VAN DYKE AV	94124	15-C7
2200	WALLACE AV	94124	15-C7
2300	YOSEMITE AV	94124	15-C7
2400	ARMSTRONG AV	94124	15-C7
2500	BANCROFT AV	94124	15-C7
2600	CARROLL AV	94124	20-C1
2700	DONNER AV	94124	20-C1
2800	EGBERT AV	94124	20-C1
2900	FITZGERALD AV	94124	20-B1
3000	GILMAN AV	94124	20-B1
3100	HOLLISTER AV	94124	20-B1
3200	INGERSON AV	94124	20-B1
3300	JAMESTOWN AV	94124	20-B1
INGERSON AV			SF
700	GIANTS DR	94124	20-C1
760	GILROY ST	94124	20-C1
800	GRIFFITH ST	94124	20-C1
770	CORONADO ST	94124	20-C1
880	HAWES ST	94124	20-B1
940	REDONDO ST	94124	20-B1
990	INGALLS ST	94124	20-B1
1110	JENNINGS ST	94124	20-B1
1200	3RD ST	94124	20-B1
INNES AV			SF
1900	RANKIN ST	94124	15-B5
2000	SELBY ST	94124	15-B5
2100	MILTON ROSS ST	94124	15-B5
1500	MENDELL ST	94124	15-C5
1600	NEWHALL ST	94124	15-C5
1610	3RD ST	94124	15-C5
1700	PHELPS ST	94124	15-C5
600	DONAHUE ST	94124	15-E7
700	EARL ST	94124	15-E7
800	FITCH ST	94124	15-D6
900	GRIFFITH ST	94124	15-D6
950	HUNTERS POINT BLVD	94124	15-D6
1000	HAWES ST	94124	15-D6
1100	INGALLS ST	94124	15-D6
1100	MIDDLEPOINT RD	94124	15-D6
400	COLEMAN ST	94124	15-E7
500	FRIEDELL ST	94124	15-E7
600	DONAHUE ST	94124	15-E7
INVERNESS DR			SF
1	SLOAT BLVD	94132	13-B6
100	OCEAN AV	94132	13-B6
200	EUCALYPTUS DR	94132	13-B6
IOWA ST			SF
700	22ND ST	94107	11-C3
IRIS AV			SF
1	MAYFAIR DR	94118	6-E6
100	EUCLID AV	94118	6-E6
IRVING ST			SF
1	ARGUELLO BLVD	94143	9-D2
1	ARGUELLO BLVD	94122	9-D2
100	2ND AV	94143	9-D2
100	2ND AV	94122	9-D2
200	3RD AV	94122	9-D2
300	4TH AV	94122	9-D2
400	5TH AV	94122	9-D2
500	6TH AV	94122	9-D2
600	7TH AV	94122	9-D2
700	8TH AV	94122	9-C2
800	9TH AV	94122	9-C2
900	10TH AV	94122	9-C2
1000	11TH AV	94122	9-C2
1100	12TH AV	94122	9-C2
1200	FUNSTON AV	94122	9-C2
1300	14TH AV	94122	9-C2
1400	15TH AV	94122	9-C2
1500	16TH AV	94122	9-C2
1600	17TH AV	94122	9-B2
1700	18TH AV	94122	9-B2
1800	19TH AV	94122	9-B2
1900	20TH AV	94122	9-B2
2000	21ST AV	94122	9-B2
2100	22ND AV	94122	9-B2
2200	23RD AV	94122	9-B2
2300	24TH AV	94122	9-B2
2400	25TH AV	94122	9-A2
2500	26TH AV	94122	9-A2
2600	27TH AV	94122	9-A2
2700	28TH AV	94122	9-A2
2800	29TH AV	94122	9-A2
2900	30TH AV	94122	9-A2
3000	31ST AV	94122	9-A2
3100	32ND AV	94122	9-A2
3200	33RD AV	94122	9-A2
3300	34TH AV	94122	8-J2
3400	35TH AV	94122	8-J2
3500	36TH AV	94122	8-J2
3540	SUNSET BLVD	94122	8-J2
3600	37TH AV	94122	8-J2
3700	38TH AV	94122	8-J2
3800	39TH AV	94122	8-J2
3900	40TH AV	94122	8-J2
4000	41ST AV	94122	8-J2
4100	42ND AV	94122	8-J2
4200	43RD AV	94122	8-H2
4300	44TH AV	94122	8-H2
4400	45TH AV	94122	8-H2
4500	46TH AV	94122	8-H2
4600	47TH AV	94122	8-H2
4700	48TH AV	94122	8-H2
4800	LA PLAYA	94122	8-H2
4900	GREAT HWY	94122	8-H2
IRWIN ST			SF
400	7TH ST	94107	11-B1
500	8TH ST	94107	11-B1
ISADORA DUNCAN LN			SF
100	TAYLOR ST	94102	6-J6
ISIS ST			SF
1	12TH ST	94103	10-J1
ISLAIS ST			SF
1	DAVIDSON AV	94124	15-B4
10	NAPOLEON ST	94124	15-B4
10	SELBY ST	94124	15-B4
	DAVIDSON AV	94124	15-B4
	RANKIN ST	94124	15-C4
	QUINT ST	94124	15-C4
ISOLA WY			SF
1	ROCKDALE DR	94127	14-E5
100	TERESITA BLVD	94127	14-E5
ITALY AV			SF
1	MISSION ST	94112	19-F1
100	LONDON ST	94112	19-F1
200	PARIS ST	94112	19-F1
300	LISBON ST	94112	19-F1
400	MADRID ST	94112	19-G1
500	EDINBURGH ST	94112	19-G1
600	NAPLES ST	94112	19-G1
700	VIENNA ST	94112	19-G1
800	ATHENS ST	94112	19-G1
900	MOSCOW ST	94112	19-G1
IVY ST			SF
200	FRANKLIN ST	94102	6-H7
300	GOUGH ST	94102	6-H7
400	OCTAVIA ST	94102	6-H7
500	LAGUNA ST	94102	6-H7
600	BUCHANAN ST	94102	6-H7
700	WEBSTER ST	94102	6-H7

J

Address	Cross Street	ZIP	City Pg-Grid
J ST			SF
50	MAHAN ST	94124	21-E1
110	I ST	94124	20-E1
170	3RD AV	94124	20-E1
270	6TH AV	94124	20-D1
300	SPEAR AV	94124	20-D1
JACK LONDON AL			SF
1	BRYANT ST	94107	7-B6
20	TABER PL	94107	7-B6
50	S PARK AV	94107	7-B6
50	S PARK AV	94107	7-B7
80	VARNEY PL	94107	7-B7
100	BRANNAN ST	94107	7-B7
JACKSON ST			SF
1	DRUMM ST	94111	7-B4
100	DAVIS ST	94111	7-B4
200	FRONT ST	94111	7-B4
300	BATTERY ST	94111	7-B4
330	CUSTOM HOUSE PL	94111	7-B4
400	SANSOME ST	94111	7-B4
400	SANSOME ST	94133	7-B4
420	BALANCE ST	94111	7-B4
420	BALANCE ST	94133	7-B4
460	HOTALING ST	94111	7-A4
460	HOTALING ST	94133	7-A4
500	MONTGOMERY ST	94111	7-A4
500	MONTGOMERY ST	94133	7-A4
530	COLUMBUS AV	94111	7-A4
530	COLUMBUS AV	94133	7-A4
600	KEARNY ST	94108	7-A4
600	KEARNY ST	94133	7-A4
620	COOPER AL	94108	7-A4
620	COOPER AL	94133	7-A4
650	WENTWORTH PL	94108	7-A4
650	WENTWORTH PL	94133	7-A4
670	BECKETT ST	94108	7-A4
670	BECKETT ST	94133	7-A4
700	GRANT AV	94108	7-A4
700	GRANT AV	94133	7-A4
720	SAINT LOUIS AL	94108	7-A4
720	SAINT LOUIS AL	94133	7-A4
730	JASON CT	94108	7-A4
730	JASON CT	94133	7-A4
740	ROSS AL	94108	7-A4
740	ROSS AL	94133	7-A4
760	DUNCOMBE AL	94108	7-A4
760	DUNCOMBE AL	94133	7-A4
810	STOCKTON ST	94108	7-A4
810	STOCKTON ST	94133	7-A4
800	SAINT JAMES AL	94108	7-A4
800	SAINT JAMES AL	94133	7-A4
820	SAINT JAMES AL	94108	7-A4
820	SAINT JAMES AL	94133	7-A4
850	BEDFORD PL	94108	7-A4
850	BEDFORD PL	94133	7-A4
870	STONE ST	94108	7-A4
870	STONE ST	94133	7-A4
880	ADELE CT	94108	7-A4
880	ADELE CT	94133	7-A4
900	POWELL ST	94108	7-A5
900	POWELL ST	94133	7-A5
970	DORIC AL	94108	7-A5
970	DORIC AL	94133	7-A5
1000	MASON ST	94108	7-A5
1000	MASON ST	94133	7-A5
1020	MARCY PL	94108	6-J5
1020	MARCY PL	94133	6-J5
1050	AUBURN ST	94108	6-J5
1050	AUBURN ST	94133	6-J5
1100	TAYLOR ST	94108	6-J5
1100	TAYLOR ST	94133	6-J5
1200	JONES ST	94109	6-J5
1300	LEAVENWORTH ST	94109	6-J5
1370	WALL PL	94109	6-J5
1400	HYDE ST	94109	6-J5
1500	LARKIN ST	94109	6-J5
1600	POLK ST	94109	6-H5
1700	VAN NESS AV	94109	6-H5
1800	FRANKLIN ST	94109	6-H5
1900	GOUGH ST	94109	6-H5
2000	OCTAVIA ST	94109	6-H5
2100	LAGUNA ST	94115	6-G5
2200	BUCHANAN ST	94115	6-G5
2300	WEBSTER ST	94115	6-G5
2400	FILLMORE ST	94115	6-G5
2500	STEINER ST	94115	6-G5
2600	PIERCE ST	94115	6-G5
2700	SCOTT ST	94115	6-F5
2800	DIVISADERO ST	94115	6-F5
2900	BRODERICK ST	94115	6-F5
3000	BAKER ST	94115	6-F5
3100	LYON ST	94115	6-F5
3200	PRESIDIO AV	94115	6-E5
3300	WALNUT ST	94118	6-E5
3400	LAUREL ST	94118	6-E5
3500	LOCUST ST	94118	5-E5
3600	SPRUCE ST	94118	5-E5
3700	MAPLE ST	94118	5-E5
3800	CHERRY ST	94118	5-D5
3900	ARGUELLO BLVD	94118	5-D5
JADE PL			SF
1	GOLD MINE DR	94131	14-F5
JAKEY CT			SF
1	HAWKINS LN	94124	15-C6
JAMESTOWN AV			SF
810	HARNEY WY	94124	20-C2
810	JAMESTOWN AVEX	94124	20-C2
1000	GRIFFITH ST	94124	20-C1
1040	CORONADO ST	94124	20-B1
1070	HAWES ST	94124	20-B1
1100	REDONDO ST	94124	20-B1
1130	INGALLS ST	94124	20-B1
1200	JENNINGS ST	94124	20-B1
1240	3RD ST	94124	20-B1
1260	KEITH ST	94124	20-B1
1300	SALINAS AV	94124	20-B1
JAMESTOWN AVEX			SF
700	HUNTERS POINT EXWY	94124	20-C2
810	JAMESTOWN AV	94124	20-C2
810	HARNEY WY	94124	20-C2
JANSEN ST			SF
1	GREENWICH ST	94133	2-J4
100	LOMBARD ST	94133	2-J4
JARBOE AV			SF
1090	MOULTRIE ST	94110	14-J5
990	ANDERSON ST	94110	14-J5
880	ELLSWORTH ST	94110	14-J5
780	GATES ST	94110	14-J5
680	FOLSOM ST	94110	14-J5
750	BANKS ST	94110	14-J5
800	PRENTISS ST	94110	14-J5
900	NEVADA ST	94110	14-J5
1000	PUTNAM ST	94110	14-J5
1100	BRONTE ST	94110	14-J5
1200	BRADFORD ST	94110	15-A5
1300	PERALTA AV	94110	15-A5
JASON CT			SF
1	JACKSON ST	94133	7-A4
JASPER PL			SF
1	GREEN ST	94133	3-A4
100	UNION ST	94133	3-A4
200	FILBERT ST	94133	3-A4
300	GREENWICH ST	94133	3-A4
JAUSS ST			SF
	JAVOWITZ ST	94129	2-E3
	MARSHALL ST	94129	2-E3
JAVA ST			SF
1	MASONIC AV	94117	10-F1
100	BUENA VISTA AV W	94117	10-F1
JAVOWITZ ST			SF
	MARINE DR	94129	2-E3
	JAUSS ST	94129	2-E3
	LIEUTENANT ALLEN ST	94129	2-E3
	LUNDEEN ST	94129	2-E3
	OLD MASON ST	94129	2-E3
JEAN WY			SF
1	ANZA ST	94118	6-E6
100	EWING TER	94118	6-E6
JEFFERSON ST			SF
1	POWELL ST	94133	2-J3
1	THE EMBARCADERO	94133	2-J3
100	MASON ST	94133	2-J3
200	TAYLOR ST	94133	2-J3
300	JONES ST	94133	2-J3
400	RICHARD HENREY DANA PL	94133	2-J3
400	LEAVENWORTH ST	94133	2-J3
500	HYDE ST	94109	2-J3
1400	WEBSTER ST	94123	2-G3
1500	FILLMORE ST	94123	2-G3
1800	SCOTT ST	94123	2-F3
1900	DIVISADERO ST	94123	2-F3
2000	BRODERICK ST	94123	2-F3
2100	BAKER ST	94123	2-F3
JENNINGS ST			SF
200	CARGO WY	94124	15-D5
300	NEWHALL ST	94124	15-D5
400	EVANS AV	94124	15-D5
400	HUNTERS POINT BLVD	94124	15-D5
400	MIDDLEPOINT RD	94124	15-D5
1500	PALOU AV	94124	15-C7
1600	QUESADA AV	94124	15-C7
1700	REVERE AV	94124	15-C7
1800	SHAFTER AV	94124	15-C7
1900	THOMAS AV	94124	15-C7
2000	UNDERWOOD AV	94124	15-C7
2100	VAN DYKE AV	94124	15-C7
2200	WALLACE AV	94124	15-C7
2300	YOSEMITE AV	94124	15-C7
2400	ARMSTRONG AV	94124	15-C7
2500	BANCROFT AV	94124	15-B7
2600	CARROLL AV	94124	15-B7
2700	DONNER AV	94124	20-B1
2800	EGBERT AV	94124	20-B1
2900	FITZGERALD AV	94124	20-B1
3000	GILMAN AV	94124	20-B1
3100	HOLLISTER AV	94124	20-B1
3200	INGERSON AV	94124	20-B1
3300	JAMESTOWN AV	94124	20-B1
3400	KEY AV	94124	20-B1
3500	LE CONTE AV	94124	20-B1
3600	MEADE AV	94124	20-B1
JERROLD AV			SF
2080	TOLAND ST	94124	15-B5
2070	LETTUCE LN	94124	15-B5
2010	MILTON ROSS ST	94124	15-B5
1900	SELBY ST	94124	15-B5
1880	RANKIN ST	94124	15-B5
1920	RANKIN ST	94124	15-B5
2010	SELBY ST	94124	15-B5
2070	MILTON ROSS ST	94124	15-B5
2100	TOLAND ST	94124	15-B5
2200	UPTON ST	94124	15-B4
2300	NAPOLEON ST	94124	15-A4
2330	BARNEVELD AV	94124	15-A4
2400	BAYSHORE BLVD	94124	15-A4
1600	NEWHALL ST	94124	15-C5
1700	PHELPS ST	94124	15-B5
1800	QUINT ST	94124	15-B5
1500	MENDELL ST	94124	15-C6
1600	3RD ST	94124	15-C6
400	COLEMAN ST	94124	15-E7
500	FRIEDELL ST	94124	15-E7
600	DONAHUE ST	94124	15-E7
700	EARL ST	94124	15-D7
800	DORMITORY RD	94124	15-D7
800	NORTHRIDGE RD	94124	15-D7
JERSEY ST			SF
1	DOLORES ST	94114	10-H4
50	CHATTANOOGA ST	94114	10-H4
100	CHURCH ST	94114	10-H4
150	VICKSBURG ST	94114	10-G4
200	SANCHEZ ST	94114	10-G4
300	NOE ST	94114	10-G4
400	CASTRO ST	94114	10-G4
500	DIAMOND ST	94114	10-G4
600	DOUGLASS ST	94114	10-G4
JESSIE ST			SF
1	1ST ST	94105	7-B5
40	ECKER ST	94105	7-B5
70	ANTHONY ST	94105	7-B5
100	2ND ST	94105	7-B6
130	NEW MONTGOMERY ST	94105	7-B6
160	ANNIE ST	94103	7-B6
200	3RD ST	94103	7-B6
300	4TH ST	94103	7-A6
400	5TH ST	94103	7-A6
400	MINT ST	94103	7-A6
410	5TH ST	94103	7-A6
420	MINT ST	94103	7-A6
500	6TH ST	94103	7-A6
600	7TH ST	94103	6-J7
800	9TH ST	94103	6-J7
900	10TH ST	94103	6-J7
1300	MCCOPPIN ST	94103	10-H1
JOHN ST			SF
1	POWELL ST	94133	7-A4
100	MASON ST	94133	7-A4
JOHN F KENNEDY DR			SF
	KEZAR DR	94117	9-E1
	CONSERVATORY DR E	-	9-D1
	MIDDLE DR E	-	9-D1
200	MIDDLE DR E	-	9-D1
	CONSERVATORY DR W	-	9-D1
	8TH AV	94118	9-C1
	S TEA GARDEN DR	94118	9-C1
	CONCOURSE DR	94118	9-C1
	10TH AV	94118	9-C1
	STOW LAKE DR	-	9-B1
	TRANSVERSE DR	-	9-A1
	30TH AV	-	9-A1
	36TH AV	-	8-J1
1300	CHAIN OF LAKES DR E	-	8-J1
1330	CHAIN OF LAKES DR W	-	8-J1
1400	S FORK DR	-	8-H1
1600	47TH AV	-	8-H1
1700	GREAT HWY	-	8-H1
JOHN F SHELLEY DR			SF
	MANSELL ST	94134	14-H7
	CAMBRIDGE ST	94134	19-J1
	MANSELL ST	94134	19-J1
JOHN MAHER ST			SF
1	FRONT ST	94111	3-B4
100	BATTERY ST	94111	3-B4
JOHN MUIR DR			SF
500	LAKE MERCED BLVD	94132	18-A2
700	SKYLINE BLVD	94132	17-J1
510	LAKE MERCED BLVD	94132	18-A2
JOHNSTONE DR			SF
20	CLARENDON AV	94131	9-E3
1	ADOLPH SUTRO CT	94131	9-E3
180	BEHR AV	94131	9-E2

Address	Cross Street	ZIP	City Pg-Grid
JOHNSTONE DR			**SF**
100	UPPER SERVICE RD	94131	9-E2
180	BEHR AV	94131	9-E2
JOICE ST			**SF**
1	PINE ST	94108	7-A5
100	CALIFORNIA ST	94108	7-A5
200	SACRAMENTO ST	94108	7-A5
300	CLAY ST	94108	7-A5
JONES ST			**SF**
	FRANCISCO ST	94133	2-J3
2450	HOUSTON ST	94133	2-J3
2530	FRANCISCO ST	94133	2-J3
2500	COLUMBUS AV	94133	2-J3
2600	BAY ST	94133	2-J3
2700	NORTH POINT ST	94133	2-J3
2800	BEACH ST	94133	2-J3
2900	JEFFERSON ST	94133	2-J3
1	MCALLISTER ST	94102	6-J6
100	GOLDEN GATE AV	94102	6-J6
200	TURK ST	94102	6-J6
300	EDDY ST	94102	6-J6
410	ELLIS ST	94102	6-J6
400	ANTONIO ST	94102	6-J6
430	STEVELOE PL	94102	6-J6
500	OFARRELL ST	94102	6-J6
600	GEARY ST	94102	6-J6
640	COLIN PL	94102	6-J6
	POST ST	94109	6-J6
	COSMO PL	94109	6-J5
800	SUTTER ST	94109	6-J5
900	BUSH ST	94109	6-J5
900	BUSH ST	94108	6-J5
1000	PINE ST	94109	6-J5
1000	PINE ST	94108	6-J5
1100	CALIFORNIA ST	94109	6-J5
1100	CALIFORNIA ST	94108	6-J5
1200	SACRAMENTO ST	94109	6-J5
1200	SACRAMENTO ST	94108	6-J5
1250	PLEASANT ST	94109	6-J5
1250	PLEASANT ST	94108	6-J5
1300	CLAY ST	94109	6-J5
1300	CLAY ST	94108	6-J5
1400	WASHINGTON ST	94109	6-J5
1400	WASHINGTON ST	94108	6-J5
1500	JACKSON ST	94109	6-J5
1500	JACKSON ST	94133	6-J5
1600	PACIFIC AV	94109	6-J4
1600	PACIFIC AV	94133	6-J4
1650	BERNARD ST	94109	6-J4
1650	BERNARD ST	94133	6-J4
1700	BROADWAY	94109	6-J4
1700	BROADWAY	94133	6-J4
1760	GLOVER ST	94109	6-J4
1760	GLOVER ST	94133	6-J4
1800	VALLEJO ST	94109	6-J4
1800	VALLEJO ST	94133	6-J4
1900	GREEN ST	94109	6-J4
1900	GREEN ST	94133	6-J4
2000	UNION ST	94133	2-J4
2100	FILBERT ST	94133	2-J4
2130	VALPARAISO ST	94133	2-J4
2200	GREENWICH ST	94133	2-J4
2300	LOMBARD ST	94133	2-J3
2400	CHESTNUT ST	94133	2-J3
JOOST AV			**SF**
10	BROMPTON AV	94131	14-G6
50	LIPPARD AV	94131	14-G6
100	ACADIA ST	94131	14-F6
200	BADEN ST	94131	14-F6
300	CONGO ST	94131	14-F6
400	DETROIT ST	94127	14-E6
600	FOERSTER ST	94127	14-E6
700	GENNESSEE ST	94127	13-E6
800	RIDGEWOOD AV	94127	13-E6
900	HAZELWOOD AV	94127	13-E6
JORDAN AV			**SF**
1	CALIFORNIA ST	94118	5-E6
100	EUCLID AV	94118	5-E6
200	GEARY BLVD	94118	5-E6
JOSEPHA AV			**SF**
1	GONZALEZ DR	94132	18-B1
100	JUAN BAUTISTA CIR	94132	18-B1
JOSIAH AV			**SF**
1	SUMMIT ST	94112	18-E1
1	MONTANA ST	94112	18-E1
60	LAKEVIEW AV	94112	18-E1
200	HOWTH ST	94112	18-E1
200	MOUNT VERNON AV	94112	18-E1
JOY ST			**SF**
1	HOLLADAY AV	94110	15-A5
100	BREWSTER ST	94110	15-A5
JUAN BAUTISTA CIR			**SF**
20	FUENTA AV	94132	18-B1
30	CRESPI DR	94132	18-B1
40	CRESPI DR	94132	18-B1
50	DIAZ AV	94132	18-B1
100	FONT BLVD	94132	18-B1
120	JOSEPHA AV	94132	18-B1
130	GRIJALVA DR	94132	18-B1
180	BUCARELI DR	94132	18-B1
1	FONT BLVD	94132	18-B1
30	FUENTA AV	94132	18-B1
JUANITA WY			**SF**
1	TERESITA BLVD	94127	13-E4
40	FOWLER AV	94127	13-E5
70	EVELYN WY	94127	13-E5
160	DEL SUR AV	94127	13-E5
250	REX AV	94127	13-D5
350	MARNE AV	94127	13-D5
360	LANSDALE AV	94127	13-D5
400	MIRALOMA DR	94127	13-D5
JUDAH ST			**SF**
1	5TH AV	94122	9-D2
1	PARNASSUS AV	94122	9-D2
100	6TH AV	94122	9-D2
200	7TH AV	94122	9-D2
300	8TH AV	94122	9-C2
400	9TH AV	94122	9-C2
500	10TH AV	94122	9-C2
600	11TH AV	94122	9-C2
700	12TH AV	94122	9-C2
800	FUNSTON AV	94122	9-C2
900	14TH AV	94122	9-C2
1000	15TH AV	94122	9-C2
1100	16TH AV	94122	9-C2
1200	17TH AV	94122	9-B2
1300	18TH AV	94122	9-B2
1400	19TH AV	94122	9-B2
1500	20TH AV	94122	9-B2
1600	21ST AV	94122	9-B2
1700	22ND AV	94122	9-B2
1800	23RD AV	94122	9-B2
1900	24TH AV	94122	9-B2
2000	25TH AV	94122	9-A2
2100	26TH AV	94122	9-A2
2200	27TH AV	94122	9-A2
2300	28TH AV	94122	9-A2
2400	29TH AV	94122	9-A2
2500	30TH AV	94122	9-A2
2600	31ST AV	94122	9-A2
2700	32ND AV	94122	9-A2
2800	33RD AV	94122	9-A2
2900	34TH AV	94122	8-J2
3000	35TH AV	94122	8-J2
3050	PINO AL	94122	8-J2
3100	36TH AV	94122	8-J2
3150	SUNSET BLVD	94122	8-J2
3200	37TH AV	94122	8-J2
3300	38TH AV	94122	8-J2
3400	39TH AV	94122	8-J2
3500	40TH AV	94122	8-J2
3600	41ST AV	94122	8-J2
3700	42ND AV	94122	8-H2
3800	43RD AV	94122	8-H2
3900	44TH AV	94122	8-H2
4000	45TH AV	94122	8-H2
4100	46TH AV	94122	8-H2
4200	47TH AV	94122	8-H2
4300	48TH AV	94122	8-H2
4400	LA PLAYA	94122	8-H2
4500	GREAT HWY	94122	8-H2
JUDSON AV			**SF**
500	PHELAN AV	94112	13-E7
600	HAZELWOOD AV	94112	13-E7
100	CIRCULAR AV	94112	14-F7
100	CIRCULAR AV	94131	14-F7
100	PAULDING ST	94131	14-F7
110	DETROIT ST	94112	14-F7
250	EDNA ST	94112	14-E7
380	FOERSTER ST	94112	14-E7
520	GENNESSEE ST	94112	13-E7
JULES AV			**SF**
1	LAKEVIEW AV	94112	18-D1
100	GRAFTON AV	94112	18-D1
200	HOLLOWAY AV	94112	13-D7
300	DE MONTFORT AV	94112	13-D7
400	DORADO TER	94112	13-D7
400	OCEAN AV	94112	13-D7
JULIA ST			**SF**
1	MISSION ST	94103	6-J7
50	MINNA ST	94103	6-J7
JULIAN AV			**SF**
1	14TH ST	94103	10-H1
100	15TH ST	94103	10-H2
200	16TH ST	94103	10-H2
JULIUS ST			**SF**
1	LOMBARD ST	94133	3-A3
100	WHITING ST	94133	3-A3
JUNIOR TER			**SF**
1	CAYUGA AV	94112	19-F1
100	SUNBEAM LN	94112	19-F1
JUNIPER ST			**SF**
1	FOLSOM ST	94103	10-J1
JUNIPERO SERRA BLVD			**SF**
1	SAINT FRANCIS BLVD	94127	13-C6
1	SAINT FRANCIS BLVD	94132	13-C6
1	SLOAT BLVD	94132	13-C6
1	PORTOLA DR	94132	13-C6
1	W PORTAL AV	94132	13-C6
1	WOODACRE DR	94132	13-C6
300	OCEAN AV	94132	13-C6
300	EUCALYPTUS DR	94132	13-C6
400	ROSSMOOR DR	94132	13-C6
500	STONECREST DR	94132	13-C7
700	WINSTON DR	94132	13-C7
800	STONECREST DR	94132	13-C7
900	LYNDHURST DR	94132	13-C7
50	SAINT FRANCIS BLVD	94127	13-C6
100	MONTEREY BLVD	94127	13-C6
200	DARIEN WY	94127	13-C6
	EUCALYPTUS DR	94127	13-C6
	EUCALYPTUS DR	94132	13-C6
	OCEAN AV	94132	13-C6
	MONCADA WY	94127	13-C6
	MONCADA WY	94132	13-C6
	WYTON LN	94127	13-C7
	WYTON LN	94132	13-C7
900	HOLLOWAY AV	94132	18-C1
1000	GARFIELD ST	94132	18-C1
1050	STRATFORD DR	94132	18-C1
1100	SHIELDS ST	94132	18-C1
1150	19TH AV	94132	18-C1
	FONT BLVD	94132	18-C2
	BROTHERHOOD WY	94132	18-C2
1560	PALMETTO AV	94132	18-C2
300	MONCADA WY	94127	13-C6
500	PALOMA AV	94127	13-C7
600	EL PLAZUELA WY	94127	13-C7
700	MERCEDES WY	94127	13-C7
	ESTERO AV	94127	13-C7
	HOLLOWAY AV	94132	18-C1
JURI ST			**SF**
1	SAN JOSE AV	94110	10-H4
JUSTIN DR			**SF**
1	COLLEGE AV	94112	14-H6
1	GENEBERN WY	94112	14-H6
80	AGNON AV	94112	14-H6
140	MURRAY ST	94112	14-H6
210	BENTON AV	94112	14-H6
400	COLLEGE AV	94112	14-H6
520	GENEBERN WY	94112	14-H6
K			
KANSAS ST			**SF**
100	ALAMEDA ST	94103	11-A1
100	HENRY ADAMS ST	94103	11-A1
200	15TH ST	94103	11-A1
300	16TH ST	94103	11-A2
400	17TH ST	94107	11-A2
500	MARIPOSA ST	94107	11-A2
600	18TH ST	94107	11-A2
700	19TH ST	94107	11-A2
800	20TH ST	94107	11-A3
1000	22ND ST	94107	11-A3
1200	23RD ST	94107	11-A3
1300	24TH ST	94107	11-A3
1400	25TH ST	94107	11-A4
1500	26TH ST	94107	11-A4
1600	MARIN ST	94124	11-A4
1700	CESAR CHAVEZ ST	94124	11-A4
KAPLAN LN			**SF**
100	CLEMENTINA ST	94103	7-B6
KAREN CT			**SF**
100	SOMERSET ST	94134	15-A7
200	HOLYOKE ST	94134	15-A7
KATE ST			**SF**
	BRYANT ST	94103	11-A1
KEARNY ST			**SF**
1900	FRANCISCO ST	94133	3-A3
2000	BAY ST	94133	3-A3
2100	THE EMBARCADERO	94133	3-A3
1700	LOMBARD ST	94133	3-A3
1700	TELEGRAPH HILL BLVD	94133	3-A3
1750	LA FERRERA TER	94133	3-A3
1800	LA FERRERA TER	94133	3-A3
	3RD ST	94108	7-A6
	MARKET ST	94108	7-A6
1	GEARY ST	94108	7-A6
30	MAIDEN LN	94108	7-A5
100	POST ST	94108	7-A5
130	VERMEHR PL	94108	7-A5
200	SUTTER ST	94108	7-A5
240	HARDIE PL	94108	7-A5
300	BUSH ST	94108	7-A5
300	BUSH ST	94104	7-A5
400	PINE ST	94108	7-A5
400	PINE ST	94104	7-A5
500	CALIFORNIA ST	94108	7-A5
500	CALIFORNIA ST	94104	7-A5
600	SACRAMENTO ST	94108	7-A5
600	SACRAMENTO ST	94111	7-A5
650	COMMERCIAL ST	94108	7-A5
650	COMMERCIAL ST	94111	7-A5
700	CLAY ST	94108	7-A5
700	CLAY ST	94111	7-A5
800	WASHINGTON ST	94108	7-A5
800	WASHINGTON ST	94111	7-A5
900	JACKSON ST	94133	7-A4
970	COLUMBUS AV	94133	7-A4
1000	PACIFIC AV	94133	7-A4
1060	NOTTINGHAM PL	94133	7-A4
1100	BROADWAY	94133	7-A4
1150	DUNNES AL	94133	7-A4
1180	FRESNO ST	94133	7-A4
1200	VALLEJO ST	94133	3-A4
1300	GREEN ST	94133	3-A4
1400	UNION ST	94133	3-A4
1500	FILBERT ST	94133	3-A4
KEITH ST			**SF**
3300	EVANS AV	94124	15-D5
3450	FAIRFAX AV	94124	15-D6
3540	BOWMAN CT	94124	15-D6
1	REBECCA LN	94124	15-D6
10	HUDSON AV	94124	15-C6
1300	NEWCOMB AV	94124	15-C6
1400	OAKDALE AV	94124	15-C6
1500	PALOU AV	94124	15-C6
1600	QUESADA AV	94124	15-C6
1700	REVERE AV	94124	15-C7
1800	SHAFTER AV	94124	15-C7
1900	THOMAS AV	94124	15-C7
2000	UNDERWOOD AV	94124	15-C7
2100	VAN DYKE AV	94124	15-C7
2200	WALLACE AV	94124	15-B7
2300	YOSEMITE AV	94124	15-B7
2400	ARMSTRONG AV	94124	15-B7
2500	BANCROFT AV	94124	15-B7
2600	CARROLL AV	94124	15-B7
1	SALINAS AV	94124	20-B1
320	JAMESTOWN AV	94124	20-B1
700	KEY AV	94124	20-B1
1730	3RD ST	94124	20-B1
1730	LE CONTE AV	94124	20-B1
3700	LE CONTE AV	94124	20-B1
KELLOCH AV			**SF**
1	VELASCO AV	94134	19-J2
200	SCHWERIN ST	94134	19-J2
KEMPTON AV			**SF**
1	ALEMANY BLVD	94132	18-C2
KENDALL DR			**SF**
	GORGAS AV	94129	2-E3
	BIRMINGHAM RD	94129	2-E4
	THORNBURG RD	94129	2-E4
	EDIE RD	94129	2-E4
KENSINGTON WY			**SF**
1	PORTOLA DR	94127	13-D5
100	ULLOA ST	94127	13-D5
200	PARK AL	94127	13-D5
300	MERCED AV	94127	13-D5
300	VASQUEZ AV	94127	13-D5
400	TARAVAL ST	94127	13-D5
KENT ST			**SF**
1	MASON ST	94133	2-J4
KENWOOD WY			**SF**
1	UPLAND DR	94112	13-D7
1	UPLAND DR	94127	13-D7
200	KEYSTONE WY	94127	13-D7
280	FAIRFIELD WY	94127	13-D7
280	MANOR DR	94127	13-D7
300	MANOR DR	94127	13-D7
400	PINEHURST WY	94127	13-C7
500	WESTGATE DR	94127	13-C7
KERN ST			**SF**
100	BROMPTON AV	94131	14-G6
200	DIAMOND ST	94131	14-G6
KEY AV			**SF**
900	BAYSHORE BLVD	94124	20-B1
1000	KEITH ST	94124	20-B1
1300	JENNINGS ST	94124	20-B1
1400	3RD ST	94124	20-B1
KEYES AV			**SF**
	PENA ST	94129	1-D4
	SAL ST	94129	1-E4
	CANBY ST	94129	1-E4
	LINCOLN BLVD	94129	1-E4
KEYSTONE WY			**SF**
1	OCEAN AV	94127	13-D7
1	OCEAN AV	94112	13-D7
100	KENWOOD WY	94127	13-D7
100	KENWOOD WY	94112	13-D7
KEZAR DR			**SF**
	STANYAN ST	94117	9-E1
	FELL ST	94117	9-E1
	OAK ST	94117	9-E1
	JOHN F KENNEDY DR	94117	9-E1
500	WALLER ST	94117	9-E1
	ARGUELLO BLVD	94117	9-D1
	3RD AV	94117	9-D1
	LINCOLN WY	94117	9-D1
KIMBALL PL			**SF**
100	SACRAMENTO ST	94109	6-J5
KING ST			**SF**
	BERRY ST	94107	7-C7
	THE EMBARCADERO	94107	7-C7
100	2ND ST	94107	7-C7
200	3RD ST	94107	7-C7
	TOWNSEND ST	94107	7-C7
100	2ND ST	94107	7-C7
200	3RD ST	94107	7-B7
300	4TH ST	94107	7-B7
400	5TH ST	94107	7-B7
500	6TH ST	94107	11-B1
600	7TH ST	94107	11-B1
600	7TH ST	94103	11-B1
700	DIVISION ST	94107	11-B1
700	DIVISION ST	94103	11-B1
KINGSTON ST			**SF**
1	SAN JOSE AV	94110	14-H5
100	MISSION ST	94110	14-H5
210	COLERIDGE ST	94110	14-H5
300	PROSPECT AV	94110	14-H5
KINZEY ST			**SF**
	RALSTON AV	94129	1-C4
	UPTON AV	94129	1-C4
KIRKHAM ST			**SF**
50	4TH AV	94143	9-D2
100	5TH AV	94122	9-D2
200	LOCKSLEY AV	94122	9-D2
200	6TH AV	94122	9-D2
300	7TH AV	94122	9-D2
400	8TH AV	94122	9-C2
500	9TH AV	94122	9-C2
600	10TH AV	94122	9-C2
700	11TH AV	94122	9-C2
800	12TH AV	94122	9-C2
900	FUNSTON AV	94122	9-C2
1000	14TH AV	94122	9-C2
1000	LURLINE ST	94122	9-C2
1100	15TH AV	94122	9-C2
1200	16TH AV	94122	9-C2
1300	17TH AV	94122	9-B2
1400	18TH AV	94122	9-B2
1500	19TH AV	94122	9-B2
1600	20TH AV	94122	9-B2
1700	21ST AV	94122	9-B2
1800	22ND AV	94122	9-B2
1900	23RD AV	94122	9-B2
2000	24TH AV	94122	9-B2
2100	25TH AV	94122	9-A2
2200	26TH AV	94122	9-A2
2300	27TH AV	94122	9-A2
2400	28TH AV	94122	9-A2
2500	29TH AV	94122	9-A2
2600	30TH AV	94122	9-A2
2700	31ST AV	94122	9-A2
2800	32ND AV	94122	9-A2
2900	33RD AV	94122	9-A2
3000	34TH AV	94122	8-J2
3100	35TH AV	94122	8-J2
3050	PINO AL	94122	8-J2
3200	36TH AV	94122	8-J2
3250	SUNSET BLVD	94122	8-J2
3300	37TH AV	94122	8-J2
3400	38TH AV	94122	8-J2
3500	39TH AV	94122	8-J2
3600	40TH AV	94122	8-J2
3700	41ST AV	94122	8-J2
3800	42ND AV	94122	8-J2
3900	43RD AV	94122	8-H2
4000	44TH AV	94122	8-H2
4100	45TH AV	94122	8-H2
4200	46TH AV	94122	8-H2
4300	47TH AV	94122	8-H2
4410	48TH AV	94122	8-H2
4400	LA PLAYA	94122	8-H2
4410	GREAT HWY	94122	8-H2
KIRKWOOD AV			**SF**
1900	RANKIN ST	94124	15-B5
2010	SELBY ST	94124	15-B5
2070	MILTON ROSS ST	94124	15-B5
2080	LETTUCE LN	94124	15-B5
2100	TOLAND ST	94124	15-B5
1500	MENDELL ST	94124	15-C6
1570	3RD ST	94124	15-C5
1600	NEWHALL ST	94124	15-C5
1700	PHELPS ST	94124	15-C5
700	EARL ST	94124	15-D7
800	DORMITORY RD	94124	15-D7
800	KISKA RD	94124	15-D7
550	FRIEDELL ST	94124	15-E7
600	DONAHUE ST	94124	15-E7
630	MARLIN CT	94124	15-E7
630	LA SALLE AV	94124	15-E7
700	EARL ST	94124	15-E7
KISKA RD			**SF**
1	INGALLS ST	94124	15-D7
100	REARDON RD	94124	15-D7
190	DORMITORY RD	94124	15-D7
190	KIRKWOOD AV	94124	15-D7
KISSLING ST			**SF**
100	11TH ST	94103	10-J1
200	12TH ST	94103	10-J1
KITTREDGE TER			**SF**
1	TURK ST	94118	6-E7
100	GOLDEN GATE AV	94118	6-E7
KNOCKASH HILL ST			**SF**
1	ULLOA ST	94127	13-D5
80	SHANGRILA WY	94127	13-D5
KNOLLVIEW WY			**SF**
1	PANORAMA DR	94131	10-E3
200	CITYVIEW WY	94131	10-E3
KNOTT CT			**SF**
100	WATT AV	94112	19-F2
KOBBE AV			**SF**
	LINCOLN BLVD	94129	1-B4
	SAFFOLD AV	94129	1-B4
1330	HARRISON BLVD	94129	1-C4
	GREENOUGH AV	94129	1-C4
	POPE ST	94129	1-C4
	TODD ST	94129	1-C4
	UPTON AV	94129	1-C4
	PARK BLVD	94129	5-C4
KRAMER PL			**SF**
70	PARDEE AL	94133	3-A4
100	GREENWICH ST	94133	3-A4
1	FILBERT ST	94133	3-A4
KRAUSGRILL PL			**SF**
1	FILBERT ST	94133	3-A4
KRONQUIST CT			**SF**
100	27TH ST	94131	14-G4
L			
LA AVANZADA			**SF**
1	DELLBROOK AV	94131	9-E3
20	PALO ALTO AV	94131	9-E3
LA BICA WY			**SF**
1	ROCKDALE DR	94127	13-E5
100	MYRA WY	94127	13-E5
LAFAYETTE ST			**SF**
70	HOWARD ST	94103	10-J1
30	NATOMA ST	94103	10-J1
1	MINNA ST	94103	10-J1
40	MISSION ST	94103	10-J1
LA FERRERA TER			**SF**
1	KEARNY ST	94133	3-A3
LA GRANDE AV			**SF**
1	AVALON AV	94112	14-H7
100	INA CT	94112	14-H7
100	MANSFIELD ST	94112	14-H7
180	DUBLIN ST	94112	19-H1
350	BRAZIL AV	94112	19-H1
630	RUSSIA AV	94112	19-H1
LAGUNA ST			**SF**
1	MARKET ST	94102	10-H1
30	HERMANN ST	94102	10-H1
100	WALLER ST	94102	10-H1
200	HAIGHT ST	94102	10-H1
250	ROSE ST	94102	10-H1
300	PAGE ST	94102	6-H7

Address	Cross Street	ZIP	City / Pg-Grid
LAGUNA ST			SF
350	LILY ST	94102	6-H7
400	OAK ST	94102	6-H7
450	HICKORY ST	94102	6-H7
500	FELL ST	94102	6-H7
520	LINDEN ST	94102	6-H7
600	HAYES ST	94102	6-H7
630	IVY ST	94102	6-H7
700	GROVE ST	94102	6-H7
730	BIRCH ST	94102	6-H7
800	FULTON ST	94102	6-H7
900	MCALLISTER ST	94102	6-H7
950	REDWOOD ST	94102	6-H7
1000	GOLDEN GATE AV	94115	6-H7
1000	GOLDEN GATE AV	94102	6-H7
1100	TURK ST	94115	6-H6
1100	TURK ST	94102	6-H6
1200	EDDY ST	94115	6-H6
1200	EDDY ST	94109	6-H6
1250	WILLOW ST	94115	6-H6
1250	WILLOW ST	94109	6-H6
1300	ELLIS ST	94115	6-H6
1300	ELLIS ST	94109	6-H6
1400	GALILEE LN	94115	6-H6
1400	GALILEE LN	94109	6-H6
1400	CLEARY CT	94109	6-H6
1500	GEARY BLVD	94115	6-H6
1500	GEARY BLVD	94109	6-H6
1600	POST ST	94115	6-H6
1600	POST ST	94109	6-H6
1650	HEMLOCK ST	94115	6-H6
1650	HEMLOCK ST	94109	6-H6
1700	SUTTER ST	94115	6-H6
1700	SUTTER ST	94109	6-H6
1800	BUSH ST	94115	6-H5
1800	BUSH ST	94109	6-H5
1900	PINE ST	94115	6-H5
1900	PINE ST	94109	6-H5
2000	CALIFORNIA ST	94115	6-H5
2000	CALIFORNIA ST	94109	6-H5
2100	SACRAMENTO ST	94115	6-H5
2100	SACRAMENTO ST	94109	6-H5
2200	CLAY ST	94115	6-H5
2200	CLAY ST	94109	6-H5
2300	WASHINGTON ST	94115	6-H5
2300	WASHINGTON ST	94109	6-H5
2400	JACKSON ST	94115	6-H5
2400	JACKSON ST	94109	6-H5
2500	PACIFIC AV	94115	6-H5
2500	PACIFIC AV	94109	6-H5
2600	BROADWAY ST	94115	6-G4
2600	BROADWAY ST	94109	6-G4
2600	BROADWAY	94109	6-G4
2700	VALLEJO ST	94123	6-G4
2800	GREEN ST	94123	6-G4
2900	UNION ST	94123	6-G4
3000	FILBERT ST	94123	2-G4
3050	HARRIS PL	94123	2-G4
3100	GREENWICH ST	94123	2-G4
3200	LOMBARD ST	94123	2-G4
3250	MAGNOLIA ST	94123	2-G4
3300	CHESTNUT ST	94123	2-G4
3400	FRANCISCO ST	94123	2-G3
3500	BAY ST	94123	2-G3
3600	NORTH POINT ST	94123	2-G3
3700	MARINA BLVD	94123	2-G3
LAGUNA HONDA BLVD			SF
200	7TH AV	94131	9-D3
200	7TH AV	94116	9-D3
230	CLARENDON AV	94116	9-D4
330	PLAZA ST	94116	9-D4
400	DEWEY BLVD	94116	13-D4
400	WOODSIDE AV	94116	13-D4
400	WOODSIDE AV	94127	13-D4
500	MERCED AV	94127	13-D4
530	VASQUEZ AV	94127	13-D4
570	VASQUEZ AV	94127	13-D4
	BALCETA AV	94127	13-D4
600	BALCETA AV	94127	13-D4
700	HERNANDEZ AV	94127	13-D4
800	IDORA AV	94127	13-D4
900	ROCKAWAY AV	94127	13-D5
900	ULLOA ST	94127	13-D5
1000	PORTOLA DR	94127	13-D5
LAGUNITAS DR			SF
1	SLOAT BLVD	94132	13-C6
30	CRANLEIGH DR	94132	13-C6
80	BEACHMONT DR	94132	13-B6
100	OCEAN AV	94132	13-B6
LAIDLEY ST			SF
1	30TH ST	94131	14-G5
90	NOE ST	94131	14-G5
110	HARPER ST	94131	14-G5
200	FAIRMOUNT ST	94131	14-H5
300	MIGUEL ST	94131	14-G5
400	MATEO ST	94131	14-G6
500	ROANOKE ST	94131	14-G6
600	CASTRO ST	94131	14-G6
LAKE ST			SF
1	ARGUELLO BLVD	94118	5-D6
100	2ND AV	94118	5-D6
200	3RD AV	94118	5-D6
300	4TH AV	94118	5-D6
400	5TH AV	94118	5-D6
500	6TH AV	94118	5-D6
600	7TH AV	94118	5-D6
700	8TH AV	94118	5-C6
800	9TH AV	94118	5-C6
900	10TH AV	94118	5-C6
1000	11TH AV	94118	5-C6
1100	12TH AV	94118	5-C6
1200	FUNSTON AV	94118	5-C6
1250	PRESIDIO BLVD	94118	5-C6
1300	14TH AV	94118	5-C6
1400	15TH AV	94118	5-C6
1500	16TH AV	94118	5-B6
1600	17TH AV	94121	5-B6
1700	18TH AV	94121	5-B6
1800	19TH AV	94121	5-B6
1900	20TH AV	94121	5-B6
2000	21ST AV	94121	5-B6
2100	22ND AV	94121	5-B6
2200	23RD AV	94121	5-B6
2300	24TH AV	94121	5-B6
2300	W CLAY ST	94121	5-B6
2400	25TH AV	94121	5-A6
2500	26TH AV	94121	5-A6
2600	27TH AV	94121	5-A6
2650	28TH AV	94121	5-A6
2700	28TH AV	94121	5-A6
2800	29TH AV	94121	5-A6
2900	30TH AV	94121	5-A6
3000	EL CAMINO DEL MAR	94121	5-A6
LAKE FOREST CT			SF
100	OAK PARK DR	94131	9-D3
LAKE MERCED BLVD			SF
1	SKYLINE BLVD	94132	12-J6
1	BERKSHIRE WY	94132	12-J6
30	SKYLINE BLVD	94132	12-J6
30	BERKSHIRE WY	94132	12-J6
170	SUNSET BLVD	94132	12-J6
250	CLEARFIELD DR	94132	13-A6
320	MIDDLEFIELD DR	94132	13-A6
	WINSTON DR	94132	13-A7
	STATE DR	94132	13-A7
470	STATE DR	94132	13-A7
100	FONT BLVD	94132	13-A7
900	BROTHERHOOD WY	94132	18-A2
1050	LAKE MERCED HILL	94132	18-A2
1190	JOHN MUIR DR	94132	18-A2
	JOHN MUIR DR	94132	18-A2
LAKE MERCED HILL			SF
	LAKE MERCED BLVD	94132	18-A2
LAKESHORE DR			SF
1	OCEAN AV	94132	12-J6
100	COUNTRY CLUB DR	94132	12-J6
300	BERKSHIRE WY	94132	12-J6
LAKESHORE PZ			SF
1	SLOAT BLVD	94132	13-A6
LAKEVIEW AV			SF
1	SAN JOSE AV	94112	18-E1
60	CAINE AV	94112	18-E1
110	MAJESTIC AV	94112	18-E1
170	MARGARET AV	94112	18-E1
220	JOSIAH AV	94112	18-E1
280	LEE AV	94112	18-E1
350	BRIGHTON AV	94112	18-D1
410	PLYMOUTH AV	94112	18-D1
480	GRANADA AV	94112	18-D1
540	MIRAMAR AV	94112	18-D1
600	CAPITOL AV	94112	18-D1
670	FAXON AV	94112	18-D1
730	JULES AV	94112	18-D1
LAKEWOOD AV			SF
1	OCEAN AV	94127	13-D7
100	FAIRFIELD WY	94127	13-D7
LAMARTINE ST			SF
1	DANTON ST	94112	14-G6
100	CAYUGA AV	94112	14-G6
LAMSON LN			SF
1	CASELLI AV	94114	10-F2
50	THORP LN	94114	10-F2
100	19TH ST	94114	10-F2
LANDERS ST			SF
1	14TH ST	94114	10-H1
100	15TH ST	94114	10-H2
150	ALERT AL	94114	10-H2
200	16TH ST	94114	10-H2
LANE ST			SF
1100	LA SALLE AV	94124	15-C6
1200	MCKINNON AV	94124	15-C6
1300	NEWCOMB AV	94124	15-C6
1400	OAKDALE AV	94124	15-C6
1500	PALOU AV	94124	15-C6
1600	QUESADA AV	94124	15-C6
1700	REVERE AV	94124	15-C6
1800	SHAFTER AV	94124	15-C7
1900	THOMAS AV	94124	15-B7
2000	UNDERWOOD AV	94124	15-B7
2100	VAN DYKE AV	94124	15-B7
2200	3RD ST	94124	15-B7
2200	WALLACE AV	94124	15-B7
2300	YOSEMITE AV	94124	15-B7
2400	ARMSTRONG AV	94124	15-B7
LANGDON CT			SF
	LINCOLN BLVD	94129	1-B3
LANGTON ST			SF
1	HOWARD ST	94103	7-A7
120	FOLSOM ST	94103	7-A7
140	DECKER AL	94103	7-A7
200	HARRISON ST	94103	7-A7
	BRYANT ST	94103	11-A1
	BRANNAN ST	94103	11-A1
LANSDALE AV			SF
1	MOLIMO DR	94127	13-E5
1	MYRA WY	94127	13-E5
100	HILLCREST CT	94127	13-E5
130	SHERWOOD CT	94127	13-E5
150	DALEWOOD WY	94127	13-E5
200	ROBINHOOD DR	94127	13-D6
300	GLOBE AL	94127	13-D6
400	ROBINHOOD DR	94127	13-D5
460	CASITAS AV	94127	13-D5
500	BENGAL AL	94127	13-D5
580	LUDLOW AL	94127	13-D5
580	DALEWOOD WY	94127	13-D5
600	JUANITA WY	94127	13-D5
LANSING ST			SF
1	1ST ST	94105	7-B6
100	GUY PL	94105	7-B6
LAPHAM WY			SF
30	ROBINSON DR	94112	19-G2
100	ROBINSON DR	94112	19-G2
200	CHICAGO WY	94112	19-G2
LAPIDGE ST			SF
1	18TH ST	94110	10-H2
100	19TH ST	94110	10-H2
LA PLAYA			SF
700	BALBOA ST	94121	4-H7
800	CABRILLO ST	94121	4-H7
900	FULTON ST	94121	8-H1
1200	LINCOLN WY	94122	8-H2
1200	MARTIN LUTHER KING JR DR	94122	8-H2
1300	IRVING ST	94122	8-H2
1400	JUDAH ST	94122	8-H2
1500	KIRKHAM ST	94122	8-H2
1600	GREAT HWY	94122	8-H2
1600	LAWTON ST	94122	8-H2
LAPU LAPU ST			SF
1	BONIFACIO ST	94107	7-B6
40	RIZAL ST	94107	7-B6
100	HARRISON ST	94107	7-B6
LARCH ST			SF
200	VAN NESS AV	94102	6-H6
300	FRANKLIN ST	94102	6-H6
LARKIN ST			SF
2900	BAY ST	94109	2-H3
3000	NORTH POINT ST	94109	2-H3
3100	BEACH ST	94109	2-H3
1	9TH ST	94102	6-J7
1	HAYES ST	94102	6-J7
1	MARKET ST	94102	6-J7
100	GROVE ST	94102	6-J7
300	MCALLISTER ST	94102	6-J6
400	GOLDEN GATE AV	94102	6-J6
500	TURK ST	94102	6-J6
600	EDDY ST	94109	6-J6
630	WILLOW ST	94109	6-J6
700	ELLIS ST	94109	6-J6
730	OLIVE ST	94109	6-J6
800	OFARRELL ST	94109	6-J6
820	MYRTLE ST	94109	6-J6
900	GEARY ST	94109	6-J6
930	CEDAR ST	94109	6-J6
1000	POST ST	94109	6-J6
1030	HEMLOCK ST	94109	6-J6
1100	SUTTER ST	94109	6-J6
1130	FERN ST	94109	6-J5
1200	BUSH ST	94109	6-J5
1250	AUSTIN ST	94109	6-J5
1260	EUREKA PL	94109	6-J5
1300	PINE ST	94109	6-J5
1400	CALIFORNIA ST	94109	6-J5
1500	SACRAMENTO ST	94109	6-J5
1600	CLAY ST	94109	6-J5
1700	WASHINGTON ST	94109	6-J5
1800	JACKSON ST	94109	6-J5
1900	PACIFIC AV	94109	6-J4
1950	BROADWAY	94109	6-J4
2100	VALLEJO ST	94109	6-J4
2200	GREEN ST	94109	6-J4
2250	ROCKLAND ST	94109	6-J4
2300	UNION ST	94109	2-J4
2400	FILBERT ST	94109	2-J4
2500	GREENWICH ST	94109	2-H4
2600	LOMBARD ST	94109	2-H4
2700	CHESTNUT ST	94109	2-H3
2800	FRANCISCO ST	94109	2-H3
LA SALLE AV			SF
1900	MCKINNON AV	94124	15-B5
1900	RANKIN ST	94124	15-B5
	SELBY ST	94124	15-B5
2100	TOLAND ST	94124	15-B5
2100	INGALLS ST	94124	15-D6
1230	WHITFIELD CT	94124	15-D6
1250	OSCEOLA LN	94124	15-C6
1310	BEATRICE LN	94124	15-C6
1340	OSCEOLA LN	94124	15-C6
1360	GARLINGTON CT	94124	15-C6
1400	NEWCOMB AV	94124	15-C6
1500	LANE ST	94124	15-C6
1520	CASHMERE ST	94124	15-C6
1600	MENDELL ST	94124	15-C6
1640	3RD ST	94124	15-C6
1700	NEWHALL ST	94124	15-C5
1800	PHELPS ST	94124	15-C5
600	KIRKWOOD AV	94124	15-E7
700	EARL ST	94124	15-E7
700	NAVY RD	94124	15-E7
LASKIE ST			SF
100	MISSION ST	94103	6-J7
LATHROP AV			SF
100	TUNNEL AV	94134	20-A2
190	WHEELER AV	94134	20-A2
290	PENINSULA AV	94134	20-B2
390	TOCOLOMA AV	94134	20-B2
490	NUEVA AV	94134	20-B2
590	GILLETTE AV	94134	20-B2
LATONA ST			SF
1	BAYVIEW ST	94124	15-B6
100	THORNTON AV	94124	15-B6
LAURA ST			SF
100	ALEMANY BLVD	94112	18-E2
1	HURON AV	94112	18-E2
100	MISSION ST	94112	18-E2
LAUREL ST			SF
10	PACIFIC AV	94118	6-E5
100	JACKSON ST	94118	6-E5
150	WASHINGTON ST	94118	6-E5
300	CLAY ST	94118	6-E5
400	SACRAMENTO ST	94118	6-E6
500	CALIFORNIA ST	94118	6-E6
530	MAYFAIR DR	94118	6-E6
600	EUCLID AV	94118	6-E6
700	LUPINE AV	94118	6-E6
LAUSSAT ST			SF
1	BUCHANAN ST	94102	10-H1
200	WEBSTER ST	94102	10-H1
200	FILLMORE ST	94117	10-G1
300	STEINER ST	94117	10-G1
LAWRENCE AV			SF
1	DE WOLF ST	94112	18-E2
30	ALEMANY BLVD	94112	18-E2
100	SEARS ST	94112	18-E2
170	HURON AV	94112	18-E2
300	MISSION ST	94112	18-E2
LAWTON ST			SF
1	LOCKSLEY AV	94122	9-D2
1	WARREN DR	94122	9-D2
100	7TH AV	94122	9-D2
200	8TH AV	94122	9-D2
250	AUTO DR	94122	9-C2
300	9TH AV	94122	9-C2
400	10TH AV	94122	9-C2
500	11TH AV	94122	9-C2
600	12TH AV	94122	9-C2
700	FUNSTON AV	94122	9-C2
850	15TH AV	94122	9-C2
900	LOMITA AV	94122	9-C2
1000	16TH AV	94122	9-C2
1100	17TH AV	94122	9-B2
1200	18TH AV	94122	9-B2
1300	19TH AV	94122	9-B2
1400	20TH AV	94122	9-B2
1500	21ST AV	94122	9-B3
1600	22ND AV	94122	9-B3
1700	23RD AV	94122	9-B3
1800	24TH AV	94122	9-B3
1900	25TH AV	94122	9-B3
2000	26TH AV	94122	9-A3
2100	27TH AV	94122	9-A3
2200	28TH AV	94122	9-A3
2300	29TH AV	94122	9-A3
2400	30TH AV	94122	9-A3
2500	31ST AV	94122	9-A3
2600	32ND AV	94122	9-A3
2700	33RD AV	94122	9-A3
2800	34TH AV	94122	8-J3
2900	35TH AV	94122	8-J3
3000	36TH AV	94122	8-J3
3050	SUNSET BLVD	94122	8-J3
3100	37TH AV	94122	8-J3
3200	38TH AV	94122	8-J3
3300	39TH AV	94122	8-J3
3400	40TH AV	94122	8-J3
3500	41ST AV	94122	8-J3
3600	42ND AV	94122	8-J3
3700	43RD AV	94122	8-H3
3800	44TH AV	94122	8-H3
3900	45TH AV	94122	8-H3
4000	46TH AV	94122	8-H3
4100	47TH AV	94122	8-H3
4200	48TH AV	94122	8-H3
4300	GREAT HWY	94122	8-H3
4300	LA PLAYA	94122	8-H3
LEAVENWORTH ST			SF
50	MCALLISTER ST	94102	6-J6
100	GOLDEN GATE AV	94102	6-J6
200	TURK ST	94102	6-J6
300	EDDY ST	94109	6-J6
300	EDDY ST	94102	6-J6
400	ELLIS ST	94109	6-J6
400	ELLIS ST	94102	6-J6
500	OFARRELL ST	94109	6-J6
500	OFARRELL ST	94102	6-J6
600	GEARY ST	94109	6-J6
600	GEARY ST	94102	6-J6
700	POST ST	94109	6-J6
800	SUTTER ST	94109	6-J5
900	BUSH ST	94109	6-J5
1000	PINE ST	94109	6-J5
1060	PANTON AL	94109	6-J5
1100	CALIFORNIA ST	94109	6-J5
1150	ACORN AL	94109	6-J5
1200	SACRAMENTO ST	94109	6-J5
1300	CLAY ST	94109	6-J5
1400	WASHINGTON ST	94109	6-J5
1500	JACKSON ST	94109	6-J5
1600	PACIFIC AV	94109	6-J4
1630	LYNCH ST	94109	6-J4
1650	BERNARD ST	94109	6-J4
1700	BROADWAY	94109	6-J4
1760	WALDO AL	94109	6-J4
1760	GLOVER ST	94109	6-J4
1800	VALLEJO ST	94109	6-J4
1900	GREEN ST	94109	6-J4
1930	MACONDRAY LN	94109	6-J4
2000	UNION ST	94109	2-J4
2000	UNION ST	94133	2-J4
2070	HAVENS ST	94109	2-J4
2070	HAVENS ST	94133	2-J4
2100	FILBERT ST	94109	2-J4
2100	FILBERT ST	94133	2-J4
2200	GREENWICH ST	94109	2-J4
2200	GREENWICH ST	94133	2-J4
2260	LURMONT TER	94109	2-J4
2260	LURMONT TER	94133	2-J4
2300	LOMBARD ST	94109	2-J4
2300	LOMBARD ST	94133	2-J4
2400	CHESTNUT ST	94109	2-J3
2400	CHESTNUT ST	94133	2-J3
2500	FRANCISCO ST	94109	2-J3
2500	FRANCISCO ST	94133	2-J3
2600	BAY ST	94109	2-J3
2600	BAY ST	94133	2-J3
2700	NORTH POINT ST	94109	2-J3
2700	NORTH POINT ST	94133	2-J3
2730	COLUMBUS AV	94133	2-J3
2800	BEACH ST	94133	2-J3
2900	JEFFERSON ST	94133	2-J3
2900	RICHARD HENREY DANA PL	94133	2-J3
LECH WALESA			SF
1	POLK ST	94102	6-J7
100	VAN NESS AV	94102	6-J7
LE CONTE AV			SF
700	KEITH ST	94124	20-B1
800	3RD ST	94124	20-B1
800	KEITH ST	94124	20-B1
900	JENNINGS ST	94124	20-B1
1020	MEADE AV	94124	20-B1
1080	BAYVIEW PARK RD	94124	20-B1
LEDYARD ST			SF
1	SILVER AV	94124	15-A6
100	MERCURY ST	94124	15-A6
200	THORNTON AV	94124	15-A6
200	VESTA ST	94124	15-A6
LEE AV			SF
1	LAKEVIEW AV	94112	18-E1
140	GRAFTON AV	94112	18-E1
280	HOLLOWAY AV	94112	18-E1
400	OCEAN AV	94112	18-E1
LEESE ST			SF
1	MISSION ST	94110	14-H6
40	PARK ST	94110	14-H6
100	RICHLAND AV	94110	14-H6
200	CRESCENT AV	94110	14-H6
LEGION CT			SF
1	ASHTON AV	94127	13-D7
100	URBANO DR N	94127	13-D7
LEGION OF HONOR DR			SF
	EL CAMINO DEL MAR	94121	4-J6
	34TH AV	94121	4-J6
	CLEMENT ST	94121	4-J6
LEIDESDORFF ST			SF
1	PINE ST	94104	7-B5
100	CALIFORNIA ST	94104	7-B5
150	HALLECK ST	94104	7-B5
200	SACRAMENTO ST	94111	7-B5
240	COMMERCIAL ST	94111	7-B5
300	CLAY ST	94111	7-B5
LELAND AV			SF
30	HAHN ST	94134	19-J2
70	SAWYER ST	94134	19-J2
120	LOEHR ST	94134	19-J2
170	BRITTON ST	94134	19-J2
190	ELLIOT ST	94134	19-J2
210	REY ST	94134	19-J2
260	SCHWERIN ST	94134	19-J2
300	DELTA ST	94134	19-J2
350	CORA ST	94134	20-A2
400	RUTLAND ST	94134	20-A2
440	PEABODY ST	94134	20-A2
490	ALPHA ST	94134	20-A2
530	DESMOND ST	94134	20-A2
600	BAYSHORE BLVD	94134	20-A2
LENDRUM CT			SF
	ARMISTEAD RD	94129	1-C3
LENOX WY			SF
1	TARAVAL ST	94127	13-D5
100	VERDUN WY	94127	13-C5
200	ULLOA ST	94127	13-C5
LEO ST			SF
20	MISSION ST	94112	14-F7
1	WATSON PL	94112	14-F7
20	ALEMANY BLVD	94112	14-F7
LEONA TER			SF
1	PRESIDIO AV	94115	6-F6
100	LYON ST	94115	6-F6
LEROY PL			SF
100	SACRAMENTO ST	94109	6-J5
LESSING ST			SF
1	LIEBIG ST	94112	18-D2
LETTERMAN DR			SF
	LOMBARD ST	94129	6-E4
	DEWITT RD	94129	6-E4
	LINCOLN BLVD	94129	2-E4
	PRESIDIO BLVD	94129	2-E4
LETTUCE LN			SF
1	JERROLD AV	94124	15-B5
	KIRKWOOD AV	94124	15-B5
LEVANT ST			SF
1	ROOSEVELT WY	94114	10-F2
20	STATES ST	94114	10-F2
90	LOWER TER	94114	10-F2
LEXINGTON ST			SF
1	SYCAMORE ST	94110	10-H2
100	18TH ST	94110	10-H2
200	19TH ST	94110	10-H2
300	20TH ST	94110	10-H3
400	21ST ST	94110	10-H3

Address	Cross Street	ZIP	City Pg-Grid
LIBERTY ST			SF
1	VALENCIA ST	94110	10-H3
100	GUERRERO ST	94110	10-H3
200	DOLORES ST	94114	10-H3
300	CHURCH ST	94114	10-H3
440	SANCHEZ ST	94114	10-G3
400	SANCHEZ ST	94114	10-G3
440	RAYBURN ST	94114	10-G3
500	NOE ST	94114	10-G3
600	CASTRO ST	94114	10-G3
LIEBIG ST			SF
1	SAN JOSE AV	94112	18-D2
1	DE LONG ST	94112	18-D2
1	LESSING ST	94112	18-D2
LIEUTENANT ALLEN ST			SF
	LYON ST	94129	2-E3
	JAVOWITZ ST	94129	2-E3
	MARSHALL ST	94129	1-E3
	SERGEANT MITCHELL ST	94129	1-E3
LIGGETT AV			SF
720	MORTON ST	94129	6-E4
700	CLARKE ST	94129	6-E4
700	SUMNER ST	94129	6-E4
710	PRESIDIO BLVD	94129	6-E4
	MORTON ST	94129	6-E4
	SANCHES ST	94129	6-E4
780	SIBLEY RD	94129	6-E4
730	VISTA CT	94129	6-E5
800	CLARKE ST	94129	6-E5
LILAC ST			SF
1	24TH ST	94110	10-J4
100	25TH ST	94110	10-J4
200	26TH ST	94110	10-J4
LILLIAN ST			SF
1	ROSIE LEE LN	94124	15-D6
100	BEATRICE LN	94124	15-D6
LILY ST			SF
1	FRANKLIN ST	94102	6-H7
100	GOUGH ST	94102	6-H7
190	OCTAVIA ST	94102	6-H7
300	LAGUNA ST	94102	6-H7
390	BUCHANAN ST	94102	6-H7
LINARES AV			SF
40	VENTURA AV	94116	9-D3
70	8TH AV	94116	9-D3
100	8TH AV	94116	9-D3
LINCOLN BLVD			SF
	MONTGOMERY ST	94129	1-D3
	TAYLOR RD	94129	1-D4
	RILEY AV	94129	1-D4
	SHERIDAN AV	94129	1-D4
	CRISSY FIELD AV	94129	1-D3
	PATTEN RD	94129	1-D4
	MCDOWELL AV	94129	1-C4
	PARK BLVD	94129	1-C4
	STOREY AV	94129	1-C4
	COWLES ST	94129	1-C3
	ARMISTEAD RD	94129	1-C3
	CRISSY FIELD AV	94129	1-C3
	LONG AV	94129	1-C3
910	HOFFMAN ST	94129	1-C3
960	ANDREWS RD	94129	1-C3
	BATTERY EAST RD	94129	1-C3
	STOREY AV	94129	1-C3
	MERCHANT RD	94129	1-C3
	RALSTON AV	94129	1-C3
	LANGDON CT	94129	1-B3
	DYNAMITE RD	94129	1-B4
40	KOBBE AV	94129	5-B4
40	BATTERY CROSBY RD	94129	5-B4
	BATTERY CHAMBERLAIN RD	94129	5-B4
	PERSHING DR	94129	5-B5
	STILLWELL DR	94129	5-B5
	BOWLEY ST	94129	5-B5
	BAKER CT	94129	5-B5
	GIBSON RD	94129	5-B5
	HOWARD RD	94129	5-B5
200	25TH AV	94121	5-B5
200	EL CAMINO DEL MAR	94121	5-B5
	BANK ST	94129	1-E4
	ANZA ST	94129	1-E4
	GRAHAM ST	94129	1-E4
	FRENCH CT	94129	1-E4
	KEYES AV	94129	1-E4
	MESA AV	94129	1-E4
970	MESA AV	94129	1-E4
970	HALLECK ST	94129	1-E4
970	FUNSTON AV	94129	1-E4
	GIRARD RD	94129	1-E4
	TORNEY AV	94129	2-E4
	PRESIDIO BLVD	94129	2-E4
	LETTERMAN DR	94129	2-E4
LINCOLN CT			SF
10	NADELL CT	94112	19-F2
10	GUTTENBERG ST	94112	19-F2
LINCOLN WY			SF
1	ARGUELLO BLVD	94122	9-D1
1	ARGUELLO BLVD	94117	9-D1
1	FREDERICK ST	94117	9-D1
100	2ND AV	94122	9-D1
100	2ND AV	94117	9-D1
250	3RD AV	94122	9-D1
250	KEZAR DR	94122	9-D1
300	4TH AV	94122	9-D1
400	5TH AV	94122	9-D1
500	6TH AV	94122	9-D1
600	7TH AV	94122	9-D1
700	8TH AV	94122	9-C1
800	9TH AV	94122	9-C1
800	MARTIN LUTHER KING JR DR	94122	9-C1
900	10TH AV	94122	9-C1
1000	11TH AV	94122	9-C1
1100	12TH AV	94122	9-C1
1200	FUNSTON AV	94122	9-C1
1300	14TH AV	94122	9-C1
1400	15TH AV	94122	9-C1
1500	16TH AV	94122	9-C1
1600	17TH AV	94122	9-B1
1700	18TH AV	94122	9-B1
1800	19TH AV	94122	9-B1
1800	CROSS OVER DR	94122	9-B1
1900	20TH AV	94122	9-B1
2000	21ST AV	94122	9-B1
2100	22ND AV	94122	9-B1
2200	23RD AV	94122	9-B1
2300	24TH AV	94122	9-B1
2400	25TH AV	94122	9-A1
2500	26TH AV	94122	9-A1
2600	27TH AV	94122	9-A1
2700	28TH AV	94122	9-A1
2800	29TH AV	94122	9-A1
2900	30TH AV	94122	9-A2
3000	31ST AV	94122	9-A2
3100	32ND AV	94122	9-A2
3200	33RD AV	94122	9-A2
3300	34TH AV	94122	8-J2
3400	35TH AV	94122	8-J2
3500	36TH AV	94122	8-J2
3550	SUNSET BLVD	94122	8-J2
3600	37TH AV	94122	8-J2
3700	38TH AV	94122	8-J2
3800	39TH AV	94122	8-J2
3900	40TH AV	94122	8-J2
4000	41ST AV	94122	8-J2
4000	CHAIN OF LAKES DR E	94122	8-J2
4100	42ND AV	94122	8-H2
4200	43RD AV	94122	8-H2
4300	44TH AV	94122	8-H2
4400	45TH AV	94122	8-H2
4500	46TH AV	94122	8-H2
4600	47TH AV	94122	8-H2
4700	48TH AV	94122	8-H2
4800	LA PLAYA	94122	8-H2
4800	MARTIN LUTHER KING JR DR	94122	8-H2
4830	GREAT HWY	94122	8-H2
4900	GREAT HWY	94122	8-H2
LINDA ST			SF
1	18TH ST	94110	10-H2
100	19TH ST	94110	10-H2
LINDEN ST			SF
200	FRANKLIN ST	94102	6-H7
300	GOUGH ST	94102	6-H7
400	OCTAVIA ST	94102	6-H7
500	LAGUNA ST	94102	6-H7
600	BUCHANAN ST	94102	6-H7
700	HAYES ST	94102	6-H7
LINDSAY CIR			SF
1	HILLVIEW CT	94124	15-C6
1	WHITNEY YOUNG CIR	94124	15-C6
LIPPARD AV			SF
1	SURREY ST	94131	14-G6
50	CHENERY ST	94131	14-G6
100	BOSWORTH ST	94131	14-G6
200	JOOST AV	94131	14-G6
LISBON ST			SF
1	SILVER AV	94112	14-G7
100	PERU AV	94112	14-G7
190	AVALON AV	94112	14-G7
200	AVALON AV	94112	14-G7
300	EXCELSIOR AV	94112	14-G7
400	BRAZIL AV	94112	19-G1
500	PERSIA AV	94112	19-G1
600	RUSSIA AV	94112	19-G1
700	FRANCE AV	94112	19-G1
800	ITALY AV	94112	19-F1
900	AMAZON AV	94112	19-F1
1000	GENEVA AV	94112	19-F1
LITTLEFIELD TER			SF
1	25TH ST	94107	11-B4
100	DE HARO ST	94107	11-B4
LIVINGSTON ST			SF
	OLD MASON ST	94129	1-D3
	MAULDIN ST	94129	1-D3
	PENNINGTON ST	94129	1-D3
	PEARCE ST	94129	1-D3
LLOYD ST			SF
1	SCOTT ST	94117	10-G1
100	CASTRO ST	94117	10-G1
LOBOS ST			SF
210	ORIZABA AV	94112	18-D1
100	CAPITOL AV	94112	18-D1
1	PLYMOUTH AV	94112	18-E1
100	CAINE AV	94112	18-E1
LOCKSLEY AV			SF
1	KIRKHAM ST	94122	9-D2
1	6TH AV	94122	9-D2
100	LAWTON ST	94122	9-D3
100	WARREN DR	94122	9-D3
LOCKWOOD ST			SF
	NIMITZ AV	94124	16-F7
	A ST	94124	16-F7
	SPEAR AV	94124	16-F7
	VAN KEUREN AV	94124	16-F7
	ROBINSON ST	94124	16-F7
	FISHER AV	94124	16-F7
	MCCANN ST	94124	16-E7
	ENGLISH ST	94124	16-E7
	DONAHUE ST	94124	16-E7
LOCUST ST			SF
1	PACIFIC AV	94118	6-E5
100	JACKSON ST	94118	6-E5
200	WASHINGTON ST	94118	6-E5
300	CLAY ST	94118	6-E5
400	SACRAMENTO ST	94118	6-E6
500	CALIFORNIA ST	94118	6-E6
LOEHR ST			SF
1	VISITACION AV	94134	19-J2
100	LELAND AV	94134	19-J2
LOMA VISTA TER			SF
1	ROOSEVELT WY	94114	10-F2
1	ROOSEVELT WY	94117	10-F2
100	ROOSEVELT WY	94114	10-F2
100	ROOSEVELT WY	94117	10-F2
LOMBARD ST			SF
1	THE EMBARCADERO	94111	3-B3
100	SANSOME ST	94133	3-A3
100	SANSOME ST	94111	3-A3
200	MONTGOMERY ST	94133	3-A3
300	WINTHROP ST	94133	3-A3
270	KEARNY ST	94133	3-A3
270	TELEGRAPH HILL BLVD	94133	3-A3
340	CHILD ST	94133	3-A3
380	JULIUS ST	94133	3-A3
400	GRANT AV	94133	3-A3
500	STOCKTON ST	94133	3-A3
550	TUSCANY AL	94133	3-A3
500	POWELL ST	94133	3-A3
610	MASON ST	94133	2-J3
600	NEWELL ST	94133	2-J4
680	COLUMBUS AV	94133	2-J4
700	JANSEN ST	94133	2-J4
800	TAYLOR ST	94133	2-J4
900	JONES ST	94133	2-J4
1000	LEAVENWORTH ST	94109	2-J4
1060	MONTCLAIR TER	94109	2-J4
1100	HYDE ST	94109	2-J4
1200	LARKIN ST	94109	2-H4
1300	POLK ST	94109	2-H4
1400	VAN NESS AV	94123	2-H4
1500	FRANKLIN ST	94123	2-H4
1600	GOUGH ST	94123	2-H4
1700	OCTAVIA ST	94123	2-H4
1800	LAGUNA ST	94123	2-G4
1900	BUCHANAN ST	94123	2-G4
2000	WEBSTER ST	94123	2-G4
2100	FILLMORE ST	94123	2-G4
2200	STEINER ST	94123	2-G4
2300	PIERCE ST	94123	2-F4
2400	SCOTT ST	94123	2-F4
2500	DIVISADERO ST	94123	2-F4
2600	BRODERICK ST	94123	2-F4
2650	RICHARDSON AV	94123	2-F4
2700	BAKER ST	94123	2-F4
	LYON ST	94129	6-F4
	RUGER ST	94129	6-F4
	LETTERMAN DR	94129	6-E4
	PRESIDIO BLVD	94129	6-E4
LOMITA AV			SF
100	16TH AV	94122	9-C3
1	ALOHA AV	94122	9-C2
100	LAWTON ST	94122	9-C2
LONDON ST			SF
200	AVALON AV	94112	14-G7
300	EXCELSIOR AV	94112	14-G7
400	BRAZIL AV	94112	14-G7
500	PERSIA AV	94112	19-G1
600	RUSSIA AV	94112	19-F1
700	FRANCE AV	94112	19-F1
750	KENNY AL	94112	19-F1
800	ITALY AV	94112	19-F1
900	AMAZON AV	94112	19-F1
1000	GENEVA AV	94112	19-F1
LONE MOUNTAIN TER			SF
1	PARKER AV	94118	5-E7
100	BEAUMONT AV	94118	5-E7
200	STANYAN ST	94118	5-E7
300	ROSSI AV	94118	5-E7
LONG AV			SF
	MARINE DR	94129	1-C3
	LINCOLN BLVD	94129	1-C3
LONGVIEW CT			SF
100	PANORAMA DR	94131	10-E4
LOOMIS ST			SF
1	BARNEVELD AV	94124	15-A5
50	MCKINNON AV	94124	15-A5
100	OAKDALE AV	94124	15-A5
120	FLOWER ST	94124	15-A5
260	WATERLOO ST	94124	15-A5
300	BOUTWELL ST	94124	15-A5
300	INDUSTRIAL ST	94124	15-A5
LOPEZ AV			SF
1	PACHECO ST	94116	9-D4
30	SOTELO AV	94116	9-D4
100	CASTENADA AV	94116	9-D4
LORAINE CT			SF
200	ANZA ST	94118	5-D6
LORI LN			SF
1	DELLBROOK AV	94131	9-E3
LOS PALMOS DR			SF
1	TERESITA BLVD	94127	14-E6
190	VERNA ST	94127	14-E6
200	FOERSTER ST	94127	14-E6
300	STANFORD HEIGHTS AV	94127	14-E6
400	BELLA VISTA WY	94127	13-E6
420	BELLAVISTA LN	94127	13-E6
500	LULU AL	94127	13-E6
700	BURLWOOD DR	94127	13-D6
600	EMIL LN	94127	13-D6
700	HAZELWOOD AV	94127	13-D6
700	GLOBE AL	94127	13-D6
LOUISBURG ST			SF
100	MARGARET AV	94112	18-E1
180	MOUNT VERNON AV	94112	18-E1
280	NIAGARA AV	94112	19-E1
400	GENEVA AV	94112	19-E1
LOWELL ST			SF
1	MISSION ST	94112	19-E2
40	MORSE ST	94112	19-E2
170	BRUNSWICK ST	94112	19-F2
230	BYRON CT	94112	19-F2
310	HANOVER ST	94112	19-F2
LOWER TER			SF
1	ROOSEVELT WY	94114	10-F2
100	LEVANT ST	94114	10-F2
180	SATURN ST	94114	10-F2
LOYOLA TER			SF
100	FULTON ST	94117	6-E7
LUCERNE ST			SF
100	BRANNAN ST	94103	7-A7
LUCKY ST			SF
1	24TH ST	94110	10-J4
100	25TH ST	94110	10-J4
200	26TH ST	94110	10-J4
LUCY ST			SF
1	THORNTON AV	94124	15-B7
100	WILLIAMS AV	94124	15-B7
LUNADO CT			SF
100	LUNADO WY	94127	13-C7
LUNADO WY			SF
	HOLLOWAY AV	94127	13-C7
80	ESTERO AV	94127	13-C7
150	LUNADO CT	94127	13-C7
200	MERCEDES WY	94127	13-C7
LUNDEEN ST			SF
	OLD MASON ST	94129	2-E3
	JAVOWITZ ST	94129	2-E3
	CROOK ST	94129	2-E3
LUNDYS LN			SF
1	COSO AV	94110	14-J4
1	MONTEZUMA ST	94110	14-J4
100	FAIR AV	94110	14-J5
150	ESMERALDA AV	94110	14-H5
200	VIRGINIA AV	94110	14-H5
LUPINE AV			SF
50	WOOD ST	94118	6-E6
330	LAUREL ST	94118	6-E6
400	DICHA AL	94118	6-E6
LURLINE ST			SF
1	FUNSTON AV	94122	9-C2
100	KIRKHAM ST	94122	9-C2
100	14TH AV	94122	9-C2
LURMONT TER			SF
1	LEAVENWORTH ST	94109	2-J4
LUSK ST			SF
100	TOWNSEND ST	94107	7-B7
LYELL ST			SF
1	BOSWORTH ST	94112	14-G6
1	BOSWORTH ST	94131	14-G6
50	BOSWORTH ST	94112	14-G6
80	STILL ST	94112	14-G6
110	STILL ST	94112	14-G6
160	CAYUGA AV	94112	14-G6
200	ALEMANY BLVD	94112	14-G6
LYNCH ST			SF
1	LEAVENWORTH ST	94109	6-J4
100	HYDE ST	94109	6-J4
LYNDHURST DR			SF
1	JUNIPERO SERRA BLVD	94132	13-C7
30	STRATFORD DR	94132	13-B7
100	DENSLOW DR	94132	13-B7
LYON ST			SF
3300	LIEUTENANT ALLEN ST	94123	2-E3
3300	LIEUTENANT ALLEN ST	94129	2-E3
3500	OLD MASON ST	94123	2-E3
3500	OLD MASON ST	94129	2-E3
2600	GREEN ST	94129	6-F5
2600	GREEN ST	94123	6-F5
2700	UNION ST	94129	6-F4
2700	UNION ST	94123	6-F4
2800	FILBERT ST	94129	6-F4
2800	FILBERT ST	94123	6-F4
2900	GREENWICH ST	94129	6-F4
2900	GREENWICH ST	94123	6-F4
3000	LOMBARD ST	94129	2-F4
3000	LOMBARD ST	94123	2-F4
3100	CHESTNUT ST	94129	2-F4
3100	CHESTNUT ST	94123	2-F4
3210	GORGAS AV	94129	2-F4
3210	GORGAS AV	94123	2-F4
3210	FRANCISCO ST	94123	2-F4
3280	RICHARDSON AV	94129	2-F4
3280	RICHARDSON AV	94123	2-F4
3280	PALACE DR	94123	2-F4
3400	BAY ST	94123	2-F4
1300	TERRA VISTA AV	94115	6-F6
1320	OFARRELL ST	94115	6-F6
	GEARY BLVD	94115	6-F6
1360	LEONA TER	94115	6-F6
1400	POST ST	94115	6-F6
1500	SUTTER ST	94115	6-F6
1600	BUSH ST	94115	6-F6
1700	PINE ST	94115	6-F6
1800	CALIFORNIA ST	94115	6-F5
1900	SACRAMENTO ST	94115	6-F5
2000	CLAY ST	94115	6-F5
2100	WASHINGTON ST	94115	6-F5
2200	JACKSON ST	94115	6-F5
2300	PACIFIC AV	94129	6-F5
2300	PACIFIC AV	94115	6-F5
2400	W BROADWAY ST	94129	6-F5
2400	W BROADWAY ST	94115	6-F5
2400	BROADWAY ST	94115	6-F5
300	FELL ST	94117	6-F7
400	HAYES ST	94117	6-F7
500	GROVE ST	94117	6-F7
600	FULTON ST	94117	6-F7
700	MCALLISTER ST	94117	6-F7
800	GOLDEN GATE AV	94115	6-F7
900	TURK ST	94115	6-F7
1	HAIGHT ST	94117	10-F1
100	PAGE ST	94117	10-F1
200	OAK ST	94117	10-F1
LYSETTE ST			SF
	SACRAMENTO ST	94109	6-J5
	CALIFORNIA ST	94109	6-J5
M			
MABINI ST			SF
1	BONIFACIO ST	94107	7-B6
100	FOLSOM ST	94107	7-B6
MABREY CT			SF
100	RICHARDS CIR	94124	15-C6
100	WHITNEY YOUNG CIR	94124	15-C6
MACARTHUR AV			SF
	FRANKLIN ST	94123	2-H3
	EL POLIN LP	94129	5-E4
850	WALLEN CT	94129	5-E4
	FERNANDEZ ST	94129	5-E4
	PORTOLA ST	94129	5-E4
	SANCHES ST	94129	5-E4
	SUMNER ST	94129	5-E4
	PRESIDIO BLVD	94129	5-E4
MACEDONIA ST			SF
1	MONTCALM ST	94110	15-A4
100	BREWSTER ST	94110	15-A4
MACONDRAY LN			SF
200	LEAVENWORTH ST	94109	6-J4
MADDUX AV			SF
1	REVERE AV	94124	15-B6
1	SILVER AV	94124	15-B6
20	ROBBLEE AV	94124	15-B6
30	QUINT ST	94124	15-B6
40	QUINT ST	94124	15-B6
70	THOMAS AV	94124	15-B6
100	TOPEKA AV	94124	15-B6
200	SCOTIA AV	94124	15-B6
MADERA ST			SF
1	ARKANSAS ST	94107	11-B3
100	WISCONSIN ST	94107	11-B3
MADISON ST			SF
1	SILVER AV	94134	14-H7
1	SILVER AV	94112	14-H7
50	ATHENS ST	94134	14-H7
50	ATHENS ST	94112	14-H7
100	PIOCHE ST	94134	14-H7
100	PIOCHE ST	94112	14-H7
150	VALMAR TER	94134	14-H7
200	SILLIMAN ST	94134	14-H7
300	FELTON ST	94134	14-H7
400	BURROWS ST	94134	14-H7
MADRID ST			SF
1	SILVER AV	94112	14-H7
100	PERU AV	94112	14-G7
200	AVALON AV	94112	14-G7
300	EXCELSIOR AV	94112	14-G7
400	BRAZIL AV	94112	19-G1
500	PERSIA AV	94112	19-G1
600	RUSSIA AV	94112	19-G1
700	FRANCE AV	94112	19-G1
800	ITALY AV	94112	19-F1
900	AMAZON AV	94112	19-F1
1000	GENEVA AV	94112	19-F2
1100	ROLPH ST	94112	19-F2
MADRONE AV			SF
1	TARAVAL ST	94127	13-C5
100	ULLOA ST	94127	13-C5
200	VICENTE ST	94127	13-C5
MAGELLAN AV			SF
1	CASTENADA AV	94116	9-D4
30	MARCELA AV	94116	9-D4
100	PLAZA ST	94116	9-D4
200	SOLA AV	94116	9-D4
290	PACHECO ST	94116	13-D4
310	DORANTES AV	94116	13-D4
310	PACHECO ST	94116	13-D4
310	DORANTES AV	94116	13-D4
400	MONTALVO AV	94116	13-C4
500	CORTES AV	94116	13-C4
600	12TH AV	94116	13-C4
MAGNOLIA ST			SF
1	LAGUNA ST	94123	2-G4
100	BUCHANAN ST	94123	2-G4
200	WEBSTER ST	94123	2-G4
MAHAN ST			SF
600	HUSSEY ST	94124	21-E1
750	H ST	94124	21-E1
900	J ST	94124	21-E1
MAIDEN LN			SF
1	KEARNY ST	94108	7-A6
100	GRANT AV	94108	7-A6
200	STOCKTON ST	94108	7-A6
MAIN ST			SF
1	MARKET ST	94105	7-B5
100	MISSION ST	94105	7-B5
200	HOWARD ST	94105	7-B5
300	FOLSOM ST	94105	7-C5
350	ELKHART ST	94105	7-C6
400	HARRISON ST	94105	7-C6
500	BRYANT ST	94105	7-C6

Address	Cross Street	ZIP	City Pg-Grid
MAJESTIC AV			SF
100	LAKEVIEW AV	94112	18-E1
200	TARA ST	94112	18-E1
MALLORCA WY			SF
1	CHESTNUT ST	94123	2-G4
100	TOLEDO WY	94123	2-G3
200	ALHAMBRA ST	94123	2-G3
230	CAPRA WY	94123	2-G3
300	BEACH ST	94123	2-G3
MALTA DR			SF
1	OSHAUGHNESSY BLVD	94131	14-F6
30	VALLETA CT	94131	14-F6
100	MERCATO CT	94131	14-F6
MALVINA PL			SF
1	DAWSON PL	94108	7-A5
1	MASON ST	94108	7-A5
MANCHESTER ST			SF
40	BESSIE ST	94110	14-J4
100	STONEMAN ST	94110	14-J4
MANGELS AV			SF
1	HAMERTON AV	94131	14-F6
50	BURNSIDE AV	94131	14-F6
100	BADEN ST	94131	14-F6
150	NORDHOFF ST	94131	14-F6
200	CONGO ST	94131	14-F6
200	CONGO ST	94127	14-F6
300	DETROIT ST	94127	14-F6
500	FOERSTER ST	94127	14-E6
600	GENNESSEE ST	94127	13-E6
700	RIDGEWOOD AV	94127	13-E6
720	BRENTWOOD AV	94127	13-E6
800	HAZELWOOD AV	94127	13-D6
850	VALDEZ AV	94127	13-D6
900	COLON AV	94127	13-D6
1000	PLYMOUTH AV	94127	13-D6
MANOR DR			SF
100	KENWOOD WY	94127	13-D7
200	UPLAND DR	94127	13-D6
300	DARIEN WY	94127	13-D6
1	OCEAN AV	94127	13-C7
100	KENWOOD WY	94127	13-C7
MANSEAU ST			SF
600	E ST	94124	21-F1
630	MORRELL ST	94124	21-E1
650	COCHRANE ST	94124	21-E1
	HUSSEY ST	94124	21-E1
670	HUSSEY ST	94124	21-E1
680	H ST	94124	20-E1
700	3RD AV	94124	20-E1
700	I ST	94124	20-E1
MANSELL ST			SF
1	SAN BRUNO AV	94134	20-A1
50	GIRARD ST	94134	20-A1
100	BRUSSELS ST	94134	20-A1
150	GOETTINGEN ST	94134	20-A1
200	SOMERSET ST	94134	20-A1
250	HOLYOKE ST	94134	20-A1
300	HAMILTON ST	94134	20-A1
350	BOWDOIN ST	94134	20-A1
400	DARTMOUTH ST	94134	20-A1
450	COLBY ST	94134	19-J1
500	UNIVERSITY ST	94134	19-J1
540	VISITACION AV	94134	19-J1
670	JOHN F SHELLEY DR	94134	19-J1
880	JOHN F SHELLEY DR	94134	19-H1
1100	BRAZIL AV	94134	19-H1
1100	PERSIA AV	94134	19-H1
MANSFIELD ST			SF
1	INA CT	94112	14-H7
1	LA GRANDE AV	94112	14-H7
100	BURROWS ST	94112	14-H7
MANZANITA AV			SF
1	MAYFAIR DR	94118	6-E6
100	EUCLID AV	94118	6-E6
MAPLE ST			SF
100	JACKSON ST	94118	5-E5
200	WASHINGTON ST	94118	5-E5
300	CLAY ST	94118	5-E5
400	SACRAMENTO ST	94118	5-E6
500	CALIFORNIA ST	94118	5-E6
MARCELA AV			SF
40	PACHECO ST	94116	9-D4
1	SOLA AV	94116	9-D4
50	MAGELLAN AV	94116	9-D4
MARCY PL			SF
1	JACKSON ST	94108	6-J5
MARENGO ST			SF
1	BAYSHORE BLVD	94124	15-A5
100	WATERLOO ST	94124	15-A5
MARGARET AV			SF
1	SUMMIT ST	94112	18-E1
100	LAKEVIEW AV	94112	18-E1
200	LOUISBURG ST	94112	18-E1
MARGRAVE PL			SF
1	VALLEJO ST	94133	7-A4
MARIETTA DR			SF
1	TERESITA BLVD	94127	14-E5
70	ENCLINE CT	94127	14-E5
110	REPOSA WY	94127	14-E5
200	ARROYO WY	94127	14-F5
500	BELLA VISTA WY	94127	14-F5
500	CUBA AL	94127	14-F5
500	TERESITA BLVD	94127	14-F5
MARIN ST			SF
900	MICHIGAN ST	94124	11-C4
1000	ILLINOIS ST	94124	11-C4
1100	3RD ST	94124	11-C4
1100	TENNESSEE ST	94124	11-C4
1300	INDIANA ST	94124	11-C4
1700	EVANS AV	94124	15-B4
2500	KANSAS ST	94124	15-A4
MARINA BLVD			SF
1	LAGUNA ST	94123	2-G3
100	BUCHANAN ST	94123	2-G3
200	WEBSTER ST	94123	2-G3
200	MARINA GREEN DR	94123	2-G3
300	FILLMORE ST	94123	2-G3
400	AVILA ST	94123	2-F3
400	CASA WY	94123	2-F3
500	MARINA GREEN DR	94123	2-F3
500	CERVANTES BLVD	94123	2-F3
500	SCOTT ST	94123	2-F3
600	DIVISADERO ST	94123	2-F3
700	BRODERICK ST	94123	2-F3
820	BAKER ST	94123	2-F3
840	DOYLE DR	94123	2-F3
870	OLD MASON ST	94123	2-F3
870	PEDESTRIAN WY	94123	2-F3
MARINA GREEN DR			SF
	MARINA BLVD	94123	2-G3
	CERVANTES BLVD	94123	2-G3
	SCOTT ST	94123	2-G3
MARINE DR			SF
	LONG AV	94129	1-C2
	SERGEANT MITCHELL ST	94129	1-E3
	MARSHALL ST	94129	2-E3
	JAVOWITZ ST	94129	2-E3
	HAMILTON ST	94129	1-D3
	PEARCE ST	94129	1-D3
	MCDONALD ST	94129	1-D3
MARION PL			SF
1	UNION ST	94133	2-J4
MARIPOSA ST			SF
400	ILLINOIS ST	94107	11-C2
400	TERRY A FRANCOIS BLVD	94107	11-C2
500	3RD ST	94107	11-C2
600	TENNESSEE ST	94107	11-C2
700	MINNESOTA ST	94107	11-C2
800	INDIANA ST	94107	11-C2
1000	PENNSYLVANIA AV	94107	11-B2
1100	MISSISSIPPI ST	94107	11-B2
1200	TEXAS ST	94107	11-B2
1300	MISSOURI ST	94107	11-B2
1400	CONNECTICUT ST	94107	11-B2
1500	ARKANSAS ST	94107	11-B2
1700	CAROLINA ST	94107	11-B2
1800	DE HARO ST	94107	11-A2
1900	RHODE ISLAND ST	94107	11-A2
2000	KANSAS ST	94107	11-A2
2100	VERMONT ST	94107	11-A2
2200	SAN BRUNO AV	94110	11-A2
2300	UTAH ST	94110	11-A2
2400	POTRERO AV	94110	11-A2
2500	HAMPSHIRE ST	94110	11-A2
2600	YORK ST	94110	11-A2
	BRYANT ST	94110	11-A2
2800	FLORIDA ST	94110	10-J2
2900	ALABAMA ST	94110	10-J2
3000	HARRISON ST	94110	10-J2
MARK LN			SF
1	HARLAN PL	94108	7-A5
100	BUSH ST	94108	7-A5
MARKET ST			SF
1	STEUART ST	94105	7-B5
1	STEUART ST	94111	7-B5
100	CALIFORNIA ST	94105	7-B5
100	CALIFORNIA ST	94111	7-B5
100	SPEAR ST	94111	7-B5
170	DRUMM ST	94105	7-B5
170	DRUMM ST	94111	7-B5
200	MAIN ST	94105	7-B5
200	MAIN ST	94111	7-B5
290	PINE ST	94105	7-B5
290	PINE ST	94111	7-B5
300	BEALE ST	94105	7-B5
300	BEALE ST	94111	7-B5
300	DAVIS ST	94111	7-B5
300	FREMONT ST	94105	7-B5
400	FREMONT ST	94111	7-B5
400	FRONT ST	94111	7-B5
500	1ST ST	94105	7-B5
500	1ST ST	94111	7-B5
500	BUSH ST	94111	7-B5
530	BATTERY ST	94105	7-B5
530	BATTERY ST	94104	7-B5
530	SUTTER ST	94105	7-B5
530	SUTTER ST	94104	7-B5
600	2ND ST	94105	7-B5
600	2ND ST	94104	7-B5
	MONTGOMERY ST	94105	7-B5
	MONTGOMERY ST	94108	7-B5
	NEW MONTGOMERY ST	94108	7-B5
630	NEW MONTGOMERY ST	94105	7-A6
630	NEW MONTGOMERY ST	94108	7-A6
660	ANNIE ST	94103	7-A6
660	ANNIE ST	94108	7-A6
670	GEARY ST	94103	7-A6
670	GEARY ST	94108	7-A6
680	3RD ST	94103	7-A6
680	3RD ST	94108	7-A6
680	KEARNY ST	94108	7-A6
700	3RD ST	94103	7-A6
700	3RD ST	94108	7-A6
740	OFARRELL ST	94103	7-A6
740	OFARRELL ST	94108	7-A6
750	GRANT AV	94103	7-A6
750	GRANT AV	94108	7-A6
800	4TH ST	94103	7-A6
800	4TH ST	94102	7-A6
800	ELLIS ST	94102	7-A6
810	STOCKTON ST	94103	7-A6
810	STOCKTON ST	94102	7-A6
900	5TH ST	94103	7-A6
900	5TH ST	94102	7-A6
900	CYRIL MAGIN ST	94102	7-A6
940	MASON ST	94103	7-A6
940	MASON ST	94102	7-A6
1000	6TH ST	94103	7-A6
1000	6TH ST	94102	7-A6
1000	GOLDEN GATE AV	94102	7-A6
1010	TAYLOR ST	94103	7-A6
1010	TAYLOR ST	94102	7-A6
1040	MCALLISTER ST	94103	6-J6
1040	MCALLISTER ST	94102	6-J6
1100	7TH ST	94103	6-J7
1100	7TH ST	94102	6-J7
	8TH ST	94103	6-J7
	8TH ST	94102	6-J7
	HYDE ST	94102	6-J7
1200	GROVE ST	94103	6-J7
1200	GROVE ST	94102	6-J7
1300	9TH ST	94103	6-J7
1300	9TH ST	94102	6-J7
1300	HAYES ST	94102	6-J7
1300	LARKIN ST	94102	6-J7
1400	10TH ST	94103	6-J7
1400	10TH ST	94102	6-J7
1400	POLK ST	94102	6-J7
1500	11TH ST	94103	6-J7
1500	11TH ST	94102	6-J7
1540	VAN NESS AV	94103	6-J7
1540	VAN NESS AV	94102	6-J7
1600	12TH ST	94103	6-H7
1600	12TH ST	94102	6-H7
1620	FRANKLIN ST	94103	6-H7
1620	FRANKLIN ST	94102	6-H7
1620	ROSE ST	94103	6-H7
1640	ROSE ST	94102	6-H7
1650	BRADY ST	94103	10-H1
1650	BRADY ST	94102	10-H1
1680	HAIGHT ST	94103	10-H1
1680	HAIGHT ST	94102	10-H1
1680	GOUGH ST	94102	10-H1
1700	GOUGH ST	94103	10-H1
1700	GOUGH ST	94102	10-H1
1720	VALENCIA ST	94103	10-H1
1720	VALENCIA ST	94102	10-H1
1800	OCTAVIA ST	94103	10-H1
1800	OCTAVIA ST	94102	10-H1
1810	MCCOPPIN ST	94103	10-H1
1810	MCCOPPIN ST	94102	10-H1
1820	PEARL ST	94103	10-H1
1820	PEARL ST	94102	10-H1
1880	GUERRERO ST	94103	10-H1
1880	GUERRERO ST	94102	10-H1
1900	LAGUNA ST	94103	10-H1
1900	LAGUNA ST	94102	10-H1
1980	DUBOCE AV	94103	10-H1
1980	DUBOCE AV	94114	10-H1
2000	DOLORES ST	94114	10-H1
2020	RESERVOIR ST	94114	10-H1
2080	14TH ST	94114	10-H1
2110	CHURCH ST	94114	10-G1
2100	15TH ST	94114	10-G2
2210	SANCHEZ ST	94114	10-G2
	16TH ST	94114	10-G2
2300	NOE ST	94114	10-G2
2400	CASTRO ST	94114	10-G2
2500	COLLINGWOOD ST	94114	10-G2
2600	DIAMOND ST	94114	10-G2
2700	EUREKA ST	94114	10-F2
2800	DOUGLASS ST	94114	10-F2
2850	STORRIE ST	94114	10-F2
2850	ORD ST	94114	10-F2
2860	HATTIE ST	94114	10-F2
2990	MERRITT ST	94114	10-F2
3060	DANVERS ST	94114	10-F2
3200	19TH ST	94114	10-F2
3370	CLAYTON ST	94114	10-F3
3370	MONO ST	94114	10-F3
3390	SHORT ST	94114	10-F3
3420	COPPER AL	94114	10-F3
3490	GLENDALE ST	94114	10-F3
3490	GRAND VIEW AV	94114	10-F3
3490	STANTON ST	94114	10-F3
3600	ROMAIN ST	94131	10-F3
3600	ROMAIN ST	94114	10-F3
3600	MORGAN AL	94131	10-F3
3600	MORGAN AL	94114	10-F3
3720	DIXIE AL	94114	10-F3
3720	DIXIE AL	94131	10-F3
	ARGENT AL	94114	10-F3
	ARGENT AL	94131	10-F3
3780	GOLDING LN	94114	10-F4
3780	GOLDING LN	94131	10-F4
3810	PORTOLA DR	94114	10-F4
3810	PORTOLA DR	94131	10-F4
3810	CORBETT AV	94131	10-F4
MARLIN CT			SF
100	KIRKWOOD AV	94124	15-E7
MARNE AV			SF
1	MIRALOMA DR	94127	13-D5
100	JUANITA WY	94127	13-D5
MARS ST			SF
1	17TH ST	94114	10-F2
100	CORBETT AV	94114	10-F2
MARSHALL ST			SF
	MARINE DR	94129	2-E3
	JAUSS ST	94129	2-E3
	LIEUTENANT ALLEN ST	94129	2-E3
	OLD MASON ST	94129	2-E3
	GORGAS AV	94129	2-E3
MARSILLY ST			SF
1	SAINT MARYS AV	94112	14-H6
100	BOSWORTH ST	94112	14-H6
MARSTON AV			SF
1	CIRCULAR AV	94112	14-F7
100	EDNA ST	94112	14-E7
MARTHA AV			SF
30	BADEN ST	94131	14-F6
70	STILLINGS AV	94131	14-F6
100	MERCATO CT	94131	14-F6
MARTIN LUTHER KING JR DR			SF
	7TH AV	-	9-C1
	BOWLING GREEN DR	-	9-C1
300	MIDDLE DR E	94118	9-C1
350	CONCOURSE DR	94118	9-C1
400	S TEA GARDEN DR	-	9-C1
580	STOW LAKE DR E	-	9-C1
500	STOW LAKE DR	-	9-B1
600	CROSS OVER DR	-	9-B1
700	TRANSVERSE DR	-	9-B1
	25TH AV	-	9-A1
	METSON RD	-	9-A1
1280	SUNSET BLVD	-	8-J1
	MIDDLE DR W	-	8-J1
1500	CHAIN OF LAKES DR E	-	8-H1
	S FORK DR	-	8-H1
	LA PLAYA	-	8-H1
	LINCOLN WY	-	8-H1
	9TH AV	-	9-C1
	LINCOLN WY	-	9-C1
MARTINEZ ST			SF
	FUNSTON AV	94129	1-E4
MARVEL CT			SF
1	32ND AV	94121	5-A6
MAR VIEW WY			SF
1	PALO ALTO AV	94131	10-E3
30	FARVIEW CT	94131	10-E3
130	AQUAVISTA WY	94131	10-E3
160	SKYVIEW WY	94131	10-E3
200	PANORAMA DR	94131	10-E3
MARY ST			SF
1	MISSION ST	94103	7-A6
1	MINT ST	94103	7-A6
30	MINNA ST	94103	7-A6
60	NATOMA ST	94103	7-A7
100	HOWARD ST	94103	7-A7
MASON ST			SF
1	MARKET ST	94102	7-A6
20	TURK ST	94102	7-A6
100	EDDY ST	94102	7-A6
200	ELLIS ST	94102	7-A6
300	OFARRELL ST	94102	7-A6
330	ELWOOD ST	94102	7-A6
400	GEARY ST	94102	7-A6
410	DERBY ST	94102	7-A6
500	POST ST	94102	7-A5
600	SUTTER ST	94102	7-A5
650	DELTA PL	94102	7-A5
700	BUSH ST	94108	7-A5
760	HOOKER AL	94108	7-A5
800	PINE ST	94108	7-A5
880	NOB HILL PL	94108	7-A5
900	CALIFORNIA ST	94108	7-A5
1000	SACRAMENTO ST	94108	7-A5
1050	EWER PL	94108	7-A5
1080	DAWSON PL	94108	7-A5
1080	MALVINA PL	94108	7-A5
1100	CLAY ST	94108	7-A5
1140	SHEPHARD PL	94108	7-A5
1140	TRUETT ST	94108	7-A5
1200	WASHINGTON ST	94108	7-A5
1300	JACKSON ST	94133	7-A4
1360	JOHN ST	94133	7-A4
1400	PACIFIC AV	94133	7-A4
1490	BROADWAY	94133	6-J4
1600	VALLEJO ST	94133	6-J4
1700	GREEN ST	94133	2-J4
1700	WINTER PL	94133	2-J4
1770	WEBB PL	94133	2-J4
1800	UNION ST	94133	2-J4
1820	KENT ST	94133	2-J4
1900	FILBERT ST	94133	2-J4
1930	VALPARAISO ST	94133	2-J4
1960	GREENWICH ST	94133	2-J4
2050	COLUMBUS AV	94133	2-J4
2100	LOMBARD ST	94133	2-J3
2200	CHESTNUT ST	94133	2-J3
2250	WATER ST	94133	2-J3
2300	FRANCISCO ST	94133	2-J3
2350	VANDEWATER ST	94133	2-J3
2400	BAY ST	94133	2-J3
2500	NORTH POINT ST	94133	2-J3
2600	BEACH ST	94133	2-J3
2700	JEFFERSON ST	94133	2-J3
	OLD MASON ST	94129	1-E3
	HALLECK ST	94129	1-E3
	BANK ST	94129	1-D3
	OLD MASON ST	94129	1-D3
	OLD MASON ST	94129	1-C3
	CRISSY FIELD AV	94129	1-C3
MASONIC AV			SF
	PRESIDIO AV	94115	6-F6
	PINE ST	94115	6-F6
	EUCLID AV	94115	6-F6
	EUCLID AV	94118	6-F6
1	GEARY BLVD	94115	6-F6
1	GEARY BLVD	94118	6-F6
100	ANZA ST	94115	6-F6
100	ANZA ST	94118	6-F6
100	OFARRELL ST	94118	6-F6
140	EWING TER	94115	6-F7
140	EWING TER	94118	6-F7
200	TURK ST	94115	6-F7
200	TURK ST	94118	6-F7
300	GOLDEN GATE AV	94117	6-F7
400	MCALLISTER ST	94117	6-F7
500	FULTON ST	94117	6-F7
600	GROVE ST	94117	6-F7
690	HAYES ST	94117	6-F7
790	FELL ST	94117	10-F1
880	OAK ST	94117	10-F1
970	PAGE ST	94117	10-F1
1070	HAIGHT ST	94117	10-F1
1160	WALLER ST	94117	10-F1
1350	FREDERICK ST	94117	10-F1
1450	JAVA ST	94117	10-F1
1510	PIEDMONT ST	94117	10-F2
1600	UPPER TER	94117	10-F2
1600	ROOSEVELT WY	94117	10-F2
MASSASOIT ST			SF
1	ESMERALDA AV	94110	15-A4
100	RUTLEDGE ST	94110	15-A4
MASSET PL			SF
1	3RD ST	94103	7-B6
MATEO ST			SF
1	BEMIS ST	94131	14-G5
90	LAIDLEY ST	94131	14-G6
190	CHENERY ST	94131	14-G6
260	ARLINGTON ST	94131	14-G6
MATTHEW CT			SF
1	ESPANOLA ST	94124	15-D6
MAULDIN ST			SF
	HAMILTON ST	94129	1-C3
	MCDONALD ST	94129	1-D3
	LIVINGSTON ST	94129	1-D3
MAYFAIR DR			SF
1	LAUREL ST	94118	6-E6
20	COLLINS ST	94118	6-E6
80	MANZANITA AV	94118	6-E6
120	IRIS AV	94118	6-E6
170	HEATHER AV	94118	5-E6
200	SPRUCE ST	94118	5-E6
MAYFLOWER ST			SF
300	HOLLADAY AV	94110	15-A5
330	FRANCONIA ST	94110	15-A5
350	PERALTA AV	94110	15-A5
370	BRADFORD ST	94110	15-A5
400	CHAPMAN ST	94110	15-A5
MAYNARD ST			SF
50	MISSION ST	94112	14-G7
50	CASTLE MANOR AV	94112	14-G7
100	CRAUT ST	94112	14-H7
200	CONGDON ST	94112	14-H7
300	GLADSTONE DR	94112	14-H7
400	TRUMBULL ST	94112	14-H7
MAYWOOD DR			SF
1	YERBA BUENA AV	94127	13-D6
100	RAVENWOOD DR	94127	13-D6
250	BRENTWOOD AV	94127	13-D6
300	EL VERANO WY	94127	13-D6
MCALLISTER ST			SF
1	MARKET ST	94102	6-J6
20	JONES ST	94102	6-J6
70	7TH ST	94102	6-J7
100	LEAVENWORTH ST	94102	6-J7
200	HYDE ST	94102	6-J7
250	BREEN PL	94102	6-J7
300	LARKIN ST	94102	6-J7
400	POLK ST	94102	6-J7
500	VAN NESS AV	94102	6-H7
600	FRANKLIN ST	94102	6-H7
700	GOUGH ST	94102	6-H7
800	OCTAVIA ST	94102	6-H7
900	LAGUNA ST	94102	6-H7
1100	WEBSTER ST	94117	6-G7
1150	CRAN PL	94117	6-G7
1200	FILLMORE ST	94117	6-G7
1290	STEINER ST	94117	6-G7
1390	PIERCE ST	94117	6-G7
1490	SCOTT ST	94117	6-G7
1590	DIVISADERO ST	94117	6-F7
1690	BRODERICK ST	94117	6-F7
1790	BAKER ST	94117	6-F7
1890	LYON ST	94117	6-F7
1990	CENTRAL AV	94117	6-F7
2100	MASONIC AV	94117	6-F7
2600	STANYAN ST	94118	5-E7
2640	PARSONS ST	94118	5-E7
2700	WILLARD ST N	94118	5-D7
2800	ARGUELLO BLVD	94118	5-D7
2500	PARKER AV	94117	5-E7
2600	STANYAN ST	94117	5-E7
MCCANN ST			SF
	ENGLISH ST	94124	16-E7
	LOCKWOOD ST	94124	16-E7
MCCARTHY AV			SF
1	ARGONAUT AV	94134	19-J2
100	BURR AV	94134	19-J2
MCCOPPIN ST			SF
1	GOUGH ST	94103	10-H1
1	OTIS ST	94103	10-H1
30	JESSIE ST	94103	10-H1
70	STEVENSON ST	94103	10-H1
100	VALENCIA ST	94103	10-H1
180	ELGIN PK	94103	10-H1
200	MARKET ST	94103	10-H1
MCCORMICK ST			SF
100	MORRELL ST	94109	6-J5

PRIMARY STREET / Address	Cross Street	ZIP	CITY Pg-Grid
MCCORMICK ST			SF
100	PACIFIC AV	94109	6-J5
MCDONALD ST			SF
	PEARCE ST	94129	1-D3
	MARINE DR	94129	1-D3
	MAULDIN ST	94129	1-D3
	OLD MASON ST	94129	1-D3
MCDOWELL AV			SF
	SCHOFIELD RD	94123	2-H3
	LINCOLN BLVD	94129	1-C4
	PARK BLVD	94129	1-C4
	PATTEN RD	94129	1-C4
	COWLES ST	94129	1-C3
	CRISSY FIELD AV	94129	1-C3
MCKINNON AV			SF
1900	LA SALLE AV	94124	15-B5
1900	RANKIN ST	94124	15-B5
2010	SELBY ST	94124	15-B5
2300	TOLAND ST	94124	15-B5
2400	UPTON ST	94124	15-A5
2490	BARNEVELD AV	94124	15-A5
2500	LOOMIS ST	94124	15-A5
1500	LANE ST	94124	15-C6
1600	MENDELL ST	94124	15-C6
1650	3RD ST	94124	15-C6
1700	NEWHALL ST	94124	15-B6
1800	PHELPS ST	94124	15-B6
MCLAREN AV			SF
1	28TH AV	94121	5-A6
50	29TH AV	94121	5-A6
100	EL CAMINO DEL MAR	94121	5-A6
MCLEA CT			SF
	9TH ST	94103	11-A1
MCRAE ST			SF
	PORTOLA ST	94129	5-E5
MEACHAM PL			SF
1	POST ST	94109	6-J6
MEADE AV			SF
700	LE CONTE AV	94124	20-B1
860	JENNINGS ST	94124	20-B1
870	NELSON AV	94124	20-B1
1000	3RD ST	94124	20-B1
MEADOWBROOK DR			SF
1	SLOAT BLVD	94132	13-A6
100	OCEAN AV	94132	13-A6
200	EUCALYPTUS DR	94132	13-A6
MEDA AV			SF
1	OTSEGO AV	94112	14-F7
100	DELANO AV	94112	14-F7
MELBA AV			SF
1	OCEAN AV	94132	13-B6
100	EUCALYPTUS DR	94132	13-B6
MELRA CT			SF
100	DELTA ST	94134	19-J2
100	SUNNYDALE AV	94134	19-J2
MELROSE AV			SF
300	FOERSTER ST	94127	14-E6
400	BELLA VISTA WY	94127	14-E6
400	BELLAVISTA LN	94127	14-E6
400	STANFORD HEIGHTS AV	94127	14-E6
500	GENNESSEE ST	94127	13-E6
600	BRENTWOOD AV	94127	13-E6
600	LULU AL	94127	13-E6
1	CONGO ST	94127	14-F6
1	CONGO ST	94131	14-F6
100	DETROIT ST	94127	14-F6
100	DETROIT ST	94131	14-F6
200	TERESITA BLVD	94127	14-F6
200	TERESITA BLVD	94131	14-F6
MENDELL ST			SF
1	CARGO WY	94124	15-C5
200	NEWHALL ST	94124	15-C5
400	EVANS AV	94124	15-C5
500	FAIRFAX AV	94124	15-C5
600	GALVEZ AV	94124	15-C5
700	HUDSON AV	94124	15-C5
800	INNES AV	94124	15-C5
900	JERROLD AV	94124	15-C6
1000	KIRKWOOD AV	94124	15-C6
1100	LA SALLE AV	94124	15-C6
1200	MCKINNON AV	94124	15-C6
1300	NEWCOMB AV	94124	15-C6
1400	OAKDALE AV	94124	15-C6
1500	3RD ST	94124	15-C6
1500	PALOU AV	94124	15-C6
2200	WILLIAMS AV	94124	15-B7
2280	YOSEMITE AV	94124	15-B7
2380	ARMSTRONG AV	94124	15-B7
2480	BANCROFT AV	94124	15-B7
2600	CARROLL AV	94124	15-B7
MENDOSA AV			SF
1	9TH AV	94116	9-C4
130	10TH AV	94116	9-C4
150	GATEVIEW CT	94116	9-C4
200	CRAGMONT AV	94116	9-C4
MERCATO CT			SF
1	BOSWORTH ST	94131	14-F6
1	ELK ST	94131	14-F6
30	MARTHA AV	94131	14-F6
50	CONGO ST	94131	14-F6
50	MALTA DR	94131	14-F6
100	STILLINGS AV	94131	14-F6
MERCED AV			SF
1	LAGUNA HONDA BLVD	94127	13-D4
70	HERNANDEZ AV	94127	13-D4
80	PACHECO ST	94127	13-D4
120	PACHECO ST	94127	13-D4
130	GARCIA AV	94127	13-D4
200	KENSINGTON WY	94127	13-D4
200	VASQUEZ AV	94127	13-D4
MERCEDES WY			SF
40	PALOMA AV	94127	13-C7
20	CEDRO AV	94127	13-C7
20	CERRITOS AV	94127	13-C7
1	LUNADO WY	94127	13-C7
20	JUNIPERO SERRA BLVD	94127	13-C7
MERCHANT RD			SF
	CRANSTON RD	94129	1-B3
	LINCOLN BLVD	94129	1-C3
	RALSTON AV	94129	1-C3
MERCHANT ST			SF
400	BATTERY ST	94111	7-B5
500	SANSOME ST	94111	7-B5
MERCURY ST			SF
1	LEDYARD ST	94124	15-A6
100	THORNTON AV	94124	15-A6
MERLIN ST			SF
1	HARRISON ST	94107	7-A7
MERRIE WY			SF
	POINT LOBOS AV	94121	4-H6
MERRILL ST			SF
1	GAVEN ST	94134	15-A6
100	SWEENY ST	94134	15-A6
200	HALE ST	94134	15-A6
300	SILVER AV	94134	15-A6
MERRIMAC ST			SF
	ILLINOIS ST	94107	11-C1
MERRITT ST			SF
1	DANVERS ST	94114	10-F2
100	MARKET ST	94114	10-F2
MERSEY ST			SF
100	23RD ST	94114	10-H3
200	24TH ST	94114	10-H3
MESA AV			SF
	LINCOLN BLVD	94129	1-E4
	HALLECK ST	94129	1-E4
	MORAGA AV	94129	5-D4
	PENA ST	94129	1-E4
	PRESIDIO BLVD	94129	1-E4
	CANBY ST	94129	1-E4
1	9TH AV	94116	9-D4
100	SANTA RITA AV	94116	9-D4
METSON RD			SF
	MARTIN LUTHER KING JR DR	-	9-A1
	MIDDLE DR W	-	9-A1
MICHIGAN ST			SF
800	24TH ST	94107	11-C3
1000	25TH ST	94107	11-C3
1600	CESAR CHAVEZ ST	94124	11-C4
1800	MARIN ST	94124	11-C4
MIDCREST WY			SF
100	CITYVIEW WY	94131	10-E4
200	PANORAMA DR	94131	10-E4
MIDDLE DR E			SF
	JOHN F KENNEDY DR	-	9-D1
	BOWLING GREEN DR	-	9-D1
	MARTIN LUTHER KING JR DR	-	9-D1
MIDDLE DR W			SF
	TRANSVERSE DR	-	9-B1
	OVERLOOK DR	-	9-A1
	METSON RD	-	9-A1
	MARTIN LUTHER KING JR DR	-	8-J1
	CHAIN OF LAKES DR E	-	8-J1
MIDDLEFIELD DR			SF
1	SLOAT BLVD	94132	13-A6
100	OCEAN AV	94132	13-A6
200	EUCALYPTUS DR	94132	13-A6
200	GELLERT DR	94132	13-A6
210	LAKE MERCED BLVD	94132	13-A6
MIDDLEPOINT RD			SF
1	INGALLS ST	94124	15-D6
1	INNES AV	94124	15-D6
30	HARE ST	94124	15-D6
90	WEST POINT RD	94124	15-D6
170	WILLS ST	94124	15-D6
220	WEST POINT RD	94124	15-D6
300	EVANS AV	94124	15-D6
300	HUNTERS POINT BLVD	94124	15-D6
300	JENNINGS ST	94124	15-D6
MIDWAY ST			SF
1	FRANCISCO ST	94133	3-A3
100	BAY ST	94133	3-A3
MIGUEL ST			SF
1	BEACON ST	94131	14-G5
230	FAIRMOUNT ST	94131	14-G5
250	BEMIS ST	94131	14-G5
320	LAIDLEY ST	94131	14-H5
	CHENERY ST	94131	14-H5
450	ARLINGTON ST	94131	14-H6
500	SAN JOSE AV	94131	14-H6
MILAN TER			SF
1	MONETA WY	94112	18-E2
100	HURON AV	94112	18-E2
MILES ST			SF
	RILEY AV	94129	1-D4
	ORD ST	94129	1-D4
MILEY ST			SF
100	BAKER ST	94123	6-F4
MILL ST			SF
1	HARKNESS AV	94134	20-A1
100	ANKENY ST	94134	20-A1
MILLER PL			SF
1	SACRAMENTO ST	94108	7-A5
MILLER RD			SF
	BELL RD	94129	1-C3
	STOREY AV	94129	1-C3
MILTON ST			SF
1	SAN JOSE AV	94112	14-G6
100	BOSWORTH ST	94112	14-G6
200	MIRANDO WY	94112	14-G6
MILTON ROSS ST			SF
1	INNES AV	94124	15-B5
	JERROLD AV	94124	15-B5
100	JERROLD AV	94124	15-B5
200	KIRKWOOD AV	94124	15-B5
MINERVA ST			SF
200	ORIZABA AV	94112	18-D1
300	CAPITOL AV	94112	18-D1
1	PLYMOUTH AV	94112	18-D1
MINNA ST			SF
1	1ST ST	94105	7-B5
40	SHAW ST	94105	7-B6
100	2ND ST	94105	7-B6
140	NEW MONTGOMERY ST	94103	7-B6
200	3RD ST	94103	7-B6
300	4TH ST	94103	7-A6
400	5TH ST	94103	7-A6
430	MARY ST	94103	7-A6
500	6TH ST	94103	7-A7
550	RUSS ST	94103	7-A7
600	7TH ST	94103	7-A7
660	JULIA ST	94103	6-J7
700	8TH ST	94103	6-J7
800	9TH ST	94103	6-J7
900	10TH ST	94103	6-J7
1000	11TH ST	94103	6-J7
1100	LAFAYETTE ST	94103	10-J1
1300	14TH ST	94103	10-J1
1400	15TH ST	94103	10-J1
MINNESOTA ST			SF
500	MARIPOSA ST	94107	11-C2
610	18TH ST	94107	11-C2
700	19TH ST	94107	11-C2
1050	22ND ST	94107	11-C3
1200	23RD ST	94107	11-C3
1300	24TH ST	94107	11-C3
1400	25TH ST	94107	11-C4
1500	26TH ST	94107	11-C4
1600	CESAR CHAVEZ ST	94107	11-C4
MINT ST			SF
1	JESSIE ST	94103	7-A6
20	JESSIE ST	94103	7-A6
100	MARY ST	94103	7-A6
100	MISSION ST	94103	7-A6
MIRABEL AV			SF
1	BESSIE ST	94110	14-J4
1	SHOTWELL ST	94110	14-J4
100	COSO AV	94110	14-J4
MIRALOMA DR			SF
1	PORTOLA DR	94127	13-D5
30	MARNE AV	94127	13-D5
70	JUANITA WY	94127	13-D5
100	BENGAL AL	94127	13-D6
200	YERBA BUENA AV	94127	13-D6
MIRAMAR AV			SF
700	EASTWOOD DR	94112	13-D6
700	WESTWOOD DR	94112	13-D6
800	NORTHWOOD DR	94112	13-D6
900	MONTEREY BLVD	94112	13-D6
1	LAKEVIEW AV	94112	18-D1
100	GRAFTON AV	94112	18-D1
200	HOLLOWAY AV	94112	13-D7
300	DE MONTFORT AV	94112	13-D7
350	OCEAN AV	94112	13-D7
400	SOUTHWOOD DR	94112	13-D7
500	EASTWOOD DR	94112	13-D7
500	WESTWOOD DR	94112	13-D7
MIRANDO WY			SF
50	ROUSSEAU ST	94112	14-G6
100	ROTTECK ST	94112	14-G6
1	CUVIER ST	94112	14-G6
50	MILTON ST	94112	14-G6
MISSION ST			SF
1	STEUART ST	94105	7-B5
1	THE EMBARCADERO	94105	7-B5
100	SPEAR ST	94105	7-B5
200	MAIN ST	94105	7-B5
300	BEALE ST	94105	7-B5
400	FREMONT ST	94105	7-B5
500	1ST ST	94105	7-B5
520	ECKER ST	94105	7-B5
530	SHAW ST	94105	7-B5
570	ANTHONY ST	94105	7-B6
600	2ND ST	94105	7-B6
640	NEW MONTGOMERY ST	94105	7-B6
670	ANNIE ST	94103	7-B6
700	3RD ST	94103	7-A6
800	4TH ST	94103	7-A6
900	5TH ST	94103	7-A6
930	MARY ST	94103	7-A6
930	MINT ST	94103	7-A6
1000	6TH ST	94103	7-A7
1100	7TH ST	94103	7-A7
1160	JULIA ST	94103	6-J7
1200	8TH ST	94103	6-J7
1250	LASKIE ST	94103	6-J7
1300	9TH ST	94103	6-J7
1330	WASHBURN ST	94103	6-J7
1360	GRACE ST	94103	6-J7
1400	10TH ST	94103	6-J7
1500	11TH ST	94103	6-J7
1570	LAFAYETTE ST	94103	10-J1
1560	S VAN NESS AV	94103	10-J1
1560	VAN NESS AV	94103	10-J1
1600	OTIS ST	94103	10-J1
1600	12TH ST	94103	10-J1
1670	PLUM ST	94103	10-J1
	DUBOCE AV	94103	10-J1
1750	ERIE ST	94103	10-H1
1790	OTIS ST	94103	10-H1
	14TH ST	94103	10-J1
	15TH ST	94103	10-J2
2000	16TH ST	94110	10-J2
2100	17TH ST	94110	10-J2
2130	CLARION AL	94110	10-J2
2160	SYCAMORE ST	94110	10-J2
2200	18TH ST	94110	10-J2
2300	19TH ST	94110	10-J2
2400	20TH ST	94110	10-J3
2470	CATHERINE CT	94110	10-J3
2500	21ST ST	94110	10-J3
2600	22ND ST	94110	10-J3
2700	23RD ST	94110	10-J3
2790	24TH ST	94110	10-J3
2890	25TH ST	94110	10-J4
3000	26TH ST	94110	10-J4
3100	CESAR CHAVEZ ST	94110	14-J4
3100	CAPP ST	94110	14-J4
3150	PRECITA AV	94110	14-H4
3180	POWERS AV	94110	14-H4
3200	FAIR AV	94110	14-H4
3200	VALENCIA ST	94110	14-H4
3290	29TH ST	94110	14-H5
3350	VIRGINIA AV	94110	14-H5
3380	GODEUS ST	94110	14-H5
3410	30TH ST	94110	14-H5
3420	EUGENIA AV	94110	14-H5
3450	KINGSTON ST	94110	14-H5
3500	CORTLAND AV	94110	14-H5
3530	SANTA MARINA ST	94110	14-H5
3530	BROOK ST	94110	14-H5
3590	RANDALL ST	94110	14-H5
3650	APPLETON AV	94110	14-H5
3740	HIGHLAND AV	94110	14-H5
3750	HIGHLAND AV	94110	14-H5
3750	LEESE ST	94110	14-H6
3790	PARK ST	94110	14-H6
3800	PARK ST	94110	14-H6
3840	RICHLAND AV	94110	14-H6
3850	RICHLAND AV	94110	14-H6
3890	COLLEGE AV	94112	14-H6
3890	CRESCENT AV	94112	14-H6
3900	COLLEGE AV	94112	14-H6
4000	COLLEGE TER	94112	14-H6
4020	SAINT MARYS AV	94112	14-H6
4040	BOSWORTH ST	94112	14-H6
4040	MURRAY ST	94112	14-H6
4190	ALEMANY BLVD	94112	14-G6
4220	TRUMBULL ST	94112	14-G6
4280	ADMIRAL AV	94112	14-G6
4280	NEY ST	94112	14-G6
4320	MAYNARD ST	94112	14-G7
4320	CASTLE MANOR AV	94112	14-G7
4350	SILVER AV	94112	14-G7
4380	TINGLEY ST	94112	14-G7
4410	AVALON AV	94112	14-G7
4410	THERESA ST	94112	14-G7
4440	COTTER ST	94112	14-G7
4470	FRANCIS ST	94112	14-G7
4490	EXCELSIOR AV	94112	14-G7
4520	SANTA ROSA AV	94112	14-G7
4560	HARRINGTON ST	94112	14-G7
4580	BRAZIL AV	94112	14-G7
4580	NORTON ST	94112	14-G7
4620	SAN JUAN AV	94112	14-G7
4620	OCEAN AV	94112	14-G7
4670	PERSIA AV	94112	14-G7
4680	RUTH ST	94112	14-G7
4700	LEO ST	94112	19-F1
4750	RUSSIA AV	94112	19-F1
4780	ONONDAGA AV	94112	19-F1
4840	FRANCE AV	94112	19-F1
4880	KENNY AL	94112	19-F1
4930	ITALY AV	94112	19-F1
4970	SENECA AV	94112	19-F1
5000	AMAZON AV	94112	19-F1
5040	GENEVA AV	94112	19-F1
4130	ROLPH ST	94112	19-F1
4170	NIAGARA AV	94112	19-F1
4180	POPE ST	94112	19-F2
4350	ALLISON ST	94112	19-F2
4350	MOUNT VERNON AV	94112	19-F2
4470	CONCORD ST	94112	19-F2
4530	OTTAWA AV	94112	19-F2
4570	FLORENTINE ST	94112	19-F2
4680	GUTTENBERG ST	94112	19-F2
4720	FOOTE AV	94112	19-F2
4940	NAGLEE AV	94112	19-E2
4970	LOWELL ST	94112	19-E2
5160	WHIPPLE AV	94112	19-E2
5260	WHITTIER ST	94112	19-E2
5260	MORSE ST	94112	19-E2
5380	FARRAGUT AV	94112	19-E2
5480	LAURA ST	94112	18-E2
5530	OLIVER ST	94112	18-E2
5570	LAWRENCE AV	94112	18-E2
5810	ACTON ST	94112	18-E2
5810	SICKLES AV	94112	18-E2
MISSION ROCK ST			SF
1	3RD ST	94107	11-C1
1	4TH ST	94107	11-C1
	TERRY A FRANCOIS BLVD	94107	11-C1
MISSISSIPPI ST			SF
1	16TH ST	94107	11-B2
1	7TH ST	94107	11-B2
100	17TH ST	94107	11-B2
200	MARIPOSA ST	94107	11-B2
300	18TH ST	94107	11-B2
400	19TH ST	94107	11-B2
500	20TH ST	94107	11-B3
700	22ND ST	94107	11-B3
1100	25TH ST	94107	11-B3
1300	CESAR CHAVEZ ST	94107	11-B4
MISSOURI ST			SF
1	16TH ST	94107	11-B2
100	17TH ST	94107	11-B2
200	MARIPOSA ST	94107	11-B2
300	18TH ST	94107	11-B2
400	19TH ST	94107	11-B2
500	20TH ST	94107	11-B3
620	SIERRA ST	94107	11-B3
700	TURNER TER	94107	11-B3
840	WATCHMAN WY	94107	11-B3
900	23RD ST	94107	11-B3
1300	CESAR CHAVEZ ST	94107	11-B4
MISTRAL ST			SF
1	HARRISON ST	94110	10-J2
100	TREAT AV	94110	10-J2
MIZPAH ST			SF
1	SUSSEX ST	94131	14-F6
100	CHENERY ST	94131	14-F6
MODOC AV			SF
1	CAYUGA AV	94112	19-E1
MOFFITT ST			SF
1	DIAMOND ST	94131	14-G5
70	FARNUM ST	94131	14-G6
300	BEMIS ST	94131	14-G6
300	ROANOKE ST	94131	14-G6
MOJAVE ST			SF
1	BRONTE ST	94110	14-J5
50	BRADFORD ST	94110	15-A5
100	PERALTA AV	94110	15-A5
MOLIMO DR			SF
100	GATUN AL	94127	14-E5
200	DORCAS WY	94127	14-E5
300	BELLA VISTA WY	94127	13-E5
390	LANSDALE AV	94127	13-E5
390	MYRA WY	94127	13-E5
600	SAINT CROIX DR	94127	13-E5
1	TERESITA BLVD	94127	14-E6
100	GATUN AL	94127	14-E6
MONCADA WY			SF
200	PALOMA AV	94127	13-C6
	JUNIPERO SERRA BLVD	94127	13-C6
1	URBANO DR N	94127	13-C7
50	CERRITOS AV	94127	13-C7
	CEDRO AV	94127	13-C7
MONETA CT			SF
1	MONETA WY	94112	19-E2
MONETA WY			SF
1	HURON AV	94112	19-E2
50	MONETA CT	94112	19-E2
90	WHIPPLE AV	94112	18-E2
140	MILAN TER	94112	18-E2
200	FARRAGUT AV	94112	18-E2
MONO ST			SF
1	19TH ST	94114	10-F2
1	CASELLI AV	94114	10-F2
50	EAGLE ST	94114	10-F3
100	MARKET ST	94114	10-F3
MONTAGUE PL			SF
1	MONTGOMERY ST	94133	3-A4
MONTALVO AV			SF
1	CASTENADA AV	94116	13-C4
100	DORANTES AV	94116	13-D4
200	MAGELLAN AV	94116	13-D4
300	DEWEY BLVD	94116	13-D4
MONTANA ST			SF
1	ORIZABA AV	94112	18-D1
80	FAXON AV	94112	18-D1
120	CAPITOL AV	94112	18-D1
220	PLYMOUTH AV	94112	18-E1
300	JOSIAH AV	94112	18-E1
300	SUMMIT ST	94112	18-E1
MONTCALM ST			SF
1	WRIGHT ST	94110	15-A4
1	YORK ST	94110	15-A4
60	BREWSTER ST	94110	15-A4
60	MULLEN AV	94110	15-A4
140	MACEDONIA ST	94110	15-A4
400	ALABAMA ST	94110	14-J4
MONTCLAIR TER			SF
1	LOMBARD ST	94109	2-J4
MONTECITO AV			SF
1	MONTEREY BLVD	94112	13-E6
100	HAZELWOOD AV	94112	13-E6
200	VALDEZ AV	94112	13-E6
300	COLON AV	94112	13-D6
350	PLYMOUTH AV	94112	13-D6
400	NORTHWOOD DR	94112	13-D6
500	EASTWOOD DR	94112	13-D6
MONTEREY BLVD			SF
1	CIRCULAR AV	94131	14-F6
100	ACADIA ST	94131	14-F6
200	BADEN ST	94131	14-F6
300	CONGO ST	94131	14-F6
500	EDNA ST	94112	14-E6
500	EDNA ST	94127	14-E6
530	EDNA ST	94112	14-E6
530	EDNA ST	94127	14-E6
600	FOERSTER ST	94112	14-E6
600	FOERSTER ST	94127	14-E6
700	GENNESSEE ST	94112	13-E6
700	GENNESSEE ST	94127	13-E6
	RIDGEWOOD AV	94112	13-E6
	RIDGEWOOD AV	94127	13-E6
800	MONTECITO AV	94112	13-E6
800	MONTECITO AV	94127	13-E6
850	HAZELWOOD AV	94112	13-E6
850	HAZELWOOD AV	94127	13-E6

PRIMARY STREET Address	Cross Street	ZIP	CITY Pg-Grid
MONTEREY BLVD			SF
900	VALDEZ AV	94112	13-D6
900	VALDEZ AV	94127	13-D6
950	COLON AV	94112	13-D6
950	COLON AV	94127	13-D6
1000	PLYMOUTH AV	94112	13-D6
1000	PLYMOUTH AV	94127	13-D6
	PLYMOUTH AV	94112	13-D6
	PLYMOUTH AV	94127	13-D6
1050	MIRAMAR AV	94112	13-D6
1050	MIRAMAR AV	94127	13-D6
1090	YERBA BUENA AV	94112	13-D6
1090	YERBA BUENA AV	94127	13-D6
1100	FAXON AV	94127	13-D6
1200	SAINT ELMO WY	94127	13-D6
1300	NORTHGATE DR	94127	13-D6
1300	SAN FELIPE AV	94127	13-D6
1400	WESTGATE DR	94127	13-D6
1450	SAN JACINTO WY	94127	13-D6
1480	SAN ALESO AV	94127	13-D6
1500	SAN ANDREAS WY	94127	13-C6
1600	SAN ANSELMO AV	94127	13-C6
1600	SANTA CLARA AV	94127	13-C6
1700	SAN BENITO WY	94127	13-C6
1800	SANTA ANA AV	94127	13-C6
1900	SAN LEANDRO WY	94127	13-C6
2000	SAN FERNANDO WY	94127	13-C6
2100	SAN RAFAEL WY	94127	13-C6
2500	JUNIPERO SERRA BLVD	94127	13-C6
MONTE VISTA DR			SF
1	19TH AV	94132	13-B6
1	BUCKINGHAM WY	94132	13-B6
MONTEZUMA ST			SF
1	SHOTWELL ST	94110	14-J4
100	COSO AV	94110	14-J4
100	LUNDYS LN	94110	14-J4
MONTGOMERY ST			SF
1600	LOMBARD ST	94133	3-A3
1600	LOMBARD ST	94111	3-A3
1700	CHESTNUT ST	94133	3-A3
1700	CHESTNUT ST	94111	3-A3
1900	FRANCISCO ST	94133	3-A3
1900	FRANCISCO ST	94111	3-A3
1230	MONTAGUE PL	94133	3-A4
1300	UNION ST	94133	3-A4
1300	SCHOOL AL	94133	3-A4
1300	ALTA ST	94133	3-A4
1300	FILBERT ST	94133	3-A4
80	LINCOLN BLVD	94129	1-D4
80	SHERIDAN AV	94129	1-D4
90	BLISS RD	94129	1-D4
90	MORAGA AV	94129	1-D4
1	MARKET ST	94108	7-B5
1	MARKET ST	94104	7-B5
1	NEW MONTGOMERY ST	94104	7-B5
20	POST ST	94104	7-B5
100	SUTTER ST	94104	7-B5
200	BUSH ST	94104	7-A5
300	PINE ST	94104	7-A5
400	CALIFORNIA ST	94104	7-A5
500	SACRAMENTO ST	94111	7-A5
530	COMMERCIAL ST	94111	7-A5
600	CLAY ST	94111	7-A5
650	TWAIN ST	94111	7-A5
710	COLUMBUS AV	94111	7-A5
710	WASHINGTON ST	94111	7-A5
800	JACKSON ST	94133	7-A4
840	GOLD ST	94133	7-A4
900	PACIFIC AV	94133	7-A4
1000	BROADWAY	94133	7-A4
1100	VALLEJO ST	94133	7-A4
1200	GREEN ST	94133	3-A4
MONTICELLO ST			SF
	HOLLOWAY AV	94127	13-C7
100	ESTERO AV	94127	13-C7
1	19TH AV	94132	18-C1
100	SARGENT ST	94132	18-C1
200	SHIELDS ST	94132	18-C1
300	GARFIELD ST	94132	18-C1
400	HOLLOWAY AV	94132	18-C1
MONUMENT WY			SF
	UPPER TER	94117	10-F2
MOORE PL			SF
1	UNION ST	94109	2-J4
MORAGA AV			SF
	INFANTRY TER	94129	1-D4
	MONTGOMERY ST	94129	1-D4
	ARGUELLO BLVD	94129	5-D4
	GRAHAM ST	94129	5-D4
	MESA AV	94129	5-D4
	FUNSTON AV	94129	5-D4
MORAGA ST			SF
200	8TH AV	94122	9-D3
250	AUTO DR	94122	9-C3
300	9TH AV	94122	9-C3
400	10TH AV	94122	9-C3
500	11TH AV	94122	9-C3
600	12TH AV	94122	9-C3
700	FUNSTON AV	94122	9-C3
1000	16TH AV	94122	9-C3
1100	17TH AV	94122	9-B3
1200	18TH AV	94122	9-B3
1300	19TH AV	94122	9-B3
1400	20TH AV	94122	9-B3
1500	21ST AV	94122	9-B3
1600	22ND AV	94122	9-B3
1700	23RD AV	94122	9-B3
1800	24TH AV	94122	9-B3
1900	25TH AV	94122	9-B3
2000	26TH AV	94122	9-A3
2100	27TH AV	94122	9-A3
2200	28TH AV	94122	9-A3
2300	29TH AV	94122	9-A3
2400	30TH AV	94122	9-A3
2500	31ST AV	94122	9-A3
2600	32ND AV	94122	9-A3
2700	33RD AV	94122	9-A3
2800	34TH AV	94122	9-A3
2900	35TH AV	94122	8-J3
3000	36TH AV	94122	8-J3
3050	SUNSET BLVD	94122	8-J3
3100	37TH AV	94122	8-J3
3200	38TH AV	94122	8-J3
3300	39TH AV	94122	8-J3
3400	40TH AV	94122	8-J3
3500	41ST AV	94122	8-J3
3600	42ND AV	94122	8-J3
3700	43RD AV	94122	8-H3
3800	44TH AV	94122	8-H3
3900	45TH AV	94122	8-H3
4000	46TH AV	94122	8-H3
4100	47TH AV	94122	8-H3
4200	48TH AV	94122	8-H3
4300	GREAT HWY	94122	8-H3
MORELAND ST			SF
100	DIAMOND ST	94131	14-G5
300	FARNUM ST	94131	14-G5
MORNINGSIDE DR			SF
1	CLEARFIELD DR	94132	13-A6
100	OCEAN AV	94132	12-J6
300	GELLERT DR	94132	13-A6
MORRELL ST			SF
1	PACIFIC AV	94109	6-J4
1	MCCORMICK ST	94109	6-J4
300	MANSEAU ST	94124	21-E1
520	E ST	94124	16-E7
600	SPEAR AV	94124	16-E7
600	FISHER AV	94124	16-E7
MORRIS RD			SF
	PARK BLVD	94129	5-C4
MORRIS ST			SF
1	HARRISON ST	94107	7-A7
100	BRYANT ST	94107	7-B7
MORSE ST			SF
1	ROLPH ST	94112	19-F2
70	ROYAL LN	94112	19-F2
110	NEWTON ST	94112	19-F2
170	CURTIS ST	94112	19-F2
180	CURTIS ST	94112	19-F2
250	POPE ST	94112	19-F2
320	ALLISON ST	94112	19-F2
380	CONCORD ST	94112	19-F2
420	FLORENTINE ST	94112	19-F2
430	FLORENTINE ST	94112	19-F2
490	GUTTENBERG ST	94112	19-F2
630	LOWELL ST	94112	19-E2
730	WHIPPLE AV	94112	19-E2
800	MISSION ST	94112	19-E2
800	WHITTIER ST	94112	19-E2
MORTON ST			SF
	LIGGETT AV	94129	6-E4
	SANCHES ST	94129	6-E4
	LIGGETT AV	94129	5-E4
780	RODRIGUEZ ST	94129	5-E4
780	PORTOLA ST	94129	5-E4
MOSCOW ST			SF
200	AVALON AV	94112	14-H7
300	EXCELSIOR AV	94112	14-H7
400	BRAZIL AV	94112	19-G1
510	PERSIA AV	94112	19-G1
630	RUSSIA AV	94112	19-G1
740	FRANCE AV	94112	19-G1
860	ITALY AV	94112	19-G2
900	AMAZON AV	94112	19-G2
1000	GENEVA AV	94112	19-G2
1000	S HILL BLVD	94112	19-G2
MOSS ST			SF
1	HOWARD ST	94103	7-A7
100	FOLSOM ST	94103	7-A7
MOULTON ST			SF
1	BUCHANAN ST	94123	2-G4
100	WEBSTER ST	94123	2-G4
200	FILLMORE ST	94123	2-G4
300	STEINER ST	94123	2-G4
MOULTRIE ST			SF
100	BERNAL HEIGHTS BLVD	94110	14-J5
200	POWHATTAN AV	94110	14-J5
300	EUGENIA AV	94110	14-J5
400	CORTLAND AV	94110	14-J5
500	JARBOE AV	94110	14-J5
600	TOMPKINS AV	94110	14-J6
700	OGDEN AV	94110	14-J6
800	CRESCENT AV	94110	14-J6
MOUNTAIN SPRINGS AV			SF
1	RACCOON DR	94114	10-E3
1	TWIN PEAKS BLVD	94114	10-E3
50	GLENBROOK AV	94114	10-E3
MOUNT VERNON AV			SF
900	GRAFTON AV	94112	18-E1
900	GETZ ST	94112	18-E1
1	WILLIAR AV	94112	18-E1
70	HOWTH ST	94112	18-E1
70	JOSIAH AV	94112	18-E1
160	LOUISBURG ST	94112	18-E1
240	TARA ST	94112	19-E1
330	SAN MIGUEL ST	94112	19-E1
330	CAINE AV	94112	19-E1
400	NAHUA AV	94112	19-E1
510	DELANO AV	94112	19-E1
590	CAYUGA AV	94112	19-F1
650	ROME ST	94112	19-F1
710	ALEMANY BLVD	94112	19-F1
780	DEL MONTE ST	94112	19-F1
790	DEL MONTE ST	94112	19-F1
830	ELLINGTON AV	94112	19-F1
840	ELLINGTON AV	94112	19-F2
900	ALLISON ST	94112	19-F2
900	MISSION ST	94112	19-F2
MOUNTVIEW CT			SF
100	PANORAMA DR	94131	14-E4
MULFORD AL			SF
100	TAYLOR ST	94108	6-J5
MULLEN AV			SF
150	BREWSTER ST	94110	15-A4
150	RUTLEDGE ST	94110	15-A4
1	BREWSTER ST	94110	15-A4
1	MONTCALM ST	94110	15-A4
150	FRANCONIA ST	94110	15-A4
200	PERALTA AV	94110	15-A4
400	ALABAMA ST	94110	14-J4
MUNICH ST			SF
100	EXCELSIOR AV	94112	19-H1
300	BRAZIL AV	94112	19-H1
450	PERSIA AV	94112	19-G1
580	RUSSIA AV	94112	19-G1
770	GENEVA AV	94112	19-G2
700	S HILL BLVD	94112	19-G2
790	ROLPH ST	94112	19-G2
870	NAYLOR ST	94112	19-G2
960	CORDOVA ST	94112	19-G2
1090	DRAKE ST	94112	19-F2
1200	CURTIS ST	94112	19-F2
1200	NAPLES ST	94112	19-F2
MURRAY ST			SF
440	HOLLY PARK CIR	94110	14-H6
400	RICHLAND AV	94110	14-H6
440	CRESCENT AV	94110	14-H6
1	BOSWORTH ST	94112	14-H6
1	MISSION ST	94112	14-H6
100	GENEBERN WY	94112	14-H6
200	COLLEGE AV	94112	14-H6
300	JUSTIN DR	94112	14-H6
MUSEUM WY			SF
200	ROOSEVELT WY	94114	10-F2
MYRA WY			SF
300	CHAVES AV	94127	13-E5
300	ROCKDALE DR	94127	13-E5
400	LA BICA WY	94127	13-E5
600	REPOSA WY	94127	14-E5
700	OMAR WY	94127	14-E5
800	AVOCA AL	94127	14-E5
900	LANSDALE AV	94127	14-E5
900	MOLIMO DR	94127	14-E5
MYRTLE ST			SF
1	LARKIN ST	94109	6-J6
100	POLK ST	94109	6-J6
200	VAN NESS AV	94109	6-H6
300	FRANKLIN ST	94109	6-H6
N			
NADELL CT			SF
1	LINCOLN CT	94112	19-F2
NAGLEE AV			SF
300	CAYUGA AV	94112	19-E2
1	MISSION ST	94112	19-E2
100	ELLINGTON AV	94112	19-E2
140	RAE AV	94112	19-E2
200	HURON AV	94112	19-E2
240	ALEMANY BLVD	94112	19-E2
NAHUA AV			SF
1	NIAGARA AV	94112	19-E1
20	SHAWNEE AV	94112	19-E1
40	MOUNT VERNON AV	94112	19-E1
70	OTEGA AV	94112	19-E1
100	DELANO AV	94112	19-E1
NANTUCKET AV			SF
1	SAN JOSE AV	94112	14-F7
NAPIER LN			SF
1	FILBERT ST	94133	3-A4
NAPLES ST			SF
1	SILVER AV	94112	14-H7
100	PERU AV	94112	14-H7
200	AVALON AV	94112	14-G7
300	EXCELSIOR AV	94112	14-G7
400	BRAZIL AV	94112	19-G1
450	PERSIA AV	94112	19-G1
580	RUSSIA AV	94112	19-G1
720	FRANCE AV	94112	19-G1
850	ITALY AV	94112	19-G1
920	AMAZON AV	94112	19-G2
1030	GENEVA AV	94112	19-G2
1080	ROLPH ST	94112	19-F2
1180	ATHENS ST	94112	19-F2
1190	ROYAL LN	94112	19-F2
1230	CURTIS ST	94112	19-F2
1230	NEWTON ST	94112	19-F2
1230	SEVILLE ST	94112	19-F2
1300	CURTIS ST	94112	19-F2
1300	MUNICH ST	94112	19-F2
NAPOLEON ST			SF
10	SELBY ST	94124	15-B4
10	ISLAIS ST	94124	15-B4
100	TOLAND ST	94124	15-B4
100	EVANS AV	94124	15-B4
300	JERROLD AV	94124	15-B4
NATICK ST			SF
1	CHENERY ST	94131	14-G6
100	WILDER ST	94131	14-G6
100	ARLINGTON ST	94131	14-G6
NATOMA ST			SF
1	FREMONT ST	94105	7-B5
20	1ST ST	94105	7-B5
100	2ND ST	94105	7-B6
130	NEW MONTGOMERY ST	94105	7-B6
400	5TH ST	94103	7-A6
430	MARY ST	94103	7-A7
500	6TH ST	94103	7-A7
550	RUSS ST	94103	7-A7
600	7TH ST	94103	7-A7
700	8TH ST	94103	6-J7
800	9TH ST	94103	6-J7
900	10TH ST	94103	6-J7
1000	11TH ST	94103	10-J1
1070	LAFAYETTE ST	94103	10-J1
1300	14TH ST	94103	10-J1
1400	15TH ST	94103	10-J1
NAUMAN RD			SF
	AMATURY LP	94129	5-D4
	WASHINGTON BLVD	94129	5-D4
NAVAJO AV			SF
1	DELANO AV	94112	19-F1
100	CAYUGA AV	94112	19-F1
NAVY RD			SF
30	GRIFFITH ST	94124	15-D7
100	EARL ST	94124	15-D7
100	LA SALLE AV	94124	15-D7
NAYLOR ST			SF
1	MUNICH ST	94112	19-G2
100	PRAGUE ST	94112	19-G2
200	WINDING WY	94112	19-G2
300	CHICAGO WY	94112	19-G2
400	BALTIMORE WY	94112	19-G2
NEBRASKA ST			SF
1	POWHATTAN AV	94110	14-J5
100	CORTLAND AV	94110	14-J5
NELLIE ST			SF
	ELIZABETH ST	94114	10-H3
1	23RD ST	94114	10-H3
NELSON AV			SF
3600	MEADE AV	94124	20-B1
NEPTUNE ST			SF
1	THORNTON AV	94124	15-B6
100	WILLIAMS AV	94124	15-B6
NEVADA ST			SF
1	POWHATTAN AV	94110	14-J5
1	BERNAL HEIGHTS BLVD	94110	14-J5
110	EUGENIA AV	94110	14-J5
140	CORTLAND AV	94110	14-J5
280	JARBOE AV	94110	14-J5
400	TOMPKINS AV	94110	14-J6
500	OGDEN AV	94110	14-J6
600	CRESCENT AV	94110	14-J6
NEWBURG ST			SF
1	27TH ST	94131	14-G4
1	CASTRO ST	94131	14-G4
100	DUNCAN ST	94131	14-G4
NEWCOMB AV			SF
1900	QUINT ST	94124	15-B5
2100	RANKIN ST	94124	15-B5
2200	SELBY ST	94124	15-B5
2300	TOLAND ST	94124	15-A5
2500	BARNEVELD AV	94124	15-A5
1300	WHITNEY YOUNG CIR	94124	15-C6
1340	LA SALLE AV	94124	15-C6
1400	KEITH ST	94124	15-C6
1500	LANE ST	94124	15-C6
1600	MENDELL ST	94124	15-C6
1640	3RD ST	94124	15-C6
1700	NEWHALL ST	94124	15-B6
1800	PHELPS ST	94124	15-B6
NEWELL ST			SF
2100	LOMBARD ST	94133	2-J3
NEWHALL ST			SF
200	MENDELL ST	94124	15-C5
400	EVANS AV	94124	15-C5
500	FAIRFAX AV	94124	15-C5
600	GALVEZ AV	94124	15-C5
700	HUDSON AV	94124	15-C5
800	INNES AV	94124	15-C5
880	3RD ST	94124	15-C5
100	JENNINGS ST	94124	15-D5
900	JERROLD AV	94124	15-C5
1000	KIRKWOOD AV	94124	15-C5
1100	LA SALLE AV	94124	15-C6
1200	MCKINNON AV	94124	15-C6
1300	NEWCOMB AV	94124	15-B6
1400	OAKDALE AV	94124	15-B6
1500	PALOU AV	94124	15-B6
1600	QUESADA AV	94124	15-B6
1700	BRIDGEVIEW DR	94124	15-B6
1700	REVERE AV	94124	15-B6
1750	BAYVIEW CIR	94124	15-B6
1800	BAYVIEW CIR	94124	15-B6
1800	BAYVIEW ST	94124	15-B6
1900	TOPEKA AV	94124	15-B6
2400	WILLIAMS AV	94124	15-B7
2440	BANCROFT AV	94124	15-B7
2500	CARROLL AV	94124	15-B7
2600	DONNER AV	94124	15-B7
2700	EGBERT AV	94124	15-B7
NEWMAN ST			SF
1	HOLLY PARK CIR	94110	14-J5
100	BENNINGTON ST	94110	14-J5
200	ANDOVER ST	94110	14-J5
NEW MONTGOMERY ST			SF
1	MARKET ST	94105	7-B5
	MARKET ST	94105	7-B5
	MONTGOMERY ST	94105	7-B5
30	STEVENSON ST	94105	7-B6
60	JESSIE ST	94105	7-B6
80	ALDRICH AL	94105	7-B6
100	MISSION ST	94105	7-B6
130	MINNA ST	94105	7-B6
160	NATOMA ST	94105	7-B6
200	HOWARD ST	94105	7-B6
NEWTON ST			SF
1	ROLPH ST	94112	19-F2
100	MORSE ST	94112	19-F2
150	BRUNSWICK ST	94112	19-F2
200	CURTIS ST	94112	19-F2
200	NAPLES ST	94112	19-F2
NEY ST			SF
1	ADMIRAL AV	94112	14-G6
1	MISSION ST	94112	14-G6
100	CRAUT ST	94112	14-H6
220	CONGDON ST	94112	14-H6
400	TRUMBULL ST	94112	14-H6
NIAGARA AV			SF
1	MISSION ST	94112	18-E1
60	ALEMANY BLVD	94112	18-E1
130	CAYUGA AV	94112	18-E1
220	DELANO AV	94112	19-E1
310	NAHUA AV	94112	19-E1
400	SAN JOSE AV	94112	19-E1
500	SAN MIGUEL ST	94112	19-E1
510	TARA ST	94112	19-E1
600	LOUISBURG ST	94112	19-F1
680	HOWTH ST	94112	19-F1
770	WILLIAR AV	94112	19-F1
900	EDGAR PL	94112	19-F1
NIANTIC AV			SF
1	SAINT CHARLES AV	94132	18-C2
1	BELLE AV	94132	18-C2
100	PANAMA ST	94132	18-C2
NIBBI CT			SF
1	GILLETTE AV	94134	20-B2
NICHOLS WY			SF
1	CAMERON WY	94124	20-C1
200	CAMERON WY	94124	20-C1
200	GRIFFITH ST	94124	20-C1
NIDO AV			SF
1	TURK ST	94115	6-F7
60	VEGA ST	94115	6-F7
NIMITZ AV			SF
600	A ST	94124	16-F7
700	LOCKWOOD ST	94124	16-F7
800	C ST	94124	16-F7
900	BLANDY ST	94124	16-F7
NOB HILL CIR			SF
1	PINE ST	94108	7-A5
NOB HILL PL			SF
1	MASON ST	94108	7-A5
NOE ST			SF
1	DUBOCE AV	94114	10-G1
100	14TH ST	94114	10-G1
150	HENRY ST	94114	10-G1
200	15TH ST	94114	10-G2
250	BEAVER ST	94114	10-G2
300	16TH ST	94114	10-G2
310	MARKET ST	94114	10-G2
400	17TH ST	94114	10-G2
450	FORD ST	94114	10-G2
500	18TH ST	94114	10-G2
550	HANCOCK ST	94114	10-G2
600	19TH ST	94114	10-G2
700	20TH ST	94114	10-G3
740	20TH ST	94114	10-G3
750	LIBERTY ST	94114	10-G3
800	21ST ST	94114	10-G3
840	HILL ST	94114	10-G3
900	22ND ST	94114	10-G3
950	ALVARADO ST	94114	10-G3
1000	23RD ST	94114	10-G3
1050	ELIZABETH ST	94114	10-G3
1100	24TH ST	94114	10-G4
1150	JERSEY ST	94114	10-G4
1200	25TH ST	94114	10-G4
1250	CLIPPER ST	94131	10-G4
1300	26TH ST	94131	10-G4
1350	CESAR CHAVEZ ST	94131	14-G4
1400	27TH ST	94131	14-G4
1450	DUNCAN ST	94131	14-G4
1500	28TH ST	94131	14-G4
1550	VALLEY ST	94131	14-G5
1600	29TH ST	94131	14-G5
1650	DAY ST	94131	14-G5
1700	30TH ST	94131	14-G5
1800	LAIDLEY ST	94131	14-G5
NORDHOFF ST			SF
1	STILLINGS AV	94131	14-F6
100	MANGELS AV	94131	14-F6
NORFOLK ST			SF
1	FOLSOM ST	94103	10-J1
100	HARRISON ST	94103	10-J1
NORIEGA ST			SF
700	14TH AV	94122	9-C3
800	15TH AV	94122	9-C3
100	8TH AV	94122	9-D3
200	9TH AV	94122	9-C3
300	10TH AV	94122	9-C3
400	11TH AV	94122	9-C3
500	12TH AV	94122	9-C3
600	FUNSTON AV	94122	9-C3
900	16TH AV	94122	9-C3
1000	17TH AV	94122	9-B3
1100	18TH AV	94122	9-B3
1200	19TH AV	94122	9-B3
1300	20TH AV	94122	9-B3
1400	21ST AV	94122	9-B3

1998 SAN FRANCISCO CROSS STREET INDEX

Address	Cross Street	ZIP	City Pg-Grid
NORIEGA ST			SF
1500	22ND AV	94122	9-B3
1600	23RD AV	94122	9-B3
1700	24TH AV	94122	9-B3
1800	25TH AV	94122	9-B3
1900	26TH AV	94122	9-A3
2000	27TH AV	94122	9-A3
2100	28TH AV	94122	9-A3
2200	29TH AV	94122	9-A3
2300	30TH AV	94122	9-A3
2400	31ST AV	94122	9-A3
2500	32ND AV	94122	9-A3
2600	33RD AV	94122	9-A3
2700	34TH AV	94122	9-A3
2800	35TH AV	94122	8-J3
2900	36TH AV	94122	8-J3
2950	SUNSET BLVD	94122	8-J3
3000	37TH AV	94122	8-J3
3100	38TH AV	94122	8-J3
3200	39TH AV	94122	8-J3
3300	40TH AV	94122	8-J3
3400	41ST AV	94122	8-J3
3500	42ND AV	94122	8-J3
3600	43RD AV	94122	8-H3
3700	44TH AV	94122	8-H3
3800	45TH AV	94122	8-H3
3900	46TH AV	94122	8-H3
4000	47TH AV	94122	8-H3
4100	48TH AV	94122	8-H3
4200	GREAT HWY	94122	8-H3
900	16TH AV	94122	9-C3
NORMANDIE TER			SF
1	BROADWAY ST	94115	6-F5
NORTHGATE DR			SF
1	UPLAND DR	94127	13-D7
100	DARIEN WY	94127	13-D6
200	MONTEREY BLVD	94127	13-D6
200	SAN FELIPE AV	94127	13-D6
NORTH POINT ST			SF
1	THE EMBARCADERO	94133	3-A3
100	GRANT AV	94133	3-A3
200	STOCKTON ST	94133	3-A3
300	POWELL ST	94133	2-J3
400	MASON ST	94133	2-J3
500	TAYLOR ST	94133	2-J3
600	JONES ST	94133	2-J3
680	COLUMBUS AV	94133	2-J3
700	LEAVENWORTH ST	94109	2-J3
800	HYDE ST	94109	2-H3
900	LARKIN ST	94109	2-H3
1000	POLK ST	94109	2-H3
1100	VAN NESS AV	94109	2-H3
1500	LAGUNA ST	94123	2-G3
1600	BUCHANAN ST	94123	2-G3
1700	WEBSTER ST	94123	2-G3
1800	FILLMORE ST	94123	2-G3
2100	SCOTT ST	94123	2-F3
2200	DIVISADERO ST	94123	2-F3
2300	BRODERICK ST	94123	2-F3
2400	BAKER ST	94123	2-F3
NORTHRIDGE RD			SF
1	INGALLS ST	94124	15-D6
1	ROSIE LEE LN	94124	16-D6
60	HARBOR RD	94124	15-D6
150	DORMITORY RD	94124	15-D6
150	JERROLD AV	94124	15-D6
NORTH VIEW CT			SF
2900	BAY ST	94109	2-H3
NORTHWOOD DR			SF
1	PLYMOUTH AV	94112	13-D6
50	MONTECITO AV	94112	13-D6
100	MIRAMAR AV	94112	13-D6
150	PIZARRO WY	94112	13-D6
200	FAXON AV	94112	13-D6
NORTON ST			SF
1	ALEMANY BLVD	94112	14-G7
100	BRAZIL AV	94112	14-G7
100	MISSION ST	94112	14-G7
NORWICH ST			SF
1	ALABAMA ST	94110	14-J4
60	HARRISON ST	94110	14-J4
NOTTINGHAM PL			SF
1	KEARNY ST	94133	7-A4
NUEVA AV			SF
200	LATHROP AV	94134	20-B2
1	BLANKEN AV	94134	20-B2
O			
OAK ST			SF
1	VAN NESS AV	94102	6-J7
100	FRANKLIN ST	94102	6-H7
200	GOUGH ST	94102	6-H7
300	OCTAVIA ST	94102	6-H7
400	LAGUNA ST	94102	6-H7
500	BUCHANAN ST	94102	6-H7
600	WEBSTER ST	94117	6-G7
700	FILLMORE ST	94117	6-G7
810	STEINER ST	94117	6-G7
800	EVA TER	94117	6-G7
900	PIERCE ST	94117	6-G7
1000	SCOTT ST	94117	6-G7
1100	DIVISADERO ST	94117	10-G1
1200	BRODERICK ST	94117	10-F1
1300	BAKER ST	94117	10-F1
1450	LYON ST	94117	10-F1
1600	CENTRAL AV	94117	10-F1
1700	MASONIC AV	94117	10-F1
1800	ASHBURY ST	94117	10-E1
1900	CLAYTON ST	94117	10-E1
2000	COLE ST	94117	10-E1
	SHRADER ST	94117	9-E1
	KEZAR DR	94117	9-E1
	STANYAN ST	94117	9-E1
	FELL ST	94117	9-E1
OAKDALE AV			SF
1400	KEITH ST	94124	15-C6
1500	LANE ST	94124	15-C6
1600	MENDELL ST	94124	15-C6
1620	3RD ST	94124	15-C6
1700	NEWHALL ST	94124	15-B6
1800	PHELPS ST	94124	15-B6
1900	QUINT ST	94124	15-B5
2000	RANKIN ST	94124	15-B5
2100	SELBY ST	94124	15-B5
2100	INDUSTRIAL ST	94124	15-B5
2200	TOLAND ST	94124	15-A5
2700	BARNEVELD AV	94124	15-A5
2720	BARNEVELD AV	94124	15-A5
2800	LOOMIS ST	94124	15-A5
2830	PATTERSON ST	94124	15-A5
2870	BAYSHORE BLVD	94124	15-A5
1000	GRIFFITH ST	94124	15-D7
1100	BALDWIN CT	94124	15-C7
1200	INGALLS ST	94124	15-C7
OAK GROVE ST			SF
1	HARRISON ST	94107	7-A7
100	BRYANT ST	94107	7-B7
OAKHURST LN			SF
1	CRESTMONT DR	94131	9-D3
50	OAK PARK DR	94131	9-D3
100	WARREN DR	94131	9-D3
OAK PARK DR			SF
1	CLARENDON AV	94131	9-E3
30	FOREST KNOLLS DR	94131	9-E3
1	WARREN DR	94131	9-D3
90	BLAIRWOOD LN	94131	9-D3
200	CHRISTOPHER DR	94131	9-D3
250	LAKE FOREST CT	94131	9-D3
300	DEVONSHIRE WY	94131	9-D3
600	OAKHURST LN	94131	9-D3
480	CHRISTOPHER DR	94131	9-D3
500	WARREN DR	94131	9-D3
OAKWOOD ST			SF
1	18TH ST	94110	10-H2
100	19TH ST	94110	10-H2
OCEAN AV			SF
1	MISSION ST	94112	14-G7
50	PERSIA AV	94112	14-G7
70	WATSON PL	94112	14-F7
100	ALEMANY BLVD	94112	14-F7
200	CAYUGA AV	94112	14-F7
300	WANDA ST	94112	14-F7
400	OTSEGO AV	94112	14-F7
500	ONONDAGA AV	94112	14-F7
560	DELANO AV	94112	14-F7
650	SAN JOSE AV	94112	14-E7
960	HOWTH ST	94112	14-E7
950	GENEVA AV	94112	13-E7
1200	PHELAN AV	94112	13-E7
1250	HAROLD AV	94112	13-E7
1320	LEE AV	94112	13-E7
1400	BRIGHTON AV	94112	13-D7
1460	PLYMOUTH AV	94112	13-D7
1500	PLYMOUTH AV	94112	13-D7
1550	GRANADA AV	94112	13-D7
1560	GRANADA AV	94112	13-D7
1620	MIRAMAR AV	94112	13-D7
1700	CAPITOL AV	94112	13-D7
1750	FAXON AV	94112	13-D7
1800	DORADO TER	94112	13-D7
1800	JULES AV	94112	13-D7
1880	ASHTON AV	94127	13-D7
1880	ASHTON AV	94112	13-D7
1950	KEYSTONE WY	94127	13-D7
2060	FAIRFIELD WY	94127	13-D7
2100	VICTORIA ST	94127	13-D7
2110	LAKEWOOD AV	94127	13-D7
2150	MANOR DR	94127	13-C7
2190	PINEHURST WY	94127	13-C7
	CERRITOS AV	94127	13-C7
2220	WESTGATE DR	94127	13-C7
2250	CEDRO AV	94127	13-C7
2280	APTOS AV	94127	13-C7
2320	SAN BENITO WY	94127	13-C6
2330	PALOMA AV	94127	13-C6
2350	SANTA ANA AV	94127	13-C6
2380	SAN LEANDRO WY	94127	13-C6
2420	SAN FERNANDO WY	94127	13-C6
	EUCALYPTUS DR	94132	13-C6
	JUNIPERO SERRA BLVD	94132	13-C6
2510	JUNIPERO SERRA BLVD	94132	13-C6
2560	WOODACRE DR	94132	13-C6
2630	LAGUNITAS DR	94132	13-C6
2700	19TH AV	94132	13-B6
2800	20TH AV	94132	13-B6
2900	21ST AV	94132	13-B6
3000	22ND AV	94132	13-B6
3030	MELBA AV	94132	13-B6
3100	23RD AV	94132	13-B6
3200	24TH AV	94132	13-B6
3300	25TH AV	94132	13-B6
3400	26TH AV	94132	13-B6
3500	INVERNESS DR	94132	13-A6
3600	FOREST VIEW DR	94132	13-A6
3700	MEADOWBROOK DR	94132	13-A6
3800	SYLVAN DR	94132	13-A6
3900	MIDDLEFIELD DR	94132	13-A6
4000	RIVERTON DR	94132	13-A6
4100	SPRINGFIELD DR	94132	13-A6
4200	EVERGLADE DR	94132	13-A6
4300	HAVENSIDE DR	94132	13-A6
4400	WESTMOORLAND DR	94132	13-A6
4500	CLEARFIELD DR	94132	13-A6
4600	MORNINGSIDE DR	94132	12-J6
4650	GELLERT DR	94132	12-J6
4700	SUNSET BLVD	94132	12-J6
4710	LAKESHORE DR	94132	12-J6
4800	COUNTRY CLUB DR	94132	12-J6
OCTAVIA ST			SF
2200	WASHINGTON ST	94109	6-H5
2300	JACKSON ST	94109	6-H5
2400	PACIFIC AV	94109	6-H5
2500	BROADWAY	94109	6-H4
2600	VALLEJO ST	94123	6-H4
2700	GREEN ST	94123	6-H4
2800	UNION ST	94123	6-H4
2900	FILBERT ST	94123	2-H4
3000	GREENWICH ST	94123	2-H4
3100	LOMBARD ST	94123	2-H4
3200	CHESTNUT ST	94123	2-H4
3300	FRANCISCO ST	94123	2-H3
3400	BAY ST	94123	2-H3
1600	SUTTER ST	94109	6-H6
1700	BUSH ST	94109	6-H5
1710	AUSTIN ST	94109	6-H5
1800	PINE ST	94109	6-H5
1900	CALIFORNIA ST	94109	6-H5
2000	SACRAMENTO ST	94109	6-H5
800	MCALLISTER ST	94102	6-H7
900	GOLDEN GATE AV	94102	6-H7
250	LILY ST	94102	6-H7
300	OAK ST	94102	6-H7
350	HICKORY ST	94102	6-H7
400	FELL ST	94102	6-H7
450	LINDEN ST	94102	6-H7
500	HAYES ST	94102	6-H7
550	IVY ST	94102	6-H7
600	GROVE ST	94102	6-H7
650	BIRCH ST	94102	6-H7
700	FULTON ST	94102	6-H7
1	MARKET ST	94102	10-H1
30	WALLER ST	94102	10-H1
100	HAIGHT ST	94102	10-H1
150	ROSE ST	94102	10-H1
200	PAGE ST	94102	6-H7
OFARRELL ST			SF
1	MARKET ST	94108	7-A6
20	GRANT AV	94108	7-A6
40	SECURITY PAC PL	94108	7-A6
100	STOCKTON ST	94108	7-A6
200	POWELL ST	94102	7-A6
240	CYRIL MAGIN ST	94102	7-A6
280	ELWOOD ST	94102	7-A6
300	MASON ST	94102	7-A6
400	TAYLOR ST	94102	7-A6
600	SHANNON ST	94102	6-J6
500	JONES ST	94102	6-J6
600	LEAVENWORTH ST	94109	6-J6
620	HARLEM AL	94109	6-J6
660	ADA CT	94109	6-J6
700	HYDE ST	94109	6-J6
800	LARKIN ST	94109	6-J6
900	POLK ST	94109	6-J6
1000	VAN NESS AV	94109	6-H6
1100	FRANKLIN ST	94109	6-H6
1100	STARR KING WY	94109	6-H6
1530	HOLLIS ST	94115	6-G6
1600	WEBSTER ST	94115	6-G6
1700	FILLMORE ST	94115	6-G6
1800	STEINER ST	94115	6-G6
1900	PIERCE ST	94115	6-G6
2000	SCOTT ST	94115	6-G6
2050	BEIDEMAN ST	94115	6-F6
2100	DIVISADERO ST	94115	6-F6
2200	BRODERICK ST	94115	6-F6
2240	SAINT JOSEPHS AV	94115	6-F6
2400	LYON ST	94115	6-F6
2500	ANZAVISTA AV	94115	6-F6
2600	ANZA ST	94115	6-F6
2600	MASONIC AV	94115	6-F6
OGDEN AV			SF
1	ANDOVER ST	94110	14-J6
110	MOULTRIE ST	94110	14-J6
210	ANDERSON ST	94110	14-J6
300	ELLSWORTH ST	94110	14-J6
400	GATES ST	94110	14-J6
500	FOLSOM ST	94110	14-J6
600	BANKS ST	94110	14-J6
700	PRENTISS ST	94110	14-J6
800	NEVADA ST	94110	14-J6
OHLONE WY			SF
1	SUSSEX ST	94131	14-G5
100	SURREY ST	94131	14-G6
OLD CHINATOWN LN			SF
1	WASHINGTON ST	94108	7-A5
OLD MASON ST			SF
870	PEDESTRIAN WY	94123	2-F3
870	MARINA BLVD	94123	2-F3
880	LUNDEEN ST	94123	2-F3
890	LYON ST	94129	2-E3
	CROOK ST	94129	2-E3
	LUNDEEN ST	94129	2-E3
	JAVOWITZ ST	94129	2-E3
	MARSHALL ST	94129	1-E3
	SERGEANT MITCHELL ST	94129	1-E3
	MASON ST	94129	1-E3
	HALLECK ST	94129	1-E3
	BANK ST	94129	1-D3
	MASON ST	94129	1-D3
	PENNINGTON ST	94129	1-D3
	LIVINGSTON ST	94129	1-D3
	MCDONALD ST	94129	1-C3
	MASON ST	94129	1-C3
OLIVE ST			SF
1	LARKIN ST	94109	6-J6
100	POLK ST	94109	6-J6
200	VAN NESS AV	94109	6-H6
300	FRANKLIN ST	94109	6-H6
OLIVER ST			SF
100	MISSION ST	94112	18-E2
OLMSTEAD ST			SF
870	SAN BRUNO AV	94134	20-A1
750	GIRARD ST	94134	20-A1
630	BRUSSELS ST	94134	20-A1
600	GOETTINGEN ST	94134	20-A1
700	BOWDOIN ST	94134	20-A1
800	DARTMOUTH ST	94134	19-J1
900	COLBY ST	94134	19-J1
1000	UNIVERSITY ST	94134	19-J1
OLYMPIA WY			SF
1	PANORAMA DR	94131	9-E3
60	DELLBROOK AV	94131	9-E3
170	DELLBROOK AV	94131	9-D3
300	CLARENDON AV	94131	9-D3
OMAR WY			SF
1	SEQUOIA WY	94127	14-E5
100	ROCKDALE DR	94127	14-E5
200	MYRA WY	94127	14-E5
ONEIDA AV			SF
1	SAN JOSE AV	94112	14-F7
200	DELANO AV	94112	19-F1
400	OTSEGO AV	94112	19-F1
300	CAYUGA AV	94112	19-F1
ONONDAGA AV			SF
1	OCEAN AV	94112	14-F7
50	OTSEGO AV	94112	14-F7
100	WANDA ST	94112	14-F7
140	CAYUGA AV	94112	19-F1
190	ROSELLA CT	94112	19-F1
220	ALEMANY BLVD	94112	19-F1
300	MISSION ST	94112	19-F1
OPAL PL			SF
100	TAYLOR ST	94102	7-A6
OPALO LN			SF
100	GOLD MINE DR	94131	14-F5
OPHIR AL			SF
1	POST ST	94109	6-J6
100	COSMO PL	94109	6-J6
ORA WY			SF
1	TOPAZ WY	94131	14-F5
100	GOLD MINE DR	94131	14-F5
ORBEN PL			SF
1	PINE ST	94115	6-G5
100	CALIFORNIA ST	94115	6-G5
ORD CT			SF
100	ORD ST	94114	10-F2
ORD ST			SF
	SHERIDAN AV	94129	1-D4
	MILES ST	94129	1-D4
1	ORD CT	94114	10-F2
50	SATURN ST	94114	10-F2
100	17TH ST	94114	10-F2
130	CORBETT AV	94114	10-F2
180	MARKET ST	94114	10-F2
180	STORRIE ST	94114	10-F2
200	18TH ST	94114	10-F2
ORDWAY ST			SF
310	SAN BRUNO AV	94134	20-A1
210	GIRARD ST	94134	20-A1
120	BRUSSELS ST	94134	20-A1
30	GOETTINGEN ST	94134	20-A1
1	SOMERSET ST	94134	20-A1
30	ANKENY ST	94134	20-A1
30	ALDER ST	94134	20-A1
OREILLY AV			SF
	TORNEY AV	94129	2-E4
	EDIE RD	94129	2-E4
ORIZABA AV			SF
600	GARFIELD ST	94132	18-D1
600	GARFIELD ST	94112	18-D1
700	HOLLOWAY AV	94132	18-D1
700	HOLLOWAY AV	94112	18-D1
100	ALEMANY BLVD	94132	18-D2
100	ALEMANY BLVD	94112	18-D2
100	BROTHERHOOD WY	94132	18-D2
100	SAGAMORE ST	94112	18-D2
60	SADOWA ST	94132	18-D2
60	SADOWA ST	94112	18-D2
200	STANLEY ST	94132	18-D2
200	STANLEY ST	94112	18-D2
230	BROAD ST	94132	18-D2
230	BROAD ST	94112	18-D2
270	FARALLONES ST	94132	18-D2
270	FARALLONES ST	94112	18-D2
300	RANDOLPH ST	94132	18-D2
300	RANDOLPH ST	94112	18-D2
310	LOBOS ST	94132	18-D1
310	LOBOS ST	94112	18-D1
370	MINERVA ST	94132	18-D1
370	MINERVA ST	94112	18-D1
	SARGENT ST	94132	18-D1
	SARGENT ST	94112	18-D1
430	MONTANA ST	94132	18-D1
430	MONTANA ST	94112	18-D1
470	THRIFT ST	94132	18-D1
470	THRIFT ST	94112	18-D1
ORTEGA ST			SF
100	8TH AV	94116	9-D3
100	8TH AV	94122	9-D3
200	9TH AV	94116	9-C3
200	9TH AV	94122	9-C3
300	10TH AV	94116	9-C3
300	10TH AV	94122	9-C3
400	11TH AV	94116	9-C3
400	11TH AV	94122	9-C3
800	14TH AV	94116	9-C3
800	14TH AV	94122	9-C3
800	15TH AV	94116	9-C3
800	15TH AV	94122	9-C3
900	16TH AV	94116	9-C3
900	16TH AV	94122	9-C3
1000	17TH AV	94116	9-B3
1000	17TH AV	94122	9-B3
1050	ANGLO AL	94116	9-B3
1050	ANGLO AL	94122	9-B3
1100	18TH AV	94116	9-B3
1100	18TH AV	94122	9-B3
1200	19TH AV	94116	9-B3
1200	19TH AV	94122	9-B3
1300	20TH AV	94116	9-B3
1300	20TH AV	94122	9-B3
1400	21ST AV	94116	9-B3
1400	21ST AV	94122	9-B3
1500	22ND AV	94116	9-B3
1500	22ND AV	94122	9-B3
1600	23RD AV	94116	9-B3
1600	23RD AV	94122	9-B3
1700	24TH AV	94116	9-B3
1700	24TH AV	94122	9-B3
1800	25TH AV	94116	9-B3
1800	25TH AV	94122	9-B3
1900	26TH AV	94116	9-A3
1900	26TH AV	94122	9-A3
2000	27TH AV	94116	9-A3
2000	27TH AV	94122	9-A3
2100	28TH AV	94116	9-A3
2100	28TH AV	94122	9-A3
2200	29TH AV	94116	9-A3
2200	29TH AV	94122	9-A3
2300	30TH AV	94116	9-A3
2300	30TH AV	94122	9-A3
2400	31ST AV	94116	9-A3
2400	31ST AV	94122	9-A3
2500	32ND AV	94116	9-A3
2500	32ND AV	94122	9-A3
2600	33RD AV	94116	9-A3
2600	33RD AV	94122	9-A3
2700	34TH AV	94116	9-A3
2700	34TH AV	94122	9-A3
2800	35TH AV	94116	8-J3
2800	35TH AV	94122	8-J3
2900	36TH AV	94116	8-J3
2900	36TH AV	94122	8-J3
2950	SUNSET BLVD	94116	8-J3
2950	SUNSET BLVD	94122	8-J3
3000	37TH AV	94116	8-J3
3000	37TH AV	94122	8-J3
3100	38TH AV	94116	8-J3
3100	38TH AV	94122	8-J3
3200	39TH AV	94116	8-J3
3200	39TH AV	94122	8-J3
3300	40TH AV	94116	8-J3
3300	40TH AV	94122	8-J3
3400	41ST AV	94116	8-J3
3400	41ST AV	94122	8-J3
3500	42ND AV	94116	8-J3
3500	42ND AV	94122	8-J3
3600	43RD AV	94116	8-H3
3600	43RD AV	94122	8-H3
3700	44TH AV	94116	8-H3
3700	44TH AV	94122	8-H3
3800	45TH AV	94116	8-H3
3800	45TH AV	94122	8-H3
3900	46TH AV	94116	8-H3
3900	46TH AV	94122	8-H3
4000	47TH AV	94116	8-H3
4000	47TH AV	94122	8-H3
4100	48TH AV	94116	8-H3
4100	48TH AV	94122	8-H3
4200	GREAT HWY	94116	8-H3
4200	GREAT HWY	94122	8-H3
OSCEOLA LN			SF
1	LA SALLE AV	94124	15-C6
100	LA SALLE AV	94124	15-C6
OSGOOD PL			SF
1	PACIFIC AV	94133	7-A4
100	BROADWAY	94133	7-A4
OSHAUGHNESSY BLVD			SF
1	PORTOLA DR	94131	14-E5
1	PORTOLA DR	94127	14-E5
1	WOODSIDE AV	94127	14-E5
420	DEL VALE AV	94131	14-F5
420	DEL VALE AV	94127	14-F5
840	MALTA DR	94131	14-F6
1000	BOSWORTH ST	94131	14-F6
OTEGA AV			SF
1	NAHUA AV	94112	19-E1
10	OTTAWA AV	94112	19-E1
OTIS ST			SF
1	MISSION ST	94103	10-J1
1	12TH ST	94103	10-J1
50	BRADY ST	94103	10-J1
100	GOUGH ST	94103	10-H1
100	MCCOPPIN ST	94103	10-H1
	DUBOCE AV	94103	10-H1
210	DUBOCE AV	94103	10-H1
270	MISSION ST	94103	10-H1
OTSEGO AV			SF
1	ONEIDA AV	94112	19-F1

PRIMARY STREET Address	Cross Street	ZIP	CITY Pg-Grid
OTSEGO AV			**SF**
100	ONONDAGA AV	94112	14-F7
160	OCEAN AV	94112	14-F7
160	MEDA AV	94112	14-F7
210	RUDDEN AV	94112	14-F7
270	SANTA YNEZ AV	94112	14-F7
380	SAN JUAN AV	94112	14-F7
500	SANTA YSABEL AV	94112	14-F7
OTTAWA AV			**SF**
10	OTEGA AV	94112	19-E1
50	DELANO AV	94112	19-E1
70	CAYUGA AV	94112	19-E1
110	ROME ST	94112	19-E1
160	ALEMANY BLVD	94112	19-F2
160	HURON AV	94112	19-F2
210	DEL MONTE ST	94112	19-F2
250	ELLINGTON AV	94112	19-F2
300	MISSION ST	94112	19-F2
OVERLOOK DR			**SF**
	MIDDLE DR W	-	9-B1
	TRANSVERSE DR	-	9-B1
OWEN ST			**SF**
	ANZA ST	94129	1-D4
	FREEMAN ST	94129	1-D4
	GRAHAM ST	94129	1-D4
OWENS ST			**SF**
1	CHANNEL ST	94107	11-B1
100	16TH ST	94107	11-B1
OXFORD ST			**SF**
1	SILVER AV	94134	14-H7
40	PIOCHE ST	94134	14-H7
180	SILLIMAN ST	94134	14-H7
310	FELTON ST	94134	14-H7
400	BURROWS ST	94134	14-H7
500	BACON ST	94134	14-J7
600	WAYLAND ST	94134	14-J7
P			
PACHECO ST			**SF**
50	DORANTES AV	94116	13-D4
50	MAGELLAN AV	94116	13-D4
100	MAGELLAN AV	94116	13-D4
200	MARCELA AV	94116	9-D4
250	CASTENADA AV	94116	9-D4
300	LOPEZ AV	94116	9-D4
410	ALTON AV	94116	9-D4
410	8TH AV	94116	9-D3
500	9TH AV	94116	9-C3
600	10TH AV	94116	9-C3
700	11TH AV	94116	9-C3
750	12TH AV	94116	9-C3
800	AERIAL WY	94116	9-C3
900	FUNSTON AV	94116	9-C3
1000	14TH AV	94116	9-C3
1100	15TH AV	94116	9-C4
1200	16TH AV	94116	9-C4
1300	17TH AV	94116	9-B4
1350	ANGLO AL	94116	9-B4
1400	18TH AV	94116	9-B4
1500	19TH AV	94116	9-B4
1600	20TH AV	94116	9-B4
1700	21ST AV	94116	9-B4
1800	22ND AV	94116	9-B4
1900	23RD AV	94116	9-B4
2000	24TH AV	94116	9-B4
2400	28TH AV	94116	9-A4
2500	29TH AV	94116	9-A4
2600	30TH AV	94116	9-A4
2700	31ST AV	94116	9-A4
2800	32ND AV	94116	9-A4
2900	33RD AV	94116	9-A4
3000	34TH AV	94116	9-A4
3100	35TH AV	94116	8-J4
3200	36TH AV	94116	8-J4
3250	SUNSET BLVD	94116	8-J4
3300	37TH AV	94116	8-J4
3700	41ST AV	94116	8-J4
3800	42ND AV	94116	8-J4
3900	43RD AV	94116	8-H4
4000	44TH AV	94116	8-H4
4100	45TH AV	94116	8-H4
4200	46TH AV	94116	8-H4
4300	47TH AV	94116	8-H4
4400	48TH AV	94116	8-H4
4500	GREAT HWY	94116	8-H4
80	MERCED AV	94127	13-D4
	DEWEY BLVD	94116	13-D4
1	EDGEHILL WY	94127	13-D5
30	GARCIA AV	94127	13-D4
50	VASQUEZ AV	94127	13-D4
PACIFIC AV			**SF**
1	FRONT ST	94111	7-B4
300	BATTERY ST	94111	7-B4
400	SANSOME ST	94133	7-B4
450	OSGOOD PL	94133	7-A4
500	MONTGOMERY ST	94133	7-A4
530	JEROME AL	94133	7-A4
600	KEARNY ST	94133	7-A4
610	COLUMBUS AV	94133	7-A4
680	BECKETT ST	94133	7-A4
700	GRANT AV	94133	7-A4
750	PELTON PL	94133	7-A4
800	STOCKTON ST	94133	7-A4
820	CORDELIA ST	94133	7-A4
900	POWELL ST	94133	7-A4
930	KEYES AL	94133	7-A4
950	WAYNE PL	94133	7-A4
1000	MASON ST	94133	7-A4
1050	SALMON ST	94133	6-J4
1050	AUBURN ST	94133	6-J4
1070	HIMMELMANN PL	94133	6-J4
1100	TAYLOR ST	94133	6-J4
1160	PHOENIX TER	94133	6-J4
1200	JONES ST	94109	6-J4
1300	LEAVENWORTH ST	94109	6-J4
1320	BURGOYNE ST	94109	6-J4
1400	HYDE ST	94109	6-J5
1460	MORRELL ST	94109	6-J5
1460	MCCORMICK ST	94109	6-J5
1500	LARKIN ST	94109	6-J5
1600	POLK ST	94109	6-H5
1700	VAN NESS AV	94109	6-H5
1800	FRANKLIN ST	94109	6-H5
1900	GOUGH ST	94109	6-H5
2000	OCTAVIA ST	94109	6-H5
2100	LAGUNA ST	94115	6-G5
2200	BUCHANAN ST	94115	6-G5
2300	WEBSTER ST	94115	6-G5
2400	FILLMORE ST	94115	6-G5
2500	STEINER ST	94115	6-G5
2600	PIERCE ST	94115	6-G5
2700	SCOTT ST	94115	6-F5
2800	DIVISADERO ST	94115	6-F5
2850	RAYCLIFF TER	94115	6-F5
2900	BRODERICK ST	94115	6-F5
3000	BAKER ST	94115	6-F5
3100	LYON ST	94115	6-F5
3100	LYON ST	94129	6-F5
3200	PRESIDIO AV	94115	6-E5
3200	PRESIDIO AV	94129	6-E5
3200	PRESIDIO BLVD	94129	6-E5
2300	WALNUT ST	94118	6-E5
2400	LAUREL ST	94118	6-E5
2500	LOCUST ST	94118	5-E5
2600	SPRUCE ST	94118	5-E5
	14TH AV	94129	5-C5
	BROWN ST	94129	5-C5
	PARK BLVD	94129	5-C5
	W PACIFIC AV	94129	5-C5
W PACIFIC AV			**SF**
	PRESIDIO BLVD	94129	6-E5
	ARGUELLO BLVD	94118	5-D5
	ARGUELLO BLVD	94129	5-D5
	PACIFIC AV	94129	5-C5
PAGE ST			**SF**
1	FRANKLIN ST	94102	6-H7
100	GOUGH ST	94102	6-H7
200	OCTAVIA ST	94102	6-H7
300	LAGUNA ST	94102	6-H7
400	BUCHANAN ST	94102	10-H1
500	WEBSTER ST	94117	10-G1
600	FILLMORE ST	94117	10-G1
700	STEINER ST	94117	10-G1
800	PIERCE ST	94117	10-G1
900	SCOTT ST	94117	10-G1
1000	DIVISADERO ST	94117	10-G1
1100	BRODERICK ST	94117	10-F1
1200	BAKER ST	94117	10-F1
1300	LYON ST	94117	10-F1
1400	CENTRAL AV	94117	10-F1
1500	MASONIC AV	94117	10-F1
1600	ASHBURY ST	94117	10-E1
1700	CLAYTON ST	94117	10-E1
1800	COLE ST	94117	10-E1
1900	SHRADER ST	94117	9-E1
2000	STANYAN ST	94117	9-E1
PAGODA PL			**SF**
1	SACRAMENTO ST	94108	7-A5
PALACE DR			**SF**
	LYON ST	94129	2-E3
	LYON ST	94123	2-E3
	DOYLE DR	94123	2-F3
	PEDESTRIAN WY	94123	2-F3
PALM AV			**SF**
1	CALIFORNIA ST	94118	5-D6
100	EUCLID AV	94118	5-D6
200	GEARY BLVD	94118	5-D6
PALMETTO AV			**SF**
700	JUNIPERO SERRA BLVD	94132	18-C2
600	CHESTER AV	94132	18-C2
700	SAINT CHARLES AV	94132	18-C2
700	ALEMANY BLVD	94132	18-C2
200	HEAD ST	94132	18-C2
350	VICTORIA ST	94132	18-C2
500	RAMSELL ST	94132	18-C2
500	WORCESTER AV	94132	18-C2
PALO ALTO AV			**SF**
200	MAR VIEW WY	94131	10-E3
200	MAR VIEW WY	94114	10-E3
230	GLENBROOK AV	94131	10-E3
230	GLENBROOK AV	94114	10-E3
300	LA AVANZADA	94131	10-E3
300	LA AVANZADA	94114	10-E3
PALOMA AV			**SF**
1	OCEAN AV	94127	13-C7
100	MONCADA WY	94127	13-C7
150	MERCEDES WY	94127	13-C7
200	JUNIPERO SERRA BLVD	94127	13-C7
PALOS PL			**SF**
1	CRESTLAKE DR	94132	13-A6
90	SLOAT BLVD	94132	13-A6
PALOU AV			**SF**
1000	GRIFFITH ST	94124	15-D7
1020	CRISP RD	94124	15-D7
1100	HAWES ST	94124	15-C7
1200	INGALLS ST	94124	15-C7
1300	JENNINGS ST	94124	15-C6
1400	KEITH ST	94124	15-C6
1500	LANE ST	94124	15-C6
1600	3RD ST	94124	15-B6
1600	MENDELL ST	94124	15-B6
1700	NEWHALL ST	94124	15-B6
1820	PHELPS ST	94124	15-B6
1870	DUNSHEE ST	94124	15-B6
1900	QUINT ST	94124	15-B6
1900	SILVER AV	94124	15-B6
2000	RANKIN ST	94124	15-B5
2110	SELBY ST	94124	15-B5
2130	INDUSTRIAL ST	94124	15-A5
2160	DORMAN AV	94124	15-A5
2300	BARNEVELD AV	94124	15-A5
PANAMA ST			**SF**
200	NIANTIC AV	94132	18-C2
PANORAMA DR			**SF**
1	CLARENDON AV	94131	9-E3
100	DELLBROOK AV	94131	10-E3
140	CLAIRVIEW CT	94131	10-E3
160	MAR VIEW WY	94131	10-E3
200	GLADEVIEW WY	94131	10-E3
230	KNOLLVIEW WY	94131	10-E3
250	STARVIEW WY	94131	9-E3
300	OLYMPIA WY	94131	9-E4
370	STARVIEW WY	94131	9-E4
400	CITYVIEW WY	94131	9-E4
500	LONGVIEW CT	94131	9-E4
600	MOUNTVIEW CT	94131	14-E4
700	MIDCREST WY	94131	14-E4
800	TWIN PEAKS BLVD	94131	14-E4
PARADISE AV			**SF**
1	BURNSIDE AV	94131	14-F6
100	ELK ST	94131	14-F6
PARAISO PL			**SF**
1	CRESTLAKE DR	94132	13-B6
90	SLOAT BLVD	94132	13-B6
PARAMOUNT TER			**SF**
	STANYAN ST	94118	5-E7
PARIS ST			**SF**
200	AVALON AV	94112	14-G7
300	EXCELSIOR AV	94112	14-G7
400	BRAZIL AV	94112	14-G7
500	PERSIA AV	94112	19-G1
600	RUSSIA AV	94112	19-G1
700	FRANCE AV	94112	19-F1
800	ITALY AV	94112	19-F1
900	AMAZON AV	94112	19-F1
1000	GENEVA AV	94112	19-F1
1100	ROLPH ST	94112	19-F1
S PARK AV			**SF**
100	JACK LONDON AL	94107	7-B7
1	JACK LONDON AL	94107	7-B6
40	2ND ST	94107	7-B6
200	3RD ST	94107	7-B7
PARK BLVD			**SF**
	LINCOLN BLVD	94129	1-C4
	MCDOWELL AV	94129	1-C4
	SCHOFIELD RD	94129	1-C4
	KOBBE AV	94129	1-C4
	HITCHCOCK ST	94129	5-C4
	AMATURY LP	94129	5-C4
70	AMATURY LP	94129	5-C4
	MORRIS RD	94129	5-C4
	WASHINGTON BLVD	94129	5-C4
	PACIFIC AV	94129	5-C5
	WASHINGTON BLVD	94129	5-C5
PARK ST			**SF**
100	MISSION ST	94110	14-H6
200	LEESE ST	94110	14-H6
300	HOLLY PARK CIR	94110	14-H6
300	HOLLY PARK CIR	94110	14-J6
400	ANDOVER ST	94110	14-J6
PARKER AV			**SF**
1	CALIFORNIA ST	94118	5-E6
100	EUCLID AV	94118	5-E6
200	GEARY BLVD	94118	5-E6
300	ANZA ST	94118	5-E7
400	LONE MOUNTAIN TER	94118	5-E7
500	TURK ST	94118	5-E7
500	TURK ST	94117	5-E7
600	GOLDEN GATE AV	94117	5-E7
700	MCALLISTER ST	94117	5-E7
800	FULTON ST	94117	5-E7
PARK HILL AV			**SF**
10	BUENA VISTA AV E	94117	10-F1
100	ROOSEVELT WY	94117	10-F1
100	15TH ST	94117	10-F1
PARKRIDGE DR			**SF**
1	CRESTLINE DR	94131	10-F3
	VISTA LN	94131	10-F4
50	VISTA LN	94131	10-F4
100	BURNETT AV	94131	10-F4
PARNASSUS AV			**SF**
1	CLAYTON ST	94117	10-E2
50	BELVEDERE ST	94117	10-E2
100	COLE ST	94117	10-E2
150	SHRADER ST	94117	10-E2
200	STANYAN ST	94117	9-E2
250	WOODLAND AV	94117	9-E2
300	WILLARD ST	94117	9-E2
350	HILLPOINT AV	94117	9-E2
400	HILLWAY AV	94143	9-D2
550	3RD AV	94143	9-D2
550	3RD AV	94122	9-D2
600	4TH AV	94143	9-D2
600	4TH AV	94122	9-D2
700	5TH AV	94143	9-D2
700	5TH AV	94122	9-D2
700	JUDAH ST	94122	9-D2
PARQUE DR			**SF**
100	GENEVA AV	94134	19-H2
220	CIELITO DR	94134	19-H2
260	ESQUINA DR	94134	19-H2
300	CARRIZAL ST	94134	19-H2
300	VELASCO AV	94134	19-H2
PARSONS ST			**SF**
1	MCALLISTER ST	94118	5-E7
100	FULTON ST	94118	5-E7
PATTEN RD			**SF**
	MCDOWELL AV	94129	1-D4
	INCINERATOR RD	94129	1-D4
	LINCOLN BLVD	94129	1-D4
PATTERSON ST			**SF**
1	FLOWER ST	94124	15-A5
50	OAKDALE AV	94124	15-A5
PATTON ST			**SF**
1	APPLETON AV	94110	14-H5
100	HIGHLAND AV	94110	14-H5
PAUL AV			**SF**
1	3RD ST	94124	20-B1
1	GILMAN AV	94124	20-B1
90	CARR ST	94124	20-B1
180	GOULD ST	94124	20-B1
250	EXETER ST	94124	20-B1
320	CRANE ST	94124	15-B7
400	WHEAT ST	94124	15-B7
470	BAYSHORE BLVD	94124	15-A7
600	SAN BRUNO AV	94134	15-A7
PAULDING ST			**SF**
1	SAN JOSE AV	94112	14-F7
30	RALEIGH ST	94112	14-F7
70	ARAGO ST	94112	14-F7
	CIRCULAR AV	94112	14-F7
	CIRCULAR AV	94131	14-F7
	JUDSON AV	94131	14-F7
PAYSON ST			**SF**
1	SAINT CHARLES AV	94132	18-C2
100	CHESTER AV	94132	18-C2
PEABODY ST			**SF**
1	LELAND AV	94134	20-A2
100	VISITACION AV	94134	20-A2
200	SUNNYDALE AV	94134	20-A2
PEARCE ST			**SF**
	MARINE DR	94129	1-D3
	HAMILTON ST	94129	1-C3
	MCDONALD ST	94129	1-D3
	LIVINGSTON ST	94129	1-D3
PEARL ST			**SF**
40	MARKET ST	94103	10-H1
60	PINK AL	94103	10-H1
100	DUBOCE AV	94103	10-H1
PEDESTRIAN WY			**SF**
	YACHT RD	94123	2-F3
	DOYLE DR	94123	2-F3
	PALACE DR	94123	2-F3
	OLD MASON ST	94123	2-F3
	MARINA BLVD	94123	2-F3
PELTON PL			**SF**
1	PACIFIC AV	94133	7-A4
PENA ST			**SF**
	MESA AV	94129	5-D4
	KEYES AV	94129	5-D4
PENINSULA AV			**SF**
290	LATHROP AV	94134	20-B2
380	BLANKEN AV	94134	20-B2
PENNINGTON ST			**SF**
	OLD MASON ST	94129	1-D3
	LIVINGSTON ST	94129	1-D3
PENNSYLVANIA AV			**SF**
100	17TH ST	94107	11-B2
200	MARIPOSA ST	94107	11-B2
300	18TH ST	94107	11-B2
400	19TH ST	94107	11-B2
500	20TH ST	94107	11-B3
700	22ND ST	94107	11-B3
900	23RD ST	94107	11-B3
1100	25TH ST	94107	11-B4
1300	CESAR CHAVEZ ST	94107	11-B4
1190	CESAR CHAVEZ ST	94107	11-B4
PENNY LN			**SF**
1	SUSSEX ST	94131	14-G6
200	DIAMOND ST	94131	14-G6
PERALTA AV			**SF**
1	HOLLADAY AV	94110	15-A4
20	HAMPSHIRE ST	94110	15-A4
70	YORK ST	94110	15-A4
100	YORK ST	94110	15-A4
170	FRANCONIA ST	94110	15-A4
200	FLORIDA ST	94110	15-A4
220	MULLEN AV	94110	15-A4
500	SAMOSET ST	94110	15-A5
510	RIPLEY ST	94110	15-A5
600	ESMERALDA AV	94110	15-A5
600	BRADFORD ST	94110	15-A5
600	ALABAMA ST	94110	15-A5
650	MAYFLOWER ST	94110	15-A5
700	POWHATTAN AV	94110	15-A5
800	CORTLAND AV	94110	15-A5
850	MOJAVE ST	94110	15-A5
900	JARBOE AV	94110	15-A5
	TOMPKINS AV	94110	15-A6
1000	PUTNAM ST	94110	14-J6
1000	CRESCENT AV	94110	14-J6
PEREGO TER			**SF**
1	BURNETT AV	94131	10-F4
PERINE PL			**SF**
1	STEINER ST	94115	6-G5
100	PIERCE ST	94115	6-G5
PERRY ST			**SF**
100	3RD ST	94107	7-B7
200	4TH ST	94107	7-B7
PERSHING DR			**SF**
1500	LINCOLN BLVD	94129	5-B5
1600	STILLWELL DR	94129	5-B5
PERSIA AV			**SF**
1	OCEAN AV	94112	14-G7
	MISSION ST	94112	14-G7
200	LONDON ST	94112	14-G7
300	PARIS ST	94112	19-G1
360	LISBON ST	94112	19-G1
410	MADRID ST	94112	19-G1
470	EDINBURGH ST	94112	19-G1
530	NAPLES ST	94112	19-G1
580	VIENNA ST	94112	19-G1
640	ATHENS ST	94112	19-G1
700	MOSCOW ST	94112	19-G1
750	MUNICH ST	94112	19-G1
810	PRAGUE ST	94112	19-H1
870	DUBLIN ST	94112	19-H1
910	SUNNYDALE AV	94112	19-H1
910	SUNNYDALE AV	94134	19-H1
1200	BRAZIL AV	94112	19-H1
1200	BRAZIL AV	94134	19-H1
1200	MANSELL ST	94134	19-H1
PERU AV			**SF**
100	LISBON ST	94112	14-G7
200	MADRID ST	94112	14-H7
300	EDINBURGH ST	94112	14-H7
400	NAPLES ST	94112	14-H7
500	VIENNA ST	94112	14-H7
600	ATHENS ST	94112	14-H7
700	VALMAR TER	94134	14-H7
700	VALMAR TER	94112	14-H7
800	AVALON AV	94134	14-H7
800	AVALON AV	94112	14-H7
800	FELTON ST	94112	14-H7
900	BURROWS ST	94134	14-H7
900	BURROWS ST	94112	14-H7
PETERS AV			**SF**
1	FAIR AV	94110	14-H4
PETER YORKE WY			**SF**
1	GEARY BLVD	94109	6-H6
1	GOUGH ST	94109	6-H6
1	STARR KING WY	94109	6-H6
100	POST ST	94109	6-H6
PETRARCH PL			**SF**
1	PINE ST	94104	7-B5
PFEIFFER ST			**SF**
100	GRANT AV	94133	3-A3
160	BELLAIR PL	94133	3-A3
200	STOCKTON ST	94133	3-A3
PHELAN AV			**SF**
1	OCEAN AV	94112	13-E7
200	JUDSON AV	94112	13-E7
230	JUDSON AV	94112	13-E7
300	STAPLES AV	94112	13-E6
400	FLOOD AV	94112	13-E6
PHELPS ST			**SF**
200	3RD ST	94124	15-C5
300	DAVIDSON AV	94124	15-C5
400	EVANS AV	94124	15-C5
500	FAIRFAX AV	94124	15-C5
600	GALVEZ AV	94124	15-C5
700	HUDSON AV	94124	15-C5
800	INNES AV	94124	15-C5
900	JERROLD AV	94124	15-C5
1000	KIRKWOOD AV	94124	15-B5
1100	LA SALLE AV	94124	15-B5
1200	MCKINNON AV	94124	15-B5
1300	NEWCOMB AV	94124	15-B6
1400	OAKDALE AV	94124	15-B6
1300	PALOU AV	94124	15-B6
1400	QUESADA AV	94124	15-B6
2400	VESTA ST	94124	15-B7
2400	WILLIAMS AV	94124	15-B7
2500	BANCROFT AV	94124	15-A7
2600	CARROLL AV	94124	15-A7
2700	DONNER AV	94124	15-A7
2800	EGBERT AV	94124	15-A7
PHOENIX TER			**SF**
1	PACIFIC AV	94133	6-J4
PICO AV			**SF**
1	ASHTON AV	94127	13-D7
100	URBANO DR N	94127	13-D7
100	URBANO DR S	94127	13-D7
PIEDMONT ST			**SF**
1	MASONIC AV	94117	10-F2
30	ASHBURY TER	94117	10-F2
30	DELMAR ST	94117	10-F2
200	ASHBURY ST	94117	10-F2
PIERCE ST			**SF**
2400	JACKSON ST	94115	6-G5
2500	PACIFIC AV	94115	6-G5
2600	BROADWAY ST	94115	6-G5
2700	VALLEJO ST	94123	6-G4
2800	GREEN ST	94123	6-G4
2900	UNION ST	94123	6-G4
3000	FILBERT ST	94123	6-G4
3100	GREENWICH ST	94123	2-G4
3200	LOMBARD ST	94123	2-F4
3300	CHESTNUT ST	94123	2-F4
3350	TOLEDO WY	94123	2-F4
3400	ALHAMBRA ST	94123	2-F4
3500	CAPRA WY	94123	2-F3
3600	BEACH ST	94123	2-F3
1600	POST ST	94115	6-G6
1700	SUTTER ST	94115	6-G6
1800	BUSH ST	94115	6-G6
1900	PINE ST	94115	6-G6
2000	CALIFORNIA ST	94115	6-G5
2050	PERINE PL	94115	6-G5

Address	Cross Street	ZIP	City Pg-Grid
PIERCE ST			**SF**
2100	SACRAMENTO ST	94115	6-G5
2200	CLAY ST	94115	6-G5
900	FULTON ST	94117	6-G7
990	MCALLISTER ST	94117	6-G7
1090	GOLDEN GATE AV	94115	6-G7
1130	ELM ST	94115	6-G7
1190	TURK ST	94115	6-G7
1290	EDDY ST	94115	6-G6
1300	ELLIS ST	94115	6-G6
1400	OFARRELL ST	94115	6-G6
100	WALLER ST	94117	10-G1
200	HAIGHT ST	94117	10-G1
300	PAGE ST	94117	10-G1
400	OAK ST	94117	6-G7
500	FELL ST	94117	6-G7
600	HAYES ST	94117	6-G7
PILGRIM AV			**SF**
1	SAN JOSE AV	94112	14-F7
PINAR LN			**SF**
1	BAKER ST	94115	6-F7
100	SAINT JOSEPHS AV	94115	6-F7
PINE ST			**SF**
1	MARKET ST	94111	7-B5
10	DAVIS ST	94111	7-B5
100	FRONT ST	94111	7-B5
200	BATTERY ST	94104	7-B5
300	SANSOME ST	94104	7-B5
340	LEIDESDORFF ST	94104	7-B5
350	CENTURY PL	94104	7-B5
370	PETRARCH PL	94104	7-B5
400	MONTGOMERY ST	94104	7-A5
450	BELDEN ST	94104	7-A5
500	KEARNY ST	94108	7-A5
510	SAINT GEORGE AL	94108	7-A5
590	QUINCY ST	94108	7-A5
570	QUINCY ST	94108	7-A5
600	GRANT AV	94108	7-A5
700	STOCKTON ST	94108	7-A5
720	DASHELLE HAMMETT ST	94108	7-A5
750	JOICE ST	94108	7-A5
800	POWELL ST	94108	7-A5
890	NOB HILL CIR	94108	7-A5
900	MASON ST	94108	7-A5
920	VINE TER	94108	7-A5
1000	TAYLOR ST	94108	6-J5
1100	JONES ST	94109	6-J5
1130	TOUCHARD ST	94109	6-J5
1200	LEAVENWORTH ST	94109	6-J5
1300	HYDE ST	94109	6-J5
1400	LARKIN ST	94109	6-J5
1500	POLK ST	94109	6-H5
1600	VAN NESS AV	94109	6-H5
1700	FRANKLIN ST	94109	6-H5
1800	GOUGH ST	94109	6-H5
1900	OCTAVIA ST	94109	6-H5
2000	LAGUNA ST	94115	6-H5
2100	BUCHANAN ST	94115	6-G5
2200	WEBSTER ST	94115	6-G5
2240	ORBEN PL	94115	6-G5
2300	FILLMORE ST	94115	6-G5
2400	STEINER ST	94115	6-G6
2500	PIERCE ST	94115	6-G6
2600	SCOTT ST	94115	6-F6
2700	DIVISADERO ST	94115	6-F6
2800	BRODERICK ST	94115	6-F6
2900	BAKER ST	94115	6-F6
3000	LYON ST	94115	6-F6
3100	MASONIC AV	94115	6-F6
3100	PRESIDIO AV	94115	6-F6
PINEHURST WY			**SF**
1	OCEAN AV	94127	13-C7
100	KENWOOD WY	94127	13-D7
200	UPLAND DR	94127	13-D7
PINTO AV			**SF**
1	ARBALLO DR	94132	18-B1
100	TAPIA DR	94132	18-B1
PIOCHE ST			**SF**
100	CAMBRIDGE ST	94134	14-H7
200	OXFORD ST	94134	14-H7
300	HARVARD ST	94134	14-H7
400	GAMBIER ST	94134	14-H7
500	MADISON ST	94134	14-H7
PIPER LP			**SF**
	DUDLEY RD	94129	5-D4
	DEEMS RD	94129	5-D5
PIXLEY ST			**SF**
1	BUCHANAN ST	94123	2-G4
100	WEBSTER ST	94123	6-G4
200	FILLMORE ST	94123	6-G4
300	STEINER ST	94123	6-G4
PIZARRO WY			**SF**
1	WESTWOOD DR	94112	13-D6
50	NORTHWOOD DR	94112	13-D6
100	FAXON AV	94112	13-D6
PLAZA ST			**SF**
1	LAGUNA HONDA BLVD	94116	9-D4
100	MAGELLAN AV	94116	9-D4
PLEASANT ST			**SF**
1	TAYLOR ST	94108	6-J5
100	JONES ST	94108	6-J5
PLUM ST			**SF**
1	S VAN NESS AV	94103	10-J1
100	MISSION ST	94103	10-J1
PLYMOUTH AV			**SF**
1600	MONTEREY BLVD	94127	13-D6
1650	MANGELS AV	94127	13-D6
1700	SAINT ELMO WY	94127	13-D6
1700	YERBA BUENA AV	94127	13-D6
1100	OCEAN AV	94112	13-D7
1230	SOUTHWOOD DR	94112	13-D7
1250	SAN RAMON WY	94112	13-D7
1360	WILDWOOD WY	94112	13-D7
1440	GREENWOOD AV	94112	13-D7
1450	NORTHWOOD DR	94112	13-D6
1510	MONTECITO AV	94112	13-D6
1600	MONTEREY BLVD	94112	13-D6
1	SICKLES AV	94112	18-D2
1	SAGAMORE ST	94112	18-D2
90	SADOWA ST	94112	18-D2
180	BROAD ST	94112	18-D2
270	FARALLONES ST	94112	18-D2
360	LOBOS ST	94112	18-D1
450	MINERVA ST	94112	18-D1
540	MONTANA ST	94112	18-D1
630	THRIFT ST	94112	18-D1
710	LAKEVIEW AV	94112	18-D1
890	GRAFTON AV	94112	18-D1
1100	HOLLOWAY AV	94112	13-D7
1200	OCEAN AV	94112	13-D7
POINT LOBOS AV			**SF**
10	40TH AV	94121	4-J6
10	GEARY BLVD	94121	4-J6
40	41ST AV	94121	4-J6
70	42ND AV	94121	4-H6
100	43RD AV	94121	4-H6
200	44TH AV	94121	4-H6
300	45TH AV	94121	4-H6
370	46TH AV	94121	4-H6
450	ALTA MAR WY	94121	4-H6
500	47TH AV	94121	4-H6
600	48TH AV	94121	4-H6
600	EL CAMINO DEL MAR	94121	4-H6
820	MERRIE WY	94121	4-G6
1080	GREAT HWY	94121	4-G6
POLARIS WY			**SF**
320	WAVERLY WY	94112	19-F2
400	POPE ST	94112	19-F2
POLK ST			**SF**
1	10TH ST	94102	6-J7
1	MARKET ST	94102	6-J7
10	FELL ST	94102	6-J7
100	HAYES ST	94102	6-J7
140	LECH WALESA	94102	6-J7
200	GROVE ST	94102	6-J7
400	MCALLISTER ST	94102	6-J7
440	REDWOOD ST	94102	6-J6
500	GOLDEN GATE AV	94102	6-J6
540	ELM ST	94102	6-J6
600	TURK ST	94102	6-J6
700	EDDY ST	94109	6-J6
730	WILLOW ST	94109	6-J6
800	ELLIS ST	94109	6-J6
840	OLIVE ST	94109	6-J6
900	OFARRELL ST	94109	6-J6
950	MYRTLE ST	94109	6-J6
1000	GEARY ST	94109	6-J6
1030	CEDAR ST	94109	6-J6
1100	POST ST	94109	6-J6
1130	HEMLOCK ST	94109	6-J6
1200	SUTTER ST	94109	6-J6
1230	FERN ST	94109	6-J5
1300	BUSH ST	94109	6-J5
1330	AUSTIN ST	94109	6-J5
1400	PINE ST	94109	6-J5
1500	CALIFORNIA ST	94109	6-H5
1600	SACRAMENTO ST	94109	6-H5
1700	CLAY ST	94109	6-H5
1800	WASHINGTON ST	94109	6-H5
1900	JACKSON ST	94109	6-H5
2000	PACIFIC AV	94109	6-H4
2100	BROADWAY	94109	6-H4
2200	VALLEJO ST	94109	6-H4
2230	BONITA ST	94109	6-H4
2300	GREEN ST	94109	6-H4
2400	UNION ST	94109	2-H4
2500	FILBERT ST	94109	2-H4
2600	GREENWICH ST	94109	2-H4
2700	LOMBARD ST	94109	2-H4
2800	CHESTNUT ST	94109	2-H4
2900	FRANCISCO ST	94109	2-H3
3000	BAY ST	94109	2-H3
3100	NORTH POINT ST	94109	2-H3
3200	BEACH ST	94109	2-H3
POLLARD PL			**SF**
1	VALLEJO ST	94133	7-A4
1	ROMOLO ST	94133	7-A4
POMONA ST			**SF**
1	BAYVIEW ST	94124	15-B6
100	THORNTON AV	94124	15-B6
POND ST			**SF**
1	16TH ST	94114	10-G2
100	17TH ST	94114	10-G2
POPE RD			**SF**
	FRANKLIN ST	94123	2-H3
	SCHOFIELD RD	94123	2-H3
	FUNSTON RD	94123	2-H3
POPE ST			**SF**
	GREENOUGH AV	94129	1-C4
	TODD ST	94129	1-C4
	KOBBE AV	94129	1-C4
1	MISSION ST	94112	19-F1
50	HOLLYWOOD CT	94112	19-F2
100	CROSS ST	94112	19-F2
190	MORSE ST	94112	19-F2
270	BRUNSWICK ST	94112	19-F2
350	HANOVER ST	94112	19-F2
370	PRAGUE ST	94112	19-F2
400	BALTIMORE WY	94112	19-F2
440	POLARIS WY	94112	19-F2
	BELLEVUE AV	94112	19-F2
POPLAR ST			**SF**
100	24TH ST	94110	10-H4
200	25TH ST	94110	10-H4
300	26TH ST	94110	10-H4
POPPY LN			**SF**
1	CONRAD ST	94131	14-G5
40	DIAMOND ST	94131	14-G5
100	SUSSEX ST	94131	14-G5
W PORTAL AV			**SF**
1	ULLOA ST	94127	13-C5
100	VICENTE ST	94127	13-C5
200	14TH AV	94127	13-C5
300	15TH AV	94127	13-C6
300	15TH AV	94132	13-C6
500	JUNIPERO SERRA BLVD	94127	13-C6
500	JUNIPERO SERRA BLVD	94132	13-C6
500	SAINT FRANCIS BLVD	94132	13-C6
500	SLOAT BLVD	94132	13-C6
500	PORTOLA DR	94132	13-C6
PORTAL PTH			**SF**
1	PORTOLA DR	94127	13-C5
1	CLAREMONT BLVD	94127	13-C5
100	SAN LORENZO WY	94127	13-C5
PORTER ST			**SF**
1	CRESCENT AV	94110	14-J6
100	BENTON AV	94110	14-J6
PORTOLA DR			**SF**
1	CORBETT AV	94114	10-F4
1	CORBETT AV	94131	10-F4
1	MARKET ST	94131	10-F4
50	DIAMOND HEIGHTS BLVD	94131	14-F4
50	BURNETT AV	94131	14-F4
220	GLENVIEW DR	94131	14-E4
470	TWIN PEAKS BLVD	94131	14-E4
540	OSHAUGHNESSY BLVD	94127	13-E4
540	WOODSIDE AV	94127	13-E4
600	TERESITA BLVD	94127	13-E4
750	FOWLER AV	94127	13-E4
700	SYDNEY WY	94127	13-E4
750	EVELYN WY	94127	13-E5
820	LAGUNA HONDA BLVD	94127	13-E5
880	DEL SUR AV	94127	13-D5
920	WAITHMAN WY	94127	13-D5
980	REX AV	94127	13-D5
1010	MIRALOMA DR	94127	13-D5
1080	KENSINGTON WY	94127	13-D5
1150	SAN PABLO AV	94127	13-D5
1150	GRANVILLE WY	94127	13-D5
1240	SANTA PAULA AV	94127	13-D5
1240	DORCHESTER WY	94127	13-D5
1300	SAN LORENZO WY	94127	13-D5
1350	PORTAL PTH	94127	13-C5
1350	CLAREMONT BLVD	94127	13-C5
1400	SANTA CLARA AV	94127	13-C5
1400	VICENTE ST	94127	13-C5
1450	TERRACE DR	94127	13-C5
1500	SAN ANSELMO AV	94127	13-C5
1500	14TH AV	94127	13-C5
1570	SAN LEANDRO WY	94127	13-C5
1600	SAN FERNANDO WY	94127	13-C6
1600	15TH AV	94127	13-C6
1700	JUNIPERO SERRA BLVD	94127	13-C6
1700	SAINT FRANCIS BLVD	94127	13-C6
1700	SLOAT BLVD	94127	13-C6
1700	W PORTAL AV	94127	13-C6
PORTOLA ST			**SF**
760	RODRIGUEZ ST	94129	5-E5
750	MCRAE ST	94129	5-E5
700	MCRAE ST	94129	5-E4
	MORTON ST	94129	5-E4
	MACARTHUR AV	94129	5-E4
POST ST			**SF**
1	MONTGOMERY ST	94108	7-B5
1	MONTGOMERY ST	94104	7-B5
100	KEARNY ST	94108	7-A5
120	ROBERT KIRK LN	94108	7-A5
200	GRANT AV	94108	7-A5
300	STOCKTON ST	94108	7-A5
400	POWELL ST	94102	7-A6
500	MASON ST	94102	7-A6
600	TAYLOR ST	94102	6-J6
600	TAYLOR ST	94109	6-J6
630	AGATE AL	94102	6-J6
630	AGATE AL	94109	6-J6
650	SHANNON ST	94102	6-J6
650	SHANNON ST	94109	6-J6
660	OPHIR AL	94102	6-J6
660	OPHIR AL	94109	6-J6
700	JONES ST	94102	6-J6
700	JONES ST	94109	6-J6
800	LEAVENWORTH ST	94109	6-J6
900	HYDE ST	94109	6-J6
920	MEACHAM PL	94109	6-J6
1000	LARKIN ST	94109	6-J6
1100	POLK ST	94109	6-J6
1200	VAN NESS AV	94109	6-H6
1300	FRANKLIN ST	94109	6-H6
1320	PETER YORKE WY	94109	6-H6
1400	GOUGH ST	94109	6-H6
1600	LAGUNA ST	94115	6-H6
1800	WEBSTER ST	94115	6-G6
1900	FILLMORE ST	94115	6-G6
1950	AVERY ST	94115	6-G6
2000	STEINER ST	94115	6-G6
2100	PIERCE ST	94115	6-G6
2200	SCOTT ST	94115	6-F6
2300	DIVISADERO ST	94115	6-F6
2330	ERKSON CT	94115	6-F6
2400	BRODERICK ST	94115	6-F6
2500	BAKER ST	94115	6-F6
2600	LYON ST	94115	6-F6
2700	PRESIDIO AV	94115	6-F6
POTOMAC ST			**SF**
100	WALLER ST	94117	10-G1
POTRERO AV			**SF**
30	DIVISION ST	94103	11-A1
30	10TH ST	94103	11-A1
50	BRANNAN ST	94103	11-A1
100	ALAMEDA ST	94103	11-A1
200	15TH ST	94103	11-A1
300	16TH ST	94103	11-A2
400	17TH ST	94110	11-A2
500	MARIPOSA ST	94110	11-A2
600	18TH ST	94110	11-A2
700	19TH ST	94110	11-A2
800	20TH ST	94110	11-A3
900	21ST ST	94110	11-A3
950	22ND ST	94110	11-A3
1000	22ND ST	94110	11-A3
1100	23RD ST	94110	11-A3
1120	23RD ST	94110	11-A3
1200	24TH ST	94110	11-A3
1280	25TH ST	94110	11-A4
	25TH ST	94110	11-A4
	SERPENTINE AV	94110	11-A4
	CESAR CHAVEZ ST	94110	11-A4
POWELL ST			**SF**
100	ELLIS ST	94102	7-A6
100	ELLIS ST	94108	7-A6
200	OFARRELL ST	94102	7-A6
200	OFARRELL ST	94108	7-A6
300	GEARY ST	94102	7-A6
300	GEARY ST	94108	7-A6
400	POST ST	94102	7-A5
400	POST ST	94108	7-A5
500	SUTTER ST	94102	7-A5
500	SUTTER ST	94108	7-A5
550	ANSON PL	94102	7-A5
550	ANSON PL	94108	7-A5
600	BUSH ST	94108	7-A5
650	FELLA PL	94108	7-A5
700	PINE ST	94108	7-A5
800	CALIFORNIA ST	94108	7-A5
900	SACRAMENTO ST	94108	7-A5
1000	CLAY ST	94108	7-A5
1100	WASHINGTON ST	94108	7-A5
1200	JACKSON ST	94133	7-A4
1230	JOHN ST	94133	7-A4
1300	PACIFIC AV	94133	7-A4
1330	FISHER AL	94133	7-A4
1400	BROADWAY	94133	7-A4
1500	VALLEJO ST	94133	7-A4
1600	GREEN ST	94133	3-A4
1700	UNION ST	94133	3-A4
1760	COLUMBUS AV	94133	3-A4
1800	FILBERT ST	94133	3-A4
1900	GREENWICH ST	94133	3-A4
2000	LOMBARD ST	94133	3-A3
2100	CHESTNUT ST	94133	3-A3
2200	FRANCISCO ST	94133	3-A3
2270	VANDEWATER ST	94133	3-A3
2300	BAY ST	94133	3-A3
2400	NORTH POINT ST	94133	2-J3
2500	BEACH ST	94133	2-J3
2600	JEFFERSON ST	94133	2-J3
2600	THE EMBARCADERO	94133	2-J3
2700	THE EMBARCADERO	94133	2-J3
POWERS AV			**SF**
1	COLERIDGE ST	94110	14-J4
100	MISSION ST	94110	14-J4
POWHATTAN AV			**SF**
300	BOCANA ST	94110	14-J5
400	WOOL ST	94110	14-J5
500	ANDOVER ST	94110	14-J5
550	MOULTRIE ST	94110	14-J5
600	ANDERSON ST	94110	14-J5
650	ELLSWORTH ST	94110	14-J5
700	GATES ST	94110	14-J5
750	FOLSOM ST	94110	14-J5
800	BANKS ST	94110	14-J5
830	PRENTISS ST	94110	14-J5
850	PRENTISS ST	94110	14-J5
900	NEVADA ST	94110	14-J5
900	BERNAL HEIGHTS BLVD	94110	14-J5
1000	NEBRASKA ST	94110	14-J5
1100	BRADFORD ST	94110	15-A5
1200	PERALTA AV	94110	15-A5
1300	FRANCONIA ST	94110	15-A5
PRADO ST			**SF**
1	AVILA ST	94123	2-F3
100	SCOTT ST	94123	2-F3
PRAGUE ST			**SF**
190	BRAZIL AV	94112	19-H1
370	PERSIA AV	94112	19-G1
550	RUSSIA AV	94112	19-G1
700	GENEVA AV	94112	19-G2
730	S HILL BLVD	94112	19-G2
760	ROLPH ST	94112	19-G2
850	NAYLOR ST	94112	19-G2
940	CORDOVA ST	94112	19-G2
1040	DRAKE ST	94112	19-F2
1070	CURTIS ST	94112	19-F2
1190	WINDING WY	94112	19-F2
1200	POPE ST	94112	19-F2
PRATT PL			**SF**
1	CALIFORNIA ST	94108	7-A5
PRECITA AV			**SF**
1	MISSION ST	94110	14-J4
100	COSO AV	94110	14-J4
200	EMMETT CT	94110	14-J4
300	SHOTWELL ST	94110	14-J4
400	FOLSOM ST	94110	14-J4
500	HARRISON ST	94110	14-J4
550	ALABAMA ST	94110	14-J4
610	FLORIDA ST	94110	15-A4
650	BRYANT ST	94110	15-A4
690	YORK ST	94110	15-A4
700	CESAR CHAVEZ ST	94110	15-A4
700	YORK ST	94110	15-A4
3050	ALABAMA ST	94110	14-J4
400	BESSIE ST	94110	14-J4
450	TREAT AV	94110	14-J4
PRENTISS ST			**SF**
50	CHAPMAN ST	94110	14-J5
100	POWHATTAN AV	94110	14-J5
200	EUGENIA AV	94110	14-J5
300	CORTLAND AV	94110	14-J5
400	JARBOE AV	94110	14-J5
500	TOMPKINS AV	94110	14-J6
600	OGDEN AV	94110	14-J6
800	CRESCENT AV	94110	14-J6
PRESCOTT CT			**SF**
100	VALLEJO ST	94133	7-A4
PRESIDIO AV			**SF**
1	PACIFIC AV	94115	6-F5
1	PRESIDIO BLVD	94115	6-F5
100	JACKSON ST	94115	6-F5
200	WASHINGTON ST	94115	6-F5
290	CLAY ST	94115	6-F5
390	SACRAMENTO ST	94115	6-F5
480	CALIFORNIA ST	94115	6-F6
590	MASONIC AV	94115	6-F6
590	PINE ST	94115	6-F6
690	EUCLID AV	94115	6-F6
690	BUSH ST	94115	6-F6
790	SUTTER ST	94115	6-F6
890	POST ST	94115	6-F6
990	LEONA TER	94115	6-F6
1000	GEARY BLVD	94115	6-F6
PRESIDIO BLVD			**SF**
520	PACIFIC AV	94129	6-F5
520	PRESIDIO AV	94129	6-F5
	W BROADWAY ST	94129	6-F5
1	W PACIFIC AV	94129	6-E5
	SIMONDS LP	94129	6-E4
	LIGGETT AV	94129	6-E4
290	SIMONDS LP	94129	6-E4
270	SHERMAN RD	94129	6-E4
210	LOMBARD ST	94129	6-E4
170	LINCOLN BLVD	94129	2-E4
170	LETTERMAN DR	94129	2-E4
	MACARTHUR AV	94129	1-E4
	BARNARD AV	94129	5-E4
70	FUNSTON AV	94129	1-E4
60	MESA AV	94129	1-E4
1	CROSS OVER DR	-	9-B1
700	FULTON ST	94118	5-C7
600	CABRILLO ST	94118	5-C7
500	BALBOA ST	94118	5-C7
400	ANZA ST	94118	5-C7
300	GEARY BLVD	94118	5-C6
200	CLEMENT ST	94118	5-C6
100	CALIFORNIA ST	94118	5-C6
200	LAKE ST	94118	5-C6
PRESIDIO TER			**SF**
1	ARGUELLO BLVD	94118	5-D5
PRETOR WY			**SF**
1	CONCORD ST	94112	19-F2
100	GUTTENBERG ST	94112	19-F2
PRICE RW			**SF**
100	UNION ST	94133	3-A4
PRIEST ST			**SF**
1	WASHINGTON ST	94109	6-J5
PRINCETON ST			**SF**
1	SWEENY ST	94134	14-J7
70	TULANE ST	94134	14-J7
140	SILVER AV	94134	14-J7
200	SILLIMAN ST	94134	14-J7
340	FELTON ST	94134	14-J7
400	BACON ST	94134	14-J7
500	WAYLAND ST	94134	14-J7
PROGRESS ST			**SF**
1	WHITNEY YOUNG CIR	94124	15-C6
PROSPECT AV			**SF**
1	COSO AV	94110	14-J4
100	FAIR AV	94110	14-J5
150	ESMERALDA AV	94110	14-J5
200	VIRGINIA AV	94110	14-H5
250	HEYMAN AV	94110	14-H5
270	EUGENIA AV	94110	14-H5
310	KINGSTON ST	94110	14-H5
370	CORTLAND AV	94110	14-H5
PROSPER ST			**SF**
1	16TH ST	94114	10-G2
100	17TH ST	94114	10-G2
PUEBLO ST			**SF**
200	VELASCO AV	94134	19-J2
PUTNAM ST			**SF**
1	CORTLAND AV	94110	14-J5
100	JARBOE AV	94110	14-J5
200	TOMPKINS AV	94110	14-J6
280	CRESCENT AV	94110	14-J6
280	PERALTA AV	94110	14-J6
300	ALEMANY BLVD	94110	14-J6

Q

Address	Cross Street	ZIP	City Pg-Grid
QUANE ST			**SF**
1	21ST ST	94110	10-H3

Address	Cross Street	ZIP	City Pg-Grid
QUANE ST			SF
100	22ND ST	94110	10-H3
200	23RD ST	94110	10-H3
300	24TH ST	94110	10-H3
QUARRY RD			SF
	FERNANDEZ ST	94129	5-E5
QUARTZ WY			SF
1	TURQUOISE WY	94131	14-F4
100	AMBER DR	94131	14-F4
QUESADA AV			SF
1900	PHELPS ST	94124	15-B6
1930	TAMPA LN	94124	15-B6
2000	QUINT ST	94124	15-B6
2030	SILVER AV	94124	15-B6
2100	RANKIN ST	94124	15-B5
2210	SELBY ST	94124	15-A5
2300	INDUSTRIAL ST	94124	15-A5
1000	FITCH ST	94124	15-D7
1100	GRIFFITH ST	94124	15-D7
1170	CRISP RD	94124	15-D7
1200	HAWES ST	94124	15-C7
1300	INGALLS ST	94124	15-C7
1400	JENNINGS ST	94124	15-C7
1500	KEITH ST	94124	15-C6
1600	LANE ST	94124	15-C6
1700	3RD ST	94124	15-C6
1800	NEWHALL ST	94124	15-C6
QUICKSTEP LN			SF
	ELLIS ST	94115	6-H6
QUINCY ST			SF
100	PINE ST	94108	7-A5
200	CALIFORNIA ST	94108	7-A5
QUINT ST			SF
1	ARTHUR AV	94124	15-C4
1	ISLAIS ST	94124	15-C4
200	CUSTER AV	94124	15-C4
220	CUSTER AV	94124	15-C5
300	DAVIDSON AV	94124	15-C5
400	EVANS AV	94124	15-C5
800	JERROLD AV	94124	15-B5
1200	NEWCOMB AV	94124	15-B5
1300	OAKDALE AV	94124	15-B6
1350	DRUMMOND AL	94124	15-B6
1500	PALOU AV	94124	15-B6
1500	SILVER AV	94124	15-B6
1600	QUESADA AV	94124	15-B6
1700	REVERE AV	94124	15-B6
1770	MADDUX AV	94124	15-B6
1800	MADDUX AV	94124	15-B6
1900	THOMAS AV	94124	15-B6
1900	TOPEKA AV	94124	15-B6
1950	SANTA FE AV	94124	15-B6
2000	SCOTIA AV	94124	15-B6
2600	BAYSHORE BLVD	94124	15-A7
2500	CARROLL AV	94124	15-A6
2400	BANCROFT AV	94124	15-A6
2500	THORNTON AV	94124	15-A6
QUINTARA ST			SF
100	10TH AV	94116	9-C4
210	CRAGMONT AV	94116	9-C4
200	12TH AV	94116	9-C4
300	12TH AV	94116	9-C4
400	FUNSTON AV	94116	9-C4
500	14TH AV	94116	9-C4
600	15TH AV	94116	9-C4
600	FANNING WY	94116	9-C4
700	16TH AV	94116	9-C4
800	17TH AV	94116	9-B4
900	18TH AV	94116	9-B4
1000	19TH AV	94116	9-B4
1100	20TH AV	94116	9-B4
1200	21ST AV	94116	9-B4
1300	22ND AV	94116	9-B4
1400	23RD AV	94116	9-B4
1500	24TH AV	94116	9-B4
1600	25TH AV	94116	9-B4
1700	26TH AV	94116	9-A4
1800	27TH AV	94116	9-A4
1900	28TH AV	94116	9-A4
2000	29TH AV	94116	9-A4
2100	30TH AV	94116	9-A4
2200	31ST AV	94116	9-A4
2300	32ND AV	94116	9-A4
2400	33RD AV	94116	9-A4
2500	34TH AV	94116	9-A4
2600	35TH AV	94116	8-J4
2700	35TH AV	94116	8-J4
2700	36TH AV	94116	8-J4
2750	SUNSET BLVD	94116	8-J4
2800	37TH AV	94116	8-J4
3000	39TH AV	94116	8-J4
3100	40TH AV	94116	8-J4
3200	41ST AV	94116	8-J4
3300	42ND AV	94116	8-J4
3400	43RD AV	94116	8-H4
3500	44TH AV	94116	8-H4
3600	45TH AV	94116	8-H4
3700	46TH AV	94116	8-H4
3800	47TH AV	94116	8-H4
3900	48TH AV	94116	8-H4
4000	GREAT HWY	94116	8-H4

R

Address	Cross Street	ZIP	City Pg-Grid
RACCOON DR			SF
	MOUNTAIN SPRINGS AV	94114	10-E3
	TWIN PEAKS BLVD	94114	10-E3
1	SAINT GERMAIN AV	94114	10-E3
80	CROWN TER	94114	10-E3
RACINE LN			SF
1	WABASH TER	94134	20-A2
100	SAN BRUNO AV	94134	20-A2
RADIO TER			SF
1	ROCKRIDGE DR	94116	9-C4
100	14TH AV	94116	9-C4
RAE AV			SF
1	WHIPPLE AV	94112	19-E2
100	NAGLEE AV	94112	19-E2
100	FARRAGUT AV	94112	19-E2
200	WHIPPLE AV	94112	19-E2
RALEIGH ST			SF
1	PAULDING ST	94112	14-F7
RALSTON AV			SF
80	STOREY AV	94129	1-C3
	RUCKMAN AV	94129	1-C4
	UPTON AV	94129	1-C4
	KINZEY ST	94129	1-C4
	GREENOUGH AV	94129	1-C4
	DYNAMITE RD	94129	1-C4
	STONE ST	94129	1-C3
	LINCOLN BLVD	94129	1-C3
	MERCHANT RD	94129	1-C3
RALSTON ST			SF
100	RANDOLPH ST	94132	18-C1
200	SARGENT ST	94132	18-C1
300	SHIELDS ST	94132	18-C1
400	GARFIELD ST	94132	18-C1
500	HOLLOWAY AV	94132	18-C1
RAMONA ST			SF
1	14TH ST	94103	10-H1
100	15TH ST	94103	10-H1
RAMSEL CT			SF
	ARMISTEAD RD	94129	1-C3
RAMSELL ST			SF
400	SHIELDS ST	94132	18-C1
500	GARFIELD ST	94132	18-C1
600	HOLLOWAY AV	94132	18-C1
200	RANDOLPH ST	94132	18-C1
300	SARGENT ST	94132	18-C1
1	PALMETTO AV	94132	18-C2
1	WORCESTER AV	94132	18-C2
100	ALEMANY BLVD	94132	18-C2
RANDALL ST			SF
1	MISSION ST	94110	14-H5
30	SAN JOSE AV	94131	14-H5
50	ARLINGTON ST	94131	14-H5
100	CHENERY ST	94131	14-H5
150	CHURCH ST	94131	14-H5
200	WHITNEY ST	94131	14-H5
250	SANCHEZ ST	94131	14-G5
300	HARPER ST	94131	14-G5
RANDOLPH ST			SF
1	ORIZABA AV	94132	18-D2
100	BRIGHT ST	94132	18-C2
200	HEAD ST	94132	18-C2
300	VICTORIA ST	94132	18-C2
400	RAMSELL ST	94132	18-C2
500	ARCH ST	94132	18-C2
600	VERNON ST	94132	18-C2
700	RALSTON ST	94132	18-C2
800	19TH AV	94132	18-C2
900	CHESTER AV	94132	18-C1
1100	19TH AV	94132	18-C1
RANKIN ST			SF
10	ISLAIS ST	94124	15-C4
100	CUSTER AV	94124	15-C4
200	DAVIDSON AV	94124	15-B4
300	EVANS AV	94124	15-B5
450	FAIRFAX AV	94124	15-B5
510	GALVEZ AV	94124	15-B5
600	INNES AV	94124	15-B5
730	JERROLD AV	94124	15-B5
1900	KIRKWOOD AV	94124	15-B5
2000	LA SALLE AV	94124	15-B5
2000	MCKINNON AV	94124	15-B5
1200	NEWCOMB AV	94124	15-B5
1300	OAKDALE AV	94124	15-B5
1400	PALOU AV	94124	15-B5
1500	QUESADA AV	94124	15-B5
1600	REVERE AV	94124	15-B6
RAUSCH ST			SF
1	HOWARD ST	94103	7-A7
100	FOLSOM ST	94103	7-A7
RAVENWOOD DR			SF
1	YERBA BUENA AV	94127	13-D6
30	FERNWOOD DR	94127	13-D6
30	ROSEWOOD DR	94127	13-D6
70	MAYWOOD DR	94127	13-D6
100	SAN JACINTO WY	94127	13-D6
RAWLES ST			SF
	SHAFTER RD	94129	6-E4
	SIMONDS LP	94129	6-E4
RAYBURN ST			SF
1	LIBERTY ST	94114	10-G3
100	21ST ST	94114	10-G3
RAYCLIFF TER			SF
100	PACIFIC AV	94115	6-F5
RAYMOND AV			SF
80	SAWYER ST	94134	19-J2
190	ELLIOT ST	94134	19-J2
300	DELTA ST	94134	19-J2
400	RUTLAND ST	94134	20-A2
490	ALPHA ST	94134	20-A2
600	BAYSHORE BLVD	94134	20-A2
REARDON RD			SF
1	KISKA RD	94124	15-D7
REBECCA LN			SF
1	KEITH ST	94124	15-C6
REDDY ST			SF
1	THORNTON AV	94124	15-B6
100	WILLIAMS AV	94124	15-B6
REDONDO ST			SF
1	INGERSON AV	94124	20-B1
100	JAMESTOWN AV	94124	20-B1
RED ROCK WY			SF
300	AMBER DR	94131	14-F4
300	DUNCAN ST	94131	14-F4
REDWOOD ST			SF
100	POLK ST	94102	6-J7
300	VAN NESS AV	94102	6-J7
600	LAGUNA ST	94102	6-H7
REED ST			SF
1	WASHINGTON ST	94109	6-J5
REGENT ST			SF
1	ALEMANY BLVD	94112	18-D2
1	SAN JOSE AV	94112	18-D2
100	CAYUGA AV	94112	18-D2
REPOSA WY			SF
1	MARIETTA DR	94127	14-E5
30	TERESITA BLVD	94127	14-E5
60	ROCKDALE DR	94127	14-E5
100	MYRA WY	94127	14-E5
RESERVOIR ST			SF
1	MARKET ST	94114	10-H1
100	CHURCH ST	94114	10-H1
RESTANI WY			SF
100	ALEMANY BLVD	94112	19-F1
RETIRO WY			SF
1	FILLMORE ST	94123	2-G3
110	CASA WY	94123	2-G3
140	RICO WY	94123	2-G3
200	BEACH ST	94123	2-G3
REUEL CT			SF
1	HUDSON AV	94124	15-C6
REVERE AV			SF
2000	MADDUX AV	94124	15-B6
2000	SILVER AV	94124	15-B6
2100	RANKIN ST	94124	15-B6
2210	SELBY ST	94124	15-A6
2300	INDUSTRIAL ST	94124	15-A5
2000	QUINT ST	94124	15-B6
1000	FITCH ST	94124	15-D7
1030	FITCH ST	94124	15-D7
1100	GRIFFITH ST	94124	15-D7
1180	CRISP RD	94124	15-D7
1200	HAWES ST	94124	15-C7
1300	INGALLS ST	94124	15-C7
1400	JENNINGS ST	94124	15-C7
1500	KEITH ST	94124	15-C6
1600	LANE ST	94124	15-C6
1670	3RD ST	94124	15-B6
1670	BAYVIEW ST	94124	15-B6
1800	BRIDGEVIEW DR	94124	15-B6
1800	NEWHALL ST	94124	15-B6
REX AV			SF
1	JUANITA WY	94127	13-D5
100	PORTOLA DR	94127	13-D5
REY ST			SF
100	SUNNYDALE AV	94134	19-J2
1	VISITACION AV	94134	19-J2
100	LELAND AV	94134	19-J2
RHINE ST			SF
1	DE LONG ST	94112	18-D2
1	GOETHE ST	94112	18-D2
100	WILSON ST	94112	18-D2
200	FLOURNOY ST	94112	18-D2
RHODE ISLAND ST			SF
1	DIVISION ST	94103	11-A1
100	ALAMEDA ST	94103	11-A1
200	15TH ST	94103	11-A1
300	16TH ST	94103	11-A2
400	17TH ST	94107	11-A2
500	MARIPOSA ST	94107	11-A2
600	18TH ST	94107	11-A2
700	19TH ST	94107	11-A2
800	20TH ST	94107	11-A3
900	SOUTHERN HEIGHTS AV	94107	11-A3
1000	22ND ST	94107	11-A3
1200	23RD ST	94107	11-A3
1300	24TH ST	94107	11-A3
1400	25TH ST	94107	11-A4
1500	26TH ST	94107	11-A4
RICE ST			SF
100	DE LONG ST	94112	18-D2
1	SAN JOSE AV	94112	18-D2
RICHARD HENREY DANA PL			SF
	JEFFERSON ST	94133	2-J3
	LEAVENWORTH ST	94133	2-J3
	FISH AL	94133	2-J3
RICHARDS CIR			SF
1	WHITNEY YOUNG CIR	94124	15-C6
1	MABREY CT	94124	15-C6
RICHARDSON AV			SF
1	LOMBARD ST	94123	2-F4
70	CHESTNUT ST	94123	2-F4
80	BAKER ST	94123	2-F4
	FRANCISCO ST	94123	2-F4
170	LYON ST	94129	2-F4
RICHLAND AV			SF
20	SAN JOSE AV	94110	14-H6
150	MISSION ST	94110	14-H6
200	LEESE ST	94110	14-H6
300	MURRAY ST	94110	14-J6
400	ANDOVER ST	94110	14-J6
RICKARD ST			SF
1	SAN BRUNO AV	94134	15-A6
100	BARNEVELD AV	94134	15-A6
200	WELDON ST	94134	15-A6
RICO WY			SF
1	RETIRO WY	94123	2-G3
100	AVILA ST	94123	2-G3
RIDGE CT			SF
1200	SADDLEBACK DR	94134	19-H2
1400	SADDLEBACK DR	94134	19-H2
RIDGEWOOD AV			SF
1	FLOOD AV	94112	13-E6
100	HEARST AV	94112	13-E6
200	MONTEREY BLVD	94127	13-E6
300	JOOST AV	94127	13-E6
400	MANGELS AV	94127	13-E6
RILEY AV			SF
130	SHERIDAN AV	94129	1-D4
200	MILES ST	94129	1-D4
130	LINCOLN BLVD	94129	1-D4
RINCON ST			SF
100	FEDERAL ST	94107	7-C6
	BRYANT ST	94107	7-C6
RINGOLD ST			SF
1	8TH ST	94103	7-A7
100	9TH ST	94103	10-J1
RIO CT			SF
1	TERESITA BLVD	94127	14-F5
100	EL SERENO CT	94127	14-F5
RIO VERDE ST			SF
1	VELASCO AV	94134	19-J2
RIPLEY ST			SF
1	PERALTA AV	94110	15-A5
100	ALABAMA ST	94110	14-J5
130	HARRISON ST	94110	14-J5
220	FOLSOM ST	94110	14-J5
RITCH ST			SF
200	BRYANT ST	94107	7-B7
300	BRANNAN ST	94107	7-B7
400	TOWNSEND ST	94107	7-B7
RIVAS AV			SF
1	GONZALEZ DR	94132	18-B1
150	GARCES DR	94132	18-B1
150	BUCARELI DR	94132	18-B1
200	VIDAL DR	94132	18-B1
RIVERA ST			SF
300	FUNSTON AV	94116	13-C4
400	14TH AV	94116	13-C4
470	15TH AV	94116	13-C4
500	15TH AV	94116	13-C4
550	CECILIA AV	94116	13-C4
600	16TH AV	94116	13-C4
700	17TH AV	94116	13-B4
800	18TH AV	94116	13-B4
900	19TH AV	94116	13-B4
1000	20TH AV	94116	13-B4
1100	21ST AV	94116	13-B4
1200	22ND AV	94116	13-B4
1400	24TH AV	94116	13-B4
1500	25TH AV	94116	13-B4
1600	26TH AV	94116	13-A4
1700	27TH AV	94116	13-A4
1800	28TH AV	94116	13-A4
1900	29TH AV	94116	13-A4
2000	30TH AV	94116	13-A4
2100	31ST AV	94116	13-A4
2200	32ND AV	94116	13-A4
2300	33RD AV	94116	13-A4
2400	34TH AV	94116	13-A4
2500	35TH AV	94116	12-J4
2600	35TH AV	94116	12-J4
2650	SUNSET BLVD	94116	12-J4
2700	37TH AV	94116	12-J4
2800	38TH AV	94116	12-J4
2900	39TH AV	94116	12-J4
3000	40TH AV	94116	12-J4
3100	41ST AV	94116	12-J4
3200	42ND AV	94116	12-J4
3300	43RD AV	94116	12-H4
3400	44TH AV	94116	12-H4
3500	45TH AV	94116	12-H4
3600	46TH AV	94116	12-H4
3700	47TH AV	94116	12-H4
3800	48TH AV	94116	12-H4
3900	GREAT HWY	94116	12-H4
RIVERTON DR			SF
1	SLOAT BLVD	94132	13-A6
20	EMERALD LN	94132	13-A6
100	OCEAN AV	94132	13-A6
200	EUCALYPTUS DR	94132	13-A6
RIVOLI ST			SF
1	BELVEDERE ST	94117	10-E2
100	COLE ST	94117	10-E2
200	SHRADER ST	94117	10-E2
300	STANYAN ST	94117	10-E2
RIZAL ST			SF
1	LAPU LAPU ST	94107	7-B6
100	TANDANG SORA	94107	7-B6
ROACH ST			SF
	GREENWICH ST	94133	2-J4
	VALPARAISO ST	94133	2-J4
ROANOKE ST			SF
1	BEMIS ST	94131	14-G6
1	MOFFITT ST	94131	14-G6
100	LAIDLEY ST	94131	14-G6
	CHENERY ST	94131	14-G6
340	ARLINGTON ST	94131	14-G6
ROBBLEE AV			SF
1	MADDUX AV	94124	15-B6
100	THOMAS AV	94124	15-B6
ROBERT KIRK LN			SF
1	POST ST	94108	7-A5
ROBINHOOD DR			SF
1	LANSDALE AV	94127	13-D5
300	LANSDALE AV	94127	13-D5
ROBINSON DR			SF
50	CANYON DR	94112	19-G2
100	LAPHAM WY	94112	19-G2
100	LAPHAM WY	94112	19-G2
ROBINSON ST			SF
	GALVEZ AV	94124	16-E7
	ENGLISH ST	94124	16-E7
	HORNE AV	94124	16-E7
	FISHER AV	94124	16-F7
	LOCKWOOD ST	94124	16-F7
ROCKAWAY AV			SF
1	LAGUNA HONDA BLVD	94127	13-D5
1	ULLOA ST	94127	13-D5
40	ROCKWOOD CT	94127	13-D5
100	ROCK AL	94127	13-D5
ROCKDALE DR			SF
500	CHAVES AV	94127	13-E5
500	MYRA WY	94127	13-E5
600	LA BICA WY	94127	13-E5
760	ISOLA WY	94127	14-E5
880	REPOSA WY	94127	14-E5
1000	OMAR WY	94127	14-E5
ROCKLAND ST			SF
1	LARKIN ST	94109	6-J4
100	EASTMAN ST	94109	6-J4
ROCKRIDGE DR			SF
1	CRAGMONT AV	94116	9-C3
30	12TH AV	94116	9-C3
30	12TH AV	94116	9-C4
30	FUNSTON AV	94116	9-C4
50	RADIO TER	94116	9-C4
100	12TH AV	94116	9-C4
ROCKWOOD CT			SF
1	ROCKAWAY AV	94127	13-D5
ROD RD			SF
	STOREY AV	94129	1-C3
	RUCKMAN AV	94129	1-C3
RODGERS ST			SF
1	FOLSOM ST	94103	7-A7
RODRIGUEZ ST			SF
770	MORTON ST	94129	5-E5
770	PORTOLA ST	94129	5-E5
ROEMER WY			SF
100	BRUNSWICK ST	94112	19-E2
ROLPH ST			SF
1	MISSION ST	94112	19-F1
90	CURTIS ST	94112	19-F1
120	PARIS ST	94112	19-F2
170	NEWTON ST	94112	19-F2
230	MADRID ST	94112	19-F2
330	MORSE ST	94112	19-F2
350	NAPLES ST	94112	19-G2
370	CORDOVA ST	94112	19-G2
470	ATHENS ST	94112	19-G2
520	SEVILLE ST	94112	19-G2
580	MUNICH ST	94112	19-G2
630	PRAGUE ST	94112	19-G2
680	S HILL BLVD	94112	19-G2
680	WINDING WY	94112	19-G2
ROMAIN ST			SF
1	DOUGLASS ST	94114	10-F3
100	GRAND VIEW AV	94114	10-F3
200	MARKET ST	94114	10-F3
300	CORBETT AV	94131	10-F3
300	CORBETT AV	94114	10-F3
ROME ST			SF
200	CAYUGA AV	94112	19-E1
100	OTTAWA AV	94112	19-E1
1	MOUNT VERNON AV	94112	19-F1
ROMOLO ST			SF
1	BROADWAY	94133	7-A4
70	FRESNO ST	94133	7-A4
100	POLLARD PL	94133	7-A4
100	VALLEJO ST	94133	7-A4
RONDEL PL			SF
1	16TH ST	94110	10-H2
ROOSEVELT WY			SF
1	14TH ST	94114	10-G1
1	14TH ST	94117	10-G1
1	ALPINE TER	94117	10-G1
100	BUENA VISTA TER	94117	10-F1
110	BUENA VISTA TER	94117	10-F1
200	15TH ST	94114	10-F1
200	15TH ST	94117	10-F1
200	PARK HILL AV	94117	10-F1
300	MUSEUM WY	94114	10-F2
300	MUSEUM WY	94117	10-F2
340	LEVANT ST	94114	10-F2
340	LEVANT ST	94117	10-F2
	LOMA VISTA TER	94117	10-F2
	UPPER TER	94117	10-F2
	MASONIC AV	94117	10-F2
400	LOMA VISTA TER	94114	10-F2
400	LOMA VISTA TER	94117	10-F2
470	CLIFFORD TER	94114	10-F2
470	CLIFFORD TER	94117	10-F2
500	LOWER TER	94114	10-F2
500	LOWER TER	94117	10-F2
550	SATURN ST	94114	10-F2
550	SATURN ST	94117	10-F2
600	17TH ST	94114	10-F2
600	17TH ST	94117	10-F2
600	URANUS TER	94117	10-F2
ROSCOE ST			SF
1	CRESCENT AV	94110	14-J6
100	BENTON AV	94110	14-J6
ROSE ST			SF
1	MARKET ST	94102	6-H7
80	GOUGH ST	94102	6-H7

PRIMARY STREET Address	Cross Street	ZIP	CITY Pg-Grid
ROSE ST			SF
200	OCTAVIA ST	94102	10-H1
300	LAGUNA ST	94102	10-H1
ROSELLA CT			SF
1	ONONDAGA AV	94112	19-F1
ROSELYN TER			SF
1	TURK ST	94118	6-E7
100	GOLDEN GATE AV	94118	6-E7
ROSEMARY CT			SF
100	25TH AV	94116	13-B5
ROSEMONT PL			SF
100	14TH ST	94103	10-H1
ROSENKRANZ ST			SF
100	BERNAL HEIGHTS BLVD	94110	14-J5
ROSEWOOD DR			SF
1	FERNWOOD DR	94127	13-D6
1	RAVENWOOD DR	94127	13-D6
100	FERNWOOD DR	94127	13-D6
ROSIE LEE LN			SF
30	LILLIAN ST	94124	15-D6
80	ESPANOLA ST	94124	15-D6
100	INGALLS ST	94124	15-D6
100	NORTHRIDGE RD	94124	15-D6
ROSSI AV			SF
1	ANZA ST	94118	5-E7
50	LONE MOUNTAIN TER	94118	5-E7
100	TURK ST	94118	5-E7
ROSSMOOR DR			SF
	JUNIPERO SERRA BLVD	94132	13-C6
10	ELMHURST DR	94132	13-C6
40	ELMHURST DR	94132	13-B6
90	19TH AV	94132	13-B6
ROTTECK ST			SF
1	BOSWORTH ST	94112	14-G6
100	MIRANDO WY	94112	14-G6
80	STILL ST	94112	14-G6
100	CAYUGA AV	94112	14-G6
ROUSSEAU ST			SF
1	SAN JOSE AV	94112	14-G6
100	BOSWORTH ST	94112	14-G6
150	MIRANDO WY	94112	14-G6
150	STILL ST	94112	14-G6
200	CAYUGA AV	94112	14-G6
250	ALEMANY BLVD	94112	14-G6
ROWLAND ST			SF
100	BROADWAY	94133	7-A4
ROYAL LN			SF
	NAPLES ST	94112	19-F2
	MORSE ST	94112	19-F2
RUCKMAN AV			SF
1240	RALSTON AV	94129	1-C3
	UPTON AV	94129	1-C3
	APPLETON ST	94129	1-C3
	ROD RD	94129	1-C3
	STOREY AV	94129	1-C3
RUDDEN AV			SF
1	OTSEGO AV	94112	14-F7
100	DELANO AV	94112	14-F7
RUGER ST			SF
	LOMBARD ST	94129	6-F4
	SHERMAN RD	94129	6-F4
	SIMONDS LP	94129	6-E4
RUSS ST			SF
100	FOLSOM ST	94103	7-A7
40	HOWARD ST	94103	7-A7
30	NATOMA ST	94103	7-A7
1	TULIP AL	94103	7-A7
20	MINNA ST	94103	7-A7
RUSSELL ST			SF
1	HYDE ST	94109	6-J4
100	EASTMAN ST	94109	6-J4
RUSSIA AV			SF
1	MISSION ST	94112	19-F1
100	LONDON ST	94112	19-G1
200	PARIS ST	94112	19-G1
300	LISBON ST	94112	19-G1
400	MADRID ST	94112	19-G1
500	EDINBURGH ST	94112	19-G1
600	NAPLES ST	94112	19-G1
700	VIENNA ST	94112	19-G1
800	ATHENS ST	94112	19-G1
900	MOSCOW ST	94112	19-G1
1000	MUNICH ST	94112	19-G1
1100	PRAGUE ST	94112	19-G1
1200	DUBLIN ST	94112	19-H1
1300	LA GRANDE AV	94112	19-H1
RUSSIAN HILL PL			SF
1	VALLEJO ST	94133	6-J4
RUTH ST			SF
1	MISSION ST	94112	14-G7
100	WATSON PL	94112	14-G7
RUTLAND ST			SF
1	SUNNYDALE AV	94134	20-A2
200	VISITACION AV	94134	20-A2
330	LELAND AV	94134	20-A2
420	RAYMOND AV	94134	20-A2
500	ARLETA AV	94134	20-A2
580	TEDDY AV	94134	20-A2
660	CAMPBELL AV	94134	20-A2
750	TUCKER AV	94134	20-A1
830	TIOGA AV	94134	20-A1
910	WILDE AV	94134	20-A1
1000	HARKNESS AV	94134	20-A1
RUTLEDGE ST			SF
100	BREWSTER ST	94110	15-A4
170	ESMERALDA AV	94110	15-A4
170	FRANCONIA ST	94110	15-A4
200	FRANCONIA ST	94110	15-A4
300	MASSASOIT ST	94110	15-A4
400	ALABAMA ST	94110	14-J4
1	HOLLADAY AV	94110	15-A4
100	MULLEN AV	94110	15-A4
S			
SABIN PL			SF
1	CALIFORNIA ST	94108	7-A5
SACRAMENTO ST			SF
100	DRUMM ST	94111	7-B5
200	DAVIS ST	94111	7-B5
300	FRONT ST	94111	7-B5
400	BATTERY ST	94104	7-B5
400	BATTERY ST	94111	7-B5
500	SANSOME ST	94104	7-B5
500	SANSOME ST	94111	7-B5
550	LEIDESDORFF ST	94104	7-B5
550	LEIDESDORFF ST	94111	7-B5
600	MONTGOMERY ST	94104	7-A5
600	MONTGOMERY ST	94111	7-A5
650	SPRING ST	94104	7-A5
650	SPRING ST	94111	7-A5
700	KEARNY ST	94108	7-A5
800	GRANT AV	94108	7-A5
820	WAVERLY PL	94108	7-A5
880	PAGODA PL	94108	7-A5
890	BROOKLYN PL	94108	7-A5
900	STOCKTON ST	94108	7-A5
940	JOICE ST	94108	7-A5
980	MILLER PL	94108	7-A5
1000	POWELL ST	94108	7-A5
1100	MASON ST	94108	7-A5
1150	SPROULE LN	94108	6-J5
1200	TAYLOR ST	94108	6-J5
1300	JONES ST	94109	6-J5
1330	LYSETTE ST	94109	6-J5
1350	LEROY PL	94109	6-J5
1380	GOLDEN CT	94109	6-J5
1400	LEAVENWORTH ST	94109	6-J5
1430	KIMBALL PL	94109	6-J5
1500	HYDE ST	94109	6-J5
1600	LARKIN ST	94109	6-J5
1700	POLK ST	94109	6-H5
1800	VAN NESS AV	94109	6-H5
1900	FRANKLIN ST	94109	6-H5
2000	GOUGH ST	94109	6-H5
2100	OCTAVIA ST	94109	6-H5
2200	LAGUNA ST	94115	6-H5
2300	BUCHANAN ST	94115	6-G5
2400	WEBSTER ST	94115	6-G5
2500	FILLMORE ST	94115	6-G5
2600	STEINER ST	94115	6-G5
2700	PIERCE ST	94115	6-G5
2800	SCOTT ST	94115	6-F5
2900	DIVISADERO ST	94115	6-F5
3000	BRODERICK ST	94115	6-F5
3100	BAKER ST	94115	6-F5
3200	LYON ST	94115	6-F5
3300	PRESIDIO AV	94115	6-F5
3400	WALNUT ST	94118	6-E5
3500	LAUREL ST	94118	6-E5
3600	LOCUST ST	94118	5-E6
3700	SPRUCE ST	94118	5-E6
3800	MAPLE ST	94118	5-E6
3900	CHERRY ST	94118	5-D6
4000	ARGUELLO BLVD	94118	5-D6
SADDLEBACK DR			SF
	RIDGE CT	94134	19-H2
	BIRCHWOOD CT	94134	19-H2
SADOWA ST			SF
210	ORIZABA AV	94112	18-D2
100	CAPITOL AV	94112	18-D2
1	PLYMOUTH AV	94112	18-D2
100	SAN JOSE AV	94112	18-D2
SAFFOLD AV			SF
	DYNAMITE RD	94129	1-B4
	KOBBE AV	94129	1-B4
SAFIRA LN			SF
1	27TH ST	94131	14-F4
SAGAMORE ST			SF
200	ALEMANY BLVD	94112	18-D2
200	BROTHERHOOD WY	94112	18-D2
200	ORIZABA AV	94112	18-D2
210	CAPITOL AV	94112	18-D2
300	PLYMOUTH AV	94112	18-D2
300	SICKLES AV	94112	18-D2
SAINT CHARLES AV			SF
1	19TH AV	94132	18-C2
100	PAYSON ST	94132	18-C2
220	ALEMANY BLVD	94132	18-C2
220	PALMETTO AV	94132	18-C2
390	NIANTIC AV	94132	18-C2
390	BELLE AV	94132	18-C2
SAINT CROIX DR			SF
1	MOLIMO DR	94127	13-E5
SAINT ELMO WY			SF
1	YERBA BUENA AV	94127	13-D6
1	PLYMOUTH AV	94127	13-D6
100	EL VERANO WY	94127	13-D6
200	MONTEREY BLVD	94127	13-D6
SAINT FRANCIS BLVD			SF
1	JUNIPERO SERRA BLVD	94127	13-C6
1	SLOAT BLVD	94127	13-C6
1	PORTOLA DR	94127	13-C6
1	W PORTAL AV	94127	13-C6
10	JUNIPERO SERRA BLVD	94127	13-C6
50	SAN RAFAEL WY	94127	13-C6
100	SAN FERNANDO WY	94127	13-C6
200	SAN LEANDRO WY	94127	13-C6
300	SANTA ANA AV	94127	13-C6
400	SAN BENITO WY	94127	13-C6
500	SANTA CLARA AV	94127	13-C6
600	SAN BUENAVENTURA WY	94127	13-C6
700	SAN ANSELMO AV	94127	13-C6
SAINT FRANCIS PL			SF
100	3RD ST	94107	7-B6
SAINT GERMAIN AV			SF
1	RACCOON DR	94114	10-E3
1	TWIN PEAKS BLVD	94114	10-E3
100	GLENBROOK AV	94114	10-E3
SAINT JOSEPHS AV			SF
10	TURK ST	94115	6-F7
1	PINAR LN	94115	6-F7
80	EDDY ST	94115	6-F7
180	TERRA VISTA AV	94115	6-F6
180	ELLIS ST	94115	6-F6
270	OFARRELL ST	94115	6-F6
400	BAKER ST	94115	6-F6
400	GEARY BLVD	94115	6-F6
SAINT MARYS AV			SF
1	MISSION ST	94112	14-H6
100	MARSILLY ST	94112	14-H6
130	COLLEGE AV	94112	14-G6
170	SAN JOSE AV	94131	14-G6
200	ARLINGTON ST	94131	14-G6
SAINT TENNY PL			SF
200	SLOAN AL	94105	7-B6
300	1ST ST	94105	7-B6
SAL ST			SF
	KEYES AV	94129	1-D4
	GRAHAM ST	94129	1-D4
SALA TER			SF
1	ELLINGTON AV	94112	19-F2
100	HURON AV	94112	19-F2
SALINAS AV			SF
340	3RD ST	94124	20-B1
320	KEITH ST	94124	20-B1
240	CARR ST	94124	20-B1
240	JAMESTOWN AV	94124	20-B1
180	GOULD ST	94124	20-B1
100	EXETER ST	94124	20-B1
180	BAYSHORE BLVD	94124	20-B1
SALMON ST			SF
1	PACIFIC AV	94133	6-J4
1	AUBURN ST	94133	6-J4
SAMOSET ST			SF
1	ESMERALDA AV	94110	15-A5
100	PERALTA AV	94110	15-A5
SAN ALESO AV			SF
1	MONTEREY BLVD	94127	13-C6
100	DARIEN WY	94127	13-C6
200	UPLAND DR	94127	13-C6
SAN ANDREAS WY			SF
1	SAN ANSELMO AV	94127	13-D6
100	MONTEREY BLVD	94127	13-D6
SAN ANSELMO AV			SF
	PORTOLA DR	94127	13-C5
	14TH AV	94127	13-C5
1	SANTA ANA AV	94127	13-C5
50	SAN BENITO WY	94127	13-C5
100	SANTA CLARA AV	94127	13-C5
150	SAN BUENAVENTURA WY	94127	13-C6
160	SANTA PAULA AV	94127	13-D6
	SAINT FRANCIS BLVD	94127	13-D6
200	SAINT FRANCIS BLVD	94127	13-D6
210	SAN ANDREAS WY	94127	13-D6
270	SAN BUENAVENTURA WY	94127	13-C6
300	MONTEREY BLVD	94127	13-C6
300	SANTA CLARA AV	94127	13-C6
SAN ANTONIO PL			SF
1	VALLEJO ST	94133	7-A4
SAN BENITO WY			SF
1	SAN ANSELMO AV	94127	13-C6
100	SAINT FRANCIS BLVD	94127	13-C6
200	MONTEREY BLVD	94127	13-C6
300	DARIEN WY	94127	13-C6
350	UPLAND DR	94127	13-C6
400	OCEAN AV	94127	13-C6
SAN BRUNO AV			SF
1	9TH ST	94103	11-A1
1	DIVISION ST	94103	11-A1
10	DIVISION ST	94103	11-A1
100	ALAMEDA ST	94103	11-A1
200	15TH ST	94103	11-A1
300	16TH ST	94103	11-A2
400	17TH ST	94110	11-A2
500	MARIPOSA ST	94110	11-A2
600	18TH ST	94107	11-A2
700	19TH ST	94107	11-A2
800	20TH ST	94107	11-A2
1000	22ND ST	94110	11-A3
1200	23RD ST	94110	11-A3
1300	24TH ST	94110	11-A3
1400	25TH ST	94110	11-A4
2100	ALEMANY BLVD	94110	15-A6
2130	ALEMANY BLVD	94110	15-A6
2210	RICKARD ST	94134	15-A6
2220	GAVEN ST	94134	15-A6
2270	SWEENY ST	94134	15-A6
2320	HALE ST	94134	15-A6
2380	SILVER AV	94134	15-A6
2490	SILLIMAN ST	94134	15-A6
2610	FELTON ST	94134	15-A7
2730	BURROWS ST	94134	15-A7
2840	BACON ST	94134	15-A7
2960	WAYLAND ST	94134	15-A7
3040	WOOLSEY ST	94134	15-A7
3120	DWIGHT ST	94134	15-A7
3120	PAUL AV	94134	15-A7
3200	OLMSTEAD ST	94134	20-A1
3290	MANSELL ST	94134	20-A1
3450	ORDWAY ST	94134	20-A1
3680	HARKNESS AV	94134	20-A1
3790	WILDE AV	94134	20-B1
3830	FRATESSA CT	94134	20-B2
3900	CAMPBELL AV	94134	20-B2
4120	EMPRESS LN	94134	20-A2
4120	SOMERSET ST	94134	20-A2
4150	WABASH TER	94134	20-A2
4150	TEDDY AV	94134	20-A2
4160	RACINE LN	94134	20-A2
4200	BAYSHORE BLVD	94134	20-A2
4200	BLANKEN AV	94134	20-A2
4200	ARLETA AV	94134	20-A2
SAN BUENAVENTURA WY			SF
1	SAN ANSELMO AV	94127	13-C6
	SAINT FRANCIS BLVD	94127	13-C6
110	SAINT FRANCIS BLVD	94127	13-C6
200	SAN ANSELMO AV	94127	13-C6
SAN CARLOS ST			SF
1	SYCAMORE ST	94110	10-H2
100	18TH ST	94110	10-H2
200	19TH ST	94110	10-H2
300	20TH ST	94110	10-H3
400	21ST ST	94110	10-H3
SANCHES ST			SF
	MACARTHUR AV	94129	5-E4
	SUMNER ST	94129	5-E4
	LIGGETT AV	94129	6-E4
	MORTON ST	94129	6-E4
SANCHEZ ST			SF
1	DUBOCE AV	94114	10-G1
100	14TH ST	94114	10-G1
150	HENRY ST	94114	10-G1
200	15TH ST	94114	10-G2
200	MARKET ST	94114	10-G2
300	16TH ST	94114	10-G2
400	17TH ST	94114	10-G2
440	DORLAND ST	94114	10-G2
450	FORD ST	94114	10-G2
500	18TH ST	94114	10-G2
550	HANCOCK ST	94114	10-G2
600	19TH ST	94114	10-G2
650	CUMBERLAND ST	94114	10-G3
400	20th ST	94114	10-G3
470	LIBERTY ST	94114	10-G3
750	LIBERTY ST	94114	10-G3
800	21ST ST	94114	10-G3
850	HILL ST	94114	10-G3
900	22ND ST	94114	10-G3
950	ALVARADO ST	94114	10-G3
1000	23RD ST	94114	10-G3
1050	ELIZABETH ST	94114	10-G3
1100	24TH ST	94114	10-G4
1150	JERSEY ST	94114	10-G4
1200	25TH ST	94114	10-G4
1250	CLIPPER ST	94131	10-G4
1300	26TH ST	94131	14-G4
1350	CESAR CHAVEZ ST	94131	14-G4
1400	27TH ST	94131	14-G4
1430	COMERFORD ST	94131	14-G4
1450	DUNCAN ST	94131	14-G4
1500	28TH ST	94131	14-G4
1550	VALLEY ST	94131	14-G5
1600	29TH ST	94131	14-G5
1650	DAY ST	94131	14-G5
1700	30TH ST	94131	14-G5
1800	RANDALL ST	94131	14-G5
SAN DIEGO AV			SF
100	DE LONG ST	94112	18-C2
SAN FELIPE AV			SF
1	SAN JACINTO WY	94127	13-D6
150	EL VERANO WY	94127	13-D6
170	MONTEREY BLVD	94127	13-D6
170	NORTHGATE DR	94127	13-D6
SAN FERNANDO WY			SF
1	PORTOLA DR	94127	13-C6
1	15TH AV	94127	13-C6
100	SAINT FRANCIS BLVD	94127	13-C6
200	MONTEREY BLVD	94127	13-C6
300	DARIEN WY	94127	13-C6
400	OCEAN AV	94127	13-C6
SAN GABRIEL AV			SF
1	SANTA ROSA AV	94112	14-F7
100	CAPISTRANO AV	94112	14-F7
SAN JACINTO WY			SF
1	SANTA PAULA AV	94127	13-D6
30	RAVENWOOD DR	94127	13-D6
80	SAN FELIPE AV	94127	13-D6
100	MONTEREY BLVD	94127	13-D6
SAN JOSE AV			SF
1	22ND ST	94110	10-H3
50	ALVARADO ST	94110	10-H3
100	23RD ST	94110	10-H3
150	ELIZABETH ST	94110	10-H3
200	24TH ST	94110	10-H4
300	25TH ST	94110	10-H4
330	JURI ST	94110	10-H4
400	26TH ST	94110	10-H4
400	CESAR CHAVEZ ST	94110	14-H4
500	27TH ST	94110	14-H4
550	DUNCAN ST	94110	14-H4
600	GUERRERO ST	94110	14-H4
640	VALLEY ST	94110	14-H5
700	29TH ST	94110	14-H5
750	DAY ST	94110	14-H5
1	30TH ST	94110	14-H5
100	KINGSTON ST	94110	14-H5
200	BROOK ST	94110	14-H5
200	DOLORES ST	94110	14-H5
200	DOLORES ST	94131	14-H5
300	RANDALL ST	94110	14-H5
300	RANDALL ST	94131	14-H5
1240	SAINT MARYS AV	94112	14-G6
1240	SAINT MARYS AV	94131	14-G6
1300	MILTON ST	94112	14-G6
1300	MILTON ST	94131	14-G6
1340	ROUSSEAU ST	94112	14-G6
1340	ROUSSEAU ST	94131	14-G6
1450	BOSWORTH ST	94131	14-G6
1450	LYELL ST	94131	14-G6
1650	TINGLEY ST	94112	14-G6
1690	THERESA ST	94112	14-G6
1730	COTTER ST	94112	14-F6
1770	CAPISTRANO AV	94112	14-F6
1790	STANDISH AV	94112	14-F7
1810	PILGRIM AV	94112	14-F7
1850	SANTA ROSA AV	94112	14-F7
1880	COLONIAL WY	94112	14-F7
1890	SANTA YSABEL AV	94112	14-F7
1900	NANTUCKET AV	94112	14-F7
1930	PAULDING ST	94112	14-F7
1950	SAN JUAN AV	94112	14-F7
1970	HAVELOCK ST	94112	14-F7
2020	SANTA YNEZ AV	94112	14-F7
2200	OCEAN AV	94112	14-F7
2210	ONEIDA AV	94112	19-F1
2240	SENECA AV	94112	19-E1
2300	GENEVA AV	94112	19-E1
2390	NIAGARA AV	94112	19-E1
2620	LAKEVIEW AV	94112	18-E1
2760	FARALLONES ST	94112	18-E2
2830	BROAD ST	94112	18-E2
2920	SADOWA ST	94112	18-D2
3000	SICKLES AV	94112	18-D2
3090	ALEMANY BLVD	94112	18-D2
3090	REGENT ST	94112	18-D2
3130	LIEBIG ST	94112	18-D2
3130	DE LONG ST	94112	18-D2
3170	RICE ST	94112	18-D2
3210	GOETHE ST	94112	18-D2
2840	BROAD ST	94112	18-E2
SAN JUAN AV			SF
1	MISSION ST	94112	14-G7
170	ALEMANY BLVD	94112	14-F7
250	CAYUGA AV	94112	14-F7
330	CAPISTRANO AV	94112	14-F7
420	OTSEGO AV	94112	14-F7
500	DELANO AV	94112	14-F7
600	SAN JOSE AV	94112	14-F7
SAN LEANDRO WY			SF
1	PORTOLA DR	94127	13-C5
100	SAINT FRANCIS BLVD	94127	13-C6
200	MONTEREY BLVD	94127	13-C6
300	DARIEN WY	94127	13-C6
400	OCEAN AV	94127	13-C6
SAN LORENZO WY			SF
1	PORTOLA DR	94127	13-D5
80	PORTAL PTH	94127	13-C5
100	SANTA MONICA WY	94127	13-C5
100	SANTA MONICA WY	94127	13-D5
SAN MARCOS AV			SF
1	DORANTES AV	94116	13-D4
100	CASTENADA AV	94116	13-D4
SAN MIGUEL ST			SF
370	MOUNT VERNON AV	94112	19-E1
370	CAINE AV	94112	19-E1
500	NIAGARA AV	94112	19-E1
SAN PABLO AV			SF
1	PORTOLA DR	94127	13-D5
100	SANTA MONICA WY	94127	13-D5
200	YERBA BUENA AV	94127	13-D5
SAN RAFAEL WY			SF
1	SAINT FRANCIS BLVD	94127	13-C6
100	MONTEREY BLVD	94127	13-C6
200	DARIEN WY	94127	13-C6
SAN RAMON WY			SF
140	PLYMOUTH AV	94112	13-D7
200	EASTWOOD DR	94112	13-D7
SANSOME ST			SF
1	SUTTER ST	94104	7-B5
100	BUSH ST	94104	7-B5
200	PINE ST	94104	7-B5
310	CALIFORNIA ST	94104	7-B5
300	HALLECK ST	94104	7-B5
360	HALLECK ST	94104	7-B5
400	SACRAMENTO ST	94111	7-B5
440	COMMERCIAL ST	94111	7-B5
500	CLAY ST	94111	7-B5
560	MERCHANT ST	94111	7-B5
600	WASHINGTON ST	94111	7-B4
700	JACKSON ST	94133	7-B4
700	JACKSON ST	94111	7-B4
740	GOLD ST	94133	7-B4
740	GOLD ST	94111	7-B4
800	PACIFIC AV	94133	7-B4
800	PACIFIC AV	94111	7-B4
850	STEVENS AL	94133	7-B4
850	STEVENS AL	94111	7-B4
900	BROADWAY	94133	7-B4
900	BROADWAY	94111	7-B4
900	BROADWAY ST	94111	7-B4
1000	VALLEJO ST	94133	3-B4
1000	VALLEJO ST	94111	3-B4
1100	GREEN ST	94133	3-B4
1100	GREEN ST	94111	3-B4
1200	UNION ST	94133	3-A4
1200	UNION ST	94111	3-A4
1300	FILBERT ST	94133	3-A4
1300	FILBERT ST	94111	3-A4
1400	GREENWICH ST	94133	3-A3

PRIMARY STREET / Address Cross Street / ZIP / CITY Pg-Grid

SANSOME ST SF
1400 GREENWICH ST 94111 3-A3
1500 LOMBARD ST 94111 3-A3
1600 CHESTNUT ST 94111 3-A3
1700 THE EMBARCADERO 94111 3-A3

SANTA ANA AV SF
1 SAN ANSELMO AV 94127 13-C5
100 SAINT FRANCIS BLVD 94127 13-C6
200 MONTEREY BLVD 94127 13-C6
300 DARIEN WY 94127 13-C6
400 OCEAN AV 94127 13-C6

SANTA BARBARA AV SF
100 HEAD ST 94112 18-C2

SANTA CLARA AV SF
1 PORTOLA DR 94127 13-C5
1 VICENTE ST 94127 13-C5
50 SANTA MONICA WY 94127 13-C5
50 YERBA BUENA AV 94127 13-C5
100 TERRACE DR 94127 13-C5
200 SAN ANSELMO AV 94127 13-C6
300 SAINT FRANCIS BLVD 94127 13-C6
400 MONTEREY BLVD 94127 13-C6
400 SAN ANSELMO AV 94127 13-C6

SANTA CRUZ AV SF
160 DE LONG ST 94112 18-C2

SANTA FE AV SF
1 SILVER AV 94124 15-A6
100 QUINT ST 94124 15-A6

SANTA MARINA ST SF
1 MISSION ST 94110 14-H5
1 BROOK ST 94110 14-H5
50 GLADYS ST 94110 14-H5
200 ELSIE ST 94110 14-H5

SANTA MONICA WY SF
1 SANTA CLARA AV 94127 13-C5
1 YERBA BUENA AV 94127 13-C5
30 SAN LORENZO WY 94127 13-D5
70 SAN LORENZO WY 94127 13-D5
100 SANTA PAULA AV 94127 13-D5
200 SAN PABLO AV 94127 13-D5

SANTA PAULA AV SF
1 PORTOLA DR 94127 13-D5
SANTA MONICA WY 94127 13-D5
100 SANTA MONICA WY 94127 13-D5
200 YERBA BUENA AV 94127 13-D6
260 SAN JACINTO WY 94127 13-D6
280 TERRACE WK 94127 13-D6
300 SAN ANSELMO AV 94127 13-D6

SANTA RITA AV SF
1 SOTELO AV 94116 9-D4
50 MESA AV 94116 13-D4
100 CASTENADA AV 94116 13-D4

SANTA ROSA AV SF
1 MISSION ST 94112 14-G7
100 ALEMANY BLVD 94112 14-G7
140 CAYUGA AV 94112 14-F7
200 CAPISTRANO AV 94112 14-F7
250 SAN GABRIEL AV 94112 14-F7
300 SAN JOSE AV 94112 14-F7

SANTA YNEZ AV SF
1 CAYUGA AV 94112 14-F7
50 CAPISTRANO AV 94112 14-F7
100 OTSEGO AV 94112 14-F7
200 DELANO AV 94112 14-F7
300 SAN JOSE AV 94112 14-F7

SANTA YSABEL AV SF
1 CAPISTRANO AV 94112 14-F7
100 OTSEGO AV 94112 14-F7
200 DELANO AV 94112 14-F7
300 SAN JOSE AV 94112 14-F7

SANTIAGO ST SF
300 14TH AV 94116 13-C4
400 15TH AV 94116 13-C4
450 CECILIA AV 94116 13-C4
500 16TH AV 94116 13-C4
600 17TH AV 94116 13-B4
700 18TH AV 94116 13-B4
800 19TH AV 94116 13-B4
900 20TH AV 94116 13-B4
1000 21ST AV 94116 13-B4
1100 22ND AV 94116 13-B4
1300 24TH AV 94116 13-B4
1400 25TH AV 94116 13-B4
1500 26TH AV 94116 13-A4
1600 27TH AV 94116 13-A4
1700 28TH AV 94116 13-A4
1800 29TH AV 94116 13-A4
1900 30TH AV 94116 13-A4
2000 31ST AV 94116 13-A4
2100 32ND AV 94116 13-A4
2200 33RD AV 94116 13-A4
2300 34TH AV 94116 13-A4
2400 35TH AV 94116 12-J4
2500 35TH AV 94116 12-J4
2550 SUNSET BLVD 94116 12-J4
2600 37TH AV 94116 12-J4
2700 38TH AV 94116 12-J4
2800 39TH AV 94116 12-J4
2900 40TH AV 94116 12-J4
3000 41ST AV 94116 12-J4
3100 42ND AV 94116 12-J4
3200 43RD AV 94116 12-H4
3300 44TH AV 94116 12-H4
3400 45TH AV 94116 12-H4
3500 46TH AV 94116 12-H4
3600 47TH AV 94116 12-H4
3700 48TH AV 94116 12-H4
3800 GREAT HWY 94116 12-H4

SANTOS ST SF
100 VELASCO AV 94134 19-H2
20 BLYTHDALE AV 94134 19-H2
1 BROOKDALE AV 94134 19-H2
50 SUNNYDALE AV 94134 19-H2

SARGENT ST SF
1 ORIZABA AV 94132 18-D1
100 BRIGHT ST 94132 18-D1
200 HEAD ST 94132 18-C1
300 VICTORIA ST 94132 18-C1
400 RAMSELL ST 94132 18-C1
500 ARCH ST 94132 18-C1
600 VERNON ST 94132 18-C1
700 RALSTON ST 94132 18-C1
800 BYXBEE ST 94132 18-C1
860 MONTICELLO ST 94132 18-C1
900 19TH AV 94132 18-C1

SATURN ST SF
1 ORD ST 94114 10-F2
100 LOWER TER 94114 10-F2
120 TEMPLE ST 94114 10-F2
200 ROOSEVELT WY 94114 10-F2

SAWYER ST SF
200 CALGARY ST 94134 19-J2
200 VELASCO AV 94134 19-J2
260 SUNRISE WY 94134 19-J2
420 SUNNYDALE AV 94134 19-J2
550 VISITACION AV 94134 19-J2
640 LELAND AV 94134 19-J2
700 RAYMOND AV 94134 19-J2

SCENIC WY SF
1 25TH AV 94121 5-A5
100 26TH AV 94121 5-A5

SCHOFIELD RD SF
POPE RD 94123 2-H3
MCDOWELL AV 94123 2-H3
APPLETON ST 94129 1-C4
PARK BLVD 94129 1-C4

SCHWERIN ST SF
1 LELAND AV 94134 19-J2
100 VISITACION AV 94134 19-J2
200 SUNNYDALE AV 94134 19-J2
320 GARRISON AV 94134 19-J2
370 KELLOCH AV 94134 19-J2

SCOTIA AV SF
1 SILVER AV 94124 15-A6
100 QUINT ST 94124 15-B6
150 MADDUX AV 94124 15-B6
200 THORNTON AV 94124 15-B6
200 BRIDGEVIEW DR 94124 15-B6

SCOTLAND ST SF
1 FILBERT ST 94133 2-J4
100 COLUMBUS AV 94133 2-J4

SCOTT ST SF
1 DUBOCE AV 94117 10-G1
50 LLOYD ST 94117 10-G1
100 WALLER ST 94117 10-G1
200 HAIGHT ST 94117 10-G1
300 PAGE ST 94117 10-G1
400 OAK ST 94117 6-G7
500 FELL ST 94117 6-G7
600 HAYES ST 94117 6-G7
700 GROVE ST 94117 6-G7
900 FULTON ST 94117 6-G7
970 MCALLISTER ST 94117 6-G7
1050 GOLDEN GATE AV 94115 6-G7
1120 TURK ST 94115 6-G7
1200 EDDY ST 94115 6-G6
1300 ELLIS ST 94115 6-G6
1400 OFARRELL ST 94115 6-G6
1500 GEARY BLVD 94115 6-G6
1600 POST ST 94115 6-G6
1700 SUTTER ST 94115 6-G6
1800 BUSH ST 94115 6-G6
1900 PINE ST 94115 6-G5
2000 CALIFORNIA ST 94115 6-G5
2100 SACRAMENTO ST 94115 6-F5
2200 CLAY ST 94115 6-F5
2300 WASHINGTON ST 94115 6-F5
2400 JACKSON ST 94115 6-F5
2500 PACIFIC AV 94115 6-F5
2600 BROADWAY ST 94115 6-F5
2700 VALLEJO ST 94123 6-F4
2800 GREEN ST 94123 6-F4
2900 UNION ST 94123 6-F4
3000 FILBERT ST 94123 6-F4
3100 GREENWICH ST 94123 2-F4
3200 LOMBARD ST 94123 2-F4
3300 CHESTNUT ST 94123 2-F4
3400 FRANCISCO ST 94123 2-F4
3400 ALHAMBRA ST 94123 2-F4
3450 BAY ST 94123 2-F3
3500 CAPRA WY 94123 2-F3
3600 NORTH POINT ST 94123 2-F3
3650 BEACH ST 94123 2-F3
3700 BEACH ST 94123 2-F3
3750 PRADO ST 94123 2-F3
3800 JEFFERSON ST 94123 2-F3
3900 MARINA BLVD 94123 2-F3
3900 MARINA GREEN DR 94123 2-F3
3900 CERVANTES BLVD 94123 2-F3

SEA CLIFF AV SF
1 25TH AV 94121 5-A5
30 25TH AV 94121 5-A5
140 26TH AV 94121 5-A5
200 27TH AV 94121 5-A5

SEAL ROCK DR SF
1 45TH AV 94121 4-H6
1 CLEMENT ST 94121 4-H6
100 ALTA MAR WY 94121 4-H6
200 EL CAMINO DEL MAR 94121 4-H6

SEARS ST SF
1 SICKLES AV 94112 18-E2
100 LAWRENCE AV 94112 18-E2

SEAVIEW TER SF
1 30TH AV 94121 5-A6
50 31ST AV 94121 5-A6

SECURITY PAC PL SF
1 OFARRELL ST 94108 7-A6

SELBY ST SF
320 NAPOLEON ST 94124 15-B4
320 ISLAIS ST 94124 15-B4
430 EVANS AV 94124 15-B4
750 INNES AV 94124 15-B5
800 JERROLD AV 94124 15-B5
840 JERROLD AV 94124 15-B5
900 KIRKWOOD AV 94124 15-B5
970 LA SALLE AV 94124 15-B5
1050 MCKINNON AV 94124 15-B5
1130 NEWCOMB AV 94124 15-B5
1210 OAKDALE AV 94124 15-B5
1290 PALOU AV 94124 15-B5
1370 QUESADA AV 94124 15-A5
1450 REVERE AV 94124 15-A5
1600 WATERVILLE ST 94124 15-A6

SEMINOLE AV SF
1 DELANO AV 94112 19-F1
100 CAYUGA AV 94112 19-F1

SENECA AV SF
1 SAN JOSE AV 94112 19-F1
80 DELANO AV 94112 19-F1
220 CAYUGA AV 94112 19-F1
270 BANNOCK ST 94112 19-F1
310 ALEMANY BLVD 94112 19-F1
340 BERTITA ST 94112 19-F1
400 MISSION ST 94112 19-F1

SEQUOIA WY SF
1 TERESITA BLVD 94127 14-E5
50 OMAR WY 94127 14-E5
100 BELLA VISTA WY 94127 14-E5

SERGEANT MITCHELL ST SF
MARINE DR 94129 1-E3
LIEUTENANT ALLEN ST 94129 1-E3
OLD MASON ST 94129 1-E3

SERPENTINE AV SF
100 POTRERO AV 94110 11-A4

SERRANO DR SF
200 FONT BLVD 94132 18-B1
300 ARELLANO AV 94132 18-B1
400 FUENTA AV 94132 18-B1
450 CARDENAS AV 94132 18-B1
VARELA AV 94132 18-B1
1 ARBALLO DR 94132 18-B1
100 TAPIA DR 94132 18-B1

SERVICE ST SF
2200 STEINER ST 94123 2-G4

SEVERN ST SF
100 23RD ST 94114 10-H3

SEVILLE ST SF
1 ROLPH ST 94112 19-G2
100 CORDOVA ST 94112 19-F2
200 NAPLES ST 94112 19-F2
200 CURTIS ST 94112 19-F2

SEWARD ST SF
1 19TH ST 94114 10-F3
80 ACME AL 94114 10-F3
100 DOUGLASS ST 94114 10-F3

SEYMOUR ST SF
1 GOLDEN GATE AV 94115 6-G7
100 TURK ST 94115 6-G7

SHAFTER AV SF
2050 ELMIRA ST 94124 15-A5
2300 INDUSTRIAL ST 94124 15-A5
2300 BARNEVELD AV 94124 15-A5
1000 FITCH ST 94124 15-D7
1100 GRIFFITH ST 94124 15-C7
1200 HAWES ST 94124 15-C7
1300 INGALLS ST 94124 15-C7
1400 JENNINGS ST 94124 15-C7
1500 KEITH ST 94124 15-C7
1600 LANE ST 94124 15-C6
1700 3RD ST 94124 15-C6

SHAFTER RD SF
RAWLES ST 94129 6-E4

SHAKESPEARE ST SF
100 DE LONG ST 94112 18-C2
120 HEAD ST 94112 18-C2

SHANGRILA WY SF
1 EDGEHILL WY 94127 13-D5
100 KNOCKASH HILL ST 94127 13-D5

SHANNON ST SF
1 OFARRELL ST 94102 6-J6
110 GEARY ST 94102 6-J6
180 COLIN PL 94102 6-J6
200 POST ST 94102 6-J6

SHARON ST SF
1 15TH ST 94114 10-G2
100 16TH ST 94114 10-G2

SHARP PL SF
1 UNION ST 94109 2-J4

SHAW ST SF
1 MISSION ST 94105 7-B5
100 MINNA ST 94105 7-B5

SHAWNEE AV SF
100 NAHUA AV 94112 19-E1
1 DELANO AV 94112 19-E1
100 CAYUGA AV 94112 19-E1

SHELDON TER SF
1 15TH AV 94122 9-C3

SHEPHARD PL SF
1 MASON ST 94108 7-A5
1 TRUETT ST 94108 7-A5

SHERIDAN AV SF
GRAHAM ST 94129 1-D4
ARGUELLO BLVD 94129 1-D4
ANZA ST 94129 1-D4
MONTGOMERY ST 94129 1-D4
TAYLOR RD 94129 1-D4
FISHER LP 94129 1-D4
ORD ST 94129 1-D4
INFANTRY TER 94129 1-D4
RILEY AV 94129 1-D4
LINCOLN BLVD 94129 1-D4

SHERIDAN ST SF
1 10TH ST 94103 10-J1
100 9TH ST 94103 11-A1

SHERMAN RD SF
PRESIDIO BLVD 94129 6-E4
RUGER ST 94129 6-E4

SHERMAN ST SF
1 FOLSOM ST 94103 7-A7
30 CLEVELAND ST 94103 7-A7
100 HARRISON ST 94103 7-A7

SHERWOOD CT SF
1 LANSDALE AV 94127 13-E6

SHIELDS ST SF
100 BRIGHT ST 94132 18-D1
200 HEAD ST 94132 18-C1
300 VICTORIA ST 94132 18-C1
400 RAMSELL ST 94132 18-C1
500 ARCH ST 94132 18-C1
600 VERNON ST 94132 18-C1
700 RALSTON ST 94132 18-C1
800 BYXBEE ST 94132 18-C1
900 MONTICELLO ST 94132 18-C1
1000 BEVERLY ST 94132 18-C1
1100 JUNIPERO SERRA BLVD 94132 18-C1

SHIPLEY ST SF
100 4TH ST 94107 7-B7
200 5TH ST 94107 7-A7
200 FALMOUTH ST 94107 7-A7
300 6TH ST 94107 7-A7

SHORE VIEW AV SF
1 36TH AV 94121 4-J6
50 37TH AV 94121 4-J6
100 38TH AV 94121 4-J6

SHORT ST SF
1 YUKON ST 94114 10-F3
100 MARKET ST 94114 10-F3

SHOTWELL ST SF
1 14TH ST 94103 10-J1
100 15TH ST 94103 10-J1
200 16TH ST 94110 10-J2
300 17TH ST 94110 10-J2
400 18TH ST 94110 10-J2
500 19TH ST 94110 10-J2
600 20TH ST 94110 10-J3
700 21ST ST 94110 10-J3
800 22ND ST 94110 10-J3
900 23RD ST 94110 10-J3
1000 24TH ST 94110 10-J4
1100 25TH ST 94110 10-J4
1200 26TH ST 94110 10-J4
1300 CESAR CHAVEZ ST 94110 14-J4
1400 PRECITA AV 94110 14-J4
1400 BESSIE ST 94110 14-J4
1400 MIRABEL AV 94110 14-J4
1430 MONTEZUMA ST 94110 14-J4
1500 STONEMAN ST 94110 14-J4

SHRADER ST SF
1 FULTON ST 94117 5-E7
100 GROVE ST 94117 5-E7
200 HAYES ST 94117 5-E7
300 FELL ST 94117 9-E1
400 OAK ST 94117 9-E1
500 PAGE ST 94117 10-E1
600 HAIGHT ST 94117 10-E1
700 WALLER ST 94117 10-E1
800 BEULAH ST 94117 10-E1
900 FREDERICK ST 94117 10-E1
1000 CARL ST 94117 10-E2
1100 PARNASSUS AV 94117 10-E2
1200 GRATTAN ST 94117 10-E2
1300 ALMA ST 94117 10-E2
1400 RIVOLI ST 94117 10-E2
1500 17TH ST 94117 10-E2
1550 CARMEL ST 94117 10-E2
1700 BELGRAVE AV 94117 10-E2

SIBERT LP SF
THOMAS AV 94129 5-D4

SIBLEY RD SF
800 VISTA CT 94129 6-E4
780 LIGGETT AV 94129 6-E4

SICKLES AV SF
100 PLYMOUTH AV 94112 18-D2
100 SAGAMORE ST 94112 18-D2
SAN JOSE AV 94112 18-D2
110 SAN JOSE AV 94112 18-D2
150 DE WOLF ST 94112 18-D2
170 ALEMANY BLVD 94112 18-E2
190 CAYUGA AV 94112 18-E2
230 SEARS ST 94112 18-E2
260 HURON AV 94112 18-E2
300 ACTON ST 94112 18-E2
300 MISSION ST 94112 18-E2

SIERRA ST SF
1 TEXAS ST 94107 11-B3
100 MISSOURI ST 94107 11-B3

SILLIMAN ST SF
1 SAN BRUNO AV 94134 15-A6
100 GIRARD ST 94134 15-A6
200 BRUSSELS ST 94134 15-A6
300 GOETTINGEN ST 94134 15-A6
400 SOMERSET ST 94134 15-A7
500 BOYLSTON ST 94134 14-J7
600 HAMILTON ST 94134 14-J7
700 BOWDOIN ST 94134 14-J7
800 DARTMOUTH ST 94134 14-J7
900 COLBY ST 94134 14-J7
1000 UNIVERSITY ST 94134 14-J7
1100 PRINCETON ST 94134 14-J7
1200 AMHERST ST 94134 14-J7
1300 YALE ST 94134 14-J7
1400 CAMBRIDGE ST 94134 14-H7
1500 OXFORD ST 94134 14-H7
1600 HARVARD ST 94134 14-H7
1700 GAMBIER ST 94134 14-H7
1800 MADISON ST 94134 14-H7
1900 VALMAR TER 94134 14-H7

SILVER AV SF
1800 SCOTIA AV 94124 15-A6
1860 CONKLING ST 94124 15-A6
1900 SANTA FE AV 94124 15-A6
2000 TOPEKA AV 94124 15-A6
2070 THOMAS AV 94124 15-B6
2100 THOMAS AV 94124 15-B6
2200 MADDUX AV 94124 15-B6
2200 REVERE AV 94124 15-B6
2300 QUESADA AV 94124 15-B6
2400 PALOU AV 94124 15-B6
2400 QUINT ST 94124 15-B6
200 ALEMANY BLVD 94112 14-G7
250 CAMELLIA AV 94112 14-G7
300 MISSION ST 94112 14-G7
410 LISBON ST 94112 14-G7
420 CRAUT ST 94112 14-G7
450 MADRID ST 94112 14-H7
490 EDINBURGH ST 94112 14-H7
510 CONGDON ST 94112 14-H7
540 NAPLES ST 94112 14-H7
580 VIENNA ST 94112 14-H7
600 MADISON ST 94112 14-H7
600 MADISON ST 94134 14-H7
700 GAMBIER ST 94112 14-H7
700 GAMBIER ST 94134 14-H7
730 HARVARD ST 94112 14-H7
730 HARVARD ST 94134 14-H7
770 OXFORD ST 94112 14-H7
770 OXFORD ST 94134 14-H7
800 CAMBRIDGE ST 94134 14-H7
830 YALE ST 94134 14-J7
870 AMHERST ST 94134 14-J7
900 PRINCETON ST 94134 14-J7
950 UNIVERSITY ST 94134 14-J7
1000 COLBY ST 94134 14-J7
1020 COLBY ST 94134 14-J7
1050 DUNSMUIR ST 94134 14-J7
1100 DARTMOUTH ST 94134 14-J7
1140 BOWDOIN ST 94134 14-J6
1160 BOWDOIN ST 94134 14-J6
1200 HAMILTON ST 94134 14-J6
1290 BOYLSTON ST 94134 14-J6
1360 SOMERSET ST 94134 15-A6
1400 MERRILL ST 94134 15-A6
1420 GOETTINGEN ST 94134 15-A6
1470 BRUSSELS ST 94134 15-A6
1510 BARNEVELD AV 94134 15-A6
1530 GIRARD ST 94134 15-A6
1600 SAN BRUNO AV 94134 15-A6
1640 BAYSHORE BLVD 94124 15-A6
1650 CHARTER OAK AV 94124 15-A6
1700 ELMIRA ST 94124 15-A6
1740 LEDYARD ST 94124 15-A6
1750 WATERVILLE ST 94124 15-A6
1800 AUGUSTA ST 94124 15-A6

SILVERVIEW DR SF
1 BAYVIEW CIR 94124 15-B6
100 BAYVIEW CIR 94124 15-B6

SIMONDS LP SF
PRESIDIO BLVD 94129 6-E4
RAWLES ST 94129 6-E4
GIBBON CT 94129 6-E4
RUGER ST 94129 6-E4

SKYLINE BLVD SF
1 SLOAT BLVD 94132 12-J6
70 LAKE MERCED BLVD 94132 12-J6
100 HERBST RD 94132 12-J6
110 LAKE MERCED BLVD 94132 12-H6
300 HARDING RD 94132 12-H7
320 GREAT HWY 94132 12-H7
350 GREAT HWY 94132 12-H7
JOHN MUIR DR 94132 17-J1

SKYVIEW WY SF
1 MAR VIEW WY 94131 10-E3
110 AQUAVISTA WY 94131 10-E4
160 GLADEVIEW WY 94131 10-E4
200 CITYVIEW WY 94131 10-E4

SLOAT BLVD SF
1 JUNIPERO SERRA BLVD 94132 13-C6
1 SAINT FRANCIS BLVD 94132 13-C6
1 PORTOLA DR 94132 13-C6
1 W PORTAL AV 94132 13-C6
80 CRANLEIGH DR 94132 13-C6
100 ARDENWOOD WY 94132 13-C6
140 LAGUNITAS DR 94132 13-C6
190 AVON WY 94132 13-B6
200 BEACHMONT DR 94132 13-B6
300 19TH AV 94132 13-B6
410 20TH AV 94132 13-B6
510 21ST AV 94132 13-B6
600 22ND AV 94132 13-B6

Address	Cross Street	ZIP	City Pg-Grid
SLOAT BLVD			SF
720	23RD AV	94132	13-B6
720	CRESTLAKE DR	94132	13-B6
760	24TH AV	94132	13-B6
790	25TH AV	94132	13-B6
800	GABILAN WY	94132	13-B6
860	26TH AV	94132	13-B6
900	PARAISO PL	94132	13-B6
970	INVERNESS DR	94132	13-A6
1000	GOLETA AV	94132	13-A6
1070	FOREST VIEW DR	94132	13-A6
1100	VALE AV	94132	13-A6
1170	MEADOWBROOK DR	94132	13-A6
1200	PALOS PL	94132	13-A6
1260	SYLVAN DR	94132	13-A6
1300	EL MIRASOL PL	94132	13-A6
1330	MIDDLEFIELD DR	94132	13-A6
1390	RIVERTON DR	94132	13-A6
1450	SPRINGFIELD DR	94132	13-A6
1500	CONSTANSO WY	94132	13-A6
1510	EVERGLADE DR	94132	13-A6
1560	LAKESHORE PZ	94132	13-A6
1600	34TH AV	94132	13-A6
1630	CLEARFIELD DR	94132	13-A6
1690	35TH AV	94132	12-J6
1800	36TH AV	94132	12-J6
1850	SUNSET BLVD	94132	12-J6
1880	37TH AV	94132	12-J6
2100	39TH AV	94132	12-J6
2120	SKYLINE BLVD	94132	12-J6
2300	41ST AV	94132	12-J6
2300	41ST AV	94116	12-J6
2400	42ND AV	94132	12-J6
2400	42ND AV	94116	12-J6
2500	43RD AV	94132	12-H6
2500	43RD AV	94116	12-H6
2600	44TH AV	94132	12-H6
2600	44TH AV	94116	12-H6
2700	45TH AV	94132	12-H6
2700	45TH AV	94116	12-H6
2820	46TH AV	94132	12-H6
2820	46TH AV	94116	12-H6
2800	47TH AV	94132	12-H6
2800	47TH AV	94116	12-H6
3000	48TH AV	94132	12-H6
3000	48TH AV	94116	12-H6
3020	GREAT HWY	94132	12-H6
3020	GREAT HWY	94116	12-H6
SOLA AV			SF
1	MAGELLAN AV	94116	9-D4
100	MARCELA AV	94116	9-D4
SOMERSET ST			SF
1	SILVER AV	94134	15-A6
100	SILLIMAN ST	94134	15-A7
200	FELTON ST	94134	15-A7
310	BURROWS ST	94134	15-A7
420	BACON ST	94134	15-A7
530	WAYLAND ST	94134	15-A7
640	WOOLSEY ST	94134	15-A7
700	KAREN CT	94134	15-A7
1	MANSELL ST	94134	20-A1
1500	ORDWAY ST	94134	20-A1
1	CAMPBELL AV	94134	20-A2
1	EMPRESS LN	94134	20-A2
1	SAN BRUNO AV	94134	20-A2
1500	CAMPBELL AV	94134	20-A2
SONOMA ST			SF
1	GREEN ST	94133	3-A4
100	UNION ST	94133	3-A4
SOTELO AV			SF
1	9TH AV	94116	9-D4
70	SANTA RITA AV	94116	9-D4
100	LOPEZ AV	94116	9-D4
SOUTHARD PL			SF
1	GREENWICH ST	94109	2-J4
SOUTHERN HEIGHTS AV			SF
50	CAROLINA ST	94107	11-B3
1	DE HARO ST	94107	11-A3
40	RHODE ISLAND ST	94107	11-A3
SOUTHWOOD DR			SF
30	PLYMOUTH AV	94112	13-D7
50	GRANADA AV	94112	13-D7
100	MIRAMAR AV	94112	13-D7
200	ELMWOOD WY	94112	13-D7
200	FAXON AV	94112	13-D7
SPARROW ST			SF
1	CALEDONIA ST	94103	10-H2
100	VALENCIA ST	94103	10-H2
SPARTA ST			SF
1	ANKENY ST	94134	20-A1
1	WARD ST	94134	20-A1
100	HARKNESS AV	94134	20-A1
SPEAR AV			SF
600	A ST	94124	16-F7
	A ST	94124	16-F7
690	A ST	94124	16-F7
690	LOCKWOOD ST	94124	16-F7
770	C ST	94124	16-F7
	BLANDY ST	94124	16-E7
830	D ST	94124	16-E7
870	FISHER AV	94124	16-E7
870	MORRELL ST	94124	16-E7
890	HORNE AV	94124	16-E7
910	COCHRANE ST	94124	16-E7
960	HUSSEY ST	94124	15-E7
1000	H ST	94124	15-E7
1000	CRISP RD	94124	15-E7
	I ST	94124	15-E7
1040	6TH AV	94124	20-D1
1200	J ST	94124	20-D1
SPEAR ST			SF
20	CALIFORNIA ST	94105	7-B5
20	MARKET ST	94105	7-B5
100	MISSION ST	94105	7-C5
200	HOWARD ST	94105	7-C5
300	FOLSOM ST	94105	7-C5
400	HARRISON ST	94105	7-C6
SPENCER ST			SF
100	16TH ST	94103	10-H2
SPOFFORD LN			SF
1	CLAY ST	94108	7-A5
100	WASHINGTON ST	94108	7-A5
SPRECKLES LAKE DR			SF
	30TH AV	-	9-A1
	36TH AV	-	8-J1
SPRING ST			SF
100	CALIFORNIA ST	94104	7-A5
200	SACRAMENTO ST	94104	7-A5
SPRINGFIELD DR			SF
1	SLOAT BLVD	94132	13-A6
20	EMERALD LN	94132	13-A6
100	OCEAN AV	94132	13-A6
200	EUCALYPTUS DR	94132	13-A6
SPROULE LN			SF
1	CALIFORNIA ST	94108	6-J5
100	SACRAMENTO ST	94108	6-J5
200	CLAY ST	94108	6-J5
SPRUCE ST			SF
1	PACIFIC AV	94118	5-E5
100	JACKSON ST	94118	5-E5
200	WASHINGTON ST	94118	5-E5
300	CLAY ST	94118	5-E5
400	SACRAMENTO ST	94118	5-E6
500	CALIFORNIA ST	94118	5-E6
530	MAYFAIR DR	94118	5-E6
600	EUCLID AV	94118	5-E6
700	GEARY BLVD	94118	5-E6
800	ANZA ST	94118	5-E6
STANDISH AV			SF
1	SAN JOSE AV	94112	14-F6
	BADEN ST	94131	14-F6
	CIRCULAR AV	94131	14-F6
STANFORD ST			SF
1	BRANNAN ST	94107	7-C7
100	TOWNSEND ST	94107	7-C7
STANFORD HEIGHTS AV			SF
100	LOS PALMOS DR	94127	14-E6
200	MELROSE AV	94127	14-E6
200	BELLA VISTA WY	94127	14-E6
200	BELLAVISTA LN	94127	14-E6
STANLEY ST			SF
1	BRIGHT ST	94132	18-D2
100	ORIZABA AV	94132	18-D2
STANTON ST			SF
100	GLENDALE ST	94114	10-F3
100	GRAND VIEW AV	94114	10-F3
100	MARKET ST	94114	10-F3
STANYAN ST			SF
1	GEARY BLVD	94118	5-E6
100	ANZA ST	94118	5-E7
130	LONE MOUNTAIN TER	94118	5-E7
150	TURK ST	94117	5-E7
150	TURK ST	94118	6-E7
160	GOLDEN GATE AV	94117	5-E7
160	GOLDEN GATE AV	94118	5-E7
200	PARAMOUNT TER	94117	5-E7
200	PARAMOUNT TER	94118	5-E7
260	MCALLISTER ST	94117	5-E7
250	MCALLISTER ST	94118	5-E7
300	MCALLISTER ST	94117	5-E7
300	MCALLISTER ST	94118	5-E7
1	FULTON ST	94117	5-E7
200	HAYES ST	94117	5-E7
300	FELL ST	94117	9-E1
440	KEZAR DR	94117	9-E1
440	FELL ST	94117	9-E1
440	OAK ST	94117	9-E1
530	OAK ST	94117	9-E1
600	PAGE ST	94117	9-E1
700	HAIGHT ST	94117	9-E1
750	WALLER ST	94117	9-E1
800	BEULAH ST	94117	9-E1
900	FREDERICK ST	94117	9-E1
1000	CARL ST	94117	9-E2
1100	PARNASSUS AV	94117	9-E2
1130	GRATTAN ST	94117	9-E2
1170	ALMA ST	94117	9-E2
1200	RIVOLI ST	94117	9-E2
1250	17TH ST	94117	9-E2
1300	BELGRAVE AV	94117	9-E2
STAPLES AV			SF
1	CIRCULAR AV	94131	14-F7
100	DETROIT ST	94112	14-F7
200	EDNA ST	94112	14-E7
300	FOERSTER ST	94112	14-E7
400	GENNESSEE ST	94112	13-E7
500	PHELAN AV	94112	13-E7
600	HAZELWOOD AV	94112	13-E7
STARK ST			SF
1	STOCKTON ST	94133	7-A4
STARR KING WY			SF
1	GEARY BLVD	94109	6-H6
1	GOUGH ST	94109	6-H6
1	PETER YORKE WY	94109	6-H6
100	FRANKLIN ST	94109	6-H6
100	OFARRELL ST	94109	6-H6
STARVIEW WY			SF
1	PANORAMA DR	94131	9-E4
200	PANORAMA DR	94131	9-E4
STATE DR			SF
	LAKE MERCED BLVD	94132	13-B7
	CAMPUS CIR	94132	13-B7
	CAMPUS CIR	94132	13-A7
	LAKE MERCED BLVD	94132	13-A7
STATES ST			SF
1	CASTRO ST	94114	10-G2
300	LEVANT ST	94114	10-F2
STEINER ST			SF
1	DUBOCE AV	94117	10-G1
100	HERMANN ST	94117	10-G1
150	GERMANIA ST	94117	10-G1
200	WALLER ST	94117	10-G1
250	LAUSSAT ST	94117	10-G1
300	HAIGHT ST	94117	10-G1
400	PAGE ST	94117	10-G1
500	OAK ST	94117	6-G7
600	FELL ST	94117	6-G7
700	HAYES ST	94117	6-G7
800	GROVE ST	94117	6-G7
900	FULTON ST	94117	6-G7
1000	MCALLISTER ST	94117	6-G7
1100	GOLDEN GATE AV	94115	6-G7
1200	TURK ST	94115	6-G6
1300	EDDY ST	94115	6-G6
1400	ELLIS ST	94115	6-G6
1500	OFARRELL ST	94115	6-G6
	GEARY BLVD	94115	6-G6
1700	POST ST	94115	6-G6
1800	SUTTER ST	94115	6-G6
1900	BUSH ST	94115	6-G6
1920	WILMOT ST	94115	6-G6
2000	PINE ST	94115	6-G5
2100	CALIFORNIA ST	94115	6-G5
2150	PERINE PL	94115	6-G5
2200	SACRAMENTO ST	94115	6-G5
2300	CLAY ST	94115	6-G5
2400	WASHINGTON ST	94115	6-G5
2500	JACKSON ST	94115	6-G5
2600	PACIFIC AV	94115	6-G5
2700	BROADWAY ST	94115	6-G5
2800	VALLEJO ST	94123	6-G4
2900	GREEN ST	94123	6-G4
3000	UNION ST	94123	6-G4
3100	FILBERT ST	94123	6-G4
3150	PIXLEY ST	94123	6-G4
3200	GREENWICH ST	94123	2-G4
3240	SERVICE ST	94123	2-G4
3260	MOULTON ST	94123	2-G4
3300	LOMBARD ST	94123	2-G4
3400	CHESTNUT ST	94123	2-G4
STERLING ST			SF
100	BRYANT ST	94107	7-B6
STEUART ST			SF
1	MARKET ST	94111	7-B5
1	MARKET ST	94105	7-B5
100	MISSION ST	94105	7-C5
100	THE EMBARCADERO	94105	7-C5
200	HOWARD ST	94105	7-C5
300	FOLSOM ST	94105	7-C5
400	HARRISON ST	94105	7-C5
400	THE EMBARCADERO	94105	7-C5
STEVELOE PL			SF
100	JONES ST	94102	6-J6
STEVENSON ST			SF
1	1ST ST	94105	7-B5
40	ECKER ST	94105	7-B5
70	ANTHONY ST	94105	7-B5
100	2ND ST	94105	7-B5
150	NEW MONTGOMERY ST	94105	7-B5
150	ANNIE ST	94103	7-A6
200	3RD ST	94103	7-A6
300	4TH ST	94103	7-A6
400	5TH ST	94103	7-A6
500	6TH ST	94103	7-A6
600	7TH ST	94103	6-J7
700	8TH ST	94103	6-J7
900	10TH ST	94103	6-J7
1100	12TH ST	94103	6-J7
1400	BRADY ST	94103	10-H1
1450	GOUGH ST	94103	10-H1
1300	MCCOPPIN ST	94103	10-H1
1400	DUBOCE AV	94103	10-H1
1400	CLINTON PK	94103	10-H1
1400	VALENCIA ST	94103	10-H1
1500	14TH ST	94103	10-H1
STILL ST			SF
1	LYELL ST	94112	14-G6
1	ROTTECK ST	94112	14-G6
50	ROUSSEAU ST	94112	14-G6
STILLINGS AV			SF
1	MARTHA AV	94131	14-F6
30	NORDHOFF ST	94131	14-F6
100	CONGO ST	94131	14-F6
150	MERCATO CT	94131	14-F6
200	VISTA VERDE CT	94131	14-F6
200	DETROIT ST	94131	14-F6
300	TERESITA BLVD	94131	14-F6
STILLMAN ST			SF
1	2ND ST	94107	7-B6
100	3RD ST	94107	7-B7
200	4TH ST	94107	7-B7
STILLWELL DR			SF
1500	LINCOLN BLVD	94129	5-B5
1600	PERSHING DR	94129	5-B5
STOCKTON ST			SF
600	CALIFORNIA ST	94108	7-A5
500	PINE ST	94108	7-A5
500	BUSH ST	94108	7-A5
	EMMA ST	94108	7-A5
	PINE ST	94108	7-A5
	CALIFORNIA ST	94108	7-A5
800	SACRAMENTO ST	94108	7-A5
900	CLAY ST	94108	7-A5
1000	WASHINGTON ST	94108	7-A5
1100	JACKSON ST	94133	7-A4
1200	PACIFIC AV	94133	7-A4
1280	STARK ST	94133	7-A4
1300	BROADWAY	94133	7-A4
1400	VALLEJO ST	94133	7-A4
1450	CARD AL	94133	3-A4
1450	COLUMBUS AV	94133	3-A4
1500	GREEN ST	94133	3-A4
1600	UNION ST	94133	3-A4
1700	FILBERT ST	94133	3-A4
1800	GREENWICH ST	94133	3-A4
1900	LOMBARD ST	94133	3-A3
2000	CHESTNUT ST	94133	3-A3
2030	PFEIFFER ST	94133	3-A3
2100	FRANCISCO ST	94133	3-A3
2200	BAY ST	94133	3-A3
2300	NORTH POINT ST	94133	3-A3
2400	BEACH ST	94133	3-A3
1	MARKET ST	94102	7-A6
10	ELLIS ST	94108	7-A6
100	OFARRELL ST	94108	7-A6
200	GEARY ST	94108	7-A6
250	MAIDEN LN	94108	7-A6
300	POST ST	94108	7-A5
370	CAMPTON PL	94108	7-A5
400	SUTTER ST	94108	7-A5
410	BUSH ST	94108	7-A5
STONE ST			SF
	RALSTON AV	94129	1-C3
	STOREY AV	94129	1-C3
1	JACKSON ST	94108	7-A5
100	WASHINGTON ST	94108	7-A5
STONECREST DR			SF
1	JUNIPERO SERRA BLVD	94132	13-C7
30	BROADMOOR DR	94132	13-C7
200	WINSTON DR	94132	13-B7
360	BROADMOOR DR	94132	13-C7
400	JUNIPERO SERRA BLVD	94132	13-C7
STONEMAN ST			SF
1	FOLSOM ST	94110	14-J4
30	MANCHESTER ST	94110	14-J4
60	SHOTWELL ST	94110	14-J4
100	BONVIEW ST	94110	14-J4
100	COSO AV	94110	14-J4
STONEYBROOK AV			SF
1	CAMBRIDGE ST	94112	14-H7
1	TRUMBULL ST	94112	14-H7
100	GLADSTONE DR	94112	14-H7
STONEYFORD AV			SF
1	CAMBRIDGE ST	94112	14-H6
100	GLADSTONE DR	94112	14-H7
STOREY AV			SF
1200	LINCOLN BLVD	94129	1-C3
	MILLER RD	94129	1-C3
	STONE ST	94129	1-C3
	BELL RD	94129	1-C3
	RALSTON AV	94129	1-C3
	WAGNER RD	94129	1-C3
	ROD RD	94129	1-C4
	RUCKMAN AV	94129	1-C4
	APPLETON ST	94129	1-C4
	LINCOLN BLVD	94129	1-C4
STORRIE ST			SF
1	MARKET ST	94114	10-F2
1	ORD ST	94114	10-F2
100	18TH ST	94114	10-F2
100	HATTIE ST	94114	10-F2
STOW LAKE DR			SF
	JOHN F KENNEDY DR	-	9-C1
	STOW LAKE DR E	-	9-B1
	MARTIN LUTHER KING JR DR	-	9-B1
STOW LAKE DR E			SF
	STOW LAKE DR	-	9-C1
	MARTIN LUTHER KING JR DR	-	9-C1
STRATFORD DR			SF
1	LYNDHURST DR	94132	13-C7
100	WYTON LN	94132	13-B7
200	HOLLOWAY AV	94132	18-B1
300	BANBURY DR	94132	18-B1
400	JUNIPERO SERRA BLVD	94132	18-C1
SUMMIT ST			SF
1	THRIFT ST	94112	18-E1
140	JOSIAH AV	94112	18-E1
140	MONTANA ST	94112	18-E1
320	MARGARET AV	94112	18-E1
SUMNER ST			SF
	MACARTHUR AV	94129	6-E4
	SANCHES ST	94129	6-E4
	LIGGETT AV	94129	6-E4
1	HOWARD ST	94103	7-A7
100	CLEMENTINA ST	94103	7-A7
SUNBEAM LN			SF
1	JUNIOR TER	94112	19-F1
SUNNYDALE AV			SF
1	BAYSHORE BLVD	94134	20-A2
260	DESMOND ST	94134	20-A2
290	DESMOND ST	94134	20-A2
340	TALBERT ST	94134	20-A2
410	PEABODY ST	94134	20-A2
490	RUTLAND ST	94134	20-A2
520	CORA ST	94134	19-J2
520	TOMASO CT	94134	19-J2
640	DELTA ST	94134	19-J2
640	MELRA CT	94134	19-J2
720	SCHWERIN ST	94134	19-J2
800	REY ST	94134	19-J2
850	GARRISON AV	94134	19-J2
1040	SAWYER ST	94134	19-J2
1120	HAHN ST	94134	19-J2
1300	SANTOS ST	94134	19-H2
2300	PERSIA AV	94134	19-H1
SUNNYSIDE TER			SF
100	FOERSTER ST	94112	14-E7
SUNRISE WY			SF
340	HAHN ST	94134	19-J2
450	SAWYER ST	94134	19-J2
SUNSET BLVD			SF
	MARTIN LUTHER KING JR DR	-	8-J1
	37TH AV	94122	8-J2
	IRVING ST	94122	8-J2
	36TH AV	94122	8-J2
	IRVING ST	94122	8-J2
	JUDAH ST	94122	8-J2
	KIRKHAM ST	94122	8-J2
	LAWTON ST	94122	8-J3
	MORAGA ST	94122	8-J3
	NORIEGA ST	94122	8-J3
	ORTEGA ST	94116	8-J3
	PACHECO ST	94116	8-J4
	QUINTARA ST	94116	8-J4
	RIVERA ST	94116	12-J4
	SANTIAGO ST	94116	12-J4
	TARAVAL ST	94116	12-J5
	ULLOA ST	94116	12-J5
	VICENTE ST	94116	12-J5
	WAWONA ST	94116	12-J5
1900	YORBA ST	94132	12-J6
	OCEAN AV	94132	12-J6
	LAKE MERCED BLVD	94132	12-J6
SURREY ST			SF
1	CHENERY ST	94131	14-F6
100	SWISS AV	94131	14-G6
200	VAN BUREN ST	94131	14-G6
230	OHLONE WY	94131	14-G6
250	LIPPARD AV	94131	14-G6
260	THOR AV	94131	14-G6
300	DIAMOND ST	94131	14-G6
400	CASTRO ST	94131	14-G6
SUSSEX ST			SF
1	CASTRO ST	94131	14-G6
1	BEMIS ST	94131	14-G6
40	PENNY LN	94131	14-G6
130	POPPY LN	94131	14-G5
200	DIAMOND ST	94131	14-G5
230	OHLONE WY	94131	14-G6
250	VAN BUREN ST	94131	14-G6
300	CONRAD ST	94131	14-G6
400	SWISS AV	94131	14-F5
450	MIZPAH ST	94131	14-F5
500	ELK ST	94131	14-F5
SUTRO HEIGHTS AV			SF
1	46TH AV	94121	4-H7
100	47TH AV	94121	4-H7
200	48TH AV	94121	4-H7
SUTTER ST			SF
	MARKET ST	94104	7-B5
1	SANSOME ST	94104	7-B5
100	MONTGOMERY ST	94104	7-B5
110	TRINITY ST	94104	7-A5
110	TRINITY ST	94108	7-A5
200	KEARNY ST	94108	7-A5
220	CLAUDE LN	94108	7-A5
300	GRANT AV	94108	7-A5
400	STOCKTON ST	94108	7-A5
500	POWELL ST	94102	7-A5
600	MASON ST	94102	7-A5
700	TAYLOR ST	94109	6-J5
800	JONES ST	94109	6-J5
900	LEAVENWORTH ST	94109	6-J5
1000	HYDE ST	94109	6-J6
1100	LARKIN ST	94109	6-J6
1200	POLK ST	94109	6-H6
1300	VAN NESS AV	94109	6-H6
1400	FRANKLIN ST	94109	6-H6
1500	GOUGH ST	94109	6-H6
1600	OCTAVIA ST	94109	6-H6
1700	LAGUNA ST	94115	6-H6
1800	BUCHANAN ST	94115	6-G6
1900	WEBSTER ST	94115	6-G6
2000	FILLMORE ST	94115	6-G6
2100	STEINER ST	94115	6-G6
2200	PIERCE ST	94115	6-G6
2300	SCOTT ST	94115	6-G6
2400	DIVISADERO ST	94115	6-F6
2500	BRODERICK ST	94115	6-F6
2600	BAKER ST	94115	6-F6
2700	LYON ST	94115	6-F6
2800	PRESIDIO AV	94115	6-F6
SWEENY ST			SF
1	SAN BRUNO AV	94134	15-A6
100	BARNEVELD AV	94134	15-A6
200	MERRILL ST	94134	15-A6
300	BOYLSTON ST	94134	14-J6
400	BOWDOIN ST	94134	14-J6
500	DARTMOUTH ST	94134	14-J6
550	DUNSMUIR ST	94134	14-J6
600	COLBY ST	94134	14-J6
650	UNIVERSITY ST	94134	14-J6
700	PRINCETON ST	94134	14-J6
800	CAMBRIDGE ST	94134	14-J6
SWISS AV			SF
1	ARBOR ST	94131	14-F5
100	SUSSEX ST	94131	14-F6
200	SURREY ST	94131	14-F6

Address	Cross Street	ZIP	Pg-Grid
SYCAMORE ST			SF
1	MISSION ST	94110	10-H2
30	SAN CARLOS ST	94110	10-H2
70	LEXINGTON ST	94110	10-H2
100	VALENCIA ST	94110	10-H2
SYDNEY WY			SF
50	ULLOA ST	94127	13-E4
100	PORTOLA DR	94127	13-E4
1	IDORA AV	94127	13-E4
SYLVAN DR			SF
1	SLOAT BLVD	94132	13-A6
100	OCEAN AV	94132	13-A6
200	EUCALYPTUS DR	94132	13-A6
T			
TABER PL			SF
1	2ND ST	94107	7-B6
100	JACK LONDON AL	94107	7-B6
200	3RD ST	94107	7-B6
TACOMA ST			SF
1	15TH AV	94118	5-C6
TALBERT CT			SF
1	VISITACION AV	94134	20-A2
TALBERT ST			SF
110	SUNNYDALE AV	94134	20-A2
290	VISITACION AV	94134	20-A2
TAMALPAIS TER			SF
1	TURK ST	94118	6-E7
100	GOLDEN GATE AV	94118	6-E7
TAMPA LN			SF
1	BRIDGEVIEW DR	94124	15-B6
100	QUESADA AV	94124	15-B6
TANDANG SORA			SF
1	BONIFACIO ST	94107	7-B6
100	RIZAL ST	94107	7-B6
TAPIA DR			SF
1	FONT BLVD	94132	13-B7
80	HOLLOWAY AV	94132	18-B1
100	FONT BLVD	94132	18-B1
120	PINTO AV	94132	18-B1
200	SERRANO DR	94132	18-B1
TARA ST			SF
100	MAJESTIC AV	94112	18-E1
170	MOUNT VERNON AV	94112	19-E1
280	NIAGARA AV	94112	19-E1
TARAVAL ST			SF
	DEWEY BLVD	94127	13-D4
	KENSINGTON WY	94127	13-D5
	CLAREMONT BLVD	94127	13-D5
1	DEWEY BLVD	94127	13-D4
1	DEWEY BLVD	94116	13-D4
50	LENOX WY	94127	13-C5
50	LENOX WY	94116	13-C5
100	WAWONA ST	94127	13-C5
100	WAWONA ST	94116	13-C5
120	CORTES AV	94127	13-C5
120	CORTES AV	94116	13-C5
150	MADRONE AV	94127	13-C5
150	MADRONE AV	94116	13-C5
200	FOREST SIDE AV	94116	13-C5
220	12TH AV	94116	13-C5
300	FUNSTON AV	94116	13-C5
400	14TH AV	94116	13-C5
500	15TH AV	94116	13-C5
600	16TH AV	94116	13-C5
700	17TH AV	94116	13-B5
800	18TH AV	94116	13-B5
900	19TH AV	94116	13-B5
1000	20TH AV	94116	13-B5
1100	21ST AV	94116	13-B5
1200	22ND AV	94116	13-B5
1300	23RD AV	94116	13-B5
1400	24TH AV	94116	13-B5
1500	25TH AV	94116	13-B5
1600	26TH AV	94116	13-A5
1700	27TH AV	94116	13-A5
1800	28TH AV	94116	13-A5
1900	29TH AV	94116	13-A5
2000	30TH AV	94116	13-A5
2100	31ST AV	94116	13-A5
2200	32ND AV	94116	13-A5
2300	33RD AV	94116	13-A5
2400	34TH AV	94116	13-A5
2500	35TH AV	94116	12-J5
2600	35TH AV	94116	12-J5
2650	SUNSET BLVD	94116	12-J5
2700	37TH AV	94116	12-J5
2800	38TH AV	94116	12-J5
2900	39TH AV	94116	12-J5
3000	40TH AV	94116	12-J5
3100	41ST AV	94116	12-J5
3200	42ND AV	94116	12-J5
3300	43RD AV	94116	12-H5
3400	44TH AV	94116	12-H5
3500	45TH AV	94116	12-H5
3600	46TH AV	94116	12-H5
3700	47TH AV	94116	12-H5
	48TH AV	94116	12-H5
	GREAT HWY	94116	12-H5
TAYLOR RD			SF
	SHERIDAN AV	94129	1-D4
	LINCOLN BLVD	94129	1-D4
TAYLOR ST			SF
2500	BAY ST	94133	2-J3
2600	NORTH POINT ST	94133	2-J3
2700	BEACH ST	94133	2-J3
2800	JEFFERSON ST	94133	2-J3
3000	THE EMBARCADERO	94133	2-J3
1	MARKET ST	94102	7-A6
20	GOLDEN GATE AV	94102	7-A6
70	OPAL PL	94102	7-A6
100	TURK ST	94102	7-A6
200	EDDY ST	94102	7-A6
300	ELLIS ST	94102	7-A6
400	OFARRELL ST	94102	7-A6
	GEARY ST	94102	6-J6
	ISADORA DUNCAN LN	94102	6-J6
560	COLIN PL	94102	6-J6
600	POST ST	94109	6-J6
600	POST ST	94102	6-J6
620	COSMO PL	94109	6-J5
620	COSMO PL	94102	6-J5
660	HOBART AL	94109	6-J5
660	HOBART AL	94102	6-J5
700	SUTTER ST	94109	6-J5
700	SUTTER ST	94102	6-J5
800	BUSH ST	94108	6-J5
820	MULFORD AL	94108	6-J5
900	PINE ST	94108	6-J5
1000	CALIFORNIA ST	94108	6-J5
1100	SACRAMENTO ST	94108	6-J5
1130	PLEASANT ST	94108	6-J5
1200	CLAY ST	94108	6-J5
1300	WASHINGTON ST	94108	6-J5
1400	JACKSON ST	94133	6-J5
1500	PACIFIC AV	94133	6-J4
1550	BERNARD ST	94133	6-J4
1600	BROADWAY	94133	6-J4
1680	FALLON PL	94133	6-J4
1700	VALLEJO ST	94133	6-J4
1800	GREEN ST	94133	6-J4
1900	UNION ST	94133	2-J4
1930	ALADDIN TER	94133	2-J4
1930	REDFIELD AL	94133	2-J4
2000	FILBERT ST	94133	2-J4
2040	VALPARAISO ST	94133	2-J4
2100	GREENWICH ST	94133	2-J4
2200	LOMBARD ST	94133	2-J3
2300	CHESTNUT ST	94133	2-J3
2300	COLUMBUS AV	94133	2-J3
2350	WATER ST	94133	2-J3
2400	FRANCISCO ST	94133	2-J3
S TEA GARDEN DR			SF
	JOHN F KENNEDY DR	94118	9-C1
	CONCOURSE DR	94118	9-C1
	MARTIN LUTHER KING JR DR	94118	9-C1
TEDDY AV			SF
1	ELLIOT ST	94134	19-J2
90	DELTA ST	94134	20-A2
190	RUTLAND ST	94134	20-A2
280	ALPHA ST	94134	20-A2
400	SAN BRUNO AV	94134	20-A2
400	WABASH TER	94134	20-A2
TEHAMA ST			SF
1	1ST ST	94105	7-B6
70	MALDEN AL	94105	7-B6
100	2ND ST	94105	7-B6
350	GALLAGHER LN	94103	7-A6
400	5TH ST	94103	7-A7
500	6TH ST	94103	7-A7
700	8TH ST	94103	7-A7
800	9TH ST	94103	6-J7
TELEGRAPH PL			SF
100	CHILD ST	94133	3-A3
TELEGRAPH HILL BLVD			SF
1	KEARNY ST	94133	3-A3
1	LOMBARD ST	94133	3-A3
TEMESCAL TER			SF
1	TURK ST	94118	5-E7
100	GOLDEN GATE AV	94118	5-E7
TEMPLE ST			SF
1	SATURN ST	94114	10-F2
100	17TH ST	94114	10-F2
TENNESSEE ST			SF
600	MARIPOSA ST	94107	11-C2
700	18TH ST	94107	11-C2
800	19TH ST	94107	11-C2
900	20TH ST	94107	11-C2
1100	22ND ST	94107	11-C3
1200	TUBBS ST	94107	11-C3
1300	23RD ST	94107	11-C3
1400	24TH ST	94107	11-C3
	25TH ST	94107	11-C3
1600	26TH ST	94107	11-C4
1700	CESAR CHAVEZ ST	94124	11-C4
1830	MARIN ST	94124	11-C4
TERESITA BLVD			SF
1	PORTOLA DR	94127	13-E4
100	JUANITA WY	94127	13-E5
200	FOWLER AV	94127	13-E5
250	EVELYN WY	94127	14-E5
260	MARIETTA DR	94127	14-E5
300	AGUA WY	94127	14-E5
320	ISOLA WY	94127	14-E5
	REPOSA WY	94127	14-E5
400	SEQUOIA WY	94127	14-E5
450	GAVIOTA WY	94127	14-E5
490	ARROYO WY	94127	14-E5
500	ARROYO WY	94127	14-E5
540	EL SERENO CT	94127	14-F5
560	RIO CT	94127	14-E5
600	BELLA VISTA WY	94127	14-E5
600	BELLA VISTA WY	94127	14-F5
600	CUBA AL	94127	14-F5
600	MARIETTA DR	94127	14-F5
700	MOLIMO DR	94131	14-F6
700	MOLIMO DR	94127	14-F6
800	FOERSTER ST	94131	14-F6
800	FOERSTER ST	94127	14-F6
850	LOS PALMOS DR	94131	14-F6
850	LOS PALMOS DR	94127	14-F6
900	STILLINGS AV	94131	14-F6
900	STILLINGS AV	94127	14-F6
1000	MELROSE AV	94127	14-E6
1080	VERNA ST	94127	14-E6
1100	FOERSTER ST	94127	14-E6
TERRACE DR			SF
1	PORTOLA DR	94127	13-C5
100	SANTA CLARA AV	94127	13-D5
200	TERRACE WK	94127	13-D5
TERRACE WK			SF
200	YERBA BUENA AV	94127	13-D5
230	TERRACE DR	94127	13-D6
280	SANTA PAULA AV	94127	13-D6
TERRA VISTA AV			SF
1	SAINT JOSEPHS AV	94115	6-F6
1	ELLIS ST	94115	6-F6
40	BAKER ST	94115	6-F6
80	FORTUNA AV	94115	6-F6
110	LYON ST	94115	6-F6
120	ENCANTO AV	94115	6-F6
160	BARCELONA AV	94115	6-F6
200	ANZAVISTA AV	94115	6-F6
TERRY A FRANCOIS BLVD			SF
	ILLINOIS ST	94107	11-C2
	MARIPOSA ST	94107	11-C2
1	MISSION ROCK ST	94107	11-C1
100	3RD ST	94107	7-C7
TEXAS ST			SF
100	17TH ST	94107	11-B2
200	MARIPOSA ST	94107	11-B2
300	18TH ST	94107	11-B2
400	19TH ST	94107	11-B2
500	20TH ST	94107	11-B3
630	SIERRA ST	94107	11-B3
700	22ND ST	94107	11-B3
1000	25TH ST	94107	11-B3
THE EMBARCADERO			SF
1800	POWELL ST	94133	2-J3
2000	TAYLOR ST	94133	2-J3
	WASHINGTON ST	94111	7-B5
270	WASHINGTON ST	94111	7-B4
500	BROADWAY ST	94111	3-B4
700	GREEN ST	94111	3-B4
800	UNION ST	94111	3-B3
1060	BATTERY ST	94111	3-B3
1090	LOMBARD ST	94111	3-A3
1220	SANSOME ST	94111	3-A3
1380	BAY ST	94133	3-A3
1490	KEARNY ST	94133	3-A3
1500	NORTH POINT ST	94133	3-A3
1610	BEACH ST	94133	3-A3
1800	JEFFERSON ST	94133	2-J3
	MISSION ST	94111	7-C5
	MISSION ST	94105	7-C5
	STEUART ST	94105	7-C5
	FOLSOM ST	94105	7-C5
	HARRISON ST	94105	7-C5
	STEUART ST	94105	7-C5
	KING ST	94107	7-C6
	BERRY ST	94107	7-C6
	BRYANT ST	94105	7-C6
	BRANNAN ST	94107	7-C6
	TOWNSEND ST	94107	7-C6
THERESA ST			SF
1	AVALON AV	94112	14-G7
1	MISSION ST	94112	14-G7
130	ALEMANY BLVD	94112	14-G7
190	CAYUGA AV	94112	14-G7
300	SAN JOSE AV	94112	14-G7
THOMAS AV			SF
	INFANTRY TER	94129	5-D4
	SIBERT LP	94129	5-D4
	ARGUELLO BLVD	94129	5-D4
2300	ELMIRA ST	94124	15-A6
2100	SILVER AV	94124	15-B6
1900	MADDUX AV	94124	15-B6
2000	QUINT ST	94124	15-B6
2050	ROBBLEE AV	94124	15-B6
1200	GRIFFITH ST	94124	15-C7
1360	HAWES ST	94124	15-C7
1550	INGALLS ST	94124	15-C7
1740	JENNINGS ST	94124	15-C7
1930	KEITH ST	94124	15-C7
2120	LANE ST	94124	15-C7
2200	3RD ST	94124	15-B6
THOMAS MELLON DR			SF
1	EXECUTIVE PARK BLVD	94134	20-B2
100	ALANA WY	94134	20-B2
THOMAS MORE WY			SF
1	BROTHERHOOD WY	94132	18-C2
1	CHUMASERO DR	94132	18-C2
THOR AV			SF
1	SURREY ST	94131	14-G6
100	CHENERY ST	94131	14-G6
THORNBURG RD			SF
	KENDALL DR	94129	2-E4
	GENERAL KENNEDY AV	94129	2-E4
THORNTON AV			SF
1	3RD ST	94124	15-B6
50	LATONA ST	94124	15-B6
90	LUCY ST	94124	15-B6
120	POMONA ST	94124	15-B6
170	CERES ST	94124	15-B6
190	FLORA ST	94124	15-B6
240	REDDY ST	94124	15-B6
290	TOPEKA AV	94124	15-B6
380	NEPTUNE ST	94124	15-B6
440	VENUS ST	94124	15-B6
460	VENUS ST	94124	15-B6
520	APOLLO ST	94124	15-B6
600	BRIDGEVIEW DR	94124	15-B6
600	SCOTIA AV	94124	15-B6
630	VESTA ST	94124	15-A6
630	LEDYARD ST	94124	15-A6
660	MERCURY ST	94124	15-A6
670	MERCURY ST	94124	15-A6
700	WATERVILLE ST	94124	15-A6
720	QUINT ST	94124	15-A6
760	ELMIRA ST	94124	15-A6
800	BAYSHORE BLVD	94124	15-A6
800	CARROLL AV	94124	15-A6
THORP LN			SF
1	LAMSON LN	94114	10-F2
100	CLOVER LN	94114	10-F2
THRIFT ST			SF
1	ORIZABA AV	94112	18-D1
90	FAXON AV	94112	18-D1
130	CAPITOL AV	94112	18-D1
240	PLYMOUTH AV	94112	18-D1
300	SUMMIT ST	94112	18-D1
TIFFANY AV			SF
20	DUNCAN ST	94110	14-H4
200	29TH ST	94110	14-H4
TILLMAN PL			SF
1	GRANT AV	94108	7-A5
TINGLEY ST			SF
1	MISSION ST	94112	14-G7
100	ALEMANY BLVD	94112	14-G7
200	CAYUGA AV	94112	14-G6
300	SAN JOSE AV	94112	14-G6
TIOGA AV			SF
1	DELTA ST	94134	20-A1
70	RUTLAND ST	94134	20-A1
200	ALPHA ST	94134	20-A1
TOCOLOMA AV			SF
190	LATHROP AV	94134	20-B2
280	BLANKEN AV	94134	20-B2
TODD ST			SF
	POPE ST	94129	1-C4
	KOBBE AV	94129	1-C4
TOLAND ST			SF
1	NAPOLEON ST	94124	15-B4
1	EVANS AV	94124	15-B4
200	GALVEZ AV	94124	15-B4
300	HUDSON AV	94124	15-B5
460	JERROLD AV	94124	15-B5
520	KIRKWOOD AV	94124	15-B5
600	LA SALLE AV	94124	15-B5
790	MCKINNON AV	94124	15-B5
890	NEWCOMB AV	94124	15-A5
1000	OAKDALE AV	94124	15-A5
TOLEDO WY			SF
1	MALLORCA WY	94123	2-G4
100	PIERCE ST	94123	2-G4
TOMASO CT			SF
100	CORA ST	94134	19-J2
100	SUNNYDALE AV	94134	19-J2
TOMPKINS AV			SF
1	ANDOVER ST	94110	14-J6
100	MOULTRIE ST	94110	14-J6
200	ANDERSON ST	94110	14-J6
300	ELLSWORTH ST	94110	14-J6
400	GATES ST	94110	14-J6
500	FOLSOM ST	94110	14-J6
600	BANKS ST	94110	14-J6
700	PRENTISS ST	94110	14-J6
800	NEVADA ST	94110	14-J6
900	PUTNAM ST	94110	14-J6
1000	BRONTE ST	94110	14-J6
1100	BRADFORD ST	94110	15-A6
1200	PERALTA AV	94110	15-A6
TOPAZ WY			SF
1	GOLD MINE DR	94131	14-G5
200	ORA WY	94131	14-F5
300	GOLD MINE DR	94131	14-F5
TOPEKA AV			SF
1	SILVER AV	94124	15-B6
110	QUINT ST	94124	15-B6
160	MADDUX AV	94124	15-B6
200	BRIDGEVIEW DR	94124	15-B6
250	APOLLO ST	94124	15-B6
270	APOLLO ST	94124	15-B6
340	VENUS ST	94124	15-B6
340	NEWHALL ST	94124	15-B6
400	THORNTON AV	94124	15-B6
TORNEY AV			SF
	LINCOLN BLVD	94129	2-E4
	OREILLY AV	94129	2-E4
TORRENS CT			SF
1	CLAY ST	94109	6-J5
TOUCHARD ST			SF
1	PINE ST	94109	6-J5
TOWNSEND ST			SF
1	KING ST	94107	7-C6
1	THE EMBARCADERO	94107	7-C6
60	COLIN P KELLY JR ST	94107	7-C7
100	2ND ST	94107	7-C7
130	STANFORD ST	94107	7-C7
180	CLARENCE PL	94107	7-C7
200	3RD ST	94107	7-B7
220	RITCH ST	94107	7-B7
240	CLYDE ST	94107	7-B7
250	LUSK ST	94107	7-B7
300	4TH ST	94107	7-B7
400	5TH ST	94107	7-B7
	6TH ST	94103	11-B1
600	7TH ST	94103	11-A1
	8TH ST	94103	11-A1
	DIVISION ST	94103	11-A1
TOYON LN			SF
1	S HILL BLVD	94112	19-G2
100	BALTIMORE WY	94112	19-G2
TRAINOR ST			SF
100	14TH ST	94103	10-J1
TRANSVERSE DR			SF
300	CROSS OVER DR	-	9-B1
200	JOHN F KENNEDY DR	-	9-B1
100	OVERLOOK DR	-	9-B1
1	MIDDLE DR W	-	9-B1
100	MARTIN LUTHER KING JR DR	-	9-B1
TREASURY PL			SF
1	BUSH ST	94104	7-B5
TREAT AV			SF
210	ALAMEDA ST	94103	10-J1
210	DIVISION ST	94103	10-J1
250	ALABAMA ST	94103	10-J1
300	15TH ST	94103	10-J1
1970	HARRISON ST	94103	10-J2
2000	HARRISON ST	94103	10-J2
400	HARRISON ST	94103	10-J2
400	16TH ST	94110	10-J2
500	17TH ST	94110	10-J2
600	18TH ST	94110	10-J2
600	19TH ST	94110	10-J2
650	MISTRAL ST	94110	10-J2
700	20TH ST	94110	10-J3
800	21ST ST	94110	10-J3
900	22ND ST	94110	10-J3
1000	23RD ST	94110	10-J3
1100	24TH ST	94110	10-J4
1200	25TH ST	94110	10-J4
1300	26TH ST	94110	10-J4
1500	PRECITA AV	94110	14-J4
TRENTON ST			SF
1	WASHINGTON ST	94108	7-A5
TRINITY ST			SF
1	BUSH ST	94104	7-A5
1	BUSH ST	94108	7-A5
100	SUTTER ST	94104	7-A5
100	SUTTER ST	94108	7-A5
TROY AL			SF
1	HYDE ST	94109	6-J5
TRUBY ST			SF
	GORGAS AV	94129	2-E4
	WINN WY	94129	2-E4
TRUETT ST			SF
1	MASON ST	94108	7-A5
1	SHEPHARD PL	94108	7-A5
TRUMBULL ST			SF
1	MISSION ST	94112	14-G6
100	CRAUT ST	94112	14-H6
200	CONGDON ST	94112	14-H6
300	NEY ST	94112	14-H6
400	MAYNARD ST	94112	14-H6
	CAMBRIDGE ST	94112	14-H6
	CAMBRIDGE ST	94134	14-H6
	STONEYBROOK AV	94134	14-H6
TUBBS ST			SF
1	TENNESSEE ST	94107	11-C3
100	INDIANA ST	94107	11-C3
TUCKER AV			SF
80	RUTLAND ST	94134	20-A2
200	ALPHA ST	94134	20-A2
TULANE ST			SF
1	PRINCETON ST	94134	14-J7
TULARE ST			SF
900	ILLINOIS ST	94124	15-C4
1000	3RD ST	94124	15-C4
1300	INDIANA ST	94124	15-C4
TUNNEL AV			SF
100	BAYSHORE BLVD	94134	20-A2
200	BLANKEN AV	94134	20-A2
280	LATHROP AV	94134	20-A2
TURK ST			SF
1	MASON ST	94102	7-A6
100	TAYLOR ST	94102	7-A6
200	JONES ST	94102	6-J6
300	LEAVENWORTH ST	94102	6-J6
400	HYDE ST	94102	6-J6
490	DODGE PL	94102	6-J6
500	LARKIN ST	94102	6-J6
600	POLK ST	94102	6-J6
700	VAN NESS AV	94102	6-H6
800	FRANKLIN ST	94102	6-H6
900	GOUGH ST	94102	6-H6
1000	LAGUNA ST	94115	6-H6
1260	WEBSTER ST	94115	6-G7
1400	FILLMORE ST	94115	6-G7
1500	STEINER ST	94115	6-G7
1600	PIERCE ST	94115	6-G7
1700	SCOTT ST	94115	6-G7
1750	SEYMOUR ST	94115	6-G7
1800	DIVISADERO ST	94115	6-F7
1900	BRODERICK ST	94115	6-F7
1940	SAINT JOSEPHS AV	94115	6-F7
2000	BAKER ST	94115	6-F7
2100	LYON ST	94115	6-F7
2170	CENTRAL AV	94115	6-F7
2250	NIDO AV	94115	6-F7
2200	MASONIC AV	94118	6-F7
2300	ANNAPOLIS TER	94118	6-E7
2400	TAMALPAIS TER	94118	6-E7
2500	ROSELYN TER	94118	6-E7
2600	KITTREDGE TER	94118	6-E7
2700	CHABOT TER	94118	6-E7
2800	TEMESCAL TER	94118	6-E7
2900	PARKER AV	94117	5-E7
2900	PARKER AV	94118	5-E7
2950	BEAUMONT AV	94117	5-E7

PRIMARY STREET Address	Cross Street	ZIP	CITY Pg-Grid
TURK ST			SF
2950	BEAUMONT AV	94118	5-E7
3000	STANYAN ST	94118	5-E7
3050	ROSSI AV	94118	5-E7
3100	WILLARD ST N	94118	5-D7
3200	ARGUELLO BLVD	94118	5-D7
3200	BALBOA ST	94118	5-D7
TURK MURPHY LN			SF
1	BROADWAY	94133	7-A4
100	VALLEJO ST	94133	7-A4
	FISHER AL	94133	7-A4
	BROADWAY	94133	7-A4
TURNER TER			SF
1	MISSOURI ST	94107	11-B3
10	MISSOURI ST	94107	11-B3
TURQUOISE WY			SF
1	AMETHYST WY	94131	14-E4
20	QUARTZ WY	94131	14-F5
200	AMBER DR	94131	14-F5
TWAIN ST			SF
600	MONTGOMERY ST	94111	7-A5
670	DUNBAR ST	94111	7-A5
TWIN PEAKS BLVD			SF
1	CARMEL ST	94114	10-F2
1	CARMEL ST	94117	10-F2
1	CLAYTON ST	94117	10-F2
50	VILLA TER	94114	10-E2
50	VILLA TER	94117	10-E2
60	GRAYSTONE TER	94114	10-E2
60	GRAYSTONE TER	94117	10-E2
60	VILLA TER	94117	10-E2
80	CROWN TER	94114	10-E2
80	CROWN TER	94117	10-E2
100	CLARENDON AV	94114	10-E3
130	MOUNTAIN SPRINGS AV	94114	10-E3
130	RACCOON DR	94114	10-E3
170	SAINT GERMAIN AV	94114	10-E3
200	BURNETT AV	94131	10-F3
230	CHRISTMAS TREE POINT RD	94131	10-F3
260	CHRISTMAS TREE POINT RD	94131	10-E3
480	PANORAMA DR	94131	14-E4
500	PORTOLA DR	94131	14-E4

U

PRIMARY STREET Address	Cross Street	ZIP	CITY Pg-Grid
ULLOA ST			SF
1	WOODSIDE AV	94127	13-E4
70	SYDNEY WY	94127	13-E4
100	SYDNEY WY	94127	13-E4
200	LAGUNA HONDA BLVD	94127	13-D5
200	ROCKAWAY AV	94127	13-D5
	WAITHMAN WY	94127	13-D5
300	KNOCKASH HILL ST	94127	13-D5
500	KENSINGTON WY	94127	13-D5
600	GRANVILLE WY	94127	13-D5
650	ALLSTON WY	94127	13-D5
700	DORCHESTER WY	94127	13-D5
800	CLAREMONT BLVD	94127	13-C5
900	W PORTAL AV	94127	13-C5
950	LENOX WY	94127	13-C5
1000	WAWONA ST	94127	13-C5
1030	WAWONA ST	94127	13-C5
1100	MADRONE AV	94127	13-C5
1200	FOREST SIDE AV	94116	13-C5
1230	FUNSTON AV	94116	13-C5
1300	14TH AV	94116	13-C5
1400	15TH AV	94116	13-C5
1500	16TH AV	94116	13-C5
1600	17TH AV	94116	13-C5
1700	18TH AV	94116	13-B5
1800	19TH AV	94116	13-B5
1900	20TH AV	94116	13-B5
2000	21ST AV	94116	13-B5
2100	22ND AV	94116	13-B5
2200	23RD AV	94116	13-B5
2300	24TH AV	94116	13-B5
2400	25TH AV	94116	13-B5
2500	26TH AV	94116	13-A5
2600	27TH AV	94116	13-A5
2700	28TH AV	94116	13-A5
2800	29TH AV	94116	13-A5
2900	30TH AV	94116	13-A5
3000	31ST AV	94116	13-A5
3100	32ND AV	94116	13-A5
3200	33RD AV	94116	13-A5
3300	34TH AV	94116	13-A5
3400	35TH AV	94116	12-J5
3500	36TH AV	94116	12-J5
3500	35TH AV	94116	12-J5
3550	SUNSET BLVD	94116	12-J5
3600	37TH AV	94116	12-J5
3700	38TH AV	94116	12-J5
3800	39TH AV	94116	12-J5
3900	40TH AV	94116	12-J5
4000	41ST AV	94116	12-J5
4100	42ND AV	94116	12-J5
4200	43RD AV	94116	12-H5
4300	44TH AV	94116	12-H5
4400	45TH AV	94116	12-H5
4500	46TH AV	94116	12-H5
4600	47TH AV	94116	12-H5
4700	48TH AV	94116	12-H5
4700	GREAT HWY	94116	12-H5
UNDERWOOD AV			SF
1200	HAWES ST	94124	15-C7
1300	INGALLS ST	94124	15-C7
1400	JENNINGS ST	94124	15-C7
1500	KEITH ST	94124	15-C7
1600	LANE ST	94124	15-B7
1700	3RD ST	94124	15-B7
UNION ST			SF
1	THE EMBARCADERO	94111	3-B4
40	FRONT ST	94111	3-B4
120	BATTERY ST	94111	3-B4
160	ICEHOUSE AL	94111	3-B4
200	SANSOME ST	94111	3-B4
250	CALHOUN TER	94133	3-A4
300	MONTGOMERY ST	94133	3-A4
350	CASTLE ST	94133	3-A4
400	KEARNY ST	94133	3-A4
430	GENOA PL	94133	3-A4
430	SONOMA ST	94133	3-A4
450	VARENNES ST	94133	3-A4
500	GRANT AV	94133	3-A4
500	BANNAM PL	94133	3-A4
520	CADELL PL	94133	3-A4
550	JASPER PL	94133	3-A4
570	PRICE RW	94133	3-A4
600	STOCKTON ST	94133	3-A4
650	COLUMBUS AV	94133	3-A4
700	POWELL ST	94133	3-A4
800	MASON ST	94133	2-J4
900	TAYLOR ST	94133	2-J4
950	MARION PL	94133	2-J4
1000	JONES ST	94109	2-J4
1000	JONES ST	94133	2-J4
1050	BLACK PL	94109	2-J4
1050	BLACK PL	94133	2-J4
1100	LEAVENWORTH ST	94109	2-J4
1150	SHARP PL	94109	2-J4
1200	HYDE ST	94109	2-J4
1260	EASTMAN ST	94109	2-J4
1280	MOORE PL	94109	6-J4
1300	LARKIN ST	94109	6-H4
1400	POLK ST	94109	6-H4
1500	VAN NESS AV	94123	6-H4
1600	FRANKLIN ST	94123	6-H4
1700	GOUGH ST	94123	6-H4
1800	OCTAVIA ST	94123	6-H4
1900	LAGUNA ST	94123	6-G4
1950	CHARLTON CT	94123	6-G4
2000	BUCHANAN ST	94123	6-G4
2100	WEBSTER ST	94123	6-G4
2200	FILLMORE ST	94123	6-G4
2300	STEINER ST	94123	6-G4
2400	PIERCE ST	94123	6-F4
2500	SCOTT ST	94123	6-F4
2600	DIVISADERO ST	94123	6-F4
2700	BRODERICK ST	94123	6-F4
2800	BAKER ST	94123	6-F4
2900	LYON ST	94123	6-F4
UNIVERSITY ST			SF
1	SWEENY ST	94134	14-J7
120	SILVER AV	94134	14-J7
170	SILLIMAN ST	94134	14-J7
280	FELTON ST	94134	14-J7
360	BURROWS ST	94134	14-J7
490	BACON ST	94134	14-J7
500	WAYLAND ST	94134	14-J7
700	WOOLSEY ST	94134	19-J1
800	DWIGHT ST	94134	19-J1
830	OLMSTEAD ST	94134	19-J1
900	MANSELL ST	94134	19-J1
UPLAND DR			SF
1	FAXON AV	94112	13-D7
1	FAXON AV	94127	13-D7
100	DARIEN WY	94127	13-D7
200	NORTHGATE DR	94127	13-D7
300	MANOR DR	94127	13-D6
400	PINEHURST WY	94127	13-D6
500	WESTGATE DR	94127	13-C6
600	SAN ALESO AV	94127	13-C6
700	APTOS AV	94127	13-C6
800	SAN BENITO WY	94127	13-C6
	DARIEN WY	94112	13-D7
	DARIEN WY	94127	13-D7
	KENWOOD WY	94112	13-D7
	KENWOOD WY	94127	13-D7
UPPER SERVICE RD			SF
	JOHNSTONE DR	94131	9-E2
UPPER TER			SF
1	BUENA VISTA AV E	94117	10-F2
1	BUENA VISTA AV W	94117	10-F2
100	MASONIC AV	94117	10-F2
100	ROOSEVELT WY	94117	10-F2
200	ASHBURY TER	94117	10-F2
300	CLIFFORD TER	94117	10-F2
460	MONUMENT WY	94117	10-F2
500	17TH ST	94117	10-F2
UPTON AV			SF
	KINZEY ST	94129	1-C4
	RALSTON AV	94129	1-C4
60	WOOL CT	94129	1-C4
70	RUCKMAN AV	94129	1-C4
1330	KOBBE AV	94129	1-C4
1330	HITCHCOCK ST	94129	1-C4
1330	WRIGHT LP	94129	1-C4
UPTON ST			SF
400	JERROLD AV	94124	15-A5
800	MCKINNON AV	94124	15-A5
URANUS TER			SF
1	17TH ST	94114	10-F2
1	ROOSEVELT WY	94114	10-F2
100	DEMING ST	94114	10-F2
URBANO DR N			SF
1	PICO AV	94127	13-D7
1	URBANO DR S	94127	13-D7
40	LEGION CT	94127	13-D7
100	VICTORIA ST	94127	13-C7
150	DE SOTO ST	94127	13-C7
200	CORONA ST	94127	13-C7
230	BORICA ST	94127	13-C7
300	MONCADA WY	94127	13-C7
400	URBANO DR S	94127	13-C7
URBANO DR S			SF
400	URBANO DR N	94127	13-C7
500	ALVISO ST	94127	13-C7
550	BORICA ST	94127	13-C7
600	CORONA ST	94127	13-C7
650	DE SOTO ST	94127	13-C7
700	VICTORIA ST	94127	13-D7
900	URBANO DR N	94127	13-D7
900	PICO AV	94127	13-D7
UTAH ST			SF
100	ALAMEDA ST	94103	11-A1
200	15TH ST	94103	11-A2
300	16TH ST	94103	11-A2
400	17TH ST	94110	11-A2
500	MARIPOSA ST	94110	11-A2
600	18TH ST	94110	11-A2
1200	23RD ST	94110	11-A3
1300	24TH ST	94110	11-A3
1400	25TH ST	94110	11-A4

V

PRIMARY STREET Address	Cross Street	ZIP	CITY Pg-Grid
VALDEZ AV			SF
1	GREENWOOD AV	94112	13-E6
100	MONTECITO AV	94112	13-E6
200	MONTEREY BLVD	94127	13-D6
300	MANGELS AV	94127	13-D6
400	BRENTWOOD AV	94127	13-D6
VALE AV			SF
100	CRESTLAKE DR	94132	13-A6
190	SLOAT BLVD	94132	13-A6
VALENCIA ST			SF
20	MARKET ST	94103	10-H1
50	MCCOPPIN ST	94103	10-H1
150	DUBOCE AV	94103	10-H1
200	CLINTON PK	94103	10-H1
200	STEVENSON ST	94103	10-H1
200	BROSNAN ST	94103	10-H1
300	14TH ST	94103	10-H1
400	15TH ST	94103	10-H1
450	SPARROW ST	94103	10-H2
500	16TH ST	94110	10-H2
600	17TH ST	94110	10-H2
630	CLARION AL	94110	10-H2
650	SYCAMORE ST	94110	10-H2
700	18TH ST	94110	10-H2
800	19TH ST	94110	10-H2
850	CUNNINGHAM PL	94110	10-H3
900	20TH ST	94110	10-H3
950	LIBERTY ST	94110	10-H3
1000	21ST ST	94110	10-H3
1050	HILL ST	94110	10-H3
1100	22ND ST	94110	10-H3
1200	23RD ST	94110	10-H3
1300	24TH ST	94110	10-H4
1400	25TH ST	94110	10-H4
1500	26TH ST	94110	10-H4
1530	CESAR CHAVEZ ST	94110	14-H4
1600	DUNCAN ST	94110	14-H4
1700	FAIR AV	94110	14-H4
1700	MISSION ST	94110	14-H4
VALERTON CT			SF
100	CAYUGA AV	94112	14-F7
VALLEJO ST			SF
	HALLECK ST	94129	1-E3
50	DAVIS ST	94111	3-B4
100	FRONT ST	94111	3-B4
200	BATTERY ST	94111	3-B4
240	COWELL PL	94111	3-B4
300	SANSOME ST	94133	7-A4
350	PRESCOTT CT	94133	7-A4
	HODGES AL	94133	7-A4
	MONTGOMERY ST	94133	7-A4
500	KEARNY ST	94133	7-A4
530	SAN ANTONIO PL	94133	7-A4
550	POLLARD PL	94133	7-A4
550	ROMOLO ST	94133	7-A4
570	MARGRAVE PL	94133	7-A4
600	GRANT AV	94133	7-A4
640	COLUMBUS AV	94133	7-A4
650	TRACY PL	94133	7-A4
700	STOCKTON ST	94133	7-A4
750	EMERY LN	94133	7-A4
770	TURK MURPHY LN	94133	7-A4
800	POWELL ST	94133	7-A4
880	WASHOE PL	94133	7-A4
900	MASON ST	94133	6-J4
920	VALLEJO TER	94133	6-J4
970	ALTA VISTA TER	94133	6-J4
980	TAYLOR ST	94133	6-J4
1060	FLORENCE ST	94133	6-J4
1070	RUSSIAN HILL PL	94133	6-J4
1100	JONES ST	94109	6-J4
1200	LEAVENWORTH ST	94109	6-J4
1300	HYDE ST	94109	6-J4
1350	WHITE ST	94109	6-J4
1400	LARKIN ST	94109	6-H4
1500	POLK ST	94109	6-H4
1600	VAN NESS AV	94109	6-H4
1600	VAN NESS AV	94123	6-H4
1700	FRANKLIN ST	94109	6-H4
1700	FRANKLIN ST	94123	6-H4
1800	GOUGH ST	94109	6-H4
1800	GOUGH ST	94123	6-H4
1900	OCTAVIA ST	94109	6-H4
1900	OCTAVIA ST	94123	6-H4
2000	LAGUNA ST	94115	6-G4
2000	LAGUNA ST	94123	6-G4
2100	BUCHANAN ST	94115	6-G4
2100	BUCHANAN ST	94123	6-G4
2200	WEBSTER ST	94115	6-G4
2200	WEBSTER ST	94123	6-G4
2300	FILLMORE ST	94115	6-G4
2300	FILLMORE ST	94123	6-G4
2400	STEINER ST	94115	6-G5
2400	STEINER ST	94123	6-G5
2500	PIERCE ST	94115	6-G5
2500	PIERCE ST	94123	6-G5
2650	SCOTT ST	94115	6-F5
2650	SCOTT ST	94123	6-F5
2700	DIVISADERO ST	94115	6-F5
2700	DIVISADERO ST	94123	6-F5
2800	BRODERICK ST	94115	6-F5
2800	BRODERICK ST	94123	6-F5
2900	BAKER ST	94115	6-F5
2900	BAKER ST	94123	6-F5
VALLEJO TER			SF
	VALLEJO ST	94133	6-J4
VALLETA CT			SF
1	MALTA DR	94131	14-F6
VALLEY ST			SF
1	SAN JOSE AV	94110	14-H4
100	DOLORES ST	94131	14-H4
200	CHURCH ST	94131	14-H4
300	SANCHEZ ST	94131	14-G5
400	NOE ST	94131	14-G5
500	CASTRO ST	94131	14-G5
600	DIAMOND ST	94131	14-G5
VALMAR TER			SF
1	MADISON ST	94134	14-H7
1	MADISON ST	94112	14-H7
60	SILLIMAN ST	94134	14-H7
60	SILLIMAN ST	94112	14-H7
100	PERU AV	94112	14-H7
200	ATHENS ST	94112	14-H7
VALPARAISO ST			SF
1	MASON ST	94133	2-J4
100	TAYLOR ST	94133	2-J4
140	ROACH ST	94133	2-J4
200	JONES ST	94133	2-J4
VAN BUREN ST			SF
1	SUSSEX ST	94131	14-G6
100	SURREY ST	94131	14-G6
VAN DYKE AV			SF
1300	INGALLS ST	94124	15-C7
1400	JENNINGS ST	94124	15-C7
1500	KEITH ST	94124	15-C7
1600	LANE ST	94124	15-B7
1700	3RD ST	94124	15-B7
1700	WILLIAMS AV	94124	15-B7
VAN KEUREN AV			SF
	FISHER AV	94124	16-E7
	D ST	94124	16-E7
	C ST	94124	16-F7
	LOCKWOOD ST	94124	16-F7
VAN NESS AV			SF
1	MISSION ST	94103	10-J1
1	S VAN NESS AV	94103	10-J1
1	MARKET ST	94102	6-J7
10	OAK ST	94102	6-J7
40	HICKORY ST	94102	6-J7
100	FELL ST	94102	6-J7
200	HAYES ST	94102	6-J7
230	LECH WALESA	94102	6-J7
300	GROVE ST	94102	6-J7
500	MCALLISTER ST	94102	6-J7
530	REDWOOD ST	94102	6-H7
600	GOLDEN GATE AV	94102	6-H6
630	ELM ST	94102	6-H6
700	TURK ST	94102	6-H6
750	LARCH ST	94102	6-H6
800	EDDY ST	94109	6-H6
850	WILLOW ST	94109	6-H6
900	ELLIS ST	94109	6-H6
930	OLIVE ST	94109	6-H6
1000	OFARRELL ST	94109	6-H6
1030	MYRTLE ST	94109	6-H6
1100	GEARY BLVD	94109	6-H6
1100	GEARY ST	94109	6-H6
1150	CEDAR ST	94109	6-H6
1200	POST ST	94109	6-H6
1230	DANIEL BURNHAM CT	94109	6-H6
1230	HEMLOCK ST	94109	6-H6
1300	SUTTER ST	94109	6-H6
1350	FERN ST	94109	6-H5
1400	BUSH ST	94109	6-H5
1430	AUSTIN ST	94109	6-H5
1500	PINE ST	94109	6-H5
1600	CALIFORNIA ST	94109	6-H5
1700	SACRAMENTO ST	94109	6-H5
1800	CLAY ST	94109	6-H5
1900	WASHINGTON ST	94109	6-H5
2000	JACKSON ST	94109	6-H5
2100	PACIFIC AV	94109	6-H5
2200	BROADWAY	94109	6-H4
2290	VALLEJO ST	94123	6-H4
2290	VALLEJO ST	94109	6-H4
2380	GREEN ST	94123	6-H4
2380	GREEN ST	94109	6-H4
2470	UNION ST	94123	2-H4
2470	UNION ST	94109	2-H4
2550	FILBERT ST	94123	2-H4
2550	FILBERT ST	94109	2-H4
2640	GREENWICH ST	94123	2-H4
2640	GREENWICH ST	94109	2-H4
2730	LOMBARD ST	94123	2-H4
2730	LOMBARD ST	94109	2-H4
2820	CHESTNUT ST	94123	2-H3
2820	CHESTNUT ST	94109	2-H3
2910	FRANCISCO ST	94123	2-H3
2910	FRANCISCO ST	94109	2-H3
3000	BAY ST	94123	2-H3
3000	BAY ST	94109	2-H3
3200	NORTH POINT ST	94123	2-H3
3200	NORTH POINT ST	94109	2-H3
S VAN NESS AV			SF
50	MISSION ST	94103	10-J1
50	VAN NESS AV	94103	10-J1
60	12TH ST	94103	10-J1
90	PLUM ST	94103	10-J1
100	HOWARD ST	94103	10-J1
250	ERIE ST	94103	10-J1
300	14TH ST	94103	10-J1
400	15TH ST	94103	10-J1
450	ADAIR ST	94103	10-J2
500	16TH ST	94110	10-J2
600	17TH ST	94110	10-J2
700	18TH ST	94110	10-J2
800	19TH ST	94110	10-J2
900	20TH ST	94110	10-J3
1000	21ST ST	94110	10-J3
1100	22ND ST	94110	10-J3
1200	23RD ST	94110	10-J3
1300	24TH ST	94110	10-J3
1400	25TH ST	94110	10-J4
1500	26TH ST	94110	10-J4
1600	CESAR CHAVEZ ST	94110	10-J4
VANDEWATER ST			SF
300	POWELL ST	94133	3-A3
400	MASON ST	94133	2-J3
VARELA AV			SF
1	HOLLOWAY AV	94132	18-B1
100	SERRANO DR	94132	18-B1
VARENNES ST			SF
1	GREEN ST	94133	3-A4
100	UNION ST	94133	3-A4
200	FILBERT ST	94133	3-A4
VARNEY PL			SF
1	JACK LONDON AL	94107	7-B7
100	3RD ST	94107	7-B7
VASQUEZ AV			SF
1	WOODSIDE AV	94127	13-D4
30	LAGUNA HONDA BLVD	94127	13-D4
70	BALCETA AV	94127	13-D4
100	GARCIA AV	94127	13-D4
100	HERNANDEZ AV	94127	13-D4
150	PACHECO ST	94127	13-D4
200	GARCIA AV	94127	13-D5
300	KENSINGTON WY	94127	13-D5
300	MERCED AV	94127	13-D5
VASSAR PL			SF
1	HARRISON ST	94107	7-B6
VEGA ST			SF
60	NIDO AV	94115	6-F7
100	ANZAVISTA AV	94115	6-F7
VELASCO AV			SF
120	KELLOCH AV	94134	19-J2
200	ARGONAUT AV	94134	19-J2
240	RIO VERDE ST	94134	19-J2
350	CALGARY ST	94134	19-J2
350	SAWYER ST	94134	19-J2
450	PUEBLO ST	94134	19-J2
550	CASTILLO ST	94134	19-H2
750	SANTOS ST	94134	19-H2
900	CARRIZAL ST	94134	19-H2
900	PARQUE DR	94134	19-H2
VENTURA AV			SF
20	CASTENADA AV	94116	9-D4
100	LINARES AV	94116	9-D3
VENUS ST			SF
1	THORNTON AV	94124	15-B6
100	TOPEKA AV	94124	15-B6
100	THORNTON AV	94124	15-B6
200	WILLIAMS AV	94124	15-B6
VERDUN WY			SF
1	CLAREMONT BLVD	94127	13-D5
60	LENOX WY	94127	13-D5
VERMEHR PL			SF
1	KEARNY ST	94108	7-A5
VERMONT ST			SF
1	DIVISION ST	94103	11-A1
100	ALAMEDA ST	94103	11-A1
200	15TH ST	94103	11-A2
300	16TH ST	94103	11-A2
400	17TH ST	94107	11-A2
500	MARIPOSA ST	94107	11-A2
600	18TH ST	94107	11-A2
700	19TH ST	94107	11-A2
800	20TH ST	94107	11-A3
1000	22ND ST	94107	11-A3
1000	22ND ST	94110	11-A3
1200	23RD ST	94110	11-A3
1300	24TH ST	94110	11-A4
1400	25TH ST	94110	11-A4
1400	26TH ST	94107	11-A4
1500	CESAR CHAVEZ ST	94107	11-A4
VERNA ST			SF
1	LOS PALMOS DR	94127	14-E6
100	TERESITA BLVD	94127	14-E6
VERNON ST			SF
100	RANDOLPH ST	94132	18-C1
200	SARGENT ST	94132	18-C1
300	SHIELDS ST	94132	18-C1
400	GARFIELD ST	94132	18-C1
500	HOLLOWAY AV	94132	18-C1

PRIMARY STREET Address	Cross Street	ZIP	CITY Pg-Grid
VESTA ST			SF
1	THORNTON AV	94124	15-B6
1	LEDYARD ST	94124	15-B6
100	PHELPS ST	94124	15-B6
100	WILLIAMS AV	94124	15-B6
VIA BUFANO			SF
1	COLUMBUS AV	94133	3-A4
100	GREENWICH ST	94133	3-A4
VICENTE ST			SF
1	PORTOLA DR	94127	13-C5
1	SANTA CLARA AV	94127	13-C5
100	W PORTAL AV	94127	13-C5
200	WAWONA ST	94127	13-C5
230	MADRONE AV	94127	13-C5
280	FOREST SIDE AV	94127	13-C5
280	FOREST SIDE AV	94116	13-C5
300	14TH AV	94127	13-C5
300	14TH AV	94116	13-C5
430	15TH AV	94116	13-C5
500	16TH AV	94116	13-C5
600	17TH AV	94116	13-C5
700	18TH AV	94116	13-B5
800	19TH AV	94116	13-B5
900	20TH AV	94116	13-B5
1000	21ST AV	94116	13-B5
1100	22ND AV	94116	13-B5
1200	23RD AV	94116	13-B5
1300	24TH AV	94116	13-B5
1400	25TH AV	94116	13-B5
1500	26TH AV	94116	13-A5
1600	27TH AV	94116	13-A5
1700	28TH AV	94116	13-A5
1800	29TH AV	94116	13-A5
1900	30TH AV	94116	13-A5
2000	31ST AV	94116	13-A5
2100	32ND AV	94116	13-A5
2200	33RD AV	94116	13-A5
2300	34TH AV	94116	13-A5
2400	35TH AV	94116	12-J5
2500	36TH AV	94116	12-J5
2550	SUNSET BLVD	94116	12-J5
2600	37TH AV	94116	12-J5
2700	38TH AV	94116	12-J5
2800	39TH AV	94116	12-J5
2900	40TH AV	94116	12-J5
3000	41ST AV	94116	12-J5
3100	42ND AV	94116	12-J5
3200	43RD AV	94116	12-H5
3300	44TH AV	94116	12-H5
3400	45TH AV	94116	12-H5
3500	46TH AV	94116	12-H5
3600	47TH AV	94116	12-H5
3700	48TH AV	94116	12-H5
VICKSBURG ST			SF
1	22ND ST	94114	10-G3
100	23RD ST	94114	10-G3
200	ELIZABETH ST	94114	10-H3
300	24TH ST	94114	10-H4
400	JERSEY ST	94114	10-H4
500	25TH ST	94114	10-H4
VICTORIA ST			SF
600	HOLLOWAY AV	94127	13-C7
700	URBANO DR S	94127	13-D7
800	URBANO DR N	94127	13-C7
900	OCEAN AV	94127	13-C7
200	RANDOLPH ST	94132	18-C1
300	SARGENT ST	94132	18-C1
400	SHIELDS ST	94132	18-C1
500	GARFIELD ST	94132	18-C1
600	HOLLOWAY AV	94132	18-C1
1	PALMETTO AV	94132	18-C2
100	ALEMANY BLVD	94132	18-C2
VIDAL DR			SF
100	FONT BLVD	94132	18-A1
30	ARBALLO DR	94132	18-A1
100	ACEVEDO AV	94132	18-A1
200	HIGUERA AV	94132	18-A1
210	HIGUERA AV	94132	18-A1
420	GARCES DR	94132	18-A1
500	ARBALLO DR	94132	18-A1
600	RIVAS AV	94132	18-A1
VIENNA ST			SF
1	SILVER AV	94112	14-H7
120	PERU AV	94112	14-H7
210	AVALON AV	94112	14-H7
300	EXCELSIOR AV	94112	14-G7
380	BRAZIL AV	94112	19-G1
470	PERSIA AV	94112	19-G1
590	RUSSIA AV	94112	19-G1
720	FRANCE AV	94112	19-G1
840	ITALY AV	94112	19-G1
900	AMAZON AV	94112	19-G2
1000	GENEVA AV	94112	19-G2
VILLA TER			SF
1	GRAYSTONE TER	94114	10-E2
1	TWIN PEAKS BLVD	94114	10-E2
20	TWIN PEAKS BLVD	94114	10-F2
200	GRAYSTONE TER	94114	10-F3
VINE TER			SF
1	PINE ST	94108	7-A5
VINTON CT			SF
1	GRANT AV	94108	7-A5
VIRGIL ST			SF
1	25TH ST	94110	10-J4
100	26TH ST	94110	10-J4
VIRGINIA AV			SF
1	MISSION ST	94110	14-H5
100	COLERIDGE ST	94110	14-H5
180	LUNDYS LN	94110	14-H5
200	PROSPECT AV	94110	14-H5
300	WINFIELD ST	94110	14-J5
400	ELSIE ST	94110	14-J5
VISITACION AV			SF
200	MANSELL ST	94134	19-J1
670	HAHN ST	94134	19-J2
750	SAWYER ST	94134	19-J2
840	LOEHR ST	94134	19-J2
930	BRITTON ST	94134	19-J2
1010	REY ST	94134	19-J2
1100	SCHWERIN ST	94134	19-J2
1200	DELTA ST	94134	19-J2
1270	CORA ST	94134	20-A2
1350	RUTLAND ST	94134	20-A2
1430	PEABODY ST	94134	20-A2
1500	TALBERT CT	94134	20-A2
1520	TALBERT ST	94134	20-A2
1600	DESMOND ST	94134	20-A2
1700	BAYSHORE BLVD	94134	20-A2
VISTA CT			SF
	SIBLEY RD	94129	6-E5
	LIGGETT AV	94129	6-E5
VISTA LN			SF
1	PARKRIDGE DR	94131	10-F3
50	PARKRIDGE DR	94131	10-F3
100	CRESTLINE DR	94131	10-F3
VISTA VERDE CT			SF
1	STILLINGS AV	94131	14-F6
1	DETROIT ST	94131	14-F6
VISTAVIEW CT			SF
1	WHITECLIFF WY	94124	15-B6
W			
WABASH TER			SF
1	SAN BRUNO AV	94134	20-A2
1	TEDDY AV	94134	20-A2
100	RACINE LN	94134	20-A2
WAGNER AL			SF
100	EDDY ST	94102	6-J6
WAGNER RD			SF
	STOREY AV	94129	1-C3
WAITHMAN WY			SF
900	ULLOA ST	94127	13-D5
1000	PORTOLA DR	94127	13-D5
WALBRIDGE AV			SF
1	GENEVA AV	94134	19-H2
WALL PL			SF
1	JACKSON ST	94109	6-J5
WALLACE AV			SF
1700	3RD ST	94124	15-B7
1700	LANE ST	94124	15-B7
1400	INGALLS ST	94124	15-C7
1500	JENNINGS ST	94124	16-C7
1600	KEITH ST	94124	15-B7
WALLEN CT			SF
	MACARTHUR AV	94129	5-E4
WALLER ST			SF
1	OCTAVIA ST	94102	10-H1
200	LAGUNA ST	94102	10-H1
200	BUCHANAN ST	94102	10-H1
300	WEBSTER ST	94117	10-H1
400	FILLMORE ST	94117	10-G1
500	STEINER ST	94117	10-G1
550	POTOMAC ST	94117	10-G1
600	PIERCE ST	94117	10-G1
650	CARMELITA ST	94117	10-G1
700	SCOTT ST	94117	10-G1
800	CASTRO ST	94117	10-G1
800	DIVISADERO ST	94117	10-G1
850	ALPINE TER	94117	10-G1
1100	BUENA VISTA AV W	94117	10-F1
1200	CENTRAL AV	94117	10-F1
1290	MASONIC AV	94117	10-F1
1300	DELMAR ST	94117	10-F1
1400	ASHBURY ST	94117	10-F1
1450	DOWNEY ST	94117	10-E1
1500	CLAYTON ST	94117	10-E1
1550	BELVEDERE ST	94117	10-E1
1600	COLE ST	94117	10-E1
1700	SHRADER ST	94117	10-E1
1880	STANYAN ST	94117	9-E1
1890	KEZAR DR	94117	9-E1
WALNUT ST			SF
1	PACIFIC AV	94115	6-E5
1	PACIFIC AV	94118	6-E5
100	JACKSON ST	94115	6-E5
100	JACKSON ST	94118	6-E5
200	WASHINGTON ST	94115	6-E5
200	WASHINGTON ST	94118	6-E5
300	CLAY ST	94115	6-E5
300	CLAY ST	94118	6-E5
400	SACRAMENTO ST	94115	6-E6
400	SACRAMENTO ST	94118	6-E6
500	CALIFORNIA ST	94115	6-E6
500	CALIFORNIA ST	94118	6-E6
WALTER ST			SF
1	DUBOCE AV	94114	10-G1
100	14TH ST	94114	10-G1
WALTER LUM PL			SF
1	CLAY ST	94108	7-A5
100	WASHINGTON ST	94108	7-A5
WALTHAM ST			SF
1	ALABAMA ST	94110	14-J5
WANDA ST			SF
1	OCEAN AV	94112	14-F7
100	ONONDAGA AV	94112	14-F7
WARD ST			SF
100	GIRARD ST	94134	20-A1
200	BRUSSELS ST	94134	20-A1
300	GOETTINGEN ST	94134	20-A1
400	SPARTA ST	94134	20-A1
400	ANKENY ST	94134	20-A1
WARNER PL			SF
1	HYDE ST	94109	6-J4
WARREN DR			SF
1	OAK PARK DR	94131	9-D3
100	ASHWOOD LN	94131	9-D3
200	OAK PARK DR	94131	9-D3
300	DEVONSHIRE WY	94131	9-D3
400	OAKHURST LN	94131	9-D3
600	LAWTON ST	94131	9-D2
600	LOCKSLEY AV	94131	9-D2
WASHBURN ST			SF
1	MISSION ST	94103	6-J7
100	HOWARD ST	94103	6-J7
WASHINGTON BLVD			SF
	CENTRAL MAGAZINE RD	94129	5-B4
	HARRISON BLVD	94129	5-B4
	COMPTON RD	94129	5-C5
	HUNTER RD	94129	5-C5
	BATTERY CAULFIELD RD	94129	5-C4
	COMPTON RD	94129	5-C4
	PARK BLVD	94129	5-C4
	NAUMAN RD	94129	5-D4
	DEEMS RD	94129	5-D5
	ARGUELLO BLVD	94129	5-D5
WASHINGTON ST			SF
	THE EMBARCADERO	94111	7-B4
1	THE EMBARCADERO	94111	7-B4
100	DRUMM ST	94111	7-B4
400	BATTERY ST	94111	7-B4
450	CUSTOM HOUSE PL	94111	7-B5
500	SANSOME ST	94111	7-B5
570	HOTALING ST	94111	7-A5
600	COLUMBUS AV	94111	7-A5
600	MONTGOMERY ST	94111	7-A5
640	DUNBAR ST	94111	7-A5
700	KEARNY ST	94108	7-A5
790	WALTER LUM PL	94108	7-A5
770	WENTWORTH PL	94108	7-A5
800	GRANT AV	94108	7-A5
830	WAVERLY PL	94108	7-A5
840	ROSS AL	94108	7-A5
860	SPOFFORD LN	94108	7-A5
870	OLD CHINATOWN LN	94108	7-A5
900	STOCKTON ST	94108	7-A5
950	TRENTON ST	94108	7-A5
970	STONE ST	94108	7-A5
1000	POWELL ST	94108	7-A5
1020	CODMAN PL	94108	7-A5
1050	WETMORE ST	94108	7-A5
1100	MASON ST	94108	7-A5
1200	TAYLOR ST	94108	6-J5
1300	JONES ST	94109	6-J5
1330	PRIEST ST	94109	6-J5
1360	REED ST	94109	6-J5
1400	LEAVENWORTH ST	94109	6-J5
1500	HYDE ST	94109	6-J5
1600	LARKIN ST	94109	6-J5
1700	POLK ST	94109	6-H5
1800	VAN NESS AV	94109	6-H5
1900	FRANKLIN ST	94109	6-H5
2000	GOUGH ST	94109	6-H5
2100	OCTAVIA ST	94109	6-H5
2200	LAGUNA ST	94115	6-H5
2300	BUCHANAN ST	94115	6-G5
2400	WEBSTER ST	94115	6-G5
2500	FILLMORE ST	94115	6-G5
2600	STEINER ST	94115	6-G5
2800	SCOTT ST	94115	6-F5
2900	DIVISADERO ST	94115	6-F5
3000	BRODERICK ST	94115	6-F5
3100	BAKER ST	94115	6-F5
3200	LYON ST	94115	6-F5
3300	PRESIDIO AV	94115	6-F5
3400	WALNUT ST	94118	6-E5
3500	LAUREL ST	94118	6-E5
3600	LOCUST ST	94118	5-E5
3700	SPRUCE ST	94118	5-E5
3800	MAPLE ST	94118	5-E5
3900	CHERRY ST	94118	5-D5
4000	ARGUELLO BLVD	94118	5-D5
WASHOE PL			SF
1	VALLEJO ST	94133	7-A4
WATCHMAN WY			SF
1	MISSOURI ST	94107	11-B3
WATER ST			SF
1	MASON ST	94133	2-J3
100	TAYLOR ST	94133	2-J3
WATERLOO ST			SF
1	LOOMIS ST	94124	15-A5
50	MARENGO ST	94124	15-A5
100	BAYSHORE BLVD	94124	15-A5
100	ALEMANY BLVD	94124	15-A5
WATERVILLE ST			SF
1	SELBY ST	94124	15-A6
100	CONKLING ST	94124	15-A6
180	AUGUSTA ST	94124	15-A6
200	SILVER AV	94124	15-A6
300	THORNTON AV	94124	15-A6
WATSON PL			SF
1	OCEAN AV	94112	14-F7
1	RUTH ST	94112	14-F7
100	LEO ST	94112	14-F7
WATT AV			SF
20	KNOTT CT	94112	19-F2
100	HANOVER ST	94112	19-F2
100	CONCORD ST	94112	19-F2
WAVERLY PL			SF
1	SACRAMENTO ST	94108	7-A5
100	CLAY ST	94108	7-A5
200	WASHINGTON ST	94108	7-A5
WAVERLY WY			SF
100	POLARIS WY	94112	19-F2
WAWONA ST			SF
1	TARAVAL ST	94127	13-C5
100	ULLOA ST	94127	13-C5
200	VICENTE ST	94127	13-C5
300	14TH AV	94127	13-C5
	15TH AV	94132	13-C5
	15TH AV	94116	13-C5
500	16TH AV	94132	13-C5
500	16TH AV	94116	13-C5
600	17TH AV	94132	13-C5
600	17TH AV	94116	13-C5
700	18TH AV	94132	13-C5
700	18TH AV	94116	13-C5
800	19TH AV	94132	13-B5
800	19TH AV	94116	13-B5
900	20TH AV	94132	13-B5
900	20TH AV	94116	13-B5
1000	21ST AV	94132	13-B5
1000	21ST AV	94116	13-B5
1100	22ND AV	94132	13-B5
1100	22ND AV	94116	13-B5
1200	23RD AV	94132	13-B5
1200	23RD AV	94116	13-B5
1300	24TH AV	94132	13-B5
1300	24TH AV	94116	13-B5
1500	26TH AV	94132	13-A5
1500	26TH AV	94116	13-A5
1700	28TH AV	94132	13-A5
1700	28TH AV	94116	13-A5
1900	30TH AV	94132	13-A5
1900	30TH AV	94116	13-A5
2200	33RD AV	94132	13-A5
2200	33RD AV	94116	13-A5
2200	ESCOLTA WY	94116	13-A5
2250	CRESTLAKE DR	94116	13-A5
2300	34TH AV	94116	13-A5
2400	35TH AV	94116	12-J5
2500	36TH AV	94116	12-J5
2550	SUNSET BLVD	94116	12-J5
2600	37TH AV	94116	12-J5
2700	38TH AV	94116	12-J5
2800	39TH AV	94116	12-J5
2900	40TH AV	94116	12-J5
3000	41ST AV	94116	12-J5
3100	42ND AV	94116	12-J5
3200	43RD AV	94116	12-H5
3300	44TH AV	94116	12-H5
3400	45TH AV	94116	12-H5
3500	46TH AV	94116	12-H5
3600	47TH AV	94116	12-H5
3700	48TH AV	94116	12-H5
WAYLAND ST			SF
100	SAN BRUNO AV	94134	15-A7
200	GIRARD ST	94134	15-A7
300	BRUSSELS ST	94134	15-A7
400	GOETTINGEN ST	94134	15-A7
500	SOMERSET ST	94134	15-A7
600	HOLYOKE ST	94134	15-A7
700	HAMILTON ST	94134	15-A7
800	BOWDOIN ST	94134	14-J7
1100	UNIVERSITY ST	94134	14-J7
1200	PRINCETON ST	94134	14-J7
1300	AMHERST ST	94134	14-J7
1400	YALE ST	94134	14-J7
1500	CAMBRIDGE ST	94134	19-J1
1600	OXFORD ST	94134	19-J1
WAYNE PL			SF
1	PACIFIC AV	94133	7-A4
90	BROADWAY	94133	7-A4
WEBB PL			SF
1	MASON ST	94133	2-J4
WEBSTER ST			SF
50	HERMANN ST	94117	10-H1
50	HERMANN ST	94102	10-H1
80	GERMANIA ST	94117	10-H1
80	GERMANIA ST	94102	10-H1
100	WALLER ST	94117	10-H1
100	WALLER ST	94102	10-H1
150	LAUSSAT ST	94117	10-H1
150	LAUSSAT ST	94102	10-H1
200	HAIGHT ST	94117	10-H1
200	HAIGHT ST	94102	10-H1
300	PAGE ST	94117	10-H1
300	PAGE ST	94102	10-H1
350	OAK ST	94117	6-H7
350	OAK ST	94102	6-H7
450	HICKORY ST	94117	6-H7
450	HICKORY ST	94102	6-H7
500	FELL ST	94117	6-G7
500	FELL ST	94102	6-G7
600	HAYES ST	94117	6-G7
600	HAYES ST	94102	6-G7
610	IVY ST	94117	6-G7
610	IVY ST	94102	6-G7
700	GROVE ST	94117	6-G7
700	GROVE ST	94102	6-G7
800	FULTON ST	94117	6-G7
800	FULTON ST	94102	6-G7
950	MCALLISTER ST	94117	6-G7
950	MCALLISTER ST	94102	6-G7
1040	GOLDEN GATE AV	94115	6-G7
1140	TURK ST	94115	6-G6
1230	EDDY ST	94115	6-G6
1320	ELLIS ST	94115	6-G6
1410	OFARRELL ST	94115	6-G6
1510	GEARY BLVD	94115	6-G6
1600	POST ST	94115	6-G6
1700	SUTTER ST	94115	6-G6
1800	BUSH ST	94115	6-G6
1850	WILMOT ST	94115	6-G6
1900	PINE ST	94115	6-G5
2000	CALIFORNIA ST	94115	6-G5
2100	SACRAMENTO ST	94115	6-G5
2200	CLAY ST	94115	6-G5
2300	WASHINGTON ST	94115	6-G5
2400	JACKSON ST	94115	6-G5
2450	BROMLEY PL	94115	6-G5
2490	PACIFIC AV	94115	6-G5
2600	BROADWAY ST	94115	6-G5
2700	VALLEJO ST	94123	6-G4
2800	GREEN ST	94123	6-G4
2900	UNION ST	94123	6-G4
3000	FILBERT ST	94123	6-G4
3050	PIXLEY ST	94123	2-G4
3100	GREENWICH ST	94123	2-G4
3150	MOULTON ST	94123	2-G4
3200	LOMBARD ST	94123	2-G4
3260	MAGNOLIA ST	94123	2-G4
3300	CHESTNUT ST	94123	2-G4
3500	BAY ST	94123	2-G3
3600	NORTH POINT ST	94123	2-G3
3800	BEACH ST	94123	2-G3
3800	JEFFERSON ST	94123	2-G3
3900	MARINA BLVD	94123	2-G3
WEDEMEYER ST			SF
	BATTERY CAULFIELD RD	94129	5-B5
	HAYS ST	94129	5-C5
	15TH AV	94129	5-C5
	14TH AV	94129	5-C5
	WYMAN AV	94129	5-C5
WELDON ST			SF
100	RICKARD ST	94134	15-A6
WELSH ST			SF
1	ZOE ST	94107	7-B7
100	4TH ST	94107	7-B7
300	5TH ST	94107	7-B7
WENTWORTH PL			SF
1	WASHINGTON ST	94108	7-A5
100	JACKSON ST	94108	7-A5
WESTBROOK CT			SF
1	HUDSON AV	94124	15-C6
WESTGATE DR			SF
1	OCEAN AV	94127	13-C7
100	KENWOOD WY	94127	13-C6
200	UPLAND DR	94127	13-C6
290	DARIEN WY	94127	13-D6
300	DARIEN WY	94127	13-D6
400	MONTEREY BLVD	94127	13-D6
WESTMOORLAND DR			SF
100	OCEAN AV	94132	13-A6
200	EUCALYPTUS DR	94132	13-A6
WEST POINT RD			SF
1	MIDDLEPOINT RD	94124	15-D6
200	MIDDLEPOINT RD	94124	15-D6
WESTSIDE DR			SF
1	GATEWAY AV	94130	3-D1
WESTVIEW AV			SF
100	CAMBRIDGE ST	94134	14-J6
WESTWOOD DR			SF
1	EASTWOOD DR	94112	13-D7
1	MIRAMAR AV	94112	13-D7
30	ELMWOOD WY	94112	13-D7
180	WILDWOOD WY	94112	13-D7
200	PIZARRO WY	94112	13-D6
200	MIRAMAR AV	94112	13-D6
200	EASTWOOD DR	94112	13-D6
WETMORE ST			SF
1	DAWSON PL	94108	7-A5
100	CLAY ST	94108	7-A5
200	WASHINGTON ST	94108	7-A5
WHEAT ST			SF
1	PAUL AV	94124	15-B7
100	BAYSHORE ST	94124	15-B7
WHEELER AV			SF
270	LATHROP AV	94134	20-A2
360	BLANKEN AV	94134	20-B2
WHIPPLE AV			SF
1	MONETA WY	94112	19-E2
80	HURON AV	94112	19-E2
150	RAE AV	94112	19-E2
160	RAE AV	94112	19-E2
230	ELLINGTON	94112	19-E2
280	MISSION ST	94112	19-E2
300	MORSE ST	94112	19-E2
WHITE ST			SF
1	VALLEJO ST	94109	6-J4
WHITECLIFF WY			SF
1	BAYVIEW CIR	94124	15-B6
40	VISTAVIEW CT	94124	15-B6
80	CLEARVIEW CT	94124	15-B6
100	BAYVIEW CIR	94124	15-B6
WHITFIELD CT			SF
1	LA SALLE AV	94124	15-D6
WHITING ST			SF
40	JULIUS ST	94133	3-A3
100	GRANT AV	94133	3-A3
WHITNEY ST			SF
1	30TH ST	94131	14-H5
100	RANDALL ST	94131	14-H5
200	FAIRMOUNT ST	94131	14-H5
300	CHENERY ST	94131	14-H5
WHITNEY YOUNG CIR			SF
1	CASHMERE ST	94124	15-C6
1	DEDMAN CT	94124	15-C6
20	YOUNG CT	94124	15-C6
50	RICHARDS CIR	94124	15-C6

PRIMARY STREET Address	Cross Street	ZIP	CITY Pg-Grid
WHITNEY YOUNG CIR			**SF**
50	MABREY CT	94124	15-C6
80	HILLVIEW CT	94124	15-C6
80	LINDSAY CIR	94124	15-C6
70	CARPENTER CT	94124	15-C6
110	HAWKINS LN	94124	15-C6
160	BELL CT	94124	15-C6
170	BASS CT	94124	15-C6
190	NEWCOMB AV	94124	15-C6
240	PROGRESS ST	94124	15-C6
300	HUDSON AV	94124	15-C6
WHITTIER ST			**SF**
1	MISSION ST	94112	19-E2
1	MORSE ST	94112	19-E2
50	CASSANDRA CT	94112	19-E2
70	CRESCIO CT	94112	19-E2
110	BRUNSWICK ST	94112	19-E2
WIESE ST			**SF**
1	15TH ST	94103	10-H2
100	16TH ST	94103	10-H2
WILDE AV			**SF**
1	ERVINE ST	94134	20-A1
60	DELTA ST	94134	20-A1
80	DELTA ST	94134	20-A1
230	RUTLAND ST	94134	20-A1
500	ALPHA ST	94134	20-A1
500	GOETTINGEN ST	94134	20-A1
540	BRUSSELS ST	94134	20-A1
580	GIRARD ST	94134	20-B1
600	SAN BRUNO AV	94134	20-B1
WILDER ST			**SF**
10	ARLINGTON ST	94131	14-G6
10	NATICK ST	94131	14-G6
40	CARRIE ST	94131	14-G6
100	DIAMOND ST	94131	14-G6
WILDWOOD WY			**SF**
560	WESTWOOD DR	94112	13-D7
580	FAXON AV	94112	13-D7
590	HOMEWOOD CT	94112	13-D7
520	PLYMOUTH AV	94112	13-D7
530	EASTWOOD DR	94112	13-D7
WILLARD ST			**SF**
1200	FREDERICK ST	94117	9-E1
1300	CARL ST	94117	9-E2
1400	PARNASSUS AV	94117	9-E2
1420	FARNSWORTH LN	94117	9-E2
1510	BELMONT AV	94117	9-E2
1600	WOODLAND AV	94117	9-E2
WILLARD ST N			**SF**
1	EDWARD ST	94118	5-D7
100	TURK ST	94118	5-E7
150	GOLDEN GATE AV	94118	5-E7
200	GOLDEN GATE AV	94118	5-E7
300	MCALLISTER ST	94118	5-E7
400	FULTON ST	94118	5-E7
WILLIAMS AV			**SF**
1	3RD ST	94124	15-B7
1	VAN DYKE AV	94124	15-B7
50	LUCY ST	94124	15-B7
100	CERES ST	94124	15-B7
120	MENDELL ST	94124	15-B7
150	REDDY ST	94124	15-B7
210	DIANA ST	94124	15-B7
250	NEPTUNE ST	94124	15-B7
260	NEWHALL ST	94124	15-B7
300	VENUS ST	94124	15-B7
350	APOLLO ST	94124	15-B7
400	PHELPS ST	94124	15-B7
400	VESTA ST	94124	15-B7
WILLIAR AV			**SF**
200	MOUNT VERNON AV	94112	18-E1
300	NIAGARA AV	94112	18-E1
WILLOW ST			**SF**
1	LARKIN ST	94109	6-J6
100	POLK ST	94109	6-J6
200	VAN NESS AV	94109	6-H6
300	FRANKLIN ST	94109	6-H6
400	GOUGH ST	94109	6-H6
600	LAGUNA ST	94115	6-H6
680	BUCHANAN ST	94115	6-H6
WILLS ST			**SF**
1	MIDDLEPOINT RD	94124	15-D6
WILMOT ST			**SF**
1	WEBSTER ST	94115	6-G6
100	FILLMORE ST	94115	6-G6
200	STEINER ST	94115	6-G6
WILSON ST			**SF**
200	RHINE ST	94112	18-D2
300	DE LONG ST	94112	18-D2
WINDING WY			**SF**
1	ROLPH ST	94112	19-G2
1	S HILL BLVD	94112	19-G2
80	NAYLOR ST	94112	19-G2
170	CORDOVA ST	94112	19-G2
230	DRAKE ST	94112	19-F2
400	PRAGUE ST	94112	19-F2
WINDSOR PL			**SF**
1	GREEN ST	94133	3-A4
WINFIELD ST			**SF**
1	COSO AV	94110	14-J5
100	ESMERALDA AV	94110	14-J5
200	VIRGINIA AV	94110	14-J5
300	EUGENIA AV	94110	14-H5
400	CORTLAND AV	94110	14-H5
WINN WY			**SF**
	DEWITT RD	94129	2-E4
	TRUBY ST	94129	2-E4
WINSTON DR			**SF**
1	JUNIPERO SERRA BLVD	94132	13-C7
20	BROADMOOR DR	94132	13-C7
70	STONECREST DR	94132	13-B7
100	19TH AV	94132	13-B7
150	20TH AV	94132	13-B7
330	BUCKINGHAM WY	94132	13-B7
500	LAKE MERCED BLVD	94132	13-A7
WINTER PL			**SF**
1	MASON ST	94133	2-J4
100	AUGUSTA AL	94133	3-A4
WINTHROP ST			**SF**
1	LOMBARD ST	94133	3-A3
100	CHESTNUT ST	94133	3-A3
WISCONSIN ST			**SF**
1	8TH ST	94107	11-B2
1	8TH ST	94103	11-B2
100	16TH ST	94107	11-B2
200	17TH ST	94107	11-B2
500	19TH ST	94107	11-B2
600	20TH ST	94107	11-B2
800	22ND ST	94107	11-B3
920	MADERA ST	94107	11-B3
1000	23RD ST	94107	11-B3
1070	CORAL RD	94107	11-B3
1080	CONNECTICUT ST	94107	11-B3
1170	CAROLINA ST	94107	11-B3
1190	25TH ST	94107	11-B4
1200	25TH ST	94107	11-B4
1260	BLAIR TER	94107	11-B4
1300	26TH ST	94107	11-B4
WISSER CT			**SF**
	WRIGHT LP	94129	1-C4
WOOD ST			**SF**
1	LUPINE AV	94118	6-E6
50	DICHA AL	94118	6-E6
100	GEARY BLVD	94118	6-E6
200	ANZA ST	94118	6-E6
WOODACRE DR			**SF**
60	JUNIPERO SERRA BLVD	94132	13-C6
100	OCEAN AV	94132	13-C6
WOODHAVEN CT			**SF**
1	FOREST KNOLLS DR	94131	9-E3
WOODLAND AV			**SF**
1	PARNASSUS AV	94117	9-E2
200	WILLARD ST	94117	9-E2
WOODSIDE AV			**SF**
1	DEWEY BLVD	94116	13-D4
1	DEWEY BLVD	94127	13-D4
1	LAGUNA HONDA BLVD	94127	13-D4
30	LAGUNA HONDA BLVD	94116	13-D4
30	LAGUNA HONDA BLVD	94127	13-D4
120	VASQUEZ AV	94116	13-D4
120	VASQUEZ AV	94127	13-D4
160	BALCETA AV	94116	13-D4
160	BALCETA AV	94127	13-D4
200	HERNANDEZ AV	94116	13-E4
200	HERNANDEZ AV	94127	13-E4
240	IDORA AV	94116	13-E4
240	IDORA AV	94127	13-E4
280	ULLOA ST	94131	13-E4
280	ULLOA ST	94127	13-E4
400	OSHAUGHNESSY BLVD	94131	13-E4
400	OSHAUGHNESSY BLVD	94127	13-E4
400	PORTOLA DR	94127	13-E4
WOODWARD ST			**SF**
1	DUBOCE AV	94103	10-H1
100	14TH ST	94103	10-H1
WOOL CT			**SF**
	UPTON AV	94129	1-C4
WOOL ST			**SF**
1	POWHATTAN AV	94110	14-J5
100	EUGENIA AV	94110	14-J5
200	CORTLAND AV	94110	14-J5
WOOLSEY ST			**SF**
100	SAN BRUNO AV	94134	15-A7
200	GIRARD ST	94134	15-A7
300	BRUSSELS ST	94134	15-A7
400	GOETTINGEN ST	94134	15-A7
500	SOMERSET ST	94134	15-A7
600	HOLYOKE ST	94134	15-A7
700	HAMILTON ST	94134	15-A7
800	BOWDOIN ST	94134	14-J7
870	DARTMOUTH ST	94134	14-J7
930	COLBY ST	94134	19-J1
1000	UNIVERSITY ST	94134	19-J1
WORCESTER AV			**SF**
1	ALEMANY BLVD	94132	18-C2
1	ARCH ST	94132	18-C2
100	RAMSELL ST	94132	18-C2
100	PALMETTO AV	94132	18-C2
WORDEN ST			**SF**
1	FRANCISCO ST	94133	3-A3
WORTH ST			**SF**
1	21ST ST	94114	10-F3
100	22ND ST	94114	10-F3
WRIGHT LP			**SF**
1330	WISSER CT	94129	1-C4
1330	HITCHCOCK ST	94129	1-C4
1330	UPTON AV	94129	1-C4
WRIGHT ST			**SF**
1	MONTCALM ST	94110	15-A4
1	YORK ST	94110	15-A4
100	HOLLADAY AV	94110	15-A4
WYMAN AV			**SF**
	14TH AV	94129	5-C5
	WEDEMEYER ST	94129	5-C5
	BROWN ST	94129	5-C5
	BELLES ST	94129	5-C5
WYTON LN			**SF**
1	JUNIPERO SERRA BLVD	94132	13-C7
30	STRATFORD DR	94132	13-B7
60	DENSLOW DR	94132	13-B7
200	19TH AV	94132	13-B7
Y			
YACHT RD			**SF**
	PEDESTRIAN WY	94123	2-F3
YALE ST			**SF**
1	SILVER AV	94134	14-J7
160	SILLIMAN ST	94134	14-J7
330	FELTON ST	94134	14-J7
500	WAYLAND ST	94134	19-J1
YERBA BUENA AV			**SF**
1	SANTA CLARA AV	94127	13-C5
1	SANTA MONICA WY	94127	13-C5
100	TERRACE WK	94127	13-D5
100	SANTA PAULA AV	94127	13-D5
150	SAN PABLO AV	94127	13-D6
200	MAYWOOD DR	94127	13-D6
230	MIRALOMA DR	94127	13-D6
250	RAVENWOOD DR	94127	13-D6
250	BAXTER AL	94127	13-D6
300	CASITAS AV	94127	13-D6
300	HAZELWOOD AV	94127	13-D6
350	BRENTWOOD AV	94127	13-D6
400	SAINT ELMO WY	94127	13-D6
400	PLYMOUTH AV	94127	13-D6
500	MONTEREY BLVD	94127	13-D6
YORBA ST			**SF**
2200	CRESTLAKE DR	94132	13-A6
2200	CRESTLAKE DR	94116	13-A6
2300	34TH AV	94132	13-A6
2300	34TH AV	94116	13-A6
2400	35TH AV	94132	12-J6
2400	35TH AV	94116	12-J6
2500	36TH AV	94132	12-J6
2500	36TH AV	94116	12-J6
2550	SUNSET BLVD	94132	12-J6
2550	SUNSET BLVD	94116	12-J6
2600	37TH AV	94132	12-J6
2600	37TH AV	94116	12-J6
2700	38TH AV	94132	12-J6
2700	38TH AV	94116	12-J6
2800	39TH AV	94132	12-J6
2800	39TH AV	94116	12-J6
2900	40TH AV	94132	12-J6
2900	40TH AV	94116	12-J6
2950	YORBA LN	94132	12-J6
2950	YORBA LN	94116	12-J6
YORK ST			**SF**
500	MARIPOSA ST	94110	11-A2
600	18TH ST	94110	11-A2
700	19TH ST	94110	11-A2
700	BRYANT ST	94110	11-A2
800	20TH ST	94110	11-A3
800	BRYANT ST	94110	11-A3
900	21ST ST	94110	11-A3
1000	22ND ST	94110	11-A3
1100	23RD ST	94110	11-A3
1200	24TH ST	94110	11-A3
1300	25TH ST	94110	11-A4
1400	26TH ST	94110	11-A4
1500	CESAR CHAVEZ ST	94110	11-A4
1500	PRECITA AV	94110	11-A4
1500	CESAR CHAVEZ ST	94110	15-A4
1500	PRECITA AV	94110	15-A4
1600	PERALTA AV	94110	15-A4
1650	MONTCALM ST	94110	15-A4
1650	WRIGHT ST	94110	15-A4
1700	HOLLADAY AV	94110	15-A4
YOSEMITE AV			**SF**
1300	HAWES ST	94124	15-C7
1340	INGALLS ST	94124	15-C7
1450	JENNINGS ST	94124	15-C7
1570	KEITH ST	94124	15-B7
1660	3RD ST	94124	15-B7
1660	LANE ST	94124	15-B7
1680	MENDELL ST	94124	15-B7
YOUNG CT			**SF**
1	WHITNEY YOUNG CIR	94124	15-C6
YOUNG ST			**SF**
	HALLECK ST	94129	1-E3
YUKON ST			**SF**
1	CASELLI AV	94114	10-F2
50	19TH ST	94114	10-F3
100	EAGLE ST	94114	10-F3
140	SHORT ST	94114	10-F3
Z			
ZAMPA LN			**SF**
1	BUCHANAN ST	94115	6-G6
ZENO PL			**SF**
1	FOLSOM ST	94105	7-C6
ZIRCON PL			**SF**
1	29TH ST	94131	14-G5
ZOE ST			**SF**
1	BRYANT ST	94107	7-B7
30	WELSH ST	94107	7-B7
70	FREELON ST	94107	7-B7
100	BRANNAN ST	94107	7-B7
#			
1ST ST			**SF**
1	BUSH ST	94105	7-B5
1	MARKET ST	94105	7-B5
40	STEVENSON ST	94105	7-B5
50	JESSIE ST	94105	7-B5
60	ELIM AL	94105	7-B5
100	MISSION ST	94105	7-B5
140	MINNA ST	94105	7-B5
170	NATOMA ST	94105	7-B5
200	HOWARD ST	94105	7-B6
220	TEHAMA ST	94105	7-B6
230	SAINT TENNY PL	94105	7-B6
260	CLEMENTINA ST	94105	7-B6
300	FOLSOM ST	94105	7-B6
370	GUY PL	94105	7-B6
390	LANSING ST	94105	7-B6
400	HARRISON ST	94105	7-C6
2ND AV			**SF**
100	LAKE ST	94118	5-D6
180	CALIFORNIA ST	94118	5-D6
200	CORNWALL ST	94118	5-D6
300	CLEMENT ST	94118	5-D6
400	GEARY BLVD	94118	5-D6
500	ANZA ST	94118	5-D7
600	BALBOA ST	94118	5-D7
700	CABRILLO ST	94118	5-D7
800	FULTON ST	94118	5-D7
1200	LINCOLN WY	94122	9-D1
1250	HUGO ST	94122	9-D2
1300	IRVING ST	94122	9-D2
2ND ST			**SF**
1	MARKET ST	94105	7-B5
40	STEVENSON ST	94105	7-B5
70	JESSIE ST	94105	7-B6
100	MISSION ST	94105	7-B6
130	MINNA ST	94105	7-B6
170	NATOMA ST	94105	7-B6
200	HOWARD ST	94105	7-B6
220	TEHAMA ST	94105	7-B6
260	CLEMENTINA ST	94105	7-B6
300	FOLSOM ST	94105	7-B6
300	FOLSOM ST	94107	7-B6
340	DOW PL	94105	7-B6
340	DOW PL	94107	7-B6
400	HARRISON ST	94105	7-B6
400	HARRISON ST	94107	7-B6
460	STILLMAN ST	94107	7-B6
500	BRYANT ST	94107	7-B6
510	TABER PL	94107	7-B6
520	FEDERAL ST	94107	7-C6
550	S PARK AV	94107	7-C6
570	DE BOOM ST	94107	7-C6
600	BRANNAN ST	94107	7-C7
700	TOWNSEND ST	94107	7-C7
750	KING ST	94107	7-C7
760	KING ST	94107	7-C7
800	BERRY ST	94107	7-C7
3RD AV			**SF**
100	LAKE ST	94118	5-D6
180	CALIFORNIA ST	94118	5-D6
200	CORNWALL ST	94118	5-D6
300	CLEMENT ST	94118	5-D6
400	GEARY BLVD	94118	5-D6
500	ANZA ST	94118	5-D7
600	BALBOA ST	94118	5-D7
700	CABRILLO ST	94118	5-D7
800	FULTON ST	94118	5-D7
1200	LINCOLN WY	94122	9-D1
1200	KEZAR DR	94122	9-D1
1250	HUGO ST	94122	9-D2
1300	IRVING ST	94143	9-D2
1300	IRVING ST	94122	9-D2
1400	PARNASSUS AV	94143	9-D2
1400	PARNASSUS AV	94122	9-D2
700	I ST	94124	20-E1
700	MANSEAU ST	94124	20-E1
900	J ST	94124	20-E1
3RD ST			**SF**
1	AVENUE OF THE PALMS	94130	3-E1
100	AVENUE B	94130	3-E1
1	MARKET ST	94103	7-A6
	KEARNY ST	94103	7-A6
	MARKET ST	94103	7-A6
40	STEVENSON ST	94103	7-A6
70	JESSIE ST	94103	7-A6
100	MISSION ST	94103	7-B6
130	MINNA ST	94103	7-B6
150	MASSET PL	94103	7-B6
200	HOWARD ST	94103	7-B6
260	CLEMENTINA ST	94103	7-B6
300	FOLSOM ST	94107	7-B6
350	SAINT FRANCIS PL	94107	7-B6
400	HARRISON ST	94107	7-B6
440	PERRY ST	94107	7-B6
470	STILLMAN ST	94107	7-B6
500	BRYANT ST	94107	7-B7
510	TABER PL	94107	7-B7
550	S PARK AV	94107	7-B7
570	VARNEY PL	94107	7-B7
600	BRANNAN ST	94107	7-B7
700	TOWNSEND ST	94107	7-C7
800	KING ST	94107	7-C7
810	KING ST	94107	7-C7
840	BERRY ST	94107	7-C7
960	TERRY A FRANCOIS BLVD	94107	7-C7
1220	4TH ST	94107	11-C1
1220	MISSION ROCK ST	94107	11-C1
1900	16TH ST	94107	11-C2
1950	17TH ST	94107	11-C2
1900	MARIPOSA ST	94107	11-C2
2000	18TH ST	94107	11-C2
2200	19TH ST	94107	11-C2
2210	20TH ST	94107	11-C3
2430	22ND ST	94107	11-C3
2650	23RD ST	94107	11-C3
2760	24TH ST	94107	11-C3
2870	25TH ST	94107	11-C4
2980	26TH ST	94107	11-C4
3100	CESAR CHAVEZ ST	94124	11-C4
3200	MARIN ST	94124	15-C4
	TULARE ST	94124	15-C4
3430	ARTHUR AV	94124	15-C4
3430	CARGO WY	94124	15-C4
3500	BURKE ST	94124	15-C5
3600	CUSTER AV	94124	15-C5
3600	PHELPS ST	94124	15-C5
3700	DAVIDSON AV	94124	15-C5
3800	EVANS AV	94124	15-C5
3900	FAIRFAX AV	94124	15-C5
4000	GALVEZ AV	94124	15-C5
4100	HUDSON AV	94124	15-C5
4200	INNES AV	94124	15-C5
4250	NEWHALL ST	94124	15-C5
4300	JERROLD AV	94124	15-C5
4400	KIRKWOOD AV	94124	15-C6
4500	LA SALLE AV	94124	15-C6
4600	MCKINNON AV	94124	15-C6
4700	NEWCOMB AV	94124	15-C6
4800	OAKDALE AV	94124	15-C6
4900	PALOU AV	94124	15-C6
4900	MENDELL ST	94124	15-C6
5000	QUESADA AV	94124	15-C6
5100	BAYVIEW ST	94124	15-B6
5100	REVERE AV	94124	15-B6
5140	SHAFTER AV	94124	15-B6
5180	THOMAS AV	94124	15-B6
5200	THORNTON AV	94124	15-B7
5240	UNDERWOOD AV	94124	15-B7
5300	WILLIAMS AV	94124	15-B7
5300	VAN DYKE AV	94124	15-B7
5380	LANE ST	94124	15-B7
5400	LANE ST	94124	15-B7
5400	WALLACE AV	94124	15-B7
5500	YOSEMITE AV	94124	15-B7
5600	ARMSTRONG AV	94124	15-B7
5700	BANCROFT AV	94124	15-B7
5800	CARROLL AV	94124	15-B7
5830	DONNER AV	94124	15-B7
5870	EGBERT AV	94124	15-B7
5900	FITZGERALD AV	94124	20-B1
6000	PAUL AV	94124	20-B1
6000	GILMAN AV	94124	20-B1
6100	HOLLISTER AV	94124	20-B1
6200	INGERSON AV	94124	20-B1
6210	SALINAS AV	94124	20-B1
	JAMESTOWN AV	94124	20-B1
	BAYSHORE BLVD	94134	20-B1
6300	JAMESTOWN AV	94124	20-B1
6400	KEY AV	94124	20-B1
6500	LE CONTE AV	94124	20-B1
6500	KEITH ST	94124	20-B1
	MEADE AV	94124	20-B1
4TH AV			**SF**
100	LAKE ST	94118	5-D6
180	CALIFORNIA ST	94118	5-D6
200	CORNWALL ST	94118	5-D6
300	CLEMENT ST	94118	5-D6
400	GEARY BLVD	94118	5-D6
500	ANZA ST	94118	5-D7
600	BALBOA ST	94118	5-D7
700	CABRILLO ST	94118	5-D7
800	FULTON ST	94118	5-D7
1200	LINCOLN WY	94122	9-D1
1250	HUGO ST	94122	9-D2
1300	IRVING ST	94122	9-D2
1400	PARNASSUS AV	94143	9-D2
1500	KIRKHAM ST	94143	9-D2
4TH ST			**SF**
1	AVENUE C	94130	3-E1
1	ELLIS ST	94103	7-A6
1	MARKET ST	94103	7-A6
20	STEVENSON ST	94103	7-A6
70	JESSIE ST	94103	7-A6
100	MISSION ST	94103	7-A6
130	MINNA ST	94103	7-A6
200	HOWARD ST	94103	7-A6
260	CLEMENTINA ST	94103	7-B6
300	FOLSOM ST	94107	7-B6
330	SHIPLEY ST	94107	7-B6
360	CLARA ST	94107	7-B7
400	HARRISON ST	94107	7-B7
430	PERRY ST	94107	7-B7
470	STILLMAN ST	94107	7-B7
500	BRYANT ST	94107	7-B7
530	WELSH ST	94107	7-B7
570	FREELON ST	94107	7-B7
600	BRANNAN ST	94107	7-B7
650	BLUXOME ST	94107	7-B7
700	TOWNSEND ST	94107	7-B7
800	KING ST	94107	7-B7
840	BERRY ST	94107	7-B7
900	CHANNEL ST	94107	7-C7
1300	3RD ST	94107	11-C1
1300	MISSION ROCK ST	94107	11-C1
1330	ILLINOIS ST	94107	11-C1
5TH AV			**SF**
100	LAKE ST	94118	5-D6
190	CALIFORNIA ST	94118	5-D6
200	CORNWALL ST	94118	5-D6
300	CLEMENT ST	94118	5-D6
400	GEARY BLVD	94118	5-D6
500	ANZA ST	94118	5-D7
600	BALBOA ST	94118	5-D7
700	CABRILLO ST	94118	5-D7
800	FULTON ST	94118	5-D7
1200	LINCOLN WY	94122	9-D1
1250	HUGO ST	94122	9-D2

Address	Cross Street	ZIP	City Pg-Grid
5TH AV			SF
1300	IRVING ST	94122	9-D2
1400	JUDAH ST	94143	9-D2
1400	JUDAH ST	94122	9-D2
1400	PARNASSUS AV	94122	9-D2
1500	KIRKHAM ST	94143	9-D2
1500	KIRKHAM ST	94122	9-D2
5TH ST			SF
1	CYRIL MAGIN ST	94103	7-A6
1	MARKET ST	94103	7-A6
30	STEVENSON ST	94103	7-A6
60	JESSIE ST	94103	7-A6
70	JESSIE ST	94103	7-A6
100	MISSION ST	94103	7-A6
130	MINNA ST	94103	7-A6
170	NATOMA ST	94103	7-A6
200	HOWARD ST	94103	7-A6
230	TEHAMA ST	94103	7-A7
260	CLEMENTINA ST	94103	7-A7
300	FOLSOM ST	94107	7-A7
330	SHIPLEY ST	94107	7-A7
370	CLARA ST	94107	7-A7
400	HARRISON ST	94107	7-B7
510	BRYANT ST	94107	7-B7
540	WELSH ST	94107	7-B7
600	BRANNAN ST	94107	7-B7
640	BLUXOME ST	94107	7-B7
700	TOWNSEND ST	94107	7-B7
800	KING ST	94107	7-B7
900	BERRY ST	94107	11-B1
6TH AV			SF
100	LAKE ST	94118	5-D6
190	CALIFORNIA ST	94118	5-D6
200	CORNWALL ST	94118	5-D6
300	CLEMENT ST	94118	5-D6
400	GEARY BLVD	94118	5-D6
500	ANZA ST	94118	5-D7
600	BALBOA ST	94118	5-D7
700	CABRILLO ST	94118	5-D7
800	FULTON ST	94118	5-D7
1200	LINCOLN WY	94122	9-D1
1250	HUGO ST	94122	9-D2
1300	IRVING ST	94122	9-D2
1400	JUDAH ST	94122	9-D2
1500	KIRKHAM ST	94122	9-D2
1500	LOCKSLEY AV	94122	9-D2
1300	SPEAR AV	94124	15-E7
1600	J ST	94124	20-D1
6TH ST			SF
1	GOLDEN GATE AV	94103	7-A6
1	MARKET ST	94103	7-A6
40	STEVENSON ST	94103	7-A6
60	JESSIE ST	94103	7-A6
100	MISSION ST	94103	7-A7
130	MINNA ST	94103	7-A7
160	NATOMA ST	94103	7-A7
200	HOWARD ST	94103	7-A7
230	TEHAMA ST	94103	7-A7
260	CLEMENTINA ST	94103	7-A7
300	FOLSOM ST	94107	7-A7
300	FOLSOM ST	94103	7-A7
330	SHIPLEY ST	94107	7-A7
330	SHIPLEY ST	94103	7-A7
360	CLARA ST	94107	7-A7
360	CLARA ST	94103	7-A7
400	HARRISON ST	94107	7-A7
400	HARRISON ST	94103	7-A7
450	AHERN WY	94107	7-A7
450	AHERN WY	94103	7-A7
500	BRYANT ST	94107	7-B7
500	BRYANT ST	94103	7-B7
600	BRANNAN ST	94107	7-B7
600	BRANNAN ST	94103	7-B7
600	BLUXOME ST	94107	7-B7
600	BLUXOME ST	94103	7-B7
700	TOWNSEND ST	94107	11-B1
700	TOWNSEND ST	94103	11-B1
1000	CHANNEL ST	94107	11-B1
1700	16TH ST	94107	11-C1
7TH AV			SF
100	LAKE ST	94118	5-D6
190	CALIFORNIA ST	94118	5-D6
200	CORNWALL ST	94118	5-D6
300	CLEMENT ST	94118	5-D6
400	GEARY BLVD	94118	5-D6
500	ANZA ST	94118	5-D7
600	BALBOA ST	94118	5-D7
700	CABRILLO ST	94118	5-D7
800	FULTON ST	94118	5-D7
	MARTIN LUTHER KING JR DR	-	9-D1
	BOWLING GREEN DR	-	9-D1
1200	LINCOLN WY	94122	9-D1
1250	HUGO ST	94122	9-D2
1300	IRVING ST	94122	9-D2
1400	JUDAH ST	94122	9-D2
1500	KIRKHAM ST	94122	9-D2
1600	LAWTON ST	94122	9-D3
1700	LAGUNA HONDA BLVD	94131	9-D3
1700	LAGUNA HONDA BLVD	94116	9-D3
7TH ST			SF
	MCALLISTER ST	94102	6-J7
1	MARKET ST	94103	6-J7
40	STEVENSON ST	94103	6-J7
80	JESSIE ST	94103	6-J7
100	MISSION ST	94103	7-A7
130	MINNA ST	94103	7-A7
170	NATOMA ST	94103	7-A7
200	HOWARD ST	94103	7-A7
300	FOLSOM ST	94103	7-A7
310	DECKER AL	94103	7-A7
340	CLEVELAND ST	94103	7-A7
400	HARRISON ST	94103	7-A7
500	BRYANT ST	94103	7-A7
	BRANNAN ST	94103	11-A1
700	TOWNSEND ST	94103	11-B1
800	KING ST	94107	11-B1
900	BERRY ST	94107	11-B1
1000	CHANNEL ST	94107	11-B1
1100	HOOPER ST	94107	11-B1
1200	IRWIN ST	94107	11-B1
1300	HUBBELL ST	94107	11-B1
1400	DAGGETT ST	94107	11-B1
1500	16TH ST	94107	11-B1
1500	MISSISSIPPI ST	94107	11-B1
8TH AV			SF
100	LAKE ST	94118	5-C6
200	CALIFORNIA ST	94118	5-C6
300	CLEMENT ST	94118	5-C6
400	GEARY BLVD	94118	5-C6
500	ANZA ST	94118	5-C7
600	BALBOA ST	94118	5-C7
700	CABRILLO ST	94118	5-D7
	FULTON ST	94118	5-D7
	JOHN F KENNEDY DR	94118	9-D1
1200	LINCOLN WY	94122	9-D2
1300	IRVING ST	94122	9-D2
1400	JUDAH ST	94122	9-D2
1500	KIRKHAM ST	94122	9-D2
1600	LAWTON ST	94122	9-D3
1700	MORAGA ST	94122	9-D3
1800	NORIEGA ST	94122	9-D3
1900	ORTEGA ST	94116	9-D3
1930	LINARES AV	94116	9-D3
	LINARES AV	94116	9-D3
2100	PACHECO ST	94116	9-D4
8TH ST			SF
1	HYDE ST	94103	6-J7
1	MARKET ST	94103	6-J7
40	STEVENSON ST	94103	6-J7
100	MISSION ST	94103	6-J7
140	MINNA ST	94103	6-J7
170	NATOMA ST	94103	6-J7
200	HOWARD ST	94103	6-J7
300	TEHAMA ST	94103	7-A7
320	CLEMENTINA ST	94103	7-A7
340	FOLSOM ST	94103	7-A7
360	RINGOLD ST	94103	7-A7
370	HERON ST	94103	7-A7
	HARRISON ST	94103	11-A1
	BRANNAN ST	94103	11-A1
500	BRYANT ST	94103	11-A1
500	BRANNAN ST	94103	11-A1
600	BRANNAN ST	94103	11-A1
690	TOWNSEND ST	94103	11-A1
700	DIVISION ST	94103	11-A1
1200	15TH ST	94107	11-B1
1200	15TH ST	94103	11-B1
1200	CAROLINA ST	94103	11-B1
1220	HOOPER ST	94107	11-B1
1220	HOOPER ST	94103	11-B1
1250	WISCONSIN ST	94107	11-B1
1260	IRWIN ST	94107	11-B2
1300	16TH ST	94107	11-B2
9TH AV			SF
100	LAKE ST	94118	5-C6
200	CALIFORNIA ST	94118	5-C6
300	CLEMENT ST	94118	5-C6
400	GEARY BLVD	94118	5-C6
500	ANZA ST	94118	5-C7
600	BALBOA ST	94118	5-C7
700	CABRILLO ST	94118	5-C7
760	GRANAT CT	94118	5-C7
800	FULTON ST	94118	5-C7
1200	LINCOLN WY	94122	9-C2
1200	MARTIN LUTHER KING JR DR	94122	9-C2
1300	IRVING ST	94122	9-C2
1400	JUDAH ST	94122	9-C2
1500	KIRKHAM ST	94122	9-C2
1600	LAWTON ST	94122	9-C3
1700	MORAGA ST	94122	9-C3
1800	NORIEGA ST	94122	9-C3
1900	ORTEGA ST	94116	9-C3
2000	PACHECO ST	94116	9-C4
2030	ALTON AV	94116	9-C4
2100	SOTELO AV	94116	9-D4
2150	MENDOSA AV	94116	9-D4
2200	MESA AV	94116	9-C4
2400	12TH AV	94116	9-C4
9TH ST			SF
1	AVENUE E	94130	3-E1
1	AVENUE D	94130	3-E1
1	AVENUE B	94130	3-E1
100	AVENUE OF THE PALMS	94130	3-E1
1	HAYES ST	94103	6-J7
1	LARKIN ST	94103	6-J7
1	MARKET ST	94103	6-J7
60	JESSIE ST	94103	6-J7
100	MISSION ST	94103	6-J7
140	MINNA ST	94103	6-J7
160	NATOMA ST	94103	6-J7
200	HOWARD ST	94103	6-J7
230	TEHAMA ST	94103	6-J7
260	CLEMENTINA ST	94103	6-J7
300	FOLSOM ST	94103	10-J1
330	RINGOLD ST	94103	10-J1
360	SHERIDAN ST	94103	11-A1
400	HARRISON ST	94103	11-A1
460	MCLEA CT	94103	11-A1
490	BRYANT ST	94103	11-A1
600	BRANNAN ST	94103	11-A1
700	SAN BRUNO AV	94103	11-A1
700	DIVISION ST	94103	11-A1
10TH AV			SF
100	LAKE ST	94118	5-C6
200	CALIFORNIA ST	94118	5-C6
300	CLEMENT ST	94118	5-C6
400	GEARY BLVD	94118	5-C6
500	ANZA ST	94118	5-C7
600	BALBOA ST	94118	5-C7
700	CABRILLO ST	94118	5-C7
	FULTON ST	94118	5-C7
	JOHN F KENNEDY DR	94118	9-C1
1200	LINCOLN WY	94122	9-C1
1300	IRVING ST	94122	9-C2
1400	JUDAH ST	94122	9-C2
1500	KIRKHAM ST	94122	9-C2
1600	LAWTON ST	94122	9-C3
1700	MORAGA ST	94122	9-C3
1800	NORIEGA ST	94122	9-C3
1900	ORTEGA ST	94116	9-C3
2000	PACHECO ST	94116	9-C4
2100	QUINTARA ST	94116	9-C4
2200	MENDOSA AV	94116	9-C4
10TH ST			SF
1	MARKET ST	94103	6-J7
1	POLK ST	94103	6-J7
40	STEVENSON ST	94103	6-J7
60	JESSIE ST	94103	6-J7
70	JESSIE ST	94103	6-J7
100	MISSION ST	94103	6-J7
150	MINNA ST	94103	6-J7
160	NATOMA ST	94103	6-J7
240	HOWARD ST	94103	6-J7
280	FOLSOM ST	94103	10-J1
340	SHERIDAN ST	94103	10-J1
380	HARRISON ST	94103	10-J1
500	BRYANT ST	94103	11-A1
560	DIVISION ST	94103	11-A1
560	POTRERO AV	94103	11-A1
11TH AV			SF
100	LAKE ST	94118	5-C6
200	CALIFORNIA ST	94118	5-C6
300	CLEMENT ST	94118	5-C6
400	GEARY BLVD	94118	5-C6
500	ANZA ST	94118	5-C7
600	BALBOA ST	94118	5-C7
700	CABRILLO ST	94118	5-C7
800	FULTON ST	94118	5-C7
1200	LINCOLN WY	94122	9-C1
1300	IRVING ST	94122	9-C2
1400	JUDAH ST	94122	9-C2
1500	KIRKHAM ST	94122	9-C2
1600	LAWTON ST	94122	9-C3
1700	MORAGA ST	94122	9-C3
1800	NORIEGA ST	94122	9-C3
1900	ORTEGA ST	94122	9-C3
2000	PACHECO ST	94116	9-C3
11TH ST			SF
1	MARKET ST	94103	6-J7
100	MISSION ST	94103	6-J7
150	MINNA ST	94103	6-J7
170	NATOMA ST	94103	10-J1
200	HOWARD ST	94103	10-J1
240	KISSLING ST	94103	10-J1
270	BURNS PL	94103	10-J1
300	FOLSOM ST	94103	10-J1
400	HARRISON ST	94103	10-J1
	BRYANT ST	94103	11-A1
12TH AV			SF
100	LAKE ST	94118	5-C6
200	CALIFORNIA ST	94118	5-C6
300	CLEMENT ST	94118	5-C6
400	GEARY BLVD	94118	5-C6
500	ANZA ST	94118	5-C7
600	BALBOA ST	94118	5-C7
700	CABRILLO ST	94118	5-C7
800	FULTON ST	94118	5-C7
1200	LINCOLN WY	94122	9-C2
1300	IRVING ST	94122	9-C2
1400	JUDAH ST	94122	9-C2
1500	KIRKHAM ST	94122	9-C2
1600	LAWTON ST	94122	9-C3
1700	MORAGA ST	94122	9-C3
1800	NORIEGA ST	94122	9-C3
1900	PACHECO ST	94116	9-C3
2000	ROCKRIDGE DR	94116	9-C3
2000	FUNSTON AV	94116	9-C3
2000	ROCKRIDGE DR	94116	9-C4
2080	ROCKRIDGE DR	94116	9-C4
2100	QUINTARA ST	94116	9-C4
2200	9TH AV	94116	9-C4
2350	MAGELLAN AV	94116	13-C4
2400	TARAVAL ST	94116	13-C4
12TH ST			SF
1	MARKET ST	94103	6-J7
70	STEVENSON ST	94103	6-J7
100	MISSION ST	94103	10-J1
100	OTIS ST	94103	10-J1
100	S VAN NESS AV	94103	10-J1
200	HOWARD ST	94103	10-J1
250	KISSLING ST	94103	10-J1
300	FOLSOM ST	94103	10-J1
330	ISIS ST	94103	10-J1
370	BERNICE ST	94103	10-J1
400	HARRISON ST	94103	10-J1
14TH AV			SF
	WYMAN AV	94129	5-C5
	WEDEMEYER ST	94129	5-C5
1	PACIFIC AV	94118	5-C6
100	LAKE ST	94118	5-C6
200	CALIFORNIA ST	94118	5-C6
300	CLEMENT ST	94118	5-C6
400	GEARY BLVD	94118	5-C6
500	ANZA ST	94118	5-C7
600	BALBOA ST	94118	5-C7
700	CABRILLO ST	94118	5-C7
800	FULTON ST	94118	5-C7
1200	LINCOLN WY	94122	9-C2
1300	IRVING ST	94122	9-C2
1400	JUDAH ST	94122	9-C2
1500	KIRKHAM ST	94122	9-C2
1500	LURLINE ST	94122	9-C2
1650	15TH AV	94122	9-C3
1720	NORIEGA ST	94122	9-C3
1750	NORIEGA ST	94122	9-C3
1780	ORTEGA ST	94116	9-C3
1780	ORTEGA ST	94122	9-C3
1910	PACHECO ST	94116	9-C3
1980	RADIO TER	94116	9-C3
2050	FANNING WY	94116	9-C4
2100	QUINTARA ST	94116	9-C4
2310	RIVERA ST	94116	13-C4
2420	SANTIAGO ST	94116	13-C4
2530	TARAVAL ST	94116	13-C5
2630	ULLOA ST	94116	13-C5
2740	VICENTE ST	94127	13-C5
2810	WAWONA ST	94127	13-C5
2850	W PORTAL AV	94127	13-C5
2900	PORTOLA DR	94127	13-C5
2900	SAN ANSELMO AV	94127	13-C5
14TH ST			SF
1	HARRISON ST	94103	10-J1
50	TRAINOR ST	94103	10-J1
100	FOLSOM ST	94103	10-J1
140	SHOTWELL ST	94103	10-J1
200	S VAN NESS AV	94103	10-J1
230	NATOMA ST	94103	10-J1
260	MINNA ST	94103	10-J1
300	MISSION ST	94103	10-H1
330	WOODWARD ST	94103	10-H1
350	JULIAN AV	94103	10-H1
350	STEVENSON ST	94103	10-H1
400	VALENCIA ST	94103	10-H1
500	GUERRERO ST	94103	10-H1
520	RAMONA ST	94103	10-H1
550	ROSEMONT PL	94103	10-H1
600	DOLORES ST	94114	10-H1
650	LANDERS ST	94114	10-H1
700	MARKET ST	94114	10-H1
710	CHURCH ST	94114	10-G1
750	BELCHER ST	94114	10-G1
770	BOYTON CT	94114	10-G1
800	SANCHEZ ST	94114	10-G1
850	WALTER ST	94114	10-G1
900	NOE ST	94114	10-G1
1000	CASTRO ST	94114	10-G1
1030	DIVISADERO ST	94114	10-G1
1030	DIVISADERO ST	94117	10-G1
1060	ROOSEVELT WY	94117	10-G1
1060	ALPINE TER	94117	10-G1
1100	BUENA VISTA TER	94117	10-G1
15TH AV			SF
	WEDEMEYER ST	94129	5-C5
100	LAKE ST	94118	5-C6
200	CALIFORNIA ST	94118	5-C6
300	CLEMENT ST	94118	5-C6
340	TACOMA ST	94118	5-C6
400	GEARY BLVD	94118	5-C7
500	ANZA ST	94118	5-C7
600	BALBOA ST	94118	5-C7
700	CABRILLO ST	94118	5-C7
800	FULTON ST	94118	5-C7
1200	LINCOLN WY	94122	9-C2
1300	IRVING ST	94122	9-C2
1400	JUDAH ST	94122	9-C2
1500	KIRKHAM ST	94122	9-C2
1550	LAWTON ST	94122	9-C2
1600	ALOHA AV	94122	9-C3
1620	ALOHA AV	94122	9-C3
1620	14TH AV	94122	9-C3
1750	NORIEGA ST	94122	9-C3
1750	SHELDON TER	94122	9-C3
1800	NORIEGA ST	94122	9-C3
1900	ORTEGA ST	94116	9-C3
2000	PACHECO ST	94116	9-C4
2100	QUINTARA ST	94116	9-C4
2100	FANNING WY	94116	9-C4
2200	RIVERA ST	94116	9-C4
2200	RIVERA ST	94116	13-C4
2300	SANTIAGO ST	94116	13-C4
2400	TARAVAL ST	94116	13-C5
2500	ULLOA ST	94116	13-C5
2600	VICENTE ST	94127	13-C5
2600	VICENTE ST	94116	13-C5
2700	WAWONA ST	94127	13-C5
2700	WAWONA ST	94132	13-C5
2800	W PORTAL AV	94127	13-C5
2900	PORTOLA DR	94127	13-C5
2900	SAN FERNANDO WY	94127	13-C5
15TH ST			SF
1	8TH ST	94103	11-B1
1	8TH ST	94107	11-B1
1	CAROLINA ST	94107	11-B1
100	DE HARO ST	94103	11-A1
200	RHODE ISLAND ST	94103	11-A1
300	KANSAS ST	94103	11-A1
400	VERMONT ST	94103	11-A1
500	SAN BRUNO AV	94103	11-A1
600	UTAH ST	94103	11-A1
700	POTRERO AV	94103	11-A1
800	HAMPSHIRE ST	94103	11-A1
1300	HARRISON ST	94103	10-J1
1400	FOLSOM ST	94103	10-J1
1450	SHOTWELL ST	94103	10-J1
1500	S VAN NESS AV	94103	10-J1
1530	NATOMA ST	94103	10-J1
1550	CAPP ST	94103	10-J1
1580	MINNA ST	94103	10-J1
1600	MISSION ST	94103	10-H1
1640	WIESE ST	94103	10-H1
1660	JULIAN AV	94103	10-H1
1680	CALEDONIA ST	94103	10-H1
1700	VALENCIA ST	94103	10-H1
1750	ALBION ST	94103	10-H1
1800	GUERRERO ST	94103	10-H1
1850	RAMONA ST	94103	10-H1
1900	DOLORES ST	94114	10-H1
1950	LANDERS ST	94114	10-H2
2000	CHURCH ST	94114	10-G2
2050	SHARON ST	94114	10-G2
2070	MARKET ST	94114	10-G2
2100	SANCHEZ ST	94114	10-G2
2200	NOE ST	94114	10-G2
2300	CASTRO ST	94114	10-G2
2400	BEAVER ST	94114	10-G2
2500	BUENA VISTA TER	94114	10-F1
2500	BUENA VISTA TER	94117	10-F1
2600	ROOSEVELT WY	94114	10-F1
2600	ROOSEVELT WY	94117	10-F1
2600	PARK HILL AV	94117	10-F1
1000	BRYANT ST	94103	11-A1
1050	FLORIDA ST	94103	10-J1
1200	ALABAMA ST	94103	10-J1
1250	TREAT AV	94103	10-J1
16TH AV			SF
100	LAKE ST	94118	5-C6
200	CALIFORNIA ST	94118	5-C6
300	CLEMENT ST	94118	5-C6
400	GEARY BLVD	94118	5-C7
500	ANZA ST	94118	5-C7
600	BALBOA ST	94118	5-C7
700	CABRILLO ST	94118	5-C7
800	FULTON ST	94118	5-C7
1200	LINCOLN WY	94122	9-C2
1300	IRVING ST	94122	9-C2
1400	JUDAH ST	94122	9-C2
1500	KIRKHAM ST	94122	9-C2
1520	LAWTON ST	94122	9-C2
1600	LAWTON ST	94122	9-C3
1650	LOMITA AV	94122	9-C3
1700	MORAGA ST	94122	9-C3
1750	NORIEGA ST	94122	9-C3
1800	NORIEGA ST	94122	9-C3
1900	ORTEGA ST	94116	9-C3
2000	PACHECO ST	94116	9-C4
2100	QUINTARA ST	94116	9-C4
2200	RIVERA ST	94116	13-C4
2300	SANTIAGO ST	94116	13-C4
2350	CECILIA AV	94116	13-C4
2400	TARAVAL ST	94116	13-C5
2500	ULLOA ST	94116	13-C5
2600	VICENTE ST	94116	13-C5
2700	WAWONA ST	94116	13-C5
16TH ST			SF
310	ILLINOIS ST	94107	11-C2
390	3RD ST	94107	11-C2
550	6TH ST	94107	11-C2
700	OWENS ST	94107	11-B2
910	MISSISSIPPI ST	94107	11-B2
910	7TH ST	94107	11-B2
1070	DAGGETT ST	94107	11-B2
1070	MISSOURI ST	94107	11-B2
1150	CONNECTICUT ST	94107	11-B2
1210	HUBBELL ST	94107	11-B2
1240	ARKANSAS ST	94107	11-B2
1270	8TH ST	94107	11-B2
1320	WISCONSIN ST	94107	11-B2
1320	WISCONSIN ST	94103	11-B2
1410	CAROLINA ST	94107	11-B2
1410	CAROLINA ST	94103	11-B2
1500	DE HARO ST	94103	11-A2
1600	RHODE ISLAND ST	94103	11-A2
1700	KANSAS ST	94103	11-A2
1800	VERMONT ST	94103	11-A2
1900	SAN BRUNO AV	94103	11-A2
2000	UTAH ST	94103	11-A2
2100	POTRERO AV	94103	11-A2
	BRYANT ST	94103	11-A2
	BRYANT ST	94110	11-A2
2500	FLORIDA ST	94110	10-J2
2500	FLORIDA ST	94103	10-J2
2600	ALABAMA ST	94110	10-J2
2600	ALABAMA ST	94103	10-J2
2700	HARRISON ST	94110	10-J2
2700	HARRISON ST	94103	10-J2
2700	TREAT AV	94110	10-J2
2700	TREAT AV	94103	10-J2
2800	FOLSOM ST	94110	10-J2
2800	FOLSOM ST	94103	10-J2
2850	SHOTWELL ST	94110	10-J2
2850	SHOTWELL ST	94103	10-J2
2900	S VAN NESS AV	94110	10-J2
2900	S VAN NESS AV	94103	10-J2
	CAPP ST	94110	10-J2
	CAPP ST	94103	10-J2
2950	CAPP ST	94110	10-J2
2950	CAPP ST	94103	10-J2
3000	MISSION ST	94110	10-H2
3000	MISSION ST	94103	10-H2
3030	WIESE ST	94110	10-H2

16TH ST — SF

Address	Cross Street	ZIP	City Pg-Grid
3030	WIESE ST	94103	10-H2
3030	HOFF ST	94110	10-H2
3030	HOFF ST	94103	10-H2
3050	JULIAN AV	94110	10-H2
3050	JULIAN AV	94103	10-H2
3060	RONDEL PL	94110	10-H2
3060	RONDEL PL	94103	10-H2
3070	CALEDONIA ST	94110	10-H2
3070	CALEDONIA ST	94103	10-H2
3100	VALENCIA ST	94110	10-H2
3100	VALENCIA ST	94103	10-H2
3150	ALBION ST	94110	10-H2
3150	ALBION ST	94103	10-H2
3160	ALBION ST	94110	10-H2
3160	ALBION ST	94103	10-H2
3200	GUERRERO ST	94110	10-H2
3200	GUERRERO ST	94103	10-H2
3230	SPENCER ST	94110	10-H2
3230	SPENCER ST	94103	10-H2
3300	DOLORES ST	94114	10-H2
3350	LANDERS ST	94114	10-H2
3400	CHURCH ST	94114	10-G2
3410	HARLOW ST	94114	10-G2
3450	SHARON ST	94114	10-G2
3460	DEHON ST	94114	10-G2
3500	SANCHEZ ST	94114	10-G2
3530	PROSPER ST	94114	10-G2
3570	POND ST	94114	10-G2
	MARKET ST	94114	10-G2
3600	NOE ST	94114	10-G2
3700	CASTRO ST	94114	10-G2
3800	FLINT ST	94114	10-G2

17TH AV — SF

Address	Cross Street	ZIP	City Pg-Grid
100	LAKE ST	94118	5-B6
100	LAKE ST	94121	5-B6
200	CALIFORNIA ST	94118	5-B6
200	CALIFORNIA ST	94121	5-B6
300	CLEMENT ST	94118	5-B6
300	CLEMENT ST	94121	5-B6
400	GEARY BLVD	94118	5-B7
400	GEARY BLVD	94121	5-B7
500	ANZA ST	94118	5-B7
500	ANZA ST	94121	5-B7
600	BALBOA ST	94118	5-B7
600	BALBOA ST	94121	5-B7
700	CABRILLO ST	94118	5-B7
700	CABRILLO ST	94121	5-B7
800	FULTON ST	94118	5-B7
800	FULTON ST	94121	5-B7
1200	LINCOLN WY	94122	9-B2
1300	IRVING ST	94122	9-B2
1400	JUDAH ST	94122	9-B2
1500	KIRKHAM ST	94122	9-B2
1600	LAWTON ST	94122	9-B3
1700	MORAGA ST	94122	9-C3
1800	NORIEGA ST	94122	9-C3
1900	ORTEGA ST	94116	9-C3
2000	PACHECO ST	94116	9-C4
2100	QUINTARA ST	94116	9-C4
2200	RIVERA ST	94116	13-C4
2300	SANTIAGO ST	94116	13-C4
2400	TARAVAL ST	94116	13-C5
2500	ULLOA ST	94116	13-C5
2600	VICENTE ST	94116	13-C5
2700	WAWONA ST	94116	13-C5

17TH ST — SF

Address	Cross Street	ZIP	City Pg-Grid
400	ILLINOIS ST	94107	11-C2
500	3RD ST	94107	11-C2
1000	PENNSYLVANIA AV	94107	11-B2
1100	MISSISSIPPI ST	94107	11-B2
1200	TEXAS ST	94107	11-B2
1300	MISSOURI ST	94107	11-B2
1400	CONNECTICUT ST	94107	11-B2
1500	ARKANSAS ST	94107	11-B2
1600	WISCONSIN ST	94107	11-B2
1700	CAROLINA ST	94107	11-B2
1800	DE HARO ST	94107	11-A2
1800	DE HARO ST	94103	11-A2
1900	RHODE ISLAND ST	94107	11-A2
1900	RHODE ISLAND ST	94103	11-A2
2010	KANSAS ST	94107	11-A2
2010	KANSAS ST	94103	11-A2
2100	VERMONT ST	94107	11-A2
2100	VERMONT ST	94103	11-A2
2200	SAN BRUNO AV	94110	11-A2
2200	SAN BRUNO AV	94103	11-A2
2300	UTAH ST	94110	11-A2
2300	UTAH ST	94103	11-A2
2400	POTRERO AV	94110	11-A2
2400	POTRERO AV	94103	11-A2
2500	HAMPSHIRE ST	94110	11-A2
	BRYANT ST	94110	11-A2
2800	FLORIDA ST	94110	10-J2
2900	ALABAMA ST	94110	10-J2
3000	HARRISON ST	94110	10-J2
3040	TREAT AV	94110	10-J2
3100	FOLSOM ST	94110	10-J2
3150	SHOTWELL ST	94110	10-J2
3200	S VAN NESS AV	94110	10-J2
	CAPP ST	94110	10-J2
3250	CAPP ST	94110	10-J2
3300	MISSION ST	94110	10-J2
3340	HOFF ST	94110	10-H2
3400	VALENCIA ST	94110	10-H2
3440	ALBION ST	94110	10-H2
3450	DEARBORN ST	94110	10-H2
3500	GUERRERO ST	94110	10-H2
3600	DOLORES ST	94114	10-H2
3640	ABBEY ST	94114	10-H2
3700	CHURCH ST	94114	10-G2
3800	SANCHEZ ST	94114	10-G2
3830	PROSPER ST	94114	10-G2
3860	POND ST	94114	10-G2
3900	NOE ST	94114	10-G2
3950	HARTFORD ST	94114	10-G2
4000	CASTRO ST	94114	10-G2
4050	COLLINGWOOD ST	94114	10-G2
4100	DIAMOND ST	94114	10-G2
4150	EUREKA ST	94114	10-F2
4200	CORBETT AV	94114	10-F2
4200	DOUGLASS ST	94114	10-F2
4300	ORD ST	94114	10-F2
4370	CORBIN PL	94114	10-F2
4400	TEMPLE ST	94114	10-F2
4450	MARS ST	94114	10-F2
4500	URANUS TER	94114	10-F2
4500	URANUS TER	94117	10-F2
4500	ROOSEVELT WY	94117	10-F2
4640	UPPER TER	94114	10-F2
4640	UPPER TER	94117	10-F2
4660	ASHBURY ST	94117	10-F2
4660	CLAYTON ST	94117	10-F2
4730	BELVEDERE ST	94117	10-E2
4810	COLE ST	94117	10-E2
4910	SHRADER ST	94117	10-E2
5000	STANYAN ST	94117	10-E2

18TH AV — SF

Address	Cross Street	ZIP	City Pg-Grid
100	LAKE ST	94121	5-B6
200	CALIFORNIA ST	94121	5-B6
300	CLEMENT ST	94121	5-B6
400	GEARY BLVD	94121	5-B6
500	ANZA ST	94121	5-B7
600	BALBOA ST	94121	5-B7
700	CABRILLO ST	94121	5-B7
800	FULTON ST	94121	5-B7
1200	LINCOLN WY	94122	9-B2
1300	IRVING ST	94122	9-B2
1400	JUDAH ST	94122	9-B2
1500	KIRKHAM ST	94122	9-B2
1600	LAWTON ST	94122	9-B3
1700	MORAGA ST	94122	9-B3
1800	NORIEGA ST	94122	9-B3
1900	ORTEGA ST	94116	9-B3
2000	PACHECO ST	94116	9-B4
2100	QUINTARA ST	94116	9-B4
2200	RIVERA ST	94116	13-B4
2300	SANTIAGO ST	94116	13-B4
2400	TARAVAL ST	94116	13-B5
2500	ULLOA ST	94116	13-B5
2600	VICENTE ST	94116	13-B5
2700	WAWONA ST	94116	13-B5

18TH ST — SF

Address	Cross Street	ZIP	City Pg-Grid
500	ILLINOIS ST	94107	11-C2
600	3RD ST	94107	11-C2
700	TENNESSEE ST	94107	11-C2
800	MINNESOTA ST	94107	11-C2
910	INDIANA ST	94107	11-C2
1100	PENNSYLVANIA AV	94107	11-B2
1200	MISSISSIPPI ST	94107	11-B2
1300	TEXAS ST	94107	11-B2
1400	MISSOURI ST	94107	11-B2
1500	CONNECTICUT ST	94107	11-B2
1600	ARKANSAS ST	94107	11-B2
1800	CAROLINA ST	94107	11-B2
1900	DE HARO ST	94107	11-A2
2000	RHODE ISLAND ST	94107	11-A2
2100	KANSAS ST	94107	11-A2
2200	VERMONT ST	94107	11-A2
2300	SAN BRUNO AV	94107	11-A2
3100	HARRISON ST	94110	10-J2
3150	TREAT AV	94110	10-J2
3200	FOLSOM ST	94110	10-J2
3250	SHOTWELL ST	94110	10-J2
3300	S VAN NESS AV	94110	10-J2
3350	CAPP ST	94110	10-J2
3400	MISSION ST	94110	10-H2
3430	SAN CARLOS ST	94110	10-H2
3470	LEXINGTON ST	94110	10-H2
3500	VALENCIA ST	94110	10-H2
3530	LAPIDGE ST	94110	10-H2
3530	DEARBORN ST	94110	10-H2
3570	LINDA ST	94110	10-H2
3600	GUERRERO ST	94110	10-H2
3650	OAKWOOD ST	94110	10-H2
3700	DOLORES ST	94114	10-H2
3800	CHURCH ST	94114	10-G2
3900	SANCHEZ ST	94114	10-G2
4000	NOE ST	94114	10-G2
4100	HARTFORD ST	94114	10-G2
4200	CASTRO ST	94114	10-G2
4300	COLLINGWOOD ST	94114	10-G2
4400	DIAMOND ST	94114	10-G2
4500	EUREKA ST	94114	10-F2
4600	DOUGLASS ST	94114	10-F2
4640	ORD ST	94114	10-F2
4690	HATTIE ST	94114	10-F2
4690	STORRIE ST	94114	10-F2
4730	CLOVER ST	94114	10-F2
4800	DANVERS ST	94114	10-F2
2400	UTAH ST	94110	11-A2
2500	POTRERO AV	94110	11-A2
2600	HAMPSHIRE ST	94110	11-A2
2700	YORK ST	94110	11-A2
	BRYANT ST	94110	11-A2
2900	FLORIDA ST	94110	10-J2
3000	ALABAMA ST	94110	10-J2

19TH AV — SF

Address	Cross Street	ZIP	City Pg-Grid
100	LAKE ST	94121	5-B6
200	CALIFORNIA ST	94121	5-B6
300	CLEMENT ST	94121	5-B6
400	GEARY BLVD	94121	5-B6
500	ANZA ST	94121	5-B7
600	BALBOA ST	94121	5-B7
700	CABRILLO ST	94121	5-B7
800	FULTON ST	94121	5-B7
1200	LINCOLN WY	94122	9-B2
1200	CROSS OVER DR	94122	9-B2
1300	IRVING ST	94122	9-B2
1400	JUDAH ST	94122	9-B2
1500	KIRKHAM ST	94122	9-B2
1600	LAWTON ST	94122	9-B3
1700	MORAGA ST	94122	9-B3
1800	NORIEGA ST	94122	9-B3
1900	ORTEGA ST	94116	9-B3
2000	PACHECO ST	94116	9-B4
2100	QUINTARA ST	94116	9-B4
2200	RIVERA ST	94116	13-B4
2300	SANTIAGO ST	94116	13-B4
2400	TARAVAL ST	94116	13-B5
2500	ULLOA ST	94116	13-B5
2600	VICENTE ST	94116	13-B5
2700	WAWONA ST	94132	13-B5
2800	BRIARCLIFF TER	94132	13-B6
2900	SLOAT BLVD	94132	13-B6
3000	OCEAN AV	94132	13-B6
3100	EUCALYPTUS DR	94132	13-B6
3200	ROSSMOOR DR	94132	13-B6
3300	MONTE VISTA DR	94132	13-B7
3300	BUCKINGHAM WY	94132	13-B7
3400	WINSTON DR	94132	13-B7
3500	BUCKINGHAM WY	94132	13-B7
3520	DENSLOW DR	94132	13-B7
3560	WYTON LN	94132	13-B7
3800	HOLLOWAY AV	94132	18-B1
3830	CRESPI DR	94132	18-B1
3870	BANBURY DR	94132	18-B1
4000	JUNIPERO SERRA BLVD	94132	18-C1
4080	BEVERLY ST	94132	18-C1
4090	RANDOLPH ST	94132	18-C1
4100	SARGENT ST	94132	18-C1
4140	MONTICELLO ST	94132	18-C1
4150	CHESTER AV	94132	18-C1
4180	BYXBEE ST	94132	18-C2
4180	RANDOLPH ST	94132	18-C2
4200	SAINT CHARLES AV	94132	18-C2

19TH ST — SF

Address	Cross Street	ZIP	City Pg-Grid
500	ILLINOIS ST	94107	11-C2
600	3RD ST	94107	11-C2
700	TENNESSEE ST	94107	11-C2
800	MINNESOTA ST	94107	11-C2
900	INDIANA ST	94107	11-C2
1100	PENNSYLVANIA AV	94107	11-B2
1200	MISSISSIPPI ST	94107	11-B2
1300	TEXAS ST	94107	11-B2
1400	MISSOURI ST	94107	11-B2
1500	CONNECTICUT ST	94107	11-B2
1600	ARKANSAS ST	94107	11-B2
1700	WISCONSIN ST	94107	11-B2
1800	CAROLINA ST	94107	11-B2
1900	DE HARO ST	94107	11-A2
2000	RHODE ISLAND ST	94107	11-A2
2100	KANSAS ST	94107	11-A2
2200	VERMONT ST	94107	11-A2
2300	SAN BRUNO AV	94107	11-A2
3100	HARRISON ST	94110	10-J2
3150	TREAT AV	94110	10-J2
3200	FOLSOM ST	94110	10-J2
3250	SHOTWELL ST	94110	10-J2
3300	S VAN NESS AV	94110	10-J2
3350	CAPP ST	94110	10-J2
3400	MISSION ST	94110	10-J2
3430	SAN CARLOS ST	94110	10-H2
3460	LEXINGTON ST	94110	10-H2
3500	VALENCIA ST	94110	10-H2
3530	LAPIDGE ST	94110	10-H2
3570	LINDA ST	94110	10-H2
3600	GUERRERO ST	94110	10-H2
3650	OAKWOOD ST	94110	10-H2
3700	DOLORES ST	94110	10-H2
2500	POTRERO AV	94110	11-A2
2600	HAMPSHIRE ST	94110	11-A2
2700	BRYANT ST	94110	11-A2
2700	YORK ST	94110	11-A2
	BRYANT ST	94110	11-A2
2900	FLORIDA ST	94110	10-J2
3000	ALABAMA ST	94110	10-J2
3020	ALABAMA ST	94110	10-J2
4900	CORBETT AV	94114	10-F2
3800	CHURCH ST	94114	10-G2
3900	SANCHEZ ST	94114	10-G2
4100	NOE ST	94114	10-G2
4100	HARTFORD ST	94114	10-G2
4200	CASTRO ST	94114	10-G2
4300	COLLINGWOOD ST	94114	10-G2
4350	DIAMOND ST	94114	10-G2
4400	DIAMOND ST	94114	10-G2
4500	EUREKA ST	94114	10-F2
4600	DOUGLASS ST	94114	10-F2
4640	LAMSON LN	94114	10-F2
4680	SEWARD ST	94114	10-F2
4700	CLOVER LN	94114	10-F2
4730	YUKON ST	94114	10-F2
4780	DANVERS ST	94114	10-F2
4800	CASELLI AV	94114	10-F2
4800	MONO ST	94114	10-F2
4850	MARKET ST	94114	10-F2

20TH AV — SF

Address	Cross Street	ZIP	City Pg-Grid
100	LAKE ST	94121	5-B6
200	CALIFORNIA ST	94121	5-B6
300	CLEMENT ST	94121	5-B6
400	GEARY BLVD	94121	5-B6
500	ANZA ST	94121	5-B7
600	BALBOA ST	94121	5-B7
700	CABRILLO ST	94121	5-B7
800	FULTON ST	94121	5-B7
1200	LINCOLN WY	94122	9-B2
1300	IRVING ST	94122	9-B2
1400	JUDAH ST	94122	9-B2
1500	KIRKHAM ST	94122	9-B2
1600	LAWTON ST	94122	9-B3
1700	MORAGA ST	94122	9-B3
1800	NORIEGA ST	94122	9-B3
1900	ORTEGA ST	94116	9-B3
2000	PACHECO ST	94116	9-B4
2100	QUINTARA ST	94116	9-B4
2200	RIVERA ST	94116	13-B4
2300	SANTIAGO ST	94116	13-B4
2400	TARAVAL ST	94116	13-B5
2500	ULLOA ST	94116	13-B5
2600	VICENTE ST	94116	13-B5
2700	WAWONA ST	94116	13-B5
2900	SLOAT BLVD	94132	13-B6
3000	OCEAN AV	94132	13-B6
3100	EUCALYPTUS DR	94132	13-B6
	BUCKINGHAM WY	94132	13-B6
3200	BUCKINGHAM WY	94132	13-B7
3280	WINSTON DR	94132	13-B7
3300	BUCKINGHAM WY	94132	13-B7

20TH ST — SF

Address	Cross Street	ZIP	City Pg-Grid
690	ILLINOIS ST	94107	11-C2
750	3RD ST	94107	11-C2
800	TENNESSEE ST	94107	11-C2
890	MINNESOTA ST	94107	11-C2
910	INDIANA ST	94107	11-C2
1200	PENNSYLVANIA AV	94107	11-B2
1300	MISSISSIPPI ST	94107	11-B2
1400	TEXAS ST	94107	11-B2
1500	MISSOURI ST	94107	11-B2
1600	CONNECTICUT ST	94107	11-B2
1700	ARKANSAS ST	94107	11-B2
1800	WISCONSIN ST	94107	11-B2
1900	CAROLINA ST	94107	11-B2
2000	DE HARO ST	94107	11-A2
2100	RHODE ISLAND ST	94107	11-A2
2200	KANSAS ST	94107	11-A2
2300	VERMONT ST	94107	11-A2
2400	SAN BRUNO AV	94107	11-A2
2600	POTRERO AV	94110	11-A2
2700	HAMPSHIRE ST	94110	11-A3
2800	YORK ST	94110	11-A3
2800	BRYANT ST	94110	11-A3
	BRYANT ST	94110	11-A3
2990	FLORIDA ST	94110	10-J3
3000	FLORIDA ST	94110	10-J3
3100	ALABAMA ST	94110	10-J3
3200	HARRISON ST	94110	10-J3
3250	TREAT AV	94110	10-J3
3300	FOLSOM ST	94110	10-J3
3350	SHOTWELL ST	94110	10-J3
3400	S VAN NESS AV	94110	10-J3
3450	CAPP ST	94110	10-J3
3500	MISSION ST	94110	10-J3
3530	SAN CARLOS ST	94110	10-H3
3570	LEXINGTON ST	94110	10-H3
3600	VALENCIA ST	94110	10-H3
3700	GUERRERO ST	94110	10-H3
3800	DOLORES ST	94114	10-H3
3900	20TH ST	94114	10-G3
4000	SANCHEZ ST	94114	10-G3
3900	CHURCH ST	94114	10-H3
4100	NOE ST	94114	10-G3
4150	HARTFORD ST	94114	10-G3
4200	CASTRO ST	94114	10-G3
4300	COLLINGWOOD ST	94114	10-G3
4350	DIAMOND ST	94114	10-G3
4400	DIAMOND ST	94114	10-G3
4500	EUREKA ST	94114	10-F3
4600	DOUGLASS ST	94114	10-F3

21ST AV — SF

Address	Cross Street	ZIP	City Pg-Grid
100	LAKE ST	94121	5-B6
200	CALIFORNIA ST	94121	5-B6
300	CLEMENT ST	94121	5-B6
400	GEARY BLVD	94121	5-B6
500	ANZA ST	94121	5-B7
600	BALBOA ST	94121	5-B7
700	CABRILLO ST	94121	5-B7
800	FULTON ST	94121	5-B7
1200	LINCOLN WY	94122	9-B2
1300	IRVING ST	94122	9-B2
1400	JUDAH ST	94122	9-B2
1500	KIRKHAM ST	94122	9-B2
1600	LAWTON ST	94122	9-B3
1700	MORAGA ST	94122	9-B3
1800	NORIEGA ST	94122	9-B3
1900	ORTEGA ST	94116	9-B3
2000	PACHECO ST	94116	9-B4
2100	QUINTARA ST	94116	9-B4
2200	RIVERA ST	94116	13-B4
2300	SANTIAGO ST	94116	13-B4
2400	TARAVAL ST	94116	13-B5
2500	ULLOA ST	94116	13-B5
2600	VICENTE ST	94116	13-B5
2700	WAWONA ST	94116	13-B5
2900	SLOAT BLVD	94132	13-B6
3000	OCEAN AV	94132	13-B6
3100	EUCALYPTUS DR	94132	13-B6

21ST ST — SF

Address	Cross Street	ZIP	City Pg-Grid
2600	POTRERO AV	94110	11-A3
2650	HAMPSHIRE ST	94110	11-A3
2700	YORK ST	94110	11-A3
	BRYANT ST	94110	11-A3
2800	FLORIDA ST	94110	10-J3
2850	ALABAMA ST	94110	10-J3
2900	HARRISON ST	94110	10-J3
2950	TREAT AV	94110	10-J3
3000	FOLSOM ST	94110	10-J3
3050	SHOTWELL ST	94110	10-J3
3100	S VAN NESS AV	94110	10-J3
3150	CAPP ST	94110	10-J3
3200	MISSION ST	94110	10-J3
3230	SAN CARLOS ST	94110	10-H3
3250	BARTLETT ST	94110	10-H3
3260	LEXINGTON ST	94110	10-H3
3300	VALENCIA ST	94110	10-H3
3400	GUERRERO ST	94110	10-H3
3420	AMES ST	94110	10-H3
3450	FAIR OAKS ST	94110	10-H3
3470	QUANE ST	94110	10-H3
3500	DOLORES ST	94114	10-H3
	CHATTANOOGA ST	94114	10-H3
3600	CHURCH ST	94114	10-G3
3700	SANCHEZ ST	94114	10-G3
3750	RAYBURN ST	94114	10-G3
3800	NOE ST	94114	10-G3
3900	CASTRO ST	94114	10-G3
4010	COLLINGWOOD ST	94114	10-G3
4100	DIAMOND ST	94114	10-G3
4200	EUREKA ST	94114	10-G3
4200	EUREKA ST	94114	10-F3
4300	DOUGLASS ST	94114	10-F3
4350	WORTH ST	94114	10-F3
4400	GRAND VIEW AV	94114	10-F3

22ND AV — SF

Address	Cross Street	ZIP	City Pg-Grid
10	W CLAY ST	94121	5-B6
100	LAKE ST	94121	5-B6
200	CALIFORNIA ST	94121	5-B6
300	CLEMENT ST	94121	5-B6
400	GEARY BLVD	94121	5-B7
500	ANZA ST	94121	5-B7
600	BALBOA ST	94121	5-B7
700	CABRILLO ST	94121	5-B7
800	FULTON ST	94121	5-B7
1200	LINCOLN WY	94122	9-B2
1300	IRVING ST	94122	9-B2
1400	JUDAH ST	94122	9-B2
1500	KIRKHAM ST	94122	9-B2
1600	LAWTON ST	94122	9-B3
1700	MORAGA ST	94122	9-B3
1800	NORIEGA ST	94122	9-B3
1900	ORTEGA ST	94116	9-B3
2000	PACHECO ST	94116	9-B4
2100	QUINTARA ST	94116	9-B4
2200	RIVERA ST	94116	13-B4
2300	SANTIAGO ST	94116	13-B4
2400	TARAVAL ST	94116	13-B5
2500	ULLOA ST	94116	13-B5
2600	VICENTE ST	94116	13-B5
2700	WAWONA ST	94116	13-B5
2900	SLOAT BLVD	94132	13-B6
3000	OCEAN AV	94132	13-B6
3100	EUCALYPTUS DR	94132	13-B6

22ND ST — SF

Address	Cross Street	ZIP	City Pg-Grid
700	ILLINOIS ST	94107	11-C3
770	3RD ST	94107	11-C3
830	TENNESSEE ST	94107	11-C3
900	MINNESOTA ST	94107	11-C3
1000	INDIANA ST	94107	11-C3
1110	IOWA ST	94107	11-C3
1200	PENNSYLVANIA AV	94107	11-B3
1300	MISSISSIPPI ST	94107	11-B3
1400	TEXAS ST	94107	11-B3
1800	WISCONSIN ST	94107	11-B3
1900	CAROLINA ST	94107	11-B3
2000	DE HARO ST	94107	11-B3
2100	RHODE ISLAND ST	94107	11-A3
2200	KANSAS ST	94107	11-A3
2300	VERMONT ST	94107	11-A3
2300	VERMONT ST	94110	11-A3
2400	SAN BRUNO AV	94110	11-A3
2600	POTRERO AV	94110	11-A3
2650	HAMPSHIRE ST	94110	11-A3
2700	YORK ST	94110	11-A3
	BRYANT ST	94110	11-A3
2800	FLORIDA ST	94110	11-A3
2850	ALABAMA ST	94110	10-J3
2900	HARRISON ST	94110	10-J3
2950	TREAT AV	94110	10-J3
3000	FOLSOM ST	94110	10-J3
3050	SHOTWELL ST	94110	10-J3
3100	S VAN NESS AV	94110	10-J3
3150	CAPP ST	94110	10-J3
3200	MISSION ST	94110	10-H3
3250	BARTLETT ST	94110	10-H3
3300	VALENCIA ST	94110	10-H3
3320	SAN JOSE AV	94110	10-H3
3400	GUERRERO ST	94110	10-H3
3420	AMES ST	94110	10-H3
3450	FAIR OAKS ST	94110	10-H3
3470	QUANE ST	94110	10-H3
3500	DOLORES ST	94114	10-H3
3550	CHATTANOOGA ST	94114	10-H3
3600	CHURCH ST	94114	10-H3
3650	VICKSBURG ST	94114	10-G3
3700	SANCHEZ ST	94114	10-G3
3800	NOE ST	94114	10-G3
3900	CASTRO ST	94114	10-G3
3970	COLLINGWOOD ST	94114	10-G3
4110	DIAMOND ST	94114	10-G3
4200	EUREKA ST	94114	10-F3

PRIMARY STREET Address	Cross Street	ZIP	CITY Pg-Grid
22ND ST			**SF**
4300	DOUGLASS ST	94114	10-F3
	WORTH ST	94114	10-F3
	HOFFMAN AV	94114	10-F3
23RD AV			**SF**
100	LAKE ST	94121	5-B6
200	CALIFORNIA ST	94121	5-B6
300	CLEMENT ST	94121	5-B6
400	GEARY BLVD	94121	5-B6
500	ANZA ST	94121	5-B7
600	BALBOA ST	94121	5-B7
700	CABRILLO ST	94121	5-B7
800	FULTON ST	94121	5-B7
1200	LINCOLN WY	94122	9-B2
1300	IRVING ST	94122	9-B2
1400	JUDAH ST	94122	9-B2
1500	KIRKHAM ST	94122	9-B2
1600	LAWTON ST	94122	9-B3
1700	MORAGA ST	94122	9-B3
1800	NORIEGA ST	94122	9-B3
1900	ORTEGA ST	94116	9-B3
2000	PACHECO ST	94116	9-B4
2100	QUINTARA ST	94116	9-B4
2400	TARAVAL ST	94116	13-B5
2500	ULLOA ST	94116	13-B5
2600	VICENTE ST	94116	13-B5
2700	WAWONA ST	94116	13-B5
2900	CRESTLAKE DR	94132	13-B6
2900	SLOAT BLVD	94132	13-B6
3000	OCEAN AV	94132	13-B6
3100	EUCALYPTUS DR	94132	13-B6
23RD ST			**SF**
800	ILLINOIS ST	94107	11-C3
860	3RD ST	94107	11-C3
930	TENNESSEE ST	94107	11-C3
1000	MINNESOTA ST	94107	11-C3
1100	INDIANA ST	94107	11-C3
1200	IOWA ST	94107	11-C3
1300	PENNSYLVANIA AV	94107	11-B3
1600	MISSOURI ST	94107	11-B3
1700	DAKOTA ST	94107	11-B3
1800	ARKANSAS ST	94107	11-B3
	WISCONSIN ST	94107	11-B3
2000	CAROLINA ST	94107	11-B3
2100	DE HARO ST	94107	11-B3
2200	RHODE ISLAND ST	94107	11-A3
2300	KANSAS ST	94107	11-A3
2400	VERMONT ST	94110	11-A3
2500	SAN BRUNO AV	94110	11-A3
2600	UTAH ST	94110	11-A3
2700	POTRERO AV	94110	11-A3
2750	HAMPSHIRE ST	94110	11-A3
2800	YORK ST	94110	11-A3
2850	BRYANT ST	94110	11-A3
	FLORIDA ST	94110	11-A3
2950	ALABAMA ST	94110	10-J3
3000	HARRISON ST	94110	10-J3
3050	TREAT AV	94110	10-J3
3100	FOLSOM ST	94110	10-J3
3150	SHOTWELL ST	94110	10-J3
3200	S VAN NESS AV	94110	10-J3
3250	CAPP ST	94110	10-J3
3300	MISSION ST	94110	10-J3
3350	BARTLETT ST	94110	10-H3
3400	VALENCIA ST	94110	10-H3
3500	SAN JOSE AV	94110	10-H3
3600	GUERRERO ST	94110	10-H3
3620	AMES ST	94110	10-H3
3650	FAIR OAKS ST	94110	10-H3
3670	QUANE ST	94110	10-H3
3700	DOLORES ST	94114	10-H3
3730	MERSEY ST	94114	10-H3
3750	CHATTANOOGA ST	94114	10-H3
3780	SEVERN ST	94114	10-H3
3800	CHURCH ST	94114	10-H3
3830	NELLIE ST	94114	10-H3
3850	VICKSBURG ST	94114	10-G3
3880	BLANCHE ST	94114	10-G3
3900	SANCHEZ ST	94114	10-G3
4000	NOE ST	94114	10-G3
4100	CASTRO ST	94114	10-G3
4200	DIAMOND ST	94114	10-G3
4250	EUREKA ST	94114	10-G3
4300	DOUGLASS ST	94114	10-F3
4400	HOFFMAN AV	94114	10-F3
4500	GRAND VIEW AV	94114	10-F3
24TH AV			**SF**
100	W CLAY ST	94121	5-B6
200	LAKE ST	94121	5-B6
200	W CLAY ST	94121	5-B6
300	CALIFORNIA ST	94121	5-B6
400	CLEMENT ST	94121	5-B6
500	GEARY BLVD	94121	5-B7
600	ANZA ST	94121	5-B7
700	BALBOA ST	94121	5-B7
800	CABRILLO ST	94121	5-B7
900	FULTON ST	94121	5-B7
1200	LINCOLN WY	94122	9-B2
1300	IRVING ST	94122	9-B2
1400	JUDAH ST	94122	9-B2
1500	KIRKHAM ST	94122	9-B2
1600	LAWTON ST	94122	9-B3
1700	MORAGA ST	94122	9-B3
1800	NORIEGA ST	94122	9-B3
1900	ORTEGA ST	94116	9-B3
2000	PACHECO ST	94116	9-B4
2100	QUINTARA ST	94116	9-B4
2200	RIVERA ST	94116	13-B4
2300	SANTIAGO ST	94116	13-B4
2400	TARAVAL ST	94116	13-B5
2500	ULLOA ST	94116	13-B5
2600	VICENTE ST	94116	13-B5
2700	WAWONA ST	94116	13-B5
2900	SLOAT BLVD	94132	13-B6
3000	OCEAN AV	94132	13-B6
3100	EUCALYPTUS DR	94132	13-B6
24TH ST			**SF**
660	MICHIGAN ST	94107	11-C3
750	ILLINOIS ST	94107	11-C3
830	3RD ST	94107	11-C3
920	TENNESSEE ST	94107	11-C3
1000	MINNESOTA ST	94107	11-C3
2100	DE HARO ST	94107	11-B3
2200	RHODE ISLAND ST	94107	11-A3
2300	KANSAS ST	94107	11-A3
2400	VERMONT ST	94110	11-A3
2500	SAN BRUNO AV	94110	11-A3
2600	UTAH ST	94110	11-A3
2700	POTRERO AV	94110	11-A3
2750	HAMPSHIRE ST	94110	11-A3
2800	YORK ST	94110	11-A3
2850	BRYANT ST	94110	11-A3
	FLORIDA ST	94110	11-A3
2950	ALABAMA ST	94110	10-J3
3000	HARRISON ST	94110	10-J3
3030	BALMY ST	94110	10-J3
3050	TREAT AV	94110	10-J3
3080	LUCKY ST	94110	10-J3
3100	FOLSOM ST	94110	10-J3
3150	SHOTWELL ST	94110	10-J3
3200	S VAN NESS AV	94110	10-J3
3220	CYPRESS ST	94110	10-J3
3250	CAPP ST	94110	10-J3
3270	LILAC ST	94110	10-J3
3300	MISSION ST	94110	10-J3
3320	OSAGE AL	94110	10-J3
3350	BARTLETT ST	94110	10-H3
3380	ORANGE AL	94110	10-H3
3440	VALENCIA ST	94110	10-H3
3490	POPLAR ST	94110	10-H3
3550	SAN JOSE AV	94110	10-H3
3600	GUERRERO ST	94110	10-H3
3650	FAIR OAKS ST	94110	10-H3
3680	QUANE ST	94110	10-H3
3700	DOLORES ST	94114	10-H3
3710	MERSEY ST	94114	10-H3
3750	CHATTANOOGA ST	94114	10-H3
3800	CHURCH ST	94114	10-H3
3850	VICKSBURG ST	94114	10-G4
3900	SANCHEZ ST	94114	10-G4
4000	NOE ST	94114	10-G4
4100	CASTRO ST	94114	10-G4
4200	DIAMOND ST	94114	10-F4
4300	DOUGLASS ST	94114	10-F4
4350	HOMESTEAD ST	94114	10-F4
4400	HOFFMAN AV	94114	10-F4
4450	FOUNTAIN ST	94114	10-F4
4500	GRAND VIEW AV	94114	10-F4
25TH AV			**SF**
30	SEA CLIFF AV	94121	5-A5
50	SCENIC WY	94121	5-A5
100	EL CAMINO DEL MAR	94121	5-A6
100	LINCOLN BLVD	94121	5-A6
200	LAKE ST	94121	5-A6
300	CALIFORNIA ST	94121	5-A6
400	CLEMENT ST	94121	5-A6
500	GEARY BLVD	94121	5-A7
600	ANZA ST	94121	5-A7
700	BALBOA ST	94121	5-A7
800	CABRILLO ST	94121	5-A7
900	CROSS OVER DR	94121	5-A7
900	FULTON ST	94121	5-A7
1	AVENUE NORTH	94121	5-A5
20	SEA CLIFF AV	94121	5-A5
1200	MARTIN LUTHER KING JR DR	-	9-B1
1200	LINCOLN WY	94122	9-B2
1300	IRVING ST	94122	9-B2
1400	JUDAH ST	94122	9-B2
1500	KIRKHAM ST	94122	9-B2
1600	LAWTON ST	94122	9-B3
1700	MORAGA ST	94122	9-B3
1800	NORIEGA ST	94122	9-B3
1900	ORTEGA ST	94122	9-B3
2100	QUINTARA ST	94116	9-B4
2200	RIVERA ST	94116	13-B4
2300	SANTIAGO ST	94116	13-B4
2400	TARAVAL ST	94116	13-B5
2500	ULLOA ST	94116	13-B5
2600	VICENTE ST	94116	13-B5
2680	ROSEMARY CT	94116	13-B5
2900	SLOAT BLVD	94132	13-B6
3000	OCEAN AV	94132	13-B6
3100	EUCALYPTUS DR	94132	13-B6
25TH ST			**SF**
700	MICHIGAN ST	94107	11-C3
800	ILLINOIS ST	94107	11-C3
900	3RD ST	94107	11-C3
1000	TENNESSEE ST	94107	11-C3
1000	MINNESOTA ST	94107	11-C3
1200	INDIANA ST	94107	11-C3
1400	PENNSYLVANIA AV	94107	11-B3
1500	MISSISSIPPI ST	94107	11-B3
	TEXAS ST	94107	11-B3
1600	DAKOTA ST	94107	11-B3
1800	CONNECTICUT ST	94107	11-B3
2000	WISCONSIN ST	94107	11-B3
2000	WISCONSIN ST	94107	11-B4
2030	LITTLEFIELD TER	94107	11-B4
2190	DE HARO ST	94107	11-B4
2200	DE HARO ST	94107	11-B4
2300	RHODE ISLAND ST	94107	11-A4
2400	KANSAS ST	94107	11-A4
2500	VERMONT ST	94110	11-A4
2600	SAN BRUNO AV	94110	11-A4
2700	UTAH ST	94110	11-A4
2800	POTRERO AV	94110	11-A4
2850	HAMPSHIRE ST	94110	11-A4
2900	YORK ST	94110	11-A4
2950	BRYANT ST	94110	11-A4
	FLORIDA ST	94110	11-A4
2930	ALABAMA ST	94110	10-J4
2980	HARRISON ST	94110	10-J4
3010	BALMY ST	94110	10-J4
3040	TREAT AV	94110	10-J4
3080	LUCKY ST	94110	10-J4
3100	FOLSOM ST	94110	10-J4
3130	HORACE ST	94110	10-J4
3160	SHOTWELL ST	94110	10-J4
3190	VIRGIL ST	94110	10-J4
3220	S VAN NESS AV	94110	10-J4
3260	CYPRESS ST	94110	10-J4
3280	CAPP ST	94110	10-J4
3320	LILAC ST	94110	10-J4
3350	MISSION ST	94110	10-J4
3380	OSAGE AL	94110	10-J4
3410	BARTLETT ST	94110	10-H4
3440	ORANGE AL	94110	10-H4
3470	VALENCIA ST	94110	10-H4
3500	POPLAR ST	94110	10-H4
3520	SAN JOSE AV	94110	10-H4
3600	GUERRERO ST	94110	10-H4
3700	FAIR OAKS ST	94110	10-H4
3800	DOLORES ST	94114	10-H4
3900	CHURCH ST	94114	10-H4
3950	VICKSBURG ST	94114	10-G4
4000	SANCHEZ ST	94114	10-G4
4100	NOE ST	94114	10-G4
4200	CASTRO ST	94114	10-G4
4300	DIAMOND ST	94114	10-G4
4400	DOUGLASS ST	94114	10-F4
4500	HOMESTEAD ST	94114	10-F4
4600	HOFFMAN AV	94114	10-F4
4700	FOUNTAIN ST	94114	10-F4
4800	GRAND VIEW AV	94114	10-F4
26TH AV			**SF**
1	SEA CLIFF AV	94121	5-A5
50	SCENIC WY	94121	5-A5
100	EL CAMINO DEL MAR	94121	5-A5
200	LAKE ST	94121	5-A6
300	CALIFORNIA ST	94121	5-A6
400	CLEMENT ST	94121	5-A6
500	GEARY BLVD	94121	5-A6
600	ANZA ST	94121	5-A7
700	BALBOA ST	94121	5-A7
800	CABRILLO ST	94121	5-A7
900	FULTON ST	94121	5-A7
1200	LINCOLN WY	94122	9-A2
1300	IRVING ST	94122	9-A2
1400	JUDAH ST	94122	9-A2
1500	KIRKHAM ST	94122	9-A2
1600	LAWTON ST	94122	9-A3
1700	MORAGA ST	94122	9-A3
1800	NORIEGA ST	94122	9-A3
1900	ORTEGA ST	94122	9-A3
2100	QUINTARA ST	94116	9-A4
2200	RIVERA ST	94116	13-A4
2300	SANTIAGO ST	94116	13-A4
2400	TARAVAL ST	94116	13-B5
2500	ULLOA ST	94116	13-B5
2600	VICENTE ST	94116	13-B5
2700	WAWONA ST	94116	13-B5
2900	SLOAT BLVD	94132	13-B6
3000	OCEAN AV	94132	13-B6
3100	EUCALYPTUS DR	94132	13-B6
26TH ST			**SF**
810	3RD ST	94107	11-C4
920	TENNESSEE ST	94107	11-C4
1030	MINNESOTA ST	94107	11-C4
1140	INDIANA ST	94107	11-C4
1700	CONNECTICUT ST	94107	11-B4
1900	WISCONSIN ST	94107	11-B4
2050	BLAIR TER	94107	11-B4
2100	DE HARO ST	94107	11-B4
2200	RHODE ISLAND ST	94107	11-A4
2300	KANSAS ST	94107	11-A4
2400	VERMONT ST	94107	11-A4
2800	HAMPSHIRE ST	94110	11-A4
2900	YORK ST	94110	11-A4
2950	BRYANT ST	94110	11-A4
3000	FLORIDA ST	94110	11-A4
3050	ALABAMA ST	94110	10-J4
3100	HARRISON ST	94110	10-J4
3160	TREAT AV	94110	10-J4
3190	LUCKY ST	94110	10-J4
3220	FOLSOM ST	94110	10-J4
3250	HORACE ST	94110	10-J4
3280	SHOTWELL ST	94110	10-J4
3310	VIRGIL ST	94110	10-J4
3340	S VAN NESS AV	94110	10-J4
3370	CYPRESS ST	94110	10-J4
3400	CAPP ST	94110	10-J4
3430	LILAC ST	94110	10-J4
3450	MISSION ST	94110	10-J4
3480	OSAGE AL	94110	10-J4
3510	BARTLETT ST	94110	10-J4
3540	ORANGE AL	94110	10-H4
3570	VALENCIA ST	94110	10-H4
3600	POPLAR ST	94110	10-H4
3620	SAN JOSE AV	94110	10-H4
3700	GUERRERO ST	94110	10-H4
3750	FAIR OAKS ST	94110	10-H4
3800	DOLORES ST	94131	10-H4
3900	CHURCH ST	94131	10-H4
4000	SANCHEZ ST	94131	10-G4
4100	NOE ST	94131	10-G4
4200	CASTRO ST	94131	10-G4
4300	DIAMOND ST	94131	10-G4
4400	DOUGLASS ST	94131	10-G4
27TH AV			**SF**
1	SEA CLIFF AV	94121	5-A5
100	EL CAMINO DEL MAR	94121	5-A5
200	LAKE ST	94121	5-A6
300	CALIFORNIA ST	94121	5-A6
400	CLEMENT ST	94121	5-A6
500	GEARY BLVD	94121	5-A7
600	ANZA ST	94121	5-A7
700	BALBOA ST	94121	5-A7
800	CABRILLO ST	94121	5-A7
900	FULTON ST	94121	5-A7
1200	LINCOLN WY	94122	9-A2
1300	IRVING ST	94122	9-A2
1400	JUDAH ST	94122	9-A2
1500	KIRKHAM ST	94122	9-A2
1600	LAWTON ST	94122	9-A3
1700	MORAGA ST	94122	9-A3
1800	NORIEGA ST	94122	9-A3
1900	ORTEGA ST	94122	9-A3
2100	QUINTARA ST	94116	9-A4
2200	RIVERA ST	94116	13-A4
2300	SANTIAGO ST	94116	13-A4
2400	TARAVAL ST	94116	13-A5
2500	ULLOA ST	94116	13-A5
2600	VICENTE ST	94116	13-A5
27TH ST			**SF**
1	SAN JOSE AV	94110	14-H4
100	GUERRERO ST	94110	14-H4
200	DOLORES ST	94131	14-H4
300	CHURCH ST	94131	14-H4
400	SANCHEZ ST	94131	14-G4
500	NOE ST	94131	14-G4
600	NEWBURG ST	94131	14-G4
600	CASTRO ST	94131	14-G4
640	KRONQUIST CT	94131	14-G4
700	DIAMOND ST	94131	14-G4
800	DOUGLASS ST	94131	14-F4
900	SAFIRA LN	94131	14-F4
28TH AV			**SF**
100	EL CAMINO DEL MAR	94121	5-A5
150	MCLAREN AV	94121	5-A6
200	LAKE ST	94121	5-A6
180	LAKE ST	94121	5-A6
300	CALIFORNIA ST	94121	5-A6
400	CLEMENT ST	94121	5-A6
500	GEARY BLVD	94121	5-A7
600	ANZA ST	94121	5-A7
700	BALBOA ST	94121	5-A7
800	CABRILLO ST	94121	5-A7
900	FULTON ST	94121	5-A7
1200	LINCOLN WY	94122	9-A2
1300	IRVING ST	94122	9-A2
1400	JUDAH ST	94122	9-A2
1500	KIRKHAM ST	94122	9-A2
1600	LAWTON ST	94122	9-A3
1700	MORAGA ST	94122	9-A3
1800	NORIEGA ST	94122	9-A3
1900	ORTEGA ST	94116	9-A3
2000	PACHECO ST	94116	9-A4
2100	QUINTARA ST	94116	9-A4
2200	RIVERA ST	94116	13-A4
2300	SANTIAGO ST	94116	13-A4
2400	TARAVAL ST	94116	13-A5
2500	ULLOA ST	94116	13-A5
2600	VICENTE ST	94116	13-A5
2700	WAWONA ST	94116	13-A5
28TH ST			**SF**
1	GUERRERO ST	94110	14-H4
100	DOLORES ST	94131	14-H4
200	CHURCH ST	94131	14-H4
300	SANCHEZ ST	94131	14-G4
400	NOE ST	94131	14-G4
500	CASTRO ST	94131	14-G4
600	DIAMOND ST	94131	14-G4
1500	DUNCAN ST	94131	14-F4
1500	DOUGLASS ST	94131	14-F4
29TH AV			**SF**
100	MCLAREN AV	94121	5-A6
200	LAKE ST	94121	5-A6
300	CALIFORNIA ST	94121	5-A6
400	CLEMENT ST	94121	5-A6
500	GEARY BLVD	94121	5-A7
600	ANZA ST	94121	5-A7
700	BALBOA ST	94121	5-A7
800	CABRILLO ST	94121	5-A7
900	FULTON ST	94121	5-A7
1200	LINCOLN WY	94122	9-A2
1300	IRVING ST	94122	9-A2
1400	JUDAH ST	94122	9-A2
1500	KIRKHAM ST	94122	9-A2
1600	LAWTON ST	94122	9-A3
1700	MORAGA ST	94122	9-A3
1800	NORIEGA ST	94122	9-A3
1900	ORTEGA ST	94116	9-A3
2000	PACHECO ST	94116	9-A4
2100	QUINTARA ST	94116	9-A4
2200	RIVERA ST	94116	13-A4
2300	SANTIAGO ST	94116	13-A4
2400	TARAVAL ST	94116	13-A5
2500	ULLOA ST	94116	13-A5
2600	VICENTE ST	94116	13-A5
29TH ST			**SF**
1	MISSION ST	94110	14-H5
50	TIFFANY AV	94110	14-H5
100	SAN JOSE AV	94110	14-H5
200	DOLORES ST	94131	14-H5
300	CHURCH ST	94131	14-H5
400	SANCHEZ ST	94131	14-G5
500	NOE ST	94131	14-G5
	CASTRO ST	94131	14-G5
600	CASTRO ST	94131	14-G5
650	ZIRCON PL	94131	14-G5
700	DIAMOND ST	94131	14-G5
30TH AV			**SF**
100	EL CAMINO DEL MAR	94121	5-A6
200	LAKE ST	94121	5-A6
250	SEAVIEW TER	94121	5-A6
300	CALIFORNIA ST	94121	5-A6
400	CLEMENT ST	94121	5-A6
500	GEARY BLVD	94121	5-A7
600	ANZA ST	94121	5-A7
700	BALBOA ST	94121	5-A7
800	CABRILLO ST	94121	5-A7
900	FULTON ST	94121	5-A7
900	FULTON ST	-	5-A7
940	SPRECKLES LAKE DR	-	9-A1
1000	JOHN F KENNEDY DR	-	9-A1
1200	LINCOLN WY	94122	9-A2
1300	IRVING ST	94122	9-A2
1400	JUDAH ST	94122	9-A2
1500	KIRKHAM ST	94122	9-A2
1600	LAWTON ST	94122	9-A3
1700	MORAGA ST	94122	9-A3
1800	NORIEGA ST	94122	9-A3
1900	ORTEGA ST	94116	9-A3
2000	PACHECO ST	94116	9-A4
2100	QUINTARA ST	94116	9-A4
2200	RIVERA ST	94116	13-A4
2300	SANTIAGO ST	94116	13-A4
2400	TARAVAL ST	94116	13-A5
2500	ULLOA ST	94116	13-A5
2600	VICENTE ST	94116	13-A5
2650	ESCOLTA WY	94116	13-A5
2700	WAWONA ST	94116	13-A5
30TH ST			**SF**
20	MISSION ST	94110	14-H5
100	SAN JOSE AV	94110	14-H5
200	DOLORES ST	94131	14-H5
250	CHENERY ST	94131	14-H5
280	CHURCH ST	94131	14-H5
300	CHURCH ST	94131	14-H5
350	WHITNEY ST	94131	14-H5
400	SANCHEZ ST	94131	14-G5
450	HARPER ST	94131	14-G5
	NOE ST	94131	14-G5
500	NOE ST	94131	14-G5
570	LAIDLEY ST	94131	14-G5
600	CASTRO ST	94131	14-G5
31ST AV			**SF**
200	SEAVIEW TER	94121	5-A6
300	CALIFORNIA ST	94121	5-A6
400	CLEMENT ST	94121	5-A6
500	GEARY BLVD	94121	5-A6
700	BALBOA ST	94121	5-A7
800	CABRILLO ST	94121	5-A7
900	FULTON ST	94121	5-A7
1200	LINCOLN WY	94122	9-A2
1300	IRVING ST	94122	9-A2
1400	JUDAH ST	94122	9-A2
1500	KIRKHAM ST	94122	9-A2
1600	LAWTON ST	94122	9-A3
1700	MORAGA ST	94122	9-A3
1800	NORIEGA ST	94122	9-A3
1900	ORTEGA ST	94116	9-A3
2000	PACHECO ST	94116	9-A4
2100	QUINTARA ST	94116	9-A4
2200	RIVERA ST	94116	13-A4
2300	SANTIAGO ST	94116	13-A4
2400	TARAVAL ST	94116	13-A5
2500	ULLOA ST	94116	13-A5
2600	VICENTE ST	94116	13-A5
2700	ESCOLTA WY	94116	13-A5
32ND AV			**SF**
1	EL CAMINO DEL MAR	94121	5-A6
300	CALIFORNIA ST	94121	5-A6
330	MARVEL CT	94121	5-A6
400	CLEMENT ST	94121	5-A6
500	GEARY BLVD	94121	5-A7
600	ANZA ST	94121	5-A7
700	BALBOA ST	94121	5-A7
800	CABRILLO ST	94121	5-A7
900	FULTON ST	94121	5-A7
1200	LINCOLN WY	94122	9-A2
1300	IRVING ST	94122	9-A2
1400	JUDAH ST	94122	9-A2
1500	KIRKHAM ST	94122	9-A2
1600	LAWTON ST	94122	9-A3
1700	MORAGA ST	94122	9-A3
1800	NORIEGA ST	94122	9-A3
1900	ORTEGA ST	94116	9-A3
2000	PACHECO ST	94116	9-A4
2100	QUINTARA ST	94116	9-A4
2200	RIVERA ST	94116	13-A4
2300	SANTIAGO ST	94116	13-A4
2400	TARAVAL ST	94116	13-A5
2500	ULLOA ST	94116	13-A5
2600	VICENTE ST	94116	13-A5
33RD AV			**SF**
400	CLEMENT ST	94121	5-A6
500	GEARY BLVD	94121	5-A7
600	ANZA ST	94121	5-A7

SAN FRANCISCO

INDEX

Address	Cross Street	ZIP	City Pg-Grid
33RD AV			**SF**
700	BALBOA ST	94121	5-A7
800	CABRILLO ST	94121	5-A7
900	FULTON ST	94121	5-A7
1200	LINCOLN WY	94122	9-A2
1300	IRVING ST	94122	9-A2
1400	JUDAH ST	94122	9-A2
1500	KIRKHAM ST	94122	9-A2
1600	LAWTON ST	94122	9-A3
1700	MORAGA ST	94122	9-A3
1800	NORIEGA ST	94122	9-A3
1900	ORTEGA ST	94116	9-A3
2000	PACHECO ST	94116	9-A4
2100	QUINTARA ST	94116	9-A4
2200	RIVERA ST	94116	13-A4
2300	SANTIAGO ST	94116	13-A4
2400	TARAVAL ST	94116	13-A5
2500	ULLOA ST	94116	13-A5
2600	VICENTE ST	94116	13-A5
2700	WAWONA ST	94116	13-A5
2700	ESCOLTA WY	94116	13-A5
34TH AV			**SF**
400	CLEMENT ST	94121	4-J6
400	LEGION OF HONOR DR	94121	4-J6
500	GEARY BLVD	94121	4-J7
600	ANZA ST	94121	4-J7
700	BALBOA ST	94121	4-J7
800	CABRILLO ST	94121	4-J7
900	FULTON ST	94121	4-J7
1200	LINCOLN WY	94122	8-J2
1300	IRVING ST	94122	8-J2
1400	JUDAH ST	94122	8-J2
1500	KIRKHAM ST	94122	8-J2
1600	LAWTON ST	94122	9-A3
1700	MORAGA ST	94122	9-A3
1800	NORIEGA ST	94122	9-A3
1900	ORTEGA ST	94116	9-A3
2000	PACHECO ST	94116	9-A4
2100	QUINTARA ST	94116	9-A4
2200	RIVERA ST	94116	13-A4
2300	SANTIAGO ST	94116	13-A4
2400	TARAVAL ST	94116	13-A5
2500	ULLOA ST	94116	13-A5
2600	VICENTE ST	94116	13-A5
2700	WAWONA ST	94116	13-A5
2800	YORBA ST	94132	13-A6
2850	ESCONDIDO AV	94132	13-A6
2890	SLOAT BLVD	94132	13-A6
35TH AV			**SF**
400	CLEMENT ST	94121	4-J6
500	GEARY BLVD	94121	4-J6
600	ANZA ST	94121	4-J7
700	BALBOA ST	94121	4-J7
800	CABRILLO ST	94121	4-J7
900	FULTON ST	94121	4-J7
1200	LINCOLN WY	94122	8-J2
1300	IRVING ST	94122	8-J2
1400	JUDAH ST	94122	8-J2
1500	KIRKHAM ST	94122	8-J2
1600	LAWTON ST	94122	8-J3
1700	MORAGA ST	94122	8-J3
1800	NORIEGA ST	94122	8-J3
1900	ORTEGA ST	94116	8-J3
2000	PACHECO ST	94116	8-J4
2100	QUINTARA ST	94116	8-J4
2200	RIVERA ST	94116	12-J4
2300	SANTIAGO ST	94116	12-J4
2400	TARAVAL ST	94116	12-J5
2500	ULLOA ST	94116	12-J5
2600	VICENTE ST	94116	12-J5
2700	WAWONA ST	94116	12-J5
2800	YORBA ST	94132	12-J6
2890	SLOAT BLVD	94132	12-J6
2100	36TH AV	94116	8-J4
2500	36TH AV	94116	12-J5
36TH AV			**SF**
400	CLEMENT ST	94121	4-J6
440	SHORE VIEW AV	94121	4-J6
500	GEARY BLVD	94121	4-J7
600	ANZA ST	94121	4-J7
700	BALBOA ST	94121	4-J7
800	CABRILLO ST	94121	4-J7
880	FULTON ST	-	8-J1
	SPRECKLES LAKE DR	-	8-J1
	JOHN F KENNEDY DR	-	8-J1
1200	LINCOLN WY	94122	8-J2
1250	SUNSET BLVD	94122	8-J2
1300	IRVING ST	94122	8-J2
1400	JUDAH ST	94122	8-J2
1500	KIRKHAM ST	94122	8-J2
1600	LAWTON ST	94122	8-J3
1700	MORAGA ST	94122	8-J3
1800	NORIEGA ST	94122	8-J3
1900	ORTEGA ST	94116	8-J3
2000	PACHECO ST	94116	8-J4
2100	35TH AV	94116	8-J4
2100	QUINTARA ST	94116	8-J4
2500	ULLOA ST	94116	12-J5
2500	35TH AV	94116	12-J5
2600	VICENTE ST	94116	12-J5
2700	WAWONA ST	94116	12-J5
2800	YORBA ST	94132	12-J6
37TH AV			**SF**
400	SHORE VIEW AV	94121	4-J6
500	GEARY BLVD	94121	4-J6
600	ANZA ST	94121	4-J7
700	BALBOA ST	94121	4-J7
800	CABRILLO ST	94121	4-J7
900	FULTON ST	94121	8-J1
1200	LINCOLN WY	94122	8-J2
1230	SUNSET BLVD	94122	8-J2
1300	IRVING ST	94122	8-J2
1400	JUDAH ST	94122	8-J2
1500	KIRKHAM ST	94122	8-J2
1600	LAWTON ST	94122	8-J3
1700	MORAGA ST	94122	8-J3
1800	NORIEGA ST	94122	8-J3
1900	ORTEGA ST	94116	8-J3
2000	PACHECO ST	94116	8-J4
2100	QUINTARA ST	94116	8-J4
2200	RIVERA ST	94116	12-J4
2300	SANTIAGO ST	94116	12-J4
2400	TARAVAL ST	94116	12-J5
2500	ULLOA ST	94116	12-J5
2600	VICENTE ST	94116	12-J5
2700	WAWONA ST	94116	12-J5
2800	YORBA ST	94132	12-J6
38TH AV			**SF**
400	CLEMENT ST	94121	4-J6
440	SHORE VIEW AV	94121	4-J6
500	GEARY BLVD	94121	4-J7
600	ANZA ST	94121	4-J7
700	BALBOA ST	94121	4-J7
800	CABRILLO ST	94121	4-J7
900	FULTON ST	94121	8-J1
1200	LINCOLN WY	94122	8-J2
1300	IRVING ST	94122	8-J2
1400	JUDAH ST	94122	8-J2
1500	KIRKHAM ST	94122	8-J2
1600	LAWTON ST	94122	8-J3
1700	MORAGA ST	94122	8-J3
1800	NORIEGA ST	94122	8-J3
1900	ORTEGA ST	94122	8-J3
2200	RIVERA ST	94116	12-J4
2300	SANTIAGO ST	94116	12-J4
2400	TARAVAL ST	94116	12-J5
2500	ULLOA ST	94116	12-J5
2600	VICENTE ST	94116	12-J5
2700	WAWONA ST	94116	12-J5
2800	YORBA ST	94116	12-J5
39TH AV			**SF**
400	CLEMENT ST	94121	4-J6
500	GEARY BLVD	94121	4-J7
600	ANZA ST	94121	4-J7
700	BALBOA ST	94121	4-J7
800	CABRILLO ST	94121	4-J7
900	FULTON ST	94121	8-J1
1200	LINCOLN WY	94122	8-J2
1300	IRVING ST	94122	8-J2
1400	JUDAH ST	94122	8-J2
1500	KIRKHAM ST	94122	8-J2
1600	LAWTON ST	94122	8-J3
1700	MORAGA ST	94122	8-J3
1800	NORIEGA ST	94122	8-J3
1900	ORTEGA ST	94122	8-J3
2100	QUINTARA ST	94116	8-J4
2200	RIVERA ST	94116	12-J4
2300	SANTIAGO ST	94116	12-J4
2400	TARAVAL ST	94116	12-J5
2500	ULLOA ST	94116	12-J5
2600	VICENTE ST	94116	12-J5
2700	WAWONA ST	94116	12-J5
2800	YORBA ST	94132	12-J6
2890	SLOAT BLVD	94132	12-J6
40TH AV			**SF**
400	CLEMENT ST	94121	4-J6
500	GEARY BLVD	94121	4-J7
500	POINT LOBOS AV	94121	4-J7
600	ANZA ST	94121	4-J7
700	BALBOA ST	94121	4-J7
800	CABRILLO ST	94121	4-J7
900	FULTON ST	94121	8-J1
1200	LINCOLN WY	94122	8-J2
1300	IRVING ST	94122	8-J2
1400	JUDAH ST	94122	8-J2
1500	KIRKHAM ST	94122	8-J2
1600	LAWTON ST	94122	8-J3
1700	MORAGA ST	94122	8-J3
1800	NORIEGA ST	94122	8-J3
1900	ORTEGA ST	94122	8-J3
2100	QUINTARA ST	94116	8-J4
2200	RIVERA ST	94116	12-J4
2300	SANTIAGO ST	94116	12-J4
2400	TARAVAL ST	94116	12-J5
2500	ULLOA ST	94116	12-J5
2600	VICENTE ST	94116	12-J5
2700	WAWONA ST	94116	12-J6
2800	YORBA ST	94116	12-J6
41ST AV			**SF**
400	CLEMENT ST	94121	4-J6
450	POINT LOBOS AV	94121	4-J6
500	GEARY BLVD	94121	4-J7
600	ANZA ST	94121	4-J7
700	BALBOA ST	94121	4-J7
800	CABRILLO ST	94121	4-J7
900	FULTON ST	94121	8-J1
1200	LINCOLN WY	94122	8-J2
1200	CHAIN OF LAKES DR E	94122	8-J2
1300	IRVING ST	94122	8-J2
1400	JUDAH ST	94122	8-J2
1500	KIRKHAM ST	94122	8-J2
1600	LAWTON ST	94122	8-J3
1700	MORAGA ST	94122	8-J3
1800	NORIEGA ST	94122	8-J3
1900	ORTEGA ST	94116	8-J3
2000	PACHECO ST	94116	8-J4
2100	QUINTARA ST	94116	8-J4
2200	RIVERA ST	94116	12-J4
2300	SANTIAGO ST	94116	12-J4
2400	TARAVAL ST	94116	12-J5
2500	ULLOA ST	94116	12-J5
2600	VICENTE ST	94116	12-J5
2700	WAWONA ST	94116	12-J6
2790	YORBA LN	94132	12-J6
2790	YORBA LN	94116	12-J6
2800	SLOAT BLVD	94132	12-J6
2800	SLOAT BLVD	94116	12-J6
42ND AV			**SF**
400	CLEMENT ST	94121	4-H6
490	POINT LOBOS AV	94121	4-H6
500	GEARY BLVD	94121	4-H7
600	ANZA ST	94121	4-H7
700	BALBOA ST	94121	4-H7
800	CABRILLO ST	94121	4-J7
900	FULTON ST	94121	8-J1
1200	LINCOLN WY	94122	8-J2
1300	IRVING ST	94122	8-J2
1400	JUDAH ST	94122	8-J2
1500	KIRKHAM ST	94122	8-J2
1600	LAWTON ST	94122	8-J3
1700	MORAGA ST	94122	8-J3
1800	NORIEGA ST	94122	8-J3
1900	ORTEGA ST	94116	8-J3
2000	PACHECO ST	94116	8-J4
2100	QUINTARA ST	94116	8-J4
2200	RIVERA ST	94116	12-J4
2300	SANTIAGO ST	94116	12-J4
2400	TARAVAL ST	94116	12-J5
2500	ULLOA ST	94116	12-J5
2600	VICENTE ST	94116	12-J5
2700	WAWONA ST	94116	12-J6
2800	SLOAT BLVD	94116	12-J6
43RD AV			**SF**
400	CLEMENT ST	94121	4-H6
470	POINT LOBOS AV	94121	4-H6
500	GEARY BLVD	94121	4-H7
600	ANZA ST	94121	4-H7
700	BALBOA ST	94121	4-H7
800	CABRILLO ST	94121	4-H7
900	CHAIN OF LAKES DR W	94121	8-H1
900	FULTON ST	94121	8-H1
1200	LINCOLN WY	94122	8-H2
1300	IRVING ST	94122	8-H2
1400	JUDAH ST	94122	8-H2
1500	KIRKHAM ST	94122	8-H2
1600	LAWTON ST	94122	8-H3
1700	MORAGA ST	94122	8-H3
1800	NORIEGA ST	94122	8-H3
1900	ORTEGA ST	94116	8-H3
2000	PACHECO ST	94116	8-H4
2100	QUINTARA ST	94116	8-H4
2200	RIVERA ST	94116	12-H4
2300	SANTIAGO ST	94116	12-H4
2400	TARAVAL ST	94116	12-J5
2500	ULLOA ST	94116	12-J5
2600	VICENTE ST	94116	12-J5
2700	WAWONA ST	94116	12-J5
2800	SLOAT BLVD	94116	12-J5
44TH AV			**SF**
400	CLEMENT ST	94121	4-H6
450	POINT LOBOS AV	94121	4-H6
500	GEARY BLVD	94121	4-H7
600	ANZA ST	94121	4-H7
700	BALBOA ST	94121	4-H7
800	CABRILLO ST	94121	4-H7
900	FULTON ST	94121	8-H1
1200	LINCOLN WY	94122	8-H2
1300	IRVING ST	94122	8-H2
1400	JUDAH ST	94122	8-H2
1500	KIRKHAM ST	94122	8-H2
1600	LAWTON ST	94122	8-H3
1700	MORAGA ST	94122	8-H3
1800	NORIEGA ST	94122	8-H3
1900	ORTEGA ST	94116	8-H3
2000	PACHECO ST	94116	8-H4
2100	QUINTARA ST	94116	8-H4
2200	RIVERA ST	94116	12-H4
2300	SANTIAGO ST	94116	12-H5
2400	TARAVAL ST	94116	12-H5
2500	ULLOA ST	94116	12-H5
2600	VICENTE ST	94116	12-H5
2700	WAWONA ST	94116	12-H5
2800	SLOAT BLVD	94116	12-H5
45TH AV			**SF**
410	SEAL ROCK DR	94121	4-H6
410	CLEMENT ST	94121	4-H6
460	POINT LOBOS AV	94121	4-H6
500	GEARY BLVD	94121	4-H7
600	ANZA ST	94121	4-H7
700	BALBOA ST	94121	4-H7
800	CABRILLO ST	94121	4-H7
900	FULTON ST	94121	8-H1
1200	LINCOLN WY	94122	8-H2
1300	IRVING ST	94122	8-H2
1400	JUDAH ST	94122	8-H2
1500	KIRKHAM ST	94122	8-H2
1600	LAWTON ST	94122	8-H3
1700	MORAGA ST	94122	8-H3
1800	NORIEGA ST	94122	8-H3
1900	ORTEGA ST	94116	8-H3
2000	PACHECO ST	94116	8-H4
2100	QUINTARA ST	94116	8-H4
2200	RIVERA ST	94116	12-H4
2300	SANTIAGO ST	94116	12-H4
2400	TARAVAL ST	94116	12-H5
2500	ULLOA ST	94116	12-H5
2600	VICENTE ST	94116	12-H5
2700	WAWONA ST	94116	12-H5
2800	SLOAT BLVD	94116	12-H5
46TH AV			**SF**
400	POINT LOBOS AV	94121	4-H6
500	GEARY BLVD	94121	4-H7
600	ANZA ST	94121	4-H7
650	SUTRO HEIGHTS AV	94121	4-H7
700	BALBOA ST	94121	4-H7
800	CABRILLO ST	94121	4-H7
900	FULTON ST	94121	8-H1
1200	LINCOLN WY	94122	8-H2
1300	IRVING ST	94122	8-H2
1400	JUDAH ST	94122	8-H2
1500	KIRKHAM ST	94122	8-H2
1600	LAWTON ST	94122	8-H3
1700	MORAGA ST	94122	8-H3
1800	NORIEGA ST	94122	8-H3
1900	ORTEGA ST	94116	8-H3
2000	PACHECO ST	94116	8-H4
2100	QUINTARA ST	94116	8-H4
2200	RIVERA ST	94116	12-H4
2300	SANTIAGO ST	94116	12-H4
2400	TARAVAL ST	94116	12-H5
2500	ULLOA ST	94116	12-H5
2600	VICENTE ST	94116	12-H5
2700	WAWONA ST	94116	12-H5
2800	SLOAT BLVD	94116	12-H5
47TH AV			**SF**
400	POINT LOBOS AV	94121	4-H6
500	GEARY BLVD	94121	4-H7
600	ANZA ST	94121	4-H7
660	SUTRO HEIGHTS AV	94121	4-H7
700	BALBOA ST	94121	4-H7
800	CABRILLO ST	94121	4-H7
900	FULTON ST	-	8-H1
	JOHN F KENNEDY DR	-	8-H1
1200	LINCOLN WY	94122	8-H2
1300	IRVING ST	94122	8-H2
1400	JUDAH ST	94122	8-H2
1500	KIRKHAM ST	94122	8-H2
1600	LAWTON ST	94122	8-H3
1700	MORAGA ST	94122	8-H3
1800	NORIEGA ST	94122	8-H3
1900	ORTEGA ST	94116	8-H3
2000	PACHECO ST	94116	8-H4
2100	QUINTARA ST	94116	8-H4
2200	RIVERA ST	94116	12-H4
2300	SANTIAGO ST	94116	12-H5
2400	TARAVAL ST	94116	12-H5
2500	ULLOA ST	94116	12-H5
2600	VICENTE ST	94116	12-H5
2650	CUTLER AV	94116	12-H5
2700	WAWONA ST	94116	12-H5
2800	SLOAT BLVD	94116	12-H5
48TH AV			**SF**
400	POINT LOBOS AV	94121	4-H6
400	EL CAMINO DEL MAR	94121	4-H6
500	GEARY BLVD	94121	4-H7
600	ANZA ST	94121	4-H7
670	SUTRO HEIGHTS AV	94121	4-H7
700	BALBOA ST	94121	4-H7
800	CABRILLO ST	94121	4-H7
900	FULTON ST	94121	8-H1
1200	LINCOLN WY	94122	8-H2
1300	IRVING ST	94122	8-H2
1400	JUDAH ST	94122	8-H2
1500	KIRKHAM ST	94122	8-H2
1600	LAWTON ST	94122	8-H3
1700	MORAGA ST	94122	8-H3
1800	NORIEGA ST	94122	8-H3
1900	ORTEGA ST	94116	8-H3
2000	PACHECO ST	94116	8-H4
2100	QUINTARA ST	94116	8-H4
2200	RIVERA ST	94116	12-H4
2300	SANTIAGO ST	94116	12-H4
2400	TARAVAL ST	94116	12-H5
2500	GREAT HWY	94116	12-H5
2500	ULLOA ST	94116	12-H5
2600	VICENTE ST	94116	12-H5
2650	CUTLER AV	94116	12-H5
2700	WAWONA ST	94116	12-H5
2800	SLOAT BLVD	94116	12-H5

1998 SAN FRANCISCO COUNTY OLD TO NEW Page Conversion List

OLD	NEW
Old 1	
A1	1 - C2
A2	1 - C3
B1	1 - D2
B2	1 - D3
C1	2 - E2
C2	2 - E3
Old 2	
A1	2 - F2
A2	2 - F3
B1	2 - H2
B2	2 - H3
C1	2 - J2
C2	2 - J3
Old 3	
A1	3 - A2
A2	3 - A3
B1	3 - B2
B2	3 - B3
Old 4	
A1	4 - H4
A2	4 - H5
A3	4 - H7
B1	4 - J4
B2	4 - J5
B3	4 - J7
C1	5 - B4
C2	5 - B5
C3	5 - B7
Old 5	
A1	5 - C4
A2	5 - C5
A3	5 - C7
B1	5 - D4
B2	5 - D6
B3	5 - D7
C1	6 - E4
C2	6 - E6
C3	6 - E7
Old 6	
A1	6 - F5
A2	6 - F6
A3	6 - F7
B1	6 - H5
B2	6 - H6
B3	6 - G7
C1	6 - J5
C2	6 - J6
C3	6 - J7
Old 7	
A1	7 - A5
A2	7 - A6
A3	7 - A7
B1	7 - B5
B2	7 - B6
B3	7 - B7
C1	7 - C5
C2	7 - C6
C3	7 - C7
Old 8	
A1	8 - H1
A2	8 - H2
A3	8 - H3
B1	8 - J1
B2	8 - J2
B3	8 - J3
C1	9 - B1
C2	9 - B2
C3	9 - B3
Old 9	
A1	9 - C1
A2	9 - C2
A3	9 - C3
B1	9 - D1
B2	9 - D2
B3	9 - D3
C1	10 - E1
C2	10 - E2
C3	10 - E3
Old 10	
A1	10 - F1
A2	10 - F2
A3	10 - F3
B1	10 - G1
B2	10 - G2
B3	10 - G3
C1	10 - J1
C2	10 - J2
C3	10 - J3
Old 11	
A1	11 - A1
A2	11 - A2
A3	11 - A3
B1	11 - B1
B2	11 - B2
B3	11 - B3
C1	11 - C1
C2	11 - C2
C3	11 - C3
Old 12	
A1	8 - H4
A2	12 - H5
A3	12 - H6
B1	8 - J4
B2	12 - J5
B3	12 - J6
C1	9 - A4
C2	13 - A5
Old 12	
C3	13 - A6
Old 13	
A1	9 - C4
A2	13 - C5
A3	13 - C6
B1	9 - D4
B2	13 - D5
B3	13 - D6
C1	9 - E4
C2	13 - E5
C3	13 - E6
Old 14	
A1	10 - F4
A2	14 - F5
A3	14 - F6
B1	10 - G4
B2	14 - G5
B3	14 - G6
C1	14 - J4
C2	14 - J5
C3	14 - J6
Old 15	
A1	15 - A4
A2	15 - A5
A3	15 - A6
B1	15 - B4
B2	15 - B5
B3	15 - B6
C1	15 - C4
C2	15 - C5
C3	15 - C6
Old 16	
A1	15 - D4
A2	15 - D5
A3	15 - D6
B1	16 - F4
B2	16 - F5
B3	16 - F6
C1	16 - G4
C2	16 - G5
C3	16 - G6
Old 17	
A1	15 - D7
A2	20 - D2
A3	20 - D3
B1	16 - F7
B2	21 - F2
B3	21 - F3
C1	16 - G7
C2	21 - G2
C3	21 - G3
Old 18	
A1	12 - H7
A2	17 - H1
A3	17 - H2
B1	12 - J7
B2	17 - J1
B3	17 - J2
C1	13 - A7
C2	18 - A1
C3	18 - A2
Old 19	
A1	13 - B7
A2	18 - B1
A3	18 - B2
B1	13 - D7
B2	18 - D1
B3	18 - D2
C1	13 - E7
C2	18 - E1
C3	18 - E2
Old 20	
A1	14 - F7
A2	19 - F1
A3	19 - F2
B1	14 - G7
B2	19 - G1
B3	19 - G2
C1	14 - H7
C2	19 - H1
C3	19 - H2
Old 21	
A1	15 - A7
A2	20 - A1
A3	20 - A3
B1	15 - B7
B2	20 - B1
B3	20 - B3
C1	15 - C7
C2	20 - C1
C3	20 - C3

1998 SAN FRANCISCO COUNTY NEW TO OLD Page Conversion List

NEW	OLD
New 1	
B4	4 - C1
C2	1 - A1
C3	1 - A2
C4	5 - A1
D2	1 - B1
D3	1 - B2
D4	1 - B2
E2	1 - C1
E3	1 - C2
E4	1 - C2
New 2	
E2	1 - C1
E3	1 - C2
E4	1 - C2
F2	2 - A1
F3	2 - A2
F4	2 - A2
G2	2 - B1
G3	2 - B2
G4	2 - B2
H2	2 - B1
H3	2 - B2
H4	2 - B2
J2	2 - C1
J3	2 - C2
J4	2 - C2
New 3	
A2	3 - A1
A3	3 - A2
A4	3 - A2
B2	3 - B1
B3	3 - B2
B4	3 - B2
C2	3 - C1
C3	3 - C1
C4	3 - C2
E1	3 - C1
E2	3 - C2
E3	3 - C2
New 4	
H4	4 - A1
H5	4 - A2
H6	4 - A3
H7	4 - A3
J4	4 - B1
J5	4 - B2
J6	4 - B2
J7	4 - B3
New 5	
A4	4 - B1
A5	4 - B2
A6	4 - B2
A7	4 - B3
B4	4 - C1
B5	4 - C2
B6	4 - C2
B7	4 - C3
C4	5 - A1
C5	5 - A2
C6	5 - A2
C7	5 - A3
D4	5 - B1
D5	5 - B2
D6	5 - B2
D7	5 - B3
E4	5 - C1
E5	5 - C2
E6	5 - C2
E7	5 - C3
New 6	
E4	5 - C1
E5	5 - C2
E6	5 - C2
E7	5 - C3
F4	6 - A1
F5	6 - A2
F6	6 - A2
F7	6 - A3
G4	6 - B1
G5	6 - B1
G6	6 - B2
G7	6 - B3
H4	6 - B1
H5	6 - B1
H6	6 - B2
H7	6 - B3
J4	6 - C1
J5	6 - C1
J6	6 - C2
J7	6 - C3
New 7	
A4	7 - A1
A5	7 - A1
A6	7 - A2
A7	7 - A3
B4	7 - B1
B5	7 - B1
B6	7 - B2
B7	7 - B3
C4	7 - C1
C5	7 - C1
C6	7 - C2
C7	7 - C3
New 8	
H1	8 - A1
H2	8 - A2
H3	8 - A3
H4	12 - A1
J1	8 - B1
J2	8 - B2
J3	8 - B3
J4	12 - B1
New 9	
A1	8 - B1
A2	8 - C2
A3	8 - C3
A4	12 - C1
B1	8 - C1
B2	8 - C2
B3	8 - C3
B4	12 - C1
C1	9 - A1
C2	9 - A2
C3	9 - A3
C4	13 - A1
D1	9 - B1
D2	9 - B2
D3	9 - B3
D4	13 - B1
E1	9 - C1
E2	9 - C2
E3	9 - C3
E4	13 - C1
New 10	
E1	9 - C1
E2	9 - C2
E3	9 - C3
E4	13 - C1
F1	10 - A1
F2	10 - A2
F3	10 - A3
F4	14 - A1
G1	10 - B1
G2	10 - B2
G3	10 - B3
G4	14 - B1
H1	10 - B1
H2	10 - B2
H3	10 - B3
H4	14 - B1
J1	10 - C1
J2	10 - C2
J3	10 - C3
J4	14 - C1
New 11	
A1	11 - A1
A2	11 - A2
A3	11 - A3
A4	15 - A1
B1	11 - B1
B2	11 - B2
B3	11 - B3
B4	15 - B1
C1	11 - C1
C2	11 - C2
C3	11 - C3
C4	15 - C1
D4	16 - A1
E4	16 - A1
New 12	
H4	12 - A1
H5	12 - A2
H6	12 - A3
H7	18 - A1
J4	12 - B1
J5	12 - B2
J6	12 - B3
J7	18 - B1
New 13	
A4	12 - C1
A5	12 - C2
A6	12 - C3
A7	18 - C1
B4	12 - C1
B5	12 - C2
B6	13 - A3
B7	19 - A1
C4	13 - A1
C5	13 - A2
C6	13 - A3
C7	19 - A1
D4	13 - B1
D5	13 - B2
D6	13 - B3
D7	19 - B1
E4	13 - C1
E5	13 - C2
E6	13 - C3
E7	19 - C1
New 14	
E4	13 - C1
E5	13 - C2
E6	13 - C3
E7	19 - C1
F4	14 - A1
F5	14 - A2
F6	14 - A3
F7	20 - A1
G4	14 - B1
G5	14 - B2
G6	14 - B3
G7	20 - B1
H4	14 - C1
H5	14 - C2
New 14	
H6	14 - C3
H7	20 - C1
J4	14 - C1
J5	14 - C2
J6	14 - C3
J7	20 - C1
New 15	
A4	15 - A1
A5	15 - A2
A6	15 - A3
A7	21 - A1
B4	15 - B1
B5	15 - B2
B6	15 - B3
B7	21 - B1
C4	15 - C1
C5	15 - C2
C6	15 - C3
C7	21 - C1
D4	16 - A1
D5	16 - A2
D6	16 - A3
D7	17 - A1
E4	16 - A1
E5	16 - A2
E6	16 - A3
E7	17 - A1
New 16	
E4	16 - B1
E5	16 - B2
E6	16 - B3
E7	17 - B1
F4	16 - B1
F5	16 - B2
F6	16 - B3
F7	17 - B1
G4	16 - C1
G5	16 - C2
G6	16 - C3
G7	17 - C1
New 17	
H1	18 - A2
H2	18 - A3
J1	18 - B2
J2	18 - B3
New 18	
A1	18 - C2
A2	18 - C3
B1	19 - A2
B2	19 - A3
C1	19 - A2
C2	19 - B3
D1	19 - B2
D2	19 - B3
E1	19 - C2
E2	19 - C3
New 19	
E1	19 - C2
E2	19 - C3
F1	20 - A2
F2	20 - A3
F3	20 - A3
G1	20 - B2
G2	20 - B3
G3	20 - B3
H1	20 - C2
H2	20 - C3
J1	20 - C2
J2	20 - C3
New 20	
A1	21 - A2
A2	21 - A3
A3	21 - A3
B1	21 - B2
B2	21 - B2
B3	21 - B3
C1	21 - C2
C2	21 - C2
C3	21 - C3
D1	17 - A2
D2	17 - A2
D3	17 - A3
E1	17 - A2
E2	17 - B2
E3	17 - B3
New 21	
E1	17 - B2
E2	17 - B2
E3	17 - B3
F1	17 - B2
F2	17 - B2
F3	17 - B3
G1	17 - C2
G2	17 - C2
G3	17 - C3

BE SURE TO VISIT OUR STORE...

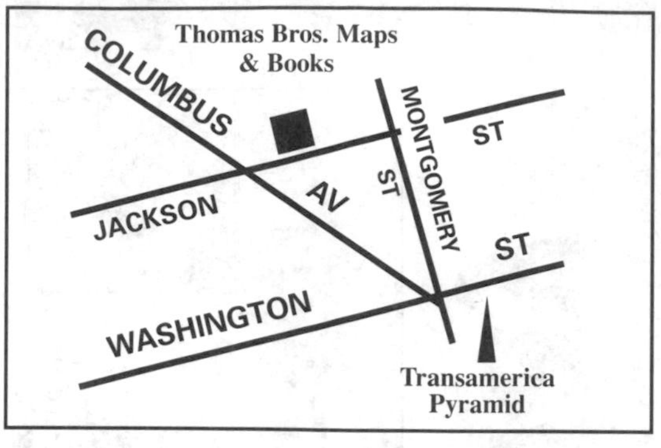

Thomas Bros. Maps® & Books

550 Jackson Street
San Francisco
CA 94133
(415) 981-7520

LOCATED IN DOWNTOWN SAN FRANCISCO AT THE ENTRANCE TO HISTORIC JACKSON SQUARE

In addition to our selection of Thomas Guides®, we offer an extensive collection of domestic and international maps, travel books and software products!

The Thomas Guide®

1998 EDITION

SAN MATEO COUNTY

ZIP

How To Use This Thomas Guide
Modo De Empleo Del Thomas Guide

To Find a City or Community:
Manera de Localizar una Ciudad o Comunidad:

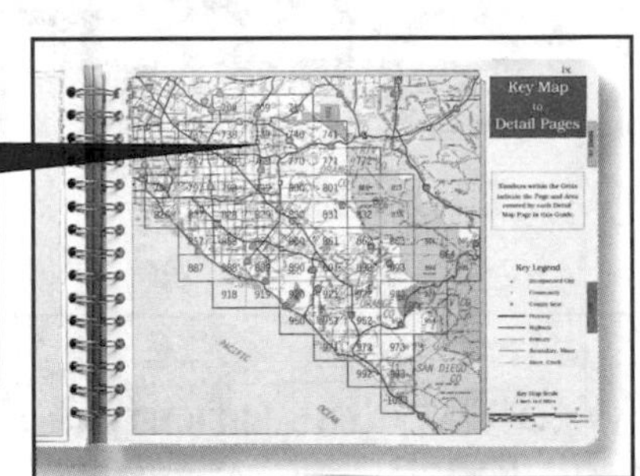

Start with the Key Map to Detail Pages, then turn to the Detail Page indicated.

Empiece con el mapa clave de páginas detalladas, luego pase a la página detallada que se indica.

or
o

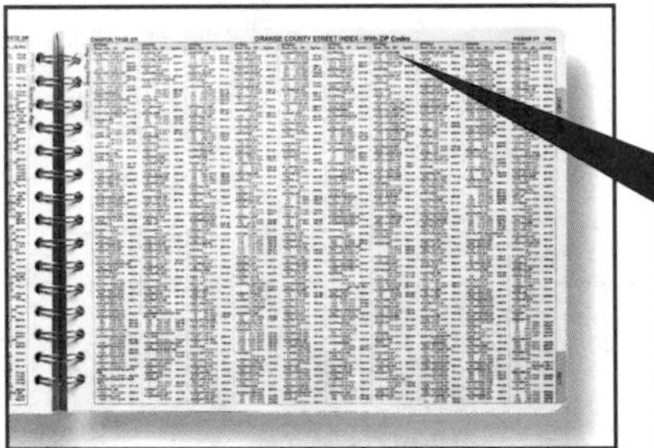

Look up the name in the Cities and Communities Index, then turn to the Detail Page indicated.

Busque el nombre en el Indice de Ciudades y Comunidades, luego pase a la página detallada que se indica.

or
o

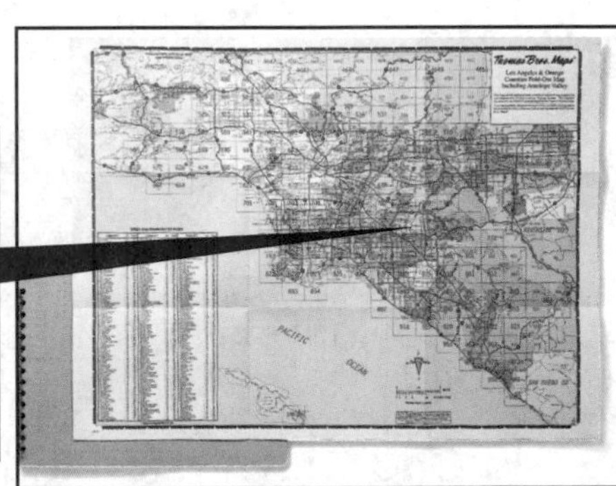

Refer to the enclosed Foldout Map and its Index, then turn to the Detail Page indicated.

Consulte el mapa desplegable y el Indice del mismo adjunto, luego pase a la página detallada que se indica.

To Find an Address:
Manera de Localizar una Dirección:

1 Look up the street name in the Street Index. If there are multiple listings, choose the proper city and/or address range. (All city abbreviations are listed in the Cities and Communities Index.)

Localice el nombre de la calle en el Indice de Calles. Si aparecen varias listas, seleccione el área apropiada de la ciudad y/o el domicilio. (Todas las abreviaturas de las ciudades figuran en la lista del Indice de Ciudades y Comunidades).

2 The street name will include a Thomas Bros. Maps Page and Grid™ where the address is located.

El nombre de la calle incluye un cuadro de Thomas Bros. Maps Page and Grid™ con el número de página y de coordenadas que indican la ubicación del domicilio.

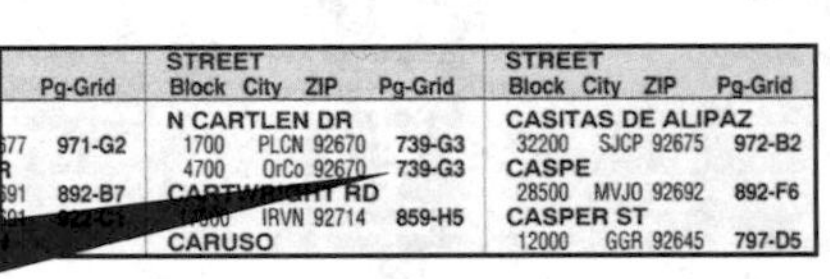

Pg-Grid	STREET Block	City	ZIP	Pg-Grid	STREET Block	City	ZIP	Pg-Grid
	N CARTLEN DR				CASITAS DE ALIPAZ			
971-G2	1700	PLCN	92670	739-G3	32200	SJCP	92675	972-B2
	4700	OrCo	92670	739-G3	CASPE			
892-B7	CARTWRIGHT RD				28500	MVJO	92692	892-F6
[illegible]	[illegible]	IRVN	92714	859-H5	CASPER ST			
	CARUSO				12000	GGR	92645	797-D5

3 Turn to the Page indicated.

Pase a la página que se indica.

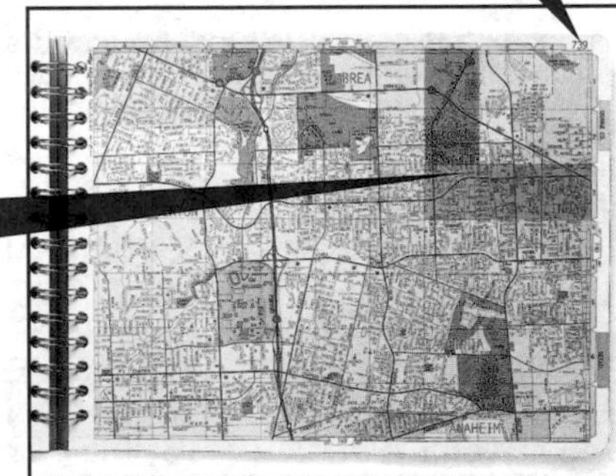

4 Locate the address by following the indicated Letter column and Number row until the two intersect. The street name is within this Grid area.

Localice el domicilio siguiendo la columna con letras y la hilera con números indicadas hasta que intersecten. El nombre de la calle se encuentra dentro de dicho cuadro.

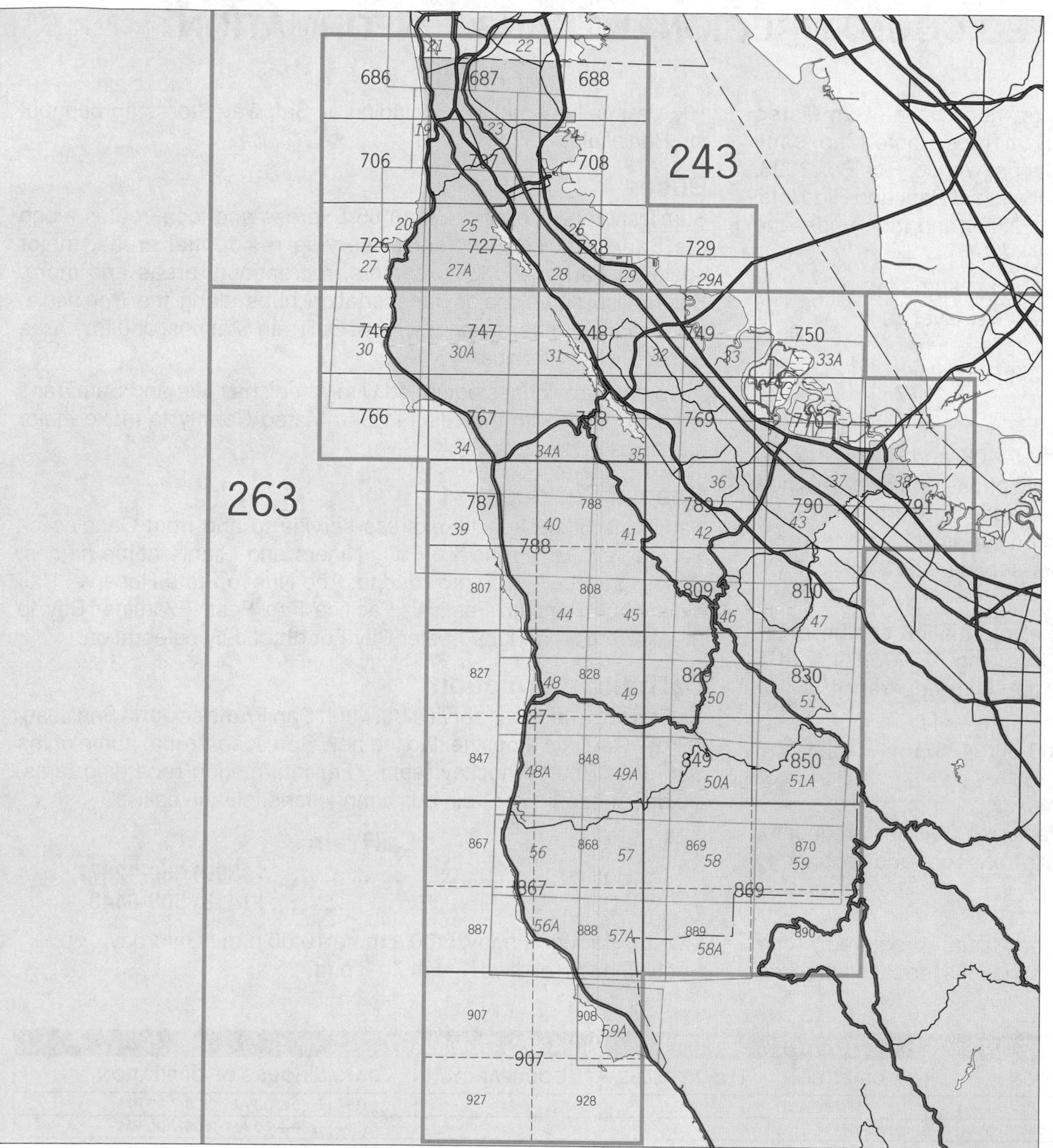

How The New Pages Work With The Old Pages

Finding New Page Numbers

This key map shows our old page layout in green and the new page layout in red. You can locate an old page number on this key map to determine the new page number.

Use of Quad-Pages

To provide important new area coverage, we have created the Quad-Page, a single map page that contains four regular pages of coverage. On the Key Map, Quad-Pages are designated by enlarged numbers in the "Quad" center, and surrounded by the page numbers of the pages included in that "Quad." Normal-size page numbers within a Quad-Page indicate that, in addition to appearing on the Quad-Page, the page is also shown in normal detail and size in the Guide. Small page numbers within the Quad-Pages indicate pages found only on Quad-Pages.

Conversion Help

As you convert to the new Thomas Bros. Maps page and grid® reference system, you may have questions or need conversion assistance. If we can be of help, please call the toll-free customer service number below for additional conversion information.

Call toll-free 1 800-899-MAPS and ask for Extension 99.

1998 SAN MATEO COUNTY REGIONAL TRANSIT INFORMATION

The transit information for this page is provided by the **San Mateo County Transit (SamTrans)**. For a SamTrans Route Map, send your request to: Sam Trans, 1250 San Carlos Avenue, P.O. Box 3006, San Carlos, CA 94070-1306. For the location of Park and Ride lots, see the Points of Interest Index in this atlas, and look under the heading *"Park & Ride"*.

Hearing Impaired (TDD) **1 (415) 508-6448**
Transbay Terminal Courtesy Phone .... Lift Receiver
BART/Daly City Courtesy Phone .... Lift Receiver
Redwood City SamTrans Depot .... Lift Receiver

TravInfo™

Area Transit Information within the 415, 510, 408, and 707 area codes is available from the new regional TravInfo phone number. This new resource provides a single source for accessing transit, traffic, rideshare, parking, freeway construction areas and other transit related information. To access this new service, call **817-1717** (no area code needed).

A 24-hour Internet site is available for information on the entire region's transit maps and timetables including AC Transit, BART. Contact the Internet site at http://server.berkeley.edu/transit/

The toll-free **Information Center** phone number is:
1-800-660-4BUS (1-800-660-4287)

Park and Ride Facilities

Park and Ride lots provided by SamTrans and Caltrans are located throughout the county to encourage public transit use and ridesharing.

Fares

Pay your bus fare when boarding. Exact change is required. Time-saving monthly passes, in various denominations, are available from 100 pass sales agencies, including all Safeway Stores, throughout the Peninsula.

Buses

SamTrans operates more than 85 Express and local routes along the San Francisco Peninsula, serving residential areas, major business parks, shopping centers, recreational areas and more. Buses also serve major transportation hubs along the Peninsula, San Francisco International Airport, CalTrain Stations, and Bay Area Rapid Transit Stations.

All routes have buses equipped with wheelchair lifts and SamTrans is cooperating with the cities in San Mateo County to make major bus stops accessible.

Special Services

SamTrans offers special express service to and from Candlestick Park for all San Francisco Forty-Niners and Giants home games. Special service is also provided to: Año Nuevo State Reserve, Half Moon Bay Pumpkin Festival, Pacifica Fog Fest, Examiner Bay to Breakers race, and the Foster City Fourth of July celebration.

CalTrain Information

CalTrain operates rail service between San Francisco and San Jose/Gilroy. CalTrain stops next to the new San Jose Arena, home of the San Jose Sharks hockey team. For information regarding fares, tickets, schedules or train/bus connections, please call:

CalTrain

Hotline **1 (800) 660-4287**
TDD **1 (415) 508-6448**

Monday through Friday, 6:00 a.m. to 10:00 p.m.; Saturday, Sunday, and Holidays, 8 a.m. to 8 p.m.

EXISTING HIGH OCCUPANCY VEHICLE (HOV) LANES SUMMARY

COUNTY	ROUTE DESCRIPTION	DIRECTION	LANE MILES	OCCUPANCY	DAYS & HOURS OF OPERATION
SAN MATEO	**US101** - Whipple Av to SC County Line	SOUTHBOUND	6.6	2+	(M-F) 5:00-9:00 AM; 3:00-7:00 PM
SAN MATEO	**US101** - SC County Line to Whipple Av	NORTHBOUND	6.6	2+	(M-F) 5:00-9:00 AM; 3:00-7:00 PM

1998 SAN MATEO COUNTY CITIES AND COMMUNITIES

ESTIMATED POPULATION INCORPORATED CITIES	637,320
ESTIMATED POPULATION UNINCORPORATED AREAS	63,780
ESTIMATED TOTAL POPULATION	701,100

COMMUNITY NAME	ABBR.	ZIP CODE	AREA SQ. MI.	EST. POP.	PAGE
ALPINE HILLS		94025			810
* ATHERTON	ATN	94027	6.00	7,375	790
BAYSHORE		94005			688
* BELMONT	BLMT	94002	4.00	25,200	769
* BRISBANE	BSBN	94005	15.00	3,210	688
BROADMOOR VILLAGE		94015			687
* BURLINGAME	BURL	94010	6.10	28,550	728
BURLINGAME HILLS		94010			728
* COLMA	CLMA	94014	2.50	1,240	687
* DALY CITY	DALY	94014	7.40	101,300	687
DEVONSHIRE		94070			769
EAST MENLO		94025			770
* EAST PALO ALTO	EPA	94303	2.50	25,050	791
EL GRANADA		94018			767
EMERALD LAKE		94062			789
FARM HILLS		94061			789
* FOSTER CITY	FCTY	94404	4.04	29,750	749
* HALF MOON BAY	HMBY	94019	8.00	10,850	787
* HILLSBOROUGH	HIL	94010	6.25	11,350	748
HILLSDALE		94403			749
KINGS MOUNTAIN		94062			788
LADERA		94025			810
LA HONDA		94020			849
LINDA MAR		94044			726
LINDENWOOD		94025			790
LOMA MAR		94021			848
LOS TRANCOS WOODS		94025			830
MENLO OAKS		94025			790
* MENLO PARK	MLPK	94025	19.00	30,550	790
* MILLBRAE	MLBR	94030	10.00	21,450	728
MIRAMAR		94019			767
MONTARA		94037			746
MOSS BEACH		94038			746
NORTH FAIR OAKS		94063			770
* PACIFICA	PCFA	94044	12.50	39,650	727
PALOMAR PARK		94062			769
PESCADERO		94060			868
* PORTOLA VALLEY	PTLV	94028	10.00	4,470	810
PORTOLA VALLEY RANCH		94025			830
PRINCETON BY THE SEA		94018			766
* REDWOOD CITY	RDWC	94061	33.60	73,200	770
REDWOOD SHORES		94065			749
ROCKAWAY BEACH		94044			726
* SAN BRUNO	SBRN	94066	5.87	40,800	707
* SAN CARLOS	SCAR	94070	4.50	28,050	769
SAN GREGORIO		94074			828
* SAN MATEO	SMTO	94401	14.60	92,200	749
-- SAN MATEO COUNTY	SMCo		552.00	701,100	
SAN PEDRO TERRACE		94044			726
SERRAMONTE		94015			707
SHARON HEIGHTS		94025			790
SHARP PARK		94044			707
SKYLINE		94062			788
SKY LONDA		94062			809
* SOUTH SAN FRANCISCO	SSF	94080	9.50	57,600	707
THE HIGHLANDS		94402			748
VALLEMAR		94044			727
VISTA VERDE		94025			830
WESTBOROUGH		94080			707
WEST MENLO PARK		94025			790
WESTRIDGE		94025			810
* WOODSIDE	WDSD	94062	14.00	5,475	789
WOODSIDE HIGHLANDS		94025			809
WOODSIDE HILLS		94062			789

* INDICATES INCORPORATED CITY

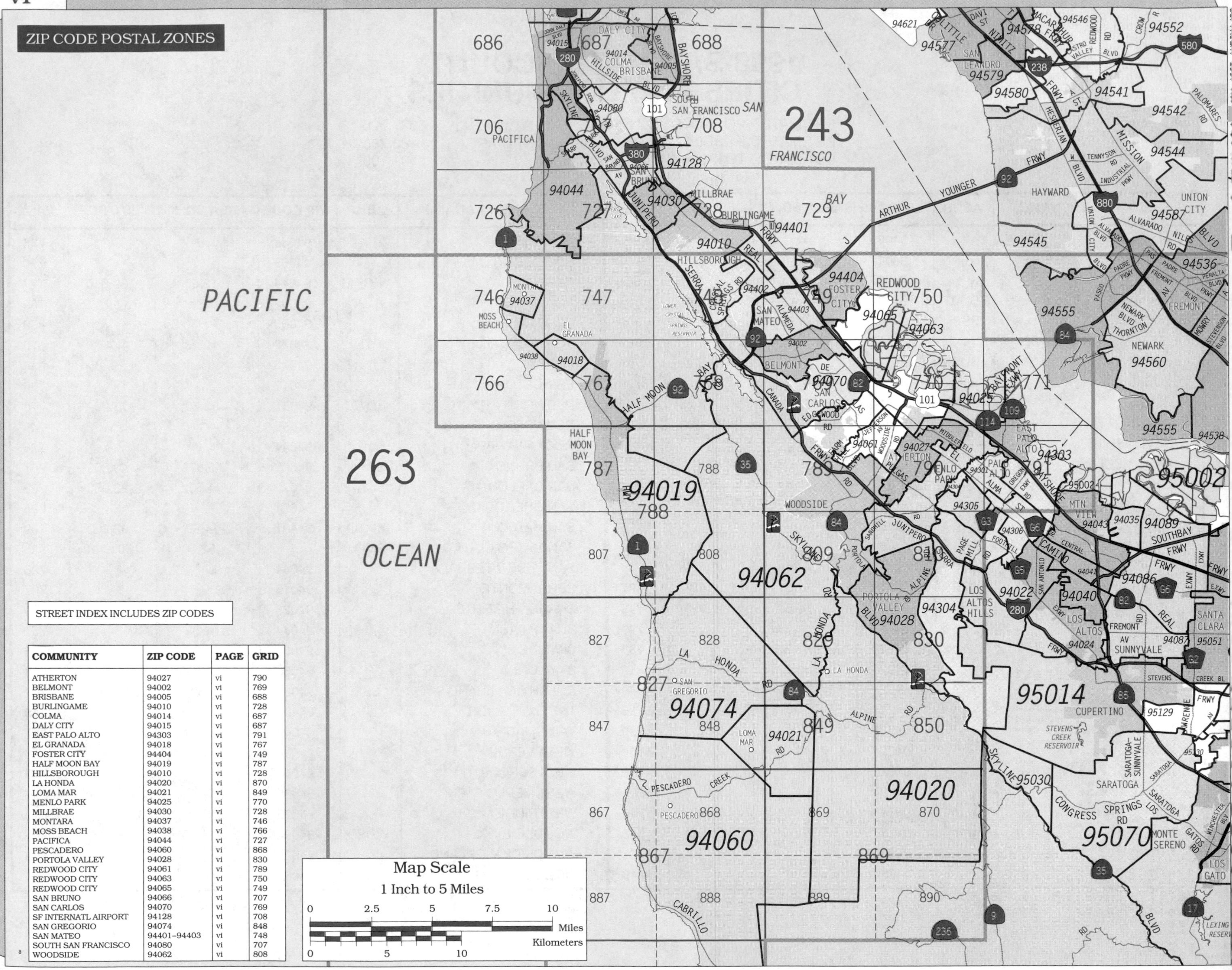

COMMUNITY	ZIP CODE	PAGE	GRID
ATHERTON	94027	vi	790
BELMONT	94002	vi	769
BRISBANE	94005	vi	688
BURLINGAME	94010	vi	728
COLMA	94014	vi	687
DALY CITY	94015	vi	687
EAST PALO ALTO	94303	vi	791
EL GRANADA	94018	vi	767
FOSTER CITY	94404	vi	749
HALF MOON BAY	94019	vi	787
HILLSBOROUGH	94010	vi	728
LA HONDA	94020	vi	870
LOMA MAR	94021	vi	849
MENLO PARK	94025	vi	770
MILLBRAE	94030	vi	728
MONTARA	94037	vi	746
MOSS BEACH	94038	vi	766
PACIFICA	94044	vi	727
PESCADERO	94060	vi	868
PORTOLA VALLEY	94028	vi	830
REDWOOD CITY	94061	vi	789
REDWOOD CITY	94063	vi	750
REDWOOD CITY	94065	vi	749
SAN BRUNO	94066	vi	707
SAN CARLOS	94070	vi	769
SF INTERNATL AIRPORT	94128	vi	708
SAN GREGORIO	94074	vi	848
SAN MATEO	94401–94403	vi	748
SOUTH SAN FRANCISCO	94080	vi	707
WOODSIDE	94062	vi	808

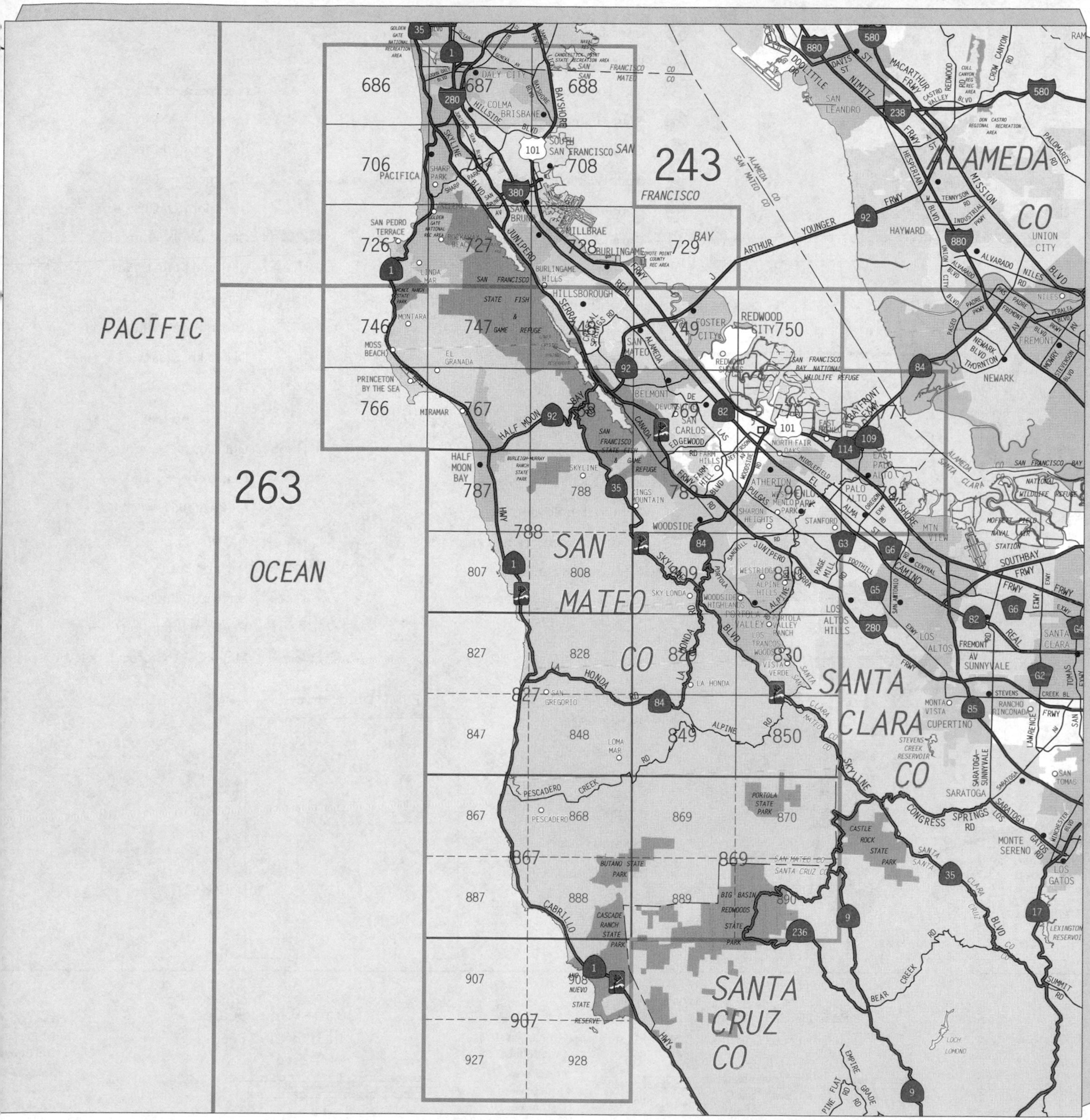

Key Map to Detail Pages

The Thomas Guide® contains several types of map pages:
Arterial, Detail, and Quad

- **263** Arterial Page– Small scale area map, shown with a wide border
- **810** Detail Page– Full scale map page, shown with a solid thin border
- **827** Quad Page– A single map page containing four interior pages at half the detail scale, shown with a bold border subdivided by thin dashed lines
- **848** Interior pages are shown only inside Quad pages

Key Legend

- Incorporated City
- Community
- County Seat
- Freeway
- Highway
- Primary
- Secondary, Minor
- River, Creek

Key Map Scale

1 Inch to 6 Miles

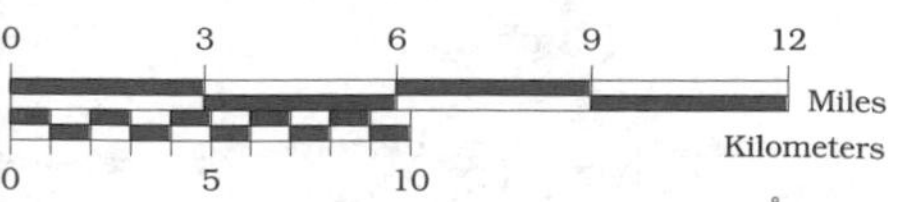

SAN MATEO CO.
ZIP
AREA
LEGEND OF MAP SYMBOLS
NORTH
Freeway
Interchange/Ramp
Highway
Primary Road
Secondary Road
Minor Road
Restricted Road
Alley
Unpaved Road
Tunnel
Toll Road
High Occupancy Veh. Lane
Stacked Multiple Roadways
Proposed Road
Proposed Freeway
Freeway Under Construction
One-Way Road
Two-Way Road
Trail, Walkway
Stairs
Railroad
Rapid Transit
Rapid Transit, Underground
City Boundary
County Boundary
State Boundary
International Boundary
Military Base, Indian Resv.
Township, Range, Rancho
River, Creek, Shoreline
Ferry
PUBLIC JR HS
GOLF COURSE
PUBLIC ELEM SCH
PUBLIC HS
PRIMARY
PARK
TUNNEL
HIGH OCCUPANCY VEHICLE LANE
PRIVATE ELEM SCH
PRIVATE HS
PRIVATE JR HS
FRWY
HIGHWAY
MINOR
ALLEY
RAIL TRANSIT
CALTRAIN
B ST
A ST
LIB
SECONDARY
FS
RAPID TRANSIT
CEM
STA
samTrans
SAN MATEO TRANSIT
CC
RESTRICTED
PO
CH
CTH
HOSP
MILITARY BASE
EXIT NUMBER
REGIONAL SHOPPING CENTER
UNDERGROUND RT
TRAIL
UNDER CONST
BOAT LAUNCH
UNPAVED
RAILROAD
SHOPPING CENTER
PROPOSED
MISSION
SEE A3
1 RIO PORTO CT
2 SAND RIVER CT
3 SMOKE RIVER WY
4 GRAND RIVER DR
Interstate
Interstate (Business)
U.S. Highway
State Highway
County Highway
State Scenic Highway
County Scenic Highway
Carpool Lane
Street List Marker
Street Name Continuation
Street Name Change
Airport
Station (Train,Bus)
Building (see List of Abbreviations page)
Building Footprint
Public Elementary School
Public High School
Private Elementary School
Private High School
Shopping Center
Fire Station
Library
Mission
Winery
Campground
Hospital
Mountain
Section Corner
Boat Launch
Gates, Locks, Barricades
Lighthouse
County Seat
County
Incorporated City
Incorporated City
Incorporated City
Incorporated City
Incorporated City
City, County, State Park
National Forest, Park
Water
Intermittent Lake, Marsh
Dry Lake, Beach
Dam
Point of Interest
Golf Course, Country Club
Cemetery
Military Base
Airport
Parking Lot
Structure Footprint
Regional Shopping Center
Major Dept. Store (List of Abbr. page)
Public Land Survey
T2S
T3S
R7W
RANCHO
TRABUCO
Detail Map Scale
1 Inch to 2400 Feet
Miles
Kilometers
Detail Grid Equivalents
1 Grid Equals:
.5 x .5 Miles
2640 x 2640 Feet
1.1 x 1.1 Inches
Arterial Map Scale
1 Inch to 5 Miles
Miles
Kilometers
Arterial Grid Equivalents
1 Grid Equals:
1 Detail Page
4.5 x 3.5 Miles
.9 x .7 Inches
"Quad-Page" Scale
1 Inch to 4800 Feet
Miles
Kilometers
"Quad Page"
Grid Equivaler
1 Grid Equal
.5 x .5 Miles
2640 x 2640 Fe
.55 x .55 Inche

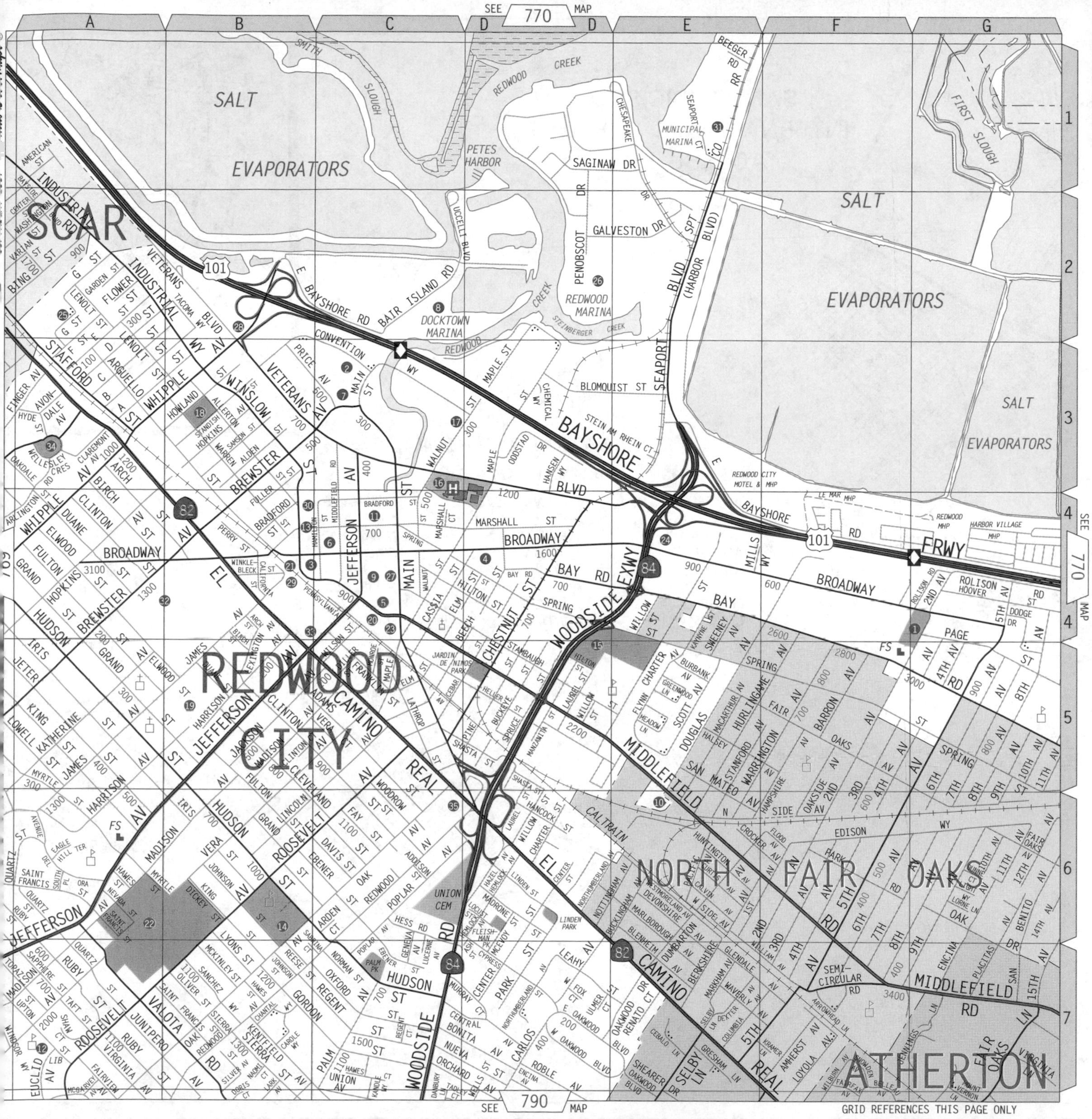

SAN MATEO CO.
ZIP
AREA

Downtown Redwood City

SEE 770 MAP

Points of Interest

1 Andrew Spinas Park	G4
2 California Highway Patrol	C3
3 Caltrain	B4
4 Chamber Of Commerce	D4
5 City Hall	C4
6 County Courthouse	C4
7 Dept Of Motor Vehicles	C3
8 Docktown Marina	C2
9 Downtown Post Office	C4
10 Fair Oaks Branch	E6
11 Fire Station	C4
12 H W Schaberg Library	A7
13 Hall Of Justice	B4
14 Hawes Park	B6
15 Hoover Park	D5
16 Kaiser Hospital	C3
17 Mervyns Plaza	C3
18 Mezes Park	B3
19 McKinley Inter School	B5
20 Police Station	C4
21 Railroad Station	B4
22 Red Morton Community Park	A6
23 Redwood City Library	C4
24 Redwood City Post Office	E4
25 Redwood Cont School	A2
26 Redwood Marina	D2
27 Redwood Plaza	C4
28 Samtrans	B2
29 Samtrans	B4
30 San Mateo County Govt Ctr	B4
31 Seaport Village North	E1
32 Sequoia High School	B4
33 Sequoia Station	B4
34 Wellesley park	A3
35 Woodside Central	C6

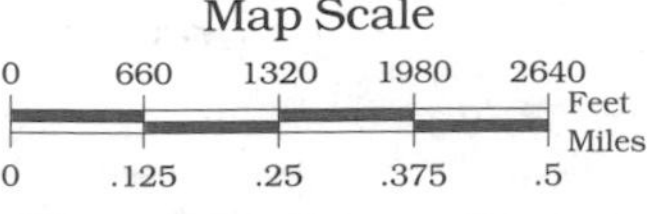

SEE 790 MAP

GRID REFERENCES THIS PAGE ONLY

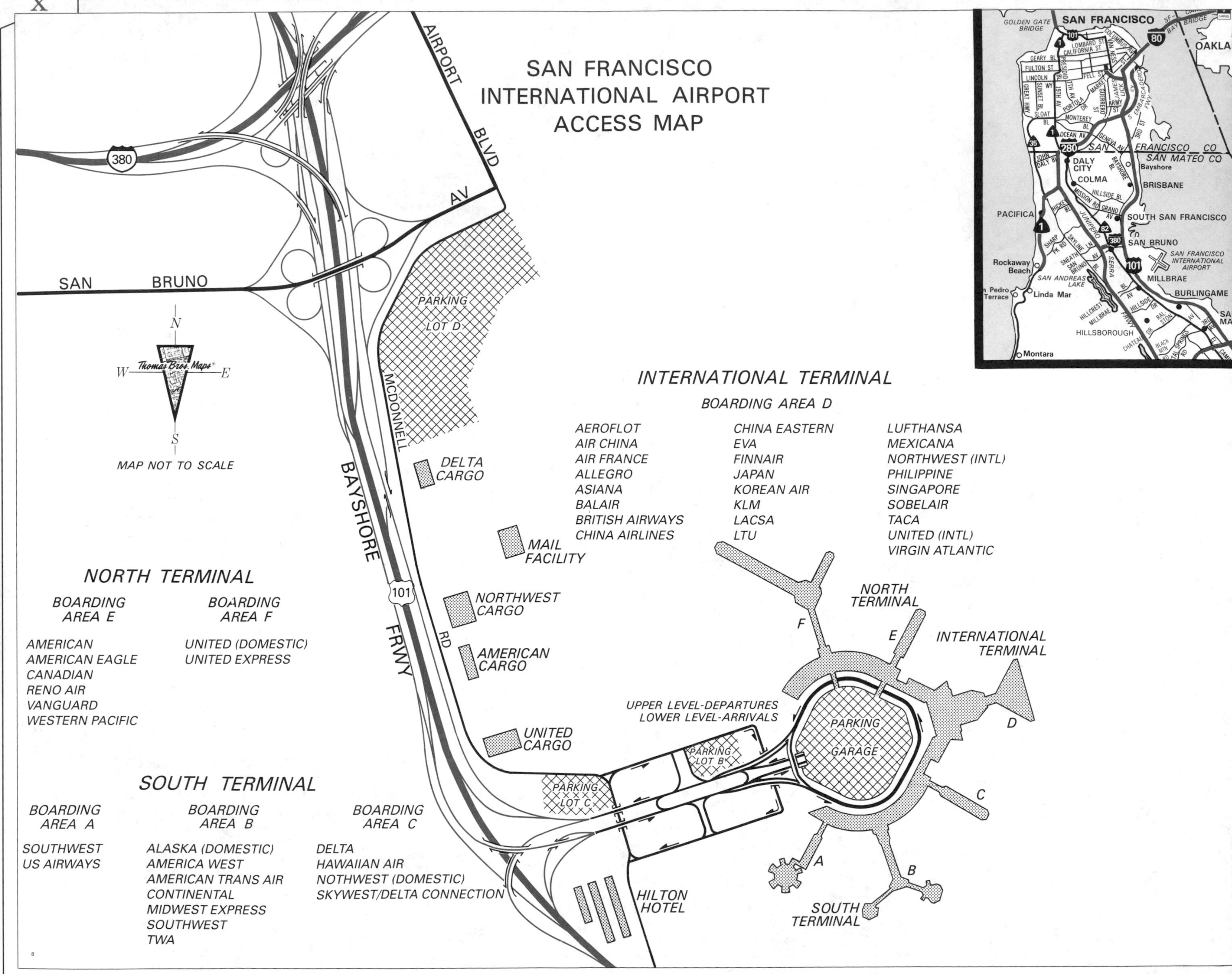
X
SAN MATEO CO.
ZIP
AREA
SAN FRANCISCO
INTERNATIONAL AIRPORT
ACCESS MAP
AIRPORT
BLVD
AV
380
SAN
BRUNO
PARKING
LOT D
N
W
E
S
Thomas Bros. Maps
MAP NOT TO SCALE
MCDONNELL
RD
BAYSHORE
FRWY
101
DELTA
CARGO
MAIL
FACILITY
NORTHWEST
CARGO
AMERICAN
CARGO
UNITED
CARGO
INTERNATIONAL TERMINAL
BOARDING AREA D
AEROFLOT
AIR CHINA
AIR FRANCE
ALLEGRO
ASIANA
BALAIR
BRITISH AIRWAYS
CHINA AIRLINES
CHINA EASTERN
EVA
FINNAIR
JAPAN
KOREAN AIR
KLM
LACSA
LTU
LUFTHANSA
MEXICANA
NORTHWEST (INTL)
PHILIPPINE
SINGAPORE
SOBELAIR
TACA
UNITED (INTL)
VIRGIN ATLANTIC
NORTH TERMINAL
BOARDING
AREA E
AMERICAN
AMERICAN EAGLE
CANADIAN
RENO AIR
VANGUARD
WESTERN PACIFIC
BOARDING
AREA F
UNITED (DOMESTIC)
UNITED EXPRESS
SOUTH TERMINAL
BOARDING
AREA A
SOUTHWEST
US AIRWAYS
BOARDING
AREA B
ALASKA (DOMESTIC)
AMERICA WEST
AMERICAN TRANS AIR
CONTINENTAL
MIDWEST EXPRESS
SOUTHWEST
TWA
BOARDING
AREA C
DELTA
HAWAIIAN AIR
NOTHWEST (DOMESTIC)
SKYWEST/DELTA CONNECTION
NORTH
TERMINAL
F
E
INTERNATIONAL
TERMINAL
D
C
B
A
SOUTH
TERMINAL
UPPER LEVEL-DEPARTURES
LOWER LEVEL-ARRIVALS
PARKING
GARAGE
PARKING
LOT B
PARKING
LOT C
HILTON
HOTEL
GOLDEN GATE
BRIDGE
SAN FRANCISCO
OAKLAN
101
80
LOMBARD ST
CALIFORNIA ST
GEARY BL
FULTON ST
LINCOLN
GREAT HWY
SUNSET BL
19TH AV
PORTOLA
SLOAT
MONTEREY
OCEAN AV
280
35
SAN FRANCISCO CO
SAN MATEO CO
DALY CITY
COLMA
Bayshore
BRISBANE
PACIFICA
SOUTH SAN FRANCISCO
SAN BRUNO
SAN FRANCISCO
INTERNATIONAL
AIRPORT
Rockaway
Beach
MILLBRAE
SAN ANDREAS
LAKE
Linda Mar
BURLINGAME
HILLSBOROUGH
Montara
380
82
1

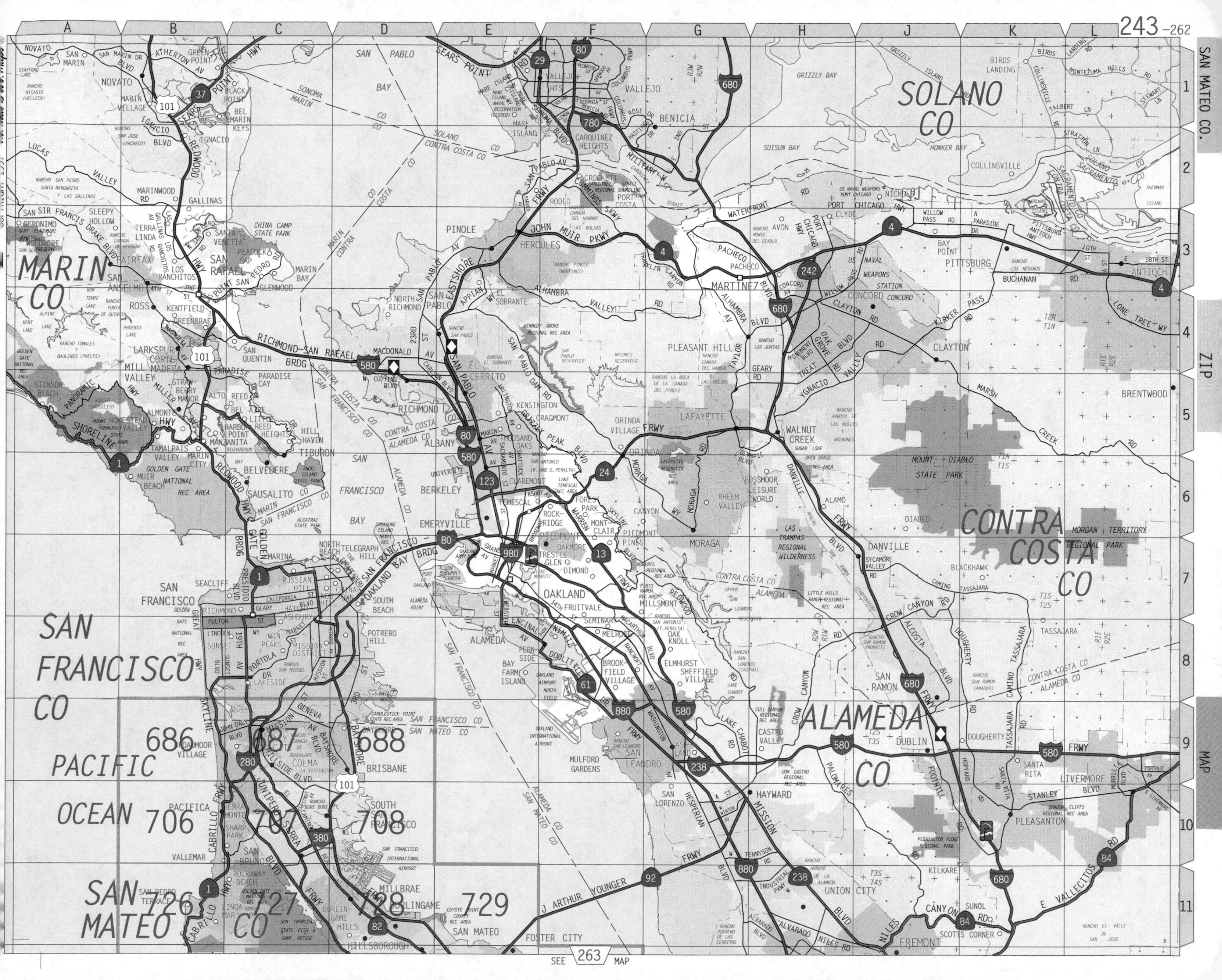
243–262
A
B
C
D
E
F
G
H
J
K
L
1
2
3
4
5
6
7
8
9
10
11
SAN MATEO CO.
ZIP
MAP
SOLANO CO
MARIN CO
CONTRA COSTA CO
SAN FRANCISCO CO
ALAMEDA CO
SAN MATEO CO
PACIFIC OCEAN
SAN PABLO BAY
SAN FRANCISCO BAY
GRIZZLY BAY
SUISUN BAY
HONKER BAY
NOVATO
SAN MARIN
IGNACIO
MARINWOOD
GALLINAS
SAN RAFAEL
FAIRFAX
SAN ANSELMO
ROSS
KENTFIELD
GREENBRAE
LARKSPUR
CORTE MADERA
MILL VALLEY
STINSON BEACH
MUIR BEACH
SAUSALITO
BELVEDERE
TIBURON
SAN QUENTIN
PARADISE CAY
CHINA CAMP STATE PARK
GOLDEN GATE NATIONAL REC AREA
MOUNT TAMALPAIS STATE PARK
ANGEL ISLAND STATE PARK
ALCATRAZ STATE PARK
VALLEJO
BENICIA
CROCKETT
RODEO
PORT COSTA
HERCULES
PINOLE
MARTINEZ
PACHECO
CONCORD
PLEASANT HILL
WALNUT CREEK
LAFAYETTE
ORINDA
MORAGA
CLAYTON
PITTSBURG
BAY POINT
ANTIOCH
BRENTWOOD
COLLINSVILLE
BIRDS LANDING
PORT CHICAGO
CLYDE
EL SOBRANTE
NORTH RICHMOND
SAN PABLO
RICHMOND
EL CERRITO
KENSINGTON
ALBANY
BERKELEY
EMERYVILLE
PIEDMONT
OAKLAND
ALAMEDA
BAY FARM ISLAND
SAN LEANDRO
SAN LORENZO
HAYWARD
CASTRO VALLEY
UNION CITY
FREMONT
NILES
SUNOL
DUBLIN
SAN RAMON
DANVILLE
ALAMO
DIABLO
BLACKHAWK
TASSAJARA
PLEASANTON
LIVERMORE
KILKARE
MOUNT DIABLO STATE PARK
MORGAN TERRITORY REGIONAL PARK
LAS TRAMPAS REGIONAL WILDERNESS
SAN FRANCISCO
DALY CITY
BRISBANE
COLMA
SOUTH SAN FRANCISCO
SAN BRUNO
PACIFICA
MILLBRAE
BURLINGAME
HILLSBOROUGH
SAN MATEO
FOSTER CITY
SAN FRANCISCO INTERNATIONAL AIRPORT
OAKLAND INTERNATIONAL AIRPORT
686
687
688
706
707
708
726
727
728
729
SEE 263 MAP

SEE 243 MAP

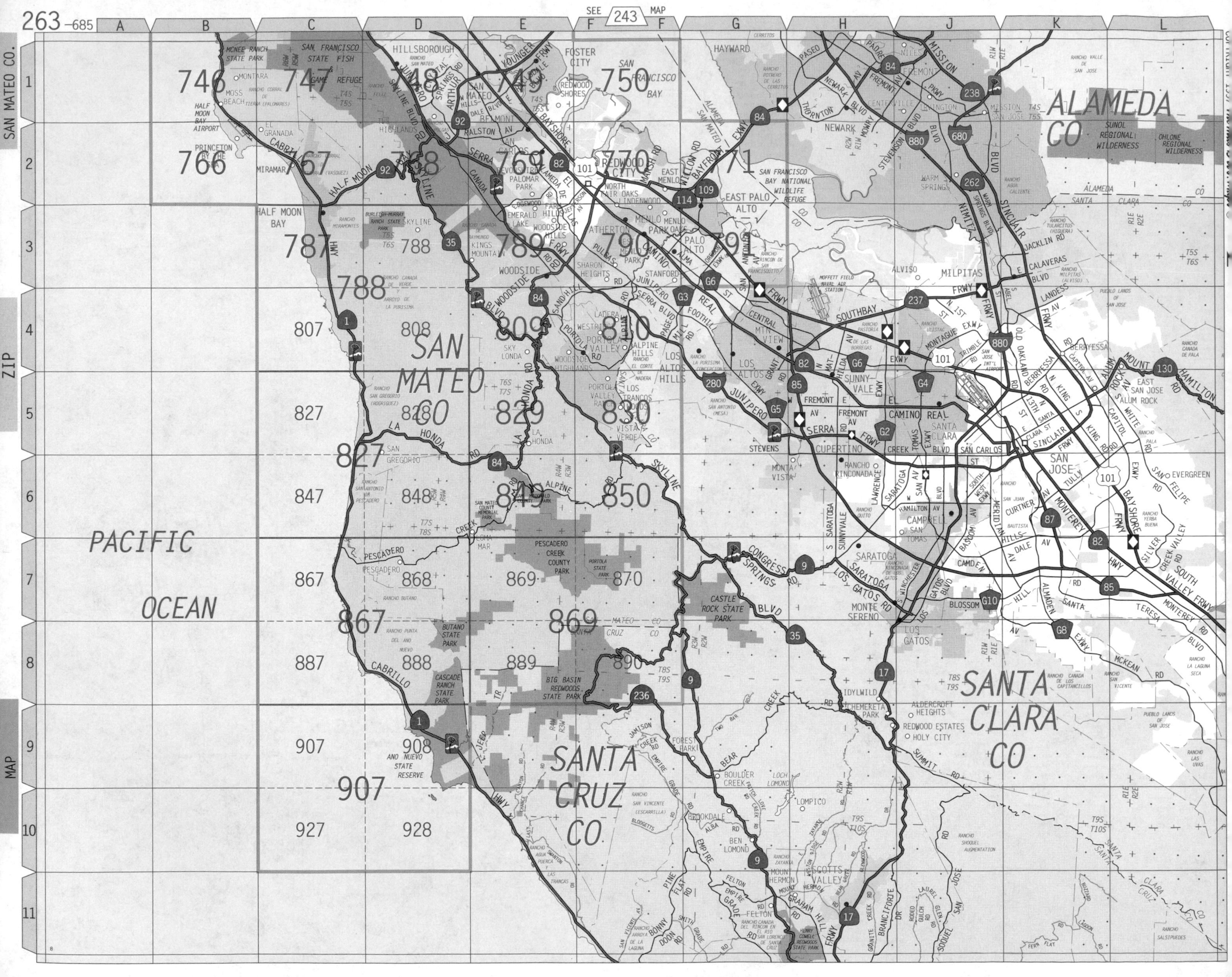
SAN MATEO CO.
ZIP
MAP
A
B
C
D
E
F
G
H
J
K
L
PACIFIC
OCEAN
SAN
MATEO
CO
SANTA
CRUZ
CO
SANTA
CLARA
CO
ALAMEDA
CO
SAN
FRANCISCO
BAY
HILLSBOROUGH
FOSTER
CITY
HAYWARD
FREMONT
NEWARK
NILES
REDWOOD
SHORES
HALF
MOON
BAY
AIRPORT
MOSS
BEACH
MONTARA
EL
GRANADA
PRINCETON
BY THE
SEA
MIRAMAR
HALF MOON
BAY
SAN
MATEO
HILLS
BELMONT
SAN
CARLOS
THE
HIGHLANDS
PALOMAR
PARK
REDWOOD
CITY
EMERALD
LAKE
WOODSIDE
HILLS
NORTH
FAIR OAKS
EAST
MENLO
EAST PALO
ALTO
LINDENWOOD
ATHERTON
MENLO
PARK
PALO
ALTO
STANFORD
KINGS
MOUNTAIN
WOODSIDE
SHARON
HEIGHTS
LADERA
PORTOLA
VALLEY
SKY
LONDA
WOODSIDE
HIGHLANDS
ALPINE
HILLS
LOS
ALTOS
HILLS
LOS
ALTOS
MTN
VIEW
SUNNY-
VALE
MOFFETT FIELD
NAVAL AIR
STATION
ALVISO
MILPITAS
WARM
SPRINGS
SUNOL
REGIONAL
WILDERNESS
OHLONE
REGIONAL
WILDERNESS
EAST
SAN JOSE
ALUM ROCK
SANTA
CLARA
SAN
JOSE
CUPERTINO
STEVENS
MONTA
VISTA
RANCHO
RINCONADA
CAMPBELL
SAN
TOMAS
SARATOGA
MONTE
SERENO
LOS
GATOS
BLOSSOM
EVERGREEN
LA
HONDA
SAN
GREGORIO
LOMA
MAR
PESCADERO
PESCADERO
CREEK
COUNTY
PARK
PORTOLA
STATE
PARK
CASTLE
ROCK STATE
PARK
BUTANO
STATE
PARK
BIG BASIN
REDWOODS
STATE PARK
CASCADE
RANCH
STATE
PARK
ANO NUEVO
STATE
RESERVE
IDYLWILD
ALDERCROFT
HEIGHTS
REDWOOD ESTATES
HOLY CITY
BOULDER
CREEK
LOCH
LOMOND
LOMPICO
BROOKDALE
BEN
LOMOND
MOUNT
HERMON
SCOTTS
VALLEY
FELTON
HENRY
COWELL
REDWOODS
STATE PARK
746
747
748
749
750
766
767
768
769
770
771
787
788
789
790
791
807
808
809
810
827
828
829
830
847
848
849
850
867
868
869
870
887
888
889
890
907
908
927
928

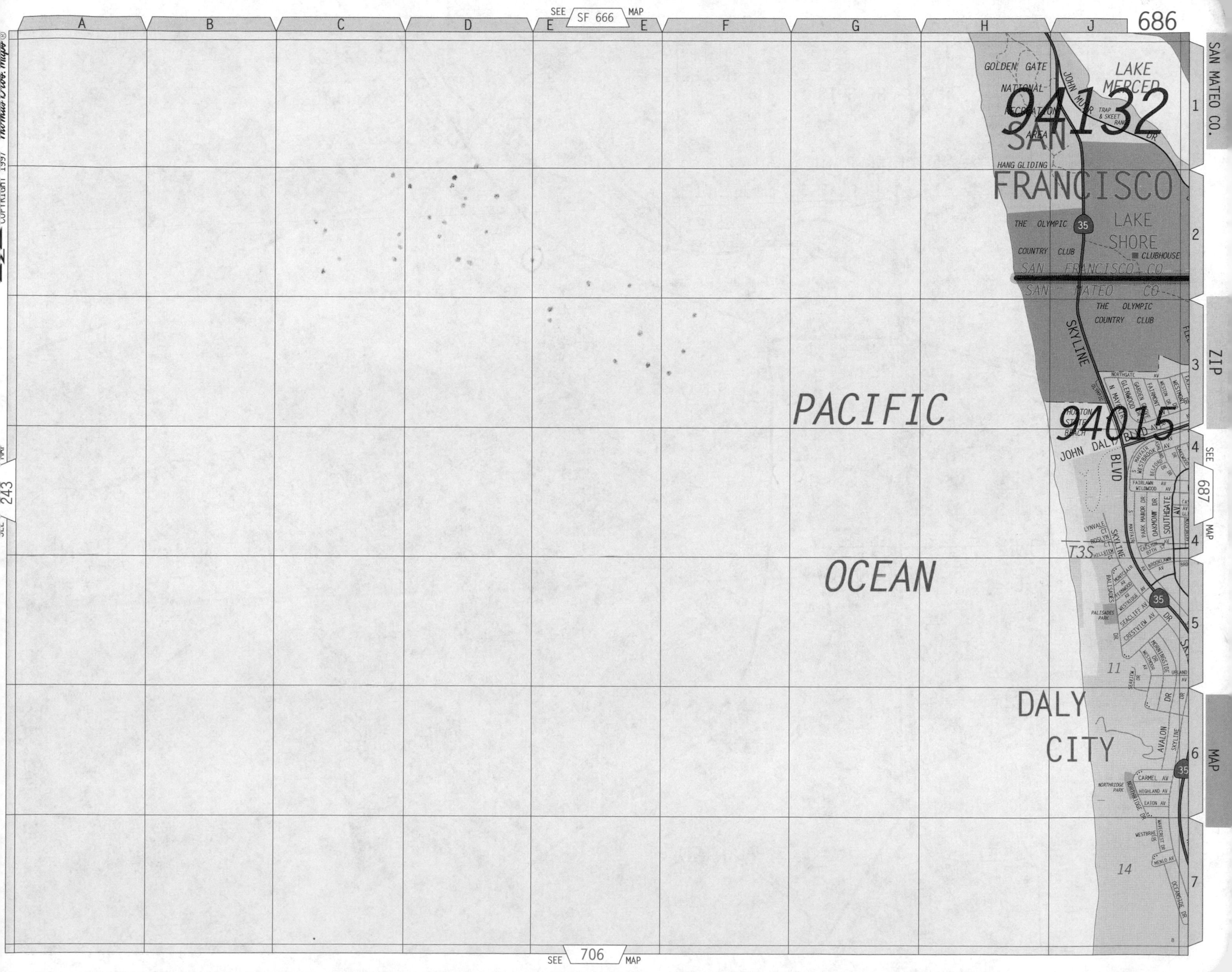
SEE SF 666 MAP
A
B
C
D
E
E
F
G
H
J
GOLDEN GATE
NATIONAL
RECREATION
AREA
HANG GLIDING
JOHN MUIR
LAKE
MERCED
TRAP & SKEET RANGE
DR
94132
SAN
FRANCISCO
THE OLYMPIC
COUNTRY CLUB
35
LAKE
SHORE
CLUBHOUSE
SAN FRANCISCO CO
SAN MATEO CO
THE OLYMPIC
COUNTRY CLUB
SKYLINE
NORTHGATE AV
PACIFIC
94015
JOHN DALY BLVD
BLVD
OCEAN
DALY
CITY
AVALON
SKYLINE
CARMEL AV
HIGHLAND AV
EATON AV
NORTHRIDGE PARK
MENLO AV
11
14
SAN MATEO CO.
ZIP
MAP
SEE 687 MAP
SEE 243 MAP
SEE 706 MAP

SEE SF 667 MAP

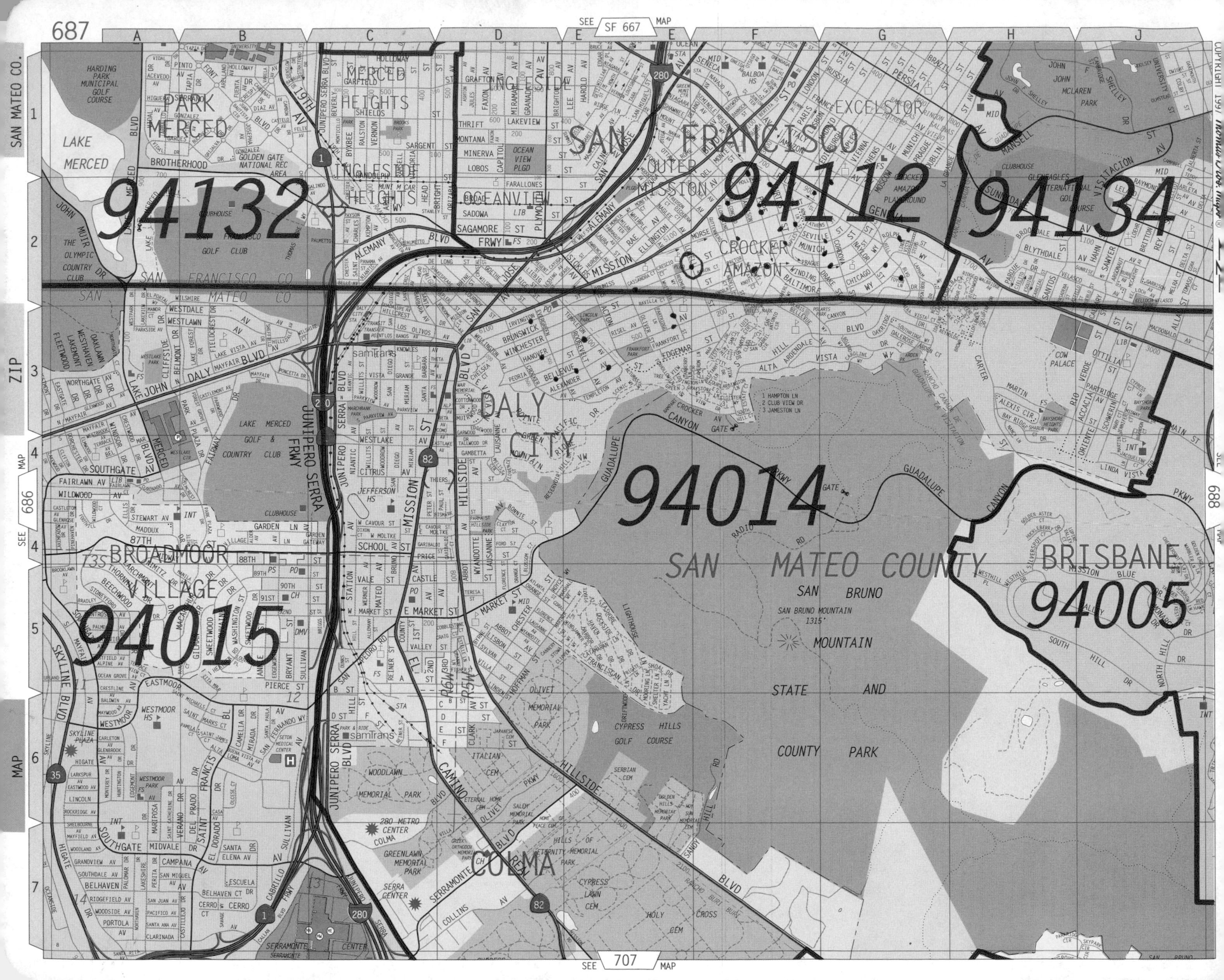

SEE 686 MAP

688

SEE 707 MAP

SEE SF 668 MAP
A
B
C
D
E
F
G
H
J
SAN MATEO CO.
ZIP
MAP
1
2
3
4
5
6
7
SEE 243 MAP
687
SAN FRANCISCO
94124
94134
94014
94005
BAYVIEW
HUNTERS
NAVAL
RESERVATION
POINT
SAN FRANCISCO
NAVAL
SHIPYARD
SOUTH BASIN
CANDLESTICK POINT
3COM PARK
(CANDLESTICK PARK)
HOME OF
SF GIANTS
&
49ERS
CANDLESTICK
POINT STATE
RECREATION
AREA
VISITACION
VALLEY
BAYVIEW
HEIGHTS
BAYSHORE
SAN FRANCISCO CO
SAN MATEO CO
SAN MATEO
COUNTY
BRISBANE
LAGOON
GUADALUPE CANAL
SAN FRANCISCO
BAY
SIERRA POINT
MARINA
1 SAN MATEO LN
2 PLACER WY
SAN BRUNO MOUNTAIN
STATE AND COUNTY PARK
SEE 708 MAP

SEE 686 MAP

A B C D E E F G H J

SAN MATEO CO.

ZIP

MAP

SEE 243 MAP

1 2 3 4 4 5 6 7

DALY CITY

MUSSEL ROCK

94015

PACIFIC OCEAN

PACIFICA

94044

LAGUNA SALADA

SHARP PARK GOLF COURSE

SHARP PARK BEACH

MORI POINT

MORIS POINT RD

FAIRWAY DR

PALMETTO AV

CABRILLO BLVD

OCEANA BLVD

MONTEREY RD

CLARENDON RD

FRANCISCO BLVD

SEE 726 MAP

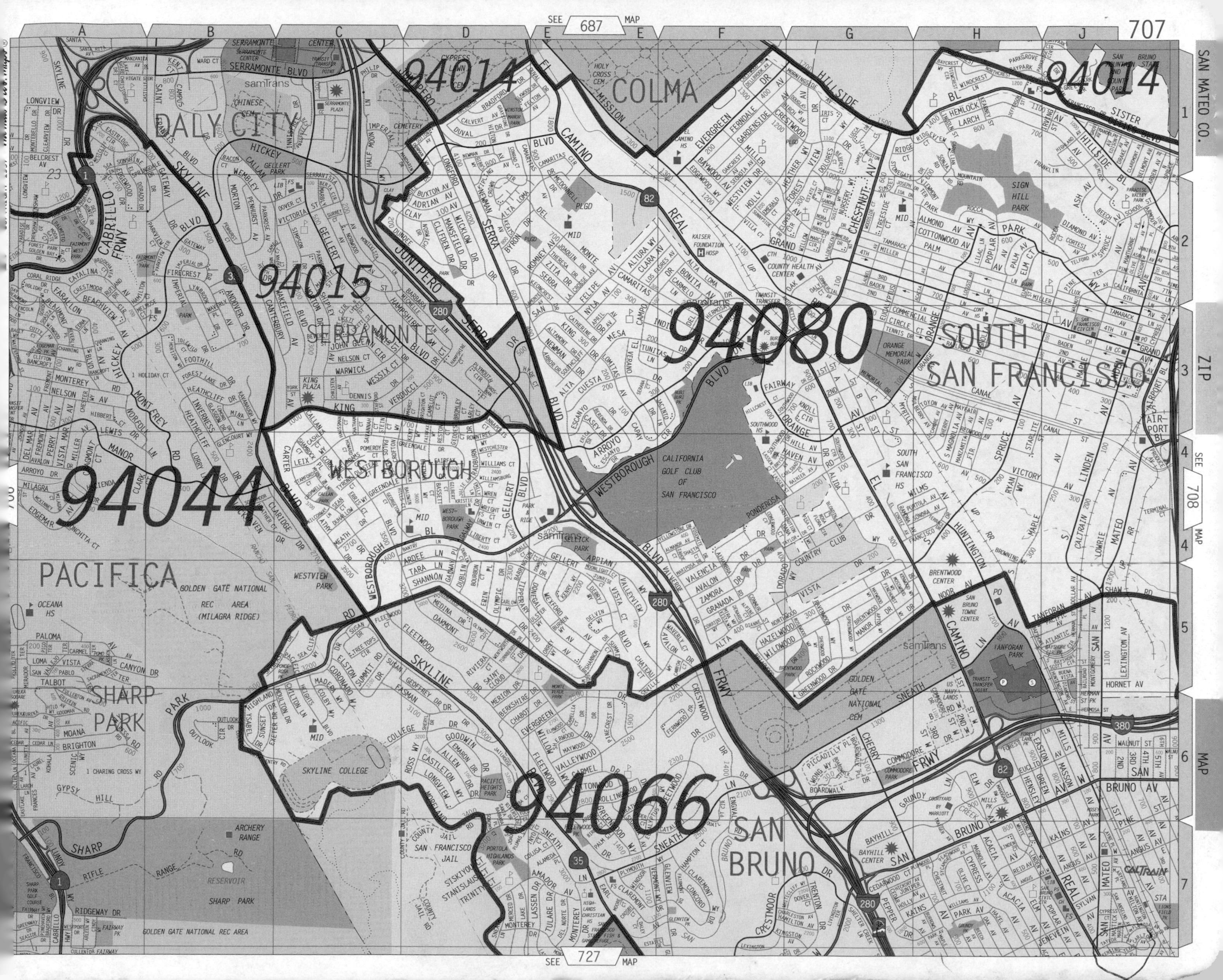
SEE 687 MAP
A
B
C
D
E
F
G
H
J
SAN MATEO CO.
ZIP
MAP
94014
94014
COLMA
DALY CITY
94015
SERRAMONTE
94080
SOUTH SAN FRANCISCO
94044
WESTBOROUGH
PACIFICA
SHARP PARK
94066
SAN BRUNO
CALIFORNIA GOLF CLUB OF SAN FRANCISCO
GOLDEN GATE NATIONAL REC AREA (MILAGRA RIDGE)
GOLDEN GATE NATIONAL REC AREA
SKYLINE COLLEGE
SAN FRANCISCO JAIL
GOLDEN GATE NATIONAL CEM
HOLY CROSS CEM
SIGN HILL PARK
ORANGE MEMORIAL PARK
TANFORAN PARK
SAN BRUNO TOWNE CENTER
BRENTWOOD CENTER
BAYHILL CENTER
SERRAMONTE CENTER
KAISER FOUNDATION HOSP
SOUTH SAN FRANCISCO HS
OCEANA HS
ARCHERY RANGE
RESERVOIR
SHARP PARK
SEE 708 MAP
SEE 706 MAP
SEE 727 MAP

SEE 688 MAP
SAN MATEO CO.
ZIP
MAP
SAN BRUNO MOUNTAIN STATE AND COUNTY PARK
94014
94080
94128
SOUTH SAN FRANCISCO
SAN FRANCISCO BAY
OYSTER COVE MARINA
OYSTER POINT
OYSTER POINT MARINA
OYSTER POINT BLVD
BAYSHORE BLVD
BAYSHORE FRWY
SISTER CITIES BLVD
AIRPORT BLVD
GATEWAY BLVD
FORBES
GRANDVIEW DR
POINT SAN BRUNO BLVD
POINT SAN BRUNO PARK
POINT SAN BRUNO
E GRAND AV
SWIFT AV
JAMIE CT
MITCHELL AV
LAWRENCE AV
LITTLEFIELD AV
HARBOR WY
SAN BRUNO CANAL
N ACCESS RD
COAST GUARD RD
FLYING TIGERS
SF COM COLLEGE AIRPORT SCHOOL
UNITED MAINTENANCE
SEAPLANE HARBOR
USCG AIR STATION
SAN FRANCISCO INTERNATIONAL AIRPORT (SEE TABLE OF CONTENTS FOR AIRPORT MAP)
ECONOMY PARKING
DELTA CARGO
BUTLER AVIATION
AMERICAN HANGAR
LIONS FIELD PARK
SAN BRUNO AV
MCDONNELL RD
SEE 707 MAP
SEE 728 MAP

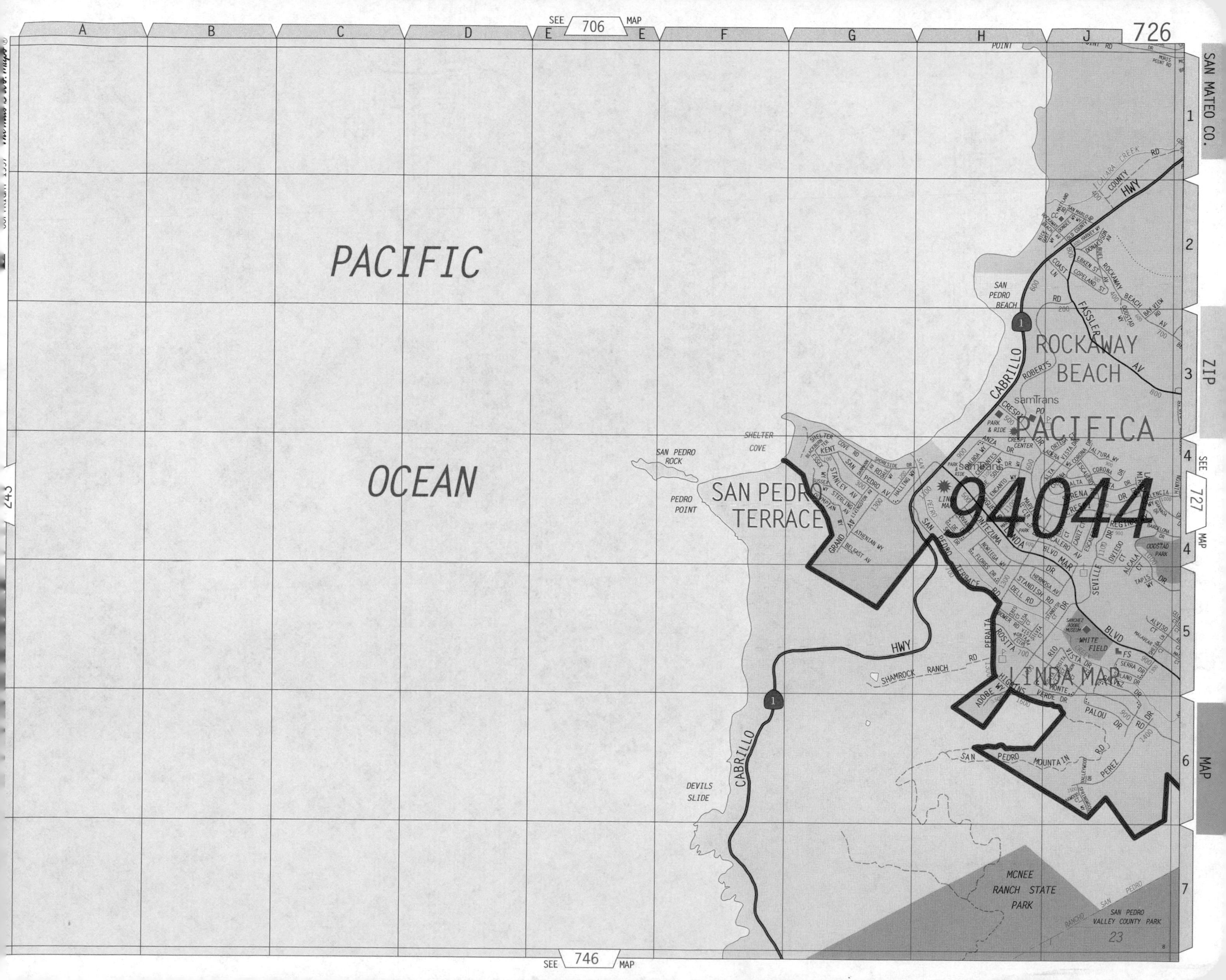
SEE 706 MAP
A
B
C
D
E
F
G
H
J
1
2
3
4
5
6
7
SAN MATEO CO.
ZIP
MAP
SEE 727 MAP
PACIFIC
OCEAN
SAN PEDRO ROCK
PEDRO POINT
SHELTER COVE
SAN PEDRO TERRACE
SAN PEDRO BEACH
ROCKAWAY BEACH
PACIFICA
94044
LINDA MAR
CABRILLO
HWY
COUNTY
SHAMROCK RANCH RD
SAN PEDRO MOUNTAIN RD
DEVILS SLIDE
MCNEE RANCH STATE PARK
SAN PEDRO VALLEY COUNTY PARK
WHITE FIELD
SANCHEZ ADOBE MUSEUM
FASSLER AV
ROCKAWAY BEACH AV
SAN PEDRO TERRACE RD
PALOU DR
PEREZ DR
OSSTAD PARK
SEE 746 MAP
243

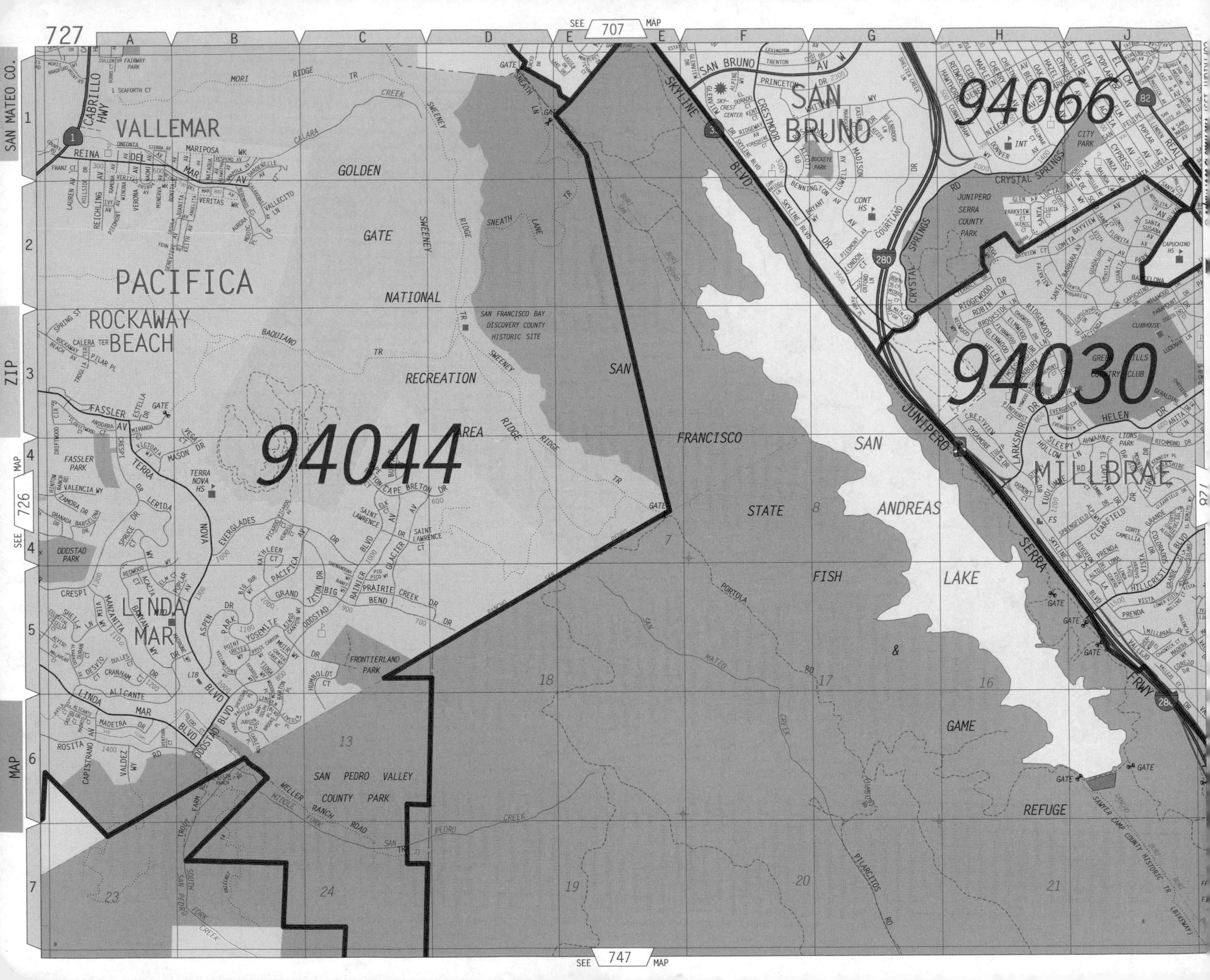
SEE 707 MAP
SAN MATEO CO.
ZIP MAP
VALLEMAR
PACIFICA
ROCKAWAY BEACH
LINDA MAR
GOLDEN GATE NATIONAL RECREATION AREA
SAN FRANCISCO BAY DISCOVERY COUNTY HISTORIC SITE
94044
SAN BRUNO
94066
94030
MILLBRAE
SAN FRANCISCO STATE FISH & GAME REFUGE
SAN ANDREAS LAKE
SAN PEDRO VALLEY COUNTY PARK
JUNIPERO SERRA COUNTY PARK
SKYLINE BLVD
JUNIPERO SERRA FRWY
CABRILLO HWY
SAWYER CAMP COUNTY HISTORIC TR (BIKEWAY)
SEE 726 MAP
SEE 747 MAP

SEE 708 MAP

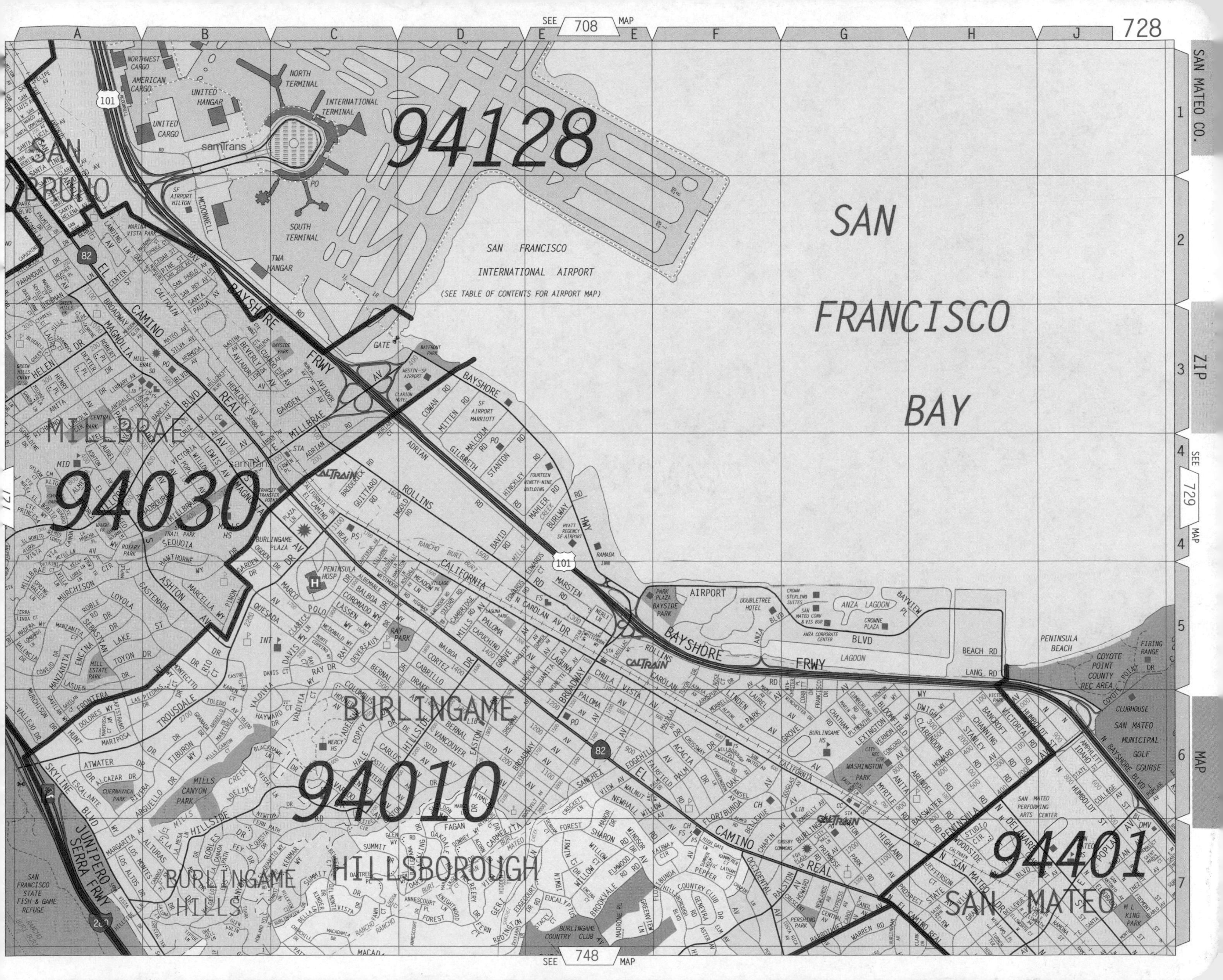

SEE 729 MAP

SEE 748 MAP

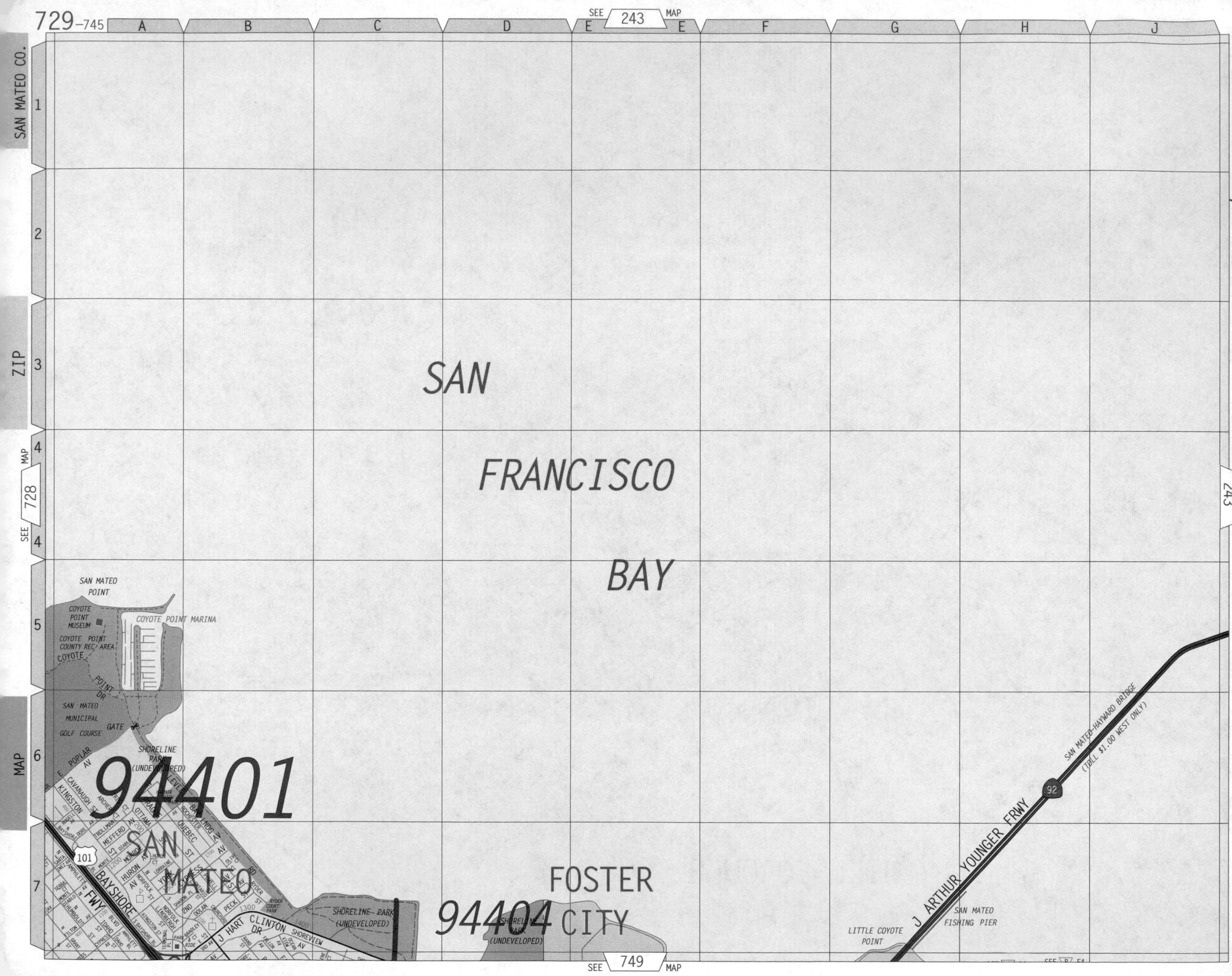

SEE 243 MAP
SAN MATEO CO.
ZIP
MAP
SEE 728 MAP
243
SAN FRANCISCO BAY
SAN MATEO POINT
COYOTE POINT MUSEUM
COYOTE POINT MARINA
COYOTE POINT COUNTY REC AREA
COYOTE POINT DR
SAN MATEO MUNICIPAL GOLF COURSE
GATE
SHORELINE PARK (UNDEVELOPED)
94401
SAN MATEO
BAYSHORE FWY
101
94404
FOSTER CITY
SHORELINE PARK (UNDEVELOPED)
J HART CLINTON DR
LITTLE COYOTE POINT
SAN MATEO FISHING PIER
J ARTHUR YOUNGER FRWY
92
SAN MATEO-HAYWARD BRIDGE (TOLL $1.00 WEST ONLY)
SEE 749 MAP

SEE 726 MAP

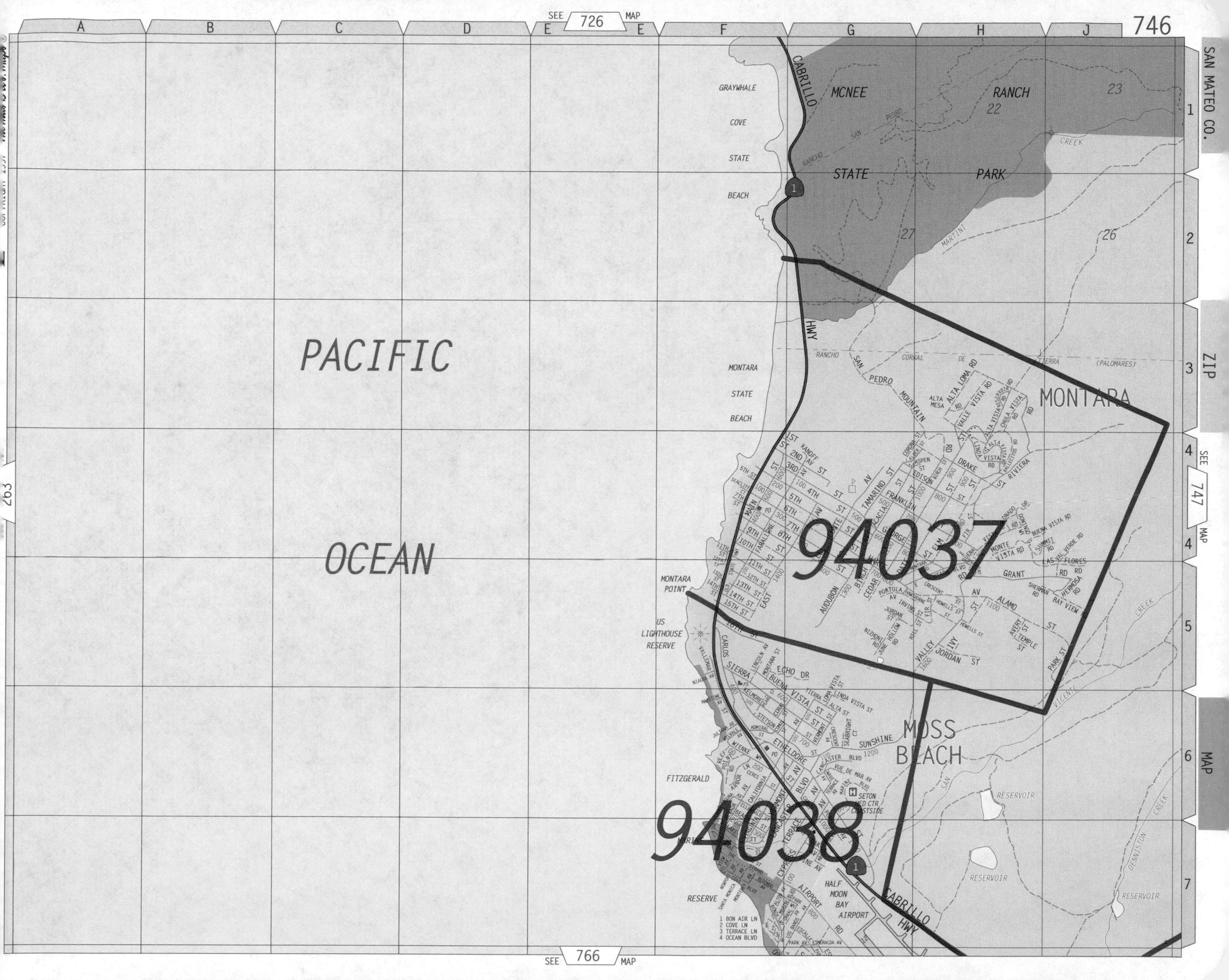

SEE 747 MAP

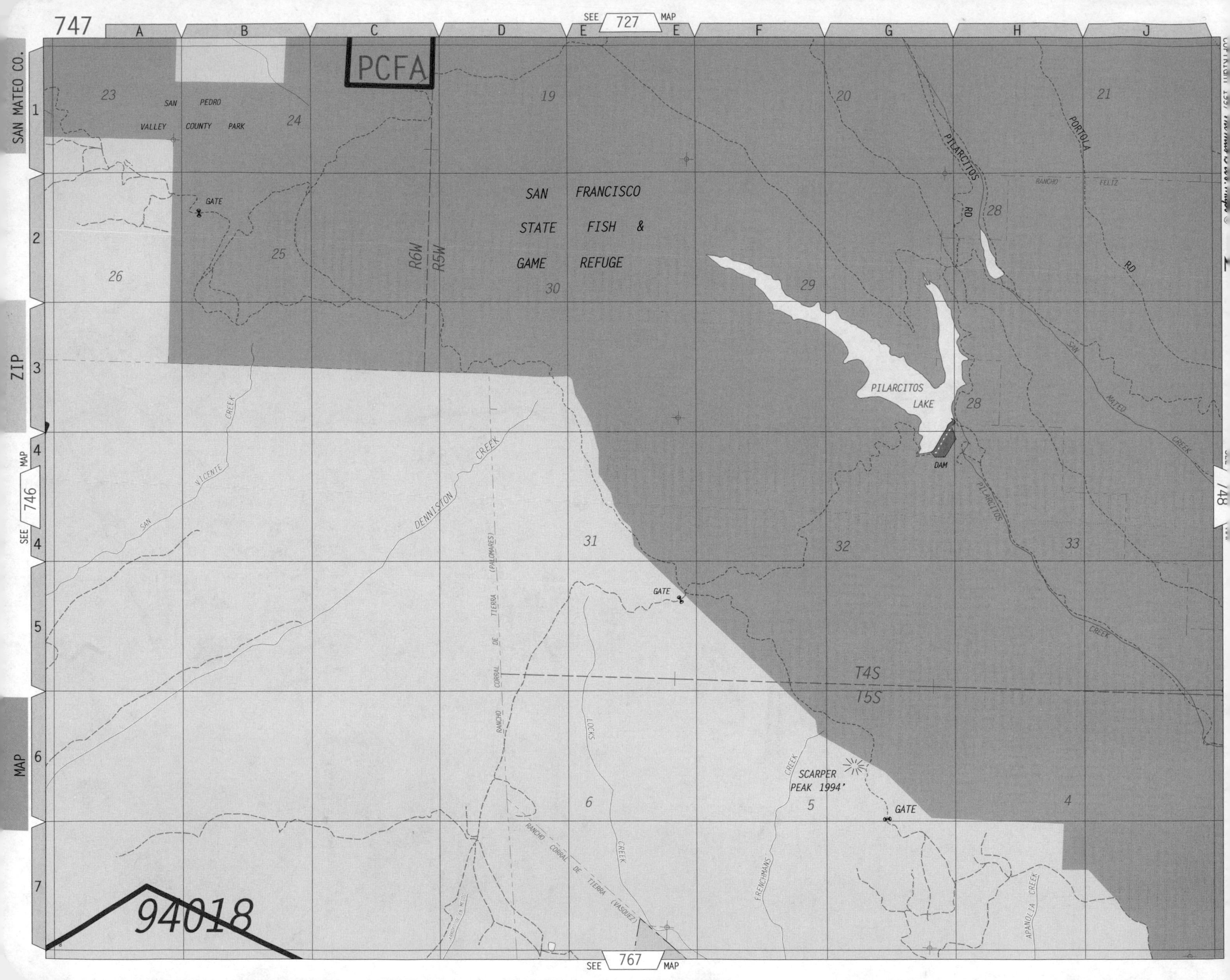

SEE 727 MAP
A
B
C
D
E
F
G
H
J
SAN MATEO CO.
ZIP
MAP
SEE 746 MAP
SEE 748 MAP
PCFA
SAN PEDRO VALLEY COUNTY PARK
SAN FRANCISCO STATE FISH & GAME REFUGE
R6W
R5W
GATE
PILARCITOS LAKE
DAM
PILARCITOS RD
PORTOLA RD
RANCHO FELIZ
SAN MATEO CREEK
PILARCITOS
SAN VICENTE CREEK
DENNISTON CREEK
RANCHO CORRAL DE TIERRA (PALOMARES)
RANCHO CORRAL DE TIERRA (VASQUEZ)
LOCKS CREEK
FRENCHMANS
CREEK
SCARPER PEAK 1994'
APANOLIA CREEK
T4S
T5S
23
24
25
26
19
30
20
21
28
29
31
32
33
6
5
4
94018
SEE 767 MAP

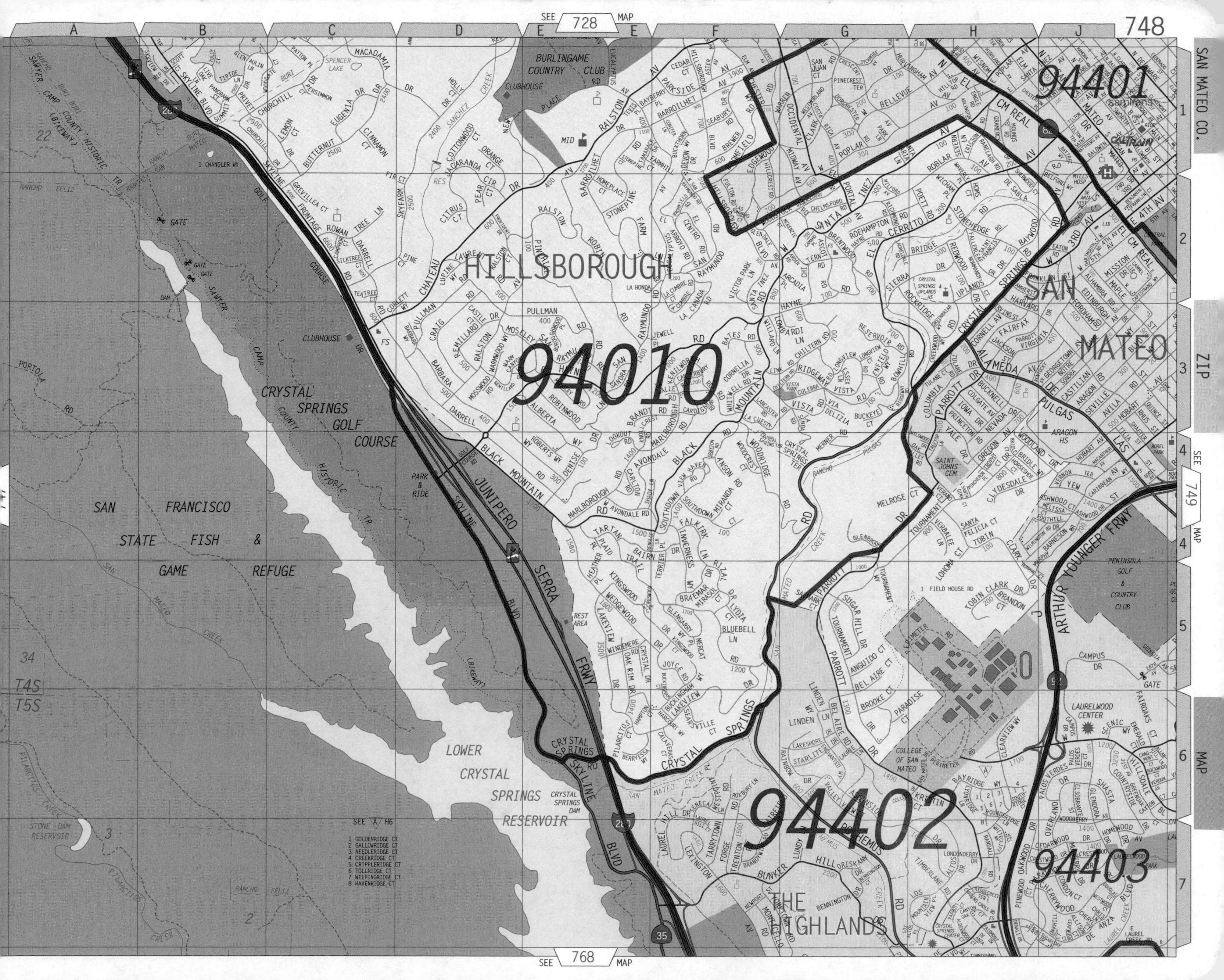
748
SEE 728 MAP
SEE 768 MAP
SEE 749 MAP
SAN MATEO CO.
ZIP
MAP
94401
94010
94402
94403
HILLSBOROUGH
SAN MATEO
BURLINGAME COUNTRY CLUB
CLUBHOUSE
CRYSTAL SPRINGS GOLF COURSE
SAN FRANCISCO STATE FISH & GAME REFUGE
LOWER CRYSTAL SPRINGS RESERVOIR
CRYSTAL SPRINGS DAM
STONE DAM RESERVOIR
SAWYER CAMP COUNTY HISTORIC TR (BIKEWAY)
PORTOLA RD
RANCHO FELIZ
JUNIPERO SERRA FRWY
SKYLINE BLVD
BLACK MOUNTAIN RD
CRYSTAL SPRINGS RD
ALAMEDA DE LAS PULGAS
J ARTHUR YOUNGER FRWY
PENINSULA GOLF & COUNTRY CLUB
COLLEGE OF SAN MATEO
LAURELWOOD CENTER
THE HIGHLANDS
CRYSTAL SPRINGS & UPLANDS HS
ARAGON HS
SAINT JOHNS CEM
PARK & RIDE
REST AREA
MILLS HOSP
CALTRAIN
T4S
T5S
SEE A H6
1 GOLDENRIDGE CT
2 GALLOWRIDGE CT
3 NEEDLERIDGE CT
4 CREEKRIDGE CT
5 CRIPPLERIDGE CT
6 TOLLRIDGE CT
7 WEEPINGRIDGE CT
8 HAVENRIDGE CT

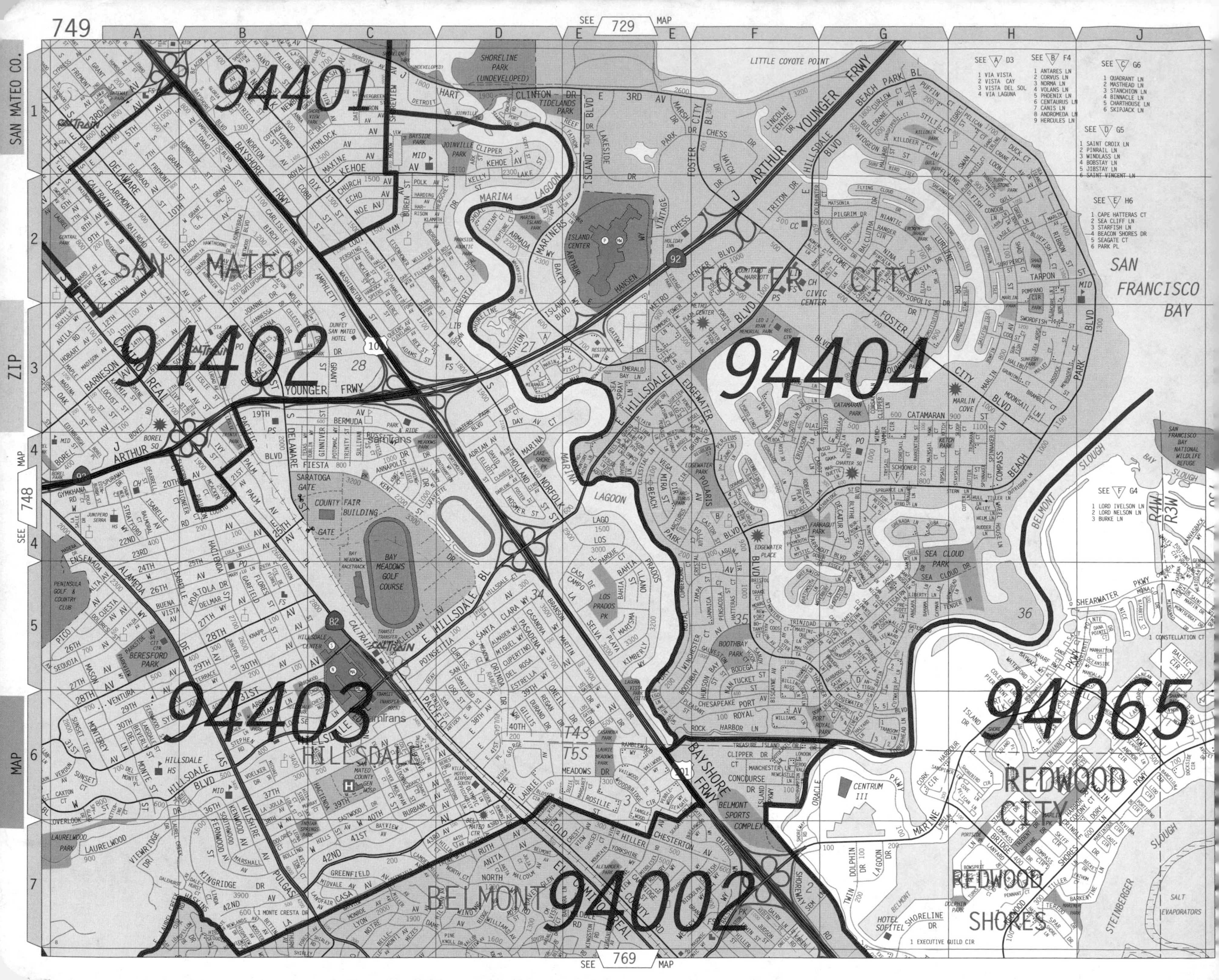

749
SEE 729 MAP
SEE 748 MAP
SEE 769 MAP
SAN MATEO CO.
ZIP
MAP
94401
94402
94403
94404
94065
94002
SAN MATEO
FOSTER CITY
HILLSDALE
BELMONT
REDWOOD CITY
REDWOOD SHORES
SAN FRANCISCO BAY
LITTLE COYOTE POINT
SHORELINE PARK (UNDEVELOPED)
MARINA LAGOON
LAGOON
BAYSHORE FRWY
J ARTHUR YOUNGER FRWY
EL CAMINO REAL
HILLSDALE BLVD
E HILLSDALE BLVD
FOSTER CITY BLVD
BEACH PARK BL
EDGEWATER BLVD
SHEARWATER PKWY
MARINE PKWY
RALSTON AV
CALTRAIN
BAY MEADOWS GOLF COURSE
COUNTY FAIR BUILDING
SARATOGA GATE
PENINSULA GOLF & COUNTRY CLUB
BERESFORD PARK
LAURELWOOD PARK
CENTRUM III
BELMONT SPORTS COMPLEX
LAKE SHORE PK
LOS PRADOS PK
SEA CLOUD PARK
MARLIN COVE
FARRAGUT PARK
EDGEWATER PLACE
BOOTHBAY PARK
CATAMARAN PARK
CIVIC CENTER
ISLAND CENTER
SAN FRANCISCO BAY NATIONAL WILDLIFE REFUGE
BELMONT SLOUGH
STEINBERGER SLOUGH
SALT EVAPORATORS
HOTEL SOFITEL
SEE A D3
1 VIA VISTA
2 VISTA CAY
3 VISTA DEL SOL
4 VIA LAGUNA
SEE B F4
1 ANTARES LN
2 CORVUS LN
3 NORMA LN
4 VOLANS LN
5 PHOENIX LN
6 CENTAURUS LN
7 CANIS LN
8 ANDROMEDA LN
9 HERCULES LN
SEE C G6
1 QUADRANT LN
2 MASTHEAD LN
3 STANCHION LN
4 BINNACLE LN
5 CHARTHOUSE LN
6 SKIPJACK LN
SEE D G5
1 SAINT CROIX LN
2 PINRAIL LN
3 WINDLASS LN
4 BOBSTAY LN
5 JIBSTAY LN
6 SAINT VINCENT LN
SEE E H6
1 CAPE HATTERAS CT
2 SEA CLIFF LN
3 STARFISH LN
4 BEACON SHORES DR
5 SEAGATE CT
6 PARK PL
SEE F G4
1 LORD IVELSON LN
2 LORD NELSON LN
3 BURKE LN
1 CONSTELLATION CT
1 EXECUTIVE GUILD CIR
1 MONTE CRESTA DR

SEE 243 MAP
750-765
A
B
C
D
E
F
G
H
J
SAN MATEO CO.
ZIP
MAP
SEE ALA 751 MAP
SAN MATEO COUNTY
ALAMEDA COUNTY
ALAMEDA SAN MATEO CO
SAN FRANCISCO BAY
SAN FRANCISCO BAY NATIONAL WILDLIFE REFUGE
BAY SLOUGH
REDWOOD CITY
SOUTH BAY SEWER AUTHORITY TREATMENT PLANT
RADIO RD
SEE A A5
1 PASSAGE LN
2 BUOY LN
3 BREAKER LN
4 CAPTAIN LN
5 GIMERL LN
6 BUCCANEER LN
7 BATTEN LN
8 CHART LN
9 KNOT LN
10 BRIGANTINE LN
11 BOSUN LN
12 GENOA DR
94065
SLOUGH
SALT EVAPORATORS
SEE A5
1 CONSTELLATION CT
2 SOVEREIGN WY
3 INTREPID LN
4 COLUMBIA WY
5 COLUMBIA CIR
6 SEA CHASE DR
7 NANTUCKET DR
8 SCHOONER BAY DR
9 PORTMAN DR
BAIR ISLAND
94063
REDWOOD POINT
STEINBERGER
SALT EVAPORATORS
CORKSCREW SLOUGH
REDWOOD CREEK
SEE 770 MAP

SEE 746 MAP
SAN MATEO CO.
ZIP
MAP
SEE 263 MAP
SEE 767 MAP
PACIFIC
OCEAN
94018
94038
PRINCETON
BY THE
SEA
HALF
MOON BAY
AIRPORT
CABRILLO
HWY
TERMINAL
AIRPORT
OCEAN
BLVD
FITZGERALD
MARINE
RESERVE
WEST
POINT
PILLAR POINT
PILLAR
POINT
HARBOR
BREAKWATER
PIER
SAN RAMON AV
ESMERALDA AV
ALVARADO
CORNELL
AV
CALIFORNIA
YALE AV
HARVARD
STANFORD
VASSAR ST
COLUMBIA
BROADWAY
PROSPECT
WY
RD
CAPISTRANO
SONORA
SEA CREST
SHELTER
COVE
HARBOUR
DR
BRIDGEPORT
BARRANCA
ST

SEE 747 MAP

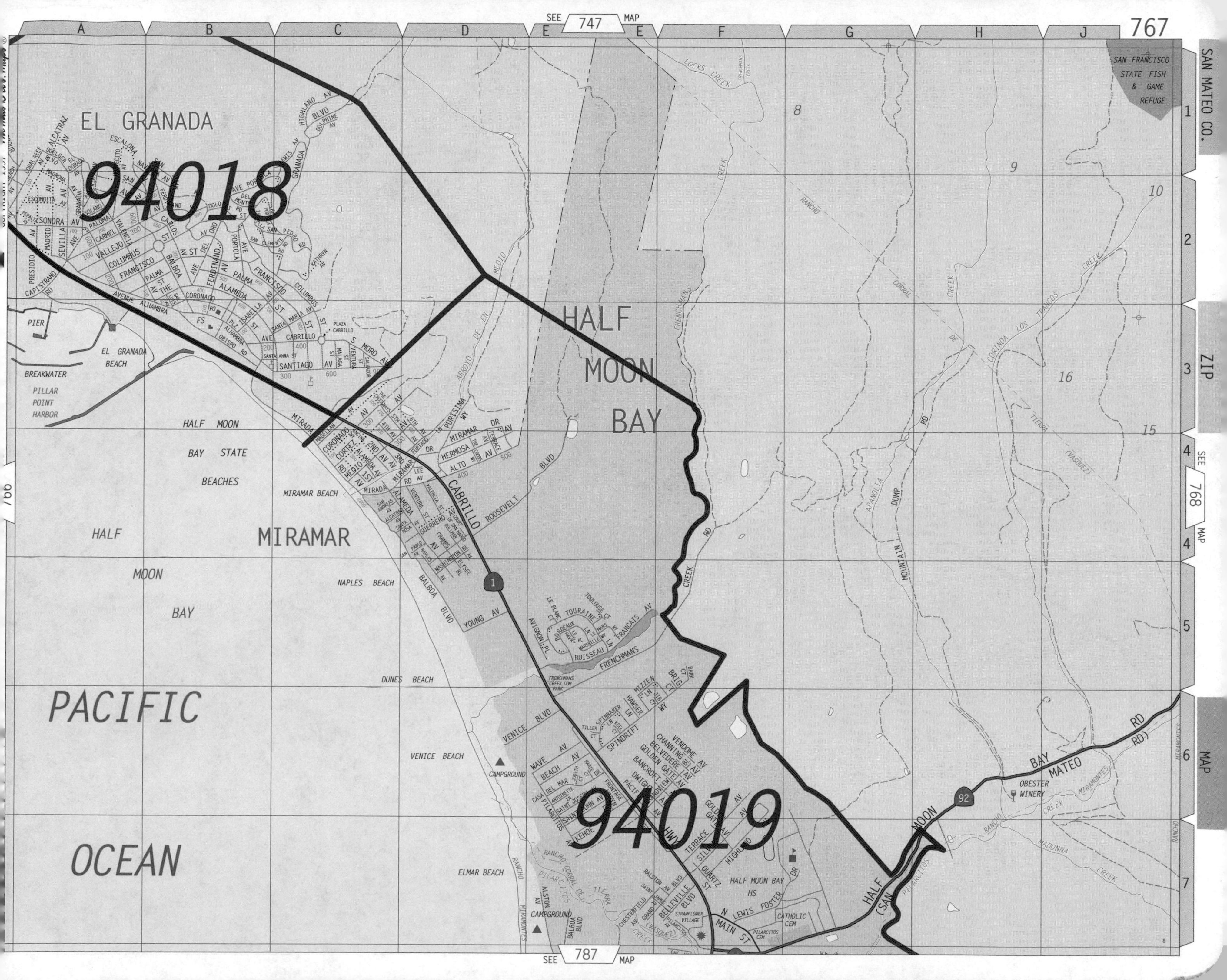

SEE 787 MAP

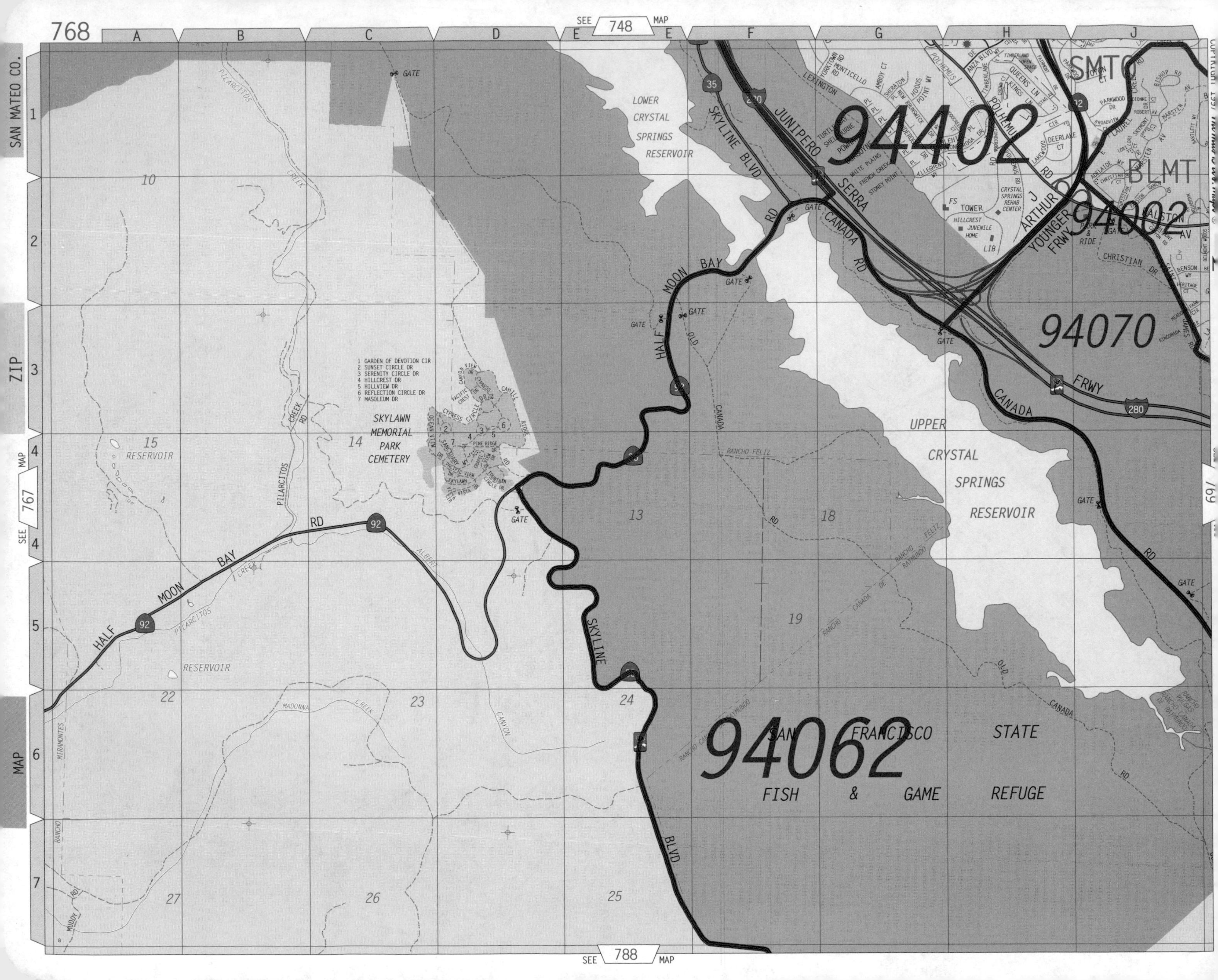

SEE 748 MAP
SAN MATEO CO.
ZIP
MAP
SEE 767 MAP
SEE 769 MAP
LOWER
CRYSTAL
SPRINGS
RESERVOIR
SKYLINE BLVD
JUNIPERO
SERRA
CANADA
RD
94402
94002
94070
94062
SMTO
BLMT
HALF
MOON
BAY
RD
GATE
1 GARDEN OF DEVOTION CIR
2 SUNSET CIRCLE DR
3 SERENITY CIRCLE DR
4 HILLCREST DR
5 HILLVIEW DR
6 REFLECTION CIRCLE DR
7 MASOLEUM DR
SKYLAWN
MEMORIAL
PARK
CEMETERY
CAHILL
RIDGE
RD
PILARCITOS
CREEK
RESERVOIR
ALBERT
CANYON
MADONNA
CREEK
MIRAMONTES
RANCHO
MUDDY
UPPER
CRYSTAL
SPRINGS
RESERVOIR
RANCHO FELIZ
OLD
CANADA
RD
FRWY
280
SAN FRANCISCO STATE
FISH & GAME REFUGE
SKYLINE
BLVD
J ARTHUR YOUNGER FRWY
CRYSTAL SPRINGS REHAB CENTER
HILLCREST JUVENILE HOME
TOWER
LIB
FS
PARK & RIDE
CHRISTIAN DR
RALSTON AV

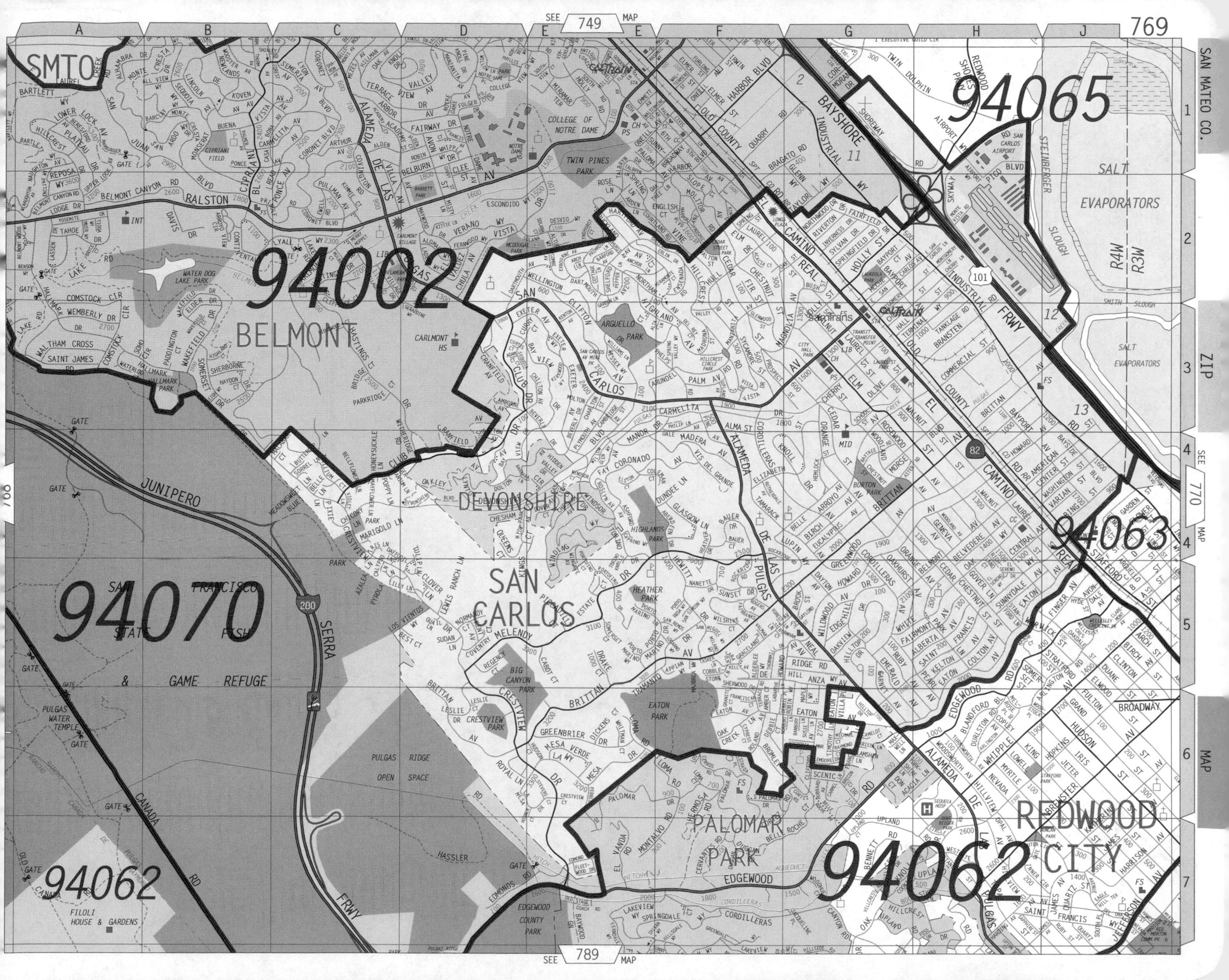

769
SEE 749 MAP
SEE 789 MAP
SEE 770 MAP
SAN MATEO CO.
ZIP
MAP
94065
94002
94070
94063
94062
BELMONT
SAN CARLOS
DEVONSHIRE
PALOMAR PARK
REDWOOD CITY
SMTO
COLLEGE OF NOTRE DAME
TWIN PINES PARK
WATER DOG LAKE PARK
CARLMONT HS
ARGUELLO PARK
HIGHLANDS PARK
HEATHER PARK
BURTON PARK
BIG CANYON PARK
CRESTVIEW PARK
EATON PARK
SAN FRANCISCO STATE FISH & GAME REFUGE
PULGAS WATER TEMPLE
PULGAS RIDGE OPEN SPACE
EDGEWOOD COUNTY PARK
FILOLI HOUSE & GARDENS
SALT EVAPORATORS
SAN CARLOS AIRPORT
BAYSHORE FRWY
JUNIPERO SERRA FRWY
ALAMEDA DE LAS PULGAS
EL CAMINO REAL
CANADA RD
EDGEWOOD RD
R4W R3W

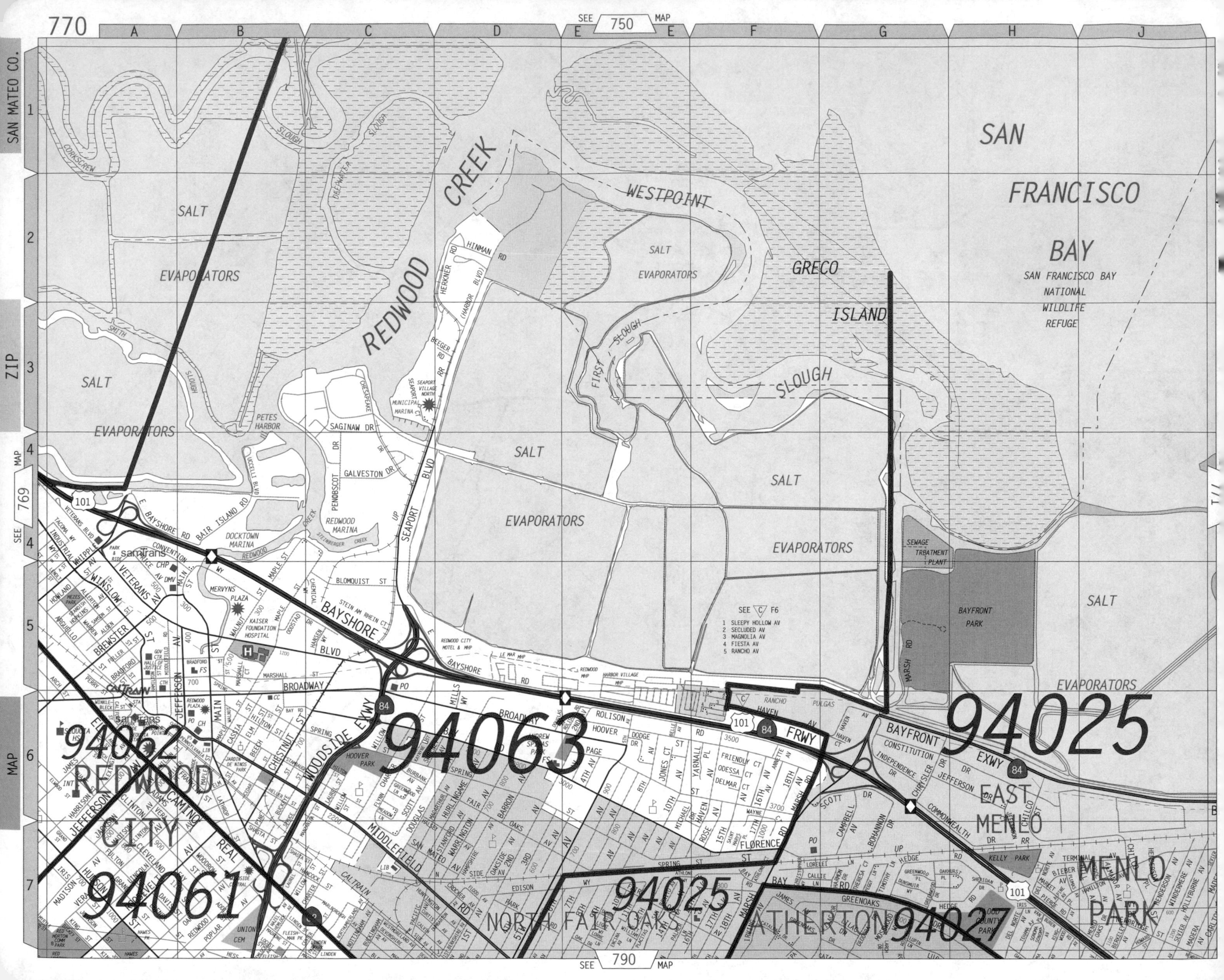
SEE 750 MAP
SAN MATEO CO.
ZIP
MAP
SEE 769 MAP
SAN
FRANCISCO
BAY
SAN FRANCISCO BAY
NATIONAL
WILDLIFE
REFUGE
REDWOOD
CREEK
WESTPOINT
GRECO
ISLAND
FIRST
SLOUGH
SALT
EVAPORATORS
SEWAGE
TREATMENT
PLANT
BAYFRONT
PARK
SEE C F6
1 SLEEPY HOLLOW AV
2 SECLUDED AV
3 MAGNOLIA AV
4 FIESTA AV
5 RANCHO AV
PETES
HARBOR
DOCKTOWN
MARINA
REDWOOD
MARINA
MERVYNS
PLAZA
KAISER
FOUNDATION
HOSPITAL
BAYSHORE
BROADWAY
WOODSIDE EXWY
MIDDLEFIELD
BAYFRONT
EXWY
94063
94062
94061
94025
94027
REDWOOD
CITY
EAST
MENLO
MENLO
PARK
NORTH FAIR OAKS
ATHERTON
SEE 790 MAP

SEE ALA 751 MAP

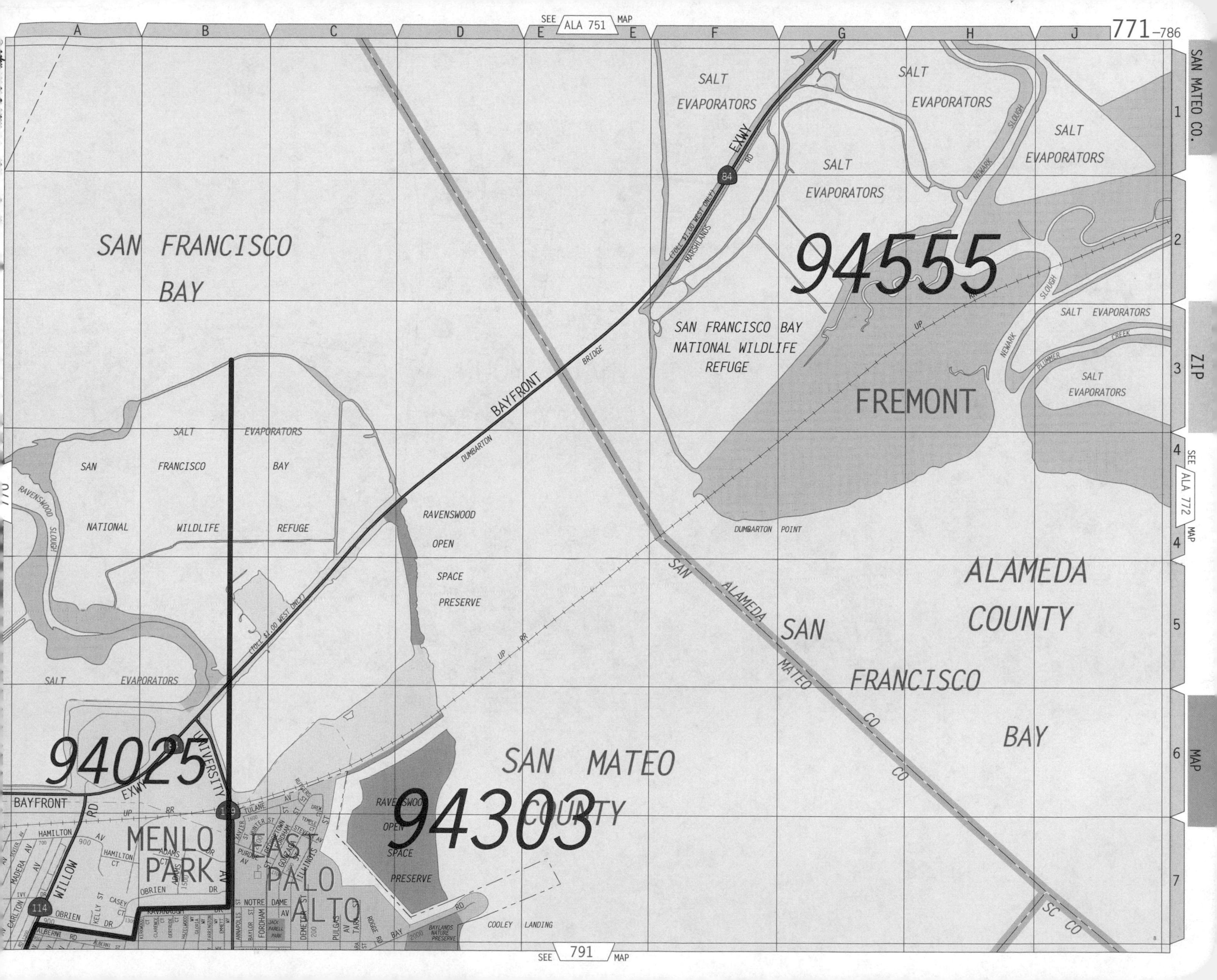

SEE ALA 772 MAP
SEE 791 MAP

SEE 767 MAP

SEE 786 MAP

SEE 788 MAP

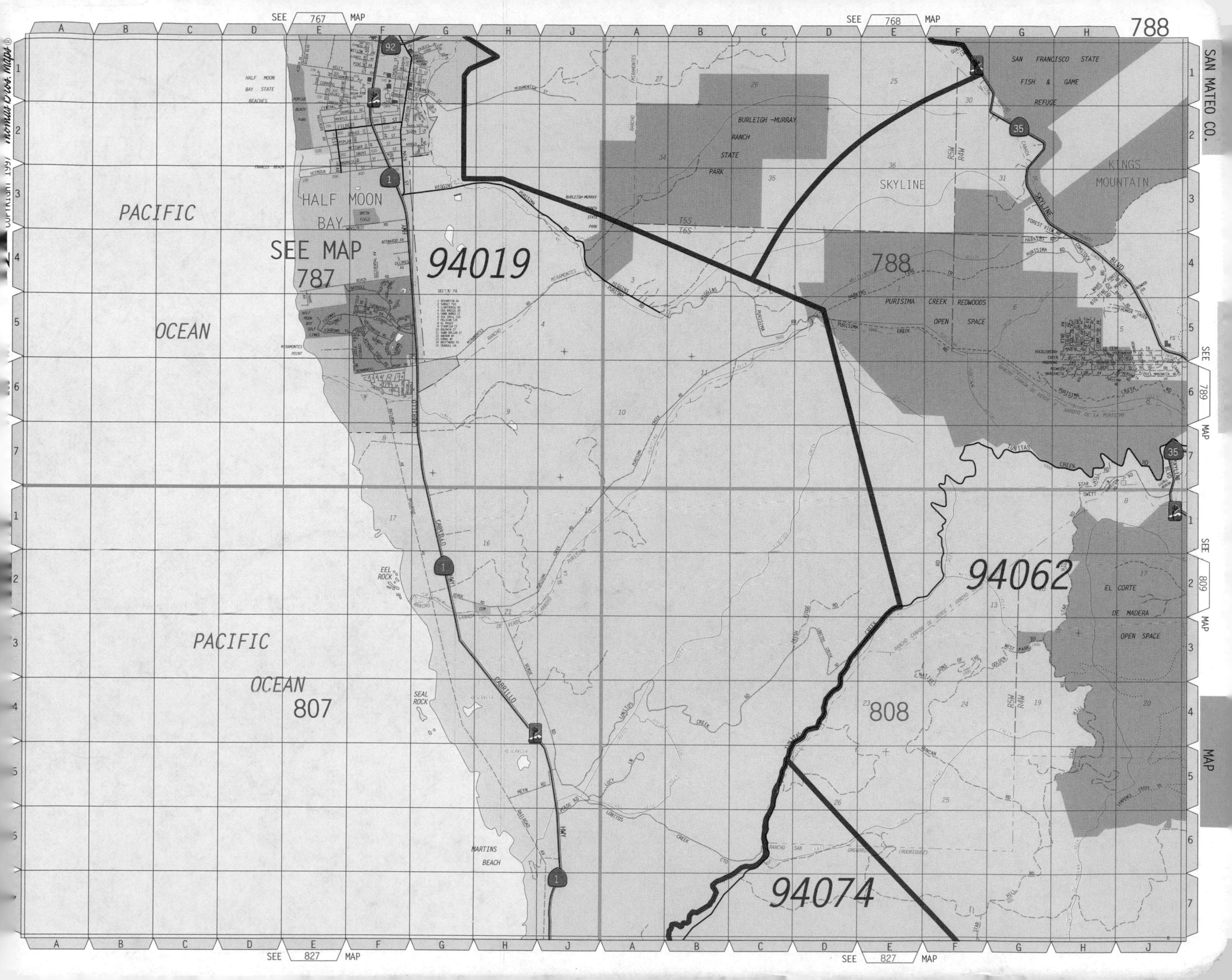
SEE 767 MAP
SEE 768 MAP
SAN MATEO CO.
HALF MOON BAY STATE BEACHES
SAN FRANCISCO STATE FISH & GAME REFUGE
BURLEIGH-MURRAY RANCH STATE PARK
SKYLINE
KINGS MOUNTAIN
PACIFIC OCEAN
HALF MOON BAY
SEE MAP 787
94019
788
PURISIMA CREEK REDWOODS OPEN SPACE
SEE 789 MAP
EEL ROCK
94062
EL CORTE DE MADERA OPEN SPACE
SEE 809 MAP
PACIFIC OCEAN
807
SEAL ROCK
808
MARTINS BEACH
94074
SEE 827 MAP
SEE 827 MAP

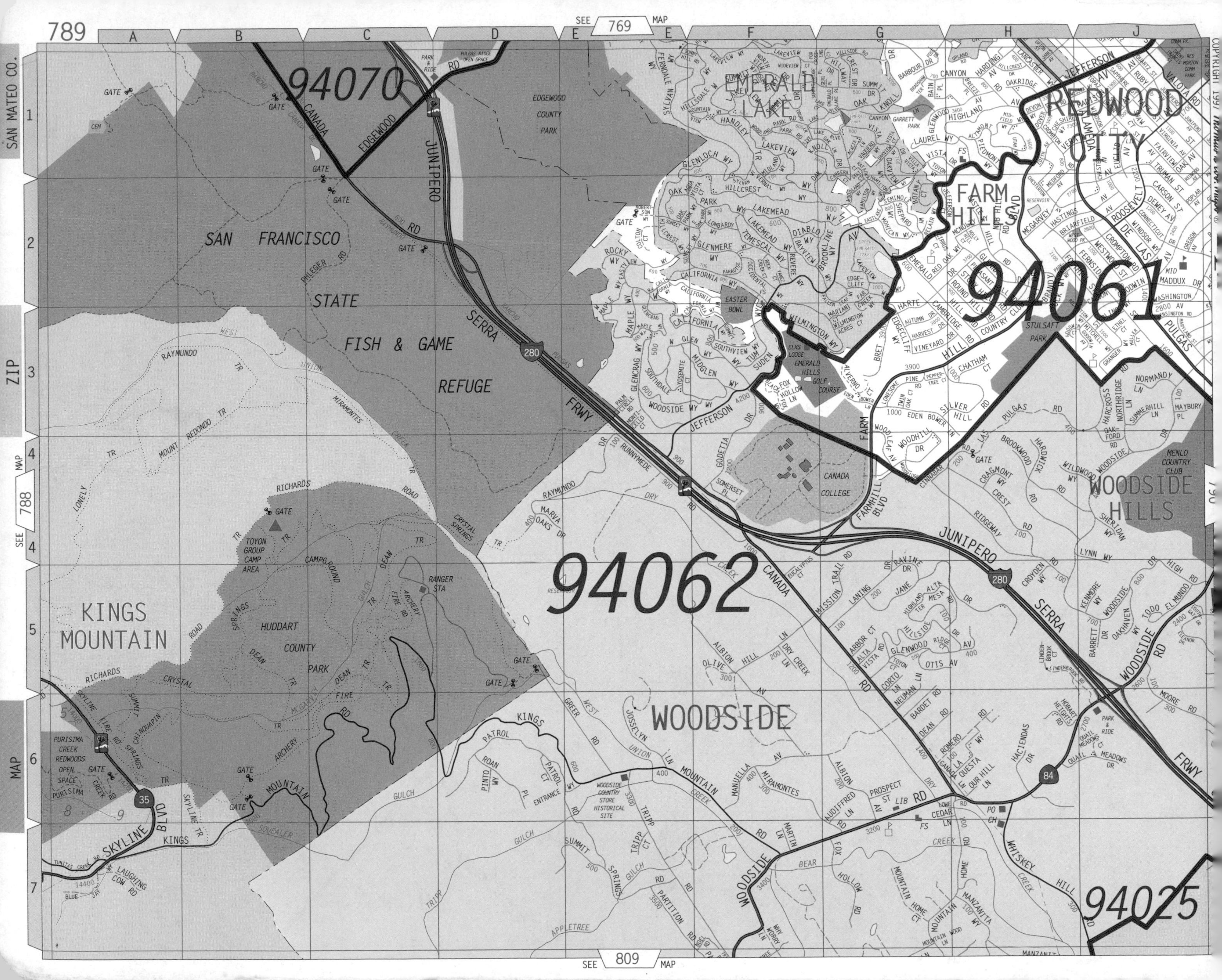
SEE 769 MAP
SEE 788 MAP
SEE 809 MAP
SAN MATEO CO.
ZIP
MAP
94070
94061
94062
94025
EMERALD LAKE
REDWOOD CITY
FARM HILLS
WOODSIDE HILLS
WOODSIDE
KINGS MOUNTAIN
SAN FRANCISCO STATE FISH & GAME REFUGE
HUDDART COUNTY PARK
EDGEWOOD COUNTY PARK
CANADA COLLEGE
EMERALD HILLS GOLF COURSE
MENLO COUNTRY CLUB
STULSAFT PARK
EASTER BOWL
TOYON GROUP CAMP AREA
RANGER STA
PURISIMA CREEK REDWOODS OPEN SPACE
JUNIPERO SERRA FRWY
WOODSIDE COUNTRY STORE HISTORICAL SITE
SKYLINE BLVD
CANADA RD
WOODSIDE RD
KINGS MOUNTAIN RD
FARM HILL BLVD
JEFFERSON AV
EDGEWOOD RD
WHISKEY HILL RD
ALAMEDA DE LAS PULGAS

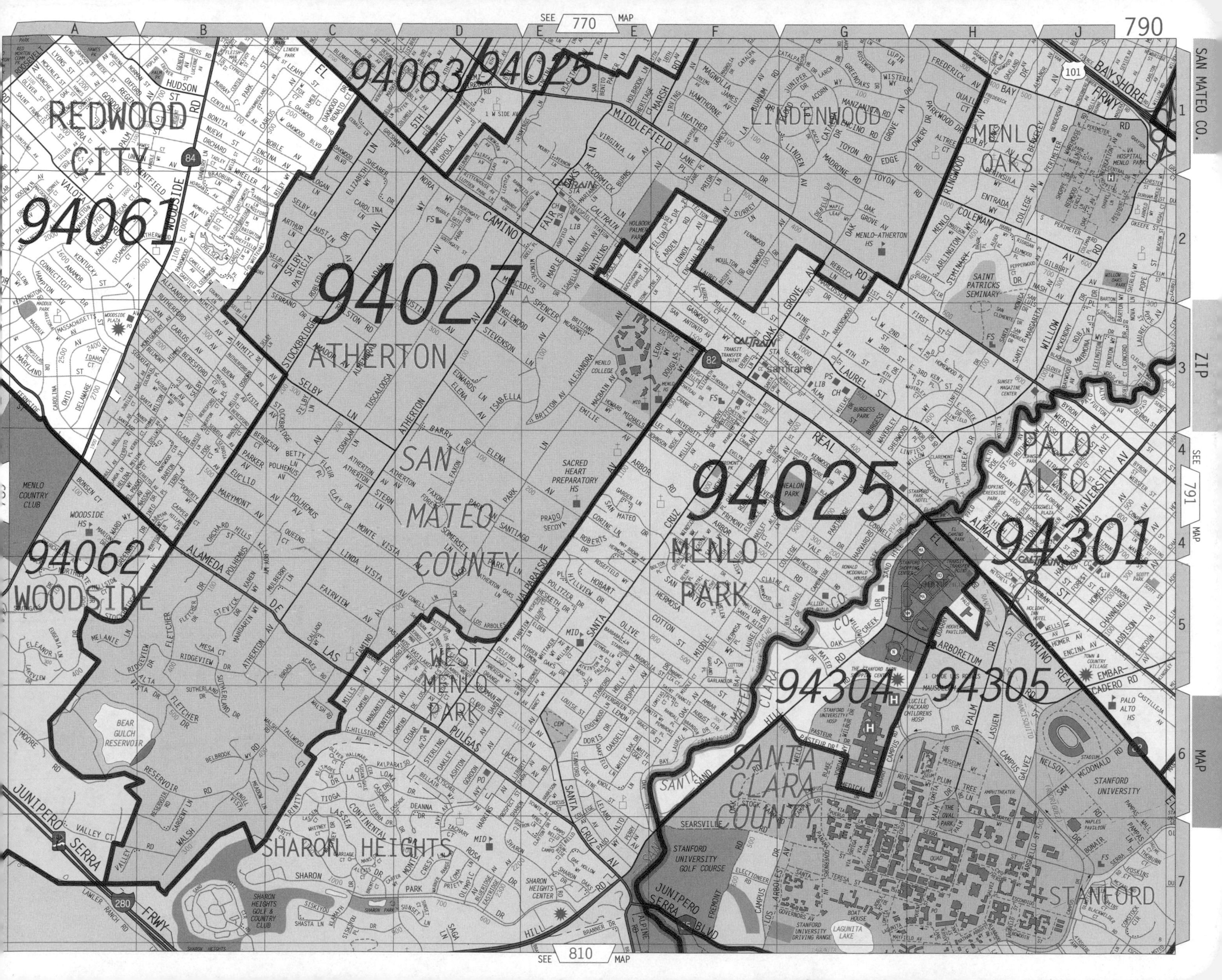

790
SEE 770 MAP
SEE 791 MAP
SEE 810 MAP
SAN MATEO CO.
ZIP
MAP
A
B
C
D
E
F
G
H
J
1
2
3
4
5
6
7
REDWOOD CITY
94061
94063
94025
94027
94062
94301
94304
94305
ATHERTON
SAN MATEO COUNTY
LINDENWOOD
MENLO OAKS
MENLO PARK
WEST MENLO PARK
PALO ALTO
WOODSIDE
SHARON HEIGHTS
SANTA CLARA COUNTY
STANFORD
STANFORD UNIVERSITY
MENLO COUNTRY CLUB
BEAR GULCH RESERVOIR
SHARON HEIGHTS GOLF & COUNTRY CLUB
STANFORD UNIVERSITY GOLF COURSE
MENLO COLLEGE
SACRED HEART PREPARATORY HS
MENLO-ATHERTON HS
SAINT PATRICKS SEMINARY
WOODSIDE HS
PALO ALTO HS
VA HOSPITAL MENLO PARK
STANFORD SHOPPING CENTER
SHARON HEIGHTS CENTER
STANFORD UNIVERSITY HOSP
LUCILE PACKARD CHILDRENS HOSP
SUNSET MAGAZINE CENTER
BURGESS PARK
HOLBROOK PALMER PARK
NEALON PARK
LAGUNITA LAKE
STADIUM
MAPLES PAVILION
EL CAMINO REAL
MIDDLEFIELD RD
ALAMEDA DE LAS PULGAS
SANTA CRUZ AV
SAND HILL RD
JUNIPERO SERRA FRWY
JUNIPERO SERRA BLVD
BAYSHORE FRWY
WOODSIDE RD
ATHERTON AV
VALPARAISO AV
UNIVERSITY AV
WILLOW RD
CALTRAIN

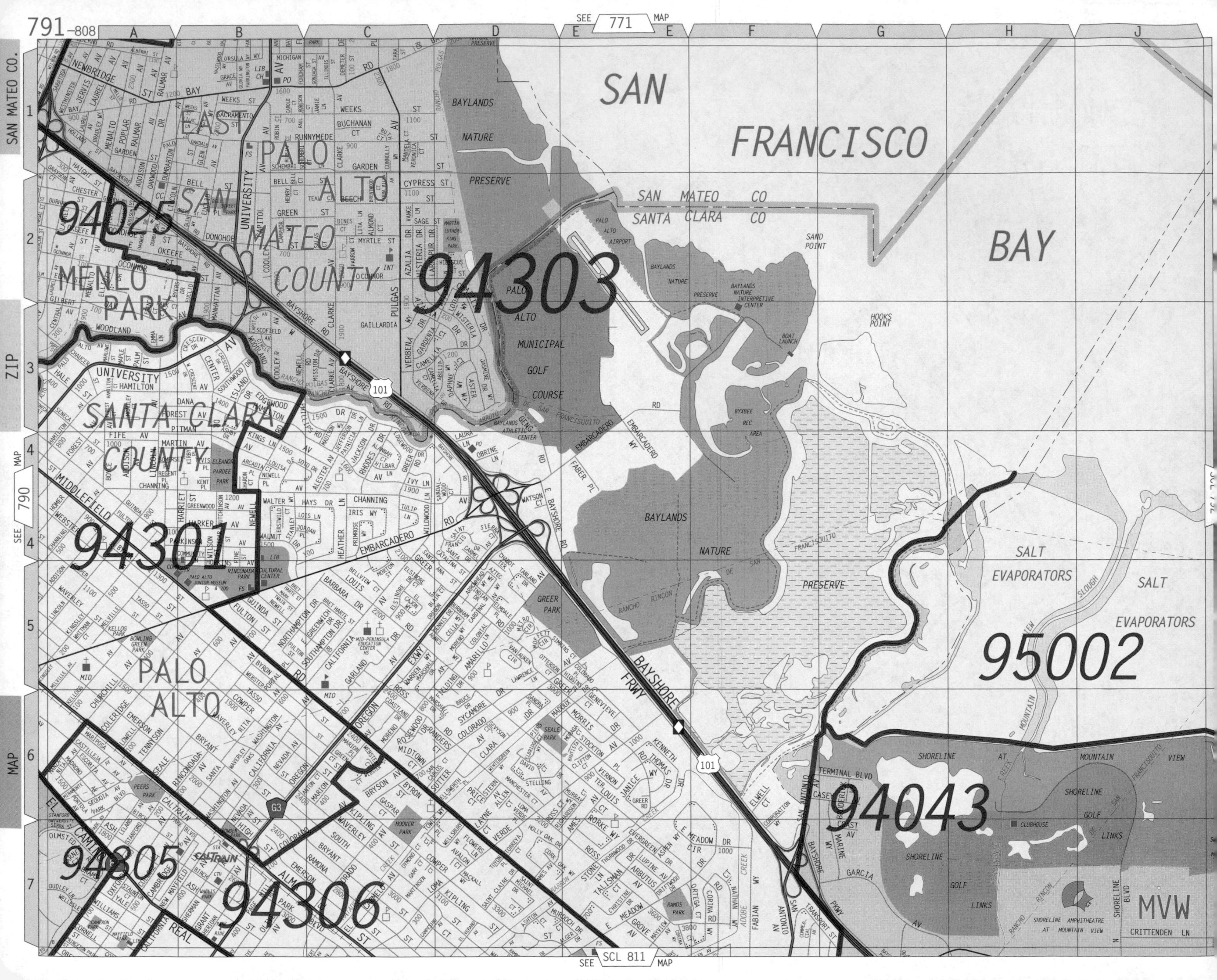

791-808
SEE 771 MAP
SEE SCL 811 MAP
SEE 790 MAP
SAN MATEO CO.
ZIP
MAP
A
B
C
D
E
F
G
H
J
1
2
3
4
5
6
7
SAN FRANCISCO BAY
EAST PALO ALTO
SAN MATEO COUNTY
SAN MATEO CO
SANTA CLARA CO
MENLO PARK
SANTA CLARA COUNTY
PALO ALTO
94025
94303
94301
94305
94306
95002
94043
MVW
BAYLANDS NATURE PRESERVE
PALO ALTO AIRPORT
PALO ALTO MUNICIPAL GOLF COURSE
BAYLANDS NATURE INTERPRETIVE CENTER
BOAT LAUNCH
SAND POINT
HOOKS POINT
BYXBEE REC AREA
SALT EVAPORATORS
SHORELINE AT MOUNTAIN VIEW
SHORELINE GOLF LINKS
CLUBHOUSE
SHORELINE AMPHITHEATRE AT MOUNTAIN VIEW
BAYSHORE FRWY
101
G3
CALTRAIN
EL CAMINO REAL
UNIVERSITY AV
EMBARCADERO RD
MIDDLEFIELD RD
OREGON EXWY
ALMA ST
SAN ANTONIO RD
CHARLESTON RD
SHORELINE BLVD
CRITTENDEN LN
GARCIA AV
TERMINAL BLVD
FABER PL
GREER PARK
SEALE PARK
PEERS PARK
HOOVER PARK
RAMOS PARK
RINCONADA PARK
ELEANOR PARDEE PARK
BOWLING GREEN PARK
CULTURAL CENTER
PALO ALTO JUNIOR MUSEUM & ZOO
MID-PENINSULA EDUCATION CENTER
MARTIN LUTHER KING PARK
BAYLANDS ATHLETIC CENTER

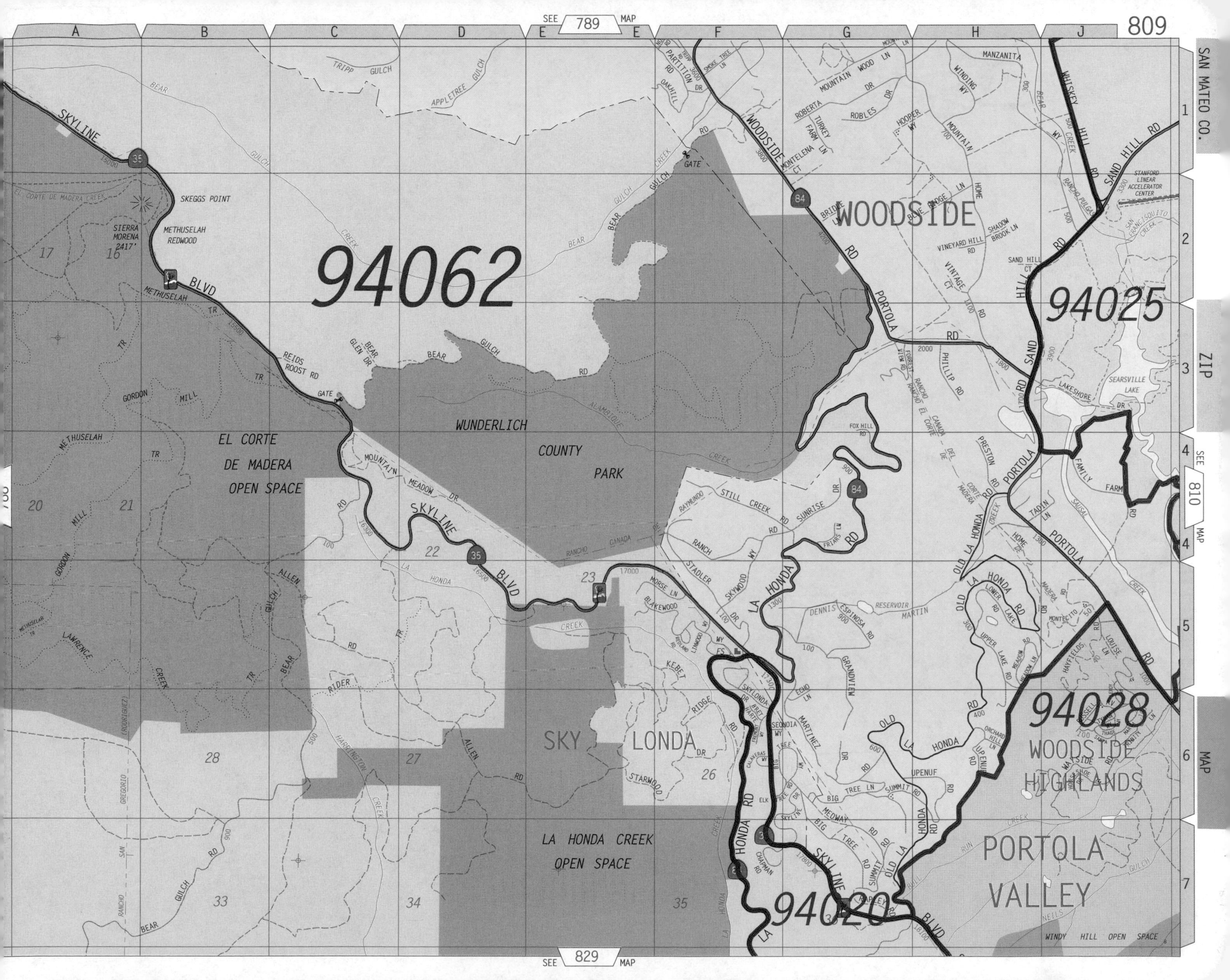
SEE 789 MAP
A
B
C
D
E
F
G
H
J
SAN MATEO CO.
ZIP
MAP
SEE 810 MAP
SEE 829 MAP
94062
94025
94028
94020
WOODSIDE
WOODSIDE HIGHLANDS
PORTOLA VALLEY
SKY LONDA
WUNDERLICH COUNTY PARK
EL CORTE DE MADERA OPEN SPACE
LA HONDA CREEK OPEN SPACE
WINDY HILL OPEN SPACE
SKEGGS POINT
SIERRA MORENA 2417'
METHUSELAH REDWOOD
SKYLINE BLVD
WOODSIDE RD
PORTOLA RD
SAND HILL RD
WHISKEY HILL RD
LA HONDA RD
OLD LA HONDA RD
STANFORD LINEAR ACCELERATOR CENTER
SEARSVILLE LAKE
GATE

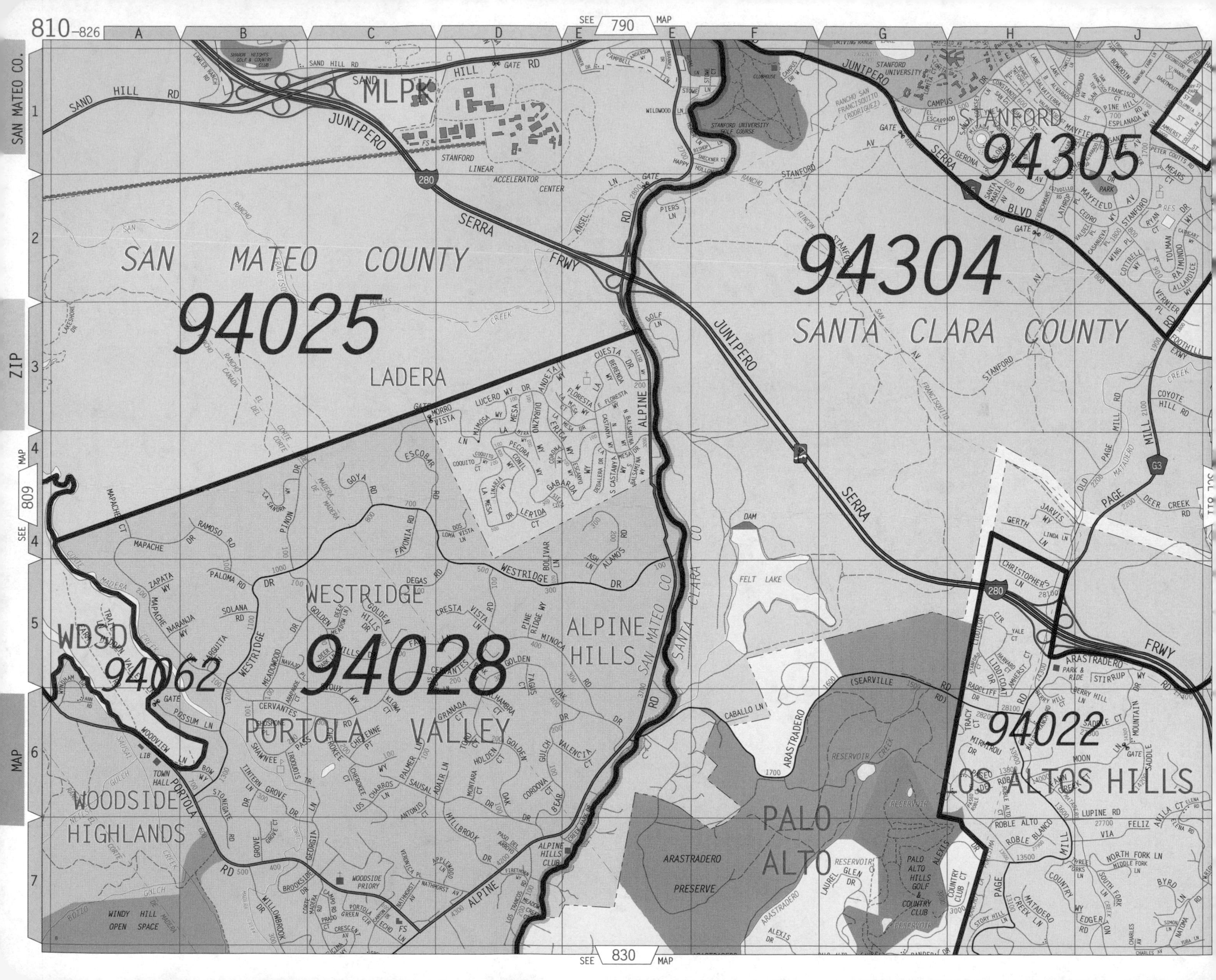
810-826
SEE 790 MAP
SEE 830 MAP
SEE 809 MAP
SAN MATEO CO.
ZIP
MAP
SAN MATEO COUNTY
94025
LADERA
MLPK
SAND HILL RD
JUNIPERO SERRA FRWY
280
STANFORD LINEAR ACCELERATOR CENTER
STANFORD UNIVERSITY GOLF COURSE
STANFORD
94305
94304
SANTA CLARA COUNTY
STANFORD AV
PAGE MILL RD
FOOTHILL EXWY
ALPINE RD
WESTRIDGE DR
WESTRIDGE
94028
PORTOLA VALLEY
ALPINE HILLS
WDSD
94062
WOODSIDE HIGHLANDS
PORTOLA RD
WINDY HILL OPEN SPACE
WOODSIDE PRIORY
FELT LAKE
ARASTRADERO RD
ARASTRADERO PRESERVE
PALO ALTO
PALO ALTO HILLS GOLF & COUNTRY CLUB
94022
LOS ALTOS HILLS
SAN MATEO CO
SANTA CLARA CO

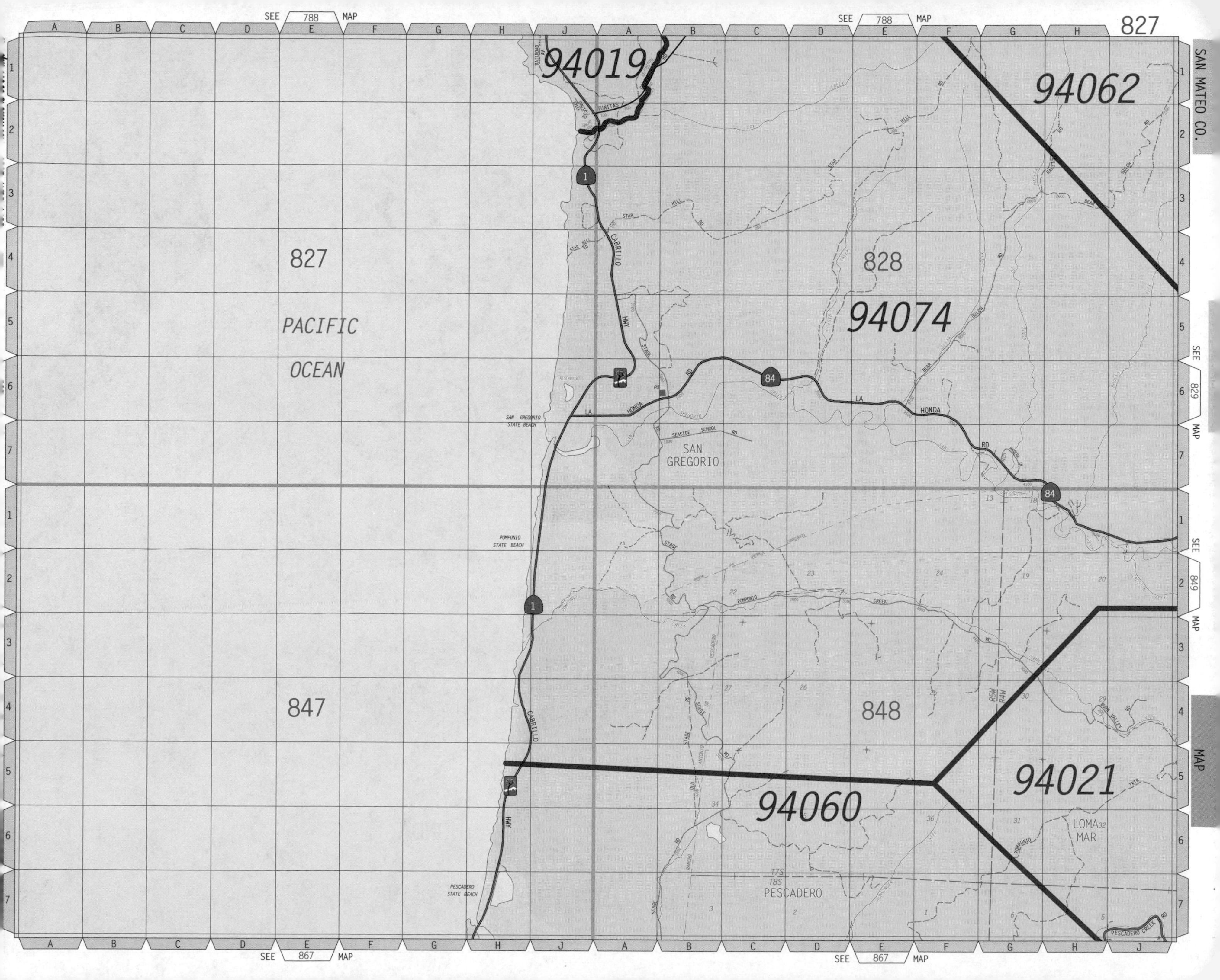
SEE 788 MAP
SEE 788 MAP
SAN MATEO CO.
94019
94062
827
828
94074
PACIFIC
OCEAN
SAN GREGORIO
SAN GREGORIO STATE BEACH
POMPONIO STATE BEACH
PESCADERO STATE BEACH
CABRILLO HWY
STAR HILL RD
STAGE RD
LA HONDA RD
SEASIDE SCHOOL RD
TUNITAS
POMPONIO CREEK RD
847
848
94060
94021
LOMA MAR
PESCADERO
SEE 829 MAP
SEE 849 MAP
MAP
SEE 867 MAP
SEE 867 MAP

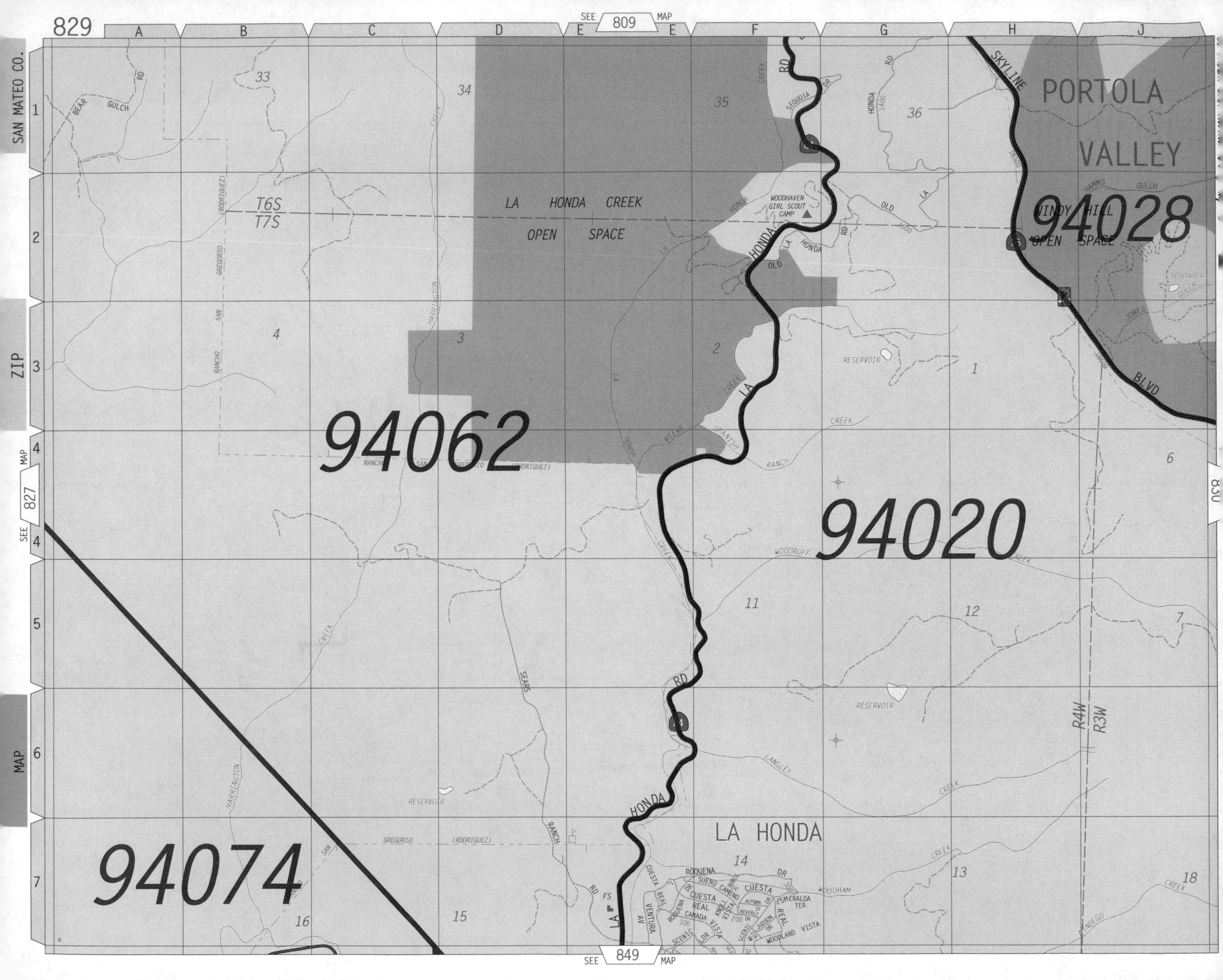
SEE 809 MAP
SAN MATEO CO.
ZIP
MAP
PORTOLA
VALLEY
94028
LA HONDA CREEK
OPEN SPACE
WOODHAVEN
GIRL SCOUT
CAMP
WINDY HILL
OPEN SPACE
T6S
T7S
94062
94020
94074
LA HONDA
SKYLINE
BLVD
R4W
R3W
RESERVOIR
SEE 827 MAP
830
SEE 849 MAP

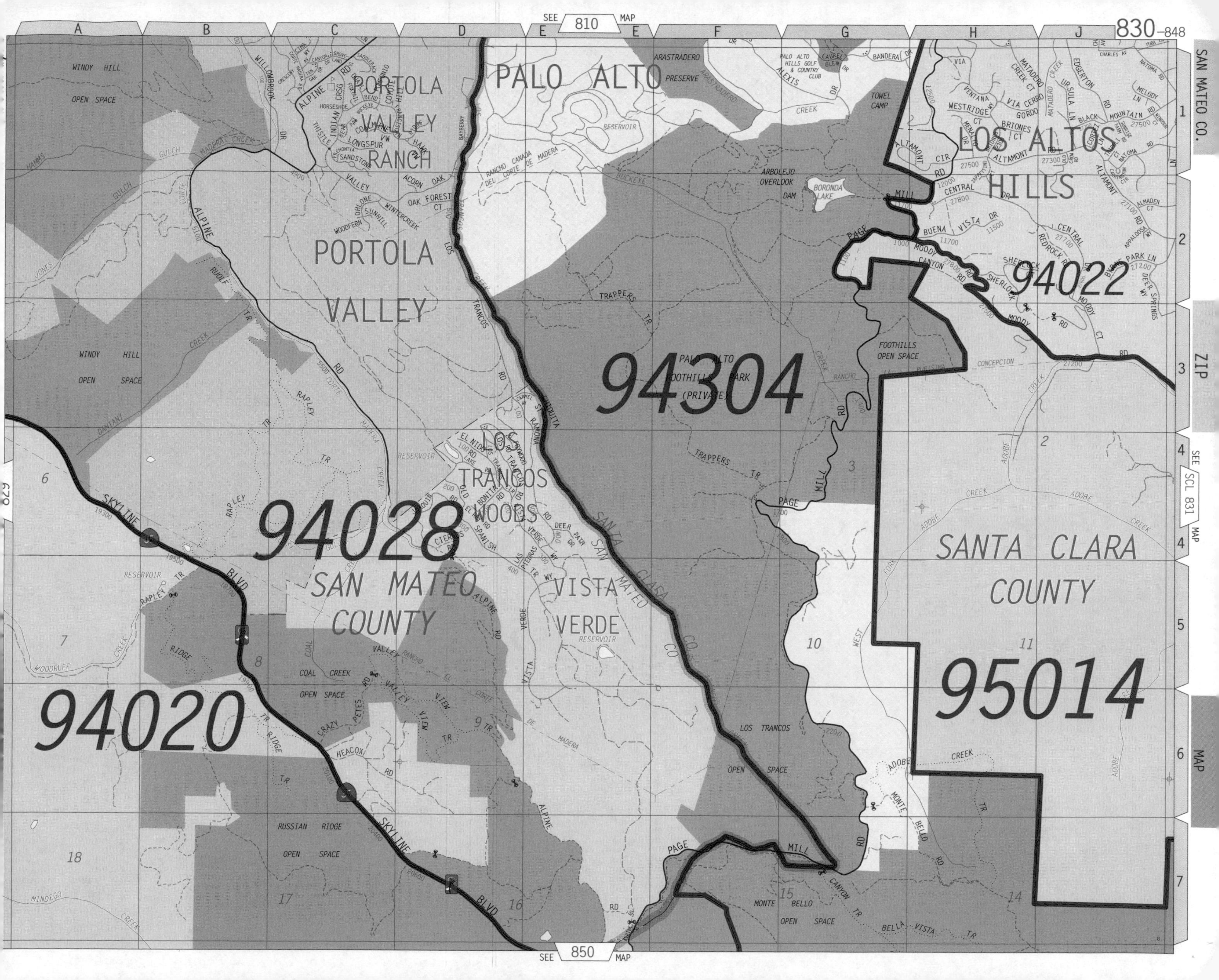
SEE 810 MAP
PALO ALTO
PORTOLA VALLEY RANCH
PORTOLA VALLEY
LOS ALTOS HILLS
94022
94304
94028
94020
95014
LOS TRANCOS WOODS
VISTA VERDE
SAN MATEO COUNTY
SANTA CLARA COUNTY
WINDY HILL OPEN SPACE
ARASTRADERO PRESERVE
PALO ALTO FOOTHILLS PARK (PRIVATE)
FOOTHILLS OPEN SPACE
COAL CREEK OPEN SPACE
RUSSIAN RIDGE OPEN SPACE
LOS TRANCOS OPEN SPACE
MONTE BELLO OPEN SPACE
SKYLINE BLVD
PAGE MILL RD
ALPINE RD
SAN MATEO CO.
ZIP
MAP
SEE SCL 831 MAP
SEE 850 MAP

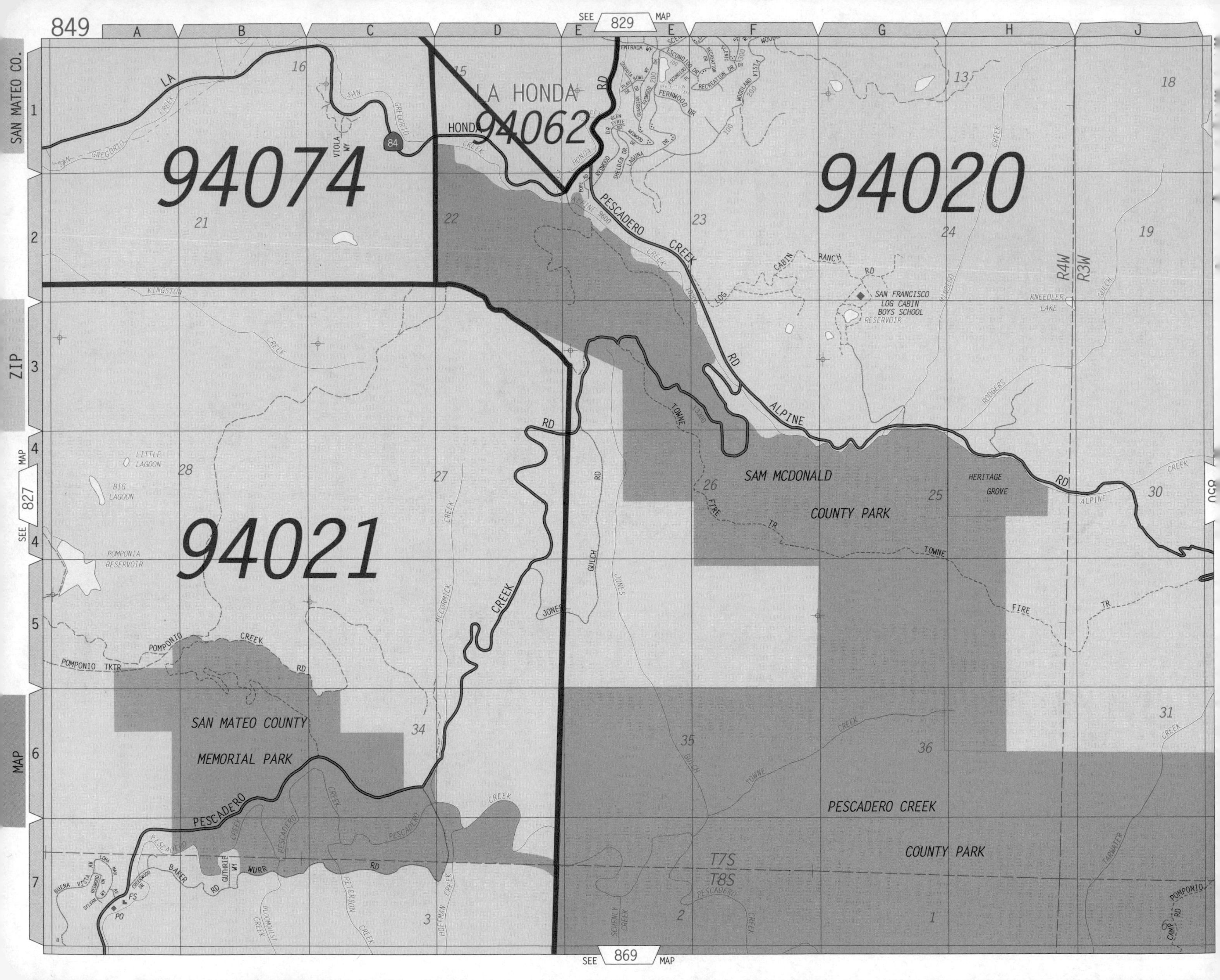
SEE 829 MAP
A
B
C
D
E
F
G
H
J
1
2
3
4
5
6
7
SAN MATEO CO.
ZIP
MAP
SEE 827 MAP
850
94074
94062
94020
94021
LA HONDA
LA HONDA RD
SAN GREGORIO CREEK
VIOLA WY
84
HONDA CREEK
PESCADERO CREEK RD
ALPINE RD
ALPINE CREEK
KINGSTON CREEK
LOG CABIN RANCH RD
SAN FRANCISCO LOG CABIN BOYS SCHOOL
RESERVOIR
KNEEDLER LAKE
R4W
R3W
ROGERS GULCH
SAM MCDONALD COUNTY PARK
HERITAGE GROVE
TOWNE FIRE TR
JONES GULCH
LITTLE LAGOON
BIG LAGOON
POMPONIA RESERVOIR
MCCORMICK CREEK
POMPONIO CREEK RD
POMPONIO TKTR
SAN MATEO COUNTY MEMORIAL PARK
PESCADERO CREEK COUNTY PARK
PESCADERO CREEK
BAKER RD
WURR RD
GUTHRIE WY
BUENA VISTA AV
LOMA MAR
REDWOOD DR
SYLVAN WY
CREEKWOOD DR
FS
PO
PETERSON CREEK
BLOOMQUIST CREEK
HOFFMAN CREEK
SCHENLY CREEK
TARWATER CREEK
POMPONIO CAMP RD
T7S
T8S
ENTRADA WY
ESCONDIDO DR
RECREATION DR
SCENIC DR
WOODLAND VISTA
FERNWOOD DR
SEQUOIA
PLAYA BOWL WY
GLEN EYRIE DR
REDWOOD DR
SHELDEN DR
LAGUNA DR
POPE RD
16
15
13
18
21
22
23
24
19
28
27
26
25
30
34
35
36
31
3
2
1

SEE 869 MAP

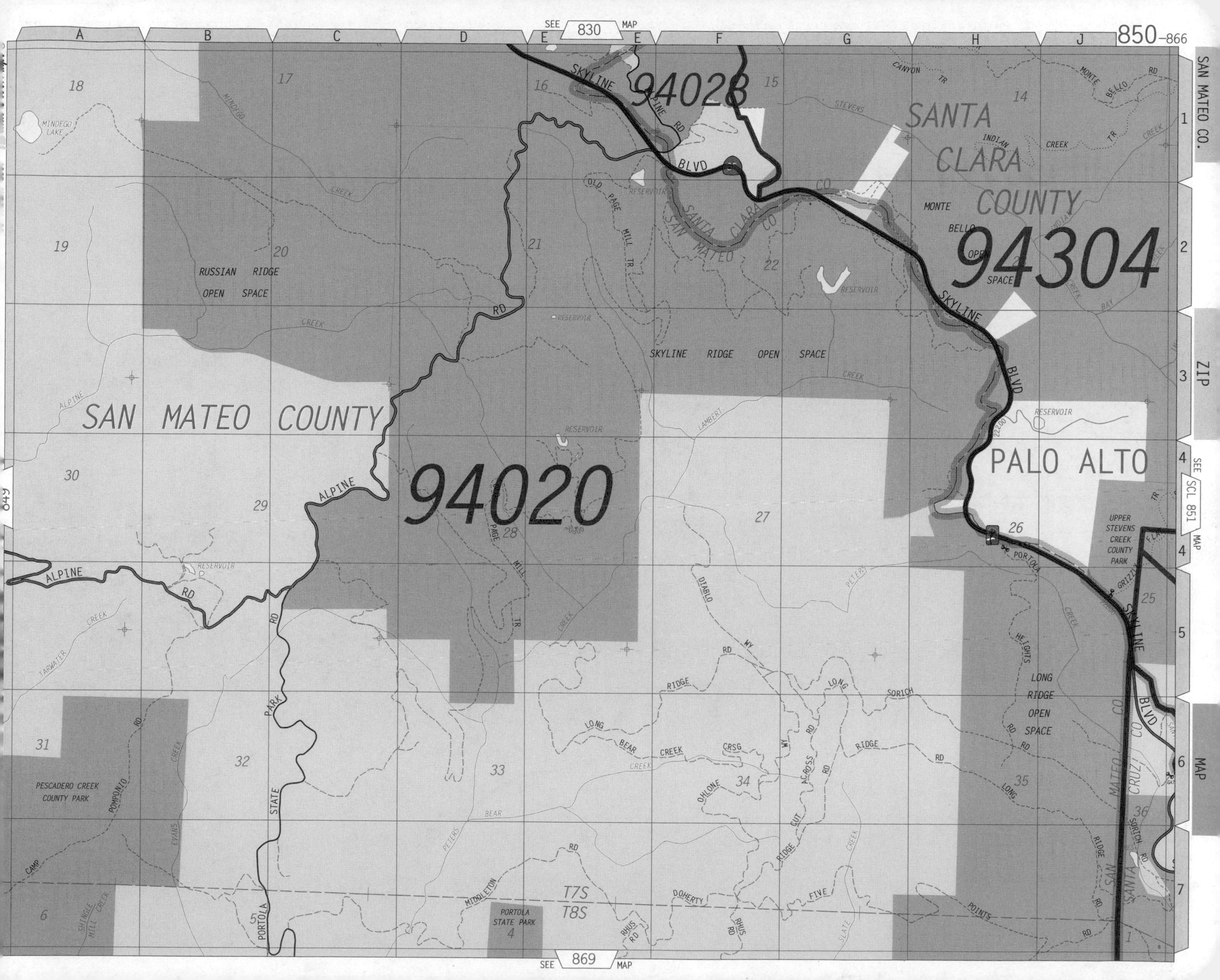
SEE 830 MAP
SAN MATEO COUNTY
SANTA CLARA COUNTY
94028
94304
94020
PALO ALTO
RUSSIAN RIDGE OPEN SPACE
SKYLINE RIDGE OPEN SPACE
MONTE BELLO OPEN SPACE
LONG RIDGE OPEN SPACE
UPPER STEVENS CREEK COUNTY PARK
PESCADERO CREEK COUNTY PARK
PORTOLA STATE PARK
MINDEGO LAKE
SKYLINE BLVD
ALPINE RD
PAGE MILL TR
OLD PAGE MILL TR
PORTOLA STATE PARK RD
T7S
T8S
SEE SCL 851 MAP
SAN MATEO CO. ZIP MAP
SEE 869 MAP

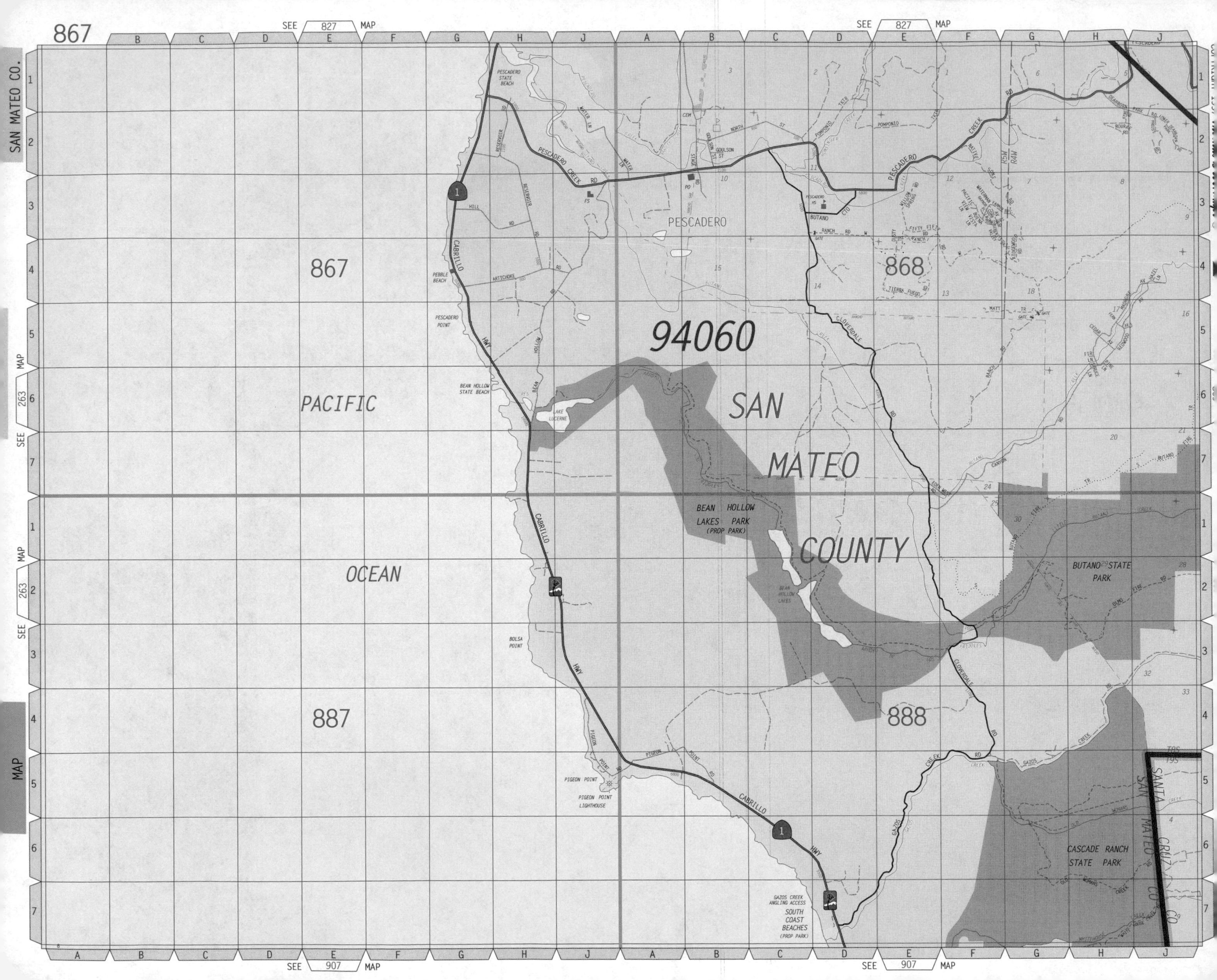
SEE 827 MAP
SEE 263 MAP
SEE 907 MAP
SAN MATEO CO.
MAP
PESCADERO STATE BEACH
PESCADERO CREEK RD
PESCADERO
CABRILLO HWY
PEBBLE BEACH
PESCADERO POINT
ARTICHOKE
BEAN HOLLOW STATE BEACH
LAKE LUCERNE
867
868
887
888
94060
SAN MATEO COUNTY
PACIFIC OCEAN
BEAN HOLLOW LAKES PARK (PROP PARK)
BEAN HOLLOW LAKES
BUTANO STATE PARK
CLOVERDALE RD
BOLSA POINT
PIGEON POINT
PIGEON POINT LIGHTHOUSE
GAZOS CREEK RD
GAZOS CREEK ANGLING ACCESS
SOUTH COAST BEACHES (PROP PARK)
CASCADE RANCH STATE PARK
SANTA CRUZ CO
SAN MATEO CO

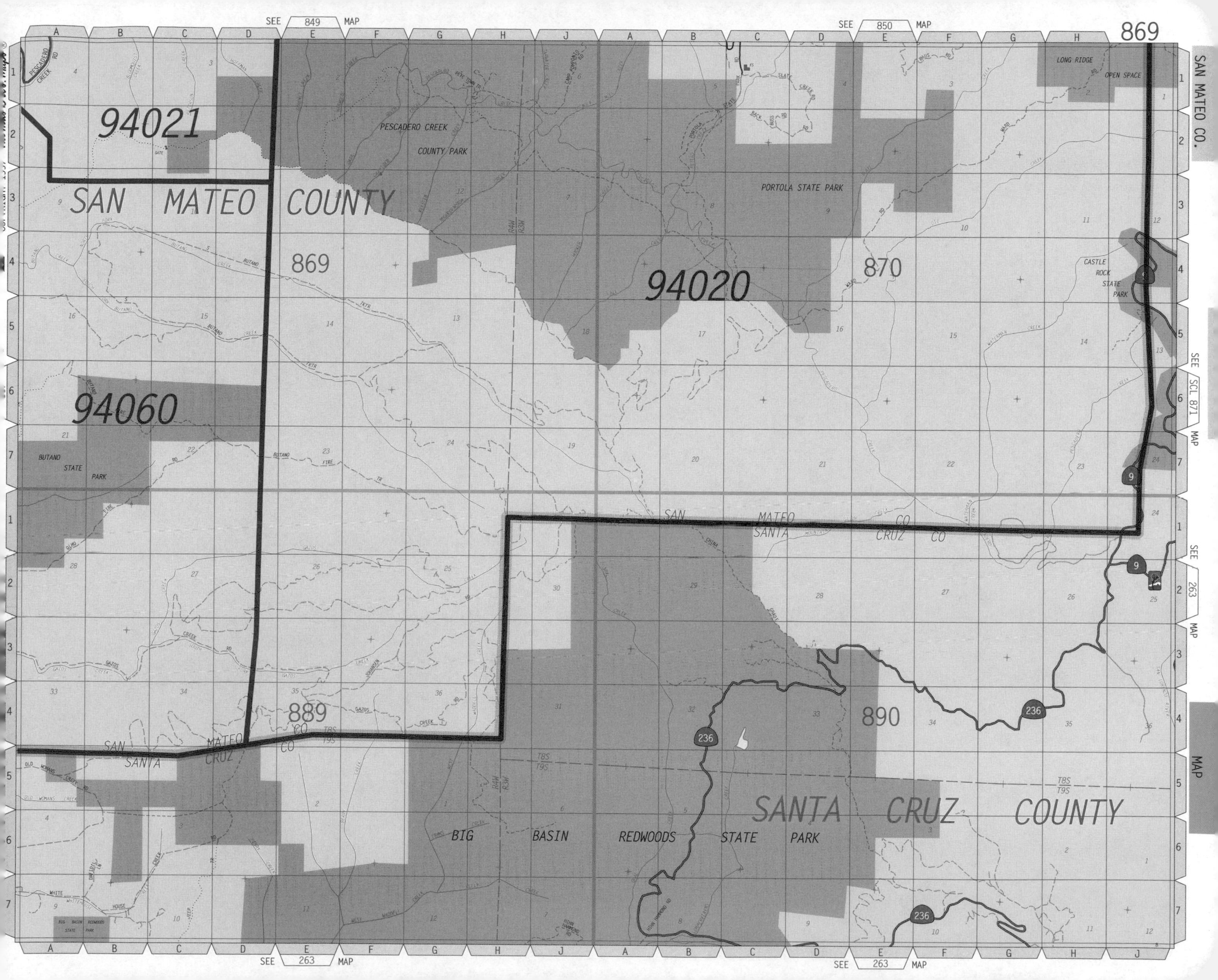
SEE 849 MAP
SEE 850 MAP
SAN MATEO CO.
94021
SAN MATEO COUNTY
PESCADERO CREEK COUNTY PARK
PORTOLA STATE PARK
LONG RIDGE OPEN SPACE
869
94020
870
CASTLE ROCK STATE PARK
94060
BUTANO STATE PARK
SEE SCL 871 MAP
SAN MATEO CO
SANTA CRUZ CO
SEE 263 MAP
889
890
SANTA CRUZ COUNTY
BIG BASIN REDWOODS STATE PARK
SEE 263 MAP
SEE 263 MAP
MAP

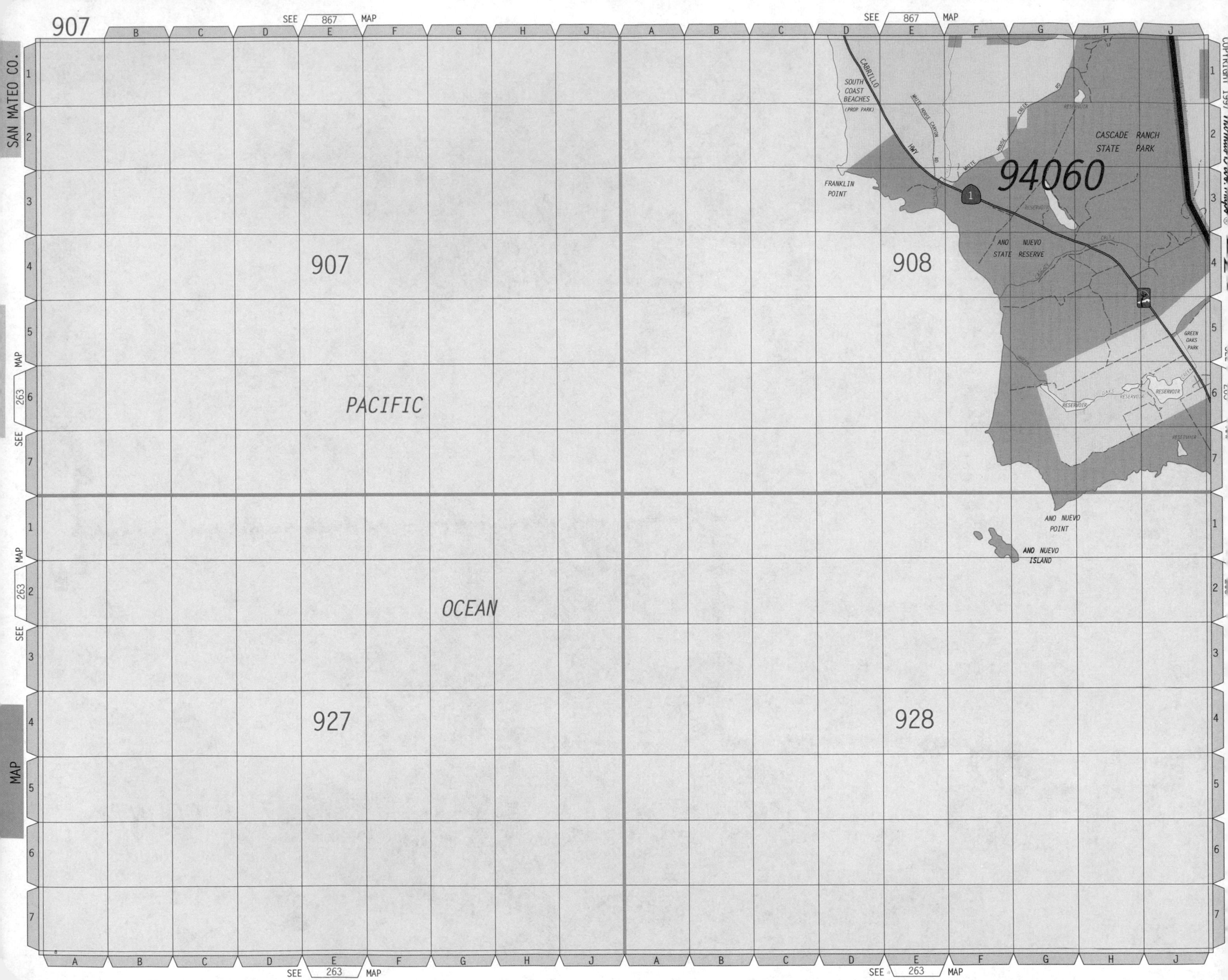
SAN MATEO CO.
SEE 867 MAP
SEE 867 MAP
SOUTH COAST BEACHES (PROP PARK)
CABRILLO HWY
FRANKLIN POINT
CASCADE RANCH STATE PARK
94060
ANO NUEVO STATE RESERVE
GREEN OAKS PARK
RESERVOIR
ANO NUEVO POINT
ANO NUEVO ISLAND
907
908
PACIFIC
OCEAN
927
928
SEE 263 MAP
SEE 263 MAP
SEE 263 MAP
SEE 263 MAP
MAP

LIST OF ABBREVIATIONS

PREFIXES AND SUFFIXES

AL	ALLEY
ARC	ARCADE
AV, AVE	AVENUE
AVCT	AVENUE COURT
AVD	AVENIDA
AVDR	AVENUE DRIVE
AVEX	AVENUE EXTENSION
BLEX	BOULEVARD EXTENSION
BL, BLVD	BOULEVARD
BLCT	BOULEVARD COURT
BRCH	BRANCH
BRDG	BRIDGE
BYPS	BYPASS
CIDR	CIRCLE DRIVE
CIR	CIRCLE
CL	CALLE
CLJ	CALLEJON
CM	CAMINO
CMTO	CAMINITO
COM	COMMON
CORR	CORRIDOR
CRES	CRESCENT
CRLO	CIRCULO
CRSG	CROSSING
CSWY	CAUSEWAY
CT	COURT
CTAV	COURT AVENUE
CTE	CORTE
CTO	CUT OFF
CTR	CENTER
CUR	CURVE
CV	COVE
D	DE
DIAG	DIAGONAL
DR	DRIVE
DVDR	DIVISION DRIVE
EXAV	EXTENSION AVENUE
EXBL	EXTENSION BOULEVARD
EXRD	EXTENSION ROAD
EXST	EXTENSION STREET
EXT	EXTENSION
EXWY	EXPRESSWAY
FRWY	FREEWAY
GDNS	GARDENS
GN	GLEN
GRN	GREEN
HWY	HIGHWAY
JCT	JUNCTION
LN	LANE
LNDG	LANDING
LP	LOOP
LS	LAS, LOS
MNR	MANOR
MTWY	MOTORWAY
OH	OUTER HIGHWAY
OVL	OVAL
OVPS	OVERPASS
PAS	PASEO
PK	PARK
PKWY	PARKWAY
PL	PLACE
PLZ, PZ	PLAZA
PT	POINT
PTH	PATH
RD	ROAD
RDEX	ROAD EXTENSION
RDGE	RIDGE
RW	ROW
SKWY	SKYWAY
SQ	SQUARE
ST	STREET
STAV	STREET AVENUE
STCT	STREET COURT
STDR	STREET DRIVE
STEX	STREET EXTENSION
STLN	STREET LANE
STLP	STREET LOOP
STPL	STREET PLACE
STXP	STREET EXPRESSWAY
TER	TERRACE
TFWY	TRAFFICWAY
THWY	THROUGHWAY
TKTR	TRUCKTRAIL
TPKE	TURNPIKE
TR	TRAIL
TUN	TUNNEL
UNPS	UNDERPASS
VIS	VISTA
VW	VIEW
WK	WALK
WY	WAY
WYPL	WAY PLACE

DIRECTIONS

E	EAST
KPN	KEY PENINSULA NORTH
KPS	KEY PENINSULA SOUTH
N	NORTH
NE	NORTHEAST
NW	NORTHWEST
S	SOUTH
SE	SOUTHEAST
SW	SOUTHWEST
W	WEST

DEPARTMENT STORES

BD	BLOOMINGDALES
BN	THE BON MARCHE
D	DIAMONDS
FN	FREDERICK & NELSON
G	GOLDWATERS
GT	GOTTSCHALKS
H	HARRIS
IM	I MAGNIN
L	LAMONTS
MA	MACY'S
ME	MERVYN'S
MF	MEIER & FRANK
MW	MONTGOMERY WARD
N	NORDSTROM
NM	NEIMAN-MARCUS
P	J C PENNEY
RM	ROBINSONS MAY
S	SEARS
SF	SAKS FIFTH AVENUE
W	WEINSTOCKS

BUILDINGS

CC	CHAMBER OF COMMERCE
CH	CITY HALL
CHP	CALIFORNIA HIGHWAY PATROL
COMM CTR	COMMUNITY CENTER
CON CTR	CONVENTION CENTER
CONT HS	CONTINUATION HIGH SCHOOL
CTH	COURT HOUSE
DMV	DEPT OF MOTOR VEHICLES
FAA	FEDERAL AVIATION ADMIN
FS	FIRE STATION
HOSP	HOSPITAL
HS	HIGH SCHOOL
INT	INTERMEDIATE SCHOOL
JR HS	JUNIOR HIGH SCHOOL
LIB	LIBRARY
MID	MIDDLE SCHOOL
MUS	MUSEUM
PO	POST OFFICE
PS	POLICE STATION
SR CIT CTR	SENIOR CITIZENS CENTER
STA	STATION
THTR	THEATER
VIS BUR	VISITORS BUREAU

OTHER COMMON ABBREVIATIONS

BCH	BEACH
BLDG	BUILDING
CEM	CEMETERY
CK	CREEK
CO	COUNTY
CTR	CENTER
COMM	COMMUNITY
EST	ESTATE
HIST	HISTORIC
HTS	HEIGHTS
LK	LAKE
MDW	MEADOW
MED	MEDICAL
MEM	MEMORIAL
MHP	MOBILE HOME PARK
MT	MOUNT
MTN	MOUNTAIN
NATL	NATIONAL
PKG	PARKING
PLGD	PLAYGROUND
RCH	RANCH
RCHO	RANCHO
REC	RECREATION
RES	RESERVOIR
RIV	RIVER
RR	RAILROAD
SPG	SPRING
STA	SANTA
VLG	VILLAGE
VLY	VALLEY
VW	VIEW

STREET Block City ZIP Pg-Grid

A

A ST
- SSF 94080 707-G3
100 MLPK 94025 790-H3
100 RDWC 94063 769-J5
100 SMCo 94014 687-C5
100 RDWC 94063 770-A5
400 CLMA 94014 687-C5
400 DALY 94014 687-C5
ABBOT AV
- DALY 94014 687-D5
ABELIA WY
100 EPA 94303 791-D3
ABERDEEN DR
100 SCAR 94070 769-F4
1300 SMTO 94402 749-B2
ABRAMS CT
- SCIC - 791-A7
ABRYAN WY
2000 SMCo 94061 790-B4
ACACIA AV
100 SBRN 94066 727-J1
200 SSF 94080 707-H2
400 SBRN 94066 707-H7
ACACIA CT
- PCFA 94044 727-A5
100 SCAR 94070 769-F2
ACACIA DR
- ATN 94027 790-G1
700 BURL 94010 728-F6
ACACIA LN
- SMCo 94062 769-G6
- SMCo 94062 789-G1
ACACIA ST
900 SMCo 94037 746-G4
ACADEMY AV
900 BLMT 94002 769-C1
ACADEMY CT
700 BLMT 94002 769-C1
ACCACIA ST
- DALY 94014 687-J3
N ACCESS RD
100 SSF 94080 708-A5
ACEVEDO AV
- SF 94132 687-A1
ACORN
- PTLV 94028 830-D2
ACORN DR
- HIL 94010 728-D7
ACORN WY
- ATN 94027 790-G1
ACTON ST
- SF 94112 687-E3
- DALY 94014 687-E3
ADA ST
700 SMTO 94401 749-B1
ADAIR LN
- PTLV 94028 810-D6
ADAM CT
- SCAR 94070 769-D3
ADAM WY
- ATN 94027 790-C2
ADAMS CT
1300 MLPK 94025 771-B7
2500 SSF 94080 707-C4
ADAMS DR
- EPA 94303 771-B7
1500 MLPK 94025 771-B7
1500 MLPK 94303 771-B7
ADAMS ST
500 RDWC 94062 770-A6
600 RDWC 94061 770-A6
1700 SMTO 94403 749-C3
ADDISON AV
100 PA 94301 790-J5
300 PA 94301 791-A4
2000 EPA 94303 791-A2
ADDISON ST
1300 RDWC 94061 770-B7
ADELAIDE WY
3200 BLMT 94002 768-J2
ADELINE DR
1500 BURL 94010 728-C6
1500 SMCo 94010 728-B6
ADMIRAL ST
100 SMCo 94038 746-F6
ADMIRALTY LN
1100 FCTY 94404 749-F2
ADMIRALTY PL
- RDWC 94065 749-J6
ADOBE DR
1300 PCFA 94044 726-H6
ADRIAN AV
100 SSF 94080 707-D2
1300 SMTO 94403 749-D4
ADRIAN CT
- BURL 94010 728-C4
ADRIAN RD
200 MLBR 94030 728-C4
1500 BURL 94010 728-D4
AFTON CT
- SMTO 94402 749-B2
AGNES WY
900 PA 94303 791-C5
AGUA VISTA CT
- SMCo 94062 789-F2
AHWAHNEE DR
800 MLBR 94030 727-J4
AIRPORT BLVD
- BURL 94010 728-F5
- SMTO 94401 728-F5
- SSF 94080 707-J3
400 SSF 94080 708-A2
S AIRPORT BLVD
- SMCo 94128 708-A5
100 SSF 94080 707-A5
100 SSF 94080 708-A4
AIRPORT ST
800 SMCo 94038 746-G7
800 SMCo 94038 766-G1
AIRPORT WY
400 SCAR 94070 769-H1
600 RDWC 94065 769-H1
ALAMEDA AV
- SMCo 94019 767-C4
2800 HMBY 94019 767-C4
ALAMEDA PL
- SBRN 94066 707-E7
ALAMEDA DE LAS PULGAS
- SMCo 94062 789-H1
- ATN 94027 790-B4
- RDWC 94062 769-H6
100 BLMT 94002 749-A5
100 SMCo 94062 769-H6
200 SMTO 94402 748-H3
200 BLMT 94002 769-C1
400 SCAR 94070 769-F4
400 SMCo 94062 769-H6
600 RDWC 94061 789-H1
1700 SMTO 94403 749-A5
1700 SMTO 94403 748-H3
1800 RDWC 94061 790-B4
1800 WDSD 94062 790-B4
2000 SMCo 94062 790-B4
2100 SMCo 94061 790-B4
3000 SMCo 94025 790-B4
3700 MLPK 94025 790-B4
ALAMEDA LAS PULGAS
400 RDWC 94062 789-J1
ALAMO ST
1100 SMCo 94037 746-H5
ALAMOS RD
- PTLV 94028 810-E5
ALANA WY
- BSBN 94005 688-B2
- SF 94134 688-B2
ALANNAH CT
- PA 94303 791-C4
ALBACORE LN
100 FCTY 94404 749-H3
ALBEMARLE WY
1500 BURL 94010 728-C5
ALBERNI ST
1000 EPA 94303 791-A1
ALBERNI ST Rt#-114
900 EPA 94303 771-A7
ALBERTA AV
100 SCAR 94070 769-H5
ALBERTA ST
- SF 94134 687-J1
ALBERTA WY
300 HIL 94010 748-E3
ALBION AV
100 WDSD 94062 789-F5
ALBRIGHT WY
2500 SSF 94080 707-E5
ALCALA CT
- PCFA 94044 726-J5
ALCATRAZ AV
- SMCo 94018 767-A1
- SMCo 94018 766-J2
- HMBY 94019 767-C4
ALCAZAR DR
3000 BURL 94010 728-A6
ALCOTT RD
200 SBRN 94066 727-F1
ALDEN CT
1200 BLMT 94002 769-D1
ALDEN ST
200 RDWC 94063 770-A5
1800 BLMT 94002 769-C1
ALDENGLEN DR
100 SSF 94080 707-G2
ALDER AV
100 SMCo 94015 687-B4
ALDER LN
400 SMTO 94403 749-B6
ALDER PL
- MLPK 94025 790-H2
ALDER ST
- SMCo 94037 746-G4
- SF 94134 688-A1
ALDERLEE WY
- SCAR 94070 769-F5
ALDERWOOD CT
1800 SMTO 94402 748-H7
ALEJANDRA AV
- MLPK 94027 790-E3
- ATN 94027 790-E3
ALEMANY BLVD
1900 SF 94112 687-E2
3200 SF 94132 687-C2
ALESTER AV
600 PA 94303 791-C4
ALEXANDER AV
- DALY 94014 687-D3
100 SMCo 94061 790-B2
ALEXANDER RD
- BSBN 94005 688-A7
ALEXIS CIR
500 DALY 94014 687-H3
ALEXIS CT
- MLPK 94025 790-C7
ALEXIS DR
3100 PA 94304 830-F1
3100 PA 94304 810-F7
3200 LAH 94022 810-G7
ALGER DR
400 PA 94306 791-D7
ALHAMBRA CT
- PTLV 94028 810-D6
ALHAMBRA DR
2600 BLMT 94002 749-B7
2600 BLMT 94002 769-A1
ALHAMBRA RD
400 SSF 94080 707-F4
500 SMTO 94402 748-J2
ALICANTE DR
1100 PCFA 94044 727-A6
ALICE LN
900 MLPK 94025 790-F4
ALIDA WY
300 SSF 94080 707-G4
300 SMCo 94080 707-G4
ALISO WY
- SMCo 94028 810-E3
ALLAN ST
400 DALY 94014 687-J3
400 SF 94134 687-J3
ALLANHILL LN
3100 SMTO 94403 748-J6
ALLARDICE WY
800 SCIC 94305 810-J2
ALLEGHENY WY
2200 SMCo 94402 768-G2
ALLEMANY ST
- DALY 94014 687-C5
ALLEN CT
700 PA 94303 791-D6
ALLEN DR
- SBRN 94066 707-D6
ALLEN RD
200 SMCo 94062 809-C5
ALLERTON AV
300 SSF 94080 708-B3
ALLERTON ST
400 RDWC 94063 770-A5
ALLISON CT
3400 SMTO 94403 748-J7
ALLISON ST
- SF 94112 687-F2
ALL VIEW WY
2600 BLMT 94002 769-B1
ALMA LN
- MLPK 94025 790-F3
ALMA ST
- MLPK 94025 790-G3
- PA 94301 790-H4
1100 PA 94301 791-B7
1500 PA 94306 791-B7
2000 SCAR 94070 769-F3
ALMADEN CT
26700 LAH 94022 830-J2
ALMADEN WY
200 SMTO 94403 749-D5
ALMANOR AV
400 SSF 94080 707-F4
1000 MLPK 94025 790-H1
1100 MLPK 94025 770-J7
ALMENAR ST
800 MLBR 94030 728-A4
ALMENDRAL AV
- ATN 94027 790-C3
ALMER RD
500 BURL 94010 728-F7
ALMERIA AV
300 SMCo 94018 767-A2
ALMOND AV
700 SSF 94080 707-H2
ALMOND CT
- EPA 94303 791-C2
ALOMAR WY
1100 BLMT 94002 769-D2
ALP AV
- DALY 94014 687-D3
ALP WY
- MLBR 94030 727-J4
ALPHA ST
- SF 94134 688-A2
ALPINE AV
- DALY 94015 687-A5
800 BURL 94010 728-F6
1100 MLPK 94025 770-H7
ALPINE CT
300 SSF 94080 707-F5
ALPINE RD
- SCIC 94028 830-E7
- SCIC 94028 850-E1
- SMCo 94020 830-D5
- PTLV 94028 810-D7
- PTLV 94028 830-C1
- SMCo 94020 849-F3
- SMCo 94020 850-C4
- SMCo 94028 810-E3
- SMCo 94028 830-D5
300 SMCo 94025 810-E3
2400 SMCo 94025 790-E7
ALPINE RD
2400 MLPK 94025 790-E7
2500 MLPK 94025 810-E3
20800 SMCo 94028 850-E1
ALPINE WY
100 SBRN 94066 727-F1
ALSACE LORAINE AV
500 HMBY 94019 787-E2
ALSTON AV
- HMBY 94019 767-E7
- HMBY 94019 787-E1
ALTA AV
500 SMTO 94403 749-A5
ALTA LN
- SCAR 94070 769-E3
ALTAIR AV
600 FCTY 94404 749-E3
ALTA LOMA AV
100 DALY 94015 687-B6
ALTA LOMA DR
100 SSF 94080 707-D2
ALTA LOMA RD
100 SSF 94080 707-E3
ALTA MESA DR
100 SSF 94080 707-E3
ALTA MESA RD
- SMCo 94037 746-H3
100 WDSD 94062 789-G5
ALTAMONT CIR
27700 SCIC 94022 830-G1
ALTAMONT DR
300 SSF 94080 707-E3
ALTAMONT RD
26600 LAH 94022 830-H1
ALTAMONT WY
3500 RDWC 94062 789-H1
ALTA VISTA DR
100 ATN 94027 790-A5
200 SMCo 94080 707-F5
300 SSF 94080 707-F5
600 PCFA 94044 726-J4
ALTA VISTA RD
100 WDSD 94062 789-G5
600 SMCo 94037 746-H4
ALTA VISTA WY
- SMCo 94014 687-F3
- DALY 94014 687-F3
ALTO AV
500 SMCo 94019 767-D4
500 HMBY 94019 767-D4
ALTO LN
- MLPK 94025 790-G4
ALTO LOMA
100 MLBR 94030 727-J5
ALTON AV
100 SMCo 94038 746-F7
ALTREE CT
- ATN 94027 790-H1
ALTSCHUL AV
900 MLPK 94025 790-D6
1000 SMCo 94025 790-D6
ALTURA WY
- SSF 94080 707-E2
900 PCFA 94044 726-J4
1500 BLMT 94002 769-E2
ALTURAS DR
100 SMCo 94010 728-A7
1500 BURL 94010 728-B7
ALTURAS WY
- DALY 94014 687-E3
ALVARADO AV
100 SMCo 94038 766-G1
1200 PCFA 94044 727-A5
1300 BURL 94010 728-C6
1400 SMCo 94010 728-C6
ALVARADO CT
700 SCIC 94305 810-J1
ALVARADO RW
500 SCIC 94305 790-H7
500 SCIC 94305 810-H1
ALVARADO ST
- BSBN 94005 688-A6
ALVERNO CT
- RDWC 94061 789-G3
ALVISO CT
- PCFA 94044 726-J5
- PCFA 94044 727-A5
ALVISO ST
- SF 94132 687-C1
AMADOR AV
- ATN 94027 790-C3
100 SBRN 94066 707-E7
AMALFI WY
400 RDWC 94065 749-J4
AMAPOLA AV
100 PCFA 94044 727-B2
AMARILLO AV
900 PA 94303 791-D5
AMAZON AV
- SF 94112 687-F1
AMBAR WY
300 MLPK 94025 790-F6
AMBER CT
- SCAR 94070 769-F6
AMBOY CT
- SMTO 94402 768-G1
AMERICAN ST
800 SCAR 94070 769-H4
AMERICAN WY
1300 SMCo 94025 790-D5
AMES AV
700 PA 94303 791-D7
AMES CT
800 PA 94303 791-E6
AMESBURY AV
600 SMTO 94402 749-B2
AMESPORT LNDG
- HMBY 94019 787-F2
AMHERST AV
- SMCo 94063 790-D1
AMHERST CT
14100 LAH 94022 810-H5
AMHERST ST
200 SMTO 94402 748-H2
2000 PA 94306 810-J1
AMHURST CT
- DALY 94015 707-D3
AMPHLETT BLVD
- SMTO 94401 729-A7
- SMTO 94401 749-B1
600 SMTO 94402 749-B1
N AMPHLETT BLVD
- SMTO 94401 729-A7
200 SMTO 94401 728-J6
AMPHLETT PL
1600 SMTO 94402 749-C2
AMY DR
- SMTO 94403 748-H7
ANACAPA LN
600 FCTY 94404 749-G5
ANAMOR ST
1600 RDWC 94061 790-A2
ANCHOR CIR
500 RDWC 94065 749-J6
ANCHOR LN
- SCAR 94070 769-E2
ANCHOR RD
400 SMTO 94404 749-D1
ANCHOR WY
- HMBY 94019 787-G5
ANDERSON WY
- MLPK 94025 790-E7
- MLPK 94025 810-E1
ANDETA WY
100 SMCo 94028 810-D3
ANDORRA CT
- PCFA 94044 727-A3
ANDOVER DR
300 PCFA 94044 707-B2
ANDROMEDA LN
800 FCTY 94404 749-H1
ANGELITA AV
100 PCFA 94044 727-B2
ANGELL CT
- SCIC - 791-A7
- SCIC 94305 790-J7
ANGUIDO CT
- HIL 94402 748-G5
ANGUS AV E
200 SBRN 94066 707-J7
500 SBRN 94066 708-A7
ANGUS AV W
- SBRN 94066 707-H7
ANITA AV
800 BLMT 94002 749-D7
ANITA CT
- BLMT 94002 749-D7
ANITA DR
200 MLBR 94030 728-A3
ANITA LN
500 MLBR 94030 728-A3
500 MLBR 94030 727-J3
ANITA RD
- BURL 94010 728-G6
ANKENY ST
- SF 94134 688-A1
ANN RD
- PTLV 94028 810-A6
ANNA ST
900 SMTO 94401 749-B1
ANNAPOLIS CT
3800 SSF 94080 707-D3
ANNAPOLIS DR
1000 SMTO 94403 749-C4
ANNAPOLIS ST
2500 EPA 94303 791-B1
2500 EPA 94303 771-B7
ANNESCOURT DR
- HIL 94010 728-D7
ANNESCOURT PL
- HIL 94010 728-D7
ANNETTE AV
1200 RDWC 94063 770-F6
ANNIE ST
1500 SMCo 94015 687-B5
1500 DALY 94015 687-B5
ANNIS RD
100 BSBN 94005 688-B7
ANSEL AV
600 BURL 94010 728-F6
ANSEL LN
- SMCo 94025 810-E2
ANSON RD
- HIL 94010 748-F4
ANTARES LN
800 FCTY 94404 749-H1
ANTIGUA LN
1400 FCTY 94404 749-G5
ANTIOCH DR
- SMTO 94403 749-D6
ANTIQUE FOREST LN
- BLMT 94002 769-E1
ANTOINETTE LN
400 HMBY 94019 767-E6
800 SSF 94080 707-F2
ANTON CT
400 PA 94301 791-B6
ANTONIO CT
- PTLV 94028 810-C7
ANZA BLVD
100 BURL 94010 728-F5
ANZA DR
900 PCFA 94044 726-H4
ANZA WY
100 SBRN 94066 727-J1
APOLLO RD
700 FCTY 94404 749-E3
APPALOOSA WY
27000 LAH 94022 830-J2
APPIAN WY
- SSF 94080 707-E4
2900 SCAR 94070 769-F5
APPLEWOOD LN
- PTLV 94028 810-C7
APRIL AV
100 SSF 94080 707-E3
APTOS WY
100 SSF 94080 707-G5
AQUARIUS LN
600 FCTY 94404 749-E4
ARA LN
600 FCTY 94404 749-E4
ARAGON BLVD
- SMTO 94401 749-A3
- SMTO 94402 749-A3
- SMTO 94402 748-J3
ARAGON CT
1000 PCFA 94044 726-J5
ARAPAHOE CT
- PTLV 94028 810-B6
ARASTRADERO RD
1500 PA 94304 810-F6
1700 SCIC 94304 810-H5
1700 PTLV 94028 810-F6
16000 LAH 94022 810-H5
ARBALLO DR
200 SF 94132 687-A1
ARBOL GRANDE CT
- SMCo 94025 790-D5
ARBOR AV
1900 BLMT 94002 769-C1
ARBOR CT
100 SBRN 94066 707-E7
100 WDSD 94062 789-G5
ARBOR DR
300 SSF 94080 707-E3
ARBOR LN
100 SMCo 94038 746-F6
100 SMTO 94403 749-B6
ARBOR RD
- MLPK 94025 790-E4
ARBORETUM RD
300 PA 94304 790-H5
400 SCIC 94305 790-H5
ARBUTUS AV
3500 PA 94303 791-E7
ARC WY
1500 BURL 94010 728-E6
ARCADIA CT
100 PCFA 94044 707-A2
ARCADIA DR
- DALY 94015 707-A2
- PCFA 94044 707-A2
ARCADIA PL
- HIL 94010 748-G2
1400 PA 94303 791-B4
ARCH LN
- SCAR 94070 769-E2
ARCH ST
- RDWC 94062 769-J5
- SF 94132 687-C2
100 RDWC 94062 770-A5
ARCHDALE CT
2200 SSF 94080 707-D4
ARCHER CT
- SMTO 94401 729-A6
ARCHERY FIRE RD
- SMCo 94062 789-C5
ARCHERY FIRE TR
- SMCo 94062 789-B6
ARCTURUS CIR
800 FCTY 94404 749-E4
ARDEE LN
2400 SSF 94080 707-D5
ARDEN AV
100 SSF 94080 707-J2
ARDEN CT
- DALY 94014 687-G3
- RDWC 94061 770-A7
- RDWC 94061 790-A1
ARDEN LN
1400 BLMT 94002 769-E2
ARDEN RD
200 MLPK 94025 790-F2
300 HIL 94010 748-G2
ARDENDALE DR
- DALY 94014 687-F3
ARELIOUS WALKER DR
2800 SF 94124 688-C1
ARELLANO AV
- SF 94132 687-B1
ARGONAUT AV
- SF 94134 687-J2
ARGUELLO BLVD
500 PCFA 94044 726-H4
ARGUELLO DR
2700 BURL 94010 728-A6
ARGUELLO ST
300 RDWC 94063 769-J4
500 SCIC 94305 790-H7
800 RDWC 94063 770-A5
ARGUS CT
800 FCTY 94404 749-E4
ARIES LN
700 FCTY 94404 749-E4
ARIZONA WY
1900 RDWC 94061 790-A3
ARK ST
1600 SMTO 94403 749-D1
ARLEEN WY
700 PCFA 94044 707-A7
700 PCFA 94044 727-A1
ARLETA AV
- SF 94134 688-A2
- SF 94134 687-J2
ARLETA WY
1000 HMBY 94019 787-F2
ARLEY CT
- DALY 94015 707-D3
ARLINGTON DR
- SSF 94080 707-D1
ARLINGTON LN
- DALY 94014 687-F3
300 SMTO 94402 748-H1
ARLINGTON RD
200 RDWC 94062 769-H6
ARLINGTON WY
- SMCo 94025 790-H2
- MLPK 94025 790-H2
ARMADA WY
2200 SMTO 94404 749-D2
ARMOUR AV
200 SSF 94080 708-A2
200 SSF 94080 707-J2
ARMSBY DR
1200 HIL 94010 728-D6
1200 BURL 94010 728-D6
ARMSTRONG AV
1200 SF 94124 688-C1
ARNOLD WY
700 HMBY 94019 787-F2
700 MLPK 94025 790-J2
ARROWHEAD LN
- SMCo 94063 790-D1
ARROWHEAD WY
1000 PA 94303 791-D5
ARROWOOD LN
100 SMTO 94403 749-B5
ARROYO AV
1100 SCAR 94070 769-G4
ARROYO CT
- SMTO 94402 748-J2
ARROYO DR
- SSF 94080 707-E4
200 PCFA 94044 707-A4
200 PCFA 94044 706-J4
ARROYO LEON DR
700 HMBY 94019 787-G2
ARROYO SECO
- MLBR 94030 727-J5
ARROYO VIEW CIR
- BLMT 94002 769-B2
ARTHUR AV
2100 BLMT 94002 769-C1
ARTHUR LN
- ATN 94027 790-C2
ARTHUR E HANSEN WY
1900 SMTO 94404 749-E2
ARTICHOKE RD
- SMCo 94060 867-H4
ARUBA LN
900 FCTY 94404 749-G4
ARUNDEL RD
- BURL 94010 728-H6
- SCAR 94070 769-E3
ASCENSION DR
1400 SMCo 94402 748-G6
ASCOT RD
300 HIL 94010 748-G2
ASH AV
600 SSF 94080 707-J2
ASH LN
100 PTLV 94028 810-E4
ASH ST
- RDWC 94061 790-B1
1800 PA 94306 791-A7
ASHBY DR
700 PA 94301 791-B3
ASHDOWN PL
- HMBY 94019 787-E5
ASHFIELD RD
- ATN 94027 790-E2
ASHFORD AV
300 SCAR 94070 769-E4
ASHLAND DR
- DALY 94015 686-J4
ASHTON AV
- MLBR 94030 728-A4
- SF 94112 687-D1
ASHTON AV
500 PA 94306 791-D7
2000 SMCo 94025 790-D6
S ASHTON AV
- MLBR 94030 728-B5
1800 BURL 94010 728-B5
ASHTON CT
3400 PA 94306 791-D7
ASHWOOD CT
1300 SMTO 94402 748-J4
ASHWOOD DR
1400 SMTO 94402 748-J4
ASPEN AV
200 SSF 94080 708-A2
200 SSF 94080 707-J2
ASPEN DR
1200 PCFA 94044 727-B5
ASPEN ST
900 SMCo 94037 746-H4
ASPEN WY
800 PA 94303 791-E7
ASSOCIATED RD
100 SSF 94080 708-A3
ASTER AV
- HIL 94010 728-F7
- HIL 94010 748-F1
ASTER RD
100 SCAR 94070 769-G4
ASTER WY
100 EPA 94303 791-D3
ATHENIAN WY
400 PCFA 94044 726-G4
ATHENS ST
300 SF 94112 687-G1
ATHERTON AV
- ATN 94027 790-C4
ATHERTON CT
100 SMCo 94061 790-B4
ATHERTON OAKS LN
- ATN 94027 790-D5
ATHERWOOD AV
- RDWC 94061 790-B2
ATHERWOOD PL
- RDWC 94061 790-B2
ATHLONE CT
- SMCo 94025 770-F7
ATHLONE WY
- SMCo 94025 770-E7
ATHY DR
3500 SSF 94080 707-C4
ATKINSON LN
1000 MLPK 94025 790-E5
ATLANTA ST
500 DALY 94014 687-D5
ATLANTIC AV
- SBRN 94066 707-J5
ATWATER DR
2900 BURL 94010 728-A6
AUDIFFRED LN
100 WDSD 94062 789-G6
AUDUBON AV
1200 SMCo 94037 746-G5
AUGUST CIR
300 MLPK 94025 790-F6
AURA VISTA
- MLBR 94030 727-J5
- PCFA 94044 706-J3
- MLBR 94030 728-A4
AURORA CT
- PCFA 94044 727-B2
AUSTIN AV
- ATN 94027 790-C2
AUTUMN DR
3800 RDWC 94061 789-G3
AUTUMN ST
200 SMCo 94020 829-F7
AVALON AV
1000 FCTY 94404 749-F5
AVALON CT
3100 PA 94306 791-D7
AVALON DR
- DALY 94015 686-J6
100 PCFA 94044 706-J4
200 PCFA 94044 707-A4
200 SSF 94080 707-F5
W AVALON DR
100 PCFA 94044 706-J4
AVENUE ALHAMBRA
200 SMCo 94018 767-A2
AVENUE BALBOA
100 SMCo 94018 767-B2
AVENUE CABRILLO
100 SMCo 94018 767-C3
AVENUE DEL ORA
400 RDWC 94062 769-J7
AVENUE DEL ORO
200 SMCo 94018 767-B2
AVENUE GRANADA
100 SMCo 94018 767-A2
AVENUE PORTOLA
- SMCo 94018 767-B2
AVERY ST
- SMCo 94037 746-H5
AVIADOR AV
- MLBR 94030 728-B3
AVIGNON PL
2000 HMBY 94019 767-D5
AVILA CT
1300 PCFA 94044 727-A6
13100 LAH 94022 810-J7
AVILA RD
- SMTO 94402 749-A3
200 SMTO 94402 748-J3
AVOCET CT
200 FCTY 94404 749-H2
AVOCET DR
- RDWC 94065 749-J6
200 RDWC 94065 750-A6
AVON ST
900 BLMT 94002 769-D1
AVONDALE AV
- RDWC 94062 769-J5
AVONDALE RD
1200 HIL 94010 748-E4
W AVONDALE RD
- HIL 94010 748-E4
AVY AV
1800 MLPK 94025 790-D6
1800 SMCo 94025 790-D6
AYRES LN
- MLPK 94025 790-E7
AYRSHIRE FARM LN
- SCIC 94305 790-J7
AZALEA AV
900 BURL 94010 728-F5
AZALEA LN
- SCAR 94070 769-C5
AZALIA DR
100 EPA 94303 791-C2
AZTEC WY
2400 PA 94303 791-D5

B

B RD W
800 SBRN 94066 707-H6
B ST
- DALY 94014 687-C6
100 RDWC 94063 769-J5
100 SSF 94080 707-G3
200 SMCo 94014 687-C6
300 CLMA 94014 687-D6
300 RDWC 94063 770-A4
N B ST
- SMTO 94401 748-J1
S B ST
100 SMTO 94401 748-J1
300 SMTO 94401 749-A2
1200 SMTO 94402 749-A2
BACK RD
- SMCo 94020 (870-C2
See Page 869)
BACON CT
- DALY 94015 707-B1
BADEN AV
100 SSF 94080 707-G2
BAFFIN CT
- FCTY 94404 749-G6
BAFFIN ST
100 FCTY 94404 749-G5
BAHAMA LN
600 FCTY 94404 749-G5
BAHIA
1800 SMTO 94403 749-E5
BAILEYANA RD
900 HIL 94010 728-D7
BAIN PL
700 RDWC 94062 789-G1
BAINBRIDGE ST
600 FCTY 94404 749-G4
BAIR ISLAND RD
500 RDWC 94063 770-B4
BAIRN DR
1400 HIL 94010 748-E4
BAKER RD
100 SMCo 94021 849-A7
BAKER ST
100 SSF 94080 708-A3
BAKER WY
900 SMTO 94404 749-D2
BALBOA AV
1000 BURL 94010 728-D5
BALBOA BLVD
- HMBY 94019 787-E1
2800 HMBY 94019 767-D5
BALBOA LN
800 FCTY 94404 749-F3
BALBOA ST
900 FCTY 94404 749-F4
BALBOA WY
100 SBRN 94066 727-J1
1100 PCFA 94044 726-H4
1300 BURL 94010 728-C5
BALCLUTHA DR
1100 FCTY 94404 749-G2
BALDWIN AV
- DALY 94015 687-A6
- SMTO 94401 748-J1
BALDWIN HILLS CT
3600 SSF 94080 707-D4
BALERI RANCH RD
14000 LAH 94022 810-H6
BALHI CT
- SF 94112 687-F1
BALLY WY
400 PCFA 94044 707-A3
400 PCFA 94044 706-J3
BALMORAL CT
2100 SMTO 94403 749-A4
N BALSAMINA WY
100 SMCo 94028 810-E3
S BALSAMINA WY
200 SMCo 94028 810-E4
BALTIC CIR
- RDWC 94065 749-J5
BALTIMORE WY
- SF 94112 687-F2
100 DALY 94014 687-F2
BANBURY DR
- SF 94132 687-B1
BANBURY LN
700 MLBR 94030 727-H3
2700 SCAR 94070 769-G6
BANCROFT AV
900 HMBY 94019 767-E6
BANCROFT LN
400 PCFA 94044 707-A3
BANCROFT RD
- BURL 94010 728-H6
BANCROFT WY
200 PCFA 94044 707-A3
200 PCFA 94044 706-J3
BANDERA DR
3100 PA 94304 830-G1
BANFF WY
- PCFA 94044 727-C5
BANNOCK ST
- SF 94112 687-F1
BANTRY LN
2400 SSF 94080 707-D4
BANYAN WY
1000 PCFA 94044 727-A5
BARBADOS LN
500 FCTY 94404 749-G5
BARBARA DR
1900 PA 94303 791-C5
BARBARA LN
- BLMT 94002 749-E7
- MLPK 94025 790-E5
- SMCo 94070 769-D4
200 DALY 94015 707-D2
BARBARA WY
300 HIL 94010 748-D3
BARBOUR DR
- RDWC 94062 769-G7
600 RDWC 94062 789-G1
BARCELONA CIR
- RDWC 94065 749-J6
BARCELONA DR
400 MLBR 94030 728-A3
400 MLBR 94030 727-J2
500 SBRN 94066 727-J2
1000 PCFA 94044 727-A4
1000 PCFA 94044 726-J4
BARCLAY AV
200 MLBR 94030 728-B3
BARCLAY WY
2600 BLMT 94002 769-B1
BARDET RD
100 WDSD 94062 789-G6
BARFORD AV
100 SCAR 94070 769-E2
BARK CT
100 HMBY 94019 767-F5
BARK DR
400 RDWC 94065 749-H6
BARKENTINE LN
400 RDWC 94065 749-H7
BARKENTINE ST
100 FCTY 94404 749-G4
BARMETTA WY
- ATN 94027 790-D2
BARNEGAT LN
400 RDWC 94065 749-J6
BARNES CT
- SCIC - 791-A7
BARNESON AV
- SMTO 94402 749-A3
300 SMTO 94402 748-J4
BARNEY AV
- ATN 94027 790-C5
- SMCo 94025 790-C5
BARNEY CT
- SMCo 94025 790-D5
BARRANCA ST
100 SMCo 94038 766-H2
BARRETT DR
- WDSD 94062 789-J5
BARRINGTON CT
2200 SSF 94080 707-D5
BARROILHET AV
- SMTO 94402 728-G7
- BURL 94010 728-G7
100 BURL 94010 748-F1
100 SMTO 94402 748-F1
200 HIL 94010 748-F1
BARROILHET DR
1100 HIL 94010 748-E2
BARRON AV
700 SMCo 94063 770-D6
BARRY LN
- ATN 94027 790-D4
BARTLETT WY
3400 BLMT 94002 769-A1
3400 BLMT 94002 768-J1
BARTON PL
- PCFA 94044 727-B6
100 MLPK 94025 790-J2

STREET	Block	City	ZIP	Pg-Grid
BARTON ST				
	1800	SMCo	94061	790-B4
BARTON WY				
	300	MLPK	94025	790-J3
BASSETT CT				
	3600	SSF	94080	707-D4
BASSETT LN				
	-	ATN	94027	790-F2
BATES RD				
	-	HIL	94010	748-F3
BATTEN LN				
	-	RDWC	94065	750-C4
BAUER CT				
	800	SCAR	94070	769-F4
BAUER DR				
	800	SCAR	94070	769-F4
BAUTISTA CT				
	900	PA	94303	791-E6
BAY CT				
	3300	BLMT	94002	749-A7
	3300	BLMT	94002	769-A1
BAY LNDG				
	-	SMTO	94401	729-B6
BAY RD				
	-	MLPK	94025	770-F7
	-	ATN	94027	770-F7
	300	ATN	94027	790-H1
	300	MLPK	94025	790-H1
	500	RDWC	94063	770-B6
	500	SMCo	94025	790-H1
	900	EPA	94303	791-A1
	1900	EPA	94303	771-D7
	2200	SMCo	94063	770-B6
	3700	SMCo	94025	770-F7
BAY ST				
	100	MLBR	94030	728-B2
BAYBERRY				
	-	PTLV	94028	830-D1
BAYBERRY LN				
	900	RDWC	94065	750-A5
BAYBERRY PL				
	-	HIL	94010	748-E1
BAYCREST WY				
	1300	SSF	94080	707-H1
BAYFRONT EXWY Rt#-84				
	-	FRMT	94555	771-D3
	-	MLPK	94025	771-A6
	-	MLPK	94025	770-G6
	-	MLPK	94303	771-D3
BAY HARBOUR DR				
	800	RDWC	94065	750-A6
BAYHILL CT				
	2100	HMBY	94019	787-F5
BAYHILL DR				
	800	SBRN	94066	707-G7
BAYHILL PL				
	-	HMBY	94019	787-F5
BAYHILL RD				
	300	HMBY	94019	787-F4
BAY LAUREL DR				
	1100	MLPK	94025	790-F5
BAYLOR ST				
	2500	EPA	94303	791-B1
	2500	EPA	94303	771-B7
BAYPARK CIR				
	-	SSF	94014	707-H1
BAYPORT AV				
	500	SCAR	94070	769-G2
BAYPORT CT				
	-	SCAR	94070	769-G2
BAY RIDGE DR				
	500	DALY	94014	687-H3
BAYRIDGE WY				
	1600	SMTO	94402	748-H6
BAYSHORE BLVD				
	-	BSBN	94005	708-B1
	-	BSBN	94080	708-B1
	-	SSF	94080	708-B1
	-	SF	94134	688-A3
	1700	SF	94124	688-A3
	3000	BSBN	94005	688-A4
	3000	DALY	94014	688-A3
N BAYSHORE BLVD				
	-	SMTO	94401	729-A7
	-	SMTO	94401	728-J6
S BAYSHORE BLVD				
	-	SMTO	94401	729-A7
	500	SMTO	94401	749-B1
N BAYSHORE CIR				
	-	SBRN	94066	707-H5
S BAYSHORE CIR				
	-	SBRN	94066	707-J5
BAYSHORE FRWY U.S.-101				
	-	BLMT	-	749-B1
	-	BLMT	-	769-G1
	-	BSBN	-	688-B3
	-	BSBN	-	708-B1
	-	BURL	-	728-F5
	-	EPA	-	791-E5
	-	EPA	-	790-J1
	-	MLBR	-	728-B2
	-	MLPK	-	770-C5
	-	MLPK	-	791-E5
	-	MLPK	-	790-J1
	-	MTVW	-	791-E5
	-	PA	-	791-E5
	-	RDWC	-	769-G1
	-	RDWC	-	770-C5
BAYSHORE FRWY U.S.-101				
	-	RDWC	-	769-G1
	-	SCAR	-	769-G1
	-	SF	-	688-B3
	-	SMCo	-	769-G1
	-	SMCo	-	769-G1
	-	SMCo	-	708-A5
	-	SMCo	-	728-B2
	-	SMTO	-	729-A7
	-	SMTO	-	728-F5
	-	SMTO	-	749-B1
	-	SMTO	-	749-B1
	-	SMTO	-	749-B1
	-	SSF	-	708-B1
BAYSHORE HWY				
	-	MLBR	94030	728-D3
	1200	BURL	94010	728-D3
BAYSHORE PKWY				
	2100	MTVW	94043	791-F7
E BAYSHORE RD				
	500	RDWC	94063	770-A4
	800	EPA	94303	791-A1
	1900	PA	94303	791-D4
	3200	SMCo	94063	770-D5
W BAYSHORE RD				
	1200	EPA	94303	791-B2
	1900	PA	94303	791-D4
BAYSIDE BLVD				
	1300	SCAR	94070	769-J4
BAYSWATER AV				
	-	BURL	94010	728-H7
	1000	SMTO	94401	728-H7
BAYTREE RD				
	100	SCAR	94070	769-G4
BAYTREE WY				
	-	SMTO	94402	748-J1
BAYVIEW AV				
	400	MLBR	94030	727-J2
	1800	BLMT	94002	749-C7
	4000	SMTO	94403	749-C7
BAYVIEW CT				
	-	MLBR	94030	727-H2
BAY VIEW DR				
	-	SCAR	94070	769-D3
	200	SMCo	94070	769-D4
BAYVIEW PL				
	-	BURL	94010	728-G5
BAY VIEW RD				
	-	SMCo	94037	746-J5
	100	PCFA	94044	726-J3
BAYVIEW WY				
	700	SMCo	94062	789-F2
BAYVIEW PARK RD				
	-	SF	94124	688-B1
BAYWALK WY				
	-	RDWC	94065	749-H5
BAYWOOD AV				
	-	HIL	94010	748-H2
	-	SMTO	94402	748-H2
	100	MLPK	94025	790-J3
	1200	SSF	94080	707-F1
BAYWOOD GN				
	-	SMCo	94062	769-E7
BAYWOOD ST				
	-	SF	94112	687-F1
BEACH AV				
	400	HMBY	94019	767-E6
BEACH BLVD				
	1500	PCFA	94044	706-J6
BEACH RD				
	300	BURL	94010	728-H5
BEACH ST				
	100	SMCo	94038	746-F6
BEACH WY				
	100	SMCo	94038	746-F7
BEACH PARK BLVD				
	-	FCTY	94404	749-G1
BEACHSIDE CT				
	-	DALY	94015	706-J2
BEACHVIEW AV				
	100	PCFA	94044	707-A2
BEACON AV				
	1200	SMTO	94401	749-B1
BEACON ST				
	100	SSF	94080	708-A5
	600	MLPK	94025	790-J2
BEACON SHORES DR				
	300	RDWC	94065	749-J2
BEAN HOLLOW RD				
	200	SMCo	94060	867-H6
BEAR CREEK CRSG				
	-	SMCo	94020	850-E6
BEAR GLEN DR				
	-	SMCo	94062	809-C3
BEAR GULCH DR				
	-	PTLV	94028	810-D6
BEAR GULCH RD				
	-	SMCo	94062	829-A1
	-	SMCo	94062	809-E2
	-	WDSD	94062	809-E2
	2300	SMCo	94062	(828-H3 See Page 827)
	2300	SMCo	94074	(828-H3 See Page 827)
BEAR PAW				
	-	PTLV	94028	830-C1
BEATTY AV				
	-	BSBN	94005	688-A3
BEAUMONT BLVD				
	100	PCFA	94044	706-J2
	200	PCFA	94044	707-A3
BECKET DR				
	500	RDWC	94065	749-J7
BEECH AV				
	400	SBRN	94066	727-H1
	400	SSF	94080	707-J2
	500	SBRN	94066	707-H7
BEECH ST				
	100	RDWC	94063	770-B6
	900	EPA	94303	791-C2
BEECHWOOD DR				
	700	DALY	94015	687-A5
	800	SMCo	94015	687-A5
BEEGER RD				
	-	RDWC	94063	770-C3
BELAIR WY				
	-	RDWC	94062	789-G2
BEL AIRE CT				
	-	HIL	94402	748-G6
BEL AIRE RD				
	1300	SMCo	94402	748-G6
	1400	HIL	94402	748-G6
BELBROOK WY				
	-	ATN	94027	790-B6
BELBURN DR				
	1600	BLMT	94002	769-D2
BELCREST AV				
	-	DALY	94015	707-A1
	100	DALY	94015	706-J1
BELFAST AV				
	400	PCFA	94044	726-G4
BELFORD DR				
	-	DALY	94015	686-J4
BELFORD WY				
	-	SMTO	94402	748-J1
BELHAVEN AV				
	-	DALY	94015	687-A7
BELHAVEN CT				
	-	DALY	94015	687-B7
BELL CT				
	-	EPA	94303	791-B2
BELL ST				
	300	EPA	94303	791-B2
BELLAIR WY				
	1100	MLPK	94025	790-D6
	1100	SMCo	94025	790-D6
BELLA VISTA DR				
	100	HIL	94010	728-C7
BELLE AV				
	-	RDWC	94063	770-E6
	-	SF	94132	687-C2
	1900	SCAR	94070	769-G4
BELLE AIR RD				
	100	SSF	94080	708-A5
BELLEAU AV				
	-	ATN	94027	790-D2
BELLEMONTI AV				
	2000	BLMT	94002	749-C7
	2000	BLMT	94002	769-C1
BELLE ROCHE AV				
	-	SMCo	94062	769-G6
BELLE ROCHE CT				
	-	SMCo	94062	769-F7
BELLEVILLE BLVD				
	300	HMBY	94019	767-F7
BELLE VISTA AV				
	100	PCFA	94044	706-J5
BELLEVUE AV				
	-	DALY	94014	687-D3
	-	SF	94112	687-F3
	1100	BURL	94010	728-F7
	1500	HIL	94010	728-F7
E BELLEVUE AV				
	-	SMTO	94401	728-H7
W BELLEVUE AV				
	-	SMTO	94402	748-G1
BELLFLOWER LN				
	-	SCAR	94070	769-C4
BELLVIEW CT				
	2100	PA	94303	791-C5
BEL MAR AV				
	-	DALY	94015	687-A4
BELMONT AV				
	100	SMCo	94061	790-B3
	100	SSF	94080	707-J2
	800	BLMT	94002	749-D7
	1100	SCAR	94070	769-H5
BELMONT DR				
	-	DALY	94015	687-B3
BELMONT CANYON RD				
	2500	BLMT	94002	769-A2
	2800	BLMT	94002	768-J2
BELMONT WOODS WY				
	2900	BLMT	94002	769-A2
BELVEDERE AV				
	-	SCAR	94070	769-H5
	900	HMBY	94019	767-E6
BELVEDERE CT				
	-	BURL	94010	728-C7
BENGLOE LN				
	-	HIL	94010	748-F4
BENITO AV				
	1300	BURL	94010	728-C6
BENJAMIN FRANKLIN CT				
	-	SMTO	94401	748-J2
BENNETT RD				
	-	RDWC	94062	769-G7
BENNINGTON AV				
	2300	SBRN	94066	727-F2
BENNINGTON CT				
	-	SMCo	94402	748-G7
BENNINGTON DR				
	-	SMCo	94402	748-G7
BENSON WY				
	2800	BLMT	94002	769-A2
	2800	BLMT	94002	768-J2
BEPLER ST				
	-	DALY	94014	687-D2
BERENDA DR				
	100	SSF	94080	707-E3
BERENDA WY				
	-	SMCo	94028	810-E3
BERENDOS AV				
	100	PCFA	94044	727-B2
BERESFORD AV				
	100	SMCo	94061	790-B3
	100	RDWC	94061	790-B3
	3400	BLMT	94002	769-A1
BERESFORD CT				
	-	SMCo	94061	790-B3
	-	SMTO	94403	749-D6
BERESFORD PL				
	-	SMCo	94061	790-B3
BERESFORD ST				
	3800	SMTO	94403	749-D6
BERGESEN CT				
	-	ATN	94027	790-B4
BERKELEY AV				
	500	SMCo	94025	790-H1
	1000	MLPK	94025	790-H1
	1100	MLPK	94025	770-J7
BERKSHIRE AV				
	-	SMCo	94063	790-C1
	200	SMCo	94063	770-D7
BERKSHIRE DR				
	700	MLBR	94030	728-A4
	700	MLBR	94030	727-J4
	2600	SBRN	94066	707-D6
BERMUDA DR				
	400	SMTO	94403	749-C3
BERNAL AV				
	-	SMCo	94038	766-G1
	1000	BURL	94010	728-C5
BERNARDO AV				
	400	HMBY	94019	787-F4
BERNI CT				
	-	MLBR	94030	728-A2
BERRYESSA WY				
	-	HIL	94010	748-E6
BERRY HILL CT				
	14100	LAH	94022	810-H5
BERRY HILL LN				
	14100	LAH	94022	810-H6
BERTA CIR				
	-	DALY	94015	707-C2
BERTITA ST				
	100	SF	94112	687-F1
BERTOCCHI LN				
	-	MLBR	94030	727-H3
BEST CT				
	700	SCAR	94070	769-D5
BETA AV				
	-	DALY	94014	687-D3
BETTINA AV				
	2200	BLMT	94002	749-B7
	2200	BLMT	94002	769-B1
	4200	SMTO	94403	749-B7
BETTMAN WY				
	3600	SSF	94080	707-D4
BETTY LN				
	-	ATN	94027	790-C4
	-	SMTO	94402	749-C3
BEVERLY AV				
	200	MLBR	94030	728-B3
BEVERLY CT				
	-	SSF	94080	707-G1
BEVERLY DR				
	-	SCAR	94070	769-E3
	200	SMCo	94020	829-F7
	200	SMCo	94070	769-E4
BEVERLY PL				
	-	PCFA	94044	707-A3
BEVERLY ST				
	-	DALY	94015	707-C3
	-	SF	94132	687-C1
	3000	SMTO	94403	749-A6
BIARRITZ CT				
	500	RDWC	94065	749-J5
BIBBITS DR				
	3900	PA	94303	791-F7
BIDDULPH WY				
	500	BLMT	94002	749-E7
BIEBER AV				
	1100	MLPK	94025	770-H7
BIG BEND DR				
	600	PCFA	94044	727-C5
BIG PINE RD				
	100	SMCo	94062	788-H5
BIG SUR WY				
	-	PCFA	94044	727-B5
BIG TREE LN				
	-	WDSD	94062	809-G6
	-	SMCo	94062	809-G6
BIG TREE RD				
	-	SMCo	94062	809-G7
	-	WDSD	94062	809-G7
BIG TREE WY				
	-	SMCo	94062	809-F6
BILLINGSGATE LN				
	200	FCTY	94404	749-F5
BILTMORE LN				
	-	MLPK	94025	790-C6
BING ST				
	900	SCAR	94070	769-J4
BINNACLE LN				
	100	FCTY	94404	749-J1
BIRCH AV				
	400	SMTO	94402	749-B2
	1200	SSF	94080	707-F1
	1900	SCAR	94070	769-G4
BIRCH CT				
	100	SBRN	94066	707-E7
BIRCH LN				
	-	PCFA	94044	706-J6
BIRCH ST				
	-	RDWC	94062	769-J5
	400	RDWC	94062	770-A6
	900	SMCo	94037	746-H4
	1800	PA	94306	791-A6
BIRCHWOOD CT				
	-	SF	94134	687-H2
BIRKDALE RD				
	-	HMBY	94019	787-F5
BISCAYNE AV				
	400	FCTY	94404	749-F6
BISHOP LN				
	-	SMCo	94025	810-F1
BISHOP RD				
	1900	BLMT	94002	768-J1
BISHOP ST				
	-	SF	94134	688-A1
BISMARK ST				
	-	DALY	94014	687-C4
BLACKBURN AV				
	100	MLPK	94025	790-J3
BLACKBURN TER				
	-	PCFA	94044	726-G4
BLACK FOX WY				
	-	RDWC	94061	789-F3
	-	WDSD	94062	789-F3
BLACKHAWK LN				
	-	SMCo	94010	728-B6
BLACK MOUNTAIN RD				
	800	HIL	94010	748-D4
	1600	SMCo	94010	748-D4
	27100	LAH	94022	830-J1
BLACKWELDER CT				
	100	SCIC	94305	790-J7
BLAIR CT				
	900	PA	94303	791-C5
BLAKE ST				
	400	MLPK	94025	790-F4
BLAKE WILBUR DR				
	900	SCIC	94305	790-G6
	900	PA	94304	790-G6
BLAKEWOOD WY				
	-	SMCo	94062	809-E5
BLANDFORD BLVD				
	800	RDWC	94062	769-H6
BLANKEN AV				
	-	SF	94134	688-A2
BLENHEIM AV				
	2700	SMCo	94063	790-C1
BLOMQUIST ST				
	300	RDWC	94063	770-C5
BLONDIN WY				
	400	SMCo	94080	707-G4
	400	SSF	94080	707-G4
BLOOM LN				
	700	HMBY	94019	787-F2
BLOOMFIELD RD				
	-	BURL	94010	728-G6
BLOSSOM CIR				
	100	SMTO	94403	749-D6
BLOSSOM CT				
	-	DALY	94014	687-D5
BLUEBELL CT				
	-	MLBR	94030	728-A3
BLUEBELL LN				
	-	HIL	94010	748-F5
BLUE BELLE LN				
	-	SCAR	94070	769-C4
BLUEFISH CT				
	300	FCTY	94404	749-H2
BLUEJAY CT				
	700	EPA	94303	791-B1
BLUE JAY WY				
	-	SMCo	94062	789-A7
BLUERIDGE AV				
	2300	MLPK	94025	790-D7
BLUE RIDGE LN				
	-	WDSD	94062	809-G2
BLYTHDALE AV				
	-	SF	94134	687-H2
BLYTHE ST				
	1100	FCTY	94404	749-G4
BOARDWALK CT				
	100	SBRN	94066	707-G6
BOARDWALK DR				
	100	SBRN	94066	707-G6
BOARDWALK PL				
	100	SBRN	94066	707-G6
	700	RDWC	94065	749-H6
BOARDWALK WY				
	-	RDWC	94065	749-H6
BOBSTAY LN				
	600	FCTY	94404	749-J1
BODEGA ST				
	300	FCTY	94404	749-F5
BOHANNON DR				
	3800	MLPK	94025	770-G7
BOLERO WY				
	-	DALY	94014	687-G3
BOLIVAR LN				
	100	PTLV	94028	810-D5
BOLTON PL				
	-	MLPK	94025	790-F5
BONAIR				
	200	SCIC	94305	790-J7
BON AIR LN				
	-	SMCo	94038	746-F7
BONITA AV				
	-	RDWC	94061	790-B1
	100	PCFA	94044	727-B2
	200	SSF	94080	707-F2
	600	MLBR	94030	727-J2
BONITA LN				
	100	FCTY	94404	749-H3
BONITA RD				
	100	SMCo	94028	830-D4
BONITA ST				
	100	SMCo	94038	766-H2
BONNIE CT				
	1400	RDWC	94061	790-A2
BONNIE LN				
	-	PCFA	94044	706-J3
BONNIE ST				
	400	DALY	94014	687-D4
BONSEN CT				
	100	SMCo	94062	790-A4
BOOTHBAY AV				
	100	FCTY	94404	749-E6
BORDEAUX LN				
	2000	HMBY	94019	767-E5
BORDEN ST				
	1600	SMTO	94403	749-C2
BOREL AV				
	-	SMTO	94402	749-A4
	400	SMTO	94402	748-J4
BOREL PL				
	-	SMTO	94402	749-A4
BORICA ST				
	-	SF	94132	687-C1
BOROUGHWOOD PL				
	-	HIL	94010	748-E3
BOSTON AV				
	1600	SMTO	94403	749-D2
BOSUN LN				
	-	RDWC	94065	750-C4
BOTANY CT				
	-	RDWC	94062	789-G2
	-	SMCo	94062	789-G2
	500	FCTY	94404	749-F5
BOUNTY DR				
	500	FCTY	94404	749-G3
BOURBON CT				
	2300	SSF	94080	707-D5
BOVET RD				
	-	SMTO	94402	749-A4
BOW WY				
	-	PTLV	94028	810-B6
BOWDOIN ST				
	600	SF	94134	688-A1
	700	SCIC	94305	790-H7
	900	SCIC	94305	810-J1
	2000	PA	94306	810-J1
BOWER RD				
	800	PCFA	94044	726-H5
BOWFIN ST				
	300	FCTY	94404	749-H3
BOWHILL RD				
	700	HIL	94010	748-G3
BOWSPRIT DR				
	300	RDWC	94065	749-H7
BOWSPRIT LN				
	100	FCTY	94404	749-G6
BOYCE AV				
	800	PA	94301	791-A4
BRADBURY LN				
	200	RDWC	94061	790-B2
BRADFORD DR				
	-	SSF	94080	707-D1
BRADFORD ST				
	200	RDWC	94063	770-A5
BRADFORD WY				
	700	PCFA	94044	707-A7
	700	PCFA	94044	727-A1
BRADLEY CT				
	-	SMCo	94061	790-B4
	1400	SMTO	94401	729-B7
BRADLEY DR				
	900	SMCo	94015	687-A5
	900	DALY	94015	687-A5
BRADLEY WY				
	1000	EPA	94303	791-A1
BRADSHAW TER				
	-	RDWC	94062	789-G1
BRADY PL				
	-	MLPK	94025	790-H2
BRAEMAR DR				
	-	HIL	94010	748-F5
BRAGATO RD				
	400	SMCo	94002	769-F1
BRAMBLE CT				
	300	FCTY	94404	749-H3
BRANDON CT				
	-	DALY	94014	687-J4
	-	HIL	94402	748-H5
BRANDON WY				
	300	MLPK	94025	790-F6
BRANDT RD				
	1300	HIL	94010	748-E3
BRANDY ROCK WY				
	3600	RDWC	94061	789-H3
BRANDYWINE RD				
	1500	SMCo	94402	748-F7
BRANNER DR				
	-	SMCo	94025	790-E7
	-	SMCo	94025	810-E1
	2300	MLPK	94025	790-E7
	2300	MLPK	94025	810-E1
BRANSON DR				
	3400	SMTO	94403	749-D5
BRANSTEN RD				
	800	SCAR	94070	769-H3
BRAZIL AV				
	600	SF	94112	687-G1
	1100	SF	94134	687-G1
BREAKER LN				
	-	RDWC	94065	750-C4
BREAKWATER DR				
	-	RDWC	94065	750-A5
BRECON CT				
	100	SMCo	94062	769-G6
BREEZE PL				
	800	RDWC	94062	789-H1
BRENT CT				
	-	MLPK	94025	790-C7
BRENTWOOD CT				
	2200	EPA	94303	791-C2
BRENTWOOD DR				
	-	SSF	94080	707-G5
BRENTWOOD RD				
	200	HIL	94010	748-G2
BRET HARTE				
	-	SMCo	94020	809-F6
BRET HARTE DR				
	3600	RDWC	94061	789-G3
BRET HARTE ST				
	1800	PA	94303	791-B5
BREWER DR				
	600	HIL	94010	748-F1
BREWSTER AV				
	300	RDWC	94063	770-A5
	900	RDWC	94062	770-A5
	1200	RDWC	94062	769-J6
	2700	SMCo	94062	769-J6
BRIAR LN				
	100	SMTO	94403	749-B6
BRIARFIELD AV				
	2500	RDWC	94061	789-H2
BRIARFIELD WY				
	400	BLMT	94002	749-E7
BRIARWOOD DR				
	400	SSF	94080	707-F5
BRIARWOOD WY				
	-	BLMT	94002	749-E7
BRIDGE CT				
	-	BLMT	94002	769-C3
BRIDGE PKWY				
	-	RDWC	94065	749-H7
BRIDGE RD				
	-	HIL	94010	748-H2
BRIDGEPORT DR				
	100	SMCo	94018	767-A2
	100	SMCo	94018	766-J1
BRIDGEPORT LN				
	600	FCTY	94404	749-F4
BRIDLE CT				
	-	HIL	94402	748-H4
BRIDLE LN				
	-	WDSD	94062	809-G2
BRIDLE WY				
	1000	HIL	94402	748-H4
BRIG CT				
	100	HMBY	94019	767-F5
BRIGANTINE LN				
	-	RDWC	94065	750-C4
BRIGGS ST				
	1500	SMCo	94015	687-C5
	1500	DALY	94015	687-C5
BRIGHT ST				
	-	SF	94132	687-D2
BRIGHTON AV				
	-	SF	94112	687-D1
BRIGHTON CT				
	-	DALY	94015	707-D3
BRIGHTON LN				
	200	RDWC	94061	790-B2
BRIGHTON RD				
	100	PCFA	94044	706-J6
	200	PCFA	94044	707-A6
BRIONES CT				
	27600	LAH	94022	830-H1
BRIONES WY				
	12300	LAH	94022	830-H1
BRISTOL CT				
	500	FCTY	94404	749-F5
BRISTOL WY				
	-	RDWC	94061	789-J3
	-	RDWC	94061	790-A3
BRITTAN AV				
	800	SCAR	94070	769-H3
BRITTANY LN				
	-	DALY	94014	687-F3
BRITTANY MEADOWS				
	-	ATN	94027	790-E3
BRITTON AV				
	100	ATN	94027	790-E3
BRITTON ST				
	-	SF	94134	687-J2
BROAD ST				
	-	SF	94112	687-D2
	200	SF	94132	687-D2
BROAD ACRES RD				
	-	ATN	94027	790-C5
BROADVIEW CT				
	3500	SMTO	94403	768-J1
BROADWAY				
	-	MLBR	94030	728-A2
	-	RDWC	94063	770-B6
	100	SMCo	94038	766-J2
	800	BLMT	94002	769-F1
	1000	BURL	94010	728-D6
	2700	RDWC	94062	770-B5
	2800	RDWC	94062	769-J6
S BROADWAY				
	-	MLBR	94030	728-B4
BRODERICK RD				
	-	BURL	94010	728-C4
BRODERICK WY				
	2700	MTVW	94043	791-G7
BROMFIELD RD				
	600	SMTO	94402	748-F1
	700	HIL	94010	748-F2
BROMLEY CT				
	-	DALY	94015	707-D3
BROMLEY DR				
	-	SCAR	94070	769-F6
	-	SMCo	94062	769-F6
BROOK ST				
	100	SCAR	94070	769-G5
BROOKDALE AV				
	-	SF	94134	687-H2
BROOKE CT				
	-	HIL	94402	748-G6
BROOKHAVEN CT				
	-	PCFA	94044	707-A2
BROOKLAWN AV				
	-	DALY	94015	687-A5
	-	DALY	94015	686-J5
BROOKLINE WY				
	3900	SMCo	94062	789-F2
BROOKS PL				
	-	PCFA	94044	727-B6
BROOKS ST				
	1700	SMTO	94403	749-C2
BROOKSIDE DR				
	100	PTLV	94028	810-B7
BROOKSIDE LN				
	800	MLBR	94030	727-H3
BROOKVALE RD				
	1800	HIL	94010	728-E7
BROOKWOOD RD				
	100	WDSD	94062	789-H4
BROSNAN CT				
	100	SSF	94080	707-G2
	500	DALY	94015	707-G2
BROTHERHOOD WY				
	500	SF	94132	687-A1
BROUGHTON LN				
	500	FCTY	94404	749-G5
BROWN ST				
	-	DALY	94014	687-H3
BROWNING WY				
	400	SSF	94080	707-H4
BRUCE AV				
	-	SF	94112	687-E1
BRUCE DR				
	800	PA	94303	791-D6
BRUCE ST				
	100	PCFA	94044	707-A4
BRUMISS TER				
	-	DALY	94014	687-E2
BRUNO AV				
	-	DALY	94014	687-C5
BRUNSWICK CT				
	3700	SSF	94080	707-D4
BRUNSWICK ST				
	-	SF	94112	687-D3
	700	DALY	94014	687-D3
BRUSCO WY				
	900	SSF	94080	707-G2
BRUSSELS ST				
	1100	SF	94134	688-A1
BRYANT CT				
	300	PA	94301	790-H4
BRYANT ST				
	100	PA	94301	790-H4
	1000	PA	94301	791-B6
	1500	DALY	94015	687-B5
	2500	PA	94306	791-C7
BRYANT WY				
	100	SBRN	94066	727-G2
BRYCE AV				
	200	SSF	94080	707-F4
BRYCE CT				
	-	BLMT	94002	769-A2
BRYCE CANYON WY				
	-	PCFA	94044	727-B5
BRYSON AV				
	500	PA	94306	791-C6
BUCARELI DR				
	-	SF	94132	687-B1
BUCCANEER LN				
	-	RDWC	94065	750-C4
BUCHANAN CT				
	-	EPA	94303	791-C1
BUCK CT				
	100	WDSD	94062	790-A5
BUCKEYE				
	-	PTLV	94028	830-C1
BUCKEYE CT				
	-	HIL	94010	748-G3
BUCKEYE ST				
	-	RDWC	94063	770-B6
BUCKINGHAM AV				
	-	SMCo	94063	790-C1
	-	SMCo	94063	770-C7
BUCKINGHAM CT				
	-	HIL	94010	748-F5
BUCKINGHAM RD				
	300	PCFA	94044	706-J6
BUCKINGHAM WY				
	1200	HIL	94010	748-F6
BUCKLAND AV				
	700	SCAR	94070	769-E2
	700	BLMT	94002	769-E2
BUCKLAND CT				
	-	SCAR	94070	769-E2
BUCKNELL DR				
	400	SMTO	94402	748-H3
BUCKTHORN WY				
	-	ATN	94025	790-E2
	-	HIL	94010	748-F1
	-	MLPK	94025	790-E2
BUDD CT				
	1500	SMTO	94403	749-D3
BUEL AV				
	400	PCFA	94044	726-J2
BUENA VISTA AV				
	-	SMCo	94021	849-A7
	-	SBRN	94066	707-J5
	200	DALY	94015	687-B6
	400	SMCo	94061	790-B3
	400	SMTO	94403	749-A5
	2300	BLMT	94002	769-B1
BUENA VISTA DR				
	11500	LAH	94022	830-H2
BUENA VISTA LN				
	-	SMCo	94060	(868-F3 See Page 867)
BUENA VISTA RD				
	-	SMCo	94037	746-H4
E BUENA VISTA RD				
	1200	SMCo	94037	746-H5
BUENA VISTA ST				
	500	SMCo	94038	746-F5
BUFFALO CT				
	-	PCFA	94044	727-C4
BUNKER HILL DR				
	2000	SMCo	94402	748-F7
	2500	SMCo	-	748-F7
BUOY LN				
	-	RDWC	94065	750-C4
BURBANK AV				
	-	RDWC	94063	770-C6
	-	SMTO	94403	749-C6
BURGESS DR				
	300	MLPK	94025	790-G4
BURGOYNE CT				
	-	SMCo	94402	768-G1
BURKE LN				
	1100	FCTY	94404	749-J4
BURLINGAME AV				
	100	BURL	94010	728-G7
BURLINGVIEW DR				
	2700	BURL	94010	728-C7
BURLWAY RD				
	700	BURL	94010	728-E4
BURNHAM CT				
	-	SCAR	94070	769-F5
BURNHAM WY				
	2400	PA	94303	791-D5
BURNING TREE CT				
	300	HMBY	94019	787-F5
BURNING TREE RD				
	2200	HMBY	94019	787-F5
BURNS AV				
	100	ATN	94027	790-E2
BURNS CT				
	800	PCFA	94044	727-A1
BURN VALLEY RD				
	300	SMCo	94021	(848-H4 See Page 827)
BURR AV				
	-	SF	94134	687-J2
BURREN WY				
	2900	SSF	94080	707-E5
BURROWS AV				
	600	SBRN	94066	707-H7
BURROWS ST				
	900	FCTY	94404	749-G4
BUSH ST				
	1100	SCAR	94070	769-G2
BUSS RD				
	-	SMCo	94020	(870-C2 See Page 869)
BUTANO CTO				
	300	SMCo	94060	(868-D3 See Page 867)
S BUTANO TKTR				
	-	SMCo	94020	869-D4
	-	SMCo	94060	869-D4
BUTANO FIRE TR				
	-	SCrC	95006	(889-J1 See Page 869)
	-	SMCo	94020	869-D7
	-	SMCo	94020	(889-F1 See Page 869)
	-	SMCo	94060	869-B6
S BUTANO FIRE TR				
	-	SMCo	94060	(868-J7 See Page 867)
	-	SMCo	94060	(888-G1 See Page 867)
BUTLER AV				
	-	SSF	94080	708-A2
BUTTERCUP LN				
	-	SCAR	94070	769-C4
BUTTERNUT DR				
	2400	HIL	94010	748-C1
BUXTON AV				
	100	SSF	94080	707-D2
BYERS DR				
	1900	MLPK	94025	791-A2
BYRD LN				
	800	FCTY	94404	749-G4
	13000	LAH	94022	810-J7
BYRNE ST				
	100	DALY	94014	687-D5
	100	SMCo	94014	687-D5
BYRNE PARK LN				
	27100	LAH	94022	830-J2
BYRON AV				
	1800	SMTO	94401	749-C1
BYRON CT				
	-	SF	94112	687-F2
BYRON DR				
	800	SSF	94080	707-D2
BYRON ST				
	100	PA	94301	790-J3
	1100	PA	94301	791-A4
	2700	PA	94306	791-C6
BYXBEE ST				
	-	SF	94132	687-C1

C

STREET	Block	City	ZIP	Pg-Grid
C ST				
	100	MLPK	94025	790-G3
	100	RDWC	94063	769-J5
	200	SSF	94080	707-G3
	300	CLMA	94014	687-D6
	300	RDWC	94063	770-A4
CABALLO LN				
	-	SCIC	94304	810-F6
CABOT CT				
	400	SSF	94080	708-B3
	800	SCAR	94070	769-E5
CABOT LN				
	800	FCTY	94404	749-F4
CABOT RD				
	400	SSF	94080	708-B3
CABRILLO AV				
	600	SCIC	94305	810-H1
	1000	BURL	94010	728-D5
CABRILLO FRWY Rt#-1				
	-	DALY	-	687-B7
	-	DALY	-	707-A2
	-	PCFA	-	706-J4
	100	PCFA	-	707-A2
	2100	DALY	-	687-B7
CABRILLO HWY Rt#-1				
	-	PCFA	94044	707-A7
	-	SMCo	-	726-F6
	-	SMCo	-	(847-H4 See Page 827)
	-	HMBY	94019	767-D4
	-	HMBY	94019	787-G7
	-	SMCo	94018	767-D4
	-	SMCo	94037	746-G1
	-	SMCo	94038	767-D4
	-	SMCo	94038	746-G7
	-	SMCo	94018	766-H1
	-	SMCo	-	746-G1
	100	PCFA	94044	727-A1
	100	PCFA	94044	726-H3
	300	SMCo	94019	767-D4
	1800	SMCo	94060	(908-D1 See Page 907)
	2100	SMCo	94038	766-H1
	2100	SMCo	-	766-H1
	4300	SMCo	94060	(888-B5 See Page 867)
	7000	SMCo	94060	(887-H1 See Page 867)
	9000	SMCo	94060	867-G4
	9500	SMCo	94019	787-G7
	9500	HMBY	94038	767-D4
	9600	SMCo	94019	(807-G1 See Page 788)
	9600			
	9600			
	1050			
	12			
	12			

STREET
Block City ZIP Pg-Grid

CADILLAC WY
1000 BURL 94010 728-E5
CADIZ CIR
- RDWC 94065 749-J7
CADIZ CT
- PCFA 94044 726-J4
CAHILL RIDGE RD
- SMCo - 768-D3
CAINE AV
- SF 94112 687-E1
CALAVERAS AV
100 PCFA 94044 727-B2
CALAVERAS CT
- HIL 94010 748-F6
CALAVERAS WY
- SMCo 94020 809-F6
CALERA TER
800 PCFA 94044 727-A3
CALGARY ST
- SF 94134 687-J3
- DALY 94014 687-J3
CALIFORNIA AV
- PA 94301 791-B6
- SMCo 94038 746-F6
100 PA 94306 791-A7
100 SMCo 94038 766-J2
100 SSF 94080 708-A3
200 SSF 94080 707-J2
500 PA 94305 791-A7
700 PA 94303 791-C5
CALIFORNIA DR
- BURL 94010 728-C4
- MLBR 94030 728-C4
CALIFORNIA ST
- RDWC 94063 770-A6
CALIFORNIA WY
500 RDWC 94062 789-E2
600 SMCo 94062 789-E2
700 WDSD 94062 789-E3
W CALIFORNIA WY
500 RDWC 94062 789-E3
500 WDSD 94062 789-E3
CALLADO WY
- ATN 94027 790-C5
CALLAN BLVD
- DALY 94015 687-B7
3500 SSF 94080 707-C3
4000 DALY 94015 707-B1
CALLIE LN
- MLPK 94025 770-F7
CALVERT AV
- SSF 94080 707-D1
CALVIN AV
2800 SMCo 94063 770-C7
CALYPSO LN
- SCAR 94070 769-C5
CAMAHO PL
- HIL 94010 748-G2
CAMARITAS AV
- SSF 94080 707-D1
CAMARITAS CIR
800 SSF 94080 707-E1
CAMBERLY WY
400 RDWC 94061 790-B2
CAMBON DR
- SF 94132 687-B1
CAMBORNE AV
- SMCo 94070 769-D3
- SCAR 94070 769-D3
CAMBRIDGE AV
200 PA 94306 791-A7
600 MLPK 94025 790-G5
CAMBRIDGE LN
100 SBRN 94066 727-F2
CAMBRIDGE RD
600 RDWC 94061 789-G3
1100 BURL 94010 728-D5
CAMBRIDGE ST
- SCAR 94070 769-E3
500 BLMT 94002 749-E7
600 SF 94134 687-J1
CAMDEN AV
4300 SMTO 94403 749-C7
CAMELIA DR
100 DALY 94015 687-B6
CAMELLIA AV
100 RDWC 94061 790-B2
CAMELLIA CT
- EPA 94303 791-C3
100 SBRN 94066 707-E6
CAMELLIA DR
1100 EPA 94303 791-D2
CAMELOT CT
- DALY 94015 707-D3
- SCAR 94062 769-G6
CAMEO CT
- DALY 94015 707-B2
CAMERON LN
- DALY 94014 687-F3
CAMERON WY
- SF 94124 688-C1
CAMEROTA WY
400 RDWC 94065 749-J5
[illegible]AMINO PZ
[illegible] SBRN 94066 707-H6
[illegible]O AL LAGO
[illegible]TN 94027 790-C5
[illegible]4025 790-C5
[illegible] CERROS
[illegible] 790-C5

CAMINO A LOS CERROS
- SMCo 94027 790-C5
1800 SMCo 94025 790-C5
CAMINO ALTO
- MLBR 94030 728-A4
CAMINO DE LAS ROBLES
- PA 94301 790-H5
CAMINO DE LOS ROBLES
- ATN 94027 790-D6
1800 SMCo 94025 790-D6
CAMINO POR LOS ARBOLES
- ATN 94027 790-D5
CAMINO VISTA CT
- BLMT 94002 749-D7
CAMPANA AV
200 DALY 94015 687-A7
CAMPBELL AV
- SF 94134 687-J1
- SF 94134 688-A1
4000 MLPK 94025 770-G7
CAMPBELL LN
- MLPK 94025 810-E1
- MLPK 94025 790-E7
CAMPESINO AV
200 PA 94306 791-C7
CAMPGROUND TR
- SMCo 94062 789-B5
CAMPHOR CT
- HIL 94010 748-C2
CAMPHOR WY
700 EPA 94303 791-B2
CAMPO RD
100 PTLV 94028 810-C7
CAMPO BELLO
- MLPK 94025 790-E7
CAMPO BELLO CT
- MLPK 94025 790-E7
CAMP POMPONIO RD
- SMCo 94020 849-J7
- SMCo 94020 850-A7
- SMCo 94020 869-J1
CAMPUS DR
100 SCIC 94305 790-G6
800 DALY 94015 707-B1
800 SCIC 94305 810-J1
2600 SMTO 94403 748-J5
CAMPUS DR E
300 SCIC 94305 810-G1
700 SCIC 94305 790-H7
CAMPUS DR W
100 SCIC 94305 790-F7
900 SCIC 94305 810-F1
900 SCIC 94304 810-F1
CANADA LN
1400 WDSD 94062 789-G6
CANADA RD
- SMCo 94062 768-H3
- SMCo 94070 768-H3
200 SMCo 94062 769-A6
200 SMCo 94070 769-A6
200 SMCo 94402 768-H3
500 SMCo 94062 789-C1
500 SMCo 94070 789-C1
800 WDSD 94062 789-F4
CANADA RD Rt#-92
- SMCo - 768-G2
- SMCo 94402 768-G2
- SMCo 94062 768-G2
CANADA COVE AV
- HMBY 94019 787-F6
CANADA VISTA
- SMCo 94020 829-E7
N CANAL ST
300 SSF 94080 707-H3
S CANAL ST
300 SSF 94080 707-J3
CANANEA AV
3100 BURL 94010 728-B7
CANANEA PL
- BURL 94010 728-B7
CANIS LN
800 FCTY 94404 749-H1
CANNERY SQ
- DALY 94014 687-D5
CANOE CT
200 RDWC 94065 749-H5
CANOGA WY
- MLBR 94030 727-H2
CANTERBURY AV
- DALY 94015 707-B2
CANTERBURY RD
1200 HIL 94010 748-F3
CANVASBACK WY
1000 RDWC 94065 749-J4
1400 RDWC 94065 750-A4
CANYON CT
- SSF 94080 707-F5
CANYON DR
- SF 94112 687-G3
- DALY 94014 687-G3
100 PTLV 94028 810-C7
200 PTLV 94028 830-C1
500 PCFA 94044 707-A5
CANYON LN
- RDWC 94062 789-G1
- SMCo 94062 789-G1

CANYON RD
- SMCo 94060 (868-F7
See Page 867)
- SMCo 94060 (888-F1
See Page 867)
600 RDWC 94062 789-H1
700 RDWC 94062 769-G7
800 SMCo 94062 769-G7
2800 BURL 94010 728-B7
2800 SMCo 94010 728-B7
27500 PA 94304 830-H2
27500 SCIC 95014 830-H2
CANYON OAK CT
1800 SMTO 94402 748-H7
CANYON VIEW DR
- SMCo - 768-D3
CAPAY CIR
- SSF 94080 707-E3
CAPE BRETON CT
- PCFA 94044 727-C4
CAPE BRETON DR
600 PCFA 94044 727-C4
CAPE COD DR
800 RDWC 94065 750-A6
CAPE HATTERAS CT
- RDWC 94065 749-J2
CAPISTRANO AV
1300 PCFA 94044 727-A6
CAPISTRANO RD
300 SMCo 94038 767-A2
300 SMCo 94038 766-J2
CAPISTRANO WY
600 SMTO 94402 748-J2
1800 BURL 94010 728-A6
E CAPISTRANO WY
500 SMTO 94402 748-J2
W CAPISTRANO WY
700 SMTO 94402 748-J2
CAPITOL AV
- SF 94112 687-D1
1900 EPA 94303 791-B2
CAPPER CT
- SMCo 94061 790-B4
CAPRI LN
500 FCTY 94404 749-G5
CAPRINO WY
300 SCAR 94070 769-E4
CAPSTAN CT
300 RDWC 94065 749-H7
CAPTAIN LN
- RDWC 94065 750-C4
CAPUCHINO AV
900 BURL 94010 728-D5
CAPUCHINO DR
- MLBR 94030 728-A2
500 MLBR 94030 727-J3
CARAVEL LN
700 FCTY 94404 749-G2
CARDENAS AV
- SF 94132 687-B1
CARDIFF LN
1000 RDWC 94061 790-B2
CARDIGAN RD
1200 HIL 94010 748-F3
CARDINAL WY
1000 PA 94303 791-D5
CARIBBEAN WY
600 SMTO 94402 748-J4
CARINA LN
800 FCTY 94404 749-F4
CARLETON AV
- DALY 94015 687-A6
CARLETON CT
1600 RDWC 94061 790-A2
CARLETON PL
- PCFA 94044 727-B6
CARLISLE DR
1100 SMTO 94402 749-B2
CARLMONT DR
2100 BLMT 94002 769-C2
CARLOS AV
100 RDWC 94061 790-B1
1300 BURL 94010 728-C6
CARLOS ST
1300 SMCo 94038 746-F5
CARLOW WY
2900 SSF 94080 707-D5
CARLSBAD CT
- SSF 94080 707-F4
CARLTON AV
200 SBRN 94066 707-J7
200 SBRN 94066 727-J1
800 MLPK 94025 771-A7
1100 MLPK 94025 790-J1
1200 MLPK 94025 770-J7
CARLTON CT
400 SSF 94080 708-B3
CARLTON RD
1400 HIL 94010 748-E4
CARMEL AV
- PCFA 94044 706-J5
- DALY 94015 686-J6
100 SMCo 94018 767-A2
200 PCFA 94044 707-A5
CARMEL CIR
500 SMTO 94402 748-J2
CARMEL DR
2300 PA 94303 791-D4
2500 SBRN 94066 707-E6

CARMEL LN
- SMCo 94062 769-G6
CARMEL RD
100 SMCo 94062 788-J6
CARMEL WY
100 SMCo 94028 830-D3
CARMELITA AV
1100 BURL 94010 728-D7
1900 HIL 94010 728-D7
2500 BLMT 94002 769-B1
CARMELITA DR
1800 SCAR 94070 769-F3
CARMELO LN
200 SSF 94080 707-F2
CARNELIAN RD
100 SSF 94080 707-H1
CAROL AV
1500 BURL 94010 728-G7
E CAROL AV
- BURL 94010 728-G7
CAROLAN AV
200 BURL 94010 728-E5
N CAROLAN AV
1300 BURL 94010 728-D5
CAROLE CT
700 EPA 94303 791-B1
CAROLE WY
1500 RDWC 94061 790-A1
CAROLINA AV
2400 RDWC 94061 790-A3
CAROLINA LN
- ATN 94027 790-C2
CAROLINE WY
- DALY 94014 687-G3
CARR ST
- SF 94124 688-B1
CARRERA CT
- SMCo 94062 789-G2
CARRIAGE CT
- MLPK 94025 790-C7
CARRINGTON CIR
27200 LAH 94022 830-J1
CARRIZAL ST
- SF 94134 687-H2
CARROLL AV
700 SF 94124 688-C1
CARSON ST
1200 RDWC 94061 789-J2
CARTER DR
3500 SSF 94080 707-C4
CARTER ST
500 DALY 94014 687-H3
500 SF 94134 687-H3
600 SMCo 94014 687-H3
CARTER WY
- MLPK 94025 790-C7
CARTIER LN
900 FCTY 94404 749-G4
CARY AV
1200 SMTO 94401 749-B1
CASA AV
- DALY 94015 687-B6
CASA BONA AV
2300 BLMT 94002 769-B1
CASA DE CAMPO
3100 SMTO 94403 749-E5
CASA DEL MAR DR
400 HMBY 94019 767-E6
CASANOVA DR
3500 SMTO 94403 749-D5
CASANUEVA PL
900 SCIC 94305 810-J2
CASCADE CT
- SMTO 94401 729-A7
1000 MLPK 94025 790-C6
CASCADE DR
1000 MLPK 94025 790-C6
CASEY AV
2500 MTVW 94043 791-F6
CASEY CT
- MLPK 94025 771-A7
CASEY DR
100 SSF 94080 707-E3
CASHLEA CT
2600 SSF 94080 707-C4
CASSANDRA CT
- SF 94112 687-E2
CASSIA ST
400 RDWC 94063 770-B6
N CASTANYA WY
100 SMCo 94028 810-E3
S CASTANYA WY
200 SMCo 94028 810-E4
CASTELO AV
- SF 94132 687-B1
CASTENADA DR
200 MLBR 94030 728-A5
1800 BURL 94010 728-A5
CASTILIAN WY
100 SMTO 94402 748-J3
CASTILLEJA AV
1400 PA 94301 791-A6
1400 PA 94301 790-J6
1500 PA 94306 791-A6
CASTILLEJO DR
- DALY 94015 687-A7
100 DALY 94015 707-A1
CASTILLO AV
1300 BURL 94010 728-C6

CASTILLO ST
- DALY 94014 687-H2
- SF 94134 687-H2
CASTLE CT
- HIL 94010 748-D3
CASTLE ST
- DALY 94014 687-C5
CASTLE WY
1100 MLPK 94025 790-F4
CASTLE HILL RD
600 RDWC 94061 789-H2
CASTLEMONT AV
- DALY 94015 687-B3
CASTLETON AV
- DALY 94015 687-A4
- DALY 94015 686-J4
CASTLETON WY
100 SBRN 94066 707-D6
CASTOR ST
800 FCTY 94404 749-F4
CASTRO CT
- BURL 94010 728-B5
1300 PCFA 94044 727-A6
CATALINA AV
100 PCFA 94044 707-A2
CATALPA AV
200 SMTO 94401 748-J1
CATALPA DR
- ATN 94027 770-F7
- ATN 94027 790-F1
CATALPA WY
2300 SBRN 94066 707-F7
CATAMARAN LN
- DALY 94014 687-E5
CATAMARAN ST
300 FCTY 94404 749-G3
CATHCART WY
1000 SCIC 94305 810-J2
CATHERINE DR
300 SSF 94080 707-E3
CATHY PL
- MLPK 94025 790-F5
CAVANAUGH ST
300 SMTO 94401 729-A6
E CAVOUR ST
- DALY 94014 687-C4
W CAVOUR ST
- DALY 94014 687-C4
CAXTON CT
3200 SMTO 94403 749-A6
3200 SMTO 94403 748-J6
CAYMAN LN
600 FCTY 94404 749-G5
CAYUGA AV
- SF 94112 687-D2
CEBALO LN
- ATN 94027 790-C1
CEDAR AV
- SMCo 94060 (868-H5
See Page 867)
300 SMCo 94062 788-H5
400 SBRN 94066 727-H1
500 SBRN 94066 707-G7
2000 SMCo 94025 790-D6
CEDAR CT
- DALY 94014 687-H2
- SF 94134 687-H2
- HIL 94010 748-F1
- SMCo 94025 790-D6
CEDAR LN
- WDSD 94062 789-G7
200 PCFA 94044 707-A6
200 PCFA 94044 706-J6
CEDAR PL
800 SSF 94080 708-A2
CEDAR ST
- RDWC 94063 770-B6
- SCAR 94070 769-F2
300 MLBR 94030 728-B2
800 SMCo 94037 746-G5
1100 PA 94301 791-B4
CEDARWOOD CT
1600 SBRN 94066 707-G7
CEDARWOOD DR
1400 SMTO 94403 748-H7
CEDARWOOD WY
1100 RDWC 94061 790-B2
CEDRO WY
700 SCIC 94305 810-J2
CELESTE DR
1600 SMTO 94402 749-B3
CELESTIAL CT
- PCFA 94044 727-A5
CELESTIAL LN
600 FCTY 94404 749-E4
CELIA CT
- PCFA 94044 727-A5
CELIA WY
900 PA 94303 791-D5
CENTAURUS LN
800 FCTY 94404 749-H1
CENTER DR
500 PA 94301 791-B3
CENTER ST
- MLBR 94030 728-A2
- RDWC 94063 770-B7
- RDWC 94061 770-B7
100 RDWC 94061 790-B1
800 SCAR 94070 769-H4

CENTER PARK LN
500 FCTY 94404 749-F3
CENTRAL AV
- RDWC 94061 790-B1
100 BURL 94010 728-G7
200 HMBY 94019 787-E2
300 MLPK 94025 791-A3
1100 SCAR 94070 769-H4
CENTRAL DR
- MLPK 94025 790-J1
27600 LAH 94022 830-H2
CERES ST
- SMCo 94038 746-F6
CERRITO AV
100 RDWC 94061 790-A4
100 SMCo 94061 790-A4
CERRITO PL
- SMCo 94061 790-A4
CERRO CT
300 DALY 94015 687-B7
CERRO DR
- DALY 94015 687-B7
CERROS MNR
- SMCo 94025 790-D5
CERVANTES RD
100 PTLV 94028 810-C5
100 SMCo 94062 769-F7
CERVANTES WY
1100 PCFA 94044 726-H4
CHABOT DR
2600 SBRN 94066 707-D6
CHABOT TER
2400 PA 94303 791-D4
CHADBOURNE AV
- MLBR 94030 728-A4
CHADBOURNE LN
1100 MLBR 94030 728-A4
CHADWICK CT
- MLBR 94030 727-J5
CHALLENGE CT
100 FCTY 94404 749-G2
CHAMPS ELYSEE BLVD
2900 HMBY 94019 767-D4
CHANDLER WY
- SMCo 94010 728-B7
- SMCo 94010 748-B1
CHANNEL DR
- RDWC 94065 750-A6
CHANNING AV
100 PA 94301 790-J5
400 PA 94301 791-A4
900 HMBY 94019 767-F6
1300 PA 94303 791-C4
CHANNING LN
500 PCFA 94044 707-A3
CHANNING RD
- BURL 94010 728-H6
CHANNING WY
300 PCFA 94044 707-A3
CHANTAL WY
- RDWC 94061 790-A1
CHAPEL LN
- MLPK 94025 790-J2
CHAPEL VIEW DR
- SMCo - 768-D4
CHAPIN AV
1400 BURL 94010 728-F7
CHAPIN LN
100 BURL 94010 728-F7
400 HIL 94010 728-F7
CHAPMAN AV
- SSF 94080 708-A2
300 SBRN 94066 727-J1
CHAPMAN RD
- SMCo 94020 809-F7
CHARING CROSS RD
1800 SMCo 94402 748-H7
1800 SMTO 94402 748-H7
CHARING CROSS WY
200 PCFA 94044 707-A6
200 PCFA 94044 706-J6
CHARLES AV
28000 LAH 94022 810-J7
28000 LAH 94022 830-J1
CHARLES LN
- SMTO 94402 749-B3
CHARLESTON AV
2200 SBRN 94066 707-F7
CHARLTON ST
- SCAR 94070 769-E3
CHART LN
- RDWC 94065 750-C4
CHARTER ST
- RDWC 94063 770-C6
800 SMCo 94063 770-C6
CHARTHOUSE LN
- FCTY 94404 749-J1
CHATEAU CT
- SSF 94080 707-E5
CHATEAU DR
- MLPK 94025 790-F3
400 HIL 94010 748-D2
CHATHAM CT
3800 RDWC 94061 789-H3
3900 SSF 94080 707-C4
CHATHAM RD
400 BURL 94010 728-G6
CHATSWORTH LN
400 RDWC 94061 790-B2

CHAUCER ST
- MLPK 94025 791-A3
400 PA 94301 791-A3
CHEBEC LN
700 FCTY 94404 749-G2
CHECKERSPOT DR
- BSBN 94005 687-J4
CHELMSFORD RD
500 HIL 94010 748-G2
CHELSEA CT
- DALY 94014 687-D3
CHELSEA WY
100 RDWC 94061 790-B2
CHEMICAL WY
- RDWC 94063 770-C5
CHEROKEE CT
- PTLV 94028 810-C6
CHEROKEE WY
100 PTLV 94028 810-C6
CHERRY AV
100 SSF 94080 707-H4
300 MLPK 94025 790-G3
400 SBRN 94066 727-H1
500 SBRN 94066 707-G6
CHERRY LN
800 SCAR 94070 769-H2
CHERRY ST
900 SCAR 94070 769-G3
CHERRYWOOD DR
1400 SMTO 94403 748-H7
CHERYL CT
3400 SMTO 94403 748-J7
CHERYL PL
- MLPK 94025 790-F5
CHESAPEAKE AV
300 FCTY 94404 749-F6
CHESAPEAKE DR
300 RDWC 94063 770-C3
CHESHAM AV
100 SMCo 94070 769-D4
100 SCAR 94070 769-D4
CHESHIRE WY
2300 RDWC 94061 789-H1
CHESS DR
- SMTO 94404 749-E2
1100 FCTY 94404 749-F1
CHESTER AV
- SF 94132 687-C2
CHESTER ST
- SMCo 94014 687-D5
- DALY 94014 687-D5
100 MLPK 94025 791-A2
300 MLPK 94025 790-J2
CHESTER WY
- HIL 94010 748-F1
300 PCFA 94044 707-A3
700 SMTO 94402 748-F1
CHESTERFIELD AV
300 HMBY 94019 767-E7
CHESTERTON AV
300 BLMT 94002 749-E7
800 RDWC 94061 789-H2
CHESTERTON PL
200 SMTO 94401 748-H1
CHESTNUT AV
- SSF 94080 707-G2
200 PA 94306 791-C7
400 SBRN 94066 727-H1
500 SBRN 94066 707-H7
CHESTNUT LN
100 SMTO 94403 749-C6
CHESTNUT ST
- SCAR 94070 769-F2
100 RDWC 94063 770-B6
1000 MLPK 94025 790-F3
CHEVY ST
800 BLMT 94002 769-D1
CHEYENNE PT
- PTLV 94028 810-C6
CHICAGO WY
- SF 94112 687-G2
CHICO CT
- PCFA 94044 726-J4
- SSF 94080 707-F3
CHICORY LN
- SCAR 94070 769-C4
CHILCO ST
1200 MLPK 94025 770-H7
CHILTERN RD
600 HIL 94010 748-G2
CHILTON AV
- SCAR 94070 769-E3
CHILTON LN
3800 SBRN 94066 707-C5
CHINA GRADE
- SCrC 95006 (890-B1
See Page 869)
- SMCo 94020 (890-B1
See Page 869)
CHINQUAPIN TR
- SMCo 94062 789-A6
CHIQUITA ST
- SMCo 94028 830-E3
CHRIS LN
3400 SMTO 94403 748-J7
CHRISTEN AV
- DALY 94015 707-C3
CHRISTIAN CT
- BLMT 94002 768-J2

CHRISTIAN DR
3900 BLMT 94002 768-J2
3900 SMCo 94070 768-J2
CHRISTINE DR
700 PA 94303 791-E7
CHRISTINE LN
- MLBR 94030 728-A3
- MLBR 94030 727-J3
CHRISTOPHER CT
- DALY 94015 707-A1
CHRISTOPHER WY
900 MLPK 94025 770-F7
CHRISTOPHERS LN
28100 LAH 94022 810-H5
CHRYSLER DR
1100 MLPK 94025 770-G6
CHRYSOPOLIS DR
800 FCTY 94404 749-G2
CHUKKER CT
100 SMTO 94403 749-A4
CHULA VISTA AV
900 BURL 94010 728-E5
CHULA VISTA DR
1000 BLMT 94002 769-D2
CHULA VISTA RD
- SMCo 94037 746-H3
CHUMASERO DR
- SF 94132 687-B1
CHURCH AV
1500 SMTO 94401 749-C2
CHURCH RD
- SMTO 94401 729-B7
CHURCH ST
300 HMBY 94019 787-F1
CHURCHILL AV
- PA 94301 790-A4
- PA 94301 791-A6
- SMCo 94062 790-A4
- PA - 790-A4
- PA 94306 791-A6
- WDSD 94062 790-A4
CHURCHILL DR
2700 HIL 94010 728-C7
2700 HIL 94010 748-B1
CIELITO DR
- SF 94134 687-H2
CIERVOS RD
- SMCo 94028 830-D4
CIMA WY
- PTLV 94028 810-C7
- PTLV 94028 830-C1
CINDY WY
700 PCFA 94044 707-A7
CINNABAR RD
200 WDSD 94062 789-G4
CINNAMON CT
- HIL 94010 748-C1
CIPRIANI BLVD
2100 BLMT 94002 749-C7
2100 BLMT 94002 769-B2
CIRCLE CT
700 SSF 94080 707-G3
CIRCLE DR
- SBRN 94066 727-G3
600 EPA 94303 791-B3
CIRCLE LN
- MLPK 94025 790-J2
CIRCLE RD
- RDWC 94062 769-H7
CIRO AV
1400 SMTO 94403 749-D4
CIRRUS CT
- RDWC 94061 789-G2
CITRUS AV
- DALY 94014 687-C4
CITRUS CT
- HIL 94010 748-D2
CITY HALL LN
1300 BURL 94010 728-G7
CITYHOMES LN
- FCTY 94404 749-E3
CITY VIEW DR
- DALY 94014 687-F3
CIVIC LN
1300 BLMT 94002 769-F1
CLAIRE PL
300 MLPK 94025 790-F5
CLARA AV
- SSF 94080 707-E2
CLARA DR
700 PA 94303 791-D6
CLAREMONT AV
- RDWC 94062 769-J5
100 SSF 94080 707-J1
CLAREMONT CT
- MLBR 94030 727-H3
CLAREMONT DR
1200 SBRN 94066 707-E7
CLAREMONT PL
- MLPK 94025 790-H4
N CLAREMONT ST
- SMTO 94401 728-H7
500 SMTO 94401 748-J1
S CLAREMONT ST
100 SMTO 94401 749-A2
100 SMTO 94401 748-J1
400 SMTO 94402 749-A2
CLAREMONT WY
300 MLPK 94025 790-H4

CLARENCE CT
- EPA 94303 771-B7
CLARENDON RD
- BURL 94010 728-H6
- PCFA 94044 706-J6
200 PCFA 94044 707-A6
CLARICE LN
2000 BURL 94010 728-C5
CLARIDGE DR
600 PCFA 94044 707-C4
CLARINADA AV
500 DALY 94015 687-A7
CLARK AV
300 DALY 94014 687-D6
300 CLMA 94014 687-D6
900 SBRN 94066 727-H1
CLARK CT
- PCFA 94044 707-A4
CLARK DR
- SMTO 94402 748-G1
- SMTO 94402 728-H7
CLARKE AV
1800 EPA 94303 791-C1
CLAUDIA AV
1300 SMTO 94403 749-D4
CLAY AV
- SSF 94080 707-D2
CLAY DR
- ATN 94027 790-C4
CLAYTON CT
- DALY 94014 687-D4
CLAYTON DR
2100 MLPK 94025 790-E7
CLEARFIELD DR
600 MLBR 94030 728-A4
600 MLBR 94030 727-J4
CLEARVIEW DR
- DALY 94015 707-A1
CLEARVIEW WY
3000 SMTO 94402 748-H6
CLEE ST
1600 BLMT 94002 769-D2
CLELAND PL
- MLPK 94025 790-J3
CLEVELAND AV
1300 SMTO 94403 749-C3
CLEVELAND ST
500 RDWC 94062 770-A7
600 RDWC 94061 770-A7
CLIFDEN DR
200 SSF 94080 707-D2
CLIFFORD AV
- SMCo 94062 769-G6
200 SCAR 94070 769-G6
CLIFFSIDE CT
- BLMT 94002 769-C3
CLIFFSIDE DR
- DALY 94015 687-A3
CLIFF SWALLOW CT
- BSBN 94005 688-A5
CLIFTON AV
200 SCAR 94070 769-E3
CLIFTON CT
3200 PA 94303 791-E6
CLIFTON DR
- DALY 94015 687-A4
CLIFTON RD
200 PCFA 94044 707-A3
200 PCFA 94044 706-J3
CLINTON CT
- RDWC 94061 770-A7
CLINTON ST
- RDWC 94062 769-J5
400 RDWC 94062 770-A6
600 RDWC 94061 770-A6
CLIPPER CT
100 BLMT 94002 749-F6
CLIPPER DR
100 BLMT 94002 749-F6
CLIPPER LN
900 FCTY 94404 749-G3
CLIPPER ST
2300 SMTO 94403 749-D1
CLIPPER WY
- DALY 94014 687-D5
CLOISTER WY
- DALY 94014 687-F3
CLOUD AV
900 MLPK 94025 790-D6
900 SMCo 94025 790-D6
CLOVELLY LN
1100 BURL 94010 728-C5
CLOVER CIR
- SSF 94080 707-F2
CLOVER LN
- SCAR 94070 769-D5
100 MLPK 94025 790-J3
CLOVERDALE RD
- SMCo 94060 (888-F3
See Page 867)
3000 SMCo 94060 (868-D5
See Page 867)
CLUB DR
- SCAR 94070 769-D3
200 SMCo 94070 769-D3
300 BLMT 94002 769-C4
CLUB VIEW DR
- DALY 94014 687-F3
CLYDESDALE DR
700 HIL 94402 748-H4

COALMINE VW
- PTLV 94028 830-C1
COAST AV
2600 MTVW 94043 791-G7
COAST LN
200 PCFA 94044 726-J2
COAST GUARD RD
- SMCo 94128 708-B5
- SSF 94080 708-B5
COASTLAND DR
700 PA 94303 791-C6
COBB LN
- SMCo 94060 (868-F3
See Page 867)
COBB ST
1100 SMTO 94401 749-B2
COBBLEHILL PL
2100 SMCo 94402 768-G1
COBBLESTONE CT
- DALY 94014 687-C5
COBBLESTONE LN
- BLMT 94002 769-E1
- SCAR 94070 769-F5
COCHRANE ST
- SF 94124 688-E1
COD ST
800 FCTY 94404 749-H3
CODO ST
100 SMCo 94038 766-H2
COGHLAN LN
- ATN 94027 790-C4
COLBY AV
900 SMCo 94025 790-H1
COLBY ST
600 SF 94134 687-J1
COLBY WY
3800 SBRN 94066 707-C6
COLEGROVE CT
- SMTO 94403 749-C6
COLEGROVE ST
3600 SMTO 94403 749-C6
COLEMAN AV
600 MLPK 94025 790-H2
800 SMCo 94025 790-H2
COLEMAN CT
- SCAR 94070 769-E4
COLEMAN PL
- MLPK 94025 790-J2
COLEPORT LNDG
- RDWC 94065 749-H5
COLERIDGE AV
100 PA 94301 791-A6
COLGATE AV
400 SMTO 94402 748-H3
COLLEGE AV
200 PA 94306 791-A7
600 MLPK 94025 790-G5
600 SMCo 94025 790-H2
1000 SMTO 94401 728-J6
1400 PA 94306 810-J1
COLLEGE DR
2800 SBRN 94066 707-C6
COLLEGE NORTH ENTRY RD
3400 SBRN 94066 707-B6
COLLEGE OF SAN MATEO DR
100 SMCo 94402 748-G6
3300 SMTO 94402 748-G6
COLLEGE VIEW WY
- BLMT 94002 769-D1
COLLINS AV
800 CLMA 94014 687-D7
1300 CLMA 94014 707-C1
COLMA BLVD
- CLMA 94014 687-C7
COLMA CREEK SERV RD
- SSF 94080 708-A4
COLONEL WY
800 HMBY 94019 787-G2
COLONIAL LN
900 PA 94303 791-D5
COLONIAL PL
- SMCo 94061 790-B3
COLORADO AV
100 PA 94306 791-D6
100 PA 94301 791-B7
700 PA 94303 791-D6
COLORADO PL
1000 PA 94303 791-E5
COLORADOS DR
- MLBR 94030 727-J4
COLTON AV
100 SCAR 94070 769-H5
COLTON CT
- RDWC 94062 789-E2
- SMCo 94062 789-E2
COLUMBIA AV
- SMCo 94063 790-D1
COLUMBIA CIR
800 RDWC 94065 750-C6
COLUMBIA DR
600 SMTO 94402 748-H3
COLUMBIA LN
800 FCTY 94404 749-F4
COLUMBIA ST
100 SMCo 94038 766-J2
2000 PA 94306 810-J1
COLUMBIA WY
800 RDWC 94065 750-C6

STREET
Block City ZIP Pg-Grid

COLUMBUS AV
1300 BURL 94010 728-C5
COLUMBUS ST
100 SMCo 94018 767-A2
COLUSA CT
100 SBRN 94066 707-D7
COMERWOOD CT
400 SSF 94080 707-F4
COMET DR
600 FCTY 94404 749-G2
COMMANDER LN
300 RDWC 94065 749-H6
COMMERCIAL AV
300 SSF 94080 707-G2
900 PA 94303 791-F7
COMMERCIAL ST
900 SCAR 94070 769-H3
COMMODORE DR
1100 SBRN 94066 707-H5
COMMODORE DR W
800 SBRN 94066 707-G6
COMMONS LN
- FCTY 94404 749-E3
COMMONWEALTH DR
100 MLPK 94025 770-G6
COMMUNITY LN
1100 PA 94301 791-A4
COMO AV
- DALY 94014 687-C3
COMPASS CIR
500 RDWC 94065 749-H7
COMPASS DR
400 RDWC 94065 749-H7
COMPASS LN
900 FCTY 94404 749-H4
COMSTOCK CIR
- SCIC 94305 790-J7
2500 BLMT 94002 769-A3
COMSTOCK RD
100 SMCo 94062 788-H4
COMUS ST
100 SMCo 94038 746-F6
CONCAR DR
- SMTO 94402 749-B3
CONCHITA CT
- PCFA 94044 707-A4
CONCORD DR
200 MLPK 94025 790-J3
CONCORD ST
- SF 94112 687-F2
CONCORD WY
600 BURL 94010 728-G6
2700 SBRN 94066 707-F7
CONCOURSE DR
100 BLMT 94002 749-F6
CONDON CT
- SMTO 94403 748-J7
CONDOR LN
900 FCTY 94404 749-H2
CONEJO DR
- MLBR 94030 728-A5
100 MLBR 94030 727-J5
CONIFER LN
- HIL 94010 748-F1
CONIL WY
300 SMCo 94028 810-D4
CONMUR ST
200 SSF 94080 707-F5
CONNECTICUT DR
1000 RDWC 94061 789-J2
1500 RDWC 94061 790-A2
CONNIE AV
600 SMTO 94402 749-B3
CONNOLLY WY
2300 EPA 94303 791-C1
CONRAD CT
- SSF 94080 707-D1
CONSTANZO ST
500 SCIC 94305 810-H1
CONSTELLATION CT
800 RDWC 94065 750-A5
800 RDWC 94065 749-J5
CONSTITUTION DR
100 MLPK 94025 770-G6
800 FCTY 94404 749-G3
CONSTITUTION SQ
300 MLBR 94030 728-B3
CONSTITUTION WY
400 SMCo 94080 707-F4
400 SSF 94080 707-F4
CONTINENTAL DR
900 MLPK 94025 790-C6
CONTINENTALS WY
1000 BLMT 94002 769-B2
CONVENTION WY
300 RDWC 94063 770-A4
COOKIE CT
100 SMCo 94062 769-G7
COOKSEY LN
700 SCIC 94305 810-H1
COOLEY AV
1900 EPA 94303 791-B2
COOS CT
500 FCTY 94404 749-F5
COPELAND ST
600 PCFA 94044 726-J2
COPLEY AV
- RDWC 94062 769-H6
COQUITO CT
- SMCo 94028 810-D4
COQUITO WY
100 SMCo 94028 810-D4
CORA ST
- SF 94134 688-A2
- SF 94134 687-J2
CORAL LN
- FCTY 94404 749-E6
CORAL PL
- DALY 94014 687-D5
CORAL ST
800 SMCo 94038 746-F6
CORAL WY
- HMBY 94019 787-G5
CORAL REEF AV
100 SMCo 94018 766-J2
100 SMCo 94018 767-A2
CORAL RIDGE DR
300 PCFA 94044 707-A2
CORBITT DR
500 BURL 94010 728-G6
CORDILLERAS AV
600 SCAR 94070 769-F3
CORDILLERAS CT
- SMCo 94062 769-F7
CORDILLERAS RD
900 SMCo 94062 769-F7
900 RDWC 94062 769-F7
CORDOVA CT
- PTLV 94028 810-D6
CORDOVA ST
- SF 94112 687-G2
500 DALY 94014 687-G2
COREY WY
300 SSF 94080 708-A4
CORINA CT
3800 PA 94303 791-F7
CORINA WY
3700 PA 94303 791-E7
CORINE LN
1300 MLPK 94025 790-E4
CORK PL
3700 SSF 94080 707-C4
CORK HARBOUR CIR
400 RDWC 94065 749-G6
CORK OAK WY
3300 PA 94303 791-D7
CORLETT WY
- HIL 94010 748-C3
CORMORANT DR
- BLMT 94002 769-G1
- RDWC 94065 769-G1
CORNELIA DR
- HIL 94010 748-F3
CORNELL AV
100 SMCo 94038 766-J2
400 SMTO 94402 748-H3
CORNELL RD
- MLPK 94025 790-G4
CORNELL ST
2000 PA 94306 791-A7
CORNISH WY
400 BLMT 94002 749-F7
CORNWALLIS LN
600 FCTY 94404 749-G5
CORONA CT
800 PCFA 94044 726-J4
CORONA DR
600 PCFA 94044 726-J4
CORONA ST
- SF 94132 687-C1
100 SMCo 94038 766-H2
900 SMCo 94037 746-G4
CORONA WY
100 SMCo 94028 810-D4
CORONADO AV
- DALY 94015 687-A4
- SCAR 94070 769-E4
100 SMCo 94019 767-C4
400 SMCo 94018 767-C4
600 SCIC 94305 810-H1
CORONADO DR
200 SMCo 94037 746-H4
CORONADO LN
700 FCTY 94404 749-F4
CORONADO ST
- SF 94124 688-B2
100 SMCo 94018 767-B3
CORONADO WY
1600 BURL 94010 728-C5
3700 SBRN 94066 707-C5
CORONET BLVD
2100 BLMT 94002 769-C1
CORPORATION WY
1000 PA 94303 791-F7
CORREAS AV
100 HMBY 94019 787-E1
CORREAS ST
500 HMBY 94019 787-F1
CORRIDO WY
400 SSF 94080 707-F5
CORRIENTE POINTE DR
800 RDWC 94065 749-J5
CORSAIR LN
900 FCTY 94404 749-G3
CORSICA LN
1200 FCTY 94404 749-G5
CORTE ALEGRE
- MLBR 94030 727-J4
CORTE ANNA
- MLBR 94030 728-B3
CORTE BALBOA
- MLBR 94030 728-B3
CORTE CAMELLIA
- MLBR 94030 727-J4
CORTE COMODA
- MLBR 94030 728-C3
CORTE DE FLORES
2600 SMTO 94403 749-B5
CORTE DEL SOL
- MLBR 94030 727-J4
CORTE DORADO
- MLBR 94030 728-A4
CORTE MADERA RD
100 PTLV 94028 830-C1
100 PTLV 94028 810-C7
CORTE NUEVA
- MLBR 94030 728-A4
CORTE PRINCESA
- MLBR 94030 728-A4
CORTESI AV
500 SSF 94080 707-J2
CORTEZ AV
100 SMCo 94019 767-C4
1000 BURL 94010 728-D5
CORTEZ LN
800 FCTY 94404 749-G3
12900 LAH 94022 830-J1
CORTEZ RD
- SMCo 94062 769-F7
CORTO LN
- WDSD 94062 789-G6
CORVUS LN
800 FCTY 94404 749-H1
COSTA RICA AV
100 BURL 94010 728-G7
100 BURL 94010 748-G1
300 SMTO 94402 748-G1
300 HIL 94010 748-G1
COTTAGE LN
- SCAR 94070 769-E2
COTTAGE GROVE AV
1400 SMTO 94401 749-B1
COTTON PL
- MLPK 94025 790-F5
COTTON ST
300 MLPK 94025 790-F5
COTTONWOOD AV
700 SSF 94080 707-H2
COTTONWOOD CT
- HIL 94010 748-D1
COTTONWOOD DR
- DALY 94014 687-D3
2400 SBRN 94066 707-E6
COTTRELL WY
900 SCIC 94305 810-J2
COUNTRY LN
- SMCo 94061 790-B2
COUNTRY WY
13300 LAH 94022 810-H7
COUNTRY CLUB CT
3000 PA 94304 810-H7
COUNTRY CLUB DR
- HIL 94010 728-F7
100 SSF 94080 707-G4
200 SMCo 94080 707-G4
3600 RDWC 94061 789-H3
COUNTRYSIDE DR
3200 SMTO 94403 748-J6
COUNTY RD
- SMCo 94062 789-A5
- SMCo 94062 788-J5
200 PCFA 94044 727-A1
200 PCFA 94044 726-J2
COUNTY ST
- DALY 94014 687-C5
COUNTY JAIL RD
- SMCo 94044 707-D7
COURT E
- DALY 94014 687-F3
E COURT LN
- FCTY 94404 749-F2
COURTLAND DR
200 SBRN 94066 727-G2
COURTLAND RD
1600 BLMT 94002 769-E2
COURT OF SAN MARCO
2900 HMBY 94019 767-D4
COVE LN
- SMCo 94038 746-F7
- RDWC 94065 749-H6
COVENTRY CT
100 SCAR 94070 769-D5
COVINGTON RD
800 BLMT 94002 769-C1
COWAN RD
800 BURL 94010 728-D3
COWELL LN
- ATN 94027 790-D5
400 SCIC 94305 810-H1
COWPENS WY
- SMTO 94402 768-G1
COWPER CT
3400 PA 94306 791-D7
COWPER ST
100 PA 94301 790-J4
800 PA 94301 791-A5
2500 PA 94306 791-C7
COYOTE HILL
- PTLV 94028 830-C1
COYOTE HILL RD
3100 SCIC 94304 810-J3
COYOTE POINT DR
1600 SMTO 94401 728-J6
1700 SMTO 94401 729-A5
COZZOLINO CT
- MLBR 94030 727-J3
CRAGMONT CT
- PCFA 94044 707-A4
- SMTO 94403 748-J6
CRAGMONT WY
- WDSD 94062 789-H4
CRAIG CT
300 DALY 94014 687-C5
CRAIG RD
500 HIL 94010 748-D3
CRANE AV
600 FCTY 94404 749-G1
CRANE ST
- SF 94124 688-B1
900 MLPK 94025 790-F3
CRANFIELD AV
- BLMT 94002 769-D4
- SMCo 94002 769-D3
- SMCo 94070 769-D3
- BLMT 94070 769-D3
600 SCAR 94070 769-D3
CRANHAM CT
- PCFA 94044 727-A5
CRATER LAKE WY
- PCFA 94044 727-B5
CRAZY PETES RD
- SMCo 94028 830-C6
CREEK AV
400 SMCo 94062 788-G5
CREEK DR
600 MLPK 94025 790-G5
E CREEK DR
100 MLPK 94025 790-H3
E CREEK PL
- MLPK 94025 790-H4
CREEK TR
- SMCo 94062 788-J5
CREEK PARK DR
- PTLV 94028 810-E7
CREEKRIDGE CT
- SMTO 94402 748-C7
CREEKSIDE DR
- HMBY 94019 787-F6
CREEKWOOD DR
100 SMCo 94021 849-A7
CREEKWOOD WY
- HIL 94010 748-H3
CRENSHAW CT
100 PCFA 94044 707-A2
CRENSHAW DR
- DALY 94015 707-A2
- PCFA 94044 707-A2
CRESCENT AV
100 BURL 94010 728-G7
100 PTLV 94028 810-C7
100 PTLV 94028 830-C1
100 SMCo 94038 746-G6
400 SMTO 94402 728-G7
400 SMTO 94402 748-G1
CRESCENT DR
- PA 94301 791-B3
E CRESCENT DR
500 PA 94301 791-B3
W CRESCENT DR
500 PA 94301 791-B3
CRESCENT ST
- SMCo 94037 746-H5
CRESCIO CT
- SF 94112 687-E2
CRESPI DR
- SF 94132 687-B1
500 PCFA 94044 726-H3
1000 PCFA 94044 727-A3
CREST DR
400 SMCo 94062 789-G1
CREST LN
2300 MLPK 94025 790-D7
CREST RD
100 WDSD 94062 789-H4
CRESTA VISTA LN
500 PTLV 94028 810-D5
CRESTLINE AV
- DALY 94015 687-A5
CRESTMOOR CIR
100 PCFA 94044 707-A2
CRESTMOOR DR
2100 SBRN 94066 707-F7
2600 SBRN 94066 727-F1
CRESTON AV
- DALY 94015 686-J4
CRESTVIEW AV
- DALY 94015 686-J5
500 BLMT 94002 749-E7
CRESTVIEW CT
100 SCAR 94070 769-E6
CRESTVIEW DR
100 SCAR 94070 769-C4
600 SMCo 94070 769-D6
700 MLBR 94030 727-H3
CRESTWOOD CT
1400 SMTO 94403 748-J7
CRESTWOOD DR
- DALY 94015 687-A3
1000 SSF 94080 707-F1
1400 SBRN 94066 707-F5
1500 SMTO 94403 748-H7
CRINGLE DR
500 RDWC 94065 749-H7
CRIPPLERIDGE CT
- SMTO 94402 748-C7
CRITTENDEN LN
- MTVW 94043 791-J7
CROCKER AV
- DALY 94014 687-D3
900 SMCo 94014 687-E3
2800 SMCo 94063 770-D7
CROCKETT LN
1700 HIL 94010 728-E6
CROCUS CT
- SMCo 94025 790-E6
CROFTON WY
3800 SSF 94080 707-C4
CROMPTON RD
600 RDWC 94061 789-H1
CROMWELL RW
2600 SSF 94080 707-C4
CRONER AV
1700 MLPK 94025 790-E5
1700 SMCo 94025 790-E5
CROSBY CT
100 SBRN 94066 707-E7
CROSS ST
- SF 94112 687-F2
CROSSWAY RD
700 BURL 94010 728-F6
CROTHERS WY
300 SCIC 94305 790-H7
CROWN CIR
- SSF 94080 707-D2
CROWN CT
- SMCo 94402 768-H1
- SMTO 94402 768-H1
CROYDEN WY
100 WDSD 94062 789-H5
CRYSTAL CT
100 SBRN 94066 727-H2
900 FCTY 94404 749-F5
CRYSTAL DR
1400 HIL 94010 748-E5
CRYSTAL ST
- SF 94112 687-D2
CRYSTAL TER
- SMCo 94010 728-B7
CRYSTAL SPRING TER
- HIL 94010 748-F4
CRYSTAL SPRINGS RD
- HIL 94010 748-H3
- SMTO 94402 748-H3
600 SBRN 94066 727-H1
1200 SMCo 94402 748-E6
1800 SMCo 94010 748-E6
1900 SMCo - 748-E6
2800 SMCo 94030 727-G3
CRYSTAL SPRINGS TER
- HIL 94010 748-G4
CRYSTAL SPRINGS TR
- SMCo 94062 789-D4
- WDSD 94062 789-D4
CUARDO AV
200 MLBR 94030 728-B3
CUESTA AV
600 SMTO 94403 749-A5
CUESTA DR
100 SSF 94080 707-E3
CUESTA REAL
- SMCo 94020 829-E7
- SMCo 94020 849-E1
CULEBRA RD
800 HIL 94010 748-G3
CULEBRA ST
100 SMCo 94038 766-H2
CULLEN DR
400 PCFA 94044 727-A1
CULVER CT
- SMTO 94403 749-C6
CUMBERLAND CT
900 FCTY 94404 749-E5
CUMBERLAND RD
400 BURL 94010 728-G6
CUNNINGHAM WY
400 SBRN 94066 727-H1
CUPERTINO WY
200 SMTO 94403 749-D5
CUPID RW
100 SBRN 94066 707-J7
CURLEW CT
200 FCTY 94404 749-G1
CURRY CT
- SCAR 94070 769-D3
CURTIS AV
2800 SMCo 94063 770-C7
CURTIS CT
- SCAR 94070 769-D3
CURTIS ST
- SF 94112 687-F2
800 MLPK 94025 790-F3
CURTIS WY
700 MLPK 94025 790-G4
CURTISS ST
3100 SMTO 94403 749-D5
CUT ACROSS RD
- SMCo 94020 850-G7
CUTTER LN
400 FCTY 94404 749-H4
CUTTER ST
300 FCTY 94404 749-H4
CUTTY CT
300 PCFA 94044 707-A3
CUTWATER LN
500 FCTY 94404 749-G6
CYGNUS LN
600 FCTY 94404 749-E4
CYPRESS AV
100 SBRN 94066 727-J1
100 SMCo 94038 746-F7
200 SSF 94080 707-J3
300 SMCo 94062 788-H5
400 HMBY 94019 787-F1
400 MLBR 94030 727-J1
400 SBRN 94066 707-H7
400 SMTO 94401 748-J1
500 SSF 94080 708-A2
600 SMTO 94401 749-A1
800 BLMT 94002 769-E1
900 SMTO 94401 729-A7
1500 BURL 94010 728-G7
CYPRESS CT
- DALY 94014 687-J3
- MLBR 94030 728-A3
- SBRN 94066 707-J7
- SCAR 94070 769-F6
CYPRESS DR
- SMCo - 768-D3
CYPRESS LN
- BSBN 94005 688-A5
- DALY 94014 687-J3
CYPRESS ST
100 RDWC 94061 790-B1
1100 EPA 94303 791-C2
CYPRESS CIRCLE DR
- SMCo - 768-D3
CYPRESS POINT RD
100 HMBY 94019 787-F5

D

D ST
100 DALY 94014 687-C6
100 RDWC 94063 769-J4
300 CLMA 94014 687-D6
300 MLPK 94025 790-G3
DAFFODIL LN
- SCAR 94070 769-C4
DAFIDIL LN
- SCrC 95006 (889-B7
See Page 869)
DAIRY LN
- BLMT 94002 749-F7
DAISY LN
400 EPA 94303 791-D2
DAISY ST
900 SMTO 94401 749-C1
DAKIN AV
1900 SMCo 94025 790-D6
DAKOTA AV
1200 SMTO 94401 749-B1
DALE AV
100 SCAR 94070 769-F3
1500 SMTO 94401 749-C1
1900 SMTO 94403 749-C1
DALE WY
1200 PCFA 94044 726-G4
DALEHURST AV
700 SMTO 94403 749-A7
DALEHURST CT
3900 SMTO 94403 749-B7
DALEROSE CT
- DALY 94014 687-G3
DALE VIEW AV
500 BLMT 94002 749-D7
DALEY CT
100 SBRN 94066 707-E7
DALHBERG AV
- PCFA 94044 706-J5
DALY CT
- SSF 94080 707-G2
DAMONTE CT
- SSF 94080 708-A1
DANA AV
1100 PA 94301 791-A3
1400 PA 94303 791-A3
DANA CT
- SSF 94080 707-F4
DANA POINTE CT
- RDWC 94065 749-J5
DANBERRY LN
- DALY 94014 687-E3
DANBURY LN
- RDWC 94061 790-B2
DANMANN AV
1200 PCFA 94044 726-G4
DAPHNE CT
- EPA 94303 791-D3
DAPHNE WY
- EPA 94303 791-D3
DARBY PL
100 SBRN 94066 727-G2
DARCY AV
- SMTO 94403 749-C6
DARCY CT
- SMTO 94403 749-C6
DARDENELLE AV
100 PCFA 94044 727-B1
DARLENE AV
1300 SMTO 94403 749-D4
DARRELL RD
200 HIL 94010 748-C2
DARTMOUTH AV
- SCAR 94070 769-D2
DARTMOUTH RD
100 SMTO 94402 748-J2
DARTMOUTH ST
600 SF 94134 687-J1
900 SF 94134 688-A1
2000 PA 94306 810-J1
DARWIN AV
1500 SMTO 94403 749-C2
DATE ST
900 SMCo 94037 746-G5
DAVEY GLEN RD
- BLMT 94002 749-D7
DAVID AV
3100 PA 94303 791-D6
DAVID CT
2300 SMTO 94403 749-D4
3100 PA 94303 791-D6
DAVID RD
900 BURL 94010 728-D4
DAVIS CT
- BURL 94010 728-B5
DAVIS DR
- BLMT 94002 769-B2
1500 BURL 94010 728-C5
DAVIS ST
1100 RDWC 94061 770-A7
DAVIT LN
600 RDWC 94065 749-J6
DAY AV
1500 SMTO 94403 749-D3
DAYTON AV
1100 SCAR 94070 769-G5
DEAN RD
100 WDSD 94062 789-G6
DEAN TR
- SMCo 94062 789-B5
DEANNA DR
1000 MLPK 94025 790-D6
DEANNE LN
300 DALY 94014 687-D5
DE ANZA AV
100 SCAR 94070 769-F5
100 RDWC 94062 769-F5
100 SCAR 94062 769-F5
DE ANZA BLVD
1400 SMTO 94403 748-J7
1800 SMTO 94402 768-H1
1900 SMTO 94402 748-J7
DE ANZA CT
- SMTO 94402 748-H7
DEARBORN PARK RD
300 SMCo 94060 (868-H1
See Page 867)
DEBBIE CT
2700 SCAR 94070 769-F6
DEBBIE LN
- BLMT 94002 749-D7
- BLMT 94002 769-D1
DEBBIE PL
2600 SCAR 94070 769-F6
DEBELL DR
- ATN 94027 790-G2
DECATUR ST
1100 FCTY 94404 749-G4
DECOTA AV
100 SMCo 94038 766-G1
DEDALERA DR
200 SMCo 94028 810-E4
DEER CREEK RD
3400 SCIC 94304 810-J4
3400 PA 94304 810-J4
DEERLAKE CT
- SMTO 94402 768-H1
DEER MEADOW LN
100 PTLV 94028 810-C5
DEER PARK LN
- PTLV 94028 810-C5
DEER PATH DR
- SMCo 94028 830-E4
DEER SPRINGS WY
27200 LAH 94022 830-J2
DEGAS RD
100 PTLV 94028 810-C5
DE KOVEN AV
2400 BLMT 94002 769-B1
DELANO AV
500 SF 94112 687-E1
DELAWARE AV
2400 RDWC 94061 790-A3
N DELAWARE ST
- SMTO 94401 748-J1
100 SMTO 94401 728-H6
S DELAWARE ST
- SMTO 94401 749-A1
400 SMTO 94402 749-A1
1900 SMTO 94403 749-B3
DEL CENTRO
100 MLBR 94030 727-J5
DE LEON LN
900 FCTY 94404 749-F4
DELFINO WY
1300 MLPK 94025 790-D5
DELL RD
800 PCFA 94044 726-H5
DELLBROOK AV
400 SSF 94080 707-F1
DEL MAR AV
100 SMCo 94038 766-G1
400 PCFA 94044 707-A4
DELMAR CT
- RDWC 94063 770-F6
DEL MAR RD
300 SMCo 94062 788-H5
DELMAR WY
200 SMTO 94403 749-B5
DEL MONTE AV
100 SSF 94080 707-E2
DEL MONTE DR
- HIL 94010 728-C7
- PCFA 94044 707-A2
DEL MONTE PL
- SMTO 94403 749-A6
DEL MONTE RD
100 SMCo 94018 767-B2
DEL MONTE ST
- SF 94112 687-F2
3000 SMTO 94403 749-A6
DEL NORTE AV
1000 MLPK 94025 770-H7
1000 MLPK 94025 790-H1
DEL NORTE DR
100 SBRN 94066 707-E7
DE LONG ST
- SF 94112 687-C2
500 DALY 94014 687-C2
S DELORES AV
400 HMBY 94019 787-F4
DEL PASO DR
- SSF 94080 707-F3
DEL PRADO DR
- DALY 94015 687-B7
DEL REY CT
- SCAR 94070 769-F3
DEL ROSA WY
200 SMTO 94403 749-D5
DELTA ST
- SF 94134 687-J2
100 SF 94134 688-A1
DELVIN WY
2200 SSF 94080 707-E5
DEMETER ST
100 EPA 94303 791-C1
200 EPA 94303 771-C7
DENALI DR
- SMTO 94403 748-H7
DENARDI WY
- SSF 94080 707-F5
DENHAM CT
- HIL 94010 728-E7
DENISE DR
- HIL 94010 748-E4
DENISE LN
400 SMCo 94061 790-B4
DENNIS DR
100 DALY 94015 707-C3
900 PA 94303 791-D5
DENSLOW DR
100 SF 94132 687-B1
DEODORA DR
- ATN 94027 790-G1
- ATN 94027 770-G7
DERBY ST
- DALY 94015 707-C2
DERECHO ST
100 SMCo 94038 766-H2
DERRY LN
500 MLPK 94025 790-F3
DERRY WY
2200 SSF 94080 707-E5
DE SABLA RD
- SMTO 94402 748-H2
- HIL 94010 748-H2
DESMOND ST
- SF 94134 688-A2
DE SOLO DR
1100 PCFA 94044 726-H4
DE SOTO AV
1300 BURL 94010 728-D6
DE SOTO DR
700 PA 94303 791-B4
DE SOTO LN
900 FCTY 94404 749-F3
DE SOTO ST
- SF 94132 687-C1
DE SOTO WY
100 SBRN 94066 727-J2
600 MLBR 94030 727-J2
DESVIO CT
- PCFA 94044 727-A5
DESVIO WY
1500 BLMT 94002 769-E2
DETROIT DR
1700 SMTO 94404 749-C1
2000 SMTO 94403 749-C1
DEVEREAUX DR
1600 BURL 94010 728-C5
DEVON DR
600 HIL 94010 748-F1
DEVON WY
3400 RDWC 94061 789-H1
DEVONSHIRE AV
2700 SMCo 94063 770-C7
2700 SMCo 94063 790-C1
DEVONSHIRE BLVD
- SCAR 94070 769-D4
100 SMCo 94070 769-D4
DEVONSHIRE CIR
- SMCo 94070 769-E4
DEWEY AV
1200 RDWC 94061 789-J2
DEWEY DR
600 FCTY 94404 749-G5
DEWEY ST
1700 SMTO 94403 749-D2
DE WOLF ST
- SF 94112 687-E2
DEXTER AV
- SMCo 94063 790-C1
DEXTER PL
- MLBR 94030 728-A3
DIABLO WY
- SMCo 94020 850-F5
700 SMCo 94062 789-F2
DIAMOND AV
500 SSF 94080 707-J2
DIAMOND ST
100 SBRN 94066 707-J5
DIANNE CT
400 SSF 94080 707-F5
DIAZ AV
- SF 94132 687-B1
DIAZ LN
900 FCTY 94404 749-F3
DICHIERA CT
- SF 94112 687-E2
DICKENS CT
- SCAR 94070 769-E6
DICKEY ST
900 RDWC 94061 770-A7
DILLER ST
- RDWC 94063 770-A6
DINES CT
- EPA 94303 791-C2
DINKLESPIEL STATION LN
- ATN 94027 790-E2
DIONNE CT
- BLMT 94002 768-J1
DIX ST
1100 SMTO 94401 749-B2
DIXON CT
- DALY 94014 687-C4
DOCKSIDE CIR
- RDWC 94065 749-J6
DOCKSIDE DR
- DALY 94014 687-E5
DODGE DR
1000 RDWC 94063 770-E6
DOELGER BLVD
100 SMCo 94018 767-A1
DOHERTY WY
100 SMCo 94061 790-B4
DOHERTY RIDGE RD
- SMCo 94020 850-F7
DOLAN AV
1500 SMTO 94401 729-B7
DOLLAR AV
100 SSF 94080 707-J5
DOLORES CT
400 SMTO 94403 749-B7
DOLORES ST
100 SMCo 94018 767-B2
700 SCIC 94305 810-H1
2300 SMTO 94403 749-A5
DOLORES WY
300 SSF 94080 707-G1
2900 BURL 94010 728-A6
DOLPHIN CT
- HMBY 94019 787-G5
DOLPHIN DR
500 PCFA 94044 706-J4
DOLPHIN ISL
300 FCTY 94404 749-H2
DOLPHINE AV
100 SMCo 94018 767-C1
DOLTON AV
100 SMCo 94070 769-D4
100 SCAR 94070 769-D4
DOMINGO WY
- SMCo 94037 746-H4
DOMINICA LN
1400 FCTY 94404 749-G5
DON CT
- SMCo 94062 769-G6
DONAHUE ST
700 SF 94124 688-C2
DONALDSON AV
400 PCFA 94044 726-J2
DONDEE WY
400 PCFA 94044 726-J2
DONEGAL AV
2300 SSF 94080 707-E5
DONNELLY AV
1200 BURL 94010 728-G7
DONNER AV
700 SF 94124 688-B1
1500 SBRN 94066 727-H1
DONNER ST
3700 SMTO 94403 749-C6
DONOHOE ST
100 MLPK 94025 791-A2
100 EPA 94303 791-A2
DORADO LN
800 FCTY 94404 749-F4
DORADO WY
300 SMCo 94080 707-F5
300 SSF 94080 707-F5
DORCHESTER DR
- DALY 94015 687-A3
DORCHESTER RD
400 SMTO 94402 748-G1
DORE AV
1200 SMTO 94401 729-A7
DORIS CT
- RDWC 94061 790-A1
DORIS DR
1800 MLPK 94025 790-E6
DORY LN
- FCTY 94404 749-F6
500 RDWC 94065 749-J6
DOS LOMA VISTA LN
- PTLV 94028 810-D4
DOUBLE ROCK ST
- SF 94124 688-C1
DOUGLAS AV
400 RDWC 94063 770-D6
400 SMCo 94063 770-D6
1100 BURL 94010 728-G6
DOUGLAS CT
3400 SMTO 94403 748-J7
DOUGLAS WY
- ATN 94027 790-F3
1200 SSF 94080 707-G1
DOVE LN
- FCTY 94404 749-H2
DOVER CT
- DALY 94015 707-C2
- SMCo 94070 769-E4
100 SBRN 94066 707-G7
DOVER LN
1100 FCTY 94404 749-F4
DOVER RD
3300 RDWC 94061 789-H1
DOWNEY CT
2200 SSF 94080 707-E5
DOWNEY WY
- HIL 94010 728-D7
DOWNING LN
700 PA 94301 790-J4
DOYLE ST
1000 MLPK 94025 790-F3
DRACO LN
600 FCTY 94404 749-E4
DRAKE AV
100 SSF 94080 707-J1
1000 BURL 94010 728-D5
DRAKE CT
500 FCTY 94404 749-F5
1000 SCAR 94070 769-E5
DRAKE ST
- DALY 94014 687-G2
- SF 94112 687-G2
700 SMCo 94037 746-H4
DRAYTON RD
- HIL 94010 748-F4
DREW CT
2800 EPA 94303 771-C6
DRIFTWOOD CIR
- PCFA 94044 727-A4
DRIFTWOOD CT
- PCFA 94044 727-A3
DRIFTWOOD DR
800 PA 94303 791-E7
DRIFTWOOD LN
- DALY 94014 687-E6
DRIFTWOOD TR
- HMBY 94019 787-G5
DRURY LN
500 SMCo 94062 789-F1
DRY CREEK LN
100 WDSD 94062 789-F5
DUANE ST
- RDWC 94062 769-J5
400 RDWC 94062 770-A6
DUBLIN CT
3100 SSF 94080 707-D4
DUBLIN DR
2900 SSF 94080 707-D5
DUBLIN ST
- SF 94112 687-G1
DUBLIN WY
2000 SMTO 94403 749-C4
DUBUQUE AV
500 SSF 94080 708-A2
DUCK CT
200 FCTY 94404 749-H1
DUDLEY LN
- SCIC - 791-A7
DUENA ST
500 SCIC 94305 790-H7
DUFFERIN AV
1100 BURL 94010 728-C5
DUGGAN CT
- SMCo 94062 769-F7
DUGGAN RD
100 SMCo 94062 769-F7
DUHALLOW WY
2600 SSF 94080 707-C4
DULLES CT
1100 PCFA 94044 727-A5

STREET
Block City ZIP Pg-Grid

DUMBARTON AV
- SMCo 94063 790-C1
100 SMCo 94063 770-C7
2000 EPA 94303 791-A2
DUMONT CT
- MLBR 94030 727-H4
DUMONT ST
4200 SMTO 94403 749-D6
DUNCAN RD
- SMCo 94062 (808-E5 See Page 788)
DUNDEE DR
100 SSF 94080 707-C2
DUNDEE LN
100 SCAR 94070 769-F4
DUNKS ST
- DALY 94014 687-C5
DUNMAN WY
- SSF 94080 707-D1
DUNNE CT
- SMCo 94025 770-E7
DUNSMUIR WY
100 MLPK 94025 770-G7
DURAN CT
- PCFA 94044 727-A5
DURAND DR
3900 SMTO 94403 749-D6
DURAZNO WY
100 SMCo 94028 810-D3
DURHAM ST
100 MLPK 94025 791-A2
300 MLPK 94025 790-J2
DURLSTON RD
800 RDWC 94062 769-H6
DUSTY TR
- SMCo 94060 (868-E4 See Page 867)
DUVAL DR
- SSF 94080 707-D1
DWIGHT AV
900 HMBY 94019 767-E6
DWIGHT RD
- BURL 94010 728-H6
DWIGHT ST
300 SF 94134 688-A1
700 SF 94134 687-J1
DYMOND CT
400 PA 94306 791-C7

E

E ST
100 RDWC 94063 769-J4
300 CLMA 94014 687-D6
300 SF 94124 688-E1
900 BLMT 94002 769-F2
EAGLE LN
1000 FCTY 94404 749-H2
EAGLE HILL TER
- RDWC 94062 769-J7
EAGLE TRACE DR
100 HMBY 94019 787-F5
EARL AV
1700 SBRN 94066 707-E7
EARL ST
700 SF 94124 688-C2
EAST AV
200 SBRN 94066 727-J1
1100 SMCo 94037 746-F5
EAST CT
- SBRN 94066 727-G3
EAST LN
200 BURL 94010 728-G6
EASTBURN CT
- SBRN 94066 727-G1
EASTGATE DR
- DALY 94015 687-A3
EASTLAKE AV
- DALY 94014 687-C4
- PCFA 94044 707-A6
EASTLAKE WY
3800 RDWC 94062 789-G2
3800 SMCo 94062 789-G2
EASTMOOR AV
- DALY 94015 687-A5
EASTMOOR RD
1100 BURL 94010 728-D5
EASTON AV
500 SBRN 94066 707-H6
EASTON DR
1500 BURL 94010 728-D6
2800 HIL 94010 728-C7
EASTRIDGE AV
2200 MLPK 94025 790-D7
EASTRIDGE CIR
- PCFA 94044 707-A1
EASTRIDGE CT
- PCFA 94044 707-A1
EASTVIEW WY
500 RDWC 94062 789-E2
500 SMCo 94062 789-E2
500 WDSD 94062 789-E2
EASTWOOD AV
- DALY 94015 687-A6
EASTWOOD DR
- SMTO 94403 749-C7
EATON AV
- DALY 94015 686-J6
300 RDWC 94062 769-G6
300 RDWC 94070 769-G6

STREET
Block City ZIP Pg-Grid

EATON AV
500 SCAR 94070 769-H5
2500 SCAR 94062 769-G6
EATON RD
200 SMTO 94402 748-J2
EATON VILLA PL
- SCAR 94062 769-G6
- RDWC 94062 769-G6
EBENER ST
1100 RDWC 94061 770-A7
1300 RDWC 94061 790-B1
EBKEN ST
300 PCFA 94044 726-J2
ECCLES AV
400 SSF 94080 708-B3
ECHO AV
1500 SMTO 94401 749-C2
ECHO DR
- SMCo 94038 746-F5
ECHO LN
- WDSD 94062 809-G6
100 PTLV 94028 810-C7
EDDINGTON LN
- DALY 94014 687-E3
EDDYSTONE CT
- RDWC 94065 749-J6
EDEN WY
- HIL 94010 728-D7
EDEN BOWER LN
900 RDWC 94061 789-G3
EDEN WEST RD
- SMCo 94060 (868-E7 See Page 867)
- SMCo 94060 (888-F1 See Page 867)
EDESSA CT
- HIL 94010 728-C7
EDGAR PL
- SF 94112 687-E1
EDGE RD
- ATN 94027 790-G1
EDGECLIFF WY
300 SMCo 94062 789-G3
400 RDWC 94061 789-G3
EDGECOURT DR
2100 HIL 94010 728-D7
EDGEHILL DR
100 SCAR 94070 769-G5
800 BURL 94010 728-E6
EDGEMAR AV
500 PCFA 94044 706-J4
600 PCFA 94044 707-A4
EDGEMAR ST
- DALY 94014 687-E3
EDGEMONT DR
- DALY 94015 687-A6
EDGERTON RD
27400 LAH 94022 830-J1
27600 LAH 94022 810-J7
EDGEWATER BLVD
500 FCTY 94404 749-E3
EDGEWOOD CT
- DALY 94014 687-D3
EDGEWOOD DR
100 PCFA 94044 707-A1
1400 PA 94301 791-B3
1500 PA 94303 791-C3
EDGEWOOD LN
1800 MLPK 94025 790-E6
EDGEWOOD RD
- RDWC 94062 769-H6
300 HIL 94010 748-F1
300 SMTO 94402 748-F1
700 SMCo 94062 769-F7
2100 SMCo 94070 769-F7
2400 SMCo 94070 789-C1
2400 RDWC 94062 789-C1
2400 SMCo 94062 789-C1
EDGEWOOD WY
1200 SSF 94080 707-F1
EDGEWORTH AV
100 SMCo 94015 687-B5
400 DALY 94015 687-B5
EDINBURGH ST
300 SF 94112 687-G1
500 SMTO 94402 748-J2
1200 SMTO 94402 749-A3
1800 SMTO 94403 749-A3
EDISON AV
100 SSF 94080 707-J1
EDISON ST
500 SMCo 94037 746-G4
2600 SMTO 94403 749-C6
EDISON WY
3000 SMCo 94063 770-D7
3200 SMCo 94025 770-D7
EDITH AV
2400 RDWC 94061 789-H1
EDMOND DR
1500 SCAR 94070 769-E7
EDMONDS RD
- SCAR 94070 769-D7
100 SMCo 94070 769-D7
EDNA DR
600 SMTO 94402 749-B3
EDNA LN
300 PCFA 94044 707-A3
EDWARDS CT
- BURL 94010 728-E5

STREET
Block City ZIP Pg-Grid

EDWARDS LN
- ATN 94027 790-D3
EDWARDS RD
1000 BURL 94010 728-D5
EGBERT AV
600 SF 94124 688-B1
EGRET LN
800 RDWC 94065 750-A6
EGRET ST
1000 FCTY 94404 749-H1
EISENHOWER ST
1600 SMTO 94403 749-C2
EL ARROYO RD
400 HIL 94010 748-F2
EL BONITO WY
- MLBR 94030 728-A4
200 MLBR 94030 727-J4
ELBRIDGE WY
800 PA 94303 791-D6
EL CAJON WY
900 PA 94303 791-C5
EL CAMINO REAL
- MLBR 94030 728-C4
1700 BURL 94010 728-C4
EL CAMINO REAL
Rt#-82
- BURL 94010 728-E6
- CLMA 94014 687-C5
- MLBR 94030 728-A2
- MLPK 94025 790-C1
- PA 94301 790-H4
- SCAR 94070 769-F2
- PA 94304 790-H4
100 ATN 94027 790-C1
100 BLMT 94002 749-D7
100 SBRN 94066 727-J1
100 SSF 94080 707-G4
100 SBRN 94066 707-G4
100 SMCo 94063 790-C1
200 DALY 94014 687-C5
200 SCIC 94305 790-H4
200 SMCo 94014 687-C5
200 PA 94305 790-H4
500 BLMT 94002 769-F2
500 HIL 94010 728-E6
700 CLMA 94014 707-E1
800 RDWC 94062 769-H3
800 RDWC 94062 770-A6
800 RDWC 94063 769-H3
800 RDWC 94063 770-A6
800 SMTO 94402 749-D7
1300 RDWC 94061 770-A6
1300 SMCo 94080 707-E1
1300 SBRN 94066 728-A2
1400 SCIC - 791-A6
1400 PA - 790-H4
1400 PA 94306 791-A6
1500 MLPK 94025 790-C1
1700 MLBR 94030 727-J1
1700 ATN 94025 790-C1
2400 PA 94306 791-A6
2600 RDWC 94063 790-C1
2600 SMCo 94063 770-A6
N EL CAMINO REAL
Rt#-82
- SMTO 94401 728-G7
- SMTO 94402 728-G7
100 SMTO 94402 748-H1
100 SMTO 94401 748-H1
800 BURL 94010 728-G7
S EL CAMINO REAL
Rt#-82
- BLMT 94002 749-A2
- SMTO 94401 748-J2
- SMTO 94402 748-J2
500 SMTO 94402 749-A2
500 SMTO 94401 749-A2
2000 SMTO 94403 749-A2
EL CAMPO DR
- SSF 94080 707-E3
EL CAPITAN DR
700 MLBR 94030 727-J4
EL CARMELO AV
100 PA 94306 791-C7
EL CENTRO RD
400 HIL 94010 748-F2
EL CERRITO AV
- SMTO 94402 748-G2
200 HIL 94010 748-G2
EL CORTEZ AV
300 SSF 94080 707-G4
ELDER AV
- MLBR 94030 728-A3
1100 MLBR 94030 727-H3
ELDER CT
- MLPK 94025 790-E5
100 SBRN 94066 707-E6
ELDER DR
- BLMT 94002 769-B3
ELDER LN
- PCFA 94044 706-J6
EL DORADO AV
- PA 94306 791-C7
100 SMCo 94018 767-A1
EL DORADO CT
100 SBRN 94066 727-F1
EL DORADO DR
200 PCFA 94044 707-A1
300 DALY 94015 687-B7

STREET
Block City ZIP Pg-Grid

N ELDORADO ST
- SMTO 94401 728-J7
- SMTO 94401 749-A1
- SMTO 94401 748-J1
S ELDORADO ST
200 SMTO 94401 749-A1
400 SMTO 94402 749-A1
ELEANOR DR
- WDSD 94062 789-J5
100 WDSD 94062 790-A5
400 ATN 94027 790-A5
1600 SMTO 94402 749-B3
ELECTIONEER RD
- SCIC 94305 790-F7
ELENA AV
- ATN 94027 790-D3
ELENA RD
27500 LAH 94022 810-J6
EL ESCARPADO CT
400 SCIC 94305 810-G1
EL GRANADA BLVD
100 SMCo 94018 767-C2
1600 SMCo - 767-C2
ELIZA CT
100 FCTY 94404 749-G2
ELIZABETH LN
700 MLPK 94025 790-F3
ELIZABETH ST
1700 SCAR 94070 769-F4
ELIZABETH WY
- ATN 94027 790-C2
ELK CT
- PCFA 94044 727-C4
ELKHORN CT
1900 SMTO 94403 749-A4
1900 SMTO 94402 749-A4
ELK TREE RD
- SMCo 94062 809-F6
ELKWOOD DR
- SSF 94080 707-D1
ELLENDALE ST
100 SMCo 94038 746-F6
ELLINGTON AV
- SF 94112 687-E2
ELLIOT ST
100 SF 94134 687-J2
ELLIOTT DR
100 MLPK 94025 791-A2
ELLIOTT ST
2300 SMTO 94403 749-D4
ELLIS DR
800 SMCo 94015 687-A4
N ELLSWORTH AV
- SMTO 94401 728-H7
- SMTO 94401 748-J1
S ELLSWORTH AV
- SMTO 94401 748-J1
400 SMTO 94401 749-A2
ELLSWORTH CT E
400 SMTO 94401 728-H7
ELLSWORTH CT W
400 SMTO 94401 728-H7
ELLSWORTH PL
700 PA 94303 791-D6
ELM AV
100 BURL 94010 748-F1
100 SBRN 94066 727-J1
100 HIL 94010 748-F1
100 BURL 94010 728-F7
100 HIL 94010 728-F7
400 SBRN 94066 707-H6
ELM CT
- PCFA 94044 727-A5
500 SSF 94080 707-H2
ELM ST
- SCAR 94070 769-F2
100 MLPK 94025 791-A2
100 RDWC 94063 770-B6
100 SMTO 94401 748-H1
300 MLPK 94025 790-J2
400 SSF 94080 707-H2
800 SMCo 94037 746-H4
ELMDALE PL
2600 PA 94303 791-D5
ELMER ST
1000 BLMT 94002 769-F1
1200 SMCo 94002 769-F1
ELMWOOD CT
100 SBRN 94066 707-E6
ELMWOOD DR
- DALY 94015 687-A4
1100 MLBR 94030 727-H3
ELMWOOD PL
- MLPK 94025 790-H2
ELMWOOD RD
1800 HIL 94010 728-E7
EL NIDO RD
100 SMCo 94028 830-D4
EL PARQUE CT
1800 SMTO 94403 749-E5
EL PASEO
- HMBY 94019 787-G5
- MLBR 94030 728-A4
EL PORTAL AV
300 HIL 94010 748-G2
300 SMTO 94402 748-G2
EL PORTAL WY
- DALY 94015 687-A2
EL PRADO AV
200 SMCo 94061 790-A4

STREET
Block City ZIP Pg-Grid

EL PRADO RD
2700 BURL 94010 728-B7
EL QUANITO WY
- BURL 94010 728-B7
EL REY RD
- SMCo 94028 830-D4
EL SERENO DR
- SCAR 94070 769-H5
EL SERENO WY
- SCAR 94070 769-H5
ELSINORE CT
900 PA 94303 791-C5
ELSINORE DR
900 PA 94303 791-C5
EL SOBRANTE ST
3300 SMTO 94403 748-J6
ELSTON CT
- SCAR 94070 769-E4
ELSTON DR
3600 SBRN 94066 707-C5
EL VANDA RD
- SMCo 94062 769-E7
EL VERANO AV
300 PA 94306 791-D7
EL VERANO WY
1500 BLMT 94002 769-D2
ELWELL CT
1000 PA 94303 791-F6
ELWOOD ST
- RDWC 94062 769-J5
300 RDWC 94062 770-A6
EMALITA CT
100 SBRN 94066 727-J2
EMARON DR
100 SBRN 94066 707-D6
EMBARCADERO RD
- SCIC 94305 790-J5
- PA 94301 790-J5
100 PA 94301 791-C4
700 PA 94303 791-C4
EMBARCADERO WY
2400 PA 94303 791-E3
EMERALD AV
100 SCAR 94070 769-G5
EMERALD CT
- SMTO 94403 748-J6
- SSF 94080 707-F2
EMERALD BAY LN
100 FCTY 94404 749-E3
EMERALD HILL RD
600 RDWC 94061 789-G2
EMERALD LAKE PL
- SMCo 94062 789-G1
EMERSON ST
100 PA 94301 790-H4
1100 PA 94301 791-A6
2500 PA 94306 791-B7
EMILIE AV
- ATN 94027 790-E3
EMILY LN
2400 SSF 94080 707-D4
EMMA LN
100 MLPK 94025 791-A3
EMMETT AV
800 BLMT 94002 769-E1
EMMETT WY
2500 EPA 94303 791-B1
2500 EPA 94303 771-B7
EMPRESS LN
- SF 94134 688-A2
ENCANTO WY
1100 PCFA 94044 726-H4
ENCHANTED WY
1300 SMCo 94402 748-G6
ENCINA AV
- PA 94301 790-J5
200 RDWC 94061 790-B1
300 ATN 94027 790-E1
300 SMCo 94063 790-E1
500 SMCo 94025 770-E7
ENCINA CT
- HIL 94010 728-E7
ENCINA DR
1200 MLBR 94030 728-A5
ENCINA WY
200 SMCo 94019 767-C3
ENCINAL AV
100 ATN 94027 790-F2
100 MLPK 94025 790-F2
100 MLPK 94027 790-F2
ENCINO RD
- ATN 94027 790-G1
ENCLINE WY
3700 BLMT 94002 769-A2
ENFIELD WY
700 HIL 94010 748-G3
ENGLE RD
- SMTO 94402 748-H1
ENGLISH CT
- BLMT 94002 769-E2
ENGVALL RD
2300 SBRN 94066 707-F6
ENSENADA RD
- SCAR 94070 769-F2
ENSENADA WY
2100 SMTO 94403 749-A5
ENSIGN LN
300 RDWC 94065 749-H7
ENTRADA WY
- SMCo 94020 829-E7

STREET
Block City ZIP Pg-Grid

ENTRADA WY
- SMCo 94020 849-E1
500 SMCo 94025 790-H2
ENTRANCE WY
- WDSD 94062 789-D6
ERICA DR
300 SSF 94080 707-E4
ERICA WY
100 SMCo 94028 810-D3
ERICKSON LN
800 FCTY 94404 749-F4
ERICSON RD
100 HIL 94010 748-H1
100 SMTO 94402 748-H1
ERIN LN
- HMBY 94019 787-G1
ERIN PL
2300 SSF 94080 707-D5
ERLIN DR
400 SCAR 94070 769-F2
ERRIS CT
3600 SSF 94080 707-C4
ERSTWILD CT
- PA 94303 791-B4
ERVINE ST
- SF 94134 688-A1
ESCALANTE WY
1600 BURL 94010 728-A6
ESCALERO AV
1000 PCFA 94044 726-H4
ESCALLE
- SMCo 94038 746-G7
ESCALONA AV
100 SMCo 94018 767-A1
ESCANYO DR
- SSF 94080 707-E3
ESCANYO WY
100 SMCo 94028 810-E4
ESCOBAR RD
100 PTLV 94028 810-C4
ESCOBITA AV
1500 PA 94306 791-A6
ESCONDIDO DR
100 SMCo 94020 849-E1
ESCONDIDO LN
1100 MLPK 94025 790-F3
ESCONDIDO PL
100 SMCo 94020 849-E1
ESCONDIDO RD
600 SCIC 94305 790-H7
800 SCIC 94305 810-J1
ESCONDIDO WY
1500 BLMT 94002 769-D2
ESOONDITA AV
- SMCo 94018 767-A2
ESCUELA DR
- DALY 94015 687-B7
ESMERALDA AV
800 SMCo 94038 746-G7
800 SMCo 94038 766-G1
ESMERALDA TER
- SMCo 94020 829-F7
ESPINOSA RD
900 WDSD 94062 809-G5
ESPLANADA WY
700 SCIC 94305 810-J1
ESPLANADE
100 PCFA 94044 706-J4
ESQUINA DR
- SF 94134 687-H2
ESSEX CT
100 SBRN 94066 727-G1
ESSEX LN
100 HIL 94010 748-G3
1100 FCTY 94404 749-G5
ESSEX WY
- PCFA 94044 726-G4
ESTATE CT
- SCAR 94070 769-E5
- SSF 94080 707-G2
600 DALY 94014 687-F3
ESTATES DR
100 SBRN 94066 707-E7
ESTELLA DR
- PCFA 94044 727-A3
ESTELLE LN
200 DALY 94014 687-D5
ESTHER LN
700 SMCo 94062 769-H7
ESTON WY
- MLBR 94030 728-A5
- MLBR 94030 727-J5
ESTRADA PL
- SMCo 94062 769-F6
ESTRELLA WY
200 SMTO 94403 749-D6
ESTUDILLO RD
100 SCIC 94305 810-H2
ETHEL CT
- RDWC 94061 789-J3
ETHELDORE ST
700 SMCo 94038 746-F6
EUCALYPTUS AV
- SSF 94080 707-G3
100 HIL 94010 748-E1
600 HIL 94010 728-E7
1900 SCAR 94070 769-G4
EUCALYPTUS CT
- WDSD 94062 789-F5

STREET
Block City ZIP Pg-Grid

EUCALYPTUS WY
2400 SBRN 94066 707-E7
EUCLID AV
- ATN 94027 790-B4
100 SBRN 94066 707-H6
1900 MLPK 94025 791-B3
2000 EPA 94303 791-B2
2100 RDWC 94061 789-J1
EUCLID PL
500 EPA 94303 791-B2
EUGENIA DR
- HIL 94010 748-C1
EUGENIA LN
- WDSD 94062 790-A5
EUREKA DR
200 PCFA 94044 707-A6
200 PCFA 94044 706-J6
EVA CT
- SMTO 94403 749-C6
EVELYN ST
900 MLPK 94025 790-F4
EVERETT AV
100 PA 94301 790-H4
EVERETT CT
500 PA 94301 790-J4
EVERGLADES DR
1000 PCFA 94044 727-B4
EVERGREEN AV
- DALY 94014 687-D3
EVERGREEN CT
- MLBR 94030 727-H3
EVERGREEN DR
200 SSF 94080 707-F1
1900 SBRN 94066 707-D6
3500 PA 94303 791-E7
EVERGREEN ST
600 MLPK 94025 790-E6
1800 SMTO 94401 749-C1
EVERGREEN WY
900 MLBR 94030 727-H3
EWELL RD
2200 BLMT 94002 769-C2
EXBOURNE AV
100 SCAR 94070 769-E2
EXCELSIOR AV
900 SF 94112 687-H1
EXECUTIVE GUILD CIR
- BLMT 94002 749-G7
- BLMT 94002 769-G1
- RDWC 94065 749-G7
- RDWC 94065 769-G1
EXECUTIVE PARK BLVD
100 SF 94134 688-B2
EXETER AV
- SCAR 94070 769-D3
EXETER DR
3500 SBRN 94066 707-B6
EXETER ST
- SF 94124 688-B1
EXETER WY
500 SCAR 94070 769-E3

F

F ST
100 DALY 94014 687-C6
100 RDWC 94063 769-J4
100 SMCo 94014 687-C6
200 CLMA 94014 687-D6
900 BLMT 94002 769-J4
900 SCAR 94070 769-J4
FABER PL
2400 PA 94303 791-E4
FABIAN WY
3700 PA 94303 791-F7
FAGAN DR
- HIL 94010 728-D7
- BURL 94010 728-D7
FAIRBANKS AV
100 SCAR 94070 769-F5
FAIRFAX AV
- ATN 94027 790-D1
300 SMTO 94402 748-H3
FAIRFAX WY
3700 SSF 94080 707-D4
FAIRFIELD CT
- SMCo 94402 748-F7
FAIRFIELD DR
200 SCAR 94070 769-G2
FAIRFIELD RD
700 BURL 94010 728-E6
FAIRLAWN AV
- DALY 94015 686-J4
- DALY 94015 687-A4
FAIRLAWN CT
- DALY 94015 687-A4
FAIRMONT AV
100 SCAR 94070 769-G5
FAIRMONT DR
- DALY 94015 686-J3
1000 SBRN 94066 707-F7
2000 SMTO 94402 748-H7
2000 SMTO 94402 768-H1
FAIR OAKS AV
2600 SMCo 94063 770-D6
3500 SMCo 94025 770-E7
FAIROAKS CT
- SMTO 94403 748-J6
FAIR OAKS LN
- ATN 94027 790-E2

STREET
Block City ZIP Pg-Grid

FAIRVIEW AV
- ATN 94027 790-C5
- DALY 94015 687-A5
1100 RDWC 94061 789-J1
FAIRVIEW PL
- MLBR 94030 727-H2
FAIRWAY CIR
600 HIL 94010 728-F7
FAIRWAY DR
- DALY 94015 687-B4
- SSF 94080 707-F3
100 HMBY 94019 787-E5
200 PCFA 94044 706-J7
300 PCFA 94044 707-A7
1600 BLMT 94002 769-D1
FAIRWAY PL
- HMBY 94019 787-E5
FALDA AV
- SMTO 94403 749-A5
FALK CT
400 MLPK 94025 791-A3
FALKIRK LN
- HIL 94010 748-F4
FALLENLEAF DR
100 HIL 94010 748-H2
FALLEN LEAF WY
900 SMCo 94062 789-G2
FALLON AV
500 SMTO 94401 729-B7
500 SMTO 94401 749-B1
FAMILY FARM RD
- WDSD 94062 809-J4
300 SMCo 94025 809-J4
FANITA WY
500 MLPK 94025 790-E6
FARALLON AV
200 PCFA 94044 707-A2
FARALLON DR
300 BLMT 94002 749-F6
FARALLONE AV
200 SMCo 94037 746-F4
FARALLONES ST
- SF 94112 687-D2
200 SF 94132 687-D2
FAR CREEK WY
900 SMCo 94062 789-G2
FARM LN
- HIL 94010 748-E2
FARM RD
100 PTLV 94028 810-A5
100 WDSD 94062 810-A5
FARM HILL BLVD
3500 RDWC 94061 789-G4
FARMHILL BLVD
4100 WDSD 94062 789-G4
FARMHILL CT
- HIL 94010 748-E1
FARMIN RD
- SMCo 94060 (868-F3 See Page 867)
FARNEE CT
2600 SSF 94080 707-C4
FARRAGUT AV
- SF 94112 687-E2
FARRAGUT BLVD
900 FCTY 94404 749-F4
FARRINGDON LN
700 BURL 94010 728-F6
FARRINGTON WY
2500 EPA 94303 791-B1
2500 EPA 94303 771-B7
FASHION ISLAND BLVD
- SMTO 94402 749-D3
1300 SMTO 94403 749-D3
1400 SMTO 94404 749-D3
FASMAN DR
3000 SBRN 94066 707-C5
FASSLER AV
300 PCFA 94044 726-J2
800 PCFA 94044 727-A3
FATHOM CT
400 RDWC 94065 749-H7
FATHOM DR
400 SMTO 94404 749-E1
FAVONIA RD
100 PTLV 94028 810-C4
FAWN CT
- HIL 94010 728-C7
FAWN LN
- PTLV 94028 810-C5
FAWN CREEK CT
27800 LAH 94022 810-H6
FAXON AV
- SF 94112 687-D1
FAXON RD
- ATN 94027 790-D4
FAXON FOREST
- ATN 94027 790-D4
FAY AV
- SCAR 94070 769-E4
- SMCo 94070 769-E4
FAY ST
1100 RDWC 94061 770-A7
FELIX AV
- SF 94132 687-B1
FELTON AV
- SSF 94080 707-D1
FELTON DR
100 MLPK 94025 790-F2

STREET
Block City ZIP Pg-Grid

FELTON PL
100 MLPK 94025 790-F2
FENNWOOD DR
- ATN 94027 790-F2
FERDINAND AV
100 SMCo 94018 767-B2
FERN AV
- SMCo 94060 (868-H5 See Page 867)
700 PCFA 94044 727-A2
FERN CT
- HIL 94010 728-D7
FERN PTH
- SMCo 94010 728-B7
FERN TR
- SMCo 94062 788-H5
FERNANDEZ WY
1100 PCFA 94044 726-H4
FERNDALE AV
200 SSF 94080 707-F1
FERNDALE WY
200 SMCo 94062 789-E7
200 SMCo 94062 789-E1
FERNSIDE ST
- RDWC 94061 790-A3
- WDSD 94062 790-A3
1000 RDWC 94061 789-J2
1600 WDSD 94062 789-J2
FERNWOOD AV
- DALY 94015 686-J5
FERNWOOD DR
- SBRN 94066 707-F6
- SMCo 94020 849-E1
1100 MLBR 94030 727-H3
FERNWOOD ST
2800 SMTO 94403 749-A6
FERNWOOD WY
1700 BLMT 94002 769-D2
FEY DR
100 SMCo 94010 728-B7
FIELDCREST DR
- DALY 94015 687-B3
FIELD HOUSE RD
- SMTO 94402 748-H5
FIELDING DR
800 PA 94303 791-D6
FIESTA AV
- SMCo 94063 770-F5
FIESTA CT
2000 SMTO 94403 749-C4
FIESTA DR
500 SMTO 94403 749-B4
FIFE AV
1000 PA 94301 791-A4
FIFTY FIFTY RD
- SMCo 94060 (868-E3 See Page 867)
FILBERT RD
- SMCo 94062 788-H6
FILBERT ST
200 HMBY 94019 787-E2
FILLMORE AV
1600 SMTO 94403 749-C2
FINGER AV
- RDWC 94062 769-J5
FIR AV
100 SSF 94080 707-H4
FIR CT
- HIL 94010 748-C1
FIR LN
- SMCo 94060 (868-H5 See Page 867)
FIR ST
- SMCo 94037 746-H4
100 SCAR 94070 769-F2
FIR VW
- SMCo 94020 829-F7
FIRECREST AV
300 PCFA 94044 707-B2
FIRETHORN WY
- PTLV 94028 810-D7
E FIRST ST
500 MLPK 94025 790-H3
FISHER ST
400 DALY 94014 687-D5
FITCH ST
2600 SF 94124 688-C1
FITZGERALD AV
500 SF 94124 688-B1
FIVE POINTS RD
- SMCo 94020 850-G7
- SMCo 94020 (870-J1 See Page 869)
FLASHNER LN
900 BLMT 94002 769-E1
FLEETWOOD CT
100 SBRN 94066 707-C5
FLEETWOOD DR
- DALY 94015 687-A3
100 SCAR 94070 769-E7
800 SMTO 94402 749-B2
2100 SBRN 94066 707-D5
3900 SSF 94080 707-D5
FLETCHER DR
- ATN 94027 790-B5
FLEUR PL
- ATN 94027 790-C4
FLINT AV
1400 SMTO 94403 749-D4

STREET
Block City ZIP Pg-Grid

FLOOD AV
2900 SMCo 94063 770-D7
FLOOD CIR
- ATN 94027 790-F1
FLORENCE LN
900 MLPK 94025 790-F4
FLORENCE ST
- DALY 94014 687-D4
400 PA 94301 790-J4
3600 SMCo 94063 770-F7
3600 RDWC 94063 770-F7
FLORENTINE ST
- SF 94112 687-F2
FLORES DR
1300 PCFA 94044 726-H4
FLORES ST
2200 SMTO 94403 749-B5
E FLORESTA WY
100 SMCo 94028 810-E3
W FLORESTA WY
200 SMCo 94028 810-E3
FLORIBUNDA AV
1200 BURL 94010 728-F7
1600 HIL 94010 728-F7
FLORIDA AV
100 SBRN 94066 707-J7
FLOURNOY ST
- DALY 94014 687-D2
100 SF 94112 687-D2
FLOWER ST
- RDWC 94063 769-J4
FLOWERS LN
3100 PA 94306 791-D7
FLYING CLOUD ISL
100 FCTY 94404 749-G2
FLYING FISH ST
900 FCTY 94404 749-G1
FLYING MIST ISL
100 FCTY 94404 749-G2
FLYNN AV
400 RDWC 94063 770-C6
FOGL CT
- SMCo 94061 790-B4
FOLGER CT
- BLMT 94002 769-D1
FOLGER DR
1500 BLMT 94002 769-D1
FOLKSTONE AV
600 SMTO 94402 749-B2
FONT BLVD
200 SF 94132 687-B1
FOOTE AV
- SF 94112 687-E1
FOOTHILL DR
600 PCFA 94044 707-B3
700 SMTO 94402 748-H4
900 SMCo 94015 687-A4
FOOTHILL EXWY
Rt#-G5
2600 SCIC 94304 810-J3
2600 PA 94304 810-J3
FOOTHILL ST
1100 RDWC 94061 789-H2
FORBES BLVD
300 SSF 94080 708-B3
FORD ST
400 DALY 94014 687-D4
FORDHAM RD
500 SMTO 94402 748-J2
FORDHAM ST
2400 EPA 94303 791-B1
2500 EPA 94303 771-C7
FORESAIL CT
200 FCTY 94404 749-G4
FOREST AV
100 PA 94301 790-J5
600 PA 94301 791-A3
1900 BLMT 94002 749-B7
2100 BLMT 94002 769-B1
FOREST CT
1000 PA 94301 791-A3
FOREST LN
- SBRN 94066 707-H6
- SCAR 94070 769-F5
100 MLPK 94025 790-E2
FOREST RD
- SMCo 94062 788-H4
FOREST GROVE DR
- DALY 94015 687-B3
FOREST LAKE DR
600 PCFA 94044 707-B3
FOREST PARK CT
200 PCFA 94044 707-A2
FOREST VIEW AV
- HIL 94010 728-D7
1500 BURL 94010 728-E7
FOREST VIEW DR
200 SSF 94080 707-G2
FOREST VIEW RD
- SMCo 94062 788-G3
FORGE RD
1400 SMCo 94402 748-F7
FORRESTAL LN
1100 FCTY 94404 749-G4
FORREST VIEW RD
- WDSD 94062 809-G3
FOSS DR
- RDWC 94062 789-G1
- RDWC 94062 769-H7
- SMCo 94062 769-H7

STREET Block City ZIP Pg-Grid

FOSTER ST
2600 SMTO 94403 749-D4
FOSTER CITY BLVD
300 FCTY 94404 749-F2
FOUNTAIN CIRCLE DR
- SMCo - 768-D4
W FOX CT
500 RDWC 94061 790-C1
FOX CROSSING CT
100 SMCo 94062 789-F1
FOX HILL RD
- SMCo 94062 809-G3
FOX HOLLOW LN
- RDWC 94061 789-F3
FOXHOLLOW LN
- DALY 94014 687-E3
FOX HOLLOW RD
100 WDSD 94062 789-G7
FOX PLAZA LN
1400 BURL 94010 728-G7
FOX SPARROW LN
- BSBN 94005 687-J5
FOXTAIL
- PTLV 94028 830-C1
FOXWOOD RD
100 SMCo 94028 830-D4
FRANCE AV
- SF 94112 687-F1
FRANCES AV
- PCFA 94044 707-A6
FRANCIS AV
1600 BLMT 94002 769-D1
FRANCIS CT
1700 BLMT 94002 769-D1
FRANCIS LN
200 RDWC 94070 769-G6
200 SCAR 94062 769-G6
200 SCAR 94070 769-G6
FRANCISCAN CT
2900 SCAR 94070 769-F6
FRANCISCAN DR
- DALY 94014 687-E5
FRANCISCAN RDGE
- PTLV 94028 830-C1
FRANCISCO BLVD
1600 PCFA 94044 706-J6
2200 PCFA 94044 707-A7
FRANCISCO DR
100 SSF 94080 707-G4
500 BURL 94010 728-G6
FRANCISCO ST
- SMCo 94018 767-A2
FRANKFORT ST
- DALY 94014 687-E3
FRANKLIN AV
- SSF 94080 707-H1
FRANKLIN ST
- RDWC 94063 770-B6
200 SMTO 94402 748-H2
500 SMCo 94037 746-G4
FRANKS LN
1400 SMCo 94025 790-D5
FRANZ CT
100 PCFA 94044 727-A1
FRATESSA CT
- SF 94134 688-A2
FREDERICK AV
- ATN 94027 790-H1
FREDERICK CT
- SMCo 94025 790-H1
FREDSON CT
- SF 94112 687-E2
FREMONT AV
200 PCFA 94044 707-A3
FREMONT PL
900 MLPK 94025 790-F4
FREMONT RD
500 SCIC 94305 790-F7
FREMONT ST
- SMCo 94037 746-H5
500 MLPK 94025 790-F4
N FREMONT ST
- SMTO 94401 728-J7
- SMTO 94401 749-A1
S FREMONT ST
- SMTO 94401 749-A1
400 SMTO 94402 749-A1
FREMONT WY
- SMCo 94020 809-F6
FREMONTIA
- PTLV 94028 830-C1
FRENCH CT
400 MLPK 94025 791-A3
FRENCH CREEK PL
- SMCo 94402 768-G2
FRENCHMANS RD
700 SCIC 94305 810-H2
FRENCHMANS CREEK RD
- HMBY 94019 767-E5
- SMCo - 767-E5
FRIARS LN
- WDSD 94062 809-G4
FRIENDLY CT
- RDWC 94063 770-F6
FRIGATE LN
- DALY 94014 687-E5
FROG VALLEY LN
200 BLMT 94002 749-F6
FRONTAGE RD
900 HMBY 94019 767-E6

FRONTERA WY
1200 MLBR 94030 728-A6
1200 BURL 94010 728-A6
FRWY I-280
- DALY - 687-C2
- DALY - 707-C1
- SF - 687-E1
- SF - 687-D2
FRWY I-380
- SBRN - 708-A6
- SBRN - 707-H6
- SMCo - 708-A6
- SSF - 708-A5
FUENTA AV
- SF 94132 687-B1
FULLER ST
300 RDWC 94063 770-A5
FULLERTON AV
400 PCFA 94044 707-A6
FULTON RD
400 SMTO 94402 748-F2
FULTON ST
- RDWC 94062 769-J6
100 PA 94301 790-J3
300 RDWC 94062 770-A7
600 PA 94301 791-A4
600 RDWC 94061 770-A7
1700 PA 94303 791-B5
FURLONG ST
1000 BLMT 94002 769-F1
FURTADO LN
400 SMCo 94019 767-D4

G

G ST
100 RDWC 94063 769-J4
GABARDA WY
100 SMCo 94028 810-D4
GAILEN AV
800 PA 94303 791-F7
GAILLARDIA WY
1100 EPA 94303 791-C3
GALINDO AV
- SF 94132 687-C2
GALLEON LN
700 FCTY 94404 749-G2
GALLEY LN
1000 FCTY 94404 749-H4
GALLOWRIDGE CT
- SMTO 94402 748-C7
GALVESTON DR
100 RDWC 94063 770-C4
GALVESTON ST
1000 FCTY 94404 749-F5
GALVEZ DR
1100 PCFA 94044 726-J5
GALVEZ ST
100 SCIC 94305 790-H6
GALWAY DR
2300 SSF 94080 707-D4
GALWAY PL
2400 SSF 94080 707-D5
GAMBETTA ST
- DALY 94014 687-D4
GARCES DR
- SF 94132 687-A1
GARCIA AV
200 HMBY 94019 787-E2
2300 MTVW 94043 791-G7
GARDEN AV
400 SBRN 94066 727-J1
GARDEN CT
- BLMT 94002 769-D2
300 PCFA 94044 706-J7
GARDEN DR
1900 BURL 94010 728-B5
GARDEN LN
- SCAR 94070 769-E3
- SMCo 94015 687-B4
- SMTO 94403 749-C6
100 MLBR 94030 728-C3
1300 MLPK 94025 790-E4
GARDEN ST
- RDWC 94063 769-J4
100 EPA 94303 791-A1
GARDEN GATEWAY
- SMCo 94015 687-B4
- DALY 94015 687-B4
GARDEN GROVE DR
- DALY 94015 686-J3
GARDENIA CT
- EPA 94303 791-D3
GARDENIA WY
100 EPA 94303 791-C3
GARDEN OF DEVOTION CIR
- SMCo - 768-C3
GARDENSIDE AV
200 SSF 94080 707-F1
GARDINER AV
- SSF 94080 708-A2
GARFIELD ST
- SF 94112 687-C1
- SF 94132 687-C1
2600 SMTO 94403 749-B5
GARIBALDI CT
- DALY 94014 687-D4
GARIBALDI ST
- DALY 94014 687-C4

GARLAND DR
100 MLPK 94025 790-F5
700 PA 94303 791-C5
GARLAND PL
- MLPK 94025 790-F5
GARNET AV
100 SCAR 94070 769-G5
GARRISON AV
- SF 94134 687-J2
GARVEY WY
- SMTO 94402 749-B3
GARWOOD DR
- DALY 94014 687-D3
GARWOOD WY
400 MLPK 94025 790-F3
GARY CT
400 PA 94306 791-C7
GASLIGHT LN
- SMCo 94070 769-E4
GASPAR CT
2700 PA 94306 791-C6
S GATE
- RDWC 94062 769-H7
GATESHEAD CT
700 FCTY 94404 749-G5
GATEWAY BLVD
200 SSF 94080 708-A3
GATEWAY DR
- DALY 94015 707-B1
- PCFA 94044 707-B1
1800 SMTO 94404 749-E3
1800 FCTY 94404 749-E3
GAVILAN CT
- MLBR 94030 728-A6
GAVILAN WY
1400 MLBR 94030 728-A6
GAYLORD ST
- SCAR 94070 769-G5
GAZOS CREEK RD
- SMCo 94060 (888-G5
See Page 867)
5200 SMCo 94060 (889-B3
See Page 869)
5400 SMCo 94020 (889-F4
See Page 869)
7500 SCrC 95006 (889-F4
See Page 869)
GEDDES CT
3900 SSF 94080 707-D4
GELLERT BLVD
300 DALY 94015 707-C2
2100 SSF 94080 707-D4
GEMINI LN
700 FCTY 94404 749-E4
GENEVA AV
- SF 94112 687-G2
500 RDWC 94061 790-B1
1300 SCAR 94070 769-H4
1600 SF 94134 687-G2
2100 DALY 94014 687-G2
3100 BSBN 94005 687-G2
3200 BSBN 94005 688-A3
3200 DALY 94014 688-A3
GENEVIEVE AV
300 PCFA 94044 727-A2
GENEVIEVE CT
3100 PA 94303 791-E6
GENEVRA RD
- HIL 94010 728-F7
GENG RD
1700 PA 94303 791-D3
GENOA DR
- RDWC 94065 749-J5
- RDWC 94065 750-C4
GEOFFREY DR
3100 SBRN 94066 707-D5
GEORGE AV
4100 SMTO 94403 749-D6
GEORGE ST
500 SMCo 94037 746-G4
GEORGETOWN AV
300 SMTO 94402 748-J3
GEORGETOWN CT
3600 SSF 94080 707-C4
GEORGETOWN ST
2700 EPA 94303 771-C7
GEORGIA AV
200 SBRN 94066 707-J7
200 SBRN 94066 727-J1
GEORGIA LN
100 PTLV 94028 810-C7
GERALDINE DR
600 MLBR 94030 728-A3
600 MLBR 94030 727-J3
GERALDINE WY
1200 BLMT 94002 769-D3
GERANIUM LN
- SCAR 94070 769-C4
GERI LN
2000 HIL 94010 728-D7
GERI PL
- SMCo 94062 789-G1
GERONA RD
400 SCIC 94305 810-H1
GERTH LN
2200 LAH 94304 810-H4
GERTRUDE CT
- EPA 94303 771-B7
GETZ ST
- SF 94112 687-E1

GIANTS DR
3000 SF 94124 688-C1
GIBBS WY
900 SSF 94080 707-D1
GIBRALTAR LN
500 FCTY 94404 749-F5
GILBERT AV
100 MLPK 94025 791-A2
300 MLPK 94025 790-J2
GILBERT CT
3600 SSF 94080 707-D4
GILBRETH RD
1500 BURL 94010 728-D4
GILLETTE AV
- SF 94134 688-B2
GILLIS DR
3900 SMTO 94403 749-D6
GILMAN AV
500 SF 94124 688-B1
GILMAN DR
1000 SMCo 94015 687-B5
1000 DALY 94015 687-B5
GILMAN ST
600 PA 94301 790-J4
GILROY ST
- SF 94124 688-C2
GIMERL LN
- RDWC 94065 750-C4
GINNIVER ST
2000 SMTO 94403 749-C4
GIRARD ST
700 SF 94134 688-A1
GLACIER AV
1000 PCFA 94044 727-C4
GLADYS AV
- BSBN 94005 688-B7
GLASGOW DR
400 PCFA 94044 707-B3
GLASGOW LN
100 SCAR 94070 769-F4
GLEN AV
1800 SBRN 94066 727-H2
GLEN PKWY
- BSBN 94005 688-A7
GLEN WY
900 HIL 94010 728-C7
2000 EPA 94303 791-B1
W GLEN WY
600 WDSD 94062 789-E3
GLEN AULIN LN
100 SMCo 94010 728-B7
100 SMCo 94010 748-B1
GLENBROOK AV
- DALY 94015 687-A6
GLENBROOK DR
- HIL 94010 748-G4
GLENBROOK LN
100 SBRN 94066 727-G1
GLENCOURT WY
300 PCFA 94044 707-B4
GLENCRAG WY
600 WDSD 94062 789-E3
GLENDALE AV
3000 SMCo 94063 790-D1
GLENDALE RD
300 HIL 94010 748-F2
300 SMTO 94402 748-F2
GLENDORA DR
1400 SMTO 94403 748-J6
GLEN EYRIE RD
- SMCo 94020 849-E1
GLENGARRY WY
- HIL 94010 748-F5
GLENLOCH WY
600 SMCo 94062 789-E1
GLENMERE WY
700 SMCo 94062 789-F2
GLENN WY
- SMCo 94002 769-G1
1500 RDWC 94061 790-A2
GLENNAN DR
500 RDWC 94061 789-H2
GLENROSE AV
- DALY 94015 687-A4
- DALY 94015 686-J4
GLENVIEW DR
700 SBRN 94066 727-F1
900 SBRN 94066 707-F7
GLENWOOD AV
100 ATN 94027 790-F2
100 DALY 94015 687-A3
100 WDSD 94062 789-G5
200 DALY 94015 686-J3
400 MLPK 94025 790-F2
3500 RDWC 94062 789-G1
GLENWOOD DR
1100 MLBR 94030 727-H3
GLENWOOD ST
300 SCAR 94070 769-F3
GLORIA CIR
- MLPK 94025 790-H2
GLORIA CT
- SF 94112 687-F1
600 SMTO 94401 749-B1
GLORIA WY
2400 EPA 94303 791-B1
2500 EPA 94303 771-B7
GLOUCESTER LN
600 FCTY 94404 749-G5

GODETIA DR
900 WDSD 94062 789-F4
GOETHE ST
- DALY 94014 687-D2
- SF 94112 687-D2
GOETTINGEN ST
800 SF 94134 688-A1
GOLDEN ASTER CT
- BSBN 94005 687-H4
GOLDEN BAY DR
200 PCFA 94044 707-A2
GOLDEN EAGLE LN
- BSBN 94005 687-J4
GOLDEN GATE AV
500 HMBY 94019 767-F6
GOLDEN HILLS DR
100 PTLV 94028 810-C5
GOLDEN OAK DR
- PTLV 94028 810-D5
GOLDENRIDGE CT
- SMTO 94402 748-C7
GOLDHUNTER CT
100 FCTY 94404 749-G2
GOLF LN
- SCIC 94304 810-E3
- SMCo 94025 810-E3
GOLF COURSE DR
- SMCo - 748-B2
- HIL - 748-B2
- SMCo 94010 748-B2
GOLF COURSE RD
6600 SMCo 94010 748-D4
GONZAGA ST
2400 EPA 94303 791-C1
2500 EPA 94303 771-C7
GONZALEZ DR
- SF 94132 687-A1
GOODMAN RD
400 PCFA 94044 707-A6
GOODWIN AV
1900 RDWC 94061 789-J2
3000 RDWC 94061 790-A2
GOODWIN CT
- RDWC 94061 789-H3
GOODWIN DR
100 SBRN 94066 707-D6
GORDON AV
800 BLMT 94002 769-E1
2000 SMCo 94025 790-D6
GORDON ST
1200 RDWC 94061 790-A1
GORDON WY
100 PCFA 94044 707-A3
GORDON MILL TR
- SMCo 94062 809-A3
GOULD ST
- SF 94124 688-B1
GOULSON ST
- SMCo 94060 (868-B2
See Page 867)
GOVER LN
1500 SCAR 94070 769-H5
GOVERNORS AV
500 SCIC 94305 790-G7
GOVERNORS BAY DR
900 RDWC 94065 750-A5
GOYA RD
100 PTLV 94028 810-C4
GRACE AV
100 EPA 94303 791-B1
GRACE DR
500 MLPK 94025 790-E6
GRACELAND AV
2400 SCAR 94070 769-F5
GRACELAND LN
- SCAR 94070 769-F5
GRAFTON AV
- SF 94112 687-D1
GRAMERCY DR
100 SMTO 94402 748-H1
GRANADA AV
- SF 94112 687-D1
GRANADA CT
- PTLV 94028 810-D6
GRANADA DR
- PCFA 94044 727-A4
300 SSF 94080 707-F5
1000 PCFA 94044 726-J4
1500 BURL 94010 728-B6
GRANADA ST
800 BLMT 94002 749-E7
1000 BLMT 94002 769-F1
GRAND AV
300 SSF 94080 707-F2
1300 PCFA 94044 726-G4
E GRAND AV
- SSF 94080 708-A3
- SSF 94080 707-J3
GRAND BLVD
- SMTO 94401 748-H1
- SMTO 94401 728-H7
300 HMBY 94019 767-E7
GRAND ST
- RDWC 94062 769-J6
400 RDWC 94062 770-A7
900 RDWC 94061 770-A7
GRAND TETON DR
1000 PCFA 94044 727-B5
GRANDVIEW AV
- DALY 94015 687-A7

GRANDVIEW BLVD
500 HMBY 94019 767-E6
GRANDVIEW DR
- WDSD 94062 809-G5
400 SSF 94080 708-C3
GRANELLI AV
100 HMBY 94019 787-E2
GRANGER WY
1500 RDWC 94061 789-J3
GRANITE CT
- SCAR 94070 769-F6
GRANT AV
100 PA 94306 791-B7
E GRANT PL
800 SMTO 94402 749-B2
W GRANT PL
800 SMTO 94402 749-B2
GRANT RD
- SMCo 94037 746-H5
N GRANT ST
- SMTO 94401 729-A7
- SMTO 94401 749-A1
100 SMTO 94401 728-J7
S GRANT ST
- SMTO 94403 749-C3
- SMTO 94401 749-A1
400 SMTO 94402 749-A1
GRAYSON CT
300 MLPK 94025 791-A1
300 MLPK 94025 790-J1
GRAYSTONE DR
- SSF 94080 707-D1
GRAYSTONE LN
- DALY 94014 687-E3
GREBE ST
1000 FCTY 94404 749-H2
GREEN AV
100 SSF 94080 708-A2
500 SBRN 94066 707-H6
GREEN CT
500 PA 94301 791-C6
GREEN RDGE
- DALY 94014 687-D4
GREEN ST
100 MLPK 94025 791-A2
100 EPA 94303 791-B2
GREENBRIAR WY
- HIL 94010 748-H3
GREENBRIER CT
- HMBY 94019 787-F5
GREENBRIER DR
1200 SCAR 94070 769-E6
GREENBRIER RD
300 HMBY 94019 787-F5
GREENDALE DR
2100 SSF 94080 707-C4
GREENDALE WY
300 SMCo 94062 769-F7
GREENFIELD AV
200 SMTO 94403 749-C7
GREENFIELD CT
- SMTO 94403 749-C7
- BLMT 94002 749-C7
GREEN HILLS CT
- MLBR 94030 728-A3
GREEN HILLS DR
200 MLBR 94030 728-A3
GREENOAK CT
3000 SMTO 94403 748-J6
3100 SMTO 94403 749-A7
GREENOAKS DR
- ATN 94027 770-F7
100 ATN 94027 790-G1
GREENPARK TER
- SSF 94014 707-J1
GREEN VIEW DR
- DALY 94014 687-E3
GREENVIEW LN
- HIL 94010 728-E7
GREENWAY DR
200 PCFA 94044 707-A7
200 PCFA 94044 706-J7
GREENWAYS DR
2100 SMCo 94062 790-A5
E GREENWICH DR
700 PA 94303 791-C5
GREENWICH LN
600 FCTY 94404 749-F5
GREENWOOD AV
800 SMTO 94402 728-G7
800 SMTO 94402 748-G1
1000 PA 94301 791-B4
1100 SCAR 94070 769-G5
GREENWOOD DR
- SSF 94080 707-G6
1000 MLPK 94025 770-G7
GREENWOOD LN
- RDWC 94063 770-C6
GREENWOOD PL
- MLPK 94025 770-G7
GREENWOOD WY
1400 SBRN 94066 707-E6
GREER RD
100 SMCo 94062 789-D6
100 WDSD 94062 789-D6
500 PA 94303 791-C4
GREGORY LN
200 RDWC 94061 790-B2
GRENADA LN
800 FCTY 94404 749-G4

GRESHAM LN
- ATN 94027 790-C1
GREVILLEA CT
- HIL 94010 748-C2
GRIFFIN AV
400 PCFA 94044 707-A6
GRIFFITH ST
1000 SF 94124 688-C1
GRIJALVA DR
- SF 94132 687-B1
GROVE AV
100 SSF 94080 707-J1
1100 BURL 94010 728-D5
3700 PA 94303 791-E7
GROVE CT
- PTLV 94028 810-B7
GROVE DR
- PTLV 94028 810-B6
GROVE ST
200 HMBY 94019 787-F2
GROVELAND ST
- PTLV 94028 830-C1
GRUNDY LN
900 SBRN 94066 707-G6
GRUNION CT
- FCTY 94404 749-H3
GUADALUPE AV
- DALY 94014 687-C2
600 MLBR 94030 727-J2
GUADALUPE CANYON PKWY
- DALY 94014 687-E4
- BSBN 94005 688-A4
300 SMCo 94014 687-E4
300 BSBN 94005 687-E4
GUARDIAN WY
- SMCo 94020 849-E1
GUERRERO AV
- HMBY 94019 767-D4
GUILDFORD AV
500 SMTO 94402 749-B2
GUINDA ST
300 PA 94301 790-J3
500 PA 94301 791-A4
1700 PA 94303 791-B5
GUITTARD RD
- BURL 94010 728-C4
GULL AV
600 FCTY 94404 749-G1
GULL RD
700 SSF 94080 708-C2
GUM ST
1600 SMTO 94402 749-B3
GUNTER LN
300 RDWC 94065 749-H7
GUTHRIE WY
- SMCo 94021 849-B7
GUTTENBERG ST
- SF 94112 687-F2
300 DALY 94014 687-F2
GYMKHANA RD
400 SMTO 94403 749-A4
GYPSY HILL RD
- PCFA 94044 707-A6

H

H ST
- SF 94124 688-E1
HACIENDA CT
- PCFA 94044 707-A4
HACIENDA ST
2200 SMTO 94403 749-B4
HACIENDA WY
600 MLBR 94030 727-J3
HACIENDAS DR
- WDSD 94062 789-H6
HADDOCK ST
800 FCTY 94404 749-H3
HADDON DR
900 SMTO 94402 749-B2
HAHN ST
- SF 94134 687-J2
HAIGHT ST
100 MLPK 94025 791-A1
HAINLINE DR
400 BLMT 94002 749-D7
HALE DR
2100 BURL 94010 728-C6
HALE ST
400 PA 94301 791-A3
HALF MOON LN
300 DALY 94015 707-C1
HALF MOON BAY RD
- HMBY 94019 767-G7
HALF MOON BAY RD Rt#-92
- HMBY 94019 787-G1
200 HMBY 94019 767-H7
300 SMCo - 767-J6
2900 SMCo - 768-E3
2900 SMCo 94062 768-E3
HALIBUT ST
1300 FCTY 94404 749-H3
HALL ST
900 SCAR 94070 769-G3
HALLING WY
1200 PCFA 94044 726-G4
HALLMARK CIR
- MLPK 94025 790-C6

HALLMARK DR
2400 BLMT 94002 769-A2
HALSEY AV
1400 SMTO 94403 749-C2
2600 SMCo 94063 770-C6
HALSEY BLVD
900 FCTY 94404 749-G4
HALYARD LN
300 FCTY 94404 749-G6
HAMILTON AV
- PA 94301 790-J5
100 MLPK 94025 770-J7
600 MLPK 94025 771-A7
700 PA 94301 791-A3
1500 PA 94303 791-B3
2200 SBRN 94066 707-F7
HAMILTON CT
- PA 94301 791-A3
- PCFA 94044 707-A3
900 MLPK 94025 771-A7
HAMILTON LN
1100 BURL 94010 728-C5
W HAMILTON RD
200 SMCo 94062 788-H7
200 SMCo 94062 (808-H1
See Page 788)
HAMILTON ST
500 RDWC 94063 770-A6
600 SF 94134 688-A1
HAMILTON WY
3700 RDWC 94062 789-G2
3700 SMCo 94062 789-G2
HAMLET ST
1700 SMTO 94403 749-C2
HAMPSHIRE AV
- DALY 94015 707-C2
400 SMCo 94063 770-D7
HAMPSHIRE CT
200 DALY 94015 707-D3
HAMPTON AV
1600 RDWC 94061 790-A2
HAMPTON CT
- HIL 94010 748-E6
100 SBRN 94066 707-F7
HAMPTON LN
1700 DALY 94014 687-F3
HANCOCK AV
1300 SMTO 94403 749-C2
HANCOCK ST
800 RDWC 94063 770-B7
HANDBURY LN
500 FCTY 94404 749-G5
HANDLEY TR
600 SMCo 94062 789-F1
HANNA WY
- MLPK 94025 790-H2
HANOVER ST
- SF 94112 687-D3
400 DALY 94014 687-D3
2000 PA 94306 810-J1
HANSEN WY
1000 RDWC 94063 770-C5
HAPPY HOLLOW LN
- SMCo 94025 810-E1
HARBOR BLVD
100 SMCo 94002 769-F1
700 BLMT 94002 769-F2
HARBOR DR
- DALY 94014 687-E5
HARBOR WY
100 SSF 94080 708-A3
HARBOR COLONY CT
500 RDWC 94065 749-H6
HARBOR SEAL CT
100 SMTO 94404 749-D3
HARBOUR DR
100 SMCo 94018 767-A1
100 SMCo 94018 766-J1
HARCOURT WY
1300 HIL 94010 748-F6
HARCROSS RD
100 RDWC 94061 789-J3
100 WDSD 94062 789-J3
HARDING AV
1800 RDWC 94062 769-H7
2000 SMTO 94403 749-C2
2000 SMCo 94062 769-H7
2300 RDWC 94062 789-H1
HARDWICK RD
100 WDSD 94062 789-H4
HARKER AV
1000 PA 94301 791-B4
HARKINS AV
2100 SMCo 94025 790-D7
2100 MLPK 94025 790-D7
HARKINS RD
100 SMCo 94062 788-G4
HARKINS FIRE TR
- SMCo 94019 788-D5
- SMCo 94062 788-D5
HARKNESS AV
- SF 94134 688-A1
HARMON DR
900 MLPK 94025 770-G7
HARNEY RD
- BSBN 94005 688-B3
- SF 94134 688-B3
HARNEY WY
- SF 94134 688-C2
- SF 94124 688-C2

HAROLD AV
- SF 94112 687-E1
HAROLD RD
- SMCo 94014 688-B7
100 BSBN 94005 688-B7
HARRIET ST
900 PA 94301 791-B4
E HARRIS AV
200 SSF 94080 708-A3
W HARRIS AV
100 SSF 94080 708-A4
HARRIS CT
200 SSF 94080 708-A3
HARRISON AV
100 RDWC 94062 770-A6
800 RDWC 94062 769-J7
2000 SMTO 94403 749-C2
HARRISON WY
- SMCo 94025 790-E6
HARROW AV
600 SMTO 94402 749-B2
HARTE AV
600 SMCo 94037 746-G4
HARTFORD AV
- SCAR 94070 769-E2
HARVARD AV
- SMCo 94038 766-H2
600 MLPK 94025 790-G5
HARVARD CT
14500 LAH 94022 810-H5
HARVARD RD
200 SMTO 94402 748-H2
HARVARD ST
2000 PA 94306 810-J1
HARVEST DR
3800 RDWC 94061 789-G3
HARVESTER DR
600 FCTY 94404 749-G2
HARVEY WY
400 PCFA 94044 726-J2
HASKINS DR
3300 BLMT 94002 749-B7
3300 SMTO 94403 749-B7
HASKINS WY
100 SSF 94080 708-C4
HASSLER RD
- SMCo 94070 769-D7
HASTINGS AV
2500 RDWC 94061 789-H2
HASTINGS DR
2200 BLMT 94002 769-C2
HASTINGS SHORE LN
200 RDWC 94065 749-H7
HATCH DR
300 FCTY 94404 749-F1
HATTERAS CT
1000 FCTY 94404 749-F5
HAUSSMAN CT
3900 SSF 94080 707-C4
HAVEN AV
700 SSF 94080 707-F4
800 RDWC 94063 770-F6
3500 MLPK 94025 770-G6
3500 SMCo 94063 770-F6
HAVEN CT
3700 MLPK 94025 770-G6
HAVEN DR
- DALY 94014 687-E5
HAVENRIDGE CT
- SMTO 94402 748-C7
HAWES CT
1500 RDWC 94061 790-A1
HAWES ST
600 RDWC 94061 769-J7
1200 RDWC 94061 790-A1
2300 SF 94124 688-B1
HAWK VW
- PTLV 94028 830-D1
HAWKSBURY LN
400 FCTY 94404 749-F5
HAWSER LN
1500 HMBY 94019 767-E6
HAWTHORNE AV
100 PA 94301 790-H4
400 SBRN 94066 727-H1
HAWTHORNE DR
- ATN 94027 790-F1
1000 SMTO 94402 749-B2
HAWTHORNE PL
600 SSF 94080 707-J2
HAWTHORNE ST
- SMCo 94037 746-G5
HAWTHORNE WY
800 MLBR 94030 728-B5
HAYDON CT
- BLMT 94002 769-B3
HAYFIELDS RD
- WDSD 94062 809-J5
- PTLV 94028 809-J5
HAYNE RD
500 HIL 94010 748-G2
HAYWARD AV
- SMTO 94401 749-A2
HAYWARD CT
- BURL 94010 728-C6
HAYWARD DR
2500 BURL 94010 728-B6
HAZEL AV
- MLBR 94030 728-A4
- RDWC 94061 770-B7

HAZEL AV
300 SBRN 94066 727-H1
500 SBRN 94066 707-H7
HAZEL LN
- SMCo 94060 (868-J4
See Page 867)
HAZELWOOD DR
- SSF 94080 707-F5
HAZELWOOD WY
2500 EPA 94303 791-B1
2500 EPA 94303 771-B7
HEACOX RD
- SMCo 94028 830-C6
HEAD ST
- SF 94112 687-C2
200 SF 94132 687-C2
HEATH CT
- DALY 94015 707-B2
HEATHCLIFF DR
300 PCFA 94044 707-B3
HEATHER CT
600 PCFA 94044 707-B4
HEATHER DR
- ATN 94027 790-F1
800 SCAR 94070 769-F4
HEATHER LN
100 PA 94303 791-C4
400 SMTO 94403 749-B6
2500 SBRN 94066 707-E6
HEATHER PL
- HIL 94010 748-E5
- MLBR 94030 728-A2
HEATHER RD
800 SMCo 94015 687-B5
HEATHER WY
300 SSF 94080 707-G2
HEDGE RD
100 MLPK 94025 770-G7
HEIDI LN
- MLBR 94030 728-A4
HELEN DR
200 MLBR 94030 728-A3
500 MLBR 94030 727-H3
HELEN PL
- MLPK 94025 790-F5
HELENA WY
2000 SMCo 94061 790-A4
HELENE CT
1800 SMTO 94401 729-C7
1800 SMTO 94401 749-C1
HELLER ST
200 RDWC 94063 770-B6
HELM LN
1000 FCTY 94404 749-H4
HEMLOCK AV
- RDWC 94061 770-B7
300 RDWC 94061 790-B1
400 SSF 94080 707-H1
500 MLBR 94030 728-B3
1400 SMTO 94401 749-C1
HEMLOCK ST
100 SCAR 94070 769-G4
HEMPSTEAD PL
1700 RDWC 94061 790-A3
HENDERSON AV
1000 MLPK 94025 790-J1
1100 MLPK 94025 770-J7
HENDERSON PL
- MLPK 94025 770-J7
HENRIK IBSEN RD
- SMCo 94062 788-J5
HENRY CT
- EPA 94303 791-B2
HENRY PL
- MLBR 94030 728-A3
HENSLEY AV
600 SBRN 94066 707-H6
HERCULES LN
800 FCTY 94404 749-H1
HERITAGE CT
- ATN 94027 790-E1
- BLMT 94002 768-J2
HERKNER RD
- RDWC 94063 770-D2
HERMAN ST
1000 SBRN 94066 707-J5
HERMOSA AV
- MLBR 94030 728-B3
400 SMCo 94019 767-D4
1200 PCFA 94044 726-H5
HERMOSA LN
- SSF 94080 707-F3
HERMOSA PL
- MLPK 94025 790-F5
HERMOSA RD
- SMCo 94037 746-J5
- SMCo 94062 769-F7
HERMOSA ST
- SBRN 94066 707-J6
HERMOSA WY
300 MLPK 94025 790-E4
HERSCHEL ST
1700 SMTO 94403 749-D2
HESKETH CT
- MLPK 94025 790-E5
HESKETH DR
- MLPK 94025 790-E5
HESS RD
1400 RDWC 94061 770-B7
1400 RDWC 94061 790-B1

SAN MATEO CO.

INDEX

STREET
Block City ZIP Pg-Grid

HESTER AV
- SF 94134 688-B2
HEWITT DR
1000 SCAR 94070 769-F4
HIAWATHA AV
100 PCFA 94044 727-B2
HIBBERT CT
- PCFA 94044 707-A3
HIBISCUS CT
400 EPA 94303 791-D2
HICKEY BLVD
100 PCFA 94044 707-A3
100 SSF 94080 707-B1
300 DALY 94015 707-B1
HICKORY AV
1600 SBRN 94066 707-G7
HICKORY LN
100 SMTO 94403 749-B6
HICKORY PL
700 SSF 94080 707-J2
HIDDEN TER
- HIL 94010 728-D7
HIDDEN OAKS DR
1100 MLPK 94025 790-E5
HIDDEN VALLEY DR
- SMCo 94070 769-E4
HIDDEN VALLEY LN
- PTLV 94028 810-A5
- WDSD 94062 810-A5
HIGATE DR
100 DALY 94015 687-A6
100 DALY 94015 707-A1
HIGGINS PL
3000 PA 94303 791-E5
HIGGINS WY
1500 PCFA 94044 726-H5
1500 SMCo - 726-H5
HIGGINS PURISIMA RD
300 HMBY 94019 787-G3
300 SMCo 94019 787-G3
2700 SMCo 94019 788-A4
HIGH RD
- WDSD 94062 790-A5
800 WDSD 94062 789-J5
HIGH ST
200 PA 94301 790-H4
2100 PA 94301 791-B7
HIGHCREST LN
1200 SSF 94080 707-H1
HIGHGATE AV
2800 BLMT 94002 749-B7
HIGH GATE LN
- HIL 94010 728-F7
HIGHLAND AV
- BURL 94010 728-G7
- DALY 94015 686-J6
- SCAR 94070 769-E2
- SMCo 94018 767-C1
- SSF 94080 707-J1
300 SMTO 94401 728-G7
500 HMBY 94019 767-F7
600 SMTO 94401 748-H1
3500 RDWC 94062 789-H1
HIGHLAND CT
- BLMT 94002 769-B3
1200 SCAR 94070 769-B3
HIGHLAND DR
3100 SBRN 94066 707-B6
HIGHLAND TER
100 WDSD 94062 789-G5
HIGHVIEW CT
600 SMTO 94403 749-B7
HIGHVIEW DR
4200 SMTO 94403 749-B7
4200 SMTO 94403 769-B1
HIGHWAY Rt#-9
- SCrC 95006 (870-J3
See Page 869)
- SCrC 95006 (890-J1
See Page 869)
- SMCo 94020 (870-J3
See Page 869)
- SMCo 94020 (890-J1
See Page 869)
HIGHWAY Rt#-236
- SCrC 95006 (890-D3
See Page 869)
HIGHWAY RD
1400 BURL 94010 728-D5
HIGUERA AV
- SF 94132 687-A1
HIHN HAMMOND RD
- SCrC 95006 (889-J7
See Page 869)
- SCrC 95006 (890-A7
See Page 869)
HILBAR LN
500 PA 94303 791-C4
HILL AV
- SCAR 94070 769-F5
700 SSF 94080 707-G4
1300 MLPK 94025 770-H7
S HILL BLVD
- SF 94112 687-G2
300 DALY 94014 687-F3
HILL RD
- SMCo 94060 867-G3
HILL ST
- DALY 94014 687-C5
- SMCo 94037 746-G5

HILL ST
- SMCo 94014 687-C5
800 BLMT 94002 769-E1
HILL WY
300 SCAR 94070 769-G5
HILLARY LN
- SMCo 94061 790-B4
HILLBARN CT
4200 SMTO 94403 749-D7
HILLBROOK DR
- PTLV 94028 810-D6
HILLCREST BLVD
- SMCo - 727-J5
- MLBR 94030 728-A4
1100 MLBR 94030 727-J5
E HILLCREST BLVD
- MLBR 94030 728-B3
HILLCREST CT
- SSF 94080 707-F3
HILLCREST DR
- SMCo - 768-C3
- DALY 94014 687-C3
400 RDWC 94062 769-G7
400 RDWC 94062 789-H1
400 SMCo 94062 769-G7
3400 BLMT 94002 769-A1
HILLCREST RD
- SCAR 94070 769-F2
400 SMTO 94402 748-F1
500 SMCo 94062 769-G7
500 RDWC 94062 769-G7
HILLCREST WY
400 SMCo 94062 789-E2
HILLER ST
100 BLMT 94002 749-E7
1000 BLMT 94002 769-F1
HILLMAN AV
1700 BLMT 94002 749-D7
1900 BLMT 94002 769-C1
HILLSBOROUGH BLVD
300 HIL 94010 748-F1
300 SMTO 94402 748-F1
800 HIL 94010 728-F7
HILLSDALE AV
- DALY 94015 687-B3
E HILLSDALE BLVD
- SMTO 94403 749-D5
600 FCTY 94404 749-F1
W HILLSDALE BLVD
- SMTO 94403 749-A6
800 SMTO 94403 748-J6
1700 SMTO 94402 748-J6
HILLSDALE CT
- SMTO 94403 749-D5
HILLSDALE PL
- SMTO 94403 749-A6
HILLSDALE WY
200 SMCo 94062 769-F7
200 SMCo 94062 789-E1
HILLSIDE AV
100 SMCo 94025 790-C6
HILLSIDE BLVD
- DALY 94014 687-D4
100 SSF 94080 708-A2
100 SSF 94080 707-J1
1000 SMCo 94014 687-D4
1300 CLMA 94014 687-D6
1400 SMCo 94014 707-G1
1700 CLMA 94014 707-G1
1700 SSF 94080 687-D6
HILLSIDE CIR
1300 BURL 94010 728-C6
HILLSIDE CT
100 WDSD 94062 790-A5
3700 SMTO 94403 749-B6
HILLSIDE DR
100 WDSD 94062 789-G5
200 PCFA 94044 727-A2
1500 BURL 94010 728-D6
1500 SMCo 94010 728-B7
HILLSIDE LN
3100 BURL 94010 728-A7
3100 SMCo 94010 728-A7
HILLSIDE RD
500 RDWC 94062 789-G1
500 SMCo 94062 789-G1
HILLTOP DR
- RDWC 94062 769-G6
- SCAR 94070 769-G5
HILLTOP RD
- SMTO 94402 748-H1
HILLVIEW AV
- RDWC 94062 769-H6
HILLVIEW CT
- BURL 94010 728-C7
- DALY 94015 686-J5
HILLVIEW DR
- SMCo - 768-C3
1100 MLPK 94025 790-E5
HILLVIEW PL
- MLPK 94025 790-E5
HILLWAY DR
300 SMCo 94062 789-G1
HILO WY
300 PCFA 94044 707-A6
HILTON AV
100 SSF 94080 707-D1
HILTON LN
100 PCFA 94044 706-J6

HILTON ST
100 RDWC 94063 770-B6
HILTON WY
100 PCFA 94044 706-J6
HIMMEL AV
1100 SMCo 94061 790-B3
HINCKLEY RD
800 BURL 94010 728-D4
HINMAN RD
- RDWC 94063 770-D2
HINTON RANCH RD
- PCFA 94044 727-A4
HOBART AV
- SMTO 94402 749-A3
200 SMTO 94402 748-J3
HOBART ST
500 MLPK 94025 790-E5
HOBART HEIGHTS RD
100 WDSD 94062 789-H6
HOFFMAN ST
- SMCo 94014 687-D5
- CLMA 94014 687-D5
300 DALY 94014 687-D5
HOLBROOK LN
- ATN 94027 790-E1
HOLDEN CT
- PTLV 94028 810-D6
HOLIDAY CT
- PCFA 94044 707-A2
- PCFA 94044 706-J2
HOLLAND ST
100 EPA 94303 791-A1
2300 SMTO 94403 749-D4
HOLLISTER AV
900 SF 94124 688-B1
HOLLOWAY AV
- SF 94112 687-C1
900 SF 94132 687-B1
HOLLY AV
200 SSF 94080 707-F2
1600 SBRN 94066 707-G7
1700 MLPK 94025 790-E6
HOLLY CT
- HIL 94010 748-D1
HOLLY RD
700 BLMT 94002 769-E1
HOLLY ST
- RDWC 94065 769-G2
- SCAR 94070 769-G2
- SMCo 94002 769-G2
- SMCo 94070 769-G2
1000 SCAR 94070 769-G2
HOLLYBURNE AV
- MLPK 94025 771-A7
1000 MLPK 94025 790-J1
1100 MLPK 94025 770-J7
HOLLY HILL CT
700 RDWC 94061 789-H2
HOLLY OAK DR
700 PA 94303 791-D7
HOLLYWOOD CT
- SF 94112 687-F2
HOLYOKE ST
- SF 94134 688-A1
HOME RD
- WDSD 94062 809-H4
HOMEPLACE CT
- HIL 94010 748-E2
HOMER AV
- PA 94301 790-J5
400 PA 94301 791-A4
HOMER LN
- SMCo 94025 810-F1
HOMEWOOD AV
1200 SMTO 94403 748-J7
E HOMEWOOD PL
- MLPK 94025 790-H3
HOMS CT
- HIL 94010 748-H2
HONEYSUCKLE LN
- SCAR 94070 769-C4
HOODS POINT WY
- SMCo 94402 768-G1
HOOPER WY
- WDSD 94062 809-G1
HOOVER AV
1500 BURL 94010 728-C6
HOOVER ST
1200 MLPK 94025 790-F3
3000 RDWC 94063 770-E6
HOPKINS AV
500 RDWC 94063 770-A5
1000 RDWC 94062 769-J6
1000 RDWC 94063 769-J6
1100 PA 94301 791-B5
HORGAN AV
- RDWC 94061 790-B2
HORIZON WY
300 PCFA 94044 707-B3
HORNET AV
200 SSF 94066 707-J5
HORSESHOE BEND
- PTLV 94028 830-C1
HORSESHOE CT
- HIL 94402 748-H4
HORSESHOE DR
- PTLV 94028 809-J6
HOSKINS CT
- SCIC 94305 790-J7

HOSMER CT
300 SCAR 94070 769-D7
HOSMER ST
2600 SMTO 94403 749-D4
HOSPITAL PZ
- MLPK 94025 790-J2
HOUNDSBRIDGE LN
- SMTO 94402 748-H6
HOWARD AV
- BURL 94010 728-H6
900 SCAR 94070 769-H4
1000 SMTO 94401 728-H6
HOWARD CT
3800 SSF 94080 707-C4
HOWARD ST
1100 MLPK 94025 770-J7
HOWARD WY
- ATN 94027 790-E3
HOWE ST
700 SMTO 94401 749-B1
HOWELLS ST
- SMCo 94037 746-H5
HOWLAND ST
200 RDWC 94063 769-J5
200 RDWC 94063 770-A5
HOWLAND HILL LN
- SMCo 94010 728-B7
HOWTH ST
- SF 94112 687-E1
HUBBARD AV
200 SMCo 94062 769-G6
HUCKLEBERRY AV
300 SMCo 94062 788-G5
HUCKLEBERRY CT
- BSBN 94005 687-H4
HUCKLEBERRY TR
- SMCo 94062 788-H5
HUDSON CT
1100 SCAR 94070 769-E6
HUDSON ST
- RDWC 94062 769-J6
500 RDWC 94062 770-A7
600 RDWC 94061 770-A7
1200 RDWC 94061 790-B1
HUDSON BAY ST
200 FCTY 94404 749-F5
HULL AV
1700 SMCo 94061 790-A3
HULL DR
1200 SCAR 94070 769-F2
HULL LN
1000 FCTY 94404 749-H4
HULME CT
- SCIC 94305 790-J7
HUMBOLDT CT
- PCFA 94044 727-C5
HUMBOLDT RD
- BSBN 94005 688-A6
HUMBOLDT ST
- BURL 94010 728-H6
- SMTO 94401 728-H6
N HUMBOLDT ST
- SMTO 94401 729-A7
- SMTO 94401 728-J6
S HUMBOLDT ST
- SMTO 94401 729-A7
- SMTO 94401 749-A1
400 SMTO 94402 749-A1
HUNT DR
1600 BURL 94010 728-A6
HUNTER ST
2700 EPA 94303 771-B7
HUNTERS POINT EXWY
- SF 94124 688-C2
HUNTINGTON AV
200 SBRN 94066 728-A1
200 SBRN 94066 727-J1
200 SBRN 94066 707-J7
1300 SSF 94080 707-H4
2800 SMCo 94063 770-C7
HUNTINGTON AV E
1000 SBRN 94066 707-J5
HUNTINGTON DR
- DALY 94015 687-A6
HURLINGAME AV
400 SMCo 94063 770-D6
HURLINGHAM AV
400 SMTO 94402 728-G7
400 SMTO 94402 748-G1
HURON AV
- DALY 94014 687-E2
100 SMTO 94401 729-A7
400 SF 94112 687-E2
HURON CT
- SMTO 94401 729-A7
HUSSEY ST
- SF 94124 688-E1
HUTCHINSON AV
900 PA 94301 791-B4
HYDE CT
- DALY 94015 707-D3
HYDE ST
- RDWC 94062 769-J5
HYDE PARK AV
100 SMCo 94070 769-D4
100 SCAR 94070 769-D4
HYDRA LN
700 FCTY 94404 749-E4

I

I ST
200 SF 94124 688-E1
IDA DR
700 SSF 94080 707-G2
IDAHO CT
2000 RDWC 94061 790-A3
N IDAHO ST
- SMTO 94401 728-J6
200 SMTO 94401 729-A7
S IDAHO ST
400 SMTO 94402 749-B1
800 SMTO 94401 729-A7
800 SMTO 94401 749-A1
IDALENE ST
- DALY 94014 687-G3
IDLEWILD CT
- PCFA 94044 707-B3
IDYLLWILD AV
1800 SMCo 94061 790-B4
IDYLLWILD CT
300 SMCo 94061 790-B4
IGNACIO ST
- SF 94124 688-C2
ILLINOIS ST
2400 EPA 94303 791-C1
2500 EPA 94303 771-C7
IMPERIAL DR
200 PCFA 94044 707-B2
IMPERIAL WY
300 DALY 94015 707-C1
INA CT
- SF 94112 687-H1
INDEPENDENCE DR
100 MLPK 94025 770-G6
INDIAN AV
600 SMTO 94401 728-J7
INDIAN CRSG
- PTLV 94028 830-C1
INDIAN DR
2400 PA 94303 791-D5
INDIO DR
100 SSF 94080 707-E3
INDUSTRIAL AV
800 PA 94303 791-G7
INDUSTRIAL RD
- SMCo 94002 769-H2
- SCAR 94070 769-H2
1400 RDWC 94063 769-H2
1400 SCAR 94063 769-H2
INDUSTRIAL WY
- BSBN 94005 688-A4
100 SSF 94080 708-A3
1300 RDWC 94063 770-A4
1500 SMCo 94062 769-G1
1500 RDWC 94063 769-G1
INGALLS ST
2500 SF 94124 688-C1
INGERSON AV
700 SF 94124 688-B1
INGLEWOOD LN
- ATN 94027 790-D3
INGOLD RD
- BURL 94010 728-C4
INNER CIR
- RDWC 94062 769-H7
INNISFREE CIR
300 DALY 94015 707-C1
INNISFREE DR
300 DALY 94015 707-C1
INTREPID LN
800 RDWC 94065 750-C6
INVERNESS DR
300 PCFA 94044 707-B3
900 SCAR 94070 769-G2
INVERNESS RD
- HMBY 94019 787-F5
INVERNESS WY
- HIL 94010 748-F4
INYO CT
100 SBRN 94066 707-E7
INYO PL
- SMCo 94061 790-B4
INYO ST
- BSBN 94005 688-A6
IOWA DR
400 SMTO 94402 748-H3
IRENE CT
100 BLMT 94002 749-D7
IRIS CT
- SMTO 94401 729-A6
- SSF 94080 707-G1
800 PCFA 94044 726-H5
IRIS LN
- MLPK 94025 770-H7
- SCAR 94070 769-C4
IRIS ST
- RDWC 94062 769-J6
500 RDWC 94062 770-A7
600 RDWC 94061 770-A7
IRIS WY
100 PA 94303 791-E7
IRISH RIDGE RD
100 SMCo 94019 (808-D3
See Page 788)
IROQUOIS TR
- PTLV 94028 810-B6

IRVING AV
- ATN 94027 770-F7
- ATN 94027 790-F1
IRVING ST
- SSF 94080 707-J1
200 SMTO 94402 748-H3
1100 SMCo 94037 746-G5
IRVINGTON ST
100 DALY 94014 687-D3
IRWIN CT
700 HIL 94010 728-E7
IRWIN DR
800 HIL 94010 728-E7
IRWIN PL
100 MLBR 94030 728-C4
IRWIN ST
1000 BLMT 94002 749-F7
1000 BLMT 94002 769-F1
ISABELLA AV
- ATN 94027 790-E2
100 SMCo 94018 767-B3
ISABELLA RD
500 SMCo 94018 767-B2
ISABELLE AV
2000 SMTO 94403 749-A4
ISLAND DR
100 PA 94301 791-B3
400 RDWC 94065 749-H6
ISLAND PKWY
- RDWC 94065 749-F6
300 BLMT 94002 749-F6
ISLAND PL
500 RDWC 94065 749-H6
ITALY AV
- SF 94112 687-F1
IVY AV
- PCFA 94044 727-A2
400 SMCo 94062 788-H5
IVY DR
200 MLPK 94025 770-J7
600 MLPK 94025 771-A7
IVY LN
1900 PA 94303 791-C4
IVY ST
- SMCo 94037 746-H5
1700 SMTO 94402 749-A3

J

J ST
- SF 94124 688-D1
JACARANDA CIR
700 HIL 94010 748-D2
JACINTO LN
- SSF 94080 707-E3
JACKLING DR
900 HIL 94010 728-D7
1200 BURL 94010 728-D7
JACKSON AV
100 RDWC 94061 770-A7
JACKSON DR
500 PA 94303 791-C4
JACKSON ST
300 SMTO 94402 748-H3
JACQUELINE CT
- DALY 94014 687-J4
JACQUELINE LN
- DALY 94014 687-J4
JACQUELINE PL
- SMCo 94062 769-G7
JAILHOUSE WY
- SBRN 94066 707-D6
JAMAICA ST
900 FCTY 94404 749-F5
JAMES AV
- RDWC 94062 789-H1
- SMCo 94062 789-H1
- ATN 94027 770-F7
- ATN 94027 790-F1
- RDWC 94063 770-A6
- RDWC 94062 770-A6
600 RDWC 94062 769-J7
JAMES CT
100 SSF 94080 707-G1
1300 SMTO 94401 749-B1
JAMES LICK FRWY U.S.-101
- SF - 688-A1
- SF - 688-A1
JAMESTON LN
- DALY 94014 687-F3
JAMESTOWN AV
800 SF 94124 688-B1
JAMESTOWN AVEX
700 SF 94124 688-C2
E JAMIE CT
400 SSF 94080 708-C4
JAMIE LN
800 EPA 94303 791-C1
JANE DR
100 WDSD 94062 789-G5
JANICE WY
3400 PA 94303 791-E6
J ARTHUR YOUNGER FRWY Rt#-92
- BLMT - 768-H2
- FCTY - 729-G7
- FCTY - 729-G7
- FCTY - 749-F2
- HIL - 748-J5

J ARTHUR YOUNGER FRWY Rt#-92
- SMCo - 768-H2
- SMCo - 768-H2
- SMCo - 748-J5
- SMTO - 749-A4
- SMTO - 748-J5
- SMTO - 768-H2
- SMTO - 749-F2
- SMTO - 748-J5
- SMTO - 768-H2
- SMTO - 749-F2
JARVIS WY
2000 LAH 94304 810-H4
JASMINE CT
- MLBR 94030 728-A3
JASMINE ST
1400 SMTO 94402 749-A3
JASMINE WY
100 EPA 94303 791-D3
JEEP TR
- SCrC 95006 (889-C7
See Page 869)
JEFFERSON AV
400 RDWC 94063 770-B6
1200 RDWC 94062 770-A7
1200 RDWC 94061 770-A7
1900 RDWC 94062 769-J7
1900 RDWC 94061 769-J7
2500 RDWC 94062 789-H1
2500 RDWC 94061 789-H1
3800 SMCo 94062 789-H1
4100 WDSD 94062 789-E3
JEFFERSON CT
- MLPK 94025 770-H6
800 SMTO 94401 728-H7
3700 RDWC 94061 789-G2
JEFFERSON DR
100 MLPK 94025 770-G6
500 PA 94303 791-C4
JEFFERSON ST
- SSF 94080 707-H1
JENEVEIN AV
- SBRN 94066 727-H1
500 SBRN 94066 707-J7
JENKINS CT
- SCIC 94305 790-J7
JENNIFER CT
- DALY 94014 687-J4
JENNINGS LN
- ATN 94027 790-D1
JENNINGS ST
2700 SF 94124 688-B1
JERVIS AV
1100 EPA 94303 791-A1
JETER ST
- RDWC 94062 769-J6
JETTY WY
- RDWC 94065 750-A5
JEWELL PL
- HIL 94010 748-F3
J HART CLINTON DR
1300 SMTO 94401 729-B7
1500 SMTO 94401 749-C1
1700 SMTO 94404 749-C1
JIB CT
- HMBY 94019 767-F6
JIBSTAY LN
500 FCTY 94404 749-J1
JOANNE DR
600 SMTO 94402 749-B3
JOAQUIN DR
500 SSF 94080 707-E2
JOAQUIN RD
- SMCo 94028 830-D4
JODY CT
- SMTO 94402 749-B3
JOHANSEN RD
- SCrC 95006 (889-F3
See Page 869)
- SMCo 94020 (889-F3
See Page 869)
JOHN DALY BLVD
400 DALY 94014 687-A3
500 DALY 94015 687-A3
800 DALY 94015 686-J4
JOHN F FORAN FRWY I-280
- DALY - 687-C2
- DALY - 687-C4
- SF - 687-E1
- SF - 687-D2
JOHN F SHELLEY DR
- SF 94134 687-H1
JOHN GLENN CIR
- DALY 94015 707-C3
JOHN MUIR DR
100 SF 94132 687-A2
100 SMCo 94015 687-A2
600 SF 94132 686-J1
JOHN PAPAN CT
- DALY 94015 707-B2
JOHNSON AV
400 PCFA 94044 707-A4
JOHNSON ST
900 RDWC 94061 770-A7
1000 RDWC 94061 790-A1
1100 MLPK 94025 790-F4
JOHNSTON ST
300 HMBY 94019 787-F2

JONES CT
1000 RDWC 94063 770-E6
JONES GULCH RD
- SMCo 94020 849-D5
- SMCo 94021 849-D5
JORDAN PL
- PA 94303 791-B4
JORDAN ST
900 SMCo 94037 746-G5
JORDAN WY
200 PA 94304 790-G6
200 SCIC 94305 790-G6
JOSEPH DR
700 SSF 94080 707-G2
JOSEPHA AV
- SF 94132 687-B1
JOSIAH AV
- SF 94112 687-E1
JOSSELYN LN
100 WDSD 94062 789-E6
JOY AV
- BSBN 94005 688-B6
JOYCE RD
- HIL 94010 748-F5
JUAN BAUTISTA CIR
- SF 94132 687-B1
JUANITA AV
100 PCFA 94044 727-B2
300 MLBR 94030 727-J2
1100 BURL 94010 728-E5
JUBILEE CT
- SMCo 94061 790-A3
JUDITH CT
- HMBY 94019 767-E6
JUDSON DR
400 SMCo 94020 829-F7
JUDSON PL
- PCFA 94044 727-B6
JUDSON ST
1000 BLMT 94002 749-F7
JULES AV
- SF 94112 687-D1
JULIA CT
- BLMT 94002 749-D7
JULIANA AV
- SMCo 94038 746-F6
JULIE LN
2300 SSF 94080 707-D4
JUNE HOLLOW RD
700 SMCo 94037 746-G5
JUNIOR TER
- SF 94112 687-F1
JUNIPER AV
200 SSF 94080 708-A2
200 SSF 94080 707-J2
1600 SBRN 94066 707-G7
JUNIPER DR
- ATN 94027 790-G1
JUNIPER ST
2800 SMTO 94403 749-B5
JUNIPERO AV
- RDWC 94061 789-J1
1200 RDWC 94061 790-A1
JUNIPERO SERRA BLVD
400 SSF 94080 707-C1
900 SF 94132 687-C1
1800 DALY 94015 687-C6
2300 DALY 94015 687-C6
3700 CLMA 94014 687-C6
4200 DALY 94015 707-D1
5000 CLMA 94014 707-C1
JUNIPERO SERRA BLVD Rt#-1
- SF 94132 687-C4
JUNIPERO SERRA BLVD Rt#-G5
- MLPK 94025 790-F7
- SCIC 94305 790-F7
- SCIC 94304 790-F7
100 SCIC 94304 810-G1
100 SCIC 94305 810-G1
JUNIPERO SERRA FRWY I-280
- DALY - 687-C7
- DALY - 687-C7
- DALY - 707-C2
- HIL - 748-D4
- HIL - 748-D4
- LAH - 810-F3
- MLBR - 728-A7
- MLBR - 727-G3
- MLPK - 810-C1
- PA - 810-F3
- SBRN - 707-C2
- SBRN - 727-G3
- SCIC - 810-F3
- SMCo - 728-A7
- SMCo - 727-G3
- SMCo - 748-D4
- SMCo - 768-F1
- SMCo - 728-A7
- SMCo - 748-D4
- SMCo - 790-A6
- SMCo - 810-C1
- SMCo - 727-G3
- SMCo - 789-D1
- SMCo - 769-A4
- SMCo - 768-F1
- SMCo - 789-D1
- SMCo - 748-D4

JUNIPERO SERRA FRWY I-280
- SMCo - 768-F1
- SSF - 707-C2
- WDSD - 789-G4
- WDSD - 790-A6
JUNIPERO SERRA FRWY Rt#-1
- DALY - 687-C3
- DALY - 687-C3
- SF - 687-C3
JUNO LN
800 FCTY 94404 749-F4
JUPITER CT
800 FCTY 94404 749-E3

K

KAINS AV
100 SBRN 94066 707-G7
KALMIA ST
1400 SMTO 94402 749-A3
KAMMERER CT
- HIL 94010 728-F7
KANDLE WY
1100 RDWC 94061 790-B1
KANOFF AV
- SMCo 94037 746-G4
KANSAS ST
1600 RDWC 94061 790-A2
KAREN CT
- BURL 94010 728-B5
KAREN RD
- SMCo 94002 749-F7
- SMCo 94002 769-F1
KAREN WY
100 ATN 94027 790-B5
KATAOKA CT
- SMCo 94062 789-G1
KATHERINE AV
500 RDWC 94062 769-J7
KATHLEEN CT
- PCFA 94044 727-B4
KATHRYN AV
100 SMCo 94018 767-C2
KATHRYNE AV
700 SMTO 94401 749-B1
KAUFFMANN CT
400 SSF 94080 708-C3
KAVANAUGH DR
1300 MLPK 94025 771-B7
1300 EPA 94303 771-B7
KAVANAUGH WY
200 PCFA 94044 707-B3
KAYNYNE ST
800 RDWC 94063 770-C6
800 SMCo 94063 770-C6
KEARNEY ST
- SSF 94080 707-H1
KEATS AV
700 SSF 94080 707-D2
KEBET RIDGE RD
- SMCo 94062 809-F5
KEDITH ST
1000 BLMT 94002 749-F7
KEEFE CT
100 SBRN 94066 727-G1
KEEL CT
100 HMBY 94019 767-E6
KEEL LN
400 RDWC 94065 749-H6
KEELSON CIR
500 RDWC 94065 749-J6
KEHOE AV
400 HMBY 94019 767-E7
1200 SMTO 94401 749-C1
1800 SMTO 94403 749-D1
KEITH AV
300 PCFA 94044 727-B2
KEITH ST
- SF 94124 688-B1
KELLOCH AV
- SF 94134 687-J2
KELLOGG AV
100 PA 94301 791-A6
KELLY AV
- HMBY 94019 787-E1
KELLY LN
- MLBR 94030 728-A5
KELLY ST
- MLPK 94025 771-A7
600 HMBY 94019 787-F1
1700 SMTO 94403 749-D2
KELMORE ST
500 SMCo 94038 746-F6
KELTON AV
100 SCAR 94070 769-H5
KELTON CT
- SMTO 94403 749-B7
KEMPTON AV
- SF 94132 687-C2
KENDALL CT
- PCFA 94044 727-B4
KENILWORTH RD
1200 HIL 94010 748-F3
KENMAR WY
- BURL 94010 728-C7
KENMORE WY
100 WDSD 94062 789-J5

KENNEDY PL
- MLBR 94030 727-J4
KENNETH DR
3300 PA 94303 791-E6
KENNY AL
- SF 94112 687-F1
KENRY WY
2200 SSF 94080 707-E5
KENSINGTON AV
400 SBRN 94066 727-J1
KENSINGTON RD
- RDWC 94061 790-A3
2700 RDWC 94061 789-J3
KENT AV
700 SCAR 94070 769-D5
KENT CT
- DALY 94015 707-B1
- SMTO 94403 749-C4
100 SBRN 94066 727-F1
KENT PL
- MLPK 94025 790-H3
- PA 94301 791-B4
KENT RD
100 PCFA 94044 726-G4
KENT ST
2200 SMTO 94403 749-C4
KENT WY
3800 SSF 94080 707-D4
KENTFIELD AV
1300 RDWC 94061 790-A1
KENTON AV
- SCAR 94070 769-E3
KENTUCKY AV
500 SMTO 94402 748-H3
KENTUCKY ST
1600 RDWC 94061 790-A2
KENWOOD AV
3600 SMTO 94403 749-B6
KENWOOD DR
500 MLPK 94025 790-G4
KENWOOD WY
200 SSF 94080 707-G5
KEONCREST DR
500 SSF 94080 707-E2
KERRI CT
100 SMCo 94061 790-A4
KESTREL CT
- BSBN 94005 687-J5
KESWICK LN
400 SMTO 94402 749-B3
KETCH CT
100 FCTY 94404 749-G4
KETTERING CT
3400 SMTO 94403 749-A6
KEY AV
900 SF 94124 688-B1
KILCONWAY LN
2700 SSF 94080 707-C4
KILLARNEY LN
1100 BURL 94010 728-C5
KILLDEER CT
200 FCTY 94404 749-G1
KILROY WY
- ATN 94027 790-B4
KIMBALL WY
100 SSF 94080 708-B4
KIMBERLY WY
3300 SMTO 94403 749-E5
KIMMIE CT
- BLMT 94002 769-C2
KINDER LN
- HIL 94010 728-C7
KING CT
- SMTO 94403 749-C6
KING DR
300 SSF 94080 707-E3
500 DALY 94015 707-C3
1100 PCFA 94044 707-C3
KING LN
700 FCTY 94404 749-G4
3800 SMTO 94403 749-C6
KING ST
- RDWC 94062 769-H6
900 RDWC 94061 770-A7
1100 RDWC 94061 790-A1
1600 BLMT 94002 769-F2
KINGRIDGE DR
3600 SMTO 94403 749-B7
KINGS CT
100 SCAR 94070 769-D5
KINGS LN
1400 PA 94303 791-B4
2000 SMCo 94402 768-H1
KINGS RD
- BSBN 94005 688-A7
KINGS CANYON WY
- PCFA 94044 727-B6
KINGSFORD LN
200 RDWC 94061 790-B2
KINGSLEY AV
100 PA 94301 790-J5
100 PA 94301 791-A5
KINGS MOUNTAIN RD
100 WDSD 94062 789-D6
600 SMCo 94062 789-A7
KINGSTON AV
2200 SBRN 94066 707-F7
2200 SBRN 94066 727-G1
KINGSTON RD
500 BLMT 94002 749-E7

STREET	Block	City	ZIP	Pg-Grid
KINGSTON ST				
	-	SMTO	94401	729-A6
KINGSWOOD CIR				
	-	HIL	94010	748-E5
KINGSWOOD CT				
	1400	HIL	94010	748-F5
KINGSWOOD DR				
	1500	HIL	94010	748-E5
KIOWA CT				
	-	PTLV	94028	810-C6
KIP LN				
	3300	BURL	94010	748-B1
KIPLING AV				
	800	SSF	94080	707-D2
KIPLING ST				
	200	PA	94301	790-J4
	2600	PA	94306	791-C6
KIRBY PL				
	-	PA	94301	791-B4
KIRKWOOD CT				
	-	EPA	94303	771-B7
KIRKWOOD WY				
	-	SCAR	94070	769-E3
KITTIE LN				
	-	BLMT	94002	769-D2
KLAMATH AV				
	2000	SMTO	94403	749-C2
KLAMATH DR				
	1000	MLPK	94025	790-C7
KLAMATH ST				
	200	BSBN	94005	688-A6
KNAPP CT				
	-	SMTO	94403	749-B5
KNIGHTSBRIDGE LN				
	-	RDWC	94061	790-B2
KNIGHTWOOD LN				
	-	HIL	94010	728-D7
KNOLL CIR				
	100	SSF	94080	707-G3
KNOLL DR				
	600	SCAR	94070	769-G4
KNOLLCREST RD				
	-	HIL	94010	748-E4
KNOLL VISTA				
	-	SMCo	94020	829-F7
	-	ATN	94027	790-B6
KNOT LN				
	-	RDWC	94065	750-C4
KNOTT CT				
	-	SF	94112	687-F2
KNOWLES AV				
	-	DALY	94014	687-C3
KOHALA AV				
	300	PCFA	94044	707-A6
KORBEL WY				
	-	BLMT	94002	749-D7
	-	BLMT	94002	769-D1
KRAMER LN				
	-	SMCo	94063	790-D1
KRISTA LN				
	-	SCAR	94062	769-G6
KRISTIE LN				
	2300	SSF	94080	707-D4
KRISTIN CT				
	100	SMCo	94402	748-H6
KYNE RD				
	-	SMCo	94060	(868-H2 See Page 867)

L

STREET	Block	City	ZIP	Pg-Grid
LABARTHE LN				
	-	SCAR	94070	769-F6
LA BURNUM RD				
	-	ATN	94027	790-F1
LA CANADA PTH				
	-	SMCo	94010	728-B7
LA CANADA RD				
	1200	HIL	94010	748-F3
LA CASA AV				
	200	SMTO	94403	749-B7
LACOUR WY				
	300	SMCo	94061	790-B3
LA CROSSE AV				
	100	SSF	94080	707-E2
LA CRUZ AV				
	-	MLBR	94030	728-B4
LA CUESTA DR				
	200	SMCo	94028	810-E3
LA CUESTA RD				
	1000	HIL	94010	748-F3
LA CUMBRE CT				
	-	HIL	94010	748-F2
LA CUMBRE RD				
	1200	HIL	94010	748-F3
LADERA WY				
	600	PCFA	94044	726-H4
	1100	BLMT	94002	769-D2
LAFAYETTE ST				
	1000	SMTO	94403	749-C4
LAGO				
	1500	SMTO	94403	749-E4
LAGOON DR				
	-	RDWC	94065	749-G7
LAGOON WY				
	100	BSBN	94005	688-B5
LA GRANADA ST				
	100	SMCo	94038	766-H2
LA GRANDE AV				
	100	SMCo	94038	766-G1
	100	SMCo	94038	746-G7
	100	SF	94112	687-G2
LAGUNA AV				
	900	BURL	94010	728-E5
S LAGUNA AV				
	-	SMCo	94038	746-F6
LAGUNA CIR				
	900	FCTY	94404	749-F4
LAGUNA DR				
	-	SMCo	94020	849-E1
LAGUNITA DR				
	500	SCIC	94305	790-G7
LA HONDA RD				
	1300	HIL	94010	748-E2
LA HONDA RD Rt#-84				
	-	SMCo	94020	829-F3
	-	SMCo	94020	849-A1
	-	SMCo	94062	829-F3
	-	SMCo	94062	849-A1
	-	SMCo	94074	829-E7
	-	SMCo	94074	849-A1
	-	SMCo	94074	(828-E6 See Page 827)
	-	SMCo	94074	827-J6
	300	WDSD	94062	809-F5
	400	SMCo	94062	809-F7
	1700	SMCo	94020	809-F5
	1700	WDSD	94020	809-F5
	4100	SMCo	94074	(848-H1 See Page 827)
LA JOLLA AV				
	400	SMTO	94403	749-B6
LAKE BLVD				
	2400	SMCo	94062	789-F1
LAKE CT				
	-	SMCo	94062	789-F1
LAKE DR				
	100	SBRN	94066	707-D7
	100	SBRN	94066	727-D1
LAKE RD				
	-	SMCo	94028	830-D4
	2200	BLMT	94002	769-A2
LAKE ST				
	100	BSBN	94005	688-B7
	1000	MLBR	94030	728-A5
	1700	SMTO	94403	749-D1
N LAKE ST				
	200	SMCo	94038	746-F7
S LAKE ST				
	-	SMCo	94038	746-F7
LAKE FOREST DR				
	-	DALY	94015	687-B3
LAKEMEAD WY				
	500	SMCo	94062	789-F2
	3900	RDWC	94062	789-F2
LAKEMEADOW DR				
	-	DALY	94015	687-A4
LAKE MERCED BLVD				
	-	SF	94132	687-A3
	100	DALY	94015	687-A3
	100	SMCo	94015	687-A3
LAKE MERCED HILL				
	-	SF	94132	687-A2
LAKEMONT DR				
	-	DALY	94015	687-A3
LAKESHIRE DR				
	200	DALY	94015	687-A7
	500	DALY	94015	707-A1
LAKESHORE DR				
	100	SMCo	94402	748-G6
	700	RDWC	94065	749-J6
	700	SMCo	94025	809-J3
	1200	SMCo	94025	810-A3
LAKESIDE AV				
	100	PCFA	94044	706-J6
LAKESIDE DR				
	300	FCTY	94404	749-E1
LAKEVIEW AV				
	-	SF	94112	687-D1
	200	PCFA	94044	706-J6
LAKEVIEW DR				
	-	DALY	94015	687-A3
	100	WDSD	94062	790-A5
	1000	HIL	94010	748-E5
LAKEVIEW LN				
	200	PCFA	94044	706-J6
LAKEVIEW WY				
	100	SMCo	94062	769-E7
	300	SMCo	94062	789-F1
	800	RDWC	94062	789-G2
	1000	RDWC	94061	789-G2
LAKE VISTA AV				
	-	DALY	94015	687-B3
LAKEWOOD CIR				
	-	SMTO	94402	768-H1
LAKEWOOD DR				
	-	DALY	94015	687-A4
	-	DALY	94015	686-J4
LA LOMA DR				
	-	SMCo	94025	790-C6
	-	MLPK	94025	790-C6
LA LOMA LN				
	100	SMCo	94010	728-B7
LA MANCHA PL				
	-	MLBR	94030	728-A4
LAMBERT AV				
	200	PA	94306	791-C7
LA MESA CT				
	-	BURL	94010	728-B7
	400	SMCo	94028	810-D3
LA MESA DR				
	100	SMCo	94010	728-B7
	100	SMCo	94028	810-D3
	1500	BURL	94010	728-B7
	3100	SCAR	94070	769-D6
LA MESA LN				
	-	BURL	94010	728-B7
LA MIRADA DR				
	900	PCFA	94044	726-J4
LAMONTE AV				
	200	SSF	94080	707-D3
LAMSHIN LN				
	-	SCAR	94062	769-G6
LANCASTER BLVD				
	400	SMCo	94038	746-G6
LANCASTER RD				
	1000	HIL	94010	748-F3
LANCASTER WY				
	400	RDWC	94062	789-H1
	600	RDWC	94061	789-H1
LANDA LN				
	-	SMCo	94061	790-A4
LANDFAIR AV				
	300	SMTO	94403	749-C7
LANDING LN				
	1100	MLBR	94030	728-A2
LANE PL				
	-	ATN	94027	790-F1
LANE ST				
	1000	BLMT	94002	769-F2
LANE A				
	-	SCIC	94305	790-H7
LANE B				
	500	SCIC	94305	810-H1
LANE C				
	500	SCIC	94305	790-H7
	500	SCIC	94305	810-H1
LANE W				
	500	SCIC	94305	790-H7
LANG RD				
	300	BURL	94010	728-H5
LANING DR				
	100	WDSD	94062	789-G5
LANSDALE AV				
	300	MLBR	94030	728-A3
LANSDALE ST				
	3000	SMTO	94403	749-A6
LANYARD DR				
	400	RDWC	94065	749-H7
LAPHAM WY				
	-	SF	94112	687-G2
LA PRENDA				
	-	MLBR	94030	727-J5
LA QUESTA DR				
	100	SMCo	94010	728-B7
LA QUESTA WY				
	100	WDSD	94062	789-H6
LARCH AV				
	400	SSF	94080	707-H1
LARCH DR				
	-	ATN	94027	770-G7
	-	ATN	94027	790-G1
LARCH LN				
	200	PCFA	94044	707-A6
	200	PCFA	94044	706-J6
LARCHMONT DR				
	600	SMCo	94015	687-A4
LARGUITA LN				
	-	PTLV	94028	810-B5
LARK AV				
	1600	RDWC	94061	790-A2
LARK LN				
	1000	FCTY	94404	749-H2
LARKSPUR AV				
	-	DALY	94015	687-A6
LARKSPUR DR				
	-	SMCo	-	727-H4
	300	EPA	94303	791-D2
	800	MLBR	94030	727-H3
	900	BURL	94010	728-F6
LA SALLE DR				
	2000	SMTO	94403	749-A4
LA SALLE RD				
	-	HIL	94010	748-F3
LA SANDRA WY				
	-	PTLV	94028	810-B4
LA SELVA				
	3000	SMTO	94403	749-E5
LA SENDA RD				
	-	HIL	94010	748-G3
LAS FLORES RD				
	-	SMCo	94037	746-H5
LA SOLANO				
	-	MLBR	94030	727-J4
LAS PIEDRAS				
	-	SMCo	94028	830-D5
LAS PIEDRAS CT				
	-	BURL	94010	728-B5
LAS PIEDRAS DR				
	2800	BURL	94010	728-A6
LAS PULGAS RD				
	400	WDSD	94062	789-H4
LASSEN CT				
	-	MLPK	94025	790-C7
	600	SSF	94080	707-F4
LASSEN DR				
	100	SBRN	94066	707-E7
	100	SBRN	94066	727-E1
	900	MLPK	94025	790-C7
	1000	BLMT	94002	769-A2
LASSEN LN				
	1000	PCFA	94044	707-A5
LASSEN ST				
	500	SSF	94080	707-F4
LASSEN WY				
	1600	BURL	94010	728-C5
LAS SOMBRAS CT				
	400	SMTO	94402	748-F2
LASUEN DR				
	1200	MLBR	94030	728-A5
LASUEN ST				
	100	SCIC	94305	790-H6
LATHAM CT				
	-	HIL	94010	728-F7
LATHROP AV				
	100	SF	94134	688-A2
LATHROP DR				
	800	SCIC	94305	810-H2
LATHROP PL				
	900	SCIC	94305	810-H2
LATHROP ST				
	-	RDWC	94063	770-B6
LAUGHING COW RD				
	100	SMCo	94062	789-A7
LAURA LN				
	100	PA	94303	791-D4
LAURA ST				
	-	SF	94112	687-E2
LAUREL AV				
	-	MLBR	94030	728-A3
	100	MLPK	94025	790-J3
	200	SSF	94080	707-G2
	300	SMCo	94062	788-H5
	400	HMBY	94019	787-E1
	400	MLPK	94025	791-A2
	500	SMTO	94401	749-A2
	700	BURL	94010	728-F6
	800	BLMT	94002	769-E1
	1000	EPA	94303	791-A1
LAUREL LN				
	400	PCFA	94044	707-A6
LAUREL PL				
	-	MLPK	94025	790-F2
LAUREL ST				
	-	ATN	94027	790-F2
	-	RDWC	94063	770-C6
	-	SCAR	94070	769-F2
	-	MLPK	94025	790-F2
LAUREL WY				
	3700	RDWC	94062	789-G1
LAUREL CREEK DR				
	3400	SMTO	94403	749-A7
E LAUREL CREEK RD				
	3000	SMTO	94403	749-A7
	3000	BLMT	94002	749-A7
	3100	SMTO	94403	769-A1
	3100	BLMT	94002	769-A1
	3500	SMTO	94403	768-J1
	3500	BLMT	94002	768-J1
	3500	SMTO	94403	748-J7
	3500	BLMT	94002	748-J7
LAURELDALE RD				
	-	HIL	94010	748-G2
LAUREL GLEN DR				
	800	PA	94304	830-G1
	800	PA	94304	810-G7
LAUREL HILL CT				
	-	SMCo	94402	748-F6
LAUREL HILL DR				
	1200	SMCo	94402	748-F7
LAURELWOOD DR				
	700	SMTO	94403	749-A7
LAUREN AV				
	200	PCFA	94044	727-A2
LAURENT RD				
	500	HIL	94010	748-D2
LAURIE LN				
	-	SMCo	94402	748-G6
LAURIE MEADOWS DR				
	-	SMTO	94403	749-D6
LAUSANNE AV				
	-	DALY	94014	687-D4
LAWLER RANCH RD				
	-	SMCo	94025	789-J7
	-	SMCo	94025	790-A7
	-	SMCo	94025	810-B1
	-	WDSD	94062	790-A7
LAWRENCE AV				
	-	SF	94112	687-E2
	200	SSF	94080	708-B4
LAWRENCE LN				
	900	PA	94303	791-D5
LAWRENCE RD				
	800	SMTO	94401	749-A1
LAWRENCE CREEK TR				
	-	SMCo	94062	809-A5
	500	SMCo	94062	(808-J5 See Page 788)
LAYNE CT				
	700	PA	94303	791-D7
LAYNE PL				
	-	SBRN	94066	707-J7
LEAFWOOD CT				
	3400	SMTO	94403	748-J7
LEAHY ST				
	500	RDWC	94061	790-C1
LE BLANC CT				
	-	HMBY	94019	767-E5
LE CONTE AV				
	700	SF	94124	688-B1
	1000	SMCo	94037	746-G4
LEE AV				
	-	SF	94112	687-E1
	400	SMCo	94019	767-D4
LEE DR				
	900	MLPK	94025	790-F3
LEEWARD LN				
	1400	FCTY	94404	749-G5
LE HAVRE PL				
	-	HMBY	94019	767-E5
LEHNING WY				
	-	BSBN	94005	688-A6
LEIGH WY				
	2600	BLMT	94002	769-B3
LEIX WY				
	2600	SSF	94080	707-C4
LELAND AV				
	-	SF	94134	687-J2
	100	SMCo	94025	790-E6
	200	PA	94306	791-A7
	300	SF	94134	688-A2
LE MANS WY				
	700	HMBY	94019	767-E5
N LEMON AV				
	1100	MLPK	94025	790-E5
LEMON CT				
	-	HIL	94010	748-C1
LEMON ST				
	400	MLPK	94025	790-E6
LEMOORE DR				
	-	SCAR	94070	769-G6
LENNOX AV				
	200	MLPK	94025	790-F2
LENOLT ST				
	1300	RDWC	94063	770-A5
	1400	RDWC	94063	769-J4
LEO CIR				
	-	SSF	94080	708-A2
	-	SSF	94080	707-J2
LEO DR				
	600	FCTY	94404	749-E3
LEON WY				
	-	ATN	94027	790-F3
LEONA ST				
	3900	SMTO	94403	749-B7
LERIDA AV				
	-	MLBR	94030	728-B3
LERIDA CT				
	-	SMCo	94028	810-D4
LERIDA WY				
	1200	PCFA	94044	727-A4
LEROY AV				
	-	PTLV	94028	809-J6
LESLIE CT				
	900	SCAR	94070	769-D6
LESLIE DR				
	-	SCAR	94070	769-D6
LESLIE ST				
	1700	SMTO	94402	749-B3
LESSING ST				
	-	SF	94112	687-D2
LEVEE RD				
	-	SMTO	94401	729-A6
LEWIS AV				
	-	MLBR	94030	728-B4
	-	SSF	94080	708-A2
	100	SMCo	94018	767-C1
LEWIS LN				
	400	PCFA	94044	707-A4
LEWIS FOSTER DR				
	100	HMBY	94019	767-F7
LEWIS RANCH LN				
	-	SCAR	94070	769-D5
LEXINGTON AV				
	100	RDWC	94062	770-A6
	300	SSF	94066	707-J5
	1400	SMCo	94402	748-F7
	1500	SMCo	94402	768-F1
LEXINGTON DR				
	200	MLPK	94025	790-J3
LEXINGTON WY				
	300	BURL	94010	728-G6
	2400	SBRN	94066	707-F7
	2400	SBRN	94066	727-F1
LIBERTY CT				
	2400	SSF	94080	707-D4
LIBERTY LN				
	700	FCTY	94404	749-G5
LIBERTY PARK AV				
	2000	SMCo	94025	790-D6
LIBRA LN				
	600	FCTY	94404	749-E3
LIBRARY AV				
	200	MLBR	94030	728-A3
LIDDICOAT CIR				
	14300	LAH	94022	810-H5
LIDDICOAT DR				
	14100	LAH	94022	810-H5
LIDO CIR				
	-	RDWC	94065	749-J6
LIDO LN				
	900	FCTY	94404	749-F3
LIDO ST				
	700	FCTY	94404	749-F3
LIEBIG ST				
	-	DALY	94014	687-D2
	-	SF	94112	687-D2
LIGHT WY				
	-	SMCo	94025	770-E7
LIGHTHOUSE LN				
	-	DALY	94014	687-E5
LIGHTHOUSE RD				
	-	HMBY	94019	787-G5
LILAC AV				
	200	SMCo	94062	788-H5
LILAC DR				
	-	ATN	94027	770-G7
LILAC LN				
	-	SSF	94080	707-H2
	300	EPA	94303	791-B1
LILLY LN				
	-	SCAR	94070	769-C5
LINARIA WY				
	-	SMCo	94028	810-D4
LINCOLN AV				
	-	DALY	94015	687-A6
	100	PA	94301	790-J5
	100	RDWC	94061	770-A7
	200	PA	94301	791-A4
	800	SMCo	94038	746-F5
	1100	BURL	94010	728-D5
	2400	BLMT	94002	769-B1
LINCOLN BLVD				
	900	PCFA	94044	727-B6
LINCOLN CIR				
	400	MLBR	94030	728-A3
LINCOLN CT				
	-	SF	94112	687-F2
LINCOLN LN				
	100	PCFA	94044	706-J3
	200	PCFA	94044	707-A3
LINCOLN PL				
	900	PCFA	94044	727-B6
LINCOLN ST				
	-	SSF	94080	707-H1
	2000	EPA	94303	791-A2
LINCOLN CENTRE DR				
	100	FCTY	94404	749-F1
LINDA CT				
	700	SMTO	94403	749-B7
LINDA LN				
	28000	LAH	94304	810-H4
LINDA MAR BLVD				
	500	PCFA	94044	726-H4
	1100	PCFA	94044	727-A6
LINDA VISTA				
	100	MLBR	94030	727-J5
LINDA VISTA AV				
	-	ATN	94027	790-C4
LINDA VISTA DR				
	100	DALY	94014	687-J4
LINDA VISTA RD				
	-	SMCo	94037	746-H4
LINDA VISTA ST				
	800	SMCo	94038	746-G6
LINDA VISTA STEPS				
	-	SF	94112	687-G2
LINDBERGH ST				
	-	SMTO	94401	729-A7
	200	SMTO	94401	749-B1
LINDEN AV				
	-	ATN	94027	790-G1
	-	MLBR	94030	727-J1
	-	SSF	94080	707-J3
	-	SBRN	94066	727-J1
	300	SBRN	94066	707-H7
	700	BURL	94010	728-F6
	700	MLBR	94030	728-B4
	900	SSF	94080	708-A2
S LINDEN AV				
	-	SSF	94080	707-J4
	300	SSF	94066	707-J4
	300	SBRN	94066	707-J4
LINDEN CT				
	700	SBRN	94066	707-H7
LINDEN LN				
	100	SMCo	94402	748-G6
LINDEN ST				
	-	SMCo	94014	687-D5
	100	RDWC	94061	770-B7
	600	DALY	94014	687-D5
LINDEN WY				
	100	SMCo	94402	748-G5
LINDENBROOK CT				
	300	WDSD	94062	789-H5
LINDENBROOK RD				
	200	WDSD	94062	789-H5
LINFIELD DR				
	400	MLPK	94025	790-G4
E LINFIELD DR				
	100	MLPK	94025	790-H3
LINFIELD PL				
	300	MLPK	94025	790-H3
LINK RD				
	900	HIL	94010	748-F3
LINWOOD WY				
	-	SMCo	94062	809-F5
LISA CT				
	800	PCFA	94044	726-H5
LISBON ST				
	400	SF	94112	687-F1
	500	SMCo	94014	687-D5
	500	DALY	94014	687-D5
LITA LN				
	-	EPA	94303	791-C2
LITTLEFIELD AV				
	200	SSF	94080	708-A4
LIVE OAK AV				
	600	MLPK	94025	790-F4
LIVE OAK LN				
	-	HIL	94010	748-B1
	500	SMCo	94062	789-F1
LIVINGSTON AV				
	1300	PCFA	94044	726-G4
LIVINGSTON PL				
	100	SSF	94080	707-G1
LIVINGSTON TER				
	2000	SBRN	94066	707-G7
LLANO ST				
	3200	SMTO	94403	749-E5
LLOYDEN DR				
	-	ATN	94027	790-D2
LLOYDEN PARK LN				
	300	ATN	94027	790-D2
LOBITOS CREEK CTO				
	1200	SMCo	94019	(808-A6 See Page 788)
	1200	SMCo	94019	(807-J5 See Page 788)
	1200	SMCo	94074	(808-A6 See Page 788)
LOBITOS CREEK RD				
	-	SMCo	94019	(808-D3 See Page 788)
	-	SMCo	94019	(807-J5 See Page 788)
LOBOS ST				
	-	SF	94112	687-D1
	200	SF	94132	687-D1
LOCARNO WY				
	1000	SCAR	94070	769-F5
LOCKHAVEN DR				
	600	PCFA	94044	707-B4
LOCUST AV				
	300	SSF	94080	707-H2
LOCUST ST				
	100	RDWC	94061	770-B7
	100	RDWC	94061	790-B1
	1400	SMTO	94402	749-A3
LODATO AV				
	-	SMTO	94403	749-B4
	-	SMTO	94402	749-B4
LODGE DR				
	3400	BLMT	94002	769-A2
LODI AV				
	1300	SMTO	94403	749-C2
	1300	SMTO	94401	749-C2
LOEHR ST				
	-	SF	94134	687-J2
LOGAN LN				
	-	ATN	94027	790-C2
LOG CABIN RANCH RD				
	-	SMCo	94020	849-F3
LOHOMA CT				
	-	HIL	94402	748-H5
LOIS LN				
	100	PA	94303	791-B4
LOLA ST				
	3700	SMTO	94403	749-B6
LOMA CT				
	700	SMCo	94062	769-F6
LOMA RD				
	-	SCAR	94070	769-E6
	-	SMCo	94062	769-F6
	-	SCAR	94062	769-E6
LOMA MAR AV				
	-	SMCo	94021	849-A7
LOMA PRIETA LN				
	2300	MLPK	94025	790-D7
LOMA VERDE AV				
	100	PA	94306	791-C7
	700	PA	94303	791-C7
LOMA VERDE PL				
	3100	PA	94303	791-D6
LOMA VISTA DR				
	-	BURL	94010	728-A7
	100	SMCo	94010	728-A7
LOMA VISTA ST				
	800	SMCo	94038	746-G6
LOMA VISTA TER				
	300	PCFA	94044	707-A5
LOMBARDI LN				
	-	MLBR	94030	728-A5
	800	HIL	94010	748-G3
LOMBARDY WY				
	600	SMCo	94062	789-F2
LOMITA AV				
	300	SBRN	94066	727-H2
	300	MLBR	94030	727-H2
LOMITA CT				
	500	MLBR	94030	727-J2
	600	SCIC	94305	810-G1
LOMITA DR				
	500	SCIC	94305	790-H6
	500	SCIC	94305	810-G1
LOMITAS AV				
	100	SSF	94080	707-E3
LOMITAS CT				
	-	MLPK	94025	790-F6
LOMOND DR				
	400	PCFA	94044	707-B3
LONDON CT				
	100	SBRN	94066	727-G2
LONDON LN				
	200	BLMT	94002	749-F6
LONDON ST				
	500	SF	94112	687-F1
LONDONDERRY DR				
	100	SMCo	94402	748-H7
LONELY TR				
	-	SMCo	94062	789-A4
	-	SMCo	94062	788-J5
LONESOME PINE RD				
	3900	RDWC	94061	789-G3
LONGFELLOW DR				
	3100	BLMT	94002	749-A7
	3100	BLMT	94002	769-A1
LONGFORD DR				
	-	SSF	94080	707-D1
LONG RIDGE RD				
	-	SMCo	94020	850-G5
LONGSPUR				
	-	PTLV	94028	830-C1
LONGVIEW CT				
	-	HIL	94010	748-G3
LONGVIEW DR				
	-	DALY	94015	707-A1
	2900	SBRN	94066	707-D6
LONGVIEW RD				
	800	HIL	94010	748-G3
LOOKOUT RD				
	-	HIL	94010	748-E4
LOON CT				
	200	FCTY	94404	749-H1
LORD IVELSON LN				
	1100	FCTY	94404	749-J4
LORD NELSON LN				
	1100	FCTY	94404	749-J4
LOREE LN				
	-	MLBR	94030	728-A5
LORELEI LN				
	-	MLPK	94025	770-F7
LORI CT				
	3200	BLMT	94002	768-J1
LORI DR				
	3200	BLMT	94002	768-J1
LORNE LN				
	-	SMCo	94025	770-E7
LORRAINE AV				
	1500	SMTO	94401	729-A7
LORRY LN				
	100	PCFA	94044	707-B4
LORTON AV				
	-	BURL	94010	728-G7
LORYN LN				
	1000	HMBY	94019	767-E6
LOS ALTOS DR				
	1500	BURL	94010	728-A7
	1700	SMCo	94402	748-H7
	2100	SMTO	94402	748-H7
LOS ALTOS PL				
	-	SMCo	94402	748-G7
LOS ARBOLES AV				
	500	SCIC	94305	790-F7
LOS BANOS AV				
	100	DALY	94014	687-C3
	100	SMCo	94038	746-G7
	100	SMCo	94038	766-G1
LOS CERROS RD				
	-	SMCo	94062	769-F6
LOS CHARROS LN				
	-	PTLV	94028	810-C6
LOS FLORES AV				
	-	SSF	94080	707-E2
LOS GATOS WY				
	400	SMTO	94403	749-E5
LOS MONTES DR				
	100	SMCo	94010	728-A7
	1600	BURL	94010	728-A7
LOS OLIVOS AV				
	-	DALY	94014	687-C3
LOS PRADOS				
	3000	SMTO	94403	749-E4
LOS ROBLES CT				
	-	SMCo	94025	790-D5
LOS ROBLES DR				
	100	SMCo	94010	728-B7
LOS TRANCOS CIR				
	100	SMCo	94028	830-D4
LOS TRANCOS RD				
	-	PA	94304	830-D2
	-	PTLV	94028	810-D7
	100	PA	94304	810-D7
	900	PTLV	94028	830-D2
	900	SMCo	94028	830-D4
LOS VIENTOS WY				
	100	SMCo	94070	769-C5
	100	SCAR	94070	769-C5
LOTUS WY				
	100	EPA	94303	791-D3
LOUIS RD				
	1900	PA	94303	791-C5
LOUISA CT				
	1500	PA	94303	791-B4
LOUISBURG ST				
	100	SF	94112	687-E1
LOUISE LN				
	100	PTLV	94028	809-J5
	100	SMTO	94403	749-B6
LOUISE ST				
	1000	MLPK	94025	790-E6
LOUVAINE DR				
	1700	SMCo	94015	687-B5
LOUVAINE PL				
	-	SMCo	94015	687-B5
LOWE RD Rt#-84				
	-	WDSD	94062	789-G6
LOWELL AV				
	100	PA	94301	791-A6
	100	SBRN	94066	727-G2
LOWELL ST				
	-	SF	94112	687-E2
	-	RDWC	94062	769-H6
	300	DALY	94014	687-E2
LOWER DEARBORN PARK RD				
	-	SMCo	94060	(868-J2 See Page 867)
LOWER LAKE RD				
	100	WDSD	94062	809-H5
LOWER LOCK AV				
	3300	BLMT	94002	769-A1
LOWER VISTA GRANDE				
	1200	MLBR	94030	727-J5
LOWERY DR				
	-	ATN	94027	790-G1
LOWRIE AV				
	1300	SSF	94080	707-J4
LOYOLA AV				
	-	SMCo	94063	790-D1
LOYOLA DR				
	200	MLBR	94030	728-A5
	1800	BURL	94010	728-A5
LUCCA DR				
	100	SSF	94080	707-G1
LUCERNE AV				
	500	RDWC	94061	790-B1
LUCERO WY				
	100	SMCo	94028	810-D3
LUCIA CT				
	100	SBRN	94066	727-H2
LUCKY AV				
	900	SMCo	94025	790-D6
LUCY LN				
	-	SMCo	94019	(808-A5 See Page 788)
	-	SMCo	94019	(807-J5 See Page 788)
LUDEMAN LN				
	-	MLBR	94030	728-A3
	300	MLBR	94030	727-J3
LUFF LN				
	400	RDWC	94065	749-H6
LULA BELLE LN				
	100	SMTO	94403	749-B4
LUNADO WY				
	-	SF	94132	687-C1
LUNDY LN				
	-	SMCo	94402	748-G7
LUNDY WY				
	100	PCFA	94044	707-A7
	700	PCFA	94044	727-A1
LUNETTA AV				
	200	PCFA	94044	707-A6
LUPIN LN				
	-	ATN	94027	770-G7
	-	ATN	94027	790-G1
LUPIN WY				
	900	SCAR	94070	769-F4
LUPINE AV				
	3500	PA	94303	791-E7
LUPINE DR				
	-	DALY	94014	687-H3
LUPINE RD				
	27700	LAH	94022	810-J6
LUPINE WY				
	-	HIL	94010	748-D2
LUPINE VALLEY CT				
	-	BSBN	94005	687-H4
LURLINE DR				
	700	FCTY	94404	749-G2
LUX AV				
	100	SSF	94080	708-A3
	100	SSF	94080	707-J2
LYALL WY				
	2300	BLMT	94002	769-C2
LYCETT CIR				
	-	DALY	94015	707-C3
LYCETT CT				
	-	DALY	94015	707-C3
N LYCETT ST				
	100	DALY	94015	707-C3
S LYCETT ST				
	100	DALY	94015	707-C3
LYDIA CT				
	-	HIL	94010	748-F5
LYME LN				
	-	FCTY	94404	749-E6
LYNBROOK DR				
	300	PCFA	94044	707-B2
LYNDHURST AV				
	100	SCAR	94070	769-E2
	200	BLMT	94002	769-E2
LYNDHURST CT				
	-	BLMT	94002	769-E2
LYNN WY				
	100	WDSD	94062	789-J4
LYNTON AV				
	100	SCAR	94070	769-D4
	100	SMCo	94070	769-D4
LYNVALE CT				
	-	DALY	94015	686-J4
LYNWOOD LN				
	900	MLBR	94030	727-H3
LYNX LN				
	800	FCTY	94404	749-F4
LYON AV				
	1900	BLMT	94002	749-C7
	2100	BLMT	94002	769-C1
LYONRIDGE LN				
	-	SMTO	94402	748-H6
LYONS ST				
	1100	RDWC	94061	790-A1
LYTTON AV				
	100	PA	94301	790-H4

M

STREET	Block	City	ZIP	Pg-Grid
MACADAMIA DR				
	900	HIL	94010	728-C7
	900	HIL	94010	748-C1
MACARTHUR AV				
	400	SMCo	94063	770-C6
	600	SMTO	94402	748-J4
MACARTHUR DR				
	500	SMCo	94015	687-B5
MACBAIN AV				
	-	ATN	94027	790-E3
MACDONALD AV				
	-	DALY	94014	687-J3
	-	DALY	94014	688-A3
MACDONALD ST				
	1400	RDWC	94061	790-A2
MACKALL WY				
	3100	PA	94306	791-D7
MADDUX DR				
	700	SMCo	94015	687-A4
	900	PA	94303	791-D6
	900	DALY	94015	687-A4
	1400	RDWC	94061	789-J2
	1500	RDWC	94061	790-A3
MADEIRA DR				
	1400	PCFA	94044	727-A6
MADERA AV				
	-	SCAR	94070	769-F4
	1000	MLPK	94025	790-J1
	1200	MLPK	94025	771-A7
	1200	MLPK	94025	770-J7
MADERA DR				
	500	SMCo	94403	749-A4
	500	SMTO	94403	749-A4
MADERA LN				
	4000	SMCo	94074	(828-G7 See Page 827)
MADERA RD				
	400	SMCo	94062	788-H5
MADERA WY				
	1300	MLBR	94030	728-A5
	1300	MLBR	94030	727-J5
	3700	SBRN	94066	707-C5
MADISON AV				
	-	SMTO	94402	749-A3
	100	RDWC	94061	770-A7
	100	SBRN	94066	727-G1
	1100	RDWC	94061	769-J7
	1600	RDWC	94061	789-J1
MADISON WY				
	-	SMCo	94025	790-H2
	500	PA	94303	791-C4
MADRID AV				
	100	SMCo	94018	767-A2
MADRID CT				
	-	MLBR	94030	728-A2
	1300	PCFA	94044	727-A6
MADRID ST				
	400	SF	94112	687-G1
MADRONA AV				
	100	SMCo	94018	767-A2
MADRONA ST				
	-	SCAR	94070	769-F3
MADRONE AV				
	-	SMCo	94038	766-G1
	-	SMCo	94060	(868-H5 See Page 867)
	-	SSF	94080	708-A2
	500	SMCo	94062	788-G6
MADRONE PL				
	-	HIL	94010	728-E7
MADRONE RD				
	-	ATN	94027	790-G1
MADRONE ST				
	100	RDWC	94061	770-B7
	200	RDWC	94061	790-C1
	300	MLBR	94030	728-A2
MADRONE TR				
	-	SMCo	94062	788-H6
MADRONE WY				
	-	PCFA	94044	727-A5
MADRONO AV				
	1500	PA	94306	791-A6
MAGELLAN AV				
	100	SMCo	94019	767-C4
MAGELLAN CT				
	400	PCFA	94044	707-A2
MAGELLAN DR				
	300	PCFA	94044	707-A2
MAGELLAN LN				
	800	FCTY	94404	749-G4
MAGNOLIA AV				
	-	SMCo	94063	770-F5
	-	SSF	94080	707-H3
	100	MLBR	94030	728-A2
	700	SBRN	94066	707-H7
	700	SBRN	94066	728-A2

STREET
Block City ZIP Pg-Grid

MAGNOLIA AV
700 SBRN 94066 727-J2
700 MLBR 94030 727-J2
1200 SCAR 94070 769-F3
S MAGNOLIA AV
- MLBR 94030 728-B4
1800 BURL 94010 728-B4
MAGNOLIA AV S
- SSF 94080 707-H4
MAGNOLIA CT
1600 MLPK 94025 790-F5
MAGNOLIA DR
- ATN 94027 790-F1
600 SMTO 94402 749-B2
MAGNOLIA ST
200 HMBY 94019 787-E2
600 MLPK 94025 790-E5
MAHAN ST
600 SF 94124 688-E1
MAHLER RD
800 BURL 94010 728-D4
MAHOGANY RW
700 SBRN 94066 707-H6
MAIDEN LN
4100 SMTO 94403 749-D6
MAIN DR
- SBRN 94066 727-G3
MAIN ST
100 BSBN 94005 688-A4
100 BSBN 94005 687-J3
100 SMTO 94401 748-J1
200 RDWC 94063 770-B5
200 SMTO 94401 749-A1
300 SMCo 94037 746-F4
N MAIN ST
100 HMBY 94019 767-F7
300 HMBY 94019 787-F1
S MAIN ST
- HMBY 94019 787-F2
MAINSAIL CT
200 FCTY 94404 749-G4
MAITLAND RD
400 PCFA 94044 726-J2
MAJESTIC AV
- SF 94112 687-E1
MAJILLA AV
1100 BURL 94010 728-F6
MAJORCA WY
2800 SCAR 94070 769-F6
MALABAR CT
- SCAR 94070 769-C4
MALAGA ST
900 SMCo 94018 767-C3
MALAVEAR CT
- PCFA 94044 726-J5
- PCFA 94044 727-A5
MALCOLM AV
100 BLMT 94002 749-D7
MALCOLM RD
800 BURL 94010 728-D4
MALLARD ST
800 FCTY 94404 749-G1
MALLET CT
1000 MLPK 94025 790-F4
MALONEY LN
600 MLPK 94025 790-F3
MALORY CT
- SMCo 94061 790-B3
MALTA LN
1200 FCTY 94404 749-F5
MANCHESTER CT
3100 PA 94303 791-D6
MANCHESTER LN
100 BLMT 94002 749-F6
MANDALAY CT
- RDWC 94065 749-J5
MANDARIN DR
300 DALY 94015 707-C1
MANDARIN WY
- ATN 94027 790-B5
MANDELA CT
1000 EPA 94303 791-C1
MANHATTAN AV
1900 EPA 94303 791-B3
MANHATTEN CT
- RDWC 94065 749-J5
MANILA WY
600 SMCo 94015 687-A5
MANOR CT
- DALY 94015 687-A3
- RDWC 94062 769-H5
MANOR DR
100 PCFA 94044 706-J3
100 SCAR 94070 769-E4
100 SSF 94080 707-G5
200 PCFA 94044 707-A4
1700 HIL 94010 728-E7
MANOR PL
- MLPK 94025 790-H3
W MANOR PZ
400 PCFA 94044 706-J3
MANSEAU ST
600 SF 94124 688-E1
MANSELL ST
- SF 94134 688-A1
400 SF 94134 687-H1
MANSFIELD DR
200 SSF 94080 707-D2
MANSION CT
- MLPK 94025 790-C7

MANUELLA AV
300 WDSD 94062 789-F6
MANZANITA AV
- DALY 94015 707-A1
- SMCo 94062 788-J6
100 SCAR 94070 769-F3
100 SSF 94080 707-H4
200 PA 94306 791-A6
1600 BLMT 94002 769-D1
2000 SMCo 94025 790-C6
MANZANITA CT
- MLBR 94030 728-A5
MANZANITA DR
1000 PCFA 94044 727-A5
1200 MLBR 94030 728-A6
MANZANITA RD
- ATN 94027 790-G1
200 SMCo 94062 788-J6
MANZANITA ST
- RDWC 94063 770-B7
MANZANITA WY
100 WDSD 94062 789-H7
100 WDSD 94062 809-H1
MAPACHE CT
- PTLV 94028 810-A4
MAPACHE DR
100 PTLV 94028 810-A4
MAPLE AV
- ATN 94027 790-E2
- SSF 94080 707-J3
400 SBRN 94066 727-H1
500 SBRN 94066 707-H7
800 BURL 94010 728-F5
S MAPLE AV
100 SSF 94080 707-H4
MAPLE PL
100 MLBR 94030 728-A5
MAPLE ST
- RDWC 94063 770-B5
400 PA 94301 791-A3
500 SMTO 94402 748-J2
1000 SMTO 94402 749-A3
MAPLE WY
- SCAR 94070 769-G6
400 WDSD 94062 789-E3
W MAPLE WY
400 WDSD 94062 789-E3
MAPLE LEAF WY
- ATN 94027 790-G2
MARBLY AV
- DALY 94015 707-C2
MARBURGER AV
3100 BLMT 94002 769-A1
MARCELLA WY
200 MLBR 94030 728-B5
MARCIE CIR
- SSF 94080 707-G2
MARCO WY
100 SSF 94080 708-A5
MARCO POLO WY
1600 BURL 94010 728-C5
MARCUSSEN DR
1000 MLPK 94025 790-G2
MARGARET AV
- BSBN 94005 688-A7
- SF 94112 687-E1
MARGARET CT
4100 SMTO 94403 749-E6
MARGARITA AV
3100 BURL 94010 728-A7
MARGATE ST
- DALY 94015 707-C2
MARGO LN
- HIL 94010 728-D6
MARIALINDA CT
- HIL 94010 728-D7
MARIANI CT
- SMCo 94062 789-G3
MARIANNA LN
- ATN 94027 790-E2
MARIE CT
- HMBY 94019 767-E6
MARIGOLD LN
- SCAR 94070 769-C4
MARIN DR
400 BURL 94010 728-G6
MARINA BLVD
- SSF 94080 708-C2
400 BSBN 94005 688-C7
MARINA CT
1500 SMTO 94403 749-D4
MARINA DR
- RDWC 94065 749-G7
MARINA WY
200 PCFA 94044 706-J7
MARINA VISTA
1500 SMTO 94404 749-D3
MARINE BLVD
100 SMCo 94038 746-G6
MARINE PKWY
100 RDWC 94065 749-G7
MARINE RD
- SMCo 94062 788-J5
MARINE WY
2600 MTVW 94043 791-G7
MARINER WY
- DALY 94014 687-D5
MARINERS ISLAND BLVD
300 FCTY 94404 749-D2

MARINERS ISLAND BLVD
300 SMTO 94404 749-D2
MARINE VIEW AV
- SMTO 94403 749-E7
300 BLMT 94002 749-E7
MARION AV
400 PA 94301 791-C6
500 PA 94306 791-C6
700 PA 94303 791-C6
MARION DR
- SMCo 94062 790-A4
MARION PL
600 PA 94301 791-C6
MARIPOSA AV
100 DALY 94015 687-A7
1500 PA 94306 791-A6
MARIPOSA CT
- BURL 94010 728-A6
MARIPOSA DR
400 SSF 94080 707-F5
2700 BURL 94010 728-A6
MARIPOSA ST
- BSBN 94005 688-A6
MARIPOSA WK
- PCFA 94044 727-B1
MARISMA
3300 SMTO 94403 749-E5
MARITIME AV
- SMCo 94038 746-F6
MARKET PL
200 MLPK 94025 770-H7
MARKET ST
600 DALY 94014 687-D5
E MARKET ST
- DALY 94014 687-C5
W MARKET ST
- DALY 94014 687-C5
MARKHAM AV
- SMCo 94063 790-C1
400 SBRN 94066 727-G1
MARK TWAIN ST
1800 PA 94303 791-B5
MARLBOROUGH AV
2600 SMCo 94063 770-C7
2700 SMCo 94063 790-C1
MARLBOROUGH RD
1100 HIL 94010 748-E4
MARLIN AV
600 FCTY 94404 749-H2
MARLIN CT
500 RDWC 94065 749-H6
MARLIN DR
500 RDWC 94065 749-J6
MARLOWE ST
400 PA 94301 791-A3
MARMONA CT
200 MLPK 94025 790-J3
MARMONA DR
200 MLPK 94025 790-J3
MARQUETTE LN
900 FCTY 94404 749-G4
MARQUITA AV
1100 BURL 94010 728-D5
MARSEILLE WY
2000 HMBY 94019 767-E5
MARSH DR
100 FCTY 94404 749-E1
MARSH RD
800 SMCo 94025 770-F6
800 ATN 94027 770-F6
900 MLPK 94025 770-G5
900 RDWC 94063 770-F6
900 SMCo 94063 770-F6
1000 SMCo 94063 790-F1
1000 ATN 94027 790-F1
1100 RDWC 94025 770-F6
MARSH RD Rt#-84
- MLPK 94025 770-F7
MARSHALL AV
900 SMTO 94403 749-B7
MARSHALL CT
600 RDWC 94063 770-B5
MARSHALL DR
800 PA 94303 791-C5
MARSHALL ST
200 RDWC 94063 770-B5
MARSHALL WY
- DALY 94014 687-D5
MARSHLANDS RD
10000 FRMT 94555 771-F2
MARSTEN AV
3500 BLMT 94002 769-A1
3500 BLMT 94002 768-J1
MARSTEN RD
1200 BURL 94010 728-E5
MARTIN AV
1200 PA 94301 791-A4
MARTIN CT
- DALY 94014 687-J4
MARTIN DR
3500 SMTO 94403 749-D5
MARTIN LN
- WDSD 94062 789-F7
MARTIN PL
100 SBRN 94066 707-J7
MARTIN ST
- DALY 94014 687-H3
MARTINEZ DR
2600 BURL 94010 728-B6

MARTINEZ RD
- WDSD 94062 809-G6
MARTINIQUE DR
500 RDWC 94065 749-J7
MARTINIQUE LN
1200 FCTY 94404 749-F5
MARTINSEN CT
400 PA 94306 791-C7
MARVA OAKS DR
100 WDSD 94062 789-D4
MARVILLA CIR
200 PCFA 94044 726-H4
MARVILLA PL
200 PCFA 94044 726-H4
MAR VISTA DR
- DALY 94014 687-F3
MARY CT
- DALY 94014 687-J3
MARYLAND PL
- SBRN 94066 707-J7
MARYLAND ST
1600 RDWC 94061 789-J3
1900 RDWC 94061 790-A3
MARY LU LN
100 SMTO 94403 749-B5
MARYMONT AV
- ATN 94027 790-B4
MASOLEUM DR
- SMCo - 768-C3
MASON DR
1100 PCFA 94044 727-B4
MASON LN
2600 SMTO 94403 749-A5
MASONIC WY
500 BLMT 94002 749-F7
600 BLMT 94002 769-E1
MASSACHUSETTS AV
- RDWC 94061 789-J3
2500 RDWC 94061 790-A3
MASSON AV
600 SBRN 94066 707-J6
MASTHEAD LN
300 FCTY 94404 749-J1
MASTICK AV
200 SBRN 94066 727-J1
300 SBRN 94066 707-J7
MATADERO CREEK CT
28600 LAH 94022 830-H1
28600 LAH 94022 810-H7
MATADERO CREEK LN
28500 LAH 94022 810-H7
MATEO AV
- DALY 94014 687-C5
- MLBR 94030 728-B3
MATSONIA DR
600 FCTY 94404 749-G2
MATT TR
- SMCo 94060 (868-F5 See Page 867)
MAUREEN AV
400 PA 94306 791-D7
MAXINE AV
1500 SMTO 94401 749-C2
MAXWELL LN
1200 RDWC 94062 769-G6
MAY BROWN AV
1100 MLPK 94025 790-E4
MAYBURY PL
100 WDSD 94062 789-J3
MAYFAIR AV
500 SSF 94080 707-H3
N MAYFAIR AV
- DALY 94015 687-A3
500 DALY 94015 686-J3
S MAYFAIR AV
100 DALY 94015 687-A3
700 DALY 94015 686-J4
MAYFAIR DR
- DALY 94015 687-B3
MAYFIELD AV
- DALY 94015 687-A7
500 SCIC 94305 790-G7
500 SCIC 94305 810-H1
MAYFLOWER LN
- SCAR 94070 769-C4
MAYVIEW AV
700 PA 94303 791-E7
MAYWOOD AV
- DALY 94015 687-A6
MAYWOOD DR
1000 BLMT 94002 769-D2
2300 SBRN 94066 707-E6
MAYWOOD LN
- MLPK 94025 790-F5
MAYWOOD WY
200 SSF 94080 707-G5
MCACKER CT
- SMTO 94402 749-B4
MCAULEY CT
1000 PA 94301 791-A3
MCCARTHY AV
- SF 94134 687-J2
MCCORMICK LN
- ATN 94027 790-E1
MCCREERY DR
- HIL 94010 728-D7
MCCUE AV
900 SCAR 94070 769-G2
MCDONALD WY
1600 BURL 94010 728-C5

MCDONNELL DR
700 SSF 94080 707-E2
MCDONNELL RD
- MLBR 94030 728-B2
- SMCo 94128 728-A1
- SMCo 94128 708-A6
MCEVOY ST
200 RDWC 94061 790-B1
300 RDWC 94061 770-B7
MCFARLAND CT
- SCIC 94305 790-J7
MCGARVEY AV
2100 RDWC 94061 789-H2
MCKENDRY DR
100 MLPK 94025 790-J3
MCKENDRY PL
300 MLPK 94025 790-J3
MCKENZIE CT
- HIL 94010 748-G2
MCKINLEY ST
1100 RDWC 94061 790-A1
1600 SMTO 94403 749-C2
MCKINNEY AV
100 PCFA 94044 707-A4
MCLAIN RD
100 BSBN 94005 688-B7
MCLELLAN AV
- SMTO 94403 749-C5
MCNULTY WY
3600 RDWC 94061 789-H2
MEADE AV
700 SF 94124 688-B1
E MEADOW CIR
1000 PA 94303 791-E7
MEADOW CT
- SMTO 94403 749-D5
E MEADOW DR
600 PA 94306 791-E7
700 PA 94303 791-E7
MEADOW LN
- ATN 94027 790-B6
- RDWC 94063 770-C6
- WDSD 94062 809-H5
- PTLV 94028 809-H5
1500 BURL 94010 728-D5
MEADOW RD
- WDSD 94062 809-H5
MEADOW CREEK CT
- PTLV 94028 810-D7
MEADOW GLEN AV
- MLBR 94030 728-A3
MEADOWOOD DR
100 PTLV 94028 810-B5
MEADOW PARK CIR
- BLMT 94002 769-A3
- BLMT 94002 768-J3
MEADOWSWEET LN
- SCAR 94070 769-C4
MEADOW VIEW PL
2100 SMTO 94403 749-C1
MEARS CT
900 SCIC 94305 810-J1
MEATH DR
2600 SSF 94080 707-C4
MEDFORD AV
2700 RDWC 94061 789-H2
MEDICAL LN
- SCIC 94305 790-G6
300 PA 94304 790-G6
MEDINA DR
2600 SBRN 94066 707-D5
MEDIO AV
100 SMCo 94019 767-C4
MEDITERRANEAN LN
200 RDWC 94065 749-J6
MEDWAY RD
- SMCo 94062 809-G6
- WDSD 94062 809-G6
MEFFERD AV
1400 SMTO 94401 729-A7
MEGANS LN
- SMCo 94062 788-H4
MELANIE LN
- ATN 94027 790-A5
MELBOURNE ST
1300 FCTY 94404 749-G5
MELENDY DR
2300 SCAR 94070 769-D5
MELISSA CIR
- DALY 94014 687-D4
MELISSA CT
700 SMTO 94402 748-J4
MELLO ST
1100 EPA 94303 791-A1
MELODY LN
12300 LAH 94022 830-J1
MELRA CT
- SF 94134 687-J2
MELROSE CT
- HIL 94010 748-G4
- PCFA 94044 707-A3
MELROSE PL
- RDWC 94062 769-H6
MELVILLE AV
100 PA 94301 791-A5
MELVIN HENRY CT
- SMCo 94061 790-A4
MEMORIAL DR
800 SSF 94080 707-G3

MEMORIAL WY
100 SCIC 94305 790-H7
MENALTO AV
1900 MLPK 94025 791-A2
2100 EPA 94303 791-A1
MENALTO DR
12200 LAH 94022 830-H1
MENDOCINO CT
100 SBRN 94066 707-E7
MENDOCINO ST
100 BSBN 94005 688-A6
MENDOCINO WY
100 RDWC 94065 749-J6
MENHADEN CT
300 FCTY 94404 749-H3
MENLO AV
- DALY 94015 686-J7
600 MLPK 94025 790-F4
MENLO OAKS DR
200 SMCo 94025 790-H2
1000 MLPK 94025 770-J7
1000 MLPK 94025 790-H2
MERCAT PL
- HIL 94010 748-F5
MERCED DR
- SBRN 94066 707-D7
- SBRN 94066 727-D1
MERCEDES LN
- ATN 94027 790-D2
MERIDIAN
- RDWC 94065 749-J5
- RDWC 94065 750-A5
MERION DR
2600 SBRN 94066 707-D6
MERION RD
- HMBY 94019 787-F5
MERNER RD
1000 HIL 94010 748-G4
MERRILL ST
1000 MLPK 94025 790-F3
MERRY MOPPET LN
2200 BLMT 94002 769-C2
MESA CT
- ATN 94027 790-B5
MESA VERDE WY
100 SCAR 94070 769-E6
METHUSELA TR
- SMCo 94062 809-A2
METHUSELAH TR
- SMCo 94062 809-A4
200 SMCo 94062 (808-J4 See Page 788)
METRO CIR
1000 PA 94303 791-D5
METRO CENTER BLVD
900 FCTY 94404 749-E3
METZGAR ST
200 HMBY 94019 787-E2
MEYN RD
- SMCo 94019 (807-H5 See Page 788)
MEZES AV
1800 BLMT 94002 749-C7
1900 BLMT 94002 769-C1
MICHAEL CT
- SCAR 94070 769-G6
MICHAEL DR
3400 RDWC 94063 770-E7
3500 SMTO 94403 749-B6
MICHAEL LN
- MLBR 94030 728-A3
- MLBR 94030 727-J3
MICHAELS WY
- ATN 94027 790-E3
MICHELLE CT
200 SSF 94080 708-B4
MICHELLE LN
300 DALY 94015 707-C2
MICHIGAN AV
1600 EPA 94303 791-B1
MIDDLE AV
600 MLPK 94025 790-F5
MIDDLE CT
- SBRN 94066 727-G2
400 MLPK 94025 790-F6
MIDDLE RD
300 BLMT 94002 749-E7
700 BLMT 94002 769-E1
MIDDLEFIELD RD
- ATN 94027 790-E1
100 PA 94301 790-E1
400 RDWC 94063 770-A5
500 MLPK 94025 790-E1
600 PA 94301 791-A4
1600 PA 94303 791-A4
2500 SMCo 94063 770-C7
2600 PA 94306 791-A4
3100 SMCo 94063 790-E1
MIDDLE FORK LN
13400 LAH 94022 810-J7
MIDDLE GATE ST
- ATN 94027 790-D2
MIDDLESEX RD
500 BLMT 94002 749-E7
MIDDLETON RD
- SMCo 94020 850-D7
MIDFIELD WY
3600 RDWC 94062 789-H1
MIDGLEN WY
800 WDSD 94062 789-F3

MIDLAND WY
700 SMCo 94062 789-F2
MIDTOWN CT
2700 PA 94303 791-C6
MIDVALE AV
300 SMTO 94403 749-C7
MIDVALE DR
- DALY 94015 687-A7
MIDWAY AV
400 SMTO 94402 748-G1
500 SMCo 94015 687-A4
MIDWAY CT
- DALY 94014 687-J3
MIDWAY DR
- DALY 94014 687-J3
MIELKE DR
400 MLPK 94025 790-G3
MILAGRA CT
- PCFA 94044 707-A4
MILAGRA DR
100 PCFA 94044 706-J4
200 PCFA 94044 707-A4
MILAN TER
- SF 94112 687-E2
MILANO WY
2700 SCAR 94070 769-F5
MILFORD AV
- HIL 94010 748-G2
MILL RD
400 SMCo 94062 788-H6
MILL ST
- SF 94134 688-A1
600 HMBY 94019 787-F1
MILLBRAE AV
- MLBR 94030 728-B4
1300 MLBR 94030 727-J5
E MILLBRAE AV
- MLBR 94030 728-C4
MILLBRAE CIR
- MLBR 94030 728-A4
MILLER AV
100 SSF 94080 707-F1
500 PCFA 94044 707-A4
1600 BLMT 94002 749-C7
MILLER CT
- SMCo 94061 790-B3
MILLIE AV
900 MLPK 94025 790-F4
MILLS AV
700 SBRN 94066 707-J6
1100 BURL 94010 728-D5
1700 BLMT 94002 749-C7
2000 SMCo 94025 790-C6
MILLS CT
1400 MLPK 94025 790-F3
MILLS ST
1200 MLPK 94025 790-F3
MILLS WY
1000 RDWC 94063 770-D6
MILLS CANYON CT
- BURL 94010 728-B6
MILLWOOD DR
100 MLBR 94030 728-A2
300 MLBR 94030 727-J3
MILTON AV
200 SBRN 94066 728-A1
200 SBRN 94066 727-J1
300 SBRN 94066 707-J7
MILTON ST
1600 SMCo 94061 790-B3
MIMOSA WY
100 SMCo 94028 810-D4
MINA LN
300 PCFA 94044 707-B3
MINDANAO DR
- RDWC 94065 749-J5
- RDWC 94065 750-A5
MINERVA AV
100 PCFA 94044 727-A2
MINERVA ST
- SF 94112 687-D1
200 SF 94132 687-D1
MINOCA RD
- PTLV 94028 810-D5
MINORCA WY
- MLBR 94030 728-A4
MIO CORTE
- MLBR 94030 728-A4
MIRA ST
100 FCTY 94404 749-E4
MIRA WY
- SMCo 94028 810-D4
MIRADA AV
600 SCIC 94305 810-H1
MIRADA DR
100 DALY 94015 687-B6
MIRADA RD
- SMCo 94019 767-C4
- SMCo 94038 767-C3
- HMBY 94019 767-C4
- HMBY 94038 767-C3
MIRADOR TER
900 PCFA 94044 707-A6
MIRAMAR
1400 SMTO 94404 749-D3
MIRAMAR AV
- SF 94112 687-D1
MIRAMAR DR
300 SMCo 94019 767-C4

MIRAMAR TER
700 BLMT 94002 769-E1
MIRAMONTE AV
100 PA 94306 791-A6
MIRAMONTE CT
- SCAR 94070 769-F2
MIRAMONTES AV
100 HMBY 94019 787-E1
MIRAMONTES RD
100 HMBY 94019 787-G5
100 SMCo 94019 787-G5
100 WDSD 94062 789-F6
MIRAMONTES ST
100 HMBY 94019 787-G1
200 SMCo 94019 787-G1
500 SMCo - 787-H1
MIRAMONTES TR
- SMCo 94062 789-C3
MIRAMONTES POINT RD
300 HMBY 94019 787-F6
MIRANDA CT
- HIL 94010 748-F4
1500 PCFA 94044 727-A3
MIRASOL CT
- HIL 94010 748-F5
MIRA VISTA CT
- DALY 94014 687-G3
MIRA VISTA WY
300 SSF 94080 707-F5
MIRIAM ST
- DALY 94014 687-C3
MIRMIROU DR
13800 LAH 94022 810-H6
MISSION CIR
- DALY 94014 687-D3
MISSION DR
- SMTO 94402 748-J2
100 EPA 94303 791-C3
MISSION RD
900 SSF 94080 707-E1
1400 CLMA 94014 707-E1
7400 CLMA 94014 687-E7
MISSION ST
4100 SF 94112 687-E2
5900 DALY 94014 687-E2
MISSION ST Rt#-82
6300 DALY 94014 687-C4
MISSION BLUE DR
- BSBN 94005 688-A4
- BSBN 94005 687-H5
MISSION HILLS DR
- DALY 94014 687-F3
MISSION TRAIL RD
- WDSD 94062 789-G5
MISTY LN
1000 BLMT 94002 769-D2
MITCHELL AV
100 SSF 94080 708-A4
MITCHELL LN
400 PA 94301 790-H5
MITCHELL WY
1400 RDWC 94061 789-J3
MITTEN RD
800 BURL 94010 728-D3
MIZZEN LN
1500 HMBY 94019 767-E6
MOANA WY
200 PCFA 94044 707-A6
200 PCFA 94044 706-J6
MODOC AV
- SF 94112 687-E1
1300 MLPK 94025 770-J7
MODOC PL
200 PCFA 94044 727-B2
MOFFETT CIR
1000 PA 94303 791-D5
MOHICAN WY
800 RDWC 94062 789-G2
MOLITOR RD
1500 BLMT 94002 769-F2
MOLONEY CT
- SMCo 94062 769-H7
E MOLTKE ST
- DALY 94014 687-C4
W MOLTKE ST
- DALY 94014 687-C4
MOLTON AV
- SCAR 94070 769-E3
MONACO DR
100 RDWC 94065 749-J5
MONARCH DR
- BSBN 94005 687-J5
MONETA CT
- SF 94112 687-E2
MONETA WY
- SF 94112 687-E2
MONO ST
- BSBN 94005 688-A6
MONROE AV
1300 SMTO 94401 729-A7
2000 BLMT 94002 749-C7
MONROE ST
100 RDWC 94063 770-B6
MONSERAT AV
2300 BLMT 94002 769-B1
MONTALVO RD
100 SMCo 94062 769-E7
MONTANA LN
- SMCo 94025 790-D5

MONTANA ST
- SF 94112 687-D1
100 SMCo 94038 746-F5
200 SF 94132 687-D1
E MONTARA BLVD
1000 SMCo 94037 746-H5
W MONTARA BLVD
- SMCo 94037 746-G5
MONTARA CT
- PTLV 94028 810-D6
MONTCLAIR AV
- DALY 94015 686-J5
MONTEBELLO DR
- DALY 94015 707-A1
MONTE BELLO RD
- PA 94304 830-G6
- PA 94304 850-J1
MONTECITO AV
100 PCFA 94044 706-J6
400 SMCo 94018 767-A2
MONTECITO RD
- WDSD 94062 809-J5
MONTECITO WY
1800 BURL 94010 728-B5
MONTE CORVINO WY
1600 BURL 94010 728-C5
MONTE CRESTA DR
2600 BLMT 94002 749-B7
2600 BLMT 94002 769-A1
MONTE DIABLO AV
- SMTO 94401 748-J1
600 SMTO 94401 728-J7
900 SMTO 94401 729-A7
MONTEGO LN
- FCTY 94404 749-E6
- SMCo 94061 790-B4
MONTELENA CT
- WDSD 94062 809-G1
MONTEREY AV
- SMCo 94038 746-F7
1000 FCTY 94404 749-F5
2000 SMCo 94025 790-C6
MONTEREY DR
- DALY 94015 687-A6
1500 SBRN 94066 707-D7
1700 SBRN 94066 727-E1
MONTEREY RD
100 PCFA 94044 706-J3
200 PCFA 94044 707-A3
MONTEREY ST
- MLBR 94030 728-B2
100 BSBN 94005 688-A6
2600 SMTO 94403 749-A6
MONTERO AV
1300 BURL 94010 728-C6
MONTE ROSA DR
600 MLPK 94025 790-D7
600 MLPK 94025 810-D1
MONTE VERDE DR
900 PCFA 94044 726-J5
MONTE VISTA AV
- ATN 94027 790-C4
MONTE VISTA LN
700 HMBY 94019 787-F2
MONTEVISTA LN
100 DALY 94015 707-C2
MONTE VISTA RD
- SMCo 94037 746-H4
100 SCAR 94070 769-H2
MONTEZUMA DR
600 PCFA 94044 726-H4
MONTGOMERY AV
900 SBRN 94066 707-J5
1200 SMCo 94061 790-B3
MONTGOMERY LN
800 SCAR 94070 769-H2
MONTGOMERY ST
900 SCAR 94070 769-G3
MONTICELLO CT
- WDSD 94062 789-E3
MONTICELLO RD
1700 SMCo 94402 748-F7
1700 SMCo 94402 768-G1
MONTICELLO ST
- SF 94132 687-C1
MONTROSE AV
- DALY 94015 687-A5
MONTSERRAT DR
- RDWC 94065 749-J5
MONTWOOD CIR
300 SMCo 94061 790-B4
MOODY CT
26800 LAH 94022 830-J2
MOODY RD
26200 LAH 94022 830-H3
26200 SCIC 96014 830-H2
MOON LN
14000 LAH 94022 810-H6
MOON GATE CT
- PCFA 94044 707-A2
MOONLIGHT CT
- SSF 94080 707-E5
MOONSAIL LN
1200 FCTY 94404 749-H3
MOORE CT
100 SBRN 94066 707-E7
MOORE RD
100 WDSD 94062 789-J6
300 WDSD 94062 790-A6

MOORING LN
- DALY 94014 687-E6
MORAGA CT
900 PA 94303 791-E6
MORELAND DR
3200 SBRN 94066 707-D6
3400 SMCo 94044 707-D6
MORENO AV
700 PA 94303 791-D5
MOREY DR
500 MLPK 94025 790-G4
MORIS POINT RD
100 PCFA 94044 706-J7
100 PCFA 94044 727-A1
100 PCFA 94044 726-J1
MORNINGSIDE AV
1100 SSF 94080 707-G1
MORNINGSIDE DR
- DALY 94015 686-J5
600 MLBR 94030 727-J4
S MORO AV
600 SMCo 94018 767-C3
MORRELL AV
800 BURL 94010 728-F6
MORRELL ST
300 SF 94124 688-E1
MORRIS DR
3100 PA 94303 791-E6
MORRO CT
500 FCTY 94404 749-F5
MORRO VISTA LN
100 SMCo 94028 810-C3
MORSE BLVD
1100 SCAR 94070 769-G4
MORSE LN
- SMCo 94062 809-E5
MORSE ST
- SF 94112 687-F2
MORTON DR
- DALY 94015 707-B2
MORTON ST
- PA 94303 791-C5
MOSCOW ST
300 SF 94112 687-G2
MOSELEY RD
300 HIL 94010 748-D3
MOSS AV
300 SMCo 94062 788-H5
MOSSWOOD LN
800 MLBR 94030 727-H3
MOSSWOOD RD
- HIL 94010 748-D3
MOSSWOOD WY
- ATN 94027 770-G7
200 SSF 94080 707-G5
MOULTON DR
- ATN 94027 790-F2
3800 SBRN 94066 707-C6
MOUNDS RD
- SMTO 94402 748-H1
MOUN REDONDO TR
- SMCo 94062 789-B3
MOUNTAIN RD
100 SSF 94080 707-H2
MOUNTAIN VW
300 DALY 94014 687-D4
MOUNTAIN DUMP RD
100 SMCo - 767-G5
MOUNTAIN HOME CT
300 WDSD 94062 789-G7
MOUNTAIN HOME RD
- WDSD 94062 789-G7
400 WDSD 94062 809-H1
MOUNTAIN MEADOW DR
- SMCo 94062 809-C4
MOUNTAIN VIEW AV
- SMTO 94403 749-E7
400 BLMT 94002 749-E7
MOUNTAIN VIEW PL
- SMCo 94402 748-H7
MOUNTAIN VIEW WY
500 SMCo 94062 789-F1
MOUNTAIN WOOD LN
- WDSD 94062 789-G7
100 WDSD 94062 809-G1
MOUNT VERNON AV
- SF 94112 687-E1
MOUNT VERNON LN
- ATN 94027 790-E1
MUDDY RD
- SMCo - 788-A1
- SMCo - 787-J1
- SMCo - 768-A7
MUIR WY
- PCFA 94044 727-B5
1000 BLMT 94002 769-A2
MUIRFIELD CIR
2600 SBRN 94066 707-D5
MUIRFIELD RD
- HMBY 94019 787-F5
MUIRWOOD DR
- DALY 94014 687-D3
MULBERRY AV
100 SSF 94080 707-H3
MULBERRY CT
- BLMT 94002 769-C2
MULBERRY DR
1700 SMTO 94403 748-J7
MULBERRY LN
- ATN 94027 790-C5

STREET
Block City ZIP Pg-Grid

PEARCE MITCHELL PL
- SCIC 94305 810-H1
PEARL AV
100 SCAR 94070 769-H5
1000 SMCo 94038 746-G6
PEARL ST
700 SMCo 94038 746-F6
PEBBLE DR
- SMCo 94062 769-E6
1300 SCAR 94070 769-E6
PEBBLEWOOD WY
1100 SMTO 94403 749-E6
PECAN CT
1600 RDWC 94061 790-A2
PECK ST
1600 SMTO 94401 729-B7
PECKS LN
100 SSF 94080 708-A2
PECORA WY
100 SMCo 94028 810-D4
PEGASUS LN
600 FCTY 94404 749-E3
PEGGY LN
900 MLPK 94025 770-G7
PELICAN CIR
- HMBY 94019 787-G5
PELICAN CT
200 FCTY 94404 749-H1
PELICAN LN
- RDWC 94065 749-H6
PEMBROKE CT
- HMBY 94019 787-F5
PEMBROKE PL
- MLPK 94025 790-F6
PENHURST AV
- DALY 94015 707-B2
PENHURST CT
100 DALY 94015 707-B2
PENINSULA AV
- BURL 94010 728-H7
- SMTO 94401 728-H7
200 SF 94134 688-A2
PENINSULA WY
900 SMCo 94025 790-H1
PENNANT CT
500 RDWC 94065 749-H7
PENNSYLVANIA AV
100 RDWC 94063 770-B6
PENOBSCOT DR
200 RDWC 94063 770-C4
PENSACOLA ST
1000 FCTY 94404 749-F5
PEORIA ST
- DALY 94014 687-D3
PEPPER AV
100 BURL 94010 728-F7
100 BURL 94010 748-F1
200 HIL 94010 728-F7
400 PA 94306 791-B7
PEPPER DR
600 SBRN 94066 707-G7
PEPPER LN
- SCAR 94070 769-E2
PEPPERTREE CT
3900 RDWC 94061 789-G3
PEPPERWOOD CT
- MLPK 94025 790-H2
PERALTA AV
- SMCo 94018 767-A2
PERALTA RD
100 PCFA 94044 726-H5
900 SMCo - 726-H5
PERCHERON PL
- HIL 94402 748-H4
900 SMTO 94402 748-H4
PEREZ DR
1400 PCFA 94044 726-J6
PERIMETER RD
- SMTO 94402 748-H5
N PERIMETER RD
- MLPK 94025 790-J1
S PERIMETER RD
600 MLPK 94025 790-J2
W PERIMETER RD
600 MLPK 94025 790-J1
600 SMCo 94025 790-J1
PERITA DR
- DALY 94015 687-A7
PERRY AV
400 PCFA 94044 707-A4
1900 SMCo 94025 790-E7
PERRY ST
- RDWC 94063 770-A5
PERSEUS LN
800 FCTY 94404 749-F4
PERSHING AV
1200 SMTO 94403 749-C2
PERSIA AV
200 SF 94112 687-G1
900 SF 94134 687-G1
PERSIMMON CT
- HIL 94010 748-C1
PESCADERO CREEK RD
- SMCo 94021 849-B7
- SMCo 94060 867-H2
1700 SMCo 94060 (868-E3
See Page 867)
4900 SMCo 94021 (868-E3
See Page 867)

PESCADERO CREEK RD
5200 SMCo 94021 (848-J7
See Page 827)
6000 SMCo 94021 869-A1
9500 SMCo 94020 849-E2
PETER ST
- DALY 94014 687-C4
PETER COUTTS RD
- SCIC 94305 810-J1
PETE TOWN TR
- SMCo 94020 869-G1
PETRINI CT
- MLBR 94030 728-A5
PHELPS RD
300 SCAR 94070 769-E3
PHILIP DR
200 DALY 94015 707-C1
PHILIP LN
- SCAR 94070 769-F3
PHILLIP RD
- WDSD 94062 809-H3
PHILLIPS RD
- PA 94303 791-C3
PHLEGER RD
- SMCo 94062 789-C2
PHOENIX LN
800 FCTY 94404 749-H1
PHYLLIS CT
- BLMT 94002 769-D1
PICARDO AV
- PCFA 94044 727-B4
PICARDO CT
- PCFA 94044 727-B4
PICCADILLY CT
- SCAR 94070 769-E5
PICCADILLY LN
4100 SMTO 94403 749-D6
PICCADILLY PL
100 SBRN 94066 707-G6
PICO AV
600 SMTO 94403 749-A5
PICO BLVD
500 SCAR 94070 769-H2
PICO TER
800 PCFA 94044 707-A5
PIEDMONT AV
100 SBRN 94066 727-G2
200 PCFA 94044 727-A2
PIEDMONT WY
800 RDWC 94062 789-H1
PIERCE RD
100 MLPK 94025 770-H7
400 MLPK 94025 790-J1
PIERCE ST
100 DALY 94015 687-B5
1700 SMTO 94403 749-C2
PIER POINT LN
- RDWC 94065 749-H5
PIERS CT
900 PA 94303 791-D6
PIERS LN
- SMCo 94025 810-E2
900 SCIC 94304 810-E2
PIGEON POINT RD
- SMCo 94060 (888-A5
See Page 867)
500 SMCo 94060 (887-J4
See Page 867)
PIKE LN
- SMTO 94403 749-D5
PILAR PL
- PCFA 94044 727-A3
PILARCITOS AV
- HMBY 94019 767-E6
- HMBY 94019 787-F1
PILARCITOS CT
- HIL 94010 748-E6
PILARCITOS RD
- SMCo - 727-G6
- SMCo - 747-G1
PILARCITOS CREEK RD
- SMCo - 768-B4
PILGRIM DR
500 FCTY 94404 749-G2
PILOT CIR
- RDWC 94065 749-J5
- RDWC 94065 750-A5
PINE AV
- SCAR 94070 769-F3
100 SSF 94080 708-A2
100 SMCo 94038 746-G7
200 SSF 94080 707-J2
400 HMBY 94019 787-F1
PINE CT
- DALY 94014 687-H3
- HIL 94010 748-D2
PINE LN
- SMCo 94060 (868-H5
See Page 867)
PINE ST
- RDWC 94063 770-B7
200 SBRN 94066 707-J7
300 MLBR 94030 728-B2
500 SBRN 94066 708-A6
1000 MLPK 94025 790-G3
1200 PA 94301 791-B5
PINE TER
500 SSF 94080 707-J2
PINECREST DR
1900 SBRN 94066 707-E6

PINECREST TER
- SMTO 94402 748-G1
PINEHAVEN DR
- DALY 94015 687-A4
PINEHAVEN WY
200 PCFA 94044 707-A7
PINE HILL RD
700 SCIC 94305 810-J1
PINEHILL RD
300 SSF 94080 708-C3
PINEHURST CT
1000 MLBR 94030 727-H3
PINEHURST LN
- HMBY 94019 787-F5
PINEHURST WY
100 SSF 94080 707-G5
PINE KNOLL DR
1500 BLMT 94002 769-D1
1700 BLMT 94002 749-D7
PINE RIDGE DR
100 SMCo - 768-D4
PINE RIDGE WY
- PTLV 94028 810-D5
PINEVIEW LN
100 MLPK 94025 790-D5
PINEWOOD CT
- SMTO 94403 748-H7
PINON AV
800 MLBR 94030 728-B5
800 BURL 94010 728-B5
PINON DR
100 PTLV 94028 810-B4
PINRAIL LN
600 FCTY 94404 749-J1
PINTA LN
700 FCTY 94404 749-G2
PINTO AV
- SF 94132 687-A1
PINTO WY
- WDSD 94062 789-D6
PIONEER CT
2000 SMTO 94403 749-A4
PIO PICO WY
- PCFA 94044 727-C5
PIRATE CV
- DALY 94014 687-E5
PISA CT
- SSF 94080 707-G4
PISCES LN
500 FCTY 94404 749-E4
PITCAIRN DR
600 FCTY 94404 749-G5
PITMAN AV
1200 PA 94301 791-A3
1400 PA 94303 791-A3
PIXIE LN
- SCAR 94070 769-C4
PIZARRO LN
900 FCTY 94404 749-F3
PLACER WY
- BSBN 94005 688-A7
PLACITAS AV
- ATN 94027 790-E1
500 SMCo 94025 770-E7
500 SMCo 94063 790-E1
PLAID PL
- HIL 94010 748-E4
PLATEAU DR
3300 BLMT 94002 769-A1
PLAYA
1900 SMTO 94403 749-E5
PLAY BOWL DR
- SMCo 94020 849-E1
PLAZA LN
900 FCTY 94404 749-E3
1500 BURL 94010 728-C4
PLAZA ALHAMBRA
500 SMCo 94018 767-B3
PLAZA CABRILLO
- SMCo 94018 767-C3
PLEASANT ST
- FCTY 94404 749-E6
PLEASANT HILL RD
900 RDWC 94061 789-H2
PLOVER ST
800 FCTY 94404 749-H2
PLUMAS AV
1400 MLPK 94025 770-H7
PLUMAS CT
100 SBRN 94066 707-D7
PLUMAS ST
- BSBN 94005 688-A6
PLUM TREE LN
100 SCIC 94305 790-H6
PLUMWOOD PL
1400 SBRN 94066 707-G7
PLYMOUTH AV
- SCAR 94070 769-E4
- SF 94112 687-D2
PLYMOUTH CIR
- DALY 94015 707-D3
PLYMOUTH LN
600 FCTY 94404 749-F4
PLYMOUTH WY
600 BURL 94010 728-G6
2600 SBRN 94066 707-E7
POE ST
300 PA 94301 790-H4
POETT RD
300 HIL 94010 748-H2

POINSETTIA AV
- SMTO 94403 749-C5
POINTE PACIFIC DR
700 DALY 94014 687-D3
POINT REYES WY
- PCFA 94044 727-B5
POINT SAN BRUNO BLVD
- SSF 94080 708-C3
POLARIS AV
600 FCTY 94404 749-F4
POLARIS WY
200 DALY 94014 687-F2
200 SF 94112 687-F2
POLHEMUS AV
200 ATN 94027 790-C4
POLHEMUS RD
- SMTO 94402 748-G7
200 SMCo 94402 748-G7
700 SMCo 94402 768-H1
700 SMTO 94402 768-H1
POLITZER DR
- MLPK 94025 790-E5
POLK AV
2000 SMTO 94403 749-C2
POLLUX CT
800 FCTY 94404 749-F4
POLO CT
1900 SMTO 94403 749-A4
POLYNESIA DR
1100 FCTY 94404 749-G2
POMEROY CT
2500 SSF 94080 707-C4
POMPANO CIR
300 FCTY 94404 749-H2
POMPONIO
- PTLV 94028 830-C1
POMPONIO TKTR
- SMCo 94021 849-A5
- SMCo 94021 (848-G6
See Page 827)
- SMCo 94060 (848-G6
See Page 827)
- SMCo 94060 (868-D2
See Page 867)
POMPONIO CREEK RD
- SMCo 94021 849-A5
- SMCo 94074 (848-C2
See Page 827)
100 SMCo 94021 (848-C2
See Page 827)
PONCE AV
2600 BLMT 94002 769-B1
PONCETTA DR
- DALY 94015 687-B3
PONDEROSA RD
- SSF 94080 707-F4
200 SMCo 94080 707-F4
POPE RD
- SMCo 94020 849-E2
POPE ST
- DALY 94014 687-F2
- SF 94112 687-F2
100 MLPK 94025 791-A3
200 MLPK 94025 790-J2
POPLAR AV
- RDWC 94061 789-J2
- MLBR 94030 728-B4
100 SBRN 94066 727-J1
100 RDWC 94061 790-B1
300 SBRN 94066 707-J7
500 SSF 94080 707-H2
1300 PCFA 94044 727-B5
1800 RDWC 94061 770-B7
2000 EPA 94303 791-A1
E POPLAR AV
- SMTO 94401 748-H1
100 SMTO 94401 728-J6
1100 SMTO 94401 729-A6
W POPLAR AV
- SMTO 94402 748-G1
POPLAR ST
100 HMBY 94019 787-E2
POPPY AV
1700 MLPK 94025 790-E6
POPPY DR
2100 BURL 94010 728-C6
POPPY LN
- SCAR 94070 769-C4
PORT DR
600 SMTO 94404 749-D1
PORTAL LN
500 FCTY 94404 749-F3
PORTAL PL
700 PA 94303 791-B6
PORTIFINO CIR
- RDWC 94065 749-J6
PORTMAN DR
800 RDWC 94065 750-C6
PORTOFINO CT
- SCAR 94070 769-E4
PORTOFINO DR
300 SCAR 94070 769-E5
PORTO FINO LN
600 FCTY 94404 749-F3
PORTOLA AV
- SMCo 94037 746-G5
- DALY 94015 687-A7
- SSF 94080 707-G4
1500 PA 94306 791-A6

PORTOLA DR
200 SMTO 94403 749-B5
PORTOLA RD
- SMCo - 727-F5
- SMCo - 748-A3
- SMCo - 747-H1
- PTLV 94028 810-A6
1000 WDSD 94062 809-G2
1000 PTLV 94028 809-J4
1700 SMCo 94025 809-H4
PORTOLA WY
100 SBRN 94066 727-J2
PORTOLA GREEN CIR
- PTLV 94028 810-C7
PORTOLA HEIGHTS RD
- SMCo 94020 850-H4
PORTOLA STATE PARK RD
- SMCo 94020 850-B7
- SMCo 94020 (870-B2
See Page 869)
PORTO MARINO DR
1000 SCAR 94070 769-E5
PORTO MARINO LN
- SCAR 94070 769-E5
PORTO MARINO WY
- SCAR 94070 769-E5
PORTO ROSA WY
2800 SCAR 94070 769-F5
PORT ROYAL AV
- FCTY 94404 749-E5
PORTSMOUTH LN
600 FCTY 94404 749-F5
PORTSMOUTH WY
2200 SMTO 94403 749-D4
PORT WALK PL
700 RDWC 94065 749-H6
POSITANO CIR
400 RDWC 94065 749-J4
POSITANO WY
400 RDWC 94065 749-J4
POSSUM LN
- PTLV 94028 810-A6
POTOMAC WY
2000 SMTO 94403 749-C4
POTTER AV
500 HMBY 94019 787-E1
POWELL ST
- SMTO 94401 729-B7
POWHATAN PL
- SMCo 94402 768-G1
PRADO CT
- PTLV 94028 810-C7
PRADO SECOYA
- ATN 94027 790-E4
PRAGUE ST
- SF 94112 687-G1
- SMTO 94401 729-A6
PRAIRIE CREEK DR
700 PCFA 94044 727-C5
PRECITA AV
100 SMCo 94038 766-G1
PRESCOTT LN
700 FCTY 94404 749-G5
PRESIDIO AV
100 SMCo 94018 767-A2
PRESTON RD
- WDSD 94062 809-H4
PRETOR WY
- SF 94112 687-F2
PREUSS RD
- SMCo 94060 (868-J2
See Page 867)
PRICE AV
500 RDWC 94063 770-A4
PRICE CT
3000 PA 94303 791-D6
PRICE ST
- DALY 94014 687-C4
PRIMROSE LN
- SCAR 94070 769-E2
PRIMROSE RD
100 BURL 94010 728-G7
PRIMROSE WY
- PA 94303 791-C4
PRINCETON AV
- SMCo 94038 766-H3
PRINCETON DR
2200 SBRN 94066 727-F1
PRINCETON RD
- MLPK 94025 790-G5
400 SMTO 94402 748-H3
PRINCETON ST
2000 PA 94306 791-A7
PRINDLE RD
2600 BLMT 94002 769-B2
PRIOR LN
200 ATN 94027 790-F2
PRIVET DR
2900 HIL 94010 748-B1
PRODUCE AV
100 SSF 94080 707-J4
100 SSF 94080 708-A4
PROMONTORY CT
500 RDWC 94065 749-H6
PROMONTORY POINT LN
700 FCTY 94404 749-E4
PROSPECT RW
600 SMTO 94401 728-G7

PROSPECT ST
- WDSD 94062 789-G6
500 SCAR 94070 769-F3
1600 BLMT 94002 769-F2
2100 MLPK 94025 790-D7
2100 SMCo 94025 790-D7
PROSPECT WY
400 SMCo 94038 766-J2
PROVIDENT DR
- HIL 94010 748-D2
PROWSHEAD LN
800 FCTY 94404 749-H5
PUEBLO ST
- DALY 94014 687-J3
- SF 94134 687-J3
PUFFIN CT
200 FCTY 94404 749-G1
PULGAS AV
1800 EPA 94303 791-C3
2500 EPA 94303 771-C7
PULLMAN AV
2100 BLMT 94002 769-C2
2900 HMBY 94019 767-D4
PULLMAN RD
400 HIL 94010 748-D3
PURDUE AV
1600 EPA 94303 771-B7
PURISIMA RD
100 SMCo 94062 788-G4
PURISIMA ST
300 HMBY 94019 787-F1
PURISIMA WY
300 SMCo 94019 767-D4
PURISIMA CREEK RD
- SMCo 94062 789-A6
1200 SMCo 94019 (808-A1
See Page 788)
1200 SMCo 94019 (807-J2
See Page 788)
1400 SMCo 94019 788-A7
2000 SMCo 94062 788-D5
PYROLA LN
- SCAR 94070 769-C5

Q

QUADRANT LN
400 FCTY 94404 749-J1
QUAIL
- PTLV 94028 830-C1
QUAIL CT
- ATN 94027 790-H1
QUAIL LN
- SCAR 94070 769-D6
- SMCo - 788-F1
QUAIL MEADOWS CT
- WDSD 94062 789-J6
QUAIL MEADOWS DR
- WDSD 94062 789-H6
QUAIL POINT CIR
2000 SBRN 94066 707-F6
QUARRY RD
100 PA 94304 790-H5
100 SCIC 94305 790-H5
300 SMCo 94002 769-F1
QUARTZ ST
400 RDWC 94062 769-J7
500 HMBY 94019 767-F7
500 RDWC 94062 789-J1
600 RDWC 94061 789-J1
QUAY LN
300 RDWC 94065 749-H7
QUEBEC ST
- SMTO 94401 729-B7
QUEEN ANNE CT
- MLBR 94030 728-A2
QUEENS AV
1300 SMTO 94403 749-C3
QUEENS CT
- ATN 94027 790-C4
200 SCAR 94070 769-D4
QUEENS LN
2000 SMCo 94402 768-H1
QUESADA WY
1600 BURL 94010 728-B5
QUILEN CT
- SCIC 94305 790-J7
QUINCE ST
1200 SMTO 94402 748-J3

R

RACINE LN
- SF 94134 688-A2
RADBURN DR
3700 SSF 94080 707-D4
RADCLIFF DR
28100 LAH 94022 810-H5
RADFORD LN
700 FCTY 94404 749-G4
RADIO RD
- SMCo 94014 687-F4
1400 RDWC 94065 750-A5
RAE AV
- SF 94112 687-E2
RAILROAD RD
300 SSF 94080 707-H3
600 HMBY 94019 787-E2
600 SMCo 94019 787-F6

RAILROAD AV
600 SMCo 94019 (807-F1
See Page 788)
1000 SMCo 94019 827-J1
1700 SMTO 94402 749-B3
N RAILROAD AV
- SMTO 94401 748-J1
S RAILROAD AV
- SMTO 94401 748-J1
100 SMTO 94401 749-A2
400 SMTO 94402 749-A2
RAILROAD PL
1000 SBRN 94066 707-J5
RAILWAY AV
1100 SMTO 94401 749-A2
1100 SMTO 94402 749-A2
RAIMUNDO WY
700 SCIC 94305 810-J2
RAINBOW DR
1300 SMCo 94402 748-G6
RAINIER AV
200 SSF 94080 707-G4
1000 PCFA 94044 727-C5
RALMAR AV
2000 EPA 94303 791-A1
2400 EPA 94303 771-A7
RALSTON AV
- RDWC 94065 749-F7
100 HMBY 94019 767-E7
400 BLMT 94002 749-F7
500 BLMT 94002 769-B2
1500 BURL 94010 728-F7
1600 HIL 94010 728-F7
1700 HIL 94010 748-E1
2800 SMCo 94070 768-J2
2900 SMTO 94402 768-J2
2900 SMCo 94402 768-J2
2900 BLMT 94002 768-J2
RALSTON CT
- HIL 94010 748-D2
RALSTON RD
- ATN 94027 790-C3
- SMCo 94074 (828-H3
See Page 827)
- SMCo 94062 (828-H3
See Page 827)
RALSTON ST
- SF 94132 687-C1
RALSTON RANCH RD
- BLMT 94002 768-J2
RAM LN
800 FCTY 94404 749-F4
RAMBLEWOOD WY
1100 SMTO 94403 749-E6
RAMBOW DR
3400 PA 94306 791-D7
RAMONA AV
100 PCFA 94044 727-A2
100 SSF 94080 707-G4
RAMONA RD
100 SMCo 94028 830-E3
RAMONA ST
200 PA 94301 790-H4
200 SMTO 94401 728-J7
300 SMTO 94401 748-J1
1100 PA 94301 791-B7
2500 PA 94306 791-B7
RAMOSO RD
100 PTLV 94028 810-B4
RAMPART WY
- DALY 94014 687-E3
RAMSELL ST
- SF 94132 687-C2
RANCH RD
- WDSD 94062 809-F4
- SMCo 94062 809-F4
S RANCH RD
700 SMCo 94060 (868-F6
See Page 867)
RANCH RD W
- SMCo 94060 (868-D3
See Page 867)
RANCHO AV
1200 MLBR 94030 727-H3
1200 PCFA 94044 727-A5
RAND ST
400 SMTO 94401 729-B7
500 SMTO 94401 749-B1
RANDALL CT
- SMCo 94015 687-B5
RANDALL PL
- MLPK 94025 790-F6
RANDALL RD
1800 SMTO 94402 748-H7
1800 SMCo 94402 748-H7
RANDERS CT
2700 PA 94303 791-C6
RANDOLPH AV
- SSF 94080 708-A2
200 SSF 94080 707-J1
RANDOLPH PL
- PCFA 94044 727-B6
RANDOLPH ST
- SF 94132 687-C2
RANDY CT
- SMCo 94061 790-A3
RANELAGH RD
300 HIL 94010 748-H1
RANGER CIR
700 FCTY 94404 749-G2

RAPLEY RD
- WDSD 94062 809-G7
RAPLEY TR
- PTLV 94028 830-C3
- SMCo 94028 830-C3
- SMCo 94020 830-B5
RAVENSCOURT RD
500 HIL 94010 748-G2
RAVENSWOOD AV
100 ATN 94027 790-G3
100 MLPK 94025 790-G3
RAVENWOOD WY
100 SSF 94080 707-G5
RAVILLA CT
- DALY 94014 687-E2
RAVINE DR
100 WDSD 94062 789-G5
RAY CT
- BURL 94010 728-C5
RAY DR
1500 BURL 94010 728-C5
RAYMOND AV
- SF 94134 687-J2
200 SF 94134 688-A2
RAYMOND CT
- SCAR 94070 769-G6
RAYMUNDO DR
100 WDSD 94062 789-D4
RAYMUNDO TR
- SMCo 94062 789-A3
RAYNOR PL
- SMCo 94060 (868-F3
See Page 867)
READ AV
2400 BLMT 94002 769-C2
REBECCA LN
- ATN 94027 790-G2
RECREATION AV
- MLPK 94025 790-J1
RECREATION DR
- SMCo 94020 829-F7
- SMCo 94020 849-F1
RECREATION WY
1300 RDWC 94061 789-H2
RED HAWK CT
- BSBN 94005 688-A5
- BSBN 94005 687-J5
REDINGTON RD
2100 HIL 94010 728-D7
REDLAND RD
- SMCo 94062 809-F5
RED LEAF CT
- DALY 94014 687-G3
RED OAK WY
3700 RDWC 94061 789-G2
REDONDO AV
- SMCo 94038 746-F7
REDONDO ST
- SF 94124 688-B1
REDONDO BEACH RD
400 HMBY 94019 787-E4
REDROCK RD
26600 LAH 94022 830-J2
REDWOOD AV
- MLPK 94025 790-J2
- RDWC 94061 789-J2
- RDWC 94061 790-A1
- SMCo 94060 (868-H5
See Page 867)
400 SBRN 94066 727-H1
500 SSF 94080 707-H3
1100 RDWC 94061 770-B7
REDWOOD DR
- SMCo 94021 849-A7
- HIL 94010 748-H2
- SMCo 94020 849-E1
REDWOOD RD
- SMCo 94062 788-H5
REDWOOD TER
- SMCo 94062 788-J4
REDWOOD WY
- ATN 94027 790-D2
- PCFA 94044 727-A5
REDWOOD SHORES PKWY
100 RDWC 94065 749-H7
100 RDWC 94065 769-H1
600 RDWC 94065 750-A5
REDWOOD SPRING RD
- SMCo 94062 788-J5
REEF DR
400 SMTO 94404 749-E1
400 FCTY 94404 749-E1
REEF POINT RD
- SMCo 94038 746-F6
REESE ST
1200 RDWC 94061 790-A1
REFLECTION CIRCLE DR
- SMCo - 768-C3
REGAL CT
700 MLPK 94025 790-J2
REGAN DR
3900 SMTO 94403 749-D6
REGENCY CT
800 SCAR 94070 769-D5
REGENT CT
900 RDWC 94061 790-B1
REGENT PL
- PA 94301 791-A4

REGENT ST
- SF 94112 687-D2
1300 RDWC 94061 790-A1
REGINA WY
900 PCFA 94044 726-J4
REGULUS ST
700 FCTY 94404 749-E5
REICHLING AV
100 PCFA 94044 727-A2
REID AV
800 SBRN 94066 707-H7
REIDS ROOST RD
- SMCo 94062 809-C3
REINA DEL MAR AV
100 PCFA 94044 727-A1
REINER ST
- DALY 94014 687-C5
- SMCo 94014 687-C5
REMILLARD DR
400 HIL 94010 748-D3
RENATO CT
- RDWC 94061 790-C1
REPOSA WY
3600 BLMT 94002 769-A2
RESERVOIR RD
- SMCo 94037 746-H3
- ATN 94027 790-B6
100 HIL 94010 748-G3
1000 SMCo 94060 867-H2
RESERVOIR HILL DR
- DALY 94014 687-D4
RESIDENT LN
- MLPK 94025 790-J2
RESSA RD
300 PCFA 94044 707-A6
RESTANI WY
- SF 94112 687-F1
RESTON CT
3900 SSF 94080 707-D4
RETIRO ST
100 SMCo 94038 766-H2
REVERE WY
800 SMCo 94062 789-F2
REX ST
1700 SMTO 94403 749-C3
REY ST
- SF 94134 687-J2
REYNA PL
- MLPK 94025 790-F5
REYNOLDS CT
- HIL 94010 728-D7
REYNOLDS ST
- DALY 94014 687-G3
RHINE ST
- SF 94112 687-D2
200 DALY 94014 687-D2
RHINETTE AV
1100 BURL 94010 728-E5
RHODES DR
500 PA 94303 791-C4
RHUS RD
- SMCo 94020 850-E7
- SMCo 94020 (870-F1
See Page 869)
RHUS ST
1200 SMTO 94402 748-J3
RIBBON ST
1300 FCTY 94404 749-H2
RICE ST
- DALY 94014 687-D2
- SMCo 94014 687-D2
RICHARDSON CT
800 PA 94303 791-D7
RICHARDS ROAD TR
- SMCo 94062 789-B4
RICHLAND CT
- SCAR 94070 769-H4
RICHMOND DR
200 MLBR 94030 728-A3
400 MLBR 94030 727-J4
RICHMOND RD
200 HIL 94010 748-G2
RICKOVER LN
1100 FCTY 94404 749-G5
RIDER TR
- SMCo 94062 809-C6
RIDGE CT
- WDSD 94062 789-G5
800 SSF 94080 707-G1
1200 SF 94134 687-H2
RIDGE LN
- SF 94112 687-E1
RIDGE RD
- SMCo 94062 788-J6
300 SCAR 94070 769-G5
1500 BLMT 94002 749-D7
RIDGECREST TER
- SMTO 94402 748-H7
RIDGEFIELD AV
- DALY 94015 687-A7
RIDGEVIEW CT
800 SSF 94080 707-H1
RIDGEVIEW DR
- ATN 94027 790-A5
RIDGEWAY AV
2600 SBRN 94066 727-F1
RIDGEWAY DR
500 PCFA 94044 707-A7
RIDGEWAY RD
- HIL 94010 748-G3

RIDGEWAY RD
100 WDSD 94062 789-H4
RIDGEWOOD CT
- BLMT 94002 769-C3
RIDGEWOOD DR
1000 MLBR 94030 727-H3
RIDGEWOOD RD
- SMCo 94060 (868-G4
See Page 867)
RIFLE RANGE RD
- PCFA 94044 707-A7
RIGEL LN
800 FCTY 94404 749-E3
RILEY WY
800 RDWC 94061 790-C2
RINCONADA CIR
- SMCo 94070 768-J3
- BLMT 94002 769-A3
- BLMT 94002 768-J3
RINCONDADA AV
100 PA 94301 791-A6
RINGWOOD AV
- SMCo 94025 790-H2
- ATN 94027 790-H1
800 MLPK 94025 790-H1
1000 MLPK 94025 770-H7
RIO CT
- BURL 94010 728-B5
RIORDAN PL
- MLPK 94025 790-H2
RIO VERDE ST
- SF 94134 687-H3
- DALY 94014 687-H3
RIO VISTA DR
900 PCFA 94044 726-J5
RISEL AV
- DALY 94014 687-E3
RITTENHOUSE AV
- ATN 94027 790-D1
RIVAS AV
- SF 94132 687-B1
RIVERA DR
2800 BURL 94010 728-A6
RIVER OAKS RD
- HMBY 94019 787-F5
RIVERSIDE DR
- SBRN 94066 707-D6
RIVERTON DR
700 MLBR 94030 727-J4
900 SCAR 94070 769-G2
RIVIERA CIR
- RDWC 94065 749-J7
RIVIERA CT
100 SBRN 94066 707-D5
RIVIERA RD
600 SMCo 94037 746-H4
RIZAL DR
100 HIL 94010 748-F5
ROAN PL
- WDSD 94062 789-D6
ROBERT AV
- BLMT 94002 768-J1
ROBERT PL
- MLBR 94030 728-A3
ROBERTA DR
- WDSD 94062 809-G1
1400 SMTO 94403 749-D3
ROBERT PEARY LN
800 FCTY 94404 749-F4
ROBERTS DR
- MLPK 94025 790-E4
ROBERTS RD
200 PCFA 94044 726-H3
ROBERTS WY
- HIL 94010 748-E3
ROBERTSON WY
500 RDWC 94062 789-E2
500 SMCo 94062 789-E2
ROBIN CT
700 EPA 94303 791-B1
ROBIN LN
800 MLBR 94030 727-H3
ROBIN RD
- HIL 94010 748-E2
ROBIN WY
- SCAR 94070 769-G6
200 MLPK 94025 790-J3
ROBINSON DR
- SF 94112 687-G2
- DALY 94014 687-G2
ROBIN WHIPPLE WY
1600 BLMT 94002 769-D1
ROBINWOOD LN
200 HIL 94010 748-E3
ROBLAR AV
100 HIL 94010 748-H1
300 MLBR 94030 728-C3
ROBLE AV
200 RDWC 94061 790-B1
600 MLPK 94025 790-F4
ROBLE DR
500 SCIC 94305 790-G7
ROBLE PL
100 SMCo 94020 829-F7
ROBLE RD
1200 MLBR 94030 728-A5
ROBLE ALTO
27900 LAH 94022 810-H7
ROBLE ALTO CT
13600 LAH 94022 810-H6

STREET
Block City ZIP Pg-Grid

ROBLE BLANCO
27900 LAH 94022 810-H7
ROBLEDA DR
- ATN 94027 790-C2
ROBLES DR
- WDSD 94062 809-G1
ROCCA AV
500 SSF 94080 707-H2
ROCCA CT
- SSF 94080 707-J2
ROCHESTER ST
- SMTO 94401 729-B6
ROCKAWAY BEACH AV
100 PCFA 94044 726-J2
700 PCFA 94044 727-A3
ROCK CREEK CT
- SMCo 94062 789-F2
ROCKFORD AV
- DALY 94015 707-A1
- DALY 94015 706-J1
ROCK HARBOR LN
- FCTY 94404 749-E6
ROCKRIDGE AV
- DALY 94015 687-A6
ROCKRIDGE RD
- HIL 94010 748-G2
100 SCAR 94070 769-F4
ROCKWOOD CT
- SMTO 94403 748-J6
ROCKWOOD DR
100 SSF 94080 707-G5
ROCK WREN LN
- BSBN 94005 687-J5
ROCKY WY
500 WDSD 94062 789-E2
RODRIQUES RD
- SMCo 94060 (868-F3
See Page 867)
ROEBLING RD
300 SSF 94080 708-B3
ROEHAMPTON RD
400 HIL 94010 748-G2
ROEMER WY
- SF 94112 687-E2
ROGELL AV
1200 SMTO 94401 729-A7
ROGELL CT
400 SMTO 94401 729-A6
ROGERS AV
100 SCAR 94070 769-F5
ROGGE RD
100 EPA 94303 791-C1
ROLAND AV
2800 SCAR 94070 769-F6
ROLISON RD
3000 MLPK 94025 770-E6
3000 RDWC 94063 770-E6
ROLLING HILLS AV
- SMTO 94403 749-B7
ROLLINGWOOD DR
2000 SBRN 94066 707-E6
ROLLINS RD
- BURL 94010 728-D4
- MLBR 94030 728-D4
ROLPH ST
- SF 94112 687-F2
ROME ST
- SF 94112 687-E1
ROMERO RD
100 WDSD 94062 789-G6
ROMNEY AV
100 SSF 94080 707-E2
RONALD CT
900 HMBY 94019 787-G2
RONDO WY
- SMCo 94025 790-D5
ROOSEVELT
- RDWC 94061 789-J1
- RDWC 94061 790-A1
ROOSEVELT AV
- DALY 94014 687-E3
100 RDWC 94061 789-J2
2000 RDWC 94061 790-A1
2100 BURL 94010 728-D6
2200 RDWC 94061 770-A7
ROOSEVELT BLVD
100 HMBY 94019 767-D4
ROQUENA DR
100 SMCo 94020 829-E7
RORKE WY
800 PA 94303 791-E6
ROSA FLORA CIR
100 SSF 94080 707-G4
ROSALITA LN
- MLBR 94030 727-J2
ROSE AV
800 SMCo 94063 770-F7
900 MLPK 94025 790-F4
900 RDWC 94063 770-F7
ROSE CT
900 BURL 94010 728-F5
ROSE LN
100 BLMT 94002 769-E2
ROSEDALE AV
1100 BURL 94010 728-D5
ROSEFIELD WY
1100 MLPK 94025 790-E4
ROSELLA CT
- SF 94112 687-F1

ROSEMARY LN
1700 RDWC 94061 790-A2
ROSEWOOD AV
900 SCAR 94070 769-G3
ROSEWOOD DR
- ATN 94027 790-G1
- ATN 94027 770-G7
700 PA 94303 791-C6
900 SMTO 94401 749-A2
2100 SBRN 94066 727-F1
ROSEWOOD WY
100 SSF 94080 707-G5
ROSILIE ST
100 SMTO 94403 749-E6
ROSITA CT N
1000 PCFA 94044 726-J5
ROSITA CT S
1000 PCFA 94044 726-J5
ROSITA RD
700 PCFA 94044 726-H5
1100 PCFA 94044 727-A6
ROSLYN AV
- SCAR 94070 769-E4
- SMCo 94070 769-E4
ROSLYN CT
- DALY 94015 686-J4
ROSS CT
800 PA 94303 791-D7
ROSS LN
200 FCTY 94404 749-F5
ROSS RD
2300 PA 94303 791-C5
ROSS ST
1100 BLMT 94002 749-D7
ROSS WY
- BSBN 94005 688-A7
- SBRN 94066 707-D6
ROSSI WY
1000 SMTO 94403 749-C4
ROTH WY
100 SCIC 94305 790-G6
ROUND HILL RD
900 RDWC 94061 789-H2
ROURKE RD
- SMCo 94060 (868-H2
See Page 867)
ROWAN TREE LN
- HIL 94010 748-C2
ROWNTREE WY
2400 SSF 94080 707-D4
ROXBURY LN
- SMCo 94402 748-F6
ROXBURY WY
500 BLMT 94002 749-E7
ROYAL AV
1300 SMTO 94401 749-B2
ROYAL LN
- SF 94112 687-F2
1100 SCAR 94070 769-D6
ROYAL PALM AV
200 SMCo 94018 766-J1
ROYCE WY
- DALY 94014 687-D5
ROZZI PL
400 SSF 94080 708-B2
RUBY AV
100 SCAR 94070 769-G5
RUBY ST
- RDWC 94061 790-A1
400 RDWC 94062 769-J7
500 RDWC 94062 789-J1
600 RDWC 94061 789-J1
RUDDER LN
1000 FCTY 94404 749-H4
RUISSEAU FRANCAIS AV
500 HMBY 94019 767-E5
RUNNING FARM LN
- SCIC 94305 790-J7
- SCIC 94305 810-J1
RUNNYMEDE RD
800 WDSD 94062 789-E4
RUNNYMEDE ST
400 EPA 94303 791-B1
RURAL LN
300 MLPK 94025 810-E1
300 SMCo 94025 810-E1
RUSSELL AV
- PTLV 94028 809-J6
RUSSELL CT
- MLPK 94025 790-J3
RUSSIA AV
- SF 94112 687-G1
RUTGERS ST
1600 EPA 94303 771-C6
RUTH AV
800 BLMT 94002 749-D7
RUTH CT
1000 EPA 94303 791-C1
RUTHERDALE AV
800 SCAR 94070 769-F4
RUTHERFORD AV
100 SMCo 94061 790-B2
RUTHVEN AV
400 PA 94301 790-H4
RUTLAND DR
500 PCFA 94044 707-A2
RUTLAND ST
- SF 94134 688-A2
500 DALY 94014 688-A2

RUTLAND ST
500 DALY 94014 687-J3
RYAN CT
- SCIC 94305 810-J2
RYAN WY
100 SSF 94080 707-H4
RYANS AL
700 MLPK 94025 790-F4
RYDER ST
200 SMTO 94401 729-B7

S

SABRINA CT
1200 RDWC 94061 790-A1
SACRAMENTO ST
500 EPA 94303 791-B1
SACRAMENTO TER
900 PCFA 94044 707-A5
SADDLE CT
27800 LAH 94022 810-J6
SADDLEBACK
2100 EPA 94303 791-C2
SADDLEBACK DR
- DALY 94014 687-G2
- SF 94134 687-G2
SADDLE MOUNTAIN DR
14200 LAH 94022 810-J6
SADOWA ST
- SF 94112 687-D2
200 SF 94132 687-D2
SAGA LN
- MLPK 94025 790-D7
- MLPK 94025 810-D1
SAGAMORE ST
200 SF 94112 687-D2
200 SF 94132 687-D2
SAGE ST
1100 EPA 94303 791-C2
SAGINAW DR
100 RDWC 94063 770-C3
SAILFISH
- HMBY 94019 787-F6
SAILFISH ISL
300 FCTY 94404 749-H3
SAINT ANDREWS LN
300 HMBY 94019 787-F4
SAINT ANDREWS RD
2100 HMBY 94019 787-F5
SAINT CATHERINE DR
200 DALY 94015 687-A7
SAINT CHARLES AV
- SF 94132 687-C2
SAINT CLAIRE DR
500 PA 94306 791-D7
SAINT CLOUD DR
2500 SSF 94080 707-D5
2500 SBRN 94066 707-D5
SAINT CROIX LN
600 FCTY 94404 749-J1
SAINT FRANCIS BLVD
- DALY 94015 687-B7
600 DALY 94015 707-B1
SAINT FRANCIS CT
500 MLPK 94025 790-F6
SAINT FRANCIS DR
2100 PA 94303 791-D4
SAINT FRANCIS PL
500 MLPK 94025 790-F6
SAINT FRANCIS RD
- HIL 94010 748-H2
SAINT FRANCIS ST
- RDWC 94061 789-J1
- RDWC 94062 769-J7
500 MLPK 94025 790-A1
600 RDWC 94061 790-A1
SAINT FRANCIS WY
100 RDWC 94062 769-H7
600 RDWC 94061 769-H7
700 RDWC 94061 789-J1
1100 SCAR 94070 769-H5
SAINT JAMES AV
500 HMBY 94019 767-E7
SAINT JAMES CT
- DALY 94015 687-B6
SAINT JAMES RD
2700 BLMT 94002 769-A3
2900 BLMT 94002 768-J2
2900 SMCo 94070 768-J2
SAINT JOHN AV
400 HMBY 94019 767-E7
SAINT JOHN CT
- SMTO 94401 728-H7
SAINT JOSEPH AV
400 HMBY 94019 767-E6
SAINT KITTS LN
1400 FCTY 94404 749-G5
SAINT LAWRENCE CT
700 PCFA 94044 727-C4
SAINT LAWRENCE DR
800 PCFA 94044 727-C4
SAINT LUCIA DR
- RDWC 94065 749-J5
SAINT MARKS CT
- DALY 94015 687-B6
SAINT MARTIN DR
- RDWC 94065 749-J5
- RDWC 94065 750-A5
SAINT MARYS CT
- SMTO 94401 728-J7

SAINT MARYS PL
- RDWC 94063 770-F7
SAINT MATTHEWS AV
- SMTO 94401 748-J1
SAINT MICHAEL CT
3300 PA 94306 791-D7
SAINT MICHAEL DR
3300 PA 94306 791-D7
SAINT MICHAELS CT
- DALY 94015 687-A6
SAINT THOMAS LN
500 FCTY 94404 749-G5
SAINT VINCENT LN
500 FCTY 94404 749-J2
SALA TER
- SF 94112 687-E2
SALADA AV
100 PCFA 94044 706-J5
SALADO DR
1500 MTVW 94043 791-G7
SALAS CT
2100 EPA 94303 791-C2
SALINAS AV
100 SF 94124 688-B1
SALISBURY WY
2200 SMTO 94403 749-C4
SALMARK CT
- HIL 94402 748-G5
SALT CT
700 RDWC 94065 749-H5
SALVADOR ST
- SMCo 94018 767-C3
SALVATIERRA ST
500 SCIC 94305 810-H1
SAM MCDONALD RD
- SCIC 94305 790-J6
SAMSON ST
200 RDWC 94063 770-A5
SAN ANDREAS AV
- HMBY 94019 767-C4
SAN ANDREAS DR
100 MLPK 94025 790-H3
SAN ANSELMO AV
100 SBRN 94066 727-J1
200 SBRN 94066 728-A1
1000 MLBR 94030 728-A1
SAN ANSELMO AV N
200 SBRN 94066 727-J1
400 SBRN 94066 707-J7
SAN ANTONIO AV
100 SBRN 94066 728-A1
100 SMCo 94128 728-A1
300 SMTO 94401 728-J7
1000 MTVW 94043 791-F7
1000 PA 94303 791-F7
1400 MLPK 94025 790-F3
1500 MTVW 94303 791-F7
SAN ANTONIO CIR
- DALY 94014 687-F3
SAN ARDO WY
2800 BLMT 94002 769-B1
SAN BENITO AV
- ATN 94027 790-E1
100 SBRN 94066 728-A1
500 SMCo 94025 770-E7
500 SMCo 94063 790-E1
SAN BENITO RD
- BSBN 94005 688-A6
SAN BENITO ST
400 HMBY 94019 787-G1
3600 SMTO 94403 749-D6
SAN BRUNO AV
- SMCo 94128 708-A6
- BSBN 94005 688-A6
3100 SF 94134 688-A1
SAN BRUNO AV E
- SMCo 94128 708-A6
100 SBRN 94066 707-J6
700 SBRN 94066 708-A6
SAN BRUNO AV W
- SBRN 94066 707-G7
2000 SBRN 94066 727-F1
SAN CARLOS AV
100 SMCo 94061 790-B3
200 SMCo 94018 767-A2
1100 SCAR 94070 769-E3
E SAN CARLOS AV
- SCAR 94070 769-G2
SAN CARLOS CT
700 PA 94303 791-C6
E SAN CARLOS LN
- SCAR 94070 769-H2
SANCHEZ AV
1100 BURL 94010 728-E6
1700 HIL 94010 728-E6
SANCHEZ WY
1100 RDWC 94061 790-A1
SAN CLEMENTE DR
200 MLPK 94025 790-H3
SAN CLEMENTE LN
600 FCTY 94404 749-G5
SAN CLEMENTE RD
- SMCo 94018 767-B2
SANCTUARY WY
- SMCo - 768-D4
SANDALWOOD CT
2000 PA 94303 791-D4
SAND DOLLAR CT
- HMBY 94019 787-G5

SAND DUNES CT
- HMBY 94019 787-G5
SANDERLING ST
1000 FCTY 94404 749-H1
SAND HILL CIR
100 MLPK 94025 790-B7
SAND HILL CT
- WDSD 94062 809-H2
SAND HILL RD
100 MLPK 94025 790-F6
500 PA 94304 790-G5
1300 SCIC 94305 790-G5
2100 SMCo 94025 790-F6
2400 MLPK 94025 810-C1
2400 SMCo 94025 810-A1
3000 SMCo 94025 809-J2
3600 WDSD 94062 809-H3
SAN DIEGO AV
- SF 94112 687-C3
100 DALY 94014 687-C3
100 SBRN 94066 728-A2
SANDPIPER CT
200 FCTY 94404 749-G1
SANDPIPER LN
- RDWC 94065 749-G6
SANDRA CT
900 SSF 94080 707-G2
SANDRA LN
- MLBR 94030 728-A3
SANDRA PL
2900 PA 94303 791-D6
SANDRA RD
- HIL 94010 748-E3
SANDSTONE
- PTLV 94028 830-C1
SANDY HILL RD
- CLMA 94014 687-E7
SANDY HOOK CT
600 FCTY 94404 749-F5
SAN FELIPE AV
- SSF 94080 707-E3
100 SBRN 94066 728-A1
200 SBRN 94066 727-J1
SAN FERNANDO WY
- DALY 94015 687-B6
SAN FRANCISCO AV
- BSBN 94005 688-A6
300 SMCo 94005 688-A6
SAN FRANCISCO CT
800 SCIC 94305 810-J1
SAN FRANCISCO TER
800 SCIC 94305 810-J1
SAN GABRIEL CIR
- DALY 94014 687-F3
SAN GABRIEL CT
- DALY 94014 687-F3
SAN JOAQUIN CT
100 SBRN 94066 707-D7
SAN JOSE AV
100 PCFA 94044 706-J6
300 MLBR 94030 728-B2
2200 SF 94112 687-E2
SAN JOSE AV Rt#-82
3200 DALY 94014 687-D3
SAN JUAN AV
- DALY 94015 687-A7
- SMCo 94025 790-D5
100 MLBR 94030 728-A2
100 SBRN 94066 728-A2
200 SMCo 94018 767-B1
SAN JUAN BLVD
2800 BLMT 94002 769-A1
SAN JUAN CT
300 SMTO 94402 748-G1
SAN JUAN ST
500 SCIC 94305 810-H1
SAN LUCAS AV
- SMCo 94038 766-G1
SAN LUIS AV
100 SBRN 94066 728-A1
100 SBRN 94066 727-J1
100 SMCo 94018 767-B2
SAN LUIS CIR
- DALY 94014 687-F3
SAN LUIS CT
- DALY 94014 687-F3
SAN LUIS DR
200 MLPK 94025 790-H2
W SAN MARCO AV
100 SBRN 94066 728-A1
100 SBRN 94066 727-J1
SAN MARLO WY
400 PCFA 94044 726-J2
SAN MATEO AV
- BURL 94010 728-F6
400 SBRN 94066 707-J5
400 SBRN 94066 727-J1
1000 SSF 94066 707-J5
1300 SSF 94080 707-J5
2600 SMCo 94063 770-C7
SAN MATEO DR
- PA 94304 790-G5
100 MLPK 94025 790-E4
N SAN MATEO DR
- SMTO 94401 728-H7
400 SMTO 94401 748-J1
S SAN MATEO DR
- SMTO 94401 748-J1
SAN MATEO LN
400 BSBN 94005 688-A7

SAN MATEO RD Rt#-92
200 HMBY 94019 767-H7
300 SMCo - 767-J6
SAN MIGUEL AV
- DALY 94015 687-A7
SAN MIGUEL LN
700 FCTY 94404 749-G5
SAN MIGUEL ST
300 SF 94112 687-E1
SAN MIGUEL WY
- SMTO 94403 749-D5
2700 SCAR 94070 769-F5
SAN NICHOLAS LN
600 FCTY 94404 749-G5
SAN PABLO AV
- HMBY 94019 767-D5
300 MLBR 94030 728-B2
SAN PABLO TER
300 PCFA 94044 707-A5
SAN PEDRO AV
200 PCFA 94044 726-G4
SAN PEDRO RD
- DALY 94014 687-C5
- SMCo 94014 687-C5
- SMCo 94018 767-B2
300 DALY 94015 687-C5
SAN PEDRO MOUNTAIN RD
- PCFA 94044 726-H6
- SMCo 94037 746-G3
- SMCo - 726-H6
SAN PEDRO TERRACE RD
700 PCFA 94044 726-H4
700 SMCo - 726-H4
SAN RAFAEL PL
700 SCIC 94305 810-H1
SAN RAMON AV
800 SMCo 94038 766-G1
SAN RAYMUNDO RD
1000 HIL 94010 748-F2
N SAN RAYMUNDO RD
100 HIL 94010 748-F2
SAN REMOS WY
1000 SCAR 94070 769-F5
SAN REY AV
300 MLBR 94030 728-B2
SAN SIMEON WY
2800 SCAR 94070 769-F5
SANTA ANA AV
- DALY 94015 687-A7
SANTA ANA ST
2200 PA 94303 791-C4
SANTA ANNA ST
- SMCo 94018 767-B3
SANTA BARBARA AV
- SF 94112 687-C2
- DALY 94014 687-C2
600 MLBR 94030 727-H2
SANTA BARBARA PL
100 SBRN 94066 707-D6
SANTA CATALINA LN
600 FCTY 94404 749-G5
SANTA CATALINA ST
2300 PA 94303 791-D4
SANTA CLARA AV
100 SBRN 94066 728-A2
100 SMCo 94061 790-A3
100 RDWC 94061 790-A3
SANTA CLARA CT
- DALY 94014 687-F3
SANTA CLARA ST
- BSBN 94005 688-A6
SANTA CLARA WY
200 SMTO 94403 749-D5
SANTA CRUZ AV
- DALY 94014 687-C2
- SF 94112 687-C2
500 MLPK 94025 790-F3
2000 SMCo 94025 790-E6
SANTA CRUZ LN
600 FCTY 94404 749-G5
SANTA DOMINGA AV
100 SBRN 94066 728-A1
100 SBRN 94066 727-J1
SANTA ELENA AV
- DALY 94015 687-B7
SANTA FE AV
800 SCIC 94305 810-J1
SANTA FELICIA CT
- HIL 94402 748-H4
SANTA FLORITA AV
400 MLBR 94030 727-J2
SANTA GINA CT
- HIL 94402 748-H4
SANTA HELENA AV
100 SBRN 94066 728-A2
200 MLBR 94030 728-A2
SANTA INEZ AV
100 SBRN 94066 728-A2
E SANTA INEZ AV
- SMTO 94401 748-H1
400 SMTO 94401 728-J7
1000 SMTO 94401 729-A7
W SANTA INEZ AV
- SMTO 94402 748-G2
100 HIL 94010 748-G2
SANTA LUCIA AV
100 SBRN 94066 728-A1
100 SBRN 94066 727-H2

SANTA LUCIA AV
900 MLBR 94030 727-H2
SANTA MARGARITA AV
100 MLPK 94025 790-H3
700 MLBR 94030 727-H2
SANTA MARIA AV
- PTLV 94028 809-J6
- PCFA 94044 706-J5
100 SBRN 94066 728-A2
200 SMCo 94018 767-C3
700 SCIC 94305 810-H2
SANTA MARIA LN
- HIL 94010 748-G1
700 FCTY 94404 749-G2
SANTA MONICA AV
- SMCo 94038 746-F7
100 MLPK 94025 790-H3
SANTA PAULA AV
- MLBR 94030 728-B3
SANTA PAULA DR
100 DALY 94015 687-B6
SANTA RITA AV
- DALY 94015 707-A1
100 PA 94301 791-B6
300 MLPK 94025 790-F5
SANTA ROSA AV
- HMBY 94019 767-C4
100 PCFA 94044 706-J6
SANTA ROSA LN
700 FCTY 94404 749-G5
SANTA SUSANA AV
600 MLBR 94030 727-J2
SANTA TERESA ST
100 SCIC 94305 790-G7
SANTA TERESA WY
500 MLBR 94030 727-J2
SANTA YNEZ ST
600 SCIC 94305 810-H1
SANTIAGO AV
- ATN 94027 790-D4
100 SMCo 94061 790-A3
200 SMCo 94018 767-C3
SANTIAGO ST
3600 SMTO 94403 749-D5
SANTOS ST
- SF 94134 687-H2
200 DALY 94014 687-H2
SAPPHIRE ST
300 RDWC 94062 769-H7
500 RDWC 94062 789-J1
600 RDWC 94061 789-J1
SARA LN
- SCAR 94070 769-F5
SARATOGA AV
1100 EPA 94303 791-A1
1300 EPA 94303 771-A7
SARATOGA DR
3200 SMTO 94403 749-B4
SARGENT LN
- ATN 94027 790-B7
SARGENT ST
- SF 94132 687-C1
SATURN CT
600 FCTY 94404 749-E3
SAUSAL DR
- PTLV 94028 810-C6
SAVAGE WY
- DALY 94015 687-B7
SAVANNAH CT
3900 SSF 94080 707-C4
SAVONA WY
400 RDWC 94065 749-J5
SAWYER ST
200 SF 94134 687-J2
SAXON WY
1100 MLPK 94025 790-F4
SCENIC CT
100 SBRN 94066 727-H2
SCENIC DR
- SMCo 94020 829-F7
- SMCo 94020 849-F1
100 SMCo 94062 789-G6
SCENIC WY
- DALY 94014 687-E3
- SMTO 94403 748-J6
SCHEMBRI CT
- EPA 94303 791-B1
SCHEMBRI LN
700 EPA 94303 791-B1
SCHOOL ST
- DALY 94014 687-C4
- SSF 94080 707-J2
200 DALY 94015 687-C4
1500 SCAR 94070 769-G3
SCHOONER ST
800 FCTY 94404 749-G4
SCHOONER BAY DR
800 RDWC 94065 750-C6
SCHWERIN ST
- SF 94134 687-J3
300 DALY 94014 687-J3
SCHWIE AL
- MLPK 94025 790-E6
SCOFIELD AV
600 EPA 94303 791-B3
SCORPIO LN
600 FCTY 94404 749-E4
SCOTT AV
500 RDWC 94063 770-C6

SCOTT CT
3000 HIL 94010 748-B1
SCOTT DR
- MLPK 94025 770-G6
SCOTT ST
- SBRN 94066 707-J5
900 PA 94301 790-J5
1600 SMTO 94403 749-D1
SEABREEZE CT
- PCFA 94044 707-A1
SEA BREEZE DR
- HMBY 94019 787-G5
SEABRIGHT CT
100 SMCo 94038 746-G6
SEABURY RD
700 HIL 94010 748-F1
SEA CHASE DR
800 RDWC 94065 750-C6
SEACLIFF AV
- DALY 94015 686-J5
SEACLIFF CT
- SMCo 94037 746-F4
SEA CLIFF LN
300 RDWC 94065 749-J2
SEA CLIFF WY
2000 SBRN 94066 707-C5
SEA CLOUD DR
700 FCTY 94404 749-G5
SEA COVE BLVD
- SMCo 94038 746-F7
SEA CREST CT
- SMCo 94018 766-J1
SEACREST CT
- DALY 94015 706-J2
SEAFORTH CT
300 PCFA 94044 707-A7
300 PCFA 94044 727-A1
SEAGATE CT
- RDWC 94065 749-J2
SEAGATE DR
100 SMTO 94403 749-E6
SEAGATE PL
- BLMT 94002 749-E7
SEAGATE WY
500 BLMT 94002 749-E6
SEAGULL LN
- HMBY 94019 787-G5
SEA HAVEN CT
- PCFA 94044 707-A1
SEA HORSE CT
300 FCTY 94404 749-H3
SEAHORSE LN
500 RDWC 94065 749-J6
SEA ISLAND LN
900 FCTY 94404 749-H1
SEAL ST
- SMTO 94403 749-D2
SEALE AV
100 PA 94301 791-A6
700 PA 94303 791-A6
SEAL POINTE DR
800 RDWC 94065 750-A6
SEAN CT
2600 SSF 94080 707-C4
SEAPORT BLVD
- RDWC 94063 770-C4
600 SMCo 94063 770-C4
SEAPORT CT
400 RDWC 94063 770-C3
SEA RANCH AV
100 SMCo 94018 766-J2
SEARS ST
- SF 94112 687-D2
SEARS RANCH RD
- SMCo 94062 829-D5
SEARSVILLE CT
- HIL 94010 748-F6
SEARSVILLE RD
- SCIC 94305 790-F7
SEARVILLE RD
1500 PA 94304 810-G5
1700 SCIC 94304 810-G5
28000 LAH 94022 810-G5
SEASCAPE DR
- HMBY 94019 787-F6
SEA SHELL CIR
- HMBY 94019 787-G5
SEASHORE DR
- EPA 94303 791-B1
SEASIDE DR
200 PCFA 94044 706-J7
200 PCFA 94044 707-A7
SEASIDE SCHOOL RD
1000 SMCo 94074 (828-B7
See Page 827)
SEA SPRAY LN
700 FCTY 94404 749-E3
SEASTORM CT
- RDWC 94065 750-A5
SEASTORM DR
- RDWC 94065 750-A5
SEAVIEW DR
- DALY 94015 686-J6
SEBASTIAN DR
200 MLBR 94030 728-A5
1600 BURL 94010 728-A5
SECLUDED AV
- SMCo 94063 770-F5
SEKI CT
- SMCo 94062 789-G2

SELBY LN
- ATN 94027 790-C2
- SMCo 94063 790-C1
1100 SMCo 94061 790-B3
W SELBY LN
1100 ATN 94027 790-C2
1400 SMCo 94061 790-B3
SEM LN
- BLMT 94002 749-F7
SEMERIA AV
2200 BLMT 94002 769-C1
SEMICIRCULAR RD
100 SMCo 94063 790-D1
SEMINARY DR
- MLPK 94025 790-H2
SEMINOLE AV
- SF 94112 687-F1
SEMINOLE WY
800 RDWC 94062 789-G2
SENECA AV
- SF 94112 687-F1
SENECA LN
1500 SMCo 94402 748-F6
SENECA ST
400 PA 94301 791-A3
400 PA 94301 790-J3
SEQUOIA AV
100 SMCo 94061 790-A3
200 PA 94306 791-A6
200 SSF 94080 707-F2
600 MLBR 94030 728-B4
700 SMTO 94403 749-A5
700 SMTO 94403 748-J5
800 BURL 94010 728-B4
1300 SBRN 94066 707-E6
SEQUOIA CT
- SCAR 94070 769-D3
SEQUOIA DR
- SMCo 94020 829-F1
- SMCo 94062 829-F1
- SMCo 94020 849-E1
SEQUOIA LN
400 SCIC 94305 790-G7
SEQUOIA WY
- PCFA 94044 727-B5
- SMCo 94061 790-B4
- SMCo 94062 809-F6
2600 BLMT 94002 749-B7
2600 BLMT 94002 769-B1
SERANA CT
- SSF 94080 707-E3
SERENA DR
700 PCFA 94044 726-J4
SERENITY CIRCLE DR
- SMCo - 768-C3
SERENITY VALLEY DR
- SMCo 94060 (868-F3
See Page 867)
SERRA AV
- MLBR 94030 728-B3
SERRA CT
- SMTO 94401 729-A7
100 SBRN 94066 727-H2
SERRA DR
300 SSF 94080 707-E2
1400 PCFA 94044 726-J5
SERRA ST
100 SCIC 94305 790-H7
700 SCIC - 791-A7
SERRAMONTE BLVD
- DALY 94015 707-B1
400 CLMA 94014 687-C7
900 CLMA 94014 707-B1
SERRANO DR
- ATN 94027 790-C2
- SF 94132 687-A1
SERRAVISTA AV
100 DALY 94015 707-C2
SEVERN LN
400 HIL 94010 748-H1
SEVIER AV
1000 MLPK 94025 790-J1
1100 MLPK 94025 770-J7
1300 MLPK 94025 771-A7
SEVILLA AV
100 SMCo 94018 767-A2
SEVILLE CT
- MLBR 94030 728-A2
SEVILLE DR
1100 PCFA 94044 726-J5
SEVILLE ST
- SF 94112 687-F2
SEVILLE WY
- SMTO 94402 749-A3
- SMTO 94402 748-J3
- SSF 94080 707-E6
SEVYSON CT
2900 PA 94303 791-D6
SEXTANT CT
800 SMTO 94404 749-D2
SEYMOUR LN
1000 MLPK 94025 790-E5
SEYMOUR ST
200 HMBY 94019 787-E3
SHAD CT
300 FCTY 94404 749-H2
SHADOW BROOK LN
- WDSD 94062 809-H2
SHADY LN
- HIL 94010 748-E4

SHAFTER ST
1200 SMTO 94402 748-J3
SHAKESPEARE ST
- DALY 94014 687-C2
100 SF 94112 687-C2
SHAMROCK CT
- MLBR 94030 728-A3
3800 SSF 94080 707-C4
SHAMROCK RANCH RD
- SMCo - 726-G5
SHANNON DR
2200 SSF 94080 707-D5
SHANNON WY
500 RDWC 94065 749-J6
SHARON AV
600 HIL 94010 728-E7
2000 BLMT 94002 769-C1
SHARON CT
- DALY 94014 687-H3
- MLPK 94025 790-D7
800 PA 94303 791-B4
SHARON PL
1500 SMTO 94401 729-A7
SHARON RD
2000 MLPK 94025 790-D7
2000 SMCo 94025 790-D7
SHARON WY
- PCFA 94044 706-J4
SHARON OAKS DR
2300 MLPK 94025 790-E7
SHARON PARK DR
100 MLPK 94025 790-C7
SHARP PARK RD
- PCFA 94044 707-A7
700 SBRN 94066 707-A7
SHASTA CT
- SSF 94080 707-F4
SHASTA DR
3300 SMTO 94403 748-J6
SHASTA LN
- MLPK 94025 790-C7
- PCFA 94044 707-A3
SHASTA ST
700 RDWC 94063 770-B7
SHAW CT
- RDWC 94061 789-J1
SHAW RD
- SBRN 94066 708-A5
200 SSF 94066 707-J5
200 SSF 94080 707-J5
200 SSF 94066 708-A5
200 SSF 94080 708-A5
SHAWNEE AV
- SF 94112 687-E1
SHAWNEE PASS
100 PTLV 94028 810-B6
SHEARER DR
- ATN 94027 790-C1
SHEARWATER ISL
200 FCTY 94404 749-G2
SHEARWATER PKWY
- RDWC 94065 749-H5
400 RDWC 94065 750-A5
SHEFFIELD DR
- DALY 94015 687-B3
SHEFFIELD LN
200 RDWC 94061 790-B2
SHEILA LN
1100 PCFA 94044 727-A5
1200 PCFA 94044 726-J5
SHELBOURNE AV
- DALY 94015 687-A7
SHELBOURNE PL
- SMCo 94402 768-G1
SHELDEN DR
- SMCo 94020 849-E2
SHELDON WY
- HIL 94010 728-D6
SHELFORD AV
- SCAR 94070 769-E2
SHELL BLVD
500 FCTY 94404 749-F2
SHELL PKWY
400 RDWC 94065 749-H5
SHELL ST
100 PCFA 94044 706-J5
SHELTER LN
- DALY 94014 687-E6
SHELTER COVE DR
100 SMCo 94018 766-J1
SHELTER COVE RD
- PCFA 94044 726-G4
SHELTER CREEK LN
- SBRN 94066 727-G1
100 SBRN 94066 707-G7
SHENANDOAH WY
- PCFA 94044 727-C5
SHEPARD WY
800 RDWC 94062 789-G2
SHERATON PL
2200 SMCo 94402 768-G1
SHERBORNE DR
2500 BLMT 94002 769-B3
SHERIDAN AV
100 PA 94306 791-B7
SHERIDAN DR
300 MLPK 94025 770-H7
SHERIDAN PL
- PCFA 94044 727-B6

STREET
Block City ZIP Pg-Grid

SHERIDAN WY
100 WDSD 94062 789-J4
SHERLOCK CT
27300 LAH 94022 830-H2
SHERLOCK RD
27000 LAH 94022 830-H2
SHERMAN AV
100 PA 94306 791-B7
800 MLPK 94025 790-D6
1100 SMCo 94025 790-D6
1500 BURL 94010 728-D6
SHERMAN RD
- SMCo 94037 746-H5
SHERWOOD CT
- HIL 94010 748-H1
- MLBR 94030 727-J5
SHERWOOD DR
2500 SBRN 94066 707-E6
2900 SCAR 94070 769-F5
SHERWOOD WY
100 SSF 94080 707-G5
300 MLPK 94025 790-G4
SHERYL DR
100 SBRN 94066 707-D6
SHIELDS ST
- SF 94132 687-C1
SHIPLEY AV
- DALY 94015 707-C2
SHIRLEY RD
2100 BLMT 94002 749-C7
2100 BLMT 94002 769-B1
SHIRLEY WY
400 MLPK 94025 790-J2
SHOAL CIR
- RDWC 94065 750-A5
SHOAL DR
- DALY 94014 687-E5
900 SMTO 94404 749-D2
SHOOTING STAR ISL
100 FCTY 94404 749-H3
SHOPPE LN
- MLPK 94025 790-J2
SHOREBIRD CIR
100 RDWC 94065 749-H6
N SHORELINE BLVD
1900 MTVW 94043 791-J7
SHORELINE CT
- SSF 94080 708-C1
SHORELINE DR
100 RDWC 94065 749-G7
100 RDWC 94065 769-G1
900 SMTO 94404 749-D3
SHORESIDE DR
- PCFA 94044 726-G4
SHOREVIEW AV
100 PCFA 94044 706-J5
1500 SMTO 94401 729-B7
1500 SMTO 94401 749-C1
2000 SMTO 94404 749-C1
2000 SMTO 94403 749-C1
SHOREWAY RD
- RDWC 94065 749-F7
- RDWC 94065 769-G1
- SCAR 94070 769-G1
1000 BLMT 94002 749-F7
1100 BLMT 94002 769-G1
SHORT ST
- PCFA 94044 707-A3
SHOSHONE PL
- PTLV 94028 810-B6
SHRATTON AV
- SMCo 94002 769-D4
- SMCo 94070 769-D4
- SCAR 94070 769-D4
SICKLES AV
100 SF 94112 687-E2
N SIDE AV
2700 SMCo 94063 770-D7
W SIDE AV
- SMCo 94063 790-C1
2800 SMCo 94063 770-C7
SIERRA AV
500 PCFA 94044 727-A1
SIERRA CT
2300 PA 94303 791-D4
SIERRA DR
200 HIL 94010 748-G2
1000 MLPK 94025 790-C6
SIERRA LN
- PTLV 94028 810-C5
SIERRA ST
400 SMCo 94038 746-F5
1200 RDWC 94061 790-A1
SIERRA TER
900 PCFA 94044 707-A5
SIERRA MORENA RD
- SMCo 94062 788-J7
SIERRA POINT PKWY
1000 BSBN 94005 688-B5
SIERRA POINT RD
- BSBN 94005 688-A6
SIESTA CT
- SMCo 94028 810-D4
SILKTREE CT
- HIL 94010 748-C2
SILVA AV
- MLBR 94030 728-B3
SILVER AV
500 HMBY 94019 767-F7
1600 RDWC 94061 790-A1

SILVER HILL RD
1000 RDWC 94061 789-G3
SILVERSPOT DR
- BSBN 94005 687-H5
SILVIA CT
800 PCFA 94044 726-H5
SIMKINS CT
2900 PA 94303 791-D5
SIMON LN
13200 LAH 94022 810-J7
SIMPSON DR
- DALY 94015 707-C2
SIOUX WY
- PTLV 94028 810-C6
SISKIYOU CT
100 SBRN 94066 707-D7
SISKIYOU DR
900 MLPK 94025 790-C7
SISKIYOU PL
- MLPK 94025 790-C7
SISTER CITIES BLVD
- SSF 94080 708-A1
200 SSF 94080 707-J1
SKIFF CIR
500 RDWC 94065 749-H7
SKIPJACK LN
100 FCTY 94404 749-J1
SKY CT
3700 SMTO 94403 749-B6
SKYFARM DR
2100 HIL 94010 728-D7
2100 HIL 94010 748-D2
SKYLAWN DR
- SMCo - 768-D4
SKYLINE BLVD
- SF 94132 686-J1
- SMCo - 748-D4
100 MLBR 94030 727-H4
500 SBRN 94066 727-F1
1600 BURL 94010 728-A6
1600 SMCo 94010 728-A6
5800 SMCo 94010 748-D4
5900 SMCo 94010 728-A6
6000 BURL 94010 748-B1
6000 SMCo 94010 748-B1
6000 HIL 94010 748-B1
SKYLINE BLVD Rt#-35
- DALY 94015 687-A5
- DALY 94015 686-J3
- SF 94132 686-J3
- SMCo - 748-E6
- SMCo - 727-F1
500 SMCo - 727-F1
500 SBRN 94066 727-F1
900 SBRN 94066 707-D5
900 SMCo - 707-D5
1100 DALY 94015 707-B1
1200 PCFA 94044 707-B1
1900 SMCo - 786-F1
2100 SMCo 94015 686-J3
2700 SSF 94080 707-D5
7500 SMCo 94062 768-E5
11400 SMCo - 788-G3
11400 SMCo 94062 788-G3
13800 SMCo 94062 789-A7
14600 SMCo 94062 (808-J1
See Page 788)
14700 SMCo 94062 809-A1
17100 WDSD 94062 809-G7
17300 SMCo 94020 809-G7
17300 WDSD 94020 809-D4
18100 PTLV 94028 809-G7
18100 SMCo 94020 829-H1
18100 PTLV 94028 829-H1
19300 SMCo 94020 830-A4
19300 PTLV 94028 830-A4
19800 SMCo 94028 830-C7
20800 SMCo 94020 850-E1
20800 SMCo 94028 850-E1
21100 SCIC - 850-E1
21100 SCIC 94028 850-E1
21200 PA 94304 850-H2
21600 SMCo 94304 850-H2
21700 PA - 850-H2
22800 SCrC 95030 850-J5
22800 SCIC 95030 850-J5
SKYLINE DR
- DALY 94015 686-J4
- SMCo 94062 809-F6
300 DALY 94015 687-A5
900 DALY 94015 707-A1
1200 DALY 94015 706-J1
SKYLINE TR
- SMCo 94062 789-A6
SKYLINE FRONTAGE RD
1900 HIL 94010 748-B1
1900 SMCo 94010 748-B1
SKYLONDA DR
- SMCo 94020 809-F5
SKYMONT CT
- BLMT 94002 768-J1
SKYMONT DR
4100 BLMT 94002 768-J1
SKYPARK CIR
- SSF 94014 687-J7
- SSF 94014 707-J1
SKYVIEW DR
1300 BURL 94010 748-B1
SKYWAY RD
600 RDWC 94065 769-H2
600 SCAR 94070 769-H2

SKYWOOD WY
- WDSD 94062 809-F5
SLATE CREEK RD
- SMCo 94020 (870-C1
See Page 869)
SLEEPY HOLLOW AV
- SMCo 94063 770-F5
SLEEPY HOLLOW LN
1100 MLBR 94030 727-H4
SLOOP CT
100 FCTY 94404 749-H4
SMOKE TREE LN
- WDSD 94062 809-F1
SNEATH LN
- PCFA 94044 727-D1
800 SBRN 94066 707-G6
3600 SBRN 94066 727-D1
3700 SMCo 94044 727-D1
SNECKNER CT
- SMCo 94025 810-F1
SNOWDEN AV
- ATN 94027 790-D1
SOHO CIR
- BLMT 94002 769-A3
SOLANA CT
- BLMT 94002 769-E2
SOLANA DR
1400 BLMT 94002 769-E2
SOLANA RD
100 PTLV 94028 810-B5
SOLANO AV
300 SMCo 94018 767-A2
SOLANO DR
1300 PCFA 94044 726-J5
SOLANO ST
- BSBN 94005 688-A6
SOMERSET CT
- BLMT 94002 769-E5
800 SCAR 94070 769-E5
SOMERSET DR
2500 BLMT 94002 769-B3
SOMERSET LN
- ATN 94027 790-D4
600 FCTY 94404 749-G5
SOMERSET PL
- PA 94301 791-A4
- WDSD 94062 789-F4
SOMERSET ST
- SF 94134 688-A1
100 RDWC 94062 769-H5
SONJA RD
100 SSF 94080 707-H1
SONOMA AV
- ATN 94027 790-H1
1000 MLPK 94025 790-H1
1000 MLPK 94025 770-H7
SONOMA CT
100 SBRN 94066 707-D6
SONOMA PL
- MLPK 94025 770-H7
SONOMA TER
800 SCIC 94305 810-J1
SONORA AV
- SMCo 94018 767-A2
- SSF 94080 707-H4
700 SMCo 94018 766-J1
SONORA DR
200 SMTO 94402 748-J3
SORICH RD
- SCrC 95030 850-J6
- SMCo 94020 850-G6
SORREL LN
- SCAR 94070 769-C4
SOTOCASTLE LN
100 BLMT 94002 749-F6
SOUTH BLVD
100 SMTO 94402 749-A3
SOUTH CT
2200 PA 94301 791-C7
2600 PA 94306 791-C7
SOUTH PL
400 RDWC 94062 769-J7
SOUTH PZ
- MLPK 94025 790-J2
SOUTH RD
300 BLMT 94002 749-D7
300 BLMT 94002 769-E1
SOUTH ST
1000 BURL 94010 728-G6
SOUTHAMPTON DR
700 PA 94303 791-B5
SOUTHAMPTON WY
2200 SMTO 94403 749-C4
SOUTHCLIFF AV
100 SSF 94080 707-E3
SOUTHDALE AV
- DALY 94015 687-A7
SOUTHDALE WY
500 WDSD 94062 789-E3
SOUTHDOWN CT
- HIL 94010 748-F4
SOUTHDOWN RD
1100 HIL 94010 748-F4
SOUTHERN FRWY I-280
- DALY 94014 687-C2
- DALY 94015 687-C4
- SF 94112 687-E1
- SF 94132 687-D2
SOUTH FORK LN
13400 LAH 94022 810-J7

SOUTHGATE AV
- DALY 94015 687-A4
400 DALY 94015 686-J4
SOUTHGATE DR
- WDSD 94062 789-J5
- WDSD 94062 790-A5
SOUTHGATE ST
- ATN 94027 790-D2
SOUTH HILL CT
200 DALY 94014 687-F3
SOUTH HILL DR
- BSBN 94005 687-H5
SOUTHMOOR DR
600 PCFA 94044 707-B4
SOUTHPORT DR
800 RDWC 94065 750-A6
SOUTHRIDGE CT
- SMTO 94402 748-H6
SOUTHRIDGE WY
- DALY 94014 687-G3
SOUTH SAN FRANCISCO DR
- SSF 94080 708-A1
- SSF 94014 708-A1
300 SSF 94014 707-H1
300 SSF 94080 707-H1
SOUTHVIEW CT
600 BLMT 94002 769-E1
SOUTHVIEW WY
700 WDSD 94062 789-F3
SOUTHWOOD AV
3600 SMTO 94403 749-B6
SOUTHWOOD CTR
100 SSF 94080 707-G4
SOUTHWOOD DR
100 PA 94301 791-B3
600 SSF 94080 707-F3
SOVEREIGN WY
800 RDWC 94065 750-C6
SPAR DR
600 RDWC 94065 749-H7
800 SMTO 94404 749-D2
SPARROW CT
- EPA 94303 791-C2
SPARTA ST
- SF 94134 688-A1
SPEAR AV
1000 SF 94124 688-D1
SPEERS AV
1300 SMTO 94403 749-C2
SPENCER LN
- ATN 94027 790-E3
SPINDRIFT WY
500 HMBY 94019 767-E6
SPINNAKER CT
200 FCTY 94404 749-H4
SPINNAKER LN
1500 HMBY 94019 767-E6
SPINNAKER PL
- RDWC 94065 749-H6
SPINNAKER ST
100 FCTY 94404 749-H4
SPIROS WY
- SMCo 94025 790-D5
SPRAGUE LN
1100 FCTY 94404 749-G4
SPRING LN
- BLMT 94002 769-E2
SPRING ST
- SMCo 94038 746-F7
- PCFA 94044 727-A3
- RDWC 94063 770-B5
1200 SCAR 94070 769-F2
2200 SMCo 94063 770-D6
SPRINGDALE DR
200 PCFA 94044 707-A2
SPRINGDALE WY
- SMCo 94062 769-E7
SPRINGFIELD DR
900 MLBR 94030 727-H4
900 SCAR 94070 769-G2
SPRINGFIELD WY
2200 SMTO 94403 749-C4
SPRING VALLEY LN
- MLBR 94030 728-A5
SPRING VALLEY WY
- SCAR 94070 769-F3
SPRINGWOOD WY
100 SSF 94080 707-G5
1200 PCFA 94044 726-J6
SPRUANCE LN
700 FCTY 94404 749-G4
SPRUCE AV
- ATN 94025 790-E2
- SSF 94080 707-J2
- MLPK 94025 790-E2
N SPRUCE AV
- SSF 94080 707-J2
400 SSF 94080 708-A2
S SPRUCE AV
- SSF 94080 707-H4
SPRUCE CT
- PCFA 94044 727-A4
SPRUCE LN
- SMCo 94060 (868-H5
See Page 867)
SPRUCE ST
- MLBR 94030 728-B2
- RDWC 94063 770-B7
200 HMBY 94019 787-E2

SPURAWAY DR
100 SMTO 94403 749-A4
SPYGLASS DR
1900 SBRN 94066 707-B5
3400 SMTO 94403 749-A6
STACEY CT
- HIL 94010 728-E7
STADLER DR
- WDSD 94062 809-F5
STAFFORD ST
- DALY 94015 707-C3
1400 SCAR 94070 769-J4
1400 RDWC 94063 769-J4
STAG AV
2000 SMCo 94402 768-H1
STAGE RD
- SMCo 94060 (868-B2
See Page 867)
1200 SMCo 94060 (848-A7
See Page 827)
1600 SMCo 94074 (848-B1
See Page 827)
7500 SMCo 94074 (828-A5
See Page 827)
STAMBAUGH ST
100 RDWC 94063 770-B6
STAMFORD CT
2600 SSF 94080 707-C4
STANCHION LN
300 FCTY 94404 749-J1
STANDISH CT
800 PCFA 94044 726-J5
STANDISH RD
800 PCFA 94044 726-H5
STANDISH ST
200 RDWC 94063 770-A5
STANFORD AV
- SCIC 94304 810-F2
100 SMCo 94025 790-E6
100 SMCo 94063 766-H3
200 PA 94306 791-A7
400 SMCo 94063 770-D7
500 SCIC - 791-A7
600 MLPK 94025 790-E6
1100 SCIC 94305 810-J2
1100 PA 94306 810-J2
1500 SMTO 94403 749-C2
STANFORD CT
900 MLPK 94025 790-E5
14100 LAH 94022 810-H5
STANFORD LN
- SCAR 94070 769-H5
STANISLAUS CT
100 SBRN 94066 707-D7
STANLEY AV
100 PCFA 94044 726-G4
STANLEY RD
- BURL 94010 728-H6
STANLEY ST
- SF 94132 687-C2
100 RDWC 94062 769-H7
STANLEY WY
900 PA 94303 791-B4
STANTON RD
800 BURL 94010 728-D4
STAR WY
- BURL 94010 728-E5
STARBOARD DR
400 RDWC 94065 749-H7
500 SMTO 94404 749-D1
STARFISH CT
- HMBY 94019 787-G5
STARFISH LN
300 RDWC 94065 749-J2
STAR HILL RD
- SMCo 94074 (828-A3
See Page 827)
- SMCo 94074 827-J4
300 SMCo 94062 (828-D3
See Page 827)
300 SMCo 94062 (808-H2
See Page 788)
STARLITE DR
100 SMCo 94402 748-G6
STARLITE ST
100 SSF 94080 707-H4
STARWOOD DR
400 SMCo 94062 809-E6
STATE ST
- SMTO 94401 728-J6
STATION AV
- DALY 94014 687-C5
STAUNTON CT
2100 PA 94306 791-A7
STAYSAIL CT
200 FCTY 94404 749-H4
STEIN CT
3900 SSF 94080 707-C4
STEIN AM RHEIN CT
- RDWC 94063 770-C5
STELLING CT
3000 PA 94303 791-D6
STELLING DR
3000 PA 94303 791-D6
STEPHEN RD
400 SMTO 94403 749-B6
STERLING AV
200 PCFA 94044 726-G4
2000 SMCo 94025 790-D6

STERLING WY
3000 RDWC 94061 789-J3
STERLING VIEW AV
500 BLMT 94002 749-D6
STERN AV
700 PA 94303 791-D6
STERN LN
- ATN 94027 790-C4
1000 FCTY 94404 749-G4
STETSON ST
400 SMCo 94038 746-F6
STEVENS AV
1700 EPA 94303 771-C7
STEVENS CT
200 SCAR 94070 769-E6
STEVENSON LN
- ATN 94027 790-D3
STEVICK DR
300 ATN 94027 790-B5
STEWART AV
700 SMCo 94015 687-A4
STILL CREEK RD
- WDSD 94062 809-F4
STILT CT
200 FCTY 94404 749-G1
STIRRUP WY
27700 LAH 94022 810-J5
STOCKBRIDGE AV
- ATN 94027 790-C3
- SMCo 94061 790-C3
2100 WDSD 94062 790-C3
STOCK FARM RD
- SCIC 94305 790-F6
STOCKTON PL
3100 PA 94303 791-E6
STONE LN
700 PA 94303 791-E7
STONEGATE DR
600 SSF 94080 707-G1
STONEGATE RD
- PTLV 94028 810-B6
STONEHEDGE RD
- HIL 94010 748-H2
STONEPINE CT
- HIL 94010 748-E1
STONE PINE LN
100 MLPK 94025 790-E3
STONE PINE RD
500 HMBY 94019 787-G1
STONEPINE RD
- HIL 94010 748-E2
STONEY CT
900 MLBR 94030 727-H4
STONEYFORD DR
600 SMCo 94015 687-A5
700 DALY 94015 687-A5
STONEY POINT PL
- SMCo 94402 768-G2
STONY HILL RD
900 RDWC 94061 789-H2
STORY HILL LN
28000 LAH 94022 810-H7
STOWA WY
- DALY 94014 687-D5
STOWE CT
- SMCo 94025 810-F1
STOWE LN
- SMCo 94025 810-E1
STRATFORD DR
100 SF 94132 687-B1
STRATFORD ST
100 RDWC 94062 769-J5
STRATFORD WY
2000 SMTO 94403 749-A4
STUDIO CIR
400 SMTO 94401 728-H7
SUDAN LN
- SCAR 94070 769-D5
SUENO CAMINO
- SMCo 94020 829-F7
SUGAR HILL DR
- HIL 94402 748-G5
SUGARLOAF DR
1600 SMTO 94403 748-J7
1600 SMTO 94403 768-J1
SULLIVAN AV
- DALY 94015 687-B5
100 SMCo 94015 687-B5
SULLIVAN ST
2000 SMTO 94403 749-C4
SUMMER AV
1100 BURL 94010 728-E5
SUMMERHILL LN
100 WDSD 94062 789-J3
SUMMER HOLM PL
- HIL 94010 728-F7
SUMMERRAIN DR
100 SSF 94080 707-G2
SUMMIT CT
- SMCo 94062 789-F1
- SSF 94080 707-E5
SUMMIT DR
100 SMCo 94062 789-F1
2100 BURL 94010 728-C7
2100 SMCo 94010 728-B7
2200 HIL 94010 728-C7
2800 SMCo 94010 748-B1
2800 HIL 94010 748-B1
W SUMMIT DR
- SMCo 94062 789-F1

SUMMIT RD
- SMCo 94037 746-H4
- SMCo 94062 788-H6
- WDSD 94062 809-G6
3100 SBRN 94066 707-C5
SUMMIT ST
- SF 94112 687-E1
SUMMIT WY
500 RDWC 94062 789-F3
500 SMCo 94062 789-F3
SUMMIT RIDGE PL
- SMCo 94062 789-G1
SUMMIT SPRINGS RD
400 WDSD 94062 789-E7
SUMMIT SPRINGS FIRE RD
- SMCo 94062 789-A6
SUNBEAM LN
- SF 94112 687-F1
SUNFISH CT
300 FCTY 94404 749-H3
SUNHILL
- PTLV 94028 830-C2
SUNNYBRAE BLVD
500 SMTO 94402 749-B2
SUNNYDALE AV
- SCAR 94070 769-H5
- SF 94134 688-A2
400 SF 94134 687-H2
2200 SF 94112 687-H2
SUNNY HILL RD
- SMCo 94062 789-E1
SUNNYSIDE DR
1000 SSF 94080 707-F2
SUNNYSLOPE AV
1300 BLMT 94002 769-E1
SUNRISE CT
- MLPK 94025 790-E7
- SMCo 94018 766-J1
- SSF 94080 707-E5
SUNRISE DR
- WDSD 94062 809-G4
SUNRISE WY
300 SF 94134 687-J2
SUNRISE FARM RD
27400 LAH 94022 830-J1
SUNSET AV
600 SSF 94080 707-G2
SUNSET CT
- MLPK 94025 790-D7
3100 SMTO 94403 749-A6
SUNSET DR
- DALY 94015 706-J2
700 SCAR 94070 769-F5
3500 SBRN 94066 707-B6
SUNSET LN
- MLPK 94025 790-D7
SUNSET TER
- HMBY 94019 787-G5
2600 SMTO 94403 749-A6
SUNSET WY
500 SMCo 94062 789-E2
SUNSET CIRCLE DR
- SMCo - 768-C3
SUNSHINE DR
100 PCFA 94044 707-A1
SUNSHINE VALLEY RD
1100 SMCo 94038 746-G6
1600 SMCo 94037 746-G6
SURF ST
100 PCFA 94044 706-J5
SURF BIRD ISL
200 FCTY 94404 749-G1
SURFPERCH ST
800 FCTY 94404 749-H2
SURREY CT
- DALY 94015 707-C2
SURREY LN
- ATN 94027 790-F2
SUSAN CT
1500 SMTO 94403 749-D3
SUSAN DR
3000 SBRN 94066 707-C5
SUSAN GALE CT
- MLPK 94025 790-C6
SUSIE LN
2800 SCAR 94070 769-G6
SUSIE WY
300 SSF 94080 707-G2
SUSSEX CT
300 BLMT 94002 749-E7
SUSSEX PL
1800 MLPK 94025 790-F2
SUSSEX WY
- RDWC 94061 789-J3
- RDWC 94061 790-A3
200 PCFA 94044 726-G4
SUTHERLAND DR
- ATN 94027 790-B5
SUTTER AV
700 PA 94303 791-C6
SUTTON AV
- SSF 94080 707-D1
SUZANNE CT
1000 HMBY 94019 787-G2
SUZIE ST
4100 SMTO 94403 749-E6
SWAN ST
900 FCTY 94404 749-H1

SWEENEY AV
800 SMCo 94063 770-C6
SWEET WILLIAM LN
- SMCo 94025 770-E7
SWEETWOOD DR
1300 SMCo 94015 687-B5
1300 DALY 94015 687-B5
SWETT RD
- SMCo 94062 788-H7
- SMCo 94062 (808-H1
See Page 788)
SWIFT AV
300 SSF 94080 708-B4
SWORDFISH ST
1200 FCTY 94404 749-H3
SYCAMORE AV
100 SMTO 94402 728-G7
100 SMTO 94402 748-G1
100 SSF 94080 707-H4
700 SBRN 94066 707-H7
SYCAMORE CT
- RDWC 94061 790-A2
SYCAMORE DR
800 PA 94303 791-D6
1000 MLBR 94030 727-H3
SYCAMORE ST
100 SCAR 94070 769-F3
SYLVAN AV
100 SBRN 94066 707-J7
100 SMTO 94403 749-A6
SYLVAN CT
- MLBR 94030 728-A4
SYLVAN DR
900 SCAR 94070 769-G2
SYLVAN ST
500 SMCo 94014 687-D5
500 DALY 94014 687-D5
SYLVAN WY
- SMCo 94021 849-A7
200 SMCo 94062 789-E7
200 SMCo 94062 789-E1
SYLVESTER RD
100 SSF 94080 708-A3

T

TACOMA WY
1500 RDWC 94063 769-J4
1500 RDWC 94063 770-A4
TADIN LN
1500 WDSD 94062 809-H4
TADLEY CT
300 RDWC 94061 790-B1
TAFT ST
900 RDWC 94061 789-J1
TAGUS CT
- PTLV 94028 810-D5
TAHOE CT
- SSF 94080 707-F4
TAHOE DR
1000 BLMT 94002 769-A2
TALBERT CT
- SF 94134 688-A2
TALBERT ST
- SF 94134 688-A3
200 DALY 94014 688-A3
400 DALY 94014 687-J3
TALBOT AV
300 PCFA 94044 707-A5
TALBRYN DR
1200 BLMT 94002 769-E2
TALBRYN LN
- BLMT 94002 769-E1
TALISMAN CT
700 PA 94303 791-E7
TALISMAN DR
800 PA 94303 791-E7
TALLWOOD CT
- ATN 94027 790-C6
TALLWOOD DR
100 DALY 94014 687-D4
TAMARACK AV
700 SCAR 94070 769-F4
TAMARACK DR
- HIL 94010 748-E1
TAMARACK LN
200 SSF 94080 707-G2
TAMARIND AV
1000 SMCo 94037 746-G4
TAMPA CT
300 FCTY 94404 749-F5
TANAGER CT
- BSBN 94005 687-J5
TANFORAN AV
- SBRN 94066 707-H5
- SSF 94080 707-H5
TANGLEWOOD WY
1100 SMTO 94403 749-E6
TANKLAGE RD
900 SCAR 94070 769-H3
TANLAND DR
1000 PA 94303 791-D5
TAN OAK DR
100 PTLV 94028 830-C1
TAPIA DR
- SF 94132 687-B1
TAPIS WY
1100 PCFA 94044 726-J5
TARA LN
2400 SSF 94080 707-D5

TARA ST
100 EPA 94303 791-C1
100 SF 94112 687-E1
100 EPA 94303 771-C7
TARPON ST
900 FCTY 94404 749-H2
TARRYTOWN RD
1400 SMCo 94402 748-F7
TARTAN TRAIL RD
1000 HIL 94010 748-E4
TASKER LN
- SCAR 94070 769-F5
TASSO ST
100 PA 94301 790-J3
1300 PA 94301 791-A5
TAURUS DR
800 FCTY 94404 749-E3
TAYLOR AV
300 SBRN 94066 707-J7
300 SBRN 94066 727-J1
TAYLOR BLVD
100 MLBR 94030 728-A4
TAYLOR DR
200 SSF 94080 707-G4
TAYLOR ST
1600 SMTO 94403 749-C2
TAYLOR WY
500 SMCo 94002 769-G2
600 SCAR 94070 769-G2
TEAL CT
- EPA 94303 791-C2
TEAL ST
600 FCTY 94404 749-G1
TEATREE CT
- HIL 94010 748-C2
TEDDY AV
- SF 94134 688-A2
- SF 94134 687-J1
TEHAMA AV
1000 MLPK 94025 770-H7
1000 MLPK 94025 790-H1
TEHAMA CT
100 SBRN 94066 727-E1
TELFORD AV
600 SSF 94080 707-J2
TEMESCAL WY
700 SMCo 94062 789-F2
TEMPLE CT
2800 EPA 94303 771-C6
TEMPLE ST
- SMCo 94037 746-H5
TEMPLETON AV
- DALY 94014 687-E3
TENDER LN
700 FCTY 94404 749-G5
TENNIS DR
800 SSF 94080 707-G3
TENNYSON AV
100 PA 94301 791-A6
700 PA 94303 791-A6
TEREDO DR
500 RDWC 94065 749-H7
TERESA ST
- DALY 94014 687-D5
TERMINAL AV
- MLPK 94025 770-H7
TERMINAL BLVD
2500 MTVW 94043 791-F6
TERMINAL CT
- SSF 94080 708-A4
- SSF 94080 707-J4
TERMINAL PL
1200 SMTO 94401 729-A7
TERMINAL WY
900 SCAR 94070 769-G3
TERRACE AV
- DALY 94015 687-A4
200 SBRN 94066 707-J7
200 SBRN 94066 727-J1
400 SMCo 94038 746-G7
400 SMCo 94019 767-D4
500 HMBY 94019 767-F7
TERRACE DR
200 SSF 94080 707-H4
1300 MLBR 94030 727-H2
1700 BLMT 94002 769-C1
TERRACE LN
- SMCo 94038 746-F7
TERRACE RD
600 SCAR 94070 769-F6
TERRACE WY
400 SMTO 94403 749-B5
TERRACE VIEW CT
- DALY 94015 687-A5
TERRA LINDA CT
- MLBR 94030 728-A5
TERRA NOVA BLVD
1000 PCFA 94044 727-A4
TERRA VILLA AV
2200 EPA 94303 791-C2
TERRIER PL
- HIL 94010 748-F5
TERRY LN
1900 SMCo 94061 790-B4
TEVIS PL
- HIL 94010 748-E1
- PA 94301 791-B4
TEXAS PL
300 SBRN 94066 727-J1

TEXAS WY
2000 SMTO 94403 749-B4
THAGE WY
- PTLV 94028 809-J6
THANE AV
600 HMBY 94019 787-E5
THATCHER LN
100 FCTY 94404 749-F5
THE ALAMEDA
200 SMCo 94018 767-B2
THE CROSS WY
500 SMCo 94019 767-D4
THE CROSSWAYS
100 SMCo 94019 767-C3
THE EMBARCADERO
500 RDWC 94065 749-J4
500 RDWC 94065 750-A4
THERESA CT
900 MLPK 94025 770-G7
THERESA DR
500 SSF 94080 707-E2
THE STRAND
- SMCo 94038 746-F7
THETA AV
- DALY 94014 687-C3
THIERS ST
- DALY 94014 687-C4
THISTLE
- PTLV 94028 830-C1
THOBURN CT
- SCIC 94305 790-J7
THOMAS AV
- BSBN 94005 688-B6
THOMAS CT
- SMTO 94401 728-J7
THOMAS DR
3300 PA 94303 791-E6
THOMAS MELLON DR
- SF 94134 688-B2
THOMAS MORE WY
- SF 94132 687-B2
THORNHILL DR
700 SMCo 94015 687-A5
2600 SCAR 94070 769-F5
THORNWOOD DR
800 PA 94303 791-E7
THREE FORKS LN
13400 LAH 94022 810-H7
THRIFT ST
- SF 94112 687-D1
200 SF 94132 687-D1
THURM AV
- SMTO 94403 749-B7
2200 BLMT 94002 749-B7
2200 BLMT 94002 769-B1
TIARA CT
- SMCo 94010 728-B7
TIBURON WY
2800 BURL 94010 728-B6
TICONDEROGA CT
- SMCo 94402 768-H1
- SMTO 94402 768-H1
TICONDEROGA DR
1900 SMCo 94402 768-G1
TIDEWATER DR
- RDWC 94065 750-A6
TIERRA ALTA ST
700 SMCo 94038 746-G6
TIERRA FUEGO RD
- SMCo 94060 (868-E4
See Page 867)
TILIA ST
1200 SMTO 94402 748-J3
TILLER CT
100 HMBY 94019 767-E6
TILLER DR
- SMTO 94404 749-D2
TILLER LN
- FCTY 94404 749-H4
400 RDWC 94065 749-H7
TILTON AV
- SMTO 94401 748-J1
700 SMTO 94401 728-J7
800 SMTO 94401 729-A7
TILTON TER
- SMTO 94401 748-J1
TIMBERHEAD LN
300 FCTY 94404 749-G6
TIMBERLANE RD
1700 SMTO 94402 748-H7
1800 SMTO 94402 748-H7
TIMBERLANE WY
1700 SMTO 94402 768-H1
1700 SMCo 94402 768-H1
TIMOTHY LN
200 RDWC 94070 769-G6
200 SCAR 94070 769-G6
900 MLPK 94025 770-G7
TINTERN LN
- PTLV 94028 810-B6
TIOGA AV
- SF 94134 688-A1
TIOGA DR
700 MLBR 94030 727-J4
2200 MLPK 94025 790-C6
TIOGA WY
- BLMT 94002 769-A2
- PCFA 94044 727-B5
TIPPERARY AV
2300 SSF 94080 707-D5

STREET
Block City ZIP Pg-Grid

TIPTOE LN
- HIL 94010 748-B1
- SMCo 94010 748-B1
100 SMCo 94010 728-B7
100 HIL 94010 728-B7
TOBIN CLARK DR
- HIL 94402 748-H4
TOCOLOMA AV
100 SF 94134 688-B2
TODO EL MUNDO
100 WDSD 94062 789-J5
TOLEDO AV
1600 BURL 94010 728-B6
TOLEDO CT
- BURL 94010 728-B6
1600 PCFA 94044 727-B6
TOLLRIDGE CT
- SMTO 94402 748-C7
TOLMAN DR
700 SCIC 94305 810-J2
TOMASO CT
- SF 94134 687-J2
TOPAZ ST
300 RDWC 94062 769-H7
500 RDWC 94062 789-J1
600 RDWC 94061 789-J1
TOPSAIL CT
200 FCTY 94404 749-G4
TORINO DR
- SMCo 94070 769-E4
300 SCAR 94070 769-E4
TORINO KNOLLS
- SCAR 94070 769-E5
TORO CT
- PTLV 94028 810-D6
TORREYA CT
700 PA 94303 791-D7
TOULOUSE CT
- HMBY 94019 767-E5
TOURAINE LN
2000 HMBY 94019 767-E5
TOURNAMENT DR
700 HIL 94402 748-H4
TOURNAMENT WY
- HIL 94402 748-G5
TOWER LN
900 FCTY 94404 749-E3
TOWER RD
- SMCo 94402 768-H2
TOWLE PL
600 PA 94306 791-D7
TOWLE WY
600 PA 94306 791-C7
TOWNE FIRE TR
- SMCo 94020 849-E3
TOYON AV
100 SSF 94080 707-H3
TOYON CT
100 WDSD 94062 789-G5
1600 SMTO 94403 768-J1
TOYON DR
900 BURL 94010 728-F6
1200 MLBR 94030 728-A5
TOYON LN
- SF 94112 687-G2
TOYON PL
600 PA 94306 791-D7
TOYON RD
- ATN 94027 790-G1
TOYON WY
800 RDWC 94062 789-G1
2300 SBRN 94066 707-F6
TRACE LN
- HMBY 94019 787-F5
TRACY CT
14000 LAH 94022 810-H6
14000 PA 94304 810-H6
TRADER LN
2200 SMTO 94404 749-E2
TRAEGER AV
- SBRN 94066 707-H6
TRAIL LN
- WDSD 94062 810-A5
TRAMANTO DR
2800 SCAR 94070 769-E6
TRANSOM LN
400 FCTY 94404 749-G6
TRANSPORT ST
3900 PA 94303 791-F7
TRAPPERS TR
- PA 94304 830-E2
TREASURE ISLAND DR
100 BLMT 94002 749-F6
TREESIDE CT
- SSF 94080 707-G2
TREETOP LN
- SMTO 94402 748-H4
TREE TOPS CIR
3000 SBRN 94066 707-C5
TREE VIEW DR
200 DALY 94014 687-E3
TRENTON DR
2200 SBRN 94066 707-G7
2400 SBRN 94066 727-F1
TRENTON PL
- SMCo 94402 748-F7
TRENTON WY
300 MLPK 94025 790-J3
600 BURL 94010 728-G6

STREET
Block City ZIP Pg-Grid

TRIDENT DR
400 RDWC 94065 749-H7
TRILLIUM CT
- SCAR 94070 769-C4
TRIMARAN CT
100 FCTY 94404 749-H4
TRINIDAD LN
400 FCTY 94404 749-F5
TRINITY CT
- MLPK 94025 790-C7
100 SBRN 94066 707-D7
TRINITY DR
1000 MLPK 94025 790-C7
TRINITY LN
- PTLV 94028 809-J6
TRINITY RD
- BSBN 94005 688-A6
TRINITY ST
2000 SMTO 94403 749-C4
TRIPOLI CT
12900 LAH 94022 830-J1
TRIPP CT
- WDSD 94062 789-E7
TRIPP RD
3300 WDSD 94062 789-E6
3600 WDSD 94062 809-F1
TRITON DR
1100 FCTY 94404 749-F2
TROGLIA TER
100 PCFA 94044 727-A3
TROLLMAN AV
1400 SMTO 94401 729-A7
TROON RD
100 HMBY 94019 787-F5
TROPHY CT
- HIL 94402 748-H4
TROUSDALE DR
- SMCo 728-B6
- SMCo 94010 728-B6
1100 BURL 94010 728-B6
TROUT FARM RD
- SMCo 727-B7
TRUDY LN
- SMCo 94025 790-D5
TRUMAN ST
1100 RDWC 94061 789-J1
TRYSAIL CT
200 FCTY 94404 749-G4
TUCKER AV
- SF 94134 688-A1
TUDOR DR
1600 MLPK 94025 790-F2
TULANE AV
1600 EPA 94303 771-B6
TULANE CT
700 SMTO 94402 748-H3
TULANE RD
200 SMTO 94402 748-H3
TULARE DR
100 SBRN 94066 707-E7
TULARE ST
- BSBN 94005 688-B6
TULIP CT
- SMCo 94010 748-B1
TULIP LN
- PA 94303 791-C4
- SCAR 94070 769-D4
100 MLBR 94030 727-H4
TUM SUDEN WY
- RDWC 94062 789-F3
- SMCo 94062 789-F3
- WDSD 94062 789-F3
TUNITAS LN
- SSF 94080 707-E3
TUNITAS CREEK RD
- SMCo 94062 789-A7
- SMCo 94019 827-J1
100 SMCo 94019 (828-A2
See Page 827)
300 SMCo 94074 (828-A2
See Page 827)
400 SMCo 94074 (808-C5
See Page 788)
2000 SMCo 94062 (808-C5
See Page 788)
2000 SMCo 94019 (808-C5
See Page 788)
4000 SMCo 94062 788-G7
W TUNITAS CREEK RD
5600 SMCo 94062 788-J7
TUNNEL AV
100 SF 94134 688-A4
500 BSBN 94005 688-A4
TUOLUMNE CT
100 MLBR 94030 727-J4
TUOLUMNE RD
1100 MLBR 94030 727-H4
TURKEY FARM LN
- WDSD 94062 809-G1
TURKS HEAD CT
- RDWC 94065 749-H7
TURKS HEAD LN
- RDWC 94065 749-H7
TURNBERRY DR
2500 SSF 94080 707-D5
2500 SBRN 94066 707-D5
TURNBERRY RD
- HMBY 94019 787-F5
TURNER TER
400 SMTO 94401 728-H7

STREET
Block City ZIP Pg-Grid

TURNER TER
400 SMTO 94401 748-H1
TURNSTONE CT
200 FCTY 94404 749-H1
TURNSWORTH AV
- RDWC 94062 769-H6
TURTLE BAY PL
- SMCo 94402 768-G1
TUSCALOOSA AV
- ATN 94027 790-C3
TWIN DOLPHIN DR
- RDWC 94065 749-G7
- RDWC 94065 769-G1
TWIN OAK CT
1000 RDWC 94061 789-G3
TYNAN WY
- PTLV 94028 809-J6
TYRONE CT
2600 SSF 94080 707-C4

U

UCCELLI BLVD
- RDWC 94063 770-B4
ULMER CT
300 RDWC 94061 790-C1
ULSTER WY
- SSF 94080 707-E5
UNION AV
1500 RDWC 94061 790-A1
UNIVERSITY AV
- PA 94301 790-J4
800 PA 94301 791-A3
1900 EPA 94303 791-B2
2500 EPA 94303 771-B7
UNIVERSITY AV Rt#-109
2600 EPA 94303 771-B6
2700 MLPK 94303 771-B6
2800 MLPK 94025 771-B6
UNIVERSITY DR
- MLPK 94025 790-F3
UNIVERSITY ST
500 SF 94134 687-J1
UNWIN CT
2400 SSF 94080 707-D4
UPENUF RD
- WDSD 94062 809-H6
UPLAND AV
- DALY 94015 687-A5
- DALY 94015 686-J5
- SCAR 94070 769-F3
UPLAND CT
200 RDWC 94062 769-G7
UPLAND RD
200 RDWC 94062 769-G7
400 SMCo 94062 769-G7
2400 SMCo 94062 789-H1
2400 RDWC 94062 789-H1
UPLANDS DR
200 HIL 94010 748-H2
UPPER LAKE RD
- WDSD 94062 809-H5
UPPER LOCK AV
3200 BLMT 94002 769-A2
UPTON ST
- SMCo 94062 789-J1
400 SMCo 94062 769-H7
500 RDWC 94062 789-J1
600 RDWC 94061 789-J1
URBAN LN
600 PA 94301 790-H5
URSA LN
800 FCTY 94404 749-F4
URSULA AV
700 PCFA 94044 727-B2
URSULA LN
27200 LAH 94022 830-J1
URSULA WY
1300 EPA 94303 791-B1
UTAH AV
100 SSF 94080 708-A4
UTAH WY
- RDWC 94062 789-H1

V

VAILWOOD PL
100 SMTO 94403 749-E6
VAILWOOD WY
1100 SMTO 94403 749-E6
VALDEFLORES DR
100 SMCo 94010 728-B7
VALDEZ AV
200 HMBY 94019 787-E1
1800 BLMT 94002 769-D2
VALDEZ PL
900 SCIC 94305 810-J2
VALDEZ WY
1500 PCFA 94044 727-A6
VALDIVIA CT
- BURL 94010 728-C6
VALDIVIA WY
2300 BURL 94010 728-B6
VALE ST
- DALY 94014 687-C5
VALENCIA AV
100 SMCo 94018 767-A2
VALENCIA CT
- PTLV 94028 810-D6

STREET
Block City ZIP Pg-Grid

VALENCIA DR
200 MLBR 94030 727-J5
200 MLBR 94030 728-A5
300 SSF 94080 707-F5
VALENCIA ST
- HMBY 94019 767-D4
VALENCIA WY
1000 PCFA 94044 726-J4
1000 PCFA 94044 727-A4
VALERGA DR
2100 BLMT 94002 769-D3
VALLECITO LN
100 PCFA 94044 727-B2
VALLECITOS RD
- SMCo 94037 746-H4
VALLEJO CT
200 MLBR 94030 727-J5
VALLEJO DR
- MLBR 94030 727-J5
200 MLBR 94030 728-A6
VALLEJO ST
100 SMCo 94018 767-A2
VALLEJO TER
700 PCFA 94044 707-A5
VALLEMAR ST
- SMCo 94038 746-F5
VALLE VISTA RD
- SMCo 94037 746-H3
VALLEY CT
- ATN 94027 790-A7
- WDSD 94062 790-A7
VALLEY DR
100 BSBN 94005 688-A5
300 BSBN 94005 687-J5
VALLEY RD
- ATN 94027 790-A7
- SCAR 94070 769-F3
VALLEY ST
- DALY 94014 687-C5
200 SMCo 94014 687-C5
VALLEY OAK
- PTLV 94028 830-C2
VALLEY VIEW AV
1600 BLMT 94002 749-D7
1600 BLMT 94002 769-D1
VALLEY VIEW CT
- SMCo 94402 748-G6
VALLEYVIEW WY
100 SSF 94080 707-E5
VALLEYWOOD DR
- PCFA 94044 726-J6
2000 SBRN 94066 707-E6
VALMAR PL
- SCAR 94070 769-F5
VALOTA RD
600 RDWC 94061 789-J1
900 RDWC 94061 790-A2
VALPARAISO AV
- ATN 94027 790-E5
- MLPK 94025 790-C6
700 MLPK 94027 790-E5
1800 SMCo 94025 790-E5
VALPARAISO ST
600 SCIC 94305 810-H1
VALVERDE DR
300 SSF 94080 707-F5
VAL VERDE RD
- SMCo 94037 746-J5
VAN AUKEN CIR
900 PA 94303 791-D5
VAN BUREN RD
100 MLPK 94025 770-H7
400 MLPK 94025 790-J1
VAN BUREN ST
1600 SMTO 94403 749-C2
VANCE LN
- EPA 94303 791-C2
VANCOUVER AV
1100 BURL 94010 728-D6
VANNESSA DR
600 SMTO 94402 749-B3
VANNIER DR
500 BLMT 94002 749-D7
500 BLMT 94002 769-D1
VAQUERO WY
100 SMCo 94062 789-G1
VARELA AV
- SF 94132 687-B1
VARIAN ST
1000 SCAR 94070 769-J4
VASCO DA GAMA
900 FCTY 94404 749-F4
VASILAKOS CT
- SMCo 94025 790-C5
VASILAKOS WY
- SMCo 94025 790-D5
VASSAR ST
100 SMCo 94038 766-J2
VAZQUES DR
700 HMBY 94019 787-G2
VEGA CIR
700 FCTY 94404 749-E4
VEGA CT
- PCFA 94044 727-B3
VELASCO AV
- DALY 94014 687-H2
- SF 94134 687-H2
VENDOME AV
- DALY 94014 687-D2
900 HMBY 94019 767-F6

STREET
Block City ZIP Pg-Grid

VENICE BLVD
400 HMBY 94019 767-D6
VENTURA AV
- SMCo 94020 829-E7
500 SMTO 94403 749-A6
VENTURA CT
- PCFA 94044 727-A6
VENTURA ST
- HMBY 94019 767-D4
900 SMCo 94018 767-C3
VENUS CT
600 FCTY 94404 749-E3
VERA AV
100 RDWC 94061 770-A7
1600 RDWC 94061 789-H1
VERA CT
- RDWC 94061 770-A6
VERANO CT
500 HIL 94402 748-H4
500 SMTO 94402 748-H4
VERANO DR
- SSF 94080 707-E3
200 DALY 94015 687-B7
VERBALEE LN
- HIL 94402 748-H4
VERBENA DR
100 EPA 94303 791-C3
VERDE RD
- SMCo 94019 (807-G2
See Page 788)
VERDUCCI CT
400 DALY 94015 707-D3
VERDUCCI DR
400 DALY 94015 707-C3
VERDUN AV
3100 SMTO 94403 749-A6
3100 SMTO 94403 748-J6
VERITAS WK
300 PCFA 94044 727-A1
VERMONT AV
200 SMCo 94038 746-F6
VERMONT CT
600 SMCo 94038 746-G6
VERMONT WY
1100 SBRN 94066 707-E7
VERNAL WY
700 SMCo 94062 789-F2
VERNIER PL
1000 SCIC 94305 810-J2
VERNON ST
- SF 94132 687-C1
VERNON TER
1100 SMTO 94402 748-J4
3300 PA 94303 791-E6
VERNON WY
600 BURL 94010 728-G6
VERONA AV
100 PCFA 94044 727-A2
VERONICA CT
1000 EPA 94303 791-C1
VERONICA PL
- PTLV 94028 810-C7
VERSAILLES DR
- MLPK 94025 790-F3
VESPERO AV
- PCFA 94044 727-B1
VESPUCCI LN
700 FCTY 94404 749-F4
VETERANS BLVD
400 RDWC 94063 769-J4
400 RDWC 94063 770-A5
VIA CANON
- MLBR 94030 728-A4
VIA CERRO GORDO
27600 LAH 94022 830-H1
VIA CORITA
27800 LAH 94022 830-J1
VIA CRESPI
400 SCIC 94305 790-G7
VIA DELIZIA
- HIL 94010 748-G3
VIA FELIZ
27600 LAH 94022 810-J7
VIA LAGUNA
1600 SMTO 94404 749-E3
VIA ORTEGA
400 SCIC 94305 790-G7
VIA PALOU
400 SCIC 94305 790-G7
VIA PUEBLO LN
100 SCIC 94305 790-G6
VIA VENTANA
12600 LAH 94022 830-H1
VIA VISTA
1400 SMTO 94404 749-D3
VICTORIA AV
- MLBR 94030 728-B4
VICTORIA DR
- ATN 94027 790-F3
VICTORIA MNR
2700 SCAR 94070 769-G6
VICTORIA RD
- BURL 94010 728-H6
VICTORIA ST
- DALY 94015 707-C2
- SF 94132 687-C2
VICTORIA WY
1500 PCFA 94044 727-A4
VICTOR PARK LN
- HIL 94010 748-F2

STREET
Block City ZIP Pg-Grid

VICTORY AV
300 SSF 94080 707-H4
VIDAL DR
- SF 94132 687-A1
VIENNA ST
300 SF 94112 687-G1
VIEW AV
- SMCo 94038 746-F7
VIEW TR
- MLBR 94030 728-A4
VIEW WY
1000 PCFA 94044 727-A5
VIEWCREST CIR
- SSF 94080 707-H1
VIEW HAVEN RD
1200 HIL 94010 748-F4
VIEWMONT TER
- SSF 94080 707-H2
VIEWRIDGE DR
800 SMTO 94403 749-A7
VILLA AV
- CLMA 94014 687-D7
900 BLMT 94002 769-C1
VILLA CT
- SSF 94080 707-F2
VILLA LN
- MLBR 94030 728-A5
VILLA ST
500 SMCo 94014 687-D5
600 DALY 94014 687-D5
VILLA TER
200 SMTO 94401 728-H7
VILLAGE CT
2200 BLMT 94002 769-C2
VILLAGE DR
1100 BLMT 94002 769-C2
VILLAGE LN
- SMCo 94015 687-B4
VILLAGE WY
200 SSF 94080 707-J3
VILLA VISTA
800 SMCo 94062 789-G1
VINE AV
300 SMCo 94062 788-H5
VINE CT
800 SMTO 94401 749-C1
VINE ST
- SCAR 94070 769-F2
100 MLPK 94025 790-E6
100 SMCo 94025 790-E6
1500 BLMT 94002 769-F2
VINEYARD DR
3800 RDWC 94061 789-G3
VINEYARD HILL RD
- WDSD 94062 809-H2
VINTAGE CT
- WDSD 94062 809-H2
VINTAGE PARK DR
300 FCTY 94404 749-E2
VIOLA WY
- SMCo 94074 849-C1
VIOLET LN
- SCAR 94070 769-C4
VIRGINIA AV
- SMCo 94038 746-F7
100 BLMT 94002 749-E7
100 BLMT 94002 769-E1
200 SMTO 94402 748-H3
1100 RDWC 94061 789-J1
1200 RDWC 94061 790-A2
VIRGINIA LN
- ATN 94027 790-E1
VISITACION AV
- BSBN 94005 688-A6
200 SF 94134 687-J2
1200 SF 94134 688-A2
VISTA AV
- SMTO 94403 749-D6
600 SCAR 94070 769-F3
E VISTA AV
- DALY 94014 687-D3
VISTA CIR
- SMCo 768-D4
VISTA CT
- SSF 94080 707-E5
500 MLBR 94030 727-J2
700 SMCo 94062 789-G1
VISTA DR
- SMCo 768-D4
400 SCAR 94070 769-F3
600 SMCo 94062 789-G1
800 RDWC 94062 789-G1
VISTA LN
- SMCo 94010 728-B6
VISTA RD
800 HIL 94010 748-G3
VISTA CAY
1900 SMTO 94404 749-H1
VISTA DEL GRANDE
- SCAR 94070 769-F4
VISTA DEL MAR
1900 SMTO 94404 749-E3
VISTA DEL SOL
1500 SMTO 94404 749-H1
VISTA GRANDE
700 MLBR 94030 727-J4
VISTA GRANDE AV
- DALY 94014 687-C3
VISTA MAR AV
400 PCFA 94044 707-A4

STREET
Block City ZIP Pg-Grid

VISTA MONTARA CIR
800 PCFA 94044 726-H5
VISTA VERDE WY
200 SMCo 94028 830-E5
VOELKER DR
400 SMTO 94403 749-B6
VOLANS LN
800 FCTY 94404 749-H1
VUE DE MAR AV
600 SMCo 94038 746-G6

W

WABASH TER
- SF 94134 688-A2
WAKEFIELD AV
- DALY 94015 707-C2
WAKEFIELD CT
- BLMT 94002 769-B3
WAKEFIELD DR
2600 BLMT 94002 769-B3
WALBRIDGE AV
- SF 94134 687-H2
WALLEA DR
500 MLPK 94025 790-F4
WALNUT AV
- ATN 94027 790-E2
300 SSF 94080 707-J3
700 HIL 94010 728-E6
700 BURL 94010 728-E6
WALNUT DR
1500 PA 94303 791-B4
WALNUT ST
- SBRN 94066 707-J6
200 RDWC 94063 770-B5
400 SCAR 94070 769-G3
700 SBRN 94066 708-A6
WALSH RD
300 ATN 94027 790-B6
WALTER HAYS DR
100 PA 94303 791-B4
WALTERMIRE ST
600 BLMT 94002 769-E1
WALTHAM CROSS
2700 BLMT 94002 769-A3
WALTON ST
- SCAR 94070 769-F2
WARBLER LN
- BSBN 94005 687-J4
WARD CT
- DALY 94015 707-B1
WARD RD
- SMCo 94020 (870-G2
See Page 869)
WARD ST
100 SF 94134 688-A1
WARD WY
2100 SMCo 94062 790-A4
WARE RD
- SMCo 94062 788-H4
WAREHOUSE RD
- MLPK 94025 790-J1
WARM CANYON WY
- HIL 94010 748-D3
WARMWOOD WY
- HIL 94010 748-D3
WARNER RANGE AV
2300 MLPK 94025 790-D7
WARREN RD
- SMTO 94402 748-G1
100 SMTO 94402 728-G7
WARREN ST
400 RDWC 94063 770-A5
WARREN WY
800 PA 94303 791-C5
WARRINGTON AV
400 SMCo 94063 770-D7
WARWICK ST
- DALY 94015 707-C3
100 RDWC 94062 769-H5
300 SCAR 94070 769-H5
WASHINGTON AV
100 PA 94301 791-B6
2000 RDWC 94061 789-J3
2400 RDWC 94061 790-A2
WASHINGTON BLVD
100 HMBY 94019 767-D5
WASHINGTON ST
- DALY 94014 687-B5
100 DALY 94015 687-B5
600 SMCo 94015 687-B5
800 SCAR 94070 769-J4
1600 SMTO 94403 749-C2
WATER LN
- SMCo 94060 (868-A2
See Page 867)
- SMCo 94060 867-J1
WATERBURY LN
600 FCTY 94404 749-F5
WATERFORD CT
- RDWC 94065 749-H5
WATERFORD ST
200 PCFA 94044 706-J3
300 PCFA 94044 707-A3
WATERLOO CT
- BLMT 94002 769-A3
WATERMAN AV
- SMCo 94060 (868-F3
See Page 867)

STREET
Block City ZIP Pg-Grid

WATERSIDE CIR
- RDWC 94065 750-A6
WATERS PARK BLVD
- SMTO 94403 749-D4
WATKINS AV
- ATN 94027 790-E2
WATSON CT
2400 PA 94303 791-D4
WATT AV
- SF 94112 687-F2
WATTIS WY
200 SSF 94080 708-A4
WAVE AV
400 HMBY 94019 767-E6
900 SMCo 94038 746-G6
WAVECREST DR
- DALY 94015 686-J7
WAVECREST RD
300 HMBY 94019 787-E3
WAVERLEY CT
- MLPK 94025 790-G3
WAVERLEY ST
100 PA 94301 790-J4
200 MLPK 94025 790-G4
900 PA 94301 791-A5
2600 PA 94306 791-C7
WAVERLEY OAKS
- PA 94301 791-B6
WAVERLY AV
3000 SMCo 94063 790-D1
WAVERLY CT
- SSF 94080 707-F5
WAVERLY PL
- HIL 94010 748-H1
500 PCFA 94044 707-B3
WAVERLY WY
- DALY 94014 687-F2
- SF 94112 687-F2
WAYLAND ST
1500 SF 94134 687-J1
WAYNE CT
- RDWC 94063 770-F6
WAYSIDE RD
- PTLV 94028 809-J6
WEBSTER CT
2500 PA 94301 791-C6
2500 PA 94306 791-C6
WEBSTER ST
- PA 94301 790-J3
700 PA 94301 791-A4
2500 PA 94306 791-C6
WEDGEWOOD DR
1500 HIL 94010 748-E5
WEEKS ST
300 EPA 94303 791-B1
WEEPINGRIDGE CT
- SMTO 94402 748-C7
WELCH RD
700 PA 94304 790-G6
1000 SCIC 94305 790-G6
WELLER RANCH RD
- SMCo 727-B6
WELLESLEY AV
1600 SMTO 94403 749-C2
WELLESLEY CRES
100 RDWC 94062 769-J5
WELLESLEY ST
1900 SCIC 791-A7
2000 PA 94306 791-A7
WELLINGTON AV
- DALY 94014 687-D3
WELLINGTON DR
- SCAR 94070 769-D2
WELLS AV
- PA 94301 790-J5
WELLS ST
800 RDWC 94061 790-B1
WELLSBURY CT
600 PA 94306 791-C7
WELLSBURY WY
600 PA 94306 791-D7
WEMBERLY DR
2700 BLMT 94002 769-A3
WEMBLEY CT
400 RDWC 94061 790-B2
WEMBLEY DR
- DALY 94015 707-B2
WENDY WY
1400 SMCo 94025 790-D5
WENTWORTH DR
2500 SSF 94080 707-D5
2500 SBRN 94066 707-D5
WERNER AV
- DALY 94014 687-C5
WERTH AV
1100 MLPK 94025 790-F5
WESSEX WY
- SCAR 94070 769-E3
400 BLMT 94002 749-E7
3100 RDWC 94061 789-H1
WESSIX CT
- DALY 94015 707-C3
WESTBOROUGH BLVD
- SSF 94080 707-C5
400 SMCo 94080 707-E4
2900 SBRN 94066 707-C5
WESTBRAE DR
- DALY 94015 686-J7
WESTBROOK AV
- DALY 94015 687-A4

STREET
Block City ZIP Pg-Grid

WESTBROOK AV
100 DALY 94015 686-J4
WESTCHESTER CT
2400 SSF 94080 707-D4
WESTCLIFF CT
- PCFA 94044 707-A1
WESTDALE AV
- DALY 94015 687-A3
WESTFIELD AV
- DALY 94015 687-A5
WESTFIELD DR
1100 MLPK 94025 790-F5
WESTGATE ST
- RDWC 94062 769-H7
WESTHAVEN DR
- DALY 94015 687-A3
WESTHILL DR
300 BSBN 94005 687-H5
WESTHILL PL
100 BSBN 94005 687-H5
WESTLAKE AV
- DALY 94014 687-C4
WESTLAWN AV
- DALY 94015 687-A3
WESTLINE DR
- DALY 94015 707-A1
- DALY 94015 706-J1
100 PCFA 94044 706-J2
WESTMINSTER AV
1100 EPA 94303 791-A1
1200 EPA 94303 771-A7
WESTMONT DR
- DALY 94015 687-A3
- DALY 94015 686-J3
WESTMOOR AV
- DALY 94015 687-A6
300 SMCo 94015 686-J5
WESTMOOR RD
1500 BURL 94010 728-C5
WESTMORELAND AV
2600 RDWC 94063 770-C7
2600 SMCo 94063 770-C7
2900 SMCo 94063 790-C1
WESTMORLAND AV
400 SMTO 94402 748-G1
WESTON DR
- DALY 94015 686-J3
WESTPARK DR
- DALY 94015 687-A3
WEST POINT AV
100 SMCo 94038 766-H2
WESTPOINT PL
- SMCo 94402 748-F6
WESTPORT DR
400 PCFA 94044 707-A7
WESTRIDGE AV
- DALY 94015 686-J5
WESTRIDGE CT
27800 LAH 94022 830-H1
WESTRIDGE DR
100 PTLV 94028 810-B5
WESTVIEW DR
200 SSF 94080 707-F2
WESTWOOD CT
3400 SMTO 94403 748-J7
WESTWOOD ST
1100 RDWC 94061 789-J2
WEXFORD AV
2200 SSF 94080 707-E5
WHARF RW
100 RDWC 94065 749-H5
WHARFSIDE RD
800 SMTO 94404 749-D2
WHEAT ST
- SF 94124 688-A1
WHEELER AV
- RDWC 94061 790-B2
200 SF 94134 688-A2
WHEEL HOUSE LN
900 FCTY 94404 749-H4
WHIPPLE AV
- SF 94112 687-E2
400 RDWC 94063 770-A5
800 RDWC 94063 769-H6
1000 RDWC 94062 769-H6
WHISKEY HILL RD
100 SMCo 94025 789-H7
100 WDSD 94062 789-H7
400 WDSD 94062 809-J1
400 SMCo 94025 809-J1
WHITAKER WY
1200 MLPK 94025 790-E5
WHITE ST
700 SMCo 94015 687-B4
WHITE WY
600 SBRN 94066 707-H7
WHITECLIFF CT
- SMTO 94402 748-H7
WHITECLIFF WY
1800 SMTO 94402 748-H7
2200 SBRN 94066 707-G7
WHITEHALL LN
200 RDWC 94061 790-B2
WHITEHORN WY
1200 BURL 94010 728-E5
WHITE HORSE CANYON RD
- SMCo 94060 (908-E1
See Page 907)

STREET
Block City ZIP Pg-Grid

WHITE HOUSE CREEK RD
- SCrC 95006 (889-A7
See Page 869)
- SCrC 95060 (888-H7
See Page 867)
- SMCo 94020 (889-A7
See Page 869)
- SMCo 94060 (888-H7
See Page 867)
- SMCo 94060 (908-F3
See Page 907)
WHITE OAK CT
- MLPK 94025 790-E6
WHITE OAK DR
1800 MLPK 94025 790-E6
WHITE OAK WY
1100 SCAR 94070 769-G5
WHITE PLAINS CT
- SMCo 94402 768-G2
WHITMAN CT
- SCAR 94070 769-E6
300 PA 94301 791-A5
WHITMAN WY
2000 SBRN 94066 727-G1
WHITNEY CT
- MLPK 94025 790-C7
WHITNEY DR
1000 MLPK 94025 790-C7
WHITTIER ST
- SF 94112 687-E2
100 DALY 94014 687-E2
WHITWELL RD
1000 HIL 94010 748-F3
WHY WORRY LN
- WDSD 94062 809-F1
- WDSD 94062 789-F7
WICHAM PL
- HIL 94010 748-H1
WICKLOW DR
200 SSF 94080 707-D2
WIDEVIEW CT
100 SMCo 94062 789-F1
WIDGEON ST
700 FCTY 94404 749-G1
WIENKE WY
100 SMCo 94038 746-F6
WILBURN AV
- ATN 94027 790-D1
WILDE AV
- SF 94134 688-A1
WILDFLOWER CT
- DALY 94014 687-H3
WILDWOOD AV
- SCAR 94070 769-G5
800 SMCo 94015 687-A4
900 DALY 94015 687-A4
900 DALY 94015 686-J4
WILDWOOD CT
- SMCo 94015 687-A4
WILDWOOD DR
- SMTO 94402 748-H3
200 SSF 94080 707-F5
WILDWOOD LN
- SMCo 94025 810-E1
600 PA 94303 791-C4
WILDWOOD WY
100 WDSD 94062 789-H4
WILLARD LN
- HIL 94010 748-F3
WILLBOROUGH PL
700 BURL 94010 728-F6
WILLIAM AV
- BSBN 94005 688-B6
3000 SMCo 94063 790-D1
WILLIAM CT
- MLPK 94025 790-E5
WILLIAMS AV
1200 SBRN 94066 707-H7
1500 BLMT 94002 749-D7
WILLIAMS CT
2400 SSF 94080 707-D4
WILLIAMS LN
- FCTY 94404 749-F6
- SCAR 94070 769-E3
WILLIAMS PL
400 SMTO 94401 728-H7
WILLIAMS ST
2000 PA 94306 791-A7
WILLIAMSBURG CT
2400 SSF 94080 707-D4
WILLIAR AV
200 SF 94112 687-E1
WILLITS ST
- DALY 94014 687-C3
WILLOW AV
- MLBR 94030 728-B4
200 SSF 94080 707-F5
400 HMBY 94019 787-E1
1500 BURL 94010 728-E6
WILLOW CT
- HIL 94010 728-E7
WILLOW LN
- BLMT 94002 769-D1
E WILLOW PL
- MLPK 94025 790-H3
WILLOW RD
- EPA 94303 790-J1
- PA 94304 790-G5
- MLPK 94025 790-J1

STREET
Block City ZIP Pg-Grid

WILLOW RD
1100 MLPK 94025 791-A1
1200 MLPK 94025 771-A7
1700 HIL 94010 728-E7
WILLOW RD Rt#-114
- MLPK 94025 791-A1
900 EPA 94303 771-A7
900 EPA 94303 791-A1
1200 MLPK 94025 771-A7
WILLOW ST
400 RDWC 94063 770-C6
800 SMCo 94063 770-C6
WILLOW WY
1700 SBRN 94066 707-E6
WILLOWBROOK DR
100 PTLV 94028 830-B1
200 PTLV 94028 810-B7
WILLOW GLEN WY
- SCAR 94070 769-E4
WILLOW SPRING RD
- SMCo 94060 (868-E3
See Page 867)
WILMINGTON RD
800 SMTO 94402 748-H4
WILMINGTON WY
900 SMCo 94062 789-F3
900 SMCo 94061 789-F3
WILMINGTON ACRES CT
- SMCo 94062 789-G3
WILMS AV
- SSF 94080 707-G4
WILSHIRE AV
- DALY 94015 687-A2
3600 SMTO 94403 749-B6
WILSHIRE CT
- DALY 94015 687-B3
100 SCAR 94070 769-F5
WILSON ST
- DALY 94014 687-D2
- RDWC 94063 770-A6
100 SF 94112 687-D2
1200 PA 94301 791-B4
WINCHESTER CT
- FCTY 94404 749-E5
WINCHESTER DR
- ATN 94027 790-E2
700 BURL 94010 728-G6
WINCHESTER PL
- BURL 94010 728-G5
WINCHESTER ST
100 DALY 94014 687-D3
WINDCREST LN
- SSF 94080 707-H1
WINDEMERE RD
- HIL 94010 748-E5
WINDERMERE AV
1000 MLPK 94025 790-J1
1100 MLPK 94025 770-J7
WINDING WY
- SCAR 94070 769-E5
- SF 94112 687-F2
- SMCo 94070 769-E5
100 WDSD 94062 809-H1
200 WDSD 94062 789-H7
1500 BLMT 94002 749-D7
WINDJAMMER CIR
1000 FCTY 94404 749-G3
WINDJAMMER PL
- DALY 94014 687-D5
WINDLASS LN
500 FCTY 94404 749-J1
WINDSOR CT
100 SBRN 94066 707-E7
100 SCAR 94070 769-E4
12200 LAH 94022 830-J1
WINDSOR DR
- HIL 94010 728-E7
- SCAR 94070 769-E4
- DALY 94015 687-A3
200 SMCo 94070 769-E4
500 MLPK 94025 790-F4
WINDSOR WY
700 RDWC 94061 789-J1
1100 MLPK 94025 790-F4
WINDWARD WY
2000 SMTO 94404 749-E3
WING PL
900 SCIC 94305 810-J2
WINGATE AV
400 SMCo 94070 769-E4
WINGED FOOT RD
- HMBY 94019 787-F5
WINKLEBLECK ST
- RDWC 94063 770-A6
WINONA AV
100 PCFA 94044 727-A2
WINSLOW ST
- RDWC 94063 770-A5
WINSTON WY
- SMCo 94061 790-B3
WINTERCREEK
- PTLV 94028 830-C2
WINTERGREEN WY
800 PA 94303 791-D6
WINWAY CIR
3500 SMTO 94403 749-C6
WINWOOD AV
200 PCFA 94044 706-J3
200 PCFA 94044 707-A3

WISNOM AV
400 SMTO 94401 748-H1
WISTERIA DR
100 EPA 94303 791-C2
WISTERIA WY
- ATN 94027 790-G1
WITHERIDGE RD
- SCAR 94070 769-D3
- SMCo 94002 769-D3
2700 BLMT 94002 769-D3
WOLFE DR
1600 SMTO 94402 749-B2
WONDERCOLOR LN
100 SSF 94080 708-A4
WONG WY
100 SBRN 94066 707-G6
WOOD LN
- MLPK 94025 790-E5
WOODBERRY AV
1300 SMTO 94403 748-J7
WOODBRIDGE CIR
100 SMTO 94403 749-E6
WOODCREEK CT
- SMCo 94402 768-H1
WOODCREST CT
- HIL 94010 748-F4
WOODFERN
- PTLV 94028 830-C2
WOODGATE CT
- HIL 94010 748-B1
WOODHILL DR
- RDWC 94061 789-G4
- RDWC 94062 789-G4
- WDSD 94062 789-G4
WOODHUE CT
- SMCo 94062 769-G7
WOODLAND AV
- DALY 94015 687-A7
500 MLPK 94025 790-J3
800 SCAR 94070 769-G4
900 MLPK 94025 791-A3
1500 EPA 94303 791-B3
WOODLAND CT
800 MLPK 94025 790-J3
WOODLAND DR
900 SMTO 94402 748-H4
900 HIL 94402 748-H4
WOODLAND PL
2500 SMCo 94062 789-F1
WOODLAND WY
3800 RDWC 94062 789-G2
3800 SMCo 94062 789-G2
WOODLAND VISTA
100 SMCo 94020 849-F1
200 SMCo 94020 829-F7
WOODLEAF AV
- RDWC 94061 789-G3
WOODRIDGE CT
- RDWC 94061 789-G4
WOODRIDGE RD
- HIL 94010 748-F4
WOODROW PL
- PCFA 94044 727-B5
WOODROW ST
- DALY 94014 687-C3
1100 RDWC 94061 770-B7
WOODSIDE AV
- DALY 94015 687-A7
WOODSIDE CT
500 SSF 94080 707-G2
WOODSIDE DR
- RDWC 94061 789-J4
- WDSD 94062 789-J4
WOODSIDE EXWY
- RDWC 770-C5
WOODSIDE EXWY Rt#-84
- RDWC - 770-C6
- RDWC - 770-C6
WOODSIDE RD Rt#-84
300 RDWC 94061 790-B2
300 SMCo 94061 790-B2
1900 RDWC 94061 770-B7
2100 WDSD 94062 790-B2
2100 SMCo 94062 790-B2
2400 WDSD 94062 789-J5
3500 WDSD 94062 809-F1
WOODSIDE WY
600 SMTO 94401 728-H7
600 WDSD 94062 789-E3
WOODSTOCK PL
- RDWC 94062 769-H6
WOODSTOCK RD
600 HIL 94010 748-F2
WOODSWORTH AV
- RDWC 94062 769-H6
WOODVIEW LN
- WDSD 94062 810-A6
WOOLSEY ST
800 SF 94134 687-J1
WOOSTER AV
2300 BLMT 94002 749-B7
2300 BLMT 94002 769-B1
4200 SMTO 94403 749-B7
WORCESTER AV
- SF 94132 687-C2
WREN CT
2400 SSF 94080 707-D4
WRIGHT CT
2400 SSF 94080 707-D4

WURR RD
- SMCo 94021 849-B7
WYANDOTTE AV
800 DALY 94014 687-D5
WYCOMBE AV
100 SCAR 94070 769-E2
WYLVALE AV
- SMCo 94038 746-F6
WYNDHAM DR
- PTLV 94028 810-A6

X

XAVIER ST
1600 EPA 94303 771-B7

Y

YACHT LN
- DALY 94014 687-E6
YALE AV
100 SMCo 94038 766-J2
YALE CT
14500 LAH 94022 810-H5
YALE DR
400 SMTO 94402 748-H3
700 HIL 94402 748-H3
YALE RD
- MLPK 94025 790-G4
YALE ST
500 SF 94134 687-J1
1900 SCIC - 791-A7
2000 PA 94306 791-A7
YANEZ CT
- SMCo 94062 789-F2
YARBOROUGH LN
200 RDWC 94061 790-B2
YARNALL PL
- RDWC 94063 770-F6
YAWL CT
100 FCTY 94404 749-G4
YELLOWSTONE DR
400 SSF 94080 707-F4
YELLOWSTONE WY
- PCFA 94044 727-B5
YEW ST
1300 SMTO 94402 748-J4
YOLO CT
100 SBRN 94066 707-D6
YORK AV
1500 SMTO 94401 729-A7
YORK ST
- DALY 94015 707-C3
YORKSHIRE CT
100 SBRN 94066 727-F1
YORKSHIRE LN
- SMCo 94062 769-G6
YORKSHIRE WY
400 BLMT 94002 749-E7
YORKTOWN RD
1600 SMCo 94402 748-F7
1600 SMCo 94402 768-G1
YOSEMITE AV
1200 SF 94124 688-C1
YOSEMITE CT
600 WDSD 94062 789-E3
YOSEMITE DR
500 SSF 94080 707-F4
900 PCFA 94044 727-B5
2600 BLMT 94002 769-A2
YOUNG AV
100 HMBY 94019 767-D5
YOUNG ST
1400 SMTO 94401 749-B1
YSABEL DR
3600 SBRN 94066 707-B6
YUBA CT
100 SBRN 94066 707-D6
YUBA LN
27800 LAH 94022 810-J7
27800 LAH 94022 830-J1

Z

ZACHARY CT
- MLPK 94025 790-D7
ZAMORA DR
300 SSF 94080 707-F5
900 PCFA 94044 727-A4
ZAPATA WY
- PTLV 94028 810-A5
ZAPPETTINI CT
- LAH 94022 830-H2
ZITA DR
500 SSF 94080 707-E2
ZITA MNR
- DALY 94015 687-B5
ZUMWALT LN
700 FCTY 94404 749-G5

#

1ST AV
- DALY 94014 687-C5
100 PCFA 94044 706-J5
200 SMCo 94063 770-D7
200 SMCo 94063 790-D1
200 SMTO 94401 748-J1
300 SMCo 94019 767-C4
500 SBRN 94066 707-J6

500 SMTO 94401 749-A1
600 HMBY 94019 787-E2
1ST LN
300 SSF 94080 707-H3
1ST ST
- SSF 94080 707-G3
100 SMCo 94037 746-F4
W 1ST ST
900 MLPK 94025 790-G2
1ST ST W
1000 SBRN 94066 707-H5
2ND AV
- DALY 94014 687-C5
- SMTO 94401 748-J2
200 PCFA 94044 706-J5
200 RDWC 94063 770-E6
200 SMCo 94063 770-D7
200 SMCo 94063 790-D1
300 SMCo 94019 767-C4
300 SMCo 94014 687-C5
400 SBRN 94066 707-J6
400 SMTO 94401 749-A1
700 HMBY 94019 787-F2
1200 SMTO 94401 729-B7
2ND LN
200 SSF 94080 707-G2
2ND ST
- SSF 94080 707-G3
100 SMCo 94037 746-G4
E 2ND ST
100 MLPK 94025 790-H3
W 2ND ST
600 MLPK 94025 790-G3
2ND ST W
1000 SBRN 94066 707-H6
3RD AV
- DALY 94014 687-D5
200 RDWC 94063 770-D7
200 SMCo 94063 770-D7
200 SMCo 94063 790-D1
300 PCFA 94044 706-J5
300 SMCo 94014 687-D5
300 SMCo 94019 767-C4
400 SBRN 94066 707-J6
600 HMBY 94019 787-F2
700 SF 94124 688-E1
E 3RD AV
- SMTO 94401 748-J2
300 SMTO 94401 749-A1
1300 SMTO 94401 729-B7
2000 FCTY 94404 749-E1
W 3RD AV
- SMTO 94402 748-J2
3RD LN
200 SSF 94080 707-G2
3RD ST
- SF 94134 688-B1
100 SMCo 94037 746-F4
5800 SF 94124 688-B1
E 3RD ST
400 MLPK 94025 790-H3
W 3RD ST
600 MLPK 94025 790-G3
3RD ST W
1000 SBRN 94066 707-H6
4TH AV
200 SMCo 94063 790-D1
300 HMBY 94019 787-F2
300 SMCo 94019 767-C3
400 PCFA 94044 706-J5
400 SMCo 94063 770-D7
500 SBRN 94066 707-J6
500 SBRN 94066 708-A7
700 RDWC 94063 770-E6
E 4TH AV
- SMTO 94401 748-J2
200 SMTO 94401 749-A1
400 SMTO 94402 749-A1
W 4TH AV
- SMTO 94402 748-J2
4TH LN
200 SSF 94080 707-G2
4TH ST
100 SMCo 94037 746-G4
E 4TH ST
600 MLPK 94025 790-G3
W 4TH ST
700 MLPK 94025 790-G3
5TH AV
- RDWC 94063 770-E6
- SMCo 94063 790-D1
300 SMCo 94019 767-C3
400 SMCo 94063 770-D7
500 PCFA 94044 706-J4
500 SBRN 94066 708-A7
600 SBRN 94066 707-J6
1200 BLMT 94002 769-F1
E 5TH AV
- SMTO 94401 749-A1
100 SMTO 94401 748-J2
100 SMTO 94402 748-J2
200 SMTO 94402 749-A1
W 5TH AV
- SMTO 94402 748-J2
5TH ST
100 SMCo 94037 746-F4
6TH AV
200 SMTO 94401 749-A2
300 SMCo 94019 767-D3

6TH AV
300 SMCo 94063 790-D1
400 SMCo 94025 770-D7
600 PCFA 94044 706-J5
600 SBRN 94066 708-A6
600 SMCo 94063 770-D7
700 SBRN 94066 707-J6
900 RDWC 94063 770-D7
1000 BLMT 94002 769-E1
1300 SF 94124 688-D1
6TH LN
100 SSF 94080 707-J2
6TH ST
100 SMCo 94037 746-F4
7TH AV
200 SMTO 94401 749-A2
400 SMCo 94025 770-E7
400 SMCo 94063 790-D1
500 SBRN 94066 708-A6
500 SMTO 94402 749-A1
700 SMCo 94063 770-E7
900 RDWC 94063 770-E7
7TH LN
200 SSF 94080 707-J2
200 SSF 94080 708-A2
7TH ST
100 SMCo 94037 746-F4
8TH AV
200 SMTO 94401 749-A2
300 SMCo 94025 770-E7
300 SMCo 94063 790-D1
700 SMCo 94063 770-E6
900 RDWC 94063 770-E6
8TH LN
200 SSF 94080 707-J2
200 SSF 94080 708-A2
8TH ST
100 SMCo 94037 746-F4
9TH AV
- SMTO 94401 749-A2
- SMTO 94402 749-A2
300 SMCo 94025 770-E7
300 SMCo 94063 790-D1
700 SMCo 94063 770-E7
9TH LN
200 SSF 94080 707-J2
200 SSF 94080 708-A2
9TH ST
100 SMCo 94037 746-F4
10TH AV
- SMTO 94401 749-A2
- SMTO 94402 749-A2
600 SMCo 94025 770-E7
800 RDWC 94063 770-E6
800 SMCo 94063 770-E7
10TH ST
200 SMCo 94037 746-F4
11TH AV
- SMTO 94401 749-A2
- SMTO 94402 749-A2
600 SMCo 94025 770-E7
800 SMCo 94063 770-E7
11TH ST
- SMCo 94037 746-F4
12TH AV
- SMTO 94402 749-A3
600 SMCo 94025 770-E7
800 SMCo 94063 770-E7
12TH ST
200 SMCo 94037 746-F5
13TH AV
- SMTO 94402 749-A3
13TH ST
200 SMCo 94037 746-F5
14TH AV
- SMTO 94402 749-A3
600 SMCo 94025 770-E7
14TH ST
200 SMCo 94037 746-F5
15TH AV
- SMTO 94402 749-A3
700 SMCo 94025 770-F7
900 RDWC 94063 770-F7
15TH ST
- SMCo 94037 746-F5
16TH AV
- SMTO 94402 749-A3
500 SMCo 94025 770-E7
500 SMCo 94063 790-E1
1000 RDWC 94063 770-F6
16TH ST
200 SMCo 94038 746-F5
17TH AV
- SMTO 94402 749-A3
500 SMCo 94025 770-F7
500 SMCo 94063 790-F1
1000 RDWC 94063 770-F7
18TH AV
- SMTO 94402 749-B3
600 SMCo 94025 770-F7
600 SMCo 94063 790-F1
1100 RDWC 94063 770-F6
19TH AV
- SMTO 94403 749-B3
19TH AV Rt# 1
1100 SF 94132 687-B1
19TH AV
4000 SF 94132 687-C1
E 20TH AV
- SMTO 94402 749-B4

E 20TH AV
- SMTO 94403 749-B4
W 20TH AV
- SMTO 94402 749-A4
- SMTO 94403 749-A4
21ST AV
- SMTO 94403 749-B4
22ND RD
- SMTO 94403 749-A4
23RD AV
- SMTO 94403 749-A4
24TH AV
- SMTO 94403 749-A5
E 25TH AV
- SMTO 94403 749-B4
W 25TH AV
- SMTO 94403 749-B5
26TH AV
200 SMTO 94403 749-A5
700 SMTO 94403 748-J5
26TH PL
- SMTO 94403 749-B5
27TH AV
- SMTO 94403 749-B5
28TH AV
- SMTO 94403 749-B5
29TH AV
- SMTO 94403 749-B5
30TH AV
- SMTO 94403 749-B5
31ST AV
- SMTO 94403 749-A6
900 SMTO 94403 748-J6
36TH AV
- SMTO 94403 749-B6
37TH AV
- SMTO 94403 749-B6
38TH AV
400 SMTO 94403 749-B7
E 38TH AV
- SMTO 94403 749-D6
W 38TH AV
- SMTO 94403 749-C6
E 39TH AV
- SMTO 94403 749-D6
W 39TH AV
- SMTO 94403 749-C6
E 40TH AV
- SMTO 94403 749-D6
W 40TH AV
- SMTO 94403 749-C7
W 41ST AV
- SMTO 94403 749-C7
E 41ST PL
- SMTO 94403 749-D6
42ND AV
- SMTO 94403 749-B7
43RD AV
- SMTO 94403 749-C7
44TH AV
100 SMTO 94403 749-D7
87TH ST
- DALY 94015 687-A4
- SMCo 94015 687-A4
1000 DALY 94015 686-J4
88TH ST
- DALY 94015 687-B4
100 SMCo 94015 687-B4
89TH ST
- DALY 94015 687-B5
400 SMCo 94015 687-B5
90TH ST
- DALY 94015 687-B5
400 SMCo 94015 687-B5
91ST ST
- DALY 94015 687-B5
92ND ST
100 DALY 94015 687-B5
100 SMCo 94015 687-B5
I-101 BAYSHORE FRWY
- BSBN - 688-B3
I-280 FRWY
- DALY - 687-C2
- DALY - 707-C1
- SF - 687-E1
- SF - 687-D2
I-280 JOHN F FORAN FRWY
- DALY - 687-C2
- DALY - 687-C4
- SF - 687-E1
- SF - 687-D2
I-280 JUNIPERO SERRA FRWY
- DALY - 687-C7
- DALY - 687-C7
- DALY - 707-C2
- HIL - 748-D4
- HIL - 748-D4
- LAH - 810-F3
- MLBR - 727-G3
- MLBR - 728-A7
- MLPK - 810-C1
- PA - 810-F3
- SBRN - 707-C2
- SBRN - 727-G3
- SCIC - 810-F3
- SMCo - 727-G3
- SMCo - 748-D4
- SMCo - 768-F1

I-280 JUNIPERO SERRA FRWY
- SMCo - 728-A7
- SMCo - 748-D4
- SMCo - 790-A6
- SMCo - 810-C1
- SMCo - 727-G3
- SMCo - 789-D1
- SMCo - 768-F1
- SMCo - 769-A4
- SMCo - 789-D1
- SMCo - 748-D4
- SMCo - 768-F1
- SSF - 707-C2
- WDSD - 789-G4
- WDSD - 790-A6
I-280 SOUTHERN FRWY
- DALY - 687-C2
- DALY - 687-C4
- SF - 687-E1
- SF - 687-D2
I-380 FRWY
- SBRN - 707-H6
- SBRN - 708-A6
- SMCo - 708-A6
- SSF - 708-A5
Rt#-G3 OREGON EXWY
- PA 94301 791-C6
- PA 94303 791-C6
300 PA 94306 791-C6
Rt#-G3 PAGE MILL RD
1800 SCIC 94305 810-J4
1800 PA 94304 810-J4
1900 SCIC 94304 810-J4
2400 LAH 94022 810-J4
Rt#-G5 FOOTHILL EXWY
2600 SCIC 94304 810-J3
2600 PA 94304 810-J3
Rt#-G5 JUNIPERO SERRA BLVD
- MLPK 94025 790-F7
- SCIC 94305 790-F7
- SCIC 94304 790-F7
100 SCIC 94304 810-G1
100 SCIC 94305 810-G1
Rt#-1 19TH AV
1100 SF 94132 687-B1
Rt#-1 CABRILLO FRWY
- DALY - 687-B7
- DALY - 707-A2
- PCFA - 706-J4
100 PCFA - 707-A2
2100 DALY - 687-B7
Rt#-1 CABRILLO HWY
- PCFA 94044 707-A7
- SMCo - 726-F6
- SMCo - (847-H4
See Page 827)
- HMBY 94019 767-D4
- HMBY 94019 787-G7
- SMCo 94018 767-D4
- SMCo 94037 746-G1
- SMCo 94038 767-D4
- SMCo 94038 746-G7
- SMCo 94018 766-H1
- SMCo - 746-G1
100 PCFA 94044 726-H3
100 PCFA 94044 727-A1
300 SMCo 94019 767-D4
1800 SMCo 94060 (908-D1
See Page 907)
2100 SMCo 94038 766-H1
2100 SMCo - 766-H1
4300 SMCo 94060 (888-B5
See Page 867)
7000 SMCo 94060 (887-H1
See Page 867)
9000 SMCo 94060 867-G4
9500 SMCo 94019 787-G7
9500 HMBY 94038 767-D4
9600 SMCo 94019 (807-G1
See Page 788)
9600 SMCo 94019 827-J1
9600 SMCo 94019 (828-A4
See Page 827)
10500 SMCo 94060 (847-H4
See Page 827)
12000 SMCo 94074 827-J2
12000 SMCo 94074 (847-H4
See Page 827)
20000 SMCo 94074 (828-A4
See Page 827)
Rt#-1 JUNIPERO SERRA BLVD
- SF 94132 687-C4
Rt#-1 JUNIPERO SERRA FRWY
- DALY - 687-C3
- DALY - 687-C3
- SF - 687-C3
Rt#-9 HIGHWAY
- SCrC 95006 (870-J3
See Page 869)
- SCrC 95006 (890-J1
See Page 869)
- SMCo 94020 (870-J3
See Page 869)
- SMCo 94020 (890-J1
See Page 869)

Rt#-35
- SMCo - 768-D4
7300 SMCo 94062 768-D4
Rt#-35 SKYLINE BLVD
- DALY 94015 687-A5
- DALY 94015 686-J3
- SF 94132 686-J3
- SMCo - 748-E6
500 SMCo - 727-F1
500 SBRN 94066 727-F1
900 SBRN 94066 707-D5
900 SMCo - 707-D5
1100 DALY 94015 707-B1
1200 PCFA 94044 707-B1
1900 SMCo - 768-F1
2100 SMCo 94015 686-J3
2700 SSF 94080 707-D5
7500 SMCo 94062 768-E5
11400 SMCo - 788-G3
11400 SMCo 94062 788-G3
13800 SMCo 94062 789-A7
14600 SMCo 94062 (808-J1
See Page 788)
14700 SMCo 94062 809-A1
17100 WDSD 94062 809-G7
17300 SMCo 94020 809-G7
17300 WDSD 94020 809-D4
18100 PTLV 94028 809-G7
18100 SMCo 94020 829-H1
18100 PTLV 94028 829-H1
19300 SMCo 94020 830-A4
19300 PTLV 94028 830-A4
19800 SMCo 94028 830-C7
20800 SMCo 94020 850-E1
20800 SMCo 94028 850-E1
21100 SCIC - 850-E1
21100 SCIC 94028 850-E1
21200 PA 94304 850-H2
21600 SMCo 94304 850-H2
21700 PA - 850-H2
22800 SCrC 95030 850-J5
22800 SCIC 95030 850-J5
Rt#-82 EL CAMINO REAL
- BURL 94010 728-E6
- CLMA 94014 687-C5
- MLBR 94030 728-A2
- MLPK 94025 790-C1
- PA 94301 790-H4
- SCAR 94070 769-F2
- PA 94304 790-H4
100 ATN 94027 790-C1
100 BLMT 94002 749-D7
100 SBRN 94066 727-J1
100 SSF 94080 707-G4
100 SBRN 94066 707-G4
100 SMCo 94063 790-C1
200 DALY 94014 687-C5
200 SCIC 94305 790-H4
200 SMCo 94014 687-C5
200 PA 94305 790-H4
500 BLMT 94002 769-F2
500 HIL 94010 728-E6
700 CLMA 94014 707-E1
800 RDWC 94062 769-H3
800 RDWC 94062 770-A6
800 RDWC 94063 769-H3
800 RDWC 94063 770-A6
800 SMTO 94402 749-D7
1300 RDWC 94061 770-A6
1300 SMCo 94080 707-E1
1300 SBRN 94066 728-A2
1400 SCIC - 791-A6
1400 PA - 790-H4
1400 PA 94306 791-A6
1500 MLPK 94027 790-C1
1700 MLBR 94030 727-J1
1700 ATN 94025 790-C1
2400 PA 94305 791-A6
2600 RDWC 94061 790-C1
2600 SMCo 94063 770-A6
Rt#-82 MISSION ST
6300 DALY 94014 687-C4
Rt#-82 N EL CAMINO REAL
- SMTO 94401 728-G7
- SMTO 94402 728-G7
100 SMTO 94402 748-H1
100 SMTO 94401 748-H1
800 BURL 94010 728-G7
Rt#-82 S EL CAMINO REAL
- BLMT 94002 749-A2
- SMTO 94401 748-J2
- SMTO 94402 748-J2
500 SMTO 94402 749-A2
500 SMTO 94401 749-A2
2000 SMTO 94403 749-A2
Rt#-82 SAN JOSE AV
3200 DALY 94014 687-D3
Rt#-84 BAYFRONT EXWY
- FRMT 94555 771-D3
- MLPK 94025 770-G6
- MLPK 94025 771-A6
- MLPK 94303 771-D3
Rt#-84 LA HONDA RD
- SMCo 94020 829-F3
- SMCo 94020 849-A1
- SMCo 94062 829-F3

Rt#-84 LA HONDA RD
- SMCo 94062 849-A1
- SMCo 94074 829-E7
- SMCo 94074 849-A1
- SMCo 94074 827-J6
- SMCo 94074 (828-E6
See Page 827)
300 WDSD 94062 809-F5
400 SMCo 94062 809-F7
1700 SMCo 94020 809-F5
1700 WDSD 94020 809-F5
4100 SMCo 94074 (848-H1
See Page 827)
Rt#-84 LOWE RD
- WDSD 94062 789-G6
Rt#-84 MARSH RD
- MLPK 94025 770-F7
Rt#-84 WOODSIDE EXWY
- RDWC - 770-C6
- RDWC - 770-C6
Rt#-84 WOODSIDE RD
300 RDWC 94061 790-B2
300 SMCo 94061 790-B2
1900 RDWC 94061 770-B7
2100 WDSD 94062 790-B2
2100 SMCo 94062 790-B2
2400 WDSD 94062 789-J5
3500 WDSD 94062 809-F1
Rt#-92 CANADA RD
- SMCo - 768-G2
- SMCo 94402 768-G2
- SMCo 94062 768-G2
Rt#-92 HALF MOON BAY RD
- HMBY 94019 787-G1
200 HMBY 94019 767-H7
300 SMCo - 767-J6
2900 SMCo - 768-E3
2900 SMCo 94062 768-E3
Rt#-92 J ARTHUR YOUNGER FRWY
- BLMT - 768-H2
- FCTY - 729-G7
- FCTY - 729-G7
- FCTY - 749-F2
- HIL - 748-J5
- SMCo - 768-H2
- SMCo - 768-H2
- SMCo - 748-J5
- SMTO - 748-J5
- SMTO - 749-A4
- SMTO - 768-H2
- SMTO - 748-J5
- SMTO - 749-F2
- SMTO - 768-H2
- SMTO - 749-F2
Rt#-92 SAN MATEO RD
200 HMBY 94019 767-H7
300 SMCo - 767-J6
Rt#-109 UNIVERSITY AV
2600 EPA 94303 771-B6
2700 MLPK 94303 771-B6
2800 MLPK 94025 771-B6
Rt#-114 ALBERNI ST
900 EPA 94303 771-A7
Rt#-114 WILLOW RD
- MLPK 94025 791-A1
900 EPA 94303 771-A7
900 EPA 94303 791-A1
1200 MLPK 94025 771-A7
Rt#-236 HIGHWAY
- SCrC 95006 (890-D3
See Page 869)
U.S.-101 BAYSHORE FRWY
- BLMT - 749-B1
- BLMT - 769-G1
- BSBN - 688-B3
- BSBN - 708-B1
- BURL - 728-F5
- EPA - 790-J1
- EPA - 791-E5
- MLBR - 728-B2
- MLPK - 770-C5
- MLPK - 790-J1
- MLPK - 791-E5
- MTVW - 791-E5
- PA - 791-E5
- RDWC - 769-G1
- RDWC - 770-C5
- RDWC - 769-G1
- SCAR - 769-G1
- SF - 688-B3
- SMCo - 769-G1
- SMCo - 769-G1
- SMCo - 708-A5
- SMCo - 728-B2
- SMTO - 728-F5
- SMTO - 729-A7
- SMTO - 749-B1
- SMTO - 749-B1
- SMTO - 749-B1
- SSF - 708-B1
U.S.-101 JAMES LICK FRWY
- SF - 688-A1
- SF - 688-A1

AIRPORTS

FEATURE NAME	Address City, ZIP Code	PAGE-GRID
HALF MOON BAY AIRPORT	CABRILLO HWY, SMCo, 94038, (650)573-3701	766 - H1
PALO ALTO AIRPORT	1925 EMBARCADERO RD, PA, 94303, (650)856-7833	791 - E2
SAN CARLOS AIRPORT	BAYSHORE FRWY, SCAR, 94070, (650)573-3700	769 - H1
SAN FRANCISCO INTERNATIONAL AIRPORT	1799 BAYSHORE HWY, SMCo, 94128, (650)876-7809	728 - D2

BEACHES & HARBORS

FEATURE NAME	Address City, ZIP Code	PAGE-GRID
BEAN HOLLOW STATE BEACH	CABRILLO HWY, SMCo, 94060	867 - G6
DUNES BEACH	HALF MOON BAY STATE BEACHES, HMBY, 94019	767 - D5
EL GRANADA BEACH	PILLAR POINT HARBOR, HMBY, 94038	767 - A3
ELMAR BEACH	HALF MOON BAY STATE BEACHES, HMBY, 94019	767 - D7
FRANCIS BEACH	HALF MOON BAY STATE BEACHES, HMBY, 94019	787 - D3
GRAYWHALE COVE STATE BEACH	CABRILLO HWY, SMCo	746 - F1
HALF MOON BAY STATE BEACHES	CABRILLO HWY & MIRADA RD, HMBY, 94019	767 - B4
MARTINS BEACH (SEE PAGE 788)	CABRILLO HWY, SMCo	807 - H6
MIRAMAR BEACH	HALF MOON BAY STATE BEACHES, HMBY, 94019	767 - C4
MONTARA STATE BEACH	CABRILLO HWY, SMCo, 94037	746 - F3
NAPLES BEACH	HALF MOON BAY STATE BEACHES, HMBY, 94019	767 - C5
PEBBLE BEACH	CABRILLO HWY, SMCo, 94060	867 - G4
PENINSULA BEACH	COYOTE POINT DR, SMTO, 94401	728 - J5
PESCADERO STATE BEACH	CABRILLO HWY, SMCo, 94060	867 - H1
POMPONIO STATE BEACH- (SEE PAGE 827)	19500 CABRILLO HWY, SMCo, 94074	847 - H1
SAN GREGORIO STATE BEACH	CABRILLO HWY & LA HONDA RD, SMCo, 94074	827 - H6
SAN PEDRO BEACH	CABRILLO HWY, PCFA, 94044	726 - H2
SHARP PARK BEACH	BEACH BLVD, PCFA, 94044	706 - J6
THORTON STATE BEACH	SKYLINE BLVD & THORNTON STATE, DALY, 94015	686 - J3
VENICE BEACH	HALF MOON BAY STATE BEACHES, HMBY, 94019	767 - D6

BUILDINGS

FEATURE NAME	Address City, ZIP Code	PAGE-GRID
DOWNTOWN BUILDINGS SEE PAGE ix		-
ANZA CORPORATE CENTER	433 AIRPORT BLVD, BURL, 94010, (650)342-5711	728 - G5
CENTRUM III	300 ORACLE PKWY, RDWC, 94065	749 - G6
ELKS LODGE	1059 WILMINGTON WY, RDWC, 94061, (650)365-1991	789 - F3
FOURTEEN NINETY-NINE BUILDING	1499 BAYSHORE HWY, BURL, 94010, (650)348-1051	728 - E4
HILLCREST JUVENILE HOME	TOWER RD, SMCo, 94402	768 - H2
MAPLES PAVILION	CAMPUS DR, SCIC, 94305, (650)723-2300	790 - J7
THE GATEWAY	651 GATEWAY BLVD, SSF, 94080	708 - A2

BUILDINGS - GOVERNMENTAL

FEATURE NAME	Address City, ZIP Code	PAGE-GRID
COURTHOUSE	GRANT & BIRCH, PA, 94306	791 - B7
HALL OF JUSTICE	401 MARSHALL ST, RDWC, 94063	770 - A5
SAN FRANCISCO JAIL	COUNTY JAIL RD, SMCo, 94044	707 - D7
SAN MATEO COUNTY COURT BUILDING	1050 MISSION RD, SSF, 94080, (650)877-5705	707 - F2
SAN MATEO COUNTY COURTHOUSE	401 MARSHALL ST, RDWC, 94063	770 - A5
SAN MATEO COUNTY GOVERNMENT CENTER	WINSLOW ST & BRADFORD ST, RDWC, 94063, (650)363-4711	770 - A5
SAN MATEO COUNTY HEALTH CENTER	OAK AV, SSF, 94080	707 - G2

CEMETERIES

FEATURE NAME	Address City, ZIP Code	PAGE-GRID
CATHOLIC CEMETERY	HALF MOON BAY RD, HMBY, 94019	767 - G7
CEMETERY	500 CANADA RD, SMCo, 94062	789 - A1
CEMETERY	JUNIPERO SERRA BLVD, DALY, 94015	707 - C1
CEMETERY	SMCo, 94019	787 - G2
CEMETERY	E LAUREL CREEK RD, SMTO, 94403	768 - J1
CEMETERY	SANTA CRUZ AV, MLPK, 94025	790 - E6
CEMETERY (SEE PAGE 867)	STAGE RD, SMCo, 94060	868 - B2
CEMETERY (SEE PAGE 788)	VERDE RD, SMCo, 94019	807 - H2
CHINESE CEMETERY	CALLAN BLVD, DALY, 94015, (650)992-4581	707 - B1
CYPRESS LAWN CEMETERY	JUNIPERO SERRA BLVD, CLMA, 94014, (415)775-0580	707 - D1
ETERNAL HOME CEMETERY	EL CAMINO REAL & OLIVET PKWY, CLMA, 94014, (650)755-5236	687 - D6
GOLDEN GATE NATIONAL CEMETERY	SNEATH LN, SBRN, 94066, (650)761-1646	707 - G6
GOLDEN HILLS MEMORIAL PARK	HILLSIDE BLVD & SERRAMONTE BLV, CLMA, 94014, (415)362-5566	687 - E6
GREEK ORTHODOX MEMORIAL PARK	1148 EL CAMINO REAL, CLMA, 94014, (650)755-6939	687 - D7
GREENLAWN MEMORIAL PARK	1100 EL CAMINO REAL, CLMA, 94014, (650)755-7622	687 - C7
HILLS OF ETERNITY MEMORIAL PARK	EL CAMINO REAL, CLMA, 94014, (650)756-3633	687 - E6
HOLY CROSS CEMETERY	MISSION RD, CLMA, 94014, (650)756-2060	707 - E1
HOME OF PEACE CEMETERY	EL CAMINO REAL, CLMA, 94014, (650)755-4700	687 - D7
HOY SUN MEMORIAL CEMETERY	HILLSIDE BLVD & SERRAMONTE BLV, CLMA, 94014, (650)757-9892	687 - E6
ITALIAN CEMETERY	EL CAMINO REAL, CLMA, 94014, (650)755-1511	687 - D6
JAPANESE CEMETERY	HILLSIDE BLVD & HOFFMAN ST, CLMA, 94014, (650)755-3747	687 - D6
OLIVET MEMORIAL PARK	1601 HILLSIDE BLVD, CLMA, 94014, (650)755-0322	687 - D5
PILARCITOS CEMETERY	HALF MOON BAY RD, HMBY, 94019	767 - F7
SAINT JOHNS CEMETERY	PARROTT DR, SMTO, 94402	748 - H4
SALEM MEMORIAL PARK	EL CAMINO REAL & SERRAMONTE BL, CLMA, 94014, (415)586-8833	687 - D6
SERBIAN CEMETERY	1801 HILLSIDE BLVD, CLMA, 94014, (650)755-2453	687 - E6
SKYLAWN MEMORIAL PARK CEMETERY	HALF MOON BAY RD, SMCo	768 - C4
UNION CEMETERY	WOODSIDE RD, RDWC, 94061	770 - B7
WOODLAWN MEMORIAL PARK	1000 EL CAMINO REAL, CLMA, 94014, (650)755-1727	687 - C6

CHAMBERS OF COMMERCE

FEATURE NAME	Address City, ZIP Code	PAGE-GRID
BELMONT CITY CHAMBER OF COMMERCE	1365 5TH AV, BLMT, 94002, (650)595-8696	769 - F1
BURLINGAME CHAMBER OF COMMERCE	290 CALIFORNIA DR, BURL, 94010, (650)344-1735	728 - G6
CHAMBER OF COMMERCE	150 PARK LN, BSBN, 94005, (415)467-7283	688 - A5
DALY CITY-COLIMA CC	355 GELLERT BLVD, DALY, 94015, (415)991-5101	707 - C1
EAST PALO ALTO CHAMBER OF COMMERCE	1491 E BAYSHORE RD, EPA, 94303, (650)462-4915	791 - A2
FOSTER CITY CHAMBER OF COMMERCE	1125 E HILLSDALE BLVD, FCTY, 94404, (650)573-7600	749 - F2
HALF MOON BAY CHAMBER OF COMMERCE	520 KELLY AV, HMBY, 94019, (650)726-8380	787 - F1
MENLO PARK CHAMBER OF COMMERCE	1100 MERRILL ST, MLPK, 94025, (650)325-2818	790 - F3
MILLBRAE CHAMBER OF COMMERCE	50 VICTORIA AV, MLBR, 94030, (650)697-7324	728 - B3
PACIFICA CHAMBER OF COMMERCE	450 DONDEE WY, PCFA, 94044, (650)355-4122	726 - J2
PALO ALTO CHAMBER OF COMMERCE	325 FOREST AV, PA, 94301, (650)324-3121	790 - J5
REDWOOD CITY CHAMBER OF COMMERCE	1675 BROADWAY, RDWC, 94063, (650)364-1722	770 - B6
SAN BRUNO CHAMBER OF COMMERCE	618 SAN MATEO AV, SBRN, 94066, (650)588-0180	707 - J7
SAN CARLOS CHAMBER OF COMMERCE	1560 LAUREL ST, SCAR, 94070, (650)593-1068	769 - H4
SAN MATEO CHAMBER OF COMMERCE	1021 S EL CAMINO REAL, SMTO, 94402, (650)341-5679	749 - A3
SAN MATEO COUNTY CONV & VIS BUR	111 ANZA BLVD, BURL, 94010, (650)348-7600	728 - G5
SOUTH SAN FRANCISCO CC	213 LINDEN AV, SSF, 94080, (650)588-1911	707 - J3

CITY HALLS

FEATURE NAME	Address City, ZIP Code	PAGE-GRID
ATHERTON CITY HALL	91 ASHFIELD RD, ATN, 94027, (650)325-4457	790 - E2
BELMONT CITY HALL	1070 6TH AV, BLMT, 94002, (415)573-2790	769 - E1
BRISBANE CITY HALL	150 PARK LN, BSBN, 94005, (650)467-1515	688 - A5
BURLINGAME CITY HALL	501 PRIMROSE RD, BURL, 94010, (650)696-7200	728 - F6
COLMA CITY HALL	235 EL CAMINO REAL, CLMA, 94014, (650)997-8300	687 - D7
DALY CITY HALL	90TH ST, DALY, 94015, (650)991-8000	687 - B5
EAST PALO ALTO CITY HALL	2415 UNIVERSITY AV, EPA, 94303, (650)853-3127	791 - B1
FOSTER CITY CITY HALL	610 FOSTER CITY BLVD, FCTY, 94404, (650)349-1200	749 - F2
HALF MOON BAY CITY HALL	510 MAIN ST, HMBY, 94019, (650)726-8270	787 - F1
HILLSBOROUGH CITY HALL	1600 FLORIBUNDA AV, HIL, 94010, (650)579-3800	728 - F7
MENLO PARK CITY HALL	701 LAUREL ST, MLPK, 94025, (650)858-3360	790 - G3
MILLBRAE CITY HALL	621 MAGNOLIA AV, MLBR, 94030, (650)259-2332	728 - B3
PACIFICA CITY HALL	170 SANTA MARIA AV, PCFA, 94044, (650)738-7300	706 - J5
PALO ALTO CITY HALL	250 HAMILTON AV, PA, 94301, (650)329-3211	790 - J5
PORTOLA VALLEY TOWN HALL	765 PORTOLA RD, PTLV, 94028, (650)851-1700	810 - A6
REDWOOD CITY HALL	1017 MIDDLEFIELD RD, RDWC, 94063, (650)780-7000	770 - B6
SAN BRUNO CITY HALL	567 EL CAMINO REAL, SBRN, 94066, (650)877-8897	707 - J7
SAN CARLOS CITY HALL	600 ELM ST, SCAR, 94070, (650)593-8011	769 - G3
SAN MATEO CITY HALL	330 W 20TH AV, SMTO, 94403, (650)377-3420	749 - A4
SOUTH SAN FRANCISCO CITY HALL	400 GRAND AV, SSF, 94080, (650)877-8500	707 - J3
WOODSIDE TOWN HALL	2955 WOODSIDE RD, WDSD, 94062, (415)851-6790	789 - H7

COLLEGES & UNIVERSITIES

FEATURE NAME	Address City, ZIP Code	PAGE-GRID
CANADA COLLEGE	4200 FARM HILL BLVD, WDSD, 94062, (650)306-3100	789 - F4
COLLEGE OF NOTRE DAME	1500 RALSTON AV, BLMT, 94002, (650)574-6444	769 - D1
COLLEGE OF SAN MATEO	1700 W HILLSDALE BLVD, SMTO, 94402, (650)574-6161	748 - H5
MENLO COLLEGE	1000 EL CAMINO REAL, ATN, 94027, (650)323-6141	790 - E3
SAINT PATRICKS SEMINARY	MIDDLEFIELD RD & SANTA MONICA, MLPK, 94025	790 - H2
SF COMM COLLEGE AIRPORT SCHOOL	N ACCESS RD, SSF, 94080	708 - C6
SAN FRANCISCO STATE UNIVERSITY	1600 HOLLOWAY AV, SF, 94132, (415)469-1111	687 - B1
SKYLINE COLLEGE	3300 COLLEGE DR, SBRN, 94066, (650)738-4100	707 - C6
STANFORD UNIVERSITY	JUNIPERO SERRA BLVD, SCIC, 94305, (650)723-2300	790 - G6

DEPARTMENT OF MOTOR VEHICLES

FEATURE NAME	Address City, ZIP Code	PAGE-GRID
DALY CITY DMV	1500 SULLIVAN AV, DALY, 94015, (650)994-5700	687 - B5
REDWOOD CITY DMV	300 BREWSTER AV, RDWC, 94063, (650)368-2837	770 - A5
SAN MATEO DMV	425 N AMPHLETT BLVD, SMTO, 94401, (650)342-5332	728 - J7

ENTERTAINMENT & SPORTS

FEATURE NAME	Address City, ZIP Code	PAGE-GRID
3COM PARK (CANDLESTICK PARK)	GIANTS DR, SF, 94124	688 - C2
BAY MEADOWS RACETRACK	2600 S DELAWARE ST, SMTO, 94403, (650)574-7223	749 - C4
COUNTY FAIR BUILDING	2495 S DELAWARE ST, SMTO, 94403, (650)574-3247	749 - C4
COW PALACE	GENEVA & RIO VERDE, DALY, 94014, (415)469-6000	687 - H3
STANFORD STADIUM	NELSON RD & SAM MCDONALD RD, SCIC, 94305, (650)723-2300	790 - J6

GOLF COURSES

FEATURE NAME	Address City, ZIP Code	PAGE-GRID
BAY MEADOWS GOLF COURSE	2600 S DELAWARE ST, SMTO, 94403, (650)341-7204	749 - C5
BURLINGAME COUNTRY CLUB	80 NEW PLACE RD, HIL, 94010, (650)342-0760	748 - E1
CALIFORNIA GOLF CLUB OF SAN-FRANCISCO	844 W ORANGE AV, SMCo, 94080, (650)589-0144	707 - F4
CRYSTAL SPRINGS GOLF COURSE	6650 GOLF COURSE DR, SMCo, (650)342-0603	748 - C3
CYPRESS HILLS GOLF COURSE	2001 HILLSIDE BLVD, CLMA, 94014, (650)992-5155	687 - E6
EMERALD HILLS GOLF COURSE	1059 WILMINGTON WY, RDWC, 94061, (650)368-7820	789 - F3
GLENEAGLES INTERNATIONAL GOLF-COURSE	2100 SUNNYDALE AV, SF, 94134, (415)587-2425	687 - H2
GREEN HILLS COUNTRY CLUB	LUDEMAN LN & LAUREL AV, MLBR, 94030, (650)588-4616	727 - J3
HALF MOON BAY GOLF LINKS	2000 FAIRWAY DR, HMBY, 94019, (650)726-4438	787 - E5
HARDING PARK MUNICIPAL GOLF COURSE	HARDING RD & SKYLINE BLVD, SF, 94132, (415)878-4427	687 - A1
LAKE MERCED GOLF & COUNTRY CLUB	2300 JUNIPERO SERRA BLVD, DALY, 94015, (650)755-2233	687 - B4
MENLO COUNTRY CLUB	2300 WOODSIDE RD, WDSD, 94062, (650)366-9910	790 - A4
PALO ALTO HILLS GOLF & COUNTRY CLUB	3000 ALEXIS DR, PA, 94304, (650)948-1800	810 - G7
PALO ALTO MUNICIPAL GOLF COURSE	1875 EMBARCADERO RD, PA, 94303, (415)856-0881	791 - D3
PENINSULA GOLF & COUNTRY CLUB	701 MADERA DR, SMCo, 94403, (650)638-2239	748 - J5
SAN FRANCISCO GOLF CLUB	JUNIPERO SERRA BLVD & BROTHERH, DALY, 94015, (415)469-4100	687 - B2
SAN MATEO MUNICIPAL GOLF COURSE	1700 COYOTE POINT DR, SMTO, 94401, (650)347-1461	728 - J6
SHARON HEIGHTS GOLF & COUNTRY CLUB	2900 SAND HILL RD, MLPK, 94025, (650)854-6422	790 - B7
SHARP PARK GOLF COURSE	SHARP PARK RD, PCFA, 94044, (650)359-3380	706 - J7
SHORELINE GOLF LINKS	2600 N SHORELINE BLVD, MTVW, 94043, (415)969-2041	791 - H7
STANFORD UNIVERSITY DRIVING RANGE	CAMPUS DR WEST & LOS ARBOLES A, SCIC, 94305, (650)323-9516	790 - G7
STANFORD UNIVERSITY GOLF COURSE	198 JUNIPERO SERRA BLVD, SCIC, 94304, (650)323-0944	790 - F7
THE OLYMPIC COUNTRY CLUB	599 SKYLINE BLVD, SMCo, 94015, (415)587-4800	686 - J3

HOSPITALS

FEATURE NAME	Address City, ZIP Code	PAGE-GRID
CRYSTAL SPRINGS REHB CENTER	35 TOWER RD, SMCo, 94402, (650)312-5200	768 - H2
KAISER FOUNDATION HOSPITAL	1150 VETERANS BLVD, RDWC, 94063, (650)299-2000	770 - B5
KAISER FOUNDATION HOSPITAL	1200 EL CAMINO REAL, SSF, 94080, (650)742-2547	707 - F2
LUCILE PACKARD CHILDRENS HOSPITAL-STAN	725 WELCH RD, PA, 94304, (650)497-8000	790 - G6
MILLS HOSPITAL	100 S SAN MATEO DR, SMTO, 94401, (650)696-4400	748 - J2
PENINSULA HOSPITAL	1783 EL CAMINO REAL, BURL, 94010, (650)696-5400	728 - C5
RONALD MCDONALD HOUSE	520 SAND HILL RD, PA, 94304, (650)325-5113	790 - G5
SAN MATEO COUNTY GENERAL HOSPITAL	222 W 39TH AV, SMTO, 94403, (650)573-2222	749 - C6
SEQUOIA HOSPITAL	170 ALAMEDA DE LAS PULGAS, RDWC, 94062, (415)367-5561	769 - H6
SETON MEDICAL CENTER	1900 SULLIVAN AV, DALY, 94015, (650)992-4000	687 - B6
SETON MEDICAL CENTER COASTSIDE	600 MARINE BLVD, SMCo, 94038, (650)728-5521	746 - G6
STANFORD UNIVERSITY HOSPITAL	300 PASTEUR DR, PA, 94304, (650)723-4000	790 - G6
VA HOSPITAL MENLO	795 WILLOW RD, MLPK, 94025, (650)493-5000	790 - J1

HOTELS & MOTELS

FEATURE NAME	Address City, ZIP Code	PAGE-GRID
AIRPORT WEST-COMFORT INN	1390 EL CAMINO REAL, MLBR, 94030, (650)952-3200	728 - A2
BEST WESTERN EL RANCHO INN	1100 EL CAMINO REAL, MLBR, 94030, (650)588-8500	728 - A2
BEST WESTERN GROSVENOR HOTEL	380 S AIRPORT BLVD, SSF, 94080, (650)873-3200	708 - A4
BEST WESTERN LOS PRADOS INN	2940 S NORFOLK ST, SMTO, 94403, (650)341-3300	749 - E4
CLARION HOTEL	401 E MILLBRAE AV, MLBR, 94030, (650)692-6363	728 - D3
COMFORT SUITES	121 E GRAND AV, SSF, 94080, (650)589-7766	708 - A3
COURTYARD BY MARRIOTT	1050 BAYHILL DR, SBRN, 94066, (650)952-3333	707 - H6
COURTYARD BY MARRIOTT	550 SHELL BLVD, FCTY, 94404, (650)377-0660	749 - F2
CROWN STERLING SUITES	150 ANZA BLVD, BURL, 94010, (650)342-4600	728 - G5
CROWNE PLAZA	600 AIRPORT BLVD, BURL, 94010, (650)340-8500	728 - G5
DOUBLETREE HOTEL	835 AIRPORT BLVD, BURL, 94010, (650)344-5500	728 - F5
DUNFEY SAN MATEO HOTEL	1770 AMPHLETT PL, SMTO, 94402, (650)573-7661	749 - C3
EMBASSY SUITES SOUTH SAN FRANCISCO	250 GATEWAY BLVD, SSF, 94080, (650)589-3400	708 - A3
GOOD NITE INN	485 VETERANS BLVD, RDWC, 94063, (415)365-5500	770 - A4
HALF MOON BAY LODGE	2400 S CABRILLO HWY, HMBY, 94019, (650)726-9000	787 - F6
HOLIDAY INN EXPRESS	350 N BAYSHORE BLVD, SMTO, 94401, (650)344-6376	729 - A7
HOLIDAY INN HOTEL	625 EL CAMINO REAL, PA, 94301, (650)328-2800	790 - H5
HOLIDAY INN SAN FRANCISCO INTL	275 S AIRPORT BLVD, SSF, 94080, (650)873-3550	708 - A4
HOLIDAY INN SAN MATEO	330 N BAYSHORE BLVD, SMTO, 94401, (650)344-3219	729 - A7
HOLIDAY INN-FOSTER CITY	1221 CHESS DR, FCTY, 94404, (650)570-5700	749 - E2
HOTEL SOFITEL	223 TWIN DOLPHIN DR, RDWC, 94065, (650)598-9000	749 - G7
HYATT REGENCY SF AIRPORT	1333 OLD BAYSHORE HWY, BURL, 94010, (650)347-1234	728 - E4
LA QUINTA INN	20 AIRPORT BLVD, SSF, 94080	707 - J4
PARK PLAZA	1177 AIRPORT BLVD, BURL, 94010, (415)342-9200	728 - F5
RAMADA INN	1250 OLD BAYSHORE HWY, BURL, 94010, (650)347-2381	728 - E4
RAMADA INN SAN FRANCISCO NORTH	245 S AIRPORT BLVD, SSF, 94080, (650)589-7200	708 - A4
RED ROOF INN	777 AIRPORT BLVD, BURL, 94010, (650)342-7772	728 - G5
RESIDENCE INN	2000 WINDWARD WY, SMTO, 94404, (650)574-4700	749 - E3
SF AIRPORT HILTON	SF INTERNATIONAL AIRPORT, SMCo, 94128, (650)589-0770	728 - B2
SF AIRPORT MARRIOTT	1800 BAYSHORE HWY, BURL, 94010, (650)692-9100	728 - D3
STANFORD PARK HOTEL	100 EL CAMINO REAL, MLPK, 94025, (650)322-1234	790 - G4
STANFORD TERRACE INN	531 STANFORD AV, PA, 94306, (650)857-0333	791 - A7
SUPER 8 LODGE	111 MITCHELL AV, SSF, 94080, (415)877-0770	708 - A4
VAGABOND INN	1640 BAYSHORE HWY, BURL, 94010, (650)692-4040	728 - E3
VILLA HOTEL AIRPORT SOUTH	4000 S EL CAMINO REAL, SMTO, 94403, (650)341-0966	749 - D6
WESTIN - SF AIRPORT	1 OLD BAYSHORE HWY, MLBR, 94030, (650)692-3500	728 - D3

LIBRARIES

FEATURE NAME	Address City, ZIP Code	PAGE-GRID
ATHERTON	2 DINKLESPEIL STATION LN, ATN, 94027, (650)328-2422	790 - E2

FEATURE NAME	Address City, ZIP Code	PAGE-GRID
BAYSHORE LIBRARY	2960 GENEVA AV, DALY, 94014, (650)991-8074	687 - J3
BELMONT	1110 ALAMEDA DE LAS PULGAS, BLMT, 94002, (650)591-8286	769 - C2
BRISBANE LIBRARY	250 VISITACION AV, BSBN, 94005, (650)467-2060	688 - A6
BURLINGAME LIBRARY	480 PRIMROSE RD, BURL, 94010, (650)342-1036	728 - G6
COLLEGE TERRACE BRANCH LIBRARY	2300 WELLESLEY ST, PA, 94306, (415)329-2298	791 - A7
DALY CITY LIBRARY	40 WEMBLEY DR, DALY, 94015, (650)991-8023	707 - B2
DALY, JOHN D LIBRARY	6351 MISSION ST, DALY, 94014, (650)991-8073	687 - D3
DOWNTOWN BRANCH LIBRARY	270 FOREST AV, PA, 94301, (650)329-2641	790 - J5
EAST PALO ALTO BRANCH LIBRARY	2415 UNIVERSITY AV E, EPA, 94303, (650)321-7712	791 - B1
EASTON BRANCH LIBRARY	1800 EASTON DR, BURL, 94010, (650)343-1794	728 - D6
FAIR OAKS BRANCH LIBRARY	2600 MIDDLEFIELD, RDWC, 94063, (650)780-7261	770 - C7
FOSTER CITY LIBRARY	1000 E HILLSDALE BLVD, FCTY, 94404, (650)574-4842	749 - F2
GRAND AVENUE LIBRARY	306 WALNUT AV, SSF, 94080, (650)877-8530	707 - J3
HALF MOON BAY LIBRARY	620 CORREAS AV, HMBY, 94019, (650)726-2316	787 - F1
HILLSDALE BRANCH LIBRARY	205 W HILLSDALE BLVD, SMTO, 94403, (650)373-4880	749 - B6
MARINA BRANCH LIBRARY	1530 SUSAN CT, SMTO, 94403, (650)377-4686	749 - D3
MENLO PARK BRANCH	ALMA ST & RAVENSWOOD AV, MLPK, 94025, (650)858-3460	790 - G3
MILLBRAE LIBRARY	1 LIBRARY AV, MLBR, 94030, (650)697-7606	728 - A3
OCEAN VIEW	111 BROAD ST, SF, 94112, (415)337-4785	687 - D2
PACIFICA BRANCH IBRARY	104 HILTON WY, PCFA, 94044, (650)355-5196	706 - J6
PALO ALTO CHILDRENS LIBRARY	1276 HARRIET ST, PA, 94301, (415)329-2134	791 - A5
PALO ALTO MAIN LIBRARY	1213 NEWELL RD, PA, 94303, (415)329-2664	791 - B4
PORTOLA VALLEY BRANCH LIBRARY	765 PORTOLA RD, PTLV, 94028, (650)851-0560	810 - A6
REDWOOD CITY BRANCH LIBRARY	1044 MIDDLEFIELD RD, RDWC, 94063, (650)780-7018	770 - B6
SAN BRUNO LIBRARY	701 ANGUS AV W, SBRN, 94066, (650)877-8878	707 - J7
SAN CARLOS LIBRARY	610 WALNUT ST, SCAR, 94070, (650)591-0341	769 - G3
SAN MATEO COUNTY LIBRARY	25 TOWER RD, SMCo, 94402, (650)312-5258	768 - H2
SAN MATEO LIBRARY	55 W 3RD AV, SMTO, 94402, (650)373-4800	748 - J2
SANCHEZ LIBRARY	1111 TERRA NOVA BLVD, PCFA, 94044, (650)359-3397	727 - B5
SCHABERG, H W LIBRARY	2140 EUCLID AV, RDWC, 94061, (650)780-7010	789 - J1
SOUTH SAN FRANCISCO LIBRARY	840 W ORANGE AV, SSF, 94080, (650)877-8525	707 - F3
VISITACION VALLEY LIBRARY	45 LELAND AV, SF, 94134, (415)337-4790	688 - A2
WESTLAKE BRANCH LIBRARY	275 SOUTHGATE AV, DALY, 94015, (650)991-8071	687 - A4
WOODSIDE PUBLIC LIBRARY	3140 WOODSIDE RD, WDSD, 94062, (650)851-0147	789 - G6

MILITARY INSTALLATIONS

FEATURE NAME	Address City, ZIP Code	PAGE-GRID
NAVAL RESERVATION	INNES AV & DONAHUE ST, SF, 94124	688 - D1
US NAVY LANDS	COMMODORE DR W & 1ST ST W, SBRN, 94066	707 - H6

MUSEUMS

FEATURE NAME	Address City, ZIP Code	PAGE-GRID
BAYLANDS NATURE INTERPRETIVE CENTER	2775 EMBARCADERO RD, PA, 94303, (650)329-2506	791 - F3
COYOTE POINT MUSEUM	COYOTE POINT DR, SMTO, 94401, (650)342-7755	729 - A5
PALO ALTO JUNIOR MUSEUM & ZOO	1451 MIDDLEFIELD RD, PA, 94301, (415)329-2111	791 - B5
SANCHEZ ADOBE MUSEUM	LINDA MAR BL & ADOBE DR, PCFA, 94044, (650)359-1462	726 - J5

OPEN SPACE PRESERVES

FEATURE NAME	Address City, ZIP Code	PAGE-GRID
ARASTRADERO PRESERVE	ARASTRADERO RD, PA, 94304	810 - E7
BAYLANDS NATURE PRESERVE	EMBARCADERO RD, EPA, 94303	791 - D2
COAL CREEK OPEN SPACE	SKYLINE BLVD, SMCo, 94028	830 - C5
EL CORTE DE MADERA OPEN SPACE	SKYLINE BLVD, SMCo, 94062	809 - B4
FITZGERALD MARINE RESERVE	BEACH WY, SMCo, 94038, (650)728-3584	746 - F7
FOOTHILLS OPEN SPACE	PAGE MILL RD, PA, 94304	830 - G3
LA HONDA CREEK OPEN SPACE	LA HONDA RD, SMCo, 94062	829 - E2
LONG RIDGE OPEN SPACE	SKYLINE BLVD, SCrC, 95030	850 - J7
LOS TRANCOS OPEN SPACE	PAGE MILL RD, PA, 94304	830 - F6
MONTE BELLO OPEN SPACE	SKYLINE BLVD, PA, 94304	850 - H2
PULGAS RIDGE OPEN SPACE	HASSLER RD, SMCo, 94070	769 - D6
PURISIMA CREEK REDWOODS OPEN SPACE	PURISIMA CREEK RD & SKYLINE BL, SMCo, 94062	789 - A6
RANCHO SAN ANTONIO OPEN SPACE	CRISTO REY DR, PA, 94304	850 - J1
RAVENSWOOD OPEN SPACE PRESERVE	HWY 84, MLPK, 94303	771 - D4
RAVENSWOOD OPEN SPACE PRESERVE	ILLINOIS ST & STEVENS AV, MLPK, 94303	771 - C6
RUSSIAN RIDGE OPEN SPACE	SKYLINE BLVD, SMCo, 94020	830 - C7
SF BAY NATIONAL REFUGE	HARBOR BLVD, RDWC, 94063	750 - A4
SKYLINE RIDGE OPEN SPACE	SKYLINE BLVD, PA	850 - H3
TIMBERLAND OPEN SPACE	QUEENS LN, SMTO, 94402	768 - H1
WINDY HILL OPEN SPACE	SKYLINE BLVD, PTLV, 94028	809 - H7

PARK & RIDE

FEATURE NAME	Address City, ZIP Code	PAGE-GRID
101/92 PARK & RIDE	HWY 92 & 101 FRWY, SMTO, 94403	749 - C3
3RD AV PARK & RIDE	3RD AV & 101 FWY, SMTO, 94401	729 - B7
CRESPI PARK & RIDE	CRESPI DR & CABRILLO HWY, PCFA, 94044	726 - H3
EDGEWOOD PARK & RIDE	EDGEWOOD RD & 280 FWY, SMCo, 94070	789 - C1
HAYNE RD PARK & RIDE	HAYNE RD & I-280 FWY, SMCo, 94010	748 - D4
PAGE MILL & ECR PARK & RIDE	EL CAMINO REAL & OREGON EXWY, PA, 94306	791 - B7
PAGE MILL & HWY 280 PARK & RIDE	PAGE MILL RD & HWY 280, LAH, 94022	810 - H5
PARK & RIDE	BAYSHORE BLVD & TUNNEL AV, BSBN, 94005	688 - B6
PARK & RIDE	JUNIPERO SERRA BLVD & D ST, DALY, 94014	687 - C6
RALSTON PARK & RIDE	HWY 92 & RALSTON AV, SMCo, 94070	768 - J2
SAMTRANS PARK & RIDE	1 ST AV & B ST, SMTO, 94401	748 - J1
SAMTRANS PARK & RIDE	LINDA MAR BLVD & CABRILLO HWY, PCFA, 94044	726 - H4
SAMTRANS PARK & RIDE	VETERANS BLVD & WHIPPLE AV, RDWC, 94063	770 - A6
SAMTRANS PARK & RIDE	WESTBOROUGH BLVD & GELLERT DR, SSF, 94080	707 - E4
SAMTRANS TRANSIT TRANSFER POINT	STANFORD SHOPPING CENTER, PA, 94304	790 - H5
WOODSIDE PARK & RIDE	WOODSIDE RD & 1-280, WDSD, 94062	789 - J6

PARKS & RECREATION

FEATURE NAME	Address City, ZIP Code	PAGE-GRID
7TH & WALNUT PARK	7TH AV & WALNUT ST, SBRN, 94066	708 - A6
7TH AV PARK	6TH AV & 7TH AV, SBRN, 94066	708 - A6
ALEXANDER PARK	OLD COUNTY RD, BLMT, 94002	749 - E7
ANDREW SPINAS PARK	BROADWAY & 2ND AV, RDWC, 94063	770 - D6
ANO NUEVO STATE RESERVE- (SEE PAGE 907)	NEW YEARS CREEK RD, SMCo, 94060, (650)879-0227	908 - G4
ARCTURUS PARK	ARCTURUS CIR, FCTY, 94404	749 - E4
ARDEN PARK	ALTA VISTA WY & ALTA ARDENDALE, DALY, 94014	687 - G3
ARGUELLO PARK	WELLINGTON DR, SCAR, 94070	769 - E3
BARRETT PARK	RALSTON AV, BLMT, 94002	769 - D2
BAYFRONT PARK	BAYSHORE HWY & E MILLBRAE AV, MLBR, 94030	728 - D3
BAYFRONT PARK	MARSH RD, MLPK, 94025	770 - H5
BAYSHORE CIRCLE PARK	N BAYSHORE CIR, SBRN, 94066	707 - J5
BAYSHORE HEIGHTS PARK	400 MARTIN ST, DALY, 94014	687 - H3
BAYSHORE PARK	45 MIDWAY DR, DALY, 94014	687 - J3
BAYSIDE PARK	AIRPORT BLVD & BAYSHORE HWY, BURL, 94010	728 - E5
BAYSIDE PARK	KEHOE AV & MEADOW VIEW PL, SMTO, 94403	749 - C1
BAYSIDE PARK	LERIDA AV & CUARDO AV, MLBR, 94030	728 - C3
BAYVIEW PARK	JAMESTOWN AV, SF, 94124	688 - B2
BELAMEDA PARK	1110 ALAMEDA DE LAS PULGAS, BLMT, 94002	769 - C2
BELL STREET PARK	BELL ST & UNIVERSITY AV, EPA, 94303	791 - B2
BELMONT SPORTS COMPLEX	ISLAND PKWY, BLMT, 94002	749 - F6
BERESFORD PARK	28TH AV & PARKVIEW WY, SMTO, 94403	749 - A5
BIG BASIN REDWOODS STATE PARK- (SEE PAGE 869)	21600 BIG BASIN WY, SCrC, 95006, (650)338-6132	890 - B6
BIG CANYON PARK	BRITTAN AV, SCAR, 94070	769 - D5
BOAT PARK	FOSTER CITY BLVD, FCTY, 94404	749 - G3
BOOTHBAY PARK	BOOTHBAY AV, FCTY, 94404	749 - F5
BOREL PARK	BOREL AV, SMTO, 94402	748 - J4
BOWDEN PARK	ALMA ST & CALIFORNIA AV, PA, 94301	791 - B7
BOWLING GREEN PARK	474 EMBARCADERO RD, PA, 94301	791 - A5
BRENTWOOD PARK	ROSEWOOD WY & BRIARWOOD DR, SSF, 94080	707 - F5
BROOKS PARK	SHIELDS ST & ARCH ST, SF, 94132	687 - C1
BUCKEYE PARK	ROSEWOOD DR & ALCOTT RD, SBRN, 94066	727 - G1
BURGESS PARK	LAUREL ST & MIEKLE DR, MLPK, 94025	790 - G3
BURI BURI PARK	1059 EL CAMINO REAL, SSF, 94080	707 - F3
BURLEIGH-MURRAY RANCH STATE PARK	HIGGINS PURISIMA RD, SMCo	788 - B2
BURTON PARK	BRITTAN AV & CEDAR ST, SCAR, 94070	769 - G4
BUTANO STATE PARK	CLOVERDALE RD, SMCo, 94060, (650)879-0173	869 - B7
BYXBEE RECREATION AREA	EMBARCADERO RD, PA, 94303	791 - F3
CALLAN PARK	CARTER DR, SSF, 94080	707 - C4
CAMERON PARK	210 WELLESLEY, PA, 94306	791 - A7
CANDLESTICK POINT STATE REC AREA	JAMESTOWN AV & HARNEY WY, SF, 94124	688 - D2
CASANOVA PARK	CASANOVA DR, SMTO, 94403	749 - E6
CASCADE RANCH STATE PARK- (SEE PAGE 867)	WHITE HOUSE CREEK RD, SMCo, 94060	888 - G6
CASTLE ROCK STATE PARK- (SEE PAGE 869)	SKYLINE BLVD, SCrC, 95006	870 - J4
CATAMARAN PARK	CATAMARAN ST, FCTY, 94404	749 - G3
CEDAR STREET PARK	CEDAR ST, SCAR, 94070	769 - F2
CENTRAL PARK	50 E 5TH AV, SMTO, 94401	748 - J2
CENTRAL PARK	PALM AV & LINCOLN CIR, MLBR, 94030	728 - A3
CIPRIANI FIELD	MONSERAT AV, BLMT, 94002	769 - B1
CITY HALL PARK	SAN CARLOS AV & ELM ST, SCAR, 94070	769 - G3
CITY PARK	CYPRESS AV & CRYSTAL SPRINGS, SBRN, 94066	727 - J1
CLAY AVENUE PARK	CLAY AV, SSF, 94080	707 - C2
COGSWELL PLAZA	BRYANT ST & LYTTON AV, PA, 94301	790 - J4
COMMODORE PARK	CHERRY AV & COMMODORE DR W, SBRN, 94066	707 - G6
CONNIE PARK	CONNIE AV, SMTO, 94402	749 - B3
COYOTE POINT COUNTY RECREATION AREA	1701 COYOTE POINT DR, SMTO, 94401, (650)573-2592	728 - J5
CRESTVIEW PARK	CRESTVIEW DR, SCAR, 94070	769 - D6
CROCKER AMAZON PLAYGROUND	GENEVA AV & MOSCOW ST, SF, 94112	687 - G2
CUERNAVACA PARK	ALCAZAR DR & HUNT DR, BURL, 94010	728 - A6
DE ANZA HISTORICAL PARK	ARROYO CT, SMTO, 94402	748 - J2
DOLPHIN PARK	QUAY LN & TURKS HEAD LN, RDWC, 94065	749 - H7
DOVE BEEGER PARK	WHIPPLE AV, RDWC, 94062	769 - H7
DUNCAN PARK	BREWSTER AV & NEVADA ST, RDWC, 94062	769 - H7
EASTER BOWL	CALIFORNIA WY & TUM SUDEN WY, RDWC, 94062	789 - F2
EATON PARK	EATON AV, SCAR, 94070	769 - E6
EDGEMAR PARK	CLIFTON RD & WINWOOD AV, PCFA, 94044	707 - A3
EDGEWATER PARK	EDGEWATER BLVD, FCTY, 94404	749 - F4
EDGEWOOD COUNTY PARK	EDGEWOOD RD & JUNIPERO SERRA F, RDWC, 94062	789 - D1
EL CAMINO PARK	100 EL CAMINO REAL, PA, 94301	790 - H4
EL PALO ALTO PARK	EL CAMION REAL & ALMA ST, PA, 94301	790 - H4
ERCKENBRACK PARK	NIANTIC DR, FCTY, 94404	749 - G2
FAIRMONT PARK	649 PARKVIEW CIR, PCFA, 94044	707 - A2
FAIRMONT WEST PARK	PALMETTO AV & MAGELLAN DR, PCFA, 94044	707 - A2
FAIRWAY PARK	CINDY WY & CULLEN DR, PCFA, 94044	707 - A7
FARRAGUT PARK	FARRAGUT BLVD, FCTY, 94404	749 - F4
FASSLER PARK	CRESPI DR, PCFA, 94044	727 - A4
FIESTA MEADOWS PARK	FIESTA DR & BERMUDA DR, SMTO, 94403	749 - C4
FIRTH PARK	GLEN PKWY & SIERRA POINT RD, BSBN, 94005	688 - A7
FLEETWOOD PARK	FLEETWOOD DR, SBRN, 94066	707 - E7
FLEISHMAN PARK	MCEVOY ST ST, RDWC, 94061	790 - B1
FLOOD COUNTY PARK	BAY RD, MLPK, 94025, (650)363-4022	770 - H7
FOREST LANE PARK	FOREST LN, SBRN, 94066	707 - H6
FRANKFORT PARK	FRANKFORT ST & OLIVER ST, DALY, 94014	687 - E3
FREMONT	SANTA CRUZ AV & UNIVERSITY DR, MLPK, 94025	790 - F4
FRENCHMANS CREEK COMMON PARK	RUISSEAU FRANCAIS AV, HMBY, 94019	767 - E5
FRONTIERLAND PARK	YOSEMITE DR & HUMBOLDT CT, PCFA, 94044	727 - C5
GARRETT PARK	CANYON LN & GLENWOOD AV, RDWC, 94062	789 - G1
GATEWAY PARK	S GRANT ST & E 3RD AV, SMTO, 94401	749 - A1
GELLERT PARK	50 WEMBLEY DR, DALY, 94015	707 - B1
GILMAN PARK	GILMAN AV & GIANTS DR, SF, 94124	688 - C1
GLENVIEW PARK	GLENVIEW DR, SBRN, 94066	707 - F7
GOLDEN GATE NATIONAL RECREATION-AREA	CABRILLO HWY, PCFA, 94044	727 - C1
GREEN HILLS PARK	MAGNOLIA AV & LUDEMAN LN, MLBR, 94030	728 - A3
GREEN OAKS PARK (SEE PAGE 907)	CABRILLO HWY, SMCo, 94060	908 - J5
GREER PARK	1098 AMARILLO AV, PA, 94303	791 - D5
GRUNDY PARK	CHESTNUT AV & PARK AV, SBRN, 94066	707 - H7
GULL PARK	GULL AV, FCTY, 94404	749 - G1
HALLMARK PARK	HALLMARK DR, BLMT, 94002	769 - B3
HARBOR VIEW PARK	MONTE DIABLO AV & ROCHESTER ST, SMTO, 94401	729 - A6
HAWES PARK	OAK AV & JOHNSON ST, RDWC, 94061	770 - A7
HEATHER PARK	MELENDY DR, SCAR, 94070	769 - E5
HERITAGE GROVE	ALPINE RD, SMCo, 94020	849 - H4
HERMAN STREET PARK	HERMAN ST & DIAMOND ST, SBRN, 94066	707 - J6
HIGHLANDS PARK	MELENDY DR & ABERDEEN DR, SCAR, 94070	769 - E4
HILLCREST CIRCLE PARK	HILLCREST RD & ARUNDEL RD, SCAR, 94070	769 - F3
E HILLSDALE PARK	CHESTNUT LN, SMTO, 94403	749 - B6
W HILLSDALE PARK	LOUISE LN, SMTO, 94403	749 - B6
HILLSIDE PARK	222 LAUSANNE AV, DALY, 94014	687 - D4
HOLBOOK PALMER PARK	WATKINS AV & MCCORMICK LN, ATN, 94027	790 - E2
HOOVER PARK	2901 COWPER AV, PA, 94306	791 - C7
HOOVER PARK	SPRING ST & CHARTER ST, RDWC, 94063	770 - C6
HOPKINS CREEKSIDE PARK	ALMA ST & PALO ALTO AV, PA, 94301	790 - H4
HUDDART COUNTY PARK	KINGS MOUNTAIN RD & SKYLINE BL, SMCo, 94062	789 - B5
INDIAN SPRINGS PARK	W 39TH AV, SMTO, 94403	749 - B7
JACK FARELL PARK	FORDHAM ST, EPA, 94303	771 - C7
JARDIN DE NINOS PARK	MIDDLEFIELD RD & CEDAR ST, RDWC, 94063	770 - B6
JOHN L CARTER MEMORIAL PARK	MAIN ST & STONE PINE RD, HMBY, 94019	787 - G1
JOHNSON PARK	EVERETT AV & WAVERLEY ST, PA, 94301	790 - H4
JOINVILLE PARK	KEHOE AV, SMTO, 94403	749 - D1
JUNIPERO SERRA COUNTY PARK	CRYSTAL SPRINGS AV, SBRN, 94066, (650)589-5708	727 - H2
KELLOCH-VELASCO PARK	KELLOCH AV & VELASCO AV, DALY, 94014	687 - J2
KELLOG PARK	EMBARCADERO RD & WAVERLY ST, PA, 94301	791 - A5
KELLY PARK	100 TERMINAL AV, MLPK, 94025, (650)322-4578	770 - H7
KETCH PARK	KETCH CT, FCTY, 94404	749 - G4
KILLDEER PARK	KILLDEER CT, FCTY, 94404	749 - G1
KING, M L PARK	725 MONTE DIABLO AV, SMTO, 94401, (650)377-4714	728 - J7
LAGUNA PARK	LAGUNA AV & GROVE AV, BURL, 94010	728 - D5
LAKESHORE PARK	1550 MARINA CT, SMTO, 94403	749 - D4
LAUREL ST PARK	LAUREL ST, SCAR, 94070	769 - G3
LAURELWOOD PARK	GLENDORA DR, SMTO, 94403	748 - J7
LAUREOLA PARK	503 OLD COUNTRY RD, SCAR, 94070	769 - G2
LAURIE MEADOWS PARK	LAURIE MEADOWS DR, SMTO, 94403	749 - E6
LINCOLN PARK	901 BRUNSWICK ST, DALY, 94014	687 - E3

FEATURE NAME	Address City, ZIP Code	PAGE-GRID
LINDEN PARK	LINDEN ST & PARK ST, RDWC, 94061	770 - C7
LIONS FIELD PARK	1ST AV, SBRN, 94066	707 - J7
LIONS PARK	TIOGA DR, MLBR, 94030	727 - J4
LOMITA PARK	500 SAN ANSELMO AV, SBRN, 94066	728 - A1
LONGVIEW PARK	WESTLINE DR, DALY, 94015	706 - J1
LOS PRADOS PARK	BAHIA, SMTO, 94403	749 - E5
MADDUX PARK	MADDUX ST & PALM AV DR, RDWC, 94061	790 - A3
MARCHBANK PARK	PARKVIEW AV & WOODROW ST, DALY, 94014	687 - C3
MARINA ISLAND PARK	MARINERS ISLAND BLVD, SMTO, 94404	749 - D2
MARINA VISTA PARK	BAY ST & SPRUCE ST, SMCo, 94128	728 - B2
MARINER PARK	TEREDO DR, RDWC, 94065	749 - H7
MARLIN PARK	MARLIN AV, FCTY, 94404	749 - H3
MARLIN PARK	NEPTUNE DR, RDWC, 94065	749 - H7
MARTIN LUTHER KING PARK	DAISY LN, EPA, 94303	791 - D2
MAYFIELD PARK	2300 COLLEGE AV & WELLESLEY ST, PA, 94306	791 - A7
MCDOUGAL PARK	VISTA DR, BLMT, 94002	769 - D2
MCLAREN, JOHN PARK	MANSELL ST & JOHN F SHELLEY DR, SF, 94134	687 - H1
MCNEE RANCH STATE PARK	CABRILLO HWY, SMCo	746 - H1
MEZES PARK	STANDISH ST & WARREN ST, RDWC, 94063, (650)780-7250	770 - A5
MILL ESTATE PARK	SEBASTIAN DR & LAKE ST, MLBR, 94030	728 - A5
MILLS CANYON PARK	ARGUELLO DR & SEBASTIAN DR, BURL, 94010	728 - B6
MISSION HILLS PARK	FRANKFORT ST & GUTTENBERG ST, DALY, 94014	687 - F3
MONTE VERDE PARK	OAKMONT DR & EVERGREEN DR, SBRN, 94066	707 - E5
NEALON PARK	802 MIDDLE AV, MLPK, 94025, (650)858-3570	790 - G4
NORTHRIDGE PARK	NORTHRIDGE DR & CARMEL AV, DALY, 94015	686 - J6
OCEAN VIEW PARK	ALSACE LORAINE AV & VALDEZ, HMBY, 94019	787 - E1
OCEAN VIEW PLAYGROUND	PLYMOUTH AV & MONTANA ST, SF, 94112	687 - D1
ODDSTAD PARK	CRESPI DR & BARCELONA DR, PCFA, 94044	727 - A4
ORANGE MEMORIAL PARK	W ORANGE AV, SSF, 94080	707 - G3
OYSTER POINT PARK	OYSTER POINT BLVD & MARINA BLV, SSF, 94080	708 - C2
PACIFIC HEIGHTS PARK	LONGVIEW DR & GOODWIN DR, SBRN, 94066	707 - D6
PALISADES PARK	PALISADES DR & WESTRIDGE AV, DALY, 94015	686 - J5
PALM PARK	HUDSON ST, RDWC, 94061	790 - B1
PALMETTO PARK	PALMETTO AV & BRIGHTON RD, PCFA, 94044	706 - J6
PALO ALTO FOOTHILLS PARK (PRIVATE)	3300 PAGE MILL RD, PA, 94304	830 - F3
PARADISE VALLEY PARK	HILLSIDE BLVD, SSF, 94080	707 - J2
PARDEE, ELEANOR PARK	851 CENTER ST, PA, 94301	791 - B4
PARK	ARGUELLO BLVD & MARVILLA PL, PCFA, 94044	726 - H4
PARK	AVALON DR & DORADO WY, SSF, 94080	707 - F4
PARK	CRESTVIEW DR, SCAR, 94070	769 - C4
PARK	DUNDEE DR, SSF, 94080	707 - D2
PARK	IMPERIAL DR, PCFA, 94044	707 - B3
PARK	LATHROP AV & TOCOLOMA AV, SF, 94134	688 - B2
PARK	LATHROP DR, SCIC, 94305	810 - J2
PARK	LYNWOOD LN, MLBR, 94030	727 - H3
PARK	OLD COUNTY RD & SAN FRANCISCO, BSBN, 94005	688 - A6
PARK	POMPANO CIR, FCTY, 94404	749 - H3
PARK	RALSTON AV, BLMT, 94002	749 - F7
PARK	SARATOGA DR, SMTO, 94403	749 - C4
PARK	SHIELDS ST & MONTICELLO ST, SF, 94132	687 - C1
PARK	SOUTHWOOD DR, SSF, 94080	707 - F4
PARK	TAMARACK LN & ELM CT, SSF, 94080	707 - H2
PARK	WILLOW LN, BLMT, 94002	769 - D1
PARK	ZAMORA DR, SSF, 94080	707 - F5
PARKSIDE AQUATIC PARK	ROBERTA DR, SMTO, 94403	749 - D2
PEERS PARK	1899 PARK BLVD, PA, 94306	791 - A6
PERSHING PARK	CRESCENT AV & NEWLANDS AV, BURL, 94010	728 - G7
PESCADERO CREEK COUNTY PARK	ALPINE RD, SMCo, 94020	849 - G6
PLAYGROUND	BRUNSWICK ST & LOWELL ST, SF, 94112	687 - E2
PLAYGROUND	BYRON DR, SSF, 94080	707 - D2
PLAYGROUND	CAYUGA AV & NAGLEE AV, SF, 94112	687 - E2
PLAYGROUND	CRESTWOOD DR, SSF, 94080	707 - G1
PLAYGROUND	MCDONNELL DR, SSF, 94080	707 - E2
POINT SAN BRUNO PARK	FORBES BLVD & SAN BRUNO BLVD, SSF, 94080	708 - D3
POLARIS PARK	POLARIS WY & CANYON DR, DALY, 94014	687 - F3
POMO PARK	CARMEL AV & CANYON DR, PCFA, 94044	707 - A5
PONDEROSA PARK	SHARP PARK RD & PACIFIC HTS BL, SBRN, 94066	707 - C5
POPLAR BEACH PARK	KELLY AV & ALSTON AV, HMBY, 94019	787 - E2
PORT ROYAL PARK	PORT ROYAL AV, FCTY, 94404	749 - F6
PORTOLA HIGHLANDS PARK	SNEATH LN, SBRN, 94066	707 - D7
PORTOLA STATE PARK	PORTOLA STATE PARK RD, SMCo, 94020, (650)948-9098	850 - D7
PORTSIDE PARK	BRIDGE PKWY, RDWC, 94065	749 - H7
POSEY PARK	SAN MATEO AV & HUNTINGTON AV, SBRN, 94066	707 - J6
PULGAS WATER TEMPLE	CANADA RD, SMCo, 94062	769 - A6
RAMOS PARK	800 E MEADOW DR, PA, 94303	791 - E7
RAY PARK	BALBOA WY & DEVERAUX DR, BURL, 94010	728 - C5
RED MORTON COMMUNITY PARK	1400 ROOSEVELT AV, RDWC, 94061, (650)780-7250	790 - A1
RINCONADA PARK	777 EMBARCADERO RD, PA, 94301	791 - B5
ROTARY PARK	S ASHTON AV & MILLBRAE AV, MLBR, 94030	728 - A4
RYAN, LEO J MEMORIAL PARK	E HILLSDALE BLVD, FCTY, 94404	749 - F3
RYDER COURT PARK	RYDER ST, SMTO, 94401	729 - B7
SAM MCDONALD COUNTY PARK	PESCADERO CREEK RD, SMCo, 94020	849 - F4
SAN BRUNO MTN STATE AND CO PARK	GUADALUPE CANYON PKWY, SMCo, 94014	687 - F5
SAN CARLOS AVENUE MINI PARK	SAN CARLOS AV, SCAR, 94070	769 - E3
SAN MATEO COUNTY MEMORIAL PARK	PESCADERO CREEK RD, SMCo, 94021, (650)879-0212	849 - B6
SAN PEDRO VALLEY COUNTY PARK	600 ODDSTAD BLVD, PCFA, 94044, (650)355-8289	727 - C6
SCHULTZ PARK	BONITO WY & CAMINO ALTO, MLBR, 94030	728 - A4
SCOTT PARK	CHANNING AV & SCOTT ST, PA, 94301	790 - J5
SEA CLOUD PARK	SEA CLOUD DR, FCTY, 94404	749 - G4
SEALE PARK	3100 STOCKTON PL, PA, 94303	791 - D6
SELLICK PARK	APPIAN WY, SSF, 94080	707 - E4
SHAD PARK	SHAD CT, FCTY, 94404	749 - H2
SHANNON PARK	DAVIT LN & SHANNON WY, RDWC, 94065	749 - J6
SHARON PARK	SHARON PARK DR & KLAMATH DR, MLPK, 94025	790 - C7
SHARP PARK	SHARP PARK RD, PCFA, 94044	707 - B7
SHOREBIRD PARK	ISLAND DR, RDWC, 94065	749 - H6
SHORELINE AT MOUNTAIN VIEW	SHORELINE BLVD, MTVW, 94043	791 - H6
SHOREVIEW PARK	950 OCEAN VIEW AV, SMTO, 94401	749 - C1
SIGN HILL PARK	ROCCA AV & POPLAR AV, SSF, 94080	707 - H2
SMITH FIELD PARK	WAVECREST RD, HMBY, 94019	787 - F3
SPUR TRAIL PARK	MAGNOLIA AV & MILLBRAE AV, MLBR, 94030	728 - B4
STAFFORD PARK	HOPKINS AV & LOWELL ST, RDWC, 94062	769 - H6
STULSAFT PARK	RECREATION WY & GOODWIN AV, RDWC, 94061	789 - H3
SUNFISH PARK	SUNFISH CT, FCTY, 94404	749 - H3
SUNNYBRAE PARK	SUNNYBRAE BLVD, SMTO, 94402	749 - B2
THE OVAL PARK	PALM DR & SERRA ST, SCIC, 94305	790 - H6
TIDELANDS PARK	J HART CLINTON DR, SMTO, 94404	749 - D1
TRAP & SKEET RANGE	JOHN MUIR DR & SKYLINE BLVD, SF, 94132	686 - J1
TRINTA PARK	LESLIE ST, SMTO, 94402	749 - B4
TURNSTONE PARK	TURNSTONE CT, FCTY, 94404	749 - H2
TWIN PINES PARK	RALSTON AV, BLMT, 94002	769 - E1
UPPER STEVENS CREEK COUNTY PARK	SKYLINE BLVD, PA, 94304	850 - J4
VICTORIA PARK	VICTORIA RD & HOWARD AV, BURL, 94010	728 - H6
VILLAGE PARK	CALIFORNIA DR & EASTMOOR RD, BURL, 94010	728 - D5
VISTA PARK	CULEBRA RD & VISTA RD, HIL, 94010	748 - G3
WALLIS PARK	GRANT AV & ASH ST, PA, 94306	791 - B7
WASHINGTON PARK	850 BURLINGAME AV, BURL, 94010, (650)344-6386	728 - G6
WATER DOG LAKE PARK	LAKE RD, BLMT, 94002	769 - B2
WAUGH PARK	HILLCREST BLVD & EL PASEO, MLBR, 94030	728 - A4
WELLESLEY CRESCENT PARK	WELLESLEY CRES, RDWC, 94062	769 - J5
WERRY PARK	DARTMOUTH ST, PA, 94306	810 - J1
WESTBOROUGH PARK	WESTBOROUGH BLVD & GALWAY DR, SSF, 94080	707 - D4
WESTLAKE PARK	149 LAKE MERCED BLVD, DALY, 94015	687 - A3
WESTMOOR PARK	123 EDGEMONT DR, DALY, 94015	687 - A6
WESTVIEW PARK	SKYLINE BLVD, PCFA, 94044	707 - C5
WESTWOOD PARK	BRIARFIELD AV & WESTWOOD ST, RDWC, 94061	789 - H2
WHITE FIELD	LINDA MAR BLVD & SEVILLE DR, PCFA, 94044	726 - J5
WILLOW OAKS PARK	500 WILLOW RD, MLPK, 94025	790 - J2
WINSTON MANOR PARK	ELKWOOD DR & DUVAL DR, SSF, 94080	707 - D1
WUNDERLICH COUNTY PARK	4040 WOODSIDE RD, SMCo, 94062, (650)851-7570	809 - E3

PERFORMING ARTS

FEATURE NAME	Address City, ZIP Code	PAGE-GRID
SAN MATEO PERFORMING ARTS CENTER	600 N DELAWARE ST, SMTO, 94401, (650)348-8243	728 - H6
SHORELINE AMPHITHEATRE AT MTN VIEW	1 AMPHITHEATRE PKWY, MTVW, 94043, (650)962-1000	791 - H7

POINTS OF INTEREST

FEATURE NAME	Address City, ZIP Code	PAGE-GRID
ALLIED ARTS GUILD	ARBOR RD & CREEK DR, MLPK, 94025, (650)325-3259	790 - G5
ALPINE HILLS CLUB	LOS TRANCOS RD, PTLV, 94028	810 - D7
BAYLANDS ATHLETIC CENTER	1900 GENG RD, PA, 94303	791 - D4
HOOVER PAVILION	QUARRY RD & PALO DR, PA, 94304	790 - H5
MAUSOLEUM	LOMITA DR & CAMPUS DR, SCIC, 94305, (650)723-2300	790 - H6
PALO ALTO CULTURAL CENTER	1313 NEWELL RD, PA, 94303, (415)329-2366	791 - B5
PIGEON POINT LIGHTHOUSE- (SEE PAGE 867)	PIGEON POINT RD, SMCo, 94060	887 - J5
SAN FRANCISCO LOG CABIN BOYS SCHOOL	LOG CABIN RANCH RD, SMCo, 94020	849 - G2
STANFORD LINEAR ACCELERATOR CENTER	2575 SAND HILL RD, SMCo, 94025, (650)926-3300	810 - D1
SUNSET MAGAZINE CENTER	MIDDLEFIELD RD & WILLOW RD, MLPK, 94025, (650)321-3600	790 - H3
US LIGHTHOUSE RESERVE	CABRILLO HWY, SMCo, 94038	746 - E5

POINTS OF INTEREST - HISTORIC

FEATURE NAME	Address City, ZIP Code	PAGE-GRID
FILOLI HOUSE & GARDENS	CANADA RD, SMCo, 94062, (650)364-2880	769 - A7
SF BAY DISCOVERY CO HIST SITE	SWEENEY RIDGE TR, PCFA, 94044	727 - D3
WAR MEMORIAL	6655 MISSION ST, DALY, 94014, (650)991-8020	687 - D3
WOODSIDE COUNTRY STORE HIST SITE	471 KINGS MOUNTAIN RD, WDSD, 94062, (650)851-7615	789 - E6

POST OFFICES

FEATURE NAME	Address City, ZIP Code	PAGE-GRID
AIRPORT BRANCH POST OFFICE	SF INTERNATIONAL AIRPORT, SMCo, 94128, (650)742-1431	728 - C2
BELMONT POST OFFICE	640 MASONIC WY, BLMT, 94002, (650)591-9471	769 - E1
BRISBANE POST OFFICE	250 OLD COUNTY RD, BSBN, 94005, (650)467-8171	688 - A6
BROADWAY STATION POST OFFICE	1141 CAPUCHINO AV, BURL, 94010, (650)343-7861	728 - E6
BURLINGAME ANNEX POST OFFICE	820 STANTON RD, BURL, 94010, (650)697-9588	728 - D4
BURLINGAME POST OFFICE	220 PARK RD, BURL, 94010, (650)342-7694	728 - G7
CAMBRIDGE STATION POST OFFICE	265 CAMBRIDGE AV, PA, 94306, (650)327-4174	791 - A7
CHESTNUT STATION POST OFFICE	36 CHESTNUT AV, SSF, 94080, (650)583-0376	707 - G3
COLMA POST OFFICE	7373 MISSION ST, DALY, 94014, (650)755-1868	687 - C5
DALY CITY POST OFFICE	1100 SULLIVAN AV, DALY, 94015, (650)756-2303	687 - B5
DOWNTOWN STATION POST OFFICE	855 JEFFERSON AV, RDWC, 94063, (650)369-5228	770 - B6
EAST PALO ALTO POST OFFICE	2197 E BAYSHORE RD, PA, 94303, (650)452-4300	791
EL GRANADA POST OFFICE	20 AVE PORTOLA, SMCo, 94018, (650)726-5000	767 -
FOSTER CITY POST OFFICE	1050 SHELL BLVD, FCTY, 94404, (650)349-5529	749 - G
HALF MOON BAY POST OFFICE	500 STONE PINE RD, HMBY, 94019, (650)726-5517	787 - F1
LINDEN AVENUE STATION POST OFFICE	322 LINDEN AV, SSF, 94080, (650)589-2242	707 - J3
LOMA MAR POST OFFICE	8150 PESCADERO CREEK RD, SMCo, 94021, (650)879-0401	849 - A7
MENLO PARK POST OFFICE	3875 BOHANNON DR, MLPK, 94025, (650)323-0038	770 - F7
MILLBRAE POST OFFICE	501 BROADWAY, MLBR, 94030, (650)697-2506	728 - B3
MONTARA POST OFFICE	215 7TH ST, SMCo, 94037, (650)728-5251	746 - F4
MOSS BEACH POST OFFICE	2315 CARLOS ST, SMCo, 94038, (650)728-3151	746 - F6
OAK GROVE STATION POST OFFICE	655 OAK GROVE AV, MLPK, 94025, (650)321-7681	790 - F3
PACIFIC POST OFFICE	50 W MANOR DR, PCFA, 94044, (650)355-4000	706 - J3
PALO ALTO	380 HAMILTON AV, PA, 94301, (650)323-1361	790 - J4
PESCADERO POST OFFICE- (SEE PAGE 867)	2020 PESCADERO CREEK RD, SMCo, 94060, (650)879-0214	868 - B3
POST OFFICE	UNIVERSITY & BAY, EPA, 94303	791 - B1
POST OFFICE F	15 ONONDAGA AV, SF, 94112, (415)334-0739	687 - F1
REDWOOD CITY POST OFFICE	1100 BROADWAY, RDWC, 94063, (650)368-4181	770 - C5
SAINT MATTHEWS STATION POST OFFICE	210 S ELLSWORTH AV, SMTO, 94401, (650)343-5618	748 - J1
SAN BRUNO POST OFFICE	1300 HUNTINGTON AV, SBRN, 94066, (650)952-2900	707 - H5
SAN CARLOS	809 LAUREL ST, SCAR, 94070, (650)591-5321	769 - G3
SAN GREGORIO POST OFFICE- (SEE PAGE 827)	7615 STAGE RD, SMCo, 94074, (650)726-1045	828 - A6
SAN MATEO POST OFFICE	1630 S DELAWARE ST, SMTO, 94402, (650)349-2301	749 - B3
STANFORD UNIVERSITY BRANCH POST-OFFICE	LAGUNITA DR & LANE W, SCIC, 94305, (650)322-0059	790 - H7
STATION A	364 WOODSIDE PZ, RDWC, 94061, (650)368-3605	790 - A3
STATION A POST OFFICE	135 W 25TH AV, SMTO, 94403, (650)345-2611	749 - B5
STATION A POST OFFICE	690 ROBERTS RD, PCFA, 94044	726 - H3
VISITATION POST OFFICE	68 LELAND AV, SF, 94134, (415)333-1150	688 - A2
VISTA GRANDE STATION	6025 MISSION ST, DALY, 94014, (415)334-7884	687 - D3
WEST MENLO PARK BRANCH POST OFFICE	2120 AVY AV, SMCo, 94025	790 - D6
WESTLAKE STATION POST OFFICE	199 SOUTHGATE AV, DALY, 94015, (650)756-1842	687 - A4
WOODSIDE POST OFFICE	2995 #200 WOODSIDE RD, WDSD, 94062, (650)851-8711	789 - H6

SCHOOLS - PRIVATE ELEMENTARY

FEATURE NAME	Address City, ZIP Code	PAGE-GRID
ALL SOULS ELEM SCHOOL	479 MILLER AV, SSF, 94080, (650)583-3562	707 - J3
ALMA HEIGHTS CHRISTIAN	1030 LINDA MAR BLVD, PCFA, 94044, (650)359-0555	726 - J5
ALPHA BEACON CHRISTIAN	750 DARTMOUTH, SCAR, 94070, (650)592-2811	769 - D2
ARMSTRONG, CHARLES	1405 SOLANA DR, BLMT, 94002, (650)592-7570	769 - E2
BEECHWOOD ELEM SCHOOL	50 TERMINAL AV, MLPK, 94025, (650)327-5052	770 - H7
BELMONT OAKS ACADEMY	2200 CARLMONT DR, BLMT, 94002, (650)593-6175	769 - C2
BRANDEIS HILLEL DAY ELEM SCHOOL	655 BROTHERHOOD WY, SF, 94132, (415)406-1035	687 - B2
CARDEN ELEM SCHOOL	2109 BROADWAY, BURL, 94010, (650)348-2131	728 - D6
CAREY ELEM SCHOOL	2101 ALAMEDA DE LAS PULGAS, SMTO, 94403, (650)345-8205	749 - A4
EL GRANADA ELEM SCHOOL	130 SANTA ANNA ST, SMCo, 94018, (650)726-2990	767 - B3
EPIPHANY ELEM SCHOOL	600 ITALY AV, SF, 94112, (415)337-4030	687 - G1
GOOD SHEPHERD ELEM SCHOOL	909 OCEANA BLVD, PCFA, 94044, (650)359-4544	706 - J4
HERITAGE CHRISTIAN ACADEMY	1305 MIDDLEFIELD RD, RDWC, 94063, (650)366-3842	770 - B6
HIGHLANDS CHRISTIAN ELEM SCHOOL	1900 MONTEREY DR, SBRN, 94066, (650)873-4090	707 - E7
HOLY ANGELS ELEM SCHOOL	20 REINER ST, SMCo, 94014, (650)755-0220	687 - C5
IMMACULATE HEART OF MARY	1000 ALAMEDA DE LAS PULGAS, BLMT, 94002, (650)593-4265	769 - C2
KEYS SCHOOL	2890 MIDDLEFIELD RD, PA, 94306, (650)328-1711	791 - C6
KROUZIAN-ZEKARIAN OF ST. GREGORY-ARMEN	825 BROTHERHOOD WY, SF, 94132, (415)586-8686	687 - B2
MATER DOLOROSA ELEM SCHOOL	1040 MILLER AV, SSF, 94080, (650)588-8175	707 - G2
NATIVITY ELEM SCHOOL	1250 LAUREL ST, MLPK, 94025, (650)325-7304	790 - F3

FEATURE NAME	Address City, ZIP Code	PAGE-GRID
	...T, 94002, (650)591-2209	769 - E1
...ARNING	..., HIL, 94010, (650)348-2272	748 - C2
...NGELS ELEM SCHOOL	... AV, BURL, 94010, (650)343-9200	728 - D6
...OF MERCY ELEM SCHOOL	...OOD DR, DALY, 94015, (650)756-3395	687 - A4
...ADY OF MOUNT CARMEL	... GRAND ST, RDWC, 94062, (650)366-6127	769 - J6
...UR LADY OF PERPETUAL HELP	80 WELLINGTON AV, DALY, 94014, (650)755-4438	687 - D3
OUR LADY OF THE VISITACION	785 SUNNYDALE AV, SF, 94134, (415)239-7840	687 - J2
PENINSULA FRENCH AMERICAN	870 N CALIFORNIA AV, PA, 94303, (650)328-2338	791 - C5
PENINSULA SCHOOL, LTD	920 PENINSULA WY, SMCo, 94025, (650)325-1584	790 - H1
PHILLIPS BROOKS ELEM SCHOOL	2245 AVY AV, MLPK, 94025, (650)854-4545	790 - D7
REDEEMER LUTHERAN ELEM SCHOOL	468 GRAND ST, RDWC, 94062, (650)366-3466	769 - J6
ROGER WILLIAMS	600 GRAND AV, SSF, 94080, (650)877-3995	707 - H2
SAINT CATHERINE OF SIENA	1300 BAYSWATER AV, BURL, 94010, (650)344-7176	728 - G7
SAINT DUNSTANS ELEM SCHOOL	1150 MAGNOLIA AV, MLBR, 94030, (650)697-8119	728 - A3
SAINT MATTHEWS EPISCOPAL	16 BALDWIN AV, SMTO, 94401, (650)342-5436	748 - J1
SAINT RAYMOND ELEM SCHOOL	1211 ARBOR RD, MLPK, 94025, (650)322-2312	790 - F4
SAINT ROBERT ELEM SCHOOL	345 OAK AV, SBRN, 94066, (650)583-5065	727 - H1
SAINT THOMAS MORE ELEM SCHOOL	50 THOMAS MORE WY, SF, 94132, (650)377-0100	687 - C2
SAINT TIMOTHY ELEM SCHOOL	1515 DOLAN AV, SMTO, 94401, (650)342-6567	729 - B7
SAINT VERONICA ELEM SCHOOL	434 ALIDA WY, SSF, 94080, (650)589-3909	707 - G4
SAN FRANCISCO CHRISTIAN	25 WHITTIER ST, SF, 94112, (415)586-1117	687 - E2
SAN FRANCISCO JUNIOR ACADEMY	66 GENEVA AV, SF, 94112, (415)585-5550	687 - F1
ST CHARLES ELEM SCHOOL	850 TAMARACK AV, SCAR, 94070, (650)593-1629	769 - F4
ST ELIZABETH SETON CATHOLIC COMM	1095 CHANNING AV, PA, 94301, (415)326-9004	791 - B4
ST GREGORY ELEM SCHOOL	2701 HACIENDA ST, SMTO, 94403, (650)573-0111	749 - B5
ST JOSEPHS ELEM SCHOOL	50 EMILIE AV, ATN, 94027, (650)322-9931	790 - E4
ST MATTHEWS CATHOLIC ELEM SCHOOL	900 S EL CAMINO REAL, SMTO, 94402, (650)343-1373	749 - A2
ST MATTHIAS SCHOOL OF RELIGION	1685 CORDILLERAS RD, RDWC, 94062, (650)366-7085	769 - G7
ST PAUL OF THE SHIPWRECK ACADEMY	1060 KEY AV, SF, 94124, (415)467-1798	688 - B1
ST PIUS ELEM SCHOOL	1100 WOODSIDE RD, RDWC, 94061, (650)368-8327	790 - B2
TRINITY EPISCOPAL ELEM SCHOOL	2650 SAND HILL RD, MLPK, 94025, (650)854-0288	810 - D1
WOODLAND ELEM SCHOOL	360 LA CUESTA DR, SMCo, 94028, (650)854-9065	810 - E3

SCHOOLS - PRIVATE HIGH

FEATURE NAME	Address City, ZIP Code	PAGE-GRID
CRYSTAL SPRINGS AND UPLANDS	400 UPLANDS DR, HIL, 94010, (650)342-4175	748 - H2
HIGHLANDS CHRISTIAN HIGH SCHOOL	1900 MONTEREY DR, SBRN, 94066, (650)873-4090	707 - E7
MENLO HIGH SCHOOL	50 VALPARAISO AV, ATN, 94027, (650)688-3863	790 - F3
MERCY HIGH SCHOOL	2750 ADELINE DR, BURL, 94010, (650)343-3631	728 - C6
MID-PENINSULA EDUCATION CENTER	870 N CALIFORNIA AV, PA, 94303, (650)493-5910	791 - C5
NOTRE DAME HIGH SCHOOL	1540 RALSTON AV, BLMT, 94002, (650)595-1913	769 - D1
SACRED HEART PREPARATORY	150 VALPARAISO AV, ATN, 94027, (650)322-1866	790 - E4
SERRA, JUNIPERO HIGH SCHOOL	451 W 20TH AV, SMTO, 94403, (650)345-8207	749 - A4
WOODSIDE PRIORY	302 PORTOLA RD, PTLV, 94028, (650)851-8221	810 - C7

SCHOOLS - PUBLIC ELEMENTARY

FEATURE NAME	Address City, ZIP Code	PAGE-GRID
ADDISON ELEM SCHOOL	650 ADDISON AV, PA, 94301, (650)322-5935	791 - A4
ALLEN, DECIMA M ELEM SCHOOL	875 ANGUS AV W, SBRN, 94066, (650)244-0165	707 - H7
ARUNDEL ELEM SCHOOL	200 ARUNDEL RD, SCAR, 94070, (650)508-7311	769 - E3
AUDUBON ELEM SCHOOL	841 GULL AV, FCTY, 94404, (650)312-7500	749 - H1
BAYSHORE ELEM SCHOOL	155 ORIENTE ST, DALY, 94014, (415)467-0442	687 - J3
BAYWOOD ELEM SCHOOL	600 ALAMEDA DE LAS PULGAS, SMTO, 94402, (650)312-7511	748 - H3
BELLE AIR ELEM SCHOOL	450 THIRD AV, SBRN, 94066, (650)244-0154	708 - A7
BELLE HAVEN ELEM SCHOOL	415 IVY DR, MLPK, 94025, (650)329-2898	770 - J7
BRENTWOOD OAKS ELEM SCHOOL	2086 CLARKE AV, EPA, 94303, (650)329-2875	791 - C2
BREWER ISLAND	1151 POLYNESIA DR, FCTY, 94404, (650)312-7532	749 - G2
BRISBANE ELEM SCHOOL	500 SAN BRUNO AV, BSBN, 94005, (650)467-0120	688 - A6
BRITTAN ACRES ELEM SCHOOL	2000 BELLE AV, SCAR, 94070, (650)593-7891	769 - G4
BROWN, MARGARET PAULINE	305 EASTMOOR AV, DALY, 94015, (650)991-1243	687 - B6
BURI BURI ELEM SCHOOL	120 EL CAMPO DR, SSF, 94080, (650)877-8776	707 - E3
CABRILLO ELEM SCHOOL	601 CRESPI DR, PCFA, 94044, (650)355-0414	726 - J3
CENTRAL ELEM SCHOOL	525 MIDDLE RD, BLMT, 94002, (650)637-4820	749 - E7
CHAVEZ, CESAR ELEM SCHOOL	2450 RALMER AV, EPA, 94303, (650)329-6700	791 - A1
CIPRIANI	2525 BUENA VISTA AV, BLMT, 94002, (415)637-4840	769 - B1
CLEVELAND ELEM SCHOOL	455 ATHENS ST, SF, 94112, (415)469-4709	687 - G1
CLIFFORD ELEM SCHOOL	225 CLIFFORD AV, SMCo, 94062, (650)366-8011	769 - G6
COLMA ELEM SCHOOL	444 E MARKET ST, DALY, 94014, (650)991-1211	687 - D5
COLUMBUS, CHRISTOPHER	60 CHRISTOPHER CT, DALY, 94015, (650)991-1206	707 - A1
CORTE MADERA	4575 ALPINE RD, PTLV, 94028, (415)851-0409	830 - C1
COSTANO ELEM SCHOOL	2695 FORDHAM ST, EPA, 94303, (650)329-2830	771 - B7
CRESTMOOR ELEM SCHOOL	2322 CRESTMOOR DR, SBRN, 94066, (650)244-0152	707 - F7
DUVENECK ELEM SCHOOL	705 ALESTER AV, PA, 94303, (650)322-5946	791 - C4
EDISON, THOMAS ELEM SCHOOL	1267 SOUTHGATE AV, DALY, 94015, (650)991-1250	687 - A7
EL CARMELO ELEM SCHOOL	3024 BRYANT ST, PA, 94306, (650)856-0960	791 - C7
EL CRYSTAL ELEM SCHOOL	201 BALBOA WY, SBRN, 94066, (650)244-0149	727 - J1
EL DORADO ELEM SCHOOL	70 DELTA ST, SF, 94134, (415)330-1537	688 - A1
EL GRANADA ELEM SCHOOL	400 SANTIAGO ST, SMCo, 94018, (650)712-7150	767 - C3
ENCINAL ELEM SCHOOL	195 ENCINAL AV, ATN, 94027, (650)326-5164	790 - F2
ESCONDIDO ELEM SCHOOL	890 ESCONDIDO RD, SCIC, 94305, (650)856-1337	810 - J1
FAIR OAKS ELEM SCHOOL	2950 FAIR OAKS AV, SMCo, 94063, (650)368-3953	770 - D7
FAIRMONT ELEM SCHOOL	290 EDGEWOOD DR, PCFA, 94044, (650)359-5473	707 - A2
FARALLONE VIEW ELEM SCHOOL	LE CONTE AV & KANOFF AV, SMCo, 94037, (650)712-7170	746 - G4
FIESTA GARDENS INTERNATIONAL	1001 BERMUDA DR, SMTO, 94403, (650)312-7737	749 - C3
FLOOD, JAMES ELEM SCHOOL	320 SHERIDAN DR, MLPK, 94025, (650)329-2890	770 - H7
FORD, HENRY ELEM SCHOOL	2498 MASSACHUSETTS AV, RDWC, 94061, (650)368-2981	790 - A3
FOSTER CITY ELEM SCHOOL	461 BEACH PARK BLVD, FCTY, 94404, (650)312-7522	749 - F4
FOX ELEM SCHOOL	3100 ST JAMES RD, BLMT, 94002, (650)637-4850	768 - J2
FRANKLIN ELEM SCHOOL	2385 TROUSDALE DR, BURL, 94010, (650)259-3850	728 - B5
GARDEN VILLAGE ELEM SCHOOL	208 GARDEN LN, SMCo, 94015, (650)991-1233	687 - B4
GARFIELD CHARTER ELEM SCHOOL	3600 MIDDLEFIELD RD, SMCo, 94063, (650)369-3759	790 - D1
GILL, JOHN ELEM SCHOOL	555 AVE DEL ORA, RDWC, 94062, (650)365-8320	769 - J7
GREEN HILLS ELEM SCHOOL	401 LUDEMAN LN, MLBR, 94030, (650)588-6485	728 - A3
GUADALUPE ELEM SCHOOL	859 PRAGUE ST, SF, 94112, (415)469-4718	687 - G2
HALL, GEORGE ELEM SCHOOL	130 SAN MIGUEL WY, SMTO, 94403, (650)312-7533	749 - D5
HARTE, BRET ELEM SCHOOL	1035 GILMAN AV, SF, 94124, (415)330-1520	688 - C1
HATCH, ALVIN S ELEM SCHOOL	MIRAMONTES ST, HMBY, 94019, (650)712-7160	787 - F1
HAWES ELEM SCHOOL	909 ROOSEVELT AV, RDWC, 94061, (650)366-3122	770 - A7
HAYS, WALTER ELEM SCHOOL	1525 MIDDLEFIELD RD, PA, 94301, (650)322-5956	791 - B5
HEATHER ELEM SCHOOL	2757 MELENDY DR, SCAR, 94070, (650)508-7303	769 - E5
HIGHLANDS ELEM SCHOOL	2320 NEWPORT ST, SMCo, 94402, (650)312-7544	748 - F7
HILLSIDE ELEM SCHOOL	1400 HILLSIDE BLVD, SSF, 94080, (650)877-8801	707 - H1
HOOVER PUBLIC ELEM SCHOOL	701 CHARTER ST, RDWC, 94063, (650)366-6236	770 - C6
HORRALL, ALBION H. ELEM SCHOOL	949 OCEAN VIEW AV, SMTO, 94401, (650)312-7550	749 - C1
KENNEDY, JOHN F ELEM SCHOOL	785 PRICE ST, DALY, 94014, (650)991-1239	687 - D4
KINGS MOUNTAIN ELEM SCHOOL	SWETT RD, SMCo, 94062, (650)712-7180	788 - J7
LA HONDA ELEM SCHOOL	SEARS RANCH RD, SMCo, 94062, (650)747-0051	829 - E7
LAS LOMITAS ELEM SCHOOL	299 ALAMEDA DE LAS PULGAS, ATN, 94027, (650)854-5900	790 - C5
LAUREL ELEM SCHOOL	316 36TH AV, SMTO, 94403, (650)312-7555	749 - B6
LAUREL ELEM SCHOOL	95 EDGE RD, ATN, 94027, (650)324-0186	790 - H1
LINCOLN ELEM SCHOOL	1801 DEVEREUX DR, BURL, 94010, (650)697-8230	728 - C5
LINDA MAR ELEM SCHOOL	830 ROSITA RD, PCFA, 94044, (650)359-2400	726 - H5
LOMITA PARK ELEM SCHOOL	200 SANTA HELENA AV, MLBR, 94030, (650)588-5852	728 - A2
LONGFELLOW ELEM SCHOOL	755 MORSE ST, SF, 94112, (415)469-4730	687 - E2
LOS CERRITOS ELEM SCHOOL	210 W ORANGE AV, SSF, 94080, (650)877-8841	707 - G3
MARTIN ELEM SCHOOL	35 SCHOOL ST, SSF, 94080, (650)877-3955	707 - J2
MCKINLEY ELEM SCHOOL	701 PALOMA AV, BURL, 94010, (650)259-3870	728 - F6
MEADOW HEIGHTS ELEM SCHOOL	2619 DOLORES ST, SMTO, 94403, (650)312-7566	749 - A5
MEADOWS ELEM SCHOOL	1101 HELEN DR, MLBR, 94030, (650)583-7590	727 - H3
MENLO OAKS ELEM SCHOOL	475 POPE ST, MLPK, 94025, (650)329-2828	790 - J2
MONTE VERDE ELEM SCHOOL	2551 SAINT CLOUD DR, SBRN, 94066, (650)877-8838	707 - E5
MUIR, JOHN ELEM SCHOOL	130 CAMBRIDGE LN, SBRN, 94066, (650)244-0143	727 - F1
NESBIT ELEM SCHOOL	500 BIDDULPH WY, BLMT, 94002, (650)637-4860	749 - E7
NIXON, LUCILLE M ELEM SCHOOL	1711 STANFORD AV, SCIC, 94305, (650)856-1622	810 - J2
NORTH HILLSBOROUGH ELEM SCHOOL	545 EUCALYPTUS AV, HIL, 94010, (650)347-4175	748 - E1
NORTH SHOREVIEW ELEM SCHOOL	1301 CYPRESS AV, SMTO, 94401, (650)312-7588	729 - A7
OAK KNOLL ELEM SCHOOL	1895 OAK KNOLL LN, MLPK, 94025, (650)854-4433	790 - E6
ODDSTAD ELEM SCHOOL	930 ODDSTAD BLVD, PCFA, 94044, (650)355-3638	727 - C5
OHLONE ELEM SCHOOL	950 AMARILLO AV, PA, 94303, (650)856-1726	791 - D5
ORION ELEM SCHOOL	3150 GRANGER WY, RDWC, 94061, (650)363-0611	789 - J3
ORMONDALE ELEM SCHOOL	200 SHAWNEE PASS, PTLV, 94028, (650)851-7230	810 - B6
ORTEGA, JOSE ELEM SCHOOL	400 SARGENT ST, SF, 94132, (415)469-4726	687 - C1
PALO VERDE ELEM SCHOOL	3450 LOUIS RD, PA, 94303, (650)856-1672	791 - E7
PANORAMA ELEM SCHOOL	25 BELLEVUE AV, DALY, 94014, (415)586-6595	687 - F3
PARK ELEM SCHOOL	161 CLARK DR, SMTO, 94402, (650)312-7577	748 - G1
PARKSIDE ELEM SCHOOL	1685 EISENHOWER ST, SMTO, 94403, (650)312-7575	749 - C2
PESCADERO ELEM SCHOOL- (SEE PAGE 867)	620 NORTH ST, SMCo, 94060, (650)879-0332	868 - B2
PONDEROSA ELEM SCHOOL	295 PONDEROSA RD, SMCo, 94080, (650)877-8825	707 - G4
PORTOLA ELEM SCHOOL	300 AMADOR AV, SBRN, 94066, (650)871-7133	707 - D7
ROLLINGWOOD ELEM SCHOOL	2500 COTTONWOOD DR, SBRN, 94066, (650)244-0146	707 - E6
ROOSEVELT ELEM SCHOOL	2223 VERA AV, RDWC, 94061, (650)369-5597	789 - J1
ROOSEVELT, FRANKLIN D	1200 SKYLINE DR, DALY, 94015, (650)991-1230	707 - A2
ROY CLOUD ELEM SCHOOL	3790 RED OAK WY, RDWC, 94061, (650)369-2264	789 - G2
SELBY LANE ELEM SCHOOL	170 SELBY LN, ATN, 94027, (650)368-3996	790 - B3
SERRA, JUNIPERO ELEM SCHOOL	151 VICTORIA ST, DALY, 94015, (650)877-8853	707 - C2
SHARP PARK ELEM SCHOOL	1427 PALMETTO AV, PCFA, 94044, (650)355-7400	706 - J5
SHERIDAN ELEM SCHOOL	431 CAPITOL AV, SF, 94112, (415)469-4743	687 - D2
SKYLINE ELEM SCHOOL	55 CHRISTEN AV, DALY, 94015, (650)877-8846	707 - C3
SOUTH HILLSBOROUGH ELEM SCHOOL	303 EL CERRITO AV, HIL, 94010, (650)344-0303	748 - H2
SPRING VALLEY ELEM SCHOOL	817 MURCHISON DR, MLBR, 94030, (650)697-5681	728 - B5
SPRUCE ELEM SCHOOL	501 SPRUCE AV, SSF, 94080, (650)877-8780	707 - J2
SUNNYBRAE ELEM SCHOOL	1031 S DELAWARE ST, SMTO, 94402, (650)312-7599	749 - B2
SUNSHINE GARDENS ELEM SCHOOL	1200 MILLER AV, SSF, 94080, (650)877-8784	707 - F1
TAFT ELEM SCHOOL	903 10TH AV, RDWC, 94063, (650)369-2589	770 - E6
TOBIAS, MARJORIE H ELEM SCHOOL	725 SOUTHGATE AV, DALY, 94015, (650)991-1246	687 - A5
TURNBULL LEARNING ACADEMY SCHOOL	715 INDIAN AV, SMTO, 94401, (650)312-7766	728 - J7
VALLEMAR ELEM SCHOOL	377 REINA DEL MAR AV, PCFA, 94044, (650)359-2444	727 - A1
VISITACION VALLEY ELEM SCHOOL	55 SCHWERIN ST, SF, 94134, (415)469-4796	687 - J2
WASHINGTON ELEM SCHOOL	801 HOWARD AV, BURL, 94010, (650)259-3880	728 - H6
WASHINGTON, GEORGE ELEM SCHOOL	251 WHITTIER ST, DALY, 94014, (650)991-1236	687 - E2
WEBSTER, DANIEL ELEM SCHOOL	425 EL DORADO DR, DALY, 94015, (650)991-1222	687 - B7
WEST HILLSBOROUGH ELEM SCHOOL	376 BARBARA WY, HIL, 94010, (650)344-9870	748 - D3
WESTLAKE ELEM SCHOOL	80 FIELDCREST DR, DALY, 94015, (650)991-1252	687 - B3
WESTVIEW ELEM SCHOOL	367 GLENCOURT WY, PCFA, 94044, (650)355-6441	707 - B4
WHITE OAKS ELEM SCHOOL	1901 WHITE OAK WY, SCAR, 94070, (650)508-7317	769 - H5
WILLOW OAKS ELEM SCHOOL	620 WILLOW RD, MLPK, 94025, (650)329-2850	790 - J2
WILSON, WOODROW ELEM SCHOOL	43 MIRIAM ST, DALY, 94014, (650)991-1255	687 - C3
WOODSIDE ELEM SCHOOL	3195 WOODSIDE RD, WDSD, 94062, (650)851-1571	789 - G7

SCHOOLS - PUBLIC HIGH

FEATURE NAME	Address City, ZIP Code	PAGE-GRID
ARAGON HIGH SCHOOL	900 ALAMEDA DE LAS PULGAS, SMTO, 94402, (650)342-7980	748 - J3
BADEN (CONT) HIGH SHCOOL	825 SOUTHWOOD DR, SSF, 94080, (650)877-8769	707 - H3
BALBOA HIGH SCHOOL	1000 CAYUGA AV, SF, 94112, (415)469-4090	687 - F1
BURLINGAME HIGH SCHOOL	400 CAROLAN AV, BURL, 94010, (650)342-8971	728 - G6
BURTON, PHILLIP & SALA HIGH SCHOOL	400 MANSELL ST, SF, 94134, (415)469-4550	688 - A1
CAPUCHINO HIGH SCHOOL	1501 MAGNOLIA AV, SBRN, 94066, (650)583-9977	727 - J2
CARLMONT HIGH SCHOOL	1400 ALAMEDA DE LAS PULGAS, BLMT, 94002, (650)595-0210	769 - D3
EL CAMINO HIGH SCHOOL	1320 MISSION RD, SSF, 94080, (650)877-8806	707 - F1
HALF MOON BAY HIGH SCHOOL	LEWIS FOSTER DR, HMBY, 94019, (650)712-7200	767 - F7
HILLSDALE HIGH SCHOOL	3115 DEL MONTE ST, SMTO, 94403, (650)574-7230	749 - A6
JEFFERSON HIGH SCHOOL	6996 MISSION ST, DALY, 94014, (650)992-4050	687 - C4
MENLO-ATHERTON HIGH SCHOOL	555 MIDDLEFIELD RD, ATN, 94027, (650)322-5311	790 - G2
MILLS HIGH SCHOOL	400 MURCHISON DR, MLBR, 94030, (650)697-3344	728 - B4
OCEANA HIGH SCHOOL	401 PALOMA AV, PCFA, 94044, (650)355-4131	707 - A5
PALO ALTO HIGH SCHOOL	50 EMBARCADERO RD, PA, 94301, (650)329-3710	790 - J6
PENINSULA CONTINUATION HIGH SCHOOL	300 PIEDMONT AV, SBRN, 94066, (650)583-3016	727 - G2
PESCADERO HIGH SCHOOL- (SEE PAGE 867)	350 BUTANO CTO RD, SMCo, 94060, (650)879-0274	868 - D3
REDWOOD HIGH (CONT)	1968 OLD COUNTY RD, RDWC, 94063, (650)369-1411	769 - J4
SAN MATEO HIGH SCHOOL	506 N DELAWARE ST, SMTO, 94401, (650)348-8050	728 - J7
SEQUOIA HIGH SCHOOL	1201 BREWSTER AV, RDWC, 94062, (650)367-9780	770 - A6
SOUTH SAN FRANCISCO HIGH SCHOOL	400 B ST, SSF, 94080, (650)877-8754	707 - G4
SOUTHWOOD HIGH SCHOOL	825 SOUTHWOOD DR, SSF, 94080, (650)877-8769	707 - F3
TERRA NOVA HIGH SCHOOL	1450 TERRA NOVA BLVD, PCFA, 94044, (650)359-3961	727 - B4
WESTMOOR HIGH SCHOOL	131 WESTMOOR AV, DALY, 94015, (650)756-3434	687 - A6
WOODSIDE HIGH SCHOOL	199 CHURCHILL AV, SMCo, 94062, (650)367-9750	790 - A4

SCHOOLS - PUBLIC INTERMEDIATE

FEATURE NAME	Address City, ZIP Code	PAGE-GRID
BURLINGAME INTERMEDIATE SCHOOL	1715 QUESADA WY, BURL, 94010, (650)259-3830	728 - B5
CUNHA, MANUEL F INTERMEDIATE SCHOOL	KELLY AND CHURCH ST, HMBY, 94019, (650)712-7190	787 - F1
FRANKLIN, BENJAMIN INTERMEDIATE-SCHOOL	700 STEWART AV, SMCo, 94015, (650)991-1202	687 - B4
LIPMAN INTERMEDIATE SCHOOL	1 SOLANO ST, BSBN, 94005, (650)467-9541	687 - J6
MCKINLEY INTERMEDIATE SCHOOL	400 DUANE ST, RDWC, 94062, (650)366-3827	770 - A6
MCNAIR, RONALD INTERMEDIATE SCHOOL	2033 PULGAS AV, EPA, 94303, (650)329-2888	791 - C2
PARKSIDE INTERMEDIATE SCHOOL	1801 NILES AV, SBRN, 94066, (650)244-0160	727 - H1
RALSTON INTERMEDIATE	2675 RALSTON AV, BLMT, 94002, (650)637-4880	769 - A2
RIVERA, FERNANDO INTERMEDIATE-SCHOOL	1255 SOUTHGATE AV, DALY, 94015, (650)991-1225	687 - A7
ROBERTSON, GARNET J INTERMEDIATE-SCHOOL	1 MARTIN ST, DALY, 94014, (415)467-5443	687 - J4

SCHOOLS - PUBLIC MIDDLE

FEATURE NAME	Address City, ZIP Code	PAGE-GRID
ABBOTT MIDDLE SCHOOL	600 36TH AV, SMTO, 94403, (650)312-7600	749 - B6
ALTA LOMA MIDDLE SCHOOL	116 ROMNEY AV, SSF, 94080, (650)877-8797	707 - E2
BAYSIDE MIDDLE SCHOOL	2025 KEHOE AV, SMTO, 94403, (650)312-7660	749 - C1
BOREL MIDDLE SCHOOL	425 BARNESON AV, SMTO, 94402, (650)312-7670	749 - A4
BOWDITCH MIDDLE SCHOOL	1450 TARPON ST, FCTY, 94404, (650)312-7680	749 - J2
BURBANK, LUTHER MIDDLE SCHOOL	325 LA GRANDE AV, SF, 94112, (415)469-4547	687 - H1
CENTRAL MIDDLE SCHOOL	828 CHESTNUT ST, SCAR, 94070, (650)508-7321	769 - G4
CROCKER, WILLIAM H MIDDLE SCHOOL	2600 RALSTON AV, HIL, 94010, (650)342-6331	748 - E1
DENMAN, JAMES MIDDLE SCHOOL	241 ONEIDA AV, SF, 94112, (415)469-4535	687 - F1
HILLVIEW MIDDLE SCHOOL	1100 ELDER AV, MLPK, 94025, (650)326-4341	790 - E5
JORDAN, DAVID STARR MIDDLE SCHOOL	750 N CALIFORNIA AV, PA, 94303, (650)494-8120	791 - C6
KENNEDY, JOHN F MIDDLE SCHOOL	2521 GOODWIN AV, RDWC, 94061, (650)365-4611	789 - J2

FEATURE NAME Address City, ZIP Code	PAGE-GRID
LA ENTRADA MIDDLE SCHOOL 2200 SHARON RD, MLPK, 94025, (650)854-3962	790 - D7
ORTEGA MIDDLE SCHOOL 1283 TERRA NOVA BLVD, PCFA, 94044, (650)359-3941	727 - A5
PACIFIC HEIGHTS MIDDLE SCHOOL 3791 PACIFIC HEIGHTS BLVD, SBRN, 94066, (650)355-6900	707 - C6
PARKWAY HEIGHTS MIDDLE SCHOOL 825 PARK WY, SSF, 94080, (650)877-8788	707 - G2
POLLICITA, THOMAS R MIDDLE SCHOOL 550 E MARKET ST, DALY, 94014, (650)991-1216	687 - D5
TAYLOR MIDDLE SCHOOL 850 TAYLOR BLVD, MLBR, 94030, (650)697-4096	728 - A4
VISITACION VALLEY MIDDLE SCHOOL 450 RAYMOND AV, SF, 94134, (415)469-4590	687 - J1
WESTBOROUGH MIDDLE SCHOOL 2570 WESTBOROUGH BLVD, SSF, 94080, (650)877-8848	707 - D4

SHOPPING CENTERS - COMMUNITY

FEATURE NAME Address City, ZIP Code	PAGE-GRID
280 METRO CENTER JUNIPERO SERRA BLVD & COLA BLV, CLMA, 94014	687 - C7
BAYHILL CENTER BAYHILL DR & CHERRY AV, SBRN, 94066	707 - G7
BEL MATEO CENTER 42ND AV & OLYMPIC AV, SMTO, 94403, (650)349-0431	749 - D7
BOREL SQUARE BOVET RD & S EL CAMINO REAL, SMTO, 94402	749 - A4
BRENTWOOD CENTER EL CAMINO REAL & S SPRUCE, SSF, 94080, (415)761-2277	707 - H5
BURI BURI WESTBOROUGH BL & CAMARITAS AV, SSF, 94080	707 - F3
BURLINGAME PLAZA MAGNOLIA AV & TROUSDALE DR, BURL, 94010	728 - B4
CARLMONT VILLAGE AVD D L PULGAS & RALSTON AV, BLMT, 94002, (415)593-8075	769 - C2
CHARTER SQUARE BEACH PARK BLVD & SHELL BLVD, FCTY, 94404	749 - G4
CRESPI CENTER 580 CRESPI DR, PCFA, 94044	726 - H4
CROSBY COMMONS BURLINGAME AV & PRIMROSE RD, BURL, 94010	728 - F7
CRYSTAL SPRINGS CENTER POLHEMUS RD & DE ANZA BLVD, SMTO, 94402	748 - H7
EDGEWATER PLACE EDGEWATER & BEACH PARK BLVD, FCTY, 94404, (650)986-0647	749 - F4
EUREKA SQUARE EUREKA DR & OCEANA BLVD, PCFA, 94044, (650)359-9896	706 - J6
KING PLAZA KING DR & CALLAN BLVD, DALY, 94015	707 - C3
LAURELWOOD CENTER HILLSDALE BLVD & CAMPUS DR, SMTO, 94403, (650)349-0431	748 - J6
LINDA MAR LINDA MAR BLVD & CABRILLO HWY, PCFA, 94044, (650)433-9300	726 - H4
LONGS PLAZA EL CAMINO REAL & HULL DR, SCAR, 94070	769 - F2
MARLIN COVE FOSTER CITY BLVD & MARLIN AV, FCTY, 94404, (650)832-1888	749 - H3
MERVYNS PLAZA HWY 101 & WALNUT ST, RDWC, 94063	770 - B5
METRO CENTER E HILLSDALE BLVD, FCTY, 94404	749 - F3
MILLBRAE SQUARE BROADWAY & MEADOW GLEN AV, MLBR, 94030	728 - A3
MILLS PARK EL CAMINO REAL & SAN BRUNO AV, SBRN, 94066, (510)392-2780	707 - H6
PACIFIC MANOR MANOR PZ, PCFA, 94044	706 - J8
REDWOOD PLAZA BROADWAY & MAIN ST, RDWC, 94063	770 - B6
SAN BRUNO TOWNE CENTER EL CAMINO REAL & NOOR AV, SBRN, 94066	707 - H5
SEAPORT VILLAGE NORTH SEAPORT BLVD & SEAPORT CT, RDWC, 94063	770 - C3
SEQUOIA STATION JEFFERSON AV & EL CAMINO REAL, RDWC, 94063	770 - A6
SERRA CENTER JUNIPERO SERRA & SERRAMONTE BL, CLMA, 94014	687 - C7
SERRAMONTE PLAZA SERRAMONTE BLVD & GELLERT BLVD, DALY, 94015	707 - C1
SHARON HEIGHTS CENTER 325 SHARON PARK DR, MLPK, 94025, (650)854-5053	790 - E7
SKYCREST CENTER SAN BRUNO AV & GLENVIEW DR, SBRN, 94066	727 - F1
SKYLINE PLAZA SOUTHGATE AV & HIGATE DR, DALY, 94015	687 - A6
STRAWFLOWER VILLAGE MAIN ST & PILARCITOS AV, HMBY, 94019	767 - F7
THE STANFORD BARN SHOPPING CENTER QUARRY RD & WELCH RD, PA, 94304	790 - G5
TOWN & COUNTRY VILLAGE EL CAMINO REAL & EMBARCADERO R, PA, 94301, (510)325-3266	790 - J5
WOODSIDE CENTRAL EL CAMINO REAL & REDWOOD AV, RDWC, 94061	770 - B7
WOODSIDE PLAZA WOODSIDE AV & KENTUCKY ST, RDWC, 94061, (650)772-7000	790 - A3

SHOPPING MALLS

FEATURE NAME Address City, ZIP Code	PAGE-GRID
HILLSDALE CENTER 60 HILLSDALE BLVD, SMTO, 94403, (650)345-8222	749 - B5
ISLAND CENTER FASHION ISLAND BLVD, SMTO, 94404, (650)570-5300	749 - E2
SERRAMONTE CENTER SERRAMONTE BLVD & CALLAN BLVD, DALY, 94015, (650)992-8686	687 - C7
STANFORD SHOPPING CENTER 180 EL CAMINO REAL, PA, 94304, (650)617-8585	790 - G5
TANFORAN PARK EL CAMINO REAL, SBRN, 94066, (650)873-2000	707 - H5
WESTLAKE CENTER 285 LAKE MERCED BLVD, DALY, 94015, (650)756-2161	687 - A3

TRANSPORTATION

FEATURE NAME Address City, ZIP Code	PAGE-GRID
BALBOA PARK STATION OCEAN AV & SAN JOSE AV, SF, 94112	687 - E1
BAYSHORE CALTRAIN STATION TUNNEL AV & VISITACION AV, SF, 94134	688 - A2
CALTRAIN ATHERTON STATION FAIR OAKS LN & DINKLESPEIL STA, ATN, 94027	790 - E2
CALTRAIN BELMONT STATION EL CAMINO REAL & RALSTON AV, BLMT, 94002	769 - E1
CALTRAIN BROADWAY STATION BROADWAY & CALIFORNIA DR, BURL, 94010	728 - E5
CALTRAIN BURLINGAME STATION BURLINGAME AV & CALIFORNIA DR, BURL, 94010	728 - G6
CALTRAIN CALIFORNIA AV STATION PARK BLVD & CALIFORNIA AV, PA, 94306	791 - B7
CALTRAIN HAYWARD PARK STATION 16TH AV, SMTO, 94402	749 - B3
CALTRAIN HILLSDALE STATION E HILLSDALE BL & EL CM REAL, SMTO, 94403	749 - C5
CALTRAIN MENLO PARK STATION STA CRUZ AV & MERRILL ST, MLPK, 94025	790 - F3
CALTRAIN MILLBRAE STATION E MILLBRAE & CALIFORNIA, MLBR, 94030	728 - C4
CALTRAIN PALO ALTO STATION UNIVERSITY AV & MITCHELL LN, PA, 94301	790 - H5
CALTRAIN REDWOOD CITY STATION BROADWAY & WINSLOW ST, RDWC, 94063	770 - A6
CALTRAIN S SAN FRANCISCO STATION DUBUQUE AV & GRAND AV, SSF, 94080	708 - A3
CALTRAIN SAN BRUNO STATION HUNTINGTON AV & SYLVAN AV, SBRN, 94066	707 - J7
CALTRAIN SAN CARLOS STATION EL CAMINO REAL & SAN CARLOS, SCAR, 94070	769 - G3
CALTRAIN SAN MATEO STATION 2ND AV & RAILROAD AV, SMTO, 94401	749 - A1
COLMA BART STATION EL CAMINO REAL & F ST, SMCo, 94014, (650)992-4398	687 - C6
DALY CITY STATION JOHN DALY BLVD & DE LONG ST, DALY, 94014	687 - C3
GREEN MUNI CENTER SAN JOSE AV & GENEVA AV, SF, 94112	687 - E1
SAMTRANS TRANSIT TRANSFER POINT 1ST AV & B ST, SMTO, 94401	748 - J1
SAMTRANS TRANSIT TRANSFER POINT AIRPORT BL & LINDEN AV, SSF, 94080	708 - A2
SAMTRANS TRANSIT TRANSFER POINT ARROYO DR & EL CAMINO REAL, SSF, 94080	707 - F3
SAMTRANS TRANSIT TRANSFER POINT BAYSHORE BLVD & TUNNEL AV, BSBN, 94005	688 - B6
SAMTRANS TRANSIT TRANSFER POINT CRESPI DR & CABRILLO HWY, PCFA, 94044	726 - H3
SAMTRANS TRANSIT TRANSFER POINT E HILLSDALE BL & EL CM REAL, SMTO, 94403	749 - C5
SAMTRANS TRANSIT TRANSFER POINT EL CAMINO REAL & JAMES AV, RDWC, 94063	770 - A6
SAMTRANS TRANSIT TRANSFER POINT EL CAMINO REAL & OAK GROVE AV, MLPK, 94025	790 - F3
SAMTRANS TRANSIT TRANSFER POINT HILLSDALE SHOPPING CENTER, SMTO, 94403	749 - C6
SAMTRANS TRANSIT TRANSFER POINT HWY 92 & 101 FWY, SMTO, 94403	749 - C3
SAMTRANS TRANSIT TRANSFER POINT JOHN DALY BLVD & DE LONG ST, DALY, 94014	687 - C3
SAMTRANS TRANSIT TRANSFER POINT JUNIPERO SERRA BLVD & D ST, DALY, 94014	687 - C6
SAMTRANS TRANSIT TRANSFER POINT LINDA MAR BLVD & CABRILLO HWY, PCFA, 94044	726 - H4
SAMTRANS TRANSIT TRANSFER POINT MURCHISON DR & EL CAMINO REAL, MLBR, 94030	728 - B4
SAMTRANS TRANSIT TRANSFER POINT OCEANA BLVD & MANOR DR, PCFA, 94044	706 - J3
SAMTRANS TRANSIT TRANSFER POINT SAN CARLOS & EL CAMINO REAL, SCAR, 94070	769 - G3
SAMTRANS TRANSIT TRANSFER POINT SERRAMONTE CENTER, DALY, 94015	707 - C1
SAMTRANS TRANSIT TRANSFER POINT TANFORAN PARK, SBRN, 94066	707 - H5
SAMTRANS TRANSIT TRANSFER POINT VETERANS BL & WHIPPLE AV, RDWC, 94063	770 - A4
SAMTRANS TRANSIT TRANSFER POINT W MANOR DR & MANOR PZ, PCFA, 94044	706 - J3
SAMTRANS TRANSIT TRANSFER POINT WESTBOROUGH BL & GELLERT BLVD, SSF, 94080	707 - D4

WINERIES

FEATURE NAME Address City, ZIP Code	PAGE-GRID
OBESTER WINERY 12341 HALF MOON BAY RD, SMCo, (650)726-9463	767 - H6

1998 OLD TO NEW Page Conversion List

OLD-NEW

…06 - F5
706 - F6
… 706 - F7
D4 726 - F1
D5 726 - F3
D6 726 - F4
E1 706 - H5
E2 706 - H6
E3 706 - H7
E4 726 - G1
E5 726 - G3
E6 726 - G4
F1 706 - J5
F2 706 - J6
F3 706 - J7
F4 726 - J1
F5 726 - J3
F6 726 - J4

Old 21
A3 686 - G1
A4 686 - G2
A5 686 - G3
A6 686 - G4
B3 686 - H1
B4 686 - H2
B5 686 - H3
B6 686 - H4
C3 686 - J1
C4 686 - J2
C5 686 - J3
C6 686 - J4
D3 687 - B1
D4 687 - A2
D5 687 - A3
D6 687 - A4
E3 687 - C1
E4 687 - C2
E5 687 - C3
E6 687 - C5
F3 687 - D1
F4 687 - D2
F5 687 - D4
F6 687 - D5

Old 22
A3 687 - E1
A4 687 - E2
A5 687 - E4
A6 687 - E5
B3 687 - F1
B4 687 - F2
B5 687 - F4
B6 687 - F5
C3 687 - G1
C4 687 - G2
C5 687 - G4
C6 687 - G5
D3 687 - J1
D4 687 - J3
D5 687 - H4
D6 687 - H5
E3 688 - A1
E4 688 - A3
E5 688 - A4
E6 688 - A5
F3 688 - B1
F4 688 - B3
F5 688 - B4
F6 688 - B5

Old 23
A1 687 - A5
A2 687 - A6
A3 707 - A1
A4 707 - A2
A5 707 - A3
A6 707 - A4
B1 687 - B5
B2 687 - B7
B3 707 - B1
B4 707 - B2
B5 707 - B3
B6 707 - B4
C1 687 - D6
C2 687 - D7
C3 707 - C1
C4 707 - C2
C5 707 - C3
C6 707 - C4
D1 687 - E6
D2 687 - E7
D3 707 - E1
D4 707 - E2
D5 707 - E3
D6 707 - E4
E1 687 - F6
E2 687 - F7
E3 707 - F1
E4 707 - F2
E5 707 - F3
E6 707 - F4
F1 687 - G6

OLD-NEW

…G7
…G1
…07 - G2
707 - G3
707 - G4

Old 24
A1 687 - H6
A2 687 - H7
A3 707 - H1
A4 707 - H2
A5 707 - H3
A6 707 - H4
B1 687 - J6
B2 687 - J7
B3 707 - J1
B4 707 - J2
B5 707 - J3
B6 707 - J4
C1 688 - B6
C2 688 - B7
C3 708 - B1
C4 708 - B2
C5 708 - B3
C6 708 - A4
D1 688 - C6
D2 688 - C7
D3 708 - C1
D4 708 - C2
D5 708 - C3
D6 708 - C4
E1 688 - D6
E2 688 - D7
E3 708 - D1
E4 708 - D2
E5 708 - D3
E6 708 - D4
F1 688 - E6
F2 688 - E7
F3 708 - E1
F4 708 - E2
F5 708 - E3
F6 708 - E4

Old 25
A1 707 - A5
A2 707 - A6
A3 707 - A7
A4 727 - A1
A5 727 - A3
A6 727 - A4
B1 707 - B5
B2 707 - B6
B3 707 - B7
B4 727 - B1
B5 727 - B3
B6 727 - B4
C1 707 - C5
C2 707 - C6
C3 707 - C7
C4 727 - C2
C5 727 - C3
C6 727 - C4
D1 707 - E5
D2 707 - E6
D3 707 - E7
D4 727 - D2
D5 727 - D3
D6 727 - D4
E1 707 - F5
E2 707 - F6
E3 707 - F7
E4 727 - F2
E5 727 - F3
E6 727 - F4
F1 707 - G5
F2 707 - G6
F3 707 - G7
F4 727 - G2
F5 727 - G3
F6 727 - G4

Old 26
A1 707 - H5
A2 707 - H6
A3 727 - H1
A4 727 - H2
A5 727 - H3
A6 727 - H4
B1 707 - J5
B2 707 - J6
B3 727 - J1
B4 727 - J2
B5 727 - J3
B6 727 - J4
C1 708 - B5
C2 708 - A6
C3 728 - A1
C4 728 - A2
C5 728 - A3
C6 728 - A4
D1 708 - C5
D2 708 - C6
D3 728 - C1
D4 728 - C2
D5 728 - C3
D6 728 - C4
E1 708 - D5
E2 708 - D6
E3 728 - D1

OLD-NEW

Old 26
E4 728 - D2
E5 728 - D3
E6 728 - D4
F1 708 - E5
F2 708 - E6
F3 728 - E1
F4 728 - E2
F5 728 - E3
F6 728 - E4

Old 27
A1 726 - C5
A2 726 - C6
A3 726 - C7
A4 746 - B1
A5 746 - B2
A6 746 - B3
B1 726 - D5
B2 726 - D6
B3 726 - D7
B4 746 - D1
B5 746 - D2
B6 746 - D3
C1 726 - E5
C2 726 - E6
C3 726 - E7
C4 746 - E1
C5 746 - E2
C6 746 - E3
D1 726 - F5
D2 726 - F6
D3 726 - F7
D4 746 - F1
D5 746 - F2
D6 746 - F3
E1 726 - G5
E2 726 - G6
E3 726 - G7
E4 746 - G1
E5 746 - G2
E6 746 - G3
F1 726 - J5
F2 726 - J6
F3 726 - J7
F4 746 - J1
F5 746 - J2
F6 746 - H3

Old 27A
A1 727 - A5
A2 727 - A6
A3 727 - A7
A4 747 - A1
A5 747 - A2
A6 747 - A3
B1 727 - B5
B2 727 - B6
B3 727 - B7
B4 747 - B1
B5 747 - B2
B6 747 - B3
C1 727 - C5
C2 727 - C6
C3 727 - C7
C4 747 - C1
C5 747 - C2
C6 747 - C3
D1 727 - D5
D2 727 - D6
D3 727 - D7
D4 747 - D1
D5 747 - D2
D6 747 - D3
E1 727 - F5
E2 727 - F6
E3 727 - F7
E4 747 - F1
E5 747 - F2
E6 747 - F4
F1 727 - G5
F2 727 - G6
F3 727 - G7
F4 747 - G1
F5 747 - G2
F6 747 - G4

Old 28
A1 727 - H5
A2 727 - H6
A3 727 - H7
A4 747 - H1
A5 747 - H2
A6 747 - H4
B1 727 - J5
B2 727 - J6
B3 727 - J7
B4 747 - J1
B5 747 - J2
B6 747 - J4
C1 728 - A5
C2 728 - A6
C3 728 - A7
C4 748 - A1
C5 748 - A2
C6 748 - A4
D1 728 - C5
D2 728 - C6
D3 728 - C7
D4 748 - C1
D5 748 - C3

OLD-NEW

Old 28
D6 748 - C4
E1 728 - D5
E2 728 - D6
E3 728 - D7
E4 748 - D1
E5 748 - D3
E6 748 - D4
F1 728 - E5
F2 728 - E6
F3 728 - E7
F4 748 - E1
F5 748 - E3
F6 748 - E4

Old 29
A1 728 - F5
A2 728 - F6
A3 728 - F7
A4 748 - F1
A5 748 - F3
A6 748 - F4
B1 728 - G5
B2 728 - G6
B3 728 - G7
B4 748 - G1
B5 748 - G3
B6 748 - G4
C1 728 - J5
C2 728 - J6
C3 728 - J7
C4 748 - J1
C5 748 - J3
C6 748 - J4
D1 729 - A5
D2 729 - A6
D3 729 - A7
D4 749 - A1
D5 749 - A3
D6 749 - A4
E1 729 - B5
E2 729 - B6
E3 729 - B7
E4 749 - B2
E5 749 - B3
E6 749 - B4
F1 729 - C5
F2 729 - C6
F3 729 - C7
F4 749 - C2
F5 749 - C3
F6 749 - C4

Old 29A
A1 729 - D5
A2 729 - D6
A3 729 - D7
A4 749 - D2
A5 749 - D3
A6 749 - D4
B1 729 - E5
B2 729 - E6
B3 729 - E7
B4 749 - E2
B5 749 - E3
B6 749 - E4
C1 729 - G5
C2 729 - G6
C3 729 - G7
C4 749 - G2
C5 749 - G3
C6 749 - G4
D1 729 - H5
D2 729 - H6
D3 729 - H7
D4 749 - H2
D5 749 - H3
D6 749 - H4
E1 729 - J5
E2 729 - J6
E3 729 - J7
E4 749 - J2
E5 749 - J3
E6 749 - J4
F4 750 - A2
F5 750 - A3
F6 750 - A4

Old 30
A1 746 - B4
A2 746 - B5
A3 746 - B6
A4 766 - B1
A5 766 - B2
A6 766 - B3
B1 746 - D4
B2 746 - C5
B3 746 - C6
B4 766 - C1
B5 766 - C2
B6 766 - C3
C1 746 - E4
C2 746 - E5
C3 746 - E6
C4 766 - E1
C5 766 - E2
C6 766 - E3
D1 746 - F4
D2 746 - F5
D3 746 - F6
D4 766 - F1

OLD-NEW

Old 30
D5 766 - F2
D6 766 - F3
E1 746 - G4
E2 746 - G5
E3 746 - G6
E4 766 - G1
E5 766 - G2
E6 766 - G3
F1 746 - H4
F2 746 - H5
F3 746 - H7
F4 766 - H1
F5 766 - H2
F6 766 - H3

Old 30A
A1 746 - J4
A2 746 - J5
A3 746 - J6
A4 766 - J1
A5 766 - J2
A6 766 - J3
B1 747 - B4
B2 747 - B5
B3 747 - B7
B4 767 - B1
B5 767 - B2
B6 767 - B3
C1 747 - C4
C2 747 - C5
C3 747 - C7
C4 767 - C1
C5 767 - C2
C6 767 - C3
D1 747 - D4
D2 747 - D5
D3 747 - D7
D4 767 - D1
D5 767 - D2
D6 767 - D3
E1 747 - F4
E2 747 - E5
E3 747 - E7
E4 767 - E1
E5 767 - E2
E6 767 - E3
F1 747 - G4
F2 747 - G6
F3 747 - G7
F4 767 - G1
F5 767 - G2
F6 767 - G3

Old 31
A1 747 - H5
A2 747 - H6
A3 747 - H7
A4 767 - H1
A5 767 - H2
A6 767 - H3
B1 747 - J5
B2 747 - J6
B3 747 - J7
B4 767 - J1
B5 767 - J2
B6 767 - J3
C1 748 - A5
C2 748 - A6
C3 748 - A7
C4 768 - A1
C5 768 - A2
C6 768 - A3
D1 748 - C5
D2 748 - B6
D3 748 - B7
D4 768 - B1
D5 768 - B2
D6 768 - B3
E1 748 - D5
E2 748 - D6
E3 748 - D7
E4 768 - D1
E5 768 - D2
E6 768 - D3
F1 748 - E5
F2 748 - E6
F3 748 - E7
F4 768 - E1
F5 768 - E2
F6 768 - E3

Old 32
A1 748 - F5
A2 748 - F6
A3 748 - F7
A4 768 - F1
A5 768 - F2
A6 768 - F3
B1 748 - G5
B2 748 - G6
B3 748 - G7
B4 768 - G1
B5 768 - G2
B6 768 - G3
C1 748 - J5
C2 748 - H6
C3 748 - H7
C4 768 - H1
C5 768 - H2
C6 768 - H3

OLD-NEW

Old 32
D1 749 - A5
D2 749 - A6
D3 749 - A7
D4 769 - A1
D5 769 - A2
D6 769 - A3
E1 749 - B5
E2 749 - B6
E3 749 - B7
E4 769 - B1
E5 769 - B2
E6 769 - B3
F1 749 - C5
F2 749 - C6
F3 749 - C7
F4 769 - C1
F5 769 - C2
F6 769 - C4

Old 33
A1 749 - D5
A2 749 - D6
A3 749 - D7
A4 769 - D1
A5 769 - D2
A6 769 - D4
B1 749 - E5
B2 749 - E6
B3 749 - E7
B4 769 - E1
B5 769 - E2
B6 769 - E4
C1 749 - G5
C2 749 - G6
C3 749 - G7
C4 769 - G1
C5 769 - G2
C6 769 - G4
D1 749 - H5
D2 749 - H6
D3 749 - H7
D4 769 - H1
D5 769 - H3
D6 769 - H4
E1 749 - J5
E2 749 - J6
E3 749 - J7
E4 769 - J1
E5 769 - J3
E6 769 - J4
F1 750 - A5
F2 750 - A6
F3 750 - A7
F4 770 - A1
F5 770 - A3
F6 770 - A4

Old 33A
A1 750 - B5
A2 750 - B6
A3 750 - B7
A4 770 - B1
A5 770 - B3
A6 770 - B4
B1 750 - D5
B2 750 - D6
B3 750 - D7
B4 770 - D1
B5 770 - D3
B6 770 - D4
C1 750 - E5
C2 750 - E6
C3 750 - E7
C4 770 - E2
C5 770 - E3
C6 770 - E4
D1 750 - F5
D2 750 - F6
D3 750 - F7
D4 770 - F2
D5 770 - F3
D6 770 - F4
E1 750 - H5
E2 750 - G6
E3 750 - G7
E4 770 - G2
E5 770 - G3
E6 770 - G4
F1 750 - J5
F2 750 - J6
F3 750 - J7
F4 770 - J2
F5 770 - J3
F6 770 - J4

Old 34
A1 766 - J4
A2 766 - J5
A3 766 - J6
A4 766 - J7
B1 767 - B4
B2 767 - B5
B3 767 - B6
B4 767 - A7
B5 787 - A1
B6 787 - A3
C1 767 - C4
C2 767 - C5
C3 767 - C6
C4 767 - C7

OLD-NEW

Old 34
C5 787 - C2
C6 787 - C3
D1 767 - D4
D2 767 - D5
D3 767 - D6
D4 767 - D7
D5 787 - D2
D6 787 - D3
E1 767 - E4
E2 767 - E5
E3 767 - E6
E4 767 - E7
E5 787 - E2
E6 787 - E3
F1 767 - G4
F2 767 - G5
F3 767 - G6
F4 767 - F7
F5 787 - F2
F6 787 - F3

Old 34A
A1 767 - H4
A2 767 - H5
A3 767 - H6
A4 767 - H7
A5 787 - H2
A6 787 - G3
B1 767 - J4
B2 767 - J5
B3 767 - J6
B4 787 - J1
B5 787 - J2
B6 787 - J3
C1 768 - A4
C2 768 - A5
C3 768 - A6
C4 788 - A1
C5 788 - A2
C6 788 - A3
D1 768 - B4
D2 768 - B5
D3 768 - B6
D4 788 - B1
D5 788 - B2
D6 788 - B3
E1 768 - D4
E2 768 - D5
E3 768 - D6
E4 788 - D1
E5 788 - D2
E6 788 - D3
F1 768 - E4
F2 768 - E5
F3 768 - E7
F4 788 - E1
F5 788 - E2
F6 788 - E3

Old 35
A1 768 - F4
A2 768 - F5
A3 768 - F7
A4 788 - F1
A5 788 - F2
A6 788 - F3
B1 768 - G4
B2 768 - G5
B3 768 - G7
B4 788 - G1
B5 788 - G2
B6 788 - G3
C1 768 - H4
C2 768 - H5
C3 768 - H7
C4 788 - H1
C5 788 - H2
C6 788 - H3
D1 769 - A4
D2 769 - A5
D3 769 - A7
D4 789 - A1
D5 789 - A2
D6 789 - A3
E1 769 - B4
E2 769 - B5
E3 769 - B7
E4 789 - B1
E5 789 - B2
E6 789 - B3
F1 769 - C4
F2 769 - C6
F3 769 - C7
F4 789 - C1
F5 789 - C2
F6 789 - C3

Old 36
A1 769 - D4
A2 769 - D6
A3 769 - D7
A4 789 - D1
A5 789 - D2
A6 789 - D3
B1 769 - E4
B2 769 - E6
B3 769 - E7
B4 789 - E1
B5 789 - E2
B6 789 - E3

OLD-NEW

Old 36
C1 769 - F5
C2 769 - F6
C3 769 - F7
C4 789 - F1
C5 789 - F2
C6 789 - F3
D1 769 - H5
D2 769 - H6
D3 769 - H7
D4 789 - H1
D5 789 - H2
D6 789 - H3
E1 769 - J5
E2 769 - J6
E3 769 - J7
E4 789 - J1
E5 789 - J2
E6 789 - J3
F1 770 - A5
F2 770 - A6
F3 770 - A7
F4 790 - A1
F5 790 - A2
F6 790 - A3

Old 37
A1 770 - B5
A2 770 - B6
A3 770 - B7
A4 790 - B1
A5 790 - B2
A6 790 - B3
B1 770 - D5
B2 770 - C6
B3 770 - C7
B4 790 - C1
B5 790 - C2
B6 790 - C3
C1 770 - E5
C2 770 - E6
C3 770 - E7
C4 790 - E1
C5 790 - E2
C6 790 - E3
D1 770 - F5
D2 770 - F6
D3 770 - F7
D4 790 - F1
D5 790 - F2
D6 790 - F3
E1 770 - G5
E2 770 - G6
E3 770 - G7
E4 790 - G1
E5 790 - G2
E6 790 - G3
F1 770 - J5
F2 770 - J6
F3 770 - J7
F4 790 - J1
F5 790 - H2
F6 790 - H3

Old 38
A1 771 - A5
A2 771 - A6
A3 771 - A7
A4 791 - A1
A5 791 - A2
A6 790 - J3
B1 771 - B5
B2 771 - B6
B3 771 - B7
B4 791 - B1
B5 791 - B2
B6 791 - B4
C1 771 - C5
C2 771 - C6
C3 771 - C7
C4 791 - C1
C5 791 - C2
C6 791 - C4
D1 771 - D5
D2 771 - D6
D3 771 - D7
D4 791 - D1
D5 791 - D2
D6 791 - D4
E1 771 - E5
E2 771 - E6
E3 771 - E7
E4 791 - E1
E5 791 - E2
E6 791 - E4
F1 771 - G5
F2 771 - G6
F3 771 - G7
F4 791 - G1
F5 791 - G2
F6 791 - G4

Old 39
B1 787 - A4
B2 787 - A5
B3 787 - A6
B4 787 - A7
B5 807 - A1
B6 807 - A2
C1 787 - C4
C2 787 - C5

OLD-NEW

Old 39
C3 787 - C6
C4 787 - C7
C5 807 - C1
C6 807 - C2
D1 787 - D4
D2 787 - D5
D3 787 - D6
D4 787 - D7
D5 807 - D1
D6 807 - D2
E1 787 - E4
E2 787 - E5
E3 787 - E6
E4 787 - E7
E5 807 - E1
E6 807 - E2
F1 787 - F4
F2 787 - F5
F3 787 - F6
F4 787 - F7
F5 807 - F1
F6 807 - F2

Old 40
A1 787 - G4
A2 787 - G5
A3 787 - G6
A4 787 - G7
A5 807 - G1
A6 807 - G2
B1 787 - J4
B2 787 - J5
B3 787 - J6
B4 787 - H7
B5 807 - H1
B6 807 - H2
C1 788 - A4
C2 788 - A5
C3 788 - A6
C4 788 - A7
C5 808 - A1
C6 808 - A2
D1 788 - B4
D2 788 - B5
D3 788 - B6
D4 788 - B7
D5 808 - B1
D6 808 - B3
E1 788 - C4
E2 788 - C5
E3 788 - C6
E4 788 - C7
E5 808 - C1
E6 808 - C3
F1 788 - E4
F2 788 - E5
F3 788 - E6
F4 788 - D7
F5 808 - D1
F6 808 - D3

Old 41
A1 788 - F4
A2 788 - F5
A3 788 - F6
A4 788 - F7
A5 808 - F1
A6 808 - F3
B1 788 - G4
B2 788 - G5
B3 788 - G6
B4 788 - G7
B5 808 - G2
B6 808 - G3
C1 788 - H4
C2 788 - H5
C3 788 - H6
C4 788 - H7
C5 808 - H2
C6 808 - H3
D1 788 - J4
D2 788 - J5
D3 788 - J6
D4 788 - J7
D5 808 - J2
D6 808 - J3
E1 789 - B4
E2 789 - B5
E3 789 - B6
E4 789 - B7
E5 809 - B2
E6 809 - B3
F1 789 - C4
F2 789 - C5
F3 789 - C6
F4 789 - C7
F5 809 - C2
F6 809 - C3

Old 42
A1 789 - D4
A2 789 - D5
A3 789 - D6
A4 809 - D1
A5 809 - D2
A6 809 - D3
B1 789 - E4
B2 789 - E5
B3 789 - E6
B4 809 - E1

OLD-NEW

Old 42
B5 809 - E2
B6 809 - E3
C1 789 - F4
C2 789 - F5
C3 789 - F6
C4 809 - F1
C5 809 - F2
C6 809 - F3
D1 789 - H4
D2 789 - H5
D3 789 - H6
D4 809 - G1
D5 809 - G2
D6 809 - G3
E1 789 - J4
E2 789 - J5
E3 789 - J6
E4 809 - J1
E5 809 - J2
E6 809 - J3
F1 790 - A4
F2 790 - A5
F3 790 - A6
F4 810 - A1
F5 810 - A2
F6 810 - A3

Old 43
A1 790 - B4
A2 790 - B5
A3 790 - B7
A4 810 - B1
A5 810 - B2
A6 810 - B3
B1 790 - C4
B2 790 - C5
B3 790 - C7
B4 810 - C1
B5 810 - C2
B6 810 - C3
C1 790 - E4
C2 790 - E5
C3 790 - E7
C4 810 - E1
C5 810 - E2
C6 810 - E3
D1 790 - F4
D2 790 - F5
D3 790 - F7
D4 810 - F1
D5 810 - F2
D6 810 - F3
E1 790 - G4
E2 790 - G5
E3 790 - G7
E4 810 - G1
E5 810 - G2
E6 810 - G3
F1 790 - H4
F2 790 - H5
F3 790 - H7
F4 810 - H1
F5 810 - H2
F6 810 - H3

Old 44
A1 807 - G3
A2 807 - G5
A3 807 - G6
A4 807 - G7
A5 827 - G1
A6 827 - G2
B1 807 - J3
B2 807 - J5
B3 807 - J6
B4 807 - H7
B5 827 - H1
B6 827 - H2
C1 808 - A3
C2 808 - A5
C3 808 - A6
C4 808 - A7
C5 828 - A1
C6 828 - A2
D1 808 - B4
D2 808 - B5
D3 808 - B6
D4 808 - B7
D5 828 - B1
D6 828 - B2
E1 808 - C4
E2 808 - C5
E3 808 - C6
E4 808 - C7
E5 828 - C1
E6 828 - C2
F1 808 - D4
F2 808 - D5
F3 808 - D6
F4 808 - D7
F5 828 - D1
F6 828 - D2

Old 45
A1 808 - F4
A2 808 - E5
A3 808 - E6
A4 808 - E7
A5 828 - E1
A6 828 - E2

OLD-NEW

Old 45
B1 808 - G4
B2 808 - G5
B3 808 - G6
B4 808 - G7
B5 828 - G1
B6 828 - G2
C1 808 - H4
C2 808 - H5
C3 808 - H6
C4 808 - H7
C5 828 - H1
C6 828 - H2
D1 808 - J4
D2 808 - J5
D3 808 - J6
D4 808 - J7
D5 828 - J1
D6 828 - J2
E1 809 - B4
E2 809 - A5
E3 809 - A6
E4 809 - A7
E5 829 - A1
E6 829 - A2
F1 809 - C4
F2 809 - C5
F3 809 - C6
F4 809 - C7
F5 829 - C1
F6 829 - C2

Old 46
A1 809 - D4
A2 809 - D5
A3 809 - D6
A4 809 - D7
A5 829 - D1
A6 829 - D2
B1 809 - E4
B2 809 - E5
B3 809 - E6
B4 809 - E7
B5 829 - E1
B6 829 - E2
C1 809 - F4
C2 809 - F5
C3 809 - F6
C4 809 - F7
C5 829 - F1
C6 829 - F2
D1 809 - G4
D2 809 - G5
D3 808 - G6
D4 809 - G7
D5 829 - G1
D6 829 - G2
E1 809 - J4
E2 809 - J5
E3 809 - J6
E4 809 - J7
E5 829 - J1
E6 829 - J2
F1 810 - A4
F2 810 - A5
F3 810 - A6
F4 810 - A7
F5 830 - A1
F6 830 - A3

Old 47
A1 810 - B4
A2 810 - B5
A3 810 - B6
A4 810 - B7
A5 830 - B1
A6 830 - B3
B1 810 - C4
B2 810 - C5
B3 810 - C6
B4 810 - C7
B5 830 - C1
B6 830 - C3
C1 810 - E4
C2 810 - D5
C3 810 - D6
C4 810 - D7
C5 830 - D2
C6 830 - D3
D1 810 - F4
D2 810 - F5
D3 810 - F6
D4 810 - F7
D5 830 - F2
D6 830 - F3
E1 810 - G4
E2 810 - G5
E3 810 - G6
E4 810 - G7
E5 830 - G2
E6 830 - G3
F1 810 - H4
F2 810 - H5
F3 810 - H6
F4 830 - H1
F5 830 - H2
F6 830 - H3

Old 48
A1 827 - G3
A2 827 - G4

OLD-NEW

Old 48
A3 827 - G5
A4 827 - G6
A5 827 - G7
A6 847 - G2
B1 827 - H3
B2 827 - H4
B3 827 - H5
B4 827 - H6
B5 827 - H7
B6 847 - H2
C1 828 - A3
C2 828 - A4
C3 828 - A5
C4 828 - A6
C5 828 - A7
C6 848 - A2
D1 828 - B3
D2 828 - B4
D3 828 - B5
D4 828 - B6
D5 828 - B7
D6 848 - B2
E1 828 - C3
E2 828 - C4
E3 828 - C5
E4 828 - C6
E5 828 - C7
E6 848 - C2
F1 828 - D3
F2 828 - D4
F3 828 - D5
F4 828 - D6
F5 828 - D7
F6 848 - D2

Old 48A
A1 847 - G3
A2 847 - G4
A3 847 - G5
A4 847 - G6
A5 847 - G7
A6 867 - G1
B1 847 - H3
B2 847 - H4
B3 847 - H5
B4 847 - H6
B5 847 - H7
B6 867 - H1
C1 848 - A3
C2 847 - J4
C3 847 - J5
C4 847 - J6
C5 847 - J7
C6 867 - J1
D1 848 - B3
D2 848 - B4
D3 848 - B5
D4 848 - B6
D5 848 - B7
D6 868 - B1
E1 848 - C3
E2 848 - C4
E3 848 - C5
E4 848 - C6
E5 848 - C7
E6 868 - C1
F1 848 - D3
F2 848 - D4
F3 848 - D5
F4 848 - D6
F5 848 - D7
F6 868 - D1

Old 49
A1 828 - E3
A2 828 - E4
A3 828 - E5
A4 828 - E6
A5 828 - E7
A6 848 - E2
B1 828 - G3
B2 828 - G4
B3 828 - F5
B4 828 - F6
B5 828 - F7
B6 848 - F2
C1 828 - H3
C2 828 - H4
C3 828 - H5
C4 828 - H6
C5 828 - H7
C6 848 - H2
D1 828 - J3
D2 828 - J4
D3 828 - J5
D4 828 - J6
D5 828 - J7
D6 848 - J2
E1 829 - A3
E2 829 - A4
E3 829 - A5
E4 829 - A6
E5 829 - A7
E6 849 - A2
F1 829 - B3
F2 829 - B4
F3 829 - B5
F4 829 - B6
F5 829 - B7

OLD-NEW

Old 49
F6 849 - B2

Old 49A
A1 848 - E3
A2 848 - E4
A3 848 - E5
A4 848 - E6
A5 848 - E7
A6 868 - E1
B1 848 - F3
B2 848 - F4
B3 848 - F5
B4 848 - F6
B5 848 - F7
B6 868 - F1
C1 848 - H3
C2 848 - H4
C3 848 - H5
C4 848 - H6
C5 848 - H7
C6 868 - H1
D1 848 - J3
D2 848 - J4
D3 848 - J5
D4 848 - J6
D5 848 - J7
D6 868 - J1
E1 849 - A3
E2 849 - A4
E3 849 - A5
E4 849 - A6
E5 849 - A7
E6 869 - A1
F1 849 - B3
F2 849 - B4
F3 849 - B5
F4 849 - B6
F5 849 - B7
F6 869 - B1

Old 50
A1 829 - C3
A2 829 - C4
A3 829 - C5
A4 829 - C6
A5 849 - C1
A6 849 - C2
B1 829 - E3
B2 829 - E4
B3 829 - E5
B4 829 - E7
B5 849 - E1
B6 849 - E2
C1 829 - F3
C2 829 - F4
C3 829 - F5
C4 829 - F7
C5 849 - F1
C6 849 - F2
D1 829 - G3
D2 829 - G4
D3 829 - G6
D4 829 - G7
D5 849 - G1
D6 849 - G2
E1 829 - J3
E2 829 - J4
E3 829 - H6
E4 829 - H7
E5 849 - H1
E6 849 - H2
F1 830 - A3
F2 830 - A4
F3 830 - A6
F4 830 - A7
F5 850 - A1
F6 850 - A2

Old 50A
A1 849 - D3
A2 849 - D4
A3 849 - D5
A4 849 - D6
A5 849 - D7
A6 869 - D1
B1 849 - E3
B2 849 - E4
B3 849 - E5
B4 849 - E6
B5 849 - E7
B6 869 - E1
C1 849 - F3
C2 849 - F4
C3 849 - F5
C4 849 - F6
C5 849 - F7
C6 869 - F1
D1 849 - G3
D2 849 - G4
D3 849 - G5
D4 849 - G6
D5 849 - G7
D6 869 - G2
E1 849 - H3
E2 849 - H4
E3 849 - H5
E4 849 - H6
E5 849 - H7
E6 869 - H2
F1 849 - J3

OLD-NEW

Old 50A
F2 849 - J4
F3 849 - J5
F4 849 - J6
F5 849 - J7
F6 869 - J2

Old 51
A1 830 - B4
A2 830 - B5
A3 830 - B6
A4 830 - B7
A5 850 - B1
A6 850 - B2
B1 830 - C4
B2 830 - C5
B3 830 - C6
B4 830 - C7
B5 850 - C1
B6 850 - C2
C1 830 - D4
C2 830 - D5
C3 830 - D6
C4 830 - D7
C5 850 - D1
C6 850 - D2
D1 830 - F4
D2 830 - F5
D3 830 - F6
D4 830 - E7
D5 850 - E1
D6 850 - E2
E1 830 - G4
E2 830 - G5
E3 830 - G6
E4 830 - G7
E5 850 - G1
E6 850 - G2
F1 830 - H4
F2 830 - H5
F3 830 - H6
F4 830 - H7
F5 850 - H1
F6 850 - H2

Old 51A
A1 850 - B3
A2 850 - B4
A3 850 - B5
A4 850 - B6
A5 850 - B7
A6 870 - B2
B1 850 - C3
B2 850 - C4
B3 850 - C5
B4 850 - C6
B5 850 - C7
B6 870 - C2
C1 850 - D3
C2 850 - D4
C3 850 - D5
C4 850 - D6
C5 850 - D7
C6 870 - D2
D1 850 - E3
D2 850 - E4
D3 850 - E5
D4 850 - E6
D5 850 - E7
D6 870 - E2
E1 850 - G3
E2 850 - G4
E3 850 - F5
E4 850 - F6
E5 870 - F1
E6 870 - F2
F1 850 - H3
F2 850 - H4
F3 850 - H5
F4 850 - H6
F5 870 - H1
F6 870 - H2

Old 56
A1 867 - G2
A2 867 - G3
A3 867 - G4
A4 867 - G5
A5 867 - G7
A6 887 - G1
B1 867 - H2
B2 867 - H3
B3 867 - H4
B4 867 - H5
B5 867 - H7
B6 887 - H1
C1 867 - J2
C2 867 - J3
C3 867 - J4
C4 867 - J5
C5 867 - J7
C6 887 - J1
D1 868 - B2
D2 868 - B3
D3 868 - A4
D4 868 - A6
D5 868 - A7
D6 888 - A1
E1 868 - C2
E2 868 - C3
E3 868 - C4

OLD-NEW

Old 56
E4 868 - C6
E5 868 - C7
E6 888 - C1
F1 868 - D2
F2 868 - D3
F3 868 - D5
F4 868 - D6
F5 868 - D7
F6 888 - D1

Old 56A
A1 887 - G2
A2 887 - G3
A3 887 - G4
A4 887 - G5
A5 887 - G6
A6 887 - G7
B1 887 - H2
B2 887 - H3
B3 887 - H4
B4 887 - H5
B5 887 - H6
B6 887 - H7
C1 887 - J2
C2 887 - J3
C3 887 - J4
C4 887 - J5
C5 887 - J6
C6 887 - J7
D1 888 - A2
D2 888 - A3
D3 888 - A4
D4 888 - A5
D5 888 - A6
D6 888 - A7
E1 888 - C2
E2 888 - C3
E3 888 - C4
E4 888 - B5
E5 888 - B6
E6 888 - B7
F1 888 - D2
F2 888 - D3
F3 888 - D4
F4 888 - D5
F5 888 - D6
F6 888 - D7

Old 57
A1 868 - E2
A2 868 - E3
A3 868 - E5
A4 868 - E6
A5 868 - E7
A6 888 - E1
B1 868 - F2
B2 868 - F3
B3 868 - F5
B4 868 - F6
B5 868 - F7
B6 888 - F1
C1 868 - H2
C2 868 - G4
C3 868 - G5
C4 868 - G6
C5 868 - G7
C6 888 - G1
D1 868 - J2
D2 868 - J4
D3 868 - J5
D4 868 - J6
D5 868 - J7
D6 888 - J1
E1 869 - A2
E2 869 - A4
E3 869 - A5
E4 869 - A6
E5 869 - A7
E6 889 - A1
F1 869 - B3
F2 869 - B4
F3 869 - B5
F4 869 - B6
F5 869 - B7
F6 889 - B1

Old 57A
A1 888 - E2
A2 888 - E3
A3 888 - E4
A4 888 - E5
A5 888 - E6
A6 888 - E7
B1 888 - F2
B2 888 - F3
B3 888 - F4
B4 888 - F5
B5 888 - F6
B6 888 - F7
C1 888 - G2
C2 888 - G3
C3 888 - G4
C4 888 - G5
C5 888 - G6
C6 888 - G7
D1 888 - J2
D2 888 - J3
D3 888 - J4
D4 888 - J5
D5 888 - J6

OLD-NEW

Old 57A
D6 888 - J7
E1 889 - A2
E2 889 - A3
E3 889 - A4
E4 889 - A5
E5 889 - A6
E6 889 - A7
F1 889 - B2
F2 889 - B3
F3 889 - B4
F4 889 - B5
F5 889 - B6

Old 58
A1 869 - C3
A2 869 - C4
A3 869 - C5
A4 869 - C6
A5 869 - C7
A6 889 - C1
B1 869 - E3
B2 869 - E4
B3 869 - E5
B4 869 - E6
B5 869 - E7
B6 889 - E1
C1 869 - F3
C2 869 - F4
C3 869 - F5
C4 869 - F6
C5 869 - F7
C6 889 - F1
D1 869 - G3
D2 869 - G4
D3 869 - G5
D4 869 - G6
D5 869 - G7
D6 889 - G1
E1 869 - H3
E2 869 - H4
E3 869 - H5
E4 869 - H6
E5 869 - H7
E6 889 - H1
F1 869 - J3
F2 869 - J4
F3 869 - J5
F4 869 - J6
F5 869 - J7
F6 889 - J1

Old 58A
A1 889 - C2
A2 889 - C3
A3 889 - C4
A4 889 - C5
A5 889 - C6
B1 889 - D2
B2 889 - D3
B3 889 - D4
B4 889 - D5
B5 889 - D6
C1 889 - F2
C2 889 - F3
C3 889 - F4
C4 889 - F5
C5 889 - F6
D1 889 - G2
D2 889 - G3
D3 889 - G4
D4 889 - G5
D5 889 - G6
D6 889 - G7
E1 889 - H2
E2 889 - H3
E3 889 - H4
E4 889 - H5
E5 889 - H6
E6 889 - H7
F1 889 - J2
F2 889 - J3
F3 889 - J4
F4 889 - J5
F5 889 - J6
F6 889 - J7

Old 59
A1 870 - B3
A2 870 - B4
A3 870 - A5
A4 870 - A6
A5 870 - A7
A6 890 - A1
B1 870 - C3
B2 870 - C4
B3 870 - C5
B4 870 - C6
B5 870 - C7
B6 890 - C1
C1 870 - D3
C2 870 - D4
C3 870 - D5
C4 870 - D6
C5 870 - D7
C6 890 - D1
D1 870 - E3
D2 870 - E4
D3 870 - E5
D4 870 - E6
D5 870 - E7

OLD-NEW

Old 59
D6 890 - E1
E1 870 - F3
E2 870 - F4
E3 870 - F5
E4 870 - F6
E5 870 - F7
E6 890 - F1
F1 870 - G3
F2 870 - G4
F3 870 - G5
F4 870 - G6
F5 870 - G7
F6 890 - G1

Old 59A
A1 908 - E2
A2 908 - E3
A3 908 - E4
A4 908 - E5
A5 908 - E6
A6 928 - E1
B1 908 - F2
B2 908 - F3
B3 908 - F4
B4 908 - F5
B5 908 - F6
B6 928 - F1
C1 908 - G2
C2 908 - G3
C3 908 - G4
C4 908 - G5
C5 908 - G6
C6 928 - G1
D1 908 - H2
D2 908 - H3
D3 908 - H4
D4 908 - H5
D5 908 - H6
D6 928 - H1
E2 908 - J3
E3 908 - J4
E4 908 - J5
E5 908 - J6
E6 908 - J7

OLD-NEW

OLD-NEW

OLD-NEW

OLD-NEW

OLD-NEW

1998 SAN MATEO NEW TO OLD Page Conversion List

NEW-OLD	
New 686	
G1	21 - A3
G2	21 - A4
G3	21 - A5
G4	21 - A6
H1	21 - B3
H2	21 - B4
H3	21 - B5
H4	21 - B6
J1	21 - C3
J2	21 - C4
J3	21 - C5
J4	21 - C6
J5	19 - A1
J6	19 - A2
J7	19 - A2
New 687	
A1	21 - D3
A2	21 - D4
A3	21 - D5
A4	21 - D5
A5	23 - A1
A6	23 - A2
A7	23 - A2
B1	21 - D3
B2	21 - D4
B3	21 - D5
B4	21 - D5
B5	23 - B1
B6	23 - B2
B7	23 - B2
C1	21 - E3
C2	21 - E4
C3	21 - E5
C4	21 - E5
C5	21 - E6
C6	23 - C2
C7	23 - C2
D1	21 - F3
D2	21 - F4
D3	21 - F5
D4	21 - F5
D5	21 - F6
D6	23 - C1
D7	23 - C2
E1	22 - A3
E2	22 - A4
E3	22 - A5
E4	22 - A5
E5	22 - A6
E6	23 - D1
E7	23 - D2
F1	22 - B3
F2	22 - B4
F3	22 - B4
F4	22 - B5
F5	22 - B6
F6	23 - E1
F7	23 - E2
G1	22 - C3
G2	22 - C4
G3	22 - C4
G4	22 - C5
G5	22 - C6
G6	23 - F1
G7	23 - F2
H1	22 - D3
H2	22 - D4
H3	22 - D4
H4	22 - D5
H5	22 - D6
H6	24 - A1
H7	24 - A2
J1	22 - D3
J2	22 - D4
J3	22 - D4
J4	22 - D5
J5	22 - D6
J6	24 - B1
J7	24 - B2
New 688	
A1	22 - E3
A2	22 - E3
A3	22 - E4
A4	22 - E5
A5	22 - E6
A6	24 - B1
A7	24 - C2
B1	22 - F3
B2	22 - F3
B3	22 - F4
B4	22 - F5
B5	22 - F6
B6	24 - C1
B7	24 - C2
C6	24 - D1
C7	24 - D2
D6	24 - E1
D7	24 - E2
E6	24 - F1
E7	24 - F2
F6	24 - F1
New 706	
F5	20 - D1
F6	20 - D2
F7	20 - D3
G5	20 - E1
G6	20 - E2

NEW-OLD	
New 706	
G7	20 - E3
H5	20 - E1
H6	20 - E2
H7	20 - E3
J1	19 - A3
J2	19 - A4
J3	19 - A5
J4	19 - A6
J5	20 - F1
J6	20 - F2
J7	20 - F3
New 707	
A1	23 - A3
A2	23 - A4
A3	23 - A5
A4	23 - A6
A5	25 - A1
A6	25 - A2
A7	25 - A3
B1	23 - B3
B2	23 - B4
B3	23 - B5
B4	23 - B6
B5	25 - B1
B6	25 - B2
B7	25 - B3
C1	23 - C3
C2	23 - C4
C3	23 - C5
C4	23 - C6
C5	25 - C1
C6	25 - C2
C7	25 - C3
D1	23 - C3
D2	23 - C4
D3	23 - C5
D4	23 - C6
D5	25 - C1
D6	25 - D2
D7	25 - D3
E1	23 - D3
E2	23 - D4
E3	23 - D5
E4	23 - D6
E5	25 - D1
E6	25 - D2
E7	25 - D3
F1	23 - E3
F2	23 - E4
F3	23 - E5
F4	23 - E6
F5	25 - E1
F6	25 - E2
F7	25 - E3
G1	23 - F3
G2	23 - F4
G3	23 - F5
G4	23 - F6
G5	25 - F1
G6	25 - F2
G7	25 - F3
H1	24 - A3
H2	24 - A4
H3	24 - A5
H4	24 - A6
H5	26 - A1
H6	26 - A2
H7	26 - A3
J1	24 - B3
J2	24 - B4
J3	24 - B5
J4	24 - B6
J5	26 - B1
J6	26 - B2
J7	26 - B3
New 708	
A1	24 - C3
A2	24 - C4
A3	24 - C5
A4	24 - C6
A5	26 - C1
A6	26 - C2
A7	26 - C3
B1	24 - C3
B2	24 - C4
B3	24 - C5
B4	24 - C6
B5	26 - C1
B6	26 - C2
B7	26 - C3
C1	24 - D3
C2	24 - D4
C3	24 - D5
C4	24 - D6
C5	26 - D1
C6	26 - D2
C7	26 - D3
D1	24 - E3
D2	24 - E4
D3	24 - E5
D4	24 - E6
D5	26 - E1
D6	26 - E2
D7	26 - E2
E1	24 - F3
E2	24 - F4
E3	24 - F5

NEW-OLD	
New 708	
E4	24 - F6
E5	26 - F1
E6	26 - F2
E7	26 - F2
New 726	
B7	27 - A3
C5	27 - A1
C6	27 - A2
C7	27 - A3
D5	27 - B1
D6	27 - B2
D7	27 - B3
E5	27 - C1
E6	27 - C2
E7	27 - C3
F1	20 - D4
F2	20 - D4
F3	20 - D5
F4	20 - D6
F5	27 - D1
F6	27 - D2
F7	27 - D3
G1	20 - E4
G2	20 - E4
G3	20 - E5
G4	20 - E6
G5	27 - E1
G6	27 - E2
G7	27 - E3
H1	20 - E4
H2	20 - E4
H3	20 - E5
H4	20 - E6
H5	27 - E1
H6	27 - E2
H7	27 - E3
J1	20 - F4
J2	20 - F4
J3	20 - F5
J4	20 - F6
J5	27 - F1
J6	27 - F2
J7	27 - F3
New 727	
A1	25 - A4
A2	25 - A4
A3	25 - A5
A4	25 - A6
A5	27A - A1
A6	27A - A2
A7	27A - A3
B1	25 - B4
B2	25 - B4
B3	25 - B5
B4	25 - B6
B5	27A - B1
B6	27A - B2
B7	27A - B3
C1	25 - C4
C2	25 - C4
C3	25 - C5
C4	25 - C6
C5	27A - C1
C6	27A - C2
C7	27A - C3
D1	25 - D4
D2	25 - D4
D3	25 - D5
D4	25 - D6
D5	27A - D1
D6	27A - D2
D7	27A - D3
E1	25 - D4
E2	25 - D4
E3	25 - E5
E4	25 - E6
E5	27A - E1
E6	27A - E2
E7	27A - E3
F1	25 - E3
F2	25 - E4
F3	25 - E5
F4	25 - E6
F5	27A - E1
F6	27A - E2
F7	27A - E3
G1	25 - F3
G2	25 - F4
G3	25 - F5
G4	25 - F6
G5	27A - F1
G6	27A - F2
G7	27A - F3
H1	26 - A3
H2	26 - A4
H3	26 - A5
H4	26 - A6
H5	28 - A1
H6	28 - A2
H7	28 - A3
J1	26 - B3
J2	26 - B4
J3	26 - B5
J4	26 - B6
J5	28 - B1
J6	28 - B2
J7	28 - B3

NEW-OLD	
New 728	
A1	26 - C3
A2	26 - C4
A3	26 - C5
A4	26 - C6
A5	28 - C1
A6	28 - C2
A7	28 - C3
B1	26 - C3
B2	26 - C4
B3	26 - C5
B4	26 - C6
B5	28 - C1
B6	28 - D2
B7	28 - D3
C1	26 - D3
C2	26 - D4
C3	26 - D5
C4	26 - D6
C5	28 - D1
C6	28 - D2
C7	28 - D3
D1	26 - E3
D2	26 - E4
D3	26 - E5
D4	26 - E6
D5	28 - E1
D6	28 - E2
D7	28 - E3
E1	26 - F3
E2	26 - F4
E3	26 - F5
E4	26 - F6
E5	28 - F1
E6	28 - F2
E7	28 - F3
F5	29 - A1
F6	29 - A2
F7	29 - A3
G5	29 - B1
G6	29 - B2
G7	29 - B3
H5	29 - B1
H6	29 - B2
H7	29 - C3
J5	29 - C1
J6	29 - C2
J7	29 - C3
New 729	
A5	29 - D1
A6	29 - D2
A7	29 - D3
B5	29 - E1
B6	29 - E2
B7	29 - E3
C5	29 - F1
C6	29 - F2
C7	29 - F3
D5	29A - A1
D6	29A - A2
D7	29A - A3
E5	29A - B1
E6	29A - B2
E7	29A - B3
F5	29A - C1
F6	29A - C2
F7	29A - B3
G5	29A - C1
G6	29A - C2
G7	29A - C3
H5	29A - D1
H6	29A - D2
H7	29A - D3
J5	29A - E1
J6	29A - E2
J7	29A - E3
New 746	
B1	27 - A4
B2	27 - A5
B3	27 - A6
B4	30 - A1
B5	30 - A2
B6	30 - A3
B7	30 - A4
C1	27 - A4
C2	27 - B5
C3	27 - B6
C4	30 - B1
C5	30 - B2
C6	30 - B3
C7	30 - B4
D1	27 - B4
D2	27 - B5
D3	27 - B6
D4	30 - B1
D5	30 - B2
D6	30 - B3
D7	30 - B3
E1	27 - C4
E2	27 - C5
E3	27 - C6
E4	30 - C1
E5	30 - C2
E6	30 - C3
E7	30 - C3
F1	27 - D4
F2	27 - D5
F3	27 - D6

NEW-OLD	
New 746	
F4	30 - D1
F5	30 - D2
F6	30 - D3
F7	30 - D3
G1	27 - E4
G2	27 - E5
G3	27 - E6
G4	30 - E1
G5	30 - E2
G6	30 - E3
G7	30 - E3
H1	27 - F4
H2	27 - F5
H3	27 - F6
H4	30 - F1
H5	30 - F2
H6	30 - F3
H7	30 - F3
J1	27 - F4
J2	27 - F5
J3	27 - F6
J4	30 - F1
J5	30A - A2
J6	30A - A3
J7	30A - A3
New 747	
A1	27A - A4
A2	27A - A5
A3	27A - A6
A4	30A - B1
A5	30A - B2
A6	30A - B3
A7	30A - B3
B1	27A - B4
B2	27A - B5
B3	27A - B6
B4	30A - B1
B5	30A - B2
B6	30A - B3
B7	30A - B3
C1	27A - C4
C2	27A - C5
C3	27A - C6
C4	30A - C1
C5	30A - C2
C6	30A - C3
C7	30A - C3
D1	27A - D4
D2	27A - D5
D3	27A - D6
D4	30A - D1
D5	30A - D2
D6	30A - D2
D7	30A - D3
E1	27A - D4
E2	27A - D5
E3	27A - D6
E4	30A - E1
E5	30A - E2
E6	30A - E2
E7	30A - E3
F1	27A - E4
F2	27A - E5
F3	27A - E6
F4	27A - E6
F5	30A - E2
F6	30A - E2
F7	30A - E3
G1	27A - F4
G2	27A - F5
G3	27A - F5
G4	27A - F6
G5	30A - F2
G6	30A - F2
G7	30A - F3
H1	28 - A4
H2	28 - A5
H3	28 - A5
H4	28 - A6
H5	31 - A1
H6	31 - A2
H7	31 - A3
J1	28 - B4
J2	28 - B5
J3	28 - B5
J4	28 - B6
J5	31 - B1
J6	31 - B2
J7	31 - B3
New 748	
A1	28 - C4
A2	28 - C5
A3	28 - C5
A4	28 - C6
A5	31 - C1
A6	31 - C2
A7	31 - C3
B1	28 - D4
B2	28 - D5
B3	28 - D5
B4	28 - D6
B5	31 - D1
B6	31 - D2
B7	31 - D3
C1	28 - D4
C2	28 - D5
C3	28 - D5

NEW-OLD	
New 748	
C4	28 - D6
C5	31 - D1
C6	31 - D2
C7	31 - D3
D1	28 - E4
D2	28 - E5
D3	28 - E5
D4	28 - E6
D5	31 - E1
D6	31 - E2
D7	31 - E3
E1	28 - F4
E2	28 - F5
E3	28 - F5
E4	28 - F6
E5	31 - F1
E6	31 - F2
E7	31 - F3
F1	29 - A4
F2	29 - A5
F3	29 - A5
F4	29 - A6
F5	32 - A1
F6	32 - A2
F7	32 - A3
G1	29 - B4
G2	29 - B4
G3	29 - B5
G4	29 - B6
G5	32 - B1
G6	32 - B2
G7	32 - B3
H1	29 - C4
H2	29 - C4
H3	29 - C5
H4	29 - C6
H5	32 - C1
H6	32 - C2
H7	32 - C3
J1	29 - C4
J2	29 - C4
J3	29 - C5
J4	29 - C6
J5	32 - C1
J6	32 - C2
J7	32 - C3
New 749	
A1	29 - D4
A2	29 - D4
A3	29 - D5
A4	29 - D6
A5	32 - D1
A6	32 - D2
A7	32 - D3
B1	29 - E4
B2	29 - E4
B3	29 - E5
B4	29 - E6
B5	32 - E1
B6	32 - E2
B7	32 - E3
C1	29 - F4
C2	29 - F4
C3	29 - F5
C4	29 - F6
C5	32 - F1
C6	32 - F2
C7	32 - F3
D1	29A - A4
D2	29A - A4
D3	29A - A5
D4	29A - A6
D5	33 - A1
D6	33 - A2
D7	33 - A3
E1	29A - B3
E2	29A - B4
E3	29A - B5
E4	29A - B6
E5	33 - B1
E6	33 - B2
E7	33 - B3
F1	29A - B3
F2	29A - B4
F3	29A - B5
F4	29A - B6
F5	33 - B1
F6	33 - C2
F7	33 - C3
G1	29A - C3
G2	29A - C4
G3	29A - C5
G4	29A - C6
G5	33 - C1
G6	33 - C2
G7	33 - C3
H1	29A - D3
H2	29A - D4
H3	29A - D5
H4	29A - D6
H5	33 - D1
H6	33 - D2
H7	33 - D3
J1	29A - E3
J2	29A - E4
J3	29A - E5
J4	29A - E6

NEW-OLD	
New 749	
J5	33 - E1
J6	33 - E2
J7	33 - E3
New 750	
A1	29A - F3
A2	29A - F4
A3	29A - F5
A4	29A - F6
A5	33 - F1
A6	33 - F2
A7	33 - F3
B5	33A - A1
B6	33A - A2
B7	33A - A3
C5	33A - B1
C6	33A - B2
C7	33A - B3
D5	33A - B1
D6	33A - B2
D7	33A - B3
E5	33A - C1
E6	33A - C2
E7	33A - C3
F5	33A - D1
F6	33A - D2
F7	33A - D3
G5	33A - E1
G6	33A - E2
G7	33A - E3
H5	33A - E1
H6	33A - E2
H7	33A - E3
J5	33A - F1
J6	33A - F2
J7	33A - F3
New 766	
B1	30 - A4
B2	30 - A5
B3	30 - A6
C1	30 - B4
C2	30 - B5
C3	30 - B6
D1	30 - B4
D2	30 - C5
D3	30 - C6
E1	30 - C4
E2	30 - C5
E3	30 - C6
F1	30 - D4
F2	30 - D5
F3	30 - D6
G1	30 - E4
G2	30 - E5
G3	30 - E6
H1	30 - F4
H2	30 - F5
H3	30 - F6
J1	30A - A4
J2	30A - A5
J3	30A - A6
J4	34 - A1
J5	34 - A2
J6	34 - A3
J7	34 - A4
New 767	
A1	30A - B4
A2	30A - B5
A3	30A - B6
A4	34 - B1
A5	34 - B2
A6	34 - B3
A7	34 - B4
B1	30A - B4
B2	30A - B5
B3	30A - B6
B4	34 - B1
B5	34 - B2
B6	34 - B3
B7	34 - B4
C1	30A - C4
C2	30A - C5
C3	30A - C6
C4	34 - C1
C5	34 - C2
C6	34 - C3
C7	34 - C4
D1	30A - D4
D2	30A - D5
D3	30A - D6
D4	34 - D1
D5	34 - D2
D6	34 - D3
D7	34 - D4
E1	30A - E4
E2	30A - E5
E3	30A - E6
E4	34 - E1
E5	34 - E2
E6	34 - E3
E7	34 - E4
F1	30A - E4
F2	30A - F5
F3	30A - F6
F4	34 - E1
F5	34 - E2
F6	34 - F3
F7	34 - F4

NEW-OLD	
New 767	
G1	30A - F4
G2	30A - F5
G3	30A - F6
G4	34 - F1
G5	34 - F2
G6	34 - F3
G7	34 - F4
H1	31 - A4
H2	31 - A5
H3	31 - A6
H4	34A - A1
H5	34A - A2
H6	34A - A3
H7	34A - A4
J1	31 - B4
J2	31 - B5
J3	31 - B6
J4	34A - B1
J5	34A - B2
J6	34A - B3
J7	34A - B4
New 768	
A1	31 - C4
A2	31 - C5
A3	31 - C6
A4	34A - C1
A5	34A - C2
A6	34A - C3
A7	34A - C4
B1	31 - D4
B2	31 - D5
B3	31 - D6
B4	34A - D1
B5	34A - D2
B6	34A - D3
B7	34A - D3
C1	31 - D4
C2	31 - D5
C3	31 - D6
C4	34A - D1
C5	34A - D2
C6	34A - E3
C7	34A - E3
D1	31 - E4
D2	31 - E5
D3	31 - E6
D4	34A - E1
D5	34A - E2
D6	34A - E3
D7	34A - E3
E1	31 - F4
E2	31 - F5
E3	31 - F6
E4	34A - F1
E5	34A - F2
E6	34A - F3
E7	34A - F3
F1	32 - A4
F2	32 - A5
F3	32 - A6
F4	35 - A1
F5	35 - A2
F6	35 - A3
F7	36 - A3
G1	32 - B4
G2	32 - B5
G3	32 - B6
G4	35 - B1
G5	35 - B2
G6	35 - B3
G7	35 - B3
H1	32 - C4
H2	32 - C5
H3	32 - C6
H4	35 - C1
H5	35 - C2
H6	35 - C3
H7	35 - C3
J1	32 - C4
J2	32 - C5
J3	32 - D6
J4	35 - D1
J5	35 - D2
J6	35 - D2
J7	35 - D3
New 769	
A1	32 - D4
A2	32 - D5
A3	32 - D6
A4	35 - D1
A5	35 - D2
A6	35 - D2
A7	35 - D3
B1	32 - E4
B2	32 - E5
B3	32 - E5
B4	35 - E1
B5	35 - E2
B6	35 - E2
B7	35 - E3
C1	32 - F4
C2	32 - F5
C3	32 - F5
C4	35 - F1
C5	35 - F2
C6	35 - F2
C7	35 - F3

NEW-OLD	
New 769	
D1	33 - A4
D2	33 - A5
D3	33 - A5
D4	33 - A6
D5	36 - A2
D6	36 - A2
D7	36 - A3
E1	33 - B4
E2	33 - B5
E3	33 - B5
E4	33 - B6
E5	36 - B2
E6	36 - B2
E7	36 - B3
F1	33 - C4
F2	33 - C5
F3	33 - C5
F4	33 - C6
F5	36 - C2
F6	36 - C2
F7	36 - C3
G1	33 - C4
G2	33 - C5
G3	33 - C5
G4	33 - C6
G5	36 - C1
G6	36 - C2
G7	36 - C3
H1	33 - D4
H2	33 - D5
H3	33 - D5
H4	33 - D6
H5	36 - D1
H6	36 - D2
H7	36 - D3
J1	33 - E4
J2	33 - E5
J3	33 - E5
J4	33 - E6
J5	36 - E1
J6	36 - E2
J7	36 - E3
New 770	
A1	33 - F4
A2	33 - F5
A3	33 - F5
A4	33 - F6
A5	36 - F1
A6	36 - F2
A7	36 - F3
B1	33A - A4
B2	33A - A5
B3	33A - A5
B4	33A - A6
B5	37 - A1
B6	37 - A2
B7	37 - A3
C1	33A - B4
C2	33A - B4
C3	33A - B5
C4	33A - B6
C5	37 - B1
C6	37 - B2
C7	37 - B3
D1	33A - B4
D2	33A - B4
D3	33A - B5
D4	33A - B6
D5	37 - B1
D6	37 - B2
D7	37 - B3
E1	33A - C4
E2	33A - C4
E3	33A - C5
E4	33A - C6
E5	37 - C1
E6	37 - C2
E7	37 - C3
F1	33A - D4
F2	33A - D4
F3	33A - D5
F4	33A - D6
F5	37 - D1
F6	37 - D2
F7	37 - D3
G1	33A - E4
G2	33A - E4
G3	33A - E5
G4	33A - E6
G5	37 - E1
G6	37 - E2
G7	37 - E3
H1	33A - E3
H2	33A - E4
H3	33A - E5
H4	33A - E6
H5	37 - F1
H6	37 - F2
H7	37 - F3
J1	33A - F3
J2	33A - F4
J3	33A - F5
J4	33A - F6
J5	37 - F1
J6	37 - F2
J7	37 - F3
New 771	

NEW-OLD	
New 771	
A5	38 - A1
A6	38 - B2
A7	38 - B3
B5	38 - B1
B6	38 - B2
B7	38 - B3
C5	38 - C1
C6	38 - C2
C7	38 - C3
D5	38 - D1
D6	38 - D2
D7	38 - D3
E5	38 - E1
E6	38 - E2
E7	38 - E3
F5	38 - E1
F6	38 - E2
F7	38 - E3
G5	38 - F1
G6	38 - F2
G7	38 - F3
New 787	
A1	34 - B5
A2	34 - B5
A3	34 - B6
A4	39 - B1
A5	39 - B2
A6	39 - B3
A7	39 - B4
B1	34 - B5
B2	34 - B5
B3	34 - B6
B4	39 - B1
B5	39 - B2
B6	39 - B3
B7	39 - B4
C1	34 - C5
C2	34 - C5
C3	34 - C6
C4	39 - C1
C5	39 - C2
C6	39 - C3
C7	39 - C4
D1	34 - D5
D2	34 - D5
D3	34 - D6
D4	39 - D1
D5	39 - D2
D6	39 - D3
D7	39 - D4
E1	34 - E4
E2	34 - E5
E3	34 - E6
E4	39 - E1
E5	39 - E2
E6	39 - E3
E7	39 - E4
F1	34 - F4
F2	34 - F5
F3	34 - F6
F4	39 - F1
F5	39 - F2
F6	39 - F3
F7	39 - F4
G1	34 - F4
G2	34A - A5
G3	34A - A6
G4	40 - A1
G5	40 - A2
G6	40 - A3
G7	40 - A4
H1	34A - A4
H2	34A - A5
H3	34A - B6
H4	40 - B1
H5	40 - B2
H6	40 - B3
H7	40 - B4
J1	34A - B4
J2	34A - B5
J3	34A - B6
J4	40 - B1
J5	40 - B2
J6	40 - B3
J7	40 - B4
New 788	
A1	34A - C4
A2	34A - C5
A3	34A - C6
A4	40 - C1
A5	40 - C2
A6	40 - C3
A7	40 - C4
B1	34A - D4
B2	34A - D5
B3	34A - D6
B4	40 - D1
B5	40 - D2
B6	40 - D3
B7	40 - D4
C1	34A - E4
C2	34A - E5
C3	34A - E6
C4	40 - E1
C5	40 - E2
C6	40 - E3
C7	40 - E4

NEW-OLD	
New 788	
D1	34A - E4
D2	34A - E5
D3	34A - E6
D4	40 - E1
D5	40 - E2
D6	40 - F3
D7	40 - F4
E1	34A - F4
E2	34A - F5
E3	34A - F6
E4	40 - F1
E5	40 - F2
E6	40 - F3
E7	40 - F4
F1	35 - A4
F2	35 - A5
F3	35 - A6
F4	41 - A1
F5	41 - A2
F6	41 - A3
F7	41 - A4
G1	35 - B4
G2	35 - B5
G3	35 - B6
G4	41 - B1
G5	41 - B2
G6	41 - B3
G7	41 - B4
H1	35 - C4
H2	35 - C5
H3	35 - C6
H4	41 - C1
H5	41 - C2
H6	41 - C3
H7	41 - C4
J1	35 - D4
J2	35 - D5
J3	35 - D6
J4	41 - D1
J5	41 - D2
J6	41 - D3
J7	41 - D4
New 789	
A1	35 - D4
A2	35 - D5
A3	35 - D6
A4	41 - D1
A5	41 - D2
A6	41 - E3
A7	41 - E4
B1	35 - E4
B2	35 - E5
B3	35 - E6
B4	41 - E1
B5	41 - E2
B6	41 - E3
B7	41 - E4
C1	35 - F4
C2	35 - F5
C3	35 - F6
C4	41 - F1
C5	41 - F2
C6	41 - F3
C7	41 - F4
D1	36 - A4
D2	36 - A5
D3	36 - A6
D4	42 - A1
D5	42 - A2
D6	42 - A3
D7	42 - A4
E1	36 - B4
E2	36 - B5
E3	36 - B6
E4	42 - B1
E5	42 - B2
E6	42 - B3
E7	42 - B3
F1	36 - C4
F2	36 - C5
F3	36 - C6
F4	42 - C1
F5	42 - C2
F6	42 - C3
F7	42 - C3
G1	36 - C4
G2	36 - C5
G3	36 - D6
G4	42 - D1
G5	42 - D2
G6	42 - D3
G7	42 - D3
H1	36 - D4
H2	36 - D5
H3	36 - D6
H4	42 - D1
H5	42 - D2
H6	42 - D3
H7	42 - D3
J1	36 - E4
J2	36 - E5
J3	36 - E6
J4	42 - E1
J5	42 - E2
J6	42 - E3
J7	42 - E3
New 790	

NEW-OLD	
New 790	
A1	36 - F4
A2	36 - F5
A3	36 - F6
A4	42 - F1
A5	42 - F2
A6	42 - F3
A7	42 - F3
B1	37 - A4
B2	37 - A5
B3	37 - A6
B4	43 - A1
B5	43 - A2
B6	43 - A3
B7	43 - A3
C1	37 - B4
C2	37 - B5
C3	37 - B6
C4	43 - B1
C5	43 - B2
C6	43 - B3
C7	43 - B3
D1	37 - B4
D2	37 - B5
D3	37 - B6
D4	43 - C1
D5	43 - C2
D6	43 - C3
D7	43 - C3
E1	37 - C4
E2	37 - C5
E3	37 - C6
E4	43 - C1
E5	43 - C2
E6	43 - C3
E7	43 - C3
F1	37 - D4
F2	37 - D5
F3	37 - D6
F4	43 - D1
F5	43 - D2
F6	43 - D3
F7	43 - D3
G1	37 - E4
G2	37 - E5
G3	37 - E6
G4	43 - E1
G5	43 - E2
G6	43 - E3
G7	43 - E3
H1	37 - F4
H2	37 - F5
H3	37 - F6
H4	43 - F1
H5	43 - F2
H6	43 - F2
H7	43 - F3
J1	37 - F4
J2	37 - F5
J3	37 - F6
J4	43 - F1
New 791	
A1	38 - B4
A2	38 - B5
A3	38 - B6
B1	38 - B4
B2	38 - B5
B3	38 - B6
C1	38 - C4
C2	38 - C5
C3	38 - C5
C4	38 - C6
D1	38 - D4
D2	38 - D5
D3	38 - D5
D4	38 - D6
E1	38 - E4
E2	38 - E5
E3	38 - E5
E4	38 - E6
F1	38 - E4
F2	38 - E5
F3	38 - E5
F4	38 - E6
G1	38 - F4
G2	38 - F5
G3	38 - F5
G4	38 - F6
New 807	
A1	39 - B5
A2	39 - B6
B1	39 - B5
B2	39 - C6
C1	39 - C5
C2	39 - C6
D1	39 - D5
D2	39 - D6
E1	39 - E5
E2	39 - E6
F1	39 - F5
F2	39 - F6
G1	40 - A5
G2	40 - A6
G3	44 - A1
G4	44 - A2
G5	44 - A2
G6	44 - A3
G7	44 - A4

NEW-OLD	
New 807	
H1	40 - B5
H2	40 - B6
H3	44 - B1
H4	44 - B2
H5	44 - B2
H6	44 - B3
H7	44 - B4
J1	40 - B5
J2	40 - B6
J3	44 - B1
J4	44 - B2
J5	44 - B2
J6	44 - B3
J7	44 - B4
New 808	
A1	40 - C5
A2	40 - C6
A3	44 - C1
A4	44 - C2
A5	44 - C2
A6	44 - C3
A7	44 - C4
B1	40 - D5
B2	40 - D5
B3	40 - D6
B4	44 - D2
B5	44 - D2
B6	44 - D3
B7	44 - D4
C1	40 - E5
C2	40 - E5
C3	40 - E6
C4	44 - E1
C5	44 - E2
C6	44 - E3
C7	44 - E4
D1	40 - F5
D2	40 - F5
D3	40 - F6
D4	44 - F1
D5	44 - F2
D6	44 - F3
D7	44 - F4
E1	40 - F5
E2	40 - F5
E3	41 - A6
E4	45 - A1
E5	45 - A2
E6	45 - A3
E7	45 - A4
F1	41 - A5
F2	41 - A5
F3	41 - A6
F4	45 - A1
F5	45 - A2
F6	45 - B3
F7	45 - B4
G1	41 - B5
G2	41 - B5
G3	41 - B6
G4	45 - B1
G5	45 - B2
G6	45 - B3
G7	45 - B4
H1	41 - C5
H2	41 - C5
H3	41 - C6
H4	45 - C1
H5	45 - C2
H6	45 - C3
H7	45 - C4
J1	41 - D5
J2	41 - D5
J3	41 - D6
J4	45 - D1
J5	45 - D2
J6	45 - D3
J7	45 - D4
New 809	
A1	41 - E4
A2	41 - E5
A3	41 - E6
A4	45 - E1
A5	45 - E2
A6	45 - E3
A7	45 - E4
B1	41 - E4
B2	41 - E5
B3	41 - E6
B4	45 - E1
B5	45 - E2
B6	45 - E3
B7	45 - E4
C1	41 - F4
C2	41 - F5
C3	41 - F6
C4	45 - F1
C5	45 - F2
C6	45 - F3
C7	45 - F4
D1	42 - A4
D2	42 - A5
D3	42 - A6
D4	46 - A1
D5	46 - A2
D6	46 - A3
D7	46 - A4

NEW-OLD	
New 809	
E1	42 - B4
E2	42 - B5
E3	42 - B6
E4	46 - B1
E5	46 - B2
E6	46 - B3
E7	46 - B4
F1	42 - C4
F2	42 - C5
F3	42 - C6
F4	46 - C1
F5	46 - C2
F6	46 - C3
F7	46 - C4
G1	42 - D4
G2	42 - D5
G3	42 - D6
G4	46 - D1
G5	46 - D2
G6	46 - D3
G7	46 - D4
H1	42 - D4
H2	42 - D5
H3	42 - D6
H4	46 - D1
H5	46 - D2
H6	46 - D3
H7	46 - E4
J1	42 - E4
J2	42 - E5
J3	42 - E6
J4	46 - E1
J5	46 - E2
J6	46 - E3
J7	46 - E4
New 810	
A1	42 - F4
A2	42 - F5
A3	42 - F6
A4	46 - F1
A5	46 - F2
A6	46 - F3
A7	46 - F4
B1	43 - A4
B2	43 - A5
B3	43 - A6
B4	47 - A1
B5	47 - A2
B6	47 - A3
B7	47 - A4
C1	43 - B4
C2	43 - B5
C3	43 - B6
C4	47 - B1
C5	47 - B2
C6	47 - B3
C7	47 - B4
D1	43 - C4
D2	43 - C5
D3	43 - C6
D4	47 - C1
D5	47 - C2
D6	47 - C3
D7	47 - C4
E1	43 - C4
E2	43 - C5
E3	43 - C6
E4	47 - C1
E5	47 - C2
E6	47 - C3
E7	47 - C4
F1	43 - D4
F2	43 - D5
F3	43 - D6
F4	47 - D1
F5	47 - D2
F6	47 - D3
F7	47 - D4
G1	43 - E4
G2	43 - E5
G3	43 - E6
G4	47 - E1
G5	47 - E2
G6	47 - E3
G7	47 - E4
H1	43 - F4
H2	43 - F5
H3	43 - F6
H4	47 - F1
H5	47 - F2
H6	47 - F3
H7	47 - F4
J1	43 - F4
J2	43 - F5
J3	43 - F6
J4	47 - F1
J5	47 - F2
New 827	
G1	44 - A5
G2	44 - A6
G3	48 - A1
G4	48 - A2
G5	48 - A3
G6	48 - A4
G7	48 - A5
H1	44 - B5
H2	44 - B6

NEW-OLD	
New 827	
H3	48 - B1
H4	48 - B2
H5	48 - B3
H6	48 - B4
H7	48 - B5
J1	44 - B5
J2	44 - B6
J3	48 - B1
J4	48 - B2
J5	48 - B3
J6	48 - C4
J7	48 - C5
New 828	
A1	44 - C5
A2	44 - C6
A3	48 - C1
A4	48 - C2
A5	48 - C3
A6	48 - C4
A7	48 - C5
B1	44 - D5
B2	44 - D6
B3	48 - D1
B4	48 - D2
B5	48 - D3
B6	48 - D4
B7	48 - D5
C1	44 - E5
C2	44 - E6
C3	48 - E1
C4	48 - E2
C5	48 - E3
C6	48 - E4
C7	48 - E5
D1	44 - F5
D2	44 - F6
D3	48 - F1
D4	48 - F2
D5	48 - F3
D6	48 - F4
D7	48 - F5
E1	45 - A5
E2	45 - A6
E3	49 - A1
E4	49 - A2
E5	49 - A3
E6	49 - A4
E7	49 - A5
F1	45 - B5
F2	45 - B6
F3	49 - B1
F4	49 - B2
F5	49 - B3
F6	49 - B4
F7	49 - B5
G1	45 - B5
G2	45 - B6
G3	49 - B1
G4	49 - B2
G5	49 - B3
G6	49 - B4
G7	49 - B5
H1	45 - C5
H2	45 - C6
H3	49 - C1
H4	49 - C2
H5	49 - C3
H6	49 - C4
H7	49 - C5
J1	45 - D5
J2	45 - D6
J3	49 - D1
J4	49 - D2
J5	49 - D3
J6	49 - D4
J7	49 - D5
New 829	
A1	45 - E5
A2	45 - E6
A3	49 - E1
A4	49 - E2
A5	49 - E3
A6	49 - E4
A7	49 - E5
B1	45 - E5
B2	45 - E6
B3	49 - F1
B4	49 - F2
B5	49 - F3
B6	49 - F4
B7	49 - F5
C1	45 - F5
C2	46 - A6
C3	50 - A1
C4	50 - A2
C5	50 - A3
C6	50 - A4
C7	50 - A4
D1	46 - A5
D2	46 - A6
D3	50 - A1
D4	50 - A2
D5	50 - A3
D6	50 - B4
D7	50 - B4
E1	46 - B5
E2	46 - B6

NEW-OLD	
New 829	
E3	50 - B1
E4	50 - B2
E5	50 - B3
E6	50 - B4
E7	50 - B4
F1	46 - C5
F2	46 - C6
F3	50 - C1
F4	50 - C2
F5	50 - C3
F6	50 - C3
F7	50 - C4
G1	46 - D5
G2	46 - D6
G3	50 - D1
G4	50 - D2
G5	50 - D3
G6	50 - D3
G7	50 - D4
H1	46 - E5
H2	46 - E6
H3	50 - E1
H4	50 - E2
H5	50 - E3
H6	50 - E3
H7	50 - E4
J1	46 - E5
J2	46 - E5
J3	50 - E1
J4	50 - E2
J5	50 - E2
J6	50 - E3
J7	50 - E4
New 830	
A1	46 - F5
A2	46 - F5
A3	46 - F6
A4	50 - F2
A5	50 - F2
A6	50 - F3
A7	50 - F4
B1	47 - A5
B2	47 - A5
B3	47 - A6
B4	51 - A2
B5	51 - A2
B6	51 - A3
B7	51 - A4
C1	47 - B5
C2	47 - B5
C3	47 - B6
C4	51 - B2
C5	51 - B2
C6	51 - B3
C7	51 - B4
D1	47 - C5
D2	47 - C5
D3	47 - C6
D4	51 - C1
D5	51 - C2
D6	51 - C3
D7	51 - C4
E1	47 - C5
E2	47 - C5
E3	47 - D6
E4	51 - D1
E5	51 - D2
E6	51 - D3
E7	51 - D4
F1	47 - D4
F2	47 - D5
F3	47 - D6
F4	51 - D1
F5	51 - D2
F6	51 - D3
F7	51 - D4
G1	47 - E4
G2	47 - E5
G3	47 - E6
G4	51 - E1
G5	51 - E2
G6	51 - E3
G7	51 - E4
H1	47 - F4
H2	47 - F5
H3	47 - F6
H4	51 - F1
H5	51 - F2
H6	51 - F3
H7	51 - F4
New 847	
G1	48 - A6
G2	48 - A6
G3	48A - A1
G4	48A - A2
G5	48A - A3
G6	48A - A4
G7	48A - A5
H1	48 - B6
H2	48 - B6
H3	48A - B1
H4	48A - B2
H5	48A - B3
H6	48A - B4
H7	48A - B5
J1	48 - C6
J2	48 - C6

NEW-OLD	
New 847	
J3	48A - C1
J4	48A - C2
J5	48A - C3
J6	48A - C4
J7	48A - C5
New 848	
A1	48 - C6
A2	48 - C6
A3	48A - C1
A4	48A - C2
A5	48A - C3
A6	48A - C4
A7	48A - C5
B1	48 - D6
B2	48 - D6
B3	48A - D1
B4	48A - D2
B5	48A - D3
B6	48A - D4
B7	48A - D5
C1	48 - E6
C2	48 - E6
C3	48A - E1
C4	48A - E2
C5	48A - E3
C6	48A - E4
C7	48A - E5
D1	48 - F6
D2	48 - F6
D3	48A - F1
D4	48A - F2
D5	48A - F3
D6	48A - F4
D7	48A - F5
E1	49 - A6
E2	49 - A6
E3	49A - A1
E4	49A - A2
E5	49A - A3
E6	49A - A4
E7	49A - A5
F1	49 - B6
F2	49 - B6
F3	49A - B1
F4	49A - B2
F5	49A - B3
F6	49A - B4
F7	49A - B5
G1	49 - B6
G2	49 - B6
G3	49A - B1
G4	49A - B2
G5	49A - B3
G6	49A - B4
G7	49A - B5
H1	49 - C6
H2	49 - C6
H3	49A - C1
H4	49A - C2
H5	49A - C3
H6	49A - C4
H7	49A - C5
J1	49 - D6
J2	49 - D6
J3	49A - D1
J4	49A - D2
J5	49A - D3
J6	49A - D4
J7	49A - D5
New 849	
A1	49 - E6
A2	49 - E6
A3	49A - E1
A4	49A - E2
A5	49A - E3
A6	49A - E4
A7	49A - E5
B1	49 - F6
B2	49 - F6
B3	49A - F1
B4	49A - F2
B5	49A - F3
B6	49A - F4
B7	49A - F5
C1	50 - A5
C2	50 - A6
C3	50A - A1
C4	50A - A2
C5	50A - A3
C6	50A - A4
C7	50A - A5
D1	50 - B5
D2	50 - B6
D3	50A - A1
D4	50A - A2
D5	50A - A3
D6	50A - A4
D7	50A - A5
E1	50 - B5
E2	50 - B6
E3	50A - B1
E4	50A - B2
E5	50A - B3
E6	50A - B4
E7	50A - B5
F1	50 - C5
F2	50 - C6

NEW-OLD	
New 849	
F3	50A - C1
F4	50A - C2
F5	50A - C3
F6	50A - C4
F7	50A - C5
G1	50 - D5
G2	50 - D6
G3	50A - D1
G4	50A - D2
G5	50A - D3
G6	50A - D4
G7	50A - D5
H1	50 - E5
H2	50 - E6
H3	50A - E1
H4	50A - E2
H5	50A - E3
H6	50A - E4
H7	50A - E5
J1	50 - E5
J2	50 - F6
J3	50A - F1
J4	50A - F2
J5	50A - F3
J6	50A - F4
J7	50A - F5
New 850	
A1	50 - F5
A2	50 - F6
A3	50A - F1
A4	50A - F2
A5	50A - F3
A6	51A - A4
A7	51A - A5
B1	51 - A5
B2	51 - A6
B3	51A - A1
B4	51A - A2
B5	51A - A3
B6	51A - A4
B7	51A - A5
C1	51 - B5
C2	51 - B6
C3	51A - B1
C4	51A - B2
C5	51A - B3
C6	51A - B4
C7	51A - B5
D1	51 - C5
D2	51 - C6
D3	51A - C1
D4	51A - C2
D5	51A - C3
D6	51A - C4
D7	51A - C5
E1	51 - D5
E2	51 - D6
E3	51A - D1
E4	51A - D2
E5	51A - D3
E6	51A - D4
E7	51A - D5
F1	51 - D5
F2	51 - D6
F3	51A - E1
F4	51A - E2
F5	51A - E3
F6	51A - E4
F7	51A - E5
G1	51 - E5
G2	51 - E6
G3	51A - E1
G4	51A - E2
G5	51A - E3
G6	51A - E4
G7	51A - E5
H1	51 - F5
H2	51 - F6
H3	51A - F1
H4	51A - F2
H5	51A - F3
H6	51A - F4
H7	51A - F5
New 867	
G1	48A - A6
G2	56 - A1
G3	56 - A2
G4	56 - A3
G5	56 - A4
G6	56 - A5
G7	56 - A5
H1	48A - B6
H2	56 - B1
H3	56 - B2
H4	56 - B3
H5	56 - B4
H6	56 - B5
H7	56 - B5
J1	48A - C6
J2	56 - C1
J3	56 - C2
J4	56 - C3
J5	56 - C4
J6	56 - C4
J7	56 - C5
New 868	
A1	48A - C6

NEW-OLD	
New 868	
A2	56 - D1
A3	56 - D2
A4	56 - D3
A5	56 - D4
A6	56 - D4
A7	56 - D5
B1	48A - D6
B2	56 - D1
B3	56 - D2
B4	56 - D3
B5	56 - D3
B6	56 - D4
B7	56 - D5
C1	48A - E6
C2	56 - E1
C3	56 - E2
C4	56 - E3
C5	56 - E3
C6	56 - E4
C7	56 - E5
D1	48A - F6
D2	56 - F1
D3	56 - F2
D4	56 - F3
D5	56 - F3
D6	56 - F4
D7	56 - F5
E1	49A - A6
E2	57 - A1
E3	57 - A2
E4	57 - A3
E5	57 - A3
E6	57 - A4
E7	57 - A5
F1	49A - B6
F2	57 - B1
F3	57 - B2
F4	57 - B2
F5	57 - B3
F6	57 - B4
F7	57 - B5
G1	49A - B6
G2	57 - C1
G3	57 - C2
G4	57 - C2
G5	57 - C3
G6	57 - C4
G7	57 - C5
H1	49A - C6
H2	57 - C1
H3	57 - C1
H4	57 - C2
H5	57 - C3
H6	57 - C4
H7	57 - C5
J1	49A - D6
J2	57 - D1
J3	57 - D1
J4	57 - D2
J5	57 - D3
J6	57 - D4
J7	57 - D5
New 869	
A1	49A - E6
A2	57 - E1
A3	57 - E1
A4	57 - E2
A5	57 - E3
A6	57 - E4
A7	57 - E5
B1	49A - F6
B2	57 - F1
B3	57 - F1
B4	57 - F2
B5	57 - F3
B6	57 - F4
B7	57 - F5
C1	50A - A6
C2	50A - A6
C3	58 - A1
C4	58 - A2
C5	58 - A3
C6	58 - A4
C7	58 - A5
D1	50A - A6
D2	50A - A6
D3	58 - A1
D4	58 - B2
D5	58 - B3
D6	58 - B4
D7	58 - B5
E1	50A - B6
E2	50A - B6
E3	58 - B1
E4	58 - B2
E5	58 - B3
E6	58 - B4
E7	58 - B5
F1	50A - C6
F2	50A - C6
F3	58 - C1
F4	58 - C2
F5	58 - C3
F6	58 - C4
F7	58 - C5
G1	50A - D6
G2	50A - D6

NEW-OLD	
New 869	
G3	58 - D1
G4	58 - D2
G5	58 - D3
G6	58 - D4
G7	58 - D5
H1	50A - E6
H2	50A - E6
H3	58 - E1
H4	58 - E2
H5	58 - E3
H6	58 - E4
H7	58 - E5
J1	50A - F6
J2	50A - F6
J3	58 - F1
J4	58 - F2
J5	58 - F3
J6	58 - F4
J7	58 - F5
New 870	
A1	51A - A6
A2	51A - A6
A3	59 - A1
A4	59 - A2
A5	59 - A3
A6	59 - A4
A7	59 - A5
B1	51A - A6
B2	51A - A6
B3	59 - A1
B4	59 - A2
B5	59 - A3
B6	59 - A4
B7	59 - A5
C1	51A - B6
C2	51A - B6
C3	59 - B1
C4	59 - B2
C5	59 - B3
C6	59 - B4
C7	59 - B5
D1	51A - C6
D2	51A - C6
D3	59 - C1
D4	59 - C2
D5	59 - C3
D6	59 - C4
D7	59 - C5
E1	51A - D5
E2	51A - D6
E3	59 - D1
E4	59 - D2
E5	59 - D3
E6	59 - D4
E7	59 - D5
F1	51A - E5
F2	51A - E6
F3	59 - E1
F4	59 - E2
F5	59 - E3
F6	59 - E4
F7	59 - E5
G1	51A - F5
G2	51A - F6
G3	59 - F1
G4	59 - F2
G5	59 - F3
G6	59 - F4
G7	59 - F5
H1	51A - F5
H2	51A - F6
H3	59 - F1
H4	59 - F2
H5	59 - F3
H6	59 - F4
New 887	
G1	56 - A6
G2	56A - A1
G3	56A - A2
G4	56A - A3
G5	56A - A4
G6	56A - A5
G7	56A - A6
H1	56 - B6
H2	56A - B1
H3	56A - B2
H4	56A - B3
H5	56A - B4
H6	56A - B5
H7	56A - B6
J1	56 - C6
J2	56A - C1
J3	56A - C2
J4	56A - C3
J5	56A - C4
J6	56A - C5
J7	56A - C6
New 888	
A1	56 - D6
A2	56A - D1
A3	56A - D2
A4	56A - D3
A5	56A - D4
A6	56A - D5
A7	56A - D6
B1	56 - D6
B2	56A - E1

NEW-OLD	
New 888	
B3	56A - E2
B4	56A - E3
B5	56A - E4
B6	56A - E5
B7	56A - E6
C1	56 - E6
C2	56A - E1
C3	56A - E2
C4	56A - E3
C5	56A - E4
C6	56A - E5
C7	56A - E6
D1	56 - F6
D2	56A - F1
D3	56A - F2
D4	56A - F3
D5	56A - F4
D6	56A - F5
D7	56A - F6
E1	57 - A6
E2	57A - A1
E3	57A - A2
E4	57A - A3
E5	57A - A4
E6	57A - A5
E7	57A - A6
F1	57 - B6
F2	57A - B1
F3	57A - B2
F4	57A - B3
F5	57A - B4
F6	57A - B5
F7	57A - B6
G1	57 - C6
G2	57A - C1
G3	57A - C2
G4	57A - C3
G5	57A - C4
G6	57A - C5
G7	57A - C6
H1	57 - D6
H2	57A - D1
H3	57A - D2
H4	57A - D3
H5	57A - D4
H6	57A - D5
H7	57A - C6
J1	57 - D6
J2	57A - D1
J3	57A - D2
J4	57A - D3
J5	57A - D4
J6	57A - D5
J7	57A - D6
New 889	
A1	57 - E6
A2	57A - E1
A3	57A - E2
A4	57A - E3
A5	57A - E4
A6	57A - E5
A7	57A - E6
B1	57 - F6
B2	57A - F1
B3	57A - F2
B4	57A - F3
B5	57A - F4
B6	57A - F5
B7	57A - F6
C1	58 - A6
C2	58A - A1
C3	58A - A2
C4	58A - A3
C5	58A - A4
C6	58A - A5
C7	58A - A6
D1	58 - B6
D2	58A - B1
D3	58A - B2
D4	58A - B3
D5	58A - B4
D6	58A - B5
D7	58A - B6
E1	58 - B6
E2	58A - B1
E3	58A - B2
E4	58A - B3
E5	58A - C4
E6	58A - C5
E7	58A - C6
F1	58 - C6
F2	58A - C1
F3	58A - C2
F4	58A - C3
F5	58A - C4
F6	58A - C5
F7	58A - C6
G1	58 - D6
G2	58A - D1
G3	58A - D2
G4	58A - D3
G5	58A - D4
G6	58A - D5
G7	58A - D6
H1	58 - E6
H2	58A - E1
H3	58A - E2

1998 SAN MATEO NEW TO OLD Page Conversion List

NEW-OLD	
New 889	
H4	58A - E3
H5	58A - E4
H6	58A - E5
H7	58A - E6
J1	58 - F6
J2	58A - F1
J3	58A - F2
J4	58A - F3
J5	58A - F4
J6	58A - F5
J7	58A - F6
New 890	
A1	59 - A6
B1	59 - A6
C1	59 - B6
D1	59 - C6
E1	59 - D6
F1	59 - E6
G1	59 - F6
New 908	
E1	57A - A6
E2	59A - A1
E3	59A - A2
E4	59A - A3
E5	59A - A4
E6	59A - A5
E7	59A - A6
F2	59A - B1
F3	59A - B2
F4	59A - B3
F5	59A - B4
F6	59A - B5
F7	59A - B6
G2	59A - C1
G3	59A - C2
G4	59A - C3
G5	59A - C4
G6	59A - C5
G7	59A - C6
H2	59A - D1
H3	59A - D2
H4	59A - D3
H5	59A - D4
H6	59A - D5
H7	59A - D6
J2	59A - D1
J3	59A - E2
J4	59A - E3
J5	59A - E4
J6	59A - E5
J7	59A - E6
New 928	
E1	59A - A6
F1	59A - B6
G1	59A - C6
H1	59A - D6

The Thomas Guide®

1998 EDITION

SANTA CLARA COUNTY

ZIP

How To Use This Thomas Guide
Modo De Empleo Del Thomas Guide

To Find a City or Community:
Manera de Localizar una Ciudad o Comunidad:

Start with the Key Map to Detail Pages, then turn to the Detail Page indicated.

Empiece con el mapa clave de páginas detalladas, luego pase a la página detallada que se indica.

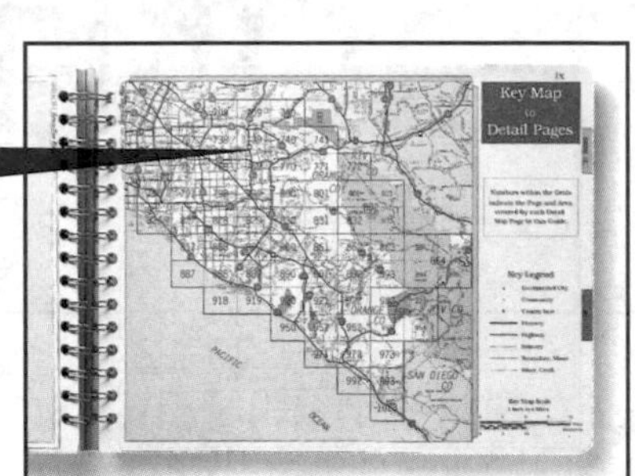

or
o

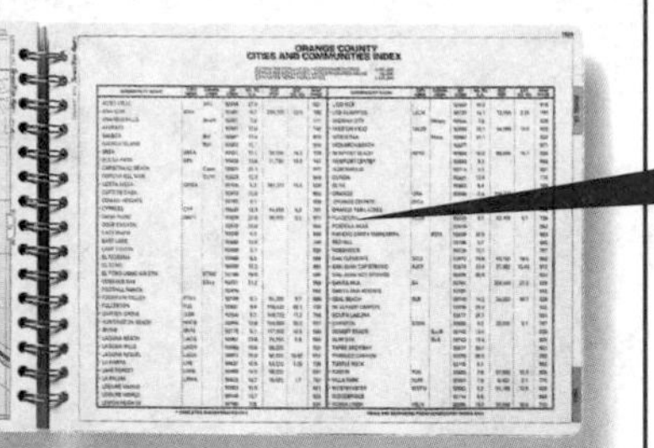

Look up the name in the Cities and Communities Index, then turn to the Detail Page indicated.

Busque el nombre en el Indice de Ciudades y Comunidades, luego pase a la página detallada que se indica.

or
o

Refer to the enclosed Foldout Map and its Index, then turn to the Detail Page indicated.

Consulte el mapa desplegable y el Indice del mismo adjunto, luego pase a la página detallada que se indica.

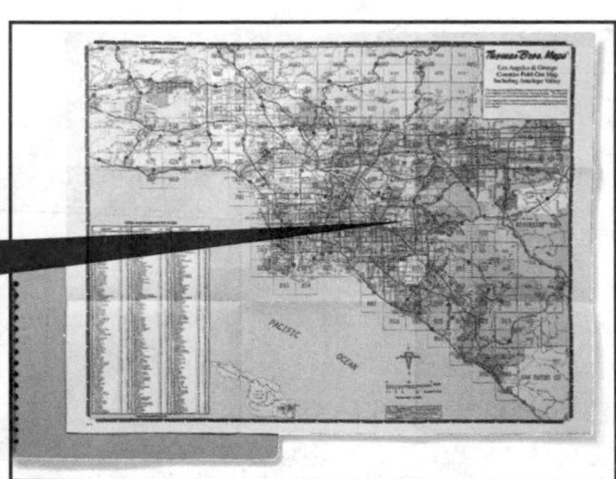

To Find an Address:
Manera de Localizar una Dirección:

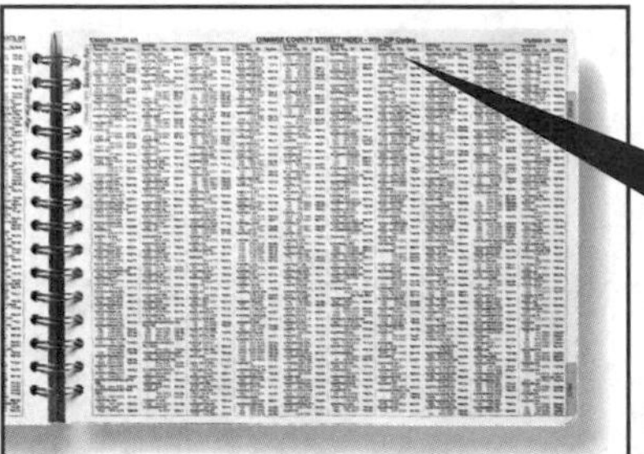

1 Look up the street name in the Street Index. If there are multiple listings, choose the proper city and/or address range. (All city abbreviations are listed in the Cities and Communities Index.)

Localice el nombre de la calle en el Indice de Calles. Si aparecen varias listas, seleccione el área apropiada de la ciudad y/o el domicilio. (Todas las abreviaturas de las ciudades figuran en la lista del Indice de Ciudades y Comunidades).

2 The street name will include a Thomas Bros. Maps Page and Grid™ where the address is located.

El nombre de la calle incluye un cuadro de Thomas Bros. Maps Page and Grid™ con el número de página y de coordenadas que indican la ubicación del domicilio.

	Pg-Grid	STREET Block	City	ZIP	Pg-Grid	STREET Block	City	ZIP	Pg-Grid
		N CARTLEN DR				CASITAS DE ALIPAZ			
77	971-G2	1700	PLCN	92670	739-G3	32200	SJCP	92675	972-B2
R		4700	OrCo	92670	739-G3	CASPE			
91	892-B7	CART[illegible] RD				28500	MVJO	92692	892-F6
[illegible]	[illegible]	[illegible]	IRVN	92714	859-H5	CASPER ST			
		CARUSO				12000	GGR	92645	797-D5

3 Turn to the Page indicated.

Pase a la página que se indica.

4 Locate the address by following the indicated Letter column and Number row until the two intersect. The street name is within this Grid area.

Localice el domicilio siguiendo la columna con letras y la hilera con números indicadas hasta que intersecten. El nombre de la calle se encuentra dentro de dicho cuadro.

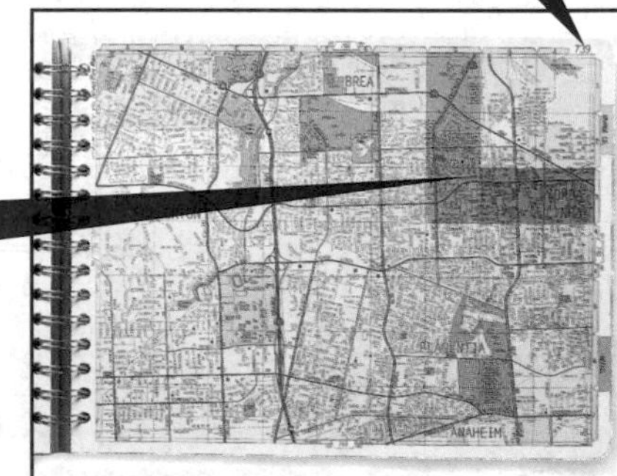

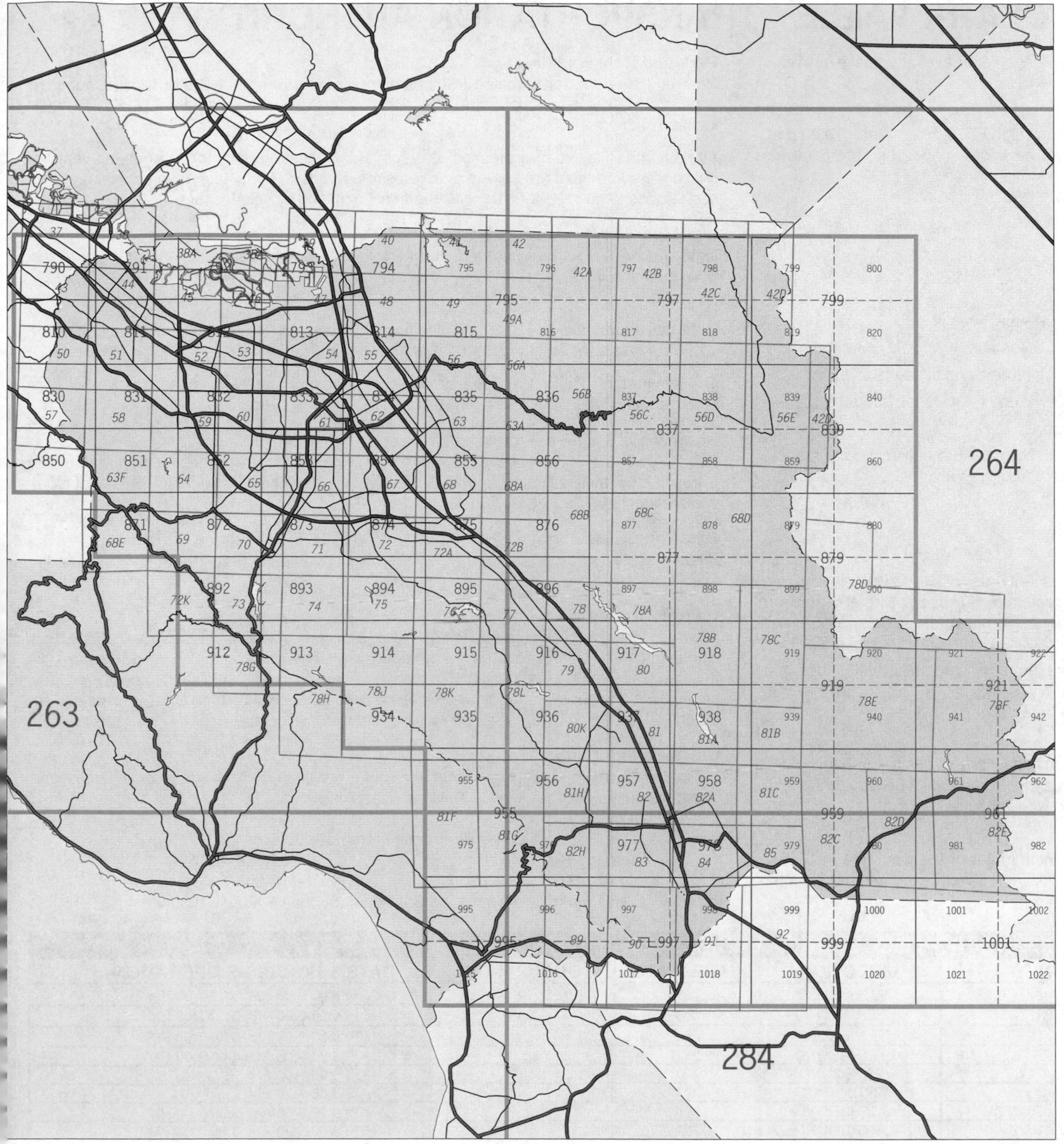

How The New Pages Work With The Old Pages

Finding New Page Numbers

This key map shows our old page layout in green and the new page layout in red. You can locate an old page number on this key map to determine the new page number.

Use of Quad-Pages

To provide important new area coverage, we have created the Quad-Page, a single map page that contains four regular pages of coverage. On the Key Map, Quad-Pages are designated by enlarged numbers in the "Quad" center, and surrounded by the page numbers of the pages included in that "Quad." Normal-size page numbers within a Quad-Page indicate that, in addition to appearing on the Quad-Page, the page is also shown in normal detail and size in the Guide. Small page numbers within the Quad-Pages indicate pages found only on Quad-Pages.

Conversion Help

As you convert to the new Thomas Bros. Maps page and grid reference system, you may have questions or need conversion assistance. If we can be of help, please call the toll-free customer service number below for additional conversion information.

Call toll-free 1 800-899-MAPS and ask for Extension 99.

1998 SANTA CLARA VALLEY TRANSPORTATION AUTHORITY

Santa Clara Valley Transportation Authority (VTA), a convenient travel alternative, provides extensive bus and light rail service throughout the county.

Personal Trip Planning

Trip Planning assistance is available to you Monday through Friday, 5:30 a.m. - 10:00 p.m. and Saturday/Sunday, 7:30 a.m. - 6:00 p.m. Please have pen, paper, and the following information ready:

- Your departure point (nearest cross streets)
- Your destination (nearest cross streets)
- Day and time you wish to travel

VTA Information: .... **(408) 321-2300**
Toll free from 415 Area Code .... **(800) 894-9908**
South County .... **(408) 683-4151**
Teleprinter for the hearing impaired .... **(408) 321-2330**
Or visit our Information Center located in downtown San Jose at 4 North Second Street.

Children under 4 years ride free with an accompanying fare paying passenger.

VTA drivers do not carry change. Please have exact change ready when boarding.

Guide dogs and signal dogs are the only pets allowed.

Monthly Flash Passes are convenient and economical. They are available for adults, youths, seniors, and the disabled. Call VTA for the locations where passes are sold.

Fares

For fares, call VTA Information at (408) 321-2300

TravInfo™

Area Transit Information within the 415, 510, 408, and 707 area codes is available from the new regional TravInfo phone number. This new resource provides a single source for accessing Transit, traffic, rideshare, parking, freeway construction areas and other transit related information. To access this new service, call **817-1717** (no area code needed).

A 24-hour Internet site is available for information on the entire region's transit maps and timetables including AC Transit, and BART. Contact the Internet site at http://server.berkeley.edu/transit/

Buses

There are 73 routes that serve Santa Clara Valley including extensions to the Menlo Park CalTrain Station (San Mateo County-SamTrans) and to the Fremont BART Station (Alameda County-BART/AC Transit). Fifty nine (59) routes are wheelchair accessible.

Express Bus Routes

VTA operates 13 Express bus routes linking residential areas of the County with Silicon Valley Industrial Centers. Major employers work with VTA to develop and refine commuter services.

Park and Ride Facilities

Park and Ride lots are located in convenient areas throughout Santa Clara County to encourage public transit use and ridesharing. Parking in the lots is free. Call VTA for a location near you.

All Park and Ride lots may be used as a convenient meeting point for carpool and vanpool passengers and most are served by Express bus routes. Many lots have special features such as passenger shelters, transit schedule signs, and bicycle lockers.

Light Rail

Light Rail Service currently extends from Santa Teresa/Almaden Valley through downtown San Jose and the Civic Center to the industrial centers along North First Street to Great America.

Light Rail operates every 10-30 minutes from 3:50 a.m. - 1:04 a.m. on weekdays and every 15-30 minutes from 5:09 a.m. - 1:04 a.m. on weekends.

The fare for Light Rail is the same as for regular fare bus routes. All passes acceptable on buses are also acceptable on Light Rail.

South County Dial-A-Ride

Door-to-door Dial-A-Ride is available within outlying areas of Morgan Hill, San Martin and Gilroy. It is not available to those who live within one-quarter mile of a transit route. For more information, call VTA.

Bikes on Buses, Light Rail

Bikes are allowed on all bus lines and Light Rail vehicles as loads permit. Call VTA for specific information.

Historic Trolleys

Restored historic trolleys operate in downtown San Jose between the San Jose Convention Center and the Civic Center. The trolleys operate every 40 minutes daily from Memorial Day to Labor Day from 11:00 a.m. to 6:00 p.m., weather permitting. Valid single ride tickets, day passes and flash passes are good on historic trolleys; special historic trolley tickets can be purchased for $1.10 by all passengers regardless of fare category.

CalTrain Information

For information regarding fares, tickets, schedules or train/bus connections, or any questions and/or comments concerning CalTrain service, please call:

The Peninsula Commute Service
Toll free Hotline **1-800-660-4287**
TDD **1-415-508-6448**
Monday - Friday 6 a.m. to 10 p.m. and Saturday - Sunday 8 a.m. to 8 p.m.

EXISTING HIGH OCCUPANCY VEHICLE (HOV) LANES SUMMARY

COUNTY	ROUTE DESCRIPTION	DIRECTION	LANE MILES	OCCUPANCY	DAYS & HOURS OF OPERATION
SANTA CLARA	**SR85** - ROUTE 237 TO ROUTE 280	SOUTHBOUND	4.1	2+	(M-F) 5:00-9:00 AM; 3:00-7:00 PM
SANTA CLARA	**SR85** - FREMONT AV TO ROUTE 237	NORTHBOUND	2.8	2+	(M-F) 5:00-9:00 AM; 3:00-7:00 PM
SANTA CLARA	**US101** - SAN MATEO CO. LINE TO BERNAL RD	SOUTHBOUND	25.2	2+	(M-F) 5:00-9:00 AM; 3:00-7:00 PM
SANTA CLARA	**US101** - BERNAL RD TO SAN MATEO CO. LINE	NORTHBOUND	24.5	2+	(M-F) 5:00-9:00 AM; 3:00-7:00 PM
SANTA CLARA	**SR237** - ROUTE 880 TO MATHILDA AV	WESTBOUND	6.0	2+	(M-F) 5:00-9:00 AM
SANTA CLARA	**SR237** - MATHILDA TO ZANKER RD	EASTBOUND	5.7	2+	(M-F) 3:00-7:00 PM
SANTA CLARA	**INT280**- MAGDALENA AV TO MERIDIAN AV	SOUTHBOUND	11.2	2+	(M-F) 5:00-9:00 AM; 3:00-7:00 PM
SANTA CLARA	**INT280**- LELAND AV TO MAGDALENA AV	NORTHBOUND	10.7	2+	(M-F) 5:00-9:00 AM; 3:00-7:00 PM

1998 SANTA CLARA COUNTY CITIES AND COMMUNITIES

ESTIMATED POPULATION INCORPORATED CITIES	1,499,085
ESTIMATED POPULATION UNINCORPORATED AREAS	108,615
ESTIMATED TOTAL POPULATION	1,607,700

COMMUNITY NAME	ABBR.	ZIP CODE	EST. POP.	PAGE
ALDERCROFT HEIGHTS		95030		913
ALUM ROCK		95127		834
ALVISO		95002		793
BELL STATION		95020		961
BERRYESSA		95132		814
CAMBRIAN VILLAGE		95124		873
* CAMPBELL	CMBL	95008	38,250	853
CHEMEKETA PARK		95030		912
COYOTE		95013		896
* CUPERTINO	CPTO	95014	43,500	852
EAST SAN JOSE		95127		835
EVERGREEN		95121		855
* GILROY	GIL	95020	33,550	977
HOLY CITY		95026		913
IDYLWILD		95030		912
* LOS ALTOS	LALT	94022	27,200	811
* LOS ALTOS HILLS	LAH	94022	7,775	811
* LOS GATOS	LGTS	95030	29,000	873
MADRONE		95037		916

COMMUNITY NAME	ABBR.	ZIP CODE	EST. POP.	PAGE
* MILPITAS	MPS	95035	59,500	794
MONTA VISTA		95014		852
* MONTE SERENO	MSER	95030	3,260	873
* MORGAN HILL	MGH	95037	27,150	937
* MOUNTAIN VIEW	MTVW	94040	71,500	811
NEW ALMADEN		95042		894
* PALO ALTO	PA	94301	58,600	791
PARADISE VALLEY		95037		936
RANCHO RINCONADA		95014		852
REDWOOD ESTATES		95044		912
RUCKER		95020		957
* SAN JOSE	SJS	95103	846,000	834
SAN MARTIN		95046		937
* SANTA CLARA	SCL	95050	98,200	833
-- SANTA CLARA COUNTY	SCIC		1,607,700	
SAN TOMAS		95008		853
* SARATOGA	SAR	95070	29,600	872
STANFORD		94305		790
* SUNNYVALE	SUNV	94086	126,000	812

*INDICATES INCORPORATED CITY

SANTA CLARA CO. | ZIP | AREA

ZIP CODE POSTAL ZONES

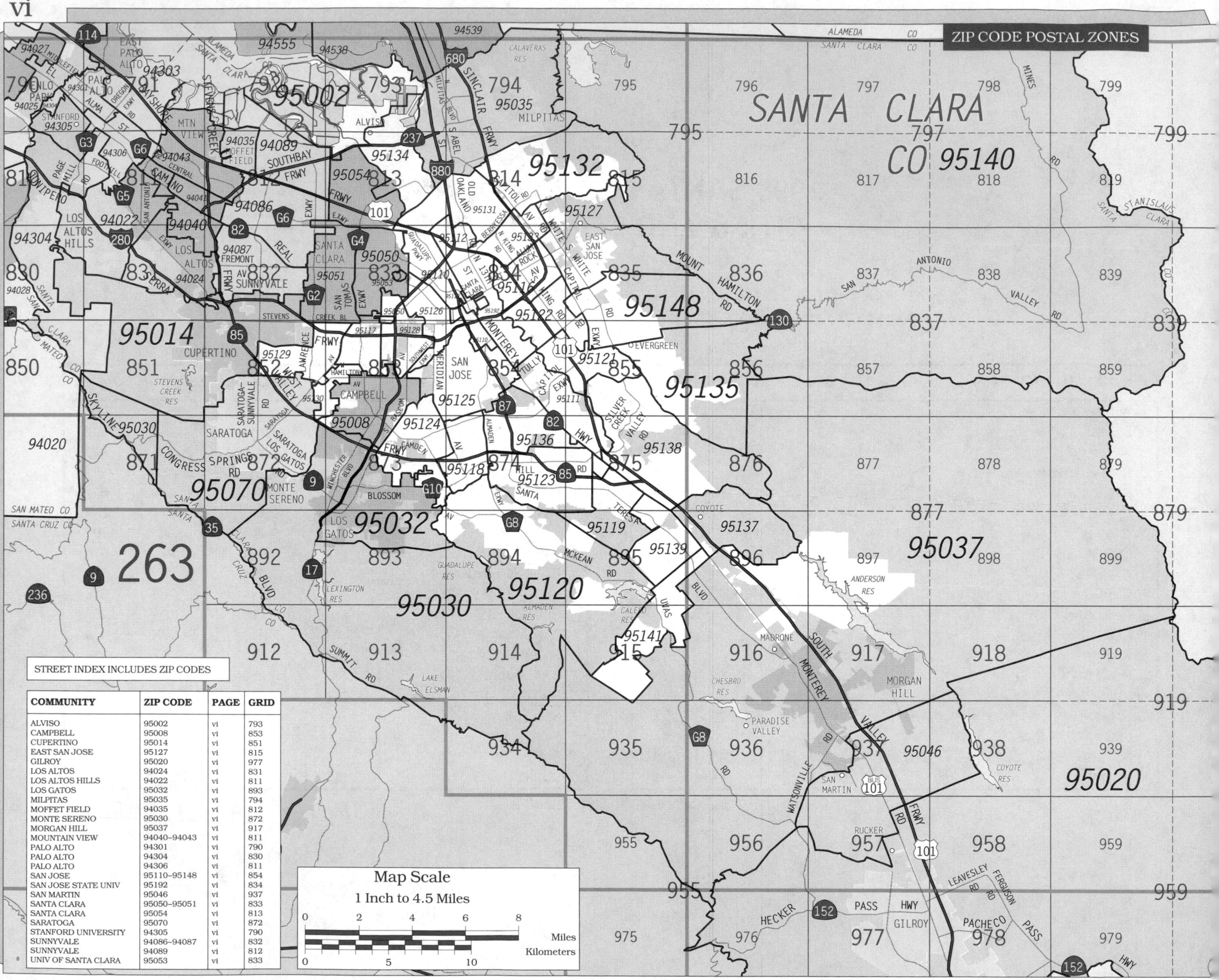

SANTA CLARA CO

STREET INDEX INCLUDES ZIP CODES

COMMUNITY	ZIP CODE	PAGE	GRID
ALVISO	95002	vi	793
CAMPBELL	95008	vi	853
CUPERTINO	95014	vi	851
EAST SAN JOSE	95127	vi	815
GILROY	95020	vi	977
LOS ALTOS	94024	vi	831
LOS ALTOS HILLS	94022	vi	811
LOS GATOS	95032	vi	893
MILPITAS	95035	vi	794
MOFFET FIELD	94035	vi	812
MONTE SERENO	95030	vi	872
MORGAN HILL	95037	vi	917
MOUNTAIN VIEW	94040–94043	vi	811
PALO ALTO	94301	vi	790
PALO ALTO	94304	vi	830
PALO ALTO	94306	vi	811
SAN JOSE	95110–95148	vi	854
SAN JOSE STATE UNIV	95192	vi	834
SAN MARTIN	95046	vi	937
SANTA CLARA	95050–95051	vi	833
SANTA CLARA	95054	vi	813
SARATOGA	95070	vi	872
STANFORD UNIVERSITY	94305	vi	790
SUNNYVALE	94086–94087	vi	832
SUNNYVALE	94089	vi	812
UNIV OF SANTA CLARA	95053	vi	833

8

Map Scale

1 Inch to 4.5 Miles

0 2 4 6 8 Miles

0 5 10 Kilometers

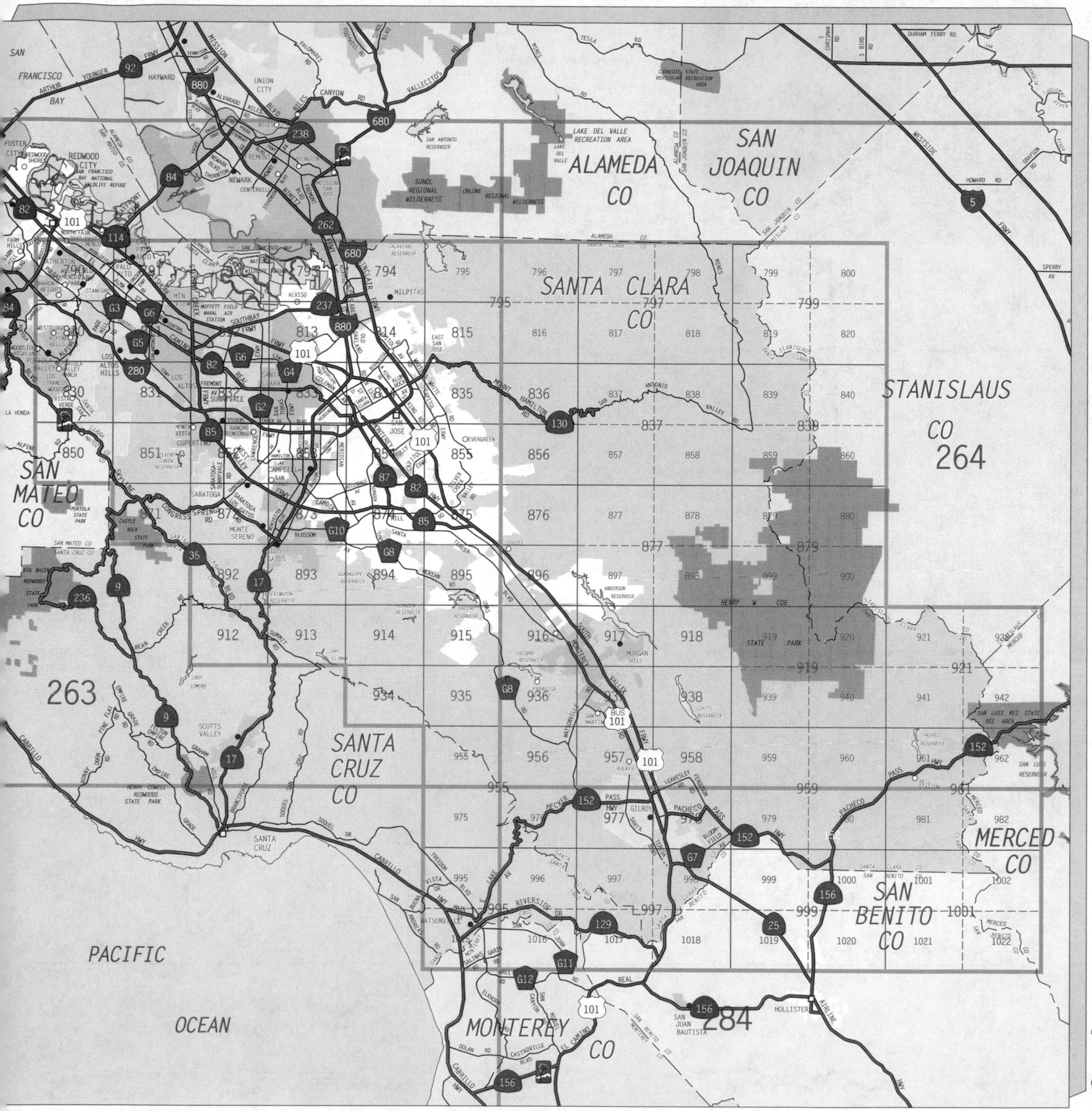

Key Map to Detail Pages

The Thomas Guide® contains several types of map pages:
Arterial, Detail, and Quad

263	**Arterial Page**– Small scale area map, shown with a wide border
810	**Detail Page**– Full scale map page, shown with a solid thin border
837	**Quad Page**– A single map page containing four interior pages at half the detail scale, shown with a bold border subdivided by thin dashed lines
838	Interior pages are shown only inside Quad pages

Key Legend

- • Incorporated City
- ○ Community
- □ County Seat
- Freeway
- Highway
- Primary
- Secondary, Minor
- River, Creek

Key Map Scale

1 Inch to 8 Miles

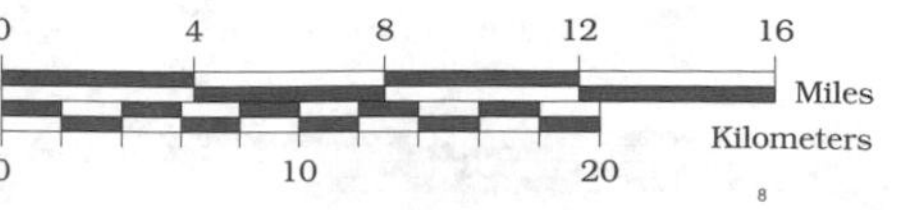

LEGEND OF MAP SYMBOLS

NORTH

SANTA CLARA CO.

ZIP

AREA

- Freeway
- Interchange/Ramp
- Highway
- Primary Road
- Secondary Road
- Minor Road
- Restricted Road
- Alley
- Unpaved Road
- Tunnel
- Toll Road
- High Occupancy Veh. Lane
- Stacked Multiple Roadways
- Proposed Road
- Proposed Freeway
- Freeway Under Construction
- One-Way Road
- Two-Way Road
- Trail, Walkway
- Stairs
- Railroad
- Rapid Transit
- Rapid Transit, Underground
- City Boundary
- County Boundary
- State Boundary
- International Boundary
- Military Base, Indian Resv.
- Township, Range, Rancho
- River, Creek, Shoreline
- Ferry

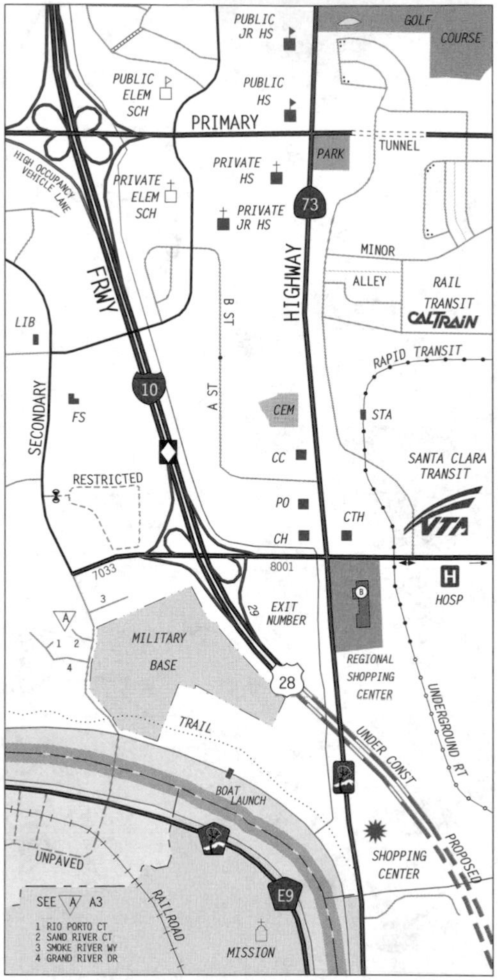

- Interstate
- Interstate (Business)
- U.S. Highway
- State Highway
- County Highway
- State Scenic Highway
- County Scenic Highway
- Carpool Lane
- Street List Marker
- Street Name Continuation
- Street Name Change
- Airport
- Station (Train,Bus)
- Building (see List of Abbreviations page)
- Building Footprint
- Public Elementary School
- Public High School
- Private Elementary School
- Private High School
- Shopping Center
- Fire Station
- Library
- Mission
- Winery
- Campground
- Hospital
- Mountain
- Section Corner
- Boat Launch
- Gates, Locks, Barricades
- Lighthouse

- County Seat
- County
- Incorporated City
- Incorporated City
- Incorporated City
- Incorporated City
- Incorporated City
- City, County, State Park
- National Forest, Park
- Water
- Intermittent Lake, Marsh
- Dry Lake, Beach
- Dam
- Point of Interest
- Golf Course, Country Club
- Cemetery
- Military Base
- Airport
- Parking Lot
- Structure Footprint
- Regional Shopping Center
- Major Dept. Store (List of Abbr. page

Public Land Survey

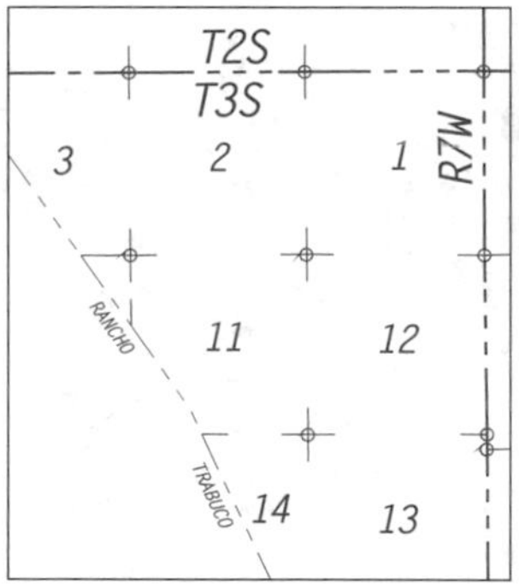

T2S
T3S
R7W
3 2 1
11 12
14 13
RANCHO
TRABUCO

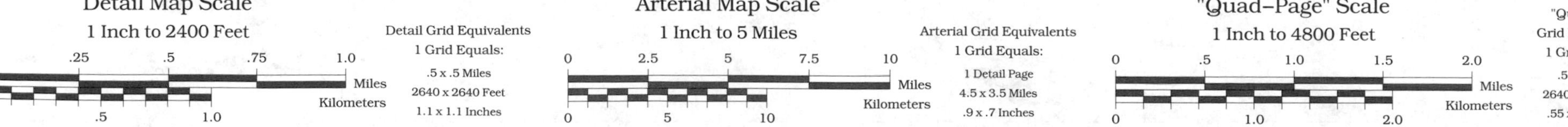

Downtown San Jose

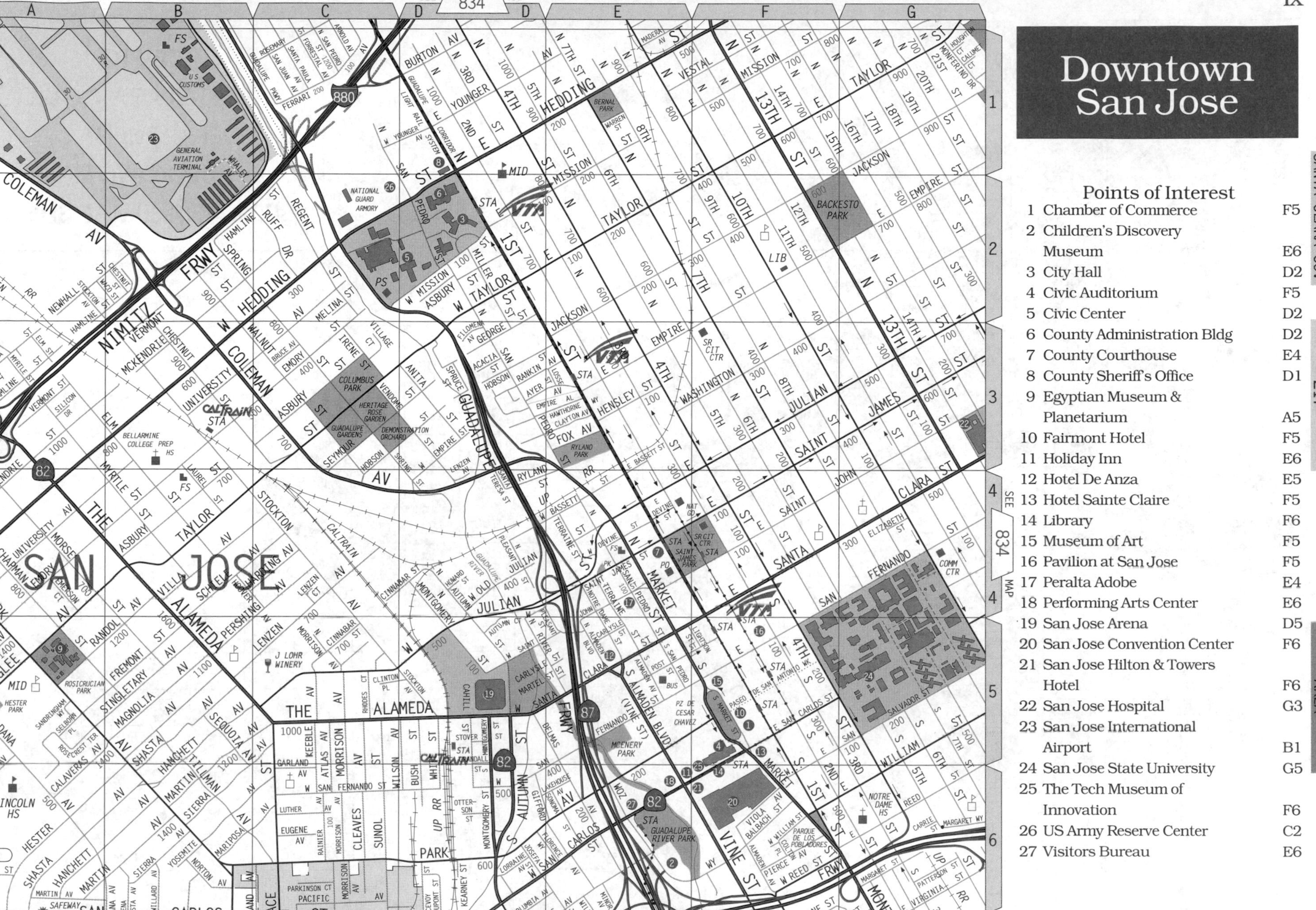

Points of Interest

1	Chamber of Commerce	F5
2	Children's Discovery Museum	E6
3	City Hall	D2
4	Civic Auditorium	F5
5	Civic Center	D2
6	County Administration Bldg	D2
7	County Courthouse	E4
8	County Sheriff's Office	D1
9	Egyptian Museum & Planetarium	A5
10	Fairmont Hotel	F5
11	Holiday Inn	E6
12	Hotel De Anza	E5
13	Hotel Sainte Claire	F5
14	Library	F6
15	Museum of Art	F5
16	Pavilion at San Jose	F5
17	Peralta Adobe	E4
18	Performing Arts Center	E6
19	San Jose Arena	D5
20	San Jose Convention Center	F6
21	San Jose Hilton & Towers Hotel	F6
22	San Jose Hospital	G3
23	San Jose International Airport	B1
24	San Jose State University	G5
25	The Tech Museum of Innovation	F6
26	US Army Reserve Center	C2
27	Visitors Bureau	E6

Map Scale

0 660 1320 1980 2640 Feet

0 .125 .25 .375 .5 Miles

KEY TO SANTA CLARA COUNTY DEPARTMENT OF PUBLIC WORKS 500FT SCALE MAP SHEETS

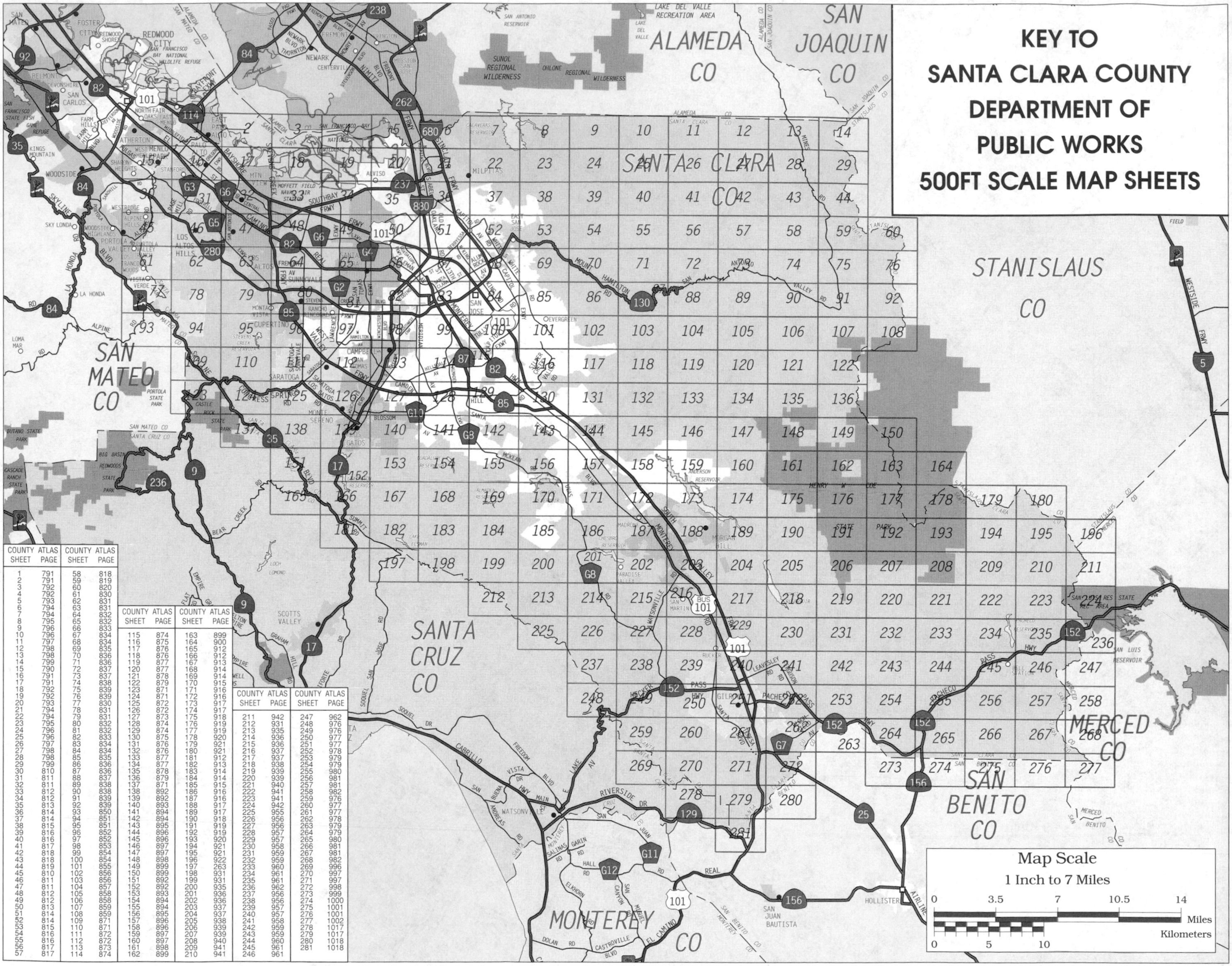

ALAMEDA CO
SAN JOAQUIN CO
SANTA CLARA CO
STANISLAUS CO
SAN MATEO CO
SANTA CRUZ CO
MERCED CO
SAN BENITO CO
MONTEREY CO

COUNTY SHEET	ATLAS PAGE	COUNTY SHEET	ATLAS PAGE
1	791	58	818
2	791	59	819
3	792	60	820
4	792	61	830
5	793	62	831
6	794	63	831
7	794	64	832
8	795	65	832
9	796	66	833
10	796	67	834
11	797	68	834
12	798	69	835
13	798	70	836
14	799	71	836
15	790	72	837
16	791	73	837
17	791	74	838
18	792	75	839
19	792	76	839
20	793	77	830
21	794	78	831
22	794	79	831
23	795	80	832
24	796	81	832
25	796	82	833
26	797	83	834
27	798	84	834
28	798	85	835
29	799	86	836
30	810	87	836
31	811	88	837
32	811	89	838
33	812	90	838
34	812	91	839
35	813	92	839
36	814	93	850
37	814	94	851
38	815	95	851
39	816	96	852
40	816	97	852
41	817	98	853
42	818	99	854
43	818	100	854
44	819	101	855
45	810	102	856
46	811	103	856
47	811	104	857
48	812	105	858
49	812	106	858
50	813	107	859
51	814	108	859
52	814	109	871
53	815	110	871
54	816	111	872
55	816	112	872
56	817	113	873
57	817	114	874

COUNTY SHEET	ATLAS PAGE	COUNTY SHEET	ATLAS PAGE
115	874	163	899
116	875	164	900
117	876	165	912
118	876	166	912
119	877	167	913
120	877	168	914
121	878	169	914
122	879	170	915
123	871	171	916
124	871	172	916
125	872	173	917
126	872	174	917
127	873	175	918
128	874	176	919
129	874	177	919
130	875	178	920
131	876	179	921
132	876	180	921
133	877	181	912
134	877	182	913
135	878	183	914
136	879	184	914
137	871	185	915
138	892	186	916
139	892	187	916
140	893	188	917
141	894	189	917
142	894	190	918
143	895	191	919
144	896	192	919
145	896	193	920
146	897	194	921
147	897	195	921
148	898	196	922
149	899	197	263
150	899	198	931
151	892	199	931
152	892	200	935
153	893	201	936
154	894	202	936
155	894	203	937
156	895	204	937
157	896	205	938
158	896	206	939
159	897	207	939
160	897	208	940
161	898	209	941
162	899	210	941

COUNTY SHEET	ATLAS PAGE	COUNTY SHEET	ATLAS PAGE
211	942	247	962
212	931	248	976
213	935	249	976
214	936	250	977
215	936	251	977
216	937	252	978
217	937	253	979
218	938	254	979
219	939	255	980
220	939	256	981
221	940	257	981
222	941	258	982
223	941	259	976
224	942	260	977
225	955	261	977
226	956	262	978
227	956	263	979
228	957	264	979
229	957	265	980
230	958	266	981
231	959	267	981
232	959	268	982
233	960	269	996
234	961	270	997
235	961	271	997
236	962	272	998
237	956	273	999
238	956	274	1000
239	957	275	1001
240	957	276	1001
241	958	277	1002
242	959	278	1017
243	959	279	1017
244	960	280	1018
245	961	281	1018
246	961		

Map Scale
1 Inch to 7 Miles

0 3.5 7 10.5 14 Miles
0 5 10 Kilometers

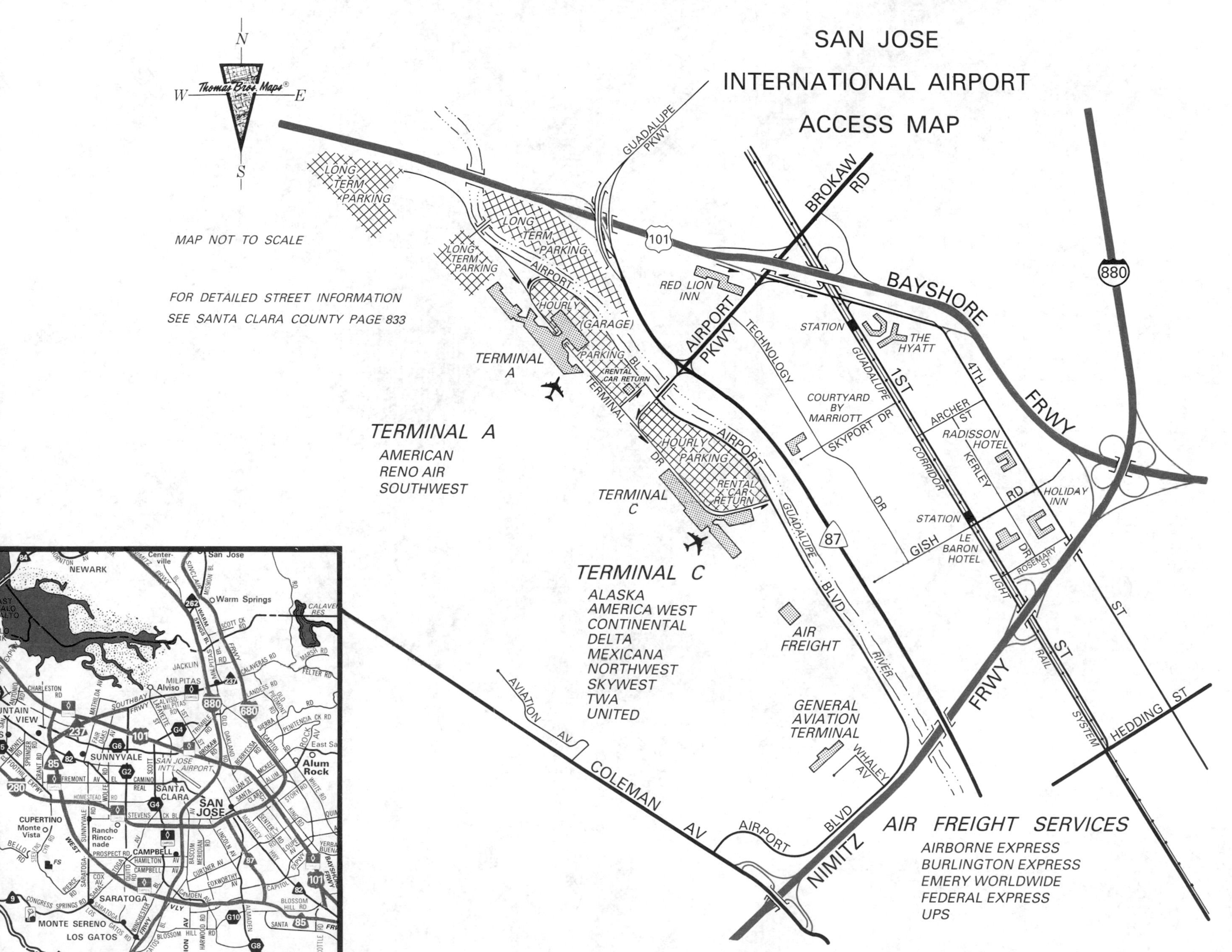
SAN JOSE
INTERNATIONAL AIRPORT
ACCESS MAP
Thomas Bros. Maps®
N
S
E
W
MAP NOT TO SCALE
FOR DETAILED STREET INFORMATION
SEE SANTA CLARA COUNTY PAGE 833
LONG TERM PARKING
HOURLY (GARAGE) PARKING
RENTAL CAR RETURN
TERMINAL A
TERMINAL C
HOURLY PARKING
TERMINAL A
AMERICAN
RENO AIR
SOUTHWEST
TERMINAL C
ALASKA
AMERICA WEST
CONTINENTAL
DELTA
MEXICANA
NORTHWEST
SKYWEST
TWA
UNITED
RED LION INN
THE HYATT
COURTYARD BY MARRIOTT
RADISSON HOTEL
HOLIDAY INN
LE BARON HOTEL
STATION
AIR FREIGHT
GENERAL AVIATION TERMINAL
AIR FREIGHT SERVICES
AIRBORNE EXPRESS
BURLINGTON EXPRESS
EMERY WORLDWIDE
FEDERAL EXPRESS
UPS
BAYSHORE FRWY
NIMITZ FRWY
AIRPORT PKWY
GUADALUPE PKWY
BROKAW RD
TECHNOLOGY DR
SKYPORT DR
ARCHER ST
KERLEY DR
GISH RD
ROSEMARY ST
GUADALUPE CORRIDOR LIGHT RAIL SYSTEM
1ST ST
4TH ST
HEDDING ST
AIRPORT BL
TERMINAL DR
GUADALUPE RIVER
AIRPORT BLVD
AVIATION AV
COLEMAN AV
WHALEY AV
101
880
87
SANTA CLARA CO.
ZIP
AREA

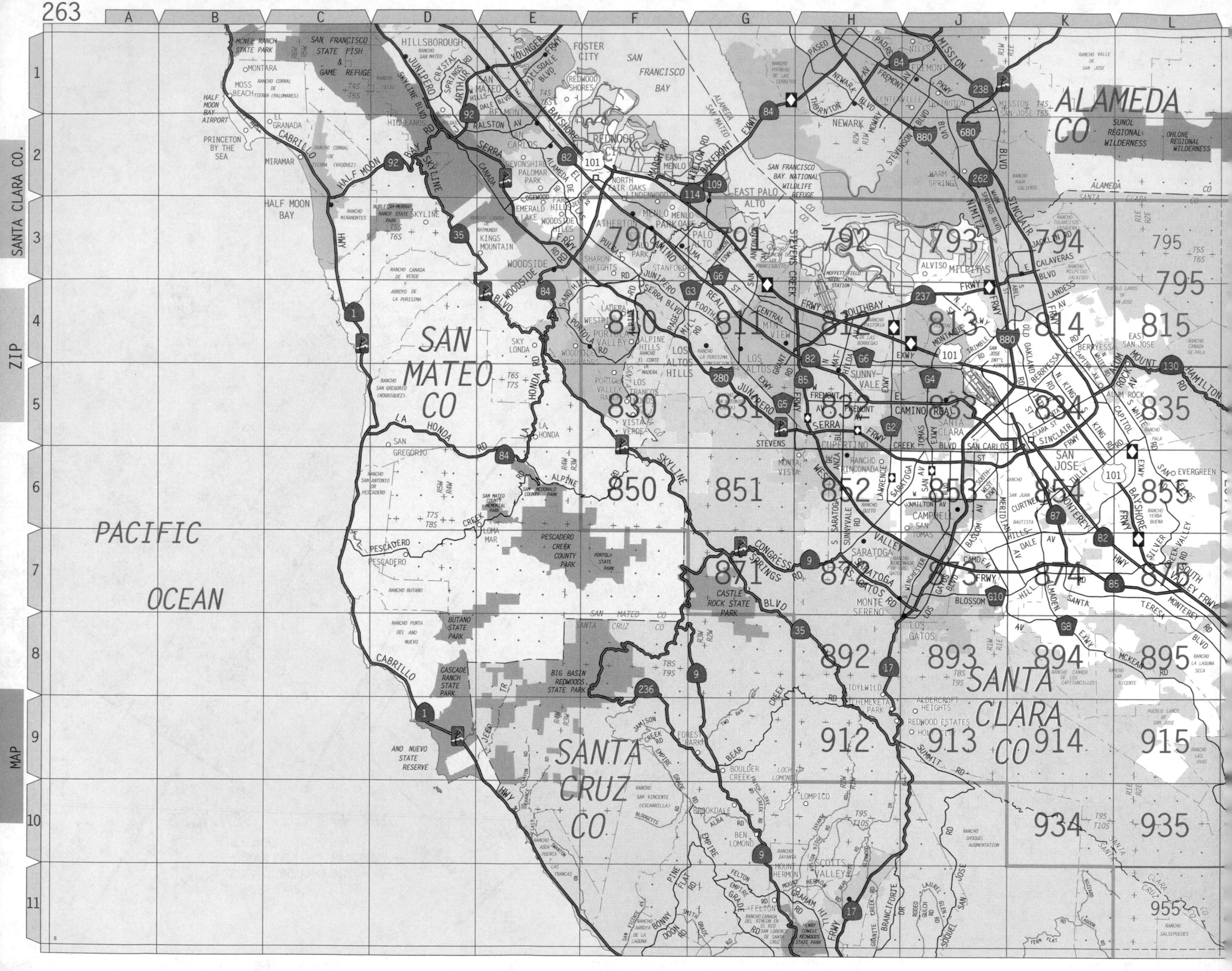
SANTA CLARA CO.
ZIP
MAP
PACIFIC
OCEAN
SAN MATEO CO
SANTA CRUZ CO
SANTA CLARA CO
ALAMEDA CO
SAN FRANCISCO BAY
790
791
792
793
794
795
810
811
812
813
814
815
830
831
832
833
834
835
850
851
852
853
854
855
871
872
873
874
875
892
893
894
895
912
913
914
915
934
935
955

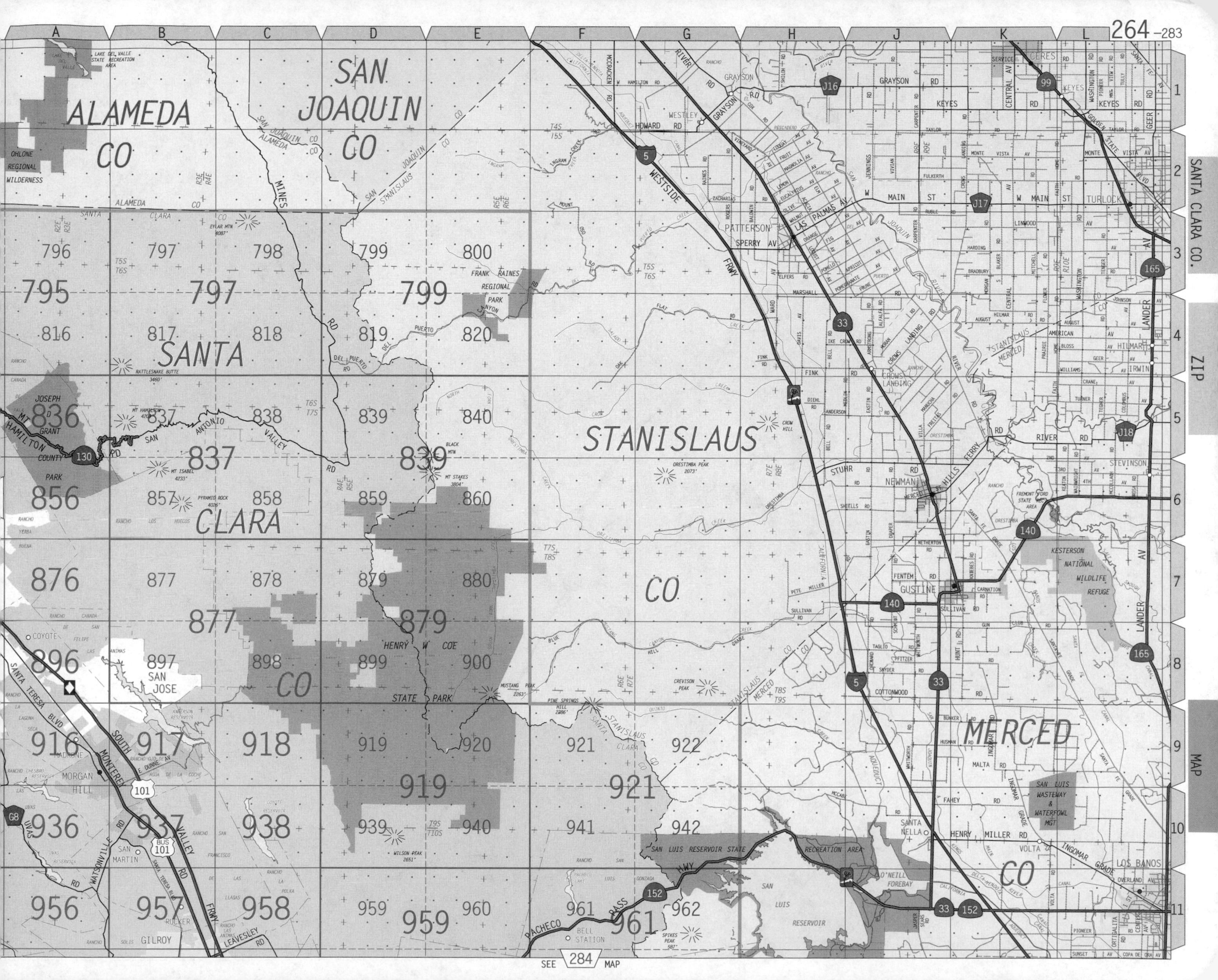
ALAMEDA CO
SAN JOAQUIN CO
SANTA CLARA
STANISLAUS CO
MERCED CO
SANTA CLARA CO. ZIP MAP
OHLONE REGIONAL WILDERNESS
LAKE DEL VALLE STATE RECREATION AREA
FRANK RAINES REGIONAL PARK
JOSEPH D GRANT COUNTY PARK
HENRY W COE STATE PARK
KESTERSON NATIONAL WILDLIFE REFUGE
SAN LUIS WASTEWAY & WATERFOWL MGT
SAN LUIS RESERVOIR STATE RECREATION AREA
O'NEILL FOREBAY
SAN LUIS RESERVOIR
PATTERSON
WESTLEY
GRAYSON
CROWS LANDING
NEWMAN
GUSTINE
HILMAR
IRWIN
STEVINSON
TURLOCK
KEYES
CERES
SANTA NELLA
VOLTA
LOS BANOS
SAN JOSE
COYOTE
MORGAN HILL
SAN MARTIN
GILROY
BELL STATION
795 796 797 798 799 800
816 817 818 819 820
836 837 838 839 840
856 857 858 859 860
876 877 878 879 880
896 897 898 899 900
916 917 918 919 920 921 922
936 937 938 939 940 941 942
956 957 958 959 960 961 962
WESTSIDE FRWY
PACHECO PASS HWY
MONTEREY RD
SANTA TERESA BLVD
INGOMAR GRADE
LANDER AV
SEE 284 MAP

SEE 264 MAP

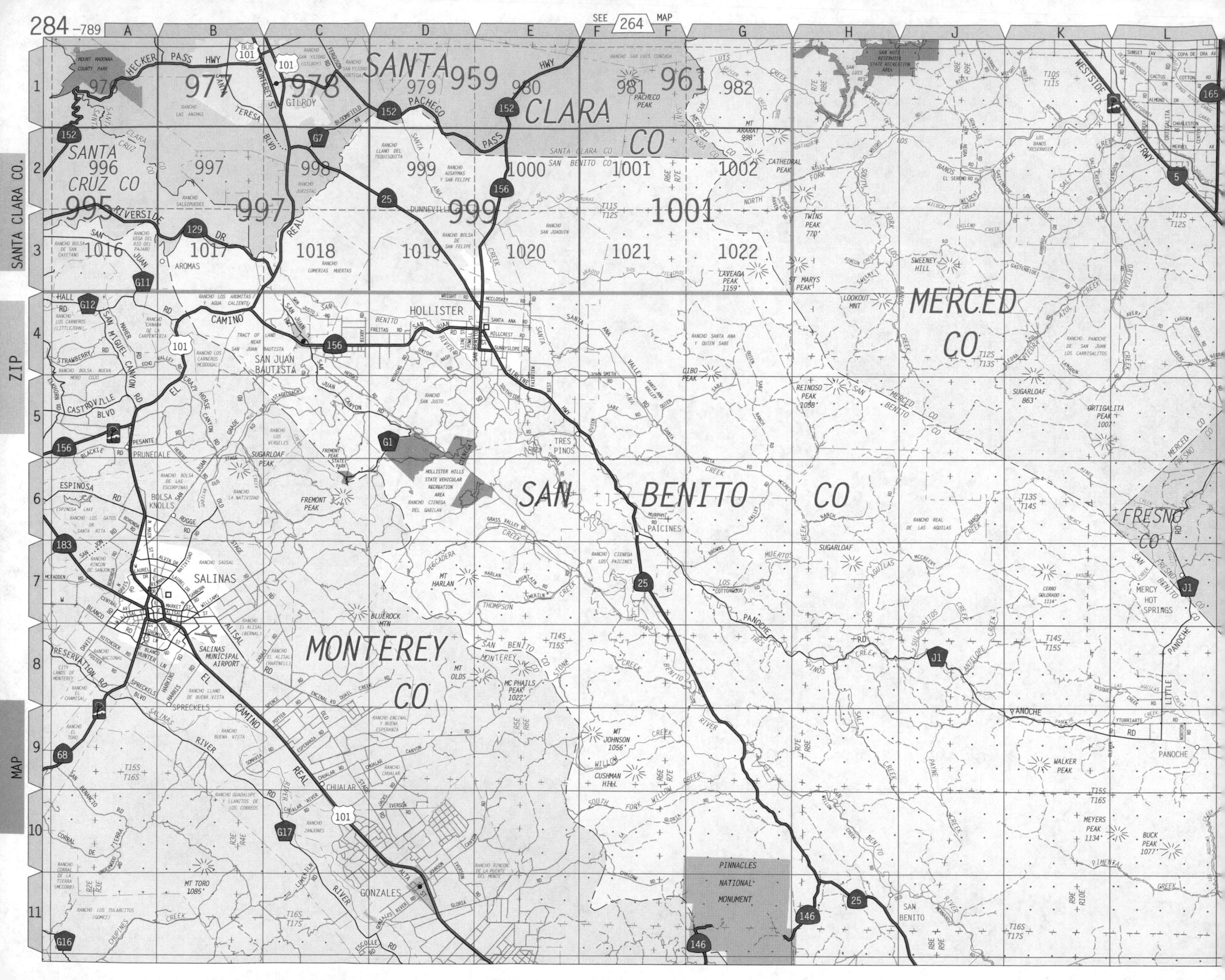
A B C D E F G H J K L
1 2 3 4 5 6 7 8 9 10 11
SANTA CLARA CO.
ZIP
MAP
SANTA CLARA CO
SANTA CRUZ CO
SAN BENITO CO
MERCED CO
MONTEREY CO
FRESNO CO
SANTA CLARA CO
SAN BENITO CO
HECKER PASS HWY
MOUNT MADONNA COUNTY PARK
GILROY
MONTEREY ST
PACHECO PASS HWY
PACHECO PEAK
MT ARARAT 998'
CATHEDRAL PEAK
TWINS PEAK 770'
SAN LUIS RESERVOIR STATE RECREATION AREA
LOS BANOS RESERVOIR
WESTSIDE FRWY
ORTIGALITA
976
977
978
979
959
980
981
961
982
995
996
997
998
999
1000
1001
1002
1016
1017
1018
1019
1020
1021
1022
DUNNEVILLE
RIVERSIDE DR
AROMAS
SWEENEY HILL
LAVEAGA PEAK 1159'
ST MARYS PEAK
LOOKOUT MNT
HOLLISTER
SAN JUAN BAUTISTA
CAMINO REAL
SAN MIGUEL CANYON RD
CASTROVILLE BLVD
STRAWBERRY RD
CRAZY HORSE CANYON RD
PRUNEDALE
PESANTE
SUGARLOAF PEAK
FREMONT PEAK STATE PARK
FREMONT PEAK
HOLLISTER HILLS STATE VEHICULAR RECREATION AREA
TRES PINOS
CIBO PEAK
REINOSO PEAK 1058'
SUGARLOAF 863'
ORTIGALITA PEAK 1007'
ESPINOSA RD
BOLSA KNOLLS
ROGGE RD
PAICINES
MT HARLAN
SUGARLOAF
CERRO COLORADO 1114'
MERCY HOT SPRINGS
SALINAS
BLUEROCK MTN
SALINAS MUNICIPAL AIRPORT
ALISAL
MT OLDS
MC PHAILS PEAK 1022'
PANOCHE RD
SPRECKELS
RESERVATION RD
SALINAS RIVER
MT JOHNSON 1056'
CUSHMAN HILL
WALKER PEAK
PANOCHE
CHUALAR
MEYERS PEAK 1134'
BUCK PEAK 1077'
CORRAL DE TIERRA
MT TORO 1085'
GONZALES
PINNACLES NATIONAL MONUMENT
SAN BENITO
ESCOLLE RD
101
152
156
25
129
183
68
G1
G7
G11
G12
G16
G17
J1
5
165
146

SEE SM 770 MAP

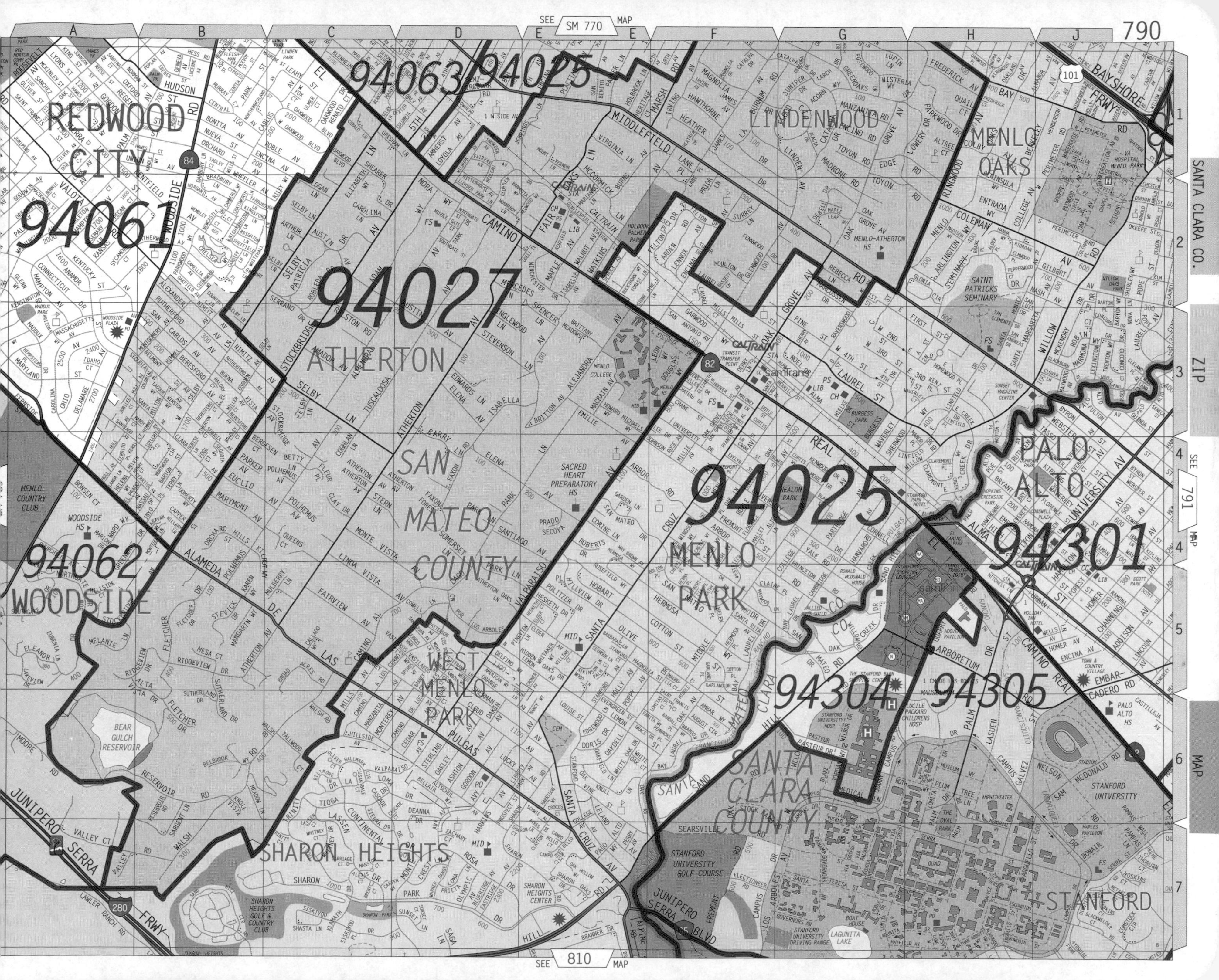

SEE 810 MAP

SEE SM 771 MAP

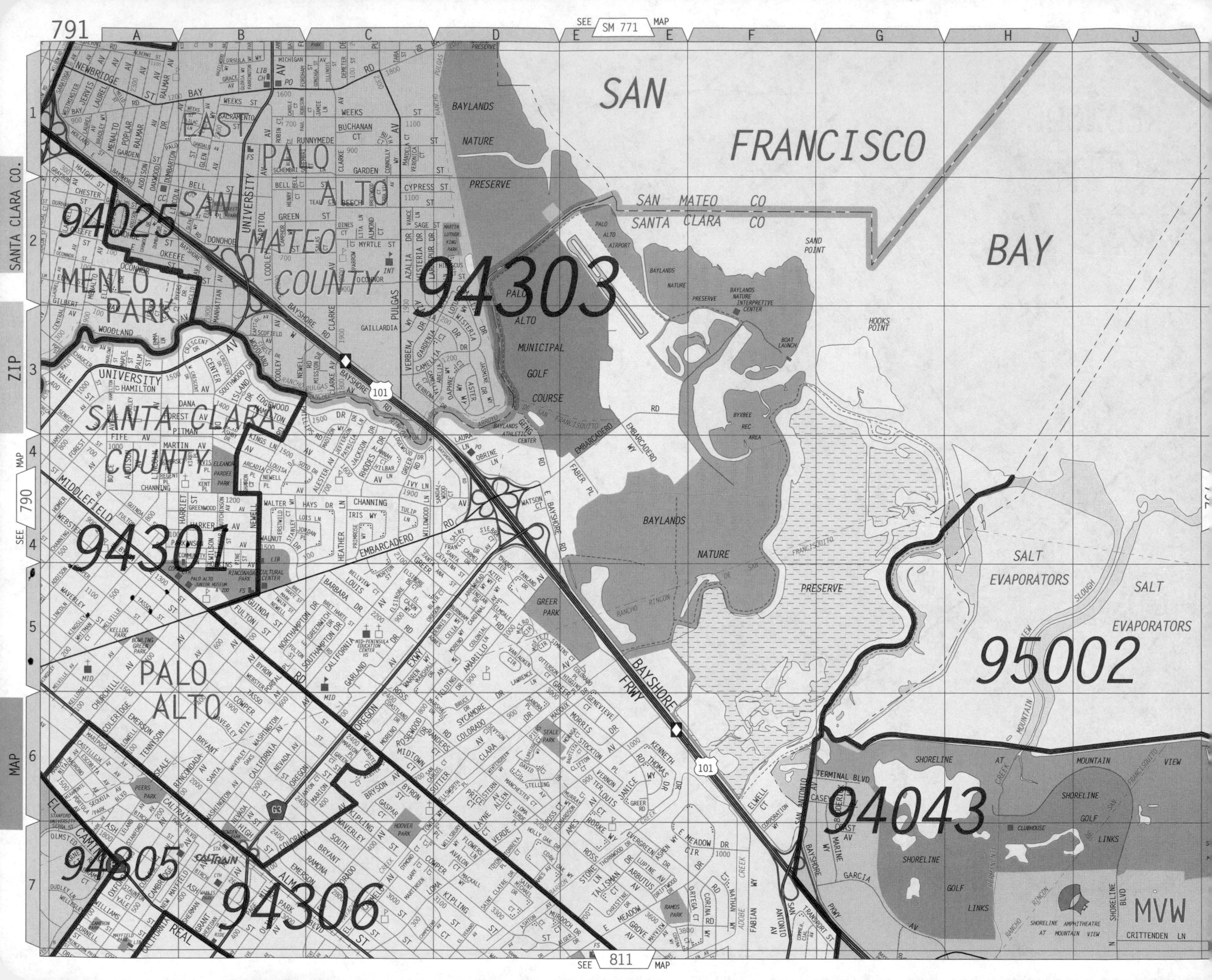

SEE 811 MAP

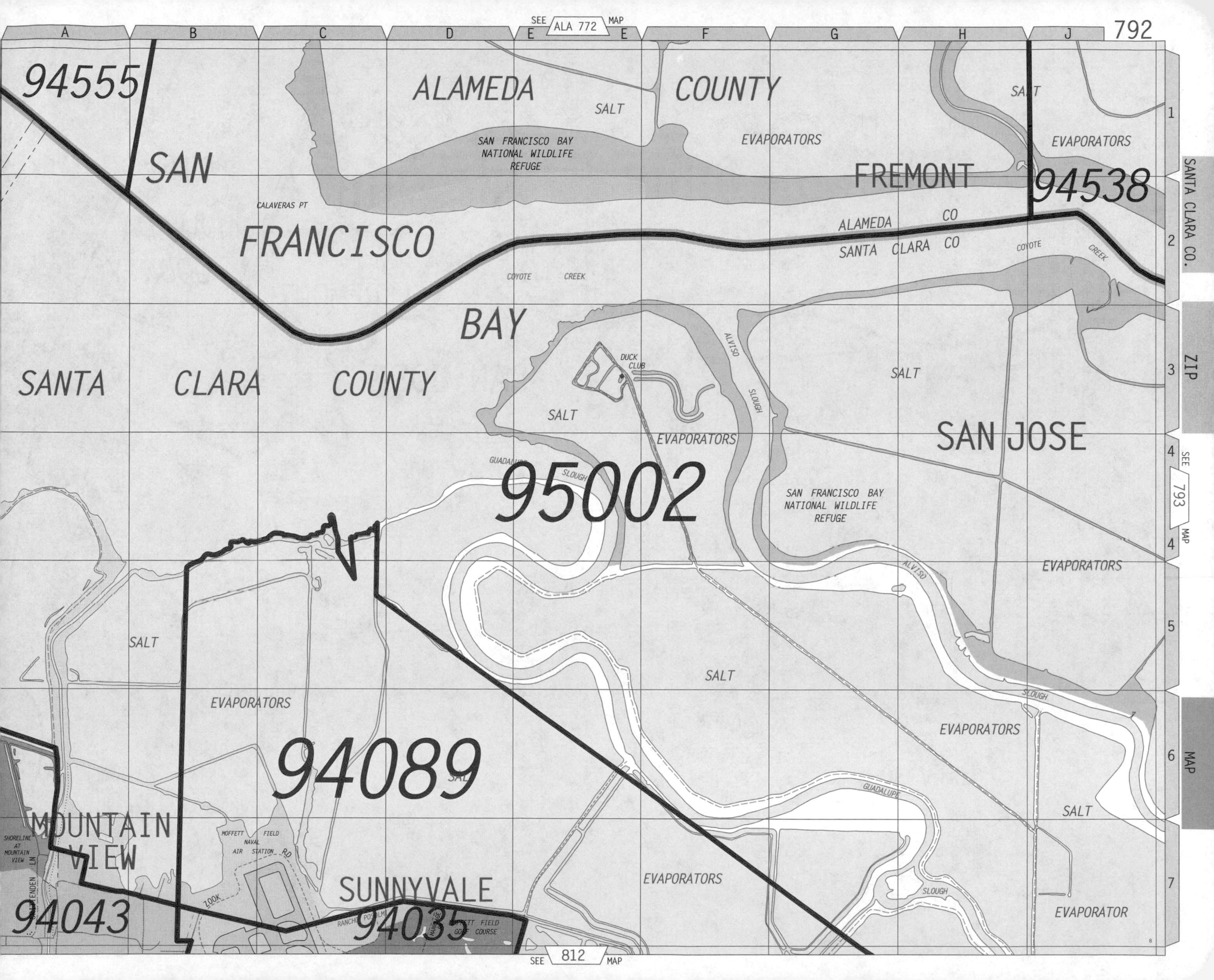
SEE ALA 772 MAP
A
B
C
D
E
E
F
G
H
J
94555
SAN
FRANCISCO
BAY
SANTA CLARA COUNTY
ALAMEDA COUNTY
SALT
EVAPORATORS
SAN FRANCISCO BAY
NATIONAL WILDLIFE
REFUGE
CALAVERAS PT
FREMONT
94538
ALAMEDA CO
SANTA CLARA CO
COYOTE CREEK
DUCK CLUB
ALVISO SLOUGH
SAN JOSE
GUADALUPE SLOUGH
95002
94089
MOUNTAIN VIEW
SHORELINE AT MOUNTAIN VIEW
94043
MOFFETT FIELD NAVAL AIR STATION
SUNNYVALE
94035
MOFFETT FIELD GOLF COURSE
EVAPORATOR
SEE 793 MAP
SEE 812 MAP
SANTA CLARA CO.
ZIP
MAP
1
2
3
4
4
5
6
7

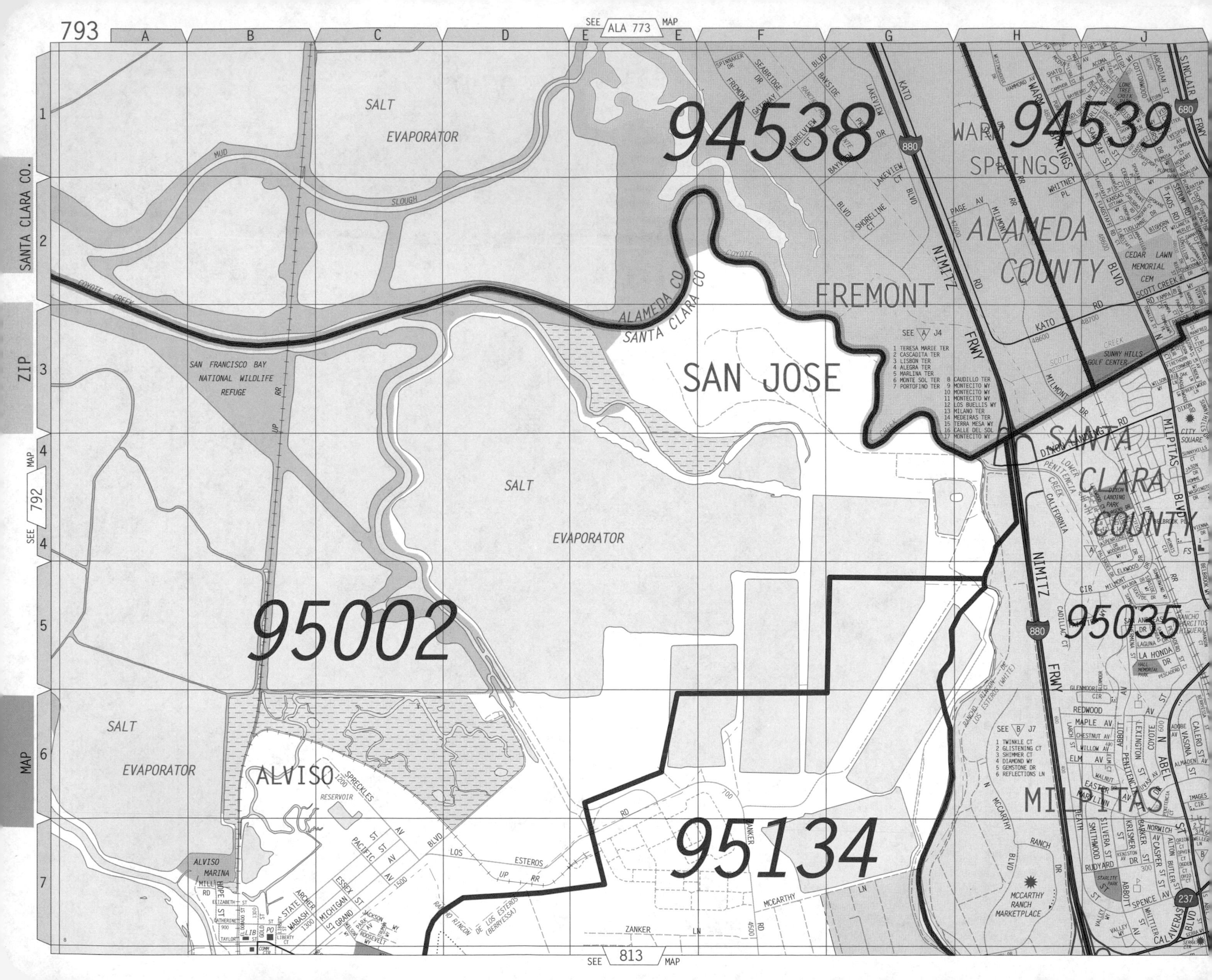
SEE ALA 773 MAP
94538
94539
95002
95035
95134
SALT EVAPORATOR
SAN FRANCISCO BAY NATIONAL WILDLIFE REFUGE
MUD SLOUGH
COYOTE CREEK
ALAMEDA CO
SANTA CLARA CO
SAN JOSE
FREMONT
WARM SPRINGS
ALAMEDA COUNTY
SANTA CLARA COUNTY
MILPITAS
ALVISO
ALVISO MARINA
NIMITZ FRWY
CEDAR LAWN MEMORIAL CEM
SUNNY HILLS GOLF CENTER
McCARTHY RANCH MARKETPLACE
SEE A J4
1 TERESA MARIE TER
2 CASCADITA TER
3 LISBON TER
4 ALEGRA TER
5 MARLINA TER
6 MONTE SOL TER
7 PORTOFINO TER
8 CAUDILLO TER
9 MONTECITO WY
10 MONTECITO WY
11 MONTECITO WY
12 LOS BUELLIS WY
13 MILANO TER
14 MEDEIRAS TER
15 TERRA MESA WY
16 CALLE DEL SOL
17 MONTECITO WY
SEE B J7
1 TWINKLE CT
2 GLISTENING CT
3 SHIMMER CT
4 DIAMOND WY
5 GEMSTONE DR
6 REFLECTIONS LN
SANTA CLARA CO.
ZIP
MAP
SEE 792 MAP
SEE 813 MAP

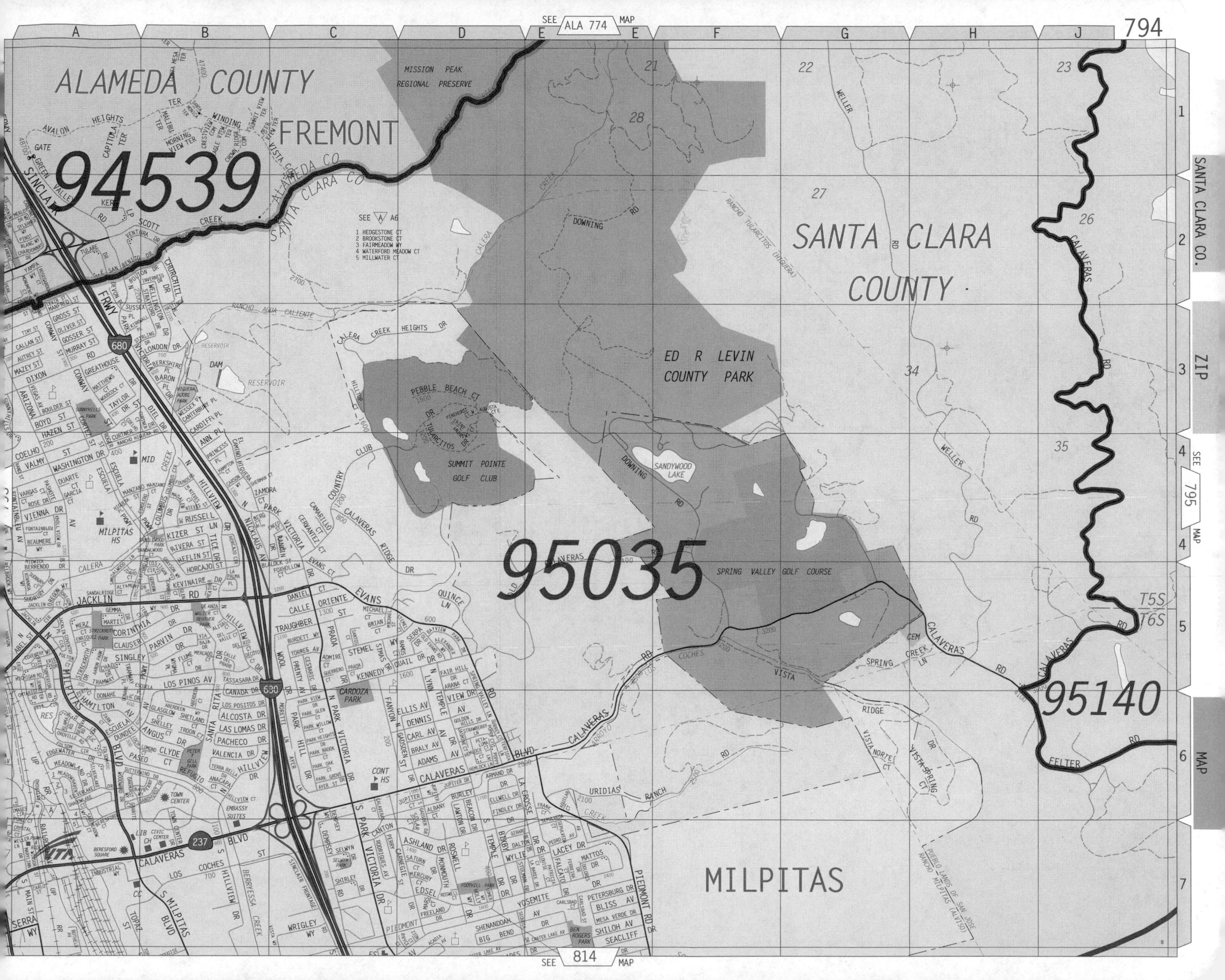

SEE ALA 774 MAP
ALAMEDA COUNTY
FREMONT
94539
MISSION PEAK REGIONAL PRESERVE
SANTA CLARA COUNTY
ED R LEVIN COUNTY PARK
SUMMIT POINTE GOLF CLUB
SANDYWOOD LAKE
SPRING VALLEY GOLF COURSE
95035
95140
MILPITAS
MILPITAS HS
CARDOZA PARK
TOWN CENTER
EMBASSY SUITES
BERESFORD SQUARE
SEE A A6
1 HEDGESTONE CT
2 BROOKSTONE CT
3 FAIRMEADOW WY
4 WATERFORD MEADOW CT
5 MILLWATER CT
CALAVERAS BLVD
CALAVERAS RD
EVANS RD
JACKLIN RD
PIEDMONT RD
FELTER RD
DOWNING RD
SANTA CLARA CO.
ZIP
MAP
SEE 795 MAP
SEE 814 MAP

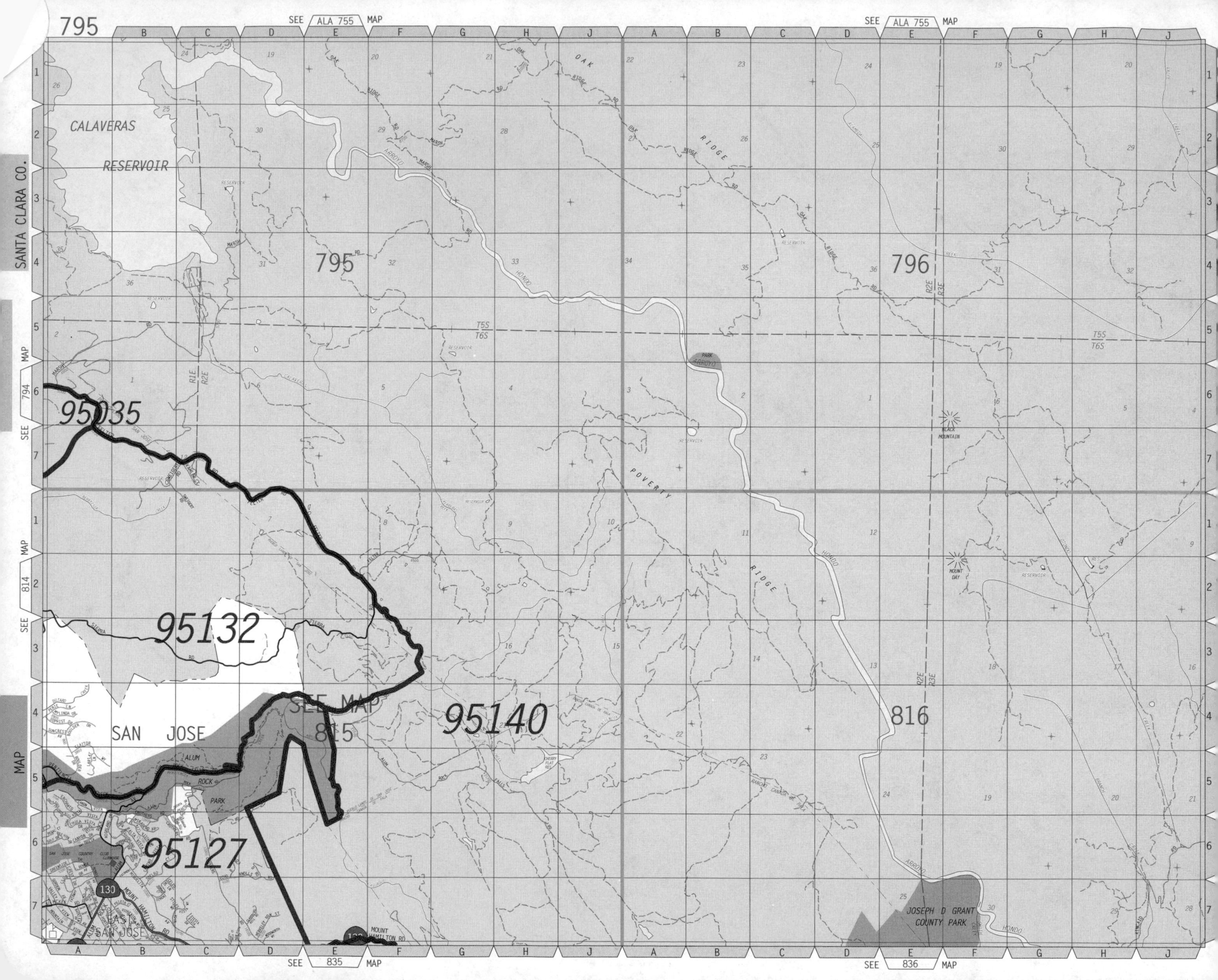
SEE ALA 755 MAP
SEE ALA 755 MAP
CALAVERAS
RESERVOIR
795
796
95035
95132
95140
95127
SEE MAP 815
816
SAN JOSE
EAST SAN JOSE
OAK RIDGE RD
POVERTY RIDGE
ARROYO HONDO
MARSH RD
ALUM ROCK
PARK
JOSEPH D GRANT COUNTY PARK
BLACK MOUNTAIN
MOUNT DAY
CHERRY FLAT RES
MOUNT HAMILTON RD
130
T5S
T6S
R1E R2E
R2E R3E
SANTA CLARA CO.
SEE 794 MAP
SEE 814 MAP
SEE 835 MAP
SEE 836 MAP

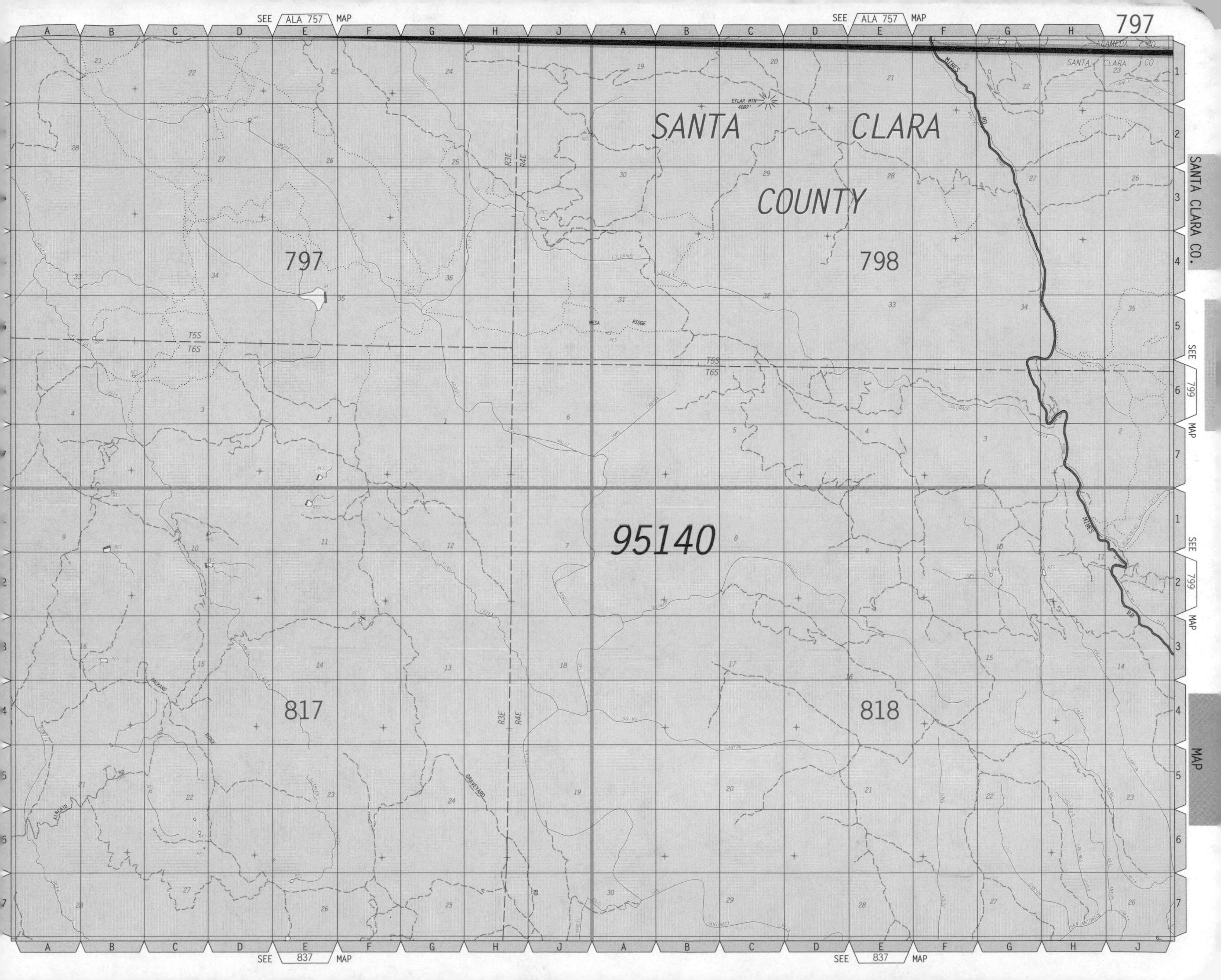
SEE ALA 757 MAP
SEE ALA 757 MAP
SANTA CLARA COUNTY
797
798
817
818
95140
EYLAR MTN 4087'
ALAMEDA CO
SANTA CLARA CO
MINES RD
COLORADO
MESA RIDGE
T5S
T6S
R3E
R4E
PACKARD RIDGE
GRAVEYARD
SPRING CANYON
SAN ANTONIO CREEK
KINCAID RD
SANTA CLARA CO.
SEE 799 MAP
SEE 799 MAP
MAP
SEE 837 MAP
SEE 837 MAP

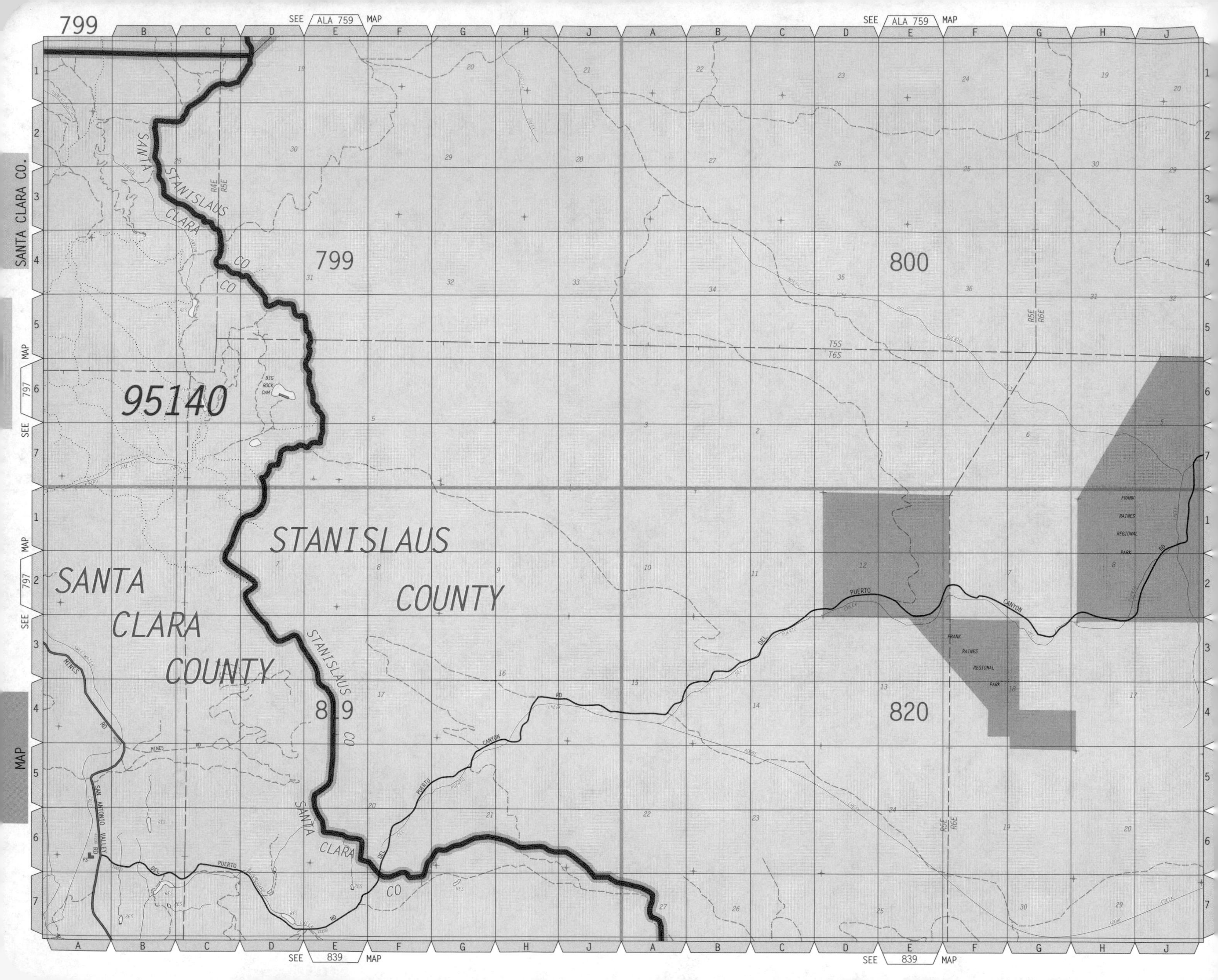

SEE ALA 759 MAP
SEE ALA 759 MAP
799
800
819
820
95140
SANTA CLARA CO.
SEE 797 MAP
SEE 797 MAP
SEE MAP
STANISLAUS
COUNTY
SANTA
CLARA
COUNTY
SANTA STANISLAUS
CLARA CO
CO
STANISLAUS CO
SANTA CLARA CO
BIG ROCK DAM
T5S
T6S
R4E R5E
R5E R6E
FRANK RAINES REGIONAL PARK
FRANK RAINES REGIONAL PARK
DEL PUERTO CANYON RD
PUERTO CANYON
MINES RD
SAN ANTONIO VALLEY RD
SEE 839 MAP
SEE 839 MAP

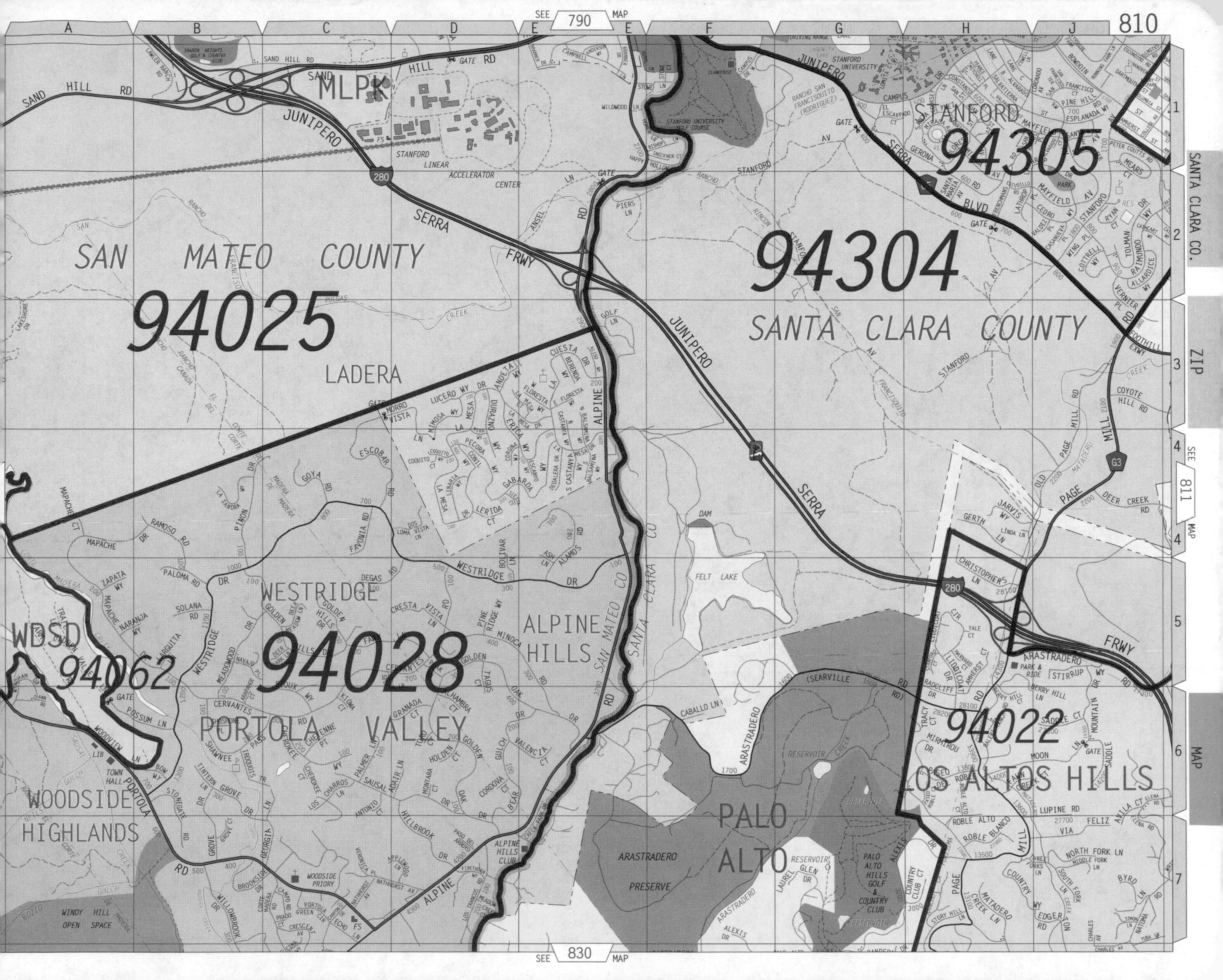
SEE 790 MAP
SEE 830 MAP
SEE 811 MAP
SANTA CLARA CO.
ZIP
MAP
MLPK
STANFORD
STANFORD UNIVERSITY
STANFORD UNIVERSITY GOLF COURSE
STANFORD LINEAR ACCELERATOR CENTER
94305
94304
94025
94028
94062
94022
SAN MATEO COUNTY
SANTA CLARA COUNTY
SAN MATEO CO
SANTA CLARA CO
LADERA
WESTRIDGE
ALPINE HILLS
PORTOLA VALLEY
WDSD
WOODSIDE HIGHLANDS
LOS ALTOS HILLS
PALO ALTO
ARASTRADERO PRESERVE
FELT LAKE
WINDY HILL OPEN SPACE
WOODSIDE PRIORY
PALO ALTO HILLS GOLF & COUNTRY CLUB
ALPINE HILLS CLUB
SHARON HEIGHTS GOLF & COUNTRY CLUB
SAND HILL RD
JUNIPERO SERRA FRWY
ALPINE RD
PORTOLA RD
ARASTRADERO RD
PAGE MILL RD
FOOTHILL EXWY
STANFORD AV
WESTRIDGE DR
280

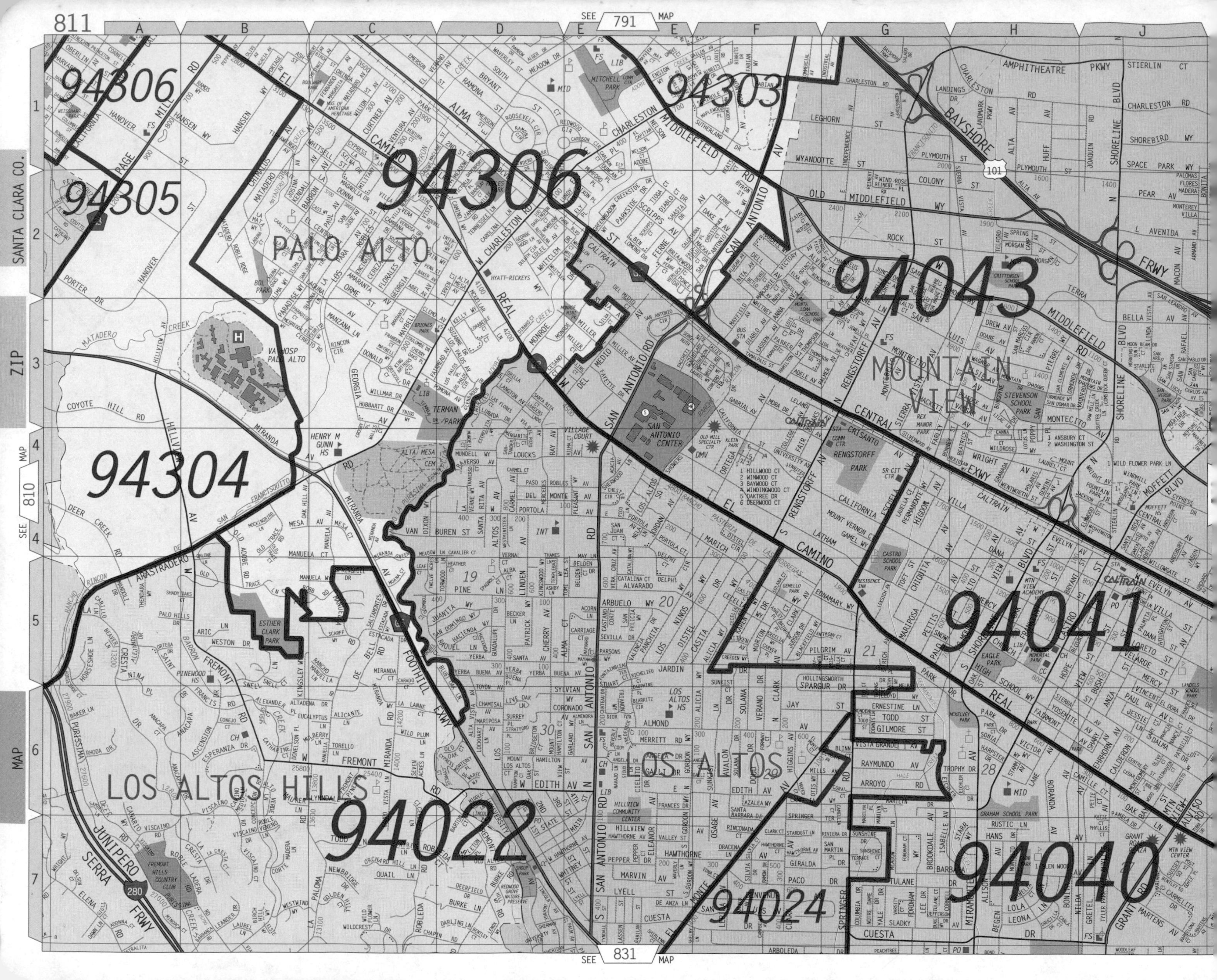
811
SEE 791 MAP
A
B
C
D
E
F
G
H
J
1
2
3
4
5
6
7
SANTA CLARA CO.
ZIP
MAP
SEE 810 MAP
94306
94305
94303
94043
94304
94041
94022
94024
94040
PALO ALTO
MOUNTAIN VIEW
LOS ALTOS
LOS ALTOS HILLS
VA HOSP PALO ALTO
HENRY M GUNN HS
SAN ANTONIO CENTER
MITCHELL PARK
RENGSTORFF PARK
TERMAN PARK
ESTHER CLARK PARK
FREMONT HILLS COUNTRY CLUB
LOS ALTOS HS
HILLVIEW COMMUNITY CENTER
AMPHITHEATRE PKWY
BAYSHORE FRWY
CHARLESTON RD
MIDDLEFIELD RD
CENTRAL EXWY
EL CAMINO REAL
ALMA ST
FOOTHILL EXWY
SAN ANTONIO RD
JUNIPERO SERRA FRWY
280
101
SEE 831 MAP

SEE 792 MAP

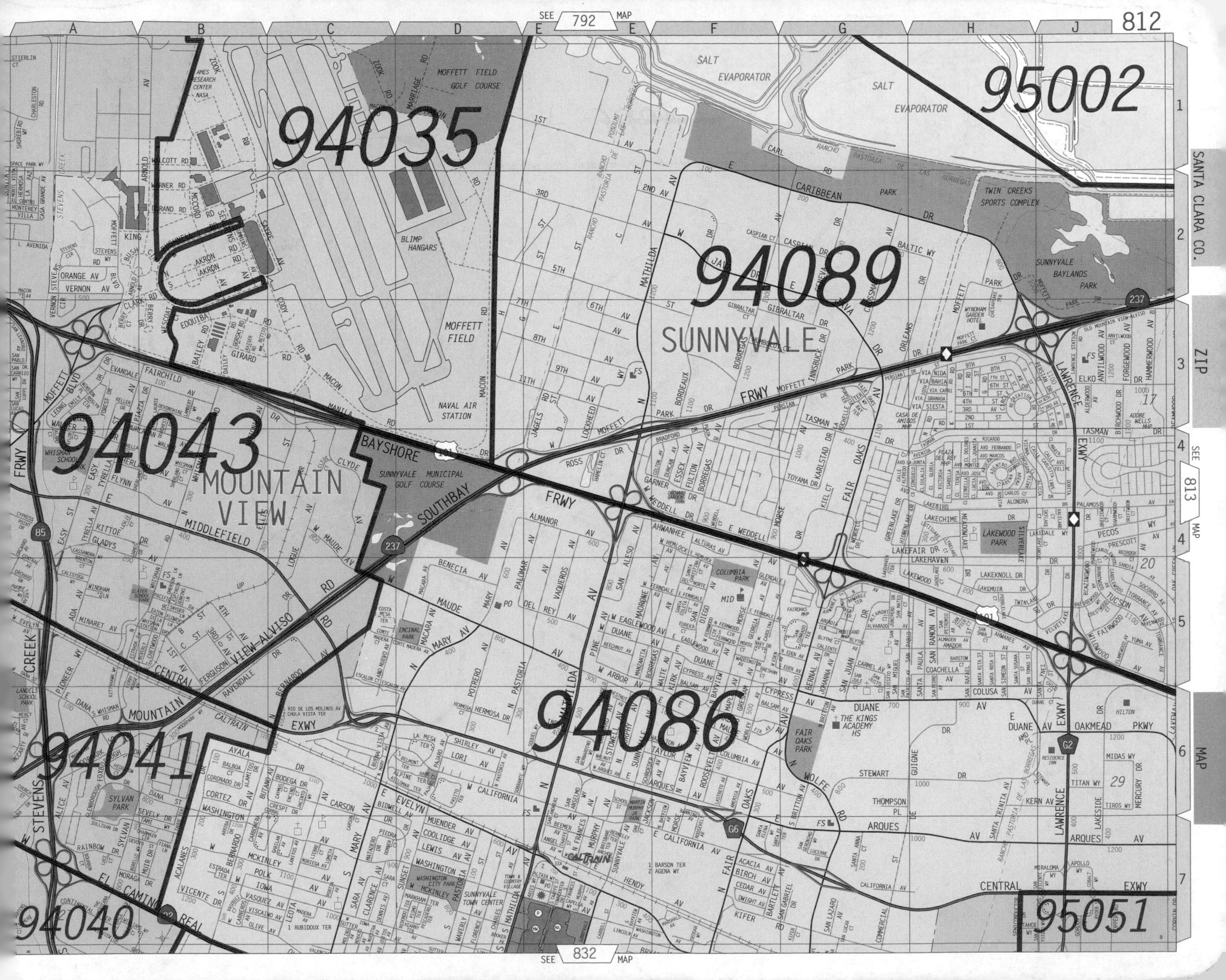

SEE 832 MAP

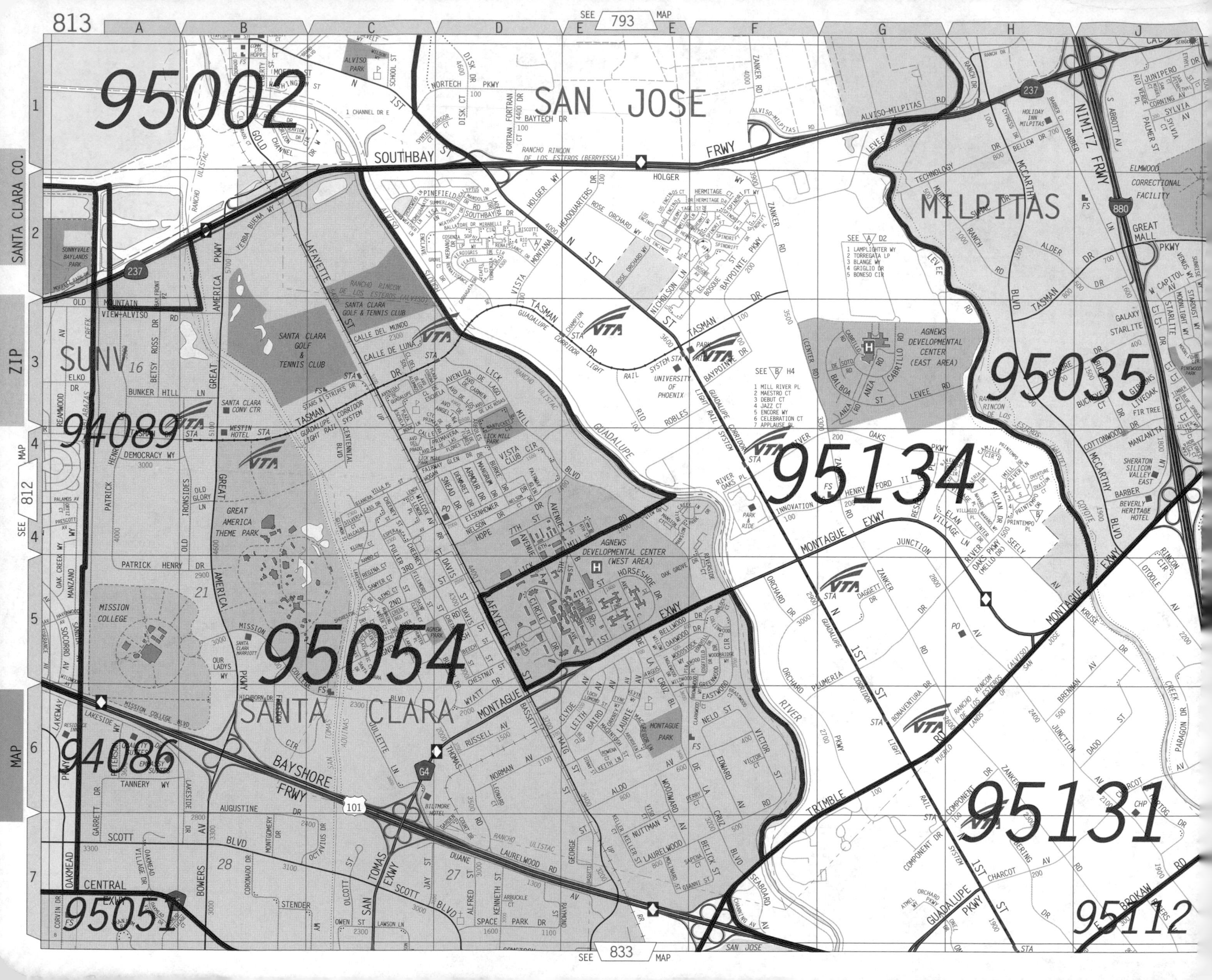

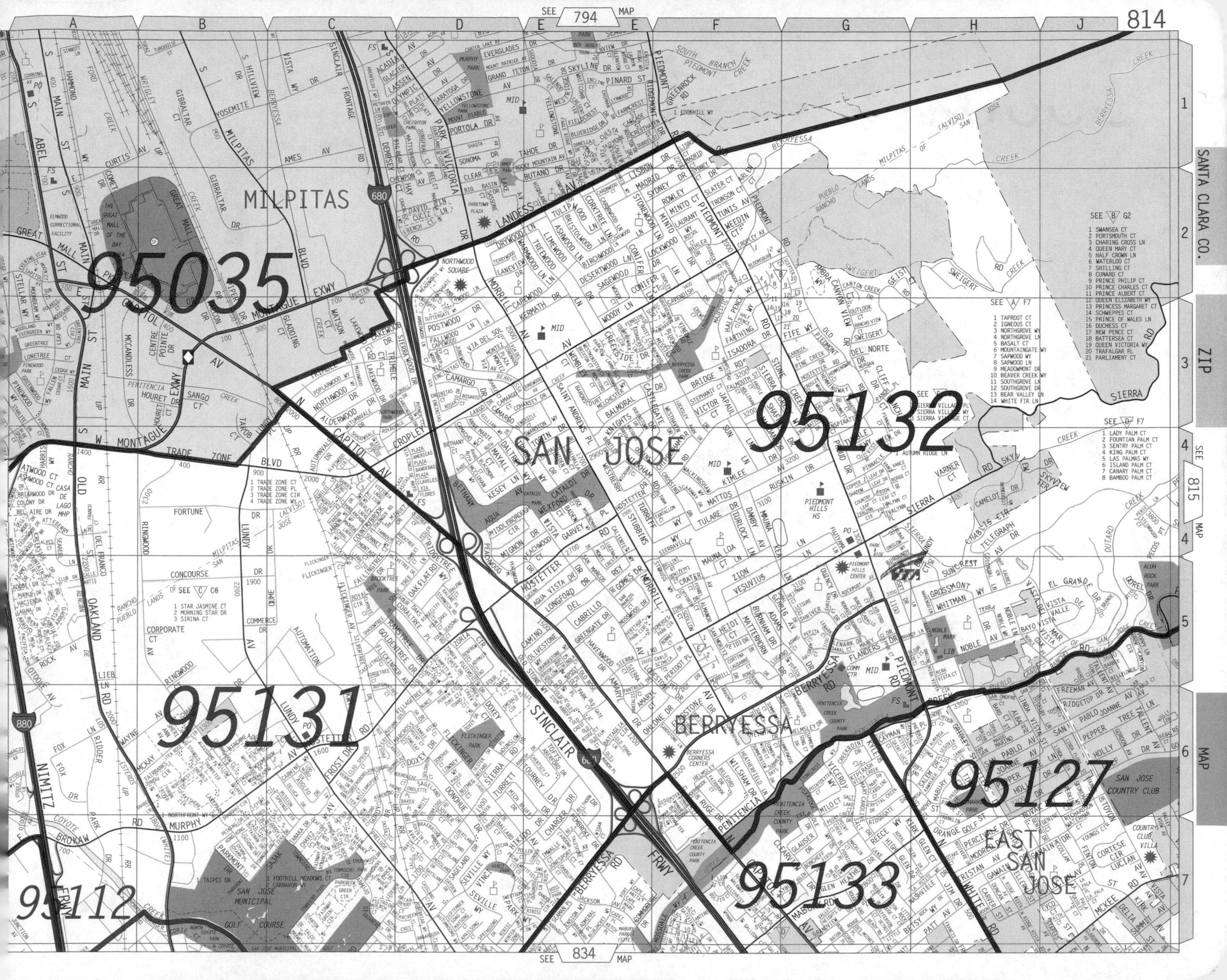

SEE 794 MAP
A
B
C
D
E
F
G
H
J
1
2
3
4
5
6
7
MILPITAS
SAN JOSE
BERRYESSA
EAST SAN JOSE
95035
95132
95131
95133
95127
95112
SANTA CLARA CO.
ZIP
MAP
SEE 815 MAP
SEE 834 MAP
GREAT MALL OF THE BAY AREA
ELMWOOD CORRECTIONAL FACILITY
MONTAGUE EXWY
CAPITOL AV
TRADE ZONE BLVD
LANDESS AV
PIEDMONT RD
BERRYESSA RD
SIERRA RD
SINCLAIR FRWY
NIMITZ FRWY
OAKLAND RD
LUNDY AV
HOSTETTER RD
MORRILL AV
MAIN ST
ABEL ST
GREAT MALL PKWY
PIEDMONT HILLS HS
PIEDMONT HILLS CENTER
BERRYESSA CORNERS CENTER
PENITENCIA CREEK COUNTY PARK
SAN JOSE COUNTRY CLUB
SAN JOSE MUNICIPAL GOLF COURSE
ALUM ROCK PARK
FLICKINGER PARK
NOBLE PARK
MURPHY PARK
NORTHWOOD SQUARE
PARKTOWN PLAZA
COUNTRY CLUB VILLA
1 TRADE ZONE CT
2 TRADE ZONE PL
3 TRADE ZONE CIR
4 TRADE ZONE WY
SEE C C6
1 STAR JASMINE CT
2 MORNING STAR DR
3 SIRINA CT
SEE B G2
1 SWANSEA CT
2 PORTSMOUTH CT
3 CHARING CROSS LN
4 QUEEN MARY CT
5 HALF CROWN LN
6 WATERLOO CT
7 SHILLING CT
8 CUNARD CT
9 PRINCE PHILIP CT
10 PRINCE CHARLES CT
11 PRINCE ALBERT CT
12 QUEEN ELIZABETH WY
13 PRINCESS MARGARET CT
14 SCHWEPPES CT
15 PRINCE OF WALES LN
16 DUCHESS CT
17 NEW PENCE CT
18 BATTERSEA CT
19 QUEEN VICTORIA WY
20 TRAFALGAR PL
21 PARLIAMENT CT
SEE A F7
1 TAPROOT CT
2 IGNEOUS CT
3 NORTHGROVE WY
4 NORTHGROVE LN
5 BASALT CT
6 MOUNTAINGATE WY
7 SAPWOOD WY
8 SAPWOOD LN
9 MEADOWMONT DR
10 BEAVER CREEK WY
11 SOUTHGROVE LN
12 SOUTHGROVE DR
13 BEAR VALLEY LN
14 WHITE FIR LN
SEE D F7
1 LADY PALM CT
2 FOUNTIAN PALM CT
3 SENTRY PALM CT
4 KING PALM CT
5 LAS PALMAS WY
6 ISLAND PALM CT
7 CANARY PALM CT
8 BAMBOO PALM CT

SEE 795 MAP

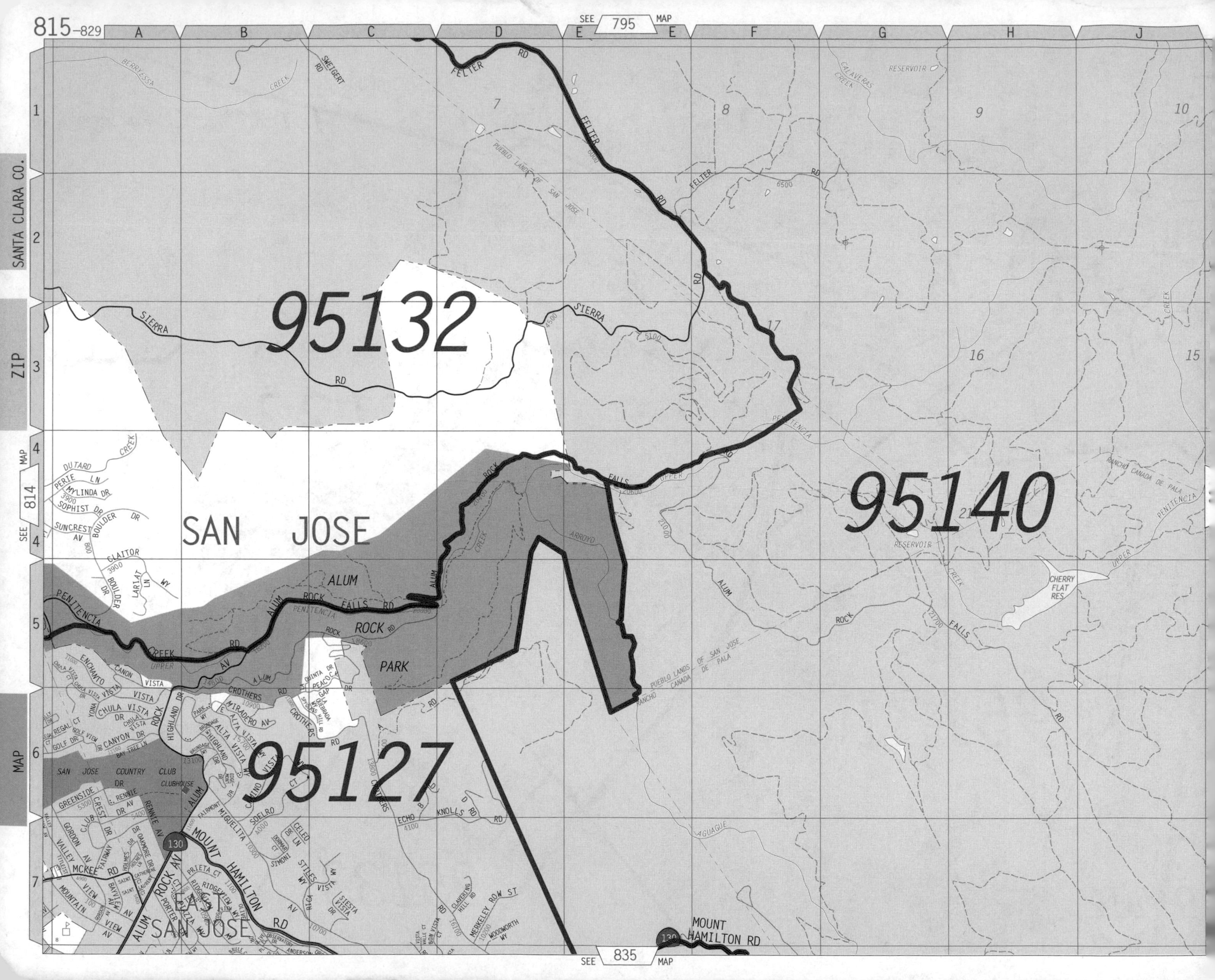

SEE 814 MAP
SEE 835 MAP

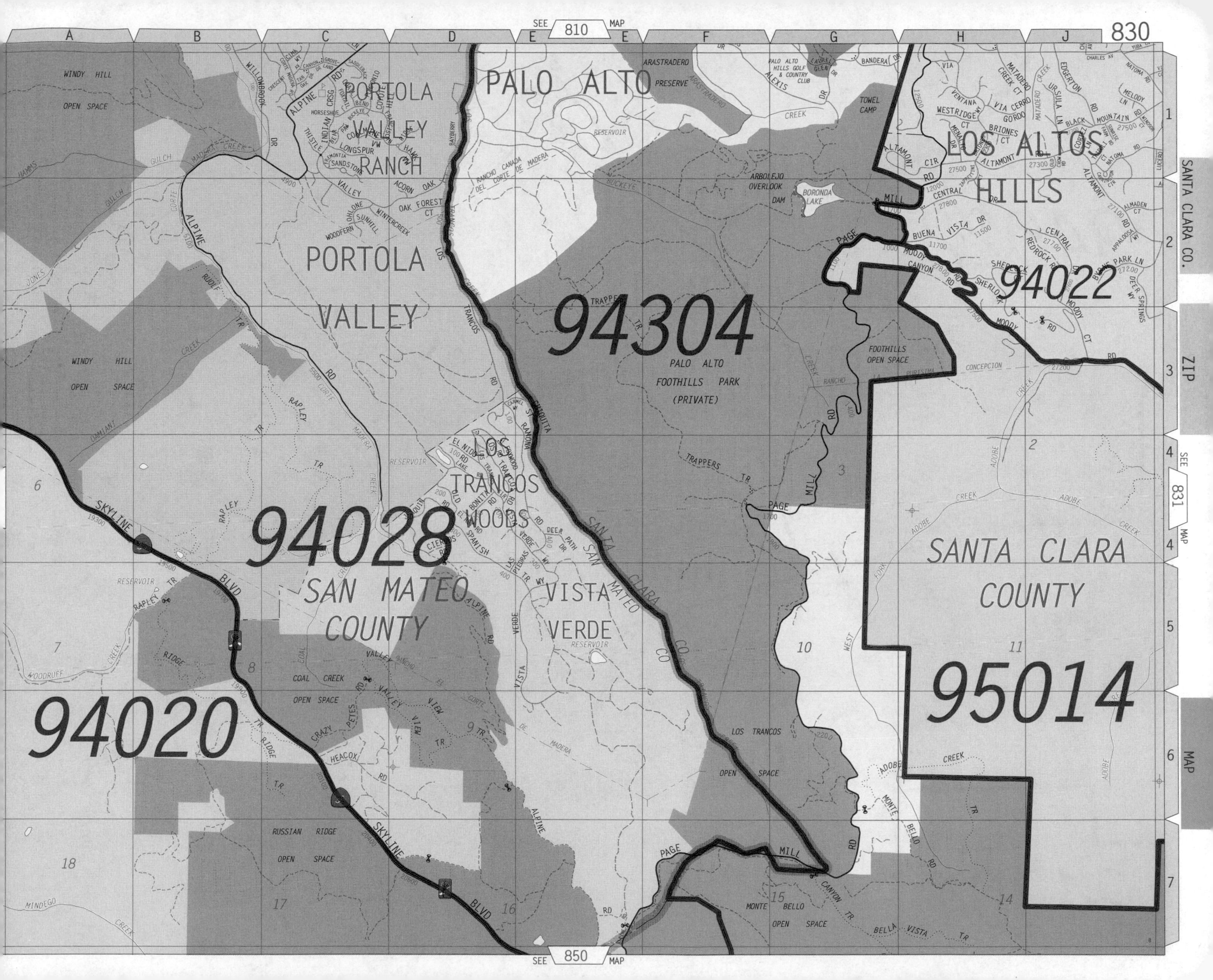
SEE 810 MAP
PORTOLA VALLEY RANCH
PALO ALTO
LOS ALTOS HILLS
PORTOLA VALLEY
94304
94022
PALO ALTO FOOTHILLS PARK (PRIVATE)
FOOTHILLS OPEN SPACE
WINDY HILL OPEN SPACE
LOS TRANCOS WOODS
94028
SAN MATEO COUNTY
VISTA VERDE
SANTA CLARA COUNTY
95014
94020
COAL CREEK OPEN SPACE
RUSSIAN RIDGE OPEN SPACE
LOS TRANCOS OPEN SPACE
MONTE BELLO OPEN SPACE
ARASTRADERO PRESERVE
PALO ALTO HILLS GOLF & COUNTRY CLUB
BORONDA LAKE
ARBOLEJO OVERLOOK
TOWEL CAMP
SKYLINE BLVD
ALPINE RD
PAGE MILL RD
LOS TRANCOS RD
SANTA CLARA SAN MATEO CO
SANTA CLARA CO.
ZIP MAP
SEE 831 MAP
SEE 850 MAP

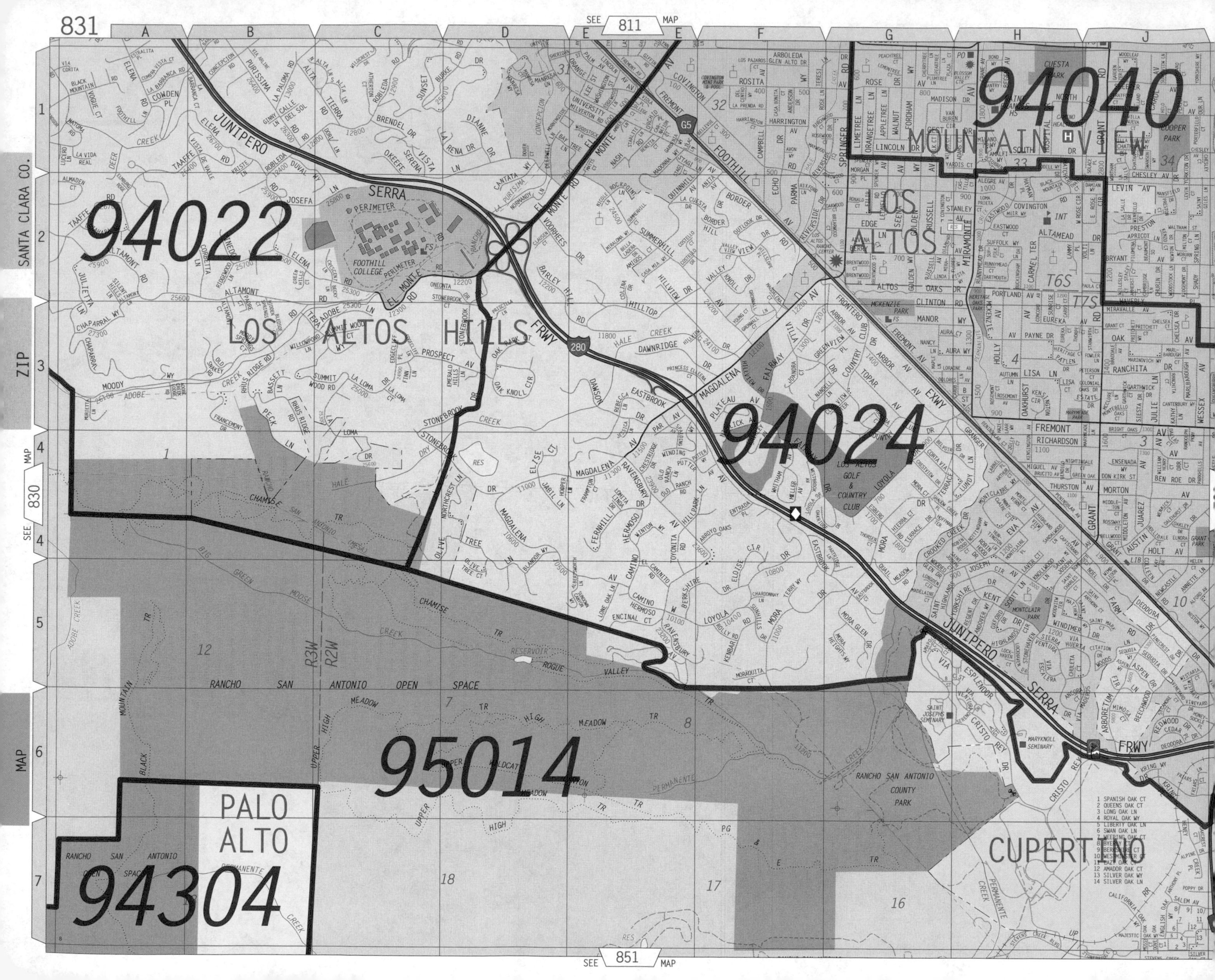

831
SEE 811 MAP
94022
LOS ALTOS HILLS
94024
LOS ALTOS
94040
MOUNTAIN VIEW
95014
PALO ALTO
94304
CUPERTINO
SANTA CLARA CO.
ZIP
MAP
SEE 830 MAP
RANCHO SAN ANTONIO OPEN SPACE
RANCHO SAN ANTONIO COUNTY PARK
FOOTHILL COLLEGE
LOS ALTOS GOLF & COUNTRY CLUB
JUNIPERO SERRA FRWY
FOOTHILL EXWY
SAINT JOSEPHS SEMINARY
MARYKNOLL SEMINARY
1 SPANISH OAK CT
2 QUEENS OAK CT
3 LONG OAK LN
4 ROYAL OAK WY
5 LIBERTY OAK LN
6 SWAN OAK LN
7 WEEPING OAK CT
8 BYERLEY CT
9 BERKSHIRE CT
10 WESTMINSTER CT
11 EAZY OAK CT
12 AMADOR OAK CT
13 SILVER OAK WY
14 SILVER OAK LN
SEE 851 MAP

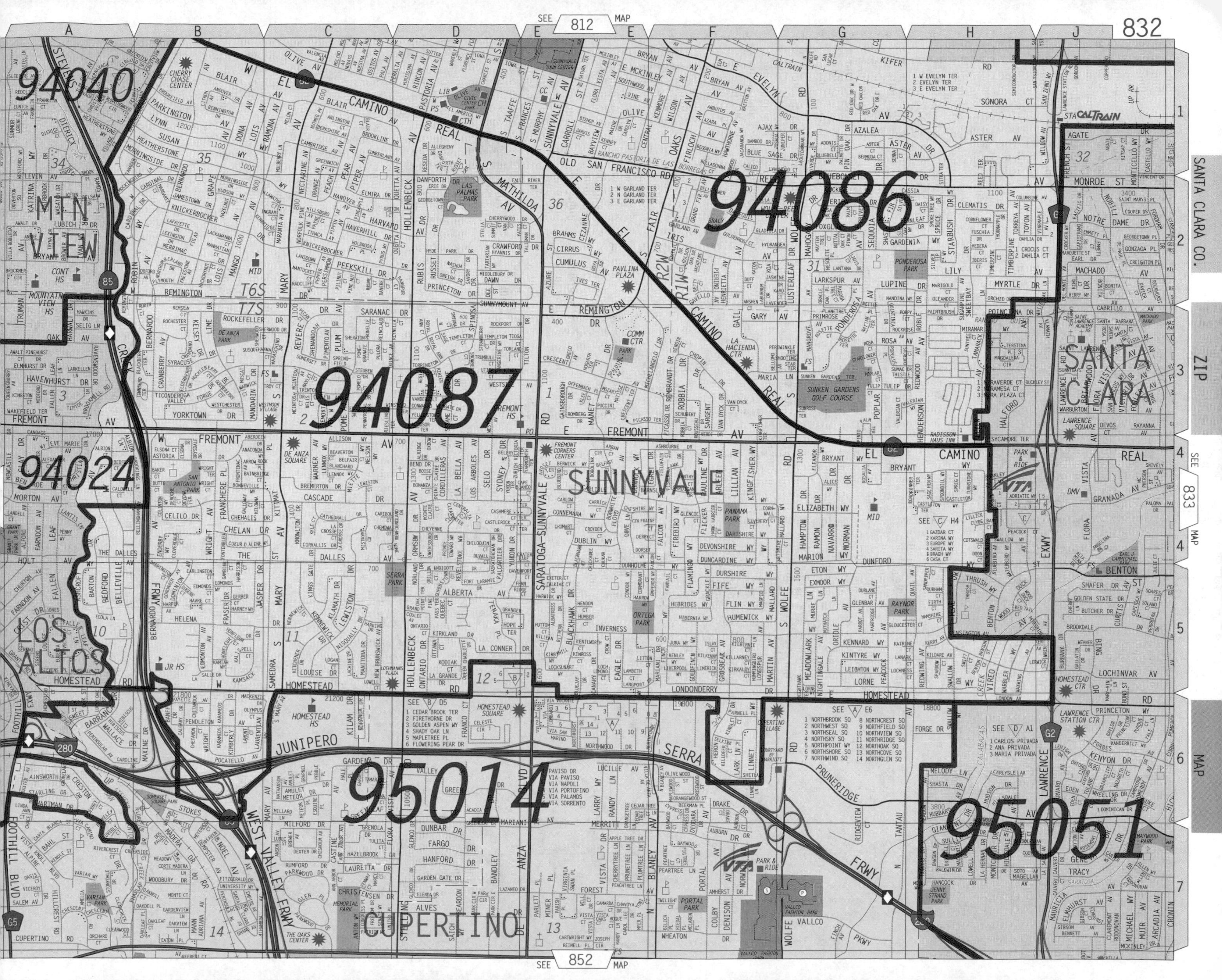
SEE 812 MAP
A
B
C
D
E
F
G
H
J
94040
94086
94087
94024
95014
95051
MTN VIEW
SUNNYVALE
SANTA CLARA
LOS ALTOS
CUPERTINO
SANTA CLARA CO.
ZIP MAP
SEE 833 MAP
SEE 852 MAP
EL CAMINO REAL
FREMONT AV
HOMESTEAD RD
REMINGTON DR
MATHILDA AV
SARATOGA-SUNNYVALE RD
WOLFE RD
LAWRENCE EXWY
JUNIPERO SERRA FRWY
WEST VALLEY FRWY
STEVENS CREEK FRWY
CALTRAIN
OLD SAN FRANCISCO RD
EVELYN AV
MONROE ST
STEVENS CREEK BLVD
FOOTHILL BLVD
DE ANZA SQUARE
FREMONT CORNERS CENTER
PAVLINA PLAZA
LAS PALMAS PARK
PONDEROSA PARK
SUNKEN GARDENS GOLF COURSE
ORTEGA PARK
RAYNOR PARK
SERRA PARK
HOMESTEAD SQUARE
HOMESTEAD HS
VALLCO FASHION PARK
PORTAL PARK
MEMORIAL PARK
THE OAKS CENTER
LAWRENCE SQUARE
LAWRENCE STATION CTR
HOMESTEAD CTR
CHERRY CHASE CENTER
SUNNYVALE TOWN CENTER
FREMONT HS
1
2
3
4
5
6
7

SEE 813 MAP

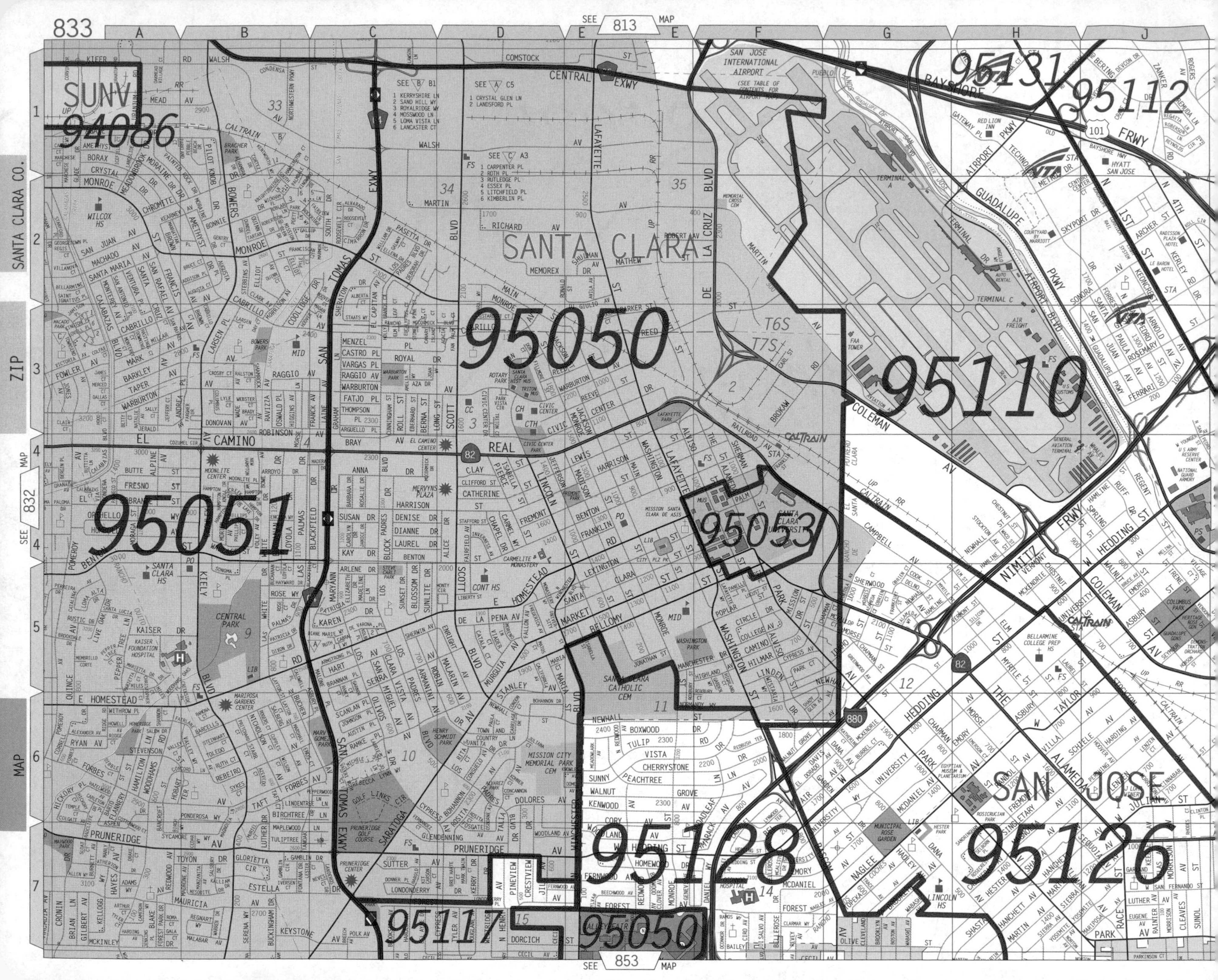

SEE 853 MAP

SEE 814 MAP

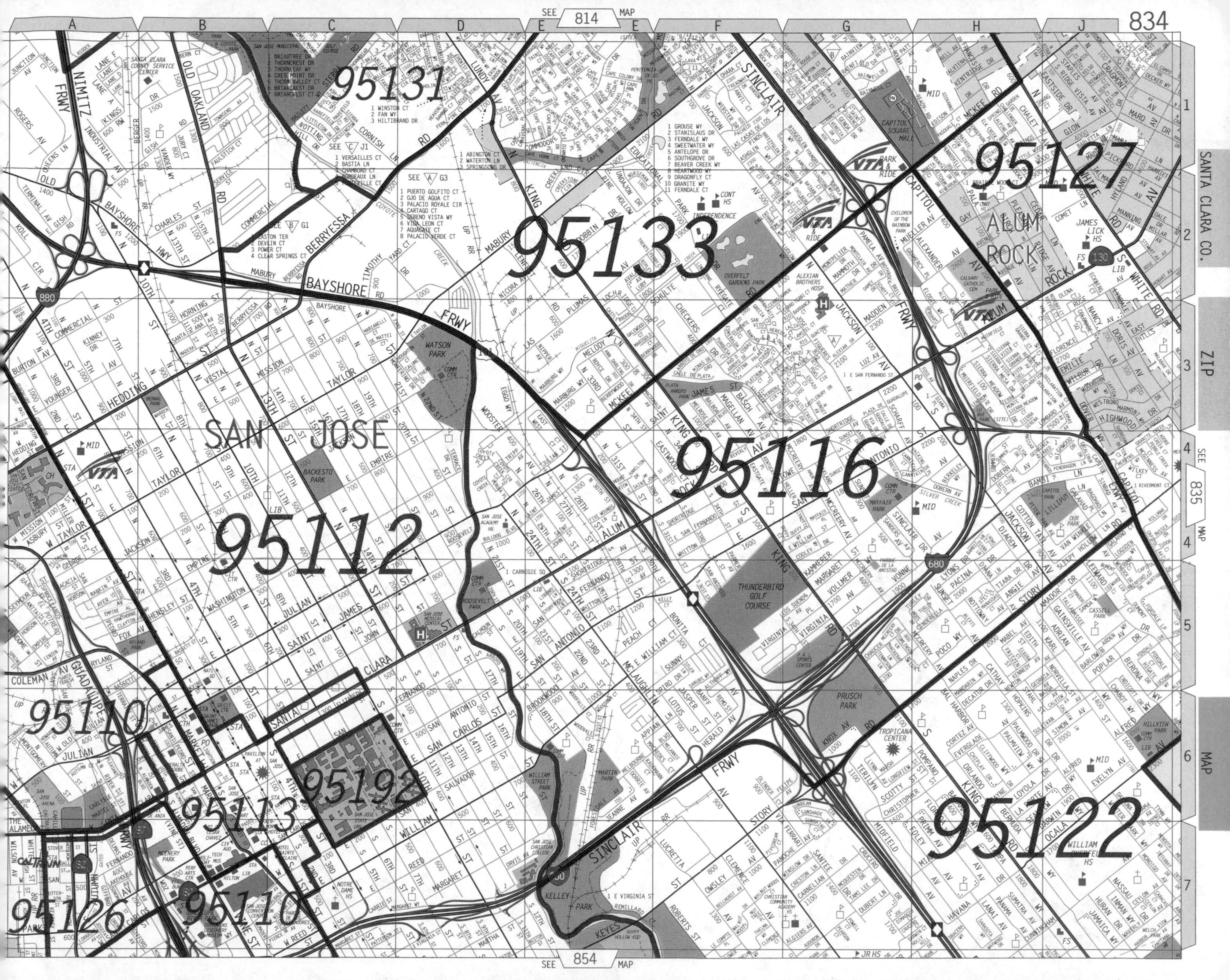

SEE 835 MAP

SEE 854 MAP

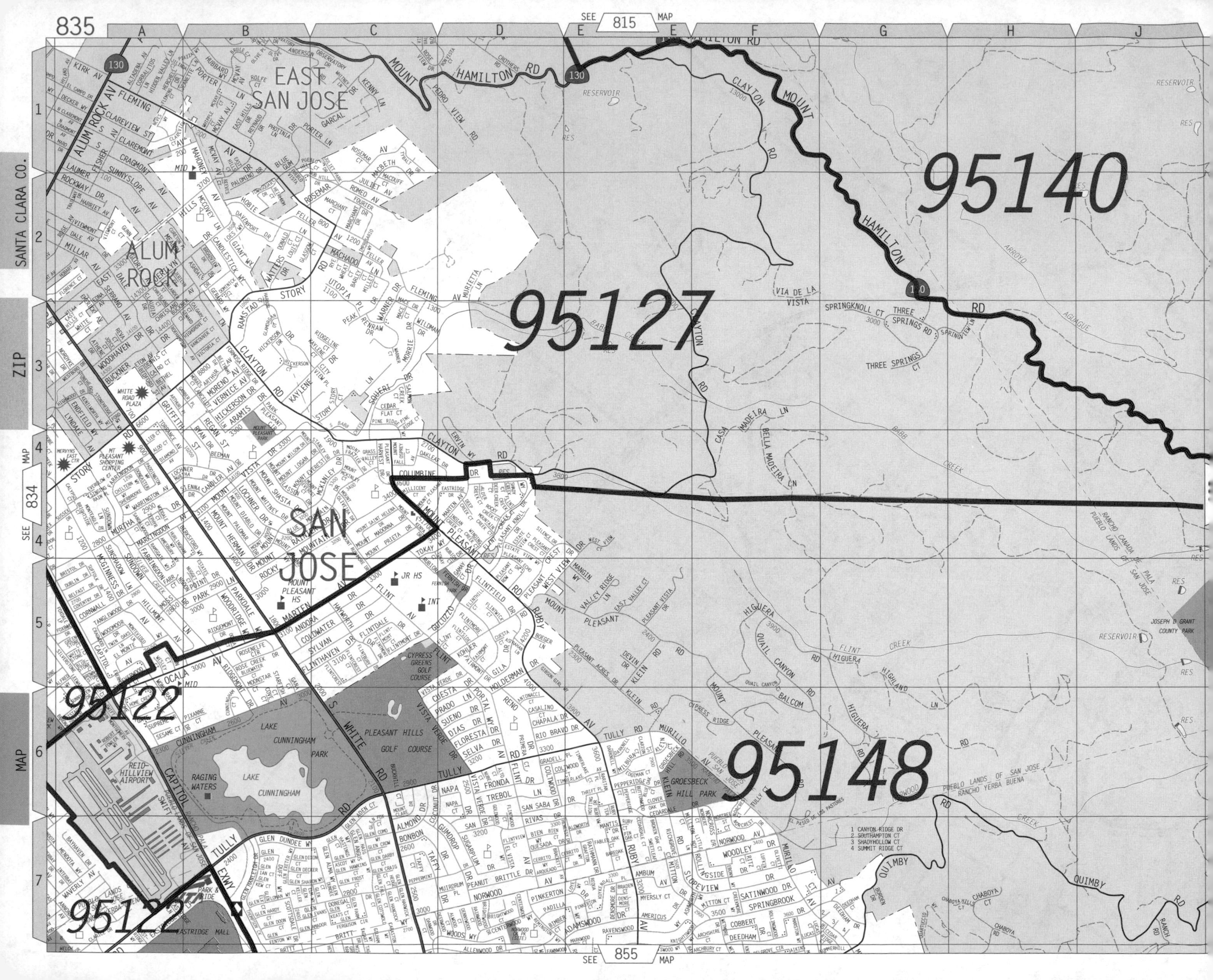
SEE 815 MAP
95140
95127
95148
95122
EAST SAN JOSE
ALUM ROCK
SAN JOSE
SANTA CLARA CO.
ZIP
MAP
SEE 834 MAP
LAKE CUNNINGHAM PARK
PLEASANT HILLS GOLF COURSE
REID-HILLVIEW AIRPORT
RAGING WATERS
CYPRESS GREENS GOLF COURSE
GROESBECK HILL PARK
JOSEPH D GRANT COUNTY PARK
EASTRIDGE MALL
MOUNT PLEASANT HS
JR HS
INT
MID
MOUNT HAMILTON RD
CLAYTON RD
STORY RD
TULLY RD
QUIMBY RD
CAPITOL EXWY
S WHITE RD
RUBY AV
1 CANYON RIDGE DR
2 SOUTHAMPTON CT
3 SHADYHOLLOW CT
4 SUMMIT RIDGE CT
SEE 855 MAP

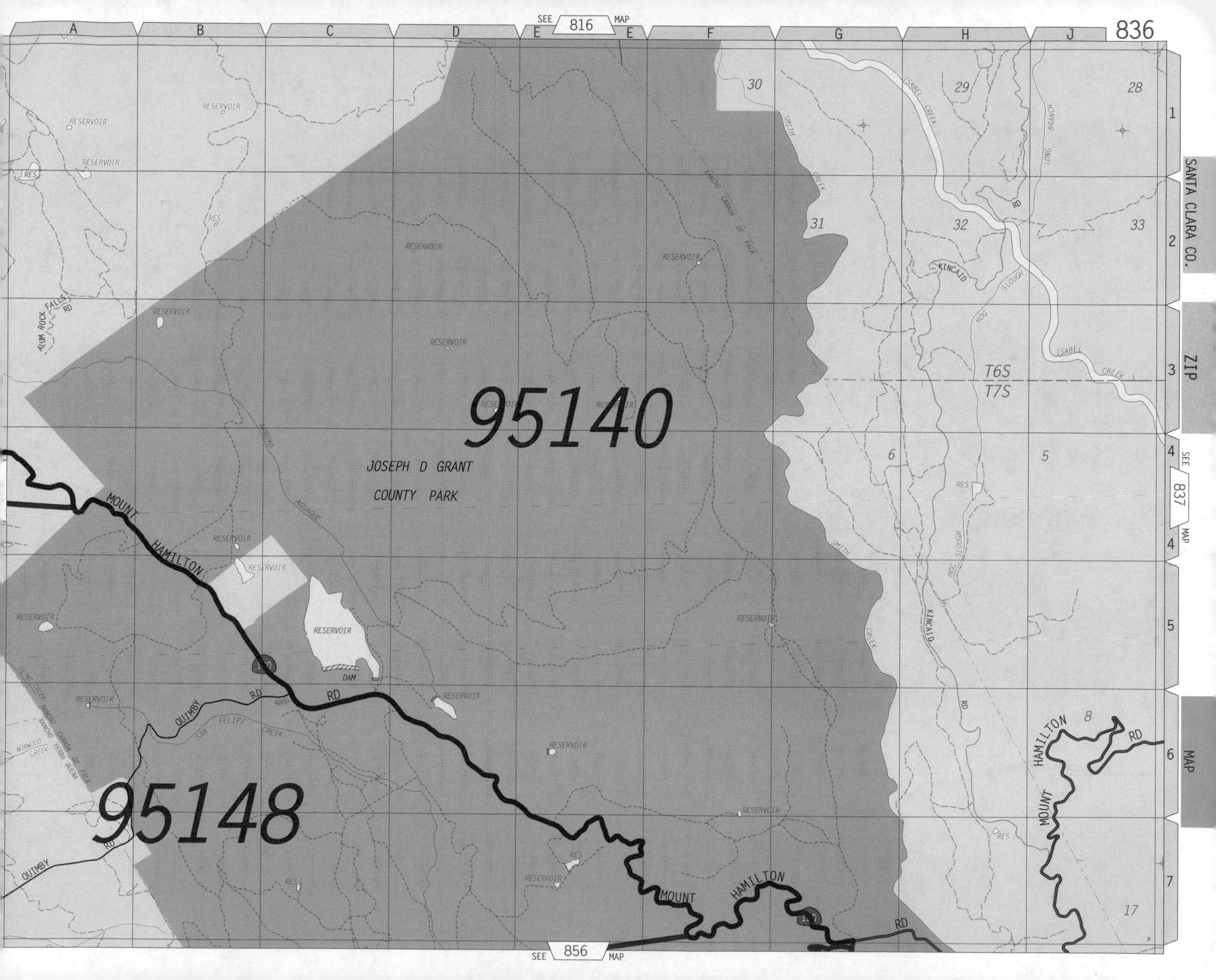
SEE 816 MAP
95140
JOSEPH D GRANT
COUNTY PARK
95148
MOUNT HAMILTON RD
QUIMBY RD
ALUM ROCK FALLS RD
ARROYO AGUAGUE
SAN FELIPE CREEK
SMITH CREEK
ISABEL CREEK
LONG BRANCH
HOG SLOUGH
KINCAID RD
RANCHO CANADA DE PALA
RANCHO YERBA BUENA
NORWOOD CREEK
RESERVOIR
RES
DAM
T6S
T7S
SANTA CLARA CO.
ZIP
MAP
SEE 837 MAP
SEE 856 MAP

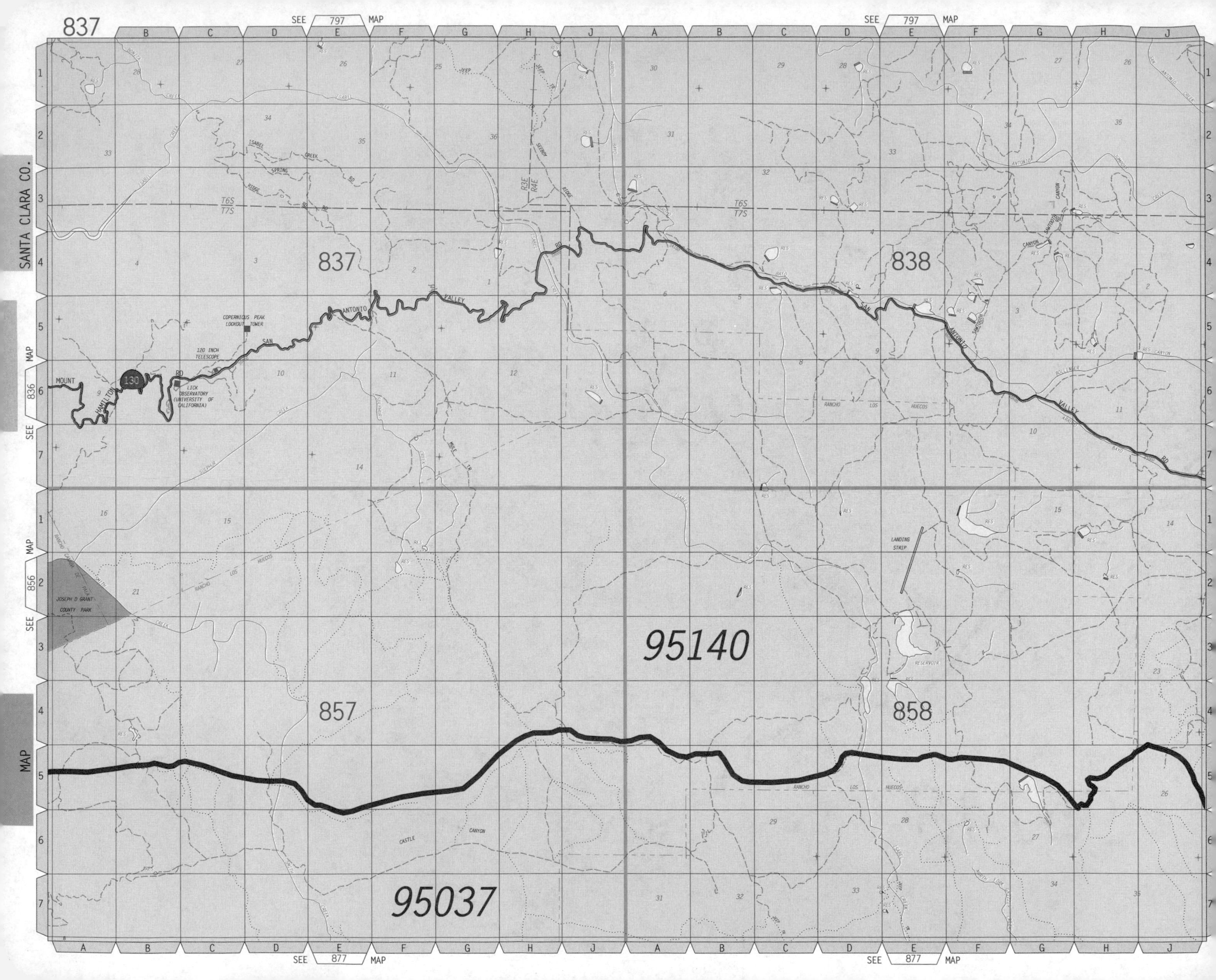

SEE 797 MAP
SANTA CLARA CO.
837
838
857
858
95140
95037
SAN ANTONIO VALLEY RD
MOUNT HAMILTON RD
130
LICK OBSERVATORY (UNIVERSITY OF CALIFORNIA)
120 INCH TELESCOPE
COPERNICUS PEAK LOOKOUT TOWER
ISABEL CREEK
SPRING RIDGE RD
SEEBOY RIDGE
JEEP TR
R3E R4E
T6S T7S
RANCHO LOS HUECOS
LANDING STRIP
RESERVOIR
JOSEPH D GRANT COUNTY PARK
CASTLE CANYON
SULPHUR CREEK
BOLLINGER CANYON
SEE 836 MAP
SEE 856 MAP
SEE 877 MAP

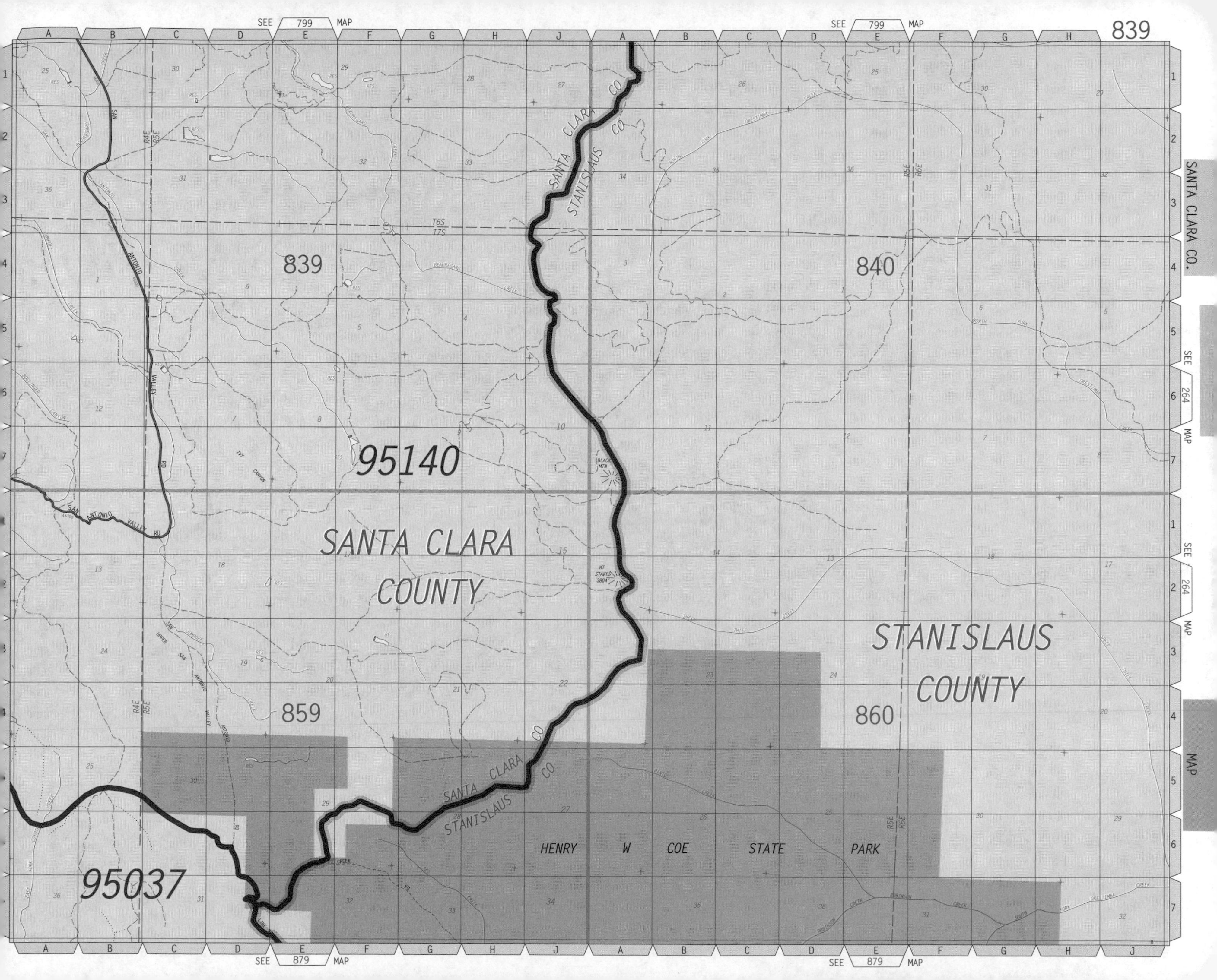
SEE 799 MAP
SEE 799 MAP
839
840
95140
SANTA CLARA COUNTY
STANISLAUS COUNTY
859
860
95037
HENRY W COE STATE PARK
SANTA CLARA CO
STANISLAUS CO
SAN ANTONIO VALLEY RD
T6S
T7S
R4E
R5E
R6E
BLACK MTN
MT STAKES 3804
SANTA CLARA CO.
SEE 264 MAP
SEE 264 MAP
SEE 879 MAP
SEE 879 MAP

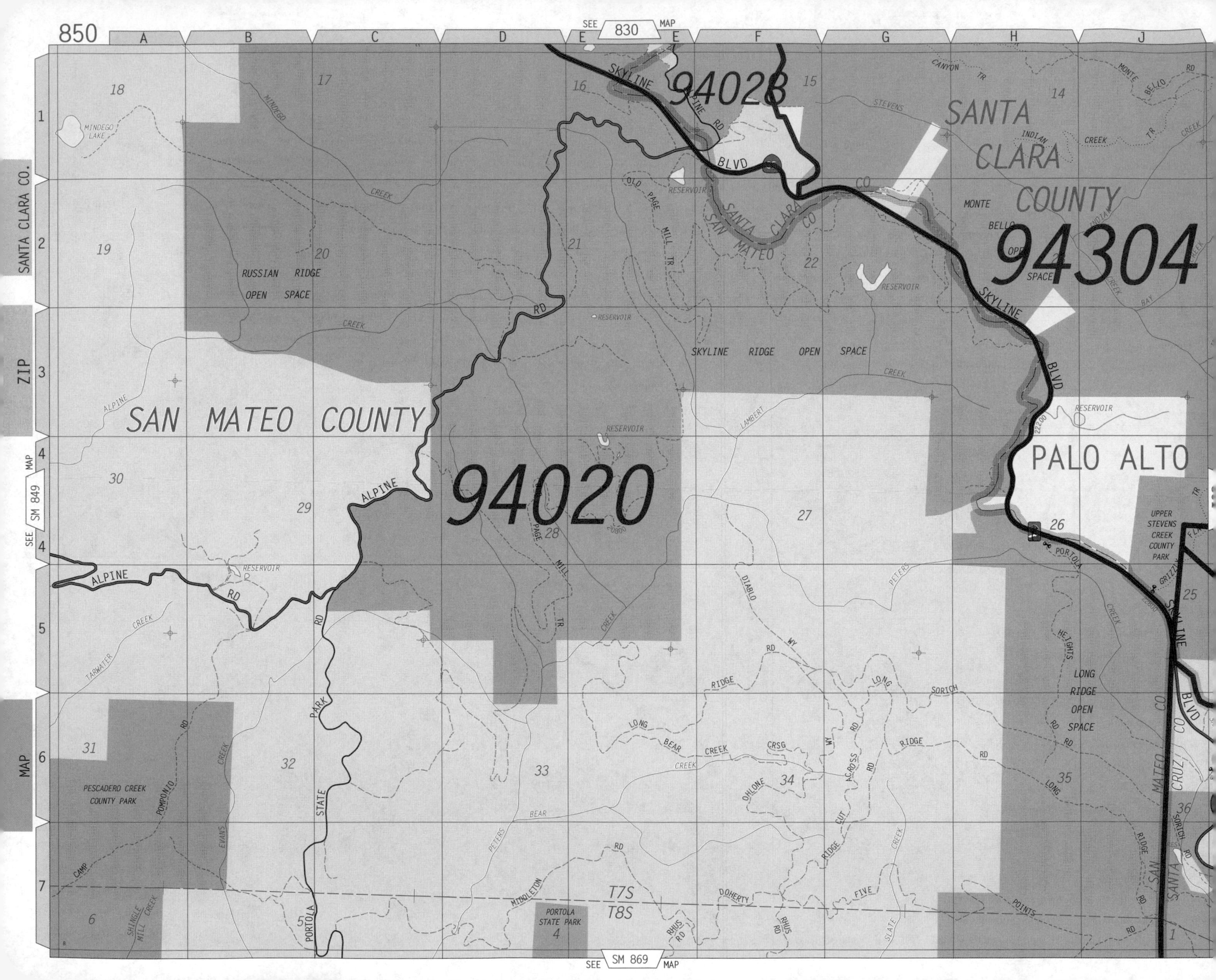
SEE 830 MAP
SAN MATEO COUNTY
SANTA CLARA COUNTY
94028
94304
94020
PALO ALTO
RUSSIAN RIDGE OPEN SPACE
SKYLINE RIDGE OPEN SPACE
MONTE BELLO OPEN SPACE
LONG RIDGE OPEN SPACE
UPPER STEVENS CREEK COUNTY PARK
PESCADERO CREEK COUNTY PARK
PORTOLA STATE PARK
MINDEGO LAKE
SKYLINE BLVD
ALPINE RD
PAGE MILL TR
OLD PAGE MILL TR
PORTOLA STATE PARK RD
RESERVOIR
T7S
T8S
SANTA CLARA CO.
ZIP
MAP
SEE SM 849 MAP
SEE SM 869 MAP

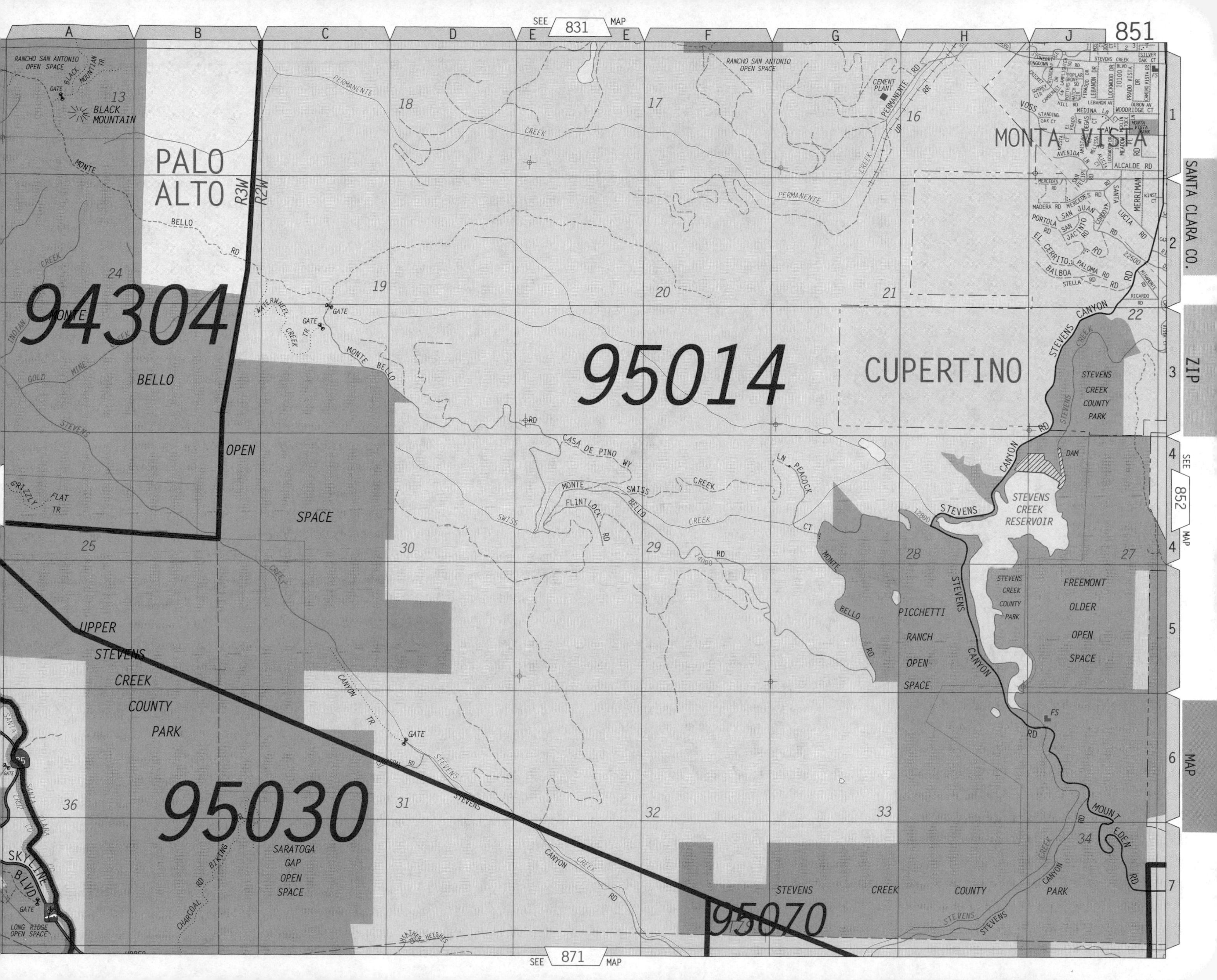
SEE 831 MAP
A
B
C
D
E
F
G
H
J
PALO ALTO
R3W
R2W
94304
95014
CUPERTINO
MONTA VISTA
95030
95070
RANCHO SAN ANTONIO OPEN SPACE
BLACK MOUNTAIN
OPEN SPACE
STEVENS CREEK COUNTY PARK
STEVENS CREEK RESERVOIR
DAM
PICCHETTI RANCH OPEN SPACE
FREEMONT OLDER OPEN SPACE
UPPER STEVENS CREEK COUNTY PARK
SARATOGA GAP OPEN SPACE
LONG RIDGE OPEN SPACE
STEVENS CREEK COUNTY PARK
CEMENT PLANT
MONTE BELLO RD
STEVENS CANYON RD
SKYLINE BLVD
MOUNT EDEN RD
CASA DE PINO WY
FLINTLOCK RD
PEACOCK LN
PERMANENTE CREEK
SANTA CLARA CO.
ZIP MAP
SEE 852 MAP
SEE 871 MAP

SEE 832 MAP

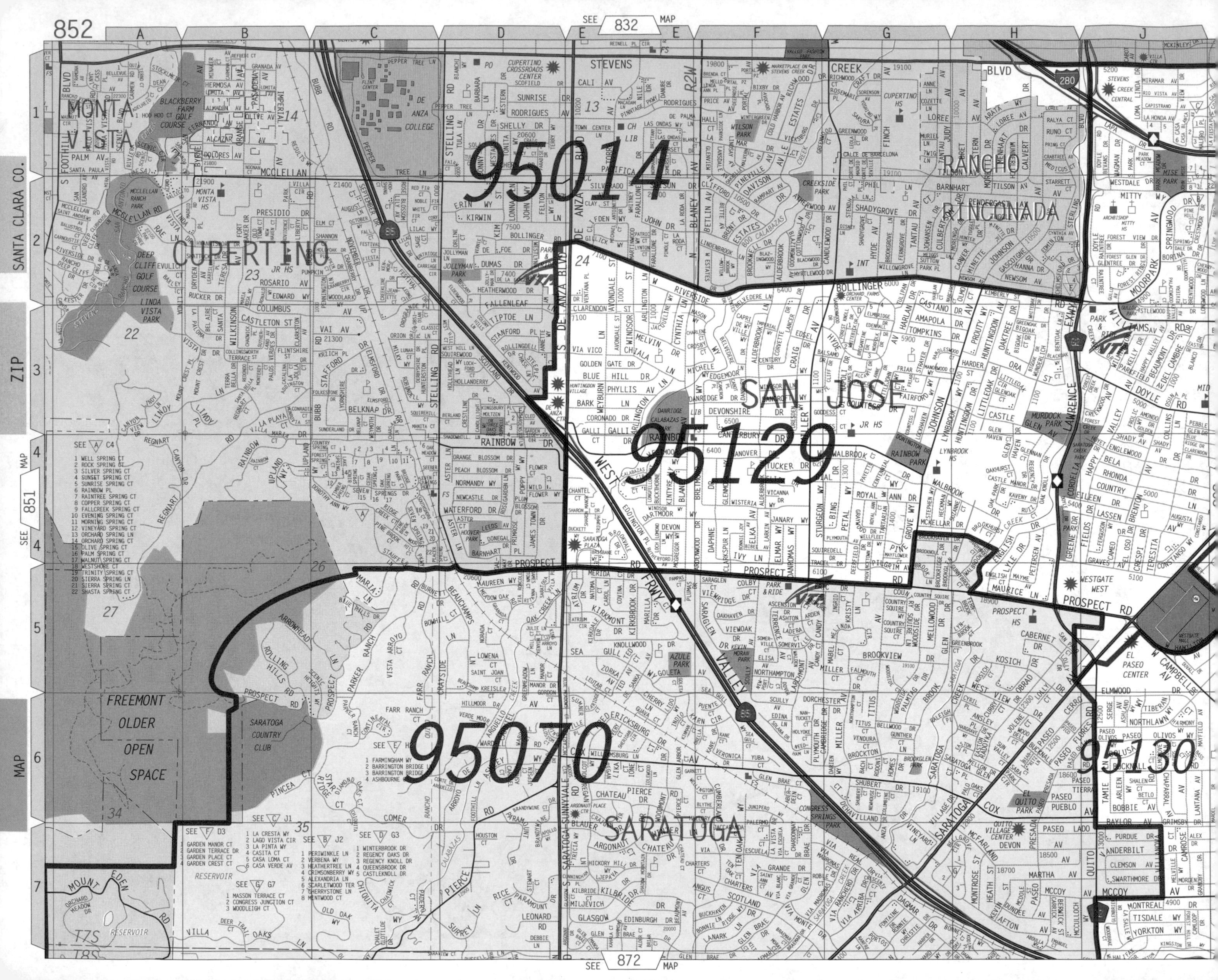

SEE 851 MAP

SEE 872 MAP

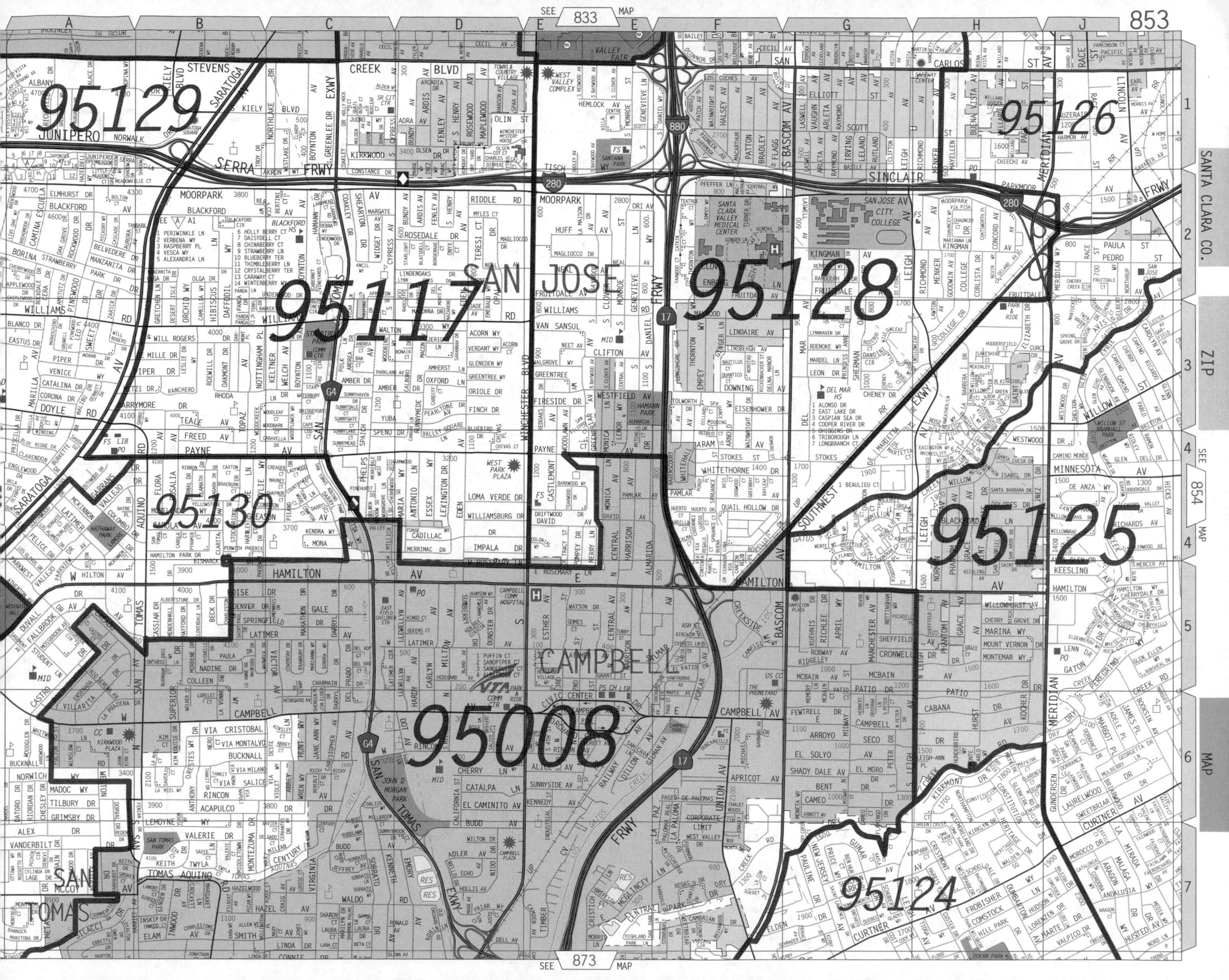
SEE 833 MAP
95129
95126
95117
SAN JOSE
95128
95130
95125
95008
CAMPBELL
95124
SANTA CLARA CO.
ZIP
MAP
SEE 854 MAP
SEE 873 MAP

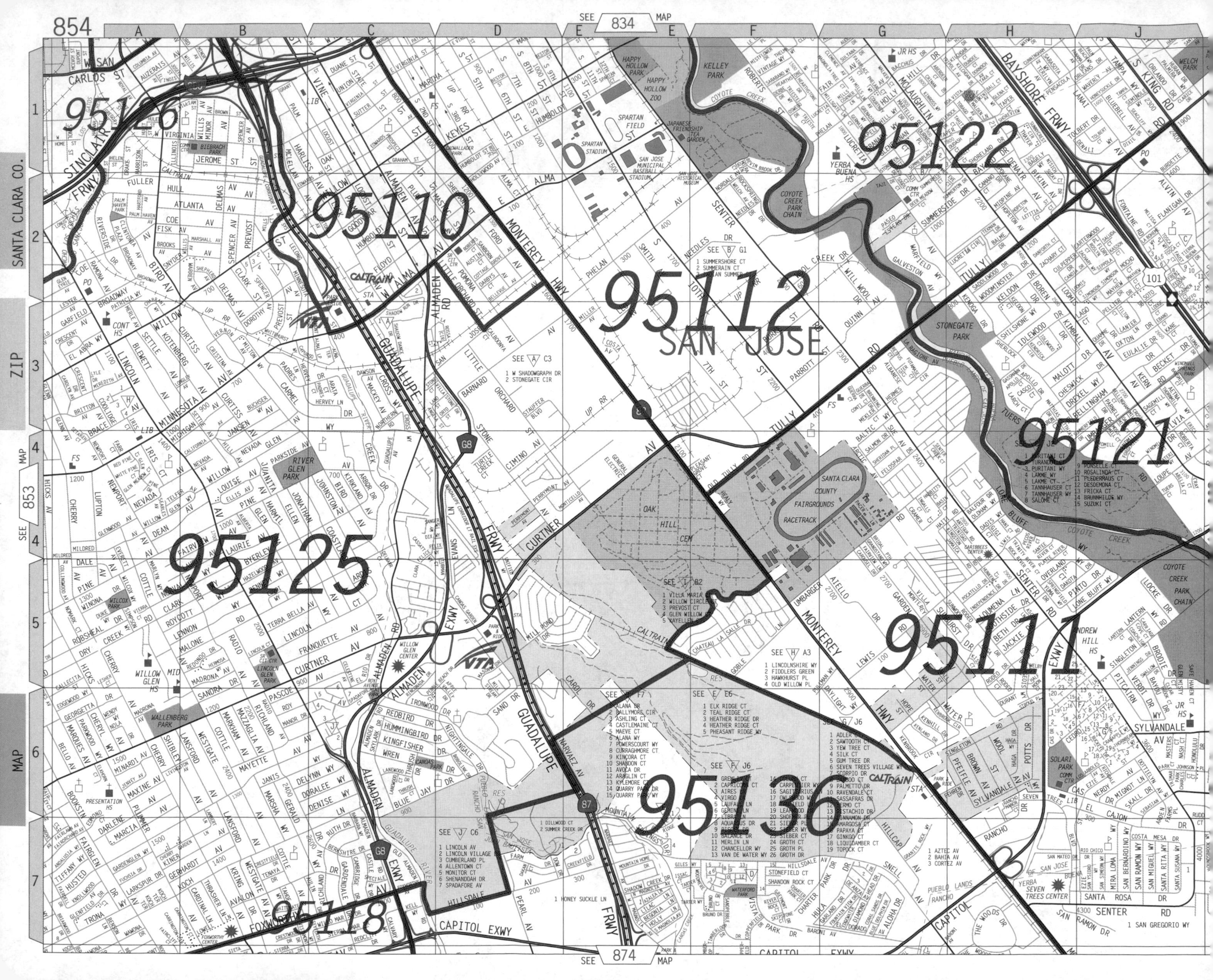
SEE 834 MAP
A
B
C
D
E
F
G
H
J
SANTA CLARA CO.
ZIP
MAP
SEE 853 MAP
95126
95110
95112
SAN JOSE
95122
95121
95125
95111
95136
95118
KELLEY PARK
HAPPY HOLLOW PARK
HAPPY HOLLOW ZOO
SPARTAN FIELD
SPARTAN STADIUM
SAN JOSE MUNICIPAL BASEBALL STADIUM
JAPANESE FRIENDSHIP TEA GARDEN
COYOTE CREEK PARK CHAIN
STONEGATE PARK
RIVER GLEN PARK
OAK HILL CEM
SANTA CLARA COUNTY FAIRGROUNDS
RACETRACK
WILLOW GLEN HS
WALLENBERG PARK
PRESENTATION HS
WILCOX PARK
YERBA BUENA HS
SOLARI PARK
YERBA SEVEN TREES CENTER
WELCH PARK
BAYSHORE FRWY
SINCLAIR FRWY
GUADALUPE FRWY
MONTEREY HWY
ALMADEN EXWY
CAPITOL EXWY
TULLY RD
CURTNER AV
SENTER RD
SEE 874 MAP

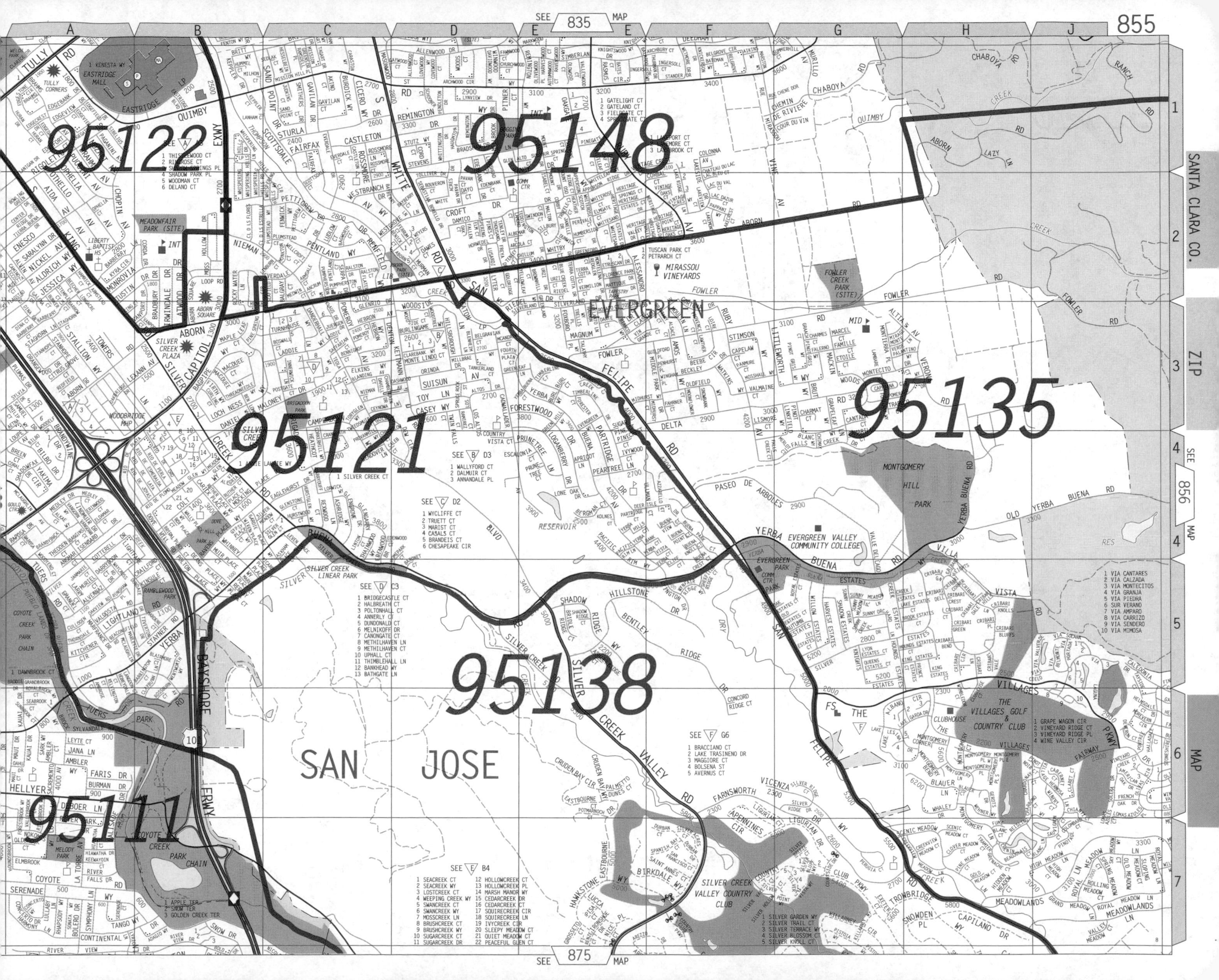
SEE 835 MAP
A
B
C
D
E
F
G
H
J
1
2
3
4
5
6
7
95122
95148
95121
95135
95138
95111
EVERGREEN
SAN JOSE
SANTA CLARA CO.
ZIP
MAP
SEE 856 MAP
EASTRIDGE MALL
TULLY CORNERS
MEADOWFAIR PARK (SITE)
SILVER CREEK PLAZA
ABORN SQUARE
MIRASSOU VINEYARDS
FOWLER CREEK PARK (SITE)
MONTGOMERY HILL PARK
EVERGREEN VALLEY COMMUNITY COLLEGE
EVERGREEN PARK
SILVER CREEK LINEAR PARK
RESERVOIR
COYOTE CREEK PARK CHAIN
MELODY PARK
THE VILLAGES GOLF & COUNTRY CLUB
CLUBHOUSE
SILVER CREEK VALLEY COUNTRY CLUB
RAMBLEWOOD PARK
BAYSHORE FRWY
CAPITOL EXWY
SAN FELIPE RD
SILVER CREEK VALLEY RD
YERBA BUENA RD
ABORN RD
QUIMBY RD
CHABOYA RD
SEE B D3
1 WALLYFORD CT
2 DALMUIR CT
3 ANNANDALE PL
SEE C D2
1 WYCLIFFE CT
2 TRUETT CT
3 MARIST CT
4 CASALS CT
5 BRANDEIS CT
6 CHESAPEAKE CIR
SEE D C3
1 BRIDGECASTLE CT
2 HALBREATH CT
3 POLTONHALL CT
4 ANNERLY CT
5 DUNDONALD CT
6 MELNIKOFF DR
7 CANONGATE CT
8 METHILHAVEN LN
9 METHILHAVEN CT
10 UPHALL CT
11 THIMBLEHALL LN
12 BANKHEAD WY
13 BATHGATE LN
SEE E B4
1 SEACREEK CT
2 SEACREEK WY
3 LOSTCREEK CT
4 WEEPING CREEK WY
5 SWANCREEK CT
6 SWANCREEK WY
7 MOSSCREEK LN
8 BRUSHCREEK CT
9 BRUSHCREEK WY
10 SUGARCREEK CT
11 SUGARCREEK DR
12 HOLLOWCREEK CT
13 HOLLOWCREEK PL
14 MARSH MANOR WY
15 CEDARCREEK DR
16 CEDARCREEK CT
17 SQUIRECREEK CIR
18 SQUIRECREEK LN
19 IVYCREEK CIR
20 SLEEPY MEADOW CT
21 QUIET MEADOW CT
22 PEACEFUL GLEN CT
SEE F G6
1 BRACCIANO CT
2 LAKE TRASINENO DR
3 MAGGIORE CT
4 BOLSENA ST
5 AVERNUS CT
1 VIA CANTARES
2 VIA CALZADA
3 VIA MONTECITOS
4 VIA GRANJA
5 VIA PIEDRA
6 SUR VERANO
7 VIA AMPARD
8 VIA CARRIZO
9 VIA SENDERO
10 VIA MIMOSA
1 GRAPE WAGON CIR
2 VINEYARD RIDGE CT
3 VINEYARD RIDGE PL
4 WINE VALLEY CIR
1 SILVER GARDEN WY
2 SILVER TRAIL CT
3 SILVER TERRACE WY
4 SILVER BLOSSOM CT
5 SILVER KNOLL CT
1 APPLE TER
2 SNOW TER
3 GOLDEN CREEK TER
1 GATELIGHT CT
2 GATELAND CT
3 FIELDGATE CT
4 SPRINGGATE CT
1 LANSPORT CT
2 LANDING CT
3 LAKEBROOK CT
1 TUSCAN PARK CT
2 PETRARCH CT
1 THISTLEWOOD CT
2 RIMROSE CT
4 SHADOW PARK PL
5 WOODMAN CT
6 DELANO CT
1 DAWNBROOK CT
1 SILVER CREEK CT
1 KENESTA WY
SEE 875 MAP

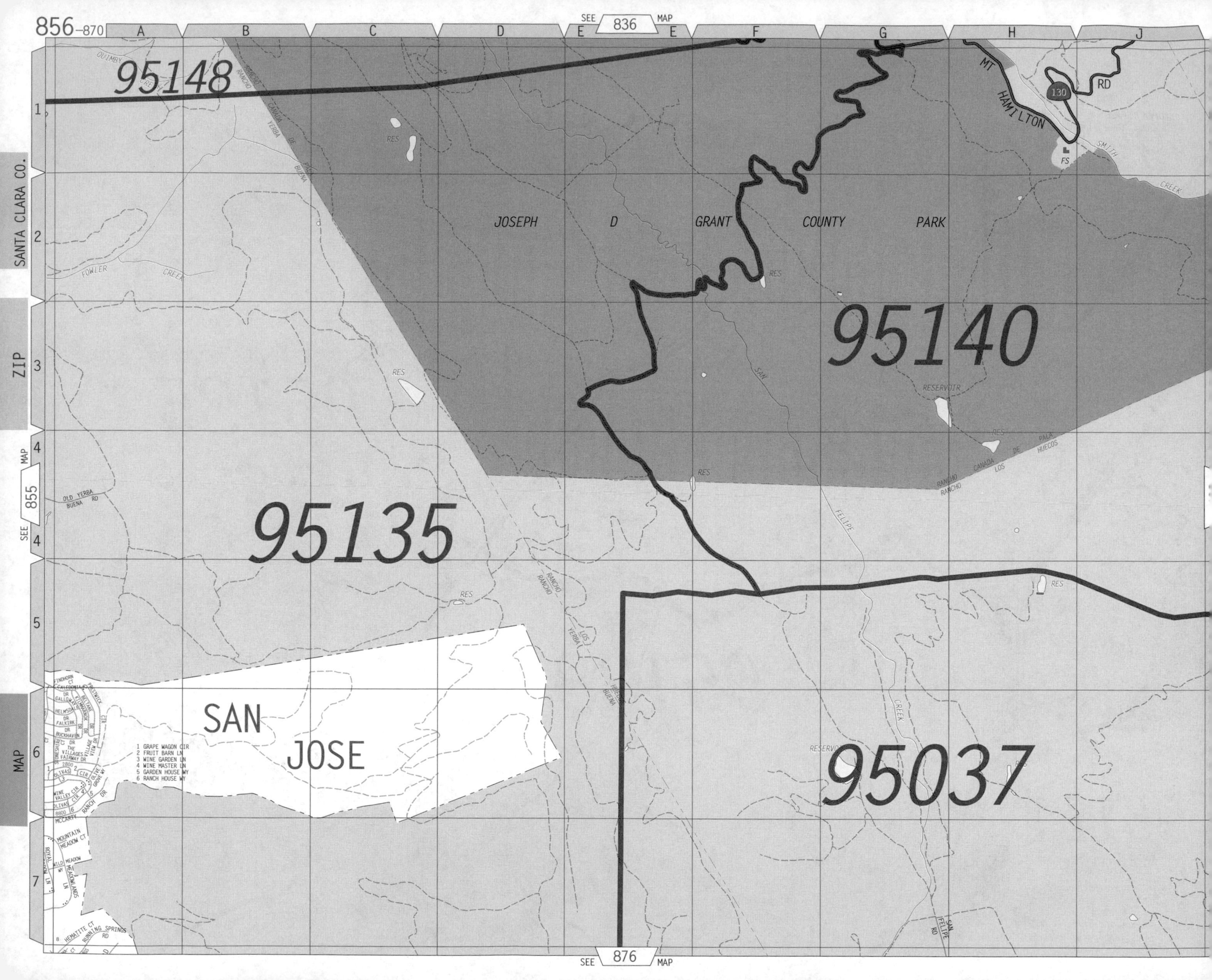
SEE 836 MAP
A
B
C
D
E
F
G
H
J
1
2
3
4
5
6
7
SANTA CLARA CO.
ZIP
MAP
SEE 855 MAP
95148
95140
95135
95037
JOSEPH D GRANT COUNTY PARK
SAN JOSE
MT HAMILTON RD
130
SMITH CREEK
FS
FOWLER CREEK
QUIMBY
RANCHO CANADA DE PALA
RANCHO CANADA LOS HUECOS
RANCHO YERBA BUENA
RANCHO LOS HUECOS
SAN FELIPE CREEK
SAN FELIPE RD
OLD YERBA BUENA RD
RES
RESERVOIR
1 GRAPE WAGON CIR
2 FRUIT BARN LN
3 WINE GARDEN LN
4 WINE MASTER LN
5 GARDEN HOUSE WY
6 RANCH HOUSE WY
FINDHORN CT
CALEDONIA
GALLOWAY
HELMSDALE
FALKIRK DR
BUCKHAVEN
STONESHIRE CT
THE VILLAGES
FAIRWAY DR
VILLAGE VIEW DR
OLIVAS CIR
WINE VALLEY CIR
RANCH DR
McCARTY
MOUNTAIN MEADOW CT
WILD MEADOW WY
MEADOWLANDS LN
ROYAL OAK LN
HEMATITE CT
RUNNING SPRINGS RD
2800
8800
SEE 876 MAP

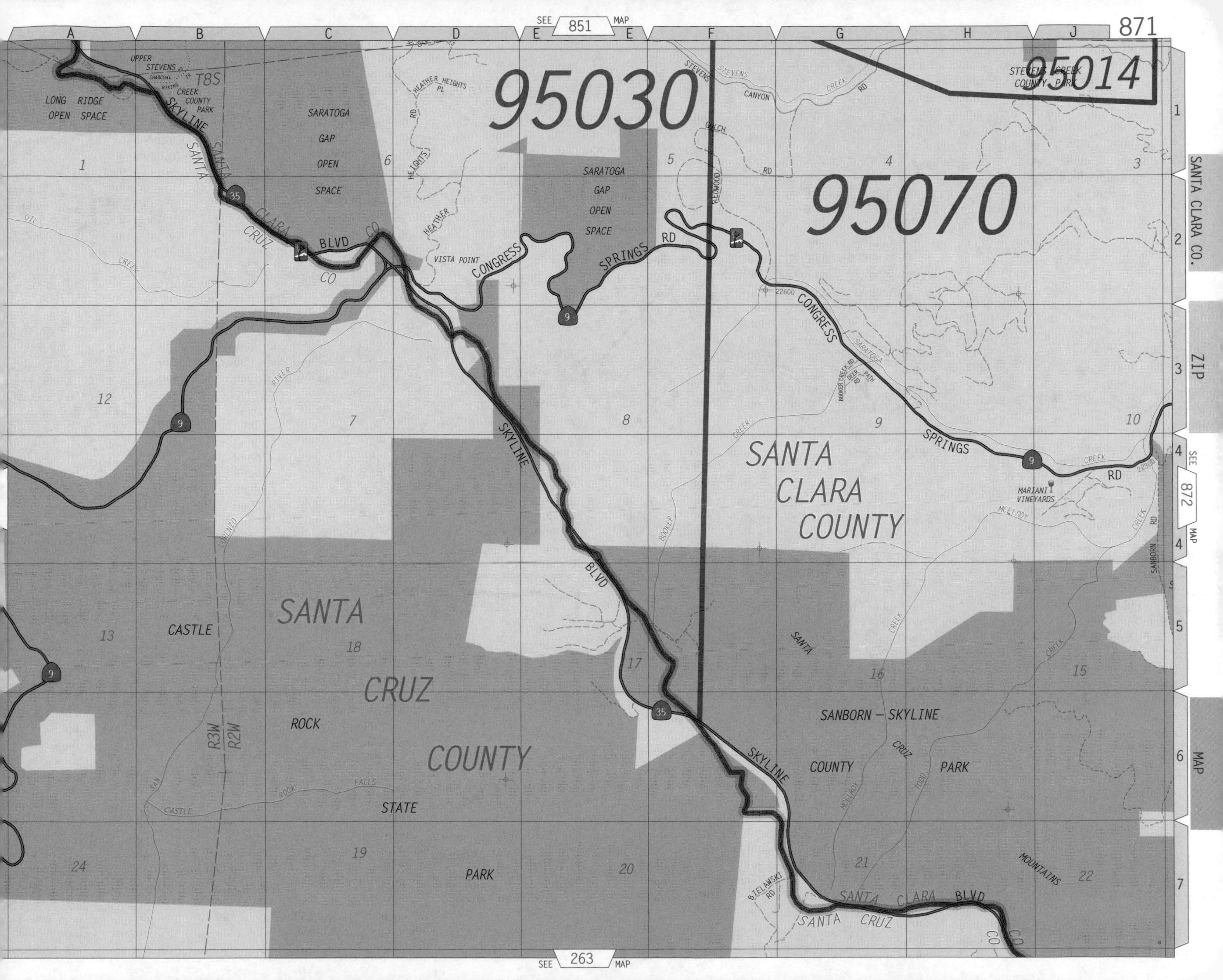
SEE 851 MAP
A
B
C
D
E
E
F
G
H
J
95030
95070
95014
UPPER STEVENS CREEK COUNTY PARK
LONG RIDGE OPEN SPACE
SARATOGA GAP OPEN SPACE
SARATOGA GAP OPEN SPACE
STEVENS CREEK COUNTY PARK
T8S
SKYLINE
SANTA CLARA
SANTA CRUZ
BLVD
CO
CO
HEATHER HEIGHTS PL
HEIGHTS RD
HEATHER
VISTA POINT
CONGRESS
SPRINGS
RD
STEVENS CANYON RD
STEVENS CREEK
GULCH RD
REDWOOD
22600
CONGRESS
SARATOGA
BOOKER CREEK RD
DEER PATH RD
SPRINGS
CREEK
RD
22300
MARIANI VINEYARDS
MCELROY
SANBORN RD
SANTA CLARA COUNTY
SANTA CRUZ COUNTY
CASTLE ROCK STATE PARK
SANBORN - SKYLINE COUNTY PARK
SKYLINE
BLVD
SANTA CRUZ
MOUNTAINS
SAN LORENZO RIVER
CASTLE ROCK FALLS
R3W
R2W
BIELAWSKI RD
SANTA CLARA BLVD
SANTA CRUZ CO
OIL CREEK
BOOKER
CREEK
TODD
MCELROY
1
2
3
4
5
6
7
8
9
10
12
13
15
16
17
18
19
20
21
22
24
SANTA CLARA CO.
ZIP
MAP
SEE 872 MAP
SEE 263 MAP

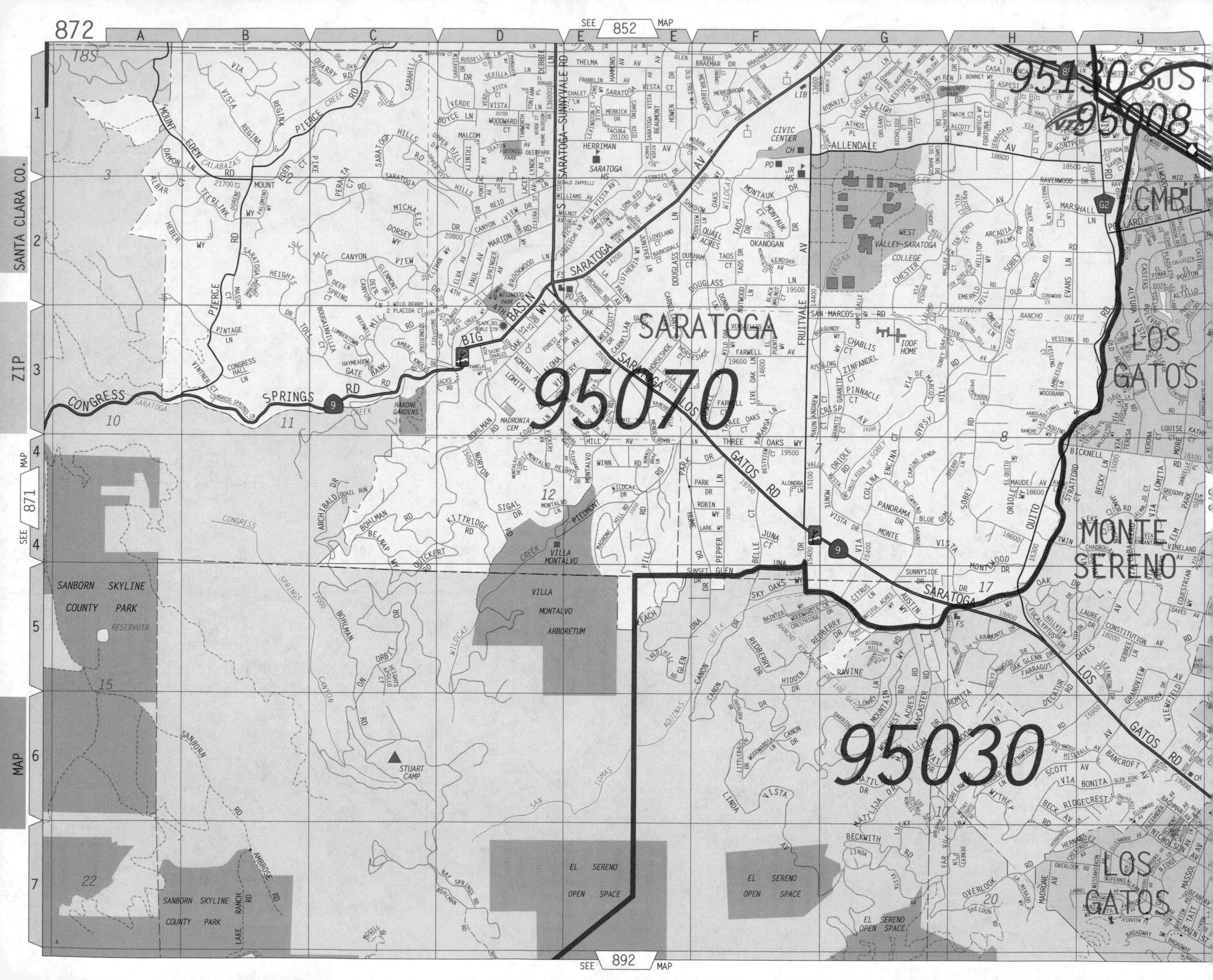

872
SEE 852 MAP
A
B
C
D
E
F
G
H
J
SANTA CLARA CO.
ZIP
MAP
SEE 871 MAP
SEE 892 MAP
SARATOGA
95070
95030
95130 SJS
95008
CMBL
LOS GATOS
MONTE SERENO
CONGRESS SPRINGS RD
SARATOGA-SUNNYVALE RD
SARATOGA AV
BIG BASIN WY
SARATOGA LOS GATOS RD
FRUITVALE AV
ALLENDALE AV
QUITO RD
PIERCE RD
MOUNT EDEN RD
SARATOGA HS
CIVIC CENTER
WEST VALLEY-SARATOGA COLLEGE
IOOF HOME
HAKONE GARDENS
MADRONIA CEM
VILLA MONTALVO
VILLA MONTALVO ARBORETUM
SANBORN SKYLINE COUNTY PARK
EL SERENO OPEN SPACE
STUART CAMP
RESERVOIR
SANBORN RD
BOHLMAN RD
SAN TOMAS AQUINAS CREEK
WILDCAT CREEK

SEE 853 MAP

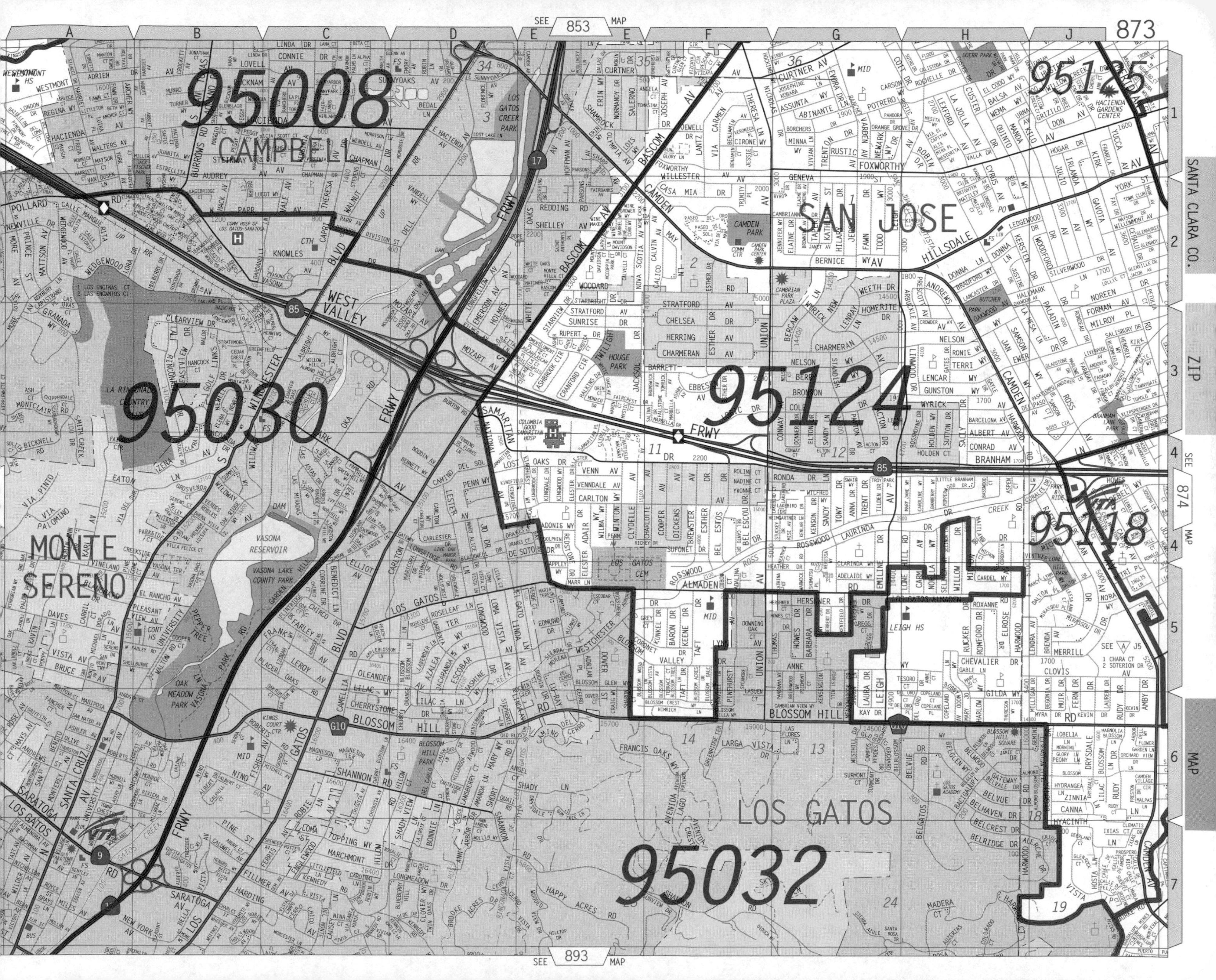

SEE 893 MAP

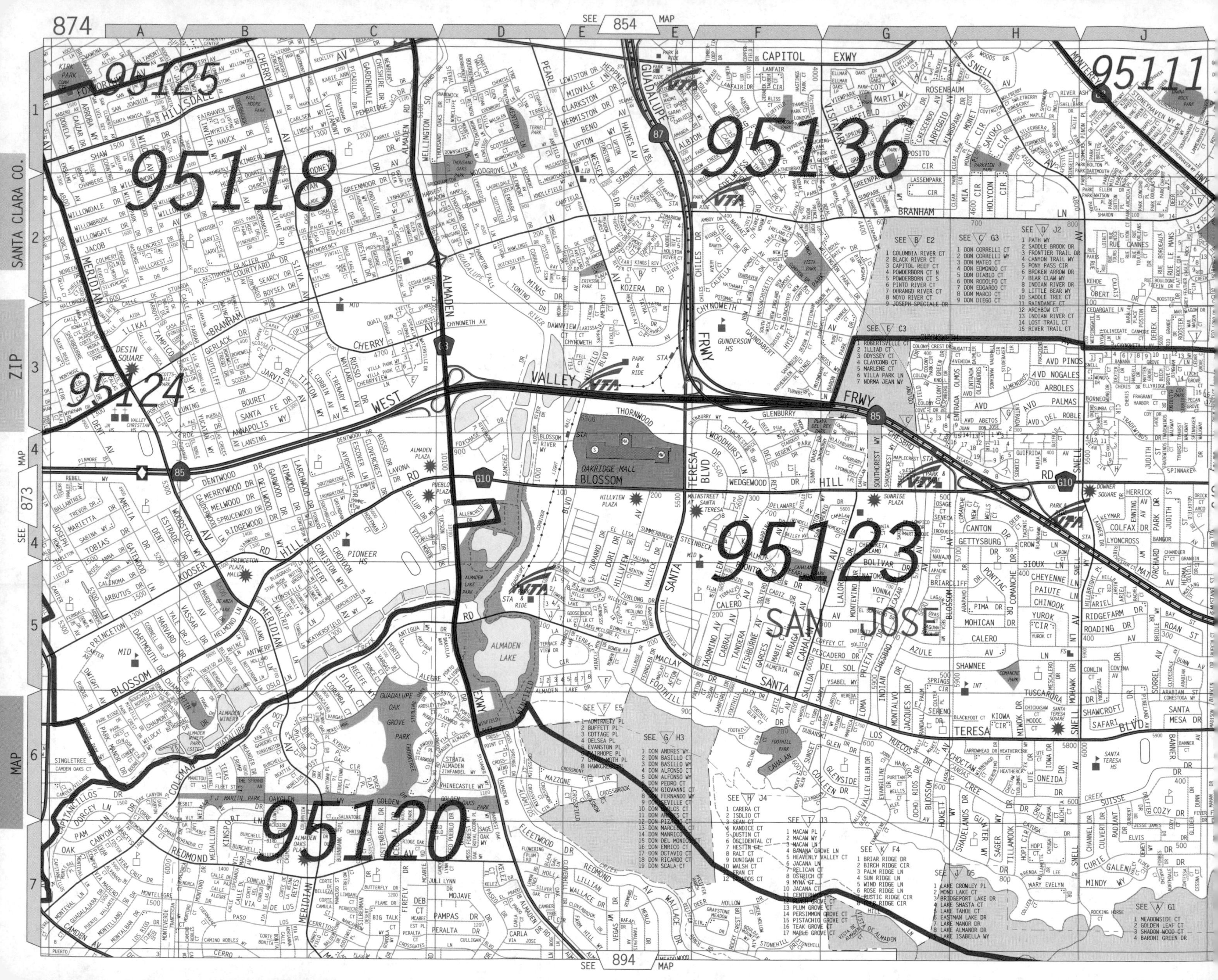

SEE 854 MAP
SEE 873 MAP
SEE 894 MAP
SANTA CLARA CO.
ZIP
MAP
A
B
C
D
E
F
G
H
J
1
2
3
4
5
6
7
95125
95118
95136
95111
95124
95123
95120
SAN JOSE
CAPITOL EXWY
BRANHAM LN
CHYNOWETH AV
WEST VALLEY FRWY
BLOSSOM HILL RD
SANTA TERESA BLVD
ALMADEN EXWY
GUADALUPE FRWY
MERIDIAN AV
HILLSDALE AV
CAMDEN AV
SNELL AV
MONTEREY HWY
OAKRIDGE MALL
ALMADEN LAKE
ALMADEN LAKE PARK
GUADALUPE OAK GROVE PARK
ALMADEN PLAZA
HILLVIEW PLAZA
SUNRISE PLAZA
DOWNER SQUARE
DESIN SQUARE
PRINCETON PLAZA MALL
MAINSTREET AT SANTA TERESA
SANTA TERESA SQUARE
PIONEER HS
GUNDERSON HS
SANTA TERESA HS
SEE B E2
1 COLUMBIA RIVER CT
2 BLACK RIVER CT
3 CAPITOL REEF CT
4 POWDERBORN CT N
5 POWDERBORN CT S
6 PINTO RIVER CT
7 DURANGO RIVER CT
8 NOYO RIVER CT
9 JOSEPH SPECIALE DR
SEE C G3
1 DON CORRELLI CT
2 DON CORRELLI WY
3 DON MATEO CT
4 DON EDMONDO CT
5 DON DIABLO CT
6 DON RODOLFO CT
7 DON EDGARDO CT
8 DON MARCO CT
9 DON DIEGO CT
SEE D J2
1 PATH WY
2 SADDLE BROOK DR
3 FRONTIER TRAIL DR
4 CANYON TRAIL WY
5 PONY PASS CIR
6 BROKEN ARROW DR
7 BEAR CLAW WY
8 INDIAN RIVER DR
9 LITTLE BEAR WY
10 SADDLE TREE CT
11 RAINDANCE CT
12 ARCHBOW CT
13 INDIAN RIVER CT
14 LOST TRAIL CT
15 RIVER TRAIL CT
SEE E C3
1 ROBERTSVILLE CT
2 ILLIAD CT
3 ODYSSEY CT
4 CLAYCOMB CT
5 MARLENE CT
6 VILLA PARK LN
7 NORMA JEAN WY
SEE F E5
1 ADMIRALTY PL
2 BUFFETT PL
3 COTTAGE PL
4 DELSEA PL
5 EVANSTON PL
SEE G H3
1 DON ANDRES WY
2 DON BASILLO CT
3 DON BASILLO WY
4 DON ALFONSO CT
5 DON ALFONSO WY
6 DON PEDRO CT
7 DON GIOVANNI CT
8 DON FERNANDO WY
SEE H J4
1 CARERA CT
2 ISDLIO CT
3 SEAN CT
4 KANDICE CT
5 DUSTIN CT
6 OCCIDENTAL CT
7 HESTIN CT
8 RALT CT
9 DUNIGAN CT
10 WALSH CT
11 JACANA CT
SEE I J3
1 MACAW PL
2 MACAW WY
3 MACAW LN
4 BANANA GROVE LN
5 HEAVENLY VALLEY CT
6 JACANA LN
SEE K F4
1 BRIAR RIDGE DR
2 BIRCH RIDGE CIR
3 PALM RIDGE LN
4 SUN RIDGE LN
5 WIND RIDGE LN
6 ROSE RIDGE LN
7 RUSTIC RIDGE CIR
8 DEER RIDGE CT
SEE J D5
1 LAKE CROWLEY PL
2 MONO LAKE CT
3 BRIDGEPORT LAKE DR
4 LAKE SHASTA CT
5 LAKE TAHOE CT
6 EASTMAN LAKE DR
7 LAKE MANOR DR
8 LAKE ALMANOR DR
9 LAKE ISABELLA WY
SEE A G1
1 MEADOWSIDE CT
2 GOLDEN LEAF CT
3 SHADOW WOOD CT
4 BARONI GREEN DR

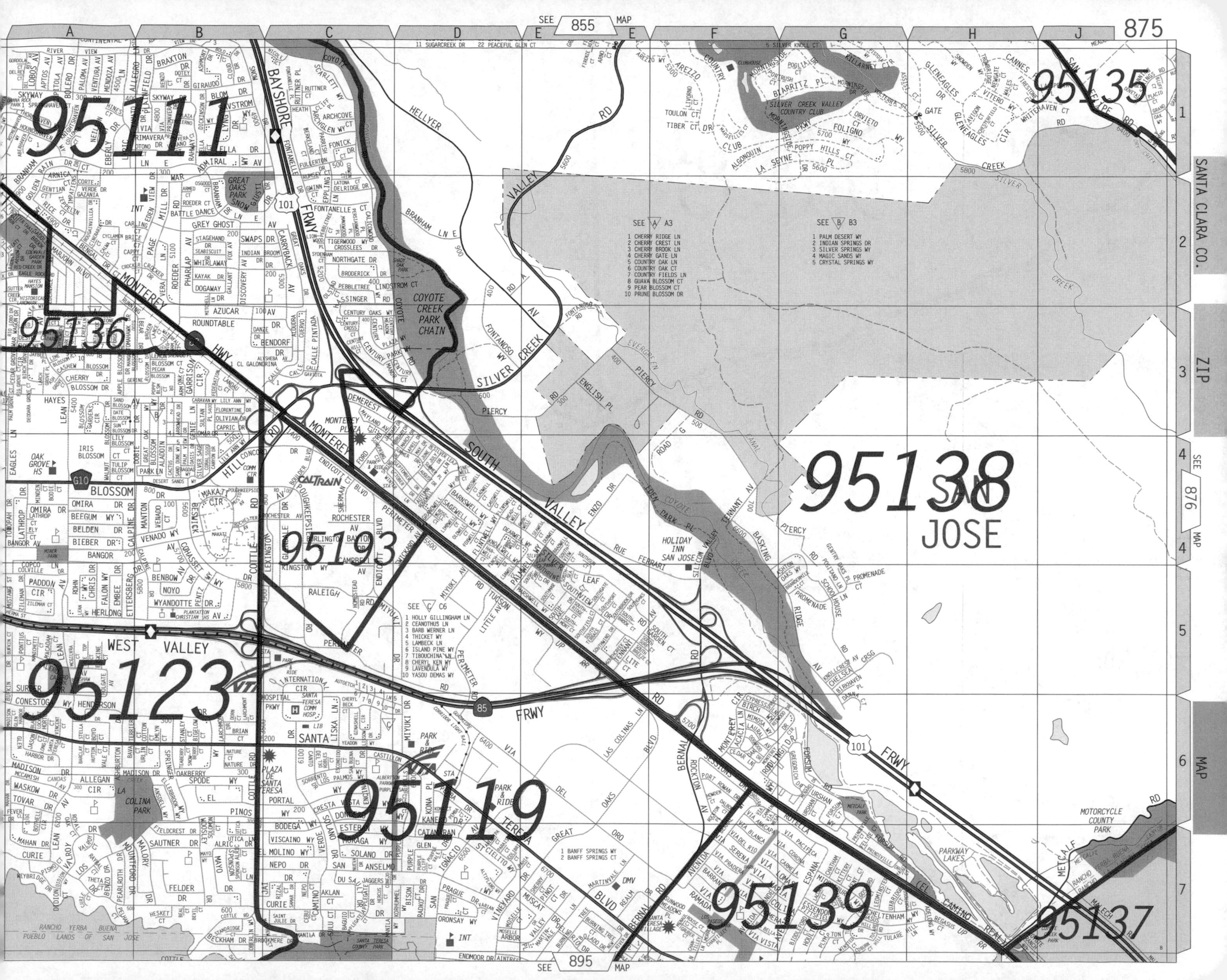
SEE 855 MAP
SEE 895 MAP
SEE 876 MAP
SANTA CLARA CO.
ZIP MAP
95111
95135
95136
95138
95193
95123
95119
95139
95137
SAN JOSE
COYOTE CREEK PARK CHAIN
GREAT OAKS PARK SNOW
SILVER CREEK VALLEY COUNTRY CLUB
MONTEREY PLAZA
HOLIDAY INN SAN JOSE
OAK GROVE HS
MINER PARK
LA COLINA PARK
PLAZA DE SANTA TERESA
SANTA TERESA COMM HOSP
MOTORCYCLE COUNTY PARK
PARKWAY LAKES
SANTA TERESA COUNTY PARK
RANCHO YERBA BUENA PUEBLO LANDS OF SAN JOSE
BAYSHORE FRWY
MONTEREY HWY
SOUTH VALLEY
FRWY
HELLYER
SILVER CREEK VALLEY RD
BRANHAM LN E
BLOSSOM HILL RD
SANTA TERESA BLVD
COTTLE RD
BERNAL RD
GREAT OAKS BLVD
MONTEREY RD
SEE A A3
1 CHERRY RIDGE LN
2 CHERRY CREST LN
3 CHERRY BROOK LN
4 CHERRY GATE LN
5 COUNTRY OAK LN
6 COUNTRY OAK CT
7 COUNTRY FIELDS LN
8 GUAVA BLOSSOM CT
9 PEAR BLOSSOM CT
10 PRUNE BLOSSOM DR
SEE B B3
1 PALM DESERT WY
2 INDIAN SPRINGS DR
3 SILVER SPRINGS WY
4 MAGIC SANDS WY
5 CRYSTAL SPRINGS WY
SEE C C6
1 HOLLY GILLINGHAM LN
2 CEANOTHUS LN
3 BARB WERNER LN
4 THICKET WY
5 LAMBECK LN
6 ISLAND PINE WY
7 TIBOUCHINA LN
8 CHERYL KEN WY
9 LAVENDULA WY
10 YASOU DEMAS WY
1 BANFF SPRINGS WY
2 BANFF SPRINGS CT

SEE 856 MAP

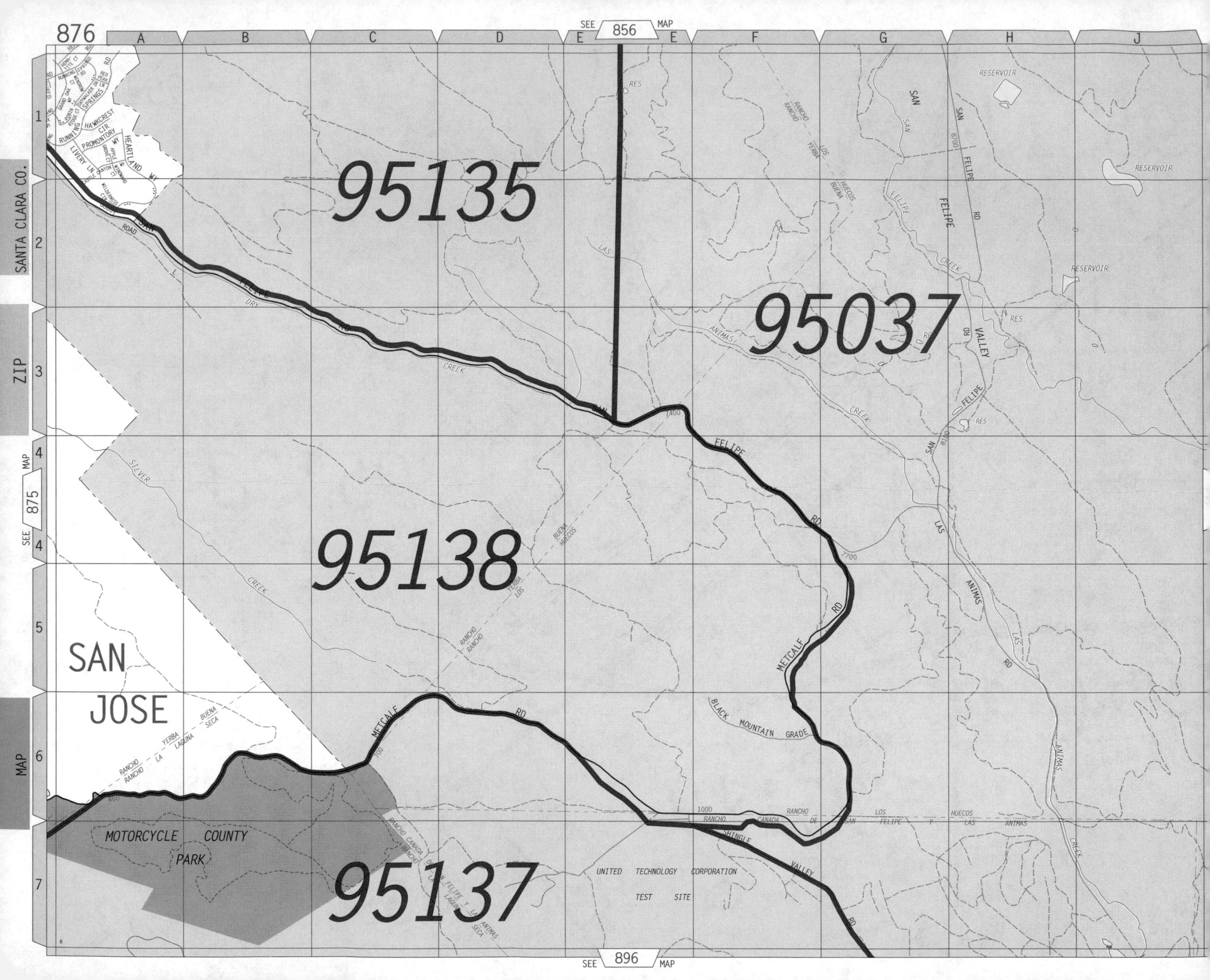

SEE 875 MAP

SEE 896 MAP

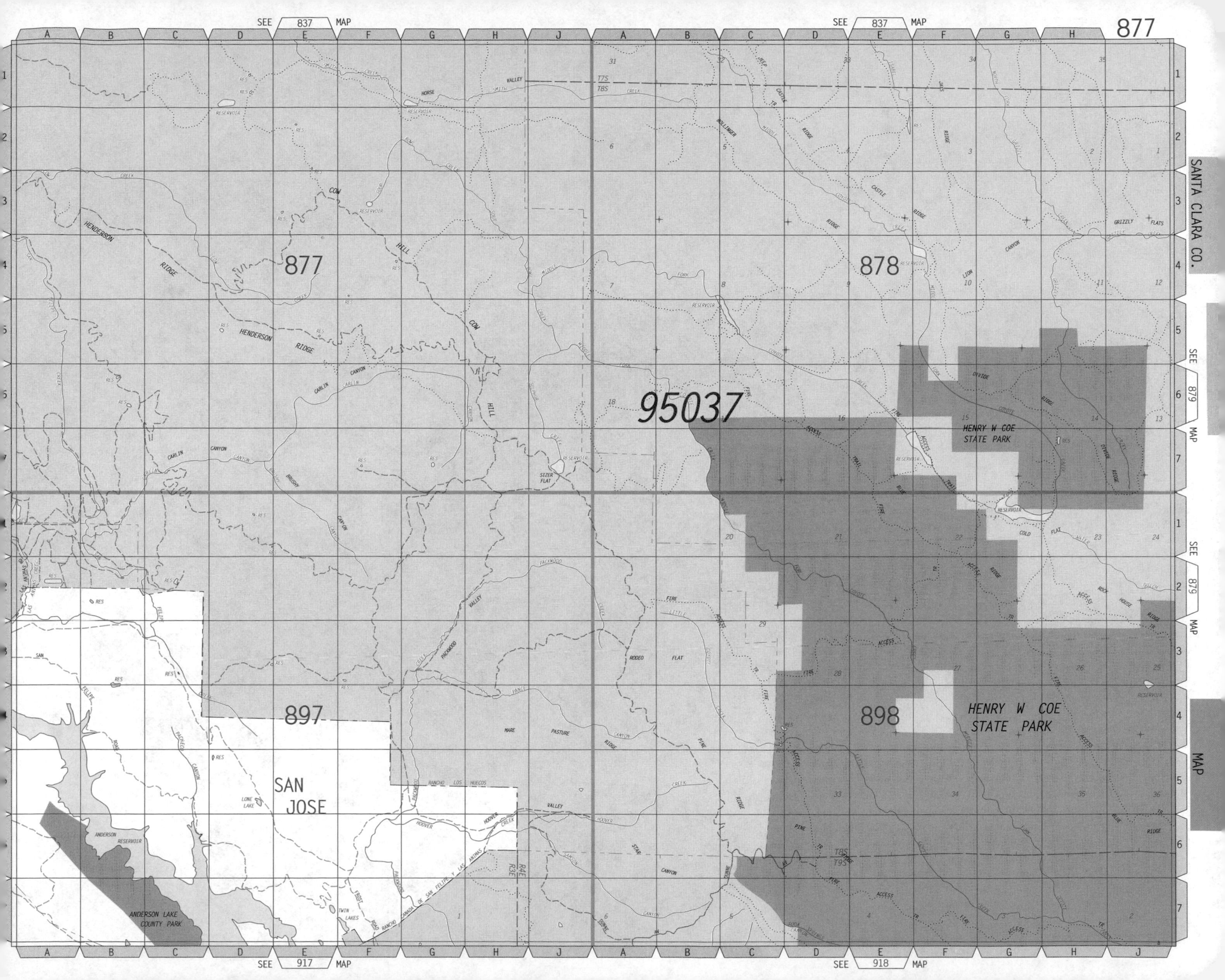
SEE 837 MAP
SEE 837 MAP
877
878
897
898
95037
SANTA CLARA CO.
SEE 879 MAP
SEE 879 MAP
SEE 917 MAP
SEE 918 MAP
MAP
HENRY W COE STATE PARK
HENRY W COE STATE PARK
SAN JOSE
ANDERSON LAKE COUNTY PARK
ANDERSON RESERVOIR
HENDERSON RIDGE
HENDERSON RIDGE
COW HILL
CARLIN CANYON
BRUSHY CANYON
SIZER FLAT
PACKWOOD VALLEY
RODEO FLAT
MARE PASTURE RIDGE
RANCHO LOS HUECOS
RANCHO CANADA DE SAN FELIPE Y LAS ANIMAS
HOOVER VALLEY
STAR CANYON
DUNNE AV
TWIN LAKES
LONE LAKE
GRIZZLY FLATS
COLD FLAT
ROCK HOUSE GULCH
DIVIDE RIDGE
CASTLE RIDGE
LION CANYON
MIDDLE RIDGE
SMITH CREEK
HORSE VALLEY
T7S
T8S
T8S
T9S
R3E
R4E

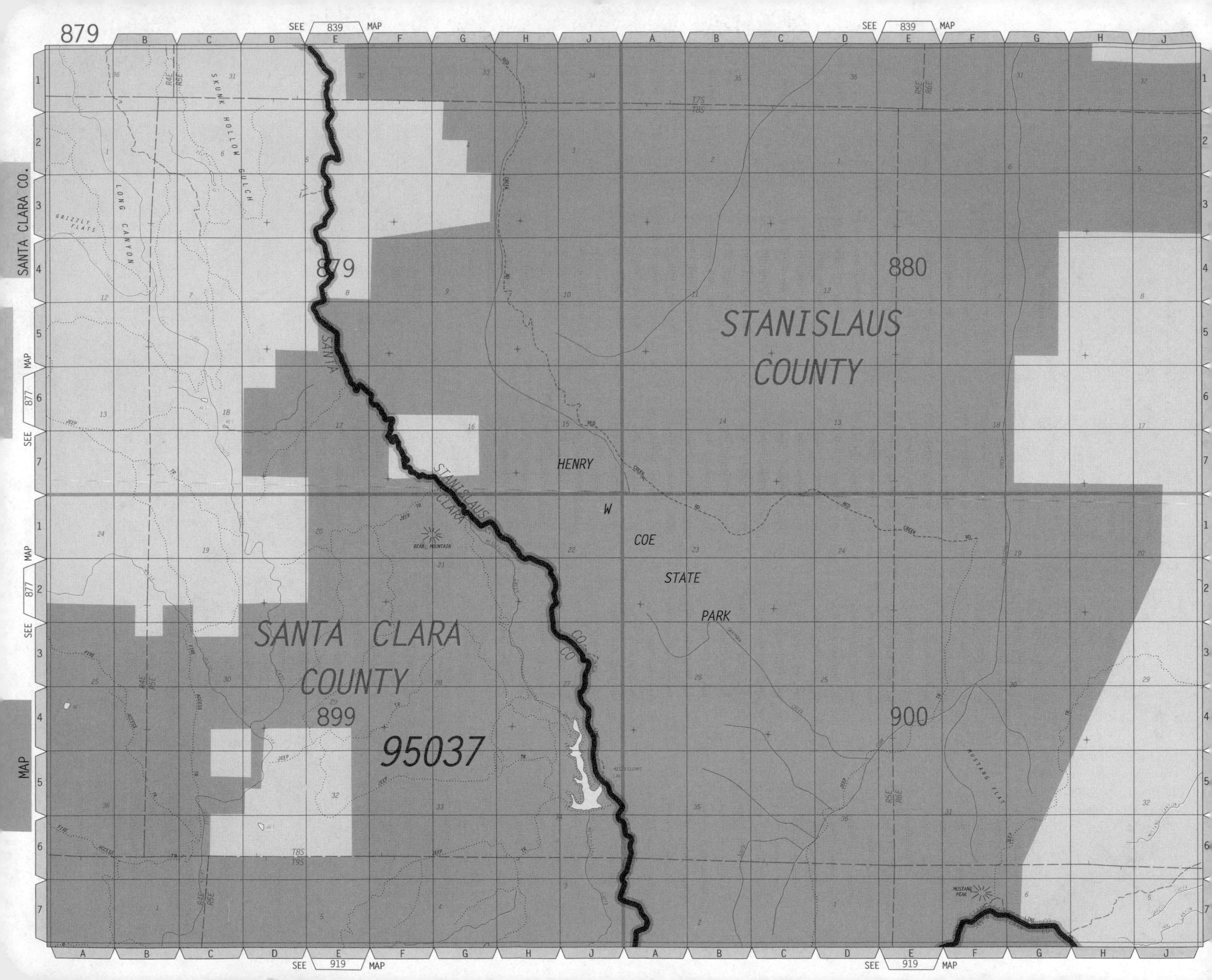
SEE 839 MAP
SEE 839 MAP
SEE 877 MAP
SEE 877 MAP
SEE 919 MAP
SEE 919 MAP
SANTA CLARA CO.
MAP
879
880
899
900
STANISLAUS COUNTY
SANTA CLARA COUNTY
95037
HENRY W COE STATE PARK
SKUNK HOLLOW GULCH
LONG CANYON
GRIZZLY FLATS
SANTA STANISLAUS
STANISLAUS CLARA
CO CO
BEAR MOUNTAIN
MUSTANG PEAK
MUSTANG FLAT
T7S
T8S
T8S
T9S
R4E R5E
R5E R6E
JEEP TR
FIRE ACCESS TR
RED CREEK RD

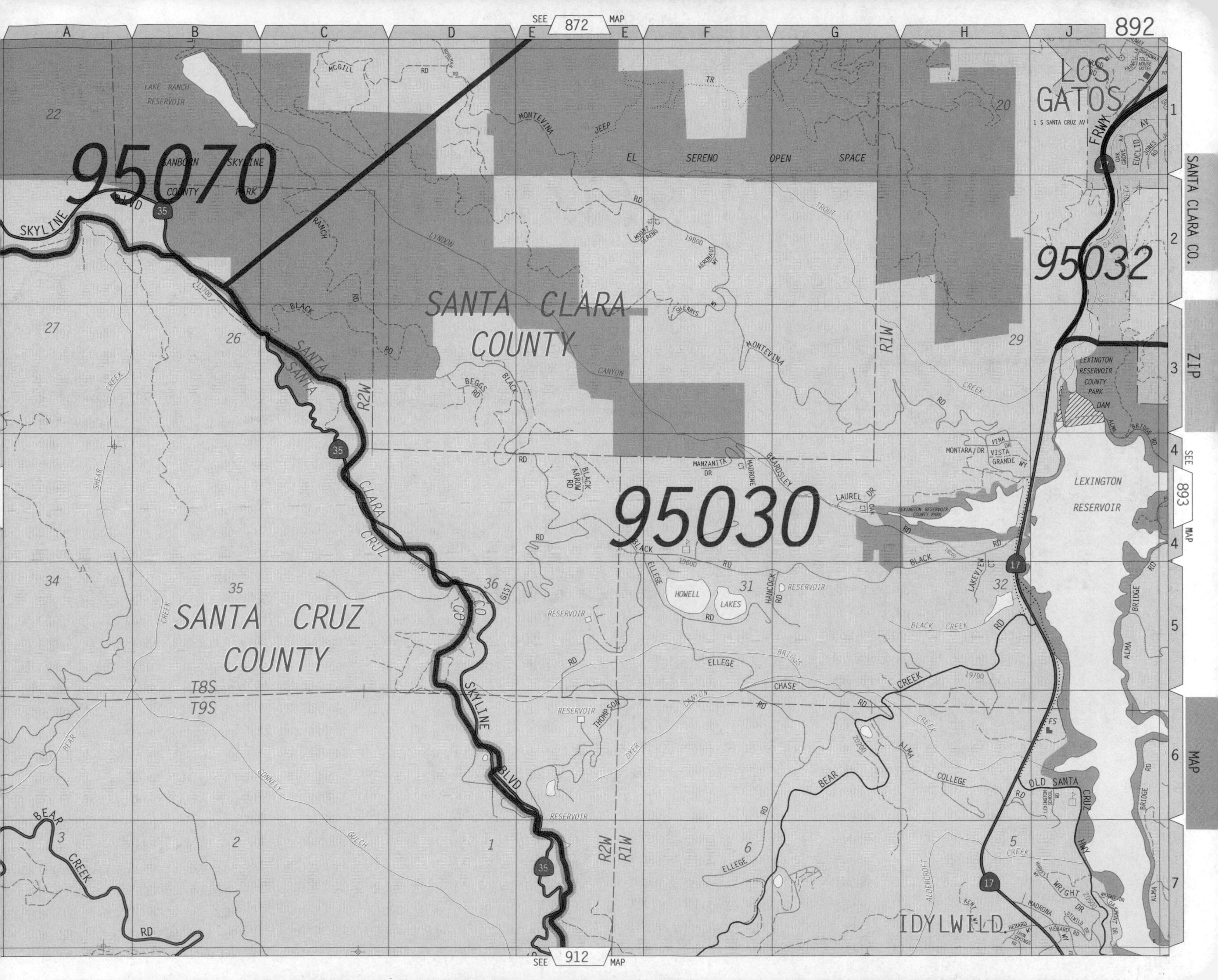
SEE 872 MAP
LOS GATOS
95070
95032
95030
SANTA CLARA COUNTY
SANTA CRUZ COUNTY
SANBORN SKYLINE COUNTY PARK
LAKE RANCH RESERVOIR
EL SERENO OPEN SPACE
LEXINGTON RESERVOIR COUNTY PARK
LEXINGTON RESERVOIR
HOWELL LAKES
IDYLWILD
SKYLINE BLVD
SANTA CRUZ CO
BLACK RD
MONTEVINA RD
BEARDSLEY
LAUREL DR
ELLEGE RD
CHASE RD
BEAR CREEK RD
ALMA BRIDGE RD
OLD SANTA CRUZ HWY
SANTA CLARA CO. ZIP MAP
SEE 893 MAP
SEE 912 MAP

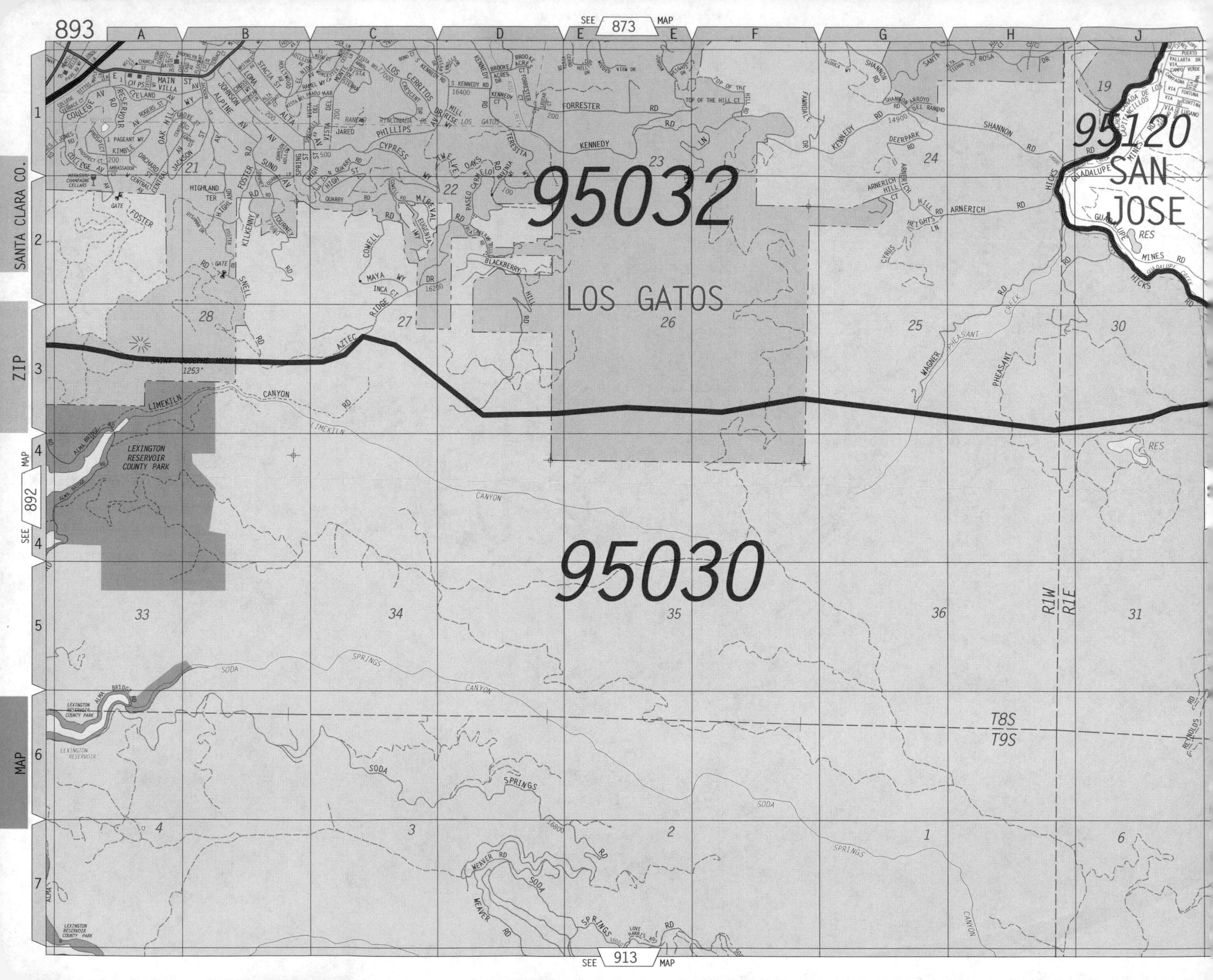

893
SEE 873 MAP
SEE 913 MAP
SEE 892 MAP
SANTA CLARA CO.
ZIP
MAP
95032
95030
95120
SAN JOSE
LOS GATOS
LEXINGTON RESERVOIR COUNTY PARK
LEXINGTON RESERVOIR
MIRASSOU CHAMPAGNE CELLARS
LIMEKILN CANYON RD
SODA SPRINGS CANYON
SODA SPRINGS RD
ALMA BRIDGE RD
KENNEDY RD
SHANNON RD
HICKS RD
ARNERICH RD
GUADALUPE MINES RD
WAGNER RD
PHEASANT CREEK
PHEASANT RD
AZTEC RIDGE RD
FORRESTER RD
TOP OF THE HILL CT
FOSTER RD
SNELL RD
BLACKBERRY HILL RD
COWELL RD
PHILLIPS RD
CYPRESS WY
WEAVER RD
REYNOLDS RD
HIGHLAND TER
MAIN ST
COLLEGE AV
T8S
T9S
R1W
R1E
1253'

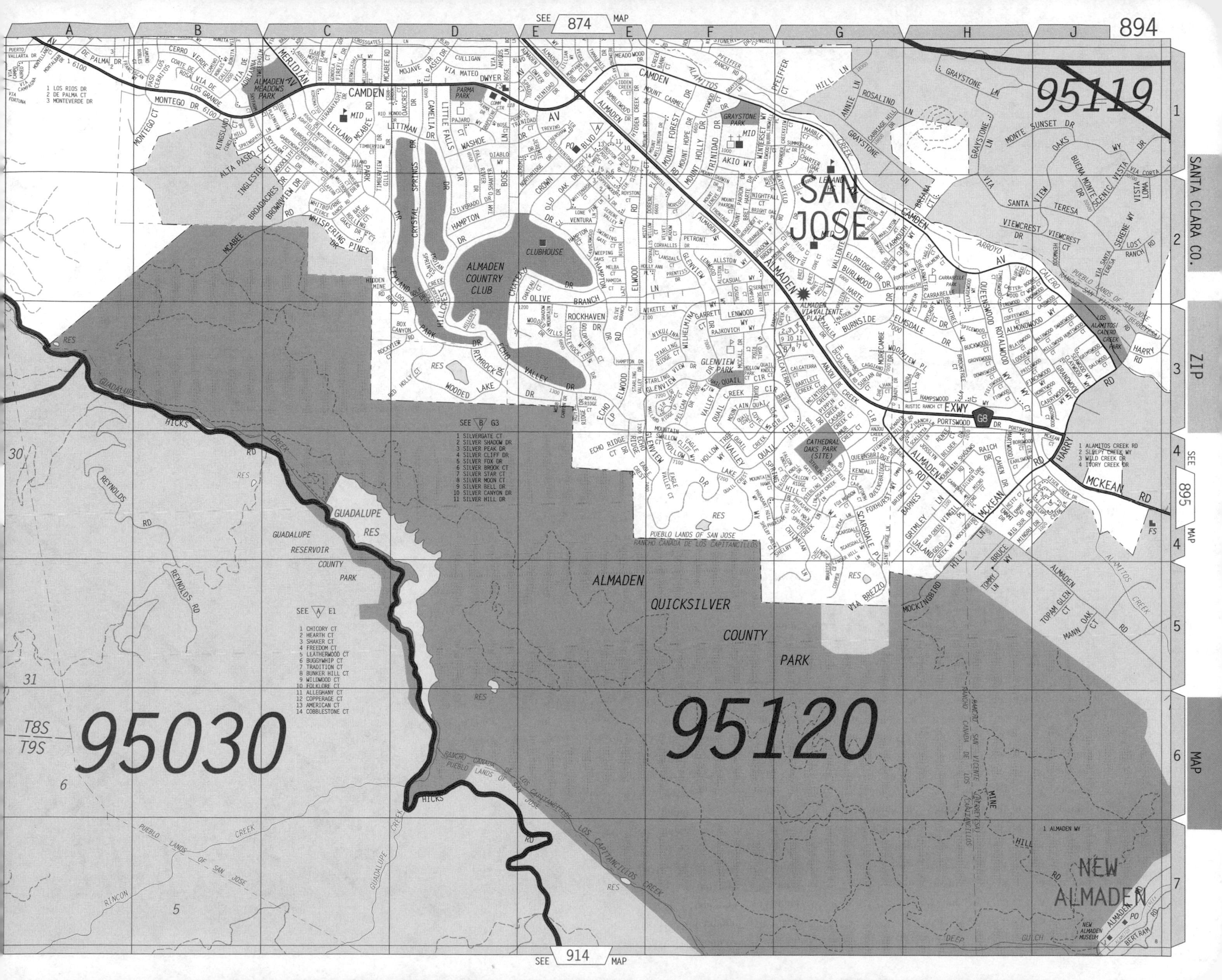
SEE 874 MAP
95119
SAN JOSE
ALMADEN COUNTRY CLUB
ALMADEN MEADOWS PARK
PARMA PARK
GRAYSTONE PARK
GLENVIEW PARK
CATHEDRAL OAKS PARK (SITE)
LOS ALAMITOS/ CALERO CREEK PARK
ALMADEN VIAVALIENTE PLAZA
CAMDEN AV
ALMADEN EXWY
MCKEAN RD
HARRY RD
HICKS RD
GUADALUPE RES
GUADALUPE RESERVOIR COUNTY PARK
ALMADEN QUICKSILVER COUNTY PARK
PUEBLO LANDS OF SAN JOSE
RANCHO CANADA DE LOS CAPITANCILLOS
95030
95120
NEW ALMADEN
NEW ALMADEN MUSEUM
SANTA CLARA CO.
ZIP MAP
T8S
T9S
SEE 895 MAP
SEE 914 MAP
1 LOS RIOS DR
2 DE PALMA CT
3 MONTEVERDE DR
SEE B G3
1 SILVERGATE CT
2 SILVER SHADOW DR
3 SILVER PEAK DR
4 SILVER CLIFF DR
5 SILVER FOX DR
6 SILVER BROOK CT
7 SILVER STAR CT
8 SILVER MOON CT
9 SILVER BELL DR
10 SILVER CANYON DR
11 SILVER HILL DR
SEE A E1
1 CHICORY CT
2 HEARTH CT
3 SHAKER CT
4 FREEDOM CT
5 LEATHERWOOD CT
6 BUGGYWHIP CT
7 TRADITION CT
8 BUNKER HILL CT
9 WILDWOOD CT
10 FOLKLORE CT
11 ALLEGHANY CT
12 COPPERAGE CT
13 AMERICAN CT
14 COBBLESTONE CT
1 ALAMITOS CREEK RD
2 SLEEPY CREEK WY
3 WILD CREEK DR
4 IVORY CREEK DR
1 ALMADEN WY

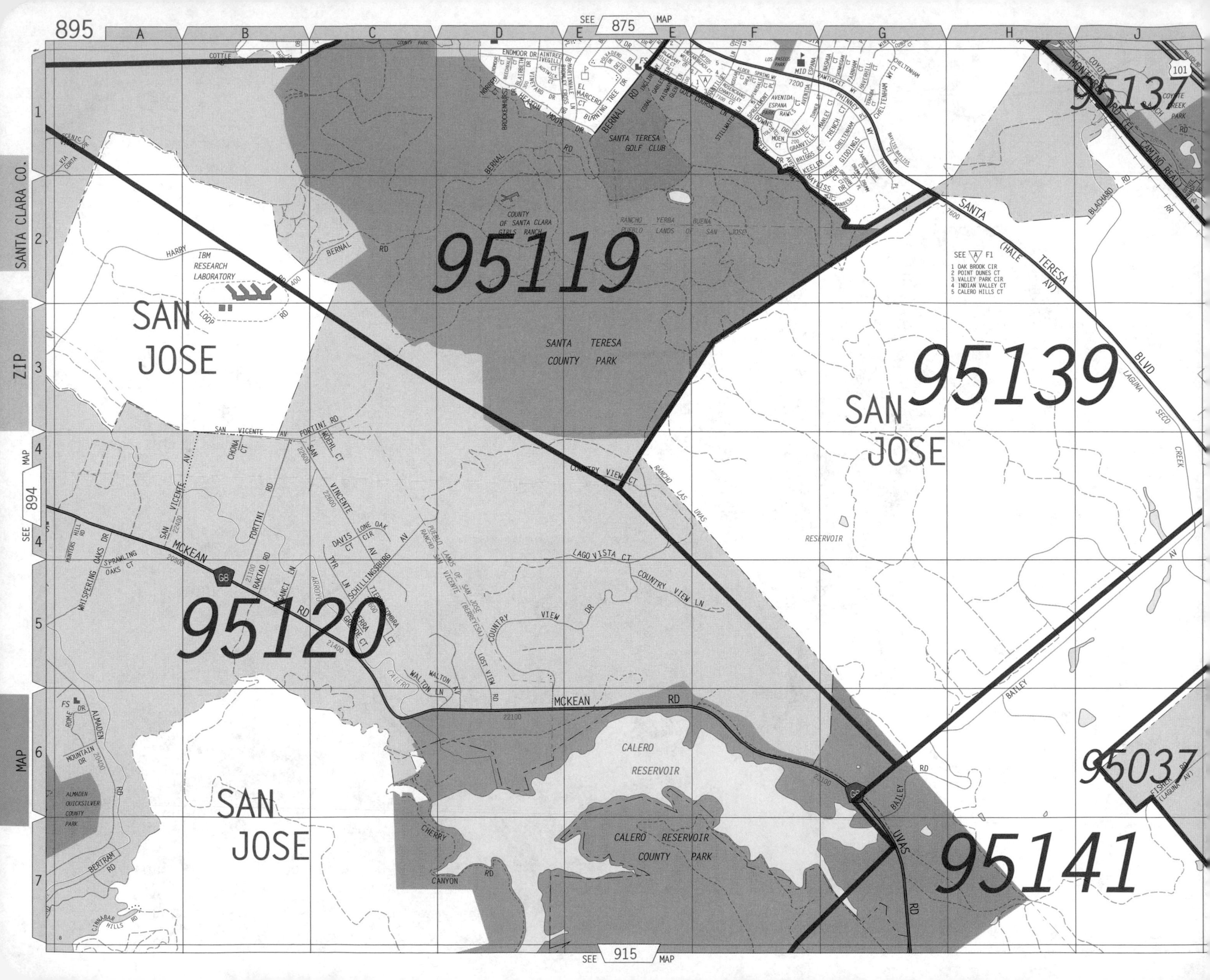
SEE 875 MAP
SEE 894 MAP
SEE 915 MAP
SANTA CLARA CO.
ZIP
MAP
95119
95120
95139
95137
95141
95037
SAN JOSE
SAN JOSE
SAN JOSE
SANTA TERESA COUNTY PARK
SANTA TERESA GOLF CLUB
COUNTY OF SANTA CLARA GIRLS RANCH
RANCHO YERBA BUENA PUEBLO LANDS OF SAN JOSE
IBM RESEARCH LABORATORY
HARRY RD
BERNAL RD
COTTLE RD
SANTA TERESA (HALE AV) BLVD
LAGUNA SECO CREEK
RESERVOIR
RANCHO LAS UVAS
SAN VICENTE AV
FORTINI RD
MCKEAN RD
COUNTRY VIEW DR
COUNTRY VIEW LN
LAGO VISTA CT
SCHILLINGSBURG AV
PUEBLO LANDS OF SAN JOSE RANCHO SAN VICENTE (BERREYESA)
LOST VIEW RD
CALERO RESERVOIR
CALERO RESERVOIR COUNTY PARK
CHERRY CANYON RD
UVAS RD
BAILEY AV
BAILEY RD
ALMADEN RD
ALMADEN QUICKSILVER COUNTY PARK
BERTRAM RD
CINNABAR HILLS RD
WHISPERING OAKS DR
SPRAWLING OAKS CT
HUNTERS HILL RD
MOUNTAIN DR
COYOTE CREEK PARK
MONTEREY RD (EL CAMINO REAL)
BLACHARD RD
SEE A F1
1 OAK BROOK CIR
2 POINT DUNES CT
3 VALLEY PARK CIR
4 INDIAN VALLEY CT
5 CALERO HILLS CT

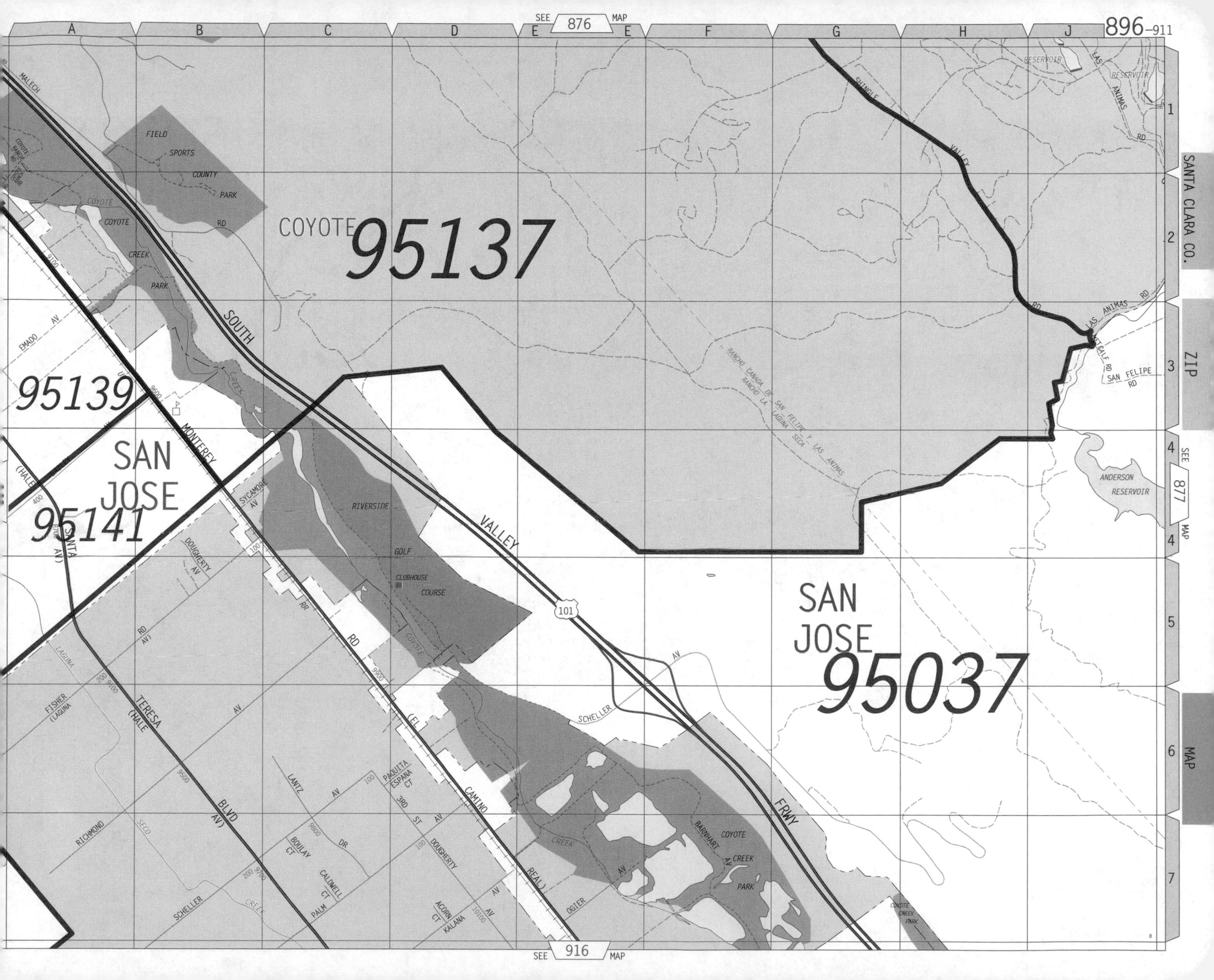
SEE 876 MAP
A
B
C
D
E
F
G
H
J
1
2
3
4
5
6
7
SANTA CLARA CO.
ZIP
MAP
SEE 877 MAP
SEE 916 MAP
COYOTE
95137
95139
95141
SAN JOSE
SAN JOSE
95037
FIELD
SPORTS
COUNTY
PARK
COYOTE
CREEK
PARK
RD
SOUTH
VALLEY
FRWY
101
MONTEREY
RD
SYCAMORE AV
DOUGHERTY AV
RIVERSIDE
GOLF
CLUBHOUSE
COURSE
SCHELLER
AV
SHINGLE
VALLEY
RD
LAS ANIMAS RD
METCALF RD
SAN FELIPE RD
RANCHO CANADA DE SAN FELIPE Y LAS ANIMAS
RANCHO LA LAGUNA SECA
ANDERSON RESERVOIR
RESERVOIR
EMADO AV
SANTA TERESA BLVD
FISHER (LAGUNA AV)
RICHMOND
SECO
SCHELLER
CREEK
LANTZ AV
PAQUITA ESPANA CT
3RD ST
BOULAY CT
CALDWELL CT
PALM
ACORN CT
KALANA AV
DOUGHERTY AV
DR
CAMINO REAL
OGIER AV
BARNHART AV
COYOTE CREEK PARK
MALECH RD

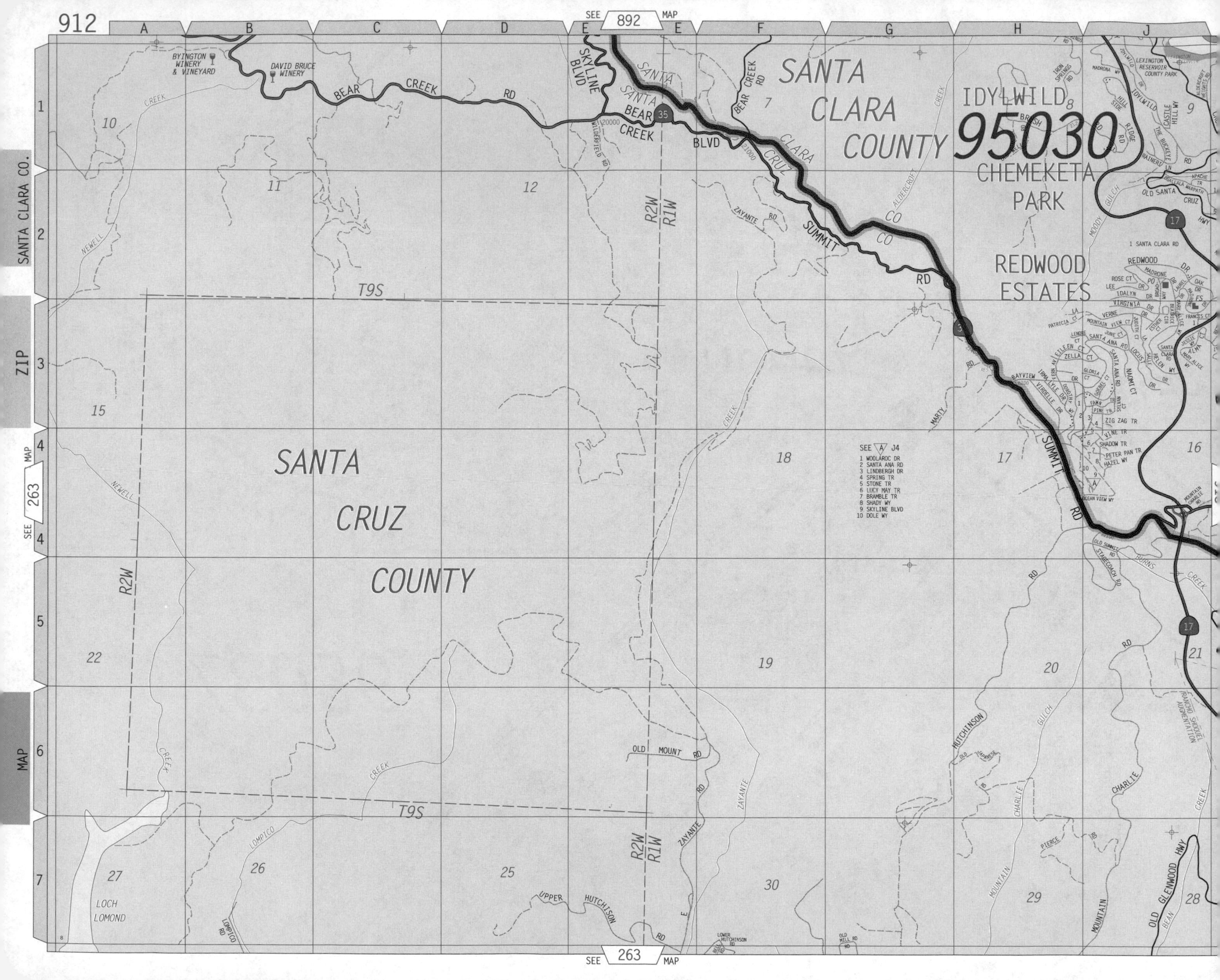
SEE 892 MAP
SANTA CLARA COUNTY
SANTA CRUZ COUNTY
IDYLWILD
95030
CHEMEKETA PARK
REDWOOD ESTATES
BYINGTON WINERY & VINEYARD
DAVID BRUCE WINERY
BEAR CREEK RD
SKYLINE BLVD
BEAR CREEK RD
SUMMIT RD
OLD SANTA CRUZ HWY
T9S
R2W
R1W
SEE A J4
1 WOOLAROC DR
2 SANTA ANA RD
3 LINDBERGH DR
4 SPRING TR
5 STONE TR
6 LUCY MAY TR
7 BRAMBLE TR
8 SHADY WY
9 SKYLINE BLVD
10 DOLE WY
OLD MOUNT RD
ZAYANTE RD
LOMPICO RD
UPPER HUTCHINSON RD
HUTCHINSON
CHARLIE
MOUNTAIN
OLD GLENWOOD HWY
LOCH LOMOND
SEE 263 MAP
SANTA CLARA CO.
ZIP
MAP

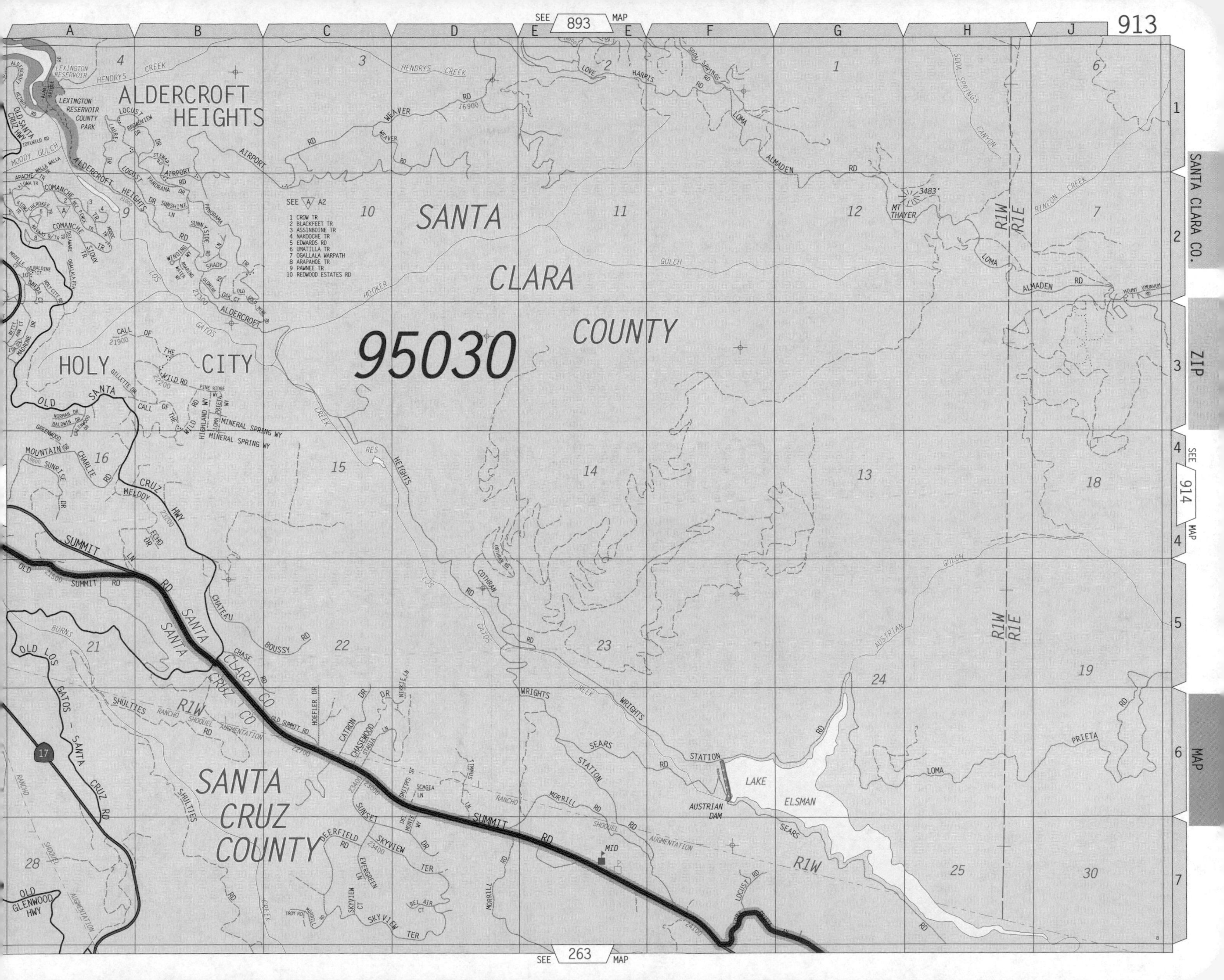
SEE 893 MAP
ALDERCROFT HEIGHTS
HOLY CITY
SANTA CLARA COUNTY
95030
SANTA CRUZ COUNTY
LEXINGTON RESERVOIR COUNTY PARK
MT THAYER 3483'
LAKE ELSMAN
AUSTRIAN DAM
SUMMIT RD
OLD SANTA CRUZ HWY
LOS GATOS - SANTA CRUZ RD
ALMADEN RD
LOMA ALMADEN RD
WEAVER RD
AIRPORT RD
WRIGHTS STATION RD
SEARS RD
LOMA PRIETA RD
SANTA CLARA CO.
ZIP
SEE 914 MAP
MAP
SEE 263 MAP

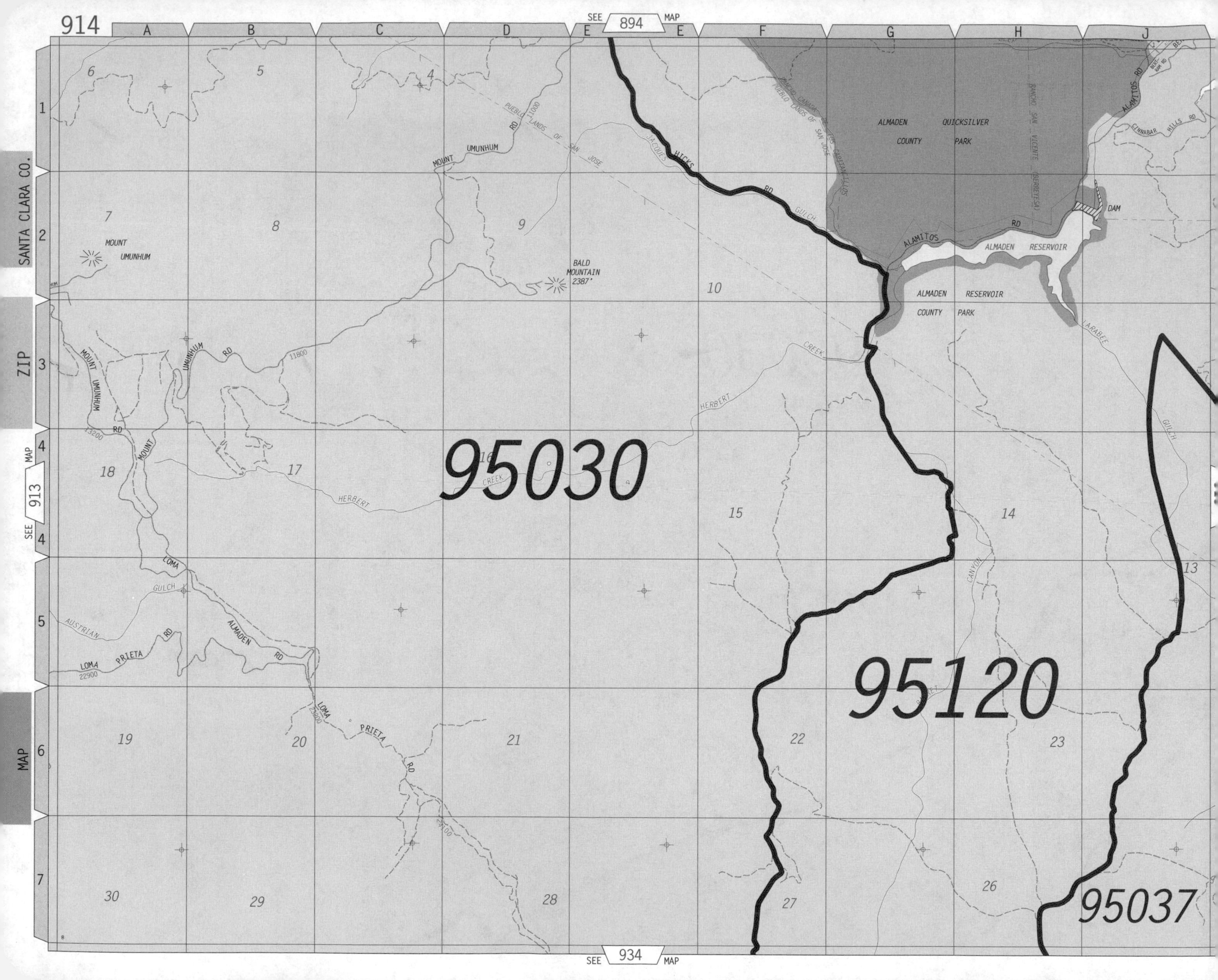
SEE 894 MAP
SEE 913 MAP
SEE 934 MAP
SANTA CLARA CO.
ZIP
MAP
95030
95120
95037
MOUNT UMUNHUM
BALD MOUNTAIN 2387'
MOUNT UMUNHUM RD
PUEBLO LANDS OF SAN JOSE
HICKS RD
JACQUES GULCH
ALMADEN QUICKSILVER COUNTY PARK
ALMADEN RESERVOIR
ALMADEN RESERVOIR COUNTY PARK
ALAMITOS RD
DAM
CINNABAR HILLS RD
HERBERT CREEK
LARABEE GULCH
CANYON
LOMA GULCH
AUSTRIAN
LOMA PRIETA RD
ALMADEN RD

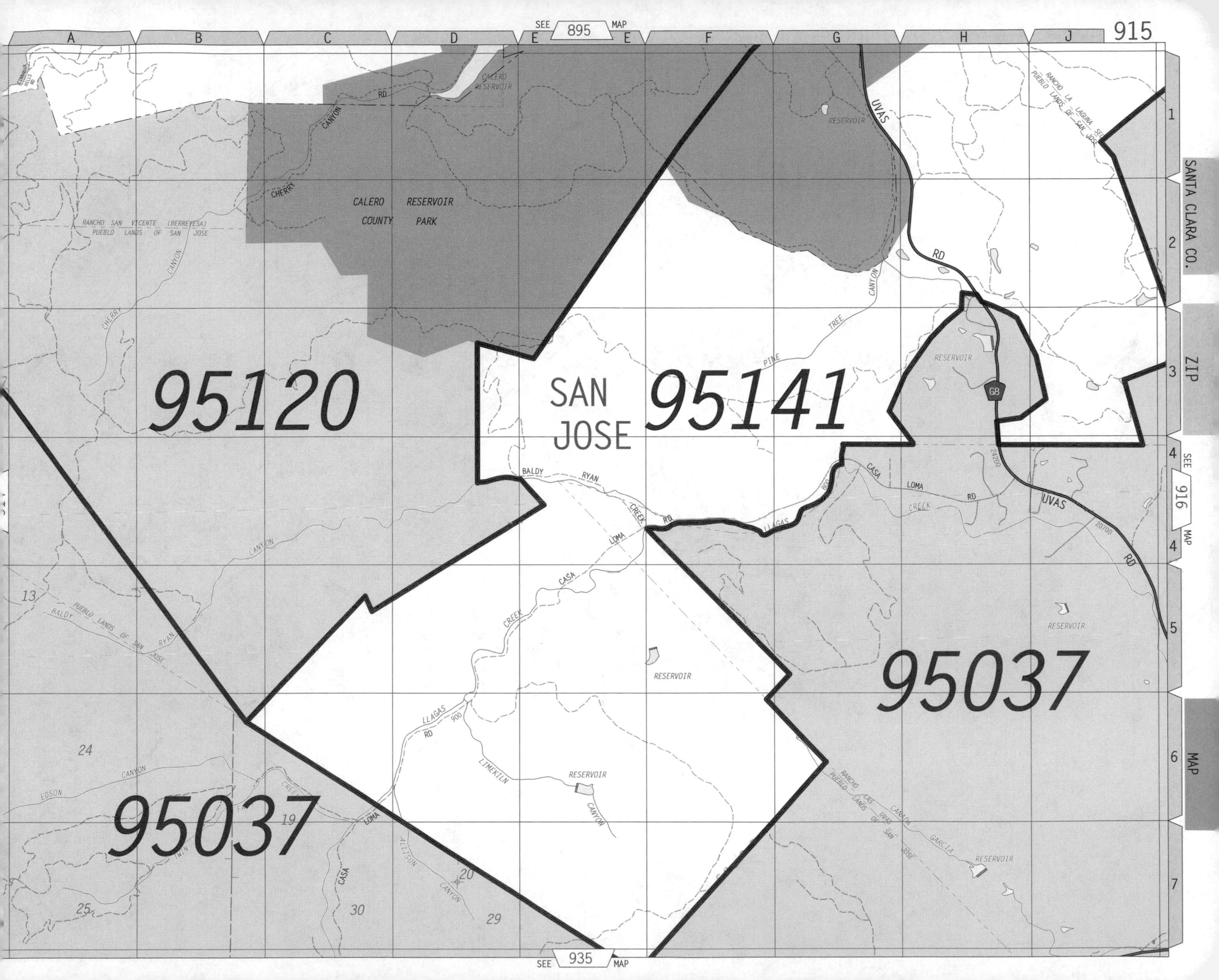

SEE 895 MAP
A
B
C
D
E
F
G
H
J
1
2
3
4
5
6
7
SANTA CLARA CO.
ZIP
MAP
SEE 916 MAP
SEE 935 MAP
95120
95141
95037
95037
SAN JOSE
CALERO RESERVOIR COUNTY PARK
CALERO RESERVOIR
RANCHO SAN VICENTE (BERREYESA) PUEBLO LANDS OF SAN JOSE
RANCHO LA LAGUNA SECA PUEBLO LANDS OF SAN JOSE
RANCHO LAS UVAS PUEBLO LANDS OF SAN JOSE
PUEBLO LANDS OF SAN JOSE
CHERRY CANYON RD
UVAS RD
UVAS CANYON
PINE TREE CANYON
BALDY RYAN CREEK RD
BALDY RYAN
CASA LOMA RD
CASA LOMA
CREEK
LLAGAS CREEK
LLAGAS RD
CANYON
LIMEKILN CANYON
EDSON CANYON
CREEK
TWIN
ALLISON CANYON
CANADA GARCIA
RESERVOIR
G8
24200
20700
900
800
13
24
19
20
25
29
30

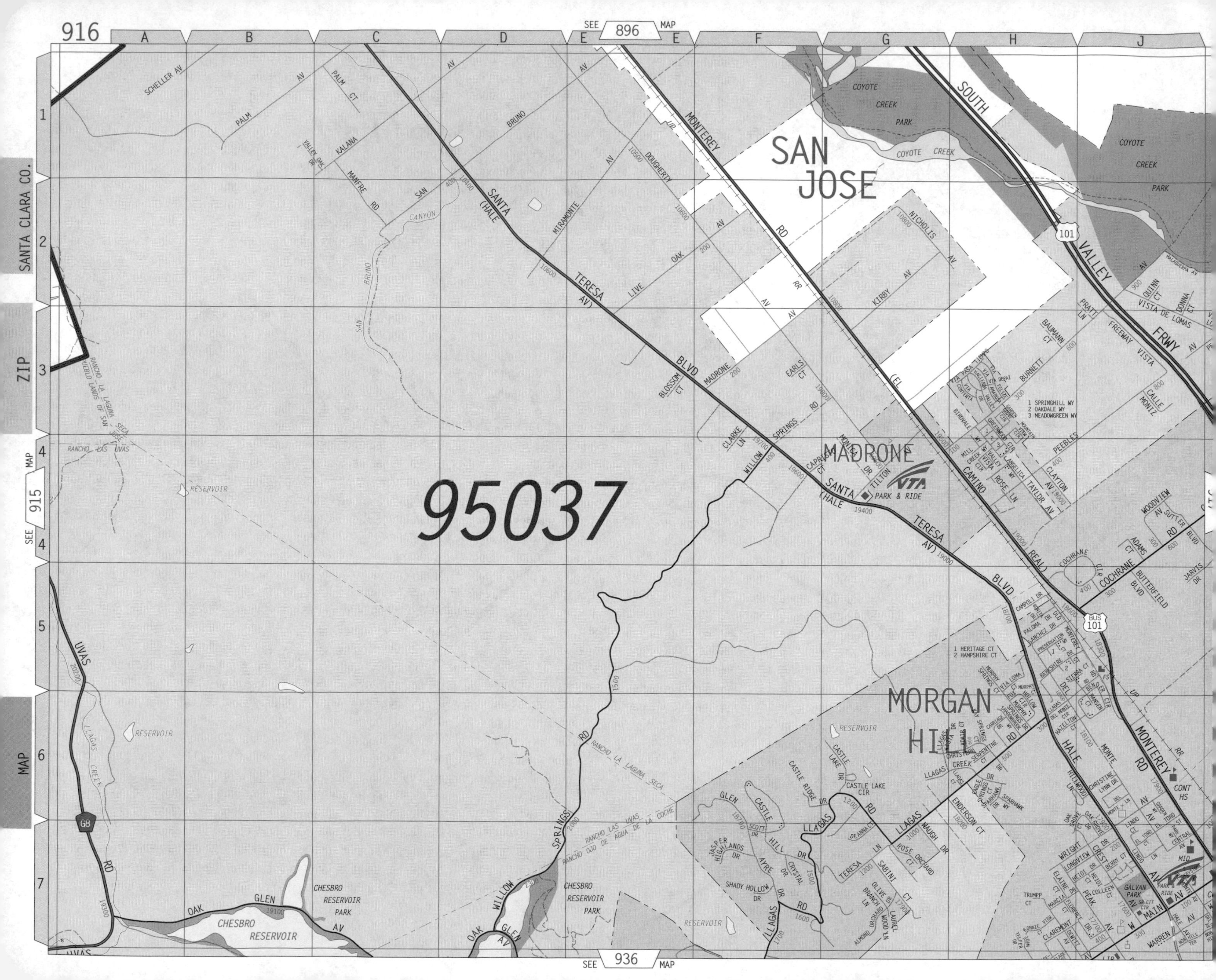

SEE 896 MAP
SEE 915 MAP
SEE 936 MAP
SANTA CLARA CO.
ZIP
MAP
95037
SAN JOSE
MADRONE
MORGAN HILL
COYOTE CREEK PARK
CHESBRO RESERVOIR
CHESBRO RESERVOIR PARK
SOUTH VALLEY FRWY
MONTEREY RD
SANTA TERESA BLVD
(HALE AV)
CAMINO REAL
WILLOW SPRINGS RD
UVAS RD
OAK GLEN AV
LLAGAS RD
COCHRANE RD
BUTTERFIELD BLVD
MAIN AV
VTA PARK & RIDE
RESERVOIR
RANCHO LAS UVAS
RANCHO LA LAGUNA SECA

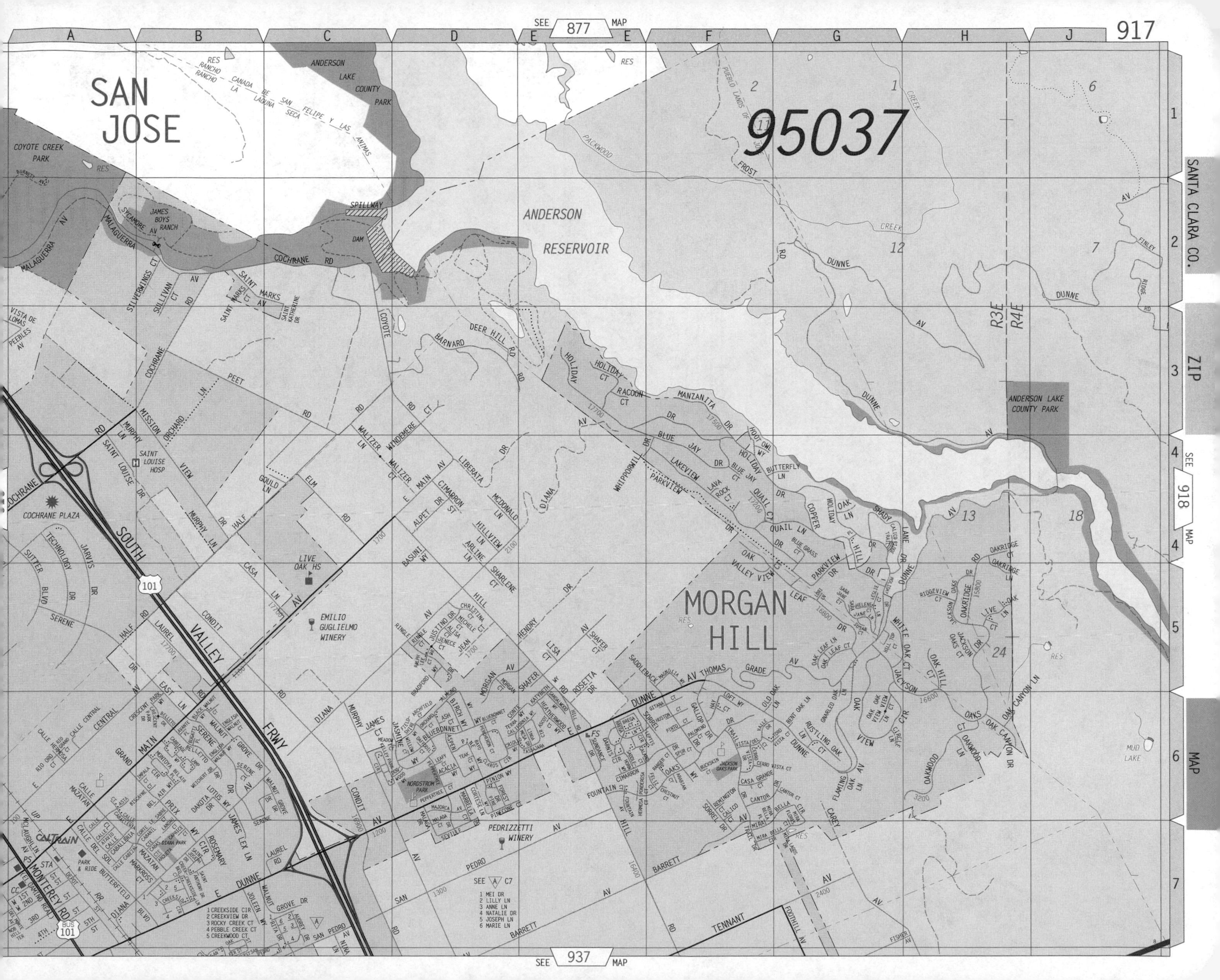
SEE 877 MAP
A
B
C
D
E
F
G
H
J
1
2
3
4
5
6
7
SAN JOSE
95037
ANDERSON LAKE COUNTY PARK
COYOTE CREEK PARK
JAMES BOYS RANCH
SPILLWAY
DAM
ANDERSON RESERVOIR
COCHRANE RD
SAINT LOUISE HOSP
COCHRANE PLAZA
SOUTH VALLEY FRWY
101
LIVE OAK HS
EMILIO GUGLIELMO WINERY
MORGAN HILL
DUNNE AV
PEDRIZZETTI WINERY
NORDSTROM PARK
JACKSON OAKS PARK
CALTRAIN
PARK & RIDE
MUD LAKE
R3E
R4E
SANTA CLARA CO.
ZIP
MAP
SEE 918 MAP
1 CREEKSIDE CIR
2 CREEKVIEW DR
3 ROCKY CREEK CT
4 PEBBLE CREEK CT
5 CREEKWOOD CT
SEE A C7
1 MEI DR
2 LILLY LN
3 ANNE LN
4 NATALIE DR
5 JOSEPH LN
6 MARIE LN
SEE 937 MAP

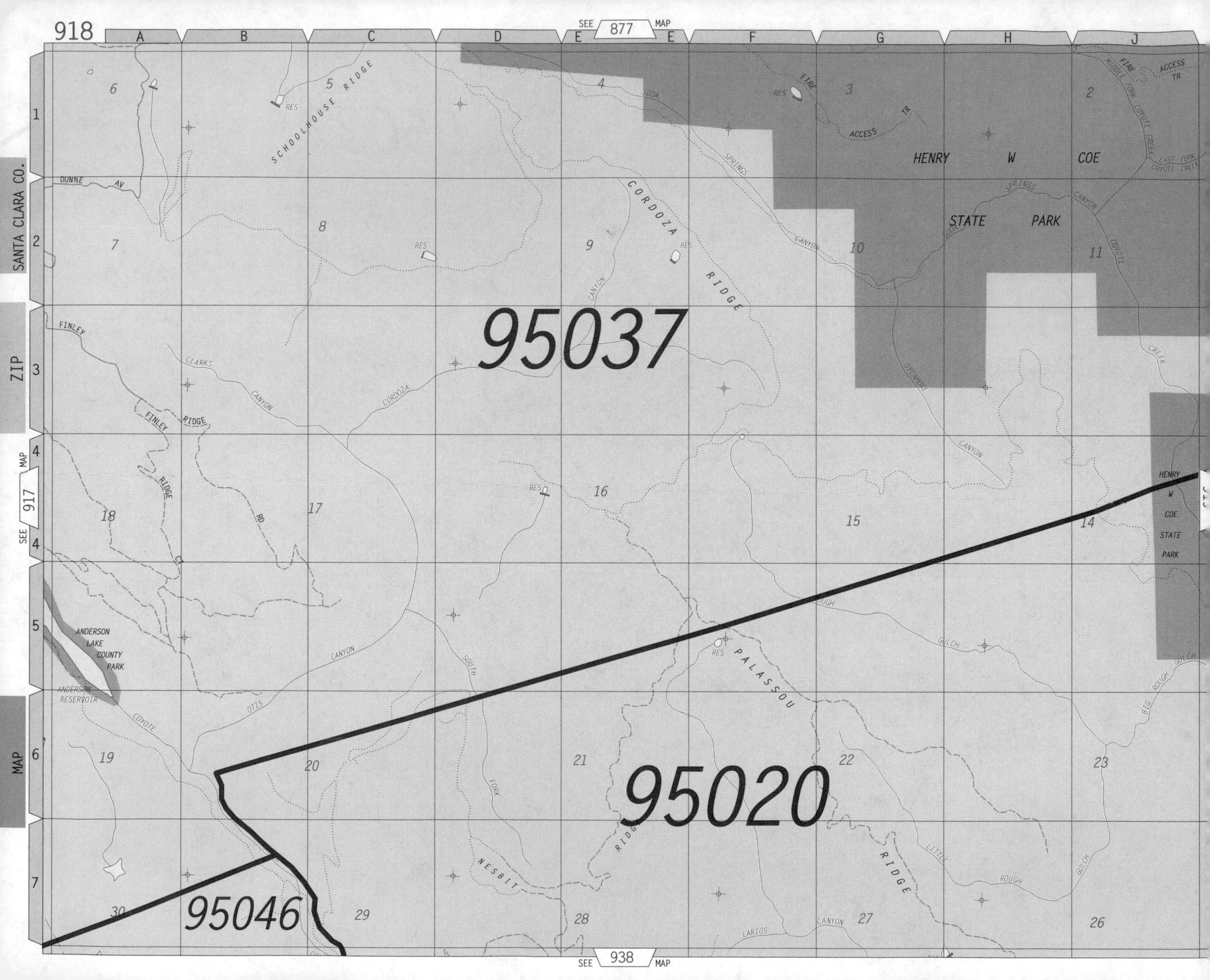
SEE 877 MAP
A
B
C
D
E
F
G
H
J
1
2
3
4
5
6
7
SANTA CLARA CO.
ZIP
MAP
SEE 917 MAP
95037
95020
95046
HENRY W COE
STATE PARK
HENRY W COE STATE PARK
ANDERSON LAKE COUNTY PARK
ANDERSON RESERVOIR
SCHOOLHOUSE RIDGE
CORDOZA RIDGE
DUNNE AV
FINLEY
FINLEY RIDGE
FINLEY RIDGE CT
CLARKS CANYON
CORDOZA CANYON
RIDGE RD
SODA SPRINGS CANYON
FIRE ACCESS TR
MIDDLE FORK COYOTE CREEK
EAST FORK COYOTE CREEK
COYOTE CREEK
SYCAMORE CANYON
ROUGH GULCH
BIG ROUGH GULCH
LITTLE ROUGH GULCH
PALASSOU RIDGE
SOUTH FORK
OTIS CANYON
COYOTE
NESBIT RIDGE
LARIOS CANYON
RES
SEE 938 MAP

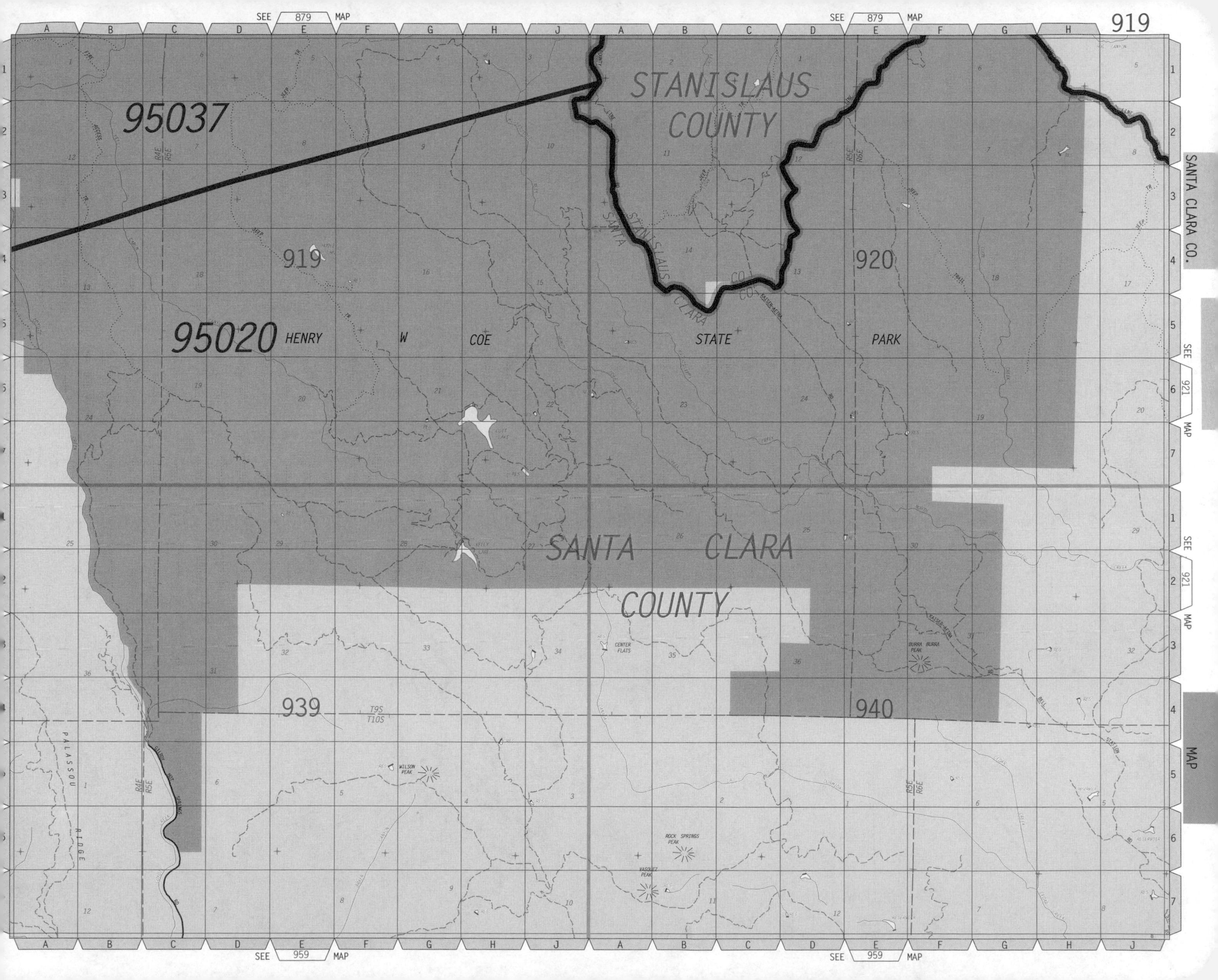
SEE 879 MAP
SEE 879 MAP
STANISLAUS COUNTY
95037
95020
HENRY W COE STATE PARK
919
920
SANTA CLARA COUNTY
939
940
SANTA CLARA CO.
SEE 921 MAP
SEE 921 MAP
MAP
CENTER FLATS
BURRA BURRA PEAK
WILSON PEAK
ROCK SPRINGS PEAK
VASQUEZ PEAK
PALASSOU RIDGE
T9S
T10S
R4E R5E
R5E R6E
SEE 959 MAP
SEE 959 MAP

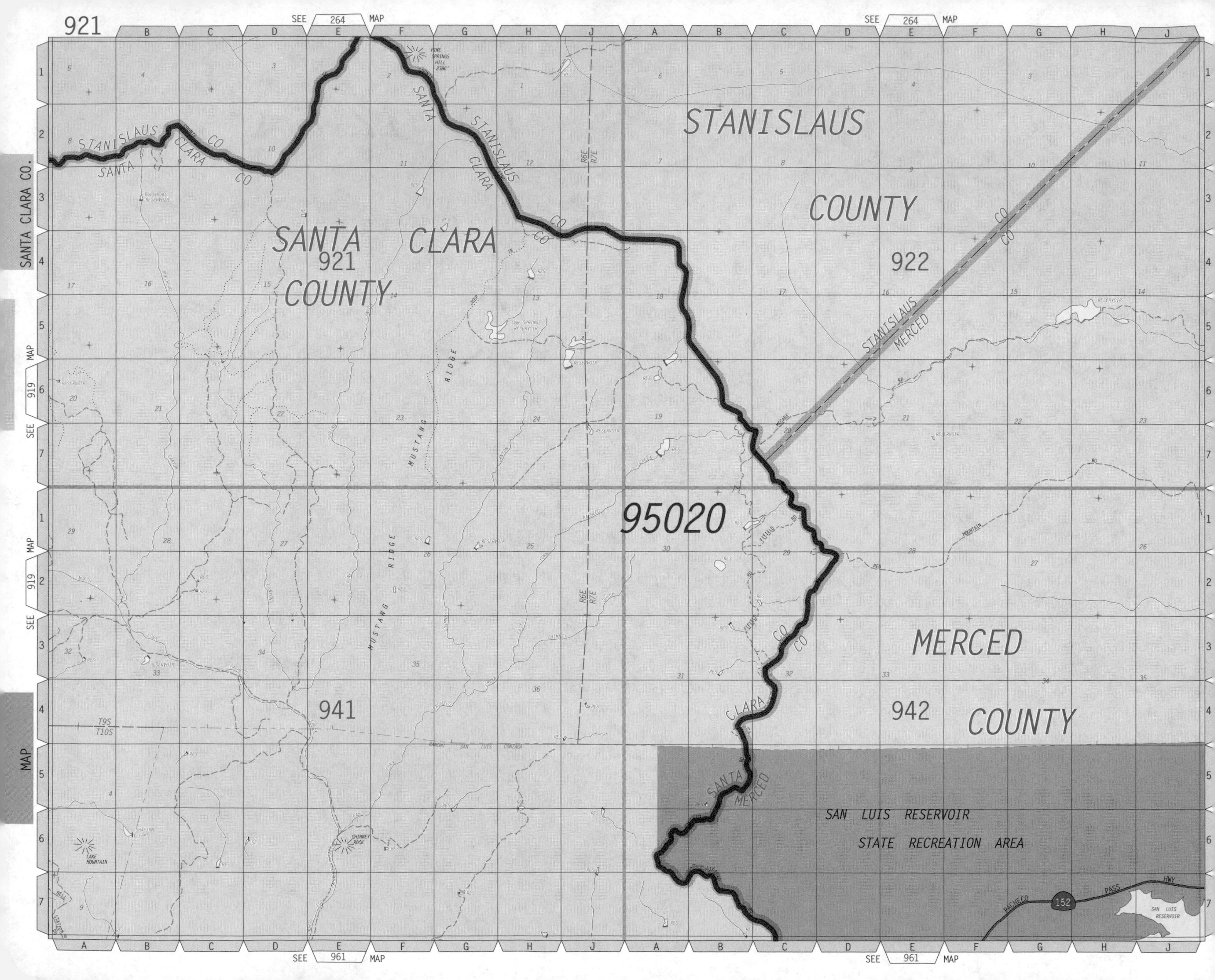
SEE 264 MAP
SEE 264 MAP
SANTA CLARA CO.
SEE 919 MAP
SEE 919 MAP
MAP
STANISLAUS COUNTY
922
SANTA CLARA 921 COUNTY
SANTA CLARA CO
STANISLAUS CO
SANTA STANISLAUS CO
SANTA CLARA CO
STANISLAUS MERCED
CO CO
PINE SPRINGS HILL 2386'
BUCKHEAD RESERVOIR
OAK SPRINGS RESERVOIR
MUSTANG RIDGE
MUSTANG RIDGE
R6E R7E
95020
MERCED 942 COUNTY
941
T9S T10S
SANTA CLARA CO CO
SANTA MERCED
SAN LUIS RESERVOIR
STATE RECREATION AREA
PACHECO PASS HWY
152
SAN LUIS RESERVOIR
LAKE MOUNTAIN
CHIMNEY ROCK
SHALLEN LAKE
SEE 961 MAP
SEE 961 MAP

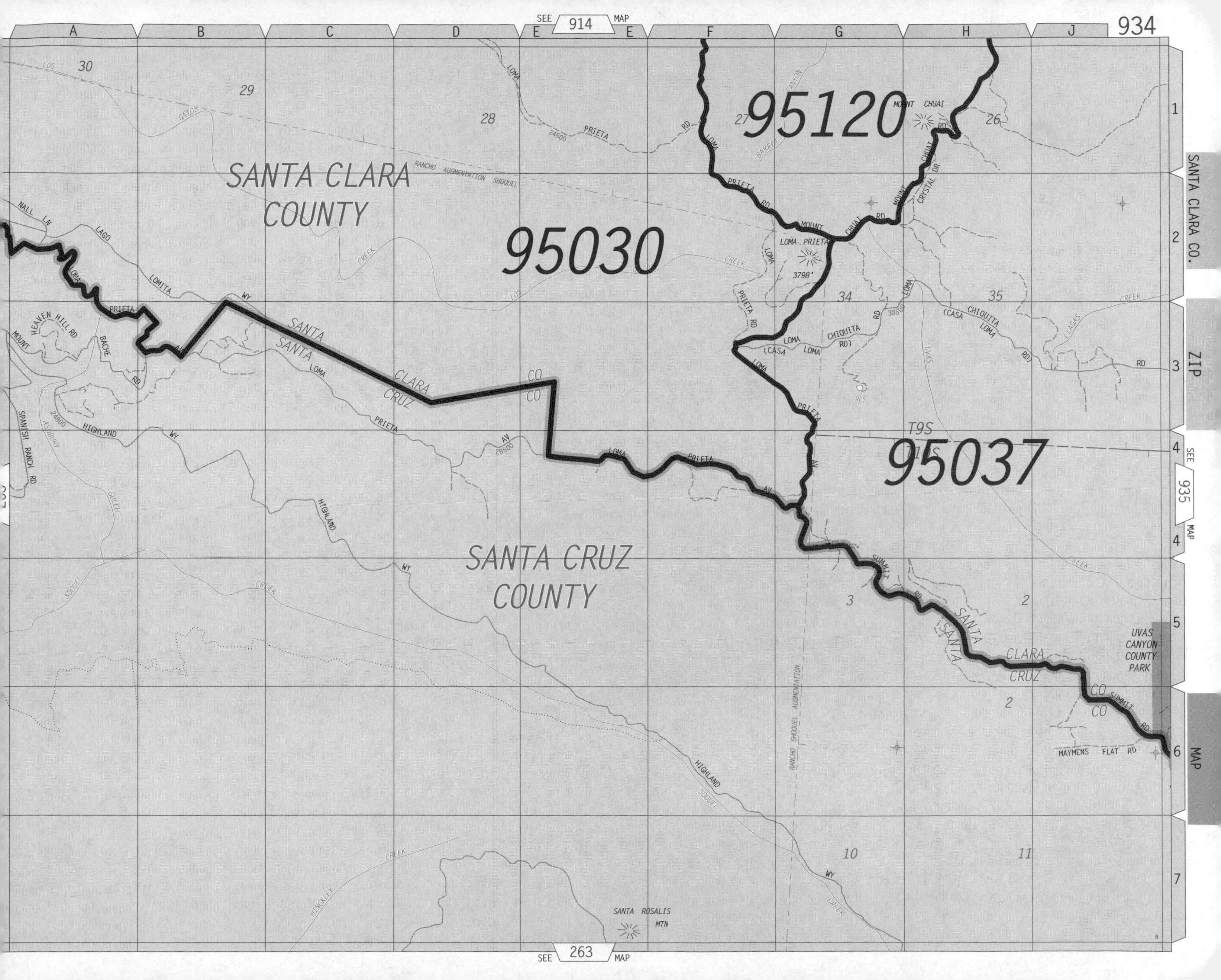

SEE 914 MAP
A B C D E E F G H J
1 2 3 4 4 5 6 7
95120
95030
95037
SANTA CLARA COUNTY
SANTA CRUZ COUNTY
MOUNT CHUAI
LOMA PRIETA
3798'
T9S
UVAS CANYON COUNTY PARK
MAYMENS FLAT RD
SANTA ROSALIS MTN
RANCHO AUGMENTATION SHOQUEL
HEAVEN HILL RD
MOUNT
BACHE RD
NALL LN
HIGHLAND WY
SPANISH RANCH RD
CRYSTAL DR
SUMMIT RD
(CASA CHIQUITA LOMA RD)
LOS GATOS CREEK
SOQUEL CREEK
HINCKLEY CREEK
SANTA CLARA CO
SANTA CRUZ CO
SANTA CLARA CO.
ZIP
MAP
SEE 935 MAP
SEE 263 MAP

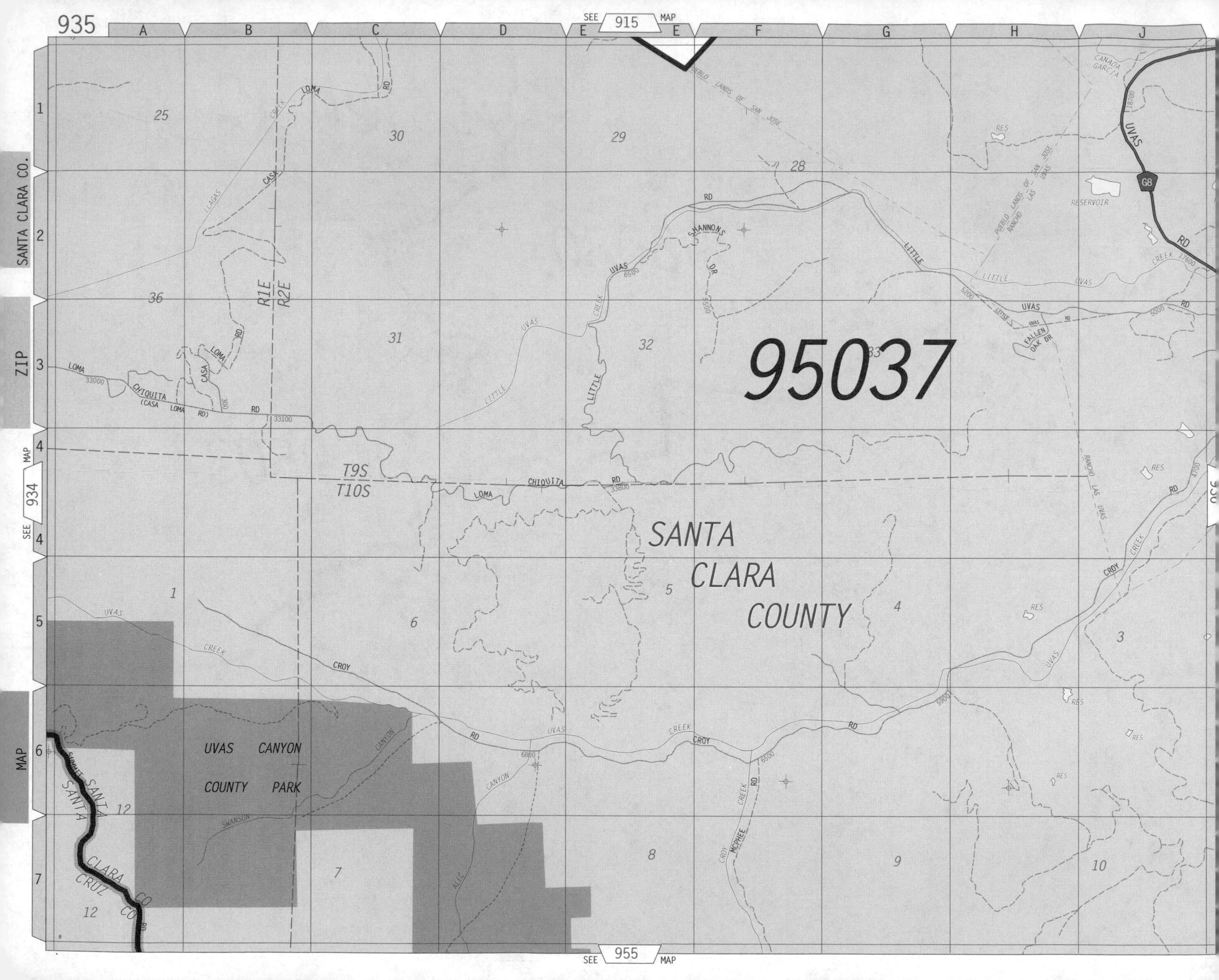

SEE 915 MAP
SEE 955 MAP
SEE 934 MAP
SANTA CLARA CO.
ZIP
MAP
95037
SANTA
CLARA
COUNTY
UVAS CANYON
COUNTY PARK
SANTA CLARA CO
SANTA CRUZ CO
CHIQUITA (CASA LOMA RD)
LOMA CHIQUITA RD
CROY RD
UVAS RD
UVAS CREEK
LITTLE UVAS CREEK
LITTLE UVAS RD
SHANNONS DR
FALLEN OAK DR
MCPHEE RD
SWANSON
ALEC
CANYON
RESERVOIR
RES
PUEBLO LANDS OF SAN JOSE
RANCHO LAS UVAS
CANADA GARCIA
LLAGAS CREEK
CASA LOMA RD
R1E
R2E
T9S
T10S
G8

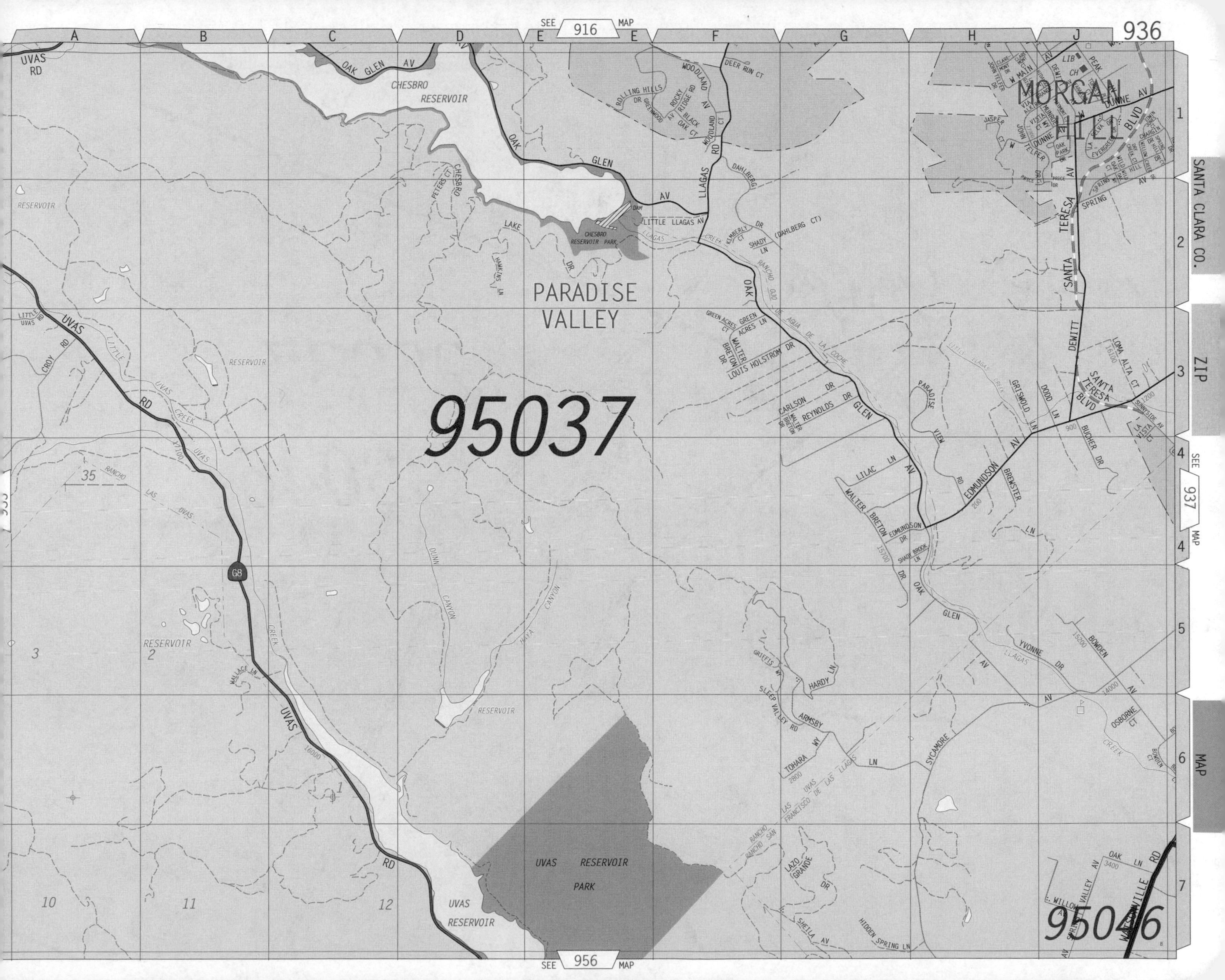
SEE 916 MAP
A
B
C
D
E
F
G
H
J
UVAS RD
OAK GLEN AV
CHESBRO RESERVOIR
MORGAN HILL
DUNNE AV
SANTA TERESA BLVD
SANTA CLARA CO.
ZIP
MAP
PARADISE VALLEY
95037
CHESBRO RESERVOIR PARK
LITTLE LLAGAS AV
LLAGAS RD
DAHLBERG
DEWITT AV
EDMUNDSON AV
UVAS CREEK
RESERVOIR
G8
DUNN CANYON
HAYA CANYON
SLEEPY VALLEY RD
ARMSBY LN
SYCAMORE AV
UVAS RESERVOIR PARK
UVAS RESERVOIR
WATSONVILLE RD
95046
SEE 937 MAP
SEE 956 MAP
1
2
3
4
5
6
7

SEE 917 MAP
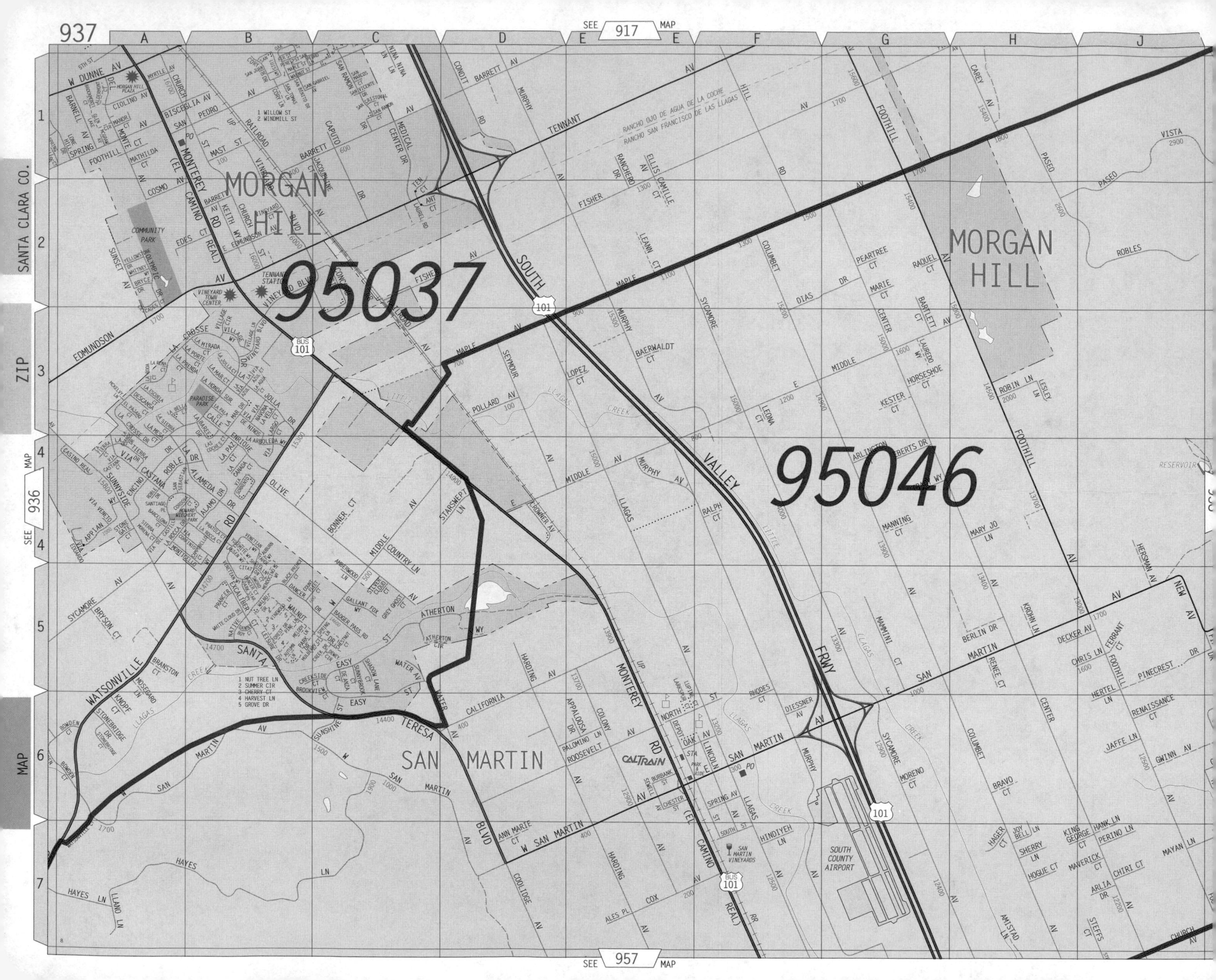

SEE 936 MAP
SEE 957 MAP

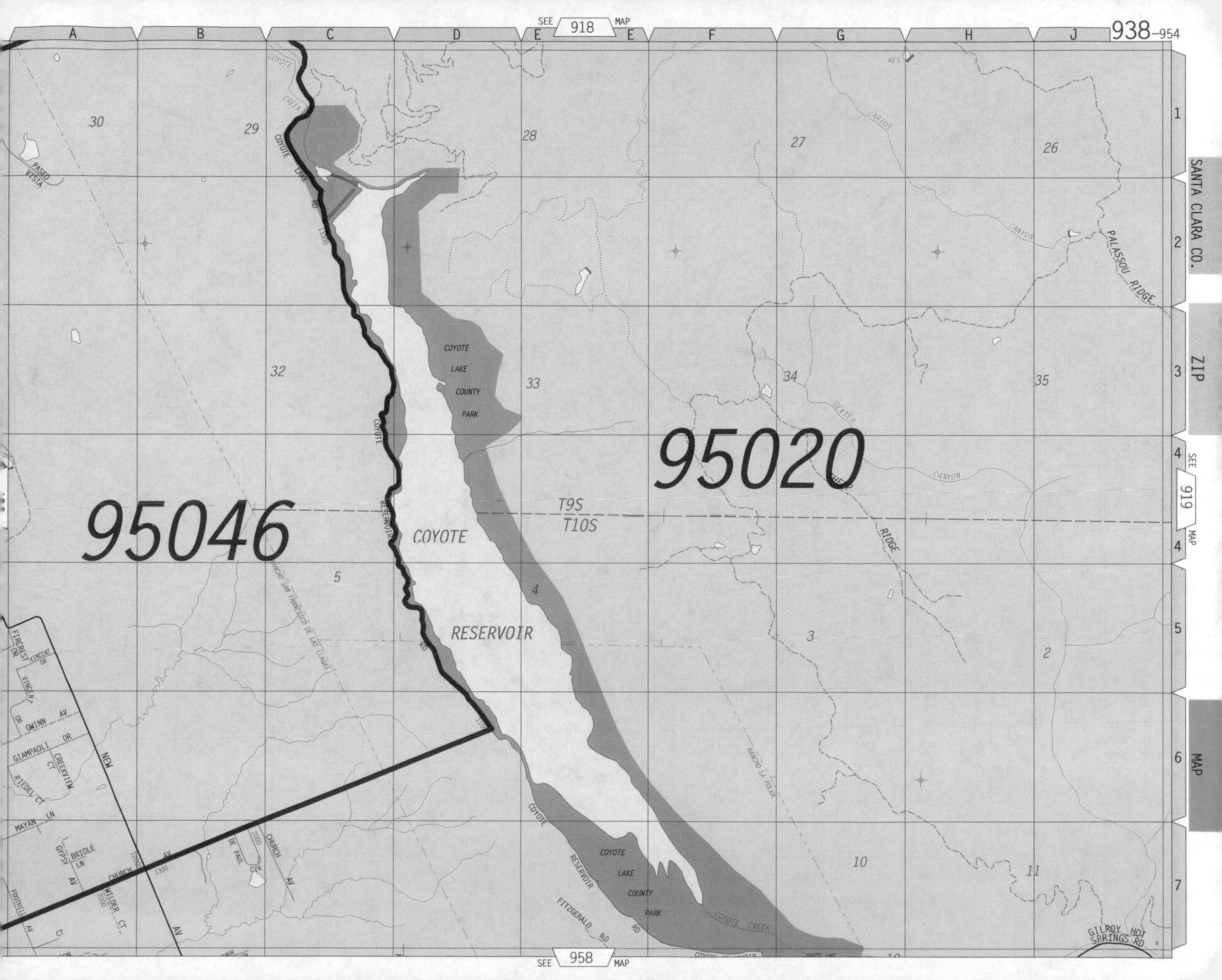
SEE 918 MAP
938-954
SANTA CLARA CO.
ZIP
MAP
SEE 919 MAP
SEE 958 MAP
95020
95046
COYOTE RESERVOIR
COYOTE LAKE COUNTY PARK
COYOTE LAKE RD
COYOTE RESERVOIR RD
COYOTE CREEK
T9S
T10S
RANCHO SAN FRANCISCO DE LAS LLAGAS
RANCHO LA POLKA
PASEO VISTA
LARIOS CANYON
PALASSOU RIDGE
DEXTER CANYON
SHEEP RIDGE
FITZGERALD RD
GILROY HOT SPRINGS RD
FIRCREST DR
VINCENT DR
GWINN AV
GIAMPAOLI DR
CREEKVIEW CT
RIEDEL CT
MAYAN LN
GYPSY AV
BRIDLE LN
CHURCH AV
NEW AV
DE PAUL CIR
WILDER CT
FOOTHILL AV
RES

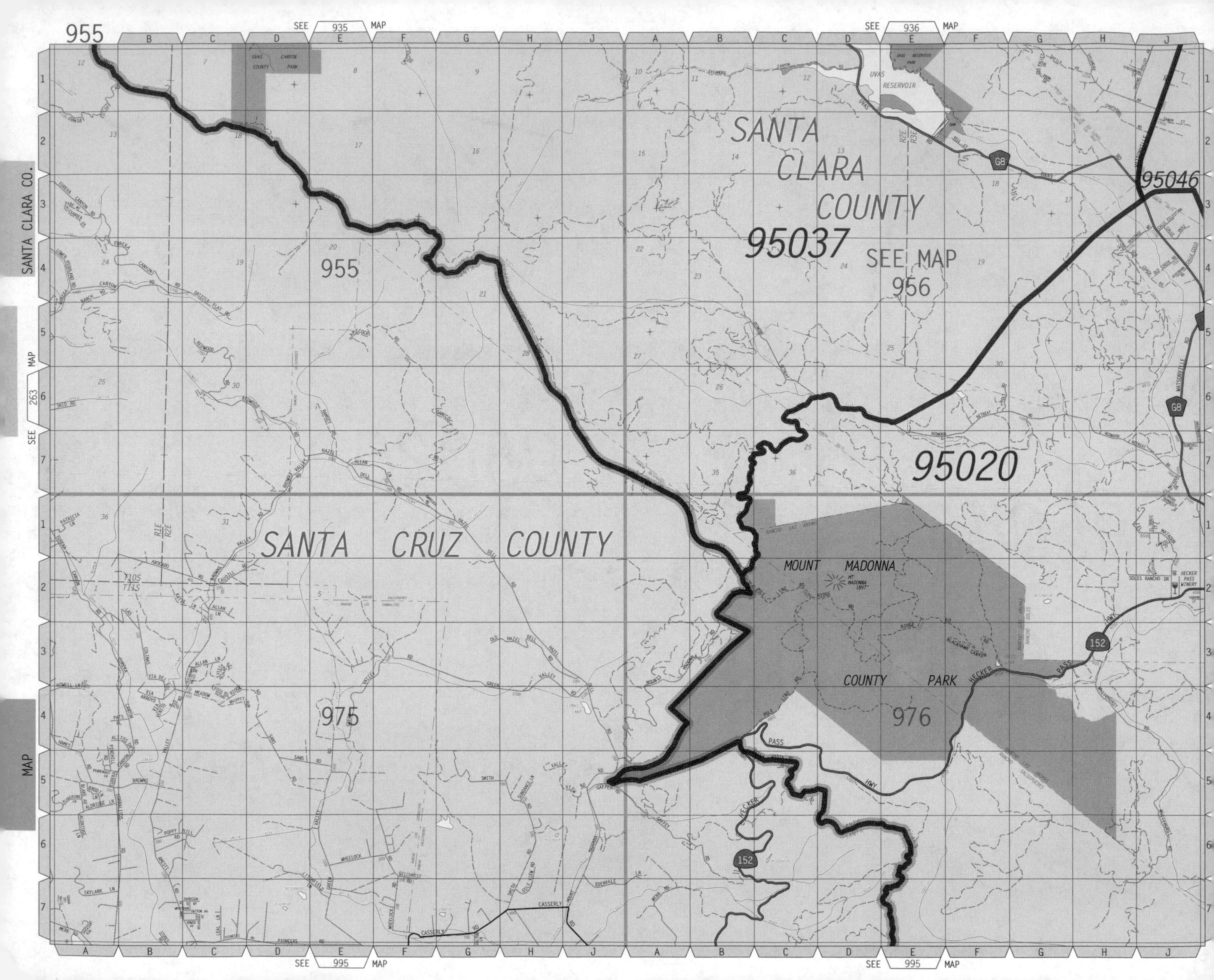
SEE 935 MAP
SEE 936 MAP
SEE 995 MAP
SEE 995 MAP
SEE 263 MAP
SANTA CLARA CO.
MAP
SANTA CLARA COUNTY
95037
SEE MAP 956
95046
95020
955
SANTA CRUZ COUNTY
975
976
MOUNT MADONNA COUNTY PARK
UVAS CANYON COUNTY PARK
UVAS RESERVOIR
HECKER PASS HWY
HECKER PASS WINERY
SOLIS RANCHO DR
WATSONVILLE RD
152
G8

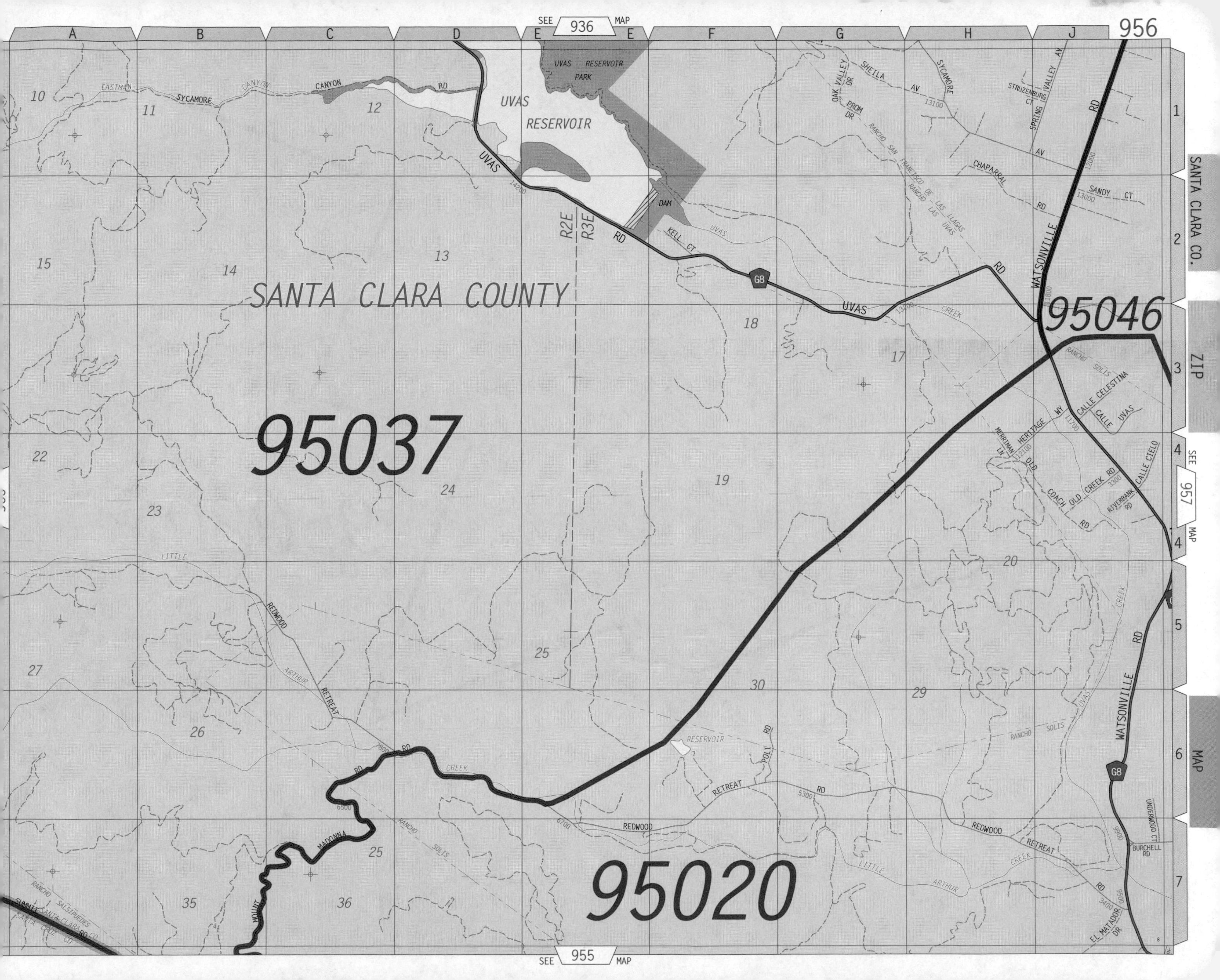
SEE 936 MAP
A
B
C
D
E
F
G
H
J
1
2
3
4
5
6
7
UVAS RESERVOIR PARK
UVAS RESERVOIR
DAM
EASTMAN
SYCAMORE
CANYON
RD
UVAS
RD
KELL CT
G8
UVAS
RD
R2E
R3E
SANTA CLARA COUNTY
95037
95046
95020
SHEILA
AV
SYCAMORE
OAK VALLEY DR
PROM DR
RANCHO SAN FRANCISCO DE LAS LLAGAS
RANCHO LAS UVAS
STRUZENBURG CT
SPRING
VALLEY
AV
CHAPARRAL
RD
SANDY CT
WATSONVILLE
RD
CREEK
RANCHO SOLIS
CALLE CELESTINA
CALLE UVAS
MERRIMAN LN
HERITAGE WY
OLD COACH RD
OLD CREEK RD
RIVERBANK RD
CALLE CIELO
LITTLE
REDWOOD
ARTHUR
RETREAT
RD
CREEK
RESERVOIR
POLI RD
RETREAT RD
REDWOOD
REDWOOD RETREAT
RD
LITTLE ARTHUR CREEK
RANCHO SOLIS
UVAS
CREEK
WATSONVILLE RD
G8
UNDERWOOD CT
BURCHELL RD
EL MATADOR DR
MADONNA
MOUNT
RANCHO SALSIPUEDES
SUMMIT
SANTA CLARA CO.
SANTA CRUZ CO.
RD
SEE 957 MAP
SANTA CLARA CO.
ZIP
MAP
SEE 955 MAP

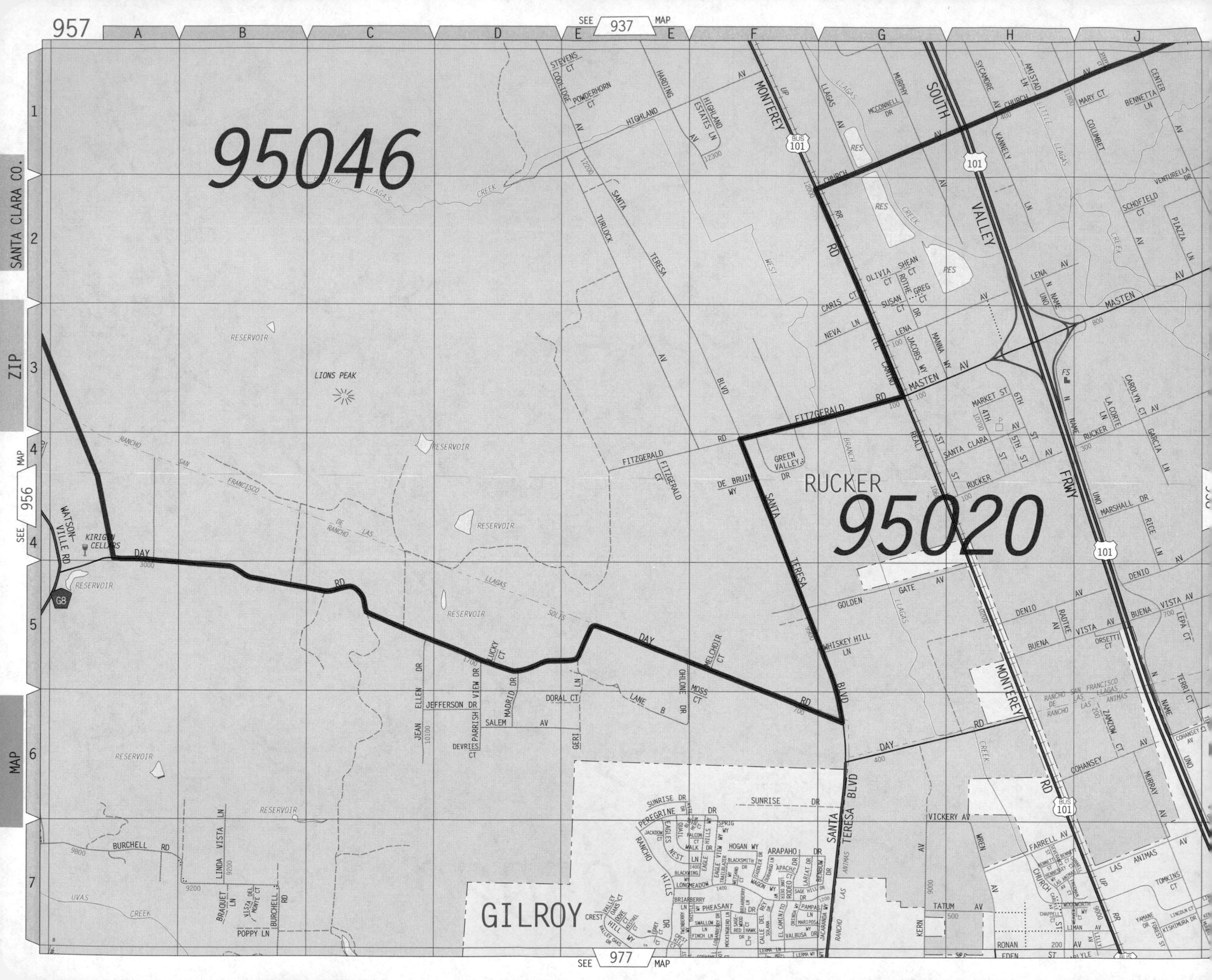
957
SEE 937 MAP
A
B
C
D
E
F
G
H
J
1
2
3
4
5
6
7
SANTA CLARA CO.
ZIP
MAP
SEE 956 MAP
95046
95020
RUCKER
GILROY
LIONS PEAK
RESERVOIR
KIRIGIN CELLARS
WATSONVILLE RD
G8
DAY RD
3000
RANCHO SAN FRANCISCO DE LAS LLAGAS
RANCHO SOLIS
WEST BRANCH LLAGAS CREEK
HIGHLAND AV
STEVENS CT
COOLIDGE AV
POWDERHORN CT
HARDING AV
HIGHLAND ESTATES LN
12300
12200
SANTA TERESA BLVD
TURLOCK AV
MONTEREY RD
UP RR
BUS 101
101
CHURCH AV
12000
LLAGAS AV
LLAGAS CREEK
MURPHY AV
McCONNELL DR
RES
SOUTH VALLEY FRWY
SYCAMORE AV
AMISTAD LN
KANNELY LN
LITTLE LLAGAS CREEK
MARY CT
COLUMBET AV
BENNETTA LN
CENTER AV
VENTURELLA DR
SCHOFIELD CT
PIAZZA LN
OLIVIA CT
SHEAN CT
ROTHE DR
GREG CT
SUSAN CT
CARIS CT
NEVA LN
LENA AV
MANNA WY
JACOBS WY
CAMINO REAL
EL CAMINO REAL
MASTEN AV
UNO NAME
N NAME
800
FS
FITZGERALD RD
FITZGERALD CT
DE BRUIN WY
GREEN VALLEY DR
WEST BRANCH
MARKET ST
4TH ST
5TH ST
6TH ST
1ST ST
SANTA CLARA AV
RUCKER AV
10700
100
300
LA CORTE LN
CAROLYN CT
GARCIA LN
MARSHALL DR
RICE LN
DENIO AV
GOLDEN GATE AV
WHISKEY HILL LN
BUENA VISTA AV
RADTKE AV
ORSETTI CT
LEPA CT
TERRI CT
COHANSEY AV
COHANSEY CT
ZAMZOW CT
MURRAY AV
700
200
400
10200
9600
LUCKY CT
MELCHOIR CT
1700
JEAN ELLEN DR
10100
PARRISH CT
VIEW DR
JEFFERSON DR
MADRID DR
SALEM AV
DEVRIES CT
DORAL CT
GERI LN
OHLONE DR
MOSS CT
LANE B
SUNRISE DR
PEREGRINE DR
EAGLES NEST LN
QUAIL
FALCON CT
HILLS WY
SPRIG WY
HOGAN WY
ARAPAHO DR
APACHE DR
BLACKSMITH DR
WAGON WY
LARIAT DR
BENBOW DR
RODEO CT
SAGE HILL DR
PAMPAS LN
VALBUSA DR
JACARANDA WY
LONGMEADOW
BRIARBERRY LN
PHEASANT DR
SMALLOW LN
FINCH LN
CALLE DEL REY
EL CAMINITO
SOLANA
MARIPOSA WY
RANCHO HILLS DR
CREST HILL WY
VALLEY OAKS CT
1400
1200
RANCHO LAS ANIMAS
LAS ANIMAS AV
VICKERY AV
WREN AV
FARRELL AV
KERN AV
TATUM AV
500
9000
CHURCH ST
WOODWORTH WY
CHAPPELL CT
LIMAN AV
LILLY
TOMKINS CT
YAMANE DR
LINCOLN CT
KISHIMURA DR
FOREST ST
RONAN AV
EDEN ST
LYLE
BURCHELL RD
9800
9200
LINDA VISTA LN
BRAQUET LN
VISTA DEL MONTE CT
BURCHELL RD
POPPY LN
UVAS CREEK
SEE 977 MAP

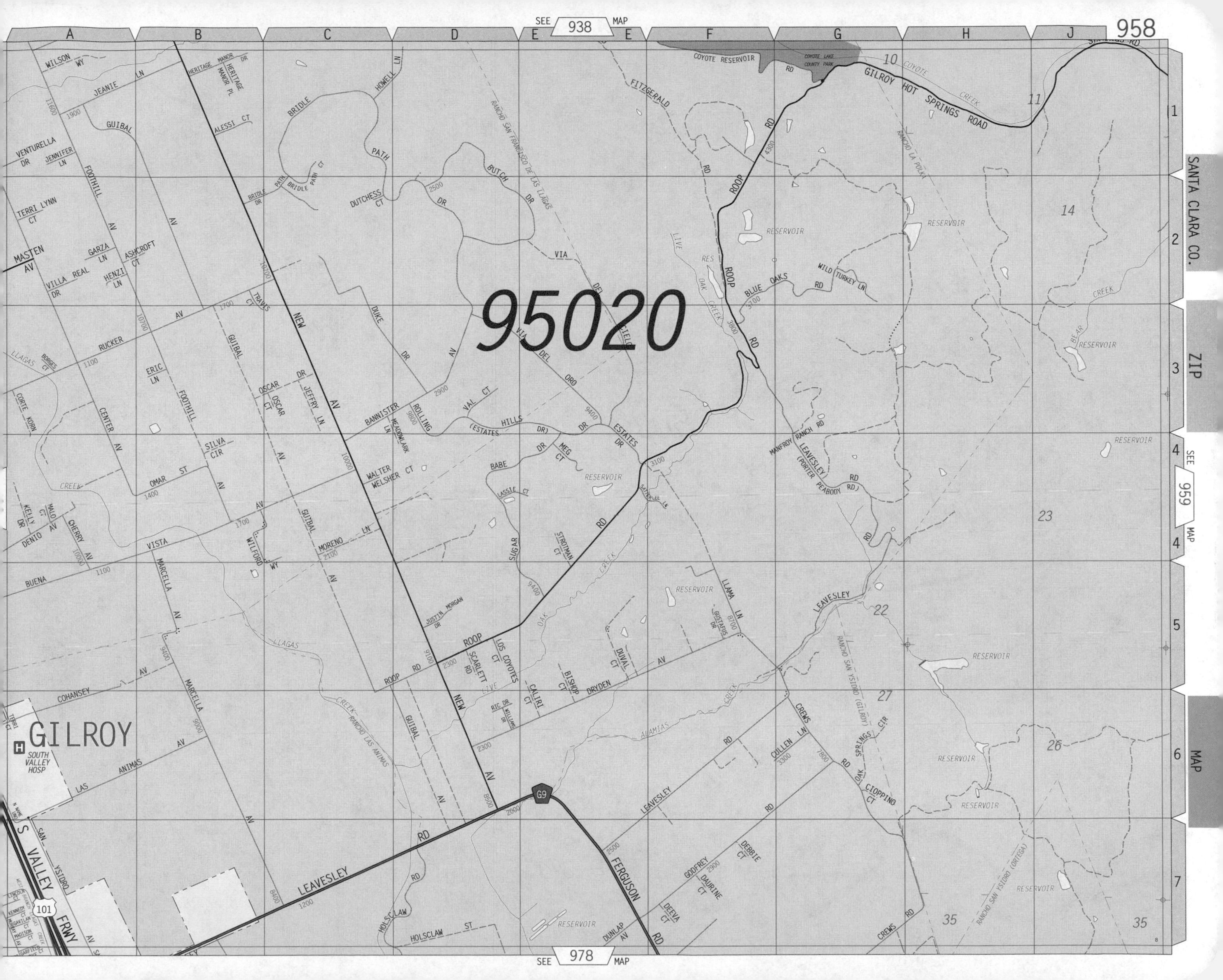

SEE 938 MAP
95020
GILROY
SOUTH VALLEY HOSP
COYOTE RESERVOIR
COYOTE LAKE COUNTY PARK
GILROY HOT SPRINGS ROAD
ROOP RD
NEW AV
LEAVESLEY RD
FERGUSON RD
SANTA CLARA CO.
ZIP MAP
SEE 959 MAP
SEE 978 MAP

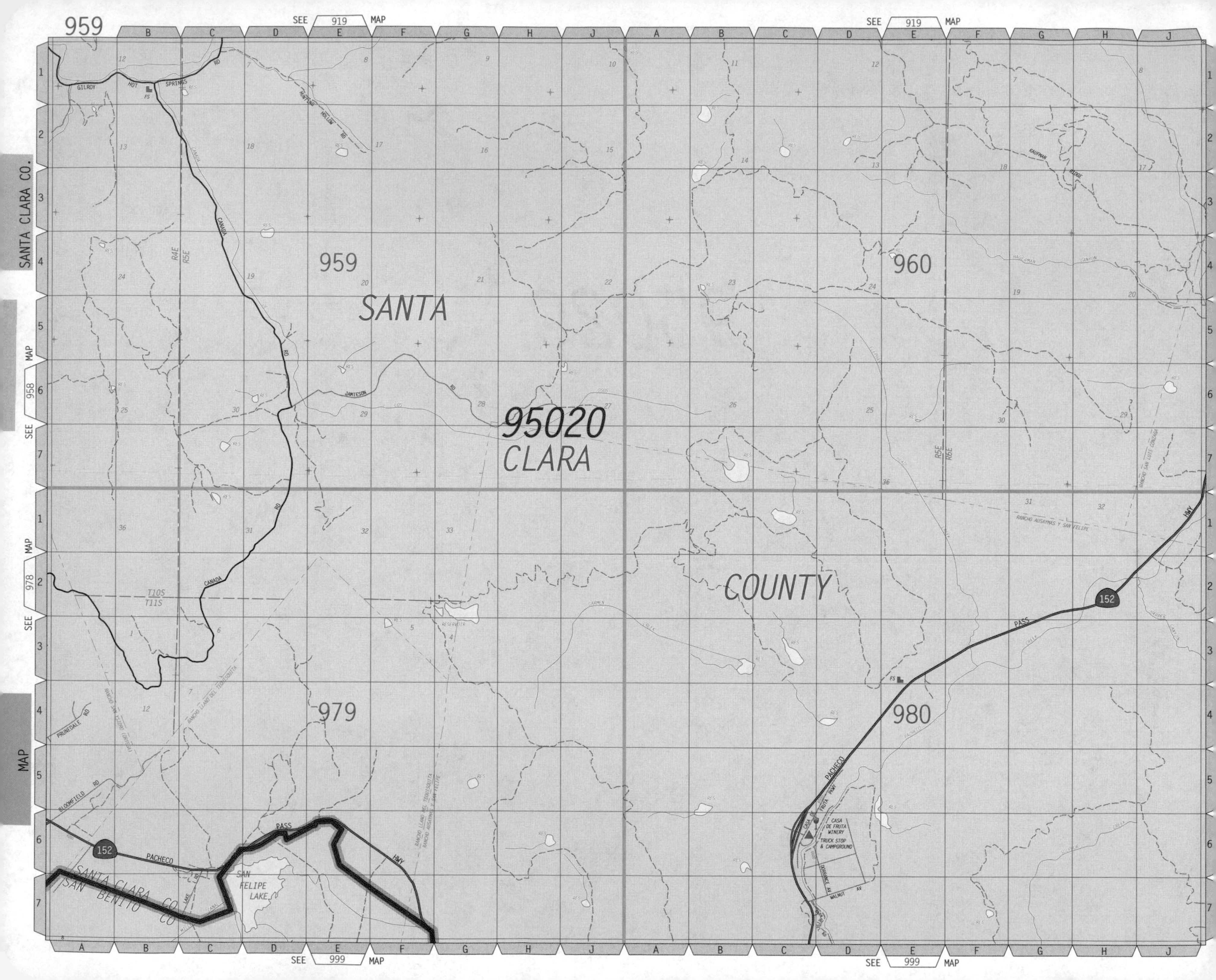
SEE 919 MAP
SEE 919 MAP
SANTA CLARA CO.
SEE 958 MAP
SEE 978 MAP
MAP
959
960
979
980
SANTA
95020
CLARA
COUNTY
GILROY HOT SPRINGS RD
HUNTING HOLLOW RD
CANADA RD
JAMESON RD
KAUFMAN RIDGE
R4E
R5E
R5E
R6E
T10S
T11S
RANCHO AUSAYMAS Y SAN FELIPE
RANCHO SAN LUIS GONZAGA
RANCHO LLANO DEL TEQUESQUITA
PRUNEDALE RD
BLOOMFIELD RD
PACHECO PASS HWY
152
SAN FELIPE LAKE
SANTA CLARA CO
SAN BENITO CO
CASA DE FRUTA PKWY
CASA DE FRUTA WINERY
TRUCK STOP & CAMPGROUND
DOMINANCE AV
WALNUT AV
RESERVOIR
CARMEN
FS
RES
SEE 999 MAP
SEE 999 MAP

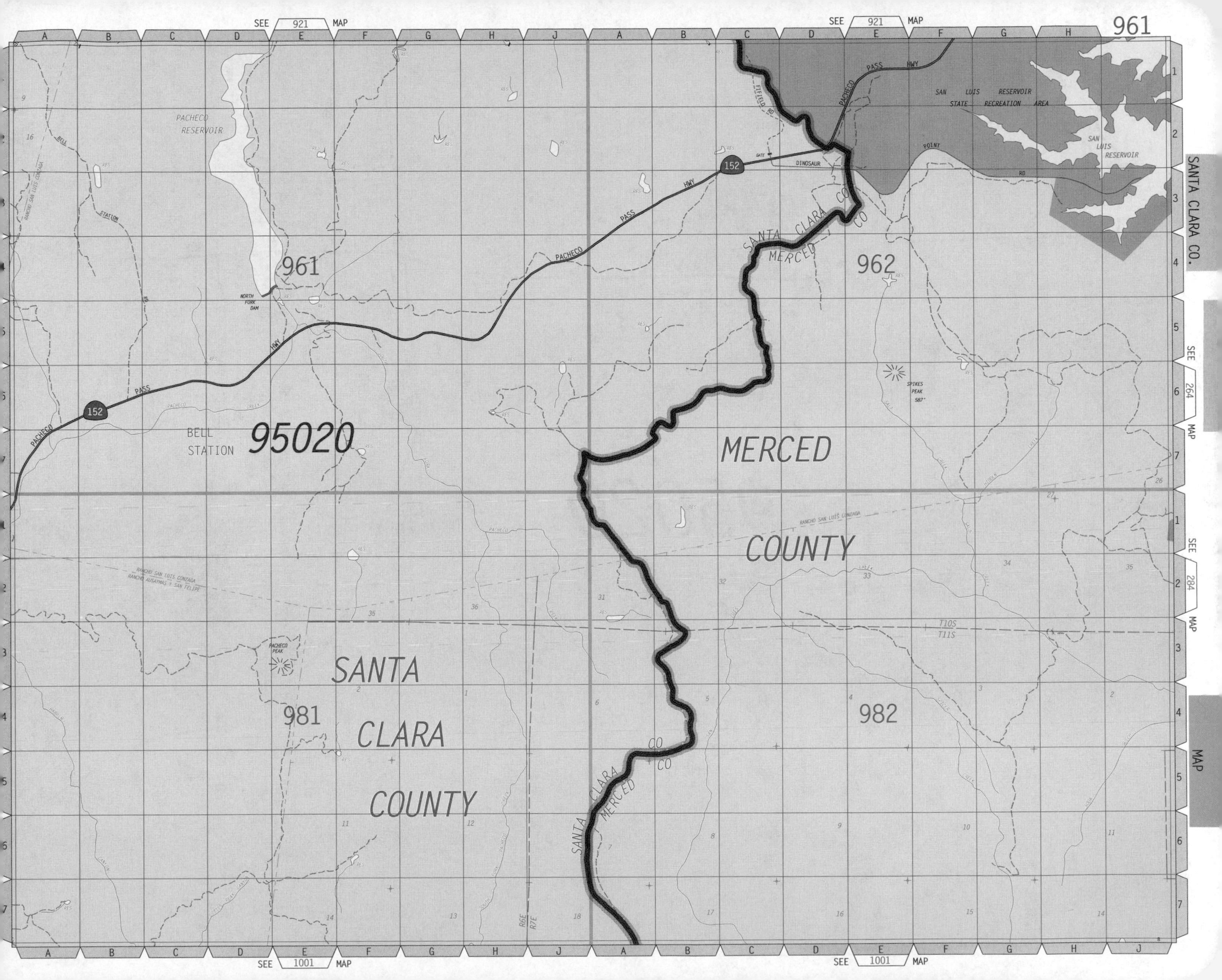
SEE 921 MAP
SEE 921 MAP
PACHECO RESERVOIR
961
NORTH FORK DAM
PACHECO PASS HWY
152
BELL STATION
95020
SAN LUIS RESERVOIR STATE RECREATION AREA
SAN LUIS RESERVOIR
FIFIELD RD
DINOSAUR POINT RD
SANTA CLARA CO
MERCED CO
962
SPIKES PEAK 587'
MERCED
COUNTY
SANTA CLARA CO.
SEE 264 MAP
SEE 284 MAP
RANCHO SAN LUIS GONZAGA
RANCHO AUSAYMAS Y SAN FELIPE
T10S
T11S
PACHECO PEAK
SANTA
CLARA
COUNTY
981
982
R6E
R7E
MAP
SEE 1001 MAP
SEE 1001 MAP

SEE 957 MAP
SEE 997 MAP
SEE 955 MAP
SANTA CLARA CO.
ZIP
MAP
GILROY
95020
WATSONVILLE RD
HECKER PASS HWY
SANTA TERESA BLVD
MONTEREY
FORTINO WINERY
LIVE OAKS WINERY
THOMAS KRUSE WINERY
SOLIS WINERY
CONROTTO WINERY
GILROY GOLF COURSE
HECKER PASS PLAZA
ST MARYS CEM
LAS ANIMAS PARK
MILLER PARK
UVAS CREEK PRESERVE
CHRISTMAS HILL PARK
GILROY HS
GAVILAN COLLEGE
UVAS CREEK
RESERVOIR

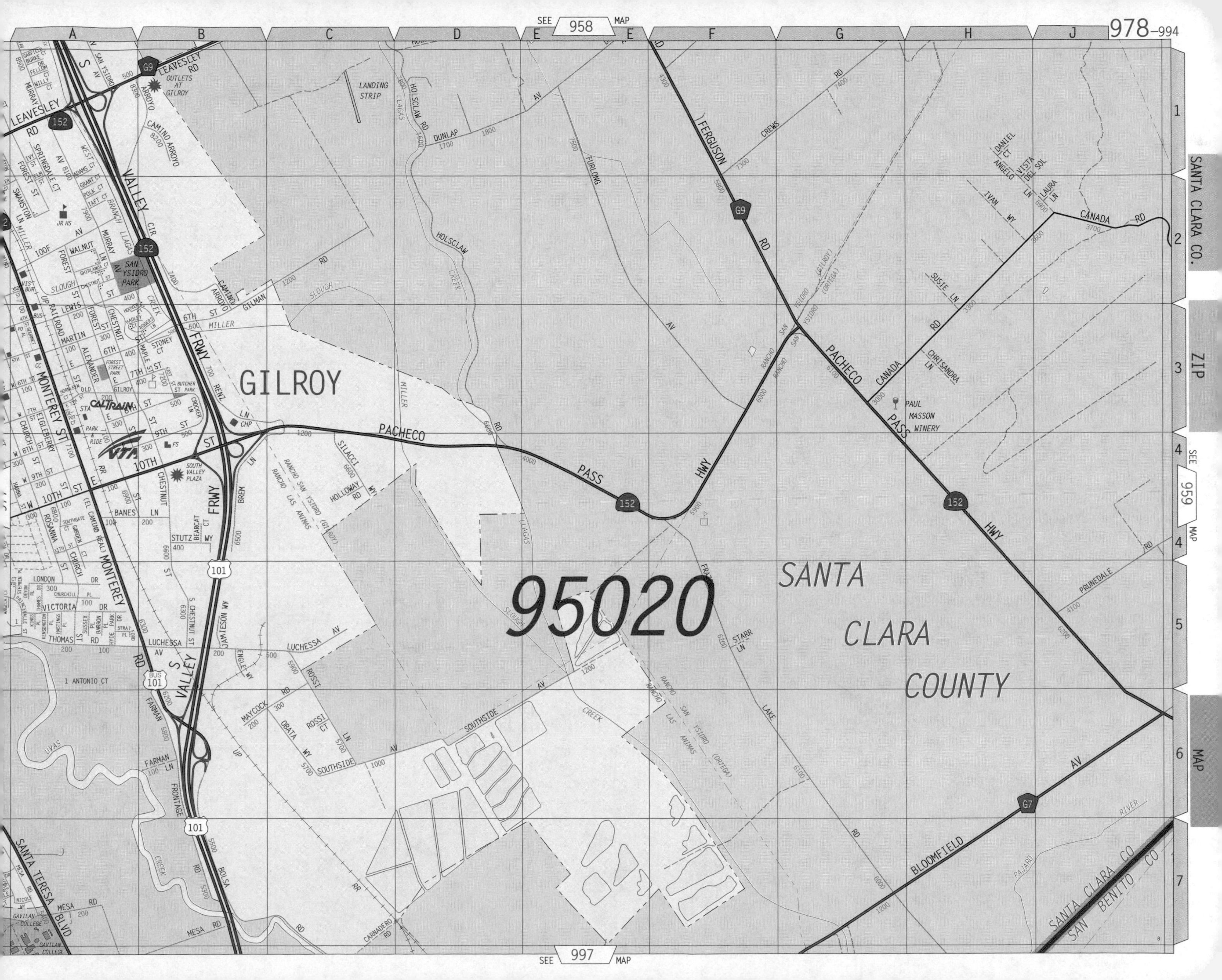

SEE 958 MAP
A
B
C
D
E
F
G
H
J
GILROY
95020
SANTA CLARA COUNTY
PACHECO PASS HWY
FERGUSON RD
CANADA RD
BLOOMFIELD AV
SOUTHSIDE AV
LUCHESSA AV
MONTEREY RD
10TH ST
LEAVESLEY RD
OUTLETS AT GILROY
LANDING STRIP
SAN YSIDRO PARK
SOUTH VALLEY PLAZA
PAUL MASSON WINERY
CALTRAIN
SANTA TERESA BLVD
GAVILAN COLLEGE
SANTA CLARA CO
SAN BENITO CO
PAJARO RIVER
UVAS CREEK
LLAGAS CREEK
SANTA CLARA CO.
ZIP
MAP
SEE 959 MAP
SEE 997 MAP

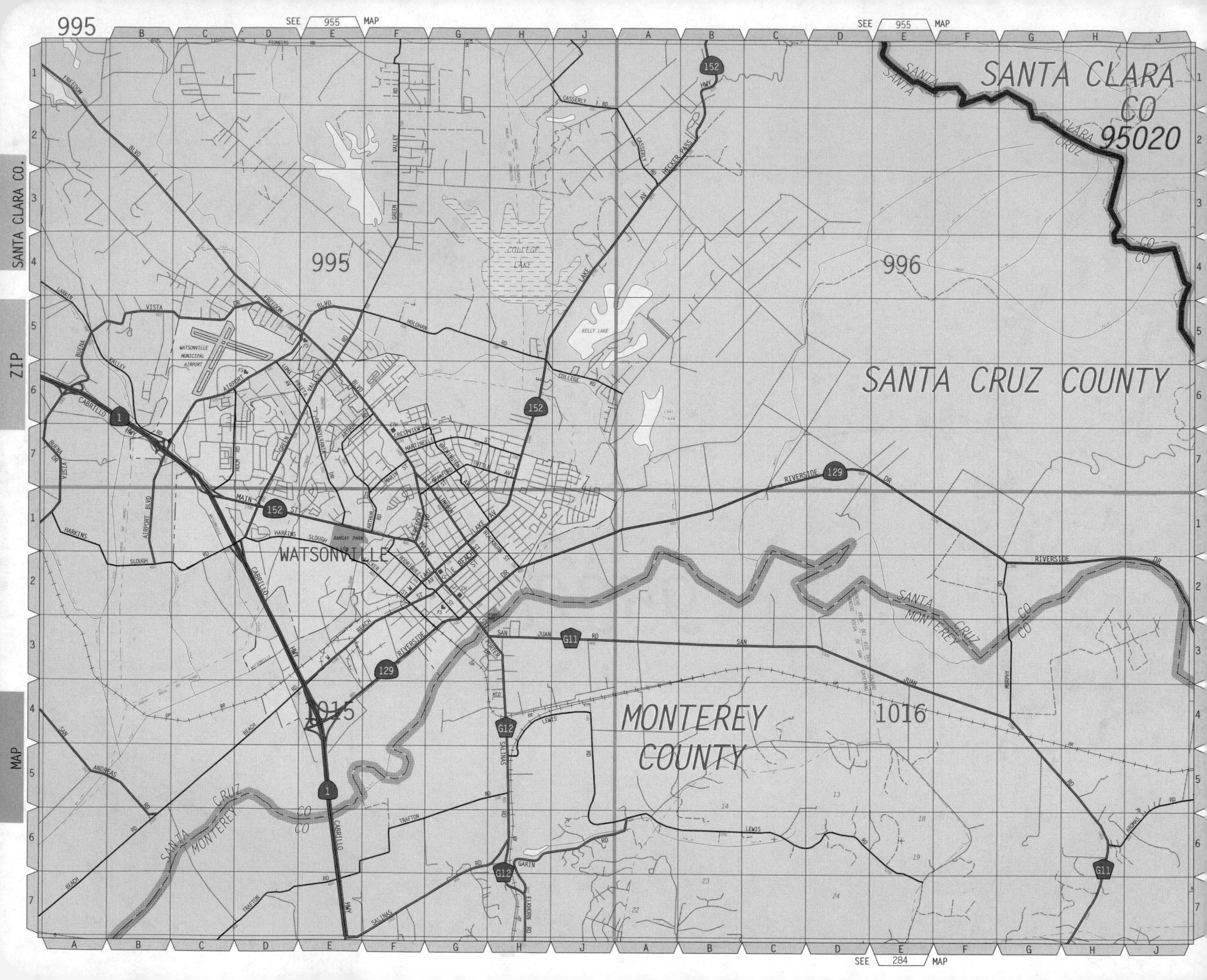
SEE 955 MAP
SEE 955 MAP
SANTA CLARA CO
95020
995
996
SANTA CRUZ COUNTY
WATSONVILLE
MONTEREY COUNTY
1015
1016
COLLEGE LAKE
KELLY LAKE
WATSONVILLE MUNICIPAL AIRPORT
RAMSAY PARK
FREEDOM BLVD
HOLOHAN RD
COLLEGE RD
CASSERLY RD
DECKER PASS
LAKE AV
MAIN ST
RIVERSIDE DR
SAN JUAN RD
SALINAS RD
LEWIS RD
CABRILLO HWY
HARKINS SLOUGH RD
AIRPORT BLVD
BUENA VISTA DR
TRAFTON RD
SAN ANDREAS RD
BEACH RD
MURPHY RD
ELKHORN RD
GARIN RD
AROMAS RD
GREEN VALLEY RD
SANTA CRUZ CO
MONTEREY CO
SEE 284 MAP
SANTA CLARA CO.
ZIP
MAP

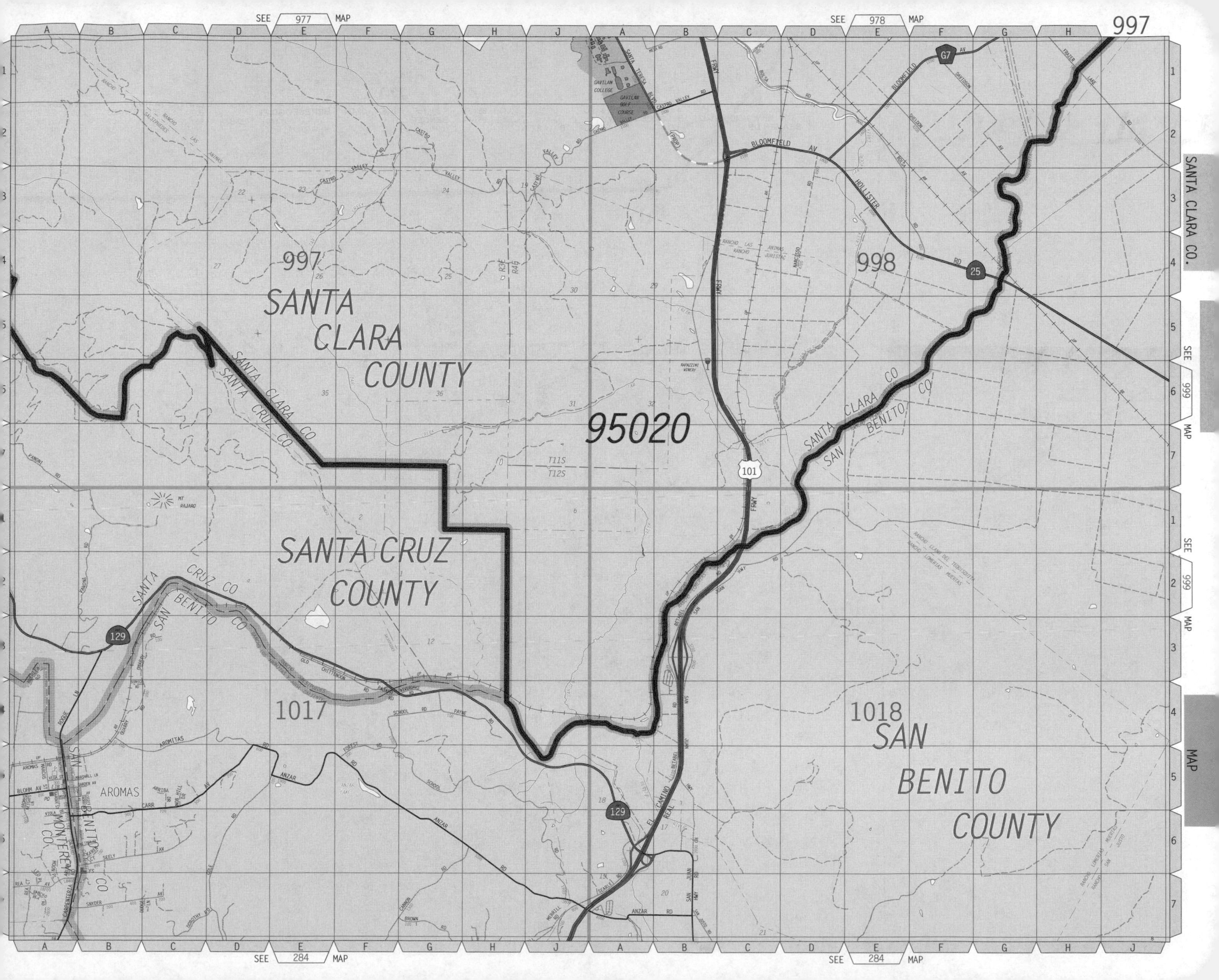
SEE 977 MAP
SEE 978 MAP
SEE 999 MAP
SEE 284 MAP
SANTA CLARA CO.
997
998
1017
1018
SANTA CLARA COUNTY
SANTA CRUZ COUNTY
SAN BENITO COUNTY
95020
SANTA CLARA CO
SANTA CRUZ CO
SAN BENITO CO
MONTEREY CO
AROMAS
GAVILAN COLLEGE
GAVILAN GOLF COURSE
BLOOMFIELD AV
HOLLISTER RD
CASTRO VALLEY RD
RAPAZZINI WINERY
MT MADONNA
ANZAR RD
EL CAMINO REAL
SAN JUAN HWY
FRWY
101
129
25
G7

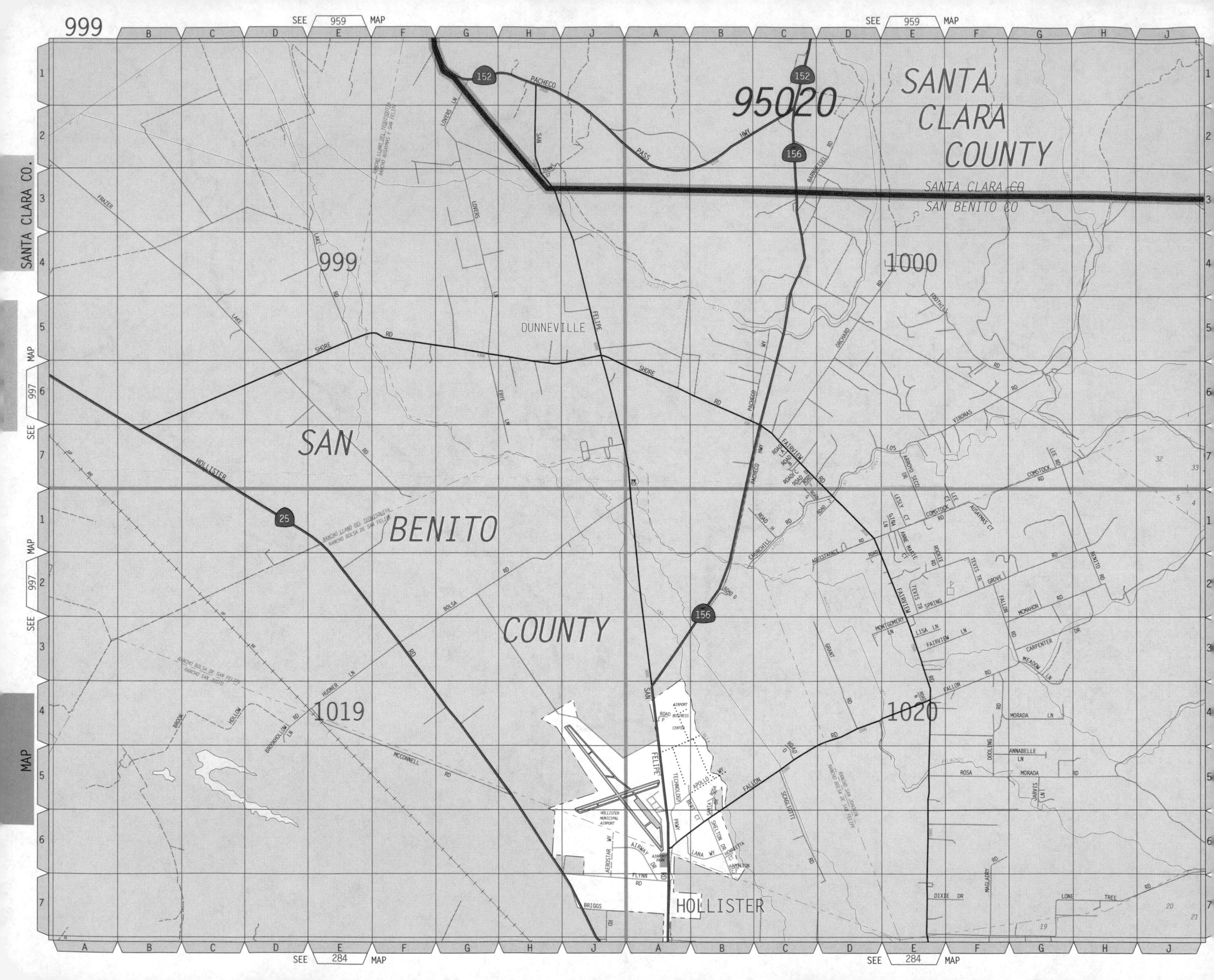
SEE 959 MAP
SEE 959 MAP
95020
SANTA CLARA COUNTY
SANTA CLARA CO
SAN BENITO CO
999
1000
1019
1020
SAN BENITO COUNTY
DUNNEVILLE
HOLLISTER
HOLLISTER MUNICIPAL AIRPORT
PACHECO PASS HWY
SAN FELIPE RD
SHORE RD
LAKE RD
FRAZER
LOVERS LN
FRYE LN
HOLLISTER RD
BOLSA RD
HUDNER LN
BROOKHOLLOW LN
MCCONNELL RD
FALLON RD
FAIRVIEW RD
VIBORAS RD
COMSTOCK RD
BENITTO RD
MCMAHON RD
CARPENTER
MEADOW DR
MORADA LN
ANNABELLE LN
ROSA
JARVIS LN
DOOLING
MAGLADRY RD
DIXIE DR
LONE TREE RD
GRANT
SCAGLIOTTI
APOLLO WY
TECHNOLOGY PKWY
AEROSTAR WY
AIRWAY DR
FLYNN RD
BRIGGS
SHELTON DR
LANA WY
ORCHARD RD
FOOTHILL
AGUISTAPACE
MONTGOMERY LN
SPRING
GROVE
TEVIS TR
LISA LN
FAIRVIEW LN
ROOKIE
ANNE MARIE
CHURCHILL
SEE 997 MAP
SEE 997 MAP
SANTA CLARA CO.
MAP
SEE 284 MAP
SEE 284 MAP

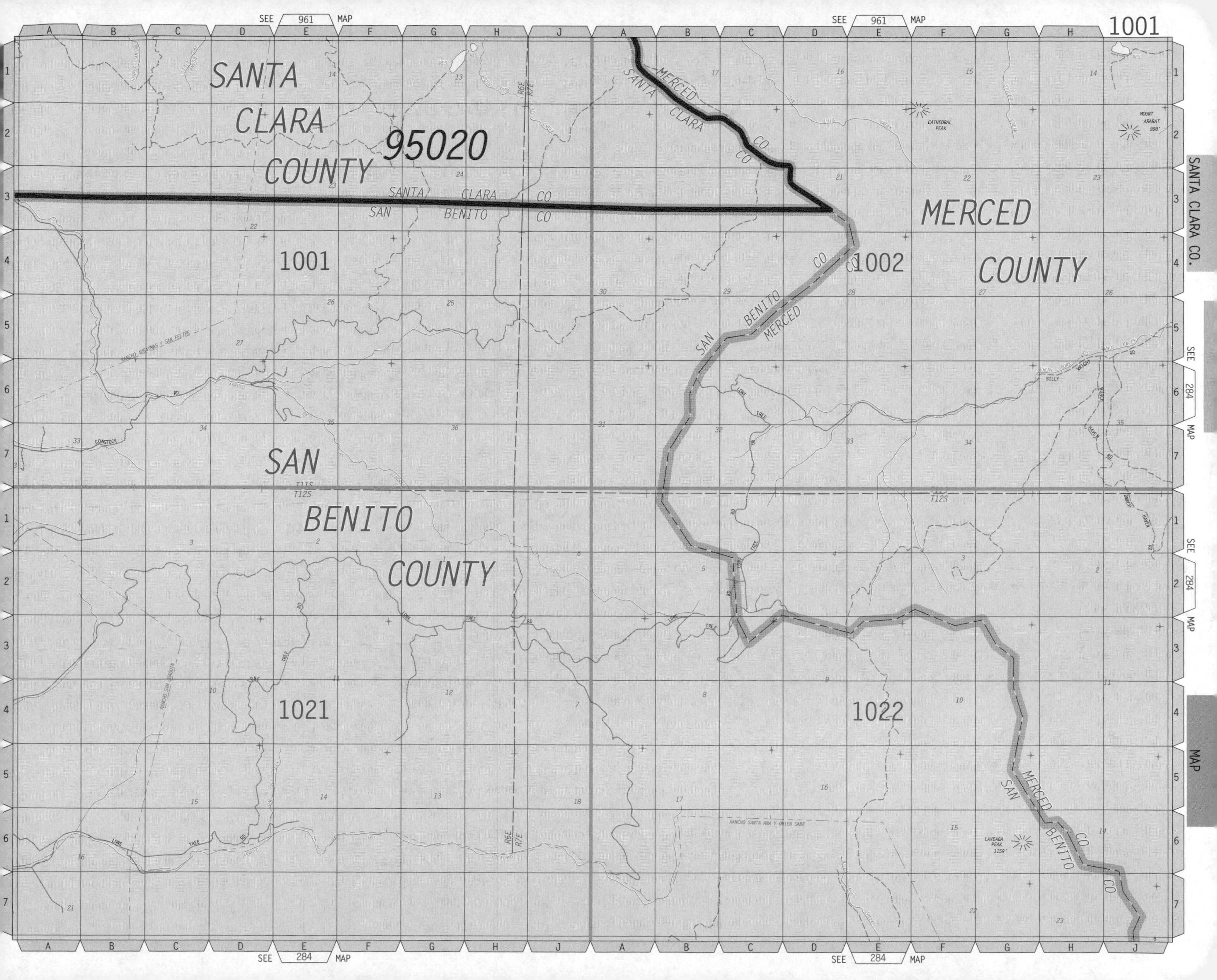
SEE 961 MAP
SEE 961 MAP
SANTA CLARA COUNTY
95020
SANTA CLARA CO
SAN BENITO CO
SANTA CLARA CO
MERCED CO
MERCED COUNTY
1001
1002
SAN BENITO COUNTY
1021
1022
CATHEDRAL PEAK
MOUNT ARARAT 998'
LAVEAGA PEAK 1159'
RANCHO AUSAYMAS Y SAN FELIPE
RANCHO SANTA ANA Y QUIEN SABE
COMSTOCK RD
LONE TREE RD
NORTH FORK
BILLY WRIGHT RD
T11S
T12S
R6E
R7E
SAN BENITO CO
MERCED CO
SANTA CLARA CO.
SEE 284 MAP
SEE 284 MAP
MAP
SEE 284 MAP
SEE 284 MAP

LIST OF ABBREVIATIONS

PREFIXES AND SUFFIXES

AL .... ALLEY
ARC .... ARCADE
AV, AVE .... AVENUE
AVCT .... AVENUE COURT
AVD .... AVENIDA
AVDR .... AVENUE DRIVE
AVEX .... AVENUE EXTENSION
BLEX .... BOULEVARD EXTENSION
BL, BLVD .... BOULEVARD
BLCT .... BOULEVARD COURT
BRCH .... BRANCH
BRDG .... BRIDGE
BYPS .... BYPASS
CIDR .... CIRCLE DRIVE
CIR .... CIRCLE
CL .... CALLE
CLJ .... CALLEJON
CM .... CAMINO
CMTO .... CAMINITO
COM .... COMMON
CORR .... CORRIDOR
CRES .... CRESCENT
CRLO .... CIRCULO
CRSG .... CROSSING
CSWY .... CAUSEWAY
CT .... COURT
CTAV .... COURT AVENUE
CTE .... CORTE
CTO .... CUT OFF
CTR .... CENTER
CUR .... CURVE
CV .... COVE
D .... DE
DIAG .... DIAGONAL
DR .... DRIVE
DVDR .... DIVISION DRIVE
EXAV .... EXTENSION AVENUE
EXBL .... EXTENSION BOULEVARD
EXRD .... EXTENSION ROAD
EXST .... EXTENSION STREET
EXT .... EXTENSION
EXWY .... EXPRESSWAY
FRWY .... FREEWAY
GDNS .... GARDENS
GN .... GLEN
GRN .... GREEN
HWY .... HIGHWAY
JCT .... JUNCTION
LN .... LANE
LNDG .... LANDING
LP .... LOOP
LS .... LAS, LOS
MNR .... MANOR
MTWY .... MOTORWAY
OH .... OUTER HIGHWAY
OVL .... OVAL
OVPS .... OVERPASS
PAS .... PASEO
PK .... PARK
PKWY .... PARKWAY
PL .... PLACE
PLZ, PZ .... PLAZA
PT .... POINT
PTH .... PATH
RD .... ROAD
RDEX .... ROAD EXTENSION
RDGE .... RIDGE
RW .... ROW
SKWY .... SKYWAY
SQ .... SQUARE
ST .... STREET
STAV .... STREET AVENUE
STCT .... STREET COURT
STDR .... STREET DRIVE
STEX .... STREET EXTENSION
STLN .... STREET LANE
STLP .... STREET LOOP
STPL .... STREET PLACE
STXP .... STREET EXPRESSWAY
TER .... TERRACE
TFWY .... TRAFFICWAY
THWY .... THROUGHWAY
TKTR .... TRUCKTRAIL
TPKE .... TURNPIKE
TR .... TRAIL
TUN .... TUNNEL
UNPS .... UNDERPASS
VIS .... VISTA
VW .... VIEW
WK .... WALK
WY .... WAY
WYPL .... WAY PLACE

DIRECTIONS

E .... EAST
KPN .... KEY PENINSULA NORTH
KPS .... KEY PENINSULA SOUTH
N .... NORTH
NE .... NORTHEAST
NW .... NORTHWEST
S .... SOUTH
SE .... SOUTHEAST
SW .... SOUTHWEST
W .... WEST

DEPARTMENT STORES

BD .... BLOOMINGDALES
BN .... THE BON MARCHE
D .... DIAMONDS
FN .... FREDERICK & NELSON
G .... GOLDWATERS
GT .... GOTTSCHALKS
H .... HARRIS
IM .... I MAGNIN
L .... LAMONTS
MA .... MACY'S
ME .... MERVYN'S
MF .... MEIER & FRANK
MW .... MONTGOMERY WARD
N .... NORDSTROM
NM .... NEIMAN-MARCUS
P .... J C PENNEY
RM .... ROBINSONS MAY
S .... SEARS
SF .... SAKS FIFTH AVENUE
W .... WEINSTOCKS

BUILDINGS

CC .... CHAMBER OF COMMERCE
CH .... CITY HALL
CHP .... CALIFORNIA HIGHWAY PATROL
COMM CTR .... COMMUNITY CENTER
CON CTR .... CONVENTION CENTER
CONT HS .... CONTINUATION HIGH SCHOOL
CTH .... COURT HOUSE
DMV .... DEPT OF MOTOR VEHICLES
FAA .... FEDERAL AVIATION ADMIN
FS .... FIRE STATION
HOSP .... HOSPITAL
HS .... HIGH SCHOOL
INT .... INTERMEDIATE SCHOOL
JR HS .... JUNIOR HIGH SCHOOL
LIB .... LIBRARY
MID .... MIDDLE SCHOOL
MUS .... MUSEUM
PO .... POST OFFICE
PS .... POLICE STATION
SR CIT CTR .... SENIOR CITIZENS CENTER
STA .... STATION
THTR .... THEATER
VIS BUR .... VISITORS BUREAU

OTHER COMMON ABBREVIATIONS

BCH .... BEACH
BLDG .... BUILDING
CEM .... CEMETERY
CK .... CREEK
CO .... COUNTY
CTR .... CENTER
COMM .... COMMUNITY
EST .... ESTATE
HIST .... HISTORIC
HTS .... HEIGHTS
LK .... LAKE
MDW .... MEADOW
MED .... MEDICAL
MEM .... MEMORIAL
MHP .... MOBILE HOME PARK
MT .... MOUNT
MTN .... MOUNTAIN
NATL .... NATIONAL
PKG .... PARKING
PLGD .... PLAYGROUND
RCH .... RANCH
RCHO .... RANCHO
REC .... RECREATION
RES .... RESERVOIR
RIV .... RIVER
RR .... RAILROAD
SPG .... SPRING
STA .... SANTA
VLG .... VILLAGE
VLY .... VALLEY
VW .... VIEW

STREET Block City ZIP Pg-Grid

A

A RD
- SUNV 94089 812-J3
4100 SCIC 95127 815-C6
A ST
- CPTO 95014 831-H6
- LALT 94024 831-H3
- SCIC 94024 831-H3
100 MLPK 94025 790-H3
AARON CT
7500 SJS 95139 895-G1
AARON PL
7500 SJS 95139 895-G1
AARON PARK DR
700 MPS 95035 794-A5
ABBEY CT
3800 SJS 95008 853-C6
ABBEY LN
200 SJS 95008 853-C6
2100 CMBL 95008 853-C6
ABBEYFIELD CT
6200 SJS 95120 874-C7
ABBEYGATE CT
4500 SJS 95124 873-J3
ABBOTT AV
100 MPS 95035 793-J6
900 CMBL 95008 873-B1
S ABBOTT AV
- MPS 95035 813-J1
ABBY WOOD CT
100 LGTS 95030 873-B2
ABDON AV
14000 SCIC 95127 814-H7
14000 SJS 95127 814-H7
ABDULLA WY
14000 SAR 95070 852-H7
ABED CT
2500 SJS 95116 834-J4
ABEL AV
4100 PA 94306 811-C2
N ABEL ST
- MPS 95035 794-A5
- MPS 95035 793-J6
S ABEL ST
- MPS 95035 793-J7
100 MPS 95035 814-A1
ABELIA CT
3000 SJS 95121 854-J4
ABELIA WY
100 EPA 94303 791-D3
ABERDEEN CT
600 MPS 95035 794-B6
1800 SJS 95122 854-G1
12800 SAR 95070 852-F6
ABERDEEN DR
900 SUNV 94087 832-B4
ABERDEEN ST
3500 SCL 95054 813-E6
ABERDEEN WY
500 MPS 95035 794-B6
ABERFELDY WY
1200 MPS 95035 814-C1
ABERFORD DR
1200 SJS 95131 814-E6
ABERHAVEN CT
- SJS 95111 875-A1
ABINANTE LN
1900 SJS 95124 873-G1
ABINGTON CT
1700 SJS 95131 834-D1
ABORN CT
2800 SJS 95148 855-D2
ABORN RD
1500 SJS 95121 855-A3
2900 SJS 95122 855-B3
3000 SJS 95148 855-F2
3300 SJS 95135 855-H1
3500 SCIC 95135 855-H1
ABORN SQUARE LOOP RD
2900 SJS 95121 855-B3
ABRA CT
200 SJS 95139 895-G2
ABRAMS CT
- SCIC - 791-A7
ABRYAN WY
2000 SMCo 94061 790-B4
ACACIA AV
- PA 94306 811-B1
800 SUNV 94086 812-F7
900 LALT 94022 811-E4
ACACIA CT
2000 SCL 95050 833-D3
ACACIA DR
- ATN 94027 790-G1
ACACIA LN
900 SJS 95138 875-F6
ACACIA ST
100 SJS 95110 834-A5
ACACIA WY
1500 MGH 95037 917-D6
ACADIA AV
1100 MPS 95035 814-C1
1200 MPS 95035 794-D7
ACADIA CT
20600 CPTO 95014 832-D6
ACALANES DR
100 SUNV 94086 812-B7
ACAPULCO DR
3700 SJS 95008 853-B6
ACOMA WY
200 FRMT 94539 793-J1
ACORN
- PTLV 94028 830-D2
ACORN CT
- SCIC 95037 896-D7
3100 SJS 95117 853-D3
ACORN LN
- LALT 94022 811-E5
ACORN WY
- GIL 95020 977-E1
- ATN 94027 790-G1
3100 SJS 95117 853-D3
ACTON CT
14800 SCIC 95124 873-G4
ACTON DR
14500 SCIC 95124 873-G3
ADA AV
100 MTVW 94043 812-A5
ADAGIO WY
600 SJS 95111 855-B7
ADAIR CT
600 MGH 95037 916-H6
ADAIR LN
- PTLV 94028 810-D6
ADAIR WY
4900 SJS 95124 873-E4
ADALINA CT
5200 SJS 95124 873-F5
ADAM WY
- ATN 94027 790-C2
ADAMO CT
4700 SJS 95136 874-E2
ADAMO DR
4600 SJS 95136 874-E2
ADAMS AV
1400 MPS 95035 794-D6
ADAMS CT
400 GIL 95020 978-A2
1100 SJS 95132 814-G5
1900 MTVW 94040 831-H1
18600 MGH 95037 916-J4
ADAMS DR
1100 SJS 95132 814-F5
ADAMS WY
3000 SCL 95051 833-A7
ADAMSWOOD DR
3100 SJS 95148 835-E7
ADDIEWELL PL
1300 SJS 95120 874-C7
1300 SJS 95120 894-C1
ADDINGTON CT
21500 CPTO 95014 852-B3
ADDISON AV
100 PA 94301 790-J5
300 PA 94301 791-A4
2000 EPA 94303 791-A2
ADDISON PL
2800 SCL 95051 833-B2
ADELAIDE WY
1900 SJS 95124 873-G5
ADELE AV
2300 MTVW 94043 811-F3
ADELE PL
1900 SJS 95125 853-J6
ADELHEID CT
10000 CPTO 95014 852-A1
ADELONG WY
- SJS 95139 875-H7
ADENTRO ARENA
- SUNV 94089 812-H4
ADLER AV
100 CMBL 95008 853-D7
ADLER CT
3600 SJS 95111 854-G6
ADMIRAL PL
2000 SJS 95133 814-E7
ADMIRALTY PL
6000 SJS 95123 874-E6
ADMIRE CT
1300 MPS 95035 794-C5
ADOBE AV
100 MPS 95035 793-J6
ADOBE CT
1400 SJS 95118 874-B2
ADOBE DR
200 SJS 95131 814-A5
ADOBE LN
25400 LAH 94022 831-C3
ADOBE PL
400 PA 94306 811-E1
ADOBE CREEK CT
1000 SJS 95127 834-J4
ADOBE CREEK LODGE RD
- LAH 94022 831-A3
ADOBE RIVER CT
4600 SJS 95136 874-E2
ADOLFO DR
1500 SJS 95131 814-C6
ADONIS CT
800 SUNV 94086 832-G1
ADONIS WY
2400 SJS 95124 873-E4
ADONNA CT
27100 LAH 94022 811-A7
ADRA AV
3400 SCIC 95117 853-D1
3400 SJS 95117 853-D1
ADRAGNA CT
4400 SJS 95136 874-H1
ADRIAN PL
100 LGTS 95032 873-E5
ADRIAN WY
1100 SJS 95122 834-J5
ADRIANA AV
10000 CPTO 95014 832-B7
ADRIATIC WY
3700 SCL 95051 832-H4
ADRIEN DR
1500 CMBL 95008 873-A1
AERONAUT WY
19400 SCIC 95030 892-F2
AEROSTAR WY
- HOLL - (1019-J6 See Page 999)
AETNA WY
2800 SJS 95121 854-J3
2800 SJS 95121 855-A3
AFTON AV
18600 SAR 95070 852-H7
AFTON CT
6000 SJS 95123 874-E5
AFUERA ARENA
- SUNV 94089 812-H4
AGAPE CT
4900 SJS 95118 873-J4
AGATE CT
2600 SCL 95051 832-J1
AGATE DR
2700 SCL 95051 833-A1
3200 SCL 95051 832-J1
AGATHA WY
3900 SJS 95136 874-E1
AGENA WY
100 SUNV 94086 812-F7
AGNES WY
900 PA 94303 791-C5
AGNEW RD
2000 SCL 95054 813-C5
AGUACATE CT
100 SJS 95116 834-D2
AGUA VISTA DR
2600 SJS 95132 814-D4
AGUILAR CT
2100 MPS 95035 794-E6
AHWANEE AV
600 SUNV 94086 812-G5
N AHWANEE TER
- SUNV 94086 812-G5
S AHWANEE TER
- SUNV 94086 812-G5
AHWANHEE AV
100 SUNV 94086 812-F4
AIDA AV
2600 SJS 95122 855-A2
AIELLO DR
2700 SJS 95111 854-G5
AIKINS WY
3500 SJS 95148 855-F1
AINSLEY CT
3800 SJS 95008 853-C6
AINSWORTH DR
10200 CPTO 95014 832-A6
10500 SCIC 94024 832-A6
AINTREE DR
6800 SJS 95119 895-D1
AIRES LN
400 SJS 95111 854-F6
AIRPORT BLVD
- WAT 95076 995-C6
- SCrC 95076 995-C6
400 SCrC 95019 995-C6
500 WAT 95019 995-C6
1100 SJS 95110 833-G1
AIRPORT PKWY
- SJS 95110 833-H2
AIRPORT RD
17000 SCIC 95030 913-B1
AIRWAY DR
- HOLL - (1020-A6 See Page 999)
AITKEN AV
2100 MTVW 94040 811-F5
AJAX DR
700 SUNV 94086 832-F1
AKINO CT
2800 SJS 95148 855-C1
AKIO WY
1000 SJS 95120 894-F1
AKLAN CT
300 SJS 95119 875-C7
N AKRON RD
- SCIC 94035 812-B2
- SCIC 94043 812-B2
S AKRON RD
- SCIC 94035 812-B2
- SCIC 94043 812-B2
AKRON WY
3700 SJS 95117 853-B2
ALADDIN DR
5400 SJS 95123 875-B4
ALAMEDA CT
2100 SJS 95126 833-G5
ALAMEDA WY
2000 SJS 95126 833-G5
ALAMEDA DE LAS PULGAS
- ATN 94027 790-B4
1800 RDWC 94061 790-B4
1800 WDSD 94062 790-B4
2000 SMCo 94062 790-B4
2100 SMCo 94061 790-B4
3000 SMCo 94025 790-B4
3700 MLPK 94025 790-B4
ALAMITOS DR
100 SUNV 94086 812-B6
ALAMITOS RD
- SCIC 95030 914-G2
21900 SCIC 95120 914-J1
ALAMITOS CREEK RD
1000 SJS 95120 894-J4
ALAMO CT
500 MTVW 94043 812-A4
ALAMO DR
600 MGH 95037 937-B4
600 SJS 95123 874-G4
600 SJS 95131 814-A5
ALAMO WY
- CPTO 95014 852-A2
ALAMOS RD
- PTLV 94028 810-E5
ALAN AV
4900 SJS 95124 873-J4
ALANA DR
400 SJS 95136 854-E6
ALANA WY
- SJS 95136 854-E6
ALANNAH CT
- PA 94303 791-C4
ALBA CT
200 LALT 94022 811-D5
800 SCIC 95127 814-H6
ALBANESE CIR
600 SJS 95111 854-G3
ALBANY CT
1500 MPS 95035 794-D6
ALBANY DR
100 SJS 95129 853-A1
ALBANY PL
7100 GIL 95020 977-H4
ALBAR CT
13900 SAR 95070 872-A1
ALBATROSS CT
- CMBL 95008 853-D5
ALBATROSS DR
1500 SUNV 94087 832-E5
ALBEMAR CT
3100 SJS 95148 855-D2
ALBERNI ST
1000 EPA 94303 791-A1
ALBERT AV
1700 SJS 95124 873-H4
ALBERT CT
100 LGTS 95032 873-B6
ALBERT DR
200 LGTS 95032 873-B6
ALBERT WY
600 CMBL 95008 853-C7
ALBERTA AV
500 SUNV 94087 832-D5
1700 SJS 95125 854-B4
ALBERTA CT
2300 SCL 95050 833-C2
ALBERTO WY
400 LGTS 95032 873-B7
ALBERTSTONE DR
4000 SJS 95130 853-B5
ALBERTSWORTH LN
10400 LAH 94024 831-E5
ALBION CT
500 SJS 95136 874-F1
1200 SUNV 94024 832-A4
ALBION DR
500 SJS 95136 874-E1
ALBION LN
1200 SUNV 94024 832-A4
ALBRIGHT CT
- LGTS 95030 873-C3
ALBRIGHT WY
- LGTS 95030 873-C3
ALBY CT
1600 SJS 95124 873-J3
ALCALDE RD
17100 CPTO 95014 851-J1
ALCALDE ST
2100 SCL 95054 813-C4
ALCANTE DR
6000 SJS 95129 852-G3
ALCAZAR AV
21700 CPTO 95014 852-B1
21900 SCIC 95014 852-B1
ALCAZAR DR
5800 SJS 95123 874-G5
ALCOSTA DR
700 MPS 95035 794-B6
ALCOTT WY
18400 SAR 95070 872-H1
ALDEAN AV
300 MTVW 94043 811-F2
ALDEN WY
3500 SJS 95117 853-C1
ALDER CT
13400 SAR 95070 852-E7
ALDER DR
500 MPS 95035 813-H2
ALDER PL
- MLPK 94025 790-H2
ALDER ST
700 GIL 95020 977-J6
ALDERBROOK LN
800 CPTO 95014 852-F2
1000 SJS 95129 852-F3
ALDER CREEK CT
1600 SJS 95148 835-D4
ALDERCROFT HEIGHTS RD
20600 SCIC 95030 913-A1
20600 SCIC 95030 912-J1
ALDERMONT CT
- MGH 95037 937-A1
ALDERNEY CT
22100 SCIC 94024 832-A6
ALDER SPRING WY
7100 SJS 95139 895-F1
ALDERWOOD AV
1200 SUNV 94089 812-J3
ALDERWOOD DR
2500 SJS 95132 814-C3
ALDO AV
400 SCL 95054 813-E6
ALDO CT
14000 SJS 95127 835-A4
ALDRICH WY
1500 SJS 95121 855-A2
ALDWORTH DR
2700 SJS 95148 835-E7
ALEGRA TER
400 MPS 95035 793-G3
ALEGRE AV
1000 LALT 94024 831-H1
ALEJANDRA AV
- MLPK 94027 790-E3
- ATN 94027 790-E3
ALEJANDRO DR
26800 LAH 94022 811-A5
ALELANTO LN
3100 SJS 95135 855-E3
ALERCHE DR
100 LGTS 95032 873-H7
ALES PL
700 SCIC 95046 937-E7
ALESSANDRO DR
3000 SJS 95135 855-E2
ALESSI CT
11000 SCIC 95020 958-B1
ALESTER AV
600 PA 94303 791-C4
ALEX DR
4400 SJS 95130 853-A7
4600 SJS 95130 852-J7
ALEXANDER AV
- SJS 95116 834-H2
100 SMCo 94061 790-B2
200 LGTS 95030 872-J7
200 MSER 95030 872-J7
ALEXANDER AV
3000 SCL 95051 833-A6
ALEXANDER CT
- SJS 95116 834-H2
1600 LALT 94024 832-A4
ALEXANDER DR
- SCrC 95076 955-A3
ALEXANDER PL
26200 LAH 94022 811-B6
ALEXANDER ST
6900 GIL 95020 978-A3
ALEXANDER WY
400 MPS 95035 794-D5
1600 LALT 94024 832-A4
ALEXANDRIA LN
4800 SJS 95129 853-B2
ALEXIAN DR
2100 SJS 95116 834-G3
ALEXIS CT
- MLPK 94025 790-C7
900 SJS 95116 834-H5
ALEXIS DR
3100 PA 94304 830-F1
3100 PA 94304 810-F7
3200 LAH 94022 810-G7
ALFORD AV
1800 LALT 94024 832-A4
1900 LALT 94024 831-J5
ALFRED ST
3000 SCL 95054 813-D7
ALFRED WY
2300 SJS 95122 834-J6
2400 SJS 95122 835-A6
ALGER DR
400 PA 94306 791-D7
400 PA 94306 811-D1
ALGIERS AV
1000 SJS 95122 834-G7
ALGONQUIN WY
5600 SJS 95138 875-F1
ALHAMBRA AV
10000 CPTO 95014 832-B7
ALHAMBRA CT
- PTLV 94028 810-D6
ALHAMBRA DR
2700 SCL 95051 833-B1
ALICANTE LN
25900 LAH 94022 811-C6
ALICE AV
- CMBL 95008 853-E6
400 MTVW 94041 812-A7
ALICE DR
1100 SCL 95050 833-D4
ALICE LN
900 MLPK 94025 790-F4
ALICE WY
900 SUNV 94087 832-G4
ALICIA CT
10400 CPTO 95014 851-J1
ALICIA WY
200 LALT 94022 811-F5
ALISA CT
17400 SCIC 95037 917-D5
ALISAL AV
1500 SJS 95125 874-A1
ALISAL CT
800 MPS 95035 794-B5
ALISO WY
- SMCo 94028 810-E3
ALISON AV
1500 MTVW 94040 811-H7
ALITOS DR
- SCrC 95076 (975-A4 See Page 955)
ALKAE CT
1200 SJS 95121 855-A4
ALKIRE AV
400 MGH 95037 936-H1
ALL AMERICA WY
700 SUNV 94086 832-D1
ALLAN LN
100 SCrC 95076 (975-C2 See Page 955)
400 SCrC 95076 955-E7
ALLARDICE WY
800 SCIC 94305 810-J2
ALLEGAN CIR
300 SJS 95123 875-A6
ALLEGHANY CT
6500 SJS 95120 894-C6
ALLEGHENY DR
600 SUNV 94087 832-D1
ALLEGRO LN
4500 SJS 95111 875-B1
ALLEN AV
5600 SJS 95123 874-F5
ALLEN CT
700 PA 94303 791-D6
3300 SCL 95051 832-J7
ALLEN WY
1000 CMBL 95008 853-B7
3100 SCL 95051 833-A7
3200 SCL 95051 832-J7
ALLENCREST DR
11700 SJS 95118 874-D4
ALLENDALE AV
18400 SAR 95070 872-G1
ALLENTOWN CT
2300 SJS 95125 854-D7
ALLENWOOD CT
2900 SJS 95148 855-D1
ALLENWOOD DR
3000 SJS 95148 855-D1
ALLEY WY
- MTVW 94040 811-F3
ALLISON WY
700 SUNV 94087 832-C4
1800 SJS 95131 814-C4
ALLSTON CT
1100 SJS 95120 894-F2
ALLSTON WY
1100 SJS 95120 894-F2
W ALMA AV
- SJS 95110 854-C2
200 SJS 95125 854-C2
ALMA CT
- LALT 94022 811-E5
1300 SJS 95112 854-D2
21500 SCIC 95030 912-J3
ALMA LN
- MLPK 94025 790-F3
ALMA LP
1400 SJS 95125 854-C3
ALMA ST
- MLPK 94025 790-G3
- PA 94301 790-H4
1100 PA 94301 791-B7
1500 PA 94306 791-B7
3000 PA 94306 811-D1
3900 MTVW 94040 811-D1
E ALMA ST
- SJS 95112 854-D2
ALMA TER
1500 SJS 95125 854-C3
ALMA BRIDGE RD
17000 SCIC 95030 892-J3
17200 SCIC 95030 893-A4
19200 SCIC 95030 913-A1
ALMA COLLEGE RD
19000 SCIC 95030 892-G6
ALMADEN AV
100 MPS 95035 793-J6
400 SJS 95110 834-B7
500 SJS 95110 854-C1
800 SUNV 94086 812-H5
21800 CPTO 95014 852-B1
S ALMADEN AV
- SJS 95113 834-B6
N ALMADEN BLVD
100 SJS 95110 834-B6
100 SJS 95113 834-B6
S ALMADEN BLVD
- SJS 95113 834-B6
- SJS 95110 834-B6
ALMADEN CT
26700 LAH 94022 830-J2
26800 LAH 94022 831-A2
ALMADEN EXWY
1500 SJS 95125 854-C6
3300 SJS 95118 854-C6
3300 SJS 95136 854-C6
ALMADEN EXWY Rt#-G8
3500 SJS 95118 874-D2
3500 SJS 95136 874-D2
4000 SJS 95118 854-C7
4000 SJS 95136 854-C7
5900 SJS 95120 874-D2
6600 SJS 95120 894-F2
8900 SJS 95123 874-D2
ALMADEN RD
1300 SJS 95110 854-C3
1300 SJS 95125 854-C3
3300 SJS 95118 874-C1
5900 SJS 95120 874-D6
6500 SJS 95120 894-E1
18800 SCIC 95120 894-J5
19700 SCIC 95120 895-A6
ALMADEN WY
21700 SCIC 95120 894-J7
ALMADEN LAKE DR
900 SJS 95123 874-D5
ALMADEN VALLEY DR
1400 SJS 95120 874-A6
ALMADEN VILLAGE RD
1100 SJS 95120 894-G3
ALMA JO CT
15100 MSER 95030 872-J4
ALMANOR AV
600 SUNV 94086 812-E4
1000 MLPK 94025 790-H1
ALMANOR CT
1300 SJS 95132 814-F5
ALMANSA CT
3200 SJS 95127 814-H6
ALMARIDA DR
500 CMBL 95008 853-F5
1000 CMBL 95128 853-E3
1100 SJS 95128 853-E3
ALMENDRA AV
200 LGTS 95030 873-A7
ALMENDRA LN
- LALT 94022 811-E6
ALMENDRAL AV
- ATN 94027 790-C3
ALMERIA DR
700 SJS 95123 874-F5
ALMOND AV
- LALT 94022 811-E6
600 LALT 94024 811-E6
ALMOND CT
- EPA 94303 791-C2
ALMOND DR
2500 SJS 95148 835-C7
ALMOND WY
1500 MGH 95037 917-D6
ALMOND BLOSSOM CT
100 LGTS 95032 873-J6
ALMOND BLOSSOM LN
1600 SJS 95124 873-H6
1700 LGTS 95032 873-H6
ALMOND HILL CT
100 LGTS 95030 873-C3
ALMOND ORCHARD DR
1200 MGH 95037 916-G7
ALMONDWOOD WY
700 SJS 95120 894-H3
ALOHA AV
14500 SAR 95070 872-D3
ALOHA DR
200 SJS 95136 854-G7
ALONDRA LN
15100 SAR 95070 872-F4
ALONSO DR
1100 SJS 95126 853-G3
ALPET DR
1900 SCIC 95037 917-D4
ALPHA CT
600 CMBL 95008 873-C1
ALPINE AV
- LGTS 95032 893-B1
200 SJS 95127 834-H1
1300 SCL 95051 833-A4
ALPINE DR
10100 CPTO 95014 832-A7
22500 CPTO 95014 831-J7
ALPINE RD
- SCIC 94028 830-E7
- SCIC 94028 850-E1
- SMCo 94020 830-D5
- PTLV 94028 810-D7
- PTLV 94028 830-C1
- SMCo 94020 850-C4
- SMCo 94028 810-E3
- SMCo 94028 830-D5
300 SMCo 94025 810-E3
2400 SMCo 94025 790-E7
2400 MLPK 94025 790-E7
2500 MLPK 94025 810-E3
20800 SMCo 94028 850-E1
ALPINE TER
900 SUNV 94086 812-C6
ALRIC CT
300 SJS 95123 875-B7
ALRIC DR
300 SJS 95123 875-B7
ALRIDGE DR
1300 SUNV 94087 832-D4
ALSACE CT
- SJS 95135 855-F3
ALTA AV
800 MTVW 94043 811-H1
ALTA CT
2200 SJS 95131 814-A5
N ALTA LN
13000 LAH 94022 831-C1
S ALTA LN
13000 LAH 94022 831-C1
ALTADENA AV
3900 SCIC 95127 835-A1
ALTADENA DR
26000 LAH 94022 811-B6
ALTA GLEN CT
1500 SJS 95125 853-J4
ALTA GLEN DR
1500 SJS 95125 853-J4
ALTA HEIGHTS CT
100 LGTS 95032 893-B1
ALTAIR WY
300 SUNV 94086 812-E7
ALTAMEAD DR
1100 LALT 94024 831-H2
ALTA MESA AV
4100 PA 94306 811-D2
ALTA MIRA DR
1000 SCL 95051 832-J4
ALTA MIRA PL
1800 SJS 95124 873-H1
ALTAMONT AV
1500 SJS 95125 874-A1
ALTAMONT CIR
27700 SCIC 94022 830-G1
ALTAMONT CT
800 SUNV 94086 812-G5
12100 LAH 94022 831-B2
ALTAMONT DR
400 MPS 95035 794-A5
ALTAMONT LN
27100 LAH 94022 831-A3
ALTAMONT RD
25300 LAH 94022 831-A2
26600 LAH 94022 830-H1
ALTA PASEO CT
6500 SJS 95120 894-B2
ALTA TIERRA CT
100 LGTS 95032 893-H1
ALTA TIERRA RD
12800 LAH 94022 831-B1
ALTA VISTA AV
100 LALT 94022 811-D6
13900 SAR 95070 872-E2
ALTA VISTA DR
100 ATN 94027 790-A5
ALTA VISTA WY
15700 SCIC 95127 815-B6
E ALTA VISTA WY
15700 SCIC 95127 815-B6
15800 SJS 95127 815-B6
ALTHAM CT
1500 SJS 95132 814-F4
ALTHOFF WY
1300 SJS 95116 834-F6
ALTIA AV
- SJS 95135 855-G3
ALTIPLANO WY
6700 SJS 95119 875-D7
ALTISSIMO PL
- SJS 95131 814-B6
ALTO CT
2500 SJS 95148 835-D6
ALTO LN
- MLPK 94025 790-G4
ALTON ST
- MPS 95035 793-J7
ALTOS OAKS DR
700 LALT 94024 831-G2
ALTO VERDE LN
12700 LAH 94022 811-B6
ALTREE CT
- ATN 94027 790-H1
ALTSCHUL AV
900 MLPK 94025 790-D6
1000 SMCo 94025 790-D6
ALTURAS AV
200 SUNV 94086 812-F4
ALTURA VISTA
100 LGTS 95030 872-J2
ALUM ROCK AV
1100 SJS 95116 834-E4
11600 SCIC 95127 815-B6
14600 SJS 95127 815-B6
ALUM ROCK AV Rt#-130
- SJS 95116 834-H3
3400 SJS 95127 834-H3
3500 SCIC 95127 834-H3
5900 SCIC 95127 834-H3
6900 SCIC 95127 835-A1
8900 SCIC 95127 815-A7
ALUM ROCK RD
16100 SJS 95127 815-B5
ALUM ROCK FALLS RD
18200 SJS 95127 815-D5
18200 SJS 95132 815-B5
20400 SCIC 95127 815-F5
20400 SCIC 95132 815-F5
20600 SCIC 95140 815-F5
22600 SCIC 95140 836-A3
ALVARADO AV
- LALT 94022 811-E5
700 SUNV 94086 812-G5
ALVARADO CT
700 SCIC 94305 810-J1
5900 SJS 95120 874-A7
13400 SAR 95070 872-H1
ALVARADO DR
2300 SCL 95051 833-C2
ALVARADO RW
500 SCIC 94305 790-H7
500 SCIC 94305 810-H1
ALVERNAZ DR
1100 SJS 95121 855-A5
ALVES CT
1100 SJS 95131 814-A4
ALVES DR
20500 CPTO 95014 832-D7
ALVESWOOD CIR
2400 SJS 95131 814-C4
ALVIENA DR
2900 SCIC 95133 834-H1
ALVIN AV
2400 SJS 95121 854-J2
2600 SJS 95121 855-A2
ALVIN ST
2400 MTVW 94043 811-F2
ALVINA CT
700 LALT 94024 831-G2
ALVISO ST
- SJS 95050 833-F5
- SCL 95050 833-E3
500 SCL 95053 833-F5
1100 SJS 95126 833-F5
ALVISO-MILPITAS RD
- MPS 95035 813-G1
1500 SJS 95134 813-F1
1500 SCIC 95134 813-G1
ALWOOD CT
2800 SJS 95148 835-D7
ALYSHEBA AV
200 SJS 95111 875-B3
AMADOR AV
- ATN 94027 790-C3
400 LALT 94024 811-F7
800 SUNV 94086 812-H5
AMADOR CT
2300 SJS 95122 834-J5
AMADOR DR
2200 SJS 95122 834-J5
AMADOR OAK CT
10000 CPTO 95014 831-J7
AMALFI WY
1900 MTVW 94040 831-H1
AMANDA AV
8500 GIL 95020 977-H1
AMANDA DR
700 SJS 95136 874-E1
AMANDA LN
100 LGTS 95032 873-D6
AMAPOLA DR
5800 SJS 95129 852-G3
AMAPOLO CT
23800 CPTO 95014 831-G5
AMARANTA AV
4000 PA 94306 811-C2
AMARANTA CT
4100 PA 94306 811-C3
AMARGOSA CT
400 SJS 95111 854-G7
AMARILLO AV
900 PA 94303 791-D5
AMARILLO CT
48700 FRMT 94539 793-J2
AMARYL CT
2500 SJS 95132 814-E6
AMARYL DR
2400 SJS 95132 814-E5
AMATO AV
- CMBL 95008 853-C5
AMBAR WY
300 MLPK 94025 790-F6
AMBASSADOR CT
200 LGTS 95032 893-A1
AMBER CT
1400 GIL 95020 977-F3
AMBER DR
3400 SJS 95117 853-C3
AMBER LN
800 LALT 94024 831-E1
AMBERGROVE DR
1400 SJS 95131 814-C7
AMBER OAK CT
100 LGTS 95030 873-B2
AMBERWOOD CT
2000 SJS 95132 814-D3
AMBERWOOD LN
2000 SJS 95132 814-D2
14700 SCIC 95037 937-C4
AMBLER CT
3900 SJS 95111 855-A6
AMBLER WY
3900 SJS 95111 855-A6
AMBLESIDE LN
18600 SAR 95070 872-H3
AMBOY DR
500 SJS 95136 874-F2
AMBRA WY
3400 SJS 95132 814-G2

STREET Block City ZIP Pg-Grid

AMBRIC KNOLLS RD
14600 SAR 95070 872-C3
AMBROSE CT
4000 SJS 95121 855-A5
AMBROSE RD
17000 SCIC 95070 872-B7
AMBUM AV
3400 SJS 95148 835-E7
AMBY DR
5400 SJS 95124 873-J6
AMD PL
- SUNV 94086 812-H6
AMELIA CT
10100 CPTO 95014 832-A7
AMELIA DR
5100 SJS 95118 874-A4
AMELIA WY
1800 SCL 95050 833-C3
AMERICA AV
300 SUNV 94086 812-F6
AMERICAN CT
6500 SJS 95120 894-C6
AMERICAN WY
1300 SMCo 94025 790-D5
AMERICAN OAK DR
8600 SJS 95135 855-J6
AMERICUS DR
3300 SJS 95148 835-E7
AMES AV
700 MPS 95035 814-C1
700 PA 94303 791-D7
AMES CT
800 PA 94303 791-E6
AMESBURY WY
1400 SJS 95127 835-A4
AMESTI RD
900 SCrC 95076 (975-B6 See Page 955)
AMETHYST CT
5000 SJS 95136 874-E3
AMETHYST DR
2100 SCL 95051 833-A1
AMHERST AV
- SMCo 94063 790-D1
AMHERST CT
3500 MTVW 94040 831-J2
14100 LAH 94022 810-H5
AMHERST DR
19600 CPTO 95014 832-F7
AMHERST LN
3200 SJS 95117 853-D3
AMHERST ST
2000 PA 94306 810-J1
AMIGOS CT
24400 SCIC 94024 831-E2
24400 LAH 94024 831-E2
AMISTAD CT
10300 CPTO 95014 851-J1
AMISTAD LN
12000 SCIC 95046 937-H7
12000 SCIC 95046 957-H1
AMONDO DR
5000 SJS 95129 852-J3
AMOS WY
4000 SJS 95135 855-F3
AMPHITHEATRE PKWY
- MTVW 94043 811-H1
AMSTEL CT
2100 SJS 95116 834-G3
AMSTUTZ DR
900 SJS 95129 853-A3
AMULET DR
21200 CPTO 95014 832-C6
AMULET PL
10600 CPTO 95014 832-C6
AMUR CT
2000 MPS 95035 793-J3
AMUR CREEK CT
1100 SJS 95120 894-G4
AMUR OAK LN
100 SJS 95116 834-G4
ANACAPA CT
700 MPS 95035 794-B6
12900 LAH 94022 811-A6
ANACAPA DR
26300 LAH 94022 811-A6
ANACONDA WY
900 SUNV 94087 832-B4
ANAMOR ST
1600 RDWC 94061 790-A2
ANA PRIVADA
1100 MTVW 94040 832-H6
ANCHOR WY
1800 SJS 95131 814-C4
ANCHOR BAY TER
100 SUNV 94086 812-E7
ANCIL WY
3500 SJS 95117 853-C2
ANCORA CT
2200 LALT 94024 831-H6

ANCRUM CT
3000 SJS 95148 855-C2
ANDALUSIA WY
1500 SJS 95125 854-A7
1500 SJS 95125 853-J7
ANDERSON CT
- MTVW 94043 811-J4
ANDERSON DR
700 LALT 94024 831-F1
ANDERSON RD
10200 SCIC 95127 815-B7
10200 SCIC 95127 835-B1
ANDERSON WY
- MLPK 94025 790-E7
- MLPK 94025 810-E1
ANDETA WY
100 SMCo 94028 810-D3
ANDORA DR
3100 SJS 95148 835-B5
ANDOVER DR
1100 SUNV 94087 832-B1
ANDOVER LN
1600 SJS 95124 873-J3
ANDOVER PL
900 GIL 95020 977-H4
ANDOVER WY
900 LALT 94024 831-H5
ANDRE AV
1100 MTVW 94040 832-A2
ANDRE CT
100 LGTS 95032 873-B7
ANDREA CT
3500 SJS 95117 853-C3
ANDREA DR
1000 SJS 95117 853-C3
ANDREA PL
1600 SCL 95051 833-B3
ANDREW CT
14800 SAR 95070 872-F3
ANDREWS AV
1800 SJS 95124 873-H2
ANDREWS CT
16100 MSER 95030 873-A6
ANDREWS ST
100 LGTS 95030 873-A6
300 MSER 95030 873-A6
ANDSBURY AV
200 MTVW 94043 811-J5
ANFIELD CT
4000 SJS 95136 874-D1
ANGEL AV
300 SUNV 94086 812-E7
ANGEL CT
100 LGTS 95032 873-D6
ANGELA CT
300 LALT 94022 811-F6
2200 SJS 95008 873-E1
6600 GIL 95020 977-J5
ANGELA DR
- LALT 94022 811-E6
ANGELA ST
1600 SJS 95125 854-C3
ANGELICA WY
- MGH 95037 916-H4
ANGELINA DR
3400 SCL 95051 832-J4
ANGELL CT
- SCIC - 791-A7
- SCIC 94305 790-J7
ANGELO LN
6900 SCIC 95020 978-H1
ANGELO WY
- SJS 95110 833-H2
ANGIE AV
2100 SJS 95116 834-H5
ANGMAR CT
1100 SJS 95121 855-A5
ANGUS CT
19900 SAR 95070 852-E7
ANGUS DR
300 MPS 95035 794-B6
ANITA AV
300 SCIC 94024 831-F2
ANITA ST
400 SJS 95110 834-A5
ANJOU CREEK CIR
7000 SJS 95120 894-G3
ANJOU CREEK CT
7100 SJS 95120 894-G3
ANN PL
600 MPS 95035 794-B4
ANN RD
- PTLV 94028 810-A6
ANNA AV
300 MTVW 94043 811-F3
ANNA DR
1900 SCL 95050 833-C4
4800 SJS 95124 873-G4

ANNABELLE LN
200 SBnC - (1020-F5 See Page 999)
ANNANDALE PL
3400 SJS 95121 855-D4
ANNAPOLIS ST
2500 EPA 94303 791-B1
ANNAPOLIS WY
1300 SJS 95118 874-B4
ANN ARBOR AV
10300 CPTO 95014 832-C7
10300 SCIC 95014 832-C7
ANN ARBOR CT
100 LGTS 95032 873-D7
10200 CPTO 95014 832-C7
ANN ARBOR DR
100 LGTS 95032 873-D7
ANN DARLING DR
300 SJS 95133 834-E3
ANNE CT
1800 SJS 95124 873-H5
ANNE LN
700 MGH 95037 917-D7
19100 SCIC 95014 852-G1
ANNE WY
100 LGTS 95032 873-G5
1800 SJS 95124 873-G5
ANNE MARIE CT
- SBnC - (1020-E1 See Page 999)
1800 SJS 95132 814-D3
ANNERLY CT
2000 SJS 95121 855-C5
ANNETTE LN
1900 LALT 94024 831-J5
ANNETTE WY
1000 CPTO 95014 852-D3
ANNIE LN
18500 SCIC 95120 894-G1
ANNIE LAURIE AV
- MTVW 94043 812-B3
ANNIE LAURIE WY
1600 SJS 95121 855-B4
ANN MARIE CT
600 SCIC 95046 937-D7
ANNONA AV
2200 SJS 96122 835-A7
ANO NUEVO AV
400 SUNV 94086 812-C5
ANSBURY CT
1000 MTVW 94043 811-H4
ANSDELL WY
6100 SJS 95123 875-B6
ANSEL LN
- SMCo 94025 810-E2
ANSHEN CT
800 SUNV 94086 832-F2
ANSLEY PL
18800 SAR 95070 852-H6
ANSON AV
10300 CPTO 95014 832-C7
ANSON CT
1700 GIL 95020 977-F1
ANT CT
- MGH 95037 937-C2
ANTELOPE DR
2300 SJS 95133 834-F1
ANTERO WY
800 SJS 95133 814-F7
ANTHONY CT
1800 MTVW 94040 811-F5
ANTHONY DR
2000 SJS 95008 853-B6
ANTHONY PL
10200 CPTO 95014 831-J7
ANTIGUA CT
5800 SJS 95120 874-C5
ANTIGUA DR
5800 SJS 95120 874-C5
ANTIGUA RD
2700 SJS 95111 854-H4
ANTIGUA WY
5700 SJS 95120 874-C5
ANTOINETTE DR
10500 CPTO 95014 852-E2
ANTON CT
400 PA 94301 791-B6
ANTON WY
10000 CPTO 95014 832-C7
ANTONACCI CT
3300 SJS 95148 835-D6
ANTONIO CT
- PTLV 94028 810-C7
600 GIL 95020 978-A5
ANTONIO LN
1300 SJS 95117 853-D4
1400 SCIC 95117 853-D4
ANTWERP LN
1200 SJS 95118 874-B5

ANVIL CT
600 SJS 95133 834-F1
ANVILWOOD AV
1200 SUNV 94089 812-J3
ANVILWOOD CT
1000 SUNV 94089 812-J3
ANZA DR
13000 SAR 95070 852-G7
ANZA RD
- SJS 95134 813-G3
ANZA ST
400 MTVW 94041 811-J6
ANZAR RD
- SBnC - (1017-E5 See Page 997)
APACHE CT
600 SJS 95123 874-G5
1500 GIL 95020 957-F7
APACHE TR
17800 SCIC 95030 913-A2
17800 SCIC 95030 912-J2
APENNINES CIR
5100 SJS 95138 855-F6
APOLLO CT
2600 SJS 95121 854-H3
APOLLO DR
2600 SJS 95121 854-H3
APOLLO WY
- HOLL - (1020-B5 See Page 999)
300 SBnC - (1020-B5 See Page 999)
1200 SUNV 94086 812-J7
12900 SAR 95070 852-D7
APOLLO HEIGHTS CT
13000 SCIC 95070 872-C5
APPALOOSA DR
13700 SCIC 95046 937-D6
APPALOOSA WY
27000 LAH 94022 830-J2
APPERSON RIDGE CT
3100 SJS 95148 855-E1
APPERSON RIDGE DR
3000 SJS 95148 855-E2
APPIAN LN
1000 SJS 95116 834-E6
APPIAN WY
1000 MGH 95037 937-A4
APPLAUSE PL
600 SJS 95134 813-F3
APPLE TER
700 SJS 95111 855-B7
APPLE BLOSSOM DR
5300 SJS 95123 875-A3
APPLEBLOSSOM LN
16400 SCIC 95032 873-C5
APPLEGATE CT
6400 SJS 95119 875-C7
APPLEGATE DR
6400 SJS 95119 875-C7
APPLE GROVE CT
7000 SJS 95135 876-A1
APPLETON DR
3500 SJS 95117 853-C2
APPLE TREE DR
20000 CPTO 95014 832-E7
APPLETREE LN
1800 MTVW 94040 831-G1
APPLE VALLEY DR
800 SJS 95125 854-D5
APPLEWOOD DR
4600 SJS 95129 853-A2
APPLEWOOD LN
- PTLV 94028 810-C7
APPLEY WY
2400 SJS 95124 873-E5
APRICOT AV
800 CMBL 95008 853-F6
APRICOT LN
100 LGTS 95030 872-J7
200 MTVW 94040 831-J2
2500 SJS 95121 855-E4
APRICOT HILL CT
14000 SAR 95070 872-H2
APRIL DR
100 SJS 95138 875-D4
APRIL WY
300 CMBL 95008 853-G5
APRILSONG CT
1700 SJS 95131 814-D7
APSIS AV
2400 SJS 95124 873-D3
APSIS CT
2300 SJS 95124 873-E3
APTOS AV
4500 SJS 95111 875-A1
APTOS BEACH CT
7100 SJS 95139 895-F1
AQUARIUS DR
500 SJS 95111 854-F7

AQUILA AV
4000 SJS 95124 873-E3
AQUINO WY
18600 SAR 95070 872-H3
AQUISTAPACE RD
100 SBnC - (1020-C2 See Page 999)
ARABIAN CT
5900 SJS 95123 874-J5
16700 MGH 95037 917-F6
ARABIAN ST
400 SJS 95123 874-J5
ARAGLIN CT
4000 SJS 95136 854-E6
ARAGON CT
2500 SJS 95125 853-J7
ARAGON WY
2400 SJS 95125 853-J7
2700 SJS 95125 873-J1
ARAM AV
300 CMBL 95128 853-F4
300 SJS 95128 853-F4
ARAMIS DR
3200 SJS 95127 835-B3
ARANA CT
1700 MPS 95035 794-D6
ARAPAHO DR
900 GIL 95020 957-F7
5700 SJS 95123 874-H5
ARAPAHOE CT
- PTLV 94028 810-B6
ARAPAHOE TR
17700 SCIC 95030 913-C2
ARASTRADERO RD
200 PA 94304 811-A5
200 LAH 94022 811-A5
400 PA 94306 811-A5
1500 PA 94304 810-F6
1700 SCIC 94304 810-H5
1700 PTLV 94028 810-F6
9600 SCIC 94304 811-A5
16000 LAH 94022 810-H5
ARATA CT
1500 SJS 95125 854-C3
ARATA WY
18800 SCIC 95014 852-H1
ARAUJO ST
1300 SJS 95131 814-C7
ARBELECHE LN
20400 SAR 95070 872-D2
ARBOL DR
4000 PA 94306 811-C2
ARBOLADO WY
18500 SAR 95070 872-H3
ARBOLEDA DR
300 LALT 94024 831-F1
ARBOL GRANDE CT
- SMCo 94025 790-D5
ARBOR AV
1200 SCIC 94024 831-G3
E ARBOR AV
200 SUNV 94086 812-F6
W ARBOR AV
100 SUNV 94086 812-E5
ARBOR CT
1200 MTVW 94040 832-A1
ARBOR DR
1600 SJS 95125 854-C4
ARBOR RD
- MLPK 94025 790-E4
ARBOR ST
8700 GIL 95020 977-H1
ARBOR DELL WY
5600 SJS 95124 873-J6
ARBORETUM DR
5200 SCIC 94024 831-J6
5300 LALT 94024 831-J6
ARBORETUM RD
300 PA 94304 790-H5
400 SCIC 94305 790-H5
ARBOR PARK CT
1300 SJS 95126 853-H3
ARBOR PARK DR
1300 SJS 95126 853-H3
ARBOR VALLEY DR
100 SJS 95119 875-D7
ARBOR VALLEY PL
200 SJS 95119 875-E7
ARBOR VISTA WY
1100 SJS 95126 853-H3
ARBUCKLE AV
3700 SJS 95124 873-H2
ARBUCKLE CT
1500 SCL 95054 813-D7
ARBUELO WY
- LALT 94022 811-E5
ARBUTUS AV
600 SUNV 94086 832-F1
3500 PA 94303 791-E7

ARBUTUS DR
1500 SJS 95118 874-A5
ARC RD
200 CMBL 95008 853-F5
ARCADIA AV
- SCL 95051 832-J7
ARCADIA DR
3300 SJS 95117 853-D1
3300 SCIC 95117 853-D1
ARCADIA PL
1400 PA 94303 791-B4
ARCADIA TER
600 SUNV 94086 812-G5
ARCADIAN ST
46200 FRMT 94539 793-J1
ARCADIA PALMS DR
14000 SAR 95070 872-H2
ARCHBOW CT
4700 SJS 95136 874-H3
ARCHBURY CT
3200 SJS 95148 855-F1
ARCHCOVE CT
400 SJS 95111 875-C1
ARCHER CT
1500 CMBL 95008 873-A1
ARCHER ST
- SJS 95112 833-J2
1300 SJS 95002 793-B7
ARCHER WY
1100 CMBL 95008 873-A1
ARCHFIELD CT
1500 MGH 95037 917-D6
1500 SCIC 95037 917-D6
ARCHGLEN WY
400 SJS 95111 875-C1
ARCHIBALD DR
15400 SCIC 95070 872-C4
ARCHSHIRE CT
3200 SJS 95148 835-F7
ARCHWOOD CIR
2900 SJS 95148 855-D1
ARCO CT
300 SJS 95123 874-J4
ARCOLA CT
3100 SJS 95148 855-D2
ARCTIC AV
2500 SJS 95111 854-G4
ARDEN CT
- RDWC 94061 790-A1
19500 SAR 95070 852-F5
ARDEN RD
200 MLPK 94025 790-F2
ARDEN WY
2300 SJS 95122 834-J5
ARDEN FARMS PL
3900 SJS 95111 854-J7
ARDENWOOD DR
1500 SJS 95129 852-F5
ARDILLA CT
2500 SJS 95128 853-F4
ARDIS AV
300 SJS 95117 853-D2
300 SCIC 95117 853-D1
ARDIS DR
2000 SJS 95125 854-C5
ARDMORE CT
19500 SAR 95070 852-F5
ARDMORE WY
5300 SJS 95118 874-A5
ARDSLEY CT
1100 SJS 95120 874-C6
AREQUIPA CT
200 SJS 95119 875-D7
AREZZO DR
5200 SJS 95138 855-E7
5200 SJS 95138 875-F1
AREZZO WY
5200 SJS 95138 875-E1
ARGONAUT CT
20200 SAR 95070 852-E7
ARGONAUT DR
20100 SAR 95070 852-E7
ARGONNE DR
13400 SAR 95070 852-D7
ARGUELLO PL
2300 SCL 95050 833-C3
ARGUELLO ST
500 SCIC 94305 790-H7
ARGUS WY
600 SCL 95054 813-E5
ARGYLE CT
1500 SJS 95132 814-F3
ARIC LN
26300 LAH 94022 811-B5
ARIEL CT
400 SJS 95123 874-J5
ARIEL DR
400 SJS 95123 874-J5
ARIES WY
100 SUNV 94086 812-E7

ARIZONA AV
1100 MPS 95035 794-A3
1900 MPS 95035 793-J3
ARIZONA WY
1900 RDWC 94061 790-A3
ARKANSAS PL
48400 FRMT 94539 793-J1
ARLEE DR
18000 MSER 95030 872-J6
ARLEEN AV
1300 SUNV 94087 832-F4
ARLEEN WY
2100 SJS 95130 852-J6
ARLEN CT
3700 SJS 95132 814-F2
ARLENE DR
2300 SCL 95050 833-C5
ARLETA AV
300 SCIC 95128 853-G1
ARLIA DR
1200 SCIC 95046 937-J7
ARLINE LN
2000 SCIC 95037 917-D4
ARLINGTON CT
900 SUNV 94087 832-C1
1400 SCIC 95046 937-G4
ARLINGTON LN
1000 SJS 95129 852-E3
ARLINGTON WY
- SMCo 94025 790-H2
- MLPK 94025 790-H2
ARLON PL
3500 MntC - (1017-A7 See Page 997)
ARMAND AV
- MTVW 94043 811-J2
ARMAND CT
1000 GIL 95020 977-H4
ARMAND DR
1700 MPS 95035 794-D6
ARMANINI AV
600 SCL 95050 833-C5
ARMDALE CT
3000 SJS 95148 855-C2
ARMED CT
300 SJS 95111 875-B2
ARMONK CT
5300 SJS 95123 875-B3
ARMOUR DR
4600 SCL 95054 813-D4
ARMSBY LN
15300 SCIC 95037 936-G6
ARMSTEAD CT
2800 SJS 95121 855-A2
ARMSTRONG PL
2400 SCL 95050 833-C5
ARNERICH RD
14000 SCIC 95032 893-H2
ARNERICH HILL CT
14500 LGTS 95032 893-G2
14500 SCIC 95032 893-G2
ARNERICH HILL RD
14500 SCIC 95032 893-G1
ARNICA CT
4900 SJS 95111 875-A2
ARNO CT
- SJS 95138 875-E1
ARNOLD AV
- MTVW 94043 812-B2
- SCIC 94043 812-A2
1200 SJS 95110 833-J3
ARNOLD DR
300 GIL 95020 977-H1
ARNOLD WY
700 MLPK 94025 790-J2
800 SJS 95128 853-F4
ARNOTT WY
1000 CMBL 95008 853-G6
AROMAS RD
- MntC - (1017-A5 See Page 997)
- MntC - (1016-J6 See Page 995)
AROMAS HEIGHTS LN
1600 MntC - (1017-A5 See Page 997)
AROMITAS RD
100 SBnC - (1017-C5 See Page 997)
ARPEGGIO AV
4200 SJS 95136 874-G1
ARQUEADO DR
3200 SJS 95148 835-D7
ARQUES AV
1200 SUNV 94086 812-J7
E ARQUES AV
100 SUNV 94086 812-E6
W ARQUES AV
100 SUNV 94086 812-E6

ARRAN CT
500 SUNV 94087 832-E4
ARRIBA CT
1500 SCIC 94024 831-G3
ARRIBA DR
- SBnC - (1017-C5 See Page 997)
200 SUNV 94086 812-B7
ARROBA WY
3000 SJS 95118 874-A1
ARROW LN
1500 SJS 95126 853-H4
ARROWHEAD DR
100 SJS 95123 874-H6
5400 SJS 95123 875-B4
ARROWHEAD LN
- SMCo 94063 790-D1
21300 SCIC 95070 852-B5
ARROWHEAD WY
1000 PA 94303 791-D5
ARROWOOD CT
600 LALT 94024 831-F1
ARROWOOD LN
2000 SJS 95130 853-A6
ARROW ROCK PL
900 SUNV 94087 832-B4
ARROYO CIR
7400 GIL 95020 978-B1
ARROYO DR
100 SJS 95131 814-A5
2400 SCL 95051 833-B4
ARROYO LN
17900 SAR 95070 852-D5
ARROYO RD
700 LALT 94024 811-G6
ARROYO WY
100 SJS 95112 834-D5
ARROYO DE ARGUELLO
12300 SAR 95070 852-D6
ARROYO DEL RANCHO
500 LGTS 95032 893-G1
ARROYO DE ORO
1700 SJS 95116 834-F3
ARROYO DE PLATINA
1800 SJS 95116 834-F3
ARROYO GRANDE WY
100 LGTS 95030 873-C4
ARROYO OAKS
11500 SCIC 94024 831-F4
ARROYO SECO DR
- SBnC - (1000-E7 See Page 999)
1000 CMBL 95008 853-G6
1500 SCIC 95125 853-G6
ARTHUR AV
3200 SJS 95127 835-B3
ARTHUR CT
3000 SCL 95051 833-A7
11700 LALT 94024 831-H4
ARTHUR LN
- ATN 94027 790-C2
ARTHUR PL
1100 SJS 95127 835-A3
ARTHUR RD
- SCrC 95076 995-E7
- WAT 95076 995-E7
ARUNDEL CT
4900 SJS 95136 874-F2
ASBURY PL
700 SCL 95051 833-B5
ASBURY ST
- SJS 95110 834-A4
300 SJS 95110 833-J5
700 SJS 95126 833-H6
ASCENSION DR
19600 SAR 95070 852-F5
26300 LAH 94022 811-B6
ASCHAUER CT
1100 SJS 95131 834-D1
ASCOT CT
2000 MGH 95037 917-E6
ASCOT LN
3000 SJS 95111 854-H5
ASH CT
100 LGTS 95030 873-A3
600 CMBL 95008 853-F5
1500 MGH 95037 917-D6
ASH LN
100 PTLV 94028 810-E4
ASH ST
- RDWC 94061 790-B1
400 PA 94306 811-B1
1800 PA 94306 791-A7
1800 SCL 95054 813-D5
ASHBOURNE CT
10700 SCIC 95014 852-C6
ASHBOURNE DR
600 SUNV 94087 832-F4
ASHBROOK CIR
4000 SJS 95124 873-E3

ASHBURTON DR
6000 SJS 95123 875-A6
ASHBURY CT
6000 GIL 95020 977-J6
ASHBY AV
4500 SJS 95124 873-F3
ASHBY DR
700 PA 94301 791-B3
ASHBY LN
100 LALT 94022 811-D5
ASHCROFT CT
1700 SCIC 95020 958-A2
ASHCROFT LN
1200 SJS 95118 874-C5
ASHCROFT WY
1100 SUNV 94087 832-A5
ASHDALE DR
10200 SCIC 95127 835-B2
ASHEBORO CT
1400 SJS 95131 814-C6
ASHER CT
3900 SJS 95124 873-E3
ASHFIELD CT
6500 SJS 95120 894-C1
ASHFIELD RD
- ATN 94027 790-E2
ASHFORD CT
1200 SJS 95131 834-C1
ASHGLEN WY
2300 SJS 95133 834-F1
ASH GROVE CT
100 SJS 95123 875-A3
ASHLAND DR
1400 MPS 95035 794-D7
ASHLAND WY
1900 SJS 95130 852-J6
ASHLER AV
- LGTS 95030 873-A6
ASHLEY CT
12800 SAR 95070 852-D6
ASHLEY PL
1000 MTVW 94040 811-F5
ASHLEY WY
20500 SAR 95070 852-D6
ASHLEY RIDGE CT
4700 SJS 95138 855-E5
ASHLING CT
- SJS 95136 854-E6
ASHLOCK CT
1100 CMBL 95008 873-A1
ASHMEADE CT
1800 SJS 95125 853-G4
ASHMONT DR
4800 SJS 95111 875-B1
ASHRIDGE LN
3800 SJS 95121 855-C4
ASHTON AV
500 PA 94306 791-D7
2000 SMCo 94025 790-D6
ASHTON CT
3400 PA 94306 791-D7
19600 SAR 95070 852-F5
ASHTON OAKS WY
700 SJS 95138 875-G5
ASHWOOD CT
- SJS 95131 814-A4
ASHWOOD LN
2000 SJS 95132 814-E2
ASHWORTH WY
3000 SJS 95148 835-E7
ASILOMAR TER
900 SUNV 94086 812-C6
ASKHAM PLACE CT
1700 SJS 95121 855-C4
ASPEN CT
4800 SJS 95124 873-H4
ASPEN DR
2900 SCL 95051 833-A7
22800 SCIC 94024 831-J5
ASPEN WY
400 SCIC 94024 831-J5
800 PA 94303 791-E7
17000 MGH 95037 917-D6
ASPENRIDGE DR
200 MPS 95035 793-J4
ASPESI CT
18600 SAR 95070 872-H1
ASPESI DR
18500 SAR 95070 872-H1
ASSINIBOINE TR
20800 SCIC 95030 913-C2
ASSISI CT
5800 SJS 95138 875-G1
ASSUNTA WY
1900 SJS 95124 873-G1
ASTER AV
900 SUNV 94086 832-G1
ASTER CT
900 SUNV 94086 832-G1
1400 CPTO 95014 852-D4

ASTER LN
1200 CPTO 95014 852-D4
ASTER WY
100 EPA 94303 791-D3
ASTORIA DR
900 SUNV 94087 832-B4
ASTRAHAN LN
2200 SJS 95148 835-D5
ASTRO CT
1900 SJS 95131 814-D6
ATHENE DR
10200 SCIC 95127 835-A3
ATHENOUR CT
1400 SJS 95120 874-A7
ATHERTON AV
- ATN 94027 790-C4
4700 SJS 95130 853-A5
4700 SJS 95130 852-J5
4800 SJS 95129 852-J4
ATHERTON CIR
14500 MGH 95037 937-C5
ATHERTON CT
100 SMCo 94061 790-B4
12800 LAH 94022 831-C1
ATHERTON DR
3000 SCL 95051 833-A7
ATHERTON WY
100 MGH 95037 937-C5
300 MGH 95046 937-C5
ATHERTON OAKS LN
- ATN 94027 790-D5
ATHERWOOD AV
- RDWC 94061 790-B2
6300 CPTO 95014 852-F2
ATHERWOOD PL
- RDWC 94061 790-B2
ATHOS PL
19300 SAR 95070 872-G1
ATKINSON LN
1000 MLPK 94025 790-E5
ATLANTA AV
300 SJS 95125 854-A2
ATLANTIC CT
4200 SCL 95054 813-C5
ATLAS AV
- SJS 95126 833-J7
ATMEL WY
- SJS 95131 813-G7
ATRIUM CIR
12200 SAR 95070 852-E5
ATRIUM DR
12000 SAR 95070 852-E5
ATTEBERRY LN
1400 SJS 95131 814-A4
ATWOOD CT
- SJS 95131 814-A4
100 LGTS 95032 873-D6
ATWOOD DR
2900 SJS 95121 855-B3
2900 SJS 95122 855-B3
AUBURN CT
19600 CPTO 95014 832-F7
AUBURN DR
19600 CPTO 95014 832-F7
AUBURN WY
200 SJS 95129 853-A1
600 MGH 95037 937-B4
AUDREY AV
900 CMBL 95008 873-B2
AUDREY DR
16700 MGH 95037 917-C7
AUDREY SMITH LN
- SAR 95070 872-E3
AUDUBON DR
1000 SJS 95122 834-G7
AUGUST CIR
300 MLPK 94025 790-F6
AUGUST DR
5600 SJS 95138 875-D4
AUGUST LN
7900 CPTO 95014 852-C2
AUGUSTA CT
- LGTS 95030 873-A6
2800 SCL 95051 833-B2
AUGUSTA CT E
1500 MPS 95035 794-D3
AUGUSTA PL
2100 SCL 95051 833-B2
AUGUSTA WY
4900 SJS 95129 852-J4
AUGUSTINE AV
15700 LGTS 95032 873-C5
AUGUSTINE DR
2400 SCL 95054 813-B6
AULIN DR
2900 SJS 95125 854-B7
AURA CT
900 LALT 94024 831-G3
AURA WY
1400 LALT 94024 831-G3

SANTA CLARA CO.

INDEX

STREET / Block City ZIP Pg-Grid

AURELIAN LN
1400 SJS 95126 853-H4
AURORA AV
700 SJS 95129 853-A2
AURORA LN
100 LGTS 95032 873-E5
AUSAYMAS CT
- SBnC - (1020-F1 See Page 999)
AUSTIN AV
- ATN 94027 790-C2
1600 LALT 94024 831-J4
AUSTIN CT
100 SJS 95110 854-D2
AUSTIN PL
2400 SCL 95050 833-C6
AUSTIN WY
18400 SCIC 95030 872-G5
18400 MSER 95030 872-H5
18800 SAR 95070 872-G5
AUSTWICK CT
6900 SJS 95119 895-D1
AUTOETCH LN
- SJS 95119 875-C5
AUTOMATION PKWY
1600 SJS 95131 814-C5
AUTREY ST
100 MPS 95035 794-A3
AUTUMN CT
400 SJS 95110 834-A6
AUTUMN LN
- SJS 95138 875-D4
200 MGH 95037 937-B5
1000 LALT 94024 831-H3
N AUTUMN ST
- SJS 95113 834-A6
- SJS 95110 834-A6
S AUTUMN ST Rt#-82
- SJS 95110 834-A7
- SJS 95113 834-A7
AUTUMN ESTATES
2800 SJS 95135 855-G5
AUTUMN GOLD DR
1900 SJS 95131 814-C6
AUTUMN RIDGE LN
1300 SJS 95132 814-G4
AUTUMNSONG WY
1100 SJS 95131 834-D1
1100 SJS 95131 814-D7
AUTUMNTREE CT
2000 SJS 95131 814-C6
AUTUMNVALE DR
2400 SJS 95131 814-C4
2500 SJS 95132 814-C4
AUTUMNWOOD CT
3000 SJS 95148 855-E1
AUZERAIS AV
400 SJS 95126 854-A1
700 SJS 95126 853-J1
AUZERIAS CT
100 LGTS 95032 873-H7
AVALANI AV
400 SJS 95133 834-E2
AVALON CT
3100 PA 94306 791-D7
AVALON DR
- LALT 94022 811-F6
1100 SJS 95125 854-B7
AVALON HEIGHTS TER
47400 FRMT 94539 794-A1
AVANTE PL
700 MGH 95037 917-B6
AVATI CT
1700 SJS 95131 814-D7
AVENIDA LN
17600 CPTO 95014 851-J1
AVENIDA ABETOS
300 SJS 95123 874-H3
AVENIDA ALMENDROS
5300 SJS 95123 874-H3
AVENIDA ALONDRA
600 SUNV 94089 812-H4
AVENIDA ARBOLES
300 SJS 95123 874-H3
AVENIDA CARLOS
- SUNV 94089 812-H4
AVENIDA CRESTA
16200 LGTS 95032 873-F7
AVENIDA DE ANGELINA
4900 SCL 95054 813-D3
AVENIDA DE CARMEN
4900 SCL 95054 813-D3
AVENIDA DE COBRE
1800 SJS 95116 834-F3
AVENIDA DE GUADALUPE
2300 SCL 95054 813-C3
AVENIDA DE LAGO
4900 SCL 95054 813-D3

AVENIDA DE LA FLORES
2100 SCL 95054 813-D4
AVENIDA DE LA ROSAS
1900 SCL 95054 813-D3
AVENIDA DE LO ALUMNOS
2200 SCL 95054 813-C3
AVENIDA DE LO ARBOLES
4800 SCL 95054 813-D3
AVENIDA DEL PRADO
- SCL 95054 813-C4
AVENIDA DEL ROBLE
300 SJS 95123 874-H3
AVENIDA DEL SOL
100 LGTS 95030 872-J2
AVENIDA ESPANA
- SJS 95139 875-G7
100 SJS 95139 895-F1
AVENIDA FELIPE
- SUNV 94089 812-J4
AVENIDA FERNANDO
- SUNV 94089 812-H4
AVENIDA GRANDE
- SUNV 94089 812-H4
- SJS 95139 875-F7
AVENIDA JOSE
- SUNV 94089 812-H4
AVENIDA LAGO
16100 LGTS 95032 873-F6
16300 SCIC 95032 873-F6
AVENIDA LA JUNTA
- SUNV 94089 812-G4
AVENIDA LEON
- SUNV 94089 812-H4
AVENIDA MANZANOS
300 SJS 95123 874-H3
AVENIDA MARCOS
- SUNV 94089 812-H4
AVENIDA MONTEZ
- SUNV 94089 812-H4
AVENIDA NOGALES
300 SJS 95123 874-H3
AVENIDA PALMAS
300 SJS 95123 874-H3
AVENIDA PINOS
300 SJS 95123 874-H3
AVENIDA PRIVADO
16100 LGTS 95032 873-F6
AVENIDA RICARDO
600 SUNV 94089 812-H4
AVENIDA ROTELLA
6800 SJS 95139 875-G6
AVENUE A
2700 SJS 95127 834-H2
2700 SCIC 95127 834-H2
3800 SCL 95134 813-D5
4300 SCL 95054 813-D5
AVENUE B
2700 SJS 95127 834-H2
2700 SCIC 95127 834-H2
3800 SCL 95134 813-E5
4300 SCL 95054 813-E5
AVENUE C
2700 SCIC 95127 834-H2
3800 SCL 95134 813-E5
AVERNUS CT
3400 SJS 95135 855-F6
AVERY CT
4900 SJS 95136 874-F2
AVERY LN
200 LGTS 95030 873-A6
AVIATION AV
- SCL 95050 833-G3
- SJS 95050 833-G3
1200 SJS 95110 833-G3
1200 SCL 95110 833-G3
AVIGON CT
5800 SJS 95138 875-H1
AVILA AV
2100 SCL 95050 833-E2
AVILA CT
13100 LAH 94022 810-J7
AVIS DR
1100 SJS 95126 853-J3
AVOCA DR
4000 SJS 95136 854-E6
AVOCADO PL
10100 CPTO 95014 852-F1
AVOCADO RD
300 SCrC 95076 (975-B2 See Page 955)
AVON CT
4200 SJS 95136 874-G1
AVON LN
18500 MSER 95030 872-H4
18500 SAR 95070 872-H4

AVON WY
500 LALT 94024 831-F1
AVONDALE ST
1000 SJS 95129 852-E3
AVOSET TER
1300 SUNV 94087 832-E4
AVY AV
1800 MLPK 94025 790-D6
1800 SMCo 94025 790-D6
AWALT CT
1500 LALT 94024 832-A3
AWALT DR
1100 MTVW 94040 832-A2
AYALA DR
1100 SUNV 94086 812-B6
AYER AV
- SJS 95110 834-A5
AYER DR
1000 GIL 95020 977-G3
AYER LN
- MPS 95035 794-C6
AYER ST
1200 MPS 95035 794-C6
AYRES LN
- MLPK 94025 790-E7
AYRSHIRE DR
5300 SJS 95118 874-C4
AYRSHIRE FARM LN
- SCIC 94305 790-J7
AZA DR
2100 SCL 95050 833-C3
AZALEA DR
800 SUNV 94086 832-G1
6900 SJS 95120 894-G3
AZALEA LN
600 SJS 95136 854-E7
AZALEA WY
400 LALT 94022 811-F6
16100 SCIC 95032 873-D5
AZALIA DR
100 EPA 94303 791-C2
AZARA PL
600 SUNV 94086 832-F1
AZEVEDO CT
600 SCL 95051 833-B6
AZTEC AV
100 SJS 95136 854-G7
AZTEC WY
2400 PA 94303 791-D5
AZTEC RIDGE DR
16200 LGTS 95032 893-C3
16200 SCIC 95032 893-C3
16200 SCIC 95030 893-C3
AZUCAR AV
- SJS 95111 875-B2
AZULE AV
600 SJS 95123 874-G5
AZURE ST
800 SUNV 94087 832-E2
AZZARELLO CT
4400 SJS 95121 855-F4

B

B RD
- SUNV 94089 812-J3
15000 SCIC 95127 815-C6
B ST
- MTVW 94043 812-B5
900 LALT 94024 831-H3
7600 CPTO 95014 831-G5
BABBS CREEK DR
700 GIL 95020 977-J6
BABERO AV
1600 SJS 95118 874-A1
BABE RUTH CT
1800 SJS 95132 814-D4
BABE RUTH DR
2700 SJS 95132 814-D4
BACCHUS DR
1100 SJS 95122 854-G1
BACH CT
12700 SAR 95070 852-G6
BACHMAN AV
100 LGTS 95030 873-A7
300 LGTS 95030 872-J6
400 MSER 95030 872-J6
BACHMAN CT
16100 LGTS 95030 872-J6
BACHMANN CT
2400 SJS 95124 853-H7
BACIGALUPI DR
100 LGTS 95032 873-H6
BADEN CT
1600 SJS 95132 814-E4
BADGER PASS RD
14600 MGH 95037 937-C5
BADGERWOOD LN
1900 MPS 95035 793-J3

BAERWALDT CT
900 SCIC 95046 937-E3
BAGDAD WY
- SJS 95123 875-B4
BAGDHAD PL
800 SJS 95116 834-J4
BAGELY WY
1300 SJS 95122 854-H1
BAGGINS CT
1200 SJS 95121 855-A4
BAGPIPE WY
1600 SJS 95121 855-B3
BAGSHAW CT
300 SJS 95123 875-A5
BAGUIO CT
6400 SJS 95119 875-C7
BAGWORTH CT
3100 SJS 95148 855-C2
BAHAMA WY
1400 SJS 95122 834-H6
BAHIA AV
100 SJS 95136 854-G7
BAHIA CT
200 SJS 95119 875-D7
BAHL ST
22200 CPTO 95014 832-A7
BAHRE LN
- SJS 95131 814-B6
BAILEY AV
400 SJS 95141 896-A4
400 SJS 95141 895-H6
2200 SJS 95128 833-F7
2200 SCIC 95128 833-F7
BAILEY RD
- SCIC 94035 812-B3
- SCIC 94043 812-B3
500 SJS 95141 895-G6
500 SJS 95139 895-G6
BAINBRIDGE CT
900 SUNV 94087 832-B4
BAINTER AV
19100 SAR 95070 872-G5
19100 SCIC 95030 872-G5
19300 SAR 95030 872-G5
BAINTER WY
19400 SCIC 95030 872-F5
BAINTREE PL
100 LGTS 95030 873-B2
BAIRD AV
700 SCL 95054 813-E6
BAKER AV
4100 PA 94306 811-C2
BAKER CT
1000 SUNV 94087 832-B4
BAKER LN
27800 LAH 94022 811-A6
BAKER PL
1900 SJS 95131 814-D6
BALANCE DR
500 SJS 95111 854-F7
BALARDO WY
3000 SJS 95148 855-E1
BALBACH ST
- SJS 95110 834-C7
BALBOA AV
- SJS 95116 834-F3
BALBOA CT
1200 SUNV 94086 812-B6
BALBOA DR
100 MPS 95035 793-J5
BALBOA RD
22500 CPTO 95014 851-J2
BALBOA ST
- SJS 95134 813-G3
BALCOM RD
3800 SCIC 95148 835-F6
BALD EAGLE WY
4300 SJS 95118 874-C2
BALDERSTONE DR
6200 SJS 95120 874-C7
BALDWIN DR
3800 SCL 95051 832-H7
21800 SCIC 95030 913-A3
BALDY RYAN CREEK
24200 SJS 95141 915-E4
24200 SCIC 95120 915-E4
BALERI RANCH RD
14000 LAH 94022 810-H6
BALFOUR DR
600 SJS 95111 854-H4
BALGRAY CT
3000 SJS 95148 855-C3
BAL HARBOR WY
1100 SJS 95122 834-H5
BALI CT
1300 SJS 95122 854-H1
BALLANTREE WY
1500 SJS 95118 874-A4
BALLARD CT
1200 SJS 95131 814-D7

BALLATORE DR
100 SJS 95134 813-D2
BALLYMORE CIR
- SJS 95136 854-E6
BALME DR
2300 SJS 95122 854-H2
BALMORAL DR
3000 SJS 95132 814-E3
BALSA AV
1700 SJS 95124 873-H1
BALSAM AV
300 SUNV 94086 812-F5
N BALSAMINA WY
100 SMCo 94028 810-E3
S BALSAMINA WY
200 SMCo 94028 810-E4
BALSAMO DR
6200 SJS 95129 852-F3
BALTIC WY
400 SJS 95111 854-G4
600 SUNV 94089 812-G2
BALUSTROL CT
22300 CPTO 95014 852-A2
BAMBI LN
2300 SJS 95116 834-H4
BAMBOO CT
500 SJS 95111 854-G6
BAMBOO DR
700 SUNV 94086 832-F1
BAMBOO PALM CT
- SJS 95133 814-J4
BAN CT
3500 SJS 95117 853-C3
BANANA GROVE LN
100 SJS 95123 874-J3
BANBERRY WY
4800 SJS 95124 873-H4
BANCROFT AV
18100 MSER 95030 872-J6
BANCROFT ST
400 SCL 95051 833-A7
BANCROFT WY
6200 SJS 95129 852-F3
BANDERA DR
3100 PA 94304 830-G1
BANDLEY DR
10000 CPTO 95014 832-D7
BANES LN
100 GIL 95020 978-A4
BANFF DR
1700 SUNV 94087 832-B6
BANFF ST
600 SJS 95116 834-F6
BANFF SPRINGS CT
7000 SJS 95139 875-E7
BANFF SPRINGS WY
100 SJS 95139 875-E7
BANGOR AV
- SJS 95123 875-A4
100 SJS 95123 874-J4
BANKHEAD WY
2500 SJS 95121 855-C5
BANK MILL RD
21000 SAR 95070 872-C3
BANNER CT
6100 SJS 95123 874-J6
BANNER DR
6100 SJS 95123 874-J6
BANNING AV
400 SUNV 94086 812-F6
BANNISTER AV
2800 SCIC 95020 958-C3
BANNOCK CIR
4700 SJS 95130 853-A7
BANTA CT
600 SJS 95136 874-F2
BANTRY CT
700 SUNV 94087 832-F4
BANYAN LN
15400 MSER 95030 872-J4
BARALAY PL
5100 SJS 95136 874-J3
BARANGA LN
14800 SAR 95070 872-F4
BARBANO AV
- CMBL 95008 853-F6
BARBARA AV
200 MTVW 94040 811-G7
BARBARA DR
200 LGTS 95032 873-G5
1300 SCL 95050 833-C4
1900 PA 94303 791-C5
BARBARA LN
- MLPK 94025 790-E5
10100 CPTO 95014 852-D1
BARBARA WY
2600 SJS 95125 854-C6
BARBEE CT
15000 SCIC 95127 814-J5

BARBER CT
300 MPS 95035 813-H1
BARBER LN
600 MPS 95035 813-H1
BARBERRY CT
1500 SJS 95121 855-A3
BARBERRY LN
1500 SJS 95121 855-A3
1700 SJS 95122 855-A2
BARB WERNER LN
6100 SJS 95119 875-D5
BARCELLS AV
2600 SCL 95051 833-B6
BARCELONA AV
1700 SJS 95124 873-H3
BARCELONA CT
400 MTVW 94040 811-J7
15400 MGH 95037 937-A4
BARCLAY CT
300 PA 94306 811-D2
6100 SJS 95123 875-A6
BARD ST
800 SCIC 95127 814-H6
800 SJS 95127 814-H6
BARDEN WY
1600 SJS 95128 853-G3
BARDUE ST
300 MntC - (1017-A5 See Page 997)
BAREOAK CT
3300 SJS 95148 835-E7
BARK LN
7000 SJS 95129 852-E3
BARKER DR
3800 SJS 95117 853-B3
BARKER ST
100 MPS 95035 793-J7
BARKLEY AV
2600 SCL 95051 833-A3
BARKSDALE CT
14200 SAR 95070 872-E2
BARKWOOD WY
2900 SJS 95128 853-E4
BARLETTA LN
3100 SCIC 95127 834-J1
3100 SJS 95127 834-J1
BARLEY CT
3500 SJS 95127 835-C2
BARLEY HILL RD
12200 LAH 94024 831-D2
BARLOW AV
2200 SJS 95122 834-J5
BARMETTA WY
- ATN 94027 790-D2
BARNARD AV
- SJS 95125 854-D3
BARNARD RD
17900 SCIC 95037 917-D3
BARNELL AV
16700 MGH 95037 937-A1
BARNES CT
- SCIC - 791-A7
BARNES LN
1100 SJS 95120 894-G4
BARNEY AV
- ATN 94027 790-C5
- SMCo 94025 790-C5
BARNEY CT
- SMCo 94025 790-D5
BARNHART AV
- SCIC 95037 896-F7
18600 SCIC 95014 852-G2
BARNHART CT
10500 SCIC 95014 852-G2
BARNHART PL
7400 CPTO 95014 852-D4
BARNHEISEL RD
100 SCIC 95020 (1000-C3 See Page 999)
500 SCIC 95020 (980-D7 See Page 959)
BARNSDALE CT
6600 SJS 95120 894-C1
BARNSLEY WY
600 SUNV 94087 832-E4
BARNSWELL WY
5700 SJS 95138 875-D4
BARON DR
5200 SJS 95124 873-F5
BARON PL
600 MPS 95035 794-B3
BARONET CT
3900 SJS 95121 855-D5
BARONI AV
100 SJS 95136 854-F7
BARONI CT
19900 SAR 95070 872-F1
BARONI GREEN DR
300 SJS 95136 874-J7

BARON PARK CT
400 SJS 95136 874-F3
BARON PARK DR
4900 SJS 95136 874-G3
BARONSCOURT WY
2900 SJS 95132 814-E3
BARRANCA DR
10800 CPTO 95014 832-A6
BARRETT AV
- MGH 95037 937-B1
800 SCIC 95037 937-D1
1200 SCIC 95037 937-D1
1300 SCIC 95037 917-D7
2000 SJS 95124 873-F3
2500 MGH 95037 917-F7
BARRINGTON CT
1100 SJS 95121 855-B5
BARRINGTON BRIDGE CT
10800 SCIC 95014 852-C6
BARRINGTON BRIDGE LN
10800 SCIC 95014 852-C6
BARRON AV
500 PA 94306 811-B2
BARRON PL
6300 GIL 95020 978-A5
BARONET CT
3900 SJS 95121 855-D5
BARONI AV
100 SJS 95136 854-F7
BARONI CT
19900 SAR 95070 872-F1
BARONI GREEN DR
300 SJS 95136 874-J7
BARON PARK CT
400 SJS 95136 874-F3
BARON PARK DR
4900 SJS 95136 874-G3
BARONSCOURT WY
2900 SJS 95132 814-E3
BARRANCA DR
10800 CPTO 95014 832-A6
BARRETT AV
- MGH 95037 937-B1
800 SCIC 95037 937-D1
1200 SCIC 95037 937-D1
1300 SCIC 95037 917-D7
2000 SJS 95124 873-F3
2500 MGH 95037 917-F7
BARRINGTON CT
1100 SJS 95121 855-B5
BARRINGTON BRIDGE CT
10800 SCIC 95014 852-C6
BARRINGTON BRIDGE LN
10800 SCIC 95014 852-C6
BARRON AV
500 PA 94306 811-B2
BARRON PL
6300 GIL 95020 978-A5
BARROW CT
2800 SJS 95121 855-A3
BARRY LN
- ATN 94027 790-D4
15900 MSER 95030 873-A5
BARRYMORE DR
4000 SJS 95117 853-A3
4100 SJS 95129 853-A3
BARSON TER
300 SUNV 94086 812-F7
BARSTOW CT
900 SUNV 94086 812-H5
BARTLETT AV
200 SUNV 94086 812-F7
BARTLETT CT
14800 SCIC 95046 937-G2
BARTLETT CREEK CT
1100 SJS 95120 894-G3
BARTO ST
400 SCL 95051 833-A6
BARTON CT
13800 LAH 94022 811-D7
BARTON DR
1400 SUNV 94087 832-A5
BARTON PL
100 MLPK 94025 790-J2
BARTON ST
1800 SMCo 94061 790-B4
BARTON WY
300 MLPK 94025 790-J3
BASALT CT
2300 SJS 95133 814-H3
BASCH AV
- SJS 95116 834-F3
BASCOM AV
- SCL 95128 833-F7
- SCL 95050 833-F7
- SJS 95050 833-F7

BASCOM AV
- SJS 95128 833-F7
100 SCIC 95128 833-F7
300 SJS 95128 853-G5
500 SCIC 95128 853-G5
700 SJS 95124 853-G5
700 SJS 95124 873-F1
1200 CMBL 95008 853-G5
1200 SJS 95125 853-G5
1500 CMBL 95125 853-G5
1800 CMBL 95128 853-G5
1800 SJS 95126 853-G5
2100 SJS 95008 853-G5
2500 SJS 95008 873-F1
2500 SCIC 95008 873-F1
2600 SCIC 95008 853-G5
S BASCOM AV
300 SJS 95128 853-G1
300 SCIC 95128 853-G1
3100 SJS 95124 873-E2
3100 SJS 95008 873-E2
3200 CMBL 95008 873-E2
3400 SCIC 95008 873-E2
3400 SCIC 95032 873-E2
BASCOM CT
100 CMBL 95008 873-E2
BASILE AV
1800 SJS 95128 853-G1
1800 SCIC 95128 853-G1
BASIN CT
500 SJS 95111 854-G4
BASKING RIDGE AV
6600 SJS 95138 875-F4
BASS CT
4800 SJS 95130 852-J6
BASSETT LN
- ATN 94027 790-F2
25700 LAH 94022 831-B3
BASSETT ST
3100 SCL 95054 813-D6
E BASSETT ST
- SJS 95112 834-B5
W BASSETT ST
100 SJS 95110 834-A6
100 SJS 95113 834-A6
BASSWOOD CT
4800 SJS 95124 873-H4
BASTIA LN
- SJS 95127 834-C1
BASUNI WY
- SCIC 96037 917-D5
BATAAN CT
400 SJS 95133 834-G2
BATEMAN WY
3500 SJS 95148 855-F1
BATES CT
3000 SJS 95148 855-E1
BATHGATE LN
3400 SJS 95121 855-C5
BATON ROUGE CT
2800 SJS 95133 814-G7
BATON ROUGE DR
2400 SJS 95133 834-G1
2400 SCIC 95133 834-G1
2500 SJS 95133 814-G7
BATTAGLIA CIR
2400 SJS 95132 814-E6
BATTERSEA CT
1700 SJS 95132 814-J3
BATTLE DANCE DR
300 SJS 95111 875-B2
BAUMANN CT
500 SCIC 95037 916-H3
BAUTISTA CT
900 PA 94303 791-E6
BAVA CT
6100 SJS 95123 875-A6
BAXLEY CT
22000 CPTO 95014 852-A2
BAXTER AV
10600 SCIC 94024 832-A6
BAY RD
300 ATN 94027 790-H1
300 MLPK 94025 790-H1
500 SMCo 94025 790-H1
900 EPA 94303 791-A1
BAY ST
300 SJS 95123 874-J5
800 MTVW 94041 811-J7
900 MTVW 94040 811-J7
BAY TER
500 SUNV 94089 812-G3
BAYARD DR
1100 SJS 95122 854-H2
BAYBERRY
- PTLV 94028 830-D1
BAYBERRY COM
- FRMT 94539 793-H1
BAYBERRY CT
3000 SJS 95148 855-D2

BAYBERRY LN
3000 SJS 95148 855-C2
BAYBERRY WY
- MPS 95035 794-A6
BAY FRONT PZ
- SCL 95002 813-A3
BAYHAVEN DR
2000 SJS 95122 835-A7
BAY LAUREL DR
1100 MLPK 94025 790-F5
BAY LAUREL LN
1100 SJS 95132 814-H5
BAYLEAF CT
800 SJS 95128 853-F4
BAYLISS CT
7400 SJS 95139 895-G1
BAYLISS DR
200 SJS 95139 895-F2
BAYLISS PL
7500 SJS 95139 895-G1
BAYLOR AV
5100 SAR 95070 852-J7
18200 SJS 95130 852-J7
BAYLOR DR
700 SCL 95051 832-J6
BAYLOR ST
2500 EPA 94303 791-B1
BAYNE PL
4300 SJS 95130 853-A4
BAYO CLAROS CIR
1800 MGH 95037 917-D6
BAYOU DR
3400 SJS 95111 854-J5
BAYO VISTA
1000 SJS 95132 814-H5
BAYPOINTE DR
100 SJS 95134 813-F3
BAYPOINTE PKWY
100 SJS 95134 813-F2
BAY RIDGE CT
1300 SJS 95120 894-C2
N BAYSHORE W
600 SJS 95112 834-C3
BAYSHORE FRWY U.S.-101
- EPA - 791-E5
- EPA - 790-J1
- MLPK - 791-E5
- MLPK - 790-J1
- MTVW - 791-E5
- MTVW - 812-C4
- MTVW - 811-G1
- PA - 791-E5
- SCL - 813-B6
- SCIC - 812-C4
- SCIC - 855-B5
- SJS - 813-B6
- SJS - 855-B5
- SJS - 875-C1
- SJS - 834-C2
- SJS - 833-G1
- SJS - 854-H1
- SUNV - 813-B6
- SUNV - 812-C4
BAYSHORE PKWY
2100 MTVW 94043 791-F7
2100 MTVW 94043 811-G1
E BAYSHORE RD
800 EPA 94303 791-A1
1900 PA 94303 791-D4
W BAYSHORE RD
1200 EPA 94303 791-B2
1900 PA 94303 791-D4
BAYSIDE CT
2300 SJS 95133 834-F2
BAYSIDE PKWY
47000 FRMT 94538 793-F1
BAYSLAND CT
1300 SJS 95131 814-D7
BAYSMILL CT
2800 SJS 95121 854-J3
BAY SPRINGS RD
18500 SCIC 95070 872-D7
BAYTECH DR
100 SJS 95134 813-D1
BAYTON DR
- SJS 95193 875-C4
BAY TREE DR
1100 GIL 95020 977-F1
BAY TREE LN
- LALT 94022 831-D1
- SCIC 95127 815-A6
BAYVIEW AV
- LGTS 95030 872-J7
200 SCIC 95127 815-A7
200 SUNV 94086 832-E1
N BAYVIEW AV
200 SUNV 94086 812-F6
S BAYVIEW AV
100 SUNV 94086 812-E7

BAYVIEW CT
- LGTS 95030 872-J7
BAYVIEW DR
- FRMT 94538 793-G1
18100 SCIC 95030 912-H3
BAYVIEW PARK DR
400 MPS 95035 794-D5
BAYWOOD AV
100 MLPK 94025 790-J3
500 SJS 95128 833-E7
S BAYWOOD AV
300 SJS 95128 853-E1
1200 CMBL 95128 853-E3
BAYWOOD CT
300 MTVW 94040 811-F4
10500 CPTO 95014 832-F7
BAYWOOD DR
10400 CPTO 95014 832-F7
BAYWOOD SQ
1800 SJS 95132 814-E3
BEACH RD
1500 WAT 95076 (1015-D4 See Page 995)
1500 SCrC 95076 (1015-D4 See Page 995)
E BEACH ST
300 WAT 95076 (1015-H1 See Page 995)
E BEACH ST Rt#-152
- WAT 95076 (1015-G2 See Page 995)
W BEACH ST
- WAT 95076 (1015-E3 See Page 995)
1000 SCrC 95076 (1015-E3 See Page 995)
BEACON DR
- MPS 95035 794-D6
BEACON LN
3300 SJS 95118 874-A1
BEACON ST
- MTVW 94040 811-F3
600 MLPK 94025 790-J2
BEACONSFIELD RD
1100 SJS 95121 855-A5
BEAL CT
6400 SJS 95123 875-B7
BEAN AV
200 LGTS 95030 873-A7
200 LGTS 95030 872-J7
BEARCAT CT
6700 GIL 95020 978-B4
BEAR CLAW WY
- SJS 95136 874-H2
BEAR CREEK BLVD Rt#-35
20000 SCrC 95030 912-E1
BEAR CREEK CRSG
- SMCo 94020 850-E6
BEAR CREEK RD
- SCrC 95030 892-A7
19500 SCIC 95030 892-G6
21500 SCIC 95030 912-F1
22200 SCrC 95030 912-C1
BEARDEN DR
1600 CMBL 95030 872-J2
BEARDON DR
10100 CPTO 95014 832-D7
10200 SCIC 95014 832-D7
BEARDSLEY RD
18200 SCIC 95030 892-F4
BEAR GULCH DR
- PTLV 94028 810-D6
BEAR PAW
- PTLV 94028 830-C1
BEAR VALLEY LN
2300 SJS 95133 834-F1
2300 SJS 95133 814-H3
BEATRICE CIR
21400 SCIC 95030 912-J3
BEATRICE CT
2000 SJS 95128 853-G3
BEATRICE LN
26900 LAH 94022 811-C7
BEATRICE ST
100 MTVW 94043 811-H4
BEATTIE CT
1300 SJS 95120 874-B6
BEAUCHAMP CT
20800 SAR 95070 852-D5
BEAUCHAMPS LN
11900 SAR 95070 852-D5
BEAUJOLAIS CT
8400 SJS 95135 855-H7
BEAULIEU CT
1200 SJS 95125 853-G4
BEAUME CT
400 MTVW 94043 811-G2
BEAUMERE WY
100 MPS 95035 794-A4

STREET
Block City ZIP Pg-Grid

BEAUMONT AV
13200 SAR 95070 852-E7
13400 SAR 95070 872-E1
BEAUMONT DR
1000 SJS 95129 852-J3
BEAUMONT SQ
3300 MTVW 94040 831-J2
BEAVEN DR
21700 CPTO 95014 832-B7
BEAVER LN
26900 LAH 94022 811-A5
BEAVER CREEK WY
700 SJS 95133 814-H3
700 SJS 95133 834-F1
BEAVERTON CT
800 SUNV 94087 832-C4
BECK AV
18400 MSER 95030 872-H6
BECK DR
1600 SJS 95130 853-B5
BECKER LN
400 LALT 94022 811-D5
BECKET DR
1200 SJS 95121 854-J3
BECKHAM DR
400 SJS 95123 875-B7
BECKLEY DR
3000 SJS 95135 855-F3
BECKWITH RD
19200 SCIC 95030 872-G7
BECKY LN
15000 MSER 95030 872-J4
25300 LAH 94022 831-C2
BEDAL LN
300 CMBL 95008 873-D1
BEDFORD AV
1300 SUNV 94024 832-A5
1300 SUNV 94087 832-A5
BEDFORD CT
1200 SUNV 94024 832-A4
BEDFORD ST
10000 SCIC 95127 835-A3
BEDIVERE DR
600 SJS 95127 814-H7
BEE CT
1000 MPS 95035 814-D2
BEEBE CIR
4000 SJS 95135 855-F3
BEECH ST
900 EPA 94303 791-C2
1800 SCL 95054 813-D5
BEECHER CT
2800 SJS 95121 855-A2
BEECH GROVE CT
5300 SJS 95123 874-J3
BEECHMONT AV
4200 SJS 95136 874-D1
BEECHNUT AV
200 SUNV 94086 812-E5
BEECHVALE CT
300 SJS 95119 895-D1
BEECHWOOD AV
2400 SJS 95128 833-E7
BEECHWOOD DR
5300 SCIC 94024 831-J6
5300 LALT 94024 831-J6
BEEGUM WY
200 SJS 95123 875-A4
BEEKMAN PL
19800 CPTO 95014 832-F6
BEEMAN DR
10300 SJS 95127 835-B4
BEEMER AV
100 SUNV 94086 812-E7
BEGEN AV
1500 MTVW 94040 811-H7
1700 MTVW 94040 831-H1
BEGGS RD
18100 SCIC 95030 892-D3
BEGONIA DR
5400 SJS 95124 873-J6
BEGONIA LN
600 SJS 95136 854-E7
BEGONIA WY
600 SUNV 94086 832-F1
BEHLER DR
3500 SJS 95132 814-F2
BELA DR
4700 SJS 95129 853-A4
4700 SJS 95129 852-J4
BEL AIR AV
2000 SJS 95126 833-F7
2000 SJS 95128 833-F7
BEL AIR CT
23400 SCrC 95030 913-D7
BEL AIR PL
600 MGH 95037 917-B6
BEL AIR WY
500 MGH 95037 917-B6

BEL AIRE CT
11000 CPTO 95014 852-B3
BEL AIRE DR
100 SJS 95131 814-A4
BEL AYRE DR
100 SCL 95117 833-C7
BELBLOSSOM WY
200 LGTS 95032 873-G6
BELBROOK CT
6500 SJS 95120 894-C1
BELBROOK PL
- MPS 95035 793-J4
BELBROOK WY
- ATN 94027 790-B6
1100 MPS 95035 793-J5
BEL CANTO DR
4900 SJS 95124 873-F4
BELCREST DR
100 LGTS 95032 873-H7
BELDEN CT
600 LALT 94022 811-E5
BELDEN DR
- LALT 94022 811-E5
200 SJS 95123 875-A4
BELDER DR
1000 SJS 95120 894-H4
BEL ESCOU DR
4900 SCIC 95124 873-F4
4900 SJS 95124 873-F4
BEL ESTOS DR
4900 SJS 95124 873-F4
15100 SCIC 95124 873-F4
BELFAIR CT
700 SUNV 94087 832-C4
BELFAST CT
500 SUNV 94087 832-E4
BELFAST DR
2700 SJS 95127 835-A5
BELFORD DR
1000 SJS 95132 814-F6
BELFRY WY
500 SUNV 94087 832-D4
BELGATOS RD
100 LGTS 95032 873-H7
BELGLEN LN
100 LGTS 95032 873-H6
BELGLEN WY
100 LGTS 95032 873-H6
BELGRAVIAN CT
2700 SJS 95121 855-D3
BELGROVE CIR
3200 SJS 95148 855-F1
BELGROVE CT
3300 SJS 95148 855-F1
BELHAVEN DR
100 LGTS 95032 873-H6
BELICK ST
3100 SCL 95054 813-F7
BELKNAP CT
1200 CPTO 95014 852-C4
BELKNAP DR
7800 CPTO 95014 852-C3
BELL AV
2900 SCIC 95133 834-H1
BELL CT
- EPA 94303 791-B2
BELL RD
13000 SCrC 95030 912-F7
BELL ST
300 EPA 94303 791-B2
BELLA CORTE
400 MTVW 94043 811-G2
BELLADONNA CT
600 SUNV 94086 832-F1
BELLAGIO DR
5600 SJS 95118 874-B5
BELLAIR WY
1100 MLPK 94025 790-D6
1100 SMCo 94025 790-D6
BELLA LADERA DR
24500 LAH 94024 831-E2
BELLA MADEIRA LN
- SCIC 95127 835-F3
BELLARMINE CT
3200 SCL 95051 833-A2
BELLA VISTA
19900 SAR 95070 872-E3
BELLA VISTA AV
100 LGTS 95032 873-B7
3400 SCL 95051 832-J3
BELLA VISTA CT
100 LGTS 95032 873-B7
3400 SCL 95051 832-J3
BELLA VISTA RD
5300 SCrC 95076 (976-C5
See Page 955)
5300 SCIC 95020 (976-B5
See Page 955)
BELLE CT
15100 SAR 95070 872-F4

BELLEAU AV
- ATN 94027 790-D2
BELLEROSE DR
300 SJS 95128 833-F7
500 SCIC 95128 833-F7
600 SCIC 95128 853-F1
800 SJS 95128 853-F1
BELLETO DR
17400 MGH 95037 917-B6
BELLEVILLE WY
1200 SUNV 94024 832-A5
1200 SUNV 94087 832-A5
BELLEVUE AV
- SJS 95110 854-D3
22300 CPTO 95014 852-A1
BELLEVUE CT
300 LALT 94024 831-F1
BELLEW DR
700 MPS 95035 813-H1
BELLFLOWER AV
600 SUNV 94086 832-F2
BELLFLOWER CT
15000 SCIC 95127 814-J5
BELLGROVE CIR
11800 SAR 95070 852-G7
BELLHURST AV
900 SJS 95122 834-F7
BELLINGHAM CT
1100 SJS 95121 854-J3
BELLINGHAM DR
1000 SJS 95121 854-J3
BELLINGHAM WY
1300 SUNV 94087 832-B4
1400 SUNV 94024 832-B4
BELLINI CT
2800 SJS 95132 814-F5
BELLIS CT
700 SJS 95123 874-G6
BELLO AV
2000 SJS 95125 854-A6
BELLOMO AV
900 SUNV 94086 832-F3
BELLOMY ST
700 SCL 95053 833-E5
700 SCL 95050 833-E5
1600 SCL 95128 833-E5
BELL STATION RD
- SCIC 95020 (941-A7
See Page 921)
- SCIC 95020 (940-H4
See Page 919)
- SCIC 95020 961-A2
BELLVIEW CT
2100 PA 94303 791-C5
BELLWOOD CT
1300 LALT 94024 831-J4
BELLWOOD DR
400 SCL 95054 813-E5
19100 SAR 95070 852-G6
BELMONT AV
100 SMCo 94061 790-B3
200 LGTS 95030 872-J7
300 MSER 95030 872-J7
BELMONT DR
400 SJS 95125 854-C3
BELMONT TER
900 SUNV 94086 812-D6
BELNAP WY
15400 SAR 95070 872-C4
15400 SCIC 95070 872-C4
BELRIDGE DR
100 LGTS 95032 873-H7
BELSHAW DR
1300 MTVW 94040 832-A2
BELTANE DR
7700 SJS 95135 856-A6
BELTHORN CT
2200 SJS 95131 814-E6
BELTRAMI DR
1100 SJS 95127 835-B3
BELVALE DR
100 LGTS 95032 873-H6
BELVEDERE DR
4200 SJS 95129 853-A2
BELVEDERE LN
1000 SJS 95129 852-F3
BELVOIR DR
1600 SCIC 94024 831-G4
BELVUE DR
- LGTS 95032 873-H6
BELWOOD CT
100 LGTS 95032 873-H6
BELWOOD LN
100 LGTS 95032 873-H6
BELWOOD GATEWAY
- LGTS 95032 873-H6
BENASSI DR
7600 GIL 95020 977-G3
BENBOW AV
100 SJS 95123 875-B5

BENBOW DR
9300 GIL 95020 957-G7
BEND AV
700 SJS 95136 874-E1
BEND DR
600 SUNV 94087 832-D4
BENDER CIR
100 MGH 95037 916-J5
BENDIGO DR
1700 LALT 94024 831-H4
BENDMILL WY
1000 SJS 95121 854-J4
BENDORF DR
100 SJS 95111 875-B3
BENECIA AV
1000 SUNV 94086 812-D5
BENEDICT LN
15400 LGTS 95032 873-C5
BENEFIT CT
400 SJS 95133 834-G2
BENETTI CT
21800 CPTO 95014 832-B7
BENGAL CT
5100 SJS 95111 875-A2
BENGAL DR
5000 SJS 95111 875-A2
BEN HUR CT
2300 SJS 95124 853-G7
BENITO RD
300 SBnC - (1020-H1
See Page 999)
BENJAMIN AV
2800 SJS 95124 873-F1
BENJAMIN CT
2900 SJS 95124 873-F1
BENJAMIN DR
2400 MTVW 94043 811-F2
BEN LOMOND DR
4000 PA 94306 811-E2
BEN LOMOND WY
3300 SJS 95121 855-B3
BENNETT AV
3400 SCL 95051 832-J7
BENNETT CT
100 GIL 95020 957-H7
BENNETT ST
100 GIL 95020 957-H7
BENNETT WY
1000 SJS 95125 854-B5
16300 LGTS 95032 873-D4
BENNETTA LN
11700 SCIC 95020 957-J1
BENNIGHOF CT
2100 SJS 95121 855-C3
BENNINGTON DR
1100 SUNV 94087 832-B1
BENNY CT
1100 SJS 95131 834-C1
BEN ROE DR
1400 LALT 94024 831-J4
1500 LALT 94024 832-A4
BENSON LN
2500 SJS 95125 854-A7
2600 SJS 95125 874-A1
BENT DR
1000 CMBL 95008 853-G6
BENTLEY AV
- LGTS 95030 873-A7
BENTLEY CT
26000 LAH 94022 811-D7
BENTLEY DR
1800 SJS 95132 814-E4
BENTLEY SQ
100 MTVW 94040 811-J7
BENTLEY RIDGE DR
- SJS 95138 855-E5
BENTOAK CT
1100 SJS 95129 852-H3
BENT OAK LN
2900 MGH 95037 917-G6
BENTOAK LN
1000 SJS 95129 852-H3
BENTON CT
1600 SUNV 94087 832-H5
BENTON ST
400 SCL 95050 833-C4
1600 SUNV 94087 832-H5
2400 SCL 95051 833-A5
3300 SCL 95051 832-H5
BENVENUE AV
300 LALT 94024 811-F7
BENZO DR
6300 SJS 95123 875-A7
BERCAW LN
14200 SJS 95124 873-G3
14200 SCIC 95124 873-G3
BERENDA WY
- SMCo 94028 810-E3
BERESFORD AV
100 SMCo 94061 790-B3

BERESFORD AV
100 RDWC 94061 790-B3
BERESFORD CT
- SMCo 94061 790-B3
100 MPS 95035 794-A7
BERESFORD PL
- SMCo 94061 790-B3
BERG CT
1100 MPS 95035 794-B4
BERGAMO CT
5600 SJS 95118 874-B5
BERGER DR
1400 SJS 95112 834-B1
BERGERAC DR
1400 SJS 95118 874-A6
BERGESEN CT
- ATN 94027 790-B4
BERGIN PL
1400 SCL 95051 833-A4
BERGMAN CT
2500 SJS 95121 855-E4
BERING DR
1800 SJS 95112 833-J1
2000 SJS 95131 813-H7
2100 SJS 95131 833-J1
BERINGER CT
1400 SJS 95125 853-G4
BERKELAND CT
4900 SJS 95111 875-C1
BERKELEY AV
500 SMCo 94025 790-H1
1000 MLPK 94025 790-H1
BERKELEY CT
22100 SCIC 94024 832-A7
BERKELEY TER
100 SUNV 94086 812-E7
BERKELEY WY
2200 SJS 95116 834-H4
BERKSFORD WY
1400 SJS 95127 835-A4
BERKSHIRE AV
- SMCo 94063 790-C1
900 SUNV 94087 832-C1
BERKSHIRE CT
10000 CPTO 95014 831-J7
18300 MGH 95037 916-H5
BERKSHIRE DR
100 MGH 95037 916-H5
1100 SJS 95125 854-C7
10200 SCIC 94024 831-E5
BERKSHIRE PL
600 MPS 95035 794-B3
BERLAND CT
7600 CPTO 95014 852-D3
BERLIN DR
1200 SCIC 95046 937-H5
BERMUDA CT
900 SUNV 94086 832-G1
BERMUDA WY
1500 SJS 95122 834-H6
BERN CT
900 SJS 95112 834-B1
BERNA ST
1600 SCL 95050 833-C3
BERNAL AV
600 SUNV 94086 812-G6
BERNAL RD
- SJS 95119 875-F6
- SJS 95138 875-F6
100 SJS 95139 875-F6
100 SJS 95139 895-E1
100 SJS 95119 895-E1
200 SCIC 95119 895-C2
500 SJS 95120 895-C2
BERNAL WY
- SJS 95119 875-F7
- SJS 95139 875-F7
BERNARDO AV
500 SUNV 94087 832-B2
1600 CPTO 95014 832-B5
N BERNARDO AV
100 MTVW 94086 812-C6
100 MTVW 94043 812-C6
S BERNARDO AV
100 MTVW 94041 812-B7
100 SUNV 94086 812-B7
BERNICE WY
1800 SJS 95124 873-G2
BERONA WY
1400 SJS 95122 834-J5
1600 SJS 95122 835-A6
BERRENDO DR
- MPS 95035 794-A5
BERRY AV
600 LALT 94024 831-G2
BERRY CT
200 MGH 95037 916-J7
600 SCIC 94043 812-A3
BERRY DR
600 SCIC 94043 812-B3

BERRY WY
3500 SCL 95051 832-J2
14500 SJS 95124 873-G3
14500 SCIC 95124 873-G3
BERRYESSA RD
600 SJS 95112 834-B3
900 SJS 95133 834-C2
1200 SJS 95131 834-C2
1800 SJS 95133 814-G5
1800 SJS 95131 814-E7
2200 SCIC 95133 814-G5
2400 SJS 95132 814-G5
BERRYESSA ST
600 MPS 95035 793-J6
BERRY HILL CT
14100 LAH 94022 810-H5
BERRY HILL LN
14100 LAH 94022 810-H6
BERRYWOOD DR
1600 SJS 95133 834-E3
BERT CT
2000 HOLL - (1020-B5
See Page 999)
BERTINI CT
3700 SJS 95117 853-C2
BERTLAND CT
1300 SJS 95131 814-D7
BERTRAM RD
21000 SCIC 95120 895-A7
21400 SCIC 95120 894-J7
21400 SCIC 95120 914-J1
BERWICK ST
13100 SAR 95070 852-H7
BERWICK WY
100 SUNV 94087 832-E4
BERWICKSHIRE WY
6400 SJS 95120 894-C1
BERYLWOOD LN
- MPS 95035 793-J3
BESS CT
1300 SJS 95128 853-F4
BEST CT
2100 SJS 95131 814-E7
BESTOR ST
200 SJS 95112 854-D1
400 SJS 95112 834-E7
BESTVIEW CT
15300 SAR 95070 872-F4
BESWICK DR
5600 SJS 95123 875-B4
BETA CT
600 CMBL 95008 853-C7
BETABEL RD
1000 SBnC - (1018-B3
See Page 997)
BETH CT
3600 SCL 95054 813-E6
BETH DR
400 SJS 95111 854-H5
BETH WY
1500 CMBL 95008 873-A1
BETHANY AV
1700 SJS 95132 814-D4
BETHANY CT
1800 SJS 95132 814-D4
BETHEL AV
10000 SCIC 95127 835-A3
BETLIN AV
800 CPTO 95014 852-F2
BETLO AV
2400 MTVW 94043 811-F2
2500 PA 94306 811-F2
BETLO CT
5000 SJS 95130 852-J6
BETSY WY
2800 SJS 95133 834-G1
2800 SJS 95133 814-G7
BETSY ROSS DR
5200 SCL 95054 813-A3
BETTE AV
800 CPTO 95014 852-F2
BETTEN CT
1000 SJS 95127 834-J4
BETTIO RD
- SCIC 94035 812-B3
BETTY CT
700 SUNV 94086 832-F2
1600 SCL 95051 833-A3
BETTY LN
- ATN 94027 790-C4
BETTY ANN CT
21500 SCIC 95030 913-A3
BEVANS DR
400 SJS 95129 852-J1
BEVERLY BLVD
1700 SJS 95116 834-F4
BEVERLY CT
200 CMBL 95008 853-C6
BEVERLY LN
100 LALT 94022 811-E6

BEVERLY ST
- MTVW 94043 812-B5
BEVIL CT
6400 SJS 95123 875-B7
BEVIN BROOK DR
1700 SJS 95112 854-F1
BEWCASTLE CT
2900 SJS 95132 814-D4
BEXLEY LNDG
1800 SJS 95131 814-C4
BIANCHI WY
10000 CPTO 95014 852-D1
BIANCO WY
3400 SJS 95135 855-E3
BIARRITZ CIR
200 LALT 94022 811-E6
BIARRITZ CT
12600 SAR 95070 852-H6
BIARRITZ LN
12600 SAR 95070 852-H6
BIARRITZ PL
5500 SJS 95138 875-F1
BIBBITS DR
3900 PA 94303 811-F1
3900 PA 94303 791-F7
BIBEL AV
6400 SJS 95129 852-F4
BICKLEY CT
5100 SJS 95136 874-E3
BICKNELL RD
600 LGTS 95030 873-A4
18000 MSER 95030 873-A4
18000 MSER 95030 872-H4
18000 LGTS 95030 872-H4
BIDDLEFORD CT
100 SJS 95139 875-G7
BIDWELL AV
900 SUNV 94086 812-C6
BIEBER DR
200 SJS 95123 875-A4
BIELAWSKI RD
- SCIC 95070 871-F7
- SCrC 95030 871-F7
BIEN CT
3300 SJS 95148 835-D7
BIEN WY
3300 SJS 95148 835-D7
BIG BASIN DR
1400 MPS 95035 814-D2
BIG BASIN WY Rt#-9
14300 SAR 95070 872-D3
BIG BEAR CT
900 MPS 95035 814-C1
BIG BEND DR
1500 MPS 95035 794-D7
BIGELOW CT
6000 SJS 95123 875-B6
BIGGS CT
600 SJS 95136 874-F2
BIGHORN CT
48700 FRMT 94539 793-J2
BIGOAK CT
1000 SJS 95129 852-H3
BIGOAK DR
5500 SJS 95129 852-H3
BIG OAK LN
- MPS 95035 793-J3
BIG SUR DR
1000 SJS 95120 894-H4
BIG TALK CT
1200 SJS 95120 874-C7
BIG WOOD DR
2900 SJS 95127 834-H2
BIKINI AV
1900 SJS 95122 854-H1
BILBO CT
1300 SJS 95121 855-A4
BILBO DR
3000 SJS 95121 855-A4
BILICH PL
10100 CPTO 95014 832-F7
BILLY WRIGHT RD
- MerC - (1002-H6
See Page 1001)
BILTMORE LN
- MLPK 94025 790-C6
BIMBER CT
3100 SJS 95148 835-D7
BIMMERLE PL
900 SJS 95123 874-E5
BING DR
800 SCL 95051 832-J5
1300 SJS 95129 852-G4
BINGHAM CT
5300 SJS 95123 874-J3
BIRCH AV
800 SUNV 94086 812-F7
1600 SJS 95125 853-H5
1600 SCIC 95125 853-H5

BIRCH DR
1600 CMBL 95008 853-F5
BIRCH LN
- SCIC 95127 834-H2
BIRCH ST
1800 PA 94306 791-A6
3300 PA 94306 811-C1
BIRCH WY
400 SCL 95051 833-A7
6200 SJS 95138 875-F6
17100 MGH 95037 917-D6
BIRCH GROVE DR
5300 SJS 95123 875-A3
BIRCH HILL WY
26600 LAH 94022 811-B7
BIRCHMEADOW CT
1300 SJS 95131 814-B6
BIRCHMEADOW LN
1300 SJS 95131 814-B6
BIRCH RIDGE CIR
100 SJS 95123 874-G7
BIRCH SPRING CT
11600 CPTO 95014 852-C4
BIRCHTREE LN
2600 SCL 95051 833-B6
BIRCH WOOD CT
100 LGTS 95030 873-A2
BIRCHWOOD CT
600 LALT 94024 831-F1
BIRCHWOOD DR
1200 SUNV 94089 812-J4
BIRCHWOOD LN
3200 SJS 95132 814-E2
BIRD AV
300 SJS 95126 854-A2
400 LGTS 95030 873-A7
400 SJS 95125 854-A2
BIRDSONG ST
500 GIL 95020 977-H1
BIRDVALE WY
- MGH 95037 916-H3
BIRKDALE WY
5000 SJS 95138 855-E7
BIRKENSHAW PL
4500 SJS 95136 874-F2
BIRKHAVEN PL
- SJS 95138 875-G5
BIRMINGHAM CT
4800 SJS 95136 874-G2
BIRMINGHAM DR
4800 SJS 95136 874-G2
BISCAYNE CT
500 MGH 95037 917-A6
BISCAYNE WY
1700 SJS 95122 834-H6
BISCEGLIA AV
- MGH 95037 937-A1
BISCOTTI PL
4000 SJS 95134 813-D2
BISHOP AV
300 SUNV 94086 832-E1
BISHOP CT
8700 SCIC 95020 958-E5
BISHOP LN
- SMCo 94025 810-F1
BISMARCK DR
1000 CMBL 95008 853-B5
1000 SJS 95130 853-B5
1000 SJS 95008 853-B5
BISON CT
6500 SJS 95119 875-D7
BITTERN DR
1300 SUNV 94087 832-E5
BITTERNUT CT
1100 SJS 95131 814-D7
BITTER OAK ST
22100 CPTO 95014 832-A6
22100 LALT 95014 832-A6
BITTERROOT PL
6700 SJS 95120 894-G2
BIXBY DR
100 MPS 95035 794-D7
19700 CPTO 95014 852-F1
BLACHARD RD
600 SJS 95139 895-J2
600 SCIC 95139 895-J2
BLACK RD
18200 SCIC 95030 892-C3
BLACK ARROW RD
- SCIC 95030 892-E4
BLACKBERRY TER
1100 SUNV 94087 832-B3
BLACKBERRY HILL RD
15000 LGTS 95032 893-D2
15000 SCIC 95032 893-D2
BLACKBIRD CT
6000 SJS 95120 874-B7
BLACKBURN AV
100 MLPK 94025 790-J3

BLACKBURN ST
100 WAT 95076 (1015-G1
See Page 995)
BLACKFEET TR
17600 SCIC 95030 913-C2
BLACKFIELD CT
1000 SCL 95051 833-C5
BLACKFIELD DR
1100 SCL 95051 833-C4
BLACKFIELD WY
1000 MTVW 94040 811-F5
BLACKFOOT CT
700 SJS 95123 874-H6
BLACKFORD AV
3700 SJS 95117 853-B2
4000 SJS 95129 853-A2
BLACKFORD CIR
4100 SJS 95117 853-B2
BLACKFORD LN
1600 SCIC 95125 853-H4
1600 SJS 95125 853-H4
BLACKHAWK CT
1400 SUNV 94087 832-E5
5600 SJS 95123 874-H4
BLACKHAWK DR
1500 SUNV 94087 832-E5
BLACKHAWK CANYON RD
4900 SCIC 95020 (976-F3
See Page 955)
BLACKLOCK CT
6000 SJS 95123 875-A6
BLACKMORE CT
1800 SJS 95132 814-D4
BLACK MOUNTAIN CT
900 LALT 94024 831-H2
BLACK MOUNTAIN RD
27100 LAH 94022 830-J1
27600 LAH 94022 831-A1
BLACK MOUNTAIN GRADE
- SCIC 95138 876-F6
BLACK OAK CT
17600 MGH 95037 936-F1
BLACK OAK LN
6100 SJS 95120 874-D7
BLACKOAK WY
5400 SJS 95129 852-H3
BLACK PRINCE CT
600 MGH 95037 937-B5
BLACK RIVER CT
4600 SJS 95136 874-G2
BLACKSMITH DR
1200 GIL 95020 957-F7
BLACKSTONE AV
1400 SJS 95118 874-B1
BLACK WALNUT CT
800 MGH 95037 917-B6
14400 SAR 95070 872-F2
BLACK WALNUT WY
800 MGH 95037 917-B6
BLACKWELDER CT
100 SCIC 94305 790-J7
BLACKWELL DR
300 LGTS 95032 873-D5
BLACKWING WY
1400 GIL 95020 957-E7
BLACKWOOD DR
6300 CPTO 95014 852-F2
BLAIR AV
800 SUNV 94087 832-B1
BLAIR CT
700 SUNV 94087 832-C1
900 PA 94303 791-C5
BLAIRBETH DR
300 SJS 95119 895-D1
BLAIRBURRY WY
500 SJS 95123 874-G4
BLAIRMORE CT
4000 SJS 95121 855-B5
BLAIRWOOD CT
700 SJS 95120 894-H3
BLAISDELL CT
700 SJS 95117 853-D2
BLAKE AV
- SCL 95051 833-A7
- SCrC 95003 (975-A5
See Page 955)
BLAKE CT
900 GIL 95020 977-H3
BLAKE ST
400 MLPK 94025 790-F4
BLAKERIDGE LN
- SCrC 95003 (975-A5
See Page 955)
BLAKE WILBUR DR
900 SCIC 94305 790-G6
900 PA 94304 790-G6
BLALOCK ST
1000 MPS 95035 794-B5

BLANCHARD DR
17500 MSER 95030 873-A5
BLANCHARD WY
700 SUNV 94087 832-C4
BLANCO DR
4600 SJS 95129 853-A3
4700 SJS 95129 852-J3
BLAND AV
100 CMBL 95008 853-D5
BLANDING AV
2100 SJS 95121 855-C3
BLANDOR WY
10500 LAH 94024 831-D5
BLANEY AV
1000 SJS 95129 852-E4
N BLANEY AV
800 CPTO 95014 852-F2
10000 CPTO 95014 832-F6
BLANEY CT
10300 CPTO 95014 852-E1
BLANGE WY
- SJS 95134 813-G2
BLAUER CT
6200 SJS 95135 855-H6
BLAUER DR
20100 SAR 95070 852-E7
BLAUER LN
6200 SJS 95135 855-H6
BLAZINGWOOD AV
800 CPTO 95014 852-F2
BLAZINGWOOD DR
900 SUNV 94089 812-J5
BLAZINGWOOD WY
19700 CPTO 95014 852-F2
BLEDSOE CT
- LAH 94022 831-B3
BLENHEIM AV
2700 SMCo 94063 790-C1
BLENHEIM LN
3400 SJS 95121 855-D3
BLEWETT AV
1100 SJS 95125 854-A3
BLINN CT
600 LALT 94024 811-G6
BLISS AV
2100 MPS 95035 794-E7
BLISS CT
500 SJS 95136 874-F1
BLOCK DR
1100 SCL 95050 833-C4
BLOM DR
500 SJS 95111 875-B1
BLOOMFIELD AV Rt#-25
1800 SCIC 95020 (998-C2
See Page 997)
BLOOMFIELD AV Rt#-G7
1000 SCIC 95020 978-H7
BLOOMFIELD DR
4200 SJS 95124 873-J3
BLOOMFIELD RD
1800 SCIC 95020 (979-A6
See Page 959)
1800 SCIC 95020 978-J6
BLOOMSBURY WY
3600 SJS 95132 814-F2
BLOSSOM AV
5600 SJS 95123 874-H5
BLOSSOM CT
300 SCIC 95037 916-E3
BLOSSOM DR
800 SCL 95050 833-C5
BLOSSOM LN
100 MTVW 94041 811-H5
20500 CPTO 95014 852-D2
BLOSSOM WY
5400 SJS 95123 875-B4
BLOSSOM ACRES DR
5400 SJS 95124 873-F6
BLOSSOM CREST WY
2100 SJS 95124 873-F6
BLOSSOM DALE DR
5400 SJS 95124 873-F6
BLOSSOM GARDENS CIR
5400 SJS 95123 875-A3
BLOSSOM GLEN WY
100 LGTS 95124 873-E5
100 SJS 95124 873-E5
100 LGTS 95032 873-E5
BLOSSOM HILL RD Rt#-G10
- LGTS 95030 873-C6
- SJS 95123 874-E4
100 SJS 95111 875-A4
200 SJS 95138 875-A4
400 LGTS 95032 873-C6
400 SCIC 95123 874-E4
700 SJS 95123 875-A4

STREET
Block City ZIP Pg-Grid

BLOSSOM HILL RD
Rt#-G10
1000 SJS 95193 875-A4
1400 SJS 95124 874-A6
1400 SJS 95124 873-F6
1600 SJS 95118 874-A6
15800 SCIC 95032 873-C6
BLOSSOM PARK LN
5600 SJS 95124 874-A6
5600 SJS 95118 874-A6
BLOSSOM RIVER DR
1000 SJS 95123 874-D4
BLOSSOM RIVER WY
1000 SJS 95123 874-D4
BLOSSOM TERRACE CT
5400 SJS 95124 873-F6
BLOSSOM TREE LN
5400 SJS 95124 873-F6
BLOSSOM VALLEY DR
200 LGTS 95032 873-E5
200 SJS 95124 873-E5
300 LGTS 95124 873-E5
BLOSSOMVIEW DR
3500 SJS 95118 874-B1
BLOSSOM VILLA WY
200 SJS 95124 873-F6
200 LGTS 95032 873-F6
BLOSSOM VISTA AV
5400 SJS 95124 873-F6
BLOSSOM WOOD DR
5400 SJS 95124 873-E6
BLUEBELL AV
2200 SJS 95122 854-J1
BLUEBELL DR
8400 GIL 95020 977-C1
BLUEBELL WY
900 SUNV 94086 832-G1
BLUEBERRY TER
500 SJS 95129 853-B2
BLUEBERRY HILL
100 LGTS 95032 873-D7
BLUEBIRD AV
1000 SCL 95051 832-H5
BLUEBIRD CT
1300 SUNV 94087 832-E4
BLUEBIRD DR
3100 SJS 95117 853-D4
BLUEBONNET CT
1900 MGH 95037 917-D6
BLUEBONNET DR
900 SUNV 94086 832-G1
BLUEBONNET WY
1400 MGH 95037 917-D6
BLUE CREEK CT
3200 SJS 95135 855-E6
BLUE DOLPHIN DR
3600 SJS 95136 854-G7
BLUEFIELD CT
500 SJS 95136 874-F1
BLUEFIELD DR
200 SJS 95136 874-G1
BLUE GRASS CT
3400 MGH 95037 917-G4
BLUEGRASS LN
5600 SJS 95118 874-B5
BLUE GUM CT
15100 SAR 95070 872-G4
BLUE GUM DR
3900 SCIC 95127 835-B1
BLUE HERON CT
9600 GIL 95020 957-E7
BLUE HILL DR
6900 SJS 95129 852-E3
BLUE HILLS DR
21200 SCIC 95070 852-C5
21300 SAR 95070 852-C5
BLUEJACKET WY
2000 SJS 95133 814-E7
BLUE JAY CT
17400 MGH 95037 917-F4
BLUEJAY CT
700 EPA 94303 791-B1
BLUE JAY DR
900 SCIC 95125 854-C6
900 SJS 95125 854-C6
17400 MGH 95037 917-F4
BLUEJAY DR
1600 SUNV 94087 832-E6
10900 CPTO 95014 832-E6
BLUE LAGOON DR
2300 SCL 95054 813-C5
BLUE MEADOWS CT
12400 SAR 95070 852-E5
BLUE MIST PL
1000 SJS 95120 894-F2
BLUE MOUNTAIN DR
3200 SJS 95127 835-B4
BLUE OAK CT
2700 SJS 95148 835-E6
BLUE OAK LN
300 SCIC 94306 811-D5
BLUE OAKS RD
3700 SCIC 95020 958-F2
BLUE PARROT CT
1200 GIL 95020 977-E2
BLUERIDGE AV
2300 MLPK 94025 790-D7
BLUE RIDGE DR
4600 SJS 95129 853-A4
4700 SJS 95129 852-J4
BLUERIDGE DR
2000 MPS 95035 814-E1
BLUERING CT
6000 SJS 95120 874-B7
BLUE ROCK CT
2500 SJS 95133 834-F1
BLUE SAGE DR
700 SUNV 94086 832-F1
BLUE SPRUCE CT
1700 MPS 95035 814-A4
BLUE SPRUCE WY
1700 MPS 95035 813-J3
BLUESTONE CT
2500 SJS 95122 835-A5
BLUEWATER CT
3000 SJS 95148 835-B5
BLUEWOOD CIR
1900 SJS 95132 814-F3
BLUFF CT
- SJS 95135 875-J1
BLUFFWOOD CT
6800 SJS 95120 894-H2
BLYTHE AV
600 SUNV 94086 812-G5
BLYTHE CT
600 SUNV 94086 812-G5
19900 SAR 95070 852-F6
BLYTHSWOOD DR
18500 SCIC 95030 872-H5
18600 MSER 95030 872-H5
BOA VISTA DR
1200 SJS 95122 854-H1
BOBBIE AV
5000 SJS 95130 852-J6
BOBBYWOOD AV
5400 SJS 95124 873-H5
BOBOLINK CIR
500 SUNV 94087 832-E4
BOBOLINK DR
2500 SJS 95125 854-D6
BOBWHITE AV
1300 SUNV 94087 832-E4
BOB WHITE PL
3300 SJS 95131 814-D7
BODEGA DR
1100 SUNV 94086 812-C6
BODEGA WY
300 SJS 95119 875-C7
BODIE CT
5600 SJS 95123 875-A4
BOEGER LN
3500 SJS 95148 835-D5
BOGALUSA CT
600 FRMT 94539 793-J2
BOHANNON DR
1900 SCL 95050 833-D6
BOHLMAN RD
14700 SAR 95070 872-C4
16400 SCIC 95070 872-C5
18700 SCIC 95070 892-D1
BOISE CT
600 SUNV 94087 832-D4
BOISE DR
3900 CMBL 95008 853-B5
3900 SJS 95130 853-B5
BOLADO DR
6900 SJS 95119 875-E7
BOLD CT
600 SJS 95111 875-B1
BOLD DR
600 SJS 95111 875-B1
BOLERO DR
4500 SJS 95111 855-A7
4500 SJS 95111 875-A1
BOLIVAR DR
600 SJS 95123 874-G5
BOLIVAR LN
100 PTLV 94028 810-D5
BOLLINGER RD
5800 SJS 95014 852-D2
5800 SCIC 95014 852-G2
6000 CPTO 95014 852-G2
6400 SJS 95129 852-D2
BOLSA RD
- SBnC - (1019-G2 See Page 999)
400 SCIC 95020 (998-C1 See Page 997)
1300 GIL 95020 978-B7
BOLSENA ST
3300 SJS 95135 855-F6
BOLTON CT
600 SJS 95129 853-A2
BOLTON DR
800 MPS 95035 794-A2
8400 GIL 95020 977-J1
BOLTON PL
- MLPK 94025 790-F5
BONACCORSO PL
600 SJS 95133 814-G7
BONAIR
200 SCIC 94305 790-J7
BONAIR CT
3400 SJS 95117 853-D3
BONANZA CT
600 SUNV 94087 832-D4
BONAVENTURA DR
2600 SJS 95134 813-G6
BONBON DR
2600 SJS 95148 835-C7
BONCHEFF DR
2700 SJS 95133 814-G7
BOND CT
100 LGTS 95032 893-C1
BOND ST
800 SCL 95051 832-J6
BOND WY
700 MTVW 94040 831-H1
BONESO CIR
4100 SJS 95134 813-G2
BONGATE CT
1400 SJS 95130 853-A4
BONITA
- MTVW 94043 811-J2
BONITA AV
- RDWC 94061 790-B1
200 SJS 95116 834-F5
900 MTVW 94040 811-H7
3400 SCL 95051 832-J2
BONITA CT
3400 SCL 95051 832-J2
BONITA DR
18700 MGH 95037 916-H5
BONITA RD
100 SMCo 94028 830-D4
BONNER CT
14900 SCIC 95037 937-C4
BONNET CT
1300 SJS 95132 814-F5
BONNET WY
13400 SAR 95070 852-G7
13500 SAR 95070 872-H1
BONNEVILLE WY
900 SUNV 94087 832-B4
BONNEY ST
100 MTVW 94043 811-G4
BONNIE CT
1400 RDWC 94061 790-A2
BONNIE DR
2500 SCL 95051 833-B2
BONNIE LN
16300 LGTS 95032 873-D7
BONNIE BRAE LN
20100 SAR 95070 872-E4
BONNIE BRAE WY
20000 SAR 95070 872-E3
BONNIE JOY AV
1500 SJS 95129 852-F4
BONNIE RIDGE WY
19700 SAR 95070 852-F7
BONNIE VIEW CT
500 MGH 95037 916-H7
BONNY DR
10100 CPTO 95014 852-D2
BONSEN CT
100 SMCo 94062 790-A4
BON VISTA CT
10000 SCIC 95127 815-C7
10000 SCIC 95127 835-D1
BOOK LN
2100 SCL 95054 813-C4
BOOKER AV
300 SUNV 94086 812-D7
BOOKER CREEK RD
24100 SCIC 95070 871-G3
BOOKSIN AV
1800 SJS 95125 853-J6
2100 SJS 95125 854-A6
2800 SJS 95125 874-A1
BOONE DR
1500 SJS 95118 874-A6
BOONEWOOD CT
700 SJS 95120 894-J2
BORANDA AV
900 MTVW 94040 811-H6
BORAX DR
2400 SCL 95051 833-A1
BORCHERS DR
1900 SJS 95124 873-G1
BORDEAUX DR
1100 SUNV 94089 812-F3
BORDEAUX LN
- SJS 95127 834-C2
BORDELAIS DR
1400 SJS 95118 874-A6
BORDEN DR
3700 SCIC 95148 835-G7
BORDENRAE CT
700 SJS 95117 853-D2
BORDER RD
1000 SCIC 94024 831-F2
BORDER HILL DR
12600 SCIC 94024 831-F2
BORDWELL CT
- SJS 95118 874-B3
BORDWELL DR
4700 SJS 95118 874-B3
BORELLO DR
2400 SJS 95128 853-F4
BORELLO WY
700 MTVW 94041 812-A7
BOREN DR
2400 SJS 95121 854-H2
BORGE CT
3400 SJS 95132 814-G4
BORGES CT
10600 SCIC 95020 958-A3
BORGWOOD CT
800 SJS 95120 894-H4
BORINA DR
4200 SJS 95129 853-A2
4600 SJS 95129 852-J2
BORNEO CIR
5200 SJS 95123 874-J3
BORREGAS AV
500 SUNV 94086 812-F5
900 SUNV 94089 812-F3
BOSCO LN
900 GIL 95020 977-G2
BOSE CT
6500 SJS 95120 894-D1
BOSE LN
6300 SJS 95120 894-D1
6600 SJS 95120 874-D7
BOSTON AV
- SJS 95128 853-G1
- SCIC 95128 853-G1
- SCIC 95128 833-G7
BOSTON POST CT
6500 SJS 95120 894-E1
BOSWALL CT
3200 SJS 95121 855-C3
BOTHELL CIR
6200 SJS 95123 875-A7
BOTHELO AV
100 MPS 95035 794-A7
BOTTLE BRUSH LN
1300 SJS 95118 874-B5
BOUCHARD DR
1400 SJS 95118 874-A6
BOUGAINVILLEA CT
14600 SAR 95070 872-C3
BOUGAINVILLEA DR
5000 SJS 95111 875-A2
BOULAY CT
- SCIC 95037 896-C7
BOULDER BLVD
- SJS 95193 875-C4
BOULDER DR
700 SJS 95132 815-A4
BOULDER ST
200 MPS 95035 794-A3
BOULDER MTN WY
6500 SJS 95120 874-F7
BOUNTIFUL ACRES WY
19100 SAR 95070 872-G5
BOURBON CT
800 MTVW 94041 812-A7
BOURET DR
1200 SJS 95118 874-B3
BOURGEOIS WY
3100 SJS 95111 854-H5
BOURNEMOUTH CT
3500 SJS 95136 874-D1
BOURNEMOUTH DR
3500 SJS 95136 874-D1
BOUVERON CT
2800 SJS 95148 855-D2
BOW WY
- PTLV 94028 810-B6
BOWDEN AV
14900 SCIC 95037 936-J5
BOWDEN CT
17000 SCIC 95037 937-A6
17000 SCIC 95037 936-J6
BOWDOIN CT
700 SCIC 94305 790-H7
900 SCIC 94305 810-J1
2000 PA 94306 810-J1
BOWDOIN ST
2200 PA 94306 811-A1
BOWE AV
1400 SCL 95051 833-B4
BOWEN AV
- SCrC 95076 (975-C7 See Page 955)
800 SJS 95123 874-E5
BOWEN CT
5900 SJS 95123 874-E5
BOWERS AV
1700 SCL 95051 833-B2
2900 SCL 95051 813-B7
3000 SCL 95054 813-B7
BOWHILL CT
20900 SAR 95070 852-C5
BOWLING LN
1600 SJS 95118 873-J4
BOWLING GREEN DR
1600 SJS 95121 855-A2
BOX CANYON RD
1300 SJS 95120 894-D3
BOXLEAF CT
400 SJS 95117 853-C1
BOXWOOD DR
2200 SJS 95128 833-E6
2400 SCL 95128 833-E6
BOYCE AV
800 PA 94301 791-A4
BOYCE LN
20700 SAR 95070 872-C1
BOYD CT
6000 SJS 95123 875-A6
BOYD ST
200 MPS 95035 794-A3
BOYNTON AV
300 SJS 95117 853-C1
BOYSEA DR
1400 SJS 95118 874-B2
BOYSOL CT
3500 SJS 95132 814-F2
BRACCIANO CT
3200 SJS 95135 855-F6
BRACE AV
1100 SJS 95125 854-A4
BRACEBRIDGE CT
1100 CMBL 95008 873-B2
BRACH WY
3600 SCL 95051 832-H4
BRACKETT AV
2800 SJS 95148 835-D7
BRADBURY DR
2900 SJS 95122 855-B3
BRADBURY LN
200 RDWC 94061 790-B2
BRADDALE AV
1400 LALT 94024 831-J3
BRADDOCK CT
1600 SJS 95125 853-G5
BRADEN CT
3300 SJS 95148 835-E7
BRADFORD DR
100 SUNV 94089 812-F4
BRADFORD WY
1600 MGH 95037 917-D6
1700 SJS 95124 873-H2
BRADLEY AV
300 SCIC 95128 853-F1
300 SJS 95128 853-F1
BRADLEY CT
- SMCo 94061 790-B4
BRADLEY WY
1000 EPA 94303 791-A1
BRADSHAW DR
3000 SJS 95148 855-D1
BRADWELL CT
100 SJS 95138 875-E4
BRADY CT
2600 SCL 95051 833-B3
BRADY PL
- MLPK 94025 790-H2
BRAEBRIDGE RD
1300 SJS 95131 814-D7
BRAEBURN CT
3900 SJS 95130 853-B4
BRAEMAR CT
19500 SAR 95070 852-F7
BRAEMAR DR
19500 SAR 95070 852-F7
19500 SAR 95070 872-F1
BRAEMER CT
1100 SJS 95132 814-F5
BRAHMS AV
2500 SJS 95122 855-A1
BRAHMS CT
1900 SJS 95122 855-A1
BRAHMS WY
100 SUNV 94087 832-E2
BRALY AV
1500 MPS 95035 794-D6
BRAMBLE TR
18100 SCIC 95030 912-G4
BRANBURY DR
100 CMBL 95008 853-C5
BRANBURY WY
900 SJS 95133 834-E1
1000 SJS 95133 814-E7
BRANDEIS CT
2900 SJS 95148 855-D4
BRANDERMILL CT
700 SJS 95138 875-G5
BRANDON WY
300 MLPK 94025 790-F6
BRANDY LN
1000 SJS 95132 814-G5
BRANDYBUCK WY
1100 SJS 95121 855-A4
BRANDYWINE CT
12900 SAR 95070 852-D6
BRANDYWINE DR
3000 SJS 95121 855-A3
12800 SAR 95070 852-D7
BRANHAM LN
100 SJS 95136 874-G2
500 SCIC 95136 874-G2
1300 SJS 95118 874-B3
1700 SJS 95124 874-B3
2000 SJS 95118 873-H4
2000 SJS 95124 873-H4
14800 SCIC 95124 873-H4
BRANHAM LN E
200 SJS 95111 875-A2
400 SJS 95138 875-D2
BRANNAN PL
2400 SCL 95050 833-C5
BRANNER DR
- SMCo 94025 790-E7
- SMCo 94025 810-E1
2300 MLPK 94025 790-E7
2300 MLPK 94025 810-E1
BRANSTON CT
14700 SCIC 95037 937-A5
BRANTLEY DR
1900 SJS 95131 814-D7
BRAQUET LN
900 SJS 95120 894-H2
BRASILIA WY
5800 SJS 95120 874-D5
BRASSWOOD CT
400 SCL 95054 813-F6
BRATER CT
1900 SJS 95131 814-D7
BRAVO CT
12700 SCIC 95046 937-H6
BRAXTON DR
600 SJS 95111 875-B1
BRAY AV
2000 SCL 95050 833-C4
BREECH AV
100 SCL 95051 833-C7
100 SCL 95051 853-C1
BREEN CT
3000 SJS 95121 855-A4
BREEZEWOOD CT
1100 SUNV 94089 812-J4
BREEZYGLEN CT
500 SJS 95133 834-F1
BREGA CT
2200 MGH 95037 917-E6
BREGA LN
2200 MGH 95037 917-E6
BREM LN
6500 GIL 95020 978-B4
BREMERTON DR
800 SUNV 94087 832-C4
BRENDA AV
5300 SJS 95124 873-J5
BRENDA CT
19900 CPTO 95014 852-F1
BRENDA LEE DR
600 SJS 95123 874-H7
BRENDEL DR
12800 LAH 94022 831-C1
BRENFORD DR
2500 SJS 95122 834-J5
BRENNAN AV
500 SJS 95131 813-H6
BRENNER WY
1500 SJS 95118 874-A5
BRENNING DR
2400 SJS 95111 854-G3
BRENT CT
- MLPK 94025 790-C7
BRENT DR
800 CPTO 95014 852-F2
BRENTON AV
1200 SJS 95129 852-J4
BRENTON CT
100 MTVW 94043 812-A5
BRENTWOOD CT
700 LALT 94024 831-G2
2200 EPA 94303 791-C2
BRENTWOOD DR
- SJS 95131 814-A5
600 SJS 95129 853-A2
600 SJS 95129 852-J3
BRENTWOOD LN
1600 GIL 95020 977-F1
BRENTWOOD PL
700 LALT 94024 831-G2
BRENTWOOD ST
1200 LALT 94024 831-G2
BRET AV
10000 SCIC 95014 852-H1
BRET COVE CT
100 SJS 95120 894-G2
BRET HARTE CT
100 SCL 95050 833-D7
BRET HARTE DR
6600 SJS 95120 894-F2
BRET HARTE ST
1800 PA 94303 791-B5
BRET HILL CT
100 SJS 95120 894-G2
BRET KNOLL CT
100 SJS 95120 894-G2
BRETMOOR WY
1100 SJS 95129 852-F4
BREWER AV
10400 CPTO 95014 832-C7
BREWINGTON AV
400 WAT 95076 995-G7
BREWSTER AV
4900 SJS 95124 873-F4
15000 SCIC 95124 873-F4
BREWSTER LN
1500 SCIC 95037 936-H4
BRIAN CT
300 SJS 95123 875-B6
1400 MPS 95035 794-C5
BRIAN LN
- SCL 95051 833-A7
BRIANA CT
900 SJS 95120 894-H2
BRIAR CT
13400 SAR 95070 852-E7
BRIARBERRY CT
1200 SJS 95131 814-D7
BRIARBERRY LN
1300 GIL 95020 957-E7
BRIARBROOK CT
3500 SJS 95132 814-F2
BRIARBUSH CT
1700 SJS 95131 814-D7
BRIARCLIFF CT
600 SCL 95051 832-J6
BRIARCLIFF DR
600 SJS 95123 874-G5
BRIARCREEK CT
1200 SJS 95131 814-C7
BRIARCREST CT
1600 SJS 95131 834-C1
BRIARCREST DR
1200 SJS 95131 834-C1
1200 SJS 95131 814-C7
BRIARGLEN DR
3900 SJS 95118 874-C1
BRIARLEAF CIR
1200 SJS 95131 834-C1
BRIARPOINT DR
1600 SJS 95131 834-C1
BRIAR RANCH LN
600 SJS 95120 894-G4
BRIAR RIDGE DR
5600 SJS 95123 874-G7
BRIARTREE DR
1400 SJS 95131 834-C1
BRIARWOOD CT
1100 LALT 94024 831-G2
BRIARWOOD DR
200 SJS 95131 814-A4
1700 SCL 95051 832-J3
2100 SJS 95125 853-J6
2600 SJS 95125 854-A7
2700 SJS 95125 874-A1
2800 SJS 95118 874-A1
BRIARWOOD WY
100 LGTS 95032 873-G6
700 SCIC 95008 853-F7
4100 PA 94306 811-E2
BRICE CT
100 SJS 95111 875-A2
BRICKWAY
- LGTS 95030 873-B6
BRIDAL PTH
- SJS 95123 854-G4
BRIDAL PLACE CT
3600 SJS 95121 855-B4
BRIDGE CT
7100 SJS 95120 894-G4
BRIDGECASTLE CT
2000 SJS 95121 855-C5
BRIDGE PARK CT
11500 CPTO 95014 852-C4
BRIDGEPORT CT
3600 SJS 95117 853-C3
BRIDGEPORT LAKE DR
5800 SJS 95123 874-G7
BRIDGET DR
700 SJS 95136 874-E1
BRIDGETON CT
100 LALT 94022 811-D6
BRIDGEWOOD WY
900 SUNV 94089 812-J5
BRIDLE LN
100 SJS 95120 894-G2
BRIDLE PATH CT
2100 SCIC 95046 938-A7
BRIDLE WY
5800 SJS 95123 874-J5
BRIDLE PATH CT
2400 SCIC 95020 958-C2
BRIDLE PATH DR
2400 SCIC 95020 958-C1
BRIDLE RIDGE CT
5000 SJS 95138 855-E5
BRIGADOON WY
3200 SJS 95121 855-C3
BRIGANTINE DR
6100 SJS 95129 852-G3
BRIGGS CT
200 SJS 95139 895-F1
BRIGGS RD
- HOLL - (1019-J7 See Page 999)
- SBnC - (1019-J7 See Page 999)
BRIGHAM RD
16200 SCIC 95030 872-G7
BRIGHTEN AV
1700 SJS 95124 873-H2
BRIGHT OAK PL
1000 SJS 95120 894-F2
BRIGHT OAKS CT
1300 LALT 94024 831-J3
BRIGHTON LN
200 RDWC 94061 790-B2
BRIGHTON PL
1000 MTVW 94040 811-F5
BRIGHTSIDE CT
1100 SJS 95127 835-A4
BRIGHTWOOD CT
3100 SJS 95148 835-D7
BRIGHTWOOD DR
2800 SJS 95148 835-D7
BRILL CT
100 SJS 95116 834-G2
BRINDOS CT
- SJS 95123 874-F7
BRIONES CT
27600 LAH 94022 830-H1
BRIONES WY
12300 LAH 94022 830-H1
BRIONNE DR
5600 SJS 95118 874-A6
BRISBANE CT
7100 SJS 95129 852-E4
BRISBANE TER
100 SUNV 94086 812-E7
BRISBANE WY
7100 SJS 95129 852-E4
BRISTLECONE CT
1400 GIL 95020 977-G3
BRISTOL DR
2700 SJS 95127 835-A5
BRISTOL WY
- RDWC 94061 790-A3
BRISTOLWOOD LN
2100 SJS 95132 814-E2
BRITT WY
2400 SJS 95148 855-B1
2500 SJS 95148 835-C7
BRITTANY CT
- SJS 95135 855-F3
9000 GIL 95020 977-H1
10200 CPTO 95014 852-E1
BRITTANY MEADOWS
- ATN 94027 790-E3
BRITTON AV
100 ATN 94027 790-E3
300 SUNV 94086 832-F1
1100 SJS 95125 854-A3
1200 SJS 95125 853-J4
N BRITTON AV
500 SUNV 94086 812-G6
S BRITTON AV
300 SUNV 94086 812-G7
BRITWELL CT
4400 SJS 95136 874-F2
BRIXTON CT
1800 SJS 95132 814-E3
BROADACRES DR
6500 SJS 95120 894-B2
BROAD ACRES RD
- ATN 94027 790-C5
BROADLEAF LN
800 SJS 95128 833-F7
BROADMOOR DR
700 SJS 95129 853-A2
BROADVIEW DR
- SCIC 95030 913-A1
10300 SCIC 95127 835-B2
BROADWAY
- LGTS 95030 892-J1
- LGTS 95030 872-J7
1000 SJS 95125 854-A2
21400 SCIC 95030 912-J2
BROADWAY CT
1000 SJS 95125 854-A2
BROADWAY ST
400 GIL 95020 977-H2
BROCASTLE WY
100 LGTS 95030 873-B4
BROCK WY
3900 SJS 95111 855-A6
3900 SCIC 95111 855-A6
BROCKENHURST DR
300 SJS 95119 895-D1
BROCKHAMPTON CT
1000 SJS 95136 874-C2
BROCKTON LN
19100 SAR 95070 852-G6
BRODERICK DR
400 SJS 95111 875-C2
BRODERICK WY
2700 MTVW 94043 791-G7
BRODIE DR
3300 SJS 95111 854-J5
3400 SJS 95111 855-A5
BRODIN LN
- SCrC 95003 (975-A5 See Page 955)
BROKAW RD
- SJS 95131 833-H1
- SJS 95110 833-H1
- SJS 95112 833-H1
200 SCL 95050 833-F3
E BROKAW RD
100 SJS 95112 833-H1
100 SJS 95131 833-H1
200 SJS 95112 813-J7
200 SJS 95131 813-J7
600 SJS 95112 814-A7
600 SJS 95131 814-A7
BROKEN ARROW DR
5000 SJS 95136 874-H2
5000 SJS 95136 875-A2
BROKEN LANCE CT
5200 SJS 95136 875-B3
BROKEN OAK CT
2800 SJS 95148 835-E7
BROMLEY CROSS DR
200 SJS 95119 895-D1
BRONSON AV
14500 SCIC 95124 873-G3
BROOK LN
19000 SAR 95070 852-G5
BROOK PL
1300 MTVW 94040 832-A2
BROOKDALE AV
1200 MTVW 94040 811-G7
BROOKDALE DR
1400 SJS 95125 853-J4
3200 SCL 95051 833-A5
3300 SCL 95051 832-J5
BROOKE ACRES CT
16200 LGTS 95032 893-D1
BROOKE ACRES DR
16200 LGTS 95032 873-D7
16200 LGTS 95032 893-D1
BROOK ESTATES CT
3000 SJS 95135 855-G5
BROOKFIELD AV
1200 SUNV 94087 832-B1
BROOK GLEN DR
- SJS 95129 852-G6
12100 SAR 95070 852-G6
BROOKGLEN DR
1300 SJS 95129 852-G5
11800 SAR 95070 852-G5
BROOKGROVE LN
800 CPTO 95014 852-G2
BROOKHAVEN DR
19000 SAR 95070 852-G4
BROOKHOLLOW DR
- SJS 95132 814-E5
BROOKHOLLOW LN
500 SBnC - (1019-D5 See Page 999)
BROOK HOLLOW RD
1000 SBnC - (1019-B4 See Page 999)
BROOKHURST CT
5600 SJS 95129 852-H4
BROOKINGS LN
- SUNV 94024 832-A4
BROOK LEAF CT
3300 SJS 95132 814-G4
BROOKLINE DR
800 SUNV 94087 832-C1
BROOKLYN AV
- LGTS 95032 893-A1
- SJS 95126 833-G7
300 SJS 95128 833-G7
1200 SCIC 95128 833-G7
1400 SCIC 95128 853-G1
BROOKMERE DR
300 SJS 95123 875-B7
BROOKMILL RD
1400 LALT 94024 832-A3
BROOKMONT CT
- MGH 95037 937-A1
BROOKNOLL CT
19100 SAR 95070 852-G4
BROOKRIDGE DR
11800 SAR 95070 852-G5
BROOKS AV
200 LGTS 95030 872-J7
500 SJS 95125 854-A2
BROOKSIDE AV
- SCL 95117 833-C7
- SCL 95117 853-C1
BROOKSIDE DR
100 PTLV 94028 810-B7
BROOKSTONE CT
- MPS 95035 794-C2
BROOKTREE CT
7100 SJS 95120 894-H3
BROOKTREE WY
7000 SJS 95120 894-H2
BROOKVALE DR
1500 SJS 95129 852-E4
BROOKVIEW CT
1000 MGH 95037 937-B6
BROOKVIEW DR
19000 SAR 95070 852-G5
BROOKWELL DR
10700 CPTO 95014 852-F2
BROOKWOOD AV
300 SJS 95116 834-E6
BROOKWOOD LN
20500 SAR 95070 872-D2
BROWER AV
3300 MTVW 94040 832-A2
BROWN AV
2000 SCL 95051 833-A2
12900 SCIC 95111 854-H6
BROWN CT
2000 SCL 95051 833-B3
BROWN RD
100 SBnC - (1017-G7 See Page 997)
BROWN ST
300 SJS 95125 854-B1
BROWNHILL CT
3200 SJS 95135 855-E2
BROWNING AV
200 SCIC 95008 873-D3
3100 SJS 95124 873-G2
BROWNS LN
14300 LGTS 95030 873-B2
BROWNSTONE CT
2500 SJS 95122 835-A5
BROWNS VALLEY RD
800 SCrC 95076 955-D7
BROWNVIEW DR
6500 SJS 95120 894-C2
BROWNWOOD WY
3600 SCL 95054 813-F6
BRUCE AV
400 SJS 95110 833-J5
17600 LGTS 95030 873-A5
17600 MSER 95030 873-A5
BRUCE CT
2800 SCL 95051 833-B2
15800 MSER 95030 873-A5
BRUCE DR
800 PA 94303 791-D6
BRUCE WY
1100 SCIC 95120 894-H5
BRUCITO AV
1100 LALT 94024 831-H4
BRUCKNER CIR
1100 MTVW 94040 832-A2
BRULE CT
14900 SCIC 95127 835-B1
BRUNDAGE WY
10900 SCIC 95127 815-B6

SANTA CLARA CO.

STREET
Block City ZIP Pg-Grid

BRUNNHILDE WY
1500 SJS 95121 854-J4
BRUNO CT
- SJS 95136 854-F7
BRUNO DR
- SJS 95136 854-F7
BRUNSWICK AV
4400 SJS 95124 873-F3
BRUSH RD
20700 SCIC 95030 912-H1
BRUSHCREEK CT
1600 SJS 95121 855-D7
BRUSHCREEK WY
1600 SJS 95121 855-D7
BRUSHGLEN WY
2300 SJS 95133 834-F2
BRUT WY
4200 SJS 95135 855-G3
BRYAN AV
400 SUNV 94086 832-E1
1100 SJS 95118 874-B2
BRYANT AV
100 MTVW 94040 831-J2
700 MTVW 94040 832-A2
BRYANT CT
300 PA 94301 790-H4
BRYANT ST
100 MTVW 94041 811-H5
100 PA 94301 790-H4
1000 PA 94301 791-B6
2500 PA 94306 791-C7
3200 PA 94306 811-D1
BRYANT WY
900 SUNV 94087 832-G4
BRYCE CT
500 MPS 95035 794-D7
BRYCE DR
300 MGH 95037 937-A2
800 SJS 95123 874-F4
BRYSON AV
500 PA 94306 791-C6
BRYSON CT
15200 SCIC 95037 937-A5
BUBB RD
800 CPTO 95014 852-C1
BUBBLINGWELL PL
6600 SJS 95120 894-F1
BUCHANAN CT
- EPA 94303 791-C1
1000 SCL 95051 833-B5
BUCHANAN DR
1100 SCL 95051 833-B4
BUCHER AV
500 SCL 95051 833-B6
BUCHER DR
15900 SCIC 95037 936-J3
BUCHSER WY
800 SJS 95125 854-B3
BUCK CT
100 WDSD 94062 790-A5
BUCKEYE
- PTLV 94028 830-C1
BUCKEYE CT
800 MPS 95035 813-J3
900 SUNV 94086 832-G2
BUCKEYE DR
500 SJS 95111 854-J6
1500 MPS 95035 813-J3
BUCKHAVEN DR
7600 SJS 95135 856-A6
BUCKHAVEN LN
19800 SAR 95070 852-F7
BUCKHILL CT
2500 SJS 95148 835-C6
BUCKINGHAM AV
- SMCo 94063 790-C1
BUCKINGHAM CT
19100 SAR 95070 872-G1
BUCKINGHAM DR
100 SCL 95051 833-B7
100 SCL 95051 853-B1
1000 LALT 94024 831-H2
3300 SJS 95118 874-C1
BUCKINGHAM PARK CT
400 SJS 95136 874-G1
BUCKLEY ST
3600 SCL 95051 832-H3
BUCKNALL RD
1600 CMBL 95008 853-A6
2000 SJS 95008 853-B6
4300 SJS 95130 853-A6
4500 SJS 95130 852-J6
18500 SAR 95070 852-H6
BUCKNAM AV
800 CMBL 95008 873-B1
BUCKNAM CT
1100 CMBL 95008 873-B1
BUCKNER DR
3400 SCIC 95127 835-A3
3400 SJS 95127 835-A3

BUCKSKIN CT
16600 MGH 95037 917-F6
BUCKTHORN WY
- ATN 94025 790-E2
- MLPK 94025 790-E2
BUCKTHORNE WY
1300 SJS 95129 852-E4
BUCKWOOD CT
800 SJS 95120 894-H3
BUDD AV
- CMBL 95008 853-C7
BUDD CT
600 CMBL 95008 853-C7
BUDDLAWN WY
600 CMBL 95008 853-C7
BUEHLER RD
- MntC - (1017-A4
See Page 997)
BUENA CREST CT
2600 SJS 95121 855-F5
BUENA KNOLL CT
2600 SJS 95121 855-F4
BUENA LUNA
1400 SJS 95128 853-F4
BUENA MONTE DR
20500 SCIC 95120 894-J1
BUENA PARK CT
4300 SJS 95121 855-F4
BUENA POINT CT
2600 SJS 95121 855-F4
BUENA VIEW CT
- SJS 95121 855-F4
BUENA VISTA AV
- GIL 95020 957-H5
100 SUNV 94086 812-C6
100 SCIC 95020 957-H5
300 SCIC 95126 853-H1
300 SJS 95126 853-H1
400 SMCo 94061 790-B3
700 SCIC 95020 958-A5
17100 LGTS 95030 873-B4
BUENA VISTA DR
- SCrC 95019 995-A5
100 SJS 95131 814-A5
100 WAT 95019 995-A5
400 SCrC 95076 995-A5
400 WAT 95076 995-A5
11500 LAH 94022 830-H2
BUFFETT PL
6000 SJS 95123 874-E6
BUFKIN CT
5800 SJS 95123 875-A5
BUFKIN DR
5900 SJS 95123 875-A6
BUGATTI CT
400 SJS 95123 874-H3
BUGATTI PL
700 MGH 95037 917-B6
BUGGYWHIP CT
6600 SJS 95120 894-C5
BULLDOG BLVD
1000 SJS 95116 834-D4
BULLION CIR
1300 SJS 95120 874-B6
BULLION CT
1400 SJS 95120 874-B6
BULLION PL
1400 SJS 95120 874-B6
BUNCE CT
1100 SJS 95132 814-G5
BUNDY AV
300 SJS 95117 853-D2
300 SCIC 95117 853-D1
BUNKER CT
2800 SJS 95121 855-A2
BUNKER HILL CT
6600 SJS 95120 894-C5
BUNKER HILL LN
2800 SCL 95054 813-A3
BURBANK DR
800 SCL 95051 832-J5
BURBANK ST
- SCIC 95046 937-E6
BURCHELL AV
5800 SJS 95120 874-B6
BURCHELL CT
5900 SJS 95120 874-B7
BURCHELL RD
8100 GIL 95020 977-B1
8100 SCIC 95020 977-B1
8900 SCIC 95020 957-A7
9800 SCIC 95020 956-J7
BURCH HAVEN RD
- MerC - (1002-H6
See Page 1001)
BURDETT WY
1100 MPS 95035 794-C5
BURDETTE DR
1600 SJS 95121 854-J1

BURDICK WY
2800 SJS 95148 855-C1
BURGESS DR
300 MLPK 94025 790-G4
BURGOYNE ST
300 MTVW 94043 811-H3
BURGUNDY CT
1200 SJS 95132 814-H5
BURGUNDY DR
3300 SJS 95132 814-G5
BURGUNDY WY
19400 SAR 95070 872-F3
BURKE DR
400 GIL 95020 978-A1
4500 SCL 95054 813-D4
BURKE LN
13200 LAH 94022 811-D7
BURKE RD
13100 LAH 94022 831-C1
13300 LAH 94022 811-D7
16700 LGTS 95032 873-J7
16700 SJS 95120 873-J7
16700 SJS 95124 873-J7
BURKE ST
400 SJS 95112 854-F3
BURKETTE DR
1200 SJS 95129 853-A4
BURL CT
2800 SJS 95121 855-E3
BURL WY
2700 SJS 95121 855-E3
BURLEY DR
1600 MPS 95035 794-D6
BURLINGAME WY
2600 SJS 95121 855-D3
BURLINGTON ST
- SJS 95193 875-C4
BURLWOOD DR
900 SJS 95120 894-G2
BURMAN DR
900 SJS 95111 855-A6
BURNBANK PL
6000 SJS 95120 874-C7
BURNETT AV
100 MGH 95037 916-H3
100 SCIC 95037 916-H3
300 SCL 95051 833-A7
1000 SCIC 95037 917-A1
BURNETT DR
20900 SAR 95070 852-C5
BURNHAM CT
100 CMBL 95008 853-B5
BURNHAM DR
1100 SJS 95132 814-F5
BURNHAM WY
2400 PA 94303 791-D5
BURNING TREE CT
6900 SJS 95119 875-E7
BURNING TREE DR
200 SJS 95119 875-E7
200 SJS 95119 895-E1
BURNLEY WY
1100 SCL 95051 832-H4
1100 SUNV 94087 832-H4
BURNS AV
100 ATN 94027 790-E2
BURNS WY
14200 SAR 95070 872-D2
BURNSIDE DR
6800 SJS 95120 894-G3
BURNTWOOD AV
1000 SUNV 94089 812-J5
BURNTWOOD CT
1100 SUNV 94089 812-J5
BURREL CT
1400 SJS 95126 833-G6
BURROWS RD
1200 CMBL 95008 873-B2
BURTON AV
- SJS 95110 834-A3
- SJS 95112 834-A3
BURTON DR
3900 SCL 95054 813-D5
BURTON RD
16100 LGTS 95032 873-D3
BUSH CIR
- SCIC 94043 812-A2
BUSH ST
- SJS 95126 834-A7
100 MTVW 94041 811-J6
BUSHNELL RD
- SCIC 94035 812-B2
- SCIC 94043 812-B2
BUSINESS CIR
2200 SJS 95128 853-F1
BUSKIRK ST
100 MPS 95035 793-J3
200 MPS 95035 794-A3
BUTANO AV
100 SUNV 94086 812-B6

BUTANO CT
6100 SJS 95123 874-G6
BUTANO DR
1600 MPS 95035 814-E2
BUTANO TER
14700 SAR 95070 872-D3
BUTCH DR
2500 SCIC 95020 958-D1
BUTCHER DR
3400 SCL 95051 832-J5
BUTLER ST
- MPS 95035 793-J7
BUTTE CT
1000 SUNV 94087 832-B4
BUTTE ST
2800 SCL 95051 833-A4
BUTTERCUP LN
1000 GIL 95020 977-G2
BUTTERFIELD BLVD
- MGH 95037 916-J5
18500 MGH 95037 917-A7
BUTTERFLY DR
1200 SJS 95120 874-C7
BUTTERFLY LN
3200 SCIC 95037 917-F4
BUTTITTA LN
1400 SCL 95051 833-A4
BUTTONWOOD CT
2700 SJS 95148 835-E6
BYERLEY AV
700 SJS 95125 854-B5
BYERLY CT
10100 CPTO 95014 831-J7
BYERS DR
1900 MLPK 94025 791-A2
BYERS ST
1000 GIL 95020 977-H3
BYINGTON DR
4800 SJS 95121 855-F5
4800 SJS 95138 855-F5
BYRD LN
13000 LAH 94022 810-J7
BYRNE AV
10000 CPTO 95014 852-B1
10300 SCIC 95014 852-B1
BYRNE PARK LN
27100 LAH 94022 830-J2
BYRON DR
1900 SJS 95124 873-G2
BYRON ST
100 PA 94301 790-J3
600 PA 94306 811-F2
1100 PA 94301 791-A4
2700 PA 94306 791-C6

C

S C RD
- SUNV 94089 812-J3
C ST
- CPTO 95014 831-H5
- MTVW 94043 812-B5
100 MLPK 94025 790-G3
1100 SUNV 94089 812-E2
CABALLO CT
1100 SJS 95132 814-G5
CABALLO LN
- SCIC 94304 810-F6
CABANA DR
1600 SCIC 95125 853-H6
CABERNET CT
8200 SJS 95135 855-J6
CABERNET DR
18700 SAR 95070 852-H5
CABERNET WY
48800 FRMT 94539 794-A2
CABERNET VINEYARDS CIR
3600 SJS 95117 853-C2
CABERNET VINEYARDS CT
900 SJS 95117 853-C2
CABOT AV
- SCL 95051 852-J1
CABOT PL
1100 SJS 95129 852-F3
CABRAL AV
5800 SJS 95123 874-F5
CABRILLO AV
600 SCIC 94305 810-H1
1200 SCL 95050 833-D3
1300 SJS 95132 814-E5
2400 SCL 95051 833-B2
3300 SCL 95051 832-J3
CABRILLO CT
2000 SCL 95051 833-B3
CABRILLO DR
800 SJS 95131 814-A5
CABRILLO HWY Rt#-1
- SCrC - 955-A6

CABRILLO HWY Rt#-1
- WAT - 995-A6
CABRILLO RD
2000 SJS 95134 813-G3
CACTUS DR
5500 SJS 95123 875-B4
CADBURRY CT
500 SJS 95123 874-G4
CADET PL
900 SJS 95133 814-E7
CADILLAC CT
900 MPS 95035 793-H5
CADILLAC DR
3100 SJS 95117 853-D4
CADIZ DR
5800 SJS 95123 874-F5
CADMILL CT
2800 SJS 95121 854-J4
CADWALLADER AV
3500 SJS 95121 855-D3
CADWELL CT
100 SJS 95138 875-D4
CAGGIANO CT
1000 SJS 95120 894-G3
CAGGIANO DR
1000 SJS 95120 894-G3
CAHALAN AV
5600 SJS 95123 874-G4
CAHALAN CT
700 SJS 95123 874-G4
CAHEN DR
7100 SJS 95120 894-H4
CAHILL ST
- SJS 95110 834-A6
- SJS 95113 834-A6
CAIRO CT
10000 SCIC 95127 835-A3
CALABAZAS BLVD
1300 SCL 95051 833-A2
CALABAZAS CT
1300 SCL 95051 833-A4
CALABAZAS CREEK CIR
6900 SJS 95129 852-E4
CALABRESE WY
1500 GIL 95020 977-F2
CALADO AV
100 CMBL 95008 853-A5
400 SJS 95130 853-A5
CALADO CT
1600 CMBL 95008 853-A5
CALAIS CT
4700 SJS 95124 874-A3
CALARO CT
2300 MGH 95037 917-E6
CALAVERAS AV
1400 SJS 95126 833-H7
CALAVERAS BLVD
1100 MPS 95035 794-D6
CALAVERAS BLVD Rt#-237
100 MPS 95035 794-A7
100 MPS 95035 793-J7
CALAVERAS CT
- MPS 95035 794-C6
CALAVERAS RD
2000 MPS 95035 794-E6
3600 SCIC 95035 794-H5
3900 SCIC 95140 794-J2
CALAVERAS RIDGE DR
800 MPS 95035 794-C4
CALBOONYA CT
1600 SJS 95125 854-D3
CALBORO DR
1000 SJS 95117 853-D3
CALCATERRA CT
1100 SJS 95120 894-G3
CALCATERRA DR
7000 SJS 95120 894-G3
CALCATERRA PL
300 PA 94306 811-E2
CALDERON AV
100 MTVW 94041 811-J6
CALDERWOOD LN
5200 SJS 95118 874-B4
CALDWELL AV
200 LGTS 95032 873-B7
CALDWELL CT
- SCIC 95037 896-C7
1200 SUNV 94024 832-A4
CALDWELL PL
700 SCL 95051 833-B5
CALEB CT
2100 SJS 95121 855-C4
CALEDONIA DR
7900 SJS 95135 855-J5
7900 SJS 95135 856-A6
CALERA CREEK HEIGHTS DR
1600 MPS 95035 794-C3

CALERO AV
200 SJS 95123 874-F5
700 SJS 95123 875-A5
CALERO ST
600 MPS 95035 793-J6
CALERO HILLS CT
7100 SJS 95139 895-H2
CALFHILL CT
- LGTS 95032 873-B6
CALGARY CT
10100 SCIC 95127 835-B3
CALGARY DR
1700 SUNV 94087 832-B6
CALHOUN ST
800 SJS 95116 834-D5
CALI AV
20400 CPTO 95014 852-E1
CALICO AV
3300 SJS 95124 873-F2
3600 SCIC 95124 873-F2
CALICO CT
700 SUNV 94086 832-F1
2600 MGH 95037 917-F6
CALICO TRAIL RDGE
- MGH 95037 917-G4
- SCIC 95037 917-G4
CALICOWOOD PL
5100 SJS 95111 875-C2
CALIDA DR
4900 SJS 95136 874-F2
CALIENTE DR
600 SUNV 94086 812-G5
CALIENTE WY
1400 SJS 95132 814-E4
CALIFORNIA AV
- PA 94301 791-B6
- SCIC 95046 937-D6
100 PA 94306 791-A7
400 SCL 95050 833-D5
500 PA 94305 791-A7
700 PA 94303 791-C5
700 PA 94304 811-A1
900 SJS 95125 854-B4
900 SUNV 94086 812-G7
1600 PA 94305 811-A1
1700 SCIC 94305 811-A1
E CALIFORNIA AV
100 SUNV 94086 812-F7
W CALIFORNIA AV
100 SUNV 94086 812-D6
CALIFORNIA CIR
1200 MPS 95035 793-H4
CALIFORNIA ST
200 CMBL 95008 853-D7
500 MTVW 94041 811-G4
1900 MTVW 94040 811-F3
CALIFORNIA OAK WY
10000 CPTO 95014 831-J7
CALINOMA DR
1500 SJS 95118 874-A5
CALIRI CT
8600 SCIC 95020 958-E5
CALISTOGA DR
1800 SJS 95124 873-H1
CALISTOGA WY
- MTVW 94043 812-A5
CALLA DR
700 SUNV 94086 832-F2
CALLADO WY
- ATN 94027 790-C5
CALLAN ST
100 MPS 95035 794-A3
CALLE ALEGRE
1400 SJS 95120 874-B7
CALLE ALFREDO
- SUNV 94089 812-G4
CALLE ALICIA
- SUNV 94089 812-H4
CALLE ALMADEN
5900 SJS 95120 874-D6
CALLE ALOUDRA
5400 SJS 95111 875-C3
CALLE ANITA
- SUNV 94089 812-H4
CALLE ARTIS
700 SJS 95131 814-A5
CALLE ASTA
300 MGH 95037 917-A6
CALLE ATAVIO
400 MGH 95037 937-A1
CALLE BONITA
6200 SJS 95120 874-B7
6200 SJS 95120 894-B1
CALLE CABALLERIA
300 MGH 95037 917-A6
CALLE CABALLERIA CT
17400 MGH 95037 917-A6

CALLE CABEZAL
300 MGH 95037 917-A7
CALLE CARLOTTA
- SUNV 94089 812-J4
CALLE CELESTINA
12300 SCIC 95020 956-J3
CALLE CENTRAL
17700 MGH 95037 917-A6
CALLE CIELO
11800 SCIC 95020 956-J4
CALLECITA
100 LGTS 95030 872-J2
CALLECITA ST
1400 SJS 95125 854-A6
CALLE CONCHITA
- SUNV 94089 812-H4
CALLE CONSUELO
- SUNV 94089 812-H4
CALLE CUERVO
200 SJS 95111 875-C3
CALLE DE AIDA
1500 SJS 95118 874-A3
CALLE DE AMOR
6000 SJS 95124 873-J7
CALLE DE ARROYO
4300 SJS 95118 874-A2
CALLE DE BARCELONA
19300 SCIC 95014 852-G1
CALLE DE CUESTANDA
1200 MPS 95035 814-E1
CALLE DE ESCUELA
4900 SCL 95054 813-C3
CALLE DE FARRAR
4300 SJS 95118 874-B3
CALLE DE FELICE
6000 SJS 95124 873-J7
CALLE DE GILDA
1400 SJS 95118 874-B3
CALLE DE GUADALUPE
- SJS 95116 834-G3
CALLE DE LA PAZ
1400 SJS 95120 874-B7
CALLE DE LAS ESTRELLA
2900 SJS 95148 855-C2
CALLE DE LAS FLORES
2900 SJS 95148 855-B2
CALLE DEL CONEJO
6100 SJS 95120 874-B7
CALLE DEL MUNDO
2300 SCL 95054 813-C3
CALLE DEL PRADO
600 MPS 95035 794-B5
CALLE DEL REY
8700 GIL 95020 977-F1
9000 GIL 95020 957-F7
CALLE DEL SOL
5100 SCL 95054 813-C3
17300 MGH 95037 917-A7
26300 LAH 94022 831-B1
CALLE DE LUCIA
4700 SJS 95124 874-A3
CALLE DE LUNA
2200 SCL 95054 813-C3
CALLE DE PLATA
1700 SJS 95116 834-F3
CALLE DE PRIMAVERA
2000 SCL 95054 813-C4
CALLE DE PROSPERO
1600 SJS 95124 873-J7
CALLE DE RICO
6000 SJS 95124 873-J7
CALLE DE STUARDA
1500 SJS 95118 874-A2
CALLE DE SUERTE
6000 SJS 95124 873-J7
CALLE DE TOSCA
4500 SJS 95118 874-A3
CALLE DE VERDE
800 SJS 95136 874-E2
CALLE DOLORES
- SUNV 94089 812-H4
CALLE DORITA
- SUNV 94089 812-J4
CALLE EL KOWALIK
1600 SJS 95124 874-A3
CALLE EL PADRE
100 LGTS 95030 873-A2
CALLE ENRIQUE
15300 MGH 95037 937-B4
CALLE ESPERANZA
6000 SJS 95120 874-B7
CALLE ESTORIA
100 LGTS 95030 873-A2
CALLE ESTRELLA
- SUNV 94089 812-H4
CALLE EULALIA
- SUNV 94089 812-H4

CALLE GALONDRINA
- SJS 95111 875-C3
CALLE GAVIOTA
300 SJS 95111 875-C3
CALLE GLORIA
- SUNV 94089 812-H4
CALLE HERMOSA
17700 MGH 95037 917-A6
CALLE ISABELLA
- SUNV 94089 812-H4
CALLE JUANITA
- SUNV 94089 812-H4
CALLE LOLITA
200 LGTS 95030 873-A2
CALLE LUCIA
- SUNV 94089 812-H4
CALLE LUPE
1000 SUNV 94089 812-J4
CALLE MARGUERITA
100 LGTS 95030 873-A2
CALLE MARIA
- SUNV 94089 812-J4
CALLE MAZATAN
17200 MGH 95037 917-A6
CALLE MESA ALTA
2000 MPS 95035 814-E2
CALLE MONIZ
19100 SCIC 95037 916-J3
CALLE MONTALVO
20200 SAR 95070 872-E3
CALLE NIVEL
100 LGTS 95030 872-J2
CALLE ORIENTE
1100 MPS 95035 794-C5
CALLE PINTADA
5400 SJS 95111 875-C3
CALLE ROSITA
- SUNV 94089 812-H4
CALLE TACUBA
13600 SAR 95070 872-E1
CALLE TERESA
- SUNV 94089 812-H4
CALLE UVAS
12100 SCIC 95020 956-J3
CALLE VENTURA
1100 SJS 95120 894-E2
CALLE VICTORIA
- SUNV 94089 812-H4
CALLE VISTA VERDE
2100 MPS 95035 814-E1
CALL OF THE WILD RD
21900 SCIC 95030 913-A3
CALMA CT
2500 SJS 95128 853-F4
CALMOR AV
5600 SJS 95123 874-F4
CALMOR CT
5600 SJS 95123 874-F5
CALOOSA CT
1700 SJS 95131 814-D7
CALPELLA DR
500 SJS 95136 874-F2
CALPINE DR
5600 SJS 95123 875-B4
CALUMET CT
1000 SJS 95112 834-D3
CALVARY WY
- SJS 95118 854-C7
CALVELLI CT
3500 SJS 95124 873-E2
CALVERT CT
200 SCL 95051 832-J7
CALVERT DR
200 SCL 95051 832-J7
10100 CPTO 95014 852-H1
10100 SCIC 95014 852-H1
CALVIEW AV
2000 SJS 95122 834-J6
CALVIEW LN
1400 SJS 95122 834-J6
CALVIN AV
3200 SJS 95124 873-F2
3600 SCIC 95124 873-F2
CALWA CT
5000 SJS 95111 875-A2
CALYPSO CT
1100 SJS 95127 835-A4
CALZAR DR
3000 SJS 95118 874-A1
CAMACHO WY
1800 SJS 95132 814-D3
CAMANO CT
1100 SJS 95122 854-H2
CAMARDA CT
20100 CPTO 95014 832-E7
CAMARGO CT
2900 SJS 95132 814-D3
CAMARGO DR
1700 SJS 95132 814-D3

CAMARILLO CT
1000 MPS 95035 794-C4
3200 SJS 95135 855-G4
CAMAS AV
400 SJS 95116 834-J3
CAMBERLEY LN
10100 CPTO 95014 851-J1
CAMBERLY WY
400 RDWC 94061 790-B2
CAMBER TREE CT
1100 SJS 95120 874-D7
CAMBRIAN DR
500 SCIC 95008 853-F7
800 SJS 95008 853-F7
CAMBRIANNA DR
1900 SJS 95124 873-F2
CAMBRIAN VIEW WY
100 LGTS 95032 873-G6
CAMBRIDGE AV
200 PA 94306 791-A7
600 MLPK 94025 790-G5
900 SUNV 94087 832-C1
CAMBRIDGE DR
500 SCL 95051 832-J6
2800 SJS 95125 854-C7
12500 SAR 95070 852-G6
CAMBRIDGE LN
3500 MTVW 94040 831-J2
CAMDEN AV
700 CMBL 95008 853-E7
700 CMBL 95008 873-E1
1000 SJS 95120 894-E1
1000 SCIC 95008 873-E1
1300 SJS 95008 873-E1
1800 SCIC 95124 873-E2
1800 SJS 95120 873-J7
1800 SJS 95124 873-E2
4200 SJS 95118 873-H3
6000 SJS 95120 874-A7
CAMDEN OAKS CT
1500 SJS 95124 874-A6
CAMDEN VILLAGE CIR
1500 SJS 95124 874-A6
1500 SJS 95124 873-J6
CAMDEN VILLAGE CT
5700 SJS 95124 874-A6
CAMELFORD WY
2600 SJS 95127 834-H1
CAMELIA DR
6400 SJS 95120 894-D1
CAMELLIA AV
100 RDWC 94061 790-B2
CAMELLIA CT
- EPA 94303 791-C3
600 LALT 94024 811-G6
CAMELLIA DR
1100 EPA 94303 791-D2
CAMELLIA TER
100 LGTS 95032 873-C6
16100 SCIC 95032 873-C6
CAMELLIA WY
500 LALT 94024 811-F6
900 SJS 95117 853-B3
CAMELOT DR
15100 SCIC 95132 814-H4
CAMEO CT
300 CMBL 95008 853-G7
CAMEO DR
1400 CMBL 95008 853-G6
1400 SJS 95129 852-J4
CAMERON PL
1100 SJS 95129 852-F3
CAMERON WY
3000 SCL 95051 833-A7
CAMILLE CIR
400 SJS 95134 813-H4
CAMILLE CT
300 MTVW 94040 811-H6
1500 SCIC 95037 937-E1
CAMINA ESCUELA
600 SJS 95129 853-A2
CAMINO DR
500 SCL 95050 833-F5
CAMINO AL LAGO
200 ATN 94027 790-C5
200 SMCo 94025 790-C5
CAMINO A LOS CERROS
- ATN 94027 790-C5
- SMCo 94027 790-C5
1800 SMCo 94025 790-C5
CAMINO ARROYO
8000 GIL 95020 978-B1
CAMINO CERRADO
1500 SJS 95128 853-F5
CAMINO DE LAS ROBLES
- PA 94301 790-H5
CAMINO DEL CERRO
100 LGTS 95032 873-E5

CAMINO DEL CERRO
100 SCIC 95032 873-E6
CAMINO DE LOS BARCOS
13900 SAR 95070 872-G1
CAMINO DE LOS ROBLES
- ATN 94027 790-D6
1800 SMCo 94025 790-D6
CAMINO DEL REY
2600 SJS 95132 814-E5
CAMINO DEL SOL
16100 LGTS 95032 873-D4
CAMINO ECCO
2600 SJS 95121 855-A2
CAMINO HERMOSO
23200 LAH 94024 831-E4
CAMINO MEDIO LN
12700 LAH 94022 811-B6
CAMINO MONDE
1500 SJS 95125 853-J4
CAMINO NOLA CT
- SJS 95132 814-E5
CAMINO PABLO
1000 SJS 95125 853-J3
CAMINO POR LOS ARBOLES
- ATN 94027 790-D5
CAMINO RAMON
1000 SJS 95125 853-J4
CAMINO RICARDO
1000 SJS 95125 853-J3
CAMINO RICO
13600 SAR 95070 872-E1
CAMINO ROBLES CT
1400 SJS 95120 874-B7
1400 SJS 95120 894-B1
CAMINO ROBLES WY
1300 SJS 95120 874-B7
1300 SJS 95120 894-B1
CAMINO VERDE DR
6000 SJS 95119 875-C7
CAMINO VISTA DR
10100 CPTO 95014 851-J1
CAMINO VISTA WY
15900 SCIC 95127 815-B6
CAMLOOP DR
2600 SJS 95130 852-J7
CAMP AV
700 MTVW 94043 811-H2
CAMP RD
6700 GIL 95020 977-G5
CAMPANA DR
4000 PA 94306 811-C2
CAMPANULA PL
4800 LGTS 95124 873-E4
CAMPBELL AV
- SCL 95050 833-G4
- SJS 95193 875-C5
500 LALT 94024 811-F7
500 LALT 94024 831-F1
1100 SJS 95126 833-G4
1200 SCL 95126 833-G4
E CAMPBELL AV
- CMBL 95008 853-E6
1500 SCIC 95125 853-G6
W CAMPBELL AV
- CMBL 95008 853-C6
1800 SJS 95008 853-C6
3900 SJS 95130 853-A6
4600 SJS 95130 852-J5
5100 SJS 95129 852-J5
CAMPBELL LN
- MLPK 94025 810-E1
- MLPK 94025 790-E7
CAMPBELL ST
900 MPS 95035 794-B5
CAMPERDOWN WY
1900 SJS 95121 855-C3
CAMPESINO AV
200 PA 94306 791-C7
CAMPHOR AV
100 FRMT 94539 793-H1
CAMPHOR CT
1800 MPS 95035 813-J4
CAMPHOR WY
700 EPA 94303 791-B2
CAMPISI CT
4500 SCIC 95020 (976-J1
See Page 955)
6800 SJS 95120 894-F2
CAMPISI WY
800 CMBL 95008 853-F5
CAMPO RD
100 PTLV 94028 810-C7
CAMPO BELLO
- MLPK 94025 790-E7
CAMPO BELLO CT
- MLPK 94025 790-E7

INDEX

STREET
Block City ZIP Pg-Grid

CAMPOBELLO CT
800 MGH 95037 937-B4
CAMPO CALLE WY
14400 SAR 95070 872-G3
CAMPOLI DR
100 SCIC 95037 916-H5
CAMPOS VERDES
100 LGTS 95032 873-G6
CAMPO VISTA LN
13800 LAH 94022 811-C7
CAMP POMPONIO RD
- SMCo 94020 850-A7
CAMPUS DR
100 SCIC 94305 790-G6
CAMPUS DR E
300 SCIC 94305 810-G1
700 SCIC 94305 790-H7
CAMPUS DR W
100 SCIC 94305 790-F7
900 SCIC 94305 810-F1
900 SCIC 94304 810-F1
CAMROSE AV
2100 SJS 95130 852-J7
CANADA DR
700 MPS 95035 794-B6
CANADA RD
3000 SCIC 95020 978-J2
5500 SCIC 95020 959-C3
CANAL WY
1800 SJS 95131 814-C4
CANARIO WY
12700 LAH 94022 811-A6
CANARY DR
1600 SUNV 94087 832-E6
CANARY LN
1200 SJS 95117 853-D4
CANARY ISLAND CT
2000 SCL 95050 833-C3
CANARY PALM CT
- SJS 95133 814-J4
CANBERRA CT
4700 SJS 95124 873-J3
CANBERRA DR
1600 SJS 95124 873-J3
CANDACE WY
1600 LALT 94024 832-A4
CANDIA DR
1100 SJS 95121 854-H2
CANDLELIGHT WY
1100 CPTO 95014 852-D3
CANDLER AV
14000 SJS 95127 835-B4
CANDLESTICK WY
500 SJS 95127 835-B2
CANDLEWOOD AV
1000 SUNV 94089 812-J5
CANDLEWOOD CT
1100 SUNV 94089 812-J4
6300 CPTO 95014 852-F2
CANDLEWOOD DR
600 CPTO 95014 852-F2
CANDY CT
12200 SAR 95070 852-F5
CANDY LN
12000 SAR 95070 852-F5
CANDY LYNN CT
6100 SJS 95120 874-D7
CANFIELD CT
800 SJS 95136 874-D2
CANMORE CT
2300 SJS 95136 874-J3
CANNA CT
1500 MTVW 94043 811-H4
CANNA LN
1600 SJS 95124 873-J6
CANNES PL
- SJS 95138 875-H1
CANNIKIN CT
200 SJS 95116 834-G4
CANNIKIN DR
200 SJS 95116 834-G4
CANNON RD
1300 SBnC - (1017-G7
See Page 997)
CANOAS GARDEN AV
2100 SJS 95125 854-D5
2400 SCIC 95125 854-D5
CANON DR
15500 SCIC 95030 872-F5
CANONGATE CT
3300 SJS 95121 855-C5
CANON VISTA
11000 SJS 95127 815-A5
11000 SCIC 95127 815-A5
CANOPY CT
- GIL 95020 977-J1
CANTADA CT
3200 SJS 95135 855-G3
CANTATA WY
25200 LAH 94022 831-D2

CANTERBURY CT
6300 SJS 95129 852-F3
CANTERBURY PL
600 MPS 95035 794-B3
CANTERBURY WY
1500 LALT 94024 831-J3
CANTO DR
4900 SJS 95124 873-J4
4900 SJS 95118 873-J4
CANTON DR
1500 SJS 95123 874-H4
1200 MPS 95035 794-C7
CANTOR CT
2700 MGH 95037 917-G6
CANTOR DR
2700 MGH 95037 917-F6
CANYON DR
100 PTLV 94028 810-C7
200 PTLV 94028 830-C1
11000 SCIC 95127 815-A6
CANYON RD
27500 PA 94304 830-H2
27500 SCIC 94304 830-H2
CANYON CREEK DR
3400 SJS 95132 814-G2
CANYON RIDGE DR
3800 SJS 95148 835-G7
CANYON RIVER CT
4700 SJS 95136 874-E2
CANYON TRAIL WY
4800 SJS 95136 874-H2
CANYON VIEW CT
3400 SJS 95132 814-G3
CANYON VIEW DR
1500 SJS 95132 814-G2
20500 SAR 95070 872-C2
22100 CPTO 95014 852-A3
CANYON VISTA CT
10800 CPTO 95014 852-A2
CAPAY CT
4600 SJS 95118 874-B3
CAPAY DR
4600 SJS 95118 874-B3
CAPE ANITA PL
900 SJS 95133 814-E7
CAPE ANN PL
1900 SJS 95133 834-E1
CAPE ASTON CT
1700 SJS 95133 834-D1
CAPE BLANCO CT
500 SUNV 94087 832-D4
CAPE BRETON PL
800 SJS 95133 834-E1
CAPE BUFFALO DR
900 SJS 95133 834-D1
CAPE CANAVERAL PL
900 SJS 95133 834-D1
CAPE COD CT
3600 SJS 95117 853-C3
CAPE COLONY DR
800 SJS 95133 834-E1
CAPE CORAL DR
1700 SJS 95133 834-E1
CAPE DIAMOND DR
800 SJS 95133 834-E1
CAPE FLATTERY PL
800 SJS 95133 834-E1
CAPE GEORGE PL
900 SJS 95133 834-E1
CAPE HATTERAS WY
1700 SJS 95133 834-E1
CAPE HILDA PL
1900 SJS 95133 834-E1
CAPE HORN CT
1700 SJS 95133 834-E1
CAPE HORN DR
1700 SJS 95133 834-E1
CAPE HORN PL
1700 SJS 95133 834-E1
CAPE JASMINE PL
1700 SJS 95133 834-E1
CAPE JESSUP DR
900 SJS 95133 834-E1
CAPE KENNEDY DR
800 SJS 95133 834-E1
CAPELAW CT
3100 SJS 95135 855-F3
CAPELLA WY
200 SUNV 94086 812-E7
CAPE MARY PL
900 SJS 95133 814-E7
CAPE MAY PL
800 SJS 95133 834-E1
CAPE MISTY DR
1700 SJS 95133 834-D1
CAPE MORRIS PL
900 SJS 95133 834-E1
CAPE POINT PL
900 SJS 95133 834-E1

CAPE TOWN PL
800 SJS 95133 834-E1
CAPE TRINITY PL
800 SJS 95133 834-E1
CAPE VERDE PL
800 SJS 95133 834-E1
CAPE VINCENT PL
800 SJS 95133 834-E1
CAPEWOOD CT
2900 SJS 95132 814-D3
CAPEWOOD LN
2800 SJS 95132 814-D3
CAPE YORK PL
800 SJS 95133 834-E1
CAPILANO DR
5700 SJS 95138 855-H7
CAPISTRANO AV
4800 SJS 95129 853-A1
4800 SJS 95129 852-J1
CAPISTRANO DR
2200 SCL 95051 832-J2
CAPISTRANO PL
100 LGTS 95030 873-A3
CAPISTRANO WY
23000 LALT 94024 831-H4
CAPITANCILLOS DR
1500 SJS 95120 874-A7
CAPITANCILLOS PL
1600 SJS 95120 874-A7
CAPITOL AV
- SJS 95116 834-J4
- SJS 95127 834-H2
200 SCIC 95127 834-H2
400 SJS 95133 834-H2
600 SCIC 95133 834-H2
1700 SJS 95127 835-A5
1800 SJS 95148 835-A5
1900 EPA 94303 791-B2
E CAPITOL AV
200 MPS 95035 814-A2
700 SJS 95132 814-A2
N CAPITOL AV
700 SJS 95133 814-F7
700 SCIC 95133 814-F7
900 SJS 95132 814-C4
1700 SJS 95131 814-C4
W CAPITOL AV
100 MPS 95035 814-A2
200 MPS 95035 813-J2
CAPITOL CT
1200 SJS 95127 834-J5
CAPITOL EXWY
100 SJS 95136 854-D7
200 SJS 95136 874-F1
700 SJS 95127 834-J4
700 SJS 95116 834-J4
1000 SJS 95111 854-G7
1000 SJS 95122 834-J4
1000 SCIC 95111 854-G7
1200 SJS 95121 854-G7
1300 SJS 95127 835-A6
1300 SJS 95122 835-A6
1300 SJS 95121 855-B3
1800 SJS 95148 835-A6
2300 SJS 95122 855-B3
2300 SJS 95148 855-B3
CAPITOLA AV
4500 SJS 95111 875-A1
CAPITOLA TER
- FRMT 94539 794-A1
CAPITOLA WY
900 SCL 95051 832-J5
CAPITOL REEF CT
4500 SJS 95136 874-G2
CAPITOL VILLAGE CIR
200 SJS 95136 874-G1
CAPPER CT
- SMCo 94061 790-B4
CAPPY CT
- SJS 95111 875-A2
CAPRI DR
1100 CMBL 95008 873-C2
14100 LGTS 95030 873-C2
CAPRI WY
6500 SJS 95129 852-F3
CAPRIANA CIR
3200 SJS 95135 855-G3
CAPRIC DR
400 SJS 95123 875-B3
CAPRICE CT
500 MGH 95037 917-B7
CAPRICORN CT
400 SJS 95111 854-F6
CAPRISTO CT
19600 SCIC 95037 916-F4
CAPURSO WY
1400 SJS 95125 854-B3
CAPUTO DR
16000 MGH 95037 937-C1

CARACAS CT
2100 SJS 95122 834-J7
CARADO CT
25700 LAH 94022 811-C5
CARASTON WY
2600 SJS 95148 835-C7
2600 SJS 95148 855-C1
CARAVAN WY
- SJS 95123 875-B3
CARAVELLA DR
3700 SJS 95117 853-B4
CARAWAY CT
4500 SJS 95129 853-B2
CARBONERA AV
100 SUNV 94086 812-B7
CARDEL WY
1700 SJS 95032 873-H5
CARDIFF CT
1100 SJS 95117 853-D3
CARDIFF LN
1000 RDWC 94061 790-B2
CARDIFF PL
600 MPS 95035 794-B4
CARDIGAN DR
700 SUNV 94087 832-F4
CARDIN AV
3300 SJS 95118 874-A1
E CARDINAL DR
900 SUNV 94087 832-A2
W CARDINAL DR
800 SUNV 94087 832-B2
CARDINAL LN
100 LGTS 95032 873-C7
2600 SJS 95125 854-B7
CARDINAL WY
1000 PA 94303 791-D5
CARDINGTON DR
2000 SJS 95132 814-D3
CARDONA WY
1200 SJS 95131 814-E7
CARDOZA CT
3400 SJS 95132 814-G3
CARERA CT
- SJS 95123 874-F6
CAREY AV
2900 SCIC 95037 937-H1
2900 SCIC 95037 917-G6
16000 MGH 95037 917-G6
E CARIBBEAN DR
200 SUNV 94089 812-G2
CARIBE WY
300 SJS 95133 834-G2
CARIBOU CT
700 SUNV 94087 832-C4
CARICK PLACE WY
3500 SJS 95121 855-B4
CARIGNANE DR
700 GIL 95020 977-J7
CARILLO LN
13400 LAH 94022 811-A5
CARIS CT
11400 SCIC 95046 957-G3
CARL AV
1500 MPS 95035 794-D6
CARL RD
- SUNV 94089 812-F1
CARL ST
300 SCL 95050 833-F3
CARLA CT
500 MTVW 94040 811-H7
1100 SJS 95120 874-D7
CARLA DR
1100 SJS 95120 874-D7
CARLA WY
700 GIL 95020 977-H1
CARLESTER DR
200 LGTS 95032 873-D4
CARLETON CT
1600 RDWC 94061 790-A2
CARLETON PL
3000 SCL 95051 833-A6
CARLING CT
100 SJS 95111 875-A2
CARLISLE WY
100 SUNV 94087 832-E4
CARLITOS CT
3700 PA 94306 811-B2
E CARLO ST
- MPS 95035 794-A7
CARLOS AV
100 RDWC 94061 790-B1
CARLO SCIMECA CT
2600 SJS 95132 814-F5
CARLO SCIMECA DR
2600 SJS 95132 814-F5
CARLOS PRIVADA
1100 MTVW 94040 832-H6
CARLOTTA CT
700 SJS 95136 874-E1

CARLOW CT
100 SUNV 94087 832-E4
CARLSBAD CT
600 MPS 95035 794-E7
CARLSBAD DR
1100 SJS 95118 874-C4
CARLSBAD RD
48500 FRMT 94539 793-J2
CARLSBAD ST
500 MPS 95035 794-E7
CARLSEN WY
1300 SJS 95118 874-B1
CARLSON CIR
3700 PA 94306 811-E1
CARLSON CT
3800 PA 94306 811-E1
CARLSON DR
16400 SCIC 95037 936-G3
CARLTON AV
100 LGTS 95032 873-D5
1100 MLPK 94025 790-J1
15000 SCIC 95124 873-E4
15000 SJS 95124 873-E4
15600 LGTS 95124 873-E4
CARLTON CT
200 LGTS 95032 873-D4
CARLTON WY
200 LGTS 95032 873-D4
CARLYLE AV
200 GIL 95020 957-H7
CARLYLE CT
200 GIL 95020 977-H1
CARLYN AV
- CMBL 95008 853-D5
CARLYSLE AV
3600 SCL 95051 832-H6
CARLYSLE ST
100 SJS 95113 834-B6
200 SJS 95110 834-A6
CARM AV
5000 SJS 95124 873-H5
5100 SJS 95032 873-H5
CARMEL AV
700 SUNV 94086 812-G5
800 LALT 94022 811-D4
CARMEL CT
900 LALT 94022 811-D4
CARMEL DR
1400 SJS 95125 854-B3
2300 PA 94303 791-D4
CARMEL ST
7200 GIL 95020 977-H1
CARMEL TER
1200 LALT 94024 831-H2
CARMEL WY
100 SMCo 94028 830-D3
1100 SCL 95050 833-D4
CARMELITA DR
100 MTVW 94040 811-J7
CARMEN CT
1400 SJS 95121 854-J2
CARMEN RD
10000 CPTO 95014 852-A1
CARMINE WY
1400 SJS 95131 814-C6
CARMONA CT
10000 CPTO 95014 852-B1
CARNABY CT
4500 SJS 95136 874-E2
CARNADERO RD
800 SCIC 95020 (998-C1
See Page 997)
800 GIL 95020 (998-C1
See Page 997)
900 SCIC 95020 978-C7
900 GIL 95020 978-C7
CARNATION CT
800 LALT 94024 831-E1
CARNATION LN
900 GIL 95020 977-G1
CARNAVON WY
1400 SJS 95131 814-C7
CARNEGIE DR
- MPS 95035 794-D7
CARNEGIE SQ
- SJS 95116 834-D5
CARNELIAN CIR
14500 SAR 95070 872-E2
CARNELIAN DR
1100 SJS 95122 834-G7
CARNELIAN GLEN CT
14500 SAR 95070 872-E3
CARNEROS AV
400 SUNV 94086 812-B7
CARNFORTH CT
1100 SJS 95120 894-G4
CARNIEL AV
12700 SAR 95070 852-D6
CARNIEL CT
12800 SAR 95070 852-D6

CARNIVAL WY
7200 SJS 95120 894-H4
CARNOT DR
1500 SJS 95126 853-H4
CARNOUSTIE CT
22300 CPTO 95014 852-A2
CAROB LN
1500 LALT 94024 831-H3
CAROBWOOD CT
3400 SJS 95132 814-E2
CAROBWOOD LN
2100 SJS 95132 814-E2
CAROL AV
2000 MTVW 94040 831-J1
CAROL DR
2400 SCIC 95125 854-E5
2400 SJS 95125 854-E5
2700 SCIC 95136 854-E5
CAROL LN
12000 SAR 95070 852-E5
CAROLA AV
900 SJS 95130 853-B4
CAROLA CT
4100 SJS 95130 853-B4
CAROLE CT
700 EPA 94303 791-B1
CAROLE WY
1500 RDWC 94061 790-A1
CAROLINA AV
600 SUNV 94086 812-F5
2400 RDWC 94061 790-A3
CAROLINA LN
- ATN 94027 790-C2
200 PA 94306 811-D2
CAROLINE DR
22000 CPTO 95014 832-A6
CAROLINE WY
4800 SJS 95124 873-H4
CAROL LEAF CT
3100 SJS 95148 855-E1
CAROL LEE DR
10100 CPTO 95014 832-E7
CAROLYN AV
1000 SJS 95125 853-J3
1000 SJS 95125 854-A3
CAROLYN CT
500 SUNV 94086 832-E1
10600 SCIC 95020 957-J3
CAROLYN DR
1100 SCL 95050 833-C4
CARON CT
900 SJS 95121 854-H3
CAROUSEL DR
- SJS 95111 854-G4
CARPENTER DR
- SBnC - (1020-G3
See Page 999)
CARPENTER PL
2000 SCL 95051 833-D1
CARPENTERIA RD
200 MntC - (1017-A7
See Page 997)
CARPENTIER WY
400 SJS 95111 854-F6
CARR AV
900 MntC - (1017-B5
See Page 997)
CARR PL
7200 GIL 95020 977-H4
CARRABELLE WY
900 SJS 95120 894-H2
CARRAGATA DR
- SJS 95134 813-D3
CARRIAGE CIR
7700 CPTO 95014 852-C2
CARRIAGE CT
- LALT 94022 811-E5
- MLPK 94025 790-C7
CARRIAGE DR
- GIL 95020 977-E1
300 SCL 95050 833-D6
18200 MGH 95037 916-H6
CARRIAGE COVE CT
3300 SJS 95111 854-J5
CARRIAGE HILL DR
18600 SCIC 95120 894-G1
CARRIAGE LAMP WY
17300 MGH 95037 917-B6
CARRICK AV
13100 SAR 95070 852-H7
CARRICK CT
500 SUNV 94087 832-E4
CARRIE ST
100 SJS 95112 834-C7
CARRIE LEE WY
1100 SJS 95118 874-B1
CARRIL CT
15500 MSER 95030 873-A5
CARRINGTON CIR
- SJS 95125 854-A7

CARRINGTON CIR
27200 LAH 94022 830-J1
CARRINGTON CT
- SJS 95125 854-A7
- SJS 95125 874-B1
CARROLL ST
100 SUNV 94086 812-F7
200 SUNV 94086 832-E1
CARRYBACK AV
5200 SJS 95111 875-C2
CARRYDUFF WY
3700 SJS 95121 855-C4
CARRYWOOD WY
700 SJS 95120 894-J3
CARSON CT
100 SUNV 94086 812-C7
CARSON DR
800 SUNV 94086 812-C6
CARSON WY
900 MPS 95035 794-B4
2700 SJS 95124 873-G1
CARTA BLANCA ST
22200 CPTO 95014 832-A7
CARTAGO CT
200 SJS 95116 834-D2
CARTER AV
- SJS 95118 874-A5
4800 SJS 95118 873-J4
CARTER WY
- MLPK 94025 790-C7
300 SCL 95051 832-J7
CARTERWOOD PL
1300 SJS 95121 854-J2
CARTWRIGHT WY
20200 CPTO 95014 832-E7
CARVER DR
10500 SCIC 95014 852-H2
10700 CPTO 95014 852-H2
CARVER PL
1100 MTVW 94040 811-F5
CARVER ST
500 SCIC 95127 814-H7
500 SJS 95127 814-H7
CARVO CT
1300 LALT 94024 831-H3
CAS DR
3500 SJS 95111 854-H6
CASA CT
1300 SCL 95051 832-H4
CASA LN
17700 MGH 95037 917-B6
17700 SCIC 95037 917-B5
CASABA CREEK CT
1100 SJS 95120 894-G3
CASA BLANCA AV
400 SJS 95129 852-J1
CASABLANCA CIR
1400 GIL 95020 977-E2
CASA BLANCA LN
18600 SAR 95070 872-H1
CASA BONITA CT
700 LALT 94024 831-F1
CASA DE FRUTA PKWY
6400 SCIC 95020 (980-C6
See Page 959)
CASA DE PINO WY
- SCIC 95014 851-E4
CASA DE PONSELLE
1500 SJS 95118 874-A3
CASA GRANDE
100 LGTS 95030 872-J2
CASA GRANDE AV
- MTVW 94043 812-A2
CASA GRANDE CT
2700 MGH 95037 917-F6
4100 SJS 95118 874-C2
CASA GRANDE WY
3900 SJS 95118 874-B2
CASALINO CT
3400 SJS 95148 835-D6
CASA LOMA CT
400 SJS 95129 852-B7
CASA LOMA RD
300 SCIC 95037 935-A3
300 SCIC 95037 915-G4
300 SJS 95141 915-G4
29000 SCIC 95037 934-F3
29000 SCIC 95030 934-F3
CASALS CT
2800 SJS 95148 855-D4
CASA MADEIRA LN
4300 SCIC 95127 835-F4
CASA MIA DR
2000 SJS 95124 873-F2
CASA MIA WY
12400 SCIC 94024 831-E2
12400 LAH 94024 831-E2
CASANUEVA PL
900 SCIC 94305 810-J2

CASA VERDE AV
4900 SJS 95129 852-B7
CASA VIEW DR
- SJS 95129 852-J1
CASCADE CT
1000 MLPK 94025 790-C6
CASCADE DR
500 SUNV 94087 832-C4
700 SJS 95129 853-A2
1000 MLPK 94025 790-C6
CASCADE ST
2200 MPS 95035 814-E1
CASCADE TER
- SUNV 94087 832-D4
CASCADES CT
300 MGH 95037 937-A2
CASCADITA TER
400 MPS 95035 793-G3
CASCO CT
2600 SJS 95121 854-H3
CASEY AV
2500 MTVW 94043 791-F6
CASEY ST
- GIL 95020 977-J1
CASEY WY
2600 SJS 95121 855-D3
CASHDAN CT
3300 SCL 95051 833-A1
CASHEW BLOSSOM DR
- SJS 95123 875-A3
CASHMERE CT
500 SUNV 94087 832-D4
CASHMERE TER
- SUNV 94087 832-D4
CASINO REAL
15700 MGH 95037 937-A4
CASITA CT
400 LALT 94022 811-F5
400 SJS 95129 852-B7
CASITA WY
400 LALT 94022 811-F5
CASITAS BULEVAR
100 LGTS 95030 872-J2
CASPER ST
- MPS 95035 793-J7
CASPIAN CT
100 SUNV 94089 812-F2
CASPIAN DR
200 SUNV 94089 812-G2
CASPIAN SEA DR
1200 SJS 95126 853-G3
CASS PL
10100 CPTO 95014 852-A1
CASS WY
3700 PA 94306 811-C2
CASSADAY CT
600 SJS 95136 874-E1
CASSANDRA WY
- MTVW 94043 812-A4
CASSATT WY
500 SJS 95125 854-C4
CASSERLY RD
100 SCrC 95076 995-J1
CASSIA WY
1000 SUNV 94086 832-G2
CASSIAR DR
1600 SJS 95130 853-B5
CASSLAND CT
1300 SJS 95131 814-D7
CASSWELL CT
100 SJS 95138 875-D4
CASSWOOD CT
700 SJS 95120 894-J3
CASTANO DR
5800 SJS 95129 852-G2
CASTANO CORTE
500 LALT 94022 811-E5
N CASTANYA WY
100 SMCo 94028 810-E3
S CASTANYA WY
200 SMCo 94028 810-E4
CASTELLO DR
6000 SJS 95120 874-C7
CASTELLO WY
2500 SCL 95051 832-J1
CASTERWOOD CT
700 SJS 95120 894-H2
CASTILE CT
2300 SJS 95125 853-J7
CASTILLEJA AV
1400 PA 94301 791-A6
1400 PA 94301 790-J6
1500 PA 94306 791-A6
CASTILLEJA CT
900 LALT 94024 831-H2
CASTILLON WY
100 SJS 95119 875-C6
CASTINE AV
10300 CPTO 95014 832-C7

CASTLE DR
2800 SJS 95125 854-C7
CASTLE WY
1100 MLPK 94025 790-F4
CASTLEBRIDGE DR
- SJS 95116 834-G3
CASTLEBROOK CT
1700 SJS 95133 834-E3
CASTLEBURY DR
1900 SJS 95116 834-G3
CASTLE CANYON WY
3100 SJS 95135 876-A2
CASTLECREST DR
- SJS 95116 834-G3
CASTLEGATE DR
1700 SJS 95132 814-E3
CASTLE GLEN AV
5400 SJS 95129 852-H3
CASTLE HILL DR
18300 MGH 95037 916-F6
CASTLE HILL WY
20500 SCIC 95030 912-J1
CASTLEKNOLL DR
6100 SJS 95129 852-C7
CASTLE LAKE CIR
1100 MGH 95037 916-G6
CASTLE LAKE DR
18600 MGH 95037 916-G6
CASTLEMAINE CT
- SJS 95136 854-E6
CASTLE MANOR DR
5400 SJS 95129 852-H4
CASTLEMONT AV
1200 SJS 95128 853-E4
CASTLE RIDGE DR
18300 MGH 95037 916-F6
CASTLEROCK CT
500 SUNV 94087 832-D4
CASTLEROCK DR
6800 SJS 95120 894-E3
CASTLEROCK TER
500 SUNV 94087 832-D4
CASTLETON CT
2500 SJS 95148 855-C1
CASTLETON DR
2500 SJS 95148 855-C1
CASTLETON ST
21500 CPTO 95014 852-B3
CASTLETON TER
1300 SUNV 94087 832-H4
CASTLETON WY
1000 SUNV 94087 832-H4
CASTLETREE CT
1700 SJS 95131 814-C5
CASTLEWOOD CT
4900 SJS 95129 852-J2
CASTLEWOOD DR
800 LGTS 95030 873-B2
4600 SJS 95129 853-A3
4600 SJS 95129 852-J2
CASTRO CT
300 CMBL 95008 853-A5
CASTRO DR
1700 CMBL 95008 853-A6
1700 SJS 95130 853-A6
CASTRO PL
2300 SCL 95050 833-C3
CASTRO ST
100 MTVW 94041 811-H5
1000 MTVW 94040 811-H5
CASTRO VALLEY RD
1100 SCIC 95020 997-G2
CASUAL CT
6800 SJS 95120 894-F2
CASUAL WY
1100 SJS 95120 894-F2
CATALA CT
600 SCL 95050 833-D5
CATALDI DR
2900 SJS 95132 814-E4
CATALINA AV
3100 SCL 95051 833-A5
CATALINA CT
- LALT 94022 811-E5
8100 GIL 95020 977-F2
11200 CPTO 95014 852-B3
CATALINA DR
4500 SJS 95129 853-A3
CATALINA WY
600 LALT 94022 811-E5
CATALONIA WY
1600 SJS 95125 853-J7
CATALPA DR
- ATN 94027 790-F1
CATALPA LN
- CMBL 95008 853-D6
CATAMARAN ST
6500 SJS 95119 875-D7
CATHARINE CT
26200 LAH 94022 811-B6

CATHAY DR
1100 SJS 95122 834-H5
CATHCART WY
1000 SCIC 94305 811-A2
1000 SCIC 94305 810-J2
CATHEDRAL DR
700 SUNV 94087 832-C4
CATHERINE CT
600 GIL 95020 977-J5
CATHERINE ST
900 SJS 95002 793-B7
1600 SCL 95050 833-D4
CATHY PL
- MLPK 94025 790-F5
CATKIN CT
800 SJS 95128 853-F2
CATRINA CT
5100 SJS 95124 873-G5
CATRON DR
23200 SCIC 95030 913-C6
CAUDILL RD
300 SCrC 95076 (975-C2
See Page 955)
CAUDILLO TER
400 MPS 95035 793-H3
CAUSEY LN
200 LGTS 95032 873-C7
CAVALIER CT
400 LALT 94022 811-D4
1800 SJS 95124 853-G7
CAVENDISH DR
3300 SJS 95132 814-F3
CAXTON CT
3900 SJS 95130 853-B4
CAYMAN PL
3100 SJS 95127 814-G6
CAYMAN WY
900 SJS 95127 814-G6
CAYMUS CT
100 SUNV 94086 812-C6
CAYUGA CT
600 SJS 95123 874-H7
CAYUGA DR
600 SJS 95123 874-H7
CEANOTHUS LN
6200 SJS 95119 875-D5
CEBALO LN
- ATN 94027 790-C1
CEBU CT
6400 SJS 95119 875-C7
CECALA DR
6000 SJS 95120 874-C7
CECELIA CT
500 LALT 94022 811-F5
CECELIA WY
2000 LALT 94022 811-F5
2000 MTVW 94040 811-F6
CECIL AV
- SCIC 95128 853-F1
- SJS 95128 853-F1
3100 SCL 95117 833-D7
3100 SCL 95117 853-C1
CEDAR AV
800 SUNV 94086 812-F7
2000 SMCo 94025 790-D6
CEDAR CT
- MPS 95035 814-A3
- SMCo 94025 790-D6
1300 GIL 95020 977-G3
CEDAR DR
500 WAT 95076 995-J7
CEDAR LN
- SCIC 95127 834-H2
6200 SJS 95138 875-F6
CEDAR PL
1400 LALT 94024 831-J6
CEDAR ST
1100 PA 94301 791-B4
CEDAR WY
- MPS 95035 814-A3
400 SCL 95051 833-B7
CEDAR BROOK
100 MTVW 94041 811-J6
CEDAR BROOK TER
20500 CPTO 95014 832-D6
CEDARCREEK CT
1600 SJS 95121 855-D7
CEDARCREEK DR
3400 SJS 95121 855-D7
CEDARCREST LN
3100 SJS 95132 814-E3
CEDAR CREST PL
100 LGTS 95030 873-B3
CEDARDALE CT
2800 SJS 95148 835-E6
CEDARDALE DR
3400 SJS 95148 835-E7
CEDAR FLAT CT
3500 SJS 95127 835-C3

STREET
Block City ZIP Pg-Grid

CEDAR GABLES DR
1100 SJS 95118 874-C2
CEDARGATE LN
100 SJS 95136 874-J3
CEDAR GROVE CIR
5300 SJS 95123 875-A3
5300 SJS 95123 874-J3
CEDARHURST LN
- SJS 95136 874-D2
CEDARMEADOW CT
1300 SJS 95131 814-B6
CEDARMEADOW LN
1700 SJS 95131 814-B6
CEDAR RIDGE CT
3000 SJS 95148 835-G7
CEDAR SPRING CT
11500 CPTO 95014 852-C4
CEDAR TREE CT
10500 CPTO 95014 832-E7
CEDAR TREE LN
20000 CPTO 95014 832-E6
CEDARVILLE LN
700 SCIC 95133 834-F1
700 SJS 95133 834-F1
CEDARWOOD DR
- SJS 95131 814-A4
CEDARWOOD LN
2100 SJS 95125 853-J6
CEDARWOOD WY
1100 RDWC 94061 790-B2
CEDRO ST
300 SJS 95111 854-H6
CEDRO WY
700 SCIC 94305 810-J2
CEFALU DR
3600 SJS 95124 873-J2
CELEBRATION CT
600 SJS 95134 813-F3
CELEO LN
10600 SCIC 95127 815-B7
CELESTE CIR
20600 CPTO 95014 832-D6
CELESTINE AV
2200 SJS 95125 854-C5
CELIA WY
900 PA 94303 791-D5
CELILO DR
1000 SUNV 94087 832-B4
CENTENNIAL BLVD
4900 SCL 95054 813-C4
CENTENNIAL CT
1300 SJS 95129 852-G4
CENTER AV
10000 SCIC 95020 958-A3
11100 SCIC 95020 957-J1
12000 SCIC 95046 937-G3
12000 SCIC 95046 957-J1
CENTER DR
500 PA 94301 791-B3
CENTER RD
3100 SJS 95134 813-F3
CENTER ST
100 RDWC 94061 790-B1
CENTERHART CT
5200 SJS 95123 874-F7
CENTER RIDGE DR
1600 SJS 95121 855-A2
CENTERWOOD CT
2800 SJS 95148 835-D7
CENTERWOOD WY
3000 SJS 95148 835-D7
CENTRAL AV
- LGTS 95032 893-A2
- MGH 95037 917-A6
- MGH 95037 916-J7
- MTVW 94043 811-J4
- RDWC 94061 790-B1
200 SUNV 94086 812-A4
200 SUNV 94086 832-E1
300 MLPK 94025 791-A3
600 MTVW 94043 812-A4
E CENTRAL AV
- MGH 95037 917-A6
- SCIC 95037 917-A6
N CENTRAL AV
- CMBL 95008 853-E5
1000 CMBL 95128 853-E3
1100 SJS 95128 853-E3
W CENTRAL AV
- LGTS 95032 893-A1
CENTRAL CT
- LGTS 95032 893-A1
CENTRAL DR
- MLPK 94025 790-J1
27600 LAH 94022 830-H2
CENTRAL EXWY
Rt#-G6
- MTVW 94041 812-B5
- MTVW 94043 812-B5
- MTVW 94086 812-B5

CENTRAL EXWY
Rt#-G6
- PA 94306 811-G3
- SCL 94086 812-H7
- SCL 95051 812-H7
- SUNV 94086 813-A7
- SUNV 94086 812-H7
100 MTVW 94043 811-G3
700 SCL 95050 833-D1
700 SCL 95054 833-D1
800 MTVW 94041 811-G3
800 SCL 95054 833-D1
2000 MTVW 94040 811-G3
2400 SCL 95051 833-D1
2700 SCL 95051 813-A7
2700 SCL 95054 813-A7
3000 SUNV 95054 813-A7
CENTRAL WY
600 SCIC 95128 853-F2
2200 SJS 95128 853-F2
CENTRALIA CT
500 SUNV 94087 832-D4
CENTRAL PARK DR
2100 CMBL 95008 853-E7
2100 SJS 95008 853-E7
CENTRE ST
- MTVW 94041 811-J6
CENTRE POINTE DR
1400 MPS 95035 814-B3
CENTURY CT
800 CMBL 95008 853-C7
CENTURY DR
300 CMBL 95008 853-C7
3400 SJS 95008 853-C7
6400 SJS 95129 852-F3
CENTURY CENTER CT
- SJS 95110 833-H2
CENTURY CROSS CT
400 SJS 95111 875-C3
CENTURY HILL CT
5400 SJS 95111 875-C3
CENTURY MANOR CT
5500 SJS 95111 875-C3
CENTURY MEADOW CT
5400 SJS 95111 875-C3
CENTURY OAKS CT
400 SJS 95111 875-C3
CENTURY OAKS WY
400 SJS 95111 875-C3
CENTURY PARK WY
5400 SJS 95111 875-C3
CENTURY PLAZA WY
5400 SJS 95111 875-C3
CERA DR
900 SJS 95129 853-A3
CEREUS CT
48400 FRMT 94539 793-J1
CEREZA DR
700 PA 94306 811-C2
CERRITO AV
100 RDWC 94061 790-A4
100 SMCo 94061 790-A4
CERRITO CT
3300 SJS 95148 835-D7
CERRITO PL
- SMCo 94061 790-A4
CERRITO WY
3200 SJS 95148 835-D7
CERRO CHICO
200 LGTS 95032 873-C7
CERRO KAMUK CT
2100 SJS 95116 834-F3
CERROS MNR
- SMCo 94025 790-D5
CERRO TERBI CT
2100 SJS 95116 834-G3
CERRO VERDE
1300 SJS 95120 894-B1
CERRO VISTA CT
2700 MGH 95037 917-F6
15900 LGTS 95032 873-D7
CERRO VISTA DR
15900 LGTS 95032 873-D7
15900 LGTS 95032 893-E1
16600 MGH 95037 917-F6
CERVANTES RD
100 PTLV 94028 810-C5
CERVANTES WY
2200 SJS 95008 853-C7
CERVANTEZ CT
1000 MPS 95035 794-C4
CESANO CT
400 PA 94306 811-D3
CESSNA CT
6300 SJS 95123 874-J7
CESTARIC DR
400 MPS 95035 794-C5
CEYLON AV
1900 SJS 95122 834-J7

CEYLON CT
2100 SJS 95122 834-J7
CEYNOWA LN
- SJS 95121 855-C3
CEZANNE DR
600 SUNV 94086 832-E2
800 SUNV 94087 832-E2
CHABLIS CIR
1100 SCL 95050 833-D4
3500 SJS 95132 814-H4
CHABLIS CT
19300 SAR 95070 872-G3
CHABOT TER
2400 PA 94303 791-D4
CHABOT WY
1400 SJS 95122 834-J5
CHABOYA CT
4200 SCIC 95148 835-H7
CHABOYA RD
3800 SJS 95148 855-G1
4000 SCIC 95148 855-H1
4000 SCIC 95148 835-H7
CHABOYA HILLS CT
4200 SCIC 95148 835-G7
CHABRANT WY
900 SJS 95125 854-A3
CHACE DR
10400 CPTO 95014 832-A7
10500 SCIC 94024 832-A7
CHAD DR
300 MPS 95035 794-A5
CHADBOURNE LN
18300 MSER 95030 872-J4
CHADWICK CT
21100 SAR 95070 852-C7
CHADWICK PL
11100 CPTO 95014 852-B3
CHADWICK ST
7200 GIL 95020 977-H4
CHALET AV
100 SJS 95127 834-H1
CHALET LN
20300 SAR 95070 872-E1
CHALET PL
100 CMBL 95008 853-F7
CHALET CLOTILDE DR
13400 SAR 95070 852-C7
CHALET WOODS CIR
100 CMBL 95008 853-F6
CHALLENGER AV
200 SJS 95127 834-H1
CHAMBERLAIN DR
3500 SJS 95121 855-C3
CHAMBERS DR
1500 SJS 95118 874-A2
CHAMBERTIN DR
5600 SJS 95118 874-A5
CHAMBERY DR
- SJS 95127 834-J1
CHAMBORD CT
- SJS 95127 834-C2
CHAMISAL AV
300 LALT 94022 811-D6
CHAMPAGNE LN
1100 SJS 95132 814-G5
CHAMPION CT
100 SJS 95134 813-E3
CHANCELLOR WY
3300 SJS 95111 854-F7
CHANDLER CT
5700 SJS 95123 874-J4
CHANDON CT
1300 SJS 95125 853-G4
CHANNEL DR
6200 SJS 95123 874-J7
CHANNEL DR E
- SJS 95002 813-C1
CHANNEL DR W
- SJS 95002 813-B1
CHANNING AV
100 PA 94301 790-J5
400 PA 94301 791-A4
1300 PA 94303 791-C4
2500 SJS 95131 813-F7
CHANT CT
2500 SJS 95122 834-J5
CHANTAL WY
- RDWC 94061 790-A1
CHANTEL CT
6800 SJS 95129 852-E4
CHANTILLEY CT
7100 SJS 95139 895-F1
CHANTILLEY LN
100 SJS 95139 875-F7
100 SJS 95139 895-F1
CHANTILLEY PL
200 SJS 95139 875-F7
CHANTRELLE CT
- GIL 95020 977-F2
CHAPALA DR
3400 SJS 95148 835-D6

CHAPARRAL AV
2200 SJS 95130 852-J6
CHAPARRAL RD
13100 SCIC 95037 956-H1
CHAPARRAL WY
27300 LAH 94022 831-A3
CHAPEL DR
1100 SCL 95050 833-D4
CHAPEL LN
- MLPK 94025 790-J2
CHAPELHAVEN CT
- SJS 95111 874-J1
CHAPEL HILL WY
900 SJS 95122 854-G1
CHAPIN RD
25500 LAH 94022 811-C7
CHAPMAN CT
500 SCL 95050 833-F5
CHAPMAN DR
400 CMBL 95008 873-C1
CHAPMAN ST
500 SJS 95126 833-G5
CHAPPELL CT
- GIL 95020 957-H7
CHARA CT
4900 SJS 95118 873-J5
CHARBONO CT
8300 SJS 95135 855-H6
CHARCOAL RD
- SCIC 95014 851-C6
- SCIC 95030 851-C6
CHARCOAL RD BIKING TR
- SCIC 95030 851-B7
- SCIC 95030 871-B1
CHARCOT AV
100 SJS 95131 814-A6
100 SJS 95131 813-J6
CHARD DR
4000 SJS 95136 874-C1
CHARDONAY CT
8000 SJS 95135 855-H6
CHARDONNAY CT
19500 SAR 95070 852-F7
48800 FRMT 94539 793-J2
CHARDONNAY DR
400 FRMT 94539 793-J2
500 FRMT 94539 794-A2
CHARDONNAY LN
10500 SCIC 94024 831-F5
CHARGER DR
2000 SJS 95131 814-E7
CHARGIN DR
300 MGH 95037 936-J1
CHARING CROSS LN
3400 SJS 95132 814-J2
CHARISE CT
1200 SJS 95120 894-G5
CHARISMA WY
1200 SJS 95131 814-B6
CHARLENE CT
6700 SJS 95129 852-E3
CHARLES AV
100 SUNV 94086 812-D7
28000 LAH 94022 810-J7
28000 LAH 94022 830-J1
CHARLES ST
- LGTS 95032 873-B7
400 SUNV 94086 832-D1
600 SJS 95112 834-B2
CHARLES CALI DR
500 SJS 95117 853-D1
CHARLESTON CT
700 PA 94303 811-E1
CHARLESTON DR
1600 SJS 95130 853-B5
1600 CMBL 95008 853-B5
CHARLESTON RD
1200 MTVW 94043 811-H1
2000 MTVW 94043 812-A1
E CHARLESTON RD
100 PA 94306 811-E1
700 PA 94303 811-E1
900 PA 94043 811-G1
900 MTVW 94043 811-G1
W CHARLESTON RD
100 PA 94306 811-D2
CHARLOTTE AV
15000 SCIC 95124 873-F4
CHARMAIN CIR
600 MTVW 94041 812-A7
CHARMAIN DR
600 CMBL 95008 853-C5
CHARMAT CT
3200 SJS 95135 855-G3
CHARMERAN AV
1800 SJS 95124 873-F3
14500 SCIC 95124 873-F3
CHARMES CT
3200 SJS 95135 855-G3

CHARMGLOW CT
2100 SJS 95121 855-C4
CHARMWOOD CT
1100 SUNV 94089 812-J4
CHARMWOOD SQ
1300 SJS 95117 853-C4
CHARNWOOD CT
1800 SJS 95132 814-E3
CHARSAN LN
11400 CPTO 95014 852-C4
CHARTER HALL CT
3500 SJS 95136 874-D1
CHARTER OAK PL
6600 SJS 95120 894-G1
CHARTER OAKS CIR
100 LGTS 95030 873-C3
CHARTER OAKS DR
200 LGTS 95030 873-C3
CHARTER PARK CT
3600 SJS 95136 854-F7
CHARTER PARK DR
3500 SJS 95136 854-F7
CHARTERS AV
19600 SAR 95070 852-F7
CHARTERS CT
19900 SAR 95070 852-E7
CHASE RD
- SCIC 95030 913-B5
19300 SCIC 95030 892-G5
CHASEWOOD DR
23200 SCIC 95030 913-C6
CHATEAU CT
6800 SJS 95120 894-E2
20100 SAR 95070 852-E7
CHATEAU DR
- LALT 94022 811-E6
- MLPK 94025 790-F3
1100 SJS 95120 894-D2
20000 SAR 95070 852-E6
CHATEAU BOUSSY RD
23500 SCIC 95030 913-B5
CHATEAU DU LAC
- SJS 95148 855-F1
CHATEAU LA SALLE DR
100 SJS 95111 854-F5
CHATHAM CT
- SJS 95139 875-G7
300 MTVW 94040 831-J1
CHATHAM WY
100 MTVW 94040 831-J1
CHATSWORTH LN
400 RDWC 94061 790-B2
CHATSWORTH PL
600 SJS 95128 853-H2
CHAUCER DR
1700 SJS 95116 834-G5
CHAUCER ST
- MLPK 94025 791-A3
400 PA 94301 791-A3
CHAUMONT DR
1500 SJS 95118 874-A6
CHAUNCEY CT
600 SJS 95128 853-H2
CHAUNCEY WY
600 SJS 95128 853-H2
CHAVEZ CT
1400 SJS 95131 814-C7
CHAVEZ WY
1300 SJS 95131 814-C7
CHAVOYA DR
20100 CPTO 95014 832-E7
CHECKERS DR
- SJS 95116 834-F3
400 SJS 95133 834-F3
CHEENEY ST
4000 SCL 95054 813-C4
CHEHALIS DR
900 SUNV 94087 832-B4
CHELAN DR
900 SUNV 94087 832-B4
CHELMSFORD DR
18400 SCIC 95014 852-H2
CHELSEA CRSG
- SJS 95138 875-G5
CHELSEA CT
1300 LALT 94024 831-J3
CHELSEA DR
1300 LALT 94024 831-J3
15000 SCIC 95124 873-F3
CHELSEA WY
100 RDWC 94061 790-B2
CHELTENHAM CT
100 SJS 95139 895-G1
CHELTENHAM PL
100 SJS 95139 895-G1
CHELTENHAM WY
- SJS 95139 875-G7
100 SJS 95139 895-G1

CHEMEKETA CT
700 SJS 95123 874-G4
CHEMEKETA DR
600 SJS 95123 874-G4
CHEMIN DE RIVIERE
3500 SJS 95148 855-F1
CHEMISE DR
900 SJS 95136 874-D1
CHEMOWA CT
700 SUNV 94087 832-C4
CHEN ST
1100 SJS 95131 834-D1
CHENEY CT
1600 SJS 95128 853-G3
CHENEY DR
1700 SJS 95128 853-G3
CHENIN BLANC DR
- FRMT 94539 793-J2
CHENIN BLANC LN
8400 SJS 95135 855-H7
CHERIS CT
5300 SJS 95123 874-J3
CHERIS DR
100 SJS 95123 874-J3
CHEROKEE CT
- PTLV 94028 810-C6
CHEROKEE TR
17600 SCIC 95030 913-A2
CHEROKEE WY
100 PTLV 94028 810-C6
CHERRY AV
200 LALT 94022 811-D5
300 MLPK 94025 790-G3
900 SJS 95126 853-J2
1000 SJS 95125 853-J3
1200 SJS 95125 854-A4
3000 SJS 95118 854-A6
3000 SJS 95118 874-B1
10000 SCIC 95020 958-A4
CHERRY CT
200 MGH 95037 937-B6
900 SJS 95126 853-J3
1300 SJS 95118 874-B2
CHERRY LN
- CMBL 95008 853-D6
900 SCL 95051 832-J5
20100 SAR 95070 852-E6
CHERRY BLOSSOM DR
- SJS 95123 875-A3
CHERRY BLOSSOM LN
- LGTS 95032 873-C6
15600 SCIC 95032 873-D6
CHERRY BROOK LN
5200 SJS 95136 875-E2
CHERRY CANYON RD
23000 SCIC 95120 895-C7
23000 SJS 95120 895-C7
23100 SJS 95120 915-C2
23500 SCIC 95120 915-C2
CHERRY CREEK CIR
800 SJS 95126 853-J2
CHERRY CREST LN
- SJS 95136 875-E2
CHERRYDALE DR
1400 SJS 95125 853-J5
CHERRY GARDEN LN
1400 SJS 95125 854-A7
CHERRY GATE LN
5200 SJS 95136 875-E2
CHERRY GLEN WY
1500 SJS 95125 853-J4
CHERRY GROVE DR
1600 SJS 95125 853-H5
1600 SCIC 95125 853-H5
CHERRY HILL CT
100 LGTS 95030 873-C4
CHERRYHILLS LN
1700 SJS 95125 853-J5
CHERRY OAKS PL
4100 PA 94306 811-C3
CHERRY RIDGE CT
- SJS 95136 875-A3
CHERRY RIDGE LN
- SJS 95136 875-E2
CHERRYSTONE CT
100 LGTS 95032 873-D6
CHERRYSTONE DR
800 LGTS 95032 873-C6
2000 SJS 95128 833-E6
CHERRYSTONE LN
4800 SJS 95129 852-B7
CHERRYTON LN
- SJS 95136 875-A3
CHERRYTREE LN
1700 MTVW 94040 831-G1
10300 CPTO 95014 832-E7
CHERRY VALLEY DR
1400 SJS 95125 853-J4
CHERRYVIEW LN
1100 SJS 95118 874-C3

CHERRY WOOD CT
100 LGTS 95030 873-B2
CHERRYWOOD CT
900 SJS 95129 853-A2
CHERRYWOOD DR
500 SUNV 94087 832-D2
4600 SJS 95129 853-A2
4600 SJS 95129 852-J2
CHERRYWOOD SQ
1300 SJS 95117 853-D4
CHERTSEY CT
1300 SJS 95131 814-E6
CHERYL DR
20600 CPTO 95014 852-D1
CHERYL PL
- MLPK 94025 790-F5
CHERYL WY
2100 SJS 95125 854-A6
CHERYL ANN CT
2700 SJS 95124 873-J1
CHERYL BECK CT
- SJS 95119 875-C6
CHERYL BECK DR
100 SJS 95119 875-C6
CHERYL KEN WY
- SJS 95119 875-D5
CHESAPEAKE CIR
2600 SJS 95148 855-D4
CHESAPEAKE PL
800 GIL 95020 977-H4
CHESAPEAKE TER
1300 SUNV 94089 812-H3
CHESBRO AV
5400 SJS 95123 874-G4
CHESBRO WY
1200 GIL 95020 977-G1
CHESBRO LAKE DR
17200 SCIC 95037 936-D1
CHESHIRE DR
3200 SJS 95118 874-C1
CHESHIRE WY
600 SUNV 94087 832-E4
CHESLEY AV
300 MTVW 94040 831-J1
CHESLEY CT
500 MTVW 94040 831-J1
CHESLEY DR
2100 SJS 95130 853-A7
CHESSINGTON DR
1200 SJS 95131 834-C1
CHESTER AV
13900 SAR 95070 872-G2
CHESTER CIR
- LALT 94022 811-E4
CHESTER ST
- LGTS 95030 873-A6
- SCIC 95046 937-E6
100 MLPK 94025 790-J2
300 MLPK 94025 790-J2
CHESTERFIELD CT
5800 SJS 95138 875-H1
CHESTERTON CIR
1600 SJS 95133 834-D1
CHESTNUT AV
- LGTS 95030 872-H7
100 SUNV 94086 812-E6
200 PA 94306 791-C7
200 PA 94306 811-C1
400 MPS 95035 793-H6
CHESTNUT CT
- MGH 95037 917-F6
- MGH 95037 937-C5
CHESTNUT ST
700 SJS 95110 833-H4
1000 MLPK 94025 790-F3
1600 SCL 95054 813-B5
6600 GIL 95020 978-A2
S CHESTNUT ST
6300 GIL 95020 978-B5
CHESTNUT PARK CT
400 SJS 95136 874-G2
CHESWICK DR
900 SJS 95121 854-H3
CHETAMON CT
1700 SUNV 94087 832-B6
CHETWOOD DR
- MTVW 94043 812-B5
CHEVALIER DR
1700 SJS 95124 873-H5
CHEVERY CT
12500 SAR 95070 852-E6
CHEWPON AV
1200 MPS 95035 814-C2
CHEYENNE DR
500 SUNV 94087 832-D4
CHEYENNE LN
400 SJS 95123 874-H5
CHEYENNE PT
- PTLV 94028 810-C6

CHIALA LN
6800 SJS 95129 852-E3
CHIANTI CT
8300 SJS 95135 855-J6
CHICAGO AV
- LGTS 95032 893-B1
CHICKADEE CT
1400 SUNV 94087 832-E5
CHICKASAW CT
500 SJS 95123 874-H6
CHICO CT
1000 SUNV 94086 812-J5
CHICORY CT
1100 SJS 95120 894-C5
CHIECHI AV
500 SJS 95126 853-H1
CHIESA DR
8100 GIL 95020 977-H2
CHIHONG DR
1400 SJS 95131 814-B7
CHILANIAN LN
1200 SJS 95120 894-G4
CHILBERG CT
400 SJS 95133 834-G2
CHILES CT
5000 SJS 95136 874-F2
CHILES DR
4900 SJS 95136 874-F2
CHILLUM CT
3100 SJS 95148 855-D2
CHILOQUIN CT
500 SUNV 94087 832-D4
CHILTERN WY
2900 SJS 95127 835-A4
CHIMALUS AV
500 PA 94306 811-B2
CHIMAY WY
3000 SJS 95135 855-G4
CHINABERRY CT
400 SJS 95129 853-B2
CHINOOK LN
400 SJS 95123 874-H5
CHIPLAY DR
1300 SJS 95122 834-H6
CHIPMAN DR
900 MPS 95035 814-E1
CHIPPENDALE CT
100 LGTS 95030 873-A3
CHIPPENHAM DR
3000 SJS 95132 814-F4
CHIQUITA AV
200 MTVW 94041 811-G5
CHIQUITA CT
12800 SAR 95070 852-C6
CHIQUITA ST
- SMCo 94028 830-E3
CHIQUITA WY
21000 SAR 95070 852-C7
CHIRCO CT
16700 LGTS 95032 873-C5
CHIRCO DR
16600 LGTS 95032 873-C5
CHIRI CT
1500 SCIC 95046 937-J7
CHISHOLM AV
10400 CPTO 95014 832-C7
CHITAMOOK CT
1700 SUNV 94087 832-B6
CHIVAS CT
3100 SJS 95117 853-D4
CHIVAS PL
3100 SJS 95117 853-D4
CHOCTAW CT
600 SJS 95123 874-H6
CHOCTAW DR
600 SJS 95123 874-G6
CHONA CT
21400 SCIC 95120 895-B4
CHOPIN AV
2600 SJS 95122 855-A2
CHOPIN DR
700 SUNV 94087 832-F3
CHRIS DR
5800 SJS 95123 875-A5
CHRIS LN
1600 SCIC 95046 937-H5
CHRISANDRA LN
7400 SCIC 95020 978-H3
CHRISLAND AV
14400 SCIC 95127 835-A3
CHRISLAND CT
10200 SCIC 95127 835-A2
CHRISMARA CT
1200 SJS 95120 874-C7
CHRISTENSEN DR
21000 CPTO 95014 832-C7
CHRISTEPH DR
18200 MGH 95037 916-G6
CHRISTIE DR
13300 SAR 95070 852-G7

CHRISTINA CT
17400 SCIC 95037 917-D5
CHRISTINA DR
1600 LALT 94024 832-A4
CHRISTINE CT
800 GIL 95020 977-J7
CHRISTINE DR
700 PA 94303 791-E7
CHRISTINE LYNN DR
100 MGH 95037 916-J6
CHRISTOBAL PRIVADA
1200 MTVW 94040 832-A1
CHRISTOPHER AV
- CMBL 95008 853-C6
CHRISTOPHER CT
800 SCL 95051 833-A5
4100 PA 94306 811-F2
CHRISTOPHER ST
1500 SJS 95122 834-G6
CHRISTOPHERS LN
28100 LAH 94022 810-H5
CHROMITE DR
2600 SCL 95051 833-A2
CHUCKWOOD DR
1300 SJS 95131 814-C7
CHUKAR CT
1400 SUNV 94087 832-E5
CHULA VISTA
11000 SCIC 95127 815-A6
CHULA VISTA CT
11300 SCIC 95127 815-A5
CHULA VISTA DR
11000 SCIC 95127 815-A5
CHULA VISTA TER
1000 SUNV 94086 812-C6
CHULETA CT
2100 LALT 94024 831-H5
CHURCH AV
- SCIC 95020 957-H1
- SCIC 95046 957-H1
800 SCIC 95046 938-A7
800 SCIC 95046 937-J7
800 SCIC 95020 938-C7
800 SCIC 95020 937-J7
CHURCH DR
1400 SJS 95118 874-B2
CHURCH ST
- MTVW 94041 811-H5
100 LGTS 95032 893-A1
100 MTVW 94041 812-A6
6400 GIL 95020 978-A3
7300 GIL 95020 977-J1
8900 GIL 95020 957-H7
16000 MGH 95037 937-A1
CHURCHILL AV
- PA 94301 790-A4
- PA 94301 791-A6
- SMCo 94062 790-A4
- PA 94306 791-A6
- WDSD 94062 790-A4
CHURCHILL DR
2100 MPS 95035 794-B2
CHURCHILL PL
100 GIL 95020 978-A5
CHURCHILL RD
- SBnC - (1020-B2
See Page 999)
CHURCHILL PARK DR
400 SJS 95136 874-F3
CHURCHWOOD CT
3100 SJS 95148 855-D1
CHURIN DR
3400 MTVW 94040 831-J2
CHURTON AV
1900 LALT 94024 832-A5
CHYNOWETH AV
100 SJS 95136 874-D3
300 SCIC 95136 874-G3
500 SJS 95123 874-G3
700 SJS 95123 875-A3
700 SJS 95136 875-A3
CHYNOWETH PARK CT
5200 SJS 95136 875-A3
CICERO WY
2800 SJS 95148 855-C1
CICERONE LN
13800 LAH 94022 811-C6
CIELITO DR
- LALT 94022 811-E6
CIELITO WY
6600 SJS 95119 875-D7
CIELO VISTA WY
4700 SJS 95129 853-A1
CIERVOS RD
- SMCo 94028 830-D4
CIMA WY
- PTLV 94028 830-C1
CIMARRON DR
2000 MGH 95037 917-E6
2300 SCL 95051 833-C2

CIMARRON ST
1900 SCIC 95037 917-D4
CIMARRON RIVER CT
- SJS 95136 874-E2
CIMINO AV
300 SJS 95125 854-D4
CINDERELLA LN
1800 SJS 95116 834-H5
CINERARIA CT
5000 SJS 95111 875-A2
CINNABAR ST
500 SJS 95110 834-A6
700 SJS 95126 833-J6
CINNABAR HILLS RD
10000 SCIC 95120 895-A7
10000 SJS 95120 895-A7
10000 SCIC 95120 915-A1
10000 SJS 95120 915-A1
10100 SCIC 95120 914-J1
10200 SJS 95120 914-J1
CINNAMON DR
500 SJS 95111 854-G7
CIOLINO AV
100 MGH 95037 937-A1
CIOPPINO CT
7700 SCIC 95020 958-G6
CIRCLE DR
- SUNV 94089 812-H3
600 EPA 94303 791-B3
700 SCL 95050 833-F5
700 SCL 95134 813-D5
CIRCLE LN
- MLPK 94025 790-J2
16400 MGH 95037 917-G6
CIRCLE HILL DR
6500 SJS 95120 894-B1
CIRO AV
100 SCIC 95128 833-F7
100 SJS 95128 833-F7
CIROLERO ST
1300 MPS 95035 794-B4
CIRONE WY
2000 SJS 95124 873-F1
CIRRUS WY
100 SUNV 94087 832-E2
CITATION CT
14900 MGH 95037 937-B5
CITATION DR
- LALT 94024 831-J5
CITRON AV
700 SUNV 94087 832-B1
CITRUS CT
500 SJS 95117 853-D2
CITRUS LN
19100 SAR 95070 872-G5
CITRUS GROVE CT
1500 SJS 95121 855-A3
CITY VIEW PL
1200 SJS 95127 835-C3
CIVIC CENTER DR
- CMBL 95008 853-E6
800 SCL 95050 833-D3
CLAIR CT
3300 SCL 95051 833-A3
CLAIRE CT
2500 MTVW 94043 811-F2
CLAIRE PL
300 MLPK 94025 790-F5
CLAITOR WY
3900 SJS 95132 815-A5
CLAMPETT CT
1500 SJS 95131 814-D5
CLAMPETT LN
1500 SJS 95131 814-D5
CLAMPETT PL
1500 SJS 95131 814-D5
CLAMPETT WY
1500 SJS 95131 814-D5
CLARA DR
700 PA 94303 791-D6
CLARA ST
14800 SCIC 95030 873-B4
14800 MSER 95030 873-B4
CLARA FELICE WY
500 SJS 95125 854-C5
CLARA VISTA AV
600 SCL 95050 833-C5
CLARDY PL
500 SJS 95117 853-C1
CLARE CT
1800 SJS 95124 873-H1
CLAREBANK WY
2500 SJS 95121 855-D3
CLAREMONT AV
- SCL 95051 832-J7
N CLAREMONT AV
- SCIC 95127 835-A1
- SCIC 95127 834-J1
100 SCIC 95127 814-J7

STREET	Block	City	ZIP	Pg-Grid
S CLAREMONT AV				
	-	SCIC	95127	835-A1
	200	SJS	95127	835-A1
CLAREMONT CT				
	-	MGH	95037	936-H1
CLAREMONT DR				
	400	MGH	95037	916-H7
	700	MGH	95037	936-H1
CLAREMONT PL				
	-	MLPK	94025	790-H4
CLAREMONT WY				
	300	MLPK	94025	790-H4
CLARENCE AV				
	200	SUNV	94086	812-C7
CLARENCE CT				
	1700	SJS	95124	853-H6
CLARENDON DR				
	4600	SJS	95129	853-A4
	4700	SJS	95129	852-J4
CLARENDON ST				
	7000	SJS	95129	852-E3
CLARET CT				
	8200	SJS	95135	855-J6
CLAREVIEW CT				
	200	SJS	95127	835-A1
CLAREVIEW ST				
	-	SCIC	95127	835-A1
	100	SJS	95127	835-A1
CLARICE DR				
	1700	SJS	95122	854-J1
	1800	SJS	95122	855-A1
	1900	SJS	95122	835-A7
CLARIDGE CT				
	20300	SAR	95070	852-E6
CLARINDA WY				
	1900	SJS	95124	873-G5
CLARION CT				
	2700	SJS	95148	835-E6
CLARITA AV				
	1400	SJS	95130	853-B4
	1500	SJS	95008	853-B4
CLARK AV				
	-	LALT	94024	811-F7
	1000	MTVW	94040	811-F5
	2000	SCL	95051	833-B2
N CLARK AV				
	200	LALT	94022	811-F6
	300	MTVW	94040	811-F6
CLARK CT				
	500	LALT	94024	811-F7
CLARK RD				
	-	MTVW	94043	812-A3
	-	SCIC	94043	812-A3
CLARK ST				
	1100	SJS	95125	854-B2
CLARK WY				
	1000	GIL	95020	977-H3
	1100	SJS	95125	854-A5
CLARKE AV				
	1800	EPA	94303	791-C1
CLARKE LN				
	200	SCIC	95037	916-F4
CLARKSPUR LN				
	1500	SJS	95129	852-F5
CLARKSTON AV				
	11000	CPTO	95014	852-B3
CLARKSTON DR				
	700	SJS	95136	874-D1
CLARKWOOD CT				
	400	SCL	95054	813-F6
CLARMAR WY				
	2000	SJS	95128	833-F7
CLASSIC CT				
	21000	CPTO	95014	852-C3
CLASSICO AV				
	-	SJS	95135	855-E3
CLAUDIA DR				
	10200	SCIC	95127	835-A2
CLAUSEN CT				
	12800	LAH	94024	831-D2
CLAUSER DR				
	400	MPS	95035	794-A5
CLAVERING HILL RD				
	4100	SCIC	95127	815-D7
CLAY DR				
	-	ATN	94027	790-C4
	1500	LALT	94024	832-A4
CLAY ST				
	1500	SCL	95050	833-D4
	20300	CPTO	95014	852-E2
CLAYBURN LN				
	1100	SJS	95121	855-B6
CLAYCOMB CT				
	1100	SJS	95118	874-G3
CLAYTON AV				
	-	SJS	95110	834-A5
	19000	SCIC	95037	916-H4
	19000	MGH	95037	916-H4
CLAYTON DR				
	2100	MLPK	94025	790-E7
CLAYTON RD				
	1100	SJS	95127	835-B3
	2700	SCIC	95127	835-F1
	3100	SJS	95148	835-C4
CLAYWOOD WY				
	6900	SJS	95120	894-J3
CLEAR BROOK CT				
	-	SJS	95111	854-J5
CLEARCREEK CT				
	22000	CPTO	95014	832-A7
CLEAR LAKE AV				
	1400	MPS	95035	814-D2
CLEAR LAKE CT				
	1100	MPS	95035	814-D1
CLEAR PARK CIR				
	200	SJS	95136	874-H2
CLEAR PARK PL				
	4300	SJS	95136	874-H1
CLEAR RIVER CT				
	4700	SJS	95136	874-E2
CLEAR SPRINGS CT				
	2400	SJS	95133	834-B2
CLEARVIEW DR				
	400	LGTS	95030	873-B3
	500	SCIC	95030	873-B3
	700	SJS	95133	814-F7
CLEARWATER CT				
	500	SUNV	94087	832-D4
CLEARWOOD CT				
	22000	CPTO	95014	832-A7
CLEAVES AV				
	-	SJS	95126	833-J7
	200	SCIC	95126	833-J7
	200	SCIC	95126	853-J1
CLELAND AV				
	-	LGTS	95032	893-A1
CLELAND PL				
	-	MLPK	94025	790-J3
CLEMATIS DR				
	1000	SUNV	94086	832-H2
	1600	SJS	95124	873-J7
CLEMENCE AV				
	1200	SJS	95122	834-F7
	1400	SJS	95122	854-G1
CLEMENCE CT				
	1400	SJS	95122	834-F7
CLEMO AV				
	4100	PA	94306	811-C3
CLEMSON AV				
	18200	SAR	95070	852-J7
CLEO AV				
	20600	CPTO	95014	852-D3
CLEO SPRINGS CT				
	1600	SJS	95131	814-C6
CLEVELAND AV				
	-	SJS	95126	833-G7
	100	SJS	95128	833-G7
	100	SCIC	95128	833-G7
	100	SCIC	95128	853-G1
CLIFDEN WY				
	20300	CPTO	95014	852-E2
CLIFF DR				
	1400	SJS	95132	814-G3
CLIFFORD CT				
	6600	CPTO	95014	852-F2
CLIFFORD DR				
	6500	CPTO	95014	852-F2
CLIFFORD LN				
	1000	MPS	95035	794-B5
CLIFFORD ST				
	1800	SCL	95050	833-D4
CLIFFWOOD DR				
	1300	SJS	95122	834-H6
CLIFTON AV				
	-	LGTS	95030	872-J7
	-	LGTS	95030	892-J1
	300	SCIC	95128	853-G1
	300	SJS	95128	853-G1
	400	CMBL	95128	853-E3
CLIFTON CT				
	3200	PA	94303	791-E6
CLINTON AV				
	3400	SCL	95051	832-J7
CLINTON PL				
	700	SJS	95126	834-A6
	700	SJS	95126	833-J6
CLINTON RD				
	800	LALT	94024	831-G3
CLINTONIA AV				
	800	SJS	95125	854-A2
CLIPPER CT				
	1100	SJS	95132	814-G5
CLISE CT				
	400	SJS	95123	875-A6
CLOGSTON CT				
	400	SJS	95133	834-G2
CLOUD AV				
	900	MLPK	94025	790-D6
	900	SMCo	94025	790-D6
CLOUD DR				
	4800	SJS	95111	875-B1
CLOVE DR				
	2200	SCIC	95128	853-F2
CLOVER AV				
	500	SJS	95128	833-E7
S CLOVER AV				
	300	SJS	95128	853-E1
	1100	CMBL	95128	853-E3
CLOVER LN				
	100	MLPK	94025	790-J3
CLOVER WY				
	100	LGTS	95032	873-D7
CLOVERBROOK DR				
	1000	SJS	95120	874-E7
CLOVERCREST DR				
	5300	SJS	95118	874-C4
CLOVERDALE CT				
	1400	SUNV	94087	832-B4
CLOVERDALE LN				
	1600	SJS	95130	853-B5
CLOVERHILL DR				
	6100	SJS	95120	874-E7
CLOVERLY CT				
	22000	SCIC	94024	832-A7
CLOVER MEADOW CT				
	-	SJS	95135	855-H7
CLOVER OAK DR				
	3400	SJS	95148	835-E6
CLOVEWOOD LN				
	3200	SJS	95132	814-E2
CLOVIS AV				
	1600	SJS	95124	873-J5
CLUB DR				
	5400	SCIC	95127	815-A7
	5400	SJS	95131	814-A5
CLUBHOUSE CT				
	4000	SJS	95135	855-H6
CLUBHOUSE LN				
	10600	CPTO	95014	852-A2
CLUB VIEW TER				
	11900	SCIC	94024	831-G3
CLYDA DR				
	2500	SJS	95116	834-H4
CLYDE AV				
	300	MTVW	94043	812-C4
	700	SCL	95054	813-E6
CLYDE CT				
	400	MTVW	94043	812-C4
	500	MPS	95035	794-B6
CLYDE BANK CT				
	1100	SUNV	94087	832-H4
CLYDELLE AV				
	4700	SJS	95124	873-E4
	15200	SCIC	95124	873-E4
CLYDESDALE AV				
	5900	SJS	95123	874-J5
COACH CT				
	1100	SJS	95120	894-E1
COACHELLA AV				
	800	SUNV	94086	812-H5
COACHLIGHT DR				
	3300	SJS	95111	854-J5
COAKLEY DR				
	400	SJS	95117	853-C2
COALBROOK DR				
	1600	SJS	95126	853-H4
COALMINE VW				
	-	PTLV	94028	830-C1
COAST AV				
	2600	MTVW	94043	791-G7
COASTLAND AV				
	1700	SJS	95125	854-C4
COASTLAND DR				
	700	PA	94303	791-C6
COBALT WY				
	300	SUNV	94086	812-J7
COBBERT DR				
	3500	SJS	95148	835-F7
COBBLESTONE CT				
	6500	SJS	95120	894-C6
COBBLESTONE DR				
	1200	CMBL	95008	853-B7
COBURN CT				
	3600	SJS	95139	875-G7
COCHISE CT				
	600	FRMT	94539	793-J2
COCHRANE CIR				
	100	MGH	95037	916-H5
COCHRANE RD				
	200	MGH	95037	916-J4
	800	MGH	95037	917-B3
	1900	SCIC	95037	917-C2
COCONUT DR				
	2500	SJS	95148	835-C7
CODY CT				
	3600	SCL	95051	832-H7
CODY LN				
	-	LALT	94022	811-E6
	14700	SAR	95070	872-E3
CODY RD				
	-	SCIC	94035	812-C2
CODY WY				
	1800	SJS	95124	853-G7
COE AV				
	400	SJS	95125	854-A2
COELHO CT				
	400	MPS	95035	794-A3
COELHO ST				
	100	MPS	95035	794-A4
COEUR D ALENE WY				
	900	SUNV	94087	832-B4
COFFEEWOOD CT				
	700	SJS	95120	894-H3
COFFEY CT				
	700	SJS	95123	874-F5
COGHLAN LN				
	-	ATN	94027	790-C4
COHANSEY AV				
	-	GIL	95020	957-J6
	-	SCIC	95020	957-H6
	700	GIL	95020	958-A6
	800	SCIC	95020	958-A6
COHANSEY DR				
	2900	SJS	95132	814-D3
COHASSET WY				
	5700	SJS	95123	875-B4
COIT DR				
	2500	SJS	95124	853-G7
	2500	SJS	95124	873-G1
COLBY AV				
	900	SMCo	94025	790-H1
	10100	CPTO	95014	832-F7
COLBY CT				
	19700	SAR	95070	852-F5
COLD HARBOR AV				
	10100	CPTO	95014	852-F1
COLDWATER DR				
	3100	SJS	95148	835-B5
COLE DR				
	14500	SCIC	95124	873-G3
	14900	SJS	95124	873-G3
COLE RD				
	100	SBnC	-	(1017-D7 See Page 997)
COLEMAN AV				
	400	SCL	95110	833-G3
	400	SJS	95110	833-G3
	600	MLPK	94025	790-H2
	800	SMCo	94025	790-H2
	900	SJS	95110	834-A5
	1200	SCL	95050	833-G3
COLEMAN PL				
	-	MLPK	94025	790-J2
COLEMAN RD				
	-	SJS	95123	874-A6
	1100	SJS	95120	874-A6
COLERAINE CT				
	600	SUNV	94087	832-E4
COLERIDGE AV				
	100	PA	94301	791-A6
COLFAX CT				
	3100	SCL	95051	833-A3
COLFAX DR				
	400	SJS	95123	874-J4
COLGATE AV				
	3200	SCL	95051	833-A6
COLIBRI CT				
	200	SJS	95119	875-D7
COLINA DR				
	12200	LAH	94024	831-E2
COLINTON WY				
	1300	SUNV	94087	832-B4
COLLEEN CT				
	300	MGH	95037	916-J7
	600	SJS	95123	874-H7
COLLEEN DR				
	600	SJS	95123	874-F6
	1800	LALT	94024	831-J4
COLLEEN WY				
	600	CMBL	95008	853-B5
COLLEGE AV				
	-	LGTS	95032	893-A1
	100	MTVW	94040	811-F4
	200	PA	94306	791-A7
	600	MLPK	94025	790-G5
	600	SMCo	94025	790-H2
	700	SCL	95050	833-F5
	900	PA	94306	811-A1
	1400	PA	94306	810-J1
COLLEGE CT				
	700	LALT	94024	831-E1
COLLEGE DR				
	300	SJS	95128	853-H2
COLLEGE RD				
	-	SCrC	95076	995-J6
COLLEGE TERRACE CT				
	-	LGTS	95032	893-A1
COLLETTE DR				
	1000	SJS	95132	814-H5
COLLINGSWORTH ST				
	21700	CPTO	95014	852-B3
COLLINGWOOD AV				
	1600	SJS	95125	854-A5
COLLINS CT				
	4300	MTVW	94040	811-E3
COLLINS LN				
	1200	SJS	95129	852-J4
COLLINWOOD CT				
	400	SCL	95054	813-F5
COLLOMIA CT				
	300	SJS	95111	875-A1
COLMERY CT				
	4000	SJS	95118	874-A2
COLMERY LN				
	1600	SJS	95118	874-A2
COLOMBARD CT				
	8300	SJS	95135	855-J7
COLOMBO DR				
	4200	SJS	95130	853-A4
	4300	SJS	95129	853-A4
COLONADE SQ				
	100	SJS	95127	834-J3
COLONIAL LN				
	900	PA	94303	791-D5
	1100	SJS	95132	814-H4
COLONIAL PL				
	-	SMCo	94061	790-B3
COLONIAL WY				
	3000	SJS	95128	853-E4
COLONIAL OAKS DR				
	1200	LALT	94024	831-H3
COLONNA AV				
	-	SJS	95148	855-F1
COLONY AV				
	1700	SCIC	95046	937-E6
COLONY CT				
	1700	GIL	95020	977-E1
COLONY DR				
	200	SJS	95131	814-A4
COLONY ST				
	1900	MTVW	94043	811-G2
COLONY WY				
	1700	GIL	95020	977-E1
COLONY COVE DR				
	400	SJS	95123	874-G3
COLONY CREST DR				
	400	SJS	95123	874-G3
COLONY FIELD DR				
	5300	SJS	95123	874-G3
COLONY GREEN DR				
	5300	SJS	95123	874-G3
COLONY HILLS LN				
	1000	CPTO	95014	852-D3
COLONY KNOLL DR				
	400	SJS	95123	874-G3
COLONY PARK CIR				
	5400	SJS	95123	874-G3
COLORADO AV				
	100	PA	94306	791-D6
	100	PA	94301	791-B7
	700	PA	94303	791-D6
COLORADO CT				
	100	LGTS	95032	873-H7
COLORADO PL				
	1000	PA	94303	791-E5
COLORVIEW CT				
	5900	SJS	95120	874-B7
COLT WY				
	1300	SJS	95121	855-B4
COLTER PL				
	6000	SJS	95123	874-G6
COLTON AV				
	1000	SUNV	94089	812-F4
COLTON PL				
	500	SJS	95110	834-C7
COLTWOOD CT				
	3400	SJS	95148	835-D6
COLTWOOD DR				
	2700	SJS	95148	835-D6
COLUMBET AV				
	11100	SCIC	95020	957-J1
	12000	SCIC	95046	937-F2
	12000	SCIC	95046	957-J1
COLUMBIA AV				
	-	SMCo	94063	790-D1
	500	SJS	95126	854-A1
	500	SUNV	94086	812-F6
COLUMBIA DR				
	1600	MTVW	94040	811-G7
COLUMBIA ST				
	2000	PA	94306	810-J1
	2200	PA	94306	811-A1
COLUMBIA RIVER CT				
	4600	SJS	95136	874-G2
COLUMBINE AV				
	1100	SUNV	94086	832-H2
COLUMBINE CT				
	8700	GIL	95020	977-E1
	19200	SAR	95070	852-G6
COLUMBINE DR				
	3500	SJS	95148	835-C4
	3500	SJS	95127	835-C4
COLUMBUS AV				
	21200	CPTO	95014	852-B3
COLUMBUS CIR				
	1300	MPS	95035	794-B4
COLUMBUS DR				
	1000	MPS	95035	794-B4
COLUMBUS PL				
	2700	SCL	95051	833-B3
COLUMN CT				
	3200	SJS	95111	854-F6
COLUSA AV				
	900	SUNV	94086	812-H5
COLUSA WY				
	1900	SJS	95130	852-J6
COLVILLE DR				
	300	SJS	95123	874-J5
	300	SJS	95123	875-A5
COMANCHE CT				
	5600	SJS	95123	874-H4
COMANCHE DR				
	5600	SJS	95123	874-H5
COMANCHE TR				
	17500	SCIC	95030	913-A2
COMER DR				
	20900	SAR	95070	852-C7
COMET DR				
	100	MPS	95035	814-A2
COMET LN				
	2900	SJS	95127	834-J2
COMMERCE DR				
	1900	SJS	95131	814-B5
COMMERCIAL AV				
	900	PA	94303	791-F7
	900	PA	94303	811-F1
COMMERCIAL CT				
	1000	SJS	95112	834-C1
COMMERCIAL ST				
	100	SUNV	94086	812-G7
	100	SJS	95112	834-B2
	1000	SJS	95133	834-B2
COMMODORE DR				
	1600	SJS	95133	834-E1
	2000	SJS	95133	814-E7
	2100	SCIC	95133	814-E7
COMMUNITY LN				
	1100	PA	94301	791-A4
COMO LN				
	3300	SJS	95118	874-A1
COMPONENT DR				
	100	SJS	95131	813-G7
COMPTON CT				
	3600	SJS	95130	853-C4
COMPTON LN				
	3600	SJS	95130	853-B4
COMSTOCK CIR				
	-	SCIC	94305	790-J7
COMSTOCK LN				
	1700	SJS	95124	853-H7
COMSTOCK RD				
	600	SBnC	-	(1000-G7 See Page 999)
	5300	SBnC	-	1001-B7
COMSTOCK ST				
	700	SCL	95054	833-D1
COMSTOCK WY				
	1800	SJS	95124	853-J7
COMSTOCK QUEEN CT				
	-	MTVW	94043	811-J3
CONCANNON CT				
	300	SCL	95050	833-D6
CONCEPCION RD				
	12200	LAH	94022	831-B1
	12300	LAH	94022	811-B7
CONCERTO DR				
	4400	SJS	95111	855-A7
CONCERTO WY				
	4400	SJS	95111	855-A7
CONCORD AV				
	700	SJS	95128	853-H2
	1300	LALT	94024	831-H3
CONCORD CIR				
	-	MTVW	94040	811-F3
	15000	MGH	95037	937-C2
CONCORD DR				
	-	SJS	95123	875-B4
	-	SJS	95193	875-B4
	200	MLPK	94025	790-J3
CONCORD LN				
	2800	SCL	95051	833-A6
CONCORD PL				
	7100	GIL	95020	977-J4
CONCORD RIDGE CT				
	-	SJS	95138	855-F6
CONCOURSE DR				
	1900	SJS	95131	814-B5
CONDENSA ST				
	2500	SCL	95051	833-B1
CONDIT RD				
	16100	MGH	95037	917-C6
	16100	SCIC	95037	917-B5
	17400	MGH	95037	937-D1
	17400	SCIC	95037	937-D1
CONDON CT				
	300	SCL	95050	833-D6
CONDOR CIR				
	5700	SJS	95118	874-A6
CONDOR CT				
	5700	SJS	95118	874-A6
CONDOR WY				
	1500	SUNV	94087	832-E5
CONEJO CT				
	26500	LAH	94022	811-B6
CONEJO DR				
	200	SJS	95119	875-C7
CONESTOGA WY				
	300	SJS	95123	874-J6
	300	SJS	95123	875-A6
CONGRESS PL				
	10000	CPTO	95014	832-C7
CONGRESS HALL LN				
	21700	SAR	95070	872-B3
CONGRESS JUNCTION CIR				
	18900	SAR	95070	852-B7
CONGRESS SPRINGS LN				
	21700	SAR	95070	872-B3
CONGRESS SPRINGS RD Rt#-9				
	-	SCrC	95030	871-D2
	20900	SAR	95070	872-A3
	21900	SCIC	95070	872-A3
	21900	SCIC	95070	871-G2
	22600	SCIC	95030	871-D2
CONIFER CT				
	1900	SJS	95132	814-E2
CONIFER LN				
	1900	SJS	95132	814-E2
CONIFER ST				
	48200	FRMT	94539	793-J1
CONIL WY				
	300	SMCo	94028	810-D4
CONISTON CT				
	1300	SJS	95118	874-B4
CONISTON WY				
	5600	SJS	95118	874-C4
CONLIN CT				
	400	SJS	95123	874-J5
CONNECTICUT DR				
	1500	RDWC	94061	790-A2
CONNELL CT				
	9000	GIL	95020	957-H7
CONNEMARA WY				
	100	SUNV	94087	832-E4
CONNIE DR				
	700	CMBL	95008	873-C1
CONNOLLY WY				
	2300	EPA	94303	791-C1
CONRAD AV				
	1700	SJS	95124	873-H4
CONRADIA CT				
	21500	CPTO	95014	852-B3
CONSTANCE DR				
	3500	SJS	95117	853-C2
CONSTANSO CT				
	1500	SJS	95129	852-J4
CONSTANSO WY				
	1400	SJS	95129	852-J4
CONSTANZO ST				
	500	SCIC	94305	810-H1
CONSTITUTION AV				
	18000	MSER	95030	872-J5
CONSTITUTION CT				
	1800	SJS	95124	853-H6
CONSTITUTION DR				
	2100	SJS	95124	853-H6
CONSUELO AV				
	2200	SCL	95050	833-D6
CONTE WY				
	1800	MGH	95037	917-D6
CONTESSA CT				
	6300	SJS	95123	874-J7
CONTI CT				
	500	SJS	95111	854-G3
CONTINENTAL CIR				
	700	MTVW	94040	812-A7
	21400	SAR	95070	852-C6
CONTINENTAL DR				
	500	SJS	95111	855-A7
	900	MLPK	94025	790-C6
CONWAY AV				
	14800	SCIC	95124	873-G4
CONWAY CT				
	14700	SCIC	95124	873-G4
CONWAY RD				
	600	SUNV	94087	832-D3
CONWAY ST				
	1600	MPS	95035	794-A3
COOK ST				
	1100	SJS	95126	833-G5
COOKSEY LN				
	700	SCIC	94305	810-H1
COOLEY AV				
	1900	EPA	94303	791-B2
COOLEY DR				
	1700	SJS	95116	834-G5
COOLIDGE AV				
	800	SUNV	94086	812-D7
	1100	SJS	95125	854-A3
	12600	SCIC	95046	957-D1
	13100	SCIC	95046	937-D7
COOLIDGE DR				
	2000	SCL	95051	833-B3
COOPER AV				
	15000	SCIC	95124	873-F4
COOPER CT				
	100	LGTS	95030	873-B5
COOPER DR				
	3300	SCL	95051	832-J2
COOPER RIVER DR				
	1100	SJS	95126	853-G3
COPAL CT				
	800	SCIC	95127	814-H6
COPCO LN				
	200	SJS	95123	875-A4
COPELAND CT				
	5400	SJS	95124	873-H6
COPELAND LN				
	5400	SJS	95124	873-H6
COPELAND PL				
	5500	SJS	95124	873-H6
COPPER RD				
	2900	SCL	95051	812-J7
	2900	SCL	95051	832-J1
COPPERAGE CT				
	6500	SJS	95120	894-C6
COPPERFIELD DR				
	4200	SJS	95136	854-F7
	4200	SJS	95136	874-F1
COPPER HILL DR				
	17000	MGH	95037	917-G4
	17000	SCIC	95037	917-G4
COPPER HILL PL				
	-	SCIC	95037	917-G4
COPPER LEAF DR				
	3300	SJS	95132	814-G4
COPPER PEAK LN				
	1100	SJS	95120	894-G5
COPPER SPRING CT				
	11500	CPTO	95014	852-A4
COPPERWOOD CIR				
	6500	SJS	95120	894-E1
COQUITO CT				
	-	SMCo	94028	810-D4
COQUITO WY				
	100	SMCo	94028	810-D4
CORA CT				
	1200	CMBL	95008	873-C1
CORAL CT				
	600	LALT	94024	811-G6
	3000	SJS	95121	855-A4
CORAL BELL CT				
	2200	GIL	95020	977-D1
CORAL CANYON DR				
	5500	SJS	95123	875-B4
CORALEE DR				
	1700	SJS	95124	873-H4
CORAL GABLES CIR				
	200	SJS	95139	895-E1
CORAL SANDS DR				
	3600	SJS	95136	854-G7
CORALTREE PL				
	1600	SJS	95131	814-C5
CORALWOOD WY				
	5700	SJS	95123	874-F5
CORBAL CT				
	3100	SJS	95148	855-F2
CORBETTA LN				
	12400	LAH	94022	831-B2
CORBIN AV				
	4900	SJS	95118	874-C3
CORBY DR				
	3100	SJS	95148	855-E2
CORCEL CT				
	16700	LGTS	95032	873-C5
CORD CT				
	2900	SJS	95148	855-D1
CORDA DR				
	2800	SJS	95122	855-B2
CORDELIA AV				
	1100	SJS	95129	852-H4
CORDILLERAS AV				
	1300	SUNV	94087	832-D4
CORDOBA WY				
	2400	SJS	95125	853-J7
CORDOVA CT				
	-	PTLV	94028	810-D6
	700	MGH	95037	937-A4
CORDOVA RD				
	10500	CPTO	95014	851-J2
CORDOY LN				
	5000	SJS	95124	873-H5
	5100	SJS	95032	873-H5
CORDWOOD CT				
	14300	SAR	95070	872-H2
CORIE CT				
	1100	SJS	95112	814-B7
CORINA CT				
	3800	PA	94303	791-F7
CORINA WY				
	3800	PA	94303	811-E1
CORINE LN				
	1300	MLPK	94025	790-E4
CORINTHIA DR				
	400	MPS	95035	794-A5
CORKERHILL WY				
	3600	SJS	95121	855-C3
CORK OAK WY				
	3300	PA	94303	791-D7
CORKTREE LN				
	2000	SJS	95132	814-E2
CORKWOOD CT				
	100	SJS	95136	874-H1
CORLISS WY				
	500	CMBL	95008	853-C6
CORLISTA DR				
	700	SJS	95128	853-H2
CORMORANT CT				
	1500	SUNV	94087	832-E5
CORNELIA CT				
	600	MTVW	94040	811-H7
CORNELL DR				
	600	SCL	95051	833-A6
	1600	MTVW	94040	811-H7
	5400	SJS	95118	874-A5
CORNELL RD				
	-	MLPK	94025	790-G4
CORNELL ST				
	2000	PA	94306	791-A7
	2200	PA	94306	811-A1
CORNFLOWER CT				
	1000	SUNV	94086	832-H2
CORNING AV				
	-	MPS	95035	814-A1
	100	MPS	95035	813-J1
CORNING DR				
	3300	SJS	95118	874-A1
CORNISH LN				
	11900	SJS	95131	834-C1
CORNWALL CT				
	800	SUNV	94087	832-G4
CORNWALL DR				
	2700	SJS	95127	835-A5
CORONA DR				
	4500	SJS	95129	853-A3
CORONA WY				
	100	SMCo	94028	810-D4
CORONACH AV				
	1500	SUNV	94087	832-B5
CORONADO AV				
	-	LALT	94022	811-D6
	600	SCIC	94305	810-H1
CORONADO CIR				
	1200	SUNV	94086	812-B6
	2900	SCL	95054	813-B7
	7000	SJS	95129	852-E3
CORONET DR				
	200	LGTS	95032	873-E5
	200	LGTS	95124	873-E5
	200	SJS	95124	873-E5
CORPORATE CT				
	2000	SJS	95131	814-B5
CORPORATE LIMIT				
	600	CMBL	95008	853-F7
CORPORATION WY				
	1000	PA	94303	791-F7
CORRAL AV				
	100	SUNV	94086	812-B6
CORRALES DR				
	4700	SJS	95136	874-D2
CORRALITOS LN				
	14800	SCIC	95127	835-A1
CORRALITOS RD				
	-	SCrC	95003	(975-A5 See Page 955)
	200	SCrC	95076	(975-A5 See Page 955)
CORRIDA CIR				
	4600	SJS	95129	853-A1
CORRINE DR				
	15400	LGTS	95032	873-C5
CORTA VIA				
	1600	SCIC	94024	831-G4
CORTE ARQUETA				
	400	MGH	95037	917-B7
CORTE BONITA				
	1300	SJS	95120	874-B7
CORTE CABANIL				
	400	MGH	95037	917-B7
CORTE CABAS				
	400	MGH	95037	917-B7
CORTE CAMULA				
	6100	SJS	95120	874-C7
CORTE DE ANNA				
	1600	SJS	95124	874-A3
CORTE DE ARBOL				
	3100	SJS	95118	874-A1
CORTE DE ARGUELLO				
	12800	SAR	95070	852-C6
CORTE DE AVELLANO				
	4700	SJS	95136	874-E2
CORTE DE BELLEZA				
	6100	SJS	95120	874-C7
CORTE DE BLANCO				
	800	SJS	95136	874-E2
CORTE DE BOLEYN				
	4300	SJS	95118	874-A2
CORTE DE CALLAS				
	1600	SJS	95124	874-A3
CORTE DE CERVATO				
	4700	SJS	95136	874-E2
CORTE DE FLORES				
	2000	SCL	95054	813-D4
	3000	SJS	95118	874-A1
CORTE DE LA REINA				
	6100	SJS	95120	874-B7
CORTE DEL CONEJO				
	6100	SJS	95120	874-B7
CORTE DE MADRID				
	10400	SCIC	95014	852-G1
CORTE DE MEDEA				
	1600	SJS	95124	874-A3
CORTE DE MOFFO				
	1500	SJS	95118	874-A3
CORTE DE PEARSON				
	1500	SJS	95124	874-A3
CORTE DE PLATA				
	800	SJS	95136	874-E2
CORTE DE PONS				
	1600	SJS	95124	874-A3
CORTE DE PRIMAVERA				
	2000	SCL	95054	813-C3
CORTE DE ROSA				
	1400	SJS	95120	894-B1
CORTE DE SEVILLE				
	10400	SCIC	95014	852-G2
CORTE DE TEBALDI				
	4200	SJS	95118	874-A3
CORTE DE THAIS				
	1400	SJS	95118	874-B3
CORTE KORN				
	10500	SCIC	95020	958-A3
CORTE MADERA AV				
	900	SUNV	94086	812-D5
CORTE MADERA CT				
	900	SUNV	94086	812-C5
CORTE MADERA LN				
	12600	LAH	94022	811-B7
	21800	CPTO	95014	832-B7
CORTE MADERA RD				
	100	PTLV	94028	830-C1
	100	PTLV	94028	810-C7
CORTESE CIR				
	3100	SJS	95127	814-J7
CORTESE LN				
	16900	SCIC	95037	917-D6
	16900	MGH	95037	917-D6
CORTE VERDE DR				
	5000	SJS	95111	875-A2
CORTEZ AV				
	100	SJS	95136	854-G7
	1700	SJS	95122	834-H6
CORTEZ DR				
	1200	SUNV	94086	812-B6
	2600	SCL	95051	833-B1
CORTEZ LN				
	12900	LAH	94022	830-J1
CORTEZ ST				
	1500	MPS	95035	794-A3
CORTINA DR				
	2900	SJS	95132	814-F5
CORTO ST				
	700	MTVW	94043	811-J4
CORTONA DR				
	-	SJS	95135	855-F2
CORUMBA CT				
	5800	SJS	95120	874-C5
CORVALLIS CT				
	1100	SJS	95120	894-F2
CORVALLIS DR				
	800	SUNV	94087	832-C4
	1100	SJS	95120	894-F2
CORVETTE DR				
	1000	SJS	95129	852-F3

STREET
Block City ZIP Pg-Grid

CORVIN DR
2900 SCL 95051 813-A7
2900 SCL 95051 833-A1
CORWIN CT
5000 SJS 95111 875-C1
CORY AV
2300 SJS 95128 833-E7
CORY CT
21000 CPTO 95014 852-C2
CORY DR
16600 MGH 95037 937-B1
CORY LN
16600 MGH 95037 937-B1
COSENZA LP
4200 SJS 95134 813-D2
COSMO AV
100 MGH 95037 937-A2
COSTA AV
- SJS 95112 854-E3
COSTA MESA DR
300 SJS 95111 854-J7
COSTA MESA TER
- FRMT 94539 794-B1
400 SUNV 94086 812-C5
COSTELLO CT
300 SCIC 94024 831-E2
COSTELLO DR
300 SCIC 94024 831-E2
COSTIGAN CIR
500 MPS 95035 794-B5
COT CT
- SJS 95117 853-D1
COTHRAN RD
- SCIC 95030 913-D4
COTSWALD CT
1100 SUNV 94087 832-H4
COTTAGE PL
6000 SJS 95123 874-E6
COTTAGE GROVE AV
- SJS 95110 854-D2
COTTERELL DR
1200 SJS 95121 855-A5
COTTLE AV
1500 SJS 95125 854-A5
COTTLE RD
- SJS 95193 875-B5
700 SJS 95123 875-B5
1800 SJS 95119 875-B5
6400 SCIC 95123 895-B1
COTTON CT
6000 SJS 95123 875-B6
COTTON PL
- MLPK 94025 790-F5
COTTON ST
300 MLPK 94025 790-F5
COTTON TAIL AV
700 SJS 95116 834-H4
COTTONWOOD CT
2900 SCL 95051 833-A6
6300 CPTO 95014 852-F2
COTTONWOOD DR
400 MPS 95035 813-J4
800 CPTO 95014 852-F2
COTTONWOOD ST
48200 FRMT 94539 793-J1
COTTRELL WY
900 SCIC 94305 810-J2
COTY WY
200 SJS 95136 874-G1
COULOMBE DR
4100 PA 94306 811-C3
COUNTESS CT
1100 SJS 95129 852-G4
COUNTESS DR
5900 SJS 95129 852-G3
COUNT FLEET CT
600 MGH 95037 937-B5
COUNTRY DR
2100 GIL 95020 977-D1
COUNTRY LN
- SMCo 94061 790-B2
4700 SJS 95129 852-J4
14600 SCIC 95037 937-C4
COUNTRY WY
13300 LAH 94022 810-H7
COUNTRYBROOK
2400 SJS 95131 814-C4
COUNTRY CLUB CT
3000 PA 94304 810-H7
COUNTRY CLUB DR
1000 MPS 95035 794-C4
1200 SCIC 94024 831-G3
COUNTRY CLUB PKWY
5300 SJS 95138 855-F7
5300 SJS 95138 875-F1
COUNTRY FIELDS LN
- SJS 95136 875-E2
COUNTRY FORGE LN
5200 SJS 95136 875-A3

COUNTRY LEAF CT
3300 SJS 95132 814-G4
COUNTRY OAK CT
5200 SJS 95136 875-E2
COUNTRY OAK LN
- SJS 95136 875-E2
COUNTRYSIDE LN
5200 SJS 95136 875-A3
COUNTRY SPRING CT
11500 CPTO 95014 852-C4
COUNTRY SQUIRE CT
12100 SAR 95070 852-G5
COUNTRY SQUIRE DR
12100 SAR 95070 852-G5
COUNTRY SQUIRE LN
12000 SAR 95070 852-G5
COUNTRY SQUIRE WY
12100 SAR 95070 852-G5
COUNTRY VIEW CT
22600 SCIC 95119 895-E4
22600 SCIC 95139 895-E4
22600 SCIC 95120 895-E4
COUNTRY VIEW DR
22500 SCIC 95120 895-D5
22600 SCIC 95139 895-D5
COUNTRY VIEW LN
22500 SCIC 95120 895-E5
COUNTRY VISTA CT
3900 SJS 95121 855-D4
COUNTRYWALK CIR
2700 SJS 95132 814-E3
COUNTRYWOOD CT
3600 SJS 95130 853-C4
COUNTY LINE RD
- SCIC 95020 (920-A1 See Page 919)
- SCIC 95020 921-F1
- SCIC 95037 (859-D7 See Page 839)
- SCIC 95037 879-E2
- SCIC 95037 (920-A1 See Page 919)
COUR DU VIN
3500 SJS 95148 855-G1
COURTLAND AV
1000 MPS 95035 814-D1
COURTLAND CT
900 MPS 95035 814-D1
COURTNEY AV
1700 SJS 95122 854-G1
COURTSIDE DR
5200 SJS 95138 855-G7
COURTYARD DR
1400 SJS 95118 874-B2
COVE CT
2000 SJS 95148 835-B6
COVENTRY CIR
800 MPS 95035 794-A5
COVENTRY CT
800 SUNV 94087 832-F4
COVENTRY DR
100 CMBL 95008 853-C5
3200 SJS 95127 835-A5
COVENTRY WY
800 MPS 95035 794-A5
COVEWOOD CT
2900 SJS 95148 855-D1
COVINA AV
- SJS 95123 874-J5
COVINA CT
12000 SAR 95070 852-E5
COVINGTON CT
100 SJS 95136 874-H1
900 LALT 94024 831-G2
COVINGTON RD
100 LALT 94024 831-E1
COWDEN PL
13100 LAH 94022 831-A1
COWELL LN
- ATN 94027 790-D5
400 SCIC 94305 810-H1
COWELL RD
14600 LGTS 95032 893-C2
16000 SCIC 95032 893-C2
COWPER CT
1500 SJS 95120 874-A7
3400 PA 94306 791-D7
COWPER ST
100 PA 94301 790-J4
800 PA 94301 791-A5
2500 PA 94306 791-C7
COX AV
- SCIC 95046 937-E7
18500 SAR 95070 852-E6
COY DR
100 SJS 95123 874-J3
COYNE CT
2100 SJS 95122 834-J7
COYOTE RD
- SCIC 95037 917-C3

COYOTE RD
400 SJS 95111 855-A7
700 SJS 95111 875-C1
700 SCIC 95111 875-C2
700 SCIC 95111 855-A7
COYOTE ST
600 MPS 95035 793-J6
COYOTE CREEK CIR
300 SJS 95116 834-D4
COYOTE CREEK CT
1200 SJS 95116 834-D4
COYOTE CREEK PL
1200 SJS 95116 834-D4
COYOTE HILL
- PTLV 94028 830-C1
COYOTE HILL RD
3100 SCIC 94304 810-J3
3100 PA 94304 811-A3
3100 SCIC 94304 811-A3
COYOTE LAKE RD
13300 SCIC 95046 938-C1
13300 SCIC 95020 938-C1
COYOTE RANCH RD
5800 SCIC 95137 875-H7
5800 SCIC 95137 895-J1
5900 SCIC 95137 896-A1
5900 SJS 95137 896-A1
5900 SJS 95137 895-J2
5900 SCIC 95137 895-J2
COYOTE RESERVOIR RD
11000 SCIC 95020 938-C3
11000 SCIC 95046 938-C3
12600 SCIC 95020 958-F1
COZETTE LN
19100 SCIC 95014 852-G1
COZUMEL CIR
2800 SCL 95051 833-A4
COZY CT
500 SJS 95123 874-J7
COZY DR
500 SJS 95123 874-J6
CRABAPPLE WY
500 SJS 95111 854-J6
CRABTREE AV
18600 SCIC 95014 852-H1
CRACOLICE WY
1200 MPS 95035 814-D2
CRAFT DR
10000 CPTO 95014 852-G1
N CRAGMONT AV
- SCIC 95127 835-A1
- SCIC 95127 834-J1
S CRAGMONT AV
- SCIC 95127 835-A1
200 SJS 95127 835-A1
CRAGWOOD LN
1500 SJS 95127 835-A5
CRAIG AV
600 CMBL 95008 853-C7
CRAIG CT
2300 MTVW 94043 811-G3
20600 CPTO 95014 852-D1
CRAIG DR
1000 SJS 95129 852-F3
CRAIG WY
100 LGTS 95032 873-E6
CRAIGEN CIR
20200 SAR 95070 852-E6
CRAILFORD CT
1300 SJS 95121 855-B5
CRAMER CT
2700 SJS 95111 854-G4
CRANBERRY AV
1100 SUNV 94087 832-B3
CRANBERRY CIR
7900 CPTO 95014 852-C2
CRANBERRY DR
900 CPTO 95014 852-C2
CRANBROOK CT
6400 SJS 95120 894-D1
CRANDALL ST
500 SJS 95110 834-A7
CRANDANO CT
1100 SUNV 94087 832-B3
CRANE AV
1700 MTVW 94040 831-H1
CRANE CT
1600 SJS 95112 833-J1
CRANE ST
900 MLPK 94025 790-F3
CRANFORD CIR
4000 SJS 95124 873-E3
CRANWORTH CIR
2000 SJS 95121 855-C4
CRATER LN
2800 SJS 95132 814-F5
CRATER LAKE AV
1500 MPS 95035 794-E7
1500 MPS 95035 814-D1

CRATER LAKE CT
500 SUNV 94087 832-D4
CRAVENS CT
300 SJS 95133 834-G2
CRAWFORD CT
7400 GIL 95020 977-H4
CRAWFORD DR
500 SUNV 94087 832-D2
7500 GIL 95020 977-G3
CRAY CT
3000 SJS 95121 854-J4
CRAYCROFT CT
48400 FRMT 94539 793-J1
CRAYCROFT DR
300 FRMT 94539 793-J1
CRAYSIDE LN
12200 SAR 95070 852-D6
CRAZY PETES RD
- SMCo 94028 830-C6
CREAGER CT
3700 SJS 95130 853-C4
CREE CT
600 SJS 95123 874-H6
CREE DR
600 SJS 95123 874-H6
CREED ST
1100 MPS 95035 794-C4
CREEDEN WY
2100 LALT 94022 811-F5
2100 MTVW 94040 811-F5
CREEK DR
- MGH 95037 937-C5
E CREEK DR
100 MLPK 94025 790-H3
N CREEK DR
200 SJS 95139 895-F1
E CREEK PL
- MLPK 94025 790-H4
CREEK BANK CT
6500 SJS 95120 894-F1
CREEK BED CT
2200 SCL 95054 813-C5
CREEKBED CT
17100 MGH 95037 917-B7
CREEK ESTATES
5100 SJS 95135 855-G5
CREEK ESTATES CT
3000 SJS 95135 855-G5
CREEKFIELD DR
600 SJS 95136 854-E7
CREEKLAND CIR
700 SJS 95133 834-E2
CREEKLINE DR
7800 CPTO 95014 852-C2
CREEKMORE WY
3100 SJS 95148 835-F7
CREEK PARK DR
- PTLV 94028 810-E7
CREEKPOINT DR
2900 SJS 95133 814-G6
CREEKSIDE CIR
17000 MGH 95037 917-B7
CREEKSIDE CT
900 MGH 95037 937-B5
17300 MSER 95030 873-A4
22000 CPTO 95014 832-A7
CREEKSIDE DR
100 PA 94306 811-E2
2700 SJS 95132 814-E3
3100 SJS 95131 814-A4
CREEKSIDE LN
400 MGH 95037 917-B7
CREEKSIDE PL
700 SCL 95051 833-A5
CREEKSIDE WY
700 CMBL 95008 853-F5
CREEKSTONE CIR
1700 SJS 95133 834-E2
CREEKVIEW CT
6600 SJS 95120 894-G1
12400 SCIC 95046 938-A6
CREEKVIEW DR
300 MGH 95037 917-B7
CREEKVIEW MDW CT
- SJS 95135 855-H7
CREEKVIEW MDW LN
- SJS 95135 855-H7
CREEKWOOD CT
300 MGH 95037 917-B7
CREEKWOOD DR
1000 SJS 95129 852-J3
CREIGHTON CT
1200 MPS 95035 814-C1
CREIGHTON PL
3300 SCL 95051 832-J2
CRENSHAW CT
6500 SJS 95120 894-E1
CRESCENDO AV
4100 SJS 95136 874-G1

CRESCENT AV
100 PTLV 94028 810-C7
100 PTLV 94028 830-C1
100 SUNV 94087 832-E3
CRESCENT CT
- CPTO 95014 832-A7
CRESCENT DR
- PA 94301 791-B3
1000 SJS 95125 854-A3
17000 LGTS 95032 893-C1
E CRESCENT DR
500 PA 94301 791-B3
W CRESCENT DR
500 PA 94301 791-B3
CRESCENT LN
25400 LAH 94022 831-C2
CRESCENT RD
10000 CPTO 95014 832-A7
CRESCENT TER
600 SUNV 94087 832-E3
CRESCENT PARK DR
17700 MGH 95037 917-B6
CRESCENT PARK WY
700 MGH 95037 917-A6
CRESENT TER
1000 MPS 95035 814-E1
CRESPI DR
1100 SUNV 94086 812-C6
1400 SJS 95129 852-J5
CREST AV
17600 MGH 95037 916-J7
CREST DR
300 SCIC 95127 815-A6
CREST LN
2300 MLPK 94025 790-D7
CRESTA VISTA LN
500 PTLV 94028 810-D5
CRESTA VISTA WY
200 SJS 95119 875-C6
CRESTBROOK DR
19600 SAR 95070 872-F1
CRESTFIELD DR
1300 SJS 95125 854-B7
CRESTHAVEN LN
1400 SJS 95118 874-B2
CRESTHAVEN ST
2200 MPS 95035 814-E1
CREST HILL CT
9000 GIL 95020 957-E7
9000 GIL 95020 977-E1
CREST HILL WY
- GIL 95020 957-E7
CRESTLINE DR
1100 CPTO 95014 852-D3
CRESTMONT DR
1800 SJS 95124 853-H7
CRESTMOOR CT
700 SJS 95129 852-J2
CRESTMOOR DR
600 SJS 95129 852-J2
CRESTOAK CT
6000 SJS 95120 874-C7
CRESTON DR
10200 CPTO 95014 832-A6
10400 SCIC 94024 832-A6
CRESTON LN
1100 SJS 95122 834-G7
CRESTPOINT DR
1200 SJS 95131 834-C1
CRESTRIDGE DR
11400 SCIC 94024 831-E4
19400 SCIC 95030 872-F5
CRESTVIEW COM
- FRMT 94539 794-B1
CRESTVIEW CT
8100 SCIC 95020 (976-J1 See Page 955)
CRESTVIEW DR
- SJS 95117 833-D7
200 SCL 95050 833-D7
1000 MTVW 94040 832-B1
1600 SCIC 94024 831-G4
CRESTWOOD CT
900 SUNV 94089 812-J5
CRESTWOOD DR
1300 SJS 95118 854-B7
CREWE CT
1800 SJS 95132 814-F3
CREWS RD
7300 SCIC 95020 978-F1
7500 SCIC 95020 958-G6
CRIBARI BEND
5400 SJS 95135 855-H5
CRIBARI CIR
5300 SJS 95135 855-H5
CRIBARI CT
5400 SJS 95135 855-H5
CRIBARI GN
5300 SJS 95135 855-H5

CRIBARI HTS
5300 SJS 95135 855-H5
CRIBARI LN
5000 SJS 95135 855-H5
CRIBARI PL
5000 SJS 95135 855-H5
CRIBARI BLUFFS
5000 SJS 95135 855-H5
CRIBARI CORNER
5200 SJS 95135 855-H5
CRIBARI CREST
5300 SJS 95135 855-H5
CRIBARI DALE
5200 SJS 95135 855-H5
CRIBARI DELL
5300 SJS 95135 855-H5
CRIBARI HILLS
5300 SJS 95135 855-H5
CRIBARI KNOLLS
5100 SJS 95135 855-H5
CRIBARI VALE
5000 SJS 95135 855-H5
CRICKET HILL RD
22800 CPTO 95014 851-J1
CRIDER CT
100 LGTS 95032 873-J7
CRIMSON DR
5900 SJS 95120 874-B7
CRIMSONBERRY WY
500 SJS 95129 852-B7
CRINAN DR
1800 SJS 95122 854-G1
CRIOLLO WY
1900 MGH 95037 917-D6
CRISANTO AV
1900 MTVW 94040 811-G3
CRISP AV
19100 SAR 95070 872-G3
CRIST DR
1900 LALT 94024 832-A5
CRISTICH LN
- CMBL 95008 853-E7
CRISTINA AV
1200 SJS 95125 854-B3
CRISTO REY DR
22500 CPTO 95014 831-H6
22500 SCIC 94024 831-H6
22900 LALT 94024 831-H6
23700 SCIC 95014 831-H6
CRITTENDEN LN
- MTVW 94043 791-J7
2000 MTVW 94043 792-A7
CROCKER CT
- SJS 95111 875-A2
CROCKER DR
- SJS 95111 875-B2
CROCKER LN
7100 GIL 95020 978-B3
CROCKER WY
2200 SCL 95051 832-J2
CROCKETT AV
600 CMBL 95008 853-B7
900 CMBL 95008 873-B1
CROCUS CT
- SMCo 94025 790-E6
1000 SUNV 94086 832-H2
CROCUS DR
4400 SJS 95136 874-F2
CROFT DR
2700 SJS 95148 855-D2
CROMART CT
100 SUNV 94087 832-E4
CRONER AV
1700 MLPK 94025 790-E5
1700 SMCo 94025 790-E5
CRONIN DR
- SCL 95051 833-A7
CRONWELL DR
1900 CMBL 95008 853-G5
1900 SCIC 95125 853-G5
CROOKED CREEK DR
11400 LALT 94024 831-G4
CROPLEY AV
2500 SJS 95132 814-F2
CROPLEY CT
3300 SJS 95132 814-F2
CROSBY CT
2700 SCL 95051 833-B3
6700 SJS 95129 852-E3
CROSBY PL
4100 PA 94306 811-C4
CROSLEY CT
3300 SJS 95132 814-G3
CROSS WY
- LGTS 95032 893-B1
1500 SJS 95125 854-C3
CROSSBOW CT
1000 SJS 95120 874-E6
CROSSBROOK CT
- SJS 95120 874-E6

CROSSFIELD CT
6000 SJS 95120 874-E6
CROSSGATES LN
1200 SJS 95120 874-C7
CROSSLEES DR
400 SJS 95111 875-C2
CROSSMAN AV
1200 SUNV 94089 812-G3
CROSSMILL CT
2800 SJS 95121 854-J3
CROSSMONT CIR
5900 SJS 95120 874-D6
5900 SCIC 95120 874-D6
CROSSMONT CT
6000 SJS 95120 874-D6
CROSSPOINT CT
1000 SJS 95120 874-D6
CROSS SPRINGS CT
1000 SJS 95120 874-D6
CROSS SPRINGS DR
1000 SJS 95120 874-D6
CROSSVIEW CIR
6000 SJS 95120 874-D6
CROSSVIEW CT
5900 SJS 95120 874-D6
CROSSWIND CT
1000 SJS 95120 874-D6
CROTHERS RD
10200 SCIC 95127 815-C6
10200 SJS 95127 815-B6
16400 SCIC 95127 835-D1
CROTHERS WY
300 SCIC 94305 790-H7
CROW AV
- SCrC 95076 (975-C7 See Page 955)
CROW CT
400 SJS 95123 874-H4
1600 SUNV 94087 832-E5
CROW LN
5600 SJS 95123 874-H4
CROW TR
17800 SCIC 95030 913-C2
CROWDER AV
1800 SJS 95124 873-H3
CROWLEY AV
1100 SCL 95051 833-B4
CROWN BLVD
6500 SJS 95120 894-E2
CROWNER AV
14400 SCIC 95046 937-D4
14500 MGH 95046 937-D4
CROWN RIDGE COM
- FRMT 94539 794-B1
CROY RD
4600 SCIC 95037 936-A3
4900 SCIC 95037 935-C5
CROYDEN CT
500 SUNV 94087 832-E4
CROYDON AV
5600 SJS 95118 874-C4
CRUCERO CT
1400 SJS 95122 834-G7
CRUCERO DR
1300 SJS 95122 834-G7
CRUDEN BAY CIR
5000 SJS 95138 855-E6
CRUDEN BAY WY
5000 SJS 95138 855-E6
CRUMP CT
5800 SJS 95120 874-B6
CRYSTAL CT
- MPS 95035 794-A7
CRYSTAL DR
2400 SCL 95051 833-A1
18000 MGH 95037 916-F7
18000 SCIC 95037 934-H2
CRYSTALBERRY TER
500 SJS 95129 853-B2
CRYSTAL CREEK DR
2900 SJS 95133 814-G6
CRYSTAL GLEN LN
800 SCL 95050 833-D1
CRYSTAL SPRINGS CT
6700 SJS 95120 894-D2
CRYSTAL SPRINGS DR
6400 SJS 95120 894-D2
CRYSTAL SPRINGS WY
- SJS 95123 875-G2
CUCIZ LN
1300 MPS 95035 814-D2
CUEN CT
3600 SJS 95136 874-D1
CUERNAVACA CT
1400 SJS 95120 874-B7
CUERNAVACA CIRCULO
1200 MTVW 94040 832-A1
CUESTA CT
3500 SJS 95148 835-D5

CUESTA DR
- LALT 94022 811-E7
100 MTVW 94040 811-G7
300 LALT 94024 811-E7
2100 MPS 95035 814-E1
3200 SJS 95148 835-C6
CUESTA DE LOS GATOS WY
100 LGTS 95032 873-B7
CULBERTSON DR
10000 SCIC 95014 852-G2
CULLEN LN
3300 SCIC 95020 958-F6
CULLIGAN BLVD
1000 SJS 95120 894-D1
1100 SJS 95120 874-D7
CULLODEN CT
1000 SJS 95121 855-A5
CULP DR
8500 GIL 95020 977-G1
CULPEPPER DR
1200 SJS 95121 854-H2
CULVERT DR
6200 SJS 95123 874-J7
CUMBERLAND AV
800 SUNV 94087 832-C1
CUMBERLAND DR
700 GIL 95020 977-H4
12700 SAR 95070 852-F6
CUMBERLAND PL
1000 SJS 95125 854-D7
CUMBRA VISTA CT
13000 LAH 94022 831-A1
CUMMINS AV
- SCIC 94035 812-B2
- SCIC 94043 812-B2
CUMULUS AV
100 SUNV 94087 832-E2
CUNARD CT
3400 SJS 95132 814-J2
CUNNINGHAM AV
1500 SJS 95122 854-H1
1500 SJS 95122 834-H7
2100 SJS 95148 835-A6
2100 SJS 95122 835-A6
CUNNINGHAM CT
2000 SJS 95148 835-B6
CUNNINGHAM PL
20400 SAR 95070 852-D7
CUNNINGHAM ST
1600 SCL 95050 833-C4
CUPERTINO RD
22200 CPTO 95014 832-A7
CUPPLES CT
600 SCL 95051 833-B6
CURCI DR
1400 SJS 95126 853-H3
CURETON PL
300 SCIC 95127 835-A2
300 SJS 95127 835-A2
CURIE CT
6400 SJS 95123 875-A7
CURIE DR
200 SJS 95119 875-C7
200 SCIC 95119 875-C7
300 SJS 95123 874-J7
400 SJS 95123 875-A7
CURLING CT
3200 SJS 95121 855-B3
CURRAGHMORE CT
4000 SJS 95136 854-E6
CURRENT DR
6200 SJS 95123 874-J7
CURRY CT
12400 SAR 95070 852-H6
CURSOR CT
- SJS 95134 813-C1
CURTIS AV
900 SCL 95051 832-J5
E CURTIS AV
- MPS 95035 814-A2
CURTIS ST
800 MLPK 94025 790-F3
CURTIS WY
700 MLPK 94025 790-G4
CURTISS AV
1100 SJS 95125 854-A3
CURTNER AV
- CMBL 95008 873-E1
100 SJS 95125 854-B5
200 PA 94306 811-C1
200 SCIC 95125 854-D4
300 SCIC 95008 873-E1
500 SJS 95008 873-G1
1600 SJS 95125 853-J7
1700 SJS 95124 853-G7
2000 SJS 95124 873-G1
CURTNER CT
400 MPS 95035 794-A3

CURTNER DR
400 MPS 95035 794-A4
CURTNER GLEN CT
2600 SJS 95008 873-F1
CUSTER DR
2500 SJS 95124 853-H7
2500 SJS 95124 873-H1
CUT ACROSS RD
- SMCo 94020 850-G7
CUTFORTH CT
1300 SJS 95132 814-F5
CYCLAMEN CT
- SJS 95111 875-A2
CYLINDA DR
3400 SJS 95130 853-A7
CYNTHIA AV
18600 SCIC 95014 852-H2
CYNTHIA LN
1000 SJS 95129 852-E3
CYNTHIA WY
2000 LALT 94024 832-A5
CYPRESS AV
- SCL 95117 833-D7
- SCL 95117 853-D1
100 SCL 95050 833-F5
300 SUNV 94086 812-F5
S CYPRESS AV
300 SJS 95117 853-C2
400 SCIC 95117 853-D1
CYPRESS CT
400 LALT 94022 811-D6
1200 GIL 95020 977-G2
10500 CPTO 95014 832-F6
CYPRESS DR
300 LALT 94022 811-D6
300 MPS 95035 813-H1
10400 CPTO 95014 832-F7
CYPRESS LN
500 CMBL 95008 853-F5
500 PA 94306 811-C1
6200 SJS 95138 875-F6
CYPRESS RDGE
2500 SCIC 95148 835-E6
CYPRESS ST
100 RDWC 94061 790-B1
1100 EPA 94303 791-C2
CYPRESS WY
16100 LGTS 95032 893-C1
CYPRESS PARK CT
400 SJS 95136 874-F1
CYPRESS POINT DR
200 MTVW 94043 812-A4
200 MTVW 94043 811-J4
CYRIL PL
18900 SAR 95070 852-H6
CYRUS AV
3000 SJS 95124 873-H1
CYRUS HEIGHTS LN
17200 SCIC 95032 893-G2

D

D RD
15000 SCIC 95127 815-D6
D ST
- MTVW 94043 812-B5
- SUNV 94089 812-H3
300 MLPK 94025 790-G3
S D ST
- SUNV 94089 812-J3
DADE CT
6400 SJS 95123 875-B7
6400 SJS 95123 895-B1
DADIS WY
600 SJS 95111 854-H4
DADO ST
600 SJS 95131 813-J6
DAFFODIL CT
700 SUNV 94086 832-F2
1400 MGH 95037 917-D6
DAFFODIL WY
700 SJS 95117 853-B3
DAGGETT DR
- SJS 95134 813-G5
DAGMAR CT
700 SJS 95136 874-E1
DAGMAR DR
19000 SAR 95070 872-H1
19000 SAR 95070 852-G7
DAHILL CT
3500 SJS 95121 855-C3
DAHLBERG CT
2100 SCIC 95037 936-F2
DAHLBERG DR
2000 SCIC 95037 936-F1
DAHLIA CT
1100 SUNV 94086 832-H2
DAHLIA DR
1100 SUNV 94086 832-H2

DAHLIA WY
15900 SCIC 95032 873-D6
15900 LGTS 95032 873-D6
DAILEY AV
700 SJS 95123 874-F4
DAILEY RD
- SCIC 94035 812-B3
- SCIC 94043 812-B3
DAIMLER CT
5300 SJS 95123 874-H3
DAISY CT
1000 SUNV 94086 832-H2
DAISY LN
400 EPA 94303 791-D2
8100 GIL 95020 977-G2
DAISYDELL CT
400 SJS 95129 853-B2
DAKAN CT
3100 SJS 95136 854-D7
DAKE AV
4100 PA 94306 811-F2
DAKIN AV
1900 SMCo 94025 790-D6
DAKOTA DR
600 SJS 95111 854-H5
700 MGH 95037 917-B6
DALBON CT
6900 SJS 95119 875-F6
DALE AV
900 MTVW 94040 812-A7
1100 MTVW 94040 832-A1
1300 SJS 95125 854-A5
DALE DR
- SCIC 95127 835-A2
- SCIC 95127 834-J2
DALEHURST DR
1600 LALT 94024 831-J4
DALEWOOD CT
700 SJS 95120 894-J3
DALLAS CT
1600 LALT 94024 831-J3
3100 SCL 95051 833-A3
DALLAS DR
200 SCIC 95008 873-E1
DALMA DR
- MTVW 94041 811-J6
DALMENY CT
6800 SJS 95120 894-H2
DALMUIR CT
2500 SJS 95121 855-D4
DALTON DR
1600 SJS 95124 873-J5
1700 MPS 95035 794-D7
DALTON LN
100 SCrC 95076 (975-G7 See Page 955)
DALTON PL
1800 SJS 95124 873-J5
DALTREY WY
1700 SJS 95132 814-D4
DAMASCUS CT
2300 SJS 95125 853-J6
DAMEY DR
2300 SJS 95116 834-G2
DAMIAN WY
900 LALT 94024 831-J2
DAMICO DR
2900 SJS 95148 855-D2
DAMON LN
13900 SAR 95070 872-A1
13900 SCIC 95070 872-A1
DANA AV
- SJS 95128 853-H1
- SJS 95126 853-H1
- SJS 95126 833-G6
- SJS 95128 833-G7
1100 PA 94301 791-A3
1400 PA 94303 791-A3
DANA ST
100 MTVW 94041 811-H4
800 MTVW 94041 812-B6
900 SUNV 94086 812-B6
E DANA ST
100 MTVW 94041 812-A6
W DANA ST
100 MTVW 94041 812-A5
DANBURY DR
1000 SJS 95129 852-F3
DANBURY LN
- RDWC 94061 790-B2
DANBY AV
1300 SJS 95132 814-F4
DANDERHALL WY
3100 SJS 95121 855-C3
DANDINI CIR
1800 SJS 95128 853-G3
DANFORTH CT
1200 SJS 95121 854-H2
DANFORTH DR
600 SUNV 94087 832-D1

STREET
Block City ZIP Pg-Grid

DANFORTH TER
700 SUNV 94087 832-D1
DANIEL CT
1200 MPS 95035 794-C5
3900 SCIC 95020 978-H1
7000 SCIC 95020 957-A7
7000 SCIC 95020 977-A1
7000 SCIC 95020 (976-J1
See Page 955)
DANIEL WY
500 SJS 95128 833-F7
3700 SCL 95051 832-H7
S DANIEL WY
300 SJS 95128 853-F1
DANIELLE PL
15000 MSER 95030 872-J4
DANIEL MALONEY DR
1700 SJS 95121 855-B3
DANNA CT
- SJS 95138 875-G6
DANNY BOY CT
900 MGH 95037 937-B5
DANRIDGE DR
6500 SJS 95129 852-E3
DANROMAS WY
1500 SJS 95129 852-F5
DANTE CT
2900 SJS 95135 855-E3
DANUBE DR
10100 CPTO 95014 852-E1
DANUBE WY
1300 SJS 95116 834-F5
DANVILLE DR
200 LGTS 95032 873-F6
DANWOOD CT
2800 SJS 95148 835-C7
DANZE DR
100 SJS 95111 875-B3
DAPHNE CT
- EPA 94303 791-D3
DAPHNE DR
1200 SJS 95129 852-F4
DAPHNE WY
- EPA 94303 791-D3
DARBYS CT
100 SJS 95110 854-D2
DARDANELLI LN
100 LGTS 95030 873-B2
DARIEN WY
12700 SAR 95070 852-G6
DARKNELL CT
3500 SJS 95148 835-E6
DARKNELL WY
2700 SJS 95148 835-E6
DARK STAR CT
14800 MGH 95037 937-B5
DARLENE AV
1400 SJS 95125 854-A7
DARLING LN
13400 LAH 94022 811-D7
DARLINGTON CT
4200 PA 94306 811-D2
DARNELL CT
2300 SJS 95133 834-F1
DARNIS CIR
2100 MGH 95037 917-E6
DARRINGTON CT
1000 SUNV 94087 832-B5
DARRYDOON CT
1200 SJS 95121 855-A5
DARRYL CT
3600 SJS 95130 853-C4
DARRYL DR
- CMBL 95008 853-C5
1300 SJS 95130 853-C4
1500 CMBL 95130 853-C4
DARTMOOR WY
5400 SJS 95129 852-E4
DARTMOUTH DR
5400 SJS 95118 874-A5
DARTMOUTH LN
1000 LALT 94024 831-H2
DARTMOUTH PL
700 GIL 95020 977-J4
DARTMOUTH ST
1000 PA 94306 810-J1
1100 PA 94306 811-A1
DARTSHIRE CT
1400 SUNV 94087 832-G4
DARTSHIRE WY
700 SUNV 94087 832-F4
DARWIN CT
300 SJS 95122 834-G7
DARWIN WY
700 SJS 95122 834-H7
DASH CT
300 SJS 95120 874-B6
DASHWOOD AV
400 SJS 95121 855-C3

DATE BLOSSOM CT
5400 SJS 95123 875-A3
DATORO DR
2100 SJS 95130 853-A7
DAUPHINE PL
200 LALT 94022 811-E6
DAURINE CT
2900 SCIC 95020 958-F7
DAVENPORT CT
500 SUNV 94087 832-D5
DAVENPORT DR
500 SJS 95127 835-B2
DAVENPORT WY
200 PA 94306 811-D2
DAVES AV
17500 MSER 95030 873-A5
17700 LGTS 95030 873-A5
17800 MSER 95030 872-J5
18200 SCIC 95030 872-H5
DAVID AV
300 CMBL 95008 853-E4
2800 SJS 95128 853-E4
3000 SJS 95008 853-E4
3100 PA 94303 791-D6
DAVID CT
3100 PA 94303 791-D6
8400 GIL 95020 977-J1
DAVID LN
1300 MPS 95035 814-D2
DAVIDSON AV
4300 SCIC 95020 (998-F1
See Page 997)
DAVIDWOOD WY
2900 SJS 95148 855-D1
DAVIS CT
22600 SCIC 95120 895-C4
DAVIS ST
1200 SJS 95126 833-F6
4000 SCL 95054 813-D5
DAVISON AV
10400 CPTO 95014 852-F2
DAWES CT
2800 SJS 95148 855-D2
DAWN DR
500 SUNV 94087 832-D2
DAWN LN
12100 LAH 94022 811-A7
DAWN WY
600 GIL 95020 977-J7
DAWNBROOK CT
3700 SJS 95111 855-A5
DAWNRIDGE DR
24200 LAH 94024 831-E3
DAWNVIEW CT
900 SJS 95136 874-D3
DAWSON AV
400 SJS 95125 854-C3
DAWSON DR
300 SCL 95051 832-H7
11600 LAH 94024 831-E3
DAY CT
2600 SCL 95051 833-B3
DAY RD
- GIL 95020 957-G6
- SCIC 95020 957-G6
700 SCIC 95046 957-A4
DAYLIGHT WY
2900 SJS 95111 854-G6
DAYO CT
2800 SJS 95148 855-D2
DAYTON AV
300 SCL 95051 832-J7
DAYTONA DR
1800 SJS 95122 834-J6
DEAN AV
1100 SJS 95125 854-A4
DEAN CT
22000 CPTO 95014 852-A1
DEANNA CT
1100 MGH 95037 916-G7
DEANNA DR
1000 MLPK 94025 790-D6
DEANS PLACE WY
3700 SJS 95121 855-B4
DE ANZA AV
100 SJS 95136 854-G7
DE ANZA BLVD
10000 CPTO 95014 832-E7
10000 CPTO 95014 852-E2
S DE ANZA BLVD
- SJS 95129 852-D3
1300 CPTO 95014 852-D3
DE ANZA CIR N
22200 CPTO 95014 852-A2
DE ANZA CIR S
22200 CPTO 95014 852-A2
DE ANZA CT
800 MPS 95035 794-B5
14500 MGH 95037 937-C5

DE ANZA LN
200 LALT 94022 811-E7
DE ANZA WY
1500 SJS 95125 853-J4
DEARBORN PL
800 GIL 95020 977-H4
DEARWELL WY
- SJS 95138 875-D4
DEB CT
1300 SJS 95120 874-C7
DEBBIE CT
3100 SCIC 95020 958-F7
DEBBIE LN
13400 SAR 95070 872-D1
20600 SAR 95070 852-D7
DEBELL DR
- ATN 94027 790-G2
DE BELL RD
14300 LAH 94022 811-C5
DEBOER LN
700 SJS 95111 855-A6
DEBORAH DR
2200 SCL 95050 833-C2
DEBRA WY
3600 SJS 95117 853-C2
DE BRUIN WY
10800 SCIC 95046 957-F4
DEBUT CT
800 SJS 95134 813-F3
DE CARLI CT
900 CMBL 95008 873-C1
DECATUR DR
1800 SJS 95122 834-H6
DECATUR RD
18400 MSER 95030 872-H6
18400 SCIC 95030 872-H6
DECKER AV
1600 SCIC 95046 937-H5
DECKER WY
- SCIC 95127 835-A1
- SCIC 95127 834-J1
DECLARATION CT
100 SJS 95116 834-H3
DECLARATION DR
2500 SJS 95116 834-H3
DECLARATION WY
100 SJS 95116 834-H3
DECORAH LN
- CMBL 95008 853-G6
DECOTO CT
900 MPS 95035 794-B6
DEDALERA DR
200 SMCo 94028 810-E4
DEE ST
800 SUNV 94087 832-D2
DEEDHAM CT
3800 SJS 95148 835-G7
DEEDHAM DR
3500 SJS 95148 835-F7
DEEP CLIFF DR
10600 CPTO 95014 852-A2
DEEP CREEK CT
1800 SJS 95148 835-D4
DEEP PURPLE WY
5400 SJS 95123 874-F3
DEEPROSE PL
10100 CPTO 95014 852-F1
DEEPWELL CT
21000 SAR 95070 872-C3
DEEPWELL LN
- LALT 94022 831-D1
DEER CT
500 SJS 95123 874-H4
DEER CANYON LN
14400 SAR 95070 872-C2
DEER CREEK CT
1700 SJS 95148 835-D4
DEER CREEK RD
3400 SCIC 94304 810-J4
3400 PA 94304 810-J4
3400 PA 94304 811-A4
DEERFIELD DR
1500 SJS 95129 852-G5
25500 LAH 94022 811-D7
DEERFIELD RD
- SCrC 95030 913-C7
DEER HILL RD
- SCIC 95037 917-D3
DEER HOLLOW CT
6500 SJS 95120 874-F7
DEER HOLLOW DR
6400 SJS 95120 874-F7
DEER ISLE DR
2700 SJS 95121 855-E4
DEERLAND CT
5900 SJS 95124 873-J7
DEER MEADOW CT
900 SJS 95122 854-G2
DEER MEADOW LN
100 PTLV 94028 810-C5

DEERPARK CT
20500 SAR 95070 872-D1
DEER PARK LN
- PTLV 94028 810-C5
DEERPARK RD
17200 SCIC 95032 893-G1
DEER PATH DR
- SMCo 94028 830-E4
DEER PATH RD
24000 SCIC 95070 871-G3
DEER RIDGE CIR
100 SJS 95123 874-G7
DEER RUN CIR
- SJS 95136 874-J2
DEER RUN CT
17900 MGH 95037 936-F1
DEER SPRING CT
14500 SAR 95070 872-C2
DEER SPRINGS WY
27200 LAH 94022 830-J2
DEER TRAIL CT
13400 SAR 95070 852-B7
DEER VIEW TER
- FRMT 94539 794-B1
DEERWOOD CT
300 MTVW 94040 811-F4
DEERWOOD DR
2800 SJS 95148 835-C7
DEEVA CT
2800 SCIC 95020 958-F7
DE FALCO WY
1300 SJS 95131 814-C7
DE FOE DR
7400 CPTO 95014 852-D2
DEGAS CT
10200 CPTO 95014 851-J1
DEGAS RD
100 PTLV 94028 810-C5
DE GUIGNE DR
300 SUNV 94086 812-G7
DEHAVILLAND CT
19400 SAR 95070 852-G6
DEHAVILLAND DR
19100 SAR 95070 852-G6
DE LA CRUZ BLVD
- SJS 95054 813-F6
- SJS 95110 813-F6
500 SCL 95054 813-E5
500 SJS 95131 813-F6
1700 SCL 95050 833-F2
2500 SJS 95050 833-F2
2900 SJS 95054 833-F2
2900 SJS 95110 833-F2
DE LA FARGE DR
7400 CPTO 95014 852-D2
DELAND AV
700 SJS 95128 853-H2
DELANO CT
1300 SJS 95121 855-B2
DE LA PENA AV
1800 SCL 95050 833-D5
DELAWARE AV
700 SJS 95123 874-F4
2400 RDWC 94061 790-A3
DELAWARE TR
20900 SCIC 95030 913-A2
DELBARR CT
2000 SJS 95125 854-C4
DELBERT WY
900 SJS 95126 853-J3
DEL CAMBRE DR
1000 SJS 95129 852-J3
DEL CANTO DR
6100 SJS 95119 875-C6
DEL CARLO CT
100 LGTS 95032 873-D6
DEL CENTRO WY
700 LALT 94024 831-F1
DEL CERRO CT
15800 LGTS 95032 873-E5
DELFINO WY
1300 MLPK 94025 790-D5
DEL FRANCO CT
2100 SJS 95131 814-A4
DEL FRANCO ST
2100 SJS 95131 814-A4
DELGADO CT
3700 SJS 95008 853-B7
DELIA ST
100 SCIC 95127 814-J7
DELL AV
400 MTVW 94043 811-F2
900 CMBL 95008 873-D1
900 CMBL 95008 853-D7
DELL CT
1600 SJS 95118 873-J4
DEL LOMA CT
4700 SJS 95008 873-A1
DEL LOMA DR
2800 SJS 95008 873-A1

DEL LOMA DR
2900 CMBL 95008 873-A1
DELLWOOD DR
- SJS 95131 814-A4
DELLWOOD WY
5200 SJS 95118 874-B4
DEL MAR AV
800 SJS 95128 853-G3
DELMAS AV
- SJS 95110 834-A7
- SJS 95113 834-A7
300 SJS 95126 834-A7
600 SJS 95125 854-B2
DEL MEDIO AV
- MTVW 94040 811-E3
DEL MEDIO CT
2700 MTVW 94040 811-E2
DEL MONTE AV
- LALT 94022 811-D4
2000 SCL 95051 832-J2
16400 MGH 95037 916-H5
17400 MGH 95037 917-A7
17900 MGH 95037 937-A1
DEL MONTE CIR
200 MGH 95037 916-H6
DEL MONTE LN
200 MGH 95037 916-J6
DEL MONTE PL
900 SJS 95117 853-D2
DEL MONTE WY
23000 SCrC 95030 913-D7
DELNA MANOR LN
1000 SJS 95128 853-F3
DELNO ST
1000 SJS 95126 833-G5
DEL NORTE AV
200 SUNV 94086 812-F5
1000 MLPK 94025 790-H1
DEL NORTE DR
3400 SJS 95132 814-G3
DE LOACH CT
1300 SJS 95125 853-G4
DEL ORO CT
600 CMBL 95008 853-C5
5500 SJS 95124 873-G6
DEL ORO DR
5400 SJS 95124 873-H6
DEL ORO PL
5500 SJS 95124 873-G6
DEL ORO WY
1100 GIL 95020 977-F1
DEL PASO AV
1700 SJS 95124 873-H3
DELPHI CIR
200 LALT 94022 811-E5
DELPHI CT
200 LALT 94022 811-E4
DEL PRADO DR
- CMBL 95008 853-C6
DEL PUERTO RD
10000 SCIC 95140 (819-B6
See Page 799)
DEL PUERTO CYN RD
- StCo - (800-J7
See Page 799)
DEL REY AV
500 SUNV 94086 812-D5
4400 SJS 95111 875-A1
DEL REY CT
300 SJS 95111 875-A1
8600 GIL 95020 977-F1
DELRIDGE DR
400 SJS 95111 875-C2
DEL RIO CT
800 MPS 95035 794-B5
DEL RIO DR
6900 SJS 95119 875-E7
6900 SJS 95119 895-E1
DEL ROBLES CT
6100 SJS 95119 875-C6
DEL ROY CT
600 CMBL 95008 853-C5
DELSEA PL
6000 SJS 95123 874-E6
DELSON CT
13100 LAH 94022 811-A7
DELTA CT
8300 GIL 95020 977-F2
DELTA DR
8000 GIL 95020 977-F2
DELTA RD
2900 SJS 95135 855-F3
DELUCA DR
1500 SJS 95131 814-C6
DEL VAILE CT
800 MPS 95035 794-B5
DELYNN WY
1100 SJS 95125 854-B6
DEMARET DR
4600 SCL 95054 813-D4

DE MARIETTA AV
1600 SJS 95126 853-G4
DE MARIETTA CT
1700 SJS 95126 853-G4
DE MATTEI CT
1000 SJS 95112 834-C3
DEMEREST LN
5400 SJS 95138 875-C3
DEMETER ST
100 EPA 94303 791-C1
DE MILLE DR
4100 SJS 95117 853-B3
4100 SJS 95129 853-B3
DEMOCRACY WY
2900 SCL 95054 813-A4
DEMPSEY RD
- MPS 95035 794-C7
400 MPS 95035 814-C1
DEMPSEY WY
- MPS 95035 794-C6
DEMPSTER AV
10200 CPTO 95014 832-B7
DENAIR AV
2200 SJS 95122 854-H1
DENALI WY
1500 SJS 95122 854-H1
DENEVI DR
2400 SJS 95130 853-A7
DENEVI LN
16500 SCIC 95030 872-H7
DENIO AV
- GIL 95020 957-H5
- SCIC 95020 957-H5
500 SCIC 95020 958-A4
DENISE DR
2000 SCL 95050 833-C4
DENISE LN
400 SMCo 94061 790-B4
DENISE WY
1100 SJS 95125 854-C6
DENISON AV
10100 CPTO 95014 832-F7
DENNIS AV
300 SUNV 94086 812-C7
1400 MPS 95035 794-D6
DENNIS CT
10100 SCIC 95127 835-A3
DENNIS DR
900 PA 94303 791-D5
DENNIS LN
1500 MTVW 94040 811-G6
DENNYWOOD CT
2800 SJS 95148 835-D7
DENSMORE CT
3300 SJS 95148 835-E7
DENSMORE DR
2800 SJS 95148 835-E7
DENT AV
4900 SJS 95118 874-A3
DENTON WY
3200 SJS 95121 855-C3
DENTWOOD DR
1200 SJS 95118 874-B4
DENVER DR
1000 CMBL 95008 853-B5
DEODAR LN
16200 MSER 95030 872-H6
DEODAR WY
200 SUNV 94086 812-F7
DEODARA DR
10400 CPTO 95014 832-F7
DEODARA GROVE CT
5300 SJS 95123 875-A3
DEODORA DR
- ATN 94027 790-G1
400 LALT 94024 831-J6
1200 SCIC 94024 831-J5
DE PALMA CT
1400 SJS 95120 894-A1
DE PALMA DR
1400 SJS 95120 894-A1
DE PALMA LN
20000 CPTO 95014 852-E1
DE PAUL CIR
2000 SCIC 95020 938-B7
DE PAUL PL
2200 SCL 95051 832-J2
DEPOT CT
- GIL 95020 978-A3
DEPOT ST
13000 SCIC 95046 937-E6
17000 MGH 95037 917-A7
DERBE DR
800 SJS 95122 854-F1
DERBY CT
600 SUNV 94087 832-E4
DERBYSHIRE DR
1000 CPTO 95014 852-C3
DEREK DR
5000 SJS 95136 874-J3

DERMOTT DR
1100 SJS 95129 853-A3
DEROCHE CT
1300 SUNV 94087 832-B4
DE ROSE WY
1400 SJS 95126 853-G3
DERRY LN
500 MLPK 94025 790-F3
DE SANKA AV
12300 SAR 95070 852-E6
DESCANSA CT
15800 MGH 95037 937-A3
DESDEMONA CT
1500 SJS 95121 854-J4
DESERT FLAME DR
6200 SJS 95120 874-C7
6300 SJS 95120 894-C1
DESERT ISLE DR
800 SJS 95117 853-B3
DESERT SANDS WY
- SJS 95123 875-B4
DESERTWOOD LN
3200 SJS 95132 814-E2
DESIN DR
4300 SJS 95118 874-C2
DES MOINES PL
600 SJS 95133 814-G7
DE SOTO AV
3600 SCL 95051 832-H7
DE SOTO DR
700 PA 94303 791-B4
2400 SJS 95124 873-D4
2400 LGTS 95032 873-D4
DE SOTO RD
- SJS 95134 813-G3
DESTRY CT
100 SJS 95136 875-A3
DE TRACY ST
1400 SJS 95128 853-E5
DETROIT CT
600 SJS 95133 814-G7
DE VARONA PL
2300 SCL 95050 833-C5
DEVCON CT
100 SJS 95112 833-J1
DEVCON DR
200 SJS 95112 833-J1
DEVERON CT
7500 SJS 95135 855-J6
DEVILLE CT
8100 GIL 95020 977-F2
DE VILLE WY
6500 SJS 95129 852-F3
DEVIN DR
2300 SCIC 95148 835-E5
E DEVINE ST
- SJS 95112 834-B6
W DEVINE ST
- SJS 95113 834-B6
100 SJS 95110 834-B6
DEVLIN CT
600 SJS 95133 834-B2
DEVON AV
18500 SAR 95070 852-H7
DEVON PL
2100 MPS 95035 794-A2
DEVON WY
6800 SJS 95129 852-E4
DEVONA TER
1300 SUNV 94087 832-B4
DEVON PARK CT
5100 SJS 95136 874-F3
DEVONSHIRE AV
- MTVW 94043 812-B3
2700 SMCo 94063 790-C1
DEVONSHIRE DR
6300 SJS 95129 852-F3
DEVONSHIRE WY
700 SUNV 94087 832-F4
DEVOS CT
3400 SCL 95051 832-J3
DEVOTO ST
800 MTVW 94041 812-A7
DEVRI CT
2500 MTVW 94043 811-F2
DEVRIES CT
10000 SCIC 95020 957-D6
DEWEY CIR
- MGH 95037 937-C5
DEWEY WY
6200 SJS 95123 874-J7
DEWITT AV
16100 SCIC 95037 936-J3
17000 MGH 95037 936-J1
17600 MGH 95037 916-H7
DEXTER AV
- SMCo 94063 790-C1
DEXTER DR
5300 SJS 95123 874-J3
21300 CPTO 95014 832-C7

DEYON PL
500 GIL 95020 978-A5
DEZAHARA WY
26800 LAH 94022 831-A2
DIABLO AV
200 MTVW 94043 811-F3
DIABLO CT
300 PA 94306 811-E2
DIABLO WY
- SMCo 94020 850-F5
1200 SJS 95120 894-D1
DIADEM DR
700 SJS 95116 834-H4
DIAL WY
5900 SJS 95129 852-F4
DIAMENTE CT
1800 SJS 95116 834-F3
DIAMOND AV
14000 SJS 95127 835-A4
DIAMOND CT
1100 LALT 94024 831-G2
DIAMOND WY
200 MPS 95035 793-H6
DIAMOND HEAD DR
3500 SJS 95136 854-G7
DIAMOND OAKS CT
21200 SAR 95070 852-C6
DIANA AV
300 MGH 95037 917-A7
800 SJS 95116 834-H5
1000 SCIC 95037 917-E4
DIANA LN
700 SJS 95116 834-H4
DIANA PL
2100 SJS 95116 834-H3
DIANE CT
8400 GIL 95020 977-H1
DIANE MARIE WY
2400 SCL 96060 833-B5
DIANNE DR
2000 SCL 95050 833-C4
12600 LAH 94022 831-D1
DIAS DR
1400 SCIC 95046 937-F2
3200 SJS 95148 835-D6
DIBBLE CT
3000 SCL 95051 833-A6
DICKENS AV
15000 SCIC 95124 873-F4
DICKINSON DR
4800 SJS 95111 875-B1
DICKINSON WY
600 SJS 95111 875-B1
DIDION CT
6300 SJS 95123 875-A7
DIDION WY
6300 SJS 95123 875-A7
DIDUCA WY
14800 SCIC 95032 873-F7
14800 SCIC 95032 893-G1
DIEL DR
1500 MPS 95035 794-B3
DIERICX CT
22300 MTVW 94040 832-A1
DIERICX DR
2500 MTVW 94040 832-A1
DIESSNER AV
500 SCIC 95046 937-F6
DI FIORE DR
800 SJS 95128 853-G2
DI GIULIO AV
900 SCL 95050 833-E2
DILLARD CT
- SJS 95128 853-F3
DILLION CT
2500 SJS 95133 814-F7
DILLON AV
- CMBL 95008 853-E6
DILLWOOD CT
800 SCIC 95136 854-D7
DINA CT
1500 SJS 95121 855-A3
DINA LN
2700 SJS 95121 855-A3
DINAHS CT
600 PA 94306 811-D3
DI NAPOLI DR
1000 SJS 95129 852-G3
DINES CT
- EPA 94303 791-C2
DINKEL CT
1100 SJS 95118 874-C3
DINKLESPIEL
STATION LN
- ATN 94027 790-E2
DINNY ST
3500 SCL 95054 813-E6
DINOSAUR POINT RD
- SCIC 95020 (962-D2
See Page 961)

DIONNE WY
900 SJS 95133 834-E1
DIOR TER
- LALT 94022 811-E6
DIPPER CIR
500 SJS 95117 853-D1
DI SALVO AV
100 SJS 95128 833-F7
200 SCIC 95128 833-F7
200 SCIC 95128 853-F1
DISCOVERY AV
5000 SJS 95111 875-B2
DISHMAN DR
17600 LGTS 95032 893-B2
DISK CT
4600 SJS 95134 813-D1
DISK DR
4700 SJS 95134 813-D1
DISNEY LN
6100 CPTO 95014 852-G2
DISTEL CIR
300 LALT 94022 811-F4
DISTEL DR
400 LALT 94022 811-E5
DITTOS LN
- LGTS 95032 893-A1
DIVISION ST
400 CMBL 95008 873-C2
E DIVISION ST
600 LGTS 95030 873-C2
600 CMBL 95008 873-C2
DIX WY
500 SJS 95125 854-C4
DIXIE DR
- SBnC - (1020-E7
See Page 999)
1600 SJS 95122 854-J1
DIXON DR
2500 SCL 95051 833-B5
DIXON PL
3800 PA 94306 811-E2
DIXON RD
- MPS 95035 793-J3
100 MPS 95035 794-A3
DIXON WY
700 LALT 94022 811-C4
DIXON LANDING RD
- FRMT 94538 793-H4
- SJS 95002 793-H4
- MPS 95035 793-H4
1600 MPS 95002 793-H4
DOANE AV
1700 MTVW 94043 811-H3
DOBBIN DR
1700 SJS 95133 834-E2
DOBERN AV
2200 SJS 95116 834-H4
DOBIE DR
- SJS 95123 875-B4
DODD LN
16100 SCIC 95037 936-J3
DODGE LN
- SBnC - (1017-C7
See Page 997)
DOGAWAY DR
100 SJS 95111 875-B2
DOGWOOD CT
800 SJS 95128 853-F4
DOGWOOD DR
6200 SJS 95138 875-F6
DOGWOOD WY
1300 MGH 95037 917-D6
DOHERTY WY
100 SMCo 94061 790-B4
DOHERTY RIDGE RD
- SMCo 94020 850-F7
DOLE WY
21600 SCIC 95030 912-G4
DOLLAR MOUNTAIN DR
200 SJS 95127 834-H1
DOLORES AV
- SCL 95128 833-D6
900 LALT 94024 831-G3
2200 SCL 95050 833-D6
21800 CPTO 95014 852-B1
21800 SCIC 95014 852-B1
DOLORES DR
400 MPS 95035 794-E7
1600 SCL 95125 853-H4
DOLORES ST
700 SCIC 94305 810-H1
DOLPHIN DR
2400 SJS 95124 873-E4
13600 SAR 95070 872-H1
DOMA DR
400 SJS 95117 853-C1
400 SCIC 95117 853-C1
DOMAINE DR
5600 SJS 95118 874-A5

DOME AV
1800 SCL 95050 833-E6
1800 SCL 95128 833-E6
DOMINICAN DR
3500 SCL 95051 832-J6
DOMINICK CT
3400 SJS 95127 835-B2
DOMINICK WY
3400 SJS 95127 835-B2
DOMINION AV
1500 SUNV 94087 832-B5
DON AV
1300 SCL 95050 833-D3
1600 SJS 95124 873-J1
DON CT
1600 MTVW 94022 811-G6
1600 MTVW 94040 811-G6
2000 SCL 95050 833-D3
DONA AV
700 SUNV 94087 832-B1
DONAHE DR
300 MPS 95035 794-A6
DONAHE PL
400 MPS 95035 794-A6
DONALD CT
3500 SJS 95127 835-B2
DONALD DR
4100 PA 94306 811-C3
DON ALFONSO CT
5500 SJS 95123 874-E6
DON ALFONSO WY
300 SJS 95123 874-E6
DON ANDRES CT
400 SJS 95123 874-E6
DON ANDRES WY
5400 SJS 95123 874-E6
DON BASILLO CT
5400 SJS 95123 874-E6
DON BASILLO WY
300 SJS 95123 874-E6
DON CARLOS CT
400 SJS 95123 874-E6
DONCASTER WY
1200 SJS 95127 835-A4
DON CORRELLI CT
400 SJS 95123 874-H2
DON CORRELLI WY
5400 SJS 95123 874-H2
DON DEL MONICO CT
5400 SJS 95123 874-E7
DONDERO WY
200 SJS 95119 875-C6
DON DIABLO CT
400 SJS 95123 874-H2
DON DIEGO CT
5400 SJS 95123 874-H2
DON EDGARDO CT
400 SJS 95123 874-H2
DON EDMONDO CT
5400 SJS 95123 874-H2
DONEGAL DR
7500 CPTO 95014 852-D4
DONELSON PL
14100 LAH 94022 811-B6
DON ENRICO CT
5500 SJS 95123 874-E7
DON FERNANDO WY
400 SJS 95123 874-E6
DON GIOVANNI CT
300 SJS 95123 874-E6
DONINGTON DR
1100 SJS 95129 852-G3
DONIZETTI CT
2800 SJS 95132 814-F5
DON JOSE WY
300 SJS 95123 874-H3
DON JUAN CIR
5300 SJS 95123 874-H4
DON KIRK ST
1300 LALT 94024 831-J4
DON MANRICO CT
5400 SJS 95123 874-E7
DON MARCELLO CT
5400 SJS 95123 874-E7
DON MARCO CT
400 SJS 95123 874-H2
DON MATEO CT
5400 SJS 95123 874-H2
DONNA CT
19200 SCIC 95037 916-J3
DONNA LN
1700 SJS 95124 873-H2
14400 SAR 95070 872-F2
DONNER CT
100 SUNV 94086 812-C7
DONNER DR
14800 SCIC 95124 873-G4
DONNER PL
2300 SCL 95050 833-C7

STREET Block City ZIP Pg-Grid

DONNORA CT
1100 SJS 95132 814-G5
DON OCTAVIO CT
5500 SJS 95123 874-E7
DONOHOE ST
100 MLPK 94025 791-A2
100 EPA 94303 791-A2
DONOHUE CT
1900 SJS 95131 814-D6
DONOHUE DR
1200 SJS 95131 814-D6
DONOVAN AV
2600 SCL 95051 833-B3
DONOVAN CT
2000 SJS 95125 853-G4
DON PEDRO CT
5500 SJS 95123 874-E6
DON PIZARRO CT
5400 SJS 95123 874-E6
DON RICARDO CT
5500 SJS 95123 874-E7
DON RODOLFO CT
5400 SJS 95123 874-H2
DON SCALA CT
5500 SJS 95123 874-E7
DON SEVILLE CT
400 SJS 95123 874-E6
DOOLING RD
- SBnC - (1020-F5
See Page 999)
DOON CT
1100 SUNV 94087 832-H4
DOORN LN
5600 SJS 95118 874-B5
DORADO LN
15500 MSER 95030 873-A5
DORAL CT
1600 SCIC 95020 957-D6
DORALEE WY
1100 SJS 95125 854-B6
DORCEY LN
1500 SJS 95120 874-A7
DORCHESTER DR
- MTVW 94043 812-B4
19400 SAR 95070 852-F6
DORCHESTER LN
1200 SJS 95118 874-C5
DORCICH ST
- SCL 95050 833-D7
3100 SCL 95117 833-D7
DOREL DR
800 SJS 95132 814-J5
900 SCIC 95132 814-J5
DORENE CT
14100 SAR 95070 872-B2
DORENE PL
6600 SJS 95120 894-F2
DORI LN
26200 LAH 94022 831-C1
DORIAN CT
800 SCIC 95127 814-H6
DORIS AV
200 SCIC 95127 834-J3
DORIS CT
- RDWC 94061 790-A1
8400 GIL 95020 977-H1
10300 SCIC 95127 834-J3
DORIS DR
1800 MLPK 94025 790-E6
DORMAR CT
10600 SCIC 95127 815-B7
DORN CT
6000 SJS 95123 875-B6
DORNOCH AV
1300 SJS 95122 854-H1
DOROTHY AV
400 SJS 95125 854-B3
DOROTHY RD
- SBnC - (1017-C7
See Page 997)
DOROTHY WY
21600 SCIC 95030 912-H3
DOROTHY ANN WY
11700 CPTO 95014 852-C4
DORRANCE AV
6500 SCIC 95020 (980-D6
See Page 959)
DORRANCE CT
1900 SJS 95125 853-J6
DORRANCE DR
1700 SJS 95125 853-J6
DORRIE AV
700 SJS 95116 834-E6
DORSET WY
600 SUNV 94087 832-E4
DORSEY WY
21000 SAR 95070 872-C2
DORVAL DR
2200 SJS 95130 853-A6

DOS LOMA VISTA LN
- PTLV 94028 810-D4
DOS PALOS CT
21800 CPTO 95014 832-B7
DOT AV
- CMBL 95008 853-D6
DOT CT
1400 SJS 95120 874-B6
DOTEY CT
600 SJS 95111 875-B1
DOTTIELYN AV
3700 SJS 95111 854-J6
DOUD DR
- LALT 94022 811-F6
DOUGHERTY AV
200 SCIC 95037 896-B4
300 SCIC 95037 916-E1
8500 SJS 95037 916-E1
17600 MGH 95037 916-E1
DOUGLANE AV
100 SCL 95117 833-D7
DOUGLAS ST
1400 SCIC 95126 853-H1
1400 SJS 95126 853-H1
DOUGLAS WY
- ATN 94027 790-F3
DOUGLASS LN
14000 SAR 95070 872-E2
DOVE CT
- GIL 95020 957-E7
DOVE LN
1400 SUNV 94087 832-E4
DOVE HILL RD
3400 SJS 95121 855-B4
DOVELA WY
3000 SJS 95118 874-A1
DOVE OAK CT
10000 CPTO 95014 831-J7
DOVER CT
100 LGTS 95032 873-E6
800 LALT 94022 831-D1
12400 SAR 95070 852-F5
DOVER ST
100 LGTS 95032 873-E5
DOVER WY
400 CMBL 95008 853-G5
10200 SCIC 95127 834-J3
DOVERTON SQ
2700 MTVW 94040 832-A2
DOVETAIL CT
- SJS 95135 875-J1
DOW DR
3000 SCIC 95136 854-D7
3000 SJS 95136 854-D7
DOWDY ST
7200 GIL 95020 977-J3
DOWNING AV
2200 SJS 95128 853-F3
2200 SCIC 95128 853-F3
DOWNING CT
1900 SCL 95051 833-A3
DOWNING LN
700 PA 94301 790-J4
DOWNING RD
800 MPS 95035 794-E4
1000 SCIC 95035 794-E2
DOWNING OAK CT
15000 LGTS 95032 873-F5
DOWNS DR
7200 SJS 95139 895-F1
DOWNSGLEN WY
500 SJS 95133 834-G1
DOWNSWICK DR
1000 SJS 95136 874-D1
DOWNSWOOD CT
800 SJS 95120 894-H3
DOXEY CT
1400 SJS 95131 814-D6
DOXEY DR
1900 SJS 95131 814-D6
DOYLE CT
4600 SJS 95129 853-A4
DOYLE DR
1400 SJS 95129 852-H4
DOYLE PL
1100 MTVW 94040 811-J7
DOYLE RD
400 SJS 95129 852-J1
4500 SJS 95129 853-A3
DOYLE ST
1000 MLPK 94025 790-F3
DRACENA LN
400 LALT 94022 811-F7
DRACENA WY
1800 SJS 95122 834-H7
DRAGONFLY CT
700 SJS 95133 834-F2
DRAGONFLY WY
700 SJS 95133 834-F1

DRAKE CT
300 SCL 95051 833-A7
19700 CPTO 95014 832-F6
DRAKE DR
19600 CPTO 95014 832-F6
DRAKE ST
400 SJS 95126 854-A1
600 SJS 95125 854-A2
DRAKES CT
100 LGTS 95032 873-D4
DRAKES BAY AV
100 LGTS 95032 873-D4
DREA RD
10900 CPTO 95014 852-A2
DRESDEN WY
1100 SJS 95129 852-F3
DREW AV
1700 MTVW 94043 811-H3
DREXEL WY
1000 SJS 95121 854-H3
DRIFTER DR
6200 SJS 95123 874-J6
DRIFTWOOD CT
1100 SUNV 94089 812-J4
DRIFTWOOD DR
800 PA 94303 791-E7
2900 SJS 95128 853-E4
DRIFTWOOD TER
1100 GIL 95020 977-G3
DRISCOLL CT
600 PA 94306 811-C3
DRUCILLA DR
500 MTVW 94040 811-H7
DRUMHEAD CT
1900 SJS 95131 814-C6
DRUMM CT
7400 SJS 95139 895-G1
DRUMM PL
7500 SJS 95139 895-G2
DRUMMOND DR
16200 SCIC 95030 872-H5
DRY BED CT
4200 SCL 95054 813-C5
DRY CREEK CT
2200 SJS 95008 853-G7
16700 MGH 95037 936-J1
DRY CREEK RD
1300 CMBL 95008 853-F7
1300 SJS 95125 854-A5
1300 SJS 95008 853-G7
1400 SJS 95125 853-J6
1400 SJS 95124 853-J6
1800 SCIC 95125 853-J6
DRY CREEK WY
2000 SJS 95124 853-H6
DRYDEN AV
2300 SCIC 95020 958-E6
10800 CPTO 95014 852-B2
DRYDEN DR
1300 SJS 95131 814-D7
DRY OAK CT
5900 SJS 95120 874-B6
DRY OAK DR
5800 SJS 95120 874-B6
DRY OAK PL
5900 SJS 95120 874-C6
DRYSDALE CT
5700 SJS 95124 873-J6
DRYSDALE DR
100 LGTS 95032 873-E6
1300 SUNV 94087 832-B4
5400 SJS 95124 873-J6
DRYTOWN PL
5900 SJS 95120 874-C6
DRYWOOD LN
3100 SJS 95132 814-D2
DRY YARD DR
500 SJS 95117 853-D2
DUANE AV
600 SUNV 94086 812-G6
800 SCL 95054 813-D7
E DUANE AV
200 SUNV 94086 812-F5
W DUANE AV
100 SUNV 94086 812-E5
DUANE CT
1000 SUNV 94086 812-H6
DUANE ST
- SJS 95110 854-C1
DUARTE CT
200 MPS 95035 794-A4
DUBANSKI DR
700 SJS 95123 874-F6
DUBERT LN
1300 SJS 95122 834-G7
DUBLIN DR
2700 SJS 95127 835-A5
DUBLIN WY
500 SUNV 94087 832-E4

DUBOIS ST
2200 MPS 95035 814-E1
DUBON AV
10100 CPTO 95014 851-J1
DUCHESS CT
3400 SJS 95132 814-J3
DUCKETT WY
1500 SJS 95129 852-E4
DUCK LAKE CT
800 SJS 95123 874-E5
DUDASH CT
1100 SJS 95122 854-H1
DUDLEY AV
500 SJS 95128 853-E2
DUDLEY LN
- SCIC - 791-A7
DUENA ST
500 SCIC 94305 790-H7
DUESENBERG DR
5300 SJS 95123 874-G3
DUET CT
6000 SJS 95120 874-C7
DUFF CT
800 SUNV 94086 832-F2
DUFFY CT
200 SJS 95116 834-F4
DUFFY WY
1700 SJS 95116 834-G4
DUGGAN DR
3900 SJS 95118 874-A2
DUKE CT
3300 SCL 95051 832-J6
DUKE DR
10200 SCIC 95020 958-C3
DUKE WY
900 MTVW 94040 811-G7
1300 SJS 95125 854-A5
DULCEY DR
4100 SJS 95136 874-G1
DULUTH CIR
300 PA 94306 811-D2
DUMAS DR
7400 CPTO 95014 852-D2
DUMBARTON AV
- SMCo 94063 790-C1
2000 EPA 94303 791-A2
2500 SJS 95124 853-H7
2600 SJS 95124 873-J1
DUMONT CIR
2400 SJS 95122 834-J5
DUMONT CT
2500 SJS 95122 834-J5
DUNBAR DR
20600 SCIC 95014 832-D7
DUNCAN AV
1000 SUNV 94089 812-F4
DUNCAN PL
3800 PA 94306 811-E1
DUNCAN ST
500 SCIC 95127 814-H7
500 SJS 95127 814-H7
DUNCANVILLE CT
700 CMBL 95008 853-F6
DUNCARDINE WY
700 SUNV 94087 832-F5
DUNDALE DR
3700 SJS 95121 855-A5
DUNDEE AV
400 MPS 95035 794-A6
18700 SAR 95070 852-H7
DUNDEE CT
1300 SJS 95122 854-H1
DUNDEE DR
2500 SCL 95051 833-B2
DUNDONALD CT
3200 SJS 95121 855-C5
DUNFORD WY
900 SUNV 94087 832-G5
1000 SCL 95051 832-G5
DUNHOLME WY
500 SUNV 94087 832-E5
DUNIGAN CT
5500 SJS 95123 874-F7
DUNLAP AV
1700 SCIC 95020 978-D1
2200 SCIC 95020 958-E7
DUNN AV
5900 SJS 95123 874-J5
DUNNE AV
- MGH 95037 917-G6
400 SCIC 95037 917-G2
2400 SCIC 95037 918-A2
2600 SCIC 95037 (898-A7
See Page 877)
E DUNNE AV
100 MGH 95037 917-E6
2000 SCIC 95037 917-E6
W DUNNE AV
- MGH 95037 936-H1
800 MGH 95037 937-A1

DUNNE ST
7100 SCIC 95020 999-H3
DUNNOCK WY
1300 SUNV 94087 832-E4
DUNRAVEN CT
600 SJS 95136 874-F2
DUNSBURRY CT
5500 SJS 95123 874-F4
DUNSBURRY WY
5500 SJS 95123 874-G3
DUNSTER DR
300 CMBL 95008 853-D5
DUNWELL CT
100 SJS 95138 875-E4
DUNWICH CT
3100 SJS 95148 855-E2
DUPONT ST
200 SJS 95126 854-A1
DURAND RD
- SCIC 94035 812-B2
- SCIC 94043 812-B2
DURANGO CT
5000 SJS 95118 874-A4
DURANGO LN
9400 GIL 95020 957-F7
DURANGO RIVER CT
4700 SJS 95136 874-G2
DURANT AV
3100 SJS 95111 854-H6
DURAZNO WY
100 SMCo 94028 810-D3
DURBAN CT
5000 SJS 95138 855-F7
DURBAN DR
1900 SJS 95138 855-F7
DURHAM CT
1000 SUNV 94087 832-H5
19900 SAR 95070 872-E2
DURHAM ST
100 MLPK 94025 791-A2
300 MLPK 94025 790-J2
DURLANE CT
900 SUNV 94087 832-G5
DURNESS PL
1000 SJS 95122 854-G1
DURSHIRE WY
600 SUNV 94087 832-F5
DU SAULT DR
6400 SJS 95119 875-C7
DUSTIN CT
- SJS 95123 874-F7
DUTCHESS CT
2400 SCIC 95020 958-C2
DUTTONWOOD LN
- MPS 95035 793-J3
DUVAL CT
3000 SCIC 95020 958-E5
DUVAL WY
26000 LAH 94022 831-B1
DUVALL CT
500 SUNV 94087 832-D4
DUVALL DR
1500 SJS 95130 853-A5
1700 SJS 95130 852-J5
DWIGHT AV
800 SUNV 94086 812-F7
5500 SJS 95118 874-A5
DWYER AV
900 SJS 95120 894-D1
DWYER CT
6400 SJS 95120 894-E1
DYMOND CT
400 PA 94306 791-C7

E

E ST
1100 SUNV 94089 812-E3
EAGLE DR
1600 SUNV 94087 832-E5
EAGLE CLIFF WY
7200 SJS 95120 894-F4
EAGLE CREST CT
7300 SJS 95120 894-E4
EAGLEHAVEN CT
- SJS 95111 874-J1
EAGLE HILLS WY
9400 GIL 95020 957-F7
EAGLEHURST DR
1700 SJS 95121 855-C4
EAGLE LAKE DR
4600 SJS 95136 874-D2
EAGLE RIDGE WY
1000 MPS 95035 814-E1
EAGLE ROCK RD
4700 SJS 95136 874-J2
4800 SJS 95136 875-A2
EAGLES LN
5400 SJS 95123 875-A4

EAGLES NEST LN
1400 GIL 95020 957-E7
EAGLE SPRINGS CT
600 MGH 95037 916-H6
EAGLE VALLEY CT
7100 SJS 95120 894-F4
EAGLE VIEW TER
- FRMT 94539 794-B1
EAGLE VIEW WY
9400 GIL 95020 957-F7
E EAGLEWOOD AV
200 SUNV 94086 812-F5
W EAGLEWOOD AV
100 SUNV 94086 812-E5
EARL AV
1000 SCIC 95126 853-J1
EARL DR
3400 SCL 95051 832-J2
EARLANDER ST
10200 SCIC 95127 835-A2
EARLINGTON CT
1000 SUNV 94087 832-B5
EARLS CT
19900 SCIC 95037 916-F3
EARLSWOOD CT
7100 SJS 95120 894-H4
EARLY MORNING LN
- SJS 95135 875-J1
- SJS 95138 875-J1
EASINGTON WY
1500 SJS 95126 853-H4
EAST CT
300 SJS 95116 834-E3
8400 GIL 95020 977-J1
EAST LN
17600 MGH 95037 917-B5
17600 SCIC 95037 917-B5
EAST ST
7200 GIL 95020 978-B3
EASTBOURNE CT
5000 SJS 95138 855-E6
EASTBOURNE DR
5100 SJS 95138 855-E7
EASTBROOK AV
1600 SCIC 94024 831-F4
11000 LAH 94024 831-E3
EASTBROOK CT
23200 SCIC 94024 831-G5
EASTER AV
400 MPS 95035 793-J6
EASTGATE AV
- SJS 95116 834-F4
EAST HILLS CT
10400 SCIC 95127 835-B1
EAST HILLS DR
2900 SCIC 95127 834-J3
3000 SJS 95127 834-J3
3100 SCIC 95127 835-B1
3100 SCIC 95127 834-J3
3400 SJS 95127 835-B1
EAST LAKE DR
1500 SJS 95126 853-G3
EASTMAN LAKE DR
5900 SJS 95123 874-G7
EASTON CT
2500 SJS 95133 834-G1
EASTON DR
500 SJS 95133 834-F1
12500 SAR 95070 852-H6
EASTON LN
2500 SJS 95133 834-G1
2500 SCIC 95133 834-G1
EASTON PL
2500 SJS 95133 834-G1
18900 SAR 95070 852-H6
EASTON TER
2500 SJS 95133 834-B2
EASTRIDGE AV
2200 MLPK 94025 790-D7
EASTRIDGE BLVD
2400 SJS 95122 855-B1
EASTRIDGE DR
100 LGTS 95032 873-D6
3500 SJS 95148 835-D4
EASTRIDGE LN
2200 SJS 95122 835-A7
EASTRIDGE LP
- SJS 95122 855-A1
200 SJS 95122 835-A7
EASTRIDGE WY
2200 SJS 95122 835-A7
EASTSIDE DR
200 SJS 95127 834-H1
200 SCIC 95127 834-H1
EASTUS DR
4600 SJS 95129 853-A3
4600 SJS 95129 852-J3
EAST VALLEY CT
3700 SCIC 95148 835-E5

EASTVIEW DR
14500 LGTS 95030 873-B3
14700 SCIC 95030 873-B3
EASTWOOD CIR
3600 SCL 95054 813-F6
EASTWOOD CT
- SJS 95116 834-F4
1000 LALT 94024 831-H2
EASTWOOD DR
900 LALT 94024 831-H2
EASY ST
- MTVW 94043 812-A4
400 MGH 95037 937-C5
1000 SCIC 95037 937-C5
EATON LN
400 MTVW 94043 812-B5
17100 MSER 95030 873-A4
EATON PL
- CPTO 95014 832-B7
EBANO CT
1300 SJS 95121 854-J3
EBBESEN AV
2100 SJS 95124 873-F3
EBBETTS DR
700 CMBL 95008 853-A7
700 CMBL 95008 873-A1
EBENER ST
1300 RDWC 94061 790-B1
EBERHARD ST
1600 SCL 95050 833-C3
EBERLY DR
4900 SJS 95111 875-A1
EBERTS DR
1600 SCIC 95046 937-G4
EBONY WY
2800 SJS 95148 835-F7
ECHO AV
100 CMBL 95008 853-D7
ECHO DR
800 LALT 94024 831-F2
22500 SCIC 95030 913-B4
ECHO LN
100 PTLV 94028 810-C7
ECHO LP
7100 SJS 95120 894-E3
ECHO KNOLLS RD
- SCIC 95140 815-C7
4100 SCIC 95127 815-C7
ECHO RIDGE CT
1200 SJS 95120 894-E4
ECHO RIDGE DR
7100 SJS 95120 894-E4
ECHO VALLEY DR
1200 SJS 95120 894-D3
ECKBERG CT
- SJS 95127 834-J2
ECKER CT
600 CMBL 95008 853-C7
ECOLA LN
- SUNV 94087 832-A5
EDALE DR
700 SUNV 94087 832-C3
EDDINGTON PL
1400 SJS 95129 852-E4
EDELEN AV
100 LGTS 95030 873-A7
EDELWEISS DR
400 SJS 95136 874-F2
EDEN AV
600 SJS 95117 853-D3
1500 CMBL 95117 853-D4
1500 CMBL 95008 853-D4
N EDEN AV
500 SUNV 94086 812-G5
S EDEN AV
500 SUNV 94086 812-G5
W EDEN AV
500 SUNV 94086 812-F5
EDEN CT
500 SCL 95051 832-J6
EDEN DR
3400 SCL 95051 832-J6
EDEN ST
500 GIL 95020 977-H1
EDENBANK CT
2900 SJS 95148 855-D2
EDENBANK DR
3000 SJS 95148 855-D1
EDENBURY LN
900 SJS 95136 874-D1
EDENHALL DR
6100 SJS 95129 852-G3
EDEN PARK PL
5800 SJS 95138 875-E4
EDENVALE AV
200 SJS 95111 875-A2
200 SJS 95136 875-A2
EDENVALE LN
- SCrC 95076 (975-J7
See Page 955)

EDEN VIEW DR
4900 SJS 95111 875-B2
EDENWOOD CT
3800 SJS 95121 855-C4
EDENWOOD DR
3800 SJS 95121 855-C5
EDES CT
100 MGH 95037 937-A2
EDGAR CT
4900 SJS 95118 874-C3
EDGE LN
700 LALT 94024 831-G2
EDGE RD
- ATN 94027 790-G1
EDGEBANK DR
1900 SJS 95122 855-A1
EDGEBROOK CT
6500 SJS 95120 894-C1
EDGECLIFF LN
12100 LAH 94022 831-C3
EDGECLIFF PL
12100 LAH 94022 831-C3
EDGECREST DR
1900 SJS 95122 855-A1
EDGEDALE CT
2500 SJS 95122 855-A1
EDGEFIELD CT
2500 SJS 95122 855-A1
EDGEFIELD DR
3600 SCL 95054 813-F5
EDGEFORT CT
1900 SJS 95122 855-A1
EDGEGATE DR
2000 SJS 95122 855-A1
EDGEHILL DR
400 SCL 95054 813-F5
EDGEHILL WY
1200 MPS 95035 814-F1
EDGEMAN CT
3500 SJS 95148 835-E6
EDGEMONT DR
10900 SCIC 95127 815-B6
EDGEMOOR WY
6300 SJS 95129 852-F3
EDGERTON RD
27400 LAH 94022 830-J1
27600 LAH 94022 810-J7
EDGESTONE CIR
1800 SJS 95122 855-A1
EDGEVIEW CT
2500 SJS 95122 855-A1
EDGEVIEW DR
1900 SJS 95122 855-A1
EDGEWATER DR
- MPS 95035 794-A6
3500 SJS 95136 854-G7
EDGEWOOD DR
1400 PA 94301 791-B3
1500 PA 94303 791-C3
EDGEWOOD LN
700 LALT 94022 831-E1
1800 MLPK 94025 790-E6
EDGEWOOD WY
1500 SJS 95125 854-A6
EDINA LN
19700 SAR 95070 852-F6
EDINBURGH DR
20000 SAR 95070 852-E7
EDISON DR
2800 SJS 95133 834-H1
2900 SCIC 95133 834-H1
E EDITH AV
- LALT 94022 811-F6
W EDITH AV
- LALT 94022 811-D6
300 LAH 94022 811-D6
EDITH ST
1100 SJS 95122 834-H5
EDLEE AV
200 PA 94306 811-D2
EDMINTON DR
18400 SCIC 95014 852-H2
EDMOND CT
1500 SJS 95125 854-A7
EDMONDS CT
1000 SUNV 94087 832-B5
EDMONDS WY
900 SUNV 94087 832-B5
EDMONTON AV
1600 SUNV 94087 832-B5
EDMUND DR
15800 LGTS 95032 873-E5
EDMUNDSON AV
- SCIC 95037 936-H4
1200 SCIC 95037 937-A3
1200 MGH 95037 937-A3
E EDMUNDSON AV
- MGH 95037 937-B2
EDMUNDSON DR
1800 SCIC 95037 936-G4

EDNA AV
- SCIC 95127 835-A3
EDNA CT
300 LALT 94022 811-F7
EDNAMARY WY
1700 MTVW 94040 811-F5
EDQUIBA RD
- SCIC 94035 812-B3
EDSEL DR
1100 MPS 95035 794-D7
6300 SJS 95129 852-F3
EDUCATIONAL PARK DR
300 SJS 95133 834-E1
EDWARD AV
3200 SCL 95054 813-F6
EDWARD WY
21500 CPTO 95014 852-B2
EDWARDS AV
- SJS 95110 854-C1
EDWARDS LN
- ATN 94027 790-D3
EDWARDS RD
17800 SCIC 95030 912-J2
EDWIN JONES CT
16800 MGH 95037 936-J1
EGGO WY
400 SJS 95116 834-D3
N EGRET CT
- GIL 95020 957-E7
S EGRET CT
- GIL 95020 957-E7
EGRET DR
1300 SUNV 94087 832-F4
EHRHORN AV
600 MTVW 94041 811-J6
EICHLER CT
1200 MTVW 94040 811-H6
EICHLER DR
900 MTVW 94040 811-G6
EIGLEBERRY ST
7000 GIL 95020 978-A3
7600 GIL 95020 977-J2
EILEEN CT
18100 SCIC 95030 912-H3
EILEEN DR
5100 SJS 95129 852-H4
EISENHOWER DR
500 SJS 95128 853-F3
1400 SCL 95054 813-D4
EL ABRA WY
1100 SJS 95125 854-A3
ELAINE CT
17800 MGH 95037 916-H7
ELAINE DR
3100 SJS 95124 873-G2
EL ALTILLO
100 LGTS 95030 872-J2
ELAM AV
1200 CMBL 95008 853-B7
ELAN VILLAGE LN
300 SJS 95134 813-G4
EL BOSQUE AV
200 SJS 95134 813-F2
EL BOSQUE DR
100 SJS 95134 813-E3
EL BOSQUE ST
100 SJS 95134 813-F2
ELBRIDGE WY
800 PA 94303 791-D6
EL CAJON DR
200 SJS 95111 854-J6
EL CAJON WY
200 LGTS 95030 873-C4
900 PA 94303 791-C5
EL CAMINITO
9200 GIL 95020 957-F7
EL CAMINITO AV
- CMBL 95008 853-D6
EL CAMINITO RD
23500 LAH 94024 831-E5
EL CAMINO WY
4000 PA 94306 811-C2
EL CAMINO GRANDE
15100 SAR 95070 872-G4
EL CAMINO HIGUERA
1100 MPS 95035 794-B4
1300 SCIC 95035 794-B4
EL CAMINO REAL
500 SJS 95037 896-B4
500 SCIC 95037 896-B4
5300 SJS 95111 875-C3
5500 GIL 95020 978-A4
5500 SJS 95138 875-C4
5800 SJS 95139 875-H7
5800 SJS 95139 896-A1
5800 SJS 95137 875-H7
5800 SJS 95137 895-H1
5900 SJS 95139 896-A2
5900 SCIC 95137 896-A2

EL CAMINO REAL
5900 SCIC 95137 895-J2
6000 SJS 95137 896-A2
6100 SJS 95141 896-B3
6200 SCIC 95020 978-A4
7900 GIL 95020 977-J2
8200 SCIC 95137 896-A3
8600 GIL 95020 957-G3
10000 SCIC 95037 896-D6
10400 SCIC 95020 957-G3
11000 SCIC 95046 957-G3
11600 MGH 95037 917-A7
12300 SCIC 95046 937-E6
13300 MGH 95037 937-E6
13900 MGH 95046 937-E6
EL CAMINO REAL Rt#-82
- MLPK 94025 790-C1
- PA 94301 790-H4
- PA 94304 790-H4
100 ATN 94027 790-C1
100 MTVW 94040 811-B1
100 MTVW 94041 811-B1
100 SMCo 94063 790-C1
200 SCIC 94305 790-H4
200 PA 94305 790-H4
300 SCL 95050 833-A4
400 SCL 95053 833-A4
1400 SCIC - 791-A6
1400 PA - 790-H4
1400 PA 94306 791-A6
1500 MLPK 94025 790-C1
1700 ATN 94025 790-C1
2400 PA 94305 791-A6
2400 SCL 95051 833-A4
2600 RDWC 94061 790-C1
2700 PA 94304 811-B1
2800 PA 94306 811-B1
3300 SCL 95051 832-J4
4300 LALT 94022 811-B1
EL CAMINO REAL U.S.-101
- SCIC 95020 (1018-A
See Page 997)
E EL CAMINO REAL Rt#-82
- SCL 95051 832-G
100 SUNV 94087 832-E
100 SUNV 94086 832-G
800 SCIC 94087 832-G
1100 SCL 94086 832-G
W EL CAMINO REAL Rt#-82
- MTVW 94040 811-F
- MTVW 94041 811-F
100 SUNV 94086 832-C
100 SUNV 94087 832-C
100 MTVW 94040 812-A
100 MTVW 94041 812-A
300 SCIC 94087 832-C
900 SUNV 94086 812-A
1100 SUNV 94087 812-A
1700 LALT 94022 811-F
EL CAMINO SENDA
15000 SAR 95070 872-G
EL CAMPO DR
- SCIC 95127 835-A
100 SCIC 95127 834-J
EL CAPITAN AV
2000 SCL 95050 833-C
EL CAPITAN PL
400 PA 94306 811-E
EL CARMELO AV
100 PA 94306 791-C
EL CENTRO
- MTVW 94043 812-A
EL CENTRO ST
3700 PA 94306 811-E
EL CERRITO RD
- CPTO 95014 851-J
3900 PA 94306 811-B
EL CERRITO WY
300 GIL 95020 977-H
1000 PA 94306 811-C
EL CODO WY
1700 SJS 95124 873-H
EL CORAL CT
1300 SJS 95118 874-C
EL CORAL WY
3900 SJS 95118 874-
ELDAMAR CT
1200 SJS 95121 855-
ELDEN DR
600 SJS 95008 853-
1900 SJS 95124 853-
ELDER AV
1100 MLPK 94025 790-
ELDER CT
- MLPK 94025 790-
500 SJS 95123 874-

SANTA CLARA CO.
INDEX

STREET Block City ZIP Pg-Grid

ELDERBERRY DR
1200 SUNV 94087 832-B3
ELDERBERRY WY
1600 SJS 95125 853-J5
ELDERWOOD CT
7600 CPTO 95014 852-D2
EL DORA DR
- MTVW 94041 812-A6
- MTVW 94041 811-J6
EL DORADO AV
100 PA 94306 791-C7
100 SJS 95136 854-G7
1600 SJS 95126 833-F6
EL DORADO CT
- SJS 95002 813-B1
20500 SAR 95070 872-D1
ELDORADO DR
1500 GIL 95020 977-F2
EL DORADO ST
1300 SJS 95002 793-B7
1500 SJS 95002 813-B1
EL DORI DR
5800 SJS 95123 874-E5
EL DORIC CT
8800 SCIC 95020 (976-J1
See Page 955)
ELDRIDGE DR
6800 SJS 95120 894-G2
ELEANOR AV
- LALT 94022 811-E7
ELEANOR DR
100 WDSD 94062 790-A5
400 ATN 94027 790-A5
ELEANOR WY
900 SUNV 94087 832-G4
ELECTIONEER RD
- SCIC 94305 790-F7
ELECTRA AV
3500 SJS 95118 874-B1
ELENA AV
- ATN 94027 790-D3
ELENA RD
25300 LAH 94022 831-A1
27000 LAH 94022 811-A7
27500 LAH 94022 810-J6
ELENA WY
100 LGTS 95030 873-B3
ELENA PRIVADA
1100 MTVW 94040 832-A1
ELENDA DR
20800 CPTO 95014 832-D7
20800 SCIC 95014 832-D7
EL ESCARPADO CT
400 SCIC 94305 810-G1
ELESTER CT
2300 SJS 95124 873-E4
ELESTER DR
4800 SJS 95124 873-E4
EL GATO LN
15500 LGTS 95032 873-E5
15500 SCIC 95032 873-E5
ELGIN LN
3300 SJS 95118 874-A1
EL GRANDE CT
3600 SJS 95132 814-J5
EL GRANDE DR
3500 SJS 95132 814-J5
ELISA AV
19700 SAR 95070 852-F5
ELISE CT
24200 LAH 94024 831-D4
ELIZABETH DR
900 SCL 95050 833-C5
ELIZABETH LN
700 MLPK 94025 790-F3
ELIZABETH ST
400 SJS 95112 834-C6
400 SJS 95113 834-C6
900 SJS 95002 793-B7
ELIZABETH WY
- ATN 94027 790-C2
900 SUNV 94087 832-G4
ELJA WY
800 SJS 95123 874-F5
ELK LN
2300 SJS 95133 814-F7
ELKA AV
1400 SJS 95129 852-F4
2400 MTVW 94043 811-F2
ELK CREEK PL
200 SJS 95127 834-H1
ELKHORN CT
2200 SJS 95125 854-A6
ELKHORN RD Rt#-G12
- MntC - (1015-H7
See Page 995)
ELKINS WY
2300 SJS 95121 855-C3
ELKO DR
1100 SUNV 94089 812-J3

ELKO DR
1200 SUNV 94089 813-A3
ELK RIDGE CT
3000 SJS 95136 854-F6
ELK RIDGE WY
500 SJS 95136 854-E7
ELKWOOD DR
1100 MPS 95035 793-J5
ELLA CT
5000 SJS 95111 875-B1
ELLA DR
400 SJS 95111 875-B1
ELLEGE RD
18400 SCIC 95030 892-F5
ELLEN AV
1700 SJS 95125 854-B4
ELLENA DR
2200 SCL 95050 833-C2
ELLENWOOD AV
- LGTS 95030 872-J7
W ELLENWOOD AV
200 MSER 95030 872-J6
200 LGTS 95030 872-J6
ELLERBROOK WY
6100 SJS 95123 875-B6
ELLERY ST
500 SCIC 95127 814-H7
500 SJS 95127 814-H7
ELLIOT AV
16500 LGTS 95032 873-C5
ELLIOT CT
2500 SCL 95051 833-B2
ELLIOT ST
2400 SCL 95051 833-B2
ELLIOTT DR
100 MLPK 94025 791-A2
ELLIOTT ST
1800 SCIC 95128 853-G1
2100 SJS 95128 853-G1
ELLIS AV
900 SJS 95125 854-B4
1500 MPS 95035 794-D6
15700 SCIC 95037 937-E1
ELLIS ST
300 MTVW 94043 812-B4
600 MTVW 94035 812-B4
600 SCIC 94035 812-B4
EL LISA DR
900 SJS 95123 874-E4
ELLMAR OAKS CT
200 SJS 95136 874-G1
ELLMAR OAKS DR
3900 SJS 95136 874-G1
ELLMAR OAKS LP
3900 SJS 95136 874-G1
ELLSWORTH PL
700 PA 94303 791-D6
ELLWELL DR
1700 MPS 95035 794-D6
ELLYRIDGE CT
200 SJS 95123 874-J3
ELLYRIDGE DR
5400 SJS 95123 874-J3
ELM AV
400 MPS 95035 793-H6
ELM CT
100 SUNV 94086 832-F1
400 MPS 95035 793-J6
21400 CPTO 95014 852-C2
ELM PK
15000 MSER 95030 873-A4
15000 MSER 95030 872-J4
ELM RD
17700 SCIC 95037 917-C4
17800 MGH 95037 917-C4
ELM ST
- LGTS 95030 873-A7
100 GIL 95020 978-A2
100 MLPK 94025 791-A2
300 MLPK 94025 790-J2
600 SJS 95126 833-H5
ELMAR WY
1500 SJS 95129 852-F5
EL MARCERO CT
6900 SJS 95119 895-E1
EL MATADOR DR
8000 SCIC 95020 (976-J1
See Page 955)
9000 SCIC 95020 956-J7
ELMBRIDGE DR
6000 SJS 95129 852-G3
ELMBROOK WY
500 SJS 95111 855-A7
ELMBURG RDGE
- LAH 94022 831-A2
ELMDALE PL
2600 PA 94303 791-D5
ELMGATE CT
2100 SJS 95148 855-E2

ELMGROVE CT
5000 SJS 95130 852-J6
ELMGROVE LN
2000 SJS 95130 852-J6
ELMHURST AV
3400 SCL 95051 832-J7
ELMHURST CT
100 SCL 95051 832-J7
ELMHURST DR
1500 LALT 94024 832-A3
4500 SJS 95129 853-A2
ELMIRA DR
800 SUNV 94087 832-C2
ELM LEAF CT
2000 SCL 95050 833-C3
EL MOLINO WY
300 SJS 95119 875-B7
EL MONTE AV
- LALT 94024 831-E1
- LALT 94022 831-E1
900 MTVW 94040 811-E7
1500 MTVW 94022 811-E7
1500 LALT 94022 811-E7
2100 LALT 94024 811-E7
N EL MONTE AV
- LALT 94022 811-G6
- LALT 94024 811-G6
EL MONTE CT
100 LALT 94022 811-F6
EL MONTE RD
- LALT 94024 831-D2
700 LALT 94022 831-D2
700 LAH 94024 831-D2
700 LAH 94022 831-D2
EL MONTE WY
2700 SJS 95127 835-A5
EL MORO DR
1200 CMBL 95008 853-G6
ELM PARK
15200 MSER 95030 872-J4
ELM PARK CT
15200 MSER 95030 872-J4
ELMSDALE DR
7000 SJS 95120 894-G3
ELMSFORD CT
1100 CPTO 95014 852-C3
ELMSFORD DR
1100 CPTO 95014 852-C3
ELMTREE CT
1800 SJS 95131 814-C5
ELMWOOD CT
100 LGTS 95030 873-A2
ELMWOOD DR
4900 SJS 95130 852-J6
ELMWOOD PL
- MLPK 94025 790-H2
ELMWOOD ST
100 MTVW 94043 811-J4
EL NIDO AV
- LGTS 95032 893-B1
EL NIDO CT
- LGTS 95032 893-C1
EL NIDO RD
100 SMCo 94028 830-D4
ELNORA CT
1400 LALT 94024 831-J4
ELODIE WY
- SJS 95116 834-H2
ELOISE CIR
10600 SCIC 94024 831-F5
EL OLIVAR
100 LGTS 95030 872-J2
EL OSO DR
1400 SJS 95129 852-J5
EL PAJARO CT
15800 MGH 95037 937-A3
EL PASEO DR
6200 SJS 95120 874-D7
6300 SJS 95120 894-D1
EL PASEO DE LOS PASTORES
3600 SCIC 95148 835-F6
EL PATIO CT
100 CMBL 95008 853-F5
EL PATIO DR
500 CMBL 95008 853-F5
EL PINAR
100 LGTS 95030 872-J2
EL PORTAL WY
200 SJS 95119 875-B6
300 SJS 95123 875-B6
EL PORTON
100 LGTS 95030 872-J2
EL PRADO AV
200 SMCo 94061 790-A4
EL PRADO CT
1100 SJS 95120 874-D7
EL PRADO DR
1100 SJS 95120 874-D7

EL PRADO WY
10200 CPTO 95014 851-J1
EL PUENTE WY
14500 SAR 95070 872-F3
EL QUITO WY
15000 SAR 95070 872-H4
EL RANCHITO WY
600 MTVW 94041 811-J6
EL RANCHO AV
17300 MSER 95030 873-B5
EL RANCHO VERDE CT
200 SJS 95116 834-G3
EL RANCHO VERDE DR
100 SJS 95116 834-F3
EL REY RD
- SMCo 94028 830-D4
EL RIO DR
800 SJS 95125 854-C5
EL ROBLE CT
5000 SJS 95118 874-B4
7600 GIL 95020 977-H3
ELROSE AV
5000 SJS 95124 873-H5
5100 SJS 95032 873-H5
EL SERENO AV
2000 LALT 94024 832-A5
EL SERENO CT
- LALT 94024 832-A5
EL SERENO DR
700 SJS 95123 874-G6
ELSIE AV
1700 MTVW 94043 811-H3
ELSIE WY
- LAH 94022 811-B7
ELSINORE CT
900 PA 94303 791-C5
ELSINORE DR
900 PA 94303 791-C5
ELSMAN CT
1400 SJS 95120 874-A7
EL SOBRANTE ST
2700 SCL 95051 833-A4
EL SOLYO AV
1000 CMBL 95008 853-G6
EL SOMBROSO DR
700 SJS 95123 874-G5
ELSONA CT
1300 SUNV 94087 832-B4
ELSONA DR
1300 SUNV 94087 832-B4
ELTON CT
14700 SCIC 95124 873-G4
ELTON DR
14800 SCIC 95124 873-G4
EL TORO CT
100 MGH 95037 916-J7
6100 SJS 95123 874-F6
EL TORO DR
300 GIL 95020 977-H2
EL TORO ST
- MGH 95037 916-J6
EL TORO WY
600 GIL 95020 977-J1
ELVA AV
14200 SAR 95070 872-D2
EL VERANO AV
100 PA 94306 811-C1
300 PA 94306 791-D7
ELVIRA CT
1200 SJS 95122 834-H5
ELVIRA ST
14000 SAR 95070 872-D2
ELVIS DR
500 SJS 95123 874-J7
EL VISTA WY
2700 SJS 95148 835-D7
ELWELL CT
1000 PA 94303 791-F6
ELWOOD CT
6600 SJS 95120 894-E1
ELWOOD DR
1300 CMBL 95008 872-J1
ELWOOD RD
6600 SJS 95120 894-E2
ELY CT
200 SJS 95123 875-A4
ELY PL
100 PA 94306 811-E1
EL ZUPARKO DR
5800 SJS 95123 874-E5
EMADO AV
600 SJS 95139 896-A3
EMAMI CT
7200 SJS 95120 894-H4
EMAMI DR
7200 SJS 95120 894-H4
EMANUEL CT
3600 SJS 95121 855-A4
18500 SAR 95070 852-H7

EMBARCADERO RD
- SCIC 94305 790-J5
- PA 94301 790-J5
100 PA 94301 791-C4
700 PA 94303 791-C4
EMBARCADERO WY
2400 PA 94303 791-E3
EMBEE DR
5800 SJS 95123 875-A5
EMERALD WY
900 SJS 95117 853-D3
EMERALD HILL
14400 SAR 95070 872-H2
EMERALD HILLS CIR
2200 SJS 95131 814-D6
EMERALD HILLS LN
12000 LAH 94022 831-D3
EMERICK AV
300 SCIC 95127 835-A2
300 SJS 95127 835-A2
EMERSON AV
1100 SCIC 95008 873-D3
EMERSON CT
700 SJS 95126 833-H6
8500 GIL 95020 977-G1
EMERSON LN
100 MTVW 94043 812-B5
EMERSON ST
100 PA 94301 790-H4
1100 PA 94301 791-A6
2500 PA 94306 791-B7
3100 PA 94306 811-C1
EMIG CT
1700 SCL 95051 832-J3
EMILIE AV
- ATN 94027 790-E3
EMILIE DR
10500 SCIC 95127 834-J3
13200 SJS 95127 834-J3
EMILINE DR
5000 SJS 95124 873-G5
EMILY DR
600 MTVW 94043 812-A3
EMLYN CT
6000 SJS 95123 875-B6
EMMA CT
900 SJS 95120 894-G4
EMMA LN
100 MLPK 94025 791-A3
EMMETT CT
2200 SCL 95051 832-J2
EMMETT PL
3400 SCL 95051 832-J2
EMMETT WY
2500 EPA 94303 791-B1
EMMONS DR
400 MTVW 94043 811-G2
EMORY AV
500 CMBL 95008 853-D7
700 CMBL 95008 873-D1
EMORY ST
200 SJS 95110 833-J5
700 SJS 95126 833-H6
1700 SJS 95128 833-F7
EMPEROR WY
1500 SUNV 94087 832-F5
EMPEY WY
600 SCIC 95128 853-F2
EMPIRE AL
- SJS 95110 834-A5
EMPIRE AV
10100 CPTO 95014 832-B7
E EMPIRE ST
- SJS 95112 834-C4
W EMPIRE ST
200 SJS 95110 834-A5
EMPRESS CT
6200 SJS 95129 852-F3
ENBORG LN
2200 SCIC 95128 853-F2
ENCHANTO VISTA
11000 SCIC 95127 815-A5
ENCINA AV
- PA 94301 790-J5
200 RDWC 94061 790-B1
300 ATN 94027 790-E1
300 SMCo 94063 790-E1
ENCINA CT
15000 SAR 95070 872-G4
ENCINA WY
2500 SCL 95051 833-B4
ENCINA GRANDE DR
600 PA 94306 811-C2
ENCINAL AV
100 ATN 94027 790-F2
100 MLPK 94025 790-F2
100 MLPK 94027 790-F2
ENCINAL CT
23200 LAH 94024 831-E5

ENCINAL DR
6100 SJS 95119 875-C6
ENCINITAS CT
2800 SJS 95132 814-D3
ENCINO CT
100 SUNV 94086 812-C6
ENCINO DR
500 MGH 95037 937-A4
ENCINO RD
- ATN 94027 790-G1
ENCLAVE DR
- SJS 95134 813-C2
ENCORE WY
600 SJS 95134 813-F3
ENDERBY WY
1000 SUNV 94087 832-B4
ENDERSON CT
18200 SCIC 95037 916-H6
ENDFIELD WY
10000 SCIC 95127 835-A3
ENDICOTT BLVD
1400 SJS 95193 875-C4
ENDICOTT DR
500 SUNV 94087 832-D2
1400 SJS 95122 834-J5
ENDMOOR CT
300 SJS 95119 895-D1
ENDMOOR DR
6700 SJS 95119 895-D1
ENESCO AV
1600 SJS 95121 855-A2
1700 SJS 95122 855-A2
ENGLE WY
6200 GIL 95020 978-B5
ENGLERT CT
300 SJS 95133 834-F2
ENGLEWOOD AV
16300 LGTS 95032 873-C7
16300 SCIC 95032 873-C7
ENGLEWOOD DR
4600 SJS 95129 853-A4
4600 SJS 95129 852-J4
ENGLISH CT
1600 SJS 95129 852-H5
ENGLISH DR
1400 SJS 95129 852-H5
ENGLISH PL
400 SCIC 95138 875-E3
ENGLISH OAK WY
10100 CPTO 95014 831-J7
ENGLISH WALNUT CT
800 MGH 95037 917-B6
ENGLISH WALNUT WY
800 MGH 95037 917-B6
ENNING AV
5600 SJS 95123 874-J4
ENOCHS ST
3600 SCL 95051 812-J7
ENOS CT
600 SCL 95051 833-B6
ENRIGHT AV
600 SCL 95050 833-D5
ENRIQUEZ CT
200 MPS 95035 794-A5
ENRIQUITA CT
700 SJS 95123 874-G5
ENSALMO AV
1600 SJS 95118 874-A1
ENSENADA DR
1500 CMBL 95008 853-A6
ENSENADA WY
1300 LALT 94024 831-J4
ENSIGN WY
700 PA 94303 811-E1
1900 SJS 95133 834-E1
1900 SJS 95133 814-E7
ENTRADA PL
11300 SCIC 94024 831-F4
ENTRADA WY
500 SMCo 94025 790-H2
ENTRADA CEDROS
5300 SJS 95123 874-H3
ENTRADA OLEANDROS
5300 SJS 95123 874-H3
ENTRADA OLMOS
5200 SJS 95123 874-H3
ENZO DR
200 SJS 95138 875-E4
EPERNAY CT
- SJS 95127 834-J1
EPPLING LN
5000 SJS 95111 875-C2
EQUESTRIAN WY
15400 MSER 95030 872-J5
ERIC DR
19300 SAR 95070 852-F5
ERIC LN
1600 SCIC 95020 958-B3
ERICA CT
2900 SJS 95121 854-J3

ERICA DR
900 SUNV 94086 832-G2
ERICA WY
100 SMCo 94028 810-D3
ERIE CIR
600 MPS 95035 794-A6
ERIE CT
700 MPS 95035 794-A5
4200 SCL 95054 813-C5
ERIE DR
300 MPS 95035 794-A5
600 SUNV 94087 832-D2
ERIE PL
700 MPS 95035 794-A5
ERIE WY
200 CMBL 95008 853-B5
ERIN WY
1000 SCIC 95008 873-E1
7500 CPTO 95014 852-D2
ERINBROOK PL
1700 SJS 95131 834-D1
ERINWOOD CT
1200 SJS 95121 855-A4
ERNESTINE LN
1300 MTVW 94040 811-G6
ERSKINE CT
5800 SJS 95123 875-A5
ERSTWILD CT
- PA 94303 791-B4
ERVIN WY
11000 SCIC 95127 835-D4
ESBERG RD
1700 SCIC 94024 831-G4
ESCALON AV
900 SUNV 94086 812-C5
ESCALON CT
1000 SUNV 94086 812-C5
ESCALONIA CT
2400 SJS 95121 855-D4
ESCANYO WY
100 SMCo 94028 810-E4
ESCAZU CT
100 SJS 95116 834-G3
ESCHENBURG DR
700 GIL 95020 977-H3
ESCOBAR AV
100 LGTS 95032 873-D5
16000 SCIC 95032 873-D5
ESCOBAR CT
100 LGTS 95032 873-E5
ESCOBAR RD
100 PTLV 94028 810-C4
ESCOBITA AV
1500 PA 94306 791-A6
ESCONDIDO CT
6100 SJS 95119 875-C6
ESCONDIDO LN
1100 MLPK 94025 790-F3
ESCONDIDO RD
600 SCIC 94305 790-H7
800 SCIC 94305 810-J1
ESCOVER LN
5300 SJS 95118 874-C4
ESCUELA AV
100 MTVW 94040 811-G4
100 MTVW 94041 811-G4
ESCUELA PKWY
400 MPS 95035 794-A4
ESCUELA PL
600 MPS 95035 794-A5
ESMERALDA CT
200 SJS 95116 834-F3
ESPADA CT
13800 SAR 95070 872-J1
ESPERANCA AV
2200 SCL 95054 813-C4
ESPERANZA DR
12800 LAH 94022 811-B6
ESPINOZA LN
100 MTVW 94043 812-B5
ESPLANADA WY
700 SCIC 94305 810-J1
ESQUIRE PL
10500 CPTO 95014 832-C6
ESSENDON WY
- SJS 95139 875-G7
ESSEX AV
1000 SUNV 94089 812-F4
ESSEX PL
1900 SCL 95051 833-D2
ESSEX ST
1400 SJS 95002 793-C7
ESSEX WY
1300 SJS 95117 853-D4
1400 SCL 95117 853-D4
ESTACADA DR
25800 LAH 94022 811-C5
ESTACADA WY
25800 LAH 94022 811-C5

ESTATE DR
1200 LALT 94024 831-H3
ESTATES CT
1600 SJS 95127 835-B5
ESTATES DR
900 CPTO 95014 852-F2
9300 SCIC 95020 958-D3
E ESTATES DR
800 CPTO 95014 852-F1
W ESTATES DR
10700 CPTO 95014 852-F2
ESTATE VIEW CT
3500 SJS 95148 835-D4
ESTATE VIEW WY
2000 SJS 95148 835-D4
ESTEBAN WY
200 SJS 95119 875-C7
ESTELLA DR
2500 SCL 95051 833-B7
ESTELLE AV
1500 SJS 95118 874-A1
ESTERLEE AV
14400 SAR 95070 872-C3
ESTHER AV
300 CMBL 95008 853-E5
ESTHER CT
21500 SCIC 95030 912-J3
ESTHER DR
4300 SCIC 95124 873-F2
4900 SJS 95124 873-F3
ESTONIA CT
600 SJS 95123 874-G4
ESTRADA DR
- MTVW 94043 812-A5
ESTRADA TER
1200 SUNV 94086 812-B7
ESTRADE DR
5200 SJS 95118 874-A4
ESTRALITA PL
13100 LAH 94022 811-A7
13100 LAH 94022 831-A1
ESTRELLITA WY
1000 LALT 94022 811-D4
1300 CMBL 95008 873-B1
ESTUDILLO RD
700 SCIC 94305 810-H2
ETHAN CT
3600 SJS 95136 874-D1
ETHYL CT
100 MPS 95035 813-J1
ETHYL ST
300 MPS 95035 813-J1
ETOILE CT
3300 SJS 95135 855-G3
ETON AV
14100 SCIC 95127 835-A3
ETON WY
900 SUNV 94087 832-G5
ETRUSCAN DR
- SJS 95135 855-E2
ETTERSBERG DR
5800 SJS 95123 875-B5
EUCALYPTUS CT
2000 SCL 95050 833-C3
EUCALYPTUS DR
300 SJS 95134 813-D2
15700 SCIC 95030 872-H5
EUCALYPTUS LN
26000 LAH 94022 811-B6
EUCLID AV
- ATN 94027 790-B4
- LGTS 95032 892-J1
1900 MLPK 94025 791-B3
2000 EPA 94303 791-B2
EUCLID PL
500 EPA 94303 791-B2
EUGENE AV
1000 SJS 95126 833-J7
EUGENE CT
1000 SUNV 94087 832-B5
EUGENIA LN
- WDSD 94062 790-A5
EUGENIA WY
2000 LALT 94024 832-A5
16400 LGTS 95032 893-C2
16400 SCIC 95032 893-C2
EULALIE DR
2600 SJS 95121 854-J3
EUNICE AV
100 MTVW 94040 831-J1
13100 MTVW 94040 832-A1
EUREKA AV
1100 LALT 94024 831-H3
EUREKA CT
200 SUNV 94086 812-F5
1200 LALT 94024 831-H3
EUREKA CANYON RD
1000 SCrC 95076 955-A3
EUROPE WY
3600 SCL 95051 832-H4

EVA AV
1200 LALT 94024 831-H4
EVA CT
2400 SJS 95008 853-B7
EVANDALE AV
- MTVW 94043 812-A3
EVANGELINE CT
6200 SJS 95123 874-G7
EVANGELINE DR
6100 SJS 95123 874-G6
EVANS CT
900 MPS 95035 794-C5
EVANS LN
1800 SJS 95125 854-D5
14300 SAR 95070 872-H2
EVANS RD
- MPS 95035 794-C5
- SCIC 95035 794-C5
EVANSTON PL
6000 SJS 95123 874-E6
EVCO CT
3200 SJS 95127 814-J7
EVELYN AV
200 SJS 95122 834-J6
E EVELYN AV
100 MTVW 94041 812-D6
100 SUNV 94086 812-D6
500 SUNV 94086 832-F1
W EVELYN AV
100 MTVW 94041 812-A5
200 MTVW 94041 811-H4
EVELYN ST
900 MLPK 94025 790-F4
EVELYN TER
- SUNV 94086 832-H1
E EVELYN TER
1000 SUNV 94086 832-H1
W EVELYN TER
900 SUNV 94086 832-H1
EVE MARIE AV
1600 LALT 94024 832-A4
EVENING SPRING CT
11500 CPTO 95014 852-A4
EVENING STAR CT
100 MPS 95035 814-A2
EVERDALE CT
2900 SJS 95148 855-C1
EVERDALE DR
2900 SJS 95148 855-C1
EVERETT AV
100 PA 94301 790-H4
200 CMBL 95008 853-E6
1600 SJS 95125 854-A4
EVERETT CT
500 PA 94301 790-J4
EVERGLADE AV
1700 SJS 95122 834-H6
EVERGLADES DR
1500 MPS 95035 814-D1
EVERGLOW CT
2900 SJS 95127 835-A4
EVERGREEN DR
3500 PA 94303 791-E7
16900 MGH 95037 936-J1
EVERGREEN LN
23000 SCrC 95030 913-C7
EVERGREEN ST
600 MLPK 94025 790-E6
EVERGREEN WY
100 MPS 95035 814-A3
2800 SJS 95121 855-E3
EVERMONT CT
1900 SJS 95148 835-A5
1900 SJS 95127 835-A5
EVERSOLE DR
2700 SJS 95133 814-G7
EVERWOOD CT
1900 SJS 95148 835-A5
1900 SJS 95127 835-A5
EVORA DR
2600 SJS 95124 873-G1
EVULICH CT
22000 CPTO 95014 852-A2
EWER DR
1700 SJS 95124 873-H3
EXCALIBER CT
14600 MGH 95037 937-B5
EXCALIBUR DR
500 SJS 95116 834-J4
EXETER CT
100 SUNV 94087 832-E5
5900 SJS 95138 855-G7
EXMOOR WY
1000 SUNV 94087 832-G5
EZIE ST
300 SJS 95111 854-J6

F

F ST
- SUNV 94089 812-H3
FABER PL
2400 PA 94303 791-E4
FABIAN DR
1700 SJS 95124 853-J7
1700 SJS 95124 873-J1
FABIAN WY
3700 PA 94303 791-F7
3700 PA 94303 811-F1
FABLED OAK CT
3300 SJS 95148 835-E7
FAHRNER CT
2900 SJS 95135 855-F3
FAIR AV
900 SJS 95122 854-G1
FAIR LN
- LGTS 95030 873-A7
FAIRBANKS AV
200 CMBL 95008 873-E2
FAIRBANKS CIR
- SJS 95131 814-B6
FAIRBROOK CT
1000 SJS 95132 814-F6
FAIRBROOK DR
1100 MTVW 94040 832-A2
FAIRCHILD DR
- MTVW 94043 812-B3
FAIRCLIFF CT
2900 SJS 95125 854-A7
2900 SJS 95125 874-A1
FAIRCREST DR
2200 SJS 95124 873-E3
FAIRDELL DR
2500 SJS 95125 854-A7
FAIRFAX AV
- ATN 94027 790-D1
2800 SJS 95148 855-C1
FAIRFAX CT
2800 SJS 95148 855-C1
FAIRFIELD AV
900 SCL 95050 833-D4
FAIRFIELD CT
200 PA 94306 811-F2
FAIRFORD CT
1100 SJS 95129 852-G3
FAIRFORD WY
1100 SJS 95129 852-G3
FAIRGLEN DR
2200 SJS 95125 854-A7
FAIRGROVE CT
2300 SJS 95125 853-J7
FAIRHAVEN CT
- MTVW 94041 811-J6
1400 SJS 95118 874-B1
FAIRHAVEN DR
1400 SJS 95118 874-B1
FAIR HILL DR
1700 MPS 95035 794-D5
FAIRHILL LN
2200 SJS 95125 853-J6
FAIRHOPE PL
6000 SJS 95123 874-E6
FAIRLANDS AV
700 CMBL 95008 873-C1
FAIRLANDS CT
1100 CMBL 95008 873-C1
FAIRLANE AV
600 SCL 95051 833-A6
FAIRLAWN AV
1600 SJS 95125 854-A7
1600 SJS 95125 853-J7
FAIRLAWN CT
2200 SJS 95125 854-A7
FAIRMEAD AV
600 PA 94306 811-C3
FAIRMEAD LN
100 LGTS 95032 873-D6
FAIRMEADOW WY
100 MPS 95035 794-C2
FAIRMONT AV
400 MTVW 94041 811-H6
FAIRMONT CT
2100 SJS 95148 835-D5
FAIRMONT DR
2100 SJS 95148 835-D5
15900 SCIC 95127 815-B7
FAIROAK CT
2400 SJS 95125 853-J7
FAIR OAKS AV
1000 SUNV 94089 812-G4
N FAIR OAKS AV
100 SUNV 94086 812-F7
900 SUNV 94089 812-F7
S FAIR OAKS AV
100 SUNV 94086 832-F2

STREET
Block City ZIP Pg-Grid

FAIR OAKS LN
- ATN 94027 790-E2
FAIR OAKS ST
100 MTVW 94040 811-F4
FAIR OAKS WY
1200 SUNV 94089 812-G3
FAIRORCHARD AV
1600 SJS 95125 854-A7
1600 SJS 95125 853-J7
FAIRPLACE CT
1700 SJS 95122 854-G1
FAIRVALLEY CT
2200 SJS 95125 853-J6
FAIRVIEW AV
- ATN 94027 790-C5
- LGTS 95030 872-J7
1000 SJS 95125 854-B5
FAIRVIEW DR
400 GIL 95020 977-J4
FAIRVIEW LN
- SBnC - (1020-E3 See Page 999)
- SJS 95111 854-G4
2400 SCL 95051 833-B2
FAIRVIEW PZ
- LGTS 95030 872-J7
FAIRVIEW RD
4900 SBnC - (1020-E2 See Page 999)
FAIRVIEW WY
300 MPS 95035 793-H5
FAIRWAY CIR
17600 LGTS 95030 873-A4
17600 MSER 95030 873-A4
FAIRWAY DR
1200 SCIC 94024 831-F3
5300 SCIC 95127 815-A7
FAIRWAY ENTRANCE DR
1300 SJS 95131 814-C7
FAIRWAY GLEN DR
2000 SCL 95054 813-C4
FAIRWAY GLEN LN
100 SJS 95139 895-E1
FAIRWAY GREEN CIR
1600 SJS 95131 814-C7
FAIRWEATHER LN
1100 SJS 95126 853-H4
FAIRWOOD AV
900 SUNV 94089 812-J5
1600 SJS 95125 853-J7
FAIRWOODS CT
20900 CPTO 95014 852-D1
FAITH CT
3200 SJS 95127 814-J7
FALCATO DR
100 MPS 95035 794-E7
FALCON AV
1400 SUNV 94087 832-F4
FALCON CT
1400 GIL 95020 957-E7
1400 SUNV 94087 832-F5
FALCON DR
1200 MPS 95035 814-B3
FALCON KNOLL CT
7000 SJS 95120 894-G4
FALCON KNOLL DR
1100 SJS 95120 894-G4
FALCON RIDGE CT
7000 SJS 95120 894-G4
FALERNO WY
- SJS 95135 855-G3
FALK CT
400 MLPK 94025 791-A3
FALKIAK CT
100 SUNV 94087 832-E5
FALKIRK DR
7600 SJS 95135 856-A6
FALL AV
1500 SJS 95127 835-C4
FALL CT
7900 CPTO 95014 852-C2
FALLBROOK AV
1600 SJS 95130 853-A5
FALLCREEK SPRING CT
11500 CPTO 95014 852-A4
FALLEN LEAF DR
1100 MPS 95035 814-A3
FALLEN LEAF LN
1400 LALT 94024 832-A3
FALLENLEAF LN
7300 CPTO 95014 852-D3
7300 SJS 95129 852-D3
FALLEN OAK CT
3200 SJS 95148 855-D2
FALLEN OAK DR
[illegible] SCIC 95037 935-H3
[illegible]INGTREE DR
[illegible] SJS 95131 814-C5

FALLING WATER CT
2300 SCL 95054 813-C5
FALLON AV
600 SCL 95050 833-D5
FALLON RD
- HOLL - (1020-B5 See Page 999)
400 SBnC - (1020-F2 See Page 999)
FALL RIVER DR
6500 SJS 95120 894-D1
FALL RIVER TER
500 SUNV 94087 832-D2
FALLS CREEK CT
3000 SJS 95135 855-F4
FALLS CREEK DR
3100 SJS 95135 855-G4
FALLSTONE CT
4500 SJS 95124 873-F3
FALLWOOD LN
2800 SJS 95132 814-D3
FALMOUTH CT
19300 SAR 95070 852-G5
FALMOUTH ST
3200 SJS 95132 814-F3
FALON WY
5800 SJS 95123 875-A5
FAMILLE CT
3300 SJS 95135 855-G3
FAN ST
1700 SJS 95131 834-D1
FAN WY
1700 SJS 95131 834-C1
FANCHER CT
100 LGTS 95030 873-A6
FANITA WY
500 MLPK 94025 790-E6
FAN PALM CT
2000 SCL 95050 833-D3
FANTAIL CT
1500 SUNV 94087 832-F5
FANWOOD CT
1700 SJS 95133 834-D1
FANYON ST
- MPS 95035 794-C6
FARADAY CT
1600 SJS 95124 873-J3
FARADAY DR
4300 SJS 95124 873-J3
FARADAY PL
4400 SJS 95124 873-J3
FARALLON DR
400 MGH 95037 936-J1
FARALLONE DR
10200 CPTO 95014 852-E2
FARAONE CT
4400 SJS 95136 874-E2
FARAONE DR
600 SJS 95136 874-E2
FARGATE CIR
1100 SJS 95131 834-C1
FARGHER DR
2800 SCL 95051 833-B3
FARGO DR
20600 SCIC 95014 832-D7
FARIS DR
900 SJS 95111 855-A6
FARLEY RD
16400 SCIC 95032 873-C5
16500 LGTS 95032 873-C5
W FARLEY RD
17400 LGTS 95030 873-A5
FARLEY ST
100 MTVW 94043 811-G4
FARM DR
700 SJS 95136 854-D7
FARM RD
- LALT 94024 831-J5
100 PTLV 94028 810-A5
100 WDSD 94062 810-A5
FARMAN LN
100 SCIC 95020 978-B6
FARMAN FRONTAGE RD
5300 GIL 95020 978-B6
5300 SCIC 95020 978-B6
FARMCREST ST
2200 MPS 95035 814-E1
FARM HILL WY
6300 SJS 95120 874-E7
14900 LGTS 95030 873-C4
FARMINGHAM WY
18400 SCIC 95014 852-C6
FARNDON AV
1800 LALT 94024 832-A4
FARNHAM CT
100 SJS 95139 895-G1
FARNSWORTH DR
2300 SJS 95138 855-F6
FARR CT
1300 SJS 95125 854-A4

FARRAGUT LN
18500 MSER 95030 872-H5
18500 SCIC 95030 872-H5
FARRAGUT WY
1900 SJS 95133 814-E7
1900 SJS 95133 834-E1
FARRELL AV
- GIL 95020 957-H7
FARRINGDON CT
1500 SJS 95127 835-A5
FARRINGDON DR
1200 SJS 95127 835-A4
FARRINGTON WY
2500 EPA 94303 791-B1
FARR RANCH CT
12300 SAR 95070 852-C6
FARR RANCH RD
12100 SAR 95070 852-C6
FARTHING WY
3200 SJS 95132 814-F3
FAR VUE LN
18900 SCIC 95030 872-H7
FARWELL AV
14600 SAR 95070 872-F3
FARWELL CT
14800 SAR 95070 872-F3
FARWELL LN
- LGTS 95030 892-J1
FATJO PL
2300 SCL 95050 833-C3
FAULSTICH CT
800 SJS 95112 834-B1
FAUST CT
2600 SJS 95121 854-J2
FAVONIA RD
100 PTLV 94028 810-C4
FAWN CT
1600 CMBL 95008 873-A1
FAWN DR
1100 CMBL 95008 873-A1
3000 SJS 95124 873-G2
FAWN LN
- PTLV 94028 810-C5
FAWN TR
18100 SCIC 95030 912-J3
FAWN CREEK CT
27800 LAH 94022 810-H6
FAWNDALE DR
15100 SCIC 95032 893-F1
FAWNWOOD CT
3100 SJS 95148 855-D1
FAXON RD
- ATN 94027 790-D4
FAXON FOREST
- ATN 94027 790-D4
FAY DR
1600 SJS 95124 873-J2
FAY WY
200 MTVW 94043 811-G3
FAYE PARK DR
5900 SJS 95123 874-E5
FAYETTE DR
2600 MTVW 94040 811-E3
FEAFEL CT
4100 SJS 95134 813-D2
FEAFEL DR
4100 SJS 95134 813-D2
FEBRUARY DR
100 SJS 95138 875-D4
FEDERATION CT
5300 SJS 95123 875-B3
FEDORA CT
1400 SJS 95121 854-J2
FEHREN DR
13000 SCIC 95111 854-G6
13000 SJS 95111 854-G6
FELDER DR
6300 SJS 95123 875-B7
FELDSPAR DR
400 SJS 95111 854-G4
FELICE CT
100 SJS 95138 875-G7
FELIPE AV
900 SJS 95122 834-F6
FELIX WY
500 SJS 95125 854-C4
FELIZ CT
16700 MGH 95037 917-F6
FELL AV
4800 SJS 95136 874-E3
FELL CT
900 SJS 95136 874-E3
FELLER AV
700 SJS 95127 835-B2
FELLOM CT
400 GIL 95020 978-A1
FELTER RD
4100 SCIC 95140 794-J6
4100 SCIC 95035 794-J6
5000 SCIC 95140 795-A7

FELTER RD
5000 SCIC 95035 795-A7
5200 SCIC 95132 795-A7
5500 SCIC 95132 815-D1
5500 SCIC 95140 815-D1
FELTON DR
100 MLPK 94025 790-F2
FELTON PL
100 MLPK 94025 790-F2
FELTON WY
10500 CPTO 95014 852-D2
FENIAN DR
2200 SJS 95008 853-B6
FENLEY AV
300 SCIC 95117 853-D1
600 SJS 95117 853-D2
FENNWOOD DR
- ATN 94027 790-F2
FENTON ST
300 SJS 95127 814-J7
600 SCIC 95127 814-J7
FENWAY CT
21000 CPTO 95014 832-C7
FENWICK WY
2900 SJS 95148 855-C2
FERGUSON DR
100 MTVW 94043 812-B5
FERGUSON RD Rt#-G9
2600 SCIC 95020 958-E7
3600 SCIC 95020 978-F1
FERGUSON WY
1400 SJS 95129 852-J4
FERN AV
18100 SCIC 95030 912-H3
FERN DR
5400 SJS 95124 873-J6
FERNANDEZ CT
400 SCL 95050 833-C6
FERNANDO AV
200 PA 94306 811-C1
FERNBROOK CT
18900 SAR 95070 852-H5
FERNCREST CT
13600 SAR 95070 872-H1
E FERNDALE AV
100 SUNV 94086 812-F5
W FERNDALE AV
100 SUNV 94086 812-E5
FERNDALE CT
700 SJS 95133 834-F2
FERNDALE DR
1500 SJS 95118 874-A5
FERNDALE WY
2300 SJS 95133 834-F1
FERNE AV
100 PA 94306 811-E2
FERNE CT
100 PA 94306 811-E2
FERNGLEN DR
5900 SJS 95123 874-E5
FERNGROVE DR
800 CPTO 95014 852-G2
FERNHILL DR
23700 LAH 94024 831-E4
FERNISH DR
1900 SJS 95148 835-D5
FERNLEAF DR
1000 SUNV 94086 832-G2
FERN PINE CT
1600 SJS 95131 834-D1
FERN RIDGE CT
500 SUNV 94087 832-D5
FERNSIDE SQ
3100 SJS 95132 814-E3
FERNSIDE ST
- RDWC 94061 790-A3
- WDSD 94062 790-A3
FERNWOOD AV
2500 SCL 95128 833-E7
2500 SJS 95117 833-D7
2500 SJS 95128 833-E7
N FERNWOOD CIR
300 SUNV 94086 812-F5
S FERNWOOD CIR
300 SUNV 94086 812-F5
W FERNWOOD CIR
600 SUNV 94086 812-F5
FERNWOOD LN
1300 GIL 95020 977-G3
FERRANT CT
13100 SCIC 95046 937-J5
FERRARI AV
- SJS 95110 833-J3
FERREIRA CT
400 MPS 95035 794-E7
FERREL CT
1300 SJS 95132 814-F5
FERRIS AV
16400 SCIC 95032 873-C7
16400 LGTS 95032 873-C7

FERRUM CT
2900 SJS 95148 855-D2
FERRY MORSE WY
100 MTVW 94041 812-A6
FESTIVAL CT
7900 CPTO 95014 852-C2
FESTIVAL DR
7700 CPTO 95014 852-C2
10900 SCIC 95014 852-C2
FETZER DR
- SJS 95125 853-G4
FEVER DR
- SJS 95123 875-A6
- SJS 95123 874-J6
FEWTRELL DR
1000 CMBL 95008 853-G6
FIDDLERS GRN
1200 SJS 95125 854-F5
FIDDLETOWN PL
5900 SJS 95120 874-C6
FIELDCREST DR
400 SJS 95123 875-B7
2000 MPS 95035 814-E1
FIELDFAIR CT
1300 SUNV 94087 832-F4
FIELDGATE CT
3200 SJS 95148 855-E1
FIELDING DR
800 PA 94303 791-D6
FIELDS DR
1400 SJS 95129 852-J4
FIELDSHIRE WY
1400 MGH 95037 917-D6
FIELDSTONE DR
14600 SAR 95070 872-C3
FIELDWOOD CT
800 SJS 95120 894-H3
FIESTA LN
7800 CPTO 95014 852-C2
FIESTA WY
- LGTS 95032 893-A1
FIFE AV
1000 PA 94301 791-A4
FIFE WY
700 SUNV 94087 832-F5
3400 SJS 95132 814-G3
FIFEWOOD CT
6500 SJS 95120 894-F1
FIFIELD RD
- SCIC 95020 (942-C1 See Page 921)
- SCIC 95020 (962-C1 See Page 961)
FIG AV
1000 SUNV 94087 832-B2
FIG GROVE CT
5300 SJS 95123 875-A3
FIG TREE CT
19800 CPTO 95014 832-F7
FIGWOOD CT
800 SJS 95120 894-H3
FIJI DR
800 SJS 95127 814-H6
FILBERT AV
700 CMBL 95008 853-B7
FILBRO DR
6600 GIL 95020 977-J5
FILICE DR
7400 GIL 95020 977-H4
FILIP RD
700 LALT 94024 831-G2
FILLIPELLI DR
900 GIL 95020 977-G2
FILLMER AV
- LGTS 95032 873-B7
FILLMORE ST
1800 SCL 95050 833-D3
4300 SCL 95054 813-C5
FILOMENA AV
100 SJS 95110 834-A5
FILOMENA CT
3300 MTVW 94040 831-J2
FINCH AV
10000 CPTO 95014 832-G7
10000 CPTO 95014 852-G1
10200 SCIC 95014 852-G1
FINCH DR
3200 SJS 95117 853-D3
FINCH LN
1400 GIL 95020 957-F7
FINCH WY
1500 SUNV 94087 832-F5
FINCHWELL CT
- SJS 95138 875-D4
FINCHWOOD WY
700 SJS 95120 894-H3
FINDHORN CT
7900 SJS 95135 856-A5
FINDLEY DR
1700 MPS 95035 794-D6

FINE DR
8800 GIL 95020 977-E1
FINEO CT
1400 SJS 95131 814-C7
FINLEY RIDGE CT
- SCIC 95037 918-A3
FINLEY RIDGE RD
- SCIC 95037 918-A3
- SCIC 95037 917-J2
FINN LN
12000 LAH 94022 831-C3
FIR AV
500 SUNV 94086 812-F6
FIR LN
400 SCIC 94024 831-J5
FIR ST
- MGH 95037 917-B7
- MGH 95037 937-B1
FIRCREST DR
12800 SCIC 95046 938-A5
FIREBIRD WY
1400 SUNV 94087 832-F4
FIREFLY DR
6200 SJS 95120 874-C7
6300 SJS 95120 894-C1
FIRENZE CT
- SJS 95138 855-E7
- SJS 95138 875-E1
FIRESIDE DR
2900 SJS 95128 853-E3
FIRESTONE CT
- SJS 95138 875-H1
FIRETHORN CT
2000 MPS 95035 793-J3
FIRETHORN ST
- MPS 95035 793-J3
FIRETHORN WY
- PTLV 94028 810-D7
FIRETHORNE DR
11000 CPTO 95014 832-D6
FIREWOOD CT
700 SJS 95120 894-H3
FIRLOCH AV
400 SUNV 94086 832-F1
E FIRST ST
500 MLPK 94025 790-H3
FIRTH CT
1000 SUNV 94087 832-H5
FIRTH WY
3200 SJS 95121 855-B3
FIR TREE CT
300 MPS 95035 813-J3
FIRWOOD DR
10000 CPTO 95014 851-J1
FISHBURNE AV
5800 SJS 95123 874-F5
FISHER AV
500 MGH 95037 937-C2
500 SCIC 95037 937-C2
1800 SCIC 95037 917-G7
4200 SCIC 95127 835-A2
16100 LGTS 95032 873-B6
FISHER RD
100 SCIC 95037 896-A6
100 SJS 95037 896-A6
200 SJS 95037 895-J6
200 SJS 95141 895-J6
FISHER HAWK DR
1300 SUNV 94087 832-F4
FISK AV
500 SJS 95125 854-A2
FITCHVILLE AV
1500 SJS 95126 853-H3
FITZGERALD CT
10900 SCIC 95046 957-E4
FITZGERALD DR
21500 CPTO 95014 832-B7
FITZGERALD RD
100 SCIC 95020 957-F3
100 SCIC 95046 957-F3
400 SCIC 95020 958-E1
700 SCIC 95020 938-E7
FIVE POINTS RD
- SMCo 94020 850-G7
FIVE WOUNDS LN
1300 SJS 95116 834-E4
FLAGG AV
400 SCIC 95128 853-F1
FLAGLER ST
500 SCIC 95127 814-H7
1800 SJS 95127 814-H7
FLAGSTAD CT
2700 SJS 95121 855-A3
FLAGSTAFF CT
48700 FRMT 94539 793-J2
FLAGSTAFF PL
48400 FRMT 94539 793-J2
FLAGSTAFF RD
48500 FRMT 94539 793-J2

FLAGSTONE DR
2500 SJS 95132 814-F6
FLAMEWOOD AV
900 SUNV 94089 812-J5
FLAMINGO DR
200 CMBL 95008 853-G7
FLAMINGO WY
1400 SUNV 94087 832-F5
FLAMING OAK LN
16300 MGH 95037 917-G6
FLANDERS DR
3100 SJS 95132 814-G5
FLANIGAN DR
1400 SJS 95121 854-J2
1500 SJS 95121 855-A2
FLANNERY ST
500 SCL 95051 833-A7
FLATER DR
3000 SJS 95148 855-C2
FLAT ROCK CIR
3400 SCL 95051 832-J3
FLAX MOSS CT
1200 SJS 95120 894-C1
FLAXWOOD ST
1100 SJS 95120 874-D6
FLEDERMAUS CT
1500 SJS 95121 854-J4
FLEET ST
5800 SJS 95120 874-B6
FLEETWOOD DR
1000 SJS 95120 874-D7
FLEMING AV
100 SJS 95127 835-C2
1200 SCIC 95127 835-C2
FLEMING CT
- SJS 95127 835-A1
FLETCHER DR
- ATN 94027 790-B5
FLEUR PL
- ATN 94027 790-C4
FLEUR DE LIS CT
3200 SJS 95132 814-G5
FLICKER WY
1300 SUNV 94087 832-F4
FLICKINGER AV
1100 SJS 95131 814-C5
FLICKINGER CT
1700 SJS 95131 814-C5
FLICKINGER PL
1700 SJS 95131 814-C5
FLICKINGER RD
1700 SJS 95131 814-C4
FLICKINGER WY
1800 SJS 95131 814-C4
FLIN WY
800 SUNV 94087 832-F5
FLINT AV
1800 SJS 95148 835-C5
2000 SCIC 95148 835-C5
FLINT CT
3300 SJS 95148 835-D5
FLINTBURY CT
2000 SJS 95148 835-C5
FLINT CREEK CT
1800 SJS 95148 835-D4
FLINT CREEK DR
3500 SJS 95148 835-D4
FLINT CREEK WY
1700 SJS 95148 835-D4
FLINTCREST CT
2000 SJS 95148 835-C5
FLINTCREST DR
2000 SJS 95148 835-C5
FLINTDALE DR
3200 SJS 95148 835-C5
FLINTFIELD DR
2000 SJS 95148 835-D5
FLINTHAVEN DR
3100 SJS 95148 835-B5
FLINTHILL CT
3400 SJS 95148 835-D5
FLINTLOCK RD
- SCIC 95014 851-E4
FLINTMONT CT
3200 SJS 95148 835-C5
FLINTMONT DR
3200 SJS 95148 835-C5
FLINTMORE CT
2100 SJS 95148 835-D5
FLINTRIDGE DR
15500 LGTS 95032 873-C5
FLINTSHIRE ST
21500 CPTO 95014 852-B3
FLINTSIDE CT
2100 SJS 95148 835-D5
FLINTVIEW CT
3200 SJS 95148 835-D7
FLINTWELL CT
100 SJS 95138 875-D4

FLINTWELL WY
- SJS 95138 875-D4
FLINTWICK CT
2000 SJS 95148 835-D5
FLINTWOOD CT
2600 SJS 95148 835-D6
FLOOD CIR
- ATN 94027 790-F1
FLOOD DR
1800 SJS 95124 873-H1
FLORA AV
1200 SJS 95117 853-B4
1300 SJS 95130 853-B4
FLORAL ST
- GIL 95020 977-H1
FLORALES DR
600 PA 94306 811-C2
FLORA VISTA AV
300 SUNV 94086 832-E1
3400 SCL 95051 832-J3
10300 SCIC 95014 832-C7
FLORENCE AV
2700 SJS 95127 834-J3
2800 SCIC 95127 834-J3
FLORENCE CT
3100 SJS 95127 835-A2
17700 MGH 95037 916-H7
FLORENCE DR
10000 SCIC 95020 958-A1
10400 CPTO 95014 832-B6
FLORENCE LN
900 MLPK 94025 790-F4
FLORENCE ST
100 SUNV 94086 812-D7
300 SUNV 94086 832-D1
400 PA 94301 790-J4
FLORENCE WY
200 SJS 95110 834-A7
1000 CMBL 95008 873-D1
FLORENCE PARK DR
2900 SJS 95135 855-E2
FLORENTINE DR
500 SJS 95123 875-B3
FLORES
- MTVW 94043 811-J2
FLORESTA DR
3200 SJS 95148 835-D6
E FLORESTA WY
100 SMCo 94028 810-E3
W FLORESTA WY
200 SMCo 94028 810-E3
FLORIDA AV
1300 SJS 95122 834-H6
FLORY DR
2400 SJS 95121 854-J2
FLOWER CT
1300 CPTO 95014 852-D4
FLOWER LN
400 MTVW 94043 812-B5
FLOWER GARDEN LN
1600 SJS 95124 873-J6
FLOWERING PEAR DR
11000 CPTO 95014 832-D6
FLOWERING PLUM RD
6100 SJS 95120 874-D7
FLOWERS LN
3100 PA 94306 791-D7
FLOYD AV
1300 SUNV 94087 832-E4
FLOYD ST
- SJS 95110 854-C2
FLUME CT
700 MPS 95035 794-B5
FLYNN AV
- MTVW 94043 812-A4
FLYNN RD
- HOLL - (1020-A7 See Page 999)
600 SBnC - (1019-J6 See Page 999)
FOGL CT
- SMCo 94061 790-B4
FOLEY AV
1100 SCL 95051 833-B4
1400 SJS 95122 834-G7
FOLIGNO WY
5700 SJS 95138 875-G1
FOLKESTONE DR
7900 CPTO 95014 852-C3
FOLKLORE CT
6600 SJS 95120 894-C5
FOLSOM CIR
400 MPS 95035 794-A6
FOLSOM CT
400 MPS 95035 794-A6
FOLSOM PL
100 MPS 95035 794-A6
FONICK DR
400 SJS 95111 875-C1
FONTAINBLEAU TER
300 LALT 94022 811-E5

FONTAINBLEU AV
1200 MPS 95035 794-A4
FONTAINBLEU CT
100 MPS 95035 794-A4
FONTAINE DR
13300 SAR 95070 852-G7
FONTAINE RD
2400 SJS 95121 854-J2
FONTANA DR
200 SCL 95051 833-B7
FONTANELLE CT
400 SJS 95111 875-C2
FONTANELLE DR
300 SJS 95111 875-C1
FONTANELLE PL
4900 SJS 95111 875-C1
FONTANOSO WY
400 SJS 95138 875-D3
FONTENAY WY
- SJS 95135 855-G3
FONTENBLEU
1400 SUNV 94087 832-B4
FONTEVILLE CT
- SJS 95127 834-C2
FOOTE AV
- CMBL 95008 853-E6
FOOTHILL AV
10000 SCIC 95020 958-A1
11800 SCIC 95020 938-A7
12000 SCIC 95046 938-A7
12000 SCIC 95046 937-H3
14500 MGH 95046 937-G1
15300 SCIC 95037 917-G7
15300 SCIC 95037 937-G1
FOOTHILL BLVD
10000 CPTO 95014 852-A1
FOOTHILL BLVD Rt#-G5
8100 CPTO 95014 832-A6
8100 LALT 94024 832-A6
8400 SCIC 94024 832-A6
8700 CPTO 94024 832-A6
FOOTHILL CT
100 MGH 95037 937-A1
800 SJS 95123 874-F6
FOOTHILL DR
700 SJS 95123 874-E5
FOOTHILL EXWY Rt#-G5
100 LALT 94022 811-C5
100 LALT 94022 831-F1
200 LALT 94024 831-F1
400 SCIC 94024 831-F1
2600 SCIC 94304 810-J3
2600 PA 94304 810-J3
2800 PA 94304 811-C5
2800 SCIC 94304 811-C5
4100 PA 94306 811-C5
4400 LALT 94024 832-A6
7100 CPTO 95014 832-A6
14000 LAH 94022 811-C5
14000 SCIC 94306 811-C5
FOOTHILL LN
12100 LAH 94022 831-A1
12800 SAR 95070 852-D6
FOOTHILL RD
200 SBnC - (1000-E4 See Page 999)
FOOTHILL GLEN CT
6000 SJS 95123 874-F6
FOOTHILL GLEN DR
6000 SJS 95123 874-F6
FOOTHILL MEADOWS CT
1400 SJS 95131 814-C7
FORBES AV
2100 SCL 95050 833-B6
2500 SCL 95051 833-A6
3200 SCL 95051 832-J6
FORBES CT
3100 SCL 95051 833-A6
FORBES DR
6200 SJS 95123 874-J7
FORD AV
1400 SJS 95110 854-D2
FORD RD
- SJS 95138 875-C4
FORDHAM CT
1500 MTVW 94040 811-G7
FORDHAM DR
2000 SCL 95051 832-J2
FORDHAM ST
2400 EPA 94303 791-B1
FORDHAM WY
1100 MTVW 94040 811-G7
1600 MTVW 94040 831-G1
FORDWELL CT
- SJS 95138 875-D4
FOREST AV
- LGTS 95030 873-B6

FOREST AV
100 PA 94301 790-J5
600 PA 94301 791-A3
2300 SJS 95050 833-E7
2300 SJS 95128 833-F7
2300 SCIC 95128 833-F7
2400 SCL 95050 833-E7
3100 SCL 95128 833-E7
3100 SJS 95117 833-C7
3100 SCL 95117 833-C7
20000 CPTO 95014 832-E7
FOREST CT
1000 PA 94301 791-A3
1800 MPS 95035 813-J4
FOREST DR
200 MGH 95037 917-D6
200 MGH 95037 937-B5
FOREST LN
100 MLPK 94025 790-E2
FOREST RD
100 SBnC - (1017-F5 See Page 997)
FOREST ST
7100 GIL 95020 978-A1
8400 GIL 95020 977-J1
8800 GIL 95020 957-J7
FORESTBROOK WY
4000 SJS 95111 855-A7
FOREST CREEK DR
1100 SJS 95129 852-J3
FORESTDALE AV
700 SJS 95116 834-E7
FORESTER CT
3800 SJS 95121 855-E3
FOREST GLEN DR
5000 SJS 95129 852-J2
FOREST HILL DR
100 LGTS 95032 873-G5
2600 SJS 95130 852-J7
FOREST HILLS DR
20400 SAR 95070 872-D3
FOREST KNOLL DR
1000 SJS 95129 852-G3
FOREST PARK DR
100 SCL 95051 833-A7
FOREST RIDGE DR
800 SJS 95129 852-J2
FOREST SPRING CT
11500 CPTO 95014 852-C4
FOREST VIEW DR
5000 SJS 95129 852-J2
FORESTWOOD DR
3800 SJS 95121 855-D3
FORGE DR
18900 CPTO 95014 832-H6
FORGEMILL CT
1000 SJS 95121 854-J4
FORGETREE CT
2000 SJS 95131 814-C5
FORGEWOOD AV
1200 SUNV 94089 812-J3
FORMAN AV
1600 SJS 95124 873-J3
FORMAN DR
500 CMBL 95008 853-F7
FORMOSA DR
1200 SJS 95131 814-B7
FORMOSA RIDGE DR
3300 SJS 95127 835-B3
FORMWAY CT
100 LALT 94022 811-F6
FORRESTAL AV
1200 SJS 95110 833-J2
FORRESTER CT
200 LGTS 95032 893-D1
FORRESTER RD
200 LGTS 95032 893-D1
FORSUM CT
100 SJS 95138 875-G6
FORSUM RD
7200 SJS 95138 875-G6
FORT BAKER DR
900 CPTO 95014 852-B2
FORTINI RD
21100 SCIC 95120 895-B4
FORT LARAMIE DR
500 SUNV 94087 832-D5
FORTRAN CT
4400 SJS 95134 813-D1
FORTRAN DR
4400 SJS 95134 813-D1
FORTROSE CT
- SJS 95139 875-H7
FORT ROYAL PL
4600 SJS 95136 874-F2
FORTUNA CT
13600 SAR 95070 872-H
FORTUNE DR
1700 SJS 95131 814-B4

STREET
Block City ZIP Pg-Grid

FOSGATE AV
2300 SCL 95050 833-D7
FOSS AV
- SJS 95116 834-H3
FOSTER CT
1500 SJS 95120 874-A7
FOSTER RD
100 LGTS 95032 893-B2
800 SCIC 95032 893-B2
18200 SCIC 95032 893-A2
FOUNDERS LN
800 MPS 95035 794-B4
FOUNDRY CT
500 SJS 95133 834-G1
FOUNTAIN AV
16600 MGH 95037 917-E6
FOUNTAIN CIR
100 SJS 95131 814-A4
FOUNTAIN CT
2100 MGH 95037 917-E6
FOUNTAIN OAKS DR
2100 MGH 95037 917-E6
FOUNTAIN PARK LN
800 MTVW 94043 811-J4
FOUNTAIN VIEW DR
3700 SJS 95136 854-G7
FOUNTIAN PALM CT
- SJS 95133 814-J4
FOURIER DR
800 SJS 95127 835-C2
FOUR OAKS CIR
1400 SJS 95131 814-D6
FOUR OAKS CT
2300 SJS 95131 814-D5
FOUR OAKS RD
1400 SJS 95131 814-D5
FOUR SEASONS CT
2300 SJS 95131 814-D5
FOURTH PLAIN CT
2700 SJS 95121 855-D3
FOWLER AV
3100 SCL 95051 833-A3
3200 SCL 95051 832-J3
FOWLER LN
1400 LALT 94024 831-J3
FOWLER RD
2800 SJS 95135 855-G2
3500 SCIC 95135 855-J2
FOWLER ST
7200 GIL 95020 977-H4
FOX AV
- SJS 95110 834-A5
W FOX CT
500 RDWC 94061 790-C1
FOX DR
1800 SJS 95131 814-A6
FOX LN
800 SJS 95131 814-A5
FOXBORO PL
3200 SJS 95135 855-E3
FOXBOROUGH DR
300 MTVW 94041 812-A6
FOXCHASE DR
900 SJS 95123 874-D4
FOXDALE CT
1500 SJS 95122 834-J5
FOXDALE DR
2400 SJS 95122 834-J5
2500 SJS 95122 835-A5
FOXDALE LP
1200 SJS 95122 835-A5
1200 SJS 95122 834-J5
FOXGLOVE CT
- GIL 95020 977-J6
FOXGLOVE DR
900 SUNV 94086 832-G2
FOXHALL LP
1900 SJS 95125 853-G4
FOX HOLLOW CIR
100 MGH 95037 916-H6
FOXHOLLOW CT
1100 MPS 95035 794-C5
FOXHURST WY
1000 SJS 95120 894-G4
FOX MEADOW CT
1100 SJS 95120 894-G4
FOXRIDGE PL
800 SJS 95133 814-G7
FOXRIDGE WY
800 SJS 95133 814-G6
FOXSWALLOW CT
900 SJS 95120 894-G2
FOXTAIL
- PTLV 94028 830-C1
FOXTAIL DR
600 SUNV 94086 832-F2
FOXWELL CT
- SJS 95138 875-D4
FOXWOOD DR
1200 SJS 95118 874-C4
FOXWOOD RD
100 SMCo 94028 830-D4
FOXWOOD WY
1200 SJS 95118 874-C4
FOXWORTHY AV
1000 SJS 95125 854-B7
1000 SJS 95136 854-C7
1000 SJS 95118 854-B7
1200 SJS 95125 874-A1
1200 SJS 95118 874-A1
1500 SJS 95120 873-G1
1500 SJS 95125 873-G1
1500 SJS 95124 873-F1
FRAGRANT HARBOR CT
200 SJS 95123 874-J3
FRAMPTON CT
25600 LAH 94024 831-E4
FRAN CT
- SJS 95123 874-F7
FRANCEMONT DR
24800 LAH 94022 831-B3
N FRANCES AV
100 SUNV 94086 812-E7
FRANCES DR
200 LALT 94022 811-E6
S FRANCES ST
100 SUNV 94086 812-E7
400 SUNV 94086 832-E1
FRANCES WY
400 MTVW 94041 811-J6
FRANCHERE PL
1300 SUNV 94087 832-B4
FRANCIS AV
1900 SCL 95051 833-A2
FRANCIS CT
17900 SCIC 95030 912-J3
FRANCIS DR
300 SJS 95133 834-H1
300 SCIC 95133 834-H1
400 SJS 95133 814-H7
400 SCIC 95133 814-H7
FRANCISCAN CT
2400 SCL 95051 833-B2
6100 SJS 95120 874-A7
FRANCISCAN RDGE
- PTLV 94028 830-C1
FRANCISCAN WY
6100 SJS 95120 874-A7
6100 SJS 95120 894-A1
FRANCISCO AV
1100 SJS 95126 853-H4
FRANCIS OAKS WY
15200 LGTS 95032 873-E6
FRANCK AV
1600 SCL 95051 833-B3
FRANCO CT
10800 CPTO 95014 832-D6
FRANDON CT
4100 PA 94306 811-C3
FRANELA DR
3000 SJS 95124 873-J1
FRANK AV
16700 LGTS 95032 873-C5
FRANK CT
2000 MPS 95035 794-E6
16900 LGTS 95032 873-C5
FRANKFURT ST
1100 SJS 95126 833-G5
FRANKLIN AV
13000 MTVW 94040 832-A1
20100 SAR 95070 872-E1
FRANKLIN CT
700 SJS 95127 814-H6
22400 MTVW 94040 832-A1
FRANKLIN ST
100 MTVW 94041 811-H5
400 SCL 95050 833-E4
700 SCL 95053 833-E4
FRANKS LN
1400 SMCo 94025 790-D5
FRANQUETTE AV
800 SJS 95125 854-B5
FRASCHINI CIR
5300 SJS 95123 874-H3
FRASER DR
1500 SUNV 94087 832-B5
FRAZER LAKE RD
5700 SCIC 95020 (998-H1
See Page 997)
5900 SCIC 95020 978-F5
6000 SBnC - 999-A3
FREDA CT
1200 CMBL 95008 873-A1
FREDERICK AV
- ATN 94027 790-H1
600 SCL 95050 833-D5
FREDERICK CT
- SMCo 94025 790-H1
100 LALT 94022 811-E6
FREDERICKSBURG CT
12200 SAR 95070 852-E6
FREDERICKSBURG DR
12100 SAR 95070 852-E6
FREED AV
3900 SJS 95117 853-B4
FREEDOM BLVD
600 WAT 95706 995-D5
1500 WAT 95019 995-D5
1800 SCrC 95019 995-D5
2300 SCrC 95076 995-A1
2900 SCrC 95003 995-A1
FREEDOM CIR
3900 SCL 95054 813-B6
FREEDOM CT
6700 SJS 95120 894-C5
FREEDOM DR
21000 CPTO 95014 832-C7
FREEDOM LN
- MTVW 94040 811-E3
FREELAND DR
1400 MPS 95035 794-D7
FREEMAN AV
14800 SCIC 95127 814-J6
14800 SJS 95127 814-J6
FREEMAN CT
9000 GIL 95020 957-H7
FREESTONE AV
1000 SUNV 94087 832-B2
FRWY Rt#-17
- CMBL - 873-D2
- CMBL - 853-F3
- LGTS - 873-D3
- LGTS - 893-A1
- LGTS - 892-J1
- SCIC - 873-D2
- SCIC - 892-J1
- SJS - 853-F3
FRWY Rt#-85
- CPTO - 852-C1
- SAR - 852-E5
- SCIC - 852-C2
- SJS - 852-D4
FRWY U.S.-101
4000 SCIC - (998-B1
See Page 997)
5200 SCIC - 978-B7
FREEWAY VISTA
19200 SCIC 95037 916-J3
FREMONT AV
- SUNV 94087 832-A3
100 LALT 94022 831-E1
100 LALT 94024 831-E1
1500 LALT 94024 832-A3
1700 SUNV 94024 832-A3
E FREMONT AV
500 SUNV 94087 832-E4
1000 SCIC 94087 832-E4
W FREMONT AV
500 SUNV 94087 832-B3
1200 SUNV 94024 832-B3
FREMONT BLVD
47000 FRMT 94538 793-F1
FREMONT PL
900 MLPK 94025 790-F4
FREMONT RD
600 SCIC 94305 790-F7
13400 LAH 94022 811-D7
W FREMONT RD
25000 LAH 94022 811-B5
FREMONT ST
500 MLPK 94025 790-F4
600 SCL 95050 833-D4
1100 SJS 95126 833-H6
FREMONT TER W
1200 SUNV 94087 832-C3
FREMONTIA
- PTLV 94028 830-C1
FREMONT PINES LN
13800 LAH 94022 811-C6
FRENCH CT
100 SJS 95139 895-G1
400 MLPK 94025 791-A3
1300 MPS 95035 814-D2
FRENCH ST
2500 SCL 95051 832-J2
2500 SUNV 94086 832-J2
FRENCHMANS RD
700 SCIC 94305 810-H2
FRENCH OAK DR
8600 SJS 95135 855-J6
FRENI CT
1400 SJS 95121 854-J2
FRESNO ST
2800 SCL 95051 833-A4
FREYA DR
2200 SJS 95148 855-D2
FRIAR CT
5900 SJS 95129 852-G3
FRIAR WY
100 CMBL 95008 853-D7
5800 SJS 95129 852-G3
FRIARS CT
2300 LALT 94024 831-J6
FRIARS LN
2300 LALT 94024 831-J6
FRICKA CT
2700 SJS 95121 854-J4
FRITZEN ST
1100 SJS 95122 834-H5
FROBISHER WY
1700 SJS 95124 853-H7
FROLIC WY
1200 SJS 95129 852-J3
FRONDA DR
3200 SJS 95148 835-D6
FRONT LN
500 MTVW 94041 811-J5
FRONTAGE RD
16500 SJS 95120 894-F2
FRONTENAC AV
1300 SUNV 94087 832-B4
FRONTERO AV
1400 SCIC 94024 831-G2
FRONTIER TRAIL DR
- SJS 95136 874-H2
2600 SJS 95136 875-A2
FROST DR
1500 SJS 95131 814-C6
FROST RD
- SCIC 95037 (897-F7
See Page 877)
- SCIC 95037 917-F1
- SJS 95037 (897-F7
See Page 877)
FRUIT BARN LN
8700 SJS 95135 856-A6
FRUITDALE AV
1100 SCIC 95128 853-F2
1400 SJS 95128 853-E2
2300 SJS 95126 853-H2
FRUITDALE CT
1600 SJS 95126 853-J2
FRUITVALE AV
13600 SAR 95070 872-F3
FRUITWOOD CT
1600 SJS 95125 853-J5
FRYE LN
5800 SBnC - 999-G6
FUCHSIA CT
8700 GIL 95020 977-G1
FUCHSIA DR
1500 SJS 95125 854-A7
FUJIKO DR
1500 SJS 95131 814-D5
FUJIKO WY
2100 SJS 95131 814-D5
FUJIYAMA LN
1300 SJS 95132 814-G4
FULBAR CT
1200 SJS 95132 814-G4
FULLER AV
300 SJS 95125 854-A2
FULLER ST
4400 SCL 95054 813-C4
FULLERTON CT
500 SJS 95111 875-C1
FULLERTON DR
400 SJS 95111 875-C1
FULTON AV
1000 SUNV 94089 812-F4
FULTON CT
400 SCL 95051 832-H7
700 MPS 95035 794-A5
FULTON ST
- CMBL 95008 853-A6
100 PA 94301 790-J3
600 PA 94301 791-A4
1700 PA 94303 791-B5
FUME BLANC CT
8500 SJS 95135 855-H7
FUNSTON DR
4100 SJS 95136 874-E1
FURLONG AV
6500 SCIC 95020 978-E1
FURLONG DR
800 SJS 95123 874-D5
FUSCHIA DR
1000 SUNV 94086 832-H2
FUSTERIA CT
200 FRMT 94539 793-H1
FUTAMASE CT
2400 SJS 95111 854-G3
FYNES CT
1100 SJS 95131 834-C1

G

G RD
- SUNV 94089 812-H3
G ST
1100 SUNV 94089 812-E3
GABARDA WY
100 SMCo 94028 810-D4
GABILAN AV
200 SUNV 94086 812-C7
GABILAN ST
400 LALT 94022 811-E7
GABLE DR
- FRMT 94539 793-H1
GABLE LN
1700 SJS 95124 873-H5
GABRIAL AV
2300 MTVW 94040 811-F3
N GADSDEN DR
- MPS 95035 794-D6
S GADSDEN DR
- MPS 95035 794-D6
GAFFEY RD
100 SCrC 95076 (976-A6
See Page 955)
GAGE CT
3900 SJS 95124 873-E3
GAIL AV
500 SUNV 94086 832-F3
GAILEN AV
700 PA 94303 811-E1
800 PA 94303 791-F7
GAILEN CT
700 PA 94303 811-F1
GAILEN LN
700 PA 94303 811-E1
GAILLARDIA WY
1100 EPA 94303 791-C3
GAINSBOROUGH DR
1200 SUNV 94087 832-E3
GAINSVILLE AV
1100 SJS 95122 834-J5
GALA CT
2900 SCL 95051 833-A7
GALAHAD AV
700 SJS 95116 834-J4
1100 SJS 95122 834-J4
GALAHAD CT
2500 SJS 95122 834-J4
GALAXY CT
400 MPS 95035 813-J3
GALE DR
700 CMBL 95008 853-C5
GALEN DR
400 SJS 95123 874-J7
GALENA DR
2700 SJS 95121 855-A2
GALEWOOD CT
1700 SJS 95133 834-E3
GALINDO CT
800 MPS 95035 814-E1
GALLANT FOX AV
5100 SJS 95111 875-B2
GALLANT FOX WY
14600 MGH 95037 937-C5
GALLATIN DR
800 SCL 95051 832-J5
GALLEON CT
600 SJS 95133 814-F7
600 SJS 95133 834-F1
GALLERIA DR
400 SJS 95134 813-H4
GALLI CT
300 LALT 94022 811-E6
7100 SJS 95129 852-E4
GALLI DR
- LALT 94022 811-E6
7000 SJS 95129 852-E4
GALLOP DR
16700 MGH 95037 917-F6
GALLOWAY CT
1400 SUNV 94087 832-B4
GALLOWAY DR
7600 SJS 95135 856-A6
GALLUP DR
2400 SCL 95051 833-B2
5600 SJS 95118 874-C4
GALVESTON AV
2100 SJS 95122 854-G2
GALVEZ ST
100 SCIC 94305 790-H6
GALWAY CT
2300 SCL 95050 833-C2
GALWAY DR
1600 CPTO 95014 852-D4
GAMAY CT
400 FRMT 94539 793-J2
3400 SJS 95148 835-D5
GAMAY DR
48800 FRMT 94539 793-J2
GAMBIER CT
1500 SUNV 94087 832-B5
GAMBLIN CIR
2600 SCL 95051 833-B7
GAMBLIN DR
2600 SCL 95051 833-B7
GAMECOCK RD
300 SCrC 95076 955-E5
GAMEL WY
1900 MTVW 94040 811-G4
GAMMA CT
600 CMBL 95008 853-C7
GANA CT
2000 SJS 95148 835-B5
GANCI LN
21100 SCIC 95120 895-B5
GANTRY WY
700 MTVW 94040 831-H1
GARBER PL
1100 SJS 95127 835-A3
GARBINI ST
8700 GIL 95020 977-J1
GARBO WY
1200 SJS 95117 853-B3
GARCAL DR
14900 SCIC 95127 835-C1
GARCES AV
5800 SJS 95123 874-F5
GARCIA AV
2300 MTVW 94043 791-G7
GARCIA CT
200 MPS 95035 794-A4
GARCIA LN
10400 SCIC 95020 957-J3
GARDEN AV
- SBnC - (1017-B5
See Page 997)
2700 SJS 95111 854-G5
2800 SCIC 95111 854-G5
GARDEN CT
6600 GIL 95020 978-A4
GARDEN DR
700 SJS 95126 833-F6
700 SJS 95128 833-F6
GARDEN LN
200 LGTS 95032 873-C4
1300 MLPK 94025 790-E4
GARDEN ST
100 EPA 94303 791-A1
GARDEN TER
2100 MTVW 94040 831-J1
GARDEN WY
- SCL 95050 833-F5
17800 MGH 95037 916-J6
GARDENA CT
10600 CPTO 95014 832-C6
GARDENA DR
21000 SCIC 95014 832-C6
21100 CPTO 95014 832-C6
GARDEN BING CIR
1900 SJS 95131 814-C4
GARDEN BING CT
1900 SJS 95131 814-C4
GARDEN COURT DR
- SCL 95054 813-D7
GARDEN CREST CT
20600 CPTO 95014 852-B7
GARDENDALE DR
2700 SJS 95125 854-C7
3000 SJS 95118 854-C7
3100 SJS 95118 874-C1
GARDEN GATE DR
20600 SCIC 95014 832-D7
GARDENGLEN WY
1500 SJS 95125 854-A7
GARDEN GROVE CIR
- MGH 95037 916-H3
GARDEN HILL DR
14900 LGTS 95030 873-C5
GARDEN HOUSE WY
8700 SJS 95135 856-A6
GARDENIA CT
- EPA 94303 791-D3
GARDENIA WY
100 EPA 94303 791-C3
800 LALT 94024 831-E1
1000 SUNV 94086 832-G2
15500 SCIC 95032 873-D5
GARDEN MANOR CT
20600 CPTO 95014 852-B7
GARDENOAK CT
6500 SJS 95120 894-C1
GARDEN PLACE CT
20700 CPTO 95014 852-B7
GARDENSIDE CIR
20600 CPTO 95014 852-D3
GARDENSIDE LN
1100 CPTO 95014 852-D3
GARDEN TERRACE DR
11400 CPTO 95014 852-B7
GARDENVIEW LN
21800 CPTO 95014 832-B7
GARDENWOOD DR
1000 SJS 95129 852-G2
GARDIE PLACE WY
3800 SJS 95121 855-B4
GARFIELD AV
1100 SJS 95125 854-A3
1100 SJS 95125 853-J3
GARFIELD CT
400 GIL 95020 958-A7
400 GIL 95020 978-A1
GARIN RD
100 MntC - (1015-H6
See Page 995)
GARLAND AV
600 SUNV 94086 832-F2
1000 SJS 95126 833-J7
GARLAND DR
100 MLPK 94025 790-F5
700 PA 94303 791-C5
3700 SJS 95136 854-G7
GARLAND PL
- MLPK 94025 790-F5
E GARLAND TER
600 SUNV 94086 832-F2
N GARLAND TER
600 SUNV 94086 832-F2
W GARLAND TER
600 SUNV 94086 832-F2
GARLAND WY
100 LALT 94022 811-E6
GARLOUGH DR
5800 SJS 95123 874-E5
GARLOUGH PL
900 SJS 95123 874-E5
GARNER CT
700 SCL 95050 833-C5
GARNER DR
100 SUNV 94089 812-E4
GARNET DR
3100 SJS 95117 853-D2
GARNETT CT
19900 SAR 95070 852-E6
GARRANS DR
1300 SJS 95130 853-A4
1300 SJS 95129 853-A4
GARRETT CT
1100 SJS 95120 894-F3
GARRETT DR
3400 SCL 95054 813-A7
GARRISON CIR
5200 SJS 95123 875-B3
GARTHWICK CT
1300 LALT 94024 831-J3
GARTHWICK DR
1300 LALT 94024 831-J3
GARVEY PL
1500 SJS 95132 814-E4
GARWOOD DR
5300 SJS 95118 874-B4
GARWOOD WY
400 MLPK 94025 790-F3
GARY AV
800 SUNV 94086 832-F3
GARY CT
100 MTVW 94041 811-J6
400 PA 94306 791-C7
GARY ST
700 GIL 95020 977-H1
GARZA LN
1600 SCIC 95020 958-A2
GASCOIGNE DR
10500 SCIC 95014 852-H2
GASPAR CT
2700 PA 94306 791-C6
GASSMANN DR
2600 SJS 95121 854-H3
GATELAND CT
3200 SJS 95148 855-E1
GATELIGHT CT
3200 SJS 95148 855-E1
GATES DR
4100 SJS 95124 873-H3
GATEVIEW CT
800 SJS 95133 814-F7
GATEVIEW DR
700 SJS 95133 814-F7
800 SJS 95133 834-F1
GATEWAY BLVD
- FRMT 94538 793-F1
GATEWAY DR
100 LGTS 95032 873-D4
GATEWAY PL
1800 SJS 95110 833-G1
GATEWOOD LN
5200 SJS 95118 874-A4
GATON DR
1600 SJS 95125 853-J5
GATTUCIO DR
4900 SJS 95124 873-J4
GAUCHO CT
1400 SJS 95118 874-B2
GAUNDABERT LN
500 SJS 95136 874-F3
600 SCIC 95123 874-F3
GAUNT AV
8200 GIL 95020 977-G2
GAVELLO AV
700 SUNV 94086 832-F2
GAVILAN CT
400 GIL 95020 958-A7
2800 SJS 95148 855-C1
GAVILAN DR
2800 SJS 95148 855-C1
GAVOTA AV
3100 SJS 95124 873-J2
GAWAIN DR
3100 SJS 95127 814-H7
GAY AV
1200 CMBL 95008 873-C1
2700 SCIC 95127 834-H2
2800 SJS 95127 834-H2
GAYLE DR
4200 SJS 95124 873-H3
GAYLOR LN
3300 SJS 95118 874-A1
GAYWOOD CT
3000 SJS 95148 855-C1
GAZANIA DR
4900 SJS 95111 875-A2
GAZDAR CT
1300 SCL 95051 832-H4
GAZELLE DR
2800 SJS 95008 873-A1
GEBHART AV
- SJS 95116 834-H3
GEHRIG AV
1100 SJS 95132 814-F5
GEIST CT
1600 SJS 95132 814-G2
GEM AV
- LGTS 95032 873-C7
GEMINI AV
200 MTVW 94043 811-H4
GEMINI CT
100 LGTS 95032 873-J6
GEMINI LN
3400 SJS 95111 854-F6
GEMMA DR
300 MPS 95035 794-A5
GEMSTONE DR
200 MPS 95035 793-H6
GENERAL ELECTRIC
- SJS 95125 854-E4
GENEVA AV
500 RDWC 94061 790-B1
GENEVA DR
1200 SUNV 94089 812-G2
3200 SCL 95051 832-J7
GENEVA RD
200 MPS 95035 794-A6
GENEVA ST
1800 SJS 95124 873-G2
GENEVIEVE CT
3100 PA 94303 791-E6
GENEVIEVE LN
500 SJS 95128 833-E7
S GENEVIEVE LN
300 SJS 95128 853-E1
GENG RD
1700 PA 94303 791-D3
GENIE LN
5400 SJS 95123 875-B4
GENINE CT
600 SJS 95127 814-J7
GENINE DR
500 SJS 95127 814-H7
GENOA DR
400 SJS 95133 834-G1
GENTIAN CT
4900 SJS 95111 875-A2
GENTRY CT
2700 SCL 95051 833-B2
GENTRY OAKS PL
6700 SJS 95138 875-G4
GEOMAX CT
4900 SJS 95118 874-C3
GEORGE ST
- SJS 95110 834-A5
900 SCL 95054 813-E7
16100 LGTS 95032 873-C6
GEORGE HOOD LN
300 PA 94306 811-D2
GEORGE OAKS DR
4400 SJS 95118 874-C2
GEORGETOWN CT
600 SUNV 94087 832-D2
GEORGETOWN PL
700 GIL 95020 977-J4
3300 SCL 95051 833-A2
3300 SCL 95051 832-J2
GEORGETTA DR
1400 SJS 95125 854-A6
1500 SJS 95125 853-J6
GEORGIA AV
500 PA 94306 811-C3
600 SUNV 94086 812-F5
2000 SJS 95122 834-H5
GEORGIA LN
100 PTLV 94028 810-C7
GEORGINIA AV
400 SJS 95116 834-H4
GERALD WY
2400 SJS 95125 854-B6
GERALDINE CT
17800 SCIC 95030 913-A2
GERALD ZAPPELLI CT
20400 SAR 95070 872-D2
GERARD WY
800 SJS 95127 835-B2
GERBER CT
900 SUNV 94087 832-B5
GERDTS DR
6200 SJS 95135 855-H6
GERHARDT AV
1400 SJS 95125 854-A7
GERI LN
200 SCIC 95020 957-E6
GERINE BLOSSOM DR
5300 SJS 95123 875-A3
GERLACK DR
1400 SJS 95118 874-B3
GERMAINE CT
1800 SJS 95122 854-G1
GERNEIL CT
14900 SAR 95070 872-E2
GERONA RD
400 SCIC 94305 810-H1
GERONIMO DR
6100 SJS 95123 874-H6
GERTH LN
2200 LAH 94304 810-H4
GEST DR
800 MTVW 94040 831-G1
GETTYSBURG DR
500 SJS 95123 874-H4
GETTYSBURG WY
700 GIL 95020 977-J4
GEYSER DR
1400 SJS 95131 814-C7
GHIRLANDA CT
7700 GIL 95020 978-A2
GIAMPAOLI DR
1900 SCIC 95046 938-A6
GIANERA ST
2000 SCL 95054 813-C4
GIANNI ST
400 SCL 95054 813-E7
GIANNINI DR
400 SCL 95051 832-H7
GIANNOTTA WY
400 SJS 95133 834-G1
GIANT WY
3400 SJS 95127 835-B2
GIBBONS CT
400 MPS 95035 813-J3
GIBRALTAR CT
100 SUNV 94089 812-F3
600 MPS 95035 814-B1
GIBRALTAR DR
200 SUNV 94089 812-F3
500 MPS 95035 814-B2
GIBSON AV
3400 SCL 95051 832-J7
GIBSON CT
3500 SCL 95051 832-J7
GIBSON GIRL WY
2300 SJS 95148 835-D5
2300 SCIC 95148 835-D5
GIDDINGS CT
100 SJS 95139 895-G1
GIER CT
700 SJS 95111 854-G3
GIFFIN RD
100 LALT 94022 831-E1
GIFFORD AV
100 SJS 95110 834-A7
300 SJS 95126 834-A7
GIGI CT
2800 SJS 95111 854-H4
GIGLI CT
12300 LAH 94022 811-A7
GIGUERE CT
600 SJS 95133 834-F2
GILA DR
3400 SJS 95148 835-D5
GILBERT AV
- SCL 95051 833-A7
100 MLPK 94025 791-A2
300 MLPK 94025 790-J2
GILCHRIST DR
800 SJS 95133 814-F7
GILCHRIST RD
100 SCrC 95076 (975-F6
See Page 955)
GILCHRIST WALKWAY
800 SJS 95133 814-F7
GILDA WY
1700 SJS 95124 873-H6
GILES WY
- SJS 95136 854-E7
GILHAM WY
2700 SJS 95148 835-C7
GILLETTE DR
21900 SCIC 95030 913-A3
GILLIAN WY
1800 SJS 95132 814-D3
GILLICK WY
20300 CPTO 95014 852-E2
GILLMOR ST
4700 SCL 95054 813-C4
GILLS DR
6500 SJS 95120 894-C2
GILMAN AV
- CMBL 95008 853-E6
GILMAN RD
1000 GIL 95020 978-B2
1200 SCIC 95020 978-B2
GILMAN ST
600 PA 94301 790-J4
GILMORE ST
1300 MTVW 94040 811-G6
GILROY HOT SPRINGS RD
4200 SCIC 95020 958-G1
5700 SCIC 95020 938-J7
6200 SCIC 95020 959-A1
10300 SCIC 95020 (939-C5
See Page 919)
GIMELLI CT
2500 SJS 95133 834-G1
GIMELLI WY
2500 SCIC 95133 834-G1
2600 SJS 95133 834-G1
GINA CT
12600 SCIC 95127 814-J5
GINA LN
- SBnC - (1020-E1
See Page 999)
GINASHELL CIR
6200 SJS 95119 875-C6
GINDEN CT
1400 CMBL 95008 853-B7
GINDEN DR
600 CMBL 95008 853-B7
GINGER LN
900 SCIC 95128 853-F2
1000 SJS 95128 853-F3
GINGERWOOD DR
1100 MPS 95035 793-J4
GINKGO CT
400 SJS 95111 854-G7
GINNY LN
26300 LAH 94022 831-B1
GION AV
4000 SCIC 95127 834-J1
GIOVANNI CT
300 SJS 95133 834-H1
GIRALDA DR
500 LALT 94024 811-F7
GIRARD DR
1700 MPS 95035 794-D7
GIRARD RD
- SCIC 94035 812-B3
GIRAUDO DR
500 SJS 95111 875-B1
E GISH RD
- SJS 95112 834-B1
W GISH RD
- SJS 95110 833-J3
- SJS 95112 833-J3
GIST RD
19800 SCIC 95030 892-D5
GITANA CT
2400 MGH 95037 917-F6
GITTLE CT
600 SJS 95116 834-H4
GIUSTI DR
5100 SJS 95111 875-B2
GLACIER DR
1100 MPS 95035 814-C1
1400 SJS 95118 874-B2
GLADDING CT
1500 MPS 95035 814-C3

STREET
Block City ZIP Pg-Grid

GLADE DR
2400 SCL 95051 833-A2
GLADIOLA DR
800 SUNV 94086 832-F2
GLADSTONE AV
1700 SJS 95124 873-J3
GLADYS AV
- MTVW 94043 812-A4
GLADYS WY
1800 SJS 95124 853-G7
GLAMORGAN CT
3400 SJS 95127 835-B3
GLASGLOW CT
400 MPS 95035 794-B6
GLASGOW CT
3500 SJS 95127 835-B2
13200 SAR 95070 852-E7
GLASGOW DR
19900 SAR 95070 852-E7
GLAUSER DR
2700 SJS 95133 814-G7
GLEASON AV
3500 SJS 95130 853-B4
GLEN CT
600 GIL 95020 977-J4
600 MPS 95035 794-B5
GLEN PL
21200 CPTO 95014 832-C7
GLEN WY
2000 EPA 94303 791-B1
GLENA CT
1300 SJS 95122 854-H1
GLEN ADEN CT
2900 SJS 95148 835-C7
GLEN ALMA WY
2500 SJS 95148 835-C7
GLEN ALTO CT
3000 SJS 95148 855-D1
GLEN ALTO DR
500 LALT 94024 831-F1
GLEN AMADOR CT
2700 SJS 95148 835-B7
GLEN ANGUS WY
2400 SJS 95148 835-C7
GLEN ARBOR CT
12700 SAR 95070 852-E6
GLEN ASCOT WY
2800 SJS 95148 835-C7
GLEN AYRE DR
18400 MGH 95037 916-F6
GLENBAR AV
900 SUNV 94087 832-G5
GLENBLAIR WY
1100 CMBL 95008 873-B1
GLENBOROUGH DR
700 MTVW 94041 812-A7
GLEN BRAE CT
20400 SAR 95070 852-F6
GLEN BRAE DR
13000 SAR 95070 852-E7
19800 SAR 95070 872-E1
GLENBRAE LN
1200 SJS 95118 874-C4
GLENBRIER DR
2600 SJS 95130 852-J7
GLENBROOK AV
1000 SJS 95125 853-J3
GLENBROOK DR
600 PA 94306 811-D3
GLENBURRY WY
500 SJS 95123 874-E3
GLENCO DR
10200 SCIC 95014 832-D7
GLENCOE CT
700 SUNV 94087 832-F4
GLEN COMO WY
2900 SJS 95148 835-C7
GLEN COTSWOLD CT
2500 SJS 95148 835-C7
GLEN CRAIG CT
2900 SJS 95148 835-C7
GLENCREST CT
1500 SJS 95118 874-A2
GLENCREST DR
1500 SJS 95118 874-A2
GLENCREST WY
1500 SJS 95118 874-A2
GLEN CROW CT
2900 SJS 95148 835-C7
GLENDALE AV
400 SUNV 94086 812-F5
3000 SMCo 94063 790-D1
GLENDALE DR
- SJS 95193 875-C4
GLEN DARBY CT
2900 SJS 95148 835-C7
GLEN DECKER CT
2800 SJS 95148 835-B7
GLEN DELL DR
1300 SJS 95125 853-J4
GLENDENNING AV
2300 SCL 95050 833-C7
GLEN DIXON CT
2800 SJS 95148 835-B7
GLEN DONEGAL DR
2700 SJS 95148 835-B7
GLEN DOON CT
2600 SJS 95148 835-B7
GLENDORA CT
6200 SJS 95123 874-F6
GLEN DUFF WY
2400 SJS 95148 835-B7
GLEN DUNDEE CT
2500 SJS 95148 835-C7
GLEN DUNDEE WY
2400 SJS 95148 835-B7
GLENEAGLES CIR
5800 SJS 95138 875-H1
GLENEAGLES DR
5800 SJS 95138 875-H1
GLEN ECHO AV
1000 SJS 95125 853-J3
18300 MSER 95030 872-J6
GLENEDEN WY
3100 SJS 95117 853-D3
GLEN ELK CT
2600 SJS 95148 835-B7
GLEN ELLEN WY
1400 SJS 95125 853-J5
GLEN ELM WY
2400 SJS 95148 835-C7
GLEN EVANS CT
2800 SJS 95148 835-B7
GLEN EXETER WY
2400 SJS 95148 835-B7
GLEN EYRIE AV
1100 SJS 95125 854-A2
1100 SJS 95125 853-J3
GLEN FALL CT
2500 SJS 95148 835-C7
GLEN FARM CT
2400 SJS 95148 835-C7
GLEN FENTON WY
2600 SJS 95148 835-B7
GLEN FERGUSON CIR
2600 SJS 95148 835-C7
GLENFIELD CT
1600 SJS 95125 854-A7
GLENFIELD DR
1600 SJS 95125 854-A7
GLENFINNAN CT
1000 SJS 95122 854-G1
GLENFINNAN DR
1000 SJS 95122 854-G1
GLEN FIRTH DR
2700 SJS 95133 814-G7
GLENFORD PARK CT
400 SJS 95136 874-F1
GLEN FOX CT
2400 SJS 95148 835-C7
GLEN FROST CT
2800 SJS 95148 835-C7
GLENGARRY DR
3800 SJS 95121 855-C4
GLENGROVE WY
3800 SJS 95121 855-C4
GLEN HAIG WY
2400 SJS 95148 835-C7
GLEN HANCOCK CT
2500 SJS 95148 835-C7
GLEN HANLEIGH DR
2400 SJS 95148 835-B7
GLEN HARBOR DR
6000 SJS 95123 875-A6
GLEN HARDY CT
2600 SJS 95148 835-B7
GLEN HARWICK CT
2500 SJS 95148 835-C7
GLEN HASTINGS CT
2500 SJS 95148 835-C7
GLEN HAVEN CT
5600 SJS 95129 852-H3
GLEN HAVEN DR
1200 SJS 95129 852-H4
GLEN HAWKINS CT
2800 SJS 95148 835-C7
GLEN HEATHER DR
2700 SJS 95133 814-G7
GLEN HEDGE CT
2500 SJS 95148 835-C7
GLEN HOLLOW WY
- SJS 95132 814-E5
GLENHURST DR
1600 SJS 95124 873-J2
GLEN IAN CT
2500 SJS 95148 835-B7
GLEN KEATS CT
2700 SJS 95148 835-C7
GLEN KELLER CT
2500 SJS 95148 835-B7
GLEN KEW CT
2500 SJS 95148 835-B7
GLENKIRK CT
2200 SJS 95124 853-H6
GLENKIRK DR
2100 SJS 95124 853-H6
GLEN LAKE CIR
- MGH 95037 937-A1
GLEN LOMAN WY
2600 SJS 95148 835-B7
GLEN MEAD CT
700 SJS 95133 814-G7
GLEN MEADOW CT
1100 SJS 95125 854-A4
GLENMONT DR
4100 SJS 95136 874-D1
21200 SAR 95070 872-C2
GLENMOOR CIR
400 MPS 95035 793-H6
GLENMOOR CT
500 MPS 95035 793-J6
GLENMOOR WY
1200 SJS 95129 852-F4
GLENN AV
400 CMBL 95008 873-C1
1100 SJS 95125 854-A3
1100 SJS 95125 853-J3
GLENN WY
1500 RDWC 94061 790-A2
GLENNAN CT
5400 SJS 95129 852-H4
GLENOAK CT
5500 SJS 95129 852-H3
GLENPARK DR
4300 SJS 95136 874-D2
GLEN PATHWAY
6800 GIL 95020 977-G4
GLEN PINE DR
1400 SJS 95125 854-A4
GLEN RIDGE AV
- LGTS 95030 872-J7
GLENRIDGE DR
900 SJS 95136 874-D1
GLENRIO DR
2500 SJS 95121 855-C3
GLENROCK CT
1600 SJS 95124 873-J7
GLENROY DR
1600 SJS 95124 873-J2
GLEN SHARON WY
2800 SJS 95148 835-B7
GLENSIDE DR
700 SJS 95123 874-G6
GLENSTONE CT
1700 SJS 95121 855-C4
GLENTREE CT
5100 SJS 95129 852-J2
GLENTREE DR
5000 SJS 95129 852-J2
GLEN UNA AV
1700 SJS 95125 854-B4
GLEN UNA DR
15400 SAR 95070 872-F5
15500 SCIC 95030 872-E5
15500 SAR 95030 872-F5
GLENVIEW AV
10300 CPTO 95014 852-F1
GLENVIEW CT
600 GIL 95020 977-J4
800 MPS 95035 814-E1
GLENVIEW DR
2100 MPS 95035 814-E1
6700 SJS 95120 894-F2
6800 GIL 95020 977-J4
GLENVILLE DR
1600 SJS 95124 873-J2
GLEN WILLOW CT
- SJS 95125 854-E5
GLEN WOOD
800 MTVW 94041 811-H7
GLENWOOD AV
100 ATN 94027 790-F2
400 MLPK 94025 790-F2
1100 SJS 95125 854-A4
1400 SJS 95125 853-J4
GLENWOOD DR
600 GIL 95020 977-J1
GLIDER DR
6100 SJS 95123 874-J7
GLISTENING CT
- MPS 95035 793-H6
GLITHERO CT
1000 SJS 95112 834-D3
GLORIA AV
300 SCIC 95127 835-A2
GLORIA CIR
- MLPK 94025 790-H2
GLORIA CT
18100 SCIC 95030 912-H3
GLORIA WY
2400 EPA 94303 791-B1
GLORIETTA CIR
2700 SCL 95051 833-B7
GLOUCESTER CT
1000 SUNV 94087 832-G5
GLOUCHESTER CT
5000 SJS 95136 874-F3
GLOWING CT
5900 SJS 95120 874-B7
GNARLED OAK LN
16700 MGH 95037 917-G6
GOBLE LN
- SJS 95111 854-F5
GODDESS CT
6200 SJS 95129 852-F3
GODFREY RD
21200 SAR 95070 872-C2
GOEBEL AV
4100 PA 94306 811-C2
GOEBEL CT
18100 SCIC 95030 912-J3
GOLD ST
- SCIC 95002 813-B1
1300 SJS 95002 793-B7
1500 SJS 95002 813-B1
GOLD CREEK CT
7200 SJS 95120 894-H4
GOLD CREEK WY
7200 SJS 95120 894-H4
GOLDEN DR
5000 SJS 95129 852-J3
GOLDEN WY
900 MTVW 94040 831-G2
1000 LALT 94024 831-G2
GOLDEN ACRE CT
1000 SJS 95136 874-C2
GOLDEN ASPEN WY
11000 CPTO 95014 832-D6
GOLDEN CREEK TER
700 SJS 95111 855-B7
GOLDEN DEW CIR
2100 SJS 95121 855-C3
GOLDEN GATE AV
1000 SCIC 95020 957-G5
GOLDEN GATE DR
7000 SJS 95129 852-E3
GOLDEN HILL CT
13600 LAH 94022 811-C7
GOLDEN HILLS DR
100 PTLV 94028 810-C5
1700 MPS 95035 794-D6
GOLDEN LEAF CT
- SJS 95136 874-J7
GOLDEN MEADOW SQ
1400 SJS 95117 853-C4
GOLDEN OAK CT
700 SUNV 94086 832-F2
GOLDEN OAK DR
- PTLV 94028 810-D5
700 SUNV 94086 832-F2
GOLDEN OAK WY
1200 SJS 95120 874-C6
GOLDENRAIN AV
200 FRMT 94539 793-H1
GOLDEN RAIN CT
200 SJS 95111 875-A1
GOLDEN RAIN DR
- SJS 95111 875-A2
GOLDENROD CIR
- GIL 95020 977-F1
GOLDENROD CT
800 SUNV 94086 832-F2
GOLDEN STATE DR
3400 SCL 95051 832-J5
GOLDENTREE DR
1600 SJS 95131 814-C5
GOLDFIELD DR
5600 SJS 95123 874-J4
GOLDFINCH WY
1500 SUNV 94087 832-F5
GOLD MEADOW CT
- SJS 95135 855-H7
GOLDPINE CT
6800 SJS 95120 894-E3
GOLDPINE WY
6800 SJS 95120 894-E3
GOLDRIDGE CT
3200 SJS 95135 855-D2
GOLD RUN WY
100 SJS 95136 874-G1
GOLDRUSH CT
1400 SJS 95131 814-D6
GOLDWOOD CT
2600 SJS 95148 835-D6
GOLETA AV
12200 SAR 95070 852-E5
GOLETA CT
12300 SAR 95070 852-E5
GOLF CT
1000 MTVW 94040 812-A7
GOLF DR
3100 SJS 95127 814-H7
3400 SCIC 95127 814-J6
3700 SCIC 95127 814-J6
4100 SJS 95127 815-A6
GOLF LN
- SCIC 94304 810-E3
- SMCo 94025 810-E3
GOLF COURSE LN
7000 SJS 95139 895-E1
7000 SCIC 95119 895-E1
GOLF CREEK DR
1300 SJS 95120 894-D2
GOLF LINKS CIR
2200 SCL 95050 833-C6
GOLF LINKS DR
14600 LGTS 95030 873-B3
14800 SCIC 95030 873-B3
GOLF VIEW DR
400 SCIC 95127 815-A6
GOLF VIEW RD
100 SCrC 95076 (975-H7
See Page 955)
GOLZIO CT
2400 SJS 95133 814-F7
GOMES CT
200 CMBL 95008 853-E5
GOMES DR
2600 SJS 95132 814-E5
GONDOLA WY
6300 SJS 95120 874-C7
6300 SJS 95120 894-C1
GONZAGA PL
3300 SCL 95051 832-J2
GONZAGA ST
2400 EPA 94303 791-C1
GOODWIN AV
700 SJS 95128 853-H2
3000 RDWC 94061 790-A2
GOODY LN
1400 SJS 95131 814-C7
GOODYEAR ST
- SJS 95110 854-C2
GOOSEBERRY CT
1200 SUNV 94087 832-B3
GOOSE LAKE CT
800 SJS 95123 874-E5
GORDOLA CT
300 SJS 95111 875-A1
GORDON AV
300 SCIC 95127 815-A7
600 SCIC 95127 814-J6
2000 SMCo 94025 790-D6
2900 SCL 95051 812-J7
2900 SCL 95051 832-J1
GORDON CT
20500 SAR 95070 852-D6
GORDON ST
1000 MPS 95035 794-B5
1200 RDWC 94061 790-A1
N GORDON WY
- LALT 94022 811-E6
S GORDON WY
- LALT 94022 811-E7
GORDY DR
1500 SJS 95131 814-C7
GORSKY RD
- SCIC 94035 812-B3
GOSFORD CT
- SJS 95139 875-G7
GOSHAWK CT
1300 GIL 95020 977-F1
GOSSER ST
300 MPS 95035 794-A3
GOULD CT
1700 SCIC 95020 938-A7
1700 SCIC 95020 958-A1
GOULD LN
18100 SCIC 95037 917-B4
GOURMET AL
7400 GIL 95020 978-A3
GOVERNORS AV
500 SCIC 94305 790-G7
GOWER DR
5300 SJS 95118 874-A5
GOYA DR
300 SUNV 94087 832-E2
GOYA RD
100 PTLV 94028 810-C4
GRAACH CT
4100 SJS 95135 855-G3
GRACE AV
100 EPA 94303 791-B1
1400 CMBL 95125 853-H5
1400 SCIC 95125 853-H5
GRACE CT
- SCIC 95125 853-H5
GRACE DR
500 MLPK 94025 790-E6
GRACKLE WY
1500 SUNV 94087 832-F5
GRADELL PL
3300 SJS 95148 835-D6
GRAFTON WY
2800 SJS 95148 835-E7
GRAHAM LN
1600 SCL 95050 833-C3
GRAHAM ST
100 SJS 95110 854-C1
GRAMERCY PL
100 SJS 95116 834-G2
GRANADA AV
3300 SCL 95051 833-A4
3300 SCL 95051 832-J4
21600 CPTO 95014 852-B1
GRANADA CT
- PTLV 94028 810-D6
3300 SCL 95051 832-J4
20700 SAR 95070 852-D5
GRANADA DR
100 MTVW 94043 811-H4
GRANADA WY
100 LGTS 95030 873-A3
900 SJS 95122 854-G1
GRAND AV
200 SJS 95126 853-J1
200 SCIC 95126 853-J1
21500 CPTO 95014 832-B7
GRAND BLVD
1200 SJS 95002 793-C7
1200 SJS 95002 813-B1
GRANDBROOK WY
800 SJS 95111 855-A5
GRANDBY DR
2400 SJS 95130 852-J7
GRAND COULEE AV
600 SUNV 94087 832-D5
GRAND FIR AV
500 SUNV 94086 832-F2
GRANDIN CT
300 SJS 95123 874-J4
GRAND MEADOW LN
6300 SJS 95135 855-J7
GRAND OAK WY
- SJS 95135 876-A1
- SJS 95135 875-J1
GRANDPARK CIR
300 SJS 95136 874-G1
GRAND PRIX WY
17200 MGH 95037 917-A6
GRANDSTAND WY
- SJS 95111 854-G4
GRAND TETON DR
1500 MPS 95035 814-D1
GRANDVIEW AV
15800 MSER 95030 872-J6
GRANDVIEW DR
2600 SCIC 95133 814-G7
2600 SJS 95133 814-G7
15800 MSER 95030 872-J6
GRANDWELL WY
- SJS 95138 875-D4
GRANDWOOD WY
6900 SJS 95120 894-J3
GRANGER AV
1700 SCIC 94024 831-H3
1700 LALT 94024 831-H3
GRANGER TER
500 SUNV 94087 832-D5
GRANITE CT
- MPS 95035 794-A6
14900 SAR 95070 872-G4
GRANITE LN
2300 SJS 95133 834-F1
GRANITE WY
800 SJS 95133 834-F2
14600 SAR 95070 872-G3
GRANITE CREEK PL
2800 SJS 95127 834-J4
GRANITE ROCK WY
100 SJS 95136 854-G7
GRANT AV
100 PA 94306 791-B7
GRANT CT
400 GIL 95020 978-A2
1300 LALT 94024 831-J3
GRANT RD
800 SBnC (1020-D3
See Page 999)
1000 MTVW 94040 811-J7
1100 LALT 94024 831-J4
1100 MTVW 94040 831-J1
1100 SCIC 94040 831-J1
2200 LALT 94024 832-A5
GRANT ST
100 CMBL 95008 853-E5
200 SJS 95110 854-B1
GRANT ST
1500 SCL 95050 833-E3
GRANT PARK LN
1800 LALT 94024 832-A4
1800 LALT 94024 831-J4
GRANVILLE CT
200 SJS 95139 895-F1
GRAPE AV
600 SUNV 94087 832-B2
GRAPELEAF WY
4200 SJS 95135 855-G3
GRAPEVINE WY
6500 SJS 95120 894-D1
GRAPE WAGON CIR
8700 SJS 95135 856-A6
8700 SJS 95135 855-J6
GRAPNEL PL
10600 CPTO 95014 832-C6
GRASS VALLEY CT
3400 SJS 95127 835-C4
GRAVES AV
5000 SJS 95129 852-J5
GRAVEYARD RD
7600 SCIC 95140 (817-G5
See Page 797)
GRAYS LN
- LGTS 95030 873-A7
GRAYSON CT
300 MLPK 94025 791-A1
300 MLPK 94025 790-J1
GRAYSON WY
500 MPS 95035 794-B4
GRAYSTONE LN
6600 SJS 95120 894-F1
6600 SCIC 95120 894-G1
GRAYSTONE MDW CIR
6400 SJS 95120 874-F7
GRAYSTONE MDW DR
6400 SJS 95120 874-F7
GRAYWOOD DR
1400 SJS 95129 852-G4
GREAT AMERICA PKWY
- SCIC 95002 813-B3
- SJS 95002 813-B3
4100 SCL 95054 813-B3
GREATHOUSE DR
400 MPS 95035 794-A3
GREAT MALL DR
100 MPS 95035 814-A2
GREAT MALL PKWY
800 MPS 95035 813-J2
800 MPS 95035 814-A2
GREAT OAK WY
5400 SJS 95123 875-B4
GREAT OAKS BLVD
- SJS 95119 875-E7
GREAT OAKS DR
5100 SJS 95111 875-C2
GRECIA CT
300 SJS 95116 834-F3
GRECO AV
1000 SUNV 94087 832-E3
GREEN CT
500 PA 94301 791-C6
GREEN ST
100 MLPK 94025 791-A2
100 EPA 94303 791-B2
GREEN ACRES CT
2100 SCIC 95037 936-F3
GREEN ACRES LN
2100 SCIC 95037 936-F3
GREENBANK CT
5300 SJS 95118 874-C4
GREENBAY CT
800 SJS 95128 853-F4
GREENBRIAR AV
1100 SJS 95128 853-E4
GREENBRIAR CT
3000 SJS 95128 853-E4
GREENBROOK CT
18900 SAR 95070 852-G5
GREEN CREEK DR
1800 SJS 95124 853-H7
GREENDALE DR
100 LGTS 95032 873-D5
GREENDALE WY
200 SJS 95129 853-A1
GREENE DR
1400 SJS 95129 852-H4
GREENFIELD PL
100 LGTS 95030 873-B3
GREENFORD CT
3100 SJS 95148 855-E2
GREENGATE DR
2400 SJS 95132 814-E5
GREEN GLEN CT
1100 SJS 95126 853-H3
GREEN HILL WY
100 LGTS 95030 873-C4
2500 SJS 95121 855-E4
GREEN HILLS CT
12000 LAH 94022 831-B2
GREENLAKE DR
300 SUNV 94089 812-G4
GREENLAND WY
3200 SJS 95135 855-E2
GREENLEAF DR
20600 CPTO 95014 832-C7
20600 SCIC 95014 832-C7
GREENLEAF LN
2800 SJS 95121 855-D3
GREENLEE DR
3500 SJS 95117 853-C1
GREENMEADOW LN
12400 SAR 95070 852-D6
GREENMEADOW WY
100 PA 94306 811-E2
500 SJS 95129 853-A2
GREENMOOR DR
1100 SJS 95118 874-C2
GREENOAK DR
5500 SJS 95129 852-H3
GREEN OAK LN
1200 LALT 94024 831-H4
GREENOAKS DR
100 ATN 94027 790-G1
GREENPARK WY
300 SJS 95136 874-G2
GREENRIDGE TER
16000 LGTS 95032 873-F6
GREENROCK RD
2500 MPS 95035 814-F1
GREENSBORO CT
1500 SJS 95131 814-C6
GREENSIDE DR
5300 SCIC 95127 815-A6
GREENSTONE CT
2500 SJS 95122 835-A5
GREENTREE CIR
- MPS 95035 814-A3
GREENTREE WY
- MPS 95035 814-A3
3000 SJS 95128 853-E3
3100 SJS 95117 853-D3
GREEN VALLEY DR
100 SCIC 95020 957-F4
GREEN VALLEY RD
- SCrC 95019 995-F3
- WAT 95019 995-D7
300 SCrC 95076 995-F3
300 WAT 95076 995-D7
48700 FRMT 94539 794-A1
48900 MPS 95035 794-A1
GREENVIEW DR
800 MTVW 94040 812-A7
800 MTVW 94040 832-A1
GREENVIEW PL
600 SCIC 94024 831-F3
GREENWAYS DR
2100 SMCo 94062 790-A5
GREENWICH AV
900 SUNV 94087 832-C1
GREENWICH CT
1300 SJS 95125 853-G4
GREENWICH DR
800 GIL 95020 977-H4
E GREENWICH DR
700 PA 94303 791-C5
GREENWOOD AV
1000 PA 94301 791-B4
1000 SJS 95126 833-G5
2100 MGH 95037 936-E1
15900 MSER 95030 872-H6
16100 SCIC 95030 872-H6
GREENWOOD CIR
- MGH 95037 916-H3
GREENWOOD CT
10300 CPTO 95014 852-F1
GREENWOOD DR
300 SCL 95054 813-F6
17500 SCIC 95030 913-A3
19300 CPTO 95014 852-G1
GREENWOOD LN
16000 MSER 95030 872-H6
16000 SCIC 95030 872-G6
GREENWOOD RD
15900 MSER 95030 872-H6
GREENWOOD WY
1500 MPS 95035 814-A3
GREER RD
500 PA 94303 791-C4
GREG CT
800 SCIC 95020 957-G2
GREGG CT
200 LGTS 95032 873-G5
GREGG DR
200 LGTS 95032 873-G5
200 LGTS 95032 873-G5
1600 SJS 95124 873-G5
GREGORICH DR
6900 SJS 95138 875-G6
GREGORY LN
200 RDWC 94061 790-B2
GREGORY PL
18200 MSER 95030 872-J4
GREGORY ST
400 SJS 95126 854-A1
500 SJS 95125 854-A2
GREMLIN CT
400 SJS 95111 854-F6
GRENACHE CT
8400 SJS 95135 855-H7
GRENADINE WY
1800 SJS 95122 854-G1
GRENOLA DR
21000 SCIC 95014 832-C7
GRESHAM AV
500 SUNV 94086 812-F6
GRESHAM CT
400 SUNV 94086 812-F5
7400 SJS 95139 895-G1
GRESHAM LN
- ATN 94027 790-C1
GRETCHEN LN
- SJS 95117 853-B3
GRETEL LN
1200 MTVW 94040 811-J7
GREY CT
2200 SJS 95124 873-E5
GREY FEATHER CIR
4900 SJS 95136 874-J3
GREY GHOST AV
200 SJS 95111 875-B2
GREY GHOST CT
500 MGH 95037 937-C5
GREYLANDS DR
1400 SJS 95125 853-G5
GREYMONT DR
3600 SJS 95136 854-F7
GREYSTONE CT
800 GIL 95020 977-G1
GRIDLEY CT
300 SJS 95127 814-J7
GRIDLEY ST
300 SJS 95127 814-H6
400 SCIC 95127 814-H7
GRIFFIS WY
15200 SCIC 95037 936-F5
GRIFFITH LN
100 CMBL 95008 853-E7
GRIFFITH PL
100 LGTS 95030 873-A6
GRIFFITH ST
10000 SJS 95127 835-A3
GRIGLIO DR
100 SJS 95134 813-G2
GRIMLEY LN
1100 SJS 95120 894-H4
GRIMSBY CT
2300 SJS 95130 852-J7
GRIMSBY DR
4400 SJS 95130 853-A7
4800 SJS 95130 852-J7
GRIMSWOOD CT
700 SJS 95120 894-J3
GRINNELL CT
300 SCL 95051 832-H7
GRISWOLD LN
16100 SCIC 95037 936-H3
GRIZILO DR
1600 SJS 95124 873-J1
GRIZZLY FLAT RD
- SCrC 95076 955-C4
GROESBECK HILL RD
3600 SJS 95148 835-E6
GRONWALL CT
1200 SCIC 94024 831-F3
GRONWALL LN
1200 SCIC 94024 831-F2
GROSBEAK AV
1600 SUNV 94087 832-F5
GROSS ST
300 MPS 95035 794-A3
GROSSETO CT
- SJS 95138 855-E7
GROSSMONT DR
3300 SJS 95132 814-H5
GROSVENOR CT
17200 MSER 95030 873-B4
GROSVENOR DR
1900 SJS 95132 814-F2
GROTH CT
3100 SJS 95111 854-F7
GROTH DR
500 SJS 95111 854-F7
GROTH PL
500 SJS 95111 854-F7
GROTON CT
800 SUNV 94087 832-C2
GROUSE WY
700 SJS 95133 834-F1
GROVE AV
3700 PA 94303 791-E7
3800 PA 94303 811-E1
GROVE CT
- SJS 95134 813-C2
- PA 94303 811-E1
- PTLV 94028 810-B7
GROVE DR
- PTLV 94028 810-B6
100 MGH 95037 937-B6
GROVE LN
700 PA 94303 811-E1
GROVE ST
- LGTS 95032 893-A1
GROVELAND DR
10600 SCIC 94024 832-A6
GROVELAND ST
- PTLV 94028 830-C1
GROVETREE CT
1500 SJS 95131 814-D5
GROVEWOOD CT
800 SJS 95120 894-H3
GRUBER CT
7100 SJS 95139 875-F7
GRUWELL PL
1000 SJS 95129 853-A3
GUADALAJARA CT
1600 SJS 95120 874-A7
GUADALAJARA DR
1500 SJS 95120 874-A7
GUADALUPE AV
1700 SJS 95125 854-C4
GUADALUPE DR
500 LALT 94022 811-D5
GUADALUPE FRWY
Rt#-87
- SCIC - 874-E1
- SCIC - 854-D6
- SJS - 854-C3
- SJS - 834-A5
- SJS - 874-E1
GUADALUPE PKWY
- SJS 95131 813-G7
- SJS 95131 833-H2
800 SJS 95110 833-H2
GUADALUPE MINES CT
6000 SJS 95120 873-J7
GUADALUPE MINES RD
6000 SJS 95120 873-J7
6600 SJS 95120 893-H2
GUANACASTE CT
200 SJS 95116 834-F2
GUAVA CT
20100 SAR 95070 852-E6
GUAVA BLOSSOM CT
- SJS 95123 875-E2
GUAYMAS CT
9000 GIL 95020 977-F1
GUERRA CT
4200 SJS 95111 854-G3
GUERRA DR
500 SJS 95111 854-G3
GUERRERO CT
1300 MPS 95035 794-C5
GUIBAL AV
8800 SCIC 95020 958-A1
GUIFRIDA AV
300 SJS 95123 874-H4
GUIFRIDA CT
5400 SJS 95123 874-H4
GUILDFORD PL
4100 SJS 95135 855-F3
GUILDHALL DR
2700 SJS 95132 814-C3
GUINDA ST
300 PA 94301 790-J3
500 PA 94301 791-A4
1700 PA 94303 791-B5
GULLO AV
900 SJS 95129 852-J2
GULUZZO DR
3300 SJS 95148 835-C5
GUMDROP DR
2500 SJS 95148 835-C7
GUM TREE DR
3500 SJS 95111 854-G6
GUM TREE LN
15600 LGTS 95032 873-E6
GUNAR DR
2200 SJS 95124 853-G7
GUNDERSEN DR
2200 SJS 95125 853-J6
GUNN CT
100 SJS 95127 835-A2
GUNSTON WY
1700 SJS 95124 873-H3
1900 SCIC 95124 873-H3

STREET
Block City ZIP Pg-Grid

GUNTER WY
6200 SJS 95123 874-H6
GUNTHER CT
19100 SAR 95070 852-G6
GURNEY CT
1100 SJS 95132 814-G5
GURRIES DR
200 GIL 95020 977-J2
GUSTAFUS DR
8700 SCIC 95020 958-F5
GWEN DR
700 CMBL 95008 853-A7
800 CMBL 95008 873-A1
GWINN AV
1700 SCIC 95046 938-A6
1700 SCIC 95046 937-J6
GWINN CT
400 SJS 95111 875-C2
GYPSY AV
12100 SCIC 95046 938-A7
GYPSY HILL RD
14600 SAR 95070 872-G4
GYPSY MOTH PL
6000 SJS 95123 874-E6
GYPSY PLACE CT
1600 SJS 95121 855-B4

H

H ST
1100 SUNV 94089 812-D3
HABBITTS CT
500 SJS 95111 854-G4
HACIENDA AV
300 CMBL 95008 873-A1
4500 SJS 95008 873-A1
E HACIENDA AV
200 CMBL 95008 873-D1
HACIENDA CT
300 LALT 94022 811-D5
1300 CMBL 95008 873-B1
HACIENDA DR
200 SJS 95131 814-A5
1000 GIL 95020 977-G3
HACIENDA WY
300 LALT 94022 811-D5
HACIENDA VALLEY DR
- MGH 95037 916-H3
HACK AV
1400 CMBL 95008 873-B2
HACKBERRY ST
48200 FRMT 94539 793-J1
HACKETT AV
1600 MTVW 94043 811-G3
HADDON WY
3200 SJS 95135 855-E3
HADEOCK CT
1600 SJS 95132 814-E4
HADLEY AV
500 SJS 95126 833-G7
HADLEY CT
400 GIL 95020 978-A3
HAGA DR
3100 SJS 95111 854-H5
8900 SCIC 95111 854-H6
HAGA WY
10300 SCIC 95111 854-H6
HAGEN CT
7300 GIL 95020 977-H4
HAGER CT
12600 SCIC 95046 937-H7
HAIG ST
3500 SCL 95054 813-E6
HAIGHT ST
100 MLPK 94025 791-A1
HAINES AV
4000 SJS 95136 874-E1
HAITI RD
500 SJS 95111 854-G4
HALBREATH CT
3200 SJS 95121 855-C5
HALE AV
7300 SJS 95139 896-A4
7300 SJS 95139 895-H2
7800 SJS 95141 896-A4
9000 SJS 95037 896-A5
14100 SCIC 95037 896-A5
14300 SCIC 95037 916-H6
14600 MGH 95037 916-H6
HALE PL
10600 CPTO 95014 832-C6
HALE ST
400 PA 94301 791-A3
HALEY CT
500 SJS 95123 874-J7
HALF RD
1000 MGH 95037 917-A5
1000 SCIC 95037 917-B4
HALF CROWN LN
3400 SJS 95132 814-J2

HALF MOON CT
3200 SJS 95111 854-H5
HALFORD AV
1200 SCL 95051 832-H3
HALF PENCE CT
1800 SJS 95132 814-F3
HALF PENCE WY
1800 SJS 95132 814-F3
HALGRIM CT
3000 SJS 95132 814-G5
HALIFAX DR
5100 SJS 95130 872-J1
HALKINS DR
4000 SJS 95124 873-E3
HALL CT
19900 CPTO 95014 852-F1
HALLADALE CT
7600 SJS 95135 855-J6
HALLBROOK DR
1500 SJS 95118 874-A3
1600 SJS 95124 873-J3
HALLCREST DR
1500 SJS 95118 874-A2
HALLECK DR
5700 SJS 95123 874-E5
HALLMARK CIR
- MLPK 94025 790-C6
HALLMARK LN
1700 SJS 95124 873-H2
HALSEY AV
300 SCIC 95128 853-F1
HAMANN DR
600 SJS 95117 853-C2
HAMELIN CT
900 SUNV 94089 812-E4
HAMES RD
100 SCrC 95003 (975-A4 See Page 955)
100 SCrC 95076 (975-A4 See Page 955)
HAMIDA CT
1200 SJS 95120 894-E2
HAMILTON AV
- CMBL 95008 853-J5
- PA 94301 790-J5
100 MTVW 94043 811-F3
500 MPS 95035 794-A6
700 PA 94301 791-A3
1400 SJS 95125 853-J5
1500 PA 94303 791-B3
1500 SCIC 95125 853-J5
1700 CMBL 95125 853-J5
E HAMILTON AV
- CMBL 95008 853-F5
800 SJS 95128 853-F5
800 CMBL 95128 853-F5
900 CMBL 95125 853-F5
900 SJS 95125 853-F5
W HAMILTON AV
- CMBL 95008 853-C5
1000 SJS 95130 853-C5
4700 SJS 95130 852-J5
4800 SJS 95129 852-J5
HAMILTON CT
- HOLL - (1020-B6 See Page 999)
- PA 94301 791-A3
HAMILTON LN
600 SCL 95051 833-A6
HAMILTON PL
1400 SJS 95125 853-G4
HAMILTON WY
1400 SJS 95125 853-J5
HAMILTON PARK DR
3900 SJS 95130 853-B4
HAMLET CT
2300 SJS 95131 814-D5
HAMLINE ST
600 SJS 95110 833-J4
900 SJS 95126 833-G5
HAMMERTON CT
5300 SJS 95118 874-C4
HAMMERWOOD AV
1200 SUNV 94089 812-J3
HAMMETT CT
- SJS 95132 814-G3
HAMMOND AV
- FRMT 94539 793-H1
HAMMOND WY
600 MPS 95035 814-A1
HAMMONS AV
13300 SAR 95070 852-E7
13400 SAR 95070 872-E1
HAMPSHIRE CT
18300 MGH 95037 916-H5
HAMPSHIRE PL
4300 SJS 95136 874-D2
HAMPSTEAD WY
1700 SJS 95132 814-F3

HAMPSWOOD CT
900 SJS 95120 894-H3
HAMPSWOOD LN
900 SJS 95120 894-H3
HAMPSWOOD WY
800 SJS 95120 894-H3
HAMPTON AV
1600 RDWC 94061 790-A2
HAMPTON CT
- LALT 94022 811-D6
900 MPS 95035 794-B4
1100 SJS 95120 894-E2
HAMPTON DR
1300 SUNV 94087 832-G4
6500 SJS 95120 894-D2
HAMPTON BROOK DR
2600 SCL 95051 833-B4
HAMPTON CREEK DR
2700 SCL 95051 833-B4
HAMPTON FALLS PL
4600 SJS 95136 874-D2
HAMPTON KNOLL DR
1300 SCL 95051 833-B4
HAMPTON LAKE DR
1300 SCL 95051 833-B4
HAMPTON PARK DR
2700 SCL 95051 833-B4
HAMRICK CT
2800 SJS 95121 855-A2
HAMSHIRE CT
1000 SUNV 94087 832-H5
HANALEI PL
4400 SJS 95118 874-B2
HANCHETT AV
1100 SJS 95126 833-H7
1500 SJS 95128 833-H7
1500 SJS 95128 853-H1
HANCOCK AV
6100 SJS 95123 874-G6
HANCOCK CT
14600 LGTS 95030 873-B3
HANCOCK DR
3700 SCL 95051 832-H7
HANCOCK RD
18500 SCIC 95030 892-F5
HANFORD DR
20600 SCIC 95014 832-D7
HANI CT
2800 SJS 95111 854-H4
HANK LN
1500 SCIC 95046 937-J7
HANNA DR
18600 SCIC 95014 852-H2
HANNA ST
7000 GIL 95020 978-A4
7100 GIL 95020 977-J1
HANNA WY
- MLPK 94025 790-H2
HANNAH ST
400 SJS 95126 854-A1
HANOVER AV
800 SUNV 94087 832-C2
HANOVER DR
6300 SJS 95129 852-F4
HANOVER ST
2000 PA 94306 811-A1
2000 PA 94306 810-J1
2200 PA 94304 811-A1
HANS AV
200 MTVW 94040 811-H7
HANS WY
300 SJS 95133 834-F2
HANSELL DR
5300 SJS 95123 874-J3
HANSEN WY
600 PA 94304 811-A1
HANSON AV
300 SJS 95117 853-D1
300 SCIC 95117 853-D1
HANSON CT
- MPS 95035 793-J5
HAPLAND CT
1300 SJS 95131 814-D7
HAPPY ACRES RD
100 LGTS 95032 873-E7
HAPPY HOLLOW LN
- SMCo 94025 810-E1
HAPPY VALLEY AV
1000 SJS 95129 852-J3
HARBOR CT
3400 SJS 95127 835-B2
HARBOR VIEW AV
1800 SJS 95122 835-A7
1800 SJS 95122 834-J7
HARDER ST
5700 SJS 95129 852-H3
HARDING AV
100 LGTS 95032 873-B7
700 SJS 95126 833-J6
3000 SCL 95051 833-A7

HARDING AV
12200 SCIC 95046 957-E1
12500 SCIC 95046 937-D5
HARDY AV
- CMBL 95008 853-D6
HARDY LN
15500 SCIC 95037 936-G5
HAREFIELD CT
1300 SJS 95131 834-C1
HAREFIELD DR
1200 SJS 95131 834-C1
HARGRAVE WY
18900 SAR 95070 852-H6
HARKER AV
1000 PA 94301 791-B4
HARKING DR
700 SUNV 94087 832-C5
HARKINS AV
2100 SMCo 94025 790-D7
2100 MLPK 94025 790-D7
HARKINS SLOUGH RD
- WAT 95076 (1015-D1 See Page 995)
- SCrC 95076 (1015-A1 See Page 995)
HARLAN CT
1000 SJS 95129 852-G2
HARLAN DR
1000 SJS 95129 852-G3
HARLEIGH CT
13700 SAR 95070 872-G1
HARLEIGH DR
13600 SAR 95070 872-G1
HARLISS AV
800 SJS 95110 854-B1
HARLOW WY
5400 SJS 95124 873-H6
HARMIL WY
1700 SJS 95125 854-B4
HARMON AV
900 SJS 95126 853-J1
HARMONY LN
400 SJS 95111 855-A7
HARMONY WY
4900 SJS 95130 852-J6
HARNEY WY
900 SUNV 94087 832-B5
HAROLD AV
- SCL 95117 833-C7
- SCL 95117 853-C1
100 SCL 95050 833-C7
HARPER AV
1000 SUNV 94087 832-B5
HARPER DR
13400 SAR 95070 852-G7
HARPSTER DR
800 MTVW 94040 811-H6
HARRIER CT
1400 SUNV 94087 832-F4
HARRIET AV
- SCIC 95127 835-A2
- SCIC 95127 834-J2
500 CMBL 95008 853-B7
700 CMBL 95008 873-A1
HARRIET ST
900 PA 94301 791-B4
HARRIETT CT
1300 CMBL 95008 873-A2
HARRINGTON AV
500 LALT 94024 831-F1
HARRINGTON CT
400 LALT 94024 831-F1
HARRIS AV
1800 SJS 95124 853-G7
HARRIS CT
2300 SJS 95124 853-H7
HARRIS WY
2300 SJS 95131 814-A4
HARRISON AV
- CMBL 95008 853-E5
HARRISON CT
1500 SUNV 94087 832-B5
HARRISON ST
600 SCL 95050 833-C4
700 SJS 95125 854-A2
HARRISON WY
- SMCo 94025 790-E6
200 SCrC 95076 (975-C7 See Page 955)
HARROW WY
600 SUNV 94087 832-E5
HARRY RD
600 SJS 95120 895-A2
600 SJS 95119 895-A2
20200 SJS 95120 894-J3
20300 SCIC 95120 894-J3
HARRY RD Rt#-G8
20400 SCIC 95120 894-J4
20400 SJS 95120 894-J4

HART AV
2300 SCL 95050 833-C5
HARTE DR
1700 SJS 95124 853-J7
HARTFORD AV
800 SJS 95125 854-A2
HARTLEY CT
1400 SJS 95130 853-B4
HARTMAN DR
22300 SCIC 94024 832-A6
22300 CPTO 95014 832-A6
HARTOG DR
1900 SJS 95131 813-J6
HARVARD AV
200 SCL 95051 832-J6
600 MLPK 94025 790-G5
600 SUNV 94087 832-C2
HARVARD CT
14500 LAH 94022 810-H5
HARVARD DR
5400 SJS 95118 874-A5
HARVARD PL
7100 GIL 95020 977-J4
HARVARD ST
2000 PA 94306 811-A1
HARVEST DR
1500 SJS 95127 835-C4
HARVEST LN
200 MGH 95037 937-B6
HARVEST ESTATES
5100 SJS 95135 855-G5
HARVEST MEADOW CT
1000 SJS 95136 874-C2
HARVEST OAK WY
6000 SJS 95120 874-D6
HARVESTWOOD CT
3000 SJS 95148 855-E1
HARVEY WY
19800 SCIC 95030 892-J7
HARWALT DR
1300 LALT 94024 832-A3
HARWELL CT
5700 SJS 95138 875-D4
HARWICK WY
100 SUNV 94087 832-E5
HARWOOD CT
100 LGTS 95032 873-H7
HARWOOD RD
4500 SJS 95124 873-H3
5200 SJS 95032 873-H5
15000 LGTS 95032 873-H7
HASSINGER RD
400 SJS 95111 875-C3
HASTINGS AV
3900 SJS 95118 874-A2
HASTINGS CT
1900 SCL 95051 833-A3
HASTINGS DR
900 MPS 95035 794-B3
HASTINGS PL
6400 GIL 95020 978-A5
HASTINGS PARK CT
3900 SJS 95136 874-F1
HATCHER CT
2200 CMBL 95008 873-E2
HATFIELD WALKWAY
4700 SJS 95124 873-E4
HATHAWAY CT
600 SJS 95136 874-F2
HATTON AV
- SCrC 95076 (975-C7 See Page 955)
HAUCK DR
1400 SJS 95118 874-B1
HAUGHTON DR
2800 SJS 95148 855-D1
HAUN CT
14900 SAR 95070 872-F4
HAVANA DR
1500 SJS 95122 834-H7
HAVEN CT
4100 SJS 95124 873-E3
HAVENHURST DR
1600 LALT 94024 832-A3
HAVENWOOD AV
1100 SUNV 94089 813-A5
1100 SUNV 94089 812-J5
HAVENWOOD DR
1300 SJS 95132 814-E5
HAVERHILL CT
100 SJS 95139 895-G1
HAVERHILL DR
700 SUNV 94087 832-C2
HAVRE CT
1000 SUNV 94087 832-B5
HAWES CT
1500 RDWC 94061 790-A1
HAWES ST
1200 RDWC 94061 790-A1

HAWK CT
1400 SUNV 94087 832-F4
HAWK VW
- PTLV 94028 830-D1
HAWKCREEK PL
6000 SJS 95123 874-E6
HAWKCREST CIR
3100 SJS 95135 876-A1
HAWKHURST PL
1200 SJS 95125 854-F5
HAWKINGTON CT
2500 SCL 95051 833-B2
HAWKINS DR
1700 LALT 94024 832-A3
HAWKINS LN
2500 SCIC 95037 936-D2
HAWKSTONE WY
5000 SJS 95138 855-E7
HAWLEY CT
5000 SJS 95118 874-A4
HAWTHORNE AV
- LALT 94022 811-E7
100 PA 94301 790-H4
400 LALT 94024 811-F7
400 SUNV 94086 832-F1
500 CMBL 95008 853-F5
W HAWTHORNE AV
- LALT 94022 811-D7
HAWTHORNE CT
500 LALT 94024 811-F7
HAWTHORNE DR
- ATN 94027 790-F1
HAWTHORNE ST
6000 GIL 95020 977-J6
HAWTHORNE WY
- SJS 95110 834-A5
HAY CT
1000 MPS 95035 814-D2
HAYDEN DR
3700 SJS 95117 853-C3
HAYES AV
- SJS 95193 875-A3
- SJS 95123 875-A3
200 SCL 95051 833-A7
HAYES LN
1900 SCIC 95046 937-A7
HAYFORD DR
1600 SJS 95130 853-B5
HAY LOFT CT
2700 MGH 95037 917-F6
HAY LOFT WY
2700 MGH 95037 917-F6
HAYMAN PL
900 LALT 94024 831-H2
HAYMEADOW DR
21000 SAR 95070 872-C3
HAYWARD DR
2500 SCL 95051 833-B5
HAYWORTH DR
1800 SJS 95148 835-C5
HAZEL AV
900 CMBL 95008 853-B7
HAZEL WY
18100 SCIC 95030 912-J4
HAZELAAR WY
1600 LALT 94024 831-H3
HAZELBROOK DR
21000 SCIC 95014 832-C7
HAZEL DELL RD
100 SCrC 95076 (975-G1 See Page 955)
800 SCrC 95076 955-E7
HAZELDELL WY
500 SJS 95129 853-A2
HAZELNUT CT
800 SUNV 94087 832-B2
HAZELTON AV
200 SUNV 94086 812-E6
HAZELTON CT
200 MGH 95037 916-H6
HAZELWOOD AV
900 CMBL 95008 853-B7
1000 SJS 95125 854-B5
3000 SCL 95051 833-A6
HAZELWOOD WY
- EPA 94303 791-B1
HAZEN ST
200 MPS 95035 794-A4
HAZLETT CT
1200 SJS 95131 834-C1
HAZLETT WY
1200 SJS 95131 834-C1
HEACOX RD
- SMCo 94028 830-C6
HEADQUARTERS DR
- SJS 95134 813-E2
HEALY WY
2400 SJS 95111 854-F4
2400 SCIC 95111 854-F4

HEARTH CT
1100 SJS 95120 894-C5
HEARTHSTONE DR
1400 SJS 95122 854-F1
HEARTHSTONE WY
800 SJS 95122 854-F1
HEARTLAND WY
6900 SJS 95135 876-A1
7100 SJS 95138 876-A1
HEARTWOOD WY
800 SJS 95133 834-F2
HEATH ST
- MPS 95035 793-H6
13000 SAR 95070 852-H7
HEATH CLIFF PL
400 SJS 95111 875-C1
HEATHCOT CT
3600 SJS 95121 855-C4
HEATHER CT
400 LALT 94022 811-D5
800 MPS 95035 794-B5
2300 MTVW 94043 811-G3
14300 SJS 95124 873-G5
HEATHER DR
- ATN 94027 790-F1
1900 SJS 95124 873-F5
HEATHER LN
1200 PA 94303 791-C4
HEATHER WY
900 GIL 95020 977-G2
HEATHERBRAY CT
400 SJS 95136 874-F2
HEATHERCREEK WY
6100 SJS 95123 874-H6
HEATHERDALE AV
1400 SJS 95050 833-F6
1400 SCL 95050 833-F6
1500 SJS 95126 833-F6
1500 SJS 95128 833-F6
HEATHERFIELD LN
1000 SJS 95132 814-F6
HEATHER HEIGHTS PL
- SCIC 95030 871-D1
HEATHER HEIGHTS RD
24600 SCIC 95030 871-D2
24600 SCIC 95030 851-D7
HEATHERKIRK CT
600 SJS 95123 874-H6
HEATHER RIDGE CT
3200 SJS 95136 854-F6
HEATHER RIDGE DR
3100 SJS 95136 854-F6
HEATHERSTONE WY
800 MTVW 94040 832-A1
900 SUNV 94087 832-B1
HEATHERTREE LN
500 SJS 95129 852-B7
HEATHERWOOD DR
7400 CPTO 95014 852-D2
HEATHERWOOD WY
17000 MGH 95037 917-E6
HEATHFIELD CT
6700 SJS 95120 894-G2
HEATHFIELD DR
6600 SJS 95120 894-F1
HEATON MOOR DR
6700 SJS 95119 895-D1
6700 SCIC 95119 895-D1
HEAVEN HILL RD
25500 SCIC 95030 934-A3
HEAVENLY BAMBOO CT
1700 SJS 95131 834-D1
HEAVENLY VALLEY CT
5300 SJS 95136 874-F7
HEBARD RD
20300 SCIC 95030 892-J7
HEBARD WY
20200 SCIC 95030 892-H7
HEBER WY
21700 SAR 95070 872-A2
HEBRIDES WY
600 SUNV 94087 832-F5
HEBRON AV
2400 SJS 95121 855-C3
HEBRON CT
3200 SJS 95121 855-C3
HECATE CT
2300 SJS 95124 873-D3
HECATE PL
2400 SJS 95124 873-D3
HECKER PASS HWY Rt#-152
- SCrC 95076 (996-A3 See Page 995)
300 GIL 95020 977-F2
1500 SCIC 95020 977-B2
4300 SCIC 95020 (976-F3 See Page 955)
5600 SCrC 95076 (976-B6 See Page 955)

HECKMAN WY
1300 SJS 95129 852-G4
HEDDA CT
3200 SJS 95127 814-H6
HEDDING ST
100 SJS 95110 833-F7
2200 SJS 95128 833-F7
E HEDDING ST
- SJS 95112 834-A3
2300 SJS 95133 834-A3
W HEDDING ST
- SJS 95110 834-A4
200 SJS 95110 833-J4
700 SJS 95126 833-G6
1700 SJS 95128 833-E7
2400 SCL 95128 833-E7
HEDEGARD AV
200 CMBL 95008 853-D5
HEDERA CT
1000 SUNV 94086 832-H2
HEDGECROFT PL
1000 SJS 95120 894-F2
HEDGEROW CT
300 MTVW 94041 812-A6
HEDGESTONE CT
- MPS 95035 794-C2
HEDLUND CT
900 SJS 95123 874-E5
HEFLIN ST
700 MPS 95035 794-B5
HEIDI CT
300 MGH 95037 916-J7
2900 SJS 95132 814-F5
HEIDI DR
300 MGH 95037 916-H7
2900 SJS 95132 814-F5
HEIMGARTNER LN
1900 SJS 95124 873-F4
HEIRLOOM CT
600 SJS 95127 835-B2
HEITMAN CT
3100 SJS 95132 814-G5
HEITZ CT
7200 SJS 95120 894-H4
HELEN AV
900 SUNV 94086 832-H4
1000 SCL 95051 832-H4
1000 SCL 94086 832-H4
HELEN CT
1900 LALT 94024 831-J5
HELEN PL
- MLPK 94025 790-F5
HELEN ST
700 SJS 95125 854-A1
HELEN WY
17900 SCIC 95030 912-J3
HELENA DR
700 SUNV 94087 832-B5
HELENA WY
2000 SMCo 94061 790-A4
HELENE CT
16900 MGH 95037 917-G5
HELENE LN
16900 MGH 95037 917-G5
HELLER WY
100 SJS 95116 834-G4
HELLYER AV
500 SJS 95111 855-A6
700 SCIC 95111 855-A6
4700 SJS 95138 855-A6
4800 SCIC 95138 855-A6
4800 SJS 95138 875-D1
HELMOND LN
1400 SJS 95118 874-B5
HELMSDALE CT
7500 SJS 95135 855-J6
HELMSDALE DR
7600 SJS 95135 856-A6
HELMSLEY DR
2600 SJS 95132 814-F6
HEMATITE CT
- SJS 95135 856-A7
- SJS 95135 876-A1
HEMLOCK AV
300 RDWC 94061 790-B1
2800 SJS 95128 853-E1
E HEMLOCK AV
100 SUNV 94086 812-F4
W HEMLOCK AV
100 SUNV 94086 812-F4
HEMLOCK CT
- MPS 95035 794-D6
100 PA 94306 811-E2
400 SCL 95054 813-F5
HEMLOCK LN
- MPS 95035 794-D6
HEMMINGWAY CT
- SJS 95132 814-G3
HEMMINGWAY RD
- SJS 95132 814-G3

HEMPSTEAD PL
1700 RDWC 94061 790-A3
HENARD WY
100 LGTS 95032 873-B7
HENDERSON AV
700 SUNV 94086 832-H4
1000 MLPK 94025 790-J1
1300 SUNV 94087 832-H4
HENDERSON DR
300 SJS 95123 875-A6
HENDON CT
500 SUNV 94087 832-E5
HENDRIX CT
4400 SJS 95124 873-J3
HENDRIX WY
4200 SJS 95124 873-J3
HENDRY DR
17300 SCIC 95037 917-E5
E HENDY AV
100 SUNV 94086 812-E7
W HENDY AV
100 SUNV 94086 812-E7
HENESSY DR
2700 SJS 95148 835-E7
HENEY CREEK PL
10300 CPTO 95014 831-J6
HENNESSEY WY
100 GIL 95020 957-H7
HENNING CT
100 LGTS 95030 873-C3
HENRIETTA AV
700 SUNV 94086 832-F2
HENRIETTA CT
- HOLL - (1020-B6 See Page 999)
N HENRY AV
100 SCL 95117 833-D7
100 SCL 95117 853-D1
300 SJS 95117 833-D7
S HENRY AV
300 SJS 95117 853-D2
300 SCIC 95117 853-D1
HENRY CT
- EPA 94303 791-B2
HENRY FORD II DR
200 SJS 95134 813-G4
HENSLEY ST
- SJS 95112 834-B5
HENWOOD RD
20500 SJS 95120 894-J2
20500 SCIC 95120 894-J2
HENZI LN
1600 SCIC 95020 958-A2
HEPPLEWHITE CT
100 LGTS 95030 872-J3
HEPPNER LN
3700 SJS 95136 874-E1
HERALD AV
1200 SJS 95116 834-F6
HERBERT DR
5200 SJS 95124 873-G5
5300 LGTS 95032 873-G5
HERBERT LN
- CMBL 95008 853-G6
HERCHELL DR
10800 SCIC 95127 835-A1
HERCUS CT
6500 SJS 95119 875-C7
HEREDIA CT
300 SJS 95116 834-F3
HERITAGE CT
- ATN 94027 790-E1
1100 LALT 94024 831-H3
2300 SJS 95124 853-H7
18500 MGH 95037 916-H5
HERITAGE DR
2200 SJS 95124 853-H6
HERITAGE WY
- GIL 95020 977-E2
12100 SCIC 95020 956-H4
HERITAGE ESTS CT
3100 SJS 95148 855-E2
HERITAGE ESTS DR
3200 SJS 95148 855-E2
HERITAGE MANOR DR
2400 SCIC 95020 958-B1
HERITAGE MANOR PL
11400 SCIC 95020 958-B1
HERITAGE OAKS CT
3200 SJS 95148 855-F2
HERITAGE OAKS DR
3400 SJS 95148 855-E2
HERITAGE PARK CIR
2600 SJS 95132 814-E5
HERITAGE POINT CT
3200 SJS 95148 855-F2
HERITAGE SPRGS CT
3100 SJS 95148 855-E2
HERITAGE VALLEY CT
3400 SJS 95148 855-F2

HERITAGE VALLEY DR
3100 SJS 95148 855-E2
HERITAGE VLG WY
- CMBL 95008 853-E5
HERLONG AV
100 SJS 95123 875-A5
HERMA ST
5600 SJS 95123 874-J5
5800 SJS 95123 875-A5
HERMES CT
600 SJS 95111 854-G3
HERMINA ST
1000 MPS 95035 793-J5
HERMISTON DR
700 SJS 95136 874-D1
HERMITAGE AV
500 SJS 95134 813-E2
HERMITAGE CT
500 SJS 95134 813-F2
HERMITAGE DR
500 SJS 95134 813-F2
HERMITAGE LN
600 SJS 95134 813-E2
HERMITAGE PL
500 SJS 95134 813-E2
HERMITAGE ST
500 SJS 95134 813-E2
HERMITAGE WY
600 SJS 95134 813-F2
HERMOSA
- MTVW 94043 812-A2
HERMOSA AV
21800 CPTO 95014 852-B1
HERMOSA CT
900 SUNV 94086 812-D6
2200 MGH 95037 917-E6
HERMOSA DR
800 SUNV 94086 812-D6
HERMOSA PL
- MLPK 94025 790-F5
HERMOSA WY
300 MLPK 94025 790-E4
1200 SJS 95125 854-B5
HERNANDEZ AV
- LGTS 95030 872-H7
400 MSER 95030 872-H7
HERNANDEZ LN
18400 MSER 95030 872-H7
HERON DR
1500 SUNV 94087 832-F6
HERRICK AV
300 SJS 95123 874-J4
HERRIMAN AV
19900 SAR 95070 872-E1
HERRING AV
15100 SCIC 95124 873-F3
HERSHNER CT
200 LGTS 95032 873-F5
HERSHNER DR
300 SJS 95124 873-G5
300 LGTS 95032 873-G5
HERSHNER WY
400 LGTS 95032 873-G5
HERSMAN AV
1300 SCIC 95046 937-J4
HERSMAN DR
1100 GIL 95020 977-G3
HERTEL LN
1600 SCIC 95046 937-J6
HERVEY LN
1400 SJS 95125 854-B3
HESKET CT
6400 SJS 95123 875-B7
HESKETH CT
- MLPK 94025 790-E5
HESKETH DR
- MLPK 94025 790-E5
HESS RD
1400 RDWC 94061 790-B1
HESSELBEIN WY
2600 SJS 95148 855-C1
HESTER AV
1100 SJS 95126 833-H7
1600 SJS 95128 833-H7
1700 SJS 95128 853-G1
HESTIN CT
- SJS 95123 874-F7
HIAWATHA CT
1000 SUNV 94087 832-B2
4300 SJS 95111 855-A7
HIAWATHA DR
700 SJS 95111 855-A7
HIBERNIA WY
700 SUNV 94087 832-F5
HIBISCUS CT
400 EPA 94303 791-D2
22000 CPTO 95014 832-A6
HIBISCUS DR
22000 CPTO 95014 832-A6

STREET
Block City ZIP Pg-Grid

HIBISCUS LN
700 SJS 95117 853-B3
HICHBORN DR
- SCL 95054 813-B6
HICKERSON CT
3500 SJS 95127 835-B3
HICKERSON DR
3200 SJS 95127 835-B3
HICKORY CT
500 SCL 95051 833-A6
HICKORY PL
400 SCL 95051 833-A6
HICKORY WY
700 SJS 95129 853-A2
HICKORY HILL WY
20200 SAR 95070 852-E7
HICKORYNUT CT
1000 SUNV 94087 832-B2
HICKS AV
1400 SJS 95125 853-J4
1700 SJS 95125 854-A5
HICKS RD
16700 LGTS 95032 873-J7
16700 LGTS 95032 893-J2
17300 SCIC 95032 893-H2
18400 SCIC 95032 894-B3
19400 SCIC 95120 894-B3
19600 SCIC 95030 894-B3
22700 SCIC 95030 914-E1
22700 SCIC 95120 914-E1
HIDALGO CT
700 MGH 95037 936-H1
2900 SJS 95125 873-J1
HIDDEN DR
15800 SCIC 95030 872-F5
HIDDEN CREEK CT
6400 SJS 95120 894-E1
HIDDEN CREEK DR
6400 SJS 95120 894-E1
HIDDEN HILL PL
15700 SCIC 95030 872-G5
HIDDEN HILL RD
15700 SCIC 95030 872-G5
HIDDENLAKE DR
300 SUNV 94089 812-G4
HIDDEN MEADOW CT
6200 SJS 95135 855-H7
HIDDEN MINE RD
1300 SJS 95120 894-C2
HIDDEN OAKS DR
1100 MLPK 94025 790-E5
HIDDEN SPRING LN
14100 SCIC 95037 936-G7
HIDDEN SPRINGS CT
- LAH 94022 831-B2
HIDDEN VALLEY LN
- PTLV 94028 810-A5
- WDSD 94062 810-A5
4000 SCIC 95127 835-A1
HIERRA CT
11500 SCIC 94024 831-G4
HIGATE DR
1500 SJS 95122 834-J5
HIGDON AV
100 MTVW 94041 811-G4
HIGGINS AV
- LALT 94022 811-F6
1600 SCL 95051 833-B3
HIGGINS PL
3000 PA 94303 791-E5
HIGH RD
- WDSD 94062 790-A5
HIGH ST
200 PA 94301 790-H4
2100 PA 94301 791-B7
17300 LGTS 95032 893-B2
HIGH GLEN DR
600 SJS 95133 814-G7
HIGHGROVE CT
14300 SCIC 95127 835-A3
HIGHLAND AV
- LGTS 95032 893-B2
- SCIC 95046 957-E1
1000 SCL 95050 833-F5
HIGHLAND CT
1000 SCL 95050 833-F5
1300 MPS 95035 814-E2
HIGHLAND DR
15700 SCIC 95127 815-A6
HIGHLAND TER
200 LGTS 95032 893-B2
HIGHLAND WY
24300 SCIC 95030 913-B4
24800 SCrC 95030 934-A3
HIGHLAND ESTATES LN
12300 SCIC 95046 957-F1
HIGHLAND OAKS DR
100 LGTS 95032 873-C4
HIGHLAND OAKS WY
100 LGTS 95032 873-C4
HIGHLAND PARK LN
2200 SJS 95008 853-E7
HIGHLANDS CIR
800 LALT 94024 831-G5
HIGHLAND VIEW CT
1400 LALT 94024 831-H4
HIGH MEADOW CT
6200 SJS 95135 855-J7
HIGH MEADOW LN
3000 SJS 95135 855-H7
HIGH SCHOOL CT
- LGTS 95032 893-A1
HIGH SCHOOL WY
800 MTVW 94041 811-H5
HIGHWAY Rt#-9
- SCrC 95030 871-C2
HIGHWAY Rt#-17
- SCIC 95030 892-J2
- SCIC 95030 912-J1
- SCIC 95032 892-J2
- SCrC 95030 913-A6
- SCrC 95030 912-J4
HIGHWAY Rt#-156
- SCIC 95020 (1000-C2 See Page 999)
HIGHWOOD DR
2600 SJS 95116 834-J4
13500 SCIC 95127 834-J3
13800 SCIC 95127 835-A3
HIGUERA PL
1300 MPS 95035 794-A4
HIGUERA RD
3800 SCIC 95148 835-F5
HIGUERA HIGHLAND LN
3900 SCIC 95148 835-G5
HIKIDO DR
1900 SJS 95131 814-D7
HILARY AV
- MTVW 94040 811-F3
HILARY DR
3000 SJS 95124 873-G2
HILBAR LN
500 PA 94303 791-C4
HILFORD CT
1100 SJS 95132 814-G5
HILL AV
1500 SJS 95125 854-B4
20100 SAR 95070 872-E4
HILL LN
18300 SJS 95120 874-G7
18300 SCIC 95120 874-G7
18400 SCIC 95120 894-G1
18400 SJS 95120 894-G1
HILL RD
15500 SCIC 95037 917-D5
15600 MGH 95037 917-E6
16500 SCIC 95037 937-F1
HILL WY
13500 LAH 94022 811-D7
HILLARY LN
- SMCo 94061 790-B4
HILLBRIGHT CIR
5700 SJS 95123 874-J5
HILLBRIGHT CT
5700 SJS 95123 874-J5
HILLBRIGHT PL
500 SJS 95123 874-J5
HILLBROOK DR
- PTLV 94028 810-D6
100 LGTS 95032 873-D6
HILLCAP AV
200 SJS 95136 854-G7
200 SCIC 95136 854-G7
HILLCREST CT
1300 SJS 95120 894-D3
HILLCREST DR
1200 SJS 95120 894-D3
HILLCREST RD
10000 CPTO 95014 832-A7
HILLMONT AV
1500 SJS 95127 835-A5
1800 SJS 95148 835-A5
HILLMOOR DR
20700 SAR 95070 852-D6
HILL PARK DR
2500 SJS 95124 853-H7
2500 SJS 95124 873-H1
HILLPARK LN
11500 SCIC 94024 831-E4
HILLROSE DR
5900 SJS 95123 874-E5
HILLSBORO AV
900 SUNV 94087 832-C2
HILLSBOROUGH WY
3400 SJS 95121 855-D3
HILLSDALE AV
- SJS 95136 854-D7
HILLSDALE AV
- SCIC 95125 854-D7
200 SCL 95051 832-H7
500 SCIC 95136 854-F7
1000 SJS 95118 854-D7
1000 SJS 95118 874-A1
1600 SJS 95120 873-H2
1600 SJS 95124 873-H2
HILLSDALE CT
3700 SCL 95051 832-H6
HILL SIDE
20500 SCIC 95030 912-J1
HILLSIDE AV
- LGTS 95032 893-B1
100 SMCo 94025 790-C6
HILLSIDE CT
100 WDSD 94062 790-A5
3300 SJS 95132 814-G4
HILLSLOPE PL
1100 SCIC 94024 831-F2
HILLSTONE DR
2100 SJS 95138 855-E5
HILL TOP CT
16800 MGH 95037 917-G5
HILLTOP CT
1500 MPS 95035 794-C3
HILLTOP DR
100 LGTS 95032 873-E7
100 LGTS 95032 893-E1
11800 LAH 94024 831-E3
HILLTOP WY
14200 SAR 95070 872-H2
HILLVALE AV
16100 MSER 95030 872-H6
HILLVIEW AV
- LALT 94022 811-E7
3200 PA 94304 811-A3
5800 SJS 95123 874-E5
HILLVIEW CT
800 MPS 95035 794-B6
24200 LAH 94024 831-E3
E HILLVIEW CT
1500 GIL 95020 977-F2
W HILLVIEW CT
1600 GIL 95020 977-F2
HILLVIEW DR
1100 MLPK 94025 790-E5
1500 LAH 94024 831-E2
1500 SCIC 94024 831-F3
18400 MSER 95030 872-H5
18400 SCIC 95030 872-H5
N HILLVIEW DR
100 MPS 95035 794-B4
S HILLVIEW DR
100 MPS 95035 794-B7
300 MPS 95035 814-B1
HILLVIEW LN
17500 SCIC 95037 917-D4
HILLVIEW PL
- MLPK 94025 790-E5
- SJS 95123 874-E5
HILLWOOD CT
300 MTVW 94040 811-F4
HILLWOOD DR
800 SJS 95129 852-J2
HILLWOOD LN
17900 MGH 95037 916-H6
HILMAR ST
500 SCL 95050 833-F5
HILO CT
2300 MTVW 94040 831-J1
HILOW CT
100 LGTS 95032 873-D6
HILOW RD
16300 SCIC 95032 873-C7
16400 LGTS 95032 873-C7
HILTIBRAND DR
1600 SJS 95131 834-C1
HILTON AV
4300 SJS 95130 853-A5
HILTON CT
1500 SJS 95130 853-A5
HIMMEL AV
1100 SMCo 94061 790-B3
HINDIYEH LN
200 SCIC 95046 937-F7
HINES CT
300 SJS 95111 875-A1
HIRABAYASHI DR
6400 SJS 95120 894-C1
HIRASAKI AV
8600 GIL 95020 977-G1
HIRASAKI CT
8600 GIL 95020 977-G1
HOBART AV
1700 SJS 95127 834-J2
1700 SCIC 95127 834-J2
3900 SCIC 95127 835-A2
HOBART CT
600 FRMT 94539 793-J1
HOBART ST
500 MLPK 94025 790-E5
HOBART TER
500 SCL 95051 833-A6
HOBIE LN
500 SJS 95127 835-B2
HOBSON ST
- SJS 95110 834-A5
400 SJS 95110 833-J5
HOCKING WY
2700 SJS 95124 873-F1
HODGES AV
400 SCIC 95128 853-F1
HOEFLER DR
23200 SCIC 95030 913-C6
HOESCH WY
900 GIL 95020 977-G1
HOFFMAN AV
1200 CMBL 95008 873-E1
HOFFMAN CT
5600 SJS 95118 874-C4
HOFFMAN TER
800 SCIC 94024 831-G4
HOGAN DR
1700 SCL 95054 813-C4
HOGAN WY
9400 GIL 95020 957-F7
HOGAR DR
1700 SJS 95124 873-J1
HOGARTH TER
400 SUNV 94087 832-E3
HOGUE CT
1100 SCIC 95046 937-H7
20100 CPTO 95014 832-E7
HOITING DR
3400 SJS 95148 835-E6
HOKETT WY
6200 SJS 95123 874-G7
HOLBROOK LN
- ATN 94027 790-E1
HOLBROOK PL
700 SUNV 94087 832-C2
HOLDEN CT
- PTLV 94028 810-D6
14200 SCIC 95124 873-H4
HOLDEN WY
14800 SCIC 95124 873-H4
HOLDERMAN DR
3300 SJS 95148 835-D6
3400 SCIC 95148 835-D6
HOLGATE AV
5900 SJS 95123 875-A6
HOLGER WY
- SJS 95134 813-D2
HOLIDAY CT
2800 MGH 95037 917-E3
13400 SAR 95070 852-H7
HOLIDAY DR
13400 SAR 95070 872-G1
17000 MGH 95037 917-E3
17000 SCIC 95037 917-G4
HOLIN WY
1700 SJS 95131 834-D1
HOLLAND CT
100 MTVW 94040 831-J1
1300 SJS 95118 874-B5
HOLLAND LN
5600 SJS 95118 874-B5
HOLLAND ST
100 EPA 94303 791-A1
HOLLANDERRY PL
7500 CPTO 95014 852-D3
HOLLENBECK AV
600 SUNV 94087 832-D2
HOLLERAN CT
1500 SJS 95132 814-F3
HOLLIDALE CT
1400 LALT 94024 831-J4
HOLLINGSWORTH DR
500 MTVW 94022 811-F5
600 LALT 94022 811-F5
HOLLIS AV
100 CMBL 95008 853-D7
HOLLISTER RD Rt#-25
- HOLL - (1019-H6 See Page 999)
- SBnC - 999-C7
1800 SCIC 95020 (998-E3 See Page 997)
HOLLOWAY RD
900 GIL 95020 978-C4
HOLLOWCREEK CT
1600 SJS 95121 855-D7
HOLLOWCREEK PL
1600 SJS 95121 855-D7
HOLLOWGATE LN
4400 SJS 95124 873-J3
HOLLOW LAKE WY
7000 SJS 95120 894-F4
HOLLOW PARK CT
1100 SJS 95120 894-F3
HOLLOW TREE WY
7000 SJS 95120 894-F4
HOLLY AV
1300 LALT 94024 831-H3
1700 MLPK 94025 790-E6
HOLLY CT
1400 GIL 95020 977-F3
HOLLY DR
3300 SCIC 95127 814-J6
3300 SJS 95127 814-J6
HOLLY LN
600 SJS 95136 854-E7
HOLLY WY
400 MPS 95035 794-D7
HOLLY ANN PL
1100 SJS 95120 894-E2
HOLLY BERRY CT
400 SJS 95129 853-B2
HOLLY BRANCH CT
2000 SCL 95050 833-C3
HOLLYBURNE AV
1000 MLPK 94025 790-J1
HOLLYCREST DR
100 LGTS 95032 873-D5
HOLLY GILLINGHAM LN
6300 SJS 95119 875-D5
HOLLYHEAD LN
1100 CPTO 95014 852-D3
HOLLY HILL DR
1000 SJS 95122 854-G1
1400 SJS 95122 834-H7
HOLLY HILL WY
100 LGTS 95030 873-C4
HOLLY HOCK CT
400 SJS 95117 853-C1
HOLLYHOCK LN
1800 GIL 95020 977-E1
HOLLY LEAF LN
5600 SJS 95118 874-B5
HOLLY OAK CIR
1100 SJS 95120 874-D7
HOLLY OAK DR
700 PA 94303 791-D7
HOLLYOAK DR
21400 CPTO 95014 852-C2
HOLLYWOOD AV
- LGTS 95032 873-B7
- SJS 95112 854-D2
17000 LGTS 95032 893-B1
HOLM RD
- WAT 95019 995-C7
- SCrC 95019 995-C7
- WAT 95076 995-C7
HOLMES AV
1000 SCIC 95008 873-D3
HOLMES DR
- SCIC 95127 815-A7
HOLMES LN
- SCIC 95127 815-A7
HOLOHAN RD
- SCrC 95076 995-F5
300 SCrC 95019 995-F5
HOLSCLAW RD
6600 GIL 95020 978-D2
6600 SCIC 95020 978-D1
7900 SCIC 95020 958-C7
HOLSCLAW ST
1800 SCIC 95020 958-D7
HOLSTON RIVER CT
4700 SJS 95136 874-E2
HOLT AV
1300 LALT 94024 831-J4
1500 LALT 94024 832-A4
HOLY CITY RD
19200 SCIC 95030 913-A2
HOLYCON CIR
4600 SJS 95136 874-H2
HOLYOKE CT
12600 SAR 95070 852-F6
W HOME ST
800 SJS 95126 854-A1
800 SJS 95126 853-J1
HOME CREST DR
1800 SJS 95148 835-A6
HOME GATE DR
1700 SJS 95148 835-A6
HOMEPARK CT
3900 SJS 95121 855-D5
HOMER AV
- PA 94301 790-J5
400 PA 94301 791-A4
HOMER LN
- SMCo 94025 810-F1
HOMERITE DR
14500 SJS 95124 873-G3
14500 SCIC 95124 873-G3
HOMES DR
12700 SAR 95070 852-G6
HOMESTEAD CT
11000 CPTO 94024 832-A6
11000 LALT 94024 832-A6
HOMESTEAD RD
- SJS 95193 875-C5
600 SCL 95050 833-F4
600 SCL 95053 833-F4
1100 SUNV 94087 832-A5
2200 LALT 94024 832-A5
2300 CPTO 94024 832-A5
22000 CPTO 95014 832-A5
E HOMESTEAD RD
100 SCL 95051 832-G6
100 SUNV 94087 832-G6
900 SCL 95050 833-D5
2500 SCL 95051 833-A6
18800 CPTO 95014 832-G6
W HOMESTEAD RD
1100 CPTO 95014 832-C5
19500 SUNV 94087 832-C5
19900 SUNV 95014 832-C5
HOMEWOOD DR
2200 SJS 95128 833-E7
E HOMEWOOD PL
- MLPK 94025 790-H3
HOMME WY
- MPS 95035 793-J4
HONEY CT
- GIL 95020 977-J1
HONEYBEE CT
8100 SCIC 95020 977-A2
HONEYCOMB LN
8100 SCIC 95020 977-A2
HONEYDALE CT
4000 SJS 95121 855-A5
HONEYSUCKLE DR
1600 SJS 95122 854-J1
HONEY SUCKLE LN
3900 SJS 95136 854-D7
HONEYSUCKLE PL
1500 LALT 94024 831-J6
HONEYWOOD CT
700 SJS 95120 894-J3
HONFLEUR CT
900 SUNV 94087 832-B6
HONFLEUR DR
1600 SUNV 94087 832-B5
HONG KONG DR
1200 SJS 95131 814-B7
HONOLULU CT
3900 SJS 95111 854-J6
HONOLULU DR
3700 SJS 95111 854-J6
HOOD CT
1600 SCL 95051 833-A3
HOO HOO CT
22300 CPTO 95014 852-A1
HOOKE LN
100 LGTS 95030 873-B3
HOOPER LN
11100 LAH 94024 831-D4
HOOSHANG CT
800 CPTO 95014 852-C2
HOOT OWL WY
17400 SCIC 95037 917-F3
17500 MGH 95037 917-F3
HOOVER AV
500 SJS 95126 833-J6
HOOVER CT
500 GIL 95020 978-A3
2100 SCL 95051 833-C2
HOOVER DR
2000 SCL 95051 833-B3
HOOVER ST
1200 MLPK 94025 790-F3
HOPE DR
1400 SCL 95054 813-D4
HOPE ST
100 MTVW 94041 811-H5
1200 SJS 95002 793-B7
3000 SCIC 95111 854-G6
3000 SJS 95111 854-G6
HOPE TER
500 SUNV 94087 832-D5
HOPETON AV
2300 SJS 95122 854-H2
HOPETON CT
1200 SJS 95122 854-H2
HOPI CIR
6200 SJS 95123 874-H7
HOPI CT
6200 SJS 95123 874-H7
HOPKINS AV
1100 PA 94301 791-B5
HOPKINS DR
1100 SJS 95122 834-H6
HOPPE ST
1000 SJS 95002 813-B1
HORACE AV
2500 SJS 95124 853-G7
HORCAJO CIR
900 MPS 95035 794-B4
HORCAJO ST
800 MPS 95035 794-B5
HORGAN AV
- RDWC 94061 790-B2
HORIZON AV
100 MTVW 94043 811-J5
HORIZON CIR
200 SJS 95002 813-B1
HORNBEAM WY
500 SJS 95111 854-J6
HORNBLOWER CT
500 SJS 95136 874-F2
HORNING ST
400 SJS 95112 834-B3
HORNLEIN CT
- GIL 95020 978-A3
HORSESHOE BEND
- PTLV 94028 830-C1
HORSESHOE CT
1700 SCIC 95046 937-G3
2800 LAH 94022 811-A5
14500 SAR 95070 872-E3
HORSESHOE DR
3800 SCL 95134 813-E5
14500 SAR 95070 872-E3
HORSESHOE LN
27000 LAH 94022 811-A5
HORTON CT
6000 SJS 95123 875-A6
HORWEDEL DR
2800 SJS 95148 855-D2
HOSKINS CT
- SCIC 94305 790-J7
HOSPITAL DR
2500 MTVW 94040 831-H1
HOSPITAL PKWY
200 SJS 95119 875-B6
HOSPITAL PZ
- MLPK 94025 790-J2
HOSTA LN
5900 SJS 95124 873-J7
HOSTETTER RD
1600 SJS 95131 814-C6
2300 SJS 95132 814-G3
HOUGHTON CT
1000 SJS 95112 834-D3
HOUGHTON ST
200 MTVW 94041 811-J5
HOULTON CT
100 SJS 95139 875-G7
HOUNDSBROOK WY
4100 SJS 95111 855-A7
HOUNDS ESTATES
5200 SJS 95135 855-G5
HOUNDS ESTATES CT
3000 SJS 95135 855-G5
HOUNDSHAVEN WY
4400 SJS 95111 874-J1
4700 SJS 95111 875-A1
HOUNSLOW DR
2100 SJS 95131 814-D6
HOURET CT
1700 MPS 95035 814-B4
HOURET DR
200 MPS 95035 814-B3
HOUSTON CT
13000 SAR 95070 852-D7
HOWARD AV
900 GIL 95020 977-G1
HOWARD CT
8500 GIL 95020 977-G1
HOWARD DR
200 SCL 95051 832-H7
HOWARD ST
400 SJS 95110 834-A6
HOWARD WY
- ATN 94027 790-E3
HOWDEN CT
6900 SJS 95119 875-F6
HOWELL AV
2900 SCL 95051 833-A6
HOWELL LN
- SCrC 95076 (975-A4 See Page 955)
2400 SCIC 95020 958-C1
HOWEN DR
13500 SAR 95070 872-E1
HOWES CT
200 LGTS 95032 873-F5
HOWES DR
100 LGTS 95032 873-G5
HOWES LN
4900 SJS 95118 873-J4
5100 SJS 95118 874-A4
HOWSON ST
- GIL 95020 977-J2
HOXETT ST
800 GIL 95020 977-H4
HOYET DR
5200 SJS 95129 852-J4
HUBBARD AV
500 SCL 95051 832-H6
HUBBARD WY
10700 SCIC 95127 835-B1
HUBBARTT DR
4100 PA 94306 811-C3
HUBBELL WY
500 LGTS 95030 873-A6
HUCKLEBERRY CT
1000 SUNV 94087 832-B3
HUDDERSFIELD CT
1500 SJS 95126 853-H3
HUDNER LN
400 SBnC - (1019-E4 See Page 999)
HUDSON DR
600 SCL 95051 832-H6
1700 SJS 95124 853-H7
HUDSON PL
700 GIL 95020 977-J4
HUDSON ST
1200 RDWC 94061 790-B1
HUDSON WY
1000 SUNV 94087 832-B2
HUERTO CT
2500 SJS 95128 853-F4
HUERTO DR
2400 SJS 95128 853-F4
HUFF AV
900 MTVW 94043 811-H1
2800 SJS 95128 853-E2
HUGO LN
1400 SJS 95118 874-B2
HULA DR
3500 SJS 95136 854-F7
HULET ST
500 SJS 95125 854-A1
HULL AV
300 SJS 95125 854-A2
1700 SMCo 94061 790-A3
HULME CT
- SCIC 94305 790-J7
HUMBER CT
500 SUNV 94087 832-E5
HUMBERSIDE CT
3100 SJS 95148 855-E2
HUMBOLDT AV
2800 SCL 95051 833-A4
HUMBOLDT CT
200 SUNV 94089 812-F3
HUMBOLDT ST
- SJS 95110 854-C2
- SJS 95112 854-D1
E HUMBOLDT ST
- SJS 95112 854-D1
HUME DR
15100 SAR 95070 872-F4
HUMEWICK WY
800 SUNV 94087 832-F5
HUMMEL CT
2400 SJS 95148 855-B1
HUMMINGBIRD DR
800 SJS 95125 854-C6
HUMMINGBIRD LN
1600 SUNV 94087 832-F5
HUNKEN DR
2900 SJS 95111 854-H5
HUNT WY
- CMBL 95008 853-C6
HUNTER PL
- SCL 95054 813-C5
HUNTER WY
18800 CPTO 95014 852-H2
HUNTERS HILL RD
20400 SCIC 95120 895-A5
HUNTERSTON PL
1000 CPTO 95014 852-C3
HUNTINGDON AV
1000 SJS 95129 852-H3
HUNTINGDON DR
1000 SJS 95129 852-H4
HUNTING HOLLOW RD
10300 SCIC 95020 959-D1
HUNTINGTON LN
2000 LALT 94024 831-H4
HUNTRIDGE LN
7700 CPTO 95014 852-C2
HUNTSFIELD CT
7000 SJS 95120 894-G4
HUNTSWOOD CT
700 SJS 95120 894-J3
HURAN CT
2500 SJS 95122 855-A1
HURAN DR
2000 SJS 95122 834-J7
2100 SJS 95122 854-J1
HURAN DR
2300 SJS 95122 855-A1
HURLINGHAM WY
1400 SJS 95127 835-A4
HURLSTONE LN
900 SJS 95120 894-G2
HURST AV
1600 SCIC 95125 853-H6
2000 SJS 95125 853-H6
2000 CMBL 95125 853-H6
HURSTGLEN WY
3800 SJS 95121 855-C4
HURSTWOOD CT
1700 SJS 95121 855-C4
HUSTED AV
1100 SJS 95125 854-A7
1600 SJS 95124 873-J1
1600 SJS 95125 853-J7
1600 SJS 95125 873-J1
HUSTON CT
2400 MGH 95037 917-F6
HUTCHINSON AV
900 PA 94301 791-B4
HUTCHINSON RD
- SCrC 95018 912-H6
- SCrC 95030 912-H6
HUTTON CT
100 SUNV 94087 832-E5
6100 SJS 95123 875-A6
HUXLEY CT
1800 SJS 95125 853-G4
HYACINTH LN
1600 SJS 95124 873-J7
HYANNIS DR
500 SUNV 94087 832-D2
HYANNISPORT DR
8000 CPTO 95014 852-B2
HYDE AV
800 CPTO 95014 852-G2
1000 SJS 95129 852-G3
HYDE CT
1600 CMBL 95030 872-J2
HYDE DR
1500 CMBL 95030 872-J2
HYDE PARK DR
400 SJS 95136 874-F3
600 SUNV 94087 832-D2
6300 GIL 95020 978-A5
HYDRANGEA CT
800 SUNV 94086 832-F2
HYDRANGEA LN
1600 SJS 95124 873-J6
HYLAND AV
4300 SCIC 95127 834-J2
4600 SJS 95127 834-J2
4800 SCIC 95127 835-A1

I

I RD
- SUNV 94089 812-H3
IBERIS CT
1000 SUNV 94086 832-H2
ICEFIELD CT
2600 SCL 95051 833-A1
IDA DR
17900 SCIC 95030 913-A3
IDA WY
2000 SJS 95124 873-E2
IDAHO CT
900 MPS 95035 794-A5
2000 RDWC 94061 790-A3
IDAHO ST
1100 SJS 95126 833-G5
1300 SCL 95050 833-G5
IDALYN DR
18000 SCIC 95030 912-J2
IDLEBROOK CT
6500 SJS 95120 894-C1
IDLEWILD CT
6500 SJS 95120 894-C1
IDLEWOOD CT
900 SJS 95121 854-H3
IDLEWOOD DR
900 SJS 95121 854-H3
IDLEWOOD LN
12700 SAR 95070 852-E6
IDYLLWILD AV
1800 SMCo 94061 790-B4
IDYLLWILD CT
300 SMCo 94061 790-B4
IDYLWILD DR
18100 SCIC 95030 892-J7
18200 SCIC 95030 912-J1
IDYLWILD RD
20400 SCIC 95030 912-J1
20600 SCIC 95030 913-A1
IGNEOUS CT
2300 SJS 95133 814-H3
ILIKAI AV
1400 SJS 95118 874-A3
ILIMA CT
800 PA 94306 811-B2
ILIMA WY
900 PA 94306 811-B3
ILLIAD CT
1100 SJS 95118 874-G3
ILLINOIS AV
400 SJS 95126 854-A1
500 SJS 95125 854-A1
ILLINOIS ST
2400 EPA 94303 791-C1
ILLSLEY CT
4400 SJS 95136 874-H1
IMAGES CIR
- MPS 95035 793-J6
100 MPS 95035 794-A6
IMPALA CT
500 MGH 95037 917-B6
IMPALA DR
3100 SJS 95117 853-D4
IMPATIENS DR
5000 SJS 95111 875-A2
IMPERIAL AV
10000 CPTO 95014 852-B1
10400 SCIC 95014 852-B1
IMPERIAL DR
6600 GIL 95020 977-J5
IMPERIAL WY
6400 SJS 95129 852-F3
IMPRESARIO WY
3500 SJS 95127 835-C2
IMWALLE CT
2000 SJS 95131 814-E7
INCA CT
16200 SCIC 95032 893-C2
INCLINE CT
2100 MPS 95035 814-E1
INCLINE WY
200 SJS 95139 895-E1
E INDEPENDENCE AV
700 MTVW 94043 811-G1
INDEPENDENCE DR
400 SJS 95111 854-H5
INDIAN AV
5600 SJS 95123 874-G6
INDIAN CRSG
- PTLV 94028 830-C1
INDIAN DR
2400 PA 94303 791-D5
INDIAN BROOM DR
300 SJS 95111 875-B2
INDIAN CREEK CT
1800 SJS 95148 835-D4
INDIAN RIVER CT
4800 SJS 95136 874-H3
INDIAN RIVER DR
4800 SJS 95136 874-H2
INDIAN SPRINGS CT
6600 SJS 95120 894-D2
INDIAN SPRINGS DR
5400 SJS 95123 875-G2
INDIAN SUMMER CT
1000 SJS 95122 854-F2
INDIAN VALLEY CT
7100 SJS 95139 895-H2
INDIAN WELLS CT
200 SJS 95139 895-E1
INDIGO DR
4200 SJS 95136 874-F2
INDIO CT
12600 SAR 95070 852-E6
INDIO WY
300 SUNV 94086 812-E6
INDUS CT
3200 SJS 95127 814-H6
INDUSTRIAL AV
800 PA 94303 791-G7
800 PA 94303 811-G1
1400 SJS 95112 834-A1
INDUSTRIAL RD
400 LGTS 95030 873-A6
INDUSTRIAL ST
300 CMBL 95008 853-E7
INDUSTRIAL WY
100 MPS 95035 794-A7
INEZ WY
500 SCIC 95117 853-D2
INGALLS CT
2700 SJS 95111 854-G4
INGERSOLL CT
3200 SJS 95148 855-F1
INGERSOLL DR
3200 SJS 95148 855-E1
INGLESIDE CT
6500 SJS 95120 894-B2
INGLEWOOD DR
500 SCL 95054 813-E5

STREET
Block City ZIP Pg-Grid

INGLEWOOD LN
- ATN 94027 790-D3
INGLIS LN
1600 SJS 95118 873-J5
INGRAM CT
200 SJS 95139 895-G2
1000 SUNV 94087 832-B2
INGRID CT
12000 SAR 95070 852-G5
INMAN WY
2000 SJS 95122 834-J7
INNERWICK LN
3300 SJS 95121 855-C3
INNOVATION DR
100 SJS 95134 813-F4
INNSBUCK DR
1200 SUNV 94089 812-G3
INSKIP DR
1400 CMBL 95008 853-B7
INSPIRATION CT
3300 SJS 95132 814-G3
INSPIRATION DR
3200 SJS 95132 814-G4
INTERBAY DR
2000 SJS 95122 835-A7
2000 SJS 95122 834-J7
INTERDALE WY
4100 PA 94306 811-D2
INTERNATIONAL CIR
200 SJS 95119 875-C5
INVERNESS AV
1100 SCL 95050 833-D4
INVERNESS CIR
1500 SJS 95124 874-A3
INVERNESS DR
700 MPS 95035 794-B2
INVERNESS WY
200 SUNV 94087 832-E5
INVICTA WY
3200 SJS 95118 874-B1
INWOOD CT
1400 CMBL 95008 853-B7
INWOOD DR
500 CMBL 95008 853-B7
INYO PL
- SMCo 94061 790-B4
ION CT
100 CMBL 95008 853-D7
IONE CT
12700 SAR 95070 852-E6
IONE DR
2700 SJS 95132 814-F6
OOF AV
- GIL 95020 978-A2
OWA AV
100 SUNV 94086 832-D1
W IOWA AV
400 SUNV 94086 832-D1
700 SUNV 94086 812-B7
OWA DR
6100 SJS 95123 874-H6
RAZU CT
200 SJS 95116 834-G3
RENE ST
700 SJS 95110 833-J5
RIS AV
600 SUNV 94086 832-F2
RIS CT
1300 SJS 95125 854-A3
RIS WY
100 PA 94303 791-C4
RIS BLOSSOM CT
100 SJS 95123 875-A4
RISH CT
900 GIL 95020 977-G2
RLANDA WY
3000 SJS 95124 873-J1
RMA LYLE DR
21600 SCIC 95030 912-H3
RONBRIDGE WY
1200 SJS 95118 874-C4
RONSHOE DR
- SJS 95138 855-E7
RONSIDE CT
3000 SJS 95132 814-E3
RON SPRINGS RD
20300 SCIC 95030 892-H7
20300 SCIC 95030 912-H1
RONSTONE CT
1100 SJS 95132 814-F6
RONWOOD DR
700 SJS 95125 854-C6
RONWOOD TER
500 SUNV 94086 832-F2
ROQUOIS CT
600 SJS 95123 874-G4
ROQUOIS TR
- PTLV 94028 810-B6
RVEN CT
500 PA 94306 811-D2

IRVING AV
- ATN 94027 790-F1
300 SCIC 95128 853-G1
300 SJS 95128 853-G1
IRWINDALE DR
2900 SJS 95122 855-B3
ISABEL DR
1600 SCIC 95125 853-H4
ISABEL CREEK RD
30000 SCIC 95140 837-D2
ISABELLA AV
- ATN 94027 790-E2
ISABELLA ST
500 SCL 95050 833-D4
ISABELLE AV
1200 MTVW 94040 811-G7
ISADORA DR
3100 SJS 95132 814-F3
ISDLIO CT
- SJS 95123 874-F6
ISENGARD DR
1200 SJS 95121 855-A4
ISHIMATSU PL
5100 SJS 95124 873-G5
ISLAND DR
100 PA 94301 791-B3
ISLAND PALM CT
- SJS 95133 814-J4
ISLAND PINE WY
6200 SJS 95119 875-D5
ISLAY CT
700 SUNV 94087 832-F5
ISSAC CT
- SJS 95136 854-E7
ITHACA AV
800 SUNV 94087 832-C2
IVALYNN CIR
3500 SJS 95132 814-G4
IVALYNN CT
3300 SJS 95132 814-G4
IVALYNN PL
3300 SJS 95132 814-G4
IVAN PL
1500 SJS 95120 874-A7
IVAN WY
3300 MTVW 94040 832-A2
6900 SCIC 95020 978-H2
IVANHOE CT
- SJS 95136 874-G3
IVEGILL CT
6800 SJS 95119 895-D1
IVERSEN CT
2600 SCL 95051 833-B7
IVES TER
400 SUNV 94087 832-E2
IVORY CREEK DR
900 SJS 95120 894-J4
IVY LN
1900 PA 94303 791-C4
6300 SJS 95129 852-F4
IVY ST
100 GIL 95020 978-A1
IVYCREEK CIR
1500 SJS 95121 855-D7
IVY ESTATES CT
2800 SJS 95135 855-G5
IVYGATE LN
3000 SJS 95136 874-J3
IVY HILL WY
100 LGTS 95030 873-C4
IVY MILLS LN
1700 SJS 95122 854-G1
IVYWOOD CT
2800 SJS 95121 855-E4
IXIAS CT
1600 SJS 95124 873-J7
IXIAS LN
5700 SJS 95124 873-J7
IZORAH WY
15700 LGTS 95032 873-C5

J

J RD
- SUNV 94089 812-H3
JABIL LN
23900 LAH 94024 831-D4
JACANA CT
5200 SJS 95123 874-F7
JACANA LN
5200 SJS 95123 874-F7
JACARANDA WY
400 SUNV 94086 832-F1
9100 GIL 95020 957-G7
16100 SCIC 95032 873-D6
JACCARANDA CT
13000 SAR 95070 852-F7
JACINTO WY
100 SUNV 94086 812-C6

JACKDOW CT
- GIL 95020 957-E7
JACKIE DR
400 SJS 95111 854-H5
JACKLIN CIR
- MPS 95035 794-A5
JACKLIN CT
- MPS 95035 794-A5
JACKLIN PL
- MPS 95035 794-A5
JACKLIN RD
- MPS 95035 794-A5
JACKPINE CT
700 SUNV 94086 832-F2
JACKS RD
20800 SAR 95070 872-D3
JACKSOL DR
14300 SJS 95124 873-E3
JACKSON AV
200 SUNV 94086 812-E7
N JACKSON AV
- SJS 95116 834-G2
300 SJS 95133 834-F1
900 SJS 95133 814-E7
900 SCIC 95133 814-E7
S JACKSON AV
- SJS 95116 834-H4
JACKSON DR
500 PA 94303 791-C4
JACKSON ST
- LGTS 95032 893-A1
- SJS 95112 834-A4
500 SCL 95050 833-D3
800 MTVW 94043 811-H4
JACKSON WY
- SJS 95002 793-C7
JACKSON OAKS CT
3600 MGH 95037 917-H5
JACKSON OAKS DR
15800 MGH 95037 917-G5
JACOB AV
1500 SJS 95118 874-A2
1700 SJS 95124 874-A2
1700 SJS 95124 873-J2
JACOBS CT
400 PA 94306 811-C2
JACOBS WY
- SCIC 95020 957-G3
JACQUELINE CT
18100 MGH 95037 937-B1
JACQUELINE WY
1000 SJS 95129 852-E3
JACQUES DR
5900 SJS 95123 874-G6
JADE AV
3200 SJS 95117 853-D3
JADELAKE CT
800 SUNV 94089 812-H5
JAFFE LN
1500 SCIC 95046 937-J6
JAGELS RD
- SUNV 94089 812-E4
JAGGERS DR
200 SJS 95119 875-C7
JAI DR
300 SJS 95119 875-C7
JALAND CT
1100 SJS 95120 894-H4
JAMAICA RD
2700 SJS 95111 854-G4
JAMAICA WY
2000 SJS 95122 834-J7
JAMES AV
- ATN 94027 790-F1
JAMES CT
1300 SCIC 95037 917-C6
3100 SCL 95051 833-A3
JAMES DR
200 MTVW 94043 812-A4
JAMES PL
1900 SJS 95125 853-J6
JAMES RD
400 PA 94306 811-D2
JAMES LEX LN
17200 MGH 95037 917-B6
JAMES TOWN CT
12000 SAR 95070 852-D5
JAMES TOWN DR
1400 CPTO 95014 852-D4
JAMESTOWN DR
1100 SUNV 94087 832-B2
JAMIE CT
100 LGTS 95032 873-H6
JAMIE LN
800 EPA 94303 791-C1
JAMIESON RD
8100 SCIC 95020 959-E6
JAMIESON WY
6300 GIL 95020 978-B5

JAMISON PL
2000 SCL 95051 833-A3
JAN DR
8700 GIL 95020 977-F1
JAN WY
4000 SJS 95124 873-H3
JANA LN
800 SJS 95111 855-A6
JANARY WY
6300 SJS 95129 852-F4
JANE LN
2300 MTVW 94043 811-G2
JANE ANN WY
- CMBL 95008 853-C6
JANELLE DR
3200 SJS 95148 855-E2
JANET AV
1900 SJS 95124 873-G2
JANICE AV
22200 CPTO 95014 852-A1
JANICE DR
1100 SCL 95050 833-C4
JANICE WY
3400 PA 94303 791-E6
JANIS WY
1100 SJS 95125 854-B6
JANKU CT
3200 SJS 95127 814-H6
JANMARIE CT
1100 SJS 95121 855-A5
JANOR CT
15200 MSER 95030 872-J4
JANSEN AV
800 SJS 95125 854-B4
JANUARY DR
100 SJS 95138 875-C4
JAPAUL LN
1400 SJS 95132 814-F3
JAPONICA WY
4600 SJS 95129 853-A1
JARDIN DR
100 LALT 94022 811-E5
200 MTVW 94040 811-E5
JARED LN
- LGTS 95032 893-C1
JARVIS AV
3000 SJS 95118 874-A1
JARVIS CT
300 SUNV 94086 832-E1
1500 SJS 95118 874-B2
JARVIS DR
400 MGH 95037 917-A4
400 MGH 95037 916-J5
JARVIS LN
700 SBnC - (1020-G5
See Page 999)
JARVIS PL
1500 SJS 95118 874-B2
JARVIS WY
2000 LAH 94304 810-H4
JASMINE CT
100 MPS 95035 794-D6
JASMINE DR
800 SUNV 94086 832-F2
JASMINE WY
100 EPA 94303 791-D3
1200 MGH 95037 917-C6
1600 SCIC 95037 917-C6
16100 SCIC 95032 873-D6
JASON CT
6100 SJS 95123 875-A6
JASON DR
- MPS 95035 793-J4
JASON WY
200 MTVW 94043 811-J5
JASPER CT
- MGH 95037 936-H1
JASPER DR
1500 SUNV 94087 832-B5
JASPER ST
600 SJS 95116 834-F6
JASPER HIGHLANDS DR
1700 MGH 95037 916-F7
E JAVA DR
200 SUNV 94089 812-G3
W JAVA DR
100 SUNV 94089 812-F2
JAY ST
500 LALT 94022 811-F6
3000 SCL 95054 813-C7
JAYBEE PL
100 SJS 95123 875-A3
JAZZ CT
800 SJS 95134 813-F3
JEAN CT
1700 SCIC 95037 917-D5
JEAN ELLEN DR
10100 SCIC 95020 957-C6

JEANETTE CT
7800 CPTO 95014 852-C2
JEANETTE LN
14800 SCIC 95127 835-A1
JEANIE LN
1900 SCIC 95020 958-A1
JEANNE AV
700 SJS 95116 834-E6
JEFFERS WY
- CMBL 95008 853-D6
JEFFERSON CT
600 SJS 95133 814-G7
JEFFERSON DR
500 PA 94303 791-C4
800 MTVW 94040 811-G7
2000 SCIC 95020 957-C6
JEFFERSON ST
200 SCL 95050 833-D4
JEFFERY AV
1400 SJS 95118 874-B1
JEFFERY CT
1700 SCL 95051 833-A3
JEFFREY AV
600 CMBL 95008 853-C7
JEFFRY LN
10200 SCIC 95020 958-C3
JENECE CT
17400 SCIC 95037 917-D5
JENKINS AV
3000 SJS 95118 874-B1
JENKINS CT
- SCIC 94305 790-J7
JENKINS LN
100 MTVW 94043 812-B5
JENKINS PL
- SCL 95051 833-A7
JENNIFER CT
300 MTVW 94040 811-F4
JENNIFER LN
1500 SCIC 95020 958-A1
JENNIFER WY
700 MPS 95035 794-A5
3000 SJS 95124 873-G2
JENNINGS DR
600 SJS 95111 854-J5
JENNINGS LN
- ATN 94027 790-D1
JENNY LIND CT
5900 SJS 95120 874-C6
JENVEY AV
1400 SJS 95125 854-A6
JEPSEN CT
12800 SAR 95070 852-D6
JERABEK CT
3900 SJS 95136 874-F1
JERALD AV
2900 SCL 95051 833-A3
JEREMIE CT
6500 SJS 95120 894-E1
JEREMIE DR
6500 SJS 95120 894-E2
JERICHO LN
3300 SJS 95117 853-D3
JERILYN CT
10200 SCIC 95127 835-A2
JERILYN DR
3400 SCIC 95127 835-A2
11700 SJS 95127 835-A2
JEROME ST
300 SJS 95125 854-B1
JERRIES DR
14000 SAR 95070 872-E2
JERVIS AV
1100 EPA 94303 791-A1
JESSE JAMES DR
500 SJS 95123 874-J7
JESSICA LN
11600 LAH 94024 831-E4
JESSICA WY
1600 SJS 95121 855-A2
JESSIE CT
2900 SJS 95124 873-F1
JESSIE LN
200 MTVW 94041 811-J6
JESSIE WY
21500 SCIC 95030 912-J3
JEWELL DR
2100 SJS 95124 873-F1
JEWELL PL
2300 MTVW 94043 811-G3
JILINDA CT
10800 SCIC 95127 835-A1
JILL AV
500 SJS 95117 833-D7
600 SCL 95050 833-D7
JIM DR
500 SJS 95133 814-H7
JIM ELDER DR
- CMBL 95008 853-C6

JIMS WY
13600 SAR 95070 872-E1
JO DR
100 LGTS 95032 873-D4
JOAN WY
1800 SCL 95050 833-C3
JOANDRA CT
500 SCIC 94024 831-F3
JOANNE AV
3300 SCIC 95127 814-H6
3400 SJS 95127 814-J6
14800 SCIC 95127 814-J6
JOAQUIN RD
- SMCo 94028 830-D4
900 MTVW 94043 811-J1
JOE DIMAGGIO CT
1400 SJS 95122 834-G7
JOEL WY
1700 LALT 94024 832-A2
JOHANNA AV
600 SUNV 94086 812-G6
JOHANSEN DR
10500 SCIC 95014 852-G2
JOHN DR
6600 CPTO 95014 852-E2
JOHN WY
800 CPTO 95014 852-D2
JOHN KIRK CT
100 CMBL 95008 853-A6
JOHN MISE CT
400 SJS 95129 852-J2
JOHN MONTGMRY DR
2500 SJS 95148 835-A6
JOHNSON AV
- LGTS 95032 893-B1
1000 SJS 95129 852-G3
1500 SAR 95070 852-G3
10200 SCIC 95014 852-H2
JOHNSON PL
2400 SCL 95050 833-C6
JOHNSON ST
1000 RDWC 94061 790-A1
1100 MLPK 94025 790-E4
JOHNSON WY
600 GIL 95020 977-J5
JOHNSON HOLLOW
100 LGTS 95032 893-B1
JOHNSTON AV
1700 SJS 95125 854-C4
JOHN TELFER DR
16900 MGH 95037 916-H7
16900 MGH 95037 936-H1
JOLEEN WY
16800 MGH 95037 917-B7
JOLENE CT
12400 SAR 95070 852-H6
JOLLY CT
1600 LALT 94024 831-H4
JOLLYMAN DR
1000 CPTO 95014 852-D2
JOLLYMAN LN
10700 CPTO 95014 852-D2
JONATHAN AV
3500 SJS 95121 855-C3
JONATHAN CT
900 CMBL 95008 873-B1
JONATHAN ST
1300 SCL 95050 833-E5
JONES AV
1700 SCL 95051 833-A3
JONES LN
1600 LALT 94024 832-A5
JONES RD
200 LGTS 95032 893-A1
200 LGTS 95032 892-J1
JONES WY
800 CMBL 95008 853-C7
JONESBORO CT
1500 SJS 95131 814-C6
JONESPORT AV
2000 SJS 95131 814-E7
JONESPORT CT
1100 SJS 95131 814-E7
JONQUIL DR
4300 SJS 95136 874-F1
JOPLIN DR
1300 SJS 95118 874-B3
JORDAN AV
- LALT 94022 811-E4
JORDAN PL
- PA 94303 791-B4
JORDAN WY
200 PA 94304 790-G6
200 SCIC 94305 790-G6
JORDAN HEIGHTS DR
15500 LGTS 95032 893-E1
JORN CT
700 SJS 95123 874-G6
JOSEFA LN
25700 LAH 94022 831-B2

JOSEFA ST
200 SJS 95110 834-A7
300 SJS 95126 834-A7
300 SJS 95126 854-A1
JOSE FIGUERES AV
- SJS 95116 834-G3
JOSEPH AV
2700 SJS 95008 873-F1
JOSEPH CIR
20100 CPTO 95014 852-E7
JOSEPH LN
700 MGH 95037 917-D7
5000 SJS 95118 874-A4
5000 SJS 95118 873-J4
JOSEPHINE AV
1900 SJS 95124 873-G1
JOSEPH SPECIALE DR
4500 SJS 95136 874-G3
JOSHUA WY
400 SUNV 94086 832-F1
JOSINA AV
600 PA 94306 811-B2
JOSSLYN DR
7100 SJS 95120 894-H4
JOY BELL LN
1100 SCIC 95046 937-H7
JOYCE CT
10200 SCIC 95127 835-A3
JOYERIN CT
1400 SJS 95131 814-D7
JOYNER CT
1300 SJS 95131 814-D6
JUANITA AV
1600 SJS 95125 854-B4
JUANITA DR
400 SCL 95050 833-D6
JUANITA WY
300 LALT 94022 811-C5
1200 CMBL 95008 873-B1
JUARCEYS CT
1500 SJS 95120 874-A7
JUAREZ AV
1600 LALT 94024 831-J4
JUAREZ CT
1900 SJS 95132 814-D3
JUBILEE CT
- SMCo 94061 790-A3
JUBILEE LN
2400 SJS 95131 814-C4
JUDITH CT
21400 SCIC 95030 912-J3
JUDITH ST
5400 SJS 95123 874-J4
JUDKINS CT
2700 SJS 95148 855-C1
JUDRO WY
3600 SJS 95117 853-C1
JUDSON DR
1000 MTVW 94040 811-F5
JUDY AV
10000 SCIC 95014 852-H1
JUERGEN DR
3500 SJS 95121 855-C3
E JULIAN ST
- SJS 95112 834-C5
1000 SJS 95116 834-E4
W JULIAN ST
100 SJS 95113 834-A6
100 SJS 95110 834-A6
600 SJS 95126 833-J6
1000 SJS 95126 834-A6
JULIANA CT
2000 SCL 95050 833-D6
JULIE CT
1000 SCL 95051 832-J5
3500 PA 94306 811-B2
JULIE LN
1500 LALT 94024 831-J3
12300 SAR 95070 852-D5
JULIET AV
800 SJS 95127 835-C2
JULIET PARK DR
700 SJS 95127 835-C1
JULIETA LN
27100 LAH 94022 831-A2
JULIETTE LN
3600 SCL 95054 813-C6
JULI LYNN DR
1200 SJS 95120 874-C7
JULIO AV
2700 SJS 95124 873-J1
JULY DR
100 SJS 95138 875-D4
JUNA CT
19500 SAR 95070 872-F4
JUNCTION AV
1700 SJS 95112 834-A1
1700 SJS 95112 814-A7
1700 SJS 95112 813-H6
1800 SJS 95131 813-H6

JUNCTION AV
2100 MTVW 94043 811-G2
2500 SJS 95134 813-G4
JUNCTION CT
1700 SJS 95112 834-A1
JUNE AV
1400 SJS 95122 834-H7
JUNE CT
18100 SCIC 95030 912-J3
JUNE DR
100 SJS 95138 875-D4
JUNE WY
14000 SAR 95070 872-E2
JUNEAU WY
- SJS 95131 814-B6
JUNEBERRY CT
100 SJS 95136 874-H1
JUNESONG WY
900 SJS 95133 834-E1
1100 SJS 95131 834-E1
JUNEWOOD AV
1800 SJS 95132 814-D3
JUNGFRAU CT
800 MPS 95035 814-D1
JUNIPER CT
400 SUNV 94086 832-G1
JUNIPER DR
- ATN 94027 790-G1
1200 GIL 95020 977-G2
JUNIPER LN
14100 SAR 95070 872-E2
JUNIPERO AV
1200 RDWC 94061 790-A1
JUNIPERO DR
100 MPS 95035 813-J1
JUNIPERO WY
19600 SAR 95070 852-F6
JUNIPERO SERRA BLVD Rt#-G5
- MLPK 94025 790-F7
- SCIC 94305 790-F7
- SCIC 94304 790-F7
100 SCIC 94304 810-G1
100 SCIC 94305 810-G1
JUNIPERO SERRA FRWY I-280
- LAH - 811-A7
- LAH - 810-F3
- LAH - 831-G5
- LALT - 831-G5
- MLPK - 810-C1
- PA - 810-F3
- SCL - 832-C6
- SCL - 852-H1
- SCIC - 831-G5
- SCIC - 832-C6
- SCIC - 810-F3
- SJS - 852-H1
- SJS - 853-A1
- SMCo - 790-A6
- SMCo - 810-C1
- SUNV - 832-C6
- WDSD - 790-A6
- CPTO - 832-C6
JUNIPERO SERRA LN
4300 SJS 95129 853-A1
JUPITER CT
600 FRMT 94539 793-J1
1400 MPS 95035 794-D6
JUPITER DR
1500 MPS 95035 794-D6
JUPITER WY
1500 MPS 95035 794-D6
JURA WY
700 SUNV 94087 832-F5
JURGENS DR
200 MPS 95035 793-J4
JURY CT
800 SJS 95112 834-B1
JUSTINE DR
3600 SJS 95124 873-H2
JUSTIN MORGAN DR
2300 SCIC 95020 958-D5
JUSTINO DR
1700 SCIC 95037 917-D5
JUSTO CT
100 CMBL 95008 853-D7

K

K RD
- SUNV 94089 812-H3
KAHALA CT
13300 SAR 95070 852-E7
KAHLER CT
1400 SCIC 95132 795-C7
KAISER DR
3000 SCL 95051 833-A5
KAISER RD
- SCIC 94035 812-B3

KAISER-AETNA RD
- SCIC 95020 (920-C5
See Page 919)
KALANA AV
- SCIC 95037 896-D7
- SJS 95037 896-D7
200 SCIC 95037 916-C1
KALISPELL CT
1600 SUNV 94087 832-B5
KALLIAM DR
2800 SCL 95051 833-B7
KAMIAH WY
900 SUNV 94087 832-B5
KAMMERER AV
1700 SJS 95116 834-G5
KAMSACK DR
1600 SUNV 94087 832-B5
KAMSON WY
200 CMBL 95008 853-D5
KANDICE CT
- SJS 95123 874-F7
KANDLE WY
1100 RDWC 94061 790-B1
KANE CT
1300 SJS 95121 854-J3
19800 SAR 95070 852-F6
KANE DR
12600 SAR 95070 852-F6
KANEKO DR
6500 SJS 95119 875-D7
KANNELY LN
11600 SCIC 95020 957-H1
KANSAS ST
1600 RDWC 94061 790-A2
KANSAS WY
100 FRMT 94539 793-J2
KARA WY
900 CMBL 95008 853-B7
900 CMBL 95008 873-B1
KARAMEOS CT
1700 SUNV 94087 832-B6
KARAMEOS DR
1700 SUNV 94087 832-B6
KAREN CT
100 SBnC - (1017-B6
See Page 997)
200 LGTS 95032 873-D7
1700 SJS 95124 873-H1
5500 GIL 95020 977-J7
KAREN DR
2300 SCL 95050 833-C5
KAREN WY
100 ATN 94027 790-B5
1000 MTVW 94040 811-F5
KARIE ANN WY
1200 SJS 95118 874-C1
KARINA CT
- SJS 95131 833-H1
KARINA WY
1300 SCL 95051 832-H4
KARL AV
14700 LGTS 95030 873-A4
14700 MSER 95030 873-A4
KARL ST
1100 SJS 95122 834-J5
KARLSTAD DR
1000 SUNV 94089 812-G4
KARMEN CT
1300 SCL 95051 832-H4
KARN CIR
19900 SAR 95070 852-E6
KARO CT
800 SUNV 94086 832-F2
KASKI CT
6100 SJS 95123 874-G6
KASSON CT
1300 SJS 95121 854-J2
KATHERINE CT
900 SJS 95126 833-G6
KATHLEEN ST
3000 SJS 95124 873-G2
KATHY CT
100 LGTS 95030 872-J3
KATHY LN
1500 LALT 94024 831-J3
17200 LGTS 95032 893-E2
KATHY WY
1100 MTVW 94022 811-G6
1100 MTVW 94040 811-G6
KATIE CT
1100 MTVW 94040 811-J7
KATIE LN
200 SCrC 95076 (975-B2
See Page 955)
KATO RD
47600 FRMT 94538 793-G1
48700 FRMT 94539 793-H3
KATON CT
700 SUNV 94086 832-F2

KATRINA WY
2500 MTVW 94040 832-A2
KATRINE CT
1000 SUNV 94087 832-G5
KATYBETH WY
1900 MGH 95037 917-E6
KAUAI DR
3700 SJS 95111 855-A6
KAUFMANN CT
700 SJS 95116 834-E6
KAVENY DR
5400 SJS 95129 852-H4
KAVIN LN
15400 MSER 95030 873-A5
15700 LGTS 95030 873-A5
KAWALKER LN
3100 SJS 95127 814-H6
KAY DR
1800 SJS 95124 873-G6
1900 LALT 94024 831-J5
2300 SCL 95050 833-C4
KAYAK DR
100 SJS 95111 875-B2
KAYBE CT
200 SJS 95139 895-F1
KAYELLEN CT
1100 SJS 95125 854-E5
KAYLA CT
2300 SJS 95124 853-G7
KAYLENE CT
1200 SJS 95127 835-B3
KAYLENE DR
3400 SJS 95127 835-B3
KAY SPRINGS CT
600 MGH 95037 916-H6
KEARNEY AV
2800 SCL 95051 833-A2
KEARNEY ST
200 SJS 95110 834-A7
KEARNY TER
800 SUNV 94086 812-D7
KEATON LP
3300 SJS 95121 855-D2
KEATS CT
600 PA 94306 811-F2
3600 SCIC 95127 834-J1
KEEBLE AV
- SJS 95126 833-J7
KEELER CT
200 SJS 95139 895-F2
KEENAN WY
1300 SJS 95125 853-G4
KEENE DR
5200 SJS 95124 873-F5
KEESLING AV
1500 SJS 95125 853-J5
1800 SCIC 95125 853-H5
KEEVER CT
- SJS 95127 834-J2
KEEWAYDIN CT
700 SJS 95111 855-A7
KEHOE CT
100 SJS 95136 874-J2
KEITH DR
1500 SJS 95008 853-B7
4100 CMBL 95008 853-A7
KEITH LN
800 SCL 95054 813-E6
KEITH WY
16100 MGH 95037 937-B2
KELDON CT
1000 SJS 95121 854-H2
KELDON DR
1000 SJS 95121 854-H3
KELEZ CT
6200 SJS 95120 874-D7
KELEZ DR
1100 SJS 95120 874-D7
KELL CT
13600 SCIC 95037 956-F2
KELL WY
- SJS 95136 854-C7
KELLER CT
3300 SCL 95054 813-E7
KELLER DR
500 MTVW 94043 812-A3
KELLER ST
3200 SCL 95054 813-E7
KELLEY PARK CIR
1200 MGH 95037 917-C6
KELLOGG AV
100 PA 94301 791-A6
KELLOGG WY
- SCL 95051 833-A7
KELLY CT
1400 SJS 95116 834-F5
KELLY DR
1000 SJS 95129 852-J3
10200 SCIC 95020 958-A4

STREET
Block City ZIP Pg-Grid

KELLY WY
500 PA 94306 811-D3
KELOWNA CT
1400 SUNV 94087 832-B4
KELSEY DR
1100 SUNV 94087 832-B3
KELSO CT
3600 SCIC 95127 834-J1
KELTNER AV
900 SJS 95117 853-C3
KELTON CT
3600 SCIC 95127 834-J1
KELTON DR
8000 GIL 95020 977-G2
KELVINGTON CT
4000 SJS 95121 855-A5
KEN CIR
200 CMBL 95008 853-D5
KENBAR RD
10200 SCIC 94024 831-F5
KENBRIDGE CT
1000 SUNV 94087 832-B2
KENBROOK CIR
- SJS 95111 854-G6
KENDALL AV
500 PA 94306 811-B2
KENDALL CT
1100 SJS 95120 894-G4
KENDLE ST
22200 CPTO 95014 832-A7
KENDRA WY
3600 SJS 95130 853-C4
KENDRICK CIR
2600 SJS 95121 854-H3
KENESTA WY
2300 SJS 95122 855-A1
KENHILL DR
3100 SJS 95111 854-G6
KENILWORTH CT
500 SUNV 94087 832-E5
KENILWORTH WY
10200 SCIC 95127 835-A3
KENISTON AV
300 MPS 95035 793-J7
KENLAND DR
3100 SJS 95111 854-G6
KENLAR DR
4900 SJS 95124 873-G4
KENLEY WY
700 SUNV 94087 832-F5
KENMAR CT
1100 SJS 95132 814-F5
KENMORE AV
300 SUNV 94086 832-F1
KENMORE CT
1000 CPTO 95014 852-C2
KENNARD WY
900 SUNV 94087 832-G5
KENNEDY AV
- CMBL 95008 853-E6
2000 SJS 95122 834-H5
KENNEDY CT
200 LGTS 95032 893-D1
400 GIL 95020 958-A7
KENNEDY DR
1300 MPS 95035 794-C5
KENNEDY RD
14900 SCIC 95032 893-G1
15200 LGTS 95032 893-D1
16200 LGTS 95032 873-D7
16600 SCIC 95032 873-C7
S KENNEDY RD
16000 LGTS 95032 873-C7
16100 LGTS 95032 893-C1
KENNEDY KNOLLS LN
100 LGTS 95032 873-D7
KENNETH AV
400 CMBL 95008 853-C7
700 CMBL 95008 873-C1
KENNETH DR
3300 PA 94303 791-E6
KENNETH ST
2900 SCL 95054 813-D7
KENNEWICK CT
800 SUNV 94087 832-C5
KENNEWICK DR
1500 SUNV 94087 832-C5
KENNEY CT
400 SUNV 94086 832-E1
KENNY LN
10100 SCIC 95127 835-C1
KENOGA DR
2400 SJS 95121 854-H2
KENOSHA AV
19500 SAR 95070 872-F2
KENPARK CT
1800 SJS 95124 853-G7
KENSINGTON AV
1100 SCL 95051 832-H5
1100 SUNV 94087 832-H5
1600 LALT 94024 831-H4
KENSINGTON CIR
1500 LALT 94024 831-H3
KENSINGTON PL
6400 GIL 95020 978-A5
KENSINGTON RD
- RDWC 94061 790-A3
KENSINGTON WY
100 SJS 95124 873-G6
100 LGTS 95032 873-G6
KENSINGTON PARK CT
400 SJS 95136 874-F1
KENSON DR
4900 SJS 95124 873-G4
KENT AV
1100 SUNV 94087 832-H5
KENT CT
- SJS 95139 875-G7
KENT DR
1900 LALT 94024 831-H5
KENT PL
- MLPK 94025 790-H3
- PA 94301 791-B4
KENT WY
20300 SCIC 95030 892-H7
KENTFIELD AV
1300 RDWC 94061 790-A1
KENTFIELD DR
5200 SJS 95124 873-G5
5300 LGTS 95032 873-G5
KENTMERE CT
400 MTVW 94040 812-A7
KENTON CT
3700 SJS 95136 874-D1
KENTON LN
3800 SJS 95136 874-D1
KENTRIDGE DR
2900 SCIC 95133 834-H1
KENTUCKY PL
- SJS 95116 834-F4
KENTUCKY ST
1600 RDWC 94061 790-A2
KENTWOOD AV
1000 CPTO 95014 852-D3
1200 SJS 95129 852-D3
KENTWOOD CT
7500 GIL 95020 977-G3
KENTWORTH WY
2600 SCL 95051 833-B1
KENWOOD AV
2200 SJS 95128 833-E6
2400 SCL 95128 833-E6
KENWOOD DR
500 MLPK 94025 790-G4
KENYON CT
3600 SCIC 95127 834-J1
18000 SAR 95070 852-D5
KENYON DR
3300 SCL 95051 832-J6
KENZO CT
3300 MTVW 94040 831-J2
KEONCREST AV
1200 SJS 95110 833-J2
KEPPLER CT
2700 SJS 95148 855-B1
KEPPLER DR
2500 SJS 95148 855-B1
KERLEY DR
1400 SJS 95112 833-J2
KERMATH DR
3100 SJS 95132 814-D3
KERN AV
1100 SUNV 94086 812-H6
2700 SJS 95121 854-J3
8100 GIL 95020 977-G2
8800 GIL 95020 957-G7
8800 SCIC 95020 957-G7
8800 SCIC 95020 977-G2
KERN CT
1200 MTVW 94040 832-A2
KERN LP
1700 FRMT 94539 794-A2
KERRI CT
100 SMCo 94061 790-A4
KERRY AV
1000 SUNV 94087 832-H5
KERRY DR
100 SCL 95050 833-D7
KERRYSHIRE LN
2600 SCL 95051 833-C1
KERSTEN DR
3400 SJS 95124 873-H2
KERWIN RANCH CT
19200 SAR 95070 872-G1
KERWOOD CT
3600 SCIC 95127 834-J1
KESEY LN
2700 SJS 95132 814-D4
KESTER CT
14400 SCIC 95046 937-G3
KESTER DR
10800 CPTO 95014 852-A2
KESTREL CT
- GIL 95020 957-E7
KESWICK CT
3600 SCIC 95127 834-J1
KETCH PL
900 SJS 95133 814-E7
KETCHUM DR
200 SJS 95127 834-H2
KETTLE CT
6600 SJS 95120 894-E1
KETTMANN RD
3300 SJS 95121 855-D3
3500 SCIC 95121 855-D3
KEVIN DR
1600 SJS 95124 873-J6
KEVIN ST
13100 SAR 95070 852-H7
KEVIN WY
3700 SCL 95054 813-E6
KEVINAIRE DR
500 MPS 95035 794-B5
KEW GARDENS CT
1400 SJS 95120 874-B6
KEYES ST
- SJS 95112 854-D1
100 SJS 95122 834-E7
400 SJS 95112 834-E7
KEYMAR DR
5600 SJS 95123 874-J4
KEYSTONE AV
2500 SCL 95051 833-B7
E KEYSTONE AV
- MGH 95037 917-A7
- MGH 95037 916-J7
KEYSTONE CT
1100 SJS 95132 814-F6
KIEL CT
1000 SUNV 94089 812-G4
KIELY BLVD
- SCL 95051 833-B5
- SCL 95051 853-B1
300 SJS 95129 853-B1
S KIELY BLVD
500 SJS 95117 853-B1
4000 SJS 95129 853-B1
KIFER CT
100 SUNV 94086 812-G7
KIFER RD
600 SUNV 94086 812-F7
900 SUNV 94086 832-G1
1100 SCL 94086 832-G1
2800 SCL 95051 833-A1
3000 SUNV 94086 833-A1
3300 SCL 95051 832-G1
KILAM DR
10800 CPTO 95014 832-C6
KILBIRNIE CT
800 SUNV 94087 832-F5
KILBRIDE CT
20300 SAR 95070 852-E7
KILBRIDE DR
20000 SAR 95070 852-E7
KILCHOAN CT
1300 SJS 95122 854-H1
KILCHOAN WY
1800 SJS 95122 854-H1
KILDARE AV
1000 SUNV 94087 832-H5
KILKENNY CT
700 SUNV 94087 832-F5
KILKENNY RD
17600 LGTS 95032 893-B2
17600 SCIC 95032 893-B2
KILLARNEY CIR
- SJS 95138 855-G7
- SJS 95138 875-G1
KILLARNEY CT
800 SUNV 94087 832-F5
KILLARNEY WY
- SJS 95138 855-G7
KILLDEER CT
1700 SUNV 94087 832-F6
KILLEAN CT
100 SUNV 94087 832-E5
KILMER AV
100 SCIC 95008 873-D3
KILMMARNOK DR
7700 SJS 95135 856-A6
KILO AV
2800 SJS 95124 873-H1
KILROY WY
- ATN 94027 790-B4
KILT CT
19600 SAR 95070 852-F7
19600 SAR 95070 872-F1
KIM CT
1400 CMBL 95008 853-B6
KIM ST
800 CPTO 95014 852-D2
KIMBALL DR
2600 SJS 95121 854-H3
KIMBER CT
2800 SJS 95124 873-H2
KIMBERLIN PL
2000 SCL 95051 833-D2
KIMBERLY CT
1400 SJS 95118 874-B2
2100 SCIC 95037 936-F2
KIMBERLY DR
1100 SJS 95118 874-B1
1700 SUNV 94087 832-B6
KIMBERLY ST
5500 SJS 95129 852-H2
KIMBLE AV
- LGTS 95032 893-A1
KIMLEE DR
3100 SJS 95132 814-F4
KIM LOUISE DR
- CMBL 95008 853-B6
100 SJS 95008 853-B6
KIMPTON CT
2400 SJS 95133 834-G1
KINCAID RD
10000 SCIC 95140 836-H2
16000 SCIC 95140 (816-J7
See Page 795)
16600 SCIC 95140 (817-A6
See Page 797)
KINCORA CT
4000 SJS 95136 854-E6
KINDRA HILL DR
7000 SJS 95120 894-H3
KINER AV
1400 SJS 95125 854-A7
KING CT
1700 SJS 95122 855-A3
2100 SCL 95051 832-J2
18000 SAR 95070 852-D5
KING RD
- SCIC 94035 812-A2
- SCIC 94043 812-A2
N KING RD
- SJS 95116 834-F3
300 SJS 95133 834-D2
800 SCIC 95133 834-D2
S KING RD
- SJS 95116 834-F4
1100 SJS 95122 834-H6
2100 SJS 95122 854-J1
2400 SJS 95121 854-J1
2400 SJS 95122 855-A2
2400 SJS 95121 855-A2
KING ST
1100 RDWC 94061 790-A1
KING ARTHURS CT
4100 PA 94306 811-C3
KINGBROOK DR
4800 SJS 95124 873-E4
KINGDALE DR
4800 SJS 95124 873-E4
KING ESTATES
3000 SJS 95135 855-G5
KING ESTATES CT
5300 SJS 95135 855-H5
KINGFIELD WY
2400 SJS 95124 873-D4
KINGFISHER DR
800 SJS 95125 854-C6
KINGFISHER TER
1200 SCIC 94087 832-F4
1200 SUNV 94087 832-F4
KINGFISHER WY
1300 SUNV 94087 832-F4
KING GEORGE CT
1200 SCIC 95046 937-H7
KINGHURST WY
4800 SJS 95124 873-E4
KINGLET CT
1700 SUNV 94087 832-F6
KINGMAN AV
1400 SJS 95128 853-G2
KING PALM CT
- SJS 95133 814-J4
KINGRIDGE DR
4800 SJS 95124 873-D4
KINGS CT
400 CMBL 95008 853-D5
KINGS LN
1400 PA 94303 791-B4
KINGS PL
6400 GIL 95020 978-A5
KINGS RW
600 SJS 95112 834-A1
KINGSBURY CT
7500 CPTO 95014 852-D3
KINGSBURY PL
7400 CPTO 95014 852-D3
KINGS CROSS WY
500 SJS 95136 874-F3
KINGSFORD LN
200 RDWC 94061 790-B2
KINGSGATE CT
2800 SJS 95132 814-D2
KINGS GATE DR
1400 SUNV 94087 832-C5
KINGSLAND CT
6500 SJS 95120 894-B1
KINGSLEY AV
100 PA 94301 790-J5
100 PA 94301 791-A5
KINGSLEY WY
14400 LAH 94022 811-B6
KINGSPARK DR
4100 SJS 95136 874-G1
KINGS RIVER CT
4700 SJS 95136 874-E2
KINGSTON CT
1600 LALT 94024 832-A3
KINGSTON RD
2700 SJS 95111 854-G4
KINGSTON WY
- SJS 95193 875-C4
4800 SJS 95130 852-J7
4800 SJS 95130 873-A1
4800 SJS 95130 872-J1
KINGSTON HILL WY
200 LGTS 95030 873-C4
KINGSWOOD WY
600 LALT 94022 811-D5
KINGTON PL
2000 SCL 95051 833-A3
KINGWOOD DR
2500 SCL 95051 833-B2
KINGWOOD WY
4800 SJS 95124 873-E4
KINMAN CT
12600 SAR 95070 852-E6
KINNEY DR
200 SJS 95112 834-A3
KINROSS CT
500 SUNV 94087 832-E5
KINROSS WY
1800 SJS 95122 854-G1
KINSPORT LN
1300 SJS 95120 874-B7
KINST CT
22500 CPTO 95014 851-J2
KINSULE CT
1300 SJS 95121 855-B5
KINTYRE WY
900 SUNV 94087 832-G5
1300 SJS 95129 852-E4
KIOWA CIR
600 SJS 95123 874-H6
KIOWA CT
- PTLV 94028 810-C6
KIOWA TR
17700 SCIC 95030 913-A2
KIPERASH CT
800 SJS 95133 814-G6
KIPERASH DR
2900 SJS 95133 814-G6
KIPLING CT
1300 SJS 95118 874-C2
KIPLING ST
200 PA 94301 790-J4
2600 PA 94306 791-C6
KIRBY AV
- SCIC 95037 916-G2
KIRBY PL
- PA 94301 791-B4
KIRBY WY
1900 SJS 95124 853-G7
1900 SJS 95124 873-F1
KIRBYHILL WY
100 SUNV 94087 832-E5
KIRCHER CT
1700 LALT 94024 832-A4
KIRK AV
- SCIC 95127 835-A1
100 SUNV 94086 812-H5
100 SJS 95127 835-A1
200 SJS 95127 814-J7
200 SCIC 95127 814-J7
KIRK CT
1600 SJS 95124 873-J3
KIRK RD
3000 SJS 95124 873-J1
4400 SJS 95124 874-A3
KIRKALDY CT
700 SUNV 94087 832-F5
KIRKBROOK DR
12000 SAR 95070 852-E5
KIRKDALE DR
12200 SAR 95070 852-E5
KIRK GLEN CT
600 SJS 95133 814-G7
KIRKHAVEN CT
- SJS 95111 874-J1
KIRKLAND AV
1700 SJS 95125 854-C4
KIRKLAND DR
600 SUNV 94087 832-D5
KIRKLYN DR
1800 SJS 95124 853-H7
KIRKMONT DR
1700 SJS 95124 853-H6
20200 SAR 95070 852-E5
KIRKORIAN WY
15500 MSER 95030 873-A5
KIRKSIDE CT
1100 SJS 95126 853-H3
KIRKWALL PL
600 MPS 95035 794-A3
KIRKWOOD DR
3300 SJS 95117 853-C1
3400 SCIC 95117 853-C1
KIRWIN LN
7400 CPTO 95014 852-D2
KISER CREEK DR
900 SJS 95120 894-J4
KISHIMURA DR
300 GIL 95020 957-J7
KISSELL CT
3100 SJS 95111 854-H5
KIT CARSON CT
100 SCL 95050 833-C7
KITCHENER CIR
1000 SJS 95121 855-A5
KITCHENER DR
1600 SUNV 94087 832-C5
KITE DR
- GIL 95020 957-E6
KITIMAT PL
1300 SUNV 94087 832-C4
KITSAP CT
2500 SCL 95051 832-J1
KITTERY CT
- SJS 95139 875-G7
KITTOE DR
100 MTVW 94043 812-A4
KITTRIDGE RD
15300 SAR 95070 872-D4
KITTYHAWK WY
100 MTVW 94041 812-A6
KIZER ST
700 MPS 95035 794-B4
KLAMATH AV
800 SCL 95051 832-J3
KLAMATH DR
1000 MLPK 94025 790-C7
1300 SJS 95130 853-B4
1500 SUNV 94087 832-C5
KLAMATH RD
200 MPS 95035 794-A6
KLAUS DR
3000 SJS 95121 855-C3
KLEE CT
700 SJS 95123 874-G6
1200 SUNV 94087 832-E3
KLEIN CT
3600 SJS 95148 835-E6
KLEIN RD
2400 SCIC 95148 835-E5
2800 SJS 95148 835-E6
KLIPSPRINGER DR
1600 SJS 95124 873-J3
KLUNE CT
2300 SCL 95054 813-C4
KNICKERBOCKER DR
600 SUNV 94087 832-A1
KNICKERSON DR
3000 SJS 95148 855-F1
KNIGHTS BRIDGE CT
3000 SJS 95132 814-E3
KNIGHTSBRIDGE LN
- RDWC 94061 790-B2
2600 SCL 95051 833-B2
KNIGHTS BRIDGE RD
2900 SJS 95132 814-E4
KNIGHTS ESTATES
5200 SJS 95135 855-G5
KNIGHTSHAVEN WY
100 SJS 95111 875-A1
KNIGHTSWOOD WY
3100 SJS 95148 835-E7
3100 SJS 95148 855-E1
KNOLL DR
12500 SCIC 94024 831-F2
KNOLLCREST AV
- SJS 95138 875-G5
KNOLLFIELD WY
800 SJS 95136 874-D2
KNOLLGLEN WY
4000 SJS 95118 874-C2
KNOLL PARK CT
6000 SJS 95120 874-C7
KNOLLS LN
16300 LGTS 95032 893-D1
KNOLL VIEW DR
1200 MPS 95035 794-A4
KNOLL VISTA
- ATN 94027 790-B6
KNOLLWELL WY
5700 SJS 95138 875-D4
KNOLLWOOD AV
1600 SJS 95125 854-A7
KNOLLWOOD DR
19900 SAR 95070 852-E5
KNOLLWOOD LN
1900 LALT 94024 831-H5
KNOPF CT
14700 SCIC 95037 937-A6
KNOWLES AV
400 SCL 95128 833-D6
400 SCL 95050 833-D6
KNOWLES DR
100 LGTS 95030 873-C2
100 CMBL 95008 873-C2
KNOWLTON DR
1400 SUNV 94087 832-C4
KNOX AV
1000 SJS 95116 834-G6
1100 SJS 95122 834-G6
KOA CT
700 SUNV 94086 832-F2
KOBARA LN
1900 SJS 95124 873-G1
KOCH LN
1100 SJS 95125 854-B7
1500 SJS 95125 874-A1
1600 SJS 95125 873-J1
KOCH TER
1500 SJS 95125 854-A7
KOCHER DR
1800 SCIC 95125 853-H6
KODIAC PL
13400 SAR 95070 852-H7
13400 SAR 95070 872-H1
KODIAK CT
600 SUNV 94087 832-D5
7100 SJS 95139 895-F1
KOHLER RD
3300 SJS 95148 835-D5
KOHNER CT
300 SCL 95050 833-D6
KOLB PL
800 SCL 95050 833-C5
KOLL CIR
1400 SJS 95112 834-A2
1400 SJS 95112 833-J2
KOLLMAR DR
2700 SJS 95127 834-J4
KOLNES CT
2500 SJS 95121 855-E4
KOMINA AV
20500 SAR 95070 872-D3
KONA CT
6500 SJS 95119 875-D6
KONA PL
- SJS 95119 875-D6
KOOSER RD
1300 SJS 95124 874-A5
1300 SJS 95118 874-A5
KOREMATSU CT
6400 SJS 95120 894-C1
KORHUMMEL WY
6500 SJS 95119 875-D7
KOSICH CT
12200 SAR 95070 852-H5
KOSICH DR
18600 SAR 95070 852-H5
KOTAKE CT
3100 SJS 95127 814-H7
KOTENBERG AV
1100 SJS 95125 854-A3
KOVANDA WY
1100 MPS 95035 794-A5
KOZERA DR
800 SJS 95136 874-E2
KOZO CT
5100 SJS 95124 873-G5
KOZO PL
5100 SJS 95124 873-G5
KRAMER LN
- SMCo 94063 790-D1
KREBS CT
1100 SJS 95131 834-D1
KREISLER CT
20700 SAR 95070 852-D5
KRING DR
2600 SJS 95125 854-B7
KRING PL
2400 LALT 94024 831-J6
KRING WY
1400 LALT 94024 831-J6
KRISMER ST
200 MPS 95035 793-J7
KRISTA CT
10300 CPTO 95014 851-J1
KRISTE LN
26000 LAH 94022 831-B2
KRISTEN CT
1000 SJS 95120 894-G3
KRISTIN RIDGE WY
800 MPS 95035 814-E1
KRISTY LN
12000 SAR 95070 852-G5
KROHN LN
13300 SCIC 95046 937-H5
KRUSE DR
2100 SJS 95131 813-J5
KRZICH PL
21300 CPTO 95014 852-C3
KUEHNIS DR
300 CMBL 95008 853-G5
KUMQUAT DR
500 SJS 95117 853-D2
KUNKEL DR
5200 SJS 95124 873-F5
KURTZ LN
5700 SJS 95123 874-E5
KUYKENDALL PL
3300 SJS 95148 835-E7
KYBURZ PL
5900 SJS 95120 874-C6
KYLE CT
1400 SUNV 94087 832-C4
KYLE ST
700 SJS 95133 814-G6
700 SJS 95127 814-G6
KYLEMORE CT
4000 SJS 95136 854-E6
KYRA CIR
1700 SJS 95122 855-A2

L

L RD
- SUNV 94089 812-H3
LA AGUA CT
200 MGH 95037 937-B3
LA ALAMEDA DR
15200 MGH 95037 937-A4
LA ALONDRA WY
700 GIL 95020 977-H2
LA ARBOLEDA WY
15300 MGH 95037 937-B4
LA BARBERA DR
800 SJS 95126 853-H3
LA BAREE DR
300 MPS 95035 794-E7
400 MGH 95037 937-B3
LA BARRANCA CT
26800 LAH 94022 831-B1
LA BARRANCA RD
13000 LAH 94022 831-A1
13100 LAH 94022 811-B7
LA BELLA AV
1300 SUNV 94087 832-D4
LA BELLA CT
15600 MGH 95037 937-A3
LA BOHEME WY
1400 SJS 95121 854-J2
LABURNUM DR
800 SUNV 94086 832-F3
LA BURNUM RD
- ATN 94027 790-F1
LA CALLE CT
3600 PA 94306 811-B2
LA CANADA CT
100 LGTS 95030 873-C4
400 MGH 95037 937-B4
LAC BLEU CT
- SJS 95148 855-F2
LAC DAZUR CT
- SJS 95148 855-F2
LAC DU VAL CT
- SJS 95148 855-F2
LACEY AV
13900 SAR 95070 872-D2
LACEY DR
2100 MPS 95035 794-E7
LACHINE DR
1600 SUNV 94087 832-C5
E LA CHIQUITA AV
16400 SCIC 95032 873-C7
W LA CHIQUITA AV
16300 SCIC 95032 873-C7
LA CIENEGA CT
100 LGTS 95030 873-C4
LACKAWANNA CT
1000 SUNV 94087 832-B2
LA COCHE WY
8300 GIL 95020 977-J1
LA CON CT
2000 SJS 95008 853-F7
LACONIA CT
- SJS 95139 875-G7
LA CONNER DR
400 SUNV 94087 832-D5
LA CORONA CT
1900 CMBL 95030 873-A2
LA CORONA DR
1900 CMBL 95030 873-A1
LA CORTE LN
10600 SCIC 95020 957-J3
LACOUR WY
300 SMCo 94061 790-B3
LA CRESTA CT
12600 LAH 94022 811-B7
LA CRESTA DR
12500 LAH 94022 811-A5
LA CRESTA WY
4700 SJS 95129 852-B7
LA CROIX CT
16500 LGTS 95032 873-D7
LA CROSSE CT
800 SUNV 94087 832-C4
LA CROSSE DR
- MGH 95037 937-A3
- MPS 95035 794-D6
1400 SUNV 94087 832-C4
LACSA CT
2100 SJS 95116 834-G3
LA CUESTA DR
200 SMCo 94028 810-E3
800 SCIC 94024 831-E2
LADDIE CT
2100 SJS 95121 855-C3
LADDIE WY
1900 SJS 95121 855-C3
LADERA CT
19600 SAR 95070 852-F5
LADERA DR
300 SJS 95134 813-D2
LADIS CT
800 SUNV 94086 832-G2
LADNER DR
5600 SJS 95123 874-J4
LA DONNA ST
3600 PA 94306 811-C2
LADYMUIR CT
2200 SJS 95131 814-D5
LADY PALM CT
- SJS 95133 814-J4
LADYWOOD CT
1300 SJS 95130 853-C4
LA ESCUELA CT
15800 MGH 95037 937-A3
LAFAYETTE DR
1100 SUNV 94087 832-B2
LAFAYETTE ST
300 SCL 95050 833-E1
600 SCL 95053 833-E4
2900 SCL 95054 833-E1
2900 SCL 95054 813-B2
3900 SCL 95134 813-D5
LAFAYETTE WY
400 SCL 95050 833-F5
LAFERN CT
6500 SJS 95120 894-C2
LA FIESTA PL
4800 SJS 95129 853-A1
LAGE DR
4600 SJS 95130 853-A7
LA GIRALDA CT
700 MGH 95037 936-H1
LAGO CT
1100 SJS 95121 854-J3
LAGO LOMITA WY
- SCIC 95030 934-A2
LAGOON WY
2400 SJS 95131 814-C4
LAGO VISTA CIR
4600 SJS 95129 853-A1
4700 SJS 95129 852-B7
LAGO VISTA CT
4600 SCIC 95120 895-E4
LA GRANDE DR
600 SUNV 94087 832-D5
700 MGH 95037 937-A4
LAGUNA AV
100 SCIC 95037 896-B4
100 SJS 95037 896-B4
200 SCIC 95037 895-J6
200 SJS 95141 895-J6
3500 PA 94306 811-B2
LAGUNA CT
3400 SCL 95051 832-J3
3500 PA 94306 811-B2
LAGUNA DR
200 MPS 95035 793-J5
200 SJS 95131 814-A5
LAGUNA OAKS PL
3700 PA 94306 811-B2
LAGUNA SECA CT
700 SJS 95123 874-G5
LAGUNA SECA WY
5800 SJS 95123 874-G5
LAGUNITA DR
500 SCIC 94305 790-G7
LAHAINA WY
4400 SJS 95118 874-B3
LA HERNAN DR
200 SCL 95051 832-H7
LA HONDA AV
5000 SJS 95129 852-J1
LA HONDA DR
200 MPS 95035 793-J5
LA HONDA SUR
15500 MGH 95037 937-B3
LAINE AV
1700 SCL 95051 833-C3
LA JENNIFER WY
800 PA 94306 811-B2
LA JOLLA AV
2700 SJS 95124 873-H1
LA JOLLA CT
11200 CPTO 95014 852-B3
15600 MGH 95037 937-B3
LA JOLLA DR
15200 MGH 95037 937-B3
E LAKE AV Rt#-152
700 WAT 95076 995-J4
1000 ScrC 95076 995-J4
W LAKE AV
- WAT 95076 (1015-F2
See Page 995)
LAKE RD
- SMCo 94028 830-D4
7000 SBnC - 999-E4
7800 SCIC 95020 (979-C7
See Page 959)
LAKE ALBANO CIR
3100 SJS 95135 855-G6
LAKE ALMANOR DR
5800 SJS 95123 874-G7
LAKEBIRD CT
4800 SJS 95124 873-F4
LAKEBIRD DR
600 SUNV 94089 812-H4
1800 SJS 95124 873-G4
LAKEBIRD PL
4800 SJS 95124 873-G4
LAKEBROOK CT
- SJS 95148 855-F1
LAKECHIME DR
300 SUNV 94089 812-H4
LAKECREST CT
- SJS 95148 855-F2
LAKE CROWLEY PL
5800 SJS 95123 874-G7
LAKEDALE WY
900 SUNV 94089 812-H4
LAKE ESTATES CT
3000 SJS 95135 855-G5
LAKEFAIR DR
600 SUNV 94089 812-G4
LAKE GARDA DR
3100 SJS 95135 855-G6
LAKEHAVEN DR
600 SUNV 94089 812-H5
LAKEHAVEN TER
600 SUNV 94089 812-G5
LAKE HENNESSY CT
5900 SJS 95123 874-E5
LAKEHOUSE AV
400 SJS 95110 834-A7
LAKE ISABELLA WY
900 SJS 95123 874-G7
LAKEKNOLL DR
700 SUNV 94089 812-H5
LAKE LESINA DR
3200 SJS 95135 855-G6
LAKE MANOR DR
5800 SJS 95123 874-G7
LAKE MCCLURE DR
800 SJS 95123 874-E5
LAKEMONT CT
- SJS 95148 855-F2
LAKEMORE CT
- SJS 95148 855-F1
LAKEMUIR DR
200 SUNV 94089 812-H5
LAKEPARK DR
1600 SJS 95148 814-B6
LAKEPORT CT
- SJS 95148 855-F1
LAKE RANCH RD
- SCL 95030 892-C1
- SCIC 95070 872-B7

STREET
Block City ZIP Pg-Grid

LAKE RANCH RD
- SCIC 95070 892-C1
LAKE RIDGE LN
- SJS 95148 855-F1
LAKE SANTA CLARA DR
4200 SCL 95054 813-C5
LAKE SHASTA CT
5900 SJS 95123 874-G7
LAKESHIRE CT
900 SJS 95126 853-H3
LAKESHORE CIR
1300 SJS 95131 814-B6
LAKESHORE DR
1200 SMCo 94025 810-A3
4200 SCL 95054 813-C5
LAKESIDE DR
- SJS 95148 855-F1
400 SUNV 94086 812-J7
600 SUNV 94086 813-A6
2800 SCL 95054 813-A6
LAKE SPRING CT
11500 CPTO 95014 852-C4
LAKE TAHOE CT
900 SJS 95123 874-G7
LAKE TRASINENO DR
3100 SJS 95135 855-F6
LAKETREE CT
1500 SJS 95131 814-D5
LAKEVIEW BLVD
47400 FRMT 94538 793-G1
LAKEVIEW CT
- FRMT 94538 793-G2
- SJS 95148 855-F2
18200 SCIC 95030 892-H5
LAKEVIEW DR
100 WDSD 94062 790-A5
17200 MGH 95037 917-F4
LAKEWAY
3000 SUNV 94086 813-A6
LAKEWOOD CT
2100 SJS 95132 814-C3
LAKEWOOD DR
600 SUNV 94089 812-G5
1900 SJS 95132 814-C3
LAKME CT
4000 SJS 95121 854-H4
LAKME WY
1400 SJS 95121 854-H4
LA LANNE CT
25600 LAH 94022 811-C6
LA LOMA CT
24900 LAH 94022 831-C3
LA LOMA DR
- SMCo 94025 790-C6
- MLPK 94025 790-C6
24900 LAH 94022 831-C3
25300 SCIC 94022 831-C3
LALOR DR
5700 SJS 95123 874-G5
LAMA WY
1600 SJS 95120 873-J1
LA MAISON DR
600 SJS 95128 853-E2
LA MAR CT
15600 MGH 95037 937-B3
19600 CPTO 95014 852-F1
LA MAR DR
15200 MGH 95037 937-B3
19600 CPTO 95014 852-F1
LA MATA WY
3500 PA 94306 811-B2
LAMBARE WY
- SJS 95135 855-G3
LAMBECK LN
6100 SJS 95119 875-D5
LAMBERT AV
200 PA 94306 791-C7
200 PA 94306 811-B1
LAMBERT LN
2500 SJS 95125 854-B6
LAMBERT WY
500 MTVW 94043 812-B3
LAMBETH CT
600 SUNV 94087 832-E5
2900 SJS 95132 814-E3
LA MESA CT
400 SMCo 94028 810-D3
5600 MGH 95037 937-A3
LA MESA DR
100 SMCo 94028 810-D3
LA MESA LN
3900 SJS 95124 873-H2
LA MESA TER
900 SUNV 94086 812-D6
LA MIEL CT
000 SJS 95008 853-B6
LA MIEL WY
100 SJS 95008 853-B6

LA MIRADA CT
15800 MGH 95037 937-B3
LA MIRADA DR
2300 SJS 95125 853-J7
LA MIRADO WY
- SCIC 95030 872-H7
LAMMERHAVEN CT
- SJS 95111 874-J1
LAMMY PL
1100 LALT 94024 831-H2
LAMOND CT
3200 SJS 95148 855-D2
LAMONT CT
1400 CMBL 95008 853-B7
1700 SUNV 94087 832-B6
LA MONTAGNE CT
100 LGTS 95030 873-B3
LAMORE DR
1400 SJS 95130 853-A4
LAMPLIGHTER SQ
10000 CPTO 95014 851-J1
LAMPLIGHTER WY
- SJS 95134 813-G2
LANA CT
800 CMBL 95008 853-C7
LANA WY
1500 HOLL - (1020-A6 See Page 999)
LANAI AV
1800 SJS 95122 834-H7
2000 SJS 95122 854-J1
LANARK CT
1000 SUNV 94087 832-G5
LANARK LN
19700 SAR 95070 852-F7
LANCASTER CT
2500 SCL 95051 833-C1
LANCASTER DR
1700 SJS 95124 873-H2
LANCASTER RD
15700 SAR 95070 872-G6
15700 SCIC 95030 872-G6
15700 MSER 95030 872-G6
LANCELOT LN
1100 SJS 95127 835-B3
LANCER DR
900 CPTO 95014 852-F3
1000 SJS 95129 852-F3
LANCEWOOD PL
100 LGTS 95030 873-B3
LANDA LN
- SMCo 94061 790-A4
LANDAU CT
500 MGH 95037 917-B7
5300 SJS 95123 875-B3
LANDELL CT
1500 LALT 94024 832-A4
LANDEROS DR
200 SCL 95051 833-C7
LANDERWOOD LN
6600 SJS 95120 894-E2
LANDESS AV
1400 MPS 95035 814-D2
1400 SJS 95132 814-D2
LANDINGS DR
1800 MTVW 94043 811-G1
LANDMARK PKWY
- MTVW 94043 811-H1
LANDSFORD PL
800 SCL 95050 833-D1
LANDSLIDE CT
2600 SCL 95051 833-A1
LANE AV
900 MTVW 94040 811-H6
LANE PL
- ATN 94027 790-F1
LANE A
- SCIC 94305 790-H7
1500 SJS 95112 834-A1
LANE B
500 SCIC 94305 810-H1
1200 SCIC 95020 957-E6
1500 SJS 95112 834-A1
LANE C
500 SCIC 94305 790-H7
500 SCIC 94305 810-H1
600 SJS 95112 834-A1
LANE D
600 SJS 95112 834-A1
LANE E
600 SJS 95112 834-A1
LANE F
600 SJS 95112 834-A1
LANEVIEW DR
3100 SJS 95132 814-D2
LANE W
500 SCIC 94305 790-H7
LANEWOOD CT
900 SJS 95125 854-C6

LANEWOOD DR
900 SJS 95125 854-C6
LANFAIR CIR
400 SJS 95136 874-F1
LANFAIR CT
600 SJS 95136 874-F1
LANFAIR DR
500 SJS 95136 874-F1
LANGDON CT
4000 SJS 95121 855-A5
LANGPORT DR
1600 SUNV 94087 832-E5
LANGPORT WY
1600 SUNV 94087 832-E5
LANGTON AV
200 LALT 94022 811-D3
LANHAM CT
2300 SJS 95148 855-B1
LANIER LN
2600 SJS 95121 854-J3
LANITOS AV
200 SUNV 94086 812-C7
LANNING CT
500 SJS 95133 834-G1
LANNING WY
2300 SJS 95133 834-F2
LANNOY CT
19900 SAR 95070 872-E1
LANO ST
400 SJS 95125 854-C3
LANSBERRY CT
100 LGTS 95032 873-D6
LANSDALE AV
10300 CPTO 95014 852-F1
LANSDALE CT
1100 SJS 95120 894-F2
LANSDOWN CT
800 SUNV 94087 832-C2
LANSFORD AV
2200 SJS 95125 854-A6
LANSING AV
1200 SJS 95118 874-B4
LANTANA AV
2100 SJS 95130 852-J6
LANTANA DR
900 SUNV 94086 832-G2
LANTERN CT
3200 SJS 95111 854-J5
LANTERN WY
3200 SJS 95111 854-J5
LANTIS LN
1700 LALT 94024 832-A4
LANTZ AV
2700 SJS 95124 873-F1
LANTZ DR
100 SCIC 95037 896-C6
LAPA DR
6000 SJS 95129 852-J1
LA PALA CT
3300 SJS 95127 814-J7
15400 MGH 95037 937-B3
LA PALA DR
200 SJS 95127 814-J7
200 SJS 95127 834-J1
LA PALA PL
3300 SJS 95127 814-J7
LA PALMA PL
600 MPS 95035 794-B5
LA PALOMA
- CMBL 95008 853-F7
LA PALOMA AV
20200 SAR 95070 872-E2
LA PALOMA DR
11000 CPTO 95014 852-B3
LA PALOMA RD
13000 LAH 94022 831-B1
13000 LAH 94022 811-C7
LA PALOMA WY
700 GIL 95020 977-H2
LA PARA AV
700 PA 94306 811-C2
LA PAZ
- MTVW 94043 812-A2
- CMBL 95008 853-F7
LA PAZ CT
400 MGH 95037 937-B4
1400 SJS 95118 874-A3
LAPAZ WY
13500 SAR 95070 872-H1
LA PETITE WY
- SJS 95133 814-G7
LA PINTA WY
4700 SJS 95129 852-B7
LA PLATA PZ
800 CMBL 95008 873-C1
LA PLAYA CT
21500 CPTO 95014 852-B3
LA PORTE AV
1700 SJS 95122 834-H6

LA PORTE CT
15800 MGH 95037 937-A3
LA PRADERA DR
1500 CMBL 95008 853-A6
LA PRENDA CT
15800 MGH 95037 937-A3
LA PRENDA RD
400 LALT 94024 831-F1
LAPRIDGE LN
3400 SJS 95124 873-E2
LA QUEBRADA WY
100 SJS 95127 815-C6
LA QUINTA DR
- SJS 95127 815-B6
LARABEE CT
5900 SJS 95120 874-B7
LA RAGIONE AV
2400 SJS 95111 854-G3
LARCH CT
2600 SJS 95121 854-H3
LARCH DR
- ATN 94027 790-G1
LARCH ST
500 MPS 95035 793-H6
LARCH GROVE PL
5300 SJS 95123 875-A3
LARCHMONT AV
12200 SAR 95070 852-F6
LARCHMONT CT
6000 SJS 95123 875-B6
LARCHMONT DR
6000 SJS 95123 875-B6
LARCHWOOD DR
5200 SJS 95118 874-B4
LA RENA CT
15900 MGH 95037 937-A3
LA RENA DR
25100 LAH 94022 831-C1
LARGA VISTA DR
14900 LGTS 95032 873-F6
LARGO DR
2700 SJS 95132 814-D3
LARGUITA LN
- PTLV 94028 810-B5
LA RHEE DR
2800 SJS 95124 873-J1
LARIAT DR
9300 GIL 95020 957-F7
LARIAT LN
600 SJS 95132 815-A5
LA RINCONADA DR
100 MSER 95030 873-B4
100 LGTS 95030 873-B2
14200 SCIC 95030 873-B3
LARIOS CT
6000 SJS 95123 874-G6
LARIOS WY
6100 SJS 95123 874-G6
LARISSA CT
900 SJS 95136 874-E3
LARK AV
1600 RDWC 94061 790-A2
16300 LGTS 95032 873-C4
16500 LGTS 95030 873-C4
LARK LN
1700 SUNV 94087 832-F6
LARK WY
19800 SAR 95070 872-F4
LARKELLEN LN
700 LALT 94024 832-A3
LARKIN AV
1400 SJS 95129 852-F4
LARKIN VALLEY RD
- WAT 95019 995-A4
- SCrC 95019 995-A4
- SCrC 95076 995-A4
LARKMEAD CT
600 SJS 95117 853-C2
LARKMEAD RD
600 SJS 95117 853-C2
LARKSPUR AV
900 SUNV 94086 832-G2
LARKSPUR CT
13400 SCIC 95046 937-E5
LARKSPUR DR
300 EPA 94303 791-D2
1500 SJS 95125 854-A7
LARKSPUR LN
8500 GIL 95020 977-E1
LARKWOOD CT
1500 MPS 95035 793-J4
LARNEL PL
11700 LALT 94024 831-H4
LA ROCCA CT
15100 MGH 95037 937-B4
LA ROCCA DR
15200 MGH 95037 937-A4
LA ROCHELLE TER
1100 SUNV 94089 812-G4

LA RODA CT
15900 MGH 95037 937-A3
20000 CPTO 95014 852-E2
LA RODA DR
10500 CPTO 95014 852-E2
LA ROSSA CIR
1500 SJS 95125 854-D3
LA ROSSA CT
200 SJS 95125 854-D3
LARRY CT
3600 SJS 95121 855-A5
LARRY WY
10500 CPTO 95014 832-E6
LARSEN CT
2600 SCL 95051 833-B3
LARSEN PL
1800 SCL 95051 833-B3
LARSENS LNDG
100 LALT 94022 811-D3
LARSON WY
1000 SJS 95117 853-B3
LA SALLE AV
200 SCL 95051 832-J7
LA SALLE DR
1000 SUNV 94087 832-B5
2600 MTVW 94040 831-J2
21400 SCIC 95030 912-J3
LA SALLE WY
2600 SJS 95130 852-J7
LA SANDRA WY
- PTLV 94028 810-B4
LAS ANIMAS AV
- GIL 95020 957-H7
600 GIL 95020 958-A6
700 SCIC 95020 958-A6
LAS ANIMAS CT
8100 GIL 95020 977-H2
LAS ANIMAS RD
- SCIC 95037 (897-A2 See Page 877)
8500 SCIC 95037 876-G4
8500 SCIC 95037 896-J1
LAS ASTAS DR
100 LGTS 95030 873-C4
LASCAR CT
2300 SJS 95124 873-E3
LASCAR PL
2400 SJS 95124 873-E3
LAS CASAS DE LOS PINOS
2300 SJS 95133 834-F1
LAS COCHES CT
400 MGH 95037 937-B4
LAS COLINAS
100 SCrC 95076 (975-B2 See Page 955)
LAS COLINAS LN
- SJS 95119 875-E6
LAS CRUCES CT
5000 SJS 95118 874-B3
LA SELVA DR
3700 PA 94306 811-C1
16900 MGH 95037 936-J1
LAS ENCANTOS CT
1900 CMBL 95030 873-A2
1900 CMBL 95030 872-J2
LA SEYNE PL
5600 SJS 95138 875-F1
LAS FLORES CT
1100 LALT 94022 811-D3
LAS FLORES LN
14800 LGTS 95032 873-G6
LA SIERRA CT
15600 MGH 95037 937-A3
LA SIERRA WY
400 GIL 95020 977-H2
LAS JOYAS CT
1900 CMBL 95030 873-A2
LAS LOMAS DR
700 MPS 95035 794-B6
LAS MIRADAS DR
200 LGTS 95030 873-C4
LAS ONDAS CT
20000 CPTO 95014 852-E1
LAS ONDAS WY
10300 CPTO 95014 852-E1
LAS PALMAS DR
800 SCL 95051 833-B5
LAS PALMAS WY
- SJS 95133 814-J4
LA SPEZIA PL
- SJS 95138 875-J1
LAS PIEDRAS
- SMCo 94028 830-D5
LAS PIEDRAS CT
1600 CMBL 95030 873-A2
LAS PLUMAS AV
1500 SJS 95133 834-E3
LASS DR
2300 SCL 95054 813-C4

LASSEN AV
200 MTVW 94043 811-F3
1100 MPS 95035 814-C1
5000 SJS 95129 852-J4
LASSEN CT
- MLPK 94025 790-C7
LASSEN DR
900 MLPK 94025 790-C7
LASSEN ST
400 LALT 94022 811-E7
LASSEN WY
15000 MGH 95037 937-B4
LASSENPARK CIR
300 SJS 95136 874-G2
LASSIE CT
3000 SCIC 95020 958-D4
LASTRETO AV
300 SUNV 94086 812-F6
LASUEN CT
100 LGTS 95032 873-F6
LASUEN ST
100 SCIC 94305 790-H6
LAS UVAS CT
100 LGTS 95030 873-A2
LASWELL AV
300 SCIC 95128 853-G1
300 SJS 95128 853-G2
LA TERRACE CIR
1000 SJS 95123 874-D5
LATHAM ST
1200 MTVW 94041 811-F4
1900 MTVW 94040 811-F4
LATHROP CT
5600 SJS 95123 875-A4
LATHROP DR
800 SCIC 94305 810-H2
5600 SJS 95123 875-A4
LATHROP PL
900 SCIC 94305 810-H2
LA TIERRA CT
15700 MGH 95037 937-A4
LA TIERRA DR
15600 MGH 95037 937-A4
LATIMER AV
3900 CMBL 95008 853-B5
4100 SJS 95130 853-A4
4500 SJS 95129 853-A4
E LATIMER AV
100 CMBL 95008 853-E5
W LATIMER AV
- CMBL 95008 853-D5
LATIMER CIR
500 CMBL 95008 853-D5
LATONA CT
400 SJS 95111 875-C2
LA TORRE AV
4200 SJS 95111 855-A7
LAUELLA CT
200 MTVW 94041 811-G4
LAUFALL LN
400 SJS 95111 854-F6
LAUMER AV
- SCIC 95127 835-A1
200 SJS 95127 835-A1
LAURA CT
800 CMBL 95008 853-C7
LAURA DR
600 CMBL 95008 853-C7
5400 SJS 95124 873-G6
LAURA LN
100 PA 94303 791-D4
200 MTVW 94043 811-F3
6900 SCIC 95020 978-J2
LAURAL AV
6200 SJS 95138 875-F6
LAURANT WY
3500 SJS 95132 814-F2
LAUREDO WY
14500 SCIC 95046 937-G3
LAUREL AV
100 LGTS 95030 872-H7
100 MLPK 94025 790-J3
400 MLPK 94025 791-A2
1000 EPA 94303 791-A1
LAUREL DR
2000 SCL 95050 833-C4
7500 GIL 95020 977-G3
16700 SCIC 95030 913-A1
18300 SCIC 95030 872-J5
18300 SCIC 95030 892-G4
21400 SCIC 95030 912-J2
LAUREL LN
26600 LAH 94022 811-B7
LAUREL PL
- MLPK 94025 790-F2
LAUREL RD
600 MGH 95037 937-C2
17000 MGH 95037 917-C7
17700 SCIC 95037 917-B5

LAUREL ST
- ATN 94027 790-F2
- MLPK 94025 790-F2
700 SJS 95126 833-H5
LAUREL WY
- MTVW 94040 811-E3
LAURELDALE LN
4400 SJS 95136 874-D2
LAURELEI AV
100 SJS 95128 833-F7
LAURELES DR
1000 LALT 94022 811-D3
LAURELGLEN CT
4000 SJS 95118 874-C2
LAUREL GLEN DR
800 PA 94304 830-G1
800 PA 94304 810-G7
LAURELVIEW CT
- FRMT 94538 793-F1
LAURELWOOD DR
1600 SJS 95125 854-J6
LAUREL WOOD LN
17900 MGH 95037 916-G7
LAURELWOOD RD
300 SCL 95054 813-D7
LAUREN DR
5400 SJS 95124 873-J6
LAURENTIAN WY
1700 SUNV 94087 832-B6
LAURETTA DR
21000 CPTO 95014 832-C7
LAURIE AV
600 SCL 95054 813-E6
1000 SJS 95125 854-B4
LAURIE JO LN
500 SCL 95050 833-C6
LAURINDA DR
1800 SJS 95124 873-G4
1800 SJS 95032 873-G4
LAURYN RIDGE CT
800 MPS 95035 814-E1
LAUSANNE CT
2800 SJS 95132 814-F5
LAUSETT AV
2000 SJS 95116 834-G4
LAVA DR
2300 SJS 95133 834-F1
LAVA WY
600 SJS 95133 834-F1
LAVA ROCK CT
3400 MGH 95037 917-F4
LAVEILLE CT
1200 SJS 95131 814-B7
LA VELA CT
300 MGH 95037 937-B3
LAVENDER DR
800 SUNV 94086 832-F3
LAVENDER LN
16300 SCIC 95032 873-D5
LAVENDULA WY
6100 SJS 95119 875-D5
L AVENIDA
1000 MTVW 94043 812-A2
1000 MTVW 94043 811-J2
LAVER CT
1900 LALT 94024 831-H5
LA VERNE DR
18600 SCIC 95030 912-H3
LA VERNE WY
800 LALT 94022 811-D4
LA VIA AZUL
200 MGH 95037 937-B3
LA VIA AZUL CT
200 MGH 95037 937-B3
LA VIDA REAL
12800 LAH 94022 831-A1
LAVINA CT
21000 SCIC 95014 832-C6
LA VISTA CT
900 MGH 95037 936-J3
13000 SAR 95070 852-F7
LA VISTA DR
13000 SAR 95070 852-F7
LAVONA DR
- SJS 95118 874-C4
LA VONNE AV
1700 SJS 95116 834-G5
LA VONNE DR
- CMBL 95008 853-B6
LAWLER RANCH RD
- SMCo 94025 790-A7
- SMCo 94025 810-B1
- WDSD 94062 790-A7
LAWNDALE AV
300 CMBL 95008 853-D5
LAWRENCE CT
1900 SCL 95051 832-J3
LAWRENCE DR
700 GIL 95020 977-H1

LAWRENCE EXWY
Rt#-G2
- SAR 95070 852-H4
- SCL 95051 832-J6
- SCL 95051 852-H4
100 SUNV 94086 812-J7
300 SJS 95014 852-H4
300 SJS 95129 852-H4
300 SCIC 95014 852-H4
800 SUNV 94087 832-J6
1000 SUNV 94089 812-J3
1800 SAR 95129 852-H4
1900 SUNV 94086 832-J6
2900 SCL 95051 812-J7
LAWRENCE LN
900 PA 94303 791-D5
LAWRENCE RD
1700 SCL 95051 832-J3
LAWRENCE STATION RD
100 SUNV 94086 832-J1
1200 SUNV 94089 812-J3
LAWSON CT
1600 SJS 95118 873-J4
LAWSON LN
2200 SCL 95054 813-C7
2200 SCL 95054 833-C1
LAWTHER CT
4000 SJS 95135 855-F3
LAWTON AV
900 SJS 95128 853-H3
LAWTON DR
- MPS 95035 794-D6
LAYNE CT
700 PA 94303 791-D7
LAYTON CT
700 SCL 95051 833-B6
LAYTON ST
700 SCL 95051 833-B5
LAYTON WY
10400 SCIC 95127 834-J3
LAZANEO DR
20300 CPTO 95014 832-D7
LAZO GRANDE DR
- SCIC 95037 936-G7
LAZY LN
3800 SCIC 95135 855-H1
LAZY OAK CT
22500 CPTO 95014 831-J7
LAZY RIVER WY
6700 SJS 95120 894-E2
LEAF CT
600 LALT 94022 811-C5
LEAFTREE CIR
1400 SJS 95131 814-C7
LEAFTREE CT
1400 SJS 95131 814-C7
LEAFWOOD LN
3200 SJS 95111 854-F6
LEAFY CT
1500 MGH 95037 917-D6
LEAHY ST
500 RDWC 94061 790-C1
LEAL LN
- SCrC 95076 (975-C7 See Page 955)
LEAN AV
5300 SJS 95123 875-A3
LEAN WY
5900 SJS 95123 875-A5
LEANDER DR
12700 LAH 94022 811-B7
LEANN CT
15300 SCIC 95037 937-E2
LEARNARD WY
8700 GIL 95020 977-F1
LEATHERWOOD CT
6700 SJS 95120 894-C5
LEAVESLEY PL
10800 CPTO 95014 852-B2
LEAVESLEY RD
2000 SCIC 95020 958-G4
LEAVESLEY RD
Rt#-152
- GIL 95020 977-J1
- GIL 95020 978-A1
LEAVESLEY RD
Rt#-G9
400 GIL 95020 978-B1
600 GIL 95020 958-C7
1100 SCIC 95020 958-C7
LE BAIN DR
2300 SJS 95130 853-A7
LEBANON AV
10200 CPTO 95014 851-J1
LEBANON DR
10100 CPTO 95014 851-J1
LE COMPTE PL
800 SJS 95122 834-F7

LEDERER CIR
1600 SJS 95131 814-C7
LEDGEWOOD DR
1700 SJS 95124 873-H2
LEE CT
- SBnC - (1020-F1 See Page 999)
LEE DR
900 MLPK 94025 790-F3
1600 MTVW 94040 811-G7
21300 SCIC 95030 912-J2
LEE RD
- SBnC - (1000-G7 See Page 999)
LEE ST
600 LALT 94022 831-E1
LEEDS AV
7500 CPTO 95014 852-D4
LEESA ANN CT
5200 SJS 95124 873-J5
LEEWARD CT
1100 SJS 95122 834-J5
LEEWARD DR
1100 SJS 95122 834-J5
1400 SJS 95122 835-A5
LE FEVRE DR
5500 SJS 95118 874-A5
LEFONT DR
1200 SJS 95131 814-B6
LE FRANC DR
5700 SJS 95118 874-B6
LEGHORN ST
1900 PA 94043 811-F1
1900 MTVW 94043 811-F1
LEHIGH DR
3500 SCL 95051 832-J6
LEIGH AV
300 SCIC 95128 853-G2
300 SJS 95128 853-G2
1000 SJS 95126 853-H2
1400 SJS 95125 853-H3
2000 CMBL 95008 853-G7
2000 SCIC 95125 853-G7
2200 SJS 95124 853-G7
2700 SJS 95124 873-G2
3500 SCIC 95124 873-G2
14400 SJS 95032 873-G6
14500 LGTS 95032 873-G6
N LEIGH AV
1500 SJS 95125 853-H5
1600 CMBL 95008 853-H5
1600 CMBL 95125 853-H5
1800 SCIC 95125 853-H5
S LEIGH AV
1800 CMBL 95008 853-H6
1800 SCIC 95125 853-H6
LEIGH CT
14400 SCIC 95124 873-G3
LEIGH ST
47900 FRMT 94539 793-J1
LEIGH-ANN PL
1900 SCIC 95125 853-H6
LEIGHTON WY
900 SUNV 94087 832-G5
LEILA CT
15400 LGTS 95032 873-D5
LEISURE CT
3100 SJS 95132 814-G5
LEISURE DR
100 MGH 95037 937-B5
LEITH AV
800 SCL 95054 813-E6
LEKSICH AV
600 MTVW 94041 811-G5
LELAND AV
100 SMCo 94025 790-E6
200 PA 94306 791-A7
300 SCIC 95128 853-G1
300 SJS 95128 853-G1
2100 MTVW 94040 811-F3
LELAND CIR
14400 SAR 95070 872-G3
LELAND PARK CT
6500 SJS 95120 894-C1
LELONG ST
1100 SJS 95110 854-B2
N LEMON AV
1100 MLPK 94025 790-E5
LEMON ST
400 MLPK 94025 790-E6
LEMON BLOSSOM CT
- SJS 95123 875-B3
LEMONTREE CT
1700 MTVW 94040 831-G1
LEMON TREE RD
1100 SJS 95120 874-D7
LEMONWOOD CT
700 SJS 95120 894-H2
LEMOYNE WY
2200 SJS 95008 853-B7

LENA AV
- SCIC 95020 957-H2
LENA DR
2700 SJS 95124 873-J1
LENARK CT
1100 SJS 95132 814-G5
LENARK DR
3100 SJS 95132 814-G5
LENCAR WY
1700 SJS 95124 873-H3
LENDRUM AV
2300 SJS 95116 834-H3
LENELLE CT
5000 SJS 95118 873-J4
LENFEST RD
600 SJS 95133 834-D2
LENN DR
1800 SJS 95125 853-J5
LENNON WY
1100 SJS 95125 854-A5
LENNOX AV
200 MLPK 94025 790-F2
LENNOX CT
800 SUNV 94087 832-C4
LENNOX WY
1300 SUNV 94087 832-C4
LENOR WY
1000 CMBL 95128 853-E4
LENORA AV
5300 SJS 95124 873-J5
LENORE CT
18200 SCIC 95030 912-H3
LENOX CT
- SCL 95054 813-C4
LENOX PL
- SCL 95054 813-C4
LENOX WY
13400 LAH 94022 811-D7
LENRAY LN
14300 SCIC 95124 873-G3
LENWOOD WY
6800 SJS 95120 894-F2
LENZEN AV
300 SJS 95110 834-A5
500 SJS 95110 833-J6
700 SJS 95126 833-J6
LENZEN CT
400 SJS 95126 833-J6
LEO AV
200 SJS 95112 854-E3
LEO DR
900 SJS 95129 853-A3
LEO PL
- MntC - (1017-A6 See Page 997)
LEOLA CT
10300 CPTO 95014 852-G1
LEOMINSTER CT
- SJS 95139 875-G7
LEON DR
2000 SJS 95128 853-G3
LEON WY
- ATN 94027 790-F3
LEONA CT
14200 SCIC 95046 937-F3
LEONA LN
500 MTVW 94040 811-H7
LEONARD CT
3300 SCL 95054 813-D6
LEONARD RD
20500 SAR 95070 852-D7
LEONELLO AV
900 LALT 94024 831-G2
LEONG CT
7800 CPTO 95014 852-C2
LEONG DR
600 MTVW 94043 812-A3
LEONTINE CT
48000 FRMT 94539 793-J1
LEOTA AV
100 SUNV 94086 812-C7
LEOTAR CT
100 LGTS 95032 893-D1
LEPA CT
700 SCIC 95020 957-J5
LEPTIS CIR
2300 MGH 95037 917-E6
LERIDA AV
300 LALT 94024 811-F7
LERIDA CT
- SMCo 94028 810-D4
LERMA LN
1200 GIL 95020 977-F1
LERMA WY
1100 GIL 95020 977-F1
LEROY AV
16700 LGTS 95032 873-C5
LERWICK CT
1100 SUNV 94087 832-H5

STREET
Block City ZIP Pg-Grid

LE SABRE CT
500 MGH 95037 917-B7
LESHER CT
1400 SJS 95125 854-A5
LESLEY LN
14000 SCIC 95046 937-H3
LESLIE CT
200 MTVW 94043 812-A4
16900 MGH 95037 917-G5
LESLIE DR
1000 SJS 95117 853-B3
LESLY CT
- SBnC - (1020-E1
See Page 999)
LESTER AV
1100 SJS 95125 854-A3
1100 SJS 95125 853-J3
LESTER CT
300 SCL 95051 833-B7
LESTER LN
100 LGTS 95032 873-D4
LETITIA CT
1200 SJS 95122 854-H2
LETITIA ST
1200 SJS 95122 854-H2
LEUTAR CT
20300 SAR 95070 852-E5
LEVEE RD
- SCIC 95035 813-G1
- SJS 95134 813-G1
LEVEN PLACE WY
3900 SJS 95121 855-C4
LEVIN AV
300 MTVW 94040 831-J2
800 MTVW 94040 832-A2
LEVIN CT
2700 MTVW 94040 831-J2
LEVIN ST
300 MPS 95035 794-A3
LEWIS AV
800 SUNV 94086 812-D7
LEWIS RD
- SJS 95111 854-H4
200 SCIC 95111 854-G5
300 MntC - (1016-C6
See Page 995)
LEWIS ST
- GIL 95020 978-A3
700 SCL 95050 833-E4
LEWISTON CT
700 SUNV 94087 832-C4
LEWISTON DR
700 SJS 95136 874-D1
1300 SUNV 94087 832-C5
LEXANN AV
1500 SJS 95121 855-A3
LEXFORD AV
2700 SJS 95124 873-H1
LEXINGTON AV
- SJS 95119 875-C5
- SJS 95193 875-C5
LEXINGTON CT
13600 SAR 95070 872-E1
18300 MSER 95030 872-E1
LEXINGTON DR
200 MLPK 94025 790-J3
1100 SUNV 94087 832-B2
1400 SJS 95117 853-D4
18200 MSER 95030 872-J5
LEXINGTON PL
700 GIL 95020 977-J4
LEXINGTON ST
600 MPS 95035 793-J6
900 SCL 95050 833-E5
LEXINGTON SCHOOL RD
19800 SCIC 95030 892-J6
LEYLAND PARK DR
6500 SJS 95120 894-C1
LEYTE CT
800 SJS 95111 855-A6
LIBERATA DR
2200 SCIC 95037 917-D4
LIBERIA CIR
1900 SJS 95116 834-G3
LIBERTY CT
- SJS 95002 793-B7
900 CPTO 95014 852-B2
LIBERTY ST
1400 SJS 95002 813-B1
1600 SJS 95002 793-B7
1900 SCL 95050 833-D5
LIBERTY OAK LN
22700 CPTO 95014 831-J7
LIBERTY PARK AV
2000 SMCo 94025 790-D6
LIBRA LN
3300 SJS 95111 854-F6
LIBRARY LN
1100 SJS 95116 834-E5

LIBRETTO CT
1800 SJS 95131 814-C4
LICK AV
1000 SJS 95110 854-C2
LICK MILL BLVD
3800 SCL 95134 813-D3
4200 SCL 95054 813-D3
LICK MILL RD
1400 SCL 95134 813-D5
1400 SCL 95054 813-D5
LIDA DR
2300 MTVW 94043 811-F3
LIDDICOAT CIR
14300 LAH 94022 810-H5
LIDDICOAT DR
14100 LAH 94022 810-H5
LIDO WY
1700 SJS 95116 834-G5
12600 SAR 95070 852-E6
LIEB CT
14000 SJS 95127 835-A4
LIEB LN
1500 SJS 95131 814-A5
LIEBELT CT
1000 SJS 95126 853-H3
LIEBRE CT
200 SUNV 94086 812-C7
LIETZ AV
1500 SJS 95118 874-A5
1500 SJS 95118 873-J5
LIGHTFARE CT
3600 SJS 95121 855-A4
LIGHTLAND RD
1100 SJS 95121 855-A5
LIGHTSON ST
- SJS 95113 834-B6
LIGURIAN CT
5200 SJS 95138 855-F6
LIGURIAN DR
5100 SJS 95138 855-G7
LIKA CT
12700 SAR 95070 852-E6
LILAC CT
7800 CPTO 95014 852-C2
LILAC LN
300 EPA 94303 791-B1
600 SJS 95136 854-E7
800 LALT 94024 831-E1
1500 MTVW 94043 811-H3
1800 SCIC 95037 936-G4
16100 SCIC 95032 873-D6
16300 LGTS 95032 873-D6
LILAC WY
700 SCIC 95032 873-C6
700 LGTS 95032 873-C6
800 CPTO 95014 852-C2
LILAC BLOSSOM LN
5600 SJS 95124 873-J6
LILLIAN AV
1300 SUNV 94087 832-F4
LILLIAN WY
6200 SJS 95120 874-E7
6400 SJS 95120 894-E1
LILLICK DR
1100 SUNV 94087 832-H4
1100 SCL 95051 832-H4
LILLIPUT LN
2500 SJS 95116 834-J4
LILLY AV
100 GIL 95020 977-J1
8700 GIL 95020 957-J7
LILLY LN
700 MGH 95037 917-D7
LILY AV
800 CPTO 95014 852-C2
1000 SUNV 94086 832-H2
LILY CT
7800 CPTO 95014 852-C2
LILY ANN WY
400 SJS 95123 875-B3
LILY BLOSSOM CT
100 SJS 95123 875-A4
LIMA CT
1500 SJS 95126 853-H3
LIMAN AV
- GIL 95020 957-H7
LIME DR
1100 SUNV 94087 832-B3
LIME BLOSSOM CT
100 SJS 95123 875-A3
LIMEKILN CANYON RD
16000 SCIC 95030 893-A3
LIMERICK CT
700 SUNV 94087 832-F5
LIMETREE LN
1800 MTVW 94040 831-G1
LIMEWELL CT
- SJS 95138 875-D4
LIMEWOOD DR
1900 SJS 95132 814-E2

LINARIA WY
- SMCo 94028 810-D4
LINBURN CT
2900 SJS 95148 855-B2
LINCOLN AV
100 PA 94301 790-J5
200 SJS 95126 853-J1
200 PA 94301 791-A4
400 SUNV 94086 812-E7
400 SCIC 95126 853-J1
500 LALT 94022 811-D7
600 LALT 94022 831-E1
900 SJS 95126 854-A3
1000 SJS 95125 854-A3
13000 SCIC 95046 937-F6
LINCOLN CT
400 GIL 95020 957-J7
800 SJS 95125 854-B5
LINCOLN DR
1100 MTVW 94040 831-G1
LINCOLN ST
400 SCL 95128 833-D4
400 SCL 95050 833-D4
2000 EPA 94303 791-A2
LINCOLN ST Rt#-152
500 WAT 95076 (1015-G1
See Page 995)
LINCOLNSHIRE WY
1100 SJS 95125 854-F5
LINCOLN VILLAGE DR
2400 SJS 95125 854-D7
LINDA AV
15500 SCIC 95032 873-D5
15900 LGTS 95032 873-E6
LINDA DR
800 CMBL 95008 873-B1
800 CMBL 95008 853-C7
LINDA LN
28000 LAH 94304 810-H4
LINDA ANN CT
22400 CPTO 95014 832-A6
LINDA ANN PL
10100 CPTO 95014 852-F1
LINDA FLORA ST
700 SCIC 95127 814-J6
LINDAHL CT
1300 SJS 95120 874-C7
LINDAIRE AV
2200 SCIC 95128 853-F3
2300 SJS 95128 853-F3
LINDA MESA DR
17000 MGH 95037 917-E6
LINDA VISTA AV
- ATN 94027 790-C4
800 MTVW 94043 811-J3
19100 SCIC 95030 872-F6
LINDA VISTA DR
10700 CPTO 95014 852-A2
LINDA VISTA LN
9200 SCIC 95020 957-B7
LINDA VISTA PL
22000 CPTO 95014 852-B2
LINDA VISTA ST
700 SCIC 95127 814-H6
LINDA VISTA WY
800 LALT 94024 831-G2
LINDBERGH AV
2200 SJS 95128 853-F3
LINDBERGH DR
21600 SCIC 95030 912-G4
LINDEN AV
- ATN 94027 790-G1
600 LALT 94022 811-D5
LINDEN DR
- SCL 95050 833-F5
1100 SJS 95126 833-F5
LINDEN LN
1900 MPS 95035 793-J3
LINDENBROOK LN
19800 CPTO 95014 852-F2
LINDENOAKS DR
3200 SJS 95117 853-D2
LINDENTREE LN
2600 SCL 95051 833-B6
LINDENWOOD DR
3600 SJS 95117 853-C2
LINDER HILL CT
1200 SJS 95120 894-G4
LINDER HILL LN
1200 SJS 95120 894-G4
LINDERO DR
3700 PA 94306 811-D1
LINDMUIR DR
3200 SJS 95121 855-A4
LINDO CT
200 MGH 95037 916-J7
LINDO LN
100 MGH 95037 916-J7
LINDSAY AV
10300 CPTO 95014 852-F1

LINDSAY WY
1300 SJS 95118 874-B1
LINDSAY ANN TER
1400 SJS 95131 814-C6
LINDSAY CREEK LN
7100 SJS 95120 894-G4
LINDSTROM CT
500 SJS 95111 875-C2
LINDY LN
21600 CPTO 95014 852-A3
LINDY PL
11300 CPTO 95014 852-B3
LINFIELD DR
400 MLPK 94025 790-G4
E LINFIELD DR
100 MLPK 94025 790-H3
LINFIELD PL
300 MLPK 94025 790-H3
LINKFIELD WY
3000 SJS 95135 855-G3
LINKHORNE CT
300 SJS 95133 834-F2
LINKSHEAD CT
3100 SJS 95148 855-D1
LINNET LN
1700 SUNV 94087 832-F6
10600 CPTO 95014 832-F6
LINNET WY
1700 SUNV 94087 832-F6
LINTON CT
3800 SJS 95121 855-C4
LINWELL CT
- SJS 95138 875-D5
LINWOOD DR
4100 SJS 95124 873-H3
LIONS CREEK DR
8700 GIL 95020 977-F1
LIONWOOD PL
400 SJS 95111 875-C2
LIQUIDAMBAR WY
400 SUNV 94086 832-G1
LIQUIDAMBER CT
400 SJS 95111 854-G7
LISA CT
- GIL 95020 977-J7
1200 LALT 94024 831-H3
2100 SCIC 95037 917-E5
LISA LN
- SBnC - (1020-E3
See Page 999)
500 SJS 95134 813-C2
1100 LALT 94024 831-H3
LISA WY
600 SJS 95130 853-C4
600 CMBL 95008 853-C4
LISBON CT
3600 SJS 95132 814-F1
LISBON DR
3400 SJS 95132 814-E2
LISBON TER
400 MPS 95035 793-G3
LISKA LN
5900 SJS 95119 875-C6
LISMORE CT
3000 SJS 95135 855-F3
LISSOW DR
- SJS 95119 875-C6
LITA LN
- EPA 94303 791-C2
LITCHFIELD LN
- SCrC 95076 (975-D6
See Page 955)
LITCHFIELD PL
2000 SCL 95051 833-D2
LITCHI GROVE CT
100 SJS 95123 874-J3
LITE CT
5900 SJS 95138 875-E5
LITTLE AV
- SJS 95119 875-D5
LITTLE BEAR WY
- SJS 95136 874-H2
LITTLE BOY LN
2600 SJS 95148 835-F7
LITTLE BRANHAM LN
1700 SJS 95124 873-H4
LITTLEBROOK DR
19000 SCIC 95030 872-F6
LITTLE FALLS DR
6400 SJS 95120 894-D1
LITTLEFIELD LN
16600 LGTS 95032 873-C7
16600 SCIC 95032 873-C7
LITTLEJOHN WY
6100 SJS 95129 852-G3
LITTLE LLAGAS AV
17200 SCIC 95037 936-E2
LITTLEMEADOW CT
4400 SJS 95129 853-A2

LITTLEOAK CIR
1100 SJS 95129 852-H3
LITTLEOAK DR
1000 SJS 95129 852-H3
LITTLE ORCHARD ST
1400 SJS 95110 854-D2
1400 SJS 95125 854-D3
LITTLE RIVER CT
4700 SJS 95136 874-E2
LITTLE ROCK CT
2800 SJS 95133 814-G7
LITTLE ROCK DR
2800 SJS 95133 814-G7
LITTLETON DR
1200 SJS 95131 834-C1
LITTLETON PL
1600 CMBL 95008 873-A1
LITTLE UVAS RD
4600 SCIC 95037 936-A3
4700 SCIC 95037 935-G2
LITTLE WOOD LN
2900 SJS 95127 834-H1
LITTLEWORTH WY
4100 SJS 95135 855-F3
LITTMAN DR
1200 SJS 95120 894-C1
LITTON CT
600 SUNV 94087 832-E5
LIVE OAK AV
- SCIC 95037 916-E2
- SJS 95037 916-E2
600 MLPK 94025 790-F4
LIVE OAK CT
3800 MGH 95037 917-H5
LIVEOAK CT
300 MPS 95035 813-J3
LIVE OAK DR
900 SCL 95051 833-A5
LIVE OAK LN
200 LALT 94022 811-D6
3700 MGH 95037 917-H5
14600 SAR 95070 872-F3
LIVE OAK WY
700 SJS 95129 853-A2
LIVERPOOL AV
1600 SJS 95124 873-J3
LIVERPOOL WY
700 SUNV 94087 832-F5
LIVERY LN
7000 SJS 95135 876-A1
LIVINGSTON AV
1400 SJS 95125 854-A6
LIVORNO CT
5400 SJS 95138 875-F1
LIZZIE LN
4400 SJS 95118 874-C2
LJEPAVA DR
20000 SAR 95070 852-E7
LLAGAS AV
12000 SCIC 95046 937-E4
12000 SCIC 95046 957-G1
LLAGAS CT
18300 MGH 95037 916-H6
LLAGAS RD
200 MGH 95037 916-H6
700 SCIC 95037 916-H6
1900 SCIC 95037 936-F2
1900 MGH 95037 936-F2
LLAGAS CREEK DR
18200 MGH 95037 916-G6
LLAGAS VISTA DR
600 MGH 95037 916-G6
LLAMA LN
8700 SCIC 95020 958-F5
LLANO LN
13900 SCIC 95046 937-A7
LLEWELLYN AV
- CMBL 95008 853-D5
LLOYD WY
1300 MTVW 94040 811-G6
LLOYDEN DR
- ATN 94027 790-D2
LLOYDEN PARK LN
300 ATN 94027 790-D2
LOBELIA LN
1600 SJS 95124 873-J6
LOBOS AV
4500 SJS 95111 875-A1
LO BUE WY
4100 SJS 95111 855-A7
LOCHBURRY CT
500 SJS 95123 874-G3
LOCHINVAR AV
1100 SUNV 94087 832-J5
3300 SCL 95051 832-J5
LOCHINVAR WY
15100 SCIC 95132 814-H4
LOCH LOMOND CT
300 MPS 95035 794-A6
500 SUNV 94087 832-E5

LOCH LOMOND LN
1500 SJS 95129 852-E4
LOCH LOMOND ST
3700 SCL 95054 813-E6
LOCHNER DR
1400 SJS 95127 835-A4
LOCHNESS CT
1000 SUNV 94087 832-G5
LOCH NESS WY
1700 SJS 95121 855-B3
LOCHRIDGE DR
300 SJS 95133 834-E3
LOCKE DR
3100 SJS 95111 854-J5
LOCKFORD CT
7500 CPTO 95014 852-D3
LOCKHART LN
100 LALT 94022 811-D6
LOCKHAVEN CT
800 LALT 94024 831-H5
LOCKHAVEN DR
800 LALT 94024 831-H5
LOCKHAVEN WY
1100 SJS 95129 852-G4
LOCKHEED WY
1100 SUNV 94089 812-E4
LOCKSLEY PARK DR
1500 SJS 95132 814-F3
LOCKSUNART WY
100 SUNV 94087 832-E5
LOCKWOOD DR
2000 SJS 95132 814-E2
10100 CPTO 95014 851-J1
LOCUST DR
17300 SCIC 95030 913-A1
21500 SCIC 95030 912-J3
LOCUST RD
24200 SCIC 95030 913-F7
LOCUST ST
100 RDWC 94061 790-B1
600 SJS 95110 854-C1
700 SCL 95050 833-F5
LODESTONE DR
1200 SJS 95132 814-E5
LODGE CT
1300 SJS 95121 854-J3
LODGEPOLE CT
1400 GIL 95020 977-G3
LODGEWOOD CT
700 SJS 95120 894-H3
LODI LN
2500 SJS 95124 853-J7
LOES WY
3400 SJS 95127 835-B2
LOGAN CT
800 SUNV 94087 832-C5
LOGAN LN
- ATN 94027 790-C2
LOGANBERRY DR
3900 SJS 95121 855-E4
8800 GIL 95020 977-F1
9000 GIL 95020 957-F7
LOGIC DR
2000 SJS 95124 873-F3
LOGSDEN WY
2500 SJS 95122 834-J4
LOGUE AV
300 MTVW 94043 812-C5
LOIRE CT
- SJS 95135 855-F3
LOIS AV
700 SUNV 94087 832-B1
LOIS LN
100 PA 94303 791-B4
LOIS ST
300 MTVW 94043 811-F3
LOIS WY
1400 SCIC 95008 873-E1
LOLA LN
600 MTVW 94040 811-H7
LOLLIE CT
1600 SJS 95124 873-J2
LOLLY CT
12400 SAR 95070 852-H6
LOLLY DR
12300 SAR 95070 852-H5
LOMA CT
- SJS 95131 814-A5
LOMA PKWY
6700 GIL 95020 977-G4
LOMA ST
16700 SCIC 95032 873-C7
LOMA ALMADEN RD
20000 SCIC 95030 913-F1
21600 SCIC 95030 914-A4
LOMA ALTA AV
- LGTS 95032 893-B1
LOMA ALTA CT
16100 SCIC 95037 936-J3

LOMA ALTA DR
3100 SCL 95051 833-A5
LOMA CHIQUITA RD
29000 SCIC 95037 934-H2
29000 SCIC 95030 934-G3
32900 SJS 95037 935-A3
LOMA LINDA DR
- SJS 95129 852-J1
LOMA PARK CT
2300 SJS 95124 853-H7
LOMA PARK DR
2200 SJS 95124 853-H7
LOMA PRIETA AV
- SCrC 95019 995-D6
- WAT 95019 995-D6
- WAT 95076 995-D6
25100 SCIC 95030 913-F7
25100 SCrC 95030 913-F7
26100 SCrC 95030 934-C3
26100 SCIC 95030 934-A2
29100 SCIC 95037 934-F3
LOMA PRIETA CT
1000 LALT 94024 831-H2
LOMA PRIETA DR
5900 SJS 95123 874-G6
LOMA PRIETA LN
2300 MLPK 94025 790-D7
LOMA PRIETA RD
- SCIC 95037 934-F2
22500 SCIC 95030 913-H6
23200 SCIC 95030 914-A5
24100 SCIC 95030 934-D1
24300 SCIC 95120 934-F1
LOMA PRIETA WY
21900 SCIC 95030 913-B3
LOMA RIO DR
14000 SAR 95070 872-E2
LOMAS LN
15700 SCIC 95030 872-G6
LOMAS AZULES CT
8700 SJS 95135 855-J7
LOMAS AZULES PL
8600 SJS 95135 855-J6
LOMA VERDE AV
100 PA 94306 791-C7
700 PA 94303 791-C7
LOMA VERDE DR
3100 SJS 95117 853-D4
LOMA VERDE PL
3100 PA 94303 791-D6
LOMA VISTA AV
15500 SCIC 95032 873-D5
LOMA VISTA CT
100 LGTS 95032 873-D5
LOMA VISTA LN
2400 SCL 95051 833-C1
LOMBARD AV
2500 SJS 95116 834-H3
LOMENT CT
2300 SJS 95124 873-E3
LOMENT PL
2400 SJS 95124 873-E3
LOMER WY
400 MPS 95035 794-D7
LOMETA AV
200 SUNV 94086 812-C7
LOMITA AV
20500 SAR 95070 872-D3
21600 CPTO 95014 852-B1
21800 SCIC 95014 852-B1
LOMITA CT
600 SCIC 94305 810-G1
LOMITA DR
500 SCIC 94305 790-H6
500 SCIC 94305 810-G1
LOMITA LINDA DR
25700 LAH 94024 831-E4
LOMITAS CT
- MLPK 94025 790-F6
LOMOND CT
13500 SAR 95070 872-F1
LOMPICO DR
600 SJS 95123 874-G4
LOMPICO RD
12600 SCrC 95018 912-B7
LONARDO AV
4300 SJS 95118 874-B2
LONDON AV
1100 SUNV 94087 832-H6
LONDON DR
200 GIL 95020 978-A5
600 MPS 95035 794-B3
4700 SJS 95008 873-A1
LONDONDERRY DR
700 SUNV 94087 832-F5
3300 SCL 95050 833-C7
LONDONDERRY PL
3300 SCL 95050 833-D7
LONDON PARK CT
400 SJS 95136 874-F1

LONE BLUFF WY
2600 SJS 95111 854-H4
LONE DEER WY
9300 GIL 95020 957-F7
LONE HILL DR
16600 MGH 95037 937-A1
LONE HILL RD
5000 SJS 95124 873-H5
11000 SJS 95032 873-H5
LONE OAK CIR
21800 SCIC 95120 895-C4
LONE OAK CT
2700 SCIC 95020 977-D2
LONE OAK DR
2400 SJS 95121 855-E4
LONE OAK LN
10400 LAH 94024 831-E5
LONE PINE LN
1100 SJS 95120 894-E2
LONETREE CT
- MPS 95035 814-A3
LONE TREE RD
1500 SBnC - (1021-G2
See Page 1001)
LONG CT
6100 SJS 95123 875-A6
LONG ST
1600 SCL 95050 833-D3
LONGACRE CT
2800 SJS 95121 855-A2
LONGBRANCH CT
1100 SJS 95126 853-G4
LONGDALE DR
3100 SJS 95124 873-H2
LONGDEN CIR
2000 LALT 94024 831-G5
LONGDOWN RD
22800 CPTO 95014 851-H1
LONGFELLOW AV
1000 SJS 95008 873-D3
LONGFELLOW CT
6900 SJS 95129 852-E4
LONGFELLOW WY
1200 SJS 95129 852-E4
LONGFORD DR
2700 SJS 95132 814-E5
LONGLEY AV
900 SJS 95125 854-A3
LONGMEADOW DR
100 LGTS 95032 873-D7
1200 GIL 95020 957-E7
LONG OAK LN
10000 CPTO 95014 831-J6
LONG RIDGE RD
- SMCo 94020 850-G5
LONGRIDGE RD
200 LGTS 95032 873-D4
LONGSHORE DR
1000 SCIC 95128 853-F3
1000 SJS 95128 853-F3
LONGSPUR
- PTLV 94028 830-C1
LONGSPUR AV
1500 SUNV 94087 832-F5
LONGVIEW DR
200 MGH 95037 916-H7
LONGVIEW ST
1600 SJS 95122 834-G6
LONGWOOD DR
15500 SCIC 95032 873-D5
LONGWOOD LN
900 SJS 95129 852-J3
LONNA LN
800 CPTO 95014 852-D2
LONUS ST
800 SJS 95126 854-A2
800 SJS 95126 853-J2
LOO LN
1400 SJS 95131 814-C6
LOOKOUT BEND
6700 SJS 95120 894-D2
LOOMIS CT
2500 SJS 95121 854-H2
LOOMIS DR
2400 SJS 95121 854-H2
LOOP RD
400 SJS 95120 895-B3
LOPEZ CT
14900 SCIC 95046 937-E3
LOPINA WY
- SJS 95129 853-A1
LOQUAT CT
13900 SAR 95070 872-J1
LORA DR
14200 LGTS 95030 873-A2
LORABELLE CT
4200 PA 94306 811-D3
LORAIN PL
100 LGTS 95030 873-B3

LORAINE AV
900 LALT 94024 831-G3
LOREE AV
18500 SCIC 95014 852-G1
LORELEI CT
1200 CMBL 95008 853-B6
LORENE CT
13000 MTVW 94040 832-A1
LORENZEN DR
1700 SJS 95124 853-H7
LORETO ST
200 MTVW 94041 811-J5
LORETTA LN
- SCIC 95008 873-D3
LORI AV
800 SUNV 94086 812-D6
LORI LN
- MGH 95037 917-G5
LORNE WY
900 SUNV 94087 832-G5
LORRAINE AV
500 SJS 95110 834-A7
LORWICK WY
1800 SJS 95121 855-C4
LOS ALAMOS DR
17800 SJS 95130 853-A4
LOS ALTOS AV
- LALT 94022 811-D6
LOS ALTOS CT
200 LALT 94022 811-D6
3800 SJS 95121 855-D3
LOS ALTOS DR
2700 SJS 95121 855-D3
LOS ALTOS SQ
- LALT 94022 811-E4
LOS ALTURAS
100 LGTS 95030 872-J3
LOS ARBOLES AV
300 SJS 95111 854-J6
500 SCIC 94305 790-F7
1300 SUNV 94087 832-D4
LOS BUELLIS WY
1400 MPS 95035 793-H3
LOS CERRITOS DR
17000 LGTS 95032 893-C1
LOS CHARROS LN
- PTLV 94028 810-C6
LOS COCHES AV
2300 SCIC 95128 853-F1
2600 SJS 95128 853-F1
LOS COCHES ST
300 MPS 95035 794-B7
LOS COYOTES CT
2500 SCIC 95020 958-D5
LOS ENCINAS CT
1600 CMBL 95030 873-A2
1600 CMBL 95030 872-J1
LOS ENCINOS AV
300 SJS 95134 813-E2
LOS ENCINOS CT
300 SJS 95134 813-E2
LOS ENCINOS DR
300 SJS 95134 813-E2
LOS ENCINOS ST
300 SJS 95134 813-E2
LOS ESTEROS RD
700 SJS 95134 793-D7
700 SJS 95002 793-D7
LOS FELICE DR
17800 SJS 95130 853-A4
17900 SJS 95129 853-A4
LOS GATOS BLVD
- SJS 95124 873-B7
- LGTS 95032 873-B7
15900 SCIC 95032 873-B7
LOS GATOS ALMADEN RD
1600 SJS 95124 873-D5
1700 SJS 95032 873-G5
1900 LGTS 95032 873-D5
16000 SCIC 95032 873-D5
LOS HUECOS DR
600 SJS 95123 874-G6
LOS NINOS WY
400 LALT 94022 811-E5
LOS OLIVOS DR
500 SCL 95050 833-C5
17900 SJS 95130 853-A4
LOS PADRES BLVD
300 SCL 95050 833-C2
LOS PADRES CT
7600 GIL 95020 977-H3
LOS PAJAROS CT
400 LALT 94024 831-F1
LOS PALMOS WY
200 SJS 95119 875-C6
LOS PALOS AV
4200 PA 94306 811-D3
LOS PALOS CIR
4200 PA 94306 811-D3

LOS PALOS CT
4100 SJS 95118 874-C2
LOS PALOS PL
4200 PA 94306 811-D3
LOS PALOS WY
1300 SJS 95118 874-B2
LOS PATIOS
100 LGTS 95030 873-A2
100 LGTS 95030 872-J2
LOS PINOS AV
500 MPS 95035 794-B5
LOS PINOS WY
300 SJS 95119 875-A7
300 SJS 95123 875-A7
LOS POSITOS DR
700 MPS 95035 794-B6
LOS RIOS CT
1500 SJS 95120 874-A7
LOS RIOS DR
1400 SJS 95120 874-A7
1500 SJS 95120 894-A1
LOS ROBLES AV
600 PA 94306 811-C2
LOS ROBLES CT
- SMCo 94025 790-D5
LOS ROBLES WY
17000 LGTS 95032 873-B7
LOSSE ST
500 SJS 95110 834-A5
LOS SERENOS ROBLES
16200 SCIC 95030 872-G6
LOS SUENOS AV
1600 SJS 95116 834-G5
LOSTCREEK CT
3200 SJS 95121 855-D7
LOST LAKE LN
- CMBL 95008 873-D1
LOST OAKS DR
2300 SJS 95124 873-D4
LOST RANCH RD
7700 SCIC 95120 894-J2
LOS TRANCOS CIR
100 SMCo 94028 830-D4
LOS TRANCOS RD
- PA 94304 830-D2
- PTLV 94028 810-D7
100 PA 94304 810-D7
900 PTLV 94028 830-D2
900 SMCo 94028 830-D4
LOST TRAIL CT
- SJS 95136 874-H3
LOST VIEW RD
7700 SCIC 95120 895-D5
LOS VIBORAS RD
- SBnC - (1000-E
See Page 999
LOTISLAKE CT
700 SUNV 94089 812-H
LOTUS LN
400 MTVW 94043 811-H
LOTUS ST
600 SJS 95116 834-F
LOTUS WY
100 EPA 94303 791-D
17300 MGH 95037 917-B
LOUCKS AV
- LALT 94022 811-D
LOUIS CT
200 SCrC 95076 (975-A
See Page 955
3500 SJS 95127 835-B
LOUIS RD
1900 PA 94303 791-C
3800 PA 94303 811-F
LOUISA CT
1500 PA 94303 791-B
LOUISE AV
900 SJS 95125 854-B
LOUISE CT
100 LGTS 95030 872-J
300 MPS 95035 794-E
600 CMBL 95008 853-C
LOUISE DR
800 SUNV 94087 832-C
LOUISE LN
2000 LALT 94024 832-A
LOUISE ST
1000 MLPK 94025 790-E
LOUIS HOLSTROM DR
2100 SCIC 95037 936-F
LOUMENA LN
400 SJS 95111 854-
LOUPE AV
900 SJS 95121 854-J
1100 SJS 95121 855-A
LOUPE CT
200 GIL 95020 977-
LOVE HARRIS RD
20000 SCIC 95030 893-
20100 SCIC 95030 913-

STREET
Block City ZIP Pg-Grid

LOVELAND CT
14200 SAR 95070 872-E2
LOVELL AV
900 CMBL 95008 873-B1
LOVELL PL
2000 SCL 95051 833-A3
LOVERS LN
6500 SBnC - 999-G2
8900 SCIC 95020 999-G2
LOVEWOOD WY
2900 SJS 95148 855-D1
LOVOI WY
1000 SJS 95125 854-B5
LOWELL AV
100 PA 94301 791-A6
LOWELL CT
700 SUNV 94087 832-C5
LOWELL DR
200 SCL 95051 832-H7
LOWELL LN
- SJS 95125 854-B7
LOWELL WY
- CMBL 95008 853-E6
LOWENA CT
20700 SAR 95070 852-D5
LOWER HIGHLAND RD
1800 SCrC 95076 955-A4
LOWER HUTCHINSON RD
200 SCrC 95030 912-F7
LOWERY DR
- ATN 94027 790-G1
LOWLAND CT
1300 MPS 95035 814-E2
LOWNEY WY
1900 SJS 95131 814-D6
LOWRY DR
3000 SJS 95118 874-B1
LOYALTON DR
700 CMBL 95008 853-A7
700 CMBL 95008 873-A1
LOYE WY
2900 SJS 95148 835-E7
LOYOLA AV
- SMCo 94063 790-D1
LOYOLA CT
1000 SCL 95051 833-B5
LOYOLA DR
500 SCIC 94024 831-F4
1100 SCL 95051 833-B4
1700 SJS 95122 834-H6
W LOYOLA DR
10100 SCIC 94024 831-F5
LU ANNE DR
100 CMBL 95008 853-B5
LUBEC ST
21400 CPTO 95014 832-C7
LUBICH DR
1200 MTVW 94040 832-A2
LUBY DR
1800 SJS 95133 834-E2
LUCAS CT
3000 SJS 95148 835-F7
LUCAS DR
3600 SJS 95148 835-F7
LUCCA PL
- SJS 95138 855-E7
LUCE CT
700 MTVW 94041 812-A7
LUCENA CT
1400 SJS 95132 814-E4
LUCENA DR
2600 SJS 95132 814-E5
LUCERNE AV
500 RDWC 94061 790-B1
LUCERNE DR
700 SUNV 94086 812-G7
LUCERNE WY
2400 SJS 95122 834-J5
LUCERO LN
12800 LAH 94022 831-A1
LUCERO WY
100 SMCo 94028 810-D3
LUCHESSA AV
- GIL 95020 978-B5
LUCHESSI CT
1100 SJS 95118 874-D2
LUCHESSI DR
1100 SJS 95118 874-C3
LUCIAN AV
3300 SJS 95127 814-J7
4000 SCIC 95127 814-J7
LUCILLE AV
20000 CPTO 95014 832-E6
LUCKY AV
900 SMCo 94025 790-D6
LUCKY CT
10200 SCIC 95046 957-D5
LUCKY RD
16200 MSER 95030 872-G7

LUCKY RD
16200 SCIC 95030 872-G7
LUCKY OAK ST
10900 CPTO 95014 832-A6
11000 CPTO 94024 832-A6
LUCOT WY
1000 CMBL 95008 873-B2
LUCRETIA AV
1100 SJS 95122 834-F7
1400 SJS 95122 854-G1
1900 SCIC 95122 854-G1
LUCRETIA CIR
900 SJS 95122 854-H2
LUCRETIA CT
1600 SJS 95122 854-F1
LUCY MAY TR
18100 SCIC 95030 912-G4
LUDLOW CT
3100 SJS 95148 855-C2
LUDLOW WY
300 SJS 95133 834-F2
LUFKIN CT
3600 SJS 95148 835-F7
LUGANO WY
2900 SJS 95132 814-F5
LUIKA PL
1600 CMBL 95008 873-A1
LUJOSO CT
1400 SJS 95128 853-F4
LUKE CT
1800 SJS 95116 834-H5
LULLABY LN
4400 SJS 95111 855-A7
LUMBERTOWN LN
21100 SAR 95070 872-C3
LUNADA DR
300 LALT 94022 811-D3
LUNAR CT
7800 CPTO 95014 852-C3
LUNDER CT
1900 SJS 95131 814-E7
LUNDY AV
900 SJS 95133 834-D1
1100 SJS 95131 834-D1
1200 SJS 95131 814-B4
LUNDY LN
- LGTS 95030 893-A1
100 PA 94306 811-D2
800 SCIC 94024 831-H4
LUNDY PL
500 SJS 95131 814-B4
500 MPS 95035 814-B4
LUNETA CT
3900 SJS 95136 874-F1
LUNETA DR
4000 SJS 95136 874-F1
LUNING DR
1300 SJS 95118 874-A3
LUPIN LN
- ATN 94027 790-G1
LUPINE AV
3500 PA 94303 791-E7
LUPINE CT
1400 GIL 95020 977-F1
1400 SCIC 95046 937-E5
1400 SJS 95118 874-B1
LUPINE DR
1000 SUNV 94086 832-G2
LUPINE RD
27700 LAH 94022 810-J6
LUPTON AV
1400 SJS 95125 854-A4
LU-RAY DR
100 LGTS 95032 873-E5
LUSARDI DR
2200 SJS 95148 855-D2
LUSTERLEAF DR
700 SUNV 94086 832-G2
LUTHER AV
1000 SJS 95126 833-J7
LUTHER DR
400 SCL 95051 833-B7
LUTHERIA WY
14200 SAR 95070 872-E2
LUX CT
3900 SJS 95136 874-F1
LUZ AV
2100 SJS 95116 834-G3
LYELL ST
- LALT 94022 811-E7
LYLE CT
2700 SCL 95051 833-B3
LYLE DR
1500 SJS 95125 854-A3
1500 SJS 95129 852-H5
LYLE LN
700 SJS 95008 873-F1
LYMEHAVEN CT
- SJS 95111 874-J1

LYNBROOK CT
18900 SAR 95070 852-H5
LYNBROOK WY
1100 SJS 95129 852-G4
LYNDALE AV
100 SCIC 95127 834-J2
100 SJS 95127 834-J2
10000 SCIC 95127 835-A3
LYNDE AV
13800 SAR 95070 872-D1
LYNDE CT
20500 SAR 95070 872-D2
LYNDON AV
- LGTS 95030 872-J7
LYNETTE WY
200 SJS 95116 834-G4
LYNFIELD LN
4200 SJS 95136 874-D2
LYNG DR
4900 SJS 95111 875-B1
LYNHURST CT
1100 SJS 95118 874-C2
LYNHURST WY
1100 SJS 95118 874-C2
LYNN AV
- MPS 95035 794-D5
1100 SJS 95122 834-G6
2000 LGTS 95032 873-F5
15000 SJS 95032 873-F5
15000 SJS 95124 873-F5
LYNN WY
1000 SUNV 94087 832-B1
LYNNDALE WY
25900 LAH 94022 811-C6
LYNNHAVEN DR
2000 SJS 95128 853-G3
LYNN OAKS DR
3200 SJS 95117 853-D2
LYNTON CT
20100 CPTO 95014 852-E2
LYNVIEW DR
3000 SJS 95148 855-D1
LYNWOOD AV
600 MTVW 94043 812-A3
LYNWOOD TER
2000 SJS 95128 833-F7
2200 MPS 95035 814-E1
LYNX CT
3700 SJS 95136 874-D1
LYNX DR
3500 SJS 95136 874-D1
LYNXWOOD CT
500 SUNV 94086 832-F1
LYONBURRY PL
500 SJS 95123 874-G4
LYONCROSS WY
400 SJS 95123 874-J4
LYON ESTATES CT
2900 SJS 95135 855-G5
LYONS CT
2200 SJS 95116 834-H4
18500 SAR 95070 872-H1
LYONS DR
2100 SJS 95116 834-H5
LYONS ST
1100 RDWC 94061 790-A1
LYONSVILLE LN
1300 SJS 95118 874-B5
LYRA ST
48800 FRMT 94539 793-H1
LYRELAKE CT
700 SUNV 94089 812-H4
LYRIC LN
4700 SJS 95111 855-A7
4700 SJS 95111 875-A1
LYTER WY
3200 SJS 95135 855-D2
LYTTON AV
100 PA 94301 790-H4

M

M RD
- SUNV 94089 812-H4
MABEL AV
2000 SJS 95122 834-H5
MABEL CT
12200 SAR 95070 852-G5
MABIE CT
5900 SJS 95123 874-F5
MABURY CT
2800 SJS 95133 814-G7
MABURY RD
600 SJS 95133 834-B2
1100 SJS 95133 834-D2
2400 SJS 95133 814-G7
3100 SJS 95127 814-H6
3200 SCIC 95127 814-H6
12200 SCIC 95133 834-D2

MACADAM CT
5800 SJS 95123 875-A5
MACADAM LN
10100 CPTO 95014 852-E1
MACARA AV
400 SUNV 94086 812-D5
MACARTHUR AV
300 SJS 95128 853-F1
300 SCIC 95128 853-F1
MACAW LN
200 SJS 95123 874-F7
MACAW PL
200 SJS 95123 874-F7
MACAW WY
5200 SJS 95123 874-F7
MACBAIN AV
- ATN 94027 790-E3
MACBETH DR
3700 SJS 95127 835-C2
MACDONALD AV
200 SJS 95116 834-E3
MACDONALD ST
1400 RDWC 94061 790-A2
MACDUEE CT
1800 SJS 95121 855-B3
MACDUEE WY
1800 SJS 95121 855-B3
MACDUFF CT
900 SJS 95127 835-C2
MACE CT
3600 SJS 95127 835-C3
MACE DR
1200 SJS 95127 835-C3
MACGREGOR LN
3500 SCL 95054 813-E6
MACHADO AV
3000 SCL 95051 833-A2
3300 SCL 95051 832-J2
3500 SUNV 94086 832-J2
MACHADO LN
1000 SJS 95127 835-C2
10000 SCIC 95127 835-C2
MACINTOSH ST
3500 SCL 95054 813-E6
MACKALL WY
3100 PA 94306 791-D7
MACKAY DR
4100 PA 94306 811-F2
MACKENZIE DR
300 SCL 95051 832-H7
900 SUNV 94087 832-B6
MACKEY AV
1500 SJS 95125 854-C3
MACKIN WOODS LN
3200 SJS 95135 855-G3
MACKLIN CT
700 SJS 95133 814-G7
MACLANE ST
200 PA 94306 811-C1
MACLAY CT
6000 SJS 95123 874-E5
14300 SAR 95070 872-G2
MACLAY DR
900 SJS 95123 874-E5
MACON AV
1000 MTVW 94043 812-A2
1000 MTVW 94043 811-J2
1000 SJS 95117 853-D3
MACON RD
- SCIC 94035 812-C1
MACREDES CT
700 SJS 95116 834-E6
MADALEN DR
1200 MPS 95035 794-B4
MADAN LN
- SCL 95051 833-C3
MADDEN AV
2300 SJS 95116 834-G3
MADDUX DR
900 PA 94303 791-D6
1500 RDWC 94061 790-A3
MADELAINE CT
2000 LALT 94024 831-G5
MADELINE DR
3300 SCIC 95127 834-J1
3400 SJS 95127 834-J1
MADELINE LN
900 SCL 95050 833-C5
MADERA
- MTVW 94043 811-J2
MADERA AV
400 SJS 95112 834-B3
400 SUNV 94086 812-C7
1000 MLPK 94025 790-J1
MADERA CT
100 LGTS 95032 873-H7
MADERA DR
2400 SCL 95051 833-C4
10300 CPTO 95014 832-B7

MADERA RD
10400 CPTO 95014 851-J2
MADISON CT
400 GIL 95020 958-A7
400 SJS 95123 875-A6
MADISON DR
300 SJS 95123 875-A6
800 MTVW 94040 831-G1
MADISON ST
200 SCL 95050 833-E4
MADISON WY
- SMCo 94025 790-H2
500 PA 94303 791-C4
MADOC WY
4400 SJS 95130 853-A6
MADONNA DR
3300 SJS 95117 853-D3
MADONNA WY
800 LALT 94024 831-E2
MADRID CT
3600 SJS 95132 814-F1
MADRID DR
2900 SCIC 95020 957-D6
3400 SJS 95132 814-E2
MADRID RD
10600 CPTO 95014 852-B2
MADRONA AV
1200 SJS 95125 854-B5
MADRONA WY
20300 SCIC 95030 892-H7
20400 SCIC 95030 912-J1
MADRONE AV
- SJS 95037 916-F3
- SCIC 95037 916-F3
200 SCL 95051 833-B7
500 SUNV 94086 812-E5
16500 LGTS 95030 872-H7
16600 SCIC 95030 872-H7
MADRONE CT
19400 SCIC 95030 892-F4
MADRONE DR
17900 SCIC 95030 913-A3
17900 SCIC 95030 912-J2
MADRONE RD
- ATN 94027 790-G1
MADRONE ST
200 RDWC 94061 790-B1
MADRONE HILL RD
15200 SAR 95070 872-E4
MADRONO AV
1600 PA 94306 791-A6
MADRUGA WY
1200 MPS 95035 814-D2
MAESTRO CT
500 SJS 95134 813-F3
MAEVE CT
- SJS 95136 854-E6
MAGDALENA AV
10200 LAH 94024 831-F3
11500 SCIC 94024 831-F3
12200 LALT 94024 831-F3
MAGDALENA CIR
1900 SCL 95051 832-H3
MAGDALENA CT
12300 SCIC 94024 831-F2
MAGELLAN AV
- SJS 95116 834-F3
3600 SCL 95051 832-H7
MAGGIO CT
1200 CMBL 95008 873-B1
MAGGIORE CT
3100 SJS 95135 855-F6
MAGIC SANDS WY
- SJS 95123 875-G2
MAGLADRY RD
100 SBnC - (1020-F7
See Page 999)
MAGLIOCCO DR
2900 SJS 95117 853-D2
3000 SJS 95128 853-E2
MAGNESON LP
100 LGTS 95032 873-C6
100 SCIC 95032 873-C6
MAGNESON TER
100 LGTS 95032 873-C6
MAGNOLIA AV
1100 SJS 95126 833-H7
N MAGNOLIA AV
- SJS 95136 854-E7
S MAGNOLIA AV
600 SJS 95136 854-E7
W MAGNOLIA AV
3900 SJS 95136 854-E7
MAGNOLIA CT
1600 MLPK 94025 790-F5
MAGNOLIA DR
- ATN 94027 790-F1
3800 PA 94306 811-C2
MAGNOLIA LN
400 SCL 95051 833-B7

MAGNOLIA ST
600 MLPK 94025 790-E5
MAGNOLIA WY
2400 MGH 95037 917-F5
MAGNOLIA BLOSSOM LN
1600 SJS 95124 873-J6
MAGNOLIA TREE CT
1700 SJS 95122 854-F1
MAGNUM DR
2900 SJS 95135 855-E3
MAGPIE LN
1500 SUNV 94087 832-F5
MAHAN DR
6100 SJS 95123 875-A6
MAHOGANY DR
700 SUNV 94086 832-G2
MAHONEY AV
200 SJS 95127 835-B1
200 SCIC 95127 835-B1
MAIDEN LN
6900 SJS 95120 894-G3
E MAIN AV
- MGH 95037 917-B6
900 SCIC 95037 917-D4
W MAIN AV
- MGH 95037 936-H1
300 MGH 95037 916-J7
MAIN ST
- LALT 94022 811-E7
600 SCL 95050 833-D2
MAIN ST Rt#-152
300 WAT 95076 (1015-C1
See Page 995)
E MAIN ST
- LGTS 95032 893-A1
S MAIN ST
- MPS 95035 794-A7
100 MPS 95035 814-A1
W MAIN ST
100 LGTS 95030 872-J7
MAIN ENTRANCE DR
1400 SJS 95131 814-C7
MAIRWOOD CT
700 SJS 95120 894-J3
MAITLAND DR
1700 SJS 95124 873-H4
MAJESTIC CT
1900 SJS 95132 814-F2
MAJESTIC WY
1700 SJS 95132 814-F3
MAJESTIC OAK WY
22700 CPTO 95014 831-J7
MAJORCA CT
6000 SJS 95120 874-B7
MAJORCA DR
1400 MGH 95037 917-D6
MAKATI CIR
5100 SJS 95123 875-B4
MAKATI CT
- SJS 95123 875-B4
MALABAR AV
2800 SCL 95051 833-B7
MALABAR DR
400 SJS 95127 834-J3
MALAGA CT
1400 MGH 95037 917-D7
MALAGA DR
2500 SJS 95125 853-J7
16900 MGH 95037 917-D6
MALAGUERRA AV
18900 MGH 95037 917-A2
19000 SCIC 95037 917-A2
19200 SCIC 95037 916-J2
MALARIN AV
600 SCL 95050 833-D5
MALCOM AV
13800 SAR 95070 872-D1
MALDEN AV
1900 SJS 95122 854-H1
MALECH RD
100 SJS 95138 875-J7
100 SCIC 95137 875-J7
100 SCIC 95137 896-A1
100 SCIC 95137 895-J1
MALERO PL
4700 SJS 95129 852-J1
MALIBU DR
1100 SJS 95129 853-A3
MALIBU TER
- FRMT 94539 794-B1
MALLARD WY
1400 SUNV 94087 832-G4
MALLARD RIDGE CIR
1400 SJS 95120 894-F3
MALLARD RIDGE CT
7100 SJS 95120 894-F3
MALLARD RIDGE DR
1400 SJS 95120 894-F3

MALLARD RIDGE LP
7200 SJS 95120 894-F3
MALLET CT
1000 MLPK 94025 790-F4
MALLORY CT
19900 SAR 95070 852-E6
MALO CT
1000 SCIC 95020 958-A4
MALONE PL
2500 SCL 95050 833-C5
MALONE RD
700 SJS 95125 854-B5
MALONEY LN
600 MLPK 94025 790-F3
MALORY CT
- SMCo 94061 790-B3
MALORY DR
6200 SJS 95123 875-B7
MALOTT DR
900 SJS 95121 854-H3
MALPAS LN
5700 SJS 95124 873-J6
MALTON CT
3100 SJS 95148 855-E2
MALVERN CT
10300 CPTO 95014 852-F1
MALVINI DR
3900 SJS 95118 874-B2
MAMMINI CT
13500 SCIC 95046 937-G5
MAMMOTH DR
2300 SJS 95116 834-G2
MANASSAS CT
2000 SJS 95116 834-H5
MANCHESTER AV
200 CMBL 95008 853-G5
MANCHESTER CT
3100 PA 94303 791-D6
MANCHESTER DR
1000 SCL 95050 833-E5
MANCUSO ST
6100 SJS 95120 874-C7
MANDA DR
2800 SJS 95124 873-H1
MANDARIN DR
1200 SUNV 94087 832-B3
MANDARIN WY
- ATN 94027 790-B6
1800 SJS 95122 834-H6
13500 SAR 95070 872-D1
MANDEL CT
1800 SJS 95131 814-D7
MANDELA CT
1000 EPA 94303 791-C1
MANDOLI DR
13400 LAH 94022 811-A5
MANDOLIN DR
300 SJS 95134 813-D2
MANDRILL CT
4700 SJS 95124 873-J3
MANET DR
1000 SUNV 94087 832-E3
MANFRE RD
10100 SCIC 95037 916-C1
MANFRED ST
100 MPS 95035 793-J3
100 MPS 95035 794-A3
MANFROY RANCH RD
3600 SCIC 95020 958-F4
MANGIN WY
2100 SCIC 95148 835-E5
MANGO AV
800 SUNV 94087 832-B2
MANGO BLOSSOM CT
5300 SJS 95123 875-A3
MANGROVE AV
800 SUNV 94086 832-G3
MANGRUM DR
4600 SCL 95054 813-D4
MANHATTAN AV
1900 EPA 94303 791-B3
MANHATTAN CT
1000 SUNV 94087 832-B2
MANHATTAN PL
2200 SCL 95051 833-A2
MANICHETTI CT
5800 SJS 95123 875-A5
MANILA DR
- MTVW 94035 812-C3
- MTVW 94043 812-C3
- SCIC 94035 812-C3
- SUNV 94089 812-C3
300 SJS 95119 875-C7
MANILA WY
6400 SJS 95119 875-C7
MANITA CT
21000 CPTO 95014 852-C3
MANITOBA DR
1600 SUNV 94087 832-C5
4700 SJS 95130 853-A7

MANITOU CT
1700 SJS 95120 874-B6
MANLEY CT
100 SJS 95139 895-G1
MANLY CT
300 SCL 95051 833-A7
MANN DR
10000 CPTO 95014 832-B7
MANNA WY
11000 SCIC 95020 957-G3
MANNING AV
- SJS 95127 834-J2
- SCIC 95127 834-J2
MANNING CT
1100 SCIC 95046 937-G4
MANN OAK CT
20000 SCIC 95120 894-J5
MANOA CT
20300 SAR 95070 852-E7
MANOR CT
100 MGH 95037 937-A1
12500 SAR 95070 852-D5
MANOR DR
1100 SJS 95126 854-B6
20500 SAR 95070 852-D5
MANOR PL
- MLPK 94025 790-H3
MANOR WY
700 LALT 94024 831-G3
MANORWOOD CT
5800 SJS 95129 852-G3
MANRESA CT
200 LALT 94022 831-D1
7500 SJS 95139 895-G2
MANRESA LN
200 LALT 94022 831-D1
MANRESA WY
500 LALT 94022 831-D1
600 LAH 94022 831-D1
MANSFIELD DR
500 MTVW 94040 831-J2
700 SJS 95128 853-G2
MANSION CT
- MLPK 94025 790-C7
500 SCL 95134 813-E4
1300 SJS 95120 894-C2
MANSION PARK DR
400 SCL 95134 813-E4
MANTECA CT
6100 SJS 95123 874-G6
MANTECA WY
13600 SAR 95070 872-H1
MANTELLI DR
500 GIL 95020 977-E1
MANTIS DR
2800 SJS 95148 835-E7
MANTON CT
1600 CMBL 95008 873-A1
MANTON DR
100 SJS 95123 875-B4
MANUELA AV
4100 PA 94306 811-C4
MANUELA CT
4200 PA 94306 811-B5
MANUELA WY
26000 PA 94306 811-B5
MANUELLA RD
4200 PA 94306 811-C6
4200 LAH 94022 811-C6
MANX AV
700 CMBL 95008 853-D7
MANXWOOD PL
5100 SJS 95111 875-C2
MANZANA LN
4000 PA 94306 811-C3
MANZANITA AV
200 PA 94306 791-A6
200 SCL 95051 833-B7
500 SUNV 94086 812-E5
2000 SMCo 94025 790-C6
MANZANITA CT
300 MPS 95035 813-J4
MANZANITA DR
3900 SJS 95117 853-B2
4200 SJS 95129 853-A2
17500 MGH 95037 917-F3
17500 SCIC 95037 917-F3
19400 SCIC 95030 892-F4
MANZANITA RD
- ATN 94027 790-G1
MANZANITA WY
18200 LGTS 95030 872-J7
MANZANO CT
600 MPS 95035 794-B4
MANZANO ST
500 MPS 95035 794-A4
MANZANO WY
1100 SUNV 94089 813-A5
MAPACHE CT
- PTLV 94028 810-A4

MAPACHE DR
100 PTLV 94028 810-A4
MAPLE AV
- ATN 94027 790-E2
400 MPS 95035 793-H6
500 CMBL 95008 853-F6
500 SUNV 94086 812-F6
700 SCIC 95037 937-E2
700 SCIC 95046 937-E2
1600 MGH 95037 937-E2
1600 MGH 95046 937-E2
MAPLE LN
1500 LALT 94024 831-G3
16700 LGTS 95032 893-A1
MAPLE ST
400 MGH 95037 937-B1
400 PA 94301 791-A3
7300 GIL 95020 978-A3
MAPLECREST CT
5500 SJS 95123 874-G4
MAPLE GROVE CT
5300 SJS 95123 874-F7
MAPLE LEAF CT
3200 SJS 95121 855-B3
MAPLE LEAF WY
- ATN 94027 790-G2
MAPLETREE PL
20500 CPTO 95014 832-D6
MAPLEWOOD AV
300 SJS 95117 853-D1
300 SCIC 95117 853-D1
700 PA 94303 811-F1
MAPLEWOOD LN
2600 SCL 95051 833-B7
MAPLEWOOD PL
700 PA 94303 811-F1
MAPLEWOOD ST
10600 CPTO 95014 832-F6
MARACAIBO DR
5800 SJS 95120 874-C6
MARANTA AV
800 SUNV 94087 832-C2
MARASCHINO DR
1000 SJS 95129 853-A3
1100 SUNV 94087 832-C3
MARATHON DR
1500 CMBL 95008 853-C5
MARBELLA CT
2200 SJS 95124 873-F3
16900 MGH 95037 917-D6
MARBELLA DR
2200 SJS 95124 873-F3
MARBLE CT
900 SJS 95120 894-G1
MARBURG WY
1500 SJS 95133 834-E3
N MARBURG WY
400 SJS 95133 834-E3
MARCEL CT
3300 SJS 95135 855-G3
MARCELLA AV
8400 SCIC 95020 958-B4
MARCELYN AV
2400 MTVW 94040 811-F2
MARCH DR
100 SJS 95138 875-D4
MARCHANT CT
3700 SJS 95127 835-C2
MARCHANT DR
3700 SJS 95127 835-C2
MARCHESE CT
3300 SCL 95051 833-A1
MARCHESE WY
2400 SCL 95051 833-A2
MARCHMONT CT
200 LGTS 95032 873-D7
MARCHMONT DR
200 LGTS 95032 873-C7
16500 SCIC 95032 873-C7
MARCIA AV
1400 SJS 95125 854-A7
MARCIA CT
100 MTVW 94041 811-J6
MARCIA DR
400 MGH 95037 916-H7
MARCO DR
1600 SJS 95131 814-C7
MARCO WY
1600 SJS 95131 814-C7
MARCONI WY
1600 SJS 95125 853-J5
MARCROSS DR
1900 SJS 95131 814-D6
MARCUS ST
200 MntC - (1017-A5
See Page 997)
MARCUSSEN DR
1000 MLPK 94025 790-G2
MARCY CT
21000 CPTO 95014 832-C7

MARCY LYNN CT
1700 SJS 95124 873-H5
MARDAN DR
1400 SJS 95132 814-F3
MARDEL LN
2000 SJS 95128 853-G3
MARDELL WY
2500 MTVW 94043 811-F2
MARDENE CT
3800 SJS 95121 855-B5
MAREE CT
6100 SJS 95123 874-G6
MARENGO LN
1100 SJS 95132 814-H5
MARE PLACE CT
3800 SJS 95121 855-B5
MARFRANCE DR
3800 SJS 95121 855-A5
MARGARET CT
900 SUNV 94087 832-B2
MARGARET LN
600 CMBL 95008 853-B7
MARGARET ST
- SJS 95112 834-D7
1700 SJS 95116 834-G5
MARGARET WY
100 SJS 95112 834-C7
MARGARITA AV
200 PA 94306 811-C1
MARGARITE CT
200 LALT 94022 811-D4
MARGATE AV
3500 SJS 95117 853-C2
MARGE WY
500 SCIC 95117 853-D2
MARGO DR
100 MTVW 94041 812-A6
MARGOT PL
1900 SJS 95125 853-J6
MARIA CT
400 SCL 95050 833-D5
MARIA LN
800 SUNV 94086 832-F3
21100 SAR 95070 852-C5
MARIA ST
200 SCL 95050 833-D5
MARIA WY
700 GIL 95020 977-H1
1300 SJS 95117 853-D4
1600 SCIC 95117 853-D4
MARIAN LN
- SCIC 95127 834-J1
MARIANELLI CT
1000 SJS 95112 834-C3
MARIANI AV
20300 CPTO 95014 832-D7
MARIANI DR
1600 SUNV 94087 832-F5
MARIANNA LN
- ATN 94027 790-E2
1500 SJS 95128 853-H2
MARIANNA WY
100 CMBL 95008 853-C5
MARIANNE CT
100 MTVW 94040 811-J7
MARIA PRIVADA
1100 MTVW 94040 832-H6
MARIA ROSA WY
10900 CPTO 95014 852-B3
MARIA TERESA CT
100 LGTS 95032 873-E5
MARICH WY
200 LALT 94022 811-F4
1700 MTVW 94040 811-F4
MARICOPA DR
100 LGTS 95032 873-D5
MARIE CT
14800 SCIC 95046 937-G2
MARIE LN
700 MGH 95037 917-D7
MARIETTA CT
800 SCL 95051 833-A6
MARIETTA DR
1500 SJS 95118 874-A4
2900 SCL 95051 833-A5
MARIGOLD CT
1000 SUNV 94086 832-H2
1700 SJS 95133 834-E3
MARIGOLD LN
8700 GIL 95020 977-G1
MARILLA AV
1000 SJS 95129 853-A3
MARILLA CT
20100 SAR 95070 852-E5
MARILLA DR
12000 SAR 95070 852-E5
MARILYN CT
1200 MTVW 94040 811-G7
MARILYN DR
700 CMBL 95008 853-C7

STREET
Block City ZIP Pg-Grid

MARILYN DR
900 MTVW 94040 811-G6
900 CMBL 95008 873-C1
MARILYN LN
14000 SAR 95070 872-H2
MARILYN PL
1300 MTVW 94040 811-G7
MARIN ST
- WAT 95076 995-F7
MARINA WY
1600 SCIC 95125 853-H5
MARINE WY
2600 MTVW 94043 791-G7
MARINER DR
900 SCIC 94043 811-J3
MARINOVICH WY
1300 LALT 94024 831-J3
MARION AV
400 PA 94301 791-C6
500 PA 94306 791-C6
700 PA 94303 791-C6
MARION DR
- SMCo 94062 790-A4
MARION PL
600 PA 94301 791-C6
MARION RD
20500 SAR 95070 872-D2
MARION WY
900 SUNV 94087 832-G4
MARIPOSA AV
- LGTS 95030 873-A6
200 MTVW 94041 811-G5
300 LALT 94022 811-D6
1100 SJS 95126 833-J7
1500 PA 94306 791-A6
MARIPOSA CT
- LGTS 95030 873-A5
MARIPOSA WY
1100 GIL 95020 957-F7
MARIST CT
2900 SJS 95148 855-D4
MARJOHN BLVD
4900 SJS 95111 875-A2
MARJORIE CT
2400 MTVW 94043 811-F3
MARJORIE DR
900 CMBL 95008 873-B1
MARK AV
2800 SCL 95051 833-A3
3300 SJS 95124 873-J2
MARKET ST
300 SCIC 95020 957-H3
700 SCL 95053 833-D5
800 SCL 95050 833-D5
N MARKET ST
- SJS 95110 834-B6
- SJS 95113 834-B6
S MARKET ST
- SJS 95113 834-B6
300 SJS 95110 834-B7
S MARKET ST Rt#-82
300 SJS 95110 834-B7
MARKHAM AV
- SMCo 94063 790-C1
2200 SJS 95125 854-B6
MARKHAM TER
800 SUNV 94086 812-D7
MARKINGDON AV
2900 SJS 95127 835-A4
MARKROSS CT
17200 MGH 95037 917-A7
MARKS AV
3500 SJS 95118 874-B2
MARK TWAIN CT
100 SCL 95050 833-D7
MARK TWAIN ST
1800 PA 94303 791-B5
MARKWOOD CT
3100 SJS 95148 835-E7
MARLA CT
6100 SJS 95124 873-J7
MARLBAROUGH AV
1400 LALT 94024 831-J3
MARLBAROUGH CT
1400 LALT 94024 831-J3
MARLBORO CT
2000 SJS 95128 853-G3
MARLBOROUGH AV
2700 SMCo 94063 790-C1
MARLENE CT
1500 SJS 95118 874-G3
MARLETTE DR
3800 SJS 95121 855-A5
MARLINA TER
400 MPS 95035 793-G3
MARLINTON CT
900 SJS 95120 894-G2
MARLOWE DR
4300 SJS 95124 873-J3

MARLOWE ST
400 PA 94301 791-A3
MARLYN WY
1700 SJS 95125 854-A5
MARMON CT
2400 SCL 95051 833-C2
MARMONA CT
200 MLPK 94025 790-J3
MARMONA DR
200 MLPK 94025 790-J3
MARMONT WY
13500 SCIC 95127 834-J3
MARO DR
- SCIC 95127 835-A1
- SCIC 95127 834-J1
MAROEL DR
2100 SJS 95130 853-A7
MARQUES AV
1900 SJS 95125 853-J5
2000 SJS 95125 854-A6
MARQUETTE DR
5400 SJS 95118 874-B5
MARQUETTE ST
3500 SCL 95051 832-J2
MARR LN
2300 SJS 95124 873-E5
MARRIAGE RD
- SCIC 94035 792-D7
- SCIC 94035 812-D1
MARS CT
400 MPS 95035 794-D7
MARSAN CT
1400 CMBL 95008 873-B1
MARSEILLES CT
1600 SJS 95138 875-F1
MARSH RD
1000 SMCo 94063 790-F1
1000 ATN 94027 790-F1
4800 SCIC 95140 795-F2
MARSH ST
1500 SJS 95122 834-G6
MARSHA WY
2400 SJS 95125 854-B6
MARSHALL AV
400 SJS 95125 854-B2
400 SUNV 94086 812-F7
MARSHALL CT
600 SCL 95051 833-B6
1700 LALT 94024 832-A5
MARSHALL DR
400 SCIC 95020 957-J4
800 PA 94303 791-C5
MARSHALL LN
200 SBnC - (1017-A5
See Page 997)
18500 SAR 95070 872-H2
MARSHGLEN CT
2300 SJS 95133 834-F2
MARSH MANOR WY
3500 SJS 95121 855-D7
MARSHWELL WY
5800 SJS 95138 875-D5
MARSTON WY
3000 SJS 95148 835-F7
3000 SJS 95148 855-F1
MARTEL ST
300 SJS 95110 834-A7
MARTELLO DR
1800 SJS 95122 854-G1
MARTEN AV
3100 SJS 95148 835-D4
3100 SJS 95127 835-B5
MARTENS AV
100 MTVW 94040 811-J7
400 MTVW 94040 812-A7
MARTHA AV
18500 SAR 95070 852-H7
MARTHA ST
- SJS 95112 854-C1
300 SJS 95112 834-D7
MARTI WY
200 SJS 95136 874-G1
MARTIL WY
300 MPS 95035 794-A5
MARTIN AV
200 SJS 95050 833-F2
200 SCL 95050 833-C2
300 SJS 95110 833-F2
1100 SJS 95126 833-H7
1200 PA 94301 791-A4
1600 SUNV 94087 832-F5
1600 SJS 95128 833-H7
1600 SJS 95128 853-H1
MARTIN ST
300 GIL 95020 978-A3
MARTINELLI ST
100 WAT 95076 995-F7
MARTINIQUE CT
600 SJS 95123 874-G4

MARTIN JUE ST
1700 SJS 95131 834-D1
MARTINSEN CT
400 PA 94306 791-C7
MARTINVALE LN
100 SJS 95119 875-E7
100 SJS 95119 895-E1
MARTINWOOD WY
10600 CPTO 95014 852-E2
MARTWOOD WY
7000 SJS 95120 894-H3
MARTY RD
21500 SCrC 95030 912-G3
MARVIN AV
- LALT 94022 811-E7
MARY AV
500 SUNV 94086 812-D5
10000 CPTO 95014 832-C7
N MARY AV
100 SUNV 94086 812-D5
S MARY AV
100 SUNV 94086 812-C7
400 SUNV 94086 832-C2
600 SUNV 94087 832-C2
10800 CPTO 95014 832-C6
MARY CT
800 CMBL 95008 853-C7
1100 SCIC 95020 957-J1
MARY WY
100 LGTS 95032 873-D6
MARY-VIN LN
800 SCL 95051 832-J6
MARY ALICE DR
100 LGTS 95032 873-D4
MARY ALICE WY
21500 SCIC 95030 912-J2
MARYANN DR
800 SCL 95050 833-C5
MARY CAROLINE CT
2900 SJS 95133 814-G6
MARY CAROLINE DR
800 SJS 95133 814-G6
MARY EVELYN DR
600 SJS 95123 874-H7
MARY JANE WY
4800 SJS 95124 873-H4
MARY JO CT
5400 SJS 95124 873-H5
MARY JO LN
1400 SCIC 95046 937-H4
MARY JO WY
5300 SJS 95124 873-H6
MARYLAND ST
1900 RDWC 94061 790-A3
MARY LEE WY
1200 SJS 95118 874-B1
MARYLINN DR
300 MPS 95035 794-A7
400 MPS 95035 793-H6
MARYMEADE LN
1600 LALT 94024 831-J4
MARYMONT AV
- ATN 94027 790-B4
MARYMONTE CT
6500 SJS 95120 894-C1
MASON WY
6700 SJS 95129 852-E3
MASONIC DR
2400 SJS 95125 854-D5
MASONWOOD ST
2700 SJS 95148 855-C1
MASSACHUSETTS AV
2500 RDWC 94061 790-A3
MASSACHUSETTS DR
4900 SJS 95136 874-F3
MASSAR AV
500 SJS 95116 834-H4
MASSIDDA CT
1600 SJS 95118 873-J4
MASSIH CT
1200 CMBL 95008 873-A1
1300 SJS 95008 873-A1
MASSOL AV
- LGTS 95030 872-J7
200 LGTS 95030 873-A7
MASSON CT
14700 SAR 95070 872-B2
MASSON TERRACE CIR
18800 SAR 95070 852-B7
MAST ST
100 MGH 95037 937-B1
MASTEN AV
100 SCIC 95020 957-G3
1200 SCIC 95020 958-A2
MASTERS CT
3700 SJS 95111 854-J6
47800 FRMT 94539 793-H1
MASTIC ST
1000 SJS 95110 854-C2

MASUDA LNDG
1800 SJS 95131 814-C4
MAT AV
300 SJS 95123 874-J5
MATADERO AV
200 PA 94306 811-C1
MATADERO CT
800 PA 94306 811-B2
MATADERO DR
100 SUNV 94086 812-C7
MATADERO CREEK CT
28600 LAH 94022 830-H1
MATADERO CREEK LN
28500 LAH 94022 810-H7
MATHER DR
2300 SJS 95116 834-G2
MATHEW ST
300 SCL 95050 833-E2
N MATHILDA AV
100 SUNV 94086 812-E6
1100 SUNV 94089 812-E2
S MATHILDA AV
100 SUNV 94086 812-D7
300 SUNV 94086 832-D2
600 SUNV 94087 832-D2
MATHILDA CT
100 MGH 95037 937-A1
MATILIJA DR
15800 SCIC 95030 872-G6
15800 MSER 95030 872-G6
MATISSE CT
1200 SUNV 94087 832-E3
MATOS CT
1800 SCL 95050 833-D5
MATSON DR
1600 SJS 95124 873-J2
MATTERHORN CT
900 MPS 95035 814-D1
MATTERHORN DR
1100 SJS 95132 814-F5
MATTHEW CT
6400 SJS 95123 875-B7
MATTHEWS CT
400 MPS 95035 794-A3
MATTHIAS CT
2700 SJS 95121 854-H3
MATTHIAS DR
2700 SJS 95121 854-H3
MATTIQUE DR
2900 SJS 95135 855-E2
MATTOS AV
3000 SJS 95132 814-F4
MATTOS DR
2200 MPS 95035 794-E7
MATTS CT
900 LALT 94024 831-E1
MATTSON AV
200 LGTS 95030 873-A2
MATZLEY CT
3100 SJS 95124 873-H2
MATZLEY DR
1700 SJS 95124 873-H2
MAUDE AV
18600 SAR 95070 872-H4
E MAUDE AV
100 SUNV 94086 812-F6
W MAUDE AV
100 SUNV 94086 812-D5
800 MTVW 94043 812-C4
MAUI CT
3900 SJS 95111 855-A6
MAUI DR
3800 SJS 95111 855-A6
MAUNA KEA LN
1300 SJS 95132 814-F4
MAUNA LOA CT
3000 SJS 95132 814-F5
MAUNEY CT
3700 SJS 95130 853-C4
MAUREEN AV
400 PA 94306 791-D7
MAUREEN WY
20700 SAR 95070 852-D5
MAURER LN
26100 LAH 94022 811-B6
MAURICE LN
1500 SJS 95129 852-H5
MAURICIA AV
2700 SCL 95051 833-A7
3200 SCL 95051 832-J7
MAVERICK CT
1300 SCIC 95046 937-H7
MAXEY DR
1100 SJS 95132 814-G5
MAXIMILIAN DR
2200 SJS 95008 853-C7
MAXINE AV
1400 SJS 95125 854-A6
MAXINE DR
400 SUNV 94086 832-E1

MAXINE DR
10700 CPTO 95014 832-B6
MAXWELL WY
1300 SJS 95131 834-C1
1400 SJS 95131 814-C7
MAY CT
- PA 94303 811-E1
MAY DR
100 SJS 95138 875-D4
MAY LN
- LALT 94022 811-E5
3400 SJS 95124 873-F2
MAYA WY
16100 SCIC 95032 893-C2
MAYALL CT
1700 SJS 95132 814-D4
MAYAN LN
1700 SCIC 95046 938-A7
12300 SCIC 95046 937-J7
MAYBELL AV
600 PA 94306 811-C3
MAYBELL WY
4100 PA 94306 811-C3
MAY BROWN AV
1100 MLPK 94025 790-E4
MAYBURY SQ
800 SJS 95133 814-G7
MAYCOCK RD
200 GIL 95020 978-B6
MAYELLEN AV
300 SJS 95126 853-H2
MAYER CT
- LALT 94022 811-F6
MAYETTE AV
1100 SJS 95125 854-B6
MAYFAIR PL
1800 SJS 95116 834-G4
MAYFIELD AV
100 MTVW 94043 811-F3
500 SCIC 94305 790-G7
500 SCIC 94305 810-H1
1900 SJS 95130 852-J6
MAYFIELD CT
4900 SJS 95130 852-J6
MAYFLOWER CT
1700 MTVW 94040 811-G5
5900 SJS 95129 852-G4
MAYGLEN CT
2800 SJS 95133 814-G7
MAYGLEN WY
2800 SJS 95133 814-G7
MAYHEW CT
1300 SJS 95121 854-J2
MAYHEW DR
1200 SJS 95121 854-J2
MAYKIRK CT
1700 SJS 95124 853-H6
MAYKIRK RD
2000 SJS 95124 853-H6
MAYLAND AV
5400 SJS 95138 875-C3
MAYLAND CT
- SJS 95138 875-C3
MAYME AV
5400 SJS 95129 852-H5
MAYMENS FLAT RD
- SCrC 95030 934-J6
MAYNARD CT
- LALT 94022 811-E5
MAYNARD WY
- LALT 94022 811-E5
MAYO DR
6200 SJS 95123 875-B7
MAYO WY
300 SJS 95123 875-B7
MAYS AV
16000 MSER 95030 873-A6
MAYSONG CT
1700 SJS 95131 814-D7
MAYSUN CT
1400 CMBL 95008 873-A1
MAYTEN WY
100 FRMT 94539 793-J1
MAYTEN GROVE CT
5300 SJS 95123 874-J3
MAYTEN TREE CT
700 SUNV 94086 832-G2
MAYVIEW AV
700 PA 94303 811-E1
700 PA 94303 791-E7
MAYWOOD AV
2200 SJS 95128 853-F3
2200 SCIC 95128 853-F3
MAYWOOD CT
900 LALT 94024 831-F1
MAYWOOD LN
- MLPK 94025 790-F5
MAZEY ST
100 MPS 95035 794-A3

MAZZAGLIA AV
2200 SJS 95125 854-B6
MAZZONE DR
900 SJS 95120 874-D6
MCABEE RD
5900 SCIC 95120 894-C1
5900 SJS 95120 874-C6
6000 SJS 95120 894-C1
MCABEE ESTATES PL
1200 SJS 95120 874-C7
MCALISTER DR
700 SJS 95128 833-F7
MCANDREW CT
2800 SJS 95121 855-D3
MCAULEY CT
1000 PA 94301 791-A3
MCBAIN AV
1000 CMBL 95008 853-G5
1600 SCIC 95125 853-G5
MCBAIN CT
100 CMBL 95008 853-G6
MCCABE RD
- SCIC 95020 (922-C7
See Page 921)
MCCALL DR
6900 SJS 95120 894-F3
MCCAMISH AV
400 SJS 95123 875-A6
MCCANDLESS DR
1300 MPS 95035 814-A3
MCCARTHY BLVD
500 MPS 95035 813-H1
N MCCARTHY BLVD
500 MPS 95035 793-H6
MCCARTHY LN
- SCIC 95134 793-F7
- SJS 95134 793-F7
MCCARTY AV
500 MTVW 94041 812-A6
MCCARTY RANCH DR
8700 SJS 95135 856-A6
MCCARTYSVILLE PL
12600 SAR 95070 852-E6
MCCLELLAN PL
10500 CPTO 95014 852-D2
MCCLELLAN RD
20500 CPTO 95014 852-A2
21800 SCIC 95014 852-B2
MCCLUHAN WY
1700 SJS 95132 814-D4
MCCLURE LN
1300 LALT 94024 831-J3
MCCOLLAM DR
500 SJS 95127 814-J7
MCCONNELL DR
12200 SCIC 95046 957-G1
MCCONNELL RD
400 SBnC - (1019-F5
See Page 999)
MCCOPPIN PARK CT
3500 SJS 95124 873-E2
MCCORD AV
- SCIC 94035 812-B2
- SCIC 94043 812-B2
MCCORMICK DR
1500 SCL 95050 833-C4
MCCORMICK LN
- ATN 94027 790-E1
MCCOVEY LN
300 SJS 95127 835-B2
MCCOY AV
1500 CMBL 95008 853-A7
1500 CMBL 95130 853-A7
2000 SJS 95130 853-A7
3200 SJS 95130 852-J7
18200 SAR 95070 852-H7
MCCREERY AV
- SJS 95116 834-G4
MCCREERY CT
1800 SJS 95116 834-G5
MCCULLOCH WY
13200 SAR 95070 852-H7
MCDANIEL AV
1400 SJS 95126 833-G6
1700 SJS 95128 833-F7
MCDOLE ST
13100 SAR 95070 852-H7
MCDONALD LN
2200 SCIC 95037 917-D4
MCDUFF AV
200 FRMT 94539 793-H1
MCEVOY ST
200 RDWC 94061 790-B1
200 SJS 95126 834-A7
200 SJS 95126 854-A1
200 SCIC 95126 854-A1
MCFARLAND AV
18500 SAR 95070 852-H7
MCFARLAND CT
- SCIC 94305 790-J7

MCGILL RD
16900 SCIC 95070 892-C1
17000 SCIC 95070 872-C7
MCGILVRA CT
5800 SJS 95123 875-A5
MCGINNESS AV
1000 SJS 95127 835-A4
1000 SJS 95127 834-J4
E MCGLINCEY LN
200 CMBL 95008 853-E7
700 CMBL 95008 873-E1
MCGRAW AV
16700 MGH 95037 937-A1
MCGREGOR WY
1000 PA 94306 811-B3
1500 SJS 95129 852-E5
MCINTOSH AV
1200 SUNV 94087 832-C3
MCINTOSH CT
1200 SUNV 94087 832-C3
MCINTOSH CREEK DR
1100 SJS 95120 894-G3
MCKAY DR
1100 SJS 95131 814-B6
1300 SCIC 95131 814-B6
MCKEAN CT
7100 SJS 95120 894-J4
MCKEAN RD
19500 SJS 95120 894-H4
MCKEAN RD Rt#-G8
19600 SJS 95120 894-J4
19600 SCIC 95120 894-J4
20000 SCIC 95120 895-A4
22200 SJS 95120 895-D6
23100 SJS 95141 895-D6
MCKEE RD
1500 SJS 95116 834-H1
1600 SJS 95133 834-H1
2800 SJS 95127 834-H1
3200 SCIC 95133 834-H1
3600 SCIC 95127 834-H1
4000 SCIC 95127 814-J7
4100 SJS 95127 814-J7
4800 SJS 95127 815-A7
4900 SCIC 95127 815-A7
MCKELLAR DR
5600 SJS 95129 852-G4
MCKELLAR LN
4200 PA 94306 811-D2
MCKELVY LN
15900 MGH 95037 937-A3
15900 SCIC 95037 937-A3
MCKENDRIE ST
300 SJS 95110 833-H5
800 SJS 95126 833-G6
MCKENDRY DR
100 MLPK 94025 790-J3
MCKENDRY PL
300 MLPK 94025 790-J3
MCKENZIE AV
1300 LALT 94024 831-H2
MCKILLOP CT
- SCL 95050 833-G5
MCKINLEY AV
200 SUNV 94086 832-E1
1400 SJS 95126 853-H3
1500 SCIC 95126 853-H3
E MCKINLEY AV
400 SUNV 94086 832-E1
W MCKINLEY AV
300 SUNV 94086 812-B7
MCKINLEY DR
2900 SCL 95051 833-A7
3300 SCL 95051 832-J7
MCKINLEY ST
1100 RDWC 94061 790-A1
MCKINNON CT
1500 SJS 95130 853-A5
MCKINNON DR
4200 SJS 95130 853-A4
MCKLINTOCK LN
10200 CPTO 95014 851-J1
MCLAREN PL
10100 CPTO 95014 832-F7
MCLAUGHLIN AV
200 SJS 95116 834-E5
900 SJS 95122 834-E5
1600 SJS 95122 854-G1
2400 SJS 95121 854-G1
3100 SJS 95121 855-A4
17600 MGH 95037 917-A6
MCLELLAN AV
700 SJS 95110 854-B1
MCMAHON RD
- SBnC - (1020-G2
See Page 999)
MCMURDIE DR
1200 CMBL 95008 873-D1
MCPHEE RD
- SCIC 95037 935-F7

MCPHEE RD
- SCIC 95037 955-F1
MC PHERSON ST
1300 SCL 95051 832-J4
MCQUESTEN DR
1300 SJS 95122 834-G7
MCVAY AV
10400 SCIC 95127 835-B1
MCVAY CT
14800 SCIC 95127 835-B1
MEAD AV
2900 SCL 95051 833-A1
MEADOW AV
500 SCL 95051 832-H7
E MEADOW CIR
1000 PA 94303 791-E7
MEADOW CT
1200 MGH 95037 917-C6
E MEADOW DR
100 PA 94306 811-D1
600 PA 94306 791-E7
700 PA 94303 791-E7
W MEADOW DR
100 PA 94306 811-D2
MEADOW LN
- SBnC - (1020-G3
See Page 999)
- ATN 94027 790-B6
300 SCIC 95127 835-A2
300 SJS 95127 835-A2
600 LALT 94022 811-C4
1400 MTVW 94040 811-G7
MEADOW PL
10300 CPTO 95014 851-J1
MEADOWBROOK DR
100 LGTS 95032 873-G6
2400 SCL 95051 833-A2
MEADOW CREEK CT
- PTLV 94028 810-D7
MEADOW CREEK DR
600 SJS 95136 874-E1
MEADOW DALE CT
400 SJS 95136 874-F1
MEADOWGATE WY
2100 SJS 95132 814-D2
MEADOW GLEN CT
1500 SJS 95121 855-B4
MEADOW GLEN WY
1400 SJS 95121 855-B4
MEADOWGREEN WY
- MGH 95037 916-H3
MEADOWHAVEN WY
200 MPS 95035 794-A6
MEADOWHURST CT
4500 SJS 95136 874-E2
MEADOWLAKE DR
200 SUNV 94089 812-H4
MEADOWLAND DR
- MPS 95035 794-A6
MEADOWLANDS LN
2900 SJS 95135 855-H7
3300 SJS 95135 856-A7
MEADOWLARK AV
1200 SJS 95128 833-E6
MEADOWLARK LN
1500 SUNV 94087 832-G5
2400 SCIC 95020 958-C3
MEADOWMONT DR
2300 SJS 95133 834-E1
2300 SJS 95133 814-H3
MEADOW OAK RD
20700 SAR 95070 852-D5
MEADOWOOD DR
100 PTLV 94028 810-B5
900 SJS 95120 894-E1
MEADOW RIDGE CIR
1300 SJS 95131 814-C7
MEADOW RIDGE RD
900 SCrC 95076 (975-C4
See Page 955)
MEADOWSIDE CT
- SJS 95136 874-J7
MEADOWVIEW LN
21800 CPTO 95014 832-B7
MEADOWVILLE CT
4400 SJS 95129 853-A2
MEADWELL CT
100 SJS 95138 875-D4
MEANDER DR
5800 SJS 95120 874-B6
MEARS CT
900 SCIC 94305 810-J1
MEDALLION DR
1300 SJS 95120 874-B7
MEDEIRAS TER
300 MPS 95035 793-H3
MEDFORD DR
1500 LALT 94024 832-A3
MEDIA WY
2600 SJS 95125 853-J7

MEDICAL LN
- SCIC 94305 790-G6
300 PA 94304 790-G6
MEDICAL CENTER DR
16100 MGH 95037 937-C1
MEDICUS CT
18600 SCIC 95014 852-H1
MEDINA CT
22600 CPTO 95014 851-J1
MEDINA LN
22700 CPTO 95014 851-J1
MEDLEY CT
1200 SJS 95121 855-A4
MEDLEY DR
1200 SJS 95121 855-A4
MEDOC CT
400 MTVW 94043 811-G3
MEDWIN CT
3000 SJS 95148 855-C2
MEG CT
9500 SCIC 95020 958-E4
MEG DR
4200 SJS 95136 874-F1
MEI DR
700 MGH 95037 917-D7
MEIGGS LN
19000 SCIC 95014 852-G2
MEKLER CT
500 SJS 95111 854-G3
MELANIE LN
- ATN 94027 790-A5
MELANNIE CT
700 SJS 95116 834-F6
MELBA CT
1200 SJS 95120 894-E2
1500 MTVW 94040 811-G6
1500 MTVW 94022 811-G6
MELBOURNE BLVD
800 SJS 95116 834-E6
MELCHESTER DR
2900 SJS 95132 814-E3
MELCHOIR CT
900 SCIC 95046 957-F5
MELINA ST
200 SJS 95110 833-J4
MELINDA CIR
12100 SAR 95070 852-G5
MELISSA CT
2500 SJS 95121 854-J2
10300 CPTO 95014 851-J1
MELLO DR
600 SJS 95134 813-H5
MELLO PL
10100 CPTO 95014 852-F1
MELLO ST
1100 EPA 94303 791-A1
MELLON DR
18900 SAR 95070 852-H6
MELLOWOOD DR
12100 SAR 95070 852-G5
MELNIKOFF DR
3000 SJS 95121 855-C5
MELODY LN
- MGH 95037 937-B5
1600 SJS 95133 834-E3
3800 SCL 95051 832-H6
12300 LAH 94022 830-J1
17000 SCIC 95030 913-A4
MELON CT
700 SUNV 94087 832-C1
MELROSE AV
- SJS 95116 834-F3
MELVILLE AV
100 PA 94301 791-A5
MELVILLE WY
2400 SJS 95130 852-J7
MELVIN DR
6800 SJS 95129 852-E3
MELVIN HENRY CT
- SMCo 94061 790-A4
MELWOOD DR
1300 SJS 95118 874-B4
MEMBRILLO CORTE
3100 SCL 95051 833-A5
MEMOREX DR
900 SCL 95050 833-D2
MEMORIAL WY
100 SCIC 94305 790-H7
MEMORY LN
100 CMBL 95008 853-G6
MEMPHIS DR
300 CMBL 95008 853-C5
MENALTO AV
1900 MLPK 94025 791-A2
2100 EPA 94303 791-A1
MENALTO DR
12200 LAH 94022 830-H1
MENARD DR
100 SJS 95138 875-G6

MENAUL CT
100 SJS 95139 875-F7
MENDELSOHN LN
14800 SAR 95070 872-E3
MENDENHALL DR
1500 SJS 95130 853-B5
MENDOCINO WY
700 MGH 95037 937-B5
MENDOTA WY
2000 SJS 95122 834-J7
2000 SJS 95122 835-A7
MENDOZA AV
4500 SJS 95111 875-A1
MENHART DR
10200 SCIC 95014 852-H1
MENKER AV
300 SJS 95126 853-H2
300 SJS 95128 853-H2
MENLO AV
600 MLPK 94025 790-F4
MENLO DR
6300 SJS 95120 874-E7
6300 SJS 95120 894-E1
MENLO OAKS DR
200 SMCo 94025 790-H2
1000 MLPK 94025 790-H2
MENORCA CT
1400 SJS 95120 874-A7
MENZEL PL
2000 SCL 95050 833-C3
MERANO DR
100 SJS 95134 813-D2
MERCADO CT
600 MPS 95035 794-B5
MERCED CT
3100 SCL 95051 833-A3
MERCEDES AV
800 LALT 94022 811-D4
MERCEDES LN
- ATN 94027 790-D2
MERCEDES RD
22700 CPTO 95014 851-J2
MERCER AV
1400 SJS 95125 853-J5
MERCURY CT
1400 MPS 95035 794-D7
MERCURY DR
400 SUNV 94086 812-J6
MERCURY ST
48100 FRMT 94539 793-J1
MERCY ST
- MTVW 94041 812-A6
- MTVW 94041 811-H5
MEREDITH AV
1100 SJS 95125 854-A3
MERIDA DR
20200 SAR 95070 852-E5
MERIDIAN AV
300 SCIC 95126 853-J2
300 SJS 95126 853-J2
600 SJS 95128 853-J2
1000 SJS 95125 853-J2
1200 SCIC 95125 853-J6
1900 SJS 95124 853-J6
2800 SJS 95124 873-J1
2800 SJS 95125 873-J1
4600 SJS 95120 873-J1
4700 SJS 95124 874-A2
4700 SJS 95118 874-A2
5800 SJS 95120 874-B7
6200 SJS 95120 894-C1
MERIDIAN WY
200 SJS 95126 853-J2
1800 MTVW 94043 811-G4
MERK RD
- SCrC 95003 (975-A
See Page 955
MERKELEY ROW ST
10200 SCIC 95127 815-D7
MERLE AV
1000 SJS 95125 854-A
MERLIN LN
500 SJS 95111 854-F7
MERLOT CT
3000 SJS 95135 855-G
MERLOT DR
400 FRMT 94539 793-J2
600 FRMT 94539 794-A
MERRIBROOK CT
19800 SAR 95070 872-F
MERRIBROOK DR
19700 SAR 95070 872-F
MERRICK DR
20200 SAR 95070 872-E
MERRILL DR
1600 SJS 95124 873-J
MERRILL LP
1600 SJS 95124 873-J
1600 SJS 95118 873-J

STREET
Block City ZIP Pg-Grid

MERRILL RD
1100 SBnC - (1017-J7
See Page 997)
MERRILL ST
1000 MLPK 94025 790-F3
MERRIMAC DR
1000 SUNV 94087 832-B2
3300 SJS 95117 853-D4
3400 CMBL 95008 853-D4
MERRIMAN LN
12400 SCIC 95020 956-H3
MERRIMAN RD
10300 CPTO 95014 851-J2
MERRITON CT
1600 SJS 95124 873-J4
MERRITT DR
19600 CPTO 95014 832-E7
MERRITT RD
100 LALT 94022 811-E6
MERRIVALE WEST SQ
1300 SJS 95117 853-C4
MERRIWEATHER LN
400 SJS 95134 813-C2
MERRY LN
1400 SJS 95128 853-E5
MERRYWOOD DR
1400 SJS 95118 874-B4
MERVYNS WY
2700 SJS 95127 834-J4
MERZ CT
200 MPS 95035 794-A5
MESA AV
800 PA 94306 811-B4
MESA CT
- ATN 94027 790-B5
800 PA 94306 811-C4
MESA DR
1100 SJS 95118 874-C4
1100 SJS 95131 814-A5
MESA RD
200 SCIC 95020 978-A7
200 SCIC 95020 (998-A1
See Page 997)
5400 GIL 95020 978-A7
5500 GIL 95020 977-J6
MESA OAK CT
900 SUNV 94086 832-G2
MESA VERDE DR
2000 MPS 95035 794-E7
MESCALERO DR
5900 SJS 95123 874-H5
MESITA WY
1800 SJS 95124 873-H1
MESQUITE DR
2800 SCL 95051 833-B7
MESQUITE PL
800 SUNV 94086 832-G2
MESSINA DR
1600 SJS 95132 814-F3
META DR
2500 SJS 95130 853-A7
METCALF RD
- SCIC 95037 896-J3
- SCIC 95137 896-J3
- SJS 95037 896-J3
100 SJS 95138 875-J7
200 SJS 95138 876-C6
300 SCIC 95137 876-F5
600 SCIC 95138 876-F5
1100 SCIC 95037 876-F5
METEOR DR
21200 CPTO 95014 832-C6
METEOR PL
10500 CPTO 95014 832-C6
METHILHAVEN CT
3300 SJS 95121 855-C5
METHILHAVEN LN
3300 SJS 95121 855-C5
METHVEN LN
1200 MPS 95035 814-C1
METLER CT
18700 SAR 95070 872-H1
METRO CIR
1000 PA 94303 791-D5
METRO DR
- SJS 95110 833-H2
MEYER CIR
3000 SJS 95121 855-B3
3000 SJS 95148 855-B3
MEYERHOLZ CT
21700 CPTO 95014 832-B7
MIA CIR
4600 SJS 95136 874-H2
MIAMI DR
1600 SJS 95122 834-H7
MICHAEL CT
1400 MPS 95035 794-C5
20300 CPTO 95014 852-E2
MICHAEL DR
200 CMBL 95008 853-F6

MICHAEL LN
15600 MSER 95030 873-A5
MICHAEL ST
600 MPS 95035 794-C5
MICHAEL WY
- SCL 95051 832-J7
MICHAELS DR
20800 SAR 95070 872-C2
MICHAELS WY
- ATN 94027 790-E3
MICH BLUFF DR
1200 SJS 95131 814-D6
MICHELANGELO DR
900 SUNV 94087 832-F3
MICHELE CT
17400 SCIC 95037 917-D5
MICHELE WY
6700 SJS 95129 852-E3
MICHELE JEAN WY
2400 SCL 95050 833-C6
MICHELLE DR
200 CMBL 95008 853-B5
MICHIGAN AV
900 SJS 95125 854-A4
1200 SJS 95002 793-C7
1600 EPA 94303 791-B1
MICHIGAN RD
200 MPS 95035 794-A5
MICHON CT
1700 SJS 95124 873-H4
MICHON DR
1700 SJS 95124 873-J4
1800 SJS 95032 873-H5
MICRO CT
1000 SJS 95120 894-H4
MICRO PL
1000 SJS 95120 894-H4
MIDAS WY
1200 SUNV 94086 812-J6
MIDDLE AV
600 MLPK 94025 790-F5
E MIDDLE AV
- MGH 95046 937-E4
100 SCIC 95046 937-G3
W MIDDLE AV
- MGH 95037 937-C4
- SCIC 95037 937-C4
MIDDLE CT
400 MLPK 94025 790-F6
MIDDLEBOROUGH CIR
2600 SJS 95132 814-D4
MIDDLEBURY DR
500 SUNV 94087 832-D2
MIDDLEBURY LN
500 LALT 94022 811-D6
MIDDLEBURY WY
7200 SJS 95139 875-G7
MIDDLEFIELD AV
- MTVW 94043 811-G2
MIDDLEFIELD RD
- ATN 94027 790-E1
100 PA 94301 790-E1
500 MLPK 94025 790-E1
600 PA 94301 791-A4
1600 PA 94303 791-A4
2600 PA 94306 791-A4
3100 SMCo 94063 790-E1
3600 PA 94306 811-E1
3600 PA 94303 811-E1
E MIDDLEFIELD RD
- SUNV 94086 812-B4
- MTVW 94043 812-B4
700 MTVW 94086 812-B4
W MIDDLEFIELD RD
500 MTVW 94043 811-H3
2200 SCIC 94043 811-H3
MIDDLE FORK LN
13400 LAH 94022 810-J7
MIDDLE GATE ST
- ATN 94027 790-D2
MIDDLE PARK DR
4000 SJS 95135 855-F3
MIDDLETON AV
1600 LALT 94024 831-J4
MIDDLETON CT
1300 LALT 94024 831-J4
MIDDLETON RD
- SMCo 94020 850-D7
MIDDLETOWN DR
2200 SJS 95008 853-B7
MIDFIELD AV
1300 SJS 95122 834-G7
MIDHURST CT
3100 SJS 95135 855-F3
MIDHURST WY
2900 SJS 95135 855-E3
MIDPINE AV
1200 SJS 95122 854-H2
MIDTOWN CT
2700 PA 94303 791-C6

MIDVALE LN
700 SJS 95136 874-E1
N MIDWAY ST
- CMBL 95008 853-G6
S MIDWAY ST
200 CMBL 95008 853-G6
MIDWICK DR
- MPS 95035 794-A4
MIELKE DR
400 MLPK 94025 790-G3
MIETTE WY
1300 SUNV 94087 832-C4
MIGNON DR
2600 SJS 95132 814-D5
MIGNOT LN
400 SJS 95111 854-J6
MIGUEL AV
1100 LALT 94024 831-H4
MIGUELITA AV
10100 SCIC 95127 815-B6
MILAN DR
400 SJS 95134 813-H4
MILANI CT
100 LGTS 95030 873-B4
MILANO TER
300 MPS 95035 793-H3
MILANO WY
1900 MTVW 94040 831-H1
MILAS CT
7400 GIL 95020 977-H3
MILBURN ST
3500 SJS 95148 835-E6
MILDRED AV
1100 SJS 95125 854-A4
MILES AV
- LGTS 95030 873-A7
MILES CT
800 SCL 95051 833-A5
MILES DR
2900 SCL 95051 833-A5
MILFORD DR
21200 CPTO 95014 832-C7
MILFORD WY
- SCIC 95127 835-A3
- SJS 95127 835-A3
MILHON CT
2600 SJS 95148 855-B1
MILITARY WY
400 PA 94306 811-C2
MILJEVICH DR
20000 SAR 95070 852-E7
MILKY WY
900 CPTO 95014 852-C3
MILL CT
18000 SAR 95070 852-D5
MILL RD
- SJS 95002 793-B7
MILL ST
- LGTS 95032 893-A1
MILLAR AV
- SJS 95127 834-J2
- SCIC 95127 834-J2
- SCIC 95127 835-A2
2800 SCL 95051 833-A3
MILLARD LN
21400 CPTO 95014 832-C6
MILLBRAE LN
200 LGTS 95030 873-B7
MILLBRAE WY
2700 SJS 95121 855-D3
MILLBROOK CT
500 CMBL 95008 853-C6
MILLBROOK DR
3000 SJS 95148 855-D1
MILL CREEK LN
500 SCL 95134 813-E4
5200 SJS 95136 875-A3
MILL CREEK WY
- MGH 95037 916-H4
MILLER AV
- SJS 95112 854-E3
600 CPTO 95014 852-F4
1000 GIL 95020 977-H4
1000 SJS 95129 852-F4
1400 CMBL 95008 873-B1
1600 SCIC 94024 831-F4
2600 MTVW 94040 811-E3
4200 PA 94306 811-E3
10300 SCIC 95014 852-F4
12000 SAR 95070 852-G6
MILLER CT
- SMCo 94061 790-B3
4300 PA 94306 811-E3
19400 SAR 95070 852-F5
MILLER ST
600 SJS 95110 834-A4
MILLET CT
3500 SJS 95127 835-C2
MILLHAVEN PL
100 SJS 95111 874-J1

MILLICENT CT
3500 SJS 95148 835-C4
MILLICH DR
500 CMBL 95008 853-C4
MILLICH LN
600 CMBL 95008 853-C4
1300 SJS 95117 853-C4
MILLIE AV
900 MLPK 94025 790-F4
MILLIGAN DR
5400 SJS 95124 873-J6
MILLION CT
2600 SJS 95148 835-E6
MILL POND DR
300 SJS 95125 854-D5
400 SCIC 95125 854-D5
MILLRICH DR
17300 LGTS 95030 873-B4
MILL RISE WY
17100 LGTS 95032 893-D1
MILL RIVER LN
400 SJS 95134 813-H4
MILL RIVER PL
400 SJS 95134 813-F3
MILLS AV
600 LALT 94022 811-F6
2000 SMCo 94025 790-C6
MILLS CT
900 SJS 95125 854-B2
1400 MLPK 94025 790-F3
MILLS ST
1200 MLPK 94025 790-F3
MILLS CORNER LN
900 SJS 95122 854-G1
MILLSGATE LN
1700 SJS 95122 854-G1
MILL STONE LN
- SJS 95136 875-A3
MILL STREAM DR
700 SJS 95125 854-D5
MILLSWOOD CT
700 SJS 95120 894-J3
MILLWATER CT
100 MPS 95035 794-C2
MILMAR WY
100 LGTS 95032 873-E5
MILMONT DR
- FRMT 94538 793-H3
1700 MPS 95035 793-J5
MILMONT ST
- FRMT 94538 793-H2
MILO CT
800 SJS 95133 814-G6
N MILPITAS BLVD
- MPS 95035 794-A5
1100 MPS 95035 793-J3
2000 FRMT 94539 793-J3
S MILPITAS BLVD
- MPS 95035 794-B7
100 MPS 95035 814-B1
MILROY PL
1600 SJS 95124 873-J3
N MILTON AV
- CMBL 95008 853-D5
S MILTON AV
400 CMBL 95008 853-D6
MILTON CT
3000 MTVW 94040 831-J2
MILTON ST
1600 SMCo 94061 790-B3
MILTON WY
1200 SJS 95125 854-B3
MILVERTON RD
600 LALT 94022 831-D1
MIMOSA CT
500 SCIC 94024 831-J6
MIMOSA WY
100 SMCo 94028 810-D4
6200 SJS 95138 875-F6
MINAKER CT
10000 CPTO 95014 852-B1
MINARDI AV
1500 SJS 95125 854-A6
MINARET AV
200 MTVW 94043 812-A5
MINAS DR
4700 SJS 95136 874-D2
MINAS DE ORO
1700 SJS 95116 834-F3
MINDEN CT
5600 SJS 95123 875-A4
MINDY WY
600 SJS 95123 874-J7
MINE HILL RD
20500 SCIC 95120 894-H6
MINER PL
10100 CPTO 95014 832-E7
MINERAL SPRING WY
- SCIC 95030 913-B3

MINES RD
25800 AlaC 94550 (798-F1
See Page 797)
47200 SCIC 95140 (819-A3
See Page 799)
48000 SCIC 95140 (798-F1
See Page 797)
MINETTE DR
10600 SCIC 95014 852-H2
MINETTE PL
10600 SCIC 95014 852-H2
MINIDOKA AV
100 SJS 95127 834-H1
MINNA WY
1900 SJS 95124 873-G1
MINNESOTA AV
200 SJS 95125 854-B2
1300 SJS 95125 853-J4
MINNIS CIR
- MPS 95035 793-J4
MINOCA RD
- PTLV 94028 810-D5
MINOCQUA CT
19700 SAR 95070 872-F2
MINOR AV
400 SJS 95126 854-B1
500 SJS 95125 854-B1
MINORCA CT
12500 LAH 94022 811-A7
MINORU DR
1000 SJS 95120 894-H4
MINTO CT
3500 SJS 95132 814-F2
MINTO DR
1900 SJS 95132 814-F2
MINTON LN
500 MTVW 94041 811-J5
MINTWOOD CT
4800 SJS 95129 852-B7
MINUET DR
1800 SJS 95131 814-C4
MINUTEMAN WY
1500 SJS 95132 814-E4
MIRA WY
- SMCo 94028 810-D4
MIRA BELLA CIR
2700 MGH 95037 917-F7
MIRA BELLA PL
16500 MGH 95037 917-F6
MIRABELLI CIR
- SJS 95134 813-D2
MIRACLE MOUNTAIN DR
5900 SJS 95123 874-E5
MIRADA AV
600 SCIC 94305 810-H1
MIRADERO AV
15000 SCIC 95127 815-B6
16000 SJS 95127 815-B6
MIRA FLORES CT
16500 MGH 95037 917-G6
MIRAFLORES WY
1200 LALT 94024 831-G2
MIRAGE WY
3200 SJS 95135 855-G3
MIRA LAGOS DR
16500 MGH 95037 917-G7
MIRA LOMA WY
3900 SJS 95111 854-J7
MIRALOMA WY
1100 SUNV 94086 812-H7
12500 LAH 94024 831-E2
MIRAMAR AV
4800 SJS 95129 852-J1
MIRAMAR WY
1100 SUNV 94086 832-H3
3700 SCL 95051 832-H3
MIRAMESA CT
3700 SCL 95051 832-H3
MIRAMONTE AV
100 PA 94306 791-A6
100 SCIC 95037 916-D2
800 MTVW 94040 811-H7
900 LALT 94024 831-H2
1600 MTVW 94040 831-H2
MIRAMONTE RD
10900 CPTO 95014 851-J2
MIRANDA AV
3200 PA 94304 811-B4
4000 PA 94306 811-C4
MIRANDA CT
14400 LAH 94022 811-C5
MIRANDA GRN
800 PA 94306 811-C5
MIRANDA RD
14000 LAH 94022 811-C6
MIRANDA WY
14300 LAH 94022 811-C5
MIRA PLAZA CT
1900 SCL 95051 832-H3

MIRASOL CT
6100 SJS 95123 874-F6
MIRASSOU DR
1600 SJS 95124 873-J5
MIRASSOU PL
1700 SJS 95124 873-J5
MIRAVALLE AV
1300 LALT 94024 831-J3
MIRAVERDE CT
3700 SCL 95051 832-H3
MIRA VISTA CIR
3300 SJS 95132 814-H5
MIRA VISTA CT
3300 SJS 95132 814-H5
MIRA VISTA RD
10200 CPTO 95014 852-A1
MIREILLE DR
5600 SJS 95118 874-A6
MIREVAL RD
16200 LGTS 95032 893-C2
16200 SCIC 95032 893-C2
16500 SCIC 95032 893-C2
MIRIAM CT
1700 SJS 95124 853-H6
MIRMIROU DR
13800 LAH 94022 810-H6
MISE AV
4900 SJS 95124 873-G4
MISSION DR
100 EPA 94303 791-C3
MISSION ST
500 SCL 95050 833-F5
E MISSION ST
- SJS 95112 834-B3
W MISSION ST
100 SJS 95110 834-A4
MISSION WY
- CMBL 95008 853-D6
21500 CPTO 95014 832-B7
MISSION COLLEGE BLVD
2000 SCL 95054 813-B5
3000 SUNV 94089 813-A6
MISSION GLEN DR
2300 SCL 95051 833-B2
MISSION GREENS DR
2600 SJS 95148 855-C1
MISSION HILL PL
2700 SJS 95148 855-C1
MISSION SPRINGS CIR
1500 SJS 95131 814-C6
MISSION SPRINGS CT
1500 SJS 95131 814-C6
MISSION VIEW DR
18500 MGH 95037 917-B3
18500 SCIC 95037 917-B3
MISTAYA CT
1400 SUNV 94087 832-C4
MISTFLOWER DR
800 SJS 95122 854-F1
MISTLETOE RD
200 LGTS 95030 872-J3
MISTY GLEN CT
- SJS 95111 854-J5
MISTY WILLOW CT
6700 SJS 95120 894-F2
MITCHELL AV
16800 LGTS 95032 873-C6
MITCHELL CT
1000 CMBL 95128 853-E4
MITCHELL LN
400 PA 94301 790-H5
5200 SJS 95111 875-B3
MITTON CT
3500 SJS 95148 835-F7
MITTON DR
2900 SJS 95148 835-E7
MITTY WY
4900 SJS 95129 852-J2
MITZI DR
4100 SJS 95117 853-A3
4100 SJS 95129 853-A3
MIWOK DR
6000 SJS 95123 874-H6
MIYUKI AV
- SJS 95119 875-D5
MIYUKI DR
1600 SJS 95193 875-C5
5700 SJS 95119 875-C5
MOANA CT
800 PA 94306 811-C5
MOCHO CT
1300 SJS 95121 854-J2
MOCKINGBIRD CT
1100 SJS 95120 894-H4
MOCKINGBIRD LN
800 PA 94306 811-B4
800 SUNV 94087 832-A2
9200 GIL 95020 957-F7

MOCKINGBIRD HILL LN
1100 SJS 95120 894-G5
10600 SCIC 95120 894-G5
MOCKING PLACE WY
1600 SJS 95121 855-B4
MODOC CT
500 SJS 95123 874-H6
MODOC TR
20900 SCIC 95030 913-A2
MODRED DR
3100 SJS 95127 814-H7
MOEN CT
7300 SJS 95139 895-F1
MOFFAT ST
1000 SJS 95002 813-B1
MOFFETT BLVD
100 MTVW 94043 811-J4
400 SCIC 94043 811-J4
500 MTVW 94043 812-A3
500 SCIC 94043 812-A2
MOFFETT CIR
1000 PA 94303 791-D5
MOFFETT PARK CT
900 SUNV 94089 812-H3
MOFFETT PARK DR
200 SUNV 94089 812-J2
1300 SUNV 94089 813-A2
W MOFFETT PARK DR
100 SUNV 94089 812-E4
MOFFO CT
1400 SJS 95121 854-J3
MOHAWK DR
5900 SJS 95123 874-H6
MOHICAN DR
600 SJS 95123 874-H5
MOIRA GLEN CT
1700 SJS 95112 854-F1
MOJAVE DR
6200 SJS 95120 874-D7
6200 SJS 95120 894-D1
MOJONERA CT
100 LGTS 95030 873-C3
MOKELUMNE PL
1200 SJS 95120 874-C6
MOLINARO ST
3100 SCL 95054 813-E7
MOLINO AV
400 SUNV 94086 812-C7
400 SUNV 94086 832-C1
MOLTZEN DR
7400 CPTO 95014 852-D3
MONA WY
3500 SJS 95008 853-C4
3500 CMBL 95008 853-C4
3500 SJS 95130 853-C4
MONACO DR
2300 SJS 95124 873-E3
MONASTERY WY
700 SCL 95050 833-D5
MONDIGO AV
2000 SJS 95122 834-J7
MONET CIR
4100 SJS 95136 874-H1
MONET PL
4300 SJS 95136 874-H1
MONETA WY
200 CMBL 95008 853-G6
MONFERINO DR
600 SJS 95112 834-C3
MONICA DR
- SCIC 95037 916-G4
MONICA LN
500 CMBL 95008 853-E4
700 SJS 95008 853-E4
1000 CMBL 95128 853-E4
MONITOR CT
2200 SJS 95125 854-D7
MONKTON CT
3000 SJS 95148 855-C2
MONMOUTH DR
200 MPS 95035 794-D7
MONO WY
100 SCL 95051 832-H7
MONO LAKE CT
5900 SJS 95123 874-G7
MONROE CT
- LGTS 95030 873-B6
MONROE DR
100 PA 94306 811-D3
100 MTVW 94040 811-D3
MONROE ST
- SUNV 94086 832-J2
- SCL 95050 833-D2
- SCL 95128 833-E5
400 SJS 95128 833-E7
500 SJS 95050 833-E7
2300 SCL 95051 833-A2
3200 SCL 95051 832-J2

S MONROE ST
300 SJS 95128 853-E1
500 SJS 95050 853-E1
MONROVIA DR
1700 SJS 95122 855-A2
1800 SJS 95121 855-A2
MONROVIA ST
21500 CPTO 95014 852-B3
MONTAGE CT
1800 SJS 95131 814-C4
MONTAGUE EXWY
- MPS 95035 814-B3
900 SJS 95132 814-B3
1300 SJS 95131 814-B3
1300 SJS 95131 813-H5
1300 MPS 95035 813-H5
MONTAGUE EXWY Rt#-G4
- SJS 95134 813-F5
400 SCL 95054 813-D6
400 SCL 95134 813-F5
600 MPS 95035 813-F5
600 SJS 95131 813-F5
1500 SCIC 95134 813-F5
W MONTAGUE EXWY
- MPS 95035 814-A4
MONTALBAN DR
1400 SJS 95120 874-A7
1400 SJS 95120 894-A1
MONTALTO DR
1500 MTVW 94040 811-H7
MONTALVO DR
5900 SJS 95123 874-G6
MONTALVO LN
20400 SAR 95070 872-D4
MONTALVO RD
14700 SAR 95070 872-E4
MONTALVO HTS CT
15200 SAR 95070 872-D4
MONTALVO HTS DR
20400 SAR 95070 872-D4
MONTALVO OAKS
20400 SAR 95070 872-D3
MONTANA CT
6400 SJS 95120 894-E1
MONTANA LN
- SMCo 94025 790-D5
MONTARA CT
- PTLV 94028 810-D6
MONTARA DR
19000 SCIC 95030 892-H4
MONTAUK CT
19600 SAR 95070 872-F2
MONTAUK DR
19500 SAR 95070 872-F2
MONTCLAIR AV
200 SJS 95116 834-G2
MONTCLAIR CT
100 LGTS 95030 872-J3
MONTCLAIR DR
300 SCL 95051 832-H7
MONTCLAIR RD
100 LGTS 95030 873-A3
200 LGTS 95030 872-J3
400 SAR 95070 872-J3
MONTCLAIRE CT
23200 LALT 94024 831-H4
MONTCLAIRE PL
1400 LALT 94024 831-H4
MONTCLAIRE WY
11400 LALT 94024 831-H4
MONTE CT
2000 MPS 95035 814-E1
21800 CPTO 95014 832-B7
MONTE DR
1100 MPS 95035 814-E1
MONTEAGLE DR
1200 SJS 95127 835-A4
MONTEBELLO AV
100 MTVW 94043 811-G3
MONTE BELLO DR
1000 GIL 95020 977-G2
MONTE BELLO RD
- PA 94304 830-G6
- PA 94304 851-A1
- PA 94304 850-J1
12800 SCIC 95014 851-C3
MONTEBELLO WY
- LGTS 95030 893-A1
MONTEBELLO OAKS CT
1500 LALT 94024 831-J3
MONTE CARLO WY
1800 SCIC 95125 853-H6
MONTECITO AV
1200 MTVW 94043 811-G3
MONTECITO CT
- SJS 95135 855-G3
MONTECITO DR
3200 SJS 95135 855-G3

MONTECITO WY
300 MPS 95035 793-H4
MONTE CRESTA WY
2800 SJS 95132 814-E4
MONTEGO CT
6400 SJS 95120 894-A1
MONTEGO DR
2600 SJS 95120 894-B1
2600 SCIC 95120 894-B1
MONTEGO LN
- SMCo 94061 790-B4
MONTELEGRE DR
1400 SJS 95120 874-A7
MONTELENA DR
3100 SJS 95135 855-E2
MONTE LINDO CT
2600 SJS 95121 855-D3
MONTELLANO CT
1600 SJS 95120 894-A1
MONTELLANO DR
1500 SJS 95120 874-A7
MONTEMAR WY
1600 SCIC 95125 853-H5
MONTEREY
- MTVW 94043 812-A2
- MTVW 94043 811-J2
MONTEREY AV
400 LGTS 95030 873-A6
2000 SMCo 94025 790-C6
2100 SCL 95051 833-A2
MONTEREY CIR
900 SJS 95138 875-F6
MONTEREY CT
1900 SCL 95051 833-A3
11200 CPTO 95014 852-B3
MONTEREY HWY Rt#-82
- SJS 95111 854-F5
- SJS 95125 854-D2
200 SCIC 95111 854-F5
700 SJS 95112 854-D2
700 SJS 95110 854-D2
3700 SJS 95136 854-F5
4100 SJS 95136 874-H1
4100 SJS 95111 874-H1
4700 SJS 95136 875-A2
4700 SJS 95111 875-A2
5100 SJS 95123 875-A2
5200 SJS 95193 875-A2
MONTEREY PL
300 LALT 94022 811-D6
MONTEREY RD
500 SJS 95037 896-B3
500 SCIC 95037 896-B3
5300 SJS 95111 875-C3
5500 GIL 95020 978-A4
5500 SJS 95138 875-C3
5800 SJS 95139 875-C3
5800 SJS 95139 895-H1
5800 SJS 95137 875-C3
5800 SJS 95137 895-H1
5900 SJS 95139 896-B3
5900 SCIC 95137 896-B3
5900 SCIC 95137 895-H1
6000 SJS 95121 896-B3
6100 SJS 95141 896-B3
6200 SCIC 95020 978-A4
8200 SCIC 95137 896-B3
8900 GIL 95020 957-H5
10000 MGH 95037 916-J6
10000 SCIC 95037 896-B3
10400 SCIC 95020 957-F1
11000 SCIC 95046 957-F1
11200 SJS 95037 916-E1
11200 SCIC 95037 916-E1
11600 MGH 95037 917-A7
12300 SCIC 95046 937-E5
12800 SCIC 95037 916-E1
13300 MGH 95037 937-A1
13900 MGH 95046 937-E5
MONTEREY ST
7000 GIL 95020 978-A3
7900 GIL 95020 977-J1
8600 GIL 95020 957-J7
MONTE ROSA DR
600 MLPK 94025 790-D7
600 MLPK 94025 810-D1
MONTE SERENO TER
- FRMT 94539 794-B1
MONTE SOL TER
400 MPS 95035 793-G3
MONTE SUNSET DR
20700 SCIC 95120 894-H1
MONTEVAL CT
1600 SJS 95120 873-J7
MONTEVAL LN
1500 SJS 95120 874-A7
MONTEVAL PL
1500 SJS 95120 874-A7

MONTE VERANO CT
- SJS 95116 834-H3
MONTE VERDE CT
1200 LALT 94024 831-H4
MONTEVERDE DR
5900 SJS 95120 874-A7
6100 SJS 95120 894-A1
MONTE VERDE LN
3200 SJS 95135 855-G3
MONTEVIDEO LN
1600 SJS 95127 835-A5
MONTE VILLA CT
100 CMBL 95008 873-E2
MONTEVINA RD
18200 SCIC 95030 892-E1
20200 SCIC 95070 892-E1
MONTEVINO DR
5800 SJS 95123 874-G5
MONTE VISTA
- MTVW 94043 812-A2
MONTE VISTA AV
- ATN 94027 790-C4
MONTE VISTA DR
15400 SAR 95070 872-G4
MONTE VISTA WY
- GIL 95020 977-H3
MONTEWOOD DR
18600 SAR 95070 872-H5
MONTEZUMA DR
2200 SJS 95008 853-B7
MONTFORD CT
1800 SJS 95132 814-E3
MONTGOMERY AV
1200 SMCo 94061 790-B3
MONTGOMERY BEND
6000 SJS 95135 855-H6
MONTGOMERY CT
6000 SJS 95135 855-H6
MONTGOMERY DR
3200 SCL 95054 813-B7
MONTGOMERY LN
- SBnC - (1020-D3
See Page 999)
5400 SJS 95135 855-H6
MONTGOMERY PL
6100 SJS 95135 855-H6
MONTGOMERY PL E
6000 SJS 95135 855-H6
MONTGOMERY PL S
6000 SJS 95135 855-H6
MONTGOMERY PL W
6000 SJS 95135 855-H6
MONTGOMERY ST
- LGTS 95030 873-A6
800 MTVW 94041 811-J6
MONTGOMERY ST Rt#-82
- SJS 95110 834-A7
N MONTGOMERY ST
100 SJS 95110 834-A6
S MONTGOMERY ST Rt#-82
- SJS 95110 834-A7
- SJS 95113 834-A7
MONTGOMERY CORNER
6000 SJS 95135 855-H6
MONTICELLO AV
200 SJS 95125 854-D4
MONTICELLO WY
2400 SCL 95051 832-J2
15100 MGH 95037 937-A4
MONTIERRA PL
3200 SJS 95135 855-G3
MONTMORENCY CT
4300 SJS 95118 874-C2
MONTMORENCY DR
1200 SJS 95118 874-B2
MONTORO CT
1400 SJS 95120 874-B7
MONTORO DR
6000 SJS 95120 874-B7
MONTOYA CIR
17400 MGH 95037 917-B6
MONTPELIER DR
2300 SJS 95116 834-G2
MONTPERE WY
18300 SAR 95070 872-H1
MONTREAL CT
4700 SJS 95130 853-A7
MONTREAL DR
4700 SJS 95130 853-A7
4800 SJS 95130 852-J7
MONTROSE AV
700 PA 94303 811-F1
MONTROSE ST
13000 SAR 95070 852-H7
MONTROSE WY
1600 SJS 95124 874-A3
MONTWOOD CIR
300 SMCo 94061 790-B4

STREET
Block City ZIP Pg-Grid

MONTY CIR
800 SCL 95050 833-C5
MONUMENT CT
500 FRMT 94539 794-A2
MOODY CT
26800 LAH 94022 830-J2
MOODY RD
25300 LAH 94022 831-A3
26200 LAH 94022 830-H3
26200 SCIC 95014 831-A3
26200 SCIC 95014 830-H2
MOODY SPRINGS CT
1200 LAH 94022 831-B3
MOON CT
1100 MPS 95035 814-A2
MOON LN
14000 LAH 94022 810-H6
MOON PL
3600 MntC - (1017-A6
See Page 997)
MOON BEAM DR
- MTVW 94043 811-J3
MOONBEAM WY
1100 MPS 95035 814-A2
MOONFLOWER CT
4100 SJS 95135 855-F3
MOON GATE PL
1000 SJS 95120 894-F2
MOON GLOW CT
700 SJS 95123 874-F3
MOONLIGHT CIR
1300 MPS 95035 813-J3
MOONLIGHT WY
1100 MPS 95035 813-J2
MOONLITE PL
2600 SCL 95051 833-B4
MOONSTAR CT
3000 SJS 95148 835-B5
MOONSTONE CT
5000 SJS 95136 874-E2
MOORBROOK DR
2600 SJS 95132 814-F6
MOORE RD
300 WDSD 94062 790-A6
MOORGLEN CT
2300 SJS 95133 834-F2
MOORPARK AV
1500 SJS 95117 853-B2
2000 SJS 95128 853-E2
2200 SCIC 95128 853-E2
4200 SJS 95129 853-B2
4600 SJS 95129 852-J2
MOORPARK WY
- MTVW 94041 812-A6
MORA CT
1700 SCIC 94024 831-G4
MORA DR
700 SCIC 94024 831-G4
2200 MTVW 94040 811-F3
11200 SCIC 95014 831-F5
MORADA LN
100 SBnC - (1020-G4
See Page 999)
MORAES CT
1100 SJS 95127 835-B3
MORAGA AV
5800 SJS 95123 874-F5
MORAGA CT
900 PA 94303 791-E6
MORAGA DR
800 MTVW 94041 812-A7
MORAGA ST
1100 SCL 95051 833-A4
MORAGA WY
200 SJS 95119 875-C7
MORA GLEN DR
23100 SCIC 94024 831-G5
MORA HEIGHTS WY
23200 SCIC 94024 831-G5
MORAINE DR
2200 SCL 95051 833-A1
MORAN DR
4300 SJS 95129 853-A3
MORAN LN
19900 SAR 95070 872-E1
MORAQUITA CT
- SCIC 94024 831-F5
MORAY CT
19500 SAR 95070 852-F7
19500 SAR 95070 872-F1
MORDEN DR
4800 SJS 95130 852-J7
MORE AV
200 SJS 95030 872-J1
200 CMBL 95030 872-J1
200 CMBL 95030 873-A2
200 LGTS 95030 873-A2
500 LGTS 95030 872-J4
MORECAMBE DR
7000 SJS 95120 894-G3

MORELAND WY
4000 SJS 95130 853-B4
MORELY CT
1100 SJS 95122 854-H1
MORENGO DR
10600 SCIC 95014 852-H2
MORENO AV
700 PA 94303 791-D5
3200 SJS 95127 835-B3
MORENO CT
12900 SCIC 95046 937-G6
MORENO LN
600 SCL 95050 833-D5
2100 SCIC 95020 958-C4
MORETTI DR
10200 SCIC 95014 852-H2
MORETTI LN
200 MPS 95035 794-C6
MOREVERN CIR
7500 SJS 95135 855-J6
MOREY DR
500 MLPK 94025 790-G4
MORGAN AV
1800 MGH 95037 917-D6
MORGAN CT
1600 MTVW 94043 811-H2
1900 MGH 95037 917-D5
MORGAN PL
700 LALT 94024 831-G1
3400 SJS 95132 814-G3
MORGAN ST
1500 MTVW 94043 811-H2
MORNING GLORY LN
1600 SJS 95124 873-J6
MORNINGSIDE
600 LALT 94022 831-D1
MORNINGSIDE DR
1000 SUNV 94087 832-A1
5500 SJS 95138 875-F1
MORNING SPRING CT
11500 CPTO 95014 852-A4
MORNING STAR DR
- SJS 95131 814-B5
MORNING SUN CT
- MTVW 94043 811-J3
MORNING VIEW TER
- FRMT 94539 794-B1
MOROCCO DR
1600 SJS 95125 853-J7
MORRENE DR
100 CMBL 95008 853-B5
MORRIE DR
3600 SJS 95127 835-C3
MORRILL AV
1100 SJS 95132 814-D2
MORRILL CT
1100 SJS 95132 814-F5
MORRILL RD
23300 SCIC 95030 913-E6
23500 SCrC 95030 913-C7
MORRIS AV
1000 SJS 95126 853-J1
MORRIS CT
2100 SJS 95126 833-G5
MORRIS DR
3100 PA 94303 791-E6
MORRIS LN
100 CMBL 95008 853-E7
MORRISON AV
100 SJS 95126 833-J7
200 SCIC 95126 833-J7
200 SCIC 95126 853-J1
200 SCL 95051 833-B3
N MORRISON AV
- SJS 95126 833-J6
MORRISON LN
300 CMBL 95008 873-C1
MORRO VISTA LN
100 SMCo 94028 810-C3
MORROW CT
- SJS 95139 875-F7
MORSE AV
200 SUNV 94086 812-F5
900 SUNV 94089 812-F4
MORSE CT
400 SUNV 94086 812-F5
MORSE LN
1600 SCL 95051 833-B4
MORSE ST
500 SJS 95126 833-G5
1800 SCL 95050 833-G5
MORTON AV
1100 SCL 95051 833-B4
1300 LALT 94024 831-J4
1400 LALT 94024 832-A4
MORTON CT
1000 MTVW 94040 811-F5
MORTON ST
- PA 94303 791-C5

MORTON WY
5600 SJS 95123 874-F4
MOSEGARD LN
14700 SCIC 95037 937-A5
MOSELLE CT
200 SJS 95119 875-D7
MOSELLE DR
6700 SJS 95119 875-D7
MOSS CT
1000 SCIC 95020 957-F5
MOSS DR
800 SJS 95116 834-G5
MOSSBROOK AV
1700 SJS 95130 853-A5
MOSSBROOK CIR
4500 SJS 95130 853-A5
MOSSCREEK LN
3300 SJS 95121 855-D7
MOSSDALE WY
2300 SJS 95133 814-F7
2300 SJS 95133 834-E1
MOSSHALL WY
3100 SJS 95135 855-F3
MOSS HOLLOW DR
2800 SJS 95121 855-B2
2800 SJS 95122 855-B2
MOSSLAND DR
1300 SJS 95131 814-D7
MOSSMILL CT
2800 SJS 95121 854-J3
MOSS OAK WY
6100 SJS 95120 874-D7
MOSS POINT DR
2800 SJS 95127 835-A5
MOSSROSE WY
- GIL 95020 977-E1
MOSSWELL CT
100 SJS 95138 875-D4
MOSSWOOD DR
2600 SJS 95132 814-E5
MOSSWOOD LN
2400 SCL 95051 833-C1
MOSSY OAK CT
10000 CPTO 95014 831-J7
MOULIN LN
- SJS 95135 855-F3
MOULTON DR
- ATN 94027 790-F2
1100 MPS 95035 814-E1
MOUNDHAVEN CT
100 SJS 95111 874-J1
MOUNTAIN DR
20300 SCIC 95120 895-A6
MOUNTAIN WY
19200 SCIC 95030 872-G6
MOUNTAIN CHARLIE RD
17500 SCIC 95030 913-A4
20700 SCIC 95030 912-J4
22500 SCrC 95030 912-J7
MOUNTAIN CREEK CT
1800 SJS 95148 835-D4
MOUNTAINGATE WY
2400 SJS 95133 814-H3
MOUNTAIN HAWK CT
- SJS 95120 894-F4
MOUNTAIN HOME DR
500 SJS 95136 854-E7
MOUNTAIN MEADOW CT
5900 SJS 95135 856-A7
MOUNTAIN QUAIL CIR
1100 SJS 95120 894-F3
MTN SHADOWS DR
1200 MTVW 94043 811-H3
MTN SHADOWS RD
1000 SJS 95120 894-H4
MTN SPRINGS DR
100 SJS 95136 854-E6
MTN SWALLOW CT
7100 SJS 95120 894-F3
MOUNTAIN VIEW AV
- SCIC 95127 815-A7
100 MTVW 94041 811-H5
200 SJS 95127 814-J7
800 LALT 94024 811-H5
900 MTVW 94040 811-H5
MOUNTAIN VIEW CIR
- MGH 95037 916-H3
MOUNTAIN VIEW CT
18000 SCIC 95030 912-J3
MTN VIEW-ALVISO RD Rt#-237
200 MTVW 94041 812-A6
500 MTVW 94043 812-A6
MOUNT BACHE RD
25000 SCrC 95030 934-A3
26100 SCIC 95030 934-A3
MOUNT BLANC WY
1600 SJS 95127 835-B4

MOUNT CARMEL DR
900 SJS 95120 894-F1
MOUNTCASTLE WY
4100 SJS 95136 874-D2
MOUNT CHUAI
24900 SCIC 95120 934-H1
24900 SCIC 95037 934-H1
MOUNT CHUAI RD
- SCIC 95030 934-G2
24700 SCIC 95120 934-G2
24700 SCIC 95037 934-G2
MOUNT CLARE DR
2900 SJS 95148 835-C7
MOUNTCLIFFE CT
3800 SJS 95136 874-D1
MOUNT CREST DR
11200 CPTO 95014 852-B3
MOUNT DARWIN DR
1000 SJS 95120 894-F2
MOUNT DAVIDSON CT
3500 SJS 95124 873-E2
MOUNT DAVIDSON DR
2200 SJS 95124 873-E2
MOUNT DIABLO AV
1400 MPS 95035 814-D1
MOUNT DIABLO DR
1400 SJS 95127 835-B4
MOUNT EDEN CT
21400 SAR 95070 872-B1
MOUNT EDEN RD
- SCIC 95014 851-J7
21700 SAR 95070 872-B1
22300 SCIC 95070 872-B1
22900 SCIC 95070 852-A7
23500 SCIC 95070 851-J7
MOUNT EL SERENO CT
19400 SCIC 95030 892-F2
MOUNT EVEREST CT
1500 SJS 95127 835-B4
MOUNT EVEREST DR
3200 SJS 95127 835-B4
MOUNTFORD DR
6200 SJS 95123 875-A7
MOUNT FOREST DR
6500 SJS 95120 894-F1
MOUNT FRAZIER DR
1400 SJS 95127 835-C4
MOUNT HAMILTON AV
- LALT 94022 811-D6
MOUNT HAMILTON CT
100 LALT 94022 811-D6
MOUNT HAMILTON RD Rt#-130
- SCIC 95127 815-B7
- SCIC 95127 835-D1
- SCIC 95140 835-G2
1000 SCIC 95140 815-E7
11700 SCIC 95127 836-B4
11700 SCIC 95140 836-J6
12000 SCIC 95148 836-B4
13100 SCIC 95135 836-F7
13400 SCIC 95135 856-H1
14000 SCIC 95140 856-H1
17200 SCIC 95140 837-A6
MOUNT HAMILTON VIEW DR
1400 SJS 95116 834-E4
MOUNT HERMAN DR
1400 SJS 95127 835-B4
MOUNT HOLLY DR
6600 SJS 95120 894-F1
MOUNT HOOD WY
3100 SJS 95127 835-B4
MOUNT HOPE DR
6600 SJS 95120 894-F1
MOUNT ISABEL CT
3100 SJS 95148 855-E1
MOUNT ISABEL DR
3100 SJS 95148 855-E1
MOUNT KENYA DR
1700 SJS 95127 835-C4
MOUNT LASSEN DR
1400 SJS 95127 835-B4
MOUNT LAUREL CT
- MTVW 94043 811-H4
MOUNT LENEVE DR
6700 SJS 95120 894-F2
MOUNT LOGAN DR
3200 SJS 95127 835-B4
MOUNT MADONNA DR
3300 SJS 95127 835-C4
MOUNT MADONNA RD
300 SCrC 95076 (976-A3
See Page 955)
6400 SCIC 95020 (976-B2
See Page 955)
6400 SCIC 95037 (976-B2
See Page 955)
6400 SCIC 95020 956-C7
6400 SCIC 95037 956-C7

MOUNT MCKINLEY CT
3400 SJS 95127 835-C4
MOUNT MCKINLEY DR
3100 SJS 95127 835-C4
MOUNT OLIVEIRA DR
1600 SJS 95127 835-C4
MOUNT OSO DR
3100 SJS 95148 855-E2
MOUNT PAKRON CT
6700 SJS 95120 894-F2
MOUNT PAKRON DR
6600 SJS 95120 894-F2
MOUNT PALOMAR DR
1400 SJS 95127 835-B4
MOUNT PLEASANT CT
3500 SJS 95148 835-C4
MOUNT PLEASANT DR
1500 SJS 95127 835-C4
1600 SJS 95148 835-C4
MOUNT PLEASANT RD
1600 SJS 95148 835-D4
1600 SJS 95127 835-D4
2200 SCIC 95148 835-E5
MOUNT PRIETA DR
3400 SJS 95127 835-C4
MOUNT RAINIER AV
1500 MPS 95035 814-D1
MOUNT RAINIER DR
3100 SJS 95127 835-B4
MOUNT ROYAL DR
6500 SJS 95120 894-F1
MOUNT RUSHMORE DR
1700 SJS 95127 835-C4
MOUNT SAINT HELENA DR
3400 SJS 95127 835-C4
MOUNT SHASTA AV
1300 MPS 95035 814-D1
MOUNT SHASTA DR
1400 SJS 95127 835-B4
MOUNT STANLEY DR
1400 SJS 95127 835-C4
MOUNT UMUNHUM RD
11000 SCIC 95030 914-D1
13600 SCIC 95030 913-J2
MOUNT VERNON CT
1900 MTVW 94040 811-G4
MOUNT VERNON DR
1600 SCIC 95125 853-H5
MOUNT VERNON LN
- ATN 94027 790-E1
MOUNT VERNON WY
7000 GIL 95020 977-J4
MOUNT VISTA DR
3100 SJS 95127 835-B4
MOUNT WELLINGTON DR
6500 SJS 95120 894-F1
MOUNT WHITNEY DR
1400 SJS 95127 835-B4
MOUNT WILSON DR
3200 SJS 95127 835-B4
MOZART AV
2600 SCIC 95032 873-D3
2600 SJS 95122 855-A1
16300 LGTS 95030 873-D2
MOZART CT
500 SUNV 94087 832-E3
MOZART WY
16400 LGTS 95030 873-D3
MOZELLE CT
17800 SCIC 95030 913-A2
MUELLER AV
2400 SJS 95116 834-G2
MUENCH CT
1300 SJS 95131 814-C7
MUENDER AV
800 SUNV 94086 812-D7
MUIR AV
- SCL 95051 832-J7
MUIR DR
700 MTVW 94041 812-B7
5400 SJS 95124 873-J6
8600 GIL 95020 977-F1
MUIR WY
1000 LALT 94024 831-H2
MUIRDRUM PL
3000 SJS 95148 835-D7
MUIRFIELD CT
- SJS 95116 834-H3
MUIRFIELD DR
- SJS 95116 834-H3
MUIRHOUSE PL
5200 SJS 95136 874-F3
MUIR PLACE CT
3800 SJS 95121 855-B4
MUIRWOOD CT
2100 SJS 95132 814-C3
MUIRWOOD WY
2000 SJS 95132 814-C3

MULBERRY CIR
2100 SJS 95125 853-J6
MULBERRY CT
- MGH 95037 937-B5
MULBERRY DR
14200 LGTS 95030 873-B2
MULBERRY LN
- ATN 94027 790-C5
800 SUNV 94087 832-C1
1600 SJS 95125 853-J6
26000 LAH 94022 811-B6
MULCASTER CT
800 SJS 95136 874-D1
MULE TR
- SCIC 95140 837-G7
MULLEN AV
- LGTS 95030 873-A7
MUMFORD PL
3800 PA 94306 811-E1
MUNDELL CT
1000 LALT 94022 811-D4
MUNDELL WY
300 LALT 94022 811-D4
MUNRO AV
1200 CMBL 95008 873-B1
MUNROE WY
17000 MGH 95037 936-J1
MURDOCH CT
3400 PA 94306 791-D7
MURDOCH DR
3400 PA 94306 791-D7
MURGUIA AV
1900 SCL 95050 833-D5
MURIEL CT
400 SCL 95051 833-B7
1100 SJS 95121 855-A5
MURIEL LN
19100 SCIC 95014 852-G1
MURIETTA LN
3700 SJS 95127 835-D2
11800 LAH 94022 831-A3
MURILLO AV
3500 SCIC 95148 835-F7
3500 SJS 95148 835-E6
3700 SJS 95148 855-G1
MURLAGAN AV
- MTVW 94043 812-A3
MURMAN CT
2900 SJS 95148 855-D2
MURPHY AV
1100 SJS 95131 814-B7
11600 SCIC 95020 957-G1
12000 SCIC 95046 957-G1
12100 SCIC 95046 937-E3
15200 SCIC 95037 917-C6
15400 MGH 95037 917-C6
16000 SCIC 95037 937-D1
N MURPHY AV
100 SUNV 94086 812-E6
S MURPHY AV
100 SUNV 94086 812-E7
400 SUNV 94086 832-E1
MURPHY CT
18400 MGH 95037 916-H5
MURPHY LN
- MGH 95037 917-A3
- SCIC 95037 917-B4
MURPHY RD
- SCrC 95076 (1016-G4
See Page 995)
MURPHY RANCH RD
500 MPS 95035 813-G2
MURPHY SPRINGS CT
18400 MGH 95037 916-H5
MURPHY SPRINGS DR
18300 MGH 95037 916-H6
MURRAY AV
7700 GIL 95020 978-A1
8600 GIL 95020 958-A7
8700 GIL 95020 957-J6
9100 SCIC 95020 957-J6
MURRAY CT
- RDWC 94061 790-B1
MURRAY ST
300 MPS 95035 794-A3
MURRAY WY
3200 PA 94303 791-E6
MURRE LN
1500 SUNV 94087 832-G5
MURTHA DR
2800 SJS 95127 835-A4
2800 SJS 95127 834-J5
MUSCAT CT
1200 SUNV 94087 832-B3
MUSCAT DR
6700 SJS 95119 875-E7
MUSETTA CT
1500 SJS 95121 855-A2
MUSEUM WY
100 SCIC 94305 790-H6

MUSTANG DR
1300 MPS 95035 814-B3
MUSTANG ST
300 SJS 95123 875-A5
300 SJS 95123 874-J5
MUSTO AV
- SJS 95123 875-B4
MYER PL
10100 CPTO 95014 832-E7
MYERSLY CT
3400 SJS 95148 835-E7
MYLES CT
3200 SJS 95117 853-D2
MYLINDA DR
3900 SJS 95132 815-A4
MYNA CT
5200 SJS 95123 874-F7
MYRA DR
1700 SJS 95124 873-J6
MYREN CT
19000 SAR 95070 872-G1
MYREN DR
13400 SAR 95070 872-G1
MYRTLE AV
- MGH 95037 937-A1
1300 SJS 95118 874-B1
MYRTLE DR
1100 SUNV 94086 832-H2
MYRTLE ST
600 SJS 95126 833-G5
900 EPA 94303 791-C2
MYRTLEWOOD DR
6300 CPTO 95014 852-F2
MYSTIC CT
4100 SJS 95124 873-E3

N

N RD
- SUNV 94089 812-H4
NADINE CT
15000 SCIC 95124 873-F4
NADINE DR
1100 CMBL 95008 853-B5
NAGLEE AV
1200 SJS 95128 833-F7
1300 SJS 95126 833-G7
NAIDA AV
2000 SJS 95122 834-H6
NAKOOCHE TR
- SCIC 95030 913-C2
NALL LN
25000 SCIC 95030 934-A2
NALOR CT
17200 LGTS 95030 873-B3
N NAME UNO
9000 GIL 95020 958-A6
9000 GIL 95020 957-J6
9500 SCIC 95020 957-H2
NAMPEYO ST
48900 FRMT 94539 793-J2
NANCARROW CT
1300 SJS 95120 874-C7
NANCARROW WY
1200 SJS 95120 874-C7
NANCY CT
100 MTVW 94041 811-J6
20600 CPTO 95014 852-D1
NANCY LN
100 SJS 95127 834-J3
200 SCIC 95127 834-J3
800 LALT 94024 831-G3
NANCY WY
- MLPK 94025 790-E6
NANDELL LN
600 SCIC 94024 831-F3
NANDINA WY
1000 SUNV 94086 832-G2
NANTUCKET CIR
- SCL 95054 813-D4
NANTUCKET CT
800 SUNV 94087 832-C2
900 SJS 95126 853-J3
12600 SAR 95070 852-F6
NANTUCKET PL
7300 GIL 95020 977-J4
NAOMI CT
1600 RDWC 94061 790-A1
4000 SJS 95136 874-E1
21600 SCIC 95030 912-J3
NAPA CT
3200 SJS 95148 835-D6
NAPA DR
3100 SJS 95148 835-D6
NAPA RIVER CT
4500 SJS 95136 874-E2
NAPLES DR
1800 SJS 95122 834-H5
NARANJA WY
- PTLV 94028 810-A5

NARCISO CT
1000 SJS 95129 852-G2
NARCISSO RD
4700 SCIC 95020 (998-D4
See Page 997)
NARVAEZ AV
3000 SJS 95125 854-D6
3200 SCIC 95136 854-D6
3600 SJS 95136 854-E7
4200 SJS 95136 874-E1
NASH AV
600 MLPK 94025 790-H2
NASH CT
3700 SJS 95111 854-J6
NASH RD
700 LALT 94024 831-E1
NASHUA CT
100 SJS 95139 895-G1
600 SUNV 94087 832-D2
NASHVILLE DR
2900 SJS 95133 814-G7
NASSAU DR
2000 SJS 95122 834-J7
2000 SMCo 94061 790-B4
NATALIE AV
1600 SCL 95051 833-A3
NATALIE CT
1600 SJS 95118 873-J4
NATALIE DR
700 MGH 95037 917-D7
NATALYE RD
14900 MSER 95030 873-B4
NATHAN CT
3700 PA 94303 791-F7
NATHAN WY
3700 PA 94303 791-F7
NATHAN ABBOTT WY
- SCIC 94305 790-H7
NATHANSON AV
10500 CPTO 95014 832-C6
NATHHORST AV
100 PTLV 94028 810-C7
NATIONAL AV
400 MTVW 94043 812-B4
14800 SJS 95124 873-D3
14800 LGTS 95032 873-D3
NATIVE DANCER DR
14700 MGH 95037 937-B5
NATOMA CT
12000 SAR 95070 852-E5
NATOMA DR
700 SJS 95123 874-G5
NATOMA RD
27200 LAH 94022 830-J1
27500 LAH 94022 831-A1
28200 LAH 94022 810-J7
NATURE CT
300 SJS 95123 875-B6
NATURE DR
300 SJS 95123 875-B6
NAUTILUS CT
2400 SJS 95128 853-F3
NAVAJO CT
600 SJS 95123 874-G4
NAVAJO LN
- LALT 94022 811-E6
NAVAJO PL
- PTLV 94028 810-B5
NAVAJO TR
17600 SCIC 95030 913-A2
NAVARO PL
400 SJS 95134 813-H4
NAVARO WY
400 SJS 95134 813-H4
NAVARRO DR
1300 SUNV 94087 832-G4
NAVLET CT
1200 SUNV 94087 832-C3
W NAVY DR
600 SUNV 94086 812-F5
NAVY PL
1900 SJS 95133 834-E1
NAZARENE WY
900 SJS 95117 853-D3
NAZARETH CT
600 SCL 95051 832-J6
NEAL AV
2700 SJS 95128 853-E2
3100 SJS 95117 853-D2
NECTAR CT
- GIL 95020 977-J1
NECTARINE AV
800 SUNV 94087 832-C2
NEDSON CT
2500 MTVW 94043 811-F2
NEEDHAM LN
19600 SAR 95070 852-F6
NEEDLES DR
400 SJS 95112 854-E2

NEET AV
2900 SJS 95128 853-E3
NEILSON CT
300 SJS 95111 875-A1
NELA LN
700 LALT 94022 811-E4
NELIS CT
1200 SUNV 94087 832-C3
NELLO DR
500 CMBL 95008 853-D7
NELO ST
400 SCL 95054 813-F6
NELSON CT
1400 SCL 95054 813-D4
3900 PA 94306 811-E1
14600 SCIC 95124 873-G3
NELSON DR
1600 SCL 95054 813-D4
3800 PA 94306 811-E1
NELSON RD
- SCIC 94305 790-J6
NELSON WY
1300 SUNV 94087 832-C4
1700 SJS 95124 873-H3
14700 SCIC 95124 873-G3
NEPO CT
6400 SJS 95119 875-C7
NEPO DR
6300 SJS 95119 875-C7
NEPTUNE CT
900 SCIC 94043 811-J4
6600 SJS 95120 894-C1
NERDY AV
300 SJS 95111 854-J6
NERISSA WY
5000 SJS 95124 873-G5
NERO CT
2000 SJS 95008 853-B6
NESBIT CT
1400 SJS 95120 874-A6
NESTA DR
3300 SJS 95118 874-A1
NESTON WY
1500 LALT 94024 831-J5
NESTORITA WY
1800 SJS 95124 873-H1
NETTLE PL
1000 SUNV 94086 832-G3
NEVA LN
14700 SCIC 95046 957-G3
NEVADA AV
100 PA 94301 791-B6
700 SJS 95125 854-A4
NEVES CT
2600 SCL 95051 833-C7
NEVES WY
3400 SJS 95127 835-A1
NEVILLE AV
2400 SJS 95130 853-A7
NEVIN WY
700 SJS 95128 853-H2
NEW AV
8500 SCIC 95020 958-C3
11600 SCIC 95020 938-A6
12000 SCIC 95046 938-A6
12600 SCIC 95046 937-J5
NEW CT
5600 SJS 95123 874-H4
NEWARK WY
2800 SJS 95124 873-G1
NEW BEDFORD CT
1500 SJS 95131 814-C7
NEWBERRY CT
4200 PA 94306 811-D2
NEWBERRY DR
3100 SJS 95118 874-C1
NEWBRIDGE DR
26000 LAH 94022 811-C7
NEWBRIDGE ST
600 MLPK 94025 790-J1
800 MLPK 94025 791-A1
800 EPA 94303 791-A1
NEW BRUNSWICK AV
1500 SUNV 94087 832-C5
NEWCASTLE CT
200 RDWC 94061 790-B2
NEWCASTLE DR
300 RDWC 94061 790-B2
1600 LALT 94024 832-A4
1800 LALT 94024 831-J5
7500 CPTO 95014 852-D4
NEW COMPTON CT
4900 SJS 95136 874-F2
NEW COMPTON DR
600 SJS 95136 874-F2
NEW DORSET CT
600 SJS 95136 874-F2
NEWELL AV
100 LGTS 95030 873-B3

NEWELL CT
100 LGTS 95030 873-B3
NEWELL PL
800 PA 94303 791-B4
NEWELL RD
- EPA 94303 791-B3
500 PA 94301 791-B4
500 PA 94303 791-B5
NEW ENGLAND CT
5000 SJS 95136 874-F3
NEWFOUNDLAND DR
1400 SUNV 94087 832-D4
NEWGATE CT
- SJS 95138 875-H1
NEWHALL ST
500 SJS 95110 833-H4
800 SCL 95128 833-F5
800 SJS 95126 833-G5
900 SJS 95128 833-E6
1400 SCL 95050 833-F5
NEW HAMPTON WY
1300 SCL 95051 833-B4
NEW HAVEN CT
900 CPTO 95014 852-B2
NEWHOUSE CT
19200 SAR 95070 852-G6
NEW IRELAND CT
600 SJS 95136 874-F2
NEW JERSEY AV
2300 SJS 95124 853-G7
2500 SJS 95124 873-G3
14200 SCIC 95124 873-G3
NEW MAYFIELD LN
200 PA 94306 791-A7
NEW PENCE CT
1700 SJS 95132 814-J3
NEWPORT AV
1300 SJS 95125 854-A4
NEWPORT CT
12400 SAR 95070 852-F5
NEW RAMSEY CT
4900 SJS 95136 874-F2
NEW RIVER DR
100 SJS 95119 875-E7
NEWSOM AV
18600 SCIC 95014 852-H2
NEWTON AV
1900 SJS 95122 834-H6
NEWTON DR
3300 MTVW 94040 831-J2
NEW TRIER AV
5000 SJS 95136 874-E2
NEWVILLE DR
500 LGTS 95030 873-A2
NEW WORLD DR
4900 SJS 95136 874-F3
NEW YORK AV
100 LGTS 95032 873-A7
NEZ PERCE TR
20800 SCIC 95030 913-A2
NIAGARA DR
1300 SJS 95130 853-B4
NIBLICK AV
11700 SCIC 94024 831-F4
NICE CT
- SJS 95138 855-E7
NICHOLAS DR
2700 SJS 95124 873-F1
NICHOLIS AV
10800 SCIC 95037 916-G2
NICHOLSON AV
200 LGTS 95030 873-A7
200 LGTS 95030 872-J7
300 MSER 95030 872-J7
500 SCL 95051 833-B6
NICHOLSON LN
- SJS 95134 813-E3
NICKEL AV
1500 SJS 95121 855-A2
NICKLAUS AV
1000 MPS 95035 794-B4
NICOLE CT
700 GIL 95020 977-J7
4800 SJS 95111 875-C1
NICOLE LN
24600 LAH 94024 831-E2
NICOLE WY
5400 GIL 95020 978-A7
5400 GIL 95020 977-J7
NICORA AV
1400 SJS 95133 834-D3
NIDO DR
300 CMBL 95008 853-D7
NIEMAN BLVD
2900 SJS 95148 855-B2
3200 SJS 95121 855-B2
NIEMAN CT
2300 SJS 95121 855-C3
NIEVES CT
1200 MPS 95035 794-B4

SANTA CLARA CO.
INDEX

STREET Block City ZIP Pg-Grid

NIEVES ST
800 MPS 95035 794-B4
NIGHTFALL CT
1000 SJS 95120 894-F2
NIGHTHAWK TER
1600 SUNV 94087 832-G6
NIGHTINGALE AV
1600 SUNV 94087 832-G6
NIGHTINGALE CT
1200 LALT 94024 831-H4
NIGHTINGALE DR
2400 SJS 95125 854-D6
2600 SCIC 95125 854-D6
NIKETTE WY
1100 SJS 95120 894-E3
NIKKIE LN
23200 SCIC 95030 913-D6
NIKULINA CT
1100 SJS 95120 894-F3
NILDA AV
1000 MTVW 94040 811-J7
NILE DR
10100 CPTO 95014 852-E1
NIMITZ AV
- RDWC 94061 790-B3
- SMCo 94061 790-B3
NIMITZ FRWY I-880
- FRMT - 793-G2
- MPS - 793-H4
- MPS - 813-J1
- SJS - 833-H5
- SJS - 834-A1
- SJS - 853-F1
- SJS - 814-A6
- SJS - 813-J1
NIMRICH LN
2100 SJS 95124 873-F6
NINA CT
100 LGTS 95032 873-C7
NINA LN
16600 SCIC 95037 917-C7
16600 SCIC 95037 937-C1
NINA PL
26800 LAH 94022 811-A5
NINO AV
400 LGTS 95032 873-B6
NINO WY
200 LGTS 95032 873-B6
NIPPER AV
500 SJS 95133 834-E3
NISICH CT
1400 SJS 95122 854-H2
NISICH DR
1300 SJS 95122 854-H1
NISQUALLY DR
700 SUNV 94087 832-C5
NITA AV
300 MTVW 94043 811-F2
NOB HILL DR
- SBnC - (1017-C5
See Page 997)
10200 SJS 95127 835-B2
15100 SCIC 95127 835-B2
NOB HILL TER
100 MGH 95037 917-A7
100 MGH 95037 916-J7
NOB HILL WY
200 LGTS 95030 873-C4
NOBILI AV
1600 SCL 95051 832-J2
NOBLE AV
1000 SJS 95132 814-H5
14600 SCIC 95132 814-H5
NOBLE CT
100 LGTS 95032 873-D6
NOBLE LN
1000 SJS 95132 814-H5
1000 SCIC 95132 814-H5
NOBLE FIR CT
21100 CPTO 95014 852-C2
NOBU DR
1500 SJS 95131 814-C6
NODDIN AV
16300 LGTS 95032 873-D4
NOEL AV
10200 CPTO 95014 832-B7
NOEL DR
1000 MLPK 94025 790-G3
1900 LALT 94024 831-J5
NOELLA WY
5000 SJS 95124 873-H5
5100 SJS 95032 873-H5
NOKOMIS DR
500 SJS 95111 855-A7
NOLA DR
2100 SJS 95125 854-A6
NOLDEN AV
400 SJS 95117 853-C1
400 SCIC 95117 853-C1

NOMARK CT
1700 SJS 95125 854-A5
NOME CT
1400 SUNV 94087 832-D4
NOONAN CT
21600 CPTO 95014 852-B1
NOONWOOD CT
7000 SJS 95120 894-J3
NORA WY
- ATN 94027 790-D2
1600 SJS 95124 873-J5
NORADA CT
20700 SAR 95070 852-D5
NORANDA DR
700 CPTO 95014 832-C6
700 SUNV 95014 832-C6
NORBERT CT
2700 SJS 95148 835-F6
NORCLIFFE CT
3700 SJS 95136 874-D1
NORCOTT CT
6700 SJS 95120 894-F2
NORCREST CT
2800 SJS 95148 835-F6
NORCREST DR
2800 SJS 95148 835-F7
NORCROSS CT
3600 SJS 95148 835-F7
NORCROSS DR
2600 SJS 95148 835-F6
NORD LN
1600 SJS 95125 853-J7
NORDALE AV
600 SJS 95112 854-F2
NORDICA CT
3900 SJS 95124 873-E3
NORDYKE DR
600 SJS 95127 835-A3
NOREEN DR
1600 SJS 95124 874-A2
1600 SJS 95124 873-J2
NORELIUS CT
1300 SJS 95120 874-B6
NORFOLK DR
1000 SJS 95129 852-G3
NORFOLK PINE AV
800 SUNV 94087 832-C2
NORIEGA AV
1000 SUNV 94086 812-C7
NORIN CT
900 SCIC 95008 873-E1
NORITA CT
2700 SJS 95127 834-H2
NORLAND DR
600 SUNV 94087 832-D5
NORMA JEAN WY
1500 SJS 95118 874-G3
NORMAN AV
1100 SCL 95054 813-D6
1400 SCIC 95125 853-H5
NORMAN DR
1200 SUNV 94087 832-G4
21500 SCIC 95030 913-A3
NORMAN ST
1300 RDWC 94061 790-A1
NORMANDALE DR
3900 SJS 95118 874-B2
NORMANDY CT
10300 CPTO 95014 852-E1
NORMANDY DR
1000 SCIC 95008 873-E1
NORMANDY LN
100 ATN 94027 790-D2
12700 LAH 94022 831-D2
NORMANDY WY
1200 SCL 95128 833-E6
1200 SCL 95050 833-E6
7500 CPTO 95014 852-D4
NORMINGTON WY
800 SJS 95136 874-D1
NORRED CT
300 SJS 95119 895-D1
NORSEMAN DR
1800 SJS 95133 834-E2
NORSTAD ST
1000 SJS 95128 853-F3
NORTECH PKWY
100 SJS 95134 813-C1
NORTH DR
100 MTVW 94040 831-H1
NORTH PZ
- MLPK 94025 790-J1
NORTH ST
- SCIC 95046 937-E6
NORTHAMPTON CT
12500 SAR 95070 852-G6
NORTHAMPTON DR
700 PA 94303 791-B5
2100 SJS 95124 853-H6
19200 SAR 95070 852-F5

NORTHBROOK SQ
20100 CPTO 95014 832-G6
NORTHCOVE SQ
20100 CPTO 95014 832-G6
NORTHCREST LN
24700 SCIC 94024 831-D4
NORTHCREST SQ
20000 CPTO 95014 832-G6
NORTHDALE CT
6300 SJS 95123 874-J7
NORTHERN RD
400 SJS 95125 854-C3
NORTHFIELD SQ
10800 CPTO 95014 832-G6
NORTHFORDE DR
10700 CPTO 95014 832-F6
NORTH FORK LN
13400 LAH 94022 810-J7
NORTHFRONT WY
- SJS 95131 814-B7
NORTHGATE DR
100 WDSD 94062 790-A5
400 SJS 95111 875-C2
NORTHGATE ST
100 ATN 94027 790-D2
NORTHGLEN SQ
20100 CPTO 95014 832-G6
NORTHGROVE LN
2300 SJS 95133 814-H3
NORTHGROVE WY
2300 SJS 95133 814-H3
NORTHHURST DR
10800 CPTO 95014 832-E6
NORTHLAKE DR
300 SJS 95117 853-C1
NORTHLAWN CT
4900 SJS 95130 852-J6
NORTHLAWN DR
4800 SJS 95130 852-J6
NORTH LOOP DR
900 SJS 95126 853-H4
NORTHOAK SQ
10800 CPTO 95014 832-G6
NORTHPOINT WY
10800 CPTO 95014 832-G6
NORTHRIDGE DR
6500 SJS 95120 894-E2
NORTHRIDGE SQ
10800 CPTO 95014 832-G6
NORTHRUP AV
1500 SUNV 94087 832-G5
NORTHRUP ST
700 SJS 95126 853-J2
700 SCIC 95126 853-J2
700 SJS 95126 853-J2
NORTHSEAL SQ
10900 CPTO 95014 832-G6
NORTHSHORE SQ
10800 CPTO 95014 832-G6
NORTHSKY SQ
10800 CPTO 95014 832-G6
NORTH STAR CIR
1900 SJS 95131 814-C4
NORTH STAR CT
2400 SJS 95131 814-C4
NORTHUMBERLAND AV
300 RDWC 94061 790-B1
NORTHUMBERLAND DR
1100 SUNV 94087 832-B2
NORTHVIEW SQ
10800 CPTO 95014 832-G6
NORTHWEST CIR
1800 SJS 95131 814-B6
NORTHWEST SQ
20100 CPTO 95014 832-G6
NORTHWESTERN PKWY
2700 SCL 95051 833-B1
NORTHWIND SQ
20000 CPTO 95014 832-G6
NORTHWOOD DR
2500 SJS 95132 814-C3
20000 CPTO 95014 832-E6
NORTON AV
- SJS 95126 833-H7
- SJS 95126 853-H1
NORTON RD
15000 SAR 95070 872-D4
NORTREE ST
3600 SJS 95148 835-F7
NORVAL WY
1100 SJS 95125 854-A5
NORVELLA ST
1300 SJS 95122 834-J5
NORWALK DR
4200 SJS 95129 853-A1
NORWICH AV
200 MPS 95035 793-J7
10200 CPTO 95014 832-F7
NORWICH WY
4400 SJS 95008 853-A6
4400 SJS 95130 853-A6

NORWOOD AV
3000 SJS 95148 835-D7
NOTRE DAME DR
1600 MTVW 94040 811-G7
3400 SCL 95051 832-J2
NOTRE DAME ST
- SJS 95110 834-B6
- SJS 95113 834-B6
NOTTINGHAM AV
- SMCo 94063 790-C1
NOTTINGHAM PL
1000 SJS 95117 853-B3
NOTTINGHAM WY
300 CMBL 95008 853-G5
1000 LALT 94024 831-H4
NOTTING HILL DR
1200 SJS 95131 834-C1
NOTTOWAY AV
2000 SJS 95116 834-H5
NOVA LN
300 MLPK 94025 790-J3
NOVAK DR
500 SJS 95127 814-H7
NOVA SCOTIA AV
3400 SJS 95124 873-E2
14200 SCIC 95124 873-E2
NOVATO AV
400 SUNV 94086 812-C7
400 SUNV 94086 832-C1
NOVEMBER DR
900 CPTO 95014 852-C2
NOYO DR
100 SJS 95123 875-B5
NOYO RIVER CT
4600 SJS 95136 874-G2
NUBE CT
2500 SJS 95148 835-D6
NUESTRA AV
400 SUNV 94086 812-C7
400 SUNV 94086 832-C1
NUEVA DR
6300 SJS 95119 875-C7
NUEVA ST
- RDWC 94061 790-B1
NUGGET CT
1600 SJS 95127 835-B5
NUNES DR
2000 SJS 95131 814-D6
NUTHATCH LN
1500 SUNV 94087 832-G5
NUTMEG AV
700 SUNV 94087 832-C1
NUTMEG CT
1900 SJS 95131 814-D6
NUTTAL OAK CT
700 SUNV 94086 832-G2
NUTTMAN ST
500 SCL 95054 813-E7
NUT TREE LN
100 MGH 95037 937-B5
NUT TREE PL
1300 SJS 95122 834-F7
NUTWOOD LN
14400 SAR 95070 872-F3

O

OAHU DR
700 SJS 95111 855-A6
OAHU LN
19100 SAR 95070 872-G1
OAK AV
- SMCo 94025 790-F6
- SCIC 95046 937-E6
200 RDWC 94061 790-A1
1300 LALT 94024 831-J3
1500 LALT 94024 832-A3
1500 LALT 94040 832-A3
1500 LALT 94040 831-J3
1600 MLPK 94025 790-J2
1600 MTVW 94040 832-A3
OAK CT
- SUNV 94086 812-E7
100 MLPK 94025 791-A3
8100 GIL 95020 977-J2
19000 SCIC 95030 892-G4
21500 SCIC 95030 913-B2
OAK DR
900 SJS 95138 875-F6
3500 SMCo 94063 790-E1
3600 ATN 94027 790-E1
17900 SCIC 95030 913-A2
18300 MSER 95030 872-H5
18300 SCIC 95030 872-H5
OAK LN
- MTVW 94040 811-J6
900 MLPK 94025 790-F4
3400 SCIC 95037 917-G4
3400 SCIC 95037 936-J7

OAK PL
14300 SAR 95070 872-E3
OAK RD
- SCIC 94305 790-F6
OAK ST
- LALT 94022 811-D6
- SJS 95110 854-C1
100 MTVW 94041 811-H5
3400 MGH 95037 917-B7
14400 SAR 95070 872-D3
OAKBERRY WY
300 SJS 95123 875-B6
OAKBLUFF CT
1100 SJS 95131 814-E7
OAKBRIDGE DR
3000 SJS 95121 855-A3
OAK BROOK CIR
200 SJS 95139 895-H2
OAK CANYON CT
1400 SJS 95120 874-A6
OAK CANYON DR
1400 SJS 95120 874-A7
16200 MGH 95037 917-H6
OAK CANYON LN
3700 MGH 95037 917-H6
3700 SCIC 95037 917-H6
OAK CANYON PL
1400 SJS 95120 874-A6
OAK CREEK DR
1300 PA 94304 790-G5
OAK CREEK LN
20500 SAR 95070 852-D5
OAK CREEK WY
1200 SUNV 94089 813-A5
OAKCREST CT
22600 CPTO 95014 831-J7
OAKCREST DR
6400 SJS 95120 894-D1
OAKDALE AV
400 EPA 94303 791-B1
OAK DALE DR
200 LGTS 95032 873-C4
OAKDALE WY
- MGH 95037 916-H3
OAKDELL DR
1600 MLPK 94025 790-E6
OAKDELL PL
900 SJS 95117 853-D3
21900 CPTO 95014 832-B7
OAK ESTATES CT
2800 SJS 95136 855-F5
OAKFIELD AV
100 RDWC 94061 790-B2
OAKFIELD LN
500 MLPK 94025 790-E6
OAK FLAT RD
2300 SJS 95131 814-D5
OAK FOREST CT
- PTLV 94028 830-D2
OAK FOREST WY
6000 SJS 95120 874-D7
OAKGATE WY
3100 SJS 95148 855-E1
OAK GLEN AV
15200 SCIC 95037 936-C1
18200 SCIC 95037 916-B7
OAKGLEN WY
1200 SJS 95120 874-B6
OAK GLENN DR
18600 SCIC 95030 872-H5
OAK GROVE AV
- ATN 94027 790-G2
- LGTS 95032 892-H3
100 MLPK 94025 790-F3
OAK GROVE CT
200 MGH 95037 916-H7
OAK GROVE DR
400 SCL 95134 813-E5
700 SJS 95129 853-A2
17900 MGH 95037 916-J6
OAK GROVE PZ
700 MLPK 94025 790-F4
OAKHAVEN DR
19700 SAR 95070 852-F5
OAK HILL AV
4100 PA 94306 811-B4
OAK HILL CT
3400 MGH 95037 917-H5
OAK HILL WY
- LGTS 95032 893-A1
OAK HOLLOW WY
- MLPK 94025 790-E7
OAKHURST AV
1300 LALT 94024 831-H3
OAKHURST CT
5500 SJS 95129 852-H4
OAKHURST DR
16200 MSER 95030 872-J6
OAKHURST WY
- MPS 95035 794-A6

OAK KNOLL CIR
24000 LAH 94024 831-D3
OAK KNOLL CT
15700 LGTS 95030 873-A5
15700 LGTS 95030 872-J5
OAK KNOLL DR
1200 SJS 95129 852-H4
15700 MSER 95030 873-A5
15700 LGTS 95030 873-A5
OAK KNOLL LN
500 MLPK 94025 790-E6
OAKLAND AV
100 SJS 95116 834-G4
1000 MLPK 94025 790-H1
OAKLAND PL
100 LGTS 95030 873-B3
OAK LEAF CT
3100 MGH 95037 917-G5
OAKLEAF CT
21900 CPTO 95014 832-B7
OAK LEAF DR
16800 MGH 95037 917-F4
OAKLEAF DR
3500 SJS 95127 835-C4
OAK LEAF LN
3000 MGH 95037 917-G5
OAKLEAF PL
10000 CPTO 95014 832-B7
OAKLEY AV
2000 SMCo 94025 790-D6
OAKLEY DR
1400 LALT 94024 831-J4
OAKMEAD PKWY
300 SUNV 94086 813-A7
1200 SUNV 94086 812-J6
OAK MEADOW CT
7700 CPTO 95014 852-C4
OAK MEADOW DR
100 LGTS 95030 873-B6
OAKMEAD VILLAGE CT
2900 SCL 95051 813-A7
2900 SCL 95051 833-A1
OAKMEAD VILLAGE DR
3000 SCL 95051 813-A7
3100 SCL 95054 813-A7
OAKMILL CT
2800 SJS 95121 854-J3
OAKMONT DR
1000 SJS 95117 853-B3
19700 SCIC 95030 892-J7
OAKMONT PL
1000 SJS 95117 853-B3
OAKMONT WY
100 LGTS 95032 873-C4
OAKMORE DR
- SCIC 95127 815-A7
OAKNOLL CT
21900 CPTO 95014 832-B7
OAK PARK CT
12100 LAH 94024 831-D3
OAK PARK DR
100 LGTS 95032 873-C4
700 MGH 95037 936-J1
5400 SJS 95129 852-H4
OAK PARK LN
2500 SJS 95008 853-F7
OAK POINT TER
1500 SUNV 94087 832-D5
OAKRIDGE CT
15600 MGH 95037 917-H4
OAKRIDGE DR
600 SCIC 94024 831-F4
OAKRIDGE LN
16900 MGH 95037 917-H5
16900 SCIC 95037 917-H5
OAK RIDGE RD
- SCIC 95140 795-E1
OAKRIDGE RD
200 SCIC 95030 872-G6
15800 MGH 95037 917-H5
OAK RIDGE WY
15200 LGTS 95030 873-B4
OAK RIM CT
100 LGTS 95032 873-C5
OAK RIM WY
100 LGTS 95032 873-C6
OAK SPRING CT
11500 CPTO 95014 852-C4
OAK SPRINGS CIR
7700 SCIC 95020 958-G6
OAKTON CT
1800 SJS 95148 835-A5
OAKTREE DR
300 MTVW 94040 811-F4
1000 SJS 95129 852-H3
OAK VALLEY DR
13000 SCIC 95037 956-G1
OAK VIEW CIR
16400 MGH 95037 917-G6

OAK VIEW CT
3200 MGH 95037 917-G6
OAK VIEW LN
3200 MGH 95037 917-G6
OAKVIEW LN
21800 CPTO 95014 832-B7
OAKVIEW RD
1100 SJS 95121 855-A5
OAKVILLE AV
10300 CPTO 95014 852-F2
OAKWOOD AV
1700 SJS 95124 873-H3
OAKWOOD BLVD
- RDWC 94061 790-C1
- ATN 94027 790-C1
E OAKWOOD BLVD
- RDWC 94061 790-C1
W OAKWOOD BLVD
200 RDWC 94061 790-C1
OAKWOOD CT
600 LALT 94024 831-G2
3200 MGH 95037 917-H6
OAK WOOD DR
100 LGTS 95030 873-B2
OAKWOOD DR
- RDWC 94061 790-C1
400 SCL 95054 813-E5
2000 EPA 94303 791-A2
OAKWOOD LN
16300 MGH 95037 917-H6
OAKWOOD PL
300 MLPK 94025 790-H1
OAKWOOD WY
200 LGTS 95032 873-C4
OASIS CT
10200 CPTO 95014 832-A7
OASIS DR
5500 SJS 95123 875-B4
OBATA WY
5700 GIL 95020 978-C6
OBERLIN ST
1900 SCIC - 791-A7
1900 SCIC 94305 811-A1
2000 PA 94306 811-A1
OBERLIN WY
6400 SJS 95123 875-B7
OBERT DR
100 SJS 95136 874-J2
OBRAD DR
12300 SAR 95070 852-H5
OBRIEN CT
100 SJS 95126 833-G5
O BRINE LN
- PA 94303 791-D4
OBSERVATORY DR
10300 SCIC 95127 815-B7
10300 SCIC 95127 835-C1
OBSIDIAN CT
7700 CPTO 95014 852-C3
OBURN CT
1500 CMBL 95008 873-B2
OCALA AV
1700 SJS 95122 834-J7
2800 SJS 95148 834-J7
2800 SJS 95148 835-A5
2800 SJS 95122 835-A5
OCALA CT
2900 SJS 95148 835-B5
OCCIDENTAL CT
- SJS 95123 874-F7
OCEAN VIEW WY
18000 SCIC 95030 912-H4
OCHO RIOS DR
6100 SJS 95123 874-G6
OCONNOR DR
200 SJS 95128 833-F7
200 SJS 95128 853-F1
400 SCIC 95128 853-F1
O CONNOR ST
400 MLPK 94025 791-C2
500 EPA 94303 791-C2
OCONNOR ST
100 MLPK 94025 791-A2
W OCONNOR ST
100 MLPK 94025 791-A2
300 MLPK 94025 790-J2
OCTAVIUS DR
3200 SCL 95054 813-B7
OCTOBER DR
5500 SJS 95138 875-D4
OCTOBER WY
7900 CPTO 95014 852-C2
ODELL PL
- ATN 94027 790-D2
ODELL WY
900 LALT 94024 831-H1
ODYSSEY CT
1100 SJS 95118 874-G3
OELLA CT
4000 SJS 95124 874-A2

OFFENBACH PL
400 SUNV 94087 832-E3
OGALLALA PTH
17600 SCIC 95030 913-A2
OGALLALA WARPATH
17600 SCIC 95030 913-C2
17700 SCIC 95030 912-J2
OGDEN CT
- MPS 95035 793-J7
OGIER AV
100 SCIC 95037 896-E7
O GRADY DR
7000 SJS 95120 894-G3
OHARA CT
2300 SJS 95133 834-F1
OHIGGINS DR
1400 SJS 95126 853-G4
OHIO AV
2400 RDWC 94061 790-A3
OHIO CT
100 MPS 95035 793-J7
OHLONE
- PTLV 94028 830-C2
OHLONE CT
100 LGTS 95030 873-B6
OHLONE DR
2500 SJS 95132 814-E6
10000 SCIC 95020 957-E5
OHLONE LN
26400 LAH 94022 811-B5
OHLONE WY
- SMCo 94020 850-F6
OJAI DR
100 SCrC 95076 (975-G3
See Page 955)
18900 SCIC 95030 872-G6
18900 MSER 95030 872-G6
OJO DE AGUA CT
2000 SJS 95116 834-D2
OKA LN
14300 LGTS 95030 873-D3
OKA RD
14400 LGTS 95030 873-C3
14500 SCIC 95030 873-C3
OKANOGAN CT
14200 SAR 95070 872-F2
OKANOGAN DR
14000 SAR 95070 872-F2
OKEEFE LN
24000 LAH 94022 831-C1
25000 LALT 94022 831-C1
OKEEFE ST
100 MLPK 94025 791-A2
300 MLPK 94025 790-J2
E OKEEFE ST
100 MLPK 94025 791-A2
100 EPA 94303 791-A2
OKINO CT
5400 SJS 95123 874-J3
OLCOTT ST
3000 SCL 95054 813-C7
OLD ABBEY PL
1300 SJS 95132 814-E6
OLD ADOBE RD
100 SAR 95070 872-J3
100 LGTS 95030 872-J3
900 PA 94306 811-B4
OLD ADOBE WY
100 LGTS 95030 872-J3
OLD ALMADEN RD
2800 SJS 95125 854-C7
3300 SJS 95136 854-C7
OLD ALTOS RD
13600 LALT 94022 811-D7
13600 LAH 94022 811-D7
OLD BAYSHORE HWY
- SJS 95110 833-H1
200 SJS 95112 833-H1
600 SJS 95112 834-A2
OLD BLOSSOM HILL RD
200 SCIC 95032 873-D6
200 LGTS 95032 873-D6
OLDBRIDGE RD
1800 SJS 95131 814-D7
OLDBROOK CT
500 SJS 95111 855-A7
OLD BROWNS VALLEY RD
- SCrC 95076 (975-C3
See Page 955)
OLD CALAVERAS RD
1900 MPS 95035 794-D5
1900 SCIC 95035 794-D5
OLD CHITTENOON RD
- SCrC 95076 (1017-E3
See Page 997)
OLD COACH RD
11900 SCIC 95020 956-H4
OLD CREEK DR
900 SJS 95120 894-G2

OLD CREEK RD
3300 SCIC 95020 956-J4
OLD CREST PL
2400 SJS 95132 814-E6
OLD CROW RD
- LAH 94022 830-J1
OLDE DR
100 LGTS 95032 873-D7
OLD ELM CT
2400 SJS 95132 814-E6
OLD ESTATES CT
2800 SJS 95135 855-G5
OLD EVANS RD
400 MPS 95035 794-D5
OLDFIELD WY
2900 SJS 95135 855-F3
OLD FORGE LN
1200 SJS 95132 814-E6
OLD GATE CT
2400 SJS 95132 814-E6
OLD GILROY ST
100 GIL 95020 978-A3
OLD GLENWOOD HWY
- SCrC 95030 912-J7
23200 SCrC 95030 913-A7
OLD GLORY LN
2800 SCL 95054 813-B4
OLD GOLD MINE RD
21500 SCIC 95030 913-B2
OLDHAM WY
600 SJS 95111 854-H4
OLD HAZEL DELL RD
100 SCrC 95076 (975-G3
See Page 955)
OLD IRONSIDES DR
4600 SCL 95054 813-B4
OLD JAPANESE RD
16400 SCrC 95030 912-H6
W OLD JULIAN ST
100 SJS 95110 834-A6
OLD LOS GATOS - SANTA CRUZ RD
- SCIC 95030 913-A5
- SCrC 95030 913-A5
OLD MANOR PL
1100 SJS 95132 814-E6
OLD MEADOW CT
6500 SJS 95135 855-J7
OLD MIDDLEFIELD WY
1700 MTVW 94043 811-F2
2400 PA 94043 811-F2
2400 PA 94306 811-F2
OLD MILL CT
6600 SJS 95120 894-E1
OLD MILL RD
100 SCrC 95018 912-G7
OLDMINE RD
21400 SCIC 95030 913-B2
OLD MONTEREY RD
18100 MGH 95037 916-H5
18700 SCIC 95037 916-H5
OLD MOUNT RD
- SCrC 95018 912-E6
OLD MOUNTAIN VIEW-ALVISO RD
- SCL 95002 813-A3
900 SUNV 94089 812-J3
1200 SUNV 94089 813-A3
3100 SCL 95054 813-A3
OLD OAK CT
400 LALT 94022 811-D6
OLD OAK DR
1100 SJS 95120 894-E2
OLD OAK LN
2800 MGH 95037 917-F6
OLD OAK WY
13300 SAR 95070 852-C7
13300 SAR 95070 872-C1
OLD OAKLAND RD
900 SJS 95112 834-B1
1000 SJS 95133 834-B1
1600 SJS 95112 814-A4
1700 SJS 95131 814-A4
OLD ORCHARD CT
100 LGTS 95032 873-G6
OLD ORCHARD DR
100 LGTS 95032 873-G6
OLD ORCHARD RD
700 CMBL 95008 853-D7
800 CMBL 95008 873-D1
OLD PAGE MILL RD
2000 SCIC 94304 810-J4
2200 PA 94304 810-J4
2200 LAH 94304 810-J4
2300 LAH 94022 810-J4
OLD PAGE MILL TR
20800 SMCo 94020 850-E2
OLD PARK PL
1300 SJS 95132 814-E5

OLD PIEDMONT RD
1400 SJS 95132 814-G3
1800 SCIC 95132 814-F1
2100 MPS 95035 814-F1
OLD POST WY
2300 SJS 95132 814-E6
OLD RANCH LN
11500 SCIC 94024 831-E4
OLD RANCH RD
11400 SCIC 94024 831-E4
OLD RIDGE CT
2400 SJS 95132 814-E6
OLD ROSE PL
1300 SJS 95132 814-E5
OLD SAN FRANCISCO RD
200 SUNV 94086 832-E1
OLD SANTA CRUZ HWY
19800 SCIC 95030 892-H6
20500 SCIC 95030 912-J2
21100 SCIC 95030 913-A1
OLD SNAKEY RD
12000 LAH 94022 831-B3
OLD SPANISH TR
100 SMCo 94028 830-D4
100 PTLV 94028 830-D4
OLD STONE PL
1300 SJS 95132 814-E6
OLD STONE WY
1300 SJS 95132 814-E5
OLD SUMMIT RD
17400 SCIC 95030 913-C6
21000 SCIC 95030 912-J4
21200 SCrC 95030 912-J4
21300 SCrC 95030 913-A4
OLD TOWN CT
900 CPTO 95014 852-B2
OLD TRACE CT
4100 PA 94306 811-B4
OLD TRACE LN
900 LAH 94022 811-B5
900 PA 94306 811-B5
OLD TRACE RD
4100 PA 94306 811-B4
OLDTREE CT
1700 SJS 95131 814-D4
OLD TREE WY
13500 SAR 95070 872-F1
OLD TULLY RD
- SJS 95112 854-F4
- SJS 95111 854-F4
- SCIC 95111 854-F4
OLDWELL CT
- SJS 95138 875-D4
OLD WELL RD
21000 SCIC 95030 912-H1
OLD WILLOW PL
1200 SJS 95125 854-F5
OLDWOOD CT
3000 SJS 95148 855-E1
OLD WOOD RD
14200 SAR 95070 872-H2
OLD YERBA BUENA RD
3200 SJS 95135 855-H4
3300 SCIC 95135 855-H4
3600 SCIC 95135 856-A4
OLEANDER AV
16100 SCIC 95032 873-C5
16300 LGTS 95032 873-C5
OLEANDER CT
1000 SUNV 94086 832-H2
OLENA CT
- SJS 95127 834-J2
OLGA DR
3900 SJS 95117 853-B2
4100 SJS 95129 853-B2
OLIN ST
3100 SJS 95117 853-D1
3100 SCIC 95117 853-D1
OLINDER CT
900 SJS 95122 834-F6
OLIVAS CIR
8700 SJS 95135 855-J6
8700 SJS 95135 856-A6
OLIVE AV
200 PA 94306 791-B7
400 PA 94306 811-B1
14500 SCIC 95037 937-B4
15000 MGH 95037 937-B4
21600 CPTO 95014 852-B1
W OLIVE AV
100 SUNV 94086 832-C1
1000 SUNV 94086 812-B7
OLIVE CT
- MTVW 94041 811-J6
OLIVE DR
10500 SCIC 95127 835-B1
10500 SCIC 95127 815-B7
OLIVE PL
- SCIC 95127 815-B7

STREET
Block City ZIP Pg-Grid

OLIVE PL
- SCIC 95127 835-B1
OLIVE ST
100 LGTS 95030 873-A6
300 MLPK 94025 790-E5
1800 SCIC 95128 833-G7
2200 SJS 95128 833-G7
OLIVE BRANCH CT
6700 SJS 95120 894-E3
OLIVE BRANCH LN
1100 SJS 95120 894-E2
18000 MGH 95037 916-G7
OLIVEGATE LN
2000 SJS 95136 874-J3
OLIVE GROVE WY
8700 SJS 95135 856-A6
OLIVER CT
- MLPK 94025 790-C6
OLIVER ST
300 MPS 95035 794-A3
1100 RDWC 94061 790-A1
OLIVE SPRING CT
11600 CPTO 95014 852-A4
OLIVESTONE WY
2600 SJS 95132 814-E5
OLIVE TREE CT
24600 LAH 94024 831-D5
OLIVETREE DR
1700 SJS 95131 814-C4
OLIVE TREE LN
24600 LAH 94024 831-C4
24700 SCIC 94024 831-C4
OLIVETTI CT
3600 SJS 95148 835-F7
OLIVEWOOD PL
3000 SJS 95148 855-E1
OLIVE WOOD ST
19900 CPTO 95014 832-F6
OLIVIA CT
11400 SCIC 95020 957-G2
OLIVIAN DR
500 SJS 95123 875-B3
OLMO CT
1000 SJS 95129 852-H2
OLMSTED RD
- SCIC 94305 810-J1
- SCIC - 791-A7
- SCIC 94305 790-J7
OLSEN DR
3100 SJS 95117 853-D1
3100 SCIC 95117 853-D1
OLSTAD CT
5300 SJS 95111 875-C2
OLYMPIA AV
1200 SCIC 95008 873-E1
1300 SJS 95008 873-E1
OLYMPIC AV
2300 MLPK 94025 790-D7
OLYMPIC DR
1100 MPS 95035 814-C1
16000 MGH 95037 937-A2
OLYMPUS CT
900 SUNV 94087 832-B6
OLYMPUS DR
1300 SJS 95129 853-A4
OMAHA CT
6200 SJS 95123 874-H6
OMAR DR
- SJS 95123 875-B4
OMAR ST
1400 SCIC 95020 958-B4
OMEGA CT
- SJS 95127 814-H6
OMEGA LN
14400 SAR 95070 872-H3
OMIRA DR
200 SJS 95123 875-A4
ONDINE CT
1000 SJS 95132 814-H5
ONEDA CT
21400 SCIC 95030 913-A2
ONEIDA DR
600 SUNV 94087 832-D2
6100 SJS 95123 874-H6
ONEL DR
2100 SJS 95131 833-H1
2100 SJS 95131 813-H7
ONE OAK LN
15400 MSER 95030 873-A5
ONEONTA DR
24900 LAH 94022 831-C2
ON ORBIT DR
15500 SCIC 95070 872-C5
ONSLOW WY
3300 SJS 95132 814-G4
ONTARIO CT
600 SUNV 94087 832-D5
ONTARIO DR
1500 SUNV 94087 832-D5
2400 SJS 95124 853-G7

ONTARIO LN
2400 CMBL 95008 853-B5
ONTARIO RD
200 MPS 95035 794-A6
ONYX CT
700 SJS 95117 853-D2
OPAL DR
700 SJS 95117 853-D3
OPENMEADOW CT
4400 SJS 95129 853-A1
OPHELIA AV
2600 SJS 95122 855-A1
OPHELIA CT
2700 SJS 95122 855-A2
OPHIR CT
- MPS 95035 793-J7
ORA ST
5400 SJS 95129 852-H3
ORACLE OAK PL
800 SUNV 94086 832-G2
ORANGE AV
400 LALT 94022 811-D7
400 LALT 94022 831-D1
800 SCIC 94043 812-A4
800 SUNV 94087 832-C2
1100 MLPK 94025 790-D5
1100 SMCo 94025 790-D5
10000 CPTO 95014 832-C2
10000 CPTO 95014 852-B1
ORANGE ST
3100 SJS 95127 814-H7
ORANGE BLOSSOM DR
7500 CPTO 95014 852-D4
ORANGE BLOSSOM LN
15700 SCIC 95032 873-D6
ORANGEBRICK WY
100 SJS 95120 894-F2
ORANGE GROVE DR
1800 SJS 95124 873-G1
ORANGESTONE WY
- SJS 95132 814-E5
ORANGETREE LN
1800 MTVW 94040 831-G1
10500 CPTO 95014 832-E7
ORANGEWOOD DR
1500 SJS 95121 855-A3
ORANGEWOOD ST
19800 CPTO 95014 832-F6
ORCHARD AV
- RDWC 94061 790-B1
100 MTVW 94043 811-J5
100 MTVW 94043 812-A4
300 SUNV 94086 812-E6
ORCHARD CT
1600 MGH 95037 917-D6
22000 CPTO 95014 832-A7
ORCHARD DR
3000 SJS 95134 813-F5
7000 GIL 95020 977-J4
ORCHARD GN
200 MTVW 94043 812-A5
ORCHARD LN
1600 MGH 95037 917-B4
ORCHARD PKWY
- SJS 95131 813-G7
2600 SJS 95134 813-F5
ORCHARD RD
1200 SCIC 95020 (1000-D5 See Page 999)
20200 SAR 95070 872-E2
ORCHARD ST
- LGTS 95032 893-A1
ORCHARD CITY DR
- CMBL 95008 853-E6
ORCHARD HILL LN
26900 LAH 94022 811-C7
ORCHARD HILLS ST
- ATN 94027 790-B4
ORCHARD MEADOW DR
20000 SCIC 95070 852-A7
ORCHARD OAK CIR
100 CMBL 95008 853-F6
ORCHARD PARK DR
5600 SJS 95123 874-J5
ORCHARD SPRING CT
11600 CPTO 95014 852-A4
ORCHARD SPRING LN
11600 CPTO 95014 852-A4
ORCHARD VIEW DR
1600 SJS 95124 873-J6
ORCHID DR
1100 SUNV 94086 832-H2
ORCHID PL
800 LALT 94024 831-E1
ORCHID WY
900 SJS 95117 853-B3
OREGOLD PL
700 SJS 95131 814-B6
OREGON AV
- RDWC 94061 790-A2

OREGON AV
100 PA 94301 791-B6
700 PA 94303 791-B6
OREGON CT
900 MPS 95035 794-A5
OREGON EXWY Rt#-G3
400 SJS 95125 854-D3
- PA 94301 791-C6
- PA 94303 791-C6
300 PA 94306 791-C6
OREGON WY
1000 MPS 95035 794-A5
ORELLA CT
12600 SAR 95070 852-F6
ORESTES WY
2000 SJS 95008 853-B6
ORI AV
2700 SJS 95128 853-E2
ORICK CT
300 SJS 95123 874-J4
ORILLA CT
1100 LALT 94022 811-D3
ORILLIA CT
1500 SUNV 94087 832-D5
ORIN CT
4100 SJS 95124 873-E3
ORINDA DR
2500 SJS 95121 855-D3
ORINDA ST
3400 PA 94306 811-C1
ORINDA WY
9100 GIL 95020 957-F7
ORIOLE AV
1500 SUNV 94087 832-G5
ORIOLE DR
3100 SJS 95117 853-D3
ORIOLE RD
14000 SAR 95070 872-G4
ORIOLE WY
15100 SAR 95070 872-H4
ORION CT
100 MPS 95035 793-J7
ORION LN
7700 CPTO 95014 852-C3
ORION PL
900 CPTO 95014 852-C3
ORKNEY AV
700 SCL 95054 813-E6
ORLANDO DR
1300 SJS 95122 834-H6
2000 SJS 95122 854-J1
ORLEANS CT
13700 SAR 95070 872-G1
ORLEANS DR
1200 SUNV 94089 812-G3
1600 SJS 95122 854-J1
ORLINE CT
10700 CPTO 95014 852-D2
ORME ST
4000 PA 94306 811-C2
ORMONDE DR
700 MTVW 94043 811-H3
ORMONDE WY
1300 MTVW 94043 811-H3
ORMSBY DR
1400 SUNV 94087 832-D4
ORMSBY CUTOFF RD
1100 SCrC 95030 955-A2
1100 SCrC 95076 955-A2
ORNELLAS DR
2000 MPS 95035 814-E1
OROGRANDE PL
7700 SCIC 95014 852-C3
7700 CPTO 95014 852-C3
OROLETTE PL
1900 SJS 95131 814-D6
ORONSAY CT
200 SJS 95119 875-D7
ORONSAY WY
200 SJS 95119 875-D7
OROPEZA CT
600 SJS 95133 834-G1
OROSI CT
200 SJS 95116 834-F3
OROSI WY
2000 SJS 95116 834-F3
OROVILLE RD
400 MPS 95035 794-A6
ORR CT
1600 LALT 94024 831-J4
ORSETTI CT
300 SCIC 95020 957-J5
ORTEGA AV
- MTVW 94040 811-F4
ORTEGA CIR
900 GIL 95020 977-G3
ORTEGA CT
3700 PA 94303 791-E7
ORTEGA DR
26800 LAH 94022 811-A5

ORTHELLO WY
2800 SCL 95051 833-A4
ORTIZ CT
1200 SUNV 94089 813-A4
ORTO ST
900 MPS 95035 794-A5
ORVIETO CT
5700 SJS 95138 875-G1
ORVIS AV
500 SJS 95112 834-D7
OSAGE AV
- LALT 94022 811-F7
OSAGE CT
600 SJS 95123 874-G4
OSBORN AV
1100 SMCo 94061 790-B3
OSBORNE AV
2300 SCL 95050 833-D7
OSBORNE CT
14900 SCIC 95037 936-J6
OSCAR CT
10200 SCIC 95020 958-C3
OSCAR DR
2000 SCIC 95020 958-B3
OSGOOD CT
400 SJS 95111 875-B2
OSITOS AV
400 SUNV 94086 812-C7
400 SUNV 94086 832-C1
OSLO LN
1300 SJS 95118 874-B5
OSPREY CT
1500 SJS 95127 835-C4
OSTENBERG DR
6000 SJS 95120 874-C7
OSTRICH CT
5200 SJS 95123 874-F7
OSUNA PL
1100 SJS 95129 852-J3
OSWALD PL
1600 SCL 95051 833-B3
OSWEGO DR
800 SJS 95122 854-F1
OTHELLO AV
2600 SJS 95122 855-A2
OTIS WY
- LALT 94022 811-F6
OTONO CT
300 SJS 95111 875-A1
OTOOLE AV
1800 SJS 95131 814-A5
2400 SJS 95131 813-J5
OTOOLE CT
8500 GIL 95020 977-G1
OTOOLE LN
- SJS 95131 814-A6
OTOOLE WY
- SJS 95131 814-A6
OTTAWA CT
1600 SUNV 94087 832-D5
OTTAWA WY
100 FRMT 94539 793-J2
2400 SJS 95130 853-A7
OTTERSON CT
2900 PA 94303 791-D5
OTTERSON ST
500 SJS 95110 834-A7
OTTO CT
900 SJS 95132 814-J5
OUR LN
2400 MTVW 94040 831-J1
OUR LADYS WY
- SCL 95054 813-B5
OUSLEY DR
1300 GIL 95020 977-F1
OUTLOOK CT
3400 SJS 95132 814-G3
OUTLOOK DR
500 SCIC 94024 831-F2
OVATION CT
700 SJS 95134 813-H4
OVERBROOK DR
3200 SJS 95118 874-B1
OVERLAND CT
600 SJS 95111 854-H5
OVERLAND WY
600 SJS 95111 854-H5
OVERLOOK DR
15900 SCIC 95030 872-F6
OVERLOOK RD
17900 SCIC 95030 872-H7
18300 MSER 95030 872-H7
18400 LGTS 95030 872-H7
OVERTURE CT
700 SJS 95134 813-H4
OWEN ST
2300 SCL 95054 813-C7
OWENS LAKE DR
800 SJS 95123 874-D5

OWEN SOUND DR
1400 SUNV 94087 832-D4
OWLSWOOD WY
400 SJS 95111 854-F6
OWSLEY AV
900 SJS 95122 834-F7
OXBOW CT
1300 SUNV 94087 832-D4
5100 SJS 95124 873-F5
OXFORD AV
200 PA 94306 791-A7
1200 SUNV 94087 832-B2
OXFORD CT
3500 SCL 95051 832-J6
OXFORD DR
900 LALT 94024 831-H5
3500 SCL 95051 832-J6
OXFORD LN
3200 SJS 95117 853-D3
OXFORD ST
1300 RDWC 94061 790-A1
OXTON DR
1100 SJS 95121 854-J3
OYAMA DR
1400 SJS 95131 814-B7
OYAMA PL
1400 SJS 95131 814-B7
OYSTER BAY DR
4700 SJS 95136 874-D2

P

PACCHETI WY
100 MTVW 94040 811-E3
PACER LN
2600 SCIC 95111 854-G4
PACHECO DR
700 MPS 95035 794-B6
2300 SJS 95133 834-F1
PACHECO HWY
- SBnC - (1000-B7 See Page 999)
PACHECO ST
1300 SCL 95051 833-A4
PACHECO WY
- SBnC - (1000-B6 See Page 999)
PACHECO PASS HWY Rt#-152
800 GIL 95020 978-C4
1400 SCIC 95020 978-G3
3000 SCIC 95020 (979-B6 See Page 959)
3700 SBnC - (979-B6 See Page 959)
4000 SCIC 95020 999-H1
6000 SCIC 95020 (980-D5 See Page 959)
8200 SCIC 95020 961-J4
PACIFIC AV
800 SCIC 95126 853-J1
1300 SJS 95002 793-C7
PACIFIC DR
400 MTVW 94043 812-B5
2300 SCL 95051 832-J2
PACIFICA DR
2000 SJS 95131 814-A5
20000 CPTO 95014 852-E1
PACIFICA WY
200 MPS 95035 793-J4
PACIFIC RIM LN
2400 SJS 95121 855-E4
PACIFIC RIM WY
4400 SJS 95121 855-E4
PACINA DR
2000 SJS 95116 834-H5
PACKING PL
200 SJS 95116 834-G4
PACO DR
400 LALT 94024 811-F7
PADDINGTON WY
1200 SJS 95127 835-A4
PADDON CIR
5800 SJS 95123 875-A5
PADERO AV
13200 SAR 95070 852-C7
PADERO CT
13200 SAR 95070 852-C7
PADILLA WY
3200 SJS 95148 835-D7
PADRE CT
12100 LAH 94022 831-B2
PADRES CT
1500 SJS 95125 854-C3
PADRES DR
1400 SJS 95125 854-B3
PAGANINI AV
2600 SJS 95122 855-A1
PAGE AV
- FRMT 94538 793-G2

PAGE ST
300 CMBL 95008 853-F6
300 SCIC 95126 853-H1
300 SJS 95126 853-H1
PAGEANT WY
- LGTS 95032 893-A1
PAGE MILL DR
100 SJS 95111 875-B2
PAGE MILL RD
100 PA 94306 791-B7
500 PA 94304 811-A2
500 PA 94305 791-B7
1000 PA 94304 830-G2
1000 SCIC 95014 830-G2
1100 PA 94305 811-A2
1200 SCIC 94305 811-A2
1600 SCIC 94305 810-H7
1600 PA 94304 810-H7
11600 LAH 94022 830-G2
11800 SCIC 94022 830-G2
12700 LAH 94022 810-H7
20800 SMCo 94028 830-F7
PAGE MILL RD Rt#-G3
1800 SCIC 94305 810-J4
1800 PA 94304 810-J4
1900 SCIC 94304 810-J4
2400 LAH 94022 810-J4
PAGODA TREE CT
800 SUNV 94086 832-G2
PAGOSA CT
48900 FRMT 94539 793-J2
PAGOSA WY
- FRMT 94539 793-J3
500 FRMT 94539 794-A2
PAINTBRUSH DR
1000 SUNV 94086 832-H3
PAINTED ROCK DR
2400 SCL 95051 833-A1
PAIUTE LN
400 SJS 95123 874-H5
PAJARO AV
200 SUNV 94086 812-D6
PAJARO CT
100 SUNV 94086 812-D6
6500 SJS 95120 894-D1
PAJARO RD
- SBnC - (1017-F4 See Page 997)
PAJARO WY
6500 SJS 95120 894-D1
PALA AV
- SJS 95127 834-H2
- SCIC 95127 834-H2
400 SUNV 94086 832-C1
PALACE DR
- SJS 95129 853-A1
PALACEWOOD CT
4900 SJS 95129 852-J2
PALACIO ESPADA CT
200 SJS 95116 834-F3
PALACIO ROYALE CIR
200 SJS 95116 834-D2
PALACIO VERDE CT
200 SJS 95116 834-D2
PALADIN DR
3900 SJS 95124 873-J2
PALAMOS AV
1100 SUNV 94089 812-J4
1200 SUNV 94089 813-A4
PALANTINO WY
3200 SJS 95135 855-G3
PALERMO CT
13000 SAR 95070 852-F7
PALISADE DR
4200 SJS 95111 855-A7
PALISADES DR
1300 MPS 95035 793-J4
PALM AV
- SJS 95037 896-C7
- LGTS 95030 872-J7
- SCIC 95037 896-C7
300 SCIC 95037 916-B1
500 LALT 94022 811-E7
500 LALT 94022 831-E1
700 RDWC 94061 790-A1
22200 CPTO 95014 852-A1
PALM CT
- MLPK 94025 790-E5
700 SUNV 94086 832-G2
9900 SCIC 95037 916-C1
PALM DR
100 PA 94305 790-H6
100 SCIC 94305 790-H6
400 SCL 95053 833-F4
PALM ST
400 PA 94301 791-A3
600 SJS 95110 854-B1
PALM BEACH WY
2000 SJS 95122 854-J1

PALMDALE CT
2500 SCL 95051 833-B2
PALM DESERT WY
- SJS 95123 875-G2
PALMER AV
100 MTVW 94043 811-G3
PALMER DR
100 LGTS 95030 873-C3
PALMER LN
- PTLV 94028 810-C6
200 SMCo 94063 790-E1
200 ATN 94027 790-E1
PALMER ST
400 MPS 95035 813-J1
PALMETTO DR
400 SUNV 94086 832-G1
500 SJS 95111 854-G6
PALMETTO DUNES CT
5000 SJS 95138 855-E6
PALM GROVE CT
5300 SJS 95123 875-A3
PALM HAVEN AV
600 SJS 95125 854-A2
PALMIRA WY
2200 SJS 95122 854-J1
PALMITA PL
200 MTVW 94041 811-J5
PALM RIDGE LN
100 SJS 95123 874-G7
PALM SPRING CT
11600 CPTO 95014 852-A4
PALM SPRINGS CIR
5900 SJS 95123 874-G6
PALMTAG DR
12300 SAR 95070 852-G6
PALM VIEW DR
5400 SJS 95123 875-B4
PALMVIEW WY
1400 SJS 95122 834-H6
PALMWELL WY
- SJS 95138 875-D5
PALMWOOD DR
1400 SJS 95122 834-H6
PALO DR
- PA 94304 790-H5
200 SCIC 94305 790-H5
PALO ALTO AV
100 PA 94301 790-J3
200 MTVW 94041 811-G5
600 MLPK 94025 790-J3
1000 PA 94301 791-A3
PALO ALTO ST
800 PA 94301 790-J3
PALO ALTO WY
1900 SMCo 94025 790-E7
PALO HILLS DR
26700 LAH 94022 811-A5
PALOMA AV
4500 SJS 95111 875-A1
PALOMA CT
23700 CPTO 95014 831-G5
PALOMA DR
100 MGH 95037 916-H5
3300 SCL 95051 833-A4
3300 SCL 95051 832-J4
PALOMA RD
- CPTO 95014 851-J2
- PTLV 94028 810-B5
PALOMAR AV
600 SUNV 94086 812-D5
PALOMAR REAL
- CMBL 95008 853-F7
PALOMAS
- MTVW 94043 811-J2
PALOMINO CT
2400 MGH 95037 917-F6
PALOMINO DR
14600 SCIC 95127 835-B2
PALOMINO LN
200 SCIC 95046 937-D6
PALOMINO WY
14000 SAR 95070 872-B2
PALO OAKS CT
18900 SAR 95070 852-H6
PALO SANTO DR
1600 CMBL 95008 853-A6
PALOS VERDES DR
11100 CPTO 95014 852-B3
15400 MSER 95030 873-A5
PALO VERDE AV
2300 EPA 94303 791-A1
PALO VERDE DR
400 SUNV 94086 832-G2
PALO VERDE WY
400 SUNV 94086 832-G1
PALO VISTA RD
10200 CPTO 95014 852-A1
PAM LN
1500 SJS 95120 874-A7

PAMELA AV
200 SJS 95116 834-G2
PAMELA DR
200 MTVW 94040 811-J6
PAMELA WY
20700 SAR 95070 872-D3
PAMLAR AV
300 CMBL 95008 853-E4
500 SJS 95128 853-F4
PAMPAS CT
20100 SAR 95070 852-E5
PAMPAS DR
1200 SJS 95120 874-C7
PAMPAS LN
300 SCIC 94305 790-J7
1100 GIL 95020 957-F7
PAMPAS WALL
600 SCIC 94305 790-J6
PANAMA AV
1800 SJS 95122 834-H7
2000 SJS 95122 854-H1
PANAMA ST
100 SCIC 94305 790-G7
PANCHITA WY
400 LALT 94022 811-E5
PANCHO CT
6300 SJS 95123 874-J7
PANDA CT
3800 SJS 95117 853-B3
PANDA DR
900 SJS 95117 853-B3
PANDA LN
900 SJS 95117 853-B2
PANDA PL
3800 SJS 95117 853-B3
PANDORA DR
1800 SJS 95124 873-G1
PANELLI PL
800 SCL 95050 833-F5
PANMURE CT
3100 SJS 95135 855-F3
PANOCHE AV
1100 SJS 95122 834-F7
PANORAMA DR
19100 SAR 95070 872-G4
20800 SCIC 95030 913-B2
PANORAMA WY
100 LGTS 95032 873-G6
PANTALIS CT
2500 SJS 95132 814-E6
PANTALIS DR
2500 SJS 95132 814-E6
PAOLO CT
1900 SJS 95131 814-D6
PAPAC WY
500 SCIC 95117 853-D2
PAPAYA CT
400 SJS 95111 854-G7
PAPPANI DR
1200 GIL 95020 977-G2
PAPPANI WY
- SJS 95148 855-F2
PAQUITA ESPANA CT
- SCIC 95037 896-C6
PAR AV
11600 SCIC 94024 831-E4
PARADISE CT
3900 PA 94306 811-B3
PARADISE DR
10300 CPTO 95014 852-D1
PARADISE WY
900 PA 94306 811-B3
PARADISE VIEW RD
1700 SCIC 95037 936-H3
PARAGON DR
2100 SJS 95131 813-J6
PARAISO CT
200 SJS 95119 875-D7
PARAMOUNT DR
12900 SAR 95070 852-D6
PARIS WY
2200 SJS 95132 814-E2
PARISH PL
10100 CPTO 95014 832-E7
PARISH WY
8100 GIL 95020 977-H2
PARK AV
- LGTS 95030 893-A1
100 PA 94306 791-A7
300 SJS 95113 834-A7
300 SJS 95110 834-A7
400 SJS 95002 793-C7
600 SJS 95126 834-A7
700 SJS 95126 833-G6
1800 SCIC 95126 833-J7
2100 SCL 95050 833-F5
2100 SJS 95050 833-F5
2800 SCL 95053 833-F5
PARK BLVD
1700 PA 94306 791-A6

PARK BLVD
3300 PA 94306 811-C1
PARK CIR
20600 CPTO 95014 832-D7
PARK CIR E
10100 CPTO 95014 832-D7
PARK CIR W
10100 CPTO 95014 832-D7
PARK CT
500 SCL 95050 833-F5
800 MTVW 94040 811-H6
PARK DR
- ATN 94027 790-D2
- MGH 95037 937-B5
100 GIL 95020 977-H1
800 MTVW 94022 811-G5
800 MTVW 94040 811-G5
15000 SAR 95070 872-E4
S PARK DR
500 SJS 95129 852-J1
PARK LN
- MLPK 94025 790-J1
- SJS 95123 875-B4
100 ATN 94027 790-D4
3000 SJS 95127 835-B5
PARK PL
20300 SAR 95070 872-E2
PARK ST
100 RDWC 94061 790-B1
PARK WY
- SCrC 95076 955-A3
16100 SCIC 95127 815-B6
16100 SJS 95127 815-B6
17700 MGH 95037 916-J7
PARK ARCADIA DR
4600 SJS 95136 874-J2
PARK BELMONT PL
- SJS 95136 874-J1
PARK BOLTON PL
100 SJS 95136 874-H1
PARK BRISTOL PL
4400 SJS 95136 874-J1
PARK BROOK CT
1100 MPS 95035 794-C6
PARK CHARLES CT
3900 SJS 95111 854-J6
PARK CHERRY PL
4500 SJS 95136 874-J2
PARK CONCORD PL
4600 SJS 95136 874-J2
PARK CREST CT
1500 SJS 95118 874-A6
PARK CREST DR
5600 SJS 95118 874-A6
PARKDALE DR
600 CMBL 95008 853-F7
600 SJS 95008 853-F7
PARKDALE WY
1600 SJS 95127 835-B5
1800 SJS 95148 835-B5
PARK DARTMOUTH PL
100 SJS 95136 874-H1
PARK DOUGLAS PL
4700 SJS 95136 874-J2
PARK ELLEN DR
100 SJS 95136 874-J2
PARKER AV
- ATN 94027 790-B4
PARKER CT
900 SCL 95050 833-E3
2900 MTVW 94043 811-F3
PARKER ST
700 SCL 95050 833-E3
2400 MTVW 94043 811-F3
PARKER RANCH CT
12400 SAR 95070 852-C6
PARKER RANCH RD
12000 SAR 95070 852-C6
PARK ESSEX PL
- SJS 95136 874-J1
PARK ESTATES WY
2800 SJS 95135 855-F5
PARKFIELD AV
5000 SJS 95129 852-J3
PARK FLETCHER PL
- SJS 95136 874-J1
PARK GLEN CT
1100 MPS 95035 794-C6
PARK GROTON PL
- SJS 95136 874-J1
PARK GROVE DR
1100 MPS 95035 794-C6
PARKHAVEN CT
3300 SJS 95132 814-F2
PARKHAVEN DR
3200 SJS 95132 814-E3
PARK HEIGHTS DR
1100 MPS 95035 794-C6
PARK HILL DR
- MPS 95035 794-C6

PARKHILLS AV
1600 LALT 94024 831-J4
PARKHURST DR
500 CMBL 95008 853-A7
PARKINGTON AV
1100 SUNV 94087 832-B1
PARKINSON AV
1000 PA 94301 791-A4
PARKINSON CT
1000 SCIC 95126 853-J1
PARK JOHNSON PL
500 SJS 95111 854-J6
PARKLAND AV
3400 SJS 95117 853-C3
PARKLAND CT
2500 SCL 95051 833-A1
PARK MANOR DR
5600 SJS 95118 874-A6
PARK MEADOW CT
500 SJS 95129 852-J1
PARK MEADOW DR
400 SJS 95129 852-J2
PARK MILFORD PL
4600 SJS 95136 874-J2
PARKMONT CT
1200 SJS 95131 814-B7
PARKMONT DR
1400 SJS 95131 814-B7
PARKMOOR AV
500 SCIC 95128 853-F1
500 SJS 95128 853-F1
1100 SJS 95126 853-H2
PARK NORTON PL
4600 SJS 95136 874-J2
PARK OAK CT
1100 MPS 95035 794-C6
PARK OXFORD PL
- SJS 95136 874-J2
PARK PAXTON PL
4400 SJS 95136 874-J1
PARK PLEASANT CIR
1300 SJS 95127 835-B3
PARK RIDGE DR
1500 SJS 95118 874-A6
PARKROW LN
2800 SJS 95132 814-E3
PARK ROYAL DR
1900 SJS 95125 853-J6
PARK SHARON DR
- SJS 95136 874-J2
PARKSIDE AV
1600 SJS 95125 854-B4
PARKSIDE CT
17300 MSER 95030 873-B4
PARKSIDE DR
100 PA 94306 811-E2
PARKSIDE LN
10200 CPTO 95014 852-F1
PARK SOMMERS WY
4400 SJS 95136 874-J2
PARK SUTTON PL
4600 SJS 95136 874-J2
N PARK VICTORIA DR
- MPS 95035 794-A3
S PARK VICTORIA DR
- MPS 95035 794-C
500 MPS 95035 814-D1
PARKVIEW AV
1500 SJS 95130 853-A
PARK VIEW DR
600 SCL 95134 813-E
1100 MPS 95035 794-C
PARKVIEW DR
17000 MGH 95037 917-G
17000 SCIC 95037 917-F
PARKVIEW GREEN CIR
1600 SJS 95131 814-C
PARK VILLA CIR
8000 CPTO 95014 852-B
PARK VILLAGE PL
- SJS 95136 874-J
PARK VISTA CIR
1800 SCL 95050 833-D
PARK WARREN PL
- SJS 95136 874-J
PARK WATSON PL
100 SJS 95136 874-J
PARKWELL CT
100 SJS 95138 875-E
PARKWEST DR
4500 SJS 95130 853-A
PARK WILLOW CT
1100 MPS 95035 794-C
PARK WILSHIRE DR
2500 SJS 95124 853-H
2500 SJS 95124 873-H
PARKWOOD DR
- ATN 94027 790-H
10100 CPTO 95014 832-C

STREET
Block City ZIP Pg-Grid

PARKWOOD WY
1000 RDWC 94061 790-B2
2100 SJS 95125 854-A6
PARLETT PL
10100 CPTO 95014 832-E7
PARLIAMENT CT
3400 SJS 95132 814-J3
PARMA DR
1100 SJS 95120 894-D1
PARMA WY
500 LALT 94024 831-F2
PARMER AV
200 SJS 95116 834-F4
PARNELL DR
2700 SJS 95121 854-J3
PARNELL PL
800 SUNV 94087 832-F6
PARQUET CT
2400 SJS 95124 853-H7
W PARR AV
600 CMBL 95008 873-B2
700 LGTS 95030 873-B2
PARR LN
200 CMBL 95008 853-D6
PARRISH CT
4900 SJS 95111 875-C1
PARRISH VIEW DR
10000 SCIC 95020 957-D6
PARROT AV
1500 SUNV 94087 832-G5
PARROTT ST
500 SJS 95112 854-F3
PARSONS AV
1300 CMBL 95008 873-E2
PARSONS CT
1300 CMBL 95008 873-E1
PARSONS WY
- LALT 94022 811-E5
PAR THREE DR
10600 CPTO 95014 852-A2
PARTRIDGE AV
600 MLPK 94025 790-G4
1500 SUNV 94087 832-G5
PARTRIDGE CT
4400 SJS 95121 855-E4
PARTRIDGE DR
1200 GIL 95020 977-F1
4000 SJS 95121 855-E3
PARTRIDGE LN
23200 SCIC 94024 831-G4
PARVIN DR
500 MPS 96036 794-B5
PASADENA AV
10000 CPTO 95014 852-B1
10000 SCIC 95014 852-B1
PASATIEMPO DR
1700 SJS 95124 873-J3
PASCOE AV
900 SJS 95125 854-B6
PASEO CARMELO
16700 LGTS 95032 893-D2
PASEO CERRO
12400 SAR 95070 852-H6
PASEO DE ARBOLES
2900 SJS 95135 855-F4
PASEO DEL ORO
2000 SJS 95124 873-F2
PASEO DEL ROBLE
13500 LAH 94022 810-H6
PASEO DEL ROBLE CT
13600 LAH 94022 810-H6
PASEO DEL SOL
2000 SJS 95124 873-F2
PASEO DE PALOMAS
500 CMBL 95008 853-F6
PASEO DE SAN ANTONIO WK
- SJS 95113 834-B6
PASEO ESTERO DR
800 SJS 95122 854-G2
PASEO FLORES
12500 SAR 95070 852-H6
PASEO LADO
18500 SAR 95070 852-H7
PASEO LAURA
100 LGTS 95030 873-D3
PASEO OLIVOS
12600 SAR 95070 852-H6
PASEO OLIVOS CT
2000 SJS 95130 852-J6
PASEO OLIVOS WY
4900 SJS 95130 852-J6
PASEO PICO
- SAR 95070 852-H6
PASEO PRESADA
12700 SAR 95070 852-H6
PASEO PUEBLO
18500 SAR 95070 852-H6
PASEO PUEBLO CT
6100 SJS 95120 874-C7
PASEO PUEBLO DR
6000 SJS 95120 874-D7
PASEO REFUGIO
300 MPS 95035 794-B6
PASEO ROBLES
2600 SCIC 95046 937-J2
PASEO TIERRA
18500 SAR 95070 852-H6
PASEO TRANQUILLO
4900 SJS 95118 873-J4
PASEO TRANQUILO
9100 SCIC 95020 (976-J1
See Page 955)
PASEO VISTA
2900 SCIC 95046 938-A1
2900 SCIC 95046 937-J1
PASETTA DR
2100 SCL 95050 833-C2
PASHOTE CT
1400 MPS 95035 794-A4
PASITO TER
100 SUNV 94086 812-D6
PASO DEL ARROYO
- PTLV 94028 810-D7
PASO LOS CERRITOS
6000 SJS 95120 874-B7
6300 SJS 95120 894-B1
PASO ROBLES AV
- LALT 94022 811-D4
PASQUALE CT
300 SJS 95133 834-H1
PASTEL LN
13300 MTVW 94040 832-A1
PASTEUR DR
100 PA 94304 790-G6
100 SCIC 94305 790-G6
PASTORIA AV
400 SUNV 94086 832-D1
N PASTORIA AV
200 SUNV 94086 812-D6
S PASTORIA AV
100 SUNV 94086 812-D7
PATCH AV
300 SCIC 95128 853-F1
PATH WY
100 SJS 95136 874-H2
PATIO CT
1200 CMBL 95008 853-G6
PATIO DR
1600 CMBL 95008 853-G6
1700 SCIC 95125 853-H6
PATLEN DR
1200 LALT 94024 831-H3
PATRIC CT
20200 CPTO 95014 852-E2
PATRICIA CT
100 MTVW 94041 811-J6
400 MPS 95035 794-E7
900 CMBL 95008 873-B1
18100 SCIC 95030 912-H3
PATRICIA DR
- ATN 94027 790-C2
2300 SCL 95050 833-C5
2500 SCL 95051 833-B5
PATRICIA LN
100 SCrC 95076 (975-A1
See Page 955)
500 PA 94303 791-C4
PATRICIA PL
- MLPK 94025 790-F5
PATRICIA WY
900 SJS 95125 854-A3
PATRICK WY
400 LALT 94022 811-D5
PATRICK HENRY DR
2900 SCL 95054 813-A4
PATRIOT WY
21000 CPTO 95014 832-C7
PATS PL
- SCrC 95076 (975-A4
See Page 955)
PATT AV
2800 SJS 95133 834-G1
2900 SCIC 95133 814-H7
2900 SJS 95133 814-H7
PATTERSON AV
- SMCo 94025 790-D5
PATTERSON ST
100 SJS 95112 834-C7
PATTON AV
300 SCIC 95128 853-F1
PAUL AV
- MTVW 94041 812-A6
- MTVW 94041 811-J6
700 PA 94306 811-C2
14200 SAR 95070 872-D2
PAULA CT
400 SCL 95050 833-D6
1200 LALT 94024 831-H2
PAULA DR
1100 CMBL 95008 853-B5
PAULA ST
800 SJS 95126 853-J2
1000 SCIC 95126 853-J2
PAULINE DR
1300 SUNV 94087 832-F4
2300 SJS 95124 853-G7
PAUL ROBESON CT
800 EPA 94303 791-B1
PAULSEN LN
200 PA 94301 790-J4
PAVAN CT
2800 SJS 95148 855-D2
PAVAN DR
3000 SJS 95148 855-D2
PAVISO DR
20400 CPTO 95014 832-E6
PAWNEE TR
20900 SCIC 95030 913-C2
PAWTUCKET WY
7300 SJS 95139 895-F1
PAXTON CT
6000 SJS 95123 874-F6
PAYETTE AV
1000 SUNV 94087 832-B6
PAYETTE CT
1300 SJS 95129 852-G4
PAYNE AV
3100 SJS 95130 853-B4
3100 SJS 95117 853-B4
3400 SJS 95128 853-E4
3400 SJS 95008 853-E4
3500 CMBL 95008 853-E4
3500 CMBL 95128 853-E4
4200 SJS 95129 853-B4
PAYNE CT
800 SUNV 94087 832-C2
PAYNE DR
1100 LALT 94024 831-H3
PAYNE RD
- SBnC - (1017-G4
See Page 997)
PAYTON AV
14800 SCIC 95124 873-G3
PEACEFUL GLEN CT
1400 SJS 95121 855-D7
PEACH AV
700 SUNV 94087 832-C2
PEACH CT
1200 SJS 95116 834-E5
PEACH TER
4900 SJS 95008 872-J1
PEACH BLOSSOM DR
7500 CPTO 95014 852-D4
PEACHBLOSSOM LN
15600 SCIC 95032 873-C5
15600 LGTS 95032 873-C5
PEACH GROVE CT
5200 SJS 95123 874-F7
PEACH HILL RD
15100 SAR 95070 872-E5
15300 SAR 95070 872-E5
15400 SCIC 95030 872-E5
PEACHTREE CT
1200 CMBL 95008 873-B2
1700 MTVW 94040 831-G1
PEACHTREE LN
2000 SJS 95128 833-E6
20000 CPTO 95014 832-E7
PEACH WILLOW CT
100 LGTS 95030 873-B2
PEACHWOOD CT
2700 SJS 95132 814-E5
PEACHWOOD DR
1600 SJS 95132 814-D4
PEACHWOOD PL
1600 SJS 95132 814-D5
PEACOCK AV
1500 SUNV 94087 832-G5
1700 MTVW 94043 811-H3
PEACOCK CT
- SCIC 95014 851-G4
3600 SCL 95051 832-H4
PEACOCK LN
16300 SCIC 95032 873-D7
PEACOCK GAP DR
4400 SJS 95127 815-C6
4400 SCIC 95127 815-C6
PEAK AV
17000 MGH 95037 936-J1
17300 MGH 95037 916-J7
PEAK DR
3500 SJS 95127 835-C3
PEAK LN
- PTLV 94028 810-D5
PEAK VIEW DR
48900 FRMT 94539 793-J2
PEANUT BRITTLE DR
3000 SJS 95148 835-D7
PEAR AV
700 SUNV 94087 832-C2
1200 MTVW 94043 811-J2
PEAR BLOSSOM CT
- SJS 95123 875-E2
PEARCE MITCHELL PL
- SCIC 94305 810-H1
PEARL AV
3000 SJS 95136 854-D7
3500 SJS 95136 874-D1
PEARLROTH DR
6300 SJS 95123 875-A7
PEARLTONE DR
3200 SJS 95117 853-D3
PEARLWOOD WY
700 SJS 95123 874-F5
PEARSON CT
1600 SJS 95122 834-G7
PEARTREE CT
15000 SCIC 95046 937-G2
19100 CPTO 95014 832-F7
PEARTREE LN
1700 MTVW 94040 831-G1
2600 SJS 95121 855-E4
19800 CPTO 95014 832-F7
PEBBLE PL
10600 CPTO 95014 832-C6
PEBBLE BEACH CT
1500 MPS 95035 794-D3
2400 SJS 95125 854-C6
PEBBLE BEACH DR
2400 SJS 95125 854-C6
2600 SCL 95051 833-B1
PEBBLE CREEK CT
200 MGH 95037 917-B7
1000 SJS 95127 834-J4
PEBBLE GLEN DR
4800 SJS 95129 852-J3
PEBBLELAKE CT
800 SUNV 94089 812-H5
PEBBLETREE CT
5100 SJS 95111 875-C2
PEBBLETREE WY
5200 SJS 95111 875-C2
PEBBLEWOOD CT
6600 SJS 95120 894-F1
PECAN CT
800 SUNV 94087 832-C3
1200 SJS 95131 814-D7
1600 RDWC 94061 790-A2
PECAN WY
700 CMBL 95008 853-B7
PECAN BLOSSOM DR
5300 SJS 95123 875-B3
PECAN GROVE CT
100 SJS 95123 874-J3
PECHIN CIR
2400 SJS 95130 853-A7
PECK LN
12000 LAH 94022 831-B3
PECORA WY
100 SMCo 94028 810-D4
PECOS PT
3800 SJS 95132 814-J5
PECOS WY
1100 SUNV 94089 812-J4
PECOS RIVER CT
600 SJS 95111 854-H4
PECTEN CT
1000 MPS 95035 814-C3
PEDRICK CT
1100 SJS 95120 894-D1
PEDRO AV
2100 MPS 95035 794-E7
PEDRO ST
900 SJS 95126 853-J2
PEDRO VIEW RD
- SCIC 95127 835-C1
PEEBLES AV
100 MGH 95037 916-H4
300 SCIC 95037 916-J3
900 SCIC 95037 917-A3
PEEKSKILL DR
700 SUNV 94087 832-C2
PEET RD
18100 SCIC 95037 917-B3
18200 MGH 95037 917-B3
PEGASUS CT
7500 SJS 95139 875-H7
PEGASUS WY
7300 SJS 95139 875-G7
PEGGY AV
1000 CMBL 95008 873-B1
PEGGY CT
1300 CMBL 95008 873-B1
PEIKING DR
1200 SJS 95131 814-B7
PELHAM CT
6400 SJS 95123 875-A7
PELICAN CT
5200 SJS 95123 874-F7
PELICAN RIDGE DR
7200 SJS 95120 894-F3
PELLEAS LN
700 SJS 95127 814-H6
PELLIER CT
1300 SJS 95121 854-J2
PELLIER DR
1200 SJS 95121 854-J3
PEMBA CT
200 SJS 95119 875-D6
PEMBA DR
6400 SJS 95119 875-D6
PEMBRIDGE CT
3400 SJS 95118 874-C1
PEMBRIDGE DR
1100 SJS 95118 874-C1
PEMBROKE DR
1100 SJS 95131 814-E6
PEMBROKE PL
- MLPK 94025 790-F6
PENA CT
500 PA 94306 811-C2
PENDERGAST AV
18700 SCIC 95014 852-H2
PENDERGAST LN
- SCrC 95076 (975-A5
See Page 955)
PENDLETON AV
900 SUNV 94087 832-B6
PENDLETON DR
2800 SJS 95148 855-D1
PENDRAGON LN
2500 SJS 95116 834-J4
PENHURST PL
4100 SJS 95135 855-F3
PENINSULA BLVD
10000 CPTO 95014 832-B7
PENINSULA WY
900 SMCo 94025 790-H1
PENINSULAR AV
1000 LALT 94024 831-H4
10700 CPTO 95014 832-A6
PENINSULAR CT
1000 LALT 94024 831-H3
PENITENCIA CT
500 MPS 95035 793-J6
PENITENCIA ST
500 MPS 95035 793-J6
PENITENCIA CREEK RD
2600 SJS 95132 814-F7
2900 SJS 95133 814-F7
3100 SJS 95127 814-F7
3400 SCIC 95132 814-F7
3600 SCIC 95132 814-F7
14800 SCIC 95127 814-F7
14900 SCIC 95127 814-F7
15300 SJS 95132 815-A5
16100 SJS 95127 815-A5
PENN AV
5000 SCIC 95124 873-E4
9800 SJS 95124 873-E4
PENN WY
200 LGTS 95032 873-D4
PENNINGTON LN
1000 CPTO 95014 852-C3
PENNSYLVANIA AV
- LGTS 95030 872-J7
PENNSYLVANIA DR
100 WAT 95076 955-E6
400 WAT 95019 955-E6
PENNY WY
1700 LALT 94024 832-A4
PENNYHILL DR
200 SJS 95127 834-H1
PENNYROYAL TER
1200 SUNV 94087 832-C3
PENROD PL
600 SJS 95116 834-J4
PENSACOLA DR
1500 SJS 95122 854-H1
PENTLAND CT
3000 SJS 95148 855-C2
PENTLAND WY
2200 SJS 95148 855-C2
PENTZ WY
5800 SJS 95123 875-B5
PENWITH AV
3900 SJS 95130 853-B4
PENWOOD ST
1700 SJS 95133 834-E1
PEONY LN
1600 SJS 95124 873-J6
PEPITA CT
3100 SJS 95132 814-G5
PEPITONE AV
1000 SJS 95110 854-C2
PEPPER AV
400 PA 94304 811-B1
400 PA 94306 791-B7
400 PA 94306 811-B1
1000 SUNV 94087 832-C2
PEPPER CT
100 LALT 94022 811-E7
PEPPER DR
- LALT 94022 811-E7
PEPPER LN
15000 SAR 95070 872-F4
PEPPERIDGE CT
2700 SJS 95148 835-E6
PEPPERIDGE DR
3400 SJS 95148 835-E6
PEPPERMINT DR
3000 SJS 95148 835-C7
PEPPER TREE CT
800 SCL 95051 833-A5
PEPPERTREE CT
1500 MGH 95037 917-D6
PEPPERTREE DR
16900 MGH 95037 917-D6
PEPPER TREE LN
- LGTS 95030 873-B5
800 SCL 95051 833-A5
3300 SCIC 95127 814-H6
3900 SCIC 95127 814-J6
3900 SJS 95127 814-J6
20800 CPTO 95014 852-C1
PEPPERWOOD CT
- MLPK 94025 790-H2
PEPPERWOOD DR
4800 SJS 95124 873-H4
PEPPERWOOD LN
2600 SCL 95051 833-B6
PERALTA AV
- LGTS 95030 872-J7
400 SUNV 94086 832-D1
PERALTA CT
1300 SJS 95120 874-C7
14100 SAR 95070 872-C2
PERALTA DR
1200 SJS 95120 874-C7
PERCHERON CT
17100 MGH 95037 917-D6
PERCIVALE DR
3100 SJS 95127 814-H7
PEREGO WY
18500 SAR 95070 872-H1
PEREGRINE CT
900 SCL 95051 832-H5
PEREGRINE DR
1200 GIL 95020 957-E7
PEREGRINO WY
1500 SJS 95125 853-J6
PERICH CT
2300 MTVW 94040 831-J1
PERIDOT DR
2600 SJS 95132 814-F5
PERIDOT PL
2600 SJS 95132 814-F5
PERIE LN
3700 SJS 95132 814-J4
3800 SJS 95132 815-A4
PERIMETER RD
- LAH 94022 831-C2
5500 SJS 95193 875-C4
6300 SJS 95119 875-C5
N PERIMETER RD
- MLPK 94025 790-J1
S PERIMETER RD
600 MLPK 94025 790-J2
W PERIMETER RD
600 MLPK 94025 790-J1
600 SMCo 94025 790-J1
PERINO LN
1500 SCIC 95046 937-J7
PERIVALE CT
3100 SJS 95148 855-E2
PERIWINKLE DR
8600 GIL 95020 977-D1
PERIWINKLE LN
4700 SJS 95129 853-B2
4700 SJS 95129 852-B7
PERIWINKLE TER
800 SUNV 94086 832-F3
PERKINS CT
100 LGTS 95030 873-B3
600 SJS 95127 814-J6
PERMANENTE RD
- SCIC 95014 851-G1
PERMANENTE WY
100 MTVW 94041 811-G4
PERNICH CT
1300 SJS 95120 874-C7
PERREIRA DR
900 SCL 95051 832-J5
900 SCL 95051 833-A5
PERRELLI ST
800 GIL 95020 977-H3
PERRIN CT
1500 SJS 95131 814-D6
PERRONE CIR
1800 SJS 95116 834-F3
PERRY AV
1900 SMCo 94025 790-E7
PERRY CT
400 SCL 95054 813-E6
1600 SJS 95116 834-F4
PERRY ST
100 MPS 95035 794-C7
PERRYMONT AV
200 SJS 95125 854-D4
400 SCIC 95125 854-D4
PERSHING AV
700 SJS 95126 833-J6
PERSIAN DR
100 SUNV 94089 812-F3
PERSIANWOOD PL
5100 SJS 95111 875-C2
PERSIMMON AV
800 SUNV 94087 832-C2
PERSIMMON PL
4600 SJS 95129 853-A2
PERSIMMON GROVE CT
5300 SJS 95123 874-F7
PERTH CT
600 MPS 95035 794-A6
PERUGIA CT
2500 SJS 95138 855-G7
PERUKA PL
300 SJS 95116 834-D4
PESCADERO CT
200 MPS 95035 793-J5
PESCADERO DR
700 SJS 95123 874-F5
PESCADERO ST
900 MPS 95035 793-J5
PESCADERO TER
300 SUNV 94086 812-D7
PESCARA CT
2600 SJS 95008 873-F1
PETAL WY
1200 SJS 95129 852-G4
PETALUMA CT
1800 MPS 95035 794-D6
S PETER CT
- CMBL 95008 853-G6
N PETER DR
- CMBL 95008 853-G6
S PETER DR
- CMBL 95008 853-G6
PETER COUTTS CIR
- SCIC 94305 811-A2
PETER COUTTS RD
- SCIC 94305 810-J1
100 SCIC 94305 811-A2
PETER PAN AV
700 SJS 95116 834-H4
PETER PAN TR
18100 SCIC 95030 912-J4
PETERS CT
- SCIC 95037 936-D2
PETERSBURG DR
2100 MPS 95035 794-E7
PETERSEN AV
1500 SJS 95129 852-H5
PETERSEN DR
1100 GIL 95020 977-G1
PETERSON CT
1200 LALT 94024 831-H3
PETERSON WY
3600 SCL 95054 813-A6
PETIE CT
1000 MTVW 94040 811-J6
PETRARCH CT
3200 SJS 95135 855-F2
PETRI PL
1600 SJS 95118 873-J5
1600 SJS 95124 873-J5
PETRONI WY
1100 SJS 95120 894-F2
PETTIGREW CT
2900 SJS 95148 855-C2
PETTIGREW DR
2200 SJS 95148 855-C2
PETTIS AV
200 MTVW 94041 811-G5
PETULLA CT
4000 SJS 95124 873-J2
PFEFFER LN
2400 SJS 95128 853-F2
2400 SCIC 95128 853-F2
PFEIFFER CT
6600 SJS 95120 894-G1
PFEIFFER RANCH RD
6300 SCIC 95120 874-F7
6300 SJS 95120 874-E7
PFEIFFER RANCH RD
6400 SJS 95120 894-F1
PFEIFLE AV
12900 SCIC 95111 854-H6
PHANTOM AV
1400 SCIC 95125 853-H5
1600 CMBL 95125 853-H5
PHARLAP AV
5000 SJS 95111 875-B2
PHARLAP DR
10000 CPTO 95014 832-B7
PHARMER RD
8400 SCIC 95020 977-A1
PHEASANT DR
1200 GIL 95020 957-F7
PHEASANT RD
18000 SCIC 95032 893-H3
18600 SCIC 95030 893-H3
PHEASANT RUN
100 SCrC 95003 (975-A7
See Page 955)
PHEASANT HILL CT
1400 SJS 95120 894-G4
PHEASANT HILL DR
1200 SJS 95120 894-F4
PHEASANT HILL WY
1300 SJS 95120 894-F4
PHEASANT RIDGE WY
- SJS 95136 854-F6
PHELAN AV
- SJS 95112 854-E2
900 SJS 95122 854-F1
PHELAN CT
1800 SJS 95122 854-G1
PHELAN WY
1100 SJS 95122 854-G1
PHELAND CT
800 MPS 95035 814-D1
PHELPS AV
1000 SJS 95117 853-C4
PHIL CT
600 CPTO 95014 852-G2
PHIL LN
19100 SCIC 95014 852-G2
19100 CPTO 95014 852-G2
PHIL PL
10500 CPTO 95014 852-G2
PHILEO CT
4900 SJS 95118 873-J4
PHILIP CT
2900 SJS 95121 855-A3
PHILLIPS AV
2600 SCL 95051 833-B4
17100 LGTS 95032 893-C1
PHILLIPS CT
1100 SCL 95051 833-B4
PHILLIPS RD
- PA 94303 791-C3
PHINNEY PL
7500 SJS 95139 895-G1
PHINNEY WY
7300 SJS 95139 895-G1
PHOENIX CT
3800 SJS 95130 853-B4
PHOENIX DR
1400 SJS 95130 853-B5
1400 CMBL 95008 853-B5
PHOTINIA LN
300 SCIC 95127 835-B1
PHYLLIS AV
900 MTVW 94040 811-J7
7000 SJS 95129 852-E3
PHYLLIS CT
1100 MTVW 94040 811-J7
PIAZZA CT
- SCIC 95127 815-A7
PIAZZA DR
500 MTVW 94043 812-B3
PIAZZA LN
11000 SCIC 95020 957-J2
PIAZZA WY
- SCIC 95127 815-A7
100 SCIC 95127 835-A1
PICADILLY DR
3200 SJS 95118 874-C1
PICADILLY PL
1400 CMBL 95008 853-G5
PICARDY PLACE CT
3300 SJS 95121 855-B4
PICASSO DR
1200 SUNV 94087 832-F4
PICASSO TER
600 SUNV 94087 832-E3
PICKFORD AV
- SCIC 95127 834-J1
PICO LN
800 LALT 94022 811-E4
PIEDMONT CT
100 LGTS 95032 873-G6
17000 MGH 95037 936-J1
PIEDMONT RD
- MPS 95035 794-E7
200 SCIC 95035 794-E7
700 MPS 95035 814-F1
900 SJS 95127 814-F2
1000 SJS 95132 814-F2
1100 SCIC 95035 814-F1
15000 SAR 95070 872-E4
PIEDRA DR
100 SUNV 94086 812-C7
PIERCE AV
- SJS 95110 834-C7
PIERCE CT
20000 SAR 95070 852-E6
PIERCE RD
- SCrC 95030 912-H7
400 MLPK 94025 790-J1
12800 SAR 95070 852-E6
13300 SAR 95070 872-B1
PIERCE ST
100 GIL 95020 977-J1
1100 SCL 95050 833-D4
PIERCE RANCH RD
1300 SJS 95120 894-C2
PIERCY RD
300 SJS 95138 875-D3
300 SCIC 95138 875-E3
PIERINO AV
700 SUNV 94086 832-F2
PIERS CT
900 PA 94303 791-D6
PIERS LN
- SMCo 94025 810-E2
900 SCIC 94304 810-E2
PIETRO DR
1300 SJS 95131 814-C7
PIETZ CT
6000 SJS 95123 874-F6
PIKE RD
13800 SAR 95070 872-C1
PILAND DR
1300 SJS 95130 853-C4
PILAR CT
5800 SJS 95120 874-C5
PILGRIM AV
1700 MTVW 94040 811-F5
5900 SJS 95129 852-G5
PILINUT CT
1000 SUNV 94087 832-C2
PILOT KNOB DR
2300 SCL 95051 833-B1
PIMA DR
600 SJS 95123 874-H5
PIMENTO AV
1100 SUNV 94087 832-C3
PINARD ST
2100 MPS 95035 814-E1
PINCEA CT
- SAR 95070 852-B6
PINE
200 CMBL 95008 853-E6
PINE AV
500 SUNV 94086 812-E5
600 SJS 95125 854-B4
PINE LN
- LALT 94022 811-D5
100 MGH 95037 937-B5
PINE ST
100 MGH 95037 937-B1
1000 MLPK 94025 790-G3
1200 PA 94301 791-B5
17000 LGTS 95032 873-B7
PINE TR
18100 SCIC 95030 912-J3
PINE WY
16900 MGH 95037 917-D6
PINEAPPLE AV
800 SUNV 94087 832-C2
PINE BROOK CT
11700 CPTO 95014 852-C4
PINE BROOK LN
11700 CPTO 95014 852-C4
PINE CONE CT
17500 MSER 95030 873-A5
PINECONE CT
1700 SCIC 95037 917-D6
1700 MGH 95037 917-D6
PINE CREEK DR
3300 SJS 95132 814-G3
PINECREST CT
2800 SJS 95121 855-E4
PINECREST DR
500 SCIC 94024 831-J5
1700 SCIC 95046 937-J5
PINEDALE CT
7200 SJS 95139 895-F1
PINEFIELD RD
300 SJS 95134 813-C2
PINEGATE WY
3200 SJS 95148 855-E1
PINE GROVE WY
1400 SJS 95129 852-G4
PINE HILL CT
4800 SJS 95129 852-J2
PINE HILL RD
700 SCIC 94305 810-J1
PINEHILL RD
- SCrC 95076 (975-A4
See Page 955)
PINE HOLLOW CIR
1700 SJS 95133 834-E2
PINEHURST AV
200 LGTS 95032 873-F6
PINEHURST CT W
1700 MPS 95035 794-D3
PINEHURST DR
1400 SJS 95118 874-B2
1600 LALT 94024 832-A3
PINEHURST SQ
1300 SJS 95117 853-C4
PINELAND AV
5900 SJS 95123 874-J5
PINE MEADOW CT
- SJS 95135 855-H7
PINEMONT DR
4700 SJS 95008 873-A1
4700 SJS 95008 872-J1
PINE NUT CT
1000 SUNV 94087 832-C2
PINE PASS TER
1500 SUNV 94087 832-D5
PINE RIDGE CT
3500 SJS 95127 835-C3
PINE RIDGE WY
- PTLV 94028 810-D5
3500 SJS 95127 835-C3
22000 SCIC 95030 913-B3
PINE SPRING CT
3200 SJS 95121 855-B3
PINE TREE AV
- SBnC - (1017-A6
See Page 997)
PINETREE TER
5000 SJS 95008 872-J1
PINEVIEW DR
300 SCL 95050 833-D7
500 SJS 95117 833-D7
PINEVIEW LN
100 MLPK 94025 790-D5
PINEVILLE AV
10300 CPTO 95014 852-F2
PINEWELL CT
5600 SJS 95138 875-D4
PINE WOOD CT
500 LGTS 95030 873-B2
PINEWOOD CT
1700 MPS 95035 814-A3
PINEWOOD DR
600 SJS 95129 853-A3
PINE WOOD LN
100 LGTS 95030 873-B2
PINEWOOD PL
1000 SJS 95129 853-A3
3700 SCL 95054 813-E5
PINEWOOD WY
1500 MPS 95035 814-A3
PINION WY
1700 MGH 95037 917-D6
PINKERTON CT
3200 SJS 95148 835-E7
PINKERTON DR
3200 SJS 95148 835-D7
PINKSTONE CT
1600 SJS 95122 835-A5
PINMORE DR
1500 SJS 95118 874-A4
1600 SJS 95118 873-J4
PINNACLE CT
3500 SJS 95132 814-G3
19300 SAR 95070 872-G3
PINNACLE DR
3300 SJS 95132 814-G4
PINNTAGE PKWY
20200 CPTO 95014 852-E1
PIN OAK CT
3400 SJS 95148 835-E7
PIN OAK DR
400 SUNV 94086 832-G1
PINOLE CT
10600 CPTO 95014 852-E2
PINON CT
700 SUNV 94086 832-G2
PINON DR
100 PTLV 94028 810-B4
PINON PL
4400 SJS 95136 874-J1
PINOT CT
200 SJS 95119 875-E7
PINOTAGE CT
8300 SJS 95135 855-J7

STREET Block City ZIP Pg-Grid

PINOT BLANC WY
600 FRMT 94539 794-A2
3200 SJS 95135 855-G3
PINOT GRIS WY
4100 SJS 95135 855-G3
PINOT NOIR CT
8000 SJS 95135 855-H6
PINTA CT
100 LGTS 95032 873-C7
PINTAIL CT
1300 SJS 95118 874-C2
PINTO CT
2400 MGH 95037 917-F6
PINTO DR
600 SJS 95111 854-H5
PINTO PALM TER
- SUNV 94086 832-G4
PINTO RIVER CT
4600 SJS 95136 874-G2
PIONEER AV
2400 SCIC 95128 853-F1
PIONEER WY
- MTVW 94041 812-A6
PIONEERS RD
- SCrC 95076 995-D1
PIPEDREAM CT
1100 SJS 95122 834-F7
PIPER AV
800 SUNV 94087 832-C2
PIPER DR
1200 MPS 95035 814-B2
4100 SJS 95117 853-A3
4100 SJS 95129 853-A3
PIPPIN AV
800 SUNV 94087 832-C2
PIPPIN CREEK CT
1100 SJS 95120 894-G3
PISA CT
- SJS 95138 855-E7
PISCES DR
3400 SJS 95111 854-F7
PISMO CT
6300 SJS 95123 875-A7
PISMO TER
300 SUNV 94086 812-D7
PISTACHIO DR
3400 SJS 95111 854-G6
PISTACHIO GROVE CT
5300 SJS 95123 874-F7
PISTOIA WY
- SJS 95138 855-G7
- SJS 95138 875-G1
PITCAIRN WY
3300 SJS 95111 854-J5
PITCH PINE CT
4300 SJS 95136 874-H1
PITMAN AV
1200 PA 94301 791-A3
1400 PA 94303 791-A3
PITNER CT
3000 SJS 95148 855-D1
PITTSFIELD WY
7200 SJS 95139 875-G7
PIXANNE CT
2600 SJS 95148 835-B6
PLACER OAKS RD
16700 LGTS 95032 873-B5
PLACER SPRING CT
11800 CPTO 95014 852-C4
PLACID CT
- SJS 95135 875-J1
PLACIDA CT
14600 SAR 95070 872-C3
PLACITAS AV
- ATN 94027 790-E1
500 SMCo 94063 790-E1
PLAINFIELD DR
4700 SJS 95111 875-B1
PLAINVIEW CT
6500 SJS 95120 894-C1
PLANETREE PL
900 SUNV 94086 832-G3
PLATEAU AV
1500 SCIC 94024 831-F3
PLATINUM CT
1800 SJS 95116 834-F3
PLATT AV
1100 MPS 95035 814-D1
PLATT CT
800 MPS 95035 814-D1
PLATTE RIVER CT
600 SJS 95111 854-H5
PLAYA DEL REY
5400 SJS 95123 874-F3
PLAZA CT
1700 MTVW 94040 831-G1
PLAZA DR
100 SUNV 94089 812-F3
800 SJS 95125 854-A2

PLAZA AMERICAS
2600 SJS 95132 814-D4
PLAZA BANDERAS
2600 SJS 95132 814-D4
PLAZA CASITAS
1700 SJS 95132 814-D4
PLAZA CLAVELES
2600 SJS 95132 814-D4
PLAZA CORONA
5000 SCL 95054 813-C3
PLAZA DE GUADALUPE
2100 SJS 95116 834-G3
PLAZA ESCUELA
4900 SCL 95054 813-C3
PLAZA INVIERNO
600 SJS 95111 875-B1
PLAZA LA POSADA
200 LGTS 95030 872-J3
PLAZA MONTEZ
1900 SJS 95132 814-D3
PLAZOLETA
100 LGTS 95030 872-J2
PLEASANT AV
- SAR 95070 872-E4
PLEASANT ST
- LGTS 95032 873-B7
- LGTS 95032 893-B1
- SJS 95110 834-A6
N PLEASANT ST
200 SJS 95110 834-A6
PLEASANT WY
800 LALT 94022 811-E4
PLEASANT ACRES DR
2300 SCIC 95148 835-E5
PLEASANT CREST CT
2000 SJS 95148 835-D4
PLEASANT CREST DR
3500 SJS 95148 835-D5
PLEASANT ECHO DR
3500 SJS 95148 835-D4
PLEASANT GROVE CT
- SJS 95112 854-E4
PLEASANT HILLS CT
7000 SJS 95139 895-E1
PLEASANT KNOLL DR
3500 SJS 95148 835-D4
PLEASANT RIDGE AV
- SCIC 95127 834-H2
PLEASANT ROW CT
3500 SJS 95148 835-D5
PLEASANT VIEW AV
17300 MSER 95030 873-A5
PLEASANT VISTA DR
3700 SCIC 95148 835-E5
PLOMOSA CT
600 FRMT 94539 793-J1
PLOMOSA RD
48500 FRMT 94539 793-J2
PLOMOSA WY
- FRMT 94539 793-J1
PLUM AV
1100 SUNV 94087 832-C3
PLUM ST
1100 SJS 95110 854-C2
PLUMAS DR
2700 SJS 95121 854-J3
2700 SJS 95121 855-A3
12000 SAR 95070 852-E5
PLUM BLOSSOM DR
7400 CPTO 95014 852-D4
PLUMERIA DR
- SJS 95134 813-F6
PLUM GROVE CT
5200 SJS 95123 874-F7
PLUMMER AV
2200 SJS 95125 854-A6
2900 SJS 95125 874-B1
2900 SJS 95118 874-B1
PLUMSTEAD CT
2200 SJS 95148 855-C2
PLUMSTEAD WY
2800 SJS 95148 855-C2
PLUM TREE LN
100 SCIC 94305 790-H6
PLUMTREE LN
900 MTVW 94040 831-G1
10200 CPTO 95014 832-E7
PLYMOUTH AV
6100 SJS 95129 852-G4
PLYMOUTH DR
800 GIL 95020 977-H4
1000 SUNV 94087 832-B2
12500 SAR 95070 852-F6
PLYMOUTH ST
1400 MTVW 94043 811-G1
PLYMPTON CT
100 SJS 95139 875-G7
POAS CIR
- SJS 95116 834-G3

POAS CT
2000 SJS 95116 834-G3
POCATELLO AV
900 SUNV 94087 832-B6
POCATELLO CT
500 SJS 95111 854-H5
POCATELLO DR
400 SJS 95111 854-H5
POCO WY
1900 SJS 95116 834-H5
POE LN
1300 SJS 95130 853-B4
POE ST
300 PA 94301 790-H4
POETT LN
2400 SCL 95051 833-B2
POGLIA CT
5600 SJS 95138 875-G1
POINCIANA DR
1100 SCL 95051 832-H3
1100 SUNV 94086 832-H3
POINSETTIA CT
4400 SJS 95136 874-H2
POINT CREEK CT
800 SJS 95133 814-G7
POINT CREEK DR
800 SJS 95133 814-G7
POINTDEXTER CT
2800 SJS 95133 814-G6
POINT DUNES CT
200 SJS 95139 895-H2
POINTE CLAIRE CT
1400 SUNV 94087 832-D4
POINTE CLAIRE DR
1300 SUNV 94087 832-D4
POKER FLAT PL
1200 SJS 95120 874-C6
POLARIS AV
200 MTVW 94043 811-H4
POLARIS CT
- MPS 95035 814-A3
POLE LINE RD
4800 SCIC 95020 (976-C2
See Page 955)
POLHEMUS AV
200 ATN 94027 790-C4
POLI RD
9200 SCIC 95020 956-F6
POLITZER DR
- MLPK 94025 790-E5
POLK AV
1000 SUNV 94086 812-B7
2400 SCL 95051 833-C7
POLK CT
400 GIL 95020 978-A2
1900 MTVW 94040 831-G1
POLK LN
1100 SJS 95117 853-C3
POLK SPRING CT
1200 SJS 95120 894-G4
POLLARD AV
100 SCIC 95046 937-D3
POLLARD CT
2100 CMBL 95030 872-J2
POLLARD RD
700 LGTS 95030 873-A2
800 CMBL 95008 873-A2
1600 CMBL 95030 873-A2
1800 LGTS 95030 872-J2
1800 CMBL 95030 872-J2
2000 SAR 95070 872-J2
POLLARD OAKS CT
- LGTS 95030 873-B2
POLLEN CT
2000 SJS 95131 814-D7
POLTONHALL CT
3200 SJS 95121 855-C5
POLTON PLACE WY
3700 SJS 95121 855-B4
POLVADERO DR
6900 SJS 95119 895-E1
POMANDER PL
6600 SJS 95120 894-G1
POME AV
1100 SUNV 94087 832-C3
POMEGRANATE CT
1100 SUNV 94087 832-C3
POMEGRANATE LN
400 SJS 95134 813-C2
POMELO CT
1100 SUNV 94087 832-C3
POMERADO DR
3200 SJS 95135 855-H3
POMERADO WY
3300 SJS 95135 855-G3
POMEROY AV
500 SCL 95051 832-J6
700 SCL 95051 833-A5
3100 SJS 95121 855-C3

POMEROY CT
3200 SJS 95121 855-C3
POMONA AV
1400 SJS 95110 854-D2
1600 SJS 95125 854-D2
4200 PA 94306 811-C3
POMPANO ST
1200 SJS 95122 834-H6
POMPEY DR
1400 SJS 95128 853-E5
POMPONIO
- PTLV 94028 830-C1
PONCE CT
5700 SJS 95120 874-C5
PONCE DR
4200 PA 94306 811-E2
POND CT
- MPS 95035 794-A7
POND WY
1900 SJS 95131 814-C4
PONDEROSA AV
700 SUNV 94086 832-G3
PONDEROSA CT
16700 MGH 95037 917-E6
PONDEROSA DR
7700 GIL 95020 977-G3
PONDEROSA TER
4900 SJS 95008 872-J1
PONDEROSA WY
2800 SCL 95051 833-A6
PONSELLE CT
2600 SJS 95121 854-J4
PONTIAC AV
13900 SAR 95070 872-D2
PONTIAC DR
5700 SJS 95123 874-H5
PONTIUS CT
5800 SJS 95123 875-A5
PONY PASS CIR
4800 SJS 95136 874-H2
POPE CT
1700 CMBL 95008 873-D2
POPE ST
100 MLPK 94025 791-A3
200 MLPK 94025 790-J2
POPEJOY CT
4800 SJS 95118 873-J4
POPLAR AV
- CMBL 95008 853-F6
100 RDWC 94061 790-B1
800 SUNV 94086 832-G3
1300 SUNV 94087 832-G3
2000 EPA 94303 791-A1
POPLAR CT
900 SUNV 94086 832-G3
POPLAR DR
2200 SJS 95122 834-J5
8700 GIL 95020 977-F1
POPLAR ST
700 SCL 95050 833-F5
POPLAR TER
4900 SJS 95008 872-J1
POPLAR GROVE SQ
22800 CPTO 95014 851-J1
POPLARWOOD WY
2500 SJS 95132 814-C3
POPPY AV
1700 MLPK 94025 790-E6
POPPY CT
100 MPS 95035 794-D6
800 SUNV 94086 832-G3
POPPY DR
22500 CPTO 95014 831-J7
POPPY LN
- SCIC 95127 814-J5
- MPS 95035 794-D6
3400 SCIC 95020 957-B7
15600 MSER 95030 873-A5
POPPY PL
400 MTVW 94043 811-H4
POPPY WY
1200 CPTO 95014 852-D4
POPPY BLOSSOM CT
5300 SJS 95123 875-B3
POPPY HILL RD
300 SCrC 95076 (975-B6
See Page 955)
POPPY HILLS CT
5700 SJS 95138 875-G1
POPULUS PL
900 SUNV 94086 832-G3
PORGY PL
1300 SJS 95128 853-F4
PORPOISE TER
500 SUNV 94089 812-G3
PORT WY
2100 SJS 95133 814-E7
PORTAGE AV
400 PA 94306 811-B1

PORTAGE MOUNTAIN DR
1500 SJS 95126 853-H4
PORTAL AV
10000 CPTO 95014 832-F7
10000 CPTO 95014 852-F1
PORTAL CT
2200 SJS 95131 814-A5
PORTAL LN
- SCL 95134 813-D5
PORTAL PL
700 PA 94303 791-B6
PORTAL PZ
19800 CPTO 95014 852-F1
PORTAL WY
2200 SJS 95148 835-D6
PORTER DR
- MntC - (1015-H3
See Page 995)
3100 PA 94304 811-A2
PORTER LN
- SCIC 95127 815-A7
300 SCIC 95127 835-B1
PORTERFIELD CT
2400 MTVW 94040 831-J1
PORTER PEABODY RD
6800 SCIC 95020 958-G4
PORTIA AV
1000 SUNV 94086 812-C7
PORTLAND AV
900 LALT 94024 831-H2
PORTO ALEGRE CT
- SJS 95120 874-D5
PORTO ALEGRE DR
5700 SJS 95120 874-C5
PORTO ALEGRE PL
1100 SJS 95120 874-D6
PORTOBELLO DR
1400 SJS 95118 874-A3
PORTOFINO TER
400 MPS 95035 793-G3
PORTOLA AV
1000 SJS 95126 833-G5
1000 SCL 95126 833-G5
1500 PA 94306 791-A6
E PORTOLA AV
- LALT 94022 811-E4
W PORTOLA AV
- LALT 94022 811-D4
PORTOLA CT
200 LALT 94022 811-E4
PORTOLA DR
1400 MPS 95035 814-D1
PORTOLA RD
- CPTO 95014 851-J2
- PTLV 94028 810-A6
PORTOLA GREEN CIR
- PTLV 94028 810-C7
PORTOLA HEIGHTS RD
- SMCo 94020 850-H4
PORTOLA STATE PARK RD
- SMCo 94020 850-B7
PORTOS CT
19200 SAR 95070 852-G7
PORTOS DR
19000 SAR 95070 872-G1
PORTOS PL
19100 SAR 95070 872-G1
PORTREE DR
7500 SJS 95135 855-J6
PORT ROWAN DR
6900 SJS 95119 875-F6
PORTRUSH CT
5600 SJS 95138 875-F1
PORTSMOUTH CT
2000 SJS 95132 814-J2
PORTSWOOD CIR
700 SJS 95120 894-H3
PORTSWOOD DR
700 SJS 95120 894-H3
POSITANO LN
6700 SJS 95138 875-G4
POSSUM LN
- PTLV 94028 810-A6
POST ST
- SJS 95113 834-B6
100 MTVW 94040 811-J7
POSTGATE CT
1900 SJS 95121 855-C3
POST OAK CIR
5900 SJS 95120 874-C6
POSTON DR
4700 SJS 95136 874-J3
POSTWOOD DR
2800 SJS 95132 814-D3
POTMARNOCH CT
5000 SJS 95138 855-E6
POTOMAC CT
600 SJS 95136 874-F2

POTOMAC DR
100 LGTS 95032 873-D5
POTOMAC PL
7100 GIL 95020 977-H4
POTRERO AV
300 SUNV 94086 812-D6
POTRERO DR
1700 SJS 95124 873-G1
POTTER CT
16700 LGTS 95032 873-C7
POTTERS HATCH CIR
10100 CPTO 95014 851-J1
POTTS DR
13000 SCIC 95111 854-H6
POUGHKEEPSIE RD
- SJS 95119 875-C4
- SJS 95193 875-C4
100 SJS 95123 875-B4
POWDERBORN CT N
4500 SJS 95136 874-G2
POWDERBORN CT S
4600 SJS 95136 874-G2
POWDERHORN CT
600 SCIC 95046 957-E1
POWELL CT
1600 SJS 95122 834-G7
POWER CT
- SJS 95133 834-B2
POWERSCOURT WY
- SJS 95136 854-E6
PRADA CT
1300 MPS 95035 794-C5
PRADA DR
400 MPS 95035 794-C5
PRADO CT
- PTLV 94028 810-C7
PRADO LN
3200 SJS 95148 835-D6
PRADO SECOYA
- ATN 94027 790-E4
PRADO VISTA DR
10100 CPTO 95014 851-J1
PRAGUE CT
6500 SJS 95119 875-D7
PRAGUE DR
100 SJS 95119 875-D7
PRAIRIE LN
2900 SJS 95127 834-H1
PRAIRIE VIEW CT
200 SJS 95127 834-H1
PRAIRIE WOOD CT
200 SJS 95127 834-H2
PRANCER CT
900 MGH 95037 937-B5
PRATOLA CT
15100 MGH 95037 937-B4
PRATT LN
600 SCIC 95037 916-J2
PRELUDE DR
1300 SJS 95131 814-C7
PRENTISS DR
1100 SJS 95120 894-F2
PRESCOTT AV
1100 SUNV 94089 812-J4
1200 SUNV 94089 813-A4
3600 SJS 95124 873-H2
PRESERVATION CT
18500 MGH 95037 916-H5
PRESERVATION DR
200 SJS 95116 834-G4
PRESERVATION WY
- MGH 95037 916-H5
PRESIDIO DR
8000 CPTO 95014 852-B2
PRESTON CT
2700 MTVW 94040 831-J2
PRESTON DR
100 MTVW 94040 831-J2
5700 SJS 95124 873-J6
PRESTWICK CIR
7700 SJS 95135 856-A5
PRESWICK CT
700 SUNV 94087 832-F6
PRETORIA CT
800 SJS 95127 814-H6
PREVOST CT
1000 SJS 95125 854-E5
PREVOST ST
800 SJS 95125 854-B2
PRICE AV
19800 CPTO 95014 852-F1
PRICE CT
3000 PA 94303 791-D6
16800 MGH 95037 936-H1
PRICE DR
16800 MGH 95037 936-J2
PRICE WY
2300 SJS 95124 853-G7
PRICEWOOD CT
700 SJS 95120 894-H3

PRIDE CT
3200 SJS 95127 814-H6
PRIDE ST
700 SJS 95127 814-H6
PRIETA CT
10900 SCIC 95127 815-B7
PRIMERA CT
2600 SJS 95148 835-D6
PRIMM AV
1400 SJS 95122 834-H6
PRIMO CT
1900 SJS 95131 814-C6
PRIMROSE AV
900 SUNV 94086 832-G3
PRIMROSE LN
1000 GIL 95020 977-G2
PRIMROSE WY
- PA 94303 791-C4
1200 CPTO 95014 852-D4
PRINCE DR
6000 SJS 95129 852-G3
PRINCE ST
200 LGTS 95030 873-A2
PRINCE ALBERT CT
3400 SJS 95132 814-J2
PRINCE CHARLES CT
3400 SJS 95132 814-J2
PRINCE EDWARD WY
1400 SUNV 94087 832-D4
PRINCE ESTATES CT
5300 SJS 95135 855-H5
PRINCE GEORGE DR
1900 SJS 95116 834-F3
PRINCE OF WALES LN
3400 SJS 95132 814-J3
PRINCE PHILIP CT
3400 SJS 95132 814-J2
PRINCE ROYAL PL
4600 SJS 95136 874-F2
PRINCESS PL
600 MPS 95035 794-B4
PRINCESS ANNE DR
900 SJS 95128 853-G3
PRINCESS ELLEENA CT
24000 LAH 94024 831-E3
PRINCESS MARGARET CT
3400 SJS 95132 814-J3
PRINCETON CT
3300 SCL 95051 832-J6
PRINCETON DR
600 SUNV 94087 832-D2
1400 SJS 95118 874-A5
PRINCETON PL
7200 GIL 95020 977-J4
PRINCETON RD
- MLPK 94025 790-G5
PRINCETON ST
2000 PA 94306 791-A7
2000 PA 94306 811-A1
PRINCETON WY
3200 SCL 95051 832-J6
PRINCEVALLE ST
6500 GIL 95020 978-A5
6500 SCIC 95020 978-A5
6600 GIL 95020 977-J3
PRINDIVILLE CT
100 SJS 95138 875-G7
PRINDIVILLE DR
7300 SJS 95138 875-G7
PRING CT
18600 SCIC 95014 852-H1
PRINTEMPO DR
600 SJS 95134 813-H4
PRINTEMPO PL
800 SJS 95134 813-H4
PRINTY AV
400 MPS 95035 794-C5
PRIOR LN
200 ATN 94027 790-F2
PRISCILLA CT
1700 MTVW 94040 811-G5
PRISCILLA DR
1200 SJS 95129 853-A4
PRISCILLA LN
12300 LAH 94022 831-D3
12300 LAH 94024 831-D3
PRITCHARD CT
700 SCL 95051 833-B6
PRITCHETT CT
1300 LALT 94024 831-J3
PRITCHETT WY
1300 LALT 94024 831-J3
PRIVADA LUISITA
100 LGTS 95030 873-B4
PRIVET CT
700 SUNV 94086 832-G2
PROM DR
- SCIC 95037 956-G1

PROMENADE CT
800 SJS 95138 875-G5
PROMENADE LN
700 SJS 95138 875-G5
PROMETHEAN WY
100 MTVW 94043 812-A5
PROMONTORY WY
3100 SJS 95135 876-A1
PRONTO DR
600 SJS 95123 874-F5
PROSPECT AV
- LGTS 95032 893-A1
100 SCIC 95032 893-A1
24600 LAH 94024 831-C3
24600 LAH 94022 831-C3
PROSPECT CT
100 LGTS 95032 893-A1
PROSPECT RD
5800 SAR 95070 852-D5
7400 CPTO 95014 852-D5
18900 SJS 95129 852-F5
21300 SCIC 95070 852-B6
PROSPECT ST
900 SJS 95110 854-C1
2100 MLPK 94025 790-D7
2100 SMCo 94025 790-D7
PROSPER AV
1100 SJS 95118 874-C2
PROSPERITY CT
1500 SJS 95131 814-C6
PROUD DR
1400 SJS 95132 814-G4
PROUTY WY
1000 SJS 95129 852-H3
PROVANMILL WY
2100 SJS 95121 855-C4
PROVENCE CT
- SJS 95135 855-F3
PROVIDENCE CT
900 CPTO 95014 852-B2
PROVINCETOWN DR
1500 SJS 95129 852-G5
PROVO CT
3100 SJS 95127 814-H6
PRUNE CT
1000 SUNV 94087 832-C2
PRUNE WY
600 SJS 95117 853-D1
PRUNE BLOSSOM DR
5300 SJS 95123 875-E2
13700 SAR 95070 872-D1
PRUNEDALE RD
4100 SCIC 95020 978-J5
4200 SCIC 95020 (979-A4
See Page 959)
PRUNELLE CT
1100 SUNV 94087 832-C3
PRUNERIDGE AV
1800 SCL 95050 833-D7
1800 SCL 95128 833-D7
1900 SJS 95117 833-D7
2500 SCL 95051 833-A7
3200 SCL 95051 832-G6
19000 CPTO 95014 832-G6
PRUNETREE CT
2400 SJS 95121 855-E4
PRUNETREE LN
4000 SJS 95121 855-D4
10300 CPTO 95014 832-E7
PUCCINI AV
2600 SJS 95122 855-A1
PUCCINI DR
500 SUNV 94087 832-E3
PUEBLA CT
1400 SJS 95118 874-B3
PUEBLO DR
200 SJS 95131 814-A5
PUEBLO HILL CT
3600 SJS 95127 835-B1
PUEBLO VISTA
10300 SCIC 95127 835-B1
10300 SJS 95127 835-B1
PUENTE CT
20000 SAR 95070 852-F6
PUERTO GOLFITO CT
500 SJS 95116 834-D2
PUERTO LIMON CT
2000 SJS 95116 834-F3
PUERTO VALLARTA DR
1500 SJS 95120 874-A7
1600 SJS 95120 894-A1
1600 SJS 95120 893-J1
PUESTA DEL SOL
100 LGTS 95030 872-J3
PUFFIN CT
- CMBL 95008 853-D5
PUGET SOUND WY
800 SJS 95133 834-E1
PULGAS AV
1800 EPA 94303 791-C3

PULLMAN WY
- SJS 95111 854-F6
PULORA CT
1100 SUNV 94087 832-C3
PUMPHERSTON CT
2200 SJS 95148 855-C2
PUMPHERSTON WY
3200 SJS 95148 855-C2
PUMPKIN CT
7900 CPTO 95014 852-C2
PUMPKIN DR
7900 CPTO 95014 852-B2
PURDUE CT
700 SCL 95051 832-J6
PURDUE DR
18200 SAR 95070 852-J7
PURDUE PL
5500 SJS 95118 874-A5
PURE CT
500 SJS 95136 874-G3
PURISSIMA AV
400 SUNV 94086 832-D1
PURISSIMA RD
26300 LAH 94022 831-B1
26600 LAH 94022 811-A6
PURITAN CT
700 SJS 95123 874-G6
PURITANI CT
2500 SJS 95121 854-H4
PURITANI WY
1400 SJS 95121 854-H4
PURPLE CLIFF CT
6500 SJS 95119 875-D7
PURPLE GLEN DR
200 SJS 95119 875-D7
PURPLE HILLS DR
6100 SJS 95119 875-D7
PURPLE KNOLL CT
6200 SJS 95119 875-C6
PURPLELEAF ST
48000 FRMT 94539 793-H1
PURPLE SAGE CT
6100 SJS 95119 875-C6
PURPLE VALE CT
6500 SJS 95119 875-D7
PUSATERI WY
1100 SJS 95121 854-J4
PUTNEY CT
1900 SJS 95132 814-D3
PUTTER AV
11500 SCIC 94024 831-E4
PUTTER WY
11600 SCIC 94024 831-E4
PYLE CT
2200 SCL 95051 833-B2
PYRAMID CT
1500 SJS 95130 853-B4
PYRUS WY
800 SUNV 94087 832-C2

Q

QUADROS LN
2000 SJS 95131 814-E7
QUAIL
- PTLV 94028 830-C1
QUAIL AV
1500 SUNV 94087 832-H5
QUAIL CT
- ATN 94027 790-H1
17200 MGH 95037 917-F4
QUAIL DR
1500 MPS 95035 794-C5
QUAIL LN
3100 MGH 95037 917-F4
25900 LAH 94022 811-C7
QUAIL ACRES
14100 SAR 95070 872-F2
QUAIL BUSH CT
400 SJS 95117 853-C1
QUAIL CANYON CT
3800 SCIC 95148 835-F5
QUAIL CANYON RD
3800 SCIC 95148 835-F5
QUAIL CLIFF WY
7000 SJS 95120 894-G3
QUAIL COVE CT
7000 SJS 95120 894-F3
QUAIL COVE WY
7000 SJS 95120 894-F3
QUAIL CREEK CIR
1000 SJS 95120 894-F3
QUAIL CREST WY
7000 SJS 95120 894-F4
QUAIL DUNES WY
7000 SJS 95120 894-G3
QUAIL HILL RD
15900 LGTS 95032 873-D6
QUAIL HOLLOW DR
- SJS 95128 853-F4

QUAIL KNOLL CT
1100 SJS 95120 894-F3
QUAIL MEADOW RD
1900 SCIC 94024 831-G5
QUAIL RIDGE CT
1100 SJS 95120 894-F3
QUAIL RUN CT
1200 SJS 95118 874-C3
15500 SCIC 95070 872-C4
QUAIL VIEW WY
1000 SJS 95120 894-F3
QUAIL WALK DR
1400 GIL 95020 957-E7
QUAMME DR
1100 SJS 95121 854-J3
QUANTICO CT
2400 SJS 95128 853-F3
QUARRY RD
100 PA 94304 790-H5
100 SBnC - (1017-B3
See Page 997)
100 SCIC 94305 790-H5
21300 SAR 95070 872-C1
N QUARRY RD
17300 LGTS 95032 893-C1
S QUARRY RD
16400 LGTS 95032 893-C2
QUARRY PARK DR
4000 SJS 95136 854-E6
QUARRY PARK WY
4000 SJS 95136 854-E6
QUARTUCCIO WY
4100 SCIC 95148 835-G7
QUARTZ WY
1400 SJS 95118 874-B2
QUEBEC CT
1500 SUNV 94087 832-D5
QUEBEC WY
1900 SJS 95124 853-G7
QUEEN ANNE DR
1000 SJS 95129 852-G3
1100 SUNV 94087 832-C3
QUEEN CHARLOTTE DR
1600 SUNV 94087 832-D5
QUEEN ELIZABETH WY
1800 SJS 95132 814-J3
QUEEN MARY CT
1900 SJS 95132 814-J2
QUEENS CT
- ATN 94027 790-C4
400 CMBL 95008 853-D5
QUEENS LN
400 SJS 95112 834-A2
QUEENSBRIDGE CT
1000 SJS 95120 894-G4
QUEENSBRIDGE WY
1000 SJS 95120 894-G4
QUEENSBROOK DR
1000 SJS 95129 852-C7
QUEENSBURRY AV
1400 LALT 94024 832-A3
QUEENS CROSSING DR
1400 SJS 95132 814-E4
QUEENS ESTATES CT
2900 SJS 95135 855-G5
QUEENS OAK CT
22600 CPTO 95014 831-J6
QUEENSTOWN CT
1500 SUNV 94087 832-D5
QUEENSTOWN DR
1700 SJS 95132 814-E3
QUEENSWOOD CT
7000 SJS 95120 894-H3
QUEENSWOOD WY
6800 SJS 95120 894-H2
QUEEN VICTORIA WY
3400 SJS 95132 814-J3
QUERCUS CT
900 SUNV 94086 832-H3
QUESADA DR
3300 SJS 95148 835-D7
QUETTA AV
700 SUNV 94087 832-D2
QUETTA CT
800 SUNV 94087 832-D2
QUICKERT RD
15400 SAR 95070 872-C5
15400 SCIC 95070 872-C5
QUICKSILVER DR
1000 SJS 95136 874-D2
QUIET CIR
1900 SJS 95132 814-E3
QUIET MEADOW CT
1400 SJS 95121 855-D7
QUILEN CT
- SCIC 94305 790-J7
QUIMBY RD
1700 SJS 95122 835-G
1700 SJS 95122 855-B
2400 SJS 95148 855-B

STREET
Block City ZIP Pg-Grid

QUIMBY RD
3600 SJS 95148 835-G7
3700 SCIC 95148 835-H7
4500 SCIC 95148 836-B6
QUINCE AV
800 SCL 95051 833-A6
1100 SUNV 94087 832-D3
QUINCE LN
500 MPS 95035 794-D5
QUINCY DR
400 MTVW 94043 811-F2
1200 SJS 95132 814-G5
QUINLAN LN
3700 SJS 95118 874-B2
QUINN AV
500 SJS 95112 854-G3
2100 SCL 95051 833-B2
QUINN CT
2100 SCL 95051 833-B2
19200 SCIC 95037 916-J2
QUINNHILL AV
200 SCIC 94024 831-E2
200 LALT 94024 831-E2
QUINTERNO CT
22200 CPTO 95014 852-A1
QUINTINIA DR
800 SUNV 94086 832-G2
QUINTO WY
2700 SJS 95124 873-H1
QUITO RD
2200 SAR 95070 872-J1
2200 SJS 95130 872-J1
QUITO RD Rt#-G2
1900 SJS 95130 852-J7
1900 SAR 95130 852-J7
1900 SAR 95070 852-J7
2200 SAR 95070 872-J1
2200 SJS 95130 872-J1
14900 LGTS 95030 872-H4
15000 MSER 95030 872-H4
15500 SCIC 95030 872-H4
QUITO OAKS WY
13900 SAR 95070 872-J2
QUME DR
2200 SJS 95131 814-C5

R

RABIA DR
5500 SJS 95123 874-H4
RACE ST
\- SJS 95126 833-J7
200 SCIC 95126 833-J7
200 SCIC 95126 853-J1
300 SJS 95126 853-J1
RACHEL CT
5700 SJS 95123 874-J5
RACOON CT
17600 MGH 95037 917-E3
RADCLIFF DR
28100 LAH 94022 810-H5
RADCLIFF WY
800 SUNV 94087 832-C2
RADCLIFFE DR
400 SCL 95051 833-A7
900 SJS 95117 853-D3
RADFORD DR
100 CMBL 95008 853-B5
RADIANT DR
6200 SJS 95123 874-J7
RADIO AV
2000 SJS 95125 854-B5
RADKO DR
6500 SJS 95119 875-D7
RADOYKA DR
12200 SAR 95070 852-H6
RADTKE AV
10000 SCIC 95020 957-H5
RAE LN
22100 CPTO 95014 852-A2
RAEBURN CT
800 SJS 95136 874-E1
RAFAEL DR
1000 SJS 95120 874-E7
RAFTON DR
4900 SJS 95124 873-J4
RAGGIO AV
2300 SCL 95050 833-C3
2400 SCL 95051 833-B3
RAHWAY DR
4700 SJS 95111 875-B1
RAICH DR
7100 SJS 95120 894-H4
RAILROAD AV
200 MPS 95035 794-A7
900 SCL 95050 833-F3
5400 MGH 95037 917-A7
5400 MGH 95037 937-B1
6100 SCIC 95037 937-C2
N RAILROAD CT
300 MPS 95035 794-A6
RAILROAD ST
7300 GIL 95020 978-A3
RAILWAY AV
\- CMBL 95008 853-E6
RAIMUNDO WY
700 SCIC 94305 810-J2
1100 SCIC 94305 811-A2
RAINBOW CT
21600 CPTO 95014 852-B4
RAINBOW DR
600 MTVW 94041 812-A7
5800 SJS 95129 852-E4
7300 CPTO 95014 852-B4
21500 SCIC 95014 852-B4
RAINBOW PL
21000 CPTO 95014 852-A4
RAINDANCE CT
\- SJS 95136 874-H2
RAINERI LN
19200 SCIC 95030 912-J1
RAINFIELD DR
2700 SJS 95133 834-G1
RAINIER AV
100 SJS 95126 833-J7
RAINTREE CT
800 SJS 95129 852-J2
RAINTREE DR
800 SJS 95129 852-J2
RAINTREE SPRING CT
11500 CPTO 95014 852-A4
RAINVIEW DR
2700 SJS 95133 834-G1
RAINWELL CT
2700 SJS 95133 834-G1
RAINWELL DR
400 SJS 95133 834-G1
RAINWOOD CT
2800 SJS 95148 835-D7
RAJKOVICH WY
1100 SJS 95120 894-F3
RAKTAD RD
21100 SCIC 95120 895-B5
RALEIGH DR
2400 SJS 95124 853-J7
RALEIGH PL
18900 SAR 95070 852-G6
RALEIGH RD
\- SJS 95193 875-C5
200 SJS 95119 875-C5
RALENE CT
1600 SJS 95131 814-D5
RALENE PL
1600 SJS 95131 814-D5
RALMAR AV
2000 EPA 94303 791-A1
RALPH CT
500 SCIC 95046 937-F4
RALPH LEE CT
1700 MGH 95037 917-D5
RALPH LEE DR
1700 MGH 95037 917-D5
RALSTON CT
2300 SJS 95148 855-C2
2600 SCL 95051 833-B3
RALSTON DR
2300 SJS 95148 855-C2
RALSTON RD
\- ATN 94027 790-C3
RALT CT
\- SJS 95123 874-F7
RALYA CT
18500 SCIC 95014 852-H1
RAMA DR
3100 SJS 95124 873-H2
RAMBLEWOOD DR
6400 SJS 95120 894-E1
RAMBO CT
2300 SCL 95054 813-C5
RAMBOW DR
3400 PA 94306 791-D7
3400 PA 94306 811-D1
RAMEL WY
100 LGTS 95032 893-B1
RAMIREZ CT
3800 SJS 95121 855-D3
RAMISH DR
2100 SJS 95131 814-D6
RAMITA CT
1400 SJS 95128 853-F5
RAMKE PL
2400 SCL 95050 833-C6
RAMON DR
200 LALT 94024 811-F7
1300 SUNV 94087 832-G4
RAMONA AV
700 SUNV 94087 832-C1
900 SJS 95125 854-A2
22300 CPTO 95014 852-A1
RAMONA CIR
3600 PA 94306 811-D1
RAMONA CT
2800 SCL 95051 833-B6
RAMONA RD
100 SMCo 94028 830-E3
RAMONA ST
200 PA 94301 790-H4
1100 PA 94301 791-B7
2500 PA 94306 791-B7
3100 PA 94306 811-D1
RAMONA WY
700 GIL 95020 977-G1
RAMOS CT
500 MPS 95035 794-D5
2700 MTVW 94040 832-A2
RAMOS WY
2100 SJS 95128 833-F7
3100 PA 94304 811-B1
RAMOSO RD
100 PTLV 94028 810-B4
RAMPART AV
10400 CPTO 95014 852-F2
RAMSDELL PL
2500 SJS 95148 855-C1
RAMSEY RD
\- SCrC 95076 955-E6
RAMSGATE WY
1400 SJS 95127 835-A4
RAMSTAD DR
3300 SJS 95127 835-B3
RAMSTREE DR
1600 SJS 95131 814-C5
RANCH CT
1400 SJS 95132 814-G3
RANCH DR
\- MPS 95035 813-H1
200 MPS 95035 793-H7
RANCH PL
3500 SJS 95132 814-G3
RANCH RD
\- SCIC 95135 855-J1
\- SCrC 95076 955-A5
4500 SCIC 95148 835-J7
4500 SCIC 95148 855-J1
RANCHERO DR
15700 SCIC 95037 937-E1
RANCHERO WY
1000 SJS 95117 853-B3
RANCH HOUSE WY
8700 SJS 95136 856-A6
RANCHITA CT
1400 LALT 94024 831-J3
RANCHITA DR
1300 LALT 94024 831-J3
RANCHO DR
\- SCIC 95111 854-H7
900 SJS 95111 854-H7
RANCHO PL
10200 CPTO 95014 852-A1
RANCHO BELLA VISTA
20100 SAR 95070 872-E3
RANCHO DEEP CLIFF DR
22300 CPTO 95014 852-A2
RANCHO HIGUERA RD
400 MPS 95035 794-A4
RANCHO HILLS CT
1700 GIL 95020 977-E1
RANCHO HILLS DR
8700 GIL 95020 977-E1
9000 GIL 95020 957-E7
RANCHO LAS CIMAS WY
18500 SAR 95070 872-H3
RANCHO MANOR CT
100 SJS 95111 854-H6
RANCHO MANUELLA LN
26000 LAH 94022 811-C5
RANCHO MCCORMICK BLVD
2000 SCL 95050 833-C3
RANCHO MCCORMICK CT
2100 SCL 95050 833-C3
RANCHO REA RD
2800 MntC - (1017-A7 See Page 997)
RANCHO REAL
8200 GIL 95020 977-F2
RANCHO VENTURA ST
22300 CPTO 95014 852-A1
RANCHO VIEW CT
3400 SJS 95132 814-G3
RANCHO VISTA CT
3300 SCIC 95020 977-B2
RANCHO VISTA DR
7800 SCIC 95020 977-C3
RAND ST
1600 MPS 95035 794-A4
RANDALL CT
6000 SJS 95123 874-G6
RANDALL PL
\- MLPK 94025 790-F6
RANDERS CT
2700 PA 94303 791-C6
RANDLESWOOD CT
5800 SJS 95129 852-G3
RANDOL AV
1100 SJS 95126 833-H6
RANDOL CREEK DR
6900 SJS 95120 894-G3
RANDOLFI PL
1100 SJS 95131 814-E7
RANDOLPH AV
3600 SCL 95051 832-H7
RANDOLPH DR
1900 SJS 95128 853-G2
1900 SCIC 95128 853-G2
RANDOLPH PKWY
1600 LALT 94024 831-J4
RANDY CT
\- SMCo 94061 790-A3
RANDY LN
10000 CPTO 95014 832-E6
RANERE CT
1000 SUNV 94087 832-C2
RANEY CT
700 SCL 95050 833-C5
RANFRE LN
19300 SAR 95070 852-G7
19300 SAR 95070 872-G1
RANGER CT
16700 MGH 95037 917-F6
RANGPUR CT
1000 SUNV 94087 832-D2
RANKIN AV
\- SJS 95110 834-A5
RANKIN DR
1000 MPS 95035 794-C4
RANSEN CT
18200 MGH 95037 916-J6
RANSON DR
600 SJS 95133 834-F1
RANWICK CT
4200 SJS 95118 874-C2
RAPLEY TR
\- PTLV 94028 830-C3
\- SMCo 94028 830-C3
\- SMCo 94020 830-B5
RAPOSA CT
1200 SJS 95121 855-A4
RAPOSA DR
1100 SJS 95121 855-A4
RAQUEL CT
400 LALT 94022 811-C5
1600 SJS 95128 853-G3
14800 SCIC 95046 937-G2
RAQUEL LN
300 LALT 94022 811-C5
RARITAN PL
2600 SJS 95148 835-E6
RASMUS CIR
3000 SJS 95148 855-E1
RASPBERRY PL
4700 SJS 95129 853-B2
RATHMANN DR
2800 SJS 95148 835-E7
RATTAN CT
600 FRMT 94539 793-J2
RATTAN TER
800 SUNV 94086 832-G3
RAVEN CT
13800 SAR 95070 872-J1
RAVENDALE CT
3400 SJS 95111 854-G6
RAVENDALE DR
200 MTVW 94043 812-B6
RAVENSBURY AV
22500 SCIC 95014 831-E5
23000 LAH 94024 831-E4
23100 SCIC 94024 831-E5
RAVENSCOURT AV
900 SJS 95128 853-F4
1000 CMBL 95128 853-F4
RAVENS PLACE WY
1500 SJS 95121 855-B4
RAVENSWOOD AV
100 ATN 94027 790-G3
100 MLPK 94025 790-G3
RAVENSWOOD DR
1400 LALT 94024 832-A3
RAVENSWOOD WY
3100 SJS 95148 855-E1
3100 SJS 95148 835-E7
RAVENWOOD DR
13700 SAR 95070 872-J1
RAVINE CT
2300 SJS 95133 834-F1
RAVINE DR
2300 SJS 95133 834-F1
RAVINE RD
15700 SCIC 95030 872-G5
RAVINIA WY
100 LGTS 95032 893-D2
RAVIZZA AV
1600 SCL 95051 833-B3
RAWLINGS DR
900 SJS 95136 874-D2
RAWLS CT
100 SJS 95139 895-F1
RAY AV
1000 LALT 94022 811-D4
RAYANNA AV
3300 SCL 95051 832-J3
RAYBAL CT
6300 SJS 95123 875-A7
RAYMOND AV
500 SCIC 95128 853-G1
600 SJS 95128 853-G1
RAYMOND ST
3000 SCL 95054 813-D7
RAYMUNDO AV
700 LALT 94024 811-G6
REA AV
18400 MntC - (1017-A7 See Page 997)
REA CT
2800 MntC - (1017-A7 See Page 997)
REA ST
7600 GIL 95020 977-H3
REALM DR
7000 SJS 95119 875-E7
REAMWOOD AV
1200 SUNV 94089 813-A4
3200 SCL 95054 813-A4
REBECCA LN
\- ATN 94027 790-G2
11600 LAH 94024 831-E3
REBECCA WY
600 SJS 95117 853-B2
REBECCA LYNN WY
2400 SCL 95050 833-C6
REBECCA PRIVADA
800 MTVW 94040 832-A1
REBEIRO AV
2600 SCL 95051 833-B6
REBEL CT
5000 SJS 95118 874-A4
REBEL WY
1500 SJS 95118 873-J4
1500 SJS 95118 874-A4
RECIFE WY
5800 SJS 95120 874-C5
RECREATION AV
\- MLPK 94025 790-J2
RECREATION DR
\- SUNV 94089 812-H3
REDBERRY DR
16300 SCIC 95030 872-F5
REDBIRD DR
800 SJS 95125 854-C6
REDBUD CT
2400 SJS 95128 853-F4
REDBUSH TER
2000 SJS 95128 833-F6
REDCLIFF CT
22500 MTVW 94040 832-A1
REDCLIFF DR
1200 SJS 95118 854-C7
1200 SJS 95118 874-C1
RED CREEK DR
4900 SJS 95136 874-J2
4900 SJS 95136 875-A2
RED CREEK RD
\- SCIC 95140 (859-E7 See Page 839)
\- StCo - (859-E7 See Page 839)
\- StCo - 879-H1
REDDING RD
\- CMBL 95008 873-E2
300 SJS 95008 873-E2
REDEN DR
4300 SJS 95130 853-A7
REDFIELD CT
1500 SJS 95121 855-A3
RED FIR CT
21100 CPTO 95014 852-C2
REDGLEN CT
3200 SJS 95135 855-E2
RED HAWK DR
1200 GIL 95020 957-F7
REDHEAD LN
\- LGTS 95032 893-B1
RED HILL RD
20000 SCIC 95030 872-E5
RED HOLLY CT
7100 SJS 95120 894-C3
REDMOND AV
900 SJS 95120 894-E1
900 SJS 95120 874-A7
REDMOND CT
1000 SJS 95120 874-E7
RED MOUNTAIN RD
\- SCIC 95020 (942-D2 See Page 921)
RED OAK DR
\- SUNV 94086 832-G1
RED OAK DR E
200 SUNV 94086 832-G1
RED OAK DR W
200 SUNV 94086 832-G1
REDOAKS DR
1100 SJS 95128 853-E4
REDONDO CT
11200 CPTO 95014 852-B3
REDONDO DR
1200 SJS 95125 854-B5
REDONDO TER
300 SUNV 94086 812-D7
RED PEAK LN
\- SJS 95135 876-A1
RED PINE CT
1100 SJS 95125 854-A4
RED RIVER WY
100 SJS 95136 875-A3
REDROCK CT
1100 SUNV 94089 812-J4
REDROCK RD
26600 LAH 94022 830-J2
REDSTONE DR
5000 SJS 95124 873-E4
RED TAIL CT
3700 SCL 95051 832-H5
REDWING AV
1600 SUNV 94087 832-H5
REDWOOD AV
\- MLPK 94025 790-J2
\- RDWC 94061 790-A1
200 MPS 95035 793-H6
200 SCL 95051 833-A7
500 SJS 95050 833-E7
500 SJS 95128 833-E7
900 SUNV 94086 832-H3
N REDWOOD AV
\- SJS 95050 833-E7
1300 SJS 95128 833-E6
S REDWOOD AV
300 SJS 95128 853-E1
REDWOOD CIR
3700 PA 94306 811-D1
REDWOOD DR
900 SJS 95138 875-F6
1400 LALT 94024 831-J6
17900 SCIC 95030 912-J2
REDWOOD LN
1300 GIL 95020 977-G3
REDWOOD RD
\- SCrC 95076 955-C5
REDWOOD WY
\- ATN 94027 790-D2
REDWOOD ESTATES RD
17800 SCIC 95030 913-C2
REDWOOD GULCH RD
13600 SCIC 95070 871-F2
13700 SCIC 95030 871-F2
REDWOOD RETREAT RD
3400 SCIC 95020 956-E7
6900 SCIC 95037 956-B5
REECE WY
2900 SJS 95133 814-G7
REED AV
700 SUNV 94086 832-F2
REED ST
300 SCL 95050 833-D3
E REED ST
\- SJS 95112 834-D7
W REED ST
\- SJS 95110 834-C7
REED TER
1000 SUNV 94086 832-H2
REEDHURST AV
3900 SJS 95118 874-A2
REESE ST
1200 RDWC 94061 790-A1
REEVE ST
900 SCL 95050 833-E3
REEVES CT
200 SCIC 95127 835-B2
REFLECTIONS LN
\- MPS 95035 793-H6
REFREDI CT
21800 CPTO 95014 852-B1
REGABY PLACE CT
3800 SJS 95121 855-B5
REGAL CT
700 MLPK 94025 790-J2
4100 SCIC 95127 814-J6
4100 SCIC 95127 815-A6
REGALO CT
1400 SJS 95128 853-F4
REGAN LN
12700 SAR 95070 852-E6
REGAN ST
10100 SJS 95127 835-B3
REGAS DR
600 CMBL 95008 853-F7
600 SJS 95008 853-F7
REGATTA LN
1600 SJS 95112 833-J1
REGENCY DR
1200 SJS 95129 852-H4
REGENCY KNOLL DR
1000 SJS 95129 852-C7
REGENCY OAKS DR
6100 SJS 95129 852-C7
REGENT CT
900 RDWC 94061 790-B1
REGENT DR
900 LALT 94024 831-H5
REGENT PL
\- PA 94301 791-A4
REGENT ST
800 SJS 95110 833-J4
1300 RDWC 94061 790-A1
REGENT PARK DR
700 SJS 95123 874-F4
REGIA CT
1100 SUNV 94087 832-D3
REGINA CT
2300 SCL 95054 813-C5
REGINA WY
1700 CMBL 95008 873-A1
1800 SJS 95008 873-A1
REGIS CT
3300 SCL 95051 833-A2
REGNART CT
21600 CPTO 95014 852-B3
REGNART RD
21500 CPTO 95014 852-A4
REGNART WY
2800 SCL 95051 833-B7
REGNART CANYON DR
11600 CPTO 95014 852-A4
REID LN
20500 SAR 95070 872-D2
REINCLAUD CT
1100 SUNV 94087 832-C3
REINELL PL
20200 CPTO 95014 832-E7
REINERT AV
2100 MTVW 94043 811-G2
REINERT RD
800 MTVW 94043 811-G2
REINOSO CT
3600 SJS 95136 874-D1
REISLING WY
8300 SJS 95135 855-H7
REMBRANDT DR
1000 SUNV 94087 832-F3
REMILLARD CT
900 SJS 95122 834-E7
REMINGTON CT
1200 SUNV 94087 832-A3
2600 MGH 95037 917-F6
3000 SJS 95148 855-D1
E REMINGTON DR
100 SUNV 94087 832-E3
W REMINGTON DR
500 SUNV 94087 832-B2
REMINGTON WY
2900 SJS 95148 835-D7
3000 SJS 95148 855-D1
REMO CT
2300 SCL 95054 813-C5
REMO ST
700 SJS 95116 834-F6
REMSEN CT
1000 SUNV 94087 832-B3
REMUDA LN
1600 SJS 95112 833-J1
RENAISSANCE CT
1700 SCIC 95046 937-J6
RENAISSANCE DR
\- SJS 95134 813-D2
RENATO CT
\- RDWC 94061 790-C1
RENEE CT
1000 SJS 95120 894-H4
1200 SCIC 95046 937-H5
RENETTA CT
800 LALT 94024 831-E1
RENFIELD WY
2300 SJS 95148 855-C2
RENFREW CT
2200 SJS 95131 814-D5
N RENGSTORFF AV
100 MTVW 94040 811-G3
100 MTVW 94043 811-G1
S RENGSTORFF AV
200 MTVW 94040 811-F4
RENICK CT
2900 SJS 95148 855-D2
RENNIE AV
\- SCIC 95127 815-A6
RENO DR
2300 SJS 95148 835-D6
RENOIR CT
1000 SUNV 94087 832-F3
RENOVA DR
400 SCIC 95128 853-F2
RENRAW DR
1200 SJS 95127 835-C3
RENTON CT
800 SJS 95123 874-E5
RENZ LN
700 GIL 95020 978-B3
RENZO CT
4700 SJS 95111 875-B1
REPUBLIC AV
100 SJS 95116 834-H3
REPUBLIC CT
2500 SJS 95116 834-H3
REPUBLIC PL
2500 SJS 95116 834-J3
REQUA CT
2900 SJS 95148 835-E7
RESEARCH PL
3000 SJS 95134 813-G4
RESEDA DR
600 SUNV 94087 832-D1
RESERVOIR RD
\- ATN 94027 790-B6
\- LGTS 95032 893-A1
RESIDENT LN
\- MLPK 94025 790-J2
RESULTS WY
\- CPTO 95014 852-B1
RETTUS CT
600 SJS 95111 854-G3
REVA CT
10200 SCIC 95127 835-A3
REVELSTOKE WY
1400 SUNV 94087 832-D5
REVERE AV
1400 SJS 95118 874-B1
REVERE DR
800 SUNV 94087 832-C3
REVERE PL
7100 GIL 95020 977-H4
REVEY AV
100 SJS 95128 853-F1
100 SCIC 95128 853-F1
100 SCIC 95128 833-F7
100 SJS 95128 833-F7
REX CIR
100 CMBL 95008 853-D5
REXFORD WY
2000 SJS 95128 853-G2
2000 SCIC 95128 853-G2
REXWOOD CT
3800 SJS 95121 855-C4
REYNA PL
\- MLPK 94025 790-F5
REYNAUD DR
14800 SCIC 95127 835-B1
REYNELLA CT
1100 SUNV 94087 832-D3
REYNOLDS CIR
400 SJS 95112 833-J1
REYNOLDS DR
16300 SCIC 95037 936-G3
REYNOLDS RD
19200 SCIC 95030 894-A4
20300 SCIC 95030 893-J6
RHAPSODY WY
4400 SJS 95111 855-A7
RHINE LN
1400 SJS 95118 874-B5
RHINECASTLE WY
1100 SJS 95120 874-D6
RHINECLIFF WY
1400 SJS 95126 853-H4
RHODA DR
3700 SJS 95117 853-B3
13200 LAH 94022 811-A6
RHODES CT
100 SJS 95126 833-J7
400 SCIC 95046 937-F6
RHODES DR
500 PA 94303 791-C4
RHODESIA WY
1500 SJS 95126 853-H4
RHONDA DR
4800 SJS 95129 852-J4
RHONE CT
400 MTVW 94043 811-G3
RHUS RD
\- SMCo 94020 850-E7
RHUS RIDGE RD
11800 LAH 94022 831-B3
12000 SCIC 94022 831-B3
RIALTO CT
400 MTVW 94043 811-G2
RIBBON DR
4000 SJS 95130 853-B4
RIBCHESTER CT
5700 SJS 95123 874-J4
RIBIER CT
1100 SUNV 94087 832-D3
RIBISI CIR
1000 SJS 95131 814-E7
RIBISI WY
1800 SJS 95131 814-D7
RIC DR
2300 SCIC 95020 958-D6
RICARDO RD
22500 CPTO 95014 851-J2
RICA VISTA WY
15600 SCIC 95127 815-B7
RICE CT
5000 SJS 95111 875-A2
20600 SAR 95070 852-D7
RICE DR
4900 SJS 95111 875-A2
RICE LN
10200 SCIC 95020 957-J4
RICE WY
5000 SJS 95111 875-A2
RICH AV
900 MTVW 94022 811-G5
900 MTVW 94040 811-G5
RICH PL
\- MTVW 94022 811-G5
\- MTVW 94040 811-G5
RICHARD AV
1400 SCL 95050 833-D2
RICHARDS AV
1400 SJS 95125 853-J4
RICHARDSON AV
1100 LALT 94024 831-H4
RICHARDSON CT
800 PA 94303 791-D7
RICHARDSON DR
3400 SJS 95127 814-J6
RICHDALE AV
400 SJS 95111 854-J6
RICHELIEU CT
300 LALT 94022 811-E6
13700 SAR 95070 872-G1
RICHEY DR
15200 SCIC 95124 873-E4
RICHFIELD DR
\- SJS 95129 853-A1
RICHGROVE CT
2800 SJS 95148 835-E7
RICHLAND AV
2200 SJS 95125 854-C7
RICHLAND DR
2200 SJS 95125 854-B6
RICHLEE DR
300 CMBL 95008 853-G5
RICHMOND AV
\- SJS 95037 896-A7
\- SCIC 95037 896-A7
300 SJS 95128 853-H2
300 SCIC 95128 853-H2
RICHTER CT
1200 MPS 95035 814-C1
RICHWOOD CT
19400 CPTO 95014 852-G1
RICHWOOD DR
10100 CPTO 95014 852-F1
RICKENBACKER ST
1100 SJS 95128 853-F3
RICKY CT
700 CMBL 95008 853-C6
RICKY DR
700 CMBL 95008 853-C6
RIDDER PARK DR
700 SJS 95131 834-A1
700 SJS 95131 814-A6
RIDDLE RD
3100 SJS 95117 853-D2
RIDGE CT
2900 SCL 95051 833-A6
RIDGE RD
700 SCL 95051 833-A6
5000 SCIC 95020 (976-C2 See Page 955)
20500 SCIC 95030 912-J1
30000 SCIC 95140 837-D3
RIDGEBROOK WY
4100 SJS 95111 855-A7
RIDGECLIFF CT
2300 SJS 95131 814-D5
RIDGE CREEK CT
11700 CPTO 95014 852-C4
RIDGECREST AV
16000 MSER 95030 872-H6
RIDGEFARM DR
400 SJS 95123 874-J5
RIDGEGATE DR
2900 SJS 95133 814-G7
RIDGEGLEN WY
2300 SJS 95133 834-G1
RIDGELEY DR
1000 CMBL 95008 853-G5
1400 SCIC 95125 853-G5
RIDGELINE CT
1200 SJS 95127 835-C3
RIDGEMONT DR
1000 MPS 95035 814-E1
1900 SJS 95148 835-B5
2900 SJS 95127 835-B5
3300 MTVW 94040 831-J2
RIDGE OAK CT
1200 SJS 95120 874-C7
RIDGETOP DR
14800 SCIC 95127 814-J6
14800 SJS 95127 814-J6
RIDGETREE WY
1600 SJS 95131 814-D4
RIDGEVIEW AV
\- SCIC 95127 815-B7
RIDGEVIEW CT
3700 MGH 95037 917-H5
10400 CPTO 95014 832-G7
10700 SCIC 95127 815-B7
RIDGEVIEW DR
\- ATN 94027 790-A5
RIDGEVIEW TER
\- SCIC 95127 815-B7
RIDGEVIEW WY
10600 SCIC 95127 815-B7
N RIDGE VISTA AV
200 SCIC 95127 814-H7
200 SJS 95127 814-H7
11900 SCIC 95127 834-H1
S RIDGE VISTA AV
300 SCIC 95127 834-J1
300 SJS 95127 834-J1
RIDGEWAY DR
8800 GIL 95020 977-E1
10100 CPTO 95014 851-J1
RIDGEWOOD DR
1300 SJS 95118 874-B4
RIDGEWOOD LN
25800 LAH 94022 831-B2
RIDING CT
6000 SJS 95124 873-J7
RIDLEY WY
1200 SJS 95125 853-J4
RIEDAL PL
10100 CPTO 95014 832-F7
RIEDEL CT
2800 SJS 95135 855-E2
12400 SCIC 95046 938-A6
RIEDEL DR
2800 SJS 95135 855-D3
RIELLY CT
700 SJS 95123 874-F4
RIESLING CT
19400 SAR 95070 872-F3
RIESLING ST
\- FRMT 94539 793-J2
RIESLING TER
1200 SUNV 94087 832-C3
RIGOLETTO DR
1700 SJS 95122 855-A2
RILEY WY
800 RDWC 94061 790-C2
RILMA CT
1000 LALT 94022 811-E4
RIMROCK DR
1300 SJS 95120 894-D3
RIMWOOD DR
5200 SJS 95118 874-B4
RINCON AV
400 SUNV 94086 832-D1
3700 CMBL 95008 853-B6
3700 SJS 95008 853-B6
4100 SJS 95130 853-B6
E RINCON AV
\- CMBL 95008 853-E6
W RINCON AV
\- CMBL 95008 853-D6
RINCON CIR
900 SJS 95131 813-J4
4100 PA 94306 811-C3
RINCONADA CT
400 LALT 94022 811-F7

STREET
Block City ZIP Pg-Grid

RINCONADA DR
2400 SJS 95125 854-C6
RINCONADA OAKS CT
100 LGTS 95030 872-J3
RINCONDADA AV
100 PA 94301 791-A6
RINEHART DR
2300 SJS 95133 834-G2
RINGLE CT
1700 MGH 95037 917-D5
RINGLE DR
17300 MGH 95037 917-D5
RINGROSE CT
1300 SJS 95121 855-B1
RINGWOOD AV
- SMCo 94025 790-H2
- ATN 94027 790-H1
800 MLPK 94025 790-H1
1400 SJS 95131 814-B4
1800 SCIC 95131 814-B4
RINGWOOD CT
1100 SJS 95131 814-B6
RIO CT
4000 SJS 95134 813-D2
RIO BARRANCA CT
2100 SJS 95116 834-G3
RIO BRAVO DR
3400 SJS 95148 835-D6
RIO CHICO DR
100 SJS 95111 854-J7
RIO DE ESMERALDA
3200 SJS 95121 855-A4
RIO DE JOYAS
3200 SJS 95121 855-A4
RIO DE LATA
3200 SJS 95121 855-A4
RIO DE LOS
MOLINOS AV
100 SUNV 94086 812-C6
RIO DE ORO
3200 SJS 95121 855-B4
RIO DE PERLA
3200 SJS 95121 855-B4
RIO DE PLATA
3200 SJS 95121 855-A4
RIO DE PLOMO
1300 SJS 95121 855-B4
RIO GRAND CT
500 MGH 95037 917-A6
RIO GRANDE DR
5200 SJS 95136 874-J3
RIO GUACIMAL CT
2100 SJS 95116 834-G3
RIO HONDO DR
1200 SJS 95120 894-C1
RIO LOBO DR
5200 SJS 95136 875-A3
RIO ORO CT
400 MGH 95037 917-A6
RIORDAN DR
2100 SJS 95130 853-A7
RIORDAN PL
- MLPK 94025 790-H2
RIO RITA WY
4700 SJS 95129 853-A1
RIO ROBLES
- SJS 95134 813-E3
RIO SERENA AV
- CMBL 95008 853-A5
200 SJS 95130 853-A5
RIO VERDE CT
4900 SJS 95118 874-A3
RIO VERDE DR
4900 SJS 95118 874-A3
RIO VERDE PL
200 MPS 95035 813-J1
RIO VISTA
100 LGTS 95030 872-J2
RIO VISTA AV
4800 SJS 95129 853-A1
4800 SJS 95129 852-J1
RIPLEY DR
500 SJS 95133 834-E2
RITA CT
2200 SCL 95050 833-D6
RITA DR
16700 MGH 95037 917-C7
RITANNA CT
20600 SAR 95070 852-D5
RITTENHOUSE AV
- ATN 94027 790-D1
RITZ CT
3600 SJS 95148 835-F7
N RIVER ST
- SJS 95113 834-A6
- SJS 95110 834-A6
RIVERA ST
700 MPS 95035 794-B4
RIVER ASH CT
- SJS 95136 874-H1

RIVERBANK RD
3300 SCIC 95020 956-J4
RIVER BED CT
2200 SCL 95054 813-C5
RIVER BIRCH CT
1600 SJS 95131 834-D1
RIVER BIRCH DR
1600 SJS 95131 834-D1
RIVERBORO PL
- SJS 95123 874-D3
RIVERCREST CT
10300 CPTO 95014 832-A7
RIVERDALE CT
13600 SAR 95070 872-H1
RIVERDALE DR
13600 SAR 95070 872-H1
RIVER FALLS DR
700 SJS 95111 855-A7
RIVERMONT CT
2600 SJS 95116 834-J4
RIVER OAKS CIR
300 SJS 95134 813-G4
RIVER OAKS PKWY
100 SJS 95134 813-F4
RIVER OAKS PL
- SJS 95134 813-F4
RIVEROAKS RD
- SBnC - (1017-G4
See Page 997)
RIVER PARK DR
700 SJS 95111 855-A7
RIVER RANCH CIR
13800 SAR 95070 872-E1
RIVER ROCK CT
400 SJS 95136 854-F7
RIVERRUN DR
2700 SCIC 95127 834-H2
2700 SJS 95127 834-H2
RIVERSIDE CT
400 SCL 95134 813-F4
RIVERSIDE DR
600 LALT 94024 831-F2
600 SJS 95125 854-A2
22300 CPTO 95014 852-A2
RIVERSIDE DR
Rt#-129
- WAT 95076 (1015-F3
See Page 995)
300 SCrC 95076 (1015-F3
See Page 995)
W RIVERSIDE WY
1000 SJS 95129 852-E2
RIVER TRAIL CT
4800 SJS 95136 874-H3
RIVER VIEW DR
300 SJS 95111 875-A1
600 SJS 95111 855-B7
RIVIERA CT
900 SJS 95129 852-J2
RIVIERA DR
100 LGTS 95030 873-B6
600 LALT 94024 811-G7
RIVIERA RD
10300 CPTO 95014 852-A1
RIVOIR DR
4000 SJS 95118 874-A2
RIXFORD LN
600 LALT 94024 831-F2
RIZAL CT
6400 SJS 95119 875-C7
ROAD A
- SBnC - (1000-C7
See Page 999)
9500 SJS 95138 875-E2
ROAD B
- SBnC - (1000-C7
See Page 999)
ROAD C
- SBnC - (1000-C7
See Page 999)
ROAD D
- SBnC - (1000-C7
See Page 999)
ROAD F
- SBnC - (1000-C7
See Page 999)
ROAD G
- SBnC - (1020-C1
See Page 999)
- SJS 95138 875-F3
ROAD H
- SBnC - (1020-C1
See Page 999)
ROADING DR
400 SJS 95123 874-J5
ROAD J
- SBnC - (1020-D1
See Page 999)

ROAD L
- SBnC - (1020-D2
See Page 999)
6900 SCIC 95138 876-A2
ROAD N
6000 SBnC - (1020-E4
See Page 999)
ROAD O
2400 SBnC - (1020-C4
See Page 999)
ROAD P
- HOLL - (1020-A4
See Page 999)
ROAD Q
- SBnC - (1020-B2
See Page 999)
ROADRUNNER TER
1300 SUNV 94087 832-H4
ROAN ST
300 SJS 95123 874-J5
ROARING WATER WY
21400 SCIC 95030 913-B2
ROBALO CT
1100 SJS 95132 814-G5
ROBB DR
4500 SJS 95118 874-B2
ROBB RD
800 PA 94306 811-B5
800 LAH 94022 811-B5
ROBBIA CT
1200 SUNV 94087 832-F4
ROBBIA DR
1000 SUNV 94087 832-F3
ROBERSON LN
400 SJS 95112 833-J1
ROBERT AV
400 SCL 95050 833-E2
ROBERTA CT
2900 SJS 95121 854-J4
ROBERT FOWLER WY
2400 SJS 95148 835-A6
ROBERTS CT
- SJS 95110 854-D2
ROBERTS DR
- MLPK 94025 790-E4
ROBERTS RD
- LGTS 95030 873-A6
16200 LGTS 95032 873-B6
ROBERTS ST
1100 SJS 95122 834-F7
1100 SJS 95122 854-F1
ROBERTSON RD
2400 SCL 95051 833-B2
ROBERTSVILLE CT
500 SJS 95118 874-G3
ROBIE LN
16200 SCIC 95032 873-C7
16200 LGTS 95032 873-C7
ROBIN CT
700 EPA 94303 791-B1
1100 SUNV 94087 832-B3
ROBIN DR
500 SCL 95050 833-C5
1800 SJS 95124 873-H1
ROBIN LN
800 CMBL 95008 853-D7
800 CMBL 95008 873-D1
2000 SCIC 95046 937-H3
ROBIN WY
100 LGTS 95032 873-C7
200 MLPK 94025 790-J3
900 SUNV 94087 832-B2
19800 SAR 95070 872-F4
ROBIN ANN DR
15300 MSER 95030 873-A5
ROBINDELL WY
7700 CPTO 95014 852-C3
ROBIN HOOD CT
1000 LALT 94024 831-H4
ROBIN HOOD DR
2000 LALT 94024 831-H4
ROBIN RIDGE CT
- SJS 95135 876-A1
ROBINSON AV
2400 SCL 95051 833-B3
ROBLAR LN
2500 SCL 95051 833-B2
ROBLE AV
200 RDWC 94061 790-B1
600 MLPK 94025 790-F4
ROBLE CT
19400 SAR 95070 852-F7
ROBLE DR
500 SCIC 94305 790-G7
600 MGH 95037 937-A4
800 SUNV 94086 832-H3
ROBLE RDGE
900 PA 94306 811-B2
ROBLE ALTO
27900 LAH 94022 810-H7

ROBLE ALTO CT
13600 LAH 94022 810-H6
ROBLE BLANCO
27900 LAH 94022 810-H7
ROBLEDA CT
26700 LAH 94022 811-C7
ROBLEDA DR
- ATN 94027 790-C2
ROBLEDA RD
12000 LAH 94022 831-C1
13000 LAH 94022 811-C7
ROBLE LADERA RD
12500 LAH 94022 811-A7
ROBLES DEL ORO
15600 SCIC 95030 872-H5
ROBLE VENENO LN
12600 LAH 94022 811-B7
ROBNICK CT
1300 CMBL 95008 873-A1
ROBSHEAL DR
1300 SJS 95125 854-A5
1300 SJS 95125 853-J5
ROBWAY AV
1100 CMBL 95008 853-G5
ROCHELLE DR
1800 SJS 95124 873-H1
ROCHESTER AV
- SJS 95123 875-B4
- SJS 95193 875-B4
ROCHESTER CT
1000 SUNV 94087 832-B3
ROCHIN CT
15900 LGTS 95032 873-E5
ROCHIN TER
15900 LGTS 95032 873-D6
15900 SCIC 95032 873-D6
ROCK AV
900 SJS 95131 814-A5
ROCK ST
1600 MTVW 94043 811-G2
ROCK CANYON CIR
900 SJS 95127 814-J5
ROCKDALE DR
900 SJS 95129 853-A3
ROCKEFELLER DR
900 SUNV 94087 832-B3
ROCKHAVEN DR
1200 SJS 95120 894-E3
ROCKHURST CT
2000 SCL 95051 832-J2
ROCKIE RD
- SBnC - (1020-E1
See Page 999)
ROCKING HORSE CT
600 SJS 95123 874-J7
ROCKLIN CT
1400 SJS 95131 814-C7
ROCKPOINT LN
- LALT 94024 831-E2
- SCIC 94024 831-E2
ROCKPORT AV
3200 SJS 95132 814-G5
ROCKPORT DR
500 SUNV 94087 832-D3
ROCKRIDGE WY
2400 SCL 95051 833-B1
ROCK RIVER CT
2900 SJS 95111 854-H4
ROCKROSE AV
1000 SUNV 94086 832-G3
ROCKROSE CT
2000 GIL 95020 977-E1
ROCK SPRING CT
11500 CPTO 95014 852-A4
ROCKSPRING DR
1700 SJS 95112 854-F2
ROCKTON AV
6900 SJS 95119 875-F6
ROCKTON PL
- SJS 95119 875-F6
ROCKTREE CT
1700 SJS 95131 814-D4
ROCKVIEW CT
6800 SJS 95120 894-C3
ROCKWAY DR
- SCIC 95127 835-A2
ROCKWOOD DR
700 SJS 95129 853-A2
ROCKY CREEK CT
3600 SJS 95148 835-D4
17000 MGH 95037 917-B7
ROCKY CREEK WY
14500 SAR 95070 872-D3
ROCKY CREST DR
6500 SJS 95120 874-F7
ROCKY GLEN CT
6100 SJS 95123 874-F6
ROCKY MOUNTAIN AV
1600 MPS 95035 814-D2

ROCKY MOUNTAIN DR
3000 SJS 95127 835-B5
ROCKY RIDGE RD
1900 MGH 95037 936-F1
ROCKY WATER LN
2900 SJS 95148 855-B3
RODEO CT
300 SJS 95111 854-H5
RODEO DR
300 SJS 95111 854-H5
9300 GIL 95020 957-F7
RODEO PL
400 SJS 95111 854-H5
RODLING DR
6900 SJS 95138 875-F6
RODLING WY
100 SJS 95138 875-F6
RODNEY DR
1100 SJS 95118 874-B2
RODONI CT
12700 SAR 95070 852-G6
RODONOVAN CT
200 SCL 95051 832-J7
RODONOVAN DR
- SCL 95051 832-J7
RODRIGUES AV
100 MPS 95035 794-C7
19800 CPTO 95014 852-D1
RODRIGUEZ ST
100 WAT 95076 (1015-F2
See Page 995)
ROEDER CT
300 SJS 95111 875-B2
ROEDER RD
4900 SJS 95111 875-B2
ROEHAMPTON AV
10000 SCIC 95127 835-A3
ROENOKE WY
2000 SJS 95128 853-G3
ROEWILL DR
1000 SJS 95117 853-B3
ROGER ST
1500 MPS 95035 794-A4
ROGERS AV
1600 SJS 95112 834-A1
1600 SJS 95112 833-J1
1600 SJS 95112 813-J7
ROGERS CT
700 SCL 95051 833-B6
ROGERS LN
7400 GIL 95020 978-B3
ROGERS ST
- LGTS 95032 893-A1
ROGGE RD
100 EPA 94303 791-C1
ROGUE LN
- SCrC 95076 (1017-A4
See Page 997)
ROHN WY
5800 SJS 95123 875-A5
ROJO PL
1400 SJS 95128 853-F5
ROLFE CT
14900 SCIC 95127 835-B1
ROLINE CT
15000 SCIC 95124 873-F4
ROLL ST
1600 SCL 95050 833-C3
ROLLINGDELL CT
1100 CPTO 95014 852-D3
ROLLINGDELL DR
7300 CPTO 95014 852-D3
7300 SJS 95129 852-D3
ROLLING GLEN CT
6000 SJS 95123 874-F6
ROLLING HILLS DR
2000 MGH 95037 936-E1
9500 SCIC 95020 958-D3
ROLLING HILLS RD
22000 SCIC 95070 852-B5
ROLLING MEADOW CT
6400 SJS 95135 855-J7
ROLLING OAKS CT
6500 SJS 95120 894-C2
ROLLING OAKS DR
6500 SJS 95120 894-C2
ROLLINGSIDE DR
3500 SJS 95148 835-F7
ROLLINGWOOD CT
3000 SJS 95148 835-F7
ROLLY RD
10200 SCIC 94024 831-F5
ROMA CT
2900 SCL 95051 833-A7
ROMBERG DR
1200 SUNV 94087 832-E3
ROME DR
20500 SCIC 95120 895-A6
ROMEO AV
10200 SJS 95127 835-C2

ROMERO ST
600 SJS 95128 853-F4
ROMFORD DR
5200 SJS 95124 873-H5
ROMITA CT
16000 MSER 95030 872-H6
RONALD AV
400 CMBL 95008 853-C7
RONALD CT
700 LALT 94024 831-G2
1600 SJS 95118 873-J4
RONALD ST
2000 SCL 95050 833-D2
RONALD WY
10900 CPTO 95014 852-B3
RONAN AV
- GIL 95020 957-H7
400 GIL 95020 977-H1
RONCO DR
2700 SJS 95132 814-F5
RONDA DR
14700 SCIC 95124 873-G4
14700 SJS 95124 873-G4
RONDEAU DR
4000 SJS 95124 873-J3
RONDEN CT
1600 MTVW 94040 811-G6
RONDO WY
- SMCo 94025 790-D5
RONIE WY
1800 SJS 95124 873-H3
RONNIE WY
13300 SAR 95070 852-G7
13400 SAR 95070 872-G1
ROOP RD
2100 SCIC 95020 958-F2
ROOSEVELT
- RDWC 94061 790-A1
ROOSEVELT AV
- SCIC 95046 937-E6
200 SUNV 94086 812-F6
2000 RDWC 94061 790-A1
ROOSEVELT CIR
- PA 94306 811-D1
2300 SCL 95051 833-C2
ROOSEVELT CT
2300 SCL 95051 833-C2
ROOSEVELT ST
900 SJS 95112 834-D4
ROOSEVELT WY
- SJS 95002 793-C7
ROOSTER CT
- SJS 95136 874-J2
ROOSTER DR
5200 SJS 95136 874-J3
RORKE WY
800 PA 94303 791-E6
ROSA AV
1000 SUNV 94086 832-G3
ROSA CT
900 SUNV 94086 832-G3
ROSALIA AV
1200 SJS 95117 853-B4
1300 SJS 95130 853-B4
1300 SUNV 94087 832-G4
ROSALIE CT
200 LGTS 95032 873-C7
ROSALIE DR
1300 SCL 95050 833-C4
ROSALIND LN
18500 SCIC 95120 894-G1
ROSALINDA CT
2600 SJS 95121 854-J4
ROSA MORADA RD
500 SBnC - (1020-F5
See Page 999)
ROSANNA ST
6700 GIL 95020 978-A4
7200 GIL 95020 977-J2
ROSARIO AV
21500 CPTO 95014 852-B2
ROSARIO CT
2800 SJS 95132 814-D3
ROSARIO DR
2800 SJS 95132 814-D3
ROSATO CT
2900 SJS 95135 855-E3
ROSE AV
400 SBnC - (1017-A5
See Page 997)
800 MTVW 94040 831-G1
900 MLPK 94025 790-F4
2800 SJS 95127 834-J3
3600 SCIC 95127 834-J2
4100 SCIC 95127 834-J2
4100 SCIC 95127 835-A2
15800 LGTS 95030 873-A6
15800 MSER 95030 873-A6
16100 MSER 95030 872-J6

E ROSE CIR
1000 LALT 94024 831-J2
W ROSE CIR
1000 LALT 94024 831-J2
ROSE CT
100 CMBL 95008 853-D6
900 SCL 95051 833-B5
17900 MSER 95030 872-J6
18000 SCIC 95030 912-J2
ROSE DR
100 MPS 95035 794-A4
ROSE LN
- LGTS 95030 873-A5
700 LALT 94024 831-F1
19000 MGH 95037 916-H4
ROSE PL
1200 SJS 95112 854-D1
ROSE WY
2500 SCL 95051 833-B5
ROSE ANNA DR
1500 SJS 95118 874-A5
ROSEBAY CT
- SJS 95127 834-J2
ROSE BLOSSOM DR
700 CPTO 95014 852-C2
ROSEBRIAR WY
1100 SJS 95131 834-D1
1100 SJS 95131 814-D7
ROSEBUD CT
1900 SJS 95128 853-G3
ROSE CREEK DR
3000 SJS 95148 835-B5
ROSECREST TER
1400 SJS 95126 833-H7
ROSEDALE DR
3200 SJS 95117 853-D2
ROSEFIELD WY
1100 MLPK 94025 790-E4
ROSEGARDEN CT
48900 FRMT 94539 794-A2
ROSEGARDEN LN
1300 CPTO 95014 852-D4
ROSELEAF CT
16300 SCIC 95032 873-D5
ROSELEAF LN
16100 SCIC 95032 873-D5
ROSEMAR AV
3600 SJS 95127 835-B2
ROSEMAR CT
700 SJS 95127 835-C1
ROSEMARIE PL
19400 CPTO 95014 852-G1
ROSEMARY CIR
17100 MGH 95037 917-B7
ROSEMARY LN
1700 RDWC 94061 790-A2
E ROSEMARY LN
- CMBL 95128 853-E5
- CMBL 95008 853-E5
2900 SJS 95008 853-E5
2900 SJS 95128 853-E5
W ROSEMARY LN
2900 CMBL 95008 853-D5
ROSEMARY ST
- SJS 95112 834-A3
- SJS 95110 833-J3
- SJS 95112 833-J3
ROSEMONT AV
1000 LALT 94024 831-H3
ROSEMONT CT
1000 LALT 94024 831-H3
ROSEMONT DR
300 SCL 95051 832-J7
ROSENBAUM AV
4100 SJS 95136 874-G1
ROSENCRANS WY
7100 SJS 95139 895-F1
ROSENELFE CIR
3000 SJS 95148 835-B5
ROSE ORCHARD CT
18100 MGH 95037 916-G7
ROSE ORCHARD WY
- SCIC 95134 813-E2
- SJS 95134 813-E2
ROSE RIDGE LN
5900 SJS 95123 874-G7
ROSETTA DR
2200 SCIC 95037 917-E6
ROSETTE CT
900 SUNV 94086 832-G3
ROSETTE TER
800 SUNV 94086 832-G3
ROSE VIEW DR
10000 SCIC 95127 835-C1
ROSEWELL CT
- SJS 95138 875-D4
ROSEWELL WY
- SJS 95138 875-D4
ROSEWOOD AV
300 SJS 95117 853-D1

ROSEWOOD AV
300 SCIC 95117 853-D1
ROSEWOOD CT
600 LALT 94024 831-F1
ROSEWOOD DR
- ATN 94027 790-G1
700 PA 94303 791-C6
ROSEWOOD ST
10600 CPTO 95014 832-F6
ROSITA AV
400 LALT 94024 831-F1
2100 SCL 95050 833-D7
ROSITA CT
2300 SCL 95050 833-D6
ROSLYN CIR
700 MTVW 94043 812-A3
ROSLYN CT
2400 SJS 95121 854-J2
ROSS AV
2800 SJS 95124 873-J3
ROSS CIR
1700 SJS 95124 873-J3
ROSS CT
800 PA 94303 791-D7
ROSS DR
300 SUNV 94089 812-E4
ROSS RD
2300 PA 94303 791-C5
ROSSBURN CT
1100 SJS 95121 855-B6
ROSS CREEK CT
100 LGTS 95032 873-E5
ROSSI CT
500 GIL 95020 978-C6
ROSSI LN
5700 SCIC 95020 978-C5
5700 GIL 95020 978-C5
ROSSMERE CT
13600 SAR 95070 872-F1
ROSSMORE CT
2900 SJS 95148 855-C1
ROSSMORE LN
2900 SJS 95148 855-C1
ROSSMORE WY
2900 SJS 95148 855-C1
ROSSMOYNE DR
14800 SCIC 95124 873-H4
ROSSOTTO DR
2400 SJS 95130 853-A7
ROSS PARK CT
4000 SJS 95118 874-B2
ROSS PARK DR
4000 SJS 95118 874-B2
ROSSWAY CT
1300 LALT 94024 831-J4
ROSSWOOD DR
1700 SJS 95124 873-G4
ROSWELL CT
300 MPS 95035 794-D7
ROSWELL DR
100 MPS 95035 794-D7
ROTH PL
2000 SCL 95051 833-D1
ROTH WY
100 SCIC 94305 790-G6
ROTHE DR
11300 SCIC 95020 957-G2
ROTHERHAVEN WY
4500 SJS 95111 875-A1
4500 SJS 95111 874-J1
ROTHLAND CT
1300 SJS 95131 814-D7
ROTHROCK DR
100 SJS 95116 834-G2
ROTTERDAM LN
5600 SJS 95118 874-B5
ROUEN CT
- SJS 95127 834-J1
ROUGH AND READY RD
400 SJS 95133 834-G1
500 SJS 95133 814-G7
ROUNDLEAF CT
1900 SJS 95131 814-C6
ROUNDTABLE DR
- SJS 95111 875-B3
ROUNDTREE CT
4800 SJS 95008 872-J1
ROUNDTREE DR
4700 SJS 95008 873-A1
4700 SJS 95008 872-J1
ROUSE CT
7100 SJS 95139 875-F7
ROUSSEAU DR
1200 SUNV 94087 832-F4
ROWENA CT
3500 SCL 95054 813-E6
ROWLEY DR
3500 SJS 95132 814-F2
ROXANNE DR
5200 SJS 95124 873-H5

ROXBURY CT
1200 SCL 95050 833-F6
ROXBURY LN
500 LGTS 95030 873-A2
ROXBURY ST
- SCL 95050 833-E6
ROX PLACE CT
3600 SJS 95121 855-B4
ROY AV
1000 SJS 95125 854-B6
ROYAL AV
300 SJS 95126 854-A1
ROYAL DR
2000 SCL 95050 833-C3
ROYAL WY
600 GIL 95020 977-J5
ROYAL ACORN PL
6000 SJS 95120 874-D7
ROYAL ACRES CT
1000 SJS 95136 874-C2
ROYAL ANN CT
1100 SUNV 94087 832-D3
1400 SJS 95129 852-G4
ROYAL ANN DR
1100 SUNV 94087 832-D3
1400 SJS 95129 852-G4
ROYALBROOK CT
800 SJS 95111 855-A6
ROYAL CREST DR
1100 SJS 95131 834-D1
1100 SJS 95131 814-C7
ROYALE PARK CT
4500 SJS 95136 874-F2
ROYALE PARK DR
400 SJS 95136 874-F2
ROYAL ESTATES CT
5000 SJS 95135 855-G5
ROYAL FOREST CT
4600 SJS 95136 874-F2
ROYAL GARDEN PL
4600 SJS 95136 874-G2
ROYAL GATE PL
400 SJS 95136 874-G2
ROYAL GLEN CT
600 SJS 95133 814-H7
ROYAL GLEN DR
600 SJS 95133 814-G7
ROYAL GROVE CT
4600 SJS 95136 874-G2
ROYAL MEADOW LN
3000 SJS 95135 855-J7
ROYAL OAK CT
6200 SJS 95123 875-A6
ROYAL OAK WY
22500 CPTO 95014 831-J6
ROYAL RIDGE CT
7000 SJS 95120 894-E3
ROYAL RIDGE DR
7000 SJS 95120 894-E3
ROYALRIDGE WY
2500 SCL 95051 833-C1
ROYALTREE CIR
2200 SJS 95131 814-C5
ROYALVALE WY
2700 SJS 95132 814-C4
ROYALWOOD WY
6800 SJS 95120 894-H3
ROYCE DR
300 SJS 95133 834-E3
ROYCE ST
100 LGTS 95030 873-A7
ROYCOTT WY
1100 SJS 95125 854-A5
ROYSTON CT
1100 SJS 95120 894-E2
RUBIDOUX TER
- SUNV 94086 812-C7
RUBION CT
3400 SJS 95148 835-D4
RUBION DR
3400 SJS 95148 835-C5
RUBIS DR
800 SUNV 94087 832-D2
RUBY AV
2300 SJS 95148 855-E1
3000 SJS 95148 835-D5
3700 SCIC 95148 835-D5
4100 SJS 95135 855-F3
RUBY CT
3400 SJS 95148 835-E7
RUBY ST
- RDWC 94061 790-A1
RUBY TER
2700 SJS 95148 835-E6
RUBY VW
2700 SJS 95148 835-E6
RUCKER AV
100 SCIC 95020 957-H4
500 SCIC 95020 958-A3

RUCKER DR
5200 SJS 95124 873-H5
5200 SJS 95032 873-H5
21800 CPTO 95014 852-B2
RUDD CT
500 SJS 95111 854-J6
RUDY CT
5700 SJS 95124 873-J6
RUDY DR
5400 SJS 95124 873-J6
RUDYARD DR
300 MPS 95035 793-J7
RUE AVATI
1300 SJS 95131 814-C6
RUE BORDEAUX
4700 SJS 95136 874-J2
RUE BOULOGNE
100 SJS 95136 874-J2
RUE CALAIS
4800 SJS 95136 874-J2
RUE CANNES
2200 SJS 95136 874-J2
RUE CHENE DOR
3500 SJS 95148 855-G1
RUE FERRARI
5800 SJS 95138 875-E4
RUE LE MANS
4700 SJS 95136 874-J2
RUE LOIRET
4800 SJS 95136 874-J2
RUE LYON CT
4700 SJS 95136 874-J2
RUE MIRASSOU
- SJS 95148 855-F1
RUE MONTAGNE
800 CMBL 95008 853-F7
RUE NICE CT
4800 SJS 95136 874-J2
RUE ORLEANS CT
4700 SJS 95136 874-J2
RUE PARIS
100 SJS 95136 874-J2
RUE TOULON CT
4800 SJS 95136 874-J2
RUE TOURS CT
4800 SJS 95136 874-J2
RUFF DR
900 SJS 95110 833-J4
RUGBY CT
1100 SJS 95120 874-C6
RUGE DR
1000 SJS 95132 814-F6
RUIZ CT
1500 SJS 95129 852-H4
RUMFORD DR
21200 CPTO 95014 832-C7
RUMSEY CT
400 SJS 95111 875-C2
RUNNING BEAR DR
5100 SJS 95136 875-A2
RUNNING FARM LN
- SCIC 94305 790-J7
- SCIC 94305 810-J1
RUNNING SPRINGS RD
- SJS 95135 856-A7
- SJS 95135 876-A1
- SJS 95135 875-J1
RUNNING WATER CT
2300 SCL 95054 813-C6
RUNNINGWOOD CIR
800 MTVW 94040 832-A1
RUNNYMEAD CT
1000 LALT 94024 831-H
RUNNYMEAD DR
1100 LALT 94024 831-H
RUNNYMEDE DR
1100 SJS 95117 853-D
RUNNYMEDE ST
400 EPA 94303 791-B
RUNO CT
18500 SCIC 95014 852-H
RUNSHAW PL
1200 SJS 95121 855-A
RUPERT DR
2300 SJS 95124 873-E
RUPPELL PL
1100 CPTO 95014 852-D
RURAL LN
300 MLPK 94025 810-E
300 SMCo 94025 810-E
RUSHMORE LN
200 LGTS 95030 873-B
RUSKIN DR
3100 SJS 95132 814-F
RUSSELL AV
900 LALT 94024 831-G
1800 SCL 95054 813-D
RUSSELL CT
- MLPK 94025 790-J
20700 SAR 95070 872-D

STREET
Block City ZIP Pg-Grid

RUSSELL LN
700 MPS 95035 794-B4
20500 SAR 95070 872-D1
RUSSET DR
800 SUNV 94087 832-D2
RUSSET TER
700 SUNV 94087 832-D1
RUSSO DR
5300 SJS 95118 874-C3
RUSTIC AV
2700 SJS 95124 873-G1
RUSTIC DR
2700 SJS 95124 873-G1
3200 SCL 95051 833-A5
RUSTIC LN
600 MTVW 94040 811-H7
RUSTIC RANCH CT
1100 SJS 95120 894-H3
RUSTIC RIDGE CIR
200 SJS 95123 874-G7
RUSTLING OAK CT
16400 MGH 95037 917-G6
RUSTLING OAK LN
16400 MGH 95037 917-G6
RUTH AV
300 MTVW 94043 811-F3
RUTH CT
1000 EPA 94303 791-C1
2800 SCL 95051 833-B6
RUTH DR
1100 SJS 95125 854-C7
RUTH CABRAL WY
2400 SCL 95050 833-C5
RUTHELMA AV
4200 PA 94306 811-D2
RUTHERFORD AV
100 SMCo 94061 790-B2
6800 SJS 95129 852-E4
RUTHERGLEN PL
5200 SJS 95136 874-F3
RUTHER PLACE CT
1600 SJS 95121 855-B4
RUTHER PLACE WY
3600 SJS 95121 855-B4
RUTHVEN AV
400 PA 94301 790-H4
RUTLAND AV
300 SCIC 95128 853-G1
RUTLEDGE PL
2000 SCL 95051 833-D2
RUTTNER CT
4900 SJS 95111 875-C1
RUTTNER PL
4900 SJS 95111 875-C1
RYAN AV
3000 SCL 95051 833-A6
RYAN CT
- SCIC 94305 810-J2
800 GIL 95020 977-H2
RYAN DR
10100 SJS 95127 835-B3
RYANS AL
700 MLPK 94025 790-F4
RYCROFT CT
7000 SJS 95120 894-H3
RYDER ST
3800 SCL 95051 812-J7
RYE CT
1000 SJS 95127 835-C2
RYEGATE CT
300 SJS 95133 834-F2
RYLAND ST
100 SJS 95110 834-A5
RYMAR CT
1000 SJS 95133 814-F6
RYMAR DR
2500 SJS 95133 814-F7
RYMAR LN
2500 SJS 95133 814-F6
RYMAR PL
1000 SJS 95133 814-F6
RYMAR TER
1000 SJS 95133 814-F7
RYMAR WY
1000 SJS 95133 814-F7

S

SABAL CT
1100 SJS 95132 814-G5
SABAL DR
1100 SJS 95132 814-G5
SABINA WY
1500 SJS 95118 874-A4
SABINI CT
17800 SCIC 95037 916-G7
17900 MGH 95037 916-G7
SABRINA CT
1200 RDWC 94061 790-A1
SACRAMENTO ST
500 EPA 94303 791-B1
SACREMENTO AV
4000 SJS 95111 855-A6
SADDLE CT
27800 LAH 94022 810-J6
SADDLEBACK
- PTLV 94028 830-C1
SADDLEBACK DR
16700 MGH 95037 917-E5
SADDLE BROOK DR
- SJS 95136 874-H2
- SJS 95136 875-A2
SADDLEHORN WY
16800 MGH 95037 917-E6
SADDLE MOUNTAIN DR
14200 LAH 94022 810-J6
SADDLER DR
9300 GIL 95020 957-F7
SADDLE TREE CT
- SJS 95136 874-H2
SADDLEWOOD DR
1000 SJS 95121 854-H2
SADIE CT
4000 SJS 95008 853-B7
SAFARI DR
400 SJS 95123 874-J6
SAFE HAVEN CT
- SJS 95111 854-J5
SAFFARIAN CT
2100 SJS 95121 855-C3
SAFFLE CT
1400 CMBL 95008 873-B1
SAGA LN
- MLPK 94025 790-D7
SAGE CT
900 CPTO 95014 852-C2
N SAGE CT
1100 SUNV 94087 832-D3
SAGE ST
1100 EPA 94303 791-C2
SAGE HEN CT
1300 SJS 95118 874-C2
SAGE HEN WY
1300 SUNV 94087 832-H4
SAGE HILL DR
1400 GIL 95020 957-F7
SAGELAND DR
1700 SJS 95131 814-D6
SAGEMEADOW CT
100 MPS 95035 794-A6
SAGEMILL CT
1200 SJS 95121 854-J3
SAGEMONT AV
4500 SJS 95130 853-A5
SAGE OAK WY
6000 SJS 95120 874-D7
SAGER WY
6200 SJS 95123 874-H7
SAGEWELL WY
5700 SJS 95138 875-D4
SAGEWOOD CT
9200 GIL 95020 957-F7
SAGEWOOD LN
3200 SJS 95132 814-E2
SAGITTARIUS LN
3200 SJS 95111 854-F6
SAGUARO CT
- SCIC 95020 977-A2
- SCIC 95020 (976-J2
See Page 955)
SAHARA WY
2000 SCL 95050 833-D3
SAICH WY
10000 CPTO 95014 832-D7
SAIDEL DR
2200 SJS 95124 873-E4
SAINT ANDREWS AV
22300 CPTO 95014 852-A2
SAINT ANDREWS CT
1700 MPS 95035 794-D3
SAINT ANDREWS PL
1700 SJS 95132 814-E3
SAINT ANN CT
19700 SAR 95070 852-F7
SAINT ANNES CT
5100 SJS 95138 855-F7
SAINT ANTHONY CT
1100 LALT 94024 831-J5
SAINT ANTHONY DR
1600 SCIC 95125 853-H5
17100 MGH 95037 917-B7
SAINT ANTHONYS PL
1600 CMBL 95008 873-E2
SAINT CATHERINE CT
5400 SCIC 95127 815-A7
SAINT CHARLES CT
1100 LALT 94024 831-H5
SAINT CHARLES ST
20700 SAR 95070 872-D3
SAINT CLAIRE CT
2200 SCL 95054 813-C5
SAINT CLAIRE DR
500 PA 94306 791-D7
SAINT CROIX CT
4200 SJS 95118 874-C2
SAINT ELIZABETH DR
800 SCIC 95126 853-H3
800 SJS 95126 853-H3
SAINT FLORENCE DR
400 SJS 95133 834-G1
SAINT FRANCIS CT
500 MLPK 94025 790-F6
7600 GIL 95020 977-G3
SAINT FRANCIS DR
1400 SCIC 95125 853-H5
2100 PA 94303 791-D4
SAINT FRANCIS PL
500 MLPK 94025 790-F6
SAINT FRANCIS RD
26400 LAH 94022 811-A5
SAINT FRANCIS ST
500 MLPK 94025 790-A1
600 RDWC 94061 790-A1
SAINT GEORGE LN
7200 SJS 95120 894-G5
SAINT GILES LN
2600 MTVW 94040 831-J2
SAINT IGNATIUS PL
3200 SCL 95051 833-A2
E SAINT JAMES ST
- SJS 95112 834-C5
1100 SJS 95116 834-F3
W SAINT JAMES ST
100 SJS 95113 834-B6
100 SJS 95110 834-B6
SAINT JOAN CT
20700 SAR 95070 852-D5
E SAINT JOHN ST
- SJS 95112 834-C5
- SJS 95113 834-C5
1100 SJS 95116 834-E4
W SAINT JOHN ST
100 SJS 95113 834-A6
100 SJS 95110 834-A6
SAINT JOSEPH AV
900 LALT 94024 831-G5
7500 SCIC 94024 831-G5
7500 CPTO 95014 831-G5
SAINT JOSEPH CT
11400 LALT 94024 831-G4
SAINT JOSEPH DR
17100 MGH 95037 917-B7
SAINT JULIE DR
300 SJS 95119 875-C7
SAINT KATHERINE DR
- MGH 95037 917-C3
- SCIC 95037 917-C3
SAINT KITTS CT
800 SJS 95127 814-G6
SAINT LAURENT CT
5400 SCIC 95127 815-A7
SAINT LAWRENCE DR
1800 SCL 95051 832-J3
2400 SJS 95124 853-G7
SAINT LOUISE DR
18500 MGH 95037 917-A4
SAINT LUCIA CT
800 SJS 95127 814-G6
SAINT MARK CT
1200 LALT 94024 831-J5
SAINT MARKS AV
18700 MGH 95037 917-B2
18700 SCIC 95037 917-B2
SAINT MARKS CT
1800 MGH 95037 917-B3
SAINT MARYS PL
3300 SCL 95051 832-J2
SAINT MATTHEW WY
1200 LALT 94024 831-J5
SAINT MICHAEL CT
3300 PA 94306 791-D7
SAINT MICHAEL DR
3300 PA 94306 791-D7
SAINT PAUL DR
1700 CMBL 95008 853-B5
SAINT REGIS DR
1500 SJS 95124 874-A3
SAJAK AV
1200 SJS 95131 814-B7
SAKURA WY
19300 CPTO 95014 852-G1
SALADO DR
1500 MTVW 94043 791-G7
1500 MTVW 94043 811-G1
SALAS CT
2100 EPA 94303 791-C2
SALBERG AV
600 SCL 95051 833-B6
SALEM AV
1600 SCIC 95020 957-D6
22300 CPTO 95014 832-A7
22500 CPTO 95014 831-J7
SALEM DR
2900 SCL 95051 833-A6
3100 SJS 95127 814-H6
SALERNO DR
900 SCIC 95008 873-E1
SALICE WY
- CMBL 95008 853-D6
SALIDA DEL SOL
6000 SJS 95123 874-F6
SALINA DR
4500 SJS 95124 873-F3
SALINAS CT
3300 SJS 95132 814-G3
SALINAS RD Rt#-G12
- MntC - (1015-H4
See Page 995)
SALISBURY DR
1600 SJS 95124 873-J3
SALLY CT
2900 SCL 95051 833-A3
SALLY DR
4400 SJS 95124 873-H4
SALMAR AV
400 CMBL 95008 853-E5
SALMON DR
400 SJS 95111 854-G4
SALMON CREEK CT
1500 SJS 95127 835-C3
SALOME CT
2600 SJS 95121 854-H4
SALSBURY DR
200 SCL 95051 833-B7
SALTAMONTES DR
14600 LAH 94022 811-C5
SALT LAKE CT
800 SJS 95133 814-G6
SALT LAKE DR
600 SJS 95133 814-G7
SALUDA CT
1300 SJS 95121 854-J2
SALVATIERRA ST
500 SCIC 94305 810-H1
SALVATORE CT
1300 SJS 95120 874-C6
SALVATORE DR
1200 SJS 95120 874-C6
SAMAR DR
6400 SJS 95119 875-C7
SAMARITAN CT
2500 SJS 95124 873-D4
SAMARITAN DR
2000 SCIC 95124 873-D3
2000 SJS 95124 873-D3
15100 LGTS 95032 873-D3
SAMARITAN PL
2300 SJS 95124 873-E4
SAM CAVA LN
400 CMBL 95008 853-E6
SAMEDRA ST
1400 SUNV 94087 832-C5
SAM MCDONALD RD
- SCIC 94305 790-J6
SAMOA WY
2300 SJS 95122 834-J5
SAMSON CT
4500 SJS 95124 873-J3
SAMSON WY
3900 SJS 95124 873-H3
SAMUEL DR
2900 SJS 95121 855-A3
SAMUEL LN
12800 LAH 94022 811-A6
SAN ALESO AV
700 SUNV 94086 812-E5
SAN ANDREAS AV
1500 SJS 95118 874-A1
SAN ANDREAS CT
100 SUNV 94086 812-E7
300 MPS 95035 793-J5
SAN ANDREAS DR
100 MLPK 94025 790-H3
200 MPS 95035 793-J5
SAN ANDREAS RD
- SCrC 95076 (1015-A4
See Page 995)
SAN ANGELO AV
400 SUNV 94086 812-E6
SAN ANSELMO WY
200 SUNV 94086 812-E6
6300 SJS 95119 875-C7
SAN ANTONIO AV
- MTVW 94040 811-F2
100 PA 94306 811-F2
700 PA 94043 811-F2
700 PA 94303 811-F2
1000 MTVW 94043 791-F7
SAN ANTONIO AV
1000 PA 94303 791-F7
1400 MLPK 94025 790-F3
1500 MTVW 94303 791-F7
SAN ANTONIO CIR
100 MTVW 94040 811-E3
SAN ANTONIO CT
200 SJS 95116 834-F5
SAN ANTONIO PL
2100 SCL 95051 833-A2
SAN ANTONIO RD
- SCIC 95037 (859-C3
See Page 839)
- SCIC 95140 (859-C3
See Page 839)
100 MTVW 94040 811-E4
N SAN ANTONIO RD
- LALT 94022 811-E6
S SAN ANTONIO RD
- LALT 94022 811-E7
E SAN ANTONIO ST
400 SJS 95112 834-D6
800 SJS 95116 834-G4
SAN ANTONIO WY
200 PA 94306 811-F2
SAN ANTONIO VLY RD
30000 SCIC 95140 837-D5
42300 SCIC 95140 839-B2
42300 SCIC 95140 (859-A1
See Page 839)
46400 SCIC 95140 (819-A5
See Page 799)
SAN ARDO DR
1500 SCIC 95125 853-H4
SAN ARDO WY
800 MTVW 94043 811-J3
SAN BENITO AV
- ATN 94027 790-E1
400 LGTS 95030 873-A6
500 SMCo 94063 790-E1
15800 MSER 95030 873-A5
SAN BENITO DR
16000 MGH 95037 937-B1
E SAN BENITO DR
1300 FRMT 94539 794-A2
SAN BENITO WY
15800 MSER 95030 873-A5
SAN BERNARDINO WY
300 SUNV 94086 812-E6
3900 SJS 95111 854-J7
SANBORN AV
1400 SJS 95110 854-D2
SANBORN RD
15500 SCIC 95070 871-J5
15800 SCIC 95070 872-A6
SAN BRUNO AV
- SCIC 95037 916-C2
- SJS 95037 916-C2
SAN BUENA CT
6100 SJS 95119 875-C6
SAN CARLOS AV
100 SMCo 94061 790-B3
700 MTVW 94043 812-A3
700 MTVW 94043 811-J3
SAN CARLOS CT
700 PA 94303 791-C6
SAN CARLOS ST
900 SCIC 95126 853-F1
900 SJS 95126 853-F1
1500 SJS 95128 853-F1
1700 SCIC 95128 853-F1
E SAN CARLOS ST
- SJS 95113 834-C7
100 SJS 95112 834-D6
W SAN CARLOS ST
- SJS 95110 834-C7
- SJS 95113 834-C7
1800 SJS 95110 854-A1
1800 SJS 95126 854-A1
1900 SCIC 95126 854-A1
W SAN CARLOS ST Rt#-82
- SJS 95113 834-A7
- SJS 95110 834-A7
1600 SJS 95126 834-A7
SAN CARRIZO WY
700 MTVW 94043 812-A3
800 MTVW 94043 811-J3
SANCHEZ DR
100 MGH 95037 916-H5
5500 SJS 95123 874-D4
5500 SJS 95136 874-D4
SANCHEZ WY
1100 RDWC 94061 790-A1
SAN CLEMENTE AV
3000 SJS 95118 874-A1
SAN CLEMENTE DR
200 MLPK 94025 790-H3
SAN CLEMENTE WY
700 MTVW 94043 811-H3
SAN CONRADO TER
600 SUNV 94086 812-G5
SAN CRISTOVAL CT
700 MGH 95037 937-C1
SAND DR
500 SJS 95125 854-D6
SANDALRIDGE CT
900 MPS 95035 794-A5
SANDALWOOD CT
600 MPS 95035 794-A4
1300 SJS 95127 835-A4
2000 PA 94303 791-D4
SANDALWOOD LN
900 MPS 95035 794-A5
1200 LALT 94024 831-H4
SANDALWOOD WY
17200 MGH 95037 917-E6
SAND BLOSSOM ST
100 SJS 95123 875-A3
SAND DUNE WY
5500 SJS 95123 875-B4
SANDERLING CT
- CMBL 95008 853-D5
SANDERS AV
400 SJS 95116 834-G4
SAND HILL CIR
100 MLPK 94025 790-B7
SAND HILL RD
100 MLPK 94025 790-F6
500 PA 94304 790-G5
1300 SCIC 94305 790-G5
2100 SMCo 94025 790-F6
2400 MLPK 94025 810-C1
2400 SMCo 94025 810-A1
SAND HILL WY
2500 SCL 95051 833-C1
SANDHURST DR
- MPS 95035 794-A6
SANDIA AV
1100 SUNV 94089 812-J5
1100 SUNV 94089 813-A5
SAN DIEGO AV
600 SUNV 94086 812-F5
SAN DOMAR DR
1300 MTVW 94043 811-H3
SAN DOMINGO WY
300 LALT 94022 811-C5
SANDPEBBLE DR
4000 SJS 95136 854-F7
SANDPIPER CT
- CMBL 95008 853-D5
1500 SUNV 94087 832-H5
SAND POINT CT
2700 SJS 95148 855-C1
SAND POINT DR
2600 SJS 95148 855-C1
SANDRA DR
1200 SJS 95125 854-B6
SANDRA PL
2900 PA 94303 791-D6
SANDRINGHAM WY
1400 SJS 95126 833-H7
SANDSTONE
- PTLV 94028 830-C1
SANDSTONE LN
1100 SJS 95132 814-F6
SANDY CT
13000 SCIC 95046 956-J2
SANDY LN
4800 SJS 95124 873-G4
4800 SCIC 95124 873-G4
SANDY CREEK LN
1700 SJS 95125 853-J5
SANDY ROCK CT
1600 SJS 95125 853-J5
SANDY ROCK LN
1600 SJS 95125 853-J5
SAN EMILION CT
- MTVW 94043 811-G3
SAN FELICIA WY
500 LALT 94022 811-E5
SAN FELIPE RD
- SJS 95037 (897-A3
See Page 877)
- SJS 95037 896-J3
3000 SJS 95135 855-D2
3000 SJS 95148 855-D2
3100 SJS 95121 855-D2
4900 SJS 95138 855-G5
6100 SJS 95138 875-J1
6100 SJS 95135 875-J1
6400 SCIC 95138 875-J1
6600 SCIC 95138 876-A2
6600 SJS 95138 876-A2
7000 SCIC 95020 999-H2
7400 SCIC 95037 876-H1
8700 SCIC 95037 856-G7
10400 CPTO 95014 851-J2
SAN FELIPE RD Rt#-156
1600 HOLL - (1020-A4
See Page 999)
2700 SBnC - (1020-A4
See Page 999)
SAN FERNANDO AV
10200 CPTO 95014 852-B1
SAN FERNANDO CT
22000 CPTO 95014 852-A1
22000 SCIC 95014 852-A1
E SAN FERNANDO ST
- SJS 95113 834-C6
100 SJS 95192 834-C6
100 SJS 95112 834-C6
900 SJS 95116 834-F4
W SAN FERNANDO ST
300 SJS 95113 834-A7
400 SJS 95110 834-A7
700 SJS 95126 834-A7
1100 SJS 95126 833-J7
SAN FILIPPO CT
1200 SJS 95128 853-E3
SANFORD AV
- CMBL 95008 853-E6
SANFORD DR
6000 SJS 95123 874-F6
SAN FRANCISCO CT
800 SCIC 94305 810-J1
5100 SJS 95138 855-F7
SAN FRANCISCO TER
800 SCIC 94305 810-J1
SAN GABRIEL AV
600 MGH 95037 937-B1
SAN GABRIEL DR
100 SUNV 94086 812-G7
SAN GABRIEL WY
1500 SCIC 95125 853-H5
SANGER WY
500 SJS 95125 854-C4
SAN GERONIMO WY
200 SUNV 94086 812-G7
SANGO CT
300 MPS 95035 814-B3
SAN GREGORIO WY
400 SJS 95111 854-J7
SAN IGNACIO AV
6200 SJS 95119 875-D7
SAN JACINTO RD
28800 CPTO 95014 851-J2
SAN JOAQUIN AV
1500 SJS 95118 874-A1
SAN JOSE AV
- SJS 95110 854-D3
- SJS 95125 854-D3
SAN JUAN AV
- SMCo 94025 790-D5
1200 SJS 95110 833-J3
3000 SCL 95051 833-A2
SAN JUAN CT
- LALT 94022 811-E4
9000 GIL 95020 977-F1
SAN JUAN DR
- MGH 95037 937-B1
600 SUNV 94086 812-G6
SAN JUAN HWY
1000 SBnC - (1018-B4
See Page 997)
SAN JUAN RD
22500 CPTO 95014 851-J2
SAN JUAN RD Rt#-G11
- MntC - (1015-H3
See Page 995)
SAN JUAN ST
500 SCIC 94305 810-H1
SAN JUAN HWY RD
2000 SBnC - (1018-B2
See Page 997)
SAN JUDE AV
700 PA 94306 811-B2
SAN JULE CT
700 SUNV 94086 812-G5
SAN JULIAN CT
- MTVW 94043 811-G3
SAN JULIAN WY
400 MTVW 94043 811-G2
SAN JUNIPERO DR
800 SUNV 94086 812-G5
SAN JUSTO CT
700 SUNV 94086 812-G5
SAN JUSTO RD
2100 SBnC - (1018-B7
See Page 997)
SAN LAZARO AV
100 SUNV 94086 812-G7
SAN LEANDRO AV
900 MTVW 94043 811-J2
900 MTVW 94043 812-A3
10500 CPTO 95014 852-A2
SAN LORENZO DR
5600 SJS 95123 874-F4
SAN LUCAR CT
100 SUNV 94086 812-G7
100 SUNV 94086 832-G1
SAN LUCAS AV
700 MTVW 94043 811-J3
800 MTVW 94043 812-A3
SAN LUCAS CT
800 MTVW 94043 811-J3
SAN LUIS AV
300 LALT 94024 811-F7
1400 MTVW 94043 811-G3
SAN LUIS DR
200 MLPK 94025 790-H2
SAN LUIS WY
16700 MGH 95037 937-B1
16700 MGH 95037 917-B7
SAN LUISITO WY
600 SUNV 94086 812-G6
SAN LUIS REY AV
3000 SJS 95118 874-A1
SAN LUPPE DR
800 MTVW 94043 812-A3
SAN MARCOS CIR
900 MTVW 94043 811-H3
SAN MARCOS CT
700 MGH 95037 937-C1
2600 SJS 95132 814-E5
SAN MARCOS DR
1300 SJS 95132 814-E5
SAN MARCOS RD
19200 SAR 95070 872-F3
SAN MARCOS WY
3400 SCL 95051 832-J3
SAN MARDO AV
3300 SCIC 95127 814-H6
SAN MARINO AV
3300 SCIC 95127 814-H6
E SAN MARTIN AV
200 SCIC 95046 937-G5
W SAN MARTIN AV
- SCIC 95046 937-A6
SAN MARTIN PL
600 LALT 94024 811-G7
SAN MATEO AV
200 LGTS 95030 873-A6
SAN MATEO CT
800 SUNV 94086 812-G5
SAN MATEO DR
- PA 94304 790-G5
- MLPK 94025 790-E4
100 SJS 95111 854-H7
SAN MIGUEL AV
600 SCL 95050 833-C5
600 SUNV 94086 812-G6
SAN MIGUEL CT
300 MPS 95035 813-J1
SAN MIGUEL ST
900 GIL 95020 977-G3
SAN MIGUEL WY
4100 SJS 95111 854-J7
SAN MORITZ DR
1100 SJS 95132 814-F5
SAN ONOFRE CT
3300 SCIC 95127 814-H6
3300 SJS 95127 814-H6
SAN PABLO AV
700 SUNV 94086 812-H5
3300 SCIC 95127 814-H6
3400 SJS 95127 814-J6
14800 SCIC 95127 814-J6
SAN PABLO CT
3700 SCIC 95127 814-J6
SAN PABLO DR
700 MTVW 94043 812-A3
700 MTVW 94043 811-J3
SAN PALO CT
18600 SAR 95070 852-H5
SAN PATRICIO AV
600 SUNV 94086 812-G6
SAN PEDRO AV
- MGH 95037 937-A1
600 SUNV 94086 812-H6
700 MGH 95037 917-C7
800 SCIC 95037 917-C7
1100 SCIC 95037 917-D7
SAN PEDRO LN
600 MGH 95037 937-B1
600 MGH 95037 917-C7
N SAN PEDRO ST
- SJS 95110 834-A4
- SJS 95110 833-J3
S SAN PEDRO ST
- SJS 95113 834-B6
SAN PETRA CT
300 MPS 95035 813-J1
SAN PETRONIO AV
800 SUNV 94086 812-H5
SAN PIER CT
800 SUNV 94086 812-H5
SAN PIERRE WY
500 MTVW 94043 811-H3
SAN RAFAEL AV
800 MTVW 94043 811-J3
2100 SCL 95051 833-A2
SAN RAFAEL CT
2000 SCL 95051 833-A3
SAN RAFAEL PL
700 SCIC 94305 810-H1
SAN RAFAEL ST
700 SUNV 94086 812-H6
SAN RAMON AV
700 SUNV 94086 812-H5
1200 MTVW 94043 811-G2
SAN RAMON CT
700 MGH 95037 937-C1
900 MTVW 94043 811-H3
SAN RAMON DR
100 SJS 95111 854-H7
16300 MGH 95037 937-C1
16500 MGH 95037 917-C7
SAN RAMON WY
4000 SJS 95111 854-J7
SAN RIVAS DR
3200 SJS 95148 835-D7
SANS RD
- SCrC 95076 (975-D4
See Page 955)
SAN SABA CT
800 SUNV 94086 812-H5
SAN SABA DR
3300 SJS 95148 835-D6
E SAN SALVADOR ST
- SJS 95113 834-D6
- SJS 95112 834-D6
100 SJS 95192 834-D6
W SAN SALVADOR ST
- SJS 95110 834-C7
SAN SEBASTIAN PL
700 MGH 95037 937-A4
SAN SIMEON DR
800 MTVW 94043 811-J3
SAN SIMEON ST
600 SUNV 94086 812-H6
SAN SIMEON WY
4000 SJS 95111 854-J7
SANTA ANA AV
400 SJS 95112 834-B3
SANTA ANA RD
18000 SCIC 95030 912-J3
SANTA ANA ST
2200 PA 94303 791-C4
SANTA ANNA CT
200 SUNV 94086 812-G7
SANTA BARBARA AV
3400 SCL 95051 832-J3
SANTA BARBARA DR
400 LALT 94022 811-F6
1600 SCIC 95125 853-H4
7500 GIL 95020 977-G3
SANTA BELLA PL
21700 CPTO 95014 852-B3
SANTA CATALINA ST
2300 PA 94303 791-D4
SANTA CHRISTINA CT
700 SUNV 94086 812-F5
SANTA CLARA AV
100 MTVW 94043 811-J4
100 SCIC 95020 957-G4
100 SMCo 94061 790-A3
100 RDWC 94061 790-A3
10000 CPTO 95014 832-B7
SANTA CLARA RD
21500 SCIC 95030 912-J3
SANTA CLARA ST
700 SCL 95053 833-D5
900 SCL 95050 833-D5
E SANTA CLARA ST
400 SJS 95113 834-C6
500 SJS 95112 834-C6
800 SJS 95116 834-C6
W SANTA CLARA ST
- SJS 95113 834-A7
100 SJS 95110 834-A7
W SANTA CLARA ST Rt#-82
500 SJS 95113 834-A7
500 SJS 95126 834-A7
SANTA COLETA CT
600 SUNV 94086 812-F5
SANTA CRUZ AV
500 MLPK 94025 790-F3
1600 SCL 95051 833-A2
2000 SMCo 94025 790-E6
N SANTA CRUZ AV
- LGTS 95030 873-A6
S SANTA CRUZ AV
100 LGTS 95030 892-J1
SANTA ELENA WY
200 SUNV 94086 812-F7
SANTA FE AV
800 SCIC 94305 810-J1
SANTA FE DR
1300 SJS 95118 874-B3
SANTA FE TER
200 SUNV 94086 812-F7
SANTA INEZ CT
1900 SCL 95051 832-J3
7600 GIL 95020 977-G3
SANTA INEZ DR
1500 SCIC 95125 853-H4
SANTA LUCIA DR
1600 SCIC 95125 853-H4
3100 SCL 95051 833-A5
SANTA LUCIA RD
10500 CPTO 95014 851-J2
SANTA MARGARITA AV
100 MLPK 94025 790-H3
3000 SJS 95118 874-A1
SANTA MARIA AV
700 SCIC 94305 810-H2
1500 SJS 95125 853-J4
3000 SCL 95051 833-A2
SANTA MARIA CT
7600 GIL 95020 977-G3
SANTA MESA DR
400 SJS 95123 874-J6
SANTA MONICA AV
100 MLPK 94025 790-H3
1500 SJS 95118 874-A1
SANTA MONICA TER
- FRMT 94539 794-B1
SANTANDER CT
200 LALT 94022 811-D4
SANTA PAULA AV
600 SUNV 94086 812-H6
1200 SJS 95110 833-J2
22300 CPTO 95014 852-A1
SANTA PAULA DR
7500 GIL 95020 977-G3
SANTA RITA AV
100 PA 94301 791-B6
300 MLPK 94025 790-F5
700 LALT 94022 811-D4
SANTA RITA CT
1000 LALT 94022 811-D3
SANTA RITA DR
300 MPS 95035 794-B6
SANTA RITA ST
700 SUNV 94086 812-H5
SANTA RITA WY
4100 SJS 95111 854-J7
SANTA ROSA AV
100 MTVW 94043 811-J4
SANTA ROSA CT
1900 SCL 95051 832-J3
SANTA ROSA DR
100 SJS 95111 854-J7
300 LGTS 95032 893-G1
300 LGTS 95032 873-G7
2000 HOLL - (1020-B6
See Page 999)
2200 SBnC - (1020-B6
See Page 999)
SANTA ROSA ST
700 SUNV 94086 812-H5
SANTA SUSANA ST
700 SUNV 94086 812-H5
SANTA SUSANA WY
4100 SJS 95111 854-J7
SANTA TERESA BLVD
5000 SCIC 95020 (998-A1
See Page 997)
5400 SCIC 95020 978-A7
5400 SJS 95136 874-E5
5500 SJS 95123 874-E5
5500 GIL 95020 978-A7
5700 SCIC 95020 977-G5
5700 GIL 95020 977-F3
5900 SJS 95123 875-C6
6200 SJS 95119 875-C6
7000 SJS 95139 875-C6
7000 SJS 95139 895-H2
7300 SCIC 95139 895-H2
7300 SCIC 95119 895-H2
7300 SJS 95139 896-A4
7800 SJS 95141 896-A4
9000 GIL 95020 957-G7
9000 SJS 95037 896-A4
9700 SCIC 95020 957-F4
9900 SCIC 95046 957-E2
14000 SCIC 95046 937-B5
14100 SCIC 95037 896-A4
14300 SCIC 95037 916-D2
14400 MGH 95037 937-B5
14400 SCIC 95037 937-B5
14500 MGH 95037 916-G4

STREET
Block City ZIP Pg-Grid

SANTA TERESA CT
6100 SJS 95123 875-A6
SANTA TERESA DR
10800 CPTO 95014 852-B3
SANTA TERESA ST
100 SCIC 94305 790-G7
300 SJS 95110 834-A5
SANTA THERESA DR
7400 GIL 95020 977-H3
SANTA TRINITA AV
300 SUNV 94086 812-H7
SANTA YNEZ ST
600 SCIC 94305 810-H1
600 SUNV 94086 812-J6
SANTA YSABEL WY
6000 SJS 95123 874-F6
SANTEE DR
1300 SJS 95122 834-G7
SANTEE RIVER CT
600 SJS 95111 854-H4
SANTIAGO AV
- ATN 94027 790-D4
100 SMCo 94061 790-A3
1900 SJS 95122 834-J7
SANTIAGO PL
800 MGH 95037 937-A4
SAN TOMAS CT
1500 SJS 95130 853-B4
SAN TOMAS EXWY
Rt#-G4
- CMBL 95008 853-C6
- SCL 95051 853-C4
- SCL 95117 833-C6
- SCL 95117 853-C4
- SJS 95008 853-C4
- SJS 95130 853-C4
100 SJS 95117 853-C4
200 SCL 95051 833-C3
200 SCL 95050 833-C6
2900 SCL 95054 813-C7
2900 SCL 95054 833-C3
SAN TOMAS LN
16600 MGH 95037 937-B1
SAN TOMAS ST
700 SUNV 94086 812-H5
SAN TOMAS AQUINO
PKWY
- SJS 95130 853-C4
N SAN TOMAS
AQUINO RD
- CMBL 95008 853-B6
200 SJS 95008 853-B6
300 SJS 95130 853-B6
1200 SJS 95117 853-B6
1200 SJS 95129 853-B6
S SAN TOMAS
AQUINO RD
100 SJS 95008 853-A7
600 SJS 95130 853-A7
700 CMBL 95008 853-A7
2100 CMBL 95008 873-B1
SANTOS CT
600 MPS 95035 794-C5
SAN VERON AV
800 MTVW 94043 811-J3
SAN VICENTE AV
22400 SCIC 95120 895-A4
22500 SJS 95120 895-B4
SAN VICENTE DR
600 MGH 95037 937-C1
SAN VICENTE WY
300 SUNV 94086 812-J7
SAN VINCENTE AV
22600 SCIC 95120 895-B4
SAN VITO CT
300 SJS 95116 834-F3
SAN YSIDRO AV
8400 GIL 95020 958-A7
8400 GIL 95020 978-A1
SAN YSIDRO WY
2900 SCL 95051 812-J7
2900 SCL 95051 832-J1
4000 SJS 95111 854-J7
SAN ZENO WY
100 SUNV 94086 832-J1
SAPENA CT
400 SCL 95054 813-E7
SAPPHIRE CT
900 SJS 95136 874-E3
SAPWOOD LN
1600 SJS 95133 814-H3
SAPWOOD WY
2300 SJS 95133 814-H3
SARA AV
300 SUNV 94086 812-C7
SARA CT
900 SUNV 94086 812-C7
SARABAND WY
800 SJS 95122 854-F1

SARAGLEN CT
19900 SAR 95070 852-F5
SARAGLEN DR
12000 SAR 95070 852-F5
SARAH CT
4000 SJS 95136 874-E1
SARAHILLS CT
21300 SAR 95070 872-C1
SARAHILLS DR
13400 SAR 95070 872-C1
SARA JANE CT
16900 MGH 95037 917-G5
SARA JANE LN
16900 MGH 95037 917-G5
SARALYNN DR
1600 SJS 95121 855-A2
SARANAC DR
700 SUNV 94087 832-C3
SARA PARK CIR
18800 SAR 95070 852-H6
SARASOTA WY
1800 SJS 95122 834-H7
2000 SJS 95122 854-H1
SARATOGA AV
- LGTS 95030 873-B7
- LGTS 95032 873-B7
- SCL 95051 833-C7
- SCL 95051 853-B1
200 SCL 95050 833-C7
300 SJS 95129 853-B1
1100 EPA 94303 791-A1
1400 SJS 95129 852-G7
1700 SAR 95070 852-G7
1700 SAR 95129 852-G7
1700 SJS 95130 852-G7
13400 SAR 95070 872-E2
SARATOGA DR
1300 MPS 95035 814-D1
SARATOGA PL
7000 GIL 95020 977-H4
SARATOGA-
SUNNYVALE RD
800 SUNV 94087 832-E5
1600 CPTO 95014 832-E5
12000 SAR 95070 852-D7
S SARATOGA-
SUNNYVALE RD
12500 SAR 95070 852-D5
13400 SAR 95070 872-D1
SARATOGA CREEK DR
12200 SAR 95070 852-G6
SARATOGA GLEN CT
12700 SAR 95070 852-H6
SARATOGA GLEN PL
18900 SAR 95070 852-G6
SARATOGA HEIGHTS
CT
14500 SAR 95070 872-B2
SARATOGA HEIGHTS
DR
21400 SAR 95070 872-B2
SARATOGA HILLS RD
20700 SAR 95070 872-C1
SARATOGA LOS
GATOS RD
- LGTS 95030 873-A6
100 LGTS 95032 873-B7
SARATOGA LOS
GATOS RD Rt#-9
17900 LGTS 95030 873-A6
17900 MSER 95030 873-A6
17900 MSER 95030 872-G5
18500 SCIC 95030 872-G5
18800 SAR 95070 872-E3
S SARATOGA
SUNNYVALE RD
13500 SAR 95070 872-D2
SARATOGA VILLA PL
12000 SAR 95070 852-D5
SARATOGA VISTA AV
13500 SAR 95070 872-E1
SARATOGA VISTA CT
20000 SAR 95070 872-E1
SARATOGA WOODS CIR
12700 SAR 95070 852-E6
SARAVIEW CT
20800 SAR 95070 852-C7
20800 SAR 95070 872-D1
SARAVIEW DR
13400 SAR 95070 872-D1
SARGENT DR
1000 SUNV 94087 832-F3
SARGENT LN
- ATN 94027 790-B7
SARGENT ST
8000 GIL 95020 977-J2
SARITA WY
1300 SCL 95051 832-H4
SARK CT
400 MPS 95035 794-A6

SARK WY
3700 SJS 95111 855-A6
SARON DR
- SJS 95116 834-G4
SASKATCHEWAN DR
1400 SUNV 94087 832-D5
SASSAFRAS DR
3400 SJS 95111 854-G6
SASSONE CT
1200 MPS 95035 814-D2
SATINWOOD DR
3600 SJS 95148 835-F7
SATTERLEE LN
8700 SCIC 95020 958-E4
SATURN AV
- FRMT 94539 793-J1
SATURN CT
1400 MPS 95035 794-D7
SATURN TER
300 SUNV 94086 832-E1
SAUSAL DR
- PTLV 94028 810-C6
SAUTNER DR
400 SJS 95123 875-B7
SAUVIGNON CT
8300 SJS 95135 855-J7
SAVAKER AV
800 SJS 95126 853-J2
SAVANNAH DR
1100 SJS 95117 853-D3
SAVENDISH CT
5200 SJS 95136 874-F3
SAVERIO CT
2100 SJS 95008 853-B6
SAVORY DR
800 SUNV 94087 832-D2
SAVOY DR
4500 SJS 95129 853-A4
SAVSTROM WY
400 SJS 95111 875-B1
SAWLEAF CT
1500 SJS 95131 814-D6
SAWLEAF ST
48200 FRMT 94539 793-J1
SAW MILL LN
- MTVW 94043 811-J3
SAWTOOTH CT
3600 SJS 95111 854-G6
SAWTOOTH CYN RD
- SCIC 95140 (838-F5
See Page 837)
SAWYER CT
2300 SCL 95054 813-C5
SAXON WY
1100 MLPK 94025 790-F4
SAXONY CT
5600 SJS 95123 874-G4
SAYOKO CIR
4200 SJS 95136 874-H1
SAYRE AV
- SCIC 94035 812-B2
SCAGIA LN
23500 SCIC 95030 913-D6
SCAGLIOTTI RD
300 SBnC - (1020-C5
See Page 999)
SCALLETTA LN
1000 SJS 95120 894-H4
SCANLAN PL
2400 SCL 95050 833-C6
SCARAWAY DR
3000 SJS 95132 814-F4
SCARFF WY
26000 LAH 94022 811-C5
SCARLETT RD
2300 SCIC 95020 958-D5
SCARLETT WY
4900 SJS 95111 875-C1
SCARLETWOOD TER
4800 SJS 95129 852-B7
SCARSBOROUGH WY
100 LGTS 95030 873-A3
SCARSDALE CT
1100 SJS 95120 894-G4
SCARSDALE PL
7100 SJS 95120 894-G4
SCARSDALE WY
7100 SJS 95120 894-G4
SCENERY CT
6500 SJS 95120 894-C1
SCENIC BLVD
10000 CPTO 95014 852-A1
SCENIC CIR
10300 CPTO 95014 852-A1
SCENIC CT
10400 CPTO 95014 852-A1
SCENIC SQ
1900 SJS 95132 814-E3
SCENIC HEIGHTS WY
21600 SCIC 95070 852-B5

SCENIC MEADOW CT
- SJS 95135 855-H7
SCENIC MEADOW LN
- SJS 95135 855-G7
- SJS 95138 855-G7
SCENIC VISTA DR
20700 SCIC 95120 894-J2
20800 SCIC 95120 895-A1
20800 SCIC 95119 895-A1
SCEPTER CT
1800 SJS 95132 814-G2
SCHALLENBERGER RD
1500 SJS 95112 814-A7
1500 SJS 95131 814-A7
SCHARFF AV
- SJS 95116 834-G3
SCHELLER AV
- SJS 95037 896-E6
100 SCIC 95037 896-B7
200 SCIC 95037 916-A1
SCHEMBRI CT
- EPA 94303 791-B1
SCHEMBRI LN
700 EPA 94303 791-B1
SCHIELE AV
700 SJS 95126 833-H6
SCHILLINGSBURG AV
21400 SCIC 95120 895-C5
SCHOFIELD CT
11700 SCIC 95020 957-J2
SCHOOL RD
1000 SBnC - (1017-F4
See Page 997)
SCHOOL ST
- SJS 95002 813-C1
100 SUNV 94086 812-E6
SCHOOLDALE DR
1800 SJS 95124 853-H7
SCHOOLHOUSE RD
700 SJS 95138 875-G5
SCHOONER CT
3000 SJS 95148 855-D1
SCHOTT ST
100 SJS 95116 834-G2
SCHRADER DR
1900 SJS 95124 853-F7
SCHROEDER AV
300 SUNV 94086 812-E6
SCHUBERT AV
2400 SJS 95124 853-G7
SCHUBERT DR
700 SUNV 94087 832-F3
SCHULTE DR
1700 SJS 95133 834-E3
SCHWEPPES CT
1800 SJS 95132 814-J3
SCHWIE AL
- MLPK 94025 790-E6
SCOFIELD AV
600 EPA 94303 791-B3
SCOFIELD DR
20500 CPTO 95014 852-D1
SCOLLON CT
1300 SJS 95132 814-F5
SCORPIO DR
300 SJS 95111 854-G6
SCOSSA AV
1300 SJS 95118 874-B3
SCOSSA CT
- SJS 95118 874-B3
SCOTCH HEATHER CT
3100 SJS 95148 855-E2
SCOTLAND DR
1100 CPTO 95014 852-D3
19400 SAR 95070 852-F7
SCOTSGLEN CT
900 SJS 95136 874-D1
SCOTT AV
- SBnC - (1017-B5
See Page 997)
18400 MSER 95030 872-H6
SCOTT BLVD
400 SCL 95050 833-D3
2900 SCL 95054 833-D3
2900 SCL 95054 813-A7
3300 SUNV 94086 813-A7
SCOTT CT
800 CMBL 95008 873-C1
SCOTT DR
1700 MGH 95037 916-F7
SCOTT LN
1900 LALT 94024 831-H5
SCOTT ST
900 PA 94301 790-J5
1500 SJS 95126 853-G1
1600 SCIC 95126 853-G1
1700 SJS 95128 853-E1
1800 SCIC 95128 853-G1
SCOTT CREEK RD
600 FRMT 94539 794-A2

SCOTT CREEK RD
600 FRMT 94539 793-J2
2200 SCIC 95035 794-A2
SCOTT ROBBINS WY
- SBnC - (1017-B5
See Page 997)
SCOTTSDALE CT
2800 SJS 95148 855-C2
SCOTTSDALE DR
2400 SJS 95148 835-B7
2500 SJS 95148 855-C1
SCOTTSFIELD DR
4300 SJS 95136 874-D2
SCOTTSVILLE CT
500 SJS 95133 834-F2
SCOTTY ST
1500 SJS 95122 834-G6
SCOUT CT
4800 SJS 95136 874-J2
SCRIPPS AV
4000 PA 94306 811-E2
SCRIPPS CT
200 PA 94306 811-E2
SCULLY AV
12000 SAR 95070 852-F5
SEABEE PL
1900 SJS 95133 834-E1
SEABISCUIT DR
200 SJS 95111 875-B2
SEABOARD AV
2500 SJS 95131 813-F7
SEABRIDGE DR
- FRMT 94538 793-F1
SEABROOK CT
800 SJS 95111 855-A6
SEABURY DR
800 SJS 95136 874-E2
SEACLIFF DR
2000 MPS 95035 794-E7
SEACLIFF WY
2300 SJS 95122 854-J1
SEACREEK CT
3200 SJS 95121 855-D7
SEACREEK WY
1600 SJS 95121 855-D7
SEAFIELD CT
3000 SJS 95148 855-C3
SEAGRAVES WY
20100 SAR 95070 872-E2
SEA GULL CT
19700 SAR 95070 852-F6
SEA GULL WY
19800 SAR 95070 852-E5
SEALE AV
100 PA 94301 791-A6
700 PA 94303 791-A6
SEAMAN PL
1000 SJS 95133 814-E7
SEAN CIR
5400 SJS 95123 874-J4
SEAN CT
- SJS 95123 874-F6
SEAN LN
5500 SJS 95123 874-J3
SEARCY DR
1300 SJS 95118 874-B2
SEAREEL LN
1400 SJS 95131 814-A4
SEARLE RD
700 SBnC - (1017-J7
See Page 997)
SEARLES AV
1500 SJS 95125 854-A4
SEARS RD
23500 SCIC 95030 913-E6
SEARSVILLE RD
- SCIC 94305 790-F7
SEARVILLE RD
1500 PA 94304 810-G5
1700 SCIC 94304 810-G5
28000 LAH 94022 810-G5
SEASIDE DR
100 MPS 95035 793-J5
SEASIDE WY
1100 MPS 95035 793-J5
SEATON AV
20600 SAR 95070 872-D1
SEAVIEW DR
300 SJS 95002 813-B1
1700 SJS 95122 834-H7
SEAWELL CT
100 SJS 95138 875-E4
SEAWOOD WY
700 SJS 95120 894-J3
SEBASIAN WY
400 SJS 95111 854-J6
SEBASTIAN CT
100 LGTS 95032 873-J6

SEBASTIAN BORELLO
DR
2800 SJS 95148 855-D2
SEBREE LN
18200 MSER 95030 872-J5
SEDLAK CT
2500 SJS 95148 855-B1
SEDUM RD
48600 FRMT 94539 793-J2
SEEBECK CT
2000 SJS 95132 814-F2
SEEBER CT
7700 CPTO 95014 852-C4
SEELY AV
- SBnC - (1017-B6
See Page 997)
2600 SCIC 95134 813-H4
2600 SJS 95134 813-H4
SEENA AV
900 LALT 94024 831-G2
SEGO CT
1600 SJS 95131 834-D1
SEGOVIA CT
3200 SJS 95127 814-H6
SEGURA CT
2900 SJS 95125 873-J1
SEIFERT AV
5600 SJS 95118 874-B4
SEINE CT
- SJS 95127 834-J1
SELBORN PL
1400 SJS 95126 833-H7
SELBY LN
- ATN 94027 790-C2
- SMCo 94063 790-C1
700 SCIC 95127 814-H6
1100 SMCo 94061 790-B3
W SELBY LN
1100 ATN 94027 790-C2
1400 SMCo 94061 790-B3
SELIG LN
1700 LALT 94024 832-A3
SELINDA LN
5000 SJS 95032 873-H4
SELINDA WY
5100 SJS 95032 873-H5
SELKIRK PL
800 SUNV 94087 832-F6
SELMAC AV
- SJS 95136 874-E1
SELO DR
1300 SUNV 94087 832-D4
SELVA DR
3200 SJS 95148 835-D6
SELWYN DR
100 MPS 95035 794-C7
SEMICIRCULAR RD
100 SMCo 94063 790-D1
SEMICONDUCTOR DR
2900 SCL 95051 812-H7
2900 SCL 95051 832-H1
2900 SCL 94086 812-H7
2900 SCL 94086 832-H1
SEMILLION DR
48800 FRMT 94539 793-J2
SEMINARY DR
- MLPK 94025 790-H2
SEMINOLE WY
- SCIC 95030 872-H5
700 PA 94303 811-F1
1600 SJS 95122 854-J1
SENATE WY
10000 CPTO 95014 832-C7
SENDA DEL VALLE
300 SCrC 95003 (975-A7
See Page 955)
SENECA CT
600 SJS 95123 874-G4
SENECA ST
400 PA 94301 791-A3
400 PA 94301 790-J3
SENEGAL CT
1300 GIL 95020 977-F1
SENNA CT
400 SUNV 94086 832-G1
SENTER RD
- SJS 95111 854-H5
1300 SJS 95112 854-F2
SENTER CREEK CT
2600 SJS 95111 854-G4
SENTINEL ST
5800 SJS 95120 874-B6
SENTRY PALM CT
- SJS 95133 814-J4
SEPTEMBER CT
800 CPTO 95014 852-C2
SEPTEMBER DR
800 CPTO 95014 852-C2
5500 SJS 95138 875-D4
SEPTEMBER SONG CT
1700 SJS 95131 814-D7

SEPULVEDA AV
2000 MPS 95035 794-E7
SEPULVEDA CT
200 MPS 95035 794-E7
SEQUESTER CT
2400 SJS 95133 814-F6
SEQUOIA AV
100 SJS 95126 833-H7
100 SMCo 94061 790-A3
200 PA 94306 791-A6
SEQUOIA DR
400 SUNV 94086 832-G2
500 MPS 95035 794-D7
600 MPS 95035 814-E1
7600 GIL 95020 977-G3
11800 SCIC 94024 831-J5
SEQUOIA LN
400 SCIC 94305 790-G7
SEQUOIA WY
- SMCo 94061 790-B4
400 SCIC 94024 831-J5
SERENA WY
100 SCL 95051 833-B7
100 SCL 95051 853-B1
SERENADE CT
600 SJS 95111 855-A7
SERENADE WY
400 SJS 95111 855-A7
SERENA VISTA CT
16200 MSER 95030 872-J6
SERENE CT
800 MGH 95037 917-B6
SERENE DR
17300 MGH 95037 917-A5
17400 SCIC 95037 917-A5
SERENE WY
21000 SCIC 95120 894-J2
SERENE VALLEY CT
1200 SJS 95120 894-E2
SERENITY CT
6800 SJS 95120 894-F2
SERENITY WY
6800 SJS 95120 894-F2
SERENO CT
17200 MSER 95030 873-B4
SERENO DR
23300 CPTO 96014 831-H6
SERENO VISTA WY
200 SJS 95116 834-D2
SERGE AV
1900 SJS 95130 852-J6
SERPA DR
1600 MPS 95035 794-D5
3000 SJS 95148 855-C2
SERPENTINE CT
600 MGH 95037 916-H6
SERRA AV
2000 SCL 95050 833-C5
SERRA CT
200 LGTS 95032 873-B6
SERRA ST
100 SCIC 94305 790-H7
700 SCIC - 791-A7
SERRA WY
- MPS 95035 793-J7
100 MPS 95035 794-A7
SERRAMONTE DR
5100 SJS 95135 855-G5
SERRANO AV
300 SCIC 95127 835-A2
SERRANO DR
- ATN 94027 790-C2
SERRAOAKS CT
13700 SAR 95070 872-H1
SERVICE RD
- SBnC - (1017-B4
See Page 997)
SERVICE ST
800 SJS 95112 834-B2
SESAME CT
1200 SUNV 94087 832-D3
2500 SJS 95148 835-A6
SESAME DR
1100 SUNV 94087 832-D3
SESSIONS DR
6800 SJS 95119 875-F6
SETAREH CT
1200 SJS 95125 854-A3
SETH CT
1000 SJS 95120 894-G3
SETTLE AV
1100 SJS 95125 854-A3
SEVELY DR
800 MTVW 94041 812-A6
SEVEN ACRES LN
14000 LAH 94022 811-C6
SEVEN SPRINGS DR
11500 CPTO 95014 852-C4
SEVEN SPRINGS LN
11500 CPTO 95014 852-C4

SEVEN SPRINGS PKWY
11700 CPTO 95014 852-C4
SEVEN TREES BLVD
3800 SJS 95111 854-H6
SEVEN TREES
VILLAGE WY
3300 SJS 95111 854-G6
SEVERANCE CT
5100 SJS 95136 874-E3
SEVERANCE DR
4900 SJS 95136 874-E3
SEVERANCE ST
9300 GIL 95020 957-H7
SEVERYNS AV
- SCIC 94035 812-B2
- SCIC 94043 812-B2
SEVIER AV
1000 MLPK 94025 790-J1
SEVILLA DR
- LALT 94022 811-E5
SEVILLA LN
20500 SAR 95070 872-D1
SEVILLE DR
1400 MGH 95037 917-D7
SEVILLE WY
1700 SJS 95131 814-D7
SEVYSON CT
2900 PA 94303 791-D6
SEWARD CT
10100 SCIC 95127 835-A3
SEWELL AV
13200 SCIC 95046 937-E6
SEYFERTH WY
3000 SJS 95118 854-C7
SEYMOUR AV
14800 SCIC 95046 937-D3
SEYMOUR LN
1000 MLPK 94025 790-E5
SEYMOUR ST
200 SJS 95110 834-A5
300 SJS 95110 833-J5
SHADELANDS DR
6100 SJS 95123 874-H7
SHADE TREE LN
2200 SJS 95131 814-C5
SHADLE AV
1100 CMBL 95008 873-B1
SHADOW CT
500 SJS 95129 853-B2
SHADOW GN
500 SJS 95129 853-A2
SHADOW TR
18100 SCIC 95030 912-J4
SHADOW BROOK DR
900 SJS 95120 894-F2
SHADOWBROOK WY
18200 MGH 95037 916-H6
SHADOW CREEK DR
600 SJS 95136 854-E7
SHADOW CREEK PL
11600 SCIC 94024 831-G4
SHADOWCREST WY
5400 SJS 95123 874-G4
SHADOW DANCE DR
100 SJS 95125 854-C3
SHADOW ESTATES
5100 SJS 95135 855-G5
SHADOWFAX DR
1200 SJS 95121 855-A4
W SHADOWGRAPH DR
100 SJS 95125 854-C3
SHADOWHILL LN
7400 CPTO 95014 852-D3
SHADOWHURST CT
4500 SJS 95136 874-E2
SHADOWLAKE CT
200 MPS 95035 794-A6
SHADOW LANE CT
14400 MGH 95037 937-C5
SHADOW LEAF DR
3300 SJS 95132 814-G4
SHADOW MOUNTAIN CT
6800 SJS 95120 894-E3
SHADOW MOUNTAIN DR
13000 SAR 95070 852-E7
SHADOW OAKS WY
13900 SAR 95070 872-E2
SHADOW PARK PL
3200 SJS 95121 855-B2
SHADOW RIDGE CT
2100 SJS 95138 855-E5
SHADOW RIDGE WY
2100 SJS 95138 855-E5
SHADOW RUN DR
400 SJS 95125 854-C3
SHADOW SPRINGS PL
3000 SJS 95121 855-B1
SHADOWTREE DR
2100 SJS 95131 814-C5

SHADOWVALE WY
2600 SJS 95132 814-C4
SHADOW WOOD CT
- SJS 95136 874-J7
SHADY AV
5000 SJS 95129 852-J4
SHADY LN
2100 SCIC 95037 936-F2
15700 LGTS 95032 873-D6
21300 SCIC 95030 913-B2
SHADY WY
21300 SCIC 95030 912-G4
SHADYBROOK CT
11900 SAR 95070 852-H4
SHADY BROOK LN
1900 SCIC 95037 936-G4
SHADY CREEK CT
1700 SJS 95148 835-D4
SHADY DALE AV
1000 CMBL 95008 853-G6
SHADY GLEN AV
1500 SCL 95050 833-F6
SHADYGROVE CT
6200 CPTO 95014 852-G2
SHADYGROVE DR
6000 CPTO 95014 852-G2
SHADYHOLLOW CT
3600 SJS 95148 835-G7
SHADY HOLLOW DR
1700 MGH 95037 916-F7
SHADY LANE DR
17000 SCIC 95037 917-G4
SHADY OAK LN
20500 CPTO 95014 832-D6
SHADY OAKS CT
26700 LAH 94022 811-A5
SHADY SPRING LN
3300 MTVW 94040 831-J2
SHADY VIEW LN
16300 LGTS 95032 873-D7
16300 SCIC 95032 873-D7
SHAFER AV
2000 MGH 95037 917-E6
2000 SCIC 95037 917-E6
SHAFER CT
- SCIC 95037 917-E5
SHAFER DR
3400 SCL 95051 832-J5
SHAFFER DR
1400 SJS 95132 814-F3
SHAKER CT
1100 SJS 95120 894-C5
SHALEN CT
5000 SJS 95130 852-J6
SHAMROCK AV
1700 SCL 95051 833-B3
SHAMROCK DR
300 SCIC 95008 873-E1
400 SJS 95008 873-E1
SHANDON CT
4000 SJS 95136 854-E6
SHANDON ROCK CT
700 SJS 95136 854-F7
SHANDWICK CT
1000 SJS 95136 874-C1
SHANG CT
3100 SJS 95127 834-H1
SHANGHAI CIR
1500 SJS 95131 814-B7
SHANGHAI CT
1200 SJS 95131 814-B6
SHANNON CT
2900 SCL 95051 833-A6
21400 CPTO 95014 852-C2
SHANNON RD
14000 SCIC 95032 893-G1
14400 LGTS 95032 893-G1
14800 SCIC 95032 873-F7
15300 LGTS 95032 873-C6
16100 SCIC 95032 873-C6
SHANNONS DR
5500 SCIC 95037 935-F2
SHARLENE CT
2100 SCIC 95037 917-D5
SHARMON PALMS LN
700 CMBL 95008 853-C7
800 CMBL 95008 873-C1
SHARON CT
- MLPK 94025 790-D7
100 LGTS 95124 873-E6
100 LGTS 95032 873-E6
800 CMBL 95008 853-C7
800 PA 94303 791-B4
SHARON DR
7000 SJS 95129 852-E4
SHARON LN
5400 SJS 95124 873-G6
SHARON RD
2000 MLPK 94025 790-D7
2000 SMCo 94025 790-D7

SHARON MANOR CT
1400 SJS 95129 852-E4
SHARON OAKS DR
2300 MLPK 94025 790-E7
SHARON PARK DR
100 MLPK 94025 790-C7
SHARP AV
200 CMBL 95008 873-E1
1400 SJS 95008 873-E1
SHARP CT
1300 CMBL 95008 873-E2
SHARY AV
700 MTVW 94041 811-J6
SHASTA AV
1100 SJS 95126 833-H7
1500 SJS 95128 833-H7
1500 SJS 95128 853-G1
SHASTA DR
3800 SCL 95051 832-H6
4100 PA 94306 811-E2
SHASTA LN
- MLPK 94025 790-C7
14900 MGH 95037 937-B4
SHASTA ST
- LALT 94022 811-D6
SHASTA FIR DR
700 SUNV 94086 832-G2
SHASTA FIR WY
- SUNV 94086 832-G2
SHASTA SPRING CT
11800 CPTO 95014 852-A5
SHATO PL
100 FRMT 94539 793-H1
SHATTUCK DR
21800 CPTO 95014 852-B2
SHAUNA LN
900 PA 94306 811-B3
SHAW DR
1500 SJS 95118 874-A1
SHAWCROFT DR
5900 SJS 95123 874-J6
SHAWN DR
1300 SJS 95118 874-B3
SHAWNEE LN
400 SJS 95123 874-H5
SHAWNEE PASS
100 PTLV 94028 810-B6
SHAWNEE PL
400 FRMT 94539 793-J1
SHAWNEE WY
300 FRMT 94539 793-J1
SHAYNOR CT
3700 SJS 95130 853-C4
SHEA CT
7200 SJS 95139 895-F1
SHEAN CT
11400 SCIC 95020 957-G2
SHEARER DR
- ATN 94027 790-C1
SHEARTON DR
600 SJS 95117 853-C2
SHEARWATER DR
6800 SJS 95120 894-H2
SHEEHAN CT
7100 SJS 95120 894-G3
SHEFFIELD AV
1500 CMBL 95008 853-G5
1600 CMBL 95125 853-G5
SHEFFIELD CT
300 CMBL 95125 853-H5
SHEFFIELD LN
200 RDWC 94061 790-B2
SHEFFIELD RIDGE CT
2100 SJS 95138 855-F5
SHEILA AV
13800 SCIC 95037 956-G1
13900 SCIC 95037 936-G7
SHEILA CT
800 CMBL 95008 873-C1
SHELBY LN
500 LALT 94024 811-F7
SHELBY CREEK CT
1300 SJS 95120 894-F4
SHELBY CREEK LN
1200 SJS 95120 894-F4
SHELDON AV
4100 SCIC 95020 (998-E2
See Page 997)
SHELDON RD
16700 SCIC 95030 872-H7
SHELLBACK PL
2000 SJS 95133 814-E7
2000 SJS 95133 834-E1
SHELLBARK DR
- SJS 95136 874-H1
SHELLBURNE WY
17400 LGTS 95030 873-A5
SHELLEY AV
2200 CMBL 95008 873-E2
2200 SJS 95124 873-E2

STREET
Block City ZIP Pg-Grid

SHELLEY AV
2200 SJS 95008 873-E2
SHELLEY CT
400 MPS 95035 794-B6
SHELLY CT
6100 SJS 95123 874-G6
SHELLY DR
20600 CPTO 95014 852-D1
SHELTON DR
1400 HOLL - (1020-B6 See Page 999)
SHELTON WY
1000 SJS 95125 853-J3
SHENADO PL
- SJS 95136 875-B3
- SJS 95123 875-B3
SHENANDOAH AV
1500 MPS 95035 794-D7
SHENANDOAH DR
800 SUNV 94087 832-C3
1000 SJS 95125 854-D7
SHEPHERD AV
400 SJS 95125 854-B2
SHERATON DR
600 SUNV 94087 832-C3
2000 SCL 95050 833-C3
SHERBOURNE DR
4300 SJS 95124 874-A3
SHERBROOKE WY
2900 SJS 95127 835-A4
SHEREE CT
12600 SCIC 95127 814-J5
SHEREEN PL
- CMBL 95008 853-C6
SHERI ANN AV
1800 SJS 95131 814-B6
SHERIDAN AV
100 PA 94306 791-B7
SHERIDAN CIR
12400 SAR 95070 852-E6
SHERIDAN PL
400 SJS 95111 854-G4
SHERIDAN ST
- LALT 94022 831-D1
SHERLAND AV
- MTVW 94043 812-A4
SHERLAND CT
300 MTVW 94043 812-B4
SHERLOCK CT
27300 LAH 94022 830-H2
SHERLOCK DR
2400 SJS 95121 854-H3
SHERLOCK RD
27000 LAH 94022 830-H2
SHERMAN AV
100 PA 94306 791-B7
800 MLPK 94025 790-D6
1100 SMCo 94025 790-D6
SHERMAN CT
- SJS 95193 875-C4
900 MPS 95035 794-B4
SHERMAN ST
400 LALT 94022 811-D7
700 SCL 95053 833-F4
900 SJS 95110 854-D2
900 SCL 95050 833-F4
SHERMAN OAKS DR
700 SJS 95128 853-G3
SHERRY CT
200 SJS 95119 875-E7
SHERRY LN
1100 SCIC 95046 937-H7
SHERRYS WY
19400 SCIC 95030 892-F3
SHERWIN AV
2100 SCL 95050 833-C5
SHERWOOD AV
1000 SJS 95126 833-G5
1200 SCL 95050 833-G5
1200 SCL 95126 833-G5
SHERWOOD CT
1100 SUNV 94087 832-B3
SHERWOOD DR
300 GIL 95020 977-H1
900 SUNV 94087 832-B3
SHERWOOD LN
800 LALT 94022 811-E4
SHERWOOD WY
300 MLPK 94025 790-G4
SHETLAND CT
500 MPS 95035 794-B6
700 SJS 95127 814-H6
SHETLAND PL
800 SUNV 94087 832-F6
SHIBLEY AV
2200 SJS 95125 854-A6
SHILLING CT
1800 SJS 95132 814-J2
SHILOH AV
2000 MPS 95035 794-E7
SHILSHONE WY
2400 SJS 95121 854-H3
SHIMMER CT
- MPS 95035 793-H6
SHINGLE VALLEY RD
- SCIC 95037 876-F7
- SCIC 95037 896-G1
- SCIC 95137 876-F7
- SCIC 95137 896-G1
- SCIC 95138 876-F7
SHIRE CT
100 LGTS 95030 873-A3
SHIRECREST CT
600 SJS 95123 874-G4
SHIRLEY AV
800 SUNV 94086 812-D6
11700 SCIC 94024 831-F4
SHIRLEY DR
1100 MPS 95035 794-C7
SHIRLEY WY
400 MLPK 94025 790-J2
SHIRLYNN CT
500 LALT 94022 811-E7
SHOFNER PL
3100 SJS 95111 854-F7
SHOLES CT
14200 LAH 94022 811-B6
SHONA CT
4000 SJS 95124 874-A2
SHOOTING STAR TER
800 SUNV 94086 832-F3
SHOPPE LN
- MLPK 94025 790-J2
SHORE RD
700 SBnC - 999-E5
SHOREBIRD WY
1100 MTVW 94043 812-A1
1100 MTVW 94043 811-J1
SHOREHAM CT
10200 SCIC 95127 834-J3
SHORELAND DR
1100 SJS 95122 854-H1
N SHORELINE BLVD
300 MTVW 94043 811-J1
1900 MTVW 94043 791-J7
S SHORELINE BLVD
100 MTVW 94041 811-H5
300 MTVW 94043 811-H5
SHORELINE CT
- FRMT 94538 793-G2
SHORESIDE CT
2300 SCL 95054 813-C5
SHOREVIEW CT
1300 SJS 95122 854-H1
SHOREWOOD LN
400 SJS 95134 813-C2
SHORT RD
15900 LGTS 95032 873-D6
SHORT HILL CT
14000 SAR 95070 872-G2
SHORTRIDGE AV
1100 SJS 95116 834-F4
SHOSHONE CT
200 SJS 95127 834-H1
SHOSHONE DR
200 SJS 95127 834-H1
SHOSHONE PL
- PTLV 94028 810-B6
SHOWERS DR
- MTVW 94040 811-E4
SHREEN CT
1600 SJS 95124 874-A2
SHRIVER CT
1200 SJS 95132 814-G5
SHRIVER DR
3100 SJS 95132 814-G5
SHUBERT CT
19300 SAR 95070 852-G6
SHUBERT DR
19200 SAR 95070 852-G6
SHULMAN AV
900 SCL 95050 833-E2
1800 SJS 95124 853-G7
SHULTIES RD
- SCrC 95030 913-A6
SHUMAKER WY
1500 SJS 95131 814-D6
SIBELIUS AV
2600 SJS 95122 855-A1
W SIDE AV
- SMCo 94063 790-C1
SIDLAW CT
4500 SJS 95136 874-F2
SIEBER CT
400 SJS 95111 854-F7
SIEBER PL
500 SJS 95111 854-F7
SIEBER WY
3200 SJS 95111 854-F7
SIENNA DR
10300 SJS 95127 835-A4
SIERRA AV
400 MTVW 94041 811-H6
1100 SJS 95126 833-H7
SIERRA CT
100 MGH 95037 916-H5
1200 SJS 95132 814-E5
2300 PA 94303 791-D4
SIERRA DR
1000 MLPK 94025 790-C6
SIERRA LN
- PTLV 94028 810-C5
SIERRA RD
1100 SJS 95131 834-C1
1300 SJS 95131 814-D6
2400 SJS 95132 814-G4
3500 SCIC 95132 814-J3
3700 SCIC 95132 814-J3
3900 SCIC 95132 815-A3
3900 SJS 95132 815-A3
5600 SCIC 95140 815-E3
SIERRA ST
1200 RDWC 94061 790-A1
SIERRA AZULE
300 LGTS 95032 873-G7
SIERRA CREEK WY
1400 SJS 95132 814-F3
SIERRA GRANDE CT
- SJS 95116 834-H3
SIERRA GRANDE WY
2500 SJS 95116 834-H3
SIERRA LINDA
100 LGTS 95030 872-J2
SIERRA MAR DR
1200 SJS 95118 874-B1
1200 SJS 95118 854-C7
SIERRA MEADOW CT
2500 SJS 95116 834-H3
SIERRA MEADOW DR
- SJS 95116 834-H3
SIERRA MESA DR
- SJS 95116 834-H3
SIERRA MONTE WY
2500 SJS 95116 834-H3
SIERRA MORENA
1100 LGTS 95032 873-E5
SIERRA MORENA CT
15400 MGH 95037 937-A4
SIERRA SERENA
2300 SJS 95116 834-H3
SIERRA SPRING CT
11700 CPTO 95014 852-A5
SIERRA SPRING LN
- CPTO 95014 852-A5
SIERRA VENTURA DR
2100 LALT 94024 831-H5
SIERRA VILLAGE CT
1100 SJS 95132 814-H3
SIERRA VILLAGE PL
1200 SJS 95132 814-H3
SIERRA VILLAGE WY
1100 SJS 95132 814-H3
SIERRAVILLE AV
1300 SJS 95132 814-F4
SIERRA VISTA AV
- MTVW 94043 811-H1
SIERRA VISTA CT
2500 SJS 95116 834-H3
SIERRA VISTA PL
- SJS 95116 834-H3
SIERRA WOOD DR
2000 SJS 95132 814-C3
SIESTA CT
- SMCo 94028 810-D4
SIESTA DR
1500 LALT 94024 831-J3
SIESTA VISTA DR
15600 SCIC 95127 815-C7
SIETA CT
1400 SJS 95118 874-B1
SIGAL DR
20600 SAR 95070 872-D4
SIGRID WY
5300 SJS 95136 874-J3
5300 SJS 95123 874-J3
SILACCI DR
800 CMBL 95008 853-A7
1400 CMBL 95008 873-A1
SILACCI WY
6600 GIL 95020 978-C4
SILBERMAN DR
6100 SJS 95120 874-C7
SILBURY CT
3100 SJS 95148 855-E2
SILCREEK DR
- SJS 95116 834-F3
SILENCE DR
2000 SJS 95148 835-D4
SILENT HILLS LN
12400 LAH 94022 831-A2
SILER LN
1200 SJS 95116 834-F5
SILICON DR
900 SJS 95126 833-H5
SILICON VALLEY BLVD
300 SJS 95138 875-F5
SILK CT
3600 SJS 95111 854-G6
SILK OAK WY
700 SUNV 94086 832-G2
SILVA AV
4300 MTVW 94040 811-E3
4300 SJS 95118 874-B2
4300 PA 94306 811-E3
SILVA CIR
10200 SCIC 95020 958-B4
SILVA CT
4300 PA 94306 811-E3
SILVER AV
1600 RDWC 94061 790-A1
SILVERA LN
- SJS 95136 874-D2
SILVERA ST
100 MPS 95035 793-J6
SILVER ACRES CT
5100 SJS 95138 855-F7
SILVERADO AV
20200 CPTO 95014 852-E2
SILVERADO DR
1200 SJS 95120 894-D2
SILVER BELL DR
6900 SJS 95120 894-D4
SILVERBERRY DR
4300 SJS 95136 874-H1
SILVER BLOSSOM CT
2200 SJS 95138 855-F7
SILVER BLUFF WY
2200 SJS 95138 855-G7
SILVER BREEZE CT
2200 SJS 95138 855-G7
SILVER BROOK CT
7000 SJS 95120 894-D4
SILVER CANYON DR
1100 SJS 95120 894-D4
SILVER CLIFF DR
6900 SJS 95120 894-D4
SILVER CLOUD CT
500 MGH 95037 937-C5
SILVER CREEK CT
1700 SJS 95121 855-C4
SILVER CREEK RD
2500 SJS 95121 855-B3
3300 SJS 95121 855-C4
5500 SJS 95138 875-H1
5800 SCIC 95138 875-H1
SILVER CREEK VALLEY RD
400 SJS 95138 875-D3
400 SJS 95111 875-D3
1200 SCIC 95138 875-D3
5000 SJS 95121 855-E5
SILVERCREST DR
1600 SJS 95118 874-A2
SILVER ESTATES
2800 SJS 95135 855-G5
SILVER FOX DR
6900 SJS 95120 894-D4
SILVER GARDEN WY
5200 SJS 95138 855-F7
SILVERGATE CT
6900 SJS 95120 894-D4
SILVER GLEN CT
1700 SJS 95121 855-B4
SILVER HILL DR
1100 SJS 95120 894-D4
SILVER HOLLOW CT
2100 SJS 95138 855-F7
SILVERIA CT
2300 SCL 95054 813-C4
SILVER KNOLL CT
2200 SJS 95138 855-F7
SILVERLAKE CT
300 MPS 95035 794-A6
SILVERLAKE DR
100 MPS 95035 794-A6
200 SUNV 94089 812-H4
SILVERLAND CT
2900 SJS 95135 855-D3
SILVERLAND DR
2900 SJS 95135 855-E3
SILVER LEAF RD
5600 SJS 95138 875-D4
SILVER LODE LN
7100 SJS 95120 894-H4
SILVER MEADOW CT
1700 SJS 95121 855-B4
SILVER MOON CT
7000 SJS 95120 894-D4
SILVER OAK CT
1100 SJS 95120 874-D7
SILVER OAK LN
22600 CPTO 95014 831-J7
SILVER OAK WY
22500 CPTO 95014 831-J7
22600 CPTO 95014 851-J1
SILVER PEAK DR
6900 SJS 95120 894-D4
SILVER PINE CT
700 SUNV 94086 832-G2
SILVER POINT WY
5300 SJS 95138 855-F7
SILVER RIDGE CT
5100 SJS 95138 855-G6
SILVER RIDGE DR
5100 SJS 95138 855-G6
SILVER SAGE
5500 SJS 95123 875-B4
SILVER SHADOW DR
1100 SJS 95120 894-D4
SILVER SPRING CT
11500 CPTO 95014 852-A4
SILVER SPRINGS WY
- SJS 95123 875-G2
SILVER STAR CT
7000 SJS 95120 894-D4
SILVERSTONE PL
1500 SJS 95122 835-A5
1700 SJS 95148 835-A5
SILVER TERRACE WY
2200 SJS 95138 855-F7
SILVERTIP CT
300 MPS 95035 813-J3
SILVER TIP WY
700 SUNV 94086 832-H2
SILVER TRAIL CT
5200 SJS 95138 855-F7
SILVERTREE DR
1600 SJS 95131 814-C5
SILVER VALE CT
2100 SJS 95138 855-F7
SILVER VISTA WY
5300 SJS 95138 855-G7
SILVERWINGS CT
1800 MGH 95037 917-A3
SILVERWOOD AV
1900 MTVW 94043 811-G4
SILVERWOOD DR
1700 SJS 95124 873-J2
SILVIA CT
200 LALT 94024 811-F7
SILVIA DR
200 LALT 94024 811-F7
SILVIA ST
8500 GIL 95020 977-G1
SIMAS DR
400 MPS 95035 794-C5
SIMBERLAN DR
3100 SJS 95148 855-E1
SIMKINS CT
2900 PA 94303 791-D5
SIMON AV
2000 SJS 95122 834-J6
SIMON LN
13200 LAH 94022 810-J7
SIMONI DR
15600 SCIC 95127 815-B7
SIMONS WY
- LGTS 95032 873-B7
SIMONSON CT
1200 SJS 95121 854-J2
SIMONSON WY
1200 SJS 95121 854-J2
SIMPSON WY
1800 SJS 95125 854-A5
SINBAD AV
800 SJS 95116 834-J4
SINCLAIR DR
400 SJS 95116 834-G4
SINCLAIR FRWY I-280
- SCIC - 853-G2
- SJS - 834-E7
- SJS - 854-A2
- SJS - 853-G2
SINCLAIR FRWY I-680
- FRMT - 794-A1
- FRMT - 793-J1
- MPS - 794-A1
- MPS - 814-E6
- SCIC - 814-E6
- SJS - 834-F1
- SJS - 814-E6
SINCLAIR FRONTAGE RD
200 MPS 95035 794-C7
400 MPS 95035 814-C1
SINGING HILL LN
14500 SAR 95070 872-H3
SINGING RAIN PL
2800 SJS 95127 835-A4
SINGLETARY AV
1100 SJS 95126 833-H7
SINGLETON LN
400 SJS 95111 854-J5
SINGLETON RD
600 SCIC 95111 854-G6
3600 SJS 95111 854-J5
SINGLETREE WY
1500 SJS 95124 874-A6
1600 SJS 95118 874-A6
SINGLEY DR
300 MPS 95035 794-A5
SINNOTT LN
100 MPS 95035 814-A1
SIOUX LN
- LALT 94022 811-E6
400 SJS 95123 874-H5
SIOUX TR
20900 SCIC 95030 913-A2
SIOUX WY
- PTLV 94028 810-C6
SIPPOLA WY
1300 SJS 95121 854-J2
SIRINA CT
- SJS 95131 814-B5
SISKIYOU DR
900 MLPK 94025 790-C7
SISKIYOU PL
- MLPK 94025 790-C7
SITKA TER
1000 SUNV 94086 832-H2
SKALL DR
400 SJS 95111 854-J6
SKID RD
- SCrC 95076 955-A6
SKIPSTONE CT
400 SJS 95136 854-F7
SKOWHEGAN CT
100 SJS 95139 895-G1
SKY LN
14700 SCIC 95032 873-F7
SKYFARM CT
6500 SJS 95120 894-B1
SKYFARM DR
6500 SJS 95120 894-C1
SKYLAKE CT
1100 SUNV 94089 812-J4
SKYLARK DR
2400 SJS 95125 854-C6
SKYLARK LN
- SCrC 95003 (975-A7 See Page 955)
SKYLINE BLVD
18000 SCIC 95030 912-G4
SKYLINE BLVD Rt#-35
11700 SCIC 95030 851-A7
11700 SCrC 95030 871-B1
11700 SCrC 95030 892-A2
11800 SCrC 95030 871-D3
12300 SCIC 95070 871-F6
13000 SCrC 95070 892-A2
13500 SCIC 95030 892-D5
19000 SCrC 95030 912-E1
19300 SMCo 94020 830-A4
19300 PTLV 94028 830-A4
19800 SMCo 94028 830-C7
20800 SMCo 94028 850-E1
20800 SMCo 94028 850-E1
21100 SCIC 94028 850-E1
21200 PA 94304 850-H2
21600 SMCo 94304 850-H2
22800 SCrC 95030 850-J5
22800 SCIC 95030 850-J5
SKYLINE DR
1900 MPS 95035 814-E1
SKY MEADOW WY
6400 SJS 95135 855-J7
SKY OAKS WY
19500 SCIC 95030 872-F5
SKYPORT DR
- SJS 95110 833-H2
SKYVIEW CT
- SCrC 95030 913-C7
SKYVIEW DR
15200 SCIC 95132 814-H4
15200 SJS 95132 814-H4
SKYVIEW TER
15300 SCIC 95132 814-J4
23400 SCrC 95030 913-C7
SKYWALKER DR
- SJS 95135 876-A1
SKYWAY DR
200 SJS 95111 874-J1
300 SJS 95111 875-A1
800 SJS 95136 874-H1
SLADKY AV
800 MTVW 94040 811-G7
SLATER CT
3600 SJS 95132 814-F2
SLEEPER AV
100 MTVW 94040 831-J1
2100 MTVW 94040 832-A1
SLEEP VALLEY RD
15600 SCIC 95037 936-F5
SLEEPY CREEK DR
7200 SJS 95120 894-J4
SLEEPY CREEK WY
7200 SJS 95120 894-J4
SLEEPY HOLLOW LN
2300 SJS 95116 834-J5
SLEEPY MEADOW CT
1400 SJS 95121 855-D7
SLIDA DR
6300 SJS 95129 852-F4
SLOAT CT
300 SCL 95051 833-A7
SLOPEVIEW DR
3500 SJS 95148 835-E7
3700 SCIC 95148 835-E7
SLOPING MEADOW CT
6500 SJS 95135 855-J7
SMITH AV
900 CMBL 95008 853-B7
1700 SJS 95112 854-E2
SMITH RD
- SCrC 95076 (975-G5 See Page 955)
SMITH CREEK DR
100 LGTS 95030 873-A3
SMITHERS DR
2700 SJS 95148 855-C1
SMITHWOOD ST
- MPS 95035 793-J7
SMITTYS ST
23500 SCIC 95030 913-D6
SMOKE RIVER CT
4600 SJS 95136 874-E2
SMOKE TREE CT
100 SJS 95136 874-H1
SMOKE TREE WY
600 SUNV 94086 832-H2
SMOKEY CT
500 CMBL 95008 853-A7
SMYRNA CT
1100 SUNV 94087 832-D3
SNEAD DR
4600 SCL 95054 813-D4
SNECKNER CT
- SMCo 94025 810-F1
SNELL AV
3500 SJS 95136 854-G7
4000 SJS 95136 874-H1
4800 SCIC 95136 874-H1
5200 SJS 95123 874-J4
SNELL CT
200 SJS 95123 874-J3
26500 LAH 94022 811-B5
SNELL LN
26500 LAH 94022 811-B5
SNELL RD
16200 SCIC 95032 893-B2
16400 LGTS 95032 893-B2
SNELL WY
5600 SJS 95123 874-J5
SNIVELY AV
3300 SCL 95051 832-J4
SNOW DR
4700 SJS 95111 855-B7
4800 SJS 95111 875-B1
SNOW ST
1200 MTVW 94041 811-G5
SNOW TER
700 SJS 95111 855-B7
SNOWBANK CT
4100 SJS 95135 855-F3
SNOWBERRY CT
1100 SUNV 94087 832-D3
6100 SJS 95123 875-B6
SNOWDEN AV
- ATN 94027 790-D1
SNOWDEN PL
5500 SJS 95138 855-H7
5600 SJS 95138 875-H1
SNOWDEN WY
5600 SJS 95138 875-H1
SNYDER AV
- SBnC - (1017-B7 See Page 997)
400 SJS 95125 854-A2
SNYDER LN
400 MTVW 94043 812-B5
SOARES CT
3300 SCL 95051 832-J5
SOBEY RD
14100 SAR 95070 872-H2
SOBEY MEADOWS CT
14000 SAR 95070 872-H2
SOBEY OAKS CT
14500 SAR 95070 872-G3
SOBRANTE WY
200 SUNV 94086 812-D6
SOBRATO CT
600 CMBL 95008 853-C7
SOBRATO DR
600 CMBL 95008 853-C7
600 CMBL 95008 873-C1
SOBRATO LN
600 CMBL 95008 853-C7
SOBRATO WY
600 CMBL 95008 853-C7
SOCORRO AV
1100 SUNV 94089 812-J5
1100 SUNV 94089 813-A5
SODA SPRINGS RD
15300 SCIC 95030 913-F1
15400 SCIC 95030 893-C6
SOELRO CT
4000 SCIC 95127 815-B7
SOGOL CT
1900 SJS 95122 854-G2
SOGOL DR
- SJS 95122 854-G1
SOLA ST
20800 CPTO 95014 852-D1
SOLACE PL
2500 MTVW 94040 831-J1
SOLANA CT
900 MTVW 94040 811-F5
SOLANA DR
- LALT 94022 811-F6
1000 MTVW 94040 811-F6
4000 PA 94306 811-C2
9200 GIL 95020 957-F7
19600 SAR 95070 852-F6
SOLANA RD
100 PTLV 94028 810-B5
SOLANO CT
3300 SCL 95051 832-J5
SOLANO DR
6200 SJS 95119 875-C6
SOLAR CT
- MPS 95035 794-D6
SOLEDAD ST
9000 GIL 95020 977-F1
SOLERA DR
8600 SJS 95135 855-J6
SOLIS DR
1300 GIL 95020 977-F1
SOLIS RANCHO DR
4900 SCIC 95020 (976-H2 See Page 955)
SOLITA CT
700 LGTS 95030 873-A4
SOLITO CT
700 SJS 95123 874-G5
SOLOMON CT
6200 SJS 95123 875-B7
SOLTERO DR
5800 SJS 95123 874-F5
SOMERSET CT
1900 LALT 94024 831-H5
10300 CPTO 95014 852-E1
SOMERSET DR
800 SUNV 94087 832-C3
1100 SJS 95132 814-G5
20000 CPTO 95014 852-E1
SOMERSET LN
- ATN 94027 790-D4
SOMERSET PL
- PA 94301 791-A4
SOMERSET PARK CIR
2600 SJS 95132 814-F5
SOMERSWORTH DR
1900 SJS 95124 853-G7
SOMERVILLE CT
19700 SAR 95070 852-F5
SOMERVILLE DR
19500 SAR 95070 852-F5
SONATA WY
4500 SJS 95111 855-A7
SONDRA WY
100 CMBL 95008 853-C5
SONG CT
1100 SJS 95131 834-D1
SONGROTH WY
13400 LAH 94022 810-J7
SONI CT
600 SJS 95116 834-H4
SONIA WY
600 MTVW 94040 811-H6
SONNET CT
1800 SJS 95131 814-C4
SONOMA AV
- ATN 94027 790-H1
1000 MLPK 94025 790-H1
SONOMA DR
1400 MPS 95035 814-D1
SONOMA PL
2600 SCL 95051 833-B5
SONOMA ST
100 SJS 95110 834-A7
SONOMA TER
800 SCIC 94305 810-J1
SONORA AV
- SJS 95110 833-H3
SONORA CT
1100 SUNV 94086 832-H1
SONUCA AV
900 CMBL 95008 873-C1
SOPHIA WY
4100 SJS 95134 813-D2
SOPHIST DR
3800 SJS 95132 815-A4
SOQUEL WY
300 SUNV 94086 812-E6
SORCI DR
3600 SJS 95124 874-A2
SORENSON AV
19300 CPTO 95014 852-G1
SORGEPARK PL
200 SJS 95127 834-H1
SORICH RD
- SCrC 95030 850-J6
- SMCo 94020 850-G6
SORREL AV
5900 SJS 95123 874-J6
SORREL DR
- MGH 95037 917-F6
SORREL WY
16600 MGH 95037 917-E6
SORRENTO CT
1900 MTVW 94040 831-H1
SORRENTO WY
200 SJS 95119 875-C6
SOTERION DR
1600 SJS 95118 873-J5
SOTO CT
1300 SJS 95121 854-J2
SOUSA LN
13300 SAR 95070 872-H1
SOUTH CT
2200 PA 94301 791-C7
2600 PA 94306 791-C7
3200 PA 94306 811-D1
SOUTH DR
100 MTVW 94040 831-H1
2300 SCL 95051 833-C2
SOUTH PZ
- MLPK 94025 790-J2
SOUTH ST
- SCIC 95046 937-F7
SOUTHAMPTON CT
3600 SJS 95148 835-G7
SOUTHAMPTON DR
700 PA 94303 791-B5
SOUTHBAY DR
300 SJS 95134 813-D2
SOUTHBAY FRWY Rt#-237
- MPS - 813-C1
- SCL - 813-C1
- SCIC - 813-C1
- SJS - 813-C1
- SUNV - 812-D4
- SUNV - 813-C1
SOUTH BREEZE CT
5900 SJS 95138 875-E5
SOUTHBRIDGE CT
5200 SJS 95118 874-C4
SOUTHBRIDGE PL
5200 SJS 95118 874-C4
SOUTHBROOK CT
5900 SJS 95138 875-E5
SOUTHBROOK DR
- SJS 95138 875-E5
SOUTHCREEK CT
- SJS 95138 875-E5
SOUTHCREST WY
5500 SCIC 95123 874-G4
5500 SJS 95123 874-G4
SOUTHFIELD CT
- SJS 95138 875-E5
SOUTH FORK LN
13400 LAH 94022 810-J7
SOUTH GARDEN CT
5900 SJS 95138 875-F5
SOUTHGATE CT
- SJS 95138 875-E5
100 GIL 95020 978-A4
SOUTHGATE DR
- WDSD 94062 790-A5
SOUTHGATE ST
- ATN 94027 790-D2
SOUTHGROVE DR
700 SJS 95133 834-F1
700 SJS 95133 814-H3
SOUTHGROVE LN
2300 SJS 95133 814-H3
SOUTHLAKE CT
- SJS 95138 875-E5
SOUTHLAKE DR
- SJS 95138 875-E5
SOUTHMAR CT
- SJS 95138 875-E5
SOUTHMONT CT
5900 SJS 95138 875-E5
SOUTHOAKS CT
5900 SJS 95138 875-E5
SOUTH PARK LN
2400 SCL 95051 833-B1
SOUTHPINE CT
- SJS 95138 875-E5
SOUTHPINE DR
5700 SJS 95138 875-E5
SOUTHPORT CT
- SJS 95138 875-E5
SOUTHRIDGE CT
5900 SJS 95138 875-E5
SOUTHSEA CT
- SJS 95138 875-E5
SOUTHSHORE CT
11600 CPTO 95014 852-C4
SOUTHSIDE AV
500 GIL 95020 978-C6
600 SCIC 95020 978-D6
SOUTHSIDE DR
- SCIC 95111 854-H5
- SJS 95111 854-H5
SOUTHSUN CT
100 SJS 95138 875-E4
SOUTH SURF CT
5900 SJS 95138 875-E5
SOUTH TERRACE CT
- SJS 95138 875-E5
SOUTH VALLEY FRWY U.S.-101
- GIL - 958-A7
- GIL - 978-A1
- MGH - 917-A4
- MGH - 916-H1
- MGH - 937-D2
- SCIC - 957-H1
- SCIC - 896-B3
- SCIC - 917-A4
- SCIC - 916-H1
- SCIC - 937-D2
- SCIC - 875-D4
- SCIC - 978-B6
- SJS - 896-B3
- SJS - 916-H1
- SJS - 875-D4
SOUTHVIEW CT
100 SJS 95138 875-E4
SOUTHVIEW DR
5700 SJS 95138 875-E5
SOUTHWEST EXWY
600 SJS 95126 853-G4
1700 SJS 95128 853-G4
SOUTHWICK CT
5100 SJS 95136 874-F3
SOUTHWIND DR
5800 SJS 95138 875-E5
SOUTHWOOD AV
400 SUNV 94086 832-E1
SOUTHWOOD DR
100 PA 94301 791-B3
1300 SJS 95129 853-A4
1300 SJS 95130 853-A4
SPACE PARK DR
1100 SCL 95054 813-D7
SPACE PARK WY
- MTVW 94043 812-A1
1200 MTVW 94043 811-J1
SPADAFORE AV
900 SJS 95125 854-D7
SPADAFORE CT
900 SJS 95125 854-C6
SPAGNOLI CT
300 LALT 94022 811-D5
SPAICH DR
1100 SJS 95117 853-C4
SPALDING AV
- SUNV 94087 832-E3
23900 SCIC 94024 831-E3
SPANISH BAY CT
1900 SJS 95138 855-F7
SPANISHGATE CT
2100 SJS 95132 814-D3

STREET
Block City ZIP Pg-Grid

SPANISH OAK CT
10000 CPTO 95014 831-J6
SPANISH RANCH RD
24000 SCrC 95030 934-A3
SPAR AV
300 SCIC 95117 853-D1
300 SJS 95117 853-D1
SPARGUR DR
500 LALT 94022 811-F6
SPARHAWK DR
600 MGH 95037 916-H6
SPARHAWK WY
18200 MGH 95037 916-H6
SPARKLING WY
1600 SJS 95125 853-J5
SPARROW CT
- EPA 94303 791-C2
1600 SUNV 94087 832-H5
SPARTAN CT
500 SJS 95112 854-E1
SPEAK LN
4800 SJS 95118 874-C2
SPECIALE WY
1100 SJS 95125 854-C7
SPENCE AV
100 MPS 95035 793-J7
SPENCER AV
700 SJS 95125 854-B1
16800 LGTS 95032 873-C7
SPENCER CT
700 MTVW 94040 831-G1
700 LALT 94024 831-G1
9000 GIL 95020 977-H1
SPENCER LN
- ATN 94027 790-E3
SPENCER WY
900 LALT 94024 831-G2
SPENO DR
3400 SJS 95117 853-C4
SPERRY LN
15000 SAR 95070 872-H4
SPICEWOOD CT
700 SJS 95120 894-H3
SPINDRIFT AV
700 SJS 95134 813-F2
SPINDRIFT DR
700 SJS 95134 813-F2
SPINDRIFT LN
800 SJS 95134 813-F2
SPINDRIFT PL
700 SJS 95134 813-F2
SPINDRIFT ST
700 SJS 95134 813-F2
SPINDRIFT WY
700 SJS 95134 813-F2
SPINNAKER DR
- FRMT 94538 793-F1
5500 SJS 95123 874-J4
SPINNAKER WALKWAY
5400 SJS 95123 874-J4
SPINOSA DR
800 SUNV 94087 832-D3
SPIRO DR
1100 SJS 95116 834-F6
SPIROS WY
- SMCo 94025 790-D5
SPODE WY
300 SJS 95123 875-B6
SPOKANE CT
48500 FRMT 94539 793-J2
SPOKANE DR
1100 SJS 95122 854-H1
SPOKANE PL
48600 FRMT 94539 793-J1
SPOKANE RD
- FRMT 94539 793-J2
SPONSON CT
6300 SJS 95123 875-B7
SPONSON LN
6200 SJS 95123 875-B7
SPOONBILL WY
1300 SUNV 94087 832-H4
SPOONWOOD CT
4200 SJS 95136 874-H1
SPOSITO CIR
200 SJS 95136 874-G1
SPRAWLING OAKS CT
20500 SCIC 95120 895-A5
SPRECKELS AV
100 LGTS 95032 893-B1
SPRECKLES AV
1200 SJS 95002 793-C6
SPRIERING DR
1500 CMBL 95008 873-E2
SPRIG CT
1300 SUNV 94087 832-H4
SPRIG WY
- GIL 95020 957-F7
SPRING AV
- MGH 95037 936-J2

SPRING AV
- SCIC 95046 937-F6
- SCIC 95037 936-J2
200 SCIC 95037 937-A1
200 MGH 95037 937-A1
SPRING DR
100 SJS 95138 875-C4
SPRING LN
- MGH 95037 937-C5
SPRING RD
30000 SCIC 95140 837-D3
SPRING ST
- LGTS 95032 893-B1
400 SJS 95110 834-A5
500 SJS 95110 833-J4
1500 MTVW 94043 811-H2
SPRING TR
18200 SCIC 95030 912-G4
SPRING BLOSSOM CT
20500 SAR 95070 852-D6
SPRINGBROOK AV
3500 SJS 95148 835-F7
3700 SCIC 95148 835-F7
SPRINGBROOK CT
2900 SJS 95148 835-F7
SPRINGBROOK LN
19000 SAR 95070 872-H3
SPRING CREEK LN
3400 SCIC 95035 794-G5
SPRINGDALE CT
8000 GIL 95020 978-A1
SPRINGDALE DR
4800 SJS 95129 852-J2
SPRINGER AV
14200 SAR 95070 872-D2
SPRINGER CT
14600 SAR 95070 872-D3
SPRINGER RD
- MTVW 94040 811-G7
- LALT 94024 811-G7
600 MTVW 94040 831-G1
600 LALT 94024 831-G1
SPRINGER TER
500 LALT 94024 811-F7
SPRINGER WY
6000 SJS 95123 875-B6
SPRINGFIELD DR
1000 SJS 95130 853-B5
3900 CMBL 95008 853-B5
SPRINGFIELD TER
800 SUNV 94087 832-C3
SPRINGFIELD WY
3100 SJS 95111 854-H5
SPRING GARDEN DR
2900 SJS 95127 834-H1
SPRING GROVE DR
900 SJS 95126 853-J3
SPRING GROVE RD
300 SBnC - (1020-E2
See Page 999)
SPRINGHAVEN CT
- SJS 95111 875-A1
SPRING HILL CT
16700 MGH 95037 936-J1
SPRINGHILL CT
13600 SAR 95070 872-H1
SPRING HILL DR
300 MGH 95037 936-J2
SPRINGHILL DR
25800 LAH 94022 811-C5
SPRING HILL WY
900 SJS 95120 894-F4
SPRINGHILL WY
- MGH 95037 916-H3
SPRINGKNOLL CT
3000 SCIC 95127 835-G3
SPRING MEADOW CT
6400 SJS 95135 855-J7
SPRINGPARK CIR
300 SJS 95136 874-G1
SPRINGPATH LN
6500 SJS 95120 894-B1
SPRINGSONG DR
1700 SJS 95131 834-D1
1700 SJS 95131 814-D7
SPRING VALLEY AV
13400 SCIC 95037 956-J1
13600 SCIC 95037 936-J7
SPRING VALLEY LN
200 MPS 95035 794-D5
SPRINGVIEW LN
3100 SCIC 95127 835-G3
SPRINGWOOD DR
600 SJS 95129 852-J2
SPROUL CT
6400 SJS 95120 894-E1
SPRUANCE CT
1300 SJS 95128 853-F4
SPRUANCE ST
1100 SJS 95128 853-F3

SPRUCE
900 SJS 95138 875-F6
SPRUCE AV
- ATN 94025 790-E2
- MLPK 94025 790-E2
SPRUCE CT
1300 GIL 95020 977-G3
SPRUCE DR
600 SUNV 94086 832-H2
SPRUCE ST
600 SJS 95110 834-A5
SPRUCEGATE CT
3200 SJS 95148 855-E1
SPRUCE HILL CT
100 LGTS 95030 873-C3
SPRUCEMONT PL
100 SJS 95139 895-F1
SPRUCE ROCK ST
3400 SJS 95121 855-D3
SPRUCEWOOD DR
1300 SJS 95118 874-B4
SPUR CT
2400 MGH 95037 917-F6
SPYGLASS HILL RD
100 SJS 95127 815-B6
SQUAREHAVEN CT
- SJS 95111 874-J1
SQUERI DR
3400 SJS 95127 835-C3
SQUIRECREEK CIR
3300 SJS 95121 855-D7
SQUIRECREEK LN
1500 SJS 95121 855-D7
SQUIREDELL DR
6100 SJS 95129 852-F4
SQUIREHILL CT
7700 CPTO 95014 852-C3
SQUIREWOOD WY
7500 CPTO 95014 852-D3
SQUIRREL HOLLOW LN
14100 SAR 95070 872-E2
STAATS WY
2000 SCL 95050 833-C3
STACEY CT
3400 MTVW 94040 831-J2
STACIA DR
2700 SJS 95124 873-J1
STACIA ST
- LGTS 95032 893-B1
STAFFORD DR
1100 CPTO 95014 852-C3
STAFFORD ST
1900 SCL 95050 833-D4
STAGECOACH RD
21200 SCrC 95030 912-J4
STAGEHAND DR
200 SJS 95111 875-B2
STAGHORN CT
1600 SJS 95121 855-A3
STAGHORN LN
1500 SJS 95121 855-A3
STAGI CT
900 LALT 94024 831-E2
STAGI LN
800 LALT 94024 831-E1
STAGIA LN
23400 SCIC 95030 913-C6
STAHL ST
1300 SJS 95122 834-H5
STALLION WY
2800 SJS 95121 855-A3
STAMM AV
600 MTVW 94040 811-H6
STANDER DR
3200 SJS 95148 855-F1
STANDING OAK CT
22900 CPTO 95014 851-J1
STANDISH DR
14500 SCIC 95124 873-G3
STANDRIDGE CT
6400 SJS 95123 875-B7
STANFIELD DR
600 CMBL 95008 853-F7
600 SJS 95008 853-F7
STANFORD AV
- SCIC 94304 810-F2
100 SMCo 94025 790-E6
200 PA 94306 791-A7
500 SCIC - 791-A7
600 MLPK 94025 790-E6
1000 SCIC 94305 811-F3
1000 PA 94306 811-F3
1100 SCIC 94305 810-J2
1100 PA 94306 810-J2
2100 MTVW 94040 811-F3
STANFORD CT
900 MLPK 94025 790-E5
14100 LAH 94022 810-H5
STANFORD PL
2300 SCL 95051 833-A2

STANFORD PL
7400 CPTO 95014 852-D3
STANFORD ST
- WAT 95076 995-G7
STANHOPE CT
1500 SJS 95121 855-A3
STANHOPE DR
2800 SJS 95121 855-A3
STANISLAUS CT
2300 SJS 95133 834-F1
STANISLAUS DR
700 SJS 95133 834-F1
STANLEY AV
900 LALT 94024 831-G2
1900 SCL 95050 833-D6
STANLEY CT
6000 SJS 95123 875-B6
STANLEY WY
900 PA 94303 791-B4
STANTON WY
1300 SJS 95131 814-C7
STANWICH RD
1600 SJS 95131 814-D5
STANWIRTH CT
1200 LALT 94024 831-J3
STANWOOD DR
1300 SJS 95118 874-B4
STAPLES AV
100 SCIC 95127 834-J1
300 SCIC 95127 814-J7
STAPLETON CT
1500 SJS 95118 874-A5
STARBIRD CIR
1100 SJS 95117 853-C3
STARBRIGHT DR
2200 SJS 95124 873-E2
STARBUSH DR
600 SUNV 94086 832-H2
STAR BUSH LN
1300 SJS 95118 874-B5
STARCREST DR
5400 SJS 95123 874-F3
STARDUST CT
1400 SCL 95050 833-D3
STARDUST LN
500 LALT 94024 811-F7
700 SJS 95123 874-F4
STARDUST WY
1100 MPS 95035 813-J2
STARFISH CT
2000 SJS 95148 835-B5
STARFLOWER CT
900 SUNV 94086 832-G3
STARGLO PL
1100 SJS 95131 814-B6
STAR JASMINE CT
- SJS 95131 814-B5
STARK WY
1400 SJS 95118 874-B2
STARLIGHT CT
700 SJS 95117 853-D2
STARLING DR
6000 GIL 95020 977-J6
22200 SCIC 94024 832-A6
22400 CPTO 95014 832-A6
22400 CPTO 94024 832-A6
STARLING RIDGE CT
1100 SJS 95120 894-F3
STARLING VALLEY DR
7000 SJS 95120 894-E3
STARLING VIEW DR
1100 SJS 95120 894-E3
STARLITE CT
- MTVW 94043 811-J3
400 MPS 95035 813-J3
48000 FRMT 94539 793-J1
STARLITE DR
1000 MPS 95035 813-J3
1600 MPS 95035 814-A3
STARLITE LN
800 LALT 94024 831-E1
STARLITE WY
100 FRMT 94539 793-J1
STARR CT
600 SCL 95051 833-B6
STARR LN
2100 SCIC 95020 978-F5
STARR WY
- MTVW 94040 811-H7
STARRETT CT
18600 SCIC 95014 852-H2
STAR RIDGE CT
12600 SAR 95070 852-C6
STARR KING CIR
3700 PA 94306 811-D1
STARS & STRIPES DR
5100 SCL 95054 813-B3
STARSWEPT LN
14800 SCIC 95037 937-D4
14900 SCIC 95046 937-D4

STARSWEPT LN
14900 MGH 95046 937-D4
STARVIEW DR
3700 SJS 95124 873-E3
STARWOOD CT
1100 SJS 95120 874-C6
STARWOOD DR
5900 SJS 95120 874-C6
STARWOOD PL
1100 SJS 95120 874-C6
STATE ST
- LALT 94022 811-D7
700 SJS 95110 854-C1
1200 SJS 95002 793-B7
STAUFFER BLVD
100 SJS 95125 854-D3
STAUFFER LN
11200 CPTO 95014 852-C4
STAUNTON CT
2100 PA 94306 791-A7
STAYNER RD
1200 SJS 95121 855-B5
STEBBINS AV
2100 SCL 95051 833-B2
STEEPLECHASE LN
1100 CPTO 95014 852-D3
STEFFS CT
12100 SCIC 95046 937-J7
12100 SCIC 95046 957-J1
STEINBAUGH CT
3800 SJS 95132 814-J4
STEINBECK DR
800 SJS 95123 874-E4
STEINHART CT
2800 SCL 95051 833-B6
STEINWAY AV
800 CMBL 95008 873-B1
STEITZ CT
900 SJS 95116 834-H5
STELLA CT
800 SUNV 94087 832-D2
6000 SJS 95123 875-A6
STELLA RD
- CPTO 95014 851-J2
STELLAR WY
1100 MPS 95035 814-A2
STELLING CT
3000 PA 94303 791-D6
STELLING DR
3000 PA 94303 791-D6
STELLING RD
800 CPTO 95014 852-D1
1000 SCIC 95014 852-D1
10000 CPTO 95014 832-D7
10100 SCIC 95014 832-D7
STEMEL CT
600 MPS 95035 794-C5
STEMEL WY
1300 MPS 95035 794-C5
STEMPLE CT
2800 SJS 95121 855-A2
STENDER WY
2200 SCL 95054 813-B7
STENDHAL LN
600 CPTO 95014 852-G2
STEPHANIE CT
3200 SJS 95132 814-F3
STEPHEN CT
6600 GIL 95020 978-A5
STEPHEN PL
6600 GIL 95020 978-A5
STEPHEN WY
1300 SJS 95129 852-G4
STEPHENIE LN
15900 LGTS 95032 873-D6
STERLING AV
2000 SMCo 94025 790-D6
STERLING BLVD
10100 SCIC 95014 852-H2
STERLING GATE CT
7000 SJS 95120 894-G4
STERLING GATE DR
1000 SJS 95120 894-G4
STERLING OAKS DR
5900 SJS 95120 874-C6
STERN AV
700 PA 94303 791-D6
10000 CPTO 95014 852-H1
10000 SJS 95014 852-H1
10000 SCIC 95014 852-H1
STERN LN
- ATN 94027 790-C4
STEUBEN DR
700 SUNV 94087 832-C3
STEVAL PL
3500 SJS 95136 874-D1
STEVENS CIR
800 SCIC 94043 812-A2
STEVENS CT
600 SCIC 95046 957-D1

STEVENS CT
1300 CMBL 95008 873-C2
3100 SJS 95148 855-E1
STEVENS LN
2900 SJS 95148 855-D1
STEVENS PL
1600 LALT 94024 832-A5
STEVENS RD
400 SCIC 94043 812-A2
STEVENS WY
800 SCIC 94043 812-A2
STEVENS CANYON RD
- SCIC 95030 851-D6
- SCIC 95030 871-F1
- SCIC 95070 871-F1
10700 CPTO 95014 851-J3
12800 SCIC 95014 851-H4
17900 SCIC 95014 871-F1
STEVENS CREEK BLVD
3100 SJS 95128 853-B1
3100 SJS 95050 853-B1
3200 SCL 95050 853-B1
3400 SCL 95117 853-B1
3400 SJS 95117 853-B1
3600 SCL 95051 853-B1
3800 SJS 95129 853-B1
4900 SJS 95129 852-E1
4900 SCL 95051 852-E1
5400 SJS 95014 852-E1
18700 SCL 95014 852-E1
18900 CPTO 95014 852-E1
18900 SCIC 95014 852-E1
22500 CPTO 95014 851-J1
23200 SCIC 95014 851-J1
23200 SCIC 95014 831-H7
STEVENS CREEK FRWY Rt#-85
- CPTO - 832-A1
- LALT - 832-A1
- MTVW - 812-A7
- MTVW - 832-A1
- SCIC - 832-A1
- SUNV - 832-A1
STEVENSON LN
- ATN 94027 790-D3
STEVENSON ST
2800 SCL 95051 833-A6
STEVICK DR
300 ATN 94027 790-B5
STEWART AV
- SJS 95127 834-J2
- SCIC 95127 834-J2
STEWART CT
1100 SUNV 94087 812-H6
13100 SAR 95070 852-D7
STEWART DR
800 SUNV 94086 812-G6
STEWART RD
- SCIC 95030 913-B1
STIERLIN CT
2000 MTVW 94043 812-A1
2000 MTVW 94043 811-J1
STIERLIN RD
100 MTVW 94043 811-J4
STILES WY
10500 SCIC 95127 815-B7
STILLWATER LN
100 SJS 95139 895-F1
STIMSON WY
3100 SJS 95135 855-F3
STIRLING DR
600 MPS 95035 794-A3
STIRRUP WY
27700 LAH 94022 810-J5
STOCKBRIDGE AV
- ATN 94027 790-C3
- SMCo 94061 790-C3
2100 WDSD 94062 790-C3
STOCKBRIDGE DR
1300 SJS 95130 853-B4
STOCK FARM RD
- SCIC 94305 790-F6
STOCKLMEIR CT
22000 CPTO 95014 852-A1
STOCKTON AV
- SJS 95126 834-A6
100 SJS 95126 833-J5
800 SJS 95110 833-H4
STOCKTON PL
3100 PA 94303 791-E6
STOESSER CT
7100 SJS 95120 894-G4
STOKES AV
10200 CPTO 95014 832-B6
STOKES ST
1400 CMBL 95128 853-F4
1400 SJS 95128 853-F4
1800 SJS 95126 853-G4
STONE AV
1700 SJS 95125 854-D3

STONE AV
2100 SCIC 95125 854-D3
STONE CT
400 SJS 95125 854-C3
STONE LN
700 PA 94303 791-E7
STONE TR
18200 SCIC 95030 912-G4
STONEBRIDGE
22700 CPTO 95014 851-J1
STONEBRIDGE CT
14600 SCIC 95037 937-A6
STONEBRIDGE DR
14700 SCIC 95037 937-A6
STONEBROOK CT
12300 LAH 94022 831-C2
STONEBROOK DR
10900 LAH 94024 831-D3
10900 SCIC 94024 831-D3
10900 LAH 94022 831-C3
STONE CANYON DR
4300 SJS 95136 874-H1
STONE CREEK DR
1400 SJS 95132 814-F3
1600 SCIC 95132 814-F3
STONECREST WY
2700 SJS 95133 814-G6
STONEFIELD CT
700 SJS 95136 854-F7
STONEGATE CIR
200 SJS 95125 854-D3
STONE GATE CT
1000 MGH 95037 937-A4
STONEGATE RD
- PTLV 94028 810-B6
STONEGLEN CT
900 SJS 95122 854-G2
STONEHAVEN DR
2000 LALT 94024 831-H5
STONEHEDGE CT
10200 SCIC 95127 835-A3
STONEHEDGE WY
10000 SCIC 95127 835-A3
STONEHILL CT
6500 SJS 95120 874-F7
STONEHILL DR
6500 SJS 95120 874-F7
STONEHURST DR
800 SCIC 95008 853-F7
800 SCIC 95008 873-F1
STONEMAG WY
600 SJS 95127 814-J6
STONE PINE CT
2000 SCL 95050 833-C3
STONE PINE LN
100 MLPK 94025 790-E3
STONERIDGE DR
14600 SAR 95070 872-C3
STONESHIRE CT
7600 SJS 95135 856-A6
STONEWOOD LN
1900 SJS 95132 814-E2
STONEY CT
500 GIL 95020 978-B3
STONEYHAVEN WY
4400 SJS 95111 874-J1
STONYBROOK RD
100 LGTS 95032 873-C7
STONYDALE DR
10100 CPTO 95014 832-A7
STONYLAKE CT
1100 SUNV 94089 812-J5
STOREY RD
300 SCrC 95076 (975-B7
See Page 955)
STORY CT
1300 SJS 95127 835-C3
STORY LN
3300 SJS 95127 835-C3
3300 SCIC 95127 835-C3
STORY RD
1200 SJS 95122 834-F7
1600 SJS 95116 834-H5
2700 SJS 95127 834-J5
3500 SJS 95127 835-B2
4000 SCIC 95127 835-B2
7500 SCIC 95127 835-B2
STORY BOOK LN
1100 SJS 95116 834-E5
STORY HILL LN
28000 LAH 94022 810-H7
STOVER ST
500 SJS 95110 834-A7
STOWE AV
1800 SJS 95116 834-F4
STOWE CT
- SMCo 94025 810-F1
STOWE LN
- SMCo 94025 810-E1

STOWELL AV
300 SUNV 94086 812-E6
STRATA ALMADEN
1100 SJS 95120 874-D6
STRATFORD AV
2200 SCIC 95124 873-F3
15000 SJS 95124 873-E3
STRATFORD CT
100 MTVW 94040 831-J1
15000 MSER 95030 872-H4
STRATFORD DR
1800 MPS 95035 794-B2
STRATFORD PL
- GIL 95020 978-A5
200 LALT 94022 811-D6
STRATFORD PK CT
400 SJS 95136 874-F2
STRATHMORE PL
100 LGTS 95030 873-B3
STRATTON PL
2100 SJS 95131 814-D6
STRAUSS WY
1300 SJS 95132 814-F5
STRAWBERRY CT
1100 SUNV 94087 832-D3
STRAWBERRY LN
500 SJS 95129 853-B2
1700 MPS 95035 794-D6
8400 GIL 95020 977-D1
STRAWBERRY PARK DR
4200 SJS 95129 853-A2
4700 SJS 95129 852-J2
STRAWFLOWER LN
5600 SJS 95118 874-B5
STRAYER DR
1000 SJS 95129 852-G3
STRELOW CT
6100 SJS 95120 874-C7
STRICKROTH DR
700 MPS 95035 794-A5
STROTMAN CT
9400 SCIC 95020 958-E4
STROUD PL
400 SJS 95111 854-H6
STRUZENBURG CT
13500 SCIC 95037 956-H1
STUART CT
- LALT 94022 811-E6
STUART DR
7500 GIL 95020 977-G4
STUBBINS WY
1400 SJS 95132 814-E4
STUCKEY DR
4900 SJS 95124 873-G4
STUDEBAKER CIR
5300 SJS 95123 874-H3
STUDENT LN
4500 SJS 95130 853-A5
STULMAN DR
300 MPS 95035 794-D7
STURGEON WY
1300 SJS 95129 852-G4
STURLA DR
2400 SJS 95148 855-C1
STUTZ WY
400 GIL 95020 978-B4
2900 SJS 95148 855-D1
SUDBURY CT
100 MPS 95035 794-A5
SUDBURY DR
- MPS 95035 794-A5
SUE AV
2500 SJS 95111 854-G3
SUENO DR
3200 SJS 95148 835-D6
SUFFOLK CT
1100 LALT 94024 831-H2
SUFFOLK DR
1300 SJS 95127 835-A5
SUFFOLK WY
1000 LALT 94024 831-H2
SUFONET DR
2100 SJS 95124 873-F4
SUGAR BABE DR
9400 SCIC 95020 958-D4
SUGARCREEK CT
3400 SJS 95121 855-D7
SUGARCREEK DR
3400 SJS 95121 855-D7
SUGAR MAPLE DR
100 SJS 95136 874-H1
SUGARPINE AV
800 SUNV 94086 832-H3
SUGAR PINE CT
2800 SJS 95121 855-E3
SUGARPLUM DR
2500 SJS 95148 835-D7
SUISSE DR
400 SJS 95123 874-J6

SUISUN AV
2500 SJS 95121 855-D3
SUISUN DR
20000 CPTO 95014 852-E2
SULLIVAN AV
1900 SJS 95122 834-H6
SULLIVAN CT
1800 MGH 95037 917-B3
SULLIVAN DR
500 MTVW 94041 812-A7
3700 SCL 95051 832-H7
SULLIVAN WY
20900 SAR 95070 872-C2
SULPHUR SPRING CT
3000 SJS 95148 855-E1
SULTAN PL
5400 SJS 95123 875-B3
SULTANA DR
1000 SJS 95122 854-G1
SULU CT
6400 SJS 95119 875-C7
SUMAC DR
1000 MPS 95035 813-H2
1000 SUNV 94086 832-G3
SUMATRA AV
1800 SJS 95122 834-H7
SUMBA CT
200 SJS 95123 874-J3
SUMMER CIR
200 MGH 95037 937-B5
SUMMER CT
2300 SJS 95116 834-H4
SUMMER DR
100 SJS 95138 875-D4
SUMMER PL
5600 SJS 95138 875-D4
SUMMER ST
2300 SJS 95116 834-H4
SUMMERAIN CT
1000 SJS 95122 854-F2
SUMMERBROOK CT
5700 SJS 95123 874-E4
SUMMERBROOK LN
800 SJS 95123 874-E4
SUMMER CREEK DR
3100 SJS 95136 854-D7
SUMMERDALE DR
1000 SJS 95132 814-F6
SUMMERDAYS CT
2800 SJS 95132 814-F6
SUMMER EVE CT
2200 SJS 95122 854-G1
SUMMERFIELD DR
- CMBL 95008 853-A7
900 SJS 95121 854-H4
SUMMERGARDEN CT
1000 SJS 95132 814-G6
SUMMERHEIGHTS DR
2700 SJS 95132 814-F6
SUMMERHILL AV
24000 LAH 94024 831-E2
24000 SCIC 94024 831-E2
24700 LALT 94024 831-E2
SUMMERHILL CT
3000 SJS 95148 855-G1
12700 SCIC 94024 831-E2
SUMMERLAND DR
400 SJS 95134 813-C2
SUMMERLEAF DR
900 SJS 95120 894-G1
SUMMERLEAF PL
900 SJS 95120 894-G1
SUMMERMIST CT
1000 SJS 95122 854-G2
SUMMERPARK CT
1000 SJS 95132 814-F6
SUMMERPLACE DR
900 SCIC 95122 854-G1
SUMMERSHORE CT
1000 SJS 95122 854-F2
SUMMERSIDE DR
900 SJS 95122 854-G2
900 SCIC 95122 854-G2
SUMMERSONG CT
1000 SJS 95132 814-G6
SUMMERTON DR
2100 SJS 95122 854-G2
SUMMERTREE CT
1000 SJS 95132 814-F6
SUMMERVIEW DR
1000 SJS 95132 814-F6
SUMMERWIND CT
1000 SJS 95132 814-F6
SUMMERWIND DR
100 MPS 95035 793-J5
SUMMERWIND WY
1100 MPS 95035 793-J5
SUMMERWINGS CT
1000 SJS 95132 814-F6

SUMMERWOOD CT
1000 SJS 95132 814-F6
SUMMIT AV
5200 SCIC 95127 814-J7
SUMMIT CT
800 SUNV 94087 832-D2
SUMMIT RD
- SCIC 95030 934-G5
- SCIC 95037 (976-B1
See Page 955)
- SCrC 95076 (976-B1
See Page 955)
100 SCIC 95037 956-A7
100 SCrC 95076 956-A7
200 SCIC 95037 955-A1
200 SCrC 95076 955-A1
900 SCrC 95030 955-A1
900 SCIC 95037 935-A6
900 SCrC 95030 935-A6
21000 SCIC 95037 934-G5
21000 SCrC 95030 934-G5
22300 SCIC 95030 912-H4
22400 SCrC 95030 913-A4
22500 SCrC 95030 913-A4
SUMMIT RD Rt#-35
21000 SCrC 95030 912-F2
21200 SCIC 95030 912-F2
SUMMIT WY
17000 LGTS 95030 873-B4
SUMMIT RIDGE CT
3600 SJS 95148 835-G7
SUMMIT VIEW TER
- FRMT 94539 794-B1
SUMMIT WOOD CT
11500 LAH 94022 831-C3
SUMMIT WOOD RD
11400 LAH 94022 831-B3
SUMNER DR
12400 SAR 95070 852-E6
SUN CT
1100 MPS 95035 814-A2
SUN LN
1500 SJS 95132 814-F3
SUNBEAM CIR
1300 SJS 95122 834-G6
SUNBERRY DR
200 CMBL 95008 853-D5
SUN BLOSSOM DR
100 SJS 95123 875-A3
SUNBROOK CT
3700 SJS 95111 855-A6
SUNBURST DR
2900 SJS 95111 854-G5
SUNCREST AV
3300 SJS 95132 814-H5
3800 SJS 95132 815-A4
SUND AV
- SCIC 95032 893-B1
100 LGTS 95032 893-B1
SUNDANCE DR
16800 MGH 95037 917-E6
SUNDANCE LN
200 SCrC 95076 (975-H5
See Page 955)
SUNDERLAND DR
7900 CPTO 95014 852-C3
SUNDOWN LN
1200 SJS 95127 835-A4
SUNDOWN CANYON W
10500 LAH 94024 831-E5
SUNFLOWER CIR
2400 GIL 95020 977-D1
SUNFLOWER LN
5600 SJS 95118 874-B5
SUN GLORY LN
2200 SJS 95124 873-F1
SUNHILL
- PTLV 94028 830-C2
SUNHILLS DR
16400 SCIC 94024 831-F5
SUNKEN GARDENS TE
900 SUNV 94086 832-G3
SUNKIST CT
300 LALT 94022 811-F5
SUNKIST LN
- LALT 94022 811-F6
SUNLAND CT
1400 SJS 95130 853-A4
SUNLITE DR
800 SCL 95050 833-C5
SUNMOR AV
1900 MTVW 94040 832-A1
SUNNY CT
1100 SJS 95116 834-F5
SUNNYARBOR CT
800 CMBL 95008 873-C1
SUNNYBROOK CT
400 CMBL 95008 853-D7
14500 MGH 95037 937-C
18900 SAR 95070 852-H

STREET
Block City ZIP Pg-Grid

SUNNYBROOK DR
400 CMBL 95008 853-C7
SUNNY CREEK DR
5100 SJS 95135 855-G5
SUNNY CREEK PL
5100 SJS 95135 855-G5
SUNNYCREST CIR
1300 SJS 95122 854-H1
SUNNYDALE CT
3500 SJS 95117 853-C3
SUNNYDAYS LN
3500 SCL 95051 832-J3
SUNNYGATE CT
3500 SJS 95117 853-C3
SUNNYGLEN DR
2500 SJS 95122 835-A6
SUNNYHAVEN DR
1100 SJS 95117 853-C3
SUNNYHILLS CT
100 MPS 95035 793-J4
SUNNYHILLS DR
1600 MPS 95035 793-J3
SUNNYLAKE CT
3500 SJS 95117 853-C4
SUNNYMEAD CT
3500 SJS 95117 853-C4
SUNNY MEADOW LN
3000 SJS 95135 855-G5
SUNNY MEADOW PL
3000 SJS 95135 855-G5
SUNNYMOUNT AV
500 SUNV 94087 832-D2
E SUNNYOAKS AV
- CMBL 95008 873-D1
W SUNNYOAKS AV
200 CMBL 95008 873-C1
SUNNY OAKS DR
5500 SJS 95123 874-F4
SUNNY ORCHARD LN
5200 SJS 95135 855-G5
SUNNYPARK CT
800 CMBL 95008 873-C1
SUNNYSIDE AV
- CMBL 95008 853-E6
15000 SCIC 95037 937-A4
15200 MGH 95037 937-A4
15800 SCIC 95037 936-J3
15800 MGH 95037 936-J3
SUNNYSIDE DR
19000 SAR 95070 872-G5
SUNNYSIDE RD
21300 SCIC 95030 913-B2
SUNNYSLOPE AV
- SCIC 95127 835-A1
100 SJS 95127 835-A1
SUNNYVALE AV
- SUNV 94086 812-E6
200 SUNV 94086 832-E1
600 SUNV 94087 832-E1
SUNNYVIEW LN
2000 MTVW 94040 831-J1
SUNNY VISTA DR
2100 SCL 95128 833-E6
2100 SJS 95128 833-E6
SUNOL ST
- SJS 95126 833-J7
200 SCIC 95126 833-J7
200 SJS 95126 853-J1
200 SCIC 95126 853-J1
300 SJS 95126 853-J1
400 SJS 95126 854-A1
SUNPARK CT
300 SJS 95136 874-G2
SUNPARK LN
300 SJS 95136 874-G2
SUNPARK PL
300 SJS 95136 874-G2
SUNRAY DR
16600 LGTS 95032 873-C5
SUN RIDGE LN
100 SJS 95123 874-G7
SUNRISE CT
- MLPK 94025 790-E7
1300 LALT 94024 831-H3
SUN RISE DR
- SJS 95002 813-B1
SUNRISE DR
- SCIC 95030 913-A4
1200 GIL 95020 957-E6
2200 SJS 95124 873-E3
20500 CPTO 95014 852-D1
SUNRISE WY
1100 MPS 95035 813-J2
SUNRISE FARM RD
7400 LAH 94022 830-J1
SUNRISE SPRING CT
1500 CPTO 95014 852-A4
SUNROSE TER
900 SUNV 94086 832-G3
SUNSET AV
100 SUNV 94086 812-D7

SUNSET AV
400 SJS 95116 834-H5
16100 MGH 95037 937-A2
16100 SCIC 95037 937-A2
N SUNSET AV
- SJS 95116 834-G3
S SUNSET AV
- SJS 95116 834-G4
SUNSET CT
- MLPK 94025 790-D7
2000 SJS 95116 834-G4
SUNSET DR
800 SCL 95050 833-C5
12700 LAH 94022 831-C1
19900 SCIC 95030 872-E5
19900 SAR 95070 872-E5
23400 SCrC 95030 913-C6
SUNSET LN
- MLPK 94025 790-D7
SUNSET GLEN DR
700 SJS 95123 874-F6
SUNSET SPRING CT
11500 CPTO 95014 852-A4
SUNSET VIEW CT
2000 SJS 95116 834-G4
SUNSHADE LN
1400 SJS 95122 834-G6
SUNSHADOW LN
1300 SJS 95127 835-A4
SUNSHINE CT
700 LALT 94024 811-G7
1400 SJS 95122 834-G7
SUNSHINE DR
700 LALT 94024 811-G7
SUNSHINE LN
17200 SCIC 95030 913-B2
SUNSHINE ST
- MGH 95037 937-B6
- SCIC 95046 937-B6
SUNSPRING CIR
5500 SJS 95138 875-C4
SUNTREE CT
900 SUNV 94086 832-H3
SUN VALLEY CT
12600 SAR 95070 852-H6
SUNVIEW DR
15200 LGTS 95032 873-F7
SUNWOOD DR
2900 SJS 95111 854-G5
SUNWOOD MDWS PL
100 SJS 95139 875-F7
SUPERIOR DR
- CMBL 95008 853-B6
SUPERIOR RD
600 MPS 95035 794-A5
SUPREME DR
1900 SJS 95148 835-A6
SURBER DR
300 SJS 95123 875-A5
SURF CT
3400 SCIC 95127 814-H6
SURIAN CT
1000 SJS 95120 894-G3
SURMONT CT
100 LGTS 95032 873-G6
SURMONT DR
100 LGTS 95032 873-G6
SURREY CIR
10200 CPTO 95014 851-J1
SURREY CT
100 MPS 95035 794-D6
SURREY LN
- ATN 94027 790-F2
13300 SAR 95070 852-D7
SURREY PL
200 LALT 94022 811-D6
2100 SJS 95008 853-F7
SUR VERANO
7200 SJS 95135 855-J5
SUSAN CT
800 GIL 95020 977-J7
800 SCIC 95020 957-G3
6000 SJS 95123 874-F6
16900 MGH 95037 917-G5
SUSAN DR
2300 SCL 95050 833-C4
SUSAN WY
1000 SUNV 94087 832-B1
SUSAN GALE CT
- MLPK 94025 790-C6
SUSIE LN
3400 SCIC 95020 978-H2
SUSQUEHANNA CT
900 SUNV 94087 832-B3
SUSSEX DR
2700 SJS 95127 835-A4
2700 SJS 95127 834-J4
SUSSEX PL
700 MPS 95035 794-A3
1800 MLPK 94025 790-F2

SUSSEX PL
6400 GIL 95020 978-A5
SUSSEX SQ
1100 MTVW 94040 811-J7
SUSSEX WY
- RDWC 94061 790-A3
SUSSEX PARK CT
5100 SJS 95136 874-F3
SUTCLIFF AV
4700 SJS 95118 874-B3
SUTHERLAND AV
11100 CPTO 95014 852-B3
SUTHERLAND DR
- ATN 94027 790-B5
3900 PA 94303 811-F1
SUTRO DR
2500 SJS 95124 873-H1
SUTTER AV
700 PA 94303 791-C6
800 SUNV 94086 832-D1
800 SUNV 94086 812-C7
2100 SCL 95050 833-C7
SUTTER BLVD
18500 MGH 95037 916-J4
18500 MGH 95037 917-A4
SUTTER ST
- SJS 95110 854-C1
SUTTER CREEK CIR
5000 SJS 95136 875-A2
SUTTER CREEK LN
- MTVW 94043 811-J3
SUTTERGATE CT
2100 SJS 95132 814-D3
SUTTERGATE WY
2900 SJS 95132 814-D3
SUTTERWIND DR
- MPS 95035 794-A6
SUTTON DR
14800 SCIC 95124 873-H4
SUTTON PARK PL
5900 CPTO 95014 852-G2
SUZANNE CT
500 PA 94306 811-D3
1300 SJS 95129 852-H4
SUZANNE DR
4200 PA 94306 811-D3
SUZAY CT
1400 SJS 95122 854-H1
SUZUKI CT
2700 SJS 95121 854-J4
SWAIN WY
1900 SJS 95124 873-G4
SWALLOW DR
600 SJS 95111 854-J5
1600 SUNV 94087 832-H5
SWALLOW LN
1400 GIL 95020 957-F7
SWALLOW WY
3700 SCL 95051 832-H4
3700 CPTO 95014 832-H6
SWANCREEK CT
3300 SJS 95121 855-D7
SWANCREEK WY
1500 SJS 95121 855-D7
SWANER DR
1200 GIL 95020 977-G2
SWANGATE WY
1600 SJS 95124 873-J3
SWAN OAK LN
10000 CPTO 95014 831-J7
SWANSEA CT
2000 SJS 95132 814-J2
SWANSON WY
2600 MTVW 94040 831-J1
SWANSTON LN
8000 GIL 95020 978-A2
8200 GIL 95020 977-J1
SWANSTON WY
1700 SJS 95132 814-E4
SWANSWOOD CT
700 SJS 95120 894-J3
SWAPS DR
300 SJS 95111 875-B2
SWARTHMORE DR
18200 SAR 95070 852-J7
SWEET DR
900 SJS 95129 853-A3
SWEETBAY DR
700 SUNV 94086 832-H3
SWEETBERRY CT
- LALT 94022 811-D6
SWEETBRIAR DR
1600 SJS 95125 853-J6
2500 SJS 95008 853-F7
2500 SCIC 95008 853-F7
2500 SCIC 95008 873-F1
SWEETGUM CT
1900 SJS 95131 814-D7
SWEETLEAF CT
2800 SJS 95148 835-E7

SWEET OAK ST
10800 CPTO 95014 832-A6
10800 LALT 95014 832-A6
11000 CPTO 94024 832-A6
SWEETWATER WY
700 SJS 95133 834-F1
SWEIGERT RD
3400 SCIC 95132 795-B7
3400 SCIC 95132 815-C1
3400 SJS 95132 814-H2
3400 SCIC 95132 814-H2
SWENSEN CT
2000 SJS 95131 814-E7
SWICKARD AV
- SJS 95193 875-D5
- SJS 95119 875-D5
SWIFT AV
2100 SJS 95148 835-A6
SWIFT CT
1600 SUNV 94087 832-H5
SWINDON CT
3100 SJS 95148 855-E2
SWINGING GATE CT
1200 SJS 95120 894-E2
SWISS CREEK LN
- SCIC 95014 851-E4
SWORD DANCER CT
14900 MGH 95037 937-B5
SYCAMORE AV
- MGH 95037 917-A2
- SCIC 95037 896-B4
12000 SCIC 95046 937-F2
12000 SCIC 95046 957-H1
13400 SCIC 95037 937-A5
13600 SCIC 95037 936-H6
15000 SCIC 95037 956-H1
SYCAMORE CT
- RDWC 94061 790-A2
300 LGTS 95032 873-F5
1200 GIL 95020 977-F1
2200 LALT 94024 831-J6
SYCAMORE DR
400 MPS 95035 813-H3
800 PA 94303 791-D6
SYCAMORE GN
1900 SJS 95125 853-J6
SYCAMORE TER
1200 SUNV 94086 832-H4
SYCAMORE WY
2800 SCL 95051 833-A7
SYCAMORE CYN RD
13400 SCIC 95037 956-B1
SYDENHAM CT
400 SJS 95111 875-C2
SYDNEY CT
3600 SJS 95132 814-F2
SYDNEY DR
1300 SUNV 94087 832-D4
3500 SJS 95132 814-E2
SYDNOR DR
800 SCIC 95008 853-F7
SYKES CT
2800 SCL 95051 833-B6
SYLVAN AV
- SJS 95050 833-E7
- SJS 95128 833-E7
300 MTVW 94041 812-A7
SYLVAN CT
21500 SCIC 95030 912-J3
SYLVAN DR
3100 SJS 95148 835-C5
SYLVANDALE AV
600 SCIC 95111 854-H6
700 SJS 95111 854-J6
700 SJS 95111 855-A6
10100 SCIC 95111 855-A6
SYLVANDALE WY
13200 SCIC 95111 854-H6
SYLVANER WY
600 FRMT 94539 794-A2
6000 SJS 95120 874-D6
SYLVIA AV
100 MPS 95035 813-J1
SYLVIA CT
300 MPS 95035 813-J1
SYLVIA DR
1200 SJS 95121 854-J4
1200 SJS 95121 855-A3
SYLVIAN WY
- LALT 94022 811-D6
SYMPHONY LN
4600 SJS 95111 855-A7
SYNTAX CT
- SJS 95002 813-C1
SYRACUSE DR
1000 SUNV 94087 832-B3

T

TAAFFE RD
26200 LAH 94022 831-A1
N TAAFFE ST
100 SUNV 94086 812-E7
S TAAFFE ST
100 SUNV 94086 812-E7
400 SUNV 94086 832-D1
TACONIC CT
5600 SJS 95123 874-H4
TADLEY CT
300 RDWC 94061 790-B1
TAFFY CT
2600 SJS 95148 835-C7
TAFFY DR
2600 SJS 95148 835-C7
TAFT AV
2600 SCL 95051 833-B6
TAFT CT
400 GIL 95020 978-A2
2600 SCL 95051 833-B6
TAFT DR
5200 SJS 95124 873-F5
TAGART DR
2600 SJS 95148 835-C7
2600 SJS 95148 855-C1
TAGLIO CT
6800 SJS 95120 894-H2
TAGUS CT
- PTLV 94028 810-D5
TAHITI CT
2000 SJS 95122 854-H1
TAHOE DR
1600 MPS 95035 814-D1
TAHOE TER
500 MTVW 94041 812-B7
TAHOE WY
2900 SJS 95125 854-B7
3600 SCL 95051 812-H7
14800 MGH 95037 937-B4
TAIDA ST
1100 SJS 95131 834-D1
TAINAN CT
1200 SJS 95131 814-B7
TAINAN DR
1400 SJS 95131 814-B7
TAINAN PL
1200 SJS 95131 814-B7
TAINI CT
1900 SJS 95133 834-E1
TAIPEI DR
1500 SJS 95131 814-B7
TAIT AV
- LGTS 95030 872-J7
100 LGTS 95030 873-A7
TAJI CT
900 SJS 95122 854-G2
TAJI DR
900 SJS 95122 854-G2
TAKA CT
1300 SJS 95122 854-H1
TALATHY WY
3200 SJS 95135 855-E3
TALESFORE CT
1100 SJS 95131 814-E7
TALIA AV
2100 SCL 95050 833-D7
TALISMAN CT
700 PA 94303 791-E7
TALISMAN DR
800 PA 94303 791-E7
800 SUNV 94087 832-E2
TALLAHASSEE DR
1100 SJS 95122 834-J5
TALLENT AV
600 SCIC 95127 814-J5
TALLMAN CT
800 SJS 95123 874-E4
TALLWOOD CT
- ATN 94027 790-C6
TALMAGE AV
- SCIC 95127 834-J1
TAMALPAIS AV
6300 SJS 95120 874-E7
6300 SJS 95120 894-E1
TAMALPAIS ST
2400 MTVW 94043 811-F3
TAMARACK AV
800 SJS 95128 833-E7
TAMARACK LN
800 SUNV 94086 832-H3
3700 SCL 95051 832-H3
TAMARIND CT
21000 SCIC 95014 832-C6
TAMBOUR WY
1800 SJS 95131 814-C4
TAMI WY
500 MTVW 94041 812-B7

TAMIE LN
2000 SJS 95130 852-J6
TAMI LEE DR
1300 SJS 95122 834-G7
TAM O SHANTER DR
6500 SJS 95120 894-D2
TAMPA CT
1600 SJS 95122 854-J1
TAMPA WY
1600 SJS 95122 834-H7
2000 SJS 95122 854-J1
TAMPICO WY
4500 SJS 95118 874-A3
TAMSON CT
15300 MSER 95030 872-J4
TAMWORTH AV
13700 SAR 95070 872-D1
TANAGER CT
900 SUNV 94087 832-A2
TANAKA DR
1300 SJS 95131 814-C7
TANBARK ST
4200 SJS 95129 853-A2
TANDERA AV
5800 SJS 95123 874-F5
TANFIELD LN
400 SJS 95111 854-F6
TANGERINE WY
1100 SUNV 94087 832-D3
TANGLEWOOD DR
2700 SJS 95127 835-A5
TANGO WY
4600 SJS 95111 855-A7
TANKERLAND CT
3500 SJS 95121 855-D3
TANKIT CT
2100 SJS 95008 853-B6
TANKIT DR
2100 SJS 95008 853-B6
TANLAND DR
1000 PA 94303 791-D5
TANNAHILL DR
6600 SJS 95120 894-E1
TANNERY WY
3100 SCL 95054 813-A6
TANNHAUSER CT
2600 SJS 95121 854-H4
TANNHAUSER WY
1400 SJS 95121 854-H4
TAN OAK DR
100 PTLV 94028 830-C1
TANOAK DR
400 SCL 95051 833-B7
TANTALLON CT
2900 SJS 95132 814-F4
TANTAU AV
800 CPTO 95014 852-G2
10000 SCIC 95014 852-G1
N TANTAU AV
10100 CPTO 95014 832-G7
TAORMINO AV
5800 SJS 95123 874-F5
TAOS CT
19600 SAR 95070 872-F2
TAOS DR
14000 SAR 95070 872-F2
TAOS RD
48600 FRMT 94539 793-J2
TAPER AV
2800 SCL 95051 833-A3
3000 SJS 95124 873-G2
TAPER CT
1300 SJS 95122 854-H1
TAPER LN
1800 SJS 95122 854-G1
TAPROOT CT
2300 SJS 95133 814-H3
TARA ST
100 EPA 94303 791-C1
TARANGA CT
7200 SJS 95139 875-G7
TAROB CT
1800 MPS 95035 814-B3
TARRYTOWN CT
600 SJS 95136 874-F2
TARTAN DR
2500 SCL 95051 833-B2
TARTARIAN WY
500 SUNV 94087 832-D2
1300 SJS 95129 852-G4
TARTER CT
- SJS 95136 854-E7
TARTER WY
- SJS 95136 854-E7
TARYN LN
8300 GIL 95020 977-F2
TASMAN CT
- SUNV 94089 812-H4
TASMAN DR
- SJS 95134 813-D3

TASMAN DR
400 SUNV 94089 812-G3
700 MPS 95035 813-H3
1200 SUNV 94089 813-A4
2100 SCL 95054 813-A4
TASSAJARA CIR
17000 MGH 95037 917-E6
TASSASARA DR
700 MPS 95035 794-B5
TASSO ST
100 PA 94301 790-J3
1300 PA 94301 791-A5
TATRA CT
800 SJS 95136 874-E3
TATRA DR
5000 SJS 95136 874-E2
TATUM AV
500 GIL 95020 957-G7
500 SCIC 95020 957-G7
TAUBEH CT
3900 SJS 95136 874-F1
TAWNYGATE WY
1600 SJS 95124 873-J3
TAYLOR AV
200 SUNV 94086 812-E6
19000 MGH 95037 916-H4
TAYLOR CT
500 MTVW 94043 812-A4
TAYLOR DR
400 MPS 95035 794-A3
TAYLOR ST
900 SJS 95002 793-B7
E TAYLOR ST
- SJS 95112 834-C3
W TAYLOR ST
- SJS 95110 834-A4
300 SJS 95110 833-H6
700 SJS 95126 833-H6
TAYSIDE CT
7500 SJS 95135 855-J5
TEABERRY CT
6100 SJS 95123 875-B6
TEAK CT
17000 MGH 95037 917-D6
TEAK GROVE CT
100 SJS 95123 875-A3
TEAKWOOD AV
800 LGTS 95030 873-B2
TEAKWOOD CT
800 LGTS 95030 873-B2
TEAKWOOD DR
3000 SJS 95128 853-E4
TEAL CT
- EPA 94303 791-C2
6100 GIL 95020 977-J6
TEAL DR
1100 SUNV 94087 832-H5
1400 SCL 95051 832-H5
TEALE AV
3900 SJS 95117 853-B3
TEAL RIDGE CT
3000 SJS 95136 854-F6
TEA ROSE CIR
1100 SJS 95131 814-B6
TEA ROSE WY
1800 SJS 95131 814-B6
TEATREE CT
600 SJS 95128 853-F2
TECHNOLOGY DR
800 MPS 95035 813-G2
1500 SJS 95110 833-H1
18400 MGH 95037 917-A4
TECHNOLOGY PKWY
2000 HOLL - (1020-A5
See Page 999)
TED AV
12300 SAR 95070 852-E5
TED CT
12300 SAR 95070 852-E5
TEDDINGTON DR
3100 SJS 95148 855-D2
TEERLINK WY
14100 SAR 95070 872-B2
TEHAMA AV
1000 MLPK 94025 790-H1
2100 SJS 95122 834-J6
TEKMAN DR
1000 SJS 95122 854-H2
TELEGRAPH DR
3500 SJS 95132 814-H4
TELFER AV
1100 SJS 95125 854-A4
TELFORD AV
700 MTVW 94043 811-H2
TEMPLE CT
3100 SCL 95051 833-A6
TEMPLE DR
900 SJS 95117 853-B3
N TEMPLE DR
- MPS 95035 794-D5

S TEMPLE DR
- MPS 95035 794-D7
TEMPLEBAR WY
600 LALT 94022 811-D5
TEMPLETON CT
600 SUNV 94087 832-D3
TEMPLETON DR
500 SUNV 94087 832-D3
TEMPLETON PL
13800 LAH 94022 811-D7
TEN CT
- MGH 95037 937-C2
TEN ACRES CT
14100 SAR 95070 872-H2
TEN ACRES RD
18800 SAR 95070 872-G2
TENAKA PL
1500 SUNV 94087 832-D5
TENAYA DR
1300 SJS 95125 854-B7
TENLEY CT
3200 SJS 95148 855-D2
TENLEY DR
3200 SJS 95148 855-D2
TENNANT AV
- MGH 95037 937-D1
- SJS 95138 875-F4
300 SCIC 95037 937-D1
2200 SCIC 95037 917-F7
2700 MGH 95037 917-F7
TENNESSEE LN
200 PA 94306 811-D2
TENNYSON AV
100 PA 94301 791-A6
700 PA 94303 791-A6
TENNYSON LN
900 SJS 95116 834-G5
TEN OAK CT
13100 SAR 95070 852-F7
TEN OAK WY
12900 SAR 95070 852-F7
TEOLA WY
2000 SJS 95121 855-C3
TEPA WY
12100 LAH 94022 831-B3
TERALBA CT
100 SJS 95139 895-G1
TERESA LN
1100 MGH 95037 916-G7
1100 SCIC 95037 916-G7
TERESA MARIE TER
1600 MPS 95035 793-G3
TERESI CT
700 SJS 95117 853-D2
TERESI LN
600 LALT 94024 831-F1
TERESITA DR
1200 SJS 95129 852-J5
TERESITA WY
100 LGTS 95032 893-D1
TERFIDIA LN
- MPS 95035 794-D6
TERILYN AV
1100 SJS 95122 834-G6
2000 SJS 95122 854-H1
TERMAN DR
4200 PA 94306 811-C3
TERMINAL AV
1400 SJS 95112 834-A2
TERMINAL BLVD
2500 MTVW 94043 791-F6
TERMINAL DR
- SJS 95110 833-G2
TERRA ALTA CT
2000 MPS 95035 814-E2
TERRA ALTA DR
1200 MPS 95035 814-E1
TERRA BELLA AV
900 MTVW 94043 811-H2
900 SJS 95125 854-B5
TERRA BELLA DR
700 MPS 95035 794-B6
11200 CPTO 95014 852-B3
TERRA CALIFORNIA WY
2000 MGH 95037 917-D6
TERRACE CT
- LGTS 95032 893-B1
700 LALT 94024 811-G7
TERRACE DR
400 SJS 95112 834-D4
700 SCIC 94024 831-G4
21500 CPTO 95014 852-B3
TERRACE LAKE DR
- SJS 95123 874-E5
TERRACE VIEW DR
- SJS 95123 874-D5
TERRA COTTA CT
3100 SJS 95135 855-E2

TERRA COTTA DR
3100 SJS 95135 855-E2
TERRAINE ST
- SJS 95113 834-B6
- SJS 95110 834-A6
TERRA MESA WY
300 MPS 95035 793-H3
TERRA NOBLE WY
1000 SJS 95132 814-H5
TERRA VILLA AV
2200 EPA 94303 791-C2
TERRAZZO CT
5800 SJS 95123 874-F5
TERRAZZO DR
700 SJS 95123 874-F5
TERRELL ST
900 SJS 95136 874-D1
TERRENCE AV
12100 SAR 95070 852-F5
TERRENO DE FLORES LN
14900 LGTS 95032 873-D4
TERRI CT
9500 GIL 95020 958-A6
9500 GIL 95020 957-J5
9500 SCIC 95020 957-J5
TERRI WY
1800 SJS 95124 873-H3
TERRIER CT
6000 SJS 95123 875-B6
TERRI LYNN CT
1400 SCIC 95020 958-A2
TERRY LN
1900 SMCo 94061 790-B4
TERRY WY
10200 CPTO 95014 852-D1
10900 SCIC 94024 831-F5
TERRYWOOD CT
3100 SJS 95132 814-D2
TERSINI CT
1800 SJS 95131 814-C7
TERSTINA PL
3700 SCL 95051 832-H3
TESORO CT
5400 SJS 95124 873-G5
TEVIS PL
- PA 94301 791-B4
TEVIS TR
100 SBnC - (1020-E2
See Page 999)
TEXAS CT
5800 SJS 95120 874-B6
THACKERAY LN
900 SJS 95116 834-G5
THADDEUS DR
2400 MTVW 94043 811-G2
THAIN WY
500 PA 94306 811-C2
THAINWOOD WY
3800 SJS 95121 855-C5
THAMES DR
1100 SJS 95129 852-G3
6500 GIL 95020 978-A5
THAMES LN
100 LALT 94022 811-D5
THAMES PARK CT
400 SJS 95136 874-F1
THATCHER CT
900 LALT 94022 831-H2
THATCHER DR
900 LALT 94024 831-H1
900 MTVW 94040 831-H1
THAYER CT
2200 SJS 95122 854-H1
7300 GIL 95020 977-H4
THE ALAMEDA
2600 SCL 95053 833-F4
3100 SCL 95050 833-F4
THE ALAMEDA Rt#-82
700 SCL 95126 833-H5
700 SJS 95126 833-H5
2100 SJS 95126 834-A7
2200 SCL 95050 833-H5
2600 SCL 95053 833-H5
THE AMERICANA
900 MTVW 94040 812-A7
THE BUCKEYE
18600 SCIC 95030 912-J1
THE DALLES AV
700 SUNV 94087 832-A4
THELMA AV
20000 SAR 95070 872-E1
THELMA WY
900 SJS 95122 834-F7
900 SJS 95122 854-F1
THENDARA WY
13400 LAH 94022 811-A5
THEO DR
1500 SJS 95131 814-B7

THEODEN CT
1100 SJS 95121 855-A4
THERESA AV
1100 CMBL 95008 873-C2
THERESA LN
2700 SJS 95124 873-F1
THE STRAND AV
1600 SJS 95120 874-B6
THETA CT
400 SJS 95123 875-A7
THE VILLAGES PKWY
2000 SJS 95135 855-G6
THE VILLAGES FAIRWAY DR
2000 SJS 95135 855-H6
2800 SJS 95135 856-A6
THE WOODS DR
3900 SJS 95136 854-H7
3900 SJS 95136 874-H1
THICKET WY
6100 SJS 95119 875-D5
THIMBLEBERRY LN
4600 SJS 95129 853-B2
THIMBLEHALL LN
3400 SJS 95121 855-C5
THISTLE
- PTLV 94028 830-C1
THISTLE CT
1000 SUNV 94086 832-G3
THISTLE DR
4400 SJS 95136 874-F1
THISTLE WY
9300 GIL 95020 957-F7
THISTLEWOOD CT
1300 SJS 95121 855-B1
THOBURN CT
- SCIC 94305 790-J7
THOMAS CT
1500 MTVW 94040 811-G6
1500 MTVW 94022 811-G6
THOMAS DR
200 LGTS 95032 873-G5
3300 PA 94303 791-E6
THOMAS RD
- SCIC 95020 978-A5
- GIL 95020 978-A5
200 SCIC 95020 977-J6
300 GIL 95020 977-J6
3300 SCL 95054 813-D6
THOMAS GRADE
2600 MGH 95037 917-F5
THOMPSON AV
100 MTVW 94043 811-F3
3300 SJS 95118 874-A1
THOMPSON CT
2300 MTVW 94043 811-G3
THOMPSON PL
900 SUNV 94086 812-G6
2300 SCL 95050 833-C3
THOMPSON RD
18400 SCIC 95030 892-E6
THOMPSON SQ
100 MTVW 94043 811-F3
THOMPSON CREEK CT
2700 SJS 95135 855-E3
3800 SJS 95135 855-E3
THORNAPPLE DR
600 SUNV 94086 832-H2
THORNBRIAR DR
1500 SJS 95131 834-C1
THORNCREST DR
1500 SJS 95131 834-C1
THORNDALE CT
1000 SJS 95121 855-A5
THORNHAVEN WY
4500 SJS 95111 875-A1
4600 SJS 95111 874-J1
THORNLEAF WY
1500 SJS 95131 834-C1
THORNMILL WY
1200 SJS 95121 854-J3
THORNTON WY
500 SJS 95128 853-F2
500 SCIC 95128 853-F3
THORNTREE CT
1100 SJS 95120 874-D6
THORNTREE DR
5900 SJS 95120 874-C6
THORNTREE PL
1100 SJS 95120 874-C6
THORN VALLEY CT
1200 SJS 95131 834-C1
THORNWOOD DR
800 PA 94303 791-E7
5300 SJS 95123 874-E3
THORP PL
- SAR 95030 872-G5
THORPE CT
1200 LALT 94024 831-H3

STREET
Block City ZIP Pg-Grid

THORSEN CT
700 SCIC 94024 831-G4
THOUSAND OAKS CT
1000 SJS 95136 874-D2
THOUSAND OAKS DR
3600 SJS 95136 874-D1
THOUSAND PINES CT
3200 SJS 95148 855-D2
THRASHER LN
2600 SJS 95125 854-B7
THREADNEEDLE WY
1800 SJS 95121 855-B3
THREE FORKS LN
13400 LAH 94022 810-H7
THREE OAKS CT
14800 SAR 95070 872-F3
THREE OAKS WY
19500 SAR 95070 872-F4
THREE SPRINGS CT
3000 SCIC 95127 835-G3
THREE SPRINGS RD
3000 SCIC 95127 835-G3
THRIFT PL
3400 SJS 95148 835-E6
THRUSH CT
1500 SCL 95051 832-H5
2600 SJS 95125 854-C6
THRUSH DR
2500 SJS 95125 854-C6
THRUSH WY
3700 SCL 95051 832-H5
THUNDERBIRD AV
1300 SUNV 94087 832-H5
1400 SCL 95051 832-H5
THUNDERBIRD WY
1800 SCIC 95125 853-H6
THURESON WY
5500 SJS 95124 873-H6
THURMAN DR
3000 SJS 95148 855-F1
THURSTON AV
1100 LALT 94024 831-H4
THURSTON ST
200 LGTS 95030 873-A6
TIA PL
1900 SJS 95131 814-E7
TIANA LN
700 MTVW 94041 812-B7
TIARA DR
2100 SJS 95116 834-H5
TIBER CT
1600 SJS 95138 875-F1
TIBERAN WY
5000 SJS 95130 852-J6
TIBOUCHINA LN
6200 SJS 95119 875-D5
TICE DR
1000 MPS 95035 794-B4
TICONDEROGA DR
800 SUNV 94087 832-B3
TICONDEROGA PL
7200 GIL 95020 977-H4
TIERRA BUENA DR
1400 SJS 95121 854-J2
1500 SJS 95121 855-A2
TIERRA GRANDE CT
21300 SCIC 95120 895-C5
TIERRA SOMBRA CT
21600 SCIC 95120 895-C5
TIFFANY WY
1600 SJS 95125 854-A7
TIFFIN DR
100 SJS 95136 874-J2
TIFTON WY
4900 SJS 95118 874-B3
TIGARA CT
3700 SJS 95136 874-D1
TIGERWOOD WY
400 SJS 95111 875-C2
TILBURY DR
4400 SJS 95130 853-A6
TILDEN DR
4800 SJS 95124 873-G4
TILLAMOOK DR
6200 SJS 95123 874-H7
TILLMAN AV
- SJS 95126 833-H7
TILSON AV
18700 SCIC 95014 852-G2
19100 CPTO 95014 852-G2
TILTON AV
- MGH 95037 916-G4
200 SCIC 95037 916-G4
TILTON CT
2600 SJS 95121 854-J3
TILTON DR
1100 SUNV 94087 832-E3
TIMBER CT
6500 SJS 95120 894-E1

TIMBER CV
- CMBL 95008 853-E7
TIMBER WY
300 MPS 95035 813-J3
TIMBER CREEK DR
1500 SJS 95131 814-D5
TIMBERCREST DR
1000 SJS 95120 894-E1
TIMBERLAKE AV
3400 SJS 95148 835-D6
TIMBERLAKE CT
2600 SJS 95148 835-E6
TIMBERLINE CT
2800 SJS 95121 855-E3
TIMBERLINE DR
3700 SJS 95121 855-E3
TIMBERLOOP DR
4200 SJS 95136 854-F7
4200 SJS 95136 874-F1
TIMBERPINE AV
600 SUNV 94086 832-H2
TIMBERPINE CT
1100 SUNV 94086 832-H2
TIMBER SPRING CT
11600 CPTO 95014 852-C4
TIMBERVIEW CT
6500 SJS 95120 894-C1
TIMBERVIEW DR
6500 SJS 95120 894-C2
TIMBERWOOD CT
6800 SJS 95120 894-H2
TIMLOTT CT
3800 PA 94306 811-C2
TIMLOTT LN
800 PA 94306 811-C2
TIMMUS LN
23400 SCIC 95030 913-D6
TIMOR CT
700 SJS 95127 814-H6
TIMOTHY DR
900 SJS 95133 834-C2
TINTERN LN
- PTLV 94028 810-B6
TINY ST
100 MPS 95035 794-A3
100 MPS 95035 793-J3
TIOGA CT
300 PA 94306 811-E2
500 SUNV 94087 832-D3
TIOGA DR
2200 MLPK 94025 790-C6
TIOGA WY
1800 SJS 95124 853-H7
TIPPAWINGO AV
3400 PA 94306 811-B1
TIPTOE LN
1500 LALT 94024 832-A3
7400 CPTO 95014 852-D3
TIROL CT
500 MPS 95035 794-A5
TIROS WY
1200 SUNV 94086 812-J6
TISCH WY
3000 SJS 95128 853-E2
TISDALE WY
5000 SJS 95130 852-J7
TITAN WY
1200 SUNV 94086 812-J6
TITLEIST CT
300 SJS 95127 815-A7
TITUS AV
12000 SAR 95070 852-G6
TITUS CT
19300 SAR 95070 852-G6
TIVERTON DR
3800 SJS 95121 855-B5
TIVOLI WY
1200 SJS 95120 894-E3
TOANO CT
1500 SJS 95131 814-D6
TOBAGO AV
1900 SJS 95122 854-H1
TOBIAS DR
1500 SJS 95118 874-A4
TOBIN DR
2900 SJS 95132 814-E4
TODD LN
25900 LAH 94022 811-C7
TODD ST
1300 MTVW 94040 811-G6
TODD WY
3000 SJS 95124 873-G2
TOFT ST
400 MTVW 94041 811-G5
TOFTS DR
1100 SJS 95131 814-E6
TOHARA WY
2800 SCIC 95037 936-G6
TOIYABE WY
2300 SJS 95133 814-F7

TOKAY CT
3400 SJS 95148 835-C4
TOKAY WY
3400 SJS 95148 835-C4
TOLBERT CT
2300 SJS 95122 854-J1
TOLBERT DR
1500 SJS 95122 854-H1
TOLEDO AV
2500 SCL 95051 833-B6
TOLIN CT
200 SJS 95139 895-F1
TOLL GATE RD
21100 SAR 95070 872-B2
TOLLIVER DR
2900 SJS 95148 855-D2
TOLMAN DR
700 SCIC 94305 810-J2
TOLWORTH DR
1000 SJS 95128 853-F3
1600 CMBL 95128 853-F3
TOMAHAWK DR
5100 SJS 95136 875-A3
TOMAHAWK PL
49000 FRMT 94539 793-J3
TOMASINA CT
2200 SJS 95008 873-E1
TOMI LEA ST
600 LALT 94022 811-E5
TOMKINS CT
300 GIL 95020 957-J7
TOMLIN WY
2200 SJS 95133 834-F2
TOMLINSON LN
900 SJS 95116 834-G5
TOMMY LN
7400 SCIC 95120 894-H5
TOMPKINS DR
5800 SJS 95129 852-G3
TOMRICK AV
4500 SJS 95124 873-F3
TONALEA ST
48900 FRMT 94539 793-J2
TONGA CT
700 SJS 95127 814-H6
TONI CT
10200 CPTO 95014 832-E7
TONI ANN PL
13500 SAR 95070 872-D1
TONINO DR
4600 SJS 95136 874-D2
TONITA WY
10300 CPTO 95014 852-D1
TONOPAH CT
48600 FRMT 94539 793-J2
TONOPAH DR
- FRMT 94539 793-J2
5600 SJS 95123 875-A4
TONY DR
4800 SJS 95124 873-G4
TOPAM GLEN CT
7400 SCIC 95120 894-J5
TOPAR AV
1400 SCIC 94024 831-G3
TOPAZ AV
1000 SJS 95117 853-B4
TOPAZ ST
100 MPS 95035 794-A7
100 MPS 95035 814-B1
TOPEKA AV
- SJS 95128 853-G1
- SCIC 95128 853-G1
- SCIC 95128 833-G7
- SJS 95128 833-G7
- SJS 95126 833-G7
TOPOCK CT
3500 SJS 95111 854-G7
TOP OF THE HILL CT
15200 LGTS 95032 893-E1
TOP OF THE HILL RD
15200 LGTS 95032 893-F1
15200 SCIC 95032 893-F1
TOPPING WY
16400 SCIC 95032 873-C7
TORELLO LN
26000 LAH 94022 811-C6
TORERO PZ
800 CMBL 95008 873-C1
TORLAND CT
500 SUNV 94087 832-D3
TORO CT
- PTLV 94028 810-D6
TORO VISTA CT
16700 MGH 95037 917-G6
TORRANCE AV
1200 SUNV 94089 812-J5
10000 SJS 95127 835-A3
TORRE AV
10000 CPTO 95014 852-E1

TORRE CT
1500 SJS 95120 874-A6
TORREGATA LP
- SJS 95134 813-G2
TORRENZIA DR
- SJS 95134 813-D2
TORRES AV
1100 MPS 95035 794-C5
TORREY CT
17200 MGH 95037 936-J1
TORREYA AV
600 SUNV 94086 832-H2
TORREYA CT
700 PA 94303 791-D7
TORRINGTON CT
1400 SJS 95120 874-B6
TORRINGTON DR
600 SUNV 94087 832-D3
TORTOLA WY
400 SJS 95133 834-G2
TORWOOD CT
500 LALT 94022 811-C5
TORWOOD LN
400 LALT 94022 811-D5
TORYGLEN WY
2100 SJS 95121 855-C3
TOSCA CT
1500 SJS 95121 854-J2
TOSCA WY
2500 SJS 95121 854-J2
TOSCANA CT
2900 SJS 95135 855-E3
TOSCANO CT
2000 MPS 95035 794-A2
TOTTENHAM CT
5000 SJS 95136 874-F3
TOULON CT
1600 SJS 95138 875-F1
TOURAINE DR
1400 SJS 95118 874-A6
TOURNEY DR
1200 SJS 95131 814-D6
TOURNEY LP
200 LGTS 95032 893-B2
TOURNEY RD
17500 LGTS 95032 893-B1
17600 SCIC 95032 893-B2
TOVAR DR
400 SJS 95123 875-A6
TOWERS LN
2900 SJS 95121 855-A3
TOWLE PL
600 PA 94306 791-D7
TOWLE WY
600 PA 94306 791-C7
TOWN AND COUNTRY LN
1900 SCL 95050 833-D6
TOWN CENTER DR
- MPS 95035 794-B6
TOWNCENTER DR
200 SUNV 94086 812-E7
TOWN CENTER LN
20300 CPTO 95014 852-E1
TOWN CLUB DR
1600 SJS 95124 873-J2
TOWNE TER
100 LGTS 95030 873-A6
TOWNSEND AV
800 SJS 95112 834-B1
1300 SJS 95131 814-C7
1700 SCL 95051 833-A3
TOWNSEND TER
- SUNV 94087 832-B3
TOWNSEND PARK CIR
1200 SJS 95131 814-C7
TOWNSQUARE DR
3500 SCIC 95127 835-B2
3500 SJS 95127 835-B2
TOY LN
2600 SJS 95121 855-D3
TOYAMA DR
400 SUNV 94089 812-G4
TOYON AV
300 LALT 94022 811-D6
300 SJS 95127 814-J6
600 SUNV 94086 832-H2
TOYON CT
3400 SCIC 95127 814-J6
3400 SJS 95127 814-J6
8700 GIL 95020 977-F1
TOYON DR
2800 SCL 95051 833-A7
15500 SCIC 95030 872-H5
TOYON PL
600 PA 94306 791-D7
TOYON RD
- ATN 94027 790-G1
TOYONITA RD
23300 LAH 94024 831-E5

TRABUCO CT
3200 SJS 95135 855-G3
TRACE AV
600 SJS 95126 833-G7
TRACEL DR
6100 SJS 95129 852-F5
TRACY CT
14000 LAH 94022 810-H6
14000 PA 94304 810-H6
TRACY DR
3200 SCL 95051 832-J7
TRACY WY
1500 SCIC 95046 937-G4
TRADAN DR
2400 SJS 95131 814-C4
TRADEWINDS CT
200 SJS 95123 874-J4
TRADEWINDS DR
200 SJS 95123 874-J3
TRADEWINDS WKWY
5400 SJS 95123 874-J4
TRADE ZONE BLVD
300 MPS 95035 814-B4
300 SJS 95131 814-B4
TRADE ZONE CIR
1900 SJS 95131 814-B4
TRADE ZONE CT
1800 SJS 95131 814-B4
TRADE ZONE PL
2400 SJS 95131 814-B4
TRADE ZONE WY
1800 SJS 95131 814-B4
TRADITION CT
6600 SJS 95120 894-C5
TRAFALGAR PL
3400 SJS 95132 814-J3
TRAFTON RD
100 MntC - (1015-F6
See Page 995)
TRAIL DR
16500 MGH 95037 917-F6
TRAIL LN
- WDSD 94062 810-A5
TRAILBLAZER WY
9300 GIL 95020 957-F7
TRAIL RUN CT
4800 SJS 95136 875-A2
TRAILWAY DR
4100 SCIC 95127 835-A2
TRAMIER CT
8300 SJS 95135 855-H7
TRAMWAY DR
200 MPS 95035 794-A5
TRAMWAY PL
400 MPS 95035 794-A5
TRANSPORT ST
3900 PA 94303 791-F7
TRAPPERS TR
- PA 94304 830-E2
TRAUGHBER ST
1100 MPS 95035 794-C5
TRAVERSO AV
300 LALT 94022 811-D4
TRAVERSO CT
400 LALT 94022 811-D4
TRAVIS CT
10400 SCIC 95020 958-B2
TREADWAY DR
2300 SJS 95133 834-F1
TREATY CT
5000 SJS 95136 875-A2
TREBOL LN
3200 SJS 95148 835-D6
TREE TOP CT
5800 SJS 95123 875-A5
TREEWOOD LN
1900 SJS 95132 814-E2
TREGO DR
4700 SJS 95118 874-B3
TRELLIS PL
3200 SJS 95135 855-E3
TRENARY WY
5000 SJS 95118 874-C3
TRENT DR
4800 SJS 95124 873-G4
TRENTON DR
700 SUNV 94087 832-C3
1900 SJS 95124 873-G1
TRENTON PL
4200 GIL 95020 977-J4
TRENTON WY
300 MLPK 94025 790-J3
TRENTS FERRY CT
500 SJS 95133 834-E2
TRESEDER CT
100 LGTS 95032 873-B7
TREVINO TER
1000 SJS 95120 894-E1
TREVISO AV
1500 SJS 95118 874-B5

TREVOR DR
1500 SJS 95118 874-A4
TRIANON WY
200 LALT 94022 811-E6
TRIBOROUGH LN
1400 SJS 95126 853-G4
TRICIA WY
20400 SAR 95070 852-E7
TRIESTE CT
1600 SJS 95122 854-F1
TRIESTE WY
1500 SJS 95122 854-F1
TRIFONE DR
900 SJS 95117 853-C3
TRIMAR CT
3900 SJS 95111 854-J6
TRIMBLE CT
2100 SJS 95132 814-C3
TRIMBLE RD
200 SJS 95131 813-G6
200 SJS 95134 813-G6
400 SCL 95134 813-G6
400 SCL 95054 813-G6
2500 SJS 95131 814-C3
2500 MPS 95035 814-C3
2500 SJS 95132 814-C3
TRINIDAD CT
6500 SJS 95120 894-D1
TRINIDAD DR
6400 SJS 95120 894-E1
TRINIDAD RD
2700 SJS 95111 854-H4
TRINITY AV
13800 SAR 95070 872-D1
TRINITY CT
- MLPK 94025 790-C7
13900 SAR 95070 872-D2
TRINITY DR
1000 MLPK 94025 790-C7
TRINITY PL
3100 SJS 95124 873-F2
TRINITY RIVER CT
2900 SJS 95111 854-H4
TRINITY SPRING CT
11700 CPTO 95014 852-A5
TRIPIANO CT
2000 MTVW 94040 831-J1
TRIPOLI AV
1800 SJS 95122 854-G1
TRIPOLI CT
12900 LAH 94022 830-J1
TRIPP AV
1200 SJS 95116 834-D4
TRISTAN AV
3100 SJS 95127 814-H7
TRITON CT
1600 SCL 95050 833-D3
TRIUMPH CT
1400 SJS 95129 852-E4
TRONA WY
1500 SJS 95125 854-A7
1600 SJS 95125 873-J1
TRONSON CT
3600 SJS 95132 814-F2
TROON CT
500 MPS 95035 794-B6
TROPHY DR
900 MTVW 94040 811-G6
TROWBRIDGE WY
5600 SJS 95138 855-G7
5800 SJS 95138 875-H1
TROY CT
900 SUNV 94087 832-C3
TROY DR
500 SJS 95117 853-B1
TROY RD
- SCrC 95030 913-C7
TROY PARK PL
1800 SJS 95124 873-G4
TRUCKEE CT
4000 SJS 95136 874-H1
TRUCKEE LN
100 SJS 95136 874-G1
TRUDEAN WY
1700 SJS 95132 814-D4
TRUDY LN
- SMCo 94025 790-D5
TRUETT CT
2900 SJS 95148 855-D4
TRUFFLE CT
3200 SJS 95148 855-E2
TRUMAN AV
1400 LALT 94024 832-A3
3300 MTVW 94040 832-A3
3500 LALT 94040 832-A3
TRUMAN WY
- SJS 95002 793-C7
TRUMBULL CT
500 SUNV 94087 832-D3

TRUMPETER PL
1200 SJS 95131 814-B6
TRUMPP CT
17800 MGH 95037 916-H7
TRYNA DR
3300 MTVW 94040 832-A2
TUBAC LN
5600 SJS 95118 874-B5
TUBBY ST
400 CMBL 95008 853-E5
TUBMAN CT
500 SJS 95125 854-D5
TUCKER DR
6300 SJS 95129 852-F4
TUCSON AV
1100 SUNV 94089 812-J5
TUCSON DR
5600 SJS 95118 874-D4
TUCSON WY
6600 SJS 95119 875-D5
TUDOR CT
1200 SJS 95127 834-J4
TUDOR DR
1600 MLPK 94025 790-F2
TUERS CT
1000 SJS 95121 854-J4
TUERS RD
2600 SJS 95121 854-H3
3200 SJS 95121 855-A5
TUGGLE AV
18700 SCIC 95014 852-H2
TUGGLE PL
10600 SCIC 95014 852-H2
TULA CT
20800 CPTO 95014 852-D1
TULA LN
10200 CPTO 95014 852-D1
TULANE CT
800 MTVW 94040 811-G7
3400 SCL 95051 832-J6
TULANE DR
600 SCL 95051 832-J6
800 MTVW 94040 811-G7
TULARCITOS DR
1200 MPS 95035 794-D3
TULARE DR
3000 SJS 95132 814-F4
48900 FRMT 94539 794-A2
TULARE HILL DR
7300 SJS 95139 875-G7
TULARE HILL LN
7400 SJS 95139 875-G7
TULARE HILL RD
7400 SJS 95139 875-G7
TULIP CT
900 SUNV 94086 832-G3
TULIP DR
1000 SUNV 94086 832-G3
TULIP LN
- PA 94303 791-C4
TULIP RD
2100 SJS 95128 833-E6
2400 SCL 95128 833-E6
TULIPAN DR
1000 SJS 95129 852-G3
TULIP BLOSSOM CT
100 SJS 95123 875-A4
TULIPTREE LN
2600 SCL 95051 833-B7
TULIPWOOD LN
3200 SJS 95132 814-E2
TULITA CT
21000 SCIC 95014 852-C7
TULLY CT
3600 SJS 95148 835-F6
TULLY RD
- SJS 95112 854-F4
- SJS 95122 854-H2
- SJS 95121 854-H2
300 SCIC 95111 854-F4
300 SJS 95111 854-H2
1600 SJS 95122 855-A1
1900 SJS 95122 835-B7
2200 SJS 95148 835-E6
2900 SCIC 95148 835-D6
3500 SCIC 95148 835-E6
TUMBLE WY
3500 SJS 95132 814-G4
TUNBRIDGE WY
6700 SJS 95120 894-G2
TUNIS AV
3600 SJS 95132 814-F2
TUOLOMNE CT
6100 SJS 95123 874-H6
TUOLUMNE DR
100 FRMT 94539 793-J2
TUPOLO DR
1600 SJS 95124 873-J3
4900 SJS 95118 873-J3

TURANDOT CT
1500 SJS 95121 854-H4
TURLEY CT
1900 SJS 95116 834-H5
TURLEY DR
800 SJS 95116 834-G5
TURLOCK AV
11400 SCIC 95046 957-E2
TURLOCK LN
1300 SJS 95132 814-F4
TURNBERRY PL
5200 SJS 95136 874-F3
TURNER CT
100 SJS 95139 895-F1
TURNER DR
700 SCIC 95128 853-F2
TURNER WY
1200 CMBL 95008 873-B1
TURNHOUSE LN
2000 SJS 95121 855-C3
TURNSTONE WY
1300 SUNV 94087 832-H4
TURNWOOD CT
3600 SJS 95130 853-C4
TURQUESA CT
200 SJS 95116 834-F3
TURQUOISE ST
300 MPS 95035 814-B1
48200 FRMT 94539 793-J1
TURRETT DR
1200 SJS 95131 814-D6
TURRIFF WY
1400 SJS 95132 814-E4
TURTLE CREEK CT
300 SJS 95125 854-D4
TURTLEROCK DR
1100 SJS 95122 854-G1
TUSCALOOSA AV
- ATN 94027 790-C3
TUSCAN PARK CT
3200 SJS 95135 855-F2
TUSCANY PL
1000 CPTO 95014 852-D2
TUSCARORA CT
5900 SJS 95123 874-J5
TUSCARORA DR
400 SJS 95123 874-H6
TUSTIN DR
1700 SJS 95122 855-A3
TUTTLE AV
500 WAT 95076 995-G7
TWAIN CT
18800 SAR 95070 872-H1
TWEED CT
19400 SAR 95070 872-F1
TWEEDHOLM CT
6200 SJS 95120 894-B1
TWEEDSMUIR CT
2100 SJS 95121 855-C4
TWELVE ACRES DR
600 LALT 94022 811-C5
TWELVE OAKS RD
100 LGTS 95032 893-D1
TWIG LN
19100 SCIC 95014 852-G1
TWILIGHT CT
19900 CPTO 95014 832-F7
TWILIGHT DR
3700 SJS 95124 873-E3
TWINBERRY WY
9200 GIL 95020 957-E7
TWIN BROOK CT
900 SJS 95126 853-J3
TWIN BROOK DR
900 SJS 95126 853-J3
TWIN CREEKS RD
18300 MSER 95030 872-H4
18500 SAR 95070 872-H4
TWIN FALLS CT
3800 SJS 95121 855-D3
TWINKLE CT
- MPS 95035 793-H6
TWINLAKE DR
200 SUNV 94089 812-H5
TWIN OAKS DR
100 LGTS 95032 873-D7
TWIN OAKS LN
2700 SJS 95127 835-A5
TWO OAKS LN
7900 SCIC 95020 977-D3
TWYLA CT
2400 SJS 95008 853-B7
TWYLA LN
3900 SJS 95008 853-B7
TYBALT DR
800 SJS 95127 835-C1
TYHURST CT
5500 SJS 95123 874-J4
TYHURST WALKWAY
5400 SJS 95123 874-J4

TYLER AV
100 SCL 95117 853-D1
100 SCL 95117 833-D7
TYLER CT
100 SCL 95051 833-A7
TYLER PARK WY
1400 MTVW 94040 811-J7
TYMN WY
1900 SJS 95122 834-J6
TYNDALL ST
400 LALT 94022 811-E7
TYNE WY
3700 SCL 95054 813-E6
TYR LN
21500 SCIC 95120 895-C4
TYRELLA AV
200 MTVW 94043 812-A4
TYRELLA CT
100 MTVW 94043 812-A4

U

ULLMAN CT
4400 SJS 95121 855-E4
ULMECA PL
- FRMT 94539 793-J1
ULMER CT
300 RDWC 94061 790-C1
ULSTER DR
2000 SJS 95131 814-D6
UMATILLA TR
17600 SCIC 95030 913-C2
UMBARGER RD
- SCIC 95111 854-F5
- SJS 95111 854-F5
300 SJS 95121 854-J4
UNDAJON DR
600 SJS 95133 834-E2
UNDERWOOD CT
9900 SCIC 95020 956-J6
UNDERWOOD DR
3700 SJS 95117 853-B2
UNIFIED WY
2200 SJS 95125 854-D4
UNION AV
1500 RDWC 94061 790-A1
2000 CMBL 95008 853-F6
2300 SJS 95008 853-F6
2400 SCIC 95008 853-F6
2600 SJS 95124 853-F6
2600 SJS 95124 873-F3
3400 SCIC 95124 873-F3
14700 SJS 95032 873-F5
14700 LGTS 95032 873-F5
UNION ST
- SJS 95110 854-C1
UNITED PL
10000 CPTO 95014 832-D7
UNIVERSITY AV
- PA 94301 790-J4
- LGTS 95030 873-B5
100 LALT 94022 811-D6
200 SJS 95110 833-H5
500 LALT 94022 831-E1
800 LALT 94024 831-E1
800 PA 94301 791-A3
800 MSER 95030 873-B5
900 SCIC 94024 831-E1
900 SJS 95126 833-G6
1700 SJS 95128 833-F7
1900 EPA 94303 791-B2
2100 MTVW 94040 811-F4
UNIVERSITY DR
- MLPK 94025 790-F3
UNIVERSITY ST
500 SCL 95050 833-D5
UNIVERSITY TER
500 LALT 94022 831-D1
UNIVERSITY WY
1600 SJS 95128 833-F7
1700 SJS 95126 833-F7
21500 CPTO 95014 832-B7
UPHALL CT
1900 SJS 95121 855-C5
UPLAND CT
11500 SCIC 95014 852-B4
UPLAND WY
11500 CPTO 95014 852-B4
11500 SCIC 95014 852-B4
UPPER HILL CT
13800 SAR 95070 872-C1
UPPER HILL DR
13800 SAR 95070 872-C1
UPPER HUTCHISON RD
- SCrC 95018 912-D7
UPTON CT
700 SJS 95136 874-E1
UPTON WY
700 SJS 95136 874-E1

URANIUM RD
100 SCL 95051 833-A1
100 SUNV 94086 833-A1
2800 SCL 95051 813-A7
URBAN LN
600 PA 94301 790-H5
URIDIAS RANCH RD
2100 MPS 95035 794-E6
2100 SCIC 95035 794-E6
URLIN CT
6100 SJS 95123 875-B6
URNA AV
1700 SJS 95124 873-H1
URSA DR
48400 FRMT 94539 793-J1
URSHAN CT
100 SJS 95138 875-G6
URSHAN WY
7200 SJS 95138 875-G6
URSULA LN
27200 LAH 94022 830-J1
URSULA WY
1300 EPA 94303 791-B1
URZI CT
2800 SJS 95135 855-E2
URZI DR
3200 SJS 95135 855-E2
USONA DR
1400 SJS 95118 874-B3
UTE CT
6100 SJS 95123 874-H6
UTE DR
6100 SJS 95123 874-H6
UTICA CT
300 SJS 95123 875-B7
500 SUNV 94087 832-D3
UTICA DR
500 SUNV 94087 832-D3
UTICA LN
300 SJS 95123 875-B7
UTICA PL
7100 GIL 95020 977-J4
UTOPIA PL
1100 SJS 95127 835-C2
UVAS AV
200 MPS 95035 793-J6
UVAS CT
700 SJS 95123 874-G5
UVAS RD Rt#-G8
12700 SCIC 95037 956-D1
15100 SCIC 95037 936-A1
18000 SCIC 95037 935-J1
19000 SCIC 95037 916-A5
20100 SCIC 95037 915-J4
23200 SJS 95141 895-G7
23500 SJS 95141 915-G1
23500 SCIC 95141 915-G1
UVAS PARK DR
7000 GIL 95020 977-G
UXBRIDGE CT
- SJS 95139 875-G7

V

VAI AV
21300 CPTO 95014 852-C
VAL CT
3000 SCIC 95020 958-D
VALBUSA DR
1100 GIL 95020 957-F
VALCARTIER DR
1400 SUNV 94087 832-D
VALDEZ PL
900 SCIC 94305 810-J
VALDOSTA RD
1100 SJS 95121 855-A
VALE AV
1400 CMBL 95008 873-C
VALE CT
6100 SJS 95123 875-A
VALE DR
300 SJS 95123 875-A
VALELAKE CT
1100 SUNV 94089 812-J
VALENCIA AV
1000 SUNV 94086 832-C
VALENCIA CT
- PTLV 94028 810-D
2300 SJS 95125 853-J
VALENCIA DR
200 LALT 94022 811-E
700 MPS 95035 794-B
VALERIAN CT
1200 SUNV 94086 832-C
VALERIAN WY
1000 SUNV 94086 832-
VALERIE CT
2200 SJS 95008 853-
VALERIE DR
3900 SJS 95008 853-

SANTA CLARA CO.

INDEX

STREET
Block City ZIP Pg-Grid

VALERI RUTH CT
500 SCL 95050 833-C6
VALHALLA CT
1700 SJS 95132 814-E4
VALHALLA DR
2900 SJS 95132 814-E4
VALLA DR
1700 SJS 95124 873-H1
VALLCO PKWY
19100 CPTO 95014 832-G7
VALLECITO RD
22000 CPTO 95014 852-A2
VALLECITOS WY
100 LGTS 95030 872-J4
VALLE DEL LAGO
- SJS 95135 855-G4
VALLEJO DR
1300 SJS 95130 853-A4
VALLE VISTA CT
19200 SAR 95070 872-G4
VALLE VISTA DR
19200 SAR 95070 872-F4
VALLEY CT
- ATN 94027 790-A7
- WDSD 94062 790-A7
700 SCL 95051 833-A6
VALLEY RD
- ATN 94027 790-A7
VALLEY ST
200 LALT 94022 811-E7
VALLEY WY
400 MPS 95035 793-J7
600 SCL 95051 833-B6
VALLEYBROOK CT
4100 SJS 95111 855-A7
VALLEY CREST CT
1500 SJS 95131 834-D1
VALLEY CREST DR
1400 SJS 95131 834-C1
VALLEY FORGE DR
700 GIL 95020 977-J4
1000 SUNV 94087 832-B3
VALLEY FORGE WY
500 SJS 95117 853-C4
500 SCIC 95117 853-C4
600 CMBL 95008 853-C4
VALLEY GLEN CT
6200 SJS 95123 874-G7
VALLEY GLEN DR
6100 SJS 95123 874-G6
VALLEY GREEN DR
20500 CPTO 95014 832-D6
VALLEYHAVEN WY
- SJS 95111 874-J1
VALLEY HEIGHTS DR
2700 SJS 95133 814-G7
VALLEY MEADOW CT
5900 SJS 95135 855-J7
VALLEY OAK
- PTLV 94028 830-C2
VALLEY OAK DR
400 SCIC 95037 916-B1
17200 MSER 95030 873-B4
VALLEY OAKS CT
- GIL 95020 957-E7
VALLEY OAKS DR
- GIL 95020 957-E7
- GIL 95020 977-E1
VALLEY PARK CIR
100 SJS 95139 895-H2
VALLEY QUAIL CIR
1100 SJS 95120 894-F3
VALLEY RIDGE LN
3700 SCIC 95148 835-E5
VALLEY SQUARE LN
3200 SJS 95117 853-D4
VALLEY VIEW AV
- SCIC 95127 815-A7
300 SCIC 95127 814-J6
VALLEY VIEW CT
1000 SCIC 94024 831-F2
3200 MGH 95037 917-F4
VALLEY VIEW DR
300 SCIC 94024 831-F2
VALLEY VIEW RD
- SCrC 95076 (975-H5 See Page 955)
VALLEY VISTA CIR
- MGH 95037 916-H4
VALLEYWOOD CT
3000 SJS 95148 855-E1
VALMAINE CT
3000 SJS 95135 855-F3
VALMY ST
100 MPS 95035 794-A4
VALOTA RD
900 RDWC 94061 790-A2
VALPARAISO AV
- ATN 94027 790-E5
- MLPK 94025 790-C6

VALPARAISO AV
700 MLPK 94027 790-E5
1800 SMCo 94025 790-E5
VALPARAISO ST
600 SCIC 94305 810-H1
VALPICO DR
1700 SJS 95124 853-J7
VALROY CT
400 SJS 95123 875-A7
VALROY DR
6200 SJS 95123 875-A7
VAN CT
800 SUNV 94087 832-D2
VAN AUKEN CIR
900 PA 94303 791-D5
VAN BUREN CIR
1800 MTVW 94040 831-G1
VAN BUREN RD
400 MLPK 94025 790-J1
VAN BUREN ST
300 LALT 94022 811-C4
VANCE CT
3400 SJS 95132 814-G4
VANCE DR
1300 SJS 95132 814-G4
VANCE LN
- EPA 94303 791-C2
VAN COTT CT
- SJS 95127 834-H3
VANCOUVER CT
14300 SCIC 95127 835-B3
VANDELL WY
400 CMBL 95008 873-D2
VANDER WY
1300 SJS 95112 834-B1
VANDERBILT CT E
1100 SUNV 94087 832-D3
VANDERBILT CT W
1100 SUNV 94087 832-D3
VANDERBILT DR
600 SUNV 94087 832-D3
4300 SJS 95130 853-A7
4300 CMBL 95008 853-A7
4800 SJS 95130 852-J7
18200 SAR 95070 852-J7
VANDERBILT WY
3300 SCL 95051 832-J6
VAN DE WATER WY
500 SJS 95111 854-F7
VAN DUSEN LN
1300 CMBL 95008 873-A2
VAN DYCK CT
800 SUNV 94087 832-F3
VAN DYCK DR
1200 SUNV 94087 832-F3
VANESSA DR
1100 SJS 95126 853-H3
VANGORN CT
3100 SJS 95121 855-A4
VANGORN WY
3300 SJS 95121 855-A4
VANONI RD
- SCrC 95076 997-A7
- SCrC 95076 (996-G7 See Page 995)
VANPORT CT
1700 SJS 95122 855-B3
VANPORT DR
2900 SJS 95122 855-B3
VAN SANSUL AV
2900 SJS 95128 853-E3
VAN WINKLE LN
2400 SJS 95116 834-J4
VAQUERO CT
13600 SAR 95070 872-C1
VAQUERO DR
700 MTVW 94043 811-J3
VAQUEROS AV
600 SUNV 94086 812-E5
VARDEN AV
2800 SJS 95124 873-G1
VARGAS CT
100 MPS 95035 794-A4
5700 SJS 95120 874-C5
VARGAS DR
1200 SJS 95120 874-C6
VARGAS PL
2300 SCL 95050 833-C3
VARIAN CT
200 SJS 95119 875-D7
VARIAN WY
22200 CPTO 95014 832-A7
VARNER CT
3400 SJS 95132 814-H4
VARSI PL
700 SCL 95053 833-F5
700 SCL 95050 833-F5
VARSITY CT
1000 MTVW 94040 811-G7

VASILAKOS CT
- SMCo 94025 790-C5
VASILAKOS WY
- SMCo 94025 790-D5
VASONA AV
500 LGTS 95030 873-B2
VASONA CT
600 LGTS 95030 873-C2
VASONA ST
600 MPS 95035 793-J6
VASONA TER
500 LGTS 95030 873-B5
VASONA OAKS DR
100 LGTS 95030 873-B5
VASONA PARK RD
- LGTS 95030 873-B6
VASQUEZ AV
1100 SUNV 94086 812-B7
VASQUEZ CT
400 SUNV 94086 812-B7
VASSAR AV
1700 MTVW 94043 811-H3
VASSAR DR
5400 SJS 95118 874-A5
VAUGHN AV
300 SJS 95128 853-G1
300 SCIC 95128 853-G1
VAUXHALL CIR
5300 SJS 95123 874-H3
VEGA ST
300 MntC - (1017-A5 See Page 997)
VEGAS AV
1700 MPS 95035 794-A3
VEGAS DR
6200 SJS 95120 874-E7
6300 SJS 95120 894-E1
VELARDE ST
200 MTVW 94041 811-J5
VELASCO DR
300 SJS 95123 874-H4
VELASQUEZ AV
- SCrC 95076 (975-C7 See Page 955)
VELVETLAKE DR
200 SUNV 94089 812-J5
VELVET MEADOW CT
6700 SJS 95120 894-F2
VENADO CT
5600 SJS 95123 875-B4
VENADO WY
100 SJS 95123 875-B4
VENDOME ST
400 SJS 95110 834-A5
600 SJS 95110 833-J5
VENDURA CT
19300 SAR 95070 852-G6
VENECIA DR
400 SJS 95133 834-G1
VENETIAN WY
15000 MGH 95037 937-B4
VENICE WY
4300 SJS 95129 853-A3
VENN AV
2300 SJS 95124 873-E4
VENNDALE AV
2300 SJS 95124 873-E4
VENNUM DR
1500 SJS 95131 814-C6
VENTANA DR
7200 SJS 95129 852-E2
VENTANA PL
7200 SJS 95129 852-E2
VENTURA AV
200 PA 94306 811-C1
4500 SJS 95111 875-A1
VENTURA CT
3900 PA 94306 811-C1
VENTURA DR
48900 FRMT 94539 794-A2
VENTURA PL
2100 SCL 95051 833-A2
VENTURELLA DR
1400 SCIC 95020 958-A1
1400 SCIC 95020 957-J2
VENUS CT
600 FRMT 94539 793-J1
VENUS WY
- MPS 95035 813-J2
VERA LN
5100 SJS 95111 875-B2
VERA CRUZ AV
600 LALT 94022 811-E5
VERA CRUZ DR
5900 SJS 95120 874-A7
VERANO CT
400 SJS 95111 875-B1
VERANO DR
200 LALT 94022 811-F6

VERBENA DR
- GIL 95020 977-E2
100 EPA 94303 791-C3
VERBENA WY
4800 SJS 95129 853-B2
4800 SJS 95129 852-B7
VERDANT WY
3100 SJS 95117 853-D3
VERDE CT
100 LGTS 95032 873-E5
20500 SAR 95070 872-D1
VERDE MOOR CT
20800 SAR 95070 852-D6
VERDES ROBLES
17200 LGTS 95030 873-B4
VERDE VISTA CT
13600 SAR 95070 872-D1
VERDE VISTA LN
20500 SAR 95070 872-D1
VERDI DR
700 SUNV 94087 832-F3
3300 SJS 95111 854-J5
VERDIGRIS CIR
4200 SJS 95134 813-D2
VERDOSA DR
4000 PA 94306 811-C2
VEREDA CT
700 SJS 95123 874-G6
VERMILION CT
3100 SJS 95135 855-E2
VERMONT ST
400 SJS 95110 833-H5
900 SJS 95126 833-H5
VERNA DR
2900 SCIC 95133 834-H1
VERNAL CT
200 LALT 94022 811-D5
VERNAL DR
1300 SJS 95130 853-B4
VERNICE AV
3200 SJS 95127 835-B3
VERNIE CT
900 CPTO 95014 852-D2
VERNIER PL
1000 SCIC 94305 810-J2
VERNON AV
500 SCIC 94043 812-A2
500 MTVW 94043 812-A2
1200 SJS 95125 854-B3
VERNON CIR
800 MTVW 94043 812-A3
VERNON TER
3300 PA 94303 791-E6
VERONA CT
100 LGTS 95030 872-J4
VERONA RD
- SJS 95135 855-H3
VERONICA CT
1000 EPA 94303 791-C1
VERONICA DR
19800 SAR 95070 852-F6
VERONICA PL
- PTLV 94028 810-C7
2000 SJS 95124 873-F1
VERSAILLES CT
- SJS 95127 834-C1
VERSAILLES DR
- MLPK 94025 790-F3
VERSAILLES WY
19600 SAR 95070 872-F3
VERWOOD DR
2400 SJS 95130 853-A7
VESCA WY
4800 SJS 95129 853-B2
VESPER AV
600 FRMT 94539 793-J1
VESSING CT
18500 SAR 95070 872-H3
VESSING RD
18500 SAR 95070 872-H3
VESTAL ST
400 SJS 95112 834-B3
VESUVIUS LN
3000 SJS 95132 814-F5
VIA ALEGRIA CT
1500 SJS 95121 855-B4
VIA ALMADEN
1100 SJS 95120 874-C6
VIA ALTO CT
13700 SAR 95070 872-H1
VIA AMAROSA
- MGH 95037 916-H3
VIA AMIGOS
6300 SJS 95120 894-D1
VIA AMPARO
7200 SJS 95135 855-J6
VIA ANACAPA
7000 SJS 95139 875-F6
VIA ARLINE
- LAH 94022 831-B1

VIA ARRIBA CT
13100 SAR 95070 852-G7
VIA ARRIBA DR
13100 SAR 95070 852-G7
VIA ARROYO
- SCrC 95076 (975-B4 See Page 955)
VIA BAHIA
- SUNV 94089 812-H3
VIA BAJA DR
700 MPS 95035 794-B5
VIA BARRANCA
7000 SJS 95139 875-F7
VIA BELLA
7200 SJS 95139 875-F7
VIA BELMONTE
7000 SJS 95135 855-J5
VIA BLANC CT
13100 SAR 95070 852-F7
VIA BLANCA
7000 SJS 95139 875-F7
VIA BONITA
18400 MSER 95030 872-J6
VIA BREZZO
7200 SJS 95120 894-G5
VIA CABALLERO
15300 MSER 95030 872-J4
VIA CALZADA
7300 SJS 95135 855-J5
VIA CAMINO CT
22100 CPTO 95014 832-A7
VIA CAMPAGNA
- SJS 95120 894-A1
- SJS 95120 893-J1
VIA CAMPINA
- SJS 95139 875-F6
VIA CAMPO AUREO
- SJS 95120 894-A1
VIA CAMPO VERDE
- SJS 95120 893-J1
VIA CANCION
1400 SJS 95128 853-F5
VIA CANTARES
7300 SJS 95135 855-J5
VIA CAPRI
- SUNV 94089 812-H3
VIA CARMELA
7100 SJS 95139 875-G7
VIA CARMEN
2800 SJS 95124 873-F1
VIA CARRIZO
7200 SJS 95135 855-J6
VIA CASTANA
15400 MGH 95037 937-A4
VIA CASTANA CT
15700 MGH 95037 937-A4
VIA CERRO GORDO
27600 LAH 94022 830-H1
VIA CIELO
7000 SJS 95135 855-H5
VIA CINCO DE MAYO
1700 SJS 95132 814-D4
VIA CODORNIZ
1400 SJS 95128 853-F4
VIA COLINA
7100 SJS 95139 875-F7
15100 SAR 95070 872-G4
VIA COLLADO
100 LGTS 95030 872-J3
VIA CONTENTA
- MGH 95037 916-H3
1400 SJS 95128 853-F5
VIA CORDURA
7000 SJS 95139 875-F6
VIA CORFINIO
15100 MGH 95037 937-A4
VIA CORITA
27800 LAH 94022 831-A1
27800 LAH 94022 830-J1
VIA CORONA
7100 SJS 95139 875-G7
VIA CORTA
20700 SCIC 95120 894-J2
20700 SCIC 95120 895-A1
VIA CORTINA
- SJS 95120 893-J1
VIA CRESCENTE CT
19200 SAR 95070 852-G7
VIA CRESPI
400 SCIC 94305 790-G7
VIA CRISTOBAL
3800 SJS 95008 853-B6
VIA DE ADRIANNA
6200 SJS 95120 874-B7
6200 SJS 95120 894-B1
VIA DE CABALLE
4700 SJS 95118 874-B3
VIA DE GUADALUPE
- SJS 95116 834-G3

VIA DE LAS ABEJAS
6100 SJS 95120 874-B7
VIA DE LA VISTA
14000 SCIC 95127 835-F2
VIA DEL CASTILLE
600 MGH 95037 937-A4
VIA DEL CIELO
9400 SCIC 95020 958-E3
VIA DEL CORONADO
3000 SJS 95132 814-D3
VIA DEL MAR
3200 SJS 95124 873-F2
VIA DEL ORO
6400 SJS 95119 875-E7
9400 SCIC 95020 958-E3
VIA DE LOS GRANDE
1300 SJS 95120 894-B1
VIA DE LOS REYES
1300 SJS 95120 874-B7
VIA DEL POZO
1000 LALT 94022 811-D4
VIA DEL RIO
7000 SJS 95139 875-F7
VIA DEL SOL
- SCrC 95076 (975-B3 See Page 955)
2900 SJS 95132 814-D3
VIA DEL SUR
15100 MSER 95030 873-A4
VIA DE MARCOS
14500 SAR 95070 872-G3
VIA DE NINOS
15300 MGH 95037 937-B3
VIA DEPAZ
- MGH 95037 916-H3
VIADER CT
600 SCL 95050 833-D5
VIA DESTE
2000 SJS 95008 853-C6
VIA DE TESOROS
100 LGTS 95030 872-J4
VIA DONDERA
1300 SCL 95051 833-A4
VIA EDUARDO
15500 MGH 95037 937-A4
VIA EL CAPITAN
1800 SJS 95124 873-H1
VIA ENCANTADA
18100 MSER 95030 872-J4
VIA ENCINITAS
2700 SJS 95132 814-D3
VIA ESCALERA
2100 LALT 94024 831-H5
VIA ESCUELA CT
13000 SAR 95070 852-F7
VIA ESCUELA DR
19500 SAR 95070 852-F7
VIA ESPLENDOR
23000 CPTO 95014 831-H5
VIA FELIZ
27600 LAH 94022 810-J7
VIA FELIZE
- MGH 95037 916-H3
VIA FERRARI
1100 SJS 95122 834-G7
VIA FLORES
1700 SJS 95132 814-D4
VIA FORTUNA
- SJS 95120 894-A1
- SJS 95120 893-J1
VIA GRANADA
- SUNV 94089 812-H3
VIA GRANDE
700 MGH 95037 936-H1
VIA GRANDE CT
13200 SAR 95070 852-F7
VIA GRANDE DR
13100 SAR 95070 852-F7
VIA GRANJA
7000 SJS 95135 855-J5
VIA HUERTA
1200 LALT 94024 831-H5
VIA JOSE
1100 SJS 95120 874-D7
VIA LAGO
100 LGTS 95030 872-J2
VIA LAGUNA
7300 SJS 95135 855-J5
VIA LA POSADA
200 LGTS 95030 872-J3
VIA LARGO CT
300 MGH 95037 937-B4
VIA LOMA CT
300 MGH 95037 916-H5
VIA LOMAS
7100 SJS 95139 875-F7
VIA LOMBARDI
20800 CPTO 95014 832-E6
VIA LOMITA
15100 MSER 95030 872-J4

VIA LUGANO
- SJS 95120 893-J1
VIA MADERO DR
5900 SJS 95120 874-A7
VIA MADEROS
2200 LALT 94024 831-H6
VIA MADRONAS CT
19400 SAR 95070 852-F7
VIA MADRONAS DR
13100 SAR 95070 852-F7
VIA MAGGIORE
- SJS 95120 893-J1
VIA MARIA
7100 SJS 95139 875-F7
VIA MATEO
1100 SJS 95120 894-D1
VIA MESA
- SJS 95139 875-F6
VIA MILANO
3800 SJS 95008 853-B6
VIA MIMOSA
7200 SJS 95135 855-J6
VIA MONTALVO
3800 SJS 95008 853-B6
VIA MONTE DR
5600 SJS 95118 874-C4
19400 SAR 95070 852-F7
VIA MONTECITOS
7200 SJS 95135 855-J5
VIA MONTEZ
3000 SJS 95132 814-D3
VIA NAPOLI
2100 SJS 95008 853-B6
20300 CPTO 95014 832-E6
VIA NAVONA
300 MGH 95037 937-B3
VIA NIDA
- SUNV 94089 812-H3
VIA ORTEGA
400 SCIC 94305 790-G7
VIA PACIFICA
7100 SJS 95139 875-G7
VIA PALAMOS
20300 CPTO 95014 832-E6
VIA PALOMA
- SJS 95120 893-J1
VIA PALOMINO
15200 MSER 95030 873-A4
15300 MSER 95030 872-J4
VIA PALOU
400 SCIC 94305 790-G7
VIA PASA TIEMPO
- MGH 95037 916-H3
VIA PAVISO
10700 CPTO 95014 832-E6
VIA PIEDRA
7300 SJS 95135 855-J5
VIA PINTO
15200 MSER 95030 873-A4
VIA PISA
1500 SJS 95128 853-H2
VIA PORTADA
7000 SJS 95135 855-J5
VIA PORTOFINO
20300 CPTO 95014 832-E6
VIA PRADERA
7000 SJS 95139 875-F7
VIA PRIMAVERA CT
500 SJS 95111 875-B1
VIA PRIMAVERA DR
300 SJS 95111 875-A1
VIA PUEBLO LN
100 SCIC 94305 790-G6
VIA RAMADA
7000 SJS 95139 875-F7
VIA RANCHERO
900 CMBL 95008 873-C1
VIA RANCHERO CT
13200 SAR 95070 852-G7
VIA RANCHERO DR
13200 SAR 95070 852-G7
VIA REAL DR
19300 SAR 95070 852-G7
VIA REGGIO CT
1900 SJS 95132 814-C4
VIA REGINA
21700 SAR 95070 872-B1
VIA ROMA
2100 SJS 95008 853-B6
VIA ROMERA
7100 SJS 95139 875-F7
VIA RONCOLE
12000 SAR 95070 852-D5
VIA SALICE
3800 SJS 95008 853-B6
VIA SAN MARINO
20300 CPTO 95014 832-E6
VIA SANTA MARIA
100 LGTS 95032 873-C7

VIA SANTA TERESA
20100 SCIC 95120 894-H2
VIA SARONNO
- SJS 95120 893-J1
VIA SENDERO
7200 SJS 95135 855-J6
VIA SERENA
7000 SJS 95139 875-F7
VIA SERENO DR
17500 MSER 95030 873-A5
VIA SIESTA
- SUNV 94089 812-H3
VIA SOLANA
7100 SJS 95135 855-J5
VIA SORRENTO
400 MGH 95037 937-B4
20300 CPTO 95014 832-E6
VIA TERESA
100 LGTS 95030 872-J4
VIA TESORO CT
19100 SAR 95070 872-G2
VIA VALIENTE
900 SJS 95120 894-G2
VIA VALVERDE
7000 SJS 95135 855-J5
VIA VAQUERO
15400 MSER 95030 872-J5
VIA VENETO
15500 MGH 95037 937-A4
VIA VENITO
100 SCrC 95076 (975-B4 See Page 955)
VIA VENTANA
12600 LAH 94022 830-H1
VIA VENTURA
23400 CPTO 95014 831-H6
VIA VICO
7200 SJS 95129 852-E3
VIA VISTA
7200 SJS 95139 875-F7
VIA VOLANTE
20300 CPTO 95014 832-E6
VICANNA DR
6300 SJS 95129 852-F4
VICAR LN
900 SJS 95117 853-C3
VICENTE DR
1200 SUNV 94086 812-B7
VICENZA WY
2300 SJS 95138 855-F6
VICEROY CT
10100 CPTO 95014 832-A7
VICEROY WY
800 SJS 95133 814-G6
900 SJS 95132 814-G6
VICKERY AV
400 SCIC 95020 957-G6
14600 SAR 95070 872-D3
VICKERY PL
14700 SAR 95070 872-E3
VICKSBURG CT
10200 CPTO 95014 852-F1
VICKSBURG DR
10100 CPTO 95014 852-F1
VICTOR AV
- CMBL 95008 853-C5
VICTOR CT
3200 SJS 95132 814-F3
3300 SCL 95054 813-F6
VICTOR PL
14100 SAR 95070 872-D2
VICTOR ST
3200 SCL 95054 813-F6
VICTOR WY
600 MTVW 94040 811-H6
VICTORIA AV
3200 SCL 95051 833-A3
3300 SCL 95051 832-J3
VICTORIA CT
2000 LALT 94024 832-A5
14300 SCIC 95127 835-B3
VICTORIA DR
- ATN 94027 790-F3
- GIL 95020 978-A5
VICTORIA LNDG
1800 SJS 95131 814-C4
VICTORIA PL
300 PA 94306 811-D2
VICTORIA TER
1300 SUNV 94087 832-D4
VICTORIA PARK DR
4000 SJS 95136 874-F1
VICTORY AV
400 MTVW 94043 811-F2
VICTORY LN
- LGTS 95030 873-A7
VIDA LEON CT
300 SJS 95116 834-D2
VIENNA DR
- MPS 95035 793-J4

VIENNA DR
- MPS 95035 794-A4
1200 SUNV 94089 812-H4
VIERRA CT
1300 SJS 95125 854-A5
VIEW DR
1700 MPS 95035 794-D6
VIEW ST
- LALT 94022 811-D6
100 MTVW 94041 811-J6
VIEWCREST CT
20200 SCIC 95120 894-J2
VIEWCREST DR
20200 SCIC 95120 894-H2
VIEWFIELD RD
15800 MSER 95030 872-J6
VIEWMONT AV
- SCIC 95127 835-A2
VIEWMONT CT
3400 SCIC 95127 835-A2
3400 SJS 95127 835-A2
VIEWOAK DR
12100 SAR 95070 852-F5
VIEW OAKS WY
20600 SCIC 95120 894-J2
VIEWPARK CIR
300 SJS 95136 874-G1
VIEWPOINT LN
10000 SJS 95120 894-G4
VIEWRIDGE DR
19700 SAR 95070 852-F5
VILLA
- MTVW 94043 812-A2
- MTVW 94043 811-J2
VILLA AV
- LGTS 95032 893-A1
700 SJS 95126 833-H6
VILLA DR
1300 SCIC 94024 831-F3
VILLA PL
2300 SCL 95054 813-C4
VILLA ST
200 MTVW 94041 811-G4
VILLA CENTRE WY
- SJS 95128 853-E1
VILLA DE ANZA AV
10600 CPTO 95014 832-F6
VILLA EAST HILLS CT
3100 SJS 95127 835-A3
VILLA FELICE CT
17100 LGTS 95030 873-B4
VILLAGE CIR
100 MGH 95037 937-B3
VILLAGE CT
200 SJS 95110 833-J4
1400 MTVW 94040 832-A1
VILLAGE DR
12900 SAR 95070 852-G7
VILLAGE LN
100 MGH 95037 937-B3
300 LGTS 95030 873-A7
VILLAGE WY
15900 MGH 95037 937-B3
VILLAGE CENTER DR
300 SJS 95134 813-H4
VILLAGE HERMOSA LN
8200 SJS 95135 855-J6
VILLAGETREE DR
2000 SJS 95131 814-D6
VILLAGE VIEW DR
7600 SJS 95135 856-A6
VILLAGEWOOD WY
6800 SJS 95120 894-H3
VILLAGIO PL
- SJS 95134 813-H4
VILLA GLEN WY
3800 SJS 95136 874-D1
VILLA MARIA CT
1000 SJS 95125 854-E5
21500 CPTO 95014 852-B3
VILLA MONTEREY
2600 SJS 95111 854-G5
VILLANOVA CT
3300 SCL 95051 833-A2
VILLANOVA RD
2100 SJS 95130 852-J7
2200 SAR 95070 852-J7
VILLA NUEVA CT
100 MTVW 94040 831-J1
VILLA NUEVA WY
2400 MTVW 94040 831-J1
VILLA OAKS LN
21700 SAR 95070 852-B7
21900 SCIC 95070 852-B7
VILLA PARK CT
500 SJS 95118 874-C3
VILLA PARK LN
- SJS 95118 874-G3

VILLA PARK WY
500 SJS 95118 874-C3
VILLA REAL
500 PA 94306 811-C2
VILLA REAL DR
1400 SCIC 95020 958-A2
VILLARITA DR
1500 CMBL 95008 853-A6
1900 SJS 95130 853-A6
VILLA ROBLEDA DR
3300 MTVW 94040 832-A2
VILLA STONE DR
1600 SJS 95125 854-D3
VILLA TERESA WY
700 SJS 95123 874-E5
VILLA VERA
4000 PA 94306 811-C2
VILLA VISTA
4000 PA 94306 811-C2
VILLA VISTA RD
- SCIC 95135 855-H4
- SJS 95135 855-H4
VILMAR AV
6000 SJS 95120 874-B7
VINA DR
18500 SCIC 95030 892-H4
VINCA CT
700 GIL 95020 977-J6
VINCENT CT
6000 SJS 95123 875-A6
VINCENT DR
200 MTVW 94041 811-J6
2000 SCIC 95046 938-A5
3300 SCL 95051 832-J1
VINCI PARK WY
1100 SJS 95131 814-D7
VINE AV
300 SUNV 94086 832-E1
2900 SJS 95148 855-F1
VINE ST
100 MLPK 94025 790-E6
100 SMCo 94025 790-E6
500 SJS 95110 834-B7
600 SJS 95110 854-C1
1400 SJS 95125 854-C1
14800 SAR 95070 872-E3
VINE TR
18100 SCIC 95030 912-J4
VINEDALE SQ
1900 SJS 95132 814-F3
VINEDO LN
25700 LAH 94022 831-B2
VINELAND AV
17300 LGTS 95030 873-A5
17300 MSER 95030 873-A5
17900 MSER 95030 872-J4
VINELAND CT
17600 MSER 95030 873-A5
VINEMAPLE AV
600 SUNV 94086 832-J2
VINEWOOD LN
100 MGH 95037 937-B5
VINEYARD BLVD
15600 MGH 95037 937-B1
VINEYARD CT
100 MGH 95037 937-B2
2200 LALT 94024 831-J5
VINEYARD DR
200 SJS 95119 875-D7
200 SJS 95119 895-D1
1500 LALT 94024 831-J6
1500 LALT 94024 832-A5
VINEYARD LN
19100 SAR 95070 852-G7
VINEYARD CREEK CT
8600 SJS 95135 855-J6
VINEYARD RIDGE CT
8600 SJS 95135 855-J6
VINEYARD RIDGE PL
8600 SJS 95135 855-J6
VINEYARD SPRING CT
11600 CPTO 95014 852-A4
VIN GRANDE CT
- SJS 95135 855-E3
VINTAGE LN
21600 SAR 95070 872-B3
VINTAGE WY
800 SJS 95122 854-F1
VINTAGE ACRES WY
- SJS 95148 855-F2
VINTAGE CREST DR
3100 SJS 95148 855-E1
VINTAGE OAKS CT
3100 SJS 95148 855-F2
VINTNER CT
14900 SAR 95070 872-B3
VINTNER WY
1600 SJS 95124 873-H4
VINYARD CT
100 LGTS 95030 872-J3

STREET Block City ZIP Pg-Grid

VIOLA AV
- SJS 95110 834-B7
VIOLA DR
3500 MntC - (1017-A6 See Page 997)
VIOLA PL
700 LALT 94024 831-E1
VIOLET WY
- GIL 95020 977-G1
2100 SJS 95008 853-C6
VIRDELLE DR
21600 SCIC 95030 912-H3
VIREO AV
1500 SUNV 94087 832-H5
3600 SCL 95051 832-H5
VIRGIL PL
1100 SJS 95120 894-H4
VIRGINIA AV
- CMBL 95008 853-C7
800 CMBL 95008 873-C1
1200 RDWC 94061 790-A2
1600 SJS 95116 834-G5
VIRGINIA CT
800 CMBL 95008 873-C1
VIRGINIA DR
18000 SCIC 95030 912-J3
VIRGINIA LN
- ATN 94027 790-E1
VIRGINIA PL
1500 SJS 95116 834-F5
E VIRGINIA ST
- SJS 95112 854-C1
100 SJS 95112 834-D7
W VIRGINIA ST
- SJS 95110 854-C1
300 SJS 95125 854-A1
VIRGINIA SWAN PL
10200 CPTO 95014 832-E7
VIRGO LN
3400 SJS 95111 854-F6
VISCAINO AV
1100 SUNV 94086 812-B7
VISCAINO CT
12600 LAH 94022 811-B7
VISCAINO DR
12600 LAH 94022 811-B7
VISCAINO PL
12800 LAH 94022 811-A7
VISCAINO RD
12600 LAH 94022 811-B6
VISCAINO WY
200 SJS 95119 875-C7
VISO CT
3300 SCL 95054 813-E6
VISTA AV
100 SCIC 95127 814-J7
200 SJS 95127 814-J7
400 PA 94306 811-C2
17600 MSER 95030 873-A5
VISTA CT
900 MGH 95037 936-H1
20200 CPTO 95014 832-E7
VISTA DR
10100 CPTO 95014 832-E7
VISTA LN
15400 LGTS 95032 873-D5
VISTA LP
5900 SJS 95124 873-J7
VISTA WY
400 MPS 95035 794-B7
400 MPS 95035 814-C1
VISTA ARROYO CT
12100 SAR 95070 852-C5
VISTA CLUB CIR
1500 SCL 95054 813-D4
VISTA CREEK DR
2900 SJS 95133 814-G6
VISTA DE ALMADEN
18600 SCIC 95120 874-G7
VISTA DE ALMADEN CT
- SJS 95120 874-G7
VISTA DEL ARBOL
200 LGTS 95032 893-C1
VISTA DEL CAMPO
100 LGTS 95032 873-C7
VISTA DEL LAGO
- LGTS 95030 872-J2
VISTA DEL MAR
100 LGTS 95032 893-C1
1000 SJS 95132 814-J5
VISTA DEL MONTE
100 LGTS 95032 873-C7
100 LGTS 95032 893-C1
VISTA DEL MONTE CT
8700 SCIC 95020 957-B7
VISTA DE LOMAS
19200 SCIC 95037 916-J3
VISTA DEL PAJARO
300 SCrC 95076 (975-C3 See Page 955)
VISTA DEL PATARO
200 SCrC 95076 (975-C4 See Page 955)
VISTA DEL PRADO
100 LGTS 95032 893-B1
VISTA DEL SOL
2500 SJS 95116 834-H3
6900 SCIC 95020 978-H1
VISTA DEL SUR DR
1700 GIL 95020 977-F2
VISTA DEL VALLE
3500 SJS 95132 814-J5
VISTA DEL VALLE CT
16700 MGH 95037 917-F6
VISTA DEL VALLE DR
2700 MGH 95037 917-F6
VISTA DE SIERRA
200 LGTS 95032 893-C1
VISTA DE VALLE
12900 LAH 94022 831-B1
VISTAGLEN CT
1700 SJS 95122 835-A6
VISTAGLEN DR
1700 SJS 95122 835-A6
VISTA GRANDE AV
700 LALT 94024 811-G6
800 MTVW 94024 811-G6
800 MTVW 94040 811-G6
VISTA GRANDE WY
18300 SCIC 95030 892-H4
VISTA KNOLL BLVD
10200 CPTO 95014 832-A7
VISTA LOMA
20700 SCIC 95120 894-J2
VISTAMONT DR
3000 SJS 95118 854-B7
3000 SJS 95118 874-C1
VISTA MONTANA
- SJS 95134 813-D2
VISTA NORTE CT
3500 MPS 95035 794-G6
3500 SCIC 95035 794-G6
VISTA OAK
1000 SJS 95132 814-J5
VISTA OAKS CT
20300 CPTO 95014 832-E7
VISTA PARK DR
4000 SJS 95136 854-F7
VISTAPARK DR
4000 SJS 95136 874-F1
VISTA REGINA
13900 SAR 95070 872-B1
VISTA RIDGE DR
200 MPS 95035 794-G6
300 SCIC 95035 794-G6
VISTA SERENA
15400 LAH 94022 831-C1
VISTA SPRING CT
500 MPS 95035 794-H6
VISTA VALLE CT
10100 SCIC 95127 815-C7
VISTA VERDE DR
2200 SJS 95148 835-D5
2200 SCIC 95148 835-C6
VISTA VERDE WY
200 SMCo 94028 830-E5
VISTAVIEW DR
3300 SJS 95132 814-G4
VITERO WY
5800 SJS 95138 875-H1
VIVIAN DR
300 LGTS 95032 873-C7
300 LGTS 95032 893-C1
VIVIAN LN
2800 SJS 95124 873-G1
VIZCAYA CIR
2100 SJS 95008 873-F1
2100 SJS 95008 853-F7
VIZCAYA WY
2100 SJS 95008 873-F1
VOGUE CT
27600 LAH 94022 831-A1
VOLLMER WY
1700 SJS 95116 834-G5
VOLTERRA CT
5800 SJS 95138 875-G1
VOLTI LN
1100 LALT 94024 831-J2
VONNA CT
700 SJS 95123 874-G5
VOORHEES DR
24500 LAH 94024 831-D2
VOSS AV
22500 CPTO 95014 851-H1
VOSS PARK LN
2000 SJS 95131 814-E7

W

WABASH AV
- SJS 95128 833-G7
100 SCIC 95128 833-G7
100 SCIC 95128 853-G1
200 SJS 95128 853-G1
WABASH ST
1200 SJS 95002 793-B7
WACO ST
1000 SJS 95110 833-H4
WADDINGTON AV
400 SUNV 94086 812-F5
WADE AV
1600 SCL 95051 833-B3
WADSWORTH AV
- LGTS 95030 872-J7
WAGMAN DR
400 SJS 95129 852-J2
WAGNER AV
1700 MTVW 94043 811-H3
WAGNER RD
17200 SCIC 95032 893-G3
WAGON WY
1200 GIL 95020 957-F7
WAIMEA CT
4400 SJS 95118 874-B2
WAINWRIGHT AV
300 SJS 95128 853-F1
300 SCIC 95128 853-F1
WAINWRIGHT DR
800 SJS 95128 853-F4
WAITE AV
500 SUNV 94086 812-F6
WAKEFIELD TER
1500 LALT 94024 832-A3
WAKE FOREST DR
700 MTVW 94043 812-A3
WALBROOK DR
5400 SJS 95129 852-G4
11800 SAR 95070 852-H5
W WALBROOK DR
5800 SJS 95129 852-G4
WALCOTT RD
- SCIC 94035 812-B1
- SCIC 94043 812-B1
WALDEN CT
12300 SAR 95070 852-F5
WALDEN SQ
2300 SJS 95124 853-H7
WALDHEIM CT
7000 SJS 95120 894-H3
WALDO RD
300 CMBL 95008 853-C7
WALES CT
- SJS 95138 875-H1
WALGLEN CT
900 SJS 95136 874-D1
WALGROVE WY
2900 SJS 95128 853-E3
WALIZER CT
17700 SCIC 95037 917-C4
WALIZER LN
17700 SCIC 95037 917-C3
WALKER CT
1800 SJS 95122 854-G1
WALKER DR
200 MTVW 94043 812-A3
WALKER ST
- WAT 95076 (1015-E2 See Page 995)
WALKINGSHAW WY
3100 SJS 95132 814-F4
WALL ST
3000 SCIC 95111 854-G5
3000 SJS 95111 854-G5
WALLACE DR
900 SJS 95120 874-E7
22000 CPTO 95014 832-A6
WALLACE LN
- SCIC 95037 936-B5
WALLACE ST
2600 SCL 95051 833-B4
WALLA WALLA TR
17700 SCIC 95030 913-A1
WALLEA DR
500 MLPK 94025 790-F4
WALLIS CT
4100 PA 94306 811-C4
WALLYFORD CT
2500 SJS 95121 855-D4
WALLY PLACE WY
3600 SJS 95121 855-B4
WALNUT AV
- ATN 94027 790-E2
- LGTS 95030 872-J7
100 SUNV 94086 812-E6
300 SCIC 95020 (980-D7 See Page 959)
20400 SAR 95070 872-D2
WALNUT CIR
10300 CPTO 95014 852-A1
WALNUT DR
- MGH 95037 937-B5
400 MPS 95035 793-J6
1200 CMBL 95008 873-C2
1500 PA 94303 791-B4
1700 MTVW 94040 831-G1
WALNUT LN
300 GIL 95020 978-A2
WALNUT ST
- MGH 95037 937-B1
500 SJS 95110 833-J5
WALNUT BLOSSOM DR
5400 SJS 95123 875-A4
WALNUT GROVE AV
1400 SJS 95050 833-F6
1400 SJS 95126 833-F6
1400 SCL 95050 833-F6
2000 SJS 95128 833-E6
2400 SCL 95128 833-E6
WALNUT GROVE DR
17300 MGH 95037 917-B6
WALNUT HILL CT
100 LGTS 95030 873-C3
WALNUT SPRING CT
11600 CPTO 95014 852-A4
WALNUT WOODS CT
1000 SJS 95122 834-F7
WALNUT WOODS DR
900 SJS 95122 834-F7
WALSH AV
600 SCL 95050 833-C1
2300 SCL 95051 833-C1
WALSH CT
- SJS 95123 874-F7
WALSH RD
300 ATN 94027 790-B6
WALTER BRETON DR
2200 SCIC 95037 936-F3
WALTER HAYS DR
100 PA 94303 791-B4
WALTERS AV
1500 CMBL 95008 873-A1
WALTER WELSHER CT
9800 SCIC 95020 958-C4
WALTHAM ST
600 MTVW 94040 831-J2
WALTON AV
21700 SCIC 95120 895-C5
WALTON LN
21700 SCIC 95120 895-C5
WALTON RD
600 LGTS 95030 873-B5
WALTON WY
3200 SJS 95117 853-C3
WALTRIP LN
5600 SJS 95118 874-B5
WAR ADMIRAL AV
300 SJS 95111 875-B2
WAR ADMIRAL WY
5000 SJS 95111 875-B1
WARBLER WY
1500 SCL 95051 832-H6
1500 SUNV 94087 832-H6
WARBURTON AV
900 SCL 95050 833-C3
2400 SCL 95051 833-A3
3300 SCL 95051 832-J3
WARD WY
2100 SMCo 94062 790-A4
13400 SAR 95070 852-G7
13400 SAR 95070 872-G1
WARDELL CT
12500 SAR 95070 852-D6
WARDELL RD
20500 SAR 95070 852-D6
WAREC WY
300 LALT 94022 811-D6
WAREHOUSE RD
- MLPK 94025 790-J1
WARFIELD WY
2200 SJS 95122 854-G2
WARM SPRINGS BLVD
48000 FRMT 94539 793-H1
WARM SPRINGS DR
2800 SJS 95127 834-H1
WARMWOOD LN
2000 SJS 95132 814-D2
WARNER AV
1300 SUNV 94087 832-C4
WARNER CT
3600 SJS 95127 835-C3
WARNER DR
3500 SJS 95127 835-C3
WARNER RD
- SCIC 94035 812-B2
- SCIC 94043 812-B2
WARNER RANGE AV
2300 MLPK 94025 790-D7
WARREN AV
100 MGH 95037 917-A7
100 MGH 95037 916-J7
1000 SJS 95125 854-B2
WARREN DR
100 SCL 95051 833-B7
WARREN ST
300 SJS 95112 834-B3
WARREN WY
800 PA 94303 791-C5
WARRING DR
700 SJS 95123 874-F4
WARRINGTON AV
2900 SJS 95127 835-A4
WAR WAGON CT
5200 SJS 95136 874-J3
WAR WAGON DR
5100 SJS 95136 874-J3
5100 SJS 95136 875-A3
WARWICK CT
900 SUNV 94087 832-B3
WARWICK DR
100 CMBL 95008 853-C5
WARWICK RD
15300 SJS 95124 873-G5
WASATCH DR
1300 MTVW 94040 832-A2
WASHINGTON AV
100 PA 94301 791-B6
100 SUNV 94086 812-B6
2400 RDWC 94061 790-A2
WASHINGTON DR
- MPS 95035 793-J4
- MPS 95035 794-A4
WASHINGTON ST
- SJS 95002 813-B1
- SCL 95050 833-E4
100 SJS 95112 834-B5
600 LALT 94022 831-E1
800 MTVW 94043 811-H4
WASHOE DR
1100 SJS 95120 894-D1
WASKOW DR
400 SJS 95123 875-A6
WATER AV
13900 SCIC 95037 937-C5
13900 SCIC 95046 937-C5
14100 MGH 95037 937-C5
WATER ST
3000 SCIC 95111 854-G5
5400 SJS 95111 854-G6
WATERBIRD WY
1000 SCL 95051 832-H5
WATERBURY CT
3600 SJS 95117 853-C3
WATERFALL CT
5200 SJS 95136 875-B3
WATERFORD DR
7500 CPTO 95014 852-D4
WATERFORD MEADOW CT
100 MPS 95035 794-C2
WATERLOO CT
3400 SJS 95132 814-J2
WATERMAN CT
3400 SJS 95127 814-J7
WATERTON LN
1100 SJS 95131 834-D1
WATERVILLE DR
4500 SJS 95118 874-C3
WATER WITCH WY
500 SJS 95117 853-D2
WATKINS AV
- ATN 94027 790-E2
WATKINS WY
4100 SJS 95135 855-F3
WATSON CT
1500 MPS 95035 814-C3
2400 PA 94303 791-D4
WATSON DR
200 CMBL 95008 853-E5
WATSONVILLE CT
16800 SCIC 95037 937-A7
16800 SCIC 95046 937-A7
WATSONVILLE RD
12300 SCIC 95046 937-A6
12300 SCIC 95037 937-A6
12600 SCIC 95046 956-J2
12600 SCIC 95037 956-J2
13400 SCIC 95046 936-J7
13400 SCIC 95037 936-J7
14600 MGH 95037 937-A6
WATSONVILLE RD Rt#-G8
8000 SCIC 95020 977-A1
9300 SCIC 95020 956-J6
9900 SCIC 95020 957-A4
12500 SCIC 95046 956-J6
WATSONVILLE RD Rt#-G8
12500 SCIC 95037 956-J6
WATTERS DR
14700 SJS 95127 835-B2
14800 SCIC 95127 835-B2
WAUGH DR
18200 SCIC 95037 916-G7
18200 MGH 95037 916-G7
WAVE PL
1900 SJS 95133 834-E1
WAVERLEY CT
- MLPK 94025 790-G3
WAVERLEY ST
100 PA 94301 790-J4
200 MLPK 94025 790-G4
900 PA 94301 791-A5
2600 PA 94306 791-C7
3300 PA 94306 811-D1
WAVERLEY OAKS
- PA 94301 791-B6
WAVERLY AV
1600 SJS 95122 854-J1
1800 SJS 95122 834-J7
2100 SJS 95122 835-A7
3000 SMCo 94063 790-D1
WAVERLY LN
200 LALT 94022 811-E7
WAVERLY PL
100 MTVW 94040 831-J2
WAVERLY ST
100 SUNV 94086 812-D7
300 SUNV 94086 832-D1
WAWONA DR
1500 SJS 95125 854-A7
1500 SJS 95125 874-A1
WAXWING AV
1500 SUNV 94087 832-H6
WAYCROSS RD
3600 SJS 95121 855-A5
WAYLAND AV
4900 SJS 95118 874-C3
WAYLAND LN
8000 GIL 95020 977-H1
WAYNE AV
1100 SJS 95131 814-A6
WAYWORD DR
1500 SJS 95122 834-H7
WEATHERLY DR
500 SJS 95134 813-D2
WEATHERSFIELD WY
1200 SJS 95118 874-B5
WEAVER CT
8900 GIL 95020 957-J7
WEAVER DR
1300 SJS 95125 853-J4
WEAVER RD
16700 SCIC 95030 893-D7
16700 SCIC 95030 913-C1
WEBB RD
- SCrC 95076 (976-A7 See Page 955)
WEBB CANYON DR
7000 SJS 95120 894-E3
7000 SCIC 95120 894-E3
WEBSTER CT
2500 PA 94301 791-C6
2500 PA 94301 791-C6
2600 SCL 95051 833-B3
WEBSTER DR
600 SJS 95133 834-F1
WEBSTER ST
100 PA 94301 790-J3
700 PA 94301 791-A4
2500 PA 94306 791-C6
WEDDELL CT
900 SUNV 94089 812-F4
E WEDDELL DR
100 SUNV 94089 812-F4
W WEDDELL DR
100 SUNV 94089 812-E4
WEDGEWOOD AV
100 LGTS 95030 873-A2
WEDGEWOOD CT
5500 SJS 95123 874-F4
WEDGEWOOD DR
700 SJS 95123 874-F4
WEEDIN CT
3600 SJS 95132 814-F2
WEEKS ST
300 EPA 94303 791-B1
WEEPING CREEK WY
3300 SJS 95121 855-D7
WEEPINGGATE LN
1000 SJS 95136 874-J3
WEEPING OAK CT
22600 CPTO 95014 831-J7
WEEPING OAKS CT
1200 SJS 95120 894-E2
WEETH DR
14500 SCIC 95124 873-G2
WEHNER DR
3400 SCL 95051 832-J5
WEHNER WY
6200 SJS 95135 855-H6
WEIBEL WY
1200 SJS 95125 853-G4
WEICHERT DR
800 MGH 95037 917-B6
WEIMAR AV
5900 SJS 95120 874-B6
WEKIVA AV
1000 CMBL 95008 873-B1
WELBURN AV
- GIL 95020 977-F1
WELBY CT
3100 SJS 95111 854-H5
WELCH AV
1000 SJS 95117 853-C3
1700 SJS 95112 854-F2
WELCH RD
700 PA 94304 790-G6
1000 SCIC 94305 790-G6
WELDON LN
1100 SJS 95131 834-D1
WELDWOOD AV
900 LGTS 95030 873-B2
WELDWOOD CT
900 LGTS 95030 873-B2
WELKER CT
- CMBL 95008 853-B6
WELLCROFT CT
3200 SJS 95148 855-C2
WELLER LN
- MPS 95035 794-A7
- MPS 95035 793-J7
WELLER RD
- SCIC 95035 794-G1
WELLESLEY CT
3500 MTVW 94040 831-J2
WELLESLEY ST
1900 SCIC - 791-A7
2000 PA 94306 791-A7
WELLFLEET WY
6000 SJS 95129 852-G4
WELLINGTON CT
19900 SAR 95070 852-E6
WELLINGTON DR
1800 MPS 95035 794-B2
WELLINGTON PL
800 CMBL 95008 853-B7
WELLINGTON SQ
3700 SJS 95136 874-C1
WELLINGTON PARK DR
4800 SJS 95136 874-G2
5000 SCIC 95136 874-G2
WELLMEADOW CT
6400 SJS 95120 894-C1
WELLS AV
- PA 94301 790-J5
WELLS CT
5600 SJS 95123 874-H4
WELLS ST
800 RDWC 94061 790-B1
WELLSBURY CT
600 PA 94306 791-C7
WELLSBURY WY
600 PA 94306 791-D7
WELL SPRING CT
11500 CPTO 95014 852-A4
WEMA WY
1700 SJS 95124 873-H1
WEMBLEY CT
400 RDWC 94061 790-B2
1800 SJS 95132 814-E3
WENDELL AV
500 CMBL 95008 873-C1
WENDOVER LN
2100 SJS 95121 855-C4
WENDY LN
13500 SAR 95070 872-G1
WENDY WY
1400 SJS 95125 854-A6
1400 SMCo 94025 790-D5
WENLOCK DR
1100 SJS 95122 834-J5
WENRICK CT
1700 LALT 94024 831-J4
WENTE PL
2000 SJS 95125 853-G4
WENTE WY
2000 SJS 95125 853-G4
WENTWORTH ST
1000 MTVW 94043 811-H4
WENTWORTH WY
1200 SJS 95121 855-B5
WENTZ DR
800 GIL 95020 977-H4
WERTH AV
1100 MLPK 94025 790-F5
WESCOAT CT
600 SCIC 94035 812-B3
600 SCIC 94043 812-B3
WESCOAT RD
400 SCIC 94035 812-B3
400 SCIC 94043 812-B3
WESLEY CT
1800 SJS 95148 835-A5
WESSEX AV
1400 LALT 94024 831-J3
WESSEX DR
4100 SJS 95136 874-E1
WESSEX PL
600 MPS 95035 794-B3
WEST CT
300 SJS 95116 834-E3
WEST RD
15900 SCIC 95030 872-G6
WESTACRES DR
10200 CPTO 95014 852-D1
WESTBERRY DR
2600 SJS 95132 814-E4
WESTBORO DR
2900 SCIC 95127 835-A3
2900 SCIC 95127 834-J3
2900 SJS 95127 835-A3
2900 SJS 95127 834-J3
WESTBRANCH DR
2700 SJS 95148 855-C2
WESTBROOK AV
11400 SCIC 94024 831-F4
WESTCHESTER DR
100 SJS 95124 873-E5
100 LGTS 95124 873-E5
100 LGTS 95032 873-E5
500 CMBL 95008 853-F7
1000 SUNV 94087 832-B3
WESTCOTT DR
14500 SAR 95070 872-E3
WEST CREEK DR
1600 SJS 95125 853-J6
WESTDALE DR
4900 SJS 95129 852-J2
WESTERN DR
10100 CPTO 95014 852-D1
WESTFIELD AV
2700 SJS 95128 853-E3
2700 CMBL 95128 853-E3
WESTFIELD DR
1100 MLPK 94025 790-F5
WESTFORD WY
2500 MTVW 94040 832-A2
WEST FORK CT
- SJS 95136 874-D2
WESTGATE AV
2200 SJS 95125 854-B6
WESTGROVE LN
2700 SJS 95148 855-C2
WESTHAVEN DR
1600 SJS 95132 814-F3
WEST HILL CT
1000 CPTO 95014 852-D3
WESTHILL DR
100 LGTS 95032 873-G6
WEST HILL LN
7600 CPTO 95014 852-D3
WESTINGHOUSE DR
47500 FRMT 94539 793-H1
WESTLAKE DR
400 SJS 95117 853-C2
WESTLYNN WY
900 CPTO 95014 852-D2
WESTMINSTER CT
1800 SJS 95132 814-E3
WESTMINSTER LN
700 LALT 94022 811-D4
WESTMINSTER AV
1100 EPA 94303 791-A1
WESTMINSTER CT
10100 CPTO 95014 831-J7
WESTMONT AV
1200 CMBL 95008 873-A1
3000 SJS 95008 873-A1
3400 SJS 95008 872-J1
4900 SJS 95130 872-J1
WESTMONT CT
900 SJS 95117 853-C3
WESTMOOR WY
6800 SJS 95129 852-E4
WESTMORELAND AV
2900 SMCo 94063 790-C1
WESTMORELAND CT
2300 SJS 95124 853-H6
WESTMORELAND DR
2100 SJS 95124 853-H6
WESTON DR
500 SJS 95008 853-A6
500 SJS 95130 853-A6
600 CMBL 95008 853-A6
26400 LAH 94022 811-B5
WESTOVER DR
13600 SAR 95070 872-G1
WESTPARK DR
2300 SJS 95124 853-H7
WESTRIDGE CT
27800 LAH 94022 830-H1
WESTRIDGE DR
100 PTLV 94028 810-B5
100 SCL 95050 833-D7
100 SCL 95117 833-D7
100 SCL 95117 853-D1
100 SJS 95117 833-D7
900 MPS 95035 814-E1
WESTSHORE CT
11600 CPTO 95014 852-A5
WESTSIDE AV
500 SUNV 94087 832-D3
WEST VALLEY DR
600 CMBL 95008 853-F7
WEST VALLEY FRWY Rt#-85
- CMBL - 873-C2
- CPTO - 832-B6
- CPTO - 852-E4
- LGTS - 873-C2
- SAR - 852-E4
- SAR - 872-H1
- SCIC - 852-E4
- SCIC - 873-C2
- SCIC - 874-C3
- SJS - 873-C2
- SJS - 872-J1
- SJS - 874-C3
- SJS - 875-A5
- SJS - 852-E4
- SUNV - 832-B6
WEST VIEW CT
3700 SCIC 95148 835-E4
WEST VIEW DR
3500 SCIC 95148 835-D5
3500 SJS 95148 835-D5
18600 SAR 95070 852-H5
WESTWIND WY
25800 LAH 94022 811-B7
WESTWOOD DR
1000 SJS 95125 853-J3
1000 SJS 95131 814-A4
7500 GIL 95020 977-G3
WETMORE DR
3000 SJS 95148 835-F7
3000 SJS 95148 855-F1
WETSAND CT
9300 GIL 95020 957-F7
WEXFORD DR
2700 SJS 95132 814-E4
WEYBRIDGE DR
500 SJS 95123 875-A7
WEYBURN LN
1000 SJS 95129 852-E3
WEYERS CT
2800 SJS 95148 835-D2
WEYMOTH DR
1200 CPTO 95014 852-C4
WHALEY AV
- SJS 95110 833-J4
WHALEY DR
6200 SJS 95135 855-H6
WHARTON CT
- SJS 95132 814-G3
WHARTON RD
- SJS 95132 814-G3
WHEAT CT
1000 SJS 95127 835-C2
WHEATON DR
19600 CPTO 95014 832-F7
WHEELER AV
- RDWC 94061 790-B2
100 LGTS 95032 873-B7
WHEELER ST
100 GIL 95020 977-J2
WHEELING DR
3300 SCL 95051 832-J6
WHEELOCK RD
- SCrC 95076 (975-E6 See Page 955)
WHEELSMAN PL
5700 SJS 95123 874-F4
WHINNEY PLACE WY
3800 SJS 95121 855-B4
WHIPPET-RUN
400 SCrC 95076 (975-C4 See Page 955)
WHIPPLE CT
14700 SCIC 95127 835-B1
WHIPPORWILL DR
2800 MGH 95037 917-E4
WHIRLAWAY DR
100 SJS 95111 875-B2
WHIRLOW PL
1100 SJS 95131 814-D7
WHISKEY HILL LN
10100 SCIC 95020 957-G5
WHISMAN CT
200 MTVW 94043 812-B4
N WHISMAN RD
- MTVW 94043 812-B4
S WHISMAN RD
100 MTVW 94041 812-A6
WHISMAN STATION DR
400 MTVW 94043 812-B5
WHISPERING ELM CT
3200 SJS 95148 855-D2
WHISPERING HLS CIR
2500 SJS 95148 855-B1
WHISPERING HLS DR
2700 SJS 95148 855-B2
WHISPERING HLS LN
2700 SJS 95148 855-B2
WHISPERING HLS LP
2600 SJS 95148 855-B1
WHISPERING HLS RD
2700 SJS 95148 855-B2
WHISPERING HLS WY
2700 SJS 95148 855-C2
WHISPERING OAKS DR
20500 SCIC 95120 895-A5
WHISPERING PINES DR
6500 SJS 95120 894-C2
WHITAKER WY
1200 MLPK 94025 790-E5
WHITBOURNE CT
1300 SJS 95120 894-C2
WHITBOURNE DR
6500 SJS 95120 894-C2
WHITBY CT
3100 SJS 95148 855-E2
WHITCLEM CT
200 PA 94306 811-E2
WHITCLEM DR
200 PA 94306 811-D2
WHITCLEM PL
300 PA 94306 811-D2
WHITCLEM WY
200 PA 94306 811-D2
WHITCOMB CT
900 MPS 95035 814-E1
WHITE CT
3100 SJS 95127 835-A3
WHITE DR
900 SCL 95051 833-B4
N WHITE RD
- SJS 95127 834-J2
- SCIC 95127 834-J2
500 SCIC 95127 814-H7
500 SJS 95133 814-H7
500 SJS 95127 814-H7
600 SJS 95133 834-J2
700 SCIC 95133 834-J2
700 SCIC 95133 814-H7
S WHITE RD
- SJS 95127 834-J2
- SCIC 95127 834-J2
300 SJS 95127 835-C6
1800 SJS 95148 835-C6
2000 SCIC 95148 835-C6
2600 SJS 95148 855-D1
WHITE ST
- SJS 95126 834-A7
WHITE ACRES DR
2700 SJS 95148 855-D
WHITEBICK DR
1000 SJS 95129 852-G
WHITE CLIFF DR
1000 SJS 95129 852-F3
WHITE CLOUD DR
900 MGH 95037 937-B5
WHITE CREEK LN
1600 SJS 95125 853-J5
WHITE FIR CT
10500 CPTO 95014 852-C
WHITE FIR LN
800 SJS 95133 814-H
WHITEGATE AV
1300 SJS 95125 854-B
WHITEHALL AV
800 SJS 95128 853-F4
1000 CMBL 95128 853-F4
WHITEHALL LN
200 RDWC 94061 790-B
WHITEHAVEN CT
6000 SJS 95138 875-H
WHITEHURST CT
1300 SJS 95125 854-B

STREET
Block City ZIP Pg-Grid

WHITEHURST RD
7400 SCIC 95020 (976-H4
See Page 955)
WHITELEAF CT
3100 SJS 95148 855-E1
WHITELEAF WY
3000 SJS 95148 855-E2
WHITEMAN AV
- SCrC 95076 (975-B7
See Page 955)
WHITEMARSH CT
1100 SJS 95120 894-E2
WHITE OAK CT
- MLPK 94025 790-E6
3300 MH 95037 917-G5
WHITE OAK DR
1800 MLPK 94025 790-E6
WHITEOAK DR
1000 SJS 95129 852-H3
WHITE OAK LN
800 SUNV 94086 832-J3
800 SCL 95051 832-J3
WHITE OAKS AV
1200 CMBL 95008 873-E3
1700 SCIC 95008 873-E3
4100 SJS 95124 873-E3
WHITE OAKS CT
1800 CMBL 95008 873-E2
WHITE PINE CT
1100 SJS 95125 854-A4
WHITEROCK CIR
1500 SJS 95125 853-J5
WHITEROCK CT
1400 SJS 95125 853-J5
WHITEROSE CT
3100 SJS 95148 855-E2
WHITEROSE DR
3200 SJS 95148 855-E2
WHITESAND CT
3200 SJS 95148 855-E2
WHITESAND DR
3000 SJS 95148 855-E2
WHITESTONE CT
2500 SJS 95122 835-A5
WHITETHORNE DR
600 SJS 95128 853-F4
900 CMBL 95128 853-F4
WHITEWOOD CT
1300 SJS 95131 814-B6
WHITEWOOD DR
1600 SJS 95131 814-B6
WHITFIELD CT
1300 SJS 95131 814-D7
WHITHAM AV
1600 SCIC 94024 831-F4
WHITMAN CT
300 PA 94301 791-A5
WHITMAN WY
3200 SJS 95132 814-H6
WHITNEY AV
- LGTS 95032 873-B7
- LGTS 95032 893-B1
WHITNEY CT
- MLPK 94025 790-C7
2400 MTVW 94043 811-F3
WHITNEY DR
1000 MLPK 94025 790-C7
2400 MTVW 94043 811-F3
WHITNEY LN
10000 SCIC 95127 835-C1
WHITNEY PL
- FRMT 94539 793-H2
WHITNEY ST
- LALT 94022 811-D7
WHITNEY WY
300 MGH 95037 937-A2
10500 CPTO 95014 852-E2
WHITS RD
- MTVW 94040 811-F3
WHITSELL ST
3500 PA 94306 811-B1
WHITTIER ST
- MPS 95035 793-J7
WHITTINGTON DR
2800 SJS 95148 855-D1
WHITTON AV
1100 SJS 95116 834-F4
WHITWOOD LN
1600 CMBL 95008 853-A6
1800 SJS 95130 853-A6
WICHITA CT
6200 SJS 95123 874-H6
WICKHAM CT
1700 SJS 95132 814-E4
WICKHAM PL
2500 SCL 95051 833-B2
WICKHAM RD
1600 SJS 95132 814-E4
WIDEN CT
1700 SJS 95132 814-E4
WIDGET DR
700 SJS 95117 853-C2
WIEUCA RD
16300 SCIC 95030 872-G6
WIGAN CT
2200 SJS 95131 814-E7
WIGWAM CT
- SJS 95136 875-B3
WILANETA AV
400 FRMT 94539 793-J2
WILBUR AV
2700 SJS 95127 834-J3
2800 SCIC 95127 834-J3
WILBURN AV
- ATN 94027 790-D1
WILCOX AV
3200 SJS 95118 874-A1
4600 SCL 95054 813-C4
WILCOX WY
1700 SJS 95125 854-A5
WILD BERRY LN
14600 SAR 95070 872-C2
WILDCAT DR
- SAR 95070 872-E4
WILDCAT WY
1500 SJS 95118 874-A6
WILD CREEK DR
7200 SJS 95120 894-J4
WILDCREST DR
13300 LAH 94022 811-C7
13300 LAH 94022 831-C1
WILDER AV
100 LGTS 95030 873-A7
WILDER CT
2000 SCIC 95020 938-A7
WILDERFIELD RD
1000 SCrC 95030 912-E1
WILDERNESS CIR
7000 SJS 95135 876-A2
WILDFLOWER CT
11600 CPTO 95014 852-D4
WILD FLOWER LN
13700 LAH 94022 811-C7
WILD FLOWER WY
7300 CPTO 95014 852-D4
WILD FLOWER PARK LN
300 MTVW 94043 811-J4
WILD IRIS DR
8700 GIL 95020 977-E1
WILDMAN DR
1300 SJS 95127 835-C3
WILD MEADOW WY
- SJS 95135 856-A7
WILD OAK CT
16700 MGH 95037 936-J1
WILD OAK WY
14500 SAR 95070 872-F3
16700 MGH 95037 936-J1
WILD PLUM LN
14100 LAH 94022 811-C6
WILDROSE CT
2300 GIL 95020 977-D1
WILDROSE WY
1400 MTVW 94043 811-H4
WILD TURKEY LN
3600 SCIC 95020 958-G2
WILDWAY
15000 LGTS 95030 873-B4
WILDWOOD AV
1200 SUNV 94089 812-J5
1200 SUNV 94089 813-A5
WILDWOOD CT
6600 SJS 95120 894-C5
WILDWOOD LN
- SMCo 94025 810-E1
600 PA 94303 791-C4
WILDWOOD WY
400 SCL 95054 813-E5
20700 SAR 95070 872-D2
WILFORD WY
9800 SCIC 95020 958-B4
WILFRED WY
1900 SJS 95124 873-G4
WILHELMINA WY
1100 SJS 95120 894-F3
WILKEY CT
2700 SJS 95127 834-J4
WILKIE CT
4100 PA 94306 811-D2
WILKIE WY
3900 PA 94306 811-C1
WILKINSON AV
10700 CPTO 95014 852-B3
WILL CT
10200 CPTO 95014 832-E7
WILLAMETTE DR
6300 SJS 95123 874-H7
WILLARD AV
300 SJS 95126 853-H1
300 SCIC 95126 853-H1
N WILLARD AV
- SJS 95126 853-H1
WILLARD CT
800 GIL 95020 977-H1
WILLARD GARDEN CT
1500 SJS 95126 853-H1
WILLESTER AV
2000 SJS 95124 873-F2
WILLIAM AV
3000 SMCo 94063 790-D1
WILLIAM CT
- MLPK 94025 790-E5
E WILLIAM CT
1100 SJS 95116 834-E5
WILLIAM DR
2200 SCL 95050 833-C2
E WILLIAM ST
- SJS 95113 834-D7
- SJS 95112 834-D7
800 SJS 95116 834-G4
W WILLIAM ST
- SJS 95110 834-C7
400 SJS 95125 854-A1
WILLIAM HENRY CT
1600 LALT 94024 831-J4
WILLIAMS AV
20300 SAR 95070 872-D2
WILLIAMS DR
8600 SCIC 95020 958-D6
WILLIAMS RD
2900 SJS 95117 853-B3
3700 SJS 95128 853-E3
4200 SJS 95129 853-A3
4600 SJS 95129 852-J3
WILLIAMS ST
2000 PA 94306 791-A7
WILLIAMS WY
800 MTVW 94040 812-A7
WILLIAMSBURG DR
3100 SJS 95117 853-D4
WILLIAMSBURG LN
20100 SAR 95070 852-E6
WILLIAMSBURG WY
700 GIL 95020 977-J4
WILLIAMSPORT DR
1500 SJS 95131 814-C6
WILLIFORD DR
2500 SJS 95133 814-F7
WILLIS AV
400 SJS 95126 854-B1
500 SJS 95125 854-B1
WILLMAR DR
4100 PA 94306 811-C3
WILLO MAR DR
1200 SJS 95118 854-C7
WILLOW AV
400 MPS 95035 793-H6
1100 SUNV 94086 832-J1
1400 SCIC 95037 936-J7
WILLOW CT
1200 GIL 95020 977-F1
1500 MGH 95037 917-D6
WILLOW DR
5000 SJS 95032 873-H5
E WILLOW PL
- MLPK 94025 790-H3
WILLOW RD
- EPA 94303 790-J1
- PA 94304 790-G5
- MLPK 94025 790-J1
1100 MLPK 94025 791-A1
WILLOW RD Rt#-114
- MLPK 94025 791-A1
900 EPA 94303 791-A1
WILLOW ST
- SJS 95110 854-C2
400 SJS 95125 854-A3
1100 SJS 95125 853-J3
1400 MGH 95037 937-B1
1400 MGH 95037 917-B7
1700 SCIC 95125 853-H4
WILLOW WY
600 SCL 95054 813-E5
WILLOWBRAE AV
1500 SJS 95125 853-J4
WILLOWBROOK DR
100 PTLV 94028 830-B1
200 PTLV 94028 810-B7
1500 SJS 95118 874-A2
WILLOWBROOK WY
10700 CPTO 95014 852-F2
WILLOW CIRCLE CT
- SJS 95125 854-E5
WILLOW CREEK CT
1700 SJS 95124 873-J1
WILLOW CREEK DR
1600 SJS 95124 873-J1
16700 MGH 95037 936-J1
WILLOWDALE DR
1500 SJS 95118 874-A2
WILLOW ESTATES
5000 SJS 95135 855-G5
WILLOWGATE DR
1500 SJS 95118 874-A2
WILLOWGATE ST
600 MTVW 94043 811-J5
WILLOW GLEN WY
400 SJS 95125 854-A4
WILLOWGROVE LN
6000 CPTO 95014 852-G2
WILLOWHAVEN CT
1500 SJS 95126 853-H3
WILLOWHAVEN DR
1100 SJS 95126 853-H3
WILLOW HILL CT
100 LGTS 95030 873-C3
WILLOWHURST AV
1600 SCIC 95125 853-H5
1700 SJS 95125 853-H5
WILLOW LAKE LN
1600 SJS 95131 814-B6
WILLOWLEAF DR
900 SJS 95128 853-G3
WILLOWMONT AV
1400 SJS 95118 874-A2
1600 SJS 95124 874-A2
1600 SJS 95124 873-J2
WILLOW OAKS DR
1500 SJS 95125 853-J4
WILLOWOOD DR
3500 SJS 95118 874-A2
WILLOWPARK DR
3500 SJS 95118 874-A2
WILLOWPOND LN
25500 LAH 94022 831-B3
WILLOW SPRINGS RD
400 SCIC 95037 916-F4
WILLOWTREE CT
1400 SJS 95118 874-B1
WILLOWVIEW DR
3500 SJS 95118 874-A2
WILL ROGERS DR
3900 SJS 95117 853-B3
4200 SJS 95129 853-A3
WILL WOOL DR
2200 SJS 95112 854-G2
WILLY CT
400 GIL 95020 978-A1
WILMA WY
4900 SJS 95124 873-E4
WILMINGTON AV
1000 SJS 95129 852-J3
WILSHAM DR
1000 SJS 95132 814-F6
WILSHIRE BLVD
1700 SJS 95116 834-F3
WILSON AV
- SJS 95126 834-A7
300 SUNV 94086 832-F1
WILSON CT
600 SCL 95051 833-B6
1900 MTVW 94040 831-G1
21800 CPTO 95014 832-B7
WILSON ST
1200 PA 94301 791-B4
WILSON WY
- MPS 95035 793-J3
- SJS 95002 793-C7
- SJS 95002 813-C1
11700 SCIC 95020 958-A1
WILTON AV
200 PA 94306 811-C1
WILTON DR
100 CMBL 95008 853-D7
WIMBLEDON CT
4000 SJS 95135 855-H5
WIMBLEDON DR
14400 LGTS 95030 873-B3
WIMBLEDON PL
1900 LALT 94024 831-J5
N WINCHESTER BLVD
- SCL 95050 833-D5
100 SCL 95050 833-E7
S WINCHESTER BLVD
300 SJS 95117 853-E4
300 SJS 95128 853-E4
700 LGTS 95030 873-B3
900 MSER 95030 873-B3
1500 CMBL 95117 853-E4
1500 CMBL 95128 853-E4
1500 CMBL 95008 853-E4
2700 CMBL 95008 873-B3
WINCHESTER DR
- ATN 94027 790-E2
WINDELL CT
700 SJS 95123 874-F4
WINDEMERE CT
2100 SCIC 95037 917-C4
WINDERMERE AV
1000 MLPK 94025 790-J1
WINDHAM LN
100 MTVW 94043 812-A5
WINDIMER DR
1200 LALT 94024 831-H5
WINDING WY
4500 SJS 95129 853-A4
11600 SCIC 94024 831-E4
21400 SCIC 95030 913-B2
WINDING CREEK CT
1800 SJS 95148 835-D4
WINDING VISTA COM
- FRMT 94539 794-B1
WINDINGWOOD CT
300 MTVW 94040 811-F4
WINDMILL CT
1100 SJS 95121 854-J4
WINDMILL ST
- MGH 95037 937-B1
WINDMILL PARK LN
300 MTVW 94043 811-J4
WIND RIDGE LN
5700 SJS 95123 874-G7
WIND ROSE PL
2100 MTVW 94043 811-G2
WINDROW CT
- SJS 95135 876-A1
WINDSOR CT
12200 LAH 94022 830-J1
WINDSOR DR
500 MLPK 94025 790-F4
WINDSOR LN
6300 SJS 95129 852-F3
WINDSOR ST
1000 SJS 95129 852-E3
WINDSOR TER
600 SUNV 94087 832-D3
WINDSOR WY
1100 MLPK 94025 790-F4
6800 SJS 95129 852-E4
WINDSOR HILLS CIR
800 SJS 95123 874-E5
WINDSOR HILLS DR
5800 SJS 95123 874-E5
WINDSOR PARK DR
4200 SJS 95136 874-F1
WINDWARD CT
7000 SJS 95135 876-A1
WINE BARREL WY
3400 SJS 95124 873-E2
WINE CASK WY
3400 SJS 95124 873-E2
WINE CORK WY
3400 SJS 95124 873-E2
WINE GARDEN LN
8700 SJS 95135 856-A6
WINE GROWER WY
2200 SJS 95124 873-E2
3200 SJS 95008 873-E2
WINE MAKER WY
2200 SJS 95124 873-E2
WINE MASTER LN
8700 SJS 95135 856-A6
WINERY CT
8000 SJS 95135 855-J6
WINE VALLEY CIR
8800 SJS 95135 855-J6
8800 SJS 95135 856-A6
WINFIELD BLVD
5500 SJS 95136 874-E3
5500 SJS 95123 874-D6
5900 SJS 95120 874-D6
WINFIELD DR
2700 MTVW 94040 831-J2
WING PL
900 SCIC 94305 810-J2
WINGATE DR
600 SUNV 94087 832-D3
WINGHAM PL
4100 SJS 95135 855-F3
WINN RD
20100 SAR 95070 872-E4
WINNEBAGO CT
6100 SJS 95123 874-H6
WINONA DR
1300 SJS 95125 854-A5
WINSLOW CT
- CMBL 95008 853-A6
WINSLOW DR
1000 SJS 95122 834-G7
WINSOR ST
- MPS 95035 794-A7
WINSTEAD TER
700 SUNV 94087 832-C3
WINSTED CT
- SJS 95139 875-G7
WINSTON CT
1000 SJS 95131 834-C1
WINSTON PL
700 MTVW 94043 812-A3
WINSTON ST
1700 SJS 95131 834-D1
WINSTON WY
- SMCo 94061 790-B3
WINTER LN
5500 SJS 95138 875-C4
19900 SAR 95070 852-E7
WINTERBERRY WY
500 SJS 95129 853-B2
WINTERBROOK DR
6100 SJS 95129 852-C7
WINTERBROOK RD
16000 LGTS 95032 873-D6
WINTERCREEK
- PTLV 94028 830-C2
WINTERGREEN DR
19700 CPTO 95014 852-F1
WINTERGREEN WY
800 PA 94303 791-D6
WINTER PARK WY
1800 SJS 95122 834-J6
WINTERSET WY
6500 SJS 95120 894-F1
WINTERSONG CT
1800 SJS 95131 814-D7
WINTON WY
4800 SJS 95124 873-E4
4800 SCIC 95124 873-E4
12100 LAH 94024 831-E4
WINWOOD CT
300 MTVW 94040 811-F4
WINWOOD WY
2900 SJS 95148 855-D1
WISSAHICKON AV
100 LGTS 95030 872-J7
WISTARIA CT
1500 LALT 94024 831-J5
WISTARIA LN
1500 LALT 94024 831-J5
WISTARIA WY
- SCL 95050 833-F5
WISTERIA DR
100 EPA 94303 791-C2
700 GIL 95020 977-J6
WISTERIA WY
- ATN 94027 790-G1
6300 SJS 95129 852-F4
WITHEY RD
16200 MSER 95030 872-H6
WITHEY HEIGHTS RD
- MSER 95030 872-H6
- SCIC 95030 872-H6
WITHROW PL
2900 SCL 95051 833-A6
WIVEN PLACE WY
3800 SJS 95121 855-B4
WIZARD CT
2000 SJS 95131 814-D6
WOBURN CT
600 MTVW 94040 831-J2
WOEHL CT
21800 SCIC 95120 895-C4
WOLCOT WY
20300 SAR 95070 852-E6
WOLFBERRY CT
100 SJS 95136 874-H1
WOLFE RD
10000 CPTO 95014 832-G7
N WOLFE RD
100 SUNV 94086 832-G1
100 SUNV 94086 812-G6
S WOLFE RD
100 SUNV 94086 832-G2
1300 SCIC 94087 832-G2
1300 SUNV 94087 832-G5
WOLLIN WY
100 LGTS 95032 873-D7
WONDERAMA DR
1900 SJS 95148 835-A5
WONG CT
5300 SJS 95123 874-J3
WONG DR
5300 SJS 95123 874-J3
WOOD GRN
800 MTVW 94041 811-J6
WOOD LN
- MLPK 94025 790-E5
WOOD RD
100 LGTS 95030 892-J1
WOOD ACRES RD
15700 SCIC 95030 872-G6
WOODALE CT
1300 SJS 95127 835-A4
WOODARD RD
15000 SCIC 95124 873-E2
15000 SJS 95124 873-E2
15900 SCIC 95008 873-D2
WOODBANK WY
18400 SAR 95070 872-H3
WOODBARK CT
3700 SJS 95117 853-B3
WOODBINE WY
1000 SJS 95117 853-C3
WOODBRAE CT
5000 SJS 95130 852-J7
WOODBRIDGE WY
400 SCL 95054 813-F5
WOODBURN WY
13500 SCIC 95127 834-J3
WOODBURY DR
21800 CPTO 95014 832-B7
WOODCLIFF CT
6500 SJS 95120 894-C2
WOODCLIFF DR
6500 SJS 95120 894-C1
WOODCOCK CT
400 MPS 95035 794-A3
WOODCREEK LN
3700 SJS 95117 853-B4
WOODCREST DR
3000 SJS 95118 874-B1
WOOD DELL CT
18700 SAR 95070 852-H6
WOOD DUCK AV
900 SCL 95051 832-H5
WOOD DUCK CT
900 SCL 95051 832-H5
WOODED GLEN DR
2000 LALT 94024 831-G4
WOODED HILLS DR
1200 SJS 95120 894-E3
WOODED LAKE DR
7000 SJS 95120 894-D3
WOODED VIEW DR
100 LGTS 95032 873-E7
200 LGTS 95032 893-E1
WOODELF DR
1300 SJS 95121 855-A3
WOODFALLS CT
1000 SJS 95116 834-E6
WOODFERN
- PTLV 94028 830-C2
WOODFLOWER WY
1100 SJS 95117 853-C4
WOODFORD DR
3500 SJS 95124 873-J2
WOODGATE CT
2900 SJS 95120 873-J1
WOODGLEN DR
2000 SJS 95130 853-A6
WOODGROVE LN
900 SJS 95136 874-D2
WOODGROVE SQ
1400 SJS 95117 853-C4
WOODHAMS RD
- SCL 95051 833-A6
- SCL 95051 853-A1
WOODHAMS OAKS PL
800 SCL 95051 833-A6
WOODHAVEN DR
14000 SCIC 95127 835-A3
14000 SJS 95127 835-A3
WOOD HILL CT
11800 CPTO 95014 852-C4
WOODHURST LN
5400 SJS 95123 874-F4
WOODING CT
2400 SJS 95128 853-F3
WOODLAND AV
400 LGTS 95030 873-A7
500 MLPK 94025 790-J3
900 MLPK 94025 791-A3
1500 EPA 94303 791-B3
1800 SCL 95050 833-D7
2200 SJS 95128 833-E7
2500 SJS 95128 833-E7
17600 MGH 95037 936-F1
WOODLAND CT
- MPS 95035 814-A3
800 MLPK 94025 790-J3
18100 MGH 95037 936-F1
18100 SCIC 95037 936-F1
WOODLAND LN
300 MTVW 94043 811-J4
WOODLAND WY
100 MPS 95035 814-A3
WOODLARK WY
7900 CPTO 95014 852-C2
WOODLAWN AV
1200 SJS 95128 853-E4
WOODLEAF CT
3700 SJS 95117 853-B3
WOODLEAF WY
2100 MTVW 94040 831-J1
WOODLEIGH CIR
18800 SAR 95070 852-B7
WOODLEY DR
3500 SJS 95148 835-F7
WOODMAN CT
1300 SJS 95121 855-B2
WOODMEADOW CT
1300 SJS 95131 814-B6
WOODMEADOW LN
1300 SJS 95131 814-B6
WOODMERE DR
4000 SJS 95136 854-F7
WOODMINSTER DR
1000 SJS 95121 854-H2
WOODMONT DR
3000 SJS 95118 874-B1
12700 SAR 95070 852-E7
WOODMOOR DR
2700 SJS 95127 835-A5
WOODRIDGE CT
22500 CPTO 95014 851-J1
WOODRIDGE WY
1600 SJS 95148 835-B5
1600 SJS 95127 835-B5
WOODRUFF DR
1200 SJS 95120 874-C7
WOODRUFF WY
200 MPS 95035 793-J4
WOODS CT
2900 SJS 95148 855-D1
WOODS LN
- LALT 94024 831-J5
- SCIC 94024 831-J5
WOODS WY
3000 SJS 95148 835-D7
WOODSIDE CT
3400 SJS 95121 855-D3
12400 SAR 95070 852-G5
WOODSIDE DR
12100 SAR 95070 852-G5
WOODSIDE LN
3300 SJS 95121 855-D3
WOODSIDE RD Rt#-84
300 RDWC 94061 790-B2
300 SMCo 94061 790-B2
2100 WDSD 94062 790-B2
2100 SMCo 94062 790-B2
WOODSON CT
1500 SJS 95118 874-B2
WOODSTOCK LN
700 LALT 94022 831-E1
3400 MTVW 94040 831-J2
WOODSTOCK WY
500 SCL 95054 813-E5
5200 SJS 95118 874-A4
WOODTHRUSH CT
900 SJS 95120 894-G2
WOODTOWN CT
1000 SJS 95116 834-E6
WOODTREE CT
3400 SJS 95121 855-D3
WOODVALE CT
1000 SJS 95116 834-E6
WOODVIEW AV
300 MGH 95037 916-J4
WOODVIEW LN
- WDSD 94062 810-A6
14100 SAR 95070 872-F2
WOODVIEW PL
900 SJS 95120 894-G3
WOODVIEW TER
1200 LALT 94024 831-H5
WOODWARD AV
3200 SCL 95054 813-E6
WOODWARD CT
20600 SAR 95070 872-D1
WOODWARD DR
- MPS 95035 794-A6
WOODWARDIA LN
19400 SCIC 95030 872-F5
WOODWORTH WY
- SCIC 95127 815-D7
- GIL 95020 957-H7
WOODY CT
1900 SJS 95132 814-E2
WOODY LN
3200 SJS 95132 814-E3
WOODYEND CT
3400 SJS 95121 855-A4
WOOL AV
12900 SCIC 95111 854-H6
WOOL DR
600 MPS 95035 794-C5
WOOLAROC DR
21600 SCIC 95030 912-G4
WOOL CREEK DR
600 SJS 95112 854-F2
WOOSLEY DR
6200 SJS 95123 875-B6
WOOSTER AV
300 SJS 95116 834-D3
WORCESTER LN
100 LGTS 95032 873-C7
WORCESTER LP
100 LGTS 95032 893-C1
WORDEN LN
14200 SAR 95070 872-E2
WORLEY AV
500 SUNV 94086 812-F6
WORTHAM CT
100 MTVW 94040 831-J2
WORTHING CT
6700 SJS 95120 894-G2
WOZ WY
- SJS 95110 834-B7
WRAIGHT AV
400 LGTS 95030 873-A7
WREN AV
900 SCL 95051 832-J5
900 SUNV 94087 832-J5
7300 GIL 95020 977-H3
8600 GIL 95020 957-H7
8800 SCIC 95020 957-H7
WREN DR
800 SJS 95125 854-C6
WREN WY
200 CMBL 95008 853-C6
300 SJS 95008 853-C7
WRIGHT AV
- MGH 95037 916-H7
900 MTVW 94043 811-H4
1200 SUNV 94087 832-B4
WRIGHT CT
1000 SUNV 94087 832-B4
WRIGHT DR
19800 SCIC 95030 892-J7
WRIGHT PL
3700 PA 94306 811-D1
WRIGHT TER
1000 SUNV 94087 832-B4
WRIGHT WY
13200 LAH 94022 811-A7
WRIGHTS STATION RD
23400 SCIC 95030 913-E6
WRIGLEY WY
800 MPS 95035 794-C7
WUNDERLICH DR
1000 SJS 95129 852-H3
10200 SCIC 95014 852-H1
WYANDOTTE DR
100 SJS 95123 875-B5
WYANDOTTE ST
2100 MTVW 94043 811-F1
WYATT DR
1500 SCL 95054 813-D6
WYCLIFFE CT
2900 SJS 95148 855-D4
WYLIE DR
1700 MPS 95035 794-D7
WYLIE WY
1300 SJS 95130 853-C4
WYMAN WY
800 SJS 95133 814-F7
WYNDHAM DR
- PTLV 94028 810-A6
1600 SJS 95124 873-J3
1600 SJS 95124 874-A3
WYNFAIR RIDGE WY
2100 SJS 95138 855-F5
WYOMA PL
500 MPS 95035 794-B5
WYRICK AV
1700 SJS 95124 873-G2
1800 SCIC 95124 873-H3

X

XAVIER CT
2000 SCL 95051 832-J2
3700 SJS 95008 853-B7

Y

YAKIMA CIR
3100 SJS 95121 855-A4
YALE CT
14500 LAH 94022 810-H5
YALE DR
1600 MTVW 94040 811-G7
5400 SJS 95118 874-A5
YALE LN
700 SCL 95051 832-J6
YALE RD
- MLPK 94025 790-G4
YALE ST
1900 SCIC - 791-A7
2000 PA 94306 791-A7
YAMADA DR
1300 SJS 95131 814-C7
YAMANE DR
200 GIL 95020 957-J7
YAMATO DR
4800 SJS 95111 875-B1
YAMPA CT
48900 FRMT 94539 793-J2
YAMPA RD
- FRMT 94539 793-J2
YAMPA WY
- FRMT 94539 793-J2
500 FRMT 94539 794-A2
YANCY DR
3000 SJS 95148 855-D2
YANKEE POINT CT
1500 SJS 95131 814-D6
YARBOROUGH LN
200 RDWC 94061 790-B2
YARD CT
1100 SJS 95133 834-C2
YARDIS CT
800 MTVW 94040 831-G1
YARMOUTH TER
1300 SUNV 94087 832-E4
YARMOUTH CT
900 SJS 95120 894-G2
YARMOUTH WY
900 SJS 95120 894-G2
YARWOOD CT
1000 SJS 95128 853-F2
YASOU DEMAS WY
- SJS 95119 875-D5
YASUI CT
100 SJS 95138 875-G7
YATES CT
800 SUNV 94087 832-E2
YEADON WY
6100 SJS 95119 875-C6
YELLOWBIRD CT
6000 SJS 95120 874-B7
YELLOWLEAF CT
3200 SJS 95135 855-D2
YELLOWSTONE AV
1400 MPS 95035 814-D1
YELLOWSTONE DR
300 MGH 95037 937-A2
3900 SJS 95130 853-B4
YELLOWSTONE TER
600 SUNV 94087 832-D3
YERBA BANK CT
- SJS 95121 855-E4
YERBA BUENA AV
- LALT 94022 811-D5
400 SCIC 94306 811-D5
2900 SJS 95135 855-E3
3600 SJS 95121 855-E3
YERBA BUENA CT
3700 SJS 95121 855-D3
YERBA BUENA PL
200 LALT 94022 811-D5
YERBA BUENA RD
800 SJS 95111 855-B5
800 SCIC 95111 855-B5
900 SCIC 95121 855-B5
900 SJS 95121 855-B5
2900 SJS 95135 855-F4
YERBA BUENA WY
2500 SCL 95054 813-B2
YERBA CLIFF CT
- SJS 95121 855-F6
YERBA HILLS CT
- SJS 95121 855-E4
YERBA SANTA AV
- LALT 94022 811-D5
YERBA SANTA CT
13800 SAR 95070 872-F1
YERBA VISTA CT
2600 SJS 95121 855-E4
YERMO CT
500 SJS 95111 854-G6
YESLER CT
2300 SJS 95131 814-D4
YEW TREE CT
3600 SJS 95111 854-G6
YNIGO WY
4200 PA 94306 811-C3
YOLANDA CT
1400 SJS 95118 874-B2
YOLO CT
- SJS 95136 874-E1
YOLO DR
3800 SJS 95136 874-F1
3800 SAR 95070 852-D6
YONA VISTA
16000 SCIC 95127 815-A6
YORK AV
1300 CMBL 95008 873-A1
YORK ST
1600 SJS 95124 873-J2
YORKSHIRE DR
900 LALT 94024 831-H5
1100 CPTO 95014 852-C3

STREET
Block City ZIP Pg-Grid

YORKSHIRE WY
2000 MTVW 94040 831-J1
YORKTON DR
2600 MTVW 94040 831-J2
YORKTON WY
5000 SJS 95130 852-J7
YORKTOWN DR
900 SUNV 94087 832-B3
7000 GIL 95020 977-H4
YOSEMITE AV
400 MTVW 94041 811-H6
1100 SJS 95126 833-H7
YOSEMITE DR
500 MPS 95035 814-B1
1400 MPS 95035 794-D7
YOSEMITE WY
100 LGTS 95032 873-B7
15000 MGH 95037 937-B4
YOSHINO PL
10100 CPTO 95014 852-G1
YOUNG CT
24100 SCIC 94024 831-F3
E YOUNGER AV
- SJS 95112 834-A3
W YOUNGER AV
- SJS 95110 834-A3
YOUNGS CIR
3400 SJS 95127 814-J7
YOUNGS CT
600 SJS 95127 814-J6
YUBA AV
3200 SJS 95117 853-C3
YUBA CT
19600 SAR 95070 852-F6
YUBA DR
700 MTVW 94041 812-A6
800 MTVW 94041 811-J7
YUBA LN
27800 LAH 94022 810-J7
27800 LAH 94022 830-J1
YUCATAN WY
4900 SJS 95118 874-B3
YUCCA AV
3000 SJS 95124 873-J1
YUKON DR
1400 SUNV 94087 832-D5
YUKON TER
1300 SUNV 94087 832-D4
YUKON WY
2200 SJS 95008 853-B7
YUKON RIVER WY
- SJS 95131 814-B6
YUMA AV
1200 SUNV 94089 812-J5
YUMA DR
3100 SJS 95111 854-H5
YUROK CIR
500 SJS 95123 874-H5
YUROK CT
500 SJS 95123 874-H5
YVETTE CT
1100 SJS 95118 874-C3
YVONNE CT
15100 SCIC 95124 873-F4
YVONNE DR
15100 SCIC 95037 936-H5

Z

ZACHARY CT
- MLPK 94025 790-D7
1200 SJS 95121 854-H2
ZACHARY WY
2400 SJS 95121 854-J2
ZAMORA CT
1000 MPS 95035 794-B4
ZAMZOW CT
200 SCIC 95020 957-J6
ZANKER LN
- SJS 95134 793-E7
ZANKER RD
1600 SJS 95112 833-J1
1900 SJS 95131 813-H6
2000 SJS 95131 813-H6
2600 SJS 95134 813-F1
3800 SJS 95134 793-F7
ZAPATA WY
- PTLV 94028 810-A5
ZAPPETTINI CT
- LAH 94022 830-H2
ZARICK DR
900 SJS 95129 853-A3
ZATON AV
400 SJS 95117 853-C1
400 SCIC 95117 853-C1
ZAYANTE RD
400 SCrC 95030 912-F2
E ZAYANTE RD
11900 SCrC 95018 912-E7
ZEKA DR
1200 SJS 95131 814-C7
ZELLA CT
18100 SCIC 95030 912-H3
ZENA AV
17100 MSER 95030 873-B4
17300 LGTS 95030 873-B4
ZEPHYR CT
1300 SJS 95127 835-A4
ZEPPELIN CT
4900 SJS 95111 875-A2
ZIG ZAG TR
18100 SCIC 95030 912-J3
ZILEMAN CT
5800 SJS 95123 875-A5
ZILEMAN DR
5800 SJS 95123 875-A5
ZINFANDEL CT
19300 SAR 95070 872-G3
ZINFANDEL ST
- FRMT 94539 793-J2
ZINFANDEL WY
1100 SJS 95120 874-D6
ZINNIA LN
1600 SJS 95124 873-J6
ZINNIA ST
8700 GIL 95020 977-G1
ZION CT
1300 MPS 95035 794-D7
ZION LN
2900 SJS 95132 814-F5
ZIRCON CT
5000 SJS 95136 874-E3
ZISCH DR
3300 SJS 95118 874-B1
ZOOK RD
- SCIC 94035 792-B7
- SCIC 94035 812-B1
- SUNV 94089 792-B7
ZORIA CIR
2200 SJS 95131 814-D5
ZORKA AV
20100 SAR 95070 852-E5
ZUNI CT
1500 SJS 95131 814-D6
ZURICH CT
1100 SJS 95132 814-G5
ZURICH TER
1300 SUNV 94087 832-D4

#

1ST AV
- MTVW 94043 812-B5
- SCIC 94035 812-E1
200 SMCo 94063 790-D1
1000 SUNV 94089 812-E1
1ST ST Rt# 152
- GIL 95020 977-J2
1ST ST
- LALT 94022 811-D7
600 SUNV 94089 812-H4
1600 SCL 95134 813-E5
10700 SCIC 95020 957-G3
N 1ST ST
- CMBL 95008 853-E6
500 SJS 95112 834-A4
500 SJS 95110 834-A4
800 SJS 95113 834-A4
1100 SJS 95112 833-J2
1100 SJS 95110 833-J2
1200 SJS 95002 813-C1
2000 SJS 95131 833-J2
2100 SJS 95131 813-H7
2600 SJS 95134 813-E2
3600 SCIC 95134 813-E2
S 1ST ST
- SJS 95113 834-B6
300 CMBL 95008 853-E6
300 SJS 95110 834-C7
500 SJS 95112 834-C7
S 1ST ST Rt# 82
600 SJS 95110 834-C7
600 SJS 95112 834-C7
W 1ST ST
- MGH 95037 917-A7
- MGH 95037 916-J7
900 MLPK 94025 790-G2
2ND AV
200 SMCo 94063 790-D1
1100 SUNV 94089 812-E2
2ND ST
- SUNV 94089 812-H3
- GIL 95020 977-H3
- LALT 94022 811-D6
2000 SCL 95054 813-C5
2000 SCL 95134 813-E5
3900 PA 94306 811-D1
E 2ND ST
100 MLPK 94025 790-H3
N 2ND ST
- CMBL 95008 853-E6
- SJS 95113 834-A3
100 SJS 95112 834-A3
S 2ND ST
- SJS 95113 834-C7
400 SJS 95112 834-C7
700 SJS 95112 854-C1
W 2ND ST
- MGH 95037 917-A7
600 MLPK 94025 790-G3
3RD AV
- MTVW 94043 812-B5
200 SMCo 94063 790-D1
1000 SUNV 94089 812-E2
3RD ST
- GIL 95020 978-A2
- LALT 94022 811-D6
- MGH 95037 917-A7
- SCIC 95037 896-D6
- GIL 95020 977-G3
2000 SCL 95054 813-C5
2000 SCL 95134 813-E5
20600 SAR 95070 872-D3
E 3RD ST
400 MLPK 94025 790-H3
N 3RD ST
- CMBL 95008 853-E5
- SJS 95113 834-B5
- SJS 95112 834-A3
S 3RD ST
- SJS 95113 834-C7
100 CMBL 95008 853-E6
300 SJS 95112 834-C7
700 SJS 95112 854-D1
W 3RD ST
600 MLPK 94025 790-G3
4TH AV
- MTVW 94043 812-B5
200 SMCo 94063 790-D1
4TH ST
- SUNV 94089 812-H3
- GIL 95020 978-A3
- LALT 94022 811-E6
- MGH 95037 917-A7
100 GIL 95020 977-H3
1600 SCL 95134 813-E5
10600 SCIC 95020 957-H3
20600 SAR 95070 872-D2
E 4TH ST
600 MLPK 94025 790-G3
N 4TH ST
- SJS 95112 834-A3
- SJS 95113 834-B5
1200 SJS 95112 833-J2
S 4TH ST
- SJS 95113 834-C6
- CMBL 95008 853-E6
- SJS 95112 834-C6
100 SJS 95192 834-C6
W 4TH ST
700 MLPK 94025 790-G3
5TH AV
- SMCo 94063 790-D1
5TH ST
- GIL 95020 978-A3
- MGH 95037 917-A7
- MGH 95037 937-A1
100 GIL 95020 977-H3
1000 SCIC 94035 812-E2
1000 SUNV 94089 812-E2
4100 SCL 95134 813-E5
10600 SCIC 95020 957-H4
20600 SAR 95070 872-D3
N 5TH ST
- SJS 95113 834-B5
- SJS 95112 834-A3
S 5TH ST
- SJS 95113 834-C7
300 SJS 95112 834-C7
800 SJS 95112 854-D1
6TH AV
300 SMCo 94063 790-D1
1000 SUNV 94089 812-E3
6TH ST
- SUNV 94089 812-H3
500 GIL 95020 978-B3
1500 SCL 95054 813-D4
10700 SCIC 95020 957-H3
14600 SAR 95070 872-D3
E 6TH ST
- GIL 95020 978-A3
N 6TH ST
- SJS 95113 834-B5
- SJS 95112 834-B4
S 6TH ST
- SJS 95113 834-C7
300 SJS 95112 834-C7
800 SJS 95112 854-D1
W 6TH ST
- GIL 95020 978-A3
100 GIL 95020 977-J3
7TH AV
400 SMCo 94063 790-D1
1000 SUNV 94089 812-D3
7TH ST
- SUNV 94089 812-H3
1700 SCL 95054 813-D4
E 7TH ST
- GIL 95020 978-A3
N 7TH ST
- SJS 95113 834-B4
- SJS 95112 834-A3
S 7TH ST
- SJS 95113 834-D7
- SJS 95112 834-D7
500 SJS 95112 854-D1
W 7TH ST
- GIL 95020 978-A3
200 GIL 95020 977-J4
8TH AV
300 SMCo 94063 790-D1
1000 SUNV 94089 812-E3
E 8TH ST
300 GIL 95020 978-A3
N 8TH ST
- SJS 95113 834-C5
- SJS 95112 834-B3
S 8TH ST
- SJS 95113 834-D7
- SJS 95112 834-D7
900 SJS 95112 854-D1
W 8TH ST
- GIL 95020 978-A4
300 GIL 95020 977-H4
9TH AV
300 SMCo 94063 790-D1
1000 SUNV 94089 812-E3
9TH ST
- SUNV 94089 812-H3
E 9TH ST
100 GIL 95020 978-B4
N 9TH ST
- SJS 95113 834-B4
- SJS 95112 834-B4
S 9TH ST
- SJS 95113 834-D7
- SJS 95112 834-D7
900 SJS 95112 854-D1
W 9TH ST
- GIL 95020 978-A4
400 GIL 95020 977-J4
10TH ST
- SUNV 94089 812-H3
E 10TH ST
- GIL 95020 978-A4
N 10TH ST
- SJS 95113 834-B4
- SJS 95112 834-B2
S 10TH ST
- SJS 95112 834-D6
- SJS 95113 834-D6
100 SJS 95192 834-D6
800 SJS 95112 854-F2
W 10TH ST
- GIL 95020 978-A4
400 GIL 95020 977-J4
11TH AV
1000 SUNV 94089 812-D3
11TH ST
- GIL 95020 978-A4
N 11TH ST
- SJS 95112 834-B3
S 11TH ST
- SJS 95112 834-D6
900 SJS 95112 854-E1
N 12TH ST
- SJS 95112 834-B3
S 12TH ST
- SJS 95112 834-D6
1000 SJS 95112 854-E1
N 13TH ST
- SJS 95112 834-B2
S 13TH ST
- SJS 95112 834-D6
N 14TH ST
- SJS 95112 834-C3
S 14TH ST
- SJS 95112 834-D6
N 15TH ST
- SJS 95112 834-B2
S 15TH ST
- SJS 95112 834-D6
16TH AV
500 SMCo 94063 790-E1
N 16TH ST
100 SJS 95112 834-C3
S 16TH ST
- SJS 95112 834-D6
17TH AV
500 SMCo 94063 790-F1
N 17TH ST
- SJS 95112 834-C3
S 17TH ST
- SJS 95112 834-D5
18TH AV
600 SMCo 94063 790-F1
N 18TH ST
100 SJS 95112 834-C3
S 18TH ST
200 SJS 95116 834-E6
N 19TH ST
100 SJS 95112 834-C3
S 19TH ST
- SJS 95116 834-D5
N 20TH ST
- SJS 95116 834-D5
100 SJS 95112 834-D3
S 20TH ST
- SJS 95116 834-D5
N 21ST ST
- SJS 95116 834-D4
300 SJS 95112 834-C3
S 21ST ST
- SJS 95116 834-E5
N 22ND ST
500 SJS 95112 834-D3
S 22ND ST
- SJS 95116 834-E5
N 23RD ST
700 SJS 95112 834-C3
S 23RD ST
- SJS 95116 834-E5
N 24TH ST
- SJS 95116 834-D4
S 24TH ST
- SJS 95116 834-E5
N 25TH ST
- SJS 95116 834-E4
N 26TH ST
- SJS 95116 834-E4
S 26TH ST
- SJS 95116 834-E5
N 27TH ST
- SJS 95116 834-E4
N 28TH ST
- SJS 95116 834-E4
S 28TH ST
- SJS 95116 834-E5
N 30TH ST
- SJS 95116 834-E4
S 30TH ST
- SJS 95116 834-E5
N 31ST ST
- SJS 95116 834-E4
S 31ST ST
- SJS 95116 834-F4
N 32ND ST
- SJS 95116 834-E4
N 33RD ST
- SJS 95116 834-E3
200 SJS 95133 834-E3
S 33RD ST
- SJS 95116 834-F4
N 34TH ST
- SJS 95116 834-E3
S 34TH ST
- SJS 95116 834-F4
I-280 JUNIPERO SERRA FRWY
- LAH - 810-F3
- LAH - 811-A7
- LAH - 831-G5
- LALT - 831-G5
- MLPK - 810-C1
- PA - 810-F3
- SCL - 832-C6
- SCL - 852-H1
- SCIC - 831-G5
- SCIC - 810-F3
- SJS - 852-H1
- SJS - 853-A1
- SMCo - 790-A6
- SMCo - 810-C1
- SUNV - 832-C6
- WDSD - 790-A6
- CPTO - 832-C6
I-280 SINCLAIR FRWY
- SCIC - 853-G2
- SJS - 834-E7
- SJS - 854-A2
- SJS - 853-G2
I-680 SINCLAIR FRWY
- FRMT - 793-J1
- FRMT - 794-A1
- MPS - 794-A1
I-680 SINCLAIR FRWY
- MPS - 814-E6
- SCIC - 814-E6
- SJS - 834-F1
- SJS - 814-E6
I-880 NIMITZ FRWY
- FRMT - 793-G2
- MPS - 793-H4
- MPS - 813-J1
- SJS - 833-H5
- SJS - 834-A1
- SJS - 853-F1
- SJS - 813-J1
- SJS - 814-A6
Rt#-G2 LAWRENCE EXWY
- SAR 95070 852-H4
- SCL 95051 832-J6
- SCL 95051 852-H4
100 SUNV 94086 812-J7
300 SJS 95014 852-H4
300 SJS 95129 852-H4
300 SCIC 95014 852-H4
800 SUNV 94087 832-J6
1000 SUNV 94089 812-J3
1800 SAR 95129 852-H4
1900 SUNV 94086 832-J6
2900 SCL 95051 812-J7
Rt#-G2 QUITO RD
1900 SJS 95130 852-J7
1900 SAR 95130 852-J7
1900 SAR 95070 852-J7
2200 SAR 95070 872-J1
2200 SJS 95130 872-J1
14900 LGTS 95030 872-H4
15000 MSER 95030 872-H4
15500 SCIC 95030 872-H4
Rt#-G3 OREGON EXWY
- PA 94301 791-C6
- PA 94303 791-C6
300 PA 94306 791-C6
Rt#-G3 PAGE MILL RD
1800 SCIC 94305 810-J4
1800 PA 94304 810-J4
1900 SCIC 94304 810-J4
2400 LAH 94022 810-J4
Rt#-G4 MONTAGUE EXWY
- SJS 95134 813-F5
400 SCL 95054 813-D6
400 SCL 95134 813-F5
600 MPS 95035 813-F5
600 SJS 95131 813-F5
1500 SCL 95054 813-F5
Rt#-G4 SAN TOMAS EXWY
- CMBL 95008 853-C6
- SCL 95051 853-C4
- SCL 95117 833-C6
- SCL 95117 853-C4
- SJS 95008 853-C4
- SJS 95130 853-C4
100 SJS 95117 853-C4
200 SCL 95051 833-C3
200 SCL 95050 833-C6
2900 SCL 95054 813-C7
2900 SCL 95054 833-C3
Rt#-G5 FOOTHILL BLVD
8100 CPTO 95014 832-A6
8100 LALT 94024 832-A6
8400 SCIC 94024 832-A6
8700 CPTO 94024 832-A6
Rt#-G5 FOOTHILL EXWY
100 LALT 94022 811-C5
100 LALT 94022 831-F1
200 LALT 94024 831-F1
400 SCIC 94024 831-F1
2600 SCIC 94304 810-J3
2600 PA 94304 810-J3
2800 PA 94304 811-C5
2800 SCIC 94304 811-C5
4100 PA 94306 811-C5
4400 LALT 94024 832-A6
7100 CPTO 95014 832-A6
14000 LAH 94022 811-C5
14000 SCIC 94306 811-C5
Rt#-G5 JUNIPERO SERRA BLVD
- MLPK 94025 790-F7
- SCIC 94305 790-F7
- SCIC 94304 790-F7
100 SCIC 94304 810-G1
100 SCIC 94305 810-G1
Rt#-G6 CENTRAL EXWY
- MTVW 94041 812-B5
Rt#-G6 CENTRAL EXWY
- MTVW 94043 812-B5
- MTVW 94086 812-B5
- PA 94306 811-G3
- SCL 94086 812-H7
- SCL 95051 812-H7
- SUNV 94086 812-H7
- SUNV 94086 813-A7
100 MTVW 94043 811-G3
700 SCL 95050 833-D1
700 SCL 95054 833-D1
800 MTVW 94041 811-G3
800 SCL 95054 833-D1
2000 MTVW 94040 811-G3
2400 SCL 95051 833-D1
2700 SCL 95051 813-A7
2700 SCL 95054 813-A7
3000 SUNV 95054 813-A7
Rt#-G7 BLOOMFIELD AV
1000 SCIC 95020 978-H7
Rt#-G8 ALMADEN EXWY
3500 SJS 95118 874-D2
3500 SJS 95136 874-D2
4000 SJS 95118 854-C7
4000 SJS 95136 854-C7
5900 SJS 95120 874-D2
6600 SJS 95120 894-F2
8900 SJS 95123 874-D2
Rt#-G8 HARRY RD
20400 SCIC 95120 894-J4
20400 SJS 95120 894-J4
Rt#-G8 MCKEAN RD
19600 SJS 95120 894-J4
19600 SCIC 95120 894-J4
20000 SCIC 95120 895-A4
22200 SJS 95120 895-D6
23100 SJS 95141 895-D6
Rt#-G8 UVAS RD
12700 SCIC 95037 956-D1
15100 SCIC 95037 936-A1
18000 SCIC 95037 935-J1
19000 SCIC 95037 916-A5
20100 SCIC 95037 915-J4
23200 SJS 95141 895-G7
23500 SJS 95141 915-G1
23500 SCIC 95141 915-G1
Rt#-G8 WATSONVILLE RD
8000 SCIC 95020 977-A1
9300 SCIC 95020 956-J6
9900 SCIC 95020 957-A4
12500 SCIC 95046 956-J6
12500 SCIC 95037 956-J6
Rt#-G9 FERGUSON RD
2600 SCIC 95020 958-E7
3600 SCIC 95020 978-F1
Rt#-G9 LEAVESLEY RD
400 GIL 95020 978-B1
600 GIL 95020 958-C7
1100 SCIC 95020 958-C7
Rt#-G10 BLOSSOM HILL RD
- LGTS 95030 873-C6
- SJS 95123 874-E4
100 SJS 95111 875-A4
200 SJS 95138 875-A4
400 LGTS 95032 873-C6
400 SCIC 95123 874-E4
700 SJS 95123 875-A4
1000 SJS 95193 875-A4
1400 SJS 95124 873-F6
1400 SJS 95124 874-A6
1600 SJS 95118 874-A6
15800 SCIC 95032 873-C6
Rt#-1 CABRILLO HWY
- WAT - 995-A6
Rt#-9 BIG BASIN WY
14300 SAR 95070 872-D3
Rt#-9 CONGRESS SPRINGS RD
- SCrC 95030 871-D2
20900 SAR 95070 872-A3
21900 SCIC 95070 871-G2
21900 SCIC 95070 872-A3
22600 SCIC 95030 871-D2
Rt#-9 HIGHWAY
- SCrC 95030 871-C2
Rt#-9 SARATOGA LOS GATOS RD
17900 LGTS 95030 873-A6
17900 MSER 95030 872-G5
17900 MSER 95030 873-A6
18500 SCIC 95030 872-G5
18800 SAR 95070 872-E3
Rt#-17 FRWY
- CMBL - 873-D2
Rt#-17 FRWY
- CMBL - 853-F3
- LGTS - 873-D3
- LGTS - 892-J1
- LGTS - 893-A1
- SCIC - 873-D2
- SCIC - 892-J1
- SJS - 853-F3
Rt#-17 HIGHWAY
- SCIC 95030 892-J2
- SCIC 95030 912-J1
- SCIC 95032 892-J2
- SCrC 95030 912-J4
- SCrC 95030 913-A6
Rt#-25 BLOOMFIELD AV
1800 SCIC 95020 (998-C2 See Page 997)
Rt#-25 HOLLISTER RD
- HOLL - (1019-H6 See Page 999)
- SBnC - 999-C7
1800 SCIC 95020 (998-E3 See Page 997)
Rt#-35 BEAR CREEK BLVD
20000 SCrC 95030 912-E1
Rt#-35 SKYLINE BLVD
11700 SCIC 95030 851-A7
11700 SCIC 95030 871-B1
11700 SCrC 95030 892-A2
11800 SCrC 95030 871-D3
12300 SCIC 95070 871-F6
13000 SCIC 95070 892-A2
13500 SCIC 95030 892-D5
19000 SCrC 95030 912-E1
19300 SMCo 94020 830-A4
19300 PTLV 94028 830-A4
19800 SMCo 94028 830-C7
20800 SMCo 94020 850-E1
20800 SMCo 94028 850-E1
21100 SCIC 94028 850-E1
21200 PA 94304 850-H2
21600 SMCo 94304 850-H2
22800 SCrC 95030 850-J5
22800 SMCo 95030 850-J5
Rt#-35 SUMMIT RD
21000 SCrC 95030 912-F2
21200 SCIC 95030 912-F2
Rt#-82 S 1ST ST
600 SJS 95110 834-C7
600 SJS 95112 834-C7
Rt#-82 S AUTUMN ST
- SJS 95110 834-A7
- SJS 95113 834-A7
Rt#-82 EL CAMINO REAL
- MLPK 94025 790-C1
- PA 94301 790-H4
- PA 94304 790-H4
100 ATN 94027 790-C1
100 MTVW 94040 811-B1
100 MTVW 94041 811-B1
100 SMCo 94063 790-C1
200 SCIC 94305 790-H4
200 PA 94305 790-H4
300 SCL 95050 833-A4
400 SCL 95053 833-A4
1400 SCIC - 791-A6
1400 PA - 790-H4
1400 PA 94306 791-A6
1500 MLPK 94027 790-C1
1700 ATN 94025 790-C1
2400 PA 94305 791-A6
2400 SCL 95051 833-A4
2600 RDWC 94061 790-C1
2700 PA 94304 811-B1
2800 PA 94306 811-B1
3300 SCL 95051 832-J4
4300 LALT 94022 811-B1
Rt#-82 E EL CAMINO REAL
- SCL 95051 832-G4
100 SUNV 94087 832-E2
100 SUNV 94086 832-G4
800 SCL 94087 832-G4
1100 SCL 94086 832-G4
Rt#-82 W EL CAMINO REAL
- MTVW 94040 811-F4
- MTVW 94041 811-F4
100 SUNV 94086 832-C1
100 SUNV 94087 832-C1
100 MTVW 94040 812-A7
100 MTVW 94041 812-A7
300 SCIC 94087 832-C1
900 SUNV 94086 812-A7
1100 SUNV 94087 812-A7
Rt#-82 W EL CAMINO REAL
1700 LALT 94022 811-F4
Rt#-82 S MARKET ST
300 SJS 95110 834-B7
Rt#-82 MONTEREY HWY
- SJS 95111 854-F5
- SJS 95125 854-D2
200 SCIC 95111 854-F5
700 SJS 95112 854-D2
700 SJS 95110 854-D2
3700 SJS 95136 854-F5
4100 SJS 95136 874-H1
4100 SJS 95111 874-H1
4700 SJS 95136 875-A2
4700 SJS 95111 875-A2
5100 SJS 95123 875-A2
5200 SJS 95193 875-A2
Rt#-82 MONTGOMERY ST
- SJS 95110 834-A7
200 SJS 95110 854-A1
Rt#-82 S MONTGOMERY ST
- SJS 95110 834-A7
- SJS 95113 834-A7
Rt#-82 W SAN CARLOS ST
- SJS 95113 834-A7
- SJS 95110 834-A7
1600 SJS 95126 834-A7
Rt#-82 W SANTA CLARA ST
500 SJS 95113 834-A7
500 SJS 95126 834-A7
Rt#-82 THE ALAMEDA
700 SCL 95126 833-H5
700 SJS 95126 833-H5
2100 SJS 95126 834-A7
2200 SCL 95050 833-H5
2600 SCL 95053 833-H5
Rt#-84 WOODSIDE RD
300 RDWC 94061 790-B2
300 SMCo 94061 790-B2
2100 WDSD 94062 790-B2
2100 SMCo 94062 790-B2
Rt#-85 FRWY
- CPTO - 852-C1
- SAR - 852-E5
- SCIC - 852-C2
- SJS - 852-D4
Rt#-85 STEVENS CREEK FRWY
- CPTO - 832-A1
- LALT - 832-A1
- MTVW - 812-A7
- MTVW - 832-A1
- SCIC - 832-A1
- SUNV - 832-A1
Rt#-85 WEST VALLEY FRWY
- CMBL - 873-C2
- CPTO - 832-B6
- CPTO - 852-E4
- LGTS - 873-C2
- SAR - 852-E4
- SAR - 872-H1
- SCL - 852-E4
- SCIC - 873-C2
- SCIC - 874-C3
- SJS - 872-J1
- SJS - 873-C2
- SJS - 874-C3
- SJS - 875-A5
- SJS - 852-E4
- SUNV - 832-B6
Rt#-87 GUADALUPE FRWY
- SCIC - 874-E1
- SCIC - 854-D6
- SJS - 854-C3
- SJS - 834-A5
- SJS - 874-E1
Rt#-114 WILLOW RD
- MLPK 94025 791-A1
900 EPA 94303 791-A1
Rt#-129 HIGHWAY
1300 SCrC 95076 (1017-D2 See Page 997)
Rt#-129 RIVERSIDE DR
- WAT 95076 (1015-F3 See Page 995)
300 SCrC 95076 (1015-F3 See Page 995)
Rt#-130 ALUM ROCK AV
- SJS 95116 834-H3
3400 SJS 95127 834-H3
Rt#-130 ALUM ROCK AV
3500 SCIC 95127 834-H3
5900 SCIC 95127 834-H3
6900 SCIC 95127 835-A1
8900 SCIC 95127 815-A7
Rt#-130 MOUNT HAMILTON RD
- SCIC 95127 815-B7
- SCIC 95127 835-D1
- SCIC 95140 835-G2
1000 SCIC 95140 815-E7
11700 SCIC 95127 836-B4
11700 SCIC 95140 836-J6
12000 SCIC 95148 836-B4
13100 SCIC 95135 836-F7
13400 SCIC 95135 856-H1
14000 SCIC 95140 856-H1
17200 SCIC 95140 837-A6
Rt#-152 1ST ST
- GIL 95020 977-J2
Rt#-152 HECKER PASS HWY
- SCrC 95076 (996-A3 See Page 995)
300 GIL 95020 977-F2
1500 SCIC 95020 977-B2
4300 SCIC 95020 (976-F3 See Page 955)
5600 SCrC 95076 (976-B6 See Page 955)
Rt#-152 E LAKE AV
700 WAT 95076 995-J4
1000 SCrC 95076 995-A3
Rt#-152 LEAVESLEY RD
- GIL 95020 977-J1
- GIL 95020 978-A1
Rt#-152 LINCOLN ST
500 WAT 95076 (1015-G See Page 995)
Rt#-152 MAIN ST
300 WAT 95076 (1015-C See Page 995)
Rt#-152 PACHECO PASS HWY
800 GIL 95020 978-C4
1400 SCIC 95020 978-G3
3000 SCIC 95020 (979-B6 See Page 959)
3700 SBnC - (979-B6 See Page 959)
4000 SCIC 95020 999-H1
6000 SCIC 95020 (980-D5 See Page 959)
8200 SCIC 95020 961-J4
Rt#-156 HIGHWAY
- SCIC 95020 (1000-C See Page 999)
Rt#-156 SAN FELIPE RD
1600 HOLL - (1020-A See Page 999)
2700 SBnC - (1020-A See Page 999)
Rt#-237 CALAVERAS BLVD
100 MPS 95035 793-J7
100 MPS 95035 794-A7
Rt#-237 MTN VIEW-ALVISO RD
200 MTVW 94041 812-A6
500 MTVW 94043 812-A6
500 MTVW 94041 811-J6
Rt#-237 SOUTHBAY FRWY
- MPS - 813-C1
- SCL - 813-C1
- SCIC - 813-C1
- SJS - 813-C1
- SUNV - 812-D4
- SUNV - 813-C1
U.S.-101 BAYSHORE FRWY
- EPA - 790-J1
- EPA - 791-E5
- MLPK - 790-J1
- MLPK - 791-E5
- MTVW - 791-E5
- MTVW - 811-G1
- MTVW - 812-C4
- PA - 791-E5
- SCL - 813-B6
- SCIC - 812-C4
- SCIC - 855-B5
- SJS - 813-B6
- SJS - 855-B5
- SJS - 875-C1
- SJS - 833-G1
- SJS - 834-C2

SANTA CLARA CO.

INDEX

SANTA CLARA CO.

INDEX

1998 SANTA CLARA POINTS OF INTEREST

AIRPORTS

FEATURE NAME	Address City, ZIP Code	PAGE-GRID
HOLLISTER MUNICIPAL AIRPORT (SEE PAGE 999)	2312 SAN FELIPE RD, HOLL	1019 - J6
PALO ALTO AIRPORT	1925 EMBARCADERO RD, PA, 94303, (650)856-7833	791 - E2
REID-HILLVIEW AIRPORT	2500 CUNNINGHAM AV, SJS, 95148, (408)929-2256	835 - A6
SAN JOSE INTERNATIONAL AIRPORT	1661 AIRPORT BLVD, SJS, 95110, (408)277-4759	833 - F1
SOUTH COUNTY AIRPORT	101 FRWY & E SAN MARTIN AV, SCIC, 95046, (408)683-4741	937 - G7
WATSONVILLE MUNICIPAL AIRPORT	WAT, 95019	995 - C6

BUILDINGS

FOR DOWNTOWN BUILDINGS SEE PAGE XIV

FEATURE NAME	Address City, ZIP Code	PAGE-GRID
IBM RESEARCH LABORATORY	LOOP DR, SJS, 95120	895 - B2
IOOF HOME	SAR, 95070	872 - G3
MAPLES PAVILION	CAMPUS DR, SCIC, 94305, (650)723-2300	790 - J7
SAN JOSE CIVIC AUDITORIUM	145 W SAN CARLOS ST, SJS, 95113, (408)277-3900	834 - B7
STANFORD LINEAR ACCELERATOR CENTER	2575 SAND HILL RD, SMCo, 94025, (650)926-3300	810 - D1

BUILDINGS - GOVERNMENTAL

FEATURE NAME	Address City, ZIP Code	PAGE-GRID
COURTHOUSE	GRANT & BIRCH, PA, 94306	791 - B7
ELMWOOD CORRECTIONAL FACILITY	701 ABEL ST, MPS, 95035, (408)299-2831	814 - A2
MILPITAS CIVIC CENTER	CALAVERAS BLVD & TOWN CENTER D, MPS, 95035	794 - B7
SANTA CLARA CIVIC CENTER	1500 WARBURTON AV, SCL, 95050	833 - D3
SANTA CLARA COUNTY COURTHOUSE	191 N 1ST ST, SJS, 95113, (408)299-2964	834 - B6
SANTA CLARA COUNTY MUNICIPAL COURT	605 W EL CAMINO REAL, SUNV, 94086, (408)739-1503	832 - D1
SANTA CLARA COUNTY SERVICE CENTER	BERGER DR, SJS, 95112	834 - B1
SANTA CLARA COURTHOUSE	1500 WARBURTON AV, SCL, 95050	833 - D3
U S CUSTOMS	AIRPORT BLVD, SJS, 95110	833 - H3
WATSONVILLE BRANCH COURT	1430 FREEDOM BLVD, WAT, 95076, (408)763-8120	995 - F6
WEST VALLEY COURTHOUSE	14205 CAPRI DR, LGTS, 95030, (408)378-3227	873 - C2

CEMETERIES

FEATURE NAME	Address City, ZIP Code	PAGE-GRID
ALTA MESA CEMETERY	695 ARASTRADERO RD, PA, 94306	811 - C4
CALVARY CATHOLIC CEMETERY	2655 MADDEN AV, SJS, 95116, (408)258-2940	834 - H2
CEDAR LAWN MEMORIAL CEMETERY	48800 WARM SPRINGS BLVD, FRMT, 94539, (510)656-5565	793 - J2
CEMETERY	CALAVERAS RD, SCIC, 95035	794 - H5
CEMETERY	SANTA CRUZ AV, MLPK, 94025	790 - E6
LOS GATOS CEMETERY	2255 LOS GATOS ALMADEN RD, SJS, 95124, (408)356-4151	873 - E5
MADRONIA CEMETERY	6TH ST, SAR, 95070	872 - D3
MEMORIAL CROSS CEMETERY	DE LA CRUZ BLVD & MARTIN AV, SJS, 95050	833 - F2
MISSION CITY MEMORIAL PARK CEMETERY	WINCHESTER BLVD, SCL, 95050, (408)984-3090	833 - D6
OAK HILL CEMETERY	300 CURTNER AV, SJS, 95125, (408)297-2447	854 - E4
ST MARYS CEMETERY	HECKER PASS HWY, GIL, 95020, (408)847-5151	977 - G2
SANTA CLARA CATHOLIC CEMETERY	490 LINCOLN ST, SCL, 95050, (408)296-4656	833 - E5
UNION CEMETERY	WOODSIDE RD, RDWC, 94061	790 - B1

CHAMBERS OF COMMERCE

FEATURE NAME	Address City, ZIP Code	PAGE-GRID
CAMPBELL CHAMBER OF COMMERCE	1628 W CAMPBELL BLVD, CMBL, 95008, (408)378-6252	853 - A6
CUPERTINO CHAMBER OF COMMERCE	20455 SILVERADO AV, CPTO, 95014, (408)252-7054	852 - E2
EAST PALO ALTO C OF C	1491 E BAYSHORE RD, EPA, 94303, (650)462-4915	791 - A2
GILROY CHAMBER OF COMMERCE	7471 MONTEREY ST, GIL, 95020, (408)842-6936	978 - A3
GILROY VISITORS BUREAU	MONTEREY ST & IOOF AVE, GIL, 95020, (408)842-6936	978 - A2
LOS ALTOS CHAMBER OF COMMERCE	321 UNIVERSITY AV, LALT, 94022, (650)948-1455	811 - D7
MENLO PARK CHAMBER OF COMMERCE	1100 MERRILL ST, MLPK, 94025, (650)325-2818	790 - F3
MILPITAS CHAMBER OF COMMERCE	75 S MILPITAS BLVD, MPS, 95035, (408)262-2613	794 - A7
MORGAN HILL CHAMBER OF COMMERCE	25 W 1ST ST, MGH, 95037, (408)779-9444	917 - A7
MOUNTAIN VIEW CHAMBER OF COMMERCE	580 CASTRO ST, MTVW, 94041, (650)968-8378	811 - H5
PAJARO VALLEY CHAMBER OF COMMERCE (SEE PAGE 995)	444 MAIN ST, WAT, 95076, (408)724-3900	1015 - G2
PALO ALTO CHAMBER OF COMMERCE	325 FOREST AV, PA, 94301, (650)324-3121	790 - J5
SAN JOSE CHAMBER OF COMMERCE	180 S MARKET ST, SJS, 95113, (408)291-5250	834 - B7
SAN JOSE CONV & VIS BUREAU	333 W SAN CARLOS ST, SJS, 95110, (408)295-9600	834 - B7
SANTA CLARA CHAMBER OF COMMERCE	1850 WARBURTON AV, SCL, 95050, (408)244-9660	833 - D3
SARATOGA CHAMBER OF COMMERCE	20460 SARATOGA LOS GATOS RD, SAR, 95070, (408)867-0753	872 - D3
SUNNYVALE CHAMBER OF COMMERCE	499 MURPHY AV, SUNV, 94086, (408)736-4971	832 - E1
US CHAMBER OF COMMERCE	1901 S BASCOM AV, CMBL, 95008, (408)371-6000	853 - F5

CITY HALLS

FEATURE NAME	Address City, ZIP Code	PAGE-GRID
ATHERTON CITY HALL	91 ASHFIELD RD, ATN, 94027, (650)325-4457	790 - E2
CAMPBELL CITY HALL	70 N 1ST ST, CMBL, 95008, (408)866-2100	853 - E5
CUPERTINO CITY HALL	10300 TORRE AV, CPTO, 95014, (408)252-4505	852 - E1
EAST PALO ALTO CITY HALL	2415 UNIVERSITY AV, EPA, 94303, (650)853-3127	791 - B1
GILROY CITY HALL	7351 ROSANNA ST, GIL, 95020, (408)848-0202	977 - J3
LOS ALTOS CITY HALL	1 N SAN ANTONIO RD, LALT, 94022, (650)348-1491	811 - E6
LOS ALTOS HILLS CITY HALL	26379 W FREMONT RD, LAH, 94022, (650)941-7222	811 - B6
LOS GATOS CITY HALL	110 E MAIN ST, LGTS, 95032, (408)354-6801	893 - A1
MENLO PARK CITY HALL	701 LAUREL ST, MLPK, 94025, (650)858-3360	790 - G3
MILPITAS CITY HALL	455 CALVAVERAS BLVD, MPS, 95035, (408)942-2374	794 - B7
MONTE SERENO CITY HALL	18041 SARATOGA-LOS GATOS RD, MSER, 95030, (408)354-6834	872 - J6
MORGAN HILL CITY HALL	17555 PEAK AV, MGH, 95037, (408)779-7259	936 - J1
MOUNTAIN VIEW CITY HALL	500 CASTRO ST, MTVW, 94041, (650)966-6300	811 - H5
PALO ALTO CITY HALL	250 HAMILTON AV, PA, 94301, (650)329-3211	790 - J5
PORTOLA VALLEY TOWN HALL	765 PORTOLA RD, PTLV, 94028, (650)851-1700	810 - A6
SAN JOSE CITY HALL	801 N 1ST ST, SJS, 95110, (408)277-4000	834 - A4
SANTA CLARA CITY HALL	1500 WARBURTON AV, SCL, 95050, (408)984-3000	833 - D3
SARATOGA CITY HALL	13777 FRUITVALE AV, SAR, 95070, (408)868-1200	872 - F1
SUNNYVALE CITY HALL	456 W OLIVE AV, SUNV, 94086, (408)738-5411	832 - D1
WATSONVILLE CITY HALL (SEE PAGE 995)	250 MAIN ST, WAT, 95076, (408)728-6005	1015 - G2

COLLEGES & UNIVERSITIES

FEATURE NAME	Address City, ZIP Code	PAGE-GRID
DE ANZA COLLEGE	21250 STEVENS CREEK BLVD, CPTO, 95014, (408)864-4567	852 - C1
EVERGREEN VALLEY COMMUNITY COLLEGE	3095 YERBA BUENA RD, SJS, 95135	855 - G4
FOOTHILL COLLEGE	12345 S EL MONTE AV, LAH, 94022, (650)949-7777	831 - C2
GAVILAN COLLEGE	5055 SANTA TERESA BLVD, SCIC, 95020, (408)847-1400	978 - A7
MARYKNOLL SEMINARY	23000 CRISTO REY DR, SCIC, 94024, (650)967-3822	831 - H6
MENLO COLLEGE	1000 EL CAMINO REAL, ATN, 94027, (650)323-6141	790 - E3
MISSION COLLEGE	3000 MISSION COLLEGE BLVD, SCL, 95054, (408)988-2200	813 - A5
SAINT JOSEPHS SEMINARY	CRISTO REY DR, CPTO, 95014	831 - G6
SAINT PATRICKS SEMINARY	MIDDLEFIELD RD & SANTA MONICA, MLPK, 94025	790 - H2
SAN JOSE CHRISTIAN COLLEGE	790 S 12TH ST, SJS, 95112, (408)293-9058	834 - D7
SAN JOSE CITY COLLEGE	2100 MOORPARK AV, SJS, 95128, (408)298-2181	853 - G2
SAN JOSE STATE UNIVERSITY	125 S 7TH ST, SJS, 95192, (408)924-1000	834 - C6
SANTA CLARA UNIVERSITY	500 EL CAMINO REAL, SCL, 95053, (408)554-4000	833 - E4
STANFORD UNIVERSITY	JUNIPERO SERRA BLVD, SCIC, 94305, (650)723-2300	790 - G6
UNIVERSITY OF PHOENIX	3590 N 1ST ST, SJS, 95134, (408)435-8500	813 - E3
WEST VALLEY-SARATOGA COLLEGE	14000 FRUITVALE AV, SAR, 95070, (408)867-2200	872 - G2

DEPARTMENT OF MOTOR VEHICLES

FEATURE NAME	Address City, ZIP Code	PAGE-GRID
GILROY DMV	8200 CHURCH ST, GIL, 95020, (408)842-6488	977 - J2
LOS GATOS DMV	600 N SANTA CRUZ AV, LGTS, 95030, (408)354-6541	873 - A6
MOUNTAIN VIEW DMV	595 SHOWERS DR, MTVW, 94040, (650)968-0610	811 - F4
SAN JOSE DMV	111 W ALMA AV, SJS, 95110, (408)277-1301	854 - D2
SANTA CLARA DMV	3665 FLORA VISTA AV, SCL, 95051, (408)277-1640	832 - J4
SANTA TERESA DMV	180 MARTINVALE LN, SJS, 95119, (408)224-4511	875 - E7

ENTERTAINMENT & SPORTS

FEATURE NAME	Address City, ZIP Code	PAGE-GRID
GREAT AMERICA THEME PARK	1 GREAT AMERICA PKWY, SCL, 95054, (408)988-1776	813 - B4
RAGING WATERS	2333 WHITE RD, SJS, 95148, (408)270-8000	835 - B6
SAN JOSE ARENA	W SANTA CLARA ST & AUTUMN ST, SJS, 95110, (408)287-9200	834 - A6
SAN JOSE CONVENTION CENTER	150 W SAN CARLOS ST, SJS, 95110, (408)277-3900	834 - B7
SAN JOSE MUNICIPAL BASEBALL STADIUM	E ALMA AV & SENTER RD, SJS, 95112	854 - E1
SANTA CLARA CONVENTION CENTER	5001 GREAT AMERICA PKWY, SCL, 95054, (408)748-7000	813 - B3
SANTA CLARA COUNTY FAIRGROUNDS	344 TULLY RD, SCIC, 95111, (408)295-3050	854 - F4
SCL COUNTY FAIRGROUNDS RACETRACK	SANTA CLARA COUNTY FAIRGROUNDS, SCIC, 95111	854 - G4
SPARTAN STADIUM	S 7TH ST & E ALMA AV, SJS, 95112, (408)924-6363	854 - E1
STADIUM	NELSON RD & SAM MCDONALD RD, SCIC, 94305, (650)723-2300	790 - J6

GOLF COURSES

FEATURE NAME	Address City, ZIP Code	PAGE-GRID
ALMADEN COUNTRY CLUB	6663 HAMPTON DR, SJS, 95120, (408)268-4653	894 - D2
BLACKBERRY FARM GOLF COURSE	22100 STEVENS CREEK BLVD, CPTO, 95014, (408)253-9200	852 - A1
CYPRESS GREENS GOLF COURSE	2050 WHITE RD, SCIC, 95148, (408)238-3485	835 - C5
DEEP CLIFF GOLF COURSE	10700 CLUBHOUSE LN, CPTO, 95014, (408)253-5357	852 - A2
FREMONT HILLS COUNTRY CLUB	ROBLE LADERA & PURISSIMA RD, LAH, 94022	811 - A7
GAVILAN GOLF COURSE (SEE PAGE 997)	5055 SANTA TERESA BLVD, SCIC, 95020, (408)848-1363	998 - A1
GILROY GOLF COURSE	2695 HECKER PASS HWY, GIL, 95020, (408)848-0490	977 - D2
LA RINCONADA COUNTRY CLUB	14595 CLEARVIEW DR, LGTS, 95030, (408)395-4220	873 - A3
LOS ALTOS GOLF & COUNTRY CLUB	1560 COUNTRY CLUB DR, SCIC, 94024, (650)948-1024	831 - G4
MENLO COUNTRY CLUB	2300 WOODSIDE RD, WDSD, 94062, (650)366-9910	790 - A4
MOFFETT FIELD GOLF COURSE	MACON RD & MARRIAGE RD, SCIC, 94035, (408)603-8026	812 - D1
PALO ALTO HILLS GOLF & COUNTRY CLUB	3000 ALEXIS DR, PA, 94304, (650)948-1800	810 - G7
PALO ALTO MUNICIPAL GOLF COURSE	1875 EMBARCADERO RD, PA, 94303, (650)856-0881	791 - D3
PLEASANT HILLS GOLF COURSE	2050 WHITE RD, SCIC, 95148, (408)238-3485	835 - C6
PRUNERIDGE GOLF COURSE	400 N SARATOGA AV, SCL, 95050, (408)248-4424	833 - C7
RIVERSIDE GOLF COURSE	9770 MONTEREY RD, SCIC, 95037, (408)463-0622	896 - C4
SAN JOSE COUNTRY CLUB	15571 ALUM ROCK AV, SCIC, 95127, (408)258-4901	815 - A6
SAN JOSE MUNICIPAL GOLF COURSE	1560 OAKLAND RD, SJS, 95131, (408)441-4653	814 - B7
SANTA CLARA GOLF & TENNIS CLUB	5155 STARS & STRIPES DR, SCL, 95054, (408)986-1666	813 - B3
SANTA TERESA GOLF CLUB	260 BERNAL RD, SCIC, 95119, (408)225-2650	895 - D3
SARATOGA COUNTRY CLUB	21990 PROSPECT RD, SAR, 95070, (408)253-0340	852 - B6
SHARON HEIGHTS GOLF & COUNTRY CLUB	2900 SAND HILL RD, MLPK, 94025, (650)854-6422	790 - C7
SHORELINE GOLF LINKS	2600 N SHORELINE BLVD, MTVW, 94043, (650)969-2041	791 - H7
SILVER CREEK VALLEY COUNTRY CLUB	5960 COUNTRY CLUB PKWY, SJS, 95138, (408)239-5775	875 - G1
SPRING VALLEY GOLF COURSE	3441 CALAVERAS RD, MPS, 95035, (408)262-1722	794 - G5
STANFORD UNIVERSITY DRIVING RANGE	CAMPUS DR WEST & LOS ARBOLES A, SCIC, 94305, (650)323-9516	790 - G7
STANFORD UNIVERSITY GOLF COURSE	198 JUNIPERO SERRA BLVD, SCIC, 94304, (650)323-0944	790 - F7
POINTE GOLF CLUB	1500 COUNTRY CLUB DR, MPS, 95035, (408)262-2500	794 - D4
SUNKEN GARDENS GOLF COURSE	1010 S WOLFE RD, SUNV, 94086, (408)732-2046	832 - G3
SUNNY HILLS GOLF CENTER	49055 WARM SPRINGS BLVD, FRMT, 94539	793 - J3
SUNNYVALE MUNICIPAL GOLF COURSE	605 MACARA AV, SUNV, 94086, (408)738-3666	812 - C4
THE VILLAGES GOLF & COUNTRY CLUB	5000 CRIBARI LN, SJS, 95135, (408)274-4400	855 - H6
THUNDERBIRD GOLF COURSE	221 S KING RD, SJS, 95116, (408)259-3355	834 - F5

HOSPITALS

FEATURE NAME	Address City, ZIP Code	PAGE-GRID
AGNEWS DEVELOPMENTAL CENTER (EAST)	ZANKER RD, SJS, 95134, (408)432-8500	813 - G3
AGNEWS DEVELOPMENTAL CENTER (WEST)	MONTAGUE EXWY, SCL, 95054, (408)432-8500	813 - D4
ALEXIAN BROTHERS HOSPITAL	225 N JACKSON AV, SJS, 95116, (408)259-5000	834 - G2
CAMINO HEALTHCARE	2500 GRANT RD, MTVW, 94040, (650)940-7000	831 - H1
COLUMBIA GOOD SAMARITAN HOSPITAL	2425 SAMARITAN DR, SJS, 95124, (408)559-2011	873 - E3
COMMUNITY HOSP OF LOS GATOS-SARATOGA	815 POLLARD, LGTS, 95030, (408)378-6131	873 - B2
KAISER FOUNDATION HOSPITAL	900 KIELY DR, SCL, 95051, (408)236-6400	833 - A5
LUCILE PACKARD CHILDRENS HOSP-STANFORD	725 WELCH RD, PA, 94304, (650)497-8000	790 - G6
OCONNOR HOSPITAL	21505 FOREST AV, SJS, 95128, (408)947-2500	833 - F7
RONALD MCDONALD HOUSE	520 SAND HILL RD, PA, 94304, (650)325-5113	790 - G5
SAINT LOUISE HOSPITAL	18500 SAINT LOUISE DR, MGH, 95037, (408)779-1500	917 - B4
SAN JOSE MEDICAL CENTER	675 E SANTA CLARA ST, SJS, 95112, (408)998-3212	834 - D5
SANTA CLARA VALLEY MEDICAL CENTER	751 BASCOM AV, SCIC, 95128, (408)299-5100	853 - F2
SANTA TERESA COMMUNITY HOSPITAL	250 HOSPITAL PKWY, SJS, 95119, (408)972-7000	875 - C6
SOUTH VALLEY HOSPITAL	9400 N NAME UNO, GIL, 95020, (408)848-2000	958 - A6
STANFORD UNIVERSITY HOSPITAL	300 PASTEUR DR, PA, 94304, (650)723-4000	790 - G6
VA HOSPITAL MENLO PARK	795 WILLOW RD, MLPK, 94025, (650)493-5000	790 - J1
VA HOSPITAL-PALO ALTO	3801 MIRANDA AV, PA, 94304, (650)493-5000	811 - B3

HOTELS & MOTELS

FEATURE NAME	Address City, ZIP Code	PAGE-GRID
AIRPORT INN INTERNATIONAL	1355 N 4TH ST, SJS, 95112, (408)453-5340	834 - A2
ARENA HOTEL	817 THE ALAMEDA, SJS, 95126, (408)294-6500	833 - J7
BEST WESTERN COUNTRY INN	16525 CONDIT RD, MGH, 95037, (408)779-0447	917 - C7
BEST WESTERN CREEKSIDE INN	3400 EL CAMINO REAL, PA, 94306, (650)493-2411	811 - C1
BEST WESTERN MOUNTAIN VIEW INN	2300 EL CAMINO REAL, MTVW, 94040, (650)962-9912	811 - E4
BEST WESTERN SAN JOSE LODGE	1440 N 1ST ST, SJS, 95112, (408)453-7750	833 - J2
BEST WESTERN SUNNYVALE INN	940 W WEDDELL DR, SUNV, 94089, (408)734-3742	812 - E4
BEVERLY HERITAGE HOTEL	1820 BARBER LN, MPS, 95035, (408)943-9080	813 - J4
BILTMORE HOTEL	2151 LAURELWOOD, SCL, 95054, (408)988-8411	813 - C6
COURTYARD BY MARRIOTT	10605 WOLFE RD, CPTO, 95014, (408)252-9100	832 - F6
COURTYARD BY MARRIOTT	1727 TECHNOLOGY DR, SJS, 95110, (408)441-6111	833 - H2
CUPERTINO INN	10889 DE ANZA BLVD, CPTO, 95014, (408)996-7700	832 - E6
DAYS INN	4200 GREAT AMERICAN PKWY, SCL, 95054, (408)980-1525	813 - B5
ECONOMY INNS OF AMERICA	270 S ABBOTT AV, MPS, 95035, (408)946-8889	813 - J1
EMBASSY SUITES	2885 LAKESIDE DR, SCL, 95054, (408)496-6400	813 - A6
EMBASSY SUITES MILPITAS	901 CALAVERAS BLVD, MPS, 95035, (408)942-0400	794 - B6
FAIRMONT HOTEL	170 S MARKET ST, SJS, 95113, (408)998-1900	834 - C7
FOREST PARK INN	375 LEAVESLEY RD, GIL, 95020, (408)848-5144	978 - A1
FOUR POINTS HOTEL	1100 N MATHILDA AV, SUNV, 94089, (408)745-6000	812 - E3
GATEWAY INN	2585 SEABOARD AV, SJS, 95131, (408)435-8800	813 - F7
HILTON	1250 LAKSIDE DR, SUNV, 94086, (408)738-4888	812 - J6
HILTON TOWERS	300 S ALMADEN BLVD, SJS, 95110, (408)287-2100	834 - B7
HOLIDAY INN HOTEL	625 EL CAMINO REAL, PA, 94301, (650)328-2800	790 - H5
HOLIDAY INN MILPITAS	777 BELLEW DR, MPS, 95035, (408)321-9500	813 - H1
HOLIDAY INN PARK CENTER PLAZA	282 S ALMADEN BLVD, SJS, 95113, (408)998-0400	834 - B7
HOLIDAY INN SAN JOSE	399 SILICON VALLEY BLVD, SJS, 95138, (408)972-7800	875 - F4
HOMEWOOD SUITES	10 TRIMBLE RD, SJS, 95131, (408)428-9900	813 - G6
HOTEL DE ANZA	233 W SANTA CLARA ST, SJS, 95110, (408)286-1000	834 - B6
HOTEL SAINTE CLAIRE	302 S MARKET ST, SJS, 95110, (408)295-2000	834 - C7
HOWARD JOHNSON	5405 STEVENS CREEK BLVD, SCL, 95014, (408)257-8600	852 - H1
HYATT SAN JOSE	1740 N 1ST ST, SJS, 95112, (408)993-1234	833 - J1
HYATT-RICKEYS	4219 EL CAMINO REAL, PA, 94306, (650)493-8000	811 - D2
INN AT MORGAN HILL	16115 CONDIT RD, MGH, 95037, (408)779-7666	937 - C1
LE BARON HOTEL	1350 N 1ST ST, SJS, 95112, (408)453-6200	833 - J2
MAPLE TREE INN	711 E EL CAMINO REAL, SUNV, 94086, (408)720-9700	832 - F2
MARIANIS INN	2500 EL CAMINO REAL, SCL, 95051, (408)243-1431	833 - B4
QUALITY SUITES	3100 LAKESIDE DR, SCL, 95054, (408)748-9800	813 - A6
RADISSON HAUS INN	1085 E EL CAMINO REAL, SUNV, 94086, (408)247-0800	832 - H4
RADISSON PLAZA HOTEL	1471 N 4TH ST, SJS, 95112, (408)452-0200	833 - J2
RAMADA INN	1217 WILDWOOD AV, SUNV, 94089, (408)245-5330	812 - J5
RED LION INN	2050 GATEWAY PL, SJS, 95110, (408)453-4000	833 - H1

FEATURE NAME Address City, ZIP Code	PAGE-GRID
RESIDENCE INN 1080 STEWART DR, SUNV, 94086, (408)720-8893	812 - J6
RESIDENCE INN 2761 S BASCOM AV, SJS, 95008, (408)559-1551	873 - F1
RESIDENCE INN 750 LAKEWAY DR, SUNV, 94086, (408)720-1000	813 - A6
RESIDENCE INN HOTEL 1854 W EL CAMINO REAL, MTVW, 94041, (650)940-1300	811 - G5
SANTA CLARA MARRIOTT 2700 MISSION COLLEGE BLVD, SCL, 95054, (408)988-1500	813 - B5
SHERATON SILICON VALLEY EAST 1801 BARBER LN, MPS, 95035, (408)943-0600	813 - J4
STANFORD PARK HOTEL 100 EL CAMINO REAL, MLPK, 94025, (650)322-1234	790 - G4
STANFORD TERRACE INN 531 STANFORD AV, PA, 94306, (650)857-0333	791 - A7
SUNDOWNER INN 504 ROSS DR, SUNV, 94089, (408)734-9900	812 - E4
SUPER 8 MOTEL 485 S MAIN ST, MPS, 95035, (408)946-1615	814 - A1
THE PRUNEYARD INN 1995 S BASCOM AV, CMBL, 95008, (408)559-4300	853 - F5
TOLL HOUSE HOTEL 140 S SANTA CRUZ AV, LGTS, 95030, (408)395-7070	892 - J1
WESTIN HOTEL 5101 GREAT AMERICAN PKWY, SCL, 95054, (408)986-0700	813 - B4
WOODFIN SUITES 635 E EL CAMINO REAL, SUNV, 94086, (408)738-1700	832 - E2
WYNDHAM GARDEN HOTEL 1300 CHESAPEAKE TER, SUNV, 94089, (408)747-0999	812 - H3

LIBRARIES

FEATURE NAME Address City, ZIP Code	PAGE-GRID
ALMADEN BRANCH 6455 CAMDEN AV, SJS, 95120, (408)268-7600	894 - D1
ALUM ROCK LIBRARY 75 S WHITE RD, SJS, 95127, (408)251-1280	834 - J2
ALVISO BRANCH LIBRARY 1060 TAYLOR ST, SJS, 95002, (650)263-3626	793 - B7
ATHERTON 2 DINKLESPEIL STATION LN, ATN, 94027, (650)328-2422	790 - E2
BERRYESSA 3311 NOBLE AV, SJS, 95132, (408)272-3554	814 - H5
BIBLIOTECA LATINO AMERICANA 690 LOCUST ST, SJS, 95110, (408)294-1237	854 - C1
CALABAZAS BRANCH LIBRARY 1230 BLANEY AV, SJS, 95129, (408)996-1535	852 - E3
CAMBRIAN BRANCH LIBRARY 1780 HILLSDALE AV, SJS, 95124, (408)269-5062	873 - H2
CAMPBELL LIBRARY 77 HARRISON AV, CMBL, 95008, (408)378-8122	853 - E5
COLLEGE TERRACE BRANCH LIBRARY 2300 WELLESLEY ST, PA, 94306, (650)329-2298	791 - A7
CUPERTINO LIBRARY 10400 TORRE AV, CPTO, 96014	852 - E1
DOWNTOWN BRANCH LIBRARY 270 FOREST AV, PA, 94301, (650)329-2641	790 - J5
EAST PALO ALTO BRANCH LIBRARY 2415 UNIVERSITY AV E, EPA, 94303, (650)321-7712	791 - B1
EAST SAN JOSE CARNEGIE LIBRARY 1102 E SANTA CLARA ST, SJS, 95116, (408)998-2069	834 - E5
EDUCATIONAL PARK LIBRARY 1770 EDUCATIONAL PARK DR, SJS, 95133, (408)272-3662	834 - F2
EMPIRE BRANCH LIBRARY 491 E EMPIRE ST, SJS, 95112, (408)286-5627	834 - C4
EVERGREEN BRANCH 2635 ABORN RD, SJS, 95148, (408)238-4434	855 - C2
GILROY LIBRARY 7387 ROSANNA ST, GIL, 95020, (408)842-8207	977 - J3
HILLVIEW BRANCH LIBRARY 2255 OCALA AV, SJS, 95122, (408)272-3100	834 - J6
LIBRARY (SEE PAGE 997) VEGA ST & CARPENERIA RD, MntC	1017 - A5
LOS ALTOS LIBRARY 13 S SAN ANTONIO RD, LALT, 94022, (650)948-7683	811 - E6
MENLO PARK BRANCH ALMA ST & RAVENSWOOD AV, MLPK, 94025, (650)858-3460	790 - G3
MILPITAS COMMUNITY 40 N MILPITAS BLVD, MPS, 95035, (408)262-1171	794 - A7
MISSION BRANCH 1098 LEXINGTON, SCL, 95050, (408)984-3154	833 - E4
MITCHELL PARK LIBRARY 3700 MIDDLEFIELD RD, PA, 94306, (650)329-2586	811 - E1
MORGAN HILL LIBRARY 17575 PEAK AV, MGH, 95037, (408)779-3196	936 - J1
MOUNTAIN VIEW LIBRARIES 585 FRANKLIN ST, MTVW, 94041, (650)903-6887	811 - H5
PALO ALTO CHILDRENS LIBRARY 1276 HARRIET ST, PA, 94301, (650)329-2134	791 - A5
PALO ALTO MAIN LIBRARY 1213 NEWELL RD, PA, 94303, (650)329-2664	791 - B4
PEARL AV BRANCH 4270 PEARL AV, SJS, 95136, (408)265-7834	874 - E1
PORTOLA VALLEY BRANCH LIBRARY 765 PORTOLA RD, PTLV, 94028, (650)851-0560	810 - A6
ROSEGARDEN BRANCH LIBRARY 1580 NAGLEE AV, SJS, 95126, (408)998-1511	833 - G6
SAN JOSE MAIN BRANCH LIBRARY 180 W SAN CARLOS ST, SJS, 95110, (408)277-4846	834 - B7
SANTA CLARA CENTRAL LIBRARY 2635 HOMESTEAD RD, SCL, 95051, (408)984-3097	833 - B5
SANTA TERESA LIBRARY 290 INTERNATIONAL CIR, SJS, 95119, (408)281-1878	875 - C6
SARATOGA COMMUNITY 13650 SARATOGA AV, SAR, 95070, (408)867-6126	872 - F1
SEVEN TREES BRANCH LIBRARY 3597 CAS DR, SJS, 95111, (408)629-4535	854 - H6
SUNNYVALE LIBRARY 665 W OLIVE AV, SUNV, 94086, (408)730-7300	832 - D1

FEATURE NAME Address City, ZIP Code	PAGE-GRID
TERMAN PARK LIBRARY 661 ARASTRADERO RD, PA, 94306, (650)329-2606	811 - C3
WEST VALLEY BRANCH LIBRARY 1243 SAN THOMAS AQUINO RD, SJS, 95117, (408)244-4747	853 - A4
WILLOW GLEN BRANCH LIBRARY 1157 MINNESOTA AV, SJS, 95125, (408)998-2022	854 - A4
WOODLAND LIBRARY 1975 GRANT RD, LALT, 94024, (650)969-6030	831 - J4

MILITARY INSTALLATIONS

FEATURE NAME Address City, ZIP Code	PAGE-GRID
MOFFETT FIELD NAVAL AIR STATION FAIRCHILD DR & DAILEY RD, SCIC, 94035	812 - D3
NATIONAL GUARD ARMORY 240 N 2ND ST, SJS, 95112	834 - B5
NATIONAL GUARD ARMORY 251 W HEDDING ST, SJS, 95110, (408)297-1974	833 - J4
U S ARMY RESERVE CENTER 155 W HEDDING ST, SJS, 95110, (408)292-4160	833 - J4

MOBILE HOME PARKS

FEATURE NAME Address City, ZIP Code	PAGE-GRID
ADOBE WELLS MOBILE HOME PARK 1220 TASMAN DR, SUNV, 94089, (408)734-8424	812 - J3
CASA DE AMIGOS MOBILE HOME PARK 1085 TASMAN DR, SUNV, 94089, (408)734-3379	812 - G3
CASA DE LAGO MOBILE HOME PARKS OAKLAND RD, SJS, 95131, (408)432-1323	814 - A4
FAIROAKS MOBILE HOME PARK 580 AHWANEE AV, SUNV, 94086, (408)736-6672	812 - G5
MOBILAND MOBILE HOME PARK 780 N FAIR OAKS AV, SUNV, 94086, (408)773-1210	812 - G5
PLAZA DEL REY MOBILE HOME PARK 1225 VIENNA DR, SUNV, 94089, (408)734-2746	812 - H4
VILLAGE OF THE FOUR SEASONS 200 FORD RD, SJS, 95138, (408)225-7255	875 - D4
WOODBRIDGE MOBILE HOME PARK SJS, 95121	855 - A3

MUSEUMS

FEATURE NAME Address City, ZIP Code	PAGE-GRID
BAYLANDS NATURE INTERPRETIVE CENTER 2775 EMBARCADERO RD, PA, 94303, (650)329-2506	791 - F3
CHILDRENS DISCOVERY MUSEUM 180 WOZ WY, SJS, 95110, (408)298-5437	834 - B7
DE SAISSET MUSEUM 500 EL CAMINO REAL, SCL, 95053, (408)554-4528	833 - F4
EGYPTIAN MUSEUM & PLANETARIUM 1342 NAGLEE AV, SJS, 95126, (408)947-3636	833 - G6
GILROY HISTORICAL MUSEUM 195 5TH ST, GIL, 95020, (408)848-0470	977 - J3
MUSEUM OF AMERICAN HERITAGE 3401 EL CAMINO REAL, PA, 94306, (650)321-1004	811 - C1
NEW ALMADEN MUSEUM 21570 ALMADEN RD, SCIC, 95120, (408)268-7869	894 - J7
PALO ALTO JUNIOR MUSEUM & ZOO 1451 MIDDLEFIELD RD, PA, 94301, (650)329-2111	791 - B5
SAN JOSE HISTORICAL MUSEUM 1600 SENTER RD, SJS, 95112, (408)287-2290	854 - F2
SAN JOSE MUSEUM OF ART 110 S MARKET ST, SJS, 95113, (408)294-2787	834 - B6
SANTA CLARA HISTORIC MUSEUM 1509 WARBURTON AV, SCL, 95050, (408)248-2787	833 - D3
THE TECH MUSEUM OF INNOVATION 145 W SAN CARLOS ST, SJS, 95113, (408)279-7150	834 - B7
TRITON MUSEUM OF ART 1505 WARBURTON AV, SCL, 95050, (408)247-3754	833 - D3

OPEN SPACE PRESERVES

FEATURE NAME Address City, ZIP Code	PAGE-GRID
ARASTRADERO PRESERVE ARASTRADERO RD, PA, 94304	830 - F1
BAYLANDS NATURE PRESERVE EMBARCADERO RD, EPA, 94303	791 - D2
COAL CREEK OPEN SPACE SKYLINE BLVD, SMCo, 94028	830 - C5
EL SERENO OPEN SPACE LINDA VISTA AV, SCIC, 95030	892 - G1
FOOTHILLS OPEN SPACE PAGE MILL RD, PA, 94304	830 - G3
FREEMONT OLDER OPEN SPACE ROLLING HILLS RD, SCIC, 95014	852 - A4
LONG RIDGE OPEN SPACE SKYLINE BLVD, SMCo, 94020	850 - H6
LOS TRANCOS OPEN SPACE PAGE MILL RD, PA, 94304	830 - F6
MISSION PEAK REGIONAL PRESERVE OFF MILL CREEK ROAD, FRMT, 94539	794 - D1
MONTE BELLO OPEN SPACE SKYLINE BLVD, PA, 94304	851 - B3
PICCHETTI RANCH OPEN SPACE STEVENS CANYON RD & MONTE BELL, SCIC, 95014	851 - H5
RANCHO SAN ANTONIO OPEN SPACE CRISTO REY DR, SCIC, 95014	831 - D5
REDWOOD GROVE NATURE PRESERVE UNIVERSITY AV & SHERMAN ST, LALT, 94022	811 - D7
RUSSIAN RIDGE OPEN SPACE SKYLINE BLVD, SMCo, 94020	830 - C7
SARATOGA GAP OPEN SPACE SKYLINE BLVD, SCrC, 95030	871 - C2
SKYLINE RIDGE OPEN SPACE SKYLINE BLVD, SCIC	850 - F2
UVAS CREEK PRESERVE UVAS PARK DR, GIL, 95020	977 - G4
WINDY HILL OPEN SPACE SKYLINE BLVD, PTLV, 94028	830 - A3

PARK & RIDE

FEATURE NAME Address City, ZIP Code	PAGE-GRID
ASCENSION PARK & RIDE PROSPECT RD & MILLER AV, SAR, 95070	852 - F5
BLOCKBUSTER VIDEO PARK & RIDE MCKEE RD & N CAPITOL AV, SJS, 95133	834 - G1
BLOSSOM HILL STATION PARK & RIDE BLOSSOM HILL RD & HWY 85, SJS, 95123	874 - G4
BRANHAM STATION PARK & RIDE BRANHAM LN & NARVAEZ AV LN, SJS, 95136	874 - F2
CAMDEN AV PARK & RIDE CAMDEN AV & HWY 85, SJS, 95118	873 - J4
CAMPBELL SENIOR CENTER PARK & RIDE W CAMPBELL AV & S WINCHESTER B, CMBL, 95008	853 - D6
CAPITOL AVENUE PARK & RIDE N CAPITOL AV & AV A, SJS, 95127	834 - H2
CAPITOL STATION PARK & RIDE CAPITOL EXPWY & NARVAEZ AV, SJS, 95136	874 - E1
CAPITOL STATION PARK & RIDE MONTEREY HWY & FEHREN DR, SJS, 95111	854 - G6
COTTLE STATION PARK & RIDE COTTLE RD & 85 FWY, SJS, 95119	875 - C5
CURTNER STATION PARK & RIDE CANOAS GARDEN AV & CURTNER AV, SJS, 95125	854 - D5
EASTRIDGE MALL PARK & RIDE TULLY RD & CAPITOL EXWY, SJS, 95122	835 - B7
FORD ROAD PARK & RIDE MONTEREY HWY & FORD RD, SJS, 95138	875 - C4
GILROY STATION PARK & RIDE MONTEREY ST & 7TH ST, GIL, 95020	978 - A3
KMART PARK & RIDE BOLLINGER RD & SARATOGA-SUNNYV, SJS, 95129	852 - D2
KMART PARK & RIDE EL CAMINO REAL & LAWRENCE EXWY, SCL, 95051	832 - H4
KMART PARK & RIDE FRUITDALE AV & SOUTHWEST EXWY, SJS, 95126	853 - H3
KMART PARK & RIDE N JACKSON AV & MCKEE RD, SJS, 95116	834 - G2
MAIN AV PARK & RIDE MAIN AV & HALE AV, MGH, 95037	916 - J7
MOORPARK AV PARK & RIDE MOORPARK AV & LAWRENCE EXPWY, SJS, 95129	852 - J3
MORGAN HILL STATION PARK & RIDE E MAIN AV & BUTTERFIELD BLVD, MGH, 95037	917 - A7
OHLONE-CHYNOWETH STA P & R CHYNOWETH AV & HWY 87, SJS, 95136	874 - E3
PAGE MILL & ECR PARK & RIDE EL CAMINO REAL & OREGON EXWY, PA, 94306	791 - B7
PAGE MILL & HWY 280 PARK & RIDE PAGE MILL RD & HWY 280, LAH, 94022	810 - H5
PARK & RIDE MONTEREY RD & HOWSON ST, GIL, 95020	977 - J2
PARK & RIDE S MAIN ST & WELLER LN, MPS, 95035	794 - A7
PIEDMONT HILLS CENTER PARK & RIDE SIERRA RD & PIEDMONT RD, SJS, 95132	814 - G4
RIVER OAKS STATION PARK & RIDE RIVER OAKS PL & N 1ST ST, SJS, 95134	813 - F4
SAN MARTIN STATION PARK & RIDE MONTEREY HWY & SAN MARTIN AV, SCIC, 95046	937 - F6
SANTA TERESA STA NORTH P & R SANTA TERESA BLVD & MIYUKI DR, SJS, 95119	875 - D6
SANTA TERESA STA SOUTH P & R SANTA TERESA BL & SAN IGNACIO, SJS, 95119	875 - D6
SARATOGA RD PARK & RIDE SARATOGA RD & SANTA CRUZ AV, LGTS, 95030	873 - A7
SNELL AVENUE STATION PARK & RIDE SNELL AV & HWY 85, SJS, 95123	874 - H4
TAMIEN STATION PARK & RIDE LELONG AV & W ALMA AV, SJS, 95110	854 - C3
TASMAN STATION PARK & RIDE TASMAN DR & N 1ST ST, SJS, 95134	813 - F3
TILTON AV PARK & RIDE TILTON AV & SANTA TERESA BLVD, SCIC, 95037	916 - G4
VALLCO FASHION PARK PARK & RIDE WOLFE RD & SERRA FRWY, CPTO, 95014	832 - F7
WINFIELD STATION PARK & RIDE COLEMAN AV & WINFIELD BLVD, SJS, 95123	874 - D5

PARKS & RECREATION

FEATURE NAME Address City, ZIP Code	PAGE-GRID
AGNEW PARK AGNEW RD, SCL, 95054	813 - C5
AIRPORT PARK (SEE PAGE 999) SAN FELIPE RD, HOLL	1020 - A6
ALBERTSON PARKWAY PURPLE HILLS DR & DONDERO WY, SJS, 95119	875 - C6
ALMADEN LAKE PARK ALMADEN EXPWY & WINFILD BLVD, SJS, 95123	874 - D5
ALMADEN MEADOWS PARK CAMDEN AV & MERIDIAN AV, SJS, 95120	894 - C1
ALMADEN QUICKSILVER COUNTY PARK ALMADEN RD & ALAMITOS RD, SCIC, 95120, (408)268-3883	894 - E5
ALMADEN RESERVOIR COUNTY PARK ALAMITOS RD, SCIC, 95120	914 - H2
ALUM ROCK PARK 16240 ALUM ROCK AV, SJS, 95132, (408)277-4661	815 - C5
ALVAREZ PARK 2280 ROSITA AV, SCL, 95050	833 - D6
ALVISO PARK WILSON WY, SJS, 95002	813 - C1
ANDERSON LAKE COUNTY PARK 18390 COCHRANE RD, SJS, 95037, (408)779-3634	917 - C1
AVENIDA ESPANA PARK RAWLS CT & DOWNS DR, SJS, 95139	895 - F1
AZULE PARK GOLETA AV, SAR, 95070	852 - E5
BACHMAN PARK BACHMAN AV & BROOKS AV, LGTS, 95030	872 - J7
BACKESTO PARK N 13TH ST & E EMPIRE ST, SJS, 95112	834 - C4
BELL STREET PARK BELL ST & UNIVERSITY AV, EPA, 94303	791 - B2
BERNAL PARK E HEDDING ST & N 7TH ST, SJS, 95112	834 - B3
BERRYESSA CREEK PARK ISADORA DR, SJS, 95132	814 - F3
BIEBRACH PARK W VIRGINIA ST & DELMAS AV, SJS, 95125	854 - B1
BLOSSOM HILL PARK BLOSSOM HILL RD, LGTS, 95032	873 - D6
BOGGINI PARK STEVENS LN & MILLBROOK DR, SJS, 95148	855 - D1
BOL PARK LAGUNA AV & LAGUNA CT, PA, 94306	811 - B2
BOULWARE PARK 390 FERNANDO AV, PA, 94306	811 - C1
BOWDEN PARK ALMA ST & CALIFORNIA AV, PA, 94301	791 - B7
BOWERS PARK 2582 CABRILLO AV, SCL, 95051	833 - B3
BOWLING GREEN PARK 474 EMBARCADERO RD, PA, 94301	791 - A5
BRACHER PARK 2700 BOWERS AV, SCL, 95051	833 - B1
BRALY PARK 704 DAFFODIL CT, SUNV, 94086, (408)732-4891	832 - F2
BRANHAM LANE PARK BRANHAM LN, SJS, 95124	873 - J3
BRIGADOON PARK BRIGADOON WY & DAN MALONEY DR, SJS, 95121	855 - C3
BRIONES PARK MAYBELL AV & CLEMO AV, PA, 94306	811 - C3
BROOKGLEN PARK BROOKGLEN DR & BROCKTON LN, SAR, 95070	852 - G6
BROOKTREE PARK FALLINGTREE DR, SJS, 95131	814 - C5
BUBB PARK BARBARA AV, MTVW, 94040	811 - H7
BURGESS PARK LAUREL ST & MIEKLE DR, MLPK, 94025	790 - G3
BUTCHER PARK CAMDEN AV & OAKWOOD AV, SJS, 95124	873 - H2
BUTCHER PARK EAST ST & OLD GILROY ST, GIL, 95020	978 - B3
BYXBEE RECREATION AREA EMBARCADERO RD, PA, 94303	791 - F3
CADWALLADER PARK S 1ST ST & KEYES ST, SJS, 95112	854 - D1
CAHALAN PARK PEARLWOOD WY & CAHALAN AV, SJS, 95123	874 - F5
CALERO PARK LEAN AV & CALERO AV, SJS, 95123	875 - A5
CALERO RESERVOIR COUNTY PARK 23201 MCKEAN RD, SCIC, 95120, (408)268-3883	895 - E7
CAMDEN PARK UNION AV & CAMDEN AV, SJS, 95124	873 - F2
CAMERON PARK 210 WELLESLEY, PA, 94306	791 - A7
CAMPBELL PARK CAMPBELL AV & GILMAN AV, CMBL, 95008	853 - F6
CANOAS PARK THRUSH DR & KINGFISHER DR, SJS, 95125	854 - C6
CAPITOL PARK BAMBI LN & PETER PAN AV, SJS, 95116	834 - J4
CARDOZA PARK KENNEDY DR, MPS, 95035	794 - C6
CARLI, STEVE PARK 1045 LOS PADRES BLVD, SCL, 95050	833 - C5
CARMICHAEL, EARL J PARK BENTON ST, SCL, 95051	832 - J4
CARRABELLE PARK CAMDEN AV & VILLAGEWOOD WY, SJS, 95120	894 - H2
CASSELL PARK LEEWARD DR & BRENFORD DR, SJS, 95122	834 - J5
CASTLE ROCK STATE PARK SKYLINE BLVD, SCIC, 95030	871 - B5
CASTRO SCHOOL PARK LATHAM ST & ESCUELA AV, MTVW, 94041	811 - G5
CATALDI PARK MORRILL AV, SJS, 95132	814 - E4
CENTRAL PARK 969 KIELY BLVD, SCL, 95051	833 - B5
CHESBRO RESERVOIR PARK OAK GLEN AV & LLAGAS RD, SCIC, 95037	936 - E2
CHILDREN OF THE RAINBOW PARK MADDEN AV & GRAMERCY PL, SJS, 95116	834 - G2
CHRISTMAS HILL PARK MILLER AV & UVAS PARK DR, GIL, 95020	977 - H5
CHYNOWETH PARK CHYNOWETH AV & EDENVALE AV, SJS, 95136	875 - A3
CIMARRON PARK ORANGE ST, SJS, 95127	814 - H6
CITY PLAZA PARK LEXINGTON & MAIN STS, SCL, 95050	833 - E4
CIVIC CENTER PARK LINCOLN ST & EL CAMINO REAL, SCL, 95050	833 - D4
CIVIC CENTER PARK S MATHILDA AV & ALL AMERICA WY, SUNV, 94086	832 - D1
CLARK, ESTHER PARK OLD TRACE LN & OLD ADOBE RD, PA, 94306	811 - B5
COE, HENRY W STATE PARK (SEE PAGE 877) DUNNE AV, SCIC, 95037, (408)779-2728	898 - F5
COGSWELL PLAZA BRYANT ST & LYTTON AV, PA, 94301	790 - J4
COLUMBIA PARK GLENDALE AV & MORSE AV, SUNV, 94086	812 - F5

SANTA CLARA CO.

INDEX

FEATURE NAME	Address City, ZIP Code	PAGE-GRID
SAN LUIS RES STATE REC AREA (SEE PAGE 961)	PACHECO PASS HWY, MerC, (209)826-1196	962 - G2
SAN TOMAS PARK	FENAN DR & LEMOYNE WY, SJS, 95008	853 - B7
SAN VERON PARK	MIDDLEFIELD RD & SAN VERON AV, MTVW, 94043	811 - J3
SAN YSIDRO PARK	MURRAY AV, GIL, 95020	978 - A2
SANBORN - SKYLINE COUNTY PARK	16055 SANBORN RD, SCrC, 95030, (408)867-9959	871 - E5
SANDLEWOOD PARK	RUSSEL LN & ESCUELA PKWY, MPS, 95035	794 - B4
SANTA TERESA COUNTY PARK	BERNAL RD, SCIC, 95119, (408)268-3883	895 - E3
SANTANA PARK	TISCH WY & BAYWOOD AV, SJS, 95128	853 - E1
SARATOGA CREEK PARK	CORDELIA AV & HOYET DR, SJS, 95129	852 - H4
SCHMIDT, HENRY PARK	SARATOGA AV & LOS PADRES BLVD, SCL, 95050	833 - D6
SCOTT PARK	CHANNING AV & SCOTT ST, PA, 94301	790 - J5
SCOTTSDALE PARK	BRANHAM LN & TAMPICO WY, SJS, 95118	874 - A3
SEALE PARK	3100 STOCKTON PL, PA, 94303	791 - D6
SELWYN PARK	SELWYN DR, MPS, 95035	794 - C7
SERRA PARK	730 THE DALLES AV, SUNV, 94087, (408)730-7506	832 - D5
SHADY OAK PARK	COYOTE RD & BRODERICK DR, SJS, 95111	875 - D2
SHARON PARK	SHARON PARK DR & KLAMATH DR, MLPK, 94025	790 - C7
SHORELINE AT MOUNTAIN VIEW	SHORELINE BLVD, MTVW, 94043	791 - H6
SHOUP PARK	400 UNIVERSITY AV, LALT, 94022	811 - D7
SILVER CREEK LINEAR PARK	SILVER CREEK & YERBA BUENA RD, SJS, 95138	855 - C5
SILVER LEAF PARK	SILVER LEAF RD & PALMWELL WY, SJS, 95138	875 - E4
SINNOTT PARK	CLEAR LAKE AV, MPS, 95035	814 - D2
SLATER SCHOOL PARK	N WHISMAN RD & 3RD AV, MTVW, 94043	812 - B5
SOLARI PARK	CAS DR & ARBOLES AV, SJS, 95111	854 - H6
SOMERSET SQUARE PARK	STOKES AV & WILSON CT, CPTO, 95014	832 - B6
STARBIRD PARK	BOYNTON AV & WILLIAMS RD, SJS, 95117	853 - C3
STARLITE PARK	ABBOTT AV & RUDYARD DR, MPS, 95035	793 - J7
STEVENS CREEK COUNTY PARK	11401 STEVENS CANYON RD, SCIC, 95014, (408)867-3654	851 - J7
STEVENSON SCHOOL PARK	MONTECITO AV & BURGOYNE ST, MTVW, 94043	811 - H3
STONEGATE PARK	KENOGA DR, SJS, 95121	854 - H3
STRAND, JENNY PARK	MONO WY & HANCOCK DR, SCL, 95051	832 - H7
STRICKROTH PARK	STRICKROTH DR & AARON PARK DR, MPS, 95035	794 - A5
SUNNYHILLS PARK	COELHO ST & CONWAY ST, MPS, 95035	794 - A3
SUNNYVALE BAYLANDS PARK	SOUTHBAY FRWY & LAWRENCE EXPW, SUNV, 94089, (408)730-7709	812 - J2
SYLVAN PARK	SYLVAN AV & GLENBOROUGH DR, MTVW, 94041	812 - A6
TAPESTRY PARK	SILVERLAND DR, SJS, 95135	855 - E2
TERMAN PARK	655 ARASTRADERO RD, PA, 94306	811 - D3
TERRELL PARK	KENTON CT & NORMINGTON WY, SJS, 95136	874 - D1
THE OVAL PARK	PALM DR & SERRA ST, SCIC, 94305	790 - H6
THOUSAND OAKS PARK	BROCKHAMPTON CT & NORMINGTON W, SJS, 95136	874 - D1
THREE OAKS PARK	RUPPELL PL & MOLTZEN DR, CPTO, 95014	852 - D3
TOWNSEND PARK	TOWNSEND PARK CIR, SJS, 95131	814 - C7
TURTLE ROCK PARK	BOA VISTA DR & MALDEN AV, SJS, 95122	854 - H1
TWIN CREEKS SPORTS COMPLEX	CARIBBEAN DR & SOUTHBAY FRWY, SUNV, 94089	812 - H2
UPPER STEVENS CREEK COUNTY PARK	SKYLINE BLVD, PA, 94304	850 - J4
UVAS CANYON COUNTY PARK	8515 CROY RD, SCIC, 95037, (408)779-9232	935 - B6
UVAS RESERVOIR PARK	UVAS RD, SCIC, 95037	936 - E7
VARIAN PARK	AMELIA CT & VARIAN WY, CPTO, 95014	832 - A7
VASONA LAKE COUNTY PARK	298 GARDEN HILL DR, LGTS, 95030, (408)356-2729	873 - B5
VILLA MONTALVO ARBORETUM	15400 MONTALVO RD, SCIC, 95070, (408)867-0190	872 - D5
VINCI PARK	VINCI PARK WY, SJS, 95131	814 - D7
VISTA PARK	NEW COMPTON DR & HYDE PARK DR, SJS, 95136	874 - F2
WALLENBERG PARK	CURTNER AV & COTTLE AV, SJS, 95125	854 - A6
WALLIS PARK	GRANT AV & ASH ST, PA, 94306	791 - B7
WARBURTON PARK	2250 ROYAL DR, SCL, 95050, (408)241-6465	833 - C3
WASHINGTON CITY PARK	880 W WASHINGTON AV, SUNV, 94086, (408)732-3479	812 - D7
WASHINGTON PARK	POPLAR ST, SCL, 95050	833 - E5
WATERFORD PARK	VISTA PARK DR & SANDPEBBLE DR, SJS, 95136	854 - F7
WATSON PARK	E JACKSON ST & N 22ND ST, SJS, 95112	834 - D3
WEISSHARR PARK	2300 DARTMOUTH ST, PA, 94306	811 - A1
WELCH PARK	1900 SANTIAGO AV, SJS, 95122	854 - J1
WERRY PARK	DARTMOUTH ST, PA, 94306	810 - J1
WESTWOOD OAKS PARK	460 LA HERNAN DR, SCL, 95051	832 - H6
WHISMAN SCHOOL PARK	EASY ST & WALKER DR, MTVW, 94043	812 - A4
WIECHERT, HOWARD PARK	VIA DEL CASTILLE, MGH, 95037	937 - A4
WILCOX PARK	WILCOX WY & DUKE WY, SJS, 95125	854 - A5
WILDWOOD PARK	4TH ST & WILDWOOD WY, SAR, 95070	872 - D2
WILLIAM STREET PARK	E WILLIAM ST & S 16TH ST, SJS, 95112	834 - E6
WILLOW OAKS PARK	500 WILLOW RD, MLPK, 94025	790 - J2
WILLOW STREET BRAMHALL PARK	WILLOW ST & CAMINO RAMON, SJS, 95125	853 - J3
WILSON PARK	PORTAL AV & WINTERGREEN DR, CPTO, 95014	852 - F1
WINDMILL SPRINGS PARK	UMBARGER RD, SJS, 95121	854 - J3
YELLOWSTONE PARK	1400 YELLOWSTONE AV, MPS, 95035	814 - D1

PERFORMING ARTS

FEATURE NAME	Address City, ZIP Code	PAGE-GRID
PERFORMING ARTS CENTER	255 S ALMADEN BLVD, SJS, 95110, (408)288-7474	834 - B7
SHORELINE AMPHITHEATRE AT MTVW	1 AMPHITHEATRE PKWY, MTVW, 94043, (650)962-1000	791 - H7
VILLA MONTALVO	15400 MONTALVO RD, SAR, 95070, (408)741-3421	872 - D4

POINTS OF INTEREST

FEATURE NAME	Address City, ZIP Code	PAGE-GRID
120 INCH TELESCOPE	MOUNT HAMILTON RD, SCIC, 95140	837 - C5
ALLIED ARTS GUILD	ARBOR RD & CREEK DR, MLPK, 94025, (650)325-3259	790 - G5
COPERNICUS PEAK LOOKOUT TOWER	MOUNT HAMILTON RD, SCIC, 95140	837 - D5
COUNTY OF SANTA CLARA GIRLS RANCH	BERNAL RD, SCIC, 95119	895 - D2
HAPPY HOLLOW ZOO	1300 SENTER RD, SJS, 95112, (408)292-8188	854 - E1
HOOVER PAVILION	QUARRY RD & PALO DR, PA, 94304	790 - H5
JAMES BOYS RANCH	SYCAMORE AV & MALAGUERRA AV, MGH, 95037	917 - B2
JAPANESE FRIENDSHIP TEA GARDEN	1300 SENTER RD, SJS, 95112, (408)277-2757	854 - E1
LICK OBSERVATORY (UNIV OF CALIF)	MOUNT HAMILTON RD, SCIC, 95140, (408)274-5062	837 - C6
MAUSOLEUM	LOMITA DR & CAMPUS DR, SCIC, 94305, (650)723-2300	790 - H6
PALO ALTO CULTURAL CENTER	1313 NEWELL RD, PA, 94303, (650)329-2366	791 - B5
SUNSET MAGAZINE CENTER	MIDDLEFIELD RD & WILLOW RD, MLPK, 94025, (650)321-3600	790 - H3
WINCHESTER MYSTERY HOUSE	1750 S WINCHESTER BLVD, SJS, 95117, (408)247-2101	853 - D1

POINTS OF INTEREST - HISTORIC

FEATURE NAME	Address City, ZIP Code	PAGE-GRID
HAYES MANSION HISTORICAL LANDMARK	EDENVALE AV & RED RIVER WY, SJS, 95136	875 - A2
HIGUERA ADOBE PARK	N PARK VICTORIA DR & WESSEX PL, MPS, 95035	794 - B3
MISSION SANTA CLARA DE ASIS	820 ALVISO ST, SCL, 95053, (408)554-4023	833 - E4
PERALTA ADOBE	175 W SAINT JOHN ST, SJS, 95110, (408)993-8182	834 - B6

POST OFFICES

FEATURE NAME	Address City, ZIP Code	PAGE-GRID
AGNEW STATION POST OFFICE	4601 LAFAYETTE ST, SCL, 95054	813 - D4
ALMADEN VALLEY STATION	6525 CROWN BLVD, SJS, 95120	894 - E1
ALVISO STATION POST OFFICE	1160 TAYLOR ST, SJS, 95002	793 - B7
BAYSIDE STATION	1750 LUNDY AV, SJS, 95131	814 - C6
BAYSIDE STATION POST OFFICE	2731 JUNCTION AV, SJS, 95134	813 - H5
BERRYESSA STATION	1315 PIEDMONT RD, SJS, 95132	814 - G4
BLOSSOM HILL STATION	5706 CAHALAN AV, SJS, 95123, (408)225-8020	874 - G4
BLOSSOM VALLEY STATION	1776 MIRAMONTE AV, MTVW, 94040	831 - H1
CAMBRIAN PARK POST OFFICE	1769 HILLSDALE AV, SJS, 95124	873 - H2
CAMBRIDGE STATION POST OFFICE	265 CAMBRIDGE AV, PA, 94306, (650)327-4174	791 - A7
CAMPBELL POST OFFICE	500 W HAMILTON AV, CMBL, 95008	853 - D5
COYOTE POST OFFICE	MONTEREY RD, SCIC, 95137, (408)463-0666	895 - J2
CUPERTINO POST OFFICE	20850 STEVENS CREEK BLVD, CPTO, 95014, (408)252-6798	852 - D1
EAST PALO ALTO POST OFFICE	2197 E BAYSHORE RD, PA, 94303	791 - D4
ENCINAL STATION POST OFFICE	526 W FREMONT AV, SUNV, 94087, (408)245-0617	832 - E3
GILROY POST OFFICE	100 CHURCH ST, GIL, 95020, (408)842-2250	978 - A3
HILLVIEW STATION POST OFFICE	2450 ALVIN AV, SJS, 95121, (408)238-1854	854 - J1
LOS ALTOS POST OFFICE	100 1ST ST, LALT, 94022, (650)948-6000	811 - D7
LOS GATOS POST OFFICE	101 S SANTA CRUZ AV, LGTS, 95030	893 - A1
MILPITAS POST OFFICE	450 S ABEL ST, MPS, 95035	814 - A1
MISSION STATION	1050 KIELY BLVD, SCL, 95051	833 - B4
MORGAN HILL POST OFFICE	16600 MONTEREY HWY, MGH, 95037, (408)779-2484	937 - B1
MOUNTAIN VIEW POST OFFICE	211 HOPE ST, MTVW, 94041, (650)967-5721	811 - J5
NEW ALMADEN	21300 ALMADEN RD, SCIC, 95120, (408)268-7730	894 - J7
OAK GROVE STATION POST OFFICE	655 OAK GROVE AV, MLPK, 94025, (650)321-7681	790 - F3
PALO ALTO	380 HAMILTON AV, PA, 94301, (650)323-1361	790 - J4
PARKMOOR STATION POST OFFICE	1545 PARKMOOR AV, SJS, 95126	853 - H1
PLAZA STATION POST OFFICE	141 S TAAFFE AV, SUNV, 94086, (408)738-1150	812 - E7
POST OFFICE (SEE PAGE 997)	BLOHM & BARDUE, MntC	1017 - A5
POST OFFICE	BROADWAY & MADRONE DR, SCIC, 95030, (408)353-1667	912 - J2
POST OFFICE	UNIVERSITY & BAY, EPA, 94303	791 - B1
ROBERTSVILLE STATION	1175 BRANHAM LN, SJS, 95118	874 - C2
SAINT JAMES PARK POST OFFICE	105 N 1ST ST, SJS, 95113	834 - B6
SAN MARTIN POST OFFICE	200 E SAN MARTIN AV, SCIC, 95046, (408)683-2252	937 - F6
SANTA CLARA POST OFFICE	1200 FRANKLIN MALL ST, SCL, 95050	833 - E4
SARATOGA POST OFFICE	19630 ALLENDALE AV, SAR, 95070	872 - E2
STANFORD UNIV BRANCH	LAGUNITA DR & LANE W, SCIC, 94305, (650)322-0059	790 - H7
STATION A POST OFFICE	364 WOODSIDE PZ, RDWC, 94061, (650)368-3605	790 - A3
STATION B POST OFFICE	1074 LINCOLN AV, SJS, 95125	854 - A2
STATION D POST OFFICE	70 S JACKSON AV, SJS, 95116	834 - H3
SUNNYVALE POST OFFICE	580 N MARY AV, SUNV, 94086, (408)732-0121	812 - D5
WEST MENLO PARK BRANCH POST OFFICE	2120 AVY AV, SMCo, 94025	790 - D6
WESTGATE STATION POST OFFICE	4285 PAYNE AV, SJS, 95117	853 - A4
WILLOW GLEN POST OFFICE	1750 MERIDIAN AV, SJS, 95126	853 - J5

SCHOOLS - PRIVATE ELEMENTARY

FEATURE NAME	Address City, ZIP Code	PAGE-GRID
ACHIEVER CHRISTIAN ELEM SCHOOL	820 IRONWOOD DR, SJS, 95125, (408)264-6789	854 - D6
ALMADEN COUNTRY ELEM SCHOOL	6835 TRINIDAD DR, SJS, 95120, (408)997-0424	894 - F1
APOSTLES LUTHERAN ELEM SCHOOL	5828 SANTA TERESA BLVD, SJS, 95123, (408)578-4800	874 - G6
CALVARY CATHEDRAL ACADEMY	2165 LUCRETIA AV, SJS, 95122, (408)298-7622	854 - G2
CAMPBELL CHRISTIAN	1075 W CAMPBELL AV, CMBL, 95008, (408)374-7260	853 - B6
CANTERBURY CHRISTIAN ELEM SCHOOL	101 N EL MONTE AV, LALT, 94022, (650)949-0909	811 - F6
CARDEN EL ENCANTO	615 HOBART TER, SCL, 95051, (414)244-5041	833 - B6
CARDEN SCHOOL OF ALMADEN SOUTH VALLEY	1921 CLARINDA WY, SJS, 95124, (408)879-1000	873 - G4
CHALLENGER ELEM SCHOOL	1185 HOLLENBECK AV, SUNV, 94087, (408)245-7170	832 - D3
CHALLENGER ELEM SCHOOL	1325 BOURET DR, SJS, 95118, (408)723-0111	874 - B3
CHALLENGER ELEM SCHOOL	880 WREN DR, SJS, 95125, (408)448-3010	854 - D6
CHRISTIAN COMMUNITY ACADEMY	1523 MCLAUGHLIN AV, SJS, 95122, (408)279-0846	834 - G7
FIVE WOUNDS ELEM SCHOOL	1390 FIVE WOUNDS LN, SJS, 95116, (408)293-0425	834 - E4
GRANADA ISLAMIC ELEM SCHOOL	3003 SCOTT BLVD, SCL, 95054, (408)980-1167	813 - D7
HARKER ACADEMY	500 SARATOGA AV, SJS, 95117, (408)249-2510	853 - B1
HILLBROOK SCHOOL	16000 MARCHMONT DR, LGTS, 95032, (408)356-6116	873 - D7
HOLY FAMILY ELEM SCHOOL	4848 PEARL AV, SJS, 95136, (408)978-1355	874 - E2
KEYS SCHOOL	2890 MIDDLEFIELD RD, PA, 94306, (650)328-1711	791 - C6
LIBERTY BAPTIST ELEM SCHOOL	2790 S KING RD, SJS, 95122, (408)274-5613	855 - A2
LOS ALTOS CHRISTIAN ELEM SCHOOL	625 MAGDALENA AV, LALT, 94024, (650)948-3738	831 - F2
LOS GATOS ACADEMY	220 BELGATOS RD, LGTS, 95032, (408)358-1046	873 - H6
LOS GATOS CHRISTIAN SCHOOL	16845 HICKS RD, LGTS, 95032, (408)268-1502	873 - J7
MID-PENINSULA JEWISH COMM SCH	655 ARASTRADERO RD, PA, 94306, (650)424-8482	811 - C3
MILPITAS CHRISTIAN ELEM SCHOOL	3435 BIRCHWOOD LN, SJS, 95132, (408)945-6530	814 - E2
MILPITAS FOOTHILL SEVENTH-DAY ADVNT	1991 LANDESS AV, MPS, 95035, (408)263-2568	814 - E2
MIRAMONTE ELEM SCHOOL	1175 ALTAMEAD DR, LALT, 94024, (650)967-2783	831 - H2
MONARCH CHRISTIAN ELEM SCHOOL	1196 LIME DR, SUNV, 94087, (408)745-7386	832 - B3
MOST HOLY TRINITY ELEM SCHOOL	1940 CUNNINGHAM AV, SJS, 95122, (408)729-3431	834 - J7
MULBERRY ELEM SCHOOL	1980 E HAMILTON AV, CMBL, 95125, (408)377-1595	853 - H5
NATIVITY ELEM SCHOOL	1250 LAUREL ST, MLPK, 94025, (650)325-7304	790 - F3
NEW COVENANT SCHOOL	220 BLAKE AV, SCL, 95051, (408)249-3993	833 - A7
OLD ORCHARD ELEM SCHOOL	400 W CAMPBELL AV, CMBL, 95008, (408)378-5935	853 - C6
PENINSULA FRENCH AMERICAN	870 N CALIFORNIA AV, PA, 94303, (650)328-2338	791 - C5
PENINSULA SCHOOL, LTD	920 PENINSULA WY, SMCo, 94025, (650)325-1584	790 - H1
PHILLIPS BROOKS ELEM SCHOOL	2245 AVY AV, MLPK, 94025, (650)854-4545	790 - D7
PINEWOOD PRIVATE SCHOOL OF LOS-ALTOS	327 FREMONT AV, LALT, 94024, (650)948-5438	831 - F1
PINEWOOD-LOWER CAMPUS	477 FREMONT AV, LALT, 94024, (650)962-9076	831 - F2
PLANTATION CHRISTIAN ELEM SCHOOL	209 HERLONG AV, SJS, 95123, (408)972-8211	875 - B5
PRIMARY PLUS	3500 AMBER DR, SJS, 95117, (408)248-2464	853 - D3
QUEEN OF APOSTLES ELEM SCHOOL	4950 MITTY WY, SJS, 95129, (408)252-3659	852 - J2
RAINBOW BRIDGE CENTER ELEM SCHOOL	1500 YOSEMITE DR, MPS, 95035, (408)945-9090	794 - D7
RAINBOW MONTESSORI ELEM SCHOOL	790 E DUANE AV, SUNV, 94086, (408)738-3261	812 - G6
RESURRECTION ELEM SCHOOL	1395 HOLLENBECK, SUNV, 94087, (408)245-4571	832 - D4
SACRED HEART ELEM SCHOOL	13718 SARATOGA AV, SAR, 95070, (408)867-9241	872 - F1
SAINT ANDREWS PRIVATE	13601 SARATOGA AV, SAR, 95070, (408)867-3785	872 - F1
SAINT CATHERINE ELEM SCHOOL	17500 S PEAK AV, MGH, 95037, (408)779-9950	916 - J7
SAINT CHRISTOPHER ELEM SCHOOL	2278 BOOKSIN AV, SJS, 95125, (408)723-7223	854 - A6
SAINT CLARE ELEM SCHOOL	725 WASHINGTON ST, SCL, 95050, (408)246-6797	833 - E4
SAINT CYPRIAN ELEM SCHOOL	195 LEOTA AV, SUNV, 94086, (408)738-3444	812 - C7
SAINT ELIZABETH SETON CATHOLIC COMM	1095 CHANNING AV, PA, 94301, (650)326-9004	791 - B4
SAINT FRANCIS CABRINI	15325 WOODWARD RD, SCIC, 95124, (408)377-6545	873 - F2
SAINT JOHN THE BAPTIST CATHOLIC ELEM	360 S ABEL ST, MPS, 95035, (408)262-8110	814 - A1
SAINT JOHN VIANNEY PRIVATE	4601 HYLAND AV, SJS, 95127, (408)258-7677	834 - J1
SAINT JOSEPH OF CUPERTINO	10120 N DE ANZA BLVD, CPTO, 95014, (650)252-6441	832 - E7
SAINT JOSEPHS ELEM SCHOOL	50 EMILIE AV, ATN, 94027, (650)322-9931	790 - E4
SAINT JOSEPHS ELEM SCHOOL	1120 MIRAMONTE AV, MTVW, 94040, (650)967-1839	811 - H6
SAINT JUSTIN ELEM SCHOOL	2655 HOMESTEAD RD, SCL, 95051, (408)248-1094	833 - B5
SAINT LAWRENCE ELEM SCHOOL	1971 SAINT LAWRENCE DR, SCL, 95051, (408)296-2260	832 - J3
SAINT LEO THE GREAT ELEM SCHOOL	1051 W SAN FERNANDO ST, SJS, 95126, (408)293-4846	833 - J7
SAINT LUCY ELEM SCHOOL	76 E KENNEDY AV, CMBL, 95008, (408)378-7454	853 - E6
SAINT MARTIN ELEM SCHOOL	597 CENTRAL AV, SUNV, 94086, (408)736-5534	832 - E1
SAINT MARTIN OF TOURS	300 OCONNOR DR, SJS, 95128, (408)287-3630	833 - F7
SAINT MARY SCHOOL	7900 CHURCH ST, GIL, 95020, (408)842-2827	977 - J2
SAINT MARYS ELEM SCHOOL	30 LYNDON AV, LGTS, 95030, (408)354-3944	873 - A7
SAINT NICHOLAS ELEM SCHOOL	12816 S EL MONTE AV, LAH, 94024, (650)941-4056	831 - E2
SAINT PATRICK ELEM SCHOOL	51 N 9TH ST, SJS, 95113, (408)283-5858	834 - C5
SAINT PIUS ELEM SCHOOL	1100 WOODSIDE RD, RDWC, 94061, (650)368-8327	790 - B2
SAINT RAYMOND ELEM SCHOOL	1211 ARBOR RD, MLPK, 94025, (650)322-2312	790 - F4
SAINT SIMON ELEM SCHOOL	1840 GRANT RD, LALT, 94024, (650)968-9952	831 - J4
SAINT STEPHENS ELEM SCHOOL	500 SHAWNEE LN, SJS, 95123, (408)365-2927	874 - H5
SAINT TIMOTHY ELEM SCHOOL	5100 CAMDEN AV, SJS, 95118, (408)265-0244	873 - J4
SAINT VICTOR ELEM SCHOOL	3150 SIERRA RD, SJS, 95132, (408)251-1740	814 - G5
SAN JOSE CHRISTIAN	1300 SHEFFIELD AV, CMBL, 95008, (408)371-7741	853 - G5

SANTA CLARA CO.

INDEX

FEATURE NAME Address City, ZIP Code	PAGE-GRID
SOUTH PENINSULA HEBREW DAY 1030 ASTORIA DR, SUNV, 94087, (408)738-3060	832 - B4
SOUTH VALLEY CHRISTIAN 145 WRIGHT AV, MGH, 95037, (408)779-8850	916 - J6
SOUTHBAY CHRISTIAN ELEM SCHOOL 1134 MIRAMONTE AV, MTVW, 94040, (650)961-5781	811 - H6
SUNSHINE CHRISTIAN ELEM SCHOOL 445 S MARY AV, SUNV, 94086, (408)736-3286	812 - C7
TRINITY EPISCOPAL ELEM SCHOOL 2650 SAND HILL RD, MLPK, 94025, (650)854-0288	810 - D1
VALLEY CHRISTIAN SCHOOL 220 KENSINGTON WY, LGTS, 95032, (408)559-4400	873 - G5
WALDORF SCHOOL OF THE PENINSULA 401 ROSITA AV, LALT, 94024, (650)948-8433	831 - F1
WEST VALLEY ELEM SCHOOL 95 DOT AV, CMBL, 95008, (408)378-4327	853 - D6
WOODLAND ELEM SCHOOL 360 LA CUESTA DR, SMCo, 94028, (650)854-9065	810 - E3
YAVNEH DAY ELEM SCHOOL 14855 OKA RD, LGTS, 95030, (408)358-3413	873 - C3

SCHOOLS - PRIVATE HIGH

FEATURE NAME Address City, ZIP Code	PAGE-GRID
ARCHBISHOP MITTY HIGH SCHOOL 5000 MITTY WY, SJS, 95129, (408)252-6610	852 - J2
BELLARMINE COLLEGE PREP 850 ELM ST, SJS, 95126, (408)294-9224	833 - H5
CHRISTIAN COMMUNITY ACADEMY 1523 MCLAUGHLIN AV, SJS, 95122, (408)279-0846	834 - F7
KINGS ACADEMY HIGH SCHOOL 562 N BRITTON AV, SUNV, 94086, (408)481-9900	812 - G6
LIBERTY BAPTIST HIGH SCHOOL 2790 S KING RD, SJS, 95122, (408)274-5613	855 - A2
LOS GATOS ACADEMY 220 BELGATOS RD, LGTS, 95032, (408)358-1046	873 - H6
MENLO HIGH SCHOOL 50 VALPARAISO AV, ATN, 94027, (650)688-3863	790 - F3
MID-PENINSULA EDUCATION CENTER 870 N CALIFORNIA AV, PA, 94303, (650)493-5910	791 - C5
MOUNTAIN VIEW ACADEMY HIGH SCHOOL 360 S SHORELINE BLVD, MTVW, 94041, (650)967-2324	811 - H5
NOTRE DAME HIGH SCHOOL 596 S 2ND ST, SJS, 95112, (408)294-1113	834 - C7
PINEWOOD HIGH SCHOOL 26800 FREMONT RD, LAH, 94022, (650)941-1532	811 - B5
PLANTATION CHRISTIAN HIGH SCHOOL 209 HERLONG AV, SJS, 95123, (408)972-8211	875 - B5
PRESENTATION HIGH SCHOOL 2281 PLUMMER AV, SJS, 95125, (408)264-1664	854 - A6
SACRED HEART PREPARATORY 150 VALPARAISO AV, ATN, 94027, (650)322-1866	790 - E4
SAINT FRANCIS HS OF MOUNTAIN VW 1885 MIRAMONTE AV, MTVW, 94040, (650)968-1213	831 - H1
SAINT LAWRENCE ACADEMY HIGH SCHOOL 2000 LAWRENCE CT, SCL, 95051, (408)296-3013	832 - J3
VALLEY CHRISTIAN HIGH SCHOOL 1570 BRANHAM LN, SJS, 95118, (408)377-5882	874 - A3
WOODSIDE PRIORY 302 PORTOLA RD, PTLV, 94028, (650)851-8221	810 - C7

SCHOOLS - PRIVATE JUNIOR HIGH

FEATURE NAME Address City, ZIP Code	PAGE-GRID
VALLEY CHRISTIAN JUNIOR HIGH SCHOOL 1570 BRANHAM LN, SJS, 95118, (408)978-9830	874 - A3

SCHOOLS - PRIVATE MIDDLE

FEATURE NAME Address City, ZIP Code	PAGE-GRID
ALMADEN COUNTRY MIDDLE SCHOOL 6835 TRINIDAD DR, SJS, 95120, (408)997-0424	894 - F1
CASTILLEJA MIDDLE SCHOOL 1310 BRYANT ST, PA, 94301, (650)328-3160	791 - A5
MENLO MIDDLE SCHOOL 50 VALPARAISO AV, ATN, 94027, (650)323-6141	790 - E3

SCHOOLS - PUBLIC ELEMENTARY

FEATURE NAME Address City, ZIP Code	PAGE-GRID
ADDISON ELEM SCHOOL 650 ADDISON AV, PA, 94301, (650)322-5935	791 - A4
ALEXANDER ROSE ELEM SCHOOL 250 ROSWELL DR, MPS, 95035, (408)495-5580	794 - D7
ALLEN ELEM SCHOOL 5845 ALLEN AV, SJS, 95123, (408)935-6205	874 - F5
ALMADEN ELEM SCHOOL 1295 DENTWOOD DR, SJS, 95118, (408)535-6207	874 - C4
ALMOND ELEM SCHOOL 550 ALMOND AV, LALT, 94022, (650)941-0470	811 - F6
ALTA VISTA ELEM SCHOOL 200 BLOSSOM VALLEY DR, LGTS, 95032, (408)356-6146	873 - E5
ANDERSON, ALEX ELEM SCHOOL 5800 CALPINE DR, SJS, 95123, (408)226-3370	875 - B5
ANDERSON, LEROY ELEM SCHOOL 4000 RHODA DR, SJS, 95117, (408)243-6031	853 - B3
APREA, LUIGI FUNDAMENTAL SCHOOL 9225 CL DL REY, GIL, 95020, (408)842-3135	957 - F7
ARBUCKLE, CLYDE ELEM SCHOOL 1970 CINDERELLA LN, SJS, 95116, (408)259-2910	834 - H5
ARGONAUT ELEM SCHOOL 13200 SHADOW MOUNTAIN DR, SAR, 95070, (408)867-4773	852 - E7
AROMAS (SEE PAGE 997) 365 VEGA ST, MntC, (408)726-5100	1017 - A5
ATHENOUR ELEM SCHOOL 5200 DENT AV, SJS, 95118, (408)265-8455	874 - A4
BACHRODT, WALTER L ELEM SCHOOL 102 SONORA AV, SJS, 95110, (408)535-6211	833 - J2
BAGBY ELEM SCHOOL 1840 HARRIS AV, SJS, 95124, (408)377-3882	853 - H7
BAKER, GUSSIE M ELEM SCHOOL 4845 BUCKNALL RD, SJS, 95130, (408)379-2101	853 - A6
BALDWIN, JULIA ELEM SCHOOL 280 MARTINVALE LN, SJS, 95119, (408)229-6302	895 - E1
BISHOP ELEM SCHOOL 450 N SUNNYVALE AV, SUNV, 94086, (408)522-8229	812 - F6
BLACKFORD ELEM SCHOOL 1970 WILLOW ST, SJS, 95125, (408)364-4221	853 - H4
BLOSSOM HILL ELEM SCHOOL 16400 BLOSSOM HILL RD, LGTS, 95032, (408)356-3141	873 - D6
BLOSSOM VALLEY ELEM SCHOOL 420 ALLEGAN CIR, SJS, 95123, (408)227-4260	875 - A6
BLUE HILLS ELEM SCHOOL 12300 DE SANKA AV, SAR, 95070, (408)257-9282	852 - E5
BOOKSIN ELEM SCHOOL 1590 DRY CREEK RD, SJS, 95125, (408)535-6213	853 - J6
BOWERS ELEM SCHOOL 2755 BARKLEY AV, SCL, 95051, (408)985-0171	833 - B3
BRACHER ELEM SCHOOL 2700 CHROMITE DR, SCL, 95051, (408)984-1682	833 - B2
BRALY ELEM SCHOOL 675 GAIL AV, SUNV, 94086, (408)983-1441	832 - F2
BRENTWOOD OAKS ELEM SCHOOL 2086 CLARKE AV, EPA, 94303, (650)329-2875	791 - C2
BRIARWOOD ELEM SCHOOL 1930 TOWNSEND AV, SCL, 95051, (408)554-6202	833 - A3
BRIONES, JUANA ELEM SCHOOL 4100 ORME AV, PA, 94306, (650)856-0877	811 - C3
BROOKTREE ELEM SCHOOL 1781 OLIVETREE DR, SJS, 95131, (408)923-1910	814 - C5
BUBB, BENJAMIN ELEM SCHOOL 525 HANS AV, MTVW, 94040, (650)965-9697	811 - H7
BULLIS-PURISSIMA ELEM SCHOOL 25890 FREMONT RD, LAH, 94022, (650)941-3880	811 - C6
BURNETT ELEM SCHOOL 85 TILTON AV, MGH, 95037, (408)779-5241	916 - G4
BURNETT, WILLIAM ELEM SCHOOL 400 FANYON ST, MPS, 95035, (408)945-2431	794 - C5
CADWALLADER ELEM SCHOOL 3799 CADWALLADER RD, SJS, 95121, (408)270-4950	855 - D3
CAPRI ELEM SCHOOL 850 CHAPMAN AV, CMBL, 95008, (408)364-4260	873 - C2
CARLTON ELEM SCHOOL 2421 CARLTON AV, SJS, 95124, (408)356-1141	873 - E4
CARSON, RACHEL ELEM SCHOOL 4245 MEG DR, SJS, 95136, (408)535-6287	874 - F1
CASSELL, SYLVIA ELEM SCHOOL 1300 TALLAHASSEE DR, SJS, 95122, (408)259-2653	834 - J5
CASTLEMONT ELEM SCHOOL 3040 E PAYNE AV, SJS, 95128, (408)364-4233	853 - E4
CASTRO, MARIANO ELEM SCHOOL 505 ESCUELA AV, MTVW, 94041, (650)964-7555	811 - G4
CEDAR GROVE ELEM SCHOOL 2702 SUGAR PLUM DR, SJS, 95148, (408)270-4958	835 - D7
CHAVEZ, CESAR ELEM SCHOOL 2000 KAMMERER AV, SJS, 95116, (408)258-5078	834 - G4
CHAVEZ, CESAR ELEM SCHOOL 2450 RALMER AV, EPA, 94303, (650)329-6700	791 - A1
CHERRY CHASE ELEM SCHOOL 1138 HEATHERSTONE WY, SUNV, 94087, (408)522-8241	832 - B1
CHERRYWOOD ELEM SCHOOL 2550 GREENGATE DR, SJS, 95132, (408)923-1915	814 - E5
CHRISTOPHER ELEM SCHOOL 565 COYOTE RD, SJS, 95111, (408)227-8550	855 - A7
COLLINS ELEM SCHOOL 10401 VISTA DR, CPTO, 95014, (650)252-6002	832 - E7
CORTE MADERA 4575 ALPINE RD, PTLV, 94028, (650)851-0409	830 - C1
CORY, BENJAMIN ELEM SCHOOL 2280 KENWOOD AV, SJS, 95128, (408)535-6219	833 - E7
COUNTRY LANE ELEM SCHOOL 5140 COUNTRY LN, SJS, 95129, (408)252-3444	852 - J4
CUMBERLAND ELEM SCHOOL 824 CUMBERLAND AV, SUNV, 94087, (408)522-8255	832 - C1
CURETON, HORACE ELEM SCHOOL 3720 E HILLS DR, SJS, 95127, (408)258-5066	835 - B2
CURTNER ELEM SCHOOL 275 REDWOOD AV, MPS, 95035, (650)945-2434	793 - J6
DARLING, ANNE ELEM SCHOOL 333 N 33RD ST, SJS, 95133, (408)535-6209	834 - E3
DAVES AV ELEM SCHOOL 17770 DAVES AV, MSER, 95030, (408)395-6311	873 - A5
DE VARGAS ELEM SCHOOL 5050 MOORPARK AV, SJS, 95129, (408)252-0303	852 - J2
DEL ROBLE 5345 AVD ALMENDROS, SJS, 95123, (408)225-5675	874 - H3
DILWORTH ELEM SCHOOL 1101 STRAYER DR, SJS, 95129, (408)253-2850	852 - G3
DORSA, ANTHONY J ELEM SCHOOL 1290 BAL HARBOR WY, SJS, 95122, (408)259-2460	834 - H6
DOVE HILL ELEM SCHOOL 1460 COLT WY, SJS, 95121, (408)270-4964	855 - B4
DUVENECK ELEM SCHOOL 705 ALESTER AV, PA, 94303, (650)322-5946	791 - C4
EASTERBROOK ELEM SCHOOL 4660 EASTUS DR, SJS, 95129, (408)253-3424	853 - A3
EDENVALE ELEM SCHOOL 285 AZUCAR AV, SJS, 95111, (408)227-7060	875 - C2
EISENHOWER ELEM SCHOOL 277 RODONOVAN DR, SCL, 95051, (408)248-4313	832 - J7
EL CARMELO ELEM SCHOOL 3024 BRYANT ST, PA, 94306, (650)856-0960	791 - C7
EL ROBLE ELEM SCHOOL 930 3RD ST, GIL, 95020, (408)842-8234	977 - H3
EL TORO ELEM SCHOOL 455 E MAIN AV, MGH, 95037, (408)779-5250	917 - A6
ELLIOT ELEM SCHOOL 470 E 7TH ST, GIL, 95020, (408)842-5618	978 - B3
ELLIS ELEM SCHOOL 550 E OLIVE AV, SUNV, 94086, (408)522-8260	832 - F1
EMPIRE GARDENS ELEM SCHOOL 1060 E EMPIRE ST, SJS, 95112, (408)535-6211	834 - D4
ENCINAL ELEM SCHOOL 195 ENCINAL AV, ATN, 94027, (650)326-5164	790 - F2
ENCINAL ELEM SCHOOL 9530 N MONTEREY RD, SJS, 95137, (408)779-5221	896 - B3
ERIKSON ELEM SCHOOL 4849 PEARL AV, SJS, 95136, (408)535-6036	874 - E2
ESCONDIDO ELEM SCHOOL 890 ESCONDIDO RD, SCIC, 94305, (650)856-1337	810 - J1
EVERGREEN ELEM SCHOOL 3010 FOWLER RD, SJS, 95135, (408)270-4966	855 - E3
FAIRMEADOW ELEM SCHOOL 500 E MEADOW DR, PA, 94306, (650)856-0845	811 - E1
FAMMATRE ELEM SCHOOL 2800 NEW JERSEY AV, SJS, 95124, (408)377-5480	873 - G1
FARIA ELEM SCHOOL 10155 BARBARA LN, CPTO, 95014, (408)252-0706	852 - D1
FARNHAM ELEM SCHOOL 15711 WOODARD RD, SJS, 95124, (408)377-3321	873 - E2
FOOTHILL ELEM SCHOOL 13919 LYNDE AV, SAR, 95070, (408)867-4036	872 - D1
FORD, HENRY ELEM SCHOOL 2498 MASSACHUSETTS AV, RDWC, 94061, (650)368-2981	790 - A3
FOREST HILL ELEM SCHOOL 4450 MCCOY AV, CMBL, 95130, (408)364-4279	853 - A7
FRANKLIN ELEM SCHOOL 420 TULLY RD, SJS, 95111, (408)283-6375	854 - F3
FROST, EARL ELEM SCHOOL 530 GETTYSBURG DR, SJS, 95123, (408)225-1881	874 - H4
GARDEN GATE ELEM SCHOOL 10500 ANN ARBOR AV, CPTO, 95014, (650)252-5414	832 - C6
GARDNER ELEM SCHOOL 502 ILLINOIS AV, SJS, 95125, (408)535-6225	854 - B1
GARFIELD CHARTER ELEM SCHOOL 3600 MIDDLEFIELD RD, SMCo, 94063, (650)369-3759	790 - D1
GLEN VIEW ELEM SCHOOL 600 W 8TH ST, GIL, 95020, (408)842-8292	977 - J4
GLIDER ELEM SCHOOL 511 COZY DR, SJS, 95123, (408)227-1505	874 - J6
GOSS, MILDRED ELEM SCHOOL 2475 VAN WINKLE LN, SJS, 95116, (408)258-8172	834 - J4
GRANT ELEM SCHOOL 470 E JACKSON ST, SJS, 95112, (408)535-6277	834 - B4
GRAYSTONE ELEM SCHOOL 6982 SHEARWATER DR, SJS, 95120, (408)535-6317	894 - H2
GUADALUPE ELEM SCHOOL 6044 VERA CRUZ DR, SJS, 95120, (408)268-1031	874 - A7
GWINN ELEM SCHOOL 95 NORTH ST, SCIC, 95046, (408)779-5219	937 - E6
HACIENDA SCIENCE/ENVIRONMENTAL MAGNET 1290 KIMBERLY DR, SJS, 95118, (408)535-6259	874 - C1
HAMAN, CW ELEM SCHOOL 865 LOS PADRES BLVD, SCL, 95050, (408)244-6893	833 - C5
HAYES ELEM SCHOOL 5035 POSTON DR, SJS, 95136, (408)227-0424	874 - J2
HAYS, WALTER ELEM SCHOOL 1525 MIDDLEFIELD RD, PA, 94301, (650)322-5956	791 - B5
HAZELWOOD ELEM SCHOOL 775 WALDO RD, CMBL, 95008, (408)364-4230	853 - C7
HELLYER, G W ELEM SCHOOL 725 HELLYER AV, SJS, 95111, (408)363-5750	855 - A6
HESTER ELEM SCHOOL 1460 THE ALAMEDA, SJS, 95126, (408)535-6235	833 - J6
HILLSDALE ELEM SCHOOL 3200 WATER ST, SJS, 95111, (408)363-5650	854 - H6
HOLLY OAK ELEM SCHOOL 2995 ROSSMORE WY, SJS, 95148, (408)270-4975	855 - C2
HOOVER, HERBERT ELEM SCHOOL 1635 PARK AV, SJS, 95126, (408)535-6274	833 - H6
HOOVER, HERBERT ELEM SCHOOL 800 BARRON AV, PA, 94306, (650)856-1377	811 - B2
HUBBARD, O S ELEM SCHOOL 1745 JUNE AV, SJS, 95122, (408)251-1296	834 - H7
HUGHES, KATHRYN ELEM SCHOOL 4949 CL DE ESCUELA, SCL, 95054, (408)988-2390	813 - C3
JACKSON ELEM SCHOOL 2700 FOUNTAIN OAKS DR, MGH, 95037, (408)779-8301	917 - F6
JORDAN ELEM SCHOOL 7743 HANNA ST, GIL, 95020, (408)842-5922	977 - J2
KENNEDY, ROBERT F ELEM SCHOOL 1602 LUCRETIA AV, SJS, 95122, (408)283-6325	854 - F1
LAKESIDE ELEM SCHOOL 19621 BLACK RD, SCIC, 95030, (408)354-2372	892 - F4
LAKEWOOD ELEM SCHOOL 750 LAKECHIME DR, SUNV, 94089, (408)522-8272	812 - H4
LANDELS, EDITH ELEM SCHOOL 115 DANA ST, MTVW, 94041, (650)965-4675	811 - J5
LANEVIEW ELEM SCHOOL 2095 WARMWOOD LN, SJS, 95132, (408)923-1920	814 - D2
LAS ANIMAS ELEM SCHOOL 8450 WREN AV, GIL, 95020, (408)842-6414	977 - H1
LAS LOMITAS ELEM SCHOOL 299 ALAMEDA DE LAS PULGAS, ATN, 94027, (650)854-5900	790 - C5
LATIMER ELEM SCHOOL 4250 LATIMER AV, SJS, 95130, (408)379-2412	853 - A5
LAUREL ELEM SCHOOL 95 EDGE RD, ATN, 94027, (650)324-0186	790 - H1
LAURELWOOD ELEM SCHOOL 4280 PARTRIDGE DR, SJS, 95121, (408)270-4983	855 - E4
LAURELWOOD ELEM SCHOOL 955 TEAL DR, SCL, 95051, (408)554-1390	832 - H5
LEXINGTON ELEM SCHOOL 19700 SANTA CRUZ HWY, SCIC, 95030, (408)354-9340	892 - J6
LIETZ ELEM SCHOOL 5300 CARTER AV, SJS, 95118, (408)264-8314	874 - A5
LINCOLN ELEM SCHOOL 21710 MCCLELLAN RD, CPTO, 95014, (408)252-4798	852 - B2
LINDA VISTA ELEM SCHOOL 100 KIRK AV, SJS, 95127, (408)258-4938	815 - A7
LOMA PRIETA ELEM SCHOOL 23800 SUMMIT RD, SCIC, 95030, (408)353-1106	913 - E7
LONE HILL ELEM SCHOOL 4949 HARWOOD RD, SJS, 95124, (408)269-1173	873 - H4
LOS ALAMITOS ELEM SCHOOL 6130 SILBERMAN DR, SJS, 95120, (408)535-6297	874 - C7
LOS ALTOS 201 COVINGTON RD, LALT, 94024, (650)941-4010	831 - E1
LOS ARBOLES ELEM SCHOOL 455 LOS ARBOLES AV, SJS, 95111, (408)363-5675	854 - J6
LOS PASEOS ELEM SCHOOL 121 AVD GRANDE, SJS, 95139, (408)578-8800	875 - F7
LOWELL ELEM SCHOOL 625 S 7TH ST, SJS, 95112, (408)535-6243	834 - D7
LOYOLA ELEM SCHOOL 770 BERRY AV, LALT, 94024, (650)964-5165	831 - G2
LUTHER BURBANK ELEM SCHOOL 4 WABASH AV, SCIC, 95128, (408)295-1813	853 - G1
LYNDALE ELEM SCHOOL 13901 NORDYKE DR, SJS, 95127, (408)251-4010	834 - J3
LYNHAVEN ELEM SCHOOL 881 S CYPRESS AV, SJS, 95117, (498)364-4215	853 - C2
MACHADO 15130 SYCAMORE AV, SCIC, 95037, (408)779-8383	936 - J6
MAJESTIC WAY ELEM SCHOOL 1855 MAJESTIC WY, SJS, 95132, (408)923-1925	814 - F3
MANN, HORACE ELEM SCHOOL 55 N 7TH ST, SJS, 95113, (408)535-6237	834 - C6
MARSHALL LANE ELEM SCHOOL 14114 MARILYN LN, SAR, 95070, (408)364-4259	872 - H2
MAYNE, GEORGE ELEM SCHOOL 1490 TAYLOR ST, SJS, 95002, (408)262-3600	813 - C1
MCAULIFFE, CHRISTA ELEM SCHOOL 12211 TITUS AV, SAR, 95070, (408)253-4696	852 - G5
MCKINLEY ELEM SCHOOL 651 MACREDES AV, SJS, 95116, (408)283-6350	834 - E6
MEADOWS, JEANNE R ELEM SCHOOL 1250 TAPER LN, SJS, 95122, (408)283-6300	854 - H1
MENLO OAKS ELEM SCHOOL 475 POPE ST, MLPK, 94025, (650)329-2828	790 - J2
MEYER, DONALD J ELEM SCHOOL 1824 DAYTONA DR, SJS, 95122, (408)258-8208	834 - J6
MEYERHOLZ ELEM SCHOOL 6990 MELVIN DR, SJS, 95129, (408)252-7450	852 - E3
MILLARD MCCOLLAM ELEM SCHOOL 3311 LUCIAN AV, SJS, 95127, (408)258-1006	814 - J7
MILLBROOK ELEM SCHOOL 3200 MILLBROOK DR, SJS, 95148, (408)270-6767	855 - D2
MILLER, GRANDIN ELEM SCHOOL 1250 S KING RD, SJS, 95122, (408)258-2214	834 - H6
MILLIKIN ELEM SCHOOL 2720 SONOMA PL, SCL, 95051, (408)554-6661	833 - B5
MINER, GEORGE ELEM SCHOOL 5629 LEAN AV, SJS, 95123, (408)225-2144	875 - A4
MONTA LOMA ELEM SCHOOL 460 THOMPSON AV, MTVW, 94043, (650)903-6915	811 - G3
MONTAGUE ELEM SCHOOL 750 LAURIE AV, SCL, 95054, (408)988-3052	813 - E6
MONTCLAIR ELEM SCHOOL 1160 SAINT JOSEPH AV, LALT, 94024, (650)967-9388	831 - H5
MONTGOMERY, JOHN J ELEM SCHOOL 2010 DANIEL MALONEY DR, SJS, 95121, (408)270-6718	855 - C3
MT PLEASANT ELEM SCHOOL 14275 CANDLER AV, SJS, 95127, (408)258-6451	835 - B4
MUIR ELEM SCHOOL 6560 HANOVER DR, SJS, 95129, (408)252-5265	852 - F4
NIMITZ ELEM SCHOOL 545 E CHEYENNE DR, SUNV, 94087, (408)736-2180	832 - D4
NIXON, LUCILLE M ELEM SCHOOL 1711 STANFORD AV, SCIC, 94305, (650)856-1622	810 - J2
NOBLE ELEM SCHOOL 3466 GROSSMONT DR, SJS, 95132, (408)923-1935	814 - H5
NODDIN ELEM SCHOOL 1755 GILDA WY, SJS, 95124, (408)356-2126	873 - H5
NORDSTROM ELEM SCHOOL 1425 E DUNNE AV, MGH, 95037, (408)779-5278	917 - D6
NORTHWOOD ELEM SCHOOL 2760 TRIMBLE RD, SJS, 95132, (408)923-1940	814 - C3
NORWOOD CREEK ELEM SCHOOL 3241 REMINGTON WY, SJS, 95148, (408)270-6726	835 - D7
OAK AVENUE ELEM SCHOOL 1501 OAK AV, LALT, 94024, (650)964-2187	831 - J3
OAK KNOLL ELEM SCHOOL 1895 OAK KNOLL LN, MLPK, 94025, (650)854-4433	790 - E6
OAK RIDGE ELEM SCHOOL 5920 BUFKIN DR, SJS, 95123, (408)578-5900	875 - A5
OHLONE ELEM SCHOOL 950 AMARILLO AV, PA, 94303, (650)856-1726	791 - D5
OLINDER, SELMA ELEM SCHOOL 890 E WILLIAM ST, SJS, 95116, (408)535-6245	834 - E6
ORCHARD ELEM SCHOOL 711 E GISH RD, SJS, 95112, (408)998-2830	834 - B1
ORMONDALE ELEM SCHOOL 200 SHAWNEE PASS, PTLV, 94028, (650)851-7230	810 - B6
OSTER ELEM SCHOOL 1855 LENCAR WY, SJS, 95124, (408)266-8121	873 - H3
PAINTER, BEN ELEM SCHOOL 500 ROUGH AND READY RD, SJS, 95133, (408)258-1458	834 - G1
PALO VERDE ELEM SCHOOL 3450 LOUIS RD, PA, 94303, (650)856-1672	791 - E7
PARADISE VALLEY ELEM SCHOOL 1400 LA CROSSE DR, MGH, 95037, (408)779-8391	937 - A3
PARKVIEW ELEM SCHOOL 330 BLUEFIELD DR, SJS, 95136, (408)226-4655	874 - G1
PAYNE, GEORGE C ELEM SCHOOL 3750 GLEASON AV, SJS, 95130, (408)241-1788	853 - C4
POMEROY ELEM SCHOOL 1250 POMEROY AV, SCL, 95051, (408)554-0834	833 - A4
POMEROY, MARSHALL ELEM SCHOOL 1505 ESCUELA PKWY, MPS, 95035, (408)945-2424	794 - A4
PONDEROSA ELEM SCHOOL 804 PONDEROSA AV, SUNV, 94086, (408)245-6009	832 - G2

FEATURE NAME	Address City, ZIP Code	PAGE-GRID
PORTAL, LOUIS ELEM SCHOOL	10300 N BLANEY AV, CPTO, 95014, (408)973-8191	832 - F7
RANDALL, ROBERT ELEM SCHOOL	1300 EDSEL DR, MPS, 95035	794 - C7
RANDOL, JAMES ELEM SCHOOL	762 SUNSET GLEN DR, SJS, 95123, (408)535-6380	874 - G6
REED ELEM SCHOOL	1524 JACOB AV, SJS, 95118, (408)535-6247	874 - B2
REGNART ELEM SCHOOL	1170 YORKSHIRE DR, CPTO, 95014, (408)253-5250	852 - C3
RIVER GLEN ELEM SCHOOL	1610 BIRD AV, SJS, 95125, (408)535-6240	854 - C4
ROD KELLEY ELEM SCHOOL	8755 KERN AV, GIL, 95020, (408)847-1932	977 - G1
ROGERS, WILLIAM R ELEM SCHOOL	2999 RIDGEMONT DR, SJS, 95127, (408)258-3686	835 - B5
ROSEMARY ELEM SCHOOL	401 W HAMILTON AV, CMBL, 95008, (408)364-4254	853 - D5
RUCKER ELEM SCHOOL	325 SANTA CLARA AV, SCIC, 95020, (408)842-6471	957 - H3
RUSKIN ELEM SCHOOL	1401 TURLOCK LN, SJS, 95132, (408)923-1950	814 - F4
SAKAMOTO ELEM SCHOOL	6280 SHADELANDS DR, SJS, 95123, (408)227-3411	874 - H7
SAN ANSELMO ELEM SCHOOL	6670 SAN ANSELMO WY, SJS, 95119, (408)578-2710	875 - D7
SAN ANTONIO ELEM SCHOOL	1855 E SAN ANTONIO ST, SJS, 95116, (408)258-8582	834 - F4
SAN MARTIN ELEM SCHOOL	100 NORTH ST, SCIC, 95046, (408)779-5220	937 - F6
SAN MIGUEL ELEM SCHOOL	777 SAN MIGUEL AV, SUNV, 94086, (408)522-8279	812 - G5
SAN YSIDRO ELEM SCHOOL	2220 PACHECO PASS HWY, SCIC, 95020, (408)842-0292	978 - F4
SANDERS, ROBERT ELEM SCHOOL	3411 ROCKY MOUNTAIN DR, SJS, 95127, (408)258-7288	835 - C4
SANTA RITA ELEM SCHOOL	700 LOS ALTOS AV, LALT, 94022, (650)941-3288	811 - D5
SANTA TERESA ELEM SCHOOL	6200 ENCINAL DR, SJS, 95119, (408)227-3303	875 - C6
SANTEE ELEM SCHOOL	1313 AUDUBON DR, SJS, 95122, (408)283-6450	834 - G7
SARATOGA ELEM SCHOOL	14592 OAK ST, SAR, 95070, (408)867-3476	872 - D3
SARTORETTE ELEM SCHOOL	3850 WOODFORD DR, SJS, 95124, (408)264-4380	873 - J2
SCHALLENBERGER ELEM SCHOOL	1280 KOCH LN, SJS, 95125, (408)535-6253	854 - B7
SCOTT LANE ELEM SCHOOL	1925 SCOTT BLVD, SCL, 95050, (408)985-1050	833 - D3
SEDGWICK ELEM SCHOOL	19200 PHIL LN, CPTO, 95014, (408)252-3103	852 - G2
SELBY LANE ELEM SCHOOL	170 SELBY LN, ATN, 94027, (650)368-3996	790 - B3
SEVEN TREES ELEM SCHOOL	3975 MIRA LOMA WY, SJS, 95111, (408)363-5775	854 - J7
SHIELDS, LESTER W ELEM SCHOOL	2851 GAY AV, SJS, 95127, (408)258-4916	834 - H2
SILVER OAKS ELEM SCHOOL	FARNSWORTH DR & SAN FELIPE RD, SJS, 95138, (408)223-4515	855 - G7
SIMONDS ELEM SCHOOL	6515 GRAPEVINE WY, SJS, 95120, (408)535-6251	894 - D1
SINNOTT, JOHN ELEM SCHOOL	2025 YELLOWSTONE AV, MPS, 95035, (408)945-2441	814 - E1
SLATER, KENNETH N ELEM SCHOOL	325 GLADYS AV, MTVW, 94043, (650)964-7392	812 - B5
SLONAKER, HARRY ELEM SCHOOL	1601 CUNNINGHAM AV, SJS, 95122, (408)259-1941	834 - H7
SMITH, KATHERINE R ELEM SCHOOL	2025 CLARICE DR, SJS, 95122, (408)270-6751	835 - A7
SPANGLER, ANTHONY ELEM SCHOOL	140 N ABBOTT AV, MPS, 95035, (650)945-5592	793 - J7
SPRING GROVE ELEM SCHOOL (SEE PAGE 999)	500 SPRING GROVE RD, SBnC, (408)637-3745	1020 - F2
SPRINGER ELEM SCHOOL	1120 ROSE AV, MTVW, 94040, (650)964-3374	831 - G1
STEVENS CREEK ELEM SCHOOL	10300 AINSWORTH DR, CPTO, 95014, (650)245-3312	832 - A7
STIPE, SAMUEL ELEM SCHOOL	5000 LYNG DR, SJS, 95111, (408)227-7332	875 - B1
STOCKLMEIR, LOUIS V ELEM SCHOOL	592 DUNHOLME WY, SUNV, 94087, (408)732-3363	832 - E5
STONEGATE ELEM SCHOOL	2605 GASSMANN DR, SJS, 95121, (408)363-5625	854 - H3
SUMMERDALE	1100 SUMMERDALE DR, SJS, 95132, (408)923-1960	814 - G6
SUTTER ELEM SCHOOL	3200 FORBES AV, SCL, 95051, (408)554-0690	832 - J6
TAYLOR, BERTHA ELEM SCHOOL	410 SAUTNER DR, SJS, 95123, (408)226-0462	875 - B7
TERRELL ELEM SCHOOL	3925 PEARL AV, SJS, 95136, (408)535-6255	874 - D1
THE DELPHI ACADEMY	445 E CHARLESTON RD, PA, 94306, (650)493-3100	811 - E1
THEUERKAUF ELEM SCHOOL	1625 SAN LUIS AV, MTVW, 94043, (650)903-6925	811 - H3
THOMAS P RYAN ELEM SCHOOL	1241 MCGINNESS AV, SJS, 95127, (408)258-4936	835 - A4
TOYON ELEM SCHOOL	995 BARD ST, SJS, 95127, (408)923-1965	814 - H6
TRACE, MERITT ELEM SCHOOL	651 DANA AV, SJS, 95126, (408)535-6257	833 - G7
VALLE VISTA ELEM SCHOOL	2400 FLINT AV, SJS, 95148, (408)238-3525	835 - D6
VAN, METER LOUISE ELEM SCHOOL	16445 LOS GATOS BLVD, LGTS, 95032, (408)356-5131	873 - C6
VARGAS ELEM SCHOOL	1054 CARSON DR, SUNV, 94086, (408)522-8267	812 - C7
VINCI PARK ELEM SCHOOL	1311 VINCI PARK WY, SJS, 95131, (408)923-1970	814 - D7
WALSH, PA ELEM SCHOOL	353 W MAIN AV, MGH, 95037, (408)779-5211	916 - J7
WASHINGTON ELEM SCHOOL	100 OAK ST, SJS, 95110, (408)535-6261	854 - C1
WELLER, JOSEPH ELEM SCHOOL	345 BOULDER ST, MPS, 95035, (408)945-2428	794 - A3
WEST VALLEY ELEM SCHOOL	1635 BELLEVILLE WY, SUNV, 94087, (408)245-0148	832 - A5
WESTWOOD ELEM SCHOOL	435 SARATOGA AV, SCL, 95050, (408)554-0308	833 - D6
WHALEY ELEM SCHOOL	2655 ALVIN AV, SJS, 95121, (408)270-6759	854 - J2
WHISMAN ELEM SCHOOL	310 EASY ST, MTVW, 94043, (650)903-6935	812 - A4
WILLIAMS ELEM SCHOOL	1150 RAJKOVICH WY, SJS, 95120, (408)535-6196	894 - F3
WILLOW GLEN ELEM SCHOOL	1425 LINCOLN AV, SJS, 95125, (408)535-6265	854 - A4
WILLOW OAKS ELEM SCHOOL	620 WILLOW RD, MLPK, 94025, (650)329-2850	790 - J2
WINDMILL SPRINGS ELEM SCHOOL	2880 AETNA WY, SJS, 95121, (408)363-5600	854 - J3
ZANKER, PEARL ELEM SCHOOL	1585 FALLEN LEAF DR, MPS, 95035, (408)945-2438	814 - A3

SCHOOLS - PUBLIC HIGH

FEATURE NAME	Address City, ZIP Code	PAGE-GRID
BLACKFORD HIGH SCHOOL	3800 BLACKFORD AV, SJS, 95117, (408)241-0330	853 - C2
BROADWAY CONTINUATION HIGH SCHOOL	1088 BROADWAY AV, SJS, 95125, (408)535-6285	854 - A3
CALAVERAS HILLS CONTINUATION	1331 CALAVERAS BLVD, MPS, 95035, (408)945-2398	794 - C6
CENTRAL HIGH (CONT)	17960 MONTEREY HWY, MGH, 95037, (408)779-5244	916 - J6
CUPERTINO HIGH SCHOOL	10100 FINCH AV, CPTO, 95014, (408)366-7380	852 - G1
DEL MAR HIGH SCHOOL	1224 DEL MAR AV, SJS, 95128, (408)298-0260	853 - G3
FOOTHILL CONTINUATION HIGH SCHOOL	230 PALA AV, SJS, 95127, (408)259-4464	834 - H2
FREMONT HIGH SCHOOL	1279 SUNNYVALE-SARATOGA RD, SUNV, 94087, (408)522-2400	832 - D3
GILROY HIGH SCHOOL	750 10TH ST, GIL, 95020, (408)847-2424	977 - J5
GUNDERSON HIGH SCHOOL	620 GAUNDABERT LN, SJS, 95136, (408)535-6340	874 - F3
GUNN, HENRY M HIGH SCHOOL	780 ARASTRADERO RD, PA, 94306, (650)354-8200	811 - C4
HILL, ANDREW HIGH SCHOOL	3200 SENTER RD, SJS, 95111, (408)227-8800	854 - J5
HOMESTEAD HIGH SCHOOL	21370 HOMESTEAD RD, CPTO, 95014, (650)522-2500	832 - C6
INDEPENDENCE HIGH SCHOOL	1776 EDUCATIONAL PARK DR, SJS, 95133, (408)729-3911	834 - F2
LEIGH HIGH SCHOOL	5210 LEIGH AV, SJS, 95124, (408)377-4470	873 - G5
LELAND HIGH SCHOOL	6677 CAMDEN AV, SJS, 95120, (408)535-6290	894 - G2
LICK, JAMES HIGH SCHOOL	57 N WHITE RD, SJS, 95127, (408)729-3580	834 - J2
LINCOLN, ABRAHAM HIGH SCHOOL	555 DANA AV, SJS, 95126, (408)535-6300	833 - G7
LIVE OAK HIGH SCHOOL	1505 E MAIN AV, MGH, 95037, (408)779-5210	917 - C5
LOS ALTOS HIGH SCHOOL	201 ALMOND AV, LALT, 94022, (650)968-6571	811 - E6
LOS GATOS HIGH SCHOOL	20 HIGH SCHOOL CT, LGTS, 95032, (408)354-2730	893 - A1
LYNBROOK HIGH SCHOOL	1280 JOHNSON AV, SJS, 95129, (408)366-7700	852 - G4
MARK TWAIN CONTINUATION HIGH SCHOOL	17421 W FARLEY RD, LGTS, 95030, (408)354-1919	873 - B5
MENLO-ATHERTON HIGH SCHOOL	555 MIDDLEFIELD RD, ATN, 94027, (650)322-5311	790 - G2
MILPITAS HIGH SCHOOL	1285 ESCUELA PKWY, MPS, 95035, (408)945-5500	794 - A4
MOFFETT HIGH SCHOOL	333 MOFFETT BLVD, MTVW, 94043, (650)940-1333	811 - J4
MONTA VISTA HIGH SCHOOL	21840 MCCLELLAN RD, CPTO, 95014, (408)366-7600	852 - B2
MOUNT PLEASANT HIGH SCHOOL	1750 S WHITE RD, SJS, 95127, (408)251-7820	835 - B5
MOUNTAIN VIEW HIGH SCHOOL	3535 TRUMAN AV, MTVW, 94040, (408)940-4600	832 - A2
MT MADONNA CONTINUATION HIGH SCHOOL	8595 CULP DR, GIL, 95020, (408)842-4313	977 - G1
NEW VALLEY CONTINUATION HIGH SCHOOL	1840 BENTON ST, SCL, 95050, (408)984-0632	833 - D5
OAK GROVE HIGH SCHOOL	285 BLOSSOM HILL RD, SJS, 95123, (408)225-9332	875 - A4
OVERFELT, WILLIAM C HIGH SCHOOL	1835 CUNNINGHAM AV, SJS, 95122, (408)259-0540	834 - J7
PALO ALTO HIGH SCHOOL	50 EMBARCADERO RD, PA, 94301, (650)329-3710	790 - J6
PEGASUS CONTINUATION HIGH SCHOOL	1776 EDUCATIONAL PARK DR, SJS, 95133, (408)729-3911	834 - F2
PIEDMONT HILLS HIGH SCHOOL	1377 PIEDMONT RD, SJS, 95132, (408)729-3950	814 - G4
PIONEER HIGH SCHOOL	1290 BLOSSOM HILL RD, SJS, 95118, (408)535-6310	874 - C4
PROSPECT HIGH SCHOOL	18900 PROSPECT RD, SAR, 95070, (408)253-1662	852 - H5
SAN JOSE ACADEMY HIGH SCHOOL	275 N 24TH ST, SJS, 95116, (408)535-6320	834 - D4
SANTA CLARA HIGH SCHOOL	3000 BENTON ST, SCL, 95051, (408)985-5900	833 - A5
SANTA TERESA HIGH SCHOOL	6150 SNELL RD, SJS, 95123, (408)578-9100	874 - J6
SARATOGA HIGH SCHOOL	20300 HERRIMAN AV, SAR, 95070, (408)867-3411	872 - E1
SHORELINE CONTINUATION HIGH SCHOOL	1299 BRYANT AV, MTVW, 94040, (408)940-4656	832 - A2
SILVER CREEK HIGH SCHOOL	3434 SILVER CREEK RD, SJS, 95121, (408)274-1700	855 - B4
WESTMONT HIGH SCHOOL	4805 WESTMONT AV, SJS, 95008, (408)378-1500	873 - A1
WILCOX, ADRIAN HIGH SCHOOL	3250 MONROE ST, SCL, 95051, (408)554-6300	833 - A2
WILLOW GLEN HIGH SCHOOL	2001 COTTLE AV, SJS, 95125, (408)535-6330	854 - A5
WOODSIDE HIGH SCHOOL	199 CHURCHILL AV, SMCo, 94062, (650)367-9750	790 - A4
YERBA BUENA HIGH SCHOOL	1855 LUCRETIA AV, SJS, 95122, (408)279-1500	854 - G1

SCHOOLS - PUBLIC INTERMEDIATE

FEATURE NAME	Address City, ZIP Code	PAGE-GRID
BERNAL INTERMEDIATE SCHOOL	6610 SAN IGNACIO DR, SJS, 95119, (408)578-5731	875 - D7
BLACH, GEORGINA P INTERMEDIATE	1120 COVINGTON RD, LALT, 94024, (650)964-1196	831 - H2
DAVIS, CAROLINE INTERMEDIATE SCHOOL	5035 EDENVIEW DR, SJS, 95111, (408)227-8550	875 - A2
EGAN, ARDIS G INTERMEDIATE SCHOOL	100 W PORTOLA AV, LALT, 94022, (650)941-6174	811 - D4
FOOTHILL INTERMEDIATE SCHOOL	1966 FLINT AV, SJS, 95148, (408)223-3750	835 - C5
HERMAN, LEONARD INTERMEDIATE SCHOOL	5955 BLOSSOM AV, SJS, 95123, (408)226-1886	874 - H5
HYDE INTERMEDIATE SCHOOL	19325 BOLLINGER RD, CPTO, 95014, (408)252-6290	852 - G2
LEYVA, GEORGE V INTERMEDIATE SCHOOL	1865 MONROVIA DR, SJS, 95122, (408)270-4992	855 - B2
MCNAIR, RONALD INTERMEDIATE SCHOOL	2033 PULGAS AV, EPA, 94303, (650)329-2888	791 - C2
QUIMBY OAK INTERMEDIATE SCHOOL	3190 QUIMBY RD, SJS, 95148, (408)270-6735	855 - E1

SCHOOLS - PUBLIC JUNIOR HIGH

FEATURE NAME	Address City, ZIP Code	PAGE-GRID
BOEGER,AUGUST JUNIOR HIGH SCHOOL	1944 FLINT AV, SJS, 95148, (408)223-3770	835 - C5
BROWNELL ACADEMY	7800 CARMEL ST, GIL, 95020, (408)842-3135	977 - J2
CUPERTINO JUNIOR HIGH SCHOOL	1650 BERNARDO AV, SUNV, 94087, (408)245-0303	832 - B5
FAIR, J WILBUR JUNIOR HIGH SCHOOL	1702 MCLAUGHLIN AV, SJS, 95122, (408)283-6400	854 - G1
KENNEDY JUNIOR HIGH SCHOOL	821 BUBB RD, CPTO, 95014, (408)253-1525	852 - B2
MILLER JUNIOR HIGH SCHOOL	6151 RAINBOW DR, SJS, 95129, (408)252-3755	852 - G3
REDWOOD MIDDLE SCHOOL	13925 FRUITVALE AV, SAR, 95070, (408)867-3042	872 - F1
SOUTH VALLEY JUNIOR HIGH SCHOOL	385 IOOF AV, GIL, 95020, (408)847-2828	978 - A2
SYLVANDALE JUNIOR HIGH SCHOOL	653 SYLVANDALE AV, SJS, 95111, (408)363-5700	854 - J6

SCHOOLS - PUBLIC MIDDLE

FEATURE NAME	Address City, ZIP Code	PAGE-GRID
BRITTON, LEWIS H MIDDLE SCHOOL	80 CENTRAL AV, MGH, 95037, (650)779-5200	916 - J7
BUCHSER, EMIL MIDDLE SCHOOL	1111 BELLOMY ST, SCL, 95050, (408)984-2900	833 - E5
BURNETT, PETER MIDDLE SCHOOL	850 N 2ND ST, SJS, 95112, (408)535-6267	834 - A4
CABRILLO MIDDLE	2550 CABRILLO AV, SCL, 95051, (408)983-2660	833 - B3
CAMPBELL MIDDLE SCHOOL	295 W CHERRY LN, CMBL, 95008, (408)364-4222	853 - D6
CASTILLERO MIDDLE SCHOOL	6384 LEYLAND PARK DR, SJS, 95120, (408)535-6385	894 - C1
CASTRO, ELVIRA MIDDLE SCHOOL	4600 STUDENT LN, SJS, 95130, (408)379-3620	853 - A5
CHABOYA MIDDLE SCHOOL	3276 FOWLER RD, SJS, 95135, (408)270-6900	855 - G3
COLUMBIA MIDDLE SCHOOL	MORSE AV, SUNV, 94086, (408)522-8247	812 - F5
CRITTENDEN MIDDLE SCHOOL	1701 ROCK ST, MTVW, 94043, (650)903-6945	811 - H2
DARTMOUTH MIDDLE SCHOOL	5575 DARTMOUTH DR, SJS, 95118, (408)264-1122	874 - A5
ENGLISH, C T MIDDLE SCHOOL	23800 SUMMIT RD, SCIC, 95030, (408)353-1123	913 - E7
FISCHER, CLYDE L MIDDLE SCHOOL	1720 HOPKINS DR, SJS, 95122, (408)258-6244	834 - J6
FISHER, RAYMOND J MIDDLE SCHOOL	17000 ROBERTS RD, LGTS, 95032, (408)356-2141	873 - B6
GEORGE, JOSEPH MIDDLE SCHOOL	277 MAHONEY DR, SJS, 95127, (408)259-2402	835 - A1
GRAHAM, ISSAC NEWTON MIDDLE SCHOOL	1175 CASTRO ST, MTVW, 94040, (650)965-9292	811 - H6
HARTE, BRET MIDDLE SCHOOL	7050 BRET HARTE DR, SJS, 95120, (408)535-6270	894 - G2
HILLVIEW MIDDLE SCHOOL	1100 ELDER AV, MLPK, 94025, (650)326-4341	790 - E5
JANE LATHROP STANFORD MIDDLE SCHOOL	480 E MEADOW DR, PA, 94306, (650)856-1713	811 - D1
JOHN MUIR MIDDLE SCHOOL	1260 BRANHAM LN, SJS, 95118, (408)535-6281	874 - C3
JORDAN, DAVID STARR MIDDLE SCHOOL	750 N CALIFORNIA AV, PA, 94303, (650)494-8120	791 - C6
LA ENTRADA MIDDLE SCHOOL	2200 SHARON RD, MLPK, 94025, (650)854-3962	790 - D7
MARKHAM, EDWIN MIDDLE SCHOOL	2105 COTTLE AV, SJS, 95125, (408)535-6227	854 - A5
MATHSON, LEE MIDDLE SCHOOL	2050 KAMMERER AV, SJS, 95116, (408)251-3232	834 - H4
MONROE MIDDLE SCHOOL	1055 S MONROE ST, SJS, 95128, (408)364-4232	853 - E3
MORRILL MIDDLE SCHOOL	1970 MORRILL AV, SJS, 95132, (408)923-1930	814 - E3
MURPHY, MARTIN MIDDLE SCHOOL	141 AVD ESPANA, SJS, 95139, (408)779-8351	895 - F1
OCALA MIDDLE SCHOOL	2800 OCALA AV, SJS, 95148, (408)923-2800	835 - B5
PALA MIDDLE SCHOOL	149 N WHITE RD, SJS, 95127, (408)258-4996	834 - J2
PETERSON MIDDLE SCHOOL	1380 ROSALIA AV, SUNV, 94087, (408)720-8540	832 - G4
PIEDMONT MIDDLE SCHOOL	955 PIEDMONT RD, SJS, 95132, (408)923-1945	814 - G5
PRICE, IDA MIDDLE SCHOOL	2650 NEW JERSEY AV, SJS, 95124, (408)377-2532	873 - G1
RANCHO MILPITAS MIDDLE SCHOOL	1915 YELLOWSTONE AV, MPS, 95035, (408)945-5561	814 - D1
ROGERS, SAMUEL C MIDDLE SCHOOL	4835 DOYLE RD, SJS, 95129, (408)253-7262	852 - J3
ROLLING HILLS MIDDLE SCHOOL	1585 MORE AV, CMBL, 95030, (408)364-4235	872 - J1
RUSSEL, THOMAS MIDDLE SCHOOL	1500 ESCUELA PKWY, MPS, 95035, (408)945-2312	794 - B4
SHEPPARD, WILLIAM L MIDDLE SCHOOL	480 ROUGH AND READY RD, SJS, 95133, (408)258-4323	834 - H1
SIERRAMONT MIDDLE SCHOOL	3155 KIMLEE DR, SJS, 95132, (408)923-1955	814 - F4
STEINBECK MIDDLE SCHOOL	820 STEINBECK DR, SJS, 95123, (408)535-6395	874 - E4
SUNNYVALE MIDDLE SCHOOL	1080 MANGO AV, SUNV, 94087, (408)522-8288	832 - B2
UNION MIDDLE SCHOOL	2130 LOS GATOS-ALMADEN RD, SJS, 95124, (408)371-0366	873 - F5

SHOPPING CENTERS - COMMUNITY

FEATURE NAME	Address City, ZIP Code	PAGE-GRID
ABORN SQUARE	CAPITOL EXPWY & ABORN RD, SJS, 95121	855 - B3
ALMADEN OAKS PLAZA	REDMOND & MERIDIAN AV, SJS, 95120, (408)478-8757	874 - B7
ALMADEN PLAZA	ALMADEN EXWY $ BLOSSOM HILL RD, SJS, 95118	874 - C4
ALMADEN VIA VALIENTE PLAZA	ALMADEN EXPWY & VIA VALIENTE W, SJS, 95120, (408)269-8273	894 - G3
ARGONAUT PLACE SHOPPING CENTER	SARATOGA-SUNNYVALE RD & BLAUER, SAR, 95070, (408)265-8955	852 - E6
BERESFORD SQUARE	N MILPITAS BLVD & CALAVERAS BL, MPS, 95035, (408)946-1550	794 - A7
BERRYESSA CORNERS CENTER	CAPITOL AV & BERRYESSA RD, SJS, 95132	814 - F6
BLOSSOM HILL SQUARE	BLOSSOM HILL RD & HARWOOD RD, LGTS, 95032, (408)478-8757	873 - H6
BLOSSOM VALLEY CENTER	1700 MIRAMONTE AV, MTVW, 94040	831 - G1
CAMBRIAN PARK PLAZA	UNION AV & CAMDEN AV, SCIC, 95124	873 - G2
CAMDEN PARK CENTER	CAMDEN AV & UNION AV, SJS, 95124	873 - F2
CAMPBELL PLAZA	WINCHESTER BLVD & BUDD AV, CMBL, 95008	853 - D7
CARIBBEES CENTER	LEWIS RD & SENTER RD, SJS, 95111, (408)225-1180	854 - H4
CHERRY CHASE CENTER	613 CHERRY CHASE CTR, SUNV, 94087, (408)736-4158	832 - B1
CITY SQUARE	N MILIPITAS BLVD & DIXON RD, MPS, 95035	793 - J3
COCHRANE PLAZA	COCHRANE RD & HWY 101, MGH, 95037	917 - A4
COUNTRY CLUB VILLA	TOYON AV & MCKEE RD, SJS, 95127, (408)251-3730	814 - J7
CUPERTINO CROSSROADS CENTER	STEVENS CREEK BLVD & DE ANZA B, CPTO, 95014	852 - D1
CUPERTINO VILLAGE	WOLFE RD & HOMESTEAD RD, CPTO, 95014, (408)255-8157	832 - F6
DE ANZA CENTER	S DE ANZA BLVD & KENTWOOD AV, SJS, 95129, (408)688-4604	852 - D3
DE ANZA SQUARE	FREMONT AV & MARY AV, SUNV, 94087, (408)738-4444	832 - C4
DESIN SQUARE	BRANHAM LN & INDIAN AV, SJS, 95118	874 - A3
DOWNER SQUARE	BLOSSOM HILL RD & SNELL RD, SJS, 95123	874 - J4
EL CAMINO CENTER	EL CAMINO REAL & SCOTT BLVD, SCL, 95050	833 - C4
EL PASEO CENTER	CAMPBELL AV & SARATOGA AV, SJS, 95130, (408)378-0247	852 - J5
FOXWORTHY CENTER	FOXWORTHY AV & CHERRY AV, SJS, 95125	854 - B7
FREMONT CORNERS CENTER	FREMONT & SARATOGA-SUNNYVALE, SUNV, 94087	832 - E4
GOULD CENTER	CAPITOL EXWY & MCLAUGHLIN AV, SJS, 95121	855 - A4
GRANT ROAD PLAZA	1040 GRANT RD, MTVW, 94040, (650)973-7180	811 - J7
HACIENDA GARDENS CENTER	MERIDIAN AV & FOXWORTHY AV, SJS, 95124	873 - J1
HAMILTON PLAZA	HAMILTON AV & BASCOM AV, CMBL, 95008, (408)255-4106	853 - G5
HECKER PASS PLAZA	HECKER PASS HWY & WESTWOOD DR, GIL, 95020, (408)847-1553	977 - G2
HILLVIEW PLAZA	SW HILLVIEW & BLOSSOM HILL RD, SJS, 95123, (408)453-7900	874 - E4
HOMESTEAD CENTER	HOMESTEAD RD & LAWRENCE EXWY, SCL, 95051, (408)249-1590	832 - J5

FEATURE NAME Address City, ZIP Code	PAGE-GRID
HOMESTEAD SQUARE HOMESTEAD & SARATOGA-SUNNYVALE, CPTO, 95014, (408)395-5560	832 - D6
HUNTINGDON VILLAGE S DE ANZA BLVD & KENTWOOD AV, SJS, 95129, (408)287-1779	852 - E3
KINGS COURT CENTER BLOSSOM HILL RD & LOS GATOS BL, LGTS, 95032	873 - C6
KIRKWOOD PLAZA CAMPBELL AV & SAN TOMAS AQUINO, CMBL, 95008, (408)379-4547	853 - A6
LA HACIENDA CENTER EL CAMINO REAL & MARIA LN, SUNV, 94086, (408)732-7300	832 - F3
LAWRENCE SQUARE EL CAMINO REAL & LAWRENCE EXWY, SCL, 95051, (650)421-7116	832 - J3
LAWRENCE STATION CENTER LAWRENCE EXWY & HOMESTEAD RD, SCL, 95051	832 - J6
LOEHMANNS PLAZA HOLLENBECK AV & HOMESTEAD RD, SUNV, 94087, (408)737-1900	832 - D5
LOS ALTOS RANCHO CENTER FOOTHILL EXPWY & SPRINGER RD, LALT, 94024	831 - F2
MAINSTREET AT SANTA TERESA SANTA TERESA BLVD & BLOSSOM HI, SJS, 95123	874 - E4
MARIPOSA GARDENS CENTER HOMESTEAD BLVD & KIELY BLVD, SCL, 95051, (650)433-9300	833 - B6
MARKETPLACE ON STEVENS CREEK STEVENS CREEK BLVD & PORTAL AV, CPTO, 95014	852 - F1
MCCARTHY RANCH MARKETPLACE MCCARTHY BLVD & RANCH DR, MPS, 95035	793 - H7
MERVYNS EAST CENTER STORY RD & MCGINNESS AV, SJS, 95127, (408)294-0868	835 - A4
MERVYNS PLAZA EL CAMINO REAL & SCOTT BLVD, SCL, 95050, (408)985-8881	833 - C4
MONTEREY PLAZA MONTEREY HWY & FORD RD, SJS, 95138, (408)327-7113	875 - C3
MOONLITE CENTER EL CAMINO REAL & KIELY BLVD, SCL, 95051	833 - B4
MORGAN HILL PLAZA MONTEREY HWY & DUNNE AV, MGH, 95037	937 - A1
MOUNTAIN VIEW CENTER EL CAMINO REAL & GRANT RD, MTVW, 94040	811 - J7
MT PLEASANT CENTER STORY RD & WHITE RD, SJS, 95127	835 - A4
NORTHWOOD SQUARE LANDESS AV & MORRILL AV, SJS, 95132, (408)946-6791	814 - D2
OLD MILL SPECIALTY CENTER 2540 CALIFORNIA ST, MTVW, 94040, (650)941-9595	811 - F4
OLD TOWN CENTER UNIVERSITY AV & SARATOGA-LOS G, LGTS, 95030	873 - A7
ORCHARD FARMS CENTER BOLLINGER RD & MILLER AV, SJS, 95129, (408)437-3011	852 - G2
OUTLETS AT GILROY 8300 ARROYO CIR, GIL, 95020, (408)842-3732	978 - B1
PARKTOWN PLAZA S PARK VICTORIA DR & LANDESS A, MPS, 95035	814 - D2
PAVILION AT SAN JOSE S 1ST ST & E SAN FERNANDO ST, SJS, 95113, (408)286-2076	834 - C6
PAVLINA PLAZA 693 E REMINGTON DR, SUNV, 94087, (408)738-1777	832 - E2
PIEDMONT HILLS CENTER SIERRA RD & PIEDMONT RD, SJS, 95132	814 - G5
PLAZA DE SANTA TERESA SANTA TERESA BLVD & COTTLE RD, SJS, 95119	875 - B6
PLAZA DEL ROBLE CENTER 4TH ST & BIG BASIN WAY, SAR, 95070, (408)371-8155	872 - D3
PRINCETON PLAZA MALL BLOSSOM HILL RD & KOOSER RD, SJS, 95118, (408)275-0550	874 - B5
PRUNERIDGE CENTER SAN TOMAS EXPWY & SARATOGA AV, SCL, 95050	833 - C7
PUEBLO PLAZA ALMADEN EXPWY & BLOSSOM HILL R, SJS, 95118, (408)997-7011	874 - D4
QUITO VILLAGE CENTER COX AV & PASEO PRESADA, SAR, 95070, (408)378-3354	852 - H6
SAFEWAY CENTER SAN CARLOS ST & SHASTA AV, SJS, 95128, (408)241-6641	853 - H1
SANTA TERESA SQUARE SANTA TERESA BLVD & SNELL AV, SJS, 95123	874 - H6
SANTA TERESA VILLAGE BERNAL RD & SANTA TERESA BLVD, SJS, 95139, (408)287-1779	875 - E7
SARATOGA PLAZA DUCKETT WY & SARATOGA-SUNNYVAL, SJS, 95129	852 - E4
SARATOGA SQUARE SARATOGA AV & KIELY BLVD, SJS, 95129	853 - B1
SERRA CENTER 200 SERRA WY, MPS, 95035, (408)263-1800	793 - J7
SEVEN TREES CENTER SENTER RD & SEVEN TREES BLVD, SJS, 95111	854 - H7
SHARON HEIGHTS CENTER 325 SHARON PARK DR, MLPK, 94025, (650)854-5053	790 - E7
SILVER CREEK PLAZA CAPITOL EXPWY & SILVER CREEK R, SJS, 95121	855 - B3
SOUTH VALLEY PLAZA CHESTNUT ST & 10TH ST, GIL, 95020	978 - B4
STEVENS CREEK CENTRAL STEVENS CREEK BLVD & HWY 280, SJS, 95129	852 - J1
SUNRISE PLAZA BLOSSOM HILL RD & CAHALAN AV, SJS, 95123, (408)371-8770	874 - G4
TENNANT STATION 628 TENNANT AV, MGH, 95037, (408)779-8484	937 - B2
THE OAKS CENTER STEVENS CREEK BLVD & HWY 85, CPTO, 95014, (650)564-8848	832 - C7
THE PRUNEYARD BASCOM AV & CAMPBELL AV, CMBL, 95008, (408)371-0811	853 - F6
THE STANFORD BARN CENTER QUARRY RD & WELCH RD, PA, 94304	790 - G5
TOWN & COUNTRY VILLAGE EL CAMINO REAL & EMBARCADERO R, PA, 94301, (510)325-3266	790 - J5
TOWN & COUNTRY VILLAGE STEVENS CREEK BLVD & WINCHESTE, SJS, 95117	853 - D1
TOWN & COUNTRY VILLAGE W WASHINGTON AV & TAAFFE ST, SUNV, 94086, (408)736-6654	812 - D7
TOWN CENTER N MILPITAS BLVD & CALAVERAS BL, MPS, 95035	794 - B6
TROPICANA CENTER STORY RD & S KING RD, SJS, 95122	834 - G6
TULLY CORNERS TULLY RD & QUIMBY RD, SJS, 95122	855 - A1
VILLA CENTER LAWRENCE EXPY & STEVENS CREEK, SCL, 95051	852 - J1
VILLAGE COURT SAN ANTONIO & EL CAMINO REAL, LALT, 94022, (650)949-0960	811 - E4
VINEYARD TOWN CENTER MONTEREY HWY & EDMUNDSON AV, MGH, 95037	937 - B2
WEST PARK PLAZA PAYNE AV & WINCHESTER BLVD, SJS, 95117	853 - D4
WEST VALLEY COMPLEX 2980 STEVENS CREEK BLVD, SJS, 95128, (408)345-4670	853 - E1
WESTGATE WEST PROSPECT RD & LAWRENCE EXPR, SJS, 95129, (408)998-7399	852 - H5
WESTMOOR VILLAGE FREMONT AV & MARY AV, SUNV, 94087, (408)245-0553	832 - C3
WHITE ROAD PLAZA STORY RD & WHITE RD, SJS, 95127	835 - A3
WILLOW GLEN CENTER ALMADEN EXWY & CURTNER AV, SJS, 95125	854 - C5
WOLFE-REED CENTER REED AV & WOLFE RD, SUNV, 94086, (408)296-3042	832 - G2
WOODSIDE PLAZA WOODSIDE AV & KENTUCKY ST, RDWC, 94061, (650)772-7000	790 - A3

SHOPPING MALLS

FEATURE NAME Address City, ZIP Code	PAGE-GRID
CAPITOL SQUARE MALL 390 N CAPITOL AV, SJS, 95133, (408)775-0717	834 - G1
EASTRIDGE MALL 1 EASTRIDGE CENTER, SJS, 95122, (408)238-3600	855 - A1
OAKRIDGE MALL 925 BLOSSOM HILL RD, SJS, 95123, (408)578-2910	874 - E4
SAN ANTONIO CENTER 2550 W EL CAMINO REAL, MTVW, 94040, (650)941-3794	811 - E3
STANFORD CENTER 180 EL CAMINO REAL, PA, 94304, (650)617-8585	790 - G5
SUNNYVALE TOWN CENTER 2502 TOWN CENTER LN, SUNV, 94086, (408)245-3270	812 - D7
THE GREAT MALL OF THE BAY AREA 341 E CAPITOL AV, MPS, 95035, (408)945-2033	814 - A2
VALLCO FASHION PARK 10123 N WOLFE RD, CPTO, 95014, (408)255-5660	832 - F7
VALLEY FAIR 2855 STEVENS CREEK BLVD, SCL, 95050, (408)248-4450	853 - E1
WESTGATE MALL 1600 SARATOGA AV, SJS, 95129, (408)379-9350	852 - J5

TRANSPORTATION

FEATURE NAME Address City, ZIP Code	PAGE-GRID
AMTRAK SAN JOSE W SANTA CLARA ST & CAHILL ST, SJS, 95110	834 - A7
AMTRAK SANTA CLARA STATION LAFAYETTE ST & TASMAN DR, SCL, 95054	813 - C3
BLOSSOM HILL VTA RAIL STATION BLOSSOM HILL RD & HWY 85, SJS, 95123	874 - G4
BONAVENTURA VTA RAIL STATION N 1ST ST & BONAVENTURA DR, SJS, 95134	813 - G6
BRANHAM VTA RAIL STATION BRANHAM LN & HWY 87, SJS, 95136	874 - F2
CALTRAIN ATHERTON STATION FAIR OAKS LN & DINKLESPEIL STA, ATN, 94027	790 - E2
CALTRAIN BLOSSOM HILL STATION MONTEREY RD & FORD RD, SJS, 95138	875 - C4
CALTRAIN CALIFORNIA AV STATION PARK BLVD & CALIFORNIA AV, PA, 94306	791 - B7
CALTRAIN CAPITOL STATION MONTEREY HWY & FEHREN DR, SJS, 95136	854 - G6
CALTRAIN CASTRO STATION W EVELYN AV & VIEW ST, MTVW, 94041	811 - J5
CALTRAIN COLLEGE PARK STATION STOCKTON AV & EMORY ST, SJS, 95110	833 - H5
CALTRAIN GILROY STATION MONTEREY ST & OLD GILROY ST, GIL, 95020	978 - A3
CALTRAIN LAWRENCE STATION LAWRENCE STA RD & LAWRENCE EXW, SUNV, 94086	832 - J1
CALTRAIN MENLO PARK STATION STA CRUZ AV & MERRILL ST, MLPK, 94025	790 - F3
CALTRAIN MORGAN HILL STATION E MAIN AV & BUTTERFIELD BLVD, MGH, 95037	917 - A7
CALTRAIN MOUNTAIN VIEW STATION S RENGSTORFF & CRISANTO AV, MTVW, 94040	811 - G4
CALTRAIN PALO ALTO STATION UNIVERSITY AV & MITCHELL LN, PA, 94301	790 - H5
CALTRAIN SAN JOSE STATION W SANTA CLARA ST & CAHILL ST, SJS, 95110	834 - A7
CALTRAIN SAN MARTIN STATION MONTEREY HWY & SAN MARTIN AV, SCIC, 95046	937 - E6
CALTRAIN SANTA CLARA STATION RAILROAD AV & FRANKLIN ST, SCL, 95050	833 - F4
CALTRAIN SUNNYVALE STATION EVELYN AV & FRANCES AV, SUNV, 94086	812 - E7
CALTRAIN TAMIEN STATION W ALMA AV & LICK AV, SJS, 95110	854 - C2
CAPITOL VTA RAIL STATION CAPITOL EXWY & HWY 87, SJS, 95136	874 - E1
CHAMPION VTA RAIL STATION TASMAN DR & CHAMPION CT, SJS, 95134	813 - E3
CIVIC CENTER VTA RAIL STATION N 1ST ST & E MISSION ST, SJS, 95112	834 - A4
COMPONENT VTA RAIL STATION N 1ST ST & COMPONENT DR, SJS, 95131	813 - G7
CONVENTION CENTER VTA RAIL STATION W SAN CARLOS ST & MARKET ST, SJS, 95110	834 - B7
COTTLE VTA RAIL STATION COTTLE RD & HWY 85, SJS, 95119	875 - C5
CURTNER VTA RAIL STATION GUADALUPE FRWY & CURTNER AV, SJS, 95125	854 - D5
GISH VTA RAIL STATION N 1ST ST & GISH RD, SJS, 95112	833 - J2
GREAT AMERICA VTA RAIL STATION TASMAN DR & GREAT AMERICA PKWY, SCL, 95054	813 - B4
GREYHOUND BUS STATION 145 S SANTA CRUZ AV, LGTS, 95030, (408)354-0766	873 - A7
GREYHOUND BUS STATION 70 ALMADEN AV, SJS, 95113, (408)295-4151	834 - B6
GREYHOUND BUS STATION 7610 MONTEREY ST, GIL, 95020, (408)847-7610	978 - A3
GREYHOUND BUS STATION CENTRAL EXPWY & MAYFIELD AV, MTVW, 94043	811 - F3
JAPANTOWN/AYER VTA RAIL STATION N 1ST ST & AYER AV, SJS, 95112	834 - A5
KARINA VTA RAIL STATION N 1ST ST & KARINA CT, SJS, 95131	833 - H1
LICK MILL VTA RAIL STATION TASMAN DR & LICK MILL BLVD, SCL, 95054	813 - C3
METRO/AIRPORT VTA RAIL STATION N 1ST ST & METRO DR, SJS, 95112	833 - H1
OAKRIDGE VTA RAIL STATION WINFIELD BLVD & BLOSSOM RIVER, SJS, 95123	874 - E4
OHLONE-CHYNOWETH VTA RAIL STATION PEARL AV & CHYNOWETH AV, SJS, 95136	874 - E3
OLD IRONSIDES VTA RAIL STATION TASMAN DR & OLD IRONSIDES DR, SCL, 95054	813 - B4
ORCHARD VTA RAIL STATION N 1ST ST & ORCHARD PKWY, SJS, 95134	813 - G5
PAS D ANTONIO VTA RAIL STATION N 1ST ST & PASEO DE SAN ANTONI, SJS, 95113	834 - B7
PAS D ANTONIO VTA RAIL STATION N 2ND ST & PASEO DE SAN ANTONI, SJS, 95113	834 - C6
RIVER OAKS VTA RAIL STATION N 1ST ST & RIVER OAKS PKWY, SJS, 95134	813 - F4
SAINT JAMES VTA RAIL STATION N 1ST ST & E SAINT JAMES ST, SJS, 95112	834 - B6
SAINT JAMES VTA RAIL STATION N 2ND ST & E SAINT JOHN ST, SJS, 95112	834 - B6
SAMTRANS TRANSIT TRANSFER POINT STANFORD SHOPPING CENTER, PA, 94304	790 - H5
SANTA CLARA VTA RAIL STATION N 1ST ST & E SANTA CLARA ST, SJS, 95113	834 - B6
SANTA CLARA VTA RAIL STATION S 2ND ST & E SANTA CLARA ST, SJS, 95113	834 - B6
SANTA TERESA VTA RAIL STATION SANTA TERESA BLVD, SJS, 95119	875 - D6
SNELL VTA RAIL STATION SNELL AV & HWY 85, SJS, 95123	874 - J4
TAMIEN VTA RAIL STATION GUADALUPE FRWY & W ALMA AV, SJS, 95110	854 - C2
TASMAN VTA RAIL STATION TASMAN DR & N 1ST ST, SJS, 95134	813 - E3
TECHNOLOGY CENTER VTA RAIL STATION WOOZ WY & W SAN CARLOS ST, SJS, 95110	834 - B7
VIRGINIA VTA LIGHT RAIL STATION W VIRGINIA ST & GUADALUPE FRWY, SJS, 95125	854 - B1
WINFIELD VTA RAIL STATION WINFIELD BLVD & COLEMAN RD, SJS, 95123	874 - D5

WINERIES

FEATURE NAME Address City, ZIP Code	PAGE-GRID
ALMADEN WINERY CHAMBERTIN RD & TOURAINE DR, SJS, 95118	874 - B6
BYINGTON WINERY & VINEYARD 21850 BEAR CREEK RD, SCrC, 95030, (408)354-1111	912 - B1
CASA DE FRUTA WINERY (SEE PAGE 959) 6680 PACHECO PASS HWY, SCIC, 95020, (408)637-0051	980 - D6
CONROTTO WINERY 1690 HECKER PASS HWY, SCIC, 95020, (408)842-3053	977 - F2
DAVID BRUCE WINERY 21435 BEAR CREEK RD, SCrC, 95030, (408)354-4214	912 - B1
EMILIO GUGLIELMO WINERY 1480 E MAIN AV, SCIC, 95037, (408)779-2145	917 - C5
FORTINO WINERY 4525 HECKER PASS HWY, SCIC, 95020, (408)842-3305	977 - A2
HECKER PASS WINERY (SEE PAGE 955) 4605 HECKER PASS HWY, SCIC, 95020, (408)842-8755	976 - J2
KIRIGIN CELLARS 11550 WATSONVILLE RD, SCIC, 95020, (408)847-8827	957 - A4
LIVE OAKS WINERY 3875 HECKER PASS HWY, SCIC, 95020, (408)842-2401	977 - B2
LOHR, J WINERY 1000 LENZEN AV, SJS, 95126, (408)288-5057	833 - J6
MARIANI VINEYARDS 23600 CONGRESS SPRINGS RD, SCIC, 95070, (408)741-2930	871 - H4
MIRASSOU CHAMPAGNE CELLARS 300 COLLEGE AV, LGTS, 95032, (408)395-3790	893 - A2
MIRASSOU VINEYARDS 3000 ABORN RD, SJS, 95135, (408)274-4000	855 - F2
PAUL MASSON WINERY PACHECO PASS HWY, SCIC, 95020	978 - G3
PEDRIZZETTI WINERY 1645 SAN PEDRO AV, SCIC, 95037, (408)779-7389	917 - D7
RAPAZZINI WINERY (SEE PAGE 997) 4350 S MONTEREY HWY, SCIC, 95020, (408)842-5649	998 - B6
SAN MARTIN VINEYARDS 13000 DEPOT ST, SCIC, 95046, (408)683-2671	937 - F7
SOLIS WINERY 3920 HECKER PASS HWY, SCIC, 95020, (408)847-6306	977 - A2
THOMAS KRUSE WINERY 4390 HECKER PASS HWY, SCIC, 95020, (408)842-7016	977 - A2

1998 SANTA CLARA OLD TO NEW Page Conversion List

OLD-NEW	
Old 37	
4	790 - B1
5	790 - B2
6	790 - B3
4	790 - C1
5	790 - C2
6	790 - C3
4	790 - E1
5	790 - E2
6	790 - E3
4	790 - F1
5	790 - F2
6	790 - F3
4	790 - G1
5	790 - G2
6	790 - G3
4	790 - H1
5	790 - H2
6	790 - H3
Old 38	
4	790 - J1
5	790 - J2
6	790 - J3
4	791 - B1
5	791 - B2
6	791 - B4
4	791 - C1
5	791 - C2
6	791 - C4
4	791 - D1
5	791 - D3
6	791 - D4
4	791 - E1
5	791 - E3
6	791 - E4
4	791 - G1
5	791 - G3
6	791 - G4
Old 38A	
1	792 - F1
2	792 - F3
3	792 - F4
4	791 - H1
5	791 - H3
6	791 - H4
1	792 - G2
2	792 - G3
3	792 - G4
4	791 - J1
5	791 - J3
6	791 - J4
1	792 - H2
2	792 - H3
3	792 - H4
4	792 - A1
5	792 - A3
6	792 - A4
1	793 - A2
2	793 - A3
3	792 - J4
4	792 - B1
5	792 - B3
6	792 - B4
1	793 - B2
2	793 - B3
3	793 - B4
4	792 - D1
5	792 - D3
6	792 - D4
1	793 - C2
2	793 - C3
3	793 - C4
4	792 - E1
5	792 - E3
6	792 - E4
Old 39	
4	793 - D2
5	793 - D3
6	793 - D4
4	793 - E2
5	793 - E3
6	793 - E4
4	793 - G2
5	793 - G3
6	793 - G4
4	793 - H2
5	793 - H3
6	793 - H4
3	793 - J1
4	793 - J2
5	793 - J3
6	793 - J4
3	794 - A1
4	794 - A2
5	794 - A3
6	794 - A4
Old 40	
3	794 - B1
4	794 - B2
5	794 - B3
6	794 - B4
3	794 - D1
4	794 - C2
5	794 - C3
6	794 - C4
3	794 - E1
4	794 - E2
5	794 - E3

OLD-NEW	
Old 40	
C6	794 - E4
D3	794 - F1
D4	794 - F2
D5	794 - F3
D6	794 - F4
E3	794 - G1
E4	794 - G2
E5	794 - G3
E6	794 - G4
F3	794 - H1
F4	794 - H2
F5	794 - H3
F6	794 - H4
Old 41	
A3	795 - A1
A4	795 - A2
A5	794 - J3
A6	794 - J4
B3	795 - B1
B4	795 - B2
B5	795 - B3
B6	795 - B4
C3	795 - C1
C4	795 - C2
C5	795 - C3
C6	795 - C4
D3	795 - D1
D4	795 - D2
D5	795 - D3
D6	795 - D4
E3	795 - F1
E4	795 - F2
E5	795 - F3
E6	795 - F4
F3	795 - G1
F4	795 - G2
F5	795 - G3
F6	795 - G5
Old 42	
A3	795 - H1
A4	795 - H2
A5	795 - H3
A6	795 - H5
B3	795 - J1
B4	795 - J2
B5	795 - J3
B6	795 - J5
C3	796 - A1
C4	796 - A2
C5	796 - A3
C6	796 - A5
D3	796 - B1
D4	796 - B2
D5	796 - C4
D6	796 - C5
E3	796 - D1
E4	796 - D2
E5	796 - D4
E6	796 - D5
F3	796 - E1
F4	796 - E2
F5	796 - E4
F6	796 - E5
Old 42A	
A2	796 - F2
A3	796 - F4
A4	796 - F6
A5	816 - F2
A6	816 - F4
B2	796 - G2
B3	796 - G4
B4	796 - G7
B5	816 - G2
B6	816 - G4
C2	796 - H2
C3	796 - H4
C4	796 - H7
C5	816 - H2
C6	816 - H4
D2	797 - A2
D3	796 - J4
D4	796 - J7
D5	816 - J2
D6	816 - J4
E2	797 - B2
E3	797 - B4
E4	797 - B6
E5	817 - B2
E6	817 - B4
F2	797 - C2
F3	797 - C4
F4	797 - C6
F5	817 - C2
F6	817 - C4
Old 42B	
A2	797 - D2
A3	797 - D4
A4	797 - D7
A5	817 - D2
A6	817 - D4
B2	797 - F2
B3	797 - E4
B4	797 - E7
B5	817 - E2
B6	817 - E4
C2	797 - G2
C3	797 - G4

OLD-NEW	
Old 42B	
C4	797 - G6
C5	817 - G2
C6	817 - G4
D2	797 - H2
D3	797 - H4
D4	797 - H6
D5	817 - H2
D6	817 - H4
E2	797 - J2
E3	797 - J4
E4	797 - J7
E5	817 - J2
E6	817 - J4
F2	798 - A2
F3	798 - A4
F4	798 - A7
F5	818 - A2
F6	818 - A4
Old 42C	
A2	798 - C2
A3	798 - B5
A4	798 - B7
A5	818 - B2
A6	818 - B4
B2	798 - D2
B3	798 - D4
B4	798 - D7
B5	818 - D2
B6	818 - C4
C2	798 - E2
C3	798 - E4
C4	798 - E7
C5	818 - E2
C6	818 - E4
D2	798 - F2
D3	798 - F4
D4	798 - F7
D5	818 - F2
D6	818 - F4
E2	798 - G2
E3	798 - G5
E4	798 - G7
E5	818 - G2
E6	818 - G4
F2	798 - H2
F3	798 - H5
F4	798 - H7
F5	818 - H2
F6	818 - H4
Old 42D	
A2	799 - A2
A3	799 - A4
A4	799 - A7
A5	819 - A2
A6	819 - A4
B2	799 - B2
B3	799 - B4
B4	799 - B7
B5	819 - B2
B6	819 - B4
C2	799 - C2
C3	799 - C5
C4	799 - C7
C5	819 - C2
C6	819 - C4
D2	799 - D2
D3	799 - D5
D4	799 - D7
D5	819 - D2
D6	819 - D4
E1	819 - H6
E2	839 - G2
E3	839 - G4
E4	839 - G6
E5	859 - G1
E6	859 - G4
F1	819 - J6
F2	839 - J1
F3	839 - H4
F4	839 - H6
F5	859 - H2
F6	859 - H4
Old 43	
A1	790 - B4
A2	790 - B5
A3	790 - B7
A4	810 - B1
A5	810 - B2
A6	810 - B3
B1	790 - C4
B2	790 - C5
B3	790 - C7
B4	810 - C1
B5	810 - C2
B6	810 - C3
C1	790 - E4
C2	790 - E5
C3	790 - E7
C4	810 - E1
C5	810 - E2
C6	810 - E3
D1	790 - F4
D2	790 - F5
D3	790 - F7
D4	810 - F1
D5	810 - F2
D6	810 - F3

OLD-NEW	
Old 43	
E1	790 - G4
E2	790 - G5
E3	790 - G7
E4	810 - G1
E5	810 - G2
E6	810 - G3
F1	790 - H4
F2	790 - H5
F3	790 - H7
F4	810 - H1
F5	810 - H2
F6	810 - H3
Old 44	
A1	790 - J4
A2	790 - J5
A3	790 - J7
A4	810 - J1
A5	810 - J2
A6	810 - J3
B1	791 - B4
B2	791 - B6
B3	791 - B7
B4	811 - B1
B5	811 - B2
B6	811 - A3
C1	791 - C5
C2	791 - C6
C3	791 - C7
C4	811 - C1
C5	811 - C2
C6	811 - C3
D1	791 - D5
D2	791 - D6
D3	791 - D7
D4	811 - D1
D5	811 - D2
D6	811 - D3
E1	791 - E5
E2	791 - E6
E3	791 - E7
E4	811 - E1
E5	811 - E2
E6	811 - E3
F1	791 - G5
F2	791 - F6
F3	791 - F7
F4	811 - F1
F5	811 - F2
F6	811 - F3
Old 45	
A1	791 - H5
A2	791 - H6
A3	791 - H7
A4	811 - H1
A5	811 - G2
A6	811 - G3
B1	791 - J5
B2	791 - J6
B3	791 - J7
B4	811 - J1
B5	811 - J2
B6	811 - J3
C1	792 - A5
C2	792 - A6
C3	792 - A7
C4	812 - A1
C5	812 - A2
C6	812 - A3
D1	792 - B5
D2	792 - B6
D3	792 - B7
D4	812 - B1
D5	812 - B2
D6	812 - B3
E1	792 - D5
E2	792 - D6
E3	792 - D7
E4	812 - D1
E5	812 - D2
E6	812 - D3
F1	792 - E5
F2	792 - E6
F3	792 - E7
F4	812 - E1
F5	812 - E2
F6	812 - E3
Old 46	
A1	792 - F5
A2	792 - F6
A3	792 - F7
A4	812 - F1
A5	812 - F2
A6	812 - F3
B1	792 - G5
B2	792 - G6
B3	792 - G7
B4	812 - G1
B5	812 - G2
B6	812 - G3
C1	792 - H5
C2	792 - H6
C3	792 - H7
C4	812 - H1
C5	812 - H2
C6	812 - H3
D1	792 - J5
D2	792 - J6

OLD-NEW	
Old 46	
D3	792 - J7
D4	812 - J1
D5	812 - J2
D6	812 - J3
E1	793 - B5
E2	793 - B6
E3	793 - B7
E4	813 - B1
E5	813 - B2
E6	813 - B3
F1	793 - C5
F2	793 - C6
F3	793 - C7
F4	813 - C1
F5	813 - C2
F6	813 - C3
Old 47	
A1	793 - D5
A2	793 - D6
A3	793 - D7
A4	813 - D1
A5	813 - D2
A6	813 - D3
B1	793 - E5
B2	793 - E6
B3	793 - E7
B4	813 - E1
B5	813 - E2
B6	813 - E4
C1	793 - F5
C2	793 - F6
C3	793 - F7
C4	813 - F1
C5	813 - F2
C6	813 - F4
D1	793 - H5
D2	793 - H6
D3	793 - H7
D4	813 - H1
D5	813 - H3
D6	813 - H4
E1	793 - J5
E2	793 - J6
E3	793 - J7
E4	813 - J1
E5	813 - J3
E6	813 - J4
F1	794 - A5
F2	794 - A6
F3	794 - A7
F4	814 - A1
F5	814 - A3
F6	814 - A4
Old 48	
A1	794 - B5
A2	794 - B6
A3	794 - B7
A4	814 - B1
A5	814 - B3
A6	814 - B4
B1	794 - C5
B2	794 - C6
B3	794 - C7
B4	814 - C2
B5	814 - C3
B6	814 - C4
C1	794 - E5
C2	794 - E6
C3	794 - E7
C4	814 - E2
C5	814 - E3
C6	814 - E4
D1	794 - F5
D2	794 - F6
D3	794 - F7
D4	814 - F2
D5	814 - F3
D6	814 - F4
E1	794 - G5
E2	794 - G6
E3	814 - G1
E4	814 - G2
E5	814 - G3
E6	814 - G4
F1	794 - H5
F2	794 - H6
F3	814 - H1
F4	814 - H2
F5	814 - H3
F6	814 - H4
Old 49	
A1	794 - J5
A2	794 - J6
A3	814 - J1
A4	814 - J2
A5	814 - J3
A6	814 - J4
B1	795 - B5
B2	795 - B6
B3	815 - B1
B4	815 - B2
B5	815 - B3
B6	815 - B4
C1	795 - C5
C2	795 - C6
C3	815 - C1
C4	815 - C2

OLD-NEW	
Old 49	
C5	815 - C3
C6	815 - C4
D1	795 - D5
D2	795 - D6
D3	815 - D1
D4	815 - D2
D5	815 - D3
D6	815 - D4
E1	795 - F5
E2	795 - F6
E3	815 - E1
E4	815 - E2
E5	815 - E3
E6	815 - E4
F1	795 - G5
F2	795 - G6
F3	815 - G1
F4	815 - G2
F5	815 - G3
F6	815 - G4
Old 49A	
A1	795 - H5
A2	795 - H7
A3	815 - H1
A4	815 - H2
A5	815 - H3
A6	815 - H4
B1	795 - J5
B2	795 - J7
B3	815 - J1
B4	815 - J2
B5	815 - J3
B6	815 - J4
C1	796 - A6
C2	796 - A7
C3	816 - A1
C4	816 - A2
C5	816 - A3
C6	816 - A4
D1	796 - C6
D2	796 - C7
D3	816 - B1
D4	816 - B2
D5	816 - B3
D6	816 - B4
E1	796 - D6
E2	796 - D7
E3	816 - D1
E4	816 - D2
E5	816 - D3
E6	816 - D4
F1	796 - E6
F2	796 - E7
F3	816 - E1
F4	816 - E2
F5	816 - E3
F6	816 - E4
Old 50	
A1	810 - B4
A2	810 - B5
A3	810 - B6
A4	810 - B7
A5	830 - B1
A6	830 - B3
B1	810 - C4
B2	810 - C5
B3	810 - C6
B4	810 - C7
B5	830 - C1
B6	830 - C3
C1	810 - D4
C2	810 - D5
C3	810 - D6
C4	810 - D7
C5	830 - D2
C6	830 - D3
D1	810 - F4
D2	810 - F5
D3	810 - F6
D4	810 - F7
D5	830 - F2
D6	830 - F3
E1	810 - G4
E2	810 - G5
E3	810 - G6
E4	810 - G7
E5	830 - G2
E6	830 - G3
F1	810 - H4
F2	810 - H5
F3	810 - H6
F4	810 - H7
F5	830 - H2
F6	830 - H3
Old 51	
A1	810 - J4
A2	810 - J5
A3	810 - J6
A4	810 - J7
A5	830 - J2
A6	830 - J3
B1	811 - A4
B2	811 - A5
B3	811 - A6
B4	811 - A7
B5	831 - A2
B6	831 - A3

OLD-NEW	
Old 51	
C1	811 - C4
C2	811 - C5
C3	811 - C6
C4	831 - C1
C5	831 - C2
C6	831 - C3
D1	811 - D4
D2	811 - D5
D3	811 - D6
D4	831 - D1
D5	831 - D2
D6	831 - D3
E1	811 - E4
E2	811 - E5
E3	811 - E6
E4	831 - E1
E5	831 - E2
E6	831 - E3
F1	811 - F4
F2	811 - F5
F3	811 - F6
F4	831 - F1
F5	831 - F2
F6	831 - F3
Old 52	
A1	811 - G4
A2	811 - G5
A3	811 - G6
A4	831 - G1
A5	831 - G2
A6	831 - G3
B1	811 - J4
B2	811 - J5
B3	811 - J6
B4	831 - J1
B5	831 - J2
B6	831 - J3
C1	812 - A4
C2	812 - A5
C3	812 - A6
C4	832 - A1
C5	832 - A2
C6	832 - A3
D1	812 - B4
D2	812 - B5
D3	812 - B7
D4	832 - B1
D5	832 - B2
D6	832 - B3
E1	812 - D4
E2	812 - D5
E3	812 - C7
E4	832 - C1
E5	832 - C2
E6	832 - C3
F1	812 - E4
F2	812 - E5
F3	812 - E7
F4	832 - E1
F5	832 - E2
F6	832 - E3
Old 53	
A1	812 - F4
A2	812 - F6
A3	812 - F7
A4	832 - F1
A5	832 - F2
A6	832 - F3
B1	812 - G4
B2	812 - G5
B3	812 - G7
B4	832 - G1
B5	832 - G2
B6	832 - G3
C1	812 - H4
C2	812 - H5
C3	812 - H7
C4	832 - H1
C5	832 - H2
C6	832 - H3
D1	812 - J4
D2	812 - J5
D3	812 - J7
D4	832 - J1
D5	832 - J2
D6	832 - J3
E1	813 - B4
E2	813 - B5
E3	813 - B7
E4	833 - B1
E5	833 - B2
E6	833 - B3
F1	813 - C4
F2	813 - C5
F3	813 - C7
F4	833 - C1
F5	833 - C2
F6	833 - C3
Old 54	
A1	813 - D4
A2	813 - D5
A3	813 - D7
A4	833 - D1
A5	833 - D2
A6	833 - D3
B1	813 - E4
B2	813 - E5

OLD-NEW	
Old 54	
B3	813 - E7
B4	833 - E1
B5	833 - E2
B6	833 - E3
C1	813 - F5
C2	813 - F6
C3	813 - F7
C4	833 - F1
C5	833 - F2
C6	833 - F3
D1	813 - H5
D2	813 - H6
D3	813 - H7
D4	833 - H1
D5	833 - H2
D6	833 - H3
E1	813 - J5
E2	813 - J6
E3	813 - J7
E4	833 - J1
E5	833 - J2
E6	833 - J3
F1	814 - A5
F2	814 - A6
F3	814 - A7
F4	834 - A1
F5	834 - A2
F6	834 - A3
Old 55	
A1	814 - B5
A2	814 - B6
A3	814 - B7
A4	834 - B1
A5	834 - B2
A6	834 - B3
B1	814 - C5
B2	814 - C6
B3	814 - C7
B4	834 - C1
B5	834 - C2
B6	834 - C3
C1	814 - E5
C2	814 - E6
C3	814 - E7
C4	834 - E1
C5	834 - E2
C6	834 - E3
D1	814 - F5
D2	814 - F6
D3	814 - F7
D4	834 - F1
D5	834 - F2
D6	834 - F3
E1	814 - G5
E2	814 - G6
E3	814 - G7
E4	834 - G1
E5	834 - G2
E6	834 - G3
F1	814 - H5
F2	814 - H6
F3	814 - H7
F4	834 - H1
F5	834 - H2
F6	834 - H3
Old 56	
A1	814 - J5
A2	814 - J6
A3	814 - J7
A4	834 - J1
A5	834 - J2
A6	834 - J3
B1	815 - B5
B2	815 - B6
B3	815 - B7
B4	835 - B1
B5	835 - B2
B6	835 - B4
C1	815 - C5
C2	815 - C6
C3	815 - C7
C4	835 - C1
C5	835 - C2
C6	835 - C4
D1	815 - D5
D2	815 - D6
D3	815 - D7
D4	835 - D1
D5	835 - D2
D6	835 - D4
E1	815 - E5
E2	815 - E6
E3	815 - E7
E4	835 - E1
E5	835 - E3
E6	835 - E4
F1	815 - G5
F2	815 - G6
F3	815 - G7
F4	835 - G1
F5	835 - G3
F6	835 - F4
Old 56A	
A1	815 - H5
A2	815 - H6
A3	815 - H7
A4	835 - H1

OLD-NEW	
Old 56A	
A5	835 - H3
A6	835 - H4
B1	815 - J5
B2	815 - J6
B3	815 - J7
B4	835 - J1
B5	835 - J3
B6	835 - J4
C1	816 - A5
C2	816 - A6
C3	816 - A7
C4	836 - A1
C5	836 - A3
C6	836 - A4
D1	816 - B5
D2	816 - B6
D3	816 - B7
D4	836 - B2
D5	836 - B3
D6	836 - B4
E1	816 - D5
E2	816 - D6
E3	816 - D7
E4	836 - D2
E5	836 - D3
E6	836 - C4
F1	816 - E5
F2	816 - E6
F3	816 - E7
F4	836 - E2
F5	836 - E3
F6	836 - E4
Old 56B	
A1	816 - F6
A2	836 - F1
A3	836 - F3
A4	836 - F5
A5	856 - F1
A6	856 - F3
B1	816 - G6
B2	836 - G1
B3	836 - G3
B4	836 - G5
B5	856 - G1
B6	856 - G3
C1	816 - H6
C2	836 - H1
C3	836 - H3
C4	836 - H5
C5	856 - H1
C6	856 - H3
D1	816 - J6
D2	836 - J1
D3	836 - J3
D4	836 - J6
D5	856 - J1
D6	856 - J3
E1	817 - B6
E2	837 - B1
E3	837 - A3
E4	837 - A6
E5	857 - A1
E6	857 - A3
F1	817 - C6
F2	837 - C1
F3	837 - C3
F4	837 - C5
F5	857 - C1
F6	857 - C3
Old 56C	
A1	817 - D6
A2	837 - D1
A3	837 - D3
A4	837 - D5
A5	857 - D1
A6	857 - D3
B1	817 - E6
B2	837 - E1
B3	837 - E3
B4	837 - E5
B5	857 - E1
B6	857 - E3
C1	817 - F6
C2	837 - F1
C3	837 - F4
C4	837 - F6
C5	857 - F1
C6	857 - F3
D1	817 - H6
D2	837 - H1
D3	837 - H3
D4	837 - H5
D5	857 - H1
D6	857 - G3
E1	817 - J6
E2	837 - J1
E3	837 - J3
E4	837 - J6
E5	857 - J1
E6	857 - J3
F1	818 - A6
F2	838 - A1
F3	838 - A3
F4	838 - A6
F5	858 - A1
F6	858 - A3
Old 56D	

OLD-NEW	
Old 56D	
A1	818 - B6
A2	838 - B1
A3	838 - B4
A4	838 - B6
A5	858 - B1
A6	858 - B3
B1	818 - C6
B2	838 - C1
B3	838 - C4
B4	838 - C6
B5	858 - C1
B6	858 - C3
C1	818 - E6
C2	838 - E1
C3	838 - D4
C4	838 - D6
C5	858 - D1
C6	858 - D3
D1	818 - F6
D2	838 - F1
D3	838 - F3
D4	838 - F6
D5	858 - F1
D6	858 - F3
E1	818 - G6
E2	838 - G1
E3	838 - G4
E4	838 - G6
E5	858 - G1
E6	858 - G3
F1	818 - H6
F2	838 - H2
F3	838 - H4
F4	838 - H6
F5	858 - H1
F6	858 - H3
Old 56E	
A1	819 - A6
A2	839 - A1
A3	838 - J4
A4	838 - J6
A5	858 - J1
A6	858 - J4
B1	819 - B6
B2	839 - B1
B3	839 - B4
B4	839 - B6
B5	859 - B1
B6	859 - B3
C1	819 - C6
C2	839 - C1
C3	839 - C4
C4	839 - C6
C5	859 - C1
C6	859 - C3
D1	819 - D6
D2	839 - D1
D3	839 - D4
D4	839 - D6
D5	859 - D1
D6	859 - D3
E1	819 - E6
E2	839 - E2
E3	839 - E4
E4	839 - E6
E5	859 - E1
E6	859 - E4
F1	819 - F6
F2	839 - F2
F3	839 - F4
F4	839 - F6
F5	859 - F1
F6	859 - F4
Old 57	
A1	830 - B3
A2	830 - B5
A3	830 - B6
A4	830 - B7
A5	850 - B1
A6	850 - A2
B1	830 - C4
B2	830 - C5
B3	830 - C6
B4	830 - C7
B5	850 - C1
B6	850 - C2
C1	830 - D4
C2	830 - D5
C3	830 - D6
C4	830 - D7
C5	850 - D1
C6	850 - D2
D1	830 - F4
D2	830 - F5
D3	830 - E6
D4	830 - E7
D5	850 - E1
D6	850 - E2
E1	830 - G4
E2	830 - G5
E3	830 - G6
E4	830 - G7
E5	850 - G1
E6	850 - G2
F1	830 - H4
F2	830 - H5
F3	830 - H6

OLD-NEW	
Old 57	
F4	830 - H7
F5	850 - H1
F6	850 - H2
Old 58	
A1	830 - J4
A2	830 - J5
A3	830 - J6
A4	830 - J7
A5	850 - J1
A6	850 - J2
B1	831 - A4
B2	831 - A5
B3	831 - A6
B4	831 - A7
B5	851 - A1
B6	851 - A2
C1	831 - B4
C2	831 - B5
C3	831 - B6
C4	831 - B7
C5	851 - B1
C6	851 - B2
D1	831 - D4
D2	831 - D5
D3	831 - D6
D4	831 - D7
D5	851 - D1
D6	851 - D2
E1	831 - E4
E2	831 - E5
E3	831 - E6
E4	831 - E7
E5	851 - E1
E6	851 - E2
F1	831 - F4
F2	831 - F5
F3	831 - F6
F4	831 - F7
F5	851 - F1
F6	851 - F2
Old 59	
A1	831 - G4
A2	831 - G5
A3	831 - G6
A4	831 - G7
A5	851 - G1
A6	851 - G3
B1	831 - J4
B2	831 - H5
B3	831 - H6
B4	831 - H7
B5	851 - H1
B6	851 - H3
C1	832 - A4
C2	832 - A5
C3	832 - A6
C4	832 - A7
C5	852 - A1
C6	852 - A3
D1	832 - B4
D2	832 - B5
D3	832 - B6
D4	832 - B7
D5	852 - B2
D6	852 - B3
E1	832 - C4
E2	832 - C5
E3	832 - C6
E4	832 - C7
E5	852 - C2
E6	852 - C3
F1	832 - D4
F2	832 - D5
F3	832 - D6
F4	832 - D7
F5	852 - D2
F6	852 - D3
Old 60	
A1	832 - F4
A2	832 - F5
A3	832 - E6
A4	832 - E7
A5	852 - E2
A6	852 - E3
B1	832 - G4
B2	832 - G5
B3	832 - G6
B4	832 - G7
B5	852 - G2
B6	852 - G3
C1	832 - H4
C2	832 - H5
C3	832 - H6
C4	832 - H7
C5	852 - H2
C6	852 - H3
D1	832 - J4
D2	832 - J5
D3	832 - J6
D4	832 - J7
D5	852 - J2
D6	852 - J3
E1	833 - B4
E2	833 - B5
E3	833 - B6
E4	853 - A1
E5	853 - A2

OLD-NEW	
Old 60	
E6	853 - A3
F1	833 - C4
F2	833 - C5
F3	833 - C6
F4	853 - C1
F5	853 - C2
F6	853 - C3
Old 61	
A1	833 - D4
A2	833 - D5
A3	833 - D6
A4	853 - D1
A5	853 - D2
A6	853 - D3
B1	833 - E4
B2	833 - E5
B3	833 - E6
B4	853 - E1
B5	853 - E2
B6	853 - E3
C1	833 - F4
C2	833 - F5
C3	833 - F6
C4	853 - F1
C5	853 - F2
C6	853 - F3
D1	833 - H4
D2	833 - H5
D3	833 - H6
D4	853 - G1
D5	853 - G2
D6	853 - G3
E1	833 - J4
E2	833 - J5
E3	833 - J6
E4	853 - J1
E5	853 - J2
E6	853 - J3
F1	834 - A4
F2	834 - A5
F3	834 - A7
F4	854 - A1
F5	854 - A2
F6	854 - A3
Old 62	
A1	834 - B4
A2	834 - B5
A3	834 - B7
A4	854 - B1
A5	854 - B2
A6	854 - B3
B1	834 - C4
B2	834 - C5
B3	834 - C7
B4	854 - C1
B5	854 - C2
B6	854 - C3
C1	834 - D4
C2	834 - D5
C3	834 - D7
C4	854 - D1
C5	854 - D2
C6	854 - D3
D1	834 - F4
D2	834 - F5
D3	834 - F7
D4	854 - F1
D5	854 - F2
D6	854 - F3
E1	834 - G4
E2	834 - G5
E3	834 - G7
E4	854 - G1
E5	854 - G2
E6	854 - G3
F1	834 - H4
F2	834 - H6
F3	834 - H7
F4	854 - H1
F5	854 - H2
F6	854 - H3
Old 63	
A1	834 - J4
A2	834 - J6
A3	834 - J7
A4	854 - J1
A5	854 - J2
A6	854 - J3
B1	835 - A4
B2	835 - A6
B3	835 - A7
B4	855 - A1
B5	855 - A2
B6	855 - A3
C1	835 - C5
C2	835 - C6
C3	835 - C7
C4	855 - C1
C5	855 - C2
C6	855 - C3
D1	835 - D5
D2	835 - D6
D3	835 - D7
D4	855 - D1
D5	855 - D2
D6	855 - D3
E1	835 - E5

OLD-NEW	
Old 63	
E2	835 - E6
E3	835 - E7
E4	855 - E1
E5	855 - E2
E6	855 - E3
F1	835 - F5
F2	835 - F6
F3	835 - F7
F4	855 - F1
F5	855 - F2
F6	855 - F3
Old 63A	
A1	835 - H5
A2	835 - G6
A3	835 - G7
A4	855 - G1
A5	855 - G2
A6	855 - G3
B1	835 - J5
B2	835 - J6
B3	835 - J7
B4	855 - J1
B5	855 - J2
B6	855 - J3
C1	836 - A5
C2	836 - A6
C3	836 - A7
C4	856 - A1
C5	856 - A2
C6	856 - A3
D1	836 - B5
D2	836 - B6
D3	836 - B7
D4	856 - B1
D5	856 - B2
D6	856 - B3
E1	836 - C5
E2	836 - C6
E3	836 - C7
E4	856 - C1
E5	856 - C2
E6	856 - C3
F1	836 - E5
F2	836 - E6
F3	836 - E7
F4	856 - E1
F5	856 - E2
F6	856 - D3
Old 63F	
A1	850 - J3
A2	850 - J4
A3	850 - J5
A4	850 - J7
B1	851 - A3
B2	851 - A4
B3	851 - A6
B4	851 - A7
B5	871 - A1
B6	871 - A2
C1	851 - B3
C2	851 - B4
C3	851 - B6
C4	851 - B7
C5	871 - B1
C6	871 - B2
D1	851 - D3
D2	851 - D4
D3	851 - D6
D4	851 - C7
D5	871 - C1
D6	871 - C2
E1	851 - E3
E2	851 - E4
E3	851 - E6
E4	851 - E7
E5	871 - E1
E6	871 - E2
F1	851 - F3
F2	851 - F5
F3	851 - F6
F4	851 - F7
F5	871 - F1
F6	871 - F2
Old 64	
A1	851 - G3
A2	851 - G5
A3	851 - G6
A4	851 - G7
A5	871 - G1
A6	871 - G2
B1	851 - H4
B2	851 - H5
B3	851 - H6
B4	851 - H7
B5	871 - H1
B6	871 - H2
C1	852 - A4
C2	852 - A5
C3	852 - A6
C4	852 - A7
C5	872 - A1
C6	872 - A2
D1	852 - B4
D2	852 - B5
D3	852 - B6
D4	852 - B7
D5	872 - B1

OLD-NEW	
Old 64	
D6	872 - B2
E1	852 - C4
E2	852 - C5
E3	852 - C6
E4	852 - C7
E5	872 - C1
E6	872 - C2
F1	852 - D4
F2	852 - D5
F3	852 - D6
F4	852 - D7
F5	872 - D1
F6	872 - D2
Old 65	
A1	852 - E4
A2	852 - E5
A3	852 - E6
A4	852 - E7
A5	872 - E1
A6	872 - E2
B1	852 - G4
B2	852 - G5
B3	852 - G6
B4	852 - G7
B5	872 - F1
B6	872 - F2
C1	852 - H4
C2	852 - H5
C3	852 - H6
C4	852 - H7
C5	872 - H1
C6	872 - H2
D1	852 - J4
D2	852 - J5
D3	852 - J6
D4	852 - J7
D5	872 - J1
D6	872 - J2
E1	853 - A4
E2	853 - A5
E3	853 - A6
E4	853 - A7
E5	873 - A1
E6	873 - A2
F1	853 - C4
F2	853 - C5
F3	853 - C6
F4	853 - B7
F5	873 - B1
F6	873 - B2
Old 66	
A1	853 - D4
A2	853 - D5
A3	853 - D6
A4	853 - D7
A5	873 - D1
A6	873 - D2
B1	853 - E4
B2	853 - E5
B3	853 - E6
B4	853 - E7
B5	873 - E1
B6	873 - E2
C1	853 - F4
C2	853 - F5
C3	853 - F6
C4	853 - F7
C5	873 - F1
C6	873 - F2
D1	853 - G4
D2	853 - G5
D3	853 - G6
D4	853 - G7
D5	873 - G1
D6	873 - G2
E1	853 - J4
E2	853 - J5
E3	853 - J6
E4	853 - J7
E5	873 - J1
E6	873 - J2
F1	854 - A4
F2	854 - A5
F3	854 - A6
F4	854 - A7
F5	874 - A1
F6	874 - A3
Old 67	
A1	854 - B4
A2	854 - B5
A3	854 - B6
A4	854 - B7
A5	874 - B1
A6	874 - B3
B1	854 - C4
B2	854 - C5
B3	854 - C6
B4	854 - C7
B5	874 - C1
B6	874 - C3
C1	854 - D4
C2	854 - D5
C3	854 - D6
C4	854 - D7
C5	874 - D1
C6	874 - D3
D1	854 - F4

OLD-NEW	
Old 67	
D2	854 - F5
D3	854 - F6
D4	854 - F7
D5	874 - F2
D6	874 - F3
E1	854 - G4
E2	854 - G5
E3	854 - G6
E4	854 - G7
E5	874 - G2
E6	874 - G3
F1	854 - H4
F2	854 - H5
F3	854 - H6
F4	854 - H7
F5	874 - H2
F6	874 - H3
Old 68	
A1	854 - J4
A2	854 - J5
A3	854 - J6
A4	854 - J7
A5	874 - J2
A6	874 - J3
B1	855 - A4
B2	855 - A5
B3	855 - A6
B4	855 - A7
B5	875 - A2
B6	875 - A3
C1	855 - C4
C2	855 - C5
C3	855 - C6
C4	855 - C7
C5	875 - C2
C6	875 - C3
D1	855 - D4
D2	855 - D5
D3	855 - D6
D4	855 - D7
D5	875 - D2
D6	875 - D3
E1	855 - E4
E2	855 - E5
E3	855 - E6
E4	875 - E1
E5	875 - E2
E6	875 - E3
F1	855 - F4
F2	855 - F5
F3	855 - F6
F4	875 - F1
F5	875 - F2
F6	875 - F3
Old 68A	
A1	855 - G4
A2	855 - G5
A3	855 - G6
A4	875 - G1
A5	875 - G2
A6	875 - G3
B1	855 - J4
B2	855 - H5
B3	855 - H6
B4	875 - H1
B5	875 - H2
B6	875 - H3
C1	856 - A4
C2	856 - A5
C3	856 - A6
C4	876 - A1
C5	876 - A2
C6	876 - A3
D1	856 - B4
D2	856 - B5
D3	856 - B6
D4	876 - B1
D5	876 - B2
D6	876 - B3
E1	856 - C4
E2	856 - C5
E3	856 - C6
E4	876 - C1
E5	876 - C2
E6	876 - C3
F1	856 - D4
F2	856 - D5
F3	856 - D7
F4	876 - D1
F5	876 - D2
F6	876 - D3
Old 68B	
A1	856 - F5
A2	856 - F7
A3	876 - F2
A4	876 - F5
A5	876 - F7
A6	896 - F2
B1	856 - G5
B2	856 - G7
B3	876 - G2
B4	876 - G5
B5	876 - G7
B6	896 - G2
C1	856 - H5
C2	856 - H7
C3	876 - H3

OLD-NEW	
Old 68B	
C4	876 - H5
C5	876 - H7
C6	896 - H2
D1	856 - J5
D2	856 - J7
D3	876 - J2
D4	876 - J5
D5	876 - J7
D6	896 - J2
E1	857 - A5
E2	857 - A7
E3	877 - A3
E4	877 - A5
E5	877 - A7
E6	897 - A2
F1	857 - C5
F2	857 - C7
F3	877 - C2
F4	877 - B5
F5	877 - B7
F6	897 - B2
Old 68C	
A1	857 - D5
A2	857 - D7
A3	877 - D2
A4	877 - D5
A5	877 - D7
A6	897 - D2
B1	857 - E5
B2	857 - E7
B3	877 - E2
B4	877 - E5
B5	877 - E7
B6	897 - E2
C1	857 - F5
C2	877 - F1
C3	877 - F3
C4	877 - F5
C5	877 - F7
C6	897 - F2
D1	857 - G5
D2	877 - G1
D3	877 - G3
D4	877 - G5
D5	877 - G7
D6	897 - G2
E1	857 - J5
E2	857 - J7
E3	877 - J3
E4	877 - J5
E5	877 - H7
E6	897 - H2
F1	858 - A5
F2	858 - A7
F3	878 - A3
F4	878 - A5
F5	878 - A7
F6	898 - A2
Old 68D	
A1	858 - B5
A2	858 - B7
A3	878 - B3
A4	878 - B5
A5	878 - B7
A6	898 - B2
B1	858 - E5
B2	858 - E7
B3	878 - E3
B4	878 - E5
B5	878 - E7
B6	898 - D2
C1	858 - G5
C2	858 - G7
C3	878 - G3
C4	878 - G5
C5	878 - G7
C6	898 - G2
D1	859 - A6
D2	879 - A1
D3	879 - A3
D4	878 - J5
D5	878 - J7
D6	898 - J2
E1	859 - C6
E2	879 - C1
E3	879 - C3
E4	879 - C5
E5	879 - C7
E6	899 - C2
F1	859 - F6
F2	879 - F1
F3	879 - E3
F4	879 - E5
F5	879 - E7
F6	899 - E2
Old 68E	
B1	871 - A3
B2	871 - A4
B3	871 - A5
B4	871 - A7
C1	871 - B3
C2	871 - B4
C3	871 - B5
C4	871 - B7
D1	871 - C3
D2	871 - C4
D3	871 - C5

OLD-NEW	
Old 68E	
D4	871 - C7
E1	871 - E3
E2	871 - E4
E3	871 - E5
E4	871 - E7
F1	871 - F3
F2	871 - F4
F3	871 - F5
F4	871 - F6
Old 69	
A1	871 - G3
A2	871 - G4
A3	871 - G5
A4	871 - G6
B1	871 - H3
B2	871 - H4
B3	871 - H5
B4	871 - H7
C1	872 - A3
C2	871 - J4
C3	871 - J5
C4	871 - J7
D1	872 - B3
D2	872 - B4
D3	872 - B5
D4	872 - B7
D5	892 - B1
D6	892 - B2
E1	872 - C3
E2	872 - C4
E3	872 - C5
E4	872 - C7
E5	892 - C1
E6	892 - C2
F1	872 - D3
F2	872 - D4
F3	872 - D5
F4	872 - D7
F5	892 - D1
F6	892 - D2
Old 70	
A1	872 - E3
A2	872 - E4
A3	872 - E5
A4	872 - E7
A5	892 - E1
A6	892 - E2
B1	872 - F3
B2	872 - F4
B3	872 - F6
B4	872 - F7
B5	892 - F1
B6	892 - F2
C1	872 - H3
C2	872 - H4
C3	872 - H6
C4	872 - H7
C5	892 - H1
C6	892 - H2
D1	872 - J3
D2	872 - J4
D3	872 - J6
D4	872 - J7
D5	892 - J1
D6	892 - J2
E1	873 - A3
E2	873 - A4
E3	873 - A6
E4	873 - A7
E5	893 - A1
E6	893 - A2
F1	873 - B3
F2	873 - B4
F3	873 - B6
F4	873 - B7
F5	893 - B1
F6	893 - B2
Old 71	
A1	873 - C3
A2	873 - C4
A3	873 - C6
A4	873 - C7
A5	893 - C1
A6	893 - C2
B1	873 - E3
B2	873 - E4
B3	873 - E6
B4	873 - E7
B5	893 - E1
B6	893 - E2
C1	873 - F3
C2	873 - F4
C3	873 - F6
C4	873 - F7
C5	893 - F1
C6	893 - F2
D1	873 - G3
D2	873 - G5
D3	873 - G6
D4	873 - G7
D5	893 - G1
D6	893 - G2
E1	873 - J3
E2	873 - J5
E3	873 - J6
E4	873 - H7
E5	893 - H1

OLD-NEW	
Old 71	
E6	893 - H2
F1	874 - A4
F2	874 - A5
F3	874 - A6
F4	874 - A7
F5	894 - A1
F6	894 - A2
Old 72	
A1	874 - B4
A2	874 - B5
A3	874 - B6
A4	874 - B7
A5	894 - B1
A6	894 - B2
B1	874 - C4
B2	874 - C5
B3	874 - C6
B4	874 - C7
B5	894 - C1
B6	894 - C2
C1	874 - D4
C2	874 - D5
C3	874 - D6
C4	874 - D7
C5	894 - D1
C6	894 - D2
D1	874 - E4
D2	874 - E5
D3	874 - E6
D4	874 - E7
D5	894 - E1
D6	894 - E2
E1	874 - G4
E2	874 - G5
E3	874 - G6
E4	874 - G7
E5	894 - G1
E6	894 - G2
F1	874 - H4
F2	874 - H5
F3	874 - H6
F4	874 - H7
F5	894 - H1
F6	894 - H2
Old 72A	
A1	874 - J4
A2	874 - J5
A3	874 - J6
A4	874 - J7
A5	894 - J1
A6	894 - J2
B1	875 - A4
B2	875 - A5
B3	875 - A6
B4	875 - A7
B5	895 - A1
B6	895 - A2
C1	875 - C4
C2	875 - B5
C3	875 - B6
C4	875 - B7
C5	895 - B1
C6	895 - B2
D1	875 - D4
D2	875 - D5
D3	875 - D6
D4	875 - D7
D5	895 - D1
D6	895 - D2
E1	875 - E4
E2	875 - E5
E3	875 - E6
E4	875 - E7
E5	895 - E1
E6	895 - E2
F1	875 - F4
F2	875 - F5
F3	875 - F6
F4	875 - F7
F5	895 - F1
F6	895 - F2
Old 72B	
A1	875 - G4
A2	875 - G5
A3	875 - G6
A4	875 - G7
A5	895 - G1
A6	895 - G2
B1	875 - H4
B2	875 - H5
B3	875 - H6
B4	875 - H7
B5	895 - H1
B6	895 - H3
C1	876 - A4
C2	876 - A5
C3	876 - A6
C4	876 - A7
C5	896 - A1
C6	896 - A3
D1	876 - B4
D2	876 - B5
D3	876 - B6
D4	876 - B7
D5	896 - B2
D6	896 - B3
E1	876 - C4

OLD-NEW	
Old 72B	
E2	876 - C5
E3	876 - C6
E4	876 - C7
E5	896 - C2
E6	896 - C3
F1	876 - D4
F2	876 - D5
F3	876 - D6
F4	876 - D7
F5	896 - D2
F6	896 - D3
Old 72K	
D1	892 - B3
D2	892 - B4
D3	892 - B5
D4	892 - A6
D5	892 - A7
D6	912 - A2
E1	892 - C3
E2	892 - C4
E3	892 - C5
E4	892 - C6
E5	892 - C7
E6	912 - C2
F1	892 - D3
F2	892 - D4
F3	892 - D5
F4	892 - D6
F5	912 - D1
F6	912 - D2
Old 73	
A1	892 - E3
A2	892 - E4
A3	892 - E5
A4	892 - E6
A5	912 - E1
A6	912 - E2
B1	892 - F3
B2	892 - F4
B3	892 - F5
B4	892 - F6
B5	912 - F1
B6	912 - F2
C1	892 - H3
C2	892 - H4
C3	892 - H5
C4	892 - H6
C5	912 - H1
C6	912 - G2
D1	892 - J3
D2	892 - J4
D3	892 - J5
D4	892 - J6
D5	912 - J1
D6	912 - J2
E1	893 - A3
E2	893 - A4
E3	893 - A5
E4	893 - A6
E5	913 - A1
E6	913 - A2
F1	893 - B3
F2	893 - B4
F3	893 - B5
F4	893 - B6
F5	913 - B1
F6	913 - B2
Old 74	
A1	893 - C3
A2	893 - C4
A3	893 - C5
A4	893 - C6
A5	913 - C1
A6	913 - C2
B1	893 - E3
B2	893 - E4
B3	893 - E5
B4	893 - E6
B5	913 - D1
B6	913 - D2
C1	893 - F3
C2	893 - F4
C3	893 - F5
C4	893 - F6
C5	913 - F1
C6	913 - F2
D1	893 - G3
D2	893 - G4
D3	893 - G5
D4	893 - G6
D5	913 - G1
D6	913 - G2
E1	893 - H3
E2	893 - H4
E3	893 - H5
E4	893 - H7
E5	913 - H1
E6	913 - H2
F1	894 - A3
F2	894 - A4
F3	894 - A5
F4	894 - A7
F5	914 - A1
F6	913 - J2
Old 75	
A1	894 - B3
A2	894 - B4

OLD-NEW	
Old 75	
A3	894 - B5
A4	894 - B7
A5	914 - B1
A6	914 - B2
B1	894 - C3
B2	894 - C4
B3	894 - C5
B4	894 - C7
B5	914 - C1
B6	914 - C2
C1	894 - D3
C2	894 - D4
C3	894 - D5
C4	894 - D7
C5	914 - D1
C6	914 - D2
D1	894 - E3
D2	894 - E4
D3	894 - E5
D4	894 - E7
D5	914 - E1
D6	914 - E2
E1	894 - G3
E2	894 - G4
E3	894 - G5
E4	894 - G7
E5	914 - G1
E6	914 - G2
F1	894 - H3
F2	894 - H4
F3	894 - H5
F4	894 - H7
F5	914 - H1
F6	914 - H2
Old 76	
A1	894 - J3
A2	894 - J4
A3	894 - J6
A4	894 - J7
A5	914 - J1
A6	914 - J2
B1	895 - A3
B2	895 - A4
B3	895 - A6
B4	895 - A7
B5	915 - A1
B6	915 - A2
C1	895 - B3
C2	895 - B4
C3	895 - B6
C4	895 - B7
C5	915 - B1
C6	915 - B2
D1	895 - D3
D2	895 - D4
D3	895 - D6
D4	895 - D7
D5	915 - D1
D6	915 - D2
E1	895 - E3
E2	895 - E4
E3	895 - E6
E4	895 - E7
E5	915 - E1
E6	915 - E2
F1	895 - F3
F2	895 - F4
F3	895 - F6
F4	895 - F7
F5	915 - F1
F6	915 - F2
Old 77	
A1	895 - G3
A2	895 - G4
A3	895 - G6
A4	895 - G7
A5	915 - G1
A6	915 - G2
B1	895 - H3
B2	895 - H5
B3	895 - H6
B4	895 - H7
B5	915 - H1
B6	915 - H2
C1	896 - A4
C2	896 - A5
C3	896 - A6
C4	896 - A7
C5	916 - A1
C6	916 - A2
D1	896 - B4
D2	896 - B5
D3	896 - B6
D4	896 - B7
D5	916 - B1
D6	916 - B2
E1	896 - C4
E2	896 - C5
E3	896 - C6
E4	896 - C7
E5	916 - C1
E6	916 - C2
F1	896 - D4
F2	896 - D5
F3	896 - D6
F4	896 - D7
F5	916 - D1

OLD-NEW	
Old 77	
F6	916 - D2
Old 78	
A1	896 - E4
A2	896 - E5
A3	896 - E6
A4	896 - E7
A5	916 - E1
A6	916 - E2
B1	896 - G4
B2	896 - G5
B3	896 - G6
B4	896 - G7
B5	916 - F1
B6	916 - F2
C1	896 - H4
C2	896 - H5
C3	896 - H6
C4	896 - H7
C5	916 - H1
C6	916 - H2
D1	896 - J4
D2	896 - J5
D3	896 - J6
D4	896 - J7
D5	916 - J1
D6	916 - J2
E1	897 - A4
E2	897 - A5
E3	897 - A6
E4	897 - A7
E5	917 - A1
E6	917 - A2
F1	897 - C4
F2	897 - C5
F3	897 - B6
F4	897 - B7
F5	917 - B1
F6	917 - B2
Old 78A	
A1	897 - D4
A2	897 - D5
A3	897 - D6
A4	897 - D7
A5	917 - C1
A6	917 - C2
B1	897 - E4
B2	897 - E5
B3	897 - E6
B4	897 - E7
B5	917 - E1
B6	917 - E2
C1	897 - F4
C2	897 - F5
C3	897 - F6
C4	897 - F7
C5	917 - F1
C6	917 - F2
D1	897 - G4
D2	897 - G5
D3	897 - G6
D4	897 - G7
D5	917 - G1
D6	917 - G2
E1	897 - H4
E2	897 - H5
E3	897 - H6
E4	897 - H7
E5	917 - H1
E6	917 - H2
F1	898 - A4
F2	898 - A5
F3	898 - A6
F4	898 - A7
F5	918 - A1
F6	918 - A2
Old 78B	
A1	898 - B4
A2	898 - B6
A3	918 - B2
A4	918 - B4
A5	918 - B6
A6	938 - B1
B1	898 - C4
B2	898 - C6
B3	918 - C2
B4	918 - C4
B5	918 - C6
B6	938 - C1
C1	898 - D4
C2	898 - D7
C3	918 - D2
C4	918 - D4
C5	918 - D6
C6	938 - D1
D1	898 - E5
D2	898 - E7
D3	918 - E2
D4	918 - E4
D5	918 - E6
D6	938 - E2
E1	898 - F5
E2	898 - F7
E3	918 - F2
E4	918 - F4
E5	918 - F7
E6	938 - F2
F1	898 - H5

1998 SANTA CLARA OLD TO NEW Page Conversion List

OLD	NEW
Old 78B	
F2	898 - H7
F3	918 - H2
F4	918 - H4
F5	918 - G7
F6	938 - G2
Old 78C	
A1	898 - J5
A2	898 - J7
A3	918 - J2
A4	918 - J4
A5	918 - J6
A6	938 - J2
B1	899 - A5
B2	899 - A7
B3	919 - A2
B4	919 - A4
B5	919 - A6
B6	939 - A2
C1	899 - B5
C2	899 - B7
C3	919 - B2
C4	919 - B4
C5	919 - B7
C6	939 - B2
D1	899 - D5
D2	899 - C7
D3	919 - C2
D4	919 - C5
D5	919 - C7
D6	939 - C2
E1	899 - E5
E2	899 - E7
E3	919 - E2
E4	919 - E4
E5	919 - D7
E6	939 - D2
F1	899 - F5
F2	899 - F7
F3	919 - F2
F4	919 - F4
F5	919 - F7
F6	939 - E2
Old 78D	
A1	879 - H4
A2	879 - G7
A3	899 - G2
A4	899 - G4
A5	899 - G7
A6	919 - G2
B1	880 - A5
B2	880 - A7
B3	900 - A2
B4	900 - A5
B5	900 - A7
B6	920 - A2
C1	880 - C5
C2	880 - C7
C3	900 - C2
C4	900 - C5
C5	900 - C7
C6	920 - C2
D3	921 - D3
D4	900 - F5
D5	900 - F7
D6	920 - F2
E3	921 - F3
E4	900 - H5
E5	900 - H7
E6	920 - H2
F3	921 - J3
F6	921 - B3
Old 78E	
A1	919 - G4
A2	919 - G6
A3	939 - G1
A4	939 - G4
A5	939 - G6
A6	959 - G1
B1	920 - A4
B2	920 - A6
B3	939 - J2
B4	939 - J4
B5	939 - J6
B6	959 - J1
C1	920 - C4
C2	920 - C6
C3	940 - C2
C4	940 - C4
C5	940 - C6
C6	960 - C1
D1	920 - F4
D2	920 - E6
D3	940 - E2
D4	940 - E4
D5	940 - E6
D6	960 - E1
E1	920 - H4
E2	920 - H7
E3	940 - H2
E4	940 - H4
E5	940 - H6
E6	960 - H2
F1	921 - A5
F2	921 - A7
F3	941 - A2
F4	941 - A4
F5	941 - A6

OLD	NEW
Old 78E	
F6	961 - A2
Old 78F	
A1	921 - D5
A2	921 - D7
A3	941 - D2
A4	941 - C4
A5	941 - C6
A6	961 - C2
B1	921 - F5
B2	921 - F7
B3	941 - F2
B4	941 - F4
B5	941 - F7
B6	961 - E2
C1	921 - H5
C2	921 - H7
C3	941 - H2
C4	941 - H4
C5	941 - H7
C6	961 - H2
D1	922 - B5
D2	922 - B7
D3	942 - B2
D4	942 - B4
D5	942 - A7
D6	962 - A2
E1	922 - D5
E2	922 - D7
E3	942 - D2
E4	942 - D4
E5	942 - D7
E6	962 - D2
F1	922 - G5
F2	922 - F7
F3	942 - F2
F4	942 - F5
F5	942 - F7
F6	962 - F2
Old 78G	
A1	912 - E3
A2	912 - E4
A3	912 - E5
A4	912 - E6
A5	912 - E7
B1	912 - F3
B2	912 - F4
B3	912 - F5
B4	912 - F6
B5	912 - F7
C1	912 - G3
C2	912 - G4
C3	912 - G5
C4	912 - G6
C5	912 - G7
D1	912 - J3
D2	912 - J4
D3	912 - J5
D4	912 - J6
D5	912 - J7
E1	913 - A3
E2	913 - A4
E3	913 - A5
E4	913 - A6
E5	913 - A7
F1	913 - B3
F2	913 - B4
F3	913 - B5
F4	913 - B6
F5	913 - B7
Old 78H	
A1	913 - C3
A2	913 - C6
B1	913 - D3
B2	913 - D6
C1	913 - E3
C2	913 - E6
D1	913 - G3
D2	913 - F6
E1	913 - H3
E2	913 - H5
F1	913 - J3
F2	913 - J5
Old 78J	
A1	914 - A3
A2	914 - A6
A3	934 - A1
A4	934 - A3
A5	934 - A5
B1	914 - B4
B2	914 - B6
B3	934 - B1
B4	934 - B3
B5	934 - B5
C1	914 - D3
C2	914 - D6
C3	934 - D1
C4	934 - C3
C5	934 - C6
D1	914 - E3
D2	914 - E6
D3	934 - E1
D4	934 - E3
D5	934 - E5
E1	914 - F4
E2	914 - F6
E3	934 - F1
E4	934 - F3

OLD	NEW
Old 78J	
E5	934 - F5
F1	914 - H3
F2	914 - H6
F3	934 - G1
F4	934 - G3
F5	934 - G6
Old 78K	
A1	914 - J3
A2	914 - J6
A3	934 - J1
A4	934 - J3
A5	934 - J5
B1	915 - A3
B2	915 - A6
B3	935 - A1
B4	935 - A3
B5	935 - A5
B6	955 - A1
C1	915 - B4
C2	915 - B6
C3	935 - B1
C4	935 - B3
C5	935 - B6
C6	955 - B1
D1	915 - C4
D2	915 - C6
D3	935 - C1
D4	935 - C3
D5	935 - C6
D6	955 - C1
E1	915 - E3
E2	915 - E6
E3	935 - E1
E4	935 - E3
E5	935 - D6
E6	955 - D1
F1	915 - F4
F2	915 - F6
F3	935 - F1
F4	935 - F3
F5	935 - F5
F6	955 - F1
Old 78L	
A1	915 - G4
A2	915 - G6
A3	935 - G1
A4	935 - G3
A5	935 - G5
A6	955 - G1
B1	915 - H4
B2	915 - H6
B3	935 - H1
B4	935 - H3
B5	935 - H6
B6	955 - H1
C1	916 - A4
C2	916 - A6
C3	935 - J1
C4	935 - J3
C5	935 - J6
C6	955 - J1
D1	916 - B4
D2	916 - B6
D3	936 - B1
D4	936 - B3
D5	936 - B5
D6	956 - B1
E1	916 - C4
E2	916 - C6
E3	936 - C1
E4	936 - C3
E5	936 - C5
E6	956 - C1
F1	916 - D4
F2	916 - D6
F3	936 - D1
F4	936 - D3
F5	936 - D5
F6	956 - D1
Old 79	
A1	916 - E3
A2	916 - E4
A3	916 - E5
A4	916 - E7
A5	936 - E1
A6	936 - E2
B1	916 - F3
B2	916 - F4
B3	916 - F5
B4	916 - F7
B5	936 - F1
B6	936 - F2
C1	916 - H3
C2	916 - H4
C3	916 - H5
C4	916 - H7
C5	936 - H1
C6	936 - H2
D1	916 - J3
D2	916 - J4
D3	916 - J5
D4	916 - J7
D5	936 - J1
D6	936 - J2
E1	917 - A3
E2	917 - A4
E3	917 - A6

OLD	NEW
Old 79	
E4	917 - A7
E5	937 - A1
E6	937 - A2
F1	917 - B3
F2	917 - B4
F3	917 - B6
F4	917 - B7
F5	937 - B1
F6	937 - B2
Old 80	
A1	917 - C3
A2	917 - C4
A3	917 - C6
A4	917 - C7
A5	937 - C1
A6	937 - C2
B1	917 - E3
B2	917 - E4
B3	917 - E6
B4	917 - E7
B5	937 - E1
B6	937 - E2
C1	917 - F3
C2	917 - F4
C3	917 - F6
C4	917 - F7
C5	937 - F1
C6	937 - F2
D1	917 - G3
D2	917 - G4
D3	917 - G6
D4	917 - G7
D5	937 - G1
D6	937 - G2
E1	917 - H3
E2	917 - H4
E3	917 - H6
E4	917 - H7
E5	937 - H1
E6	937 - H2
F1	918 - A3
F2	918 - A4
F3	918 - A6
F4	918 - A7
F5	938 - A1
F6	938 - A2
Old 80K	
A1	936 - E3
A2	936 - E4
A3	936 - E5
A4	936 - E6
A5	936 - E7
A6	956 - E1
B1	936 - F3
B2	936 - F4
B3	936 - F5
B4	936 - F6
B5	936 - F7
B6	956 - F1
C1	936 - H3
C2	936 - H4
C3	936 - H5
C4	936 - H6
C5	936 - H7
C6	956 - H1
D1	936 - J3
D2	936 - J4
D3	936 - J5
D4	936 - J6
D5	936 - J7
D6	956 - J1
E1	937 - A3
E2	937 - A4
E3	937 - A5
E4	937 - A6
E5	937 - A7
E6	957 - A1
F1	937 - B3
F2	937 - B4
F3	937 - B5
F4	937 - B6
F5	937 - B7
F6	957 - B1
Old 81	
A1	937 - C3
A2	937 - C4
A3	937 - C5
A4	937 - C6
A5	937 - C7
A6	957 - C1
B1	937 - E3
B2	937 - E4
B3	937 - E5
B4	937 - E6
B5	937 - E7
B6	957 - E1
C1	937 - F3
C2	937 - F4
C3	937 - F5
C4	937 - F6
C5	937 - F7
C6	957 - F1
D1	937 - G3
D2	937 - G4
D3	937 - G5
D4	937 - G6
D5	937 - G7

OLD	NEW
Old 81	
D6	957 - G1
E1	937 - H3
E2	937 - H4
E3	937 - H5
E4	937 - H6
E5	937 - H7
E6	957 - H2
F1	938 - A3
F2	938 - A4
F3	938 - A5
F4	938 - A6
F5	938 - A7
F6	958 - A2
Old 81A	
A1	938 - B3
A2	938 - B4
A3	938 - B5
A4	938 - B6
A5	938 - B7
A6	958 - B2
B1	938 - C3
B2	938 - C4
B3	938 - C5
B4	938 - C6
B5	938 - C7
B6	958 - C2
C1	938 - D3
C2	938 - D4
C3	938 - D5
C4	938 - D6
C5	958 - D1
C6	958 - D2
D1	938 - E3
D2	938 - E4
D3	938 - E5
D4	938 - E6
D5	958 - E1
D6	958 - E2
E1	938 - F3
E2	938 - F4
E3	938 - F5
E4	938 - F6
E5	958 - F1
E6	958 - F2
F1	938 - G3
F2	938 - G4
F3	938 - G5
F4	938 - G6
F5	958 - G1
F6	958 - G2
Old 81B	
A1	938 - J3
A2	938 - J4
A3	938 - J5
A4	938 - J7
A5	958 - J1
A6	958 - J2
B1	939 - A3
B2	939 - A4
B3	939 - A5
B4	939 - A7
B5	959 - A1
B6	959 - A2
C1	939 - B3
C2	939 - B4
C3	939 - B5
C4	939 - B7
C5	959 - B1
C6	959 - B2
D1	939 - C4
D2	939 - C5
D3	939 - C6
D4	939 - C7
D5	959 - C1
D6	959 - C2
E1	939 - D4
E2	939 - D5
E3	939 - D6
E4	939 - D7
E5	959 - D1
E6	959 - D2
F1	939 - E4
F2	939 - E5
F3	939 - E6
F4	939 - E7
F5	959 - E1
F6	959 - E2
Old 81C	
A1	958 - J3
A2	958 - J4
A3	958 - J5
A4	958 - J6
A5	958 - J7
A6	978 - J1
B1	959 - A3
B2	959 - A4
B3	959 - A5
B4	959 - A6
B5	959 - A7
B6	979 - A1
C1	959 - B3
C2	959 - B4
C3	959 - B5
C4	959 - B6
C5	959 - B7
C6	979 - B1
D1	959 - C3

OLD	NEW
Old 81C	
D2	959 - C4
D3	959 - C5
D4	959 - C6
D5	959 - C7
D6	979 - C1
E1	959 - D3
E2	959 - D4
E3	959 - D5
E4	959 - D6
E5	959 - D7
E6	979 - D1
F1	959 - E3
F2	959 - E4
F3	959 - E5
F4	959 - E6
F5	959 - E7
F6	979 - F1
Old 81F	
B1	955 - A3
B2	955 - A5
B3	955 - A7
B4	975 - A3
B5	975 - A5
B6	975 - A7
C1	955 - B3
C2	955 - B5
C3	955 - B7
C4	975 - B3
C5	975 - B5
C6	975 - B7
D1	955 - C3
D2	955 - C5
D3	955 - C7
D4	975 - C3
D5	975 - C5
D6	995 - D1
E1	955 - D3
E2	955 - E5
E3	975 - E1
E4	975 - E3
E5	975 - E5
E6	995 - E1
F1	955 - F3
F2	955 - F5
F3	975 - F1
F4	975 - F3
F5	975 - F5
F6	975 - F7
Old 81G	
A1	955 - G3
A2	966 - G5
A3	955 - G7
A4	975 - G3
A5	975 - G5
A6	975 - G7
B1	955 - H3
B2	955 - H5
B3	955 - H7
B4	975 - H3
B5	975 - H5
B6	975 - H7
C1	955 - J3
C2	955 - J5
C3	955 - J7
C4	976 - A3
C5	976 - A5
C6	976 - A7
D1	956 - B3
D2	956 - B5
D3	976 - B1
D4	976 - B3
D5	976 - B5
D6	976 - B7
E1	956 - C3
E2	956 - C5
E3	956 - C7
E4	976 - C2
E5	976 - C5
E6	976 - C7
F1	956 - D3
F2	956 - D5
F3	956 - D7
F4	976 - D2
F5	976 - D5
F6	976 - D7
Old 81H	
A1	956 - E2
A2	956 - E3
A3	956 - E5
A4	956 - E6
A5	956 - E7
A6	976 - E1
B1	956 - F2
B2	956 - F3
B3	956 - F5
B4	956 - F6
B5	956 - F7
B6	976 - F1
C1	956 - H2
C2	956 - H3
C3	956 - H5
C4	956 - H6
C5	956 - H7
C6	976 - H1
D1	956 - J2
D2	956 - J3
D3	956 - J5

OLD	NEW
Old 81H	
D4	956 - J6
D5	956 - J7
D6	976 - J1
E1	957 - A2
E2	957 - A3
E3	957 - A5
E4	957 - A6
E5	957 - A7
E6	977 - A1
F1	957 - B2
F2	957 - B3
F3	957 - B5
F4	957 - B6
F5	957 - B7
F6	977 - B1
Old 82	
A1	957 - C2
A2	957 - C3
A3	957 - C5
A4	957 - C6
A5	957 - C7
A6	977 - C1
B1	957 - E2
B2	957 - E4
B3	957 - E5
B4	957 - E6
B5	957 - D7
B6	977 - D1
C1	957 - F2
C2	957 - F4
C3	957 - F5
C4	957 - F6
C5	957 - F7
C6	977 - F1
D1	957 - G2
D2	957 - G4
D3	957 - G5
D4	957 - G6
D5	957 - G7
D6	977 - G1
E1	957 - H3
E2	957 - H4
E3	957 - H5
E4	957 - H6
E5	957 - H7
E6	977 - H1
F1	958 - A3
F2	957 - J4
F3	957 - J5
F4	957 - J6
F5	967 - J7
F6	977 - J1
Old 82A	
A1	958 - B3
A2	958 - B4
A3	958 - B5
A4	958 - A6
A5	958 - A7
A6	978 - A1
B1	958 - C3
B2	958 - C4
B3	958 - C5
B4	958 - C6
B5	958 - C7
B6	978 - C1
C1	958 - D3
C2	958 - D4
C3	958 - D5
C4	958 - D6
C5	958 - D7
C6	978 - D1
D1	958 - E3
D2	958 - E4
D3	958 - E5
D4	958 - E6
D5	958 - E7
D6	978 - E1
E1	958 - F3
E2	958 - F4
E3	958 - F5
E4	958 - F6
E5	958 - F7
E6	978 - F1
F1	958 - G3
F2	958 - G4
F3	958 - G5
F4	958 - G6
F5	958 - G7
F6	978 - G1
Old 82C	
A1	959 - G4
A2	959 - G6
A3	979 - G1
A4	979 - G3
A5	979 - G5
A6	979 - G7
B1	959 - H4
B2	959 - H6
B3	979 - H1
B4	979 - H3
B5	979 - H5
B6	979 - H7
C1	959 - J4
C2	959 - J6
C3	979 - J1
C4	979 - J3
C5	979 - J5

OLD	NEW
Old 82C	
C6	979 - J7
D1	960 - A4
D2	960 - A6
D3	980 - A1
D4	980 - A3
D5	980 - A5
D6	980 - A7
E1	960 - B4
E2	960 - B6
E3	980 - B1
E4	980 - C3
E5	980 - C5
E6	980 - C7
F1	960 - D4
F2	960 - D6
F3	980 - D1
F4	980 - D3
F5	980 - D5
F6	980 - D7
Old 82D	
A1	960 - E4
A2	960 - E6
A3	980 - E1
A4	980 - E3
A5	980 - E5
A6	980 - E7
B1	960 - F4
B2	960 - F6
B3	980 - F1
B4	980 - F3
B5	980 - F5
B6	980 - F7
C1	960 - G4
C2	960 - G6
C3	980 - G1
C4	980 - G3
C5	980 - H5
C6	1000 - H1
D1	960 - H4
D2	960 - J6
D3	980 - J1
D4	980 - J3
D5	980 - J5
D6	1000 - J1
E1	961 - A4
E2	961 - A6
E3	981 - A1
E4	981 - A3
E5	981 - A5
E6	981 - A7
F1	961 - B4
F2	961 - B6
F3	981 - B1
F4	981 - B3
F5	981 - B5
F6	981 - B7
Old 82E	
A1	961 - C4
A2	961 - C6
A3	981 - C1
A4	981 - D3
A5	981 - D5
A6	1001 - D1
B1	961 - E4
B2	961 - F6
B3	981 - F1
B4	981 - F3
B5	981 - F6
B6	1001 - F1
C1	961 - H4
C2	961 - H6
C3	981 - H1
C4	981 - H3
C5	981 - H6
C6	1001 - J1
D1	962 - A4
D2	962 - B6
D3	982 - B1
D4	982 - B4
D5	982 - B6
D6	1002 - B1
E1	962 - D4
E2	962 - D6
E3	982 - D1
E4	982 - D4
E5	982 - E6
E6	1002 - E1
F1	962 - F4
F2	962 - G6
F3	982 - G2
F4	982 - G4
F5	982 - G6
F6	1002 - G1
Old 82H	
A1	976 - E2
A2	976 - E3
A3	976 - E4
A4	976 - E5
A5	976 - E7
A6	996 - E1
B1	976 - F2
B2	976 - F3
B3	976 - F4
B4	976 - F5
B5	976 - F7
B6	996 - F1
C1	976 - H2

OLD	NEW
Old 82H	
C2	976 - H3
C3	976 - H4
C4	976 - H5
C5	976 - H7
C6	996 - H1
D1	976 - J2
D2	976 - J3
D3	976 - J4
D4	976 - J5
D5	976 - J7
D6	996 - J1
E1	977 - A2
E2	977 - A3
E3	977 - A4
E4	977 - A5
E5	977 - A7
E6	997 - A1
F1	977 - B2
F2	977 - B3
F3	977 - B4
F4	977 - B6
F5	977 - B7
F6	997 - B1
Old 83	
A1	977 - C2
A2	977 - C3
A3	977 - C4
A4	977 - C6
A5	977 - C7
A6	997 - C1
B1	977 - D2
B2	977 - D3
B3	977 - D4
B4	977 - D6
B5	977 - D7
B6	997 - D1
C1	977 - F2
C2	977 - F3
C3	977 - F4
C4	977 - F6
C5	977 - F7
C6	997 - F1
D1	977 - G2
D2	977 - G3
D3	977 - G4
D4	977 - G6
D5	977 - G7
D6	997 - G1
E1	977 - H2
E2	977 - H3
E3	977 - H4
E4	977 - H6
E5	977 - H7
E6	997 - H1
F1	977 - J2
F2	977 - J3
F3	977 - J4
F4	977 - J6
F5	977 - J7
F6	997 - J1
Old 84	
A1	978 - A2
A2	978 - A3
A3	978 - A5
A4	978 - A6
A5	978 - A7
A6	998 - A1
B1	978 - C2
B2	978 - C3
B3	978 - C5
B4	978 - C6
B5	978 - C7
B6	998 - C1
C1	978 - D2
C2	978 - D3
C3	978 - D4
C4	978 - D6
C5	978 - D7
C6	998 - D1
D1	978 - E2
D2	978 - E3
D3	978 - E4
D4	978 - E6
D5	978 - E7
D6	998 - E1
E1	978 - F2
E2	978 - F3
E3	978 - F4
E4	978 - F6
E5	978 - F7
E6	998 - F1
F1	978 - G2
F2	978 - G3
F3	978 - G4
F4	978 - H6
F5	978 - H7
F6	998 - H1
Old 85	
A1	978 - H2
A2	978 - H3
A3	978 - J4
A4	978 - J6
A5	978 - J7
A6	998 - J1
B1	979 - A2
B2	979 - A3
B3	979 - A4

OLD	NEW
Old 85	
B4	979 - A6
B5	979 - A7
B6	999 - A1
C1	979 - B2
C2	979 - B3
C3	979 - B4
C4	979 - B5
C5	979 - B7
C6	999 - B1
D1	979 - C2
D2	979 - C3
D3	979 - C4
D4	979 - C5
D5	979 - C7
D6	999 - C1
E1	979 - D2
E2	979 - D3
E3	979 - D4
E4	979 - E5
E5	979 - E7
E6	999 - E1
F1	979 - F2
F2	979 - F3
F3	979 - F4
F4	979 - F5
F5	979 - F6
F6	999 - F1
Old 89	
A1	996 - E3
A2	996 - E5
A3	996 - E7
A4	1016 - E2
A5	1016 - E4
A6	1016 - E6
B1	996 - F3
B2	996 - F5
B3	996 - F7
B4	1016 - F2
B5	1016 - F4
B6	1016 - F7
C1	996 - G3
C2	996 - G5
C3	996 - G7
C4	1016 - G2
C5	1016 - G5
C6	1016 - G7
D1	996 - J2
D2	996 - J5
D3	996 - J7
D4	1016 - J2
D5	1016 - J4
D6	1016 - H7
E1	997 - A2
E2	997 - A5
E3	997 - A7
E4	1017 - A2
E5	1017 - A4
E6	1017 - A7
F1	997 - B3
F2	997 - B5
F3	997 - B7
F4	1017 - B2
F5	1017 - B4
F6	1017 - B7
Old 90	
A1	997 - C3
A2	997 - C5
A3	997 - C7
A4	1017 - C3
A5	1017 - C5
A6	1017 - C7
B1	997 - D3
B2	997 - D5
B3	997 - D7
B4	1017 - D3
B5	1017 - D5
B6	1017 - D7
C1	997 - F2
C2	997 - F5
C3	997 - F7
C4	1017 - F2
C5	1017 - F5
C6	1017 - F7
D1	997 - G3
D2	997 - G5
D3	997 - G7
D4	1017 - G2
D5	1017 - G5
D6	1017 - G7
E1	997 - H3
E2	997 - H5
E3	997 - H7
E4	1017 - H2
E5	1017 - H5
E6	1017 - H7
F1	998 - A3
F2	998 - A5
F3	998 - A7
F4	1017 - J3
F5	1017 - J5
F6	1017 - J7
Old 91	
A1	998 - B3
A2	998 - B5
A3	998 - B7
A4	1018 - B2
A5	1018 - B5

OLD	NEW
Old 91	
A6	1018 - B7
B1	998 - C3
B2	998 - C5
B3	998 - C7
B4	1018 - C2
B5	1018 - C5
B6	1018 - C7
C1	998 - D3
C2	998 - D5
C3	998 - D7
C4	1018 - D3
C5	1018 - D5
C6	1018 - D7
D1	998 - F2
D2	998 - E5
D3	998 - E7
D4	1018 - E3
D5	1018 - E5
D6	1018 - E7
E1	998 - G2
E2	998 - G5
E3	998 - G7
E4	1018 - G2
E5	1018 - G5
F1	998 - H2
F2	998 - H5
F3	998 - H7
F4	1018 - H2
F5	1018 - H5
F6	1018 - H7
Old 92	
A1	998 - J3
A2	998 - J5
A3	998 - J7
A4	1018 - J2
A5	1018 - J5
A6	1018 - J7
B1	999 - A3
B2	999 - A5
B3	999 - A7
B4	1019 - A3
B5	1019 - A5
B6	1019 - A7
C1	999 - C2
C2	999 - C5
C3	999 - C7
C4	1019 - B3
C5	1019 - B5
C6	1019 - B7
D1	999 - D2
D2	999 - D5
D3	999 - D7
D4	1019 - D2
D5	1019 - D5
D6	1019 - D7
E1	999 - E2
E2	999 - E5
E3	999 - E7
E4	1019 - E2
E5	1019 - E5
E6	1019 - E7
F1	999 - F3
F2	999 - F5
F3	999 - F7
F4	1019 - F2
F5	1019 - F5
F6	1019 - F7

1998 SANTA CLARA NEW TO OLD Page Conversion List

NEW-OLD	
New 790	
B1	37 - A4
B2	37 - A5
B3	37 - A6
B4	43 - A1
B5	43 - A2
B6	43 - A3
B7	43 - A3
C1	37 - B4
C2	37 - B5
C3	37 - B6
C4	43 - B1
C5	43 - B2
C6	43 - B3
C7	43 - B3
D1	37 - B4
D2	37 - B5
D3	37 - B6
D4	43 - C1
D5	43 - C2
D6	43 - C3
D7	43 - C3
E1	37 - C4
E2	37 - C5
E3	37 - C6
E4	43 - C1
E5	43 - C2
E6	43 - C3
E7	43 - C3
F1	37 - D4
F2	37 - D5
F3	37 - D6
F4	43 - D1
F5	43 - D2
F6	43 - D2
F7	43 - D3
G1	37 - E4
G2	37 - E5
G3	37 - E6
G4	43 - E1
G5	43 - E2
G6	43 - E2
G7	43 - E3
H1	37 - F4
H2	37 - F5
H3	37 - F6
H4	43 - F1
H5	43 - F2
H6	43 - F2
H7	43 - F3
J1	38 - A4
J2	38 - A5
J3	38 - A6
J4	44 - A1
J5	44 - A2
J6	44 - A2
J7	44 - A3
New 791	
A1	38 - B4
A2	38 - B5
A3	38 - B6
A4	44 - B1
A5	44 - B2
A6	44 - B2
A7	44 - B3
B1	38 - B4
B2	38 - B5
B3	38 - B5
B4	38 - B6
B5	44 - B2
B6	44 - B2
B7	44 - B3
C1	38 - C4
C2	38 - C5
C3	38 - C5
C4	38 - C6
C5	44 - C1
C6	44 - C2
C7	44 - C3
D1	38 - D4
D2	38 - D5
D3	38 - D5
D4	38 - D6
D5	44 - D1
D6	44 - D2
D7	44 - D3
E1	38 - E4
E2	38 - E5
E3	38 - E5
E4	38 - E6
E5	44 - E1
E6	44 - E2
E7	44 - E3
F1	38 - E4
F2	38 - E5
F3	38 - E5
F4	38 - E6
F5	44 - F1
F6	44 - F2
F7	44 - F3
G1	38 - F4
G2	38 - F4
G3	38 - F5
G4	38 - F6
G5	44 - F1
G6	45 - A2
G7	45 - A3
H2	38A - A4

NEW-OLD	
New 791	
H3	38A - A5
H4	38A - A6
H5	45 - A1
H6	45 - A2
H7	45 - A3
J1	38A - B4
J2	38A - B4
J3	38A - B5
J4	38A - B6
J5	45 - B1
J6	45 - B2
J7	45 - B3
New 792	
A1	38A - C4
A2	38A - C4
A3	38A - C5
A4	38A - C6
A5	45 - C1
A6	45 - C2
A7	45 - C3
B1	38A - D4
B2	38A - D4
B3	38A - D5
B4	38A - D6
B5	45 - D1
B6	45 - D2
B7	45 - D3
C2	38A - E4
C3	38A - E5
C4	38A - E6
C5	45 - E1
C6	45 - E2
C7	45 - E3
D2	38A - E4
D3	38A - E5
D4	38A - E6
D5	45 - E1
D6	45 - E2
D7	45 - E3
E2	38A - F4
E3	38A - F5
E4	38A - F6
E5	45 - F1
E6	45 - F2
E7	45 - F3
F1	38A - A1
F2	38A - A1
F3	38A - A2
F4	38A - A3
F5	46 - A1
F6	46 - A2
F7	46 - A3
G1	38A - B1
G2	38A - B1
G3	38A - B2
G4	38A - B3
G5	46 - B1
G6	46 - B2
G7	46 - B3
H2	38A - C1
H3	38A - C2
H4	38A - C3
H5	46 - C1
H6	46 - C2
H7	46 - C3
J2	38A - D1
J3	38A - D2
J4	38A - D3
J5	46 - D1
J6	46 - D2
J7	46 - D3
New 793	
A2	38A - D1
A3	38A - D2
A4	38A - D3
A5	46 - D1
A6	46 - D2
A7	46 - D3
B1	38A - E1
B2	38A - E1
B3	38A - E2
B4	38A - E3
B5	46 - E1
B6	46 - E2
B7	46 - E3
C1	38A - F1
C2	38A - F1
C3	38A - F2
C4	38A - F3
C5	46 - F1
C6	46 - F2
C7	46 - F3
D1	39 - A3
D2	39 - A4
D3	39 - A5
D4	39 - A6
D5	47 - A1
D6	47 - A2
D7	47 - A3
E1	39 - B3
E2	39 - B4
E3	39 - B5
E4	39 - B6
E5	47 - B1
E6	47 - B2
E7	47 - B3
F1	39 - C3

NEW-OLD	
New 793	
F2	39 - C4
F3	39 - C5
F4	39 - C6
F5	47 - C1
F6	47 - C2
F7	47 - C3
G1	39 - C3
G2	39 - C4
G3	39 - C5
G4	39 - C6
G5	47 - C1
G6	47 - C2
G7	47 - C3
H1	39 - D3
H2	39 - D4
H3	39 - D5
H4	39 - D6
H5	47 - D1
H6	47 - D2
H7	47 - D3
J1	39 - E3
J2	39 - E4
J3	39 - E5
J4	39 - E6
J5	47 - E1
J6	47 - E2
J7	47 - E3
New 794	
A1	39 - F3
A2	39 - F4
A3	39 - F5
A4	39 - F6
A5	47 - F1
A6	47 - F2
A7	47 - F3
B1	40 - A3
B2	40 - A4
B3	40 - A5
B4	40 - A6
B5	48 - A1
B6	48 - A2
B7	48 - A3
C1	40 - B3
C2	40 - B4
C3	40 - B5
C4	40 - B6
C5	48 - B1
C6	48 - B2
C7	48 - B3
D1	40 - B3
D2	40 - B4
D3	40 - B5
D4	40 - B6
D5	48 - B1
D6	48 - B2
D7	48 - B3
E1	40 - C3
E2	40 - C4
E3	40 - C5
E4	40 - C6
E5	48 - C1
E6	48 - C2
E7	48 - C3
F1	40 - D3
F2	40 - D4
F3	40 - D5
F4	40 - D6
F5	48 - D1
F6	48 - D2
F7	48 - D3
G1	40 - E3
G2	40 - E4
G3	40 - E5
G4	40 - E6
G5	48 - E1
G6	48 - E2
G7	48 - E3
H1	40 - F3
H2	40 - F4
H3	40 - F5
H4	40 - F6
H5	48 - F1
H6	48 - F2
H7	48 - F3
J1	40 - F3
J2	41 - A4
J3	41 - A5
J4	41 - A6
J5	49 - A1
J6	49 - A2
J7	49 - A3
New 795	
A1	41 - A3
A2	41 - A4
A3	41 - A5
A4	41 - A6
A5	49 - A1
A6	49 - A2
A7	49 - A2
B1	41 - B3
B2	41 - B4
B3	41 - B5
B4	41 - B6
B5	49 - B1
B6	49 - B2
B7	49 - B2
C1	41 - C3

NEW-OLD	
New 795	
C2	41 - C4
C3	41 - C5
C4	41 - C6
C5	49 - C1
C6	49 - C2
C7	49 - C2
D1	41 - D3
D2	41 - D4
D3	41 - D5
D4	41 - D6
D5	49 - D1
D6	49 - D2
D7	49 - D2
E1	41 - E3
E2	41 - E4
E3	41 - E5
E4	41 - E6
E5	49 - E1
E6	49 - E2
E7	49 - E2
F1	41 - E3
F2	41 - E4
F3	41 - E5
F4	41 - E5
F5	49 - E1
F6	49 - E2
F7	49 - E2
G1	41 - F3
G2	41 - F4
G3	41 - F5
G4	41 - F5
G5	49 - F1
G6	49 - F2
G7	49 - F2
H1	42 - A3
H2	42 - A4
H3	42 - A5
H4	42 - A5
H5	42 - A6
H6	49A - A2
H7	49A - A2
J1	42 - B3
J2	42 - B4
J3	42 - B5
J4	42 - B5
J5	42 - B6
J6	49A - B2
J7	49A - B2
New 796	
A1	42 - C3
A2	42 - C4
A3	42 - C5
A4	42 - C5
A5	42 - C6
A6	49A - C2
A7	49A - C2
B1	42 - D3
B2	42 - D4
B3	42 - D5
B4	42 - D5
B5	42 - D6
B6	49A - D2
B7	49A - D2
C1	42 - D3
C2	42 - D4
C3	42 - D5
C4	42 - D5
C5	42 - D6
C6	49A - D1
C7	49A - D2
D1	42 - E3
D2	42 - E4
D3	42 - E5
D4	42 - E5
D5	42 - E6
D6	49A - E1
D7	49A - E2
E1	42 - F3
E2	42 - F4
E3	42 - F5
E4	42 - F5
E5	42 - F6
E6	49A - F1
E7	49A - F2
F1	42A - A2
F2	42A - A2
F3	42A - A2
F4	42A - A3
F5	42A - A3
F6	42A - A4
F7	42A - A4
G1	42A - B2
G2	42A - B2
G3	42A - B2
G4	42A - B3
G5	42A - B3
G6	42A - B4
G7	42A - B4
H1	42A - C2
H2	42A - C2
H3	42A - C2
H4	42A - C3
H5	42A - C3
H6	42A - C4
H7	42A - C4
J1	42A - D2
J2	42A - D2

NEW-OLD	
New 796	
J3	42A - D2
J4	42A - D3
J5	42A - D3
J6	42A - D4
J7	42A - D4
New 797	
A1	42A - D2
A2	42A - D2
A3	42A - D2
A4	42A - D3
A5	42A - D3
A6	42A - D4
A7	42A - D4
B1	42A - E2
B2	42A - E2
B3	42A - E2
B4	42A - E3
B5	42A - E3
B6	42A - E4
B7	42A - E4
C1	42A - F2
C2	42A - F2
C3	42A - F2
C4	42A - F3
C5	42A - F3
C6	42A - F4
C7	42A - F4
D1	42B - A2
D2	42B - A2
D3	42B - A2
D4	42B - A3
D5	42B - A3
D6	42B - A4
D7	42B - A4
E1	42B - B2
E2	42B - B2
E3	42B - B2
E4	42B - B3
E5	42B - B3
E6	42B - B4
E7	42B - B4
F1	42B - B2
F2	42B - B2
F3	42B - B2
F4	42B - B3
F5	42B - B3
F6	42B - B4
F7	42B - B4
G1	42B - C2
G2	42B - C2
G3	42B - C2
G4	42B - C3
G5	42B - C3
G6	42B - C4
G7	42B - C4
H1	42B - D2
H2	42B - D2
H3	42B - D2
H4	42B - D3
H5	42B - D3
H6	42B - D4
H7	42B - D4
J1	42B - E2
J2	42B - E2
J3	42B - E2
J4	42B - E3
J5	42B - E3
J6	42B - E4
J7	42B - E4
New 798	
A1	42B - F2
A2	42B - F2
A3	42B - F2
A4	42B - F3
A5	42B - F3
A6	42B - F4
A7	42B - F4
B1	42B - F2
B2	42C - A2
B3	42C - A2
B4	42C - A3
B5	42C - A3
B6	42C - A4
B7	42C - A4
C1	42C - A1
C2	42C - A2
C3	42C - A2
C4	42C - A3
C5	42C - A3
C6	42C - A4
C7	42C - A4
D1	42C - B1
D2	42C - B2
D3	42C - B2
D4	42C - B3
D5	42C - B3
D6	42C - B4
D7	42C - B4
E1	42C - C1
E2	42C - C2
E3	42C - C2
E4	42C - C3
E5	42C - C3
E6	42C - C4
E7	42C - C4
F1	42C - D1
F2	42C - D2

NEW-OLD	
New 798	
F3	42C - D2
F4	42C - D3
F5	42C - D3
F6	42C - D4
F7	42C - D4
G1	42C - E1
G2	42C - E2
G3	42C - E2
G4	42C - E3
G5	42C - E3
G6	42C - E4
G7	42C - E4
H1	42C - F1
H2	42C - F2
H3	42C - F2
H4	42C - F3
H5	42C - F3
H6	42C - F4
H7	42C - F4
J1	42C - F1
J2	42C - F2
J3	42C - F2
J4	42C - F3
J5	42C - F3
J6	42C - F4
J7	42C - F4
New 799	
A1	42D - A1
A2	42D - A2
A3	42D - A2
A4	42D - A3
A5	42D - A3
A6	42D - A4
A7	42D - A4
B1	42D - B1
B2	42D - B2
B3	42D - B2
B4	42D - B3
B5	42D - B3
B6	42D - B4
B7	42D - B4
C1	42D - C1
C2	42D - C2
C3	42D - C2
C4	42D - C3
C5	42D - C3
C6	42D - C4
C7	42D - C4
D1	42D - D1
D2	42D - D2
D3	42D - D2
D4	42D - D3
D5	42D - D3
D6	42D - D4
D7	42D - D4
E1	42D - D1
E2	42D - D2
E3	42D - D2
E4	42D - D3
E5	42D - D3
New 810	
B1	43 - A4
B2	43 - A5
B3	43 - A6
B4	50 - A1
B5	50 - A2
B6	50 - A3
B7	50 - A4
C1	43 - B4
C2	43 - B5
C3	43 - B6
C4	50 - B1
C5	50 - B2
C6	50 - B3
C7	50 - B4
D1	43 - C4
D2	43 - C5
D3	43 - C6
D4	50 - C1
D5	50 - C2
D6	50 - C3
D7	50 - C4
E1	43 - C4
E2	43 - C5
E3	43 - C6
E4	50 - C1
E5	50 - C2
E6	50 - C3
E7	50 - C4
F1	43 - D4
F2	43 - D5
F3	43 - D6
F4	50 - D1
F5	50 - D2
F6	50 - D3
F7	50 - D4
G1	43 - E4
G2	43 - E5
G3	43 - E6
G4	50 - E1
G5	50 - E2
G6	50 - E3
G7	50 - E4
H1	43 - F4
H2	43 - F5
H3	43 - F6
H4	50 - F1

NEW-OLD	
New 810	
H5	50 - F2
H6	50 - F3
H7	50 - F4
J1	44 - A4
J2	44 - A5
J3	44 - A6
J4	51 - A1
J5	51 - A2
J6	51 - A3
J7	51 - A4
New 811	
A1	44 - B4
A2	44 - B5
A3	44 - B6
A4	51 - B1
A5	51 - B2
A6	51 - B3
A7	51 - B4
B1	44 - B4
B2	44 - B5
B3	44 - B6
B4	51 - B1
B5	51 - B2
B6	51 - B3
B7	51 - C4
C1	44 - C4
C2	44 - C5
C3	44 - C6
C4	51 - C1
C5	51 - C2
C6	51 - C3
C7	51 - C4
D1	44 - D4
D2	44 - D5
D3	44 - D6
D4	51 - D1
D5	51 - D2
D6	51 - D3
D7	51 - D4
E1	44 - E4
E2	44 - E5
E3	44 - E6
E4	51 - E1
E5	51 - E2
E6	51 - E3
E7	51 - E3
F1	44 - F4
F2	44 - F5
F3	44 - F6
F4	51 - F1
F5	51 - F2
F6	51 - F3
F7	51 - F3
G1	45 - A4
G2	45 - A5
G3	45 - A6
G4	52 - A1
G5	52 - A2
G6	52 - A3
G7	52 - A3
H1	45 - A4
H2	45 - A5
H3	45 - A6
H4	52 - A1
H5	52 - A2
H6	52 - B3
H7	52 - B3
J1	45 - B4
J2	45 - B5
J3	45 - B6
J4	52 - B1
J5	52 - B2
J6	52 - B3
J7	52 - B3
New 812	
A1	45 - C4
A2	45 - C5
A3	45 - C6
A4	52 - C1
A5	52 - C2
A6	52 - C3
A7	52 - C3
B1	45 - D4
B2	45 - D5
B3	45 - D6
B4	52 - D1
B5	52 - D2
B6	52 - D3
B7	52 - D3
C1	45 - E4
C2	45 - E5
C3	45 - E6
C4	52 - E1
C5	52 - E2
C6	52 - E3
C7	52 - E3
D1	45 - E4
D2	45 - E5
D3	45 - E6
D4	52 - E1
D5	52 - E2
D6	52 - E3
D7	52 - E3
E1	45 - F4
E2	45 - F5
E3	45 - F6
E4	52 - F1

NEW-OLD	
New 812	
E5	52 - F2
E6	52 - F3
E7	52 - F3
F1	46 - A4
F2	46 - A5
F3	46 - A6
F4	53 - A1
F5	53 - A2
F6	53 - A2
F7	53 - A3
G1	46 - B4
G2	46 - B5
G3	46 - B6
G4	53 - B1
G5	53 - B2
G6	53 - B2
G7	53 - B3
H1	46 - C4
H2	46 - C5
H3	46 - C6
H4	53 - C1
H5	53 - C2
H6	53 - C2
H7	53 - C3
J1	46 - D4
J2	46 - D5
J3	46 - D6
J4	53 - D1
J5	53 - D2
J6	53 - D2
J7	53 - D3
New 813	
A1	46 - D4
A2	46 - D5
A3	46 - D6
A4	53 - D1
A5	53 - D2
A6	53 - D2
A7	53 - E3
B1	46 - E4
B2	46 - E5
B3	46 - E6
B4	53 - E1
B5	53 - E2
B6	53 - E2
B7	53 - E3
C1	46 - F4
C2	46 - F5
C3	46 - F6
C4	53 - F1
C5	53 - F2
C6	53 - F2
C7	53 - F3
D1	47 - A4
D2	47 - A5
D3	47 - A6
D4	54 - A1
D5	54 - A2
D6	54 - A2
D7	54 - A3
E1	47 - B4
E2	47 - B5
E3	47 - B5
E4	47 - B6
E5	54 - B2
E6	54 - B2
E7	54 - B3
F1	47 - C4
F2	47 - C5
F3	47 - C5
F4	47 - C6
F5	54 - C2
F6	54 - C2
F7	54 - C3
G1	47 - C4
G2	47 - C5
G3	47 - C5
G4	47 - C6
G5	54 - C2
G6	54 - C2
G7	54 - C3
H1	47 - D4
H2	47 - D5
H3	47 - D5
H4	47 - D6
H5	54 - D2
H6	54 - D2
H7	54 - D3
J1	47 - E4
J2	47 - E5
J3	47 - E5
J4	47 - E6
J5	54 - E1
J6	54 - E2
J7	54 - E3
New 814	
A1	47 - F4
A2	47 - F4
A3	47 - F5
A4	47 - F6
A5	54 - F1
A6	54 - F2
A7	54 - F3
B1	48 - A4
B2	48 - A4
B3	48 - A5
B4	48 - A6

NEW-OLD	
New 814	
B5	55 - A1
B6	55 - A2
B7	55 - A3
C1	48 - B4
C2	48 - B4
C3	48 - B5
C4	48 - B6
C5	55 - B1
C6	55 - B2
C7	55 - B3
D1	48 - B4
D2	48 - C4
D3	48 - B5
D4	48 - B6
D5	55 - C1
D6	55 - C2
D7	55 - C3
E1	48 - C3
E2	48 - C4
E3	48 - C5
E4	48 - C6
E5	55 - C1
E6	55 - C2
E7	55 - C3
F1	48 - D3
F2	48 - D4
F3	48 - D5
F4	48 - D6
F5	55 - D1
F6	55 - D2
F7	55 - D3
G1	48 - E3
G2	48 - E4
G3	48 - E5
G4	48 - E6
G5	55 - E1
G6	55 - E2
G7	55 - E3
H1	48 - F3
H2	48 - F4
H3	48 - F5
H4	48 - F6
H5	55 - F1
H6	55 - F2
H7	55 - F3
J1	49 - A3
J2	49 - A4
J3	49 - A5
J4	49 - A6
J5	56 - A1
J6	56 - A2
J7	56 - A3
New 815	
A1	49 - A3
A2	49 - A4
A3	49 - A5
A4	49 - A6
A5	56 - A1
A6	56 - B2
A7	56 - B3
B1	49 - B3
B2	49 - B4
B3	49 - B5
B4	49 - B6
B5	56 - B1
B6	56 - B2
B7	56 - B3
C1	49 - C3
C2	49 - C4
C3	49 - C5
C4	49 - C6
C5	56 - C1
C6	56 - C2
C7	56 - C3
D1	49 - D3
D2	49 - D4
D3	49 - D5
D4	49 - D6
D5	56 - D1
D6	56 - D2
D7	56 - D3
E1	49 - E3
E2	49 - E4
E3	49 - E5
E4	49 - E6
E5	56 - E1
E6	56 - E2
E7	56 - E3
F1	49 - E3
F2	49 - E4
F3	49 - E5
F4	49 - E6
F5	56 - E1
F6	56 - E2
F7	56 - E3
G1	49 - F3
G2	49 - F4
G3	49 - F5
G4	49 - F6
G5	56 - F1
G6	56 - F2
G7	56 - F3
H1	49A - A3
H2	49A - A4
H3	49A - A5
H4	49A - A6
H5	56A - A1

NEW-OLD	
New 815	
H6	56A - A2
H7	56A - A3
J1	49A - B3
J2	49A - B4
J3	49A - B5
J4	49A - B6
J5	56A - B1
J6	56A - B2
J7	56A - B3
New 816	
A1	49A - C3
A2	49A - C4
A3	49A - C5
A4	49A - C6
A5	56A - C1
A6	56A - C2
A7	56A - C3
B1	49A - D3
B2	49A - D4
B3	49A - D5
B4	49A - D6
B5	56A - D1
B6	56A - D2
B7	56A - D3
C1	49A - D3
C2	49A - D4
C3	49A - D5
C4	49A - D6
C5	56A - D1
C6	56A - E2
C7	56A - E3
D1	49A - E3
D2	49A - E4
D3	49A - E5
D4	49A - E6
D5	56A - E1
D6	56A - E2
D7	56A - E3
E1	49A - F3
E2	49A - F4
E3	49A - F5
E4	49A - F6
E5	56A - F1
E6	56A - F2
E7	56A - F3
F1	42A - A5
F2	42A - A5
F3	42A - A6
F4	42A - A6
F5	56B - A1
F6	56B - A1
F7	56B - A2
G1	42A - B5
G2	42A - B5
G3	42A - B6
G4	42A - B6
G5	56B - B1
G6	66B - B1
G7	56B - B2
H1	42A - C5
H2	42A - C5
H3	42A - C6
H4	42A - C6
H5	56B - C1
H6	56B - C1
H7	56B - C2
J1	42A - D5
J2	42A - D5
J3	42A - D6
J4	42A - D6
J5	56B - D1
J6	56B - D1
J7	56B - D2
New 817	
A1	42A - D5
A2	42A - D5
A3	42A - D6
A4	42A - D6
A5	56B - D1
A6	56B - E1
A7	56B - E2
B1	42A - E5
B2	42A - E5
B3	42A - E6
B4	42A - E6
B5	56B - E1
B6	56B - E1
B7	56B - E2
C1	42A - F5
C2	42A - F5
C3	42A - F6
C4	42A - F6
C5	56B - F1
C6	56B - F1
C7	56B - F2
D1	42B - A5
D2	42B - A5
D3	42B - A6
D4	42B - A6
D5	56C - A1
D6	56C - A1
D7	56C - A2
E1	42B - B5
E2	42B - B5
E3	42B - B6
E4	42B - B6
E5	56C - B1

NEW-OLD	
New 817	
E6	56C - B1
E7	56C - B2
F1	42B - B5
F2	42B - B5
F3	42B - B6
F4	42B - C6
F5	56C - C1
F6	56C - C1
F7	56C - C2
G1	42B - C5
G2	42B - C5
G3	42B - C6
G4	42B - C6
G5	42B - C6
G6	56C - C1
G7	56C - C2
H1	42B - D5
H2	42B - D5
H3	42B - D6
H4	42B - D6
H5	42B - D6
H6	56C - D1
H7	56C - D2
J1	42B - E5
J2	42B - E5
J3	42B - E6
J4	42B - E6
J5	42B - E6
J6	56C - E1
J7	56C - E2
New 818	
A1	42B - F5
A2	42B - F5
A3	42B - F6
A4	42B - F6
A5	42B - F6
A6	56C - F1
A7	56C - F1
B1	42C - A5
B2	42C - A5
B3	42C - A5
B4	42C - A6
B5	42C - A6
B6	56D - A1
B7	56D - A1
C1	42C - B5
C2	42C - B5
C3	42C - B5
C4	42C - B6
C5	42C - B6
C6	56D - B1
C7	56D - B1
D1	42C - B5
D2	42C - B5
D3	42C - B5
D4	42C - B6
D5	42C - B6
D6	56D - C1
D7	56D - C1
E1	42C - C5
E2	42C - C5
E3	42C - C5
E4	42C - C6
E5	42C - C6
E6	56D - C1
E7	56D - C1
F1	42C - D5
F2	42C - D5
F3	42C - D5
F4	42C - D6
F5	42C - D6
F6	56D - D1
F7	56D - D1
G1	42C - E5
G2	42C - E5
G3	42C - E5
G4	42C - E6
G5	42C - E6
G6	56D - E1
G7	56D - E1
H1	42C - F5
H2	42C - F5
H3	42C - F5
H4	42C - F6
H5	42C - F6
H6	56D - F1
H7	56D - F1
J1	42C - F5
J2	42C - F5
J3	42D - A5
J4	42D - A6
J5	42D - A6
J6	56E - A1
J7	56E - A1
New 819	
A1	42D - A5
A2	42D - A5
A3	42D - A5
A4	42D - A6
A5	42D - A6
A6	56E - A1
A7	56E - A1
B1	42D - B5
B2	42D - B5
B3	42D - B5
B4	42D - B6
B5	42D - B6

NEW-OLD	
New 819	
B6	56E - B1
B7	56E - B1
C1	42D - C5
C2	42D - C5
C3	42D - C5
C4	42D - C6
C5	42D - C6
C6	56E - C1
C7	56E - C1
D1	42D - D5
D2	42D - D5
D3	42D - D5
D4	42D - D6
D5	42D - D6
D6	56E - D1
D7	56E - D1
E6	56E - E1
E7	56E - E1
F6	56E - F1
F7	56E - F1
G6	42D - E1
G7	42D - E1
H6	42D - E1
H7	42D - E1
J6	42D - F1
J7	42D - F1
New 830	
A7	57 - A4
B1	50 - A5
B2	50 - A5
B3	50 - A6
B4	57 - A2
B5	57 - A2
B6	57 - A3
B7	57 - A4
C1	50 - B5
C2	50 - B5
C3	50 - B6
C4	57 - B2
C5	57 - B2
C6	57 - B3
C7	57 - B4
D1	50 - C5
D2	50 - C5
D3	50 - C6
D4	57 - C1
D5	57 - C2
D6	57 - C3
D7	57 - C4
E1	50 - D5
E2	50 - D5
E3	50 - D6
E4	57 - D1
E5	57 - D2
E6	57 - D3
E7	57 - D4
F1	50 - D5
F2	50 - D5
F3	50 - D6
F4	57 - D1
F5	57 - D2
F6	57 - D3
F7	57 - D4
G1	50 - E4
G2	50 - E5
G3	50 - E6
G4	57 - E1
G5	57 - E2
G6	57 - E3
G7	57 - E4
H1	50 - F4
H2	50 - F5
H3	50 - F6
H4	57 - F1
H5	57 - F2
H6	57 - F3
H7	57 - F4
J1	51 - A4
J2	51 - A5
J3	51 - A6
J4	58 - A1
J5	58 - A2
J6	58 - A3
J7	58 - A4
New 831	
A1	51 - B4
A2	51 - B5
A3	51 - B6
A4	58 - B1
A5	58 - B2
A6	58 - B3
A7	58 - B4
B1	51 - C4
B2	51 - C5
B3	51 - C6
B4	58 - C1
B5	58 - C2
B6	58 - C3
B7	58 - C4
C1	51 - C4
C2	51 - C5
C3	51 - C6
C4	58 - C1
C5	58 - C2
C6	58 - C3
C7	58 - C4
D1	51 - D4

NEW-OLD	
New 831	
D2	51 - D5
D3	51 - D6
D4	58 - D1
D5	58 - D2
D6	58 - D3
D7	58 - D4
E1	51 - E4
E2	51 - E5
E3	51 - E6
E4	58 - E1
E5	58 - E2
E6	58 - E3
E7	58 - E4
F1	51 - F4
F2	51 - F5
F3	51 - F6
F4	58 - F1
F5	58 - F2
F6	58 - F3
F7	58 - F4
G1	52 - A4
G2	52 - A5
G3	52 - A6
G4	59 - A1
G5	59 - A2
G6	59 - A3
G7	59 - A4
H1	52 - B4
H2	52 - B5
H3	52 - B6
H4	59 - B1
H5	59 - B2
H6	59 - B3
H7	59 - B4
J1	52 - B4
J2	52 - B5
J3	52 - B6
J4	59 - B1
J5	59 - B2
J6	59 - B3
J7	59 - B4
New 832	
A1	52 - C4
A2	52 - C5
A3	52 - C6
A4	59 - C1
A5	59 - C2
A6	59 - C3
A7	59 - C4
B1	52 - D4
B2	52 - D5
B3	52 - D6
B4	59 - D1
B5	59 - D2
B6	59 - D3
B7	59 - D4
C1	52 - E4
C2	52 - E5
C3	52 - E6
C4	59 - E1
C5	59 - E2
C6	59 - E3
C7	59 - E4
D1	52 - E4
D2	52 - E5
D3	52 - E6
D4	59 - F1
D5	59 - F2
D6	59 - F3
D7	59 - F4
E1	52 - F4
E2	52 - F5
E3	52 - F6
E4	60 - A1
E5	60 - A2
E6	60 - A3
E7	60 - A4
F1	53 - A4
F2	53 - A5
F3	53 - A6
F4	60 - A1
F5	60 - A2
F6	60 - A3
F7	60 - A4
G1	53 - B4
G2	53 - B5
G3	53 - B6
G4	60 - B1
G5	60 - B2
G6	60 - B3
G7	60 - B4
H1	53 - C4
H2	53 - C5
H3	53 - C6
H4	60 - C1
H5	60 - C2
H6	60 - C3
H7	60 - C4
J1	53 - D4
J2	53 - D5
J3	53 - D6
J4	60 - D1
J5	60 - D2
J6	60 - D3
J7	60 - D4
New 833	
A1	53 - E4

NEW-OLD	
New 833	
A2	53 - E5
A3	53 - E6
A4	60 - E1
A5	60 - E2
A6	60 - E3
A7	60 - E4
B1	53 - E4
B2	53 - E5
B3	53 - E6
B4	60 - E1
B5	60 - E2
B6	60 - E3
B7	60 - E4
C1	53 - F4
C2	53 - F5
C3	53 - F6
C4	60 - F1
C5	60 - F2
C6	60 - F3
C7	60 - F4
D1	54 - A4
D2	54 - A5
D3	54 - A6
D4	61 - A1
D5	61 - A2
D6	61 - A3
D7	61 - A4
E1	54 - B4
E2	54 - B5
E3	54 - B6
E4	61 - B1
E5	61 - B2
E6	61 - B3
E7	61 - B3
F1	54 - C4
F2	54 - C5
F3	54 - C6
F4	61 - C1
F5	61 - C2
F6	61 - C3
F7	61 - C3
G1	54 - D4
G2	54 - D5
G3	54 - D6
G4	61 - D1
G5	61 - D2
G6	61 - D3
G7	61 - D3
H1	54 - D4
H2	54 - D5
H3	54 - D6
H4	61 - D1
H5	61 - D2
H6	61 - D3
H7	61 - D3
J1	54 - E4
J2	54 - E5
J3	54 - E6
J4	61 - E1
J5	61 - E2
J6	61 - E3
J7	61 - E3
New 834	
A1	54 - F4
A2	54 - F5
A3	54 - F6
A4	61 - F1
A5	61 - F2
A6	61 - F3
A7	61 - F3
B1	55 - A4
B2	55 - A5
B3	55 - A6
B4	62 - A1
B5	62 - A2
B6	62 - A3
B7	62 - A3
C1	55 - B4
C2	55 - B5
C3	55 - B6
C4	62 - B1
C5	62 - B2
C6	62 - B3
C7	62 - B3
D1	55 - C4
D2	55 - C5
D3	55 - C6
D4	62 - C1
D5	62 - C2
D6	62 - C3
D7	62 - C3
E1	55 - C4
E2	55 - C5
E3	55 - C6
E4	62 - C1
E5	62 - C2
E6	62 - C2
E7	62 - C3
F1	55 - D4
F2	55 - D5
F3	55 - D6
F4	62 - D1
F5	62 - D2
F6	62 - D2
F7	62 - D3
G1	55 - E4
G2	55 - E5

NEW-OLD	
New 834	
G3	55 - E6
G4	62 - E1
G5	62 - E2
G6	62 - E2
G7	62 - E3
H1	55 - F4
H2	55 - F5
H3	55 - F6
H4	62 - F1
H5	62 - F2
H6	62 - F2
H7	62 - F3
J1	56 - A4
J2	56 - A5
J3	56 - A6
J4	63 - A1
J5	63 - A2
J6	63 - A2
J7	63 - A3
New 835	
A1	56 - B4
A2	56 - B5
A3	56 - B6
A4	63 - B1
A5	63 - B2
A6	63 - B2
A7	63 - B3
B1	56 - B4
B2	56 - B5
B3	56 - B5
B4	56 - B6
B5	63 - B2
B6	63 - B2
B7	63 - B3
C1	56 - C4
C2	56 - C5
C3	56 - C5
C4	56 - C6
C5	63 - C2
C6	63 - C2
C7	63 - C3
D1	56 - D4
D2	56 - D5
D3	56 - D5
D4	56 - D6
D5	63 - D1
D6	63 - D2
D7	63 - D3
E1	56 - E4
E2	56 - E5
E3	56 - E5
E4	56 - E6
E5	63 - E1
E6	63 - E2
E7	63 - E3
F1	56 - E4
F2	56 - F5
F3	56 - F5
F4	56 - F6
F5	63 - F1
F6	63 - F2
F7	63 - F3
G1	56 - F4
G2	56 - F5
G3	56 - F5
G4	56A - A6
G5	63A - A1
G6	63A - A2
G7	63A - A3
H1	56A - A4
H2	56A - A4
H3	56A - A5
H4	56A - A6
H5	63A - A1
H6	63A - B2
H7	63A - B3
J1	56A - B4
J2	56A - B4
J3	56A - B5
J4	56A - B6
J5	63A - B1
J6	63A - B2
J7	63A - B3
New 836	
A1	56A - C4
A2	56A - C4
A3	56A - C5
A4	56A - C6
A5	63A - C1
A6	63A - C2
A7	63A - C3
B1	56A - D4
B2	56A - D4
B3	56A - D5
B4	56A - D6
B5	63A - D1
B6	63A - D2
B7	63A - D3
C1	56A - E4
C2	56A - E4
C3	56A - E5
C4	56A - E6
C5	63A - E1
C6	63A - E2
C7	63A - E3
D1	56A - E4
D2	56A - E4

NEW-OLD	
New 836	
D3	56A - E5
D4	56A - E6
D5	63A - E1
D6	63A - E2
D7	63A - E3
E1	56A - F3
E2	56A - F4
E3	56A - F5
E4	56A - F6
E5	63A - F1
E6	63A - F2
E7	63A - F3
F1	56B - A2
F2	56B - A2
F3	56B - A3
F4	56B - A3
F5	56B - A4
F6	56B - A4
F7	56B - A5
G1	56B - B2
G2	56B - B2
G3	56B - B3
G4	56B - B3
G5	56B - B4
G6	56B - B4
G7	56B - B5
H1	56B - C2
H2	56B - C2
H3	56B - C3
H4	56B - C3
H5	56B - C4
H6	56B - C4
H7	56B - C5
J1	56B - D2
J2	56B - D2
J3	56B - D3
J4	56B - D3
J5	56B - D4
J6	56B - D4
J7	56B - D5
New 837	
A1	56B - E2
A2	56B - E2
A3	56B - E3
A4	56B - E3
A5	56B - E4
A6	56B - E4
A7	56B - E5
B1	56B - E2
B2	56B - E2
B3	56B - E3
B4	56B - E3
B5	56B - E4
B6	56B - F4
B7	56B - F5
C1	56B - F2
C2	56B - F2
C3	56B - F3
C4	56B - F3
C5	56B - F4
C6	56B - F4
C7	56B - F5
D1	56C - A2
D2	56C - A2
D3	56C - A3
D4	56C - A3
D5	56C - A4
D6	56C - A4
D7	56C - A5
E1	56C - B2
E2	56C - B2
E3	56C - B3
E4	56C - B3
E5	56C - B4
E6	56C - B4
E7	56C - B5
F1	56C - C2
F2	56C - C2
F3	56C - C3
F4	56C - C3
F5	56C - C4
F6	56C - C4
F7	56C - C5
G1	56C - C2
G2	56C - C2
G3	56C - D3
G4	56C - D3
G5	56C - D4
G6	56C - D4
G7	56C - D5
H1	56C - D2
H2	56C - D2
H3	56C - D3
H4	56C - D3
H5	56C - D4
H6	56C - D4
H7	56C - D5
J1	56C - E2
J2	56C - E2
J3	56C - E3
J4	56C - E3
J5	56C - E4
J6	56C - E4
J7	56C - E5
New 838	
A1	56C - F2
A2	56C - F2

NEW-OLD	
New 838	
A3	56C - F3
A4	56C - F3
A5	56C - F4
A6	56C - F4
A7	56C - F5
B1	56D - A2
B2	56D - A2
B3	56D - A3
B4	56D - A3
B5	56D - A4
B6	56D - A4
B7	56D - A5
C1	56D - B2
C2	56D - B2
C3	56D - B3
C4	56D - B3
C5	56D - B4
C6	56D - B4
C7	56D - B5
D1	56D - C2
D2	56D - C2
D3	56D - C3
D4	56D - C3
D5	56D - C4
D6	56D - C4
D7	56D - C5
E1	56D - C2
E2	56D - C2
E3	56D - C3
E4	56D - C3
E5	56D - C4
E6	56D - D4
E7	56D - D5
F1	56D - D2
F2	56D - D2
F3	56D - D3
F4	56D - D3
F5	56D - D4
F6	56D - D4
F7	56D - D5
G1	56D - E2
G2	56D - E2
G3	56D - E3
G4	56D - E3
G5	56D - E4
G6	56D - E4
G7	56D - E5
H1	56D - F2
H2	56D - F2
H3	56D - F3
H4	56D - F3
H5	56D - F4
H6	56D - F4
H7	56D - F4
J1	56E - A2
J2	56E - A2
J3	56E - A3
J4	56E - A3
J5	56E - A4
J6	56E - A4
J7	56E - A4
New 839	
A1	56E - A2
A2	56E - A2
A3	56E - A3
A4	56E - A3
A5	56E - A4
A6	56E - A4
A7	56E - A4
B1	56E - B2
B2	56E - B2
B3	56E - B3
B4	56E - B3
B5	56E - B4
B6	56E - B4
B7	56E - B4
C1	56E - C2
C2	56E - C2
C3	56E - C3
C4	56E - C3
C5	56E - C4
C6	56E - C4
C7	56E - C4
D1	56E - D2
D2	56E - D2
D3	56E - D3
D4	56E - D3
D5	56E - D4
D6	56E - D4
D7	56E - D4
E1	56E - E2
E2	56E - E2
E3	56E - E3
E4	56E - E3
E5	56E - E4
E6	56E - E4
E7	56E - E4
F1	56E - F2
F2	56E - F2
F3	56E - F3
F4	56E - F3
F5	56E - F4
F6	56E - F4
F7	56E - F4
G1	42D - E2
G2	42D - E2
G3	42D - E3

NEW-OLD	
New 839	
G4	42D - E3
G5	42D - E4
G6	42D - E4
G7	42D - E4
H1	42D - E2
H2	42D - E2
H3	42D - F3
H4	42D - F3
H5	42D - F4
H6	42D - F4
H7	42D - F4
J1	42D - F2
J2	42D - F2
J4	42D - F3
New 850	
A1	57 - A5
A2	57 - A6
B1	57 - A5
B2	57 - A6
C1	57 - B5
C2	57 - B6
D1	57 - C5
D2	57 - C6
E1	57 - D5
E2	57 - D6
F1	57 - D5
F2	57 - D6
G1	57 - E5
G2	57 - E6
H1	57 - F5
H2	57 - F6
J1	58 - A5
J2	58 - A6
J3	63F - A1
J4	63F - A2
J5	63F - A3
J6	63F - A3
J7	63F - A4
New 851	
A1	58 - B5
A2	58 - B6
A3	63F - B1
A4	63F - B2
A5	63F - B3
A6	63F - B3
A7	63F - B4
B1	58 - C5
B2	58 - C6
B3	63F - C1
B4	63F - C2
B5	63F - C3
B6	63F - C3
B7	63F - C4
C1	58 - C5
C2	58 - D6
C3	63F - D1
C4	63F - D2
C5	63F - D2
C6	63F - D3
C7	63F - D4
D1	58 - D5
D2	58 - D6
D3	63F - D1
D4	63F - D2
D5	63F - D2
D6	63F - D3
D7	63F - D4
E1	58 - E5
E2	58 - E6
E3	63F - E1
E4	63F - E2
E5	63F - E2
E6	63F - E3
E7	63F - E4
F1	58 - F5
F2	58 - F6
F3	63F - F1
F4	63F - F2
F5	63F - F2
F6	63F - F3
F7	63F - F4
G1	59 - A5
G2	59 - A5
G3	64 - A1
G4	64 - A2
G5	64 - A2
G6	64 - A3
G7	64 - A4
H1	59 - B5
H2	59 - B5
H3	59 - B6
H4	64 - B2
H5	64 - B2
H6	64 - B3
H7	64 - B4
J1	59 - B5
J2	59 - B5
J3	59 - B6
J4	64 - B1
J5	64 - C2
J6	64 - C3
J7	64 - C4
New 852	
A1	59 - C5
A2	59 - C5
A3	59 - C6
A4	64 - C1

NEW-OLD	
New 852	
A5	64 - C2
A6	64 - C3
A7	64 - C4
B1	59 - D5
B2	59 - D5
B3	59 - D6
B4	64 - D1
B5	64 - D2
B6	64 - D3
B7	64 - D4
C1	59 - E5
C2	59 - E5
C3	59 - E6
C4	64 - E1
C5	64 - E2
C6	64 - E3
C7	64 - E4
D1	59 - F5
D2	59 - F5
D3	59 - F6
D4	64 - F1
D5	64 - F2
D6	64 - F3
D7	64 - F4
E1	60 - A4
E2	60 - A5
E3	60 - A6
E4	65 - A1
E5	65 - A2
E6	65 - A3
E7	65 - A4
F1	60 - B4
F2	60 - B5
F3	60 - B6
F4	65 - B1
F5	65 - B2
F6	65 - B3
F7	65 - B4
G1	60 - B4
G2	60 - B5
G3	60 - B6
G4	65 - B1
G5	65 - B2
G6	65 - B3
G7	65 - B4
H1	60 - C4
H2	60 - C5
H3	60 - C6
H4	65 - C1
H5	65 - C2
H6	65 - C3
H7	65 - C4
J1	60 - D4
J2	60 - D5
J3	60 - D6
J4	65 - D1
J5	65 - D2
J6	65 - D3
J7	65 - D4
New 853	
A1	60 - E4
A2	60 - E5
A3	60 - E6
A4	65 - E1
A5	65 - E2
A6	65 - E3
A7	65 - E4
B1	60 - E4
B2	60 - E5
B3	60 - E6
B4	65 - E1
B5	65 - E2
B6	65 - F3
B7	65 - F4
C1	60 - F4
C2	60 - F5
C3	60 - F6
C4	65 - F1
C5	65 - F2
C6	65 - F3
C7	65 - F4
D1	61 - A4
D2	61 - A5
D3	61 - A6
D4	66 - A1
D5	66 - A2
D6	66 - A3
D7	66 - A4
E1	61 - B4
E2	61 - B5
E3	61 - B6
E4	66 - B1
E5	66 - B2
E6	66 - B3
E7	66 - B4
F1	61 - C4
F2	61 - C5
F3	61 - C6
F4	66 - C1
F5	66 - C2
F6	66 - C3
F7	66 - C4
G1	61 - D4
G2	61 - D5
G3	61 - D6
G4	66 - D1
G5	66 - D2

NEW-OLD	
New 853	
G6	66 - D3
G7	66 - D4
H1	61 - D4
H2	61 - D5
H3	61 - D6
H4	66 - D1
H5	66 - D2
H6	66 - E3
H7	66 - E4
J1	61 - E4
J2	61 - E5
J3	61 - E6
J4	66 - E1
J5	66 - E2
J6	66 - E3
J7	66 - E4
New 854	
A1	61 - F4
A2	61 - F5
A3	61 - F6
A4	66 - F1
A5	66 - F2
A6	66 - F3
A7	66 - F4
B1	62 - A4
B2	62 - A5
B3	62 - A6
B4	67 - A1
B5	67 - A2
B6	67 - A3
B7	67 - A4
C1	62 - B4
C2	62 - B5
C3	62 - B6
C4	67 - B1
C5	67 - B2
C6	67 - B3
C7	67 - B4
D1	62 - C4
D2	62 - C5
D3	62 - C6
D4	67 - C1
D5	67 - C2
D6	67 - C3
D7	67 - C4
E1	62 - C4
E2	62 - C5
E3	62 - D6
E4	67 - D1
E5	67 - D2
E6	67 - D3
E7	67 - D4
F1	62 - D4
F2	62 - D5
F3	62 - D6
F4	67 - D1
F5	67 - D2
F6	67 - D3
F7	67 - D4
G1	62 - E4
G2	62 - E5
G3	62 - E6
G4	67 - E1
G5	67 - E2
G6	67 - E3
G7	67 - E4
H1	62 - F4
H2	62 - F5
H3	62 - F6
H4	67 - F1
H5	67 - F2
H6	67 - F3
H7	67 - F4
J1	63 - A4
J2	63 - A5
J3	63 - A6
J4	68 - A1
J5	68 - A2
J6	68 - A3
J7	68 - A4
New 855	
A1	63 - B4
A2	63 - B5
A3	63 - B6
A4	68 - B1
A5	68 - B2
A6	68 - B3
A7	68 - B4
B1	63 - B4
B2	63 - C5
B3	63 - C6
B4	68 - C1
B5	68 - C2
B6	68 - C3
B7	68 - C4
C1	63 - C4
C2	63 - C5
C3	63 - C6
C4	68 - C1
C5	68 - C2
C6	68 - C3
C7	68 - C4
D1	63 - D4
D2	63 - D5
D3	63 - D6
D4	68 - D1
D5	68 - D2

NEW-OLD	
New 855	
D6	68 - D3
D7	68 - D4
E1	63 - E4
E2	63 - E5
E3	63 - E6
E4	68 - E1
E5	68 - E2
E6	68 - E3
E7	68 - E4
F1	63 - F4
F2	63 - F5
F3	63 - F6
F4	68 - F1
F5	68 - F2
F6	68 - F3
F7	68 - F4
G1	63A - A4
G2	63A - A5
G3	63A - A6
G4	68A - A1
G5	68A - A2
G6	68A - A3
G7	68A - A4
H1	63A - B4
H2	63A - B5
H3	63A - B6
H4	68A - B1
H5	68A - B2
H6	68A - B3
H7	68A - B4
J1	63A - B4
J2	63A - B5
J3	63A - B6
J4	68A - B1
J5	68A - B2
J6	68A - B3
J7	68A - B3
New 856	
A1	63A - C4
A2	63A - C5
A3	63A - C6
A4	68A - C1
A5	68A - C2
A6	68A - C3
A7	68A - C3
B1	63A - D4
B2	63A - D5
B3	63A - D6
B4	68A - D1
B5	68A - D2
B6	68A - D3
B7	68A - D3
C1	63A - E4
C2	63A - E5
C3	63A - E6
C4	68A - E1
C5	68A - E2
C6	68A - E3
C7	68A - E3
D1	63A - E4
D2	63A - E5
D3	63A - F6
D4	68A - F1
D5	68A - F2
D6	68A - F3
D7	68A - F3
E1	63A - F4
E2	63A - F5
E3	56B - A6
E4	68A - F1
E5	68B - A1
E6	68A - F3
E7	68B - A2
F1	56B - A5
F2	56B - A6
F3	56B - A6
F4	68B - A1
F5	68B - A1
F6	68B - A1
F7	68B - A2
G1	56B - B5
G2	56B - B6
G3	56B - B6
G4	68B - B1
G5	68B - B1
G6	68B - B1
G7	68B - B2
H1	56B - C5
H2	56B - C6
H3	56B - C6
H4	68B - C1
H5	68B - C1
H6	68B - C1
H7	68B - C2
J1	56B - D5
J2	56B - D6
J3	56B - D6
J4	56B - D6
J5	68B - D1
J6	68B - D1
J7	68B - D2
New 857	
A1	56B - E5
A2	56B - E6
A3	56B - E6
A4	56B - E6
A5	68B - E1

1998 SANTA CLARA NEW TO OLD Page Conversion List

NEW-OLD	
New 857	
A6	68B - E1
A7	68B - E2
B1	56B - F5
B2	56B - F6
B3	56B - F6
B4	56B - F6
B5	68B - F1
B6	68B - F1
B7	68B - F2
C1	56B - F5
C2	56B - F6
C3	56B - F6
C4	56B - F6
C5	68B - F1
C6	68B - F1
C7	68B - F2
D1	56C - A5
D2	56C - A5
D3	56C - A6
D4	56C - A6
D5	68C - A1
D6	68C - A1
D7	68C - A2
E1	56C - B5
E2	56C - B5
E3	56C - B6
E4	56C - B6
E5	68C - B1
E6	68C - B1
E7	68C - B2
F1	56C - C5
F2	56C - C5
F3	56C - C6
F4	56C - C6
F5	68C - C1
F6	68C - C1
F7	68C - C2
G1	56C - D5
G2	56C - D5
G3	56C - D6
G4	56C - D6
G5	68C - D1
G6	68C - D1
G7	68C - D2
H1	56C - D5
H2	56C - D5
H3	56C - D6
H4	56C - D6
H5	68C - D1
H6	68C - D1
H7	68C - D2
J1	56C - E5
J2	56C - E5
J3	56C - E6
J4	56C - E6
J5	68C - E1
J6	68C - E1
J7	68C - E2
New 858	
A1	56C - F5
A2	56C - F5
A3	56C - F6
A4	56C - F6
A5	68C - F1
A6	68C - F1
A7	68C - F2
B1	56D - A5
B2	56D - A5
B3	56D - A6
B4	56D - A6
B5	68D - A1
B6	68D - A1
B7	68D - A2
C1	56D - B5
C2	56D - B5
C3	56D - B6
C4	56D - B6
C5	68D - A1
C6	68D - A1
C7	68D - A2
D1	56D - C5
D2	56D - C5
D3	56D - C6
D4	56D - C6
D5	68D - B1
D6	68D - B1
D7	68D - B2
E1	56D - D5
E2	56D - D5
E3	56D - D6
E4	56D - D6
E5	68D - B1
E6	68D - B1
E7	68D - B2
F1	56D - D5
F2	56D - D5
F3	56D - D6
F4	56D - D6
F5	68D - B1
F6	68D - B1
F7	68D - B2
G1	56D - E5
G2	56D - E5
G3	56D - E6
G4	56D - E6
G5	68D - C1
G6	68D - C1

NEW-OLD	
New 858	
G7	68D - C2
H1	56D - F5
H2	56D - F5
H3	56D - F6
H4	56D - F6
H5	68D - C1
H6	68D - C1
H7	68D - C2
J1	56E - A5
J2	56E - A5
J3	56E - A6
J4	56E - A6
J5	68D - D1
J6	68D - D1
J7	68D - D2
New 859	
A1	56E - A5
A2	56E - A5
A3	56E - A6
A4	56E - B6
A5	68D - D1
A6	68D - D1
A7	68D - D2
B1	56E - B5
B2	56E - B5
B3	56E - B6
B4	56E - B6
B5	68D - D1
B6	68D - D1
B7	68D - D2
C1	56E - C5
C2	56E - C5
C3	56E - C6
C4	56E - C6
C5	68D - E1
C6	68D - E1
C7	68D - E2
D1	56E - D5
D2	56E - D5
D3	56E - D6
D4	56E - D6
D5	68D - E1
D6	68D - E1
D7	68D - E2
E1	56E - E5
E2	56E - E5
E3	56E - E6
E4	56E - E6
E5	68D - F1
E6	68D - F1
E7	68D - F2
F1	56E - F5
F2	56E - F5
F3	56E - F6
F4	56E - F6
F5	68D - F1
F6	68D - F1
F7	68D - F2
G1	42D - E5
G2	42D - E5
G3	42D - E6
G4	42D - E6
H1	42D - F5
H2	42D - F5
H3	42D - F6
H4	42D - F6
New 871	
A1	63F - B5
A2	63F - B6
A3	68E - B1
A4	68E - B2
A5	68E - B3
A6	68E - B4
A7	68E - B4
B1	63F - C5
B2	63F - C6
B3	68E - C1
B4	68E - C2
B5	68E - C3
B6	68E - C4
B7	68E - C4
C1	63F - D5
C2	63F - D6
C3	68E - D1
C4	68E - D2
C5	68E - D3
C6	68E - D4
C7	68E - D4
D1	63F - D5
D2	63F - D6
D3	68E - D1
D4	68E - D2
D5	68E - D3
D6	68E - D4
D7	68E - D4
E1	63F - E5
E2	63F - E6
E3	68E - E1
E4	68E - E2
E5	68E - E3
E6	68E - E4
E7	68E - E4
F1	63F - F5
F2	63F - F6
F3	68E - F1
F4	68E - F2
F5	68E - F3

NEW-OLD	
New 871	
F6	68E - F4
F7	68E - F4
G1	64 - A5
G2	64 - A6
G3	69 - A1
G4	69 - A2
G5	69 - A3
G6	69 - A4
G7	69 - A4
H1	64 - B5
H2	64 - B6
H3	69 - B1
H4	69 - B2
H5	69 - B3
H6	69 - B4
H7	69 - B4
J1	64 - C5
J2	64 - C6
J3	69 - C1
J4	69 - C2
J5	69 - C3
J6	69 - C4
J7	69 - C4
New 872	
A1	64 - C5
A2	64 - C6
A3	69 - C1
A4	69 - C2
A5	69 - C3
A6	69 - C4
A7	69 - D4
B1	64 - D5
B2	64 - D6
B3	69 - D1
B4	69 - D2
B5	69 - D3
B6	69 - D3
B7	69 - D4
C1	64 - E5
C2	64 - E6
C3	69 - E1
C4	69 - E2
C5	69 - E3
C6	69 - E3
C7	69 - E4
D1	64 - F5
D2	64 - F6
D3	69 - F1
D4	69 - F2
D5	69 - F3
D6	69 - F3
D7	69 - F4
E1	65 - A5
E2	65 - A6
E3	70 - A1
E4	70 - A2
E5	70 - A3
E6	70 - A3
E7	70 - A4
F1	65 - B5
F2	65 - B6
F3	70 - B1
F4	70 - B2
F5	70 - B3
F6	70 - B3
F7	70 - B4
G1	65 - B5
G2	65 - B6
G3	70 - B1
G4	70 - B2
G5	70 - B3
G6	70 - B3
G7	70 - C4
H1	65 - C5
H2	65 - C6
H3	70 - C1
H4	70 - C2
H5	70 - C3
H6	70 - C3
H7	70 - C4
J1	65 - D5
J2	65 - D6
J3	70 - D1
J4	70 - D2
J5	70 - D3
J6	70 - D3
J7	70 - D4
New 873	
A1	65 - E5
A2	65 - E6
A3	70 - E1
A4	70 - E2
A5	70 - E3
A6	70 - E3
A7	70 - E4
B1	65 - F5
B2	65 - F6
B3	70 - F1
B4	70 - F2
B5	70 - F2
B6	70 - F3
B7	70 - F4
C1	65 - F5
C2	66 - A6
C3	71 - A1
C4	71 - A2
C5	71 - A2

NEW-OLD	
New 873	
C6	71 - A3
C7	71 - A4
D1	66 - A5
D2	66 - A6
D3	71 - A1
D4	71 - A2
D5	71 - A2
D6	71 - A3
D7	71 - A4
E1	66 - B5
E2	66 - B6
E3	71 - B1
E4	71 - B2
E5	71 - B2
E6	71 - B3
E7	71 - B4
F1	66 - C5
F2	66 - C6
F3	71 - C1
F4	71 - C2
F5	71 - C2
F6	71 - C3
F7	71 - C4
G1	66 - D5
G2	66 - D6
G3	71 - D1
G4	71 - D2
G5	71 - D2
G6	71 - D3
G7	71 - D4
H1	66 - E5
H2	66 - E6
H3	66 - E6
H4	71 - E2
H5	71 - E2
H6	71 - E3
H7	71 - E4
J1	66 - E5
J2	66 - E6
J3	66 - E6
J4	71 - E2
J5	71 - E2
J6	71 - E3
J7	71 - E4
New 874	
A1	66 - F5
A2	66 - F6
A3	66 - F6
A4	71 - F2
A5	71 - F2
A6	71 - F3
A7	71 - F4
B1	67 - A5
B2	67 - A5
B3	67 - A6
B4	72 - A1
B5	72 - A2
B6	72 - A3
B7	72 - A4
C1	67 - B5
C2	67 - B5
C3	67 - B6
C4	72 - B1
C5	72 - B2
C6	72 - B3
C7	72 - B4
D1	67 - C5
D2	67 - C5
D3	67 - C6
D4	72 - C1
D5	72 - C2
D6	72 - C3
D7	72 - C4
E1	67 - D5
E2	67 - D5
E3	67 - D6
E4	72 - D1
E5	72 - D2
E6	72 - D3
E7	72 - D4
F1	67 - D5
F2	67 - D5
F3	67 - D6
F4	72 - D1
F5	72 - D2
F6	72 - D3
F7	72 - D4
G1	67 - E5
G2	67 - E5
G3	67 - E6
G4	72 - E1
G5	72 - E2
G6	72 - E3
G7	72 - E4
H1	67 - F5
H2	67 - F5
H3	67 - F6
H4	72 - F1
H5	72 - F2
H6	72 - F3
H7	72 - F4
J1	68 - A4
J2	68 - A5
J3	68 - A6
J4	72A - A1
J5	72A - A2
J6	72A - A3

NEW-OLD	
New 874	
J7	72A - A4
New 875	
A1	68 - B4
A2	68 - B5
A3	68 - B6
A4	72A - B1
A5	72A - B2
A6	72A - B3
A7	72A - B4
B1	68 - C4
B2	68 - C5
B3	68 - C6
B4	72A - C1
B5	72A - C2
B6	72A - C3
B7	72A - C4
C1	68 - C4
C2	68 - C5
C3	68 - C6
C4	72A - C1
C5	72A - C2
C6	72A - C3
C7	72A - C4
D1	68 - D4
D2	68 - D5
D3	68 - D6
D4	72A - D1
D5	72A - D2
D6	72A - D3
D7	72A - D4
E1	68 - E4
E2	68 - E5
E3	68 - E6
E4	72A - E1
E5	72A - E2
E6	72A - E3
E7	72A - E4
F1	68 - F4
F2	68 - F5
F3	68 - F6
F4	72A - F1
F5	72A - F2
F6	72A - F3
F7	72A - F4
G1	68A - A4
G2	68A - A5
G3	68A - A6
G4	72B - A1
G5	72B - A2
G6	72B - A3
G7	72B - A4
H1	68A - B4
H2	68A - B5
H3	68A - B6
H4	72B - B1
H5	72B - B2
H6	72B - B3
H7	72B - B4
J1	68A - B4
J2	68A - B5
J3	68A - B6
J4	72B - B1
J5	72B - B2
J6	72B - B3
J7	72B - B4
New 876	
A1	68A - C4
A2	68A - C5
A3	68A - C6
A4	72B - C1
A5	72B - C2
A6	72B - C3
A7	72B - C4
B1	68A - D4
B2	68A - D5
B3	68A - D6
B4	72B - D1
B5	72B - D2
B6	72B - D3
B7	72B - D4
C1	68A - E4
C2	68A - E5
C3	68A - E6
C4	72B - E1
C5	72B - E2
C6	72B - E3
C7	72B - E4
D1	68A - F4
D2	68A - F5
D3	68A - F6
D4	72B - F1
D5	72B - F2
D6	72B - F3
D7	72B - F4
E1	68B - A2
E2	68B - A3
E3	68B - A3
E4	68B - A4
E5	68B - A4
E6	72B - F3
E7	68B - A5
F1	68B - A2
F2	68B - A3
F3	68B - A3
F4	68B - A4
F5	68B - A4
F6	68B - A5

NEW-OLD	
New 876	
F7	68B - A5
G1	68B - B2
G2	68B - B3
G3	68B - B3
G4	68B - B4
G5	68B - B4
G6	68B - B5
G7	68B - B5
H1	68B - C2
H2	68B - C3
H3	68B - C3
H4	68B - C4
H5	68B - C4
H6	68B - C5
H7	68B - C5
J1	68B - D2
J2	68B - D3
J3	68B - D3
J4	68B - D4
J5	68B - D4
J6	68B - D5
J7	68B - D5
New 877	
A1	68B - E2
A2	68B - E3
A3	68B - E3
A4	68B - E4
A5	68B - E4
A6	68B - E5
A7	68B - E5
B1	68B - F2
B2	68B - F3
B3	68B - F3
B4	68B - F4
B5	68B - F4
B6	68B - F5
B7	68B - F5
C1	68B - F2
C2	68B - F3
C3	68B - F3
C4	68B - F4
C5	68B - F4
C6	68B - F5
C7	68B - F5
D1	68C - A2
D2	68C - A3
D3	68C - A3
D4	68C - A4
D5	68C - A4
D6	68C - A5
D7	68C - A6
E1	68C - B2
E2	68C - B3
E3	68C - B3
E4	68C - B4
E5	68C - B4
E6	68C - B5
E7	68C - B5
F1	68C - C2
F2	68C - C3
F3	68C - C3
F4	68C - C4
F5	68C - C4
F6	68C - C4
F7	68C - C5
G1	68C - D2
G2	68C - D3
G3	68C - D3
G4	68C - D4
G5	68C - D4
G6	68C - D4
G7	68C - D5
H1	68C - D2
H2	68C - D3
H3	68C - E3
H4	68C - E4
H5	68C - E4
H6	68C - E4
H7	68C - E5
J1	68C - E2
J2	68C - E3
J3	68C - E3
J4	68C - E4
J5	68C - E4
J6	68C - E4
J7	68C - E5
New 878	
A1	68C - F2
A2	68C - F3
A3	68C - F3
A4	68C - F4
A5	68C - F4
A6	68C - F4
A7	68C - F5
B1	68D - A2
B2	68D - A3
B3	68D - A3
B4	68D - A4
B5	68D - A4
B6	68D - A5
B7	68D - A5
C1	68D - A2
C2	68D - A3
C3	68D - A3
C4	68D - A4
C5	68D - A4
C6	68D - A5

NEW-OLD	
New 878	
C7	68D - A5
D1	68D - B2
D2	68D - B3
D3	68D - B3
D4	68D - B4
D5	68D - B4
D6	68D - B4
D7	68D - B5
E1	68D - B2
E2	68D - B3
E3	68D - B3
E4	68D - B4
E5	68D - B4
E6	68D - B4
E7	68D - B5
F1	68D - B2
F2	68D - B3
F3	68D - B3
F4	68D - B4
F5	68D - B4
F6	68D - C4
F7	68D - C5
G1	68D - C2
G2	68D - C3
G3	68D - C3
G4	68D - C4
G5	68D - C4
G6	68D - C4
G7	68D - C5
H1	68D - C2
H2	68D - C3
H3	68D - C3
H4	68D - C4
H5	68D - C4
H6	68D - C4
H7	68D - C5
J1	68D - D2
J2	68D - D3
J3	68D - D3
J4	68D - D4
J5	68D - D4
J6	68D - D4
J7	68D - D5
New 879	
A1	68D - D2
A2	68D - D3
A3	68D - D3
A4	68D - D4
A5	68D - D4
A6	68D - D4
A7	68D - D5
B1	68D - D2
B2	68D - D3
B3	68D - E3
B4	68D - E4
B5	68D - E4
B6	68D - E4
B7	68D - E5
C1	68D - E2
C2	68D - E3
C3	68D - E3
C4	68D - E3
C5	68D - E4
C6	68D - E4
C7	68D - E5
D1	68D - E2
D2	68D - E3
D3	68D - E3
D4	68D - E3
D5	68D - E4
D6	68D - E4
D7	68D - E5
E1	68D - F2
E2	68D - F3
E3	68D - F3
E4	68D - F3
E5	68D - F4
E6	68D - F4
E7	68D - F5
F1	68D - F2
F2	68D - F3
F3	68D - F3
F4	68D - F3
F5	68D - F4
F6	68D - F4
F7	68D - F5
G4	78D - A1
G5	78D - A1
G6	78D - A2
G7	78D - A2
H4	78D - A1
H5	78D - A1
H6	78D - A2
H7	78D - A2
J4	78D - B1
J5	78D - B1
J6	78D - B2
J7	78D - B2
New 880	
A4	78D - B1
A5	78D - B1
A6	78D - B2
A7	78D - B2
B4	78D - B1
B5	78D - B1
B6	78D - B2
B7	78D - B2

NEW-OLD	
New 880	
C4	78D - C1
C5	78D - C1
C6	78D - C1
C7	78D - C2
D4	78D - C1
D5	78D - C1
D6	78D - C1
D7	78D - C2
New 892	
A1	69 - D5
A2	69 - D6
A3	72K - D1
A4	72K - D2
A5	72K - D3
A6	72K - D4
A7	72K - D5
B1	69 - D5
B2	69 - D6
B3	72K - D1
B4	72K - D2
B5	72K - D3
B6	72K - D4
B7	72K - D5
C1	69 - E5
C2	69 - E6
C3	72K - E1
C4	72K - E2
C5	72K - E3
C6	72K - E4
C7	72K - E5
D1	69 - F5
D2	69 - F6
D3	72K - F1
D4	72K - F2
D5	72K - F3
D6	72K - F4
D7	72K - F5
E1	70 - A5
E2	70 - A6
E3	73 - A1
E4	73 - A2
E5	73 - A3
E6	73 - A4
E7	73 - A5
F1	70 - B5
F2	70 - B6
F3	73 - B1
F4	73 - B2
F5	73 - B3
F6	73 - B4
F7	73 - B5
G1	70 - C5
G2	70 - C6
G3	73 - C1
G4	73 - C2
G5	73 - C3
G6	73 - C4
G7	73 - C5
H1	70 - C5
H2	70 - C6
H3	73 - C1
H4	73 - C2
H5	73 - C3
H6	73 - C4
H7	73 - C5
J1	70 - D5
J2	70 - D6
J3	73 - D1
J4	73 - D2
J5	73 - D3
J6	73 - D4
J7	73 - D5
New 893	
A1	70 - E5
A2	70 - E6
A3	73 - E1
A4	73 - E2
A5	73 - E3
A6	73 - E4
A7	73 - E5
B1	70 - F5
B2	70 - F6
B3	73 - F1
B4	73 - F2
B5	73 - F3
B6	73 - F4
B7	73 - F5
C1	71 - A5
C2	71 - A6
C3	74 - A1
C4	74 - A2
C5	74 - A3
C6	74 - A4
C7	74 - A4
D1	71 - A5
D2	71 - B6
D3	74 - B1
D4	74 - B2
D5	74 - B3
D6	74 - B4
D7	74 - B4
E1	71 - B5
E2	71 - B6
E3	74 - B1
E4	74 - B2
E5	74 - B3
E6	74 - B4

NEW-OLD	
New 893	
E7	74 - B4
F1	71 - C5
F2	71 - C6
F3	74 - C1
F4	74 - C2
F5	74 - C3
F6	74 - C4
F7	74 - C4
G1	71 - D5
G2	71 - D6
G3	74 - D1
G4	74 - D2
G5	74 - D3
G6	74 - D4
G7	74 - D4
H1	71 - E5
H2	71 - E6
H3	74 - E1
H4	74 - E2
H5	74 - E3
H6	74 - E4
H7	74 - E4
J1	71 - E5
J2	71 - E6
J3	74 - E1
J4	74 - E2
J5	74 - E3
J6	74 - E4
J7	74 - F4
New 894	
A1	71 - F5
A2	71 - F6
A3	74 - F1
A4	74 - F2
A5	74 - F3
A6	74 - F4
A7	74 - F4
B1	72 - A5
B2	72 - A6
B3	75 - A1
B4	75 - A2
B5	75 - A3
B6	75 - A4
B7	75 - A4
C1	72 - B5
C2	72 - B6
C3	75 - B1
C4	75 - B2
C5	75 - B3
C6	75 - B4
C7	75 - B4
D1	72 - C5
D2	72 - C6
D3	75 - C1
D4	75 - C2
D5	75 - C3
D6	75 - C4
D7	75 - C4
E1	72 - D5
E2	72 - D6
E3	75 - D1
E4	75 - D2
E5	75 - D3
E6	75 - D3
E7	75 - D4
F1	72 - D5
F2	72 - D6
F3	75 - D1
F4	75 - D2
F5	75 - E3
F6	75 - E3
F7	75 - E4
G1	72 - E5
G2	72 - E6
G3	75 - E1
G4	75 - E2
G5	75 - E3
G6	75 - E3
G7	75 - E4
H1	72 - F5
H2	72 - F6
H3	75 - F1
H4	75 - F2
H5	75 - F3
H6	75 - F3
H7	75 - F4
J1	72A - A5
J2	72A - A6
J3	76 - A1
J4	76 - A2
J5	76 - A3
J6	76 - A3
J7	76 - A4
New 895	
A1	72A - B5
A2	72A - B6
A3	76 - B1
A4	76 - B2
A5	76 - B3
A6	76 - B3
A7	76 - B4
B1	72A - C5
B2	72A - C6
B3	76 - C1
B4	76 - C2
B5	76 - C3
B6	76 - C3

NEW-OLD	
New 895	
B7	76 - C4
C1	72A - C5
C2	72A - C6
C3	76 - C1
C4	76 - C2
C5	76 - C3
C6	76 - D3
C7	76 - D4
D1	72A - D5
D2	72A - D6
D3	76 - D1
D4	76 - D2
D5	76 - D3
D6	76 - D3
D7	76 - D4
E1	72A - E5
E2	72A - E6
E3	76 - E1
E4	76 - E2
E5	76 - E2
E6	76 - E3
E7	76 - E4
F1	72A - F5
F2	72A - F6
F3	76 - F1
F4	76 - F2
F5	76 - F2
F6	76 - F3
F7	76 - F4
G1	72B - A5
G2	72B - A6
G3	77 - A1
G4	77 - A2
G5	77 - A2
G6	77 - A3
G7	77 - A4
H1	72B - B5
H2	72B - B5
H3	72B - B6
H4	77 - B2
H5	77 - B2
H6	77 - B3
H7	77 - B4
J1	72B - B5
J2	72B - C5
J3	72B - C6
J4	77 - C2
J5	77 - C2
J6	77 - C3
J7	77 - C4
New 896	
A1	72B - C5
A2	72B - C5
A3	72B - C6
A4	77 - C2
A5	77 - C2
A6	77 - C3
A7	77 - C4
B1	72B - D5
B2	72B - D5
B3	72B - D6
B4	77 - D2
B5	77 - D2
B6	77 - D3
B7	77 - D4
C1	72B - E5
C2	72B - E5
C3	72B - E6
C4	77 - E1
C5	77 - E2
C6	77 - E3
C7	77 - E4
D1	72B - F5
D2	72B - F5
D3	72B - F6
D4	77 - F1
D5	77 - F2
D6	77 - F3
D7	77 - F4
E1	68B - A5
E2	68B - A6
E3	68B - A6
E4	78 - A1
E5	78 - A2
E6	78 - A3
E7	78 - A4
F1	68B - A5
F2	68B - A6
F3	68B - A6
F4	78 - A1
F5	78 - B2
F6	78 - B3
F7	78 - B4
G1	68B - B5
G2	68B - B6
G3	68B - B6
G4	78 - B1
G5	78 - B2
G6	78 - B3
G7	78 - B4
H1	68B - C5
H2	68B - C6
H3	68B - C6
H4	78 - C1
H5	78 - C2
H6	78 - C3
H7	78 - C4

NEW-OLD	
New 896	
J1	68B - D5
J2	68B - D6
J3	68B - D6
J4	78 - D1
J5	78 - D2
J6	78 - D3
J7	78 - D4
New 897	
A1	68B - E5
A2	68B - E6
A3	68B - E6
A4	78 - E1
A5	78 - E2
A6	78 - E3
A7	78 - E4
B1	68B - F5
B2	68B - F6
B3	68B - F6
B4	78 - F1
B5	78 - F2
B6	78 - F3
B7	78 - F4
C1	68B - F5
C2	68B - F6
C3	68B - F6
C4	78 - F1
C5	78 - F2
C6	78A - A3
C7	78A - A4
D1	68C - A5
D2	68C - A6
D3	68C - A6
D4	78A - A1
D5	78A - A2
D6	78A - A3
D7	78A - A4
E1	68C - B5
E2	68C - B6
E3	68C - B6
E4	78A - B1
E5	78A - B2
E6	78A - B3
E7	78A - B4
F1	68C - C5
F2	68C - C6
F3	68C - C6
F4	78A - C1
F5	78A - C2
F6	78A - C3
F7	78A - C4
G1	68C - D5
G2	68C - D6
G3	68C - D6
G4	78A - D1
G5	78A - D2
G6	78A - D3
G7	78A - D4
H1	68C - E5
H2	68C - E6
H3	68C - E6
H4	78A - E1
H5	78A - E2
H6	78A - E3
H7	78A - E4
J1	68C - E5
J2	68C - E6
J3	68C - E6
J4	78A - E1
J5	78A - E2
J6	78A - E3
J7	78A - E4
New 898	
A1	68C - F5
A2	68C - F6
A3	68C - F6
A4	78A - F1
A5	78A - F2
A6	78A - F3
A7	78A - F4
B1	68D - A5
B2	68D - A6
B3	68D - A6
B4	78B - A1
B5	78B - A1
B6	78B - A2
B7	78B - A2
C1	68D - A5
C2	68D - A6
C3	68D - A6
C4	78B - B1
C5	78B - B1
C6	78B - B2
C7	78B - B2
D1	68D - B5
D2	68D - B6
D3	68D - B6
D4	78B - C1
D5	78B - C1
D6	78B - C2
D7	78B - C2
E1	68D - B5
E2	68D - B6
E3	68D - B6
E4	78B - D1
E5	78B - D1
E6	78B - D2
E7	78B - D2

NEW-OLD	
New 898	
F1	68D - C5
F2	68D - C6
F3	68D - C6
F4	78B - E1
F5	78B - E1
F6	78B - E2
F7	78B - E2
G1	68D - C5
G2	68D - C6
G3	68D - C6
G4	78B - F1
G5	78B - F1
G6	78B - F2
G7	78B - F2
H1	68D - C5
H2	68D - C6
H3	68D - C6
H4	78B - F1
H5	78B - F1
H6	78B - F2
H7	78B - F2
J1	68D - D5
J2	68D - D6
J3	68D - D6
J4	78C - A1
J5	78C - A1
J6	78C - A2
J7	78C - A2
New 899	
A1	68D - D5
A2	68D - D6
A3	68D - D6
A4	78C - B1
A5	78C - B1
A6	78C - B2
A7	78C - B2
B1	68D - E5
B2	68D - E6
B3	68D - E6
B4	78C - C1
B5	78C - C1
B6	78C - C2
B7	78C - C2
C1	68D - E5
C2	68D - E6
C3	68D - E6
C4	78C - D1
C5	78C - D1
C6	78C - D2
C7	78C - D2
D1	68D - E5
D2	68D - E6
D3	68D - E6
D4	78C - D1
D5	78C - D1
D6	78C - D2
D7	78C - D2
E1	68D - F5
E2	68D - F6
E3	68D - F6
E4	78C - E1
E5	78C - E1
E6	78C - E2
E7	78C - E2
F1	68D - F5
F2	68D - F6
F3	68D - F6
F4	78C - F1
F5	78C - F1
F6	78C - F2
F7	78C - F2
G1	78D - A2
G2	78D - A3
G3	78D - A3
G4	78D - A4
G5	78D - A4
G6	78D - A5
G7	78D - A5
H1	78D - A2
H2	78D - A3
H3	78D - A3
H4	78D - A4
H5	78D - A4
H6	78D - A5
H7	78D - A5
J1	78D - B2
J2	78D - B3
J3	78D - B3
J4	78D - B4
J5	78D - B4
J6	78D - B5
J7	78D - B5
New 900	
A1	78D - B2
A2	78D - B3
A3	78D - B3
A4	78D - B4
A5	78D - B4
A6	78D - B5
A7	78D - B5
B1	78D - B2
B2	78D - B3
B3	78D - B3
B4	78D - B4
B5	78D - B4
B6	78D - B5
B7	78D - B5

NEW-OLD	
New 900	
C1	78D - C2
C2	78D - C3
C3	78D - C3
C4	78D - C4
C5	78D - C4
C6	78D - C5
C7	78D - C5
D1	78D - C2
D2	78D - C3
D3	78D - C3
D4	78D - C4
D5	78D - C4
D6	78D - C4
D7	78D - C5
E4	78D - D4
E5	78D - D4
E6	78D - D4
E7	78D - D5
F4	78D - D4
F5	78D - D4
F6	78D - D4
F7	78D - D5
G4	78D - D4
G5	78D - D4
G6	78D - D4
G7	78D - D5
H4	78D - E4
H5	78D - E4
H6	78D - E4
H7	78D - E5
J4	78D - E4
J5	78D - E4
J6	78D - E4
J7	78D - E5
New 912	
A1	72K - D5
A2	72K - D6
B1	72K - D5
B2	72K - D6
C1	72K - E5
C2	72K - E6
D1	72K - F5
D2	72K - F6
E1	73 - A5
E2	73 - A6
E3	78G - A1
E4	78G - A2
E5	78G - A3
E6	78G - A4
E7	78G - A5
F1	73 - B5
F2	73 - B6
F3	78G - B1
F4	78G - B2
F5	78G - B3
F6	78G - B4
F7	78G - B5
G1	73 - C5
G2	73 - C6
G3	78G - C1
G4	78G - C2
G5	78G - C3
G6	78G - C4
G7	78G - C5
H1	73 - C5
H2	73 - C6
H3	78G - C1
H4	78G - C2
H5	78G - C3
H6	78G - C4
H7	78G - C5
J1	73 - D5
J2	73 - D6
J3	78G - D1
J4	78G - D2
J5	78G - D3
J6	78G - D4
J7	78G - D5
New 913	
A1	73 - E5
A2	73 - E6
A3	78G - E1
A4	78G - E2
A5	78G - E3
A6	78G - E4
A7	78G - E5
B1	73 - F5
B2	73 - F6
B3	78G - F1
B4	78G - F2
B5	78G - F3
B6	78G - F4
B7	78G - F5
C1	74 - A5
C2	74 - A6
C3	78H - A1
C4	78H - A1
C5	78H - A2
C6	78H - A2
C7	78H - A3
D1	74 - B5
D2	74 - B6
D3	78H - B1
D4	78H - B1
D5	78H - B2
D6	78H - B2
D7	78H - B3

NEW-OLD	
New 913	
E1	74 - B5
E2	74 - B6
E3	78H - C1
E4	78H - C1
E5	78H - C2
E6	78H - C2
E7	78H - C3
F1	74 - C5
F2	74 - C6
F3	78H - D1
F4	78H - D1
F5	78H - D2
F6	78H - D2
F7	78H - D3
G1	74 - D5
G2	74 - D6
G3	78H - D1
G4	78H - D1
G5	78H - D2
G6	78H - D2
G7	78H - D3
H1	74 - E5
H2	74 - E6
H3	78H - E1
H4	78H - E1
H5	78H - E2
H6	78H - E2
H7	78H - E3
J1	74 - F5
J2	74 - F6
J3	78H - F1
J4	78H - F1
J5	78H - F2
J6	78H - F2
J7	78H - F3
New 914	
A1	74 - F5
A2	74 - F6
A3	78J - A1
A4	78J - A1
A5	78J - A2
A6	78J - A2
A7	78J - A3
B1	75 - A5
B2	75 - A6
B3	78J - B1
B4	78J - B1
B5	78J - B2
B6	78J - B2
B7	78J - B3
C1	75 - B5
C2	75 - B6
C3	78J - B1
C4	78J - B1
C5	78J - B2
C6	78J - B2
C7	78J - C3
D1	75 - C5
D2	75 - C6
D3	78J - C1
D4	78J - C1
D5	78J - C2
D6	78J - C2
D7	78J - C3
E1	75 - D5
E2	75 - D6
E3	78J - D1
E4	78J - D1
E5	78J - D2
E6	78J - D2
E7	78J - D3
F1	75 - E5
F2	75 - E6
F3	78J - E1
F4	78J - E1
F5	78J - E2
F6	78J - E2
F7	78J - E3
G1	75 - E5
G2	75 - E6
G3	78J - F1
G4	78J - F1
G5	78J - F2
G6	78J - F2
G7	78J - F3
H1	75 - F5
H2	75 - F6
H3	78J - F1
H4	78J - F1
H5	78J - F2
H6	78J - F2
H7	78J - F3
J1	76 - A5
J2	76 - A6
J3	78K - A1
J4	78K - A1
J5	78K - A2
J6	78K - A2
J7	78K - A3
New 915	
A1	76 - B5
A2	76 - B6
A3	78K - B1
A4	78K - B1
A5	78K - B2
A6	78K - B2
A7	78K - B3

NEW-OLD	
New 915	
B1	76 - C5
B2	76 - C6
B3	78K - C1
B4	78K - C1
B5	78K - C2
B6	78K - C2
B7	78K - C3
C1	76 - D5
C2	76 - D6
C3	78K - D1
C4	78K - D1
C5	78K - D2
C6	78K - D2
C7	78K - D3
D1	76 - D5
D2	76 - D6
D3	78K - D1
D4	78K - D1
D5	78K - D2
D6	78K - E2
D7	78K - E3
E1	76 - E5
E2	76 - E6
E3	78K - E1
E4	78K - E1
E5	78K - E2
E6	78K - E2
E7	78K - E3
F1	76 - F5
F2	76 - F6
F3	78K - F1
F4	78K - F1
F5	78K - F2
F6	78K - F2
F7	78K - F3
G1	77 - A5
G2	77 - A6
G3	78L - A1
G4	78L - A1
G5	78L - A2
G6	78L - A2
G7	78L - A3
H1	77 - B5
H2	77 - B6
H3	78L - B1
H4	78L - B1
H5	78L - B2
H6	78L - B2
H7	78L - B3
J1	77 - C5
J2	77 - C6
J3	78L - C1
J4	78L - C1
J5	78L - C2
J6	78L - C2
J7	78L - C3
New 916	
A1	77 - C5
A2	77 - C6
A3	78L - C1
A4	78L - C1
A5	78L - C2
A6	78L - C2
A7	78L - C3
B1	77 - D5
B2	77 - D6
B3	78L - D1
B4	78L - D1
B5	78L - D2
B6	78L - D2
B7	78L - D3
C1	77 - E5
C2	77 - E6
C3	78L - E1
C4	78L - E1
C5	78L - E2
C6	78L - E2
C7	78L - E3
D1	77 - F5
D2	77 - F6
D3	78L - F1
D4	78L - F1
D5	78L - F2
D6	78L - F2
D7	78L - F3
E1	78 - A5
E2	78 - A6
E3	79 - A1
E4	79 - A2
E5	79 - A3
E6	79 - A4
E7	79 - A4
F1	78 - B5
F2	78 - B6
F3	79 - B1
F4	79 - B2
F5	79 - B3
F6	79 - B4
F7	79 - B4
G1	78 - B5
G2	78 - B6
G3	79 - B1
G4	79 - B2
G5	79 - B3
G6	79 - B3
G7	79 - B4
H1	78 - C5

NEW-OLD	
New 916	
H2	78 - C6
H3	79 - C1
H4	79 - C2
H5	79 - C3
H6	79 - C3
H7	79 - C4
J1	78 - D5
J2	78 - D6
J3	79 - D1
J4	79 - D2
J5	79 - D3
J6	79 - D3
J7	79 - D4
New 917	
A1	78 - E5
A2	78 - E6
A3	79 - E1
A4	79 - E2
A5	79 - E3
A6	79 - E3
A7	79 - E4
B1	78 - E5
B2	78 - E6
B3	79 - F1
B4	79 - F2
B5	79 - F3
B6	79 - F3
B7	79 - F4
C1	78A - A5
C2	78A - A6
C3	80 - A1
C4	80 - A2
C5	80 - A2
C6	80 - A3
C7	80 - A4
D1	78A - A5
D2	78A - A6
D3	80 - B1
D4	80 - B2
D5	80 - B2
D6	80 - B3
D7	80 - B4
E1	78A - B5
E2	78A - B6
E3	80 - B1
E4	80 - B2
E5	80 - B2
E6	80 - B3
E7	80 - B4
F1	78A - C5
F2	78A - C6
F3	80 - C1
F4	80 - C2
F5	80 - C2
F6	80 - C3
F7	80 - C4
G1	78A - D5
G2	78A - D6
G3	80 - D1
G4	80 - D2
G5	80 - D2
G6	80 - D3
G7	80 - D4
H1	78A - E5
H2	78A - E6
H3	80 - E1
H4	80 - E2
H5	80 - E2
H6	80 - E3
H7	80 - E4
J1	78A - E5
J2	78A - E6
J3	80 - E1
J4	80 - E2
J5	80 - E2
J6	80 - E3
J7	80 - E4
New 918	
A1	78A - F5
A2	78B - A3
A3	80 - F1
A4	80 - F2
A5	80 - F2
A6	80 - F3
A7	80 - F4
B1	78B - A3
B2	78B - A3
B3	78B - A4
B4	78B - A4
B5	78B - A4
B6	78B - A5
B7	78B - A5
C1	78B - B3
C2	78B - B3
C3	78B - B4
C4	78B - B4
C5	78B - B4
C6	78B - B5
C7	78B - B5
D1	78B - C3
D2	78B - C3
D3	78B - C4
D4	78B - C4
D5	78B - C4
D6	78B - C5
D7	78B - C5
E1	78B - D3

NEW-OLD	
New 918	
E2	78B - D3
E3	78B - D3
E4	78B - D4
E5	78B - D4
E6	78B - D5
E7	78B - D5
F1	78B - E3
F2	78B - E3
F3	78B - E3
F4	78B - E4
F5	78B - E4
F6	78B - E5
F7	78B - E5
G1	78B - F3
G2	78B - F3
G3	78B - F3
G4	78B - F4
G5	78B - F4
G6	78B - F5
G7	78B - F5
H1	78B - F3
H2	78B - F3
H3	78B - F3
H4	78B - F4
H5	78B - F4
H6	78B - F5
H7	78B - F5
J1	78C - A3
J2	78C - A3
J3	78C - A3
J4	78C - A4
J5	78C - A4
J6	78C - A5
J7	78C - A5
New 919	
A1	78C - B3
A2	78C - B3
A3	78C - B3
A4	78C - B4
A5	78C - B4
A6	78C - B5
A7	78C - B5
B1	78C - C3
B2	78C - C3
B3	78C - C3
B4	78C - C4
B5	78C - C4
B6	78C - C5
B7	78C - C5
C1	78C - D2
C2	78C - D3
C3	78C - D3
C4	78C - D4
C5	78C - D4
C6	78C - D5
C7	78C - D5
D1	78C - D2
D2	78C - D3
D3	78C - D3
D4	78C - D4
D5	78C - D4
D6	78C - D5
D7	78C - E5
E1	78C - E2
E2	78C - E3
E3	78C - E3
E4	78C - E4
E5	78C - E4
E6	78C - E5
E7	78C - F5
F1	78C - F2
F2	78C - F3
F3	78C - F3
F4	78C - F4
F5	78C - F4
F6	78C - F5
F7	78C - F5
G1	78D - A5
G2	78D - A6
G3	78D - A6
G4	78E - A1
G5	78E - A1
G6	78E - A2
G7	78E - A2
H1	78D - A5
H2	78D - A6
H3	78D - A6
H4	78E - A1
H5	78E - A1
H6	78E - A2
H7	78E - A2
J1	78D - B5
J2	78D - B6
J3	78D - B6
J4	78E - B1
J5	78E - B1
J6	78E - B2
J7	78E - B2
New 920	
A1	78D - B5
A2	78D - B6
A3	78D - B6
A4	78E - B1
A5	78E - B1
A6	78E - B2
A7	78E - B2
B1	78D - B5

NEW-OLD	
New 920	
B2	78D - B6
B3	78D - B6
B4	78E - B1
B5	78E - B1
B6	78E - B2
B7	78E - B2
C1	78D - C5
C2	78D - C6
C3	78D - C6
C4	78E - C1
C5	78E - C1
C6	78E - C2
C7	78E - C2
D1	78D - C5
D2	78D - C6
D3	78D - C6
D4	78E - C1
D5	78E - C1
D6	78E - C2
D7	78E - C2
E1	78D - D5
E2	78D - D6
E3	78D - D6
E4	78E - D1
E5	78E - D1
E6	78E - D2
E7	78E - D2
F1	78D - D5
F2	78D - D6
F3	78D - D6
F4	78E - D1
F5	78E - D1
F6	78E - D2
F7	78E - D2
G1	78D - D5
G2	78D - D6
G3	78D - D6
G4	78E - D1
G5	78E - E1
G6	78E - E2
G7	78E - E2
H1	78D - E5
H2	78D - E6
H3	78D - E6
H4	78E - E1
H5	78E - E1
H6	78E - E2
H7	78E - E2
J1	78D - E6
J2	78D - E6
J3	78D - E6
J4	78E - E1
J5	78E - E1
J6	78E - E2
J7	78E - E2
New 921	
A1	78D - F5
A2	78D - F6
A3	78D - F6
A4	78E - F1
A5	78E - F1
A6	78E - F2
A7	78E - F2
B1	78D - F5
B2	78D - F6
B3	78D - F6
B4	78E - F1
B5	78E - F1
B6	78E - F2
B7	78E - F2
C1	78D - D2
C2	78D - D3
C3	78D - D3
C4	78F - A1
C5	78F - A1
C6	78F - A2
C7	78F - A2
D1	78D - D2
D2	78D - D3
D3	78D - D3
D4	78F - A1
D5	78F - A1
D6	78F - A2
D7	78F - A2
E1	78D - D2
E2	78D - D3
E3	78D - D3
E4	78F - B1
E5	78F - B1
E6	78F - B2
E7	78F - B2
F1	78D - E2
F2	78D - E3
F3	78D - E3
F4	78F - B1
F5	78F - B1
F6	78F - B2
F7	78F - B2
G1	78D - E2
G2	78D - E3
G3	78D - E3
G4	78F - B1
G5	78F - B1
G6	78F - B2
G7	78F - B2
H1	78D - F2
H2	78D - F3

NEW-OLD	
New 921	
H3	78D - F3
H4	78F - C1
H5	78F - C1
H6	78F - C2
H7	78F - C2
J1	78D - F2
J2	78D - F3
J3	78D - F3
J4	78F - C1
J5	78F - C1
J6	78F - C2
J7	78F - C2
New 922	
A1	78D - F2
A3	78D - F3
A4	78F - D1
A5	78F - D1
A6	78F - D2
A7	78F - D2
B4	78F - D1
B5	78F - D1
B6	78F - D2
B7	78F - D2
C4	78F - D1
C5	78F - D1
C6	78F - D2
C7	78F - D2
D4	78F - E1
D5	78F - E1
D6	78F - E2
D7	78F - E2
E4	78F - E1
E5	78F - E1
E6	78F - E2
E7	78F - E2
F4	78F - F1
F5	78F - F1
F6	78F - F2
F7	78F - F2
G4	78F - F1
G5	78F - F1
G6	78F - F2
G7	78F - F2
New 934	
A1	78J - A3
A2	78J - A4
A3	78J - A4
A4	78J - A4
A5	78J - A5
A6	78J - A5
A7	78J - A6
B1	78J - B3
B2	78J - B4
B3	78J - B4
B4	78J - B4
B5	78J - B5
B6	78J - B5
B7	78J - B6
C1	78J - C3
C2	78J - C3
C3	78J - C4
C4	78J - C4
C5	78J - C5
C6	78J - C5
C7	78J - C6
D1	78J - C3
D2	78J - C3
D3	78J - C4
D4	78J - C4
D5	78J - C5
D6	78J - D5
D7	78J - D6
E1	78J - D3
E2	78J - D3
E3	78J - D4
E4	78J - D4
E5	78J - D5
E6	78J - D5
E7	78J - D6
F1	78J - E3
F2	78J - E3
F3	78J - E4
F4	78J - E4
F5	78J - E5
F6	78J - E5
F7	78J - E6
G1	78J - F3
G2	78J - F3
G3	78J - F4
G4	78J - F4
G5	78J - F5
G6	78J - F5
G7	78J - F6
H1	78J - F3
H2	78J - F3
H3	78J - F4
H4	78J - F4
H5	78J - F5
H6	78J - F5
H7	78J - F6
J1	78K - A3
J2	78K - A3
J3	78K - A4
J4	78K - A4
J5	78K - A5
J6	78K - A5
J7	78K - A6

NEW-OLD	
New 935	
A1	78K - B3
A2	78K - B3
A3	78K - B4
A4	78K - B4
A5	78K - B5
A6	78K - B5
A7	78K - B6
B1	78K - C3
B2	78K - C3
B3	78K - C4
B4	78K - C4
B5	78K - C5
B6	78K - C5
B7	78K - C6
C1	78K - D3
C2	78K - D3
C3	78K - D4
C4	78K - D4
C5	78K - D5
C6	78K - D5
C7	78K - D6
D1	78K - E3
D2	78K - E3
D3	78K - E4
D4	78K - E4
D5	78K - E5
D6	78K - E5
D7	78K - E6
E1	78K - E3
E2	78K - E3
E3	78K - E4
E4	78K - E4
E5	78K - E5
E6	78K - E5
E7	78K - E6
F1	78K - F3
F2	78K - F3
F3	78K - F4
F4	78K - F4
F5	78K - F5
F6	78K - F5
F7	78K - F6
G1	78L - A3
G2	78L - A3
G3	78L - A4
G4	78L - A4
G5	78L - A5
G6	78L - A5
G7	78L - A6
H1	78L - B3
H2	78L - B3
H3	78L - B4
H4	78L - B4
H5	78L - B5
H6	78L - B5
H7	78L - B6
J1	78L - C3
J2	78L - C3
J3	78L - C4
J4	78L - C4
J5	78L - C5
J6	78L - C5
J7	78L - C6
New 936	
A1	78L - C3
A2	78L - C3
A3	78L - C4
A4	78L - C4
A5	78L - C5
A6	78L - D5
A7	78L - D6
B1	78L - D3
B2	78L - D3
B3	78L - D4
B4	78L - D4
B5	78L - D5
B6	78L - D5
B7	78L - D6
C1	78L - E3
C2	78L - E3
C3	78L - E4
C4	78L - E4
C5	78L - E5
C6	78L - E5
C7	78L - E6
D1	78L - F3
D2	78L - F3
D3	78L - F4
D4	78L - F4
D5	78L - F5
D6	78L - F5
D7	78L - F6
E1	79 - A5
E2	79 - A6
E3	80K - A1
E4	80K - A2
E5	80K - A3
E6	80K - A4
E7	80K - A5
F1	79 - B5
F2	79 - B6
F3	80K - B1
F4	80K - B2
F5	80K - B3
F6	80K - B4
F7	80K - B5
G1	79 - B5

NEW-OLD	
New 936	
G2	79 - B6
G3	80K - B1
G4	80K - C2
G5	80K - C3
G6	80K - C4
G7	80K - C5
H1	79 - C5
H2	79 - C6
H3	80K - C1
H4	80K - C2
H5	80K - C3
H6	80K - C4
H7	80K - C5
J1	79 - D5
J2	79 - D6
J3	80K - D1
J4	80K - D2
J5	80K - D3
J6	80K - D4
J7	80K - D5
New 937	
A1	79 - E5
A2	79 - E6
A3	80K - E1
A4	80K - E2
A5	80K - E3
A6	80K - E4
A7	80K - E5
B1	79 - F5
B2	79 - F6
B3	80K - F1
B4	80K - F2
B5	80K - F3
B6	80K - F4
B7	80K - F5
C1	80 - A5
C2	80 - A6
C3	81 - A1
C4	81 - A2
C5	81 - A3
C6	81 - A4
C7	81 - A5
D1	80 - B5
D2	80 - B6
D3	81 - B1
D4	81 - B2
D5	81 - B3
D6	81 - B4
D7	81 - B5
E1	80 - B5
E2	80 - B6
E3	81 - B1
E4	81 - B2
E5	81 - B3
E6	81 - B4
E7	81 - B5
F1	80 - C5
F2	80 - C6
F3	81 - C1
F4	81 - C2
F5	81 - C3
F6	81 - C4
F7	81 - C5
G1	80 - D5
G2	80 - D6
G3	81 - D1
G4	81 - D2
G5	81 - D3
G6	81 - D4
G7	81 - D5
H1	80 - E5
H2	80 - E6
H3	81 - E1
H4	81 - E2
H5	81 - E3
H6	81 - E4
H7	81 - E5
J1	80 - E5
J2	80 - E6
J3	81 - E1
J4	81 - E2
J5	81 - E3
J6	81 - E4
J7	81 - E5
New 938	
A1	80 - F5
A2	80 - F6
A3	81 - F1
A4	81 - F2
A5	81 - F3
A6	81 - F4
A7	81 - F5
B1	78B - A6
B2	78B - A6
B3	81A - A1
B4	81A - A2
B5	81A - A3
B6	81A - A4
B7	81A - A5
C1	78B - B6
C2	78B - B6
C3	81A - B1
C4	81A - B2
C5	81A - B3
C6	81A - B4
C7	81A - B5
D1	78B - C6

1998 SANTA CLARA NEW TO OLD Page Conversion List

NEW-OLD	NEW-OLD	NEW-OLD	NEW-OLD	NEW-OLD	NEW-OLD	NEW-OLD	NEW-OLD	NEW-OLD	NEW-OLD	NEW-OLD	NEW-OLD	NEW-OLD	NEW-OLD	NEW-OLD	NEW-OLD	NEW-OLD	NEW-OLD	NEW-OLD	NEW-OLD	NEW-OLD
New 938	**New 940**	**New 941**	**New 955**	**New 957**	**New 958**	**New 960**	**New 962**	**New 976**	**New 977**	**New 979**	**New 981**	**New 982**	**New 997**	**New 999**	**New 1017**	**New 1019**				
D2 78B - C6	A2 78E - B3	G3 78F - B3	F3 81F - F1	C3 82 - A2	J4 81C - A2	F4 82D - B1	C4 82E - E1	B4 81G - D5	H5 83 - E3	E5 85 - E4	B5 82D - F5	H6 82E - F5	H6 90 - E2	E6 92 - E2	D1 90 - B3	A1 92 - B3				
D3 81A - C1	A3 78E - B4	G4 78F - B4	F4 81F - F1	C4 82 - A2	J5 81C - A3	F5 82D - B2	C5 82E - E1	B5 81G - D5	H6 83 - E4	E6 85 - E5	B6 82D - F5	H7 82E - F5	H7 90 - E3	E7 92 - E3	D2 90 - B4	A2 92 - B4				
D4 81A - C2	A4 78E - B4	G5 78F - B4	F5 81F - F2	C5 82 - A3	J6 81C - A4	F6 82D - B2	C6 82E - D2	B6 81G - D5	H7 83 - E5	E7 85 - E5	B7 82D - F6	**New 995**	J1 83 - F6	F1 85 - F6	D3 90 - B4	A3 92 - B4				
D5 81A - C3	A5 78E - B4	G6 78F - B5	F6 81F - F2	C6 82 - A4	J7 81C - A5	F7 82D - B3	C7 82E - D2	B7 81G - D6	J1 82 - F6	F1 82C - A3	C1 82E - A3	A1 81F - B6	J2 90 - F1	F2 92 - F1	D4 90 - B5	A4 92 - B5				
D6 81A - C4	A6 78E - B5	G7 78F - B5	F7 81F - F3	C7 82 - A5	**New 959**	G1 78E - E6	D1 78F - E5	C1 81G - E3	J2 83 - F1	F2 85 - F1	C2 82E - A3	B1 81F - C6	J3 90 - F1	F3 92 - F1	D5 90 - B5	A5 92 - B5				
D7 81A - C5	A7 78E - B5	H1 78F - C2	G1 78L - A6	D1 81 - B6	A1 81B - B5	G2 78E - E6	D2 78F - E6	C2 81G - E4	J3 83 - F2	F3 85 - F2	C3 82E - A4	C1 81F - C6	J4 90 - F2	F4 92 - F2	D6 90 - B6	A6 92 - B6				
E1 78B - D6	B1 78E - C3	H2 78F - C3	G2 81G - A1	D2 82 - B1	A2 81B - B6	G3 82D - C1	D3 78F - E6	C3 81G - E4	J4 83 - F3	F4 85 - F3	C4 82E - A4	D1 81F - D6	J5 90 - F2	F5 92 - F2	D7 90 - B6	A7 92 - B6				
E2 78B - D6	B2 78E - C3	H3 78F - C3	G3 81G - A1	D3 82 - B2	A3 81C - B1	G4 82D - C1	D4 82E - E1	C4 81G - E5	J5 83 - F3	F5 85 - F4	C5 82E - A5	E1 81F - E6	J6 90 - F2	F6 92 - F2	E1 90 - C3	B1 92 - C3				
E3 81A - D1	B3 78E - C4	H4 78F - C4	G4 81G - A1	D4 82 - B2	A4 81C - B2	G5 82D - C2	D5 82E - E1	C5 81G - E5	J6 83 - F4	F6 85 - F5	C6 82E - A5	F1 81F - F6	J7 90 - F3	F7 92 - F3	E2 90 - C4	B2 92 - C4				
E4 81A - D2	B4 78E - C4	H5 78F - C4	G5 81G - A2	D5 82 - B3	A5 81C - B3	G6 82D - C2	D6 82E - E2	C6 81G - E5	J7 83 - F5	F7 85 - F5	C7 82E - A6	G1 81G - A6	**New 998**	G1 82C - A6	E3 90 - C4	B3 92 - C4				
E5 81A - D3	B5 78E - C4	H6 78F - C5	G6 81G - A2	D6 82 - B4	A6 81C - B4	G7 82D - C2	D7 82E - E2	C7 81G - E6	**New 978**	G1 82C - A3	D1 82E - A3	H1 81G - B6	A1 84 - A6	H1 82C - B6	E4 90 - C5	B4 92 - C5				
E6 81A - D4	B6 78E - C5	H7 78F - C5	G7 81G - A3	D7 82 - B5	A7 81C - B5	H1 78E - E6	E1 78F - E5	D1 81G - F3	A1 82A - A6	G2 82C - A4	D2 82E - A3	J1 81G - C6	A2 90 - F1	J1 82C - C6	E5 90 - C5	B5 92 - C5				
E7 81A - D5	B7 78E - C5	J1 78F - C2	H1 78L - B6	E1 81 - B6	B1 81B - C5	H2 78E - E6	E2 78F - E6	D2 81G - F4	A2 84 - A1	G3 82C - A4	D3 82E - A4	**New 996**	A3 90 - F1	**New 1000**	E6 90 - C6	B6 92 - C6				
F1 78B - E6	C1 78E - C3	J2 78F - C3	H2 81G - B1	E2 82 - B1	B2 81B - C6	H3 82D - D1	E3 78F - E6	D3 81G - F4	A3 84 - A2	G4 82C - A5	D4 82E - A4	A1 81G - C6	A4 90 - F2	A1 82C - D6	E7 90 - C6	B7 92 - C6				
F2 78B - E6	C2 78E - C3	J3 78F - C3	H3 81G - B1	E3 82 - B2	B3 81C - C1	H4 82D - D1	E4 82E - E1	D4 81G - F5	A4 84 - A3	G5 82C - A5	D5 82E - A5	B1 81G - D6	A5 90 - F2	B1 82C - D6	F1 90 - C3	C1 92 - C3				
F3 81A - E1	C3 78E - C4	J4 78F - C4	H4 81G - B1	E4 82 - B2	B4 81C - C2	H5 82D - D2	E5 82E - E1	D5 81G - F5	A5 84 - A3	G6 82C - A6	D6 82E - A5	C1 81G - E6	A6 90 - F2	C1 82C - E6	F2 90 - C4	C2 92 - C4				
F4 81A - E2	C4 78E - C4	J5 78F - C4	H5 81G - B2	E5 82 - B3	B5 81C - C3	H6 82D - C2	E6 82E - E2	D6 81G - F5	A6 84 - A4	G7 82C - A6	D7 82E - A6	D1 81G - F6	A7 90 - F3	D1 82C - F6	F3 90 - C4	C3 92 - C4				
F5 81A - E3	C5 78E - C4	J6 78F - C5	H6 81G - B2	E6 82 - B4	B6 81C - C4	H7 82D - C2	E7 82E - E2	D7 81G - F6	A7 84 - A5	H1 82C - B3	E1 82E - B3	E1 82H - A6	B1 84 - B6	E1 82D - A6	F4 90 - C5	C4 92 - C5				
F6 81A - E4	C6 78E - C5	J7 78F - C5	H7 81G - B3	E7 82 - B5	B7 81C - C5	J1 78E - E6	F1 78F - F5	E1 81H - A6	B1 82A - B6	H2 82C - B4	E2 82E - B3	E2 89 - A1	B2 91 - A1	F1 82D - B6	F5 90 - C5	C5 92 - C5				
F7 81A - E5	C7 78E - C5	**New 942**	J1 78L - C6	F1 81 - C6	C1 81B - D5	J2 78E - E6	F2 78F - F6	E2 82H - A1	B2 84 - B1	H3 82C - B4	E3 82E - B4	E3 89 - A1	B3 91 - A1	G1 82D - C6	F6 90 - C6	C6 92 - C6				
G1 78B - F6	D1 78E - C3	A1 78F - D2	J2 81G - C1	F2 82 - C1	C2 81B - D6	J3 82D - D1	F3 78F - F6	E3 82H - A2	B3 84 - B2	H4 82C - B5	E4 82E - B4	E4 89 - A2	B4 91 - A2	H1 82D - C6	F7 90 - C6	C7 92 - C6				
G2 78B - F6	D2 78E - C3	A2 78F - D3	J3 81G - C1	F3 82 - C2	C3 81C - D1	J4 82D - D1	F4 82E - F1	E4 82H - A3	B4 84 - B3	H5 82C - B5	E5 82E - B5	E5 89 - A2	B5 91 - A2	J1 82D - D6	G1 90 - D3	D1 92 - D3				
G3 81A - F1	D3 78E - C4	A3 78F - D3	J4 81G - C1	F4 82 - C2	C4 81C - D2	J5 82D - D2	F5 82E - F1	E5 82H - A4	B5 84 - B3	H6 82C - B6	E6 82E - B5	E6 89 - A3	B6 91 - A2	**New 1001**	G2 90 - D4	D2 92 - D4				
G4 81A - F2	D4 78E - C4	A4 78F - D4	J5 81G - C2	F5 82 - C3	C5 81C - D3	J6 82D - D2	F6 82E - F2	E6 82H - A4	B6 84 - B4	H7 82C - B6	E7 82E - B6	E7 89 - A3	B7 91 - A3	A1 82D - E6	G3 90 - D4	D3 92 - D4				
G5 81A - F3	D5 78E - C4	A5 78F - D4	J6 81G - C2	F6 82 - C4	C6 81C - D4	J7 82D - D2	F7 82E - F2	E7 82H - A5	B7 84 - B5	J1 82C - C3	F1 82E - B3	F1 82H - B6	C1 84 - B6	B1 82D - F6	G4 90 - D5	D4 92 - D5				
G6 81A - F4	D6 78E - C5	A6 78F - D5	J7 81G - C3	F7 82 - C5	C7 81C - D5	**New 961**	G1 78F - F5	F1 81H - B6	C1 82A - B6	J2 82C - C4	F2 82E - B3	F2 89 - B1	C2 91 - B1	C1 82E - A6	G5 90 - D5	D5 92 - D5				
G7 81A - F4	D7 78E - C5	A7 78F - D5	**New 956**	G1 81 - D6	D1 81B - E5	A1 78E - F6	G2 78F - F6	F2 82H - B1	C2 84 - B1	J3 82C - C4	F3 82E - B4	F3 89 - B1	C3 91 - B1	D1 82E - A6	G6 90 - D6	D6 92 - D6				
H1 78B - F6	E1 78E - D3	B1 78F - D2	A1 78L - D6	G2 82 - D1	D2 81B - E6	A2 78E - F6	G3 78F - F6	F3 82H - B2	C3 84 - B2	J4 82C - C5	F4 82E - B4	F4 89 - B2	C4 91 - B2	E1 82E - B6	G7 90 - D6	D7 92 - D6				
H2 78B - F6	E2 78E - D3	B2 78F - D3	A2 81G - D1	G3 82 - D2	D3 81C - E1	A3 78E - F6	G4 82E - F1	F4 82H - B3	C4 84 - B3	J5 82C - C5	F5 82E - B5	F5 89 - B2	C5 91 - B2	F1 82E - B6	H1 90 - E3	E1 92 - E3				
H3 81A - F1	E3 78E - D4	B3 78F - D3	A3 81G - D1	G4 82 - D2	D4 81C - E2	A4 82D - E1	G5 82E - F1	F5 82H - B4	C5 84 - B3	J6 82C - C6	F6 82E - B5	F6 89 - B3	C6 91 - B2	G1 82E - B6	H2 90 - E4	E2 92 - E4				
H4 81A - F2	E4 78E - D4	B4 78F - D4	A4 81G - D2	G5 82 - D3	D5 81C - E3	A5 82D - E2	G6 82E - F2	F6 82H - B4	C6 84 - B4	J7 82C - C6	F7 82E - B6	F7 89 - B3	C7 91 - B3	H1 82E - C6	H3 90 - E4	E3 92 - E4				
H5 81A - F3	E5 78E - D4	B5 78F - D4	A5 81G - C2	G6 82 - D4	D6 81C - E4	A6 82D - E2	G7 82E - F2	F7 82H - B5	C7 84 - B5	**New 980**	G1 82E - B3	G1 82H - C6	D1 84 - C6	J1 82E - C6	H4 90 - E5	E4 92 - E5				
H6 81A - F4	E6 78E - D5	B6 78F - D5	A6 81G - C2	G7 82 - D5	D7 81C - E5	A7 82D - E2	**New 975**	G1 81H - C6	D1 82A - C6	A1 82C - D3	G2 82E - B3	G2 89 - C1	D2 91 - C1	J2 82E - C6	H5 90 - E5	E5 92 - E5				
H7 81B - A4	E7 78E - D5	B7 78F - D5	A7 81G - C3	H1 81 - E5	E1 81B - F5	B1 78E - F6	A1 81F - B3	G2 82H - C1	D2 84 - C1	A2 82C - D4	G3 82E - B4	G3 89 - C1	D3 91 - C1	**New 1002**	H6 90 - E6	E6 92 - E6				
J1 78C - A6	F1 78E - D3	C1 78F - D2	B1 78L - D6	H2 81 - E6	E2 81B - F6	B2 78E - F6	A2 81F - B4	G3 82H - C2	D3 84 - C2	A3 82C - D4	G4 82E - B4	G4 89 - C2	D4 91 - C2	A1 82E - C6	H7 90 - E6	E7 92 - E6				
J2 78C - A6	F2 78E - D3	C2 78F - E3	B2 81G - D1	H3 82 - E1	E3 81C - F1	B3 82D - F1	A3 81F - B4	G4 82H - C3	D4 84 - C3	A4 82C - D5	G5 82E - B5	G5 89 - C2	D5 91 - C2	B1 82E - D6	J1 90 - F3	F1 92 - F3				
J3 81B - A1	F3 78E - D4	C3 78F - E3	B3 81G - D1	H4 82 - E2	E4 81C - F2	B4 82D - F1	A4 81F - B5	G5 82H - C4	D5 84 - C3	A5 82C - D5	G6 82E - B5	G6 89 - C3	D6 91 - C2	B2 82E - D6	J2 90 - F4	F2 92 - F4				
J4 81B - A2	F4 78E - D4	C4 78F - E4	B4 81G - D2	H5 82 - E3	E5 81C - F3	B5 82D - F1	A5 81F - B5	G6 82H - C4	D6 84 - C4	A6 82C - D5	G7 82E - B6	G7 89 - C3	D7 91 - C3	C1 82E - D6	J3 90 - F4	F3 92 - F4				
J5 81B - A3	F5 78E - D4	C5 78F - E4	B5 81G - D2	H6 82 - E4	E6 81C - F4	B6 82D - F2	A6 81F - B5	G7 82H - C5	D7 84 - C5	A7 82C - D6	H1 82E - C3	H1 82H - C6	E1 84 - D6	C2 82E - D6	J4 90 - F5	F4 92 - F5				
J6 81B - A3	F6 78E - D5	C6 78F - E5	B6 81G - D2	H7 82 - E5	E7 81C - F5	B7 82D - F2	A7 81F - B6	H1 81H - C6	E1 82A - D6	B1 82C - E3	H2 82E - C3	H2 89 - C1	E2 91 - D1	D1 82E - E6	J5 90 - F5	F5 92 - F5				
J7 81B - A4	F7 78E - D5	C7 78F - E5	B7 81G - D3	J1 81 - E5	F1 78E - A6	C1 78F - A6	B1 81F - C3	H2 82H - C1	E2 84 - D1	B2 82C - E4	H3 82E - C4	H3 89 - C1	E3 91 - D1	D2 82E - E6	J6 90 - F6	F6 92 - F6				
New 939	G1 78E - E3	D1 78F - E2	C1 78L - E6	J2 81 - F6	F2 78E - A6	C2 78F - A6	B2 81F - C4	H3 82H - C2	E3 84 - D2	B3 82C - E4	H4 82E - C4	H4 89 - C2	E4 91 - D2	E1 82E - E6	J7 90 - F6	F7 92 - F6				
A1 78C - B6	G2 78E - E3	D2 78F - E3	C2 81G - E1	J3 82 - F1	F3 82C - A1	C3 82E - A1	B3 81F - C4	H4 82H - C3	E4 84 - D3	B4 82C - E5	H5 82E - C5	H5 89 - C2	E5 91 - D2	E2 82E - E6	**New 1018**					
A2 78C - B6	G3 78E - E4	D3 78F - E3	C3 81G - E1	J4 82 - F2	F4 82C - A1	C4 82E - A1	B4 81F - C5	H5 82H - C4	E5 84 - D3	B5 82C - E5	H6 82E - C5	H6 89 - C3	E6 91 - D2	F1 82E - E6	A1 90 - F3					
A3 81B - B1	G4 78E - E4	D4 78F - E4	C4 81G - E2	J5 82 - F3	F5 82C - A2	C5 82E - A1	B5 81F - C5	H6 82H - C4	E6 84 - D4	B6 82C - E5	H7 82E - C6	H7 89 - C3	E7 91 - D3	F2 82E - E6	A2 90 - F4					
A4 81B - B1	G5 78E - E4	D5 78F - E4	C5 81G - E2	J6 82 - F4	F6 82C - A2	C6 82E - A2	B6 81F - C5	H7 82H - C5	E7 84 - D5	B7 82C - D6	J1 82E - C3	J1 82H - D6	F1 84 - E6	G1 82E - F6	A3 90 - F4					
A5 81B - B3	G6 78E - E5	D6 78F - E5	C6 81G - E2	J7 82 - F5	F7 82C - A3	C7 82E - A2	B7 81F - C6	J1 81H - D6	F1 82A - E6	C1 82C - E3	J2 82E - C3	J2 89 - D1	F2 91 - D1	G2 82E - F6	A4 90 - F5					
A6 81B - B3	G7 78E - E5	D7 78F - E5	C7 81G - E3	**New 958**	G1 78E - A6	D1 78F - A6	C1 81F - D3	J2 82H - D1	F2 84 - E1	C2 82C - E4	J3 82E - C4	J3 89 - D1	F3 91 - D1	H1 82E - F6	A5 90 - F5					
A7 81B - B4	H1 78E - E3	E1 78F - E2	D1 78L - F6	A1 81 - F5	G2 78E - A6	D2 78F - A6	C2 81F - D4	J3 82H - D2	F3 84 - E2	C3 82C - E4	J4 82E - C4	J4 89 - D2	F4 91 - D2	H2 82E - F6	A6 90 - F6					
B1 78C - C6	H2 78E - E3	E2 78F - E3	D2 81G - F1	A2 81 - F6	G3 82C - A1	D3 78F - A6	C3 81F - D4	J4 82H - D3	F4 84 - E3	C4 82C - E4	J5 82E - C5	J5 89 - D2	F5 91 - D2	**New 1016**	A7 90 - F6					
B2 78C - C6	H3 78E - E3	E3 78F - E3	D3 81G - F1	A3 82A - A1	G4 82C - A1	D4 82E - A1	C4 81F - D5	J5 82H - D4	F5 84 - E3	C5 82C - E5	J6 82E - C5	J6 89 - D3	F6 91 - D2	E1 89 - A3	B1 91 - A3					
B3 81B - C1	H4 78E - E4	E4 78F - E4	D4 81G - F2	A4 82A - A2	G5 82C - A2	D5 82E - A1	C5 81F - D5	J6 82H - D4	F6 84 - E4	C6 82C - E5	J7 82E - C6	J7 89 - D3	F7 91 - D3	E2 89 - A4	B2 91 - A4					
B4 81B - C1	H5 78E - E4	E5 78F - E4	D5 81G - F2	A5 82A - A3	G6 82C - A2	D6 82E - A2	C6 81F - D5	J7 82H - D5	F7 84 - E5	C7 82C - E6	**New 982**	**New 997**	G1 84 - E6	E3 89 - A4	B3 91 - A4					
B5 81B - C3	H6 78E - E5	E6 78F - E5	D6 81G - F2	A6 82A - A4	G7 82C - A3	D7 82E - A2	C7 81F - C6	**New 977**	G1 82A - F6	D1 82C - F3	A1 82E - D3	A1 82H - E6	G2 91 - E1	E4 89 - A5	B4 91 - A5					
B6 81B - C3	H7 78E - E5	E7 78F - E5	D7 81G - F3	A7 82A - A5	H1 78E - A6	E1 78F - B6	D1 81F - E3	A1 81H - E6	G2 84 - F1	D2 82C - F4	A2 82E - D3	A2 89 - E1	G3 91 - E1	E5 89 - A5	B5 91 - A5					
B7 81B - C4	J1 78E - E3	F1 78F - F2	E1 80K - A6	B1 81A - A5	H2 78E - A6	E2 78F - B6	D2 81F - E4	A2 82H - E1	G3 84 - F2	D3 82C - F4	A3 82E - D4	A3 89 - E1	G4 91 - E2	E6 89 - A6	B6 91 - A6					
C1 78C - D6	J2 78E - E3	F2 78F - F3	E2 81H - A1	B2 81A - A6	H3 82C - B1	E3 78F - B6	D3 81F - D4	A3 82H - E2	G4 84 - F3	D4 82C - F4	A4 82E - D4	A4 89 - E2	G5 91 - E2	E7 89 - A6	B7 91 - A6					
C2 78C - D6	J3 78E - E3	F3 78F - F3	E3 81H - A2	B3 82A - A1	H4 82C - B1	E4 82E - B1	D4 81F - D5	A4 82H - E3	G5 84 - F3	D5 82C - F5	A5 82E - D5	A5 89 - E2	G6 91 - E2	F1 89 - B3	C1 91 - B3					
C3 81B - D1	J4 78E - E4	F4 78F - F4	E4 81H - A3	B4 82A - A2	H5 82C - B2	E5 82E - B1	D5 81F - D5	A5 82H - E4	G6 84 - E4	D6 82C - F5	A6 82E - D5	A6 89 - E3	G7 91 - E3	F2 89 - B4	C2 91 - B4					
C4 81B - D1	J5 78E - E4	F5 78F - F4	E5 81H - A3	B5 82A - A3	H6 82C - B2	E6 82E - B2	D6 81F - D5	A6 82H - E4	G7 84 - E5	D7 82C - F6	A7 82E - C6	A7 89 - E3	H1 84 - F6	F3 89 - B4	C3 91 - B4					
C5 81B - D3	J6 78E - E5	F6 78F - F5	E6 81H - A4	B6 82A - A4	H7 82C - B3	E7 82E - B2	D7 81F - D6	A7 82H - E5	H1 81C - A6	E1 82D - A3	B1 82E - D3	B1 82H - F6	H2 91 - F1	F4 89 - B5	C4 91 - B5					
C6 81B - D3	J7 78E - E5	F7 78F - F5	E7 81H - A5	B7 82A - B6	J1 78E - B6	F1 78F - B6	E1 81F - E3	B1 81H - F6	H2 85 - A1	E2 82D - A3	B2 82E - D3	B2 89 - F1	H3 91 - F1	F5 89 - B5	C5 91 - B5					
C7 81B - D4	**New 941**	G1 78F - F2	F1 80K - B6	C1 81A - B5	J2 78E - B6	F2 78F - B6	E2 81F - E4	B2 82H - F1	H3 85 - A2	E3 82D - A4	B3 82E - D4	B3 89 - F1	H4 91 - F2	F6 89 - B6	C6 91 - B6					
D1 78C - E6	A1 78E - F3	G2 78F - F3	F2 81H - B1	C2 81A - B6	J3 82C - C1	F3 78F - B6	E3 81F - E4	B3 82H - F2	H4 85 - A3	E4 82D - A4	B4 82E - D4	B4 89 - F2	H5 91 - F2	F7 89 - B6	C7 91 - B6					
D2 78C - E6	A2 78E - F3	G3 78F - F3	F3 81H - B2	C3 82A - B1	J4 82C - C1	F4 82E - B1	E4 81F - E5	B4 82H - F3	H5 84 - F4	E5 82D - A5	B5 82E - D5	B5 89 - F2	H6 91 - F2	G1 89 - C3	D1 91 - C3					
D3 81B - E1	A3 78E - F3	G4 78F - F4	F4 81H - B3	C4 82A - B2	J5 82C - C2	F5 82E - B1	E5 81F - E5	B5 82H - F4	H6 84 - F4	E6 82D - A5	B6 82E - D5	B6 89 - F3	H7 91 - F3	G2 89 - C4	D2 91 - C4					
D4 81B - E1	A4 78E - F4	G5 78F - F4	F5 81H - B3	C5 82A - B3	J6 82C - C2	F6 82E - B2	E6 81F - E5	B6 82H - F4	H7 84 - F5	E7 82D - A6	B7 82E - D6	B7 89 - F3	J1 85 - A6	G3 89 - C4	D3 91 - C4					
D5 81B - E3	A5 78E - F4	G6 78F - F5	F6 81H - B4	C6 82A - B4	J7 82C - C3	F7 82E - B2	E7 81F - E6	B7 82H - F5	J1 81C - A6	F1 82D - B3	C1 82E - D3	C1 83 - A6	J2 92 - A1	G4 89 - C5	D4 91 - C5					
D6 81B - E3	A6 78E - F5	G7 78F - F5	F7 81H - B5	C7 82A - B5	**New 960**	G1 78F - B6	F1 81F - F3	C1 82 - A6	J2 85 - A1	F2 82D - B3	C2 82E - D3	C2 90 - A1	J3 92 - A1	G5 89 - C5	D5 91 - C5					
D7 81B - E4	A7 78E - F5	**New 955**	G1 80K - C6	D1 81A - C5	A1 78E - B6	G2 78F - C6	F2 81F - F4	C2 83 - A1	J3 85 - A2	F3 82D - B4	C3 82E - D4	C3 90 - A1	J4 92 - A2	G6 89 - C6	D6 91 - C6					
E1 78C - F6	B1 78E - F3	A1 78K - B6	G2 81H - C1	D2 81A - C6	A2 78E - B6	G3 78F - C6	F3 81F - F4	C3 83 - A2	J4 85 - A3	F4 82D - B4	C4 82E - D4	C4 90 - A2	J5 92 - A2	G7 89 - C6	D7 91 - C6					
E2 78C - F6	B2 78E - F3	A2 81F - B1	G3 81H - C2	D3 82A - C1	A3 82C - D1	G4 82E - B1	F4 81F - F5	C4 83 - A3	J5 85 - A4	F5 82D - B5	C5 82E - D5	C5 90 - A2	J6 92 - A2	H1 89 - D3	E1 91 - D3					
E3 81B - F1	B3 78E - F3	A3 81F - B1	G4 81H - C3	D4 82A - C2	A4 82C - D1	G5 82E - B1	F5 81F - F5	C5 83 - A4	J6 85 - A4	F6 82D - B5	C6 82E - D5	C6 90 - A2	J7 92 - A3	H2 89 - D4	E2 91 - D4					
E4 81B - F1	B4 78E - F4	A4 81F - B1	G5 81H - C3	D5 82A - C3	A5 82C - D2	G6 82E - B2	F6 81F - F5	C6 83 - A4	J7 85 - A5	F7 82D - B6	C7 82E - D6	C7 90 - A3	**New 999**	H3 89 - D4	E3 91 - D4					
E5 81B - F2	B5 78E - F4	A5 81F - B2	G6 81H - C4	D6 82A - C4	A6 82C - D2	G7 82E - B2	F7 81F - F6	C7 83 - A5	**New 979**	G1 82D - C3	D1 82E - E3	D1 83 - B6	A1 85 - B6	H4 89 - D5	E4 91 - D5					
E6 81B - F3	B6 78E - F5	A6 81F - B2	G7 81H - C5	D7 82A - C5	A7 82C - D3	H1 78F - C6	G1 81G - A3	D1 82 - B6	A1 81C - B6	G2 82D - C3	D2 82E - E3	D2 90 - B1	A2 92 - B1	H5 89 - D5	E5 91 - D5					
E7 81B - F4	B7 78E - F5	A7 81F - B3	H1 80K - C6	E1 81A - D5	B1 78E - C6	H2 78F - C6	G2 81G - A4	D2 83 - B1	A2 85 - B1	G3 82D - C4	D3 82E - E4	D3 90 - B1	A3 92 - B1	H6 89 - D6	E6 91 - D6					
F1 78C - F6	C1 78F - A3	B1 78K - C6	H2 81H - C1	E2 81A - D6	B2 78E - C6	H3 78F - C6	G3 81G - A4	D3 83 - B2	A3 85 - B2	G4 82D - C4	D4 82E - E4	D4 90 - B2	A4 92 - B2	H7 89 - D6	E7 91 - D6					
F2 78C - F6	C2 78F - A3	B2 81F - C1	H3 81H - C2	E3 82A - D1	B3 82C - E1	H4 82E - C1	G4 81G - A5	D4 83 - B3	A4 85 - B3	G5 82D - C5	D5 82E - E5	D5 90 - B2	A5 92 - B2	J1 89 - D3	F1 91 - E3					
F3 78E - A4	C3 78F - A3	B3 81F - C1	H4 81H - C3	E4 82A - D2	B4 82C - E1	H5 82E - C1	G5 81G - A5	D5 83 - B4	A5 85 - B4	G6 82D - C5	D6 82E - E5	D6 90 - B2	A6 92 - B2	J2 89 - D4	F2 91 - E4					
F4 78E - A4	C4 78F - A4	B4 81F - C1	H5 81H - C3	E5 82A - D3	B5 82C - E2	H6 82E - C2	G6 81G - A5	D6 83 - B4	A6 85 - B4	G7 82D - C6	D7 82E - E5	D7 90 - B3	A7 92 - B3	J3 89 - D4	F3 91 - E4					
F5 81B - F2	C5 78F - A4	B5 81F - C2	H6 81H - C4	E6 82A - D4	B6 82C - E2	H7 82E - C2	G7 81G - A6	D7 83 - B5	A7 85 - B5	H1 82D - C3	E1 82E - E3	E1 83 - B6	B1 85 - C6	J4 89 - D5	F4 91 - E5					
F6 78E - A5	C6 78F - A5	B6 81F - C2	H7 81H - C5	E7 82A - D5	B7 82C - E3	J1 78F - C6	H1 81G - B3	E1 82 - B6	B1 81C - C6	H2 82D - C3	E2 82E - E3	E2 90 - B1	B2 92 - B1	J5 89 - D5	F5 91 - E5					
F7 81B - F4	C7 78F - A5	B7 81F - C3	J1 80K - D6	F1 81A - E5	C1 78E - C6	J2 78F - C6	H2 81G - B4	E2 83 - B1	B2 85 - C1	H3 82D - C4	E3 82E - E4	E3 90 - B1	B3 92 - C1	J6 89 - D6	F6 91 - E6					
G1 78E - A3	D1 78F - A3	C1 78K - D6	J2 81H - D1	F2 81A - E6	C2 78E - C6	J3 78F - C6	H3 81G - B4	E3 83 - B2	B3 85 - C2	H4 82D - C4	E4 82E - E4	E4 90 - B2	B4 92 - C2	J7 89 - D6	F7 91 - E6					
G2 78E - A3	D2 78F - A3	C2 81F - D1	J3 81H - D2	F3 82A - E1	C3 82C - E1	J4 82E - C1	H4 81G - B5	E4 83 - B3	B4 85 - C3	H5 82D - C5	E5 82E - E5	E5 90 - B2	B5 92 - C2	**New 1017**	G1 91 - E3					
G3 78E - A4	D3 78F - A3	C3 81F - D1	J4 81H - D2	F4 82A - E2	C4 82C - E1	J5 82E - C1	H5 81G - B5	E5 83 - B4	B5 85 - C4	H6 82D - C5	E6 82E - E5	E6 90 - B2	B6 92 - C2	A1 89 - E3	G2 91 - E4					
G4 78E - A4	D4 78F - A4	C4 81F - D1	J5 81H - D3	F5 82A - E3	C5 82C - E2	J6 82E - C2	H6 81G - B5	E6 83 - B4	B6 85 - C4	H7 82D - C6	E7 82E - E5	E7 90 - C3	B7 92 - C3	A2 89 - E4	G3 91 - E4					
G5 78E - A5	D5 78F - A4	C5 81F - D2	J6 81H - D4	F6 82A - E4	C6 82C - E2	J7 82E - C2	H7 81G - B6	E7 83 - B5	B7 85 - C5	J1 82D - D3	F1 82E - F3	F1 83 - C6	C1 85 - D6	A3 89 - E4	G4 91 - E5					
G6 78E - A5	D6 78F - A5	C6 81F - D2	J7 81H - D5	F7 82A - E5	C7 82C - E3	**New 962**	J1 81G - C3	F1 82 - C6	C1 81C - D6	J2 82D - D3	F2 82E - F3	F2 90 - C1	C2 92 - C1	A4 89 - E5	G5 91 - E5					
G7 78E - A5	D7 78F - A5	C7 81F - D3	**New 957**	G1 81A - F5	D1 78E - C6	A1 78F - D6	J2 81G - C4	F2 83 - C1	C2 85 - D1	J3 82D - D4	F3 82E - F4	F3 90 - C1	C3 92 - C1	A5 89 - E5	G6 91 - E6					
H1 78E - A3	E1 78F - B3	D1 78K - E6	A1 80K - E6	G2 81A - F6	D2 78E - C6	A2 78F - D6	J3 81G - C4	F3 83 - C2	C3 85 - D2	J4 82D - D4	F4 82E - F4	F4 90 - C2	C4 92 - C2	A6 89 - E6	G7 91 - E6					
H2 78E - A3	E2 78F - B3	D2 81F - E1	A2 81H - E1	G3 82A - F1	D3 82C - F1	A3 78F - D6	J4 81G - C5	F4 83 - C3	C4 85 - D3	J5 82D - D5	F5 82E - F5	F5 90 - C2	C5 92 - C2	A7 89 - E6	H1 91 - F3					
H3 78E - A4	E3 78F - B3	D3 81F - E1	A3 81H - E2	G4 82A - F2	D4 82C - F1	A4 82E - D1	J5 81G - C5	F5 83 - C4	C5 85 - D4	J6 82D - D5	F6 82E - F5	F6 90 - C2	C6 92 - C2	B1 89 - F3	H2 91 - F4					
H4 78E - A4	E4 78F - B4	D4 81F - E1	A4 81H - E2	G5 82A - F3	D5 82C - F2	A5 82E - D1	J6 81G - C5	F6 83 - C4	C6 85 - D4	J7 82D - D6	F7 82E - E5	F7 90 - C3	C7 92 - C3	B2 89 - F4	H3 91 - F4					
H5 78E - A5	E5 78F - B4	D5 81F - E2	A5 81H - E3	G6 82A - F4	D6 82C - F2	A6 82E - D2	J7 81G - C6	F7 83 - C5	C7 85 - D5	**New 981**	G1 82E - F3	G1 83 - D6	D1 85 - E6	B3 89 - F4	H4 91 - F5					
H6 78E - A5	E6 78F - B5	D6 81F - E2	A6 81H - E4	G7 82A - F5	D7 82C - F3	A7 82E - D2	**New 976**	G1 82 - D6	D1 81C - E6	A1 82D - E3	G2 82E - F3	G2 90 - D1	D2 92 - D1	B4 89 - F5	H5 91 - F5					
H7 78E - A5	E7 78F - B5	D7 81F - E3	A7 81H - E5	H1 81B - A5	E1 78E - D6	B1 78F - D5	A1 81G - C3	G2 83 - D1	D2 85 - E1	A2 82D - E3	G3 82E - F4	G3 90 - D1	D3 92 - D1	B5 89 - F5	H6 91 - F6					
J1 78E - B3	F1 78F - B3	E1 78K - E6	B1 80K - F6	H2 81B - A6	E2 78E - D6	B2 78F - D6	A2 81G - C4	G3 83 - D2	D3 85 - E2	A3 82D - E4	G4 82E - F4	G4 90 - D2	D4 92 - D2	B6 89 - F6	H7 91 - F6					
J2 78E - B3	F2 78F - B3	E2 81F - E1	B2 81H - F1	H3 81C - A1	E3 82D - A1	B3 78F - D6	A3 81G - C4	G4 83 - D3	D4 85 - E3	A4 82D - E4	G5 82E - F5	G5 90 - D2	D5 92 - D2	B7 89 - F6	J1 92 - A3					
J3 78E - B4	F3 78F - B3	E3 81F - E1	B3 81H - F2	H4 81C - A2	E4 82D - A1	B4 82E - D1	A4 81G - C5	G5 83 - D4	D5 85 - E4	A5 82D - E5	G6 82E - F5	G6 90 - D2	D6 92 - D2	C1 90 - A3	J2 92 - A4					
J4 78E - B4	F4 78F - B4	E4 81F - E1	B4 81H - F2	H5 81C - A3	E5 82D - A2	B5 82E - D1	A5 81G - C5	G6 83 - D4	D6 85 - E5	A6 82D - E5	G7 82E - F5	G7 90 - D3	D7 92 - D3	C2 90 - A4	J3 92 - A4					
J5 78E - B4	F5 78F - B4	E5 81F - E2	B5 81H - F3	H6 81C - A4	E6 82D - A2	B6 82E - D2	A6 81G - C5	G7 83 - D5	D7 85 - E5	A7 82D - E6	H1 82E - F3	H1 83 - E6	E1 85 - E6	C3 90 - A4	J4 92 - A5					
J6 78E - B5	F6 78F - B5	E6 81F - E2	B6 81H - F4	H7 81C - A5	E7 82D - A3	B7 82E - D2	A7 81G - C6	H1 82 - E6	E1 81C - F5	B1 82D - F3	H2 82E - F3	H2 90 - E1	E2 92 - E1	C4 90 - A5	J5 92 - A5					
J7 78E - B5	F7 78F - B5	E7 81F - E3	B7 81H - F5	J1 81B - A5	F1 78E - D6	C1 78F - E5	B1 81G - D3	H2 83 - E1	E2 85 - E1	B2 82D - F3	H3 82E - F4	H3 90 - E1	E3 92 - E1	C5 90 - A5	J6 92 - A6					
New 940	G1 78F - B3	F1 78K - F6	C1 81 - A6	J2 81B - A6	F2 78E - D6	C2 78F - E6	B2 81G - D4	H3 83 - E2	E3 85 - E2	B3 82D - F4	H4 82E - F4	H4 90 - E2	E4 92 - E2	C6 90 - A6	J7 92 - A6					
A1 78E - B3	G2 78F - B3	F2 81F - F1	C2 82 - A1	J3 81C - A1	F3 82D - B1	C3 78F - E6	B3 81G - D4	H4 83 - E3	E4 85 - E3	B4 82D - F4	H5 82E - F5	H5 90 - E2	E5 92 - E2	C7 90 - A6	**New 1019**					

BE SURE TO VISIT OUR STORE...

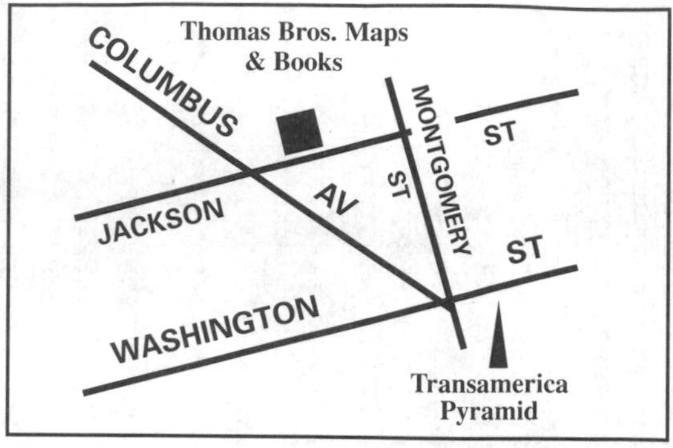

Thomas Bros. Maps® & Books

550 Jackson Street
San Francisco
CA 94133
(415) 981-7520

Located in Downtown San Francisco at the Entrance to Historic Jackson Square

In addition to our selection of Thomas Guides®, we offer an extensive collection of domestic and international maps, travel books and software products!

Thomas Bros. Maps®
SINCE 1915
1-800-969-3072
http://www.thomas.com

1998 The Thomas Guide
NORTHERN VIRGINIA & THE BELTWAY
METROPOLITAN BAY AREA Thomas Guide
GEOFINDER
CALIFORNIA
ROAD ATLAS AND DRIVER'S GUIDE
PACIFIC NORTHWEST
ROAD ATLAS AND DRIVER'S GUIDE
1998 The Thomas Guide
PRINCE GEORGE'S COUNTY & THE BELTWAY
1998 The Thomas Guide
METROPOLITAN WASHINGTON DC
The Thomas Guide CD-ROM
1998 Los Angeles & Orange Counties
The Thomas Guide
1998 Los Angeles/Orange Counties
Street Guide and Directory
The Thomas Guide CD-ROM
1998 Washington D.C. Metro Area
GEOFINDER
Thomas Bros. Maps
Express Maps